Travel Clinic
383-1554

PAGE 54

ON THE ROAD

YOUR COMPLETE DESTINATION GUIDE
In-depth reviews, detailed listings
and insider tips

PAGE 1155

SURVIVAL GUIDE

Women
& Solo
Travellers

THIS EDITION WRITTEN AND RESEARCHED BY

Sarina Singh,

Michael Benanav, Lindsay Brown, Stuart Butler, Mark Elliott, Katja Gaskell,
Trent Holden, Abigail Hole, Kate James, Amy Karafin, Anirban Mahapatra,
Bradley Mayhew, Daniel McCrohan, John Noble, Kevin Raub

welcome to
India

Soul Stirring

Bamboozling. There's simply no other word that captures the enigma that is India. With an ability to inspire, frustrate, thrill and confound all at once, India presents an extraordinary spectrum of encounters for the traveller. Some of these can be challenging, particularly for the first-time visitor: the poverty is confronting, Indian bureaucracy can be exasperating and the crush of humanity sometimes turns the simplest task into an energy-zapping battle. Even veteran travellers find their sanity frayed at some point, yet this is all part of the India experience. Love it or loathe it – and most visitors see-saw between the two – India will jostle your entire being. It's a place that fires the imagination and stirs the soul like nowhere else on earth.

Spectacularly Diverse

With its in-your-face diversity – from snow-dusted mountains to sun-washed beaches, tranquil temples to frenetic bazaars, lantern-lit villages to software-supremo cities – it's hardly surprising that this country has been dubbed the world's most multidimensional. For those seeking spiritual sustenance, India has oodles of sacrosanct sites and thought-provoking philosophies, while history buffs will stumble upon gems from the past almost everywhere – grand vestiges of former empires serenely peer over swarming streets and crumbling fortresses loom high above plunging ravines. Meanwhile, aficionados of the great outdoors can paddle in the shimmering waters

India bristles with an eclectic melange of ethnic groups; an intoxicating cultural cocktail for the traveller. With such astonishing diversity, you will be taken on a journey that will linger in your mind long after you've left her shores.

(left) Elephant Festival dancer, Jaipur (p108)
(below) Buffalo-riding on the banks of the Ganges, Varanasi (p383)

of one of many beautiful beaches, scout for big jungle cats on blood-pumping wildlife safaris, or simply inhale pine-scented air on meditative forest walks. And then there are the festivals. With its vibrant mix of religious denominations, India is home to a formidable array of celebrations – from larger-than-life extravaganzas with caparisoned elephants and body-twisting acrobats to pint-sized harvest fairs paying homage to a locally worshipped deity.

Too Delicious

Brace yourself – you're about to jump on board one of the wildest culinary trips of your life! Frying, simmering, sizzling, kneading and flipping a deliciously diverse variety of regional dishes, feasting your way through the subcontinent is certainly one hell of a ride. The hungry traveller can look forward to a bountiful smorgasbord of tasty delights, ranging from the spicy goodness of masterfully marinated chicken drumsticks in North India to the simple splendour of squidgy rice dumplings in the steamy south. So what are you waiting for? Roll up your sleeves, put on your chomp-chomp hat and rumble your way down India's gastronomic highway!

Top Experiences ›

External boundaries shown reflect the requirements of the Government of India. Some boundaries may not be those recognised by neighbouring countries. Lonely Planet always tries to show on maps where travellers may need to cross a boundary (and present documentation) irrespective of any dispute.

ELEVATION

	6000m
	5000m
	4000m
	3000m
	2000m
	1000m
	0

Darjeeling
Quintessential hill station, famed for tea (p487)

Amritsar
Sikhism's revered Golden Temple (p213)

Agra
Home to the iconic Taj Mahal (p350)

Khajuraho
Sensuous sculptures adorn exquisite temples (p623)

Varanasi
Intense spirituality by the Ganges River (p383)

Ladakh
Starkly beautiful Himalayan mountainscapes (p243)

Udaipur
Ochre-shaded hills encircling pretty palaces (p154)

Jaisalmer
Majestic fort and desert camel safaris (p182)

CHINA
TIBET

Lhasa

Gyantse

Thimphu Valley

BHUTAN
Thimphu

Gangtok
Sikkim

Darjeeling
Siliguri

Jaldhapara Wildlife Sanctuary

Guwahati

Shillong
Meghalaya

Dibrugarh

Arunachal Pradesh
Itanagar

Kaziranga National Park

Nagaland
Kohima

Imphal
Manipur

Aizawl

West Bengal

BANGLADESH
Agartala
Dhaka

NEPAL
Kathmandu

Mt Everest (8848m)

Annapurna (8090m)

Gorakhpur

Bihar
Muzaffarpur
Patna

Gaya
Bodhgaya

Jharkhand

Great Himalaya Range

Nanda Devi (7816m)

Nainital

Uttar Pradesh
Lucknow
Kanpur

Ayodhya
Bareilly

Allahabad (Tirth Raj Prayag)

Varanasi

Satna
Khajuraho

Madhya Pradesh

Shivpuri

Gwalior
Jhansi

Agra
Mathura

Ganges
Jamuna

Keoladeo Ghana National Park

Corbett Tiger Reserve

Haridwar
Dehra Dun
Uttarakhand

Himachal Pradesh
Shimla
Manali
Kullu
Dharamsala

Great Himalaya Range

K2 (Godwin Austin) (8611m)

Under Administration of China

Jammu & Kashmir

Leh
Ladakh
Padum
Zanskar
Kargil

Srinagar

Kishtwar

Under Administration of Pakistan

Jammu

Dalhousie
Pathankot

Punjab
Chandigarh
Amritsar
Attari
Firozpur
Bathinda

Haryana
Hansi
Churu

Delhi

Jaipur
Ajmer

Rajasthan
Bikaner

Ranthambhore National Park

Chittorgarh (Chittor)

Bundi
Kota

Udaipur (Chittor)

Mt Abu

Jodhpur

Barmer

Jaisalmer

Great Thar Desert

Great Rann of Kutch

Gujarat

TAJIKISTAN
Dushanbe

AFGHANISTAN
Kabul

PAKISTAN
Islamabad

Shantiniketan

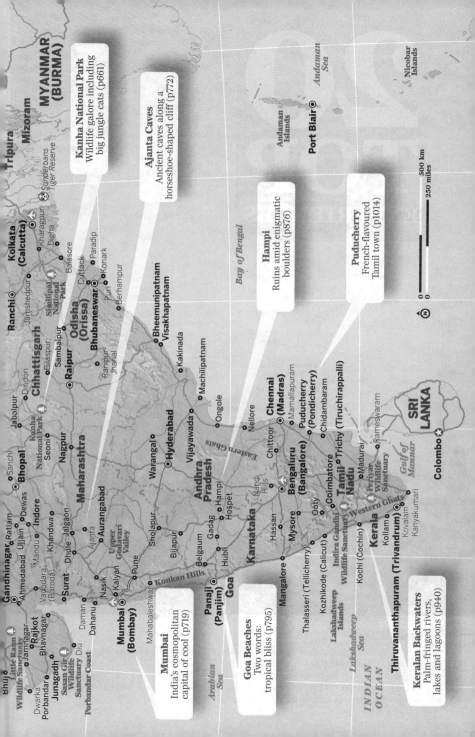

Kanha National Park
Wildlife galore including big jungle cats (p661)

Ajanta Caves
Ancient caves along a horseshoe-shaped cliff (p772)

Hampi
Ruins amid enigmatic boulders (p876)

Puducherry
French-flavoured Tamil town (p1014)

Mumbai
India's cosmopolitan capital of cool (p719)

Goa Beaches
Two words: tropical bliss (p795)

Keralan Backwaters
Palm-fringed rivers, lakes and lagoons (p940)

MYANMAR (BURMA)

Tripura
Mizoram

Sunderbans Tiger Reserve

Kolkata (Calcutta)
Kharagpur
Digha

Ranchi
Jamshedpur

Chhattisgarh
Dindori
Bilaspur
Sambalpur
Raipur
Ranipur Jharial

Odisha (Orissa)
Bhubaneswar
Simlipal National Park
Balasore
Paradip
Cuttack
Puri
Konark
Berhampur

Bheemunipatnam
Visakhapatnam
Kakinada
Machilipatnam

Bay of Bengal

Andaman Sea

Nicobar Islands

Andaman Islands

Port Blair

500 km
250 miles

N

Chennai (Madras)
Mamallapuram
Puducherry (Pondicherry)
Chidambaram

Eastern Ghats

Nellore
Ongole
Chittoor

Andhra Pradesh
Hyderabad
Vijayawada
Warangal

Maharashtra
Jabalpur
Bhopal
Sanchi
Kanha National Park
Seoni
Nagpur
Dewas
Indore
Mandu
Khandwa
Ujjain
Ratlam

Gandhinagar
Ahmedabad
Vadodara (Baroda)
Surat
Dhule
Jalgaon
Nasik
Aurangabad
Ajanta
Upper Godavari Valley
Sholapur
Bijapur
Gadag
Hampi
Hospet

Little Rann Wildlife Sanctuary
Rajkot
Jamnagar
Bhavnagar
Junagadh
Sasan Gir Wildlife Sanctuary
Diu
Dwarka
Porbandar
Porbandar Coast
Bhuj
Daman
Dahanu

Mahabaleshwar
Kalyan
Pune
Konkan Hills
Belgaum
Hubli

Mumbai (Bombay)

Panaji (Panjim)
Goa

Arabian Sea

Mangalore

Karnataka
Hassan
Mysore

Bengaluru (Bangalore)
Nandi Hills

Coimbatore
Ooty
Indira Gandhi Wildlife Sanctuary

Tamil Nadu
Trichy (Tiruchirappalli)
Madurai
Periyar Wildlife Sanctuary
Rameswaram

Western Ghats
Kochi (Cochin)
Kollam
Kovalam
Kanyakumari

Kerala
Thiruvananthapuram (Trivandrum)

Thalasseri (Tellicherry)
Kozhikode (Calicut)
Lakshadweep Islands

Lakshadweep Sea

INDIAN OCEAN

SRI LANKA
Colombo

Gulf of Mannar

20 TOP EXPERIENCES

Taj Mahal

1 Don't let fears of tour buses or hordes of visitors get you thinking you can skip the Taj – you can't. Even on a crowded, hot day, this world wonder (p350) is still the 'Crown of Palaces', a monument to love whose very walls seem to resound with the emperor Shah Jahan's adoration of his beloved Mumtaz Mahal, the 'Gem of the Palace'. The marble mausoleum is inlaid with calligraphy, precious and semiprecious stones, and intricate flower designs representing paradise.

FELIX HUG / LONELY PLANET IMAGES ©

Backwaters of Kerala

2 It's unusual to find a place as gorgeous as Kerala's backwaters (p940): 900km of interconnected rivers, lakes and lagoons lined with tropical flora. And if you do, there likely won't be a way to experience it that's as peaceful and intimate as a few days on a teak-and-palm-thatch houseboat. Float along the water – maybe as the sun sets behind the palms, maybe while eating to-die-for Keralan seafood, maybe as you fall asleep under a twinkling sky – and forget about life on land for a while.

Holy Varanasi

3 Everyone in Varanasi (p383) seems to be dying or praying or hustling or cremating someone or swimming or laundering or washing buffaloes in the city's sewage-saturated Ganges. The goddess river will clean away your sins and help you escape from that tedious life-and-death cycle – and Varanasi is the place to take a sacred dip. So take a deep breath, put on a big smile for the ever-present touts, go to the holy water and get your karma in order.

BRENT WINEBRENNER / LONELY PLANET IMAGES ©

Alluring Darjeeling

4 Up in a tippy-top nook of India's far northeast is storied Darjeeling (p487). It's no longer a romantic mountain hideaway, but the allure remains. Undulating hills of bulbous tea trees are pruned by women in bright-coloured dresses; the majestic Himalaya peek through puffy clouds as the sun climbs out from behind the mountains; and little alleys wend their way through mountain mist, past clotheslines and monasteries. Ride the 'toy train' and drink it all in – the tea and the town's legendary enchantment.

GREG ELMS / LONELY PLANET IMAGES ©

Caves of Ajanta

5 They may have been ascetics, but the 2nd-century-BC monks who created the Ajanta caves (p772) had an eye for the dramatic. The 30 rock-cut forest grottoes punctuate the side of a horseshoe-shaped cliff, and originally had individual staircases leading down to the river. The architecture and towering stupas made these caves inspiring places in which to meditate and live, but the real bling came centuries later, in the form of exquisite carvings and paintings depicting Buddha's former lives. Makes living in a cave look pretty good.

KEREN SU / LONELY PLANET IMAGES ©

ANDERS BLOMQVIST / LONELY PLANET IMAGES ©

Dreamy Hampi

6 Today's surreal boulderscape of Hampi (p876) was once the glorious and cosmopolitan Vijayanagar, capital of a powerful Hindu empire. Still glorious in ruins, its temples and royal structures combine sublimely with the terrain: giant rocks balance on skinny pedestals near an ancient elephant garage; temples tuck into crevices between boulders; and round coracle boats float by rice paddies and bathing buffaloes near a gargantuan bathtub for a queen. Watching the sunset cast a rosy glow over the dreamy landscape, you might just forget what planet you're on.

Riding the Rails

7 India's quintessential journey is still the long train ride. Domestic flights are increasingly common, but as the train's 20 million daily passengers will tell you, you can't watch the Indian landscape change from dry valley to lush mountain forest to lime-green rice paddies on a plane. The train's also where you can hang out with families and other domestic travellers, learning about Indian culture the old-fashioned way – over a cup of tea, to the rhythm of the rails.

CHRISTER FREDRIKSSON / LONELY PLANET IMAGES ©

Puducherry Savoir Faire

8 A little pocket of France in Tamil Nadu? Pourquoi pas? In this former French colony (p1014), yellow houses line cobblestone streets, grand cathedrals are adorned with architectural frou-frou, and the croissants are the real deal. But Puducherry's also a Tamil town – with all the history, temples and hustle and bustle that go along with that – and a classic retreat town, too, with the Sri Aurobindo Ashram at its heart. Turns out that yoga, pain chocolat, Hindu gods and colonial-era architecture make for an atmospheric melange.

Cuppa in a Hill Station

9 The valleys, deserts, and palm-lined beaches are all well and good, but it can get hot down there! India's princes and British colonials long used the country's cool mountain towns as refuges from the summer heat, and today the hill stations still have lush forests, crisp mountain air and picturesque tea plantations. Curl up under a blanket with a steaming cup of local tea, look out over misty hills at swooping mountain birds, and experience India's cool side.

Neighbourhood Markets

10 Shopaholics: be careful not to lose control. Those with no interest in shopping: get in touch with your consumerist side. India's markets have something you want, guaranteed (though you may not have known this beforehand), with a fun haggle to go with it. The range of technicolour saris, glittering gold and silver bling, mounds of rainbow vermilion, aromatic fresh spices, stainless-steel head massagers, bangles and bobby pins, motorcycle bumper stickers, heaping piles of fruit, Bollywood-star-silkscreened pajamas, and marigold and coconut offerings is, well, astounding.

Goan Beaches

11 There might be no better place in the world to be lazy than on one of Goa's spectacular beaches (p795). With palm-tree groves on one side of the white sands and gently lapping waves on the other, the best of the beaches live up to your image of a tropical paradise. But it's not an undiscovered one: the sands are also peppered with fellow travellers and beach-shack restaurants. Goa's treasures are for social creatures and fans of creature comforts who like their seafood fresh and their holidays easy.

Mumbai's Architectural Visions

12 Mumbai (p719) has always absorbed everything in her midst and made them her own. The architectural result is a heady mix of buildings with countless influences. The art deco and modern towers are flashy, but it's the eclectic Victorian-era structures – the neo-Gothic, Indo-Saracenic and Venetian Gothic hodgepodge – that have come to define Mumbai and make her the flamboyant beauty that she is. All those spires, gables, arches and onion domes make for a pleasant walk through the city's past.

DALLAS STRIBLEY / LONELY PLANET IMAGES ©

Safaris

13 You have to be lucky to spot a tiger in India, but it can be done. Even if you don't see any, you'll enjoy wandering one of India's many forest wildlife reserves on the back of an elephant, surrounded by birds and butterflies. Or just forget the tigers and elephants and go for camels: desert safaris around Jaisalmer (p190) and Bikaner (p196) involve riding atop the tall, goofy animals and camping out among dunes under star-packed skies.

Streets Alive

14 At first it might be overwhelming – dust will get in your eyes, honking in your ears, people in your way – but you'll adjust. And when you do, you'll find insanely good food being fried in carts, trucks painted with baroque designs, flower garlands sold by friendly vendors, cars, rickshaws and bicycles dancing to a rhythm only they can hear, people speaking several of India's 1500-plus languages and, of course, cows – those sweet, stubborn animals that Gandhi called the 'mother to millions of Indian mankind'.

RICHARD I'ANSON / LONELY PLANET IMAGES ©

Himalayan Mountains & Monasteries

DAVID ELSE / LONELY PLANET IMAGES ©

15 Up north, where the air is cooler and crisper, quaint hill stations give way to snow-topped peaks. Here, the cultural influences came not by coasts but via mountain passes. Tibetan Buddhism thrives, and multilayered monasteries emerge from the forest or steep cliffs as vividly and poetically as the sun rises over golden Khangchendzonga (p543). Weathered prayer flags on forest paths blow in the wind, the sound of monks chanting reverberates in meditation halls, and locals bring offerings and make merit, all in the shadow of the mighty Himalaya.

Sexy Khajuraho

16 Some say that the sensuous carvings on Khajuraho's temples (p623) depict the Kama Sutra, or Tantric practices for initiates; others, that they're educational models for children or allegories for the faithful. But pretty much everyone agrees that they're naughty and fun to look at. Want to see a nine-person orgy? Men getting it on with horses? Hot nymphs? Khajuraho's your chance. Once the titillation passes, you'll notice that the carving and architecture of these thousand-year-old temples are exquisite, and the magical feeling of being in 11th-century India pleasantly absorbing.

Festive Parades

17 India knows festivals, and it has been perfecting the parade for, oh, a few millennia. It usually starts with the far-off sound of the trumpets, then the drums and, before you know it, there's a mass of humanity, marching brass bands (often in fine traditional regalia: jodhpurs, turbans, the works), a chariot, and then a dozen or a hundred bejewelled and caparisoned elephants. The giant creatures may be wearing solid-gold headdresses, bearing canopied goddesses or carrying silk, pompommed parasols high overhead as they march languorously to the beat.

Jaisalmer's Desert Mirage

18 Rising like a sandcastle from the deserts of Rajasthan, the 'Land of Kings', Jaisalmer's 12th-century citadel (p183) looks more like something from a dream than reality. The enormous golden sandstone fort, with its crenellated ramparts and undulating towers, is a fantastical structure, even while camouflaged against the desert sand. Inside, an ornate royal palace, fairytale *havelis* (traditional residences), intricately carved Jain temples and narrow lanes conspire to create the world's best place to get lost.

Amritsar's Golden Temple

19 The Sikhs' holiest of shrines, the Golden Temple (p213) is a magical place designed for people of all religions to worship. Seeming to float atop a glistening pool named for the 'nectar of immortality', the temple is a gorgeous structure, made even more so by its extreme goldness (the lotus-shaped dome is gilded in the real thing). Even when crowded with happy pilgrims, the temple is peaceful, with birds singing outside and the lake gently lapping against the godly abode.

Delhi

20 India's capital has had several incarnations over the last few thousand years, which partly explains why there's so much going on here. Dust, noise and chaos aside, Delhi (p56) is full of stunning architecture, culture (its residents come from all over the country), good food and even better shopping. The Mughal legacy is one of its biggest attractions: Old Delhi is all crumbling splendour, with the majestic Jama Masjid, the massive Red Fort and other monuments of the historic Mughal capital adorning the old city like royal jewels.

need to know

Currency
» Indian Rupees (₹)

Language
» Hindi and English

When to Go

Leh
GO Jul–Sep

Delhi
GO Nov–Mar

Kolkata (Calcutta)
GO Nov–Mar

Mumbai (Bombay)
GO Nov–Feb

Bengaluru (Bangalore)
GO Nov–Mar

Desert, dry climate
Mild to hot summers, cold winters
Tropical climate, rain year-round
Tropical climate, wet dry seasons
Warm to hot summers, mild winters

High Season
(Dec–Mar)

» Pleasant weather, mostly. Peak tourists. Peak prices.

» In December and January northern cities can get cold, bitterly so in the far north.

» It starts heating up in February.

Shoulder Season
(Jul–Nov)

» July to early September is the prime time to visit Ladakh.

» India's southeast coast (and southern Kerala) experiences heavy rain any time from October to early December.

Low Season
(Apr–Jun)

» April is hot; May and June even hotter. Competitive hotel prices.

» From June the monsoon sweeps from south to north. Fatiguing humidity.

» Beat the heat (but not the crowds) in the cool hills.

Your Daily Budget

» Prices (especially accommodation) vary widely across the country – consult regional chapters for on-the-ground costs.

Budget

» Stay at cheap guesthouses with shared bathrooms, or hostels.

» Eat at roadside stalls or basic restaurants.

» Travel locally by bus, occasionally autorickshaw.

Midrange

» Good accommodation (with private bathrooms) and restaurants.

» Travel locally by autorickshaw and taxi.

Top end

» Accommodation and dining out – the sky is the limit!

» Hire a car with driver – but don't miss the adventure of an autorickshaw ride.

Money

» Most urban centres have ATMS. It's wise to carry cash or travellers cheques as back-up. MasterCard and Visa are the most widely accepted credit cards.

Visas

» Most people travel on the standard six-month tourist visa. Tourist visas are valid from the date of issue, not the date you arrive in India.

Mobile Phones

» Getting connected can be complicated in some states due to security issues. To avoid expensive roaming costs get hooked up to the local mobile-phone network.

Driving

» Don't do it. Hiring a car with driver doesn't cost a fortune and India has expansive rail, bus and air connections.

Websites

» **Lonely Planet** (www.lonelyplanet.com/india) Destination information, the popular Thorn Tree Travel Forum and more.

» **Incredible India** (www.incredibleindia.org) Official India tourism site.

» **World Newspapers** (www.world-newspapers.com/india.html) Links to India's English-language publications.

» **Art India** (www.artindia.net) Performing arts information, especially dance and music.

» **Templenet** (www.templenet.com) Temple talk.

Exchange Rates

Australia	A$1	₹45
Canada	C$1	₹45
Euro zone	€1	₹63
Japan	¥100	₹55
New Zealand	NZ$1	₹33
UK	UK£1	₹73
US	US$1	₹45

For current exchange rates see www.xe.com

Important Numbers

From outside India, dial your international access code, India's country code then the number (minus '0', only used when dialling domestically).

Country code	91
International access code	00
Ambulance	102
Fire	101
Police	100

Arriving in India

» **Delhi, Mumbai, Chennai, Kolkata**
India's major international airports have prepaid-taxi booths. These enable you to book a fixed-price taxi (including luggage), thus avoiding commission or other scams. Some terminals also have train, bus and/or autorickshaw options. Many hotels will arrange airport pick-ups with advance notice. These are often complimentary with top-end hotels. For further details, see p98 (Delhi), p752 (Mumbai), p998 (Chennai) and p469 (Kolkata).

Don't Leave Home Without...

» Getting a visa (p1173) and travel insurance (p1166)
» Seeking advice about vaccinations (p1188)
» Nonrevealing clothes (both sexes) – covering up is respectful, and essential at holy sites
» Well-concealed money belt
» Sunscreen and sunglasses
» Small torch for poorly lit streets and/or power cuts
» Earplugs – noise can be a nuisance
» Slip-on shoes – handy for visiting sacred sites
» Expecting the unexpected – India loves to toss up surprises

if you like...

Forts & Palaces

India's long history is riddled with tales of conquest and domination, mostly by guys trying to get – or keep – the region's many literal and figurative jewels. Today their forts are serene, with artfully crumbling facades and spectacular views.

Rajasthan Kingly Rajasthan is studded with an outrageous number of magnificent fortresses and elegant palaces. Chittorgarh and Jaisalmer are rightly the most popular forts, while Udaipur and Jaipur palaces are surreally romantic (p104)

Maharashtra The land of Shivaji is almost as much of a fort junkie as Rajasthan, with defensive masterpieces like Daulatabad, camouflaged on a hilltop, and Janjira, an island fortress (p757)

Hyderabad The rugged Golconda Fort, whose gem vault once stored the Hope and Koh-i-Noor diamonds, complements the ethereal palaces of the City of Pearls (p894)

Bidar Fort So weathered and peaceful, you'll just have to trust that it was the seat of a powerful sultanate (p889)

Grand Temples

No one does temples like India – from psychedelic technicolor Hindu towers to silently grand Buddhist cave temples and Amritsar's gold-plated fairy-tale Sikh shrine.

Golden Temple The queen of Sikh temples floats like a shining gem over a pool in Amritsar. As Sikhism's most important shrine, it has good vibes to match (p213)

Tamil Nadu Tamil Nadu is temple heaven, with towering, fantastical structures – like Madurai's Sri Meenakshi Temple (p1036) – that climb to the sky in busy rainbows of sculpted gods

Rajasthan It's hard to decide who's better at ridiculously beautiful temple carving: the Hindus or the Jains. Rajasthan's Jain temples, especially at Jaisalmer (p183), Ranakpur (p167) and Mt Abu (p168), are pretty amazing – the stone-architecture equivalent of princesses draped in piles of exquisite jewelry

Ajanta & Ellora Ancient, vast, sculpted caves. Because monks like beautiful sculpture, too (p764)

Ancient Ruins

You don't get to be a 5000-year-old civilisation without having lots of atmospheric ruins peppered around the place. Each region in India has seen many cultures and empires pass through and leave their architectural marks, making for easy time travel.

Hampi The rosy-hued temples and palaces of what was once the mighty capital of Vijayanagar scatter here among other-worldly-looking boulders and hilltops (p876)

Mandu Many of the tombs, palaces, monuments and mosques on Mandu's 20-sq-km green plateau are among India's finest Afghan architecture. The Jahaz Mahal, aka Ship Palace, is an odd beauty (p654)

Nalanda This 1600-year-old university once enrolled 10,000 monks and students from as far afield as China and Greece. You can tell what a sophisticated operation – and a lovely campus – it was by the monasteries, temples and stupas that lie today, still elegant, in ruins (p522)

» Jama Masjid (p66), Delhi

City Sophistication

It's true that most Indians live in villages, but city people here had attained high planes of sophistication when classiness was just a glimmer in the West's eye. India's cities have great arts scenes, excellent restaurants and heaps of style.

Mumbai Mumbai has it all – fashion, film, art, dining and a nightlife scene that's just crazy – on an elaborate stage of fanciful architecture and water views (p719)

Delhi Also an urban sophisticate, Delhi has Mughal attractions (gorgeous tombs and the awesome Jama Masjid, among others) to go with its exceedingly good shopping, museums and street food (p56)

Kolkata Long known for its poetic and political tendencies, Kolkata also has colonial-era glam and sublime cuisine – while several prominent gods look on (p442)

Hyderabad The ancient architecture of several excessively wealthy dynasties sits just across town from a refined restaurant, nightlife and arts scene (p905)

Bazaars

Shoppers, get ready. Indian megamalls may be popping up like monsoon frogs, but the age-old bazaar – with its mix of crowds and spices, garbage and flowers, altars and underwear – is still where it's at.

Old Delhi Just about everything you can think of is for sale in the old Mughal-era bazaars. Some of India's best street food – and oldest restaurants – are in Chandni Chowk, which translates to 'moonlit square' (p94)

Goa Tourist flea markets have become huge events at several spots on the north coast, while the local bazaars of Panaji (Panjim) and, especially, Margao make for excellent wandering (p795)

Mumbai The megalopolis has several old, characterful markets handily dedicated to themes: Mangaldas (fabric), Zaveri (jewellery), Crawford (meat and produce) and Chor (random antique things) (p748)

Mysore Devaraja Market is about 125 years old and filled with about 125 million flowers, fruits and vegetables (p852)

Beaches

India's coastlines are diverse and gorgeous, with lots of personality. Several beaches in Goa and Kerala are downright paradisiacal, while elsewhere, the shoreline is more tinselled and all about long strolls and snack carts.

Kerala Kovalam and Varkala, with their crescent-shaped white-sand beaches, palm trees, lighthouse (Kovalam) and dramatic cliffs (Varkala), are a vision (p919)

Goa Everything they say about the beaches is true. Even when overrun with travellers, they're still lovely somehow. Vagator and Palolem are two of the prettiest, as is Gokarna, just nearby in Karnataka (p795)

East Coast Puri, in Odisha, and Visakhapatnam, in Andhra Pradesh, are more fun than precious: think esplanades, balloon-wallahs and extended families on holiday kicking back and eating candy floss (p594 and p911)

Mumbai Beaches? In Bombay? We say yes. Hit Girguam Chowpatty, eat strange and exciting local delicacies, people-watch, and see how hot-pink the sunset can get (p727)

» Cruising the backwaters (p940) near Alappuzha (Alleppey), Kerala

Hill Stations

India is blessed with lots of warm sunshine and lots of hills to escape from it. Locals – and especially royalty and colonials – have fled to nearby hills for ages, laying the foundations for today's hill-station resort culture.

Shimla The British, Shimla's founders, moved their capital here every summer. Today it's a sweet mix of forest trails and city bazaars, colonial-era architecture and rhododendrons (p282)

Tamil Nadu The Tamil hill stations of the Western Ghats are full of lush, misty pine forests, little tea houses, cardamom plantations and British touches (p1044)

Uttarakhand Mussoorie has Raj-era architecture, Himalayan views and walking trails galore; Nainital has those too, plus a gigantic volcanic lake at the centre of town (p408)

Matheran A popular weekend retreat for Mumbaikars, Matheran is not only scenic and car-free but it has a narrow-gauge toy train plying the 21km to the main road (p780)

Boat Tours

India has such a diverse collection of waterways that the cruising possibilities are endless. From canoes to bamboo rafts and pedal boats to steamships, there are lots of ways to experience the aquatic life, Indian style.

Kerala Kerala's all about the water: days of languorous drifting on the backwaters around Alappuzha (Alleppey), canoe tours from Kollam and bamboo-raft tours in Periyar Wildlife Sanctuary (p919)

Gujarat Coral reef cruises leave at high tide in Marine National Park. Octopuses, corals, sea horses, anemones and puffer fish are just a few of the creatures floating around (p709)

Uttar Pradesh Dawn tours of the ghats at Varanasi and sacred river cruises in Chitrakut, Mathura and Allahabad are a peaceful way to navigate Uttar Pradesh's chaotic holiness (p345)

Assam Four- to 10-night steam-boat cruises are offered along the mighty Brahmaputra River, as it meanders through the Northeast on its way from Tibet to Bangladesh (p550)

Traveller Enclaves

Sometimes you don't want to be out exploring exciting sights and challenging yourself. Sometimes you just want to chill with other travellers: find travel partners, exchange stories, talk about strange bowel events. There are places for that.

Hampi The stunning beauty of Hampi's landscape and architecture makes everyone want to stay for a while, which has led to a well-developed traveller community (p876)

Arambol Goa is one big traveller enclave, but Arambol may be its epicentre. Lots of shops and services combine in a gorgeous beach and cheap sleeps; no wonder we all end up there sooner or later (p824)

Yoga Centres Those with an eye towards well-being will feel right at home in Rishikesh, Mysore or Pune, which all have major international yoga centres – and concomitant hang-outs (p417, p852 and p783)

Paharganj It's got faults for sure, but skanky Paharganj couldn't be more convenient or better suited to making friends (p83)

If you like... Motorcycling
The mountain pass between Manali and Ladakh or Spiti may be the most spectacular motorcycle ride of your life. (p311)

If you like... Cycling
Go for a peaceful roll around the ruins of Bidar Fort and Bahmani tombs. (p889)

Arts & Crafts

Practically every little town, village and, in some cases, family here has its own tradition of Tantric painting, silk weaving, camel-hide decorating, mirrored embroidering, 24-carat-gold jewellery design, silver-inlaid gunmetal bangle-making, or other art you won't find anywhere else.

Jewellery Indians like bling – always have – and silver's an old favourite. Odisha's *tarakasi*, a kind of filigree work, is stunning, while Karnataka's *bidri* is made with blackened metal

Fabric The number of textile traditions here is astounding. Gujarati and Rajasthani villages specialise in embroidery with tiny mirrors – like jewellery for your clothes (p669 and p104)

Painting Folk paintings in the Bihari style known as Mithila (or Madhubani) colourfully depict village scenes. The style is ancient but looks surprisingly contemporary (p506)

Mountains

India has several beautiful mountain ranges that would be knockouts anywhere else. But here, there's really only one range that matters – the Himalaya – and the only question is how to approach it.

Ladakh The trekking and the views are excellent in Ladakh, whose name means 'land of high passes' and whose landscape is usually described as resembling the moon (p243)

Lahaul & Spiti Green Lahaul and dryer, more rugged Spiti are separated from the rest of Himachal Pradesh by seasonal mountain passes. Himalaya peaks are all around, as are monasteries stacked in piles along the cliffs (p336)

Sikkim Khangchendzonga, the world's third-highest mountain and Sikkim's big attraction, is the hub around which all travel here seems to revolve. Early-morning views from Pelling or from treks to Goecha La and Dzongri are the way to do it (p526)

Wildlife Safaris

India has tigers and leopards, and they do come out sometimes, but you'll definitely see elephants, antelope, bison, one-horned rhinos and deer if you play your cards right. Trips are by jeep or elephant.

Madhya Pradesh & Chhattisgarh This is tiger country, and tiger-spotting elephant and jeep safaris are offered in several national parks (p610)

Assam Pobitora National Park is the world's rhinoceros capital. Seeing them involves going by boat to the elephant station followed by an hour's ride on a lumbering elephant (p553)

Kerala The prettiest animal reserve in one of India's prettiest states, Wayanad Wildlife Sanctuary has jeep safaris into the 345-sq-km park, one of the few places where you have a good chance of spotting wild elephants (p972)

Gujarat The only wild Asiatic lions – along with various other animals and 300 species of birds – live in the Sasan Gir Wildlife Sanctuary, which offers jeep safaris (p699)

month by month

Top Events

1 **Carnival,** January or February

2 **Trekking,** May–June and September–October

3 **Ganesh Chaturthi,** August or September

4 **Navratri** and **Dussehra,** September or October

5 **Diwali,** October or November

Many festivals follow the Indian lunar calendar (a complex system based on astrology) or the Islamic calendar (which falls about 11 days earlier each year; 12 days earlier in leap years), and therefore change annually relative to the Gregorian calendar. Contact local tourist offices for exact festival dates, as many are variable.

January

Post-monsoon cool lingers throughout the country, with downright cold in the mountains. Pleasant weather and several festivals make it a popular time to travel (book ahead!), while Delhi hosts big Republic Day celebrations.

 Free India
Republic Day commemorates the founding of the Republic of India on 26 January 1950; the biggest celebrations are in Delhi, which holds a huge military parade along Rajpath, and the Beating of the Retreat ceremony three days later.

 Kite Festival
Sankranti, the Hindu festival marking the sun's passage into Capricorn, is celebrated in many ways across India – from banana-giving to dips in the Ganges to cockfights. But it's the mass kite-flying in Gujarat, Andhra Pradesh, Uttar Pradesh and Maharashtra that steal the show.

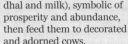 **Southern Harvest**
The Tamil festival of Pongal, equivalent to Sankranti, marks the end of the harvest season. Families in the south prepare pots of *pongal* (a mixture of rice, sugar, dhal and milk), symbolic of prosperity and abundance, then feed them to decorated and adorned cows.

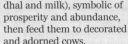 **Celebrating Saraswati**
On Vasant Panchami, Hindus dress in yellow and place books, musical instruments and other educational objects in front of idols of Saraswati, the goddess of learning, to receive her blessing. As the holiday follows the Indian lunar calendar, it may fall in February.

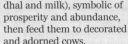 **Pilgrimage, Size: Extra-Large**
There are several versions of the huge Hindu pilgrimage, Kumbh Mela, held every few years, but all involve mass devotion – mass as in tens of millions of people. The next group dip in the Ganges is in Allahabad in January/February 2013.

February

The weather is comfortable in most nonmountainous areas, with summer heat starting to percolate, especially in the south (up to Maharashtra and West Bengal). It's still peak travel season; sunbathing and skiing are still on.

 The Prophet Mohammed's Birthday
The Islamic festival of Eid-Milad-un-Nabi celebrates the birth of the Prophet Mohammed with prayers and processions, especially in Jammu & Kashmir. It falls in the third month of the Islamic Calendar: around 4 February (2012), 24 January (2013) and 13 January (2014).

 Tibetan New Year
Losar is celebrated by Tantric Buddhists all over India –

particularly in Himachal Pradesh, Sikkim, Ladakh and Zanskar – for 15 days, with the most important festivities during the first three. Losar is usually in February or March, though dates can vary between regions.

🏃 Skiing the Northern Slopes

Jammu & Kashmir (when peaceful), Himachal Pradesh and Uttarakhand have some fine skiing and snowboarding opportunities for all levels (at some of the ski world's lowest costs). Snow season tends to be January to March, with February a safe bet.

✨ Shivaratri

This day of Hindu fasting recalls the *tandava* (cosmic victory dance) of Lord Shiva. Temple processions are followed by the chanting of mantras and anointing of linga (phallic images of Shiva). Shivaratri can also fall in March.

✨ Carnival in Goa

The four-day party kicking off Lent is particularly big in Goa. Sabado Gordo, Fat Saturday, starts it off with parades of elaborate floats and costumed dancers and the revelry continues with street parties, concerts and general merrymaking.

March

The last month of the main travel season, March is full-on hot in most of the country, with rains starting in the northeast. Wildlife is easier to spot as animals come out to search for water, and Holi lends a festive air.

✨ Holi

One of North India's most ecstatic festivals; Hindus celebrate the beginning of spring according to the lunar calendar, in either February or March, by throwing coloured water and *gulal* (powder) at anyone within range. On the night before Holi, bonfires symbolise the demise of the evil demoness Holika.

🏃 Wildlife-Watching

When the weather warms up, water sources dry out and animals have to venture into the open to find refreshment – your chance to spot elephants, deer and, if you're lucky, tigers and leopards. See p1146 and visit www.sanctuaryasia.com for detailed info.

✨ Rama's Birthday

During Ramanavami, which lasts anywhere from one to nine days, Hindus celebrate the birth of Rama with processions, music, fasting and feasting, readings and enactments of scenes from the Ramayana and, at some temples, ceremonial weddings of Rama and Sita idols.

April

The heat has officially arrived in most places, which means you can get great deals and avoid tourist crowds. The northeast, meanwhile, is wet, but it's peak time for visiting Sikkim and upland West Bengal.

✨ Easter

The Christian holiday marking the Crucifixion and Resurrection of Jesus Christ is celebrated simply in Christian communities with prayer and good food. It's nowhere near as boisterous as Carnival, earlier in the year, but good vibes abound. Easter may also be in March.

✨ Mahavir's Birthday

Mahavir Jayanti commemorates the birth of Jainism's 24th and most important *tirthankar* (teacher and enlightened being). Temples are decorated and visited, Mahavir statues are given ritual baths, processions are held and offerings are given to the poor. The festival can also fall in March.

May

In most of the country it's hot. Really hot. Festivals slow down as the humidity builds up in anticipation of the rain. Hill stations are hopping, though, and in the mountains, it's premonsoon trekking season.

✨ Buddha's Birthday

Commemorating the Buddha's birth, nirvana (enlightenment) and parinirvana (total liberation from the cycle of existence, or passing away), Buddha Jayanti is quiet but moving: devotees dress simply, eat vegetarian food, listen to dharma talks and visit monasteries or temples.

🏃 Northern Trekking

May and June, the months preceding the rains in the northern mountains, are surprisingly good times for trekking, with sunshine and temperate weather. Consider Himachal Pradesh, Jammu & Kashmir and Uttarakhand; see p33 for more info.

Mango Madness

Mangoes are indigenous to India, which might be why they're so ridiculously good here (seriously, it's ridiculous). The season starts in March, but in May the fruit is sweet, juicy and everywhere. A hundred varieties grow here, but the Alphonso is known as 'king'.

June

June's not a popular travel month in India, unless you're trekking up north. The rainy season, or premonsoon extreme heat, have started just about everywhere else.

Odisha's Festival of Chariots

During Rath Yatra (Car Festival), effigies of Lord Jagannath (Vishnu incarnated as lord of the world) and his siblings Balarama and Subhadra are carried through towns on massive chariots, most famously in Puri, Odisha (Orissa; p585). Millions turn out to see them.

July

Now it's really raining almost everywhere, with many remote roads being washed out. Consider visiting Ladakh, where the weather's surprisingly fine, or do a rainy-season meditation retreat, an ancient Indian tradition.

Snake Festival

The Hindu festival Naag Panchami is dedicated to Ananta, the serpent upon whose coils Vishnu rested between universes. Women return to their family homes and fast, while serpents are venerated as totems against flooding and other evils. Falls in July or August.

Brothers & Sisters

On Raksha Bandhan (Narial Purnima), girls fix amulets known as *rakhis* to the wrists of brothers and close male friends to protect them in the coming year. Brothers reciprocate with gifts and promises to take care of their sisters.

Ramadan (Ramazan)

Thirty days of dawn-to-dusk fasting mark the ninth month of the Islamic calendar. Muslims traditionally turn their attention to God, with a focus on prayer and purification. Ramadan begins around 20 July (2012), 9 July (2013) and 28 June (2014).

August

It's still high monsoon season, but it's prime time in Ladakh. Some folks swear by visiting tropical areas, like Kerala or Goa, at this time of year: the jungles are lush, green and glistening in the rain.

Independence Day

This public holiday on 15 August marks the anniversary of India's independence from Britain in 1947. Celebrations are a countrywide expression of patriotism,

with flag-hoisting ceremonies (the biggest one is in Delhi), parades and patriotic cultural programs.

Celebrating the Buddha's Teaching

Drupka Teshi commemorates Siddhartha Gautama's first teaching, in which he explained the Four Noble Truths to disciples in Sarnath. Celebrations are big in Sikkim, with prayers in Gangtok's Deer Park and a yak race. The festival may also fall in July.

Krishna's Birthday

Janmastami celebrations can last a week in Krishna's birthplace, Mathura (p368); elsewhere the festivities range from fasting to *puja* (prayers) and offering sweets, to drawing elaborate *rangoli* (rice-paste designs) outside the home. Janmastami is sometimes in July.

Parsi New Year

Parsis celebrate Pateti, the Zoroastrian new year, especially in Mumbai. Houses are cleaned and decorated with flowers and *rangoli,* the family dresses up and eats special fish dishes and sweets, and offerings are made at the Fire Temple.

Eid al-Fitr

Muslims celebrate the end of Ramadan with three days of festivities, beginning 30 days after the start of the fast. Prayers, shopping, gift-giving and, for women and girls, *mehndi* (henna designs) may all be part of the celebrations.

September

The rain begins to ease up (with temperatures still relatively high), with places like Rajasthan all but finished with the monsoon. The second trekking season begins midmonth in the Himalaya and runs through October.

Ganesh's Birthday

Hindus celebrate Ganesh Chaturthi, the birth of the elephant-headed god, with verve, particularly in Mumbai. Clay idols of Ganesh are paraded through the streets before being ceremonially immersed in rivers, tanks (reservoirs) or the sea. Ganesh Chaturthi may also be in August.

October

Some showers aside, this is when India starts to get its travel mojo on. October, aka shoulder season, brings festivals, mostly good weather with reasonably comfy temperatures, and lots of post-rain greenery and lushness.

Gandhi's Birthday

The national holiday of Gandhi Jayanti is a solemn celebration of Mohandas Gandhi's birth, on 2 October, with prayer meetings at his cremation site in Delhi (Raj Ghat; p67). Schools and businesses close for the day.

Water, Water Everywhere

Water bodies are full up after the rains, making for spectacularly gushing white-water falls that will slow to a trickle in the coming months. This is also the season for rafting in some areas; visit www.india rafting.com.

Durga Puja

The conquest of good over evil, exemplified by the goddess Durga's victory over buffalo-headed demon Mahishasura. Celebrations occur around the time of Dussehra, particularly in Kolkata (p457), where thousands of images of the goddess are displayed then ritually immersed in rivers and water tanks.

Navratri

This Hindu 'Festival of Nine Nights' leading up to Dussehra celebrates the goddess Durga in all her incarnations. Special dances are performed, and the goddesses Lakshmi and Saraswati are also celebrated. Festivities are particularly vibrant in Gujarat and Maharashtra. Navratri sometimes falls in September.

Dussehra

Colourful Dussehra celebrates the victory of the Hindu god Rama over the demon-king Ravana and the triumph of good over evil. Dussehra is big in Kullu (p300), where effigies of Ravana are ritually burned, and Mysore (p852), which hosts one of India's grandest parades.

Festival of Lights

In the lunar month of Kartika, in October or November, Hindus celebrate Diwali (Deepavali) for five days, giving gifts, lighting fireworks, and burning butter and oil lamps (or hanging lanterns) to lead Lord Rama home from exile. One of India's prettiest festivals.

Eid al-Adha

Muslims commemorate Ibrahim's readiness to sacrifice his son to God by slaughtering a goat or sheep and sharing it with family, the community and the poor. It will be held around 26 October in 2012, 15 October in 2013 and 4 October in 2014.

November

The climate is blissful in most places, but the anomalous southern monsoon is sweeping Tamil Nadu and some of Kerala. It's a good time to be anywhere low altitude, notwithstanding, as the temperatures are just right.

Guru Nanak's Birthday

Nanak Jayanti, birthday of Guru Nanak, founder of Sikhism, is celebrated with prayer readings, *kirtan* (Sikh devotional singing) and processions for three days, especially in Punjab and Haryana. The festival may also be held on 14 April, thought to be Nanak's actual 1469 birth date.

Muharram

During this month of grieving and remembrance, Shiite Muslims commemorate the martyrdom of the Prophet Mohammed's grandson Imam, an event known as Ashura, with beautiful processions. It begins around 15 November (2012), 4 November (2013) and 25 October (2014).

Beach the Crowds

December and January really have the best beach weather, but if you like a little space with your sea, go in November or February, when the cocohuts have been built, the rains are over and it's sunny but not too hot.

December

December is peak tourist season for a reason: the weather's glorious (except for the chilly mountains), the humidity's low, the mood is festive and the beach is sublime.

Weddings

Marriage season peaks in December, and you may see a *baraat* (bridegroom's procession), replete with white horse and fireworks, on your travels in the north. Across the country, loud music and spectacular parties are the way they roll, with brides in *mehndi* and pure gold.

Birding

Many of India's 1000-plus bird species (including exhibitionists like pink flamingos) perform their winter migration from November to January or February, and excellent birdwatching spots are peppered across the country; www.birding.in is an excellent resource.

Camel Treks in Rajasthan

The cool winter (November to February) is the time to mount a camel and ride through the Rajasthani sands. See the Thar Desert from a whole new perspective: observe gazelles, cook dinner over an open fire and camp out in the dunes.

Christmas Day

Christians celebrate the birth of Jesus Christ on 25 December. The festivities are especially big in Goa and Kerala, with musical events, elaborate decorations and special Masses, while Mumbai's Catholic neighbourhoods become festivals of lights.

itineraries

Whether you've got six days or 60, these itineraries provide a starting point for the trip of a lifetime. Want more inspiration? Head online to lonelyplanet. com/thorntree to chat with other travellers.

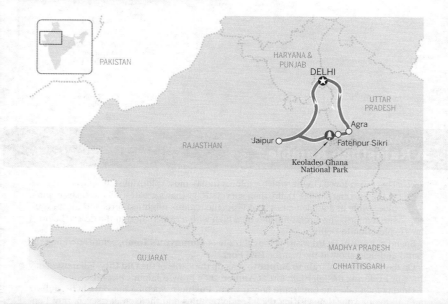

One Week
The Golden Triangle

One route is so well loved it even has a name: the Golden Triangle. This classic Delhi–Agra–Jaipur trip can be squeezed into a single week.

Spend a day or two in **Delhi** finding your feet and seeing the big-draw sights, such as the magnificent Mughal **Red Fort** and **Jama Masjid**, India's largest mosque. Then catch a convenient train to **Agra** to spend a day being awed by the world's most extravagant monument to love, the **Taj Mahal**, and exploring the mighty **Agra Fort**. Only an hour away is **Fatehpur Sikri**, a beautiful Mughal city dating from the apogee of Mughal power. It is amazingly well preserved and deserves a full day of exploring.

If you have time, take a rural respite at **Keoladeo Ghana National Park**, one of the world's foremost bird reserves. Having relaxed at this beautiful and rewarding place, you can then take a train to **Jaipur**. Spend a couple of days in and around Rajasthan's hectic, dusky-pink capital, seeing the **City Palace** and **Amber Fort**, and stocking up on blue pottery, dazzling jewellery and Rajasthani puppets before heading back to Delhi.

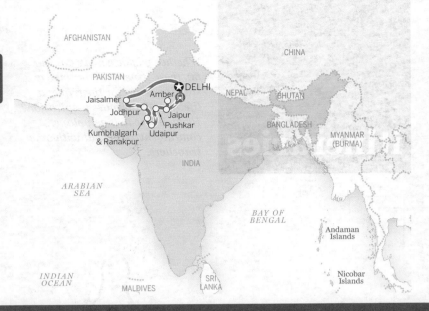

Two Weeks
A Rajasthan Ramble

This much-loved circuit, which explores India's most colourful state, starts and ends in the bustling capital, Delhi, then surveys Rajasthan's greatest hits: it takes in pink, blue, white and golden cities, and visits the region's mightiest forts and most exquisite temples. The circuit finishes on a high with a camel safari in the desert, before a day's exploration in Delhi.

Spend day one in **Delhi**, visiting the calm site of **Humayun's Tomb**, before attending the sound-and-light show at the historic **Red Fort**.

On day two, take the train to **Jaipur** to soak up the sights of the **Old City**. Fill most of day three by exploring the fairy-tale fort at **Amber**, then browse Jaipur's **bazaars**.

On day four, take the bus to the holy town of **Pushkar**. Spend a few days here, chilling out and taking your time visiting the lakeside **temples** and then, on day seven, travel onward to graceful **Udaipur**. Again, you can relax and sightsee for a couple of days. Make time for an extravagant meal at the palace on the **lake**.

Next, on day nine, take a taxi and visit **Kumbhalgarh** and the temple at **Ranakpur** en route to the Blue City, **Jodhpur**. In Jodhpur you can admire the pastel-painted houses and magnificent **Mehrangarh Fort**

On day 11, take the bus or train through the desert to the ancient fortress of **Jaisalmer** to relive your *Arabian Nights* fantasies on a **camel safari** in the dunes. Finally, on day 13, make your way back to Delhi, where you can visit the **Jama Masjid**, dive into the surrounding **bazaars** and finish off with some last-minute **shopping**.

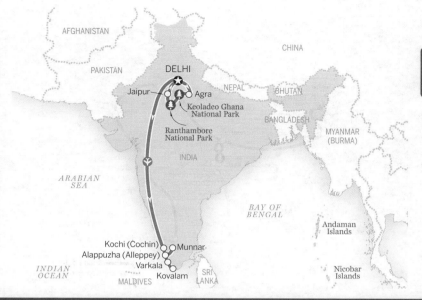

A Taste Of North & South

For a smattering of the north, and a sprinkling of the south, this trip is ideal. Wallow in the cultural and artistic wealth of Delhi, Agra and Rajasthan before flying south for some serene relaxation, including boating in tranquil backwaters, yoga, massage and the beach.

Start by visiting the sights of **Delhi**, such as the **Red Fort**, **Qutb Minar** and **Humayun's Tomb**, then head to **Agra** and the **Taj Mahal**, **Agra Fort** and **Fatehpur Sikri**. Next, if you have time, stop at **Keoladeo Ghana National Park** to see the rich birdlife, and then **Ranthambore National Park** to spot tigers and explore the wild jungle setting, before heading to the confounding Pink City of **Jaipur**. Visit **Amber Fort**, browse the amazing **bazaars** of Jaipur and peek from behind the shutters at the **Hawa Mahal** before returning to Delhi to start the southern part of your trip.

Prepare to relax: fly south to **Kochi** (Cochin), where you can stay in a gorgeous ex-colonial mansion in evocative Fort Cochin, catch a **Kathakali performance**, and spend a couple of nights exploring this exotic spice port with its historic **synagogue**, **Chinese fishing nets**, and delicious restaurants, as well as the remarkable **Kerala Folklore Museum**. The next delight is launching off into the **backwaters of Kerala**. The main launch point is from **Alappuzha** (Alleppey), from where you can take a slow cruise in a houseboat, watching life on the water, kicking back and sleeping under the stars. If you have time, you could head for the hills, staying in a remote hideaway, trekking around the tea plantations, visiting spice gardens and discovering the breathtaking views around **Munnar**. Next stop, the beach: try the less-visited sands around **Varkala**, with its backpacker vibe, dramatic sea-cliffs and long sandy beaches, or the more mainstream town of **Kovalam**. To experience Zen-like calm before taking your return flight from Kochi, do yoga and meditation at a local ashram and revel in **Ayurvedic treatments** such as synchronised massage.

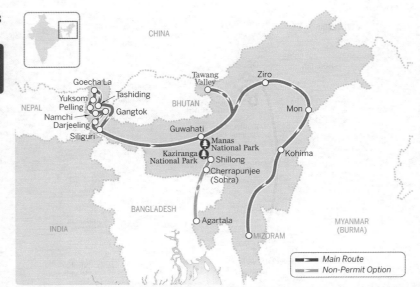

One Month
Sikkim & The Northeast States

Surprisingly few people explore mountainous Sikkim and the tribal heartland of India's Northeast States. You have the chance to get even further from the tourist circuit in tribal Nagaland, Mizoram and Arunachal Pradesh, providing you can obtain the required permits. You will need to plan your trip in advance and have a clear idea of your schedule. Also make sure you are aware of the security risks.

Obtain a Sikkim permit in **Siliguri** or in **Darjeeling**, where you can sample India's most famous **teas** while enjoying the glories of the classic Indian hill station. Then head to **Gangtok**, the Sikkimese capital, and visit the surrounding **Buddhist monasteries**, situated along tortuous lanes that cut through mountainous forested landscape.

Veer to **Namchi** to see the giant statues of Shiva and Padmasambhava perched on their hilltops, and to **Pelling**, to see the inspiring views of the white-peaked **Khangchendzonga** and the beautiful **Pemayangtse Gompa**, ringed by gardens and monks' cottages. Take the week- or 10-day-long trek from **Yuksom** to **Goecha La**, a 4940m pass with incredible views. Exit Sikkim via **Tashiding**, with yet more wonderful views and another beautifully set gompa, before returning to Siliguri for the journey east to Assam.

In **Guwahati**, the Assamese capital, arrange tours and permits for the Northeast States: the remote areas of Arunachal Pradesh, Nagaland, Mizoram and Manipur. If you can't get a permit, try this loop: from Guwahati, head to **Manas** and **Kaziranga National Parks** to spot rare wildlife. Detour to sleepy **Shillong**, and the waterfalls and incredible living root bridges of **Cherrapunjee** (Sohra). From **Agartala**, capital of Tripura, head by air or land to Bangladesh.

With the right permits, head from Guwahati to Arunachal Pradesh for the stunning Buddhist monastery in the **Tawang Valley**, or the tribal villages near **Ziro**, where the elder Apatani women have dramatic facial tattoos and nose plugs. A Nagaland permit opens up fascinating tribal villages around **Mon**, rugged countryside dotted by traditional longhouses and remote settlements, and the capital **Kohima**. Manipur permits are rarely granted, but there's a fair chance of eyeing Mizo culture in **Mizoram**.

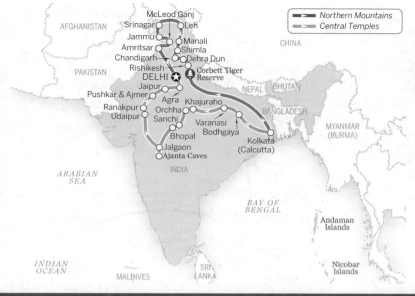

Two/Three Weeks
Central Temples

> Discover some of India's most spiritual places in this trip around Bihar, Madhya Pradesh, Rajasthan and Uttar Pradesh.

Start your trip in the cultured yet chaotic city of **Kolkata**, and then travel west to **Bodhgaya**, the birthplace of Buddhism and where Buddha attained enlightenment. Roll across the plains to the sacred city of **Varanasi**, one of India's holiest places, then to **Khajuraho**, where temples drip with erotic carvings.

Head southwest through the tranquil village of **Orchha**, with its imposing 17th-century palaces, to **Sanchi**, where Emperor Ashoka embraced Buddhism. In **Bhopal** catch the train to **Jalgaon**, a jumping-off point for the wonderful **Ajanta Caves**.

You could then head upwards through Rajasthan, stopping in whimsical **Udaipur**, with its lakes and palaces, before visiting the extraordinary Jain temples of **Ranakpur**. Next stop is the holy pilgrimage town of **Pushkar**, then a trip to **Dargah** at nearby **Ajmer**, one of India's most holy Islamic sites. After this you can make your way to **Jaipur**, from where you can catch the train to Agra's **Taj Mahal**. From here it's a short trip to **Delhi** for some last-minute sightseeing and shopping before flying home.

Two Weeks
Northern Mountains

> This northern exploration takes in some of India's most sumptuous views. It starts in Kolkata (Calcutta), draws a snaking line through some of the highlights of West Bengal, Uttar Pradesh, Himachal Pradesh, Ladakh, Kashmir and Punjab, and finishes up in Delhi. Time your schedule so that the last leg through Ladakh falls between July and October, when the mountain passes are open.

Pass a few days enjoying the atmosphere and food in **Kolkata**, the busy and frenetic cultural metropolis that is home to the **Victoria Memorial**. Next, dash northwest to spot tigers in **Corbett Tiger Reserve** and practise yoga in India's New Age capital, **Rishikesh**. Connect through **Dehra Dun** and **Chandigarh** to **Shimla**, India's premier hill station, where you can relax or trek into the hills.

Bus it to **Manali** for some adrenalin-charged activities, then ride the mountain bus to Buddhist city **Leh**. If the political situation allows, head to **Srinagar** in Kashmir, then through **Jammu** to **McLeod Ganj**, home of the Dalai Lama and India's centre of Tibetan Buddhism.

It's a relatively short trip southwest to **Amritsar**, with its shimmering **Golden Temple** before one last train ride to Delhi.

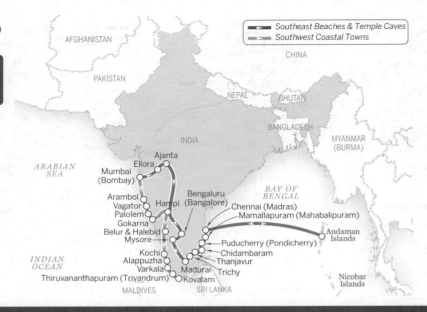

Southeast Beaches & Temple Caves
Southwest Coastal Towns

Two Weeks
Southwest Coastal Towns

> This laid-back trip meanders along some of India's finest beaches and most charismatic southwest towns, and also offers some stunning cultural and temple stops.

Start at Mumbai's **Chowpatty Beach** with a plate of *bhelpuri* (crisp fried thin rounds of dough) while looking out over the Arabian Sea. Cruise to the stunning rock-cut temples on **Elephanta Island**, then travel south by train to beach-blessed **Goa**. Enjoy the best of the sand at **Arambol**, **Vagator** and **Palolem**, then continue along the coast to the sacred town of **Gokarna**. Next, veer inland to the ruined Vijayanagar temples at **Hampi** and the Hoysala temples of **Belur** and **Halebid**.

Head further south, along the coast, to the enigmatic ex-colonial melting pot **Kochi** for a **Kathakali performance** and to feel the palpable history of this ancient, laid-back port. Cruise Kerala's languorous backwaters from **Alappuzha** via canoe or houseboat, before dipping your toes in the warm waters around beach resorts **Varkala** or **Kovalam**, and visiting off-the-track museums at **Thiruvananthapuram** (Trivandrum) before flying out.

Two/Three Weeks
Southeast Beaches & Caves

> Mumbai is the borderline between north and south, and the easiest starting point for exploring India's steamy southern tip. Time your trip to avoid the monsoon – the sunniest skies are from October to February.

Kick off shopping, eating and drinking in cosmopolitan **Mumbai** before heading inland to **Ellora** and **Ajanta** to marvel at Maharashtra's finest cave art.

Travel inland to wonderful **Hampi**, with its temple ruins and giant boulders. Rub shoulders with yuppies in the bars of **Bengaluru** (Bangalore), smell the incense in spicy **Mysore** with its extravagant **Maharaja's Palace**, and feast on a banana-leaf **thali**. Zoom south to the awesome Sri Meenakshi Temple in **Madurai**, then return north through the temple towns of **Trichy**, **Thanjavur** and **Chidambaram**.

Next, head for the coast and the decadent grace of hectic, French-flavoured **Puducherry** (Pondicherry). For desert-island beach splendour, visit the sun-soaked **Andaman Islands**. Stop off at the ruins of **Mamallapuram** (Mahabalipuram) by sunset, then dine in Tamil Nadu's busy capital, **Chennai** (Madras), before heading home.

Booking Trains

Air-Conditioned 1st Class (1AC)

The most expensive class of train travel; two- or four-berth compartments with locking doors and meals included.

Air-Conditioned 2-Tier (2AC)

Two-tier berths arranged in groups of four and two in an open-plan carriage. The bunks convert to seats by day and there are curtains for some semblance of privacy.

Air-Conditioned 3-Tier (3AC)

Three-tier berths arranged in groups of six in an open-plan carriage; no curtains.

AC Executive Chair

Comfortable, reclining chairs and plenty of space; usually found on Shatabdi express trains.

AC Chair

Similar to the Executive Chair carriage but with less fancy seating.

Sleeper Class

Open plan carriages with three-tier bunks and no AC; the open windows afford great views.

Unreserved 2nd Class

Wooden or plastic seats and a lot of people – but cheap!

Travelling on an Indian train is a reason to travel all by itself. India's rail network is one of the world's most extensive and the prices are very reasonable. Bookings open 90 days before departure and seats fill up quickly – an estimated 17 to 20 million people travel by train in India *every day*. Trains and seats come in a variety of classes and not all classes are available on every train. New to the rails are eight women-only trains, which service New Delhi, Mumbai (Bombay), Chennai (Madras) and Kolkata (Calcutta). Express and mail trains usually have general (2nd class) compartments with unreserved seating and more comfortable compartments that you can reserve.

Shatabdi express trains are same-day services with seating only; Rajdhani express trains are long-distance overnight services between Delhi and state capitals with a choice of 1AC, 2AC, 3AC and 2nd class. In all classes, a padlock and a length of chain are useful for securing your luggage to the baggage racks; the higher sleeper categories provide bedding, but it doesn't hurt to bring your own. Some cities also have suburban train networks, but these are very crowded during peak hours.

So if you have a route mapped out and dates locked in, you can book your train tickets before you even arrive in the country. Here's the low-down on how to do it.

Booking Tickets

Booking online is the easiest way to buy train tickets. The railway reservation system is open from 1.30am to 11.30pm every day

TRAIN PASSES

The IndRail Pass permits unlimited rail travel for the period of its validity, but it offers limited savings and you must still make reservations. Passes are available for one to 90 days of travel. The easiest way to book these is through the IndRail pass agency in your home country; it can also book any necessary train reservations for you. Overseas travel agencies and station ticket offices in major Indian cities also sell the pass – click on the Information/International Tourist link on www.indianrail.gov.in for further details, including prices. There's no refund for either lost or partially used tickets.

(IST) so keep this in mind when trying to book online, particularly if you are abroad. The following websites all issue e-tickets, which are valid for train travel. You may have to show your passport as ID along with the printout of your booking reference when you are on the train. The following websites all accept international credit cards.

Indian Railway Catering and Tourism Corporation Limited (www.irctc.co.in) Set up by the Ministry of Railways, here you can book regular trains as well as tourist trains such as the *Deccan Odyssey*. The site can often be overloaded.

Cleartrip (www.cleartrip.com) An excellent, easy-to-use and reliable website that charges a small fee (₹20) on top of the regular ticket price.

Make My Trip (www.makemytrip.com) Similar to Cleartrip, with very good reports from travellers.

Yatra (www.yatra.com) This travel booking website has an Indian version (www.yatra.in) and a UK site (www.yatra.com/UK/index.html).

Reservations

You must make a reservation for all chair-car, sleeper, 1AC, 2AC and 3AC carriages. No reservations are required for general (2nd class) compartments. Bookings are strongly recommended for all overnight journeys and if you plan on travelling during Indian holidays or festivals. For more information on trains, tickets and fares, see p1185.

RAILWAY RAZZLE DAZZLE

India offers an enticing choice of luxurious train journeys for tourists. Fares usually include accommodation on board, tours, admission fees and all or most meals, and there are normally child concessions – enquire when booking.

» **Palace on Wheels** (www.palaceonwheels.net) Operates week-long tours of Rajasthan, departing from Delhi. Running from August to April, the total fare per person is US$4830/3610/3250 for single/double/triple cabins, except for August when it's US$3605/2708/2456. Book ahead as tickets can sell out 10 months in advance for peak periods.

» **Royal Rajasthan on Wheels** (www.royalrajasthanonwheels.com) Runs one-week trips from September to April starting and finishing in Delhi. The total fare per person is US$11,200 for a super deluxe suite and US$6370/9100 for single/twin occupancy of deluxe suites.

» **Deccan Odyssey** (www.deccan-odyssey-india.com) Offers seven nights covering the main tourist spots of Maharashtra and Goa. From October to March, fares per person per night start at US$650/500/425 for single/double/triple occupancy (US$500/390/315 in September and April).

» **Golden Chariot** (www.thegoldenchariot.co.in) Takes visitors through Karnataka in style. Two tour packages are available: Bengaluru (Bangalore)–Bengaluru (Monday to Monday) and Bengaluru–Goa (Monday to Sunday). Rates per person for the seven-night tour are US$4795/3465/2800 for single/double/triple occupancy.

» **Mahaparinirvan Express** (aka Buddhist Circuit Special; www.irctc.co.in) Running October to March, tours Buddhist sites over eight days, starting in Delhi. It costs US$150/125/105 in 1st/2nd/3rd class per person per night on a twin-share basis (single-occupancy hotel rooms can be arranged at an extra charge). For a private twin cabin, the First AC Coupe costs US$168 per person per night.

Trekking

Best Himalayan Treks

Jammu & Kashmir The high, dry and rugged ranges rising in Ladakh (p243) boast a bounty of unforgettable treks.

Himachal Pradesh Alpine bliss is attainable throughout the state, including on the trek from McLeod Ganj to Bharmour (p328).

Uttarakhand Under the gleaming white crown of Nanda Devi, India's highest peak, head to the Kumaon region for the Milam Glacier trek (p440).

Sikkim Gape at Khangchendzonga (8586m), the world's third-highest mountain, on the Goecha La trek (p548).

Other Best Treks

Cultural Immerse yourself in high mountain Buddhist life on the Homestay Trail (p342) in Himachal Pradesh's remote Spiti Valley.

Karnataka Explore the serene hills and forests of Kodagu (p866).

Kerala Check out tigers, elephants and boar in Periyar Wildlife Sanctuary (p945).

Least-Trekked Hike tough terrain in the isolated, northeast mountain state of Arunachal Pradesh (p564), where only an intrepid few venture.

Sacred In Uttarakhand, join Hindu pilgrims on treks to Kedarnath Temple (p426), hike with Sikhs up to Hem Kund or circumnavigate Kinner Kailash (6050m) in Himachal Pradesh's Kinnaur Valley (p343).

Tamil Nadu The hill station Ooty (p1052) is popular for relaxing forest hikes.

When To Go

With India's diverse variety of terrain and altitudes, there's no single time throughout the country that's best for trekking; seasonal conditions vary greatly depending on what region you're in. In the Himalaya the monsoon makes things tough (you're better off heading to Ladakh or Spiti) and winter trekking is not advisable – unless you want to tackle the frozen-river Chadar Route in Ladakh's Zanskar region (p241) and (p252).

Best Times

» **Mid-September–late October** Once the monsoons clear out, searing blue skies usually bless the Himalaya. While nights at high altitude may dip below freezing, days are usually sunny and warm. Facilities and services (and some roads) in many mountain regions close for winter in October or November, so if you hope to trek then, check in advance to see what will be open.

» **May–June** The two months before monsoon are also great for mountain trekking. Trails to some sacred sites, such as those on the Char Dham in Uttarakhand and Amarnath Cave in Kashmir (p231), can be packed with pilgrims. In the lowlands, this season can be ridiculously hot.

» **December–March** The most comfortable season to trek in South India.

Avoid

» **Mid-July–mid-September** Trekking during the monsoon ranges from uncomfortable to deadly. In the Himalaya there are landslides, and jungle treks can be forbiddingly muddy. Most days in the Himalaya, the peaks are obscured by thick clouds, greatly diminishing the rewards trekkers seek for their efforts. One major exception is Uttarakhand's famous Valley of Flowers National Park (p428), which draws most of its visitors during the rainy season, when its dazzling botanical carpet spreads most vibrantly across the valley floor.

Why Go?

India offers world-class trekking opportunities, particularly in the Himalaya, where staggering views of snow-clad peaks, traditional tribal villages, sacred Hindu sites, ancient Buddhist monasteries and blazing fields of wildflowers are just some of the features that make for extraordinary alpine experiences. Routes range in difficulty from easy half-day jaunts to strenuous multiweek expeditions.

The Low-down

» With a commercial trekking industry that's far less developed than in neighbouring Nepal, many places still feel wild and relatively unspoiled.

» Trekking lodges are only found on a handful of routes, so you often have to carry a tent, stove and sleeping bag, but you can usually hire porters to do the schlepping for you.

» If you opt to go with a trekking company, some gear will probably be supplied. Specify *everything* that's included before you sign up, and get it in writing if possible.

» Wherever you go, make sure you have any permits you may need. See On the Road chapters for region-specific permit information and recommended adventure outfitters.

Route Planning

» High-quality maps of the Indian Himalaya are difficult to find in-country. On the internet, you can buy or download topographical maps at various scales, which are good for planning and good enough for navigating (if you're experienced at reading them).

GETTING HIGH SAFELY

Throughout the Himalaya, plan in some extra days to acclimatise while en route to high-altitude destinations. Acute Mountain Sickness is a serious risk on trails over 3000m (see p1193). These mountains deserve your respect – don't try to trek beyond your physical or technical abilities.

PEAK BAGGING

Mountaineers need permission from the Indian Mountaineering Foundation (IMF; www.indmount. org) in Delhi to climb most peaks over 6000m. Expedition fees start at US$1000 and rise with the height of the peak and number of people on your team. Fortunately, some high summits don't require exorbitant climbing fees, particularly in Ladakh, Lahaul, Spiti and Sikkim. The four-day ascent of Stok Kangri (6120m) is one of the most popular treks in India, providing an affordable but rewarding taste of high-altitude mountaineering (p250).

» On popular pilgrims' trails, it's nearly impossible to get lost. On less travelled routes, tracks with no signage can split or vanish altogether, so hiring a local guide can be super-helpful.

» Lonely Planet's detailed *Trekking in the Indian Himalaya* is a great resource for planning and following trekking routes.

Packing

☐ Bring gear and clothing that's appropriate for the conditions you expect to encounter.

☐ On well-established trails heavy hiking boots are overkill, but on remote mountain tracks they can be lifesavers.

☐ First-aid and water-purification supplies are often essential.

☐ Raingear is a must, and warm layers are crucial for comfort at altitude.

☐ Remember sunscreen!

Trekking Ethics

» As anywhere, follow low-impact trekking protocols (you know the mantra – leave only footprints, take only photographs – see www.nols. edu/Int/principles.shtml for more details).

» In India, it's important to cook over stoves, since local people rely on limited fuelwood sources for their own sustenance.

» People live throughout the Indian Himalaya; even in remote spots, you may encounter a shepherd camp (beware of their dogs).

» Respect local cultural sensibilities by dressing modestly; asking permission before snapping photos; remembering that while local hospitality may be endless, the food supply might not be; and refraining from giving gifts to children.

Yoga, Spas & Spiritual Pursuits

Ashrams

India has hundreds of ashrams – places of communal living established around the philosophies of a guru (a spiritual guide or teacher). Programs usually involve discourse, yoga and/or meditation.

Ayurveda

Ayurveda is the ancient science of Indian herbal medicine and holistic healing, which uses natural treatments, massage and other therapies.

Buddhist Meditation

There are plenty of courses and retreats offering *vipassana* (mindfulness meditation) and Buddhist philosophy; some require a vow of silence and many also ban smoking, alcohol and sex.

Spa Treatments

Pampering opportunities abound in India; choices range from a simple massage to a full day of beautification (and relaxation) at luxurious health centres.

Yoga

Yoga's roots lay firmly in India and you'll find hundreds of schools to suit all levels.

Travellers with an interest in spirituality or alternative therapies will find an array of courses and treatments in India that strive to heal mind, body and spirit. Some offer spiritual enlightenment within five-star accommodation while others offer basic dwellings and require a vow of silence. Meditation, ayurveda and especially yoga are attracting an ever-increasing number of visitors. So whether you're seeking a guru or just a really good massage, India almost guarantees instant karma.

Ashrams

Many ashrams have made a name for themselves – both within India and abroad – thanks to their charismatic (and sometimes controversial) gurus. Some programs are more intensive than others and codes of conduct vary so make sure you're willing to abide by them before committing. Many people visit India specifically to spend time at an ashram – literally a 'place of striving' – for spiritual and personal enrichment. However, a little caution is required. Some ashrams tread a fine line between spiritual community and personality cult, and there have been reports of questionable happenings at ashrams, often of a sexual nature.

Choosing an ashram will depend on your spiritual leanings. All ashrams have a code of conduct, and visitors are usually required to adhere to strict rules, which may include a certain dress code, a daily regimen of yoga or meditation, and charitable work at social projects run by the ashram. Ashrams are generally run as charitable projects and a donation is appropriate to cover the expenses of your food, accommodation and the running costs of the ashram. Most ashrams accept new residents without advance notice, but call ahead to make sure.

Where To Go

For a gentle introduction into ashram life, try one of the numerous ashrams in Rishikesh (p420) or Haridwar (p414), which tend to be more foreigner-orientated and less austere. Alternatively, try one of the following recommendations:

Kerala

» **Matha Amrithanandamayi Mission** (p940) painted pink, this is famed for its female guru Amma, 'The Hugging Saint'.

Andhra Pradesh

» **Prasanthi Nilayam** (p918) was the ashram of the controversial but phenomenally popular guru Sri Sathya Sai Baba, who passed away in 2011.

Maharashtra

» Sevagram houses the **Brahmavidya Mandir Ashram** (p777), established by Gandhi's disciple Vinoba Bhave, and the **Sevagram Ashram** (p777), founded by Gandhi himself. In Pune there is the **Osho Meditation Resort** (p787), which runs on the teachings of its founder, Osho.

Tamil Nadu

» **Sri Aurobindo Ashram** (p1014), founded by the famous Sri Aurobindo, has branches around India. The rural **Isha Yoga Center** (Coimbatore; p1050) offers residential courses and retreats.

Ayurveda

Ayurvedic treatment aims to restore balance in the body through two main methods: *panchakarma* (internal purification) and herbal massage.

Where To Go

There are clinics, resorts and colleges across India where you can learn ayurvedic techniques or enjoy an ayurvedic massage. The following are just some recommendations; see the regional chapters for more details.

Goa

» Ayurvedic-style massage is offered in almost every beach town on a seasonally changing basis. The **Ayurvedic Natural Health Centre** (p814) in Saligao is a reputable school with professional courses, as well as short- and long-term treatments.

Gujarat

» Ayurvedic therapy and courses in yoga and naturopathy are conducted at the famous **Ayurvedic University** (p707). Courses last from six weeks to one year.

Karnataka

» The **Chiraayu Ayurvedic Health & Rejuvenation Centre** in Bengaluru (p842) is *the* place to head to for serious diagnosis and treatment, while the more upmarket **Soukya** runs excellent programs in ayurvedic therapy and yoga. In Mysore (p874), the **Indus Valley Ayurvedic Centre**, which derives its therapies from ancient scriptures and prescriptions, is just one of several well-being options. Gokarna (p874) is home to the fancy **SwaSwara** resort.

Kerala

» Most towns and villages in Kerala offer ayurvedic treatments. The **Eden Garden Retreat** in Varkala (p945) is popular and offers single treatments and packages. In Kollam (p936, the **Janakanthi Panchakarma Centre** has seven- to 21-day treatment packages as well as drop-in treatments. See also Kovalam (p936), Periya (p972) and Kochi (p955).

Buddhist Meditation

Whether you want an introduction to Buddhism or are seeking something more spiritual, there are numerous courses, classes and retreats on offer. Public teachings are given by the Dalai Lama and 17th Karmapa at certain times of year in McLeod Ganj – visit www.dalailama.com/page.60.htm for the schedule.

Where To Go

McLeod Ganj is the centre for Tibetan Buddhist teaching but there are other places you can study. See the Maharashtra (p763), Andhra Pradesh (p898), Gujarat (p713) and Tamil Nadu (p991) chapters for recommendations in addition to those listed following.

Himachal Pradesh

» In McLeod Ganj (p321) the **Library of Tibetan Works & Archives** offers Buddhist philosophy courses, while the **Vipassana Meditation Centre** runs strict 10-day retreats. The **Tushita Meditation Centre** runs introductory courses on Buddhist philosophy and meditation, as well as more advanced courses.

Jammu & Kashmir

» The **Mahabodhi International Meditation Centre** in Ladakh (p249) holds three- or 10-day courses in *vipassana* meditation.

Bihar

» There are several options in Bodhgaya (p517). **Tergar Monastery** is a good place to head for an introduction to Tibetan Buddhism, while the **Bodhgaya Vipassana Meditation Centre** runs intensive 10-day *vipassana* courses twice a month throughout the year. The **International Meditation Centre** offers more informal courses. A three-day commitment is preferred.

Mumbai

» One-, 10- and 20-day *vipassana* courses are offered at the impressive **Global Pagoda** (p731). Even longer courses (up to 60 days) are periodically offered for advanced students.

Spa Treatments

There are spas all over India, from ayurvedic hospitals to fancy health centres at five-star resorts (see regional chapters for top-end hotel recommendations). Be cautious of dodgy one-on-one massages by private (often unqualified) operators, particularly in tourist towns – seek recommendations from fellow travellers and trust your instincts.

Tibetan Buddhist areas have their own herbal-medicine tradition – *amchi* – based on a mixture of astrology and treatments with herbs from the Himalaya. Despite the arrival of Western medicine, *amchi* is still a popular form of treatment in parts of Ladakh and Himachal Pradesh; see p321 and p340.

Where To Go

This is just a sprinkling of recommended options.

Delhi

» Experience the full ayurvedic treatment at the **Lambency Spa** or the **Amatra Spa** (p77)

at the Ashok Hotel, where the who's who of Delhi goes to get pampered.

Madhya Pradesh & Chhattisgarh

» The **Jiva Spa** at Usha Kiran Palace (p616) offers massages, scrubs and wraps in beautiful surrounds. In Bhopal there's the excellent **Jehan Numa Palace Hotel** (p616), and in Orchha (p620) both the **Amar Mahal** and **Orchha Resort** offer good-quality ayurvedic massage treatments and hold yoga classes.

Mumbai

» Experience the pampering of pamperings at one of Mumbai's finest spas, the **Kaya Kalp**, located inside the ITC Maratha hotel (p740).

Uttarakhand

» In Haridwar, the **Haveli Hari Ganga** (p414) boasts an ayurvedic health spa and yoga classes in a spectacular setting on the Ganges.

Yoga

You can practise yoga almost anywhere in India. Some outfits are more reputable than others (especially in tourist towns). Seek recommendations from travellers and local tourist offices, and visit several to find one that suits your needs and ability. Many ashrams also offer yoga courses.

Where To Go

The following are just some of the numerous possibilities; for more options see the regional chapters, including Anjuna (p819), Arambol (p824) and Mandrem (p823) in Goa. Also see Vashisht (p313) and McLeod Ganj (p320) in Himachal Pradesh, and Rishikesh (p420) and Haridwar (p412) in Uttarakhand. In Rajasthan, you can practise yoga in Udaipur (p159), Pushkar (p140), and Jaipur (p113).

Karnataka

» World-renowned courses in *ashtanga,* hatha and Iyengar yoga and meditation are held in Mysore (p856). These centres require at least a month's commitment on your part. Register well in advance.

Kerala

» The **Sivandanda Yoga Vedanta Dhanwantari Ashram** (p927) is renowned for its hatha yoga course. Courses run for a minimum of two weeks, with the daily routine starting at 5.30am. Varkala (p945) and Kochi (p972) are also popular places for yoga.

Madhya Pradesh & Chhattisgarh

» Yogi Sudarshan Dwiveda (p629) is the most revered of a number of yogis in Khajuraho. In Orchha, **Amar Mahal** and **Orchha Resort** (p620) both run daily classes.

Maharashtra

» Yogic healing – a combination of yoga and naturopathic therapies – is held at the **Kaivalyadhama Yoga Hospital** (p782) in Lonavla. Advanced Iyengar yoga courses (for experienced practitioners only) are offered at famous **Ramamani Iyengar Memorial Yoga Institute** (p787) in Pune.

Volunteering

Choosing an Organisation

Consider how your skill set may benefit an organisation and community, and choose a cause that you're passionate about.

Time Required

Think realistically about how much time you can devote to a project. Some charities offer week-long placements but you're more likely to be of help if you commit for at least a month.

Money

Often giving up your time is not enough; many charities will expect volunteers to cover their own costs including accommodation, food and transport.

Working 9 to 5

Make sure you know what you're signing up to; many volunteer programs expect you to work full-time, five days a week.

Transparency

Ensure that the organisation you choose is reputable and transparent about how they spend their money. Where possible, get feedback from former volunteers.

Many charities and international aid agencies work in India and there are numerous opportunities for volunteers. It may be possible to find a placement after you arrive in India, but charities and nongovernment organisations (NGOs) normally prefer volunteers who have applied in advance and been approved for the kind of work involved.

There are some excellent local charities and NGOs, some of which have opportunities for volunteers; for listings check www.indianngos.com. The **Concern India Foundation** (☎011-26224482/3; www.concernindiafoundation.org; Room A52, 1st fl, Amar Colony, Lajpat Nagar 4) may be able to link volunteers with current projects around the country; contact it well in advance for information. In Delhi, the magazine *First City* lists various local NGOs that welcome volunteers and financial aid.

Aid Programs in India

The following are listings of programs in India that may have opportunities for volunteers; it's best to contact them before turning up on their doorstep. Donations may also be welcomed.

Caregiving

There are numerous opportunities for volunteer work in this field, particularly those with a medical, health or teaching background.

Delhi

» There are two branches of Mother Teresa's Kolkata (Calcutta)-based order, **Missionaries of Charity** (☎011-65731435; www.motherteresa.org; 1 Magazine Rd), in Delhi, which welcome volunteers (weekdays only). In Kolkata (p448) there are volunteering opportunities at several care homes. There are also branches in Jaipur (☎0141-2365804; Vardhman Path, C-Scheme) and Chennai (☎044-25956928; 79 Main Rd, Royapuram).

Kolkata

» **Calcutta Rescue** (☎/fax 033-22175675; www.calcuttarescue.org; 4th fl, 85 Collins St) provides medical care and health education for the disadvantaged of Kolkata and other parts of West Bengal. There are six- to nine-month openings for experienced professionals; contact staff for current vacancies.

» The **Samaritans** (☎033-22295920; http://thecalcuttasamaritans.org; 48 Ripon Rd) welcomes caring listeners and donations.

Madhya Pradesh & Chhattisgarh

» **Sambhavna Trust** (☎0755-2730914; www.bhopal.org; Bafna Colony, Berasia Rd) was established to help victims of the 1984 Bhopal Disaster – see the boxed text on p637.

Maharashtra

» **Sadhana Village** (☎020-25380792; www .sadhana-village.org; Priyankit, 1 Lokmanya Colony, Pune) is a residence for intellectually disabled adults; minimum commitment of two months for volunteers.

Rajasthan

» **Disha** (☎0141-2393319; www.dishafoundation .org; Disha Path, Nirman Nagar-C, Jaipur) assists people with cerebral palsy and other neural conditions. Volunteers who are physiotherapists, speech therapists, special education, sports, arts and crafts professionals, and vocational counsellors are needed.

» The NGO **Marwar Medical & Relief Society** (☎0291-2545210; www.mandore.com; c/o Mandore Guesthouse, Dadwari Lane) runs educational, health, environmental and other projects in villages in the Jodhpur district. Short- or long-term volunteers are welcome.

Community

Many community volunteer projects work to provide health care and education to villages.

Andhra Pradesh

» The **Confederation of Voluntary Associations** (☎040-24572984; www.cova network.org; 20-4-10, Charminar, Hyderabad) is an umbrella organisation for around 800 NGOs in Andhra Pradesh. Volunteers are matched by their skills; long-term volunteers preferred.

Bihar & Jharkhand

» The **Root Institute for Wisdom Culture** (☎0631-2200714; www.rootinstitute.com) is a Buddhist meditation centre (see p517) that provides free health care to villagers. Skilled volunteers are occasionally needed to train local health workers.

» **The Village Experience Program** (☎0631-2227922; www.peoplefirstindia.net) accepts volunteers every July and August to work alongside teachers and staff on health care programs in village schools and with street children.

Delhi

» The **Hope Project** (☎011-24353006; www.hopeprojectindia.org; 127 Basti Hazrat, Nizamuddin) runs a community health centre, a creche, a nonformal school, vocational training courses, a thrift and credit program, and a women's micro-enterprise unit, and welcomes volunteers.

Karnataka

» In Bengaluru, **Equations** (☎080-25457607; www.equitabletourism.org; 415, 2nd C Cross, 4th Main Rd, OMBR Layout, Banaswadi Post) promotes 'holistic tourism' and protects local communities from exploitation through lobbying, local training programs and research publications.

» Across the river from Hampi, the **Kishkinda Trust** (☎08533-267777; www.thekishkindatrust .org; Royal St, Anegundi) devotes itself to social empowerment and sustainable community development through a number of avenues, such as rural tourism.

Madhya Pradesh & Chhattisgarh

» **Friends of Orchaa** (☎9993385405; www .orchha.org) is a nonprofit organisation that works to improve the livelihoods of villagers in Ganj, which visitors can contribute to by volunteering or by taking part in its excellent homestay program (p622).

Mumbai

» The **Concern India Foundation** (☎022-22852270; www.concernindia.org; 3rd fl, Ador House, 6 K Dubash Marg) supports development-oriented organisations to establish sustainable projects run by local people. Six months minimum; many of the field jobs require Hindi.

Rajasthan

» In Bikaner, **Action Formation Education Voyage** (AFEV; ☎9829867323; www.afevinde.com; Pause Cafe, Bihari Temple, KEM Rd, Bikaner) works on a host of projects, including plastic-bag recycling, a small orphanage, street cleaning and equitable tourism. Food and accommodation provided.

» The **URMUL Trust** (☎0151-2523093; urmultrust@datainfosys.net; Urmul Bhawan, Ganganagar Rd, Bikaner) provides primary health care and education to desert dwellers in arid western Rajasthan. Volunteer placements (minimum one month) are available in English teaching, health care and other work.

» **Seva Mandir** (☎0294-2451041; www.sevamandir.org; Old Fatehpura, Udaipur) is an NGO working in southern Rajasthan on projects including afforestation, water resources, health, education, and empowerment of women and village institutions.

Tamil Nadu

» In Chennai, the **Rejuvenate India Movement** (RIM; ☎044-22235133; www.rejuvenateindiamovement.org) can arrange short- and long-term placements for skilled volunteers on development projects run by partner NGOs in Tamil Nadu.

Uttarakhand

» The grassroots **Rural Organisation for Social Elevation** (ROSE; ☎05963-241081; www.rosekanda.info) is based in Kanda village, near Bageshwar. Volunteers live with a local family for one to six months, helping out with cooking, teaching, field work and building projects.

West Bengal

» **Human Wave** (☎033-26852823; http://humanwave-volunteer.org) runs community development and health schemes in West Bengal; short-term volunteer opportunities are available.

» The **Makaibari Tea Estate** (☎9832447774; www.volmakaibari.org; volunteerinmakaibari@gmail.com), near Kurseong, accepts volunteers, particularly in fields of primary school teaching

and organic farming. Contact Nayan Lama for details.

Design & Restoration

Those with craft skills should look at one of the following:

Jammu & Kashmir

» The **Tibet Heritage Fund** (www.tibetheritagefund.org) is working on the preservation of old Leh in Ladakh. Those qualified and experienced in art restoration or architecture might be able to help (check its website).

Madhya Pradesh & Chhattisgarh

» Volunteers with design and craft knowledge are welcome at **Saathi** (☎942529152; saathibastar@yahoo.co.in; Kondagaon, Chhattisgarh), an organisation that encourages tribal people in the production of terracotta, woodcarving and metalwork.

Environment & Conservation

The following are just some of the charities focused on environmental education and sustainable development:

Andaman Islands

» **ANET** (Andaman & Nicobar Environmental Team; ☎03192-280081; www.anetindia.org; North Wandoor) is an environmental NGO that accepts volunteers to assist with activities from field projects to general maintenance.

Himachal Pradesh

» The Kaza-based NGO **Ecosphere** (☎01906-222724; www.spitiecosphere.com; Old Bazaar, Kaza, Spiti) has partnered with a number of villages to create a sustainable tourism infrastructure. Volunteers (two-week commitment required) live in homestays and work on ecofriendly construction projects (p342)

Jammu & Kashmir

» The **International Society for Ecology & Culture** (www.isec.org.uk) works to promote sustainable development in rural parts of Ladakh and offers one-month placements on rural farms.

» The **Ladakh Ecological Development Group** (☎01982-253221; www.ledeg.org; Ecology Centre, Leh) is a local NGO involved in environmental education and sustainable development.

AGENCIES OVERSEAS

There are so many international volunteering agencies it can be bewildering try-ing to assess which ones have ethical policies. Agencies offering short projects in a number of countries are almost always tailoring projects to the volunteer rather than finding the right volunteer for what needs to be done. Look for projects that will derive benefits from your existing skills. To find sending agencies in your area, read Lonely Planet's *Volunteer: a Traveller's Guide*, the *Big Trip* and the *Career Break Book*, or try one of the following agencies.

» **Ethical Volunteering** (www.ethicalvolunteering.org) has some excellent guidelines for choosing an ethical sending agency.

» **Voluntary Service Overseas** (VSO; www.vso.org.uk) is a British organisation that places volunteers in various professional roles, though the time commitment can be up to several years.

» **Indicorps** (www.indicorps.org) matches volunteers to projects across India in all sorts of fields, particularly social development. There are special fellowships for people of Indian descent living outside India.

» **Jamyang Foundation** (www.jamyang.org) may be able to arrange volunteer place-ments for experienced teachers in Zanskar and Himachal Pradesh.

» **Mondo Challenge** (www.mondochallenge.org/india) has opportunities, from teach-ing to community projects, for volunteers in West Bengal hill towns, although it's not cheap.

» **Himalayan Education Lifeline Programme** (HELP; www.help-education.org) is a British-based charity that can organise placements for volunteer teachers at schools in Sikkim.

» **Kerala Link** (www.kerala-link.org) is a UK-registered charity that places volunteers at one of its partner institutions located in rural Kerala, including a special-needs children's school.

Karnataka

» **Ashoka Trust for Research in Ecology & the Environment** (ATREE; ✆080-23635555; www.atree.org; Royal Enclave, Sriramapura, Jakkur Post, Bengaluru) takes volunteers who have experience or a keen interest in conservation and environmental issues.

Maharashtra

» **Nimbkar Agricultural Research Institute** (✆02166-222396; www.nariphaltan.org; Phaltan-Lonand Rd, Tambmal, Phaltan) focuses on sustainable development, animal husbandry and renewable energy. Volunteer internships lasting two to six months are available for agriculture, engineering and science graduates to assist with the research.

Tamil Nadu

» In Kotagiri, the **Keystone Foundation** (www.keystone-foundation.org; PB 35 Groves Hill Rd, Kotagiri) strives to improve environmental conditions in the Nilgiris while working with, and creating better living standards for, indigenous communities.

Uttarakhand

» **Eco Development Committee** runs conservation projects between June and September in Ghangaria Village, in the Valley of Flowers. Contact the Nature Interpretation Centre (p428).

Teaching

Volunteering in Jammu and the Kashmir Valley is complicated by the security situa-tion, but there are various opportunities in Zanskar and Ladakh. Many Buddhist mon-astery schools need experienced teachers of English for long-term volunteer placements.

Bihar & Jharkhand

» Volunteers are sometimes required for **Prajna Vihar School**, a nonprofit village school just south of the Mahabodhi Temple in Bihar. For information, contact the **Burmese Vihar** (✆0612-2200721).

Himachal Pradesh

» **Himalayan Buddhist Cultural School** (☑01902-251845; palkithakur@yahoo.com) has placements for experienced teachers who are willing to volunteer for six months or more. Contact staff in advance.

» The **Kullu Project** (☑94181-02083; www .kulluproject.web.officelive.com) arranges volunteers to work with schools and orphanages in the Kullu Valley.

West Bengal & Darjeeling

» **Hayden House** (☑0354-2253228; radhakarky@gmail.com, www.haydenhouse.org) in Darjeeling accepts volunteers for a minimum two- to three-month stay, especially doctors, nurses, teachers, or those with experience or interest in handicraft marketing and product design. It can connect you with teaching in a rural school near Kalimpong, or in a Montessori school in Darjeeling.

Working with Animals

From stray dogs to olive ridley turtles, opportunities for animal lovers are plentiful.

Andhra Pradesh

» **Blue Cross of Hyderabad** (☑040-23544355; www.bluecrosshyd.in; Rd No 35, Jubilee Hills, Hyderabad) runs a large shelter with over 1000 animals. It works to rescue and adopt sick animals, and vaccinate and sterilise stray dogs. Volunteers can help care for shelter animals (dogs, cats and livestock), or in the office.

» **Karuna Society for Animals & Nature** (☑08555-287214; www.karunasociety.org; 2/138C Karuna Nilayam, Prasanthi Nilayam Post, Anantapur) rescues and treats sick, abandoned and mistreated animals. Volunteers can help with caretaking operations; a one-month, full-time minimum commitment is needed, as are rabies vaccinations.

Goa

» **International Animal Rescue** (IAR; ☑2268328/272; www.internationalanimalrescue. org; Animal Tracks, Madungo Vaddo, Assagao) runs its Animal Tracks rescue facility in Assagao, and visitors and volunteers (both short- and long-term) are always welcome to assist vets and tend to sick strays.

» The animal welfare group **GAWT** (see p831) also has volunteer opportunities.

Mumbai

» The **Welfare of Stray Dogs** (☑022-64222838; www.wsdindia.org; Yeshwant Chambers, B Bharocha Rd, Kala Ghoda) works to improve the lives of street dogs. Volunteers can walk dogs, mind kennels, treat animals (training and rabies shot required), manage stores, educate kids in school programs or fundraise.

Odisha

» The **Wildlife Society of Odisha** (☑0674-2311513; www.wildlifeorissa.org; A320, Sahid Nagar, Bhubaneswar) may accept volunteers to help with its work to save endangered species in Odisha, especially the olive ridley turtle (also see p603).

Rajasthan

» The animal hospital, **Animal Aid Unlimited** (☑9784005989, 9950531639; www .animalaidunlimited.com; Badi Village, Udaipur), accepts volunteers to help injured, abandoned or stray animals. Make an appointment before visiting. There's no minimum period, although trained veterinarians should commit for at least a few weeks. (See also p159.)

» The laudable animal hospital, **Help in Suffering** (☑0141-3245673; www.his-india.org .au; Maharani Farm, Durgapura, Jaipur), welcomes qualified voluntary vets (three-, six-, 12-month commitments). Apply first in writing.

Working with Children

The following are just a selection of the many excellent charities working with children in India.

Delhi

» **Salaam Baalak Trust** (☑011-23681803; www.salaambaalaktrust.com; Chandiwalan, Main Bazaar, Paharganj) provides shelter, food, education and other support to Delhi's homeless street children. Volunteer English teachers, doctors and computer experts are welcome. Another way you can help is by taking a tour with a street child. (See p80.)

Goa

» **Children Walking Tall** (☑09822-124802; www.childrenwalkingtall.com, 'The Mango House', near Vrundavan Hospital, Karaswada, Mapusa) has opportunities for volunteer child care workers, teachers and medics at its projects for homeless children and orphans near Mapusa (minimum three months). Every volunteer needs a criminal-background check.

HANDY WEBSITES

» **World Volunteer Web** (www.worldvolunteerweb.org) Information and resources for volunteering around the world.

» **Working Abroad** (www.workingabroad.com) Volunteer and professional work opportunities in over 150 countries.

» **Worldwide Volunteering** (www.worldwidevolunteering.org.uk) Enormous database offering information on worldwide volunteering opportunities.

» **El Shaddai** (☑6513286/7; www.childrescue.net; El Shaddai House, Socol Vaddo, Assagao) aids impoverished and homeless children. A one-month commitment is required and volunteers undergo a rigorous vetting process, which can take up to six months, so apply well in advance.

Mumbai

» **Child Rights & You** (CRY; ☑022-23096845; www.cry.org; 189A Anand Estate, Sane Guruji Marg, Mahalaxmi) fundraises for more than 300 projects India-wide. Volunteers can assist with campaigns (online and on the ground), research, surveys and media. A six-week commitment is required.

» **Saathi** (☑022-23009117; www.saathi.org; Agripada Municipal School, Farooque Umarbhouy Lane, Agripada) works with adolescent youths living on the street. Volunteers should be willing to commit to at least three months and work full-time (six days per week). Those interested in working directly with adolescents should speak some Hindi. You can take a tour of the neighbourhood where Saathi works for a ₹1000 donation.

» The **Vatsalya Foundation** (☑022-24962115; www.thevatsalyafoundation.org; Anand Niketan, King George V Memorial, Dr E Moses Rd, Mahalaxmi) works with Mumbai's street children, focusing on rehabilitation into mainstream society. There are long- and short-term opportunities in teaching and sports activities.

Rajasthan

» **Ladli** (☑9829011124; www.ladli.org; 74 Govindpuri, Rakdi, Sodala, Jaipur) provides vocational training for abused, orphaned and destitute children. Volunteers work in child care and teach English; placements last from a week to a year.

Tamil Nadu

» The NGO **Rural Institute for Development Education** (RIDE; ☑044-27268223; www.rideindia.org) works with villages around Kanchipuram to remove children from forced labour and into transition schools. Volunteers can contribute in teaching, administrative and support roles.

Uttar Pradesh

» The **Learn for Life Society** (www.learn-for-life.net), which can be contacted through the **Brown Bread Bakery** (☑0542-2403566; www.brownbreakbakery.com), has volunteer opportunities at its small school for disadvantaged children

Working with Women

See www.indianngos.com for more charities working to empower and educate women.

Mumbai

» Volunteers can support English and art classes, design workshops or do research or data analysis at **Apne Aap Women Worldwide** (☑022-23004201; www.apneaap.org; Chandramani Budh Vihar Municipal School, ground fl, 13th Lane, Kamathipura), an anti-trafficking organisation that provides learning and livelihood training to women's and teenage girls' groups. There are also volunteer possibilities with its offices in Kolkata, Bihar and Delhi.

Rajasthan

» The **Sambhali Trust** (☑0291-2512385; www.sambhali-trust.org; c/o Durag Niwas Guest House, 1st Old Public Park, Raika Bagh, Jodhpur) works to empower disadvantaged women and girls in Jodhpur city and Setrawa village. Volunteers can teach and help organise workshops on topics like health, women's rights and nutrition.

Travel With Children

Best Regions for Kids

Delhi A fun city for exploring the quirky National Rail Museum, Shankhar's International Dolls Museum and Sulabh International Museum of Toilets, along with plenty of comfy hotels and good food of all culinary persuasions.

Rajasthan A kaleidoscopic state replete with fairy-tale palaces, blue cities and pink cities fit for little princes and princesses, open-air astrological observatories for stargazers, desert camel treks for older kids and a plethora of colourful festivals.

Ladakh Families can take it easy in laid-back Leh, while high-altitude treks amid incredible, otherworldly lunar landscapes suit those with older children.

Himachal Pradesh Take pony rides and high teas in charming, colonial British-era hill stations; go zorbing or rafting in Manali, and experience monks, mantras and multicoloured prayer wheels in McLeod Ganj.

Goa Gorgeous white-sand beaches make Goa the perfect family choice for lazing the days away with swimming, sand castles, boat trips and an excursion out to a spice plantation (near Ponda to bathe with an elephant).

Kerala Backwater houseboat adventures, elephant spotting at wildlife reserves, tea picking in firefly-studded plantations and serious beach time await beside the Arabian Sea.

Fascinating, frustrating, thrilling and fulfilling; India is every bit as much a great adventure for children as it is for parents. Though the sensory overload may be overwhelming for younger kids and even short journeys by bus or train can prove rigorous for the entire family, the colours, scents, sights and sounds of India more than compensate by setting young imaginations ablaze. Gaze at twinkling Diwali candles with your under-10s, dig your heels into white-sand beaches while your toddlers build a sand temple or two; tuck into family-sized thalis at a bus station lunch joint; or trek the Himalayan byways with your teenagers: perfect moments like these make the occasional aches and pains of Indian travel worthwhile.

A Warm Welcome

In many respects, travel with children in India can be a delight, and warm welcomes are frequent. Hotels will almost always come up with an extra bed or two, and restaurants with a familiar meal. Railway porters will produce boiled sweets from their pockets; clucking old ladies will pinch rosy toddler cheeks; domestic tourists will thrill at taking a photograph or two beside your bouncing baby.

But while all this is fabulous for outgoing children it may prove tiring, or even disconcerting, for those of a more retiring disposition. The key as a parent on the road in India is to stay alert to children's needs and to remain firm in fulfilling them. Remember, though, that the attention your children will inevitably receive is almost always good natured; kids are the centre of life in many Indian households, and your own will be treated just the same.

Eating

You'll usually find something to satisfy sensitive childhood palates, but if you're travelling in the most family-friendly regions of India, such as Rajasthan, Himachal Pradesh, Goa, Kerala or the big cities, feeding your brood is easier. Here you will find familiar Western dishes in abundance. While on the road, easy portable snacks such as bananas, samosas, *puri* (puffy dough pockets) and packaged biscuits (Parle G brand are a perennial hit) will keep diminutive hunger pangs at bay. Adventurous eaters and vegetarian children, meanwhile, will delight in experimenting with the vast range of tastes and textures available at the Indian table: *paneer* (unfermented cheese) dishes, simple dhals (mild lentil curries), creamy kormas, buttered naans (tandoori breads), pilaus (rice dishes) and Tibetan *momos* (steamed or fried dumplings) are all firm favourites, while few children, no matter how culinarily unadventurous, can resist the finger food fun of a vast South Indian dosa (paper-thin lentil-flour pancake) served up for breakfast.

Sleeping

India offers such an array of accommodation options – from beach huts to heritage boutiques to five-star fantasies – that you're bound to be able to find something that will appeal to the whole family. Even the swishest of hotels are almost always child-friendly, as are many budget hotels, whose staff will usually rustle up an extra mattress or two; some places won't mind cramming several children into a regular-sized double room along with their parents. Travelling with a baby, it can make sense to pack the lightest possible travel cot you can find (companies such as KidCo make excellent pop-up tent-style beds) since hotel cots may prove precarious. If your budget stretches to it, a good way to maintain familial energy levels is to mix in a few top-end stays throughout your travels. The very best five stars come equipped with children's pools, games rooms and even children's clubs, while an occasional night with a warm bubble bath, room service macaroni cheese and the Disney channel will revive even the most disgruntled young traveller's spirits.

On the Road

Travel in India, be it by taxi, local bus, train or air, can be arduous for the whole family. Plan fun, easy days to follow longer bus or train rides, pack plenty of diversions (iPads or laptops with a stock of movies downloaded make invaluable travel companions, as do the good old-fashioned story books, cheap toys and games available widely across India), but most of all don't be put off: it might take you a while to get there (and there are few words more daunting than 'delay' to already frazzled parents), but chances are it will be well worth it when you do.

Health

The availability of a decent standard of health care varies widely in India, and is better in traveller-frequented parts of the country where it's almost always easy to track down a doctor at short notice (most hotels will be able to recommend a reliable one), and prescriptions are quickly and cheaply filled over the counter at numerous pharmacies. Diarrhoea can be serious in young children; rehydration is essential and seek medical help if persistent or accompanied by fever. Heat rash, skin complaints such as impetigo, insect bites or stings can be treated with the help of a well-equipped first aid kit. See Health (p1188).

Children's Highlights
Best Fairy-tale Splendours

» **Jaisalmer** Revel in *Arabian Nights* grandeur in Jaisalmer's centuries-old Old Fort on the edge of the Thar desert.

» **Hampi** Make like the Flintstones on the boulder-strewn shores of the Tungabhadra River, crossable by coracle; explore magical ancient ruins, and stop for a tasty dosa at the riverside Mango Tree.

» **Udaipur** Explore impossibly romantic palaces galore, take a riding excursion with the aptly named Princess Trails, and spoil your children rotten with a stay at the glorious Lake Palace Hotel.

» **Orchha** Wander the crumbling palaces and battlements of little-known Orccha, not far from the rather more adult-oriented attractions of Khajuraho. Have a swim in the river, and fulfil every little girl's Cinderella fantasies with a stay in one of the palaces.

Before You Go

Remember to visit your doctor to discuss vaccinations, health advisories and other health-related issues involving your children well in advance of travel. For more tips on travel in India, and first-hand accounts of travels in the country, pick up Lonely Planet's *Travel with Children* or visit the Thorn Tree Forum at lonelyplanet.com.

What to Pack

If you're travelling with a baby or toddler, there are several items worth packing in quantity: disposable or washable nappies, nappy rash cream (Calendula cream works well against heat rash too), extra bottles, a good stock of wet wipes, infant formula and jarred or rehydratable food. You can get all these items in many parts of India too, but often prices are at a premium and brands may not be those you recognise. Another good idea is a fold-up baby bed; a stroller, though, is optional, as there are few places with pavements even enough to use it successfully. For older children, make sure you bring good sturdy footwear, a hat or two, a few less-precious toys – that won't be mourned if lost or damaged – and a swimming jacket, life jacket or water wings for the sea or pool. Finally child-friendly insect repellent and sun lotion are a must.

Best Natural Encounters

» **Tiger Parks, Madhya Pradesh** Delve deep into the jungle or roam the plains at the tiger parks of Kanha, Pench or Bandhavgarh. You might not see a tiger, but there's plenty of other wildlife worth spotting.

» **Elephants in Karnataka** Visit these pachyderms at the Dubare Forest Reserve near Madikeri; get busy bathing and feeding them, and then hop on for a ride.

» **Goa's dolphins** Splash out on a dolphin-spotting boat trip from almost any Goan beach to see them cavorting among the waves.

» **Hill Station Monkeys** Head up to Shimla or Matheran for close encounters with the monkeys that will readily sneak into your bedroom and steal your precious packet of Hobnobs if you give them half a chance. Be cautious – these feisty simians can be aggressive and are known to bite unsuspecting visitors.

Funnest Forms of Transport

» **Autorickshaw, Old Delhi** Hurtle at top speed to create a scene worthy of Indiana Jones in the colourful, congested, incredibly atmospheric alleyways off Old Delhi's Chandni Chowk.

» **Toy Train, Darjeeling** Ride the seven-hour diesel toy train past colourful mountain villages and gushing waterfalls to witness mountain peaks so jagged and towering they look like illustrations straight from the pages of the Brothers Grimm.

» **Hand-pulled rickshaw, Matheran** A narrow-gauge toy train takes visitors most of the way up to this cute, monkey-infested hill station, after which your children can choose to continue to the village on horseback or in a hand-pulled rickshaw.

» **Backwater boat, Allapuzha** Take a cruise or rent a houseboat to troll Kerala's beautiful, mangrove-infested backwaters. If you happen to hit town on the second Saturday in August, take the kids along to see the spectacular Nehru Trophy snake boat race.

Best Beachfront Kick-backs

» **Palolem, Goa** Hole up in a beachfront palm-thatched hut and watch your kids cavort at beautiful Palolem beach, featuring the shallowest, safest waters in Goa.

» **Patnem, Goa** Just up the leafy lane from Palolem, quieter Patnem draws scores of long-stayers with children to its nice sand beach and cool, calm, child-friendly beach restaurants.

» **Havelock Island** Splash about in the shallows at languid Havelock Island, part of the Andaman Island chain, where, for older children, there's spectacular diving on offer.

regions at a glance

Rajasthan

Palaces ✓✓✓
Arts ✓✓✓
Wildlife ✓✓

Haryana & Punjab

Art ✓✓✓
Borders ✓✓
Cuisine ✓✓

Delhi

Food ✓✓✓
Shopping ✓✓✓
Mughal Sites ✓✓✓

Food
This is one of the best places in India to eat, from cutting-edge creative Indian cuisine in luscious five-star hotels, to fresh-from-the-fire, impossibly delectable Dilli-ka-Chaat (Delhi street food).

Shopping
All of India's riches sparkle in Delhi's bazaars and emporiums. Plus you can browse designer boutiques, 19th-century musical instrument shops and some of the country's best bookstores.

Mughal Sites
Wander around Delhi's Red Fort and Old Delhi, and you'll gain a sense of the glories of the Mughal empire. Humayun's Tomb was the precursor to the Taj Mahal.

p56

Palaces & Forts
The architectural legacy of the maharajas is this state's signature attraction. Forts, palaces and gardens are scattered across Rajasthan's mountains and deserts.

Arts & Crafts
From exquisite miniature paintings and jewellery fit for royalty to camel-hide shoes and everyday clothing and utensils, the traditional arts and crafts of Rajasthan will fill your shopping list.

Wildlife Wonders
Rajasthan is surprisingly rewarding for wildlife watchers. Former royal hunting reservations are now national parks where you can spot tigers, crocodiles, deer and bird life.

p104

Art & Architecture
Chandigarh hosts the quirky Nek Chand Fantasy Rock Garden where whimsy and recycling has created a spectacular dream world. Amritsar's Golden Temple is the heart of Sikh worship.

Border Bravado
Not many national borders are tourist attractions. The Attari–Wagah border is unexpectedly entertaining, where border guards of India and Pakistan camp it up with cock-comb headgear and goose steps.

Cuisine
The home of butter chicken and basmati rice, Haryana and Punjab are proud of their agricultural assets and food culture.

p199

Jammu & Kashmir (including Ladakh)

Landscapes ✓✓✓
Trekking ✓✓✓
Spiritual ✓

Himachal Pradesh

Buddhism ✓✓✓
Sports ✓✓✓
Hill Stations ✓✓

Uttar Pradesh & the Taj Mahal

Architecture ✓✓✓
Religion ✓✓✓
Ghats ✓✓✓

Uttarakhand

Trekking ✓✓✓
Yoga ✓✓✓
Wildlife ✓✓✓

Ladakh
The high-altitude deserts, craggy canyons and dazzlingly blue mountain lakes are magnificent for their own sake. But they're made all the more photogenic in Ladakh by villages of earth-brick homes, emerald-green fields and fortress-like monasteries.

Homestay Trekking
High-altitude hikes made easier (minimal baggage) and culturally fascinating by sleeping and eating in traditional Ladakhi farmsteads.

Spiritual Srinagar
Once a cradle of Indian Buddhism, Srinagar now has a Muslim suffused with Sufi spirituality and, according to some, is home to the grave of Jesus Christ.

p222

Buddhism
With the Dalai Lama and some 80,000 other Tibetan exiles living around Dharamsala, plus the ancient but still active monasteries along the Lahaul and Spiti Valleys, Himachal abounds with Buddhist art, architecture, ritual, philosophy and meditation.

Mountain Sport
Himachal's mountains may offer the best combination of awe and accessibility anywhere in India. Trekking routes criss-cross the state, and rock climbing, rafting, mountain biking, skiing, snowboarding and paragliding are all on the menu.

Hill Stations
An inviting blend of colonial-era holiday-town and bustling Indian bazaar is found in Shimla, Himachal's charming capital city.

p278

It's not all about the Taj
OK, so the Taj Mahal is breathtaking, but UP's architectural treasure trove boasts plenty besides: check out Lucknow, Allahabad and Fatehpur Sikri.

Eclectic Mix
Two of Hinduism's seven holy cities, two of Buddhism's four most sacred pilgrimage centres and two modern cities inextricably linked to powerful Islamic pasts.

Spirituality Intensified
Holy rivers pack the biggest spiritual punch. Visitors are bowled over by the religious fervour displayed at riverside ghats in Allahabad, Chitrakut and Varanasi.

p345

Trekking
Uttarakhand's trekking trails wind beneath India's highest peaks to sacred Hindu sites, remote glaciers and rolling alpine meadows where shepherds tend their flocks.

Yoga
People from around the world head to Rishikesh for a spiritual tune-up, where all types of breathing, stretching and mind-clearing are taught by masters.

Wildlife
See tigers, leopards and wild elephants in the steamy jungles of Corbett Tiger Reserve and the forests of Rajaji National Park. In Uttarakhand's northern national parks, like Gangotri and Valley of Flowers, look for snow leopards and Himalayan bears.

p401

Kolkata (Calcutta)

Contrasts ✓✓✓
Bengali Food ✓✓
Architecture ✓

Contrasts

Yes, there's in-your-face poverty, but this is also India's cultural and intellectual capital, a place that's disarmingly human for a mega-city.

Cuisine

Eating seafood in many parts of India can be a recipe for disaster. But in Kolkata, fantastic fresh fish and prawns are central to a rich, delicious cuisine that deserves to be far more widely known.

Colonial-era Buildings

Kolkata (as Calcutta) was the capital of British India, so it's not surprising to find colonial-era buildings that are world beaters of the genre.

p442

West Bengal & Darjeeling

Hill Stations ✓✓✓
Tigers ✓✓✓
Hotels ✓

Hill Stations

Darjeeling is perhaps the quintessential Himalayan hill station, dotted with colonial-era buildings and even a gentleman's club, all recalling the faded ghosts of the past. The state also has some spectacular mountain views.

Tigers

Watch the awesome Bengal tiger in its eponymous habitat. Nearly 300 big cats roam the mangrove jungles of the Sunderbans.

Heritage Hotels

Raj-era guesthouses, colonial residences and the odd tea estate now offer historic accommodation, ranging in tone from restored grandeur to melancholy neglect. Enjoy high tea or sip a G&T.

p474

Bihar & Jharkhand

Religion ✓✓✓
Ruins ✓✓
Wildlife ✓✓

Powerful Pilgrimages

Buddhist pilgrims the world over flock to Bodhgaya, where Siddhartha Gautama – Buddha – attained enlightenment underneath a bodhi tree.

Ancient Booksmarts

The Unesco ruins at the ancient University of Nalanda, date back to the 5th century, and are the biggest of a plethora of early Buddhist relics scattered around Rajgir and Bodhgaya.

Wild Elephants on Parade

Jharkhand's Betla National Park is one of the easiest spots to find wild elephants in India, but an overnight here amid its serene bamboo thickets and rich evergreens is a welcomed respite, even if pachyderms prove evasive.

p506

Sikkim

Views ✓✓✓
Monasteries ✓✓
Trekking ✓

Mountain Views

Sikkim's northern fringe of Himalayan peaks guarantees epic views, whether you take a jeep trip up to the Alpine-style valleys of the border with Tibet or savour the views from a hotel balcony in Pelling.

Monasteries

This former Buddhist kingdom is dotted with impressive Tibetan-style monasteries, home to Buddha statues, chanting lines of maroon-robed monks and prayer flags fluttering serenely in the mountain breezes.

Trekking

Khanchengdzonga draws trekkers like bears to Himalayan honey. The choicest trail here is the Goecha La trek, which gives the closest views you'll ever get of the world's third-highest peak.

p526

Northeast Tribal States

Tribes ✓✓✓
Wildlife ✓✓
Adventure ✓✓✓

Tribes

From headhunting Naga tribes to the delicately tattooed and pierced Apatani women, the northeast is India's tribal heartland and ethnically one of the most fascinating places in Asia.

Wildlife

The one-horned Indian rhino is only the most glamorous of a roll call of exotic animals that fill this region's magnificent national parks, which feature the highest biodiversity in India.

Adventure

These remote frontier lands where India, Tibet and Southeast Asia collide are only just starting to open up to tourism, thus giving wannabe explorers a genuine opportunity to go where few have trodden before.

p550

Odisha

Temples ✓✓✓
Tribal Tours ✓✓✓
Wildlife ✓✓✓

Medieval Architecture

Odisha once boasted temples in the thousands. Today, much of the best-preserved medieval Kalinga architecture has survived unscathed in the numerous temples in the area.

Adivasi Markets

The tribal markets of Onkadelli and Chatikona are fascinating highlights of Western Odisha, where Adivasi tribes still thrive, staunchly clinging to a fiercely traditional way of life.

Gorgeous Gorges & Supersized Crocs

Odisha is a hotbed for nature lovers: beaches, tiger reserves, mangrove forests and wetlands, and a varied tangle of flora and fauna abound.

p584

Madhya Pradesh & Chhattisgarh

Tigers ✓✓✓
Temples ✓✓✓
Adventure ✓✓✓

Prowling the Plains

Madhya Pradesh is the king of the jungle when it comes to tiger parks. Bandhavgarh gives you your best chance of spotting a tiger, but serious wildlife enthusiasts should head for the forests of Kanha.

Khajuraho's Just for Starters

The raunchy relief work on the World Heritage–listed Khajuraho temples steals the show but visit Orchha, Maheshwar, Omkareshwar and Ujjain for more temple-tastic treats.

Trekking & Biking

And rafting and waterskiing and parasailing: Madhya Pradesh suits outdoor adventurers down to the ground, up to the sky and into the rivers.

p610

Gujarat

Wildlife ✓✓
Crafts ✓✓
Mountains ✓

Wildlife

Asia's only wild lions, India's only wild asses, antelopes, gazelles and rare and spectacular birds can be seen with relative ease in Gujarat's national parks and wildlife sanctuaries.

Crafts

Gujarati embroiderers, weavers, printers and dyers, especially in the western region of Kachchh (Kutch), produce some of the most colourful, intricate textiles in India.

Sacred Mountains

In this predominantly flat state, it's not surprising that the few mountains act as spiritual magnets. You can join Hindu or Jain pilgrims on their treks up stunning, temple-topped peaks such as Shatrunjaya, Girnar and Pavagadh.

p669

Mumbai (Bombay)

Buildings ✓✓✓
Food ✓✓✓
Nightlife ✓✓✓

Gothic Revivals & Colonial Relics

The British left behind beautiful colonial-era architecture, highlighted by Chhatrapati Shivaji Terminus, the High Court and the University of Mumbai.

Culture & Cuisine

Mumbai's collision of cultures means it's a haven for foodies. A kaleidoscope of flavours from all over India vie for tastebud attention with imported cuisines the world over.

Bollywood & Booze

As India's financial powerhouse and home to the world's most prolific film industry, Mumbai unapologetically parties its ass off... The country's wildest bars, clubs and exclusive Bollywood bashes showcase a tipsier side of India.

p719

Maharashtra

Caves ✓✓✓
Beaches ✓✓
Wine ✓✓

Caves

The World Heritage Sites of Ajanta and Ellora house exquisite collections of cave paintings and rock sculptures dating back to India's golden ages.

Beaches

Strung out along Maharashtra's Konkan Coast are some of the most secluded but beautiful beaches, custom-made for romantics, adventurers, loners and philosophers alike.

Wine

Nasik, the *grand cru* of India's up-and-coming wine industry, proudly flaunts a few world-class drops in the many excellent cellars around town.

p757

Goa

Beaches ✓✓✓
Food ✓✓
Architecture ✓✓✓

Beaches

They're so beautiful, they're almost a cliché, but even the most off-the-beaten-path travellers can't resist Goa's stunning beachscapes. Many are backed by shady palm-tree groves – an echo of Goa's lush interior.

Food

Goa has fresh, fresh seafood and a tradition of preparing it in brilliant ways, often with coconut. Sometimes it's the random beach shack that does it best.

Architecture

Portuguese colonialism's most attractive legacy may be its pretty buildings. Mansions in Quepem and Chandor, houses in Panaji, Old Goa's grand religious structures, and little homes and churches across the state are pure eye candy.

p795

Karnataka & Bengaluru

Temples ✓✓✓
Parks ✓✓
Cuisine ✓✓

Temples

From the Hoysala beauties at Belur, Halebid and Somnathpur to the electric Virupaksha Temple in Hampi or quaint shrines in Gokarna and Udupi, Karnataka is strewn with fantastic temples that overwhelm you with their ambience and ritual fineries.

National Parks

The Nilgiri Biosphere Reserve boasts some of the most pristine forests in India, and there's abundant wildlife to be sighted in national parks such as Bandipur, Kabini and Nagarhole.

Cuisine

Start off with the delectable Udupi vegetarian thali, then move on to some fiery Mangalorean seafood, washing it all down with fresh draught in beer-town Bengaluru.

p835

Andhra Pradesh

Religion ✓✓✓
Food ✓✓
Beaches ✓

Religious Sites

Attracting more pilgrims than anywhere else in the world, Hindus flock to Sri Venkateswara Temple at Tirumala. There are ancient ruins of once-flourishing Buddhist centres across the state, while Hyderabad has some truly grand Islamic architecture.

Food

Synonymous with Hyderabad, biryani is a local obsession. The taste will leave you salivating long after your departure. Meanwhile 'hyderabadi haleem' has been patented so that it can't be served unless it meets strict quality standards.

Beaches

Visakhapatnam has a gorgeous stretch of coastline. Tourism is geared towards the domestic market, bringing a unique and festive atmosphere.

p891

Kerala

Backwaters ✓✓✓
Food ✓✓✓
Wildlife ✓✓

Backwaters

Kerala's backwaters are vast lakes and long canals that spread like tendrils inland. It's one of India's most relaxing and beautiful experiences to stay overnight on a houseboat or take a canoe trip.

Food

Delicious, delicate cuisine flavoured with coconut and myriad spices – Kerala's table is born of a melting pot of influences and remarkable geography.

Wildlife

Kerala has a concentration of inland national parks, where, amid lush mountainous landscapes, you can spot wild elephants, tigers, lions, birds and other wildlife.

p919

Tamil Nadu & Chennai

Temples ✓✓✓
Hill Stations ✓✓
Hotels ✓

Temples

The amazing architecture, daily rituals and colourful festivals of Tamil Nadu's Hindu temples draw pilgrims from around India; major temples have soaring *gopurams* (gateway towers) and intricately carved *mandapas* (pavilions).

Hill Stations

The hill stations of the Westerns Ghats offer wonderfully cool weather, the chance to hike out to gorgeous mountain vistas, bustling festival seasons and cosy colonial-era guesthouses with open fires.

Heritage Hotels

Restored spots to lay your head include the picturesque houses of Puducherry's French Quarter, the grand old palace hotels of the hill stations and the teak-and-tile Chettiar mansions of the south.

p981

Andaman Islands

Diving ✓✓✓
Beaches ✓✓✓
Tribal Groups ✓✓

Diving/ Snorkelling

Exploring the underwater jungles of coral and tropical fish is what lures most visitors to the islands; perfect for beginners or dive masters alike.

Beaches

Whether you're searching for that picture-postcard beach, or kilometres of deserted coastline – here you'll find some of the nicest beaches in India.

Ethnic groups

An anthropologist's dream, the Andamans are home to fascinating tribal groups; some still literally living in the Stone Age. Most reside on outlying islands, which tourists are prohibited from visiting, but elsewhere you'll encounter an interesting mix of South and Southeast Asian settlers.

p1061

Look out for these icons:

 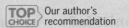 Our author's recommendation

A green or sustainable option

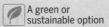 No payment required

See the Index for a full list of destinations covered in this book.

On the Road

Delhi

Best Places to Eat

» Saravana Bhavan (p89)

» Bukhara (p90)

» Indian Accent (p92)

» Monsoon (p90)

» Olive (p92)

» Gunpowder (p91)

» Rajdhani (p89)

Best Places to Stay

» Shanti Home (p85)

» Devna (p86)

» Bnineteen (p86)

» Cottage Yes Please (p83)

Why Go?

Medieval mayhem, the New India, stately maiden aunt: give it a chance and this schizophrenic capital could capture your heart. Yes, it's aggravating, polluted and hectic, but hey – nobody's perfect.

Like a subcontinental Rome, India's capital is punctuated by vestiges of lost empires: ancient forts freckle the suburbs; Old Delhi was once the capital of Islamic India; the British built New Delhi, with its exaggerated avenues; and even-newer Delhi features utopian malls linked by potholed roads. These disparate, codependent elements are all now gloriously intertwined via the new metro system.

There are also magnificent museums, temples, mosques, and a busy cultural scene – and shopaholics, you are home: all the riches of India twinkle in Delhi's emporiums.

Prepare yourself to tuck into some of the subcontinent's finest food, including the famous *Dilli-ka-Chaat* (Delhi street food) – which, rather like the city itself, jumbles up every flavour in one bite.

When to Go
Delhi

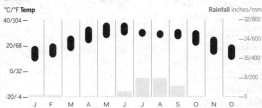

Oct–Mar Delhi at its best – the weather is bright and sunny but not too hot.

May–Aug These are the months to avoid – it's hot and humid.

Jun–Sep Monsoon season (heaviest from July to September) is also worth avoiding if you can.

Top Tips

» Ensure your taxi or autorickshaw driver has taken you to the hotel/shop you requested, as some try to offload passengers at places where they receive commission.

» Decline offers from taxi or auto drivers to take you to hotels/shops of their choice.

» Avoid chatty young men who hang around touristy spots, some of whom claim humbly to be students wanting to improve their English.

» Don't believe the helpful chaps who try to direct you to a 'tourist office' around Connaught Place. There is only one Government of India tourist office, at 88 Janpath.

» Carry small denominations (below ₹50) as drivers often have a lack of change.

» Ignore touts who surreptitiously dirty your shoe and offer to clean it at a price.

DON'T MISS

One of Delhi's most mystical and atmospheric experiences is to hear *qawwali* singers and musicians perform devotional songs at the **Hazrat Nizam-ud-din Dargah**. This is a beautiful Islamic holy shrine, where song performances take place after sunset prayers on Thursday. The air is thick with incense and the shrine thronged with pilgrims.

Delhi's Top Festivals

» To check dates contact India Tourism Delhi (p98).

» Delhi celebrates Diwali and Dussehra (Durga Puja) with particular verve.

» Republic Day (26 Jan, Rajpath, p71) Incorporates a spectacular military parade.

» Beating of the Retreat (29 Jan, Rajpath, p71) The closing of the Republic Day celebrations is marked by the Beating of the Retreat – more military pageantry. Tickets are essential for both events and are available at India Tourism Delhi.

» Independence Day (15 Aug, Red Fort, p62) India celebrates its Independence from Britain in 1947 and the prime minister addresses the nation from the Red Fort ramparts.

» Qutb Festival (Oct/Nov, Qutb Minar, p102) Held over several days, featuring Sufi singing and classical dance performances.

» Delhi International Arts Festival (DIAF, Dec) Three weeks of exhibitions, performing arts, films, literature and culinary events at Delhi-wide venues.

MAIN POINTS OF ENTRY

Indira Gandhi International Airport, New Delhi train station, Old Delhi train station, and the Inter State Bus Terminal (ISBT).

Fast Facts

» Population: 12.8 million

» Area: 1483 sq km

» Area code: ☑011

» Main languages: Hindi and English

» Sleeping prices: **$** below ₹1000, **$$** ₹1000 to ₹5000, **$$$** above ₹5000

Planning Your Trip

» Book accommodation ahead at http://hotels.lonelyplanet.com

» Call your hotel to confirm the day before you arrive

» Book train tickets for longer journeys at least a week ahead on www.indianrail.gov.in

Resources

» Delhi Tourism (http://delhitourism.nic.in/delhitourism/index.jsp) lists government-rated homestays and recommended tourist agencies.

» A free AA map is available in many places but, for street-by-street detail, Delhi newsstands sell the excellent 245-page *Eicher City Map* (₹340).

Delhi Highlights

1 Experience the sometime splendour of the **Red Fort** (p62), a sandstone queen bee overlooking the Old Delhi hive

2 See the great Mughal tomb that inspired the Taj Mahal, **Humayun's Tomb** (p67)

3 Explore the greenery-surrounded **Qutb Minar** (p102), in a Delhi suburb.

4 Hear qawwali singers at **Hazrat Nizam-ud-din Dargah** (p69)

5 Sample delicious **Dilli-ka-Chaat** (p87). Delhi's famous street food

6 Take an early-morning ride around Old Delhi with **DelhiByCycle** (p80), ending at **Karim's** (p87)

See Old Delhi Map (p64)

Yamuna River

Dr KB Hedgewar Marg

Red Fort 1

Ring Rd (MG Rd)

Lothian Cemetery

Delhi by Cycle 6

Dilli-ka-Chaat 5

Chandni Chowk

Chawri Bazaar

Qutb Rd

See Paharganj Map (p76)

New Delhi Train Station

Minto Bridge

Shivaji Bridge Train Station

Rajiv Chowk (Connaught Place)

Barakhamba Road

See Connaught Place Map (p72)

High Tea at the Imperial 7

See New Delhi & Around Map (p68)

Pusa Hill Forest

Upper Ridge Rd

Prithviraj Rd

India Gate

Khan Market

Mandi House

Pragati Maidan

Tilak Bridge Train Station

Hindi Park

Indraprastha Marg

Indraprastha

Pragati Maidan Train Station

Hapur Bypass

Boating Lake

KAKA NAGAR

SUNDER NAGAR

Central Secretariat

Udyog Bhawan

Motilal Nehru Place

PRESIDENT'S ESTATE

Mughal Gardens

WillingdonCres

DIPLOMATIC ENCLAVE

Delhi Polo Club

Mahavir Jayanti Park

NEW RAJENDRA NAGAR

Rajendra Place

Rajendra Nagar

Pusa Rd

Patel Rd

Patel Nagar

PATEL NAGAR

Patel Nagar Train Station

Shadipur

KAROL BAGH

Karol Bagh

Jhandewalan

Kishan Ganj Train Station

Sarai Rohilla Train Station

Sadaar Bazaar Station

SADAR BAZAR

RAM NAGAR

Phulbangash

Pratap Nagar

SABZI MANDI

Sabzi Mandi Train Station

Daya Basti

Shastri Nagar

Inderlok

Kirti Nagar

Kirti Train Station

New Rohtak Rd

Grand Trunk Rd

Ring Rd

Keshav Puram

Kanhiya Nagar

ASHOK VIHAR

KAMLA NAGAR

Delhi University

Civil Lines

CIVIL LINES

Tis Hazari

Kashmiri Gate

Delhi Train Station (Old Delhi)

OLD DELHI

PARDA BAGH

DARYAGANJ

PAHARGANJ

Minto Bridge

MEENA BAGH

NEW DELHI

SEELAMPUR

Shastri Park

Seelampur

Welcome

Marginal Bandh Rd

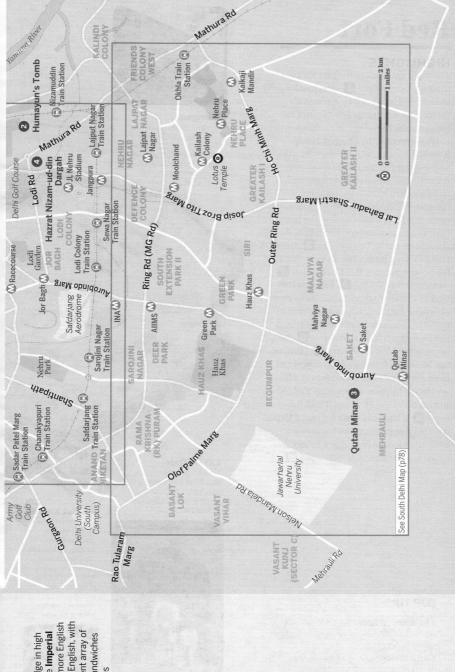

7 Indulge in high tea at the **Imperial** (p84) – more English than the English, with a decadent array of dainty sandwiches and cakes

Red Fort

HIGHLIGHTS

The main entrance to the Red Fort is through Lahore Gate **1** – the bastion in front of it was built by Aurangzeb for increased security. You can still see bullet marks from 1857 on the gate.

Walk through the Chatta Chowk (Covered Bazaar), which once sold silks and jewellery to the nobility; beyond it lies Naubat Khana **2**, a russet-red building, also known as Hathi Pol (Elephant Gate) because visitors used to dismount from their elephants or horses here as a sign of respect. From here it's straight on to the Diwan-i-Am **3**, the Hall of Public Audiences. Behind this are the private palaces, the Khas Mahal **4** and the Diwan-i-Khas **5**. Entry to this Hall of Private Audiences, the fort's most expensive building, was only permitted to the highest official of state. Nearby is the Moti Masjid (Pearl Mosque) **6** and south is the Mumtaz Mahal **7**, housing the Museum of Archaeology, or you can head north, where the Red Fort gardens are dotted by palatial pavilions and old British barracks. Here you'll find the *baoli* **8**, a spookily deserted water tank. Another five minutes' walk – across a road, then a railway bridge – brings you to the island fortress of Salimgarh **9**.

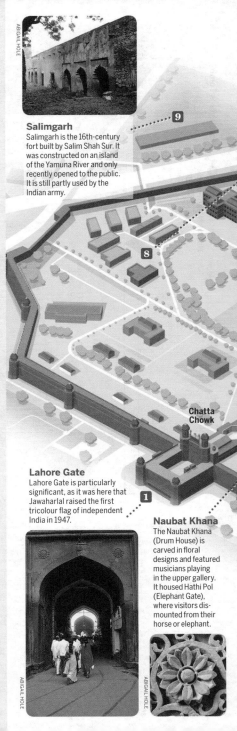

9

Salimgarh
Salimgarh is the 16th-century fort built by Salim Shah Sur. It was constructed on an island of the Yamuna River and only recently opened to the public. It is still partly used by the Indian army.

8

Chatta Chowk

Lahore Gate
Lahore Gate is particularly significant, as it was here that Jawaharlal raised the first tricolour flag of independent India in 1947.

1

Naubat Khana
The Naubat Khana (Drum House) is carved in floral designs and featured musicians playing in the upper gallery. It housed Hathi Pol (Elephant Gate), where visitors dismounted from their horse or elephant.

TOP TIPS

» **To avoid crowds**, get here early or late in the day; avoid weekends and public holidays.

» **An atmospheric way** to see the Red Fort is by night; you can visit after dark if you attend the nightly Sound-&-Light Show.

Baoli

The Red Fort step well is seldom visited and is a hauntingly deserted place, even more so when you consider its chambers were used as cells by the British from August 1942.

Moti Masjid

The Moti Masjid (Pearl Mosque) was built by Aurangzeb in 1662 for his personal use. The domes were originally covered in copper, but the copper was removed and sold by the British.

KIMBERLEY COOLE/LONELY PLANET IMAGES ©

Diwan-i-Khas

This was the most expensive building in the fort, consisting of white marble decorated with inlay work of cornelian and other stones. The screens overlooking what was once the river (now the ring road) were filled with coloured glass.

Baidon Pavilion

Zafar Mahal

Hammam

5

6

4

Rang Mahal

Mumtaz Mahal

7

3

2

Pit Stop

To refuel, head to Paratha Gali Wali, a food-stall-lined lane off Chandni Chowk noted for its many varieties of freshly made *paratha* (traditional flat bread).

Delhi Gate

← NORTH

Diwan-i-Am

These red sandstone columns were once covered in shell plaster, as polished and smooth as ivory, and in hot weather heavy red curtains were hung around the columns to block out the sun. It's believed the panels behind the marble throne were created by Florentine jeweller Austin de Bordeaux.

ABIGAIL HOLE

Khas Mahal

Most spectacular in the Emperor's private apartments is a beautiful marble screen at the northern end of the rooms; the 'Scales of Justice' are carved above it, suspended over a crescent, surrounded by stars and clouds.

ABIGAIL HOLE

DELHI IN...

Two Days

Acclimatise gently at tranquil sites, such as the **National Museum** (p70), **Gandhi Smriti** (p73) and **Humayun's Tomb** (p67). In the evening head to **Hazrat Nizam-ud-din Dargah** (p69) to hear the Sufis sing *qawwalis*.

On day two, ramble around Old Delhi's **Red Fort** (p62), then scoff *jalebis* (fried sweet 'squiggles'), launch into the old city's action-packed **bazaars** (p95) and visit the mighty **Jama Masjid** (p66). Afterwards, grab an autorickshaw south to **Connaught Place** (p75) for a bite to **eat** (p89) and to explore the hassle-free, treasure-trove **government emporiums** (p95).

Four Days

Follow the itinerary above, then on the third day wander around **Qutb Minar** (p102) and **Mehrauli** (p103) before indulging in some quiet meditation at the **Bahai House of Worship** (p75). In the evening, watch the mesmerising **Dances of India** (p94), then kick back at a **bar** (p92).

On day four, wonder at the glories in the laid-back **Crafts Museum** (p70) and nearby **Purana Qila** (p73). Then head to **Hauz Khas** (p77) to wander around the forgotten tank and mausoleum, and browse in its boutiques.

History

Delhi hasn't always been India's capital but, as a gateway city, it has long played a pivotal role. It was built on the plains near a fording point on the Yamuna River, and on the route between western and Central Asia and Southeast Asia. It's believed to be the site of the fabled city of Indraprastha, which featured in the Mahabharata more than 3000 years ago, but historical evidence suggests that the area has been settled for a mere 2500 years.

At least eight known cities have been founded here. The first four cities of Delhi were to the south, around the area where the Qutb Minar now stands. The fifth Delhi, Firozabad, was at Firoz Shah Kotla, while Emperor Sher Shah created the sixth at Purana Qila (both in present-day New Delhi). The Mughal emperor, Shah Jahan, constructed the seventh Delhi in the 17th century; his Shahjahanabad roughly corresponds to Old Delhi today. In 1911, the British announced the shifting of their capital from Kolkata (Calcutta) and proceeded to build New Delhi, which was inaugurated in 1931. Only 16 years later, the British were out, and Delhi became the capital of an independent India.

Since Independence, the capital has prospered. The downside of this boom is chronic overcrowding, housing shortages, pollution, traffic congestion, and ever more extreme contrasts between rich and poor.

◉ Sights

Most sights in Delhi are easily accessible via metro. Note that many places are closed on Monday.

OLD DELHI

Medieval-seeming Old Delhi is a crazy hubbub that bombards the senses. Set aside at least half a day to do this fascinating area justice. All of the following attractions feature on Map p64.

Red Fort (Lal Qila)   FORT

(Indian/foreigner ₹10/250, video ₹25, combined museum ticket ₹5; ⊙9am-6pm Tue-Sun; ⓂChandni Chowk) This massive fort is a sandstone shadow of its former self; but it's the best place in Delhi to imagine the Mughal city's sometime splendour. It dates from the peak of the dynasty's power, a time of unparalleled pomp: of eunuchs, ceremonial elephants, palanquins, and buildings lined with precious stones.

The walls of the fort extend for 2km and vary in height from 18m on the river side to 33m on the city side. Shah Jahan constructed the fort between 1638 and 1648, but never completely moved his capital from Agra to his new city of Shahjahanabad, because he was deposed and imprisoned in Agra Fort by his son Aurangzeb.

Mughal reign from Delhi was short; Aurangzeb was the first and last great Mughal emperor to rule from here. Subsequent rulers, sapped by civil war, were unable to maintain the fort properly, and slums within the walls were thronged with impoverished imperial descendants. By the 19th century it was already much dilapidated. Following the 1857 First War of Independence, the British cleared all but the most important buildings to make way for ugly barracks and army offices.

The 10m-deep moat, which has been dry since 1857, was originally crossed on creaky wooden drawbridges, replaced with stone bridges in 1811.

Since Independence many landmark political speeches have taken place at the fort, and every year on Independence Day (15 August) it hosts the prime minister's address to the nation.

Lahore Gate

The fort's main gate is so named because it faces towards Lahore, now in Pakistan. The gate is a potent symbol of modern India: during the fight for Independence, there was a nationalist aspiration to see the Indian flag flying over the gate – a dream that became reality in 1947.

You enter the fort through here and immediately find yourself in the vaulted arcade known as the **Chatta Chowk** (Covered Bazaar). The tourist-trap arcade once sold rather more exclusive items to the royal household – silks, jewellery and gold.

The arcade leads to the **Naubat Khana** (Drum House), where musicians used to perform. There's an **Indian War Memorial Museum** upstairs, full of fearsome weaponry and phallic shells.

Diwan-i-Am

In the **Hall of Public Audiences** the emperor would hear disputes from his subjects. Many of the precious stones set above the emperor's throne were looted following the First War of Independence. The hall was restored following a directive by Lord Curzon, the viceroy of India between 1898 and 1905.

Diwan-i-Khas

The white marble **Hall of Private Audiences** was the luxurious chamber where the emperor would hold private meetings. The centrepiece was once the magnificent solid-gold and jewel-studded Peacock Throne, looted from India by Persia's Nadir Shah in 1739. In 1760 the Marathas removed the hall's silver ceiling.

Royal Baths

Next to the Diwan-i-Khas are the hammams (baths) – three large rooms surmounted by domes, with a fountain in the centre – one of which was set up as a sauna. The floors were once inlaid with more pietra dura and the rooms were illuminated through stained-glass roof panels.

Shahi Burj

This modest, three-storey, octagonal tower to the northeastern edge of the fort was once Shah Jahan's private working area. From here, cooling water, known as the *nahr-i-bihisht* (river of paradise), used to flow south through the Royal Baths, the Diwan-i-Khas, the Khas Mahal and on to the Rang Mahal.

Moti Masjid

The small, enclosed, marble **Pearl Mosque** is next to the baths. Its outer walls are oriented exactly in symmetry with the rest of the fort, while the inner walls are slightly askew, so that the mosque is correctly orientated to Mecca.

Other Features

The **Khas Mahal**, south of the Diwan-i-Khas, was the emperor's private palace. It was divided into rooms for worship, sleeping and living, with carved walls and painted ceilings.

The **Rang Mahal** (Palace of Colour), further south again, took its name from its vividly painted interior, now long gone. This was the residence of the emperor's chief wife and is where he dined. On the floor in the centre there's an exquisitely carved marble lotus; the water flowing along the channel from the Shahi Burj would end up here.

Relics from the Mughal era are displayed at the **Museum of Archaeology** in the **Mumtaz Mahal**, once the women's quarters, still further south along the eastern wall. In one of the British-built barracks there's also the interesting **Museum of India's Struggle for Freedom**, with some dramatic life-size dioramas,

It's worth seeking out the deserted **baoli** (step well). A short walk away is **Salimgarh** (☉10am-5pm) built by Salim Shah Suri in 1546. Few visitors make it over here to see the ruined mosque and broad, much restored walls – it's still partly occupied by the Indian army and was only opened to the public in 2008.

The old walled city of **Shahjahanabad** stretches west from the Red Fort. It was at one time surrounded by a sturdy defensive wall, only fragments of which now exist. The **Kashmiri Gate**, to the north, was the scene of desperate fighting when the British retook Delhi during the 1857 First War of Independence.

Old Delhi

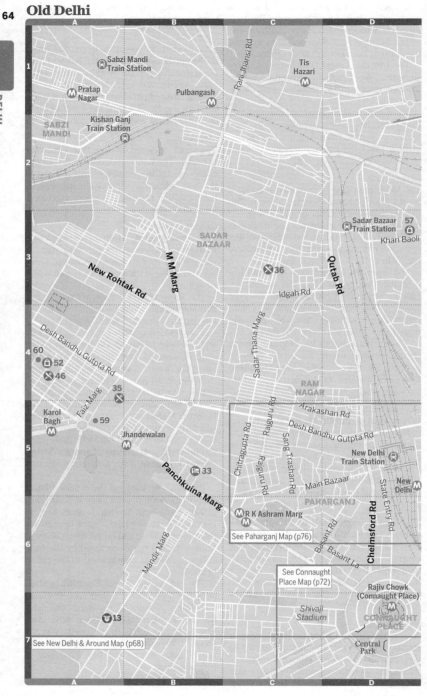

Sabzi Mandi Train Station

Pratap Nagar

Pulbangash

Rani Jhansi Rd

Tis Hazari

SABZI MANDI

Kishan Ganj Train Station

SADAR BAZAAR

Sadar Bazaar Train Station · 57
Khari Baoli

New Rohtak Rd

M M Marg

Qutab Rd

⊗ 36

Idgah Rd

Desh Bandhu Gutpta Rd

Sadar Thana Marg

60
🔒 52
⊗ 46

Faiz Marg

35 ⊗

RAM NAGAR

Karol Bagh

● 59

Jhandewalan

Arakashan Rd

Rajguru Rd

Chittragupta Rd

Desh Bandhu Gutpta Rd

Sang Trashan Rd

New Delhi Train Station

Rajguru Rd

Panchkuina Marg

33

Main Bazaar

State Entry Rd

New Delhi

PAHARGANJ

R K Ashram Marg

See Paharganj Map (p76)

Mandir Marg

Basant Rd

Chelmsford Rd

Basant La

See Connaught Place Map (p72)

Rajiv Chowk (Connaught Place)

Shivaji Stadium

CONNAUGHT PLACE

13

See New Delhi & Around Map (p68)

Central Park

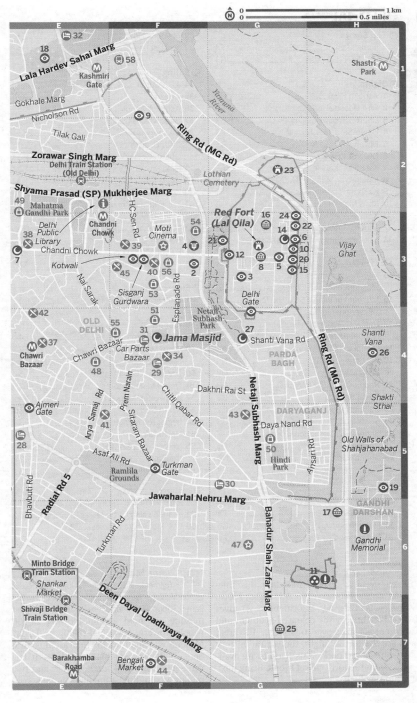

Old Delhi

Sound-&-Light Show

Each evening (except Monday) this one-hour **show** (admission ₹60; ⊙in English 7.30pm Nov-Jan, 9pm May-Aug, 8.30pm rest of yr) gives Red Fort history the coloured-spotlight and portentous-voice-over treatment. It's great to see the fort by night, though the history lesson is a tad ponderous. Tickets are available from the fort's **ticket kiosk**. Bring mosquito repellent.

TOP CHOICE **Jama Masjid**   MOSQUE
(camera, video each ₹200; tower ₹100; ⊙non-Muslims 8am-½hr before sunset, minaret 9am-5.30pm; MChandni Chowk) India's largest mosque can hold a mind-blowing 25,000 people. Towering over Old Delhi, the 'Friday Mosque' was Shah Jahan's final architectural opus, built between 1644 and 1658. It has three gateways, four angle towers and two minarets standing 40m high, and is con-

structed of alternating vertical strips of red sandstone and white marble. You can enter from gate 1 or 3.

For an extra charge you can climb the narrow southern minaret (notices say that unaccompanied women are not permitted), up 121 steps, for incredible views. From the top of the minaret, you can see one of the features that architect Edwin Lutyens incorporated into his design of New Delhi – the Jama Masjid, Connaught Place and Sansad Bhavan (Parliament House) are in a direct line.

Visitors should remove their shoes at the top of the stairs. There's no charge to enter the mosque, but you'll have to pay the camera charge whether you want to use your camera or not.

Chandni Chowk
AREA

Old Delhi's backbone is the madcap Chandni Chowk or 'moonlight place', a wide avenue thronged by crowds, hawkers and rickshaws. In the time of Shah Jahan, a canal ran down its centre, lined by peepal and neem trees – at night the waters reflected the moon, hence the name. Tiny bazaar-crammed lanes snake off the broadway like clogged arteries. At the eastern (Red Fort) end of Chandni Chowk, there's the 16th-century **Digambara Jain Temple** (☉5am-noon & 6-9pm) (remove shoes and leather before entering). The fascinating **bird hospital** (donations appreciated; ☉8am-9pm) here was founded in 1939 and is run by the Jains, who believe in the preservation of all life. Only vegetarian birds are admitted, though carnivores are treated as outpatients. The upstairs pigeons' section brings to mind Hitchcock's *The Birds*.

The western end of Chandni Chowk is marked by the mid-17th-century **Fatehpuri Masjid**, named after one of Shah Jahan's wives. It offers a striking tranquility after the craziness of the street. After the 1857 First War of Independence the mosque was sold to a Hindu merchant, who used it as a warehouse, but it was later returned to local Muslims.

There's a CNG shuttle service (small green buses) between Digambara Jain Temple and Fatehpuri Masjid (₹5).

Sunehri Masjid
MOSQUE

South of the Red Fort is the 18th-century Sunehri Masjid. In 1739 Nadir Shah, the Persian invader, stood on its roof and macabrely watched his soldiers conduct a bloody massacre of Delhi's inhabitants.

Raj Ghat
MONUMENT

South of the Red Fort, on the banks of the Yamuna River, a simple square platform of black marble marks the spot where Mahatma Gandhi was cremated following his assassination in 1948. It's inscribed with what are said to have been his final words, 'Hai Ram' (Oh, God), and has a hushed, peaceful atmosphere, set amid tranquil lawns.

Jawaharlal Nehru, the first Indian prime minister, was cremated just to the north, at **Shanti Vana** (Forest of Peace), in 1964. Nehru's daughter, Indira Gandhi, who was assassinated in 1984, and grandsons Sanjay (who died in 1980) and Rajiv (assassinated in 1991) were also cremated in this vicinity.

Nicholson Cemetery
CEMETERY

(9am-5pm) Close to the Kashmiri Gate is this 3-hectare forgotten corner of Delhi. It's named after John Nicholson, who died in 1857 and is buried here amid a sea of British graves that hint at fascinating stories. At the time he was described as the 'Hero of Delhi' but author William Dalrymple calls him an 'imperial psychopath' in *The Last Mughal*. Northwest of here is the British-erected **Mutiny Memorial**, dedicated to the soldiers who died during the First War of Independance. Near the monument is an **Ashoka Pillar**; like the one in Firoz Shah Kotla, it was brought here by Firoz Shah.

FREE **National Gandhi Museum** MUSEUM (🖉23311793; ☉9.30am-5.30pm Tue-Sun) Contains photos and some of Gandhi's belongings.

NEW DELHI & AROUND

All of the attractions in this section feature on Map p68.

TOP CHOICE **Humayun's Tomb** HISTORIC BUILDING (Indian/foreigner ₹10/250, video ₹25; ☉dawn-dusk; ⓂJLN Stadium) This tomb is the city's most sublime sight, and the one the Obamas were taken to visit when they were in Delhi. A beautiful example of early Mughal architecture, this tomb was built in the mid-16th century by Haji Begum, the Persian-born senior wife of the second Mughal emperor Humayun. The tomb brought Persian style to Delhi, but the two-tone combination of red sandstone and white marble is entirely local, showing the complementary merging of the different cultures. Various elements in the design of Humayun's Tomb – a squat building with high arched entrances that let in light, topped by a bulbous dome and

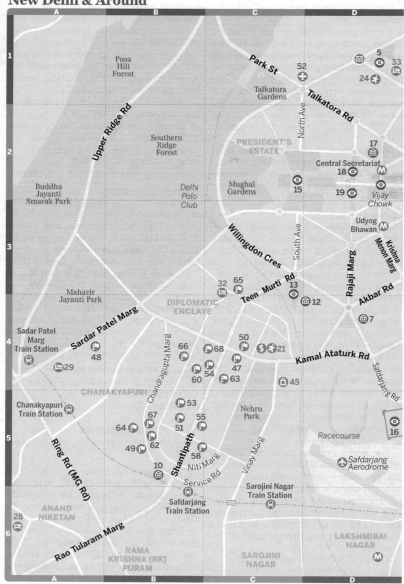

surrounded by 12 hectares of formal gardens –
were to be refined in the years that followed
to eventually create the magnificence of
Agra's Taj Mahal.

Other beautiful tombs dot the complex,
including that of the emperor's favourite
barber, as well as one belonging to Haji Begum herself and the tomb of Isa Khan – a
fine example of Lodi architecture through a
gate to the left of the entrance. The magnificent Mughal gardens are a magical place
to wander, particularly towards sunset.

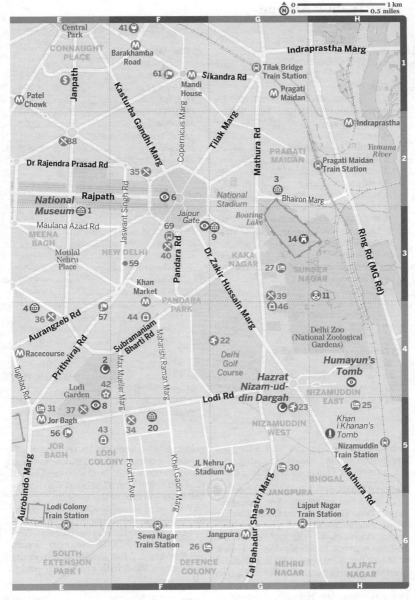

TOP CHOICE **Hazrat Nizam-ud-din Dargah**   SACRED SITE

(⊘24hr) Amid a tangle of alleys, and attracting hordes of devotees, is the vibrant marble shrine of the Muslim Sufi saint, Nizam-ud-din Chishti. He died in 1325, aged 92, but the mausoleum has been revamped several times, and dates from 1562. Other tombs include the later grave of Jahanara (daughter of Shah Jahan), and the renowned Urdu poet, Amir Khusru. It's one of Delhi's most extraordinary pleasures to experience the buzz around the site and hear Sufis sing *qawwali* at around sunset, just after evening prayers on Thursdays and feast days.

National Museum   MUSEUM
(☏23019272; www.nationalmuseum india.gov.in; Janpath; Indian ₹10, foreigner incl English, French or German audio guide ₹300, Hindi audio guide ₹150; camera Indian/foreigner ₹20/300; ◷10am-5pm Tue-Sun; Ⓜ Central Secretariat) An overview of India's last 5000 years, this is a splendid museum – perfect for a rainy day and not so large that it overwhelms. Exhibits include rare relics from the Harappan Civilisation, including some fascinating mundane items such as tweezers and hairpins from around 2700 BC, Central Asian antiquities including many artefacts from the Silk Route, a mesmerising collection of jewel-bright miniature paintings, exquisite old coins including pure gold examples from the 1st century, woodcarving, textiles, musical instruments, and Indus jewellery made from shells and bones. Give yourself at least a few hours – preferably half a day – to explore this museum.

You'll need some identification to obtain an audio guide. Video cameras are prohibited.

Next door is the **Archaeological Survey of India** (☏23019108; asi.nic.in; Janpath; ◷9.30am-1pm & 2-6pm Mon-Fri) which stocks publications about India's main archaeological sites.

FREE **Crafts Museum**   MUSEUM
(☏23371641; Bhairon Marg; ◷10am-5pm Tue-Sun; Ⓜ Pragati Maidan) This is a tree-shaded treasure trove of a museum. The galleries contain more than 20,000 exhibits from around India, including metalware, woodwork, tribal masks, paintings, terracotta figurines and

richly coloured textiles. The fascinating items display the application of art to everyday life, from village toys to a huge 18th-century wooden Gujarati *jharokha* (elaborate balcony). Artisans demonstrate their skills and sell their products. The on-site **shop** is particularly good. Photography is only allowed with prior permission.

Lodi Garden PARK
(Lodi Rd; ☺6am-8pm Oct-Mar, 5am-8pm Apr-Sep; ⓂKhan Market) Lodi garden is Delhi's loveliest escape, popular with everyone from power-walking politicians to canoodling couples. The gardens are dotted by the crumbling **tombs** of the Sayyid and Lodi rulers, including the impressive 15th-century **Bara Gumbad**, and inhabited by fluttering butterflies, stalking peacocks and all sorts of birds.

If you want serenity, avoid Sunday.

National Gallery of Modern Art ART GALLERY
(☎23382835; ngmaindia.gov.in; Jaipur House; Indian/foreigner ₹10/150; ☺10am-5pm Tue-Sun; ⓂKhan Market) This gallery has a fantastic new wing alongside the Maharaja of Jaipur's former place. It includes all the great modern Indian masters, such as the fascinating 'Company Paintings', which were provided by local artists to suit their new British patrons, beautiful works by Amrita Sher-Gil and Nobel Prize–winner Rabindranath Tagore (who started painting aged 67), and stunning pieces by FN Souza and MF Husain. Photography isn't allowed.

Rajpath AREA
Rajpath (Kingsway) is the imposing approach to New Delhi. It hosts the huge Republic Day parade every 26 January and the Beating of the Retreat on 29 January.

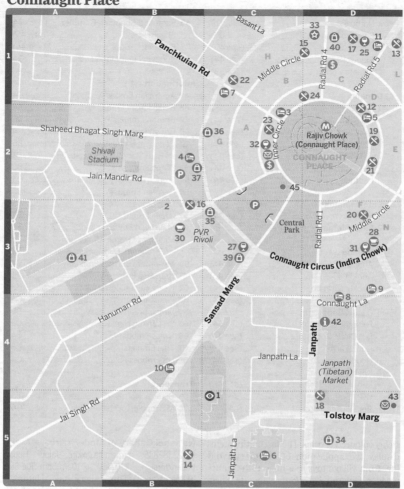

Raj-appointed English architect Edwin Lutyens constructed New Delhi between 1914 and 1931, when the British moved their capital here from Calcutta. His designs were intended to spell out in stone the might of the British empire – but 16 years later, the British were out on their ear. New Delhi became the powerhouse of the new Republic.

At the western end of Rajpath is the official residence of the president of India, the Rashtrapati Bhavan (President's House), built in 1929. Pre-Independence, this 340-room palace was the viceroy's residence. At the time of Mountbatten, India's last viceroy,

the number of servants employed here was staggering. There were 418 gardeners alone, 50 of whom were boys employed to chase away birds. To its west, the Mughal Gardens occupy 130 hectares; it's only open (admission free; photography prohibited) to the public for several days in February/March – for dates contact India Tourism Delhi.

Rashtrapati Bhavan is flanked by the mirror-image, dome-crowned North and South Secretariat buildings, housing government ministries, which have over 1000 rooms between them. The three buildings sit upon a small rise, known as Raisina Hill.

At Rajpath's eastern end is **India Gate**. This 42m-high stone memorial arch, designed by Lutyens, pays tribute to around 90,000 Indian army soldiers who died in WWI, the Northwest Frontier operations of the same time and the 1919 Anglo-Afghan War.

Sansad Bhavan (Parliament House), a circular, colonnaded structure 171m in diameter, stands at the end of Sansad Marg.

Purana Qila   FORT
(Old Fort; ☑24353178; Mathura Rd; Indian/foreigner ₹5/100, video ₹25; ⊙dawn-dusk; ⓂPragati Maidan) With its massive walls and impressive gateways, Purana Qila was built by Af-

ghan ruler Sher Shah during his reign (1538-45), before the emperor Humayun (whom he had previously defeated) regained control of India. The site is thought to be that of ancient Indraprastha

Entering from the south gate you'll see the graceful octagonal, red-sandstone tower, the **Sher Mandal**, later used by Humayun as a library. It was while hurriedly descending the stairs of this tower in 1556 that he slipped and sustained injuries from which he later died. Just beyond it is the 1541 **Qila-i-Kuhran Mosque** (Mosque of Sher Shah), which delicately combines black-and-white marble with the more easily available deep red sandstone.

A popular, picturesque **boating lake** has been created from the former moat, with pedaloes for hire.

FREE **Gandhi Smriti**   MUSEUM
(☑23012843; 5 Tees January Marg, camera free, video prohibited; ⊙10am-1.30pm & 2-5pm Tue-Sun, closed every 2nd Sat of month; ⓂRacecourse) This poignant memorial is where Mahatma Gandhi was shot dead by a Hindu zealot on 30 January 1948. Concrete footsteps represent Gandhi's final steps and lead to the spot where he died, marked by a small pavilion known as the Martyr's Column.

The impressive indoor museum has photographs, paintings and dioramas depicting scenes from Gandhi's life, including some whizz-bang interactive exhibits.

Gandhi had been staying in the house as a guest, and spent the last 144 days of his life here. In the room he occupied, his meagre possessions are on display, such as his walking stick, spectacles, spinning wheel and chappals (sandals).

Gurdwara Bangla Sahib   SIKH TEMPLE
(Ashoka Rd; ⊙4am-9pm; ⓂShivaji Stadium) The Gurdwara Bangla Sahib is an important Sikh shrine and a constant hive of activity. Topped with gold onion domes, it was constructed at the site where the eighth Sikh guru, Harkrishan Dev, spent several months in 1664. This guru dedicated most of his time to helping the destitute and sick and was revered for his healing powers. At the back of the gurdwara (Sikh temple) is a huge tank, surrounded by a graceful colonnade. The water is said to have curative properties. Devotional songs are sung throughout the day.

Safdarjang's Tomb   HISTORIC BUILDING
(Aurobindo Marg; Indian/foreigner ₹5/100, video ₹25; ⊙dawn-dusk; ⓂJor Bagh) Built by the

Nawab of Avadh for his father, Safdarjang, this grandiose mid-18th-century tomb is one of the last examples of Mughal architecture. It's a fantastical work of overwrought mannerism, which seems reflect the final throes of the great empire.

FREE **Indira Gandhi Memorial Museum** MUSEUM
(☎23010094; 1 Safdarjang Rd; ⊙9.30am-4.45pm Tue-Sun; Ⓜ Racecourse) The former residence of Indira Gandhi is now a fascinating museum, displaying artefacts, photos and newspaper clippings, as well as personal belongings, including the blood-stained sari she was wearing when she was assassinated in 1984. Some of the rooms are preserved as they were, an interesting window into the understated elegance of her life. Another section is devoted to her son Rajiv, also assassinated in 1991 by a suicide bomber. Fragments of the clothes he was wearing and, even more poignantly, his trainers, are

on display. On the way out, you'll pass an enclosed crystal pathway that marks Gandhi's final footsteps before her murder.

Nehru Memorial Museum & Planetarium   MUSEUM

(☎23016734; ⏾9am-5.15pm Tue-Sun) Teen Murti Bhavan is the former residence of Jawaharlal Nehru (India's first prime minister), and was previously Flagstaff House, home to the British commander-in-chief. Just off Teen Murti Rd, it has been converted into a must-see museum for those interested in the Independence movement. Some rooms have been preserved as Nehru left them, and there's a wealth of photographs, though some contextualisation would come in handy.

In the grounds is a recently renovated planetarium (☎23014504; http://nehruplanetarium.org; 45min show ₹50; ⏾in English 11.30am & 3pm).

Tibet House   MUSEUM

(☎24611515; 1 Lodi Rd; admission ₹10; ⏾9.30am-1pm & 2-5.30pm Mon-Fri; MJLN Stadium) Tibet House has a small museum displaying ceremonial items, including sacred manuscripts, sculptures and old *thangkas* (Tibetan paintings on cloth). All were brought out of Tibet when the Dalai Lama fled following Chinese occupation. Photography prohibited.

The **bookshop** sells Buddhist books, chanting CDs, prayer flags and *katas* (sacred Tibetan scarves).

National Zoological Gardens   ZOO

(☎24359825; Mathura Rd; Indian/foreigner ₹10/50, video ₹50; ⏾9am-5pm Sat-Thu; MPragati Maidan) Wildly popular with families and couples, this is India's biggest zoo, set in 86 hectares. There are white Bengal tigers, Himalayan black bears, rhinos, wolves, elephants and some spectacular birds.

CONNAUGHT PLACE AREA
New Delhi's colonnaded heart is commercial centre Connaught Place (CP; Map p72), named after George V's uncle who visited in 1921. Its streets radiate from the central circle, divided into blocks and devoted to shops, banks, restaurants, hotels and offices.

Often creating confusion, the outer circle is technically called Connaught Circus (divided into blocks from G to N) and the inner circle Connaught Place (divided into blocks from A to F). There's also a Middle Circle. In 1995 the inner and outer circles were re-named Rajiv Chowk and Indira Chowk respectively, but these names are rarely used.

Touts are especially rampant in Connaught Place.

Jantar Mantar   HISTORIC SITE

(Map p72; Sansad Marg; Indian/foreigner ₹5/100; ⏾9am-dusk; MPatel Chowk) The most eccentric of all Delhi's inner-city structures, Jantar Mantar is an odd collection of huge curved terracotta buildings, a giant playground which makes for great photo opps. 'Jantar Mantar' may mean the equivalent to 'abracadabra' in Hindi, but the site was constructed in 1725 for scientific purposes – it's the earliest of Maharaja Jai Singh II's five observatories. It's dominated by a huge sundial and houses other instruments plotting the course of heavenly bodies.

OTHER AREAS
Bahai House of Worship (Lotus Temple)   TEMPLE

(Map p78; ☎26444029; Kalkaji; ⏾9.30am-5.30pm Tue-Sun; MKalkaji Mandir) This extraordinary temple is shaped like the sacred lotus flower and is a wonderful place to seek some otherworldly peace. Designed by Iranian-Canadian architect Fariburz Sahba in 1986, it has 27 immaculate white-marble petals. The Bahai philosophy revolves around universal peace and the elimination of prejudice, and adherents of all faiths are welcome to pray or meditate silently according to their own religion.

Refrain from speaking in the temple; photography inside is prohibited.

Akshardham Temple   TEMPLE

(www.akshardham.com; Noida turning, National Hwy 24; ⏾9am-6pm Tue-Sun Oct-Mar, 10am-7pm Tue-Sun Apr-Sep; MAkshardham) The Hindu Swaminarayan Group's controversially ostentatious Akshardham Temple, on Delhi's outskirts, has something of a Disney feel. Inaugurated in 2005, it's made of salmon-coloured sandstone with an interior carved from white marble in giddying detail. It contains around 20,000 carved deities, and reflects traditional Orissan, Gujarati, Mughal and Rajasthani architectural elements. Outside there are 148 carved elephants, each different.

Allow at least half a day to do it justice (weekdays are less crowded) as there's lots to see, including a boat ride through 10,000 years of Indian history, elaborate animatronics telling stories of the life of Swaminarayan, and musical fountains.

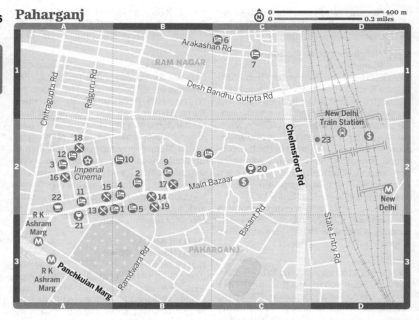

Paharganj

**Lakshmi Narayan Temple
(Birla Mandir)** TEMPLE
(Map p64; Mandir Marg; ⊙6am-9pm; MRK Ashram
Marg) West of Connaught Place, the Orissan-
style Lakshmi Narayan Temple, a rather
overexcited red-and-cream confection, was
erected in 1938 by the wealthy industrialist
BD Birla. It was inaugurated by Gandhi as a

temple for all castes; a sign on the gate says,
'Everyone is Welcome'.

National Rail Museum MUSEUM
(Map p68; ✆26881816; www.nationalrailmuseum.
org; Chanakyapuri; admission adult/child ₹20/10,
video ₹100; ⊙9.30am-5pm Tue-Sun Oct-Mar, to 7pm
Apr-Sep) Trainspotters and kids will adore this
museum, with around 30 locomotives and old

carriages. Exhibits include an 1855 steam engine, still in working order, and various oddities including the skull of an elephant that charged a train in 1894, and lost.

There's also the 10-minute **Joy Train** ride (adult/child ₹10/5), and **boating** is also possible (adult/child ₹30/15).

Hauz Khas
AREA

Hauz Khas means 'royal tank', named after a 13th-century reservoir built by Allauddin Khilji. The artificial lake was once the water source for Siri Fort – the second city of Delhi – and now is a beautiful blue-green expanse that feels forgotten by the modern city. Overlooking it are Firoz Shah's 14th-century domed madrasa (religious school) and his tomb (Map p78), which were once covered in brilliantly painted white plaster and topped by gold domes. Some Lodi and Tughlak tombs also dot the area, which whirls with grass-green parakeets and other birds. This is a fascinating, secluded place to explore, and neighbouring Hauz Khas village (Map p78) is one of Delhi's artiest enclaves, filled with upmarket boutiques, quirky bars and curio shops.

Shankar's International Dolls Museum
MUSEUM

(Map p64; ☑23316970; www.childrensbooktrust.com; Nehru House, Bahadur Shah Zafar Marg; adult/child ₹15/5; ⊙10am-5.30pm Tue-Sun) From Spanish bullfighting figurines to Indian bridal dolls, this remarkable museum has 6500 dolls from 85 countries.

Coronation Durbar Site
HISTORIC SITE

In a desolate field, north of Old Delhi, stands a lone obelisk. Here, in 1877 and 1903, the great durbars, featuring Indian nobility, paid homage to the British monarch. In 1911, King George V was declared emperor of India here.

Kotla Firoz Shah
HISTORIC SITE

(Map p64; Indian/foreigner ₹5/100, video ₹25; ⊙dawn-dusk; Ⓜ Pragati Maidan) Firozabad (the fifth city of Delhi) was built by Firoz Shah in 1354. Its ruins, including a mosque and step well, can be found at Kotla Firoz Shah, off Bahadur Shah Zafar Marg. Visit on a Thursday afternoon when crowds come to pray, light candles and leave bowls of milk to appease Delhi's djinns (invisible spirits or genies) that are reputed to inhabit the kotla. In the fortress/palace is a 13m-high sandstone **Ashoka Pillar** inscribed with Ashoka's edicts (and a later inscription).

⬦ Sulabh International Museum of Toilets
MUSEUM

(☑25031518; www.sulabhtoiletmuseum.org; Sulabh Complex, Mahavir Enclave, Palam Dabri Rd; admission free; ⊙10am-5pm Mon-Sat) This quirky museum houses toilet-related paraphernalia dating from 2500 BC to modern times. It's not just a curiosity: Sulabh International has done extraordinary work in the field of sanitation, developing pour-flush toilets and bio-gas plants, and educating the children of 'manual scavengers' (whose job is to remove the crap from dry toilets) for other work. A guided tour (free) brings the loos to life.

🏃 Activities

TOP CHOICE / Amatrra Spa
SPA

(Map p68; ☑24122921; www.amatrraspa.com; Ashok Hotel, Chanakyapuri; ⊙9am-10pm; Ⓜ Racecourse) The most legendarily luxurious of all Delhi's luxury spas, Amatrra is the A-list place to be pampered. There's a cover charge of ₹1000 for nonguests; massages, such as 'Asian Blend', cost from ₹3000, and there are many other treatments, like 'Sparkle Body Scrub' (₹3500).

Delhi Golf Club
GOLFING

(Map p68; ☑24307100; www.delhigolfclub.org; Dr Zakir Hussain Marg; weekdays/weekends US$50/70; ⊙sunrise-sunset; Ⓜ Jor Bagh) Dates from 1931 and has beautiful, well-tended fairways; weekends are busy.

Kerala Ayurveda
AYURVEDA

(Map p78; ☑41754888; www.keralaayurveda.biz; E-2 Green Park Extn; ⊙8am-8pm; Ⓜ Green Park) For *abhyangam* (oil treatment; ₹1200 for 45 minutes), plus other Ayurvedic therapies, try this place.

Lambency Spa
SPA

(Map p78; ☑40587983; www.chandansparsh.com; M-24 Greater Kailash II; ⊙9am-9pm) Here you can have a top-of-the-range manicure and pedicure (₹1000) or one-hour body massage (from ₹1000). Prices don't include tax.

Jaypee Vasant Continental Hotel
SWIMMING

(Map p78; ☑26148800; Basant Lok complex, Vasant Vihar; per person ₹1202) Escape the summer heat at this five-star hotel pool.

Siri Fort Sports Complex
SWIMMING

(Map p78; ☑26496657; day membership Indian/foreigner ₹40/100; ⊙Apr-Sep; Ⓜ Green Park) Olympic-sized swimming pool plus a toddler pool.

DELHI

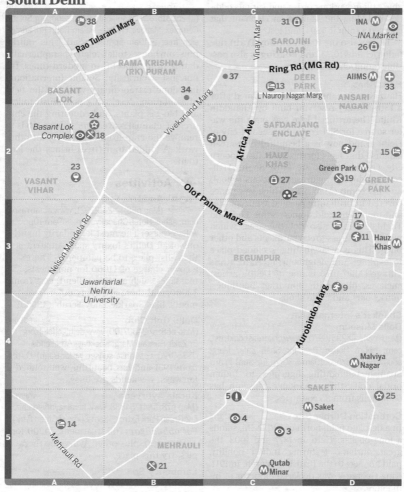

🎓 Courses

Tannie Baig COOKING

(☎9899555704; baig.murad@gmail.com; 2hr lesson ₹3200; Ⓜ Hauz Khas) The elegant Tannie, who runs Treetops Guest House in Hauz Khas has written 16 cookery books. A two-hour cooking lesson sounds pricey, but it's a flat rate for up to five people. If you stay at the guesthouse, lessons are half price.

Parul Puri COOKING

(Map p68; ☎9810793322; www.koneone.com; Ⓜ Jangpura) K-One One (p85) runs two-hour classes with a focus on cuisine from

North India regions. The charge is ₹1200 per person; book at least two days in advance.

Central Hindi Directorate LANGUAGE

(☎26103160; hindinideshalaya.nic.in; West Block VII, RK Puram; 60hr course ₹6000) Runs basic Hindi courses (minimum numbers apply) of 60 hours (two hours daily, three lessons per week).

Dhyan Foundation MEDITATION, YOGA

(☎26253374; www.dhyanfoundation.com) Various yoga and meditation options based in South Extension II.

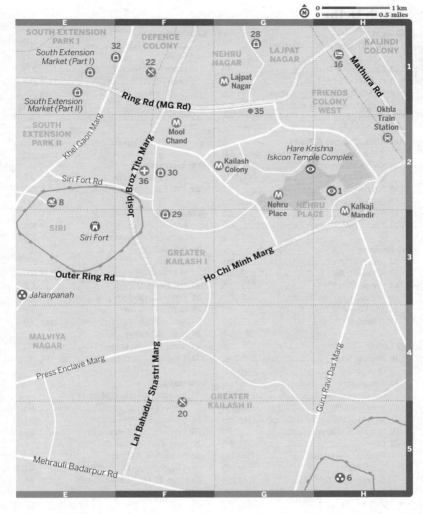

Morarji Desai National Institute of Yoga MEDITATION, YOGA
(Map p68; ☎23721472; www.yogamdniy.com; 68 Ashoka Rd; ⓜPatel Chowk) Offers one-year diploma courses that include pranayama and hatha yoga as well as meditation.

Sri Aurobindo Ashram MEDITATION, YOGA
(☎26858563; Aurobindo Marg; classes per month ₹500) Yoga and meditation, morning, afternoon and evening, three days a week.

Studio Abhyas MEDITATION, YOGA
(☎26962757, bookings Monica 9810522624; F-27 Green Park) Yoga classes combining *asanas* (fixed body positions) and pranayama,

meditation classes, and Vedic chanting classes (evenings or by appointment).

Tushita Meditation Centre MEDITATION
(☎26513400; 9 Padmini Enclave, Hauz Khas) Tibetan/Buddhist meditation sessions on Monday and Fridays at 6.30pm. Donations are appreciated.

ⓖ Tours

Delhi is a spread-out city so taking a tour makes sense, although you can feel rushed at some sites. Avoid Monday when many sites are shut. Admission fees and camera/video charges aren't included in tour prices

South Delhi

below, and rates are per person. Book several days in advance as minimum numbers may be required. India Tourism Delhi (p98) can arrange multilingual, government-approved guides (from ₹150/300 per half-/full day).

TOP **DelhiByCycle** CYCLING
CHOICE (☏9811723720; www.delhibycycle.com; ₹1250; ☉6.45-10am) Run by Jack Leenaars, a journalist from the Netherlands, this is a fantastic way to see Delhi. There's the Shah Jahan Tour around the back lanes and bazaars of Old Delhi, and the Raj Tour around New Delhi. Tours start early to avoid the traffic and the price includes chai and a Mughal breakfast.

Salaam Balaak Trust WALKING
(Map p76; ☏23584164, 9910099348; www.salaambaalaktrust.com; Gali Chandiwali, Paharganj; suggested donation ₹200; Ⓜ RK Ashram Marg) This charitable organisation offers two-hour 'street walks' with a twist – your guide is a former (Trust-trained) street child, who will show you first-hand what life is like for inner-city homeless kids. The

money goes to the Trust to assist children on the streets.

Hope Project
WALKING

(Map p68; ☎24353006; www.hopeproject india.org; 127 Hazrat Nizamuddin; 90min walk ₹150) Ninety-minute walks around the basti (slum) of Nizamuddin, which surrounds the Dargah, learning about the area. It's a poverty-stricken place, so can be shocking as well as insightful. The walk fee goes towards supporting the Hope Project's work. Wear modest clothing as this is a very traditional area.

Delhi Tourism & Transport Development Corporation
BUS TOURS

(DTTDC; delhitourism.nic.in) Baba Kharak Singh Marg (Map p72; ☎23363607; ⊘7am-9pm); international airport (☎25675609; ⊘8am-9pm) Bus tours (₹310 AC) of New Delhi (9am to 2pm) and Old Delhi (2.15pm to 5.15pm). Also runs the new air-conditioned **Hop-on, Hop-off (HOHO) Bus Service** (☎1280; ₹300; ⊘every 30 min, 7.30am-8pm Tue-Sun), which passes by all Delhi's major sights. Same-day trips to Agra (₹1100 AC) run three times a week while three-day tours of Agra and Jaipur (₹6350, via rail) operate twice weekly.

Old Delhi Walks
WALKING

(Intach; ☎24641304; www.intachdelhichapter. org; tour ₹50) Intach runs a walking tour (approximately two hours) every month with an expert guide, exploring different areas, such as Chandhi Chowk, Nizamuddin, Hauz Khas, and Mehrauli. Customised tours are also possible. Book ahead.

🛏 Sleeping

It's wise to book in advance, as Delhi's most salubrious places can fill up in a flash, leaving new arrivals easy prey for commission sharks. Most hotels offer pick-up from the airport with advance notice.

Be warned that street din can be diabolical – request a quiet room and keep earplugs handy. Also, room quality in less expensive hotels can vary radically so try to inspect a few rooms first. Delhi's budget bunch tend to offer dreary rooms, bathrooms in need of a good scrub and patchy service. Most backpackers head for hyperactive Paharganj, a touristy pocket near the New Delhi train station that has some of the city's cheapest beds.

Midrange prices have rocketed upwards over recent years, so homestays are becoming an attractive alternative. For details of government-approved places contact India

Tourism Delhi, or check www.incredible indianhomes.com and www.mahindrahome stays.com.

Long-term stayers could consider renting a furnished apartment – check ads in the latest *Delhi City Guide, Delhi Diary* and local newspapers. Two good websites are www. speciality-apartments.com and www.delhi escape.net.

Hotels with a minimum tariff of ₹1000 charge 12.5% luxury tax and some also whack on a service charge (5% to 10%). Taxes aren't included in this chapter unless indicated and all rooms have private bathrooms unless otherwise stated. Most hotels have a noon checkout and luggage storage is usually possible (sometimes for a small charge).

It's a good idea to call or email ahead to confirm your booking 24 hours before you arrive.

NORTH DELHI

OLD DELHI

Few foreign tourists stay in teeming Old Delhi – those who do will probably attract a bit of innocuous attention.

Maidens Hotel
HOTEL $$$

(Map p64; ☎23975464; www.maidenshotel.com; Sham Nath Marg; r from ₹15,000; ❄@☒; Ⓜ Civil Lines) Set in a 3.2-hectare garden, Maidens is a graceful wedding cake of a hotel, built in 1903. Lutyens stayed here while supervising the building of New Delhi. The high-ceilinged rooms are traditional and well equipped, and some have good views.

Hotel Bombay Orient
HOTEL $

(Map p64; ☎23242691; s/d ₹400/625; ❄; Ⓜ Chawri Bazaar) Set on the busy bazaar leading from the Jama Masjid's south gate. You'll need to book ahead here. It's one of the old city's best budget bets but, even so, don't expect too much and request one of its newer rooms.

Hotel Broadway
HOTEL $$

(Map p64; ☎43663600; www.hotelbroadwaydelhi .com/; 4/15 Asaf Ali Rd; s/d incl breakfast ₹2495/4495; ❄@; Ⓜ New Delhi) Semiluxurious Broadway, between the old and new cities, has some rooms with views over Old Delhi. Room standards vary (some are sleek and smart), so look at a few. Nos 44 and 46 have been kitschly kitted out by French designer Catherine Lévy, as has the Chor Bizarre restaurant, and there's the atmospheric, if divey, 'Thugs' bar upstairs.

Delhi Metro Map

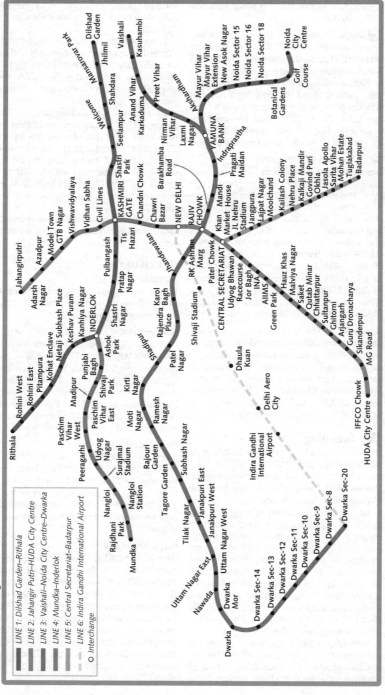

LINE 1: Dilshad Garden–Rithala
LINE 2: Jahangir Putri–HUDA City Centre
LINE 3: Vaishali–Noida City Centre–Dwarka
LINE 4: Mundka–Inderlok
LINE 5: Central Secretariat–Badarpur
LINE 6: Indira Gandhi International Airport
O Interchange

Hotel New City Palace

HOTEL $

(Map p64; ☎23279548; www.hotelnewcitypalace.in; d ₹400-500, tr ₹600, q ₹700-1300; ✳; Ⓜ Chawri Bazaar) A palace it's not, but this has an amazing location overlooking the Jama Masjid (some rooms have views over the mosque), snug rooms, bathrooms that could do with a good scrub but are bearable, and friendly reception.

Ginger

HOTEL $$

(Map p64; ☎1800 209 3333; www.gingerhotels.com; Rail Yatri Niwas; r incl tax ₹1300; ✳ @; Ⓜ New Delhi) Offers reasonably smart rooms that are ideal for business travel on the cheap. It is in an ugly building in a desolate-feeling location that's nevertheless a few minutes' walk from New Delhi train station. There's a 24-hour restaurant.

PAHARGANJ AREA

With its bumper-to-bumper budget lodgings, Paharganj – with its seedy reputation for drugs and dodgy characters – isn't everyone's cup of *chai,* though it's certainly got a lively feel. Grot aside, it's walking distance from New Delhi train station and close to the hub of Connaught Place – and it's *the* place to tap into the backpacker grapevine. Paharganj has some of Delhi's cheapest places to sleep, but sun-starved, grimy cells are depressingly common, and hot water erratic.

Despite drastic street-widening measures that forced many businesses to destroy their encroaching facades in preparation for the Commonwealth Games, Main Bazaar remains overwhelmingly congested. Thus, taxi-wallahs may (understandably) refuse to drop you at your hotel's doorstep; however, most are a short walk from the train station. All the following are close to metro stop RK Ashram Marg unless otherwise stated. Note this stop is more convenient for the Main Bazaar than metro stop New Delhi, as from the latter you have to walk all the way through the busy station. The following accommodation features on Map p76.

TOP CHOICE Cottage Yes Please

HOTEL $

(☎23562300; cottageyesplease@yahoo.co.in; 1843 Laxmi Narayan St; d ₹900; ✳ @) Around the corner from Cottage Crown Plaza is this place, its sibling, and one of the best deals in Paharganj, with a range of glitzy, clean rooms, with TVs, fridges, brassware fans and stained glass windows.

Hotel Grand Godwin

HOTEL $$

(☎23546891; www.godwinhotels.com; 8502/41 Arakashan Rd, Ram Nagar; s/d incl breakfast ₹2300/2600; ✳ @ 🛜; Ⓜ New Delhi) Located north of Main Bazaar in Ram Nagar, the Grand Godwin is the best midrange choice in this area, with smart rooms, a snazzy lobby, glass-capsule lift and room service. Godwin Deluxe at number 15 is a more upmarket hotel, owned by the same management.

Hotel Amax Inn

HOTEL $

(☎23543813; www.hotelamax.com; 8145/6 Arakashan Rd; s ₹400-450, d ₹550-750, AC s ₹650, d ₹750-850; ✳ 🛜; Ⓜ New Delhi) Away from the main bazaar, this chilled place is fantastic value, with nice clean rooms and bathrooms, tucked away in a lane off Arakashan Rd. There's a small roof terrace and wi-fi in reception.

Hotel Namaskar

GUESTHOUSE $

(☎23583456; www.hotelnamaskar.com; 917 Chandiwalan, Main Bazaar; r ₹350/500/600, AC d ₹600; ✳ 🛜) This old favourite is run by two amiable brothers. Rooms are spartan – you get what you pay for, but they're usually freshly painted and the colour scheme is bound to tickle you pink. Car hire can be arranged, and wi-fi is available courtesy of the net cafe next door (₹100 per 24 hours).

Cottage Ganga Inn

HOTEL $$

(☎23561516; cottagegangainn@yahoo.co.in; 1562 Bazar Sangtra shan; s/d ₹800/1100; ✳ @ 🛜) Popular with overlanders, this hotel is tucked away off the Main Bazaar in a courtyard, located next to a nursery school. It is clean, comfortable and a great deal for Paharganj.

Ajay Guest House

GUESTHOUSE $$

(☎23583125; www.anupamhoteliersltd.com; 5084 Main Bazaar; s/d ₹900/1000; ✳ @) Ajay is more promising than it appears from its hallways. Fresh coats of paint mean rooms look bright and snazzy, and some have colourful geometric detailing. Bathrooms are clean and colourfully tiled.

Hotel Rak International

HOTEL $

(☎23562478; hotelrakint@yahoo.co.in; Tooti Chowk, Main Bazaar; s/d ₹450-750, ₹550-850; ✳) Tucked off the main bazaar and overlooking a messy little courtyard with a temple, the modest rooms at this popular hotel have marble floors, TVs, wardrobes, small dressing tables and...windows!

Vivek Hotel

HOTEL $

(☎46470555; www.vivekhotel.com; Main Bazaar; r ₹600-1000; ✳ @) This multistorey favourite has a good range of rooms – cheaper ones are reasonable and clean and the more expensive even have a small window with a view.

Metropolis Tourist Home HOTEL $$
(📞23561794; www.metropolistravels.com; 1634 Main Bazaar; s/d incl tax from ₹1000/1250; ❋ @) Rooms (some with tight balconies) here are simple and characterless but come with smooth tiled floors, TVs and fridges. The rooftop restaurant is an added bonus.

Major's Den GUESTHOUSE $
(📞23589010; s/d ₹500/600; ❋) In a quietish sidestreet, the friendly Den has no-frills, bearably clean rooms, with cleanish walls; not all have windows.

Hare Krishna Guest House GUESTHOUSE $
(📞41541341; 1572 Main Bazaar; r from ₹300) Scuffed but bearable rooms.

Hare Rama Guest House GUESTHOUSE $
(📞23561301; Main Bazaar; s/d from ₹300/400; ❋) Grotty but bearable rooms, tucked in behind the bazaar.

MAJNU-KA-TILLA

The antidote for anyone who's got the big-city blues, this mellow enclave (aka Tibetan Colony), a block intercut by narrow lanes, is a long way from the centre, but good for a little Lhasa vibe. It's packed with travel agents, cyber cafes and trinket markets, and you'll rub shoulders with maroon-clad Buddhist monks, curio vendors, local residents and rather a lot of beggars. It's tricky to find though, north of the ISBT (bus station), and its rubbish problem makes Paharganj look tidy. From the centre, take the metro to Vidhan Sabha, then take a rickshaw.

Wongdhen House GUESTHOUSE $
(📞23816689;wongdhenhouse@hotmail.com;r₹575, without bathroom ₹375; ❋) The pick of the Majnu-ka-Tilla bunch has basic but good-sized, clean rooms. The rooftop has views over the Yamuna and the tasty restaurant rustles up everything from banana pancakes to Tibetan noodles (and does room service).

NEW DELHI & AROUND

CONNAUGHT PLACE AREA

CP properties are unbeatably central, but you pay a premium for the location. These listings feature on Map p72 and are close to metro stop Rajiv Chowk.

TOP CHOICE **Imperial** HOTEL $$$
(📞23341234; www.theimperialindia.com; Janpath; s/d ₹15,000/17,500; ❋@🛜⛱) The inimitable, Raj-era Imperial marries Victorian colonial classicism with gilded art deco, houses an impressive collection of 17th- and 18th-century paintings, and has hosted ev-

eryone from princesses to pop stars. The high-ceilinged rooms have it all, from French linen and puffy pillows to marble baths and finely crafted furniture. There's a great bar, **1911**, which is perfect for high tea.

Radisson Marina HOTEL $$$
(📞43582610; www.hotelpalaceheights.com; 26-28 D-Block; s/d ₹6500/7000; ❋@🛜) CP's flashest hotel, the Radisson's update of the old Hotel Marina is nice, with sleek, stylish all-mod-con rooms, two restaurants and a cool bar, the **Connaught**.

Park HOTEL $$$
(📞23744000; www.theparkhotels.com; 15 Parliament St; s/d from ₹12,000/14,000; ❋@🛜⛱) Conran-designed, with lots of modern flair, and has a smashing spa, breezily chic restaurant and a great poolside bar.

Hotel Palace Heights HOTEL $$$
(📞43582610; www.hotelpalaceheights.com; 26-28 D-Block; s/d ₹6500/7000; ❋@🛜) Connaught Place's most accessibly priced boutique hotel has sleek rooms with gleaming white linen, black lampshades and caramel padded headboards. There's an excellent restaurant and 24-hour room service.

Corus HOTEL $$$
(📞43652222; www.hotelcorus.com; 49 B-Block; s/d from ₹6000/6500; ❋@) This has clean, swish, compact rooms, with dazzling white sheets. More money buys you a lot more space. But readers report mixed service and occasional problems with hot water. There's an attractive restaurant, **Bonsai**, good for a drink, with outdoor seating in a white-pebbled courtyard.

Hotel Alka HOTEL $$$
(📞23344328;www.hotelalka.com;P-Block;s/dfrom ₹2950/5000; ❋) Alka's cramped standard rooms are overpriced but comfortable, some with wood-panelled walls. More money buys more pizazz, including grrrroovy leopard-skin-themed rooms. There's a good vegetarian restaurant.

Prem Sagar Guest House GUESTHOUSE $$
(📞23345263; www.premsarguesthouse.com; 1st fl, 11 P-Block; s/d from ₹3000/3500; ❋@) This is a reliable choice. The 12 snug rooms aren't flash, but they're clean, with TV, fridge and wardrobe. There's a pot-plant filled outdoor area, and internet in reception.

Ringo Guest House GUESTHOUSE $
(📞23310605; ringo_guest_house@yahoo.co.in; 17 Scindia House, Connaught Lane; s/d ₹350/550, without bathroom ₹350/450)

Sunny Guest House GUESTHOUSE $
(📞23312909; sunnyguesthouse1234@hotmail.com; 152 Scindia House, Connaught Lane; s/d ₹400/500, without bathroom ₹200/350)

WEST OF CONNAUGHT PLACE

If you like home-style lodgings you will love these hassle-free places but be aware that they fill up fast – so you should book ahead.

TOP CHOICE **Shanti Home** HOTEL $$$
(📞41573366; www.shantihome.com; A-1/300 Janakpuri; r incl tax & breakfast from ₹8500; ✳@🛜; MJanakpuri West) Though in an off-the-radar location in West Delhi, this is close to the metro station and is a gorgeous hotel with beautifully decorated rooms and an excellent rooftop restaurant. Spa treatments are available.

Master Guest House GUESTHOUSE $$
(📞28741089; www.master-guesthouse.com; R-500 New Rajendra Nagar; s/d incl tax & breakfast from ₹2500/3500; ✳@🛜; MRajendra Place) Run by an obliging couple, this polished suburban residence is somewhat out of the way, and has three thoughtfully furnished, characterful rooms with smart, spotless bathrooms. There's a leafy rooftop terrace.

Bajaj Indian Home Stay GUESTHOUSE $$$
(📞25736509; www.bajajindianhomestay.com; 8A/34 WEA Karol Bagh; s/d/tr incl tax & breakfast ₹4000/5000/6300; ✳@; MKarol Bagh) It doesn't feel like a homestay, but this highly professional place has 10 well-decorated rooms. The tariff has almost doubled in recent years, but includes complimentary tea/coffee, local telephone calls and airport transfers. There's a rooftop restaurant.

Ess Gee's GUESTHOUSE $$
(📞5725403; www.essgees.net; 12/9 East Patel Nagar; d incl breakfast ₹1250; ✳@; MPatel Nagar) An out-of-the-way, somewhat dowdy guesthouse (no signboard), with shrines in the hallways, this may bring back fond memories of grandma's place – ask to look at a few of the rooms as some are better than others.

Yatri House GUESTHOUSE $$
(📞23625563; www.yatrihouse.com; 3/4 Panchkuian Marg; s/d from ₹4000/4500; ✳@🛜; MRK Ashram Marg) Central yet serene, Yatri is less homey than some of its peers, with spacious rooms that have flat-screen TVs. It is fronted by a small garden and backed by a courtyard with wrought-iron furniture. Price includes an airport pick-up and drop-off, free internet, local calls, tea and coffee and afternoon snack. It's only 200m to the metro.

CHANAKYAPURI & ASHOKA ROAD

Youth Hostel HOSTEL $
(Map p68; 📞26871969; www.yhaindia.org; 5 Nyaya Marg, Chanakyapuri; dm/s/d ₹275/450/900, with AC ₹600/650/1300; ✳@) The dormitory is good value (YHA membership costs ₹100 per year), pretty clean, basic and centrally located – it's in the diplomatic enclave.

YWCA Blue Triangle Family Hostel HOSTEL $$
(Map p68; 📞23360133; www.ywcaofdelhi.org; Ashoka Rd; dm ₹600, s/d incl tax & breakfast ₹1485/2585; ✳@; MPatel Chowk) Despite having an institutional vibe and hint of eau de mothball, this Y (men and women) is central and has reasonable rooms.

LODI, DEFENCE COLONY & NIZAMUDDIN

ITC Maurya HOTEL $$$
(Map p68; 📞26112233; www.starwoodhotels.com; Sardar Patel Marg; s/d ₹13,500/15,000; ✳@🛜🏊) This is where the Obamas stayed when they were in town in 2010. In the diplomatic enclave, it offers all creature comforts, and excellent service. Luxuriate in high thread counts and dine at a clutch of sterling restaurants, including **Bukhara**.

K-One One GUESTHOUSE $$
(Map p68; 📞43592583; www.parigold.com; K-11 Jangpura Extn; s/d incl breakfast ₹3500/4000; ✳@🛜; MJangpura) Set in a peaceful enclave, the four rooms are spacious and painted in jewel-bright hues, with good bathrooms and LCD TVs, and there's a cool roof terrace dotted by red-painted pots. The owner offers the Parul Puri cooking lessons.

Colonel's Retreat GUESTHOUSE $$
(Map p68; 📞9999720024; D-418, Defence Colony; s/d incl breakfast ₹3500/3800; ✳@🛜; MLajpat Nagar) With four smart, nicely furnished rooms, this is a bright and well-kept option in a Delhi suburb. It's handily close to the metro.

Lutyens Guest House GUESTHOUSE $$$
(Map p68; 📞24625716; www.lutyensguesthouse.com; 39 Prithviraj Rd; d incl tax & breakfast from ₹8000; ✳@🛜🏊; MRacecourse) This great rambling house is an atmospheric green oasis. The garden is great – lawns, flowers and fluttering parrots – but rooms are basic, and rates have sky-rocketed in recent years, and it's now absurdly overpriced. However, it's a good place to stay with kids.

SOUTH DELHI

TOP CHOICE **Bnineteen** GUESTHOUSE **$$$**
(Map p68; ☑41825500; www.bnineteen.com; B-19 Nizamuddin East; d from ₹7500; ❄@) Secluded, and located in fascinating Nizamuddin East, with fabulous views over Humayun's Tomb from the rooftop, this gorgeous place shows an architect's touch. The rooms are spacious and cool, and great for long stayers, with a state-of-the-art shared kitchen on each floor.

Manor HOTEL **$$$**
(Map p78; ☑26925151; www.themanordelhi.com; 77 Friends Colony (West); d incl breakfast from ₹8500; ❄@) If you're looking for a more intimate alternative to Delhi's opulent five stars, this 16-room boutique hotel is it. Off Mathura Rd, set amid manicured lawns, the renovated bungalow combines contemporary luxury with caramel-hued elegance that seems from another era. The restaurant, **Indian Accent**, is superb, and lush lawns and a sun-warmed terrace complete the picture.

Treetops GUESTHOUSE **$$**
(Map p78; ☑9899555704; baig.murad@gmail.com; R-8, Hauz Khas Enclave; d incl breakfast ₹4000; ❄@🛜; Ⓜ Hauz Khas) The elegant home of a hospitable couple, journalist Murad Baig and his wife Tannie, who is a cookery writer and teacher, this has two lovely large rooms opening onto a leafy roof terrace – truly in the treetops. It's minutes from the metro and Tannie gives cookery lessons (see p78). There's a cheaper, single (also en suite) room which occupies the apartment's study (₹2500). Dinner is available (₹300).

Amarya Haveli GUESTHOUSE **$$$**
(Map p78; ☑41759267; www.amaryagroup.com; Hauz Khas Enclave; s/d ₹6500/6900; ❄@; Ⓜ Hauz Khas) The French owners of Amarya Haveli have created a haven in Hauz Khas, a boutique place that is funkily furnished with Indian artefacts, carved furniture and textiles, and has an appealing roof terrace swathed in pink and orange. They also opened in 2010 the even-more-chic **Amarya Villa** (D-179 Defence Colony; Ⓜ Lajpat Nagar), with slightly more expensive rooms (same contact details).

Home Away from Home HOMESTAY **$$**
(Map p78; ☑26560289; permkamte@sify.com; 1st fl, D-8 Gulmohar Park; s/d incl breakfast from ₹2000/2200; ❄; Ⓜ Green Park) This stylish apartment, in a classy suburb, is home to Mrs Kamte and she keeps the place in a gleaming condition. There are just two rooms, each tasteful, antique-decorated and with small balconies; there's a midnight curfew.

TOP CHOICE **Devna** GUESTHOUSE **$$$**
(Map p68; ☑24355047; www.newdelhiboutiqueinns.com; 10 Sunder Nagar; d ₹5500; ❄) Fronted by a pretty garden, gloriously pretty Devna is one of Delhi's most charismatic choices, with four curio- and antique-furnished rooms. Those opening onto the terrace upstairs are the best.

AIRPORT AREA

New Delhi Bed & Breakfast HOMESTAY **$$**
(☑2689 4812; www.newdelhibedandbreakfast.com; C8/8225 Vasant Kunj; s/d ₹3000/3500; @) Renu Dayal's welcoming homestay has two cosy double rooms (one en suite) in her elegant house in a leafy enclave, only 10 minutes' drive from the airport.

Inn at Delhi HOMESTAY **$$**
(Map p68; ☑24113234; www.innatdelhi.com; s/d ₹3500/4500; ❄@🛜) Between the city and the airport, in a smart area close to the diplomatic enclave, this is a good choice for single women. Your hosts are a professional couple, the rooms are spacious and comfortable and, upstairs, one has an impressive wooden carved bed from Rajasthan.

Chhoti Haveli HOMESTAY **$$**
(Map p78; ☑2612 4880; http://chhotihaveli.com; A1006, Pocket A, Vasant Kunj; s/d ₹3100/3500; ❄@) Set in a block of low-rise apartments, in a quiet, leafy area near the airport, this well-kept place offers nicely decorated rooms; there are lots of plants, with little touches such as petals adorning the steps.

Radisson Hotel HOTEL **$$$**
(☑26779191; www.radisson.com/newdelhiin; National Hwy 8; s/d from ₹11,500/12,500; ❄@🛜⌖) Radisson's rooms are business-hotel comfortable. But oh, what a joy to lie down on soft linen and orthopaedic beds after a long-haul flight. On site are Chinese, kebab and Italian restaurants.

✕ Eating

Delhiites love to eat, and visitors will find plenty of delicious options, ranging from ramshackle stalls serving delicious kebabs to top-of-the-range temples of excellence.

Most midrange and all upmarket restaurants charge a service tax of around 10%, while drinks taxes can suck a further 20%

EAT & DUST

Pamela Timms is a Delhiite food writer and blogs at eatanddust.wordpress.com. She can sometimes be persuaded to do food walks in Old Delhi (pamelatimms@gmail.com). Here are some of her top tips.

The Delhi street food I can never resist in the cooler months when Delhi's (particularly Old Delhi's) street food is at its most appealing:

» *Daulat ki chaat*, which is only available in the winter, is a not-too-sweet frothed milk, whisked overnight and, allegedly, set with the morning dew. Vendors bearing huge great platters of it can be seen all over Old Delhi from November to February.

» Roasted and spiced sweet potato *(shakarkandi)* served with slices of star fruit, lime juice and masala is wonderful, available all over Delhi.

» I find it very difficult to walk by the *aloo tikka* vendors. These deep-fried stuffed potato patties a great for filling awkward gaps between meals.

» For possibly the best kebabs in Delhi, head to **Moinuddin** (Map p64; Lal Kuan nr crn Gali Qasimjan; ⓜChawri Bazaar) for melt-in-the-mouth buffalo.

» For a wonderful Korma, chicken and lamb, go to **Ashok and Ashok** (Map p64; 42 Subhas Chowk, Sadar Thana Rd, Sadar Bazaar, Old Delhi; ⓜSadar Bazaar).

» If you have a sweet tooth, stop at the old and famous Jalebiwala (p88). Their deep fried fritters drenched in sugar syrup are about as good as sugar-hits get.

» If *kheer* (rice pudding) is more to your taste, go to **Bade Mian's** (Map p64; Lal Kuan; ⓜChawri Bazaar) shop in Lal Kuan.

» Also near Chawri Bazaar is the legendary **Kuremal ice cream shop** (Map p64; Kucha Pati Ram, off Sitaram Bazaar; ⓜChawri Bazaar) with flavours such as mango, pomegranate and falsa.

(alcoholic) or 12.5% (nonalcoholic) from your moneybelt. Taxes haven't been included in this chapter unless indicated.

Telephone numbers have only been provided for restaurants where reservations are recommended.

NORTH DELHI

OLD DELHI
The following eateries are featured on Map p64.

Karim's   MUGHLAI $
(mains   ₹27-110; ⊗7am-midnight)   Old   Delhi
(ⓜChawri Bazaar); Nizamuddin West (168/2 Jha House Basti) Down a lane across from the Jama Masjid's south gate (No 1), legendary Karim's has been delighting Delhi folk with divine Mughlai cuisine since 1913. The chefs prepare brutally good (predominantly non-veg) fare: try the *burrah* (marinated mutton) kebab. There's a newer branch close to Nizamuddin.

Haldiram's   FAST FOOD $$
(mains ₹50-140; ⊗9.30am-10.30pm); Old Delhi (Chandni Chowk; ⓜChandni Chowk); Connaught Place (Map p72; 6 L-Block; ⓜRajiv Chowk) This clean, bright cafeteria-sweet shop is a handy spot for a top-notch thali (₹156), choley bhature and other morsels, some tasty South Indian cuisine, or *namkin* (savouries) and *mithai* (sweets) on the dash. Try the *soan papadi* (flaky sweet with almond and pistachio).

Chor Bizarre   KASHMIRI $$
(⌨23273821; Hotel Broadway, 4/15 Asaf Ali Rd; mains ₹240-500; ⊗7.30-10.30am, noon-3.30pm & 7.30-11.30pm; ⓜNew Delhi) A dimly lit, atmospheric place, filled with eccentric clutter, Chor Bizarre (meaning 'thieves market') offers particularly delicious Kashmiri cuisine. It's popular with tourists and locals

Paratha Wali Gali   STREET FOOD $
(parathas ₹15-35; ⓜChandni Chowk) Head to this foodstall-lined lane off Chandni Chowk for delectable *parathas* (traditional flat bread) fresh off the *tawa* (hotplate). Stuffed varieties include *aloo* (potato), *mooli* (white radish), smashed pappadams and crushed *badam* (almond), all served with a splodge of tangy pickles. Some of the foodstalls have seating.

Jalebiwala
STREET FOOD **$**

(Dariba Corner, Chandni Chowk; jalebis per kg ₹250; Ⓜ Chandni Chowk) Calories schmalories! Century-old Jalebiwala does Delhi's – if not India's – finest *jalebis* (deep-fried, syrupy squiggles), so pig out and worry about your waistline tomorrow.

Al-Jawahar
MUGHLAI **$$**

(mains ₹20-120; ⏱7am-midnight; Ⓜ Chawri Bazaar) Next door to Karim's, this offers brighter surroundings for Mughlai cuisine. It serves similar and cheaper, if less legendary, fare (some swear it's even better). You can watch the naan being deftly made at the front of the shop.

Moti Mahal
NORTH INDIAN **$$**

(☎23273661; 3704 Netaji Subhash Marg, Daryaganj; mains ₹110-250; ⏱noon-midnight) This faded, family-oriented restaurant has been wooing diners with its Indian food for some six decades. It's famed for its butter chicken and dhal Makhani. There's live *qawwali* Wednesday to Monday (8pm–midnight).

Ghantewala
SWEETS **$**

(Chandni Chowk; mithai per kg from ₹220; Ⓜ Chandni Chowk) Delhi's most famous sweetery, 'the bell ringer' has been churning out *mithai* (Indian sweets) since 1790. Try some *sohan halwa* (ghee-dipped gram flour biscuits).

Bikanerwala
FAST FOOD **$**

(snacks ₹8-60; ⏱7am-midnight; Ⓜ Chandni Chowk) This bright little canteen offers tasty snacks such as *paratha* (stuffed bread) and *channa bhatura* (spicy chickpeas with fried puffed bread).

PAHARGANJ AREA

Yielding wobbly results, Paharganj's menus are of the mix-it-up variety, serving anything from Israeli to Italian, Mughlai to Mexican. The eateries are nothing fancy but are cheap and abuzz with chattering travellers.

The following places are along, or just off, Main Bazaar (Map p76) and near the RK Ashram Metro Stop.

Sita Ram Dewan Chand
STREET FOOD **$**

(2246 Chuna Mandi; half/full plate ₹17/30; ⏱8am-6pm) Pran Kohli now runs this place, which his grandfather started over 60 years ago. It's a basic and devoted to just one dish: *chole* (spicy chickpeas) accompanied by delicious, freshly made *paratha* stuffed with spices and paneer.

Tadka
INDIAN **$**

(4986 Ram Dwara Rd; mains ₹70-85; ⏱noon-11pm) Nothing flash, but one of the best bets in Paharganj: a simple, clean and tasty pure veg restaurant. Try the *saag paneer* (spinach and cottage cheese) and Tadka dhal.

Malhotra
MULTICUISINE **$$**

(1833 Laxmi Narayan St; mains ₹90-425) Snug, smartish Malhotra offers tasty Indian, continental and Chinese food that keeps it busy with a mix of locals and backpackers.

Sam's Café
MULTICUISINE **$$**

(Vivek Hotel, 1534-1550 Main Bazaar; mains ₹90-190) On Vivek Hotel's ground floor and (much more atmospheric) rooftop, Sam's does reasonble breakfasts and is a tranquil place to hang; it's usually packed with travellers. The pizzas are a good bet.

Metropolis Restaurant & Bar
MULTICUISINE **$$$**

(Metropolis Tourist Home, 1634 Main Bazaar; mains ₹225-500) On a rooftop, this crammed, humming travellers' haunt is one of the more upmarket in the area, with an encyclopedic, have-a-go-at-anything menu. It serves alcohol.

Madan Café
CAFE **$**

(Main Bazaar; mains ₹20-45) Cash crisis? Tuck into a basic thali for just ₹40 at this basic veg cafe; outside tables are ideal for watching the human traffic. Facing is the similar **Khosla Café**.

Kitchen Café
CAFE **$**

(Hotel Shelton, 5043 Main Bazaar; mains ₹55-150) This cane-furnished, plant-strewn rooftop restaurant is a relaxing place to kill time over the usual world-ranging menu.

KAROL BAGH

Angan
INDIAN **$**

(Map p64; Chowk Gurudwara Rd; mains ₹60-125; Ⓜ Karol Bagh) A small but buzzing canteen-style pitstop for Indian and South Indian food, plus yummy snacks (try the *channa bhatura*).

Roshan di Kulfi
ICE CREAM **$**

(Map p64; Gafal Market, Ajmal Khan Rd; kulfi ₹45; Ⓜ Karol Bagh) A Delhi institution for its scrumptious *kulfi* (pistachio-, cardamom- or saffron-flavoured frozen milk dessert). Also has good *golgappas* (small fried bread filled with water, tamarind, chilli, chaat masala, potato, onion and chickpeas) and lassi.

CONNAUGHT PLACE AREA

The following eateries appear on Map p72, unless otherwise indicated, and are closest to Metro Rajiv Chowk, unless otherwise stated.

TOP CHOICE | Saravana Bhavan   SOUTH INDIAN $
(mains ₹55-120; ⊗8am-10.30pm) Connaught Place (15 P-Block); Janpath (Map p72; 46 Janpath); Karol Bagh (Map p72; 8/54 Desh Bandhu Gupta Rd; MKarol Bagh) Massively popular, Tamil Saravana has a fast-food feel, but food is by no means junk: dosas, *idlis* and other southern specialities, accompanied by delectable coconut chutneys. Inventive sweets include cucumber-seed *ladoos* (sweet balls). Finish with a South Indian coffee.

Rajdhani   INDIAN $$
(1/90 P-Block; thalis from ₹125-249; ⊗noon-3.30pm & 7-11pm) Opposite PVR Rivoli Cinema, this pristine, nicely decorated two-level place serves up excellent-value delicious vegetarian Gujarati and Rajasthani thalis, to grateful local and foreign punters.

Nizam's Kathi Kabab   FAST FOOD $$
(5 H-Block; kebabs ₹110-150) This takeaway eatery has some seating and creates masterful kebabs and *kathi* rolls (kebab wrapped in *paratha*). It's always busy with kebab-loving hoards.

Andhra Pradesh Bhawan Canteen   SOUTH INDIAN $
(Map p68; 1 Ashoka Rd; veg thalis ₹80; ⊗noon-3pm; MPatel Chowk) A hallowed bargain: tasty unlimited South Indian thalis at cheap-as-chips prices; nonveg is also available. It's canteen-style, delicious and hugely popular.

Chinese   CHINESE $$$
(☎65398888; 14/15 F-Block; mains ₹300-1200; ⊗lunch & dinner) Popular with Chinese diplomats, here the Hunan chef serves up authentic cuisine, such as Hunan smoked lamb or *gong boa ji ding* (chicken with onion, chilli, peanut and hot garlic sauce) in a wow-factor calligraphy-decorated interior.

United Coffee House   MULTICUISINE $$$
(15 E-Block; mains ₹300-400; ⊗10am-midnight) Oozing old-world charm and full of characters that look as elderly as the fixtures and fittings, this classic 1940s restaurant is a splendid spot to slow the pace. It has a long menu covering everything from pizza to *paneer* (cottage cheese). Try the butter chicken. It's great for an afternoon drink too (small Kingfisher ₹165).

Zen   CHINESE $$$
(25 B-Block; mains ₹229-400; ⊗11am-11pm) A high-ceilinged place with a dash of old-style glitz – its walls are quilted like a Chanel handbag – this has a venerable Chinese menu, including tasty dishes such as crispy sesame lamb and Szechwan prawns, with a few Japanese and Thai cameos.

Kwality   INDIAN $$
(7 Regal bdg; mains ₹200-350; ⊗noon-11pm) Charmingly old-school, with its waiters clad in dark-red jackets, Kwality's speciality is *channa bhatura*, but you might want to try some other hits, such as *malai* kofta or *murgh malai kebab* (chicken and cheese). A Kingfisher beer will set you back a refreshing ₹90.

Véda   INDIAN $$$
(☎41513535; 27 H-Block; mains ₹300-700; ⊗noon-midnight) Head here for atmosphere: fashion designer Rohit Baal created this sumptuous interior – dim red lighting, neo-Murano chandeliers, and twisted gold-a-go-go. Mughlai and North West Frontier specialities are on the menu (try the tandoori grilled lamb chops or the Parsi sea bass). A DJ plays (loudly) in the lounge bar. They also do a mean margharita.

Wenger's   BAKERY $
(16 A-Block; cakes/pizza from ₹40/85; ⊗10.45am-7.45pm) Legendary Wenger's has been baking since 1926 when it was opened by a South African expat. It's always buzzing and there's a great array of sweet and savoury treats, including perfect patties.

Sagar Ratna   SOUTH INDIAN $
(dishes ₹60-120); Connaught Place (15 K-Block; mains ₹60-120); Defence Colony (Map p78; 18 Defence Colony Market; MLajpat Nagar) Another dosa dreamland, with expertly prepared dosas, *idlis*, *uttapams* (savoury rice pancakes) and other smashing southern goodies, plus thalis.

Embassy   INDIAN $$
(11 D-Block; mains ₹160-380; ⊗10am-11pm) A long-time favourite, gracious and old-fashioned, featuring Indian and continental creations.

Zāffrān   MUGHLAI $$$
(mains ₹230-400; ⊗noon-3.30pm & 7pm-midnight); Connaught Place (☎43582610; Hotel Palace Heights, 26-28 D-Block); Greater Kailash (Map p78; 2 N-Block) An excellent restaurant serving Mughlai cuisine and designed to feel like a bamboo-shuttered terrace.

Kake-da-Hotel MUGHLAI $$

(☎9136666820; 74 M-Block; mains ₹80-110; ⏱11.30am-midnight) This simple *dhaba* (snack bar) is a basic hole in the wall that's popular with local workers for its butter chicken and other Mughlai Punjabi dishes.

Kerala House SOUTH INDIAN $

(3 Jantar Mantar Rd; meal ₹30; ⏱1-3pm; Ⓜ Patel Chowk) The staff canteen at Kerala House was, at the time of writing, housed in part of the underground car park, but don't let this put you off. It's open to the public and tasty meals here are a bargain, including unlimited rice, sambar, a couple of veg dishes and pickle.

Tao PAN-ASIAN $$$

(8 E-Block; mains ₹189-429; ⏱11am-11pm) Sleek and swish, but with something of the feel of an upmarket airport dining option, this is a popular place for its dim sum, Japanese, Thai and Chinese cuisine.

Nirula's ICE CREAM $

(14 K-Block Connaught Place) Drop into Nirula's for its hot chocolate fudge ice cream, every Delhiite's favourite flavour.

DIPLOMATIC ENCLAVE & CHANAKYAPURI AREA

Bukhara NORTH INDIAN $$$

(Map p68; ☎26112233; ITC Maurya, Sadar Patel Marg; mains ₹600-800; ⏱lunch & dinner; ❋) Considered Delhi's best restaurant, this rustic place serves Northwest Frontier-style cuisine. Its tandoor and dhal are particularly renowned. Clinton and Obama have eaten here. Reservations are essential (taken between 7pm and 8pm).

Monsoon INDIAN $$$

(Map p68; ☎23710101; Le Meridien, Janpath; mains around ₹600-1000; ❋; Ⓜ Patel Chowk) With waterfall plate-glass windows, this is a wow-factor restaurant for sampling some creative Indian cuisine. Enjoy beautifully presented, taste-sensation dishes such as *millefeuille* of sole with mint chutney, and sumptuous pistachio *kulfi* to finish off.

Dhaba PUNJABI $$$

(Map p68; ☎23010211; The Claridges, Chanakyapuri, 12 Aurangzeb Rd; mains ₹400-500; ⏱11.30am-4pm & 7pm-midnight) Claridges does Punjabi highway cuisine, complete with kitsch 'roadside' decor (try the balti meat and fish or chicken tikka).

LODI COLONY & PANDARA MARKET

The eateries below feature on Map p68.

Lodi Garden Restaurant MEDITERRANEAN $$$

(Lodi Rd; mains ₹395-895; ⏱lunch & dinner; Ⓜ Jor Bagh) Set in an elegant garden shaded by trees hung with lanterns, and with a fountain made out of watering cans, beside Lodi Garden. The menu and clientele are remarkably non-Indian, but it's good for Mediterranean and Lebanese cuisine (think lamb chops with mint and tamarind, and herb-crusted Manali trout). Brunch (₹1399) is available at weekends.

All American Diner FAST FOOD $$

(India Habitat Centre, Lodi Rd; mains ₹120-270; Ⓜ JLN Stadium) Make like it's 1950s USA and head down to the cherry-red booths and bar stools of the All American, to eat stars-and-stripes classics, from buttermilk pancakes to hot dogs, and work the jukebox. Or try the Habitat's cheap-and-cheerful food court **Eatopia**, with good *chaat*, Chinese and Indian food.

Pandara Market INDIAN $$$

(Ⓜ Khan Market) This market has a little horseshoe of restaurants popular among night owls – most are open daily from noon to 1am or 2am. Highlights: **Pindi** (mains ₹130-370), serving tasty Mughlai Punjabi food since 1948; **Gulati** (mains ₹140-480), which has a North Indian focus amid the beige and mirrored decor; **Chicken Inn** (mains ₹150-430) flasher than the name suggests, and a popular choice for Indian and Chinese; and **Havemore** (mains ₹160-390), a snug, smartish spot, serving Indian food with a venerable veg selection.

SOUTH DELHI

KHAN & SUNDER NAGAR MARKETS

If you're shopping at the Khan (Ⓜ Khan Market) or Sunder Nagar Markets, there are some great places to top up your tank.

Amici ITALIAN $$$

(Map p68; Khan Market; mains ₹300-400; ⏱lunch & dinner) This sleek, calm jewel of a cafe serves up splendid pizzas and tasty burgers. It has a soothing biscuit-coloured walls and a palpable sense of style. The only thing missing is a booze licence.

Sidewok ASIAN FUSION $$$

(Map p68; ☎46068122; Khan Market; mains ₹225-475; ⏱11am-11.30pm) Sleek Sidewok dishes up top-notch Asian cuisine, amid dark slatted wood and Japanese minimalism. Try the delicious Vietnamese spring rolls.

Khan Chacha
MIDDLE EASTERN $$
(Map p68; Khan Market; snacks ₹110-160; ☺noon-11pm) Chacha has gone chi-chi, the prices have doubled, and it has lost something of its original charm in the process. But all is not lost – it still turns out pretty lipsmacking roti-wrapped mutton/chicken/paneer. There is now plentiful seating, set under nail-formed lamps that look like torture implements.

Mamagoto
ASIAN FUSION $$$
(Map p68; ☑45166060; 1st fl, Middle Lane, Khan Market; mains ₹325-500; ☺12.30pm-12.30am) The name means 'to play with food' in Japanese, the decor is prettily kitsch and the food is fun – a meal can span snow peas and green bean salad, lamb sticky rice and date rolls with vanilla ice cream.

Baci
ITALIAN $$$
(Map p68; ☑41507445; Sunder Nagar Market; mains ₹360-700; ☺11am-1am) Reasonable Italian cuisine and good coffee is served up here in grown-up surroundings, either at the informal cafe or in the sleek upstairs restaurant. On Thursday there's live jazz from 8pm. Cocktails are ₹385.

Kitchen
PAN-ASIAN $$
(Map p68; ☑41757960; Khan Market; mains ₹269-399) A buzzing, small, backstreet all-rounder, simply and chicly decorated. Kitchen offers tasty dishes such as Thai red curry with rice, yummy *pad thai* and fine fish and chips.

Nathu's
INDIAN $
(mains ₹27-105; Sunder Nagar (Map p68; Sunder Nagar Market); Connaught Place (Map p64; 23-25 Bengali Market) Famous sweet shop serving up yummy *chaat* (snacks), *namkin* (savouries) and *mithai* (sweets), plus good thalis (₹130).

Sweets Corner
SWEETS & SNACKS $
(Map p68; Sunder Nagar Market; mains ₹16-90) Next door to Nathu's, this is another popular canteen-style eatery, with a terrace out the front where local families tuck into *chaat*, sweets, South Indian dishes and thalis.

Basil & Thyme
ITALIAN $$$
(Map p68; Santushti Enclave; mains ₹375-435;☺11am-6pm Mon-Sat) A chic yet simple white-washed restaurant that buzzes with expats and locals, here for the reasonable Mediterranean cooking.

TOP CHOICE Gunpowder
SOUTH INDIAN $$
(Map p78; ☑26535700; 22 Hauz Khas Village; mains ₹80-300; ☺noon-3pm & 7.30-11pm Tue-Sun; Ⓜ Hauz Khas) You reach this cool place up numerous flights to the 3rd floor. The setting is great: a simple room with wicker chairs that opens onto huge views over the greenery of Hauz Khas. The food is fit to match, with dishes such as Kerala-style vegetable korma, toddy-shop *meen* (fish) curry, and sweet-and-sour pumpkin. Bookings are essential.

Evergreen
INDIAN $
(Map p78; S29-30 Green Park Market; mains ₹50-115; ☺8am-10.30pm; Ⓜ Green Park) Since 1963 Evergreen has been keeping punters happy with its snacks, *chaat* and South Indian dishes. It's a hugely popular, bright, clean two-level place that's perfect for a quick lunch or dinner.

VASANT VIHAR

Punjabi by Nature
PUNJABI $$$
(Map p78; ☑41516666; Basant Lok complex; mains ₹425-650; ☺12.30pm-1am) Served against a masculine backdrop featuring murals of turbaned men, this place offers ravishingly delicious Punjabi food. Mop up flavour-packed sauces with *rumali roti* (paper-thin chapatis) or thick garlic naan. Go on, try the vodka *golgappas!*

Arabian Nites
KEBAB $$
(Map p78; 59 Basant Lok complex; snacks ₹70-230; ☺10.30am-11pm) This teeny takeaway (there are a few inside seats) does mighty good chicken shawarma.

GREATER KAILASH I

Moti Mahal
MUGHLAI $$
(Map p78; 30 M-Block; mains ₹140-450; ☺lunch & dinner Wed-Mon) Smarter than the Old Delhi original and popular with well-off families for its North Indian and Mughlai cooking.

GREATER KAILASH II

Diva
ITALIAN $$$
(Map p78; ☑29215673; M-Block; mains ₹500-950; ☺lunch & dinner) Chef Ritu Dalmia's *molto chic* Italian restaurant is an intimate space on two levels, with white tablecloths, plate-glass windows, and a wood-fired oven behind glass. Cooking is superlative, imaginative and delicious. *Avanti!*

Smokehouse Grill
MULTICUISINE $$$
(Map p78; ☑41435530; 2 VIPPS Center, LSC Masjid Moth; mains around ₹600-800; ☺7.30pm-1am)

Another uberhip hangout, suffused in minimalist chic, with lots of good, smoked(!) food on the menu. Try the smoked melon mojitos, and leave room for the divine chocolate soufflé. On Friday and Saturday nights there's a DJ playing everything from '80s to Bhangra.

Not Just Parathas   NORTH INDIAN $$

(Map p78; 84 M-Block; dishes ₹80-300; ⏱noon-midnight) Yes, this cheery place offers not just *parathas* but, with 120 types on the menu, you've gotta go for the speciality, be they Tawa-fried or roasted tandoori and stuffed with *palak* (spinach), chicken tikka or *aloo gobi* (potato and cauliflower), to name a few.

DEFENCE COLONY & FRIENDS COLONY

TOP CHOICE **Indian Accent**   INDIAN $$$

(Map p78; ☎26925151; Manor Hotel, 77 Friends Colony; tasting menu veg/nonveg ₹1875/1975) Overlooking the hotel veranda and lush lawns, this is a remarkable restaurant with inspired creative Indian cuisine. Expect starters such as baked paneer pinwheel and indian coriander pesto, and main dishes such as masala wild mushrooms and water chestnut paper-roast dosai.

Swagath   SOUTH INDIAN $$$

(Map p78; Defence Colony Market; mains ₹235-645; ⏱11am-midnight; MLajpat Nagar) Supremely scrumptious Indian fare with a focus on Mangalorean and Chettinad cuisine (especially seafood), this smart six-floor restaurant swarms with well-heeled locals, here for the excellent *dhal-e-Swagath* (lentil curry), delicious *surmai rawas* (fish), butter pepper garlic, butter chicken and similarly satiating dishes.

SAKET & MEHRAULI

Olive   MEDITERRANEAN $$$

(Map p78; ☎29574443; One Style Mile, Mehrauli; tasting lunch menu from ₹495, dinner mains from ₹575; ⏱noon-12pm; MQutab Minar) Uberchic, the original Olive has reopened, much to the delight of the Delhi in-crowd. The *haveli* setting, decorated in rustic beach-house chic, with its mismatched antiques, is unlike anywhere else in Delhi. As well as creative Mediterranean dishes, the menu includes pasta and pizzas – as tasty as the clientele.

🍷 Drinking

Whether it's cappuccino and pastries for breakfast, or beer and kebabs for supper, Delhi's cool cafes and buzzing bars deliver. Most Delhi bars double up as both restaurants and nightclubs. The scene might not be huge, but as the sun goes down, the party

starts, particularly from Wednesday to Saturday night. A smart-casual dress code (no shorts, vests or flip-flops) applies at most places.

The fancier bars are overflowing with domestic and foreign booze, but taxes can pack a nasty punch (alcoholic 20%, nonalcoholic 12.5%); taxes aren't included here unless stated. Most bars have two-for-one happy hours from around noon till 8pm or on certain days.

NEW DELHI & AROUND

Latitude   CAFE

(Map p68; Khan Market; ⏱11.30am-10.30pm; MKhan Market) Above the exclusively priced Good Earth homewares store, this is Khan Market's prettiest cafe, with sparkly chandeliers and handpainted walls. It's a good place for a chi-chi light lunch and to pretend you're not in Delhi.

Café Turtle   CAFE

Greater Kailash Part I (Map p78; N-Block); Khan Market (Map p68; 2nd fl, Full Circle Bookstore; ⏱9.30am-9.30pm; MKhan Market) This bookish, boho cafe ticks all the boxes when you're in the mood for coffee and gateau (the 'gooey chocolate cake' is a triumph).

Big Chill   CAFE

(Map p68; Khan Market; ⏱noon-11.30pm; MKhan Market) Khan Market has two film-poster-lined branches of BC, packed with chattering, well-manicured, wholesome folk. The menu is a telephone directory of continental, Indian and other dishes.

Café Oz   CAFE

(Map p68; Khan Market; ⏱9am-midnight; MKhan Market) A busy Australian cafe, this has reasonable food and Delhi's best coffee, including flat whites.

Indian Coffee House   CAFE

(Map p72; Mohan Singh Place; ⏱9am-9pm; MRajiv Chowk) Stuck-in-time Indian Coffee House is down at heel, but serves up basic, cheap snacks and south Indian coffee (₹13!) and has a 2nd-floor terrace.

PAHARGANJ

The following are on Map p76, and close to Metro RK Ashram.

Open Hand Cafe   CAFE

(Main Bazaar; ⏱8am-10pm; MRK Ashram Marg) Bringing a touch of class to Paharganj, this South African-owned, two-level cafe has a chic, arty feel, sculptural chairs, good coffee and yummy cheesecake.

Gem
BAR

(Main Bazaar) In this dark, wood-panelled dive, a large Kingfisher costs a bargain ₹102 (including tax). Upstairs has more atmosphere. The snacks are good too.

My Bar
BAR

(Main Bazaar; ⊙10am-12.30pm) Another dark and dingy bar where the main charm is the cheap beer (Kingfisher costs ₹72 for 330ml) and the chance to hang out with other backpackers.

Metropolis Restaurant & Bar
BAR

(Metropolis Tourist Home, 1634 Main Bazaar; ⊙7am-11pm) This hotel's rooftop restaurant is a breezier choice than Gem, with al fresco drinking on its terrace and a 330cl Kingfisher for ₹80.

CONNAUGHT PLACE AREA
The following venues are located on Map p72, close to Metro Rajiv Chowk, and most have happy hours during the daytime.

1911
BAR

(Imperial Hotel, Janpath) Named after the year in which Delhi was proclaimed British India's capital, this is the ultimate neocolonial treat. Sip cocktails, while being overlooked by oil-painted Maharajas (drinks ₹650 plus).

Aqua
BAR

(Park Hotel, 15 Parliament St; ⊙11am-1am) A chic poolside bar, this see-and-be-seen place is a perfect bolthole after visiting Jantar Mantar or shopping in Connaught Place. There's seating overlooking the pool, or white-clad, curtained daybeds on which to lounge. A Kingfisher costs ₹225, and you can munch on mezze, kebabs or Lebanese snacks.

Cha Bar
CAFE

(Map p72; Oxford Bookstore, Statesman House, 148 Barakhamba Rd; ⊙10am-7.30pm Mon-Sat, noon-7.30pm Sun; MBarakhamba Rd) After browsing at the Oxford, pop into Cha for a tea with a view (over CP). More than 75 flavours to choose from, and the blueberry muffins are fab too.

@live
LIVE MUSIC

(12 K-Block) Intimate and smart without being formal, @live has a cool gimmick: a live jukebox. The band plays from 8.30pm, and there's a song menu, so you choose the songs from a list including the Bee Gees, Bob Dylan and Sir Cliff. The band mightn't be the most dynamic you've seen, but they're great, and it's a fun night out (food's good too).

Q'BA
BAR

(1st fl, 42 E-Block) Connaught Place's swishest watering hole has a Q-shaped bar, dim lighting, leather chairs and Chesterfield sofas. Upstairs is the fine-dining restaurant (from 7pm) and there's a roof terrace, ideal on sultry evenings.

24/7
BAR

(Lalit Hotel, Maharaja Rajit Singh Marg; ⊙24hr) Every now and again, a 24-hour bar comes in extremely handy. This is at the Lalit hotel, so if you're hankering after a Martini at 5am you can drink it somewhere defiantly unseedy.

Costa
CAFE

(Map p72; L-Block, Connaught Place; ⊙9am-11pm; MRajiv Chowk) Arguably the best of the coffee chains, a dapper downtown cafe with strong coffee, delicate teas, English-toffee milkshakes and good cakes.

Café Coffee Day
CAFE

Connaught Place (Map p72; 11 N-Block, Connaught Place; ⊙9am-11pm; MRajiv Chowk); Khan Market (Map p68; MKhan Market). You know what you're getting at CCD: cappuccinos, Americanised cheery staff and brownies. But sometimes that's what you need. Citywide branches galore.

Pind Balluchi
BAR

(Regal Bldg; ⊙noon-11pm) This location has undergone yet another makeover, and this time emerged as a high-kitsch 'village restaurant' complete with a fake central tree. It still has possibly CP's cheapest beers and cocktails (Kingfisher ₹120, cocktails from ₹120).

Blues
BAR

(18 N-Block) A dark den with reasonably priced beers. The brick walls are plastered with the likes of Jimi Hendrix and other less-recognisable figures. With its cheerily unhip soundtrack (think Sonny and Cher), this is a lively, snob-free zone.

Rodeo
BAR

(12 A-Block) In the mood for saloon doors, tequila, saddle barstools and staff in cowboy hats? Then easygoing Rodeo is for you, partner. Cocktails cost from ₹275, but give the nachos a miss.

SOUTH DELHI
The following drinking venues are on Map p78.

Kunzum Travel Cafe
CAFE

(Map p78; Hauz Khas Village; ⊙11am-7.30pm Tue-Sun; 🛜; MHauz khas) This unique cafe is run by travel authors and photographers and has a pay-what-you-like policy, self-service French-press coffee and tea, and travel books and magazines to browse. You can also BYO drinks and food and put your iPod in the dock!

Love Hotel
BAR

(2nd fl, MGF Metropolitan Mall; ☉1pm-1am; ⓂSaket) In a mall, but worth seeking out nonetheless: the Love Hotel adjoins **Ai**, an exclusive, popular and chic Japanese restaurant, and occupies a little open terrace. The food is excellent and the atmosphere is best here when there's a party going on – check local listings for what's on. Cocktails cost around ₹400.

Shalom
BAR

Greater Kailash I (18 N-Block; ☉noon-1am); Vasant Vihar (4 D-Block) This loungey bar–restaurant, with wooden furniture and whitewashed walls, is one of the doyennes of the Delhi loungebar scene. As well as wine, beers, cocktails (around ₹400) and nightly DJs, there's top-notch Mediterranean fare.

Urban Pind
BAR

(4 N-Block, Greater Kailash I; ☉noon-1am) Three-floored, this has cushy flocked sofas, mock-Khajuraho carvings and nightly DJs. Tuesday is Salsa night, with free lessons from 9pm, while expats and diplomats flock on a Thursday for the all-you-can-drink deal.

Red Monkey
BAR

(☑24618358; 7 Defence Colony Market; ☉4pm-1am; ⓂLajpat Nagar) A small cosy bar, this is a buzzy if unexciting choice in the Defence Colony. Cocktails cost ₹300-500 and it's worth making it for happy Monday, where it's two-for-one.

☆ Entertainment

To access Delhi's dynamic arts scene, check local listings (see p98). October and March is the 'season', with happenings (often free) nightly.

TLR
LIVE MUSIC

(www.tlrcafe.com; Hauz Khas Village; ☉11am-1am; ⓂHauz Khas) Delhi's coolest and most boho hangout, TLR (The Living Room) is in laid-back Hauz Khas Village. It's worth the trek: a 2nd-floor bar with live music, jam sessions and other events from 9pm most evenings. It has a tiny stage complete with a three-piece suite. Meals are also available and cocktails cost from ₹400. If there's something on, book a table or arrive early.

Attic
CULTURAL PROGRAM

(Map p72; ☑23746050; www.theatticdelhi.org; 36 Regal bdg; ⓂRajiv Chowk) Small arts space, with regular free classical concerts and talks. There are also explorations of forgotten foods and 'food meditation' (where participants eat in silence and then have a discussion) – these sessions cost ₹100 and should be booked in advance.

Dances of India
DANCE

(Map p64; ☑26234689; Parsi Anjuman Hall, Bahadur Shah Zafar Marg; ₹400; ☉6.45pm) A one-hour performance of regional dances that includes Bharata Natyam (Tamil dance), Kathakali, bhangra and Manipuri.

Haze
LIVE MUSIC

(8 Basant Lok, Visant Vihar; ☉3pm-midnight) A hip yet unpretentious haunt, this moody, intimate, inexpensive jazz bar has real soul and is *the* place to see live Indian blues and jazz at weekends.

Habitat World
CULTURAL PROGRAM

(Map p68; ☑43663333; www.habitatworld.com; India Habitat Centre, Lodi Rd) Check out the Visual Arts Gallery's excellent temporary exhibitions.

India International Centre
CULTURAL PROGRAM

(Map p68; ☑24619431; 40 Max Mueller Marg) The IIC holds regular free exhibitions, talks and cultural performances.

PVR Plaza Cinema
CINEMA

(Map p72; ☑41516787; H-Block, Connaught Place)

PVR Priya Cinema
CINEMA

(Map p78; www.pvrcinemas.com; Basant Lok complex, Vasant Vihar)

PVR Saket (Anupam 4)
CINEMA

(Map p78; www.pvrcinemas.com; Saket Community Centre, Saket)

🔒 Shopping

From bamboozling bazaars to *bijoux* boutiques, Delhi is a fantastic place to shop. There's an astounding array of wonderful stuff: handicrafts, textiles, clothing, carpets, jewellery and a kaleidoscope of saris.

Away from the emporiums and other fixed-price shops, put on your haggle hat. Many taxi and autorickshaw drivers earn commissions (via your inflated purchase price) and may not take you to the most reputable stores, either, making it best to decline their shopping suggestions.

For dependable art gallery recommendations (many of which sell exhibits), check *First City* and *Time Out*.

Old Delhi's **bazaars** (Map p64; MChandni Chowk) are a headspinning assault on the senses: an aromatic muddle of flowers, urine, incense, chai, fumes and frying food. They're busiest (and best avoided) on Monday and Friday and during other afternoons. Come at around 11.30am when most shops have opened and the jostling is bearable.

For silver jewellery (some gold) head for **Dariba Kalan**, near the Sisganj Gurdwara. Nearby **Kinari Bazaar** (literally 'trimmings market') is famous for *zari* (gold-thread weaving) and *zardozi* (gold embroidery), and is the place to head for your bridal trousseau. The **cloth market** sells swathes of uncut material and linen, while electrical gadgets are the speciality of **Lajpat Rai Market**. **Chowri Bazaar** is the wholesale paper and greeting-card market. Nearby, **Nai Sarak** deals in wholesale stationery, books and saris.

Near the Fatehpuri Masjid, on Khari Baoli, is the nose-numbing **Spice Market**, ablaze with powdery piles of scarlet-red chilli powder and burnt-orange turmeric, as well as pickles, tea and nuts. As it's a wholesale market, spices here rarely come hermetically sealed – for these, go to Roopak's in Karol Bagh.

The **Daryaganj Book Market**, north of Delhi Gate, is a bookworm's delight (Sunday afternoons).

NORTH DELHI

Chandni Chowk
CLOTHING

(Map p64; Old Delhi; ☺Mon-Sat; MChandni Chowk) Pure pandemonium, this is the old city's famed shopping strip, with endless haphazard traffic, stores selling a mishmash of saris, Nehru suits, glittering shoes and electrical goods. There are roadside tailors and locksmiths, hawkers selling birdseed, labourers catching a snooze amid the chaos and half-dead dogs everywhere you look. Some stores open from around 10am to 7pm, others from noon to 9pm.

New Gramophone House
MUSIC STORE

(Map p64; ☎23271524; Pleasure Garden Market; ☺10am-9pm Mon-Sat; MChandni Chowk) Opposite Moti Cinema, this is a 1st-floor wonderland of vintage Bollywood records (₹50 to ₹200) and even older gramophones.

Main Bazaar
MARKET

(Map p76; Paharganj; ☺around 10am-9pm Tue-Sun; MRK Ashram Marg) The backpacker-oriented spine of Paharganj is the perfect place to pick up bargains in the form of T-shirts, bags, costume jewellery, essential oils, incense and more. Although the Main Bazaar is officially closed on Monday, many of the shops remain open during the tourist season.

Karol Bagh Market
MARKET

(Map p64; ☺around 10am-7pm Tue-Sun; MKarol Bagh) This brash middle-class market shimmers with all things sparkly, from dressy *lehanga choli* (skirt-and-blouse sets) to princess-style shoes. Get spice-happy at

Roopak's (6/9 Ajmal Khan Rd), two neighbouring shops with similar spices (around ₹60 to ₹100 per 100g and well packed).

CONNAUGHT PLACE

Central Cottage Industries Emporium
HANDICRAFTS

(Map p72; ☎23326790; Janpath; MRajiv Chowk) This government-run, fixed-price multilevel Aladdin's cave of India-wide handicrafts is a great place to shop: woodcarvings, silverware, jewellery, pottery, papier mâché, brassware, textiles (including shawls), beauty products and heaps more.

State Emporiums
HANDICRAFTS

(Map p72; Baba Kharak Singh Marg; ☺11am-7pm Mon-Sat; MRajiv Chowk) These neighbouring state government emporiums showcase products from different states, from Rajasthan to Bihar. Set aside several hours for these fabulous shops.

Shop
CLOTHING & HOMEWARES

(Map p72; 10 Regal Bldg, Sansad Marg; ☺9.30am-7pm Mon-Sat; MRajiv Chowk) There are lovely homewares and clothes (including children's clothes) from all over India in this chic boutique with reasonable fixed prices.

Khadi Gramodyog Bhawan
HANDICRAFTS

(Map p72; Regal Bldg, Sansad Marg; ☺10.30am-7.15pm Mon-Sat; MRajiv Chowk) Best known for its excellent *khadi* (homespun cloth) clothing, including good-value shawls, but also worth a visit for its handmade paper, incense, spices, henna and lovely natural soaps.

Oxford Bookstore (Statesman House) BOOKSTORE
(Map p72; 14 G-Block, Connaught Place; ☺10am-9.30pm Mon-Sat, 11am-9.30pm Sun; MRajiv Chowk) A fantastic bookshop where you could spend hours. It also sells some good gifts, such as handmade paper notebooks. Attached is the **Cha Bar**.

People Tree HANDICRAFTS
(Map p72; Regal Bldg, Sansad Marg; ☺10.30am-7pm Mon-Sat; MRajiv Chowk) The blink-and-you'll-miss-it People Tree sells cool, etching-style or embroidered T-shirts, many featuring Indian gods, as well as skirts, dresses, shirts (for men and women), shoulder bags, costume jewellery and books.

Soma HOMEWARES
(Map p72; 1st fl, 44 K-Block, Connaught Place; ☺10am-8pm; MRajiv Chowk) Situated opposite PVR Plaza Cinema, 1st-floor Soma stocks brilliant block-printed textiles at reasonable prices: anything from scarves to pyjamas, cushion covers to children's clothing.

Marques & Co MUSIC STORE
(Map p72; 14 G-Block, Connaught Place; ☺10.30am-1.30pm & 2-6.30pm Mon-Sat; MRajiv Chowk) This vintage music shop (since 1918) houses polished guitars (from ₹3000), tablas (from ₹6000) and harmonicas (from ₹300) in stuck-in-time glass cabinets. Sheet music is also available.

Janpath Market MARKET
(Map p72; Janpath; ☺10.30am-7.30pm Mon-Sat; MRajiv Chowk) Aka the Tibetan Market, this touristy strip sells the usual trinkets: shimmering mirrorwork textiles, colourful shawls, brass oms, and dangly earrings and trinkets galore. It has some good finds if you rummage through the junk. Haggle hard.

Rikhi Ram MUSIC STORE
(☎23327685; www.rikhiram.com; 8A G-Block, Connaught Place; ☺11.30am-8pm Mon-Sat; MRajiv Chowk) A beautiful old shop, selling professional classic and electric sitars, tablas and more.

M Ram & Sons CLOTHING
(Map p72; ☎23416558; 21 E-Block, Connaught Place; ☺10am-8pm Mon-Sat; MRajiv Chowk) Men's suits from ₹4000 (excluding material), ladies long skirts from ₹500 (excluding material). Tailoring is possible in 24 hours.

SOUTH DELHI

Khan Market MARKET
(Map p68; ☺around 10.30am-8pm Mon-Sat; MKhan Market) Favoured by expats and Delhi's elite, the boutiques in this enclave are devoted to fashion, books, homewares, and gourmet groceries. For handmade paperware check out **Anand Stationers**. For a fantastic range of English-language fiction and nonfiction head to **Full Circle Bookstore** and **Bahri Sons**. There's a TARDIS-like branch of **Fabindia** (p97), **Anokhi**, wow-factor homewares store **Good Earth** (featuring London-style prices) and the excellent **Silverline**, which does attractive, reasonable silver and gold jewellery.

Dilli Haat HANDICRAFTS
(Map p78; Aurobindo Marg; admission ₹15; ☺10.30am-10pm; MINA) Located opposite the colourful INA Market, this open-air food-and-crafts market sells regional handicrafts; bargain hard. Tasty on-site food stalls cook up regionally diverse cuisine. Avoid the busy weekends.

Hauz Khas Village ANTIQUES & CLOTHING
(Map p78; ☺11am-7pm Mon-Sat; MHauz Khas) This arty little enclave is packed with designer Indian-clothing boutiques, art galleries and furniture shops. It's a great place to find superb old Bollywood posters. Try Country Collection for antique and new furniture (they'll post overseas), and Cotton Curios for handprinted *kameez* (women's tunics) and soft furnishings.

C Lal & Sons HANDICRAFTS
(Map p68; 9/172 Jor Bagh Market; ☺10.30am-7.30pm; MJor Bagh) After sightseeing at Safdarjang's tomb, drop into kindly Mr Lal's 'curiosity shop'. Much loved by Delhi-based diplomats for its dazzling Christmas-tree decorations, it also sells handicrafts such as papier mâché and carvings.

Timeless BOOKSTORE
(Map p78; ☎24693257; 46 Housing Society, Part I) Hidden in a back lane (ask around), Timeless has a devoted following for its quality coffee-table books, from Indian textiles to architecture.

Sarojini Nagar Market CLOTHING
(Map p78; ☺around 11am-8pm Tue-Sun; MINA) Rummage here for good-value Western-style clothes (seek out the lanes lined exclusively with clothing stalls) that have been dumped here either because they were an export surplus or from a cancelled line. Check for faults. Bargain hard.

Sunder Nagar Market
HANDICRAFTS, TEA

(Map p68; ⊙around 10.30am-7.30pm Mon-Sat) Just south of Purana Qila, this genteel enclave specialises in Indian and Nepali handicrafts and 'antiques' (most are replicas). There are two outstanding teashops here: **Regalía Tea House** (⊙10am-7.30pm Mon-Sat, 11am-5pm Sun); and its neighbour **Mittal Tea House** (⊙10am-7.30pm Mon-Sat, 10am-4.30pm Sun). They stock similar products and offer complimentary tea tastings. There's plenty on offer, from fragrant Kashmiri kahwa (green tea with cardamom; ₹110 per 100g) to the finest of teas, Vintage Musk (₹700 per 100g) and Royal Muscatel (₹600 per 100g). The white tea (₹600/350 per 100g organic/nonorganic) is said to contain more antioxidants than green tea, while dragon balls (₹35-80 each) are a visual thrill when brewed.

Santushti Shopping Complex
HOMEWARES, CLOTHING

(Map p68; Santushti Enclave; ⊙10am-7pm Mon-Sat) This enclave across from the Ashok hotel is an unusually relaxing, if expensive, place to browse and shop, with stores such as **Anokhi**, **Good Earth** and **Shyam Ahuja** (which sells carpets), housed in appealing little pavilions in a landscaped area.

M-Block & N-Block Markets
MARKET

(Map p78; Greater Kailash I; ⊙Wed-Mon) This two-part upmarket shopping enclave is perhaps best known for the awesome mothership of **Fabindia**. Also worth checking out is the clothes store **Anokhi** (N-Block) and the big branch of the lovely **Full Circle Bookstore**, complete with a Café Turtle.

Fabindia
CLOTHING, HOMEWARES

GKI (Map p78; www.fabindia.com; 7 N-Block Market; ⊙10am to 7.30pm); Khan Market (Map p68; Above shop 20 & 21; ⓂKhan Market); Connaught Place (Map p72; Upper Ground fl, 28 B-Block; ⓂRajiv Chowk) Readymade clothes that won't look odd back home, plus great tablecloths, cushion covers, curtains and other homewares.

Nalli Silk Sarees
CLOTHING

Greater Kailash (Map p78; ☑24629926; Greater Kailash II; ⊙10am-8.30pm); Connaught Place (Map p72; 7/90 P-Block; ⓂRajiv Chowk) This multistorey sari emporium is a kaleidoscope of silk varieties, specialising in those from South India. Prices range from ₹1000 to ₹30,000.

Lajpat Nagar Central Market
MARKET

(Map p78; ⊙around 11am-8pm Tue-Sun; ⓂLajpat Nagar) This market attracts bargain-hunting locals on the prowl for household goods, clothing and jewellery. Look out for the local *mehndiwallahs,* who paint beautiful henna designs.

Delhi Musical Stores
MUSIC STORE

(Map p64; ☑23276909; www.indianmusical instruments.com; 1070 Paiwalan, Old Delhi; ⊙10am-6.30pm Mon-Sat; ⓂPatel Chowk) Opposite Jama Masjid's Gate No 3. Check the website for details.

OCM Suitings
CLOTHING

(Map p68; ☑24618937; Khan Market; ⊙11am-8pm Mon-Sat; ⓂKhan Market) Men's wool suits from ₹9000 to ₹22,000 (including material); ankle-length skirts from ₹500 (excluding material). Suits take around 7 to 10 days.

ⓘ Information
Dangers & Annoyances

HOTEL TOUTS Taxi-wallahs at the international airport frequently act as touts. These sneaky drivers will try to persuade you that your hotel is full, poor value, overbooked, dangerous, burned down or closed, or even that there are riots in Delhi. Their intention is to take you to a hotel where they'll get some commission. Some will even 'kindly' take you to a 'tourist office' where a colleague will phone your hotel on your behalf, and corroborate the driver's story. In reality, of course, he's talking to his mate in the next room. Alternatively, the driver may claim that he's lost and stop at a travel agency for directions. The agent supposedly dials your hotel and informs you that your room is double-booked, and 'helpfully' finds you another hotel where he'll get commission and you get a high room rate.

Tell persistent taxi drivers that you've paid for your hotel in advance, have recently confirmed the booking, or have friends/relatives waiting for you there. If they continue, ask that they stop the car so that you can write down the registration plate number. Just to be sure, call or email to confirm your hotel booking, if possible, 24 hours before check-in.

TRAVEL AGENT TOUTS Be cautious with travel agencies, as many travellers every year report being overcharged and underwhelmed by unscrupulous agents. To avoid grief, ask for traveller recommendations, or ask for a list of recommended agents from the India Tourist office (88 Janpath). *Think twice before parting with your money.* Choose agents who are members of accredited associations such as the Travel Agents Association of India and the Indian Association of Tour Operators.

Be especially careful if booking a multistop trip out of Delhi. Lonely Planet often gets letters from travellers who've paid upfront and then found out there are extra expenses, they've been overcharged, or the accommodation is terrible. Given the number of letters we've received from unhappy travellers, it's also best not to book tours to Kashmir from Delhi.

TRAIN STATION TOUTS These touts are at their worst at New Delhi train station. Here they may try to prevent you reaching the upstairs International Tourist Bureau and divert you to a local (over-priced and often unreliable) travel agency. Make the assumption that the office is *never* closed (outside the official opening hours; see p99) and has not shifted. It's still in its regular place on the 1st floor, close to the Paharganj side of the station.

Other swindlers may insist that your ticket needs to be stamped or checked (for a hefty fee) before it is considered valid. Some may try to convince wait-listed passengers that there is a charge to check their reservation status – don't fall for it.

For more info on Scams & Touts, see p1156.

Internet Access

Internet cafes are mushrooming, with centres in Khan Market, Paharganj and Connaught Place, among others, usually charging around ₹35 per hour, ₹5 to print a page and ₹25 to scan/write a CD. Reviewed places with wi-fi are indicated with .

Media

To check out what's on, grab *Delhi Diary* (₹10). Fab monthly magazine *First City* (₹50) has comprehensive listings/reviews, ranging from theatre to so-now bars, while *Time Out Delhi* (₹40) is a hip take on the city. Publications are available at newsstands and bookshops.

Medical Services

Pharmacies are ubiquitous in most markets.

All India Institute of Medical Sciences (Aiims; Map p78; ☑26588500; www.aiims.edu; Ansari Nagar; Ⓜ AIIMS)

Apollo Hospital (☑26925858; Mathura Rd, Sarita Vihar)

Dr Ram Manohar Lohia Hospital (Map p68; ☑23365525; Baba Kharak Singh Marg)

East West Medical Centre (Map p78; ☑24690429; www.eastwestrescue.com; B-28 Greater Kailash Part I) Opposite N-Block Market; this is one of the easier options if you have to make an insurance claim.

Money

There are ATMs almost everywhere you look in Delhi. Many travel agents and money changers, including Thomas Cook, can do international money transfers.

Baluja Forex (Map p76; ☑41541523; 4596 Main Bazaar, Paharganj; ◷9am-7.30pm) Does cash advances on MasterCard and Visa.

Central Bank of India (Map p68; ☑26110101; Ashok Hotel, Chanakyapuri; ◷24hr)

Thomas Cook International airport (☑25653439; ◷24hr); Janpath (Map p68; ☑23342171; Hotel Janpath, Janpath; ◷9.30am-7pm Mon-Sat)

Post & Telephone

Delhi has tons of telephone kiosks where you can make cheap local, interstate and international calls.

DHL (Map p72; ☑23737587; Mercantile Bldg, ground fl Tolstoy Marg; ◷8am-8pm Mon-Sat) Organises international air freight.

Post office Connaught Place (Map p72; 6 A-Block; ◷8am-8pm Mon-Sat); New Delhi main post office (Map p68; ☑23364111; Baba Kharak Singh Marg; ◷10am-1pm & 1.30-4pm Mon-Sat) Poste restante available at the main post office; ensure mail is addressed to GPO, New Delhi – 110001.

Tourist Information

Beware Delhi's many dodgy travel agencies and 'tourist information centres'. Do *not* be fooled – the only official tourist information centre is India Tourism Delhi. Touts may (falsely) claim to be associated with this office.

For Indian regional tourist offices' contact details ask at India Tourism Delhi, or dial directory enquiries on ☑197.

India Tourism Delhi (Government of India; Map p72; ☑23320008/5; www.incredible india.org; 88 Janpath; ◷9am-6pm Mon-Fri, to 2pm Sat) Gives tourist-related advice as well as a free Delhi map and brochures. Has a list of recommended agencies and bed & breakfasts. Their special branch investigates tourism-related complaints.

❶ Getting There & Away

Delhi is a major international gateway. It's also a centre for domestic travel, with extensive bus, rail and air connections. Delhi's airport can be prone to thick fog in December and January (often disrupting airline schedules), making it wise not to book back-to-back flights during this period.

Air

International and domestic flights all leave from and arrive at the airport's gleaming new Terminal 3. For flight inquiries, call the **international airport** (☑0124-3376000; www.newdelhi airport.in). At the new Terminal 3 there are 14 'nap & go' rooms with wi-fi, a desk, TV and bed (₹315/hr).

Apart from public buses, there are comfortable private bus services (including sleepers), leaving from central locations, but their schedules vary (enquire at travel agencies or your hotel). Example routes are Delhi to Jammu (₹500, 15 hours) and McLeon Ganj (₹650, 14 hours). Himachal Pradesh Tourism Development Corporation (HPTDC) also runs a bus for Dharamsala from Connaught Place. There are buses to Agra, but the train is much easier and quicker.

DESTINATION	ONE-WAY FARE (₹)	DURATION (HR)	DEPARTURES
Amritsar	500-665 (B)	10	hourly 5.30am-9.30pm
Chandigarh	180/345-515 (A/B)	5	every 30min 6am-1.50am
Dehra Dun	179/278-460 (A/B)	7	hourly 5am-11pm
Dharamsala	395/500-780 (A/B)	12	hourly 4.30am-11pm
Kullu	490/830-1050 (A/B)	13	9am
Manali	490/830-1050 (A/B)	15	hourly 1-10pm
Shimla	310/580-860	10	hourly 5am-10.30pm

A – ordinary, B – deluxe AC

For comprehensive details of domestic air routes, see *Excel's Timetable of Air Services Within India* (₹55), available at newsstands. When making reservations request the most direct (quickest) route. Note that airline prices fluctuate and website bookings with some carriers can be markedly cheaper.

DOMESTIC ARRIVALS & DEPARTURES Check-in at the airport for domestic flights is one hour before departure.

DOMESTIC AIRLINES The **Air India office** (3 Safdarjung Airport; 9.30am-5.30pm) is in South Delhi. To confirm flights dial 1407.

Other domestic airlines:

Jagson Airlines (Map p72; 23721593; Vandana Bldg, 11 Tolstoy Marg)

Kingfisher Airlines (Map p72; 23730238; 42 N-Block, Connaught Place)

INTERNATIONAL ARRIVALS The arrivals hall has 24-hour money-exchange facilities, ATM, prepaid taxi and car-hire counters, a tourist information counter, cafes and bookshops.

INTERNATIONAL DEPARTURES At the check-in counter, ensure you collect tags to attach to hand luggage (mandatory to clear security later).

Bus

Bikaner House (Map p68; 23383469; Pandara Rd), near India Gate, operates good state-run buses. These are the best buses for Jaipur (super deluxe/Volvo ₹325/625, six hours, hourly); Udaipur (₹750, 15 hours, one daily); Ajmer (₹400, nine hours, three daily); and Jodhpur (₹500, 11 hours, one daily).

Delhi's main bus station is the **Inter State Bus Terminal** (ISBT; Map p64; 23860290; Kashmiri Gate; 24hr), north of the (Old) Delhi train station. It has a 24-hour left-luggage facility (₹14 per bag). This station is chaotic so arrive at least 30 minutes ahead of your departure time. State-government bus companies (and their counters) at the ISBT include the following (timetables are online):

Delhi Transport Corporation (23865181; dtc.nic.in; Counter 34)

Haryana Roadways (23861262; hartrans.gov.in; Counter 35)

Himachal Roadways (23868694; Counter 40)

Punjab Roadways (23867842; www.punjabroadways.gov.in; Counter 37)

Rajasthan Roadways (23386658, 23864470; Counter 36)

Uttar Pradesh Roadways (23868709; Counter 33)

Train

For foreigners, it's easiest to make ticket bookings at the helpful **International Tourist Bureau** (Map p76; 23405156; 1st fl, New Delhi train station; 8am-8pm Mon-Sat, to 2pm Sun). Do *not* believe anyone – including porters – who tells you it has shifted, closed or burnt down and don't let anyone stop you from going to the 1st floor of the *main* building for bookings. When making reservations here, if you are paying in rupees you may have to provide back-up money-exchange certificates (or ATM receipts), so take these with you just in case. You can also pay in travellers cheques: in Thomas Cook US dollars, euros or pounds sterling, Amex US dollars and euros, and US dollars in Barclays cheques. Any change is given in rupees. Bring your passport.

When you arrive, complete a reservation form, then wait to check availability at the Tourism Counter in the office. You can then queue to pay for the ticket at one of the other counters.

There are two main stations in Delhi – (Old) Delhi train station (Map p64) in Old Delhi, and New Delhi train station (Map p64) at Paharganj; make sure you know which station serves your destination (New Delhi train station is closer to Connaught Place). If you're departing from the Delhi train station, allow adequate time to meander through Old Delhi's snail-paced traffic.

There's also the Nizamuddin train station (Map p68), south of Sunder Nagar, where various trains (usually for south-bound destinations) start or finish.

Railway porters should charge around ₹30 per bag.

There are many more destinations and trains than those listed in the boxed text, p101 – check the Indian Railways Website (www.indianrail.gov.in) consult *Trains at a Glance* (₹45), available at most newsstands, or ask tourist office staff.

ⓘ Getting Around

The metro system has transformed getting around the city, making it incredibly easy to whizz out to places that were once a long traffic-hampered struggle to reach. Most of Delhi's main sights lie close to a metro station. Local buses get horrendously crowded so the metro, autorickshaws and taxis are desirable alternatives. Keep small change handy for fares.

To/From the Airport

Many international flights arrive at ghastly hours, so it pays to book a hotel in advance and notify it of your arrival time.

PRE-ARRANGED PICK-UPS If you arrange an airport pick-up through a travel agency or hotel, it's more expensive than a prepaid taxi from the airport due to the airport parking fee (up to ₹140) and ₹80 charge for the person collecting you to enter the airport arrivals hall. Sometimes drivers are barred from arrivals for security reasons, in which case most will wait outside Gates 4–6.

METRO The new high-speed metro line is the best way to get to/from the airport, and runs between New Delhi train station and Dwarka Sector 21, via Shivaji Stadium, Dhaula Kuan NH8 (Mahipalpur station) and Indira Gandhi International station (Terminal 3). Trains operate every 10 minutes from 5am to 1am.

BUS Air-conditioned deluxe buses run to the airport about every 40 minutes from ISBT Kashmere Gate, via the Red Fort, LNJP Hospital, New Delhi Station Gate 2, Connaught Place, Parliament Street and Ashoka Rd (₹50). There are several other routes, one of which goes via Saket and Vasant Kunj; another calls at Hauz Khas and Vasant Vihar.

TAXI There is a **Delhi Traffic Police Prepaid Taxi counter** (☑helpline 23010101; www.delhitrafficpolice.nic.in) inside the arrivals building. It costs about ₹310 to Connaught Place, plus a 25% surcharge between 11pm and 5am.

You'll be given a voucher with the destination on it – insist that the driver honours it. Never surrender your voucher until you get to your destination; without that docket the driver won't get paid.

You can also book a prepaid taxi at the **Megacabs** counter inside the arrivals building at both the international and domestic airports. It costs around ₹600 to the centre, but you get a cleaner, car with air-con, and you can pay by credit card.

Car

HIRING A CAR & DRIVER Numerous operators offer chauffeur-driven cars. The following companies get positive reports from travellers. Each has an eight-hour, 80km limit per day. All offer tours beyond Delhi (including Rajasthan) but higher charges apply for these. The rates below are only for travel within Delhi. Beware of frauds/touts claiming association with these companies or insisting their offices have closed.

Kumar Tourist Taxi Service (Map p72; ☑23415930; kumartaxi@rediffmail.com; 14/1 K-Block, Connaught Place; non-AC/AC per day ₹800/900; ⊙9am-9pm) Near the York Hotel. Tiny office run by two brothers, Bittoo and Titoo. Their rates are among Delhi's lowest.

Metropole Tourist Service (Map p68; ☑24310313; www.metrovista.co.in; 224 Defence Colony Flyover Market; non-AC car per day from ₹850; ⊙7am-7pm) Under the Defence Flyover Bridge (on the Jangpura side).

Cycle-Rickshaw & Bicycle

Cycle-rickshaws are still in use in parts of Old Delhi, though they have been banned in Chandni Chowk to reduce congestion. Let's hope they're not banned in other areas, as they're the best way to get around Old Delhi – the drivers are wizards at weaving through the crowds. Tips are appreciated for this gruelling work.

Cycle-rickshaws are also banned from the Connaught Place area and New Delhi, but they're handy for commuting between Connaught Place and Paharganj (about ₹30).

The largest range of new and secondhand bicycles for sale can be found at **Jhandewalan Cycle Market** (Map p64).

Metro

Delhi's marvellous metro (Map p82) has efficient services with arrival/departure announcements in Hindi and English. Two carriages on each train are designated women-only – look for the pink signs on the platform. The trains can get very busy, particularly at peak commuting times (around 9-10am and 5-6pm).

DESTINA-TION	TRAIN NO & NAME	FARE (₹)	DURA-TION (HR)	FREQUENCY	DEPAR-TURES & TRAIN STATION
Agra	12280 *Taj Exp*	75/263 (A)	3	1 daily	7.10am HN
	12002A *Bhopal Shatabdi*	370/700 (B)	2	1 daily	6.15am ND
Amritsar	12013 *Shatabdi Exp*	645/1200 (B)	5½	1 daily	4.30pm ND
	12029/12031 *Swarna/Amritsar Shatabdi*	600/1145 (B)	5½	1 daily	7.20am ND
Bengaluru	12430 *Bangalore Rajdhani*	2100/2740/4580 (C)	34	4 weekly	8.50pm HN
Chennai	12434 *Chennai Rajdhani*	2075/2700/4500 (C)	28	2 weekly	4pm HN
	12622 *Tamil Nadu Exp*	528/1429/1960/3322 (D)	33	1 daily	10.30pm ND
Goa (Madgaon)	12432 *Trivndrm Rajdhani*	2035/2615/4370 (C)	25½	2 weekly	11am HN
Haridwar	12017 *Dehradun Shatabdi*	435/825 (B)	4½	1 daily	6.50am ND
Jaipur	12958 *ADI SJ Rajdani*	605/775/1285 (C)	5	6 weekly	7.55pm ND
	12916 *Ashram Exp*	175/434/581/969 (D)	5¾	1 daily	3pm OD
	12015 *Shatabdi Exp*	465/885 (B)	4¾	6 weekly	6.05am ND
Khajuraho	12448 *Nizamud-din-Khajuraho Exp*	269/802 (E)	10¼	3 weekly	8.15pm HN
Lucknow	12004 *Lko Swran Shatabdi*	700/1360 (B)	6¼	1 daily	6.15am ND
Mumbai	12952 *Mumbai Rajdhani*	1495/1975/3305 (C)	16	1 daily	4.30pm ND
	12954 *Ag Kranti Rajdani Exp*	1495/1975/3305 (C)	17¼	1 daily	4.55pm HN
Udaipur	12963 *Mewar Exp*	320/801/1087/1821 (D)	12	1 daily	7.05pm HN
Varanasi	12560 *Shivganga Exp*	320/806/1095/1805 (D)	13	1 daily	6.45pm ND

Train stations: ND – New Delhi, OD – Old Delhi, HN – Hazrat Nizamuddin

Fares: A – 2nd class/chair car; B – chair car/1st-class AC; C – 3AC/2AC/1st-class AC; D – sleeper/3AC/2AC/1st-class AC; E – sleeper/3AC

Tokens (₹8 to ₹30) are sold at metro stations; there are also one-/three-day (₹70/200) 'tourist cards' for unlimited short-distance travel; or a Smart Card (₹50, refundable when you return it), which can be recharged for amounts from ₹50 to ₹800 – fares are 10% cheaper than paying by token.

For the latest developments (plus route maps) see www.delhimetrorail.com or call ☏23417910.

AUTORICKSHAW RATES

To gauge fares vis-à-vis distances, the following list shows one-way (official) rates departing from Janpath's pre-paid autorickshaw booth. Taxis charge around double.

DESTINATION	COST (₹)
Bahai House of Worship	100
Humayun's Tomb	50
Karol Bagh	50
Old Delhi train station	50
Paharganj	30
Purana Qila	30
Red Fort	50
Defence Colony	65

Motorcycle

For motorcycle rental details, see p1183.

Radiocab

If you have a local mobile number, you can call a radiocab. These air-conditioned cars are clean, efficient, and use reliable meters. They charge ₹20 per km. After calling the operator, you'll receive a text with your driver's registration number, then another to confirm arrival time (book 20 to 30 minutes in advance). You can also book online.

Some companies:

Easycabs (☏43434343; www.easycabs.com)

Megacabs (☏41414141; www.megacabs.com)

Quickcabs (☏45333333; www.quickcabs.in)

Taxi & Autorickshaw

All taxis and autorickshaws have meters but they are often 'not working' or drivers refuse to use them (so they can overcharge). If the meter isn't an option, agree on a fare before setting off. If the driver won't agree, look for one who will. From 11pm to 5am there's a 25% surcharge for autorickshaws and taxis.

Otherwise, to avoid shenanigans, catch an autorickshaw from a prepaid booth:

Janpath (Map p72; 88 Janpath; ⊘11am-8.30pm) Outside the India Tourism Delhi office.

New Delhi train station car park (Map p76; ⊘24hr)

Palika Bazaar's Gate No 2 (Map p72; Connaught Place; ⊘11am-7pm)

GREATER DELHI

TOP CHOICE **Qutb Minar** — HISTORIC SITE

(Map p78; ☏26643856; Indian/foreigner ₹10/250, video ₹25; ⊘sunrise-sunset; MQutab Minar) The beautiful religious buildings of the Qutb Minar complex form one of Delhi's most spectacular sights. They date from the onset of Islamic rule in India, and tell of tumultuous rises and falls in stone. Today on Delhi's outskirts, once these constructions formed the heart of the Muslim city.

The Qutb Minar itself is a mighty, awesome tower of victory, which closely resembles similar Afghan towers, and was also used as a minaret. Muslim sultan Qutb-ud-din began its construction in 1193, immediately after the defeat of the last Hindu kingdom in Delhi. It's nearly 73m high and tapers from a 15m-diameter base to a mere 2.5m at the top.

The tower has five distinct storeys, each marked by a projecting balcony. The first three storeys are made of red sandstone, the 4th and 5th storeys are of marble and sandstone. Qutb-ud-din built only to the 1st storey. His successors completed it and then, in 1326 it was struck by lightning. In 1368, Firoz Shah rebuilt the top storeys and added a cupola. An earthquake brought the cupola crashing down in 1803 – it was replaced with another in 1829, which was later removed.

There's a **Decorative Light Show** (Indian/foreigner ₹20/250; ⊘6.30-8pm) nightly. The Qutb Festival takes place here every October/November.

Be warned that Qutb Minar gets crowded on weekends.

Quwwat-ul-Islam Masjid

At the foot of the Qutb Minar stands the first mosque to be built in India, known as the Might of Islam Mosque. Also constructed in 1193, with various additions over the centuries, this building symbolises in stone the ascendance of one religious power over another. The original mosque was built on the foundations of a Hindu temple, and an inscription over the east gate states that it was built with materials obtained from demolishing '27 idolatrous temples' – it's possible to see many Hindu and Jain elements in the decoration.

Altamish, Qutb-ud-din's son-in-law, surrounded the original mosque with a cloistered court between 1210 and 1220.

Iron Pillar

This 7m-high pillar stands in the courtyard of the mosque and it was here a long time prior to the mosque's construction. A six-line Sanskrit inscription indicates that it was initially erected outside a Vishnu temple, possibly in Bihar, and was raised in memory of Chandragupta II, who ruled from AD 375 to 413.

What the inscription does not tell is how it was made, for the iron in the pillar is of exceptional purity. Scientists have never discovered how the iron, which has not rusted after some 2000 years, could be cast using the technology of the time.

Alai Minar

When Ala-ud-din made his additions to the mosque he also conceived a far more ambitious construction program. He aimed to build a second tower of victory, exactly like the Qutb Minar, but twice as high! By the time of his death the tower had reached 27m and no one was willing to continue his over-ambitious project. The incomplete tower, a solid stack of rubble, stands to the north of the Qutb Minar and the mosque.

Other Features

Ala-ud-din's exquisite **Alai Darwaza** gateway is the main entrance to the whole complex. It was built of red sandstone in 1310 and is just southwest of the Qutb Minar. The **tomb of Imam Zamin** is beside the gateway, while the **tomb of Altamish**, who died in 1235, is by the northwestern corner of the mosque. The largely ruined **madrasa of Ala-ud-din** stands at the rear of the complex.

There are some **summer palaces** in the area and also the **tombs** of the last kings of Delhi, who succeeded the Mughals. An empty space between two of the tombs was intended for the last king of Delhi, who died in exile in Yangon, Burma (Myanmar), in 1862, following his implication in the 1857 First War of Independence.

Tughlaqabad   FORT
(Map p78; Indian/foreigner ₹5/100, video ₹25; ◷8.30am-5.30pm; ⓂTughlaqabad) Crumbling Tughlaqabad was the third city of Delhi. This mammoth, battered-looking stronghold, with 6.5km of walls and 13 gateways, was built by Ghiyas-ud-din Tughlaq. Its construc-

tion was said to have sparked a quarrel with the saint Nizam-ud-din: when the Tughlaq ruler refused the workers whom Nizam-ud-din wanted for work on his shrine, the saint cursed the king, warning that his city would be inhabited only by shepherds. Later, this was indeed the case.

Later, when Ghiyas-ud-din was returning from a military campaign, Nizam-ud-din again prophesised doom for him, telling his followers, 'Delhi is a long way off'. And it was: the king was killed on his way towards Delhi in 1325.

The metro runs to Tughlaqabad.

FREE Mehrauli Archaelogical Park   HISTORIC PARK
(Map p78; ◷dawn-dusk; ⓂQutab Minar) There's an entrance a few hundred metres to the left of that to Qutb Minar as you face it – walk down a narrow road which leads into the park. It's a rambling forest, once a hunting ground for the Mughals, then a favoured spot for colonial officers. It's dotted by extraordinary monuments, and has an undiscovered feel. The major monuments include **Jamali Kamali** (sunrise-sunset), a mosque, alongside which lies a small building containing two tombs: that of Jamali, a sufi saint, and Kamali, his unknown male friend, obviously important enough to be buried alongside him. Ask the caretaker to unlock the building to see the well-preserved painting within. A short walk from here is the dizzying **Rajon ki Baoli**, a majestic 16th-century step-well with an Escheresque sweeping flight of steps.

Garden of the 5 Senses   PARK
(Map p78; admission ₹15; ◷8am-9pm; ⓂSaket) This relaxing garden, an 8-hectare landscaped park inaugurated in 2003, is filled with intriguing contemporary sculptures, formal gardens and features such as wind chimes and lily ponds. Its discreet corners make it a favourite of canoodling couples. There are several upmarket restaurants and bars close to Gate 3.

ⓘ Getting There & Away

The metro extends to Qutb Minar, but the entrance is a couple of kilometres away along busy, broad roads from the station, so catch a rickshaw (₹30).

Rajasthan

Why Go?

Rajasthan, the Land of Kings, is aptly named. It is indeed a fabulous realm of maharajas and their majestic forts and lavish palaces. While its people-charged cities throb with the crowds and chaos of emerging India, the treasures of the past hold pride of place in mind and spirit The romantic remnants of a rich and glorious past have earned Rajasthan a place on most travellers' wish lists. Yet there is much more to this iconic region of the subcontinent. It is a land of desert dunes and jungle, camel trains and tigers, glittering jewels, vivid colours and a vibrant culture. There are enough festivals here to fill a calendar and an artist's palette, and the shopping and cuisine are nothing short of spectacular. In short, Rajasthan just about has it all; it is the must-see state of India, brimming with varied, startling and incredible attractions.

Best Places to Eat

» Niro's (p117)
» LMB (p119)
» Ambrai (p163)
» Indique (p178)

Best Places to Stay

» Hotel Pearl Palace (p115)
» Haveli Braj Bushanjee (p149)
» Khem Villas (p146)
» Inn Seventh Heaven (p141)
» Apani Dhani (p132)

When to Go

Jaipur

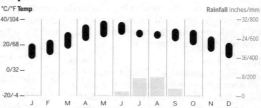

Oct Ranthambhore National Park reopens for tiger safaris.

Oct/Nov Don't miss the Pushkar Camel Festival, featuring camels (of course) and culture.

Mar Jaipur's famous Elephant Festival precedes the typically boisterous Holi celebrations.

Food

As with the rest of the north, Mughal-influenced curries and smoky tandoori food is extremely popular, but there are a few favourites with a regional twist that are worth hunting down. Kachori is a masala-dahl-filled, deep-fried package that hits the spot for an uncomplicated street snack. A favourite Rajasthani meal is *gatta*, gram-flour dumplings cooked in a yoghurt sauce. For refreshment you can't go past a thick and creamy *makhania* (saffron-flavoured) lassi, or a light, fragrant *kheer* (rice pudding).

DON'T MISS

In Jaipur, the **City Palace** is at the centre of a cluster of 'don't miss' sights, including the fascinating **Jantar Mantar**, **Hawa Mahal** and **Iswari Minar Swarga Sal**. For more vestiges of Maharaja high life check out Udaipur's **City Palace** and **Lake Palace**.

Nature lovers can't miss the birdlife at **Keoladeo Ghana National Park** nor the very real chance of spotting a tiger at **Ranthambhore National Park**.

Rajasthan has a surfeit of spectacular fortresses including the desert citadel of **Jaisalmer Fort** and Jodhpur's imposing **Mehrangarh**. You must also take a day trip out to spectacular **Amber Fort**.

Top State Festivals

» Desert Festival (Feb, Jaisalmer, p182) A chance for moustache twirlers to compete in the Mr Desert contest.

» Elephant Festival (Mar, Jaipur, p108) Parades, polo and human-versus-elephant tugs-of-war.

» Gangaur (Mar/Apr, Jaipur, p108) A statewide festival honouring Shiva and Parvati's love, celebrated with particular fervour in Jaipur.

» Mewar Festival (Mar/Apr, Udaipur, p160) Udaipur's version of Gangaur, with free cultural events and a colourful procession down to the lake.

» Teej (Aug, Jaipur, p108, & Bundi, p147) Honours the arrival of the monsoon, and Shiva and Parvati's marriage.

» Dussehra Mela (Oct, Kota, p151) Commemorates Rama's victory over Ravana (the demon king of Lanka). It's a spectacular time to visit Kota – the huge fair features 22m-tall firecracker-stuffed effigies.

» Marwar Festival (Oct, Jodhpur, p172, & Osian, p181) Celebrates Rajasthan heroes through music and dance; one day is held in Jodhpur, the other in Osiyan.

» Pushkar Camel Fair (Oct/Nov, Pushkar, p142) The Pushkar Camel Fair is the most famous festival in the state; it's a massive congregation of camels, horses and cattle, traders, pilgrims and tourists.

MAIN POINTS OF ENTRY

Jaipur International Airport, Jaipur train station, Jaipur main bus station.

Fast Facts

» Population: 68.6 million

» Area: 342,239 sq km

» Capital: Jaipur

» Main languages: Hindi and Rajasthani

» Sleeping prices: **$** below ₹1000, **$$** ₹100 to ₹5000, **$$$** above ₹5000

Top Tips

» Carry small denominations (below ₹50) as drivers often have a lack of change.

» Call your hotel to confirm the day before you arrive.

» Book train tickets for longer journeys at least a week ahead

Resources

» Festivals of India (www.festivalsofindia.in)

» Incredible India (www.incredibleindia.org)

» (Rajasthan Tourism Development Corporation www.rtdc.in)

Rajasthan Highlights

1 Cross the desert on a camel and explore the sandstone fort at **Jaisalmer** (p182)

2 Kick back in the pastel-hued pilgrimage town of **Pushkar** (p139)

3 Wander through the colourful bazaars of the pink, chaotic capital of **Jaipur** (p108)

4 Spot a tiger in the lush jungle and explore a magical clifftop fortress at **Ranthambhore National Park** (p145)

5 Listen to the blue city's secrets from the soaring ramparts of Jodhpur's magnificent fortress, **Mehrangarh** (p173)

6 Indulge in the romance of **Udaipur** (p154), with its gorgeous lake vistas and labyrinthine palace

7 Explore the forgotten towns and discover the crumbling frescoed *havelis* of **Shekhawati** (p132)

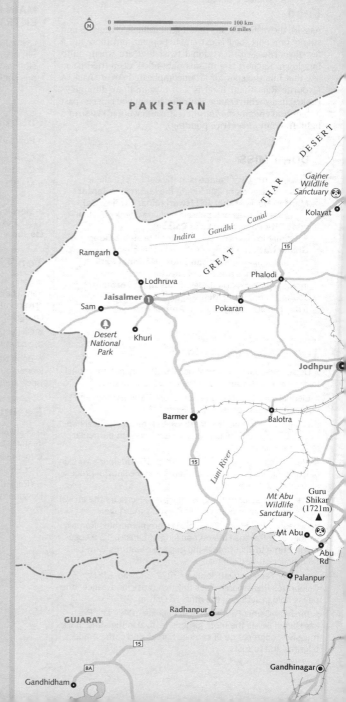

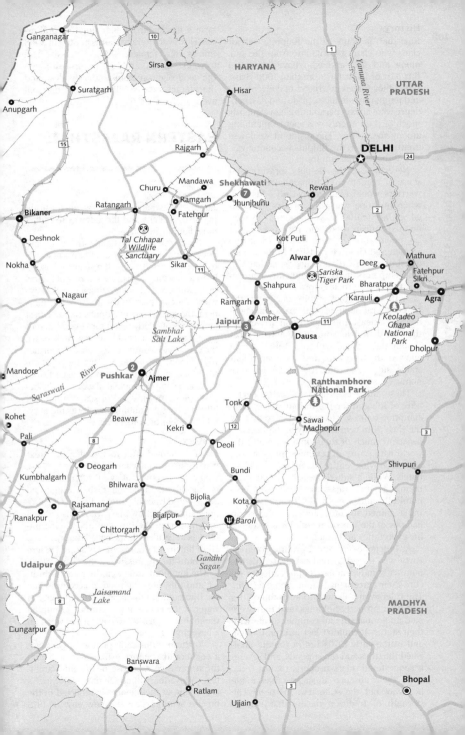

History

Rajasthan is home to the Rajputs, warrior clans who claim to originate from the sun, moon and fire, and who have controlled this part of India for more than 1000 years. While they forged marriages of convenience and temporary alliances, pride and independence were always paramount; consequently much of their energy was spent squabbling among themselves. The resultant weakness eventually led to the Rajputs becoming vassals of the Mughal empire.

Nevertheless, the Rajputs' bravery and sense of honour were unparalleled. Rajput warriors would fight against all odds and, when no hope was left, chivalry demanded *jauhar* (ritual mass suicide). The men donned saffron robes and rode out to face the enemy (and certain death), while the women and children perished in the flames of a funeral pyre. It's not surprising that Mughal emperors had such difficulty controlling this part of their empire.

With the Mughal empire declining, the Rajputs gradually clawed back independence – at least until the British arrived. As the British Raj inexorably expanded, most Rajput states allied with the British, which allowed them to continue as independent states, subject to certain political and economic constraints.

These alliances proved to be the beginning of the end for the Rajput rulers. Consumption took over from chivalry so that, by the early 20th century, many of the maharajas spent much of their time travelling the world with scores of retainers, playing polo and occupying entire floors of expensive hotels. While it suited the British to indulge them, the maharajas' profligacy was economically and socially detrimental. When India gained its independence, Rajasthan had one of the subcontinent's lowest rates of life expectancy and literacy.

At Independence, India's ruling Congress Party was forced to make a deal with the nominally independent Rajput states to secure their agreement to join the new India. The rulers were allowed to keep their titles and their property holdings, and they were paid an annual stipend commensurate with their status. It couldn't last forever, though, and in the early 1970s Indira Gandhi abolished the titles and the stipends, and severely sequestered rulers' property rights.

In their absence Rajasthan has made headway, but the state remains poor. The strength of tradition means that women have a particularly tough time in rural areas. However, literacy stands at 60% in 2008 (males 76%, females 44%), a massive rise from 18% in 1961 and 39% in 1991, although the gender gap remains India's widest, and the literacy rate is still below the national average of around 65%.

EASTERN RAJASTHAN

Jaipur

☎ 0141 / 3.21 MILLION

Jaipur, Rajasthan's capital, is an enthralling historical city and the gateway to India's most flamboyant state.

The city's colourful, chaotic streets ebb and flow with a heady brew of old and new. Careering buses dodge dawdling camels, leisurely cycle-rickshaws frustrate swarms of motorbikes, and everywhere buzzing autorickshaws watch for easy prey. In the midst of this mayhem, the splendours of Jaipur's majestic past are islands of relative calm evoking a different pace and another world. At the city's heart, the City Palace continues to house the former royal family, the Jantar Mantar, the royal observatory, maintains a heavenly aspect, and the honeycomb Hawa Mahal gazes on the bazaar below. And just out of sight, in the arid hill country surrounding the city, is the fairytale grandeur of Amber Fort.

History

Jaipur is named after its founder, the great warrior-astronomer Jai Singh II (1688–1744), who came to power at age 11 after the death of his father, Maharaja Bishan Singh. Jai Singh could trace his lineage back to the Rajput clan of Kachhwahas, who consolidated their power in the 12th century. Their capital was at Amber (pronounced amer), about 11km northeast of present-day Jaipur, where they built the impressive Amber Fort (p125).

The kingdom grew wealthier and wealthier, and this, plus the need to accommodate the burgeoning population and a paucity of water at the old capital at Amber, prompted the maharaja in 1727 to commence work on a new city – Jaipur.

Northern India's first planned city, it was a collaborative effort using his vision and the impressive expertise of his chief architect, Vidyadhar Bhattacharya. Jai Singh's grounding in the sciences is reflected in the precise symmetry of the new city. In 1876

Maharaja Ram Singh had the entire Old City painted pink (traditionally the colour of hospitality) to welcome the Prince of Wales (later King Edward VII). Today all residents of the Old City are compelled by law to preserve the pink facade.

◉ Sights

Consider buying a **composite ticket** (Indian/foreigner ₹50/300), which gives you entry to Amber Fort, Central Museum, Jantar Mantar, Hawa Mahal and Narhargarh, and is valid for two days from time of purchase.

OLD CITY (PINK CITY)

The Old City is partially encircled by a crenellated wall punctuated at intervals by grand gateways. The major gates are Chandpol (*pol* means 'gate'), Ajmer Gate and Sanganeri Gate. Avenues divide the Pink City into neat rectangles, each specialising in certain crafts, as ordained in the *Shilpa-Shastra*. The main bazaars in the Old City include Johari Bazaar, Tripolia Bazaar, Bapu Bazaar and Chandpol Bazaar; see the walking tour (p114) or Shopping (p120) for more details of these bazaars.

City Palace
PALACE

(Indian/foreigner incl camera & audio guide ₹75/300, video camera ₹200, Chandra Mahal tour ₹2500; ☺9.30am-5pm) A complex of courtyards, gardens and buildings, the impressive City Palace is right in the centre of the Old City. The outer wall was built by Jai Singh, but within it the palace has been enlarged and adapted over the centuries. Despite the gradual development, the whole is a striking blend of Rajasthani and Mughal architecture.

The price of admission also gets you in to Jaigarh Fort (see p125; a long climb above Amber Fort). This is valid for two days.

Mubarak Mahal

Entering through Virendra Pol, you'll see the Mubarak Mahal (Welcome Palace), built in the late 19th century for Maharaja Madho Singh II as a reception centre for visiting dignitaries. Its multiarched and colonnaded construction was cooked up in an Islamic, Rajput and European stylistic stew by the architect Sir Swinton Jacob. It now forms part of the **Maharaja Sawai Mansingh II Museum**, containing a collection of royal costumes and superb shawls, including Kashmiri *pashmina* (wool shawls). One remarkable exhibit is Sawai Madho Singh I's capacious clothing. It's said he was a cuddly 2m tall, 1.2m wide and 250kg.

Diwan-i-Khas (Sarvatobhadra)

Set between the Armoury and the Diwan-i-Am art gallery is an open courtyard known in Sanskrit as Sarvatobhadra. At its centre is a pink-and-white, marble-paved gallery that was used as the Diwan-i-Khas (Hall of Private Audience), where the maharajas would consult their ministers. Here you can see two enormous silver vessels, 1.6m tall and reputedly the largest silver objects in the world; Maharaja Madho Singh II, as a devout Hindu, used these vessels to take holy Ganges water to England.

Diwan-i-Am

Within the lavish Diwan-i-Am (Hall of Public Audience) is the **art gallery**. Exhibits include a copy of the entire Bhagavad Gita handwritten in tiny script, and miniature copies of other holy Hindu scriptures, which were small enough to be easily hidden in the event that Mughal zealot Aurangzeb tried to destroy the sacred texts.

The Armoury

The Anand Mahal Sileg Khana – the Maharani's Palace – houses the Armoury, which has one of the best collections of weapons in the country. Many of the ceremonial weapons are elegantly engraved and inlaid belying their grisly purpose.

Pitam Niwas Chowk & Chandra Mahal

Located towards the palace's inner courtyard is Pitam Niwas Chowk. Here four glorious gates represent the seasons. The **Peacock Gate** depicts autumn, with zigzagging patterns and peacock motifs – around the doorway are five beautiful repeated peacock bas reliefs in all their feathered glory.

Beyond this *chowk* (square) is the private palace, the Chandra Mahal, which is still the residence of the descendants of the royal family and where you can take a 45-minute guided **tour** (₹2500) of select areas.

Jantar Mantar
HISTORIC SITE

(Indian/foreigner ₹ 20/100 incl audio guide, optional guide Hindi/English ₹200/250; ☺9am-4.30pm) Adjacent to the City Palace is Jantar Mantar, an observatory begun by Jai Singh in 1728 that resembles a collection of bizarre sculptures. The name is derived from the Sanskrit *yanta mantr*, meaning 'instrument of calculation', and in 2010 it was added to India's list of World heritage Sites.

Jai Singh liked astronomy even more than he liked war and town planning. Before constructing the observatory he sent scholars abroad to study foreign constructs. He built

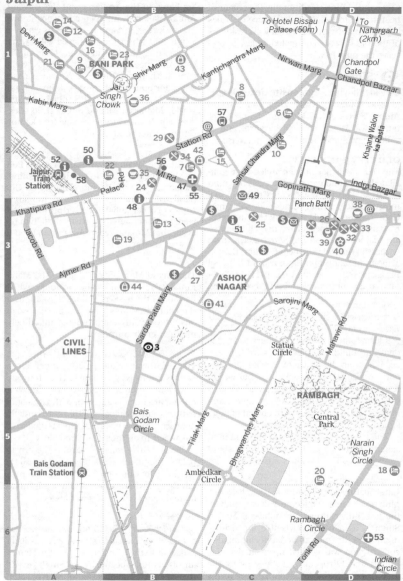

five observatories in total, and this is the largest and best preserved (it was restored in 1901). Others are in Delhi, Varanasi and Ujjain. No traces of the fifth, the Mathura observatory, remain.

Each construction within Jantar Mantar has a specific purpose, for example, measuring the positions of the stars, altitude and azimuth, and calculating eclipses. Paying for the half-hour to one-hour guide is worthwhile if you wish to learn how each fascinating instrument works.

honeycombed hive that rises a dizzying five storeys. Constructed in 1799 by Maharaja Sawai Pratap Singh to enable ladies of the royal household to watch the life and processions of the city. The top offers stunning views over Jantar Mantar and the City Palace one way, and over Siredeori Bazaar the other.

There's also a small **museum** (⊘9am-4.30pm Sat-Thu), with miniature paintings and some rich relics, such as ceremonial armour, which help evoke the royal past.

Entrance to the Hawa Mahal is from the back of the complex. To get here, return to the intersection on your left as you face the Hawa Mahal, turn right and then take the first right again through an archway.

NEW CITY
By the mid-19th century it became obvious that the well-planned city was bulging at the seams. During the reign of Maharaja Ram Singh (1835–80) the seams ruptured and the city burst out beyond its walls. The maharaja commissioned the landscaping of the Ram Niwas Public Gardens, on Jawaharlal Nehru (J Nehru) Rd, and the uproarious splendour of Albert Hall, built in honour of the Prince of Wales' 1876 visit, which now houses the Central Museum.

Central Museum   MUSEUM
(Albert Hall; Indian/foreigner ₹20/150, audio guide Hindi/English ₹80/110; ⊘9.30am-5pm) The museum is housed in the spectacularly florid Albert Hall, south of the Old City. It was designed by Sir Swinton Jacob, and combines elements of English and North Indian architecture. The grand old building hosts an eclectic array of tribal dress, clay models of yogis in various positions, dioramas, puppets, sculptures, miniature paintings, carpets, musical instruments and even an Egyptian mummy.

⬤ RC Museum of Indology   MUSEUM
(Prachyavidya Path, 24 Gangwell Park; Indian/foreigner incl guide ₹20/40; ⊘8am-6pm) This ramshackle, dusty treasure trove is an extraordinary private collection. It contains folk-art objects and other pieces – there's everything from a manuscript written by Aurangzeb and a 200-year-old mirrorwork swing from Bikaner to a glass bed (for a short queen). The museum is signposted off J Nehru Rd, south of the Central Museum.

Philatelic Bureau & Museum   MUSEUM
(Main Post Office, MI Rd; admission free; ⊘10am-5pm Mon-Sat) At the rear of the main post

Hawa Mahal   HISTORIC BUILDING
(Palace of the Winds; Indian/foreigner incl camera ₹10/50, audio guide Hindi/English ₹80/110, guide ₹200; ⊘9am-5pm) Jaipur's most distinctive landmark, the Hawa Mahal is an extraordinary, fairy-tale, pink-sandstone, delicately

Jaipur

office, this interesting little museum has historical stamps, telegrams and artefacts, including brass belt buckles and badges for Mail Runners and Packers. Even the Mail Peon could wear a badge with pride.

CITY EDGE

Nahargarh   HISTORIC BUILDING
(Tiger Fort; ☎5148044; Indian/foreigner ₹10/30; ☺10am-5pm) Built in 1734 and extended in 1868, sturdy Nahargarh overlooks the city

from a sheer ridge to the north. An 8km-long road runs up through the hills from Jaipur, or the fort can be reached along a zigzagging 2km-long footpath, which starts northwest of the Old City. The views are glorious – it's a great sunset spot, and there's a restaurant that's perfect for a beer.

Royal Gaitor
HISTORIC SITE

(Gatore ki Chhatryan; Indian/foreigner ₹20/30; ⊙9am-5pm) The royal cenotaphs, just outside the city walls, beneath Nahargarh, are an appropriately restful place to visit and feel remarkably undiscovered. The stone monuments are beautifully and intricately carved. Maharajas Pratap Singh, Madho Singh II and Jai Singh II, among others, are honoured here. Jai Singh II has the most impressive marble cenotaph, with a dome supported by 20 carved pillars.

The **cenotaphs of the maharanis of Jaipur** (Maharani ki Chhatri; Amber Rd; Indian/foreigner ₹20/30; ⊙9am-5pm) are also worth a visit. They lie between Jaipur and Amber, opposite the Holiday Inn.

Galta & Surya Mandir
HINDU TEMPLE

Perched between the cliff faces of a rocky valley, Galta is a desolate, if evocative, place. It is also known as the **Monkey Temple** and you will find hundreds of monkeys living here – bold and aggressive macaques and more graceful and tolerable langurs. You can purchase peanuts at the gate to feed to them, but be prepared to be mobbed by teeth-baring primates.

The temple houses a number of sacred tanks, into which some daring souls jump from the adjacent cliffs. The water is claimed to be 'several elephants deep' and fed from a spring that falls through the mouth of a sculptured cow.

On the ridge above Galta is the Surya Mandir (Temple of the Sun God), which rises 100m above Jaipur and can be seen from the eastern side of the city. A 2.5km-long walking trail climbs up to the temple from Suraj Pol, or you can walk up from the Galta side.

🏃 Activities

Several hotels will let you use their pool for a daily fee; try the pool at the **Narain Niwas Palace Hotel** (p117; admission ₹150).

Kerala Ayurveda Kendra
AYURVEDA

(☑5106743; www.keralaayurvedakendra.com; F-30 Jamnalal Bajaj Marg; ⊙8am-noon & 4-8pm) Is Jaipur making your nerves jangle? Get help through Ayurvedic massage and therapy. Massages (male masseur for male clients and female masseur for female clients) cost from ₹500 for 55 minutes. It offers free transport to/from your hotel.

🍴 Courses

Sakshi
BLOCK PRINTING

(☑2731862; Laxmi Colony; ⊙shop 8.30am-8.30pm, factory 9am-6pm) You can do block-printing courses in nearby Sanganer village, around 16km south of Jaipur. Costs depend on numbers of students; contact Sakshi for more details.

Kripal Kumbh
BLUE POTTERY

(☑2201127; B18A Shiv Marg, Bani Park) Free lessons in blue pottery (although it's not possible during the monsoon, from late June to mid-September). Advance bookings are essential.

Dhamma Thali Vipassana Meditation Centre
MEDITATION

(☑2680220; www.thali.dhamma.org) Located in beautiful surrounds, Dhammathali Vipas-

---

DON'T MISS

ISWARI MINAR SWARGA SAL

(Heaven-Piercing Minaret; Indian/foreigner ₹5/10, camera ₹10; ⊙9am-4.30pm) Piercing the skyline near the City Palace is the unusual Iswari Minar Swarga Sal, just west of Tripolia Gate. The minaret was erected by Jai Singh's son Iswari, who later ignominiously killed himself by snakebite (in the Chandra Mahal) rather than face the advancing Maratha army – 21 wives and concubines then did the necessary noble thing and committed *jauhar* (ritual mass suicide by immolation) on his funeral pyre. You can spiral to the top of the minaret for excellent views over the Old City. The entrance is around the back of the row of shops fronting Chandpol Bazaar – take the alley 50m west of the minaret along Chandpol Bazaar or go via the Atishpol entrance to the City Palace compound, 150m east of the minaret.

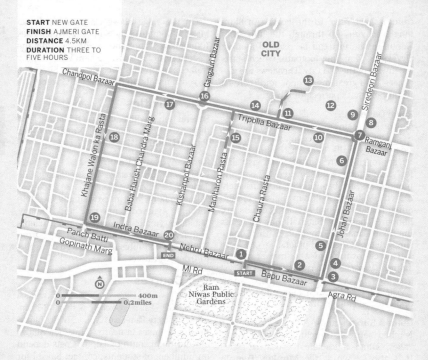

OLD CITY

Chandpol Bazaar

Gangauri Bazaar

Siredeori Bazaar

Tripolia Bazaar

Ramganj Bazaar

Khajane Walon ka Rasta

Baba Harish Chandra Marg

Kishanpol Bazaar

Maniharon Rasta

Chaura Rasta

Johari Bazaar

Indra Bazaar

Panch Batti
Gopinath Marg

Nehru Bazaar

END

MI Rd

START

Bapu Bazaar

Agra Rd

N

0   400m
0   0.2miles

Ram Niwas Public Gardens

Walking Tour
Pink City

❯ Entering the Old City from ❶ **New Gate**, turn right into ❷ **Bapu Bazaar**, inside the city wall. Brightly coloured bolts of fabric, *jootis* (traditional shoes) and aromatic perfumes make the street a favourite destination for Jaipur's women. At the end of Bapu Bazaar you'll come to ❸ **Sangane-ri Gate**. Turn left into ❹ **Johari Bazaar**, the jewellery market, where you will find jewellers, goldsmiths and also artisans doing highly glazed *meenakari* (enamelling), a speciality of Jaipur.

Continuing north you'll pass the famous ❺ **LMB Hotel**, and the ❻ **Jama Masjid**, with its tall minarets, and the bustling ❼ **Badi Chaupar**. Be very careful crossing the road here. To the north is ❽ **Siredeori Bazaar**, also known as Hawa Mahal Bazaar. The name is derived from the spectacular ❾ **Hawa Mahal**, a short distance to the north. Turning left on ❿ **Tripolia Bazaar**, you will see a lane leading to the entrance to the Hawa Mahal. A few hundred metres west is ⓫ **Tripolia Gate**. This is the

main entrance to the ⓬ **Jantar Mantar** and ⓭ **City Palace**, but only the maharaja's family may enter here. The public entrance is via the less-ostentatious Atishpol (Stable Gate), a little further along.

After visiting the City Palace complex, head back to Tripolia Bazaar and resume your walk west past ⓮ **Iswari Minar Swarga Sal**, which is well worth the climb for the view. Cross the bazaar at the minaret and head west. The next lane on the left is ⓯ **Maniharon ka Rasta**, the best place to buy colourful lac (resin) bangles.

Back on Tripolia Bazaar, continue west to cross ⓰ **Choti Chaupar** to ⓱ **Chandpol Bazaar** until you reach a traffic light. Turn left into ⓲ **Khajane Walon ka Rasta**, where you'll find marble and stoneware carvers at work. Continue south until you reach a broad road, just inside the city wall, ⓳ **Indra Bazaar**. Follow the road east towards ⓴ **Ajmer Gate**, the end of this tour.

sana Meditation Centre runs courses (for a donation) in meditation for both beginners and more-advanced students throughout the year.

Maharaja Sawai Mansingh Sangeet Mahavidyalaya
MUSIC & DANCE

(☑2611397; www.sangeetmahavidyalaya.org; Chandni Chowk, City Palace) Lessons in music and dance are available behind Tripolia Gate. Tuition is given in traditional Indian instruments, such as tabla, sitar and flute.

⟳ Tours

RTDC
SIGHTSEEING

(☑22020778; tours@rtdc.in; RTDC tourist information bureau, Platform 1, Jaipur train station; ⊙8am-6.30pm Mon-Sat) Offers half-/full-day tours of Jaipur and its surrounds (₹150/200. The full-day tours (9am to 6pm) take in all the major sights (including Amber Fort), with a lunch break at Nahargarh. The lunch break can be as late as 3pm, so have a big breakfast. Rushed half-day tours are confined to the city limits (8am to 1pm, 11.30am to 4.30pm and 1.30pm to 6.30pm) – some travellers recommend these, as you avoid the long lunch break. Fees don't include admission charges. The **Pink City by Night tour** (₹250) departs at 6.30pm, explores several well-known sights, and includes dinner at Nahargarh Fort. Tours depart from Jaipur train station; the company also picks up and takes bookings from the RTDC Hotel Teej, RTDC Hotel Gangaur and the Tourist Information Bureau at the main bus station.

🛏 Sleeping

Prepare yourself to be besieged by autorickshaw and taxi drivers when you arrive by train or bus. If you refuse to go to their choice of hotel, many will either snub you or will double the fare. To avoid this annoyance, go straight to the prepaid autorickshaw and taxi stands at the bus and train stations. Even better, many hotels will pick you up if you ring ahead.

From May to September, most midrange and top-end hotels offer bargain rates, dropping prices by 25% to 50%.

AROUND MI ROAD

TOP CHOICE **Hotel Pearl Palace**
HOTEL **$**

(☑2373700, 9414236323; www.hotelpearlpalace.com; Hari Kishan Somani Marg, Hathroi Fort; dm ₹175, r ₹350-1200; ✹@⧠) There's quite a range of rooms to choose from – small, large, shared bath, private bath, some balconied, some with AC or fan cooled, and all are spotless. Congenial hosts Mr and Mrs Singh offer all manner of services including free pick-up (8am to 11pm only), moneychanging and travel services. Rightfully popular; advance booking is highly recommended.

Pearl Palace Heritage
HOTEL **$$**

(☑2375242; 9829404055; www.pearlpalaceheritage.com; 54 Gopal Bari, lane 2; r ₹1500-1800; ✹@⧠) The second hotel for the successful Pearl Palace team is a midrange hotel with several special characteristics and great attention to detail. Stone carvings adorn the halls and each room re-creates an individual cultural theme such, as a village hut, a sandstone fort, or a mirror-lined palace boudoir.

Atithi Guest House
GUESTHOUSE **$**

(☑2378679; atithijaipur@hotmail.com; 1 Park House Scheme Rd; s ₹650-1100, d ₹750-1200; ✹@⧠) This well-presented guesthouse, set between MI and Station Rds, offers strikingly clean, simple rooms around a quiet courtyard. It's central but peaceful, and the service is friendly and helpful. There's a spotless kitchen and restaurant (guests only), and you can also dine on the very pleasant rooftop terrace.

Hotel Arya Niwas
HOTEL **$$**

(☑4073456; www.aryaniwas.com; Sansar Chandra Marg; s from ₹900, s/d with AC from ₹1800/1150; ✹@⧠) Just off Sansar Chandra Marg, behind a high-rise tower, this is a very popular travellers' haunt, with a travel desk, bookshop and yoga lessons. The spotless rooms vary in layout and size so check out a few. There's an extensive terrace facing a soothing expanse of lawn for relaxing.

Sheraton Rajputana Hotel
HOTEL **$$$**

(☑5100100; www.itcwelcomgroup.in; Palace Rd; r incl breakfast from ₹7500; ✹@⧉) Ritzy and comfortable and staffed to the hilt, this grand hotel is a high-walled oasis in an otherwise scruffy part of town near the train station. There is an enormous pool, a select shopping arcade and several plush dining options. The rack rates are heavily discounted if the hotel isn't full, particularly April to September.

Alsisar Haveli
HERITAGE HOTEL **$$**

(☑2368290; www.alsisar.com; Sansar Chandra Marg; s/d from ₹3400/4300; ✹⧉) Another genuine heritage hotel that has emerged from a gracious 19th-century mansion. Alsisar Haveli is set in beautiful green gardens, and boasts a lovely swimming pool and a wonderful dining room. Its bedrooms don't disappoint either, with elegant Rajput arches and antique furnishings.

Dera Rawatsar
HOTEL $$

(☑2200770; www.derarawatsar.com; D194, Vijay Path; r ₹2800-3800, ste ₹4500; ❄@🗚🏊) Situated off the main drag and close to the bus station, this quiet hotel is managed by three generations of women of a gracious Bikaner noble family. The hotel has a varying range of lovely decorated rooms, sunny courtyards and home-style Indian meals. It is an excellent choice for solo female travellers.

Nana-ki-Haveli
HERITAGE HOTEL $$

(☑2615502; www.nanakihaveli.com; Fateh Tiba, Moti Dungri Marg; r ₹1800-3000; ❄) Found off Moti Dungri Marg is this tucked-away, tranquil place with attractive, comfortable rooms decorated with traditional flourishes (discreet wall painting, wooden furniture). It's hosted by a lovely family and is a good choice for solo female travellers.

Karni Niwas
HOTEL $

(☑2365433; www.hotelkarniniwas.com; C5 Motilal Atal Marg; s ₹600-1100, d ₹650-1200; ❄@🗚) Tucked behind Hotel Neelam, this friendly hotel has clean, cool and comfortable rooms, often with balconies. There is no restaurant, but there are relaxing plant-decked terraces to enjoy room service on. The owner shuns commissions for rickshaw drivers and free pick-up from the train or bus station is available.

Jwala Niketan
GUESTHOUSE $

(☑5108303; www.jwala-niketan.com; C6 Motilal Atal Marg; s ₹150-650, d ₹200-800; ❄) This quiet yet centrally located guesthouse (behind the large Hotel Neelam) has a range of good-value, clean but very basic pastel-toned rooms. There is no restaurant, but meals can be delivered to your room from the nearby cheap and multicuisine Mohan Restaurant, or you can sample the family's vegetarian fare.

Krishna Palace
HOTEL $

(☑2201395; www.krishnapalace.com; E26 Durga Marg, Bani Park; r ₹550-1250; ❄@🗚) Krishna Palace is an overly managed hotel with some boisterous staff; however, there are some quiet corners and a relaxing lawn to retreat to with a book. It's convenient to the train station (free pick up) and the generally spacious rooms are maintained to an adequate standard.

Hotel Anuraag Villa
HOTEL $

(☑2201679; www.anuraagvilla.com; D249 Devi Marg; s ₹600-1850, d ₹790-1850; ❄@🗚) This quiet and comfortable option has no-fuss, spacious rooms (there are three grades) and an extensive lawn where you find some quiet respite from the hassles of sightseeing. It has a recommended restaurant with its kitchen on view, and efficient, helpful staff.

Retiring rooms
RAILWAY RETIRING ROOM $

(male-only dm ₹70, s without bathroom ₹150, s/d ₹225/450, r with AC ₹750-1000; ❄) Located upstairs at the train station and very handy if you're catching an early-morning train. Rooms are well worn but surprisingly neat and clean. Make reservations on the inquiries number (☑131).

BANI PARK

The Bani Park area is relatively peaceful (away from the main roads), about 2km west of the Old City (northwest of MI Road).

TOP CHOICE Madhuban
HERITAGE HOTEL $$

(☑2200033; www.madhuban.net; D237 Behari Marg, Bani Park; s ₹1700-2300, d ₹1900-3600; ❄@🏊) Madhuban is an elegant, heritage hotel-guesthouse run by the convivial Dicky and his family. It features a range of bright, spotless, antique-furnished rooms, including a suite with a Jacuzzi. Most guests gravitate quickly to the peaceful lawn where they can drink tea, read a newspaper over breakfast, watch a puppet show at night or just pat the dog. Money-changing and travel services are available, as is free pick-up from the bus or train station.

Umaid Bhawan
HERITAGE HOTEL $$

(☑2206426; www.umaidbhawan.com; Kali Das Marg, via Bank Rd, Bani Park; s ₹1400-2400, d ₹1600-2800, ste ₹4000; ❄@🏊) This mock-heritage hotel, behind the Collectorate in a quiet cul-de-sac, is extravagantly decorated in traditional style. Rooms are stately, full of marble and carved furniture, and the rooftop restaurant is wonderful. Free pick-up is available from the train or bus station and all taxes and breakfast are included in the tariff.

Shahpura House
HERITAGE HOTEL $$

(☑2203069; www.shahpurahouse.com; D257 Devi Marg, Bani Park; s/d from ₹3000/3500, ste from

₹4500; ❄@☎☒) Elaborately built and decorated in traditional style, this heritage hotel offers immaculate rooms, some with balconies, featuring murals, coloured-glass lamps, flat-screen TVs and even ceilings covered in small mirrors (in the suites). There's an inviting swimming pool and an elegant rooftop terrace that stages cultural shows.

Jas Vilas   HOTEL $$
(✆2204638; www.jasvilas.com; C9 Sawai Jai Singh Hwy, Bani Park; s/d ₹3500/3800; ❄@☎☒) This small but impressive hotel was built in 1950 and is still run by the same charming family. It offers 11 spacious rooms, most of which face the large sparkling pool set in a romantic courtyard. Three garden-facing rooms are wheelchair accessible. In addition to the relaxing courtyard and lawn, there is a cosy dining room and management will help with all onward travel planning.

Hotel Meghniwas   HOTEL $$
(✆4060100; www.meghniwas.com; C9 Sawai Jai Singh Hwy; standard/deluxe r ₹3000/3800, ste ₹4200; ❄@☒) In a building erected by Brigadier Singh in 1950 and run by his gracious descendants, this very welcoming hotel has comfortable and spotless rooms, with traditional carved-wood furniture and leafy outlooks. The standard rooms are good, but the suite does not measure up to expectations. There's a first-rate restaurant and an inviting pool set in a pleasant lawn area.

OLD CITY
Hotel Bissau Palace   HERITAGE HOTEL $$
(✆2304391; www.bissaupalace.com; outside Chandpol; r from ₹3000-6000; ❄@☎☒) This is a worthy choice if you want to stay in a palace on a budget. It's actually just outside the city walls, less than 10 minutes' walk from Chandpol (a gateway to the Old City), where there is a very earthy produce market. The hotel has oodles of heritage atmosphere, with lots of antique furnishings and mementos, such as moustached photos and hunting paraphernalia. It feels a bit rundown, however, and could do with a lick of paint.

Samode Haveli   HERITAGE HOTEL $$$
(✆2632370; www.samode.com; Gangapol; s/d incl breakfast from €190/215, ste from €250; ❄@☒) Tucked away in the northeast corner of the Old City is this charming 200-year-old building, once the town house of the *rawal* (nobleman) of Samode, Jaipur's prime minister. Rooms have large beds and most have

private terraces. The standard rooms are more ordinary but still manage to charm.

Hotel Kailash   HOTEL $
(✆2577372; Johari Bazaar; s/d ₹500/575, without bathroom ₹330/360) This hotel, opposite the Jama Masjid, is one of the few budget digs within the Old City. The cheapest rooms are little more than windowless cells and the shared bathrooms can be challenging, but the bigger doubles with attached bath are adequate.

RAMBAGH ENVIRONS
Rambagh Palace   HERITAGE HOTEL $$$
(✆2211919; www.tajhotels.com; Bhawan Singh Marg; r from ₹27,500; ❄@☒) This splendid palace was once the Jaipur pad of Maharaja Man Singh II and, until recently, his glamorous wife Gayatri Devi. Veiled in 19 hectares of gardens, there are fantastic views across the immaculate lawns. Nonguests can join in the magnificence by dining in the lavish restaurants or drinking tea on the gracious veranda. At least treat yourself to a drink at the spiffing Polo Bar (p119).

Narain Niwas Palace Hotel   HERITAGE HOTEL $$
(✆2561291; www.hotelnarainniwas.com; Narain Singh Rd; s/d incl breakfast from ₹4000/4500, ste from ₹8100; ❄@☒) In Kanota Bagh, just south of the city, this genuine heritage hotel has a wonderful ramshackle splendour. There's a lavish dining room with liveried staff, an old-fashioned veranda on which to drink tea, and antiques galore. The high-ceilinged rooms are varyingly atmospheric and the bathrooms also vary greatly – so inspect before committing. You will find a large secluded pool, heavenly spa and sprawling gardens complete with peacocks out the back.

✗ Eating
AROUND MI ROAD

TOP CHOICE Niro's   INDIAN $$
(✆2374493; MI Rd; mains ₹110-350; ⊙10am-11pm) Established in 1949, Niro's is a long-standing favourite on MI Road that continues to shine. Escape the chaos of the street by ducking into its cool, clean, mirror-ceiling sanctum to savour veg and nonveg Indian cuisine. Classic Chinese and Continental food are available but the Indian menu is definitely the pick.

Four Seasons VEGETARIAN $$
(☎2373700; D43A Subhas Marg; mains ₹100-210; ☺noon-3.30pm & 6.30-11pm) Four Seasons is one of Jaipur's best vegetarian restaurants and being pure vegetarian there's no alcohol. It's a vastly popular place on two levels, with a glass wall to the kitchens. There's a great range of dishes on offer, including tasty Rajasthani specialities, dosas and a selection of pizzas.

Little Italy ITALIAN $$
(☎4022444; 3rd fl, KK Square, C-11, Prithviraj Marg; mains ₹165-200; ☺noon-3.30pm & 6.30-11pm) Easily the best Italian restaurant in town, Little Italy is part of a small national chain that offers excellent vegetarian pasta, risotto and wood-fired pizzas in cool, contemporary surroundings. The menu is extensive and includes some Mexican items and first-rate Italian desserts.

Moti Mahal Delux NORTH INDIAN $$
(☎4017733; MI Rd; mains ₹140-300; ☺11am-4pm & 7-11pm) The tantalising menu features a vast range of veg and nonveg, including seafood and succulent tandoori dishes. Snuggle into a comfortable booth and enjoy the ambience, spicy food and, last but not least, a delicious *pista kulfi* (pistachio-flavoured sweet similar to ice cream). Beer and wine available.

Peacock Rooftop Restaurant MULTICUISINE $$
(☎2373700; Hotel Pearl Palace, Hari Kishan Somani Marg, Hathroi Fort; mains ₹35-120; ☺7am-11pm) This multilevel rooftop restaurant at the popular Hotel Pearl Palace gets rave reviews for its excellent and inexpensive cuisine (Indian, Chinese and Continental) and relaxed ambience. The mouthwatering food, attentive service, whimsical furnishings and romantic view towards Hathroi Fort make this a first-rate restaurant and the economical prices all the more unbelievable.

Dāsaprakash SOUTH INDIAN $$
(☎2371313; Kamal Mansions, MI Rd; mains ₹90-200; ☺11am-11pm) Part of a renowned chain, Dāsaprakash specialises in South Indian cuisine including thalis and several versions of *dosa* and *idli* (rice cake). Afterwards you can choose from a wonderful selection of cold drinks and over-the-top ice-cream sundaes.

Surya Mahal SOUTH INDIAN $$
(☎2362811; MI Rd; mains ₹90-170; ☺8am-11pm) Near Panch Batti is this popular option specialising in South Indian vegetarian food; try the delicious *masala dosa,* and the tasty *dhal makhani* (black lentils and red kidney beans). There are also Chinese and Italian dishes, and good ice creams, sundaes and cool drinks.

Handi Restaurant NORTH INDIAN $$
(☎2364839; MI Rd; mains ₹140-300; ☺noon-3.30pm & 6.30-11pm) Handi has been satisfying customers for years. It's opposite the main post office, tucked at the back of the Maya Mansions, offering scrumptious tandoori and barbecued dishes and rich Mughlai curries. In the evenings it sets up a smoky kebab stall at the entrance to the restaurant. Good vegetarian items are also available. No beer.

Natraj VEGETARIAN $$
(☎2375804; MI Rd; mains ₹85-200; ☺9am-11pm) Not far from Panch Batti is this classy vegetarian place, which has an extensive menu featuring North Indian, Continental and Chinese cuisine. Diners are blown away by the potato-encased vegetable bomb curry. There's a good selection of thalis and South Indian food – the *dosa paper masala* is delicious – as well as Indian sweets.

Copper Chimney INDIAN $$
(☎2372275; Maya Mansions, MI Rd; mains ₹100-220; ☺noon-3pm & 6.30-11pm) Copper Chimney is casual, almost elegant and definitely welcoming, with the requisite waiter army and a fridge of cold beer. It offers excellent veg and nonveg Indian cuisine, including aromatic Rajasthani specials. There is also Continental and Chinese food and a small selection of Indian wine, but the curry and beer combos are hard to beat.

Rawat Kachori FAST FOOD $
(Station Rd; kachori ₹40, lassis ₹25) For great Indian sweets (₹10 or ₹120 to ₹300 per kg) and famous *kachori* (potato masala in fried pastry case), head to this exceedingly popular place. A delicious milk crown should fill you up for the afternoon.

Hotel Kanji SWEETS $
(Station Rd; sweets per kg ₹120-340) Across the road from Rawat Kachori, Kanji also has a fabulous array of sweets.

Bake Hut BAKERY $
(Arvind Marg, off MI Rd; cakes ₹25-100; ☺9am-10pm Mon-Sat) An extremely busy bakery that does a roaring trade in sweet cakes and various breads. It's attached to the back of the Surya Mahal restaurant.

Jal Mahal
SWEETS $

(MI Rd; ice creams ₹12-110; ☺10am-midnight) This packed little takeaway ice-cream parlour has some inventive concoctions, from the earthquake to the after ate.

Baskin Robbins
SWEETS $

(Sanjay Marg; ice creams ₹20-150; ☺noon-11.30pm) Tucked into the edge of the Hotel Gangaur's compound is this pint-sized ice-cream pit stop.

OLD CITY

TOP CHOICE LMB
VEGETARIAN $$

(☎2560845; Johari Bazaar; mains ₹95-190; ☺11.30am-3.30pm & 7-11pm) Laxmi Misthan Bhandar, LMB to you and me, is a *sattvik* (pure vegetarian) restaurant in the Old City that's been going strong since 1954. A welcoming AC refuge from frenzied Johari Bazaar, LMB is also an institution with its singular decor, attentive waiters and extensive sweet counter. The menu opens with a warning from Krishna about people who like *tamasic* (putrid and polluted food), which gets you into the *sattvik* mood. Try the Rajasthan thali followed by the signature *kulfa*, a fusion of *kulfi* and *falooda* with dry fruits and saffron.

Ganesh Restaurant
VEGETARIAN $

(☎2312380; Nehru Bazaar; mains ₹50-90; ☺9.30am-11pm) This pocket-sized outdoor restaurant is in a fantastic location on the top of the Old City wall near New Gate. The cook is in a pit on one side of the wall, so you can check out your pure vegetarian food being cooked. If you're looking for a local eatery with fresh tasty food, such as *paneer butter masala*, you'll love it. There's an easy-to-miss signpost, but no doubt a stallholder will show you the narrow stairway.

Drinking

TOP CHOICE Lassiwala
LASSI

(MI Rd; ☺7.30am till sold out) This famous, much-imitated institution, opposite Niro's, is a simple place that whips up fabulous, creamy lassis at ₹14/28 for a small/jumbo clay cup. Get there early to avoid disappointment! Will the real Lassiwala please stand up? It's the one that says 'Shop 312' and 'Since 1944', directly next to the alleyway. Imitators spread to the right as you face it.

Indian Coffee House
CAFE

(MI Rd; coffee ₹11-15; ☺8am-9.30pm) Set back from the street, down an alley, this tradition-al coffee house (a venerable co-op owned institution) offers a very pleasant cup of filtered coffee in very relaxed surroundings. Aficionados of Indian Coffee Houses will not be disappointed by the fan-cooled ambience. Inexpensive samosas, pakoras and *dosas* grace the snack menu.

Reds
BAR

(☎4007710; 5th fl, Mall 21, Bhagwandas Marg; ☺11am-midnight Sun-Fri, 11am-1.30pm Sat) Over-looking the Raj Mandir cinema and MI Rd with views to Tiger Fort, slick Reds is a great place to kick back with a drink or take a meal. Drop into one of the low-slung, red-and-black couches with a beer (bottled or draught), cocktail or mocktail and enjoy the sound system.

Polo Bar
BAR

(Rambagh Palace Hotel, Bhawan Singh Rd; ☺noon-midnight) A spiffing watering hole adorned with polo memorabilia and arched, scal-loped windows framing the neatly clipped lawns. A bottle of beer costs ₹350 to ₹450 and cocktails around ₹450.

Café Coffee Day
CAFE

(Country Inn Hotel, MI Rd; coffee ₹50-90) The fran-chise that successfully delivers espresso to coffee addicts, as well as the occasional iced concoction and muffin, has several branches in Jaipur. In addition to this one, sniff out the brews at Paris Point on Sawai Jai Singh Hwy (aka Collectorate Rd), and near the exit point at Amber Fort.

☆ Entertainment

Jaipur isn't a big late-night party town, although many hotels put on some sort of evening music, dance or puppet show. English-language films are occasionally screened at some cinemas in Jaipur – check the cinemas and local press for details.

Raj Mandir Cinema
CINEMA

(☎2379372; Baghwandas Marg; admission ₹50-110; ☺reservations 10am-6pm, screenings 12.30pm, 3.30pm, 6.30pm & 9.30pm) Just off MI Rd, Raj Mandir is *the* place to go to see a Hindi film in India. This opulent cinema looks like a huge pink cream cake, with a meringue au-ditorium and a foyer somewhere between a temple and Disneyland. Bookings can be made one hour to seven days in advance at window Nos 7 and 8 – this is your best chance of securing a seat, although forget it in the early days of a new release. Alter-natively, sharpen your elbows and join the queue when the current booking office opens 45 minutes before curtain up. Avoid the very cheapest tickets, which are very close to the screen.

Chokhi Dhani THEME PARK
(✆2225001; Tonk Rd; adult/child aged 3-9 incl dinner ₹350/200) Chokhi Dhani means 'special village' and this mock Rajasthani village, 20km south of Jaipur, lives up to its name. As well as the restaurants, where you can enjoy an oily Rajasthani thali, there is a bevy of traditional entertainment. You can wander around and watch traditional tribal dancers setting fire to their hats, children balancing on poles and dancers dressed in lion costumes lurking in a wood. A return taxi from Jaipur, including waiting time, will cost about ₹600.

🛍 Shopping

Jaipur is a shopper's paradise. You'll have to bargain hard though – shops have seen too many cash-rich, time-poor tourists. Shops around major tourist centres, such as the City Palace and Hawa Mahal, tend to be pricier. Also commercial buyers come here from all over the world to stock up on the amazing range of jewellery, gems, artefacts and crafts that come from all over Rajasthan.

Most of the larger shops can pack and send your parcels home for you – although it may be slightly cheaper if you do it yourself (see p165) it's generally not worth the hassle.

The city is still loosely divided into traditional artisans quarters. The Pink City Walking Tour (p114) will take you through some of these.

Bapu Bazaar is lined with saris and fabrics, and is a good place to buy trinkets. **Johari Bazaar** (⊗closed part of Sun) and **Siredeori Bazaar** are where many jewellery shops are concentrated, selling gold, silver and highly glazed enamelwork known as *meenakari*, a Jaipur speciality. You may also find better deals for fabrics with the cotton merchants of Johari Bazaar.

Kishanpol Bazaar is famous for textiles, particularly *bandhani* (tie-dye). **Nehru Bazaar** also sells fabric, as well as jootis, trinkets and perfume. MI Rd is another good place to buy jootis. The best place for bangles is Maniharon ka Rasta, near the Shree Sanjay Sharma Museum.

Plenty of factories and showrooms are strung along the length of Amber Rd, between Zorawar Singh Gate and the Holiday Inn, to catch the tourist traffic. Here you'll find huge emporiums selling block prints, blue pottery, carpets and antiques; but these shops are used to busloads swinging in to blow their cash, so you'll need to wear your bargaining hat.

Rickshaw-wallahs, hotels and travel agents will be getting a hefty cut from any shop they steer you towards. Many unwary visitors get talked into buying things for resale at inflated prices, especially gems. Beware of these get-rich-quick scams.

JAIPUR'S GEMS

Jaipur is famous for precious and semiprecious stones. There are many shops offering bargain prices, but you do need to know your gems. The main gem-dealing area is around the Muslim area of Pahar Ganj, in the southeast of the Old City. Here you can see stones being cut and polished in workshops tucked off narrow backstreets.

There is a **gem testing laboratory** (www .gtjaipur.info; ⊗10am-5.15pm Mon-Sat) in the Rajasthan Chamber Bhawan on MI Rd. Deposit gems before noon and receive an authenticity certificate on the same day between 4.30pm and 5.15pm. Certification charges start at ₹550 for a single stone.

Kripal Kumbh HANDICRAFTS
(✆2201127; B18A Shiv Marg, Bani Park; ⊗10am-6pm) This is a showroom in a private home and a great place to buy Jaipur's famous blue pottery produced by the late Mr Kripal Singh, his family and his students. Ceramics go for anything from ₹30 (for a paperweight) to ₹25,000 (for a large vase).

Rajasthali HANDICRAFTS
(MI Rd; ⊗11am-7.30pm Mon-Sat) The state-government emporium, opposite Ajmeri Gate, is packed with quality Rajasthani artefacts and crafts, including enamelwork, embroidery, pottery, woodwork, jewellery, colourful puppets, block-printed sheets, cute miniatures, brassware, mirror work and more, but it has an air of torpor that doesn't make shopping much fun.

Mojari CLOTHING
(Shiv Heera Marg; ⊗11am-6pm Mon-Sat) Named after the traditional decorated shoes of Rajasthan, Mojari is a UN-supported project that helps rural leatherworkers, traditionally among the poorest members of society. There is a wide range of footwear available, including embroidered, appliquéd and open-toed shoes, mules and sandals. Mojari also has a small collection of covetable leather and felt bags.

GEM SCAMS – A WARNING

If you believe any stories about buying anything in India to sell at a profit elsewhere, you'll simply be proving (once again) that old adage about separating fools from their money. Precious stones are favourites for this game. Merchants will tell you that you can sell the items back home for several times the purchase price, and will even give you the (often imaginary) addresses of dealers who will buy them. You may also be shown written statements from other travellers documenting the money they have made, even photographs of the merchants shaking hands with their so-called business partners overseas. Don't be taken in, it's all a scam. The gems you buy will be worth only a fraction of what you pay. Often the scams involve showing you real stones and then packing up worthless glass beads to give you in their place. Don't let greed cloud your judgment.

Tip: beware of anyone who wants to become your best friend in areas that see a lot of tourists, eg hotel and shopping strips and transport hubs.

Anokhi   CLOTHING
(www.anokhi.com; 2nd fl, KK Square, C-11, Prithviraj Marg; ⊙9.30am-8pm Mon-Sat, 11am-7pm Sun) Anokhi is a classy, upmarket boutique that's well worth visiting – there's a wonderful little cafe on the premises and an excellent bookshop in the same building. Anokhi sells stunning high-quality textiles, such as block-printed fabrics, tablecloths, bed covers, cosmetic bags and scarves, as well as a range of well-designed, beautifully made clothing that combines Indian and Western influences.

Jodhpur Tailors   CLOTHING
(www.jodhpurtailors.com; 9 Ksheer Sagar Hotel, Motilal Atal Rd; ⊙9am-8.30pm Mon-Sat, 9am-5pm Sun) You can have a beautiful pair of jodhpurs (₹2500) made in preparation for your visit to the Blue City. Or you can just go for a made-to-measure suit (₹7000 to ₹15000) or shirt (₹700 to ₹900).

The Silver Shop   JEWELLERY
(Hotel Pearl Palace, Hari Kishan Somani Marg, Hathroi Fort; ⊙6-10pm) A trusted jewellery shop backed by the hotel management that hosts the store, and offering a money-back guarantee on all items. Find it under the peacock canopy in the hotel's Peacock Rooftop Restaurant.

ℹ Information

Internet Access

Many places provide internet access, including most hotels and guesthouses. However fast or slow, it'll set you back about ₹25 per hour.

Dhoom Cyber Café (MI Rd; per hr ₹25) Enter through an arch into a quiet courtyard just off the main drag.

Mewar Cyber Café & Communication (Station Rd; per hr ₹25; ⊙8am-11pm) Near the main bus station.

Medical Services

Most hotels can arrange a doctor on-site. At **Galundia Clinic** (☎2361040, 9829061040; dagalundia@doctor.com; MI Rd), **Dr Chandra Sen** (☎9829061040) is on 24-hour call.

Good hospitals include:

Santokba Durlabhji Hospital (☎2566251; Bhawan Singh Marg)

Sawai Mansingh Hospital (☎2560291; Sawai Ram Singh Rd)

Money

There are plenty of places to change money, including numerous hotels, and masses of ATMs, most of which accept foreign cards, including **HDFC** (Ashoka Marg & Sawai Jai Singh Hwy), **HSBC** (Sardar Patel Marg), **ICICI** (ground fl, Ganpati Plaza, MI Rd), **IDBI** (Sawai Jai Singh Hwy), **State Bank of India** (Hotel Om Tower) and **Standard Chartered** (Bhagwat Bhavan, MI Rd), which are open 24 hours.

Thomas Cook (☎2360940; Jaipur Towers MI Rd; ⊙9.30am-6pm Mon-Sat) Changes cash and travellers cheques.

Post

DHL Express (☎2361159; www.dhl.co.in; G8 Geeta Enclave, Vinobha Rd; ⊙10am-8pm) This reliable international courier also has a small and friendly office (but dealing in cash payments only) beside the Standard Chartered bank on MI Rd. To get to the head office, take the alley beside the small office for about 50m to the Geeta Enclave building. Ensure that you ask to pay customs charges for the destination country upfront.

Main post office (☎2368740; MI Rd; ⊙8am-7.45pm Mon-Fri, 10am-5.45pm Sat) A cost-effective and efficient (though you will inevitably get a little frustrated with the back-and-forth) institution. Parcels need to be wrapped according to the rules, so stand back and watch the parcel-packing wallah (10am to 4pm Monday to Saturday) in the foyer, who will pack, stitch and wax seal your parcels for a reasonable fee.

Tourist Information

The Tourism Assistance Force (police) is stationed at the train and bus stations, the airport and at Jaipur's major tourist sights.

Foreigners' Regional Registration Office (FRRO; ✆2618508; City Palace Complex; ⊙10am-5pm Mon-Sat) Any applications for visa extensions should be lodged at the FRRO at least one week before the visa expires. It is somewhat hard to find behind the Hawa Mahal, so ask around. The likelihood you'll get an extension on a tourist visa is slight – see p1174 for more details.

Government of India Tourist Office (GITO; ✆2372200; Khasa Kothi Circle; ⊙9am-6pm Mon-Fri) Inside the Hotel Khasa Kothi compound (go through the arch and look to the left). Provides brochures on places all over India.

RTDC Tourist Reception Centre Main branch (✆5155137; www.rajasthantourism .gov.in; Room 21, former RTDC Tourist Hotel; ⊙9.30am-6pm Mon-Fri); airport (✆2722647); Amber Fort (✆2530264); Jaipur train station (✆2200778; Platform 1; ⊙24hr); main bus station (✆5064102; Platform 3; ⊙10am-5pm Mon-Fri) Has maps and brochures on Jaipur and Rajasthan.

❶ Getting There & Away

Air

For details of international airlines, see p1175.

Offices of domestic airlines:

Air India/Indian Airlines (✆2743500; www. indian-airlines.nic.in; Nehru Place, Tonk Rd)
IndiGo (✆2743500; www.goindigo.in; airport)

Jet Airways (✆5112225; www.jetairways.com; Room 112, Jaipur Tower, MI Rd; ⊙9.30am-6pm Mon-Sat)
Kingfisher Airlines (✆4030372; www.flyking fisher.com; Usha Plaza, MI Rd; ⊙9.30am-5.30pm Mon-Sat, 10am-3pm Sun).

Bus

Rajasthan State Road Transport Corporation (RSRTC, aka Rajasthan Roadways) buses all leave from the **main bus station** (Station Rd), picking up passengers at Narain Singh Circle (you can also buy tickets here). There is a left-luggage office at the main bus station (₹10 per bag for 24 hours), as well as a prepaid autorickshaw stand.

Deluxe or private buses are far preferable to RSRTC Blue Line or Star Line or local buses, which stop in small villages and are usually crowded bone rattlers with questionable safety. Deluxe buses all leave from Platform 3, tucked away in the right-hand corner of the bus station, and seats may be booked in advance from the **reservation office** (✆5116032), which is within the main bus station.

For long journeys, the RSRTC Volvo and Gold Line buses are easily the most comfortable and safe AC services. There is a cluster of private offices along Motilal Atal Rd, near the Polo Victory Cinema.

Car

You can arrange car and driver hire directly with the driver at the taxi stand at the train station. Usually the drivers need only a day's notice for a long trip. A much easier way to do this is to utilise the services provided by your hotel. Most hotels will be able to contact drivers (with cars) that are known to the hotel. These drivers value the work they obtain through the hotels and that provides you with greater security and service standards. A reasonable price is non-AC/AC ₹7/8 per kilometre, with a 250km minimum per day and an overnight charge of ₹150 per night.

DOMESTIC FLIGHTS FROM JAIPUR

There are plenty of domestic flights from Jaipur, mostly run by Indian Airlines, Kingfisher Airlines and Jet Airways, who offer similar prices. Other airlines serving Jaipur include IndiGo and SpiceJet. Fares and schedules vary widely and these are just indicative fares at the time of writing.

DESTINATION	FARE (US$)	DURATION
Ahmedabad	110	1hr
Delhi	55	40min
Jodhpur	100	40min
Kolkata (Calcutta)	145	2hr
Mumbai (Bombay)	70	1½hr
Udaipur	110	1¾hr

DESTINATION	FARE (₹)	DURATION (HR)	FREQUENCY
Agra	195, AC 370	5½	11 daily
Ajmer	110, AC 200	2½	13 daily
Bharatpur	128*	4½	5 daily
Bikaner	190	8	hourly
Bundi	160, AC 220	5	5 daily
Chittorgarh	210, AC 335	7	6 daily
Delhi	325, AC 425-600	5½	at least hourly
Jaisalmer	430	15	daily
Jhunjhunu	140	5	half-hourly
Jodhpur	240, AC 350	7	every 2 hours
Kota	255, AC 370	5	hourly
Mt Abu	AC 531	13	daily
Nawalgarh	95	4	hourly
Pushkar	120	3	daily (direct)
Sawai Madhopur	110	6	2 daily
Udaipur	300, AC 605	10	6 daily

* To take an AC bus to Bharatpur you must pay the full Agra fare on an Agra-bound bus and alight at Bharatpur.

Motorcycle

You can hire, buy or fix a Royal Enfield Bullet (and lesser motorbikes) at **Rajasthan Auto Centre** (☑2568074; www.royalenfieldsaleem.com; Sanjay Bazaar, Sanganeri Gate), the cleanest little motorcycle workshop in India. To hire a 350cc Bullet costs ₹500 per day (including helmet) within Jaipur. If you take the bike outside Jaipur it costs ₹600 per day.

Train

The efficient **railway reservation office** (☑135; ⊘8am-2pm & 2.15-8pm Mon-Sat, 8am-2pm Sun) is to your left as you enter Jaipur train station. It's open for advance reservations only (more than five hours before departure). Join the queue for 'Freedom Fighters and Foreign Tourists' (counter 769). See the table (p124) for details of routes and fares.

For same-day travel, buy your ticket at the northern end of the train station on **Platform 1, window 10** (⊘closed 6-6.30am, 2-2.30pm & 10-10.30pm). The railway inquiries number is ☑131.

Station facilities on Platform 1 include an RTDC tourist information bureau, Tourism Assistance Force (police), a cloakroom for left luggage (₹10 per bag per 24 hours), retiring rooms (p115), restaurants and AC waiting rooms for those with 1st class and 2AC train tickets.

ⓘ Getting Around

To/From the Airport

There are no bus services from the airport, which is 12km southeast of the city. An autorickshaw/taxi costs at least ₹200/350 for the 15km journey into the city centre, or there's a prepaid taxi booth inside the terminal.

Autorickshaw

There are prepaid autorickshaw stands at the bus and train stations. Rates are fixed by the government, which means you don't have to haggle. In other cases you should be prepared to bargain hard.

Cycle-Rickshaw

You can do your bit for the environment by flagging down a lean-limbed cycle-rickshaw rider. Though it can be uncomfortable watching someone pedalling hard to transport you, this *is* how they make a living. A short trip costs about ₹30.

Taxi

There are unmetered taxis available which will require negotiating a fare or you can try **Mericar** (☑4188888; www.mericar.in; flagfall incl 3km ₹50, afterwards per km ₹11, 25% night surcharge 10pm-5am). It's a 24-hour service and taxis can hired for sightseeing for four-/six-/eight-hour blocks costing ₹550/850/1050.

MAJOR TRAINS FROM JAIPUR

DESTINATION	TRAIN NO & NAME	FARE (₹)	DURA-TION (HR)	DEPARTURE
Agra	12308 Jodhpur-Howrah Express	160/385/515 (A)	4¾	2.10am
Agra	12966 Udaipur-Gwalior Express	90/305/385/515/840 (B)	4¼	6.10am
Ahmedabad	12958 Ahmedabad SJ Rajdhani Express	890/1215/2055 (C)	9½	12.35am
Ahmedabad	12916 Ahmedabad Ashram Express	280/730/990/1650 (D)	11	8.45pm
Ajmer	12015 Ajmer Shatabdi	270/530 (E)	2	10.40pm (Thu-Tue)
Ajmer	19708 Aravalli Express	120/245/330 (A)	2½	8.30am
Ajmer	12195 Intercity Express	65/222 (F)	2	9.40am
Ajmer	09622 Intercity Express	65/222 (F)	2	2.15pm
Bikaner	12468 Intercity Express	115 (G)	7	3.45pm
Delhi	12016 Shatabdi	535/1015 (D)	5	5.50pm (Thu-Tue)
Delhi	14060 Jaisalmer-Delhi Express	90/155/410/550 (H)	6	5am
Delhi	12413 Jaipur-Delhi Express	100/175/440/590/970 (I)	5	4.30pm
Jaisalmer	14059 Delhi-Jaisalmer Express	145/255/680/930/1555 (I)	13	11.55pm
Jodhpur	12465 Ranthambhore Express	100/180/355/450 (J)	5½	5pm
Jodhpur	14059 Delhi-Jaisalmer Express	90/160/415/565/940 (I)	5½	11.55pm
Sawai Madhoper	12956 Jaipur-Mumbai Express	140/275/355/585 (D)	2	2.10pm
Sawai Madhoper	12466 Intercity Express	65/140/225/275 (J)	2¼	10.55am
Udaipur	12965 Jaipur-Udaipur Express	125/215/435/545/735/1230 (K)	9½	10.25pm

Fares: A – sleeper/3AC/2AC, B – 2nd class/AC chair/3AC/2AC/1AC, C – 3AC/2AC/1AC, D – sleeper, 3AC, 2AC, 1AC, E – AC chair/1AC, F – 2nd class/AC chair, G – 2nd class, H – 2nd class/sleeper/3AC/2AC, I – 2nd class/sleeper/3AC/2AC/1AC, J – 2nd class/sleeper/AC chair/3AC, K – 2nd class/sleeper/AC chair/3AC/2AC/1AC.

Around Jaipur

AMBER

The formidable, magnificent, honey-hued fort-palace of Amber (pronounced Amer), an ethereal example of Rajput architecture, rises from a rocky mountainside about 11km northeast of Jaipur. Amber was the former capital of Jaipur state.

Amber was built by the Kachhwaha Rajputs, who hailed from Gwalior, in present-day Madhya Pradesh, where they reigned for over 800 years. With war booty they financed construction of the fort-palace at Amber, which was begun in 1592 by Maharaja Man Singh, the Rajput commander of Akbar's army. It was later extended and completed by the Jai Singhs before the move to Jaipur on the plains below.

◉ Sights

Amber Fort   HISTORIC SITE
(Indian/foreigner ₹25/200, guide ₹200, audio guide Hindi/English/various European/various Asian ₹100/150/200/250; ☺8am-6pm, last entry 5.30pm) This magnificent fort is more of a palace, built from pale yellow and pink sandstone and white marble, and divided into four main sections, each with its own courtyard.

You can trudge up to the fort from the road in about 10 minutes (cold drinks are available at the top). A seat in a jeep up to the fort costs ₹200 return. Riding up on elephant back (₹900 per two passengers; ☺8-11am & 3.30-5.30pm) is very popular, however.

If you walk or ride an elephant you will enter Amber Fort through Suraj Pol (Sun Gate), which leads to the Jaleb Chowk (Main Courtyard), where returning armies would display their war booty to the populace – women could view this area from the veiled windows of the palace. The ticket office is directly across the courtyard from Suraj Pol. If you arrive by car you will enter through Chand Pol (Moon Gate) on the opposite side of Jaleb Chowk. Hiring a guide or grabbing an audio guide is highly recommended as there are very few signs and many blind alleys.

From Jaleb Chowk, an imposing stairway leads up to the main palace, but first it's worth taking the steps just to the right, which lead to the small Siladevi Temple (photography prohibited; ☺6am-noon & 4-8pm). Every day from the 16th century until 1980 (when the government banned the practice), a goat was sacrificed here.

Heading back to the main stairway will take you up to the second courtyard and the Diwan-i-Am (Hall of Public Audience), which has a double row of columns, each topped by a capital in the shape of an elephant, and latticed galleries above.

The maharaja's apartments are located around the third courtyard – you enter through the fabulous Ganesh Pol, decorated with mosaics and sculptures. The Jai Mandir (Hall of Victory) is noted for its inlaid panels and multimirrored ceiling. Carved marble relief panels around the hall are fascinatingly delicate and quirky, depicting cartoon-like insects and sinuous flowers.

Opposite the Jai Mandir is the Sukh Niwas (Hall of Pleasure), with an ivory-inlaid sandalwood door and a channel that once carried cooling water right through the room. From the Jai Mandir you can enjoy fine views from the palace ramparts over picturesque Maota Lake below.

The zenana (women's quarters) surrounds the fourth courtyard. The rooms were designed so that the maharaja could embark on his nocturnal visits to his wives' and concubines' respective chambers without the others knowing, as the chambers are independent but open onto a common corridor.

Anokhi Museum of Hand Printing   MUSEUM
(Anokhi Haveli, Kheri Gate; child/adult ₹15/30, camera/video ₹50/150; ☺10.30am-4.30pm Tue-Sat, 11am-4.30pm Sun, closed 1 May-15 Jul) Just beyond Amber Fort, in Amber town, is this interesting museum that documents the art of hand-block printing and runs hands-on demonstrations.

❶ Getting There & Away
There are frequent (crowded) buses to Amber from near the Hawa Mahal in Jaipur (₹10, 25 minutes). An autorickshaw/taxi will cost at least ₹150/550 for the return trip. RTDC city tours (see p115) include Amber Fort.

JAIGARH
A scrubby green hill – Cheel ka Teela (Mound of Eagles) – rising above Amber, is topped by the imposing fortress of Jaigarh (Indian/foreigner ₹25/75, camera or video ₹50, car ₹50, Hindi/English guide ₹150/200; ☺9am-5pm). This massive fort was planned by Jai Singh I, but what you see today dates from the reign of Jai Singh II. Punctuated by whimsically hatted lookout towers, the fort was never captured and is a splendid example of grand 18th-century defences, without the palatial frills that are found in many other Rajput forts. It has water reservoirs, residential areas, a puppet theatre and the world's largest wheeled cannon, Jaya Vana.

The fort is a steep uphill walk (about 1km) from Amber and offers great views from the Diwa Burj watchtower.

Admission is free if you have a ticket to Jaipur's City Palace that is less than two days' old.

SANGANER
The large village of Sanganer is 16km south of Jaipur, and has a ruined palace, a group of Jain temples with fine carvings (to which entry is restricted) and two ruined tripolias (triple gateways). The main reason to visit, however, is to see its handmade paper and block-printing shops, workshops and facto-

ries (most shops can be found on or just off the main drag, Stadium Rd), where you can see the products being made by hand.

Best of all in Sanganer is walking down to the riverbank to see the brightly coloured fabrics drying in the sun.

For block-printed fabrics and blue pottery, there are a number of shops, including **Sakshi** (2731862; Laxmi Colony; shop 8.30am-8.30pm, factory 9am-6pm). You can see the block-printing workshop here, and even try your hand at block printing. It also runs courses in block printing and blue pottery (see p113).

ℹ Getting There & Away

Local buses leave from the Ajmeri Gate in Jaipur for Sanganer every few minutes (₹10, one hour). To Bagru, there are daily buses from Sanganer (₹26, 1½ hours).

Bharatpur

05644 / POP 263,800

Bharatpur is famous for its Unesco-listed Keoladeo Ghana National Park (p128), a wetland and significant bird sanctuary. Apart from the park, Bharatpur has a few historical vestiges, though it would not be worth making the journey for these alone. The town is dusty, noisy and not particularly visitor friendly

Keoladeo Ghana National Park lies 3km to the south of Bharatpur's centre.

◉ Sights

Lohagarh   HISTORIC BUILDING
Lohagarh, the early-18th-century Iron Fort, was so named because of its sturdy defences. Today still impressive, though also forlorn and derelict, it occupies the entire small artificial island in the town centre. The main entrance is the **Austdhatu (Eight-Metal) Gate** – apparently the spikes on the gate are made of eight different metals.

Maharaja Suraj Mahl, constructor of the fort and founder of Bharatpur, built two towers, the **Jawahar Burj** and the **Fateh Burj**, within the ramparts to commemorate his victories over the Mughals and the British. The fort also contains three much-decayed palaces within its precincts.

One of the palaces, centred on a tranquil courtyard, houses a seemingly forgotten **museum** (admission ₹10, free Mon, camera/video ₹10/20, no photography inside museum; 10am-4.30pm Sat-Thu). Downstairs is a Jain

sculpture gallery that includes some beautiful 7th- to 10th-century sculpture, and most spectacularly, the palace's original *hammam* (bathhouse), which retains some fine carvings and frescoes.

🛏 Sleeping & Eating

Don't be pressured by touts at Bharatpur train or bus stations. Most hotels can also can arrange guides and offer binocular and bike hire. Guests usually eat in the hotel they are staying at and most places offer a *thali* (all-you-can-eat meal) for between ₹80 and ₹180. All of the following options are within easy walking distance of the national park entrance, except for Shagun Guest House.

TOP CHOICE **Birder's Inn**   HOTEL **$$**
(227346; www.birdersinn.com; Bird Sanctuary Rd; s/d incl breakfast from ₹1600/2100; ✳@🛜🏊) The Birder's Inn is rightly the most popular base for exploring the park. The atmospheric stone and thatch-roof restaurant is a great place for a meal and to compare birdwatching stories. The rooms are airy, spacious and nicely decorated with LCD TVs, and are well set back from the road in well-tended gardens.

Hotel Sunbird   HOTEL **$$**
(225701; www.hotelsunbird.com; Bird Sanctuary Rd; s/d from ₹1700/2000, cottages ₹2200/2500; ✳) Another well-run and popular place next door to Birder's Inn. Rooms are clean and comfortable, and there's an appealing garden bar and restaurant with a good range of tasty dishes and cold beer. Packed lunches and guided tours for the park are available.

Kiran Guest House   GUESTHOUSE **$**
(223845; www.kiranguesthouse.com; 364 Rajendra Nagar; r ₹150-300, with AC ₹750; ✳) Managed by eager-to-please brothers, this guesthouse delivers great value with seven simple, spacious, clean rooms and a pleasant rooftop where you can eat tasty home cooking. It's on a quiet road not far from the park. Nature guiding and free pick up from the Bharatpur train and bus stations are offered.

Hotel Bharatpur Ashok   HOTEL **$$**
(222722; www.theashokgroup.com; s/d ₹2700/3000; ✳✳@) This lodge, run by the Indian Tourism Development Corporation (ITDC), is 1km inside the park and 8km from the Bharatpur train station. It's looking a little faded, and service is typically lax. However, the comfortable, quiet rooms have

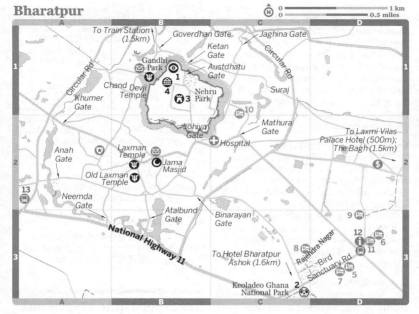

balconies with swing seats and there's a bar downstairs. The multicuisine restaurant's handy if you want something to eat while within the park (nonguests are welcome).

Laxmi Vilas Palace Hotel HOTEL **$$$**
(☎223523; www.laxmivilas.com; Kakaji-ki-Kothi, Old Agra Rd; s/d/ste ₹4400/4800/6100; ✳@☈) This exquisite heritage hotel, about equidistant between the national park and the town centre, was once owned by the younger son of Maharaja Jaswant Singh. Arched ceilings and heavy old furniture make for atmospheric rooms, set around a courtyard.

The Bagh HOTEL **$$$**
(☎225415; www.thebagh.com; Old Agra Rd; s/d from ₹6000/7500; ✳@☈) A picturesque hotel 2km from town, the Bagh has 23 elegant rooms spread out in separate pavilions nestled in a former royal orchard. All rooms boast cool marble floors, antique furnishings and wonderful bathrooms. The 4-hectare garden is over 200 years old and has masses of birds if you're feeling too lazy to go to the park.

Royal Guest House HOTEL **$**
(☎9414315457; www.royalguesthousebharatpur. com; r ₹250-750; ✳@) The ultrakeen management, who live on the premises, also do

Bharatpur

⊙ Sights

moneychanging and run an internet cafe here. The rooms are all very clean and fresh, and the rooftop restaurant is cosy. Guests can use a kitchen for self-catering, and have free access to the internet.

Falcon Guest House HOTEL $

(223815; falconguesthouse@hotmail.com; Gori Shankur Colony; r ₹300-1600; ✳@) The Falcon may well be the pick of a bunch of hotels all in a row and all owned by the same extended family. It is a well-kept, snug place to stay, run by the affable Mrs Rajni Singh. Her husband, Tej, is an ornithologist and he's happy to answer any bird-related questions. Flavoursome home-cooked food is served in the garden restaurant.

Spoonbill Hotel & Restaurant HOTEL $

(223571; www.hotelspoonbill.com; Gori Shankur Colony; s ₹150-600, d ₹200-700; ✳) The original Spoonbill has a variety of different rooms – all good value and clean, if a bit worn. The hotel has excellent food (mains ₹30 to ₹150), with curd from the family cow and Rajasthani delicacies, such as *churma* (sugar, cheese and dried fruit fried in butter), the royal dish of Rajasthan. There's often a campfire in winter.

Shagun Guest House GUESTHOUSE $

(9828687488; rajeev_shagun@hotmail.com; s/d ₹120/150, without bathroom ₹100) It doesn't get much more basic than this. Down a lane inside Mathura Gate, you will find yourself well off the bird trail with a little tree-shaded courtyard and friendly locals keen for a chat. The affable owner is knowledgeable about the park and conducts village tours.

❶ Information

Main post office (⊙10am-1pm & 2-5pm Mon-Sat) Near Gandhi Park.

Royal Forex (New Civil Lines; ⊙6am-10pm;@) Moneychanger that has expanded into the hotel and internet cafe business (per hour ₹40).

Tourist Reception Centre (222542; ⊙9.30am-6pm Mon-Fri) About 700m from the park entrance; sells maps of Bharatpur (₹10).

❶ Getting There & Away

Bus

There are regular buses to various places, including Agra (₹55, 1½ hours), Fatehpur Sikri (₹30, one hour), Jaipur (₹110, 4½ hours), Deeg (₹25, one hour) and Alwar (₹60, four hours). Buses leave from the main bus station, but also drop off and pick up passengers at the bus stop at the crossroads by the Tourist Reception Centre.

Train

The 19023/4 *Janata Express* leaves New Delhi (sleeper ₹120) at 1.05pm and arrives in Bharatpur at 5.30pm. It leaves Bharatpur at 8.10am, arriving in the capital at 12.50pm. The 12925/6 *Paschim Express* leaves New Delhi (sleeper/3AC/2AC/1AC ₹140/315/410/675) at 4.55pm and arrives in Bharatpur at 7.40pm. It leaves Bharatpur at 6.15am, arriving in the capital at 10.55pm.

There are several trains daily to Sawai Madhopur (sleeper/3AC/2AC/1AC ₹140/325/425/700), including the 12094 *Golden Temple Mail*, which departs at 10.40am and arrives at Sawai Madhopur at 1.05pm and then continues to Kota and Mumbai (Bombay).

To Agra (2nd class/sleeper/ AC chair/3AC/2AC/1AC ₹47/140/195/240/310/505), the 12966 *Udaipur–Gwalior Express* departs at 9.05am, arriving at Agra Cantt at 10.15am.

❶ Getting Around

An auto- or cycle-rickshaw from the bus station to the tourist office and most of the hotels should cost around ₹30 (₹35 from the train station).

Keoladeo Ghana National Park

This famous bird sanctuary and **national park** (Indian/foreigner ₹55/400, video ₹400; ⊙6am-6pm Apr-Sep, 6.30am-5pm Oct-Mar) has long been recognised as one of the world's most important bird breeding and feeding grounds. In a good monsoon season over one-third of the park can be submerged, hosting over 360 species within its 29 sq km. The marshland patchwork is a wintering area for aquatic birds, including visitors from Afghanistan, Turkmenistan, China and Siberia.

Keoladeo originated as a royal hunting reserve in the 1850s. It continued to supply the maharajas' tables with fresh game until as late as 1965. In 1982 Keoladeo was declared a national park and it was listed as a World Heritage Site in 1985.

Visiting the Park

The best time to visit is from October to February, when you will see many migratory birds.

Admission entitles you to one entrance per day; if you want to spend the day inside the park, carry plenty of drinking water, as birdwatching is thirsty work.

One narrow road (no motorised vehicles are permitted past checkpoint 2) runs through the park, and countless embankments thread their way between the shallow wetlands.

Only government-authorised cycle-rickshaws (recognisable by the yellow license plate) are allowed beyond checkpoint 2. You don't pay an admission fee for the drivers, but they charge ₹70 per hour. Some are very knowledgeable. However, these cycle-rickshaws can only travel along the park's larger tracks.

An excellent way to see the park is by hiring a bike/mountain bike (₹25/40 per six hours) at the park entrance. Having a bike is a wonderfully quiet way to travel, and allows you to avoid bottlenecks and take in the serenity on your own. You get a map with your entrance ticket.

Alwar

📞 0144 / POP 313,300

Alwar is perhaps the oldest of the Rajasthani kingdoms, forming part of the Matsya territories of Viratnagar in 1500 BC. It became known again in the 18th century under Pratap Singh, who pushed back the rulers of Jaipur to the south and the Jats of Bharatpur to the east, and who successfully resisted the Marathas. It was one of the first Rajput states to ally itself with the fledgling British empire, although British interference in Alwar's internal affairs meant that this partnership was not always amicable.

It's the nearest town to **Sariska Tiger Reserve**.

⊙ Sights

Bala Qila   HISTORIC BUILDING
This imposing fort, with its 5km ramparts, stands 300m above the city, its fortifications hugging the steep incline. Predating the time of Pratap Singh, it's one of the few forts in Rajasthan built before the rise of the Mughals, who used it as a base for attacking Ranthambhore. Now in ruins, unfortunately, the fort houses a radio transmitter station and parts can only be visited with permission from the superintendent of police. However, this is easy to get: just ask at the superintendent's office in the City Palace Complex.

City Palace Complex   HISTORIC BUILDING
Below the fort sprawls the colourful and convoluted City Palace, or Vinay Vilas Mahal, with massive gates and a tank reflecting a symmetrical series of ghats and pavilions.

Hidden within the City Palace is the excellent **Alwar Museum** (Indian/foreigner ₹5/50; ☺10am-5pm Tue-Sun). Its eclectic exhibits evoke the extravagance of the maharajas' lifestyle: stunning weapons, stuffed Scottish

SURAJ MAHL'S PALACE, DEEG

Deeg is a small, rarely visited, dusty tumult of a town. At its centre stands an incongruously glorious palace edged by stately formal gardens. **Suraj Mahl's Palace** (Indian/foreigner ₹5/100; ☺9.30am-5.30pm Sat-Thu) is one of India's most beautiful and carefully proportioned palace complexes. Pick up a map and brochure at the entrance and note that photography is not permitted in some of the *bhavans* (buildings).

Built in a mixture of Rajput and Mughal architectural styles, the 18th-century **Gopal Bhavan** is fronted by imposing arches to take full advantage of the early-morning light. Downstairs is a lower storey that becomes submerged during the monsoon as the water level of the adjacent tank, **Gopal Sagar**, rises. It was used by the maharajas until the early 1950s, and contains many original furnishings, including faded sofas, huge *punkas* (cloth fans) that are over 200 years old, chaise longues, a stuffed tiger, elephant-foot stands, and fine porcelain from China and France.

The **Keshav Bhavan** (Summer or Monsoon Pavilion) is a single-storey edifice with five arches along each side. Tiny jets spray water from the archways and metal balls rumble around in a water channel imitating monsoon thunder. Deeg's massive walls (which are up to 28m high) and 12 vast bastions, some with their cannons still in place, are also worth exploring. You can walk up to the top of the walls from the palace.

Deeg is about 36km north of Bharatpur, and is an easy day trip (and there's nowhere good to stay) from Bharatpur or Alwar by car. All the roads to Deeg are rough and the buses crowded. Frequent buses run to and from Alwar (₹45, 2½ hours) and Bharatpur (₹25, one hour).

pheasants, royal ivory slippers, erotic miniatures, royal vestments, a solid silver table and stone sculptures, such as an 11th-century sculpture of Vishnu.

Cenotaph of Maharaja
Bakhtawar Singh
HISTORIC BUILDING

This double-storey edifice, resting on a platform of sandstone, was built in 1815 by Maharaja Vinay Singh in memory of his father. To gain access to the cenotaph, take the steps on the far left when facing the palace. The cenotaph is also known as the Chhatri of Moosi Rani, after one of the mistresses of Bakhtawar Singh who performed *sati* (self-immolation) on his funeral pyre – after this act she was promoted to wifely status.

🛏 Sleeping & Eating

As not many tourists stop here, Alwar's hotels are mostly aimed at budget business travellers and are not particularly good value.

Alwar Hotel
HOTEL $$

(**TOP CHOICE**)

(☎2700012; www.alwarhotel.com; 26 Manu Rd; s/d incl breakfast ₹1750/2500, ste ₹2850; ❄@🛜) Set back from the road in a neatly manicured garden, this well-run hotel has spacious, renovated and comfortable rooms. This is easily the best option in town, and staff can be helpful with general information and sightseeing advice. Tours to Sariska and visits to sporting and swimming clubs can be arranged.

Hotel Aravali
HOTEL $

(☎2332883; www.hotelaravali.co.in; Nehru Rd; s/d from ₹450/500, with AC from ₹850/950; ❄@🛜) This is also one of the town's better choices, but nevertheless is a bit like *Fawlty Towers* without the humour. Its room options stretch to midrange, though rowdy guests can be a problem. If the hotel isn't full request a quiet room. There's a summer-only pool. Turn left out of the train station and it's about 100m down the road.

Prem Pavitra Bhojnalaya
INDIAN $

(☎2700925; Old Bus Stand; mains ₹40-70; ⊙10am-10pm; ❄) Alwar's renowned restaurant has been going since 1957. It is in the heart of the old town and serves fresh, tasty pure veg food – try the delicious *aloo parathas* (bread stuffed with spicy potato) and *palak paneer* (unfermented cheese cubes in spinach puree). Do finish off with the special *kheer* (creamy rice pudding).

Angeethi
MULTICUISINE $

(Alwar Hotel, Manu Rd; mains ₹50-100; ⊙Tue-Sun; ❄) Alwar Hotel's restaurant serves first-rate Indian, Continental and Chinese food; the South Indian selection is particularly good. It's slightly gloomy in the restaurant but you can eat in the pleasant gardens.

ℹ Getting There & Away

Bus

From Alwar there are numerous buses to Sariska (₹21, 1½ hours, half-hourly 5.15am to 8.30pm), which go on to Jaipur (₹80, four hours). There are also frequent (bumpy) services to Bharatpur (₹50, four hours) for Keoladeo Ghana National Park, and Deeg (₹45, 2½ hours). Buses to Delhi take two different routes (₹95, via Tijara/Ramgarh four/five hours, half-hourly).

Car

A return taxi to Sariska Tiger Reserve (including a stop at Siliserh) will cost you around ₹1150.

Train

The 2015/6 *Shatabdi Express* passes through Alwar. It departs for Ajmer (AC chair/1st class ₹435/830, four hours) at 8.39am and stops at Jaipur (₹320/605) at 10.45am. For Delhi, it departs at 7.30pm (₹335/640, 2½ hours). The 2461 *Mandore Express* to Jodhpur (2AC/3AC ₹793/578, 10½ hours) departs Alwar at 9.45pm.

Sariska Tiger Reserve

☑0144

Enclosed within the dramatic, shadowy folds of the Aravallis, the **Sariska Tiger Reserve** (Indian/foreigner ₹60/450, vehicle ₹250; ⊙ticket sales 7am-3.30pm Oct-Mar, 6.30am-4pm Apr-Sep, park closes at sunset) is a tangle of remnant semideciduous jungle and craggy canyons sheltering streams and greenery. It covers 866 sq km (including a core area of 498 sq km), and is home to peacocks, monkeys, majestic sambars, nilgai, chital, wild boars and jackals.

Although Project Tiger has been in charge of the sanctuary since 1979, there has been a dramatic failure in tiger protection. In 2004 there were an estimated 18 tigers in the park; however, this was called into question after an investigation by the WWF. That report prompted the federal government to investigate what has happened to the tigers of Sariska.

Sariska is in any case a fascinating sanctuary. Unlike most national parks, it opens year-round, although the best time to spot wildlife is November to March, and you'll see most wildlife in the evening.

💿 Sights

Besides wildlife, Sariska has some fantastic sights within the park or around its peripheries, which are well worth seeking out. If you take a longer tour, you can ask to visit one or more of these. A couple of them are also accessible by public bus.

Kankwari Fort   HISTORIC BUILDING

Deep inside the sanctuary, this imposing small jungle fort, 22km away from Sariska, offers amazing views over the plains of the national park, dotted with red mud-brick villages. A four- to five-hour jeep safari (one to five passengers plus guide) to Kankwari Fort from the Forest Reception Office near the reserve entrance costs ₹1600, plus guide fee (₹150).

Bhangarh   HISTORIC SITE

Around 55km from Sariska, beyond the inner park sanctuary and out in open countryside, is this deserted, well-preserved, notoriously haunted city. It was founded in 1631 by Madho Singh, and had 10,000 dwellings, but was suddenly deserted about 300 years ago for reasons that remain mysterious.

Bhangarh can be reached by a bus that runs twice daily through the sanctuary (₹35) to nearby Golaka village. Check what time the bus returns, otherwise you risk getting stranded.

☞ Tours

Private cars, including taxis, are limited to sealed roads. The best way to visit the park is by 4WD gypsy (open-topped, takes five passengers), which can explore off the main tracks. Gypsy safaris start at the park entrance and you'll be quoted ₹1050 for three hours, or ₹3200 for a full day. They can take up to five people. Guides are available (₹150 for three hours).

Bookings can be made at the **Forest Reception Office** (📞2841333; Jaipur Rd), directly opposite the Hotel Sariska Palace, which is where buses will drop you.

🛏 Sleeping & Eating

TOP CHOICE Alwar Bagh   HOTEL $$

(📞2885231; www.alwarbagh.com; r & tent ₹2800, ste ₹3500; ; 🏢🏊) This is a very peaceful option located in the village of Dhawala, between Alwar (14km) and Sariska (19km). It can arrange pick-up and drop-off from Alwar, and can also arrange safaris of Sariska. The bright heritage-style hotel boasts traditional styling, spotless rooms and romantic tents, an organic orchard, a garden restaurant (breakfast/lunch/dinner ₹150/350/350) and a gorgeous swimming pool.

RTDC Hotel Tiger Den   HOTEL $$

(📞2841342; s/d incl breakfast & lunch or dinner; ₹1290/1850, with AC ₹2150/2800; 🏢) Hotel Tiger Den is a quasi-Soviet block, backed by a rambling garden. Accommodation and meals are drab, but the rooms have balconies and occupy a pleasant setting close to

---

SARISKA'S TIGER TALE

Sariska Tiger Reserve has taken centre stage in one of India's most publicised wildlife dramas. It wasn't until 2005 that it was revealed that the tiger population here had been eliminated.

An enquiry into the crisis recommended fundamental management changes before tigers should be reintroduced to the reserve. Extra funding was proposed to cover relocation of villages within the park as well as increasing the protection force. Action on the recommendations has been slow and incomplete despite extensive media coverage and a high level of concern in India.

Nevertheless, tigers from Ranthambhore National Park were moved by helicopter to Sariska. The first pair were airlifted in 2008. By 2010 five tigers had been transferred; however, in November 2010 the male of the original pair was found dead in suspicious circumstances. Later it was confirmed that it had been poisoned. Authorities pointed the finger at local villagers who are not supportive of the reintroduction. The underlying problem – the inevitable battle between India's poorest and ever-expanding village populace with rare and phenomenally valuable wildlife on their doorstep – remains largely unresolved despite official plans to relocate and reimburse villagers.

Only time will tell if this reintroduction is successful – another big concern is that the reintroduced tigers are all closely related – but, as things stand, Sariska remains a sad indictment of tiger conservation in India, from the top government officials down to the underpaid forest guard.

the reserve entrance. Bring a mosquito net or repellent.

Sariska Tiger Heaven HOTEL **$$**
(☑224815; www.sariskatigerheaven.com; s/d with full board ₹3500/4000, with AC ₹4000/5000; ❄☀) This is an isolated place about 3km west of the bus stop at Thanagazi village and free pick-up is on offer. Rooms are set in stone-and-tile cottages and have big beds and windowed alcoves. Staff can arrange jeeps and guides to the park and pick-up from Jaipur (₹1200).

❶ Getting There & Away

Sariska is 35km from Alwar, a convenient town from which to approach the reserve. There are frequent (and crowded) buses from Alwar (₹21, one to 1½ hours, at least hourly) and on to Jaipur (₹75). Buses stop in front of the Forest Reception Office.

Shekhawati

Far less visited than other parts of Rajasthan, the Shekhawati region is most famous for its extraordinary painted *havelis* (traditional, ornately decorated residences), highlighted with dazzling, often whimsical, murals. Part of the region's appeal and mystique is due to these works of art being found in tiny towns, connected to each other by single-track roads that run through lonely, arid countryside. Today it seems curious that such care, attention and financing was lavished on these out-of-the-way houses, but from the 14th century onwards, Shekhawati's towns were important trading posts on the caravan routes from Gujarati ports.

What makes the artwork on Shekhawati's *havelis* so fascinating is the manner in which their artists combined traditional subjects, such as mythology, religious scenes and images of the family, with contemporary concerns, including brand-new inventions and accounts of current events, many of which these isolated painters rendered straight from their imagination.

❶ Getting Around

The Shekhawati region is crisscrossed by narrow, dusty roads and all towns are served by government or private buses and jam-packed shared jeeps. To zip from town to town more speedily and in greater comfort, hire a taxi for the day. The usual rate for a non-AC taxi is ₹5 to ₹7 per kilometre with a minimum charge of 250km per day.

NAWALGARH
☑01594 / POP 60,000

Nawalgarh is a small town almost at the very centre of the region, and thus makes a great base for exploring. It boasts several fine *havelis*, a colourful, mostly pedestrianised bazaar and some excellent accommodation options.

◉ Sights

Dr Ramnath A Poddar Haveli Museum MUSEUM
(www.poddarhavelimuseum.org; admission ₹100, camera ₹30; ◔8.30am-6.30pm) Built in 1902 on the eastern side of town, this is one of the region's few buildings to have been thoroughly restored. The paintings of this *haveli* are defined in strong colours, as they must have looked when new. On the ground floor are several galleries on Rajasthani culture, including examples of different schools of Rajasthani painting, turbans, tablas and polystyrene forts.

⊂ァ Tours

Ramesh Jangid at **Apani Dhani** (☑222239; www.apanidhani.com) and his son Rajesh at **Ramesh Jangid's Tourist Pension** (☑224060; www.touristpension.com) are keen to promote sustainable rural tourism, in part by organising village treks, camel-cart safaris and informative guided tours.

🛏 Sleeping & Eating

TOP CHOICE **Apani Dhani** GUESTHOUSE **$$**
(☑222239; www.apanidhani.com; s/d from ₹995/1350) This award-winning ecotourism venture is a delightful and relaxing place. Rooms are in traditional, cosy mud-hut bungalows, enhanced by thatched roofs and comfortable beds, around a bougainvillea-shaded courtyard. It's on the west side of the Jaipur road. Multilingual Ramesh Jangid runs the show and 5% of the room tariff goes to community projects.

TOP CHOICE **Ramesh Jangid's Tourist Pension** GUESTHOUSE **$**
(☑224060; www.touristpension.com; s/d from ₹400/450) The guesthouse, run by genial Rajesh, Ramesh's son, offers homey, clean accommodation in spacious rooms with big beds. Pure veg meals, made with organic ingredients, are available (including a delectable vegetable thali for ₹180). The family also arranges all sorts of tours around Shekhawati.

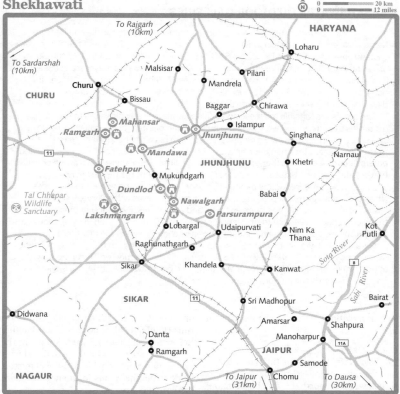

0   20 km
0   12 miles

Shekhawati Guesthouse   GUESTHOUSE $

(☎224658; www.shekhawatiguesthouse.com; s/d ₹400/500, cottages s/d ₹ 700/800, r with AC ₹1000; ✳@) This friendly guesthouse is more like a homestay run by a very friendly couple. There are six rooms in the main building plus five atmospheric, thatch-roofed, mud-walled cottages in the garden. The restaurant has received awards for its delicious organic food and we heartily recommend the kheer (rice pudding). It's 4km east of the bus stand (₹60 by taxi). Pick-up from the bus or train station can be arranged, as can cooking lessons.

DS Bungalow   GUESTHOUSE $

(☎9983168916; s ₹350-450, d ₹400-500) Run by a friendly, down-to-earth couple, this simple place with boxy air-cooled rooms is a little out of town on the way to Roop Niwas Palace. The restaurant's home cooking is decent; a full veg/nonveg dinner comes in at at ₹250/300.

ⓘ Getting There & Away

Bus

There are RSRTC buses between Nawalgarh and Jaipur (₹85, 3½ hours, every 15 minutes). There's also a daily deluxe bus to Jaipur departing at 8am (₹120, three hours). Buses run to Fatehpur (₹30, hourly) and Mandawa (₹20, every 45 minutes).

JHUNJHUNU

☎01592 / POP 131,000

Shekhawati's most important commercial centre has a different atmosphere from the smaller towns, with lots of traffic, concrete and hustle and bustle as befits the district headquarters.

◉ Sights

Rani Sati Temple   HINDU TEMPLE

(admission free, ⊙4am-10pm) In the northeast corner of town is the enormous, multistorey Rani Sati Temple, notorious and hugely popular for commemorating an act of *sati*

In the 18th and 19th centuries, shrewd Marwari merchants lived frugally and far from home while earning money in India's new commercial centres. They sent the bulk of their vast fortunes back to their families in Shekhawati to construct grand *havelis* (traditional, ornately decorated mansions) to show their neighbours how well they were doing and to compensate their families for their long absences. Merchants competed with one another to build ever more grand edifices – homes, temples, step-wells – which were richly decorated, both inside and out, with painted murals.

The artists responsible for these acres of decoration largely belonged to the caste of *kumhars* (potters) and were both the builders and painters of the *havelis*. Known as *chajeras* (masons), many were commissioned from beyond Shekhawati – particularly from Jaipur, where they had been employed to decorate the new capital's palaces – and others flooded in from further afield to offer their skills. Soon, there was a cross-pollination of ideas and techniques, with local artists learning from the new arrivals.

Haveli walls were frequently painted by the *chajeras* from the ground to the eaves. Often the paintings mix depictions of the gods and their lives with everyday scenes featuring modern inventions, such as trains and aeroplanes, even though these artists themselves had never seen them. Hence, Krishna and Radha are seen in flying motorcars and Europeans can be observed inflating hot-air balloons by blowing into them.

For a full rundown on the history, people, towns and buildings of the area, try tracking down a copy of *The Painted Towns of Shekhawati* by Ilay Cooper, which can be picked up at bookshops in the region or Jaipur. Another good book, available locally, is *Shekhawati: Painted Townships* by Kishore Singh.

(self-immolation) by a merchant's wife in 1595.

Khetri Mahal
HISTORIC BUILDING
(admission ₹20) A series of tiny laneways at the western end of Nehru Bazaar (a short rickshaw drive north of the bus station) leads to the imposing Khetri Mahal, a small palace dating from around 1770 and once one of Shekhawati's most sophisticated and beautiful buildings. Unfortunately, it now has a desolate, forlorn atmosphere, but the architecture remains a superb open-sided collection of intricate arches and columns. There are good views over the town from here, stretching across to the old Muslim quarter, Pirzada Mahalla, and its mosques.

⚡ Courses
If you are interested in tuition in traditional Shekhawati painting, contact Laxmi Kant Jangid at the Hotel Jamuna Resort or Hotel Shiv Shekhawati. Laxmi also runs hands-on cookery courses at Hotel Jamuna Resort; these cost around ₹300 per person.

🛏 Sleeping & Eating

TOP CHOICE Hotel Jamuna Resort   HOTEL $$
(☎512696; www.hoteljamunaresort.com; s/d from ₹1500/2000, d with AC from ₹1200; ❋@☎) Perched on a hill overlooking town and operated by Laxmi Kant Jangid (who also runs Hotel Shiv Shekhawati), Hotel Jamuna Resort has all that you need. Rooms in the older wing are either vibrantly painted with murals or decorated with traditional mirror-work, while the rooms in the new wing are modern and airy.

Hotel Shiv Shekhawati   HOTEL $
(☎232651; www.shivshekhawati.com; Khemi Shakti Rd; s/d from ₹600/800; ❋@) East of the town centre, Shiv Shekhawati is the best budget option with plain but squeaky-clean rooms. It's 600m from the private bus stand in a quiet area on the eastern edge of town. The affable owner, Laxmi Kant Jangid (usually found at Hotel Jamuna Resort), is a wealth of knowledge on the villages of Shekhawati and tours can be organised here.

ⓘ Information
Tourist Reception Centre (☎232909; ◷10am-5pm Mon-Fri) Out of the town centre at the Churu Bypass Rd, Mandawa Circle. The office has helpful, cheery staff, but all they can provide are a few brochures and a basic map of the town and region.

ⓘ Getting There & Away
Regular buses run between Jhunjhunu and Jaipur (₹80, four hours). Numerous buses go to Mandawa (₹15, one hour) and Nawalgarh (₹20, one hour).

FATEHPUR

☎01571 / POP 89,000

Established in 1451 as a capital for Muslim nawabs, Fatehpur was their stronghold for centuries before it was taken over by the Shekhawati Rajputs in the 18th century. It's a busy little town, with masses of *havelis,* many in a sad state of disrepair, but with a few notable exceptions.

Haveli Nadine Prince (☎231479; www.cultural-centre.com; adult/child ₹100/50; ⊙10am-7pm) has been restored to its former dazzling glory and the admission includes a detailed guided tour. The 1802 building is owned by French artist Nadine Le Prince, who has turned it into an art gallery and cultural centre, and has done much to publicise the plight of Shekhawati.

Some other Fatehpur highlights include the nearby **Jagannath Singhania Haveli**; the **Mahavir Prasad Goenka Haveli** (often locked, but with superb paintings); **Geori Shankar Haveli**, with mirrored mosaics on the antechamber ceiling; **Harikrishnan Das Sarogi Haveli**, with a colourful facade and iron lacework; and **Vishnunath Keria Haveli**, which depicts Radha and Krishna in flying gondolas.

🛏 Sleeping & Eating

Haveli Cultural Centre Guest House & Art Cafe   BOUTIQUE HOTEL **$**
(☎233024; www.cultural-centre.com; r from ₹800; dishes ₹50-150) This extraordinarily restored *haveli* and cultural centre has opened up its artist residence rooms to travellers with several traditional-style rooms overlooking the central courtyard. Tariff is room only, with breakfast ₹150 and dinner ₹300. To just visit the Art Café you'll have to pay to get into the *haveli,* but this is a good option for a light lunch. It's a cosy place with low tables, serving food such as omelettes, toast and rum-blazed bananas, as well as Indian snacks.

ℹ Getting There & Around

At the private bus stand, on the Churu–Sikar road, buses leave for Jhunjhunu (₹25, one hour) and Mandawa (₹20, one hour). From the RSRTC bus stand, which is further south down this road, buses leave for Jaipur (₹80, 3½ hours, every 15 minutes).

MANDAWA

☎01592 / POP 20,717

Mandawa is the preferred base for travellers to Shekhawati. Settled in the 18th century and fortified by the dominant merchant families, it remains a relatively subdued market town, though the very young, very persistent touts are surprisingly forceful.

Binsidhar Newatia Haveli (now the State Bank of Bikaner & Jaipur) has curious paintings on its outer eastern wall – a boy using a telephone, a European woman in a chauffeur-driven car, and the Wright brothers in flight. The **Gulab Rai Ladia Haveli**, southwest of the fort, has some defaced erotic images.

🛏 Sleeping & Eating

Hotel Shekhawati   HOTEL **$**
(☎9314698079; www.hotelshekwati.com; r ₹350-1800; ❋@) Near Mukundgarh Rd, the only real budget choice in town is run by a retired bank manager and his son (who's also a registered tourist guide). Bright, comically bawdy murals painted by artistic former guests give the rooms a splash of colour. Tasty meals are served on the peaceful rooftop, and competitively priced camel, horse and jeep tours can also be arranged.

Hotel Mandawa Haveli   HERITAGE HOTEL **$$**
(☎223088; www.hotelmandawa.com; s/d/ste from 1450/1950/4250;❋) Close to Sonathia Gate and Subhash Chowk, this hotel is set in a glorious, restored 19th-century *haveli* with rooms surrounding a painted courtyard. The cheapest rooms are small, so it's worth splashing out on a suite, filled with arches, window seats and countless small windows.

Hotel Castle Mandawa   HERITAGE HOTEL **$$$**
(☎223124; www.castlemandawa.com; s/d from ₹4000/4500; ❋@≋) Mandawa's large upmarket hotel in the town's converted fort attempts a slightly twee medieval atmosphere but is still a swish and generally comfortable choice. Some rooms are far better appointed than others (the best are the suites in the tower, with four-poster and swing beds), so check a few before you settle in.

ℹ Getting There & Away

There are buses to Nawalgarh (₹20, 45 minutes), Fatehpur (₹20, one hour), Bissau (₹18, 1½ hours) and Ramgarh (₹25, 1½ hours).

Ajmer

☎0145 / POP 557,000

Ajmer is a bustling chaotic city around 130km southwest of Jaipur. It surrounds the tranquil lake of Ana Sagar, and is itself ringed by rugged Aravalli hills. Ajmer is

RAJASTHAN EASTERN RAJASTHAN

Rajasthan's most important site in terms of Islamic history and heritage. It contains one of India's most important Muslim pilgrimage centres – the shrine of Khwaja Muin-ud-din Chishti, a venerated Sufi saint who founded the Chishtiya order, the prime Sufi order in India today. As well as some superb examples of early Muslim architecture, Ajmer is also a significant centre for the Jain religion, possessing an amazing golden Jain temple. However, most travellers just use Ajmer as a stepping stone to nearby Pushkar, a supremely sacred town to Hindus and a former hippy hang-out.

◉ Sights

Ana Sagar   LAKE
This large lake, created in the 12th century by damming the River Luni, is set against the blue-grey hills that are reflected on its oily surface. On its bank are two green parks, the **Subash Bagh** and **Dault Bagh**, containing a series of marble pavilions erected in 1637 by Shah Jahan.

Dargah of Khwaja Muin-ud-din Chishti   SUFI SHRINE
(www.dargahajmer.com; ⏲5am-9pm winter, 4am-9pm summer) This is the tomb of a Sufi saint Khwaja Muin-ud-din Chishti, who came to Ajmer from Persia in 1192 and died here in 1236. The tomb gained its significance during the time of the Mughals – many emperors added to the buildings here. Construction of the shrine was completed by Humayun, and the gate was added by the Nizam of Hyderabad. Akbar used to make the pilgrimage to the dargah from Agra every year.

You have to cover your head in certain parts of the shrine, so remember to take a scarf or cap, although there are plenty for sale at the colourful bazaar leading to the dargah, along with floral offerings and delicious toffees.

The first gate is the **Nizam Gate**, built in 1915 up some steps to protect it from the rains. The green and white mosque, **Akbari Masjid**, on the right was constructed by Akbar in 1571 and is now Moiniua Usmania Darul-Uloom, an Arabic and Persian School for religious education. The second gate was built by Shah Jahan, and is often called the Nakkarkhana because it has two large *nakkharas* (drums) fixed above it.

The third gate, **Buland Darwaza**, dates from the 16th century. It's tall – about 28m high – and whitewashed, and leads into the dargah courtyard. Flanking the entrance of the courtyard are the *degs* (large iron cauldrons), one donated by Akbar in 1567, the other by Jehangir in 1631, for offerings for the poor.

The saint's tomb has a marble dome, and the tomb inside is surrounded by a silver platform. Pilgrims believe that the saint's spirit will intercede on their behalf in matters of illness, business or personal problems, so the notes and holy string attached to the railings around are thanks or requests.

Pilgrims and Sufis come from all over the world on the anniversary of the saint's death, The Urs, in the seventh month of the lunar calendar, Jyaistha.

Adhai-din-ka-Jhonpra　　　HISTORIC SITE
Beyond the dargah, on the town outskirts, are the extraordinary ruins of the Adhai-din-ka-Jhonpra (Two-and-a-Half-Day Building) mosque. According to legend, construction in 1153 took 2½ days. Others say it was named after a festival lasting 2½ days. It was built as a Sanskrit college, but in 1198 Mohammed of Ghori seized Ajmer and converted the building into a mosque by adding a seven-arched wall covered with Islamic calligraphy in front of the pillared hall.

Although in need of restoration, it's an exquisite piece of architecture, with soaring domes, pillars and a beautiful arched screen, largely built from pieces of Jain and Hindu temples.

Taragarh　　　FORT
(Star Fort; admission free; ⊙sunrise to sunset) About 3km and a steep 1½-hour climb beyond the Adhai-din-ka-Jhonpra mosque, the ancient Taragarh commands a superb view over the city (accessible by car). Built by Ajaipal Chauhan, the town's founder, it saw lots of military action during Mughal times and was later used as a British sanatorium.

Nasiyan (Red) Temple　　　JAIN TEMPLE
(Prithviraj Marg; admission ₹10; ⊙8am-4.30pm) This marvellous Jain temple was built in 1865. It's also known as the Golden Temple, due to its amazing display – its double-storey temple hall is filled with a huge golden diorama depicting the Jain concept of the ancient world, with 13 continents and oceans, the intricate golden city of Ayodhya, flying peacock and elephant gondolas, and gilded elephants with many tusks.

Akbar's Palace　　　MUSEUM
Not far from the main post office, Akbar built this imposing building in 1570 – partly as a pleasure retreat, but mainly to keep an eye on pesky local chiefs. This is just part of the original impressive fortifications. It houses the underwhelming government museum (Indian/foreigner ₹5/50; ⊙9.45am-5.15pm Tue-Sun), with a small collection of old weapons, miniature paintings, ancient rock

inscriptions and stone sculptures that date back to the 8th century.

🛏 Sleeping

Haveli Heritage Inn   HOTEL $
(☑2621607; www.haveliheritageinn.com; Kutchery Rd; r ₹650-1850; ❄) Set in a 140-year-old *haveli*, this is a welcoming city-centre oasis and arguably Ajmer's best budget choice. The high-ceilinged rooms are spacious, simply decorated, air-cooled and set well back from the busy road. There's a pleasant, grassy courtyard and the hotel is infused with a family atmosphere, complete with home-cooked meals.

Badnor House   GUESTHOUSE $$
(☑2627579; www.badnorhouse.com; Civil Lines; d incl breakfast ₹2500, ste ₹2800; ❄) This guesthouse provides an excellent opportunity to stay with a delightful family. The down-to-earth hospitality includes three new heritage-style doubles and an older-style, spacious and comfortable self-contained suite with a private courtyard.

Mansingh Palace   HOTEL $$$
(☑2425956; www.mansinghhotels.com; Circular Rd; s/d from ₹4600/5400, ste ₹9000; ❄@≋) This modern place, on the shores of Ana Sagar, is rather out of the way, but has attractive and comfortable rooms, some with views and balconies. The hotel has a shady garden, a bar and a good restaurant, the Sheesh Mahal.

Hotel Ajmeru   HOTEL $
(☑2431103; Khailand Market; s/d from ₹500/600, with AC ₹900/1100; ❄) This hotel with a veg restaurant and small tidy rooms can be found just past the narrow Kotwali Gate off Prithviraj Marg. It's convenient to the train station, Jain Temple and Dargah.

🍴 Eating

Honeydew   MULTICUISINE $$
(☑2622498; Station Rd; mains ₹90-290; ⊙9am-11pm) The Honeydew offers a great selection of veg and nonveg Indian, Chinese and Continental food in a pleasant, clean, relaxed, but overly dim, atmosphere. It has long been one of Ajmer's best, and is the restaurant of choice for Mayo College students' midterm treat. The ice cream, milkshakes and floats will keep you cool.

Madina Hotel   NORTH INDIAN $
(Station Rd; mains ₹30-100; ⊙9am-11pm) Handy if you're waiting for a train (it's opposite the station), this simple, open-to-the-street eatery cooks up cheap veg and nonveg fare, with specialities such as chicken Mughlai and *rumali roti* (huge paper-thin chapati).

Elite   VEGETARIAN $
(☑2429544; Station Rd; mains ₹50-105; ⊙11am-11pm) Elite has a welcoming ambience attracting families to feast on the town's best value thali (₹66), as well as South Indian and tandoori veg.

ℹ Information

Bank of Baroda (Prithviraj Marg) Changes travellers cheques and does credit-card advances.

Bank of Baroda ATM (Station Rd) By the entrance to Honeydew restaurant.

HDFC ATM (Sadar Patel Marg)

Main post office (Prithviraj Marg; ⊙10am-1pm & 1.30-6pm Mon-Sat) Less than 500m from the train station.

Satguru's Internet (60-61 Kutchery Rd; per hr ₹20; ⊙9am-10pm)

State Bank of India (Civil Lines) Changes travellers cheques and foreign currency and has an ATM.

Tourist Reception Centre train station (⊙9am-6pm); RTDC Hotel Khadim (☑2627426; ⊙9am-6pm Mon-Fri);

ℹ Getting There & Away

Bus

There are frequent RSRTC buses of various grades and comfort leaving from the busy main bus stand to destinations listed in the following table. Fares quoted are for express and/or AC services either Gold Line or Volvo. The enquiry number is ☑2429398.

In addition, there are numerous private buses to these destinations – many companies have offices on Kutchery Rd.

DESTINATION	FARE (₹)	DURATION (HR)
Agra	232	10
Ahmedabad	311	13
Bharatpur	195	8
Bikaner	155	8
Bundi	110	5
Chittorgarh	115	5
Delhi	265/570 AC	9
Indore	250	12
Jaipur	110/200 AC	2½
Jaisalmer	315	10

DESTINATION	FARE (₹)	DURATION (HR)
Jodhpur	125/300 AC	6
Kishangarh	20	15
Pushkar	10	½
Udaipur	170/200 AC	8

Train

There are no tourist quotas for many Ajmer trains, so book early. Use the services of an agent or go to booth 5 at the train station's **reservations office** (◷8am-2pm & 2.15-8pm Mon-Sat, 8am-2pm Sun).

Ajmer is a busy station on the Delhi–Jaipur–Ahmedabad–Mumbai line. The 12016/5 *Shatabdi Express* runs between Ajmer and Delhi (AC chair/1st class ₹645/1200, four hours) via Jaipur (₹300/575). It leaves Delhi at 6.05am and arrives in Ajmer at 12.45pm. Going the other way, the train leaves Ajmer at 3.50pm, arriving in Jaipur at 5.35pm and in Delhi at 10.45pm. There's also the 12957 *Rajdhani Express* to Delhi (3AC/2AC/1AC ₹660/880/1480, seven hours), which leaves Ajmer at 12.40am.

The 19105/6 *Delhi–Ahmedabad Mail* departs from Ajmer at 8.45pm and arrives in Delhi (sleeper/3AC/2AC/1AC ₹200/525/725/1200) at 5.20am. Heading for Gujarat, the train leaves Ajmer at 7.30am and arrives in Ahmedabad (₹227/608/832/1385) at 6.40pm.

The 12195/6 *Ajmer Agra Fort City Express* leaves at 2.50pm, arriving in Agra Fort (2nd class/AC chair ₹111/393) at 9.30pm via Jaipur (₹65/222, 4.55pm).

The 12992 *Ajmer Udaipur City Express* leaves at 4.15pm, arriving in Udaipur (2nd class/AC chair ₹100/347) at 9.30pm via Chittorgarh (₹75/263, 7.15pm).

Pushkar

⌂0145 / POP 14,789

Pushkar has a magnetism all of its own, and is quite unlike anywhere else in Rajasthan. It's a prominent Hindu pilgrimage town and devout Hindus should visit at least once in their lifetime. The town curls around a holy lake, said to have appeared when Brahma dropped a lotus flower. It also has one of the world's few Brahma temples. With 52 bathing ghats and 400 milky-blue temples, the town literally hums with regular *pujas* (prayers) generating an episodic soundtrack of chanting, drums and gongs, and devotional songs.

The result is a muddle of religious and tourist scenes. The main street is one long bazaar, selling anything to tickle a traveller's fancy, from hippy-chic tie-dye to didgeridoos. Despite the commercialism and banana pancakes, the town remains enchantingly small and authentically mystic.

Pushkar is only 11km from Ajmer but separated from it by Nag Pahar, the Snake Mountain.

⊙ Sights

Temples HINDU TEMPLE

Pushkar boasts hundreds of temples, though few are particularly ancient, as they were mostly desecrated by Aurangzeb and subsequently rebuilt.

Brahma Temple

Most famous is the Brahma Temple, said to be one of the few such temples in the world as a result of a curse by Brahma's consort, Saraswati. The temple is marked by a red spire, and over the entrance gateway is the *hans* (goose symbol) of Brahma. Inside, the floor and walls are engraved with dedications to the dead.

Saraswati Temple

The one-hour trek up to the hilltop Saraswati Temple overlooking the lake is best made before dawn (to beat the heat and capture the best light), though the views are fantastic at any time of day.

Pap Mochani (Gayatri) Temple

The sunrise views over town from the closer Pap Mochani (Gayatri) Temple, reached by a track behind the Marwar bus stand, are also well worth the 30-minute climb.

Ghats BATHING GHAT

Fifty-two bathing ghats surround the lake, where pilgrims bathe in the sacred waters. If you wish to join them, do it with respect. Remember, this is a holy place: remove your shoes and don't smoke, kid around or take photographs.

Some ghats have particular importance: Vishnu appeared at **Varah Ghat** in the form of a boar, Brahma bathed at **Brahma Ghat**, and Gandhi's ashes were sprinkled at **Gandhi Ghat** (formerly Gau Ghat).

🏃 Activities

The following hotels allow nonguests use of their swimming pools: Jagat Palace Hotel (₹300 per person), Hotel Navaratan Palace (₹100) and Green Park Resort (₹30).

Shannu's Riding School HORSE RIDING

(☑2772043; http://shannus.weebly.comm; Panch Kund Marg; ride/lessons per hr ₹350) Long-

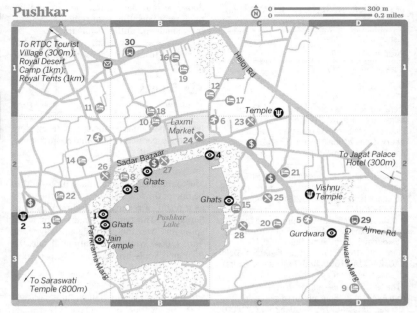

time Pushkar resident Marc can organise riding lessons and horse safaris on his graceful Marwari steeds. On top of that you can also stay here, nice and close to the horses.

Dr NS Mathur   REFLEXOLOGY
(☎2622777, 9828103031; Ajmer Rd; ◷10.30am-6.30pm) Provides back, hand and foot reflexology (from ₹250), which will most certainly take your mind off any pains you might have had. The doctor also teaches reiki and his daughter teaches yoga and provides beauty treatments.

Roshi Hiralal Verma   REIKI, YOGA
For reiki, yoga and shiatsu, Roshi is based at the Ambika Guesthouse. Costs depend on the duration and type of session.

📖 Courses

Saraswati Music School   MUSIC
(☎2773124; Mainon Ka Chowk) Teaches classical *tabla* (drums), flute, singing and *kathak* (classical dance). For music, contact Birju on ☎9828297784, who's been playing for around 20 years, and charges from ₹350 for two hours. He often conducts evening performances (7pm to 8pm), and also sells instruments. For dance, contact Hemant on ☎9829333548.

Cooking Bahar   COOKING
(☎2773124; www.cookingbahar.com; Mainon Ka Chowk) Part of the Saraswati Music School family, Deepa conducts three-hour cooking classes that cover three vegetarian courses.

Dr NS Mathur   REIKI
(☎2622777, 9828103031; Ajmer Rd; ◷10.30am-6.30pm) Reflexologist Dr NS Mathur is also a teacher of reiki (I/II/III ₹1500/3000/10,000).

🧭 Tours
Camel Safaris
Plenty of people in Pushkar offer **camel safaris** (around ₹175 per hour), which are a good way to explore the starkly beautiful landscape – a mixture of desert and the rocky hills – around town. It's best to ask your hotel, a travel agent or other travellers to recommend somebody who organises good trips.

For longer camel treks, Pushkar makes a convenient starting point. Trips start at around ₹700 per day, and head out to Jodhpur (six to seven days) and Jaisalmer (10 to 12 days). See p190 for general details about camel treks. Numerous operators line Panch Kund Marg.

RAJASTHAN PUSHKAR

🛏 Sleeping

Owing to Pushkar's status among backpackers, there are far more budget options than midrange, though many have a selection of midrange-priced rooms. At the time of the camel fair, prices multiply up to five times and it's essential to book several weeks, even months ahead.

TOP CHOICE Inn Seventh Heaven BOUTIQUE HOTEL **$$**
(📞5105455; www.inn-seventh-heaven.com; Chotti Basti; r ₹550-2400; ❄@) You enter this lovingly converted *haveli* through heavy wooden doors into an incense-perfumed courtyard, centred with a marble fountain. There are just 12 individually decorated rooms on three levels, with traditionally crafted furniture and comfortable beds. On the roof you'll find the excellent Sixth Sense restaurant as well as sofas and swing chairs for relaxing with a book.

Hotel Pushkar Palace HOTEL **$$$**
(📞2773001; www.hotelpushkarpalace.com; s/d from ₹4225/5150, ste ₹10,850; ❄@) Once belonging to the maharaja of Kishangarh, this top-end hotel boasts a romantic lakeside setting. Rooms have carved wooden furniture and beds, and the suites look directly onto the lake. There's also a pleasant outdoor dining area overlooking the lake.

Jagat Palace Hotel HOTEL **$$**
(📞2772953; www.hotelpushkarpalace.com; Ajmer Rd; s/d ₹3575/4225; ❄@) This is a lovely heritage-style hotel in new but traditional-style buildings resembling a palace. It's in a quiet spot on the town's outskirts and offers romantic bedrooms with carved wooden furniture and lovely bathrooms. There are tempting packages including meals and low-season discounts.

Hotel Everest HOTEL **$**
(📞2773417; www.pushkarhoteleverest.com; r ₹200-600, with AC ₹850; ❄@) This welcoming budget hotel is secreted in the quiet laneways north of Sadar Bazaarand, is convenient to the bazaar and the mela ground. The rooms are variable in size, colourful and spotless, and the beds are comfortable. The roof is a pleasant retreat for meals or relaxation.

Hotel Shannu's Ranch Inn BOUTIQUE HOTEL **$**
(📞2772043; http://shannus.weebly.com; Panch Kund Marg; r ₹600, ste ₹1200) Especially for horse lovers but not exclusively so, this relaxed, family-run hotel is just a short walk from the lake. There is a large garden compound featuring

PUSHKAR CAMEL FAIR

Come the month of Kartika, the eighth lunar month of the Hindu calendar and one of the holiest, Thar camel drivers spruce up their ships of the desert and start the long walk to Pushkar in time for Kartik Purnima (Full Moon). Each year around 200,000 people converge here, bringing with them some 50,000 camels, horses and cattle. The place becomes an extraordinary swirl of colour, sound and movement, thronged with musicians, mystics, tourists, traders, animals, devotees and camera crews.

Trading begins a week before the official fair (a good time to arrive to see the serious business), but by the time the RTDC *mela* (fair) starts, business takes a back seat and the bizarre sidelines (snake charmers, children balancing on poles etc) jostle onto centre stage. Even the cultural program is bizarre: moustache contests, turban-tying contests, or seeing how many people can balance on a camel.

It's hard to believe, but this seething mass is all just a sideshow. Kartik Purnima is when Hindu pilgrims come to bathe in Pushkar's sacred waters. The religious event builds in tandem with the camel fair in a wild, magical crescendo of incense, chanting and processions to dousing day, the last night of the fair, when thousands of devotees wash away their sins and set candles afloat on the holy lake.

Although fantastical, mystical and a one-off, it must be said that it's also crowded, touristy, noisy (light sleepers should bring earplugs) and tacky. Those affected by dust and/or animal hair should bring appropriate medication. However, it's a grand epic, and not to be missed if you're anywhere within camel-spitting distance.

It usually takes place in October or November and because dates can change the following are indicative only: 2 to 10 November 2011, 20 to 28 November 2012, 9 to 17 November 2013 and 1 to 8 November 2014.

the family home, separate guest accommodation and, of course, the stables housing Marc's beloved Marwari horses. The large suites easily accommodate a family of five.

Hotel Kanhaia Haveli HOTEL $
(☎2772146; http://pushkarhotelkanhaia.com; Chotti Basti; r ₹200-1200, s/d without bathroom ₹150/200; ❉@) With a vast range of rooms from cheap budget digs to AC suites you are sure to find a room and price that suits. As you spend more dosh the rooms get bigger and lighter with more windows and even balconies.

Bharatpur Palace HOTEL $
(☎2772320; bharatpurpalace_pushkar@yahoo.co.in; r ₹200-800; ❉) This rambling old building occupies one of the best spots in Pushkar, on the upper levels adjacent to Ghandi Ghat. It features aesthetic blue-washed simplicity: bare as bones rooms with unsurpassed views of the holy lake. There's a variety of rooms with or without bathrooms, running hot water and AC. Room 1 is the most romantic place to wake up: it's surrounded on three sides by the lake.

Sun-n-Moon HOTEL $
(☎2772883; r ₹400) With a neohippy vibe, the Sun-n-Moon has a lovely, serene courtyard surrounding a bodhi tree and a small shrine. It's a very quiet and relaxing place to stay in inexpensive, simple but clean rooms with excellent food.

Shri Shyam Krishna Guesthouse GUESTHOUSE $
(☎2772461; skguesthouse@yahoo.com; Sadar Bazaar; s/d ₹300/500, without bathroom ₹200/300) Housed in a lovely old blue-washed building with lawns and gardens, this guesthouse has ashram austerity and genuine friendly management. Some of the cheaper rooms are cell-like, though all share the simple, authentic ambience.

Hotel Navaratan Palace HOTEL $
(☎2772145; www.pushkarnavaratanpalace.co.in; s/d from ₹300/400, with AC from ₹600/700; ❉≋) Located close to the Brahma Temple, this hotel has a lovely enclosed garden with a fabulous pool (₹100 for nonguests), children's playground and pet tortoises. The rooms are clean, small and crammed with carved wooden furniture.

Pushkar Inn's Hotel HOTEL $$
(☎2772010; hotelpushkarinns@yahoo.com; Pushkar Lake; s/d ₹650/700, r with AC ₹1200; ❉) A charming little hotel comprising a row of clean and bright rooms, backed by a garden

and orchard, which catch the breeze from the lake, and that is mostly good, though some wafts are less than holy. The best rooms have lake views.

Hotel New Park
HOTEL $$

(☑2772464; www.newparkpushkar.com; Panch Kund Marg; s/d ₹1050/1200; ✳@✉) This quiet hotel is blissfully rural, located among fields of red roses, but still an easy walk to/from the lake. Smart, modern rooms with TVs and balconies overlook an inviting pool, gardens and a backdrop of hills.

Green Park Resort
HOTEL $$

(☑2773532; www.greenparkpushkar.com; Gurdwara Marg; s/d ₹800/1200; ✳✉) This welcoming place has 18 spiffy rooms all with marble floors, comfy beds and satellite TV. The swimming pool is big and inviting (₹30 for nonguests) and there's a relaxing rooftop restaurant. It's only a 10-minute stroll to town along a shady country lane.

Hotel Paramount Palace
HOTEL $

(☑2772428; hotelparamountpalace@hotmail.com; Bari Basti; r ₹200-1000) Perched on the highest point in town overlooking an old temple, this welcoming hotel has excellent views over the town and lake (and lots of stairs). The rooms vary widely. The best rooms (106, 108, 109) have lovely balconies, stained glass and are good value; smaller rooms can be dingy. There's a dizzyingly magical rooftop terrace.

Milkman Guesthouse
GUESTHOUSE $

(☑2773452; vinodmilkman@hotmail.com; Mali Mohalla; r ₹200-700, without bathroom ₹100; ✳@🛜) Milkman is a cosy guesthouse in a backstreet location with a relaxing rooftop retreat featuring the Ooh-la-la Café and a lawn with high-altitude tortoises. The widely varying rooms are all brightly decorated with paintings and though some of the cheaper rooms are small and doorways are low, the bright colours, cleanliness and friendly family atmosphere keep this place cheerful.

Hotel White House
GUESTHOUSE $

(☑2772147; www.pushkarwhitehouse.com; r ₹250-650, with AC ₹650-1350; ✳@) This place is indeed white with spotless rooms, though some rooms are decidedly on the small side and the stairwells are narrow and steep. There is good traveller fare and fine views from the plant-filled rooftop restaurant. Yoga is offered.

Mayur Guest House
GUESTHOUSE $

(☑2772302; www.mayurguesthouse.com; Holi ka Chowk; r ₹200-700, s without bathroom ₹100)

A pleasant blue-washed place, with neat, unspectacular rooms around a tiny leafy courtyard. Upstairs rooms have balconies and there's a cheerful welcome and more views from the rooftop.

Hotel Diamond
HOTEL $

(☑9829206787; Holi ka Chowk; r ₹300, s without bathroom ₹150-200) In a quiet part of town, Diamond has tiny cell-like rooms around a small tranquil courtyard. The better rooms with attached bathrooms are upstairs.

TOURIST VILLAGE

During the camel fair, the RTDC and many private operators set up a sea of tents near the fairground. You're advised to book ahead. These all have private bathroom.

RTDC Tourist Village
LUXURY TENTS $$

(☑2772074; s/d huts from ₹4500/5000, s/d tents from ₹6000/6500; ✳) This option has various permanent huts and semipermanent tents that are usually booked out by tour groups well in advance. Rates include all meals.

Royal Tents
LUXURY TENTS $$$

(www.jodhpurheritage.com; tents s/d ₹14,500/16,500; ✳) Owned by the former royal family of Jodhpur, these are probably the most luxurious tents you'll ever come across, with comfy beds, verandahs and deck chairs, and running hot and cold water. Note that meals cost extra.

Royal Desert Camp
LUXURY TENTS $$$

(☑2772001; www.hotelpushkarpalace.com; tents s/d ₹10,000/11,500; ✳) Further away from the fairground than Royal Tents, but another super luxurious option run by owners of Jagat Palace Hotel and Hotel Pushkar Palace. Again, note that meals are extra.

✖ Eating

Pushkar has plenty of atmospheric eateries with lake views and menus reflecting backpacker tastes and preferences. Strict vegetarianism, forbidding even eggs, limits the range of ingredients, but the cooks usually make up for this with imagination and by using fresh ingredients.

TOP CHOICE Sixth Sense
MULTICUISINE $

(Inn Seventh Heaven, Chotti Basti; mains ₹50-180; ⊙8.30am-4pm & 6-10pm) This chilled rooftop restaurant is a great place to head even if you didn't score a room in its popular hotel. Indian seasonal vegetables and rice, vegetable sizzlers, pasta and pizzas are all excellent. As are the filter coffee and fresh juice blends. Its ambience is immediately relaxing and the pulley apparatus that delivers the delicious food from the ground-floor kitchen is enthralling. Save room for the desserts, such as the excellent homemade tarts.

Little Italy
ITALIAN $
(Panchkund Marg; mains ₹80-200; ⊙10am-11pm) This superb garden restaurant has excellent thin-crust, wood-fired pizzas and imported pasta with tasty sauces. As well as homemade pesto and gnocchi, there are some Indian and Israeli dishes and fresh ground Keralan coffee.

Sunset Café
MULTICUISINE $
(mains ₹75-200; ⊙7.30am-midnight) Right on the eastern ghats, this cafe has sublime lake views. It offers the usual traveller menu, including curries, pizza and pasta, plus there's a German bakery serving OK cakes. The lakeshore setting is perfect at sunset and gathers a crowd.

Out of the Blue
MULTICUISINE $
(mains ₹50-180; ⊙8am-11pm) Distinctly a deeper shade of blue in this sky-blue town, Out of the Blue is a new addition to the horde of lakeview restaurants. The menu ranges from noodles and *momos* (Tibetan dumplings) to pizza, pasta and pancakes. A nice touch is the espresso coffee, which can also be enjoyed at street level.

Honey & Spice
MULTICUISINE $
(Laxmi Market off Sadar Bazaar; mains ₹75-120; ⊙7am-7pm) Run by a friendly man who is a mine of information, this tiny breakfast and lunch place has delicious South Indian coffee and home-made banana cake. Soups and hearty vegetable stews served with brown rice are thoroughly healthy.

Raju Terrace Garden Restaurant
MULTICUISINE $
(Sadar Bazaar; mains ₹40-90; ⊙10am-10pm) This relaxed rooftop restaurant serves lots of dishes for the homesick (for example, shepherd's pie, pizza and baked potatoes) and rather tame Indian food. It's on a pleasant terrace that's filled with pot plants and fairy lights and has great views of the lake. Note the service can be super slow.

Om Shiva
MULTICUISINE $
(☑5105045; mains ₹70-150; ⊙7.30am-late) This traveller stalwart continues to satisfy with its ₹80 buffet. Wood-fired pizzas and espresso coffee are new additions to the try-anything menu.

Baba Restaurant
MULTICUISINE $
(☑2772858; mains ₹60-120; ⊙8am-10pm) Tucked away, east of Sadar Bazaar, and open to the street, Baba has good pizzas and Israeli food and a chilled atmosphere.

Shopping
Pushkar's Sadar Bazaar is lined with enchanting little shops and is a good place for picking up gifts. Many of the vibrant textiles come from the Barmer district south of Jaisalmer. There's plenty of silver and beaded jewellery catering to foreign tastes, and some old tribal pieces, too. Coloured glass lamps are another appealing buy (you can ponder trying to get them home intact), as are embroidered and mirrored wall hangings. The range of Indian-music CDs makes this market an excellent place for sampling local tunes.

Information
Post office (off Heloj Rd,⊙9.30am-5pm) Near the Marwar bus stand.
Punjab National Bank ATM (Sadar Bazaar; ⊙9.30am-5pm Mon-Fri, to 4pm Sat) ATM inside branch accepts Cirrus and MasterCard but not Visa cards. There's a second ATM near the SBBJ ATM (north of the Brahma temple).
State Bank of Bikaner & Jaipur (SBBJ; Sadar Bazaar; ⊙10am-4pm Mon-Fri, to 12.30pm Sat) Changes travellers cheques and cash. The SBBJ ATM accepts international cards.
Thomas Cook (Sadar Bazaar; ⊙9.30am-6.30pm Mon-Sat) Changes cash and travellers cheques and also does train and flight ticketing.
Tourist Reception Centre (☑2772040; ⊙10am-5pm) In the grounds of RTDC Hotel Sarovar; staff will give out a free map.

Dangers & Annoyances
Priests – some genuine, some not – will approach you near the ghats and offer to do a *puja* (prayer) for which you'll receive a 'Pushkar passport' (a red ribbon around your wrist). Others proffer flowers (to avoid trouble, don't take any flowers you are offered). Some of these priests genuinely live off the donations of others and this is a tradition that goes back centuries. Others can be pushy and aggressive. Walk away if you feel bullied and agree on a price before taking a ribbon or flowers.

During the camel fair, Pushkar is besieged by pickpockets working the crowded bazaars. You can avoid the razor gang by not using thin-walled daypacks and by carrying your daypack in front of you. Fortunately, there is very little motorised traffic in the main bazaar, making it a pleasurable place to explore at leisure – though watch out for stray motorbikes.

Getting There & Away

Frequent buses to/from Ajmer (₹8, 30 minutes) stop on the road heading eastwards out of town; other buses leave from the Marwar bus stand to the north.

Local travel agencies sell tickets for private buses – you should shop around. These buses generally leave from Ajmer, but the agencies should provide you with free connecting transport. Those that leave from Pushkar usually stop for an hour or more in Ajmer anyway. Be warned that some buses (particularly those via Jodhpur) don't go all the way; in spite of promises, they'll involve a change of bus *and* an extra fare. Some destinations and fares from Pushkar:

DESTINATION	FARE (₹)	DURATION (HR)
Ajmer	express/local 8/7	½
Bundi	117	6
Delhi	ordinary/sleeper 200/300	10½
Jaipur	120	4
Jaisalmer	ordinary/sleeper 240/340	10½
Jodhpur	120	5

The post office will book train tickets for services out of Ajmer for about ₹15 commission. For around ₹50 private agencies do the same, including transfer to Ajmer.

Getting Around

There are no autorickshaws, but it's a breeze to get around on foot. Another good option is to hire a bicycle (₹30 per day) or a motorbike (₹200 to ₹250 per day, helmet ₹30 per day). Try **Shree Ganpati Motorbike Hire** (☑2772830; Brahma Rd), whose bikes have an all-Rajasthan tourist permit. A *wallah* can carry your luggage on a *thela* (hand-drawn cart) to/from the bus stand for around ₹30.

Ranthambhore National Park

☑ 07462

This famous national park, open from October to June, is the best place to spot wild tigers in Rajasthan. Comprising 1334 sq km of wild jungle scrub hemmed in by rocky ridges, at its centre is the amazing 10th-century Ranthambhore Fort. Scattered around the fort are ancient temples and mosques, hunting pavilions, crocodile-filled lakes and vine-covered *chhatris*. The park was a maharajas' hunting ground until 1970 – a curious 15 years after it had become a sanctuary.

Project Tiger has been in charge of the tiger population since 1979, but the project's difficulties were thrown into sharp relief when government officials were implicated in poaching in 2005. Getting an accurate figure on the number of tigers comes down to who you believe – the park probably has around 32 tigers, after the relocation of five tigers to Sariska Tiger Reserve (see p131).

Seeing a tiger is partly a matter of luck; you should plan on two or three safaris to improve your chances. But remember there's plenty of other wildlife to see including more than 300 species of birds.

It's 10km from the town of Sawai Madhopurto to the first gate and another 3km to the main gate and Ranthambore Fort. Accommodation is stretched out along the road from the town to the park. The train station is in the heart of Sawai Madhopur, just south of the main bazaar.

⊙ Sights

Safaris take place in the early morning and late afternoon. The mornings can be very chilly in the open vehicles, so bring some warm clothes. The best option is to travel by jeep gypsy. You still have a good chance of seeing a tiger from the canter, though sometimes other passengers can be rowdy.

Safaris (Indian/foreigner per person in gypsy ₹500/890, in canter ₹425/812; video camera ₹400) take three hours. In October canters and gypsies leave at 6.30am and 2.30pm; from November to January they leave at 7am and 2pm; from February to March they leave at 6.30am and 2.30pm; from April to May they leave at 6am and 3pm; and from May to June they leave at 6am and 3.30pm.

Be aware that the rules for booking safaris (and prices) are prone to change. Seats in gypsies and canters can be reserved on the official website (www.rajasthanwildlife.in). If you book online you will need to pay the balance at the Forest Office on the day of the safari or risk being cancelled. Cancelled seats are subsequently made available for direct booking. A single gypsy and five canters are also kept for direct booking at the **Forest Office** (Ranthambhore Rd; ⊙5.30am-7am & noon-2pm). Demand often outstrips supply during holiday seasons. Direct bookings on the day of the safari are best done through your hotel, which will send someone down to the Forest Office to obtain your ticket and naturally this will incur a small fee. This is the easiest way to do it, even though there is a dedicated window for foreigners at the Forest Office. If you do decide to do it yourself, be prepared for plenty of jostling and confusion.

🛏 Sleeping

TOP CHOICE Khem Villas BOUTIQUE HOTEL $$$
(☎252099; www.khemvillas.com; Ranthambhore Rd; s/d incl all meals & taxes ₹8000/9500, tents ₹10,600/14,000, cottages ₹14,000/17,000; ❄) This splendid option has been created by the Singh Rathore family – the patriarch Fateh Singh Rathore is lauded as the driving force behind the conservation of the tiger at Ranthambhore. His son Goverdhan, and his daughter-in-law Usha, run this impressive ecolodge set in 22 acres of organic farmland and re-afforested land. The accommodation ranges from rooms in the colonial-style bungalow to luxury tents to sumptuous stone cottages.

Hotel Tiger Safari Resort HOTEL $$
(☎221137; www.tigersafariresort.com; d incl breakfast ₹1280-1600; ❄@❄) This is one of the best options for those on a budget, with the helpful management adept at organising safaris, wake-up calls and early breakfasts before the morning safari. They can also organise pick-up and drop-off from the train station and sightseeing trips to the fort. The spacious doubles and so-called 'cottages' (larger rooms with bigger bathrooms) face a well-kept garden and small pool.

Hotel Ranthambhore Regency HOTEL $$$
(☎221176; www.ranthambhor.com; r ₹5500, s/d incl meals from US$135/165; ❄@❄) This is a very professional place that caters to tour groups but can still provide a good service to independent travellers. It has immaculate, well-appointed rooms (think marble floors, flat-screen TVs etc), which would rate as suites in most hotels.

Hotel Aditya Resort HOTEL $
(☎9414728468; www.adityaresort.com; r ₹400, without bathroom ₹250, with AC ₹750; ❄) This friendly place represents good value for money. There are just six simple, unadorned rooms and a cute rooftop restaurant. The keen young staff will help organise safari bookings.

Hotel Ankur Resort HOTEL $$
(☎220792; www.hotelankurresort.com; r incl breakfast ₹1500, cottages ₹2000; ❄@❄) Ankur Resort is another hotel that is good at organising safaris, wake-up calls and early breakfasts for tiger spotters. Standard rooms are clean and comfortable with TVs, if fairly unadorned. The cottages boast better beds and a settee overlooking the surrounding gardens with its inviting pool.

RTDC Castle Jhoomar Baori HOTEL $$
(☎220495; www.rtdc.in; s/d incl breakfast ₹3300/4300, ste ₹6000; ❄) This is a stunningly set hilltop former royal hunting lodge, about 7km from the train station (you can spot it from the train). The multichamber rooms are loaded with character, although they're a bit shabby in true RTDC style. Open-rooftop areas add appeal.

RTDC Vinayak Hotel HOTEL $$
(☎221333; www.rtdc.in; s/d ₹1900/2800, tents ₹1700/2600, with AC ₹2600/3500; ❄) This RTDC complex is close to the park entrance and, although institutional in atmosphere, has bright and spacious rooms generally better than typical RTDC rooms. The tents on concrete bases are less appealing. There's a nice lawn area and a campfire is lit in the winter.

🔒 Shopping

Dastkar Craft Centre HANDICRAFTS
(Ranthambhore Rd; ⊙10am-8pm) This workshop and outlet located beyond the park entrance, near Khem Villas, is well worth a visit. The organisation helps to empower low-caste village women, who gain regular income through selling their textile and embroidery work. Many attractive handicrafts are on sale, including saris, scarves, bags and bedspreads. There is another outlet about 3km from the train station. Beware of imitators.

ℹ Information

Bank of Baroda ATM (Bazariya Market) Located 200m northwest of the train station.

Post office (Sawai Madhoper) Located 400m northeast of the train station.

Project Tiger office (☎223402; Ranthambhore Rd) The office is 500m from the train station. Don't expect much in the way of information.

State Bank of Bikaner & Jaipur (SBBJ) The place to change cash or travellers cheques, also with an ATM. There's another ATM east of the entrance in the train station building and one on Hamir Circle near the start of Ranthambhore Rd.

Tiger Track (☑222790; Ranthambhore Rd; per hr ₹60; ◷7am-10.30pm) Near Ankur Resort Hotel. Offers internet access and a good range of books.

Tourist Reception Centre (☑220808; Train station; ◷9.30am-6pm Mon-Fri) This friendly office has a good, although not to scale, map of Sawai Madhopur and the park.

❶ Getting There & Away

Bus

Firstly, trains are preferable on all routes. Buses to Jaipur (₹110, six hours, four daily) via Tonk (₹44), and to Kota (₹86, five hours) via Bundi (₹74, 3½ hours) leave from the Bundi bus stand near the petrol station close to the overpass. Travelling to Bharatpur by bus invariably involves a change in Dausa (on the Jaipur–Bharatpur road). Buses to Jaipur (₹85, six hours) via Dausa (₹65, five hours) leave from the roundabout near the main post office.

Train

At Sawai Madhopur train station there's a computerised **reservation office** (◷8am-8pm Mon-Sat, to 2pm Sun).

The 12956 *Jaipur-Mumbai Express* departs Jaipur at 2.10pm, arriving at Sawai Madhopur (sleeper/3AC/2AC/1AC ₹140/275/355/585) at 4pm. Going the other way (No 12955) it departs Sawai Madhopur at 10.45am arriving at Jaipur at 12.50pm. The 12466 *Intercity Express* leaves Jaipur at 10.55am, arriving at Sawai Madhopur (2nd class/sleeper/AC chair/3AC ₹65/140/225/275) at 1.15pm. Going the other way, the 12465 *Ranthambhore Express* departs Sawai Madhopur at 2.40pm and reaches Jaipur at 4.40pm.

The 12903 *Golden Temple Mail* leaves Sawai Madhopur at 12.30pm, stopping at Bharatpur (sleeper/3AC/2AC/1AC ₹140/322/424/699) at 3pm and continuing to arrive at Delhi (₹187/469/628/1051) at 6.30pm. From Delhi (No 12904), it leaves at 7.40am, stopping at Bharatpur at 10.40am and arriving at 1pm. It then departs at 1.05pm and arrives at Kota (₹140/265/323/526) at 2.25pm. Another convenient train to Kota is the 19037/8 *Avadh Express*. It leaves Sawai Madhopur at 9.10am and arrives in Kota (sleeper/3AC/2AC ₹120/235/293) on Monday, Wednesday, Friday and Saturday at 10.50am. Going the other way, it departs from Sawai Madhopur at 4.20pm, arriving in Agra (₹130/335/454) at 9.50pm on Tuesday, Wednesday, Friday and Sunday.

❶ Getting Around

Bicycle hire is available in the main bazaar (around ₹30 per day). Autorickshaws are available at the train station; the journey to Ranthambhore Rd will cost around ₹40.

SOUTHERN RAJASTHAN

Bundi

☑0747 / POP 88,312

A captivating town with narrow lanes of Brahmin-blue houses, lakes, hills, bazaars and a temple at every turn, Bundi is dominated by a fantastical palace of faded-parchment cupolas and loggias rising from the hillside above the town. Though popular with travellers, Bundi attracts nothing like the tourist crowds of cities like Jaipur or Udaipur, nor are its streets choked with noisy, polluting vehicles or dense throngs of people. Few places in Rajasthan retain so much of the magical atmosphere of centuries past.

A group of Chauhan nobles from Ajmer, pushed south in the 12th century by Mohammed of Ghori, wrested the Bundi area from the Mina and Bhil tribes and made Bundi the capital of their kingdom, known as Hadoti.

◉ Sights

Bundi Palace   PALACE

(Garh Palace; Indian/foreigner ₹10/100, camera/video ₹50/100; ◷8am-5pm) This extraordinary, partly decaying edifice – described by Kipling as 'the work of goblins rather than of men' – almost seems to grow out of the rock of the hillside it stands on. Though large sections are still closed up and left to the bats, the rooms that are open hold a series of fabulous, fading turquoise-and-gold murals that are the palace's chief treasure. The palace was constructed in the reign of Rao Raja Ratan Ji Heruled (Ratan Singh; 1607–31) and added to by his successors.

If you are going up to Taragarh as well as the palace, get tickets for both at the palace entrance. Once inside the palace's Hathi Pol (Elephant Gate), climb the stairs to the Ratan Daulat or Diwan-e-Aam, a hall of public audience with a white marble coronation throne. You then pass into the Chhatra Mahal, added by Rao Raja Chhatra Shabji in 1644, with some fine but rather weathered

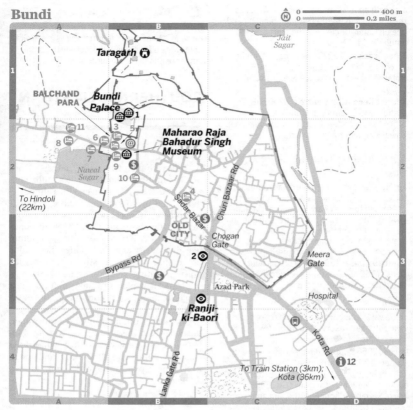

murals. Stairs lead up to the Phool Mahal (1607), whose murals include an immense royal procession, and then the Badal Mahal (Cloud Palace; also 1607), with Bundi's very best murals, including a wonderful Chinese-inspired ceiling, divided into petal shapes and decorated with peacocks and Krishnas.

FREE Chitrasala PALACE
(Ummed Mahal; ⊙dawn-dusk) To reach this small 18th-century palace built by Rao Ummed Singh, exit through Bundi Palace's Elephant Gate and walk round the corner uphill. Above the palace's garden courtyard are several rooms covered in beautiful paintings. There are some great Krishna images, including a detail of him sitting up a tree playing the flute after stealing the clothes of the *gopis* (milkmaids). The back room to the right is the Sheesh Mahal, badly damaged but still featuring some beautiful inlaid

glass, while in the front room there's an image of 18th-century Bundi itself.

Taragarh FORT
(Star Fort; Indian/foreigner ₹10/100, camera/video ₹50/100; ⊙8am-5pm) The ramshackle, partly overgrown 1354 Taragarh fort, on the hilltop above the palace, is great to ramble around – but take a stick to battle the overgrown vegetation, help the knees on the steep climb and provide confidence when surrounded by testosterone-charged macaques.

Maharao Raja Bahadur Singh Museum MUSEUM
(admission ₹50, camera ₹50; ⊙9am-1pm & 2-5pm) This museum is housed in the Moti Mahal, where the current royal descendants live. It is an extraordinary celebration of the lives of the more recent royal members. The first hall is stuffed with stuffed wildlife, chiefly tigers shot by Indian, British and American luminaries.

Baoris
NOTABLE BUILDINGS

Bundi has around 60 beautiful *baoris* (step-wells), some right in the town centre. The majesty of many of them is unfortunately diminished by their lack of water today – a result of declining groundwater levels – and by the rubbish that collects in them which no one bothers to clean up. The most impressive, **Raniji-ki-Baori** (Queen's Step-Well), is 46m deep and decorated with sinuous carvings, including the avatars of Lord Vishnu. The **Nagar Sagar Kund** is a pair of matching step-wells just outside the old city's Chogan Gate.

Old City
AREA

It's great to explore the ancient winding streets, gateways and bazaars of the old city, as well as the more touristic Balchand Para area below the palace. Bundi has more than 200 temples, and the market area just outside the Chogan Gate, around Nagar Sagar Kund, is the most vibrant area of town.

✲✲ Festivals

A visit in August or September might reward you with a glimpse of the cheerful festival of **Kajli Teej**, celebrating the arrival of the monsoon and a good chance to see local artists perform, while October or November sees **Bundi Utsav**, a cultural festival complete with music, dance, fireworks, a turban-tying competition and more, blaze through Bundi's quiet streets.

🛏 Sleeping & Eating

Most accommodation clusters in the Balchand Para area beneath the palace. Guesthouses and hotels provide the main eating options and many of them happily serve nonguests as well as guests. Most places will pick you up from the train station or bus stand if you call ahead. Bundi was once a dry town, so it's not a place for evening revelry; however, a cold beer can usually be arranged.

TOP CHOICE ⟩ Haveli Braj Bhushanjee
HERITAGE HOTEL **$$**

(📞2442322; www.kiplingsbundi.com; r ₹500-4500; ❄🈂) This rambling, authentic, 200-year-old *haveli* is run by the very helpful and knowledgeable Braj Bhushanjee family, descendants of the former prime ministers of Bundi. It's an enchanting place with original stone interiors (plenty of low doorways), splendid rooftop views, beautiful, well-preserved murals, and all sorts of other historic and valuable artefacts. The terrific range of accommodation includes some lovely, recently modernised rooms that are still in traditional style.

Hotel Bundi Haveli
BOUTIQUE HOTEL **$$**

(📞2447861; http://hotelbundihaveli.com; r ₹1000-2500, ste ₹4000; ❄) The exquisitely renovated Bundi Haveli certainly leads the pack in terms of up-to-date style and sophistication. Yes, it is very comfortable and relaxed and there's a lovely rooftop dining area boasting palace views and an extensive, mainly Indian menu (mains ₹90 to ₹250).

Haveli Katkoun
GUESTHOUSE **$**

(📞2444311; http://havelikatkoun.free.fr; s from ₹350, d ₹500-1800; ❄) Just outside the town's west gate, Katkoun is a totally revamped *haveli*. It boasts large, spotless rooms with superb views of the lake or palace and has a good courtyard restaurant (mains ₹65 to ₹200).

Kasera Heritage View   HERITAGE HOTEL $$
(☎2444679; www.kaseraheritageview.com; s/d ₹800/1000, AC from ₹1500/1800; ❋) Another revamped *haveli*, Kasera has an incongruously modern lobby but offers a range of slightly more authentic rooms. The welcome is friendly, it's all cheerfully decorated, the rooftop restaurant has great views, and discounts of 40% to 50% are frequently offered.

RN Haveli   GUESTHOUSE $
(☎2443278, 9784486854; rnhavelibundi@yahoo .co.in; Rawle ka Chowk; r ₹300-400, without bathroom ₹150-200, AC ₹1000-1200; ❋) This is an old, rambling house with a grassy garden, recently decorated rooms and delectable, home-cooked, vegetarian meals (mains ₹60 to ₹80). Run by a dynamic mother-and-two-daughters team, it's a place where solo female travellers will feel comfortable at once.

Hadee Rani Guest House   GUESTHOUSE $
(☎2442903; hadeeranipg@yahoo.com; Sadar Bazar; s ₹150-700, d ₹200-800) A friendly, enthusiastic family runs this three-centuries-old *haveli* with rooms of varied sizes up and down its staircases. It has a very good multicuisine restaurant (mains ₹50 to ₹200, thali ₹100 or ₹180).

Bundi Vilas   HERITAGE HOTEL $$
(☎5120694; www.bundivilas.com; r incl breakfast ₹2500-3000; ❋@) This 300-year-old *haveli* has been tastefully renovated with Jaisalmer sandstone, earth-toned walls and deft interior design. Rooms are medium sized, except for two larger ones next to the restaurant.

Shivam Tourist Guest House   GUESTHOUSE $
(☎2447892, 9214911113; www.shivam-bundi.co.in; r ₹250-800; ❋) Rooms are good and clean if a trifle Spartan. The energetic, talkative hosts offer good veg meals on the rooftop, plus classes in cooking, henna design and Hindi.

Haveli Uma Megh   GUESTHOUSE $
(☎2442191; haveliumamegh@yahoo.com; r ₹200-600) Has plenty of dilapidated charm, with wall paintings, alcoves and a lakeside garden for candlelit dinners (mains ₹40 to ₹60, thali ₹80 to ₹200). The pricier rooms are spacious.

ⓘ Information

There's an Axis Bank ATM on Sadar Bazar and a State Bank ATM west of Azad Park.

Front Page Cyber Cafe (Balchand Para; per hr ₹40; ◷8am-10pm) One of the less expensive places to check your email, and it has decent connections.

Tourist office (☎2443697; Kota Rd; ◷9.30am-6pm Mon-Fri) This very helpful office has bus and train schedules, and offers free maps and helpful advice on most practical questions you can toss at it.

ⓘ Getting There & Away

Bus

Bus journeys to and from Bundi are bone-rattlers, although the recently made four-lane Hwy 76, which you hit about halfway to Chittorgarh, has improved journeys in that direction. 'Express' government buses from the bus stand run to Kota (₹24, one hour, every 15 minutes), Chittorgarh (₹100, four hours, two evening buses), Udaipur (₹175, six hours, two evening buses), Ajmer (₹111, four hours, half-hourly), Jaipur (₹120, five hours, half-hourly), Sawai Madhopur (₹60, 4½ hours, four daily), Jodhpur (₹160, 10 hours, three daily), Delhi (₹270, 11 hours, three daily) and Indore (₹175, 12 hours, 8am and 11am). For Pushkar, change buses at Ajmer.

Private sleeper buses with similar seat prices to government buses launch around 10pm for Chittorgarh, Udaipur, Ajmer and Delhi (one each), but they are for thrill-seekers and sadomasochists only.

Train

The station is 4km south of the old city; trains are fewer but smoother and sometimes quicker than buses. The 12963 *Mewar Express* departs at 2.04am for Chittorgarh (sleeper/3AC/2AC/1AC ₹150/288/371/608, 2¾ hours) and Udaipur (₹167/399/527/874, 5¼ hours). In the other direction the 12964 *Mewar Express* leaves at 10.50pm for Delhi's Nizamuddin station (₹242/609/817/1375, 7¾ hours), stopping at Kota, Sawai Madhopur and Bharatpur en route. Two other trains go to Chittorgarh: the 59812 *Haldighati Passenger* at 7.20am (sleeper ₹90, 3¼ hours), and the 29020 *Dehradun Express* at 9.38am (sleeper/2AC/1AC ₹130/341/558, 3¼ hours). Eastbound, the 59811 *Haldighati Passenger* at 5.50pm heads to Sawai Madhopur (sleeper ₹90, 5½ hours) and Agra (₹119, 12 hours); the 29019 *Nimach–Kota Express* at 5.21pm heads to Kota, Sawai Madhopur (sleeper/2AC/1AC ₹130/362/593, four hours), Bharatpur and Delhi Nizamuddin (₹202/787/1325, 12 hours).

ⓘ Getting Around

Bicycles are an ideal way to get around this area. They are available at many guesthouses for around ₹30 or ₹40 per day. You can also hire motorbikes for ₹200 to ₹300 per day.

An autorickshaw to the train station costs ₹50 to ₹70 by day and ₹100 to ₹120 by night.

You can rent taxis for ₹700 to ₹1200 per day through your accommodation.

Kota

📞0744 / POP 695,899

Kota is an industrial and commercial town on Rajasthan's only permanent river, the Chambal, mainly worth visiting for its spectacular palace within the walled old city south of the centre. Originally part of the Bundi princedom, Kota separated in 1624 and subsequently became a larger and more powerful city and state than Bundi. Kishore Sagar lake marks the approximate centre of town.

◉ Sights & Activities

City Palace & Fort   PALACE, FORT
The fort and the palace within it make up one of the largest such complexes in Rajasthan. This was the royal residence and centre of power, housing the Kota princedom's treasury, courts, arsenal, armed forces and state offices. Some of its buildings are now used as schools. The **City Palace** (Indian/foreigner ₹10/100, camera/video ₹50/100; ⊙10am-4.30pm Sat-Thu), entered through a gateway topped by rampant elephants, contains the excellent **Rao Madho Singh Museum**, where you'll find all the stuff necessary for a respectable Raj existence – silver furniture, an old-fashioned ice-cream maker and ingenious, beautiful weapons. The oldest part of the palace dates from 1624. Downstairs is an elegant durbar (royal audience) hall with beautiful mirror work, while the elegant, small-scale apartments upstairs dance with exquisite, beautifully preserved paintings, particularly the hunting scenes for which Kota is renowned.

Boat Trips   BOATING
The Chambal River upstream of Kota is part of the Darrah National Park and once you escape the city it's beautiful, with lush vegetation and craggy cliffs on either side. It's an opportunity to spot birds, gharials (those thin-snouted, fish-eating crocodiles), muggers (those keep-your-limbs-inside-the-boat crocodiles) and possibly sloth bears. A 20-minute jaunt costs ₹40 per person; longer trips for up to six people are ₹1000 an hour. Boats start from **Chambal Gardens** (Indian/foreigner ₹2/5), 1.5km south of the fort on the river's east bank, and normally operate from 10.30am to sunset.

✦✦ Festivals & Events

If you happen to hit Kota in October or November, check whether your visit coincides with the city's huge **Dussehra Mela**, during which massive effigies are built then spectacularly set aflame.

🛏 Sleeping & Eating

All the hotels listed here, except Palkiya Haveli, are in the northern half of town between Kishore Sagar and the train station.

TOP CHOICE
Palkiya Haveli   HERITAGE HOTEL $$
(📞2387497; www.alsisar.com; palkiyahaveli@yahoo.com; Mokha Para; s/d ₹1800/2300, ste ₹2600; ✳)
This is an exquisite *haveli* that has been in the same family for 200 years. Set in a deliciously peaceful corner of the old city about 800m east of the City Palace, it's a lovely, relaxing place to stay, with welcoming hosts, a high-walled garden and a courtyard with a graceful neem tree. There are impressive murals and appealing heritage rooms, and the food is top notch.

Brijraj Bhawan Palace Hotel   HERITAGE HOTEL $$
(📞2450529; brijraj@dil.in; off Collectorate Circle, Civil Lines; s/d ₹2500/3550, ste ₹3700/4600; ✳)
High above the Chambal River, this charismatic hotel was built to house the British Residency and is still home to the head of the Kota royal house. The enormous, classically presented rooms, admittedly not refurbished very recently, open onto lofty verandas and terraces overlooking the river. The intimate dining room (for guests only) is, unlike those in most palaces, homey rather than grand.

Hotel Navrang   HOTEL $
(📞2323294; Collectorate Circle, Civil Lines; s/d ₹450/550, with AC ₹750/950; ✳) The Navrang's rooms are worn but good-sized and comfortable and arranged around a modern internal courtyard. The attached vegetarian **New South Indian Restaurant** (mains ₹50-90; ⊙9am-11pm) is OK, if slow.

ℹ Information

Tourist Reception Centre (📞2327695; RTDC Hotel Chambal; ⊙9.30am-6pm Mon-Sat) About 250m north of Kishore Sagar.

ℹ Getting There & Away

Bus
The central bus stand is just east of the Bundi Rd river bridge, 1km north of Kishore Sagar.

'Express' government buses head to Ajmer (₹133, six hours, half-hourly), Bundi (₹24, one hour, every 15 minutes), Chittorgarh (₹120, four hours, five daily), Jaipur (₹149, six hours, half-hourly), Jodhpur (₹225, 10 hours, six daily), Udaipur (₹195, seven hours, nine daily) and Delhi (₹224, 12 hours, eight daily). There's an AC deluxe bus to Jaipur (₹255, five hours) at 2.30pm, and a Volvo AC bus to Jaipur (₹370, five hours) and Delhi (₹900, 11 hours) at 11pm.

Train

Kota is on the main Mumbai–Delhi train route via Sawai Madhopur, so there are plenty of trains to choose from.

❶ Getting Around

Minibuses link the train station and central bus stand (₹6). An autorickshaw should cost ₹30 for this journey; there's a prepay place at the station.

Chittorgarh (Chittor)

✒ 01472 / POP 96,028

Chittorgarh, the fort *(garh)* at Chittor, is the greatest in Rajasthan, and is well worth re-shuffling an itinerary to explore. It rises from the plains like a huge rock island, nearly 6km long and surrounded on all sides by 150m-plus cliffs. Wandering around the plateau on top is like being on an island in the sky, or a gigantic boat, dotted with a collection of sublimely beautiful stone buildings. Chittorgarh's history epitomises Rajput romanticism, chivalry and tragedy, and it holds a special place in the hearts of many Rajputs. Three times Chittorgarh was under attack from a more powerful enemy; each time, its people chose death before dishonour, performing *jauhar.* The men donned saffron martyrs' robes and rode out from the fort to certain death, while the women and children immolated themselves on huge funeral pyres.

The first of Chittor's three great disasters occurred in 1303 when the Delhi sultan Ala-ud-din Khilji besieged the fort – according to legend, in order to capture the beautiful Padmini, the wife of the Mewar king Ratan Singh. When defeat was inevitable, the men rode out to die and the Rajput noblewomen, including Padmini, committed *jauhar.* Mewar recaptured the fort in 1326 and under Rana Kumbha (1433-68), a poet and musician as well as a military leader, Chittorgarh reached its cultural peak and Mewar attained its territorial zenith.

A siege by Bahadur Shah, the sultan of Gujarat, in 1535, precipitated the second great *jauhar,* in which, it's thought, 13,000 Rajput women and 32,000 Rajput warriors died. The final sacking of Chittor came just 33 years later, in 1568, when the Mughal emperor Akbar took the fort. Once again, the odds were overwhelming, and again the women performed *jauhar,* while 8000 orange-robed warriors rode out to certain death. On this occasion, Rana Udai Singh II fled to Udaipur, where he established a new capital for Mewar. In 1616, Jehangir returned Chittor to the Rajputs. There was no attempt at resettlement, though it was restored in 1905.

◉ Sights

TOP CHOICE **Chittorgarh Fort**   FORT

(Indian/foreigner ₹5/100; ☉sunrise-sunset) A zig-zag ascent of more than 1km leads through six outer gateways to the main gate on the

---

MAJOR TRAINS FROM KOTA

DESTINATION	TRAIN NUMBER & NAME	FARE (₹)	DURATION (HR)	DEPARTURE
Chittorgarh	29020 *Dehradun Express*	130/395/650 (A)	3¼	9am
Delhi (Nizamuddin)	12964 *Mewar Express*	230/576/770/1294 (B)	6½	11.55pm
Jaipur	12955 *Mumbai-Jaipur Express*	163/390/512/852 (B)	4	8.52am
Mumbai	12904 *Golden Temple Mail*	349/913/1237/2078 (B)	15	2.35pm
Sawai Madhopur	12059 *Shatabdi*	87/240 (C)	1¼	6am
Udaipur	12963 *Mewar Express*	179/433/573/955 (B)	6	1.25am

Fares: A – sleeper/2AC/1AC, B – sleeper/3AC/2AC/1AC, C – 2nd class/AC chair.

western side, the **Ram Pole** (the former back entrance). Inside Ram Pole is a village of perhaps 4000 people that occupies a small northwestern part of the fort. (Turn right here for the ticket office.) The rest of the plateau is deserted except for the wonderful palaces, towers and temples that remain from its heyday, with the addition of a few more recent temples. A loop road runs around the plateau, which has a deer park at the southern end.

There is a **Sound & Light Show** (Indian/foreigner ₹75/200; ☉sunset) at the Rana Kumbha Palace. The commentary is in English on days when the Palace on Wheels and Royal Rajasthan on Wheels tourist trains hit Chittor (Tuesday and Friday at research time).

Rana Kumbha Palace

Past the ticket office, you arrive almost immediately at this ruined palace group, which takes its name from the 15th-century ruler who renovated and added to earlier palaces on this site. The complex includes elephant and horse stables and a Shiva temple. Across from the palace is the **Sringar Chowri Temple**, a Jain temple built by Rana Kumbha's treasurer in 1448 and adorned with attractive, intricate carvings of elephants, musicians and deities.

Meera & Kumbha Shyam Temples

Both these temples southeast of the Rana Kumbha Palace were built by Rana Kumbha in the ornate Indo-Aryan style, with classic, tall *sikharas* (spires). The Meera Temple, the smaller of the two, is now associated with the mystic-poetess Meerabai, a 16th-century Mewar royal who was poisoned by her brother-in-law but survived due to the blessings of Krishna. The Kumbha Shyam Temple is dedicated to Vishnu and its carved panels illustrate 15th-century Mewar life.

Tower of Victory

The glorious Tower of Victory (Jaya Stambha), symbol of Chittorgarh, was erected by Rana Kumbha in the 1440s, probably to commemorate a victory over Mahmud Khilji of Malwa. Dedicated to Vishnu, it rises 37m in nine exquisitely carved storeys, and you can climb the 157 narrow stairs (the interior is also carved) to the 8th floor, from where there's a good view of the area.

Below the tower, to the southwest, is the Mahasati area where there are many *sati* (suicide by immolation) stones – this was the royal cremation ground and was also where 13,000 women committed *jauhar* in 1535. The **Samidheshwar Temple**, built

EXPLORING THE FORT

A typical vehicular exploration of the fort takes two to three hours. Guides charging around ₹350 for up to four hours are available for either walking or autorickshaw tours, usually at the ticket office. Make sure you get a government guide (they carry a guide licence).

in the 6th century and restored in 1427, is nearby. Notable among its intricate carving is a Trimurti (Three-Faced) figure of Shiva.

Gaumukh Reservoir

Walk down beyond the Samidheshwar Temple and at the edge of the cliff is a deep tank, the Gaumukh Reservoir, where you can feed the fish. The reservoir takes its name from a spring that feeds the tank from a *gaumukh* (cow's mouth) carved into the cliffside.

Padmini's Palace

Continuing south, you reach the **Kalika Mata Temple**, an 8th-century sun temple damaged during the first sack of Chittorgarh and then converted to a temple for the goddess Kali in the 14th century. Padmini's Palace stands about 250m further south, beside a small lake with a central pavilion. Legend relates that, as Padmini sat in this pavilion, Ala-ud-din Khilji saw her reflection in mirrors from the palace, and this glimpse convinced him to destroy Chittorgarh in order to possess her.

Surajpol & Tower of Fame

Surajpol, on the fort's east side, was the main gate and offers fantastic views across the empty plains. A little further north, the 24m-high Tower of Fame (Kirtti Stambha) is older (dating from 1301) and smaller than the Tower of Victory. Built by a Jain merchant, the tower is dedicated to Adinath, the first Jain *tirthankar* (one of the 24 revered Jain teachers) and is decorated with naked figures of various other *tirthankars,* indicating that it is a monument of the Digambara (sky-clad) order. Next door is a 14th-century Jain temple.

🛏 Sleeping & Eating

The modern town of Chittor below the fort's west side is an ordinary place, and its accommodation options are ordinary too. The best places to stay in the area are two heritage hotels in villages to the east.

Alternatively you can visit Chittorgarh as a long day-trip from Udaipur or as a half-day stopover between Udaipur and Bundi.

Castle Bijaipur HERITAGE HOTEL $$
(✆276351; www.castlebijaipur.com; r incl breakfast from ₹2500; ✳✦≋) This is a fantastically set 16th-century palace apparently plucked from the whimsy of Udaipur and dropped into a rural retreat 41km by road east of Chittorgarh. It's a great place to settle down with a good book, compose a fairy-tale fantasy or just laze around. Rooms are romantic and luxurious, and there is a pleasant garden courtyard and an airy restaurant serving Rajasthani food. Reservations should be made through the website or Chittorgarh's Hotel Pratap Palace. The owners can arrange transfer from Chittor as well as horse and jeep safaris, birdwatching, cooking classes, massage and yoga.

Bassi Fort Palace HERITAGE HOTEL $$
(✆225321; www.bassifortpalace.com; s/d incl breakfast ₹2000/2200) A glorious 450-year-old meringue of a place in Bassi village, 25km northeast of Chittorgarh. It's a peaceful spot with 18 lovely rooms sporting attractive murals and antique furnishings including bedside lamps made from chain-mail helmets. Buses to Bassi (₹13, 30 minutes) leave Chittorgarh's central bus stand about every half-hour.

Hotel Pratap Palace HOTEL $$
(✆240099; www.hotelpratappalacechittaurgarh.com; r ₹800-1000, AC s ₹1250-2500, d ₹1550-3000; ✳@) This is Chittor's best and friendliest option, with a wide range of rooms, a convenient location and travel-savvy staff. The more expensive rooms have window seats and leafy outlooks, and even a big mural (Room 209).

Hotel Nandan Palace HOTEL $$
(✆243314; hotel.nandanpalace2@gmail.com; Station Rd; s/d from ₹1900/2200; ✳@) New in 2010, this is a step up from other options near the train station, a business hotel with good-sized rooms in shades of orange and apricot, a lift and an Indian restaurant (mains ₹60 to ₹100). Discounts are often available.

Hotel Amber Plaza HOTEL $
(✆248862; 32 Kidwai Nagar; r without/with AC ₹500/900; ✳) Down a quietish street near the bus stand, this has quite comfy, medium-sized rooms with bright decorations (eg large posters of Versailles) and a restaurant.

ℹ Information

You can access an ATM and change money at the **SBBJ** (Bhilwara Rd), and there's an ATM at **SBI** (Bundi Rd).

Mahavir Cyber Cafe (Collectorate Circle; per hr ₹25; ◷8am-10pm)

Tourist Reception Centre (✆241089; Station Rd; ◷10am-1.30pm & 2-5pm Mon-Sat) Friendly and helpful, with a town map and brochure to give out.

ℹ Getting There & Away
Bus

'Express' services from the bus stand head to Delhi (₹354, 14 hours, two daily), Ajmer (₹120, four hours, frequent), Jaipur (₹180 to ₹192, seven hours, 19 daily), Udaipur (₹72, 2½ hours, half-hourly), Bundi (₹100, four hours, 10am) and Kota (₹120, four hours, eight daily), among other places. There are also a few 'deluxe' services to Jaipur (₹225).

Train

At least six daily trains head to Udaipur, including the 12963 *Mewar Express* at 7.20am (sleeper/3AC/2AC/1AC ₹150/280/344/561, 2¼ hours) and the 12992 *Ajmer–Udaipur Express* at 7.35pm (2nd class/AC chair ₹70/223, two hours). For Bundi there are four daily trains, including the 12964 *Mewar Express* at 8.50pm (sleeper/3AC/2AC/1AC ₹150/288/371/608, two hours) and the 29019 *Nimach–Kota Express* at 2.55pm (sleeper/2AC/1AC ₹130/341/558, 2½ hours).

The 12966 *Udaipur–Gwalior Super Express* leaves Chittorgarh at 12.35am and arrives in Jaipur (2nd class/sleeper/AC chair/3AC/2AC/1AC ₹112/191/376/467/619/1036) at 6am. There are also six or more trains daily to Ajmer.

ℹ Getting Around

It's about 6km from the train station to the fort (4km from the bus stand), and a further 9km to make a full loop around the fort (7km if you don't go south of Padmini's Palace). Autorickshaws charge around ₹200 from the bus or train station to go around the fort and come back (including waiting time). You'll have to haggle, and make sure it's clear that you're going to visit the sights and have time to look around.

Udaipur

✆0294 / POP 389,317

Beside shimmering Lake Pichola, with the ochre and purple ridges of the wooded Aravalli Hills stretching away in every direction, Udaipur has a romantic setting unmatched in Rajasthan and arguably in all India. Fantastical palaces, temples, *havelis* and count-less narrow, crooked, colourful streets add the human counterpoint to the city's natural charms. It's tag of 'the most romantic spot on the continent of India' was first applied in 1829 by Colonel James Tod, the East India Company's first Political Agent in the region. Today the romance is wearing ever so slightly thin as Udaipur strains to exploit it for tourist rupees. In the parts of the city nearest the lake, almost every building is a hotel, shop, restaurant, travel agent – or all four rolled into one – and noisy, dirty traffic clogs some of the streets that were made for people and donkeys.

Take a step back from the hustle, how-ever, and Udaipur still has its magic, not just in its marvellous palaces and monuments but in its matchless setting, the tranquil-lity of boat rides on the lake, the bustle of its ancient bazaars, the quaint old-world feel of its better hotels, its tempting shops, and lovely countryside to explore on wheels, feet or horseback.

Udaipur was founded in 1568 by Mahara-na Udai Singh II following the final sacking of Chittorgarh by the Mughal emperor Ak-bar. This new capital of Mewar had a much less vulnerable location than Chittorgarh. Mewar still had to contend with repeated invasions by the Mughals and, later, the Marathas, until British intervention in the early 19th century. This resulted in a treaty that protected Udaipur from invaders while allowing Mewar's rulers to remain effective-ly all powerful in internal affairs. The ex-roy-al family remains influential and in recent decades has been the driving force behind the rise of Udaipur as a tourist destination.

◉ Sights

Lake Pichola   LAKE
Limpid and large, Lake Pichola reflects the cool grey-blue mountains on its rippling mirror-like surface. It was enlarged by Ma-harana Udai Singh II, following his founda-tion of the city, by flooding Picholi village, which gave the lake its name. The lake is now 4km long and 3km wide, but remains shallow and dries up in severe droughts. The City Palace complex, including the gardens at its south end, extends nearly 1km along the lake's eastern shore.

The lake is allegedly home to a handful of crocodiles, believed to reside near un-inhabited sections of the shore (making it an unappealing option for swimming and wading).

Boat rides (adult/child 30min ₹200/100, 1hr ₹300/150, sunset ₹500/250; ☺10am-5pm) leave roughly hourly from Rameshwar Ghat in the City Palace gardens. Note that you also have to pay ₹25 to enter the City Palace complex. The one-hour trips (including sunset trips) make a stop at Jagmandir Island.

Jagniwas Island
The world-famous Lake Palace hotel island of Jagniwas is about 15,000 sq metres in size, entirely covered by the opulent palace built by Maharana Jagat Singh II in 1754. Once the royal summer palace, it was greatly ex-tended and converted into the **Lake Palace hotel** in the 1960s by Maharana Bhagwat Singh, and is now in the hands of the Indi-an-owned Taj hotel group. One of the world's top luxury hotels, with gleaming courtyards, lotus ponds and a pool shaded by a mango tree, it has been largely responsible for put-ting Udaipur on the international tourist map. You may also remember it from that classic Bond movie, *Octopussy,* along with the Shiv Niwas Palace and the Monsoon Pal-ace. The Taj Lake Palace doesn't welcome ca-sual visitors: the only time nonguests might be able to experience its magic is during the quietest seasons (eg May and June) when the hotel sometimes accepts outside reserva-tions for lunch or dinner.

Jagmandir Island
The palace on Jagmandir Island, about 800m south of Jagniwas, was built by Ma-harana Karan Singh in 1620, added to by his successor Maharana Jagat Singh, and then changed very little until the last few years when it was partly converted into another (small) hotel. When lit up at night it has more romantic sparkle to it than the Lake Palace. With its entrance flanked by a row of enormous stone elephants, the island has an ornate 17th-century tower, the Gol Ma-hal, carved from bluestone and containing a small exhibit on Jagmandir's history, plus a garden and lovely views across the lake. As well as the seven hotel rooms, the island has a restaurant, bar and spa, which are open to visitors.

TOP CHOICE **City Palace**   PALACE
(www.eternalmewar.in; adult/child ₹25/15, not charged if visiting City Palace Museum; ☺7am-11pm) Surmounted by balconies, towers and cupolas towering over the lake, the

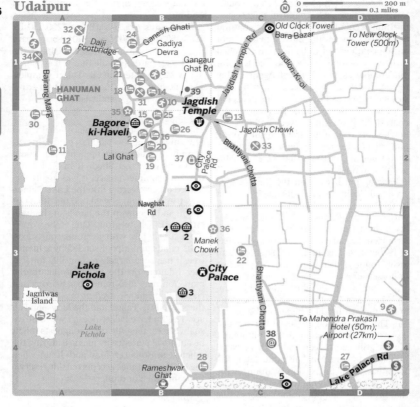

imposing City Palace is Rajasthan's largest palace, with a facade 244m long and 30.4m high. Construction was begun by Maharana Udai Singh II, the city's founder, and it later became a conglomeration of structures built and extended by various maharanas, though it still manages to retain a surprising uniformity of design.

You can enter the complex at the **Badi Pol** (Great Gate; 1615) at the palace's north end, or at the **Sheetla Mata Gate** on Lake Palace Rd. Tickets for the City Palace Museum are sold at both entrances. At Badi Pol you can rent an audio guide in English, French, German or Spanish for ₹250, or hire a human guide for ₹150 for up to five people.

Inside the Badi Pol, eight **arches** on the left commemorate the eight times maharanas were weighed here and their weight in gold or silver distributed to the lucky locals. You then pass through the three-arched **Tripolia Gate** (1711) into a large courtyard,

Manek Chowk. Spot the large tiger-catching cage, which worked rather like an oversized mousetrap, and the smaller one for leopards.

City Palace Museum

(adult/child ₹50/30, camera or video ₹200; ☺9.30am-5.30pm, last entry 4.30pm) The main part of the palace is open as the City Palace Museum, with rooms extravagantly decorated with mirrors, tiles and paintings and housing a large, varied collection of artefacts. It's entered from **Ganesh Chowk**, which you reach from Manek Chowk.

The City Palace Museum begins with the **Rai Angan** (Royal Courtyard), the very spot where Udai Singh met the sage who told him to build a city here. Rooms along one side contain historical paintings including several of the Battle of Haldighati (1576), in which Mewar forces under Maharana Pratap, one of the great Rajput heroes, gallantly fought the army of Mughal emperor Akbar to a stalemate. As you move through the palace, highlight spots include the **Baadi Mahal** (1699) where a pretty central garden gives fine views over the city. **Kishan (Krishna) Vilas** has a remarkable collection of miniatures from the time of Maharana Bhim Singh (1778–1828). The story goes that Bhim Singh's daughter Krishna Kumari drank a fatal cup of poison here to solve the dilemma of rival princely suitors from Jaipur and Jodhpur who were both threatening to invade Mewar if she didn't marry them. The **Surya Choupad** boasts a huge, ornamental sun – the symbol of the sun-descended Mewar dynasty – and opens into **Mor Chowk** (Peacock Courtyard) with its lovely mosaics of peacocks, the favourite Rajasthani bird. The south end of the museum comprises the **Zenana Mahal**, the royal ladies' quarters built in the 17th century. It now contains a long picture gallery with lots of royal hunting scenes. The Zenana Mahal's central courtyard, **Laxmi Chowk**, contains a beautiful white pavilion and a stable of howdahs, palanquins and other people carriers.

Crystal Gallery & Durbar Hall
(adult/child incl audio guide & drink ₹500/300; ☺9am-7pm) The Crystal Gallery houses rare crystal that Maharana Sajjan Singh ordered from F&C Osler & Co in England in 1877. The maharana died before it arrived, and all the items stayed forgotten and packed up in boxes for 110 years. The extraordinary, extravagant collection includes crystal chairs, sofas, tables and even beds. Below, and included on the same admission ticket – along with tea or a soft drink in the Gallery Restaurant – is the grand Durbar Hall, one of India's vastest and most lavish royal reception halls, with some of the country's hugest chandeliers. Tickets are available at the city palace gates or the Crystal Gallery entrance.

Government Museum
(admission free; ☺10am-5pm Tue-Sun) Entered from Ganesh Chowk, this has a splendid collection of jewel-like miniature paintings of the Mewar school and a turban that belonged to Shah Jahan, creator of the Taj Mahal. Stranger exhibits include a stuffed monkey holding a lamp.

Jagdish Temple   HINDU TEMPLE
(☺5.30am-2pm & 4-10pm) Entered by a steep, elephant-flanked flight of steps 150m north of the City Palace's Badi Pol entrance, this busy Indo-Aryan temple was built by Maharana Jagat Singh in 1651. The wonderfully carved main structure enshrines a black stone image of Vishnu as Jagannath, Lord of the Universe; there's a brass image of the Garuda (Vishnu's man-bird vehicle) in a shrine facing the main structure.

Bagore-ki-Haveli   NOTABLE BUILDING
(admission ₹30; ☺10am-5pm) This gracious 18th-century *haveli,* set on the water's edge in the Gangaur Ghat area, was built by a Mewar prime minister and has been carefully restored. There are 138 rooms set around courtyards, some arranged to evoke the period during which the house was inhabited, and others housing cultural displays, including – intriguingly enough – the world's biggest turban. The *haveli* also houses an interesting art gallery, featuring contemporary and folk art, and an eclectic selection of world-famous monuments lovingly carved out of polystyrene.

Sajjan Garh (Monsoon Palace)   PALACE
Perched on top of a distant mountain like a fairy-tale castle, this melancholy, neglected late 19th-century palace was constructed by Maharana Sajjan Singh. Originally an astronomical centre, it became a monsoon palace and hunting lodge. Now government owned, it's in a sadly dilapidated state but visitors stream up here for the marvellous views, particularly at sunset. It's 5km west of the old city as the crow flies, about 9km by the winding road. At the foot of the hill you enter the 5-sq-km **Sajjan Garh Wildlife Sanctuary** (Indian/foreigner ₹10/80, car ₹60, camera/video free/₹200). A good way to visit is with the daily sunset excursion in **taxi No RJ-27-TA 2108** (☏9784400120; per person ₹200), a minivan, which leaves Udaipur's Gangaur Ghat at 5pm daily; the charge does not include the sanctuary fees. Autorickshaws charge ₹200 including waiting time for a round trip to the sanctuary gate, which they are not allowed to pass. Taxis ferry people the final 4km up to the palace for ₹100 per person.

Vintage & Classic Car Collection   MUSEUM
(Garden Hotel, Garden Rd; admission ₹150, incl lunch or dinner ₹250; ☺9am-9pm) The maharanas' car collection makes a fascinating diversion, for what it tells about their elite lifestyle and for the vintage vehicles themselves. Housed in the former state garage are 22 splendid vehicles, including a seven-seat 1938 Cadillac complete with purdah system, the beautiful 1934 Rolls-Royce Phantom used in *Octopussy* and the Cadillac convertible that whisked Queen Elizabeth II to the airport in 1961. If you enjoy a vegetarian thali, the combined museum-and-meal ticket is a very good option (lunch 11.30am to 3pm, dinner 7.30pm to 10pm).

Saheliyon-ki-Bari   GARDEN
(Garden of the Maids of Honour; admission ₹5; ☺8am-7pm) In the north of the city, the Saheliyon-ki-Bari was built by Sangram Singh II in 1710. This small, quaint ornamental garden was laid out for the enjoyment of 48 women attendants who came as part of a princess' dowry and has beautiful, well-maintained fountains (water shortages permitting), kiosks, marble elephants and a delightful lotus pool.

🏃 **Activities**

Horse Riding
The wooded hills, villages and lakes around Udaipur make lovely riding country. Several operators offer horse rides from a couple of hours to multiday safaris. Expect to pay about ₹900 for a half-day ride, including lunch or snacks and transport to/from your hotel.

ANIMAL AID UNLIMITED

This spacious **animal refuge** (☑9950531639, 9829596637; www.animalaidunlimited .com) treats around 250 street animals a day (mainly dogs, donkeys and cows) and answers more than 3000 emergency rescue calls a year. The refuge welcomes volunteers and visitors: make contact in advance to fix a time between 9am and 5pm any day. It's in Badi village, 7km northwest of Udaipur: a round trip by autorickshaw, including waiting time, costs around ₹250. Call Animal Aid Unlimited if you see an injured or ill street animal in Udaipur.

Krishna Ranch   HORSE RIDING
(☑9828059505; www.krishnaranch.com) In beautiful countryside near Badi village; experienced owner-guide Dinesh Jain leads most trips himself.

Princess Trails   HORSE RIDING
(☑3096909, 9829042012; www.princesstrails. com; city office Boheda Haveli, Kalaji Goraji) A recommended Indian-German operation offering extended horse safaris and half-day nature rides.

Massage

Ayurvedic Body Care   AYURVEDA
(☑2413816; www.ayurvedicbodycare.com; 39 Lal Ghat; ☺10.30am-9pm) A small and popular old-city operation offering ayurvedic massage at reasonable prices, including a 15-minute head or back massage (₹250) and a 45-minute full-body massage (₹750). It also has ayurvedic products such as oils, moisturisers, shampoos and soaps for sale.

Walking

Exploring the surrounding countryside and villages on foot is a fantastic way to see rural and tribal life while taking in some beautiful scenery.

Mountain Ridge   WALKING
(☑3291478, 9602192902; www.mountainridge .in; Sisarma; half-day trek per person ₹650) This British-run homestay 6km west of town has pioneered country walking around Udaipur. The trips, with local tribal guides, include morning pick-up in Udaipur, lunch and a ride back to town afterwards.

⚡ Courses

Cooking

Spice Box   COOKING
(☑2424713; www.spicebox.co.in; 38 Lal Ghat; 2-3hr class ₹750) Shakti Singh from this spice, tea, oils and incense shop offered Udaipur's orig-

inal cooking classes and they are still recommended. Recipes are all vegetarian but the curries are good with meat too.

Queen Cafe   COOKING
(☑2430875; 14 Bajrang Marg; 2/4hr class ₹900/1400) The four-hour introductory class with Meenu, composer of many of this little eatery's delicious dishes, encompasses a grand 14 veg items.

Shashi Cooking Classes   COOKING
(☑9929303511; www.shashicookingclasses. blogspot.com; Sunrise Restaurant, 18 Gangaur Ghat Rd; 4hr class ₹500) Readers rave about Shashi's high-spirited classes (maximum four students), teaching many fundamental Indian dishes.

Music

Prem Musical Instruments   MUSIC
(☑2430599; 28 Gadiya Devra; per hr ₹200) Rajesh Prajapati (Bablu) is a successful local musician who gives sitar, tabla and flute lessons. He also sells and repairs those instruments and can arrange performances.

Painting

Hotel Krishna Niwas   PAINTING
(☑2420163; www.hotelkrishnaniwas.com; 35 Lal Ghat; 2hr class ₹600) Jairaj Soni is a renowned artist who teaches miniature and classical painting.

Ashoka Arts   PAINTING
(Hotel Gangaur Palace, Gadiya Devra; per hr ₹150) Here you can learn the basics of classic miniature painting.

☞ Tours

City tours (per person excl admission charges ₹140) run by the Rajasthan Tourism Development Corporation (RTDC) leave at 8.30am from the RTDC Hotel Kajri by Shastri Circle (400m northeast of Delhi Gate), and take in the main sights in 4½ hours.

Contact the Tourist Reception Centre for more information.

✯ Festivals & Events

In March or April the procession-heavy **Mewar Festival** is Udaipur's own version of the springtime Gangaur festival, with free cultural programmes.

🛌 Sleeping

Accommodation clusters where most people want to stay – close to the lake, especially on its eastern side in and near the narrow street Lal Ghat. This area is a tangle of streets and lanes (some quiet, some busy and noisy), close to the City Palace and Jagdish Temple. It's Udaipur's tourist epicentre and the streets are strung not just with lodgings but also with tourist-oriented eateries and shops whose owners will be doing their best to tempt you in.

Directly across the water from Lal Ghat, Hanuman Ghat has a slightly more local vibe and often better views, though you're certainly not out of the touristic zone.

Discounts are often available outside the peak tourist seasons.

To bypass rapacious rickshaw drivers looking for commissions from hotels, use the prepaid autorickshaw stands outside the train and bus stations (if they are operating). If you're heading for the Lal Ghat area to find accommodation, you can avoid discussions about individual lodgings by taking a rickshaw to the nearby Jagdish Temple, which should cost ₹30.

LAL GHAT AREA

Jagat Niwas Palace Hotel HERITAGE HOTEL **$$**
(☑2420133; www.jagatniwaspalace.com; 23-25 Lal Ghat; r ₹1750-3950, ste ₹6350; ❄@🛜) This leading midrange hotel set in two converted lakeside *havelis* takes the location cake. The lake-view rooms are charming, with carved wooden furniture, cushioned window seats and pretty prints. Non-lake-facing rooms are almost as comfortable and attractive, and considerably cheaper. The building is full of character with lots of attractive sitting areas, terraces and courtyards, and it makes the most of its position with a picture-perfect rooftop restaurant.

Jaiwana Haveli HOTEL **$$**
(☑2411103; www.jaiwanahaveli.com; 14 Lal Ghat; s/d ₹1890/1990; ❄@🛜) Professionally run by two helpful, efficient brothers, this smart

midrange option has spotless, unfussy rooms with good beds, some decorated with attractive block-printed fabrics. Book corner room 11, 21 or 31 for views.

Poonam Haveli HOTEL **$$**
(☑2410303; www.hotelpoonamhaveli.com; 39 Lal Ghat; r ₹800-1600, ste ₹2000; ❄@🛜) A fairly modern place decked out in traditional style, friendly Poonam has 16 spacious, spotlessly clean rooms with big beds and spare but tasteful decor, plus pleasant sitting areas. None of the rooms enjoy lake views, but the rooftop restaurant does, and boasts 'real Italian' pizzas among the usual Indian and traveller fare.

Nukkad Guest House GUESTHOUSE **$**
(☑2411403; nukkad_raju@yahoo.com; 56 Ganesh Ghati; r ₹300-500, s/d without bathroom ₹100/200; @) Always busy with travellers, Nukkad has a relaxed atmosphere and a sociable, breezy, upstairs restaurant with very good Indian and international dishes (mains ₹60 to ₹85). Your hosts Raju and Kala are most helpful and you can join afternoon cooking classes and morning yoga sessions without stepping outside the door. Rooms are simple, fan-cooled, very clean and good value; there's plenty of hot water and many rooms have cushioned window seats.

Mewar Haveli HOTEL **$$**
(☑2521140; www.mewarhaveli.com; 34-35 Lal Ghat; r ₹990-1620; ❄@🛜) Mewar is a good midranger with excellent staff who oversee sun-filled rooms with good beds. It has a nice, clean, fresh feel, with bright fabrics and wall paintings. All rooms are AC and most have lake views.

Pratap Bhawan Paying Guest House GUESTHOUSE **$**
(☑2560566; 12 Lal Ghat; r ₹500-800) A curving marble staircase leads up from the wide lobby to large, sparkling-clean rooms with good, big bathrooms and in many cases cushioned window seats. Recently taken over by friendly new management, this place will probably get even better.

Hotel Minerwa HOTEL **$**
(☑2523471; www.hotelminerwaudaipur.com; 5/13 Gadiya Devra; r ₹300-700, with AC ₹900; ❄@🛜) A good-value, new-on-the-scene budget bet with clean rooms that is proving pretty popular. Rooms improve in size, decor and views as you go up the price scale: a few have lake glimpses. The pleasant, well-priced, two-level roof restaurant has a floor-cushion zone.

Hotel Baba Palace
HOTEL $$

(☎2427126; www.hotelbabapalace.com; Jagdish Chowk; s ₹950, d ₹1400-2800; 🖵🛜) This slick hotel has spotless, fresh rooms with decent beds behind solid doors, and offers free train station or airport pick-ups. It's eye to eye with Jagdish Temple so many of them have interesting views; all rooms have AC and TVs. On top there's the first-rate Mayur Rooftop Cafe.

Hotel Lake Ghat Palace
HOTEL $$

(☎2521636; http://lakeghatpalace.com; 23/165 Lal Ghat; s ₹600-800, d ₹500-1900; 🖵🛜) Some of the smart, biggish rooms at this travellers' hot spot have views, others have balconies, and all are decorated with stained glass. The rooms are set around a small atrium, about six storeys high and hung with plants; there are splendid views from the roof and a good multicuisine restaurant (mains ₹60 to ₹120).

Jheel Palace Guest House
GUESTHOUSE $$

(☎2421352; www.jheelguesthouse.com; 56 Gangaur Ghat; r ₹1800-2800; 🖵) Right on the lake edge (when the lake is full), Jheel Palace has three nice rooms with little balconies and four-poster beds, and three more ordinary ones. All are AC. Staff are accommodating and hands-off, and there's a good Brahmin pure veg rooftop restaurant (no beer).

Hotel Krishna Niwas
HOTEL $$

(☎2420163; www.hotelkrishnaniwas.com; 35 Lal Ghat; d ₹1350-1650; 🖵@) Run by an artist family, Krishna Niwas has smart, clean, all AC rooms; those with views are smaller, and some come with balconies. There are splendid views from the rooftop, and a decent restaurant. Or you can eat your own cooking after taking a lesson here.

Lalghat Guest House
GUESTHOUSE $

(☎2525301; lalghat@hotmail.com; 33 Lal Ghat; dm ₹100, r ₹400-1500; 🖵@) This mellow guesthouse by the lake was one of the first to open in Udaipur, and it's still a sound choice, with an amazing variety of older and newer rooms. Most rooms have lake views and those in the older part of the building generally have more character. There's a small kitchen for self-caterers.

Kankarwa Haveli
HERITAGE HOTEL $$

(☎2411457; www.kankarwahaveli.com; 26 Lal Ghat; s ₹1100-1650, d ₹1250-2200; 🖵@🛜) This is one of Udaipur's few hotels that are genuine old *havelis*. It's right by the lake, and the whitewashed rooms, set around a courtyard, have a lovely simplicity with splashes of colour.

The pricier ones look right onto Lake Pichola; the cheapest lack AC.

Hotel Gangaur Palace
HERITAGE HOTEL $

(☎2422303; www.ashokahaveli.com; Gadiya Devra; s ₹400-2000, d ₹500-2500; 🖵) This elaborate, faded *haveli* is set around a stone-pillared courtyard, with a wide assortment of rooms on several floors. It's gradually moving upmarket and rooms range from windowless with flaking paint to bright and recently decorated with lake views. The hotel also boasts an in-house palm reader, an art school, the good Cafe Namaste and a rooftop restaurant.

Hotel Pichola Haveli
HOTEL $$

(☎2413653; info@picholahaveli.com; 64 Gangaur Ghat; s/d ₹1200/1500; 🖵@🛜) A sound choice with medium-sized heritage-style rooms, friendly and helpful management, and a quiet location. Lake Pichola, across the street, is visible from some rooms and the pleasant rooftop restaurant.

HANUMAN GHAT AREA
Amet Haveli
HERITAGE HOTEL $$

(☎2431085; www.amethaveliudaipur.com; s/d/ste ₹4000/5000/6000; 🖵@🛜🏊) This 350-year-old heritage building on the lake shore has delightful rooms with cushioned window seats and coloured glass with little shutters. They're set around a pretty little courtyard and pond. Splurge on one with a balcony or giant bathtub. One of Udaipur's most romantic restaurants, Ambrai, is part of the hotel.

Dream Heaven
GUESTHOUSE $

(☎2431038; www.dreamheaven.co.in; Hanuman Ghat; r ₹150-600; 🖵) A deservedly popular place to come to a halt, with spick-and-span rooms featuring wall hangings and paintings. Bathrooms are smallish, though some rooms have a decent balcony and/or views. The food at the rooftop restaurant (dishes ₹40 to ₹90), which overlooks the lake and shows Udaipur at its best, is fresh, tasty and highly recommended – the perfect place to chill out on a pile of cushions.

Udai Kothi
HOTEL $$$

(☎2432810; www.udaikothi.com; Hanuman Ghat; r ₹4000-10,000; 🖵@🛜🏊) A bit like a five-storey wedding cake, Udai Kothi is a glittery, modern building with lots of traditional touches – cupolas, interesting art and fabrics, window seats in some rooms, marble bathrooms and carved-wood doors in others, and thoughtful touches such as bowls of floating flowers. The apex is the roof terrace, where you can dine well and swim in Udaipur's *only* rooftop pool (nonguests ₹300).

LAKE PALACE ROAD AREA

TOP CHOICE **Mahendra Prakash Hotel**　　HOTEL $$
(🗷2419811; www.hotelmahendraprakash.com; r ₹1400-3000; ❋@🗑🏊) Spacious gardens, spick-and-span rooms well furnished in traditional style, a cheery atmosphere and friendly staff are the name of the game at the very well-run Mahendra Prakash. There's a fabulous lawn (nonguests ₹100), a decent restaurant and a lawn with tortoises. Rooms at the top have private balconies and City Palace views.

Kumbha Palace　　GUESTHOUSE $
(🗷2422702, 9828059505; www.hotelkumbha palace.com; 104 Bhattiyani Chotta; r ₹300-450, with AC ₹900; ❋@) This excellent place run by a Dutch-Indian couple is tucked up a quiet lane off busy Bhattiyani Chotta and is backed by a lovely lush lawn. The 10 rooms are simple but comfortable (just one has AC), and the restaurant knows how to satisfy homesick travellers. The owners also run Krishna Ranch, where excellent horse riding and cottage accommodation are on offer.

Rangniwas Palace Hotel　　HERITAGE HOTEL $$
(🗷2523890; www.rangniwaspalace.com; Lake Palace Rd; s ₹880-2200, d ₹990-2500, ste s/d ₹3000/3500; ❋🏊🗑) This 19th-century palace boasts plenty of heritage character and a peaceful central garden with a small pool. The quaint rooms in the older section are the most appealing, while the suites – full of carved wooden furniture and terraces with swing seats – are divine.

CITY PALACE

Shiv Niwas Palace Hotel　　HERITAGE HOTEL $$$
(🗷2528016; www.hrhhotels.com; City Palace Complex; r ₹12,000, ste ₹24,000-80,000; ❋@🗑🏊) This hotel, in the former palace guest quarters, has opulent common areas like its pool courtyard, bar and lovely lawn garden with a 30m-long royal procession mural. Some of the suites are truly palatial, filled with fountains and silver, but the standard rooms are not great value. Go for a suite, or just go for a drink, meal, massage, or swim in the gorgeous marble **pool** (nonguests ₹300; ⊙9am-6pm). Rates drop dramatically from April to September.

OTHER AREAS

TOP CHOICE **Taj Lake Palace**　　HERITAGE HOTEL $$$
(🗷2428800; www.tajhotels.com; r ₹37,500-43,500, ste from ₹150,000; ❋@🗑🏊) The icon of Udaipur, this romantic white-marble palace seemingly floating on the lake is extraordinary, with open-air courtyards, lotus ponds and a small, mango-tree-shaded pool. Rooms are hung with breezy silks and filled with carved furniture. Service is superb. Access is by boat from the hotel's own jetty in the City Palace gardens. Rates can vary a lot with season and demand: check the website.

TOP CHOICE **Udaivilas**　　HOTEL $$$
(🗷2433300; www.oberoihotels.com; r ₹35,000-40,500, ste ₹180,00-250,000; ❋@🗑🏊) In lovely grounds running down to the northwest shore of Lake Pichola, 2km west of the old city by road, Udaivilas' butter-sculpture domes are breathtaking. It's a beautifully designed, luxurious but personal hotel that doesn't spare the glitz or gold leaf, and the suites and many rooms even come equipped with private or semiprivate pools. The hotel houses three fine restaurants and a plush spa.

Mountain Ridge　　HOMESTAY $$
(🗷3291478, 9602192902; www.mountainridge. in; Sisarma; r incl breakfast & dinner ₹1950-3950; 🏊) This country homestay run by a resident Briton makes a great alternative to the city noise and hustle, and a good base for exploring the Udaipur countryside. It's a lovely stone-built house with five spacious rooms and great views, perched on a hilltop near Sisarma village, 6km from the city centre. Guided hikes and birdwatching, yoga, yummy food and free cooking lessons are all available here. An autorickshaw/taxi from town costs around ₹100/300.

🍴 Eating

Udaipur has scores of sun-kissed rooftop cafes, many with mesmerising lake views but often with uninspired multicuisine fare. Fortunately there's also a healthy number of places putting a bit more thought into their food, and the beer is plentiful.

LAL GHAT AREA

Jagat Niwas Palace Hotel　　INDIAN $$
(🗷2420133; 23-25 Lal Ghat; mains ₹120-300; ⊙6.30am-10.30am, noon-3.30pm & 7-10pm) A wonderful, classy, rooftop restaurant with superb lake views, delicious Indian cuisine

and good service. Choose from an extensive selection of rich curries (tempered for Western tastes) – mutton, chicken, fish, veg – as well as the tandoori classics. There's a tempting cocktail menu and the beer is icy. It's wise to book ahead for dinner.

Lotus Cafe
MULTICUISINE $

(15 Bhattiyani Chotta; dishes ₹50-120; ☺9am-10.30pm) This funky little restaurant plucks out fabulous chicken dishes (predominantly Indian), plus salads, baked potatoes and plenty of vegetarian fare. It's ideal for meeting and greeting other travellers, with a mezzanine to loll about on and cool background sounds.

Cafe Edelweiss
CAFE $

(73 Gangaur Ghat Rd; snacks ₹30-80; ☺7am-7pm) The Savage Garden restaurant folks run this itsy piece of Europe that appeals to homesick and discerning travellers with superb baked goods and good coffee. If sticky cinnamon rolls, squidgy blueberry chocolate cake, spinach-and-mushroom quiche or apple strudel don't appeal, give it a miss.

Cafe Namaste
CAFE $

(Gadiya Devra; cakes, pies, breakfast dishes ₹20-80; ☺7.30am-9.30pm) A European-themed streetside cafe at the Gangaur Palace Hotel that delivers the goods with scrumptious muffins, apple pies, cinnamon rolls, brownies etc. And to wash it down there is coffee from a shiny silver espresso machine (₹40 to ₹70) taking pride of place. The noisy street is a minus.

HANUMAN GHAT AREA

TOP CHOICE Ambrai
NORTH INDIAN $$

(☑2431085; Amet Haveli hotel; mains ₹145-325; ☺12.30-3pm & 7.30-10.30pm) The cuisine at this scenic restaurant – at lake-shore level, looking across to Lake Palace Hotel, Lal Ghat and the City Palace – does justice to its fabulous position. Highly atmospheric at night, Ambrai feels like a French park, with its wrought-iron furniture, dusty ground and large shady trees, and there's a terrific bar to complement the dining.

Jasmin
MULTICUISINE $

(mains ₹50-80) Very tasty vegetarian dishes are cooked up here in a lovely, quiet, open-air spot looking out on the quaint Daiji footbridge. There are plenty of Indian options, and some original variations on the usual multicuisine theme including Korean and Israeli dishes. The ambience is super-relaxed and service friendly.

Queen Cafe
INDIAN $

(14 Bajrang Marg; mains ₹60-75; ☺8am-10pm) This homey little eatery with just a couple of tables serves up fabulous home-style Indian vegetarian dishes. Try the pumpkin curry with mint and coconut, and the Kashmir pulao with fruit, vegies and coconut. Don't pass on the chocolate desserts either!

CITY PALACE

Note that you have to pay ₹25 to enter the City Palace complex if you're not staying in one of its hotels.

Paantya Restaurant
MULTICUISINE $$$

(☑2528016; Shiv Niwas Palace Hotel; mains ₹500-1400) Most captivating in the evening, this semiformal restaurant in the ritzy Shiv Niwas Palace has indoor seating, but if the weather's warm enough it's best out in the open-air courtyard by the pool. Indian classical music is performed nightly, and the food is great. For local flavour try the very tasty *laal maas dhungar*, a Rajasthani spiced and smoked mutton dish.

Gallery Restaurant
CONTINENTAL $$$

(Durbar Hall; Durbar tea ₹325; ☺9am-6pm) Alongside the splendiferous Durbar Hall, this elegant little restaurant has beguiling views across Lake Pichola. It does snacks and a Continental lunch, but the time to come is between 3pm and 5pm when you can indulge in afternoon tea with cakes and the all-important scones, jam and cream.

OTHER AREAS

1559 AD
MULTICUISINE $$$

(☑2433559; PP Singhal Marg; mains ₹200-650; ☺11am-11pm) Waiters in embroidered-silk waistcoats serve up lovely Indian, Thai and Continental dishes in elegant surroundings at this secluded restaurant near the southeastern side of Fateh Sagar Lake. There are garden tables as well as several different rooms with just a few candlelit tables in each, and Indian classical music in the evenings. Includes a coffee shop with the best coffee we tasted in Udaipur.

Savage Garden
MEDITERRANEAN $$

(☑2425440; 22 Inside Chandpol; mains ₹190-320; ☺11am-11pm) Savage Garden has a winning line in soups and chicken and homemade pasta dishes with assorted sauces, though portions aren't huge. There are some Middle

Eastern influences too. The setting is atmospheric, in a 250-year-old *haveli* with indigo walls and bowls of flowers, and tables in alcoves or a pleasant courtyard.

Natraj Hotel   GUJARATI $
(New Bapu Bazaar; thali ₹70; ☺10.30am-3.30pm & 6.15-10.30pm) Famous throughout town for its delicious all-you-can-eat vegetarian Gujarati thalis, this place has been filled to the brim for two decades with devout locals, who arrive to chow down on its huge portions of cheap, fresh food. It's tucked away in a backstreet 1.5km northeast of the City Palace, but definitely worth the hunt.

🍷 Drinking

Most guesthouses have a roof terrace serving up cold Kingfishers with views over the lazy waters of Lake Pichola, but for a real treat try the top-end hotels. Note that you have to pay ₹25 to enter the City Palace complex if you're not staying in one of its hotels.

Panera Bar   BAR
(Shiv Niwas Palace Hotel; Kingfisher or Indian whisky ₹250-275; ☺11.30am-10pm) Sink into plush sofas surrounded by huge mirrors, royal portraits and beautiful paintwork, or sit out by the pool, and be served like a maharaja.

Sunset Terrace   BAR
(Fateh Prakash Palace Hotel; ☺7am-10.30pm) On a terrace overlooking Lake Pichola, this is perfect for a sunset gin and tonic. It's also a restaurant, with live music performed every night.

☆ Entertainment

Dharohar   DANCE
(☑2523858; Bagore-ki-Haveli, Gangaur Ghat; admission ₹60, camera ₹50; ☺7pm) The beautiful Bagore-ki-Haveli hosts the best (and most convenient) opportunity to see Rajasthani folk dancing, with nightly shows of colourful, energetic Mewari, Bhil and western Rajasthani dances, by talented performers.

Mewar Sound & Light Show   SOUND & LIGHT SHOW
(Manek Chowk, City Palace; lower/upper seating English show ₹150/400, Hindi show ₹100/200; ☺7pm Sep-Feb, 7.30pm Mar-Apr, 8pm May-Aug) Fifteen centuries of intriguing Mewar history are squeezed into one atmospheric hour of commentary and light switching – in English from September to April, in Hindi other months.

🛍 Shopping

Tourist-oriented shops – selling miniature paintings, wood carvings, silver and other jewellery, bangles, traditional shoes, spices, leather-bound handmade-paper notebooks, ornate knives, camel-bone boxes and a large variety of textiles – line the streets radiating from Jagdish Chowk. There are more on Bajrang Marg near Hanuman Ghat. Udaipur is known for its local crafts, particularly its miniature paintings in the Rajput-Mughal style, but finding an authentic artist takes a collector's eye.

Be prepared to bargain hard in these areas, as most places will probably quote you a ridiculous opening price: as a rule of thumb, aim to pay around 50% of the initial asking price.

The local market area extends east from the old clock tower at the north end of Jagdish Temple Rd, and buzzes loudest in the evening. Foodstuffs are mainly found around the new clock tower at the east end of the bazaar area.

Numerous shops clustered around Lal Ghat purvey and exchange guidebooks, nonfiction and fiction about Rajasthan and India, in English and other languages.

Rajasthali   HANDICRAFTS
Chetak Circle (26 Chetak Circle; ☺10.30am-7.30pm Mon-Sat); old city (City Palace Rd; ☺10am-6.30pm) This government fixed-price emporium is worth dropping into to gauge handicraft prices. The branch at Chetak Circle, 1km north of the old clock tower, has a pretty representative range of Rajasthan crafts.

ℹ️ Information

Emergency

Police (☑2414600, 100) There are police posts at Surajpol, Hatipol and Delhi Gate.

Internet Access

You can surf the internet at plenty of places, particularly around Lal Ghat, for ₹30 per hour. Many places double as travel agencies, bookshops, art shops etc.

BA Photo N Book Store (69 Durga Sadan; ☺10am-11pm)

Lake City (Lal Ghat; ☺9am-11pm)

Medical Services

GBH American Hospital (☑3056000; www.gbhamericanhospital.com; 101 Kothi Bagh, Bhatt Ji Ki Bari, Meera Girls College Rd) Modern, reader-recommended private hospital with

24-hour emergency service, about 2km north-east of the old city.

Money

There are lots of ATMs, including Axis Bank and State Bank ATMs on City Palace Rd near Jagdish Temple; HDFC, ICICI and State Bank ATMs near the bus stand; and two ATMs outside the train station. Places to change currency and travellers cheques include the following:

Sai Tours & Travels (168 City Palace Rd; ☺8am-9pm)

Thomas Cook (Lake Palace Rd; ☺9.30am-6pm Mon-Sat)

Post

DHL (1 Town Hall Rd; ☺10am-7pm Mon-Sat) Has a free collection service within Udaipur.

Post office (City Palace Rd; ☺9.30am-1pm & 2-5.30pm Mon-Sat) Beside the City Palace's Badi Pol ticket office, 1.5km northeast of the City Palace.

Tourist Information

Tourist Reception Centre (☎2411535; Fateh Memorial Bldg; ☺10am-5pm Mon-Sat) Not situated in the most convenient position, 1.5km east of the Jagdish Temple (although only about 500m from the bus stand), this place dishes out a limited amount of brochures and information.

ⓘ Getting There & Away

Air

Air India (☎2410999; www.airindia.com; 222/16 Mumal Towers, Saheli Rd) Flies to Mumbai daily and to Delhi via Jodhpur also daily.

Jet Airways (☎2561105; www.jetairways.com; Blue Circle Business Centre, Madhuban) Flies direct to Delhi daily, and Mumbai once or twice daily.

Kingfisher Airlines (☎1800 2093030; www .flykingfisher.com; 4/73 Chetak Circle) has daily flights to Delhi, Mumbai and Jaipur, with the Jaipur flight continuing to Jodhpur from about October to March.

Bus

Frequent **Rajasthan State Road Transport Corporation** (RSRTC) buses travel from the main bus stand near the Udaipol gate to other Rajasthani cities, as well as Delhi, Agra and Ahmedabad. If you use these buses, take an express or one of the infrequent deluxe services as the ordinary buses take an incredibly long time and can be very uncomfortable. The best RSRTC buses are the air-conditioned Volvo services, which run once a day on just a few routes.

Private buses, mostly leaving from Station Rd a little south of the main bus stand, operate to destinations including Kota (seat/sleeper ₹150/200, seven hours), Bundi (₹160/220, seven hours), Jaipur (₹180/280, seven to eight hours), Jodhpur (₹180/250, five to eight hours), Agra (₹300/400, 13 hours), Delhi (₹450/800, 12 hours), Ahmedabad (₹160/260, five hours), Mumbai (₹400/600, 15 hours) and Mt Abu (seat ₹150, four hours). AC buses costing around 50% more are available to Jaipur, Delhi, Ahmedabad and Mumbai; Mumbai even has some Volvo AC services (seat/sleeper around ₹1200/1500). You can get tickets from plenty of travel agencies, hotels and guesthouses, though you may find commission charges are lower at the ticket offices near the departure area.

Taxi

Most hotels, guesthouses and travel agencies can organise you a car and driver to just about anywhere you want. A typical round-trip day

RSRTC BUSES FROM UDAIPUR

DESTINATION	FARE (EXPRESS/DE-LUXE/VOLVO, ₹)	APPROXIMATE DURATION (HR)	FREQUENCY
Agra	415/456/-	14	2 daily
Ahmedabad	157/170/390	5	hourly, 4am-11pm
Ajmer	161/201/-	7	every 30 minutes
Bundi	160/-/-	6	4 daily, 4.30-9.30am
Chittorgarh	70/81/-	2½	every 30 minutes, 5.30am-11.30pm
Delhi	406/456/1207	15	4
Jaipur	235/285/685	9	hourly
Jodhpur	145/160/400	6-8	10 daily
Kota	170/204/-	7	every 30 minutes, 5am-9.30pm
Mt Abu	127/-/-	4	about every 30 minutes, 5am-4pm

outing in a non-AC car costs around ₹800 to Eklingji and Nagda, ₹1400 to Chittorgarh, and ₹1400 to Ranakpur and Kumbhalgarh. One-way trips to Mt Abu, Ahmedabad, Bundi via Chittorgarh, or Jodhpur via Kumbhalgarh and Ranakpur are around ₹2500 (this includes a charge for the driver's trip back to Udaipur).

Train

The computerised main **ticket office** (☉8am-8pm Mon-Sat, 8am-2pm Sun) at the station has a window for foreign tourists and other special categories of passenger.

The 12964 *Mewar Express* departs Udaipur at 6.15pm and arrives in Delhi's Nizamuddin station (sleeper/3AC/2AC/1AC ₹315/816/1102/1846) at 6.30am, via Chittorgarh, Bundi, Kota, Sawai Madhopur and Bharatpur.

The 12966 *Udaipur–Gwalior Super Express* departs Udaipur at 10.20pm and arrives in Gwalior (sleeper/3AC/2AC/1AC ₹324/844/1142/1915) at 12.45pm, via Chittorgarh, Ajmer, Jaipur (₹224/559/747/1255, 7½ hours) and Bharatpur.

The 12991 *Udaipur–Ajmer Express* departs at 6.15am and arrives in Ajmer (2nd class/AC chair ₹109/362) at 11.40am, via Chittorgarh (₹70/223, two hours).

The 19943 *Udaipur–Ahmedabad Express* departs at 7.25pm and reaches Dungarpur (sleeper/2AC ₹130/314) at 10.56pm and Ahmedabad (₹162/554) at 4.25am.

ℹ Getting Around

To/From the Airport

The airport is 25km east of town, about 900m south of Hwy 76 to Chittorgarh. A prepaid taxi to the Lal Ghat area costs ₹400.

Autorickshaw

These are unmetered, so you should agree on a fare before setting off – the normal fare anywhere in town is around ₹30.

Bicycle & Motorcycle

A cheap and environmentally friendly way to buzz around is by bike; many guesthouses can arrange bikes to rent, costing around ₹50 per day. Scooters and motorbikes, meanwhile, are great for exploring the surrounding countryside. **Heera Cycle Store** (☉7.30am-9pm), just off Gangaur Ghat Rd, hires out bicycles/mountain bikes/mopeds/scooters/motorbikes/Bullets for ₹50/100/200/350/350/450 per day (with a deposit of US$50/100/200/300/400/500); you must show your passport and driving licence.

Around Udaipur

KUMBHALGARH

☏02954

About 80km north of Udaipur, **Kumbhalgarh** (Indian/foreigner ₹5/100; ☉9am-6pm) is a fantastic, remote fort, fulfilling romantic expectations and vividly summoning up the chivalrous, warlike Rajput era. One of the many forts built by Rana Kumbha (r 1433–68), under whom Mewar reached its greatest extents, the isolated fort is perched 1100m above sea level, with endless views melting into the blue distance. The journey to the fort, along twisting roads through the Aravalli Hills, is a highlight in itself.

Kumbhalgarh was the most important Mewar fort after Chittorgarh, and the rulers, sensibly, used to retreat here in times of danger. Not surprisingly, Kumbhalgarh was only taken once in its entire history. Even then, it took the combined armies of Amber, Marwar and Mughal emperor Akbar to breach its strong defences, and they only managed to hang on to it for two days.

The fort's thick walls stretch about 36km; they're wide enough in some places for eight horses to ride abreast and it's possible to walk right round the circuit (allow two days). They enclose around 360 intact and ruined temples, some of which date back to the Mauryan period in the 2nd century BC, as well as palaces, gardens, step-wells and 700 cannon bunkers.

The large and rugged Kumbhalgarh Wildlife Sanctuary can be visited from Kumbhalgarh and most accommodation here can organise jeep, horse or walking trips in the sanctuary.

⊨ Sleeping & Eating

Aodhi HOTEL **$$$**
(☏242341; www.eternalmewar.in; r ₹6000, ste ₹7000, meals ₹400-1000; ✳@⬤◈✸) Just under 2km from the fort is this luxurious and blissfully tranquil hotel with an inviting pool, rambling gardens and winter campfires. The spacious rooms, in stone buildings, all boast their own palm-thatched terraces, balconies or pavilions, assorted wildlife, and botanical art and photos. Nonguests can dine in the restaurant, where good standard Indian fare is the pick of the options on offer, or have a drink in the cosy Chowpal Bar. Room rates plummet from April to September.

Kumbhal Castle
HOTEL $$

(☎242171; www.thekumbhalcastle.com; Fort Rd; s/d ₹2000/2400, super deluxe ₹2500/2900, meals ₹250-500; ❉☀) The modern Kumbhal Castle, 2km from the fort, has plain but pleasant white rooms featuring curly iron beds, bright bedspreads and window seats, shared balconies and good views.

Karni Palace Hotel
HOTEL $$

(☎242033; www.karnipalace.com; Bus Stand Rd, Kelwara; s/d ₹500/750, with AC ₹800/1200, ste ₹1500/2000; ❉) In the town of Kelwara, 7km south of Kumbhalgarh, this hotel backs onto lovely cornfields. Rooms are clean and adequately comfortable, with bathtubs in the bathrooms and balconies overlooking the main street, and there's a rooftop restaurant.

❶ Getting There & Away
Buses leave Udaipur bus stand at 5.15am, 8.15am and 2.30pm for Kelwara (₹50, three hours), 7km south of the fort, from where you can continue by autorickshaw or jeep. Hiring a taxi from Udaipur means you can visit both Ranakpur and Kumbhalgarh in a day: the round trip costs around ₹1400 (or ₹1600 with AC).

RANAKPUR
☎02934

At the foot of a remote, steep, wooded escarpment of the Aravalli Hills, Ranakpur (camera/video ₹50/150; ☉Jains 6am-7pm, non-Jains noon-5pm) is one of India's biggest and most important Jain temple complexes. It's 75km northwest of Udaipur, and 12km west of Kumbhalgarh as the crow flies (but 50km by road, via Saira). The main temple, the Chaumukha Mandir (Four-Faced Temple), is dedicated to Adinath, the first Jain *tirthankar* (depicted in the many Buddha-like images in the temple), and was built in the 15th century in milk-white marble. An incredible feat of Jain devotion, this is a complicated series of 29 halls, 80 domes and 1444 individually engraved pillars.

The interior is covered in knotted, lovingly wrought carving, and has a calming sense of space and harmony. Shoes, cigarettes and leather articles must be left at the entrance; menstruating women are asked not to enter.

Also exquisitely carved and well worth inspecting are two other Jain temples, dedicated to **Neminath** (22nd *tirthankar*) and **Parasnath** (23rd *tirthankar*), both within the complex, and a nearby **Sun Temple**. About 1km from the main complex is the **Amba Mata Temple**.

🛏 Sleeping & Eating
Shivika Lake Hotel
HOTEL $$

(☎285078; www.shivikalakehotel.com; r ₹600-1600, tent ₹1200; ❉@☀) Two kilometres north of the temple, Shivika is a welcoming, rustic, family-run hotel that provides free pick-ups and drops at the bus stop near the temple. You can stay in small, cosy rooms amid leafy gardens, or safari-style tents. Two tents have prime positions beside beautiful Nalwania Lake.

Aranyawas
HOTEL $$

(☎02956-293029; www.aranyawas.com; r incl breakfast ₹3500; ❉@☀) In beautifully secluded, tree-shaded grounds just off Hwy 32, 12km south of the temple, Aranyawas has 28 attractive rooms in stone-built cottages. They are not fancy but neat and tasteful, with pine furnishings and, in most cases, balconies overlooking a small river and hills. There's a large pool surrounded by broad, stone-paved terraces, and the inside-and-outside restaurant (mains ₹150 to ₹250) is a lovely place to stop for an Indian meal.

Ranakpur Hill Resort
HOTEL $$

(☎286411; www.ranakpurhillresort.com; Ranakpur Rd; s ₹2000-3500, d ₹2500-4000, s/d tent ₹2000/2500; ❉@☀) A well-run hotel with a nice pool in grassy gardens, around which

---

WORTH A TRIP

KUMBALGARH WILDLIFE SANCTUARY

Ranakpur is a great base for exploring the hilly, densely forested **Kumbhalgarh Wildlife Sanctuary** (Indian/foreigner ₹20/160, jeep or car ₹130, camera/video free/₹400, guide per day ₹200; ☉dawn-dusk), which extends over some 600 sq km to the northeast and southwest. It's known for its leopards and wolves, although the chances of spotting antelopes, gazelles, deer and possible sloth bears are higher, especially from March to June. You will certainly see some of the sanctuary's 200-plus bird species. Some of the best safaris and treks are offered (to guests and nonguests) by Shivika Lake Hotel: options include three-hour jeep safaris (per person ₹650), a three-hour forest and lake walk (₹300), a one-way trek to Kumbhalgarh (about five hours; ₹650) and a two-night camping trip, with one jeep safari included, for ₹3500 (all prices are per person, with a two-person minimum).

are attractive, all-AC rooms sporting marble floors, stained glass and floral wall paintings. It's 3.5km north of the temple along Hwy 32.

Maharani Bagh Orchard Retreat HOTEL $$$
(☑285105; www.jodhanaheritage.com; s/d ₹4500/5500; ※@≋) Maharani Bagh (Queen's Garden) is set in lush grounds with its own 1.5km walking trail. Accommodation is in colourful, spacious cottages with verandahs and there's a beautiful pool. It's down a short lane from Hwy 32, 4km north of the temple.

❶ Getting There & Away

Buses to Ranakpur leave roughly hourly from the bus stand in Udaipur (₹70, three hours), and 10 times daily from the central bus stand in Jodhpur (₹109, four to five hours). The stop in Ranakpur is outside the temple: you should either ask to be dropped at your accommodation or arrange for a pick-up on arrival. Buses from Ranakpur to both Udaipur and Jodhpur leave every one to two hours; the best services are the expresses, at around 7am, 2pm, 4pm and 6pm to both destinations.

Mt Abu

☑02974 / POP 22,045 / ELEV 1200M

Rajasthan's only hill station sits among green forests on the state's highest mountain at the southwestern end of the Aravalli Range and close to the Gujarat border.

Quite unlike anywhere else in Rajasthan, Mt Abu provides Rajasthanis, Gujaratis and a steady flow of foreign tourists with respite from scorching temperatures and arid beige terrain elsewhere. It's a particular hit with honeymooners, middle-class families from Gujarat and others from that alcohol-dry state in search of a beverage more potent than lassi.

Mt Abu town sits towards the southwest end of the plateau-like upper part of the mountain, which stretches about 19km from end to end and 6km from east to west. The town is surrounded by the flora- and fauna-rich, 289-sq-km Mt Abu Wildlife Sanctuary, which extends over most of the mountain from an altitude of 300m upwards.

The mountain is of great spiritual importance for both Hindus and Jains and has over 80 temples and shrines, most notably the exquisite Jain temples at Delwara, built between 400 and 1000 years ago.

Try to avoid arriving in Diwali (October or November) or the following two weeks, when prices soar and the place is packed. Mt Abu also gets pretty busy from mid-May to mid-June, before the monsoon. This is when the Summer Festival hits town, with music, fireworks and boat races. In the cooler months, you will find everyone wrapped up in shawls and hats; pack something woolly

Mt Abu

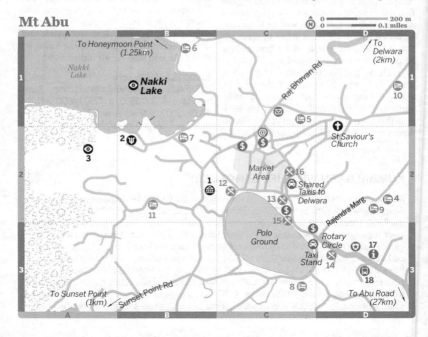

to avoid winter chills in poorly heated hotel rooms.

Sights & Activities

Nakki Lake
LAKE

Scenic Nakki Lake, the town's focus, is one of its biggest attractions. It's so named because, according to legend, it was scooped out by a god using his *nakh* (nails). Some Hindus thus consider it a holy lake. It's a pleasant stroll around the perimeter – the lake is surrounded by hills, parks and strange rock formations. The best known, **Toad Rock**, looks just like a toad about to hop into the lake. The 14th-century **Raghunath Temple** (⊘dawn-dusk) stands near the lake's south shore.

Sunset Point
VIEWPOINT

Sunset Point is a popular and lovely place to watch the brilliant setting sun, though distinctly unromantic unless being thrust red roses, bags of peanuts or Polaroid cameras gets you into a loving mood. Hordes stroll out here every evening to catch the end of the day, the food stalls and all the usual jolly hill-station entertainment.

Brahma Kumaris Peace Hall & Museum
MEDITATION, MUSEUM

The white-clad people you'll see around town are either armed forces or members of the **Brahma Kumaris World Spiritual University** (www.bkwsu.com, www.brahmakumaris.com), a worldwide organisation whose headquarters are here in Mt Abu. Brahma Kumaris teaches that all religions lead to God

and are equally valid, and that the principles of each should be studied. Its aim is the establishment of universal peace through 'the impartation of spiritual knowledge and training of easy raja yoga meditation'. Tens of thousands of followers come to Mt Abu each year for intense meditation or outreach training courses.

For many the teachings are intensely powerful; there are over 800 branches in 130 countries. For others, it gives off a New Age–sect vibe. You can find out more for yourself by paying a visit to the university's **Universal Peace Hall** (Om Shanti Bhawan; ⊘8am-6pm), just north of Nakki Lake, where free 30-minute tours are available, including an introduction to the Brahma Kumaris philosophy.

The organisation also runs the small **World Renewal Spiritual Museum** (admission free; ⊘8am-8pm) in the town centre, the entrance of which is labelled 'Gateway to Paradise'. The museum outlines Brahma Kumaris' teachings through kitschy dioramas and maxims like 'Man was never a beast nor will he ever become a beast, but he has now become worse than a beast'.

Tours

The RSRTC runs full-day (₹83) and half-day (₹45) bus tours of Mt Abu's main sights, leaving from the bus stand at 9.30am and 1pm respectively (times may vary). Admission and camera fees and the ₹20 guide fee are extra. Make reservations at the **enquiries counter** (☑235434) at the main bus stand.

Mt Abu

🛌 Sleeping

Mt Abu seems to consist mostly of hotels. Room rates can double or worse during the peak seasons – mid-May to mid-June, Diwali and Christmas/New Year – but generous discounts are often available at other times in midrange and top-end places. If you have to come here at Diwali, you'll need to book way ahead and you won't be able to move for crowds. Most hotels have an ungenerous 9am check-out time.

Connaught House HERITAGE HOTEL **$$**
(☑238560; www.jodhanaheritage.com; Rajendra Marg; s/d incl breakfast ₹4000/5000; ❄@) Connaught House is a charmingly stuck-in-time colonial bungalow that looks like an English cottage, with lots of sepia photographs, dark wood, angled ceilings and a gorgeous shady garden. The five rooms in the original 'cottage' have most character – and big colonial-era baths. The other five sit in a newer building with good views from their own verandahs.

Shri Ganesh Hotel HOTEL **$**
(☑237292; lalit_ganesh@yahoo.co.in; dm ₹150-200, without bathroom ₹100, s ₹300, d ₹400-1200;

@) Deservedly the most popular budget spot, Shri Ganesh is well set up for travellers, with an inexpensive cafe, a small internet room and plenty of helpful travel information. Rooms are well used but kept clean. Some have squat toilets and limited hours for hot water; clothes washing is not allowed. Daily forest walks and cooking lessons are on offer.

Hotel Lake Palace HOTEL **$$**
(☑237154; http://savshantihotels.com; r ₹2000-2800; ❄❄⊛) Spacious and friendly, Lake Palace has an excellent location, with small lawns overlooking the lake. Rooms are simple, uncluttered, bright and clean. All have AC and some have semiprivate lake-view terrace areas. There are rooftop and garden multicuisine restaurants too.

Kishangarh House HERITAGE HOTEL **$$**
(☑238092; www.royalkishangarh.com; Rajendra Marg; s/d cottage room ₹2500/3000, deluxe ₹4000/4500; ⊛) The former summer residence of the maharaja of Kishangarh has been successfully converted into a heritage hotel. The deluxe rooms in the main building are big, with extravagantly high ceilings.

DON'T MISS

DELWARA TEMPLES

These remarkable Jain temples (donations welcome; ⊙Jains 6am-6pm, non-Jains noon-6pm) are Mt Abu's most remarkable attraction and feature some of India's finest temple decoration. They predate the town of Mt Abu by many centuries and were built when this site was just a remote mountain fastness. It's said that the artisans were paid according to the amount of dust they collected, encouraging them to carve ever more intricately. Whatever their inducement, there are two temples here in which the marble work is dizzyingly intense.

The older of the two is the **Vimal Vasahi**, on which work began in 1031 and which was financed by a Gujarati chief minister named Vimal. Dedicated to the first *tirthankar*, Adinath, it took 1500 masons and 1200 labourers 14 years to build, and allegedly cost ₹185.3 million. Outside the entrance is the **House of Elephants**, featuring a procession of stone elephants marching to the temple, some of which were damaged long ago by marauding Mughals. Inside, a forest of beautifully carved pillars surrounds the central shrine, which holds an image of Adinath himself.

The **Luna Vasahi Temple** is dedicated to Neminath, the 22nd *tirthankar*, and was built in 1230 by the brothers Tejpal and Vastupal for a mere ₹125.3 million. Like Vimal, the brothers were both Gujarati government ministers. The marble carving here took 2500 workers 15 years to create, and its most notable feature is its intricacy and delicacy, which is so fine that, in places, the marble becomes almost transparent. It's difficult to believe that this huge lace-like filigree started life as a solid block of marble.

As at other Jain temples, leather articles (belts as well as shoes) have to be left at the entrance, and menstruating women are asked not to enter. No photography is permitted.

Delwara is about 2.5km north of Mt Abu town centre: you can walk there in less than an hour, or hop aboard a shared taxi (₹5 per person) from up the street opposite Chacha Cafe. A taxi all to yourself should be ₹50, or ₹150 round trip with one hour's waiting.

TREKKING AROUND MT ABU

Getting off the well-worn tourist trail and out into the forests and hills of Mt Abu is a revelation. This is a world of isolated shrines and lakes, weird rock formations, fantastic panoramas, nomadic villagers, orchids, wild fruits, plants used in ayurvedic medicine, sloth bears (which are fairly common), langurs, 150 bird species and even the occasional leopard.

Mt Abu–born Mahendra Dan ('Charles') of **Mt Abu Treks** (⌂9414154854; www.mount -abu-treks.blogspot.com; Hotel Lake Palace) is a passionate and knowledgable nature lover who leads excellent tailor-made treks ranging from three or four hours close to Mt Abu (₹300 per person) to overnight treks to nomad villages beyond Guru Shikhar (up to ₹1500 per person including meals). There's a two-person minimum, and on some routes wildlife sanctuary entrance fees (Indian/foreigner ₹20/160) and/or transport costs (minimum ₹250 for a car drop and pick-up) have to be paid too.

The cottage rooms at the back are smaller but cosier. There is a delightful sun-filled drawing room and the lovely terraced gardens are devotedly tended.

Honey Dew Paying Guest House　　　GUESTHOUSE **$$**
(⌂238429; off Raj Bhavan Rd; r ₹1500) Honey Dew sits at the top of the central area, near the post office. Its five rooms, around a courtyard-like area, are unostentatious but comfy, clean, well kept and good sized – and decorated with a touch of modern art for a change.

Mushkil Aasan　　　GUESTHOUSE **$$**
(⌂235150; r ₹1000-1500) A lovely guesthouse nestled in a tranquil vale in the north of town, with nine homey decorated rooms and a small garden above a stream. Home-style Gujarati meals are available, and check-out is a civilised 24 hours.

Hotel Saraswati　　　HOTEL **$**
(⌂238887; r ₹590-1000; ❄⌂) Saraswati is a reasonably appealing place in a peaceful setting behind the polo ground. Rooms are big enough and in varied states of repair: see a few of the 36 on offer before you decide. Hot water is only available from 7am to 11am. The restaurant serves good Gujarati thalis (₹80).

Hotel Panghat　　　HOTEL **$**
(⌂238886; r ₹450-500) The rooms are plain and worn, with squat toilets and unheated showers, but the lake is across the street and some rooms overlook it. There's a good rooftop with a swing, and management is friendly and obliging.

✗ Eating

Most holidaymakers here are Gujarati – hence the profusion of sweet veg thali restaurants.

Sankalp　　　SOUTH INDIAN **$**
(Hotel Maharaja; mains ₹50-120; ⌂9am-11pm) A branch of a quality Gujarat-based chain serving up excellent South Indian vegetarian fare. Unusual fillings like pineapple or spinach-cheese-garlic are available for its renowned dosas and *uttapams* (savoury South Indian rice pancake), which come with multiple sauces and condiments. Order *masala papad* (wafer with spicy topping) for a tasty starter.

Kanak Dining Hall　　　INDIAN **$**
(Gujarati/Punjabi thali ₹90/100; ⌂11.30am-3pm & 7-10.30pm) The excellent all-you-can-eat thalis are contenders for Mt Abu's best meals; there's seating indoors in the busy dining hall or outside under a canopy. It's conveniently near the bus stand for the lunch break during the all-day RSRTC tour.

Chacha Cafe　　　MULTICUISINE **$**
(dishes ₹60-120; ⌂) A very neat, bright eatery with red-check table cloths and welcome AC. The presentable fare ranges over dosas, pizzas, vegetarian burgers, cashew curry and biryanis.

Sher-e-Punjab Hotel　　　PUNJABI **$**
(mains ₹60-160) This place in the market area has bargain Punjabi food. Plenty of regular veg and nonveg curries that won't stretch the budget.

Arbuda　　　INDIAN **$**
(Arbuda Circle; mains ₹65-90) This big restaurant is set on a sweeping open terrace filled with chrome chairs. It's popular for

its Gujarati, Punjabi and South Indian food.

Information

There are State Bank ATMs on Raj Bhavan Rd, opposite Hotel Samrat International and outside the Tourist Reception Centre, and a Bank of Baroda ATM on Lake Rd.

Union Bank of India (Main Market; ⊙10am-3pm Mon-Fri, 10am-12.30pm Sat) The only bank changing travellers cheques and currency.

Yani-Ya Cyber Zone (Raj Bhavan Rd; internet per hr ₹30; ⊙9am-10pm) There are also a couple of cybercafes down in the market area below here.

Getting There & Away

Access to Mt Abu is by a dramatic 28km road that winds its way up thickly forested hillsides from the town of Abu Road on Hwy 14, about 140km west of Udaipur. The nearest train station is at Abu Road. Some buses from other cities go all the way up to Mt Abu; others only go as far as Abu Road. Buses (₹22, one hour) run between Abu Road and Mt Abu bus stands roughly hourly in each direction from about 6am to 7pm. A taxi from Abu Road to Mt Abu is ₹300 by day or ₹400 by night: make it clear you want to be taken to your hotel and not just Mt Abu bus stand.

There's a charge of ₹10 for each person (including bus passengers) and car as you enter Mt Abu.

Bus

Public buses from the main bus stand go to Udaipur (₹137, 4½ hours, four daily), Jodhpur (₹150, six hours, one daily), Jaisalmer (₹220, 10 hours, one daily), Jaipur (₹480, 11 hours, one AC bus daily) and Ahmedabad (₹130, seven hours, nine daily). Private bus companies, serving similar destinations at usually slightly higher prices, have ticket offices on the street near the bus stand.

MT ABU PRECAUTIONS

Unless you are in a group, it is very unwise to visit Sunset Point or Honeymoon Point any time other than sunset when lots of people will be around. It is also unwise to walk off the streets alone – for example along some of the paths shown on Tourist Reception Centre maps. Muggings and at least one murder have happened in recent years to people who ignored these precautions.

Train

Abu Road station is on the line between Delhi and Mumbai via Ahmedabad. An autorickshaw from Abu Road train station to Abu Road bus stand costs ₹10. Mt Abu has a **railway reservation centre** (⊙8am-2pm), above the tourist office, with quotas on most of the express trains.

Around Mt Abu

GURU SHIKHAR

At the northeast end of the Mt Abu plateau, 17km by the winding road from the town, rises 1722m-high Guru Shikhar, Rajasthan's highest point. A road goes almost all the way to the summit and the **Atri Rishi Temple**, complete with a priest and fantastic, huge views. A popular spot, it's a highlight of the RSRTC tour; if you decide to go it alone, a jeep will cost ₹500 return.

WESTERN RAJASTHAN

Jodhpur

✆0291 / POP 846,400

Mighty Mehrangarh, the muscular fort that towers over the Blue City of Jodhpur, is a magnificent spectacle and an architectural masterpiece. Around Mehrangarh's feet, the old city, a jumble of Brahmin-blue cubes, stretches out to the 10km-long, 16th-century city wall. The 'Blue City' really is blue! Inside is a tangle of winding, glittering, medieval streets, which never seem to lead where you expect them to, scented by incense, roses and sewers, with shops and bazaars selling everything from trumpets and temple decorations to snuff and saris. Traditionally, blue signified the home of a Brahmin, but non-Brahmins have got in on the act, too. As well as glowing with a mysterious light, the blue tint is thought to repel insects.

Modern Jodhpur stretches well beyond the city walls, but it's the immediacy and buzz of the old Blue City and the larger-than-life fort that capture travellers' imaginations. This crowded, hectic zone is also Jodhpur's main tourist shopping and eating area, and it often seems you can't speak to anyone without them trying to sell you something. Areas of the old city further west, such as Navchokiya, are just as atmospheric, with far less hustling.

DESTINATION	TRAIN NUMBER & NAME	FARE (₹)	DURATION (HR)	DEPARTURE
Ahmedabad	19224 *Jammu Tawi-Ahmedabad Express*	130/312/415 (B)	4½	11.10am
Bhuj	14311 *Ala Hazrat Express*	245/644/876 (B)	13	1.35am Wed, Fri, Sat, Sun
	14321 *Bareilly-Bhuj Express*	197/511/694 (B)	9	1.35am Mon, Tue, Thu
Jaipur	19707 *Aravalli Express*	204/529/717 (B)	9	10.02am
Jodhpur	19223 *Ahmedabad-Jammu Tawi Express*	153/386/519	4¾	3.22pm

Fares: B – sleeper/3AC/2AC.

History

Driven from their homeland of Kannauj, east of Agra, by Afghans serving Mohammed of Ghori, the Rathore Rajputs fled west around AD 1200 to the region around Pali, 70km southeast of Jodhpur. They prospered to such a degree that in 1381 they managed to oust the Pratiharas of Mandore, 9km north of present-day Jodhpur. In 1459 the Rathore leader Rao Jodha chose a nearby rocky ridge as the site for a new fortress of staggering proportions, Mehrangarh, around which grew Jodha's city: Jodhpur.

Jodhpur lay on the vital trade route between Delhi and Gujarat. The Rathore kingdom grew on the profits of opium, sandalwood, dates and copper, and controlled a large area which became cheerily known as Marwar (the Land of Death) due to its harsh topography and climate. It stretched as far west as what's now the India–Pakistan border area, and bordered with Mewar (Udaipur) in the south, Jaisalmer in the northwest, Bikaner in the north and Jaipur and Ajmer in the east.

◉ Sights & Activities

TOP CHOICE **Mehrangarh** FORT
(www.mehrangarh.org; museum admission adult/senior & student incl camera & audio guide ₹300/250, video ₹200; ⊙9am-5.30pm) Rising perpendicular and impregnable from a rocky hill that itself stands 120m above Jodhpur's skyline, Mehrangarh is one of the most magnificent forts in India. The battlements are 6m to 36m high and as the building materials were chiselled from the rock on which the fort stands, the structure merges with its base. Still run by the Jodhpur royal family, Mehrangarh is chock-full of history and legend.

Mehrangarh's main entrance, at the northeast gate, Jaipol, is a 300m walk up from Hill View Guest House in the old city. Or you can take a winding 5km autorickshaw ride (around ₹80). The audio tour, included with the museum ticket, is in multiple languages and requires a deposit of passport, credit/debit card or ₹2000.

The **Jaipol** was built by Maharaja Man Singh in 1808 following his defeat of invading forces from Jaipur. Past the ticket office, the 16th-century **Dodh Kangra Pol** was an external gate before the Jaipol was built, and still bears the scars of 1808 cannonball hits. Through here, the main route heads up to the left, through the 16th-century **Imritiapol** and then the **Loha Pol**, the fort's original entrance, with iron spikes to deter enemy elephants. Just inside the gate are two sets of small handprints, the *sati* (self-immolation) marks of royal widows who threw themselves on their maharajas' funeral pyres – the last to do so were widows of Maharaja Man Singh in 1843.

Past Loha Pol you'll find a cafe and the Surajpol gate, which gives access to the museum. Once you've visited the museum, continue up to the panoramic **ramparts**, which are lined with impressive antique artillery.

Museum

This beautiful network of stone-latticed courtyards and halls, formerly the fort's palace, is a superb example of Rajput architec-

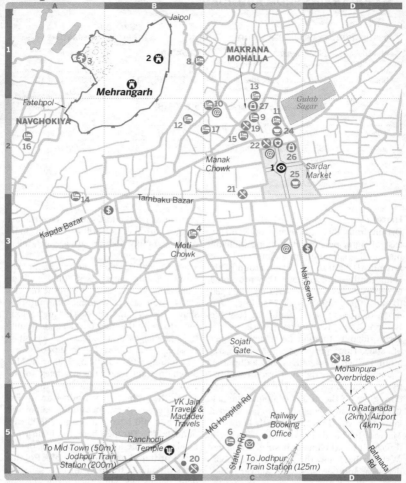

ture, so finely carved that it often looks more like sandalwood than sandstone.

The galleries around **Shringar Chowk** (Anointment Courtyard) display India's best collection of elephant howdahs and Jodhpur's royal palanquin collection.

One of the two galleries off **Daulat Khana Chowk** displays textiles, paintings, manuscripts, headgear and the curved sword of the Mughal emperor Akbar; the other gallery is the armoury. Upstairs are a **gallery of miniature paintings** from the sophisticated Marwar school and the beautiful 18th-century **Phul Mahal** (Flower Palace), whose

19th-century wall paintings depict the 36 moods of classical ragas as well as royal portraits; the artist took 10 years to create them using a curious concoction of gold leaf, glue and cow's urine.

Takhat Vilas was the bedchamber of Maharaja Takhat Singh (r 1843–73), who had just 30 maharanis and numerous concubines. Its beautiful ceiling is covered with Christmas baubles. You then enter the extensive zenana, whose lovely latticed windows (from which the women could watch the goings-on in the courtyards) are said to feature over 250 different de-

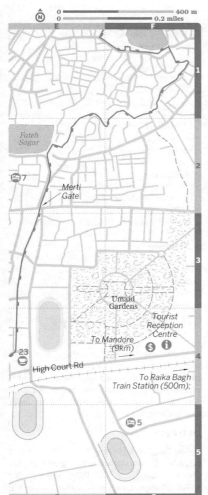

Jaswant Thada
HISTORIC BUILDING

(Indian/foreigner ₹15/30, camera/video ₹25/50; ☺9am-5pm) This milky white marble memorial to Maharaja Jaswant Singh II, sitting above a small lake 1km northeast of Mehrangarh, is an array of whimsical domes. It's a welcome, peaceful spot after the hubbub of the city, and the views across to the fort and over the city are superb. Built in 1899, the cenotaph has some beautiful *jalis* (carved marble lattice screens) and is hung with portraits of Rathore rulers going back to the 13th century.

Clock Tower & Markets
LANDMARK

The century-old clock tower is an old city landmark surrounded by the vibrant sounds, sights and smells of Sardar Market, which is marked by triple gateways at its north and south ends. The narrow, winding lanes of the old city spread out in all directions from here. Westward, you plunge into the old city's commercial heart, with crowded alleys and bazaars selling vegetables, spices, sweets, silver and handicrafts.

Umaid Bhawan Palace
PALACE

Take a rickshaw or taxi to this hill-top palace, 3km southeast of the old city, sometimes called the Chittar Palace because local Chittar sandstone was used to build it. Building began in 1929 and the 365-room edifice was designed by the British architect Henry Lanchester for Maharaja Umaid Singh. It took over 3000 workers 15 years to complete, at a cost of around ₹11 million. The building is mortarless, and incorporates 100 wagon loads of Makrana marble and Burmese teak in the interior. Apparently the construction of this over-the-top palace began as a royal job-creation program during a time of severe drought.

The current royal incumbent, Gaj Singh II (known as Bapji), still lives in part of the building. Most of the rest has been turned into a suitably grand hotel.

Most interesting in the **museum** (Indian/foreigner ₹15/50; ☺9am-5pm) are the photos showing the elegant art deco design of the palace interior. Look out for some of the maharaja's highly polished classic cars displayed on the lawn in front of the museum.

signs. Here you'll find the **Cradle Gallery**, exhibiting the elaborate cradles of infant princes, and the 17th-century **Moti Mahal** (Pearl Palace), which was the palace's main durbar hall for official meetings and receptions, with gorgeously colourful stained glass.

Flying Fox

(www.flyingfox.asia; 1/6 zips ₹330/1330; ☺9am-4pm) This two-hour circuit of six zip lines flies back and forth over walls, bastions and lakes on the north side of Mehrangarh. Safety standards are good and 'awesome' is the verdict of most who dare.

Tours

Most guesthouses and hotels can lay on city tours by autorickshaw (half-day/day around ₹350/700) or taxi (around ₹500/1000). If you prefer to organise your own taxi, there's a stand outside the main train station.

Further afield, tours to Bishnoi and craft-making villages south of Jodhpur are popular (see p181).

🎎 Festivals & Events

In September or October Jodhpur hosts the colourful **Marwar Festival**, which includes polo and a camel tattoo.

🛏 Sleeping

The old city has something like 100 guesthouses, most of which scramble for your custom within half a kilometre of Sardar Market and its landmark clock tower. Many midrange and top-end options are found outside the old city, especially in the Ratanada area (about 2km south), and on Circuit House Rd (1km southeast).

If a rickshaw driver is clamouring to take you to a particular guesthouse or hotel, it's probably because he is aiming to receive a commission from them. There's a growing anti-commission movement among hoteliers here, but some still pay your rickshaw or taxi driver an absurd 50% of what you pay for your room. Don't believe drivers, or strangers on the street, who tell you the place you want has closed, is full, is under repair, is far from the centre etc.

Many lodgings can organise a pick-up from the train station or bus stops, even at night, if you call ahead. Otherwise, for most places in the old city, you can avoid nonsense by getting dropped at the clock tower and walking from there.

OLD CITY

TOP
CHOICE **Singhvi's Haveli**   GUESTHOUSE **$**
(📞2624293; www.singhvihaveli.com; Ramdevji-ka-Chowk, Navchokiya; r ₹300-1800; ✳@🛜) This red-sandstone, family-run, 500-odd-year-old *haveli* is an understated gem. It's in Navchokiya, one of the most atmospheric yet least touristy parts of the old city, beneath the western end of Mehrangarh (which you can enter by the Fatehpol gate). Run by a friendly Jain family, Singhvi's has 13 individual rooms, ranging from the simple to the magnificent Maharani Suite with 10 windows and a fort view. The relaxing and romantic vegetarian restaurant is decorated with sari curtains and floor cushions.

**Krishna Prakash Heritage
Haveli**   HERITAGE HOTEL **$$**
(📞2633448; www.kpheritage.net; Nayabas, Killikhana; s/d standard ₹850/1050, deluxe incl breakfast

₹1550/1750, ste incl breakfast ₹2450-3500; ✳✥)
This multilevel heritage hotel right under
the fort walls is a good-value and peaceful
choice. It has prettily painted furniture and
murals and rooms are well proportioned;
the deluxe ones are a bit more spruced up,
generally a bit bigger, and set on the upper
floors, so airier. There's an undercover swimming pool and a relaxing terrace restaurant.

Pal Haveli
HERITAGE HOTEL $$

(📞3293328; www.palhaveli.com; Gulab Sagar; r
incl breakfast ₹2500-4000; ✳@) This stun-
ning *haveli,* the best and most attractive
in the old city, was built by the Thakur of
Pal in 1847. There are 21 charming, spa-
cious rooms, mostly large and elaborately
decorated in traditional heritage style, sur-
rounding a cool central courtyard. The fam-
ily still lives here and can show you its small
museum. Three restaurants serve excellent
food and the rooftop Indique boasts unbeat-
able views.

Raas
BOUTIQUE HOTEL $$$

(📞2636455; www.raasjodhpur.com; Tunvarji-ka-
Jhalra, Makrana Mohalla; incl breakfast r ₹15,000-
18,000, ste ₹26,000; ✳🛜✥) Developed from
a 19th-century city mansion, Jodhpur's
first contemporary-style boutique hotel is a
splendid retreat of clean, uncluttered style,
hidden behind a big castle-like gateway. If
you fancy a change from the heritage aesthetic that prevails in Rajasthan's top-end
hotels, Raas' clean, uncluttered style and
subtle lighting are just the ticket. The red-
stone-and-terrazzo rooms are not massive,
but they come with plenty of luxury touches
and have balconies with great Mehrangarh
views.

Haveli Inn Pal
HERITAGE HOTEL $$

(📞2612519; www.haveliinnpal.com; Gulab Sagar;
r incl breakfast ₹2050-2550; ✳@) The smaller,
12-room sibling of Pal Haveli. It's accessed
through the same grand entrance, but is
located around to the right in one wing of
the grand *haveli.* It's a simpler heritage ex-
perience, with comfortable rooms and lake
or fort views from the more expensive ones.
Discounts are often available for single oc-
cupancy.

Hill View Guest House
GUESTHOUSE $

((📞2441763; r ₹150-400) Perched just below the
fort walls, this is run by a friendly, enthusi-
astic, no-hassle, Muslim family, who'll make
you feel right at home. Rooms are basic, clean
and simple, all with bathrooms, and the ter-

race has a great view over the city. Good,
home-cooked veg and nonveg food is on offer.

Blue House
GUESTHOUSE $

(📞2621396; bluehouse36@hotmail.com; Dabga-
ron-ki-Gali, Moti Chowk; r ₹250-1800; ✳@) Cer-
tainly blue, this rambling old house run by
a friendly Jain family is a reliable bet. It has
a big range of individually decorated rooms
and some very steep stairs. The two top-floor
rooms (₹900 each) are good value.

Shahi Guest House
GUESTHOUSE $$

(📞2623802; www.shahiguesthouse.net; Gandhi
St, City Police; r ₹900-2200; ✳🛜) Shahi is an
interesting guesthouse developed from a
350-year-old zenana. There's lots of cool
stone, and narrow walkways surrounding
a petite courtyard. The six rooms are individual and cosy, and the family is charming.
There is a delightful rooftop restaurant with
views.

Hotel Haveli
HOTEL $$

(📞2614615; www.hotelhaveli.net; Makrana Mohalla;
r ₹500-2200; ✳@🛜) This 250-year-old build-
ing inside the walled city is a popular, effi-
cient and friendly place. Rooms vary greatly
and are individually decorated with colour
themes and paintings; many have semibal-
conies and fort views. The rooftop vegetari-
an restaurant, Jharokha, has excellent views
and nightly entertainment.

Yogi's Guest House
GUESTHOUSE $

(📞2643436; www.yogiguesthouse.com; Naya Bass,
Manak Chowk; r ₹350-1200; ✳@) Yogi's is a
classic travellers' hangout that's moving up-
market, with many refurbished rooms but
also still plenty of budget options. Set in a
500-year-old *haveli* near the base of the fort
walls, it's a friendly place painted blue and
other bright colours. The rooms are smart
and clean; some have AC and/or views.

Shivam Paying Guest House
GUESTHOUSE $

(📞2610688; shivamgh@hotmail.com; Makrana
Mohalla; r ₹200-700, without bathroom ₹150; ✳)
Near the clock tower, this quiet, hassle-
free option run by a helpful family has
cosy rooms, steep staircases and a lovely
little rooftop restaurant.

Pushp Paying Guest House
GUESTHOUSE $

(📞2648494; sanukash2003@yahoo.co.in; Pipli-
ki-Gali, Naya Bass, Manak Chowk; r ₹200-600;
✳@🛜) A small guesthouse with five clean,
colourful rooms with windows. There's
an up-close view of Mehrangarh from its
rooftop restaurant.

Heritage Kuchaman Haveli
HERITAGE HOTEL $$

(2547787; www.kuchamanhaveli.com; inside Merti Gate; r ₹1550-2950, ste ₹3750; ✳@🛜🏊) This recently renovated 19th-century *haveli* is a rare midrange option in the old city. It's a well-proportioned building, but the rooms are rather dull.

TRAIN STATION AREA

Govind Hotel
HOTEL $

(2622758; www.govind-hotel.com; Station Rd; r ₹350-900; ✳@🛜) Well set up for travellers, with helpful management, an internet cafe and a location convenient to the Jodhpur train station. All rooms are clean and tiled, with fairly smart bathrooms. There's a rooftop restaurant and coffee shop with excellent espresso and cakes.

SOUTH OF THE OLD CITY

Devi Bhawan
HERITAGE HOTEL $$

(2511067; www.devibhawan.com; Ratanada; r ₹1800-2300; ✳@🛜🏊) A charming hotel surrounding a verdant oasis shaded by majestic neem trees. As well as being the most peaceful place in Jodhpur it is also excellent value. There's a superb pool and a good **restaurant** (veg/nonveg thali ₹175/200; ⏲7-10am & 8-10pm). Rooms are spacious, clean, comfortable and decorated with colourful textiles and traditional furnishings.

Ratan Vilas
HERITAGE HOTEL $$

(2613011; www.ratanvilas.com; Loco Shed Rd, Ratanada; r ₹2000-2950; ✳@🛜) Built in 1920, this beauty from a bygone era is quintessential colonial India, with manicured lawns, spacious, spotless and solidly tasteful rooms, and exceptional staff who prepare wonderful meals.

Durag Niwas Guest House
GUESTHOUSE $

(2512385; www.durag-niwas.com; 1st Old Public Park Lane, Raika Bagh; rooftop per person ₹100, r ₹350-1000; ✳) A friendly place set away from the hustle of the old city. Good home-cooked veg and nonveg dishes are available, and there's a cushion-floored, sari-curtained area on the roof for relaxing. Management offers cultural tours and the opportunity to do volunteer work with the Sambhali Trust.

Newtons Manor
GUESTHOUSE $$

(2670986; www.newtonsmanor.com; 86 Jawahar Colony, Ratanada; r ₹1395-1595; ✳🛜) This family home has eight elegant guest rooms fussily decorated with lots of antique furniture.

It offers excellent home cooking, though pride of place goes to the good-sized billiard table. There's an eternally ungrateful tiger in the sitting room.

Ajit Bhawan
HERITAGE HOTEL $$$

(2513333; www.ajitbhawan.com; Circuit House Rd; r ₹10,000-17,000; ✳@🏊) Behind the gracious main heritage building, built in 1927 for Maharajadhiraj Ajit Singh (younger brother of Maharaja Umaid Singh), the accommodation is a series of comfortable thatched stone cottages with traditional furnishings. There's a sensational swimming pool and a fine-dining restaurant with live Rajasthani folk music in the evenings.

Vivanta Hari Mahal
HOTEL $$$

(2439700; www.vivantabytaj.com; 5 Residency Rd; r ₹14,500-16,500, ste ₹27,500; ✳@🛜🏊) Run by the Taj Group, this is a luxurious modern hotel with traditional Rajasthani flourishes, 2km south of the train station. It has very spacious common areas, including a bar, a big, inviting courtyard swimming pool and some lovely artwork. Decent discounts are often available for online bookings.

Umaid Bhawan Palace
HERITAGE HOTEL $$$

(2510101; www.tajhotels.com; Umaid Bhawan Rd; r ₹26,500-43,500, ste ₹41,000-150,000; ✳@🏊) This massive art deco palace, still the royal residence, is constructed from honey sandstone and white marble and is located 3km southeast of the old city. It's so immense it feels rather like a parliament building or a university (ie not all that cosy). It has luxurious rooms of course and numerous sporting facilities, including a magnificent indoor swimming pool.

🍴 Eating

It's often convenient to eat in your guesthouse or hotel restaurant (which is usually on the roof, with a fort view), but there are also a number of places well worth going out to.

TOP CHOICE Indique
INDIAN $$

(3293328; Pal Haveli, Gulab Sagar; mains ₹200-275) This candle-lit rooftop restaurant at the Pal Haveli hotel is the perfect place for a romantic dinner. Even murky Gulab Sagar glistens at night and the views to the fort, clock tower and Umaid Bhawan are superb. The food covers traditional tandoori, biryanis and North Indian curries, and you won't be disappointed by the old favourites –

butter chicken and rogan josh. On your way up, drop into the delightful 18 Century Bar, with saddle stools and enough heritage paraphernalia to have you ordering pink gins.

Nirvana
INDIAN $$

(1st fl, Tija Mata ka Mandir, Tambaku Bazar; mains ₹90-130, regular/special thali ₹160/250) Sharing premises with a Rama temple, 300m from the clock tower, Nirvana has both an indoor cafe covered in 150-year-old wall paintings of the Ramayana story, and a rooftop eating area with panoramic views. The Indian vegetarian food is among the most delicious you'll find in Rajasthan, and the thalis are wonderful. The special thali is truly enormous and easily enough for two. Continental as well as Indian breakfasts are served in the cafe.

Jharokha
MULTICUISINE $

(Hotel Haveli, Makrana Mohalla; mains ₹60-90) The rooftop terraces of the Hotel Haveli host one of the best vegetarian restaurants in Jodhpur. As well as the excellent food and views there's nightly entertainment in the form of traditional music and dance. The dishes include Rajasthani specialities and traditional North Indian favourites, plus pizza, pasta and pancakes for the homesick.

Jhankar Choti Haveli
MULTICUISINE $

(Makrana Mohalla; mains ₹70-110; 🛜) Stone walls, big cane chairs, prettily painted woodwork and whirring fans set the scene at this semi-open-air travellers' favourite. It serves up good Indian vegetarian dishes plus pizzas, burgers and baked cheese dishes.

On the Rocks
INDIAN $$

(📞5102701; Circuit House Rd; mains ₹115-325; 🕐12.30-3.30pm & 7.30-11pm) This leafy garden restaurant, 2km southeast of the old city, is very popular with locals and tour groups. It has tasty Indian cuisine, including lots of barbecue options and rich and creamy curries, plus a small playground and a cave-like bar (open 11am to 11pm) with a dance floor (for couples only).

Omelette Shop
CAFE $

(Sardar Market; dishes ₹15-25) Located beside the northern gate of Sardar Market, this spot goes through 1000 to 1500 eggs a day. The egg man has been doing his thing here for over 30 years. Three tasty, spicy boiled eggs cost ₹15, and a two-egg masala and cheese omelette with four pieces of bread is ₹25.

Kalinga Restaurant
MULTICUISINE $

(off Station Rd; mains ₹105-270) This restaurant near Jodhpur train station is smart and popular. It's in a dimly lit setting and has AC, a well-stocked bar, and tasty veg and non-veg North Indian tandooris and curries. Try the *lal maans,* a mouthwatering Rajasthani mutton curry.

Mid Town
INDIAN $

(off Station Rd; mains ₹70-120, thali ₹110-150; 🕐7am-11pm) This clean, AC restaurant does great veg food, including some Rajasthani specialities, and some particular to Jodhpur, such as *chakki-ka-sagh* (wheat dumpling cooked in rich gravy), *bajara-ki-roti pachkuta* (*bajara* wheat roti with local dry vegetables) and kabuli (vegetables with rice, milk, bread and fruit).

Priya Restaurant
INDIAN $

(181-182 Nai Sarak; mains ₹50-73) If you can handle the traffic fumes, this street-facing place has a certain cheerful clamour, and serves up reliable North and South Indian cuisine. The thalis (₹89) are good and there are sweets, too.

🍷 Drinking

Shri Mishrilal Hotel
CAFE

(Sardar Market; lassi ₹20; 🕐8am-10pm) Just inside the southern gate of Sardar Market, this place is nothing fancy but whips up the most superb creamy *makhania* lassis. These are the best in town, probably in all of Rajasthan, possibly in all of India.

Coffee drinkers will enjoy the precious beans and espresso machines at the deliciously air-conditioned **Cafe Sheesh Mahal** (Pal Haveli; 🕐10am-9pm); the rooftop coffee shop at the **Govind Hotel** (Station Rd); and, for those who need their dose of double-shot espresso, a branch of **Café Coffee Day** (Ansal Plaza, High Court Rd; 🕐10am-11pm).

🛍 Shopping

Plenty of Rajasthani handicrafts are available, with shops selling textiles and other wares clustered around Sardar Market and along Nai Sarak (you'll need to bargain hard).

Jodhpur is famous for antiques, with a concentration of showrooms along Palace Rd, 2km southeast of the centre. These warehouse-sized shops are fascinating to wander around, but they're well known to Western antique dealers, so you'll be hard-pressed to find any bargains. Also remember that the trade in antique architectural fixtures may be contributing to the desecration of India's cultural heritage (beautiful old *havelis* are often ripped apart for their doors and window frames). Restrictions apply to the export of Indian items over 100 years old. However, most of these showrooms deal in antique reproductions, and can make a piece of antique-style furniture and ship it home for you. The best bets for quality replica antiques are **Ajay Art Emporium** (Palace Rd) **Rani Handicrafts** (www.ranihandicrafts.com; Palace Rd), and **Rajasthan Arts & Crafts House** (www.rachindia.com; Palace Rd). These shops also have more portable and often less expensive items than furniture, such as textiles, carvings and silverware.

MV Spices   FOOD & DRINK
(www.mvspices.com) Nai Sarak (107 Nai Sarak; ◷9.30am-10pm); Sardar Market (209B Vegetable Market; ◷10am-9pm) The clock tower area has several tourist-oriented spice shops. This one has genuine spices and good service.

Sambhali Boutique CLOTHING, ACCESSORIES
(Makrana Mohalla; ◷10.30am-8pm) This small but interesting shop sells goods made by women who have learned craft skills with the Sambhali Trust.

Krishna Art & Crafts   HANDICRAFTS
(1st fl, Tija Mata ka Mandir, Tambaku Bazar) A good place to gain knowledge of traditional garments. It also has a large range of carpets and shawls.

Krishna Book Depot   BOOKSTORE
(Sardar Market; ◷10.30am-7.30pm) Stocks an impressive range of secondhand and new books, including Lonely Planet titles.

ℹ Information

There are ATMs all over the city, including State Bank ATMs at Jodhpur train station, on Nai Sarak, next to the Tourist Reception Centre (High Court Rd) and near Shahi Guest House. There's also an ICICI Bank ATM on Nai Sarak.

Main post office (Station Rd; ◷9am-4pm Mon-Fri, 9am-3pm Sat, stamp sales only 10am-3pm Sun)

Net Hut (Makrana Mohalla; internet per hr ₹30; ◷9.30am-11pm)

Om Forex (Sardar Market; internet per hr ₹30; ◷9am-10pm) Also exchanges currency and travellers cheques.

Police (Sardar Market; ◷24hr) Small police post inside the market's north gate.

State Bank of India (off High Court Rd; ◷10am-4pm Mon-Fri, 10am-1pm Sat) Changes currencies and travellers cheques; east of Umaid Gardens.

Tourist Reception Centre (☑2545083; High Court Rd; ◷9am-6pm Mon-Fri) Offers a free map and willingly answers questions.

ℹ Getting There & Away

Air

Jet Airways (☑5102222; www.jetairways.com; Residency Rd) and **Indian Airlines** (☑2510758; www.indian-airlines.nic.in; Circuit House Rd) both fly daily to Delhi and Mumbai, with Indian Airlines' Mumbai flights stopping at Udaipur on the way.

Bus

Destinations served from the RSRTC **Central Bus Stand** (Raika Bagh) include Ajmer (non-AC/AC ₹133/217, 4½ hours, half-hourly), Bikaner (₹145, 5½ hours, hourly), Delhi (₹379, 13 hours, four daily), Jaipur (express/deluxe/AC ₹197/239/346, seven hours, half-hourly), Jaisalmer (₹155, 5½ hours, 11 daily), Pushkar (₹125, five hours, five daily), Mt Abu (₹172, 5½ hours, three daily) and Udaipur (₹157, six to eight hours, 10 daily). Comfortable Volvo AC buses head off to Ajmer (₹300) and Jaipur (₹500) at 1am, and to Jaipur and Delhi (₹1100) at 4pm.

Numerous private bus companies, including Mahadev Travels, Jain Travels and VK Jain Travels, have offices on the street leading from Jodhpur train station to the Ranchodji Temple. They serve destinations such as Jaisalmer (₹150), Udaipur (₹160), Bikaner (₹140), Jaipur (₹180), Ajmer (₹120), Mt Abu (₹200) and Ahmedabad (₹260). Hotels and guesthouses will get you tickets for about ₹30 commission. Private buses leave from various locations around 2km southwest of Jodhpur train station, including Bombay Motors Circle, Kalpatru Cinema and Residency Rd – about ₹60 by autorickshaw from the clock tower.

Taxi

You can organise taxis for intercity trips, or longer, through most accommodation places, or deal direct with drivers. There's a taxi stand outside Jodhpur train station. A reasonable price is ₹6 per kilometre (for a non-AC car), with a minimum of 250km per day. The driver will charge at least ₹100 for overnight stops and will charge for his return journey.

Train

The computerised **booking office** (Station Rd; ◷8am-8pm Mon-Sat, 8am-1.45pm Sun) is 300m northeast of Jodhpur train station. There's a tourist quota (Window 786).

Most trains from the east stop at the Raika Bagh station before heading on to the main station, which is handy if you're heading for a hotel on the eastern side of town.

To Jaisalmer, the 14059 *Delhi–Jaisalmer Express* departs at 6.10am, arriving in Jaisalmer (2nd class/sleeper/3AC/2AC/1AC ₹100/165/419/566/944) at 11.45am. The 14810 *Jodhpur–Jaisalmer Express* departs every night at 11pm, arriving at 5am.

To Delhi, the 12462 *Mandore Express* leaves Jodhpur at 7.30pm, reaching Jaipur (sleeper/3AC/2AC/1AC ₹188/458/608/1015) at 12.40am, and Delhi (₹282/723/975/1627) at 6.25am. The 12466 *Intercity Express* departs at 5.55am, reaching Jaipur (2nd class/sleeper/AC chair/3AC ₹110/188/369/458) at 10.45am, and Sawai Madhopur (₹133/227/453/567) at 1.15pm. There are several daily trains to Bikaner, including the 14708 *Ranakpur Express* departing at 10.45am and arriving in Bikaner (sleeper/3AC/2AC ₹156/395/531) at 4.40pm.

For Karachi (Pakistan), the 14889 *Thar Express*, alias the *Jodhpur–Munabao Link Express*, leaves Bhagat Ki Kothi station, 4km south of the main station, at 1am on Saturday only, reaching Munabao on the India–Pakistan border at 7am. There you undergo lengthy border procedures before continuing to Karachi (assuming you have a Pakistan visa) in a Pakistani train, arriving about 2am on Sunday. Accommodation is 2nd class and sleeper only, with a total sleeper fare of around ₹400 from Jodhpur to Karachi. In the other direction the Pakistani train leaves Karachi at about 11pm on Friday, and Indian train 14890 leaves Munabao at 7pm on Saturday, reaching Jodhpur at 11.50pm. Schedules can be erratic, so check in Jodhpur for departure times and stations.

❶ Getting Around

To/From the Airport
The airport is 5km south of the city centre, about ₹200/100 by taxi/autorickshaw.

Autorickshaw
Autorickshaws between the clock tower area and the train stations or central bus stand should be about ₹35.

Around Jodhpur

The mainly arid countryside around Jodhpur is dotted with surprising lakes, isolated forts and palaces, and intriguing villages. It's home to a clutch of fine heritage hotels where you can enjoy the slower pace of rural life.

MANDORE
Situated 7km north of the centre of Jodhpur, Mandore was the capital of Marwar prior to the founding of Jodhpur. Only a few traces of the ancient seat of power remain, but the lush **Mandore Gardens** (☉9am-5.30pm), with their monuments and museum, make an appealing and relaxing excursion from Jodhpur (it's thronged with local tourists at weekends). Buses to Mandore (₹8) run about every five minutes from Jodhpur. You can catch them at a stop just east of the Tourist Reception Centre on High Court Rd.

OSIAN
This ancient Thar Desert town, 65km north of Jodhpur, was an important trading centre between the 8th and 12th centuries. It was dominated by the Jains, whose wealth left a legacy of exquisitely sculptured, well-preserved temples. The **Mahavira Temple** (Indian/foreigner free/₹10, camera/video ₹50/100; ☉6am-8.30pm) surrounds an image of the 24th *tirthankar* (great teacher), formed from sand and milk. **Sachiya Mata Temple** (☉6am-7.15pm) is an impressive walled complex where both Hindus and Jains worship.

Prakash Bhanu Sharma, a personable Brahmin priest, has an echoing **guesthouse** (☏02922-274331, 9414440479; s/d without bathroom ₹250/300), geared towards pilgrims, opposite the Mahavira Temple.

🖉**Gemar Singh** (☏9460585154; www.hacra.org), a native of Bhikamkor village northwest of Osian, arranges camel safaris, homestays, camping, desert walks and jeep trips in the deserts around Osian and their Rajput and Bishnoi villages. His trips receive rave reviews. The cost is around ₹1000 per person per day (minimum two people), including bus transfer from Jodhpur.

RSRTC buses run about hourly to/from Jodhpur (local/express ₹33/36, 1½ hours) and Phalodi (local/express ₹44/49, two hours). Trains between Jodhpur and Jaisalmer (three daily each way) also stop here. A return taxi from Jodhpur costs about ₹900.

SOUTHERN VILLAGES
A number of traditional villages are strung along and off the Pali road southeast of Jodhpur. Most hotels and guesthouses in Jodhpur offer tours to these villages. It's a well-worn trail and a lot depends on how good your guide is: a typical four-hour, 90km tour to the Bishnoi villages of Khejadali and Guda (east of the main road) and

the non-Bishnoi craft-making villages of Salawas (west of the road) and Kakani (on the road) costs ₹500 or ₹600 per person (minumum two people). A recommended Jodhpur-based operator is **Bishnoi Village Safari** (☑9829126398; www.bishnoivillagesafari .com), run by Deepak Dhanraj.

Many visitors are surprised by the density, and fearlessness, of wildlife such as blackbuck, bluebulls (nilgai), chinkara gazelles and desert fox around the Bishnoi villages. The Bishnoi are a Hindu sect who hold all animal life sacred. The 1730 sacrifice of 363 villagers to protect khejri trees is commemorated in September at **Khejadali** village, where there is a memorial to the victims fronted by a small grove of khejri trees.

ROHET

Rohet Garh (☑02936-268231; www.rohetgarh .com; s/d ₹4000/5000, ste ₹7500; ❄@☎☀☲), in Rohet village, 40km south of Jodhpur on the Pali road, is one of the area's most appealing heritage hotels. This 350-year-old, lovingly tended manor has masses of character and a tranquil atmosphere, which obviously helped Bruce Chatwin when he wrote *The Songlines* here, and William Dalrymple when he began *City of Djinns* in the same room, No 15. Rohet Garh has a gorgeous colonnaded pool, charming green gardens, great food and lovely, individual rooms. It also possesses a stable of fine Marwari horses and organises rides from two-hour evening rides (₹1500) to six-day back-country treks, sleeping in luxury tents.

Mihir Garh (☑9829023453; www.mihirgarh. com; ste incl full board & village safari ₹24,000; ❄@☎☀☲), the latest pride and joy of the family who own Rohet Garh, rises out of the plains 17km to the west of its sibling like a fantasy desert castle. Opened in 2009, this is the ultimate Rajasthan chill-out spot. It has just nine huge, all-different suites, equipped with contemporary amenities (including plunge pool or Jacuzzi) and beautiful Rajasthani artefacts. Three specialist chefs (Continental, Indian and desserts) cater to your personal culinary preferences, and you can relax in the infinity pool or the spa.

One of the strangest temples in all India stands 8km south of Rohet beside the Pali road, near Chotila village. The deity at **Om Bana Temple** is a garland-decked Enfield Bullet motorcycle, known as Bullet Baba. The story goes that local villager Om Bana died at this spot in the 1980s when his motorbike skidded into a tree. The bike was taken to the local police station, but then mysteriously twice made its own way back to the tree, and travellers along the road started seeing visions of Om Bana – inevitably leading to the machine's deification.

Buses to Rohet (₹29, one to 1½ hours) leave Jodhpur's Central Bus Stand about every 15 minutes. A taxi is around ₹800.

Jaisalmer

☑02992 / POP 58,286

The fort of Jaisalmer is a breathtaking sight: a massive sandcastle rising from the sandy plains like a mirage from a bygone era. No place better evokes exotic camel-train trade routes and desert mystery. Ninety-nine bastions encircle the fort's still-inhabited twisting lanes. Inside are shops swaddled in bright embroideries, a royal palace and numerous businesses looking for your tourist rupee. Despite the commercialism it's hard not to be enchanted by this desert citadel. Beneath the ramparts the narrow streets of the old city conceal magnificent *havelis*, all carved from the same golden-honey sandstone as the fort – hence Jaisalmer's designation as the Golden City.

A city that has come back almost from the dead in the past half-century, Jaisalmer may be remote but it's certainly not forgotten – indeed it's one of Rajasthan's biggest tourist destinations, and few people come here without climbing onto a camel in the surrounding Thar Desert. Competition to get *your* bum into a camel saddle can be fierce, with some operators adopting unpleasant hard-sell tactics (see the boxed text, p190, for more on camel safaris).

Jaisalmer celebrates its desert culture in January or February each year with the action-packed **Desert Festival**, featuring camel races, camel polo, folk music, snake charmers, turban-tying contests and the famous Mr Desert competition. Many events take place at the Sam sand dunes.

History

Jaisalmer was founded way back in 1156 by a leader of the Bhati Rajput clan named Jaisal. The Bhatis, who trace their lineage back to Krishna, ruled right through to Independence in 1947.

The city's early centuries were tempestuous, partly because its rulers relied on looting for want of other income, but by the 16th century Jaisalmer was prospering from its strategic position on the camel-train routes between India and Central Asia. It eventually established cordial relations with the Mughal empire. Maharawal Sabal Singh, in the mid-17th century, expanded the Jaisalmer princedom to its greatest extents by annexing areas that now fall within the administrative districts of Bikaner and Jodhpur.

Under British rule the rise of sea trade (especially through Mumbai) and railways saw Jaisalmer's importance and population decline. Partition in 1947, with the cutting of trade routes to Pakistan, seemingly sealed the city's fate. But the 1965 and 1971 wars between India and Pakistan gave Jaisalmer new strategic importance, and since the 1960s the Indira Gandhi Canal to the north has brought revitalising water to the desert.

Today tourism and the area's many military installations are the pillars of the city's economy.

◉ Sights

TOP CHOICE Jaisalmer Fort   FORT

Founded in 1156 by the Rajput ruler Jaisal and reinforced by subsequent rulers, Jaisalmer Fort was the focus of a number of battles between the Bhatis, the Mughals of Delhi and the Rathores of Jodhpur. You enter the fort from its east side and pass through four massive gates on the zigzagging route to the upper part. The fourth gate opens into a large square, Dashera Chowk, where Jaisalmer Fort's uniqueness becomes apparent: this is a living fort, with about 3000 people residing within its walls. It's honeycombed with narrow, winding lanes which are lined with houses and temples – along with a large number of handicraft shops, guesthouses, restaurants and massage/beauty parlours. Watch your bags and pockets as you wander around the fort – there have been some incidents of theft.

Fort Palace

(Indian/foreigner incl audio guide & camera ₹30/250; video ₹50/150; ⊙8am-6pm Apr-Oct, 9am-6pm Nov-Mar) Towering over the fort's main square, and partly built on top of the Hawa Pol (the fourth fort gate), is the former rulers' elegant seven-storey palace. The 1½-hour audio-guide tour, available in six languages, is worthwhile but you must deposit ₹2000 or your passport/driver's licence/credit card. Highlights include the mirrored and painted Rang Mahal (the bedroom of the 18th-century ruler Mulraj II), a gallery of finely wrought 15th-century sculptures

Touts work the buses heading to Jaisalmer from Jodhpur, hoping to steer travellers to guesthouses or hotels in Jaisalmer where they will get a commission. On arrival in Jaisalmer, most buses are surrounded by a swarm of touts baying for your attention. If an autorickshaw driver has a sign with the name of the accommodation you want, by all means take the free ride offered (after checking that it is free). Otherwise, don't believe anyone who offers to take you 'anywhere you like' for just a few rupees, and do take with a fistful of salt any claims that the hotel you want is 'full', 'closed' or 'no good any more'.

Also be very wary of offers of rooms for ₹100 or similar absurd rates. Places offering such prices are almost certainly in the camel-safari hard-sell game and their objective is to get you out of the room and on to a camel as fast as possible. If you don't take up their safari offers, the room price may suddenly increase or you might be told there isn't a room available any more.

Touts are less prevalent on the trains, but the same clamour for your custom ensues outside the station once you have arrived.

donated to the rulers by the builders of the fort's temples, and the spectacular 360-degree views from the rooftop. One room contains an intriguing display of stamps from the former Rajput states.

Jain Temples

(admission ₹30, camera/video/mobile phone ₹70/120/30; ⊙7am-1pm) Within the fort walls is a mazelike, interconnecting treasure trove of seven beautiful yellow-sandstone Jain temples, dating from the 15th and 16th centuries. The intricate carving rivals that of the marble Jain temples in Ranakpur and Mt Abu, and has an extraordinary quality because of the soft, warm stone. Shoes and all leather items must be removed before entering the temples.

Chandraprabhu is the first temple you come to inside. Dedicated to the eighth *tirthankar*, whose symbol is the moon, it was built in 1509 and features fine sculpture in the *mandapa*, whose intensely sculpted pillars form a series of *toranas*. To the right of Chandraprabhu is the tranquil **Rikhabdev**

RAJASTHAN WESTERN RAJASTHAN

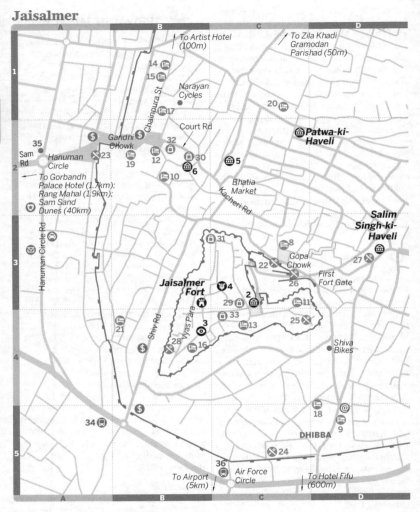

temple, with fine sculptures around the walls, protected by glass cabinets, and pillars beautifully sculpted with *apsaras* and gods. Behind Chandraprabhu is **Parasnath**, which you enter through a beautifully carved *torana* culminating in an image of the Jain *tirthankar* at its apex. A door to the south leads to small **Shitalnath**, dedicated to the 10th *tirthankar,* whose image is composed of eight precious metals. A door in the north wall leads to the enchanting, dim chamber of **Sambhavanth** – in the front courtyard, Jain priests grind sandalwood in mortars for devotional use. Steps lead down to the **Gyan**

Bhandar, a fascinating, tiny, underground library founded in 1500, which houses priceless ancient illustrated manuscripts. The remaining two temples, **Shantinath** and **Kunthunath**, were both built in 1536 and feature plenty of sensual carving.

Laxminarayan Temple

The Hindu Laxminarayan Temple, in the centre of the fort, is simpler than the Jain temples and has a brightly decorated dome. Devotees offer grain, which is distributed before the temple. The inner sanctum has a repoussé silver architrave around its en-

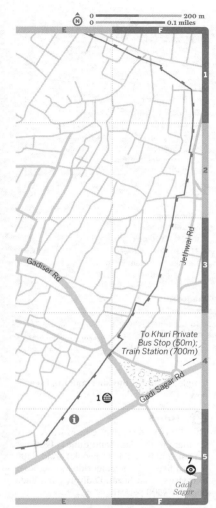

Map scale: 0 — 200 m / 0 — 0.1 miles

To Khuri Private Bus Stop (50m); Train Station (700m)

Gadiser Rd

Jethwai Rd

Gadi Sagar Rd

Gadi Sagar

lace. It is divided into five sections and was built between 1800 and 1860 by five Jain brothers who made their fortunes in brocade and jewellery. It's most impressive from the outside, though the first of the five sections is open as the privately owned **Kothari's Patwa-ki-Haveli Museum** (Indian/foreigner ₹50/120, camera/video ₹40/70; ⊙8.30am-7pm), which richly evokes 19th-century life.

Salim Singh-ki-Haveli HISTORIC BUILDING
(admission incl guide ₹20, camera/video ₹20/50; ⊙8am-7pm May-Sep, 8am-6pm Oct-Apr) This 18th-century *haveli* has an amazing, distinctive shape. The top storey spreads out into a mass of carving, with graceful arched balconies surmounted by pale blue cupolas. Salim Singh was a notorious 19th-century prime minister of Jaisalmer whose ill treatment of the area's Paliwal Brahmin community led them to abandon their 84 villages and move elsewhere.

Nathmal-ki-Haveli HISTORIC BUILDING
(admission ₹20; ⊙8am-7pm) This late-19th-century *haveli* also used to be a prime minister's house and is still partly inhabited. It has an extraordinary exterior, dripping with carvings and the 1st floor has some beautiful paintings using 1.5kg of gold. A doorway is surrounded by 19th-century British postcards and there's a picture of Queen Victoria. The left and right wings were the work of two brothers, whose competitive spirits apparently produced this virtuoso work – the two sides are similar, but not identical.

Museums

Desert Cultural Centre & Museum MUSEUM
(Indian/foreigner ₹20/50, camera/video ₹20/50; ⊙9am-8pm) Next to the Tourist Reception Centre, this interesting little museum has material in English and Hindi on the history of Rajasthan's different princely states, and exhibits on traditional Rajasthani culture. Features include Rajasthani music (with video), textiles and a *phad* scroll painting. It also hosts nightly half-hour **puppet shows** (Indian/foreigner ₹30/50, camera/video ₹20/50; ⊙6.30pm, 7.30pm) with English commentary.

Thar Heritage Museum MUSEUM
(off Court Rd; admission ₹40) This privately run museum near Gandhi Chowk also has an intriguing assortment of Jaisalmer area artefacts. It's brought alive by the guided tour you'll probably get from its founder, local historian and folklorist LN Khatri. Opening

trance, and a heavily garlanded image enshrined within.

Havelis

Inside the fort but outside it, too (especially in the streets to the north), Jaisalmer is replete with the fairy-tale architecture of *havelis* – gorgeously carved stone doorways, *jali* (carved lattice) screens, balconies and turrets.

Patwa-ki-Haveli HISTORIC BUILDING
The biggest fish in the *haveli* pond is Patwa-ki-Haveli, which towers over a narrow lane, its intricate stonework like honey-coloured

Jaisalmer

Top Sights

Jaisalmer Fort	B3
Patwa-ki-Haveli	C2
Salim Singh-ki-Haveli	D3

Sights

1 Desert Cultural Centre & Museum	E4
2 Fort Palace Museum	C3
3 Jain Temples	B4
4 Laxminarayan Temple	C3
5 Nathmal-ki-Haveli	C2
6 Thar Heritage Museum	B2
7 Tilon-ki-Pol	F5

Sleeping

8 Hotel Fort View	C3
9 Hotel Gorakh Haveli	D5
10 Hotel Jaisal Palace	B2
11 Hotel Killa Bhawan	C3
12 Hotel Nachana Haveli	B2
13 Hotel Paradise	C4
14 Hotel Pleasant Haveli	B1
15 Hotel Renuka	B1
16 Hotel Siddhartha	B4
17 Hotel Swastika	B1
18 Hotel The Royale Jaisalmer	D5
19 Mandir Palace Hotel	B2
20 Residency Centre Point	C1
21 Shahi Palace	B4

Eating

22 Bhang Shop	C3
23 Chandan Shree Restaurant	A2
24 Desert Boy's Dhani	C5
25 Free Tibet	C4
26 Jaisal Italy	C3
27 Natraj Restaurant	D3
Saffron	(see 12)
28 Sun Set Palace	B4
The Trio	(see 19)

Shopping

29 Bellissima	C3
30 Desert Handicrafts Emporium	B2
31 Hari Om Jewellers	C3
32 Jaisalmer Handloom	B2
33 Light of the East	C4

Transport

34 Bus Stand	A5
35 Hanuman Travels	A2
36 Private Bus Stand	C5
Swagat Travels	(see 35)

hours are variable, but if it's closed, you should find Mr Khatri at his shop, Desert Handicrafts Emporium, nearby on Court Rd.

Other Attractions

Gadi Sagar LAKE

This stately 14th-century tank, southeast of the city walls, was Jaisalmer's vital water supply until 1965, and because of its importance it is surrounded by many small temples and shrines. It's a waterfowl favourite in winter, but can almost dry up before the monsoon. The lake's large catfish population swarms in a writhing mass to the shore whenever someone is tossing breadcrumbs. **Boat hire** (8am-9pm) costs ₹50 to ₹100 for 30 minutes.

The attractive **Tilon-ki-Pol** gateway that straddles the road down to the tank is said to have been built by a famous prostitute. When she offered to pay to have it constructed, the maharawal refused permission on the grounds that he would have to pass under it to go down to the tank, which would be beneath his dignity. While he was away, she built the gate anyway, adding a Krishna temple on top so the king could not tear it down.

Tours

The Tourist Reception Centre runs sunset tours to the Sam sand dunes (₹200 per person, minimum four people). Add ₹100 if you'd like a short camel ride too. Another tour visits Amar Sagar, Lodhruva and Bada Bagh for ₹500 per car.

Sleeping

Staying in the fort is the most atmospheric and romantic chocie, but you should be aware of the pressure tourism is exerting on the fort's infrastructure (see the boxed text, p187). There is a wide choice of good places to stay outside the fort. Rates at many places fluctuate with the seasons: if there's a festival on, rooms are expensive and scarce, but at slow times most places offer big discounts. You'll get massive discounts between April and August, because Jaisalmer is hellishly hot then.

OUTSIDE THE FORT

Desert Moon
GUESTHOUSE $

([🖉]250116, 9414149350; www.desertmoonguest house.com; Achalvansi Colony; s ₹700-800, d ₹800-1000; [❄]) On the northwest edge of town, 1km from Gandhi Chowk, Desert Moon is in a peaceful location beneath the Vyas Chhatari sunset point. The guesthouse is run by a friendly Indian-Kiwi couple who offer free pick-up from the train and bus stations. The 11 rooms are cool, clean and comfortable ,and the rooftop vegetarian restaurant has fort and *chhatri* views.

Hotel Pleasant Haveli
HOTEL $$

([🖉]253253; www.pleasanthaveli.com; Chainpura St; r ₹1200-2000, ste ₹2000-3250; [❄][📶]) Recently renovated, this welcoming place has lots of lovely carved stone, a beautiful rooftop and just a handful of spacious, attractive, colour-themed rooms, all with bathroom and AC.

Residency Centre Point
GUESTHOUSE $

([🖉]/fax 252883; residency_guesthouse@yahoo. com; Kumbhara Para; r ₹450) Near the Patwa-ki-Haveli, this friendly, family-run guesthouse has five clean, spacious doubles in a lovely 250-year-old building. Rooms vary in size – budget by price but midrange in quality. The rooftop restaurant has superb fort views and offers home-cooked food.

Hotel Fifu
HOTEL $$

([🖉]254317; www.fifutravel.com; Bera Rd; r incl breakfast ₹2650; [❄][📶]) Down a dusty lane on the south edge of town, this hotel is a little out of the way, though the beautiful, colour-themed sandstone rooms afford a very peaceful and pleasant stay. The rooftop has tremendous views and a great vegetarian restaurant.

Hotel Nachana Haveli
HERITAGE HOTEL $$

([🖉]252110; www.nachanahaveli.com; Gandhi Chowk; s/d ₹2500/3000; [❄][@]) This 280-year-old royal *haveli,* set around three courtyards – one with a tinkling fountain – is a fascinating hotel. The raw sandstone rooms have arched stone ceilings and the ambience of a medieval castle. They are sumptuously and romantically decorated, though some lack much natural light.

Hotel Gorakh Haveli
HOTEL $$

([🖉]9982657525; www.hotelgorakhhaveli.com; Dhibba; s/d ₹1000/1500, with AC ₹1500/2500; [❄]) A pleasantly low-key spot south of the fort, Gorakh Haveli is a modern place built with traditional sandstone and some attractive carving. Rooms are comfy and spacious, staff are amiable, and there's a reasonable multicuisine rooftop restaurant.

Hotel Renuka
HOTEL $

([🖉]252757; hotelrenuka@rediffmail.com; Chainpura St; r ₹200-750; [❄][@]) Spread over three floors, Renuka has squeaky clean rooms – the best have balconies, bathrooms and AC. It's been warmly accommodating guests since 1988, so management knows its stuff. The roof terrace has great fort views and a good restaurant.

[📷] Artist Hotel
HOTEL $

([🖉]252082; www.artisthotel.info; Artist Colony; s ₹150-250, d ₹250-500, tr with AC ₹1000; [❄]) This friendly, Austrian-and-Indian-run establishment helps support – and maintain the artistic traditions of – formerly nomadic musicians and storytellers who are now settled in the same area of town. There are great fort views from the roof, where frequent musical

---

A CASTLE BUILT ON SAND

A decade ago the whole structure of Jaisalmer Fort was in danger of being undermined by water leakage from its antique drainage system. The main problem: material progress, in the form of piped water for the fort's inhabitants – something undreamt of when the fort was built. Three of the ancient bastions had collapsed and parts of the fort palace were leaning at an alarming rate.

Since then, British-based **Jaisalmer in Jeopardy** (www.jaisalmer-in-jeopardy.org) and several Indian organisations, including the **Indian National Trust for Art & Cultural Heritage** (INTACH; www.intach.org), have raised funds and carried out much-needed conservation works to save the fort. Most important has been the renewal of the fort's drainage system and repaving of the streets, as well as repair works inside the fort palace.

While the fort is no longer in imminent danger of subsiding, it remains a delicate structure. Thoughtless, often illegal, building work remains a threat to parts of its structure. Visitors should be aware of the fort's fragile nature and conserve resources, especially water, as much as possible.

events take place, and a very good range of European and Indian dishes (mains ₹85 to ₹220) is served. Rooms vary, but are clean and comfortable, with small bathrooms.

Shahi Palace
HOTEL $

(☏255920; www.shahipalacehotel.com; off Shiv Rd; r ₹550-2050; ✻@) A modern building in traditional style with some lovely carved sandstone, Shai Palace has attractive rooms, though a limited number have natural light. The cheaper rooms are mostly in two annexes along the street, **Star Haveli** and **Oasis Haveli**. The rooftop restaurant (mains ₹80 to ₹200) is excellent.

Mandir Palace Hotel
HERITAGE HOTEL $$$

(☏252788; www.mandirpalace.com; Gandhi Chowk; s/d ₹4500/5000, ste ₹8000-10,000; ✻☎☀) Jaisalmer's erstwhile royal family still lives in this sprawling 18th-century palace just inside the town walls. Some rooms are full of character, but the newer ones have less character, and staff can be distant.

Hotel Fort View
HOTEL $

(☏252214; Gopa Chowk; r ₹150-400) A friendly stalwart of the budget scene, close to the fort gate. The cheapest rooms are small and in the back, but clean. Rooms 21 and 31 have fort views. There's a popular fort-facing multicuisine restaurant (mains ₹50 to ₹80).

Hotel The Royale Jaisalmer
HOTEL $$

(☏252601; www.royalejaisalmer.com; Dhibba; r ₹1850-2500; ✻@☀) A good choice for its spacious, colourful, traditionally decorated rooms, multicuisine rooftop restaurant and neat pool in the rear courtyard.

Hotel Swastika
HOTEL $

(☏252483; swastikahotel@yahoo.com; Chainpura St; dm ₹100, s/d/tr ₹200/300/400, r with AC ₹600; ✻) In this well-run place the only thing you'll be hassled about is to relax. Rooms are plain, quiet, clean and good value.

Hotel Jaisal Palace
HOTEL $

(☏252717; www.hoteljaisalpalace.com; near Gandhi Chowk; s ₹600-1050, d ₹750-1250; ✻) This is a well-run, good-value hotel, though the rooms tend to be smallish and characterless.

IN THE FORT

Hotel Killa Bhawan
BOUTIQUE HOTEL $$$

(☏251204; www.killabhawan.com; 445 Kotri Para; r incl breakfast ₹3850-9400; ✻) A cute mini-labyrinth of a place combining three old houses set right on the fort walls. French-owned and designed, it has vividly coloured rooms,

attractive little sitting areas and all sorts of intriguing arts and crafts.

Hotel Paradise
HOTEL $$

(☏252674; www.paradiseonfort.com; r ₹300-2000, with AC from ₹1050; ✻@) Right above the fort's southern walls, Paradise has great terraces for lounging, eating and drinking, and nice clean rooms, many with views.

Hotel Siddhartha
HOTEL $

(☏253614; r ₹500-700) Just past the Jain temples, little Siddhartha has well-kept, stone-walled rooms; some with street or panoramic views and some have no views.

OUTSIDE TOWN

Fort Rajwada
HOTEL $$$

(☏253233; www.fortrajwada.com; Jodhpur-Barmer Link Rd; s/d ₹5400/7000, ste from ₹12,500; ✻@☎☀) Two kilometres east of town, off the Pokaran road, this large, modern but traditional-style place was built according to the ancient Indian design principles of *vaastu,* which is similar to feng shui. An opera designer created the interior, so it's suitably dramatic. Rooms are well equipped, though not huge, and there's a nice pool.

Gorbandh Palace Hotel
HOTEL $$$

(☏253801; www.hrhhotels.com; Sam Rd; r ₹6000; ✻@☎☀) Two kilometres west of Hanuman Circle, this grandiose modern hotel with large if unimaginative gardens is a good bet for families. It's constructed with traditional design elements from local sandstone. There's a superb pool (nonguests ₹200), a classy spa and a good bookshop. Rooms aren't huge, though some have balconies or terraces.

✕ Eating

As well as the many hotel-rooftop eateries, there's a good number of other places to enjoy a tasty meal, often with a view.

Desert Boy's Dhani
INDIAN $

(Dhibba; mains ₹70-90; ⊙8am-10pm) This is a walled-garden restaurant where tables are spread around a large, stone-paved courtyard with a big tree. Rajasthani music and dance is performed from 8pm to 10pm nightly, and it's a very pleasant place to eat excellent, good-value Rajasthani and other Indian veg dishes.

Jaisal Italy
ITALIAN $$

(First Fort Gate; mains ₹120-170) Though it's run by the same family as the Bhang Shop, you won't have to worry about bhang pizzas. Instead you'll find superb all-veg bruschetta, antipasti, pasta, pizza, salad and desserts, plus Spanish omelettes, served in an exotically decorated indoor restaurant (cosy in winter, deliciously air-conditioned in summer) or on a delightful terrace atop the lower fort walls, with cinematic views.

Sun Set Palace
MULTICUISINE **$**
(Fort; mains ₹60-120) This restaurant has cushions and low tables on an airy terrace on (as the name implies) the fort's west side. Pretty good vegetarian Indian dishes are prepared, as well as Chinese and Italian options.

Natraj Restaurant
MULTICUISINE **$$**
(mains ₹110-270) This is an excellent place to eat, and the rooftop has a satisfying view of the upper part of the Salim Singh-ki-Haveli next door. The veg and nonveg food, including tandoori and curries, as well as Chinese and Continental dishes, is consistently excellent, as is the service.

Saffron
MULTICUISINE **$$**
(Gandhi Chowk; mains ₹70-180) On the spacious roof terrace of Hotel Nachana Haveli, the veg and nonveg food here is excellent and it's a particularly atmospheric place in the evening. The Indian food is hard to beat, though the Italian comes a close second.

Free Tibet
MULTICUISINE **$$**
(Fort; mains ₹70-140; ⊗8am-9pm) It's multicuisine here, with everything from French baguettes to moussaka, but the speciality is Tibetan, including good noodle soups and *momos* (dumplings). It's near the fort's southeast corner, with good views from window tables.

The Trio
MULTICUISINE **$$**
(☑252733; Gandhi Chowk; mains ₹100-190) Under a tented roof atop the wall of the Mandir Palace, this long-running Indian, Chinese and Continental restaurant offers reliably good veg and nonveg dishes. The thalis and tandoori items are excellent, and the restaurant has a lot more atmosphere than most places in town. Traditional musicians play in the evening and there's a great fort view.

Chandan Shree Restaurant
INDIAN **$**
(near Hanuman Circle; mains ₹50-90, thalis ₹60-140) An always busy dining hall churning out a huge range of tasty, spicy South Indian, Gujarati, Rajasthani, Punjabi and Bengali dishes.

Bhang Shop
CAFE **$**
(Gopa Chowk; medium/strong lassi ₹50/60) Outside the First Fort Gate, this 'shop' (not the most attractive establishment in town) offers lassis of different strengths as well as bhang cookies, cakes and sweets; camel-safari packs are a speciality. Note that bhang doesn't agree with everyone (see p1167).

🛍 Shopping
Jaisalmer is famous for stunning embroidery, bedspreads, mirror-work wall hangings, oil lamps, stonework and antiques. Watch out when buying silver items: the metal is sometimes adulterated with bronze.

Hari Om Jewellers
HANDICRAFTS
(Chougan Para, Fort; ⊗10am-8.30pm) This family of silversmiths makes beautiful, delicate silver rings and bracelets featuring world landmarks and Hindu gods. Asking prices for rings start at ₹1800 (at a rate of ₹300 per day's work).

Jaisalmer Handloom
HANDICRAFTS
(Court Rd; www.jaisalmerhandloom.com; ⊗9am-8pm) Has a big array of bedspreads, tapestries, clothing (ready made and custom-made, including silk) and other textiles, made by its own workers and others, and doesn't belabour you with too much of a hard sell.

Light of the East
SOUVENIRS
(Tewata Para, Fort; ⊗8am-9pm) An enthralling little shop selling crystals and rare mineral specimens.

Desert Handicrafts Emporium
HANDICRAFTS
(Court Rd; ⊗9am-8pm) With some unusual jewellery, paintings and all sorts of textiles, this is one of the most original of numerous craft shops around town.

Bellissima
HANDICRAFTS
(Fort; ⊗8am-9pm) This small shop near the Fort's main square sells beautiful patchworks, embroidery, paintings, bags, rugs, cushion covers and all types of Rajasthani art. Proceeds assist women.

ℹ Information

Internet Access
There are several internet cafes in the fort, but not so many outside it. Typical cost is ₹40 per hour.

SOCH it (Dhibba; internet per hr ₹40; ⊗7.30am-10pm)

Money
ATMs include State Bank and SBBJ near Hanuman Circle, SBBJ and ICICI Bank on Shiv Rd, and State Bank outside the train station.

RAJASTHAN WESTERN RAJASTHAN

Trekking around by camel is the most evocative and fun way to sample Thar Desert life. Don't expect dune seas, however – the Thar is mostly arid scrubland sprinkled with villages and wind turbines, with occasional dune areas popping out here and there. You will often come across fields of millet, and children herding flocks of sheep or goats whose neck-bells tinkle in the desert silence – a welcome change after the sound of belching camels.

Most trips now include jeep rides to get you to less frequented areas. An alternative to Jaisalmer is to base yourself in Khuri, 48km southwest, where some good safaris are available and you're already in the desert when you start.

Before You Go

Competition between safari organisers is cut-throat and standards vary. Most hotels and guesthouses are very happy to organise a camel safari for you. While many provide a good service, some may cut corners and take you for the kind of ride you didn't have in mind. A few low-budget hotels in particular exert considerable pressure on guests to take 'their' safari. Others specifically claim 'no safari hassle'.

You can also organise a safari directly with one of the several reputable specialist agencies in Jaisalmer. Since these agencies depend exclusively on safari business it's particularly in their interest to satisfy their clients. It's a good idea to talk to other travellers and ask two or three operators what they're offering.

A one-night safari, leaving Jaisalmer in the afternoon and returning next morning, with a night on some dunes, is a minimum to get a feel for the experience: you'll probably get 1½ to two hours riding each day. You can trek for several days or weeks if you wish. The longer you ride, the more you'll gain understanding of the desert's villages, oases, wildlife and people.

The best known dunes, at Sam (40km west of Jaisalmer) and Khuri, are always crowded in the evening and are more of a carnival than a back-to-nature experience. 'Nontouristy' and 'off the beaten track' trips take you to other areas, usually southwest from Jaisalmer to the area between Sam and Khuri, or beyond Khuri.

With jeep transfers included, typical rates are between ₹550 and ₹750 per person per day. This should include three meals a day, plus as much mineral water and as many blankets as you need, and often thin mattresses. Check that there will be one camel for each rider. You can pay for greater levels of comfort (eg tents, better food), but always get it all down in writing.

You shouldn't have to pay for a full day if you're returning after breakfast on the last day. One-night safaris starting in the afternoon and ending the following morning are normally charged as about 1½ days.

Thomas Cook (Gandhi Chowk; ☺9.30am-7pm Mon-Sat, 10am-5pm Sun) A reliable moneychanger, changing travellers cheques and cash, and providing credit- and debit-card advances.

Post
Main post office (Hanuman Circle Rd; ☺10am-5pm Mon-Sat)

Tourist Information
Tourist Reception Centre (☎252406; Gadi Sagar Rd; ☺9.30am-6pm) This friendly office has a free (if rather old) town map and various brochures. Staff will helpfully answer all sorts of questions.

Getting There & Away

Air
The airport, 5km south of town, opens and closes intermittently due to border tensions with Pakistan. In early 2011 it was closed. The most recent flights were operated by **Kingfisher Airlines** (www.flykingfisher.com) to Jodhpur.

Bus
RSRTC buses leave from a stand just off Shiv Rd on the south side of town. There are buses to Jodhpur (ordinary/express ₹125/155, 5½ hours, 15 daily), Bikaner (₹130/162, seven hours, four daily) and Jaipur (semi-deluxe ₹375, 12 hours, 5.30pm).

Private buses mostly leave from a yard near Desert Boy's Dhani, south of the fort. You can

What to Take

Women should consider wearing a sports bra, as a trotting camel is a bumpy ride. A wide-brimmed hat (or Lawrence of Arabia turban), long trousers, long-sleeved shirt, insect repellent, toilet paper, torch, sunscreen, water bottle (with a strap), and some cash (for a tip to the camel men, if nothing else) are also recommended. It can get cold at night, so if you have a sleeping bag bring it along, even if you're told that lots of blankets will be supplied. During summer, rain is not unheard of, so come prepared.

Which Safari?

» **Ganesh Travels** (☑250138; ganeshtravel45@hotmail.com; Fort) Run by camel owners from the villages and has a good basic rate of ₹550 per day. Most shorter trips are in the Bersiala area, 50km to 60km southwest of Jaisalmer.

» **Sahara Travels** (☑252609; sahara_travels@yahoo.com; Gopa Chowk) Its office is just outside the First Fort Gate. This agency gets good reviews and is run by the proudly bearded and moustachioed LN Bissa, alias Mr Desert. Trips may circle the area around Sam, or head out beyond Khuri. The normal daily rate is ₹700.

» **Trotters** (☑9414469292; www.trotterscamelsafarijaisalmer.com; Gopa Chowk) Trotters has a daily rate of ₹750 but provides very reliable service. Its one-night, off-the-beaten-track option costs between ₹900 and ₹1500 depending on your departure and return times.

There are several other options, including hotel-organised safaris. Note that recommendations here should not be a substitute for doing your own research. Whichever agency you go for, insist that all rubbish is carried back to Jaisalmer.

In the Desert

Camping out at night, huddling around a tiny fire beneath the stars and listening to the camel drivers' songs, is magical.

There's always a long lunch stop during the hottest part of the day. At resting points the camels are unsaddled and hobbled; they'll often have a roll in the sand before limping away to browse on nearby shrubs, while the camel drivers brew chai or prepare food.

Take care of your possessions, particularly on the return journey. Any complaints you do have should be reported, either to the **Superintendent of Police** (☑252233), the Tourist Reception Centre, or the intermittently staffed Tourist Assistance Force posts inside the First Fort Gate and on the Gadi Sagar access road.

The camel drivers will expect a tip or gift at the end of the trip; don't neglect to give them one.

book through your accommodation (which adds ₹30 to the fare) or direct with the bus company ticket offices, most of which are at Hanuman Circle, including Swagat Travels, which has buses to Jodhpur (seat/sleeper ₹150/250, 16 daily), Bikaner (₹150/250, three daily), Ahmedabad (₹350/450, 12 hours, 5.30pm) and Udaipur (₹350/450, 12 hours, 3.30pm), and Hanuman Travels, with services to Jaipur (₹280/380, 4.30pm) and Bhuj (₹400/800, 15 hours, 2.30pm). These prices are for direct buses; some agencies may also sell tickets requiring a change of bus at Jodhpur, and some travellers have found themselves in Jodhpur with a useless onward ticket, so do clarify what you're getting.

Taxi

One-way taxis should cost about ₹1800 to Jodhpur, ₹2500 to Bikaner or ₹4500 to Udaipur. There is a stand on Hanuman Circle Rd.

Train

The **train station** (◷ticket office 8am-8pm Mon-Sat, 8am-1.45pm Sun) is on the eastern edge of town, just off the Jodhpur road.

Two daily express trains leave for Jodhpur. The 14809 *Jaisalmer–Jodhpur Express* (sleeper/3AC ₹165/419) departs at 11.15pm, reaching Jodhpur at 5.20am. The 14060 *Jaisalmer–Delhi Express* leaves at 4.30pm, reaching Jodhpur (sleeper/3AC/2AC ₹165/419/566) at 9.50pm, and continues to Jaipur (₹262/693/945,

10½ hours from Jaisalmer) and Delhi (₹331/888/1215, 18½ hours).

Trains 14703 and 14701 leave Jaisalmer at 10.40am and 10.45pm respectively for Bikaner (sleeper ₹168, 5½ hours).

ⓘ Getting Around

Autorickshaw

Official rates (first kilometre ₹11, each subsequent kilometre ₹6, minute of waiting ₹0.20) are posted at some autorickshaw stands. That adds up to about ₹25 from the train station to Gandhi Chowk, for example, but you may have to bargain hard to get this price.

Bicycle

A good way to get around town is by bicycle. There are a number of hire places, including **Narayan Cycles** (near Gandhi Chowk; per hr/day ₹10/40).

Car & Motorcycle

It's possible to hire taxis or jeeps from the stand on Hanuman Circle Rd. To Khuri, the Sam sand dunes or Lodhruva, expect to pay ₹500 return including a wait of about an hour or so. A full day of sightseeing around Jaisalmer is around ₹1000.

Shiva Bikes (Dhibba; scooter/motorbike per day ₹300/400) is a licensed hire place with adequate motorbikes and scooters for exploring town and nearby sights (helmets and area maps included).

Around Jaisalmer

SAM SAND DUNES

The silky **Sam sand dunes** (admission vehicle/camel ₹50/80), 41km west of Jaisalmer along a good sealed road (maintained by the Indian army), are one of the most popular excursions from the city. The band of dunes is about 2km long and is undeniably one of the most picturesque in the region. Some camel safaris camp here, but many more people just roll in for sunset, to be chased across the sands by dressed-up dancing children and tenacious camel owners offering short rides. Plenty more people stay overnight in one of the couple of dozen tent resorts near the dunes. All in all the place acquires something of a carnival atmosphere from late afternoon till the next morning, making it somewhere to avoid if you're after a solitary desert sunset experience.

If you're organising your own camel ride on the spot, expect to pay ₹200 to ₹300 for a one-hour sunset ride, but beware of tricks from camel men such as demanding more money en route.

KHURI

☑ 03014

The village of Khuri, 48km southwest of Jaisalmer, has quite extensive dune areas attracting their share of sunset visitors, and a lot of mostly smallish 'resorts' offering the same sort of overnight packages as Sam. It also has a number of low-key guesthouses where you can stay in tranquillity in a traditional-style hut with clay-and-dung walls and thatched roof, and venture out on interesting camel trips in the relatively remote and empty surrounding area. Khuri is within the **Desert National Park** which stretches over 3162 sq km southwest of Jaisalmer to protect part of the Thar ecosystem, including wildlife such as the desert fox, desert cat, chinkara gazelle, nilgai or bluebull (a large antelope), and some unusual bird life including the endangered great Indian bustard.

🛏 Sleeping & Eating

Badal House   HOMESTAY $

(☑9660535389; per person incl full board r or hut ₹300) Here you can stay in a family compound in the centre of the village with a few spotlessly clean, mud-walled, thatch-roofed huts and equally spotless rooms (one with its own squat toilet), and enjoy good home cooking. Former camel driver Badal Singh is a charming, gentle man who charges ₹500 for a camel safari with a night on the dunes. He doesn't pay commission so don't let touts warn you away.

Gangaur Guest House   GUESTHOUSE $

(☑7742547711, 9929296900; hameersingh@yahoo.com; huts per person from ₹500, tent per person ₹1000) One of the closest lodgings to the main dunes (on the south side of the village), this has yet another circle of snug huts. Prices are for packages including a camel ride, dinner with traditional dance entertainment and breakfast. Wildlife jeep tours (per person per day ₹500) as well as overnight camel safaris in the less touristy area east of Khuri are on offer.

Arjun Family   GUESTHOUSE $

(☑274132; arjunguesthouse@yahoo.co.in; per person incl full board huts/r ₹150/200) A couple of doors from Badal House, this is another friendly family offering very clean lodgings, home-cooked meals and inexpensive safaris. Rooms have attached bathroom, huts don't.

Getting There & Away

Private buses to Khuri (₹30, one hour) leave from the Barmer road corner in the southeast of Jaisalmer at about 10.30am, 11.30am, 3.30pm and 5pm. You may be approached by camel-safari touts en route.

Bikaner

♪ 0151 / POP 529.007

Bikaner is a vibrant, dust-swirling desert town with a fabulous fort and an energising outpost feel. It's less dominated by tourism than many other Rajasthan cities, though it has plenty of hotels and a busy camel-safari scene, which is attracting more and more travellers looking to avoid the Jaisalmer hustle. Bikaner's atmospheric walled old city sits in what's now the southwest of the city, with the main train station (Bikaner Junction) and Junagarh fort to its northeast, in what's more or less the centre of town.

Few people come to Bikaner without taking a trip out to the notorious Karni Mata Temple at Deshnok, 30km south, where pilgrims worship thousands of holy rats.

Around the full moon in January or very late December, Bikaner celebrates its three-day **Camel Festival**, with one day of events at the Karni Singh Stadium and two days out at Ladera, 45km northeast of the city.

History

The city was founded in 1488 by Rao Bika, a son of Rao Jodha, Jodhpur's founder, though the two Rathore ruling houses later had a serious falling out over who had the right to keep the family heirlooms. It grew fast as a staging post on the great caravan trade routes from the late 16th century onwards, and flourished under a friendly relationship with the Mughals, but declined as they did in the 18th century. By the 19th century the area was markedly backward, but managed to turn its fortunes around by hiring out camels to the British during the Afghan War. In 1886 it was the first desert princely state to install electricity.

☉ Sights

TOP CHOICE Junagarh FORT

(Indian/foreigner ₹30/200, video ₹100, audio guide incl camera ₹250; ☉10am-5.30pm, last entry 4.30pm) This most impressive fort was constructed between 1589 and 1593 by Raja Rai Singh, ruler of Bikaner and a general in the army of the Mughal Emperor Akbar. You enter through the Karan Prole gate on the east side and pass through three more gates before the ticket office for the palace-museum.

The admission price includes a group tour in Hindi and/or English with an official guide. The one-hour tours leave every 15 to 20 minutes. The audio guide (requiring an identity document as a deposit), available in English, French, German and Hindi, is very informative and allows you to visit at a more leisurely pace.

The beautifully decorated **Karan Mahal** was the palace's Diwan-i-Am (Hall of Public Audience), built in the 17th and 18th centuries. **Anup Mahal Chowk** has lovely carved *jarokhas* (balcony-windows) and *jali* screens, and was commissioned in the late 17th century by Maharaja Anup Mahal. Rooms off here include the sumptuous **Anup Mahal**, a hall of private audience with walls lacquered in red and gold, and the **Badal Mahal** (Cloud Palace), whose walls are beautifully painted with blue cloud motifs and red and gold lightning.

The **Gaj Mandir**, the suite of Maharaja Gaj Singh (r 1745–87) and his two top wives, is a fantastic symphony of gold paint, colourful murals, sandalwood, ivory, mirrors, niches and stained glass. From here you head up to the palace roof to enjoy the views and then down eventually to the superb **Ganga Durbar Hall** of 1896, with its pink stone walls covered in fascinating relief carvings. You then move into **Maharaja Ganga Singh's office** and finally the **Vikram Vilas Durbar Hall**, where pride of place goes to a WWI De Havilland DH-9 biplane bomber.

Old City AREA

The old city still has a medieval feel despite the motorbikes and autorickshaws. This labyrinth of narrow, winding streets conceals a number of fine old *havelis,* and a couple of notable Jain temples (**Bhandasar Temple** and **Sandeshwar Temple**), and makes for an interesting wander, on which we guarantee you will get lost at least once. The main entrance from the city centre is the triple-arched Kothe Gate, surrounded by a bustling commercial area.

Sri Sadul Museum MUSEUM

(Indian/foreigner ₹25/50, camera/video free/₹150; ☉10am-5.30pm) In the grounds of the royal Lallgarh Palace (now a hotel), about 2km northeast of Junagarh, this well-presented museum celebrates the history of Bikaner's Rathore royal family. You can see Maharaja Sadul Singh's 1940s railway carriage,

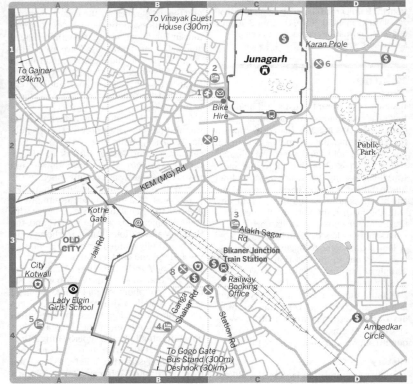

Maharaja Karni Singh's golf clubs and hairbrush, a nice collection of Bikaner school miniatures, and lots of shooting photos right down to the medals of contemporary Princess Rajyashree Kumari, who excelled in target shooting rather than wildlife shooting.

🛏 Sleeping

Hotels and guesthouses are scattered all round town. If you're arriving by train in the early morning, check whether you'll have to pay extra for occupying the room before noon.

Bhanwar Niwas HERITAGE HOTEL $$$
(☎2529323; www.bhanwarniwas.com; Rampuria St, Old City; s ₹4000-5000, d ₹5000-6000, ste ₹14,000; ❀@) This superb hotel has been developed out of the beautiful Rampuria Haveli – a gem in the old city, 300m southwest of the City Kotwali police station. It has 26 all-different, spacious and delightfully deco-

rated rooms, featuring stencil-painted wallpaper, marble or mosaic floors and antique furnishings. Comfortable common rooms drip with antiques and are arranged around a large internal courtyard, which doubles as a venue for cultural events.

Hotel Desert Winds HOTEL $$
(☎2542202; www.hoteldesertwinds.in; s ₹900-1100, d ₹1100-1300; ❀@) This lovely hotel with spotless, spacious rooms and a friendly, relaxed atmosphere is 1km northeast of the fort. It's owned by a retired deputy director of Rajasthan Tourism and his family, who can give you plenty of info about the city.

Bhairon Vilas HERITAGE HOTEL $$
(☎2544751, 9928312283; http://hotelbhaironvilas. tripod.com; s ₹1000-1800, d ₹1300-2100; ❀@☎) This hotel on the west side of Junagarh is run by a former Bikaner prime minister's great-grandson. Rooms are mostly large and are eclectically decorated with antiques,

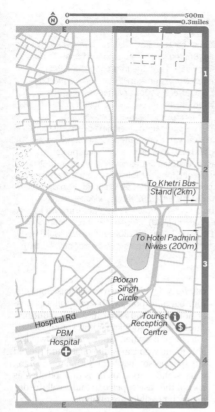

descendants of Bikaner prime ministers. The AC rooms are spacious, plain and airy, though some of the external paintwork needs attention. It's a two-minute walk from the main train station (via the station's 'foot over bridge'); self-catering is also possible.

Vijay Guest House GUESTHOUSE **$**
(☎2231244, 9829217331; www.camelman.com; Jaipur Rd; s ₹300-1000, d ₹400-1200; a) About 4km east of the centre, this is a home away from home with 10 spacious, light-filled rooms and a friendly family. Owner Vijay is a camel expert and a recommended safari operator. This is an ideal base for taking a safari, with good home-cooked meals (₹125 to ₹200), which you can eat inside or in the garden. As well as camel trips, they offer free pick-up and drop-off from the train and bus stations, and jeep outings to Deshnok and other sights around Bikaner.

Hotel Padmini Niwas HOTEL **$**
(☎2522794; padmini_hotel@rediffmail.com; 148 Sadul Ganj; r without/with AC ₹850/1050; ❋@⊠) A fabulous place to unwind away from the rush of the city. Padmini Niwas has clean, carpeted rooms and a chilled-out, helpful owner. The lawn area is a revelation, boasting one of the town's few outdoor pools.

Hotel Marudhar Heritage HOTEL **$**
(☎2522524; hmheritage2000@hotmail.com; Ganga Shahar Rd; s ₹400-1200, d ₹500-1500; ❋@)

gold-threaded curtains and old family photographs (some of the wiring and fittings seem to be of the same vintage). Three-hour city tours with government-authorised guides (₹200) and a range of camel and jeep safaris are on offer.

Laxmi Niwas Palace HERITAGE HOTEL **$$$**
(☎2202777; www.laxminiwaspalace.com; s ₹7700-9900, d ₹8800-11,000, ste ₹18,000-25,000; ❋@❂) Located 2km north of the city centre, this pink-sandstone hotel is part of the royal palace, dating from 1902. It has opulent interiors with lovely stone carving. Rooms are mostly large, elegant and evocative, and the bar and billiards room are overlooked by skins, heads and photos of deceased wildlife.

Hotel Jaswant Bhawan HOTEL **$$**
(☎2548848; www.hoteljaswantbhawan.com; s/d ₹600/800, with AC ₹1000/1200; ❋@) This is a pleasant, quiet, welcoming place run by

BIKANER SAFARIS

Bikaner is an excellent alternative to the Jaisalmer camel safari scene and increasingly popular with travellers. There are fewer people running safaris here, so the hassle factor is quite low. Camel trips tend to focus on desert villages and the interesting wildlife.

Three days and two nights is a common camel-safari duration, but half-day, one-day and short overnight trips are all possible. If you're after a serious camel trek, go for a cross-country trip to Kichan (about six days), famous for its concentration of large, graceful demoiselle cranes from September to March, or Jaisalmer (two weeks).

Typical prices are around ₹1000 to ₹1200 per person per day including overnight camping, with tents, mattresses, blankets, meals, mineral water, one camel per person, a camel cart to carry the gear (and sometimes tired riders), and a guide in addition to the camel men. Many trips start at Raisar, about 8km east of Bikaner, or Deshnok, 30km south.

The two most popular operators, both reliable and long established, are the Camel Man (☑2231244, 9829217331; www.camelman.com; Vijay Guest House, Jaipur Rd), run by Vijay Singh Rathore, and Vino Desert Safari (☑2270445, 9414139245; www.vinodesertsafari.com; Vino Paying Guest House, Ganga Shahar), run by Vinod Bhojak. The French-run NGO AFEV (☑9829867323; www.afevinde.com; Pause Café, KEM Rd) offers desert horse-cart and bike trips as well as camel safaris. Vinayak Desert Safari (☑2202634; www.vinayakdesertsafari.com; Vinayak Guest House) does appealing jeep safaris (per person per day ₹1500) focusing on desert animals and birds.

This is a friendly, well-run and good-value option a short walk from the main train station. There are plain and comfortable rooms with TV and phone to suit most budgets. You may wish to avoid the carpeted rooms which are a bit musty. Checkout is 24 hours after you check in.

Vinayak Guest House GUESTHOUSE $
(☑2202634; vinayakguesthouse@gmail.com; r ₹150-800, s without bathroom ₹100; ✳@) This place offers six varied and clean rooms in a quiet family house with a little sandy garden. On offer are a free pick-up service, good home-cooked food, cooking lessons, bicycles (per day ₹25), and camel safaris and wildlife trips with Vinayak Desert Safari. It's just 400m north of Junagarh fort.

Vino Paying Guest House GUESTHOUSE $
(☑2270445, 9414139245; www.vinodesertsafari.com; Ganga Shahar; s ₹150-200, d ₹250-350; @✉) This guesthouse is in a family home 3km south of the main train station. It's a cosy choice and is the base of one of Bikaner's best camel-safari operations. It's excellent value, and the family is enthusiastic, helpful and welcoming. They also serve up good home-cooked food and offer free cooking classes. It's opposite Gopeshwar Temple; they'll pick you up for free from the main train station.

Shanti House GUESTHOUSE $
(☑2543306; inoldcity@yahoo.com; New Well, near City Kotwali; r ₹250-400; @) This is a tiny old-city *haveli* with a narrow staircase and just four bargain rooms with squat toilets, bucket hot water and some nice wall paintings. The bustle of old Bikaner is at your doorstep. The helpful owner, Gouri, is a knowledgeable guide who can walk you around the old city (per person per hour ₹30). Free cooking classes and station pickups (a good idea as it's not the easiest place to find – call the day before if possible) are offered.

Hotel Harasar Haveli HOTEL $$
(☑2209891; www.harasar.com; near Karni Singh Stadium; r ₹500-2000) Most rickshaw-wallahs will want to bring you to this hotel, 1km northeast of Junagarh fort, which is notorious for its commission-paying tactics. So it's a good place to meet other travellers. The 38 plain rooms cover a big range in price, size and cleanliness. There's a decent rooftop restaurant.

✗ Eating

Gallops MULTICUISINE $$
(mains ₹200-400; ⊙10.30am-10pm) This modern-ish cafe-restaurant close to the Junagarh entrance is known as 'Glops' to rickshaw-wallahs. There are snacks such as pizzas, pakoras and sandwiches, and a good range of Indian and Chinese veg and non-veg dishes. You can sit outside or curl up in an armchair in the air-conditioned interior with a cold beer, espresso coffee or fuming hookah.

Pause Café
CAFE $

(KEM Rd; dishes ₹30-70; ☺10am-10pm; 📶) A travellers' hang-out with a nice garden setting and internet (per hour ₹20, wi-fi per hour ₹10), French-run Pause serves up soups, chips, cheese toast, salads, rice and dhal, a daily vegetarian dish, banana lassi and real coffee. It's run by the NGO AFEV (p41) and is also the contact point for AFEV's 'equitable-tourism' camel safaris.

Heeralal's
INDIAN $

(Station Rd; mains ₹50-110; ☺noon-10.30pm) This bright and hugely popular 1st-floor restaurant serves up pretty good veg and nonveg Indian dishes, plus a few Chinese and pizzas (but unfortunately no beer), amid large banks of plastic flowers.

Palace Garden Restaurant
INDIAN, CHINESE $$

(Hotel Laxmi Niwas; mains ₹110-240; ☺7.30-10pm) This excellent garden restaurant at one of Bikaner's best hotels is a lovely place to eat – at least until the nights become too chilly. The fare spans South Indian, veg and nonveg North Indian, and Chinese, and if you're lucky there will be live music.

Bhanwar Niwas
INDIAN $$

(☎2529323; Rampuria St, Old City; set lunch/dinner ₹350/375; ☺lunch & dinner) A splendid place to eat, this beautiful hotel welcomes nonguests to its veg dining hall (reservations are essential). You can have a drink before dinner in the courtyard.

Laxmi Hotel
INDIAN $

(Station Rd; mains ₹40-80, thali ₹60-100) A simple place, Laxmi is open to the street and dishes up tasty, fresh vegetarian thalis. You can see the roti being flipped in front of you.

Amber Restaurant
INDIAN $

(Station Rd; mains ₹75-115, thali ₹51-105; ☺8am-10.30pm) It has a staid, no-nonsense look, but Amber is well regarded and popular for veg fare. To one side is an Indian sweets counter, to the other an ice-cream parlour.

ℹ Information

You'll find a State Bank ATM outside the main train station, and Bank of Baroda ATMs opposite the station and next to the Tourist Reception Centre. There are several cybercafes on Ganga Shahar Rd.

Cyber Station (internet per hr ₹20; ☺6.30am-11pm)

Lake Palace Trade & Travels (Junagarh; ☺9am-6pm Mon-Sat) Just inside the fort

entrance; changes currency and travellers cheques.

Main post office (☺9am-4pm Mon-Fri, 9am-2pm Sat) Near Bhairon Vilas hotel.

Modi Cyber Cafe (Station Rd; internet per hr ₹20; ☺9.30am-9.30pm) Under a Vadilal (ice cream) sign.

Tourist Reception Centre (☎2226701; ☺9.30am-6pm Mon-Fri) This very helpful and friendly office (near Pooran Singh Circle) can answer most tourism-related questions and provide transport schedules and a map-brochure.

ℹ Getting There & Away

Bus

The RSRTC's Central Bus Stand is 1.5km northeast of Junagarh fort. If your bus is coming from the south, you can ask the driver to let you out closer to the city centre. RSRTC buses depart for Jodhpur (₹143, 5½ hours, half-hourly), Jaipur (₹191, seven hours, hourly 5am to 6pm) via Fatehpur and Sikar, Udaipur (₹289, 13 hours, 4.30pm), Delhi (₹287, 11 hours, three daily) via Mandawa (₹117, five hours), Jhunjhunu (₹130, five hours, two daily) and Ajmer (₹156, seven hours, seven daily).

Private buses and their ticket offices mostly congregate along the southern wall of the fort. Destinations include Jaisalmer (seat/sleeper ₹140/200, seven hours, 5.30am, 3pm and 10pm), Jodhpur (₹150/200, six daily), Jaipur (₹150/200, 11 daily), Delhi (₹250/300, 7.30pm, 8pm and 8.30pm), Ajmer (₹150/200, 10pm and 11pm)and Pushkar (₹150/180, seven hours, 9pm, 10pm and 11pm). Private buses to Fatehpur, Nawalgarh and Mandawa leave about every half-hour, 10am to 7pm, from a stop on the Jaipur road known as the Khetri bus stand. A private bus to Amritsar (seat/sleeper ₹300/350, 15 hours, 5.45pm) leaves from Ambedkar Circle.

Train

The main train station is Bikaner Junction, with a **computerised reservations office** (☺8am-8pm Mon-Sat, 8am-2pm Sun) in a separate building just east of the main station building. A couple of other useful services go from Lalgarh Junction station in the north of the city.

To Jaipur, the 09733 *Hanumangarh–Kota Special* leaves at 10.17pm (sleeper/3AC/2AC ₹188/487/659, seven hours) and the 12467 *Intercity Express* leaves at 5.30am (2nd class ₹123, 6¾ hours), both from Bikaner Junction. For Jodhpur the 14707 *Ranakpur Express* departs Bikaner Junction at 9.30am (sleeper/3AC/2AC ₹156/395/531, five hours). The 15610 *Avadh–Assam Express* leaves Lalgarh Junction at 7.45pm for Delhi (sleeper/3AC/2AC ₹262/693/945, 11½ hours). To Jaisalmer (sleeper ₹168, six hours), the

14702 *Bikaner–Jaisalmer Express* leaves Bikaner Junction at 11.35pm, and the 14704 *Lalgarh–Jaisalmer Express* leaves Lalgarh Junction at 7.20am.

❶ Getting Around

An autorickshaw from the train station to Junagarh fort should cost ₹30, but you'll probably be asked for more.

Bikaner Motorbikes & Bicycle Hire (www.bikanermotorbikesbicyclehirerentalcenter.com; ☻9am-7pm), by the roundabout 600m northeast of Junagarh fort, rents out 18-gear mountain bikes for ₹300 per day, ordinary gearless bikes for ₹50, 125cc and 150cc motorbikes for ₹400 and 180cc motorbikes for ₹600. Motorbikes come with a clean helmet! It also offers interesting guided day and half-day desert rides by bike or motorbike.

Around Bikaner

NATIONAL RESEARCH CENTRE ON CAMELS

The **National Research Centre on Camels** (🕿0151-2230183; Indian/foreigner ₹10/20, camera ₹20, rides ₹20; ☻2-6pm) is 8km southeast of central Bikaner, beside the Jodhpur–Jaipur Bypass. While here you can visit baby camels, go for a short ride and look around the small museum. There are about 400 camels, of three different breeds. The British Army had a camel corps drawn from Bikaner during WWI. Guides are available for ₹50-plus.

The on-site Camel Milk Parlour doesn't look much but can whip up a lassi for ₹5. The round trip, including a half-hour wait at the camel farm, is around ₹150 for an autorickshaw or ₹300 for a taxi.

DESHNOK

 **Karni Mata Temple** (camera/video ₹20/50; ☻4am-10pm) at the village of Deshnok, 30km south of Bikaner, is extraordinary even by Indian standards. Most travellers coming to Bikaner make a beeline here. According to legend, Karni Mata, a 14th-century incarnation of Durga, asked Yama, the god of death, to restore life to her drowned son, Lakhan. When Yama refused, Karni Mata decreed that all members of her family would be reincarnated as *kabas* (rats), and that these *kabas* would return as members of her family. The mass of holy rodents running around the temple is not for the squeamish. It's considered auspicious to have one run across your feet – and sighting one of the few white *kabas* at the temple also augurs well for your spiritual progress.

Buses to Deshnok (₹20, 40 minutes) leave the main and Gogo Gate bus stands in Bikaner every 20 minutes. There are also several trains from Bikaner Junction station.

A return taxi/autorickshaw from Bikaner with a one-hour wait costs ₹500/280.

Haryana & Punjab

Best Places to Eat

» Moti Mahal Deluxe (p218)
» Pomodoro (p206)
» Brothers' Dhaba (p218)
» Bhoj (p205)

Best Places to Stay

» Aura Vaseela (p205)
» Grand Hotel (p215)
» Mrs Bhandari's Guest House (p215)
» Hotel Satyadeep (p205)

Why Go?

Haryana and Punjab comprise the Indian half of the erstwhile Punjab region that was tumultuously split when India and Pakistan separated in 1947. Punjab (translating to 'Five Waters') is named after the five rivers of this fertile 'rice bowl' and 'bread basket': the Beas, Jhelum, Chenab, Ravi and Sutlej.

Hindi-speaking, primarily Hindu Haryana split from Punjabi-speaking, primarily Sikh Punjab in 1966, but they still share a capital, Chandigarh. Apart from its prodigious manufacturing and agriculture industries, and the precocious Delhi satellite of Gurgaon, Haryana is best known for the Hindu holy site of Kurukshetra.

Punjab is the home of the Sikhs, butter chicken and bhangra (music/dance). Here, *Sat Sri Akal* replaces *Namaste* as the preferred greeting, and Sikh gurdwaras outnumber Hindu temples as places of worship. Tourists and worshippers flock to Amritsar's gleaming Golden Temple, while nationalists and the curious join in the fun at Attari–Wagah's entertaining border-closing ceremony on the India–Pakistan border.

When to Go
Chandigarh

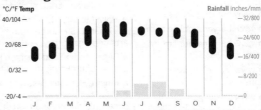

Feb–Mar Colourful kites take to the air to welcome spring during the festival of Basant.

Mar Holla Mohalla is a three-day celebration of the Khalsa (Sikh brotherhood) at Anandpur Sahib.

Dec Amritsar throbs and swivels during the three-night International Bhangra Festival.

Fast Facts

» Population: 25.3 million (Haryana), 27.7 million (Punjab)

» Area: 44,212 sq km (Haryana), 50,362 sq km (Punjab)

» Capital: Chandigarh

» Main languages: Hindi (Haryana), Punjabi (Punjab)

» Sleeping prices: **$** below ₹1000, **$$** ₹1000 to ₹5000, **$$$** above ₹5000

Top Tips

Hotels in Chandigarh and Amritsar quickly fill during weekends and festivals (book ahead). Attari is a train station near the border at Wagah, but transport from there to the border-closing ceremony is virtually nonexistent, so organise transport from Amritsar.

Resources

» www.punjabgovt.nic.in

» www.haryana-online.com

» www.haryanatourism.com

» www.citcochandigarh.com

» www.chandigarh.nic.in

» www.nrisabhapunjab.in

» www.nrizone.in

Food

Punjab is a food-lover's paradise. Not only is this region home to nutty, long-grain basmati rice, that quintessential accompaniment to spicy curries, it also nurtures much of India's wheat thanks to the green revolution of the 1960s. Punjabi cooks quickly embraced the cuisine of the Mugals and their renowned barbecue techniques using the ingenious and simple tandoor clay oven. Sizzling tandoori chicken is only beaten for popularity by the world-famous butter chicken; but you should also savour the tandoori vegetables, the various dhal (lentil) dishes and the locally famous Amritsari fried fish.

DON'T MISS

Join the pilgrimage to Sikhism's serene **Golden Temple** in Amritsar. Spend some time circumambulating the sacred lake, Amrit Sarovar, partaking *prasad* and generally joining in. Sikhism prides itself on its open and inclusive outlook to all religions and all peoples. Witness the gilded temple during an ethereal sunrise, moody sunset, and when it is sparkling and illuminated at night.

Cheer with pumped-up patriots as they watch Indian and Pakistani soldiers try to out-stomp, out-scowl and out-salute each other at Attari–Wagah's fantastical **border-closing ceremony**.

When in Chandigarh, explore the whimsical world of **Nek Chand Fantasy Rock Garden**. Reputed to be one of India's top tourist attractions, this recycled wonder world will enthral the kids and may even provide a few ideas for home projects!

Top State Festivals

» Kila Raipur Sports Festival (Rural Olympics; www.ruralolympics.net; Feb, Kila Raipur, near Ludhiana, p212) Three days of rural 'sports': bullock-cart races, kabaddi, strongman contests, folk dancing and more.

» Surajkund Crafts Mela (1–15 Feb, Surajkund, p210) Visiting artisans showcase and sell colourful handicrafts among food stalls and cultural performances.

» Holla Mohalla (Mar, Anandpur Sahib, p211) Celebration of the Khalsa (Sikh brotherhood): kirtan (Sikh hymns), martial-arts demonstrations and re-enactments of past battles.

» Baba Sheikh Farid Aagman Purb Festival (Sep, Faridkot, p212) Cultural performances to commemorate the Sufi saint.

» Pinjore Heritage Festival (early Oct, Pinjore Gardens, p209) Three-day festival with music and dance performances, handicraft and food stalls.

» Harballabh Sangeet Sammelan (www.harballabh.org; late Dec, Jalandhar, p212) Four-day music festival (in existence for over 130 years) showcasing Indian classical instrumentalists and vocalists.

» Gita Jayanti (Nov/Dec, Kurukshetra, p210) One week of cultural events celebrating the Bhagavad Gita's anniversary.

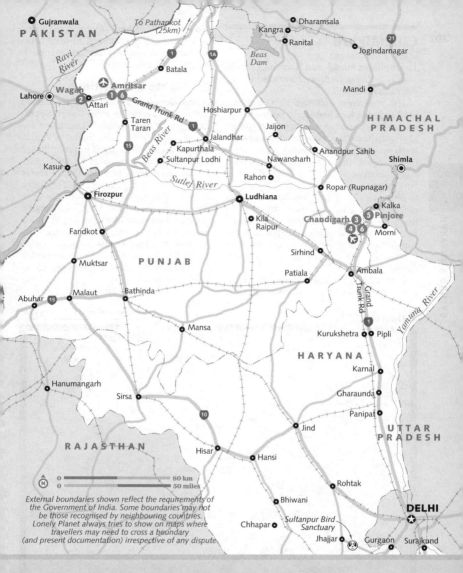

Haryana & Punjab Highlights

1 Immerse yourself in the soul-soothing splendour of Amritsar's divine **Golden Temple** (p213), Sikhism's holiest site

2 Watch Indian and Pakistani border guards compete with high kicks, quick marches and foot stomps at Attari–Wagah's entertaining

border-closing ceremony (p220)

3 Tumble into the maze-like alternate reality of Chandigarh's **Nek Chand Fantasy Rock Garden** (p203) where household items are recycled into imaginative art

4 Explore Le Corbusier's uber-structured modernist

metropolis of **Chandigarh** (p202)

5 Pause at **Pinjore Gardens** (p209), one of India's finest Mughal-era walled gardens

6 Savour the delights of Punjabi and Mughlai cuisine in the excellent restaurants of **Chandigarh** (p206) and **Amritsar** (p218)

Chandigarh

📞 0172 / POP 1,064,700

The capital of Punjab and Haryana, Chandigarh is a Union Territory controlled by the central government.

The modernist architect Le Corbusier's radical design for Chandigarh polarises critics, and this anomaly among Indian cities also splits travellers. Some dislike its rather soulless grid and impersonal scale, while others enjoy the city's broad, tree-lined roads, angular sense of order and use of street signs.

Although Chandigarh may lack the colour and chaos so typical of subcontinental cities, it does offer a clean and green respite from urban pandemonium, is home to the wonderfully wacky Nek Chand Fantasy Rock Garden, and has some of the state's yummiest places to eat.

Chandigarh is divided into a series of sectors that are numbered. The main shopping area is located in Sector 17, while most hotels and restaurants are situated in neighbouring Sectors 22 and 35. The train station is 8km from the city centre.

◉ Sights & Activities

Capital Complex   NOTABLE BUILDINGS
The imposing concrete **High Court**, **Secretariat** and **Vidhan Sabha** (Legislative Assembly), all in Sector 1 and shared by Punjab and Haryana, were designed by Le Corbusier.

The High Court opened in 1955. A visit inside may be possible from Monday to Friday with prior permission from the Chandigarh Tourism office (p209); bring your passport. The internal ramp, the wavy overhanging roof and the colourful supporting slabs are the main features. You can walk around to the symbolic **Open Hand** sculpture, another creation of the workaholic Le Corbusier. It symbolises an 'open to give, open to receive' message of peace.

Chandigarh

You must enter the High Court via the car park. On the way is the small **High Court Museum** (admission free; ☺10am-5pm Mon-Sat) containing assorted memorabilia including original Le Corbusier sketches and the handcuffs worn by Nathuram Godse, Mahatma Gandhi's assassin (see boxed text, p1096). Most exhibits are on the 1st floor. On request, there's a free guided tour.

To visit the huge Secretariat and the Vidhan Sabha obtain a permit from the Architecture Department in the **UT Secretariat** (☏2741620; Sector 9-D).

Nek Chand Fantasy Rock Garden

ART GALLERY

(www.nekchand.com; adult/child ₹10/5; ☺9am-6pm Oct-Mar, to 7pm Apr-Sep) Entering this Chandigarh icon, a 25-acre garden, is like falling down a rabbit hole into the labyrinthine interior of one man's mind. Created by Nek Chand (see the boxed text, p204), cleverly using recycled junk and organic ma-

HARYANA & PUNJAB CHANDIGARH

Chandigarh

⊚ **Sights**
1 Bougainvillea Garden C1
2 Chandigarh Architecture Museum B2
3 Government Museum & Art
   Gallery B2
4 High Court D1
5 High Court Museum D1
6 Le Corbusier Centre C4
7 National Gallery of Portraits B3
   Natural History Museum .... (see 2)
8 Nek Chand Fantasy Rock Garden D2
9 Open Hand Sculpture D1
10 Rose Garden B2
11 Secretariat C1
12 Sukhna Lake Paddle Boats D2
13 UT Secretariat B2
14 Vidhan Sabha D1

⊜ **Sleeping**
15 AB's D4
16 Hotel City Heart Premium B3
17 Hotel Divyadeep A4
18 Hotel Kwality Regency A3
19 Hotel Mountview B2
20 Hotel Satyadeep A4
21 Hotel Shivalikview A3
22 Hotel Sunbeam A4
23 Piccadily Hotel A4
24 Taj Chandigarh B2

⊗ **Eating**
   AB's .... (see 15)
25 Aroma A4
26 Barista Crème A3
   Bhoj .... (see 17)
   Ghazal .... (see 28)
27 Hot Millions Salad Bar &
   Restaurant B3
28 Mehfil B3
   Moti Mahal .... (see 28)
29 Picadilly Blue Ice Bar &
   Restaurant A3

   Pomodoro .... (see 23)
30 Punjab Grill B3
31 Sagar Ratna A3
   Sai Sweets .... (see 20)
   Swagath .... (see 15)
   Yangtse .... (see 21)

⊜ **Drinking**
   English Garden Bar .... (see 28)
32 Java Dave's B2
   Lava Bar .... (see 24)
   Oriental Lounge .... (see 15)
   Vintage Terrace Lounge Bar .... (see 19)

⊛ **Entertainment**
33 Kiran Cinema B3
   Neelam Cinema .... (see 29)
34 Tagore Theatre B4

⊝ **Shopping**
35 Anokhi C3
36 Fabindia B3
37 Khadi Ashram B3
   Music World .... (see 29)
38 Music World B4
   Phulkari .... (see 37)
39 Suvasa C3

Information
40 Chandigarh Tourism A4
41 Haryana Tourism B3
   Himachal Tourism .... (see 40)
   Shri Gurudev .... (see 27)
   Uttar Pradesh Tourism .... (see 40)
   Uttarakhand (Uttaranchal)
      Tourism .... (see 40)

Transport
   Inter State Bus Terminal (ISBT) . (see 40)
42 Jet Airways B3
43 Prepaid Autorickshaws A3

terials, the garden is a curious maze of interlinking courtyards, twisting walkways and staircases suddenly emerging into valleys with crashing waterfalls or amphitheatres overrun by figures made of china shards. No material is wasted, from electrical sockets to colourful wire, glass and even broken bangles, in the legions of men, animals, archways and walls, with broken-art faces around almost every corner.

Wear comfortable shoes and arrive early on weekends to beat the crowds.

Sukhna Lake   LAKE
Another aspect of Le Corbusier's masterplan is this landmark **artificial lake** (⊙8am-10pm) replete with **paddle boats** (2-seaters per 30min ₹50; ⊙8.30am-5.30pm). Ornamental gardens, a children's playground and the **Mermaid Pub & Restaurant** (meals ₹70-150; ⊙11am-11pm) complete the fun. Sunday afternoons can get crowded.

GALLERIES
Government Museum & Art Gallery   ART GALLERY
(☑2740261; Sector 10-C; admission ₹10,; ⊙10am-4.30pm Tue-Sun, free guided tours 11am & 3pm Tue-Sun, films 11am & 3pm Sun) This gallery has a sizeable collection, including *phulkari* (embroidery work) wraps made by Punjabi village women, metal work, Indian miniature paintings, contemporary art and Gandhara Buddhist sculptures. Your ticket includes admission to the Chandigarh Architecture Museum and Natural History Museum.

FREE **National Gallery of Portraits**   ART GALLERY
(☑2720261; Sector 17-B; ⊙10am-5pm Tue-Sun, free guided tour 11am-3pm) Located behind the State Library, it displays photos and paintings illustrating the country's independence movements.

MUSEUMS
Chandigarh Architecture Museum   MUSEUM
(City Museum; ☑2743626; Sector 10-C; admission ₹10; ⊙9.45am-5pm Tue-Sun) This museum uses photos, letters, models, newspaper reports and architectural drawings to provide revealing insights into the city's planning and development.

Natural History Museum   MUSEUM
(☑2740261; Sector 10-C; admission ₹10; ⊙10am-4.30pm Tue-Sun) Next door is the National History Museum, less interesting for its fossilised dinosaur skulls than its Cro Magnon man using an electric torch to illuminate his cave art!

FREE **Le Corbusier Centre**   MUSEUM
(☑2777077; www.lecorbusiercentrechd.org; Sector 19-B; ⊙10am-1pm & 2.15-5pm Tue-Sun) This

JUNK ART GENIUS

Following Independence, as refugees flooded across the Pakistan border and a newly liberated India made the bold statement that was Chandigarh, one of the new city's road inspectors, a diminutive arrival from Pakistan called Nek Chand, was struck by the amount of waste generated as villages were cleared in the construction of Chandigarh. Chand hauled this matter back to his jungle home and gave it a second life as sculptural material.

Eventually he had tens of thousands of forms made of urban and industrial waste, as well as local stone, created by his own hands and the slow forces of nature. His battalions of water women, pipers, chai drinkers, monkeys, cheeky stick men wearing tea-cup hats, dancing women and other characters steadily multiplied in secretly sculpted spaces.

Chand's efforts weren't officially discovered until 15 years after they began, when a government survey crew stumbled upon them in 1973. The unauthorised garden was illegally occupying government land and should technically have been demolished, but fortunately the local council recognised the garden as a cultural asset. Chand was given 50 labourers and paid a salary so he could devote himself to the project.

Today, the garden is said to receive over 2000 visitors a day. There's a **Nek Chand Foundation** (www.nekchand.com), raising funds and recruiting volunteers.

Chand had no formal education beyond high school. 'In my childhood I used to build mud houses and other toys.' He is said to be influenced by modernist masters such as Le Corbusier and Gaudi, but he is clear on the main source of his ideas: 'they are a gift from God.'

will especially appeal to those interested in urban planning. Through old documents, sketches and photos, this place chronicles the work of Chandigarh's chief architect. There's a black-and-white photo of a suit-and-bow-tie-attired Le Corbusier on a paddle boat, as well as some fascinating letters, including one from Jawaharlal Nehru to the Chief Minister of Punjab dated 4 November 1960, part of which states, 'I do hope that you will not overrule Corbusier. His opinion is of value.'

PARKS & GARDENS
In line with Le Corbusier's vision of a garden city, Chandigarh is dotted with verdant parks. These include the **Rose Garden** (Sector 16), which has over 1500 rose varieties, and **Bougainvillea Garden** (Sector 3). Less central are the **Terraced Garden** (Sector 33) and the **Garden of Fragrance** (Sector 36), the latter with sweet-scented varieties such as jasmine and damask rose.

☞ Tours

A double-decker **tourist bus** (☏2703839, 4644484; ticket ₹50; ⏱10am-1.30pm & 2.30-5.30pm) runs two daily half-day trips from outside the Hotel Shivalikview (buy ticket from conductor) to the Rose Garden, Government Museum & Art Gallery, Nek Chand Fantasy Rock Garden and Sukhna Lake.

🛏 Sleeping

Chandigarh fails to excite on the accommodation front, especially when it comes to value for money. To stay with a family, contact the Chandigarh Tourism office (p209) for details about its Bed & Breakfast scheme (rooms from ₹1000).

TOP CHOICE Aura Vaseela HOTEL $$
(☏01762-287575; www.auravaseela.com; Nadiali Village; s/d from ₹2899/3199, cottages from ₹3599/3899; ✱@☀) Run by a dynamic duo, Gags and Jeeva, this stress-banishing 'ethnic countryside resort' may be tricky to find (pick-ups possible with advance notice) given its secluded location (around 4.5km from the centre), but the effort is well rewarded. Tastefully appointed accommodation is in traditional-style (modern) cottages or rooms in the classy main complex, and tariffs include bed, tea and breakfast. Amenities and activities include a paintball field, gym, craft gallery, museum, restaurant and bar.

Hotel Satyadeep HOTEL $
(☏2703103; hddeepsdeep@yahoo.com; Sector 22-B; s ₹700-900, d ₹800-1000; ✱@) Upstairs from the affiliated Sai Sweets shop, this is the most traveller-friendly budget option in town. Run by the courteous Vikramjit, the rooms aren't fancy but are well maintained and adequately comfortable – it's a sound choice for solo women.

Hotel Divyadeep HOTEL $
(☏2705191; Sector 22-B; s ₹700-900, d ₹800-1000; ✱) This is Satyadeep's sister hotel, and another reliable choice that is convenient to the bus station and Sector 17 (CBD). The cheaper rooms have smaller dimensions but are just as well kept as the more expensive rooms.

Hotel Sunbeam HOTEL $$
(☏2708100; www.hotelsunbeam.com; Sector 22-B; s/d from ₹2295/2695; ✱@) Sunbeam's rooms and service adequately shine, despite being a little dowdy decorated. They're reasonably furnished and have satellite TV, including the news channels BBC and CNN. The 24-hour coffee shop, the Pillars, has a restaurant atmosphere, while the restaurant-bar, the Ambassador (mains ₹175 to ₹495), is dimly lit for surreptitious quaffing of cocktails.

Piccadily Hotel HOTEL $$
(☏2707571; www.thepiccadily.com; Sector 22-B; s/d from ₹3850/4850; ✱@☎) This ageing but appealing three-star property offers complimentary breakfast, contemporary rooms with LCD TV, minibar, sofa, writing desk, tea-and-coffee-making facilities, safe, and satiny bedcovers. It's worth asking for a discount and, with two restaurants, you don't have to travel far for a decent meal. Graze on Italian faves at Pomodoro (p206) or a curry at Currys.

Kaptain's Retreat HOTEL $$
(☏5005599; www.kaptainsretreat.com; Sector 35-B; s/d ₹2190/2490, ste ₹3190; ✱) Owned by cricketing icon Kapil Dev, this 10-room hotel is filled with cricket paraphernalia, including signed cricket bats and coloured-glass objets d'art. For unenthusiastic pace bowlers, there's a relaxing bar-restaurant downstairs. The rooms aren't superluxe but are comfy, cosy with heavy wooden furnishings and shuttered windows.

AB's HOTEL $$
(☏6577888; Sector 26; r from ₹2800; ✱) Above its namesake restaurant (p207), rooms are clean and modern, although the cheaper ones are a bit space-frugal. Rooms also boast flatscreen

TV and tea-and-coffee-making facilities, and guests are just a dash away from the stylish subterranean Oriental Lounge (p208).

Hotel Kwality Regency
HOTEL $$

(✆/fax 2720204; Sector 22-A; s/d ₹1795/1995, deluxe ₹2395/2695; ❀) The 14 agreeable rooms have individual character, although the cheapest are small and sun starved (consider upgrading if you need a window). Nevertheless, the marble-adorned deluxe rooms are good value (for Chandigarh), with TV, scatter rugs, writing desk and electronic safe. There's a cosy bar and multicuisine restaurant behind the lobby.

Hotel Mountview
HOTEL $$$

(✆4671111; www.citcochandigarh.com/mountview; Sector 10-B; s/d incl breakfast from ₹7000/8000; ❀@🖰🏊) This hotel has well-presented rooms with flatscreen TV, tea-and-coffee-making facilities, minibars, safes and easy-on-the-eye interiors. There's a health club, good restaurants (including 24-hour cafe) and the slick Vintage Terrace Lounge Bar (p208).

Hotel Shivalikview
HOTEL $$

(✆4672222; www.citcochandigarh.com/shivalikview; Sector 17-E; s/d incl breakfast & dinner ₹4250/5050; ❀@) CITCO's midrange hotel has functional and comfortable, if somewhat humdrum rooms, each with TV, writing desk and cool tiled floors. As well as the good-value 'meal deal', there's a business centre, beauty salon and the popular Chinese restaurant, Yangtse (p207).

Taj Chandigarh
HOTEL $$$

(✆6613000; www.tajhotels.com; Sector 17-A; r from ₹9000; ❀@🖰🏊) Although not as uber-luxurious as we've come to expect of the Taj, this place is still suitably svelte and 25% weekend discounts add to the appeal. Plush, big-windowed rooms boast ergonomic furniture, minibars, flatscreen TV, electronic safes and round-the-clock concierge services. There are several restaurants, the Lava Bar (p208), spa (dare to try the 'warrior massage') and a 24-hour business centre.

Hotel City Heart Premium
HOTEL $$

(✆2724203; cityhearthotels.com; Sector 17-C; s/d ₹2395/2795; ❀@🖰) A reasonable and, as the name suggests, central choice. Its modernish rooms don't really meet the expectations of the midrange price tag, but they are adequately spacious and comfortable with flatscreen TV, and there's a helpful travel desk.

✗ Eating

Thanks to the locals' love of food, the hungry traveller is well catered for in Chandigarh, with new eateries ever sprouting. You'll find a particularly impressive knot of restaurants in Sectors 17, 26 and 35. Telephone numbers are given for places where reservations are advisable.

TOP CHOICE Punjab Grill
NORTH INDIAN $$$

(✆4029444; Sector 17-C; mains ₹425-600; ⊙11am-3.30pm & 6pm-midnight; ❀) Step inside this chic black, gold and glass restaurant where smoking tandoors deliver succulent veg and nonveg delights such as spicy *boti kebab* (charcoal-grilled marinated mutton) and tandoori *gobi* (cauliflower). Curries include the meat Punjab grill, where lamb tikka is first roasted then curried with fresh herbs to create a mouth-watering dish. Finish off with deliciously cool *kheer* (creamy rice pudding).

Khyber
INDIAN $$

(✆2607728; Sector 35-B; mains ₹90-285; ❀) Drop downstairs, past a scowling Clint Eastwood, to the nonsmoking Wild West Bar in the basement, before diving into flavoursome Northwest Frontier–style cuisine at the restaurant. It does startlingly good *dhal Bukhara* (slow-simmered curried lentils) and Pathan kebab (lava stone–roasted lamb).

Pomodoro
ITALIAN $$

(✆2707571; Piccadily Hotel, Sector 22-B; mains ₹245-345; ⊙11.30am-3.30pm & 7pm-midnight; ❀) This cosy basement restaurant serves traditional Italian food in a sleek setting. Authentic minestrone, pastas, thin-crust pizzas, risottos, grilled meats and to-die-for desserts like tiramisu and panacotta make Pomodoro a *numero uno* choice. There's also an impressive wine list.

Sagar Ratna
SOUTH INDIAN $

(Sector 17-E; mains ₹75-150; ⊙8am-11pm; ❀) This all-veg chain restaurant does South Indian specialities with aplomb, from first-rate dosas (thin lentil-flour pancakes) to satiating, good-value thalis. The cool *dahi idli* (spongy rice cake) is a tummy-soothing yoghurty elixir.

Bhoj
NORTH INDIAN $

(Sector 22-B; standard/choti thali ₹140/110; ⊙7.30am-10.30pm; ❀) A travellers' favourite, this is an unpretentious spot to fuel up on a hearty North Indian veg thali. The thali ingredients change throughout the day and you can augment the chapattis with rice for a nominal ₹10, or light eaters can order the smaller *choti* thali.

Hot Millions Salad Bar & Restaurant
MULTICUISINE $$

(☎2723222; 1st fl, Sector 17-D; mains ₹175-380; ⏰10am-midnight; ❄) This is the best of its city-wide branches and is popular for its salad buffet (soups, veg/nonveg salads and desserts, ₹284 per person). The higgledy-piggledy à la carte menu has everything from Tex-Mex and Chinese to Indian and Italian. It's advisable to book at this busy upstairs restaurant with attentive staff.

Yangtse
CHINESE $$

(☎4672222; Hotel Shivalikview, Sector 17-E; mains ₹150-390; ⏰12.30-3pm & 7.30-11.30pm; ❄) Sporting panoramic city views from its lofty heights, this is one of Chandigarh's best Chinese restaurants. Chicken Sichuan, eggplant in garlic sauce, spicy honey chicken, chilli garlic noodles...decisions, decisions! All desserts come with ice cream; try the fried apple Cantonese style or date pancakes.

Piccadilly Blue Ice Bar & Restaurant
MULTICUISINE $$$

(☎2703338; Sector 17-E; mains ₹175-750; ⏰11am-11pm; ❄) A contemporary, split-level restaurant with a cool-blue decor and slick service that is suitable for an unhurried predinner drink followed by well-executed multicuisine dishes. Menu items range from Thai fish curry to burgers and chicken stroganoff; barbecued prawns top the menu at ₹750.

Barista Crème
MULTICUISINE $$

(Sector 17; mains ₹130-250; ⏰8am-11pm; ❄) In addition to the usual cakes and superb coffee, this franchise has table service, Continental breakfasts, including croissants and eggs, and a good range of pastas and pizzas for later in the day.

Mehfil
MULTICUISINE $$

(Sector 17-C; mains ₹140-300; ⏰11am-midnight; ❄) Indian, Chinese and Continental food served in comfortable surrounds, with the *murg tawa* (Punjabi-style chicken) and *methi murg* (chicken with fenugreek) among the standouts. Spice aficionados may find some dishes too tame.

Ghazal
MULTICUISINE $$

(☎2704448; Sector 17-C; meals ₹195-395; ⏰8am-11.30pm; ❄) A Chandigarh stalwart, grand Ghazal has an admirable Indian, Continental and Chinese menu. *Ghazal special murg* (cream-based chicken) or *bhuna gohst* (mutton) is nicely washed down with draught beer. Vegetarians are well catered for.

Moti Mahal
INDIAN $$

(☎5073333; Sector 17-C; mains ₹145-250; ⏰10.30am-11.30pm; ❄) Scrummy North Indian favourites; the butter chicken, *aloo jeera* (spiced potatoes), chicken masala and *palak paneer* (unfermented cheese chunks in spiced pureed spinach) get the thumbs up. Good variety of piping-hot Indian breads.

AB's
INDIAN $$

(☎2795666; Sector 26; mains ₹195-525; ⏰11am-midnight; ❄) Settle back at suave AB's (specialising in Punjabi, Kashmiri and Mughlai cuisine) and savour the likes of *tabakh maaz* (spicy, marinated mutton ribs), *paneer achari* (slow flame-cooked, spice-and-pickle-marinated unfermented cheese) and *jungli gosht* (spicy tomato-based mutton).

Swagath
INDIAN $$

(☎5000444; Sector 26; mains ₹195-575; ⏰11am-midnight; ❄) Stellar Indian food with a focus on Mangalorean and Chettinad recipes. Seafood – prawns, squid, crab and a tasty fish *gassi* (coconut-based curry) – is artfully prepared, and the *murg malai tikka* (clay oven-cooked marinated chicken) isn't bad either.

Sai Sweets
SWEETS $

(Sector 22-B; sweets ₹10-35) Apart from an awesome array of *mithai* (Indian sweets), humble Sai Sweets has *namkin* (savoury nibbles) and more substantial snacks like plump samosas and *channa bhatura* (fried Indian-style bread with spiced chickpeas).

Aroma
MULTICUISINE $

(Sector 22; mains ₹50-150; ❄) Open 24 hours, this bustling concoction of fast-food joints includes a Café Coffee Day, Nik's Bakery (croissants, burgers, cakes, hot dogs, pizzas), Coccoberry (ice cream), Sundaram's (South Indian) and Yo!China (Chinese). Seating is shared; how they keep track of your order and bill is a mystery.

🍷 Drinking
Watering holes range from the seedy to the swish, the better ones flaunting a great selection of domestic and foreign booze. Women are less likely to get hassled if they're with a male companion.

Zinc Lounge
BAR

(Sector 26; ⏰11am-4.30pm & 7.30-11pm; ❄) Steely suave Zinc attracts Chandigarh's pretty people. There's a show-off wine list that includes Indian, Australian, Spanish and French labels. Cocktailers can sup mint juleps, cosmopolitans, margaritas and 'Indian sangria' (ginger-infused).

Vintage Terrace Lounge Bar BAR
(Hotel Mountview, Sector 10-B; ☉11am-11pm; ❋) One of the best in the hotel-bar category, with comfy chairs, a big-screen TV and plenty of choice: wine, beer, cocktails, mocktails, spirits and liqueurs. The peckish can nibble fish fingers (₹400).

Lava Bar BAR
(Taj Chandigarh Hotel, Sector 17-A; ☉11am-11.30pm; ❋) With lava lamps and a retro vibe, this small bar celebrates an 'amoebic ambiance in a hot modern way'. Rejoice this fact with expensive bubbles, ie Dom Perignon...or maybe not. Thank heavens there's plenty of (affordable) beer such as Corona. There's a DJ from 7pm on Wednesday, Thursday, Friday and Saturday.

Oriental Lounge BAR
(Sector 26; ☉11am-midnight; ❋) Below AB's restaurant (p207), this chi-chi lounge-bar is a most civilised spot to slow the pace. There's imported beer and mint tequilas, among other things, while the pan-Asian food menu has an impressive range, from glass noodle soup to crab cakes. Happy hour noon to 6pm.

English Garden Bar BAR
(Sector 17-C; ☉11am-midnight; ❋) A basement bar below Mehfil restaurant, it doesn't exactly bring an English garden to mind, but is OK for a draught beer. A tad gloomy it may be, but snooty it is not.

Opposite the entrance to the Hotel Mountview, **Café Coffee Day** (Sector 10-D; snacks from ₹45; ❋) and **Java Dave's** (Sector 10-D; cakes from ₹55; ❋) continue trying to out-froth and out-bake each other on the cappuccino and cake fronts.

☆ Entertainment

Tagore Theatre (☏2724278; Sector 18-B) hosts music, dance and theatrical performances.

Movies (mainly Hindi) are screened at the **Kiran Cinema** (☏2705082; Sector 22-D) and **Neelam Cinema** (☏2703600; Sector 17-D), while a mix of Bollywood and Hollywood is shown at the multiplex **Fun Cinemas** (☏9888997806; Fun Republic shopping centre, Mani Majra).

🛍 Shopping

The central section of Sector 17 is the main shopping and entertainment area.

Anokhi CLOTHING
(www.anokhi.com; Sector 7-C, Inner Market; ☉10.30am-7pm Mon-Sat) Beautiful block-printed textiles.

Fabindia CLOTHING
(www.fabindia.com; Sector 9-C; ☉10am-8pm) Gorgeous garments (Indian-meets-Western style) and homewares.

Khadi Ashram CLOTHING
(Sector 17-C; ☉10.30am-2pm & 3.30-8pm Mon-Sat) Homespun textiles and herbal beauty products (soaps include water lily, aloe vera and mint).

Music World MUSIC STORE
(Sectors 17-E & 18-D; ☉10am-9.30pm) CDs (from ₹40) and DVDs (from ₹60).

Phulkari HANDICRAFTS
(Sector 17-C; ☉10.30am-2pm & 3.30-8pm Mon-Sat) Government of Punjab emporium with everything from handicrafts to jootis (traditional slip-in shoes).

Suvasa CLOTHING
(Inner Market, Sector 8-B; ☉10.30am-7.45pm) Quality block-printed fabrics that include toiletry bags and *salwar kameez* (traditional dresslike tunic and trouser combination for women).

🛈 Information

Internet Access
Each of the central sectors has an internet cafe. **Cyber-22** (Sector 22-C; per hr ₹20; ☉9.30am-10pm)

Left Luggage
Bus station (Sector 17; per day ₹25; ☉24hr)

Medical Services
PGI Hospital (☏2746018; Post Graduate Institute, Sector 12-A)
Silver Oaks Hospital (☏5094125; Phase 9, Sector 63, Mohali) Reputable private hospital.

Money
ATMs are plentiful and easy to find.
Thomas Cook (☏6610907; Sector 9-D; ☉9.30am-6pm Mon-Sat) Changes foreign currency and travellers cheques. International transfers.

Photography
Shri Gurudev (☏2704534; Sector 17-D; ☉9.30am-6pm)

Post
Main post office (☏2702170; Sector 17; ☉9.30am-4pm Mon-Sat)

HARYANA & PUNJAB

Tourist Information

Chandigarh Tourism (2703839; 1st fl, Sector 17-B bus station; ☺9.30am-6pm)

Haryana Tourism (☑2702957; Sector 17-B; ☺9am-5pm Mon-Fri)

Himachal Tourism (☑2708569; 1st fl, Sector 17-B bus station; ☺10am-5pm Mon-Sat, closed 2nd Sat of month)

Uttar Pradesh & Uttarakhand (Uttaranchal) Tourism (☑2707649; 2nd fl, Sector 17-B bus station; ☺10am-5pm Mon-Sat, closed 2nd Sat of month)

❶ Getting There & Away

Air

The first stage of an international airport was scheduled for completion around 2013 at the time of research, although the first international flights may start before this date. The following have daily flights to Delhi (one way ₹3000) and Mumbai (Bombay; ₹7700).

Air India (Indian Airlines) (☑1800227722; www.airindia.in; Sector 34-A)

Jet Airways (☑2741465; www.jetairways.com; Sector 9-D)

Kingfisher Airlines (☑9302795005; www.flykingfisher.com; airport)

Bus

Half a dozen companies operate buses leaving from the Inter State Bus Terminal (ISBT) in Sector 17. Buses to Anandpur Sahib and Amritsar leave from the ISBT in Sector 43.

Regular buses run to Patiala (₹45, three hours), Sirhind (₹30, two hours), Anandpur Sahib (₹45, 2½ hours), Amritsar (₹150, seven hours), Dharamsala (ordinary/deluxe ₹200/350, eight hours), Manali (ordinary/deluxe ₹300/400, 11 hours), Haridwar (₹145, six hours), Delhi (₹180, 5½ hours) and Shimla (₹130, four hours).

Train

A **reservation office** (☑2720242; ☺8am-8pm Mon-Sat, to 2pm Sun) is on the 1st floor of the bus terminal at Sector 17. Prepaid autorickshaws from there to the train station cost around ₹100.

Three fast trains connect Delhi and Chandigarh daily: the 12005/6 and 12011/12 *Kalka Shatabdi Express* (AC chair/1AC ₹420/800, 3½ hours) and the 12057/8 *Una Jan Shatabdi Express* (2nd class/AC chair ₹107/345, four hours).

Half a dozen trains (including the above) go to Kalka (AC chair/1AC ₹210/430, 35 minutes), from where four daily trains (2nd class/1st class ₹48/228, five hours) rattle up the mountain to Shimla.

❶ Getting Around

Chandigarh is spread out but, with its cycle paths and parks, was built for cycling. The Chandigarh Tourism office hires out bicycles (₹100 per eight hours); bicycles are also available for hire at Sukhna Lake (p204) for the same cost but with a (refundable) ₹500 deposit.

Cycle-rickshaw rates within town vary from around ₹30 to ₹50, depending on the distance travelled.

Taxis charge around ₹200 to the airport. Two reputable taxi companies are **Indus Cab** (☑4646464) and **Mega Cab** (☑4141414), with both charging around ₹15 per kilometre. For local sightseeing, including Pinjore (Yadavindra) Gardens, the Chandigarh Tourism office can arrange taxis (₹900 per eight hours, 80km limit).

For car (with driver) hire, expect to pay around ₹800/950 for non-AC/AC per eight hours with an 80km limit (after 80km non-AC/AC ₹5/6 per km).

Around Chandigarh

PINJORE (YADAVINDRA) GARDENS

These reconstructed 17th-century Mughal-era walled **gardens** (☑01733-230759; admission ₹20; ☺7am-10pm) are built on seven levels with water features (that sometimes operate) and enjoy panoramic views of the Shivalik Hills.

Founded and designed by Nawab Fidai Khan, who also designed Badshahi Mosque in Lahore (Pakistan), the gardens served as a retreat for the Mughal kings and their harems. Nowadays there's an annual **heritage festival** (see p200) here.

At the gardens is the pleasant Mughal-style **Bajrigar Motel** (☑01733-231877; r ₹1900-2250, ste 5000; ✴), which has excellent and spotless comfy rooms and free garden entry for its guests. All are welcome at the motel's restaurant, **Golden Oriel** (veg/nonveg thali ₹120/140; ☺7am-11pm).

In the centre of the gardens, near the small **Jal Mahal**, which was under restoration when we visited, is a cluster of small cafes (snacks ₹30 to ₹150).

To get here from Chandigarh, catch a bus (₹20, one hour, frequent).

MORNI HILLS

Haryana's only hill station gazes across the hazy plains to the Shivalik and Kasauli Hills in nearby Himachal Pradesh. Morni's leafy heights are a great escape from the rat race, but weekends can get busy.

Located 10km from Morni village, **Hosh & Josh Hills 'n' Thrills** (☑01733-201150; Tikka

Tal; adult/child ₹50/30; ⊘9am-7pm) amusement park promises to keep the kids entertained.

Mountain Quail Tourist Resort (☑01733-250166; r ₹900-1800) is run by Haryana Tourism and boasts neat, wood-panelled rooms with hilltop views and a multicuisine restaurant and bar.

Lake View Camping Complex (☑01733-250166; Tikka Tal; dm ₹150, r ₹1500, camping per person per night ₹600) has a picturesque lakeside location and very good rooms with water-facing balconies. Tents include sleeping bags and use of shared bathrooms. Overlooking the lake is a terrace **restaurant** (mains ₹60-290).

There are daily buses from Chandigarh to Morni (₹45, two hours). Mountain Quail is 2km before the village, from where there is transport to Tikka Tal.

HARYANA

Haryana's name means either 'Abode of God' or 'green home' depending on whether you believe its first syllable refers to Hari, one of Lord Vishnu's aliases, or *hara,* Hindi for green.

The Haryana state government has motel-restaurants along the main roads; **Haryana Tourism** (www.haryanatourism.gov.in) Chandigarh (☑0172-2702957; Sector 17-B; ⊘9am-5pm Mon-Fri); Delhi ☑011-23324910; Chanderlok Bldg, 36 Janpath; ⊘9am-5pm Mon-Fri, to 1pm Sat) can supply further details.

Kurukshetra (Thanesar)

☑01744 / POP 163,000

Kurukshetra, or more correctly, the town of Thanesar in the district of Kurukshetra, will appeal to tourists with an interest in history and religion. According to Hindu teachings, Brahma created the universe here, and Krishna delivered his epic Bhagavad Gita sermon, offered as advice to Arjuna (p1108) before he fought the 18-day Mahabharata battle in which good triumphed over evil. The district takes its name from its founder Kuru, the Aryan king who offered his limbs to Vishnu in order to establish a land of ethics and values.

The **Sri Krishna Museum** (Pehowa Rd; admission ₹15; ⊘10am-5pm) has ancient and modern representations of this heroic incarnation of Vishnu.

Next door is the **Kurukshetra Panorama & Science Centre** (Pehowa Rd; admission ₹15, camera ₹20; ⊘10am-5.30pm). Upstairs, an air-

brushed sky flares behind vultures picking at severed heads in the diorama relaying the Mahabharata battle. The ground floor has interactive science exhibits.

Just 500m away, India's largest water tank, the ghat-flanked **Bhramasarovar**, was, according to Hindu holy texts, created by Lord Brahma. It attracts throngs during solar eclipses and **Gita Jayanti**, anniversary of the Bhagavad Gita (see p200).

Another 6km away is Jyotisar, where the **banyan tree** is said to be an offshoot of the one under which Krishna delivered the Bhagavad Gita. There's a one-hour Hindi (English on request) **sound-and-light show** (adult/child ₹20/15; ⊘sunset Tue-Sun).

Sheikh Chaheli's tomb (Indian/foreigner ₹5/100; ⊘9am-5pm Tue-Sun), 2.3km from the Sri Krishna Museum, is where this Sufi saint is buried with his family in sandstone-and-marble mausoleums.

Neelkanthi Krishna Dham Yatri Niwas (☑291615; Pehowa Rd; r ₹900-1950; ❋⚛) offers the best accommodation option, with charmless but otherwise fine rooms; the attached **tourist office** (☑293570; ⊘9.30am-5pm Tue-Sat) is of limited help.

There are daily buses to Delhi (₹125, three hours) and Patiala (₹60, 1½ hours).

South & West of Delhi

SURAJKUND

Some 30km south of downtown Delhi, this sleepy village bursts into life during the two-week **Surajkund Crafts Mela** (see p200).

Surajkund is named after the 10th-century **sun pool** built by Raja Surajpal, leader of the sun-worshipping Tomars.

Most visitors are Delhi day-trippers, but if you wish to stay here Haryana Tourism has three hotels, the best being **Hotel Rajhans** (☑0129-2512318; r ₹3500; ❋⚛). The midrange options are **Hermitage** (☑0129-25112313; r ₹1500; ❋) and the better **Sunbird Motel** (☑0129-2512312; non AC/AC r ₹1000/1500; ❋).

During the mela there are several daily buses from Delhi (₹50, two hours). A taxi charges around ₹900 (return).

SULTANPUR BIRD SANCTUARY

This 145-hectare **sanctuary** (Indian/foreigner ₹5/40, camera/video ₹25/500; ⊘6.30am-6pm Apr-Sep, to 4.30pm Oct-Mar) plays host to over 250 bird species, including painted storks, Demoiselle cranes, cormorants, spotted sandpipers, mallards and plovers. Its fluctuating population of woodland, shallow-water and deep-water birds includes an estimated 150 resident species and roughly 100 visiting species from Europe, Afghanistan, Siberia and elsewhere. The best time to visit is October to March.

Unfortunately accommodation is limited to the **Rosy Pelican Guest House** (☏0124-2375242; r from ₹3500; ❋), which has passable but overpriced rooms. Note that the tariff includes three meals. The Guest House's restaurant is open to everyone.

Sultanpur is 46km southwest of Delhi and getting there is tougher than spotting a red-crested pochard! There are irregular, bone-shaking buses (₹40, one hour). It's better to hire a taxi (return ₹1400).

PUNJAB

Anandpur Sahib
☏01887 / POP 17,000

The Sikhs' holiest site after the Golden Temple has several historical gurdwaras. An important pilgrimage site for more than 300 years, it was founded by ninth Sikh guru Tegh Bahadur in 1664, before the Mughal emperor Aurangzeb beheaded him for refusing to convert to Islam. His son, Guru Gobind Singh, founded the Khalsa (Sikh brotherhood) here in 1699, and **Holla Mohalla** (see p200) celebrates its anniversary.

The **Kesgarh Sahib** is the largest gurdwara and has a number of holy weapons on display, some of them in the hands of the guards. The smaller gurdwara **Sis Ganj** marks the spot where Guru Tegh Bahadur's head was cremated after it was brought back from Delhi. Some 500m from town is **Anandgarh Sahib**, where a flight of steps leads to a fort on the roof. From here you can see the five-petal form (inspired by the five warrior-saints in the Khalsa) of the **Khalsa Heritage Complex**. This impressive museum complex, with informative exhibits showcasing Sikhism's vibrant history and culture, has been under construction for over a decade but was nearing completion when we visited. For further details click www.khalsaheritagecomplex.org.

Kishan Haveli (☏01887-232650; Academy Rd; r ₹600-1000; ❋) is set in spacious grounds and has an uncommercial, ramshackle charm. This mellow countryside retreat, around 1.5km from town, has comfortable rooms and a simple restaurant (meals ₹80).

Gurdwaras also provide accommodation and meals (donations appreciated), though they are often full.

The bus and train stations are 300m apart on the main road outside town. Buses leave frequently for Chandigarh (₹45, two hours) and every hour to Amritsar (₹100, five hours).

The overnight 14553/4 *Delhi–Una Himachal Express* train connects Delhi with Anandpur Sahib (sleeper/3AC/2AC ₹165/430/590, eight hours, daily). It departs Delhi at 10.15pm and on the return leg it departs Anandpur Sahib at 10pm.

Sirhind
☏01763 / POP 73,800

If you happen to be passing through this small town, sites of interest include the **Aam Khas Bagh**, a Mughal-era walled garden, and the **Gurdwara Fatehgarh Sahib**, which commemorates the 1704 martyrdom of the two youngest sons of the 10th Sikh guru, Gobind Singh. Entombed alive by the Mughals for refusing to convert to Islam, they are honoured at the three-day **Shaheedi Jor Mela** held here every December. There's also **Rauza Sharif**, the marble mausoleum of Muslim saint Shaikh Ahmad Faruqi Sirhindi, which draws pilgrims during the **Urs** festival (August).

If you have to stay overnight, the **Sahil Motel** (☏01763-228392; r from ₹1250; ❋) is your best bet.

Buses connect Sirhind with Patiala (₹20, one hour) and Chandigarh (₹30, two hours).

Patiala
☏0175 / POP 364,000

Once the capital of an independent Sikh state that was established by Baba Ala Singh as the Mughals weakened, Patiala is today a modest town that sees just a trickle of travellers. It's well known for its kite flying during the **Basant** festival and, of course, the Patiala peg (see the boxed text, p212).

The crumbling **Qila Mubarak fort** looks like it could have been transported from the desert to its position in the bazaar. There's an **arms gallery** (admission ₹10; ◷10.30am-5pm Tue-Sun) in its 1859 Durbar Hall which displays antique weapons.

Moti Bagh Palace (Sheesh Mahal; admission ₹10; ◷10.30am-5pm Tue-Sun) has a gallery containing ivory figurines, stuffed animals, musical instruments and more. Nearby, the Old Moti Bagh Palace houses a **sports museum** (admission free, ID required; ☉10.30am-1pm & 2-5.30pm Mon-Fri) with exhibits that include memorabilia relating to Punjabi sprinting hero Milkha Singh, 'the Flying Sikh'.

It is said that those who pray at the **Dukh Niwaran Gurdwara** (☉dawn-dusk), located near the bus stand, are relieved of suffering.

The **Baradari Palace** (Rajinder Kothi; ☑2304433; www.neemranahotels.com; Baradari Garden area; r ₹3500-5500; ❄) is a grand heritage-hotel, Punjab's most graceful place to stay and a perfect stopover for anyone belting out the Delhi–Amritsar road trip. Dripping with old-world charm, this restored property boasts high ceilings, period furnishings and wide, relaxing terraces that overlook lovely gardens. Note that most rooms are in the upper bracket of the quoted range.

Patiala's other hotel options are grungy, and solo women may feel uncomfortable. The best of the bunch are the midrange **Hotel Narain Continental** (☑2212846; www.hotelnarain.com; Mall; r from ₹1575; ❄), locally known as Hotel NC, and cheaper **Green's Hotel** (☑2213071; Mall; r ₹600; ❄), both of which have unexciting furniture-scarred rooms and matter-of-fact service.

Daily buses connect Patiala and Sirhind (₹20, one hour).

Northern Punjab

A major textile centre, **Ludhiana** is also the headquarters of Hero Cycles, which manufactures upward of four million bicycles annually. This big city is a convenient base from which to attend the **Kila Raipur Sports Festival** (see p200).

Jalandhar survived sacking by Mahmud of Ghazni nearly 1000 years ago and later became an important Mughal city. Nowadays it's a commercial hub and the venue for the **Harballabh Sangeet Sammelan** (see p200). It's also a good base from which to visit **Kapurthala**, which was the home of the young Spanish flamenco dancer Anita Delgado, who married (wealthy) Maharaja Jagatjit Singh Bahadurmaharaja (a story that inspired the Javier Moro novel, *Passion India*).

Faridkot was once capital of a Sikh state of the same name and has a 700-year-old **fortress**. The 13th-century poet and Sufi Baba Sheikh Farid lived here, and he is honoured by a festival (see p200). His belief in equality influenced Guru Nanak (see the boxed text, p1110) and some of his poems are in the Sikh holy book, the Guru Granth Sahib.

Amritsar

☑0183 / POP 1.25 MILLION

Founded in 1577 by the fourth Sikh guru, Ram Das, Amritsar is home to Sikhism's holiest shrine, the spectacular Golden Temple. The gold-plated gurdwara glitters in the middle of its sacred pool of placid water and draws millions of pilgrims from all over the world. A welcome escape from the frenetic bazaars, this gilded temple is rated by many tourists as a glowing highlight of their visit to India. Regrettably, the same can't be said for the hyperactive streets! Indeed, Amritsar's crush of fuming mechanical traffic, especially in the people-packed old city, can be downright frazzling.

The Mughal emperor Akbar granted the original site for the city, but an Afghan, Ahmad Shah Durani, sacked Amritsar in 1761 and destroyed the temple. It was rebuilt in 1764, and in 1802 was roofed with gilded

---

A PATIALA PEG

In the early 1900s a tent-pegging contest took place in Patiala between the teams of the viceroy and the sports-mad maharaja of Patiala. Tent-pegging is the curious sport of spearing tent pegs out of the ground with a lance from the back of a galloping horse.

Desperate to win and fearful of the wrath of their maharaja, the Patialan team invited their opponents to drinks the night before the match. The British were plied with larger-than-usual measures (or pegs) of whisky, while the tent pegs were changed – smaller ones for the viceroy's team and larger ones for the Patialans. The maharaja's team won but the viceroy's team complained to the maharaja about the size of the pegs. The maharaja (not realising that the complaint referred to the tent pegs) replied that in Patiala, well known for its hospitality, the pegs (of whisky) were always larger than elsewhere. Even today an extra-large measure of whisky is known all over India as a Patiala peg.

copper plates by Maharaja Ranjit Singh and became known as the Golden Temple.

During unrest in Punjab in the early 1980s, separatists seeking to create an independent Sikh homeland occupied the Golden Temple. The army flushed them out in 1984 in a controversial military action that damaged the temple and fuelled violent Sikh-Hindu clashes in Punjab and beyond that left thousands (predominantly Sikhs) dead.

The old city, which includes the Golden Temple and bazaars, is located to the southeast of the train station and is surrounded by a circular road, once the site of the city's massive walls. Modern Amritsar, north of the train station, contains the majority of the upmarket hotels and Lawrence Rd, which is a popular eating and shopping street. The bus station is located 2km east of the train station.

◉ Sights & Activities

Golden Temple   SIKH TEMPLE
(⊙dawn-around 10pm) True to Sikhism's inclusive nature, everyone is welcome at the Sikhs' holiest shrine. As when at any sacred site, dress and behave respectfully. Everyone must remove their shoes and socks, wash their feet (walk through the shallow footbaths) and cover their head; scarves can be borrowed (no charge) and there are also plenty of people selling them for ₹10 – an inexpensive souvenir of your visit. Tobacco and alcohol are strictly prohibited. Temple officials request tourists not to casually dangle their feet in the (holy) water tank but, rather, to sit cross-legged. Photography is only permitted from the **Parkarma**, the marble walkway surrounding the pool.

Volunteers are constantly washing the floor – watch your step, as surfaces can get slippery.

There's an **information office** (☎2553954; ⊙7am-8pm) near the main entrance.

Donations should be placed in one of the donation boxes in the temple precincts.

The temple's architecture is a blend of Hindu and Islamic styles but with unique distinctions. The golden dome (said to be gilded with 750kg of gold) represents an inverted lotus flower, a symbol of Sikh devotees' aim to live a pure life.

A causeway (Gurus' Bridge) leads to the two-storey marble temple, **Hari Mandir Sahib** (or Darbar Sahib). This stands in the middle of the sacred pool, **Amrit Sarovar**

(Pool of Nectar), which gave the town its name. The lower parts of the marble walls are decorated with inlaid flower and animal motifs in the pietra dura (marble inlay) style of the Taj Mahal.

Priests inside the temple keep up a continuous chant in Gurmukhi from the Sikh holy book and this is broadcast around the temple complex by loudspeakers. The original copy of the Sikh holy book, the **Guru Granth Sahib**, is kept under a shroud in the Hari Mandir Sahib during the day and returns ceremoniously to the Akal Takhat at night. Ceremony times are 5am and 9.40pm in winter, and 4am and 10.30pm in summer.

Upstairs, in the main entrance clock tower, the **Sikh Museum** (admission free; ⊙7am-7pm summer, 8am-6pm winter) vividly shows the grisly history of those Sikhs martyred by the Mughals, the British and Mrs Indira Gandhi.

The **Akal Takhat**, where the Shiromani Gurdwara Parbandhak Committee (SGPC), or Sikh Parliament, traditionally meets, was heavily damaged when it was stormed by the Indian army in 1984. The Indian government later repaired it; however, the Sikhs, appalled by the army's actions in the first place, pulled it down and rebuilt it themselves.

Completed in 1784, the octagonal **Baba Atal Tower** commemorates Atal Rai, the son of sixth Sikh guru Har Gobind. After Atal performed a miracle, bringing back to life a playmate who had died of a snake bite, his father scolded him for interfering with the ways of god. The repentant youngster committed suicide on this spot in return for the life he had saved. The nine storeys each represent one year of Atal's short life.

Guru-Ka-Langar is the free (donations appreciated) community dining room, a feature of all Sikh temples as a mark of unity among people of all religions, creeds and nationalities. The massive kitchens (one has a chapati machine) prepare vegetarian meals for an estimated 60,000 to 80,000 pilgrims a day (more during holy festivals). A truly incredible feat! All are welcome to join the masses eating on the floor and we highly recommend the experience (feel free to help volunteers with the washing up).

Try to visit the Golden Temple several times, particularly around dawn and dusk, to fully appreciate the varying light cast upon it at different times of the day.

To learn more about Sikhism, read p1110.

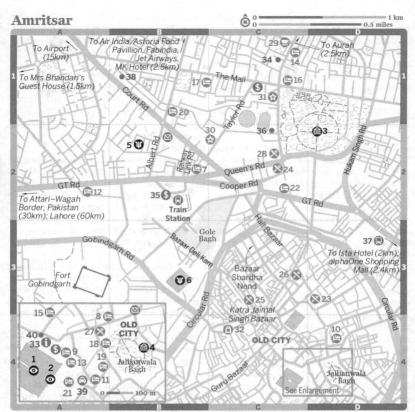

Jallianwala Bagh
HISTORIC SITE

(☻6am-9pm summer, 7am-8pm winter) Near the Golden Temple, this poignant park commemorates those Indians killed or wounded here by the British authorities in 1919 – see the boxed text, p216. Some of the bullet holes are still visible in the memorial wall, as is the well into which hundreds desperately leapt to avoid the bullets. There's an eternal (24-hour) flame of remembrance. The park also contains the **Martyrs' Gallery** (☻6am-9pm summer, 7am-8pm winter) exhibiting firsthand reports and pictures.

Maharaja Ranjit Singh Panorama (Ram Bagh)
MUSEUM

(admission ₹10; ☻9am-9pm Tue-Sun) Within the grounds of the Ram Bagh park is the extraordinary Maharaja Ranjit Singh Panorama, dedicated to the 'Lion of Punjab' (1780–1839). Upstairs is the larger-than-life panorama, replete with booming sound effects (think screaming men and horses in pitch battle),

depicting various battle scenes including the maharaja's 1818 conquest of the fort at Multan. Kids, especially those with a penchant for war, will love it. Exhibits downstairs include colour paintings and dioramas.

Shoes must be removed and cameras aren't permitted inside.

Mata Temple
HINDU TEMPLE

(Model Town, Rani-ka-Bagh; ☻dawn-dusk) This labyrinthine Hindu cave temple commemorates the bespectacled 20th-century female saint Lal Devi. Women wishing to become pregnant come here to pray. The circuitous route to the main shrine passes through ankle-deep waterways, low tunnels, staircases, walkways and caves, the last of which turns out to be the inside of a cave-like divine mouth.

Sri Durgiana Temple
HINDU TEMPLE

(Gobindgarh Rd; ☻dawn-dusk) Dedicated to the goddess Durga, this 16th-century temple, surrounded by a holy water tank, is a Hindu version of the Golden Temple, sometimes known as the Silver Temple for its carved silver doors. Try to visit when there are soothing bhajans (devotional songs); held daily from around 7.30am to 9.30am and 6.30pm to 8.30pm.

⟳ Tours

Sanjay from the Grand Hotel runs reputable and good-value tours that include the Attari–Wagah border closing ceremony, Mata Temple and a night visit to the Golden Temple from ₹500 per person. Day tours can also include the Golden Temple, Jallianwala Bagh and Sri Durgiana Temple. Customised tours to Dharamsala, Dalhousie and Manali can also be arranged.

Sleeping

Most of Amritsar's budget digs are in the old city's boisterous bazaar, not far from the Golden Temple. Bring earplugs!

TOP CHOICE **Grand Hotel**   HOTEL **$$**
(☏2562424; www.hotelgrand.in; Queen's Rd; s/d from ₹1000/1200; ❄@🛜) This three-star hotel, close to the train station, is deservedly popular. The rooms aren't exactly grand but are certainly comfortably appointed and well kept. They, along with a restaurant (mains ₹50 to ₹250), the Bottoms Up Pub (see p218), and a breezy veranda with tables and chairs (perfect at beer o'clock), fringe a leafy garden. The amiable owner, Sanjay, is a reliable source of information and can arrange sightseeing trips (including to the Attari–Wagah border closing ceremony).

Mrs Bhandari's Guest House GUESTHOUSE **$$**
(☏2228509; http://bhandari_guesthouse.tripod.com; 10 Cantonment; camping ₹ 200, s/d from ₹1500/1800; ❄@🏊) Legacy of the much-loved Mrs Bhandari (1906–2007), this earthy, ecoconscious guesthouse is set on

THE JALLIANWALA BAGH MASSACRE

Unrest in Amritsar was sparked by the controversial Rowlatt Act (1919), which gave British authorities 'emergency' powers to imprison without trial Indians suspected of sedition. Hartals (general strikes) were organised in protest, and escalated into rioting and looting. Three British bank managers were murdered in reprisal attacks following the killing of Indian protestors by the British.

Brigadier-General Reginald Dyer was called upon to return order to the city. On 13 April 1919 (Baisakhi Day), over 5000 Indians were holding a peaceful demonstration in Jallianwala Bagh, an open space surrounded by high walls. Dyer arrived with 150 troops and without warning ordered his soldiers to open fire. Some six minutes later, more than 400 people were dead and a further 1500 were wounded.

The exact number of final fatalities is unknown, but estimated to be upwards of 1500, including women and children.

Dyer's action was supported by some of his British colleagues but described as 'a savage and inappropriate folly' by Sir Edwin Montague, the Secretary of State for India. It galvanised Indian nationalism – Gandhi responded with his program of civil disobedience, announcing that 'cooperation in any shape or form with this satanic government is sinful'.

Richard Attenborough's acclaimed film *Gandhi* dramatically re-enacts the massacre and subsequent enquiry.

spacious green grounds northwest of Fort Gobindgarh. The comfy rooms bring back memories of grandma's place and will appeal to those seeking a calm, uncommercial atmosphere. Overlanders with their own tents can camp and park, while train travellers can organise pick-up from the train station. The main house is filled with charming old treasures like the century-old wood stove in the gorgeous kitchen. Set meals and an à la carte menu are available (mains ₹120 to ₹440).

Ista Hotel HOTEL $$$
(☎2708888; www.istahotels.com; GT Rd; s/d from ₹9000/9500; ✴@🤶🏊) Amritsar's only five-star hotel, sits beside a bright shopping mall, alphaOne, 3km east of the interstate bus terminus. Fans of five-star hotels may be a little underwhelmed by the smallish standard rooms, but will adore the pool and the pampering Ista Spa, which has quite a reputation. Room, meal and spa packages are available. Thai and Chinese cuisine is available in Thai Chi Restaurant and teppanyaki is available in Collage, the hotel's multicuisine restaurant (mains ₹160 to ₹400).

Tourist Guesthouse GUESTHOUSE $
(☎2553830; bubblesgoolry@yahoo.com; 1355 GT Rd; dm/s/d ₹100/150/300; @) This stalwart is a backpacker institution (especially with overlanders). The rooms may be scuffed and bare but have high ceilings and fans, and you're paying peanuts! There is a go-with-the-flow vibe, helpful staff, secure parking, a small garden and simple restaurant. All rooms are equipped with TVs, hot water and air coolers.

Hotel Grand Legacy HOTEL $$
(☎5069991; www.grandlegacy.net; 8 GT Rd, Model Town; s/d incl breakfast ₹3600/4600 ✴@) Fifty-two attractive rooms boast leather chairs, writing desk, LCD TV, minibar, tea-and-coffee-making facilities and electronic safe. There's also a gym, round-the-clock coffee shop, travel desk, business centre, the Moti Mahal Deluxe restaurant (p218) and, for a cocktaily escapade, Behind Bars, with its zebra-print chairs and icy cold beer. Room discounts are readily offered depending on occupancy.

Hotel City Heart HOTEL $$
(☎2545186; www.hotelcityheartamritsar.com; opposite Jallianwala Bagh; r from ₹1400; ✴@🤶) City Heart is a sophisticated choice in the old city with tidy rooms, flatscreen TVs and soft mattresses. Even the bottom-of-the-range rooms are a soothing respite from the frenetic streets. The attached Café Heart restaurant (mains ₹80 to ₹300) has cool desserts, curries and a great outlook onto vibrant Golden Temple Rd.

Hotel Indus HOTEL $$
(☎2535900; www.hotelindus.com; Sri Hamandir Sahib Marg; r from ₹1550; ✴🤶) The dramatic million-dollar view of the Golden Temple

from the rooftop is reason alone to stay at this modern-style hotel. Apart from being smallish, rooms are otherwise fine with two (303 and 304; ₹2116) boasting spectacular temple vistas – book ahead!

MK Hotel
HOTEL $$

(✆2504610; www.mkhotel.com; Ranjit Ave; s/d incl breakfast ₹3000/4600, ste ₹7000; ❋@✸) One of Amritsar's best four-star hotels, elegant MK has all the in-room comforts to make your stay relaxing and pampered. There is a business centre, multicuisine restaurant (mains ₹115 to ₹400), 24-hour coffee shop, health club and bar.

Hotel Ritz Plaza
HOTEL $$

(✆2562836; www.ritzhotel.in; 45 The Mall; s/d incl breakfast ₹3500/4700, ste ₹5700; ❋@✸) Particularly popular with business travellers and tour groups, the well-furnished rooms (either marble or timber flooring) come with TV, tea-and-coffee-making facilities, sofas and minibars. Standard rooms vary so check a few. On-site is a relaxing bar, round-the-clock cafe and multicuisine restaurant.

MK Sood Guesthouse
HOTEL $

(✆5093376; r ₹650; ❋) MK's rooms all have AC, are good sized and well maintained with decent bathrooms and comfy beds. All this, along with the helpful staff, make it a reasonably good choice near the Golden Temple.

Hotel Grace
HOTEL $

(✆2559355; www.hotelgrace.net; 35 Brahma Buta Market; r with AC ₹800-1450, without AC ₹600; ❋) Rooms are mostly repainted, refurbished and are fair at this price, all come with TV and straightforward furnishings. Partial Golden Temple views are to be had from the rooftop.

Hotel Le Golden
HOTEL $$

(✆5028000; www.hotellegolden.com; r from ₹1350; ❋) A reasonable choice near the Golden Temple, rooms are tidy (if somewhat squishy) and the rooftop cafe has squinty temple views. Newly refurbished rooms on the 3rd floor will be the pick of the bunch.

Sri Guru Ram Das Niwas
PILGRIMS' REST HOUSE $

(dm free but donations appreciated, r with/without AC ₹300/100; ❋) To stay in the huge accommodation blocks for pilgrims and visitors to the Golden Temple, check in at Guru Arjan Dev Niwas. Foreigners are generally accommodated in the dorm at Sri Guru Ram Das Niwas next door. Rooms and dorms are ba-sic, with shared bathrooms. Please respect the requested three-day stay limit.

Hotel Lawrence
HOTEL $$

(✆2400105; www.lawrenceamritsar.com; 6 Lawrence Rd; s/d incl breakfast ₹2700/3500; ❋) Don't let the facade put you off. This mid-ranger is a welcome retreat from the bustle of Lawrence Rd, with contemporary rooms that have either marble or carpeted floors. It will pay to check rooms for road noise and thin mattresses. Multicuisine restaurant.

Hotel MC International
HOTEL $$

(✆2222901; www.hotelmcinternational.com; The Mall; s/d incl breakfast ₹2800/3200; ❋@) This midranger has unadorned contemporary rooms, somewhat lifted by the incredibly bright bed covers and sparkling bathrooms. There is a 24-hour coffee shop and business centre but the advertised gym, beauty parlour and bar are all still on the planning board.

Mohan International Hotel
HOTEL $$

(✆3010100; www.mohaninternationalhotel.com; Albert Rd; s/d incl breakfast ₹3000/4000; ❋✸) The ageing Mohan has seen better days, but is an option if you can't get a bed elsewhere. Rooms are a mixed bag (some in better shape than others), all adequately comfortable with flatscreen TV. Ensure the AC works in summer!

Other options near the Golden Temple include:

Hotel Holy City
HOTEL $

(✆5068111; www.hotelholycity.co.in; Parag Das Chowk; r ₹600-1850; ❋) Not far from the Golden Temple, featuring mostly modest boxy rooms with scuffed walls. However, several refurbished deluxe rooms are attractively decorated in coordinated colours and have a fresh feel.

Hotel Sita Niwas
HOTEL $

(✆2543092; www.hotelniwas.com; d from ₹350, without bathroom ₹250) The basic rooms are oversized shoeboxes but with hard-to-beat prices. More money buys bigger rooms.

Lucky Guest House
HOTEL $

(✆2542175; Mahna Singh Rd; r with/without AC from ₹700/500; ❋) The basic rooms are a bit pokey and it is worth paying ₹100 more for the deluxe versions. More of a fall-back option than a first choice.

Hotel Golden Tower
HOTEL $$

(✆2534446; www.hotelgoldentower.com; Phawara Chowk; r from ₹1250; ❋) Another hotel with location at the top of its list of charms, this no-frills midrange option has sparsely decorated but reasonable rooms with TV and fridge.

Hotel CJ International
HOTEL $$

(☎2543478; www.cjhotel.net; r from ₹1550; ❄@) The rooms are blandly comfortable and the staff can be brusque, but the draw is its proximity to the Golden Temple (pre-book one of the five temple-facing rooms on level three).

✘ Eating

Amritsar is famous for its *dhabas* (snack bars) such as **Punjab Dhaba** (Goal Hatti Chowk), **Kesar Da Dhaba** (Passian Chowk) and **Brothers' Dhaba** (Town Hall Chowk), all with (mainly Indian) thali meals averaging ₹65 to ₹110, and open early to late. Brothers' is the current favourite. Hotels and restaurants in the (holy) Golden Temple locale don't serve alcohol; elsewhere your beer may be disguised in a napkin.

The city is also famous for its 'Amritsari' (deep-fried fish with lemon, chilli, garlic and ginger); sniff out the stalls frying it up (especially prevalent in the old city).

Moti Mahal Deluxe
NORTH INDIAN $$

(☎5069991; Hotel Grand Legacy, GT Rd, Model Town; mains ₹130-350; ⏰9am-11.30pm; ❄) Moti Mahal enjoys a well-deserved reputation for expertly prepared North Indian cuisine (especially tandoori). Consider the tasty *murgh makhani* (butter chicken) and *diwani handi* (mixed vegies in a roulette of fenugreek and mint). Icy cold Kingfisher beer is available.

Crystal Restaurant
MULTICUISINE $$

(☎2225555; Cooper Rd; mains ₹140-250; ⏰11am-11.30pm; ❄) Rated by many as one of Amritsar's best restaurants, Crystal boasts all sorts of yummy global favourites, from lasagne to fish curry. Book ahead, especially on weekends. There are two 'Crystals' (one upstairs and one downstairs), apparently due to a family split...we're equally divided when it comes to judging which is best. Guess you'll just have to try both!

Astoria Food Pavillion
MULTICUISINE $

(mains ₹140-325; ⏰noon-11pm; ❄) It sounds like a food court, but it is in fact a pleasant multicuisine restaurant near the MK Hotel, cooking up a mishmash of dishes, from chicken Patiala and veg biryani to poached fish and spinach cannelloni. Head upstairs to the sister restaurant, Oka (mains ₹120 to

₹300) where pizza, pasta, stir-fry and burgers are cooked fresh right in front of you.

Sagar Ratna
SOUTH INDIAN $

(Queen's Rd; mains ₹50-110; ⏰9am-11pm; ❄) An easygoing South Indian veg restaurant with fresh lime sodas that will quench the most savage summer thirst. Excellent southern specialities (*idlis, dosas, uttapams* etc) with a sprinkling of North Indian and Chinese dishes.

Neelam's
MULTICUISINE $

(mains ₹35-90; ⏰9am-10.30pm) Not far from the Golden Temple, this unassuming eatery is a convenient spot to cool your heels over a banana lassi. The have-a-go-at-anything menu includes pizzas, burgers, soups, dosas, *aloo paratha* and, for breakfast, honey muesli.

Aurah
CAFE $

(B-Block, Ranjit Ave; mains ₹150-250; ⏰11.30am-11.30pm; ❄) Alongside a Subway franchise is this chilled-out cafe, delighting diners with global goodies: glass-noodle salad, lemongrass chicken skewers, risotto, crispy lotus stems, lettuce wraps with sweet chilli dressing, pasta, Caesar salad and, for the mother of all sugar fixes, the 'chocolate trip'.

Punjabi Rasoi
MULTICUISINE $

(mains ₹45-85; ⏰9am-11.30pm) A stone's throw away from the Golden Temple, this unpretentious, fan-cooled, all-veg restaurant rustles up reasonable Indian, Continental and Chinese fare.

alphaOne Foodcourt
FAST FOOD $

(GT Rd; mains ₹45-85; ⏰10am-10pm) On the 2nd floor of the alphaOne shopping mall, adjacent to the Ista Hotel and about 3km east of the interstate bus terminus, is this clean and cool food court. Purchase a cash card at the counter to then purchase the food from the various stalls, including North Indian, South Indian, Chinese, ice creams etc. Take the cash card back to the counter to get any change remaining on the card.

Drinking

Bottoms Up Pub
BAR

(Grand Hotel, Queen's Rd) A mixed crowd of travellers and locals are attracted to this congenial bar by the icy cold, glycerine-free, draught Kingfisher beer and the seriously delicious snacks and meals from the Grand Hotel's excellent kitchen.

Café Coffee Day CAFE
(Phawara Chowk; snacks from ₹45;) One of the ubiquitous espresso coffee franchises with savoury and sweet munchies, decent coffee and brain-freezing cold concoctions. Other branches are on Lawrence Rd and inside the alphaOne shopping mall.

☆ Entertainment

The **Aaanaam** (2210949; Taylor Rd) and **Adarsh** (2565249; MMM Rd) cinemas screen Hindi (and occasionally English) movies. Consult newspapers for session details.

🛍 Shopping

Wandering around the skinny alleys of the old city bazaars is a head-spinning assault on the senses. There are shops selling everything from devotional ornaments to jootis; a good place for jootis is around Gandhi Gate (Hall Gate), where they start at ₹200. Katra Jaimal Singh Bazaar is full of *salwar kameez* and saris, while the city's more modern shops can be found along Lawrence and Mall Rds.

alphaOne (GT Rd; ⊙10am-10pm;) Western-style shopping mall with food court (p218) and international brand shops.

Fabindia (2503102; www.fabindia.com; 30 Ranjit Ave; ⊙10am-8pm) Contemporary-meets-traditional Indian textiles and homewares store.

ℹ Information

Internet Access
Cyber Swing (Old city; per hr ₹40; ⊙9.30am-10pm) Upstairs from Punjabi Rasoi restaurant.

Medical Services
Fortis Escort Hospital (2573901; Majitha Verka Bypass)

Money
Amritsar has an ever-mushrooming supply of ATMs.

HDFC (Golden Temple branch; ⊙9.30am-3.30pm Mon-Sat) Exchanges travellers cheques and currencies; has an ATM.

ICICI ATM (Lawrence Rd) Also has an ATM in the old city beside Hotel City Heart.

Photography
The following studios sell memory cards and camera batteries.

SS Colour Lab (2401515; 104 Lawrence Rd; ⊙10am-9pm Mon-Sat)

Unique Colour Lab (2223263; MMM Rd; ⊙10am-9.30pm Mon-Sat, 2-8.30pm Sun) Next door to the Indian Academy of Fine Arts.

Post
Main post office (2566032; Court Rd; ⊙9am-3pm Mon-Fri, to 2pm Sat)
Post office (Phawara Chowk; ⊙9am-7pm Mon-Sat)

Tourist Information
Tourist office (2402452; Train station exit, Queens Rd; ⊙9am-5pm Mon-Sat) Has good free maps covering Punjab and Amritsar.

ℹ Getting There & Away

Air
Amritsar's Sri Guru Ram Dass Jee International Airport services domestic and international flights. One-way flights to Delhi/Mumbai cost around ₹3200/7800

Air India (2508122; www.airindia.in; MK Hotel, Ranjit Ave)

Indian Airlines (2213392; www.indianair lines.nic.in; 39A Court Rd)

Jet Airways (2508003; www.jetairways .com; Ranjit Ave)

Kingfisher Airlines (080-39008888; www .flykingfisher.com; airport)

Bus
The main interstate bus terminus is on GT Rd about 2km north of the Golden Temple. Frequent buses leave for Delhi (non-AC/AC ₹305/665, 10 hours), Chandigarh (non-AC/AC ₹175/150, seven hours), Pathankot (₹65, three hours) and Jammu (₹120, six hours).

To Himachal Pradesh, at least one bus travels daily to Dalhousie (₹165, six hours), Dharamsala (₹165, six hours), Shimla (₹265, 10 hours) and Manali (₹380, 14 hours).

Private buses, with similar fares to the above, depart daily for Delhi from near the train station at 10pm. Other private buses, including to Chandigarh and Jammu, depart from Gandhi Gate.

Train
Apart from the train station, a less busy **train reservation office** (⊙8am-8pm, to 2pm Sun) is at the Golden Temple.

The fastest train to Delhi is the twice-daily *Shatabdi Express* (5.10am service chair car/executive ₹570/1095, 5pm service ₹675/1260, 5¾ hours). A daily Amritsar–Howrah Mail run links Amritsar with Lucknow (sleeper/3AC/2AC ₹310/825/1158, 16½ hours), Varanasi (₹365/998/1373, 22 hours) and Howrah (₹489/1346/1857, 37 hours).

ℹ Getting Around
A free bus service runs from the train station and the bus stand to the Golden Temple every 20

minutes from 4.30am to 9.30pm. The buses are bright yellow and almost always full. Otherwise, from the train station to the Golden Temple a cycle-rickshaw costs around ₹30, an autorickshaw ₹50 and a taxi (📞01835151515) ₹120. To the airport, an autorickshaw costs ₹200 and a taxi ₹500.

India–Pakistan Border at Attari–Wagah

People come to the border, 30km west of Amritsar, for two reasons: to enjoy the late afternoon border-closing ceremony (see the boxed text, p221) or to use the crossing between India and Pakistan (see the boxed text, p220).

Return taxis (official ones have yellow number plates) from Amritsar to the border cost around ₹800 to ₹950 and take about one hour (price includes waiting time). Shared taxis (return per person ₹85) also run to the border-closing ceremony from the dining-hall entrance to the Golden Temple. They leave about two hours before the ceremony starts and squeeze in eight passengers.

You can travel to the border by autorickshaw but you run the risk of being stopped by the police, as it's illegal for autorickshaws to travel beyond Amritsar's city precincts.

Also, the local train to Attari will leave you 2km from the action with few options other than walking to get to the border.

By far and away the easiest option is to take a trip organised by a hotel. Most hotels can arrange trips to the border; one reliable option is the Grand Hotel (p215), which also takes nonguests with advance notice.

Pathankot

📞0186 / POP 190,000

For travellers, the dusty frontier town of Pathankot is a transport hub for neighbouring Himachal Pradesh and Jammu.

Hotel Venice (📞2225061; www.venicehotel india.com; Dhangu Rd; r from ₹1780; ✳) has the best accommodation and restaurants. There are also hotels on Railway Rd and for those with ongoing rail tickets, there's the train station retiring rooms (d ₹200).

The bus station (📞2254435; Gurdaspur Rd) is 500m from the Pathankot Junction train station and 3km from Chakki Bank train station.

Buses go to Amritsar (₹65, 2½ hours), Jammu (₹70, 2½ hours), Chamba (₹80, 3½ hours), Dalhousie (₹65, 2½ hours), Dharamsala (₹65, 2½ hours), Manali (₹300, 10½ hours), Chandigarh (₹150, six hours) and Delhi (₹320, 11 hours).

CROSSING INTO PAKISTAN

Border Hours

The border is open from 10am to 4pm daily, but get there at least half an hour before it closes.

Foreign Exchange

There's a State Bank of India (◷10am-5pm Mon-Sat) which exchanges currency, but it's a tiny branch so play it safe and change money in Amritsar.

Onward Transport

From Wagah (Pakistan) there are buses and taxis to Lahore, 30km away.

Sleeping & Eating

If you have to stay overnight, there's the Aman Umeed Tourist Complex (📞9780953882; Wagah border; r from ₹1500; ✳), which has just three rooms and a restaurant (mains ₹90 to ₹190).

There are small stalls selling snacks and cold drinks.

Visas

Visas are theoretically available at the Pakistan embassy in Delhi; however, travellers are strongly urged to apply for a visa in their home country, where the process is usually more straightforward (see also p1177).

BORDERLINE ENTERTAINMENT

Every late afternoon, just before sunset, members of the Indian and Pakistani military meet at the border to engage in a 30-minute display of pure theatre. The flag-lowering, closing-of-the-border ceremony is a fusion of orderly colonial-style pomp, comical goose-stepping and, considering the two countries' rocky relationship, stunning demonstration of harmony. So popular is this event, that grandstands have been specially constructed to accommodate the patriotic throngs.

The ceremony starts at around 4.15pm in winter and 5.15pm in summer (but double-check, given that timings vary according to sunset). Cameras are permitted (free) but bags, large and small, are banned (although this is haphazardly enforced).

It's worth getting here early to avoid the stampede when the crowd charges along the chicken run leading to the grandstands. It's about a 10-minute walk from where vehicles drop you to the seating area. Foreigners are allowed to sit at the front stalls (behind the VIP area, which is closest to the border).

Prior to the ceremony, the stony-faced soldiers mill about with the air of self-conscious debutantes and the real action is that of the spectators, some parading the Indian flag. Loud music and a compère pump up the crowd's patriotic fervour. The Pakistanis are equally vociferous, except during Ramadan, when their stands are noticeably quieter.

Then, with a bellow from the guardroom, a squad stomps out, shoulders square, moustaches twirled and eyes bulging. The drill is to parade up and down as dramatically as possible, preceded by a kick so high the soldier looks in danger of concussing himself. The high-octane march to the border, vaguely reminiscent of Monty Python's 'Ministry of Silly Walks' sketch, rouses thunderous applause from the audience and repetitive chants of 'Hindustan zindabad!' (Long live India!).

The gates are flung open and commanding officers of both countries shake hands and salute (blink and you'll miss it). Then, the flags of both countries are simultaneously lowered and folded and the gates slammed shut. The border is now closed for the night.

Several daily express trains leave for Delhi (sleeper/2AC/1AC ₹212/772/1300, 11 hours), Amritsar (chair ₹40, three hours) and Jammu (chair ₹47, three hours). The Kangra Valley narrow-gauge line leaves from Pathankot Junction train station (see the boxed text, p330).

Taxis to Amritsar/Dharamsala cost around ₹1500/1700.

Jammu & Kashmir (including Ladakh)

Includes »

Why Go?

Welcome to three incredibly different worlds in one state. For most foreigners, J&K's greatest attractions are the Himalayan lands of Ladakh and Zanskar, with their disarmingly friendly Tibetan Buddhist people, timeless monasteries, arid canyons and soaring snow-topped mountains. But neither area is easily accessible, especially outside midsummer.

Hordes of domestic visitors make pilgrimages to temples around Hindu Jammu and love Muslim Kashmir for its cool summer air and alpine scenery. Srinagar's romantic houseboat accommodation is another drawcard. However, political volatility remains a concern. Disputes over Kashmir caused three 20th-century wars and intercommunal strife still breaks out sporadically. Always check the security situation before travelling to Jammu or Srinagar but, even if things look dodgy there, you can expect Ladakh to be as meditatively calm as ever.

Best Buddhist Monasteries

» Lamayuru (p268)

» Diskit (p269)

» Chemrey (p273)

» Thiksey (p272)

» Karsha (p242)

Best Mountain Scenery

» Pangong Tso (p276)

» Dal Lake, Srinagar (p235)

» Shyok Valley (p270)

» Manali–Leh road (p274)

When to Go

Leh

[Climate chart showing temperature (°C/°F) and rainfall (inches/mm) by month January–December]

Jun & Sep
Ideal for Srinagar and Sonamarg; roads to Ladakh can be blocked.

Jul–Aug
Perfect for Ladakh; Pahalgam overflows with pilgrims; rain drenches Jammu.

Winter
Skiing at Gulmarg. Ladakh, only accessible by air, has festivals but no tourists.

Food

A full traditional Kashmiri *wazawan* (feast) can have dozens of courses, notably mutton-based dishes like *goshtaba* (pale mutton balls in saffron-yoghurt curry), *tabak maaz* (fried lamb's ribs) and mildly spicy rogan josh (rich, vividly red-coloured mutton curry). Kashmiri chefs also serve deliciously aromatic cheese-based curries and seasonal *nadir* (lotus stems) typically served in *yakhni* (a curd-based sauce made mildly minty with fennel).

Ladakh's Tibetan favourites include salt-tea, *momos* (dumplings) and *thukpa* (noodle soup) though a more genuinely Ladakhi dish is *skiu*, a stew incorporating flakes of homemade barley 'pasta'. Ladakh's barley-beer, chhang, is available at rural homestays but not for general sale.

DON'T MISS

Buddhist **Ladakh** is India at its most beguilingly human and scenically stunning, a rugged high-altitude desert softened with Tibetan temples, irrigated paddies and mesmerising mountain lakes. Come in summer when the rest of sweltering India is drenched in monsoons. But allow ample contingency time for acclimatisation, cancelled planes and roads that can suffer lengthy closures caused by landslides.

Top State Festivals

Hindu festivals are celebrated in Jammu, Muslim ones in the Kashmir Valley and Buddhist temple festivals abound in Ladakh and Zanskar. The latter, held around local monasteries, typically feature masked dances and village fairs that are colourful but lengthy, slow-moving affairs. Those held in winter, eg at Spituk (January), Stok (March) and Thiksey (November), see few foreigners but summer ones, like those at Lamayuru (June), Hemis (July) and Takthog (July), can feel overloaded with camera-toting tourists. Exact dates vary with the lunar calendar.

» Losar (Dec) Ladakhi New Year, celebrated in Buddhist homes and gompas with feasts, rituals and dances.

» Dosmoche (Feb-early Mar, widespread) Buddhist New Year. Masked dances; effigies representing the evil spirits of the old year are burnt or cast into the desert.

» Matho Nagrang (Feb-Mar, Matho, p262) Monastery oracles perform blindfolded acrobatics and ritual mutilations.

» Ladakh Festival (1-15 Sep, Leh, p244) Unrepentantly touristy but entertaining cycle of events including a carnivalesque opening parade, Buddhist dances, polo, music and archery.

MAIN POINTS OF ENTRY

Srinagar, Jammu and Leh have commercial airports. Jammu has the only major railhead. By road, Ladakh is only accessible in summer over tortuous mountain roads from Srinagar and Manali.

Fast Facts

» Population: 12.5 million

» Area: 222,236 sq km

» Capitals: Srinagar (summer), Jammu (winter), Leh (Ladakh)

» Main languages: Kashmiri, Urdu, Ladakhi, Balti

» Sleeping prices: **$** below ₹1000, **$$** ₹1000 to ₹5000, **$$$** above ₹5000

Top Tip

Check the security situation before heading to the Kashmir Valley but don't let troubles in Srinagar deter you from visiting ever-calm Ladakh.

Resources

» **News** www.greaterkashmir.com, www.dailyexcelsior.com, www.kashmirtimes.com, www.kashmirherald.com

» **Traveller Forum** www.indiamike.com/india/jammu-and-kashmir-f30

» **Tourism** www.jktourism.org, www.ladakhtourism.in

» **Rare maps** http://blankonthemap.free.fr

» **Ladakh Homestays** www.himalayan-homestays.com

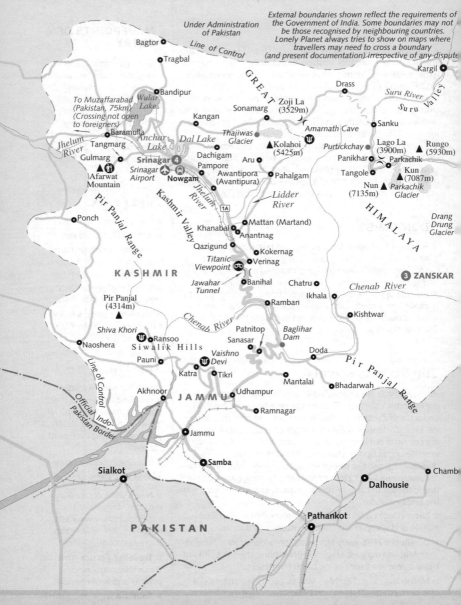

External boundaries shown reflect the requirements of the Government of India. Some boundaries may not be those recognised by neighbouring countries. Lonely Planet always tries to show on maps where travellers may need to cross a boundary (and present documentation) irrespective of any dispute

Jammu & Kashmir Highlights

1 Murmur meditative mantras in the mural-decked gompas (Tibetan Buddhist monasteries) of the **Indus Valley** (p272)

2 Escape India's humid summer heat in entrancing **Leh** (p244), a low-key traveller hub with dusty medieval backstreets, a Potala-style palace and a deep sense of ecological awareness

3 Experience the stark magnificence of **Ladakh** or **Zanskar** on an unforgettable high-altitude trek (p252)

Turtuk • • Chalunka • Panamik
Pinchamik
Dha • Skuru (Khar) ✈ Sumur
Hanu-Do • Hunder • Tirit
Indus River Diskit • Rongo
Road closed to foreigners Skurbuchan Khardung
Shargol Khalsi *Shyok River*
Mulbekh Lamayuru Khardung La
Hansukot (Heniskot) (5602m) **Nubra Valley ⑤**
Rangdum Sisir La Alchi **①** Phyang
(4850m) **Indus Valley** Spituk **② Leh** Chang La
Singge La Zingchen Thiksey (5289m)
(5050m) Takthog Durbuk Tangtse
Nerak *Zanskar River* *Markha River* Stok Kangri Chemrey *Lukung* **Pangong Tso ⑤**
Pensi La (6121m) Hemis • Karu Spangmik
(4401m) *Stod River* Upshi Man Merak
Zanskar Range **Stok Range** Rumtse Himya *No foreigners allowed beyond this point*
Pidmo Taglang La *Indus River* Chushul
Phey (5359m) *Kiari Army Camp*
Karsha *Tso Kar*
Sani Stongde **③ LADAKH** Horlamkong La Chumathang
Padum ⚠ Bardan (4712m) Kidmang *Mahe Police Checkpoint*
Mune Sumdo
Raru Ishar **RUPSU** Puga Mahe
Tsetang ⚠ *Phuktal* Pang ⛵ Kyamayur La Gompa Nyoma
Yal Purne Lachlung La (5125m) *Tso Kiagar*
Tetha (5060m) Gamabarma La
RANGE Tanze Nakila Pass (5101m)
Lookout Kargyak Yalangyau La
Lakong *Bharatpur* (4920m) Korzok
Shingo (Shinkun) La ⚠ ⚠ *Sarchu* *Chang-Pa Nomad Camp* *Tso Moriri*
(5090m) *Patseo* (summer)
Ramjak Chika Baralacha La
Tandi Jispa (4950m)
Udaipur Gemur Darcha *Zingzingbar*
Darcha Checkpoint
Gondla Keylong **LAHAUL** **CHINA TIBET**
HIMACHAL PRADESH Khoksar
McLeod Ganj *Rohtang Pass*
Dharamsala Manali
Naggar **SPITI** Kaza
Kullu Tabo

Under Administration of China

Ⓝ 0 ———————— 50 km
0 ———————— 30 miles

---

④ Enjoy an amusingly caricatured Raj-type experience relaxing on a deluxe Dal Lake houseboat in **Srinagar** (p236)

⑤ Gawp at the mountain-valley scenery backing surreally blue **Pangong Tso** (p276) or the splendid **Nubra Valley** (p269)

JAMMU & THE KASHMIR VALLEY

Predominantly Hindu Jammu swelters at the edge of the Indian plains, north of which seemingly endless layers of alpine peaks start unfolding. Hemmed deep within those mountains is the fabled Kashmir Valley where tin-roofed villages guard terraced paddy fields delineated by orchards and pin-straight poplars. Proudly independent-minded Kashmiris mostly follow a Sufi-based Islamic faith, worshiping in distinctive box-shaped mosques which, traditionally, feature a small central spire rather than dome or minaret. Many Kashmiris have startlingly green eyes and in winter keep warm by clutching a kangri (wicker fire-pot holder) beneath their flowing grey-brown pheran (woollen capes).

Once the very vision of tranquillity, the Kashmir Valley has been scarred by violence ever since Indian Independence. The India-Pakistan wars left greater Kashmir painfully divided, while Kashmiris' longing for more meaningful autonomy has resulted in waves of civil unrest and resultant curfews that periodically cripple the valley's tourist industry.

History

Geologists and Hindu mystics agree that the 140km-long Kashmir Valley was once a vast lake. Where they disagree is whether it was drained by a post-Ice Age earthquake or by Lord Vishnu and friends to kill a lake demon.

In the 3rd century BC the Hindu kingdom of Kashmir became a major centre of Buddhist learning under Emperor Ashoka. For centuries Kashmir's Buddhist artists travelled across the Himalaya, creating monastery murals like those at Alchi.

In the 13th and 14th centuries AD Islam arrived in Kashmir through the inspiration of peaceable Sufi mystics. Later some Muslim rulers, like Sultan Sikandar 'Butshikan' (r 1389–1413), set about the destruction of Hindu temples and Buddhist monasteries. However, others like the great Zain-ul-Abidin (r 1423–74) encouraged such religious and cultural tolerance that medieval visitors reported finding it hard to tell Hindus and Muslims apart. Relative open-mindedness continued under Mughal emperor Akbar (1556–1605), whose troops took Kashmir in 1586. The Mughals saw Kashmir as their Xanadu and developed a series of extravagant gardens around Srinagar that partially survive today.

When the British arrived in India, Jammu and Kashmir was a loose affiliation of independent kingdoms, nominally controlled by the Sikh rulers of Jammu. In 1846, after the British had defeated the Sikhs, they handed Kashmir to Maharaja Gulab Singh in return for a yearly tribute of six shawls, 12 goats and a horse. Singh's autocratic Hindu-Dogra dynasty ruled until Independence, showing an infamous disregard for the welfare of the Muslim majority. Many citizens were little better than slaves, liable for service as unpaid porters or labourers at the whim of local landowners.

PARTITION & CONFLICT

As Partition approached in 1947, although Jammu and Kashmir's population was majority Muslim, the (jailed) popular leader of the predominantly Islamic opposition favoured joining India. Hindu Maharaja Hari Singh favoured Kashmiri independence but failed to make a definitive decision. Finally, to force the issue, Pashtun tribesmen, backed by the new government in Pakistan, attempted to grab the state by force. They were within a day or so of reaching virtually unprotected Srinagar when, in the nick of time, India's first Prime Minister, Nehru, himself a Kashmiri Hindu, airlifted in Indian troops, sparking the first India-Pakistani war. The invaders were pushed out of the Kashmir Valley but Pakistan retained control of Baltistan, Muzaffarabad and the valley's main access routes. Kashmir has remained divided ever since along a tenuous UN-demarcated border, known as the Line of Control. A proposed referendum to let Kashmir's people decide (for Pakistan or India) never materialised and Pakistan invaded again in 1965, triggering another protracted conflict.

Although most Indian Kashmiris would prefer to be independent of both India *and* Pakistan, the conflict became a cause célèbre for pro-Pakistani Islamic radicals. A militant fringe turned to armed rebellion, countered with brutal force by the Indian Army, stoking a cycle of increasing resentment. By 1990 the state was awash with fighters, some from Kashmir but rather more from Afghanistan and Pakistan, whose brand of fundamentalist Sunni Islam jarred significantly with Kashmir's native Sufi-based forms of broad-minded spirituality.

Kashmir was placed under direct rule from Delhi in 1990, triggering the bloodiest years of unrest. Massacres and bomb attacks by militants were countered by brutal counter-insurgency tactics from the Indian armed forces with significant human rights abuses reported on both sides.

In 1998 India and Pakistan's nuclear weapons tests brought regional tensions almost to breaking point and resulted in the brief 1999 'Kargil War', a high-altitude Pakistani incursion. However, after a cease-fire, increasing autonomy for Kashmir was matched by a significant reduction in tensions, while the tragic 2005 earthquake helped bring the Indian and Pakistani governments a little closer and some relief aid was allowed to cross the Line of Control.

With militant attacks dwindling, domestic tourist numbers had been increasing rapidly until disturbances in 2008 (over an arcane land dispute at Amarnath) and June 2010 (after the shooting of juvenile stone-throwers). Each resulted in months of strikes, violence, curfews and the closing of the Jammu-Srinagar road. The 2010 events stirred up deeply felt popular resentment towards the heavy Indian military presence and the situation is likely to remain highly unpredictable for the forseeable future.

Meanwhile, ever-peaceful Ladakh is angling for Union status (like Chandigarh) so that it can finally divorce itself from Kashmir's troubles, with which it has no real connection.

Jammu

📞 0191 / POP 612,000 / ELEV 327M

Sweaty Jammu is J&K's winter capital and main rail hub. It's a major 'base camp' for floods of Hindu *yatri* (pilgrims) en route to Katra and Amarnath (p231) but foreign visitors are rare.

⊙ Sights

Jammu dubs itself as the 'city of temples'. Although few of these are historically compulsive, many offer a joyously colourful festival of kitsch that helps justify a one-day stop en route to Srinagar. Attractions are widely spread and given the heat it's a great idea to take one of the autorickshaw drivers' ₹300 inclusive four-hour 'tours'.

Mubarak Mandi   PALACE, MUSEUM
Crowning a hilly maze of bustling if architecturally neutral 'old town', Mubarak Mandi is the extensive former palace complex of Jammu's 19th-century maharajas. Later used as government offices and now severely neglected, it's a fascinatingly maudlin sight whose only functioning section is the **Dogra Art Gallery** (foreigner/Indian ₹50/10; ⊙10am-5pm Tue-Sun). Occupying the former Durbar Hall (painted a ghastly pink), that's actually more museum than gallery and features bronzes, armaments, instruments, 9th-century carvings and Kushan coins.

Amar Mahal   PALACE, MUSEUM
(www.karansingh.com/amml; foreigner/Indian ₹45/10; ⊙9am-12.50pm & 2-5.50pm Tue-Sun, to 4.50pm Apr-Sep) The last official residence of Jammu royalty, this very European brick-and-stone mansion has fine wooden balconies, a token castle tower and a cliff-top setting with sweeping valley views. Visiting the few open rooms takes barely five minutes,

JAMMU & KASHMIR (INCLUDING LADAKH) JAMMU

SAFETY IN KASHMIR

Kashmir's history as a political football between India and Pakistan plus the delicate relationship between nationalist Muslims and Jammu Hindus creates a cauldron of intercommunal tensions. When things are calm, Kashmir is probably safer than most places in India but even then, army presence at banks, offices and religious sites can feel intrusive (don't take photos of anything military without express permission). Strikes and outbursts of stone-throwing can erupt after a firebrand speech or controversial arrest. Tourists are very rarely targeted directly, but buses, bus stations and pilgrim groups are vulnerable; at times of tension, consider hiring private transport, travelling very early in the morning, and avoiding hotspots like Baramulla, Sopore, Anantnag or Srinagar's Old City. Occasionally the Srinagar-Jammu highway is closed completely. During troubles, local newspapers often print timetables indicating which days businesses will open, but prolonged strikes and curfews can mean closures for days on end, making it hard to buy food, change money etc. And it's hardly conducive to a holiday mood, though relaxing on a Srinagar houseboat you could easily forget that there was any problem at all. Use common sense and avoid public demonstrations, political rallies and military installations.

Before travelling, consult a wide range of resources to get a feel of the situation, keeping in mind that every view of the debate sounds 'biased' to someone.

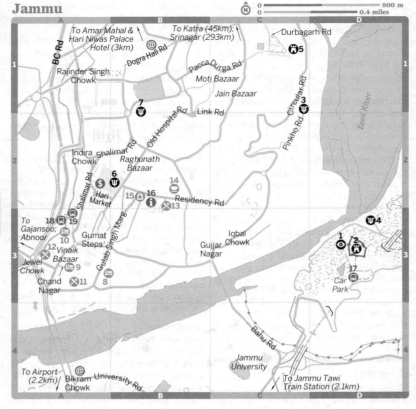

but if you've paid, don't miss peeping through a guarded rear window to see the raja's canopied throne, supposedly made of solid gold.

Raghunath Mandir HINDU TEMPLE
(Raghunath Bazaar; ⏰6-11.30am & 6-9.30pm) Marking the heart of the older city, this 19th-century Rama temple complex is fronted by partly gilded temple-spires and surrounded by pavilions containing thousands of what look like grey pebbles set in concrete; in fact, these are saligrams (ammonite fossils) symbolically representing the myriad deities of the Hindu pantheon.

Ranbireshwar Mandir HINDU TEMPLE
(Shalimar Rd) This large if architecturally unremarkable temple enshrines a large collection of lingams, some in opalescent crystal.

Gupawala Mandir HINDU TEMPLE
(Pinkho Rd) Tucked behind shawl stalls in an easy-to-miss side valley, this small complex

comprises tunnels and glitteringly colourful Krishna and Shiva caves.

Bahu Fort Area FORT
Across the Tawi River the low-slung, completely renovated walls of 19th-century **Bahu Fort** now enclose a **Kali temple**, while the lawn outside covers a subterranean **aquarium** (adult/child ₹20/10; ⏰11am-9pm Tue-Sat, to 8pm Sun), less interesting for its minor fish collection than for the fact that you enter through the gaping mouth of a giant carp.

Nearby is **Har-ki-Paori Mandir**, a family of giant, concrete gods in a modern, Disneyesque style. Viewed across the river from here, the vast scale of the cliff-top Mubarak Mandi becomes apparent.

🛏 Sleeping

Hotels are spread all over town but Vaishno Devi pilgrims fill virtually every bed during peak *yatra* (pilgrimage) periods (early summer, early October). Basic budget options are plentiful around Vinaik Bazaar (a block southeast of the bus station) but names like Hotel Touch Wood give a premonition of their chancy nature. If booking Jammu accommodation through online discounters be aware that many hotels offered are 45km away in Katra.

Fortune Riviera   HOTEL $$
(☏2561415; www.fortunehotels.in; Gulab Singh Marg; s/d from ₹4195/4410; ❋@❋) Jammu's most stylish address includes a glass elevator in the four-story atrium, Empire State bedposts and slight hints of oriental minimalism in the flower arrangements.

Hari Niwas Palace Hotel   HERITAGE HOTEL $$
(☏2543303; www.hariniwaspalace.com; s/d from ₹2860/3320, deluxe ₹3850/4950; ❋❋) With maharaja connections and elements of princely style, this all-white 20th-century palace has a fine cliff-top setting beside the Amar Mahal Palace. Deluxe rooms are professionally appointed but cheaper 'Palace Mews' units are below ground level and overall upkeep is a little flawed given the prices. Indoor pool.

Hotel Samrat   HOTEL $$
(☏2547402; s/d from ₹1650/1760; ❋@) The neatest of numerous options as you leave the bus station, Samrat's best rooms (single/double ₹2090/2200) are brand new with high ceilings, lashings of marble and Chagall prints on wooden back-boards.

Green View Hotel   GUESTHOUSE $
(☏2573906; 69 Chand Nagar; s from ₹150, d ₹300-500; ❋) This budget standby is a little quieter, friendlier and more accustomed to foreigners than most Vinaik Bazaar options. Certainly the cheap singles are miserable coffin-boxes but most doubles come with cold-shower bathroom, air-cooler and even windows. For ₹500 there's AC and new tiling. It's hidden at the end of a dead-end side lane east of Jewel Chowk.

Vaishnavi Dham   PILGRIM HOSTEL $
(☏2473275; www.maavaishnodevi.org; Railway Rd; dm/d ₹60/650; ❋) Although primarily for *yatri,* this large, modern hostel accepts non-pilgrims out of season. It's immediately on the right as you leave the train station's large forecourt square.

✖ Eating & Drinking

Between Jewel Chowk and Vinaik Bazaar are several inexpensive **dhabas** (snack bars), a fast-food place, wine shops and two bars. **City Square Mall** has Domino's Pizza and four other air-conditioned restaurants. Residency Rd has a wide range of options from cheap fish barbecues (near Raghunath Mandir) to AC vegetarian restaurants to ever-reliable **Café Coffee Day** opposite KC Plaza.

Wazwan   KASHMIRI $$
(☏2579554; Residency Rd; veg/non-veg mains ₹110/210; ⊘12.30-4pm & 7-10pm) Filigree lamps, wood panelling and draped crewel

canopies set the scene for a range of classic Kashmiri specialities. It's hidden within the accommodation block behind J&K Tourism.

Falak INDIAN $$

(2520770; www.kcresidency.com; 7th fl, KC Residency Hotel, Residency Rd; mains veg/non-veg ₹175/255, rice ₹100; ⊘12.30-10.45pm) This jerkily revolving hotel restaurant serves a faultless if pricey range of enticing pan-Indian cuisine. Add 22.5% to prices (for tax/service charge).

❶ Information

Cyber Point (Jewel Chowk; per hr ₹25; ⊘9am-10pm) Sweaty but cheap and central internet access.

J&K Tourism (2548172; www.jktdc.org; Residency Rd; ⊘8am-8pm) Refreshingly air-conditioned reception centre. Just west is a well-presented **government arts emporium** and an English-language **bookshop**.

SBI (Hari Market; ⊘10am-4pm Mon-Fri) Exchanges currency and travellers cheques. ATM.

❶ Getting There & Away

Air
The following all fly to Delhi (from ₹2250, one hour) and Srinagar (from ₹2250, 35 minutes). Air India also flies to Leh on Mondays and Fridays.

Air India (2456086; www.indianairlines.in; J&K Tourism complex; ⊘10am-4.45pm Mon-Sat)

GoAir (www.goair.in)

IndiGo (www.goindigo.in)

JetLite (www.jetlite.com)

SpiceJet (www.spicejet.com)

Bus & Jeep
Private buses and shared jeeps depart from a chaotic strip in the shadow of the BC Rd (NH1A Hwy) overpass. Public buses use the big, rotting concrete bus station complex immediately east.

Amritsar Up to 30 buses daily (₹117, six hours) via Pathankot in Punjab (₹59, 2½ hours).

Chamba Bus (₹170, seven hours, 8.05am).

Dalhousie Bus (₹160, six hours, 8am).

Delhi Public buses 13 times daily (₹360, 12 hours) plus many private services leaving between 5pm and 10.30pm (seat/sleeper ₹500/800).

Dharamsala Direct bus at 8.30am (₹170, six hours) or take an Amritsar service and change at Pathankot. Taxis cost around ₹4000.

Katra Buses, minibuses and taxis (₹31/60/800, 1½ hours) regularly depart from both bus and train stations.

Srinagar Buses run by day, by night or not at all depending on the security situation. Shared/chartered jeeps (from ₹400/3000) depart early morning from both bus and train stations.

Train
Jammu Tawi, Jammu's main train station, is well south of the river, 5km from the bus station.

Agra Indore-bound *Malwa Express* (12920) departs at 9am (sleeper/3AC/2AC ₹270/792/1087).

Amritsar *Muri Express* (18102) departs at 2.30pm (₹124, four hours).

Delhi *Shalimar Express* (14646) departs at 9pm (sleeper/3AC/2AC ₹237/668/924, 14 hours).

Udhampur Local trains (₹11) 7.45am and 5pm, *Jammu Mail* (₹23) 10.25am. Line extension to Katra due 2012, to Srinagar in 2017 crossing the Chenab River on the world's tallest rail-bridge.

❶ Getting Around

AUTORICKSHAWS Short hops ₹30, train station to bus station ₹70, to airport ₹100.

MINIBUS Overloaded minibuses and curiously stretched 'Matadors' charge ₹5 per hop: route 117 links bus and train stations, 108 to the fort, 'Satwari' minibuses pass the airport.

Jammu To Srinagar

The well-paved Jammu–Srinagar road has many scenic points and is kept open year-round, but it's also exceedingly busy, a thundering conveyerbelt of trucks and army convoys that jams up entirely during hartals (strikes) and when landslides block the passes. Be prepared to fly at such times.

Leaving Jammu, the road climbs through a bizarre landscape of wooded hilly chunks that seem to have been diced by an overenthusiastic divine sous-chef preparing a never-finished geological recipe. Approaching Tikri, a hulking, multishouldered mountain looms distantly ahead. Accessed from nearby Katra, that mountain's latter-day **Vaishno Devi Shrine** (www.maavaishnodevi.org) is one of India's busiest pilgrim sites but its appeal is hard to understand for most non-Hindus.

Between Udhampur and Srinagar, the road winds up a vertical kilometre into mature coniferous woodlands where, between Kud and Patnitop (Km110) lies a sprinkling of **resort hotels** (d low season/rack rate ₹700/2500).

The main road zigzags back down almost as far as the controversial billion-dollar Baglihar Dam before winding back up to the 2531m Jawahar Tunnel, where foreigners must fill in lengthy forms for entering/leaving Kashmir (curious, given that you're already within J&K). The **Titanic Viewpoint** (Km208), 2km beyond the tunnel, provides sweeping views across the vast mountain-rimmed **Kashmir Valley**, with its beautiful poplar-edged rice terraces. Another viewpoint at Km213 surveys **Verinag**, one of three local villages to sport Mughal Gardens. Most traffic makes a tea stop in **Qazigund**, full of saffron sellers and shops selling locally produced cricket bats.

At times of unrest, a common troublespot is **Khanabal/Anantnag** where the Lidder Valley branches off towards the pine-framed pilgrim-tourist resort of Pahalgam.

At the roadside in **Awantipora** (Avantipura; Km266), 30km before Srinagar, is the chunky ruin of 9th-century **Avantisvara Vishnu Temple** (Indian/foreigner ₹5/100; ⊘dawn-dusk). The stone blocks are massive with numerous column bases but most carvings have long since been defaced. The essentially similar but even less complete **Avantisvara Shiva Temple** (Km226.9) can be visited on the same ticket.

Straggling between Km279 and Km281, dusty **Pampore** is India's saffron capital. The violet crocuses, whose yellow stamens produce the saffron, bloom colourfully in October around Km275.

PAHALGAM
POP 6000 / ELEV 2740M

Surrounded by high peaks, the Lidder and Seshnag rivers tumble down picturesque, deep-cut mountain valleys covered with giant conifers. Where they meet, the scene is marred by the sprawling low-rise resort town of **Pahalgam** (www.pahalgam.com) that overflows with Amarnath-bound *yatri* in summer. Heading up the Lidder valley towards Aru you'll swiftly get away from the worst pilgrim crowds and, further into the mountains, the region offers superb trekking potential. However, compared to Ladakh, prices are very high, fellow hikers hard to find and the alpine scenery feels less exotic. Also be aware that access roads to Pahalgam pass through areas particularly prone to violence during times of instability in Kashmir. Get advice before departing.

Accommodation prices fluctuate up to 600%, peaking in July. Choice is vast though most places close in winter. Main concentrations are around the bus stand (where there's an ATM and essentially useless tourist office) and along the main road towards Chandanwari, notably 4km east in Laripora where the brand new **Hotel Pine Spring** (☑243386; www.hotelpinespring.com; s/d ₹4400/5500) makes an unusually successful attempt at modernist hip design. Directly across the quiet laneway **Himalaya House** (☑243072; www.himalayafunandtours.com; rear houses ₹1200, front houses ₹1500-2500) is a spic-and-span, homely place with a lawn-garden forming an island in a pretty section of river. Unlike most cheaper Pahalgam places, the owners are accustomed to foreigners but might try to nudge you into an expensive trekking deal.

The most convivial eateries, **Troutbeat** (fish meals ₹350) and coffee shop **Log Inn** (veg mains from ₹110, espresso ₹50) front the venerable **Pahalgam Hotel** (www.pahalgamhotel.com) in the upper bazaar area. Much closes down in winter.

Srinagar
☑0194 / POP 988,000 / ELEV 1730M

Indulgent houseboats on placid Dal Lake, famous Mughal gardens, distinctive Kashmiri wooden mosques and a mild summer climate

---

AMARNATH

Far from the nearest road, in a mountain cave at **Amarnath**, a natural stone lingam becomes opalescently encrusted with ice and is believed to wax and wane with the phases of the moon. Seen as symbolising Lord Shiva, it's the destination for a vastly popular summer *yatra* (Hindu pilgrimage). Joining the chaotic swarm is an unforgettable experience but it's certainly not a peaceful or meditative country hike. All prospective *yatri* (pilgrims, hikers) must sign up through **SASB** (www.shriamarnathjishrine.com; ⊘Jul-Aug), be suitably equipped for potentially subzero conditions and be ready for intrusive security: both blizzards and Kashmiri militants have killed pilgrims in the past.

There are two approach routes. From Pahalgam it's a 16km taxi ride to Chandanwari then a 36km, three-day hike. Alternatively, from the vast Baltal Camp near Sonamarg (p239) it's a 14km walk to the cave. Wealthier pilgrims complete the journey by pony, helicopter (₹7600 return) or *dandy* (palanquin).

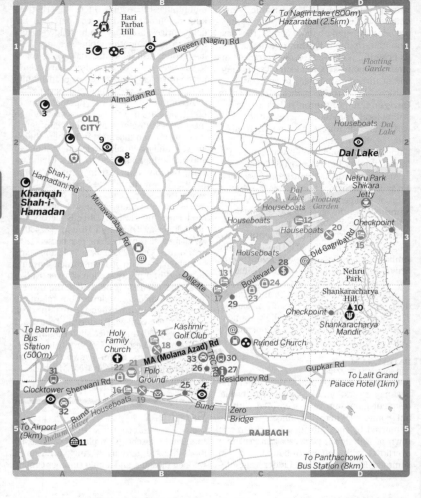

combine to make Srinagar one of India's top domestic tourist attractions. Except, that is, when intercommunal tensions erupt. Sadly, such eruptions have proved depressingly frequent and throughout summer 2010 paralysing strikes and curfews effectively shut down the city altogether. Visiting Srinagar without thoroughly checking the latest security situation would be foolhardy (see boxed text, p227).

Srinagar's three main areas converge around Dalgate, where the southwestern nose of Dal Lake passes through a lock gate. Northwest lies the Old City, largely out-of-bounds during curfews. The commercial centre, southwest around Lal Chowk, can also face major disruptions but the Boulevard, facing a major concentration of houseboats, is usually comparatively calm as are the Mughal gardens, strung out over several kilometres around the lake further east.

☉ Sights

Sitting and watching waterborne life go by from a houseboat's carved wooden veranda is one of Srinagar's great pleasures.

OLD CITY

When visiting mosques, follow normal Islamic formalities (dress modestly, remove shoes) and ask permission before entering or taking interior photos. Women will usually be expected to cover their hair and use a separate entrance.

Khanqah Shah-i-Hamadan MOSQUE
(Khanqah-e-Muala; Khawaja Bazaar area) This distinctively spired 1730s Muslim meeting hall is one of Srinagar's most beautiful with both frontage and interiors covered in papier-mâché reliefs and elaborately coloured *khatam-band* (faceted wood panelling). Non-Muslim visitors can peek through the door but may not enter. The building stands on the site of one of Kashmir's first mosques, founded by Persian saint Mir Sayed Ali Hamadani who had arrived in 1372, one of 700 refugees fleeing Timur's conquest of Iran. He is said to have converted 37,000 people to Sufi Islam, and it's likely that his retinue introduced Kashmiris to the Persian art of fine carpet-making.

Jama Masjid MOSQUE
(Nowhatta) This mighty 1672 mosque has room for thousands of devotees between 378 roof-support columns, each fashioned from the trunk of a single deodar tree. Monumental brick gatehouses mark the four cardinal directions. Bags and cameras are prohibited.

Pir Dastgir Sahib SACRED SITE
(Khanyar Chowk area; ⊘4am-10pm) This large, fanciful Sufi shrine has a spired tower, wooden filigree work outside and a colourfully faceted interior with some beautiful papier-mâché work around a series of graves that flash with fairy lights.

Rozabal SACRED SITE
A minute's stroll northwest from Pir Dastgir Sahib, facing the four-level brick tower of Rozabal Mosque, is the small, green **Rozabal Shrine** (Ziyarat Hazrati Youza Asouph). Visually it's utterly insignificant. Yet a highly controversial theory claims that the shrine's

JESUS IN KASHMIR?

To many the theory sounds crackpot or even blasphemous but several authors have claimed that Jesus' 'lost years' (between his youth and the start of his ministry when he was 30) were spent in India where Buddhism moulded his ideas. This theory gained a lot of publicity in the 1890s when Russian traveller/spy Nicolas Notovitch 'discovered' supposedly corroborating documents at Hemis Gompa (Ladakh), described in his book *Unknown Life of Jesus Christ*. The Hemis documents have since gone missing.

The Koran (surah 4, verses 156–157) suggests that Jesus' death on the cross was a 'grievous calumny' and that 'they slew him not'. Khwaja Nazir Ahmad's *Jesus in Heaven & Earth* further postulates that Jesus (as Isa, Yuz Asaf or Youza Asouph) retired to Kashmir post-crucifixion and was buried in Srinagar. Holger Kersten's *Jesus lived in India*, widely sold in Indian traveller bookshops, agrees and even gives a floor-plan of that tomb at Rozabal in Srinagar. The roughly four-million-strong Ahmadiyya sect (who consider themselves Muslim but are not recognised as such by some Islamic communities) also subscribe to the idea of Jesus dying in Kashmir (www.alislam.org/topics/jesus), seeing Christ's mortality as underlining his role as human prophet.

crypt holds the grave of Jesus Christ. Supposedly, a sarcophagus here features carved feet punctured by half-moon 'crucifixion marks'. Tourists aren't encouraged and in reality you're unlikely to be granted access but the very act of discovering this little place is highly thought-provoking and might inspire you to read more deeply about the fascinating subject of Jesus' historical career.

Naqshband Sahib   SACRED SITE
(Khanyar Chowk area) This beautifully proportioned but uncoloured 17th-century shrine was built in Himachal Pradesh style with alternating layers of wood and brick to dissipate the force of earthquakes.

HARI PARBAT HILL
The imposing 18th-century **Hari Parbat Fort** is visible from virtually anywhere in Srinagar but closed to the public, for military use. It crowns a prominent hill that Hindus believe was originally the island from which Vishnu and Sharika (Durga) defeated Jalodbhava, Kashmir's mythical lake demon. On the hill's mid-slopes, Muslims pay homage at the large **Makhdoom Sahib Shrine**, reached by beggar-lined steps that pass the ruined 1649 stone mosque of **Akhund Mullah Shah**. The steps start a few hundred metres beyond the scant remains of Srinagar's **Old City walls** (built by Akbar in the 1590s) and the large **Chetipacha Gurdwara** (Sikh Temple).

CENTRAL SRINAGAR
Sri Pratap Singh Museum   MUSEUM
(2312859; http://spsmuseum.org; Indian/foreigner ₹10/50; ⊙10am-4pm Tue-Sun) Accessed by a footbridge across the Jhelum River then

by shimmying through frightening coils of razor wire, this richly endowed historical museum features Mughal papier-mâché work, weaponry and traditional Kashmiri costumes. An impressive new exhibition hall is nearing completion. Bring ID.

Kashmir Government Arts
Emporium   HISTORIC BUILDING
(2452783; Bund; ⊙10am-5.30pm Mon-Sat) The century-old half-timbered former British Residency Building (restored 2004) is now used as an elegant fixed-price craft showroom where, without sales pressure, you can peruse Kashmiri copperwork, rugs, crewel (embroidered bedcovers) and intricately carved furniture. Information boards make the place more museum than shop. The building is army-guarded and flanked by curious gatehouses that seem transported from an Oxford College.

AROUND DAL LAKE
Shankaracharya Hill   VIEWPOINT, SACRED SITE
(⊙7.30am-5pm) Thickly forested Shankaracharya Hill is topped by a small Shiva temple built from hefty blocks of visibly ancient grey stone. Previously known as Takht-i-Sulaiman (Throne of Solomon), it's now named for a sage who reached enlightenment here in 750AD, but signs date the octagonal structure as 5th-century and the site is even older. Some claim, controversially, that a previous temple here was once renovated by Jesus and St Thomas. Access is by a winding 5.5km road from Nehru Park (₹150 return by autorickshaw). Walking isn't advisable, given the population of wild bears. The temple

is five minutes up a stairway from a police checkpoint where you must leave phones and cameras before reaching the panoramic views of Srinagar and Dal Lake.

Parks & Gardens GARDENS
Srinagar's famous gardens date back to the Mughal era. Most have a fundamentally similar design with terraced lawns, fountain pools and carefully manicured flowerbeds interspersed with mighty *chinar* (plane trees), pavilions and mock fortress facades.

Built for Nur Jahan by her husband Jehangir, **Shalimar Bagh** (adult/child ₹10/5; ☉9am-dusk Apr-Oct, 10am-dusk Nov-Mar) is the most famous garden. However, **Nishat Bagh** (adult/child ₹10/5; ☉9am-dusk Sat-Thu) is more immediately impressive, with steeper terracing and a lake-facing panorama.

FREE **Pari Mahal** (☉dawn-dusk) is set amid palace ruins high above the lakeshore. The ensemble looks intriguing when floodlit at night and viewed from afar. By day, making the long, steep autorickshaw ride is worthwhile more for the lake views than for the gardens themselves. Bring ID for serious police checks on your way. En route you'll pass the petite **Cheshmashahi Garden** (adult/child ₹10/5; ☉8am-8pm) and the extensive, less formal **Botanical Garden** (adult/child ₹10/5; ☉8am-dusk Sat-Thu).

Hazratbal MOSQUE, AREA
Several kilometres north of the Old City, Srinagar's main university area extends around the large, white-domed **Hazratbal Mosque**. This 20th-century building enshrines Kashmir's holiest relic, the **Moi-e-Muqqadas**, supposedly a beard hair of the Prophet Mohammed. Hazratbal's original mosque was built to house it when the Naqshband Sahib proved too small for the many pilgrims. In December 1963 the hair briefly disappeared in still-unexplained circumstances, nearly sparking civil war.

The mosque backs onto Dal Lake through heavily guarded prayer lawns. Surrounding **market areas** sell lotus pods and vast Kashmiri fried *puris* (flat dough that puffs up when fried).

🛏 Sleeping
Staying on a houseboat (p236) is one of the city's main attractions, but you might prefer to sleep at least the first night in a hotel while carefully selecting a suitable boat. Dozens of large, forgettable hotels along the Boulevard charge around ₹5000 per night in season but far, far less during troubles. Several hotels subcontract rooms to government departments or the army, making for an odd ambience. Many others rely primarily on noisy, self-catering groups of domestic tourists, especially in summer and during Bengali holidays (May and October). Useful lower midrange options are dotted along Old Gagribal Rd and around Dalgate. Srinagar's most deluxe option is the new Taj Vivanta (www.tajhotels.com).

Hotel Swiss GUESTHOUSE $
(☑2472766; www.swisshotelkashmir.com; Old Gagribal Rd; foreigners d ₹450-850, Indians ₹1200-1800; @) The Swiss has reliably good-value budget accommodation at prices that are discounted for foreigners. There's a peaceful lawn, free fast internet and bicycle hire available. But most of all it's the tirelessly helpful Sufi-spiritual manager which makes the place so congenial. The area stays calm during curfews.

Lalit Grand Palace HERITAGE HOTEL $$$
(☑2501001; www.thelalit.com/Srinagar; ste from ₹20,000) Vast period suites in the Maharaja's 1910 palace and a wing of (slightly) cheaper new rooms are all beautifully set above hectares of manicured lawns. The Durbar Hall features royal portraits and one of the world's largest handmade carpets.

JAMMU & KASHMIR (INCLUDING LADAKH) SRINAGAR

DON'T MISS

DAL LAKE
Whether you sleep on one of its wonderful time-warp houseboats or just stroll along the Boulevard savouring the sunset, beautifully serene Dal Lake is likely to be your main memory of Srinagar. Mirror-flat waters beautifully reflect the misty peaks of the Pir Panjal mountains while gaily painted *shikaras* glide by. These are gondolalike boats, hand-powered with heart-shaped paddles and used to transport goods to market, children to school, and visitors on explorative tours of the lake's floating communities. Nehru Park is a good starting point for visiting the early-morning floating vegetable market and canal-like passages link all the way to Nagin Lake.

Srinagar's signature houseboats first appeared in colonial times, because the British were prohibited from owning land. Most houseboats you'll see are less than 30 years old but the best **deluxe** ones are still palatial, with chandeliers, carved walnut panels, *khatamband* (wooden patchwork) ceilings and chintzy sitting rooms redolent of the 1930s Raj era. **Category A** boats are comfy but less grand. Lower categories often lack interior sitting areas. **Category D** boats hopefully stay afloat. Better houseboats typically have three double bedrooms; when the political climate drives tourists away you're likely to get the whole boat to yourself, chef and all.

Choosing from 1400 boats is challenging. Some owners are super-friendly families, others are crooks – ask fellow travellers for recent first-hand recommendations. For most visitors, staying on a houseboat is a relaxing Srinagar highlight. But others report feeling cheated, being held virtual hostage ('kidnapped' passport, external dangers exaggerated, etc), or suffering inappropriate advances from houseboat staff.

Things to watch out for

» Don't prepurchase houseboat packages; never book in Delhi.

» Thoroughly check out houseboats in person before agreeing to or paying anything.

» Get a clear, possibly written, agreement stating what the fees cover.

» Don't be pressured into giving 'charity' donations.

» Don't sign up for overpriced treks or excursions (prices are usually far lower in Ladakh).

» Beware isolated or less friendly houseboats. Trust your instincts.

» Don't leave valuables unattended.

» Don't leave your passport with the boat owner.

» Tell a friend, hotelier or the Houseboat Owners Association (☑2450326; www. houseboatowners.org; TRC Rd; ⊙10am-5pm Mon-Sat) where you're staying.

Choosing the Area

The boats facing the **Boulevard** offer a good variety, close together, so you can visit a wide selection by *shikara* (gondolalike boat) before choosing. Just drop into the ones that take your fancy (the boatman will probably nudge you towards those that give him better commission). Their proximity to shore makes it relatively easy to hail a *shikara* should you need to 'escape'.

A second row of boats directly behind in **Golden Dal Lake** (eg the **California Group**) is still easily accessible but quieter, with sunset views. Houseboats further out offer beguiling solitude but leave you prey to pressures from owners. **Nagin Lake** houseboats also suffer somewhat from isolation but readers have recommended several groups including **Mount View**. In almost any location, visits from *shikara*-borne souvenir sellers are an unavoidable irritation.

Prices

Officially prices are 'set', between ₹1100 (category D) and ₹4500 (deluxe) for a double room including all meals, but when occupancy is low you might only pay a fraction of that.

Always double-check what's included and how much: food and drink (only dhal-and-rice? Is tea extra?), heating, *shikara* transfers and/or use of a canoe (once or unlimited?). Ideally get this in writing. Check the price of extras – 'hidden charges' can amount to hundreds of dollars.

Sumptuous. When occupancy is low you might get half-price walk-in rates.

New Zeenath Guest House   GUESTHOUSE $
(☑2474070; off Dalgate; r ₹400-800) Compact, but sparklingly clean with new tile-floored rooms above a doctors' clinic.

Noor Guest House   GUESTHOUSE $
(☑2450872; off Dalgate; d ₹400-500, without bathroom ₹150-250) Cheaper rooms are in a creaky but characterful old wooden house and newer ones have thin hardboard divider walls but the family owners are

kind and the front room gets canal views. Limited free laundry.

Hotel Akbar HOTEL **$$**
(☑2500507; hotelakbar.com; d ₹1500-2500) Trump cards are the manicured garden with trellises of blooming vines and the quiet yet central, lakeside location. Older rooms are wood panelled and a little musty but newer ones are fresher with geysers in bathrooms.

Hotel Broadway HOTEL **$$$**
(☑2459001; www.hotelbroadway.com; s/d ₹5750/7000; @🛜❄) Behind a drab concrete-slab facade, the atmosphere is unexpectedly warm, rooms are ageing but well-tended business-style affairs and the outdoor swimming pool is sparkling clean. Off-season rates ₹4000 or less.

Residency HOTEL **$$$**
(☑2473702; www.hotelresidencykashmir.com; Residency Rd; s/d/ste ₹4500/5500/7500; 🛜) A glass elevator whisks you up through a reverberant shopping-mall atrium to this small but professional business hotel.

✕ Eating & Drinking

Srinagar's Muslim mores mean that alcohol isn't served in restaurants and there are just a tiny handful of bars, mostly in upmarket hotels.

Mughal Darbar KASHMIRI **$$**
(☑2476998; Residency Rd; mains ₹150-300; ⊘10am-10pm) Widely considered the city's best place to indulge in top quality Kashmiri delicacies. The better of the two separately managed dining rooms is upstairs above the bakery section.

Coffea Arabica MULTICUISINE **$$**
(MA Rd; meals ₹150-250; ⊘9am-10pm) Behind a half-timbered facade, this spacious modern eatery has various fast-food-style serving stations (Arabic, Chinese, Italian, coffee-and-cake) and a little bookshop.

Nathu's Sweets INDIAN **$**
(Blvd; mains ₹40-130, thalis ₹150; ⊘8am-midnight) Brighter and more inviting than most of the basic *dhabas* dotted along the Boulevard serving inexpensive, filling veggie meals including dosas and grilled sandwiches.

Cafe Robusta CAFE
(MA Rd; ⊘9.30am-9pm; 🛜) Srinagar's hip young set sip a selection of coffees or share sundaes and smoothies in a pseudo-Western

upstairs lounge with chess and pictionary to play. All-day wi-fi ₹50.

Dar Bar BAR
(⊘10am-10pm; cocktails from ₹350) The little bar of the Lalit Grand Palace Hotel has indulgent lawn views towards Dal Lake.

Wine Shop TAKEAWAY BOOZE
(Heemal Hotel Shopping Complex, Boulevard) Rare takeaway outlet for alcoholic beverages.

🛍 Shopping

The Boulevard has several emporia flogging Kashmiri souvenirs, including elegantly painted papier-mâché boxes and carved walnut woodwork, plus cashmere and pashmina shawls, originally popularised in Europe by Napoleon's wife Josephine. Saffron, cricket bats and dried fruits are widely sold around Lal Chowk. Carpet-selling 'factories' line the road to Shalimar Bagh targeting tour groups. Unless you know how to assess carpet values, consider erring instead towards much cheaper chain-stitched *gabbas* (Kashmiri rugs with appliqué) or floral *namdas* (felted wool carpets). Be aware that your guide, driver or even hotelier may be getting hefty commissions unless you show up without 'help'. The Kashmir Government Arts Emporium is an exception with fixed, marked prices.

Kashmir Government Arts Emporium HANDICRAFTS
(☑2452783; Bund; ⊘10am-5.30pm Mon-Sat) In a historic building (p234). It has a less glamorous branch upstairs on the Boulevard.

Gulshan Books BOOKSTORE
(Residency Rd; ⊘9am-8pm Mon-Sat) Stocks a wide selection of English-language books including plenty on Kashmiri history and politics.

ⓘ Information

Most banks, shops and offices shut for Muslim prayers around lunchtime on Friday: if you have urgent business, get it done by Thursday to be safe.

ATMs are widespread, especially on Residency Rd, but during prolonged curfews they might run out of funds. Beware of freelance moneychangers offering improbably good rates – you're likely to get forged banknotes.

Euphoria (Old Gagribal Rd; internet per 30min/hr ₹20/30; ⊘9am-10pm) Internet access.

Skybiz Internet (Dalgate; internet per hr ₹30; ⊘9am-8pm)

Tourism Reception Centre (☑2456291; www.jktourism.org, www.jktdc.org) With perseverance you might actually find answers to your questions. Supposedly open 24hr but don't count on it.

Transcorp International (Boulevard; ◷9.30am-6pm Mon-Sat) Half-hidden between hotels Sunshine and Dal View, this moneychanger offers good cash rates.

❶ Getting There & Away

Air

Srinagar's sparkling new airport is 1.2km behind a high security barrier where there can be long queues for baggage and body screening. You'll need to show an air ticket (or e-ticket confirmation print-out) to get through so don't come to the airport hoping to buy a ticket on departure. The barrier opens at 7.15am but on curfew days (usually safer before 6.30am) it's still wise to arrive earlier and wait rather than getting caught in strikes or stone-throwing en route.

The following all fly to Delhi and/or Jammu. Air India also flies to Leh on Wednesdays.

Air India (☑2450247; www.airindia.in; Boulevard)

GoAir (www.goair.in)

IndiGo (www.goindigo.in)

Jet Airways (☑2480801; Residency Rd)

JetLite (www.jetlite.com)

Kingfisher (www.flykingfisher.com)

SpiceJet (www.spicejet.com)

Bus

Everything is highly dependent upon security measures and road conditions so double-check carefully.

J&K SRTC bus station (☑2455107) has buses to Kargil (₹413, 10 hours), Jammu (class B/A bus ₹200/280, nine hours) and Leh (₹799, two days) all at 6.30am. **Batmalu bus station**, west of centre has services thrice daily to Sonamarg, frequent to Tangmarg for Gulmarg. **Panthachowk bus station**, 8km south of centre has various buses to Pampore and Anantnag (change for Pahalgam).

Given sufficient custom, the Tourism Reception Centre runs day-return excursions to mountain 'resorts' Sonamarg (₹193, 87km northeast), Gulmarg (₹186, 52km west) and Pahalgam (₹193, 100km southeast), all departing at 8.30am.

Jeep

Check security and road conditions.

Shared jeeps depart from **Tourist Taxi Stand 1** to Kargil (per person/jeep ₹620/4340, 5am) and to Jammu (₹500/4500, 6.30am to 9am). Somewhat cheaper jeeps and minibuses to Jammu start from near the clocktower at Lal Chowk.

Jeep hire one-way/return costs: Pahalgam ₹1900/2100, Sonamarg ₹1600/1900, Gulmarg ₹1200/1500.

Train

Local services only: Qazigund–Anantnag–Srinagar–Baramulla.

❶ Getting Around

Even when there's no official curfew, don't rely on being able to find an autorickshaw or boatman after 8pm, when Srinagar becomes eerily silent.

TO/FROM THE AIRPORT Airport buses (₹40) run very sporadically. Prepaid, fixed-price taxis cost ₹350 to town. During curfews and strikes expect to pay around ₹500 to reach the airport and leave at dawn to avoid getting blocked en route.

AUTORICKSHAWS From ₹25 for short hops, ₹50 across town, around ₹600 for a full-day tour including Mughal gardens, Old City and Hazratbal.

BOAT *Shikaras* charge ₹20 for short houseboat-to-shore hops. Posted per-hour rates (₹300) are very negotiable.

MINIBUSES Overcrowded. Destination boards only in Urdu. Useful routes include Lal Chowk–Hazratbal and Lal Chowk–Shalimar Bagh via Dal Lake's south bank and Nishat Bagh.

Gulmarg

☑01954 / ELEV 2730M

Pine-fringed Gulmarg is the nearest India gets to a ski resort. It's not so much a town as a twisting 4km-long loop of road ringing the undulating 'Meadow of Flowers' for which it's named. The meadow is given some visual focus by the demure 1890s Anglican **Church of St Mary's** sitting on a lonely hillock. It's accessed off the dead-end road linking historic **Gulmarg Golf Club** (admission ₹5, driving range ₹450) to the resort's oldest cottage-hotels, the 1888 **Nedous Hotel** (www.nedoushotels.com) and the 1965 neo-colonial style **Hotel Highlands Park** (www.hotelhighlandspark.com). Without being really luxurious, both have pleasant garden settings and lounges decorated with trophies and animal hides (₹50 for tea, no alcohol served).

However, the only reason to come to Gulmarg is to venture up through the backing stands of mature pines towards the bald ridge of **Mt Afarwat**. This can be done on foot or with ponies (₹300 per hour) but is easiest using the two-stage **Gondola** (cable car 1st/2nd stage ₹150/250) that whisks you to 3747m for outstanding clear-day views, reputedly encompassing Nanga Parbat (the world's ninth-highest mountain across in Pakistan). The gondola's base-station is around 1km west of the bus stand.

Gulmarg offers over 40 accommodation choices. In July, musty, ageing rooms average ₹2000, newer ones over ₹5000 a night. Prices dip around 20% in winter and fall massively lower during troubles in Srinagar and in less popular months, like September. For skiers and hikers the most convenient accommodation is located on the rise just north of the gondola. Here, the new **Heevan Retreat** (☑254455; www.ahadhotelsandresorts.com; d/ste ₹5000/6500, incl half-board ₹6250/7750) is head and shoulders above most competition. Fresh pine interiors are inlayed with crewel embroidery panels and there's a wonderfully cosy lounge.

On the same hill the untidy **Pine Palace** (☑254466; d ₹2500-3800) is the only hotel with a public bar (beers ₹200) and bakes fresh pizzas on Tuesday nights.

The other side of the gondola, **Hotel Green Heights** (☑254404; hotelgreenheights gulmarg@yahoo.com; d winter/peak season ₹1000/2750) has seriously ageing rooms that are far

---

SKIING AT GULMARG

In season (mid-December to mid-March) Gulmarg is famed amongst serious skiers for its high-altitude powder. However, weather conditions can be unreliable, only a small section of piste is groomed, rescue facilities are limited and avalanche prevention is hamstrung by military restrictions on explosives and weather data. For regularly updated snow and safety conditions, consult http://gulmargsnowsafety.com.

Apart from beginners' drag-lifts on the meadow, ski access is by the **Gondola** (day pass ₹ 1000), which closes down when winds blow over 35km/h and whenever Kashmir has curfews. Quality equipment can be hired from **Kashmir Alpine** (☑254638; www.kashmiralpine.com) outside Hotel Highlands Park and from the **Indian Institute of Skiing and Mountaineering** (IISM; ☑214037; www.iismgulmarg.com), 1.5km from the gondola in the conspicuous new octagonal building near the army camp.

---

from charming but they're big and currently (at troubled time of research ₹300) about the cheapest you'll find in Gulmarg.

ℹ **Getting There & Away**

Buses and more frequent shared jeeps run from Batmalu Bus Station in Srinagar to Tangmarg (summer/winter ₹45/55). Change there for Gulmarg (₹20/30), around 13km beyond on hairpins through the pine forest.

By private jeep, day returns from Srinagar cost around ₹1800 per vehicle.

Sonamarg

☑0194 /POP 800/ ELEV 2800M

A beautiful 200km drive between Srinagar and Sonamarg takes you from alpine valleys over the double loops of the 3529m **Zoji La**, a spectacular pass that becomes treacherously muddy after rain, then descends into a series of high-sided valleys. Windows on the vehicle's south side offer the best views.

Though ugly in itself, the jerry-built one-street strip settlement of **Sonamarg** occupies a memorable mountain-valley setting and could make for a great trekking base. Many Indian tourists get their first taste of snow here by walking or pony-riding two hours towards the **Thajiwas Glacier**, which rises on a spectacularly soaring mountain crag. The access track is 5km down a lane that starts 2km west of Sonamarg, opposite the area's best accommodation, **Hotel Snowland** (☑2417262; hotel.snowland@yahoo.com; s/d/ste from ₹2900/3300/4400) whose brand-new deluxe rooms (from ₹3600) are fashionably appointed if not overly large.

Sonamarg town has a strip of boxy restaurants, almost all offering poorly maintained guest rooms for around ₹1500 in season, bargainable to ₹350 when occupancy is low. Even the newest (Hotel International, Hotel Sonamarg) are already conspicuously battered by the endless procession of pilgrim-tourists who start their *yatra*-hike to Amarnath's famous ice lingam (p231) from **Baltal Camp**, a summer-only mayhem of tents, shacks and even a mobile ATM machine.

Buses to Srinagar depart Sonamarg at 7.30am, 9.30am and 12.30pm (₹80, 2½ hours). Alternatively take shared/private jeeps (₹120/1200), possibly changing en route at Kangan. Eastbound buses are often full by the time they reach Sonamarg, so for Kargil consider chartering a taxi/jeep or returning to Srinagar to get a seat.

JAMMU & KASHMIR (INCLUDING LADAKH) SONAMARG

DRAS

📞 0194 / POP 2000 / ELEV 3280M

Muslim Dras (Km147) is a miserable parade of shop-houses and army bases marring an otherwise attractive, upland valley. One day it might make a good hiking base but as it's so close to the Line of Control, strolling carelessly into the mountains here could get you shot. On 9 January 2005, Dras meteorologists recorded a freak temperature of -60°C and ever since the town has touted itself as the world's second-coldest place (after Oymyakon in Sakha-Yakutia, Russia). Local tourists visit various battlefields of the 1999 Indo-Pakistan conflict. Just east of town at Km148.2, notice a small collection of very battered ancient carvings gathered by the roadside.

KARGIL & ZANSKAR

Ladakh's less visited 'second half' comprises remote, sparsely populated Buddhist Zanskar and the slightly greener Suru Valley, where villagers predominantly follow Shia-Islam, as they do in the regional capital Kargil. Scenery reaches some truly majestic mountain climaxes.

Kargil

📞 01985 / POP 10,700 / ELEV 2817M

Most travellers only stop in Ladakh's second 'city' to change transport between Leh and Srinagar or Zanskar. After the calm and charm of Buddhist Ladakh, Muslim Kargil feels grimy and mildly hassled, though the feeling's only very relative. Slow-motion **internet cafes** (per hr ₹80) and an ATM are conveniently found within the three central blocks along bustling Main Bazaar (aka Imam Khomeini Chowk, Khumani Chowk). Tucked behind the main bus stand is a Kafkaesque **Tourist Reception Centre** (📞232721; ⊙10am-4pm Mon-Sat).

Central, down-at-heel budget options include the ageing **J&K TDC Tourist Bungalow** (📞232328; d ₹200) right beside the tourist office. Follow a well-signed alley from the main drag to find **Hotel Greenland** (📞232324; r old/new ₹800/1500), a popular choice with Westerners seeking fellow Zanskar-bound travellers. Its cheaper rooms are old if passable, the new block unexpectedly well appointed and fair value. **Hotel Caravanserai** (📞232237; r standard/deluxe ₹1000/1800), hidden 500m up Hospital Rd from Main Bazaar, has decent views from upper storeys and rooms that are quiet and

clean but hardly luxurious. Bargaining can save around 35% in many Kargil hotels.

Numerous simple restaurants line Main Bazaar but finding non-meat options can be challenging.

ⓘ Getting There & Away

The jeep stand (Hospital Rd) and bus station are one block apart, linked via a narrow alley of butchers' and barbers' shops. Both are a short distance off Main Bazaar towards the river. The minibus station is 300m further west. Kargil's only operative petrol pump is 2.5km up the Leh road from the main river bridge (nearest alternatives at Kangan and Wakha).

LEH Buses (from ₹300, 10 hours) depart at 4.30am, driving via Mulbekh (1½ hours) and Lamayuru (around five hours). Shared jeeps (₹600) leave around 7am.

MULBEKH Minibuses (₹30) leave at 2pm, 3pm and 4pm from the minibus stand, returning next morning.

SRINAGAR Buses (from ₹330, 10 hours) and share taxis (₹600, seven hours) usually leave around either 2pm or 1am. Hire your own jeep (₹5000) if you want to leave at a much more sociable hour and enjoy the beautiful if occasionally nail-biting scenery.

SURU VALLEY The 11am Parkachik and 1pm Panikhar buses start from the minibus station. The 6.30am Panikhar bus departs from outside the post office on Main Bazaar.

ZANSKAR Leh-Kargil-Padum buses run approximately thrice weekly, supposedly departing Kargil bus station around 1am but timetables are infamously idiosyncratic. Consider gathering a group and hiring a jeep to Padum (₹10,000, 14 hours): start before dawn or consider overnighting at Rangdum. Double-check that your driver has Zanskar-endorsed permits from the drivers' cooperative.

Around Kargil

MULBEKH
📞 01985

High on a dizzying pyramidal crag, a pair of two-monk gompas and mud-brick tower-stumps are all that remain of Mulbekh's medieval castle. However, the 45-minute zigzag climb is rewarded by symphonic views across gently terraced barley fields to the Zanskar Mountains, rising with Grand Canyon majesty in a series of angular cliffs and crags. Access is easiest driving up a 2.8km spaghetti of crumbling asphalt lane starting 100m west of **Chamba Gompa** (Km243.2), a tiny 1975 shrine guarding a resplendent 8m-high Maitreya-Buddha relief that's over 1000 years old. Opposite are three forgettable roadhouse hotel-restaurants. For much more atmospheric accommodation, the venerable old **Karzoo Guest House** (☏270027; Km242.3; s/d without bathroom ₹200/300) offers carpet-mat sleeping spaces in a traditional Ladakhi homestay. In a pleasant garden further west is Mulbekh's most comfortable option, **Maitreya Guest House** (☏270035; Km241.3; per person ₹600), which oddly charges the same for decent en suite rooms as for low-ceilinged ones with shared bathrooms.

SHARGOL

Little **Shargol Gompa** is built onto a cliffside, its minuscule prayer chamber lit by a single flickering butter lamp. Access is via a ladder then through the sole monk's kitchen. The site is distantly visible from Km238 on the Leh-Kargil road but reached from Km235.5 on 1.6km of unpaved lane. Before hiking up the short, steep approach path, check in at the new Lower Monastery building.

Suru Valley

The main Kargil-Zanskar road winds prettily through rustic Muslim villages in the fertile Suru Valley. High valley walls and mountain backdrops reach a thrilling climax approaching **Panikhar** with views of spiky, ever snow-capped **Nun** (7135m) and **Kun** (7087m). A steep but satisfying day-trek crosses the 3900m Lago La from the Panikhar bypass road then descends to **Parkachik**.

Despite the area's great scenic grandeur, traveller infrastructure is limited to rarely used **J&K Tourist Bungalows** (d ₹200-300) at Sanku, Panikhar, Tangole, Parkachik and lonely Purtickchay – which has perfectly framed Nun-Kun views. Each bungalow's *chowkidar* (caretaker) can rustle up extremely basic dinners and Sanku has very simple tea-stall shops but you'd be well advised to bring your own supplies.

Buses to Kargil leave Panikhar at 5am and 11am, Parkachik at 7am. Taxis aren't available and, for Zanskar, transport is generally limited to highly uncertain hitch-hiking.

Zanskar

Majestically rugged, the greatest attraction of this mountain-hemmed Ladakhi-Buddhist valley is simply getting there, preferably on a trek. Beware that Zanskar has no money-changing banks nor any official petrol stations (though Padum's taxi union has its own supply). If camping, be prepared for very cold nights even in summer. As for winter, see the boxed text, below.

RANGDUM
POP 280 / ELEV 3670M

Set in a wild, big-sky valley, wind-scoured Rangdum is the first Buddhist village heading for Zanskar. Rangdum's tiny cluster of low-rise Ladakhi houses and communications masts isn't attractive in itself. However, 7000m mountains Nun and Kun rise spectacularly white-capped to the west while **Rangdum Gompa** (admission ₹50), 5km east, looks like a tiny floating island backed by an arid pastiche of oddly contorted strata. The gompa's 25 yellow-hatted monks are outnumbered by monastery donkeys who sleep inside at night.

Beside the slightly hidden police checkpost, Rangdum's three basic teahouses can organise beds in village homes for around ₹300. There's also a central **J&K Tourism Bungalow** (d ₹200). In marvellously scenic isolation, 2km beyond the village, **Nun-Kun Deluxe Camp** (d ₹2500) has bedded tents with shared outside toilets and sometimes offers drop-in bargain rates from ₹700, (₹1200 with meals).

RANGDUM TO PADUM

Rugged **Pensi La** (4401m) is the pass dividing the Suru and Zanskar Valleys. Just beyond are spectacular views encompassing the long, glistening-white **Drang Drung glacier**. Further down, the Zanskar Valley broadens with several small villages in grassy parcels of farmland hemmed by sheer mountain walls. **Phey** has a small gompa and homestay. At **Sani**, Zanskar's oldest gompa is a small, two-storey prayer hall

ZANSKAR IN WINTER

In winter Zanskar is essentially cut off. Nonetheless, every February, intrepid travellers (along with Zanskar's teachers returning from their winter break) arrive here on the unique **Chadar Trek**. Much of the route is along the frozen Zanskar River, crossing side streams on precarious snow-bridges and camping in rock caves en route. While there are no high-altitude stages, you'll need serious winter equipment and an experienced local guide who can 'read' the ice.

ringed by a tunnelled cloister and a white-washed stone wall studded with stupas.

PADUM
📞 01983 / POP 1500 / ELEV 3505M

After the rigours and beauty of getting here, Zanskar's dusty little capital is rather an anti-climax. Despite an impressive mountain back-drop, central Padum is essentially a character-less crossroads within a block of which you'll find the bus/share-taxi stand, phone offices, an internet cafe, a **Tourist Office** (☏245017; ⏰10am-4pm Mon-Sat) and most of Padum's dozen hotel-guesthouses. The main road then straggles 700m south past a sizeable 1991 **mosque** to the crumbling little 'old town' and a hillock of stupas and water-eroded boulders. More traditional **Pibiting** village, 2km north, has a small gompa dwarfed by a large hilltop stupa topped with a beacon lamp.

🏃 Activities

Zanskar's top activity is trekking in or out. Guides, tents and provisions are essential for such multiday routes on which high-lights include the isolated monasteries at Lingshet or Phuktal. To find **horsemen** (per horse per day from ₹400) as guides/porters, ask at the simple camping ground opposite the Tourist Office or agencies like **Zanskar Trek** (☏245136) along the road to the mosque. To avoid hiking within the stark, sun-blasted Padum Valley you could give the horses two days' head start, then drive to Hanumil/Itchar, trailheads for Honupatta/Darcha.

🛏 Sleeping & Eating

Most hotels close from late October to June, except when pre-booked for winter trekking groups. There's a simple camping ground opposite the Tourist Office, which has an ac-ceptable **Tourist Bungalow** (d ₹200).

Hotel Ibex   GUESTHOUSE $
(☏245214; d ₹700) Room standards vary, but there's a pleasant setting around a sheltered garden courtyard and a convivial restaurant. Similarly priced Kailash and Changthang Hotels nearby look outwardly smarter but lack the traveller vibe.

Mont-Blanc Guest House   HOMESTAY $
(☏245183; r ₹400, without bathroom ₹250) Friendly place with four traditionally fur-nished rooms and possibly a free glass or three of chhang (barley beer).

Gakyi Hotel   RESTAURANT $
(s/d from ₹700/900) Good-looking, well-furnished if slightly musty rooms beneath Padum's glitziest restaurant.

① Getting There & Away

Until the Darcha-Padum-Chiling road is com-pleted, years hence, public transport to Zanskar remains very limited.

BUS The unpredictable Padum-Kargil-Leh bus takes around 18 hours to Kargil (₹300). It only runs a few times weekly (keep asking!).

JEEP Jeep hire to Kargil from Padum costs ₹8000 (while Kargil to Padum is ₹10,000 – taxi-union rules don't allow return trips) per vehicle, whether done in one gruelling 14-hour drive or with an overnight stop en route. Other one-way/ return rates from Padum: Karsha ₹600/750; Zangla ₹2000/3000, Rangdum ₹4000/6000.

AROUND PADUM

Zanskar's largest Buddhist monastery, **Karsha Gompa** dates back to at least the 10th century. It's a jumble of whitewashed blocks rising almost vertically up the red rock of a mountain cliff across the valley from Padum. Concrete steps lead to the monastery's up-per cloister and prayer hall with its cracked old murals and wobbly wooden columns. It's a great vantage point from which to sur-vey Karsha's old-fashioned homes, barley fields and threshing circles worked by dzo (cow-yak half-breed). Three homestay-style 'guesthouses' all come with shared local toilets. One daily bus (₹15) leaves Padum at 4pm, returning from Karsha next morning at 8am. Walking from Padum takes around two hours across the exposed plain.

For a fine half-day excursion from Padum, drive to Zangla admiring the curled, contort-ed geological strata that are especially strik-ing above **Rinam** and **Shilingskit** villages. A trip highlight is **Stongde Gompa** crowning a bird's-eye perch some 300m above the valley, 12km from Padum. The entrance to **Zangla** is guarded by a small hilltop **fortress-palace ruin**. See http://.csomasroom.kibu. hu for details about volunteering to help save it. At the far end of the village there's a small, friendly Buddhist **nunnery**.

The road south from Padum passes **Bardan Gompa**, spectacularly sat on a rocky outcrop above the valley. Appealing little **Raru** village has two tiny eateries and a very basic homestay. The road ends near the rock-perched village of **Itchar** (aka Khor) whose homestay is in the highest house, beside a tiny gompa, with great views.

PHUKTAL & BEYOND

Partly damaged by heavy snows in 2010, **Phuktal Gompa** remains one of Zanskar's most photogenic monasteries, built up against a cliff face beneath a gaping cave en-trance. It contains a sacred spring and some

700-year-old murals in the Alchi style. The monastery guesthouse, a fair distance beneath the gompa, has five rooms with real beds and even a shower.

There's no road – trekking to Phuktal (possible in one long day, better in two) is easiest using the south-bank trail. There are bridges at **Dorzong** and **Purne**, both with homestay/guesthouse, though space is limited.

Rather than returning to Padum, many trekking groups continue to **Darcha** on the Manali road (around four days) but you'll need proper gear and a guide to cross the 4980m Shingo-La.

LADAKH

Spectacularly jagged, arid mountains enfold this magical, Buddhist ex-kingdom. Picture-perfect gompas dramatically crown rocky outcrops amid whitewashed stupas and meditational *mani* walls topped with mantra-inscribed pebbles. Colourful fluttering prayer flags spread their spiritual messages metaphorically with the mountain breeze. Prayer wheels spun clockwise release more merit-making mantras. Gompa interiors are colourfully awash with murals and statuary of numerous bodhisattvas.

Ladakh's remarkably well-balanced traditional society has much to teach the West in terms of ecological awareness. While most Ladakhis are cash poor, traditional mud-brick homesteads are large, comfortable and self-sufficient in fuel and dairy products, organic vegetables and barley used to make *tsampa* (roast barley flour) and chhang. Such self-sufficiency is an incredible achievement given the short growing season and very limited arable land in this upland desert, where precious water supplies must be laboriously channelled from glacier-melt mountain streams.

History
Ladakh's (now-deposed) royal family traces its dynasty back 39 generations to 975AD. They took the name Namgyal ('Victorious') in 1470 when their progenitor Lhachen Bhagan, ruling from Basgo, conquered a competing Ladakhi kingdom based at Leh/Shey. Although Ladakh had been culturally 'Tibetanised' in the 9th century, Buddhism originally arrived in an Indian form that's visible in ancient temple craftsmanship at Alchi. Over time, however, different Buddhist sects struggled for prominence, with the Tibetan Gelukpa order eventually becoming the majority philosophy after its introduction in the 14th century by Tibetan pilgrim Tsongkhapa (who left a curious relic at Spituk).

Ladakh's greatest king, Sengge Namgyal (r 1616–42) gained riches by plundering gold

REACHING LADAKH

There are only three route options and all suffer a significant degree of uncertainty, so always build several days' flexibility into your plans. Visit websites www.leh.nic.in or http://vistet.wordpress.com to check which seasonal roads are open.

Zanskar is essentially cut off altogether in winter except by ice-trek.

Air

Flights (year-round) are dramatically scenic, but can be cancelled at short notice. Although flying into Leh means you're likely to suffer mild altitude problems on arrival, the Delhi–Manali–Leh drive is arguably worse as you'll cross passes over 5000m. Flying is the only way to reach Ladakh once roads close in winter.

Manali–Leh Road

Fabulously beautiful but gruellingly rough (minimum 22 hours), the road is frequently subject to landslides and is generally closed from October to May. Travelling southbound reduces the risk of altitude problems on high passes and has other advantages (see p274).

Srinagar–Leh Road

This route is less physically painful and lower altitude but also less spectacular than Leh–Manali. Landslides are possible on the Zoji La, which gets dangerously slippery after rain. Transport can stop altogether during serious political disturbances in Kashmir and the road is generally closed from November to May.

reserves from western Tibet and re-established a capital at Leh. Ladakh remained an independent kingdom until the 1840s when the Namgyals lost power and the region was annexed by the Jammu maharajas.

Since Independence Ladakh has been ruled as a (now semi-autonomous) sub-district of J&K. That's a culturally odd situation for this 'little Tibet' which is one of the last undisturbed Tantric Buddhist societies on earth. Tourism was first permitted in 1974 but, while globalised economics and climate change have certainly caused many problems, including dangerous population shifts, the traditional lifestyle has proved unexpectedly robust, while locally relevant technologies, such as solar energy and Trombe walls, are starting to improve rural living standards.

Ladakh is famed for crystal-blue skies and enjoys sunshine an average of 300 days a year. But storms can brew suddenly and heavy rain, while very rare, can cause devastating (if localised) mudslides. The worst in decades hit during August 2010, killing around 200 people and rendering thousands homeless. At the time of writing, recovery was well under way.

Climate

Ladakh's short tourist season (July to early September) typically sees pleasantly mild T-shirt weather by day, with slightly crisp, occasionally chilly nights. However, on higher treks night-time temperatures can dip below –5°C even in midsummer. By September snow is likely on higher ground although major passes usually stay open till October. In winter temperatures can fall below –20°C and most tourist infrastructure closes.

Language

Though they use the same script, the Tibetan and Ladakhi languages are significantly different. The wonderfully all-purpose word *jule* (pronounced *joo*-lay) means 'hello', 'goodbye', 'please' and 'thanks'. To the greeting *khamzang*, simply reply *khamzang*. *Zhimpo-rak* means 'it's delicious'. Rebecca Norman's excellent *Getting Started in Ladakhi* (₹200) has more phrases and useful cultural tips.

⚡ Activities

In summer Ladakh is an adventure playground for outdoor types. Thanks to Leh's vast range of agents, making arrangements is very easy for climbing, rafting, high-altitude trekking or jeep tours.

Leh

📞 01982 / POP 28,640 / ELEV 3520M

Few places in India are at once so traveller-friendly and yet so enchanting and hassle-free as mountain-framed Leh. Dotted with stupas and crumbling mud-brick houses, the Old Town is dominated by a dagger of steep rocky ridge topped by an imposing Tibetan-style palace and fort. Beneath, the bustling bazaar area is draped in a thick veneer of tour agencies, souvenir shops and pizza restaurants but a web of lanes quickly fans out into a green suburban patchwork of irrigated barley fields. Here gushing streams and narrow footpaths link traditionally styled Ladakhi buildings with flat roofs, sturdy walls and ornate wooden window frames. Leh's a place that's all too easy to fall in love with, but take things easy on arrival. The altitude means that most visitors initially suffer mild headaches and breathlessness. To prevent this becoming full-blown Acute Mountain Sickness (AMS, p1193), drink plenty of ginger tea and avoid strenuous exertion at first. Climbing Palace Ridge or Shanti Stupa on your two days in Leh is unwise unless you're already altitude-acclimatised.

◉ Sights

CENTRAL LEH

Leh's major monuments are perched on the stark rocky ridge that forms the town's mesmerising visual focus.

LADAKH PERMITS

You'll need an **inner line permit** to visit Nubra Valley, Pangong Tso, Dha-Hanu, Tso Moriri and the Upper Indus (beyond Upshi).

Such permits, valid for seven days and unextendable, are effortlessly obtained within one working day through Leh travel agencies for around ₹150. You're supposed to have a group (at least two people) to apply but, once you have the permit, travelling alone is rarely prevented. Agencies organise multiple copies of your passport, visa and permit, to give to police checkpoints en route, but making extra copies can prove wise. Whether or not a permit is required, always carry your passport; as Ladakh's a border region, checkpoints are fairly common on rural roads.

Leh Palace
PALACE

(Map p249; Indian/foreigner ₹5/100; ☉dawn-dusk) Bearing a passing similarity to the Potala Palace in Lhasa (Tibet), this nine-storey dun-coloured palace took shape under 17th-century king Sengge Namgyal. Essentially it has been unoccupied since the Ladakhi royals were stripped of power and shuffled off to Stok in 1846. Today the very sturdy walls are mostly unadorned and a few interior sections remain in a state of partial collapse; only the palace prayer room gives any sense of former grandeur. Nonetheless it's gently thrilling to weave your way through the maze of dark corridors, hidden stairways and makeshift ladders to reach the rooftop for great views across the city. Carry a torch (flashlight) and watch out for holes in the floor.

Palace Gompas
BUDDHIST TEMPLES

A trio of photogenic religious structures guard the imposing palace entrance. The courtyard of the 1840 Soma Gompa is used in summer for traditional dances (Map p249; admission ₹200; ☉5.30pm). Behind, the colourfully muralled Chandazik Gompa (Chenrezi Lhakhang; admission ₹20; ☉7am-6pm) celebrates the full pantheon of 1000 Buddhas (of which 996 have yet to be born). The main attractions of the red, 1430 Chamba Lhakhang (Map p249; admission ₹20; ☉7am-6pm) are the medieval mural fragments between the inner and outer walls. Its central chamber enthrones a very gaudy three-storey Maitreya statue, reworked in 1957.

Tsemo Fort
CASTLE RUIN

(Map p249; admission ₹20; ☉dawn-dusk) Visible from virtually everywhere in Leh, 16th-century Tsemo (Victory) Fort is a defining landmark that crowns the top of Palace Ridge. Up close, it's surprisingly small and the shattered walls contain little more than flapping prayer flags but scrambling around them provides a precarious frisson. Directly beneath, Tsemo Gompa consists of two little 15th-century **temple buildings**, one enshrining an 8m-tall gold-faced Maitreya. An alternative descent slithers down to a **collection of stupas** in Chubi.

Old Town
AREA

Behind Leh's fanciful Jama Masjid (Sunni men's mosque; Map p249), the winding alleys and stairways of Old Town burrow between and beneath a series of eroded chortens (stupas) and traditional mud-brick Ladakhi houses. Belatedly, many finer structures are

being restored and a new Central Asian Museum (Map p249; www.tibetheritagefund.org/pages/projects/ladakh/central-asian-museum.php) is under construction, styled like a tapered fortress tower. That's in a courtyard opposite Datun Sahib (Map p249), a sacred tree supposedly planted in 1517 by a Sikh mystic, though others claim it grew magically from the walking staff of Staksang Raspa, guru to Ladakh's great king Sengge Namgyal.

A tunnel-passage leads up to the beautifully reconstructed 17th-century Munshi Mansion (Map p249), once the residence of the Ladakhi royal secretary and now housing the Lamo Arts Centre (☏251554; www.lamo.org.in).

The squat Guru Lhakhang Shrine (Map p249) contains newly repainted murals and a fierce-looking **Guru Rinpoche statue**. A short rocky scramble above, prominent Namgyal Stupa (Map p249) is just outside the palace walls.

Informative small-group walking tours (per person ₹300; ☉9.30am & 3pm, Tue, Thu & Sat) dawdle around the Old Town starting from Lala's Art Cafe (p257), where you should prebook. Although advertised as lasting two hours, sometimes they take double that.

Chowkhang Gompa
BUDDHIST TEMPLE

Hidden in a large courtyard behind Main Bazaar (Map p249), the small, 20th-century Chowkhang Gompa has a gilt-roofed prayer room strung with hundreds of prayer flags. It's the headquarters of the Ladakh Buddhist Association.

Women's Alliance
CULTURAL PROGRAM

(Map p249; ☏250293; www.womensalliance ladakh.org, www.isec.org.uk/pages/ladakh.html; ☉10am-5pm Mon-Sat) To learn more about the admirable balance between man and nature in traditional Ladakhi society, consider attending one of ISEC's relevant film screenings here (the venue might change). At 11am there's a varying programme, at 1pm *Economics of Happiness* and at 3pm the excellent hour-long documentary *Ancient Futures: Learning from Ladakh*. Films are often followed by a group discussion. Donation appropriate.

NORTH OF CENTRE

Leh's rural qualities, its remarkable network of canal-streams and its impressive mountain setting become swiftly apparent as you wander north. A relatively short yet captivating route follows crooked footpaths and lanes to little Sankar Gompa (Map p246;

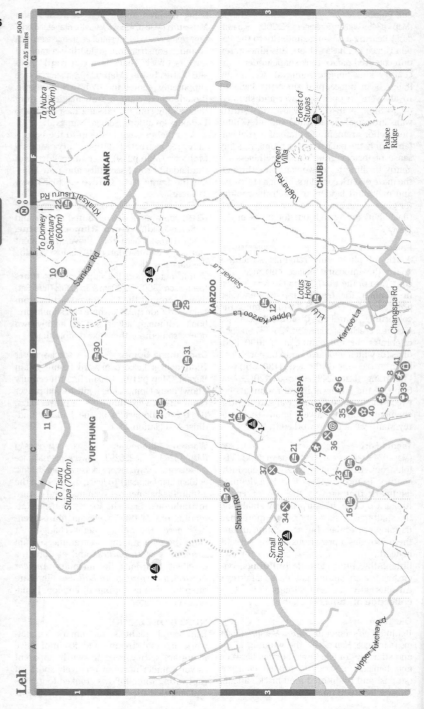

Leh

0   500 m
0   0.25 miles

SANKAR

To Nubra
(230km)

Forest of
Stupas

Green Villa

CHUBI

Palace Ridge

Khaksal/Tisruri Rd

To Donkey
Sanctuary
(600m)

22

10

Sankar Rd

3

KARZOO

29

12

Upper Karzoo La

Sankar La

Lotus Hotel

Karzoo La

Changspa Rd

30

31

25

14

1

CHANGSPA

38

35

6

8

41

5

40

39

21

7

36

@

23

9

11

YURTHUNG

To Tisuru
Stupa (700m)

37

26

Shanti Rd

34

16

Small
Stupas

4

Upper Tukcha Rd

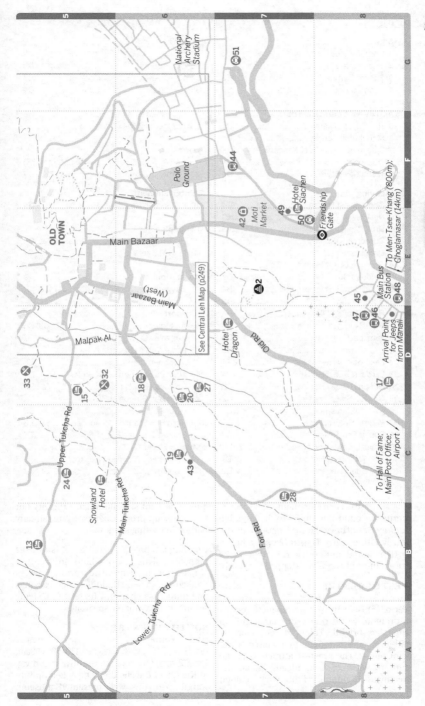

National Archery Stadium

51

44

Polo Ground

Hotel Siachen

49

50

Friendship Gate

42

Moti Market

Main Bazaar

OLD TOWN

Main Bazaar (West)

See Central Leh Map (p249)

Main Bus Station

To Men-Tsee-Khang (800m); Choglamasar (14km)

48

45

46

47

2

Arrival Point for Jeeps from Manali

Hotel Dragon

Malpak Al

Old Rd

33

32

18

15

27

20

17

To Hall of Fame; Main Post Office; Airport

Upper Tukcha Rd

24

Snowland Hotel

Main Tukcha Rd

19

43

28

Fort Rd

13

Lower Tukcha Rd

Leh

admission ₹30). Then, for memorable views, continue around 1km uphill to the laudable **Donkey Sanctuary** (Korean Temple Rd) or the nearby 11th-century **Tisuru Stupa**, a bulky, partly-restored mud-brick ruin that looks like a half-built *ziggurat* (stepped pyramid).

WEST OF CENTRE

Shanti Stupa   VIEWPOINT
(Map p246) Built in 1991 by Japanese monks to promote world peace, this large, hilltop stupa has brightly coloured reliefs on its mid-levels and is topped by a spired white hemisphere. The greatest attraction is the stunning view of Leh. Ideally, make the breathless 15-minute climb when golden afternoon light still illuminates the city but the steps up from Changspa are already bathed in cooling shadow.

Gomang Stupa   SACRED SITE
(Map p246) This one-of-a-kind, 9th-century stupa rises in concentric serrated layers flanked by ancient Buddhist rock carvings and numerous chortens. Its peaceful, shady setting feels genuinely spiritual.

SOUTH OF CENTRE

Hall of Fame   MUSEUM
(off Map p246; Indian/foreigner ₹10/50; ⊙9am-1pm & 2-7pm) Overlooking the airport runway at Km428 of the chokingly busy Leh-Spituk-Kargil road, this well presented museum

mostly commemorates the various high-altitude battles fought with Pakistan during the 20th century. Two afterthought rooms feature Ladakhi culture and nature.

Nezer Latho
VIEWPOINT, SACRED SITE

(Map p246) This mysterious whitewashed cube, topped by a sheaf of juniper twigs, is the shrine of Leh's guardian deity. It sits atop a rocky outcrop offering superb 360-degree views over the city through colourful strings of prayer flags, a five-minute climb from Hotel Dragon.

🏃 Activities, Courses & Tours

Cycling
CYCLING

For an exhilarating yet effortless excursion take a jeep ride up to Khardung La (the 'world's highest road-pass', p269) and let gravity bring you back down. Actually, given the potholes of the uppermost 15km you might prefer to start from South Pullu army camp from which all 25km to Leh are well paved. The ₹700 to ₹900 per person fee includes bike hire, permit and support vehicle (minimum group-size four). Book through **Summer Holidays** (Map p249; ☎252651; Zangsti Rd) or **Himalayan Bikers** (Map p246; ☎250937; www.himalayan-biker.com; Changspa). Both also rent mountain bikes (per day ₹350 to ₹550).

Gephel Shadrupling
MEDITATION

(www.ladakh-gsn-nuns.org; Ayu-Sabu) This tiny nunnery, around 6km from Leh, runs five-day meditation courses. The suggested donation of ₹500 per day includes bed-space and food. It's very hard to find but Choglamsar-based taxi-driver **Hassan** (☎9419243576) knows the way.

Mahabodhi Centre
YOGA, MEDITATION

(Map p246; ☎251162; www.mahabodhi-ladakh.org; Changspa Lane; 90min yoga class ₹150-250) Daily except Sundays there's a meditation session (by donation) and several 1½-hour yoga classes in a variety of styles. Book here for

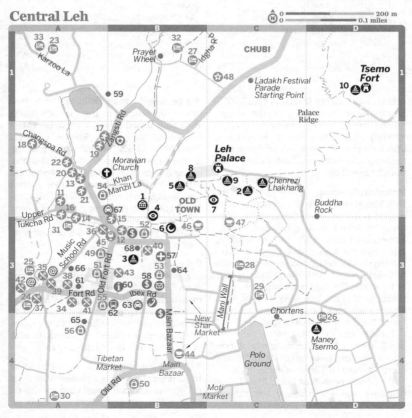

Central Leh
Ⓝ 0 — 200 m
0 — 0.1 miles

residential courses (3/10 days ₹3000/7000) in *vipassana* meditation at the organisation's much bigger Meditation Centre, approximately 1km north of Km464.2 in Choglamsar where Sunday 'introduction-to-meditation' sessions cost ₹500 including bus transfer from Leh.

Mountain Climbing MOUNTAINEERING
Stok Kangri (6120m) is the triangular snow-capped peak usually visible straight across the valley from Leh. As a 'trekking peak' it's accessible to those with minimal climbing experience but scaling its uppermost slopes still requires ice axes, crampons, considerable fitness and a guide with groups roped together for safety. Pre-climb acclimatisation is essential as AMS can be a serious worry. Many agencies offer Stok Kangri packages generally taking five days from Stok or Zingchen.

Ladakh has over 100 other climbable peaks above 6000m, many rarely, if ever, scaled. **Venture Equipment** (Map p249) and other Changspa outfits rent climbing gear.

Per-person **peak fees** range from US$50 (trekking peaks) to US$400 according to peak height. Peaks over 7000m require spe-cial permission from Delhi and thus take months of preparation. However, any others are usually issued in minutes through **IMF**'s Leh representative, **Sri Sonam Wangyal** (Map p249; ☑252992; www.indmount.org; Changspa Rd) whose house-office is tucked incongruously into the Mentokling Restaurant yard. The youngest man to scale Everest back in 1965, he happily shows off his medals and recounts climbing yarns. You'll need six copies of your passport and visa plus details of your guide. Agencies can apply on your behalf.

Open Ladakh MEDITATION
(Map p249; ☑9906981026; www.openladakh.com; Hemis Complex, 1st fl, unit 23) Runs one-hour **meditation sessions** at 4pm Monday to Thursday, a Wednesday all-day workshop on understanding Buddhism (₹300), weekend *vipassana* residential retreats in Stok (₹2000) and monthly meditation treks.

Rafting & Kayaking OUTDOOR ADVENTURE
In summer, numerous agencies offer daily rafting excursions through glorious canyon scenery. You can also follow in a kayak for

around 50% extra. Prepare to get very wet. There are two main routes, **Phey to Nimmu** – grade II (beginners) from ₹1000; and **Chiling to Nimmu** – grade III, tougher, from ₹1400; kayakers must be experienced.

Rimo (Map p249; ☑253348; www.rimoriver expeditions.com; Zangsti Rd) has very helpful staff and offers two-day kayaking courses for beginners and a twice-yearly expedition making a full four-day rafting descent of the Zanskar river from near Padum (US$728 inclusive). **Splash Adventures** (☑254870; www.splashladakh.com) Central (Map p249; Zangsti Rd) Changspa (Map p246; Changspa Rd) is another useful contact.

Trekking & Jeep Safaris   OUTDOOR ADVENTURE
Countless agencies offer trekking packages (p252) and jeep tours. Few seem systematically bad but many are very inconsistent. In reality, a deciding factor is often which agent happens to have a group leaving on the day you need. The ones we've listed here proved competent and/or were warmly recommended by travellers. For multi-day jeep hires, agencies can put together a fare-sharing

group, organising permits, vehicle and driver. Five per jeep is optimal for comfort versus expense. Most popular excursions are Pangong Tso or the Nubra/Shyok Valleys. Book at least 24 hours ahead.

Shayok Tours & Travels (Map p249; ☑9419342346, 9419888902; shayoktravels@rediffmail.com; Changspa Rd) Frank, trustworthy and helpful. Can organise inner line permits for travellers on motorbikes.

Yama Adventures (Map p246; ☑250833; www.yamatreks.com; Changspa Rd) Consistent recommendations from several readers underlining their eco-credentials.

Ladakh Tour Escort (Map p249; ☑255825; Zangsti) Honest and obliging.

Snow Leopard Trails (Map p249; ☑252074; Hotel Kang-Lha-Chen Complex, Zangsti Rd)

Little Tibet (Map p249; ☑252951; www.little tibetladakh.com; Zangsti Rd)

Ladakh Eco Adventure (Map p249; ☑252951; www.ladakh-eco-adventures.com)

Bargain value, thrillingly scenic treks can take you into magical roadless villages, through craggy gorges and across dazzlingly stark mountain passes.

Seasons

The season is essentially July and August. Storms occasionally interrupt itineraries and snow is possible from early September. In February you could attempt the challenging Chadar ice-trek (p241).

Preparation

As most trekking routes start around 3500m (often climbing above 5000m) proper acclimatisation is essential to avoid AMS (p1193). You could acclimatise with 'baby' treks or by adding extra (less interesting) days to the core treks, for instance starting from Lamayuru, Spituk or Martselang rather than Hinju/Photoksar, Zingchen or Shang Sumdo.

Book a jeep transfer from your finishing point or choose to end up somewhere with public transport (eg Stok).

Horse Treks

At these altitudes carrying heavy packs is much more exhausting than many anticipate so consider engaging packhorses (the accompanying horseman can often double as a guide) or do a 'homestay trek' (see below). Agencies will happily arrange all-in packages with horses, guides, food and (often old) camping gear starting from around $35 per person per day. If you're self-sufficient (tent, food) it's often possible to find your own horseman from ₹300 per horse per day, but prices rise considerably during August (harvest season) and many horsemen are contracted to agencies, so even at Lamayuru or Padum you'll need patience. If booking horses or trekking late in the season, expect to pay for the necessary extra days' travel between trailhead and stables (for many agency horses, that's Spituk).

Homestay Treks

Rural homestays and/or parachute cafes are now available along many (though not all) popular trekking routes, reducing or negating the need to carry significant supplies and camping gear. Such homestays (typically ₹400/700 per single/double including simple meals) provide a fascinating window into local culture; you'll generally eat with the family in their traditional kitchen, their pots and pans proudly displayed above the Aga-style winter stove. You might even be able to help harvesting or planting the family fields. Mud-brick rooms generally have rugs and blankets for bedding, some have solar-battery electric lamps. On popular routes it's probably worth paying the ₹50 extra to have Leh agencies (listed on www.himalayan-homestays.com) book bed-space for you. However, given the lack of telephones, such 'bookings' are essentially just notes in Ladakhi asking a host to

🛏 Sleeping

Leh has hundreds of guesthouses and around 60 hotels. Conditions in rock-bottom places are usually simple rather than sleazy, though room standards can vary significantly within each property so, when possible, look before you book. Many budget places won't take advance bookings. If all our suggestions are full, there are dozens of other decent budget options, especially in Changspa and Karzoo.

Often, better guesthouses (around ₹700) are preferable to lacklustre ₹2200 hotels with ill-fitting carpets, saggy beds and faux veneer panelling. A few slap on 10% service fees.

Hot water is typically provided either morning or evening (sometimes both) using wood-fired boilers. Water can take up to 10 minutes to run warm, wasting a precious resource. An ecofriendly alternative is to request hot water by bucket or use it less often. Geysers are likely to be more common and power cuts less frequent once the Alchi hydro-power dam comes online (probably 2012). Many guesthouses will provide towels on request. Toilet paper is rarely included and usually should NOT be flushed (use the plastic bin).

Most accommodation closes in winter. A few hotels and family guesthouses do stay

give you priority. In Rumbak and Sham villages it's generally OK to turn up unannounced. Engaging a guide (typically ₹800 per day) is worthwhile for security, route-finding and to better appreciate social interactions en route. Useful contacts:

» **Ladakhi Women's Travel Company** (Map p249; ☑250973; www.ladakhiwomenstravel .com; Hemis Complex, 1st fl, unit 14, Leh; ☺10am-7pm) Female run, but male customers accepted. Recommended but only four guides available.

» **Hemis National Park Guide Service** (Map p249; ☑256207; hemis_npark@yahoo.co.in; Hemis Complex, 1st fl, unit 11, Leh; ☺9am-1pm & 2-7pm) Dozens of guides available.

Which Trek?

Popular options:

DAYS	ROUTE	HOMESTAYS?	HIGH PASSES	SEE
2	Zingchen-Rumbak-Stok	plenty	4900m	p262
2	Hinju-Sumdho Chinmu-Sumdha Do	yes, limited space	4950m	p268
2-4	Itchar-Phuktal-Itchar	yes, limited space	no	p242
3+	Chiling-Skiu (Markha Valley)-Yurutse/ Rumbak-Zingchen	yes	4920m	p262
5+	Chiling-Kaya-Markha-Hankar-Nimaling-Shang Sumdo	yes (or tent-camp)	5030m	p263
5 (8)	(Rumtse)-Tso Khar-Korzok	no	four (seven)	p277
6 (8)	(Padum)-Itchar-Darcha including Phuktal	some days	5090m	p242
5 (9)	(Lamayuru-Honupatta)-Photoksar-Lingshet-Hanumil-(Padum)	some days	at least four	p267

For something relatively easy, Zingchen–Rumbak–Yurutse–Zingchen makes a great one- or two-day sampler from Leh, Markha Valley routes before Nimaling have no passes to cross and Sham (p265) 'treks' are little more than road walks between attractive old villages.

Further Information

» Lonely Planet's *Trekking in the Indian Himalaya*
» Trailblazer's *Trekking in Ladakh*
» www.myhimalayas.com/travelogues/ladakh.htm.

open, the latter often charging ₹100 extra for heating and offering only bucket water since pipes freeze.

CENTRAL LEH

The following accommodation features on Map p249.

Travellers' House GUESTHOUSE **$**
(☑250419; thetravellershouse@gmail.com; Karzoo Lane; d ₹500-600) Eight well-kept guest rooms with geyser-equipped bathrooms face the friendly family's attractive traditional home and vegetable patch. Great castle views from the flat roof. There are several other great-value choices on the same quiet lane, including the nearby **Hotel Saser** (☑250162; Karzoo Lane; d ₹600-1000).

New Royal Guest House GUESTHOUSE **$**
(☑252956; Idgha Rd; d ₹800, without bathroom ₹600) A notch above many hotels, the rooms have smart fittings, wood-effect floors and bathrooms with designer shower-heads. The upper-floor balcony has a swing seat perusing mountain *and* fortress views.

Palace View Guest House GUESTHOUSE **$**
(☑250773; palace.view@hotmail.com; d from ₹450, without bathroom ₹200-300) First opened in

1975, this upliftingly lived-in family place has garden seating, two sitting rooms and a roof-top with brilliant views of the palace ridge. Rooms are simple with ageing but clean linen, the cheapest using camp-beds. Bath-rooms have geysers. The owners are friendly and conscientious. Ladakhi dinners available if you order by 5pm. Open year-round.

Pangong Hotel HOTEL $$
(☑254655; www.pangongladakh.com; Chulung Lane; s/d ₹2000/2210; @☎) Despite a few signs of wear, the Pangong is comparatively stylish with attractive pine cladding in pub-lic areas. The best rooms are on the top floor with rooftop terraces. Wi-fi per hour/day costs ₹100/500.

Namgyal Guest House GUESTHOUSE $
(☑253307; d ₹400, s/d/tr without bathroom ₹150/200/300) En suite rooms have var-nished log ceilings, geyser and sit-down flush toilet, though some seem dusty and have foam beds. Many have views of Stok Kangri and the Maney Tsermo stupas. Cheaper rooms are simple but recently re-painted and share three bathrooms (seatless toilets) in a cube of traditional old building.

Old Ladakh Guest House GUESTHOUSE $
(☑252951; www.littletibetladakh.com; d ₹400-600, without bathroom s/d ₹200/300) Picked out with distinctive crimson timbers, there's a central courtyard, traditional kitchen/breakfast room and phenomenal rooftop view. Downstairs rooms are dingily claustrophobic, others are bright if worn; room 304 has roof terrace and settees. New annex under construction.

Indus Guest House GUESTHOUSE $
(☑252502; masters _ adv@yahoo.co.in; Malpak Al-ley; d ₹300-700; ☎) All 16 rooms are en suite, the water heated all day by a furnace burn-ing waste (cardboard, cow-dung etc). Little shared terraces have fortress views and the semi-enclosed courtyard is peacefully tree-shaded. Food, served on request, is mostly sourced from the well-travelled family's or-ganic farm. Original treks available.

Hotel Tso-Kar HOTEL $$
(☑255763; www.lehladakhhotel.com; Fort Rd; d from ₹1000) Rooms have newly re-tiled bathrooms but otherwise aren't quite as attractive as the seductively colonnaded courtyard might imply.

Rehela Guest House HOMESTAY $
(☑250969; Tsemoview Alley; d ₹400-500, without bathroom ₹200-300) Small, partly solar-powered homestay with bright unfussy rooms, free drinking water and use of the kitchen/laundry tap.

Peace Guest House GUESTHOUSE $
(☑253514; r ₹400) Very central yet quietly tucked away in a hidden garden, this new bungalow has five good value, gleamingly clean rooms each with decent bathrooms.

NORTH OF CENTRE

Karzoo becomes delightfully rural towards the north and west and has some of Leh's best-value budget accommodation but there are no shops or restaurants and at night it's a long, dark walk home from town if you're as far out as Sankar or Yurthung. The follow-ing accommodation features on Map p246.

TOP CHOICE Royal Ladakh HOTEL $$
(☑251646; www.hotelroyalladakh.com; Upper Karzoo Ln; s/d ₹1800/2450; ☎) Behind the manicured lawn, whitewashed facade and traditionally carved wooden window frames lies a stylishly appointed modern hotel with fine linen, flat-screen TVs and 1960s-retro bathrooms. Virtually every room has oodles of space and inspiring views of either Stok Kangri or Tsemo Fort.

Dumbang Villa GUESTHOUSE $
(☑9419219416; Sankar Ln; d ₹300-600) One of Leh's best value guesthouses, this new bun-galow is set in peaceful gardens with wide panoramic views. Fair-sized rooms come with wicker seats, log ceilings and good bathrooms (hot water by bucket).

Tse-Tan Guest House GUESTHOUSE $
(☑250510; tsetan_n@yahoo.com; Upper Changspa; r without bathroom ₹200-300) Worth the walk for large, airy rooms sharing very clean bathrooms with geysers. There are perfect-ly framed mountain views from the upper front rooms and the adorable host family plies guests with endless mint tea. Other peaceful family guesthouses costing under ₹300 include friendly **Zee Guest House** (☑251131; r without bathroom ₹250) and **Nur-boo Guest House** (☑9419340947; s/d without bathroom ₹200/300), where you'll be serenad-ed by the sound of rushing water.

Gomang Guest House GUESTHOUSE $
(☑252657; Old Karzoo; r without bathroom ₹200-300) A warren of wobbly stairways links simple rooms sharing Ladakhi and Western bathrooms. A big plus is the pair of 1st-floor sitting areas overlook Gomang Stupa.

Lak Rook Guest House GUESTHOUSE $

(✓252987; Sankar; s/d ₹300/350, s/d/tr without bathroom ₹200/250/300) This cult traveller favourite is a large, ramshackle Ladakhi farmhouse almost lost within its vast organic vegetable garden. Friendly owners and good food but be prepared for lumpy ageing mattresses, paper-bag lampshades and other minor inconveniences. Ladakhi toilet available.

Oriental Guest House HOTEL, GUESTHOUSE $

(✓253153; www.oriental-ladakh.com; Shanti Rd; r ₹600-1000, without bathroom ₹150/250; ☺year-round; @) This self-contained 70-room complex on the edge of Changspa uses solar heating, has a lobby-library with internet, a central lawn and both traditional and modern glass-fronted kitchens, the latter serving a full-scale restaurant. Rooms range from very basic, through fair-value ₹600 doubles to newer ₹1000 versions with sizes and views that vary.

Deskit Villa GUESTHOUSE $$

(✓253498; Sankar; d incl breakfast ₹1200) But for the typically undulating carpets, rooms would be adorable with marble-floored bathrooms and private balconies (in some). An attraction is the thatched gazebo in the raised garden offering comfortable outdoor reading space. Includes breakfast

Druk Ladakh HOTEL $$$

(✓251702; Yurthung; s/d/ste ₹3400/4400/6400; ☎) Echoing acres of marble, carved wood and crimson furniture lead to relatively indulgent new rooms with parquet floors, flat screen TVs and closable shower booths. Luxuries even run to free toilet paper.

WEST OF CENTRE

Pleasant, if traffic-clogged, Fort Rd and Changspa Rd are conveniently full of cafes, internet travel agencies and tourist shops. The Tukcha roads are quieter while side lanes take you swiftly into another, altogether more peaceful world with dozens of decent sleeping options available. The following accommodation features on Map p246.

Padma Hotel HOTEL $$

(✓252630; www.padmaladakh.net; d ₹1850-2200; @☎) Hidden in a large garden, the eco-aware Padma has attractively appointed new hotel rooms with fan, bed lamps, good linen and simple bathrooms using solar-heated water. The upstairs restaurant and common balconies enjoy fine mountain views, there's a library, ₹8 water refills and free wi-fi. The guesthouse section (d ₹600) with shared bathrooms occupies the family's traditional Ladakhi house, complete with traditional kitchen and chapel/meditation room.

Gangs-Shun HOMESTAY $

(✓252603; morup_lee@yahoo.co.in; Upper Tukcha Rd; d ₹600-700, f ₹800) Five guest rooms above an attractive new family home come with good beds, quality parquet flooring and attached bathrooms that are better quality than in most Leh hotels. Shared upper terrace.

Chow Guest House GUESTHOUSE $

(✓252399; d ₹400, without bathroom ₹250) Sparkling clean, airy budget rooms with good mattresses and log ceilings in two new but unobtrusive buildings set in a beautiful flower-filled garden down a narrow path from Changspa Rd.

Jamspal Guest House GUESTHOUSE $

(✓251272; Mayflower Alley; r ₹400-500, without bathroom ₹200-300) Super-friendly family place, with large garden, shrine and traditional-style sitting room. Simple but central, and open year-round.

Norzin Holiday Home GUESTHOUSE $

(✓252022; norzinholidays@gmail.com; Upper Tukcha Rd; r ₹500-600, without bathroom s/d ₹200/300) Unusually well-kept local home with roof terrace, garden seating and a grapevine dominating the glassed-in veranda. Free drinking water refills, welcoming family.

Haldupa Guest House GUESTHOUSE $

(✓251374; Upper Tukcha Rd; r ₹400-500, without bathroom ₹250) One airy, cheaper room (with shared squat) is inside the wonderfully authentic original house, home to an utterly enchanting local family. The rest are compact but brand new with good bathrooms in a separate block facing the garden.

Hotel Gawaling International HOTEL $$

(✓253252; www.hotelgawaling.com; s/d/deluxe ₹1980/2640/2970; @☎) Rooms are better maintained than at most other Leh hotels with parquet floors and good bathrooms albeit offering minimal toiletries. Each has a balcony (huge in deluxe rooms) facing attractively rural scenery and the whole complex is serenaded by a flowing river. Wi-fi is free, internet ₹100 per hour. Road access from Upper Tukcha Rd.

Ladakh Residency
HOTEL $$$

(☏254111; www.ladakhresidency.com; Changspa Rd; s/d/ste ₹3850/4950/6600; 🛜) This brand-new layered collage of wooden balconies and marble floors is one of the few wheelchair-friendly buildings in Ladakh, though it feels disproportionately large for Changspa and a carpark fills most of what should be the garden.

Hotel Namgyal Palace
HOTEL $$

(☏256356; namgyalpalace.com; Fort Rd; s/d/ste ₹1570/2180/3630; 🛜) The facade's clashing mix of silvered windows and Tibetan woodwork is eye-catching if discordant. Rooms have well-appointed bathrooms (including toiletries) and seats in the bay windows from which to contemplate mountain panoramas (upper floor rooms). Better than most in this price range but there are some minor housekeeping niggles.

Poplar Eco-Resort
ECORESORT $$

(☏253518; poplar_ecoresort@yahoo.com; Shenam Rd; s/d ₹1600/2200, full board ₹2450/3300) Lost in the birdsong of an overgrown apricot orchard are a series of two-room cottages, each pair sharing a veranda with wicker chairs. Rooms have good tiled bathrooms with all-day hot water, though beds are soft and decor is mostly lacking. Most food and juice served is sourced from the organic garden.

Lardakh Guest House
HOMESTAY $

(☏250480; s/d/view without bathroom ₹150/200/300) From the wobbly old pillars to the rooftop shrine, this is the absolute archetype of a classic Ladakhi house but it makes few concessions to Western comfort and the bathroom is in the big, attractive garden.

Hotel Grand Willow
HOTEL $$

(☏251835; www.hotelgrandwillow.net; Fort Rd; s/d ₹1600/2200) Three floors of carved balconies fold around a small, neat garden area. Recently re-painted rooms have ceiling mouldings and silky bedcovers and although a little dark, come with good new bathrooms. Discounts possible.

SOUTH OF CENTRE

Noisy Old Road has several lacklustre midrange options and package tour places, of which only a couple are recommended.

Hotel Grand Dragon
HOTEL $$$

(Map p246; ☏250786; www.thegranddragonladakh.com; Old Rd, Shenam; s/d/ste ₹6050/7150/11,000; 🛜) Leh's only really international-standard hotel, the Grand Dragon is professionally appointed with functioning lift, fitting carpets and rooms approximating to business standards (safe and fridge in suites). However, it's away from shops down a busy road and there's an ugly foreground to the mountain views. Open year-round. Wi-fi ₹300/1600 per hour/day.

Lha-Ri-Sa Resort
HOTEL $$

(☏252423; www.ladakh-lharisa.com; s/d/ste ₹2800/3380/6000) Strikingly designed, the soaring atrium is held aloft on temple-like pillars. Raised walkways between apple trees link large, high-ceilinged rooms with 1940s-retro walnut furniture. This is arguably Leh's best hotel but it's 3km south of town via unpleasantly busy major roads so you'll need wheels to go almost anywhere of interest. Ample parking.

✗ Eating

Traveller cafes abound, Israeli and Chinese options supplementing curries, banana pancakes, tandoori pizzas and Tibetan favourites but curiously few restaurants offer true Ladakhi food (try Chopsticks or request it at family guesthouses). Many eateries, including Changspa's numerous garden-restaurants, close from mid-September to July, their owners often decamping to Goa.

CENTRAL LEH

You won't need a guide to find the numerous rooftop and Tibetan/Chinese restaurants dotted all along Main Bazaar but while there are a few decent options, food tends to be better and gardens more inviting if you head out along Fort Rd or into Changspa. Self caterers can buy fresh produce from the vegetable market (Old Fort Rd) or from colourfully dressed women along Main Bazaar. Fresh-baked bread rounds (₹3) are sold hot from traditional wood-fired tandoori bakeries behind Jama Masjid.

The following eateries feature on Map p249.

Chopsticks
ASIAN $$

(Fort Rd; mains ₹60-180, rice ₹55) This 3rd-floor pan-Asian restaurant is one of Leh's most stylish eateries. Their 'Wonderwok' stir-fries and Thai green curry are excellent and prices are very fair, given the high quality of service.

Norlakh
TIBETAN $

(Main Bazaar; mains ₹40-100, momos ₹50-95, rice ₹30) The best of several town-centre options with mildly trendy decor touches and great pure-veg Tibetan food. Try the cheese-and-spinach *momos* or special *gyathuk* (a rich noodle soup). It's upstairs and easy to miss hidden behind a willow tree almost opposite Ladakh Bookshop.

Pumpernickel German Bakery
BAKERY CAFE **$**

(Zangsti Rd; meals ₹70-180) Behind the simple bakery counter (good strudels) is a merrily ramshackle dining room with Ladakhi wooden columns and a full multicuisine menu.

Gesmo
MULTICUISINE **$**

(Fort Rd, curries ₹40-100, rice ₹35) Old-fashioned traveller haunt, with gingham tablecloths, checkerboard ceilings, and a range of cakes, breakfasts and good-value meals from curries to yak-cheese pizza.

Tenzin Dickey
TIBETAN **$**

(Fort Rd, mains ₹40-70) Cosy if unpretentious eatery serving generous portions of excellent vegetarian Tibetan and Chinese food at sensible prices. Try the delectable cheese *kothay* (like Japanese *gyoza*).

Summer Harvest
MULTICUISINE **$$**

(Fort Rd; mains ₹70-120, rice ₹30-90) Tourist favourite with pseudo-traditional lacquered-wood columns and dangling mod-Chinese lamps. Our malai kofta was divine but *momos* were bullet-proof. Service charge 10%.

Lamayuru Restaurant
MULTICUISINE **$**

(Fort Rd; curries ₹30-80, rice ₹25) Plain but reliable backpacker place for good inexpensive Indian, Chinese and international snacks, all vegetarian. A ₹70 thali is available till 7pm.

Dolphin Bakery
CAFE **$**

(Malpak Alley; mains ₹40-120) Cakes and snack meals served in the open air at a simple triangle of a tree-shaded, streamside terrace.

CHANGSPA
The following eateries feature on Map p246.

TOP CHOICE Bon Appetit
MULTICUISINE **$$**

(☏251533; mains ₹180-350; ⊘11am-late) By far Leh's most imaginative restaurant is a stylish exercise in Ladakhi minimalist architecture and offers a wide panorama of the southern mountains. A limited but thoroughly scrumptious selection of artistically prepared dishes includes sublime cashew chicken in pesto sauce.

Calabria
MULTICUISINE **$**

(Changspa Rd; mains ₹45-90, rice ₹30, pastas ₹160-180) The decor wins no prizes and traffic outside can be annoying but the vegetarian Indian and Chinese fare is consistently excellent, sensibly priced and obligingly served. Pastries and real espressos (₹30) are available, electricity willing.

Café Jeevan
MULTICUISINE **$**

(Booklovers Retreat; Changspa Rd; meals ₹70-140) Despite the comparatively sophisticated appearance, prices aren't significantly higher than most bog-standard traveller pads. A glass-sided kitchen turns out high quality vegetarian meals in a wide range of cuisines, including some of Leh's best pizza. There's also a two-case bookshop and a covered roof terrace.

Amego
KOREAN **$$**

(mains ₹85-400; ⊘9am-8pm Mon-Sat) A wide range of very authentic Korean specialities served in a rural farmhouse setting surrounded by barley fields.

Wonderland Restaurant
MULTICUISINE **$**

(Changspa Lane; meals ₹70-190, rice ₹30) The brick-thick menu is a veritable dictionary of cuisines covering virtually all bases. The rooftop offers indoor and outdoor seating, limited views and respite from traffic noise. Prices are reasonable. Real coffee served.

Otsal Restaurant
MULTICUISINE **$**

(Changspa Rd; mains ₹40-90, pizza ₹90-130) Serenaded by a gurgling stream, this pleasant backpacker retreat includes rooftop seating plus an indoor area of floor mats and colourful Tibetan tables.

🍷 Drinking

Many garden and rooftop restaurants serve beer, but it's almost never on the menu: ask the waiter. Bon Appetit has a cocktail menu and pours a mean mojito (₹170). For takeaway booze the handy **Indus Wine Shop** (Map p249; Ibex Rd; ⊘10am-1pm & 3-9pm) is closed on the 8th, 10th and 15th days of the Tibetan calendar.

TOP CHOICE Lala's Art Cafe
CAFE

(Map p249; Old Town; ⊘8.30am-7.30pm) A tiny, brilliantly restored mud-brick Old Town house with trip-you-up stone steps and an open roof terrace serving great Italian coffee and scrumptious cake-of-the-day. Read the newspapers then check out the ancient carved steles in the ground floor shrine section.

Elements
GARDEN CAFE

(Map p246; Changspa Rd; ⊘noon-late) The idiosyncratic food is almost as full of herbs as the clients' cigarettes in this popular open-air chillout. Adobe-style low walls separate cushioned ground-spaces, there's an open fire on colder evenings and after the mountain views have faded into darkness, movies or music vids are often projected. Open unusually late. Beer available.

Zoya Cafe
CAFE

(Map p249; Old Town; ⊘9am-7pm) Handy as a landmark when climbing to the palace or as a tea-stop when returning, entry is disconcertingly through a typical local home but the 360-degree rooftop views are unparalleled anywhere in Leh.

Desert Rain
CAFE

(Map p249; New Shar Market; ⊘9am-9pm Mon-Sat) Relaxed Western-style cafe serving good coffee and various teas with plenty of (predominantly Christian) books to read. Film nights on Saturdays around 5.30pm.

Il Forno
RESTAURANT-BAR

(Map p249; Zangsti Rd) One of several gastronomically lacklustre rooftop restaurants above Main Bazaar where town views and (sometimes cold) beer are the main attractions. The thin-crust, wood-oven pizzas (₹140–190) are OK too.

☆ Entertainment

KC Garden Restaurant
CINEMA RESTAURANT

(Map p246; Changspa Rd) One of Changspa's liveliest evening spots. Open-air movies are projected (around 8pm most nights) and KC's is also the pickup point for monthly all-night parties (₹400 including transport) on full-moon nights May to August.

Traditional Ladakhi Song-&-Dance Shows
CULTURAL PROGRAM

(Map p249; admission R200; ⊘5.30pm) Tourist-oriented performances on summer evenings outside Soma Gompa, partly visible for free from the ridge behind.

🔒 Shopping

Many colourful souvenir shops and **Tibetan Refugee Markets** (Map p249) sell wide selections of *thangkas,* Ladakhi hats, 'antiques' and heavy turquoise jewellery, as well as Kashmiri shawls and various Nepali, Tibetan and Chinese knick-knacks.

Several bookshops are well stocked with postcards, novels, spiritual works and books on Ladakh, Kashmir and Tibet.

LEDeG
HANDICRAFTS

(Ladakh Ecological Development Group; Map p249; www.ledeg.org; ⊘9.30am-6pm Mon-Sat) Sells crafts and clothes that are locally produced (see www.himalayanhandicrafts.org) and generally very fair value. Behind (except weekends) you can peruse their display of renewable energy devices and visit their one-room exhibition featuring a typical Ladakhi kitchen scene.

LEH ECO AWARENESS

Water is precious – those streams you see cascading beside virtually every lane aren't a sign of plenty but an elaborate network of irrigation that keep Leh from reverting to dusty mountain desert. Anything you can do to save water is a positive step. One move among guesthouses is to encourage eco-aware clients to use traditional Ladakhi long-drop toilets. These recycle human waste into compost with earth occasionally sprinkled over the latest 'deposits'. These brilliant inventions prevent sewerage from polluting streams while avoiding the terrible water wastage of flush toilets. But don't put anything nonbiodegradeable down the hole. Remember whatever goes in will end up on the farmer's field in a year or two.

To save Leh from vanishing under a sea of plastic bottles, refills of pressure-boiled, purified water are provided by environmental organisations **Dzomsa** (Map p249 & Map p246; refill ₹7; ⊘8am-10.30pm) – which has branches on Changspa Rd, Fort Rd and Main Bazaar – and **LEDeG** (Map p249; ☎253221; www.ledeg.org; refill ₹5; ⊘9.30am-6pm Mon-Sat). Both also offer recycling and disposal services for paper, bottles and batteries while Dzomsa also offers an eco-friendly laundry service (₹70 per kg).

Sensitive travellers are encouraged to buy locally sourced foods, eg apricots and *tsestalulu* (sea buckthorn) juice instead of imported chocolate and packaged soft drinks. Get these and other local fruit products at Dzomsa or **Ladag Apricot Store** (Map p249; ⊘9am-6pm).

Ladakh Bookshop
BOOKSHOP

(Ladakh Ecological Development Group; Map p249; Main Bazaar) Hidden upstairs near the SBI ATM, it's the best stocked of the bookshops. It publishes locally relevant works and stocks Olizane's pricey, slightly flawed but indispensible *Ladakh Trekking Maps* (www.abram. ch/lzmmaps.php) for ₹1300 per sheet.

Women's Alliance
HANDICRAFTS

(Ladakh Ecological Development Group; Map p249; www.womensallianceladakh.org; ⊙10am-5pm Mon-Sat) Sells similar wares to LEDeG.

Handicrafts Industrial Cooperative Shop
HANDICRAFTS

(Ladakh Ecological Development Group; Map p249; Old Fort Rd; ⊙10am-5pm Mon-Fri) This shop and Wamda Wood Carving sell wooden *choktse* tables carved with images of mythical beasts.

Wamda Wood Carving
HANDICRAFTS

(Ladakh Ecological Development Group; Map p249; Old Fort Rd; ⊙9am-6pm).

Harish
MUSIC STORE

(Map p246; Changspa Rd) Sells local and Western musical instruments.

Gol Market
MARKET

(Ladakh Ecological Development Group; Map p249; Old Rd; ⊙9am-5.30pm) A good first place to look for prosaic items of cheap clothing plus bags and limited camping supplies.

Moti Market
MARKET

(Map p246) Bigger than Gol market but less central.

Leh Ling
BOOKSHOP

(Ladakh Ecological Development Group; Map p249; Main Bazaar)

Otdan
BOOKSHOP

(Ladakh Ecological Development Group; Map p249; Zangsti Rd)

Book Worm
BOOKSHOP

(Ladakh Ecological Development Group; Map p249; Old Fort Rd) Buys and sells secondhand volumes.

ⓘ Information

Noticeboards all over town have adverts for tours, treks and activities.

Dozens of internet cafes all charge ₹90 per hour. Connection speeds vary randomly even at the same place and power cuts can prove annoying. There's a wide choice along Changspa Lane, around Dolphin Bakery (Fort Rd) and near Il Forno (Main Bazaar). Some bigger hotels offer wi-fi but virtually all charge extra and coverage rarely stretches beyond the lobby.

There are numerous moneychangers on Changspa Rd and Main Bazaar. Compare rates carefully. Leh's two ATMs are the only ones in Ladakh and are often over-stretched. Keep back-up cash for emergencies.

Central post office (Main Bazaar; ⊙10am-4.30pm Mon-Sat)

Cyber Station (Fort Rd; internet per hr ₹90; ⊙9am-11pm) One floor below Chopsticks, this unusually comfy internet cafe has a generator, satellite connection and serves great coffee (₹40) and free black tea.

Het Ram Vinay Kumar pharmacy (Map p249; Main Bazaar; ⊙9.30am-8pm)

J&K Forex (1st fl, Himalaya Complex, Main Bazaar; ⊙8.30am-4pm Mon-Fri, to 1pm Sat) Good exchange rates, better still for travellers cheques. ATM on Ibex Rd.

Men-Tsee-Khang (www.men-tsee-khang.org; ⊙8.30am-1pm & 2-5.30pm Mon-Fri & 1st & 3rd Sat). Amchi (Tibetan herbal medicine) consultations with no appointment required; average ₹180 including prescribed herbal drugs. Their one room **museum** (admission ₹5) displays medicinal herbs, clinical thangkas and minerals (lapis lazuli, tiger eye etc) used in making 'precious pills'. It's 800m south of the bus station.

Oxygen Bar (Map p249; KC Garden Restaurant; per min ₹20) Breath pure oxygen to relieve altitude sickness, or just for the buzz.

SBI (Main Bazaar; ⊙10am-4pm Mon-Fri, to 1pm Sat) The upstairs exchange desk can be chaotic and long queues are common at the 24-hour ATM outside.

Tourist office (Map p249; ☑253462; www.ladakhtourism.in; Ibex Rd; ⊙10am-4pm Mon-Sat) General info, listings and very approximate maps.

ⓘ Getting There & Away

Air

Delhi-Leh flights rarely cost under ₹11,500 in summer but in winter ₹4000 is possible. Unusually, Leh's airline offices sometimes undercut online prices.

Air India (Map p246; ☑252076; Fort Rd; ⊙10am-1pm & 2-4.30pm) Leh–Delhi (₹11,661), via Srinagar (₹7354, Wednesday) or via Jammu (₹8053, Monday and Friday). Fly to Jammu for Dharamsala.

Jet Airways (Map p249; ☑250999; Main Bazaar; ⊙10am-1pm & 2-5pm) Leh–Delhi daily in August. Frequency drops gradually to twice weekly in February.

Kingfisher (www.flykingfisher.com) Leh–Delhi daily in summer.

Bus & Shared Jeep

KARGIL Bus (₹300, 10 hours) departs 4.30am from the Polo Ground (Map p246). Faster shared jeeps (per seat/vehicle ₹600/4500) leave around 7am from outside Hotel Siachen ('Old Bus Station'). Make arrangements one day before.

SRINAGAR J&K SRTC bus (₹707, 19 hours) from main bus station (Map p246) at 3pm. Shared jeeps (front/back seats ₹1500/1300, 15 hours) depart from the 'Old Bus Station' around 5pm. Book by 8am that morning to get a good seat. Leh–Srinagar road closed November to May.

MANALI J&K SRTC buses (ordinary/deluxe ₹585/850, two days) depart Leh's main bus sta-tion around 4.30am. More comfortable HPTDC buses (₹1500, two days) leave at 5am from outside J&K Bank (Ibex Rd, Leh) and must be pre-booked at **HPTDC** (Map p249; 94518460071; Fort Rd; 9.30am-1pm & 2-7pm), upstairs oppo-site Chopsticks. Jeeps take at least 22 hours. See boxed text, p274, for details. The route is gorgeous but strenuous so you might prefer to fly one way (to/from Delhi) rather than doing it twice.

For other destinations, see below.

BUSES TO/FROM LEH

The following use Leh's main bus station, 700m south of the town centre. The short-est walk to get there from town uses a toilet-scented footpath starting opposite Hotel Dragon. Alternatively cut through the stepped bazaar from Friendship Gate.

DESTINATION	FARE (₹)	DURATION	DEPARTURES
Alchi	60	3hr	8am (return 3pm)
Chemrey	35	1½hr	use Sakti buses
Choglamsar	8	15min	frequent
Chiling	55	2½hr	9am Wed & Sun (return 1pm)
Chitkan*	164	8hr	8am Tue, Fri, Sun (return Wed, Sat, Mon)
Dha*	151	7hr	9am both directions
Diskit/Hunder**	116	6hr	6am Tue, Sat (return Sun, Wed)
Hemis	40	2hr	9.30am (return noon)
Hemis Shukpachan*	78	4hr	2pm (return 8.30am) via Yangthang
Keylong	475	17hr	4.30am
Khalsi*	88	4½hr	3pm each way
Lamayuru	150	5½hr	use Chitkan or Srinagar buses
Likir Gompa	50	2hr	4pm (return 6.30am)
Matho	20	40min	9am, 2pm, 5pm
Pangong Tso	150	8hr	6.30am Sat using Chushul-Merak bus
Phey	13	30min	noon, 4.30pm (return 8am, 1pm)
Phyang	20	40min	7am, 8am, 9am, 3pm, 4pm
Rumtse*	72	3hr	4pm, alternate days
Sakti	40	1¾hr	8.15am, noon, then half-hourly till 5pm (return frequent 7am-9am, 12.30pm, 3.30pm)
Shang Sumdo	50	3hr	3pm (return 8am)
Shey	15	25min	use Thiksey or Sakti buses
Spituk	10	15min	one or two hourly till 7pm
Stakna	15	40min	Thiksey buses terminate nearby
Stok	15	30min	8am, 2pm, 4.30pm (return 9am, 3pm, 5.30pm)
Thiksey	20	30min	half-hourly 7.30am-6.30pm
Tia*	85	4½hr	noon
Timishgan*	78	4hr	11am (return 8am)
Wanla*	111	5hr	8.30am Tue, Thu, Sun

* LBOC Bus (252792), **J&K SRTC (252085), other minibus (253262)

DESTINATION	ONE WAY (₹)	RETURN (₹)
Alchi	1330	1729
Basgo	819	1064
Chiling	1767	2287
Hemis	948	1232
Kargil	4709	6552
Keylong	11,000	14,300
Lamayuru	2579	3353
Likir	1125	1463
Matho	663	862
Manali	13,547	17,611
Nimmu	737	958
Phey	327	425
Phyang	511	664
Shang Sumdo	1175	1558
Shey	279	363
Spituk	204	266
Srinagar	9773	12,700
Stakna	686	892
Stok Palace	376	492
Sumur	3465	4504
Thiksey	442	574
Wanla	2562	3330

Combining destinations reduces the total price, eg: Leh–Stok–Matho–Stakna–Leh ₹1251.

Taxi & Charter-Jeeps

Published in an annually updated booklet, fares (p261) are the same for taxis and charter-jeeps and include reasonable stopping time en route for photos/visits. Longer waits are charged (₹160/650/1251 per hour/half-day/full day), extra overnight stops add ₹350. Unplanned diversions from the agreed routing can cause unexpected difficulties so plan carefully.

INDUS VALLEY Monastery villages make interesting day trips: engage a driver at one of Leh's three main taxi-van stands or add sights as extra stops to longer jeep tours.

JEEP TOURS For multiday jeep hire, agencies can put together a fare-sharing group, organising permits, vehicle and driver. Five per jeep is optimal for comfort versus expense. Most popular excursions are Pangong Tso or the Nubra/Shyok Valleys. Book at least 24 hours ahead.

Motorcycle

Several companies along Music School Rd and Main Bazaar (west) hire motorcycles for between ₹500 and ₹800 per day. Double-check insurance and fittings.

ⓘ Getting Around

TO/FROM AIRPORT The airport's well-guarded terminal is at Km430 of the Leh-Spituk

PETROL IN LADAKH

Ladakh's only petrol stations are at Leh, Choglamsar, Serthi (Km440.5, near Karu), Diksit, Spituk, Phyang junction, Khaltse, Mulbekh and Kargil. Even those don't always have anything to sell so, if driving, carry plenty of spare fuel.

highway, 4km south of centre. Taxi transfers cost ₹150/190 to central Leh/Changspa. Passing public minibuses to town cost only ₹5 but are usually packed full.

TAXI Leh's little micro-van taxis charge from ₹75 per hop. Flagging down rides rarely works; go to a taxi stand to make arrangements.

South of Leh

🖉01982

To visit Stok and Matho and then return to Leh via Thiksey and Shey, you'll need a vehicle that's small enough to cross the very narrow Indus River bridge at Stakna.

STOK

Ladakh's former royal family now keeps a low profile life, dividing its time between a private mansion in Manali and the stately **Stok Palace** (admission ₹50; ⊙9am-1pm & 2-7pm May-Oct). Vaguely potala-like and with colourful window frames, the three-storey palace is undoubtedly photogenic despite a giant telecommunication tower that looms directly behind. Inside, the handful of rooms that are opened to visitors display family treasures, including the queen's ancient turquoise-and-gold *yub-jhur* (crown) and a sword that the king's oracle managed to bend into a knot, Uri Geller–style. The palace's attractively appointed **cafe** (tea ₹15, sandwiches ₹60) has open terrace seating with gorgeous views.

Across from the palace, a short alley leads to the 350-year-old **Stok Abagon** (suggested donation ₹20), the decrepit former home of the royal physician (bring a torch).

Stok's peaceful main lane winds up past whitewashed farmhouses, crumbling old stupas and, after 1.4km, bypasses the modest **Stok Gompa**, where royal oracles make predictions about the future during Stok's important **Guru Tse-Chu festival** (February/March). Another kilometre south, buses from Leh terminate at a pair of simple food shacks known as the **trekking point**. Ten minutes' walk upstream from here on the path towards Rumbak, the village's last house is the misnamed **Hotel Kangri** (🖉20 1009; per person half-board ₹350), a very authentic homestay with wall murals and a full-blown Ladakhi kitchen.

Along the main road about 200m north of the trekking point, **Yarsta Guest House** (🖉242087; d half-board ₹700) is set in a garden amid poplar trees. Two top-floor rooms with beds and plenty of windows share a clean, tiled bathroom.

Commanding a fine valley panorama around 2km north of the palace beside the Leh road, isolated **Hotel Skittsal** (🖉242051; www.skittsal.com; s/d ₹1500/2180) has a neo-traditional facade and giant Buddha seated in the garden. However corridors are straight from *The Shining* and dated rooms have rucked carpets.

MATHO

Sakya-Buddhist **Matho Gompa** (🖉246085; admission ₹20) is perched on a colourfully stratified ridge above Matho village. Most of the early-15th-century monastery has been replaced by more modern structures in recent years and the top-floor museum is only one room. However, it's still well worth the bumpy trip from Leh for the scenery en route and the exceptional valley views. During the monastery's famous **Matho Nagrang festival** (February/March), a pair of monk-oracles performs daring physical challenges while effectively blindfolded by mop-wigs, 'seeing' only through the fearsome 'eyes' painted on their chests. They also engage in ritual acts of self-mutilation and make predictions for the coming year.

SPITUK & ZINGCHEN

Founded in the late 14th century as See-Thub ('Exemplary') Monastery, impressive **Spituk Gompa** (admission ₹20) is incongruously perched overlooking the end of Leh airport: don't photograph the militarily sensitive runway – soldiers are watching. The gompa's multiple mud-brick buildings tumble merrily down a steep hillock towards Spituk village on the Indus riverbank. Overlooked by the gilt-roofed **Skudung Lhakhang**, a photogenic courtyard leads to the very colourful **Dukhang** containing a yellow-hatted statue of Tsongkhapa (1357–1419) who spread Gelukpa Buddhism. A Buddha statue on the other side of the room's main image supposedly incorporates an odd relic: Tsongkhapa's nose-bleed. On the very top of the gompa hill is a three-tiered **latho** (spirit shrine) and the small **Palden Lama temple** hiding veiled deities in a smoke-blackened rear section.

For treks, the pretty two-house oasis of **Zingchen** (Zinchan, Jingchian) makes a much better starting point than Spituk village, as the first 10km of the Spituk–Zingchen road is a sun-blistered masochistic slog. A Leh–Zingchen taxi ride (₹1300) should allow stops at Spituk Gompa and at photogenic spots in the monumentally stark canyonlands that start 6km before Zingchen.

Zingchen has a homestay, campsite and parachute cafe. There's no bus but, with a little patience, hitching a (paid) ride back to Leh is often possible with vehicles that arrive to drop off trekkers.

RUMBAK & YURUTSE
Roadless **Rumbak** (4050m) is a magical village with a high proportion of closely packed traditional homes, almost all of which offer homestay beds. It's around three hours' riverside hike from Zingchen. The route is mostly easy to follow given a decent map: where in doubt, follow donkey droppings and cross any bridge you see. At a lone summer parachute cafe take the left valley (half an hour) to Rumbak, or continue for one hour to **Yurutse** (4200m), an eerie one-house hamlet/homestay flanked by little stupas. Yurutse has a dribbling, drinkable spring and enjoys a perfectly framed view of Stok Kangri (6121m) through a cleft valley opposite.

Next day from Yurutse you could trek across the 4920m Ganda La in around six hours to **Shingo** village (two farms, both homestays), possibly continuing three hours further to **Kaya/Skiu** in the Markha Valley. Alternatively from Rumbak, a similarly strenuous trek crosses the equally high **Stok La** (Namling La) pass and reaches Stok in around seven hours (turn left and descend at the second mini-pass). If there's cloud on either pass don't hike without a guide.

LOWER ZANSKAR VALLEY
For a feast of stark, colourful geology, turn off the old Leh-Nimmu road at Km400 then take the riverside ledge road up the deep **Zanskar River** canyon.

The two house hamlet of **Sumdha Do**, where three- to five-day treks from Lamayuru, Wanla or Hinju typically culminate, has a summer tea-tent and the loveable **Tashi Khangsar** homestay.

At first glance tiny **Chiling** seems limited to a teahouse and the boxy shop-cafe **Kongma Restaurant**, where trekkers should pay the **Hemis National Park fee** (₹20 per day). The village proper is on a fertile plateau above to the right. All six families here offer homestays.

Chiling village was founded by the families of Nepali copper craftsmen. They originally arrived in Ladakh to build Shey Palace's classic Buddha statue and never went home. The handicraft continues, though today typical products are roughly turned-out heartshaped spoons (around ₹150). One of the best

known smiths is wizened old Ishay Namgyal whose house has a sizeable forge area in its yard. Finding the place takes you past some timeless old mud-brick buildings with a serrated dry-peak backdrop.

If trekking into the **Markha Valley**, continue 4km further south to the river confluence then cross the Zanskar on a dangling-basket ropeway contraption. A disputed road bridge, planned to replace this, remains half-built.

MARKHA VALLEY
Very well trodden tracks between diffuse roadless villages make this Ladakh's most popular trekking area. There are fort ruins at **Markha** and **Hankar** and several seasonal parachute cafes. Homestays exist in virtually every settlement but before hiking across the Kongmaru La (5050m), those without camping gear will need to spend a night at Nimaling tent-camp. From Nimaling allow nine hours walking to Shang Sumdo via Chokdo (seven hours). Both places have homestays and there's an 8am bus to Leh from Shang Sumdo. Allow at least five days for the Chiling–Nimaling–Shang Sumdo loop, including transport to/from Leh. Or simply explore the valley out-and-back from Chiling. Nicholas Eakins' full-colour *Markha Valley Trekking and Homestay Guide* (₹450) is useful.

West of Leh

PHYANG
Pretty Phyang is an emerald splash of treehemmed barley fields layered for miles up a side valley with stupendous views back towards the snow-topped pyramid of Stok Kangri. The white-and-ochre **Phyang Gompa** (admission ₹25) photogenically dominates the village, its west wing currently under fullscale reconstruction following earthquake damage. Behind, dzo graze their meadows and a beautiful lane follows a rock escarpment past traditional homes to Phyang's only accommodation (1.5km), the delightful **Hidden North Guest House** (☑226007; Phyang Tsakma; www.hiddennorth.com; campsite/ site & tent hire ₹100/150, d ₹800, without bathroom ₹500). Set in a mountain-facing sunflower garden, unfussy rooms are immaculately maintained and room 8 has Stok Kangri views. You might be tempted to stay awhile. Meals are available, filtered drinking water is free and off-beat treks can be organised.

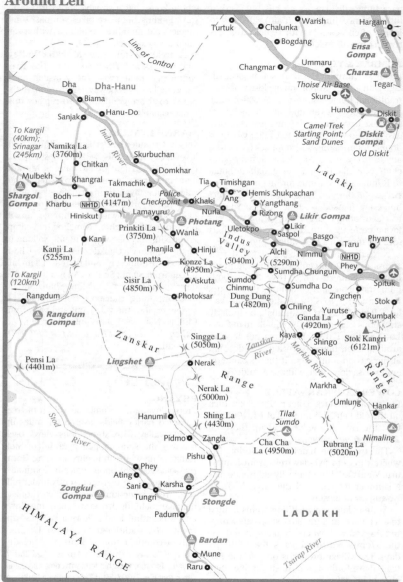

BASGO

Capital of lower Ladakh until the Ladakhi kingdoms united in 1470, Basgo's ancient chortens whisper hints of its antiquity. Rising above the village on a surreal collection of eroded earthen pinnacles are remnant stubs of once-great **citadel walls**, along with a largely derelict mud-walled **palace** and two brilliant **temples** (admission ₹20). The upper **Chamba Gompa** has spectacularly restored mural work covering walls and ceilings around a cartoonlike two-storey statue

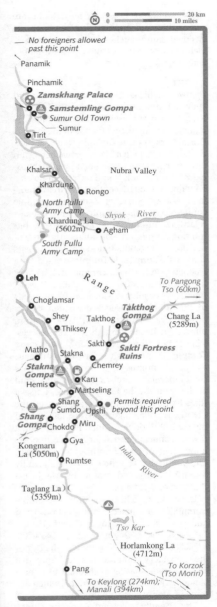

No foreigners allowed past this point

Panamik

Pinchamik

Zamskhang Palace

Samstemling Gompa

Sumur Old Town

Sumur

Tirit

Khalsar

Nubra Valley

Khardung

Rongo

North Pullu Army Camp

Shyok River

Khardung La (5602m)

Agham

South Pullu Army Camp

Leh

Range

To Pangong Tso (60km)

Choglamsar

Shey

Takthog

Takthog Gompa

Chang La (5289m)

Thiksey

Matho

Stakna

Sakti

Sakti Fortress Ruins

Stakna Gompa

Chemrey

Hemis

Karu

Martseling

Shang

Permits required beyond this point

Shang Gompa

Sumdo

Upshi

Chokdo

Miru

Kongmaru La (5050m)

Gya

Rumtse

Taglang La (5359m)

Tso Kar

Horlamkong La (4712m)

Pang

To Korzok (Tso Moriri)

To Keylong (274km); Manali (394km)

of Maitreya, whose expression embodies the spirit of detachment. Within the palace complex is the darker and even more atmospheric **Sar-Zung Temple** hosting another outsized Maitreya statue and a library of wrapped scriptures.

LIKIR

Surveying a grand section of mountain ridge, lower Likir has better value accommodation than at Alchi, making it a possible starting point for visiting the region. Around 4km above the main village, **Likir Gompa** (☉8am-1pm & 2-6pm summer, 10am-1pm & 2-4pm winter) very photogenically covers a hillside with archetypal Ladakhi buildings. Though founded in 1065, its current incarnation originated in the 15th century. The first prayer hall to the right on entry has seats allocated for both the Dalai Lama and his brother, Likir's honorary head lama. After two more colourful prayer halls you climb to the crammed-full, one-room **museum** (admission ₹20). The gompa is backed by a giant gilded 20th-century **Maitreya statue** that looks impressive from afar, less so once you notice its peeling gold paint.

For great photos of the gompa complex framed between barley fields and old chortens, descend for 10 minutes on the rocky footpath signed to the Old Likir Guesthouse.

There are half a dozen accommodation choices in lower Likir. Designed vaguely like a Chinese temple, **Hotel Lhukhil** (☏227137; www.hotellhukhil.com; d ₹1200-1800) has painted wall motifs, en suite bathrooms and mountain views from most rooms. There's oodles of outdoor sitting space and rates include breakfast and dinner.

Norboo Lagams Chow Guest House (☏227145; without bathroom d ₹200, dinner/breakfast ₹60/50) has compact but new, neat rooms hidden at the back of a farm-garden off the Yangthang road. Note that the only toilet is in the traditional house behind where there's also an ornate Ladaki kitchen-dining room.

Lotos Guest House (☏227177; per person incl meals ₹300), almost opposite Hotel Lhukhil, is relatively new and neat for a homestay. It has decent beds, dorm style in two rooms, but the toilet is in the yard.

Directly above the gompa are two homestay-guesthouses in traditional homesteads, each including breakfast and dinner in a wonderfully authentic Ladakhi dining room. **Chhuma Guest House** (☏9906973732; per person ₹200) has great views from two perfectly located if tatty mattress-on-floor rooms. Five minutes' walk beyond, **Dolker Guest House** (☏227141; per person ₹300) is similar but has real beds in the best, top-corner room.

SHAM

A few kilometres north of the main NH1D, the parallel 'Sham' route links several picturesque Ladakhi villages between Likir and Timishgan. The stark arid scenery here reaches some grand Nevada-style crescendos and the route is used as a homestay 'baby trek' to walkers who don't want to cross major passes. Daily bus connections mean you could do any one-day section then give up as you please. However, be aware that most of the trek is a road walk (only Hemis-Shukpachan to Ang is roadless) and there's minimal shade so hike early before the sun is high.

In timeless little **Yangthang**, sturdy old houses fit together, forming an architecturally cohesive square around a tiny shrine. Set in barley fields backed by a jagged horizon of saw-toothed mountains, the village has four traditional if basic **homestays** (per person ₹300) with floor mattresses and meals included. **Padma Guest House** (☎08991-922129) has fine views, its corner dorm-room overlooking the chasm that descends steeply to Rizong, a two-hour hike when the trail hasn't been washed away.

Central **Hemis Shukpachan** is a curiously medieval little knot of houses clustered around a central rocky hillock. Around 1km beyond at the village's northwest edge is a famous grove of **ancient juniper trees** beside the footpath leading towards Ang/Timishgan (a half-day walk). There are nearly a dozen widely scattered guesthouses and homestays. It's 10km west of Yangthang by a painfully bumpy jeep track.

The former co-capital of 14th-century lower Ladakh, **Timishgan** (Tingmosgan, Temisgam) sits at the centre of a very large, green Y-shaped valley stretching several kilometres to Ang (northeast) and Tia (northwest). It was here in 1864 that Ladakh signed treaties with Tibet allowing for formalised trade missions.

The mostly contemporary main **monastery** sits on a high, central rocky crag climbed by a large remnant section of fortress curtain-wall. There are two more small gompas in **Tia** which has an architecturally interesting central core. Central Timishgan and parts of **Ang** also have several fine old traditional Ladakhi houses offering basic **homestays** (incl food ₹200-400). Around 1km northeast of Timishgan's central junction, the **Namra Hotel** (☎229033; www.namrahotel.com; s/d/deluxe ₹1600/2200/2450) is far and away the Sham route's top accommodation option. Set in relaxing parasol-decked gardens, attractive common areas have bench seats and photos of local scenes. Rooms are reasonably well appointed, albeit with occasional damp patches and soft mattresses. Deluxe rooms have balcony areas with monastery views.

ALCHI

Central Alchi is 4km down a dead-end spur lane that leaves the Leh-Kargil road at Km370. This rural village has become a regional tourism magnet thanks to the famous **Chhoskhor Temple Complex** (foreigner/Indian ₹50/20; ⏲8am-1pm & 2-6pm), reached by an obvious pedestrian lane lined by guesthouses, souvenir peddlers and a German Bakery. Founded in the 11th century by 'Great Translator' Lotsava Ringchen Zangpo, the temple complex (no photography allowed) looks relatively uninteresting from outside but interior murals are considered the crowning glory of Ladakh's Indo-Tibetan art. Visits start with **Sumrtsek Temple** fronted by a wooden porch whose carving style is very much Indian rather than Tibetan. Inside, murals cover all three levels with hundreds of little Buddhas. Oversized wooden statues of Maitreya, Manjushri and Avalokitesvara burst their heads through into the inaccessible upper storey. Next along, **Vairocana Temple** is impressive for its mandalas: as antique murals in the rear chamber, as contemporary exercises in coloured sand at the front. In the **Lotsa Temple**, Lotsava Ringchen Zangpo himself appears as the slightly reptilian figure to the left behind the central Buddha cabinet. Beneath him, a row of comical-faced figures underline the importance of taking nothing too seriously. The **Manjushri Temple** enshrines a joyfully colourful four-sided statue of Manjushri (Buddha of Wisdom).

In summer Alchi has nearly a dozen accommodation choices. Many close from mid-September. **Heritage Guest House** (☎227125; dikit1920@gmail.com; d ₹400-800, without bathroom ₹250-300) right at the exit of the monastery complex, has an impressive carved facade that leads through to a marble floored interior courtyard, off which are some of Alchi's best-value rooms.

The friendly, colourful **Choksor Guest House** (☎227084; r ₹500-600), with shrine room and open roof-terrace, is set in a flower garden 800m back towards Leh from central Alchi. Next door the sadly derelict, once-grand **Lonpo House** was formerly home to the Ladakhi King's local tax collector.

Hotel Potala (☎205030; downstairs/upstairs
d ₹350/600) is fair value and central, with en
suite bathrooms set in a small garden and
hollyhocks enlivening gravel sitting areas.

At **Lotsava Summer Camp** (☎227129; d
₹300-500) close-packed bedded tents share
a bathroom block. Prices are reduced if you
forgo the by-bucket option of hot water.

ULETOKPO & RIZONG

From pretty **Uletokpo** village, an erosion-
prone lane leaves the Leh-Khalsi highway
and climbs 6km along a narrow gorge. It
dead-ends at the photogenic 19th-century
Rizong Gompa (admission by donation; ☺7am-
1pm & 1.30-6pm), stepped handsomely up an
amphitheatre of rocky cliff. A steep, sometimes treacherous footpath continues up to
Yangthang.

Uletokpo has three tourist camps. The
best value if least manicured is **West Ladakh
Camp** (☎9419178555; d ₹1500) where octagonal bedded tents in an apricot orchard come
with shower, toilet and clamshell glass wash-
basins. Add ₹1000 for all meals. **Uley Ethnic
Resort** (☎227208) has many overpriced tent
rooms but is building sturdy new river-view
cabins with solar-heated bathrooms.

KHALSI

Comparatively bustling Khalsi has shops,
taxis, PCO phone booths, two basic **restau-
rant-hotels** (d ₹500) and several other eateries including relatively convivial **Samyas
Garden Restaurant** (mains ₹50-140, rice ₹40).
Taxis charge around ₹700 to Lamayuru or
Phanjila. Hitch-hiking westbound, it's generally easier to start from the checkpoint
2km west.

DHA-HANU

Foreigners with prearranged **permits** (apply in Leh) may take the lovely, increasingly
dramatic Indus Valley road northwest of
Khalsi as far as Dha. Just before reaching the
walnut-growing village of **Domkhar**, look
across the river for fine views of terraced
Takmachik. Picturesque **Skurbuchan** village is topped by a rickety gompa-fort overlooking the Indus canyon. Scattered ancient
petroglyphs are inscribed on brown, time-
polished roadside rocks (eg at Km55.9) but
they're small, hard to spot and some are
latter-day imitations. From **Sanjak** a side
road cuts through a sharp gorge to Chitkan.
Kargil-bound shared jeeps (₹150) via Chitkan depart at 6.30am from near Sanjak's

bridge where there are teahouses and single
guesthouse.

Dha (pop 250) is a centre of the Brokpa
people (see boxed text, right). Though outnumbered these days by 'one pen' kids, a few
Brokpa people still wear pearly button ear
decorations and traditional hats, with older
women tying their hair in long triple-stranded
braids reminiscent of knotted dreadlocks.

The bus from Leh sputters to an unexpected halt at a middle-of-nowhere lay-by, from
where Dha village is a 10-minute walk via the
small footpath immediately opposite. Amid
Dha's tomato gardens, apricot orchards and
huddles of rough stone barns you'll pass
mud-floored **Skybapa Guest House** (dm/d
₹200/400). It's simple with shared squat toilets across the yard, but a great feature is the
outdoor dining area shaded by a vast grapevine that thrives in Dha's unexpectedly warm
microclimate. Friendly owners make their
own organic wine.

With linguistic help, other homestays can
be arranged in Dha or in less striking **Bia-
ma**, 3km back towards Leh, where there's
also an overpriced roadside tent-camp.

A two-day Leh-Dha return jeep-excursion
costs ₹4631 per vehicle. The three-day circuit
Leh–Dha–Chitkan–Kargil–Lamayuru–Leh
costs ₹10,200. Foreigners are not allowed to
use the Dha–Battalik–Kargil road.

YAPOLA VALLEY

Several classic villages that were previously
only accessible to trekkers have recently become accessible with new (if often washed-
out) jeep roads.

Perched above **Wanla** village on a towering knife-edge ridge is the tiny, medieval **Wanla Gompa** (www.achiassociation.org;

LOST TRIBES

The facial features of the Brokpa (aka
Drokpa or Dard, 'people of the pastures') have led to speculation that the
tribe was descended from Alexander
the Great's invasion force or even a
lost tribe of Israel. However, based on
their dialect, they are thought to have
immigrated to Dha-Hanu from Gilgit/
Baltistan (just across what is now the
India–Pakistan border) around a millennium ago. Some Brokpas still follow
an animist faith that incorporates
elements of the ancient Bon religion,
precursor of Tibetan Buddhism.

admission ₹20; ☉dawn-dusk), flanked by tower remnants of a now-destroyed 14th-century fortress. The monastery's carved porch is reminiscent of Alchi's and its spookily dark prayer-chamber contains three large statues backed by ancient smoke-blackened murals and naive statuettes. If hiking in from Lamayuru you'll pass close to some desultory hot springs 4km west of Wanla but they aren't worth a special excursion. Hidden **Rongstak Guest House** (per person incl meals ₹400) is the most attractive of three homestays in Wanla proper but the area's most convivial accommodation choice is the very well kept **Tarchit Camp** (☑254866, 9419243601; per person incl meals ₹450), 2km beyond Wanla beside the Phanjila road. There are homestay mattress spaces in a traditional family dining room, one new private room and a sizeable camping area (₹100) with separate horse-tethering. **Singey La Camp** (per person ₹100) at **Phanjila** has a garden restaurant and three mat-on-floor sleeping spaces.

At the top of pretty **Hinju** village there's a recommended **homestay** with traditional Ladakhi kitchen. A fabulous two-day trek to Sumdha Do on the Chiling road can be done as a homestay **trek** (guide essential) if you're prepared to do a long, strenuous first day, crossing the 4950m Konze La for breathtaking views then sleeping at Sumdho Chinmu.

South of Phanjila a seriously rough jeep track follows the spectacular **Yapola Gorge** to its fork then veers right to **Honupatta**, a tight-knit village with three basic homestays tucked away in the upper section. Mudslides often block vehicular traffic on the track beyond which climbs the 4805m Sisir-La for sensational views of ridges and rocky spires before descending to **Photoksar**. Most **Zanskar-bound treks** follow this jeep road but, on foot, it's reputedly possible to hike an alternative route down the Yapola Gorge's left fork via Askuta camp, at least when water levels are low. Finding a suitably experienced guide might prove hard.

LAMAYURU
☑01982 / ELEV 3390M

Set among mountain-backed badlands, low-paced Lamayuru is one of Ladakh's most memorable villages and an ideal place to break the Kargil–Leh journey.

☉ Sights & Activities

Picturesque homes huddle around a crumbling hilltop that's pitted with caves and topped by the ultra-photogenic **Yungdrung**

Gompa (admission ₹50). Behind glass within the gompa's main prayer hall is a tiny cave in which 11th-century mystic Naropa meditated. Before that, legend claims, this whole area had been the bottom of a deep lake whose waters receded miraculously thanks to the powerful prayers of Buddhist saint Arahat Nimagung. Sculpted by time into curiously draped forms, the sands of that former lake-bed now form 'moonland' landscapes beside the new Leh road around 1km east of town.

Lamayuru is traditionally the starting point for some of Ladakh's greatest treks (to Zanskar, Chiling etc). Although new roads mean that walkers can now choose to reach advance trailheads (Honupatta/Photoksar, Hinju etc) by jeep, Lamayuru remains the most hopeful place for organising your own packhorses/donkeys (₹330 per day including driver), sometimes possible within a day or two. Guesthouses can help or ask **Royal Caravan Trek** (☑9469384434) at the bus stand who can also arrange jeep charters and, in extremis, currency exchange (terrible rates).

🛏 Sleeping & Eating

Lamayuru only gets electricity from 7.30pm to 11pm and some guesthouse rooms lack powerpoints. Accommodation prices will probably rise if/when Kashmir stabilises and transit tourist numbers recover.

Hotel Moonland   HOTEL $
(☑224551; d ₹600-800) Lamayuru's best hotel is set in a garden at the first hairpin, 400m beyond the bus stop. Rooms offer little in terms of decor but have tiled bathrooms and hot showers while the agreeable restaurant has postcard-perfect views back towards the monastery complex. Limited menu.

Dragon Guest House   GUESTHOUSE $
(☑224501; d ₹500, without bathroom ₹300) Simpler rooms are a decent size in a big, clean traditional house with olde-worlde Ladakhi kitchen. A few newer rooms come with geyser-equipped private bathroom and the pleasant garden restaurant serves nonguests too.

Tharpaling Guest House   GUESTHOUSE $
(☑224516; d ₹300, without bathroom ₹200, half-board ₹500/400) Ever-smiling matriarch Tsiring Yandol gives this place a jolly family feel, serving communal dinners in a dining room that's new but with traditional-style painted motifs.

Hotel Niranjana   MONASTERY HOTEL $
(☎224555; r without bathroom ₹400-600) The main selling point is its location right beside the monastery complex, ideal for those attending 5.30am prayers. Above a dark, cavernous restaurant, rooms are bland but comfy enough, many with fine views. Clean shared bathrooms have geysers.

❶ Getting There & Away
Daily Kargil–Leh buses briefly stop in Lamayuru sometime between 9am and 10am in both directions. Chitkan–Leh buses stop eastbound around 11am Monday, Wednesday and Saturday. Khalsi has more choice of buses.

WEST OF LAMAYURU
From Lamayuru, the NH1D road zigzags up towards Iguanodon-back spires that tower impressively over the **Fotu La** (4147m). At Km281 a rough 12km spur road leads to Kanji with its small but very historic **Chuchik-Zhal Temple** (www.achiassociation.org). After **Hansukot** (Heniskot; Km282), with its tourist bungalow and vague fortress ruins, a comparatively wide, fertile valley extends as far as **Khangral** (Km268) where passports are checked beside the Chitkan-Dha road junction. The NH1D then crosses the **Namika La** (3760m pass) and descends into the glorious **Wakha Valley** continuing to Kargil via **Mulbekh** (p240) and **Shargol** (p241).

Nubra Valley
☎01980
The deep valleys of the Shyok and Nubra Rivers offer tremendous yet accessible scenery (permit required) with green oasis villages surrounded by thrillingly stark scree slopes, boulder fields and harsh arid mountains. Visiting from Leh by chartered jeep, including Panamik, Diskit, Hunder and everything in between, costs ₹6931 per vehicle (or ₹7331 if you add Ensa Gompa). While it's possible to do all that in two days, lengthy view stops are the main attraction so taking a third day is recommended and costs no extra. You'll certainly need that extra day (or more) if adding in Turtuk (around ₹3000 extra).

KHARDUNG LA
ELEV 5602M
Zigzagging up a stark bare-rock mountain from Leh, it takes around 1½ hours to reach 5602m **Khardung La** (Km39), disputably claimed to be the world's highest motorable pass. Celebrate by sipping a cuppa at the pass-top canteen, buy T-shirts at the souve-

nir shop or, if your altitude acclimatisation allows, get dizzy clambering five minutes to a viewpoint through a chaos of prayer flags and boulders. Beyond Khardung La, as the road descends northbound alongside a gurgling stream, keep your eyes open for Himalayan marmots and grazing dzo. Permits are checked at army camps at Km24 and Km53.

KHARDUNG
The yak-herding village of Khardung (Km71) is a two-centred shelf of barley fields and scattered Ladakhi buildings set within a jaw-dropping bowl of arid crags, giant tiger-paw bluffs and the distantly glimpsed teeth of snow-mountains. Tiny roadside **shop-cafes** (dhal ₹20) dish up delicious dhal while **Cho Guest House** (per person ₹400) offers mattresses on the floor of a large room with en suite squat toilet. Prices include breakfast, dinner and tea.

Beyond Khardung, the road descends through Grand Canyon scenery towards the impressively wide **Shyok Valley**, where soaring red-brown cliff-mountains rise from the gleaming grey-white sand of the floodplain.

DISKIT
ELEV 3144M
Schizophrenic Diskit has two very different centres. Nubra's biggest settlement, **Central Diskit**, is a comparatively unattractive place by Ladakh's very high standards, but it has the area's **bus/taxi stand**, a useful **bazaar**, a **tourist reception centre** and the region's only **petrol pump** (1km north towards Hunder). Follow the bazaar east to a small roundabout then turn right to find the power-cut prone **NI Internet cafe** (per hr ₹100).

This lane leads 1.5km further south rejoining the main road at Old Diskit.

◉ Sights
Old Diskit is a hamlet full of prayer wheels, mani walls and clusters of old stupas with a collapsing little old temple and a derelict Ladakhi mansion-palace.

Directly above Old Diskit, a 2km spaghetti of hairpins winds up to the 17th-century **Diskit Gompa** (admission ₹20), a brilliant jumble of Tibetan-style box buildings piled higgledy-piggledy up a steep rocky peak that ends in a toe-curlingly vertical chasm. On an intermediate hill, the access road passes a gigantic (32m) full-colour **Statue of Chamba** (Maitreya-Buddha), formally inaugurated by the Dalai Lama in July 2010.

🛏 Sleeping & Eating

OLD DISKIT

Lhasthang Guest House & Restaurant
HOTEL $

(☑220165, 9469176104; d ₹600, without bathroom ₹350) Directly beneath the gompa turning, this new, sparkling-clean place has big expansion plans, Buddha views from its open roof-terrace and excellent bathrooms with geysers.

Sunrise Guest House
GUESTHOUSE $

(☑220011; r ₹500, without bathroom ₹250; ☺year-round) Reached through a 'tunnel stupa', this ageing stalwart has decent-sized guestrooms and is set in a small sunflower garden amid scattered Buddhist ruins. Two newer rooms have private bathrooms.

CENTRAL DISKIT

Several decent options lie in quiet lanes conveniently close to the bazaar.

Spangla Guest House
GUESTHOUSE $

(☑220022; d without bathroom ₹250-300) Neatly set in a rose and vegetable garden beside NI Internet, this female-run guesthouse is lovingly maintained, there's a traditional-style dining room and the shared bathrooms have geysers.

Sand Dune Guest House
GUESTHOUSE $

(☑220022; r ₹400-600, without bathroom ₹200-250) Shaded by apricot trees, the garden courtyard makes a pleasant oasis from the nearby bazaar. Rooms vary considerably in size and style but all are well kept and the family is friendly.

❶ Getting There & Away

Leh-bound shared jeeps (₹300, 4½ hours) leave frequently between 6am and 9am. From Leh, these start near the *zabakhana* (abattoir, Map p246). Buses to Diskit depart from virtually every main Nubra village before 7am, returning from Diskit after lunch. A morning bus runs from Diskit to Sumur.

HUNDER (HUNDUR)

Lost in greenery and closely backed by soaring valley cliffs, Hunder village is a popular overnight stop 10km from Diskit.

◉ Sights & Activities

Hunder Gompa contains a large gilded Chamba statue and a crude trail climbs to a precarious little ridgetop **fort**. Photogenic **sand dunes** starting 3km east of the village (500m from the army camp) can be explored on touristy **Bactrian camel rides** (per 15min ₹150, one-way to Diskit ₹700). Host camels are reputedly offspring of animals that plied the Ladakh–Xinjiang caravans up until the closure of the India-China border in the 1940s. Hunder's dunes aren't exactly Sahara-sized but the landscape can prove disorientating so, if attempting to walk back to Diskit, bring plenty of water, stick relatively near to the road and beware following dead-end camel tracks into impenetrable thorn thickets.

🛏 Sleeping & Eating

Hunder has around a dozen garden guesthouses, mostly clumped into two loose groupings around 1.4km apart, with Himalayan and Snow Leopard lying in between. The first, lower group (Karma, Mehreen, Olgok, Padma) is around 1km north of the army camp. The second forms Hunder's vague 'centre' where the village lane turns a right-angle beside Jamshed Guesthouse. About 200m further there's a small grocery shop on the paved side lane that runs to the Ibex and Goba guesthouses. Arrange meals with your accommodation or eat in Diskit.

Three seriously overpriced 'luxury' camps charge ₹3300 full-board for bedded tents with outside shared bathrooms.

Goba Guest House
GUESTHOUSE $

(☑221083; d from ₹200) Choose upper options with private bathroom, especially room 8 (₹600) which has wraparound windows and a terrace with views. Staff are remarkably obliging, the setting is lovely and the food is reliably good.

Ibex Guest House
GUESTHOUSE $

(☑9469264242; d ₹600) Set in an unusually neat garden, this new bungalow home offers super-clean en suite rooms off a tiled central dining area.

Karma Inn
HOTEL $$

(☑221042; karmaleh@yahoo.co.in; d ₹2000, half-board ₹2600) Ten spacious, comparatively smart rooms with big bathrooms, firm beds and bay-window seating overlook an extensive garden backed by a panorama of mountains. Coming from Diskit, follow signs towards the 'Organic Camp', around 2km before central Hunder.

Snow Leopard Guest House
GUESTHOUSE $

(☑221097; r ₹500-800) Hunder's biggest and busiest guesthouse encloses a splendid central garden. Older rooms have traditional ceilings and squat toilets, newer rooms are bigger with sit-down loos.

Olgok Guest House HOMESTAY GUESTHOUSE $
(☎221092; d ₹600) Three excellent new rooms with sparkling clean bathrooms in an unremarkable concrete bungalow set in a large if scrappy garden near Karma Inn. The nearby **Padma** is similar.

Himalayan Guest House GUESTHOUSE $
(☎221131; r ₹450, without bathroom ₹300) Tucked into a warren of village footpaths, rooms here are fairly standard but the welcome is heartfelt.

BEYOND HUNDER
Since June 2010, permits allow you to drive 90km beyond Hunder following the turbulent **Shyok valley** along its scenically magnificent route to Turtuk. It cascades through a narrow canyon to tiny **Changmar** after which the raw-rock cliff-mountains become even more impressive. The rare, green splashes of village beyond are culturally and linguistically Balti rather than Ladakhi. Visitors are extremely rare and can expect considerable attention. The two biggest Balti villages, **Bogdang** and **Turtuk**, both have attractive centres that are almost invisible from the road. To reach central Turtuk, cross the bridge towards Tyakshi (closed to tourists) then turn immediately left. After 500m cross back on a conspicuous green footbridge and walk five minutes along a very scenic upper pathway to find **Maha Guest House** (☎248040; extremeadvindia@gmail.com; with/without windows ₹700/600, meals ₹100). While a tad pricey given the shared flush squat toilet, it's new, very clean and the owners speak English. On the main road Turtuk's only other accommodation option is **Turtuk Holiday** (☎248103; s/d ₹919/1335, half-board ₹1366/2191), nine bedded tents sharing a trio of outside bathrooms. Turtuk's three minuscule 'restaurants' can only manage instant noodles.

The Turtuk-Hunder road is almost entirely asphalted. The drive takes under three hours eastbound but westbound allow far longer as at least nine military check posts en route will entertain you with their interminable bureaucracy. You'll need a dozen permit photocopies.

SUMUR & PANAMIK
The Nubra River proper descends towards the Shyok from the heavily disputed Siachen Glacier, the world's highest battleground (between India and Pakistan). With standard Nubra permits foreigners can take the recently asphalted road as far as Hargam Bridge.

NUBRA NAMES

Note that on many maps, the names for several western Nubra settlements don't correspond at all with local reality.

ON MAPS	LOCALLY USED
Thoise village	Terchey
Khar	Skuru
Yaglung	Changmar
Biadango	Bogdang

At Km12 the road bypasses **Tirit village**, with views across the valley to a long **waterfall** spurting out of the bare rock-face. Spooky **Zonzhar Gompa** is a small ruin atop a roadside knoll at Km16.5. At first sight **Sumur** (Km22.5) seems little more than the trio of uninspired restaurants at a road junction. However to explore Sumur proper turn right here following the pleasantly green 'link' road past J&K Bank. After 2km, leading past several well-spaced guest houses and prayer wheels, turn left at a road fork and wind up another 1.5km to find the colourful if extensively rebuilt **Samstemling Gompa** (donation appropriate, ◷6am-6pm). The gompa is alternatively accessible by driving a 2km asphalted spur road from Km25 on the main road, ie the northern end of intriguing **Tegar** (Tiger) village. Directly overlooking that junction, the eerie rubble of Nubra's former royal citadel leads up to the largely intact three-storey shell of **Zamskhang Palace** (unguarded). Cautiously climb to the roof for stunning valley views.

Pinchamik (Km29) is a timeless hamlet full of prayer wheels, chortens and costumed old folk carrying baskets full of greens on their backs.

Panamik (Km44–48) is a diffuse low-rise hamlet with a sprinkling of budget guest houses. At the southern end are two famous but utterly forgettable dribbles of ferric-orange hot spring. Bathing is possible. Panamik's main attraction is the scenery of surrounding valleys, best appreciated from the bridge just west of **Hargam** (Km49). Since 2010, permits allow you to cross that bridge and double back down a very rough road (part stream) towards little **Ensa Gompa**. However, Ensa's single resident monk seems far from excited to see visitors, and the small, partly collapsing buildings are less interesting than the hair-raising 25-minute access trek along red-rock ledges from the nearest driveable track (a road is planned eventually).

JAMMU & KASHMIR (INCLUDING LADAKH) NUBRA VALLEY

📥 Sleeping & Eating

Most guesthouses can arrange simple meals (around ₹80) and allow camping (₹100) in their gardens.

SUMUR

Near J&K Bank, almost at the main junction, **AO Guest House** (☑223506; r ₹250-400) is convenient for buses and is set in a garden of roses and hollyhocks. The best rooms are on the rooftop.

Some 600m up Sumur Link Rd are peaceful **Saser Guest House** (☑223501; d without/with bathroom ₹200/400) and similar **K,Sar Guest House** (☑9469177479; d ₹300, dm/d without bathroom ₹120/200), both pleasant low-rise houses set in garden-fields which is where you'll find the shared bathrooms for the cheaper rooms. K,Sar has a bright dorm room and generous meals are served family style at a central communal table.

Around 300m further, **Namgyal Guest House** (☑223505, 9419887505; d without/with view ₹600/700, without bathroom ₹350) is an attractive two-storey building where the best rooms have good tiled bathrooms and survey distant mountains across the organic vegetable garden.

A former traveller favourite, the basic **Largyal Guest House** (☑223537) is due to re-open in 2011 with at least one new ensuite room.

Where the link road forks after 2km, head right to find Sumur's two 'luxury' camps. **Mystic Meadows** (☑9419178944; d ₹1500, full board ₹3000) has bedded tents complete with a pebble-floored toilet set around a verdant vegetable garden. **Silk Route Cottages** (☑253439; d ₹2200, full board ₹3300) features claustrophobically tight-packed cottages, some made of bamboo, others of bamboo-clad concrete.

TEGAR

Tegar has two hotels, both slightly smarter than Sumur's guest houses but at vastly higher prices. Both are off the main road around Km24.5. **Hotel Yarabtso** (☑223544; s/d ₹1606/1784, full board ₹2160/2920) has the more impressive traditional-style facade and sits in farm-sized grounds but bathrooms at **Rimo Hotel** (☑223528; kesarbardam@hotmail.com; s/d ₹1700/1900, full board ₹3100/3300) are more polished. Standards vary between rooms at either hotel so look at a few.

PANAMIK

Panamik has five budget guest houses. **Nebula** (☑247013; Km44.3; d ₹350) has the best kept rooms and its shared bathroom is indoors. **Bangka** (☑247044; Km44.7; d ₹250) and

Charon (☑247011; Km43.8; d ₹300) have family vibes with some rooms good, others less so. Toilets are in their attractive gardens. **Hot Springs Guest House** (☑247043; without/with bathroom ₹300/400) is the only Panamik place so far with ensuite bathrooms but despite the floral setting, its rooms are lacklustre. **Saser Restaurant** (☑247021; Km44.8; d ₹300) has three small but decent rooms sharing an indoor squat loo but it lacks personality.

East of Leh

Permits are required for Pangong Tso or to continue east of Upshi.

SHEY

Once one of Ladakh's royal capitals, Shey is an attractive, pond-dappled oasis from which rises a central dry rocky ridge, inscribed with roadside **Buddha carvings** (Km459). Along the rising ridge-top, a series of **fortress ruins** bracket the three-storey, 17th-century **Naropa Royal Palace** whose wholesale reconstruction is nearing completion. The palace **temple** (admission ₹20; ⊗6am-6pm) contains a highly revered 7.5m-tall gilded-copper **Buddha**, originally installed in 1645. The upper door opens to his inscrutably smirking face, a rarely open hall below views his torso.

For the most photogenic views of Shey's palace ridge, walk part-way along the access track to the simple, semi-dormant **Besthang Guest House** (☑267556; r without bathroom ₹300) then turn around.

Experienced teachers are in demand for volunteer work at the local, architecturally innovative, ecofriendly **Druk White Lotus School** (www.dwls.org).

THIKSEY

Glorious **Thiksey Gompa** (☑267011; admission ₹30, video ₹100; ⊗6am-1pm & 1.30-6pm, festival Oct/Nov) is one of Ladakh's biggest and most recognisable monasteries. Covering a large rocky outcrop with layered Tibetan-style buildings, it's a veritable monastic village incorporating shops, a school, restaurant and hotel. The **main gompa** starts with a prayer chamber containing a 14m-high Buddha whose expression is simultaneously peaceful, smirking and vaguely menacing. Smaller but much more obviously ancient is the **Gonkhang** (Protectors' Temple) and little rooftop **library**. A **museum** hidden away beneath the monastery restaurant displays well-labelled Tantric artefacts, some carved from human bones. Notice the 10 weapons symbolically used to combat evil spirits.

Thiksey has an interesting dawn *puja* but it has become disproportionately popular with tourists who, in summer, often outnumber the monks.

Pedestrian access is a steep climb from near Km455. By car it's a 1.5km loop starting from Km454.2 where monastery-run **Chamba Hotel** (☑267005; d ₹1500, without bathroom ₹500) has fair-value if unexotic older courtyard rooms and newer, relatively plush en suite rooms within a traditionally styled two-storey building. The monastery itself also has some **guest rooms** (upper/lower r without bathroom ₹500/300) beneath the gompa museum.

STAKNA

Small but visually impressive, the 1618 **Stakna Gompa** (admission ₹30; ☺8am-7pm) crowns a rocky outcrop that rises like an island out of the Indus Valley floor. Off the gompa's small central courtyard, four rooms with vivid new Tantric murals can be visited. Behind the main prayer hall, sub-shrines retain 400-year-old sandalwood statues, original frescoes and statuettes of the Bhutanese lamas who founded the monastery. From the Leh–Thiksey bus terminus (Km449), the complex is 1.7km away (less on foot), crossing the Indus on a narrow suspension bridge decked with prayer flags then climbing a winding access road.

HEMIS

The 1672 **Hemis gompa** (www.drukpa-hemis.org; admission ₹100; ☺8am-1pm & 2-6pm) is the spiritual centre of Ladakh's **Drukpa Buddhists** (www.drukpa.org). Documents supposedly found here were used to support Jesus-in-India conspiracists' notion that Christ visited Kashmir (p234). However, for all its fame, the main monastery has a rectilinear exterior that lacks the vertically stacked perfection of Chemrey or Thiksey. Inside, the fine central courtyard has plenty of colourfully detailed timbers but the main prayer hall is undergoing long-term reconstruction and the Guru Lhakhang's 8m-high statue of Padmasambhava is garish. The monastery's extensive museum has some very precious religious treasures mixed in with spurious tiger skins, swords and a bra-shaped wooden cup-case.

The annual **Tse-Chu festival** (☺Jul) sees three days of masked dances and every 12th year (next in 2016) the festival culminates in the unfurling of Hemis' famous three-storey-high, pearl-encrusted *thangka*.

Below the gompa, timeless Hemis village spills out of a craggy red-rock canyon with mountain and valley panoramas as you descend the winding 7km back to Karu, passing a pair of astonishingly long *mani* walls.

SHANG

Many visitors end their Markha trek (p263) in the barley fields around diffuse **Shang Sumdo**. However, few visitors venture 5km up the side valley to **Shang** above which a tiny but extremely dramatic **gompa** rises on a prominent crag with many semiderelict mud-brick houses around its base. The stark, riverside road from Karu (15km) is being asphalted.

Towards Pangong Tso

Chemrey and Takthog can be visited independently but permits are required for serene Pangong Tso, arguably Ladakh's loveliest lake. The whole route is scenically magnificent and constantly varied with serrated peaks, trickling streams, horse meadows, reflective ponds and drifting sands. Parched dry desert mountains form dazzling ochre counterpoints to the deep blue skies, some remaining snow-dusted even in August.

You'll cross the **Chang La** (5289m), India's third-highest motorable pass and probably the only one offering free cups of tea (courtesy of the Indian Army).

All but 20km of the Leh–Lukung road is now asphalted allowing masochistic tourists to pack a basic Pangong Tso experience into an exhaustingly long day trip. However, it's vastly more pleasurable to stay the night in pretty **Spangmik** or, more adventurously, in enchanting **Merak**. Foreigners can't (yet) visit Chushul nor the fabled 17th-century Hanle Palace.

One/two day jeep tours from Leh cost ₹5160/6143 (per vehicle) to Spangmik, ₹5960/7300 to Merak. A minivan excursion Leh–Chemrey–Takthog–Hemis–Leh costs ₹1785.

Km readings are initially from Karu (add 35km for Leh) then reset to zero at Tangtse (Km81). Petrol is not available beyond Karu.

CHEMREY

Spectacularly viewed across barley fields and buckthorn bushes, Chemrey village is dominated by the beautifully proportioned **Thekchhok Gompa** (admission ₹20; ☺festival Nov) covering a steep hillock with a maze of pathways and Tibetan buildings. Above the

Utterly beautiful but exhaustingly spine-jangling, this is a ride you won't forget. The Upshi–Keylong section crosses four passes over 4900m, and then there's the infamously unpredictable Rohtang Pass before Manali. Although the road is 'normally' open from June to late September, unseasonable snow or major landslides can close it for days (or weeks). There's no petrol station for 365km between Karu and Tandi (8km south of Keylong). When the road is open, straight-through jeeps should take 22 to 25 exhausting hours. Most travel agencies plus the **Ladakh Taxi Operators Cooperative** (Map p246; ☑252723;☺6am-7.30pm) organise shared through-jeeps (back/middle ₹1300/1500) departing around midnight. Hiring your own jeep (approximately ₹15,000 per vehicle) with at least one overnight stop means you can have more space and more time for photo stops.

Bus services (p259) take two days overnighting in Keylong.

Which Direction is Best?

Southbound you'll be better acclimatised for high altitude sleeps (Pang or Sarchu); you could visit Tso Moriri en route; and, if there's a major landslide on the Rohtang Pass, you could 'escape' by walking two hours down to Mahri, a group of cafes jammed with day-trip tourist traffic from Manali.

Northbound jeep rental can prove much cheaper from Manali, if you find Ladakhi vehicles returning otherwise empty.

Which Overnight Stop(s)?

» Overnighting in **Sarchu** handily breaks the journey into two roughly equal sections but the altitude can cause problems. Private minibuses overnighting at Sarchu Tent Camps run sporadically; tickets are usually sold through **Vajra Voyages** (☑9906999135; Main Bazaar, Leh) and **Tiger Eye Adventure** (☑01902252718; www.tigereyeadventure.com; Old Manali).

» **Keylong**, **Jispa** or **Gemur** offer more comfortable accommodation and significantly lower altitude but Leh–Keylong is a very long day's ride (around 14/17 hours by jeep/bus).

» To make a three-day ride you might stop at **Pang** plus **Keylong**. However at Pang (4634m) facilities are rudimentary and there are altitude worries if you're not acclimatised.

» Other lonelier parachute cafes offer handy rest stops for acclimatised cyclists.

Km by Km to Keylong

» **Km425 Upshi**: shops, teahouses. The southbound Manali road leaves the Indus Valley.

» **Km410 Miru**: village with shattered fortress and numerous stupas. Beyond is a beautiful, narrow valley edged with serrated vertical mineral strata in alternating layers of vivid red-purple and ferrous green.

» **Km398 Gya**: picturesque village. Across the river is another crumbling crag-top fortress.

» **Km394 Rumtse**: last village for 250km. Then lonely rough road climbs through numerous hairpins to **Taglang La** (5359m), claimed to be the world's second-highest road pass (after Khardung La). South of Taglang La, the wide Moray Plains are edged with smooth peaks.

appealingly wobbly 17th-century prayer hall, the **Lama Lhakhang** has murals blackened to semi-invisibility by butter-lamp smoke. On the penultimate floor the **Guru Lhakhang** has contrastingly vivid colours and a 3m-high golden Padmasambhava statue en-

crusted with turquoise ornamentation. The monastery access lane starts from near Km8.

SAKTI & TAKTHOG
Branching off at Km10.4, a paved side-lane passes through **Sakti**, a spread-out village of gently terraced fields, waterlogged meadows

» **Km341** Jeep track signposted 'Pastureland Camp' leads towards **Tso Kar**, a sizeable lake ringed by round-topped, snow-speckled mountains.

» *Km297** **Pang** (4634m): a gaggle of similar **parachute cafes** (bed space ₹100). For serious altitude problems, the army camp's **AMS unit** 800m away provides free oxygen.

» **Km287** The road rises through a memorable, spiky-edged canyon before crossing **Lachung La** (5035m).

» *Km270** **Dolma Tibetan** (per person ₹100): a lonely, basic parachute cafe with a few mattresses laid on stony ground. Thereafter the road crosses **Nakeela La** (4915m), descends the 21 switchbacks of the **Gata Loops** then trundles through two very photogenic valleys featuring Cappadocia-style erosion formations.

» **Km222** **Sarchu**: 'wine' shop plus 10 parachute cafes, many offering ₹100 communal bed-spaces. Better than most options, **Mount View Dhaba** (tr/q ₹500/800) rents whole bedded tents but there's still no bathroom.

» *Km216–214** **Sarchu Tent Camps**: six more upmarket camps almost side-by-side along an attractive grassy valley. Most have bedded tents with attached toilets and tap/wash-basin though size and quality vary both between and within properties. Marginally the most attractive tents are at **Antrek Camp** (www.antrek.co.in; Km214.3; bed/half-board ₹2000/2800) but a better deal and almost as good are the smaller 'standard' tents (₹1000/2000) at orange-topped **Goldrop** (www.ladakhmanali.com/camping.htm; Km215.1) whose hard toilet floors are more comfy than stone cobbles or mud floors.

» *Km197** **Bharatpur**: eight **parachute cafes** (bed-space ₹100-150) in a lovely high-altitude valley. **Biru Dhaba** has the sturdiest stone-sided communal sleeping tent.

» *Km176** **Zingzingbar Restaurant**: one of three *dhabas* on the long steady descent from 4850m **Baralacha Pass**.

» **Km174** Surreally isolated tyre repair tent.

» **Km169** **Zingzingbar road-camp**.

» *Km159.5** **Hozer Café** (bed-space ₹200): sleeps 15. An opal blue pond reflects the mountains. Around 2.5km from **Patsio Camp**.

» *Km143** **Darcha Bridge**, passport check and several *dhabas* including **Lhasa Food Corner** (bed-space ₹80) at the bridge's south side: friendly, female-run, has an unusually clean outdoor toilet. After a few days asking around it's possible to find **horses** for the trek to Zanskar (p242). Buses are generally full by the time they reach Darcha but, heading south, standing for the 30km to Keylong isn't too bad.

» *Km139–138** **Jispa**: has three roadside hotels; **Padma Lodge** (d ₹1000-1400) is the best value.

» *Km134** **Gemur**: pretty little Lahaul village whose single three-room hotel, **Gemoor Khar** (☎9459103910; www.hotelsnowviewmanali.com/gemoor.htm; tent/d/lux ₹1000/1320/1650) is a British-style house with exposed stone walls and flagged bathrooms.

» *Km115** **Keylong** (p338): the first real town. Plenty of hotels.

* accommodation available (very basic communal sleeping spaces unless otherwise indicated)

and dry-stone walls. The lane skirts Sakti's shattered stone **fortress** ruins (also visible from the main road above) and after nearly 5km, passes beside **Takthog (Dakthok) Gompa** (donation appropriate; ☉festival Jul), the region's only Nyingmapa monastery. The name Takthog ('stone roof') refers to a pair of small but highly revered cave-shrines in which the great sage Padmasambhava supposedly meditated during the 8th century. These smoke-blackened prayer chambers now form part of the monastery's attractive older section, directly opposite the tin-roofed **Tourist Bungalow** (s/d ₹300/500) where four simple rooms have en suite squat toilets and share a kitchen.

TANGTSE

Dishevelled central Tangtse is an anticlimax after the surrounding scenic glory. However, 2km beyond, the main road squeezes through a rocky cleft behind which clings **Tangtse Gompa**. The colourful main monastery is a recent construction but a hidden stairway leads down to an intriguing 800-year-old cube of 'old gompa' with blackened murals and a mysterious shaft of sunlight cutting through the incense smoke.

Marginally the best of Tangtse's six guesthouse-restaurants is perfectly central **Dothguling Guest House** (✆9469368805; d ₹600) with a pleasant Tibetan-style dining room and private bathrooms in half of the guestrooms. **Zamserling Guest House** (d ₹800), in a garden 800m east of town, has the finest location and pretty gompa views but overpriced rooms are very basic, with outside toilets.

PANGONG TSO

A **permit** is required to visit **Pangong Tso**, a giant lake, whose surreal palate of vivid blues can't fail to impress, backed as it is by colourful mineral swirls and rolling snow-brushed mountains. Whether you're driving or strolling, the views change constantly, emphasised by natural reflecting pools and occasional foregrounds of makeshift cairns. At one point, a sand-spit jutting into the turquoise waters creates an almost Caribbean beach scene near **Lukung**, the lake's most accessible point. Set back from the lake's salt-whitened western end, there's no village here, just an army hut plus a trio of makeshift **cafes**. They're mostly popular with day trippers who have no time to go further but all offer overnight options; sleeping spaces in **Pangong Restaurant** (₹150), dreary box rooms at **Pangtso Padma** (d ₹700) and misnamed 'luxury' tents (with tap and simple wc) at **Martsemik** (s/d ₹2000/2200).

Further east, a bumpy unpaved road continues to pretty **Spangmik** whose well-spaced mud-brick houses climb steadily amid gold-green barley fields and mazes of dry-stone walls. It's a wonderful place to unwind, meet part-time nomads and maybe stroll 30 minutes up to the lonely, very modest **Gontserboom Gompa**. Virtually all of Spangmik's 10 farmsteads offer a **homestay**

(per person ₹100-250) – usually just three to six mattresses laid side by side on the floor and (at best) sharing an outdoor toilet. None have showers. Most can serve simple meals (around ₹50) given a little warning. Places further away from the lake-shore generally have better views and more traditional interiors. Of these, **Gongma Homestay** (dm/d/tent ₹200/500/500) has outstandingly obliging hosts, an unusually clean outside toilet and three twin-bedded tents in addition to typically simple rooms. Nearer the lake **Wonderland Camp** (tw tent ₹400) is a good deal with bedded tents and shared sit-down toilets. Closest to the shore, **Padma** (tr ₹300) is a four-room blockhouse with three lie-on-the-floor box rooms. It's beside Spangmik's only 'restaurant', a **parachute tent** (dishes ₹25-40) serving omelettes, instant noodles and dhal-rice.

If you must have an attached toilet choose between **Pangong Tso Resort** (✆9568505530; www.campsofladakh.com; d half-board ₹3300), Spangmik's low-rise concrete eyesore, or **Camp Watermark** (✆9968420496; www.campsofladakh.com; d full board ₹3500), an arc of unexceptional bedded tents attractively situated near the water's edge at the entrance to Spangmik. Both feel seriously overpriced.

Beyond Spangmik the lakeside track gets much rougher but remains every bit as beautiful especially after **Man**, approaching the similar but more extensive village of **Merak**. Backed by some of the lake's most memorable mountain ridges, Merak only opened to foreigners in 2010 and remains little visited. Permits don't allow you to go further but the lake itself stretches way beyond into areas under Chinese control. As yet Merak has no formal tourist facilities but for ₹150 per person **Twang Rigzen Amchi** can find you a sleeping space at the traditional medicine clinic while **Chawang Tunduk** offers homestay beds if you can track him down, price 'negotiable'.

Tso Moriri & Eastern Indus Valley

ELEV 4595M

Permits, required to reach Tso Moriri and the upper Indus, are checked at Upshi. Beyond, the Indus flows through a stark, sharp-cut rocky valley with occasional villages eking out an existence from small oases of irrigated barley fields. The most significant settlement is **Chumathang**. All that most travellers see here is a rag-tag handful of cheap restaurant shacks around some messy hot-spring pools: Chumathang village itself is hidden away above the road some 2km beyond. Foreigner permits currently allow you to continue 43km up the Indus beyond Mahe Bridge to the **Loma Bend** army checkpoint. The route is asphalted and passes through some mesmerising desert scenery and oxbow lakelands. However, apart from the twin-horned gompa at **Nyoma**, there's little else in the way of specific sights and the long drive can feel anticlimactic. At Mahe Bridge, most travellers swing south to **Tso Moriri**, a vast, mildly brackish lake. In the area you stand a good chance of seeing kiang (wild ass), foxes and marmots, and of meeting nomadic Chang-Pa (Khampa) people herding their pashmina goats and yaks. But the high altitude can cause trouble and the overall experience is arguably less satisfying than visiting Pangong Tso.

KORZOK

Tiny Korzok village is Tso Moriri's only significant settlement. Set on a slope around 500m back from the grassy lakeshore, its mud-brick buildings have a scrappy half-finished look and first impressions are off-putting. But the backdrop of snow-topped mountains is attractive and the lake's ever-changing colours are photogenic. Some 3km up the jeep road behind town, a grassy valley bowl is dotted in summer with the tents and animal enclosures of a seasonal **Chang-Pa nomad camp**.

Korzok has seven active homestays/guesthouses each a little dusty and basic with shared bathrooms and cold water usually in buckets. Most are clean enough but consider bringing your own sleeping bag. Relatively good choices are **Mentok Guest House** (d ₹300, with view ₹500) and **Crane Homestay** (same prices), both with sit-down toilets on the same floor as the best view-rooms. **Lake View GH & Restaurant** (☑9419345362; d without bathroom ₹500) has comparatively airy

guestrooms but the squat toilet is upstairs. **Goose Homestay** (dm ₹150) has a lake-view dorm with floor mattresses and simple food included in the deal.

The only option with en suite bathroom facilities is **Tsomoriri Camp & Resort** (☑01982-254855 in Leh; www.campsofladakh .com; d ₹2000, full board ₹3700), five overpriced hut-rooms and a line of 'luxury tents', whose touted view of the lake is marred by fences and new boxy buildings.

Downhill from the village gompa on the opposite (south) edge of town are four more tent-camps. All have shared outdoor bathroom blocks and prices that seem to vary at whim (₹500 to ₹1500 for essentially identical double tents).

Lhasa Restaurant, a makeshift parachute cafe beside the central gompa, produces simple meals (from ₹40) and has ₹50 mattress-on-floor bed spaces in the rear tent section.

Trekking from Tso Kar to Korzok takes four to five days. Constant high altitude, four passes over 4700m and subzero nights make for an unusually arduous trek. You'll need pre-arranged guides, horses and good-quality camping equipment. Landscapes are broad pastureland valleys rolling up to very high but mostly smooth-topped mountains quite unlike Ladakh's signature arid, spiked peaks. No permanent villages en route.

❶ Getting There & Away

BUS Departs Leh (₹219) at 6.30am on the 10th, 20th and 30th of each month, returning next morning.

JEEP A three-day, one-way excursion from Leh to Keylong/Manali (₹16,241/19,058) via Mahe, Korzok (first night), Tso Kar and Pang/Sarchu (second night) is only possible southbound since permits must be issued in Leh. A return jeep charter (Leh–Korzok–Leh) takes two days and costs ₹7035 per vehicle (via the Indus Valley both ways), or ₹7800 returning cross-country via Puga, Tso Kar lake and Tanglang-La (very bumpy). Add ₹2000 extra for Loma Bend.

Himachal Pradesh

Why Go?

With spectacular peaks and gorgeous river valleys, Himachal is India's outdoor adventure playground. From trekking and climbing to rafting, paragliding and skiing, if it can be done in the mountains, it can be done here. Yet Himachal offers much more than just a shot of alpine adrenaline.

Across the state, traditional Himachali culture flourishes amid Himalayan landscapes. Villages perched on staggering slopes enchant with fairy tale wood-and-stone architecture and the easygoing grace of the people who live there. Elsewhere, hill stations appeal with colonial-era charm, while groovy backpacker magnets lure with their legendary local charas.

In many places, you might think you've stumbled into Tibet. But the ancient Buddhist monasteries, troves of Buddhist arts, and the home-away-from-home of the Dalai Lama are just another part of the essence of Himachal.

Best Places to Eat

» Moonpeak Thali (p324)
» Lazy Dog Lounge (p309)
» Indian Coffee House (p286)
» Jakhu Temple (p283)

Best Places to Stay

» Chonor House Hotel (p322)
» Chapslee (p284)
» Norling Guest House (p328)
» Veer Guest House (p307)

When to Go
Manali

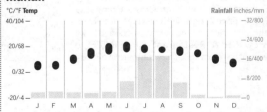

Jan/Feb Tibetan New Year is celebrated across Himachal.	**May–Jun & Mid-Sep–Oct** Outside the monsoon season is perfect for trekking.	**Nov–Apr** Great for skiers, but snow blocks the high passes to the Lahaul and Spiti Valleys.

Food

Himachal is the best place in India to get a taste of authentic Tibetan cuisine. *Momos* (steamed or fried dumplings), *thukpas* (noodle soups) and breads made from *tsampa* (barley flour) are found virtually everywhere. Tasty and cheap, these dishes hit the spot when you're not in the mood for curry.

Carnivores enjoy traditional Himachali food, which frequently features chicken or fresh trout from the region's streams. Most vegetarian specialities are flavourful dhal-based concoctions, often mixed with yoghurt, paneer or potatoes. Himachal is also known for producing India's finest apples, harvested in autumn.

DON'T MISS

McLeod Ganj isn't called 'Little Lhasa' just because it's the seat of the Tibetan government-in-exile; it's infused with a living blend of ancient and contemporary Tibetan culture, from arts to religion to food. The nearby **Norbulingka Institute** is among the best places in the world to see exquisite Tibetan crafts being handmade by masters and their apprentices.

Further east, Himachal's stretch of the **Great Himalayan Circuit** – a demanding and sometimes terrifying road – crosses towering mountain passes as it traverses the **Lahaul and Spiti Valleys**. A remote land of rugged, elemental beauty, you'll find countless trekking opportunities near some of the highest villages and Buddhist monasteries on earth. A favourite gateway to this region is **Manali**, Himachal's outdoor adventure capital, with activities from the relaxed (walking) to the intense (mountaineering or heli-skiing) to the absurd (zorbing).

Top State Festivals

» Losar (Jan/Feb, McLeod Ganj, p316, Lahaul, p337, Spiti p339) Tibetan New Year is celebrated with processions, music and dancing, and masked performances by monks in Tibetan Buddhist monasteries.

» Ladarcha Fair (Aug, Kaza, p340) An ancient trade fair celebrated in Spiti, with Buddhist dances, mountain sports and bustling rural markets.

» Phulech Festival (Sep/Oct, Kalpa, p293, Sangla p292) Villagers throughout Kinnaur fill temple courtyards with flowers of intoxicating fragrance; oracles perform sacrifices and make predictions for the coming year.

» Dussehra (Oct, Kullu, p300) An intense celebration of the defeat of the demon Ravana, with a huge parade led by the chariot of Raghunath (Rama).

» International Himalayan Festival (10-12 Dec, McLeod Ganj, p316) Celebrating the Dalai Lama's Nobel Peace Prize, this festival promotes peace and cultural understanding with Buddhist dances and music.

MAIN POINTS OF ENTRY

Shimla, Dharamsala and towns in the Kullu Valley are connected to Delhi by direct buses and air services. A long and wild road connects Manali to Leh, in Ladakh.

Fast Facts

» Population: 6.9 million
» Area: 55,673 sq km
» Capital: Shimla
» Main languages: Hindi, Pahari, Punjabi
» Sleeping prices: **$** below ₹800, **$$** ₹801 to ₹2000, **$$$** above ₹2000

Top Tip

If travelling between the Spiti and Kinnaur Valleys, foreigners must obtain an easy-to-get Inner Line Permit in Kaza (see the boxed text p340), Rekong Peo (p293) or Shimla (see the boxed text p287). Permits are also required for some Tibetan-border-area treks.

Resources

» Himachal Tourism (www .hptdc.gov.in)
» US Military maps (www .lib.utexas.edu/maps/ams /india), useful for trekking
» Online bus info and booking (www.hrtc.gov .in), (www.hptdc.nic.in /bus.htm)

Himachal Pradesh Highlights

1 Take the toy train up to **Shimla** (p289), one of India's favourite hill stations

2 Earn karma credits by volunteering with the Tibetan refugees of **McLeod Ganj** (p323)

3 Ski, trek, climb, paraglide or raft in the backpacker playground of **Manali** (p304)

4 Chill out in the **Parvati Valley** (p297) and trek to the mountain village of **Malana** (p297)

5 Get off the tourist trail and visit centuries-old temples in **Chamba** (p333) and **Bharmour** (p336)

6 Cross the spectacular mountain passes of Rohtang La and Kunzum La to the incredibly remote **Spiti Valley** (p339)

7 Visit charming villages with awesome Himalayan views in the upper **Kinnaur Valley** (p290)

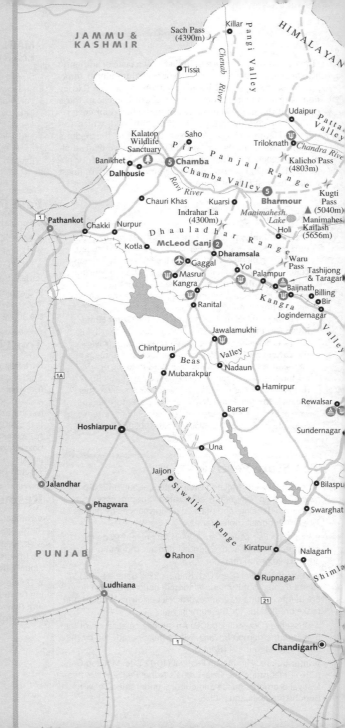

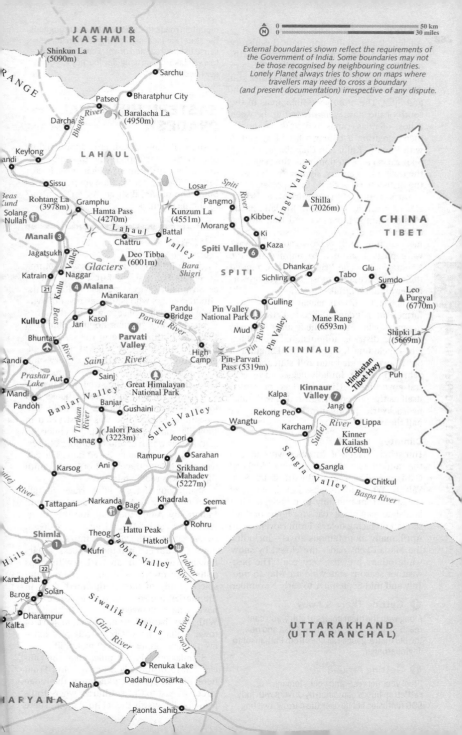

History

Ancient trade routes dominate the history of Himachal Pradesh. Large parts of northern Himachal were conquered by Tibet in the 10th century, and Buddhist culture still dominates the mountain deserts of Lahaul and Spiti. The more accessible areas in the south of the state were divvied up between a host of rajas, ranas and *thakurs* (noblemen), creating a patchwork of tiny states, with Kangra, Kullu and Chamba at the top. Sikh rajas came to dominate the region by the early 19th century, signing treaties with the British to consolidate their power.

During the 19th century the British started creating little bits of England in the hills of Shimla, Dalhousie and Dharamsala. Shimla later became the British Raj's summer capital, and narrow-gauge railways were pushed through to Shimla and the Kangra Valley. The British slowly extended their influence until most of the region was under Shimla's thrall.

The state of Himachal Pradesh was formed after Independence in 1948, liberating many villages from the feudal system. In 1966 the districts administered from Punjab – including Kangra, Kullu, Lahaul and Spiti – were added and full statehood was achieved in 1971. Initially neglected by central government, Himachal has reinvented itself as the powerhouse of India, with huge hydroelectric plants providing power for half the country.

Climate

Himachal is a land of extremes, with some of the rainiest spots in India (around McLeod Ganj) as well as some of the driest (the Spiti Valley). When monsoons drench much of the state from mid-July to mid-September, landslides can block roads for hours or days, so plan on facing delays. From November to April, many mountainous areas – including the Manali-Leh road – are closed by snow, while others are just very cold! The best-weather seasons statewide are May to mid-July and mid-September to early November.

❶ Getting There & Away

Along with the main points of entry, you can reach Shimla by toy train from Kalka and ride the old metre-gauge rail lines from Pathankot to Jogindarnagar.

❶ Getting Around

Steel your nerves – and your stomach – as rattletrap buses captained by drivers with Indy 500 fantasies hurtle over the narrow, twisting mountain roads that connect towns throughout the state. For local sightseeing it often makes sense to hire a car and driver. For a price, any taxi will take you on a full-day journey to your next destination.

EASTERN HIMACHAL PRADESH

Eastern Himachal Pradesh is dominated by Shimla, the state capital, and the mountainous district of Kinnaur, which spreads east to the Tibetan border then loops north to Spiti. The official district website is http://hpshimla.nic.in.

Shimla

📝 0177 / POP 144,900 / ELEV 2205M

Until the British arrived, there was nothing at Shimla but a sleepy forest glade known as Shyamala (a local name for Kali – the Hindu goddess who is the destroyer of evil). Then a Scottish civil servant named Charles Kennedy built a summer home in Shimla in 1822 and nothing was ever the same again. By 1864 Shimla had developed into the official summer capital of the Raj. Every summer until 1939, the entire government of India fled here from the sweltering heat of the plains, with all their clerks' books and forms filled out in triplicate. When the Kalka–Shimla railway line was constructed in 1903, Shimla's status as India's premier hill station was assured, and a number of prestigious schools are now based here. The city was even briefly the capital of Punjab until the map was redrawn in 1966.

Strung out along a 12km ridge, Shimla is an engaging blend of holiday town and Indian city. Along the Mall and the Ridge, vacationers stroll around licking ice-cream cones, gazing at the views or into store windows. Cascading down the hillsides, bazaars flowing with local life are packed with shops selling hardware, stationery, fabric and spices. Many of the handpainted signs in the market are so retro they look like they haven't been changed since the British left. With cars banned from the main part of town, walking anywhere is truly pleasant – even when huffing and puffing uphill.

Shimla sprawls for miles, but the official centre of town is Scandal Point. From here, the flat open area known as the Ridge stretches east to Christ Church, where trails lead uphill towards the Jakhu Temple. There are some good forest walks nearby, and a jagged line of snow-covered peaks is clearly visible from April to June, and in October and November.

The long, winding, pedestrian-only Mall runs west and east from Scandal Point. Downhill is Cart Rd, with the train station, the Inter State Bus Terminal (ISBT) and taxi stands. A passenger lift provides a quick route between the Mall and Cart Rd, or you can go via the maze of alleyways of the Middle Bazar and Lower Bazar.

At the bus or train stations you will be besieged by porters offering to carry your luggage uphill for ₹50 to ₹80. Most double as touts, and hotels will increase your room tariff to cover their commission.

◉ Sights & Activities

Jakhu Temple   HINDU TEMPLE
Shimla's most famous temple is dedicated to the Hindu monkey god Hanuman; it's therefore appropriate that hundreds of rhesus macaques loiter around harassing devotees for *prasad* (temple-blessed food offerings). Set atop a hill awash in devotional music, the temple houses a small shrine surrounded by funky relief murals of Hanuman performing feats from the Ramayana. The dining hall serves delicious all-you-can-eat plates of dhal, rice and *sabzi* (vegetables) from 10am to 4pm (donations appreciated), so coordinate your visit with your hunger! Getting here involves a steep 30-minute hike to the top of a hill, starting at the east end of the Ridge. Primate alert: the monkeys on this route can be a menace! Consider renting a walking stick at the start of the walk (from ₹10) to discourage them. Taxis from either stand charge around ₹300 return.

Himachal State Museum & Library   MUSEUM
(Indian/foreigner ₹10/50, camera/video ₹100/1500; ⊙10am-1.30pm & 2-5pm Tue-Fri, Sun & 2nd Sat each month) About 2.5km west of Scandal Point and a stiff walk up to the telecommunications mast, the state museum is home to an impressive collection of miniatures from Kangra and Rajasthan, as well as Chamba embroidery, coins and jewellery, temple carvings, paintings of Shimla, and various weapons.

Viceregal Lodge & Botanical Gardens   HISTORIC BUILDING
(Indian/foreigner ₹20/50; ⊙9.15am-1pm & 2-5pm, to 7pm May-Jul, tours every 30min) Built as an official residence for the British viceroys, the Viceregal Lodge looks like a cross between Harry Potter's Hogwarts School and the Tower of London. Every brick used in its construction was hauled up here by mule. Today it houses the Indian Institute of Advanced Study, but you can take a guided tour of the buildings. Tickets cost ₹20 if you just want to look around the gardens.

Opposite the lodge entrance is the **Himalayan Bird Park** (admission ₹5; ⊙10am-5pm), where you can see the iridescent monal pheasant, Himachal's state bird, among others.

The lodge is a 4.5km walk west from Scandal Point along the Mall, but it is poorly signposted, so you should try to aim for the telecommunications mast, then stick to the largest road.

Christ Church   CHURCH
(☑2652953; the Ridge; ⊙services in English 9am Sun) This very English church dominates the top of the ridge and is the second-oldest church in northern India (the oldest is in Ambala in Haryana). Built between 1846 and 1857, it contains Raj-era memorials and fine stained glass. There's still a small Sunday service held here.

Other Temples   HINDU/SIKH TEMPLES
The most popular temple for locals is the small **Shiv Mandir**, just below the Ridge – crowds of school children drop in before and after school, and sadhus wait on the steps, soliciting donations.

About 1km west of the Ridge is the Bengali hut-style **Kali Bari Mandir** (temple), enshrining an image of Kali as Shyamala. Vaishnavites gather at the modernist **Ram Mandir**, just above the bus stand in Middle Bazar, while Sikhs attend the huge white **Sri Guru Singh Sabha Gurdwara** near the ISBT.

Historic Buildings   HISTORIC BUILDING
The Ridge is lined with grand examples of British architecture, including the **Town Hall**, oddly reminiscent of the mansion in Hammer Horror films, and the mock-Tudor folly housing the **post office**. The **Gaiety Theatre** should house shows again after renovations are complete, but for now check out the fabulous auditorium. At the west end of the Mall are the grand mock-Gothic **Offices of the Accountant General**. Above Shimla on the way to the Jakhu Temple, you can peek through the gates of **Rothney Castle**, former home of Allan Octavian Hume, which housed Asia's largest collection of stuffed birds during the 19th century.

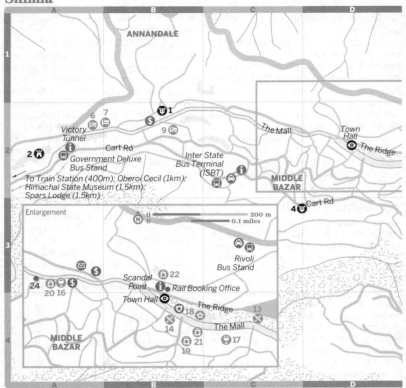

Walking

WALKING

About 4km northwest of Scandal Point is **The Glen**, a former playground of British colonialists, selected for its similarity to the Scottish highlands. The road here passes through the flat green meadow at **Annandale**, once the site of a famous racecourse, and a popular venue for cricket and polo matches.

There's an interesting temple and excellent views at **Prospect Hill**, about 4km west of Shimla. About 5km away on the Shimla–Kalka railway line, **Summer Hill** has pleasant, shady walks. Pretty **Chadwick Falls** (67m high) are 2km further west, best visited just after the monsoon. About 3km east of Lakkar Bazar, the village of **Sanjauli** has a Durga temple and a small Buddhist monastery run by Gelugpa monks.

⏚ Tours

The HPTDC tourist office organises daily sightseeing bus tours of villages around Shimla. The tours leave from the Rivoli bus stand

at around 10.30am. Seats cost ₹160 to ₹250. Contact the office for current itineraries.

The taxi unions also offer one-day sightseeing tours to Kufri, Naldehra, Fagu and Mashobra (₹1000), and to Mashobra, Naldehra and Tattapani (₹1250).

🛏 Sleeping

Hotels in Shimla charge steep rates during the peak tourist season (April to June, October, November and Christmas). At all other times, ask about discounts. In winter, heating can usually be provided for an extra charge. Touts abound in Shimla – claims that hotels are full or closed should be taken with a grain of salt.

Chapslee   HERITAGE HOTEL **$$$**
(☏2802542; www.chapslee.com; d with full board ₹12,500-20,000; ❄) For the full Raj treatment, the outrageously ostentatious former home of Raja Charanjit Singh of Kapurthala is perched atop Elysium Hill, about 4km north

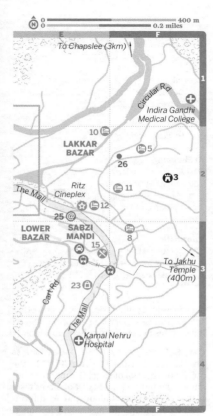

tures mirrored ceilings, timber panelling and harem-style curtains, though all rooms look (and smell) different, so check out a few. The roof terrace has unbeatable views of Shimla, and prices halve in the off season.

YMCA
HOTEL $

(☏2650021; ymcashimla@yahoo.co.in; s/d incl breakfast ₹750/1000, without bathroom ₹370/500; @) Up the steps beside the Ritz Cineplex, the expansive, bright-red YMCA takes all comers, regardless of age, religion or gender. Rooms are pleasant and clean, and there's an internet cafe, lockers for valuables (₹20), a weight room and table tennis. Book ahead April to July.

Le Royale
HOTEL $$$

(☏2651002; le_royale@hotmail.com; Jakhu Rd; r ₹2000-3500) Perched on the track up to Jakhu Temple, this boutique hotel has plenty of charm, with tastefully furnished rooms. It's close to the Ridge but tucked away enough to feel private. The Green Leaf restaurant is good and there are mountain views from the garden.

Oberoi Cecil
HOTEL $$$

(☏2804848; www.oberoicecil.com; the Mall; s/d from ₹12,750/14,250, ste from ₹25,750; ❄@⏾❄) Along the Mall about 2km west of Scandal Point, this grand high-rise is Shimla's glitziest five-star hotel. Colonial grandeur outside gives way to luxurious comforts within, and the cavernous colonial-style central atrium has a gorgeous bar and restaurant, open to nonguests. There's wi-fi throughout.

Hotel White
HOTEL $$

(☏2656136; www.hotelwhiteshimla.com; Lakkar Bazar; r ₹1000-1350, ste from ₹1600) Northeast of Scandal Point through the bustling bazaar, this place is well run and priced right – rates are fixed all year. No two rooms are the same, but all are clean and comfortable. The huge suites here are perfect for families.

Hotel Amar Palace
HOTEL $

(☏2804055; d ₹500-1700) Off the road up to Jakhu Temple, Amar Palace has a wide range of rooms. Some are pristine, with fresh wood panelling, loveseats and marble sinks. Others are slated for an upgrade so see a few, since some of the cheaper rooms are nicer than the expensive ones. Most have great valley views and prices are negotiable.

Hotel Gulmarg
HOTEL $

(☏2653168; gulmarghotel@yahoo.com; r ₹660-1600; ste from 2000; ❄) Found below the Mall

of Shimla. The exclusive mountain retreat is crammed with chandeliers, tapestries, Afghan carpets, big-game trophies, Mughal ceramics, baroque furniture and pieces of Victoriana. There are just six sumptuous bedrooms, all with completely original fittings, plus a library, card room, sun lounge, tennis courts and – of course – a croquet lawn.

TOP CHOICE Spars Lodge
GUESTHOUSE $

(☏2657908; Museum Rd; s/d ₹660/990; @) On the little road up to the museum, Spars is a real travellers' hotel with an inviting, homey feel. It's bright, clean and airy with a lovely sunny dining room upstairs. The owners are welcoming and the cafe serves great food, including local trout.

Hotel Doegar
HOTEL $$

(☏2811927; www.hoteldoegar.com; the Ridge; d ₹1000-2500) Many of Shimla's hotels turn on the chintzy honeymoon charm, but Doegar does it with aplomb. The disco decor fea-

and spread over several buildings and annexes, this huge honeymoon hotel offers a mixed bag, from plain, boxlike singles to gloriously chintzy doubles with round beds and mirrored ceilings to palatial family suites. Low-season discount is up to 50%.

Hotel Classic   HOTEL $
(☎2653078; d ₹660-880) Classic is a worn but welcoming place and the location is handy for the train station and Scandal Point. The lower rooms with windows facing out over the valley and Annandale meadow are more expensive, but all rooms have TV and hot water. Some were being renovated at the time of research.

Hotel Dalziel   HOTEL $
(☎2652691; www.hoteldalziel.com; the Mall; d ₹550-900) Dalziel advertises heritage on a budget, and it's hard to argue with this claim. Well located at the west end of the Mall, the old building – a former colonial bungalow – has a lodge-like lounge area and faded rooms in varying states of cleanliness. All have TV and hot water.

✖ Eating

Befitting a holiday town and state capital, Shimla has plenty of places to eat, especially along the Mall and the Ridge. As well as the formal restaurants, there are dozens of Indian fast-food places in Middle Bazar serving samosas, potato cakes, *channa puri* (spiced chickpeas and puffed fried bread) and other snacks. Unless otherwise stated, the following eateries are open from 10am to 10pm.

Cafe Sol   MULTICUISINE $$
(the Mall; dishes ₹140-400; ⊙11am-10pm) In the atrium on the roof of Hotel Combermere but entered straight off the Mall, Sol serves tasty plates of Mexican, Italian and Mediterranean food, and has the best cake selection in Shimla. At the time of research, unsecured wi-fi networks were accessible here.

Baljee's   INDIAN $$
(the Mall; mains ₹70-240) Opposite the Town Hall, Baljee's gets packed with Indian families, many of whom come for the snacks and South Indian specialities. Breakfasts of omelettes, toast and dosas are good, and there's a popular counter selling Indian sweets.

⟨TOP CHOICE⟩ Indian Coffee House   CAFE $
(the Mall; dishes ₹20-35; ⊙8.30am-9.30pm) A Shimla institution, the Indian Coffee House is like an old boys' club with its ageing booths, uniformed waiters and blackboard menu. It's the most atmospheric place in town for breakfast, cheap dosas and coffee (don't even ask for tea!).

Ashiana   INDIAN $$
(the Ridge; dishes ₹65-230; ⊙9am-10pm) In a fanciful circular building on the Ridge, this is an almost elegant restaurant and a good people-watching spot. As well as tasty In-

dian dishes there are sizzlers, Chinese and a few Thai favourites. In Ashiana's basement, Goofa serves similar food at slightly cheaper prices, but with no views.

Cecil Restaurant
MULTICUISINE $$$
(☎2804848; the Mall; mains from ₹400, breakfast/dinner buffet ₹650/950) For a formal night out, look no further than the colonial elegance of the Cecil Restaurant at the Oberoi. An à la carte menu is available but there are sumptuous buffets for breakfast and dinner. Book ahead. There's also a casual garden restaurant, or you can opt for a drink in the atrium lobby bar.

🍷 Drinking

Himani's
BAR
(the Mall) The neon and marble decor is straight out of the 1980s, but Himani's is a good place for a casual drink or plate of chicken tikka. The top-floor terrace overlooking the Mall is perfect on a sunny afternoon.

Devico's Bar
BAR
(the Mall; 10am-10pm) Head upstairs above Café Coffee Day for a beer or cocktail in this casual bar with couches, chairs and stools.

🛍 Shopping

Local holidaymakers head to the bustling Lakkar Bazar to haggle for wood and handloom souvenirs, but Middle Bazar, on the way down to the bus station, is more interesting. You can buy everything here from tin pots and peacock feathers to henna kits to bangles. Fruit and veg are sold at the heaving Sabzi Mandi at the bottom of the hill. For well-made, knock-off brand-name clothes, head to the Tibetan Clothes Market, behind the tourist office.

Carpets, shawls and other Himachal souvenirs are sold at Himachal Emporium (☎2011234; the Mall; ⊙Mon-Sat), while Tibetan souvenirs are sold at the Tibetan Handloom Shop (☎2808163; the Mall), aiding Tibetan refugees.

For English-language books and maps of the region, try Asia Book House (the Mall; ⊙10am-8.30pm) or Minerva Bookshop (☎2803078; the Mall; ⊙10.30am-8pm).

ℹ Information

Laws exist banning plastic bags, littering, smoking and spitting in public places; police can hit offenders with a ₹500 fine.

Emergency
Indira Gandhi Medical College (☎2803073; the Ridge, Circular Rd; 24hr)
Tourist police (☎2812344; Scandal Point)

Internet Access
There are a few internet places along the Mall; for wi-fi, try to jump on the occasional unsecured network that filters into some of the restaurants and cafes around town.
Asian & International Travels (the Mall; per hr ₹30; ⊙9am-9pm) Cramped place on the Mall.
Interwebs (the Mall; per hr ₹30, wi-fi ₹60; ⊙9.30am-9.30pm) The best of the bunch on the Mall, and the rare wi-fi hotspot in Shimla.
Play World Cybercafe (the Mall; per hr ₹30; ⊙9am-8.30pm)

Money
If you're heading out to Kinnaur, Spiti and Lahaul, stock up on rupees in Shimla. Numerous 24-hour ATMs are dotted around Scandal Point and the Mall.
Punjab National Bank (the Mall; ⊙10am-4pm Mon-Fri, to 1pm Sat) Changes major currencies in cash and travellers cheques.
State Bank of India (the Mall; ⊙10am-4pm Mon-Fri, to 1pm Sat) West of Scandal Point; has an ATM opposite.
State Bank of India ATM (Scandal Point)

Post
Main post office (the Ridge) Looks after parcels and poste restante. There are several suboffices west along the Mall.

INNER LINE PERMITS IN SHIMLA

Permits for travel from Rekong Peo to Tabo in Spiti are issued by the office of the Additional District Magistrate (☎2657005; ⊙10am-1.30pm & 2-5pm Mon-Sat, closed 2nd Sat each month), in the Collectorate Building, which is down a couple of flights of steps from the Mall about 200m west of Scandal Point. Permits (₹200) are usually issued within 30 minutes. You'll need two passport photos, copies of your passport identity and visa pages, and a letter from a local travel agency stating that they're taking responsibility for you (₹100-200). At this office, permits are only given to groups of four or more, so find other travellers to connect with or get your papers in Rekong Peo (p293) or Kaza (see the boxed text p340), where restrictions are looser.

Tourist Information

HPTDC tourist office (Himachal Pradesh Tourist Development Corporation; ☎2652561; www.hptdc.gov.in; Scandal Point; ◷9am-8pm, to 6pm Aug, Sep & Dec-Mar) Helpful for advice, brochures and booking HPTDC buses, hotels and tours, along with a railway booking window. There are satellite booths by the Inter State Bus Terminal and the Victory Tunnel.

Travel Agencies

Great Escape Routes (☎5533037; www.greatescaperoutes.com; 6 Andi Bhavan, Jakhu) Specialises in trekking and adventure tours around Shimla and throughout North India. Hires out mountain bikes for ₹500 per day and has an internet cafe.

YMCA Tours & Treks (☎9857102657; www.himalayansites.com; Shimla YMCA, the Ridge) The affable and knowledgeable Anil Kumar runs day trips around Shimla as well as treks throughout Himachal and Uttarakhand.

ⓘ Getting There & Away

Air

Jubbarhatti airport, 23km south of Shimla, is served by **Kingfisher Airlines** (☎1800 2093030; www.flykingfisher.com). Weather permitting, there are daily flights from Shimla to Delhi. **Jagson Airlines** (☎2625177; www.jagsonairline.com) flies to Kullu on Monday, Wednesday and Friday.

Bus

The HPTDC and private travel agencies offer overnight deluxe buses to Delhi (₹760, nine hours), plus morning and evening buses to Manali (₹500, 10 hours) in season (April to June, October and November). They depart from the deluxe bus stand near Victory Tunnel. There are also four HRTC Volvo buses to Delhi (₹775, nine hours) each day, along with three AC deluxe (₹520) and three semi-deluxe (₹300) rides. Deluxe/semi-deluxe buses head to Manali (₹455/325, 10 hours) a few times daily. The government buses leave from the large and chaotic **Inter State Bus Terminal** (☎2656326; Cart Rd). Make reservations at counter 9 and get information at counter 8, or do both at the booth by the HPTDC Tourist Office at Scandal Point. See the boxed text below for services.

Regular buses to Chail (₹50, 2½ hours), Naldehra (₹25, one hour) and Tattapani (₹50, 2½ hours) leave from the small Rivoli (Lakkar Bazar) bus stand, north of the Ridge.

Taxi

The **Kalka-Shimla Taxi Union** (☎2658225) has its stand near the ISBT, while **Vishal Himachal**

BUSES FROM SHIMLA

DESTINATION	FARE (₹)	DURATION (HR)	FREQUENCY
Chamba	440	14	four daily
Chandigarh	180/320 (ordinary/deluxe)	four	every 15 minutes
Dehra Dun	240	nine	three daily
Delhi	280/520 (ordinary/deluxe)	nine	hourly
Dharampur (for Kasauli)	85	2½	regularly
Dharamsala	295	10	five daily
Haridwar	265	10	five daily
Jammu	410	12	4.10pm 5.30pm
Kullu	385	8½	five daily
Manali	440	10	five daily
Mandi	165	six	hourly
Nahan	150	five	four daily
Narkanda	65	two	regularly
Paonta Sahib	170	seven	five daily
Rampur	150	five	hourly
Rekong Peo	265	10	hourly
Rohru	160	six	regularly
Sangla	270	10	7.30am
Sarahan	170	eight	three daily

DESTINATION	ONE-WAY FARE (₹)
Airport	750
Chail	1150
Chandigarh	1750
Dehra Dun	3600
Dharamsala/McLeod Ganj	3600/3800
Kasauli	1400
Kullu	3000
Manali	3700
Naldehra	700
Narkanda	1250
Rekong Peo	4000
Sarahan	3400
Tattapani	1250

Taxi Operators Union (☎2805164) operates from the bottom of the passenger lift. Share taxis are available to Kalka between noon and 2pm (₹275). Taxis from the train station or the ISBT to the passenger lift cost around ₹70. There's another taxi stand next to the Rivoli bus stand.

Train

One of the little joys of Shimla is getting to or from it by the narrow-gauge toy train from Kalka, just north of Chandigarh. Although the steam trains are long gone, it's a scenic four- to six-hour trip, passing through 103 tunnels as it creeps up through the hills. Tiny Shimla train station is 1.5km west of Scandal Point on Cart Rd – about a 15-minute uphill walk. The left-luggage office is open 9am to 5pm.

Ordinary trains (1st/2nd class ₹189/16) run downhill to Kalka at 8.30am, 2.25pm and 6.15pm, returning at 4am, 6am and 12.15pm. To travel in style, catch the posh *Shivalik Express* at 5.40pm (returning at 5.30am; ₹280, 1st class only) or the *Himalayan Queen* at 10.30am (returning at 4pm; ₹167, chair car only). All 1st-class prices include food.

The *Himalayan Queen* service connects with the *Himalayan Queen* trains to and from Delhi (chair car/2nd class ₹284/75). The train from Delhi's Nizammudin station leaves at 5.25am, departing from New Delhi station at 5.50am.

There's a rail booking office next to the tourist office on the Ridge (◷9am-4pm), or you can book at the train station.

❶ Getting Around

The only way to get around central Shimla is on foot. Fortunately, there's a two-part **lift** (per person ₹7; ◷8am-10pm, till 9pm Jul-Sep) connecting the east end of the Mall with Cart Rd, a 15-minute walk east of the ISBT. Taxis from the train station to the bottom of the lift cost about ₹100.

Around Shimla

SHIMLA TO TATTAPANI

About 12km north of Shimla, the small village of **Mashobra** has an old colonial church and some pleasant walks among deodar trees.

About 15km north of Mashobra, **Naldehra** is famous chiefly for the **Naldehra Golf Course** (☎0177-2747739; www.naldehragolf .com; green fees Indian/foreigner ₹250/500, club hire ₹250; ◷7am-6pm), established in 1905 by British viceroy Lord Curzon. Set among tall cedars – some of which stand directly between the tee and green – it's a challenging course. Hire a caddy (₹40/70 for nine/18 holes) or you won't know where you're going. Ponies can be hired for treks along the ridge and there are pine-scented walks.

At the golf course, **Hotel Golf Glade** (☎0177-2747739; d ₹1500-1600) is an upmarket HPTDC property offering smart hotel rooms around an inviting restaurant and bar.

TATTAPANI
☎01907 / ELEV 656M

About 30km below Naldehra, on the banks of the Sutlej River, tiny Tattapani is known for its steaming **sulphurous springs**, which once spilled out onto a sandy river beach. By the time you read this they, along with the once-great Spring View Guest House, should be submerged beneath the Sutlej thanks to a dam that's being built about 35km downstream.

The village has several **temples** linked to the cult of Rishi Jamdagam, and you can walk to **sacred Shiva caves** and former **palaces**. Ask directions locally or at New Spring View Guest House.

If you've come for the waters, your only option is the spa at the fancy new **Hotel Hot Spring** (☏230736; www.hotelhotspring.in; r ₹3000-6000;✳), which is moderately luxurious (it's got an elevator!) if relatively soulless. You can soak in the pools as a non-guest (₹100-350) and stay at the **New Spring View Guest House** (☏230711; www.newspringview. com; r without/with AC ₹500/1200; ✳) just down the road, which has simple, bright and immaculate rooms and a good inexpensive restaurant.

Buses leave from Tattapani to Shimla every hour or so for much of the day.

NARKANDA
☏01782 / ELEV 2708M

About 65km northeast of Shimla, Narkanda is a nondescript truck-stop town for most of the year, but from January to March it transforms into a modest ski resort. The HPTDC offers three-/five-/seven-day skiing packages from ₹2739/4565/6391, including accommodation, meals, equipment and tuition, but not transport – see www.hptdc.nic. in for dates.

On the busy main road in the village centre, **Hotel Mahamaya Palace** (☏242448; r ₹500-900) has a suitably alpine mood, or try **HPTDC Hotel Hatu** (☏242430; www.hotelha tu.tripod.com; d ₹1200-2100), off the main road, with pleasant gardens, snug rooms and a restaurant and bar.

PABBAR VALLEY
☏01781 / ELEV 1400M

Running northeast to Kinnaur, the calm Pabbar Valley is easily accessible from Shimla by public bus. Set in rolling fields at the mouth of the valley, the Durga temple at **Hatkoti** was founded in the 8th century AD. Built in classic Kinnauri style, the slate-roofed temples attract large numbers of Shaivite pilgrims during the Chaitra Navratra and Asvin Navratra festivals in April and October. Pilgrims' quarters are available at the temple or you can stay at the **HPTDC Hotel Chanshal** (☏240661; dm ₹100, d ₹800-1000; ✳), 10km north of Hatkoti towards Rohru.

Local buses connect Hatkoti to **Jubbal**, 29km west, which has a fanciful slate-roofed palace built by the former Rana of Jubbal.

SOUTH OF SHIMLA

The hilltop village of **Chail**, 65km south of Shimla, lays claim to the world's highest cricket ground, a 3km walk from town. As well as forest strolls, there's a **wildlife park** abundant with deer and birds. Stay at **Hotel Pineview** (☏248349; r from ₹200) or **Palace Hotel** (☏248141; palace@hptdc.in; r ₹1600-8500; ✳) a former maharaja's pad, luxurious in a Raj-era way.

Continuing southeast, **Renukaji** (Renuka Lake) is Himachal's largest lake and site of the week-long **Renuka Mela** festival each November, honouring the goddess Renukaji. The lake is an hour by bus from **Nahan**, which is well-connected to Shimla.

Virtually on the Uttarakhand state line, **Paonta Sahib** is famous as the one-time home of Guru Gobind Singh, the 10th Sikh guru. The sprawling **Paonta Sahib Gurdwara** is set on banks of the Yamuna River where Gobind Singh got off his horse. You can eat at the gurdwara and stay in its guestrooms (donation encouraged), or head for the nearby **Hotel Yamuna** (☏222341; d ₹700-900, with AC ₹1400-2000; ✳), which could use a paint job but has very friendly management. There are hourly morning buses to Shimla (₹200, seven hours) and plenty of services to Dehra Dun (₹40, two hours).

Kinnaur Valley

The old Hindustan–Tibet Hwy – built by the British as a sneaky invasion route into Tibet – runs northeast from Shimla through the Kinnaur Valley, providing access to mountain villages with slate-roofed temples, the vast apple orchards, and some of Eastern Himachal's grandest views. The Kinnauris, or Kinners, are proud Aryan people who mainly survive from farming and apple growing. You can recognise Kinners all over India by their green felt *basheri* hats.

To truly appreciate Kinnaur, you have to leave the main road, much of which currently feels like an endless construction zone due to the multiple dam projects that are turning the powerful Sutlej River into a massive generator. With an easy-to-obtain inner line permit (see p293) you can travel onwards to the mountain deserts of the Spiti Valley.

For much of the year, Kinnaur is a relaxed rural retreat, but that all changes in September/

October when Bengali holidaymakers flood into Kinnaur from the plains. Simultaneously, the annual apple harvest lures hundreds of fruit wholesalers from right across India. At this time it can be impossible to find a room anywhere in Kinnaur, especially in popular spots such as Kalpa and the Sangla Valley.

For more information on the Kinnaur Valley, visit the local government website at http://hpkinnaur.nic.in.

RAMPUR
📞 01782 / ELEV 1005M

The gateway to Kinnaur, this bustling little town was once the capital of the Bushahr rajas. Today, Rampur is mainly a place to change buses, but if you decide to stick around, check out the delightful, terraced and turreted **Padam Palace**, built in 1925 for the maharaja of Bushahr; only the garden is open to visitors.

The huge **Lavi Fair** is held yearly in the second week of November, attracting traders and pilgrims from remote villages.

🛏 Sleeping & Eating

Rampur isn't the ideal spot to overnight in Kinnaur, but there is cheap lodging if you get stuck.

Hotel Satluj View　　　　　HOTEL $
(📞233924; r ₹300-550) Just behind the temple across the road from the bus station and down a flight of stairs, cheap rooms are grubby holes, while the more expensive ones are clean and pleasant, with big windows overlooking the river. The restaurant (mains ₹50-200) is the best place to eat near the bus station.

Hotel Bushehar Regency　　　HOTEL $$
(📞234103; d ₹1200-1400, with AC ₹1800-2100; ❄) This standard HPTDC property on the western edge of Rampur has spacious rooms and a decent restaurant.

❶ Getting There & Away

Rampur's chaotic bus station has frequent services to Rekong Peo (₹100, five hours) and Shimla (₹150, five hours) via Narkanda. Buses to Sarahan (₹45, two hours) leave every two hours. Three daily buses run to Sangla (₹105, five hours).

SARAHAN
📞 01782 / ELEV 1920M

The former summer capital of the Bushahr kingdom, Sarahan is dominated by the fabulous **Bhimakali Temple** (⊙7am-8pm), built from layers of stone and timber to absorb the force of earthquakes. There are two towers here, one built in the 12th century, and a newer tower from the 1920s containing a highly revered shrine to Bhimakali (the local version of Kali) beneath a beautiful silver-filigree canopy.

There are some strict entry rules. Male visitors must wear a cap (which can be borrowed inside the temple), shoes must be removed, smoking is banned, and cameras and leather goods like belts and wallets must be left with the guards. Behind the temple is a small display of ancient ceremonial horns, lamps and weaponry, and across the courtyard is the squat **Lankra Vir Temple**, where human sacrifices were carried out right up to the 18th century. The tradition lives on in a tamer form in the Astomi ritual during October's **Dussehra** celebration, when a menagerie of animals is sacrificed to Bhimakali, including goats, chickens and buffalo.

There are peaceful walks in the surrounding hills – stroll downhill to the **Buddhist gompa** in Gharat village, or gird yourself for the treks on the slopes of **Bashal Peak**. The flamboyant **palace** of the last maharaja of Bushahr is just behind the Bhimakali Temple.

🛏 Sleeping & Eating

For such a tiny village, Sarahan has some good places to stay. Apart from the temple guesthouse, all hotels offer significant discounts out of season (August and December to March).

Temple Guesthouse　　　　　HOTEL $
(📞274248; dm ₹50, r ₹250-350) The obvious place to stay is within the ancient temple precinct and, unlike most temple accommodation, rooms here are far from gloomy and austere. Dorm rooms are basic, but the upper-storey rooms are bright and airy, with hot water.

Hotel Trehan's　　　　　　HOTEL $$
(📞274205; r ₹880-1200) Run by a friendly family, rooms here have carved ceilings, big windows, TV and cheap tapestries of Indian epics that give the place a touch of character. Shared terraces have great views of the valley and the mountains beyond it.

❶ Getting There & Away

Direct buses run to Shimla from Sarahan (₹200, eight hours) via Rampur (₹45, two hours) at 8am, 11.45am and 1.30pm. The 8am bus continues on to Haridwar. From early morning to late afternoon, there's a regular service to Rampur and Jeori (₹20, 45 minutes), the junction on the main road from where you can catch buses to other destinations. Note that times are approximate and buses may leave earlier than scheduled. Taxis from Jeori to Sarahan cost ₹350.

SANGLA

☎ 01786 / ELEV 2680M

The Sangla, or Baspa, Valley is a deeply carved cleft between burly mountain slopes, where evergreen forests rise to alpine meadows crowned by snowy summits. Down below churns the frothy Sangla River. Villages here, especially further up the valley, feature houses and temples built in traditional Kinnauri wood-and-stone-style. The area is best avoided during the busy Dussehra (Durga Puja) season, when it's overrun by Indian vacationers. The hair-raising road to the valley begins at Karcham on the Rekong Peo–Shimla Hwy, passing the gushing outflow pipes from a big hydroelectric plant.

The largest village in the valley, Sangla was once a fairy-tale village of low wooden houses and slate-roofed temples looking out over a pristine valley, but the so-called benefits of hydroelectricity are changing all that. Wooden houses are being rebuilt in concrete and new hotels are springing up on every corner. You'll have to head into the hills to find the serenity that the valley was once famous for, though there are neck-craning views of Kinner Kailash from here and a few guesthouses set in blissfully peaceful gardens. Walk down to the lower village to admire the old stone houses and Hindu and Buddhist temples. The **Bering Nag Temple** forms the centrepiece of the annual **Phulech Festival** in September.

Sleeping & Eating

All hotels are booked solid during Durga Puja, but ask about discounts outside of September and October, which comprise the main tourist season.

Braham Villa Guest House GUESTHOUSE $
(☎ 9459385863; r ₹300-400) A two minute walk up a trail from the main road, this four-room, family-run place surrounded by orchards and gardens has enormous, clean rooms; the ones upstairs have carved wooden ceilings. There are long, gorgeous views up the valley from the shared terrace.

Sangla Resort GUESTHOUSE $
(☎ 242201; d ₹650-900) Uphill from the bridge near the town centre, this is one of Sangla's most appealing places. A stone chalet is set in peaceful gardens and surrounded by orchards. Rooms are spotless and the shared terrace and balconies have great valley views.

Baspa Guesthouse HOTEL $
(☎ 9805649350; d ₹400-660) Run by a genial Kinnauri family, centrally-located Baspa offers a range of decent rooms with wood panelling and enough mirrors to satisfy Narcissus. There are good views from the upper floors.

The bus stand has half a dozen identical 'Tibetan restaurants' serving *momos* (Tibetan dumplings), *thukpa* (Tibetan noodle soup), chow mein, fried rice and Indian snacks.

ℹ Getting There & Away

Buses run in the morning to Rampur (₹100, five hours) and there are two daily buses to Rekong Peo (₹50, three hours), one in the morning, the other at about 3pm. Local buses run up the valley to Chitkul (₹30, 1½ hours) at around noon and 5pm. Buses run to Shimla (₹250, eleven hours) at 6.30am and 5.30pm.

Share jeeps can take you up to Chitkul (₹40, one hour) or down to Karcham (₹45, 1½ hours), on the main Shimla–Rekong Peo bus route. Taxis cost ₹1000 to Rekong and ₹1600 to Sarahan.

AROUND THE SANGLA VALLEY

Clinging to a rocky spur 2km above Sangla, the village of **Kamru** was the former capital of the kingdom of Bushahr. The village is modernising rapidly but there are some impressive slate and stone houses and temples. The village is dominated by the tower-style **Kamakhya Devi Fort**, the former home of the *thakurs* of Bushahr (shoes and leather items should be removed and heads must be covered). Kamru is reached by a sealed road through apple and walnut orchards, starting just west of the bridge into Sangla.

Further up the valley from Sangla are the smaller villages of **Rakcham** (3050m), 14km from Sangla, and **Chitkul** (3450m) another 10km up the road. The last stop on the old trade route to Tibet – and an increasingly popular stop for backpackers – Chitkul is easily the most scenic settlement along the Sangla. A tiny wooden hamlet, it sits in a meadow above the treeline with full-on views of Rani Khanda Mountain up the valley. There are easy walks along the river and strenuous scrambles into the hills; this is where the trail circumabulating Kinner Kailash descends into the Sangla Valley.

A handful of basic guesthouses in Chitkul have rooms from ₹100-300; among the best of the bunch is **Thakur Guest House** (r ₹250), with stone walls and carpeted floors. Buses leave Chitkul at 6am and 2pm, going through Sangla (₹30, one hour) all the way to Rekong Peo (₹60, 3½ hours).

REKONG PEO

☎ 01786 / ELEV 2290M

Rekong Peo is the main administrative centre for Kinnaur and an important transport hub, but the main reason to visit is as a stepping stone to the pretty village of Kalpa, or to obtain a permit for onward travel to Tabo in Spiti. A steep walk above town near the radio mast is the **Kinnaur Kalachakra Celestial Palace** (Mahabodhi Gompa), with a 10m-high statue of Sakyamuni and great views across to Kinner Kailash (6050m).

Known to locals as 'Peo', the town is spread out along a looping road about 10km above the Hindustan–Tibet Hwy. Most hotels are around the main bazaar at the bottom of town or uphill from the bus stand. A set of concrete steps connects the bus stand and bazaar.

There is nowhere to change money, but the State Bank of India ATM in the main bazaar accepts international cards.

The **Tourist Information Centre** (☎ 222897; ⊙ 10am-5pm Mon-Sat, closed 2nd Sat of month) below the bazaar provides some local information but is mainly kept busy as a rail reservation office. There's also an internet cafe (per hour ₹50) here. This is the place to arrange **inner line permits** for onward travel to Tabo in Spiti. The office issues permits (₹350) within a few hours. It's best to show up as early in the day as possible. You'll need a couple of passport-sized photos and copies of your passport identity and visa pages. Solo travellers may run into minor hassles getting permits here since the powers-that-be prefer groups of two or more, so if you're alone you can streamline the process by hooking up with someone else just for paperwork purposes.

In the main bazaar, **Little Chef Restaurant** (per hr ₹40; ⊙ 8am-10pm) has internet access.

🛏 Sleeping & Eating

Ridang Hotel
HOTEL $

(☎ 9816820767; d ₹300-900) The best of several hotels lining the main bazaar, Ridang has a range of tidy rooms, some carpeted and all with TV. There's also a good restaurant.

Hotel Mehfil
INDIAN $$

(ITBP Rd; mains ₹45-230) Uphill from the bazaar, near the start of the steps up to the bus stand, Mehfil serves some of the coldest beer in North India, and a big range of veg and nonveg food. Eat on the restaurant side to avoid the local drunks in the bar.

❶ Getting There & Away

The bus stand is 2km from the main bazaar by road or 500m by the steps that start by the police compound at the top of ITBP Rd.

Buses run roughly hourly to Shimla (₹265, 10 hours) from 4am to 7pm, via Jeori (for Sarahan; ₹90, four hours) and Rampur (₹120, five hours). To Sangla there are direct buses at 9.30am, 1pm and 4pm (₹50, 2½ hours) or you can take any bus heading south and change at Karcham (₹25, one hour).

For Spiti, there's a 7am bus to Kaza (₹250, 11 hours) via Nako (₹125, five hours) and Tabo (₹200, nine hours). A second bus leaves for Tabo at 4pm, and another heads only as far as Nako at noon. You need an inner line permit to travel this route – see left.

Local buses run hourly from the main bazaar to Kalpa (₹10, 30 minutes), or you can take a chartered taxi (₹200) or shared taxi (₹30). Taxis charge ₹1000 to Sangla and ₹4000 to Shimla or Kaza.

KALPA

☎ 01786 / ELEV 2960M

Reached by a winding road above Rekong Peo, Kalpa is a little gem. Majestic views of the Kinner Kailash massif grab your eyeballs and don't let go. The surrounding orchards and forest provide easy walks, or you can just wander the narrow cobbled streets. There are several simple guesthouses here, plus a growing number of modern hotels on the ridge above town.

According to legend, this was the winter home of Shiva, and there are some impressive Kinnauri-style temples in the **Narayan-Nagini** temple complex, plus a colourful **Buddhist temple** at the top of the village. In September/October, villagers pile wildflowers in the centre of the village as part of the annual **Phulech Festival**.

🛏 Sleeping & Eating

The following hotels are booked solid during the Durga Puja holiday season (September/October) and offer discounts at other times.

Hotel Blue Lotus
HOTEL $

(☎ 226001; r ₹350-900) Hard to beat for its combination of convenience, quality and price, this friendly place has a range of rooms and a wide, sunny terrace facing directly across to the mountains – ideal for a breakfast or just hanging out in a state of Himalayan-inspired awe.

Hotel Rollingrang
HOTEL $

(☎ 9816421102; d ₹500-600, without bathroom ₹300) Up in a peaceful spot on the hillside above the village, rooms here are spacious and sparkling clean, with enormous bathrooms. The best have balconies with perfect mountain views. In all, it's great value.

Hotel Kinner Villa   HOTEL $$
(☎226006; r ₹1800) Reached via a 1km walk through orchards and farmland beyond the village, Kinner Villa is the pick of Kalpa's guesthouses. Rooms have superb mountain views and there are heated lounges with big windows facing the valley for winter.

For meals, try the restaurant at the Blue Lotus or the string of *dhabas* (snack bars) on the road down to the Buddhist temple.

ⓘ Getting There & Away
Local minibuses run throughout the day between Kalpa and Rekong Peo (₹10, 30 minutes), or you can take a taxi (₹30/200 shared/chartered) or walk – follow the well-worn stepped path rather than the winding road. If heading to the Sangla Valley, catch the 'Chitkul Express' direct from Kalpa at around 9am, stopping in Sangla (₹60, three hours) and Chitkul (₹90, five hours).

CENTRAL HIMACHAL PRADESH

Central Himachal is dominated by the Kullu and Parvati Valleys – famous for the production of woollen shawls and charas. The area is popular with hippies, honeymooners, trekkers and adrenaline junkies, and is home to Manali, one of the state's main travellers' centres. This is also the main route northwards, and many people continue from Manali over Rohtang La (3978m) to Lahaul, Spiti and Ladakh.

For more information on Kullu district, see the websites www.kullu.net and http://hpkullu.nic.in.

Mandi
☎01905 / POP 27,400 / ELEV 800M

Formerly a trading stop on the salt route to Tibet, Mandi is the gateway to the Kullu Valley and the junction of the main roads from Kullu, Chandigarh and Pathankot. It's no tourist town, and it feels more Punjabi than Himalayan, with a large Sikh community and a sticky air reminiscent of the plains. Sprawling around the confluence of the Beas River and the Suketi Khad stream, the town is dotted with ancient Shaivite temples – at

least 81, according to official figures – and you can do a day trip into the hills to visit the holy lakes at Rewalsar and Prashar.

Mandi is centred on a sunken shopping complex called Indira Market, arranged around a pretty garden square, with the steps leading to the Raj Mahal Palace on one side. The bus stand is on the east side of the Beas River, a ₹15 autorickshaw ride away. Though not a top-shelf destination, it's a nice place to stop and get off the tourist trail for a few days.

◎ Sights & Activities

Bhutnath Mandir   HINDU TEMPLE
Along the river, this brightly painted temple dating from the 7th century AD is the focal point for the animated **Shivaratri Festival** in February, honouring Lord Shiva.

Other River Temples   HINDU TEMPLES
If you follow Bhutnath Bazar to the river, you'll find bathing ghats with a giant statue of **Hanuman** and a long avenue of carved stone *sikharas* (Hindu temple-spires). Most impressive are the **Panch Bahktar** and **Triloknath** mandirs, facing each other across the river. Also worth seeking out is the **Akardash Rudar** mandir, near the British-built bridge over the Beas.

Rani Amrit Kaur Park   PARK
Perched at the top of Tarna Hill is **Rani Amrit Kaur Park**, with superb views and the colourful **Syamakali Temple**, decorated with paintings of ferocious incarnations of Kali. You can walk the 5km from town or take an autorickshaw (₹50).

🛏 Sleeping & Eating

There are several hotels and places to eat conveniently lining Indira Market.

Evening Plaza Hotel   HOTEL $
(☎225123; d from ₹500, with AC ₹990; ❄) Right on the main square, this is reliable value offering clean rooms with TVs and a resident moneychanger. Front-facing rooms are best but the noisiest.

Raj Mahal Palace Hotel   HERITAGE HOTEL $$
(☎222401; www.rajmahalpalace.com; r from ₹900, with AC ₹1700, ste ₹2000-3200; ❄) Mandi's most romantic hotel, this refurbished heritage place occupies part of the palace of Mandi's royal family. The rooms are bright, cosy and clean, some with the air of a colonial hunting lodge, some with a modern

chalet design. The **Garden Restaurant** here (mains ₹60 to ₹160, open 7am to 11pm) is the best in town, set under trees, with a choice of indoor and outdoor dining, excellent veg and nonveg food and the Copacabana Bar.

Treat Restaurant   SOUTH INDIAN **$**
(Indira Market; dishes ₹30-130) On the lower level of the market square, this small but swish restaurant is a popular meeting spot and serves up Chinese and South Indian food in air-conditioned comfort. They've got good omelettes and decent coffee for breakfast.

ℹ Information

There isn't anywhere to change travellers cheques, but there are international ATMs at the State Bank of India and HDFC around the market square, while the Evening Plaza Hotel can change US dollars (cash). There are several internet cafes around the square.

ℹ Getting There & Away

Bus

The bus station is across the river in the eastern part of town. Local buses run to Rewalsar (₹25, 1½ hours, hourly) until early evening from Indira Chowk, below the Raj Mahal Hotel.

Taxi

Taxis at the bus station charge ₹1000 to Kullu, ₹800 to Bhuntar airport and ₹600 for a return trip to Rewalsar. Expect to pay around ₹1500 per day for longer trips to the Banjar Valley and Great Himalayan National Park.

Rewalsar Lake

📞 01905 / ELEV 1350M
High in the hills about 24km southwest of Mandi, the sacred lake of Rewalsar is revered by Buddhists, Hindus and Sikhs. The Indian scholar Padmasambhava departed from Rewalsar in the 8th century AD to spread Buddhism to Tibet, and Hindus, Buddhists and Sikhs came together here in the 17th century to plan their resistance against ethnic cleansing by the Mughals.

Today it's home to the ochre-red **Drikung Kagyu Gompa**, with an active *thangka* (Tibetan cloth painting) school, academy of Buddhist studies and a large, central Sakyamuni statue. Just beyond is the pale blue **gurdwara** (Sikh temple) built in honour of Guru Gobind Singh in the 1930s. In the other direction, the **Tso-Pema Ogyen Heru-kai Nyingmapa Gompa** has artful murals and atmospheric *pujas* (offerings or prayers) in the morning and afternoon. Uphill from the lake is the towering white **Zigar Drukpa Kagyud Institute**, with outsized statues of tantric deities. A 12m-high statue of Padmasambhava surveys his kingdom from the hillside. On the far side of the lake are a number of small **Hindu temples** dedicated to the sage Rishi Lomas, who was forced to do penance here as a dedication to Shiva.

Local taxi drivers can arrange tours to other temples and viewpoints around the lake, including the **Padmasambhava Cave** on the ridge, where Padmasambhava allegedly meditated (you can also walk here from the lakeshore).

At the ghats on the northwestern side of the lake is a remarkable fish-feeding frenzy where hundreds of fish practically jump out of the water to get to the puffed rice being thrown in by pilgrims.

🛏 Sleeping & Eating

Hotel Lotus Lake   HOTEL **$**
(📞 240239; hlotuslake@yahoo.com; r ₹350-600) Facing the lake, this spotless modern place is Buddhist-run and the bright rooms, with TV and hot water, are a bargain.

BUSES FROM MANDI

DESTINATION	FARE (₹)	DURATION (HR)	FREQUENCY
Aut	45	one	half-hourly
Bhuntar	70	two	half-hourly airport
Chandigarh	190	six	10 daily
Delhi	320/625 (ordinary/deluxe)	12	10 daily
Dharamsala	165	six	six daily
Kullu	85	2½	half-hourly
Manali	125	four	half-hourly
Shimla	165	six	hourly

Drikung Kagyu Gompa Guesthouse HOTEL $
(☑240364; www.dk-petsek.org; r without bathroom ₹100-200) The guesthouse at the red gompa has simple but cosy quarters for pilgrims and nonpilgrims. Bucket hot water is included. There's a shared terrace with peaceful lake views.

There are several *dhabas* and simple Buddhist restaurants. **Ema Ho Coffee Shop** (drinks & snacks ₹15-40), at the entrance to the Drikung Kagyu Gompa, helps support the monastery with the coffees, teas and fresh baked pastries it serves. **Kora Community Cafe** (meals ₹30-80), near Hotel Lotus Lake, is good for coffee, Tibetan snacks and veg thali.

❶ Getting There & Away

Frequent buses go to Rewalsar from Mandi (₹25, 1½ hours), making for an easy day trip. A taxi from Mandi costs ₹450/600 one way/return.

Mandi To Kullu

About 15km south of Kullu near the village of Bajaura is **Basheshar Mahadev**, the largest stone temple in the Kullu Valley. Built in the 8th century AD and intricately carved, the temple is a larger version of the classic hutstyle *sikhara* seen all over the Kullu Valley.

Hidden away in the hills between Mandi and Bajaura is scenic **Prashar Lake** (2730m), home to the striking, pagoda-style **Prashara Temple**, built in the 14th century in honour of the sage Prashar Rishi. Prashar is an 8km walk from the village of Kandi on the Mandi–Bajaura road, accessible by local bus (ask for times at the bus stand).

Southeast of Mandi is the little-visited **Banjar Valley**, offering peaceful walks and trips to unspoiled villages. The town of **Banjar** has a few simple hotels, and you can hike the steep 6km to the village of **Chaini** to see one of the tallest temple towers in Himachal – damaged by an earthquake in 1905 but still impressive at seven storeys. A popular longer walk is the trek to the 3223m **Jalori Pass**.

Great Himalayan National Park

This 750-sq-km **national park** (☑01902-265320; www.greathimalayannationalpark.com; per day Indian/foreigner ₹10/200, camera ₹50/150, video ₹2500/5000) was established in 1984 to preserve the home of 180 species of birds and rare mammals, such as black bears, brown bears, musk deer and the ever-elusive snow leopard. The park also runs programs that provide a sustainable income for people living on the periphery of the conservation area.

Wildlife is best spotted on a three- to eight-day organised trek, accompanied by a park ranger. Arrangements can be made through the park rangers at the Sai Ropa Tourist Centre, 5km before Gushaini, or with private companies in Manali.

To get here, catch any bus on the Mandi-Manali route to Aut, then take a taxi to the park entrance.

Bhuntar
☑01902

Bhuntar is a highway town with the main airport for the Kullu Valley (the airport is smack in the centre of town, by the Beas River) and a handful of hotels catering to airline passengers. This is also the junction town for buses to the beautiful Parvati Valley. Most travellers merely pass through on the road to or from Manali or Kasol, or stay at Kullu, 10km down the road.

Bhuntar has a State Bank of India ATM, which is the last place you're able to get cash with plastic if you're headed to the Parvati Valley.

🛏 Sleeping & Eating

There are a few choices opposite the airport, and 500m north in the main bazaar.

Hotel Bala Ji Inn HOTEL $
(☑265096; d ₹500-1250) By the junction where the road forks to the Kullu and Parvati Valleys, rooms here are clean and modern. The rooftop terrace has great views of the river.

Hotel Amit HOTEL $
(☑265123; d ₹550-1550) Next door to the Bala Ji, Amit offers smarter rooms with surprisingly stylish furnishings. There's also a good restaurant downstairs.

There are several *dhabas* at the bus stand, or more-substantial meals are available at **Malabar Restaurant** (mains ₹40-120), opposite the airport.

❶ Getting There & Away

Air

The airport is next to the bus stand. **Kingfisher Air** (www.flykingfisher.com) has a daily flight to Delhi.

Jagson Airlines (✆265222; www.jagsonair
lines.com; Bhuntar airport; ⊗8am-5pm) has
short-hop flights from Delhi to Bhuntar and on
to Dharamsala on Tuesday, Thursday and Saturday, and from Delhi to Bhuntar via Shimla on
Monday, Wednesday and Friday. Baggage limit is
a measly 10kg.

Bus

There are very regular services to Manali (₹50,
three hours), Kullu (₹13, 30 minutes) and Mandi
(₹68, two hours). Buses to other destinations
pass through three hours after leaving Manali.
For the Parvati Valley, there are regular services
to Manikaran (₹40, three hours) via Kasol (₹35,
2½ hours) and Jari (₹25, one hour).

Taxi

The taxi stand is next to the bus stand. Fares
include Jari (₹550), Kasol (₹750), Kullu (₹300),
Manali (₹1100), Mandi (₹1400) and Manikaran
(₹900).

Parvati Valley

✆01902
The Parvati River winds from the highway
at Bhuntar to the hot springs at Manikaran
and beyond, and the sublime surrounding
valley is a popular traveller hang-out. Over
the years the Parvati Valley has developed
a well-deserved reputation for its wild and
cultivated crops of charas – as well as its
natural beauty. A couple of villages along
the river have been transformed into hippie resorts, offering cheap accommodation,
international food and a nonstop reggae
soundtrack to crowds of dreadlocked and
taffeta-skirted travellers. There are some
excellent treks in the area – including the
trek to the intriguing mountain village of
Malana, over the Chandrakani Pass to Naggar, or across the Pin-Parvati Pass to Spiti.
For safety reasons, solo trekking is not recommended – see the boxed text, p298.

JARI & MALANA

About halfway along the Parvati Valley, **Jari**
is a busy little village straddling the highway,
but it's the quietest of the traveller hang-
outs in the valley. Most travellers stay above
the village in the peaceful hamlet of Mateura
Jari – it's worth the hike up to it.

Jari is the starting point for the trek to the
mountain village of **Malana**, though a road
now goes most of the way there – you can
arrange a taxi in Jari, Kasol or Manikaran.
Malana was once an isolated sprawl of traditional wood and stone houses, but about
half of them burned in a fire in 2008 and
some have been replaced by cinder block
boxes. The villagers have their own unique
caste system and, while Hindu, each February they perform a Muslim ritual, slaughtering and eating a sheep. Charas is an integral
part of their religious practice.

Visitors no longer need to wait on the outskirts of the village to be invited in, but once
inside you must obey a litany of esoteric rules
or face minimum fines of ₹1000. For example,
it's forbidden to touch any of the villagers or
their belongings, including homes, temples
or buildings – they want nothing soiled by
the spiritually impure hands of low-caste
or non-Hindus. To get the most out of the
cultural experience and avoid breaking any
rules, it's worthwhile to visit with a knowledgeable guide (₹3000, including transport).

There are a few guesthouses above the village proper, where foreigners are welcome
to stay overnight for around ₹150. A taxi
(₹750 one-way from Jari) will take you to
the end of the road, from where it's a steep
one-hour walk up to the village. Carry your
passport as you must show it to security at
the hydroelectric plant. It's also possible to
walk the 17km all the way to Malana, both
from Jari and from Kasol.

For guide services to Malana or for
any trekking around the Parvati Valley,
contact **Negi's Himalayan Adventure**
(✆9816081894; www.negis-himalayan-adventure.
com) in Jari. Owner Chhape Negi is head of
the area's mountain rescue team (meaning if
travellers or locals go missing in the hills, he
gets the call), so he's as reliable as it gets. He
also runs a museum with shelves full of traditional artefacts from Malana along with a
small guesthouse in the village of Chowki,
across the river from Jari.

🛏 Sleeping & Eating

Most guesthouses are a steep 1.5km walk
above Jari through cornfields to the beautifully serene hamlet of Mateura Jari – follow
the guesthouse signs from the main road.
None have private bathrooms.

Village Guest House   GUESTHOUSE $
(✆9805190051; r ₹100) This large, welcoming guesthouse is the first place you come
to in Mateura Jari, with a big walled garden
and rooms in several old village houses.
The owners are charming and the spotless
rooms are a bargain. Meals are available.

Just uphill from Village Guest House, near
some ornate wooden temples, are the
laid-back **Chandra Place Guesthouse**

WARNING – DEADLY VACATIONS

Since the mid-1990s more than two dozen foreign tourists have 'disappeared' from the Kullu and Parvati Valleys. While some got too deep into the high-stakes local drug trade and crossed the wrong people, others became lost or fatally injured while trekking alone through the confusing and rugged mountain terrain.

If you plan to head into the hills, especially around the Parvati Valley, we recommend going with a guide who can steer you away from natural – and human – hazards. It's a good idea to let your hotel know where you are going and when you plan to return, avoid walking alone, and be cautious about befriending *sadhus* (holy people) or others wandering in the woods. So go, hike, and enjoy this incredible area – just be smart about it, for your mother's sake!

(☎9805969606; r ₹100), with an awesome covered porch with blissful views, and **Rooftop Guesthouse** (☎275434; r ₹100), both offering a pleasant, villagey vibe.

❶ Getting There & Away

Buses from Bhuntar to Manikaran stop in Jari (₹25, one hour). A one-way taxi between Bhuntar and Jari is around ₹550.

KASOL

☎01902

Spread out along the lovely Parvati River and with mountain views to the northeast, Kasol is the main traveller hang-out in the valley. It's a small village, but with reggae bars, traveller restaurants, internet cafes and cheap guesthouses catering to a largely hippie/Israeli crowd, it's like Vashaisht or Old Manali – without the large town attached. You'll either love it or loathe it. Still, it's an easy base from which to explore the valley and chill out. The village is divided into Old Kasol on the Bhuntar side of the bridge, and New Kasol on the Manikaran side, but there's little to distinguish between the two sides.

Kasol has plenty of internet cafes charging ₹40 per hour, and several travel agents will happily change cash and travellers cheques.

From Kasol, it's a demanding four-hour walk to the mountain village of **Rashol**, where there are a couple of basic guesthouses.

🛏 Sleeping & Eating

Most guesthouses close down for winter from November to April.

Old and New Kasol have loads of traveller restaurants serving cakes and identical menus of traveller fare – **Moon Dance Cafe & German Bakery** and **Evergreen Restaurant** are good choices.

Alpine Guest House   HOTEL $
(☎273710; alpinehimachal@gmail.com; d ₹400-600, q ₹800) One of the best places in town, this sturdy brick-and-timber place is set among pine trees next to the river in Old Kasol. Lawns and terraces provide space for swapping travel stories, and spacious rooms bask in the natural sounds of river and forest.

Taji Place   HOTEL $
(☎9816461684; d ₹200-400, cottage ₹700) A big pink house in a sweet littttle meadow down by the river in New Kasol, Taji has a range of tidy rooms, a couple of well-equipped cottages in the garden, and a private hot spring.

Panchali Holiday Home   HOTEL $
(☎273095; r ₹400-1200) Set back from the main road, this modern hotel has rooms with TVs, phones and geysers. They don't have a ton of character, but they're clean and comfortable. Front rooms have nice balconies, and some have an extra bed perfect for a child.

Bhoj Restaurant   MULTICUISINE $
(mains ₹50-150) The loungey furniture, funky music and great food make this a popular hang-out in Old Kasol. A full menu of Indian, Chinese and continental includes local river trout and desserts like 'Hello to the Queen'.

Little Italy   ITALIAN $
(mains ₹60-120) Pizzas and pasta dishes are better than average at this 1st-floor restaurant, and you can get a cold beer.

❶ Getting There & Away

Buses from Bhuntar to Manikaran pass through Kasol (₹25, 2½ hours). Fares at the taxi stand near the bridge in Kasol include Manikaran (₹100), Jari (₹200), Bhuntar (₹600), Kullu (₹800) and Manali (₹1600).

MANIKARAN

☎ 01902 / ELEV 1737M

With steam rising from the enormous temple beside the Parvati River, Manikaran is famous for its hot springs and is an important place of pilgrimage for Sikhs and Hindus. The name means 'Jewel from the Ear' – according to local legend, a giant snake stole earrings from Parvati while she was bathing, then snorted them out into the ground. This released the hot springs that bubble beneath. The water emerging from the ground is hot enough to boil rice (as high as 94°C) and it has to be cooled with river water for bathing. Locals claim it can cure everything from rheumatism to bronchitis.

The town is centred on the enormous multistorey **Sri Guru Nanak Ji Gurdwara**, which was built in 1940 by Sant Baba Narain Har Ji and lurks behind a veil of steam on the north side of the river. It's a temple with bathing pools and a 'hot cave', which is like a steam room. The shrine inside is revered by both Hindus and Sikhs and receives a steady stream of pilgrims.

There are baths with separate facilities for men and women in the village, too, with water diluted to a bearable temperature. The village also has several temples, including the stone hut–style **Raghunath Mandir**, and the ornate wooden **Naini Devi Temple**. Keep an eye out for pots of rice and bags of potatoes boiling in the vents, fumaroles and springs around the village and gurdwara.

🛏 Sleeping & Eating

Manikaran is much less traveller-oriented than Kasol, but there are several budget guesthouses near the gurdwara. Most hotels are on the north side of the river in the main village, reached by a suspension bridge from the bus stand. Note that alcohol is banned on the gurdwara side of the river.

Fateh Paying Guesthouse　　　HOTEL $
(☎ 9816894968; r ₹200) Signposted down an alley in the old part of the village, this big blue house has nice simple rooms, welcoming owners and a cool vibe. The rooftop terrace is set among the pitched stone roofs of old village homes.

Padha Family Guest House　　　HOTEL $
(☎ 9418408073; d ₹100-250) In the bazaar just before the gurdwara, this recommended budget place has a range of simple rooms with shared and attached bathrooms. Some have great river views, some have balconies. Downstairs is a good restaurant and a square plunge pool full of spring water.

Country Charm Hotel　　　HOTEL $
(☎ 9805683677; d ₹500-600) On the south side of the river near the bus stand, Country

HIMACHAL PRADESH PARVATI VALLEY

PIN-PARVATI VALLEY TREK

Best attempted from mid-September to mid-October, this strenuous but rewarding six to nine day trek crosses the snow-bound Pin-Parvati Pass (5319m) to the Pin Valley in Spiti. There's no accommodation en route so you'll have to be self-sufficient or go with a trekking agency from Kasol or Manali (see p305). The stages described here may be different than those preferred by your trekking agency – many take more days to do shorter stages – but this is a good baseline to work from, especially for independent trekkers.

The trail starts at Pulga – easily accessible by bus or taxi from Manikaran. From Pulga, the route ascends through forest and pasture to Thakur Khan. Two more days through an arid alpine zone takes you to High Camp for an overnight stop before attempting the pass. A challenging tramp over snow and scree will take you up to the ridge, then down into the Pin Valley. The final stage easily could be broken up to allow for two days hiking through the Pin Valley National Park to the village of Mud, which has a daily bus connection to Kaza.

STAGE	ROUTE	DURATION (HR)	DISTANCE (KM)
1	Pulga to Khir Ganga	four to five	10
2	Khir Ganga to Thakur Khan	six	15
3	Thakur Khan to Mantalai	seven	16
4	Mantalai to High Camp	four	12
5	High Camp to Pin Valley Camp via Pin-Parvati Pass	five to six	12
6	Pin Valley Camp to Mud	eight	20

Charm has views across to the village and gurdwara. Rooms are comfortable, with spotless bathrooms. The upstairs balconies practically hang out over the river.

Holy Palace Restaurant　　MULTICUISINE $
(mains ₹50-135) Travellers and pilgrims are lured here by the cosy surroundings, pop soundtrack and a broad menu of Indian, Chinese and continental veg and nonveg food.

❶ Getting There & Away

Buses run regularly between Manikaran and Bhuntar (₹35, 2½ hours), via Kasol (₹5, 15 minutes). For Manali, change in Kullu or Bhuntar. Day trips by taxi can be arranged in Manali, Kullu or Bhuntar.

From Manikaran, taxis charge ₹100 to Kasol, ₹900 to Bhuntar, ₹1000 to Kullu and ₹1700 to Manali.

Kullu

📞01902 / POP 18,300 / ELEV 1220M

Kullu is the administrative capital of the Kullu Valley and marks the beginning of the ascent to Manali. Although there's not a great deal of interest in the town itself, Kullu makes a gritty change from the hippie holiday resorts found elsewhere in the valley. In October, Kullu hosts one of the largest and loudest **Dussehra** festivals in India. Over 200 idols are paraded into town from surrounding temples, led by a huge *rath* (chariot) holding the statue of Lord Raghunath from the Raghunath Temple in Sultanpur. Simultaneously, a week-long carnival and market is held on the *maidan* (parade ground), with entertainment such as acrobats and musicians. With some 30,000 devotees hitting town, accommodation is scarce, but it's an easy day trip from Manali or even Kasol.

Kullu is divided in two by the Sarvari River. The southern part of town has the taxi stand, tourist office and most restaurants and hotels. The bus station and Raghunath Temple are north of the river – take the shortcut down through the bazaar below the Hotel Shobla International.

◉ Sights & Activities

Raghunath Temple　　HINDU TEMPLE
The pre-eminent temple in Kullu is the **Raghunath Temple**, which enshrines a revered idol that's paraded through town during Dussehra. To get there, take either of the two tracks leading uphill opposite the bus station and look for the gateway near the imposing **Raja Rupi**, the former palace of the rajas of Kullu.

Other Temples　　HINDU TEMPLES
There are several important temples in the surrounding hills, accessible by taxi or local bus (ask for times at the bus stand). About 3km from Kullu, in the village of Bhekhli, the **Bhekhli Temple** (Jagannathi Devi Temple) offers an impressive vista over Kullu and the valley.

Gijleshwar Mahadev　　HINDU TEMPLE
Reached via a 3km trek from Chansari, 11km southeast of Kullu on the east bank of the Beas, the hilltop temple of **Bijleshwar Mahadev** (Bijli Mahadev) is surmounted by a 20m wooden pole that attracts divine blessings in the form of lightning. The surge of power shatters the stone Shiva lingam inside the temple, which is then glued back together with butter.

☞ Tours

The **Kullu Taxi Operators' Union** (📞222332) offers sightseeing tours from the taxi stand for around ₹1000.

🛏 Sleeping & Eating

Hotel Vikrant　　HOTEL $
(📞222756; d ₹300-600) Centrally located down a quiet alley behind the maidan, Vikrant is a good budget choice. Wood panelling and blue carpeting give rooms a simple charm. Those on the upper floors are bigger and brighter than those on the ground floor, but all have TVs and hot showers.

Hotel Aaditya　　HOTEL $
(📞9857062618; d ₹380-770) Just across the footbridge from the bus station at the southern end of the bazaar, Aaditya tries harder than most in this price range, with quality bedframes and oddly fancy bathroom fixtures. The best are the top-floor rooms with balconies overlooking the river.

Hotel Shobla International　　HOTEL $$
(📞222800; www.shoblainternational.com; r ₹1650-2200, ste ₹2750-3850; ❄) Although this is the best of the business hotels in Kullu's centre, rooms in this modern hotel near the bazaar are clean but nothing special. There's a good restaurant and bar downstairs.

✕ Eating

There are numerous *dhabas* clustered around the taxi stand and bus station, and

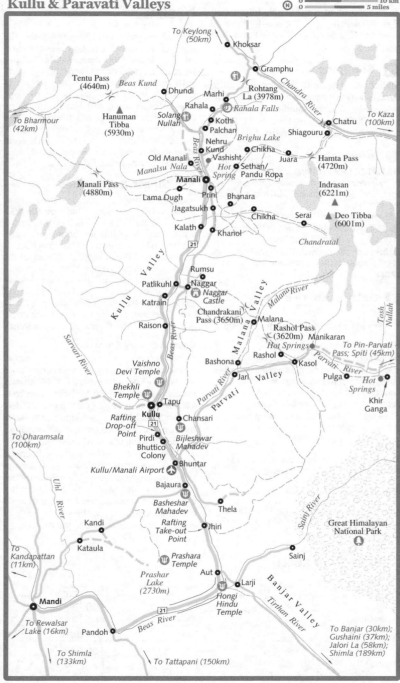

plenty of cheap eats in the narrow bazaar. The restaurant at Hotel Shobla International-al is also worth trying. For non-Indian food, head for **Hot Stuff** or **Planet Food**, both near the tourist office.

Shopping

Kullu has several outlets selling the valley's famous shawls, or you can buy at the source at the huge Bhuttico hand-loom centre just south of Kullu – see boxed text, p304. There's another Bhuttico Store in Akhara Bazaar.

Information

The **HPTDC tourist office** (☏222349; ☉10am-5pm) is near the taxi stand on the maidan. It's useful for booking deluxe HPTDC buses, which leave from outside.

The main post office is uphill from the taxi stand. There are internet cafes on the main road in Dhalpur charging ₹30 per hour.

There's an international ATM at the State Bank of India, south of the maidan, and another in the bazaar.

Getting There & Away

Air

The airport for Kullu is 10km south at Bhuntar.

Bus

On the north side of the Sarvari River, the bus station has frequent services around the valley. Buses from Manali to destinations outside the Kullu Valley arrive in Kullu about 1½ hours after departure – see p312 for more details.

See the boxed text below for useful buses around the valley.

Taxi

The taxi stand on the maidan books tours and charter trips – a day of sightseeing costs ₹1000.

Getting Around

Autorickshaws provide services around Kullu; trips in town should cost around ₹30.

Naggar

☏01902 / ELEV 1760M

Centred on imposing Naggar Castle, the slumbering village of Naggar was the capital of Kullu for 1500 years. Russian painter Nikolai Roerich settled here in the early 20th century, ensuring a steady stream of Russian tourists. The village lies on the back road between Kullu and Manali but everything of interest is around the castle, 2km uphill. There are several small internet cafes and, although it's an easy day trip from Manali, there are some decent guesthouses and restaurants around the castle.

◉ Sights & Activities

Naggar Castle   HISTORIC BUILDING
(foreigner ₹15; ☉7am-10pm) Built by the Sikh rajas of Kullu in 1460, this beautiful fort is a fine example of the alternating stone and timber style of Himachali architecture. It was converted into a hotel in 1978 when the last raja fell on hard times. There's a tiny one-room **museum** downstairs, and the **Jagtip-ath Temple** in the courtyard houses a slab of stone said to have been carried here by wild bees. The best way to experience the castle is to stay here, and there's also a restaurant.

**Roerich Gallery & Urusvati
Museum**   MUSEUM
The main road through the village continues for 2km to **Roerich Gallery** (☏248290; www.roerichtrust.org; adult/child combined admission to folk & art museum ₹30/20, camera/video ₹25/60; ☉10am-1pm & 1.30-6pm Tue-Sun, to 5pm Nov-Mar), the former home of eccentric Russian painter Nikolai Roerich, who died in Naggar in 1947. The lower floors display some of Roerich's surreally colourful paintings, while the upper floors preserve the artist's private rooms. Roerich was also the brains behind the Ro-erich Pact, a treaty signed by more than 60 countries guaranteeing the preservation of cultural monuments around the world.

BUSES FROM KULLU

DESTINATION	FARE (₹)	DURATION (HR)	FREQUENCY
Aut	35	1½	every 15min
Bhuntar	13	30min	every 10min Airport
Manali	45	1½	every 10min
Mandi	82	2½	every 10min
Manikaran	60	three	hourly

DESTINATION	FARE (₹)
Bhuntar	300
Jari	700
Kasol	850
Manali	800
Mandi	1200
Manikaran	900
Naggar	600

A five-minute walk uphill from the gallery is the **Urusvati Himalayan Folk & Art Museum** (admission with the gallery ticket), which houses the painter's personal collection of ethnological artefacts and photos of the Roerich family.

Temples HINDU TEMPLES
Heading down the track beside the castle, you'll pass the handsome 11th-century **Vishnu Mandir**, covered in ornate carvings. Downhill past the tiny post office is the **Gauri Shankar Temple**, dedicated to Shiva and surrounded by smaller temples devoted to Narayan (an incarnation of Vishnu). Just below Roerich Gallery is the pagodalike **Tripura Sundari Devi Temple**, surrounded by carved wooden outbuildings. High up on the ridge above Naggar, the **Murlidhar Krishna Temple** is reached by a woodland path beyond the Roerich Gallery.

Trekking TREKKING
Naggar is the starting point for the excellent three-day trek to Malana village and Jari via Chandrakhani Pass (3660m). Ravi Sharma at Poonam Mountain Lodge is an experienced operator who can organise this trek, as well as all-inclusive longer treks around the Kullu Valley to Manikaran, Lahaul and Spiti and Ladakh for around ₹1700 per day. Jeep safaris cost around ₹2500 per day.

🛏 Sleeping & Eating

Hotels are clustered around the castle or there's a village-style guesthouse downhill in the small hamlet of Chanalti Naggar.

Castle Hotel HERITAGE HOTEL **$$$**
(☑248316; www.hptdc.gov.in; d ₹1200-4000) The most atmospheric accommodation in town is the castle itself. Wood and stone corridors open onto a wide variety of rooms, some original and decked out in colonial finery, others completely refurbished. The views

from valley-side rooms are superb. Even if the hotel isn't within your budget, there's a good restaurant and terrace overlooking the valley.

Poonam Mountain Lodge HOTEL **$**
(☑248248; www.poonamlodge.com; r ₹300-400; @) Just below the castle, the wood-panelled rooms at this well-kept lodge are cosy and comfortable, and the owner, Ravi Sharma, is a mine of local trekking information. For longer stays you can rent his traditional stone-and-timber two-storey house in the nearby village for ₹5000 a month.

Chanderlok Guesthouse GUESTHOUSE **$**
(☑248213; d ₹250) Though the rooms here are more basic than at any other place listed, Chanderlok's outdoor garden and lawn opens up into a cool 1500-year-old stone temple complex. Cheaper rooms have bucket hot water and mattresses on the floor, slumber-party style; the best rooms have real beds and geysers.

Hotel Ragini HOTEL **$$**
(☑248185; raginihotel@hotmail.com; r ₹700-1200; @) Ragini is a clean, modern hotel that's popular for its bright rooms with parquet floors and balconies, and its garden. The rooftop restaurant serves great food, and there's an ayurvedic healing spa if your chakras need a tweak.

La Purezza ITALIAN **$**
(meals ₹50-120; ◷11am-10pm, closed winter) On the road to Roerich Gallery, this rooftop cafe serves surprisingly good pizza, pasta and fresh trout. Bring patience.

❶ Getting There & Away

Local buses run regularly between Manali and Naggar from 6am to 6pm (₹20, one hour). A return taxi from Manali to Naggar costs ₹650, and from Kullu it's ₹750.

SHOPPING FOR SHAWLS

The Kullu Valley is famous for its shawls, and the highway between Bhuntar and Manali is lined with scores of shops, showrooms and emporiums dedicated to selling traditional Kullu shawls. The shawls are woven on wooden hand-looms using wool from sheep, pashmina goats or angora rabbits. This is one of the main industries in the Kullu Valley and it provides an income for thousands of local women, many of whom have organised themselves into shawl-weaving cooperatives. You can tour several of these around Kullu and buy shawls directly from the women who make them.

With so much competition, the sales pressure in touristy places can be fairly overbearing and you'll have to haggle hard for a bargain. For high quality without the hard sell, head to the nearest branch of **Bhuttico** (www.bhutticoshawls.com), the Bhutti Weavers' Cooperative, which has showrooms in Manali, Kullu, Bhuntar and other major towns around the state. Established in 1944 by a group of village women, Bhuttico charges fixed prices, so it's a good place to gauge price and quality. Expect to pay upwards of ₹400 for lambswool, from ₹1400 for angora, from ₹3300 for pashmina and ₹6800 for the exquisitely embroidered shawls worn by village women.

Manali

📞01902 / POP 4400 / ELEV 2050M

With super views of the Dhauladhar and Pir Panjal Ranges, and the fast-flowing Beas River running through the town, Manali is a year-round magnet for tourists. Backpackers come to hang out in the hippy villages around the main town; adventure tourists come for trekking, paragliding, rafting and skiing; and Indian honeymoon couples or families come for the cool mountain air and their first taste of snow on a day trip to Rohtang La. Over the years, many tourists have been lured here by the famous Manali charas, which is seriously potent stuff. Though in Old Manali it's smoked fairly openly, it's still illegal and local police do arrest people for possession (or hit them for bribes).

As the main jumping-off point for Ladakh, Spiti and Lahaul, it makes sense to unwind here for a few days before continuing the long journey into the mountains. Daily buses and jeeps to Leh, Keylong and Kaza leave from approximately June to October. Most travellers stay in the villages of Vashisht or Old Manali, which have a laid-back vibe and plenty of services, but close for winter from sometime in October to May.

Manali's main street is the Mall, part of the highway that runs into town. The bus and taxi stands are here and most hotels and restaurants are on alleys to the west. Two roads run north from Manali along the Beas River – one to Old Manali on the west bank and one to Vashisht and the Rohtang La on the east bank.

◉ Sights & Activities

Hadimba Temple HINDU TEMPLE

(Map p306) Also known as the Dhungri Temple, this ancient wood and stone mandir was erected in 1553. Pilgrims come here from across India to honour Hadimba, the wife of Bhima from the Mahabharata. The walls of the temple are covered in woodcarvings of dancers, and horns of bulls and ibex adorn the walls. Grisly animal sacrifices are carried out in May for the three-day **Dhungri Mela**. Photo-wallahs loiter around the temple offering souvenir photos in traditional costume, with your arm around a yak or angora rabbit.

Ghatotkach, the son of Hadimba and Bhima, is worshipped in the form of a **sacred tree** near the temple. Villagers make offerings of knives, goat horns, and tin effigies of animals, people and houses.

Hadimba is a 20-minute walk northwest of Manali, or you can take an autorickshaw (₹50).

Buddhist Monasteries BUDDHIST TEMPLES

There's a small Tibetan colony just south of the town centre. The **Himalayan Nyinmapa Buddhist Temple** (Map p308; ⊗6am-6pm) contains a two-storey statue of Sakyamuni, the historical Buddha.

Further along the same lane is the more traditional **Gelukpa Cultural Society Gompa** (Map p308; ⊗6am-6pm), with an atmospheric prayer room crammed with statues of bodhisattvas, revered lamas and Buddhist deities. There's also a small workshop producing Tibetan carpets.

Old Manali AREA

About 2.5km above the Mall on the far side of the Manalsu Nala stream, Old Manali still has some of the feel of an Indian mountain village once you get past the core backpacker zone. There are some remarkable old houses of wood and stone, and the towering **Manu Maharishi Temple** (off Map p306) is built on the site where Manu is said to have meditated after landing the boat that saved humanity. A trail to Solang Nullah (11km) runs north from here through the village of Goshal (2km).

Nature Parks PARKS

A large grove of deodars (cedars) on the banks of the Beas has been set aside as a **nature park** (Map p308; admission ₹10; ⏲9am-7pm), with a small aviary of Himalayan birds, including the monal pheasant, Himachal's state bird. South of the centre is the similar **Van Vihar Park** (Map p308; admission ₹10; ⏲8am-7pm, to 5pm in winter).

Tours

In season, the HPTDC offers day tours by bus to Rohtang La (₹290) and Manikaran and the Parvati Valley (₹330), if there are enough takers. Private travel agencies offer similar bus tours.

The **Him-Anchal Taxi Operators Union** (Map p308; ☎252120; the Mall) has fixed-price tours, including Rohtang La (₹1900), Solang Nullah (₹600) and Naggar (₹650).

Adventure Tour Operators

The following places are reliable and well established and can arrange treks, tours and adventure activities – see boxed text, p311, for popular options.

Antrek Tours & Travel OUTDOOR ADVENTURE

(Map p308; ☎252292; www.antrek.co.in; 1 Rambagh, the Mall)

Arohi Travels OUTDOOR ADVENTURE

(Map p308; ☎254421; www.arohieco adventures) Located off the Mall, and also has an office at Hotel Arohi in Vashisht (Map p306).

Himalayan Adventurers OUTDOOR ADVENTURE

(Map p308; ☎252750; www.himalayanadventurersindia.com; 44 the Mall)

TOP CHOICE **Himalayan Extreme Center** OUTDOOR ADVENTURE

(Map p306; ☎9816174164; www.himalayan-extreme-center.com) With one office in Old Manali and one in Vashisht, your one-stop shop for any adventure activity.

North Face Adventure Tours OUTDOOR ADVENTURE

(Map p308; ☎254041; www.northfaceindia.com; the Mall)

Tiger Eye Adventure OUTDOOR ADVENTURE

(Map 000; ☎252718; www.tigereyeadventure.com; Old Manali) Especially recommended for transport to Leh.

Sleeping

Manali has some of the best-value accommodation in the state, though prices are highest during the peak seasons of April to June, September, October and Christmas. At other times, discounts are standard, but bargain anyway. Heating is rare in Manali so be prepared to dive under a blanket to stay warm.

Few backpackers choose to stay in central Manali unless planning to catch an early bus – the best budget places, by far, are a short distance north in the villages of Old Manali and Vashisht.

Manali also has some fine upmarket hotels and all are found along Circuit House Rd, heading uphill to Old Manali.

MANALI

Sunshine Guest House GUESTHOUSE $

(Map p306; ☎252320; Circuit House Rd; r ₹400) This rambling, wooden Raj-era mansion will appeal to lovers of unfussy colonial character rather than modern comforts. Enormous rooms with fireplaces (firewood is extra) and giant bathrooms may be a bit draughty, but the balconies, sunrooms and overgrown garden are straight out of a storybook.

Johnson Hotel HOTEL $$$

(Map p308; ☎253764; www.johnsonhotel.in; Circuit House Rd; d ₹2750-3200; ❄@📶) One of several places named in honour of the Raj-era landowner Jimmy Johnson. This is a classy wood-and-stone hotel that has snug heritage rooms, a century-old lodge and lovely gardens, as well as an excellent restaurant. Everything's in immaculate shape, making this a high-end place that's worth the price.

Negi's Hotel Mayflower HOTEL $$$

(Map p306; ☎252104; www.negismayflower.com; Club House Rd; r ₹3000; ❄@) Mayflower is a stately wooden lodge with cascading balconies and cosy but luxurious wood-panelled rooms, some with open fireplaces (firewood costs extra). The lawns and gardens are a good place to relax in the afternoon.

Manali & Vashisht

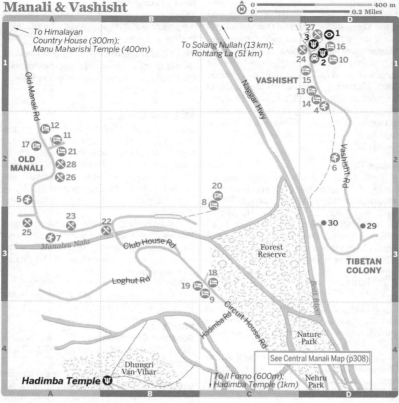

Pushpak Hotel
HOTEL $

(Map p308; ☎253656; d ₹300) Down an alley opposite the bus station, this is one of the better budget places along the Mall. Rooms have surprisingly nice carpeting and those overlooking the street have great light. The ones toward the back are quieter.

Johnson Lodge
HOTEL $$$

(Map p308; ☎251523; www.johnsonslodge.com; Circuit House Rd; d ₹2900, cottage ₹6350; ❄@) Built in wood and timber in the traditional Himachal style, but slick and contemporary inside, this towering hotel boasts bright, designer rooms that are starting to show some wear, as well as luxurious two- and three-bedroom cottages.

Banon Resorts
HOTEL $$$

(Map p306; ☎253026; www.banonresortsmanali. com; d ₹4500-6000, cottages from ₹12,000; ❄🛜) This luxury hotel is the most comfortable in Old Manali. Centrally heated rooms in the main hotel are spacious but surprisingly plain, while the two-bedroom cottages are the last word in luxurious peace and privacy.

Hotel Snow View
HOTEL $$$

(Map p308; ☎252684; www.snowviewhotelmanali. com; d ₹1800-2500; ❄) Right in the centre of town, Snow View is a comfortable, if bland, business hotel that's got one thing to boast about – an elevator! – along with all the mod cons you would expect for the price, plus a bar and restaurant.

OLD MANALI

Uphill from Manali on the far side of the Manaslu Nala stream, Old Manali is a well-established traveller centre and has Manali's best budget accommodation. Hotels are spread over a kilometre or more from the stream northwards to the village proper, but most are in an enclave about halfway along. Most places close down in late October when many locals head to Goa for the winter.

TOP CHOICE **Veer Guest House**   HOTEL $
(Map p306; ☏252710; veerguesthouse@hotmail.
com; r ₹400-700; @) Set in a pretty garden,
long-running Veer is one of Old Manali's
best-value hotels. Rooms in the quaint lime-
green original section with wood-plank
flooring have plenty of character, while new
rooms at the front are bright and slick, with
TVs and private balconies. Staff is easygoing
and helpful, and there's a great little restaurant and an internet cafe.

Drifters' Inn   HOTEL $
(Map p306; ☏9805033127; www.driftersinn.in; r
₹500-800; @⦿) This relative newcomer in
Old Manali does it right, with stylish rooms
with quality wood furnishings and outdoor
terraces on every floor. If you don't need TV,
stick to the cheaper rooms. There's a laid-
back cafe downstairs.

Himalayan Country House   GUESTHOUSE $
(off Map p306; ☏252294; www.himalayancountry
house.com; Old Manali; r ₹600-1000) Ensconced
at the end of the road in Old Manali, this
four-storey stone and timber hotel overlooks
the slate roofs of village homes and across
to the mountains. It's beautifully designed,
with traditional carved doors and compact
wood-panelled rooms opening on to shared

balconies with the best valley views of any
hotel on this side of the Beas.

Mountain Dew Guesthouse   HOTEL $
(Map p306; ☏9816446366; d ₹300-400) This yellow three-storey hotel has good-sized rooms
and nice balconies where laptop users can
sometimes catch the wi-fi signal from the
attached coffee shop. It's all-around good
value for Old Manali.

**Apple View Paying Guest
House**   GUESTHOUSE $
(Map p306; ☏253899; r without bathroom ₹200)
Up a pathway behind the HPTDC Club
House, this delightful village guesthouse is
set on a peaceful garden plot among apple
orchards. The rooms are basic but well
cared for, and the upstairs patio is perfect
for hanging out. If full, try the similar **Up
Country Lodge** (Map p306; ☏252257; d ₹200-
400) next door.

Dragon Guest House   HOTEL $
(Map p306; ☏252290; www.dragontreks.com; Old
Manali; r ₹400-1000, ste from ₹2500; ❄@⦿) A
one-time backpackers' place moving upmarket, Dragon has a beautful stone-and-wood
facade and an orchard out front. Some of the
less expensive rooms don't quite live up to

Central Manali

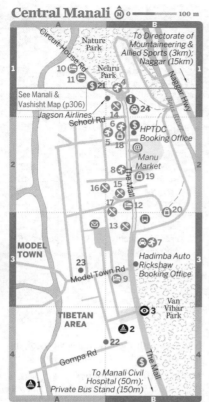

Central Manali

◎ Sights
1 Gelukpa Cultural Society Gompa	A4
2 Himalayan Nyinmapa Buddhist Temple	B4
3 Van Vihar Park Entrance	B4

◉ Activities, Courses & Tours
4 Antrek Tours & Travel	B1
5 Arohi Travels	B2
6 Himalayan Adventurers	B2
7 Him-Anchal Taxi Operators Union Tours	B3
8 North Face Adventure Tours	B2

🛏 Sleeping
9 Hotel Snow View	B3
10 Johnson Hotel	A1
11 Johnson Lodge	A1
12 Pushpak Hotel	B2

🍴 Eating
13 Chopsticks	B3
Johnson's Cafe	(see 10)
14 Khyber	B1
15 Manali Sweets	B2
16 Mayur	A2
17 Peace Cafe	B2

🛍 Shopping
18 Bhuttico	B2
19 Bhuttico	B2
20 Tibet Art Collections	B2
Tibet Emporium	(see 18)

Information
21 Trans Corp Forex	A1

Transport
22 Himalayan Inder Motors	B4
23 Life Adventure Tours	A3
Manali Luxury Coach Owners Association	(see 24)
24 Taxi Booking Desk	B1

the exterior, but the spacious suites at the top are 'honeymoon' standard. There's a good restaurant, an internet cafe, and a reliable travel agency for treks and tours.

✖ Eating

Manali has some fine Indian and international restaurants, and there are lots of cheap travellers' cafes in Old Manali and Vashisht. Most restaurants serve trout sourced from local farms.

MANALI

Mayur   INDIAN/MULTICUISINE **$$**
(Map p308; Mission Rd; dishes ₹70-250; ⊗9am-11pm) Locals rate Mayur highly for its well-prepared North and South Indian specialities. Downstairs is traditional Indian, in decor as well as cuisine, while the contemporary upstairs bistro serves dishes such as croquettes, chicken stroganoff and, oddly, Marmite toast.

Il Forno   ITALIAN **$$**
(off Map p306; Hadimba Rd; mains ₹140-270; ⊗12.30-10.30pm) Perched on a hillside near Hadimba Temple, Il Forno is a genuine Italian restaurant in a superb Himachal stone and timber building. The wood-fired pizzas, calzone, lasagne and pasta dishes are prepared by a Veronese chef and you can enjoy an espresso or beer with wonderful valley views from the garden terrace.

Johnson's Cafe
CONTINENTAL $$

(Map p308; Circuit House Rd; dishes ₹120-350; ⊙8am-10.30pm) The restaurant at Johnson Hotel is one of the best in town for European food, with dishes like lamb and mint gravy, smoked chicken, and fig and apple crumble. The restaurant-bar is cosy, but on warm evenings or sunny afternoons, the garden terrace is the place to be.

Chopsticks
ASIAN $$

(Map p308; the Mall; dishes ₹60-270; ⊙7.30am-10.30pm) The most popular traveller choice along the Mall in Manali town, this intimate Tibetan-Chinese-Japanese place is always busy. Naturally there are Indian dishes here, too, along with local trout. Cold beers and fruit wines are also served. Arrive early to secure a table in the evening.

Khyber
AFGHANI $$

(Map p308; the Mall; dishes ₹80-250; ⊙8am-midnight) Upstairs by the main junction, this darkened bar and restaurant is central Manali's best place for a cold beer or bottle of fruit wine or cider. The food is also good – the speciality is meat-heavy Punjabi and Afghani cuisine but there's also Chinese, continental, and tandoori trout. Drinks are reasonably priced, and the booths are a good place to huddle.

Peace Cafe
MULTICUISINE $$

(Map p308; Siyali Mahadev Market; mains ₹70-200; ⊙8.30am-10pm) Down an alley near the post office, this cosy 1st-floor Tibetan-run restaurant serves possibly Manali's biggest range of global food, from *momos* to Japanese noodles, and local river trout to Hong Kong lamb. Service is friendly and efficient.

Manali Sweets
SWEETS $

(Map p308; snacks from ₹10; ⊙from 7am) Manali's favourite *dhaba* (snack bar), serving Indian sticky sweets, hot chai, samosas and hot veg snacks from early morning to late at night.

OLD MANALI

There are numerous garden restaurants serving all the usual suspects – pizzas, pita-bread wraps, *momos,* banana pancakes, apple pie – from early morning to late evening. All these places close by the start of November. Popular backpacker restaurants include **Shiva Garden Cafe** (Map p306) and **Blue Elephant Cafe** (Map p306) near the river, both serving decent traveller fare for ₹50 to ₹120.

Lazy Dog Lounge
FUSION $$

(Map p306; mains ₹70-300; ⊙) This restaurant/bar overlooking the river features big plates of fresh and flavourful international food that's steps above typical backpacker fare. Sit on chairs, benches or floor cushions in a space that's classy yet earthy, or relax in the outdoor garden. The beer (₹120-230) and wine (₹180-1250) lists are plenty long and the desserts will sate your sweet tooth.

Dylan's Toasted & Roasted
CAFE $

(Map p306; www.dylanscoffee.com; drinks & snacks ₹20-100; ⊙10am-8pm Mon-Sat) Manali's mellowest hang-out, this hole-in-the-wall cabin-style coffeeshop in Old Manali serves the best espresso coffee in town, cinnamon tea, hearty breakfasts, garlic cheese toast and wicked desserts like chocolate-chip cookies and 'Hello to the Queen'. DVD movies are shown in an adjoining room.

Veer Restaurant
MULTICUISINE $

(Map p306; mains ₹60-150; ⊙8am-10pm) Located at Veer Guest House, this relaxed restaurant has garden tables with umbrellas outside and cushions on the floor inside. Most nights a Bollywood movie is playing on the TV. The barbecued chicken is a treat and service is good-humoured.

Pizza Olive
ITALIAN $$

(Map p306; mains ₹80-160; ⊙9am-10pm) The aromas wafting from the pizza oven give this place an authentic Italian feel and the pizzas and pasta dishes don't disappoint. You can eat indoors or out in the garden.

Drinking

Restaurants double as bars to form the centre of nightlife in Manali, and most serve alcohol. Himachal's bounteous orchards produce huge quantities of apples, pears, plums and apricots, some of which are fermented locally and made into alcoholic cider and perry (pear cider) and a wide range of strong fruit wines. In Manali town, the best places for a beer or fruit wine are Khyber and Chopsticks. The upmarket Johnson Hotel, Johnson Lodge and Banon Resort also have good bars.

In Old Manali, most traveller cafes serve beer. In Vashisht, Rainbow Cafe is the place to be.

Shopping

Manali is crammed with souvenir shops selling souvenirs from Himachal, Tibet and Ladakh – most are open from 10am to 7pm. **Tibet Art Collections** (Map p308; 252974; NAC

OUTDOOR ACTIVITIES IN MANALI

Manali is the adventure sports capital of Himachal Pradesh, and all sorts of outdoor activities can be organised through tour operators in town (see Tours, p305).

Fishing

The rivers of the Kullu and Parvati Valleys are rich in trout and mahseer. The season runs from March to June and October to November, and rods and tackle can be hired from agencies in Manali; daily fishing licences from HPTDC cost ₹100. Top spots include the upper tributaries of the Beas and Parvati Rivers at Kasol.

Jeep Safaris

Jeep safaris can be arranged to Ladakh, Lahaul and Spiti for around ₹2600 per day, visiting monasteries, mountain passes and glacial lakes, with accommodation in tents or village guesthouses.

Mountain Biking

Though you may think that the steep slopes around Manali would have some prime mountain biking, you'll probably have to take a car to most tracks that are worth riding. Agencies offer bike hire for ₹450 to ₹850 per day (and can give current info on routes) or you can organise tours to Ladakh, Spiti and Lahaul. One audacious day trip is the descent from the Rohtang La – buses and taxis can transport you and your bike to the pass, then you can freewheel down. On all high-altitude routes, take time to acclimatise.

Mountaineering

Mountaineering training can be arranged through the **Directorate of Mountaineering & Allied Sports** (off Map p306; ☑250337; www.adventurehimalaya.org), in Aleo, 3km south of Manali. Basic eight-day mountaineering courses run between May and October for ₹3400/13,000 (Indian/foreigner), including food, accommodation, guides and training. The courses cover essential trekking techniques and a series of local ascents. Local agencies can arrange expeditions to Hanuman Tibba (5930m) and Deo Tibba (6001m).

Paragliding

Paragliding is popular at Solang Nullah from April to October. Short flights start at ₹700 for a two-minute flight, but adventure tour operators can organise longer flights from surrounding take-off points for ₹1500 to ₹3000.

Rafting

White-water rafting trips on the Beas River can be arranged in Manali, starting from Pirdi, 3km downriver from Kullu. There is 14km of Grade II and III white water between Pirdi and

Market) has a good choice, while **Tibet Emporium** (Map p308; ☑252431; the Mall) stocks Tibetan knick-knacks and funky T-shirts.

Shawls are sold all over Manali. A good place to start is at the cooperative **Bhuttico** (Map p308; ☑260079; the Mall), which charges fair, fixed prices and has another store located in Manu Market. Several other cooperatives have shops around the Mall.

ℹ️ Information

Internet Access

Many travel agencies offer internet access, and there are numerous internet cafes in Old Manali and Vashisht charging ₹30 to ₹40 per hour. The following places are in town.

Cafe Digital (Map p308; Manu Market; per hr ₹50; ⊙8am-11pm)

Himgiri Adventure & Tours (Map p308; the Mall; per hr ₹50; ⊙9.30am-9.30pm)

Medical Services

Manali Civil Hospital (off Map p308; ☑253385) Just south of town.

Money

Banks in Manali don't offer foreign exchange but there are private moneychangers, and the State Bank of India has two international ATMs – the one at the bank branch south of the pedestrian

the take-out point at Jhiri; trips cost around ₹600 per person. Book through travel agents or directly at Pirdi.

Rock Climbing

The cliffs at Solang, Aleo and Vashisht have a good range of bolted and traditional routes ranging from French 6a to 6c (British 5a to 6a). Himalayan Extreme Center (p305) in Vashisht offers day trips for ₹1500/900 per full-/half-day, including all equipment. Independent climbers should bring a selection of slings, nuts and cams (particularly in the smaller sizes) and a 30m or 60m rope.

Skiing & Snowboarding

From January to March, the village of Solang Nullah transforms into Himachal's main ski and snowboarding resort. Skiing and showboarding equipment can be hired through tour operators in Manali or accommodation places in Solang Nullah for ₹500 per day. Year-round high-altitude skiing expeditions can be arranged on virgin powder (experienced skiers only) through Himalayan Extreme Center for around ₹2500 per day (trips last three to five days). Costly heli-skiing trips to high-altitude powder can be arranged through Himachal Heli Adventures (☑9816025899; www.himachal.com).

Walking & Trekking

Manali is a popular starting point for organised mountain treks. Most agencies offer multiday treks for around ₹2500 per day, all-inclusive. Popular options include Beas Kund (three days), the Pin-Parvati Trek from the Parvati Valley to Spiti (eight days) and the Hamta Pass (4270m) to Lahaul (five days).

Plenty of shorter walks are possible from Manali, though the usual rules on safe trekking apply – tell someone where you are going and never walk alone. The 13km hike up the western side of the Beas River to Solang Nullah is a pleasing alternative to the bus, or you can trek 6km to the snowline above Lama Dugh meadow along the Manalsu Nala stream.

Zorbing

During summer, the ski slope at Solang Nullah is a popular place for zorbing – basically, rolling downhill inside a giant inflatable ball. You can make arrangements in Manali or in Solang Nullah – expect to pay ₹300 for a roll down the hill.

Other Activities

Other activities available in the area include horse riding (₹900 per day) and canyoning (₹2400 per day). Quad bike rides around Solang Nullah cost ₹500 for a quick 4km round or ₹1500 per hour. Short hot-air balloon rides are sometimes organised from Solang Nullah during summer.

mall has shorter queues. If you are heading north to Ladakh, Lahaul or Spiti, change some extra money here.

Trans Corp Forex (Map p308; The Mall; ☺9.30am-7.30pm) Changes cash and cheques.

Post

Manali sub-post office (Map p308; Model Town; ☺9.30am-5.30pm Mon-Sat) For poste restante and parcels (before 2pm only).

Tourist Information

HPTDC booking office (Map p308; ☑252116; the Mall; ☺7am-8pm, 9am-5pm in winter) Can book seats on HPTDC buses, and rooms in HPTDC hotels.

Tourist office (Map p308; ☑253531; the Mall; ☺8am-9pm, 10am-5pm Mon-Sat in winter) Helpful for brochures and local information. You can book train tickets at the railway booking office (open 8am to 1.30pm Monday to Saturday) next door.

ⓘ Getting There & Away

Air

Manali's closest airport is 50km south at Bhuntar. You can book seats at travel agencies in Manali or at **Jagson Airlines** (Map p308; ☑252843; www.jagsonairlines.com; the Mall).

Bus

The bus station has a **booth** (Map p308; ✆252323; ⊗5am-7pm) for advance bookings.

Luxury buses are run by the **HPTDC** (Map p308; ✆252116; the Mall) and **Manali Luxury Coach Owners Association** (Map p308; ✆253816; the Mall). Tickets can be bought from their offices or from travel agencies thronging the Mall.

KULLU & PARVATI VALLEYS Buses go to Kullu every 30 minutes (₹45, 1½ hours), continuing to Mandi (₹125, four hours) via the airport at Bhuntar (₹60, two hours). Regular local services run to Naggar (₹25, one hour) from 6am to 6pm. For the Parvati Valley, change at Bhuntar.

LEH From 15 July to 15 September, buses make the bone-shaking ascent to Leh in two exhausting but spectacular days, with a stopover en route at Keylong or Sarchu. Bring a shawl or warm clothing and be alert to the symptoms of Acute Mountain Sickness (see p1193 for more info).

Government buses (₹610) leave at 1pm, with an overnight stop in Keylong. Private buses run till around mid-October, charging about ₹1700 and stopping at Keylong or Sarchu.

LAHAUL & SPITI The Rohtang La, on the road between Manali and Keylong, is normally open from June to late October and the Kunzum La, between Manali and Spiti, is open from July to mid-October (exact dates depend on snow conditions). Note that Rohtang La is usually closed Tuesdays for road maintenance; some buses leave early enough to beat the closure but if you plan on heading north on a Tuesday check this out in advance. This route is also particularly susceptible to closure – sometimes for days – due to bad weather.

In season, there are regular buses to Keylong between 4am and 10.30am (₹130, six hours). Shared jeeps to Keylong can sometimes be found near the bus stand at around 8am or 9am for ₹300 per seat. For Spiti, buses leave for Kaza (₹230, 10 hours) at 5am and 6am; the 5.30am service continues to Tabo (₹295, 13 hours).

DELHI & CHANDIGARH The most comfortable options for Delhi are the daily HPTDC buses to the Himachal Tourism office on Janpath in Delhi. The AC Volvo coach leaves at 5.30pm (₹1190).

All buses run via Chandigarh (₹450, 10 hours). Book at the HPTDC booking office.

Private travel agencies run similar services to Delhi's Paharganj, but make sure you're getting a deluxe bus all the way through to Delhi.

Government buses run regularly from the bus stand till mid-afternoon; the fare to Delhi is ₹465/810/1050 (ordinary/deluxe/AC). Volvos depart at 5.45am and 4pm.

OTHER DESTINATIONS In season, HPTDC and private companies run buses to Shimla (₹450, 10 hours) and Dharamsala/McLeod Ganj (₹450, 10 hours).

For details of public buses see the boxed text below.

Taxi

The **Him-Anchal Taxi Operators Union** (Map p308; ✆252120; the Mall) has share minibuses to Leh (₹1600, 14 hours) at 2am from July to mid-October; book a day in advance. In season, travel agents can usually help organise share jeeps. Seats cost the same if you disembark at Keylong. Share jeeps to Kaza are rare and cost about ₹800. Sightseeing trips to the Rohtang La cost ₹1900.

Other one-way fares:

DESTINATION	FARE (₹)
Bhuntar airport	1000
Dharamsala	3500
Kaza	6000
Keylong	4200
Kullu	700 (950 via Naggar)
Leh	15,000
Manikaran	1500
Naggar	650
Solang Nullah	600

❶ Getting Around

Autorickshaw

Autos run to Old Manali and Vashisht for ₹50. If you can't find an auto in the street, head to the

PUBLIC BUSES FROM MANALI

DESTINATION	FARE (₹)	DURATION (HR)	FREQUENCY
Amritsar	420	17	1.45pm & 3.30pm
Dehra Dun	460	16	11am, 6.30pm & 8.30pm
Dharamsala	295	10	7.45am & 7pm
Haridwar	450	17	11am, 12.30pm, 3pm & 8.30pm
Jammu	440	12	4pm
Shimla	305/440 (ordinary/deluxe)	10	5 daily

Hadimba Auto Rickshaw Booking Office (Map p308; ☑253366; the Mall).

Motorcycle

Many people tackle the mountain passes to Ladakh or Spiti on bought or rented bikes. The **Enfield Club** (Map p306; ☑251094; Vashisht Rd), by the turn-off to Vashisht, does Enfield repairs and sells secondhand machines.

Several places rent out motorbikes, but make sure the price includes third-party insurance. The going rate per day is ₹600 for a 500cc Enfield, ₹400 for a 350cc Enfield and ₹350 for a 100cc to 150cc Yamaha, Honda or Bajaj. Reliable rental places include the following:

Anu Auto Works (Map p306; ☑9816163378; Vashisht Rd)

Himalayan Inder Motors (Map p308; ☑9816113973; Gompa Rd)

Life Adventure Tours (Map p308; ☑253825; Diamond Hotel, Model Town Rd)

Around Manali

VASHISHT

☑01902

About 3km north of Manali on the slopes east of the Beas River, Vashisht (Map p306) is a village in its own right, but, much like Old Manali on the other side of the river (but even quieter), it's a satellite of Manali and is a popular travellers' hang-out. Indian tourists mostly come here to bathe in the hot springs and tour the temples, while foreign tourists largely come here for the cheap accommodation, chilled atmosphere and charas. Most guesthouses close down for the winter from late October.

There are some interesting old wood and stone houses with ornate carving beyond the public baths, and a number of typically Himachali temples in the middle of the village. Vashisht is far more compact than Old Manali – travel agencies, moneychangers, traveller restaurants and internet cafes line the single street, all within a few minutes' walk.

◉ Sights & Activities

Vashisht Mandir   HINDU TEMPLE
(Map p306) Dedicated to the sage Vashisht, the ancient stone Vashisht Mandir has **public baths** (admission free; ⊙5am-9pm) with separate areas for men and women, or there are open-air baths just uphill. The hotsprings area is always busy with locals doing their laundry or washing dishes. Nearby are similar temples to **Shiva** and **Rama**, and there's a second Vashisht mandir at the back

of the village, built in the two-storey Kinnauri style.

Activities

Travel agencies can arrange treks and other adventure activities around the valley (see the boxed text p311).

Along the walking track down to the Beas, orange-roofed **Shri Hari Yoga Ashram** (☑9418047038; ⊙closed Oct-Apr) offers daily yoga classes for beginners at 10am, and advanced classes at 8am and 4.30pm (₹100 to ₹150).

🛏 Sleeping

Most places close from late October to April. Prices listed here can double in the peak season (April to June, September and October).

Dharma Guest House   HOTEL $
(Map p306; ☑252354; r ₹200-1000; @) Up a steep path above Rama Temple, this huge and expanding place has rooms in all budgets, and the hike up is rewarded with the best valley views from any hotel on either side of the Beas River. The older wing has basic but clean rooms that get more expensive as you get higher, while the new section has spacious deluxe rooms with TV, hot water and balconies.

Hotel Surabhi   HOTEL $
(Map p306; ☑252796; www.surabhihotel.com; d ₹400-1000) One of several big modern places on the main road but facing out over the valley, Surabhi is excellent value. Spacious, clean rooms have balconies with great mountain and river views and all have TVs and hot water. This is one place where you don't really need to spring for the more expensive rooms.

Hotel Arohi   HOTEL $
(Map p306; ☑254421; www.arohiecoadventures.com; d ₹500-900; ❄) Run by experienced and welcoming mountaineer, trekker and tour operator, Mr Thakur, Arohi has midrange standard rooms with TVs and geysers and views from everywhere, including the restaurant.

Hotel Brighu   HOTEL $
(Map p306; ☑253414; d ₹350-450, ste 800) This big old-fashioned wood and stone place has some interesting rooms with velour bedheads, and huge timber balconies with valley views. Although faded, rooms are carpeted and clean, with TV and hot water. The big family suite is a great deal.

Kalptaru Guest House
GUESTHOUSE **$**

(Map p306; ☑9418845343; d ₹200) This big old village house above the temple has plenty of character. Rooms are simple, but there's a nice garden patio where the air is filled with the sound of the gushing springs just below. Upstairs rooms have nice views over the village.

✗ Eating

Vashisht has several good traveller cafes and hotel restaurants. Most close down for the winter by November.

Rainbow Cafe
MULTICUISINE **$$**

(Map p306; mains ₹70-150; ⊘8am-10pm) Most people end up at this rooftop Vashisht institution at the end of an evening. Come here for decent traveller fare – breakfast, *momos*, yak cheese pasta, pizzas and thalis, as well as cold beers and an endless reggae soundtrack. There's an internet cafe downstairs.

Freedom Cafe
MULTICUISINE **$**

(Map p306; mains ₹50-150; ⊘7.30am-11pm) It's hard to resist the fun of this colorful outdoor cafe-on-stilts, which serves clay-oven pizzas and Thai, Mexican and Israeli dishes.

World Peace Cafe
MULTICUISINE **$$**

(Map p306; mains ₹65-155; ⊘8am-10pm) On the rooftop at Hotel Surabhi, this popular choice has cushions on the floor, a menu of Italian, Mexican and Israeli food, and views across to the Dhauladhar range from a huge patio. If you play an instrument, bring it to the open jams on Wednesday and Sunday nights.

Fuji Restaurant
JAPANESE **$**

(Map p306; mains ₹60-110; ⊘8am-10pm Mon-Sat) On the rooftop of Negi's Paying Guesthouse, past the temple, this authentic Japanese veg place specialises in noodles and miso soup.

ⓘ Getting There & Away

Autorickshaws charge ₹50 for the journey between Vashisht and Manali; don't rely on being able to get a lift back to Manali later than 7pm. On foot it's about 30 minutes; take the trail near the Himalayan Extreme Center past the Shri Hari Yoga Ashram and down to the banks of the Beas River. Coming uphill, the trail begins about 200m north of the Vashisht turn-off.

HAMTA PASS TREK

Easily accessible from Manali, this four- or five-day trek crosses the 4270m Hamta Pass over the Pir Panjal. The trailhead is the village of Prini, accessible by bus on the Manali–Naggar road, but it's camping all the way so it's best to take an organised trek.

From Prini, the route climbs through pine forests to Sethan, then open meadows to Chikha. A waterfall campground gives time to acclimatise before reaching the foot of the pass at Juara. The climb to the pass is steep and tiring but there are sublime snow-peak views from the top. On the descent, you can possibly push on to Chatru or break the journey with a riverside camp at Shiagouru. From Chatru, road transport runs north to Ladakh, east to Spiti and south to Manali.

STAGE	ROUTE	DURA-TION (HR)	DISTANCE (KM)
1	Prini to Sethan/ Pandu Ropa	5-6	8
2	Sethan/Pandu Ropa to Juara	4-5	10
3	Juara to Shia-gouru via Hamta Pass	7-8	10
4	Shiagouru to Chatru	3-4	8

SOLANG NULLAH
☑01902

About 13km north of Manali, Solang Nullah is Himachal's favourite winter ski resort. From January to March, skiers and snowboarders can enjoy 1.5km of alpine-style runs, taking a brand new gondola up to 3200m. A small drag-lift runs up the beginners' slopes. With the impressive backdrop of snowcapped Friendship Peak, it's also a year-round 'beauty spot', with a carnival-like atmosphere in summer.

Adventure-tour companies in Manali and hotels in Solang Nullah run ski and snowboard courses and rent out equipment – expect to pay ₹500 per day, plus ₹300 for use of the ski lifts. If you're up for an adventure in fashion, mangy winter clothing and slightly tired ski gear can be rented at dozens of wooden huts on the road between Solang Nullah and Manali.

In summer, Solang Nullah meadow, (which becomes a mud pit during the monsoon) is booming with Indian day-trippers taking pony rides (from ₹150), quad-bike rides (from ₹500), zorbing (from ₹300) and paragliding (from ₹700 for a tame flight down the slope). The surrounding hills are also good for walking – the Shiva temple 3km above the village is a popular destination.

Solang Nullah village has an alpine feel in the winter months: there are a few chalet-style guesthouses with heaters and hot showers. At other times it's an OK base for local trekking, but it's close enough to Manali that there's no real need to stay here. If you do, try **Hotel Iceland** (☏256008; www. icelandsolang.com; r ₹500-3000), a genuine ski lodge with great rooms, equipment rental, restaurant and bar.

Buses to Solang Nullah (₹15, one hour) leave Manali at 8am, 9.30am, 2pm and 4pm, heading back immediately on arrival. A taxi from Manali is ₹600, or it's a two-hour walk from Old Manali. Snow may make the road impassable in January and February, which usually means walking the 3km from the village of Palchan on the highway.

WESTERN HIMACHAL PRADESH

Western Himachal Pradesh is most famous as the home of the Tibetan government in exile, near Dharamsala, but consider travelling further afield to the fascinating Chamba Valley. The official website for Kangra district is http://hpkangra.nic.in, while the official Chamba Valley site is http://hpchamba. nic.in.

Dharamsala

☏01892 / POP 19,800 / ELEV 1219M

Dharamsala is best known as the home of the Dalai Lama, but the grubby market town where the buses pull in is actually Lower Dharamsala. The Tibetan government in exile is based just uphill in Gangchen Kyishong, and travellers make a beeline further uphill to the remarkably busy little traveller town of McLeod Ganj, also known as Upper Dharamsala. The bus station, a small museum and the bustling Kotwali Bazar can be found in Dharamsala, but otherwise it's just a place to pass through on your way to McLeod or Bhagsu.

The **State Bank of India** (☉10am-4pm Mon-Fri, to 1pm Sat) accepts travellers cheques and changes cash, and there's an ATM about 50m up the street.

◎ Sights

Museum of Kangra Art MUSEUM
(Indian/foreigner ₹10/50; ☉10am-5pm Tue-Sun) The Museum of Kangra Art near the bus station displays some fine miniature paintings from the Kangra school, along with temple

carvings, fabrics and embroidery, weapons and palanquins belonging to local rajas.

🛏 Sleeping & Eating

There are a few sleeping options if you have an early bus in the morning.

Kashmir House HERITAGE HOTEL **$$**
(☏222977; d ₹1200-2200) A short hike up the hill towards Gangchen Kyishong, this well-run heritage hotel once belonged to the maharaja of Jammu and Kashmir.

Hotel Dhauladhar HOTEL **$$$**
(☏224926; r ₹1500-3000) Way better than Dharamsala's budget dives, rooms are comfortable if overpriced.

Hotel Paradise HOTEL **$**
(☏224207; Kotwali Bazar; r ₹250) A short walk uphill from the bus stand, rooms range from glorified prison cells to spartan but cleanish.

Andey's Midtown Restaurant MULTICUISINE **$$**
(mains ₹100-300; ☉10am-10.30pm) Dharamsala's best restaurant. Come for kebabs, rich curries, burgers and a fine veg or nonveg thali, and sit on a horse saddle at the bar in the back.

❶ Getting There & Away

Air

See p326 for details of air services to the area.

Bus

There's a regular shuttle service from Dharamsala bus station to McLeod Ganj (₹10, 35 minutes) about every half-hour till about 7pm. For Delhi there's a deluxe Volvo bus at 8pm (₹785, 12 hours). See the boxed text p316, for other services.

Taxi

The **taxi stand** (☏222105) is up some steep steps from the bus stand. Shared jeeps (₹10 per person, 30 minutes) to McLeod Ganj leave when full. Day tours covering less than 80km can be arranged for ₹1400 per day.

Fixed one-way fares:

DESTINATION	FARE (₹)
Gaggal airport	400
Jawalamukhi	700
Kangra	500
Masrur	900
McLeod Ganj	150
Palampur	700

BUSES FROM DHARAMSALA

DESTINATION	FARE (₹)	DURATION (HR)	FREQUENCY
Amritsar	165	7	5am
Chamba	210	8	six daily
Dalhousie	150	6	7.30am & 12.15pm
Dehra Dun	375	13	9pm
Delhi	290-785	12	11 daily
Gaggal	12	30min	frequently
Jammu	160	5	9.45am
Jawalamukhi	60	1½	hourly
Kangra	20	1	frequently
Kullu	210	9	four daily
Manali	250	10	four daily
Mandi	150	6	five daily
Palampur	40	2	frequently
Pathankot	100	3½	hourly
Shimla	280-430	10	seven daily

Train

The nearest train station is Kangra Mandir, on the slow narrow-gauge line from Pathankot to Jogindarnagar – see the boxed text p330. Reservations for other services from Pathankot can be made at the **Rail Reservation Centre** (☑226711; Hotel Dhauladhar; ⊙8am-2pm Mon-Sat).

McLeod Ganj

☑01892 / ELEV 1770M

When travellers talk of heading up to Dharamsala (to see the Dalai Lama...), this is where they mean. Around 4km above Dharamsala town – or 10km via the main bus route – McLeod Ganj is the headquarters of the Tibetan government in exile and the residence of His Holiness the 14th Dalai Lama. Along with Manali, it's the big traveller hang-out in Himachal Pradesh, with many budget hotels, trekking companies, internet cafes, restaurants and shops selling Tibetan souvenirs. Naturally, there's a large Tibetan population here, many of whom are refugees, so you'll see plenty of maroon robes about, especially when the Dalai Lama is in residence.

McLeod (named after David McLeod, Lieutenant-Governor of Punjab) was established in the mid-1850s as a British garrison and it served as an administration centre for the colonial government until the earthquake of 1905. It was a backwater until 1960, when the Dalai Lama claimed asylum here following the Chinese invasion of Tibet.

Since then, McLeod has become a centre for the study of Buddhism and Tibetan culture. There are all sorts of holistic activities and courses on offer, and lots of travellers come here to volunteer on community projects that focus on the refugee community.

Waterproof clothing is handy for McLeod Ganj: it rains a lot. Many shops and businesses are closed on Monday.

From the Main Chowk, Jogibara Rd runs south to Gangchen Kyishong and Dharamsala; Temple Rd runs south to the Tsuglagkhang Complex; Bhagsu Rd runs east to Bhagsu, Tipa Rd runs northeast to the Tibetan Institute of Performing Arts; and Dharamkot Rd runs north to Dharamkot.

Buses now arrive and depart from a new depot about 200m north of the Main Chowk, just past the autorickshaw stand and the shared jeep lot, on the lower road that heads toward the Church of St John in the Wilderness and Dal Lake. The taxi stand is located on Mall Rd.

⊙ Sights

Tsuglagkhang Complex   BUDDHIST TEMPLE
(Temple Rd; Central Chapel; ⊙nonresidents 5am-8pm) The main focus of visiting pilgrims, monks and many tourists is the Tsuglagkhang,

comprising the *photang* (official residence) of the Dalai Lama, the Namgyal Gompa, Tibet Museum and the Tsuglagkhang itself.

The revered Tsuglagkhang is the exiles' equivalent of the Jokhang Temple in Lhasa. Sacred to Avalokitesvara (Chenrezi in Tibet), the Tibetan deity of compassion, it enshrines a 3m-high gilded statue of the Sakyamuni Buddha, flanked by Avalokitesvara and Padmasambhava, the Indian scholar who introduced Buddhism to Tibet. The Avalokitesvara statue contains several relics rescued from the Jokhang Temple during the Cultural Revolution.

Next to the Tsuglagkhang is the **Kalachakra Temple**, built in 1992, which contains mesmerising murals of the Kalachakra (Wheel of Time) mandala, specifically linked to Avalokitesvara, currently represented on earth by the Dalai Lama. Sand mandalas are created here annually on the fifth day of the third Tibetan month. Photography is allowed in the Tsuglagkhang, but not in the Kalachakra Temple. Note that during teachings, cameras, mobile phones, cigarettes and lighters are not permitted in the temple.

The remaining buildings form the **Namgyal Gompa**, where you can watch monks debate most afternoons, sealing points of argument with great flourish, a foot stamp and a theatrical clap of the hands. The monastery bookshop has a good selection of Buddhist texts, and you can enjoy cakes and vegetarian food at Namgyal Cafe.

Just inside the main entry gate is the **Tibet Museum** (admission ₹5; ⊙9am-5pm), telling the story of the Chinese occupation and the subsequent Tibetan exodus through photographs, interviews and video clips. A visit here is a must for anyone staying in McLeod Ganj.

Most Tibetan pilgrims make a *kora* (ritual circuit) of the Tsuglagkhang Complex, which must be carried out in a clockwise direction. Take the downhill road to the left at the entrance to the temple and follow the winding path leading off to the right. It passes through forest strewn with prayer flags before emerging back on Temple Rd.

Secretariat of the Tibetan Government in Exile
MUSEUM

Inside the government compound at Gangchen Kyishong, the **Library of Tibetan Works & Archives** (Secretariat Complex; www.ltwa.net; ⊙9am-1pm & 2-5pm Mon-Sat, closed 2nd & 4th Sat of month) preserves the Tibetan texts spared from the Cultural Revolution. Many have since been translated into English and other European languages. Regular visitors can become temporary members (₹50 per month; passport needed for ID) to access the collection.

Upstairs is a fascinating **cultural museum** (admission ₹10; ⊙9am-1pm & 2-5pm Mon-Sat, closed 2nd & 4th Sat each month) with statues, old Tibetan artefacts and books and some astonishing three-dimensional mandalas in wood and sand. Also worth a visit is the **Nechung Gompa**, home to the Tibetan state oracle.

Tibetan Medical & Astrological Institute (Men-Tsee-Khang)
AMCHI

Established to preserve the ancient arts of *amchi* (traditional Tibetan medicine) and astrology, the **Men-Tsee-Khang** (☏223113; www.men-tsee-khang.org; Gangchen Kyishong) is a five-minute walk below the Secretariat. There's a library and training college, and if you know the exact time you were born, you can have a whole life horoscope prepared in English.

The **Men-Tsee-Khang Museum** (admission ₹5; ⊙9am-1pm & 2-5pm Mon-Sat) has fascinating displays on traditional Tibetan medicine, told via preserved specimens and illustrative *thangkas*.

MEETING THE DALAI LAMA

Meeting face to face with the Dalai Lama is a lifelong dream for many travellers and certainly for Buddhists, but private audiences are rarely granted. Put simply, the Dalai Lama is too busy with spiritual duties and running the government in exile to meet everyone who comes to Dharamsala. Tibetan refugees are automatically guaranteed an audience, but travellers must make do with the occasional public teachings held at Gangchen Kyishong during the monsoon (July/August), after Losar (Tibetan New Year) in February/March and on other occasions, depending on his schedule. For annual schedules and just about everything you need to know about His Holiness, check out www.dalailama.com. To attend, you have to register with your passport and two passport photographs, at the **Branch Security Office** (☏221560; Bhagsu Rd; ⊙9am-1pm & 2-5pm Mon-Sat, closed 2nd & 4th Sat each month). Sign up a few days before the teaching begins for the best chance of getting in.

McLeod Ganj

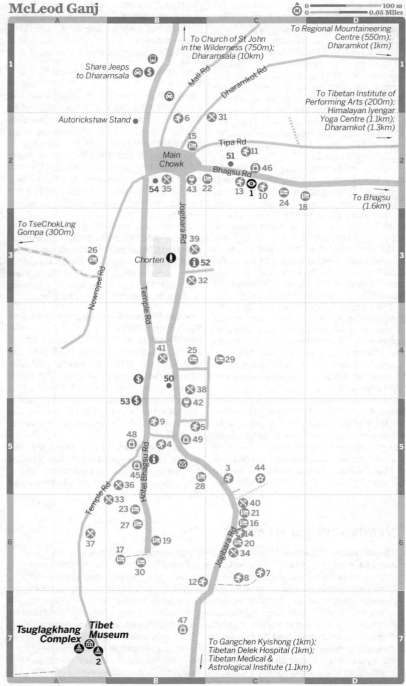

To Church of St John
in the Wilderness (750m);
Dharamsala (10km)

To Regional Mountaineering
Centre (550m);
Dharamkot (1km)

Share Jeeps
to Dharamsala

Mall Rd

Dharamkot Rd

To Tibetan Institute of
Performing Arts (200m);
Himalayan Iyengar
Yoga Centre (1.1km);
Dharamkot (1.3km)

Autorickshaw Stand

6

31

15

Tipa Rd

51

11

Main
Chowk

Bhagsu Rd

46

54 35

43 22

13 1 10

24

18

To Bhagsu
(1.6km)

To TseChokLing
Gompa (300m)

26

Chorten

39

52

32

Temple Rd

Naurowji Rd

41

25

29

50

38

53

42

9

5

48

4

49

Hotel Bhagsu Rd

45 36

28

3

44

33

23

40

21

16

14

20

34

27

37

17

19

30

12

8 7

47

Tsuglagkhang
Complex

Tibet
Museum

2

To Gangchen Kyishong (1km);
Tibetan Delek Hospital (1km);
Tibetan Medical &
Astrological Institute (1.1km)

Jogibara Rd

HIMACHAL PRADESH WESTERN HIMACHAL PRADESH

TseChokLing Gompa BUDDHIST TEMPLE
At the base of a long flight of steps off of Nowrojee Rd, this peaceful gompa was built in 1987 to replace the original Dip Tse Chokling Gompa in Tibet, destroyed in the Cultural Revolution. Home to a small order of Gelukpa monks, the prayer hall enshrines a statue of Sakyamuni in a magnificent jewelled headdress.

McLeod Ganj

In October of 1950, about a year after Mao Zedong declared the founding of the People's Republic of China, Chinese troops invaded Tibet. At the time, Tibet was an independent state led by the Dalai Lama. A year later, in October 1951, Lhasa, the Tibetan capital, fell. After resistance simmered for years in the countryside, protests against the Chinese occupation broke out on the streets of Lhasa in 1959. As the Chinese Army squelched the uprising, it fired upon Norbulingka, the Dalai Lama's summer palace. Believing his life or his freedom was at risk, the Dalai Lama secretly fled across the Himalayas to India, where he received asylum.

China says its army was sent to Tibet as liberators, to free Tibetans from fuedal serf-dom and improve life on the vast high plateau. It hasn't worked out that way. While the commonly quoted figure of 1.2 million Tibetans killed since 1950 is seriously disputed – even by Western scholars – no independent observers question the reality of the suf-fering and human rights abuses, as well as huge losses to Tibet's cultural legacy, that have occurred under Chinese occupation. Each year, at least 2500 Tibetans risk the dangerous, clandestine crossing over the mountains into India, and it's estimated that about 130,000 refugees are now living outside their homeland. Most come first to the Dharamsala area, where they find support from their community, their government-in-exile and a legion of NGOs. About 80,000 exiles live around Dharamsala today.

If you're interested in volunteering with the Tibetan community, see the boxed text on p323.

Gu Chu Sum Movement Gallery GALLERY
(Jogibara Rd; admission free; ⊘2-5pm Mon, Wed & Fri) Run by a local charity that works with former political prisoners, this houses an exhibition of photos telling the story of political oppression in Chinese-occupied Tibet.

Environmental Education Centre LEARNING CENTRE
(Bhagsu Rd; ⊘8.30am-7pm Mon-Sat) Estab-lished by the Tibetan Welfare Office, this centre provides education on environmen-tal issues. You can refill your water bottle, and the adjacent **Green Shop** (Bhagsu Rd; ⊘10am-5pm Tue-Sun) sells handmade paper and other organic products.

Church of St John in the Wilderness CHURCH
Just off the main road into McLeod, this church has handsome stained-glass win-dows dating from the British era. It's open on Sunday mornings for the weekly ser-vice. The cemetery contains the graves of many victims of the 1905 earthquake.

🏃 Activities

Alternative Therapies, Yoga & Massage
McLeod Ganj has dozens of practitioners of holistic and alternative therapies, some legitimate and some making a fast buck at the expense of gullible travellers. Adverts for courses and sessions are posted on notice-boards all over McLeod Ganj and in *Contact* magazine, but talking to other travellers is a better way to find the good practitioners.

Lha (☑220992; www.lhasocialwork.org; Temple Rd; ⊘10am-5pm Mon-Fri) runs yoga classes from 5pm to 6.30pm (₹100 per session) and also offers reliable massage treatments.

Universal Yoga Centre (☑9418291929; www.vijaypoweryoga.com; Yongling School, Jogibara Rd) gets good reports for drop-in yoga class-es and longer courses.

Walks

Short walks around McLeod include the 2km stroll to **Bhagsu** and the 3km walk northeast to **Dharamkot** for uplifting views south over the valley and north towards the Dhauladhar Ridge. You can do a loop to Bhagsu, across to Dharamkot and back down to McLeod in a few hours.

About 4km northwest of McLeod Ganj on Mall Rd, peaceful **Dal Lake** is home to the **Tibetan Children's Village** (☑221348; www.tcv.org.in; ⊘9.30am-5pm Mon-Fri), which provides free education for some 2000 refu-gee children. Visitors are welcome and there may be opportunities for volunteers. The lake itself has a small Hindu temple and there are great views from **Naddi** just uphill.

A popular longer walk is the one- or two-day return trip through boulder fields and rhododendron forests to **Triund** (2900m), a 9km walk past Dharamkot. Triund has a simple rest house and you can stop overnight and stroll up to the glacier at Laka Got (3350m) before turning back to McLeod Ganj. There's a scenic route along the gorge from the waterfall at Bhagsu. From Triund, you can trek to **Indrahar La** (4300m) and the Chamba Valley.

Trekking

It's possible to trek from McLeod Ganj to the Kullu, Chamba, Lahaul and Spiti Valleys, and there are several agencies in town that can make the necessary arrangements. The most popular route crosses the 4300m Indrahar La over the Dhauladhar to Bharmour (p328). All-inclusive treks costs around ₹1500 to ₹2000 per person, per day.

Uphill from the bus stand on the road to Dharamkot, the **Regional Mountaineering Centre** (☏221787; ⊙10am-5pm Mon-Sat) can arrange treks and adventure activities and offers courses and expeditions on set dates. It can also provide a list of registered guides and porters.

Other reliable trekking operators:

Eagle's Height Trekkers   TREKKING
(☏221097; www.trekking.123himachal.com; Mall Rd) Also runs birdwatching tours and jeep safaris.

High Point Adventure   TREKKING
(☏220718; www.trek.123himachal.com; Hotel Bhagsu Rd) Highly recommended, with some of the best prices in town.

⇌ Courses

Yoga, Meditation & Philosophy

Several organisations offer long-term courses in Buddhist philosophy and meditation. They have strict rules on silence, alcohol and smoking.

Himalayan Iyengar Yoga Centre   YOGA
(☏221312; www.hiyogacentre.com; Tipa Rd; ⊙Apr-Oct) Five-day courses start every Thursday (₹3000).

Tushita Meditation Centre   MEDITATION
(☏221866; www.tushita.info; ⊙registration 9.30-11.30am & 12.30-4pm Mon-Sat) Near Dharamkot, Tushita offers 10-day residential retreats in Buddhist philosophy, courses for advanced students and shorter programs, including drop-in meditation – see the website for course dates.

Vipassana Meditation Centre   MEDITATION
(☏221309; www.sikhara.dhamma.org; ⊙registration 4-5pm) Located in Dharamkot, this centre runs strict 10-day retreats on *vipassana* (mindfulness meditation) from April to November.

Library of Tibetan Works & Archives   BUDDHISM
(☏222467; itwa.net) At the Gangchen Kyishong complex, there are Buddhist philosophy courses for ₹200 per month, plus ₹50 registration.

Cooking

Cooking courses in McLeod Ganj cover everything from South Indian dosas to chocolate *momos*. Book the following courses one day in advance:

Bhimsen's Cooking Class   COOKING
(Jogibara Rd; classes ₹200; ⊙11am-1pm & 4-6pm) Courses in North and South Indian cooking.

Lhamo's Kitchen   COOKING
(☏9816468719; Bhagsu Rd; classes ₹300, 3-day courses ₹550; ⊙10.30am-12.30pm, 5-7pm) Recommended courses in vegetarian Tibetan cooking.

AMCHI

Amchi (traditional Tibetan medicine) is a centuries-old holistic healing practice and a popular treatment for all kinds of minor and persistent ailments. There are several clinics around town, including **Men-Tsee-Khang Clinic** (☏221484; Tipa Rd; ⊙9am-1pm & 2-5pm Mon-Sat, closed 2nd & 4th Sat each month) and **Dr Lobsang Khangkar Memorial Clinic** (☏220811; ⊙9am-noon & 2-5pm Mon-Sat), near the post office.

The most popular practitioner in town is the former physician to the Dalai Lama, **Dr Yeshi Dhonden** (⊙8am-1pm), whose tiny clinic is squirreled away off Jogibara Rd, down an alley past Ashoka Restaurant. No appointment is necessary: you arrive at 8am and collect a token and approximate consultation time. You come back with a sample of urine, which, along with a quick examination, is all the doctor needs to prescribe the appropriate herbal pills. Many locals and expats swear by his treatments.

For an insight into *amchi*, visit the Tibetan Medical & Astrological Institute (Men-Tsee Khang; p317).

Sangye's Kitchen COOKING
(✔9816164540; Jogibara Rd; classes ₹250; ◷10am-noon & 4-6pm Thu-Tue) Tibetan treats, with a different menu daily. Next to Tashi Choeling Monastery.

Nisha's Indian Cooking Course COOKING
(✔9318877674; www.indiancookingcourse.com; Taste of India Restaurant, Jogibara Rd; courses ₹700) Three-day veg and nonveg North Indian courses.

Language

Inside the Gangchen Kyishong complex, the **Library of Tibetan Works & Archives** (✔222467; www.ltwa.net; ◷classes Mon-Sat) runs long-term Tibetan-language courses for beginners and experienced students for ₹250 per month, plus a ₹50 registration fee.

Lha (✔220992; Temple Rd; ◷10am-5pm Mon-Fri) offers private Tibetan-language tuition for ₹100 per hour.

There are several independent Tibetan teachers – check *Contact* magazine for details. Classes run by **Pema Youton** (✔9418603523) get good reports.

Massage

The recommended **Tibetan Universal Massage** (✔9816378307; www.tibetanmassage.com; Jogibara Rd) offers training in traditional Tibetan massage. Courses run for five afternoons on set dates and cost ₹1500.

★ Festivals & Events

Performances of traditional lhamo (Tibetan opera) and musical theatre are held on special occasions at the **Tibetan Institute of Performing Arts** (TIPA; ✔221478; www.tibetanarts.org), east of Main Chowk. The annual **Opera Festival** is held in February or March, while the **TIPA Anniversary Festival** takes place in August.

In December or January, McLeod celebrates **Losar** with processions and masked dances at local monasteries. The Dalai Lama often gives public teachings at this time. The Dalai Lama's birthday on 6 July is also celebrated with aplomb.

From 10 to 12 December, McLeod Ganj hosts the **International Himalayan Festival** to commemorate the Dalai Lama's Nobel Peace Prize, featuring cultural troupes from all the Himalayan nations.

🛏 Sleeping

Popular places fill up quickly; advance bookings are advised year-round, especially from April to June, October and November.

TOP CHOICE Chonor House Hotel HOTEL $$$
(✔221006; www.norbulingka.org; s/d from ₹2300/2900, ste ₹2800/3500; @) Hidden down a track off Hotel Bhagsu Rd, Chonor House is a real gem. It's run by the Norbulingka Institute (p328), and rooms are decked out with its wonderful handicrafts and fabrics. Each room has a Tibetan theme that runs from the bedspreads to the murals on the walls. There's also a lovely garden, shop, restaurant and net cafe.

Green Hotel HOTEL $$
(✔221200; www.greenhotel.biz; Bhagsu Rd; r from ₹800, @☎) A long-time traveller favourite, Green has a diverse range of sunny, stylish rooms in two buildings, some with valley and mountain views. The busy restaurant and internet cafe here feel like the hip place to be.

Pema Thang Guest House GUESTHOUSE $$
(✔221871; www.pemathang.net; Hotel Bhagsu Rd; d ₹825-1155; ❄☎) A tasteful Tibetan-style guesthouse, with a great restaurant and spacious, well-lit rooms with comforting, homey furnishings. The one single room (₹650) is an ideal writer's haven.

Om Hotel HOTEL $
(✔221313; omhotel@hotmail.com; Nowrojee Rd; d with/without bathroom ₹375/200) Conveniently located down a lane below the main square, the friendly family-run Om has pleasing rooms with good views and a great little terrace restaurant that catches the sunset over the valley. This might be the best deal in town.

Zambala House HOTEL $$$
(✔221121; www.zambalahouse.com; Hotel Bhagsu Rd; d ₹2000-2900; ☎) Still feeling fresh-out-of-the-box, this place down the same lane as Chonor House is has spacious modern rooms with the best bathrooms in town. The views from the upper floor balconies are so good you might never turn on the flat screen TV.

Hotel Ladies Venture HOTEL $
(✔9816235648; shantiazad@yahoo.co.in; Jogibara Rd; s ₹200, d ₹250-500) Named by the previous lady owners, this peaceful green-and-yellow hotel welcomes all with wraparound balconies, flower pots, a range of tidy rooms and lovely mountain views from the rooftop terrace.

Cheryton Cottage Guest House HOTEL $
(✔221993; tcheryl_89@yahoo.com; Jogibara Rd; d ₹700, apt ₹1500) In the garden behind

McLeod Ganj has more volunteering opportunities than anywhere else in Himachal Pradesh. Travellers can get involved in short-term volunteering such as English-language conversation classes or cleaning up litter, but for longer-term placements always look for a position that matches your existing skills. Volunteers generally make their own arrangements for accommodation and meals.

One of the best places to start is **VolunteerTibet** (☎220894; www.volunteertibet.org; Jogibara Rd; ⊙10am-1.30pm & 2-5pm Mon-Fri), a community organisation that arranges placements in areas of need – eg teaching, computer training and social services. Volunteers with two months or more to spare are preferred, but short-term spots can also be arranged.

Lha (☎220992; www.lhasocialwork.org; Temple Rd; ⊙10am-5pm Mon-Fri) also arranges placements at a variety of local community projects, including those for English- and French-language teachers, grant writers or website developers.

Hope Education Centre (☎9218947689), off Jogibara Rd, runs conversational English classes for Tibetan refugees from 4.30pm to 6pm Monday to Friday, often held informally over coffee at Cafe Oasis. Anyone is welcome to turn up.

Learning & Ideas for Tibet (☎9418794218; www.learningandideasfortibet.org; Jogibara Rd; ⊙9am-5pm) has a variety of positions, including teaching and editing the autobiographies of Tibetan political prisoners and exiles.

Tibetan Settlement Office (☎221059; www.twodhasa.org; Bhagsu Rd; ⊙9am-1pm & 2-5pm Mon-Sat, closed 2nd & 4th Sat each month) can provide advice on other opportunities for volunteers around McLeod Ganj, including environmental efforts such as their Clean Upper Dharamsala Project.

Many organisations seeking volunteers also advertise in the free magazine *Contact*. The magazine itself looks for volunteers to help with writing, proofreading or design.

Chocolate Log, Cheryton has four peaceful rooms with a relaxing outdoor space. The four-room apartment next door is fully self-contained. While the new owners don't run things quite as tightly as the previous ones, it's still good value.

Hotel Tibet　　　　　　　　HOTEL **$$**
(☎221587; htdshala@sancharnet.in; Bhagsu Rd; r ₹600-1000; ❉) A short walk from the bus stand, this place has the feel of an upmarket hotel yet it's at almost budget prices. It's run by the Tibetan government, and has a good restaurant and bar. All rooms have TV and hot water; credit cards accepted.

Takhyil Hotel　　　　　　　　HOTEL **$**
(☎221152; Jogibara Rd; r ₹400-600) A calm vibe and tidy rooms with TVs and hot showers add up to a good package at this Tibetan-run hotel that's just downhill from the chorten.

Hotel Bhagsu　　　　　　　　HOTEL **$$**
(☎221091; Hotel Bhagsu Rd; d ₹1200-2400; ❉) On the road above the bazaar and Tsuglagkhang, this popular HPTDC hotel has a solid Raj-era feel and attractively decorated rooms, some with valley views.

Asian Plaza Hotel　　　　　　HOTEL **$$$**
(☎220655; www.asianplazahotel.com; Main Chowk; d ₹1800-3500, ste ₹3200) Opposite the noisy bus stand, this is a clean and modern business-type hotel with all the conveniences you would expect for the price but little in the way of charm.

Tibetan Ashoka Guest House　　HOTEL **$**
(☎221763; d with/without bathroom ₹350/100) Off Jogibara Rd, down an alley near the chorten (Tibetan for stupa), this big place looks out on the valley and catches plenty of sunlight. Its clean, simple rooms fill up in season, but advance reservations aren't accepted.

Loseling Guest House　　GUESTHOUSE **$**
(☎9218923305; d ₹250-350) Down the same alley as Tibetan Ashoka Guest House, Loseling is run by a Tibetan monastery based in Karnataka. It's a good cheapie and all rooms have a hot shower; cheaper ones have squat toilets.

Kareri Lodge　　　　　　　　HOTEL **$$**
(☎221132; karerihl@hotmail.com; Hotel Bhagsu Rd; r ₹770-1100; ❉) Squeezed in among a string of more-upmarket hotels, Kareri has

five well-worn but clean rooms, some with huge windows and prime views. There's a good vibe here, helped by the friendly manager who offers a reliable trekking service.

Hotel Mount View
HOTEL $

(☑221382; Jogibara Rd; ₹300-500) A tidy Kashmiri-run hotel offering a range of good rooms that extend well back from the street to reveal valley views from the rear balconies. The owners run a trekking outfit and tours to Pahalgam in Kashmir, but be sure to check that conditions in the area are safe before signing up.

Kunga Guesthouse
GUESTHOUSE $

(☑221180; Bhagsu Rd; d ₹300-600) Above Nick's Italian Kitchen, Kunga's clean rooms are popular and offer reasonable value.

🍴 Eating

Restaurants

McLeod Ganj is crammed with backpacker restaurants serving identical traveller menus – pizzas, pasta, omelettes, Indian and Chinese staples – and commendable attempts at European and Mexican food. For a quick snack, local women sell *momos* and *tingmo* (steamed Tibetan bread) around the chorten and at the entrance to the Tsuglagkhang.

TOP CHOICE Moonpeak Thali
INDIAN $$

(Temple Rd; mains ₹70-200; ⊙9am-10.30pm; 🛜) With a stylishly understated dining room and a tasteful blend of Tibetan and Indian artwork, this new place might just have the best food in town. Among the culinary highlights is the Himachali Thali, a sampler of regional dishes. To reach the tables on the rooftop terrace, you walk through the kitchen – and it's clean! •

Oogo's Cafe Italiano
ITALIAN $$

(Jogibara Rd; mains ₹60-150) This cute hole-in-the-wall place serves up mainly Italian fare, but with a few surprises – waffles, baked potatoes, intriguing pasta dishes like 'chicken vodka' and even grilled lamb chops. The atmosphere is warm and busy and there are tempting desserts, as well as a bookshelf full of reading material.

Green Hotel
MULTICUISINE $

(Bhagsu Rd; mains ₹50-100; ⊙6.30am-9.30pm; @🛜) This traveller-oriented hotel restaurant with comfy chairs and couches serves good vegetarian food and the earliest breakfasts in town. The internet cafe and wi-fi are a bonus.

🍴 Common Ground Cafe
ASIAN FUSION $$

(Dharamkot Rd; www.commongroundsproject.com; mains ₹60-100; ⊙11am-9pm) The mission of the NGO that runs this restaurant is to promote understanding between Tibetan and Chinese people, and food is used symbolically here. The menu is a sizzling variety of cross-cultural dishes, served in a pleasingly laid-back atmosphere.

McLlo Restaurant
MULTICUISINE $

(Main Chowk; mains ₹125-225; ⊙10am-10pm) Crowded nightly and justifiably popular, this big place above the noisy main square serves a mind-boggling menu of Indian, Chinese and international fare, including pizzas and pasta. It's also one of the best places to enjoy an icy cold beer (₹115), and it has cider and wines.

Peace Cafe
TIBETAN $

(Jogibara Rd; dishes ₹30-55; ⊙7.30am-9.30pm) This cosy little cafe is always full of monks chatting and dining, and tasty Tibetan *momos*, chow chow (stir-fried noodles with vegetables or meat) and *thukpa*.

🍴 Lung Ta
JAPANESE $

(Jogibara Rd; mains ₹40-60; ⊙noon-8.30pm Mon-Sat) The set menu changes daily at this popular, nonprofit, vegetarian Japanese restaurant. Food and ambience are authentic and many Japanese travellers come here for a taste of home.

Nick's Italian Kitchen
ITALIAN $

(Bhagsu Rd; meals ₹50-100; ⊙7am-9pm) At Kunga Guesthouse, Nick's has been serving up tasty vegetarian pizzas, pasta and gnocchi for years. Follow up with heavenly desserts like chocolate brownies with hot chocolate sauce. Eat inside by candlelight or out on the terrace.

Taste of India
INDIAN $

(Jogibara Rd; mains ₹60-130) This tiny place has just five tables and is often full of diners savouring North Indian veg and nonveg curries. Chicken dishes can be unsatifyingly skimpy.

Tsongkha
TIBETAN $

(Jogibara Rd; dishes ₹40-90; ⊙from 8am) A simple but popular Tibetan restaurant with a great rooftop terrace looking out over the chorten and valley, plus an indoor dining room for chilly days.

Snow Lion Restaurant   TIBETAN $
(Jogibara Rd; dishes ₹45-70; ⊙7.30am-9.30pm)
Behind the Snow Lion guesthouse, this is
another good place to come for *momos,*
thukpa and *tingmo.*

Jimmy's Italian Kitchen   ITALIAN $
(Jogibara Rd; dishes ₹60-130) Jimmy's is a well-
established Italian place with a new location
upstairs opposite the chorten. Authentic pizzas with real pepperoni, and a good range of
pasta dishes.

✎ Namgyal Cafe   CAFE $
(snacks ₹30-80; ⊙10am-10pm Tue-Sun) Located
at Namgyal Gompa (part of the Tsuglagkhang Complex), this cafe serves cakes and
vegetarian food. It also provides vocational
training for refugees.

Cafes

McLeod has some of the best cafes in North
India, with several places serving good
espresso coffee, cappuccino and English-
style tea.

Beans Cafe   CAFE $$
(Main Chowk; coffees/mains ₹ 30/70-150;
⊙8.30am-9.30pm; @🛜) This two-level coffee
house serves up satisyingly strong java
and has a mixed menu of full meals and
yummy desserts. You can get on one of
their computers or bring your laptop.

Moonpeak Espresso   CAFE $
(Temple Rd; coffees & meals ₹30-100; ⊙7am-
8pm; 🛜) A little bit of Seattle, transported
to India. Come for excellent coffee, cakes,
imaginative sandwiches and dishes like
poached chicken with mango, lime and
coriander sauce.

Mandala Wifi Coffee House   CAFE $
(Temple Rd; snacks ₹25-90; ⊙7am-8pm; 🛜)
Next to Moonpeak, Mandala has an even
more inviting terrace and serves tasty
wraps, sandwiches and coffee.

Khana Nirvana   CAFE $
(www.khananirvana.org; Temple Rd; meals ₹35-
85) Up a steep stairway, this community
cafe is a relaxed hang-out serving healthy
vegetarian breakfasts, soups and salad,
pita sandwiches, burritos and organic tea.
There's local entertainment most nights.

🍸 Drinking & Entertainment

McLeod's bars are mostly clustered around
the main *chowk* (town square) and charge
around ₹115 for a big bottle of beer. The
best choices for a drink are McLlo Restau-

rant and **X-cite**, both in the bus stand area.
Hotel Tibet, **Aroma** (Jogibara Rd) and Hotel
Mount View also have bars. Takeaway beer
(₹80) and spirits (from ₹70) are available
from several small **liquor stores**, including
one right opposite the bus stand.

✎ Khana Nirvana   CULTURAL PROGRAM
(www.khananirvana.org; Temple Rd) Cool commu-
nity cafe with a program of arts and enter-
tainment most nights. There's an open-mic
night on Monday, documentary films about
Tibet on Tuesday, and Tibetan speakers on
Sunday.

Tibetan Music Trust   LIVE MUSIC
(📞9805661031; www.tibetanmusictrust.org; ad-
mission by donation) Performances of Tibetan
folk music are held with varying regularity
at Yonglings School, off Jogibara Rd. The live
shows feature demonstrations of traditional
regional Tibetan instruments and song. It's
a great cultural and educational experience.

🔒 Shopping

Dozens of shops and stalls sell Tibetan ar-
tefacts, including *thangkas,* bronze statues,
metal prayer wheels, bundles of prayer flags,
Tibetan horns and gemstone rosary beads.
Some are Tibetan-run, but many are run by
Kashmiri traders who apply a fair amount
of sales pressure. Several local cooperatives
offer the same goods without the hassle.

Bookworm (📞221465; Hotel Bhagsu Rd;
⊙9am-6.30pm Tue-Sun) and **Hills Bookshop**
(📞220008; Bhagsu Rd; ⊙10am-9.30pm) are
good general bookstores, while **Namgyal**
Bookshop (📞221492; Tsuglagkhang Complex;

☺9.30am-noon & 1-6pm Tue-Sun) specialises in Buddhist texts.

Tibetan Handicrafts Cooperative Centre
HANDICRAFTS

(☎221415; Jogibara Rd; ☺8.30am-5pm Mon-Sat) Employs newly arrived refugees in the weaving of Tibetan carpets. You'll pay around ₹6000 for a 0.9m by 1.8m wool carpet in traditional Tibetan colours and you can watch the weavers in action. For made-to-order clothing, head over the road to the Tailoring Section.

Stitches of Tibet
HANDICRAFTS

(☎221527; www.tibetanwomen.org; Jogibara Rd; ☺10am-5pm Tue-Sun) This organisation offers a similar tailoring service to that of the Tibetan Handicrafts Centre of Tibet, providing work for newly arrived women refugees.

TCV Handicraft Centre
HANDICRAFTS

(☎221592; www.tcvcraft.com; Temple Rd; ☺10am-5pm Tue-Sun) Has a huge range of Tibetan souvenirs at fixed prices. Sales benefit the Tibetan Children's Village.

❶ Information

Media
Contact (www.contactmag.org) is an informative, free local magazine that contains some useful listings, as well as details regarding courses and volunteer work. It's also a useful website.

Tibetan Review provides coverage of Tibetan issues, as does the *Tibetan Bulletin*, the official journal of the government in exile.

Medical Services
Traditional Tibetan medicine known as *amchi* is a popular form of treatment in McLeod Ganj – see p321.

Tibetan Delek Hospital (☎222053; Gangchen Kyishong; consultations ₹10; ☺outpatient clinic 9am-1pm & 2-5pm).

Money
Several places around town offer Western Union money transfers.

HDFC ATM (Lower Rd; ☺24hr) Located upstairs at the new bus depot.

State Bank of India (Temple Rd; ☺10am-4pm Mon-Fri, to 1pm Sat) Has a busy international ATM.

Thomas Cook (Temple Rd; ☺9.30am-6.30pm)

Post
Post office (Jogibara Rd; ☺9.30am-5pm Mon-Fri & to noon Sat, parcel post to 1pm Mon-Fri) Poste restante and parcels.

Tourist Information
HPTDC tourist office (☎221205; Hotel Bhagsu Rd; ☺10am-5pm, closed Sun in Jul-Aug & Dec-Mar) Offers maps and guides, and can also make bookings for HPTDC hotels and buses around Himachal.

Information Office of Central Tibetan Administration (☎222457; www.tibet.net; Jogibara Rd; ☺9am-5.30pm Tue-Sun) For information on Tibetan issues.

Travel Agencies
Numerous travel agencies can book train and bus tickets, and can also arrange tours and treks.

Himachal Travels (☎221428; himachaltravels@sancharnet.in; Jogibara Rd)

Himalaya Tours & Travels (☎220714; www.akupema.net/himalaya; Bhagsu Rd)

❶ Getting There & Around

Many travel agencies in McLeod Ganj will book train tickets for services out of Pathankot for a fee. See p316 for train services in the Kangra Valley.

Air
McLeod Ganj's nearest airport is at Gaggal, 15km southwest of Dharamsala. **Kingfisher** (www.flykingfisher.com) flies to Delhi daily at 1pm. Book at a travel agency.

Autorickshaw
Autorickshaws are useful for getting around the immediate area – the autorickshaw stand is just north of the bus stand. Sample fares include Bhagsu (₹30), Jogibara (₹50), Dal Lake (₹60) and Dharamkot (₹50).

Bus
While the new bus terminal is now just north of the autorickshaw stand, the ticket office is still at McLeod's main square. There, you can book Himachal Roadways Transport Corporation (HRTC) buses up to a month in advance. Travel agencies can book seats on deluxe private buses to Delhi (₹800, 12 hours, 6.30pm), Manali (₹500, 10 hours, 8pm) and other destinations, and there are regular long-haul buses from Dharamsala. For more details on buses from McLeod Ganj see the table, p327.

Taxi
McLeod's **taxi stand** (☎221034) is on Mall Rd, north of the Main Chowk. To hire a taxi for the day, for a journey of less than 80km, expect to pay ₹1400.

Fares for short hops include Gangchen Kyishong (₹80), Dharamkot (₹80), Dharamsala's Kotwali Bazaar (₹150), Dharamsala bus station (₹170), Norbulingka Institute (₹350) and the

DESTINATION	FARE (₹)	DURATION (HR)	FREQUENCY
Dehra Dun	325	13	8pm
Delhi	325	12	4am, 6pm, 7pm (ordinary); 4.30pm, 7.45pm (deluxe); 7.30pm (AC)
Manali	255	11	6am, 6.30am, 5pm
Pathankot	65	4	five daily

airport (₹600). Return fares are about a third more, while longer fares are similar to those charged by the taxi stand in Dharamsala – see p315.

Around McLeod Ganj

BHAGSU & DHARAMKOT
📞 01892

Through pine trees to the north and east of McLeod lie the villages of Dharamkot and Bhagsu, which can both be visited on a pleasant half-day hike, or as an alternative accommodation base. Bhagsu (Bhagsunag) in particular is developing into a travellers' hot spot. The village has a cold spring with **baths**, a small **Shiva temple** built by the raja of Kangra in the 16th century, and a gaudy **temple** with stairways passing through the open mouths of a cement crocodile and lion. Head uphill a bit and you'll enter a backpackerland heavy with Hebrew signage, where you can lounge in cafes, take drumming lessons and yoga classes, and forget that there's a crisis in Tibet. Continuing through Bhagsu, you can walk on to Dharamkot and back to McLeod, or climb up to Triund alongside a gushing **waterfall**.

Various alternative therapies are available in the backpacker enclave. The **Buddha Hall** (📞221749; www.buddhahall.com) has courses in reiki, yoga and Indian classical music. Bhagsu has half a dozen internet cafes and travel agencies.

🛏 Sleeping

BHAGSU

Oak View Guesthouse   GUESTHOUSE $
(📞221530; d ₹350) Clean guesthouse on the path to Upper Baghsu with a classic backpacker vibe – right down to the Bob Marley flag in the common lounge area. All rooms have hot water and TV.

Sky Pye Guesthouse   GUESTHOUSE $
(📞220497; d ₹300-800; @) A little further up the hill from Oak View, Sky Pye is another good-value traveller hang-out that's often full. There are views from the terrace and from some rooms, and there's an internet cafe and a cute little restaurant with low tables and cushions on the floor.

DHARAMKOT

Dharamkot is much more low-key than Bhagsu, but has a small knot of guesthouses near the Himalayan Iyengar Yoga Centre.

Kamal Guesthouse   GUESTHOUSE $
(📞226920; d with/without bathroom ₹200/75) Friendly five-room guesthouse with roof terrace.

New Blue Heaven Guesthouse   HOTEL $
(📞221005; www.hotelnewblueheaven.com; d ₹ 350-880; @) Spotless carpeted rooms with TV, hot water and balconies overlooking the valley make this a solid choice. Upper-floor rooms have the best views.

🍴 Eating

Bhagsu is full of busy German bakeries and backpacker cafes serving falafel, hummus and Tibetan food.

Ashoka International Restaurant ASIAN $
(mains ₹30-140; ⊙lunch & dinner) Bhagsu's best Indian and Chinese food is served in a smart dining room with a choice of floor cushions or normal tables.

Oasis Cafe   MULTICUISINE $$
(mains ₹80-150; ⊙breakfast, lunch & dinner) In front of the Oak View Guesthouose you'll find this inviting dining space with a Thai/Israeli/Italian emphasis on the menu.

SIDHIBARI & TAPOVAN
About 6km from Dharamsala, the little village of Sidhibari is the adopted home of Ogyen Trinley Dorje, the 17th Karmapa of Tibetan Buddhism, who fled to India in 2000. Although his official seat is Rumtek

Monastery in Sikkim, the young leader of the Kagyu (Black Hat) sect has been banned from taking up his seat for fear this would upset the Chinese government.

The temporary seat of the Karmapa is the large **Gyuto Tantric Gompa** (☎01892-236637; www.kagyuoffice.org) in Sidhibari. Public audiences take place here on Wednesday and Saturday at 2.30pm; foreign visitors are welcome but security is tight and bags, phones and cameras are not allowed inside the auditorium.

Nearby is the **Tapovan Ashram**, a popular spiritual retreat for devotees of Rama, with a colourful Ram Mandir, a giant black Shiva lingam and a 6m-high statue of Hanuman.

Regular local buses run from Dharamsala to Sidhibari (₹5, 15 minutes) or you can take a taxi for ₹250 return. Tapovan is a 2km walk south along a quiet country road.

NORBULINGKA INSTITUTE
☎01892

About 6km from Dharamsala, the wonderful **Norbulingka Institute** (☎246405; www.norbulingka.org; ☺8am-6pm) was established in 1988 to teach and preserve traditional Tibetan art forms, including woodcarving, statue-making, *thangka* painting and embroidery. The centre produces expensive but exquisite craftworks, including embroidered clothes, cushions and wall hangings, and sales benefit refugee artists. Also here are delightful Japanese-influenced **gardens** and a central **Buddhist temple** with a 4m-high gilded statue of Sakyamuni. Next to the shop is the **Losel Doll Museum** (Indian/foreigner ₹5/20; ☺9am-5.30pm), with quaint puppet dioramas of Tibetan life. A short walk behind the complex is the large **Dolma Ling** Buddhist nunnery. On Sundays and the second Saturday of each month the workshops are closed but the rest of the grounds are open.

Set in the gorgeous Norbulingka gardens, **Norling Guest House** (☎246406; normail@norbulingka.org; s/d from ₹1400/1800) offers fairy-tale rooms decked out with Buddhist murals and handicrafts from the institute, and arranged around a sunny atrium. Meals are available at the institute's Norling Cafe.

To get here, catch a Yol-bound bus from Dharamsala and ask to be let off at Sidhpur (₹5, 15 minutes), near the Sacred Heart School, from where it's a 15-minute walk. A taxi from Dharamsala will cost ₹300 return.

MCLEOD GANJ TO BHARMOUR TREK

This popular six- to seven-day route crosses over the Indrahar La (4300m) to the ancient village of Bharmour in the Chamba Valley. The pass is open from September to early November and you can start this trek, and make all arrangements, in McLeod Ganj or Bharmour.

From McLeod, take an autorickshaw along the Dharamkot road, then walk on through pine and rhododendron forests to Triund, where there's a simple rest house. The next stage climbs to the glacier at Laka Got (3350m) and continues to the rocky shelter known as Lahes Cave. With an early start the next day, you can cross the Indrahar La – and be rewarded with astounding views – before descending to the meadow campground at Chata Parao.

The stages on to Bharmour can be tricky without a local guide. From Chata Parao, the path moves back into the forest, descending over three days to Kuarsi, Garola and finally to Bharmour, where you can catch buses on to Chamba. Alternatively, you can bail out and catch a bus at several places along the route.

STAGE	ROUTE	DURATION (HR)	DISTANCE (KM)
1	McLeod Ganj to Triund	4-5	9
2	Triund to Lahesh Cave	4-5	8
3	Lahesh Cave to Chata Parao over Indrahar La	6	10
4	Chata Parao to Kuarsi	5-6	15
5	Kuarsi to Chanauta	6-7	16
6	Chanauta to Garola	5-6	12
7	Garola to Bharmour	5-6	14

Southwest Of Dharamsala

KANGRA
☎01892 / ELEV 734M

The former capital of the princely state of Kangra, this bustling pilgrim town is an easy day trip from McLeod Ganj. Hindus visit to pay homage at the **Brajeshwari Devi Temple**, one of the 51 *Shakti peeths,* the famous temples marking the sites where body parts from Shiva's first wife, Sati, fell after the goddess was consumed by flames. The Brajeshwari temple marks the final resting place of Sati's left breast (see p443 for more on the legend). It's reached through an atmospheric bazaar winding uphill from the main road, lined with shops selling *prasad* and religious trinkets.

On the far side of town, an ₹80 autorickshaw ride from the bus stand, the impregnable-looking **Kangra Fort** (Nagar Kot; Indian/foreigner ₹5/100; ⊘dawn-dusk) soars above the confluence of the Manjhi and Banganga Rivers. The fort was used by Hindu rajas, Mughal warlords and even the British before it was finally toppled by the earthquake of 1905. On clear days, head to the battlements for views north to the mountains and south to the plains. A small **museum** at the fort has stone carvings from temples inside the compound and miniature paintings from the Kangra School.

Royal Hotel & Restaurant (☎265013; royalhotel@rediffmail.com; r ₹400-500), on the main road between the steps of the main temple and the bus stand, has neat, tiled rooms with hot showers, plus a decent restaurant.

For meals, eat at your hotel or try one of the many *dhabas* in the centre of town and along the bazaar that runs up to Brajeshwari Devi.

ℹ Getting There & Away

Kangra's bus stand is 1.5km north of the temple bazaar, a ₹25 autorickshaw ride from the centre. There are frequent buses to Dharamsala (₹20, one hour), Palampur (₹35, 1½ hours), Pathankot (₹70, three hours) and Jawalamukhi (₹30, 1½ hours).

Trains pull into Kangra Mandir station, 3km east of town, and Kangra station, 5km south. Travellers have reported problems getting an autorickshaw from the stations in town.

Taxis in Kangra charge ₹200 to Gaggal airport, ₹350 to Dharamsala, and ₹500 to McLeod Ganj, Jawalamukhi or Masrur.

MASRUR

A winding road runs southwest from Gaggal through pleasant green hills to the 10th-century **temples** (Indian/foreigner ₹5/100; ⊘dawn-dusk) at Masrur. Although badly damaged by the 1905 earthquake, the *sikharas* owe more than a passing resemblance to the Hindu temples at Angkor Wat in Cambodia. You can climb to the upper level for mountain views.

The easiest way to get here is by taxi from Dharamsala (₹1200 return), or you can get as far as Lunj (₹25, 1½ hours) from Dharamsala by public bus and take a local taxi for the last few kilometres.

JAWALAMUKHI
☎01970

About 34km south of Kangra is the town **temple** of Jawalamukhi, the goddess of light, worshipped in the form of a natural-gas eternal flame issuing from the rocks. The temple is one of the 51 *Shakti peeths,* marking the spot where the tongue of Shiva's first wife, Sati, fell after her body was consumed by flames. The gold dome and spire were installed by Maharaja Ranjit Singh, the 'Lion of Punjab', who purportedly never went into battle without seeking a blessing from the temple.

Hotel Jawalaji (☎222280; d ₹600-800, with AC ₹1300-2000; ❄) is a superior HPTDC property, with well-loved rooms, conveniently located for walks to the temple and outlying countryside.

Buses to Dharamsala (₹50, 1½ hours) and Kangra (₹30, 1½ hours) leave all day from the stand below the road leading up to the temple. Taxis charge ₹700/1000 one way/return from McLeod Ganj.

Dharamsala To Mandi

PALAMPUR
☎01894 / ELEV 1249M

About 30km southeast of Dharamsala, Palampur is a small junction town surrounded by tea plantations and rice fields. A short trek from town takes you to the pretty waterfall in **Bundla Chasm**, or you can pass a few hours observing the tea-making process at the **Palampur Tea Cooperative** (☎230220; ⊘10.30am-12.30pm & 1.30-4.30pm Tue-Fri), about 2km south of town on the main road between Kangra and Mandi.

HPTDC Hotel Tea-Bud (☎231298; d ₹900-2000), 1km north of Main Bazar on the edge of town, has large grounds and a good restaurant; rooms are spacious and well kept. The more-expensive rooms are in a newer block but the old ones aren't bad.

The bus station is 1km south of Main Bazar; an autorickshaw from the centre costs ₹20. Buses leave all day for Dharamsala (₹40, two hours). A taxi from Dharamsala costs ₹700. Palampur is a stop on the Pathankot-Jogindarnagar rail line. If taking the bus from here to Mandi, the best views are from the right-side seats.

BAIJNATH

☎ 01894 / ELEV 1010M

The small town of Baijnath, set on a mountain-facing ridge 46km southeast of Dharamsala, is an important pilgrimage destination. In the middle of the village is the exquisitely carved **Baidyanath Temple**, sacred to Shiva in his incarnation as Vaidyanath, Lord of the Physicians, dating from the 8th century. Thousands of pilgrims make their way here for the **Shivaratri Festival** in late February and early March.

Most people visit on a day trip, or a stop on the journey from Mandi to Dharamsala. The Pathankot-Jogindarnagar rail line passes through Paprola, about 1km west of the main bus stand.

TASHIJONG & TARAGARH

About 5km west of Baijnath, and 2km north from the Palampur road, the village of Tashijong is home to a small community of Drukpa Kagyud monks and refugees. The focus of life here is the impressive **Tashijong Gompa**, with several mural-filled prayer halls and a carpet-making, *thangka*-painting and woodcarving cooperative.

About 2km south of Tashijong, at Taragarh, is the extraordinary **Taragarh Palace** (☎01894-242034, ☎in Delhi 011-24692317; www .taragarh.com; r ₹4000-5500; ❈☞), the summer palace of the last maharaja of Jammu and Kashmir. Now a luxury hotel, this elegant country seat is full of portraits of the Dogra royal family, Italian marble, crystal chandeliers, tiger skins and other ostentatious furnishings. It's set in beautiful grounds with a pool and tennis courts. The restaurant serves lavish buffet meals (₹300 to ₹500).

Both villages can be reached on the buses that run along the Mandi–Palampur Hwy – just tell the bus driver where you want to get off.

BIR & BILLING

About 9km east of Baijnath, a road winds uphill to the village of Bir (1300m), a small Tibetan colony with three peaceful **gompas** that welcome passing visitors, and Billing (2600m), a famous launch pad for paragliding and hang-gliding. In 1992 the world record of 132.5km for an out-and-return flight was set here. International teams come to challenge the record every May for the **Himalayan Hang-Gliding Rally**, while paragliders compete in the **Himalayan Open** in autumn.

A taxi from McLeod Ganj to Billing will cost ₹900. Alternatively, travel by bus or train to Jogindarnagar (on the route to Mandi) and take a taxi there for ₹400 return.

Chamba Valley

The Chamba Valley is a splendidly isolated valley system, cut off from the Kangra Valley by the Dhauladhar Range and from Kashmir by the Pir Panjal. This area was ruled for centuries as the princely state of Chamba, the most ancient state in North India. Even though good roads connect Chamba with Pathankot and Kangra, surprisingly few travellers make it out here, with even fewer continuing up the valley beyond the old hill station of Dalhousie.

DALHOUSIE

☎ 01899 / POP 10,500 / ELEV 2036M

With its plunging pine-clad valleys and distant mountain views, Dalhousie is another of those cool mountain retreats that the British left behind. Since independence, the colonial mansions have been joined by the posh Dalhousie Public School and numerous modern hotels catering to honeymooners from the plains, along with the obligatory army cantonment. There's not

KANGRA VALLEY TOY TRAIN

A lumbering narrow-gauge train runs east from Pathankot, providing a scenic, if slow, back route to Kangra (2½ hours), Palampur (four hours), Baijnath (6½ hours) and Jogindarnagar (nine hours). There are seven trains a day – two as far as Jogindarnagar and five as far as Baijnath. Ordinary trains cost ₹42 or less to any destination on the route, but carriages are crammed with passengers and seats cannot be booked in advance. Board early to grab a window seat and enjoy the views en route.

a lot to do here other than stroll around admiring the views.

Quite a few Tibetan refugees have made a home in Dalhousie and there are painted **rock carvings** of Buddhist deities along the south side of the ridge. You can also visit the British-era churches of **St John** and **St Francis**, set among the pines at opposite ends of the ridge.

Unusually for a hill station there are few truly steep roads, but Dalhousie is spread far enough to be exhausting. The market areas at Subhash Chowk and Gandhi Chowk are linked by lanes – Thandi Sarak (Cold Rd), and Garam Sarak (Hot Rd). The latter lane receives more sunshine. The bus stand area, with several good hotels, is about 2km north.

Street lighting is limited so carry a torch at night.

🛏 Sleeping

Dalhousie has more than 100 hotels spread across various ridges and lanes. Most are either old or just look old. High season runs from April to July, and Christmas to New Year, and there's a mid-season from September to late October; expect at least 50% off at other times.

Hotel Grand View HERITAGE HOTEL **$$$**
(☎240760; www.grandviewdalhousie.in; d ₹1800-2000, ste ₹2500-4500) The Grand has great rooms loaded with colonial character, including four-poster beds, bathrooms with dressing rooms attached. And it more than lives up to its name. The stately 1920s hotel is surrounded by gardens gazing across to views of the Pir Panjal peaks, and the spacious Raj-inspired rooms open out to sunny glass-panelled hallways. There's a spa with sauna, jacuzzi and exercise room.

Hotel Crags GUESTHOUSE **$**
(☎242124; Garam Sarak; r ₹400-700, cottage ₹800) For colonial character and valley views, Crags is the pick of the budget places – listed rates are half this price most of the year. Down some steps from the Subhash Chowk end of Garam Sarak, this big old house has huge rooms and a large front terrace offering spectacular views of the valley – the upper-floor rooms with front sitting room are easily the best and there's a self-contained cottage.

Youth Hostel Dalhousie HOSTEL **$**
(☎242189; yh_dalhousie@rediffmail.com; dm ₹100, r ₹250; ☻) A 200m walk down a back lane opposite the bus stand, Dalhousie's hostel is spotless and run with military precision.

Dorms are single sex, showers are hot, and facilities include internet access, free wi-fi and a dining hall. YHA rules include a 10pm curfew, no alcohol, and vacating of rooms from 10am to 12.30pm for cleaning. There can also be noisy school groups – but it's a welcoming place with fixed rates all year.

Hotel Mount View HOTEL **$$$**
(☎242120; www.hotelmountview.com; Club Rd; r ₹2400-3100, ste ₹3400-4200) There's an undeniable Raj-era charm to this delightful hotel, full of dark-wood finishes and period furnishings. Less expensive rooms are smallish but well equipped; some bigger rooms are spacious but offer less than they should for the price. There are good valley views from the well-tended garden terrace.

🍴 Eating

Both Subhash Chowk and Gandhi Chowk have places to eat. Most restaurants are open from 9am to 10pm. None of Dalhousie's hotels are licensed to serve alcohol.

Kwality Restaurant INDIAN **$$**
(Gandhi Chowk; dishes ₹75-180) Regarded as Dalhousie's best independent restaurant, the extensive veg and nonveg menu covers Indian and Chinese as well as burgers, pizza and sizzlers.

Lovely Restaurant INDIAN **$**
(Gandhi Chowk; mains ₹50-130; ⏲9am-10pm) Has the typical list of Indian and Chinese plates, along with Bollywood movies playing on the flatscreen TV.

The restaurants at Hotel Grand View and Mount View near the bus stand offer a charming colonial dining experience and multicuisine menus. For cheap eats, there are several Punjabi *dhabas* on the south side of Subhash Chowk.

🛍 Shopping

Close to Gandhi Chowk on Garam Sarak, you'll find fair-priced Kullu shawls and hats at **Bhuttico** (☎240440; ⏲10am-6pm Mon-Sat) and a good selection of Tibetan carpets and handicrafts at the **Tibetan Refugee Handicraft Centre** (☎240607; ⏲10am-6pm Wed-Mon). Just up from the bus stand, the **Tibetan Market** sells textiles, clothing and trinkets for the holiday crowd.

ℹ Information

At the Tibetan Market and near Gandhi Chowk there are internet cafes charging ₹40 an hour.
HPTDC tourist office (☎242225; ⏲10am-5pm Apr-Jul, closed Sun Aug-Mar) Opposite the bus stand; helpful staff can advise on bus times.

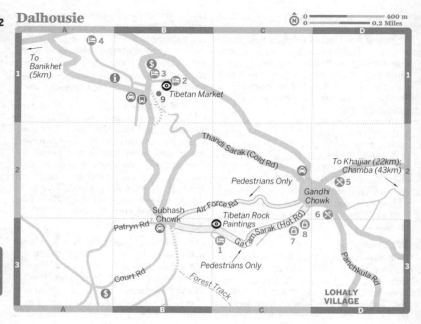

State Bank of India (☉24hr) International ATM, near the bus stand.

Trek-n-Travels (☏242160; Tibetan Market) Near the bus stand; can arrange treks around Chamba Valley from ₹800 per day.

❶ Getting There & Away

BUS The booking office at the bus stand is invariably closed, but the tourist office next door can help with bus information; for long-distance services, there are many more options from Banikhet, a major transport hub about 10 minutes ride from Dalhousie (bus/taxi ₹10/150). Four buses run to Chamba (₹70, two hours); two through Khajjiar (₹30, one hour). For more-frequent Chamba buses, head to Banikhet first. See the table, p333, for direct services.

TAXI There are unionised taxi stands with fixed fares at Subhash Chowk, Gandhi Chowk and the bus stand. From the bus stand, you'll pay ₹50 to Subhash Chowk and ₹100 to Gandhi Chowk. Other one-way fares:

DESTINATION	FARE (₹)
Bharmour	2500
Chamba	930 (1150 return)
Dharamsala	2050
Kalatop	520 (930 return)
Khajjiar	620 (720 return)
Pathankot	1550

AROUND DALHOUSIE

KALATOP WILDLIFE SANCTUARY

Midway between Dalhousie and Chamba, accessible by taxi or public bus, the forested hills around Khajjiar are preserved as the **Kalatop Wildlife Sanctuary**. The pine forests provide excellent walking country and you have a chance of spotting langur monkeys, barking deer and black bears. Buses between Dalhousie and Khajjiar pass the park entrance at **Lakkar Mandi**.

KHAJJIAR

India's so-called 'Mini Switzerland', this grassy bowl-shaped *marg* (meadow), 22km from Dalhousie, is ringed by pines and thronged by Indian holidaymakers. In among the *dhabas* on one side is the **Khajjinag Temple**, with fine woodcarvings and crude effigies of the five Pandavas, installed here in the 16th century.

In season, **pony rides** around the meadow and its small central lake cost from ₹100, and **zorbing** in giant inflatable balls costs from ₹200 for a quick roll. Since there are no big slopes as such, you get pushed along – not exactly high adrenaline!

There are a handful of fast-food restaurants and several hotels, but most travellers make a day trip here by bus from Chamba (₹25, 1½ hours) or Dalhousie (₹30, one

Dalhousie

hour). Buses run on this route about five times a day. If you do decide to stay, the best option is the **HPTDC Hotel Davdar** (📞236333; ₹1100-2000).

CHAMBA
📞01899 / POP 20,700 / ELEV 996M

Ensconced in the valley of the fast-flowing Ravi River, the charming capital of Chamba district is dominated by the former palaces of the local maharajas. The princely state of Chamba was founded in AD 920 by Raja Sahil Varman and it survived for 1000 years until it finally fell to the British in 1845. Every year since 935, Chamba has celebrated the annual harvest with the **Minjar Festival** in July/August, in honour of Raghuvira (an incarnation of Rama).

Although en route to Bharmour and popular trekking country, Chamba is well off the tourist radar, giving it the feeling of an everyday but surprisingly mellow Indian town. The de facto centre of town is the open grassy sports field known as the Chowgan, the focus for festivals, impromptu cricket matches, picnics and promenades. Most places of interest are tucked away in the alleyways of Dogra Bazar, which runs uphill past the maharaja's palace.

👁 Sights & Activities

Lakshmi Narayan Temple Complex   HINDU TEMPLE

Opposite the Akhand Chandi Palace are six **sikharas** dating from the 10th to the 19th centuries, built in the Himachal stone-hut style and covered in carvings. The largest (and oldest) is dedicated to Lakshmi Narayan (Vishnu). In front is a distinctive Nepalistyle pillar topped by a statue of Vishnu's faithful servant, the man-bird Garuda. The remaining temples are sacred to Radha Krishna, Shiva, Gauri Shankar, Triambkeshwar Mahdev and Lakshmi Damodar. The compound has a small **museum** (admission free; ⏰11am-5pm Mon-Sat) displaying religious artefacts.

Other Temples   HINDU TEMPLES

On the hilltop above the Rang Mahal, reached via a set of steps near the bus stand, or by taxi along the road to Jhumar, the stone **Chamunda Devi Temple** features impressive carvings of Chamunda Devi (Durga in her wrathful aspect) and superior views of Chamba and the Dhauladhar. About 500m north along the road to Saho, the **Bajreshwari Devi Temple** is a handsome hut-style mandir with exquisite effigies of Bajreshwari (an incarnation of Durga) set into plinths around the walls.

Between the two is a small shrine to **Sui Mata**, a local princess who gave her life to appease a water spirit that was causing a terrible drought in Chamba. The goddess

HIMACHAL PRADESH CHAMBA VALLEY

BUSES FROM DALHOUSIE

DESTINATION	FARE (₹)	DURATION (HR)	FREQUENCY
Amritsar	120	6	6am
Delhi	370/590	12	3pm/7.30pm (ordinary/deluxe)
Dharamsala	130	6	7am, 11.50am & 2pm
Jammu	120	6	10am
Pathankot	70	3	10 daily
Shimla	350	12	12.45pm

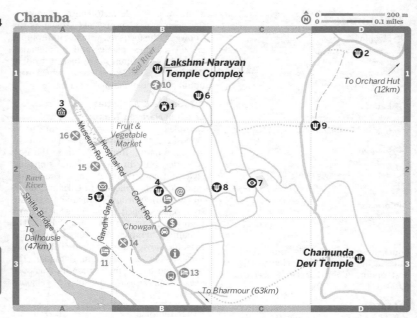

is highly venerated by local women and the four-day **Sui Mata Mela** is celebrated each April on the Chowgan in her honour.

By the Chowgan is the 11th-century **Harirai Mandir**, sacred to Vishnu. Dotted nearby Akhand Chandi Palace are similar stone temples to **Radha Krishna**, **Sitaram** (Rama) and **Champavati**, daughter of Raja Sahil Varman, worshipped locally as an incarnation of Durga.

Historic Buildings   HISTORIC BUILDINGS
Uphill from the Chowgan and lording over the town is the unmissable stately white **Akhand Chandi Palace**, the former home of the Chamba raja. Built in 1764, the central Darbar Hall is reminiscent of many civic buildings in Kathmandu. It now houses a postgraduate college; you can peek inside during school hours.

A few blocks southeast is the fortresslike, rusty-coloured **Rang Mahal** (Old Palace), which once housed the royal granary and treasury and now houses a handicrafts shop.

Bhuri Singh Museum   MUSEUM
(☑222590; Museum Rd; Indian/foreigner ₹10/50, camera ₹50; ⊙10am-5pm Tue-Sun, closed 2nd Sat each month) Founded in 1908 and named after the Chamba ruler of that time, this museum has a wonderful collection of miniature paintings from the Chamba, Kangra and Basohli schools, plus wood carvings, weapons, *rumals,* intriguing copper-plate inscriptions, relics from the rajas and ornately carved fountain slabs from around the Chamba Valley. There's detailed labelling in English.

☞ Tours
Near the Lakshmi Narayan complex, **Mani Mahesh Travels** (☑222507, 9816620401; manimaheshtravels@yahoo.com) can arrange treks with guides and porters in the foothills of the Pir Panjal and Dhauladhar (₹1500 to ₹2000 per person, per day, depending on altitude), as well as informative tours of Chamba's temples (from ₹550).

🛏 Sleeping
Unlike Dalhousie, Chamba is not a tourist town, so hotel prices vary little by season.

TOP CHOICE Orchard Hut   GUESTHOUSE $
(☑9418020401; orchardhut@hotmail.com; r ₹500-850) About 12km from Chamba in the tranquil Saal Valley, this friendly village guesthouse is a peaceful place to immerse in the countryside. Great homecooked meals are served and there are some sweet walks in the area. Staff at Mani Manesh Travels in Chamba will arrange transfers.

Chamba

Hotel Aroma Palace   HOTEL **$$**
(☏225177; www.hotelaromapalacechamba.com; s/d from ₹550/700, deluxe r ₹1000-3300; @ 🛜) Uphill from the taxi stand and past the courthouse, this modern place has a range of tidy rooms, an internet cafe, a restaurant and a sunny terrace with views over Chowgan. The cheaper rooms are disappointing – you can't swing a cat in the single rooms and others have their own bathroom outside off the hall – but if you pay a bit more you get the real deal.

Chamba House Guesthouse   GUESTHOUSE **$**
(☏222564; Gopal Nivas; d ₹350-700) With fine views over the Ravi River from its balcony, this creaky heritage building near Gandhi Gate is Chamba's best budget bolthole. Rooms are quaint, with wood floors, giving it a homey cottage feeling. The manager speaks little English, but it's very welcoming.

Jimmy's Inn   HOTEL **$**
(☏224748; r ₹200-400) If you're really pinching rupees, head to Jimmy's, across from the bus stand.

✖ Eating & Drinking

Chamba is known for its *chukh* – a chilli sauce consisting of red and green peppers, lemon juice and mustard oil, served as a condiment in most restaurants. Chamba's most interesting restaurants are clustered together just south of the museum.

[TOP CHOICE] Park View Restaurant   INDIAN **$**
(Museum Rd; dishes ₹30-110; ⊗8am-11pm) Up a flight of stairs, the low-ceilinged dining room feels like someone's attic. The veg and nonveg food is fantastic – order some *jheera* (cumin) rice and curd and a copper pail of dhal on the side, or chicken cooked twelve different ways (including lemon chicken).

Jagan Restaurant   INDIAN **$**
(Museum Rd; dishes ₹30-180) It's nothing flash but Jagan offers the tasty Chamba speciality *chamba madhra* (kidney beans with curd and ghee) for ₹65, plus a good selection of veg curries and chicken dishes. The top-floor Madhusala Bar is a no-frills place to have a beer and gaze over the town through glassless windows.

Cafe Ravi View   INDIAN **$$**
(Chowgan; mains ₹40-250; ⊗9am-9pm) In a circular hut overlooking the Ravi River, this HPTDC-run snack house is worth a visit as much for the icy-cold beers and outdoor terrace as for the food. It serves a good range of Indian and Chinese veg food – including dosas and bargain veg thalis (₹40).

🛍 Shopping

Housed in the Rang Mahal, the **Himachal Emporium** (☏222333; ⊗10am-5pm Mon-Sat) sells Chamba's famous *rumals* – pieces of cloth finely embroidered in silk, with a perfect mirror image of the same pattern on the reverse side and no evidence of knots or loose threads. Prices start at ₹300.

ℹ Information

There's an international ATM at the State Bank of India, near the court house.

Cyberia (per hr ₹30; ⊗9am-8pm Mon-Sat) Near Hotel Aroma Palace; has broadband connection and helpful staff.

Himachal Tourist Office (☏224002; Court Rd; ⊗10am-5pm Mon-Sat) In the yellow building in the courtyard of Hotel Iravati. Has limited local information but lots of brochures.

Post office (Museum Rd; ⊗9.30am-5.30pm Mon-Sat)

ℹ Getting There & Away

Six daily buses make the hair-raising run to Bharmour (₹70, three hours), though the road can be temporarily blocked by rockfalls. The best views on this route are from seats on the left side. Buses for Dalhousie run every two hours (₹60, 2½ hours), some going via Khajjiar (₹30, 1½ hours). There are also buses to Dharamsala (₹175, eight hours).

Official taxi fares include Khajjiar (₹700 return), Bharmour (₹1200/1500 one way/return), Dalhousie (₹1000) and Dharamsala (₹2500).

BHARMOUR
🕿 01895 / ELEV 2195M

Hovering on the edge of a seemingly bottomless valley, the charming mountain village of Bharmour is reached by a mountain road as scenic as it is perilous, winding 65km east of Chamba. This ancient slate-roofed settlement was the capital of the princely state of Chamba until AD 920, and there are fascinating temples and treks to surrounding mountain passes. In fact, you can trek from here all the way to McLeod Ganj. The villages around Bharmour are home to the seminomadic Gaddis, pastoralists who move their flocks up to alpine pastures during the summer, and descend to Kangra, Mandi and Bilaspur in winter.

◉ Sights & Activities

Chaurasi Temples　　HINDU TEMPLE
Reached through the bazaar leading uphill from the jeep stand, the **Chaurasi temples** are some of Himachal's finest. Built in the classic stone-*sikhara* style, with wide slate canopies, the Shaivite temples are spread over a flagstone courtyard that doubles as an outdoor classroom for local schools. Highlights of the compound are the towering **Manimahesh Temple**, built in the 6th century AD, and the squat **Lakshna Devi Temple**, featuring an eroded but wildly carved wooden doorway.

Trekking　　TREKKING
Treks from Bharmour can be arranged through the **Himalayan Travelling Agency** (🕿 225059), by the HP State Coop Bank in the bazaar, and the **Directorate of Mountaineering & Allied Sports** (🕿 225036), on the track above the jeep stand. Expect to pay around ₹1500 a day, for food, tents, guides and porters. The trekking season lasts from May to late October.

Trekking destinations include Keylong and Udaipur in Lahaul, Baijnath and McLeod Ganj in the Kangra Valley, and the popular trek to the sacred lake at Manima-

hesh, a three-day, 35km hike above Bharmour. In August/September, pilgrims take a freezing dip in Manimahesh Lake as part of the **Manimahesh Yatra** in honour of Lord Shiva.

🛏 Sleeping & Eating

As well as hotel restaurants, there are several *dhabas* on the path to the Chaurasi temples.

Chaurasi Hotel & Restaurant　　HOTEL $
(🕿 225615; r ₹500-900, mains ₹45-160) You can't miss this blazing red multistorey building on the temple road. Though carpets are a little ratty, this is a good-value hotel with generous-sized rooms offering soaring views over the valley, especially from the top-floor room with balcony. The multicuisine restaurant here is Bharmour's best.

Chamunda Guest House　　GUESTHOUSE $
(🕿 225056; r ₹300) This pink village house with purple balconies only has bucket hot water, but rooms are comfortable enough for the price. Run by a friendly family, it's on the lower road from the jeep stand.

ℹ Getting There & Away

Buses leave every few hours for the rugged trip to Chamba (₹65, three hours), but expect delays due to landslides. If you want to get a seat, board early! For the ride to Chamba, the best views are from the right side of the bus. Taxis charge ₹1100 but you can bargain at the jeep stand.

LAHAUL & SPITI

This vast, desolate corner of Himachal Pradesh is also one of the most sparsely populated regions on earth. Lahaul is a relatively green valley north of the Rohtang La, but as you travel east into Spiti the landscape transforms into a rugged network of interlocking river valleys hidden in the rain shadow of the Himalaya. It's 12,000 sq km of snow-topped mountains and high-altitude desert, punctuated by tiny patches of greenery and villages of whitewashed mud-brick houses clinging to the sides of rivers and meltwater streams.

As in Zanskar and Ladakh, Buddhism is the dominant religion, though there are small pockets of Hinduism in Lahaul, where many temples are sacred to Buddhist and Hindu deities. According to legend, some monasteries in Lahaul were founded personally by Padmasambhava, the Indian monk who converted Tibet to Buddhism in the 8th century AD.

Manali is the main gateway to Lahaul and Spiti. A seasonal highway runs north over the Rohtang La (3978m) to Keylong, the capital of Lahaul, continuing to Ladakh over the mighty Baralacha La (4950m) and Tanglang La (5328m). Side roads branch west to the little-visited Pattan Valley and east to Spiti over the 4551m Kunzum La.

Growing numbers of travellers are visiting Lahaul and Spiti as part of the Great Himalayan Circuit from Kashmir to Kinnaur. The Rohtang La, Baralacha La and Tanglang La are normally open from June to late October, while the Kunzum La to Spiti is accessible from July to October, with exact dates depending on snow conditions. At other times, the entire region is virtually cut off from the outside world, except for the rugged Hindustan–Tibet Hwy from Kinnaur.

For more information on Lahaul and Spiti, visit the local government website at http://hplahaulspiti.gov.in.

Losar, the Tibetan New Year, is celebrated in villages throughout Lahaul and Spiti in January or February, depending on the lunar calendar.

History

Buddhism arrived in Lahaul and Spiti during the 8th century AD with the Indian missionary Padmasambhava. By the 10th century, upper Lahaul, Spiti and Zanskar had been incorporated into the vast Guge kingdom of western Tibet. The Great Translator, Ringchen Zangpo, founded a series of centres of Buddhist learning along the Spiti Valley, including Tabo, one of the most remarkable Buddhist monasteries in North India.

After the kings of Ladakh were defeated by Mongol-Tibetan armies in the 18th century, the region was divided and ruled by various Rajas, then fell under the British administration. Yet it maintained strong links with Tibet right up until the Chinese occupation in 1949.

Since then, there has been a major resurgence in the cultural and religious life of Spiti, aided by the work of the Tibetan government in exile in Dharamsala. The gompas of Lahaul and Spiti are being restored, and money from tourism and hydroelectricity is improving living conditions for the farming communities who get snowed in here each winter.

Climate

Lahaul and Spiti have a markedly different climate from the rest of Himachal Pradesh. The limited rainfall and high altitude – mostly above 3000m – ensures desperately cold conditions in winter. Even in summer, temperatures rarely rise above 15°C, and winter temperatures can plummet below -30°C! On the plus side, when monsoons are drenching the rest of the state, it's usually sunny here.

Realistically, the region is only open to travellers when the mountain passes are open, from early June/July to late October. Whenever you travel, bring plenty of clothing for cold weather.

Lahaul

Separated from the Kullu Valley by the 3978m Rohtang La and from Spiti by 4551m Kunzum La, Lahaul is greener and more developed than Ladakh and Spiti, but most travellers whistle straight through on the road between Manali and Leh, missing most of what Lahaul has to offer. The capital, Keylong, is an easy stop on the popular Leh to Manali bus trip and you can detour to a number of mountain villages and medieval monasteries that are blissfully untouched by mass tourism.

Normally, government buses between Manali and Leh run from mid-July to mid-September; at the time of research, these services were suspended due to catastrophic landslides. By the time you read this, we expect them to be up and running again. Private buses and shared minivans operate from late June to mid-October. Services as far as Keylong continue until the Rohtang La closes in November, and buses east to Kaza stop when the Kunzum La closes in October. Check the status of the passes before visiting late in the season – once the snows arrive, you might be stuck for the winter.

MANALI TO KEYLONG

From Manali the road to Leh strikes north along the Beas River valley and climbs slowly through pine forests and switchbacks to the bare rocky slopes below snow-clad **Rohtang La** (3978m). The name literally translates as 'pile of dead bodies' – a reference to the hundreds of travellers who have frozen to death here over the centuries. At the pass, look out for the small, dome-shaped temple that marks the source of the Beas River.

On the far side of the pass, the road plunges spectacularly down into the awesome

Lahaul Valley, a rugged landscape of soaring crags, alpine meadows and mesmerising waterfalls plunging from glacial heights. About 66km northwest of Manali, the tiny hamlet of Gramphu marks the turn-off to Spiti. There is only one building in Gramphu – a rustic stone *dhaba* beside a stream where you'll have to wait for the bus if you're heading to Kaza from Keylong.

Khoksar, 5km northwest of Gramphu, has several *dhabas* and a police checkpoint where foreigners must show their passports. The road passes through a sheer-sided valley, hemmed in by skyscraping rocky peaks.

About 18km before Keylong, Gondla is famous for its eight-storey tower fort, built from alternating layers of stone and timber. Once the home of the local *thakur,* the fort is no longer occupied, but it's still an impressive sight. Try to visit during the lively Gondla Fair in July. From Gondla, you can hike 4km to the village of Tupchiling to visit historic Guru Ghantal Gompa, allegedly founded by Padmasambhava. Although crumbling, the gompa contains ancient murals and wooden statues of bodhisattvas (Buddhist enlightened beings).

PATTAN VALLEY

About 8km south of Keylong at Tandi, a side road branches northwest along the Pattan Valley towards Udaipur. Overlooking the Chenab River, it's a peaceful spot with a few basic hotels and the plain-looking Markula Devi Temple, which hides fabulous wooden panels depicting scenes from the Mahabharata and Ramayana, carved in the 12th century.

From Udaipur, you can backtrack 9km along the valley to the squat stone temple at Triloknath, where Hindus worship the idol inside as Shiva while Buddhists venerate it as Avalokitesvara. It's a major pilgrimage site for both religions during the Pauri Festival in August.

KEYLONG

01900 / ELEV 3350M

The capital of Lahaul stretches along one side of the green Bhaga Valley just below the Manali–Leh Hwy, and it's a popular overnight stop for many buses plying that route. Hence many travellers only see Keylong briefly and in the dark, but a longer stay reveals grand mountain views, a laid-back village lifestyle and plenty of scenic walks; for tips on day hikes, visit Brokpa Adventure (9418165176) in the bazaar.

The bus stand is off the highway, just above the main bazaar. At the south end of town is the sort-of-interesting Lahaul & Spiti Tribal Museum (10am-5pm Tue-Sun), with traditional costumes, old dance masks and treasures from local gompas. There is a State Bank of India ATM at the north end of the bazaar.

Keylong celebrates the annual Lahaul Festival in July with a big, bustling market and various cultural activities.

Sleeping & Eating

There are a few hotels around the bus stand, and more about five minutes walk into town.

Hotel New Gyespa HOTEL $

(222207; r ₹400) The best choice of hotels by the bus stand, rooms at the New Gyespa actually seem fairly new. Windows give good light, and some have views of the valley. Every room has TV and hot water.

Hotel Tashi Deleg HOTEL $$

(222450; r ₹850-1750) Through the main bazaar, this big white place is Keylong's nicest hotel. Rooms on upper floors cost more, but all open out onto a balcony with mountain and valley views. The restaurant serves good Indian, Chinese and Tibetan food (meals ₹40 to ₹100), as well as cold beers.

Lamayuru Restaurant INDIAN $

(mains ₹40-140; 7am-11pm) A popular local restaurant down in the bazaar, you'll find a long list of Indian and Chinese staples, along with a full breakfast menu.

Aside from the hotel restaurants, there are plenty of *dhabas* on the highway and along the bazaar. For Tibetan food, Pau Gomba Sonju Dhaba (mains ₹40; 7am-7pm) has yummy soup, momos and noodle dishes.

Getting There & Away

Keylong is the official overnight stop for government buses travelling between Manali and Leh, so there are regular services in both directions when the mountain passes are open – typically June to October. Through bookings are only taken in Manali, so arrange a seat the day before, if you break the journey.

Normally, buses to Leh (15 hours) leave at 5am, arriving at about 8pm the same evening. At the time of research, these services were suspended due to massive landslides in Ladakh.

There around six daily buses to Manali (₹135, six hours). There's no direct bus to Kaza in Spiti: take the 5.30am bus and change at Gramphu (₹60, two hours); the bus from Manali to Kaza pulls in around 8.30am.

For the Pattan Valley, there are six daily buses to Udaipur (₹65, two hours).

AROUND KEYLONG

About 3km above Keylong is **Shashur Gompa**, dedicated to the Zanskari lama Deva Gyatsho. The original 16th-century gompa is now enshrined inside a modern gompa, with fine views over the valley. Frenetic masked *chaams* (ritual masked dances performed by Buddhist monks in gompas to celebrate the victory of good over evil and of Buddhism over pre-existing religions) are held here every June or July, depending on the Tibetan calendar. The path to the gompa cuts uphill behind the old bus stand – stick to the rough dirt path until you see the white chortens visible on the ridge.

Propped up on stilts on the far side of the valley, the 900-year-old gompa at **Khardong** is a steep two-hour walk from Keylong. Maintained by an order of Drukpa Kagyud monks and nuns, the monastery enshrines a mighty prayer wheel said to contain a million strips of paper bearing the mantra *'om mani padme hum'* (hail to the jewel in the lotus). The surrounding scenery is magnificent and there are excellent frescoes, but you'll have to track down a monk or nun to open the doors. To get to the monastery, head through the bazaar, follow the stepped path down to the hospital and take the bridge over the Bhaga River, from where it's a 4km slog uphill.

Perched on the side of the valley above the village of Satingri, the ancient **Tayul Gompa** has elegant mural work and a 4m-high statue of Padmasabhava, flanked by his two manifestations, Sighmukha and Vijravarashi. Tayul is about 6km from Keylong, reached by a fairly long day-hike.

About 20km northeast of Keylong, the pretty village of **Jispa** is a popular overnight stop for mountain bikers and motorcyclists. There's a small and interesting **folk museum** (admission ₹25; ☺9am-6pm) on the main road and a 2km walk south is the 16th-century **Ghemur Gompa**, where a famous masked 'devil dance' is held in July.

For accommodation, there's the extremely inviting **Hotel Ibex Jispa** (☏01900-233203; www.hotelibexjispa.com; dm/d ₹150/1800) on the main road.

Spiti

Separated from the fertile Lahaul Valley by the soaring 4551m Kunzum La, Spiti is another piece of Tibet transported to India. Villages are few and far between in this serrated, rocky landscape and they arrive like mirages – clusters of whitewashed homes nestled on the arid valley floor or perched in nooks on the slopes a thousand feet up. Even more impressive are the Buddhist monasteries built high on the sides of the valley and dwarfed by the sheer scale of the surrounding terrain. Local farmers eke out a living on the small strip of greenery that hugs the banks of the Spiti River and in isolated hamlets far above it.

In many ways Spiti is even more rugged and remote than Ladakh, but buses run over the Kunzum La from Manali from July to October, and the Hindustan–Tibet Hwy to Tabo is theoretically open all year. A steady stream of motorcyclists and mountain bikers pit their machines against some of the most challenging roads in India. Most people start in Manali or Keylong and exit the valley at Rekong Peo in Kinnaur, but a few travellers go against the flow and travel west to Keylong or Ladakh. Sections of the road are frequently washed away by floods and landslides, especially between Nako and Rekong Peo, so build some extra time into your itinerary in case of delays.

In either direction, an inner line permit is required for the stretch from Tabo to Rekong Peo – see the boxed text, p340.

GRAMPHU TO KAZA

From the *dhaba* at **Gramphu**, the road to Spiti follows the dramatic Chandra River gorge, which was carved by glaciers as the Himalaya thrust upwards 50 million years ago.

At **Battal**, a rough track runs 14km north to lovely **Chandratal** (Moon Lake), a tranquil glacial pool set among snow peaks at 4270m. From June to September you can probably stay in comfortable tents (per person inc meals ₹550) on the lakeshore, but these are operated on a year-to-year basis so there's no guarantee they'll be there when you arrive. This is also the starting point for treks to nearby **Bara Shigri** (Big Glacier), one of the longest glaciers in the Himalaya, but the route is treacherous and it's best to travel with an experienced guide.

From Battal, the road leaves the river and switchbacks precipitously up to **Kunzum La** (4551m), the watershed between the Spiti and Lahaul Valleys. Buses perform a respectful circuit of the stupas strewn with fluttering prayer flags at the top before continuing down into the Spiti Valley. An alternative 10.5km trail to Chandratal starts at the pass, continuing to Baralacha La on the Manali–Leh road in three strenuous days.

The first village of any size is **Losar**, a cluster of concrete and mud-brick houses in scrubby vegetation on the valley floor, where there's a passport check. A couple of basic guesthouses allow you to break the journey here; the friendly **Samsong Cafe & Guesthouse** (r with/without bathroom ₹600/200) has simple but clean rooms and hot meals.

The final stretch to Kaza follows the edge of the Spiti River, passing the large **Yangchen Choling** nunnery at Pangmo, and the **Sherab Choling** monastery school at Morang. Experienced teachers may be able to arrange volunteer teaching placements at these schools through the US-based **Jamyang Foundation** (www.jamyang.org).

KAZA
📞01906 / ELEV 3640M

The capital of Spiti, Kaza sits on the eroded flood plain of the Spiti River and is the biggest settlement you'll encounter in this empty corner of the state. Still, it's relatively small, feeling like a frontier town with an easygoing pace. The setting is wonderfully rugged – jagged mountains rise on either side and the river coils across the valley floor like twisted locks of Medusa's hair. The colourful new **Sakya Gompa** dominates the high road in New Kaza – where the town's administrative centre is located – while the ramshackle bazaar and whitewashed buildings of Old Kaza spread out on the other side of the stream that divides the town.

Most people stay at least one night to arrange the inner line permit for travel beyond Tabo. Kaza is also the starting point for trips to Ki Gompa and Kibber and treks into the mountains. The well-organised bus and jeep stand is below the bazaar in the old village.

In August, villagers from across Spiti descend on Kaza for the **Ladarcha Fair**. All sorts of goods are bought and sold and traders wear their finest clothes.

🛏 Sleeping & Eating

There are a surprising number of guesthouses squirrelled away close to the bus and taxi stands in Old Kaza, as well as a few places along the highway and across the stream in New Kaza. Most places close down by November.

Sakya Abode HOTEL $
(📞222256; r ₹500-600) On the main road in New Kaza, near the gompa, this is one of the best values in town. With a modest combination of character and class, it looks like it should cost more. Bright, comfy rooms open onto shared terraces that overlook a grassy-

lawned courtyard, and the restaurant is inviting (and appears remarkably hygienic).

Hotel Mandala HOTEL $
(📞222757; d ₹450) Right next to the taxi stand, Mandala is the cleanest budget option in Old Kaza. Run by a friendly family, there's a good restaurant and the location is handy.

Zanchuk Guest House HOTEL $
(📞9418537545; r without/with bathroom ₹150/500) Near the footbridge between Old and New Kaza, this popular backpacker guest house has good views from a sunny terrace. Rooms are rough around the edges, but prices for those with bathrooms are definitely negotiable.

Banjara Kunphen Retreat HOTEL $$
(📞222236; www.banjaracamps.com; d ₹2000; ☉May-Oct) This modern set-up near the police station in New Kaza will appeal to travellers looking for extra comfort. Rooms are bright and tastefully furnished but are overpriced and smell a bit like mothballs.

Dragon Restaurant MULTICUISINE $$
(Old Kaza; ₹ 60-200) Near the top end of the bazaar, the Dragon has an outdoor terrace where you can enjoy the usual *momos,* pizza and Chinese. Don't believe they've got chicken until you see it.

Sachin Kunga Restaurant MULTICUISINE $$
(Old Kaza; Mains ₹60-150) In the heart of the bazaar, this upstairs restaurant does the typical travellers' menu a little bit better than

---

INNER LINE PERMITS IN KAZA

To travel between Tabo in Spiti and Rekong Peo in Kinnaur, travellers need an inner line permit. This is easily arranged in Kaza – free permits are usually issued in around twenty minutes by the **Assistant District Commissioner's Office** (📞222202; ☉10.30am-5pm Mon-Sat, closed 2nd Sat each month) in New Kaza – look for the big green-roofed building behind the hospital. You'll need two passport photos and photocopies of the identity and visa pages from your passport. Solo travellers have no problems getting permits here. Permits can also be obtained in Rekong Peo and Shimla.

some other places around town. Its bright pink walls nudge the mood in a cheery direction.

As well as the hotel restaurants, there are several traveller-friendly restaurants in the old bazaar.

ℹ Information
There is nowhere to change money, but there is a new State Bank of India ATM in the bazaar. The couple of internet cafes in the bazaar charge ₹80/hour. The post office is just below the gompa in New Kaza. Inner line permits for travel to Kinnaur are easy to arrange – see the boxed text, opposite .

Ecosphere (☎222724; www.spitiecosphere. com) Arranges village homestays, tours and volunteer opportunities in Spitian villages. See the boxed text, p342.

Spiti Holiday Adventure (☎222711; www.spiti holidayadventure.com; Main Bazaar) Organises all-inclusive mountain treks from two to nine days for around ₹2500 per person per day, as well as jeep safaris and monastery tours.

ℹ Getting There & Away
BUS The bus station is at the bottom of the old town, just off the main road or reached on foot through the bazaar. There are buses to Manali (₹230, 10 hours) at 4.30am and 7am. For Keylong, change at Gramphu (₹155, eight hours). A bus leaves for Rekong Peo (₹255, 12 hours) at 7.30am, passing through Sichling (for Dhankar; ₹30, one hour) and Tabo (₹55, two hours). There's a second Tabo bus at 2pm.

There's a single daily bus to Kibber (₹25, 50 minutes) via Ki (₹20, 30 minutes) at 5pm, but it doesn't return until 8.30am, making a taxi the sensible way to visit these spots unless you want spend the night at one of them.

For the Pin Valley, buses to Mud (₹60, two hours) leave at 4pm.

TAXI The local taxi union is based a few metres from the bus stand, or you can make arrangements at your hotel. Fixed rates include Tabo (₹1200, 1½ hours), Keylong (₹6000, seven hours), Manali (₹6000, nine hours) and Rekong Peo (₹5000, 10 hours). Day trips include Ki and Kibber (₹900 return) and Dhankar and the Pin Valley (one way/return ₹900/1200). A seat in a shared jeep to Manali is usually easy to arrange, but not so easy going the other way; enquire at the taxi stand and turn up early.

KI
On the road up to the village of Kibber, about 12km from Kaza, the tiny village of Ki is dominated by the whitewashed buildings of **Ki Gompa** (☺6am-7pm). Set atop a 4116m-high hillock, this is the largest gompa in Spiti and the views from the top are ex-

tremely photogenic. Around 300 monks, including many students from surrounding villages, live here. An atmospheric *puja* is held in the new prayer hall every morning at around 7am (8am in winter). On request, the monks will open up the original medieval prayer rooms, full of *thangkas,* Buddhist texts printed on cloth, and the bed slept in by the Dalai Lama on his visits in 1960 and 2000. Dance masks are brought out for the annual **Ki chaam** festival (June/July) and again in February/March for **Losar**.

The monks offer some basic four-bed **rooms** (☎01906-262201; dm without bathroom ₹150); the price includes meals and cold water.

KIBBER
☎01906
A further 8km above Ki, this charming village of traditional whitewashed homes was once a stop on the overland salt trade. Catch your breath because at 4205m, Kibber once laid claim to being the highest village in the world with a drivable road and electricity, but tiny Gada village, a few hundred metres higher up the gorge, now has both power and a road – and the title belongs to a Tibetan village anyway. The surrounding snow-covered landscape is incredibly beautiful and desolate and you can walk to other, roadless, villages along the edge of the gorge that are even more remote.

The villagers are friendly but passing tour groups have created a small amount of child begging in the village. Resist the urge to hand out sweets, pens and cash; if you want to help, donate to the village school instead.

🛏 Sleeping & Eating
There are several village guesthouses offering rooms and meals. Most have bucket hot water (for ₹10 to ₹15) and most close down for the winter in early October.

Norling Home Stay GUESTHOUSE $
(r without/with bathroom ₹ 200/300) At the far end of the village, rooms in this tradtional whitewashed home are easily the best in town – clean, light and airy. Those with private bath have geysers.

Serkong Guesthouse GUESTHOUSE $
(☎226222; r without bathroom ₹150-200) Rooms here are neat and clean, and the bohemian front terrace has couches and old photos of Spiti.

Norling Guest House HOTEL $
(☎226242; r without bathroom ₹250-350) On the road into the village, this friendly place has

HIMACHAL PRADESH SPITI

SUSTAINABLE SPITI

While tourism brings money and development to remote rural areas like Spiti, it can also do unintentional damage to fragile cultures and ecosystems. Recognising this, a number of villages here are parterning with Ecosphere, a Kaza-based NGO, to create a home-grown sustainable tourism industry.

Homestays (per night ₹500, including meals) have been set up in six villages, five of which are linked into a week-long trekking route called the Homestay Trail. Visitors get a taste of authentic Spitian life, sleeping in traditional whitewashed houses and eating homecooked food. From the villages, wildlife-watching hikes offer a chance of spotting the Spitian wolf – the world's oldest wolf species; scenic bliss is guaranteed. Trained guides (per day ₹600), which are recommended but not required, translate and explain about the culture and the land.

Part of the homestay fee supports the host family; part of it is deposited into a village fund and used for something that benefits the community as whole – like restoring the local Buddhist monastery, which is the heart of their cultural life. If you can spare two weeks or more, you can volunteer on ecofriendly projects, like building greenhouses used as solar home-heating systems, which reduce fuelwood consumption and cut soot emissions that settle on nearby glaciers and speed their melting.

For more information on Spitian homestays, treks, volunteer opportunities and grass-roots environmental initiatives, visit Ecosphere's website (www.spitiecosphere.com) or drop by their office in Old Kaza's bazaar (☑222724). Refill your bottle with filtered water while you're there.

the best restaurant in town, but rooms look like they're coming apart at the seams.

DHANKAR

Southeast of Kaza, the snaking Spiti River merges with the Pin River, creating a single ribbon of grey in the midst of dust-coloured badlands. Perched high above the confluence is the tiny village of Dhankar, the former capital of the Nono kings of Spiti.

The 1200-year-old **Dhankar Gompa** (admission ₹25; 8am-6pm) hangs on the edge of a cliff, wedged surreally between rocky pinnacles above the village. The lower monastery building has a silver statue of Vajradhara (the Diamond Being), and there's a second prayer hall on the hilltop, with exquisite medieval murals of Sakyamuni, Tsongkhapa and Lama Chodrag.

Just downhill is a small **museum** (admission ₹25; ⊘8am-6pm) with costumes, instruments, old saddles and Buddhist devotional objects. In November, Dhankar monks celebrate the **Guktor Festival** with energetic masked dances.

Above the gompa are the ruins of the mud-brick **fort** that sheltered the entire population of the Nono kingdom during times of war, and an hour's climb uphill is the scenic lake of **Dhankar Tso**, offering epic views towards the twin peaks of **Mane Rang** (6593m).

Dhankar is a steep 10km walk or drive from the village of Sichling on the Kaza–Tabo Hwy. You can stay at a terrific **guesthouse** (dm ₹150, r ₹300-700) at the monastery, where most of the red-carpeted rooms have walls of windows with picture-postcard views. Food in the restaurant is fresh and tasty, and can be taken on a terrrace with mesmerising vistas.

Buses from Kaza to Tabo pass through Sichling (₹25, one hour) or you can do a day trip by taxi from Kaza for ₹800.

PIN VALLEY NATIONAL PARK

Running south from the Spiti Valley, the wind-scoured Pin Valley National Park (1875 sq km) is famous as the 'land of ibex and snow leopards', though sightings of either species are rare. From July to October, a popular eight-day trek runs from here over the 5319m Pin-Parvati Pass to the Parvati Valley near Kullu.

The road to the Pin Valley branches off the Kaza–Tabo Hwy about 10km before Sichling, climbing through winter meadows to the cluster of whitewashed farmhouses at **Gulling**. About 2km above Gulling at Kungri, the 600-year-old **Ugyen Sanag Choling Gompa** has old prayer rooms and a huge new monastery with vivid murals of protector deities, including the many-eyed archer Rahula and one-eyed Ekajati, the Guardian of Mantras. There's also a small **museum** (admission ₹25; ⊙10am-6pm) with ethnological and religious displays and plain, clean **rooms** (r without bathroom ₹250).

Southwest of Gulling, **Sagnam** marks the turn-off to the village of **Mud**, trailhead for the trek over the Pin-Parvati Pass and an increasingly popular hang-out for the Israeli backpacker crowd. There are some scenic day hikes around the valley and a handful of cheap guesthouses by the main road, as well as the modern **PWD Resthouse** (r without bathroom ₹200-300), below the hospital.

Buses run daily from Kaza to Mud (₹50, two hours), stopping in Gulling (₹30, 1¼ hours) and Sagnam (₹38, 1½ hours). Taxis in Kaza charge ₹900 to Sagnam and ₹1500 to Mud.

TABO
☑01906

About 47km east of Kaza, tiny Tabo is the only other town in the Spiti Valley. The setting, hemmed in by scree slopes, is windblown and dramatic, and the ridge above town is riddled with **caves** used as meditation cells by local lamas.

The village is completely dominated by **Tabo Gompa** (admission by donation; 6am-10pm), a World Heritage Site preserving some of the finest Indo-Tibetan art in the world. Founded in AD 996, the gompa's fantastically adorned sanctuaries, which are generally open from 9am to 5pm, were painted by some of the best Buddhist muralists of the era. Beyond the intricate madalas and scenes of gods and demons, the moody chambers are graced with life-size stucco statues of bodhisattvas and detailed wood carvings. The modern gompa outside the ancient compound has a well-attended morning *puja* at 6.30am, and the monastery guesthouse contains a **Buddhist library** (admission free; ⊙10-noon & 2-4pm Jun-Sep) and a small **religious museum** (admission ₹20, camera/video ₹25/50; ⊙8.30am-5pm Mon-Sat).

🛏 Sleeping & Eating

Guesthouses in Tabo are clustered around the gompa, or strung out along the main road.

Tashi Khangsar Hotel   HOTEL $
(☑94188-17761; vaneetrana23@gmail.com; r/tent site from ₹300/200) The light and inviting rooms here surround a lawn where tables sit shaded beneath a large parachute canopy. There's a small lending library, a good res-

taurant, a flat grassy area for tent camping, and a relaxed vibe, all adding up to a solid value.

Zion Cafe   HOTEL $
(meals ₹40-70) Spitian and Tibetan specialities are done well at this mellow place, with a well-windowed dining room and small outdoor terrace. Four comfortable rooms are also available here (₹300 for a double).

Millennium Monastery Guesthouse HOTEL $
(☑223315; dm ₹50, r with/without bathroom from ₹400/250) Run by the monastery, this ageing but popular place has decent rooms around a bright central courtyard. Rooms have piped hot water for washing, but guests are asked to refrain from smoking, drinking alcohol and other activities that might offend monastic sensibilities.

Dewachen Retreat   HOTEL $$$
(☑233301; www.banjaracamps.com; r from ₹2800; ⊙May-Oct) Tabo's most upmarket accommodation rents its tasteful rooms to passing travellers when it isn't booked out by groups. It also has a good restaurant that's open to nonguests.

ⓘ Getting There & Away

At the time of writing, the road was open from Tabo through to Rekong Peo, with the odd landslide or other random event holding up traffic. There are buses to Kaza (₹45, two hours) at around 9am and 4pm, which may actually depart an hour earlier or a few hours later, if at all. There's a daily bus to Rekong Peo (₹200, nine hours) at 9am, going through Nako (₹80, four hours) but since this originates in Kaza it can be overfull. Taxis charge ₹1250 to Kaza (1½ hours), ₹2000 to Nako (three hours) and ₹5000 to Rekong Peo (nine hours).

TABO TO REKONG PEO

One of India's scariest but most sublime mountain roads, the Tabo–Rekong Peo Hwy in Kinnaur is an adventure. In theory, this highway is open year-round, providing the only winter access to the Spiti Valley; however, the Sutlej River frequently floods, washing away parts of the precarious road, and snowfalls can occasionally cut off this route in winter, so it's worth checking if the road is intact before heading east of Tabo. You will need to show your passport and inner line permit at Sumdo and Jangi. Some of the following places are technically in Kinnaur, but they are covered here because they form part of the Spiti circuit.

From Tabo, the road follows the narrowing Spiti Valley, passing villages full of apple orchards, before soaring over the ridge into the valley of the Sutlej River. If you're on a bus, this may well be the most dangerous and knee-trembling road in India – even diehard travellers have been known to gulp and ponder the possibilty of an afterlife as the bus skids around hairpin bends with millimetres to spare. The views of the Spiti River flashing hundreds of metres below and the road ahead zigzagging across the mountainside are mesmerising. Views are best – but scariest – from the right side window seats.

Overnight stops used to be forbidden, but travellers now have fourteen days to complete the trip. The first permit checkpost is at **Sumdo**. Just before that, if you've got your own transport, look for the turn-off to **Giu**, a village where you can see the mummified remains of a Buddhist monk who died over 500 years ago. The mummy still has hair and fingernails and, according to local lore, spurted blood when unearthed by the shovels of an ITBP construction crew in 2004.

Beyond **Sumdo**, the main highway starts its ascent into the hills at **Chango**, which has several Buddhist temples.

The first settlement with accommodation is **Nako**, an other-timely village of stone and mud-brick houses and a popular stop for motorcyclists. Even if you're on the bus, this is a great place to break the journey and a gem of a destination in itself. The village is centred on a small sacred lake, behind which rise towering rock-strewn mountains criss-crossed by trails to high stupas, an old monastery and ridges with commanding vistas – it's perfect terrain for short or extended day hikes. In town, you'll find the 11th-century buildings of **Nako Gompa**, containing some fine Tabo-style murals and sculptures. The whole scene is a sweet first or final glimpse of Spiti.

There are several simple guesthouses offering rooms for around ₹200-500, or there's the posher **Reo Purgil Hotel** (☏01785-236339; d ₹500-800). Better still is the bright **Lake View Guest House** (r ₹400-500), a short walk through the village overlooking the lake.

The final stage of the journey passes through greener country in the narrow gorge of the Sutlej River. The village of **Puh** marks the official crossing into Kinnaur and there are two colourful gompas belonging to the Drukpa sect.

There are more monasteries and temples at **Khanum**, near Spillo, founded by Ringchen Zangpo in the 10th century. **Jangi** marks the end of the permit zone and the starting point of the *parikrama* (ceremonial circumnavigation) around Kinner Kailash (6050m). The village has a number of Kinnauri-style temples and you can continue 14km uphill to visit the Buddhist monastery at **Lippa**. An inner line permit is required, even if you just do a day trip here from Rekong Peo.

Uttar Pradesh & the Taj Mahal

Best Places to Eat

» Tunday Kabab (p373)
» Brown Bread Bakery (p392)
» Joney's Place (p361)
» Pizzeria Vaatika Cafe (p393)
» Indian Coffee House (p380)

Best Places to Stay

» Hotel Ganges View (p391)
» Lucknow Homestay (p371)
» Ganpati Guesthouse (p390)
» Hotel Sheela (p358)

Why Go?

There's no doubting the star attraction here. Agra's Taj Mahal – the most visited sight in India by some distance – is a wonder to behold and leaving Uttar Pradesh (UP) without seeing it would be a bit like drinking *chai* without spoonfuls of sugar: absurd.

Those who linger in this enormous state, however, soon find that it's the unmistakeable spirituality of UP, rather than its magnificent architecture, that leaves the longest-lasting impression.

The buildings left by the Mughals, the Nawabs and the British are certainly worth admiring, but it's the religious fervour that sweeps you off your feet at some Hindu temples, the contemplative aura that emanates from ancient Buddhist stupas and the serenity of waking up before dawn to watch locals perform *puja* (offerings or prayers) at a holy riverside ghat that create the truly unforgettable moments of a trip to this part of India.

When to Go

Agra

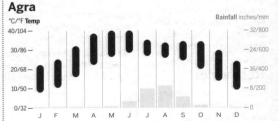

| **Sep–Oct** Monsoon rains are mostly over, temperatures have cooled, but not too much. | **Nov–Feb** Winter days are comfortable but nights are nippy; sights can be overcrowded. | **Mar–Apr** The evening chill has mostly gone but the raging mid-summer heat has yet to materialise. |

Fast Facts

» Population: 199.6 million

» Area: 231,254 sq km

» Capital: Lucknow

» Language: Hindi

» Sleeping prices: $ below ₹500, $$ ₹500 to ₹2500, $$$ above ₹2500

Top Tip

Touts in Agra and Varanasi can be voracious. When arriving by train or a bus, try to look as if you know what you're doing, even if you don't. Ignore anyone who approaches you in the station; just head straight for the prepaid autorickshaw booth (opposite the main entrance) or find a rider yourself outside the station on a quieter road where you're more likely to get a fair deal.

Resources

» Uttar Pradesh Tourism (www.up-tourism.com)

» Agra District (www.agra.nic.in)

» Varanasi District (www.varanasi.nic.in)

» (Virtual tour of the Taj Mahal) www.taj-mahal.net

Food

Mughlai cuisine – rich, meaty and impossibly tasty – is the order of the day across much of Uttar Pradesh, with the best restaurants often attached to the top hotels in the big cities. Lucknow is the undisputed king of UP cuisine. You'll find some excellent Mughlai kitchens here as well as great *chaat* (snacks) and some simply sumptuous kebabs (p374).

DON'T MISS

There are two things you mustn't leave Uttar Pradesh without doing: seeing the **Taj Mahal** at sunset and taking a dawn boat ride along the Ganges in the holy city of **Varanasi**.

Top State Festivals

» Magh Mela (Jan/Feb, Allahabad, p377) A huge annual religious fair that transforms into the world's largest human gathering, the Kumbh Mela, every 12th year (next in 2013).

» Holi (Feb/Mar, Mathura and Vrindavan, p368) This national festival is celebrated with particular fervour around Mathura and Vrindavan, spiritual home of Krishna.

» Purnima (Apr/May, Sarnath, p396) Also known as Vesak, Buddha Jayanti or, informally, Buddha's birthday, Purnima actually celebrates the birth, enlightenment and death of Buddha. Sarnath, just outside Varanasi, takes on a particularly festive air on this day, when Buddhists from many countries take part in a procession and a fair is held.

» Janmastami (Aug/Sep, Mathura, p368) You can barely move here during Krishna's birthday, when temples are swathed in decorations and musical dramas about Krishna are performed.

» Ram Lila (Sep/Oct, Varanasi, p388) Every year since the early 1800s the Ram Lila, a lengthy version of the Ramayana, has been performed beside Ramnagar Fort in Varanasi. The epic saga of Rama's marriage to Sita and his battle against the demon king Ravana is performed mainly by Brahmin youths aided by masks, music, dancing and giant papier-mâché figures.

» Eid al-Fitr (Dec/Jan, Fatehpur Sikri, p365) Join the happy crowds in the bazaar and mosque at Fatehpur Sikri, near Agra, for the end-of-Ramadan celebrations.

History

Over 2000 years ago this region was part of Ashoka's great Buddhist empire, remnants of which can be found in the ruins at the pilgrimage centre of Sarnath near Varanasi. Muslim raids from the northwest began in the 11th century, and by the 16th century the region was part of the Mughal empire, with its capital in Agra, then Delhi and, for a brief time, Fatehpur Sikri.

Following the decline of the Mughal empire, Persians stepped in briefly before the nawabs of Avadh rose to prominence in the central part of the region. The nawabs were responsible for turning Lucknow into a flourishing centre for the arts, but their empire came to a dramatic end when the British East India Company deposed the last nawab, triggering the First War of Independence (Indian Uprising) of 1857. Agra was later merged with Avadh and the state became known as United Province. It was renamed Uttar Pradesh after Independence and has since been the most dominant state in Indian politics, producing half of the country's prime ministers, most of them from Allahabad. The local population doesn't seem to have benefited much from this, though, as poor governance, a high birth rate, a low literacy rate and an erratic electricity supply have held back economic progress in UP in the past 60 years.

In 2000 the mountainous northwestern part of the state was carved off to create the new state of Uttaranchal.

Agra

📞 0562 / POP 1,321,410

The magical allure of the Taj Mahal draws tourists to Agra like moths to a wondrous flame. And despite the hype, it's every bit as good as you've heard. But the Taj is not a stand-alone attraction. The legacy of the Mughal empire has left a magnificent fort and a liberal sprinkling of fascinating tombs and mausoleums. There's also fun to be had in the bustling *chowks* (marketplaces), some of which border on the chaotic.

The downside comes in the form of hordes of rickshaw-wallahs, touts, unofficial guides and souvenir vendors, whose persistence can be infuriating at times.

Many tourists choose to visit Agra on a whistle-stop day trip from Delhi. This is a shame. There is much more of interest here than can be seen in that time. In fact, you can enjoy several days' sightseeing with side trips to the superb ruined city of Fatehpur Sikri and the Hindu pilgrimage centre of Mathura.

Agra sits on a large bend in the holy Yamuna River. The fort and the Taj, 2km apart, both overlook the river on different parts of the bend. The main train and bus stations are a few kilometres southwest.

The labourers and artisans who toiled on the Taj set up home immediately south of the mausoleum, creating the congested network of alleys known as Taj Ganj, now a popular area for budget travellers.

History

In 1501 Sultan Sikander Lodi established his capital here, but the city fell into Mughal hands in 1526, when Emperor Babur defeated the last Lodi sultan at Panipat. Agra reached the peak of its magnificence between the mid-16th and mid-17th centuries during the reigns of Akbar, Jehangir and Shah Jahan. During this period the fort, the Taj Mahal and other major mausoleums were built. In 1638 Shah Jahan built a new city in Delhi, and his son Aurangzeb moved the capital there 10 years later.

In 1761 Agra fell to the Jats, a warrior class who looted its monuments, including the Taj Mahal. The Marathas took over in 1770, but were replaced by the British in 1803. Following the First War of Independence of 1857, the British shifted the administration of the province to Allahabad. Deprived of its administrative role, Agra developed as a centre for heavy industry, quickly becoming famous for its chemicals industry and air pollution, before the Taj and tourism became a major source of income.

⊙ Sights & Activities

The entrance fee for Agra's five main sights – the Taj, Agra Fort, Fatehpur Sikri, Akbar's Tomb and Itimad-ud-Daulah – is made up of charges from two different bodies, the Archaeological Survey of India (ASI) and the Agra Development Association (ADA). Of the ₹750 ticket for the Taj Mahal, ₹500 is a special ADA ticket, which gives you small savings on the other four sights if visited on the same day. You'll save ₹50 at Agra Fort and ₹10 each at Fatehpur Sikri, Akbar's Tomb and Itimad-ud-Daulah. You can buy this ₹500 ADA ticket at any of the five sights. Just say you intend to visit the Taj later that day.

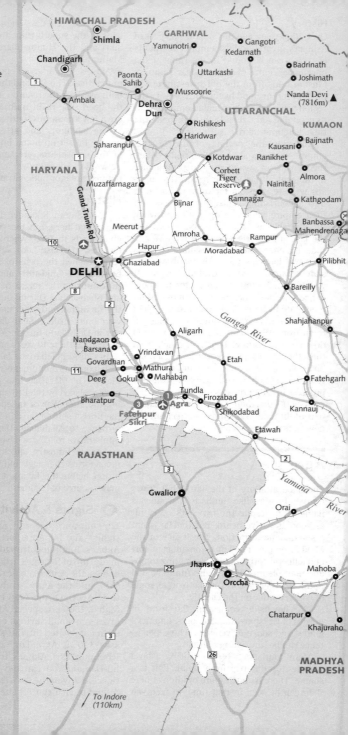

Uttar Pradesh Highlights

1 Be inspired as the sunrise illuminates the Taj Mahal in **Agra** (p347) before returning for the oh-so romantic sunset view

2 Take a pre-dawn boat ride along the River Ganges to witness **Varanasi** (p383) at its spiritual best

3 Stand in awe beside immense Mughal monuments in the ruined city of **Fatehpur Sikri** (p365)

4 Sign up for the Heritage Walking Tour in **Lucknow** (p370), the best way to see the old town

5 Escape the chaos of the cities at the pilgrimage centre of **Kushinagar** (p398), Buddha's final resting place

6 Experience the spirituality of Varanasi, without the hassle, at the more chilled-out riverside ghats of **Chitrakut** (p381)

7 Be rowed out to the confluence of two holy rivers in **Allahabad** (p377), and imagine 70 million people doing the same during the Kumbh Mela festival

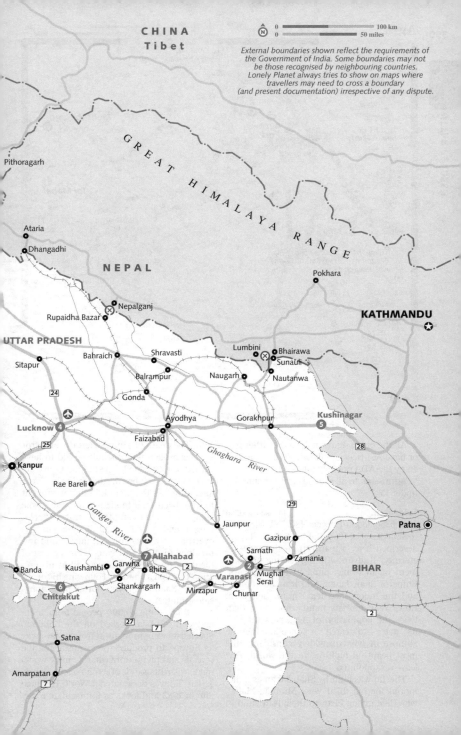

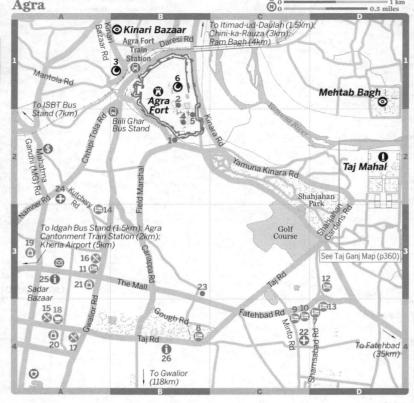

All the other sights in Agra are either free or have ASI tickets only which aren't affected by the ADA one-day offer.

Admission to all sights is free for children under 15.

Taj Mahal HISTORIC BUILDING

(Map p360; Indian/foreigner ₹20/750, video ₹25; ⊗dawn-dusk Sat-Thu) Rabindranath Tagore described it as 'a teardrop on the cheek of eternity', Rudyard Kipling as 'the embodiment of all things pure', while its creator, Emperor Shah Jahan, said it made 'the sun and the moon shed tears from their eyes'. Every year, tourists numbering more than twice the population of Agra pass through its gates to catch a once-in-a-lifetime glimpse of what is widely considered the most beautiful building in the world. Few leave disappointed.

The Taj was built by Shah Jahan as a memorial for his third wife, Mumtaz Mahal, who died giving birth to their 14th child in 1631. The death of Mumtaz left the emperor so heartbroken that his hair is said to have turned grey virtually overnight. Construction of the Taj began the following year and, although the main building is thought to have been built in eight years, the whole complex was not completed until 1653. Not long after it was finished Shah Jahan was overthrown by his son Aurangzeb and imprisoned in Agra Fort where, for the rest of his days, he could only gaze out at his creation through a window. Following his death in 1666, Shah Jahan was buried here alongside Mumtaz.

In total, some 20,000 people from India and Central Asia worked on the building. Specialists were brought in from as far away as Europe to produce the exquisite marble screens and pietra dura (marble inlay work) made with thousands of semiprecious stones.

The Taj was designated a World Heritage Site in 1983 and looks as immaculate today as when it was first constructed – though it underwent a huge restoration project in the early 20th century. In 2002, having been gradually discoloured by city pollution, it was spruced up with an ancient face-pack recipe known as *multani mitti* – a blend of soil, cereal, milk and lime once used by Indian women to beautify their skin. Now only nonpolluting vehicles are allowed within a couple of hundred metres of the building.

Entry & Information

Note: the Taj is closed every Friday to anyone not attending prayers at the mosque.

The Taj can be accessed through the west, south and east gates. Tour groups tend to enter through the east and west gates. Independent travellers tend to use the south gate, which is nearest to Taj Ganj, the main area for budget accommodation and generally has shorter queues than the west gate. The east gate has the shortest queues of the lot, but this is because the ticket office is inconveniently located a 1km walk away at Shilpgram, a dire government-run tourist centre. There are separate queues for men and women at all three gates.

Cameras and videos are permitted but you cannot take photographs inside the mausoleum itself, and the areas in which you can take videos are quite limited.

If you keep your Taj ticket you get small entry-fee reductions when visiting Agra Fort, Fatehpur Sikri, Akbar's Tomb or the Itimad-ud-Daulah on the same day.

From the south gate, entry to the inner compound is through a very impressive, 30m red sandstone **gateway** on the south side of the forecourt, which is inscribed with verses from the Quran.

Inside the Grounds

Once inside, the **ornamental gardens** are set out along classical Mughal *charbagh* (formal Persian garden) lines – a square quartered by watercourses, with an ornamental marble plinth at its centre. When the fountains are not flowing, the Taj is beautifully reflected in the water.

TAJ MAHAL MYTHS

The Taj is a Hindu Temple

The well-publicised theory that the Taj was in fact a Shiva temple built in the 12th century and only later converted into Mumtaz Mahal's famous mausoleum was developed by Purushottam Nagesh Oak. In 2000 India's Supreme Court dismissed his petition to have the sealed basement rooms of the Taj opened to prove his theory. Oak also claims that the Kaaba, Stonehenge and the Papacy all have Hindu origins.

The Black Taj Mahal

The story goes that Shah Jahan planned to build a negative image of the Taj Mahal in black marble on the opposite side of the river as his own mausoleum, and that work began before he was imprisoned by his son Aurangzeb in Agra Fort. Extensive excavations at Mehtab Bagh have found no trace of any such construction.

Craftsmen Mutilations

Legend has it that, on completion of the Taj, Shah Jahan ordered that the hands of the project's craftsmen be chopped off, to prevent them from ever building anything as beautiful again. Some even say he went so far as to have their eyes gouged out. Thankfully, no historical evidence supports either story.

Sinking Taj

Some experts believe there is evidence to show that the Taj is slowly tilting towards and sinking into the riverbed due to the changing nature of the soil beside an increasingly dry Yamuna River. The Archaeological Survey of India has dismissed any marginal change in the elevation of the building as statistically insignificant, adding that it has not detected any structural damage at its base in the seven decades since its first scientific study of the Taj was carried out, in 1941.

The Taj Mahal itself stands on a raised marble platform at the northern end of the ornamental gardens, with its back to the Yamuna River. Its raised position means that the backdrop is only sky – a masterstroke of design. Purely decorative 40m-high white **minarets** grace each corner of the platform. After more than three centuries they are not quite perpendicular, but they may have been designed to lean slightly outwards so that in the event of an earthquake they would fall away from the precious Taj. The red sandstone **mosque** to the west is an important gathering place for Agra's Muslims. The identical building to the east, the **jawab**, was built for symmetry.

The central Taj structure is made of semitranslucent white marble, carved with flowers and inlaid with thousands of semiprecious stones in beautiful patterns. A perfect exercise in symmetry, the four identical faces of the Taj feature impressive vaulted arches embellished with pietra dura scrollwork and quotations from the Quran in a style of calligraphy using inlaid jasper. The whole structure is topped off by four small domes surrounding the famous bulbous central dome.

Directly below the main dome is the **Cenotaph of Mumtaz Mahal**, an elaborate false tomb surrounded by an exquisite perforated marble screen inlaid with dozens of different types of semiprecious stones. Beside it, offsetting the symmetry of the Taj, is the **Cenotaph of Shah Jahan**, who was interred here with little ceremony by his usurping son Aurangzeb in 1666. Light is admitted into the central chamber by finely cut marble screens. The real tombs of Mumtaz Mahal and Shah Jahan are in a locked basement room below the main chamber and cannot be viewed.

Agra Fort   FORT

(Map p350; Indian/foreigner ₹20/300, video ₹25; ☉dawn-dusk) With the Taj Mahal overshadowing it, one can easily forget that Agra has one of the finest Mughal forts in India. By visiting the fort and Taj on the same day you get a ₹50 reduction in ticket price. Construction of the massive red-sandstone fort, on the bank of the Yamuna River, was begun by Emperor Akbar in 1565. Further additions were made, particularly by his grandson Shah Jahan, using his favourite building material – white marble. The fort was built primarily as a military structure, but Shah Jahan transformed it into a palace, and later it became his gilded prison for eight years after his son Aurangzeb seized power in 1658.

The ear-shaped fort's colossal double walls rise over 20m in height and measure 2.5km in circumference. The Yamuna River originally flowed along the straight eastern edge of the fort, and the emperors had their own bathing ghats here. It contains a maze of buildings, forming a city within a city, including vast underground sections, though many of the structures were destroyed over the years by Nadir Shah, the Marathas, the Jats and finally the British, who used the fort as a garrison. Even today, much of the fort is used by the military and so is off-limits to the general public.

The **Amar Singh Gate** to the south is the sole entry point to the fort these days and where you buy your entrance ticket. Its dogleg design was meant to confuse attackers who made it past the first line of defence – the crocodile-infested moat.

A path leads straight from here up to the large **Moti Masjid** (Pearl Mosque), which is always closed. To your right, just before you

DON'T MISS

TAJ MUSEUM

Within the Taj complex, on the western side of the gardens, is the small but excellent **Taj Museum** (admission ₹5; ⊙10am-5pm Sat-Thu), housing a number of original Mughal miniature paintings, including a pair of 17th-century ivory portraits of Emperor Shah Jahan and his beloved wife Mumtaz Mahal. You also find here some very well preserved gold and silver coins dating from the same period, plus architectural drawings of the Taj and some nifty celadon plates, said to split into pieces or change colour if the food served on them contains poison.

reach Moti Masjid, is the large open **Diwan-i-Am** (Hall of Public Audiences), which was used by Shah Jahan for domestic government business, and features a throne room where the emperor listened to petitioners. In front of it is the small and rather incongruous **grave of John Colvin**, a lieutenant-governor of the northwest provinces who died of an illness in the fort during the 1857 First War of Independence.

A tiny staircase just to the left of the Diwan-i-Am throne leads up to a large courtyard. To your left, is the tiny but exquisite **Nagina Masjid** (Gem Mosque), built in 1635 by Shah Jahan for the ladies of the court. Down below was the **Ladies' bazaar**, where the court ladies bought goods.

On the far side of the large courtyard, along the eastern wall of the fort, is **Diwan-i-Khas** (Hall of Private Audiences), which was reserved for important dignitaries or foreign representatives. The hall once housed Shah Jahan's legendary Peacock Throne, which was inset with precious stones including the famous Koh-i-noor diamond. The throne was taken to Delhi by Aurangzeb, then to Iran in 1739 by Nadir Shah and dismantled after his assassination in 1747. Overlooking the river and the distant Taj Mahal is **Takhti-i-Jehangir**, a huge slab of black rock with an inscription around the edge. The throne that stood here was made for Jehangir when he was Prince Salim.

Off to your right from here (as you face the river) is **Shish Mahal** (Mirror Palace), with walls inlaid with tiny mirrors. At the time of research it had been closed for some

ⓘ BEST TIMES TO SEE THE TAJ

The Taj is arguably at its most atmospheric at **sunrise**. This is certainly the most comfortable time to visit, with far fewer crowds. **Sunset** is another magical viewing time. You can also view the Taj for five nights around **full moon**. Entry numbers are limited, though, and tickets must be bought a day in advance from the **Archaeological Survey of India office** (Map p350; ☏2227263; www.asi.nic.in; 22 The Mall; Indian/foreigner ₹510/750). See its website for details. Note, this office is known as the Taj Mahal Office by some rickshaw riders.

One final word of advice; whatever you do, don't plan your trip around seeing the Taj on a Friday, as the whole complex is closed to anyone not attending Friday prayers at the mosque inside the Taj grounds.

Taj Mahal

TIMELINE

1631 Emperor Shah Jahan's beloved third wife, Mumtaz Mahal, dies in Buhanpur while giving birth to their 14th child. Her body is initially interred in Buhanpur itself, where Shah Jahan is fighting a military campaign, but is later moved, in a golden casket, to a small building on the banks of the Yamuna River in Agra.

1632 Construction of a permanent mausoleum for Mumtaz Mahal begins.

1633 Mumtaz Mahal is interred in her final resting place, an underground tomb beneath a marble plinth, on top of which the Taj Mahal will be built.

1640 The white-marble mausoleum is completed.

1653 The rest of the Taj Mahal complex is completed.

1658 Emperor Shah Jahan is overthrown by his son Aurangzeb and imprisoned in Agra Fort.

1666 Shah Jahan dies. His body is transported along the Yamuna River and buried underneath the Taj, alongside the tomb of his wife.

1908 Repeatedly damaged and looted after the fall of the Mughal empire, the Taj receives some long-overdue attention as part of a major restoration project ordered by British viceroy Lord Curzon.

1983 The Taj is awarded Unesco World Heritage Site status.

2002 Having been discoloured by pollution in more recent years, the Taj is spruced up with an ancient recipe known as *multani mitti* – a blend of soil, cereal, milk and lime once used by Indian women to beautify their skin.

Today More than three million tourists visit the Taj Mahal each year. That's more than twice the current population of Agra.

DANIEL MCCROHAN

Go Barefoot
Help the environment by entering the mausoleum barefoot instead of using the free disposable shoe covers.

Pishtaqs
These huge arched recesses are set into each side of the Taj. They provide depth to the building while their central, latticed marble screens allow patterned light to illuminate the inside of the mausoleum.

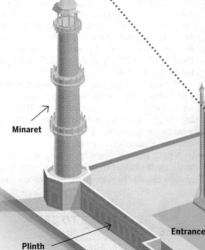

Minaret

Entrance

Plinth

Marble Relief Work
Flowering plants, thought to be representations of paradise, are a common theme among the beautifully decorative panels carved onto the white marble.

DANIEL MCCROHAN

Be Enlightened
Bring a small torch into the mausoleum to fully appreciate the translucency of the white marble and semiprecious stones.

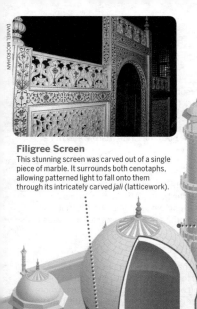

Filigree Screen
This stunning screen was carved out of a single piece of marble. It surrounds both cenotaphs, allowing patterned light to fall onto them through its intricately carved *jali* (latticework).

Central Dome
The Taj's famous central dome, topped by a brass finial, represents the vault of heaven, a stark contrast to the material world, which is represented by the square shape of the main structure.

Yamuna River

NORTH →

Pietra Dura
It's believed that 35 different precious and semi-precious stones were used to create the exquisite pietra dura (marble inlay work) found on the inside and outside of the mausoleum walls. Again, floral designs are common.

Calligraphy
The strips of calligraphy surrounding each of the four pishtaqs get larger as they get higher, giving the impression of uniform size when viewed from the ground. There's also calligraphy inside the mausoleum, including on Mumtaz Mahal's cenotaph.

Cenotaphs
The cenotaphs of Mumtaz Mahal and Shah Jahan, decorated with pietra dura inlay work, are actually fake tombs. The real ones are located in an underground vault closed to the public.

TOP TAJ VIEWS

Inside the Taj Grounds

You may have to pay ₹750 for the privilege, but it's only when you're inside the grounds themselves that you can really get up close and personal with the world's most beautiful building. Don't miss inspecting the marble inlay work (pietra dura) inside the *pishtaqs* (large arched recesses) on the four outer walls. And don't forget to bring a small torch with you so that you can shine it on similar pietra dura work inside the dark central chamber of the mausoleum. Note the translucency of both the white marble and the semi-precious stones inlaid into it.

From Mehtab Bagh

Tourists are no longer allowed to wander freely along the riverbank on the opposite side of the Yamuna River, but you can still enjoy a view of the back of the Taj from the 16th-century Mughal park Mehtab Bagh, with the river flowing between you and the mausoleum. A path leading down to the river beside the park offers the same view for free, albeit from a more restricted angle.

Looking Up from the South Sank of the River

This is a great place to be for sunset. Take the path that hugs the outside of the Taj's eastern wall and walk all the way down to the small temple beside the river. You should be able to find boat hands down here willing to row you out onto the water for an even more romantic view. Expect to pay them around ₹100 per boat. For safety reasons, it's best not to wander down here on your own for sunset.

On a Rooftop Cafe in Taj Ganj

Perfect for sunrise shots, there are some wonderful photos to be had from the numerous rooftop cafes in Taj Ganj. We think the cafe on Saniya Palace Hotel is the pick of the bunch, with its plant-filled design and great position, but many of them are good. And all offer the bonus of being able to view the Taj with the added comfort of an early-morning cup of coffee.

From Agra Fort

With a decent zoom lens you can capture some fabulous images of the Taj from Agra Fort, especially if you're willing to get up at the crack of dawn to see the sun rising up from behind it. The best places to picture it from are probably Musamman Burj and Khas Mahal, the octagonal tower and palace where Shah Jahan was imprisoned for eight years until his death.

time due to restoration, although you could peek through cracks in the doors at the sparkling mirrors inside.

Further along the eastern edge of the fort you'll find **Musamman Burj** and **Khas Mahal**, the wonderful white-marble octagonal tower and palace where Shah Jahan was imprisoned for eight years until his death in 1666, and from where he could gaze out at the Taj Mahal, the tomb of his wife. When he died, Shah Jahan's body was taken from here by boat to the Taj. The now closed **Mina Masjid**, set back slightly from the eastern edge, was his private mosque.

The large courtyard here is **Anguri Bagh**, a garden that has been brought back to life in recent years. In the courtyard is an innocuous-looking entrance – now locked – that leads down a flight of stairs into a two-storey labyrinth of underground rooms and passageways where Akbar used to keep his 500-strong harem.

Continuing south, the huge red-sandstone Jehangir's Palace was probably built by Akbar for his son Jehangir. It blends Indian and Central Asian architectural styles, a reminder of the Mughals' Afghani cultural roots. In front of the palace is **Hauz-i-Jehangir**, a huge bowl carved out of a single block of stone, which was used for bathing. Walking past this brings you back to the main path to Amar Singh Gate.

You can walk here from Taj Ganj, or its ₹20-30 in a cycle-rickshaw.

Akbar's Mausoleum
HISTORIC BUILDING

(Indian/foreigner ₹10/110, video ₹25; ⊘dawn-dusk) This outstanding sandstone and marble tomb commemorates the greatest of the Mughal emperors. The huge courtyard is entered through a stunning gateway. It has three-storey minarets at each corner and is built of red sandstone strikingly inlaid with white-marble geometric patterns.

The mausoleum is at Sikandra, 10km northwest of Agra Fort. Buses (₹20, 45 minutes) heading to Mathura from Biili Ghar bus stand go past the mausoleum.

Itimad-ud-Daulah
HISTORIC BUILDING

(Map p350; Indian/foreigner ₹10/110, video ₹25; ⊘dawn-dusk) Nicknamed the Baby Taj, the exquisite tomb of Mizra Ghiyas Beg should not be missed. This Persian nobleman was Mumtaz Mahal's grandfather and Emperor Jehangir's *wazir* (chief minister). His daughter Nur Jahan, who married Jehangir, built the tomb between 1622 and 1628 in a style similar to the tomb she built for Jehangir near Lahore in Pakistan.

It doesn't have the same awesome beauty as the Taj, but it's arguably more delicate in appearance thanks to its particularly finely carved *jali* (marble lattice screens). This was the first Mughal structure built completely from marble, the first to make extensive use of pietra dura and the first tomb to be built on the banks of the Yamuna, which until then had been a sequence of beautiful pleasure gardens.

You can combine a trip here with Chini-ka-Rauza, Mehtab Bagh and Ram Bagh, all on the east bank. A cycle-rickshaw covering all four should cost about ₹200 return from the Taj, including waiting time. An autorickshaw (auto) will be at least double.

Chini-ka-Rauza
HISTORIC BUILDING

(Map p350; ⊘dawn-dusk) This Persian-style riverside tomb of Afzal Khan, a poet who served as Shah Jahan's chief minister, was built between 1628 and 1639. Rarely visited, it is hidden away down a shady avenue of trees on the east bank of the Yamuna. Bright blue tiles, which once covered the whole mausoleum, can still be seen on part of the exterior, while the interior is painted in floral designs.

Mehtab Bagh
PARK

(Map p350; Indian/foreigner ₹5/100; ⊘dawn-dusk) This park, originally built by Emperor Babur as the last in a series of 11 parks on the Yamuna's east bank, long before the Taj

was conceived, fell into disrepair until it was little more than a huge mound of sand. To protect the Taj from the erosive effects of the sand blown across the river, the park was reconstructed in recent years and is now one the best places from which to view the great mausoleum. The gardens in the Taj are perfectly aligned with the ones here, and the view of the Taj from the fountain directly in front of the entrance gate is a special one.

It used to be possible to sneak down the side of this park to the riverbank and view the Taj for free in a peaceful, natural ambience of buffaloes and wading birds. You can still reach the riverbank, but guards and a barbed-wire fence prevent you from walking freely along the water's edge.

Jama Masjid
MOSQUE

(Map p350; Jama Masjid Rd) This fine mosque, built in the Kinari Bazaar by Shah Jahan's daughter in 1648, and once connected to Agra Fort, features striking marble patterning on its domes.

Kinari Bazaar
MARKET

(Map p350; ⊘dawn-late) The narrow streets behind Jama Masjid are a crazy maze of overcrowded lanes bursting with colourful markets. There are a number of different bazaars here, each specialising in different wares, but the area is generally known as Kinari Bazaar as many of the lanes fan out from Kinari Bazaar Rd. You'll find clothing, shoes, fabrics, jewellery, spices, marble work, snack stalls and what seems like 20 million other people. Amazingly, there is somehow room for buffaloes and even the odd working elephant to squeeze their way through the crowds. Even if you're not buying anything, just walking the streets is an experience in itself. Don't forget to look up from time to time at the old wooden balconies above some of the shop fronts. As with all crowded markets, take extra care of your belongings here.

Swimming Pools
SWIMMING

Hotels allowing nonguests to use their pools include Atithi (₹300), Yamuna View (₹350), Park Plaza (₹350), Amar (₹400) – with slide! – and Clarks Shiraz (₹500).

☞ Tours

UP Tourism
COACH TOURS

(incl entry fees Indian/foreigner ₹400/1700); Agra Cantonment train station (off Map p350; ✆2421204; ⊘7am-10pm); Taj Rd (Map p350; ✆2226431;

TAKE A BREAK: FIVE RELAXING RETREATS

Touts, vendors and rickshaw-wallahs can be pretty draining in Agra, particularly around the big sights. Here are some ideas for how to escape their attentions.

Garden Retreat

Wandering around any of the half-ruined Mughal gardens of Agra can make a pleasant change from the noisy, bustling city streets. Try Mehtab Bagh or Ram Bagh. In summer, it's best to visit in the cool of the morning. Alternatively, sit in the shade of the wonderfully peaceful garden restaurant at Hotel Sheela, just a stone's throw from the Taj Mahal's east gate.

Rooftop Retreat

You'll be almost physically dragged off the street by over-keen owners trying to ensure you choose theirs, but once you're actually sitting down at a rooftop cafe in Taj Ganj you'll have all the peace and quiet you could wish for, plus fabulous views of the Taj. Saniya Palace Hotel is our favourite.

Rickshaw Retreat

Find a cycle-rickshaw with a deep, comfy, padded seat, agree to pay the rider ₹100–200 for a half-day tour of the city then sit back and watch Agra roll past you. The beauty of this retreat is that rickshaw riders don't bother tourists who are already in a rickshaw.

Poolside Retreat

For a total escape, pack your swimmers and head to one of Agra's more expensive hotels for a day by the pool. Fees for nonguests are typically ₹300–500.

Coffee Break

For a quick break, slip inside Café Coffee Day by the east gate of the Taj. Yes, it's a chain and, yes, it's relatively expensive, but it has AC and it's the only place in Taj Ganj that sells proper fresh coffee.

---

agrauptourism@gmail.com; 64 Taj Rd; ◷10.30am-5pm Mon-Sat) UP Tourism runs daily coach tours that leave Agra Cantonment train station at 10.30am, after picking up passengers arriving from Delhi on the *Taj Express*. The tour includes the Taj Mahal, Agra Fort and Fatehpur Sikri with a 1¼-hour stop in each place. Tours return to the station so that day trippers can catch the *Taj Express* back to Delhi at 6.55pm. Contact either of the UP Tourism offices to book a seat, or just turn up at the train station tourist office at 9.45am to sign up for that day.

🛏 Sleeping

The main place for budget accommodation is the bustling area of Taj Ganj, immediately south of the Taj, while there's a high concentration of midrange hotels further south, along Fatehabad Rd. Sadar Bazaar, an area boasting good quality restaurants, offers another option.

Ask at the UP Tourism office for the latest list of recommended homestays. The qual-

ity of accommodation in the homestays here is generally pretty good, but locations are rarely central. Prices range from ₹2000 to ₹4000 per room.

TAJ GANJ AREA

TOP CHOICE **Hotel Sheela**   HOTEL $

(Map p360; ☎2331194; www.hotelsheelaagra.com; Taj East Gate Rd; d ₹400-600, with AC ₹800;❋@) If you're not fussed about looking at the Taj Mahal 24 hours a day, this superb budget option could be just the ticket. Rooms are simple (no TVs here), but spotless and come with towel, soap and loo roll – a nice touch for a cheapie. Best of all they're set around a beautifully landscaped garden with singing birds, plenty of shade and a pleasant restaurant area. Book ahead.

Hotel Kamal   HOTEL $$

(Map p360; ☎2330126; hotelkamal@hotmail.com; Taj South Gate; d ₹600, with AC ₹1000;❋) The smartest of the hotels in Taj Ganj proper, Kamal has very clean, comfortable rooms with nice touches such as framed photos of the Taj on the walls and rugs on the tiled floors. Some rooms also have sofas. The rooftop restaurant has a decent Taj view, albeit slightly obscured by a tree.

Shanti Lodge HOTEL $
(Map p360; 🖄2231973; shantilodge2000@yahoo.co.in; Taj South Gate; r ₹200-1200; ❄@) There's a huge mixed bag of rooms at this Taj Ganj old-timer; some shoddy, with dodgy bathrooms; some much smarter and cleaner. The ones round the back in the newer block are worth asking for, but check a few rooms before you commit. The rooftop restaurant here has one of the best views of the Taj.

Saniya Palace Hotel HOTEL $
(Map p360; 🖄3270199; saniyapalaceemailid@gmail.com; Taj South Gate; d ₹400, without bathroom ₹200, with AC ₹800) Set back from the main strip down a tiny alleyway, this place has more character than its rivals, with marble floors and Mughal-style framed carpets hung on the walls. The rooms (apart from the cramped bathroomless cheapies) are clean and big enough, although the bathrooms in the non-AC rooms are miniscule. The very pleasant, plant-filled rooftop restaurant has a fabulous view of the Taj.

Hotel Sidhartha HOTEL $
(Map p360; 🖄2230901; www.hotelsidhartha.com; Taj West Gate; d ₹400, with AC ₹800; ❄@) First opened its doors in 1986 and still going strong. The 18 very smart double rooms are bright and clean and are set around a small, leafy courtyard, which has an OK restaurant. Hot water is available for all the rooms but only the AC ones have hot-water showers.

Oberoi Amar Vilas HOTEL $$$
(off Map p360; 🖄2231515; www.oberoihotels.com; Taj East Gate Rd; d ₹35,000-40,500, ste ₹75,000-261,000; ❄@≋) If money is no object, look no further. By far the best hotel in Agra, this place oozes style and luxury. Elegant interior design is suffused with Mughal themes, a composition carried over into the exterior fountain courtyard and swimming pool, both of which are set in a delightful water garden. All rooms (and even some bathtubs) have wonderful views of the Taj, as do the two excellent restaurants and classy cocktail bar, all of which are open to nonguests.

Taj Plaza HOTEL $$
(off Map p360; 🖄2232515; www.hoteltajplaza.com; Taj East Gate Rd; s/d ₹800/1200, with AC ₹2000/3000, ❄@) This former good-quality

budget hotel has been stretched into a mid-range price bracket in recent years. You won't be disappointed if you stay here – rooms are clean, have TV and some come with Taj views – but you won't write home about it. Still, it's a whole lot closer to the Taj than most hotels in the same price range.

FATEHABAD ROAD AREA

Howard Park Plaza HOTEL $$$
(Map p350; 🖄4048600; www.sarovarhotels.com; Fatehabad Rd; s/d/ste ₹6000/7000/12,000; ❄@🛜≋) Rooms in this very welcoming hotel are decked out in elegant dark-wood furniture and stylish decorative tiling. Bathrooms are a little on the compact side for this price, but still very smart. There's an unusual splash-shaped pool out the back, a small gym, and a spa offering a whole range of ayurvedic treatments. Wi-fi-enabled throughout.

Hotel Amar HOTEL $$$
(Map p350; 🖄4008402; www.hotelamar.com; Fatehabad Rd; s ₹3000-4500, d ₹3400-4500, ste ₹6000-8000; ❄@≋) Smart, wi-fi-enabled rooms come with big TV and clean bathrooms, but the real treat here is the pool area, complete with a lush green lawn and a 3.5m-tall water slide.

Amar Yatri Niwas HOTEL $$
(Map p350; 🖄2233030; www.amaryatriniwas.com; Fatehabad Rd; s ₹1500-2500, d ₹1800-2800; ❄@🛜) Sandwiched between a Costa Coffee and a Pizza Hut (but don't let that put you off), this place has had a recent makeover so that even the standard rooms are now smart, clean and come with modern furnishings and bright bathrooms. Be warned, wi-fi is chargeable at the ludicrous rate of ₹100 per hour!

Mansingh Palace HOTEL $$$
(Map p350; 🖄2331771; www.mansinghhotels.com; Fatehabad Rd; s/d from ₹7000/8000; ❄@≋) The service isn't up to scratch for the quality of this hotel, but if you can put up with the grumpy staff on reception you'll find plush rooms inside a complex crammed with Mughal design themes and exotic furnishings. The garden has an interestingly shaped pool and outdoor BBQ area. There's a gym and the quality **Sheesh Mahal** restaurant has live *ghazals* (Urdu songs) nightly.

Hotel Atithi HOTEL $$
(Map p350; 🖄2330878; www.hotelatithiagra.com; Fatehabad Rd; s ₹2400-2900, d ₹2900-3800; ❄@≋) Simple but comfortable rooms are a

UTTAR PRADESH

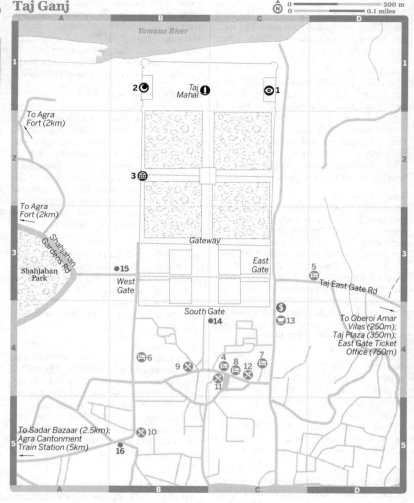

Taj Ganj

0 ——————— 200 m
0 ——————— 0.1 miles

Yamuna River

To Agra
Fort (2km)

To Agra
Fort (2km)

Shahjahan Gardens Rd

Shahjahan
Park

Taj Mahal

Gateway

West
Gate

East
Gate

South Gate

Taj East Gate Rd

To Oberoi Amar
Vilas (250m);
Taj Plaza (350m);
East Gate Ticket
Office (750m)

To Sadar Bazaar (2.5km);
Agra Cantonment
Train Station (5km)

---

decent size, while the white-tiled bathrooms are clean, if a little old fashioned. Guests can use the lovely public swimming pool next door for free.

SADAR BAZAAR AREA

Tourists Rest House HOTEL **$**
(Map p350; ☎2463961; dontworrychickencurry@hotmail.com; Kutchery Rd; d ₹250-550, with AC ₹750; ❄@) Very clean rooms of varying sizes come with tiled floors, TV and hot water and are set around a peaceful plant-filled, palm-shaded courtyard restaurant. Owners speak English and French and are very helpful. Phone

ahead for a free pick-up. Otherwise, it's ₹30 in a cycle-rickshaw from the train station.

Clarks Shiraz Hotel HOTEL **$$$**
(Map p350; ☎2226121; www.hotelclarksshiraz.com; 54 Taj Rd; s/d from ₹6500/7000; ❄@🛜🏊) One of Agra's original five-star hotels has seen some recent renovation. The standard doubles are still nothing special, but marble-floored deluxe versions are excellent and all bathrooms have been retiled so are spotless. There are two very good restaurants, three bars, a gym, a shaded garden pool area and ayurvedic massages. Some rooms have distant Taj views.

Taj Ganj

Hotel Yamuna View
HOTEL **$$$**

(Map p350; ☎2462990; www.hotelyamunaviewagra
.com; 6B The Mall; s/d from ₹4800/5500; ❊@🛜🖳)
A pool in the garden, a water feature in the
grand sunken lobby, a plush Chinese restau-
rant and some spacious rooms with gleam-
ing bathrooms make this friendly hotel in a
quiet part of Sadar Bazaar worth the splurge.
It also has a 24-hour cafe. The free wi-fi is in
the lobby only.

✕ Eating

Dalmoth is Agra's famous version of *nam-
kin* (spicy nibbles). *Peitha* is a square sweet
made from pumpkin and glucose that is fla-
voured with rosewater, coconut or saffron.
You can buy it all over Agra. From October
to March look out for *gajak,* a slightly spicy
sesame-seed biscuit strip.

TAJ GANJ AREA
This lively area directly south of the Taj has
plenty of budget rooftop restaurants, where
menus appear to be carbon copies of one
another. None are licensed but most will
find you a beer if you ask nicely and drink
discreetly.

Joney's Place
MULTICUISINE **$**

(Map p360; mains ₹40-90; ⊙5am-10.30pm)
Open at the crack of dawn, this pocket-
sized, brightly painted, travellers' institution
whipped up its first creamy lassi in 1978 and
continues to please despite having to cook its
meals in what must be the smallest restau-
rant kitchen in Agra. Everything they do here
is good, but the cheese and tomato 'jayfelles'
(toasted sandwich), the banana lassi and the
malai kofta get consistently good reviews.

Taj Cafe
MULTICUISINE **$**

(Map p360; mains ₹45-90; ⊙6.30am-11pm) Up
a flight of steps and overlooking Taj Ganj's
busy street scene, this friendly, family-run
restaurant is a nice choice if you're not
fussed about Taj views. There's a good choice
of breakfasts, thalis (₹70-120) and pizza
(₹130-170), and the lassis here are even bet-
ter than at Joney's Place.

Saniya Palace Hotel
MULTICUISINE **$$**

(Map p360; mains ₹70-200; ⊙6am-11pm) With
cute tablecloths, dozens of potted plants and
a bamboo pergola for shade, this is the most
pleasant rooftop restaurant in Taj Ganj. It
also has the best rooftop view of the Taj bar
none. Again, it's the usual mix of Western
dishes and Western-friendly Indian dishes
on offer, including set breakfasts, pizza and
pancakes.

Esphahan
NORTH INDIAN **$$$**

(off Map p360; ☎2231515; Oberoi Amar Vilas ho-
tel; Taj East Gate Rd; mains ₹1000-1400; ⊙dinner)
Agra's best hotel has now opened the doors
of its top-notch Indian restaurant to non-
guests. There are only two sittings each even-
ing, at 7pm and 9.30pm, so booking a table
is essential. The menu is small but exquisite,
specialising in Mughlai cuisine with unusual
offerings such as quail curry. We couldn't
afford the ₹2500-thali, but it's bound to be
extraordinarily good.

Hotel Sheela
MULTICUISINE **$$**

(Map p360; mains ₹60-200; ⊙7am-10pm) Actually the menu here is a bit limited compared
to others in Taj Ganj, meaning this isn't the
best spot for an evening meal. It's fine for
breakfast or a lunchtime snack, though –
and, let's face it, no one comes here specifically for the food. They come for the wonderfully peaceful garden retreat that makes it
hard to believe you're 100m from one of the
biggest tourist attractions in the world.

Shanti Lodge Restaurant   MULTICUISINE $$

(Map p360; mains ₹50-150; ⏱6.30am-10.30pm) The rooftop Taj view here is superb so this is a great place for breakfast or a sunset beer. There's some shade for hot afternoons, although it's not as comfortable as nearby Saniya Palace. The only let-down is the menu which, although not bad, lacks invention. Banana pancakes, anyone?

Yash Cafe   MULTICUISINE $

(Map p360; mains ₹30-130) This chilled-out 1st-floor cafe has wicker chairs, sports channels on TV, DVDs shown in the evening and a good range of meals, from good-value set breakfasts to thali (₹55) and pizza (₹80–150). It also offers a shower and storage space (₹50 for both) to day visitors.

Shankar Restaurant   INDIAN $

(Map p360; mains ₹25-50; ⏱9am-10pm) Those who are bored of the multicuisine Western-friendly tourist restaurants in Taj Ganj, and are after something a bit more down to earth, should head round the corner to the *dhabas* (snack bars) near the autorickshaw stand. Most are little more than shacks serving up simple Indian dishes. Shankar is as basic as any, but is friendly and has an English menu.

SADAR BAZAAR

This area offers better quality restaurants and makes a nice change from the please-all, multicuisine offerings in Taj Ganj.

Lakshmi Vilas   SOUTH INDIAN $

(Map p350; Taj Rd; meals ₹40-90;❄) This no-nonsense, plainly decorated, nonsmoking restaurant is *the* place in Agra to come for affordable South Indian fare. Treats include *idli* (spongy, round, fermented rice cake), *vada* (doughnut-shaped, deep-fried lentil savoury), *uttapam* (thick, savoury rice pancake) and more than 20 varieties of dosa (large savoury crepe), including a family special that is 1.2m long! The thali meal (₹88), served noon–3.30pm and 7–10.30pm, is very good indeed.

Dasaprakash   SOUTH INDIAN $$

(Map p350; ✆2363535, 1 Gwalior Rd; meals ₹90-150; ⏱11am-10.45pm; ❄) Highly recommended by locals for consistently good South Indian vegetarian food, Dasaprakash whips up spectacular unlimited thalis (₹100–225), dosa and a few token continental dishes. The ice-cream desserts (₹90–125), which take up a whole page of the two-page menu, are another speciality. Comfortable booth seating and wood-lattice screens make for intimate dining.

Vedic   NORTH INDIAN $$

(Map p350; ✆2250041, 1 Gwalior Rd; meals ₹140-200; ⏱11.30am-11pm; ❄) This classy new restaurant with modern decor but a traditional ambience has a mouth-wateringly good North Indian veg menu, with paneer (unfermented cheese) dishes featuring highly. The paneer tikka masala is particularly good. There's also a range of delicious vegetarian kebabs.

Mughal Room   NORTH INDIAN $$$

(Map p350; ✆2226121; 54 Taj Rd; mains ₹295-950; ⏱lunch & dinner) The best of four eating options at Clarks Shiraz Hotel, this top-floor restaurant serves up sumptuous Mughlai cuisine with a distant view of the Taj and

---

ⓘ STAYING AHEAD OF THE SCAMS

As well as the usual commission rackets and ever-present gem import scam (see p1156), some specific methods to relieve Agra tourists of their hard-earned include:

Rickshaws

When taking an auto or cycle-rickshaw to the Taj, make sure you are clear which gate you want to go to when negotiating the price. Otherwise, almost without fail, riders will take you to the roundabout at the south end of Shahjahan Gardens Rd – where expensive tongas (horse-drawn carriage) or camels wait to take tour groups to the west gate – and claim that's where they thought you meant. Autos cannot go right up to the Taj because of pollution rules, but they can get a lot closer than this.

Fake Marble

Lots of 'marble' souvenirs are actually alabaster, or even just soapstone. The mini Taj Mahals are always alabaster because they are too intricate to carve quickly in marble.

Agra Fort. Remember, though, you won't be able to see either at night. There's also live classical music here every evening.

Tourists Rest House
MULTICUISINE $

(Map p350; ☑2363961; Kutchery Rd; meals ₹45-80) The courtyard garden restaurant here is often full of chattering travellers enjoying the candle-lit atmosphere around the small fountain, and the all-veg menu is decent.

Brijwasi
SWEETS $

(Map p350; Sadar Bazaar; sweets from ₹220/kg, meals ₹75-120; ⊙8am-10.30pm; ✳) Mouthwatering selection of traditional Indian sweets, nuts and biscuits on the ground floor, with a decent-value Indian restaurant upstairs.

🍷 Drinking & Entertainment

A night out in Agra tends to revolve around sitting at a rooftop restaurant with a couple of bottles of beer. None of the restaurants in Taj Ganj are licensed, but they can find alcohol for you if you ask nicely, and don't mind if you bring your own drinks, as long as you're discreet. You can catch live Indian classical music and *ghazals* (Urdu love songs) at restaurants in several of Agra's top-end hotels, most of which also have bars, albeit of the rather soulless variety.

Café Coffee Day
CAFE

(Map p360; ⊙6am-8pm) This AC-cooled branch of the popular cafe chain is the closest place to the Taj selling proper coffee (from ₹39). Also does cakes and snacks. There's another branch in Sadar Bazaar (Map p350).

Amar Vilas Bar
BAR

(off Map p360; Oberoi Amar Vilas hotel, Taj East Gate Rd; ⊙noon-midnight) For a beer (₹300) or cocktail (₹500) in sheer opulence, look no further than the bar at Agra's best hotel. A terrace opens out to views of the Taj.

🔒 Shopping

Agra is well known for its marble items inlaid with coloured stones, similar to the pietra dura work on the Taj. Sadar Bazaar, the old town and the area around the Taj are full of emporiums. Taj Mahal models are all made of alabaster rather than marble. Very cheap ones are made of soapstone, which scratches easily.

Other popular buys include rugs, leather and gemstones, though the latter are imported from Rajasthan and are cheaper in Jaipur.

Subhash Emporium
HANDICRAFTS

(Map p350; ☑2850749; 18/1 Gwalior Rd) This expensive but honest marble-carving shop has been knocking up quality pieces for more than 35 years. Watch artisans at work in the entranceway before delving into the stock out the back. Small marble boxes start at about ₹500.

Kinari Bazaar
MARKET

(Map p350; ⊙dawn-late) This is just one market of many in a crowded tangle of streets in the old town, selling everything from textiles and handicrafts to fruit and produce.

Subhash Bazaar
MARKET

Skirts the northern edge of Agra's Jama Masjid and is particularly good for silks and saris.

Khadi Gramodyog
CLOTHING

(Map p350; ☑2421481; MG Rd; ⊙10.30am-7pm) Stocks simple, good-quality men's Indian clothing made from the homespun *khadi* fabric famously recommended by Mahatma Gandhi (p1132). No English sign: on Mahatma Gandhi (MG) Rd, look for the *khadi* logo of hands clasped around a mud hut.

Modern Book Depot
BOOKS

(Map p350; ☑2225695; Sadar Bazaar; ⊙10.30am-9.30pm, closed Tue) Great selection of novels, plus Lonely Planet guides, at this 60-year-old establishment.

ℹ Information

Taj Ganj is riddled with **internet cafes** (per hr ₹20-40). Many have webcams for Skype use, and some let you use your own laptop. Some also have CD-burning facilities for **digital photography** (per disc ₹50-100).

Emergency
Tourist police (☑2421204; Agra Cantonment train station; ⊙24hr) The guys in sky-blue uniforms are based just outside the train station, but it's easier to go through the tourism office inside where they often hang out.

Medical Services
Amit Jaggi Memorial Hospital (Map p350; ☑2230515; www.ajmh.in; Vibhav Nagar, off Minto Rd) Private hospital recommended by readers.

District Hospital (Map p350; ☑2466099) Government-run local hospital on Mahatma Gandhi (MG) Rd.

Money

ATMs are all over the city. There's only one close to the Taj, though; just by the east gate.

State Bank of India (⊙10am-4pm Mon-Fri, to 1pm Sat) Changes cash and travellers cheques.

Post

Main post office (Map p350; The Mall; ⊙10am-5pm Mon-Sat, Sunday speed-post only) Has a handy 'facilitation office' for foreigners.

Tourist Information

Government of India Tourism (Map p350; ☑2226378; www.incredibleindia.org; 191 The Mall; ⊙10am-5.30pm Mon-Fri, to 2pm Sat) Very helpful branch; has brochures on local and India-wide attractions and can arrange guides (half/full day ₹500/700).

UP Tourism Agra Cantonment train station (off Map p350; ☑2421204; ⊙7am-10pm); Taj Rd (Map p350; ☑2226431; agrauptourism@gmail. com; 64 Taj Rd; ⊙10.30am-5pm Mon-Sat) The friendly train station branch has round-the-clock help and advice, and is the place to contact the tourist police. Either branch can arrange guides (half/full day ₹600/750).

ⓘ Getting There & Away

Air

Kingfisher Airlines (☑2400693; www.flyking fisher.com; airport; ⊙10am-5pm) has one daily flight to Delhi (from ₹2000, one hour, 3pm). Agra's Kheria airport is in Indian Air Force territory so you won't get in without your name being on the list of those who have booked flights for that day. You'll have to purchase your ticket online or over the phone.

Bus

Some services from **Idgah bus stand** (off Map p350):

Delhi non-AC/AC ₹149/226, five hours, frequent, 24 hours (non-AC)/6am–6pm (AC)

Fatehpur Sikri ₹27, one hour, every 30 minutes, 6am–5pm

Gwalior ₹82, three hours, frequent, 5am–1am

Jaipur ₹159, six hours, frequent, 6am–1am

Jhansi ₹141, six hours, four daily: 5am, 6am, 7am and 11.30am

Services from **ISBT bus stand** (off map p350) include Dehra Dun (seat/sleeper ₹512/574, 11 hours, at 8pm and 8.30pm, both AC).

Biili Ghar bus stand (Map p350) serves Mathura (₹42, 90 minutes, every 30 minutes, 6am–7pm).

Shared autos (₹10) run between Idgah and Biili Ghar bus stands. To get to ISBT, take the AC public bus from Agra Cantt train station to Dayalbagh (₹20) but get off at Baghwan Talkies (₹15), from where shared autos (₹5) can take you to ISBT.

Train

Train is easily the quickest way to travel to/ from Delhi, Varanasi, Jaipur and Khajuraho (p365). Most trains leave from **Agra Cantonment (Cantt) train station** (off Map p350; ☑2421204), although some go from Agra Fort station (Map p350).

Express trains are well set up for day trippers to/from Delhi (see table below) but trains run to Delhi all day. If you can't reserve a seat, just buy a 'general ticket' for the next train (about ₹60), find a seat in Sleeper class then upgrade when the ticket collector comes along. Most of the time, he won't even make you pay any more.

For Orchha, catch one of the many daily trains to Jhansi (sleeper ₹150, 3hrs), then take a shared auto to the bus stand (₹5) from where shared autos run all day to Orchha (₹10).

ⓘ Getting Around

Autorickshaw

Agra's green-and-yellow autorickshaws run on CNG (compressed natural gas) rather than petrol, and so are less environmentally destructive. Just outside Agra Cantonment train station

DELHI–AGRA TRAINS – DAY TRIPPERS

TRIP	TRAIN NO & NAME	FARE (₹)	DURATION (HR)	DEPARTURES
New Delhi-Agra	12002 *Shatabdi Exp*	370/700*	2	6.15am (except Fri)
Agra-New Delhi	12001 *Shatabdi Exp*	400/745*	2	8.30pm (except Fri)
Hazrat Nizamuddin-Agra	12280 *Taj Exp*	75/263**	3	7.10am
Agra-Hazrat Nizamuddin	12279 *Taj Exp*	75/263**	3	6.55pm

*chair/1AC; **2nd/chair

DESTINATION	TRAIN NO & NAME	FARE (₹)	DURATION (HR)	DEPARTURES
Gorakhpur*	19037/19039 Avadh Exp	249/672/920	15½	10pm
Jaipur*	14853/14863 Marudhar Exp	135/349/474	5	6.15am (except Thu)
Khajuraho	12448 UP SMPRK KRNTI	207/526**	8	11.20pm (Tue, Fri, Sun)
Kolkata (Howrah)	13008 UA Toofan Exp	394/1079**	31	12.40pm
Lucknow	13238/13240 MTJ PNBE Exp	161/422/574	6½	11.30pm
Mumbai (CST)	12138 Punjab Mail	410/1098/1501	23	8.55am
Varanasi	13238/13240 MTJ PNBE Exp	262/707/969	12	11.30pm

Fares are sleeper/3AC/2AC; *leaves from Agra Fort station; **sleeper/3AC only

is the **prepaid autorickshaw booth** (⊘24hr) which gives you a good guide for haggling elsewhere. Note, autos aren't allowed to go to Fatehpur Sikri. Sample prices: Fatehabad Rd ₹50; ISBT bus stand ₹80; Sadar Bazaar ₹40; Sikandra ₹80; Taj Mahal ₹50; half-day (four-hour) tour ₹200; full-day (10-hour) tour ₹400.

Cycle-Rickshaw

Prices from the **Taj Mahal** include: Agra Cantonment train station ₹40-50; Agra Fort ₹20; Bijli Ghar bus stand ₹30; Fatehabad Rd ₹20; Kinari Bazaar ₹30; Sadar Bazaar ₹30; haf-day tour ₹150–200.

Taxi

Outside Agra Cantonment train station the **prepaid taxi booth** (⊘24hr) gives a good idea of what taxis should cost. Prices include: Delhi ₹2500; Fatehabad Rd ₹150; Sadar Bazaar ₹70; Taj Mahal ₹150; half-day (four-hour) tour ₹450; full-day (eight-hour) tour ₹650.

Around Agra

FATEHPUR SIKRI
☑ 05613 / POP 28,750

This magnificent fortified ancient city, 40km west of Agra, was the short-lived capital of the Mughal empire between 1571 and 1585, during the reign of Emperor Akbar. Akbar visited the village of Sikri to consult the Sufi saint Shaikh Salim Chishti, who predicted the birth of an heir to the Mughal throne. When the prophecy came true, Akbar built his new capital here, including a stunning mosque – still in use today – and three palaces for each of his favourite wives, one a Hindu, one a Muslim and one a Christian. The city was an Indo-Islamic masterpiece, but erected in an area that suffered from water shortages and so was abandoned shortly after Akbar's death.

It's easy to visit this World Heritage Site as a day trip from Agra, but there are a couple of decent places to stay, and the colourful bazaar in the village of Fatehpur, just below the ruins, as well as the small village of Sikri, a few kilometres north, are worth exploring. Also, the red-sandstone palace walls are at their most atmospheric, and photogenic, at sunset.

The bus stand is at the eastern end of the bazaar. Walking another 1km northeast will bring you to Agra Gate and the junction with the main Agra–Jaipur road, from where you can catch buses.

⊙ Sights

The palace buildings lie beside the Jama Masjid mosque. Both sit on top of a ridge that runs between the small villages of Fatehpur and Sikri. Official guides, hired from the ticket office, will show you around for ₹125. There are other ruins scattered all over this area, all of which can be viewed for free. Colourful Fatehpur Bazaar also deserves some of your time.

Jama Masjid   MOSQUE

This beautiful, immense mosque was completed in 1571 and contains elements of Persian and Indian design. The main en-

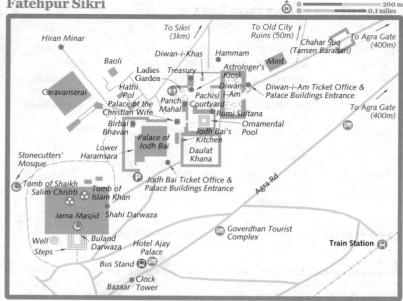

trance, at the top of a flight of stone steps, is through the spectacular 54m-high **Buland Darwaza** (Victory Gate), built to commemorate Akbar's military victory in Gujarat.

Inside the courtyard of the mosque is the stunning white-marble **tomb of Shaikh Salim Chishti**, which was completed in 1581 and is entered through a door made of ebony. Inside it are brightly coloured flower murals while the canopy is decorated with mother-of-pearl shell. Just as Akbar came to the saint four centuries ago hoping for a son, childless women visit his tomb today and tie a thread to the *jali*, which are among the finest in India. To the right of the tomb lie the gravestones of family members of Shaikh Salim Chishti and nearby is the entrance to an underground tunnel (barred by a locked gate) that reputedly goes all the way to Agra Fort! Behind the entrance to the tunnel, on the far wall, are three holes, part of the ancient ventilation system. You can still feel the rush of cool air forcing its way through them. Just east of Shaikh Salim Chisti's tomb is the red-sandstone **tomb of Islam Khan**, the final resting place of Shaikh Salim Chisti's grandson and one-time governor of Bengal.

On the east wall of the courtyard is a smaller entrance to the mosque – the **Shahi Darwaza** (King's Gate), which leads to the palace complex.

Palaces & Pavilions   PALACES
(Indian/foreigner ₹20/260, video ₹25; ⊙dawn-dusk) The first of the palace buildings you enter from the south is the largest, the **Palace of Jodh Bai**, and the one-time home of Akbar's Hindu wife, said to be his favourite. Set around an enormous courtyard, it blends traditional Indian columns, Islamic cupolas and turquoise-blue Persian roof tiles.

Just outside, to the left of Jodh Bai's former kitchen, is the **Palace of the Christian Wife**. This was used by Akbar's Goan wife Mariam, who gave birth to Jehangir here in 1569. Like many of the buildings in the palace complex, it contains elements of different religions, as befitted Akbar's tolerant religious beliefs. The domed ceiling is Islamic in style, while remnants of a wall painting of the Hindu god Shiva can also be found.

Continuing anticlockwise will bring you to the **Ornamental Pool**. Here, singers and musicians would perform on the platform above the water while Akbar watched from the pavilion in his private quarters, known as **Daulat Khana** (Abode of Fortune). Behind the pavilion is the **Khwabgah** (Dream House), a sleeping area with a huge stone bunk bed. Nowadays the only sleeping done here is by bats, hanging from the ceiling. The small room in the far corner is full of them!

Heading north from the Ornamental Pool brings you to the most intricately carved structure in the whole complex, the tiny, but elegant Rumi Sultana, the palace built for Akbar's Turkish Muslim wife.

Just past Rumi Sultana is Pachisi Courtyard where Akbar is said to have played the game *pachisi* (an ancient version of ludo) using slave girls as pieces.

From here you can step down into Diwan-i-Am (Hall of Public Audiences), a large courtyard (which is now a garden) where Akbar dispensed justice by orchestrating public executions, said to have been carried out by elephants trampling to death convicted criminals.

The Diwan-i-Khas (Hall of Private Audiences), found at the northern end of the Pachisi Courtyard, looks nothing special from the outside, but the interior is dominated by a magnificently carved stone central column. This pillar flares to create a flat-topped plinth linked to the four corners of the room by narrow stone bridges. From this plinth Akbar is believed to have debated with scholars and ministers who stood at the ends of the four bridges.

Next to Diwan-i-Khas is the Treasury, which houses secret stone safes in some corners (one has been left with its stone lid open for visitors to see). Sea monsters carved on the ceiling struts were there to protect the fabulous wealth once stored here. The so-called Astrologer's Kiosk in front has roof supports carved in a serpentine Jain style.

On one corner of the Ladies Garden is the impressive Panch Mahal, a pavilion whose five storeys decrease in size until the top one consists of only a tiny kiosk. The lower floor has 84 columns, all different.

Walking past the Palace of the Christian Wife once more will take you west to Birbal Bhavan, ornately carved inside and out, and thought to have been the living quarters of one of Akbar's most senior ministers. The Lower Haramsara, just to the south, housed the royal stables.

Plenty of ruins are scattered behind the whole complex, including the Caravanserai, a vast courtyard surrounded by rooms where visiting merchants stayed, and the bizarre 21m-tall Hiran Minar, a tower decorated with hundreds of stone representations of elephant tusks, which is said to be the place where Akbar's favourite execution elephant died. Badly defaced carvings of elephants still guard Hathi Pol (Elephant Gate), while the remains of the small Stonecutters' Mosque and a hammam (bath) are also a short stroll away. Other unnamed ruins can be explored north of what is known as the Mint but is thought to have in fact been stables, including some in the interesting village of Sikri to the north.

Sleeping & Eating

Fatehpur Sikri's culinary speciality is *khataie,* the biscuits you can see piled high in the bazaar.

Hotel Ajay Palace   GUESTHOUSE $
(☑282950; Agra Rd; d ₹200) This very friendly family guesthouse has three simple but neat and tidy double rooms with marble floors and sit-down flush toilets. It's also a very popular lunch stop (mains ₹30–70). Sit on the rooftop at the large, elongated marble table and enjoy a view of the village streets with the Jama Masjid towering above. Non-guests can store luggage (₹10) here while they visit the ruins.

Goverdhan Tourist Complex   HOTEL $
(☑282643;   www.hotelfatehpursikriviews.com; Agra Rd; d ₹400, with AC ₹700; ✳@✶) Brightly painted, spotless rooms set around a very well-kept garden. There's communal balcony and terrace seating, free internet and wi-fi, and the restaurant is decent (meals ₹50 to ₹120).

ⓘ Information

Dangers & Annoyances

Take no notice of anyone who gets on the Fatehpur Sikri–Agra bus before the final stop at Idgah bus stand, telling you that you have arrived at the city centre or the Taj Mahal. You haven't. You're still a long rickshaw ride away, and the man trying to tease you off the bus is, surprise surprise, a rickshaw driver.

ⓘ Getting There & Away

Buses run to Agra's Idgah Bus Stand from the bazaar every half hour, from 6am to 5.30pm. If you miss those, walk to Agra Gate and wave down a Jaipur–Agra bus on the main road. They run regularly, day and night.

For Bharatpur (₹15, 40 minutes) or Jaipur (₹140, 4½ hours), wave down a westbound bus from Agra Gate.

Trains for Agra Fort Station (₹6, one to two hours) leave Fatehpur Sikri at 4.53am, 10.28am, 2.10pm (to Agra Cantonment station), 3.56pm and 8.17pm. Just buy a 'general' ticket at the station and pile in.

Mathura

📞 0565 / POP 319,235

Famed for being the birthplace of the much-loved Hindu god Krishna, Mathura is one of Hinduism's seven sacred cities and attracts floods of pilgrims, particularly during **Jan-mastami** (Krishna's birthday) in August/September. The town is dotted with temples from various ages and the stretch of the sacred Yamuna River which flows past here is lined with 25 ghats, best seen at dawn, when many people take their holy dip, and just after sunset, when hundreds of candles are sent floating out onto the river during the evening *aarti* ceremony.

Mathura was once a Buddhist centre with 20 monasteries that housed 3000 monks but, after the rise of Hinduism, and later sackings by Afghan and Mughal invaders, today all that's left of the oldest sights are the beautiful sculptures recovered from ruins, now on display in the archaeological museum.

◉ Sights

Kesava Deo Temple   HINDU TEMPLE
(Shri Kirshna Janmbhoomi; ⊙5.30am-8.30pm) Among the foundations of the mural-filled temple complex is a small, bare room with a slab of rock on which Krishna is said to have been born, some 3500 years ago.

Surrounding the temple are gardens and Krishna souvenir shops. Next door is **Katra Masjid**, a mosque built by Aurangzeb in 1661 on the site of a temple he ordered to be destroyed. The mosque is now guarded round the clock by soldiers to prevent a repeat of the tragic events at Ayodhya in 1992 (p376).

Archaeological Museum   MUSEUM
(Museum Rd; Indian/foreigner ₹5/25, camera ₹20; ⊙10.30am-4.30pm Tue-Sun) The rooms that aren't empty in this large museum house superb collections of religious sculptures by the Mathura school, which flourished from the 3rd century BC to the 12th century AD.

Mathura & Vrindavan

Mathura & Vrindavan

Vishram Ghat & Around   AREA

A string of ghats and temples lines the Yamuna River north of the main road bridge. The most central and most popular is **Vishram Ghat**, where Krishna is said to have rested after killing the tyrannical King Kansa. Boats gather along the banks here to take tourists along the Yamuna (₹50 per half hour). Beside the ghat is the 17m **Sati Burj**, a four-storey tower built by the son of Behari Mal of Jaipur in 1570 to commemorate his mother's *sati* (self-immolation on her husband's funeral pyre).

Gita Temple   HINDU TEMPLE

(⊘dawn-dusk) This serene marble temple, on the road to Vrindavan, has the entire Bhagavad Gita written on a red pillar in the garden.

🛏 Sleeping & Eating

Agra Hotel   HOTEL $

(📞2403318; Bengali Ghat; s ₹250-300, d ₹400-450, with AC ₹700-750, tr ₹600-850; ❄) This area, with narrow lanes winding their way down to the ghats and temples that line the Yamuna River, is easily the most interesting place to stay. Rooms here are basic but have character and some overlook the river, while staff members are very welcoming. The restaurant has a small menu of veg dishes (₹18–30) and thalis (₹50–60) plus tea, coffee and toast.

Hotel Brijwasi Royal   HOTEL $$

(📞2401224; www.brijwasiroyal.com; Station Rd; s/d incl breakfast from ₹1950/2350; ❄@) Clean comfortable rooms come with either marble floors or carpets. All have TV, fridge and bathtub, while some overlook a buffalo pond out the back. The restaurant (meals ₹95 to ₹135), with a striking Krishna mural, does good quality Indian veg dishes and South Indian breakfasts and is deservedly popular. There's also a bar (beer from ₹110).

ℹ Information

Near New bus stand is a **State Bank of India** (Station Rd; ⊘10.30am-4pm Mon-Fri, to 1.30pm Sat) which has a 1st-floor money-exchange desk and an ATM outside. There's a small **internet cafe** (per hr ₹30; ⊘8.30am-1.30pm & 3.30-8pm) opposite the main entrance to Shri Krishna Janmbhoomi.

ℹ Getting There & Around

BUS The so-called **New bus stand** has regular buses to Delhi (₹110, four hours) and Agra (₹41, 90 minutes) that run throughout the day and night. Tempos (large autorickshaws) charge ₹10 for the 10km Mathura–Vrindavan run.

TRAIN Regular trains go to Delhi (class/chair ₹58/68, three hours), Agra (₹35/50, one hour), and Bharatpur (₹25/40, 45 minutes). The Bharatpur trains continue to Sawai Madhopur (for Ranthambore National Park, two hours) and Kota (5½ hours).

369

Vrindavan

📞0565 / POP 56,618

The village of Vrindavan is where the young Krishna is said to have grown up. Pilgrims flock here from all over India and, in the case of the Hare Krishna community, from all over the world. Dozens of temples, old and modern, dot the area. They come in all shapes and sizes and many have their own unique peculiarities, making a visit here more than just your average temple hop.

The **International Society for Krishna Consciousness** (Iskcon; 📞2540343; www .iskcon.com), also known as the Hare Krishnas, is based at the **Krishna Balaram temple complex**, accessed through a beautiful white-marble gate, which houses the tomb of Swami Prabhupada (1896–1977), the founder of the Hare Krishna organisation. Several hundred foreigners attend courses and seminars here annually. The temple is closed to the public at various times of the day, most significantly from noon to 4pm. It's possible to stay at the **guesthouse** (📞2540021; d ₹600-1500) at the back of the temple complex, where you'll also find the clean, cool and healthy **New Govinda's Restaurant** (mains ₹60-110; ⊘8am-3pm & 5.30-9.30pm), which does Indian veg dishes, pasta, cakes, shakes, salads and soups. There's a small **bakery** beside it.

The cavernous, red sandstone **Govind Dev Temple**, built in 1590 by Raja Man Singh of Amber, has cute bells carved on its pillars. Resident monkeys here are as cheeky as any in India. We caught one running off with a lady's purse and saw another sitting in the rafters wearing a pair of sunglasses!

The 10-storey **Pagal Baba Temple** (admission ₹2), a fairytale-castle lookalike, has an amusing succession of animated puppets and dioramas in glass cases on the ground floor, which depict scenes from the lives of Rama and Krishna.

The glittery **Krishna Temple**, at the town's entrance, is modern and adorned with mirrors, enamel art and chandeliers. On the right is a fake **cave passageway** (admission ₹3) where you walk past a long

UTTAR PRADESH VRINDAVANUTTAR PRADESH VRINDAVAN

line of slightly moving tableaux depicting scenes from Krishna's life.

Rangaji Temple, dating from 1851, Radha Ballabh Temple, built in 1626, Madan Mohan Temple and Nidhivan Temple are also worth a visit.

ℹ Information

There is an **information office** (☉10am-1pm & 5-8.30pm) in the Krishna Balaram temple complex which has lists of places to stay in Vrindavan and can help with booking Gita (studies in the Bhagavad Gita, an ancient Hindu scripture) classes.

There's an **ATM** beside the temple and an **internet cafe** (per hr ₹20; ☉9am-9pm) opposite.

ℹ Getting There & Around

Most temples are open from dawn to dusk and admission is free, but they are well spread out so a cycle-rickshaw tour is a good way to see them. Expect to pay ₹100-150 for a half-day tour.

Tempos, shared autos and buses all charge ₹10 from Vrindavan to Mathura.

Lucknow

📞0522 / POP 2.27 MILLION

Liberally sprinkled with British Raj-era buildings – including the famous Residency – and boasting two superb mausoleums, the capital of Uttar Pradesh has enough to keep history buffs interested without attracting the hordes of tourists that sometimes make sightseeing tiresome.

The city rose to prominence as the home of the nawabs of Avadh (Oudh) who were great patrons of the culinary and other arts, particularly dance and music. Lucknow's reputation as a city of culture, gracious living and rich cuisine has continued to this day. And eating out is still a major highlight of a visit to the city, especially if you like kebabs!

In 1856 the British annexed Avadh, exiling Nawab Wajid Ali Shah to a palace in Kolkata (Calcutta). The disruption this caused was a factor behind the First War of Independence of 1857, culminating in the dramatic Siege of Lucknow at the Residency.

Lucknow's commercial centre, known as Hazratganj, contains much of the city's accommodation and restaurants and is centred on Mahatma Gandhi (MG) Rd.

⊙ Sights

Residency   HISTORIC SITE

(Indian/foreigner ₹5/100, video ₹25; ☉dawn-dusk) The large collection of gardens and ruins that makes up the Residency offers a fascinating historical glimpse of the beginning of the end for the British Raj. Built in 1800, the Residency became the stage for the most dramatic events of the 1857 First War of Independence, the Siege of Lucknow, a 147-day siege that claimed the lives of thousands. The compound has been left as it was at the time of the final relief and the walls are still pockmarked from bullets and cannon balls.

The focus is the well-designed museum (admission ₹5; ☉8am-4.30pm Tue-Sun) in the main Residency building, which includes a scale model of the original buildings. Downstairs are the huge basement rooms where many of the British women and children lived throughout the siege.

The cemetery around the ruined St Mary's church is where 2000 of the defenders were buried, including their leader, Sir Henry Lawrence, 'who tried to do his duty' according to the famous inscription on his weathered gravestone.

Bara Imambara   HISTORIC BUILDING

(Hussainabad Trust Rd; Indian/foreigner ₹20/300; guide ₹75; ☉dawn-dusk) This colossal tomb is worth seeing in its own right, but the highly unusual labyrinth of corridors inside its upper floors make a visit to this *imambara* (tomb dedicated to a Shiite holy man) particularly special. The ticket price includes entrance to Chota Imambara, the clock tower and the *baradari* (summer palace), all walking distance from here.

The complex is accessed through two enormous gateways which lead into a huge courtyard. On one side is an attractive **mosque**, on the other a large **baori** (step-well) which can be explored. Bring a torch (flashlight). At the far end of the courtyard is the huge central hall, one of the world's largest vaulted galleries. *Tazias* (small replicas of Imam Hussain's tomb in Karbala, Iraq) are stored inside and are paraded around during the Shiite mourning ceremony of Muharram.

But it's what's beyond the small entrance – intriguingly marked 'labyrinth' – to the left of the central hall, that steals the show. It leads to the **Bhulbhulaiya**, an enticing network of narrow passageways that winds its way inside the upper floors of the tomb's structure, eventually leading out to rooftop balconies. As with the step-well, it's handy to have a torch.

Just beyond the Bara Imambara is the unusual but imposing gateway Rumi Darwaza, said to be a copy of an entrance gate in Istanbul. 'Rumi' (relating to Rome) is the term Muslims applied to Istanbul when it was still Byzantium, the capital of the Eastern Roman empire. Over the road is the beautiful white mosque **Tila Wali Masjid**, a deceptively shallow building built in 1680. The interior is repainted every year over the original designs.

On the short walk from here to Chota Imambara, a turning to your right leads to the banks of the Gomti River where you'll find some **bathing ghats**. Boat hands wait here to row visitors across the river (per boat ₹100 return).

Chota Imambara
HISTORIC BUILDING

(Hussainabad Imambara; Hussainabad Trust Rd; admission with Bara Imambara ticket; ⊙dawn-dusk) About 500m beyond the Bara Imambara, through a second beautiful gateway, is another tomb that was constructed by Mohammed Ali Shah in 1832, who is buried here, alongside his mother. Smaller than the Bara Imambara but adorned with calligraphy, it has a more serene and intimate atmosphere.

Mohammed's silver throne and red crown can be seen here as well as countless chandeliers and some brightly decorated *tazias*. In the garden is a water tank and two replicas of the Taj Mahal that are the **tombs** of Mohammed Ali Shah's daughter and her husband. A traditional **hammam** is off to one side.

Outside the complex, the decaying watchtower on the other side of the road is known as **Satkhanda** (Seven Storey Tower), although it has only four storeys because construction was abandoned in 1840 when Mohammed Ali Shah died.

The 67m red-brick **clock tower** (admission with Bara Imambara ticket; ⊙dawn-dusk), the tallest in India, was built in the 1880s. Nearby is a **baradari** (summer palace; admission with Bara Imambara ticket; ⊙7am-6.30pm), a striking red-brick building, built in 1842, which overlooks an artificial lake and houses portraits of the nawabs.

Old Town
AREA

Getting lost in the crazy maze of alleyways in some of the city's older districts is a highlight of a trip to Lucknow. The bazaars in these tight lanes, overlooked by centuries-old buildings, some quite exquisite, are where traders have made their livings for generations. One great area to explore is **Aminabad**; take a rickshaw to Tunday Kebab (Lucknow's most famous kebab restaurant) then, after dining on possibly the world's greatest mutton kebabs, step out into the lanes and get lost.

Chowk, northwest of here, is even older and crazier. Everything, it seems, is made and sold here, from the impossibly thin edible silver foil that sweets are wrapped in to Lucknow's renowned *chikan* embroidery. The alleyways centre on a 1km street that runs north-south between two old gateways, **Gol Darawza** and **Akbari Darwaza**. Gol Darwaza is walking distance from Bara Imambara; head towards Chota Imambara, take the first left then fork right. Alternatively get up early and take the excellent Heritage Walking Tour run by UP Tourism.

☞ Tours

UP Tourism
WALKING

(☑2615005; Hotel Gomti, 6 Sapru Marg; 2hr tour ₹10; ⊙10am-5.30pm Mon-Sat, tours 7am) This fabulous two-hour Heritage Walking Tour could well turn out to be the best ₹10 you ever spend. Meet your English-speaking guide outside Tila Wali Masjid then follow him first around the mosque, then the Bara Imambara (you won't need to pay an entrance fee at this time of the morning), before delving in to the architectural delights of Chowk. This is a great way to get your bearings amongst Chowk's maze of alleys before returning on your own in the evening when things really get started.

This tour had only just started at the time of research, so check with UP Tourism at Gomti Hotel to see that it's still running as stated here.

🛏 Sleeping

Lucknow Homestay
🏆 TOP CHOICE | HOMESTAY $

(☑2235460; naheed2k@gmail.com; 110D Mall Ave; r incl breakfast ₹450;🖥) This delightful family homestay in a leafy neighbourhood is run by the very welcoming Naheed and her family. The 11 rooms are simple but large and comfortable, and two have private bathrooms. You may need to call for directions as Mall Ave is a bit of a maze. The house number isn't marked, but you enter through a small green garden gate. A sign reading 'Munni's Dream' is above the front door. To help non English-speaking rickshaw riders understand where you're going, try to draw out the word Mall; 'Ma-ah-luh'.

Hotel Clarks Avadh
HOTEL $$$

(☑2620131; www.clarksavadh.com; 8 MG Rd; r from ₹8000; ☀@🖥) Lucknow's top hotel displays a cool elegance and restrained decor. Slick

(Map of Lucknow with labels: Chota Imambara, Bara Imambara, Chowk, CHOWK, Shah Mina Rd, Gomti River, Residency, Vishwa Vidyalaya Rd, Botanical Gardens, Rana Pratap Marg, Ashok Marg, Cricket Stadium, HAZRATGANJ, Hakim Abdul Aziz Rd, Victoria St, Nadan Mahal Rd, Subhash Marg, Nabi Ullah Rd, J Narain Rd, Hospital Rd, Mahatma Gandhi (MG) Rd, Ram Tirth Marg, KAISERBAGH, Bisheshwar Nath Rd, Ganaprasad Marg, AMINABAD, Janpath Market, Christ Church, Lucknow Zoo, Park Rd, Kalidas Marg, Aishbagh Rd, Subhash Marg, Aminabad Rd, Buddha Rd, CHARBAGH, Guru Govind Singh Marg, Station Rd, Saroini Naidu Marg, Vivekanand Marg, Vikramaditya Marg, The Mall, Haider Canal, Buddha Rd, Lucknow Junction Train Station, Charbagh Train Station, Kanpur Rd, Mall Ave, To Alambagh Bus Station (3km); Amausi Airport (15km))

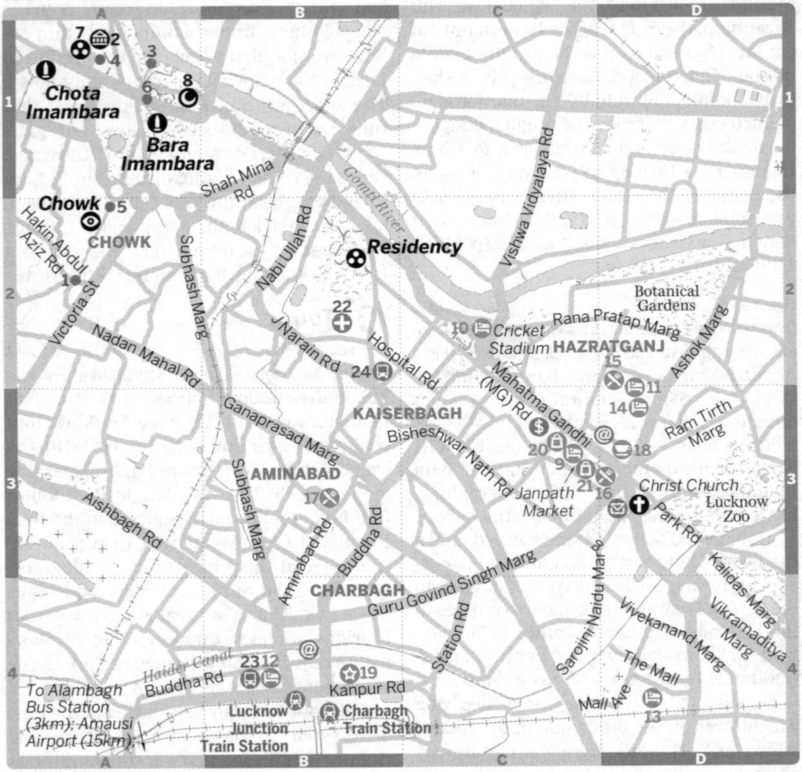

rooms have bathtubs and views of either the Gomti River or the cricket stadium. The elevated outdoor pool is superb, and there's a gym, a jazzy bar and the wonderful top-floor restaurant, Falaknuma.

Hotel Mayur HOTEL $

(☎2451824; Subhash Marg; s ₹275-350, d ₹350-450, with AC ₹550/650; ✷) Good-value rooms in this well-run establishment are basic but come with cable TV and some have huge bathrooms. Definitely one of the better cheapies near the train station.

Hotel Gomti HOTEL $$

(☎2620624; hotelgomti@up-tourism.com; 6 Sapru Marg; r from ₹650, with AC from ₹1200; ✷) AC rooms are decent, but the cheaper rooms, with air coolers, are a bit musty. All rooms come reasonably well equipped, though, with TV, sofa, table and chairs. A restaurant, a bar with a garden and a UP Tourism office are all here too.

Capoor's HOTEL $$

(☎4954300; www.hotelcapoors.com; 52 MG Rd; s/d from ₹1500/1700; ✷) Although perfectly located in the heart of Hazratganj, Capoor's is in need of a refit. Rooms have a homely feel, and there's an old-fashioned ambience about the place, but the carpets aren't the cleanest and the bathrooms are underwhelming for this price. **Nawab's Restaurant** (⊙7am-3.30pm & 7pm-11.15pm; mains ₹100 to ₹250) is very popular, however, and you won't forget the neon-tastic Strokes Sports Bar in a hurry.

Tekarees Inn HOTEL $$

(☎4016241; www.tekareesinn.com; 17/3 Ashok Marg; s/d/ste ₹1700/2300/2600; ✷) Neat and tidy business hotel with marble floors in decent-sized twin rooms. Bathrooms are spartan but clean.

✗ Eating

The refined palates of the nawabs left Lucknow with a reputation for rich Mughlai cuisine, and the city's dinner tables are heavily influenced by the Arab world. Lucknow is famous for its biryani dishes as well as its wide range of kebabs (p374). It's also known for *dum pukht* – the 'art' of steam pressure cooking, in which meat and vegetables are cooked in a sealed clay pot. Huge *rumali roti* (paper-thin chapatis; *rumali* means handkerchief) are served in many small Muslim-style restaurants in the old city. They arrive folded up and should be eaten with a goat or lamb curry like *bhuna ghosht* or rogan josh.

The popular dessert *kulfi faluda* (ice cream with long chickpea-flour noodles) is served in several places in Aminabad. The sweet orange-coloured rice dish known as *zarda* is also popular.

Like many Indian cities, Lucknow has a fine array of *chaat,* savoury snacks typically served in mini *puris* (flat dough that puffs up when deep fried).

TOP
CHOICE **Tunday Kabab**   NORTH INDIAN **$**
(just off Aminabad Rd; dishes ₹20-60; ⏱11.30am-12.30am) Tucked away down a small street in the bustling Aminabad district, this re-nowned, 100-year-old kebab shop serves up delicious plates of mutton biryani, ke-babs and tandoori chicken. The mutton ke-bab here is impossibly delicious. Consider coming along early to give yourself time for a wander around the bazaar here, a prime location for picking up *chikan* (delicately embroidered muslin cloth). Rickshaw riders know how to find this place. You'll find other Tunday Kabab restaurants around the city, but they're all copies.

Moti Mahal Restaurant   INDIAN **$$**
(75 MG Rd; mains ₹40-90 & ₹70-130; ⏱11am-11pm; ❄) Downstairs is perfect for breakfast or lunch, with its dosa and coffee as well as some Chinese noodle dishes. Come evening, head upstairs for more refined dining in the good-quality, low-lit AC restaurant. You could do worse here than try the Lucknow *dum aloo* (potatoes stuffed with nuts and paneer in a tomato-based sauce) followed by *kulfi faluda*.

Royal Cafe   MUGHLAI **$$**
(MG Rd; chaat ₹10-50, mains ₹100-250) Even if you don't step inside this excellent restau-rant, don't miss its exceedingly popular *chaat* (spicy snack) stand at the front where mixed

LUCKNOW'S TOP FIVE KEBABS

Kakori Kebab

Originates from Kakori, a small town outside Lucknow. Legend has it that the old and toothless Nawab of Kakori asked his royal *bawarchi* (chef) to make kebabs that would simply melt in the mouth. So these kebabs are made adding papaya as a tenderizer to raw mincemeat and a mix of spices. They are then applied to skewers and barbecued over charcoals.

Galawat Kebab

This is the mouthwatering creation that is served up in Lucknow's most famous kebab restaurant, Tunday Kabab. There it is simply referred to as a mutton kebab, and in other restaurants it is often called Tunday. Galawat is the name of the tenderizer that's used for these kebabs. Essentially, they are the same as kakori kebabs except that rather than being barbecued they are made into patties and shallow fried in oil or ghee.

Shami Kebab

Raw mincemeat is boiled with spices and black gram lentil. It is then ground on stone before being mixed with finely chopped onions, coriander leaves and green chillies. Shaped into patties, it is then shallow fried like seekh kebabs.

Pasanda Kebab

Fillets (pasanda) of beef or mutton are marinated with papaya and salt before yoghurt, spices, ginger, garlic paste and finally roasted gram flour are added. The marinated meat is then added to heated ghee and bay leaves and cooked slowly on a charcoal fire.

Nargisi Kebab

A mix of mincemeat, roasted gram flour (which acts as a binder) and spices is coated over boiled eggs and gently tied with thread. After each egg has been deep fried, the thread is removed and the egg cut lengthwise so that it resembles the *nargis* (the flower of Narcissus, or daffodil).

chaats are served in an *aloo* (potato) basket or in mini *puris*. Inside you can dine on fine Mughlai cuisine, some mouth-watering kebabs and even pizza.

Brindavan
SOUTH INDIAN **$$**

(Sapru Marg; mains ₹45-75, thalis ₹90; ⏰11am-11pm) This smart 1st-floor restaurant has good service and a modest but delicious south Indian menu including *idli, vada, uttapam, thali* and more than 20 varieties of dosa. There's a huge window along the far wall allowing you to eat overlooking the street scenes below.

Falaknuma
MUGHLAI **$$$**

(Hotel Clarks Avadh, 8 MG Rd; mains ₹210-525) Lucknow's best hotel also lays claim to having one of its best restaurants. The stylish rooftop dining room has fabulous bird's-eye views and serves up sumptuous Nawab cuisine, such as *kakori* (minced mutton) and *galawat* (minced goat) kebabs. There's a small bar area (beer from ₹200) if you just want to enjoy the views.

 Drinking & Entertainment

Indian Coffee House
CAFE

(Ashok Marg; ⏰8am-10pm) This 60-year-old branch of this Indian institution has gone fusion (Indian Coffee House purists steer clear!), meaning you can now dine on dishes from around the world (pizza, noodles etc) whilst having your morning coffee. Nearby Café Coffee Day and Barista do better coffee but at much higher prices (coffee from ₹46).

Strokes Sports Bar
BAR

(Capoor's, MG Rd; ⏰11am-11pm, till 3am Sat) With metallic decor, zebra-print chairs, ultraviolet lights and a backlit bar, this must be one of the strangest places in India to come to watch the latest cricket match on TV. Gets pretty lively at weekends.

Rabindralaya Auditorium
THEATRE

(☎2635670; Kanpur Rd) Opposite the two train stations, this auditorium hosts a variety of cultural shows, including classical music, dance and theatrical performances, all free of charge. It's often used by schools, however, so is not always open to the public. Call ahead.

Tashna Bar   BAR
(Hotel Gomti; Sapru Marg; ⊙11am-midnight) Has the usual AC bar with little atmosphere found in many hotels, but the added attraction of a beer garden on a well-tended lawn.

 Shopping

Lucknow is famous for *chikan,* an embroidered cloth worn by men and women. It is sold in a number of shops in the bazaars near Tunday Kebab, in the maze of streets in Chowk and in the small, traffic-free Janpath Market, just south of MG Rd in Hazratganj.

Sugandhco   PERFUME
(www.sugandhco.com; D-4 Janpath Market; ⊙midday-7.30pm Mon-Sat) A family business since 1850, the sweet-scented Sugandhco sells attar (pure essence oil extracted from flowers by a traditional method) in the form of women's perfume and men's cologne (from ₹20) as well as incense sticks (from ₹15).

Ram Advani Bookshop   BOOKSTORE
(📞2223511; Mayfair Bldg, MG Rd; ⊙10am-7.30pm Mon-Sat) This Lucknow institution is worth visiting just to meet the fantastically friendly and exceedingly knowledgeable 90-year-old Mr Advani, who owns the place. Be aware, though, that he takes his siestas very seriously and is rarely seen between noon and 4pm. There's a strong collection of books on Lucknow history here as well as some popular India-based contemporary literature.

ℹ️ Information

Internet Access
Cyber Cafe (Buddha Rd; per hr ₹20; ⊙8am-10pm)
Cyber City (per hr ₹25; ⊙9am-9pm) At the end of an alley off MG Rd.

Medical Services
Balrampur District Hospital (📞2224040; Hospital Rd) The emergency department is to the right as you enter the complex.

Money
Foreign-friendly ATMs are dotted around Hazratganj. There's also one at the train station and the airport.
ICICI (MG Rd, Hazratganj; ⊙8am-8pm Mon-Sat) Approximately 100m northwest of Ram

Avandi Bookshop. Changes travellers cheques (Monday to Friday only, 10am-5pm) and cash and has an ATM.

Post
Main post office (MG Rd; ⊙24hr) Grand Rajera architecture.

 Getting There & Away

Air
Amausi airport is 15km southwest of Lucknow. **Jet Airlines** (📞2434009; Amausi airport; ⊙7am-7pm) is one of a number of airlines that has offices at the airport. Daily flights include Delhi (around ₹3000), Kolkata (₹4000) and Mumbai (Bombay; ₹5000).

Bus
Long-distance buses leave from **Alambagh bus station**, 4km southwest of the town centre. Non-AC services include: Faizabad (₹91, four hours); Allahabad (₹131, 5½ hours); Gorakhpur (₹188, eight hours); Varanasi (₹197, eight hours); and Agra (₹237, nine hours). Two or three AC buses run each day to each of these destinations. They are one or two hours quicker, but cost more than twice the price. Regular local buses (₹5) run to Alambagh bus station from **Charbagh bus stand**, near the train station.

  Kaiserbagh bus stand also has hourly services to Faizabad and Gorakhpur as well as buses to Rupaidha (seven hours), a rickshaw ride away from the rarely used Nepal border crossing of Jamunaha.

Train
The two main stations, **Charbagh** and **Lucknow Junction**, are side by side. Services (above) for most major destinations leave from Charbagh, including several daily to Agra, Varanasi, Faizabad, Gorakhpur and New Delhi. Lucknow Junction handles the one daily train to Mumbai.

ℹ️ Getting Around

To/From the Airport
An autorickshaw to Amausi airport from the prepaid taxi stand outside the train station costs ₹105 and takes about 30 minutes.

Local Transport
A short cycle-rickshaw ride is ₹20. From the train station to the Residency costs about ₹40, as does the trip from Hazratganj to Bara Imambara. An autorickshaw from the train station to the Bara Imambara is about ₹80. A half-day (four-hour) autorickshaw tour covering all the main sights costs ₹255 from the prepaid taxi stand at the train station. A full-day tour is ₹510.

DESTINATION	TRAIN NO & NAME	FARE (₹)	DURATION (HR)	DEPARTURES
Agra	13237/13239 *PNBE-MTJ Exp*	161/422/574	6	11.55pm
Allahabad	14210 *Intercity Exp*	244*	4	7.30am
Faizabad	13010 *Doon Exp*	120/238/319	2½	8.35am
Gorakhpur	15708 *ASR-KIR Exp*	146/380/516	5	12.55am
Jhansi	11016 *Kushinagar Exp*	150/393/534	6½	12.40am
Kolkata (Howrah)	13006 *ASR-HWH Mail*	347/947/1302	20½	10.55am
Mumbai (CST)**	12533 *Pushpak Exp*	422/1131/1547	24	7.45pm
New Delhi	0429 *LKO NDLS*	212/564/772	9	10.50pm
Varanasi	14236 *BE-BSB Exp*	161/422/481***	7½	11.15pm

Fares are sleeper/3AC/2AC; *chair class only; **leaves from Lucknow Junction; ***sleeper/3AC/first class

Ayodhya

📞05278 / POP 49,593

With monkeys galore, the usual smattering of cows and even the odd working elephant, the relatively traffic-free streets of Ayodhya would be an intriguing place to spend some time even if it wasn't for the religious significance of the place. This is not only the birthplace of Rama, and as such one of Hinduism's seven holy cities, nor just the birthplace of four of Jainism's 24 *tirthankars* (religious teachers), this is also the site of one of modern India's most controversial religious disputes.

Ayodhya became tragically synonymous with Hindu extremism in 1992, when rioting Hindus tore down the Babri Masjid, a mosque built by the Mughals in the 15th century, which Hindus claimed stood on the site of an earlier Rama temple, marking Lord Rama's birthplace. Hindus built Ram Janam Bhumi in its place. Tit-for-tat reprisals soon followed, including reactionary riots across the country that led to more than 2000 deaths, and the problem eventually reached the High Court. Archaeological investigations were carried out at the site and, in September 2010, the Allahabad High Court ruled that the site should be split equally between three religious groups; two Hindu, one Muslim. At the time of research, the Muslim group Sunni Waqf Board, had vowed to appeal against the decision. In the meantime, security around the Ram Janam Bhumi remains incredibly tight.

The slightly larger town of Faizabad, 7km away, is the jumping-off point for Ayodhya and where you'll find more accommodation. From the Faizabad bus stand, turn left onto the main road where you'll find tempos (₹8) to Ayodhya.

◉ Sights

A 20-minute tempo ride from Faizabad brings you to Ayodhya, where you can make a walking tour of the temples.

Hanumangarhi   TEMPLE
(☉dawn-dusk) This is one of the town's most popular temples, and is the closest of the major temples here to the main road. Walk up the 76 steps to the ornate carved gateway and the fortresslike outer walls, and join the throng inside offering *prasad* (temple-blessed food).

Dashrath Bhavan   TEMPLE
(☉dawn-dusk) A further 200m up the side road from Hanumangarhi, this temple is approached through a colourful entranceway. The atmosphere inside is peaceful, with musicians playing and orange-clad sadhus reading scriptures.

Kanak Bhavan   TEMPLE
(Palace of Gold; ☉8.30-11.30am & 4.30-7pm) A few minutes' walk straight on from Dashrath Bhavan is this impressive, ancient but often rebuilt palace-cum-temple.

Ram Janam Bhumi   TEMPLE
(☉7-11am & 2-6pm) If you turn left at Dashrath Bhavan, when coming from Hanumanghari, you soon reach the highly contentious temple that marks the birthplace of Rama.

Security here is staggering. You must first show your passport then leave all belongings apart from your passport and money in nearby lockers. You are then searched several times before being accompanied through a caged corridor that leads to a spot 20m away from a makeshift tent of a shrine, which marks Rama's birthplace.

FREE **Ramkatha Museum**   MUSEUM
(☻10.30am-4.30pm Tue-Sun) A five-minute walk on the other side of the main road from the above-mentioned temples brings you to Ramkatha Museum, a large yellow-and-red building with paintings and ancient sculptures. Every evening except Monday the museum hosts free **performances** (☻6-9pm) of the Ram Lila (a dramatic re-enactment of the battle between Lord Ram and Ravan, as described in the Hindu epic, the Ramayana).

🛏 Sleeping & Eating

Hotel Shan-e-Avadh   HOTEL $
(✆223586; shane_avadh@yahoo.com; Faizabad; s ₹250-500, with AC ₹850-1400, d ₹275-600, with AC ₹950-1700; ❄) There's a huge range of rooms at this well-run establishment in Faizabad, and even the cheapest ones are neat and spacious, if a little basic. There's also a good **restaurant** (mains ₹55-150). This place is popular so try to book ahead. Turn left out of the bus stand and it's on your right after a few hundred metres.

Ramdhan Guest House   HOTEL $
(✆232791, 9415917626; Ayodhya; d ₹200-400, with AC ₹650-750; ❄) This pink hotel, with green-and-blue pastel interior, is the most fun place to stay in Ayodhya. Rooms are basic (tap-and-bucket showers, squat toilets) but are a good size and clean. There's no restaurant but friendly staff will whip up a thali (₹30 to ₹70) and some chai. From the path leading up to Hanumangarhi, walk back towards Faizabad, take the second left, walk for about 200m and it's on your left, just after Cyber Zone internet cafe.

Hotel Krishna Palace   HOTEL $$
(✆221367; www.krishnapalace.in; Faizabad; s ₹500-600, with AC ₹990-1200, d ₹700-850, with AC ₹1250-1600; ❄) If Shan-e-Avadh is full, this clean and comfortable hotel is a strong alternative in Faizabad. Also has a good **restaurant** (mains ₹70-140; ☻7am-10.30pm) and a small **bar** (beer ₹70; ☻1pm to 10.30pm). Turn left out of the bus stand, then first right, then left at the small roundabout, left again and it's on your left.

❶ Information

There's an HDFC Bank **ATM** 100m from Hotel Krishna Palace. **Cyber Zone** (per hr ₹20; ☻10am-9pm) is an internet cafe just past Hotel Shan-e-Avadh. There's another one close to Ramdhan Guest House.

❶ Getting There & Away

From Faizabad bus stand, buses run to Lucknow (₹91, three hours), Gorakhpur (₹101, five hours) and Allahabad (₹107, five hours).

Daily trains include Lucknow (13307 *Gangas-utlej Express*, sleeper/3AC/2AC ₹120/238/319, four hours, 11.13am), Varanasi (13010 *Doon Express*, sleeper/3AC/2AC ₹120/306/413, five hours, 11.15am) and Delhi (14205 *Faizabad-Delhi Express*, ₹252/678/930, 12 hours, 9.30pm).

A cycle-rickshaw from the bus stand to the train station is ₹10 to ₹20.

Allahabad

📞 0532 / POP 1,049,579

For all its importance in Hindu mythology, Indian history and modern politics, Allahabad is a surprisingly relaxed city that offers plenty in terms of sights, but little in the way of in-yer-face hassle.

Brahma, the Hindu god of creation, is believed to have landed on earth in Allahabad, or Prayag as it was originally known, and to have called it the king of all pilgrimage centres. Indeed, Sangam, a river confluence on the outskirts of the city, is the most celebrated of India's four Kumbh Mela locations. The vast riverbanks here attract tens of millions of pilgrims every six years for either the Kumbh Mela or the Ardh (Half) Mela, but every year there is a smaller Magh Mela.

Of more immediate interest to casual visitors are Allahabad's grand Raj-era buildings, its Mughal fort and tombs, and the historic legacy of the Nehru family.

Allahabad's Civil Lines is a district of broad avenues, Raj-era bungalows, hotels, restaurants and coffee shops. The Civil Lines bus stand – the main bus terminal – is also here. This area is divided from Chowk, the crowded, older part of town, by the railway line. Sangam is 4km southeast of the city centre.

◉ Sights & Activities

Sangam   SACRED SITE
This is the particularly auspicious point where two of India's holiest rivers, the Ganges and the Yamuna, meet one of Hinduism's mythical rivers, the Saraswati. All year round,

UTTAR PRADESH

Allahabad

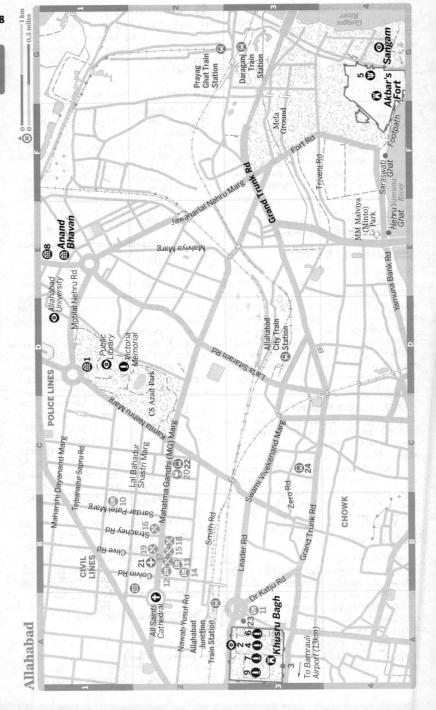

CIVIL LINES

POLICE LINES

CHOWK

Khusru Bagh

Akbar's Fort

Anand Bhavan

Sangam

All Saints Cathedral

Allahabad Junction Train Station

Allahabad City Train Station

Prayag Ghat Train Station

Daraganj Train Station

Allahabad University

Victoria Memorial

Public Library

CS Azad Park

Mela Ground

MM Malviya (Minto) Park

Nehru Yamuna Ghat

Saraswati Ghat

Footpath

Ganges River

Yamuna River

Maharshi Dayanand Marg
Tejbahadur Sapru Rd
Colvin Rd
Olive Rd
Strachey Rd
Sardar Patel Marg
Lal Bahadur Shastri Marg
Mahatma Gandhi (MG) Marg
Kamla Nehru Marg
Motilal Nehru Rd
Jawaharlal Nehru Marg
Malviya Marg
Grand Trunk Rd
Fort Rd
Triveni Rd
Yamuna Bank Rd
Smith Rd
Leader Rd
Swami Vivekenand Marg
Zero Rd
Grand Trunk Rd
Dr Katju Rd
Lata Sitaram Rd
Nawab Yusuf Rd

To Bamrauli Airport (33km)

1 km
0.5 miles

pilgrims row boats out to this holy spot, but their numbers increase dramatically during the annual **Magh Mela**, a six-week festival held between January and March, which culminates in six communal 'holy dips' (p380). Every 12 years the massive **Kumbh Mela** (p1103) takes place here, attracting millions of people, while the **Ardh Mela** (Half Mela) is held here every six years.

In the early 1950s, 350 pilgrims were killed in a stampede to the soul-cleansing water (an incident re-created vividly in Vikram Seth's immense novel *A Suitable Boy*). The last Ardh Mela, in 2007, attracted more than 70 million people – the largest-ever human gathering. The next Kumbh Mela will take place in 2013. Expect a big one.

Old boat hands will row you out to the sacred confluence for around ₹50 per person, or ₹250–500 per boat.

Around the corner from Sangam (skirt the riverbank around the front of Akbar's Fort) are the Saraswati and Nehru Ghats, home to a nightly *aarti* (an auspicious lighting of lamps/candles).

Akbar's Fort & Patalpuri Temple   FORT
Built by the Mughal Emperor Akbar, this 16th-century fort on the northern bank of the Yamuna has massive walls with three gateways flanked by towers. Most of it is occupied by the Indian army and cannot be visited, but a small door in the eastern wall by Sangam leads to one part you can enter, the underground Patalpuri temple (admission by donation; ⊙7am-5pm). This unique temple is crowded with all sorts of idols – pick up some coins from the change dealers outside so you can leave small offerings as you go. You may be pressured into giving ₹100 at some shrines. A few coins are perfectly acceptable.

Outside the temple – though its roots can be seen beneath ground – is the Undying Banyan Tree from which pilgrims used to leap to their deaths, believing it would liberate them from the cycle of rebirth.

Khusru Bagh   PARK
This intriguing park, surrounded by huge walls, contains four highly impressive Mughal tombs (admission free; ⊙dawn-dusk). One is that of Prince Khusru, the eldest son of Emperor Jehangir, who tried to assassinate his father but was blinded and imprisoned, finally dying in 1622. If Khusru's coup had succeeded, his brother, Shah Jahan, would not have become emperor and the Taj Mahal would not exist.

A second tomb belongs to Shah Begum, Khusru's mother (Jehangir's first wife), who committed suicide in 1603 with an opium overdose because of the ongoing feud be-

ℹ️ DIP DATES

The following are the auspicious bathing dates for upcoming mela to be held at Sangam in Allahabad. The 2013 event will be a full-blown Kumbh Mela (see p1103).

2012	2013	2014	2015
9 Jan	14 Jan	14 Jan	5 Jan
14 Jan	27 Jan	16 Jan	14 Jan
23 Jan	10 Feb	30 Jan	20 Jan
28 Jan	15 Feb	4 Feb	24 Jan
7 Feb	25 Feb	14 Feb	3 Feb
20 Feb	10 Mar	28 Feb	17 Feb

tween her son and his father. Between these two, a third, particularly attractive tomb was constructed by **Nesa Begum**, Khusru's sister, although was never actually used as a tomb. A smaller structure, called **Tamolon's Tomb**, stands to the west of the others, but its origin is unknown.

Anand Bhavan MUSEUM
(Indian/foreigner ₹10/50; ⏱9.30am-5pm Tue-Sun) This picturesque two-storey building is a shrine to the Nehru family, which has produced five generations of leading politicians from Motilal Nehru to the latest political figure, Rahul Gandhi. This stately home is where Mahatma Gandhi, Jawaharlal Nehru and others successfully planned the overthrow of the British Raj. It is full of books, personal effects and photos from those stirring times. Indira Gandhi was married here in 1942.

Allahabad Museum MUSEUM
(Indian/foreigner ₹5/100; Kamla Nehru Marg; ⏱10.30am-4.45pm Tue-Sun) This extensive museum in the grounds of a pleasant park has archaeological and Nehru family items, modern paintings, miniatures and ancient sculptures.

🛏️ Sleeping

Royal Hotel HOTEL $
(☎2427201; Nawab Yusuf Rd; r ₹150-350) This wonderful old building, near the train station, used to be royal stables but was converted into a hotel by the King of Kalakankar, a former princely state, after he was refused entry into a British-run hotel nearby.

It's basic and very run down, but has bags of character. The rooms (with 6m-high ceilings) and their bathrooms, are absolutely enormous. Has 24-hour checkout.

Hotel Prayag HOTEL $
(☎2656416; Noorullah Rd; s ₹250-400, d ₹350-450, with AC ₹800-900; ❄️@) South of the train station, this large, well-equipped, well-run place with an internet cafe and ATM has a wide variety of rooms, so look before you leap into one. It's pretty old-fashioned and rooms are basic, especially the non-AC ones. Note: the shared bathrooms are tap-and-bucket jobs.

Hotel Tepso HOTEL $$
(☎2561408; MG Marg; dm ₹250, s/d ₹700/900; ❄️) Small clean rooms arranged around a neat little patio courtyard are on the pricey side, but come with TV and AC. The 12-bed dorm also has its own bathroom. There's a small children's playground in the front garden beside the spotless Jade Garden Restaurant. Has 24-hour checkout.

Grand Continental HOTEL $$$
(☎2260631; www.birhotel.com; Sardar Patel Marg; s ₹3000-4500, d ₹4000-5500, ste ₹6000-8000; ❄️@🛜🏊) Rooms are a bit old fashioned, with carpeted floors and nonmatching furniture, but they're larger than other top-end choices in town, and staying here means you can use the delightful swimming pool, housed in a beautiful open-air marble courtyard. There's also a good quality restaurant and a bar where evening *ghazal* performances are held. Wi-fi is free.

Hotel Valentines HOTEL $$
(☎2560030; 7/3/2b Clive Rd, off MG Marg; d ₹1500-1900; ❄️) Not as romantic as the name suggests, but smart, comfortable rooms have TV, AC, carpeted floors and big bathrooms with towels and toiletries provided.

🍴 Eating

Allahabadians have a sweet tooth and MG Marg is lined with shops selling ice creams, shakes, cakes and sweets. Outdoor eating is all the rage, with some stalls along MG Marg setting up tables and chairs on the footpath in the evening.

TOP CHOICE **Indian Coffee House** CAFE $
(MG Marg; coffee from ₹13; mains ₹20-32; ⏱8am-9pm) This large, airy 50-year-old coffee hall is a top choice for breakfast, with waiters

in fan-tailed headgear serving up delicious south Indian fare – dosa, *idli, uttapam* – as well as eggs, omelettes and toast.

Shahenshah INDIAN $
(MG Marg; mains ₹20-80; ⏰11am-10.30pm) Watch young chefs frying up their creations from a couple of stalls set around a half open-air seating area with plastic tables and chairs and a high corrugated iron roof. This is no-nonsense, cheap eating, but it's popular with the locals so there's a nice atmosphere. The menu includes *uttapam, paratha* (flaky bread made with ghee and cooked on a hotplate), a few Chinese dishes, pizza and some absolutely cracking dosa. The fruit beer isn't alcoholic.

Aao Ji Haryana Dhaba INDIAN $
(MG Marg; mains ₹20-80; ⏰9am-11pm) This airy fan-cooled shack is run by friendly staff and serves up great-value south Indian breakfasts as well as thalis (₹40-55) and north Indian curries.

El Chico MULTICUISINE $$
(MG Marg; mains ₹100-240; ⏰noon-3pm & 7.30-11pm; ❄) A swish restaurant with a reliable Indian, Chinese and continental menu, including fish dishes and sizzlers. Next door, **El Chico Takeaway** (snacks ₹12-60; ⏰9am-10.30pm) tempts diners with ice creams, cakes, cookies and savoury snacks.

Kamdhenu Sweets SWEETS $
(MG Marg; snacks ₹5-25; ⏰9am-10pm) Very popular snack shop selling delicious homebaked sweets (from ₹240 per box) as well as cakes, samosas, sandwiches and ice cream (from ₹25).

Jade Garden INDIAN $$
(Hotel Tepso, MG Marg; mains ₹100-250; ⏰11am-11pm; ❄) Spotless hotel restaurant with attentive black-tie staff serving Indian, Chinese, nonveg sizzlers, salads and tandoori.

 Drinking

Patiyala Peg Bar BAR
(Grand Continental hotel, Sardar Patel Marg) Has live *ghazal* music nightly from 7.30pm.

Rahi Ilawart Tourist Bungalow BAR
(⏰11am-11pm)

 Information

ATMs dot the Civil Lines area.

Apollo Clinic (☑3290507; MG Marg; ⏰8am-8pm) A modern private medical facility with 24-hour pharmacy.

Cyber Cafe (per hr ₹20; ⏰9am-9pm) Behind Shahenshah restaurant.

Post office (Sarojini Naidu Marg; ⏰9am-5pm Mon-Sat)

UP Tourism (☑2408873; rtoalld_upt@yahoo.co.in; 35 MG Marg; ⏰10am-5pm Mon-Sat) At the Rahi Ilawart Tourist Bungalow. Very helpful.

 Getting There & Away

Air
Bamrauli airport is 15km west of Allahabad. **Air India** (☑2581370; ⏰incoming flights), at the airport, has daily flights to Delhi from ₹4500, except on Sunday. An autorickshaw to the airport costs ₹150 to ₹200, a taxi about ₹350.

Bus
From the **Civil Lines bus stand** regular buses run to Varanasi (₹85, three hours), Lucknow (₹130, five hours), Faizabad (₹110, five hours) and Gorakhpur (₹180, eight hours). More comfortable AC buses are much less frequent and about twice the price. To get to Delhi or Agra, change in Lucknow, or take a train.

For hourly buses to Chitrakut (₹82, four hours, 3am to 9pm), head to **Zero Road bus stand**.

Train
Allahabad Junction is the main station. A few daily trains run to Lucknow, Varanasi, Delhi, Agra and Kolkata. Frequent trains also run to Satna from where you can catch buses to Khajuraho. Also see p382.

 **Getting Around**

Cycle-rickshaws (₹20 for a short trip) are plentiful. The train station is your best bet for autos. A return auto to Sangam should cost around ₹150. Consider hiring one for half a day (₹300, four hours) to take in more of the sights. Vikrams (large shared autos) hang about on the south side of the train station. Destinations include Zero Road Bus Stand (₹5) and Sangam (₹10).

Chitrakut
☑05198 / POP 22,294
Known as a mini Varanasi because of its many temples and ghats, this small, peaceful town on the banks of the River Mandakini is the stuff of Hindu legends. It is here that Hinduism's principal trinity – Brahma, Vishnu and Shiva – took on their incarnations. It is also the place where Lord Rama is believed to have spent 11½ years of his 14-year exile after being banished from his birthplace in Ayodhya at the behest of a jealous stepmother.

HANDY TRAINS FROM ALLAHABAD

DESTINATION	TRAIN NO & NAME	FARE (₹)	DURATION (HR)	DEPARTURES
Agra	12403 ALD MTJ Exp	220/561/755	7½	11.30pm
Kolkata (Howrah)	12312 Kalka Mail	318/841/1142	14	5.30pm
Lucknow	14209 ALD-LKO Intercity	244*	4½	3.20pm
New Delhi	12559 Shiv Ganga Exp	277/723/979	9	10.30pm
Satna	13201 Rajendra-Nagar Exp	120/287/387	4½	8.25am
Varanasi	15017 Gorakhpur Exp	120/243/326	4	8.35am

Fares are sleeper/3AC/2AC; *AC chair only

Today Chitrakut attracts throngs of pilgrims, giving the area a strong religious quality, particularly by Ram Ghat, the town's centre of activity, and at the holy hill of Kamadgiri, 2km away.

Dozens, sometimes hundreds, of devotees descend onto Ram Ghat to take holy dips at dawn before returning at the end of the day for the evening *aarti*. **Rowboats** wait here to take you across to the opposite bank (₹5), which is actually in Madhya Pradesh, or to scenic spots along the river. The 2km-trip to the Glass Temple (₹100 return), a building covered in religious mosaics made with thousands of pieces of coloured glass, is popular. During the day, many people make their way to Kamadgiri (₹5 by tempo), a hill revered as the holy embodiment of Lord Rama. A 5km-circuit (90 minutes) around the base of the hill takes you past prostrating pilgrims, innumerable monkeys and temples galore.

The most enjoyable place to stay in Chitrakut is Pitra Smiviti Vishramgrah (☏9450223214; Ram Ghat; r ₹350, without bathroom ₹200). Rooms built just in front of Bada Math, a 300-year-old red-stone palace, are very basic, but lead out onto a huge shared balcony overlooking Ram Ghat. Look for the word 'Lodge' painted on the balcony. There are more comfortable rooms at UP Tourist Bungalow (☏224219; dm ₹125-300, s/d/tr with AC ₹750/800/950; ❄), which also has an OK restaurant (mains ₹40-70; ☺6am-midnight).

Shared minivans and tempos ply the 10km route from the train station to Ram Ghat (₹8), passing the bus stand (2km from the train station) and the UP Tourist Bungalow (1km before Ram Ghat).

With the exception of buses to Allahabad (₹82, four hours), which run regularly all day,

buses in Chitrakut are notoriously unreliable. There *should* be a couple a day to both Varanasi (₹160, seven hours) and Khajuraho (₹76, four hours), leaving at around midday, but they don't always materialise. For Varanasi, you're better off changing in Allahabad. For Khajuraho, you will probably have to change once, twice or even three times, via either Satna or Banda, Mahoba and Chhatarpur.

Trains tend to pass through Chitrakut at stupid o'clock. Ones you may consider anyway are: Agra (12189 *Mahakaushal Exp* sleeper/3AC/2AC ₹226/577/780, nine hours, 11.24pm), Varanasi (11107 *Bundelkhand Exp*, ₹143/391/504, seven hours, 3.52am) and Khajuraho (21108 *BSB-KURJ Link E*, ₹120/297/400, four hours, 1.03am Tuesday, Thursday and Sunday).

Jhansi

☏0510 / POP 420,665

Jhansi is mostly used by travellers on their way to Orchha, Gwalior or Khajuraho, all in Madhya Pradesh. The fort here is of some interest, but otherwise there's little reason to linger.

History

When the raja here died in 1853, his widow and successor, Rani Lakshmibai, was forcibly retired by the British (a controversial law allowed them to take over any princely state under their patronage if the ruler died without a male heir). During the First War of Independence four years later, Rani Lakshmibai was at the forefront of Jhansi's rebellion. The British contingent here was massacred, but the following year the British retook Jhansi. The rani fled to Gwalior. In a fatal last stand she rode out against the

British disguised as a man and subsequently became a heroine of Indian Independence.

◎ Sights

Jhansi Fort   HISTORIC BUILDING
(Indian/foreigner ₹5/100, video ₹25; ◷dawn-dusk) Built in 1613 by Maharaja Bir Singh Deo of Orchha, Jhansi Fort still bears signs of the blood-letting that took place within its double walls and moat, once inhabited by crocodiles. These days its shaded lawns make for pleasant strolls and there are some good views of the city and surrounding rocky outcrops.

Near the flag turret is a parapet, over which the fleeing Rani Lakshmibai, with her adopted son mounted behind her, rode her horse. The horse is said to have died, but the story still seems incredible looking at the steep, rocky slope 15m below.

⌂ Sleeping & Eating

There are a number of cheap places around the bus station where you can grab a snack on the run.

Hotel Samrat   HOTEL $
(◢2444943; Elite Rd; s/d from ₹400/500, with AC from ₹775/875; ❄) This well-run hotel, walking distance from the train station, has decent rooms, all with TV and private bathroom, although the cheaper ones have squat toilets. Turn left out of the station then right at the roundabout.

Red Tomato   INDIAN $$
(Hotel Samrat; Elite Rd; mains ₹50-150; ◷7am-10.30pm; ❄) This smart, clean restaurant at Hotel Samrat has a good choice of breakfasts plus curries and kebabs.

❶ Information

Madhya Pradesh Tourism (◢2442622; ◷10am-6pm) On Platform 1 at the train station; has leaflets and mini guides to the area's popular destinations.

Net Blast (per hr ₹20; ◷9am-9pm) Internet cafe 200m from Hotel Samrat. Left out of train station, left at roundabout, on right.

State Bank of India (Elite Rd; ◷10am-4pm Mon-Fri, 10am-1pm Sat) Changes money and travellers cheques; there's an ATM outside the train station.

❶ Getting There & Away

Bus

Buses for Khajuraho leave from the bus stand (₹120, five to six hours) at 6am, 7am, 8am, 9am, 11am, noon and 2pm.

Regular buses go to Gwalior (₹70, three hours, 9am-10pm).

Train

Several daily trains run to Gwalior, Agra and Delhi. In addition to the middle-of-the-night, thrice-weekly fast train to Khajuraho, there is also one daily slow train that leaves at 7.20am, takes around five hours and costs ₹30 for a 'general' ticket. See p383.

❶ Getting Around

Tempos run all the main routes in Jhansi. Prices include: train station to bus station ₹8; train station to Hotel Samrat ₹2; bus station to Jhansi Fort ₹5; and bus station to Orchha ₹10. Autos cost up to 10 times more.

Varanasi

◢0542 / POP 1.2 MILLION

Brace yourself. You're about to enter one of the most blindingly colourful, unrelentingly chaotic and unapologetically indiscreet places on earth. Varanasi takes no prisoners. But if you're ready for it, this may just turn out to be your favourite stop of all.

HANDY TRAINS FROM JHANSI

DESTINATION	TRAIN NO & NAME	FARE (₹)	DURATION (HR)	DEPARTURE
Agra	12137 *Punjab Mail*	147/355/471	3½	2.30pm
Delhi	12615 *Grand Trunk Exp*	204/519/697	6½	11.40pm
Gwalior	12137 *Punjab Mail*	140/240/309	1½	2.30pm
Mumbai	12138 *Punjab Mail*	379/1010/1378	19	12.35pm
Varanasi	11107 *Bundelkhand Exp*	229/615/842	12½	10.30pm

Fares are sleeper/3AC/2AC

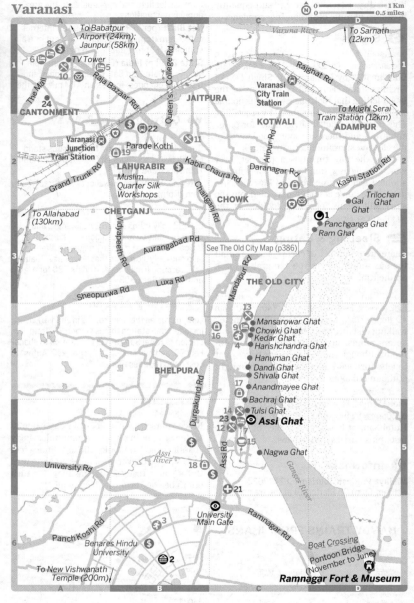

Also known at various times in history as Kashi (City of Life) and Benares, this is one of the world's oldest continually inhabited cities and is regarded as one of Hinduism's seven holy cities. Pilgrims come to the ghats lining the River Ganges here to wash away a life-time of sins in the sacred waters or to cremate their loved ones. It's a particularly auspicious place to die, since expiring here offers moksha (liberation from the cycle of birth and death), making Varanasi the beating heart of the Hindu universe. Most visitors agree it's a magical place, but it's not for the faint-hearted. Here the most intimate rituals of life and death take place in public and the sights, sounds and smells in and around the ghats – not to mention the almost constant attention from touts – can be overwhelming. Persevere. Varanasi is unique, and a walk along the ghats or a boat ride on the river will live long in the memory.

The old city of Varanasi is situated along the western bank of the Ganges and extends back from the riverbank ghats in a labyrinth of alleys called *galis* that are too narrow for traffic. They can be disorienting, but the popular hotels and restaurants are usually signposted and, however lost you become, you will eventually end up at a ghat and get your bearings. You can walk all the way along the ghats, apart from during and immediately after the monsoon, when the river level is too high.

Most places of interest, and much of the accommodation, are in the old city. Behind the station is the peaceful Cantonment area, home to most of the top-end hotels.

History

Thought to date back to around 1200 BC, Varanasi really rose to prominence in the 8th century AD, when Shankaracharya, a reformer of Hinduism, established Shiva worship as the principal sect. The Afghans destroyed Varanasi around AD 1300, after laying waste to nearby Sarnath, but the fanatical Mughal emperor Aurangzeb was the most destructive, looting and destroying almost all of the temples. The old city of Varanasi may look antique, but few buildings are more than a couple of hundred years old.

◉ Sights

Ghats   GHATS

Spiritually enlightening and fantastically photogenic, Varanasi is at its brilliant best by the ghats, the long stretch of steps leading down to the water on the western bank of the Ganges. Most are used for bathing but there are also several 'burning ghats' where bodies are cremated in public. The main one is

Manikarnika: you'll often see funeral processions threading their way through the backstreets to this ghat. The best time to visit the ghats is at dawn when the river is bathed in a mellow light as pilgrims come to perform *puja* (literally 'respect'; offering or prayers) to the rising sun, and at sunset when the main *ganga aarti* (river worship ceremony) takes place at Dasaswamedh Ghat.

About 80 ghats border the river, but the main group extends from Assi Ghat, near the university, northwards to Raj Ghat, near the road and rail bridge.

A boat trip along the river provides the perfect introduction, although for most of the year the water level is low enough for you to walk freely along the whole length of the ghats. It's a world-class 'people-watching' stroll as you mingle with the fascinating mixture of people who come to the Ganges not only for a ritual bath but also to wash clothes, do yoga, offer blessings, sell flowers, get a massage, play cricket, wash their buffaloes, improve their karma by giving to beggars or simply hang around.

Southern Stretch

Assi Ghat (Map p384), the furthest south of the main ghats, and one of the biggest, is particularly important as the River Assi meets the Ganges near here and pilgrims come to worship a Shiva lingam (phallic image of Shi-

va) beneath a peepul tree. Evenings are particularly lively, as the ghat's vast concreted area fills up with hawkers and entertainers. It's a popular starting point for boat trips and there are some excellent hotels here.

Nearby **Tulsi Ghat** (Map p384), named after a 16th-century Hindu poet, has fallen down towards the river but in the month of Kartika (October/November) a festival devoted to Krishna is celebrated here. Next along, **Bachraj Ghat** (Map p384) has three Jain temples. A small Shiva temple and a 19th-century mansion built by Nepali royalty, sit back from **Shivala Ghat** (Map p384), built by the local maharaja of Benares. The **Dandi Ghat** (Map p384) is used by ascetics known as Dandi Panths, and nearby is the very popular **Hanuman Ghat** (Map p384).

Harishchandra Ghat (Map p384) is a cremation ghat – smaller and secondary in importance to Manikarnika, but one of the oldest ghats in Varanasi. Above it, **Kedar Ghat** (Map p384) has a shrine popular with Bengalis and South Indians. **Mansarowar Ghat** was built by Raja Man Singh of Amber and named after the Tibetan lake at the foot of Mt Kailash, Shiva's Himalayan home.

Old City Stretch

Varanasi's liveliest and most colourful ghat is **Dasaswamedh Ghat** (Map p386), easily

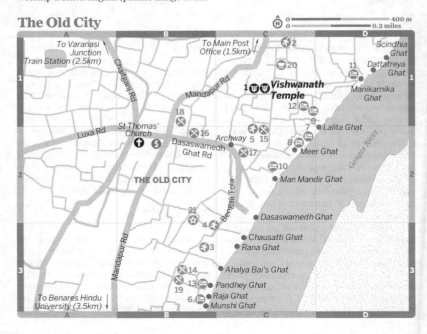

The Old City

reached at the end of the main road from Godaulia Crossing. The name indicates that Brahma sacrificed *(medh)* 10 *(das)* horses *(aswa)* here. In spite of the oppressive boat owners, flower sellers and touts trying to drag you off to a silk shop, it's a wonderful place to linger and people-watch while soaking up the atmosphere. Every evening at 7pm an elaborate *ganga aarti* ceremony with *puja,* fire and dance is staged here.

Just south of here is **Someswar Ghat** (Lord of the Moon Ghat), said to be able to heal diseases. The **Munshi Ghat** (Map p386) is very photogenic, while **Ahalya Bai's Ghat** (Map p386) is named after the female Maratha ruler of Indore.

Just north of Dasaswamedh Ghat, Raja Man Singh's **Man Mandir Ghat** (Map p386) was built in 1600, but was poorly restored in the 19th century. The northern corner of the ghat has a fine stone balcony. Nearby **Meer Ghat** (Map p386) leads to a Nepali temple, which has erotic sculptures.

Manikarnika Ghat (Map p386), the main burning ghat, is the most auspicious place for a Hindu to be cremated. Dead bodies are handled by outcasts known as *doms,* and are carried through the alleyways of the old city to the holy Ganges on a bamboo stretcher swathed in cloth. The corpse is doused in the Ganges prior to cremation. Huge piles of firewood are stacked along the top of the ghat; every log is carefully weighed on giant scales so that the price of cremation can be calculated. Each type of wood has its own price, sandalwood being the most expensive. There is an art to using just enough wood to completely incinerate a corpse.

You can watch cremations but always show reverence by behaving respectfully. Photography is strictly prohibited.

You're almost guaranteed to be led by a priest, or more likely a guide, to the upper floor of a nearby building from where you can watch cremations taking place, and then asked for a donation (in dollars) towards the cost of wood. If you don't want to make a donation, don't follow them.

Above the steps here is a tank known as the **Manikarnika Well**. Parvati is said to have dropped her earring here and Shiva dug the tank to recover it, filling the depression with his sweat. The **Charanpaduka**, a slab of stone between the well and the ghat, bears footprints made by Vishnu. Privileged VIPs are cremated at the Charanpaduka, which also has a temple dedicated to Ganesh.

Dattatreya Ghat (Map p386) bears the footprint of the Brahmin saint of that name in a small temple nearby. **Scindhia Ghat** (Map p386) was originally built in 1830, but was so huge and magnificent that it collapsed into the river and had to be rebuilt.

Northern Stretch

Continuing north from Scindhia Ghat, you soon reach **Ram Ghat** (Map p384), which

The Old City

THE VARANASI SHAKEDOWN

If you thought the touts and rickshaw-wallahs were annoying in Agra, wait till you get to Varanasi. The attention here, particularly around the ghats and the Old City, is incredible: you will have to put up with persistent offers from touts and drivers of 'cheapest and best' boat trips, guides, tour operators, travel agents, silk shops and money changers (to name a few). Take it in good humour but politely refuse. Don't take photos at the 'burning' ghats and resist offers to 'follow me for a better view', where you'll be pressured for money and possibly be placed in an uncomfortable situation.

was built by a maharaja of Jaipur. Just beyond it **Panchganga Ghat** (Map p384), as its name indicates, is where five rivers are supposed to meet. Dominating the ghat is Aurangzeb's smaller mosque, also known as the **Alamgir Mosque** (Map p384), which he built on the site of a large Vishnu temple. **Gai Ghat** (Map p384) has a figure of a cow made of stone. **Trilochan Ghat** (Map p384) has two turrets emerging from the river, and the water between them is especially holy. Just north of here, **Raj Ghat** was the ferry pier until the road and rail bridge was completed.

Vishwanath Temple   HINDU TEMPLE

(Golden Temple; Map p386) There are temples at almost every turn in Varanasi, but this is the most famous of the lot. It is dedicated to Vishveswara – Shiva as lord of the universe. The current temple was built in 1776 by Ahalya Bai of Indore; the 800kg of gold plating on the tower and dome was supplied by Maharaja Ranjit Singh of Lahore 50 years later.

The area is full of soldiers because of security issues and communal tensions. Bags, cameras and mobile phones must be deposited in lockers (₹25-50) before you enter the alleyway it's in. Non-Hindus are not allowed inside the temple itself, although this is not always strictly enforced.

On the northern side of Vishwanath Temple is the **Gyan Kupor Well** (Well of Knowledge; Map p386). The faithful believe drinking its water leads to a higher spiritual plane, though they are prevented from doing so by a strong security screen. Non-Hindus are also not allowed to enter here, and here the rule is enforced more strictly.

Benares Hindu University   HISTORIC SITE

(BHU; Map p384; www.bhu.ac.in) Long regarded as a centre of learning, Varanasi's tradition of top-quality education continues today at Benares Hindu University, established in 1916. The wide tree-lined streets and parkland of the 5-sq-km campus offer a peaceful atmosphere a world away from the city outside. On campus is **Bharat Kala Bhavan** (Map p384; ☏316337; Indian/foreigner ₹10/100, camera ₹50; ⊙10.30am-4.30pm Mon-Sat, 7.30am-1pm May-Jun), a roomy museum with a wonderful collection of miniature paintings, as well as 12th-century palm-leaf manuscripts, sculptures and local history displays.

The attractive **New Vishwanath Temple** (off Map p384; ⊙4am-noon & 1-9pm), unlike most temples in Varanasi, is open to all, irrespective of religion.

Ramnagar Fort & Museum   MUSEUM

(Map p384; ☏2339322; museum admission ₹7; ⊙9am-noon & 2-5.30pm) This crumbling but impressive 17th-century fort and palace, on the eastern bank of the Ganges, is a beautiful place to watch the sun set over the river. It also houses an eccentric museum. There are vintage American cars, jewel-encrusted sedan chairs, a superb weaponry section and an extremely unusual astrological clock. The current maharaja, Anant Narayan Singh – still known in these parts as the Maharaja of Benares despite such royal titles being officially abolished in 1971 – continues his family tradition of attending the annual month-long **Ram Lila drama festival** (p346) held in the streets behind the fort.

Boats operate a shuttle service across the river (₹10 return, 10 minutes) between 5am and 8pm, but from November to June you can also cross on the somewhat unsteady pontoon bridge. A boat all the way back to Dasaswamedh Ghat is ₹200-300.

🏃 Activities

Nonguests can use the outdoor **swimming pools** (Map p384) at Hotel Surya (₹200), Hotel Clarks Varanasi (₹300) and Gateway Hotel Ganges (₹350).

River Trips   BOATING

A dawn rowing boat ride along the Ganges is a quintessential Varanasi experience. The early morning light is particularly inspiring, and all the colour and clamour of pilgrims bathing and performing *puja* unfolds before you. An hour-long trip south from Dasaswamedh Ghat to Harishchandra Ghat and back is popular, but be prepared to see a burning corpse at Harishchandra. Early evening is also a good time to be on the river, when you can light a lotus flower candle (₹10) and set it adrift on the water before watching the nightly *ganga aarti* ceremony (7pm) at Dasaswamedh Ghat directly from the boat.

Boats, available at most ghats, cost about ₹100 per person per hour, but be prepared for some hard bargaining.

Another trip worth considering is the lazy one-hour motorboat trip to Ramnagar Fort, which should cost around ₹100 per person from Dasaswamedh Ghat.

Many guesthouses offer boat trips, although they're more expensive than dealing with the boatmen directly.

Hotel Surya MASSAGE
(Map p384; ☑2508465; www.hotelsuryavns.com; The Mall; massage from ₹300; ⊙8am-8pm) Offers perhaps the best-value massage treatments in Varanasi.

Learn for Life Society VOLUNTEERING
(Map p386; ☑2403566, 6450232; www.learn-for-life.net) This small charity, contacted through the nearby Brown Bread Bakery, has established a small school for disadvantaged children, and travellers are welcome to turn up and help out. The charity also runs a women's empowerment group, offering fairly paid work to local women, some of whom are mothers of the school's students. The women make produce such as jams and pickles, which travellers can buy from Brown Bread Bakery. See the website for more details.

Saraswati Education Center VOLUNTEERING
(Map p386; ☑9839105112; www.varanasivolunteer .blogspot.com; D.32/22 Hathiphatak, Bengali Tola Lane) This reader-recommended NGO runs a school for around 40 to 50 children whose families don't have the money to provide them with a proper education. The school runs classes in English, Maths and Science as well as activities such as music, art and games. Volunteers are welcomed for help with teaching and supervising.

🔁 Courses

Beware of 'fake' yoga teachers who are mainly interested in hands-on lessons with young females.

Yoga Training Centre YOGA
(Map p386; ☑9919857895; www.yogatrainingcentre .com, yoga_sunil@hotmail.com; Sakarkand Gali; 2hr class ₹200; ⊙8am, 10am & 4pm) Yoga master Sunil Kumar runs classes three times a day on the 3rd floor of a small backstreet building near Meer Ghat. He teaches an integrated blend of hatha, Iyengar, pranayama and ashtanga, and serious students can continue on certificate and diploma courses. This place is highly recommended by travellers.

Ankit Music House INDIAN MUSIC
(Map p386; ☑9336567134; ankitmusichouse@hot mail.com; 5/15 Sakarkand Gali; per hr ₹150 to ₹250) In the same building as the Yoga Training Centre, in the alleys near Meer Ghat, this friendly place offers classical music tuition. Instructors Bablu and Vijay can also give advice on buying musical instruments.

Bhasha Bharati Language Institute LANGUAGE
(Map p386; ☑9839076805; www.bhashabharati. com; 19/8 Thatheri Bazaar, Chowk; per hr ₹300) This long-running language institute, housed in a charming old courtyard, offers small classes. You must book at least a one-week block of classes including at least two hours per day. All-inclusive family homestays – staying in the courtyard building where classes are taught, and including six hours of tuition a day – can be arranged (from ₹13500). Book courses two weeks in advance.

Pragati Hindi LANGUAGE
(Map p384; (☑9335376488; pragatihindi@yahoo. com; B-7/176 Kedar Ghat) Readers recommend

---

DON'T MISS

VARANASI'S TOP FIVE GHATS

» **Dasaswamedh Ghat** (p386) Especially for the evening *ganga aarti* ceremony

» **Manikarnika Ghat** (p387)– Varanasi's primary cremation ghat

» **Assi Ghat** (p386) Large and lively, especially early evening

» **Harishchandra Ghat** (p386) Another prominent cremation ghat

» **Panchganga Ghat** (p388) Dominated by Alamgir Mosque

the flexibility of the one-to-one classes taught here by the amiable Rajeswar Mukherjee (Raju). Private classes start from ₹200 per hour. Call ahead, or just drop in, to meet Raju and arrange a schedule. Walk up the lane opposite Kedar Ghat and take the first left.

International Music Centre Ashram   INDIAN MUSIC
(Map p386; ☑2452303; keshavaraonayak@hotmail.com; per hr ₹200) This family-run centre is hidden in the tangle of backstreets off Bengali Tola. It offers sitar, tabla, flute and classical dance tuition, and performances are held every Saturday and Wednesday evening at 8pm (₹100). There's a small, easy-to-miss sign on Bengali Tola directing you here. If you can't find it, there are loads of **musical-instrument shops** on Bengali Tola (Map p386), many of which offer tuition.

Yoga Education Training Society   YOGA
(www.varanasiindiango.jimdo.com; 2hr class ₹150-300) Founder of Saraswati Education Center, Somit Dutta, also runs this society.

International Centre   VARIOUS
(Map p384; ☑2368130; trraobhu@hotmail.com; ⊙10am-5pm Mon-Fri) If you're interested in studying at Benares Hindu University, contact this centre. Courses on offer include Hindi, Sanskrit, yoga, ayurveda studies, and weaving and handicraft.

☞ Tours

UP Tourism Office   CITY TOUR
(☑2506670; Varanasi Junction train station; half-/full day tour per person ₹900/1400; ⊙7am-7pm) If time is short, UP Tourism can arrange guided tours by taxi of the major sites, including a 5.30am boat ride and an afternoon trip to Sarnath.

🛏 Sleeping

The majority of Varanasi's budget hotels – and some midrange gems – are concentrated in the most interesting part of the city – the tangle of narrow streets back from the ghats along the River Ganges. There's a concentration around Assi Ghat, while others are in the crazy, bustling northern stretch of alleys between Scindhia and Meer Ghat, part of an area we refer to as the Old City.

Varanasi has an active paying-guest house scheme with more than 100 family homes available for accommodation from ₹200 to ₹2000 a night. UP Tourism has a full list.

OLD CITY AREA

TOP CHOICE Ganpati Guesthouse   GUESTHOUSE $
(Map p386; ☑2390059; www.ganpatiguesthouse.com; Meer Ghat; r ₹700-1000; r without bathroom ₹350-550, @🛜) Loads more character than next-door Hotel Alka, which is also a great choice, this old red-brick building has a pleasant, shaded, wi-fi-enabled courtyard as well as plenty of balcony space dotted around offering fine river views. Nicely painted rooms are colourful and clean and the ones facing out onto the Ganges (₹550) are lovely and spacious.

Hotel Alka   GUESTHOUSE $
(Map p386; ☑2401681; www.hotelalkavns.com; Meer Ghat; r ₹450-750, with AC ₹800-1700;❉@) An excellent ghat-side option, Alka has pretty much spotless rooms that open onto, or overlook a large, plant-filled courtyard. In the far corner, a terrace juts out over Meer Ghat for one of the best views in all of Varanasi, a view shared from the balconies of the pricier rooms.

Uma Guesthouse   GUESTHOUSE $
(Map p386; ☑2403566, 9628698015; brown breadbakery@yahoo.com; d ₹300, s/d without bathroom ₹150/250,) Part of the Learn for Life Society run by the excellent Brown Bread Bakery, this homely place has basic but clean rooms that are looked after by some of the women involved with the charity. A percentage of your bill goes to the charity that runs the school behind the guesthouse. Bookings should be made through the bakery, where you can also ask about volunteering or donating.

Shanti Guest House   GUESTHOUSE $
(Map p386; ☑2392568; varanasishanti@yahoo.com; Manikarnika Ghat; d ₹200-350, with AC from ₹500; ❉@🛜) Big, bold and bright yellow, Shanti is as popular as ever. Rooms are basic – often nothing more than a bed in a stone-floor room – but this place is well looked after (even the communal bathrooms are clean). In any case, it's the very high, 24-hour rooftop restaurant with pool table and fabulous views of the Ganges that really pulls in the punters. Wi-fi isn't free.

Kedareswar   HOTEL $$
(Map p384; ☑2455568; www.kedareswarguesthouse.com; Chowki Ghat; d ₹600, with AC ₹1000-1600;❉) Housed in a brightly painted, aquamarine green building, this friendly place has small but immaculate rooms with spar-

kling bathrooms. There's only one cheaper non-AC room, so it might be worth phoning ahead. Chowki Ghat is right beside Kedar Ghat.

Vishnu Rest House
GUESTHOUSE $

(Map p386; ☑2455238; Pandhey Ghat; r from ₹200) Accessed through a small courtyard with family homes coming off it, or directly from Pandhey Ghat itself, this simple guesthouse is a pleasant place to stay. Some rooms are poky and not the cleanest, but the atmosphere is friendly and the stone terrace overlooking the ghat is a winner.

Shiva Ganges View Paying Guest House
GUESTHOUSE $$

(Map p384; ☑2450063; www.varanasiguesthouse.com; Mansarowar Ghat; r ₹2000-2500, with AC ₹3000; ste ₹5000 ✳) Next to Lotus Lounge Restaurant, this delightful, bright-red brick building is part of the city's paying-guest house scheme. Rooms here ooze character, with central double beds, high ceilings, chunky door and window shutters, and some attractive ornaments on shelves. All have river views and spotlessly clean bathrooms. Home-cooked food is also available. The one downside – the manager can be a bit pushy.

Eden Halt
GUESTHOUSE $

(Map p386; ☑2454612; Raja Ghat; d ₹400-500 , s/d without bathroom ₹200/300) This friendly, pocket-sized guesthouse only has four rooms. Two have private bathrooms, two have river views. All are simple, but spacious and come with interesting alcoves and built-in shelving (just in case you bring along your favourite ornaments). A simple roof terrace overlooks peaceful Raja Ghat, but be prepared to fight monkeys for space on it.

Rashmi Guest House
HOTEL $$$

(Map p386; ☑2402778; www.rashmiguesthouse.com; rashmiguesthouse@sify.com; Man Mandir Ghat; d ₹2500-6500; ✳@) Sparkling white-tiled corridors and marble staircases lead to clean and modern rooms, which are small but smart. Many have views of Man Mandir Ghat, although the excellent rooftop Dolphin Restaurant offers the best views of all. Ayurvedic massage (₹1250) is also available.

Puja Guest House
GUESTHOUSE $

(Map p386; ☑2405027; www.pujaguesthouse.com; Lalita Ghat; r from ₹350, without bathroom from ₹150; @) Hidden away up an alley overlooking Lalita Ghat, this towering building offers extremely basic, but clean enough, cheap rooms. The rooftop restaurant is one of Varanasi's tallest, with superb 180-degree views of the river and free sitar-and-tabla performances every evening from 8pm.

ASSI GHAT AREA

TOP CHOICE ### Hotel Ganges View
HOTEL $$

(Map p384; ☑2313218; www.hotelgangesview.com; Assi Ghat; r ₹1000, with AC ₹3000; ✳) Simply gorgeous, this beautifully restored and maintained colonial-style house overlooking Assi Ghat is crammed with books, artwork and antiques. Rooms are spacious and immaculate and there are some charming communal areas in which to sit and relax, including a lovely 1st-floor garden terrace. Book ahead.

Palace on Ganges
HOTEL $$$

(Map p384; ☑2315050; palaceonganges@indiatimes.com; Assi Ghat; d ₹2500-3500; ✳@) Each room in this immaculate heritage accommodation is individually themed on a regional Indian style, using antique furnishings and colourful design themes. The colonial, Rajasthan and Jodhpur rooms are among the best. The spa and massage centre (Ayur Arogyam) is also very good.

DON'T MISS

VARANASI'S TOP FIVE RIVERSIDE RETREATS

» **Pizzeria Vaatika Cafe** (p393) Tree-shaded veranda overlooking Assi Ghat.

» **Lotus Lounge** (p392) Laid-back yet chic.

» **Hotel Ganges View** (p391) Sip tea in style from the gorgeous first-floor garden terrace.

» **Puja Guest House** (p391) Offers 180-degree rooftop views with live classical music every evening.

» **Vishnu Rest House** (p391) Simple stone terrace sandwiched between Pandhey Ghat and a colourful temple.

Chaitanya Guest House GUESTHOUSE $
(Map p384; ☑2313686; Assi Ghat; s/d ₹350/400, d with AC ₹800; ❋) In complete contrast to next-door Sahi River View Guesthouse, Chaitanya has just four rooms: a single, two doubles and a double with AC. All are comfortable, with high ceilings and clean bathrooms, and are well looked after by friendly staff.

Sahi River View Guesthouse GUESTHOUSE $
(Map p384; ☑2366730; sahi_rvgh@sify.com; Assi Ghat; r from ₹250, with AC from ₹625; ❋) There's a huge variety of rooms at this friendly place. Most are good quality and clean, and some have interesting private balconies. Each floor has a pleasant communal seating area with river view, creating a great feeling of space throughout.

CANTONMENT AREA

Hotel Surya HOTEL $$
(Map p384; ☑2508465; www.hotelsuryavns.com; 20/51 The Mall; s/d ₹600/800, with AC from ₹1200/1500; ❋@☎☀) Varanasi's cheapest hotel with a swimming pool, Surya has OK modern rooms, built around a huge lawn area that includes a laid-back Middle Eastern–style cafe (**Mango Tree**). There's a nice swimming pool area, a quality restaurant (**Canton Royale**) housed in a 150-year-old heritage building, and a recommended massage centre. Wi-fi costs ₹60.

Gateway Hotel Ganges HOTEL $$$
(Map p384; ☑2503001; www.thegatewayhotels.com; Raja Bazaar Rd; r ₹9000-10,500, ste ₹11,500-13,500; ❋@☎☀) Varanasi's best hotel is set in five hectares of beautiful gardens with fruit trees, a tennis court, a pool, an outdoor yoga centre and the old maharaja's guest-house. You can walk, cycle or take a ride in a maharaja's buggy around the grounds. Inside, rooms are luxurious, service is top class and there are two fine restaurants, two bars and a luxury spa treatment centre (massages from ₹900). Note, prices rise by about 20% around Christmas and New Year.

Hotel Clarks Varanasi HOTEL $$$
(Map p384; ☑2501011; www.clarkshotels.com; The Mall; s/d from ₹5000/5500; ❋@☎☀) The executive rooms are enormous, with their own private dining areas, but standard rooms are smart rather than luxurious. Service is excellent, though, as is the main restaurant, and the garden out the back has a delightful tear-drop-shaped swimming pool shaded by bamboo and palm trees. There's also a 24-hour cafe. Note, wi-fi costs ₹600 per day!

Eating

Look out for locally grown *langda aam* (mangoes) in summer or *sitafal* (custard apples) in autumn. *Singhara* is a blackish root that tastes like water chestnut.

OLD CITY AREA

TOP CHOICE Brown Bread Bakery MULITCUISINE $$
(Map p386; 17 Tripura Bhairavi; mains ₹75-230; ☉7am-10pm; @) Not only does this place lead the way socially and environmentally – it supports a local school, runs a women's empowerment group and uses organic produce wherever possible – but the food is also terrific. The fabulous menu includes more than 20 varieties of cheese and more than 30 types of bread, cookies and cakes as well as main courses from around the world. The ambience is spot on too, with seating on cushions around low tables and live classical music performances in the evenings. Admittedly, it's pricier than most, but part of the profits go to the charity Learn for Life (p389). Those with bad backs might like to try their other branch **Brownie** (Map p384), which has regular chairs and tables and the same great menu.

Madhur Milan Cafe INDIAN $
(Map p386; Dasaswamedh Ghat Rd; mains ₹24-60; ☉8am-10pm) Popular with locals, this no-nonsense restaurant serves up a range of good-value, mostly south Indian dishes, including dosa, *idli* and *uttapam*, and *paratha*. Thalis start from ₹45, and they have lassis.

Lotus Lounge MULTICUISINE $$
(Map p384; Mansarowar Ghat; mains ₹90-200; ☉8am-10pm) A great place to chill, this laid-back, half-open-air restaurant, with broken-tile mosaic flooring and wicker chairs, has a terrace that juts out over Mansarowar Ghat. The menu's a mixed bag, with fresh coffee, set breakfasts, salads, pasta and curries.

Keshari Ruchikar Byanjan INDIAN $$
(Map p386; Dasaswamedh Ghat Rd; mains ₹60-110; ☉9am-10.30pm) This 1st-floor veg restaurant, specialising in both North and South Indian cuisine, is the nicest place to eat along this busy market street and is popular with local families. The ground-floor *chaat* stall (chaat from ₹15) is also a big hit.

VSR SOUTH INDIAN $
(Map p386; 25/2 Ganga Mahal; mains from ₹25; ☉6.30am-9.30pm) This locals' favourite, right

next to Apsara Restaurant, serves up excellent-value south Indian food (dosa, *idli* and *uttapam*) in an airy, fan-cooled hall. Between breakfast (6.30am–10am) and dinner (6pm–9.30pm), it's thalis only (from ₹35).

Apsara Restaurant   MULTICUISINE $
(Map p386; 24/42 Ganga Mahal; mains ₹35-80) This cosy AC restaurant has cushioned seats, good music and friendly staff. The multi cuisine menu includes Indian, Chinese, continental, Japanese, Israeli and Korean food, and there's a small rooftop area.

Dolphin Restaurant   INDIAN $$$
(Map p386; Rashmi Guest House, Man Mandir Ghat; mains ₹110-300) Quality food, quality location; Dolphin – the rooftop restaurant at Rashmi Guest House – is perched high above Man Mandir Ghat and is a fine place for an evening meal. Watch food being prepared through the glass-walled kitchen by the AC restaurant, or sit out on the breezy balcony.

Phulwari   MULTICUISINE $$
(Map p386; Chowk Rd; mains ₹45-100; ⊙8.30am-10.30pm) Set back from noisy Chowk Rd in a shaded courtyard beside an old temple, this place makes an unusual change from all the rooftop restaurants nearby. Its speciality is Mediterranean, but Phulwari also does Indian and Chinese plus coffee and lassis.

ASSI GHAT AREA

TOP CHOICE Pizzeria Vaatika Cafe   MULTICUISINE $$
(Map p384; Assi Ghat; pizza ₹65-100; ⊙7am-10pm) Sit in the shady garden terrace overlooking Assi Ghat while you munch your way through top-notch pizza baked in a wood-fired oven. None of that thick-crust nonsense here – it's all thin and crispy, as every pizza should be. Don't forget to leave some room for the delicious apple pie.

Haifa Restaurant   MIDDLE EASTERN $$
(Map p384; Hotel Haifa, Assi Ghat; mains ₹50-120; ⊙7.30am-9.30pm) Specialises in Middle Eastern food – humus, falafel, even a Middle Eastern thali! – but also does Indian and Chinese like everywhere else.

CANTONMENT AREA

Canton Restaurant   INDIAN $$$
(Map p384; Hotel Surya, The Mall; mains ₹100-300; ⊙7am-11pm) Housed in a 150-year-old heritage building, Hotel Surya's excellent main restaurant has a colonial elegance, and

on warm evenings you can eat out on the large lawn. The menu includes high-quality Indian dishes as well as some Chinese and continental.

Varuna Restaurant   NORTH INDIAN $$$
(Map p384; Gateway Hotel Ganges, Raja Bazaar Rd; mains ₹200-1450; ⊙lunch & dinner) As you'd expect from Varanasi's best hotel, this is one of the city's top restaurants. Elegant without being stuffy, Varuna's specialities include classic North Indian and Afghan dishes, the sumptuous maharaja thali and tandoor kebabs. There's live sitar and tabla music every evening.

Eden Restaurant   INDIAN $$$
(Map p384; Hotel Pradeep, Kabir Chaura Rd; mains ₹110-250) Hotel Pradeep's rooftop restaurant, complete with garden, manicured lawns and wrought-iron furniture, is a lovely place for a candle-lit evening meal. Note that staircase-weary waiters will be very appreciative if you order at the ground-floor AC restaurant behind the lobby before heading up to the roof. The good-quality Indian menu is the same in both restaurants.

Drinking & Entertainment

Wine and beer shops are dotted discreetly around the city, usually away from the river. Note that it is frowned upon to drink alcohol on or near the holy Ganges. For bars, head to midrange and top-end hotels away from the ghats.

There's nightly live **classical music** at Brown Bread Bakery, Puja Hotel and Varuna Restaurant at Gateway Hotel Ganges, to name but a few.

The International Music Centre Ashram (Map p390) has small **performances** (₹100) on Wednesday and Saturday evenings.

TOP CHOICE Aum Cafe   CAFE
(Map p384; www.touchoflight.us; ⊙7am-5.30pm Tue-Sun; 🖥) Run by a friendly American woman who has been coming to India for more than 20 years, this cute and colourful cafe has fabulously fresh juices, coffee and lassis as well as some delicious snacks and sandwiches. The back of the menu lists the ayurvedic qualities of all the ingredients used. There's also massage therapies and body piercing available. Up the steps from Assi Ghat.

Open Hand   CAFE
(Map p384; www.openhandonline.com; ⊙8am-8pm Mon-Sat; 🖥) A cafe-cum-gift shop with fresh coffee and juices and a range of cakes and

DON'T MISS

NO 1 LASSI IN ALL VARANASI

Your long, thirsty search for the best lassi in town is over. Look no further than **Blue Lassi** (Map p386; lassis ₹10-30; ☺9am-11.30pm), a tiny, hole-in-the-wall yoghurt shop that has been churning out the freshest, creamiest, fruit-filled lassis for more than 70 years. The grandson of the original owner still works here, sitting by his lassi-mixing cauldron in front of a small room with wooden benches for customers and walls plastered with messages from happy drinkers; most of whom seem to be Korean. All four flavours – plain, banana, apple and mango – are delicious (it's worth coming here four times to try them all!), but we think the apple one, flecked with fresh apple shreds, just about tops the bunch.

snacks plus a few main courses. There's free wi-fi plus a large selection of gorgeous handicrafts (jewellery, toys, clothing) made in the local community.

Prinsep Bar BAR
(Map p384; Gateway Hotel Ganges, Raja Bazaar Rd; ☺midday-11pm) For a quiet drink with a dash of history try this tiny bar, named after James Prinsep, who drew wonderful illustrations of Varanasi's ghats and temples. Beers start at ₹225, cocktails ₹200.

Mango Tree CAFE
(Map p384; ☑2508465; www.hotelsuryavns.com; 20/51 The Mall) This laid-back cafe in the garden at Hotel Surya is a relaxing place where you can smoke hookah pipes (₹100) while sipping a beer.

Shopping

Varanasi is justifiably famous for silk brocades and beautiful Benares saris, but being led by touts and rickshaw drivers to a silk shop is all part of the Varanasi shuffle and virtually everyone involved will try to rip you off. Don't believe much of what the silk salesmen tell you about the relative quality of products, even in government emporiums. Instead, shop around and judge for yourself.

Varanasi is also a good place to shop for sitars (starting from ₹3000) and tablas (from ₹2500). The cost depends primarily on the type of wood used. Mango is cheapest, while teak and vijaysar (a wild Indian herb, the bark of which is used in ayurvedic medicine) are of the highest quality.

Ingenious locally made toys, Bhadohi carpets, brass ornaments, perfumes and textiles are other popular purchases.

Baba Blacksheep SILK
(Map p384; ☑2454342; Bhelpura; 9am-8pm) Trustworthy, non-pushy and frequently recommended by our readers, this is a great place to come for silks (scarves/saris from ₹250/3000) and pashminas (shawls from ₹1300).

Benares Art & Culture HANDICRAFTS
(Map p384; Shivala Rd; ☺10am-8pm Mon-Sat) This centuries-old *haveli* (traditional, ornately decorated residence) stocks quality carvings, sculptures, paintings and wooden toys all made by local artists. Prices are fixed.

Khadi Gramodyog CLOTHING
(Map p384; Khabir Chaura Rd; ☺7am-10pm Mon-Sat) Stocks shirts, kurta pyjamas, saris and head scarves, all made from the famous homespun *khadi* fabric. There's another branch, called **Shri Gandhi Ashram Khadi** (Map p384), on the 1st floor of the row of shops opposite the post office. Both can arrange next-day tailoring services.

Mehrotra Silk Factory SILK
(Map p384; ☑2200189; www.mehrotrasilk.com; ☺10am-8pm) Tucked away down a tiny alleyway near the main train station, this pocket-sized, fixed-priced shop is a fun place to buy silk scarves (from ₹250), saris (from ₹1600) and bedspread sets (from ₹5000).

Information

Internet cafes are everywhere; ₹20 per hour is the going rate. Guesthouses tend to charge double. Wi-fi is becoming more and more popular. Places that didn't have it during our research may well do by the time you read this. Some charge. Many don't. There are several **ATMs** scattered around town. We've marked some on our maps.

Heritage Hospital (Map p384; ☑2368888; www.heritagehospitals.com; Lanka) English-speaking staff and doctors; 24-hour pharmacy in reception. Casualty to the right.

Main post office (Map p384; ☑2331398; Kabir Chaura Rd; ☺10am-7pm Mon-Sat, parcels 10am-4pm) Known as GPO by some rickshaw riders;

best PO for sending parcels abroad. Small post offices are dotted around the city. The Cantonment area (Map p384) has a large one.

State Bank of India (Map p384; 2343742; The Mall; ⏱10am-2pm & 2.30-4pm Mon-Fri, 10am-1pm Sat) Changes travellers cheques and cash.

Tourist Police (Map p384; ⏱2506670; UP Tourism office, Varanasi Junction train station; ⏱6am-7pm) Tourist police wear sky-blue uniforms.

UP Tourism (Map p384; Varanasi Junction train station; ⏱2506670; ⏱9am-5pm) The patient Mr Umashankar at the office inside the train station has been dishing out reasonably impartial information to arriving travellers for years; he's a mine of knowledge, so take advantage of it if you arrive here by train. Can give details of Varanasi's paying-guesthouse scheme and guided tours.

❶ Getting There & Away

Air

Indian Airlines (Map p384; ⏱10am-5pm Mon-Sat) airport (⏱ 2622494); Cantonment office (⏱2502529) has direct flights to Delhi (around ₹3000, daily), Mumbai (₹5000, daily), Kathmandu (₹7800, Tuesday, Thursday, Saturday and Sunday) and Khajuraho (₹3000, Monday, Wednesday and Friday). Other airlines are based at the airport.

Bus

The main **bus stand** is opposite Varanasi Junction train station. Popular destinations are listed below. Allahabad and Lucknow are also served by one or two AC buses that are more comfortable but cost at least twice the price.

Allahabad ₹82, three hours, every 30 minutes

Faizabad ₹160, seven hours, daily at 6am, 7am, 8am, 1.30pm and 2pm

Gorakhpur ₹144, seven hours, every 30 minutes

Lucknow ₹197, seven to eight hours, about every hour

Train

Luggage theft has been reported on trains to and from Varanasi so you should take extra care. A few years ago there were reports of drugged food and drink, so it's probably still best to politely decline any offers from strangers.

Varanasi Junction train station (Map p384), also known as Varanasi Cantonment (Cantt) train station, is the main station. Foreign tourist quota tickets (p1187) must be purchased at the helpful **Foreign Tourist Centre** (⏱8am-8pm Mon-Sat, 8am-2pm Sun), a ticket office just past the UP Tourism office, on your right as you exit the station.

There are several daily trains to Allahabad, Gorakhpur and Lucknow. A few daily trains leave for New Delhi and Kolkata, but only two daily trains goes to Agra. The direct train to Khajuraho only runs on Monday, Wednesday and Saturday. On other days, go via Satna from where you can catch buses to Khajuraho.

To/From Nepal

From Varanasi's bus stand there are regular services to Sunauli (₹206, 10 hours, 7am-8.30pm).

By train, go to Gorakhpur then transfer to a Sunauli bus.

Indian Airlines has four weekly flights to Kathmandu (₹7800). Nepali visas are available on arrival.

HANDY TRAINS FROM VARANASI

DESTINATION	TRAIN NO & NAME	FARE (₹)	DURATION (HR)	DEPARTURES
Agra	13237/13239 *PNBE MTJ Exp*	252/678/930	13	4.45pm
Allahabad	11094 *Mahangari Exp*	120/277/373	3	11.30am
Gorakhpur	15003 *Chaurichaura Exp*	132/340/460	6½	12.35am
Jabalpur	11062/11066 *MFP/DBG-LTT Exp*	212/562/772	10½	11.20pm
Khajuraho	21108 *BSB-Kurj Link E*	200/531/725	12	5.10pm*
Kolkata (Howrah)	12334 *Vibhuti Exp*	306/806**	14	6.10pm
Lucknow	14235 *BSB-BE Exp*	161/422/481***	7¼	11.45pm
New Delhi	12559 *Shiv Ganga Exp*	306/806/1095	12½	7.15pm

All fares are sleeper/3AC/2AC; *Mon, Wed, Sat only; **sleeper/3AC; ***sleeper/3AC/1st class

❶ Getting Around

To/From the Airport

An autorickshaw to **Babatpur airport**, 22km northwest of the city, costs ₹200. A taxi is about ₹400.

Bicycle

You can hire bikes (per day ₹20) from a small **cycle repair shop** (Map p384) near Assi Ghat.

Cycle-Rickshaw

Rough prices from Dasaswamedh Ghat Rd include: Assi Ghat ₹20, Benares Hindu University ₹40 and Varanasi Junction train station ₹30. Be prepared for hard bargaining.

Taxi & Autorickshaw

Prepaid booths for autorickshaws and taxis are directly outside Varanasi Junction train station and give you a good benchmark for prices around town. First pay a ₹5 administration charge at the booth then take a ticket which you give to your driver, along with the fare, once you've reached your destination. Fares include:

Airport auto/taxi ₹200/400
Assi Ghat auto/taxi ₹70/200
Dasaswamedh Ghat auto/taxi ₹60/150
Godaulia (by St Thomas' Church) auto ₹50
Ramnagar Fort auto ₹140
Sarnath auto/taxi ₹80/250
Half-day tour (four hours) auto ₹300
Full-day tour (eight hours) auto ₹600

Sarnath

☑0542

Buddha came to Sarnath to preach his message of the middle way to nirvana after he achieved enlightenment at Bodhgaya and gave his famous first sermon here. In the 3rd century BC emperor Ashoka had magnificent stupas and monasteries erected here as well as an engraved pillar. When Chinese traveller Xuan Zang dropped by in AD 640, Sarnath boasted a 100m-high stupa and 1500 monks living in large monasteries. However, soon after, Buddhism went into decline and, when Muslim invaders sacked the city in the late 12th century, Sarnath disappeared altogether. It was 'rediscovered' by British archaeologists in 1835.

Today it's one of the four important sites on the Buddhist circuit (along with Bodhgaya, Kushinagar and Lumbini in Nepal) and attracts followers from around the world. An easy day trip from Varanasi, Sarnath is also a peaceful place to stay.

◉ Sights

Dhamekh Stupa & Monastery Ruins
HISTORIC SITE

(Indian/foreigner ₹5/100, video ₹25; ◷dawn-dusk) Set in a peaceful park of monastery ruins is the impressive 34m **Dhamekh Stupa**, which marks the spot where the Buddha preached his first sermon. The floral and geometric carvings are 5th century AD, but some of the brickwork dates back as far as 200 BC.

Nearby is a 3rd-century BC **Ashoka Pillar** with an edict engraved on it. It once stood 15m tall and had the famous four-lion capital (now in the museum) perched on top of it, but all that remains are five fragments of its base.

Chaukhandi Stupa
SACRED SITE

(◷dawn-dusk) This large ruined stupa dates back to the 5th century AD, and marks the spot where Buddha met his first disciples. The incongruous tower on top of the stupa is Mughal and was constructed here in the 16th century to commemorate the visit of Emperor Humayun.

Mulgandha Kuti Vihar
BUDDHIST TEMPLE

(☑2585595; ◷4-11.30am & 1.30-8pm; photo ₹20, video ₹50) This modern temple was completed in 1931 by the Mahabodhi Society. Buddha's first sermon is chanted daily, starting between 6pm and 7pm depending on the season. A **bodhi tree** growing outside was transplanted in 1931 from the tree in Anuradhapura, Sri Lanka, which in turn is said to be the offspring of the original tree in Bodhgaya under which Buddha attained enlightenment.

Archaeological Museum
MUSEUM

(admission ₹5; ◷9am-6pm) This fully modernised, 100-year-old sandstone museum houses wonderfully displayed ancient treasures such as the very well preserved 3rd-century BC lion capital from the Ashoka pillar, which has been adopted as India's national emblem, and a huge 2000-year-old stone umbrella, ornately carved with Buddhist symbols.

🛏 Sleeping

TOP CHOICE Agrawal Paying Guest House
GUESTHOUSE **$$**

(☑2595316; r ₹500-600, with AC ₹900) Peaceful place with a refined owner and spotless rooms overlooking a beautiful garden.

Jain Paying Guest House
GUESTHOUSE **$**

(☑2595621; d ₹300) Simple but friendly.

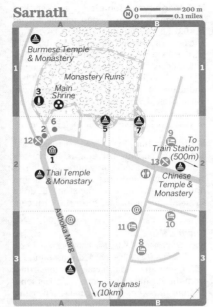

N 0 —— 200 m
0 —— 0.1 miles

Burmese Temple & Monastery

Monastery Ruins

Main Shrine

To Train Station (500m)

Thai Temple & Monastary

Chinese Temple & Monastery

Ashoka Marg

To Varanasi (10km)

way back you can snag a lift in a shared auto or *vikram* (large autorickshaw; ₹10-20) but you may have to change on the outskirts of the city. Some trains running between Varanasi and Gorakhpur also stop here. Trains for Sarnath leave Varanasi Junction at 6.50am, 11.10am, 12.15pm, 4pm, 5pm and 6.35pm. Returning to Varanasi, trains leave Sarnath at 8.43am, 9.47am, 11.31am, 11.58am, 2.48pm, 6.53pm and 9.13pm. The journey takes around 20 minutes and a 'general' ticket for an unreserved second-class seat will cost you just a few rupees.

You can stay in very basic rooms, with shared bathrooms, at these monasteries:

Tibetan Temple & Monastery
(dm ₹100)

Japanese Temple & Monastery
(dm by donation) Has one five-bed dorm.

✕ Eating

Vaishali Restaurant INDIAN $
(mains ₹20-100; ⊙7am-9pm) Large 1st-floor restaurant serving mostly Indian dishes, but some Chinese too.

Green Hut MULTICUISINE $
(meals ₹40-90; ⊙8.30am-8.30pm) A breezy open-sided cafe-restaurant offering dosa, snacks and chicken dishes.

❶ Information

Power cuts mean **internet cafes** (per hr ₹20; ⊙8am-8pm) are unreliable, but we've marked a couple of options on the map.

❶ Getting There & Away

Local buses to Sarnath (₹10, 40 minutes) pass in front of Varanasi Junction train station, but you may wait a long time for one. An auto-rickshaw costs about ₹100 from Varanasi's Old City. Some cycle-rickshaw-wallahs are willing to do the trip (₹80), but tip generously. On the

Gorakhpur

📞 0551 / POP 624,570

There's little to see in Gorakhpur itself, but this well-connected transport hub is a short hop from the pilgrimage centre of Kushinagar – the place where Buddha died – making it a possible stopover on the road between Varanasi and Nepal.

⊨ Sleeping & Eating

Hotel Adarsh Palace HOTEL $
(📞2201912; hotel.adarshpalace@rediffmail.com; Railway Station Rd; dm ₹150, s ₹300-450, d ₹600, with AC ₹800-900; ❄) There are loads of budget hotels opposite the train station, but this smarter-than-average one, 200m to the left as you leave the station, has something for everyone. The 10-bed dorm has lockers above each bed, cheap singles come with TV and bathroom and there are some decent-quality AC rooms too. As with most hotels here, checkout is 24 hours.

New Varden Restaurant
INDIAN $

(mains ₹20-70, thalis ₹35-60; ☺8am-10pm)
Right opposite the train station, this is popular with travellers and will box up your order for onward journeys.

ℹ Information

UP Tourism (☑2335450; ☺10am-5pm Mon-Sat) is inside the train station. There's an **internet cafe** (per hour ₹20; ☺10am-11pm) opposite the train station, below Hotel Varden.

For the main bus stand, come out of the train station and keep walking straight for about 300m. For Varanasi buses you need the Katchari bus stand, about 3km further south.

ℹ Getting There & Away

Frequent bus services run from the main bus stand to Faizabad (₹84, five hours), Kushinagar (₹36, two hours) and Sunauli (₹67, three hours). Buses to Varanasi (₹120, seven hours) leave from the Katchari bus stand.

There are six daily trains to Varanasi (sleeper/3AC, ₹132/340, 5½ hours), including one slower, cheaper night train (No 55149, seven hours, 11.15pm). A number of daily trains also leave for Lucknow (sleeper/3AC ₹146/380, six hours) and Delhi (₹312/823, 13 hours) and one for Agra Fort (No 19038/19040, ₹249/672, 1.15pm, 15½ hours). The **train ticket reservation office** is 500m from the train station; to the right of the station as you exit.

Kushinagar

☑05564 / POP 17,982

One of the four main pilgrimage sites marking Buddha's life – the others being Lumbini (Nepal), Bodhgaya and Sarnath – Kushinagar is where Buddha died. There are several peaceful, modern temples where you can stay, chat with monks or simply contemplate your place in the world, and there are three main historical sights, including the simple but wonderfully serene stupa where Buddha is said to have been cremated.

◉ Sights & Activities

Ramabhar Stupa
SACRED SITE

Architecturally, this half-ruined, 15m-high stupa is little more than a large, dome-shaped clump of red bricks, but there is an unmistakable aura about this place which is hard to ignore. This is where Buddha's body is said to have been cremated and monks and pilgrims can often be seen meditating by the palm-lined path that leads around the stupa.

Mahaparinirvana Temple
BUDDHIST TEMPLE

The highlight of this modest temple, rebuilt in 1927 and set among extensive lawns and ancient ruins with a circumambulatory path, is its serene 5th-century reclining Buddha, unearthed in 1876. Six metres long, it depicts Buddha on his ancient death-bed and is one of the world's most moving Buddhist icons. Behind the temple is an ancient 19m-tall stupa, and in the surrounding park is a large bell erected by the Dalai Lama.

Mathakuar Temple
BUDDHIST TEMPLE

This small shrine, set among monastery ruins, marks the spot where Buddha is said to have made his final sermon and now houses a 3m-tall blue-stone Buddha statue, thought to date from the 10th century AD.

Buddha Museum
MUSEUM

(Indian/foreigner ₹3/10, photography ₹20; ☺10.30am-4.30pm Tue-Sun) Exhibits Buddhist relics, sculptures and terracottas unearthed from the Kushinagar region, as well as some Tibetan *thangkas* (rectangular cloth paintings) and Mughal miniature paintings.

Wat Thai complex
TEMPLE

(☺9-11.30am & 1.30-4pm) Features an elaborate temple, beautifully maintained gardens with bonsai-style trees, a monastery and a temple containing a gilded Buddha. There's also a Sunday school and health clinic, each of which welcomes visitors.

Yama Cafe
WALKING

(walk incl guide, food, water & return transport ₹750) The cafe runs a so-called Holy Hike, a 13km-walk that takes in some of the area's historical sights as well as local villages and a school in the surrounding farmland.

🛏 Sleeping & Eating

Lotus Nikko Hotel
HOTEL $$$

(☑274403; s/d ₹3800/4500; ❄) The best value of Kushinagar's top-end hotels, Lotus Nikko has huge, spotless rooms with dining table, sofa and chairs. There's a **restaurant** (mains ₹90-145; ☺7.30am-9.30pm) and a Japanese bath house.

[TOP CHOICE] Yama Cafe
MULTICUISINE $

(mains ₹25-55; ☺7am-8pm) Run by the welcoming Mr and Mrs Roy, this Kushinagar institution has a traveller-friendly menu which includes toast, omelettes, fried rice and *thukpa* (Tibetan noodle soup) and is the best place to come for information about the area.

Some of the temples which have basic accommodation for pilgrims also welcome tourists, including the following:

Linh Son Temple   PILGRIMS' REST HOUSE $
(tr ₹250) Simple, clean triples with private bathroom and hot water.

Japan-Sri Lanka Buddhist Centre   PILGRIMS' REST HOUSE $
(📞273044; tr ₹400) Set up for large groups, so call ahead, but has decent quality, clean rooms.

Tibetan Temple   PILGRIMS' REST HOUSE $
(r without bathroom by donation) Rooms are run down, but the place is welcoming.

ℹ️ Information

You'll find a couple of private money changers here, but no ATMs. Internet connections were too temperamental to bother with when we were here.

ℹ️ Getting There & Away

Frequent buses to Gorakhpur (₹36, two hours, until 7pm) will pick you up at the yellow archway.

Sunauli & the Nepal Border

📞05522

Sunauli is a dusty town that offers little more than a bus stop, a couple of hotels, a few shops and a border post. The border is open 24 hours and the crossing is straightforward (p399) so most travellers carry on into Nepal without stopping here. There are more facilities in the Nepali part of Sunauli; Bhairawa, a further 4km north, is a more substantial town.

Buses drop you just a few hundred metres from the Indian immigration office, so you can ignore the cycle-rickshaws.

If you're coming from Nepal but miss the last bus to Gorakhpur, then **Hotel Indo-Nepal** (📞238142; dm/d ₹100/350), by the bus stand, has basic rooms set around a cool courtyard. Its simple **restaurant** (mains ₹25-100; thali ₹60-150; ⊘6.30am-10pm) makes a nice lunch stop even if you don't stay.

If you're leaving India, the very helpful **Nepal Tourism Board information centre** (📞0977 1520197; ⊘10am-5pm Sun-Fri) is on your right, in no-man's land.

CROSSING INTO NEPAL

Border Hours

The border is open 24 hours but closes to vehicles at 10pm, and if you arrive in the middle of the night you may have to wake someone to get stamped out of India.

Foreign Exchange

There's nowhere to change money in Sunauli, but there are foreign-exchange places just across the border on the Nepal side. Small denominations of Indian currency are accepted for bus fares on the Nepal side.

Onward Transport

Buses and shared jeeps leave all day until around 8pm from the Nepal side of the border for Kathmandu (NRs500, six hours) and Pokhara (NRs500, eight hours). A taxi to Kathmandu costs around NRs15,000. Shared autorickshaws or jeeps (NRs10) can take you from the border to Bhairawa, 4km away, where you can also catch buses to Kathmandu and Pokhara for the same prices, as well as to Buddha's birthplace, Lumbini (NRs35, one hour).

Visas

Multiple-entry visas (15-/30-/60-day US$25/40/80 – cash, not rupees) are available at the immigration post just across the border. You will need two recent passport photos. At the time of research, travellers leaving India were being prevented from re-entering within two months. Some travellers reported being able to get round this rule by showing proof of an imminent international flight leaving from an Indian city. Others reported being able to pay (US$10) the Indian Embassy in Kathmandu for special dispensation to re-enter earlier.

The Nepali side of Sunauli has a few cheap hotels, outdoor restaurants and a more upbeat atmosphere, but most travellers prefer to stay in Bhairawa, or get straight on a bus to Kathmandu or Pokhara.

Regular buses run from Sunauli to Gorakhpur (₹67, three hours, until 7pm) from where you can catch trains to Varanasi. A few morning (4.30am to 10.30am) and afternoon (4.30pm to 7pm) buses run direct to Varanasi (₹208, 10 hours), but it's a long, bumpy ride.

Be wary of buying 'through' tickets from Kathmandu or Pokhara to Varanasi. Some travellers report being intimidated into buying another ticket once over the border. Travelling in either direction, it's better to take a local bus to the border, walk across and take another onward bus (pay the conductor on board). Travellers have also complained about being pressured into paying extra luggage charges for buses out of Sunauli. You shouldn't have to.

Uttarakhand

Best Places to Eat

» Kasmanda Palace
Restaurant (p411)

» Little Buddha Cafe (p422)

» Imperial Square (p410)

» Prakash Lok (p415)

Best Places to Stay

» Palace Belvedere (p433)

» Kasmanda Palace Hotel
(p409)

» Infinity Resorts (p432)

Why Go?

Soaring Himalayan peaks and steamy lowland jungles. Revered temples and renowned ashrams. Peaceful hill stations and busy cities. Uttarakhand is truly a *thali* of a state, with some of India's best trekking, yoga schools, holiday towns and wildlife watching all tucked into this little corner of the country.

Hindus think of Uttarakhand as *Dev Bhoomi* – the Land of Gods – and the dramatic terrain is covered with holy mountains, lakes and rivers. Twisting roads and high-altitude hiking trails lead to spectacular pilgrimage sites where tales from the Hindu epics are set. And something of these ancient stories seems to have been absorbed by the land, which exudes a subtle sense of actually being sacred – even to ultra-orthodox agnostics. Many travellers flock here for this vibe, finding it a powerful place to pursue a spiritual practice.

Others come here for the tigers!

When to Go
Rishikesh

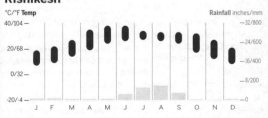

Apr–mid-Jun
The best season for tiger spotting at Corbett Tiger Reserve.

Jul–mid-Sep
Monsoons may make travel difficult; Valley of Flowers bloom is best July-August.

Mid-Sep–Oct
The perfect time to trek the Himalayas.

Fast Facts

» Population: 10.1 million

» Area: 51,125sq km

» Capital: Dehra Dun

» Main languages: Hindi, Garhwali, Kumaoni

» Sleeping prices: **$** below ₹800, **$$** ₹800 to 1800, **$$$** above ₹1800

Top Tip

If travelling through the hills or mountains, get to buses early to claim a window seat. The landscape, much of which you'll never stop to explore, is gorgeous.

Resources

» US Military maps (www .lib.utexas.edu/maps/ams /india), useful for trekking.

» Background on the Chipko movement (http:// nandadevi.prayaga.org /chipko.html), the original 'tree-huggers'.

» Read up on Transcendental Meditation (www .tm.org), founded by Maharishi Mahesh Yogi.

Food

Not famous for its food, cuisine in Uttarakhand is typically North Indian. The most variety is found in Mussoorie, Rishikesh, Nainital and Dehra Dun. A warning to meat-eaters: towns with top-tier religious significance are all-vegetarian, all the time.

DON'T MISS

Every evening around sunset, hundreds of Hindu worshippers converge at **Haridwar's Har-ki-Pairi Ghat** to perform *puja* (prayer offering) on the Ganges canal. Leaf baskets filled with a fragrant rainbow of flower petals, each softly lit by a candle nestled in the centre, are launched onto the water; this river of flickering flames carries the prayers of the faithful downstream. Beautiful and intense, this might be the most potent scene of archetypal 'India' in all of Uttarakhand.

Just north of Haridwar, follow the footsteps of The Beatles to **Rishikesh**, the world-renowned spiritual-seekers' city, where you'll surely find a yoga or meditation course to suit your needs – whether you're a serious practitioner or an undisciplined dabbler.

Spanning the northern half of the state are the mighty **Himalayas**. A vast land of soaring, snowy summits and rolling alpine meadows – plus a chance to see snow leopards and meet tribal herders – Uttarakhand is a **trekking** paradise. Choose between busy pilgrims' trails on the Char Dham route or remote wilderness where you'll hardly see another soul.

Top State Festivals

» Magh Mela (Jan & Feb, Haridwar, p412) Hundreds of thousands of pilgrims come to bathe in the soul-cleansing Ganges during this huge annual religious fair. The Ardh Kumbh Mela is held every six years; and millions of pilgrims attend the mega Kumbh Mela every 12 years.

» International Yoga Festival (Mar, Rishikesh, p421) Yoga and meditation masters from around the world converge and give demonstrations and lectures.

» Shivaratri (usually Mar, Tapkeshwar Temple, p406) A festival celebrated in style with carnival rides and stalls at a picturesque riverside cave temple on the outskirts of Dehra Dun.

» Nanda Devi Fair (Sep, Almora, p437) During this five-day fair, thousands of devotees parade the image of the goddess around and watch dancing and other cultural shows.

Uttarakhand Highlights

1 Visit the temple at **Gangotri** and trek beyond it to **Gaumukh**, the source of the holy Ganges River (p425)

2 Float a candle down the Ganges at the gorgeous nightly ceremony at Haridwar's **Har-ki-Pairi Ghat** (p412)

3 Scout for rare Bengal tigers and ride an elephant in **Corbett Tiger Reserve** (p430)

4 Get your asanas and chakras sorted at **Rishikesh**, the yoga and ashram capital of the universe (p417)

5 Cool off in a scenic Raj-era hill station in **Mussoorie** (p408) or **Nainital** (p432)

6 Trek to the sublime **Valley of Flowers** and nearby **Hem Kund** for an unforgettable combo of the scenic and sacred (p428)

7 Immerse yourself in a mind-blowing Himalayan landscape while trekking the **Kuari Pass** (p430) through **Nanda Devi National Park (Sanctuary)**

History

Uttarakhand consists of the culturally distinct Garhwal (in the west) and Kumaon (east) districts. Over the centuries various dynasties have dominated the region, including the Guptas, Kuturyi and Chand *rajas* (kings). In the 18th century the Nepalese Gurkhas attacked first the kingdom of Kumaon, then Garhwal, prompting the British to step in and take most of the region as part of the Treaty of Sigauli in 1817.

After Independence, the region was merged with Uttar Pradesh, but a vocal separatist movement follwed, and the present-day state of Uttaranchal was formed in 2000. In 2007 it was officially renamed Uttarakhand, a traditional name meaning 'northern country'.

Climate

Look at the altitude to get an idea of likely temperatures in this state of elevation extremes. Trekking the Himalayas is possible from May to October, but can be extremely dangerous between July and mid-September, during the monsoon. Heavy rains at that time can also make roads impassable for days. Hill stations can be visited all year, but winters there are freezing cold. Low-lying Rishikesh and Haridwar are most comfortable from October to March.

ℹ Information

Most towns in the region have an Uttarakhand Tourism office, however the main responsibility for the region's tourism rests with the **Garhwal Mandal Vikas Nigam** (GMVN; www.gmvnl.com), which covers the Garhwal district; and **Kumaon Mandal Vikas Nigam** (KMVN; www.kmvn.org), which covers the Kumaon district.

ℹ Getting Around

Tough old government buses are the main means of travelling around Uttarakhand. In addition, crowded share jeeps (often called 'sumos') criss-cross the state, linking remote towns and villages to important road junctions. Pay 10 times the share-taxi rate and you can hire the whole vehicle and travel in comfort. Roads that snake through the hills can be nerve-racking and stomach-churning.

Dehra Dun

🖉 0135 / POP 527,859 / ELEV 700M

Perhaps best known for the institutions the British left behind – the huge Forest Research Institute Museum, the Indian Military Academy, the Wildlife Institute of India and the Survey of India – the capital of Uttarakhand is a hectic, congested city sprawling in the Doon Valley between the Himalayan foothills and the Siwalik Range. Be prepared to encounter assertive beggars in the city center.

A once green and pleasant town of rice and tea gardens, Dehra Dun has lost much of its charm, but you don't have to go far out of the city centre to find relief from the traffic. Rishikesh and Mussoorie are both just over an hour away, so most travellers merely pass through, but Dehra Dun is worth a stop for its lively Paltan Bazaar and vibrant Tibetan community south of the city in Clement Town. It's also a transit point for Himachal Pradesh.

◉ Sights & Activities

Great Stupa & Buddha Statue   BUDDHIST TEMPLE

The region around Dehra Dun is home to a thriving Tibetan Buddhist community, mainly focused on the **Mindrolling Monastery** (🖉2640556; www.mindrolling.org), about 10km south of the centre in Clement Town. Everything about the monastery is on a grand scale: it boasts a large college, manicured gardens and the five-storey **Great Stupa** (admission free; ⊙5am-9pm). At over 60m, it's believed to be the world's tallest stupa and contains a series of shrine rooms displaying relics, murals and Tibetan art. Presiding over the monastery is the impressive 35m-high gold **Buddha Statue**, dedicated to the Dalai Lama.

The streets around the monastery have several Tibetan-run guesthouses and cafes. Take *vikram* (large tempo) 5 from the city centre (₹10). An autorickshaw costs about ₹150.

Forest Research Institute Museum   NOTABLE BUILDING

(🖉2759382; www.icfre.org; admission ₹10, guide ₹50; ⊙9.30am-1pm & 1.30-5.30pm) The prime attraction of this museum is the building itself. Set in a 5 sq km park, the institute – where most of India's forest officers are trained – is larger than Buckingham Palace and is one of the Raj's grandest buildings. Built between 1924 and 1929, and designed by CG Blomfield, this red-brick colossus has Mughal towers, perfectly formed arches and Roman columns in a series of quadrangles edged by elegant cloisters. Six huge halls have displays on every aspect of forestry in India that look like leftovers from a middle school science fair. Highlights include beau-

tiful animal, bird and plant paintings by Afshan Zaidi, exhibits on the medicinal uses of trees, and a cross-section of a 700-year-old deodar tree. A return autorickshaw from the city centre, including waiting time, costs around ₹250. Or take *vikram* 8 (from Gandhi Rd) or *vikram* 6 (from Connaught Place) and get out at the institute's entry gate.

Ram Rai Darbar   MAUSOLEUM
(Paltan Bazaar; admission free; ☉dawn-dusk) This unique mausoleum is made of white marble, and the four smaller tombs in the garden courtyard are those of Ram Rai's four wives. Ram Rai, the errant son of the seventh Sikh guru, Har Rai, was excommunicated by his father. He formed his own Udasi sect, which still runs schools and hospitals. When Ram Rai died in 1687, Mughal emperor Aurangzeb ordered the building of the mausoleum. A free communal lunch of dhal, rice and chapatis is offered to anyone who wants it, although a donation is appreciated.

Survey of India Museum   MUSEUM
(Survey Chowk; admission free; ☉10.30am-5pm Mon-Fri) Instruments used to accomplish the monumental task of mapping India in the 19th century are on display here, including some designed for the mission by its leader, George Everest. Among them are beautiful transits and scopes of gleaming brass, and a bar made partly of iron, partly of brass, which allowed surveyors to compensate for inaccuracies in their measurements, caused by the expansion and contraction of their instruments due to heat and cold. Small placards tell snippets of the story of one of the most impressive geographical feats ever achieved.

The museum, however, is not officially opened to the public. To get permission to see it, go to the Surveyor General's office at the Survey of India compound in Harthibarkala. There, you'll have to write a brief letter explaining why you want to view the collection. Permits are given only to those

Dehra Dun

with an academic or professional interest in the subject – like a geography student or a historian – but proof of your vocation or college major isn't demanded.

Tapkeshwar Temple   HINDU TEMPLE
(⊘dawn-dusk) In a scenic setting on the banks of the Tons Nadi River, you'll find an unusual and popular Shiva shrine inside a small, dripping cave, which is the site of the annual **Shivaratri** festival. Turn left at the bottom of the steps for the main shrine. Cross the bridge over the river to visit another one, where you have to squeeze through a narrow cave to see an image of Mata Vaishno Devi. The temple is about 5km north of the centre. Take a rickshaw for ₹300 roundtrip.

🛏 Sleeping

There are plenty of cheapies along the Haridwar road outside the train station, some charging as little as ₹250 a double, but the better places can be found along Gandhi Rd and Rajpur Rd. There are also some cheap guest houses in the Tibetan colony at Clement Town.

Samar Niwas Guest House   GUESTHOUSE $$
(📞2740299; www.samarniwas.com; M-16 Chanderlok Colony; d ₹800-1500; ❄@) This charming four-room guesthouse, in a peaceful residential area just off Rajpur Rd, is as cosy and welcoming as it gets. The owners are descendants of the Tehri royal family, but the rulers of the house seem to be the friendly pugs that roam the comfortable lounge-cum-lobby. Rooms are well-appointed, but beds are a bit hard.

Devaloka House   HOTEL $
(📞9759862769; Clement Town; s/d/tr ₹250/350/450) Part of the Mindrolling Monastery complex, the spotless white rooms here are above the semicircular arcade looking across to the monumental Great Stupa and gardens. Rooms have TV, hot water, a small balcony and tiled floors. Check in at Norjin Restaurant.

Hotel President   HOTEL $$$
(📞2657082; www.hotelpresidentdehradun.com; 6 Astley Hall, Rajpur Rd; s ₹2250-2500, d ₹2500-2800; ❄) This Dehra Dun institution is one of the classiest hotels in town, despite being sandwiched within the complex of shops, restaurants and fast-food spots called Astley Hall. Rooms are thoroughly modern and even the least expensive have fridges, safes and complimentary slippers. There's a good restaurant, a coffee shop and the Polo Bar.

Hotel Saurab   HOTEL $
(📞2728042; hotelsaurab@hotmail.com; 1 Raja Rd; s/d from ₹550/700, with AC from ₹1200/1600; ❄) With midrange quality at a near-budget price, this neatly furnished, comfortable hotel just off Gandhi Rd is a great deal. All rooms have hot water and TVs, and there's a multicuisine restaurant.

Hotel GP Grand   HOTEL $
(📞2625555; 68 Gandhi Rd; s/d from ₹750/900; ❄) If you want to be near the train station, you can't get much closer or cleaner than the GP Grand.

🍴 Eating

Dehra Dun has an eclectic range of restaurants, but by far the best hunting ground is along Rajpur Rd, northeast of the clock tower.

The Astley Hall precinct is popular for fast food and has a couple of upmarket bars.

Kumar Vegetarian & South Indian Restaurant
INDIAN $$

(15B Rajpur Rd; mains ₹50-150; ⊙lunch & dinner; ❀) This popular, sparkling clean restaurant serves what surely comes close to the Platonic Form of a masala dosa, which is the main reason locals flock here. Other Indian dishes are also cooked to near perfection and even the Chinese food is quite good. The waitstaff are very attentive.

Motimahal
INDIAN $$

(7 Rajpur Rd; mains ₹110-300; ⊙lunch & dinner; ❀) Locals consistently rate Motimahal as one of the best midrange diners along Rajpur Rd. An interesting range of vegetarian and nonvegetarian includes Goan fish curry and Afghani *murg* (chicken), along with traditional South Indian fare and Chinese food.

Lakshmi Restaurant
SOUTH INDIAN $

(Paltan Bazaar; mains ₹22-44; ⊙10.30am-9pm) If you're looking for fast, cheap and tasty, Lakshmi is your place. Near the top of Paltan Bazaar, the busy, blue-walled dining room is a classic Indian restaurant. Dosas and lassis are the specialties, plus chow mein and a few other South Indian snacks.

 Drinking

Maa Cozy Coffee Lounge
CAFE

(76 Rajpur Rd; ⊙11am-11pm) A hip Arabian-style lounge where you can smoke a fruit sheesha (water pipe from ₹210) while reclining on cushions and rugs. Has a big range of tea, coffee and cold drinks.

Polo Bar
BAR

(6 Astley Hall, Rajpur Rd; ⊙11am-11pm) One of the more salubrious of Dehra Dun's many hotel bars, this one is at Hotel President.

Barista
CAFE

(15a Rajpur Rd; drinks & snacks ₹10-50; ⊙9am-11pm) A popular modern cafe with board games and an excellent bookshop next door.

 Shopping

The congested but virtually traffic-free street through **Paltan Bazaar**, running south from the clock tower, is a popular spot for an evening stroll. Here you can pick up everything from cheap clothing and souvenirs to camping and trekking gear.

Among the best bookshops in town are **Natraj Booksellers** (17 Rajpur Rd; ⊙10.30am-1.30pm & 3-8pm Mon-Sat), which gives plenty

of shelf to local author Ruskin Bond, and **English Book Depot** (☑2655192; www.english bookdepot.com; 15 Rajpur Rd; ⊙10am-8pm), attached to the Barista coffee shop.

Though the **Survey of India Map Counter** (⊙9am-5.30pm Mon-Fri; maps ₹20-70) in Harthibarkala is mostly good for being told which topographical maps you're not allowed to buy, you can pick up trekking maps that aren't bad for getting from village to village, but are worthless for backcountry navigation.

 Information

Emergency
Ambulance ☑2650102
Police ☑2653333

Internet Access
iWay (Hotel Grand, Shri Laxmi Plaza, 64 Gandhi Rd; per hr ₹30; ⊙10am-8pm)
Netzone (per hr ₹25; ⊙9am-9pm) Located one block southeast of the clock tower.

Medical Services
Doon College Hospital (☑2760330; General Mahadev Singh Rd)

Money
The banks that are located on Rajpur Rd exchange travellers cheques and currency, and there are numerous ATMs that accept foreign credit cards.

Post
Main post office (Rajpur Rd; ⊙10am-6pm Mon-Fri, 10am-1pm Sat)

Tourist Information
Uttarakhand Tourism office (☑2653217; 45 Gandhi Rd; ⊙10am-5pm Mon-Sat) The local tourist office, attached to the Hotel Drona. There's also a tourist-information counter at the train station.

 Getting There & Away

Air
Kingfisher Airlines (www.flykingfisher.com) flies from Delhi to Dehra Dun's Jolly Grant Airport – about 20km east of the city on the Haridwar road – at 10:50am and 3pm. Flights to Delhi depart at 12:25pm and 4:20pm. A taxi to/from the airport costs ₹550, or take the AC coach for ₹100 (call the Uttarakhand Tourism office for details).

Bus
Nearly all long-distance buses arrive and depart from the huge, modern Interstate Bus Terminal (ISBT), 5km south of the city centre. To get

BUSES FROM DEHRA DUN

The following buses depart from the Interstate Bus Terminal (ISBT).

DESTINATION	FARE (₹)	DURATION (HR)	FREQUENCY
Chandigarh	150	6	hourly btwn 4am & 10pm
Delhi (deluxe)	290/392AC	7	hourly btwn 4am & 10.30pm
Delhi (standard)	200	7	hourly btwn 4am & 10.30pm
Dharamsala	380/700AC	14	12.30pm & 5pm (AC)
Haridwar	50	2	half-hourly
Joshimath	300	12	5.30am
Manali	425	14	3pm
Nainital	275	12	7 per day
Ramnagar	200	7	7 per day
Rishikesh	35	1½	half-hourly
Shimla	240	10	6am, 8am, 10am, 11.30pm
Uttarkashi	225	8	5am & 8am

there take a local bus (₹5), *vikram* 5 (₹10) or an autorickshaw (₹100). A few buses to Mussoorie leave from here but most go from the **Mussoorie bus stand** (₹35, 1½ hours, half-hourly between 6am & 8pm) next to the train station. Some head to Mussoorie's Picture Palace bus stand while others go to the Library bus stand across town. Private buses to Joshimath (₹250, 12 hours, departs 7am) and Uttarkashi (₹190, 9 hours, departs 8.15am & 1pm) leave from the **Parade Ground bus stand**. For more bus details, see the table, p408.

Taxi
A taxi to Mussoorie costs ₹510, while a share taxi should cost ₹100 per person; both can be found in front of the train station. Taxis charge ₹810 to Rishikesh and ₹960 to Haridwar.

Train
Dehra Dun is well connected by train to Delhi, and there are a handful of services to Lucknow, Varanasi, Chennai (Madras) and Kolkata (Calcutta). The quickest service linking Dehra Dun and Delhi is the daily *Shatabdi Express* (chair/executive ₹390/780), which leaves New Delhi train station at 6.50am and reaches Dehra Dun at 12.40pm. The return trip leaves Dehra Dun at 5pm.

The daily *Mussoorie Express* (sleeper/3AC/2AC ₹130/365/508, 11 hours) is an overnight service that leaves Delhi Sarai Rohilla station at 9.05pm. The return trip leaves Dehra Dun at 9.30pm.

The overnight *Dehradun-Amritsar Express* (sleeper/3A ₹127/356, 12 hours) to Amritsar departs daily at 7.40pm.

 ### Getting Around

Hundreds of eight-seater *vikrams* (₹3 to ₹10 per trip) race along five fixed routes (look at the front for the number). Most useful is *vikram* 5, which runs between the ISBT stand, the train station and Rajpur Rd, and as far south as the Tibetan colony at Clement Town. *Vikram* 1 runs up and down Rajpur Rd above Gandhi Park, and also to Harthibarkala (check with the driver to see which route he's on). Autorickshaws cost ₹30 for a short distance, ₹100 from ISBT to the city centre or ₹120 per hour for touring around the city.

Mussoorie

☎ 0135 / POP 29,319 / ELEV 2000M

Perched on a ridge 2km high, the 'Queen of Hill Stations' vies with Nainital as Uttarakhand's favourite holiday destination. When the mist clears, views of the green Doon Valley and the distant white-capped Himalayan peaks are superb, and in the hot months the cooler temperatures and fresh mountain air make a welcome break from the plains below. Although Mussoorie's main bazaars can at first seem like a tacky holiday camp for families and honeymooners, there are plenty of walks in the area, interesting Raj-era buildings, and an upbeat atmosphere.

Established by the British in 1823, Mussoorie became hugely popular with the Raj set. The ghosts of that era linger on in the architecture of the churches, libraries, hotels and summer palaces. The town is swamped with visitors between May and July, but at other times many of the 300 hotels have vacancies and their prices drop dramatically.

Central Mussoorie consists of two developed areas: Gandhi Chowk (also called Library Bazaar) at the western end, and the livelier Kulri Bazaar and Picture Palace at the eastern end, linked by the (almost) traffic-free 2km Mall. Beyond Kulri Bazaar a narrow road leads 5km to the settlement of Landour.

◉ Sights & Activities

Gun Hill   VIEWPOINT
From midway along the Mall, a **cable car** (return ₹55; ☺8am-9pm May-Jul & Oct, 10am-6pm Aug-Sep & late Nov-Apr) runs up to Gun Hill (2530m), which, on a clear day, has views of several big peaks. A steep path also winds up to the viewpoint. The most popular time to go up is an hour or so before sunset and there's a minicarnival atmosphere in high season with kids' rides, food stalls, magic shops and honeymooners having their photos taken in Garhwali costumes.

Walks   WALKING
When the clouds don't get in the way, the walks around Mussoorie offer great views. **Camel's Back Rd** is a popular 3km promenade from Kulri Bazaar to Gandhi Chowk, and passes a rock formation that looks like a camel. There are a couple of good mountain viewpoints along the way, and you can ride a horse (one way/return ₹200/250) along the trail if you start from the Gandhi Chowk end. An enjoyable, longer walk (5km one way) starts at the **Picture Palace Cinema**, goes past **Union Church** and the clock tower to Landour and the Sisters' Bazaar area.

West of Gandhi Chowk, a more demanding walk is to the **Jwalaji Temple** on Benog Hill (about 18km return) via Clouds End Hotel. The walk passes through thick forest and offers some fine views. A slightly shorter walk is to the abandoned **Everest House** (12km return), former residence of Sir George Everest, first surveyor-general of India and namesake of the world's highest mountain. **Trek Himalaya** (☏2630491; Upper Mall; ☺9.30am-8pm) can organise guides for around ₹650 a day.

Jawahar Aquarium   AQUARIUM
(The Mall; admission ₹15; ☺9am-9pm) Just up from the cable-car station, this aquarium is Mussoorie's newest attraction. Kids might like it, but your local pet shop is more impressive.

Courses

Mussoorie is home to many schools and colleges, including the **Landour Language School** (☏2631487; www.landourlanguageschool.com; Landour; ☺1st Mon in Feb-2nd Fri in Dec). One of India's leading schools for teaching conversational Hindi at beginner, intermediate and advanced levels. Group classes are ₹175 per hour, and private tutorials are ₹275 per hour. There's an enrolment fee of ₹250, and course books are an extra ₹2000.

☞ Tours

GMVN Booth   SIGHTSEEING
(☏2631281; Library bus stand; ☺10am-5pm Mon-Sat) GMVN organises a number of local bus tours, including to Kempty Falls (three-hour tour ₹70), and Dhanoltri, Surkhanda Devi Temple and Mussoorie Lake (full-day tour ₹160). Tours can also be booked at the Utterakhand Tourist office on the Lower Mall.

Trek Himalaya   TREKKING
(☏2630491; www.trekhimalaya.com; Upper Mall; ☺9.30am-8pm) For around ₹2500 per day, long-time local trekker Neelambar Badoni organises three-day treks to unspoilt Nagtibba, as well as customised treks to Dodital, Har-ki-Dun and Gaumukh Glacier, and safaris as far as Ladakh.

⌷ Sleeping

Peak season is summer (May to July) when hotel prices shoot to ridiculous heights. There's a midseason during the honeymoon period around October and November, and over Christmas and New Year. At other times you should be able to get a bargain. The following prices are for midseason, unless otherwise specified.

Budget places are few (you'll find some dives near Picture Palace), but most hotels drop their rates to almost budget levels out of season.

TOP CHOICE **Kasmanda Palace Hotel**   HERITAGE HOTEL $$$
(☏2632424; www.kasmandapalace.com; d ₹4000-6500, low-season discount 20%) Located off the Mall, this is Mussoorie's most romantic hotel. The white Romanesque castle was built in 1836 for a British officer and was bought by the Maharaja of Kasmanda in 1915. The red-carpeted hall has a superb staircase

flanked by moth-eaten hunting trophies (the tiger and leopard skins are a sad anachronism). All of the rooms have charm but the wood-panelled and antique-filled Maharaja Room is the royal best. There's also a separate cottage with six renovated contemporary-style rooms. The formal dining room and pretty garden area complete the picture.

Hotel Broadway   HOTEL $
(📞2632243; Camel's Back Rd, Kulri Bazaar; d ₹600-1200, low-season discount 50%) The best of the budget places by a country mile, this historic 1880s wooden hotel with colourful flowerboxes in the windows oozes character without sacrificing comfort. It's in a quiet location but close to the Mall. Room 1 has good views and lovely sunlit bay windows.

Hotel Padmini Nivas   HERITAGE HOTEL $$$
(📞2631093; www.hotelpadmininivas.com; The Mall; d ₹1875-2400, ste ₹2850-3300; @) Built in 1840 by a British colonel and then bought by the Maharaja of Rajpipla, this green-roofed heritage hotel has real old-fashioned charm. Large rooms with quaint sun rooms, suites and even a private cottage are well appointed and beautifully furnished. The dining room, with its antique furniture, is an outstanding feature, and the whole place is set on 2 hectares of landscaped gardens.

✖ Eating

Most of Mussoorie's best eating places are at the Kulri Bazaar and Picture Palace end of town. True to the holiday feel there are lots of fast-food places, and most hotels have their own restaurants. A branch of the popular **Barista** coffee shops is at Gandhi Chowk and there's a **Café Coffee Day** in Kulri Bazaar.

Imperial Square   CONTINENTAL $$
(📞2632632; Gandhi Chowk; mains ₹120-320; ☺7.30am-11pm; 📶) The tastefully understated Imperial, with huge windows overlooking Gandhi Chowk, scores high on everything – decor, service and, most importantly, food. The menu is strong on Continental dishes, with long lists of chicken platters and sizzlers, plus big toasted vegetarian or nonvegetarian sandwiches perfect for lunch. For breakfast you can even have waffles. There's an attached **hotel** (d ₹4000, off-season discount 30%) with excellent rooms with valley views.

Lovely Omelette Centre   FAST FOOD $
(The Mall, Kulri Bazaar; mains ₹35-60; ☺8am-9pm) Mussorie's most famous eatery is also its smallest – a cubbyhole along the Mall that serves what many say are the best omelettes in India (a Facebook page for the restaurant started by an omelette lover

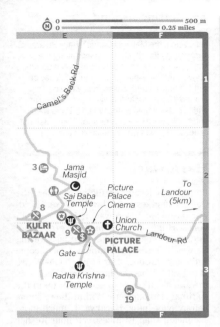

has over 2000 friends). The specialty is the cheese omelette, with chilies, onions and spices, served over toast, but the maestro at the frying pan will whip up a chocolate omelette on request.

**Kasmanda Palace
Restaurant** MULTICUISINE **$$**
(☑2632424; mains ₹110-350) The regal restaurant at this Raj-era hotel (found north of the Mall) is the perfect escape from Mussoorie's holiday bustle. The wood-panelled dining room is intimate but not stuffy, and the garden restaurant is fine for a lazy lunch or summer evening. The food lives up to the setting with North and South Indian dishes, as well as Continental (moussaka and pastas) and Chinese.

Tavern MULTICUISINE **$$**
(The Mall, Picture Palace; mains ₹90-300; ⊙11am-11pm) Run by the same family that owns the Imperial Square, this is a long-time favourite place to dine and hang out, with a global range of food from crispy roast lamb to Goan fish curry and just about everything in between. The decor is a bit British pub, but staff are welcoming and there's live music in the evening. Beer (₹160) and cocktails are available at the bar.

Kalsang Friends Corner TIBETAN **$$**
(The Mall, Kulri Bazaar; mains ₹70-150; ⊙11.30am-10.30pm) Tibetan-run, Kalsang has a longer list of *momos* than you might think possible – and they're done right. Also strong on Thai food, this place is deservedly popular for its coconut curries, Thai papaya salad and noodles.

🛍 Shopping

There's a **Tibetan Market** (The Mall; ⊙from 9am) with cheap clothing and other goods. Mussoorie has a wonderful collection of magic shops, where you can buy cheap but baffling magic tricks and whacky toys – great gifts for kids. These shops are scattered mainly along the Mall and at Gun Hill.

ℹ Information

Internet Access

Connexions (The Mall, Kulri Bazaar; per hr ₹60; ◷10.30am-10.30pm) Above the Tavern.

Money

Axis Bank ATM (The Mall and Gandhi Chowk)

Bank of Baroda ATM (Kulri Bazaar)

State Bank of India ATM (The Mall, Kulri Bazaar)

Trek Himalaya (🕿2630491; Upper Mall; ◷9.30am-8pm) Exchanges major currencies and travellers cheques at a fair rate.

Post

Main post office (🕿2632206; Upper Mall, Kulri Bazaar; ◷9am-5pm Mon-Sat)

Tourist Information

GMVN booth (🕿2631281; Library bus stand; ◷10am-5pm Mon-Sat) Can book local tours, treks and far-flung rest houses.

Uttarakhand Tourism office (🕿2632863; Lower Mall; ◷10am-5pm Mon-Sat) Near the cable-car station.

ℹ Getting There & Away

Bus

Frequent buses leave from Dehra Dun's Mussoorie bus stand (next to the train station) for Mussoorie (₹35, 1½ hours). Some go to the **Picture Palace bus stand** (🕿2632259) while others go to the **Library bus stand** (🕿2632258) at the other end of town – if you know where you're staying it helps to be on the right bus. The return trip takes an hour. There are no direct buses to Rishikesh or Haridwar – change at Dehra Dun.

Mussoorie provides access to the mountain towns of Garhwal, but direct buses are not frequent. Head to the Library bus stand for buses and jeeps heading north. For Yamunotri, take a local bus to Barkot (₹140, 3½ hours), then another to Hanuman Chatti (₹60, 2½ hours), from where there are jeeps. The trip to Sankri for the Har-ki Dun trek also requires a combination of buses and share jeeps. For Uttarkashi, leave from the Tehri bus stand on the way to Landour and change at Chamba.

Taxi

From taxi stands at both bus stands you can hire taxis to Dehra Dun (₹510) and Rishikesh (₹1300), or jeeps to Uttarkashi (₹2700). A shared taxi to Dehra Dun should cost ₹100 per person.

Train

The **Northern Railway booking agency** (🕿2632846; Lower Mall, Kulri Bazaar; ◷8-11am & noon-3pm Mon-Sat, 8am-2pm Sun) books tickets for trains from Dehra Dun and Haridwar.

ℹ Getting Around

Central Mussoorie is very walkable – for a hill station, the Mall and Camel's Back Rd are surprisingly flat. Cycle-rickshaws along the Mall cost ₹20, but can only go between Gandhi Chowk and the cable-car station. A full day of sightseeing around Mussoorie by taxi costs around ₹2000, including visits to the popular and overdeveloped **Kempty Falls**, 15km west, and to **Dhanoltri** – a serene spot 25km east, set in deodar forests with Himalayan views.

Haridwar

🕿01334 / POP 220,433 / ELEV 249M

Propitiously located at the point where the Ganges emerges from the Himalaya, Haridwar (also called Hardwar) is Uttarakhand's holiest Hindu city, and pilgrims arrive here in droves to bathe in the often fast-flowing Ganges. The sheer numbers of people gathering around Har-ki-Pairi Ghat give Haridwar a chaotic but reverent feel – as in Varanasi, it's easy to get caught up in the spiritual clamour here. Within the religious heirarchy of India, Haridwar is much more significant than Rishikesh, an hour further north, and every evening the river comes alive with flickering flames as floating offerings are released onto the Ganges.

Dotted around the city are impressive temples, both ancient and modern, *dharamsalas* (pilgrims' guesthouses) and ashrams, some of which are the size of small villages. Haridwar is busy during the *yatra* (pilgrimage) season from May to October, and is the site of the annual Magh Mela religious festival.

Haridwar's main street is Railway Rd, becoming Upper Rd, and runs parallel to the Ganges canal (the river proper runs further to the east). Generally only cycle-rickshaws are allowed between Laltarao Bridge and Bhimgoda Jhula (Bhimgoda Bridge), so vehicles travel around the opposite bank of the river. The alleyways of Bara Bazaar run south of Har-ki-Pairi Ghat.

◉ Sights & Activities

Har-ki-Pairi Ghat   GHAT

Har-ki-Pairi (The Footstep of God) is where Vishnu is said to have dropped some heavenly nectar and left behind a footprint. As such, it is very sacred to Hindus, and is the place to wash away your sins. Pilgrims bathe here in its often fast currents and donate money to the priests and shrines.

The ghat sits on the western bank of the Ganges canal, and every evening hundreds

of worshippers gather for the *ganga aarti* (river worship ceremony). Officials in blue uniforms collect donations (and give out receipts) and, as the sun sets, bells ring out a rhythm, torches are lit, and leaf baskets with flower petals inside and a candle on top (₹10) are lit and put on the river to drift away downstream.

Tourists can mingle with the crowd to experience the rituals of an ancient religion that still retains its power in the modern age. Someone may claim to be a priest and help you with your *puja* before asking for ₹200 or more. If you want to make a donation, give it to a uniformed collector, or put money in a charity box.

The best times to visit the ghat are early morning or just before dusk.

Mansa Devi & Chandi Devi Temples   HINDU TEMPLES

Take the **cable car** (return ₹48; ☺7am-7pm Apr-Oct, 8.30am-6pm Nov-Mar) to the crowded hilltop temple of **Mansa Devi**, a wish-fulfilling goddess. The path to the cable car is lined with stalls selling packages of *prasad* (food offering used in religious ceremonies) to take up to the goddess on the hill. You can walk up (1.5km) but beware of *prasad*-stealing monkeys. Photography is forbidden in the temple.

Many visitors and pilgrims combine this with a **cable car** (return ₹117; ⊘8am-6pm) up Neel Hill, 4km southeast of Haridwar, to **Chandi Devi Temple**. The temple was built by Raja Suchet Singh of Kashmir in 1929. Pay ₹165 at Mansa Devi and you can ride both cable cars and take an AC coach between the two temples.

Tours

From his office next to Chitra Talkies cinema, Sanjeev Mehta of **Mohan's Adventure Tours** (☑9412022966, 9319051335; www.mohansadventure.in; Railway Rd; ⊘8am-10.30pm) can organise any kind of tour, including trekking, fishing, birdwatching, cycling, motorcycling and rafting. An accomplished wildlife photographer, he specialises in five-hour safaris (₹2350 per person) around Rajaji National Park. Sanjeev also runs three-day trips to Corbett Tiger Reserve (from ₹7000). Tours operate year-round.

🛏 Sleeping

Haridwar has loads of hotels catering to Hindu pilgrims. The busiest time of year is the *yatra* season from April to November – outside this time you should have no problem finding a room at discounts of 20% to 50%. For details on staying at an ashram, see the boxed text below.

Jassa Ram Rd and the other alleys running off Railway Rd have plenty of budget hotels and although some of the fancy foyers and neon signs may raise your hopes, none are great. Rishikesh has far superior budget accommodation.

Down by the ghats are a number of similar high-rise hotels that are recommended mainly for the location and views, and are popular with middle-class pilgrims.

TOP CHOICE Haveli Hari Ganga   HERITAGE HOTEL **$$$**
(☑226443; www.havelihariganga.com; 21 Ram Ghat; r ₹4000-5000; ✳🖥) Hidden away in Bara Bazaar, but right on the Ganges, this superb 1918 *haveli* (traditional, ornately decorated residence) is Haridwar's finest hotel. Airy courtyards, marble floors, hanging flower baskets and balconies overlooking the river give it a regal charm. Room rates include breakfast, steam bath, yoga and the hotel's own *ganga aarti* on its private ghat. The Ganges laps one terrace, and downstairs an ayurvedic health spa offers treatments as well as yoga classes. It's hard to find, so call ahead for a pick-up.

Yatri Niwas   HOTEL **$$**
(☑226004; www.yatriniwas.com; Upper Rd; r ₹1000) Just a few minutes walk from Har-ki-Pairi Ghat and the Mansa Devi cable car, this place is set back from the road around a surprisingly quiet courtyard. Rooms are good value, with nice wooden furnishings, glass and steel light fixtures, flat-screen TVs and modern bathrooms.

Bhaj-Govindam   HOTEL **$$**
(☑261682; www.bhajgovindam.com; Upper Rd; huts ₹800, d from ₹1800; ✳) Located on Upper Rd about 100m north of Bhimgoda Jhula, Bhaj-Govindam is in a wonderful spot with river frontage on the banks of the Ganges. Set around a grassy garden and with an am-

---

HARIDWAR'S ASHRAM STAYS

Most travellers make a beeline for Rishikesh to partake in yoga and spirituality and to stay in an ashram, but Haridwar has several serious ashrams where you'll be surrounded by longer-term practitioners and a less commercial feel. The two most accessible to foreigners:

Shri Prem Nagar Ashram (☑226345; www.manavdharam.com; Jwalapur Rd) This large ashram was founded by Hansji Maharaj, who died in 1966. His extraordinary mausoleum features a pyramidical blue ceiling with eight steps representing the seven holy rivers and the sea. Silent meditation takes place at 5am and singing prayers are at 7.30pm. The ashram has its own cows, ayurvedic medicine factory and bookshop, as well as a huge, pillarless meeting hall and a ghat facing the Ganges. Plain rooms (from ₹300) have fans, private bathrooms and hot water.

Mohyal Ashram (☑9219441137; mohans_india@yahoo.com; Rishikesh Rd; d ₹650, with AC ₹1200; ✳) More a yoga retreat than an ashram, Mohyal has peaceful lawns, marble floors and a meditation and yoga hall with wonderful acoustics. The spotless, almost luxurious accommodation includes meals and occasional classes. This is not a strict ashram (although smoking, alcohol and meat are prohibited), and casual guests are welcome.

biance that's classy yet casual, rooms are as comfortable as you'd expect for the price, with some of the best mattresses in town. There are also a couple of worn reed huts you can stay in.

Hotel Swagat Palace HOTEL $
(☎221581; Jassa Ram Rd; d with/without AC ₹950/450; ❄) Rooms here are large and clean, with tiled floors. Each has its own quirks, so check out a few, but all in all it's decent value and close to the train and bus stations. Ask for a discount and you will probably get it.

🍴 Eating & Drinking

Being a holy city, only vegetarian food and nonalcoholic drinks are available.

Hoshiyar Puri INDIAN $
(Upper Rd; mains ₹40-70; ⊙11am-4pm & 7pm-4am) Established in 1937, this place still has a loyal (and well-deserved) local following. The *dal makhani* (Kashmiri beans and lentils), *lacha paratha* (layered fried bread), *aloo gobi* (potato-and-cauliflower curry) and *kheer* (rice pudding) are lip-smackingly good.

Big Ben Restaurant MULTICUISINE $$
(Hotel Ganga Azure, Railway Rd; mains ₹80-150; ⊙8.30am-10.30pm) Watch the passing parade through the big windows and enjoy some of Haridwar's best food in this restaurant of mirrors, soft music and polite staff. It's a solid choice for breakfast, with good coffee. There's wi-fi in the adjoining lobby.

Haveli Hari Ganga Restaurant INDIAN $$$
(☎226443; www.havelihariganga.com; 21 Ram Ghat; dinner buffet ₹450; ⊙8.30-11pm) The Indian vegetarian buffet at this lovely heritage hotel is the classiest in Haridwar.

Prakash Lok LASSI $
(Bara Bazaar; lassis ₹20). Don't miss a creamy lassi at this Haridwar institution, known for its ice-cold, best-you'll-ever-have lassis served in tin cups. Just about anyone in the Bara Bazaar can point you to it.

ℹ️ Information

Internet Access
There are a number of internet places on Railway Rd near the train station and down the side lanes, but most have only one or two terminals. These places have more.
Hillway Internet (Jassa Ram Rd; per hr ₹30; ⊙9am-10.30pm)

Internet Zone iWay (Upper Rd; per hr ₹30; ⊙10am-8.30pm)

Medical Services
Rishikul Ayurvedic Hospital (☎221003; Railway Rd) A long-established medical college and hospital with a good reputation.

Money
Sai Forex (Upper Rd; ⊙10am-9pm) Changes cash and travellers cheques for a commission of 1%.
State Bank of India ATM (Railway Rd)

Post
Main post office (Upper Rd; ⊙10am-6pm Mon-Sat)

Tourist Information
GMVN tourist office (☎224240; Railway Rd; ⊙10am-5pm Mon-Sat)
Uttarakhand Tourism office (☎265304; Rahi Motel, Railway Rd; ⊙10am-5pm Mon-Sat)

ℹ️ Getting There & Away

Haridwar is well connected by bus and train, but book ahead for trains during the pilgrimage season (May to October).

Bus
For details of major bus routes from Haridwar, see the table, p416.

Private deluxe buses and sleeper buses run to Delhi (deluxe/Volvo ₹175/400), Agra (seat/sleeper ₹240/295), Jaipur (₹375/475) and Pushkar (₹400/500). They leave from a stand around the corner from the GMVN tourist office by the gurdwara (Sikh temple), and any travel agent in town can make a booking.

Taxi & Vikram
The main taxi stand is outside the train station on Railway Rd. Destinations include Chilla (for Rajaji National Park, ₹510), Rishikesh (₹700, one hour) and Dehra Dun (₹1000), but it's usually possible to arrange a taxi for less than these official rates. You can hire private jeep Sumos to go to one or all of the pilgrimage sites on the Char Dham between April and October. One-way rates for Gangotri, Yamnotri and Badrinath are ₹6520 each; Kedarnath costs ₹5500; a 9-day tour of all four is ₹17,150.

Shared *vikrams* run up and down Railway Rd (₹10) and to Rishikesh (₹30, one hour) from Upper Rd at Laltarao Bridge, but for that trip buses are more comfortable. You can hire the whole thing to Rishikesh's Lakshman Jhula for ₹400.

Train
The trains listed in the table on p417 run daily, except as indicated.

BUSES FROM HARIDWAR

The following buses depart from the UP Roadways bus stand on Railway Rd.

DESTINATION	FARE (₹)	DURATION (HR)	FREQUENCY
Agra	300	12	early morning
Almora	370	10	early morning & 5.30pm
Chandigarh	140	10	hourly
Dehra Dun	44	2	half-hourly
Delhi	140	6	half-hourly
Dharamsala	350	15	2.30pm & 4.30pm
Jaipur	310	12	early morning
Nainital	300	8	early morning & evening
Ranikhet	230	10	6am & 5pm
Rishikesh	22	1	half-hourly
Shimla	255	14	1.30am, 12.30pm & 5.30pm
Uttarkashi	200	10	5.30am, 7.30am & 9.30am

In the *yatra* (pilgrimage) season from May to October, the following buses run from the GMOU bus stand on Railway Rd. During monsoon season (July to mid-September), service is occasionally suspended. For current info, call ☑9897924247 for the Gangotri route and ☑9364936474 for Kedarnath and Badrinath buses.

DESTINATION	FARE (₹)	DURATION (HR)	FREQUENCY
Badrinath (via Joshimath)	325	15	4.15am & 5am
Gangotri	300	10	5am
Kedarnath	235	10	5.30am & 7am

ⓘ Getting Around

Cycle-rickshaws cost ₹10 for a short distance and ₹30 for longer hauls, such as from the Haridwar train station to Har-ki-Pairi. Hiring a taxi for three hours to tour the local temples and ashrams costs around ₹700; an autorickshaw costs ₹300.

Rajaji National Park

ELEV 300-1000M

This unspoilt **park** (www.rajajinationalpark.in; admission Indian/foreigner per day ₹150/600; ◷15 Nov-15 Jun), covering 820 sq km in the forested foothills near Haridwar, is best known for its wild elephants, numbering around 450 at last count.

As well as elephants, the park contains some 15 tigers and 100 leopards. Although they're not easily seen, they have thousands of chital (spotted deer) and hundreds of sambars (India's largest species of deer) to feed on. A handful of rarely seen sloth bears are hidden away. Some 300 species of birds also add interest.

Rajaji's forests include the traditional winter territory of over 1000 families of nomadic Van Gujjar buffalo herders – most of whom have been evicted from the park against their will. For more on this and other issues affecting the unique Van Gujjar tribe, visit www.sophiaindia.org.

The village of **Chilla**, 13km northeast of Haridwar, is the base for visiting the park. At the Forest Ranger's office, close to the tourist guesthouse at Chilla, you can pick up a brochure, pay entry fees and organise a jeep. These take up to eight people and cost ₹700 for the standard safari (plus a ₹100 entry fee for the vehicle). Elephant rides are no longer offered at Rajaji.

Before visiting, contact the **GMVN tourist office** (Map p413; ☑2244240; Railway Rd, Haridwar; ◷10am-5pm Mon-Sat) and **Mohan's Adventure Tours** (Map p413; ☑220910; www.mohansadventure.in; Railway Rd, Haridwar; ◷8am-

DESTINATION	TRAIN	FARE (₹)	DURATION (HR)	DEPARTURE/ ARRIVAL
Delhi (Old Delhi Station)	Mussoorie Express	sleeper/3AC/2AC 147/384/522	8¾	11.10pm/7.55am
Delhi (New Delhi Station)	Shatabdi Express	chair car/executive 512/950	4½	6.13pm/10.45pm
Delhi (New Delhi Station)	Jan Shatabdi Express	2nd class/chair car 110/352	4½	6.22am/11.15am
Lucknow	Doon Express	sleeper/3AC/2AC 212/564/772	10	10.15pm/8.15am
Varanasi	Doon Express	sleeper/3AC/2AC 298/811/1112	18	10.15pm/4.10pm
Kolkata/Howrah	Doon Express	sleeper/3AC/2AC 423/1152/1587	32	10.15pm/7am (two nights later)
Amritsar	Jan Shatabdi	2nd class/chair car 140/457	7	2.35pm/9.45pm
Amritsar	Dehra Dun– Amritsar Express	sleeper/3AC/1st class 192/503/580	9¾	9.40pm/7.25am
Haldwani (for Nanital and Almora)	Dehra Dun–Kath- godam Express	sleeper/2AC/1AC 146/516/860	6½	12.20am/6.50am

10.30pm), which offers abridged safaris even when the park is officially closed. These are five-hour trips (₹2350 per person) that include being taken on a short safari, hopefully seeing a parade of wild elephants, and maybe visiting a Van Gujjar forest camp. If you're lucky, Sanjeev might take you to see his legally adopted orphaned elephant.

🛏 Sleeping & Eating

The Chilla Guesthouse (☎0138-226678; r with AC Indian/foreigner ₹1500/3000; ❄) is the GMVN rest house and the most comfortable place to stay in Chilla. There's a good restaurant here and a pleasant garden.

Within the park there are nine historic but basic forest rest houses at Asarohi, Beribara, Kansrao and Motichur (₹1000/2000 per Indian/foreigner), as well as Chilla, Phandowala and Ranipur (₹750/1500 per Indian/ foreigner). If you're staying at one of the rest houses, the park entry fee is valid for three days. The 1883 forest rest house in Chilla has three rooms downstairs and a suite upstairs with a balcony, while the one at Kansrao has retained its original features. No food is available (except in Chilla) and if you don't have your own transport you will have to make a special arrangement with a jeep driver. To book a forest rest house, contact the director at the Rajaji National Park Office (☎/fax 0135-2621669; 5/1 Ansari Marg, Dehra Dun). Mohan's Adventure Tours (see p414) can also make bookings.

There's also a new safari resort in the park north of Chilla, Camp King Elephant (☎9871604712; cottage per Indian/foreigner from ₹4000/$110), with solar electricity, private bathrooms, full meal service and optional jeep tours.

❶ Getting There & Away

Buses to Chilla (₹20, one hour) leave the GMOU bus stand in Haridwar every hour from 7am to 2pm. The last return trip leaves Chilla at 5.30pm. Taxis charge ₹510 one way for the 13km journey.

Rishikesh

☎0135 / POP 79,591 / ELEV 356M

Ever since the Beatles rocked up at the ashram of the Maharishi Mahesh Yogi in the late '60s, Rishikesh has been a magnet for spiritual seekers. Today it styles itself as the 'Yoga Capital of the World', with masses of ashrams and all kinds of yoga and meditation classes. Most of this action is north of the main town, where the exquisite setting on the fast-flowing

UTTARAKHAND

Rishikesh

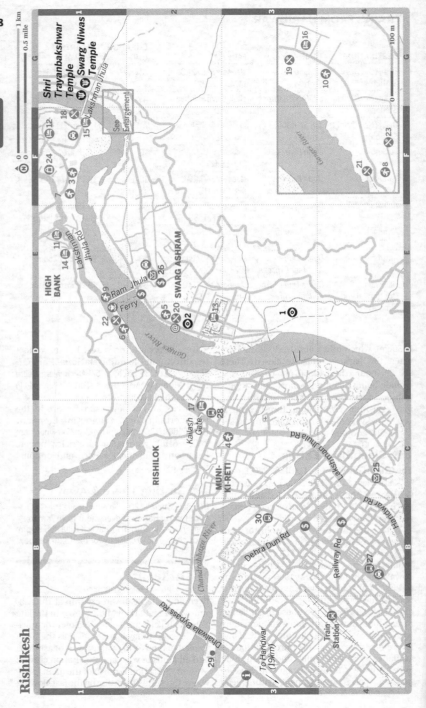

Shri Trayambakshwar Temple

Swarg Niwas Temple

Lakshman Jhula

See Enlargement

Ram Jhula

Ferry

HIGH BANK

Lakshman Jhula Rd

SWARG ASHRAM

Ganges River

RISHILOK

Kailash Gate

MUNI-KI-RETI

Dehra Dun Rd

Chandrabhaga River

Dhalwala Bypass Rd

To Haridwar (19km)

Lakshman Jhula Rd

Haridwar Rd

Railway Rd

Train Station

Ganges River

1 km

0.5 mile

Ganges, surrounded by forested hills, is conducive to meditation and mind expansion. In the evening, the breeze blows down the valley, setting temple bells ringing as sadhus (spiritual men), pilgrims and tourists prepare for the nightly *ganga aarti*.

Rishikesh is very New Age: you can learn to play the sitar or tabla on your hotel roof; try laughing yoga; practise humming or gong meditation; experience crystal healing and all styles of massage; have a go at chanting mantras; and listen to spiritually uplifting CDs as you sip ayurvedic tea with your vegetarian meal.

But it's not all spirituality and contorted limbs. Rishikesh is now a popular whitewater rafting centre, backpacker hang-out, and gateway to treks in the Himalaya.

Rishikesh is divided into two main areas: the crowded, unattractive downtown area (Rishikesh town), where you'll find the bus and train stations as well as the Triveni Ghat; and the riverside communities 2km upstream around Ram Jhula and Lakshman Jhula, where most of the accommodation, ashrams,

restaurants and travellers are ensconced. The two *jhula* (suspension bridges) that cross the river are pedestrian-only. Swarg Ashram, located on the eastern bank, is the traffic-free 'spiritual centre' of Rishikesh, while High Bank, west of Lakshman Jhula, is a small enclave popular with backpackers.

◎ Sights

Lakshman Jhula & Around   AREA
The defining image of Rishikesh is the view across the Lakshman Jhula hanging bridge to the huge, 13-storey wedding-cake temples of **Swarg Niwas** and **Shri Trayanbakshwar**. Built by the organisation of the guru Kailashanand, they resemble fairyland castles and have dozens of shrines to Hindu deities on each level, interspersed with jewellery and textile shops. Sunset is an especially good time to photograph the temples from the bridge itself, and you'll hear the bell-clanging and chanting of devotees in the morning and evening. Shops selling devotional CDs add to the cacophony of noise on this side of the river.

Markets, restaurants, ashrams and guest-houses sprawl on both sides of the river; in recent years the area has grown into the busiest and liveliest part of upper Rishikesh.

Swarg Ashram
AREA

A pleasant 2km south of Lakshman Jhula along the path skirting the east bank of the Ganges leads to the spiritual community of Swarg Ashram, made up of temples, ashrams, a crowded bazaar, sadhus and the bathing ghats where religious ceremonies are performed at sunrise and sunset. The colourful, though rather touristy, *ganga aarti* is held at the riverside temple of the **Parmarth Niketan Ashram** every evening at sunset, with singing, chanting, musicians and the lighting of candles.

Maharishi Mahesh Yogi Ashram
HISTORIC BUILDING

Just south of Swarg Ashram, slowly being consumed by the forest undergrowth, is what's left of the original Maharishi Mahesh Yogi Ashram. It was abandoned in 1997 and is now back under the control of the forest department. However, the shells of many buildings, meditation cells and lecture halls can still be seen, including Maharishi's own house and the guest house where the Beatles stayed and apparently wrote much of the *White Album*.

🏃 Activities

Yoga & Meditation

Rishikesh styles itself as the yoga capital of the world, and yoga and meditation are the buzzwords here. Teaching and yoga styles vary tremendously, so check out a few classes before committing yourself to a course. If you want to get started, virtually every hotel offers one-hour yoga sessions for around ₹100, but ashram stays are the best way to truly immerse yourself in the spiritual vibe. Many places also offer ayurvedic massage.

Sri Sant Seva Ashram
MIXED YOGA

(☏2430465; www.santsewaashram.com; Laksh-man Jhula; d ₹150-600, with AC ₹1000; @) Over-looking the Ganges in Lakshman Jhula, the large rooms here are popular, so book ahead. The more expensive rooms have balconies with river views. The yoga classes are mixed styles and open to all. Beginner (₹100) and intermediate and advanced (₹200) sessions run daily. There are also courses in reiki, ayurvedic massage and cooking.

Omkarananda Ganga Sadan
IYENGAR YOGA

(☏2430763; www.iyengaryoga.in; Lakshman Jhula Rd; r with/without AC ₹850/280, minimum 3-day stay) Also on the river, at Ram Jhula, this ash-ram has comfortable rooms and specialises in Iyengar yoga classes at the Patanjala Yoga Kendra centre. There are daily classes (except Sunday; ₹250) and intensive seven- to 10-day courses (₹800) on offer from October to May. The ashram has its own ghat and evening *ganga aarti*.

Sivananda Ashram
YOGA, MEDITATION

(☏2430040; www.sivanandaonline.org; Lakshman Jhula Rd) Founded by Swami Shivananda, this ashram is run by the Divine Life Society. Free yoga and meditation classes are available every morning, but two months' advance notice is required if you want to stay here – email the ashram through its website.

Parmarth Niketan Ashram
HATHA YOGA

(☏244008; www.parmarth.com; Swarg Ashram; r ₹600) Dominating the centre of Swarg Ashram and drawing visitors to its evening *ganga aarti* on the riverbank, Parmarth has a wonderfully ornate and serene garden courtyard. The price includes a room with a private bathroom, all meals and hatha yoga lessons.

Rafting, Kayaking & Trekking

A number of companies offer full- and half-day rafting trips, putting in upstream and paddling back to Rishikesh. Some also offer multiday rafting trips, staying at raft-ing camps along the river bank. The offi-cial rafting season runs from 15 September to 30 June. A half-day trip starts at about ₹800 per person, while a full day costs from ₹1500. Most companies also offer all-inclusive Himalayan treks to places such as Kuari Pass, Har-ki Dun and Gangotri from around ₹2300 per day.

De-N-Ascent Expeditions
KAYAKING, TREKKING

(☏2442354; www.kayakhimalaya.com; Tapovan Sarai, Lakshman Jhula) Specialist in kayaking lessons and expeditions. Learn to paddle and eskimo roll with an experienced instructor, or go on multiday kayaking or rafting adventures. Also organises trekking trips.

GMVN Trekking & Mountaineering Division
TREKKING

(☏2430799; www.gmvnl.com; Lakshman Jhula Rd, Muni-ki-Reti; ⊙10am-5pm) Can arrange high-altitude treks in the Garhwal Himalaya and hires out trekking equipment, guides and porters.

Red Chilli Adventure TREKKING, RAFTING
(☏2434021; www.redchilliadventure.com; Lakshman Jhula Rd; ⏱9am-9pm) Reliable outfit offering Himalayan trekking and rafting trips throughout Uttarakhand and to Himachal Pradesh and Ladakh.

Walks & Beaches

An easy, 15-minute walk to two small **waterfalls** starts 3km north of Lakshman Jhula bridge on the south side of the river. The start is marked by drink stalls and a roadside shrine, and the path is easy to find. Four-wheel-drive taxis cost ₹100 from Lakshman Jhula.

On the other side of the river, it's about 2km north to the signposted walk to lovely **Neer Garh Waterfall** (admission ₹30), from where it's a 20-minute uphill walk.

For a longer hike, follow the dedicated pilgrims who take water from the Ganges to offer at **Neelkantha Mahadev Temple**, a 7km, approximately three-hour walk along a forest path from Swarg Ashram.

🍃 Courses

Look out for flyers around Lakshman Jhula, Swarg Ashram and High Bank advertising music tuition and concerts.

Om Rudra Cultural Society (☏98376 54284; rudradance@rediffmail.com; Swarg Ashram; ⏱Sep-May) is run by an enterprising couple and offers *kathak* (classical) dance, flute, tabla or Hindi lessons.

Sachdeva Language Service (☏98971 03808; sachdevalanguage@yahoo.com.uk; Lakshman Jhula; per hr ₹150) offers casual one-on-one Hindi language instruction.

✦ Festivals & Events

In the first week of March, Rishikesh hosts the **International Yoga Festival** (www.international yogafestival.com), attracting swamis and yoga masters from around the world for discourses and lectures. Most of the action is centred on the Parmarth Niketan Ashram in Swarg Ashram. Check the festival website for dates.

🛏 Sleeping

Most of the accommodation is spread on both sides of the river around Lakshman Jhula; there are a handful of hotels among the ashrams at Swarg Ashram and directly across the river around Ram Jhula, and some good budget places at High Bank. For ashram stays, see p420.

Midrange and top-end hotels are in relatively short supply in budget-minded Rishikesh.

HIGH BANK

This small, leafy travellers' enclave is a 20-minute walk up the hill from Lakshman Jhula and has some of the best backpacker accommodation in Rishikesh. All of the following places are clean, relaxed and good value. It gets pretty rowdy during peak season from November to March.

New Bhandari Swiss Cottage HOTEL $
(☏2435322; www.newbhandariswisscottage.com; d ₹300-800, AC cottages ₹1200-1800; ❄@) One of the last places on the High Bank lane, this is a large, popular place with rooms ranging from clean and simple to simply impressive. There's a massage centre, a good restaurant, and a helpful travel desk in their internet cafe.

High Bank Peasants Cottage HOTEL $$
(☏2431167; d ₹600-800, with AC ₹1500-2000; ❄@🛜) A High Bank original, this is the

---

THE MAHARISHI & THE BEATLES

In February 1968 Rishikesh hit world headlines when the Beatles and their partners stayed at Maharishi Mahesh Yogi's ashram in Swarg Ashram, following an earlier visit by George Harrison. Ringo Starr and his wife didn't like the vegetarian food, missed their children and left after a couple of weeks, but the others stayed for a month or two. They relaxed and wrote tons of songs, many of which ended up on their double album *White Album*. But rumours of the Maharishi's demands for money and his behaviour towards some female disciples eventually disillusioned all of them. 'You made a fool of everyone,' John Lennon sang about the Maharishi. In later years, Harrison and Paul McCartney said, on record, that the rumours were unfounded. The original ashram is now abandoned, but nearly 40 years on, idealistic foreigners still swarm into Rishikesh seeking spiritual enlightenment from teachers and healers in their tranquil ashrams scattered along the Ganges River.

most upmarket accommodation here (it's closer to midrange than budget). Lovely gardens feature flowering trees and giant cacti, there are wicker chairs on the balconies, and the spacious rooms are neatly furnished.

Bhandari Swiss Cottage   HOTEL $
(2432939; www.bhandariswisscottage.com; r ₹150-600, ste with AC ₹1500; ✳@) The first place you come to, this is a well-run backpacker favourite with rooms in several budgets – the higher up you stay, the higher the price. Rooms with big balconies have expansive views of the river backed by green mountains. Excellent little restaurant, internet cafe and yoga classes.

LAKSHMAN JHULA
There are several good budget options on both sides of the river here, which is the liveliest part of Rishikesh.

Divine Ganga Cottage   HOTEL $
(2442175; www.divindgangacottage.com; r ₹300-600; ✳@) Tucked away from the hubbub and surrounded by small rice paddies and local homes with gardens, the huge upstairs terrace has supreme river views. Sweet rooms for the price have nice beds, and some have writing tables. There's an ayurvedic spa and yoga instruction on some days.

Hotel Surya   HOTEL $
(2433211; www.hotelsuryalaxmanjhula.com; s/d ₹150/250) Above the Coffee Day, Surya is great value. Some rooms have balconies overlooking the river and all are good-sized and clean, though there are signs that mice like it here too. The management is friendly and helpful.

Hotel Ishan   HOTEL $
(2431534; narendra_u@hotmail.com; r ₹250-700; @) This long-running riverfront place near Lakshman Jhula looks a bit rough, but has a wide range of clean rooms, some with balconies overlooking the river. The top-floor room with TV and balcony has a prime view.

SWARG ASHRAM & MUNI-KI-RETI
If you're serious about yoga and introspection, stay at one of Swarg's numerous ashrams. Otherwise, there's a knot of guest houses a block back from the river towards the southern end of Swarg.

Green Hotel   HOTEL $$
(2434948; www.hotelgreen.com; Swarg Ashram; d with/without AC ₹1300/750; ✳@) In a small enclave of hotels down an alleyway, the newly renovated Green has bright rooms with tasteful furnishings, hot showers and flat-screen TVs. There are peaceful views of the hills – but not the river – from the rooftop terrace. Hallways on some floors are connected by wooden bridges over the atrium. The sibling Green View Hotel around the corner is a bit cheaper (₹500-900) but not as nice.

Vasundhara Palace   HOTEL $$$
(2442345; www.vasundharapalace.com; Muni-ki-Reti; s/d ₹2950/3550, ste ₹5500; ✳✳) Rishikesh's top riverside hotel, this modern high-rise has luxurious, tastefully designed rooms, an elegant restaurant, and a rooftop pool and health spa with river views – unfortunately, views from the rooms are blocked by apartments.

Hotel Rajpalace   HOTEL $
(2440079; rajholidays@hotmail.com; Swarg Ashram; d ₹450-650, with AC from ₹1000; ✳) This is a small but well-run hotel with clean rooms and friendly staff. The rooftop terrace has views, and facilities include a yoga hall and a travel agent offering tours and activities.

✗ Eating
Virtually every restaurant in Rishikesh serves only vegetarian food, but there are lots of travellers' restaurants whipping up various interpretations of Continental and Israeli food, as well as Indian and Chinese.

LAKSHMAN JHULA
TOP CHOICE Little Buddha Cafe   MULTICUISINE $$
(mains ₹70-140; ⊘8am-11pm) This funky treehouse-style restaurant has an ultraloungey top floor, tables overlooking the Ganga, and really good international food. Pizzas are big and the mixed vegetable platter is a serious feast. It's one of the busiest places in Lakshman Jhula, for good reasons.

Devraj Coffee Corner   CAFE $
(snacks & mains ₹30-100; ⊘8am-9pm) Perched above the bridge and looking across the river to Shri Trayanbakshwar temple, this German bakery is a sublime spot for a break at any time of the day. The coffee is the best in town and the menu ranges from specialties like brown bread with yak cheese to soups and sizzlers, along with the usual croissants and apple strudel. There's a good new and used bookshop next door.

Pyramid Cafe   MULTICUISINE $
(mains ₹35-95; ⊘8am-10.30pm; 🛜) Sit on cushions inside pyramid-shaped tents and choose

from a menu of home-cooked Indian food, plus a few Tibetan and Western dishes including pancakes. The family that runs it is super friendly and they also rent out a peaceful, well-kept pyramid tent with a double bed and attached bath (₹250). At the time of research, this was the only cafe in Rishikesh that had wi-fi (per hour ₹ 20). Bonus!

Ganga Beach Restaurant MULTICUISINE **$**
(mains ₹60-120; ⊙8am-10pm) Great riverside location with a spacious terrace and big menu including crepes and ice-cold lassis.

Lucky Restaurant INDIAN **$**
(mains ₹40-100; ⊙9am-10pm) An awesome riverside garden shaded by a huge tree and a cushioned area.

La Bella View MULTICUISINE **$**
(mains ₹60-120; ⊙9m-11pm) A good menu and a split personality: upstairs is more refined, with tables overlooking the river, while the cushioned downstairs area has a hippie-den vibe.

SWARG ASHRAM & RAM JHULA
Madras Cafe INDIAN **$**
(Ram Jhula; mains ₹50-120) This local institution dishes up tasty South and North Indian vegetarian food, thalis, a mean mushroom curry, whole-wheat pancakes and the intriguing Himalayan 'health *pilau*', as well as super-thick lassis.

Green Italian Restaurant ITALIAN **$$**
(Swarg Ashram; mains ₹60-150) Wood-fired vegetarian pizzas and imported pastas including gnocchi and cannelloni keep the customers coming back to this spotless, glass-fronted restaurant in the heart of Swarg.

HIGH BANK
Backpackers gather at the popular restaurants on High Bank. This is the only area in town where you'll find meat on the menu.

Oasis Restaurant MULTICUISINE **$$**
(mains ₹45-190) At New Bhandari Swiss Cottage, this place has some character, with candlelit tables in the garden and hanging lanterns inside. The menu covers oodles of world cuisines, from Mexican and Thai to Israeli and Tibetan, and features a number of chicken dishes including a delicious chilli chicken. Great desserts include apple crumble.

Shopping
Swarg Ashram is the place to go for bookshops, ayurvedic herbal medicines, clothing, handicrafts and tourist trinkets such as jewellery and Tibetan singing bowls, though there are also plenty of stalls around Lakshman Jhula. Many stalls sell *rudraksh mala* (the strings of beads used in *puja*), made from the nuts of the rudraksh tree, which originally grew where Shiva's tears fell. Beads with *mukhi* (different faces) confer various blessings on the wearer.

If you need outdoor gear, your best bet is **Adventure Compass** (9899297904; www.adventurecompass.com; Badrinath Rd, Lakshman Jhula), which stocks everything from sleeping bags and carabiners to climbing harnesses and trekking boots.

ℹ️ Information
Dangers & Annoyances
Travellers should be cautious of being befriended by sadhus – while many sadhus are on genuine spiritual journeys, the orange robes have been used as a disguise by fugitives from the law since medieval times.

The current in some parts of the Ganges is very strong, and as inviting as a dip from one of the beaches may seem, people drown here every year. Don't swim out of your depth.

Women walking alone may be at risk.

Internet Access
Internet access is available all over town, usually for ₹20 or ₹30 per hour.

Blue Hills Travels (Swarg Ashram; per hr ₹30; ⊙8am-10pm)

Lucky Internet (Lakshman Jhula; per hr ₹30; ⊙8.30am-10pm) Wi-fi access.

Red Chilli Adventure (Lakshman Jhula Rd; per hr ₹30; ⊙9am-9pm) Surf with a view.

Medical Services
Himalayan Institute Hospital (2471133; ⊙24hr) The nearest large hospital, 17km along the road to Dehra Dun and 1km beyond Jolly Grant airport.

Shivananda Ashram (2430040; www.sivanandaonline.org; Lakshman Jhula Rd) Provides free medical services and a pharmacy.

Money
Several travel agents around Lakshman Jhula and Swarg Ashram will exchange travellers cheques and cash.

Axis Bank ATM (Swarg Ashram)
Bank of Baroda ATM (Dehra Dun Rd)
State Bank of India ATM (Swarg Ashram & Dehra Dun Rd)

Post
Main post office (Ghat Rd; ⊙10am-4pm Mon-Fri, 10am-1pm Sat) Near Triveni Ghat.

Post office (Swarg Ashram; ◷10am-4pm Mon-Fri, 10am-1pm Sat)

Tourist Information
Uttarakhand Tourism office (☎2430209; Dhalwala Bypass Rd; ◷10am-5pm Mon-Sat) Inconveniently located out on the road to Haridwar, it's in the same building as the GMVN Yatra office. It has a few brochures and can book tours.

ⓘ Getting There & Away

Bus
There are regular buses to Haridwar and Dehra Dun; for Mussoorie change at Dehra Dun. Buses run north to pilgrimage centres during the *yatra* season (April to November), and to Joshimath and Uttarkashi year-round. See the table below for details.

Private deluxe buses to Delhi (₹350, seven hours) leave from Kailash Gate, just south of Ram Jhula, at 1.30pm and 9.30pm. There's also one direct overnight bus daily from Rishikesh to Dharamsala (₹1100) at 4pm.

Private night buses to Jaipur (seat/sleeper ₹700/900, 13 hours), Agra (₹600/700, 12 hours) and Pushkar (₹700/900, 16 hours) can be booked at travel agents in Lakshman Jhula, Swarg Ashram and High Bank, but they leave from Haridwar (see p415).

Share Jeeps & Taxi
Share jeeps leave, when overfull, from the corner of Dehra Dun Rd and Dhalwala Bypass Rd, to Uttarkashi (₹180, five hours) and Joshimath (₹250, eight hours), mostly early in the morning, starting from 4am.

From the taxi stand near the main bus stand, official taxi rates are: Haridwar (₹500), Dehra Dun (₹650, 1½ hours) and Uttarkashi (for Gangotri; ₹2000, seven hours).

There are also taxi stands at Ram Jhula and Lakshman Jhula (west bank), charging ₹550 to Haridwar, ₹800 to Dehra Dun, ₹2300 to Uttarkarshi and ₹3500 to Joshimath. Although these rates are fixed, on long-distance trips you can usually get a cheaper rate by asking around at travel agents and guesthouses.

Vikrams charge ₹300 to make the trip to Haridwar.

Train
Bookings can be made at the **reservation office** (◷8am-6pm Mon-Sat, to 2pm Sun) at the train station, or at travel agents around Lakshman Jhula and Swarg Ashram (for a fee). Only a handful of slow trains run from Rishikesh to Haridwar, so it's usually better to go by bus or taxi.

ⓘ Getting Around

Shared *vikrams* run from the downtown Ghat Rd junction up past Ram Jhula (₹10 per person) and the High Bank turn-off to Lakshman Jhula. To hire the entire *vikram* from downtown to Ram Jhula should cost ₹80, and from Ram Jhula to High Bank or Lakshman Jhula is ₹40.

To get to the eastern bank of the Ganges you either need to walk across one of the suspension bridges or take the **ferry** (one way/return ₹10/15; ◷7.30am-6.45pm) from Ram Jhula.

On the eastern bank of the Ganges, taxis and share jeeps hang around to take passengers to waterfalls and Neelkantha temple, but it's a 16km trip by road to get from one side of the river to the other.

Motorcycles (Enfields and Yamahas) and mopeds can be hired for ₹300 to ₹600 a day around the Lakshman Jhula area. There are no specific shops – you just hire from private owners – so there's no insurance; ask around at guesthouses or look for rental signs.

BUSES FROM RISHIKESH

The following buses depart from the main bus stand (A) or the *yatra* bus stand (B). The latter leave when full.

DESTINATION	FARE (₹)	DURATION (HR)	FREQUENCY
Dehra Dun (A)	33	1½	half-hourly
Delhi (A)	167/265 ordinary/deluxe	7	half-hourly
Gangotri (B)	250	12	btwn 4am & 7am or 9am
Haridwar (A)	22	1	half-hourly
Joshimath (B)	230	10	btwn 4am & 7am or 9am
Kedarnath (B)	210	12	btwn 4am & 7am or 9am
Yamnotri (B)	230	12	btwn 3am & 7am
Uttarkashi (B)	150	7	btwn 3am & 12pm

Uttarkashi

📞 01374 / POP 16,220 / ELEV 1158M

Uttarkashi, 155km from Rishikesh and the largest town in northern Garhwal, is a major stop on the road to Gangotri Temple and the Gaumukh Glacier trek, so it's an obvious place to break your journey and stock up on supplies at the local market. Guides and porters can also be arranged here.

There's a State Bank of India ATM in the market.

The town is probably best known for the **Nehru Institute of Mountaineering** (📞222123; www.nimindia.net; ⊙10am-5pm), which trains many of the guides running trekking and mountaineering outfits in India. The centre has a museum and outdoor climbing wall. Basic and advanced mountaineering and adventure courses are open to all – check the website for details and admission information. Across the river from the main market.

Uttarkashi also hosts the annual **Makar Sakranti** festival in January.

There are plenty of hotels and *dhabas* (snack bars) around the bus stand and in the nearby market.

Monal Guest House   HOTEL $

(📞222270; www.monaluttarkashi.com; Kot Bungalow Rd; s/d/q/ste from ₹400/500/1350/1500; @) Off the Gangotri road 3km north of town, about 100m from the office that issues permits to Gamukh, this hillside hotel feels like a large comfortable house with lean, airy rooms, a big-windowed restaurant and peaceful garden setting.

Hotel Govind Palace   HOTEL $

(📞223815; near bus stand; s/d from ₹ 200/300) One of the best value choices if you've got to catch an early morning bus. It's got good beds, hot showers, TVs and helpful management.

Shangri-La Restaurant   MULTICUISINE $

(mains ₹30-125; ⊙9am-9pm) In the main bazaar, this restaurant has the most diverse menu in Uttarkashi: pizza, veggie burgers and banana pancakes as well as Indian and Tibetan food.

Buses depart in the morning for Gangotri (₹90, six hours), Haridwar (₹175, eight hours, at 7am), and Dehradun (₹190, nine hours) via Rishikesh (₹160, seven hours). There are buses to Hanuman Chatti, for Yamunotri Temple, at 7.45am and 10am (₹115, seven hours), and multiple services to Sangam Chatti, for Dodi Tal, until 3pm (₹10, one hour).

Garhwal Temple Treks

GANGOTRI TEMPLE & GAUMUKH GLACIER TREK

📞 01377 / ELEV 3042M

In a remote setting at an altitude of 3042m, Gangotri temple is one of the holiest places in India. Near the source of the Ganges (known as the Bhagirathi until it reaches Deoprayag), the shrine is dedicated to the origin of Hinduism's most sacred river – nearby is the rock on which Shiva is said to have received the flowing waters in his matted locks.

Erected by Gorkha commander Amar Singh Thapa in the 18th century, the temple – for a site of such significance – is surprisingly underwhelming. Unless you're a devout Hindu, to get a real sense of awe for the place you'll probably have to trek from Gangotri to the true source of the river, at **Gaumukh**, 18km upstream. There, the water flows out of **Gangotri Glacier** beneath the soaring west face of **Baghirathi Parvat** (6856m), with the peak of **Shivling** (the 6543m 'Indian Matterhorn') towering to the south.

Don't be daunted by the trek – the trail rises gradually and is totally solid. Fourteen kilometres (four to six hours) up the trail, at **Bhojbasa** (3790m), there's a **GMVN Tourist Bungalow** (dorm beds ₹300) and other basic lodging; Gaumukh is 4km (1½ hours) past that. On clear days, the best time to visit the source is early-to-mid-afternoon, when it's out of the shadows. Porters (₹500 each way) and horses (one way/return ₹850/1250) can be hired in Gangotri. More ambitious hikers with their own gear often continue to the gorgeous meadow at **Tapovan**, 6km beyond Gaumukh.

Before trekking to Gaumaukh, you must get a permit from the **District Forest Office** (📞222444), 3km north of the Uttarkashi bus stand. It's valid for two days and costs ₹150/600 per Indian/foreigner (then ₹50/250 for each extra day). Access to Gaumukh is limited to 150 people per day. Bring a copy of your passport ID page and visa.

Gangotri village has plenty of guesthouses, ashrams and *dharamsalas* charging ₹300 or less per room. There's also a **GMVN Tourist Bungalow** (📞22221; dm ₹150, d ₹400-900). When hungry, follow the Indian families to the **Hotel Gangaputra Restaurant** (mains ₹ 45-100; ⊙7am-11pm), which is busy for a good reason.

Buses run from Gangotri to Uttarkashi (₹90, six hours) and, during peak season, to Rishikesh (₹250, 12 hours). Share jeeps (₹150) also run between Gangotri and Uttarkashi.

YAMUNOTRI TEMPLE TREK
ELEV 3185M

Yamunotri Temple is tucked in a tight gorge close to the source of the Yamuna, Hinduism's second most sacred river after the Ganges. For pilgrims, Yamunotri is the least visited and so least developed of the *char dham* temples, but once you get to the trailhead it's an easy trek in.

The 5km, two-hour hike begins where the road ends at **Janki Chatti**, 6km beyond the village of **Hanuman Chatti** (2400m). At Yamunotri Temple there are several hot springs where you can take a dip, and others where pilgrims cook potatoes and rice as *prasad*. One kilometre beyond the temple, the Yamuna River spills from a frozen lake of ice and glaciers on the **Kalinda Parvat** mountain at an altitude of 4421m, but this is a very tough climb that requires mountaineering skills.

Across the river from Janki Chatti is the pretty village of **Kharsali**, which is worth a stroll if you've got the time.

Accommodation is available at basic guesthouses or the **GMVN tourist lodges** (www.gmvnl.com) in Yamunotri, Janki Chatti and Hanuman Chatti.

Buses only go as far as Hanuman Chatti, where you need to catch a share jeep to Janki Chatti (₹30). During peak *yatra* season buses run from Dehra Dun, Mussoorie and Rishikesh to Hanuman Chatti, but the most frequent transport services originate in Barkot. From Janki Chatti, share jeeps go to Barkot (₹60, two hours); from Hanuman Chatti, buses go to Barkot (₹50, 2½ hours) and Uttarkashi (₹115, seven hours) for those heading to Gangotri.

HAR-KI-DUN VALLEY TREK

The wonderfully remote Har-ki-Dun (3510m) is a botanical paradise criss-crossed by glacial streams and surrounded by pristine forests and snowy peaks. The area is preserved as **Govind Wildlife Sanctuary & National Park** (Indian/foreigner up to 3 days ₹50/350, subsequent days ₹20/175). You might be lucky enough to glimpse the elusive snow leopard above 3500m.

The trail begins at Sankri (also called Saur), and there are **GMVN Tourist Bungalows** (dm/d ₹150/450) at Sankri, Taluka and Osla, but you have to stay in a Forest Department rest house or camp in the valley itself. It's a 38km hike to Har-ki-Dun, which takes three days – or two days if you take a share jeep to Taluka. A side trip to Jamdar Glacier takes another day. The trek can be busy during June and October.

To get to Sankri, take a bus or a share jeep from Gandhi Chowk in Mussoorie. If you cannot find a bus or share jeep going all the way, go as far as you can and then catch other buses or share jeeps.

KEDARNATH TEMPLE TREK
☑ 01364 / ELEV 3584M

Kedarnath is revered as the source of the Mandakini River, but this magnificent temple is primarily dedicated to the hump that Shiva (who had taken the form of a bull) left behind when he dove into the ground to escape the Pandavas. Other portions of Shiva's body are worshipped at the other four Panch Kedar shrines, which are hard to reach but can be visited: the arms at Tungnath; the face at Rudranath; the navel at Madmaheshwar; and the hair at Kalpeshwar. The actual source of the Mandakini River is 12km past Kedarnath.

THE CHAR DHAM

The *char dham* of Garhwal refers to the four ancient temples that mark the spiritual sources of four sacred rivers: the Yamuna (Yamunotri), the Ganges (Gangotri), the Mandakini (Kedarnath) and the Alaknanda (Badrinath). Every year during the *yatra* (pilgrimage) season from April to November, hundreds of thousands of dedicated Hindu pilgrims make these important treks – the exact dates the temples are open are announced each year by local priests.

Religious tourism is big business and numerous buses, share jeeps, porters, ponies and palanquins are on hand for transport, along with a well-established network of budget guesthouses, ashrams and government rest houses. As a result, getting to these temples is easy enough without the need for a guide or carrying supplies. Only Gangotri and Badrinath temples can be visited without having to undertake a trek.

The temple was originally built in the 8th century by Guru Shankara, who is buried behind the shrine. The surrounding scenery is superb, but Kedarnath attracts 100,000 pilgrims every year, which means plenty of people, noise and litter. The site is so auspicious that pilgrims used to throw themselves from one of the cliffs behind the temple in the hope of instantly attaining *moksha* (liberation).

The tough 14km uphill trek to the temple (3584m) takes six hours on foot (five hours on a pony) and begins at Gaurikund, which has basic accommodation and a **GMVN Tourist Bungalow** (☑269202; dm ₹200, d ₹600-990). Stalls store luggage, and porters and ponies can be hired. The wide, paved trail to the temple is lined with *dhabas* and chai stalls.

There is more pilgrim accommodation available near the temple, including the **GMVN Tourist Bungalow** (☑263218; dm ₹200, d ₹640-800).

Buses run from Gaurikund to Rishikesh (₹190, 12 hours), or you can use share jeeps to make the same journey. Get off at Rudraprayag for connections to Joshimath, Badrinath and the eastern Kumaon district.

Joshimath

☑01389 / POP 13,202 / ELEV 1845M

As the gateway to Badrinath Temple and Hem Kund, Joshimath sees a steady stream of Hindu and Sikh pilgrims from May to October. And as the base for the Valley of Flowers, the Kuari Pass and Nanda Devi treks, and Auli ski resort, it attracts adventure travellers year-round.

Reached from Rishikesh by a hair-raising mountain road that hugs steep-sided valleys for the final few hours, Joshimath is a ramshackle two-street town and a rather ugly administrative centre full of rusting rooftops, erratic power supply and limited places to eat. Although the mountain views are lost from the town itself, it's only a short cable-car ride from here to magnificent views of Nanda Devi.

Activities

Trekking

Kuari Pass and Nanda Devi are two of the most popular treks from Joshimath. You need a permit and a registered guide to undertake these treks. There are three excellent operators in town who can organise everything.

Adventure Trekking   OUTDOOR ADVENTURE
(☑9837937948; www.thehimalayanadventures. com; Main Bazaar) Treks of anything from two to 10 days can be arranged here for around US$45 per person per day, as well as white-water rafting, skiing and mountain climbing. The owner, Santosh, is helpful and runs a guesthouse on the way up to Auli (r ₹1000 to ₹2000).

Eskimo Adventures   OUTDOOR ADVENTURE
(☑222630; eskimoadventures@rediffmail.com) Offers treks and rock-climbing expeditions from ₹1500 per day, and equipment rental (for trekking and skiing), as well as white-water rafting trips on the Ganges.

Himalayan Snow Runner   OUTDOOR ADVENTURE
(☑9412082247; www.himalayansnowrunner.com) Recommended outfit for trekking (from ₹1900 per day), skiing and adventure activities. The owner, Ajay, also takes cultural tours to Bhotia and Garhwali villages, and runs a guesthouse in his home in Mawari village, 5km from Joshimath (d ₹1060).

🛏 Sleeping & Eating

There are lots of cheap lodgings and a few hotels scattered around town. Joshimath's trekking outfits also operate upmarket homestay-style guesthouses that are worth considering.

Hotel New Kamal   HOTEL $
(☑221891; r ₹300) Small and clean with bucket hot water and TV, one of the better cheapies in the town center.

Hotel Snow Crest   HOTEL $$
(☑222344; www.snowcrest.co.in; d ₹1750) A few steps up the road to the Auli ropeway, it's clean and cosy but very overpriced. Rates are usually reduced by 40% (except in May and June).

Hotel Kamet   HOTEL $
(☑222155; d ₹200-900) Decent enough central budget option, but check a few rooms to find the least worn. There's a new, modern annexe in the back with rooms from ₹1000.

There are several *dhabas* in the main bazaar, all serving similar vegetarian thalis and dosas from ₹20 to ₹90.

ⓘ Information

There's a **GMVN Tourist Office** (☑222181; ⏰10am-5pm Mon-Sat) located just north of the town (follow the Tourist Rest House sign off Upper Bazaar Rd), and there's a State Bank of India

ATM that accepts foreign cards. Tour companies also have internet services.

ℹ Getting There & Away

Although the main road up to Joshimath is maintained by the Indian army, and a hydroelectric plant on the way to Badrinath has improved that road, the area around Joshimath is inevitably prone to landslides, particularly in the rainy season from mid-June to the end of August.

Buses run to Badrinath (₹50, two hours) at 6.30am, 9am, 11.00am, 2pm and 4.00pm, departing from the Badrinath bus stand at the far end of Upper Bazar Rd. Take the same buses to Govindghat (₹25, one hour), which is the start of the treks to the wonderful Valley of Flowers and dramatic Hem Kund. Share jeeps (₹60) do the same trip, departing from the jeep stand in the same spot. Hiring the whole jeep costs ₹600.

Buses run from Joshimath to Rishikesh (₹230, 10 hours) and Haridwar (₹250, 11½ hours) about every hour between 4am and 7am. They leave from outside the tiny **GMOU booth** (Upper Bazaar Rd; ⊙4am-8pm), where you can also book tickets.

During *yatra* season you can also catch an 8am bus directly to Gaurikund (₹185, 12 hours) for Kedarnath Temple. To get to the eastern Kumaon region take any Rishikesh bus to Karnaprayag (₹75, 3½ hours), from where local buses and share jeeps can take you along the beautiful road – that often feels like a charming country lane – towards Kausani, Bageshwar and Almora. You may have to change buses at Gwaldam (₹65, 3½ hours), to get to where you're going.

Around Joshimath

AULI
☏ 01389 / ELEV 3019M

Rising above Joshimath, 14km by road – and only 4km by the gondola-style cable car – Auli is India's premier ski resort. But you don't have to visit in winter to do some hiking and enjoy the awesome views of Nanda Devi (India's highest peak) from the top of the cable-car station.

As a ski resort, Auli is hardly spectacular, with gentle 5km-long slopes, one 500m rope tow (₹100 per trip) that runs beside the main slope, and an 800m chairlift (₹200) that connects the upper and lower slopes. The snow is consistently good, though, and the setting is superb. The season runs from January to March and equipment hire and instruction can be arranged here or in Joshimath.

The state-of-the-art **cable car** (return ₹500; ⊙every 20min 8am-6.50pm), India's longest, links Joshimath to the upper slopes

above Auli. There's a cafe, of sorts, at the top, serving hot chai and tomato soup.

There are just two places to stay at Auli and both hire out ski equipment and provide ski lessons.

The **Cliff Top Club Resort** (☏223217, in Delhi 011-25616679; www.nivalink.com/clifftop; studio ₹4500, ste ₹7500, f ₹9500) wouldn't look out of place in the Swiss Alps, with its solid timber interior finish, cosy atmosphere and spacious rooms, some with views of Nanda Devi. Meals and all-inclusive ski packages are available.

If on a tighter budget, stay at the perfectly acceptable **GMVN Tourist Rest House** (☏223208; www.gmvnl.com; dm ₹250, huts ₹2500, d ₹3000) at the start of the chairlift.

Valley of Flowers & Hem Kund Trek

British mountaineer Frank Smythe stumbled upon the Valley of Flowers in 1931. 'In all my mountain wandering,' he wrote, 'I have not seen a more beautiful valley where the human spirit may find repose.' The *bugyals* (high-altitude meadows) of tall wildflowers are a glorious sight on a sunny day, rippling in the breeze, and framed by mighty 6000m mountains that have glaciers and snow decorating their peaks all year.

The 300 species of flowers make the valley a unique and valuable pharmaceutical resource that may soon be a World Heritage Site. Unfortunately, most flowers bloom during the monsoon season in July and August, when the rains make access difficult and hazardous. There's a widespread misconception that the valley isn't worth visiting outside of peak flower season, but even without its technicolour carpet it's still ridiculously beautiful. And you may find you have it all to yourself.

To reach the 87-sq-km **Valley of Flowers National Park** (Indian/foreigner up to 3 days ₹40/600, subsequent days ₹20/175; ⊙6am-6pm May-Oct, last entry 3pm) requires a full-day trek from Govindghat to the village of Ghangaria, less than 1km from the park. The fabled valley begins 2km uphill from the ticket office, and continues for another 5km. Tracks are easy to follow. No overnight stay is permitted here (or at Hem Kund) so you must stay in Ghangaria.

A tougher trek from Ghangaria involves joining the hundreds of Sikh pilgrims toiling up to the 4300m **Hem Kund**, the sacred lake surrounded by seven peaks where Sikh guru Gobind Singh is believed to have meditated in a previous life. The pilgrim season runs from around 1 June to 1 October. Ponies (₹350) are available if you prefer to ride up the 6km zigzag track.

Also called Govinddham, **Ghangaria** is a one-street village in a wonderful deodar forest with a busy market, a handful of budget hotels and mediocre restaurants, hundreds of ponies, a pharmacy and a doctor. Water and electricity supplies are erratic.

Hotel Pritam (☎0199-1322031; s/d ₹200/300) is one of the better budget places to stay. **Hotel Priya** (d from ₹200) is good, too.

Ghangaria is a scenic but strenuous 14km uphill trek from Govindghat, which takes four to seven hours depending on your pace. You can quicken the trip and help the local economy by hiring a pony (₹437) through the Eco Development Committee office at the bridge over the Alaknanda River. The return trip takes four to five hours. You don't need to carry food because there are *dhabas* and drink stalls along the way serving the army of pilgrims heading to Hem Kund.

Despite the distances and grades of the trails, treks to Ghangaria, the Valley of Flowers and Hem Kund are often undertaken by small children and people with weak legs or lungs – they ride up in a wicker chair hauled on the back of a *kandi* man (from ₹400) or reclining in a *dandi* litter (from ₹5000), carried on the shoulders of four men like the royalty of old.

At **Govindghat** you can stay at the huge **gurdwara** (payment by donation), where VIP rooms are basic, or the **Hotel Bhagat** (☎01381-225226; d ₹600), up on the main road between Joshimath and Badrinath, with very clean rooms and meals available.

All buses and share jeeps between Joshimath and Badrinath stop in Govindghat, so you can easily find transport travelling in either direction, though this trickles off later in the day and stops dead at night.

Badrinath & Mana Village

☎01381 / ELEV 3133M

Basking in a superb setting in the shadow of snow-topped Nilkantha, **Badrinath Temple** appears almost lost in the tatty village that surrounds it. Sacred to Lord Vishnu, this vividly painted temple is the most easily accessible and popular of the *char dham* temples. It was founded by Guru Shankara in the 8th century, but the current structure

is much more recent. Below the temple are hot springs that reach a scalding 40°C and serve as a laundry for locals.

A scenic 3km walk beyond Badrinath along the Alaknanda River (cross over to the temple side to pick up the path), past fields divided by dry-stone walls, leads to tiny but charismatic **Mana Village**. The village is crammed with narrow stone laneways and traditional houses of varying designs – some have slate walls and roofs while others are wooden with cute balconies. You can wander around and watch the village ladies knitting colourful jerseys or hauling loads of fodder while the men tend goats or play cards or carom billiards. Carpets (₹200 for a small square, ₹2000 for bigger ones), blankets, jerseys, hats and gloves are all on sale.

Just outside the village in a small cave is the tiny, 5000-year-old **Vyas Temple**. Nearby is **Bhima's Rock**, a natural rock arch over a river that is said to have been made by Bhima, strongest of the Pandava brothers, whose tale is told in the Mahabharata. The 4km hike along the Alaknanda to the 145m **Vasudhara Waterfall** has a great reward-to-effort ratio, with views up the valley of the Badrinath massif jutting skyward like a giant fang. The villagers migrate to somewhere warmer and less remote – usually Joshimath – between November and April.

From the large bus station at the entrance to Badrinath, buses run to Govindghat, Joshimath and Gaurikund (for Kedarnath) during *yatra* season, but check scheduled departure times or you may end up stranded.

🛏 Sleeping & Eating

Badrinath can easily be visited in a day from Joshimath if you get an early start, but it's a serene place to spend the night and there are plenty of places to stay and eat here during the pilgrimage season. Budget guesthouses are generally discounted to ₹200 a room outside the short peak season of May and June.

Hotel Charan Paduka　　HOTEL **$**
(☎9411554098; r ₹150) Right behind the bus stand, it's friendly and clean enough for the price, with bucket hot water.

Jagirdar Guest House　　HOTEL **$**
(☎9457646148; r ₹500) In a stone building on the temple side of the river, this is a good place in a quiet spot out of the fray of pilgrims.

Hotel Snow Crest　　HOTEL **$$$**
(☎9412082465; www.snowcrest.co.in; r ₹2000-6000) Overpriced but modern and clean, rooms have heaters, TVs and geysers.

Brahma Kamal INDIAN $
(meals ₹30-80) Directly opposite the temple overlooking the river, this is a popular restaurant.

Kuari Pass Trek

Also known as the Curzon Trail (though Lord Curzon's party abandoned its attempt on the pass following an attack of wild bees), the trek over the Kuari Pass (3640m) was popular in the Raj era. It's still one of Uttarakhand's finest and most accessible treks, affording breathtaking views of the snow-clad peaks around Nanda Devi – India's highest mountain – while passing through the outer sanctuary of Nanda Devi National Park. The trailhead is at Auli and the 75km trek to Ghat past lakes, waterfalls, forests, meadows and small villages takes five days, though it's possible to do a shorter version that finishes in Tapovan in three days. A tent, guide, permit and your own food supplies are necessary, all of which can be organised easily in Joshimath.

Auli can be reached by bus or cable car from Joshimath. From Ghat, share jeeps (₹40, 1½ hours) go to Nandaprayag, and from there buses run to Joshimath or southwest to Rishikesh and Haridwar.

For other trekking options within the fabulous Nanda Devi, you must go with a registered guiding company. Check details with trekking outfitters in Joshimath or Rishikesh.

Corbett Tiger Reserve

☏ 05947 / ELEV 400-1210M

This famous **reserve** (☉15 Nov-15 Jun, Jhirna zone open year-round) was established in 1936 as India's first national park. It's named for legendary tiger hunter Jim Corbett (1875-1955), who put Kumaon on the map with his book *The Man-Eaters of Kumaon*. The British hunter was greatly revered by local people for shooting tigers that had developed a taste for human flesh, but he eventually shot more wildlife with his camera than with his gun.

The reserve Jim Corbett established inspired the India-wide Project Tiger program, which started in 1973 and saw the creation of 22 other reserves. Tiger sightings take some luck as the 175 or so tigers in the reserve are neither baited nor tracked. Your best chance of spotting one is late in the season (April to mid-June), when the forest cover is low and animals come out in search of water.

Notwithstanding tiger sightings, few serious wildlife enthusiasts will leave disappointed, as the 1318-sq-km park has a variety of wildlife and birdlife in grassland, sal forest and river habitats, and a beautiful location in the foothills of the Himalaya on the Ramganga River. Commonly seen wildlife include wild elephants (200 to 300 live in the reserve), sloth bears, langur monkeys (black face, long tail), rhesus macaques (red face and backside), peacocks, schools of otters and several types of deer including chital (spotted deer), sambars, hog deer and barking deer. You might also see leopards, mugger crocodiles, gharials, monitor lizards, wild boars and jackals. The Ramganga Reservoir attracts large numbers of migrating birds, especially from mid-December to the end of March, and over 600 species have been spotted here.

The **reception centre** (☏251489; www.corbettnationalpark.in; Ranikhet Rd; ☉6am-4pm), where you must get your park entry permit and can sign up for a day trip or overnight safari, is located on the main road in the town of Ramnagar, almost opposite the bus stand. From 15 November to 15 June the entry fee (₹200/900 per Indian/foreigner) covers three days and grants access to the entire park. Single-day permits (valid for four hours) are available for every zone except Dikhala (₹100/450 per Indian/foreigner). On top of that, there's the jeep vehicle fee (₹500/1500 per Indian/foreigner overnight, ₹250/500 for a single day).

Of Corbett's five zones – Bijrani, Dhikala, Domunda, Jhirna and Sonanadi – Dhikala is the highlight of the park. Forty-nine kilometres northwest of Ramnagar and deep inside the reserve, this is the designated core area, where the highest concentration of the animals you probably hope to see are found. It's only open from 15 November to 15 June to overnight guests or as part of a one-day tour booked through the reception centre.

Jhirna, in the southern part of the reserve, is the only zone that remains open all year. Short jeep safaris can be organised in Ramnagar, but your chances of seeing serious megafauna there are iffy. In certain years, depending on conditions, some of the other zones open in October, but the only way to find out is to contact the reception centre.

Two-hour elephant rides (₹300/1000 per Indian/foreigner) are available only at Dhikala and Bijrani, at 6am and 4pm on a first-come, first-served basis.

Be sure to bring binoculars (you can hire them at park gates) and plenty of mosquito repellent and mineral water. If you're interested in the life of Jim Corbett, his former house at Kaladhungi, 26km southeast of Ramnagar, is now a **museum** (admission ₹50; ☺8am-5pm).

☞ Tours

The reception centre in Ramnagar runs daily **bus tours** (Indian/foreigner ₹1000/2000) to Dhikala at 5.30am and 12pm.

Four-wheel drives or the smaller Maruti Gypsies can be hired at the reception centre in Ramnagar, or through your accommodation or a tour agency. The jeep owners have formed a union, so in theory the rates are fixed (on a per jeep basis, carrying up to six people). Half-day safaris (leaving in the morning and afternoon) should cost ₹1000 to Bijrani, ₹1000 to Jhirna, or ₹1500 to Domunda, excluding the entry fees for you and your guide. Full-day safaris cost double. Trips to Dhikala cost ₹2500. Check prices at the reception centre and at your hotel before hiring a jeep.

🛏 Sleeping & Eating

For serious wildlife viewing, Dhikala – deep inside the reserve – is the best place to stay, though the prices for foreigners are exorbitant. Book through the reception centre in Ramnagar at least one month in advance, except where indicated. The town of Ramnagar has budget accommodation, while upmarket resorts are strung out along the road skirting the eastern side of the park between Dhikuli and Dhangarhi Gate.

DHIKALA

Easily the cheapest beds in the park are at **Log Huts** (dm Indian/foreigner ₹200/400), resembling 3AC train sleepers, with 24 basic beds (no bedding supplied). **Tourist Hutments** (Indian/foreigner ₹1250/2500) offer the best value accommodation in Dhikala and sleep up to six people. Dhikala has a couple of restaurants serving vegetarian food. No alcohol is allowed in the park.

The **New Forest Rest House** (r ₹1250/2500), three **cabins** (₹1250/2500) and the VIP **Old Forest Rest House** (r ₹1500/3000 or ₹2500/5000) can all be booked at the reception centre in Ramnagar. **Annexe** (r ₹1000/2000) can be booked through the **Uttarakhand Tourism Development Board** (UTDB; ☎011-23319835) in Delhi.

ELSEWHERE IN THE RESERVE

Small rest houses in the park are at Kanda, Sultan Mailini and Jhirna (₹600/1400 per Indian/foreigner), Lohachaur, Halduparao, Morghatti, Sendhikal, Mudiapani, Rathuadhab, Pakhro and Dhela (₹400/800). The following are some other places to stay.

Bijrani Rest House　　　　　HOTEL $$
(s/d Indian ₹500/1000, foreigner ₹1250/2500) The first place in from Amdanda Gate; meals and elephant rides available.

Gairal Rest House　　　　　HOTEL $$$
(r Indian/foreigner from ₹1250/2500) On the Ramnagar River, accessed from Dhangarhi Gate; meals available.

Sarapduli Rest House　　　　HOTEL $$$
(r Indian/foreigner ₹2000/4000) Also has a good location in the reserve's core area.

Khinnanauli Rest House　　　HOTEL $$$
(r Indian/foreigner ₹5000/12000) VIP lodging near Dhikala, deep in the reserve.

RAMNAGAR

A busy, unappealing town, Ramnagar has plenty of facilities, including internet cafes (₹30 per hr), ATMs (State Bank of India ATM at the train station, and a Bank of Baroda ATM on Ranikhet Rd) and transport connections – mostly along Ranikhet Rd.

TOP CHOICE Corbett Motel　　　HOTEL $
(☎9837468933; karansafaris@yahoo.co.in; tent ₹400, d/tr ₹500/600) Set in a beautiful mango orchard only a few hundred metres from the train station, Ramnagar's best budget accommodation is a world away from the traffic-clogged centre and offers exceptional service and hospitality. You can stay in sturdy tents or basic but spotless rooms, and the restaurant serves fine food. The owner, Karan, is a well-known local naturalist and can organise jeep safaris into the park. Call ahead for a pick-up.

Krishna Nidhi Corbett Inn　　HOTEL $$
(☎251225; Ranikhet Rd; dm ₹300, d with/without AC ₹1600/600; ❄) Clean, spacious rooms with balconies or verandas make this a good midrange option at the northern end of Ramnagar's main street. The manager can help organise safaris.

Hotel Anand　　　　　　　HOTEL $
(☎254385; Ranikhet Rd; s/d ₹300/500) A noisy budget option located about 100m from the bus stand, Anand has average rooms with bucket hot water and TV – however many of the rooms only have windows onto a corridor. Its **Delhi Darbar Restaurant** (mains

₹50-100; ☻7am-11pm) is one of the cleanest, quietest places to eat in town, with a typical Indian menu plus pizzas.

NORTH OF RAMNAGAR

Half a dozen upmarket African-style safari resorts are strung along the Ramnagar-Ranikhet road that runs along the reserve's eastern boundary. Most are around a settlement called Dhikuli – not to be confused with Dhikala! When most of the reserve is closed (15 June to 15 November), discounts of up to 50% are offered. Rates given here are for a room only, but most have packages that include meals and safaris. All places have resident naturalists, recreational facilities, restaurants and bars.

Tiger Camp HOTEL $$$
(☎2551963; www.tiger-camp.com; r ₹2050/2500, cottages ₹3050; ❄) This intimate, excellent-value resort is nestled in a shady jungle-style garden by the Kosi River, 8km from Ramnagar. Cosy cottages and bungalows have modern facilities, and nature walks and village tours are offered.

Infinity Resorts HOTEL $$$
(☎251279; www.infinityresorts.com; Dhikuli; s/d incl breakfast from ₹6000/8000; ❄☇) The most impressive of the resorts in this area, Infinity has luxurious rooms, a roundhouse with restaurant and bar, and a swimming pool in a lovely garden backing onto the Kosi River (where you can see hordes of golden mahseer fish).

Corbett Hideaway HOTEL $$$
(☎284132; www.corbetthideaway.com; Dhikuli; cottages ₹11,000-22,000; ❄☇) The luxurious ochre cottages offer privacy, the riverside garden is relaxing, and there's a poolside bar and thatched restaurant at this quality resort, 12km north of Ramnagar.

❶ Getting There & Away

Buses run almost hourly from Ramnagar to Delhi (₹150, seven hours), Haridwar (₹113, six hours) and Dehra Dun (₹150, seven hours). For Nainital (₹71, 3½ hours) there are four direct buses, or take one to Kaladhungi and change there. Buses to Ranikhet (₹77, 4½ hours) leave every couple of hours in the morning, and some continue to Almora. Frequent buses run to Haldwani (₹35, two hours).

Ramnagar train station is 1.5km south of the main reception centre. The nightly *Corbett Park Link Express* (sleeper/2AC ₹107/417) leaves Delhi at 10.40pm, arriving in Ramnagar at 4.55am. The return trip leaves Ramnagar at 9.40pm, arriving in Old Delhi at 4.15am. For other destinations, change at Moradabad.

Nainital

☏05942 / POP 39,840 / ELEV 1938M

Crowded around a deep, green volcanic lake, Nainital is Kumaon's largest town and favourite hill resort. It occupies a steep forested valley around the namesake lake Naini and was founded by homesick Brits reminded of the Cumbrian Lake District. Disaster struck here in December 1880, when a major landslide buried a hotel and 150 people, creating the memorial recreation ground now known as the Flats.

Plenty of hotels are set in the forested hills around the lake, there's a busy bazaar, and a spider's web of walking tracks covers the forested hillsides to viewpoints overlooking the distant Himalayan peaks. For travellers, it's a good place to kick back and relax, eat well, go horse riding or paddling on the lake. In peak seasons – roughly May to mid-July and October – Nainital is packed to the gills with holidaying families and honeymooners, and hotel prices skyrocket.

Tallital (Lake's Foot) is at the southeastern end of the lake where you'll find the bus stand and the main road heading east towards Bhowali. The 1.5km promenade known as the Mall leads to Mallital (Lake's Head) at the northwestern end of the lake. Most hotels, guest houses and restaurants are strung out along the Mall between Mallital and Tallital.

◉ Sights & Activities

Naini Lake SIGHTSEEING
This pretty lake is Nainital's centrepiece and is said to be one of the emerald green eyes of Shiva's wife, Sati (*naina* is Sanskrit for eye). **Naina Devi Temple**, rebuilt after the 1880 landslide, is on the precise spot where the eye is believed to have fallen. Nearby is the **Jama Masjid** and a **gurdwara**. You can walk around the lake in about an hour – the southern side is more peaceful and has good views of the town.

Boatmen will row you around the lake for ₹160 (₹95 one way) in the brightly painted gondola-like boats, or the **Nainital Boat Club** (Mallital; ☻10am-4pm) will sail you round for ₹250. Pedal and rowing boats can also be hired for ₹100 per hour.

Snow View & Cable Car VIEWPOINT
A **cable car** (adult/child return ₹150/100; ☻8am-7pm May & Jun, 10.30am-4pm Jul-Apr) runs up to the popular Snow View at 2270m, which (on

clear days) has panoramic Himalayan views, including of Nanda Devi. The ticket office is at the bottom. At the top you'll find the usual food, souvenir and carnival stalls, as well as **Mountain Magic** (rides ₹30-100), an amusement park with kids' entertainment including bumper cars, trampolines and a flying fox.

A highlight of the trip to Snow View is hiking to viewpoints such as **Cheena/Naina Peak**, 4km away. Local guides may offer to lead you on walks. One such guide, Sunil Kumar (🖉9411196837), has plenty of experience as a trekker and birdwatcher and can take you on day walks (₹550), or overnight walks where you stay in local villages (₹1400).

If you want to get up to Snow View for sunrise, taxis charge ₹180.

Tiffin Top & Land's End   HORSE RIDING,WALKING
A 4km walk west of the lake brings you to Tiffin Top (2292m), also called Dorothy's Seat. From there, it's a lovely 30-minute walk to Land's End (2118m) through a forest of oak, deodar and pine. Mangy horses gather west of town on the road to Ramnagar to take you on rides to these spots. A three-hour ride costs about ₹490, but you can take shorter rides (eg Tiffin Top for ₹70). Touts for these rides will no doubt accost you in Mallital near the ropeway.

Nainital Zoo   ZOO
This high-altitude hillside **zoo** (admission ₹25, with camera ₹25; ☉10am-5pm Tue-Sun) has some large enclosures containing Himalayan animals, Siberian tigers, leopards and lots of pheasant species. It's a steep 20-minute walk from the Mall or a ₹50 taxi ride.

Rock Climbing & Trekking   OUTDOOR ADVENTURE
The enthusiasts at **Nainital Mountaineering Club** (🖉235051; Mallital; per day ₹600) offer rock-climbing courses on an artificial tower and at the rock-climbing area, a 15m-high rock outcrop to the west of the town.

Snout Adventures (🖉231749; www.snout adventure.co.in; Ashok Cinema Bldg, Mallital) is a recommended outfit offering treks in the Kumaon and Garhwal mountains (from ₹3000 per day, all inclusive), rock-climbing courses (₹600 per day) and adventure camps.

For information on KMVN's rest houses and trekking packages, visit **KMVN Parvat Tours** (🖉235656; www.kmvn.org; Tallital; ☉9am-7pm).

👉 Tours

Travel agencies along the Mall such as **Hina Tours & Travel** (🖉235860; www.nainital

hinatours.com) and **Anamika Travels** (🖉9720180161) offer bus tours of the local lakes and trips to Corbett National Park.

🛏 Sleeping

Nainital is packed with hotels but they fill up fast in peak seasons, making it hard to find a bargain at those times. The prices given below are for the main peak season; virtually all hotels offer around 50% discounts in the low season. The main peak season is generally 1 May to 30 June, and some hotels have a semipeak in October, at Diwali (October/November) and at Christmas.

A few of the following hotels have budget-range prices in the low season.

TOP CHOICE **Palace Belvedere**   HERITAGE HOTEL **$$$**
(🖉237434; www.palacebelvedere.com; Mallital; s/d/ste from ₹4500/5200/7000; 🛜) Built in 1897, this was the summer palace of the rajas of Awagarh. Animal skins and old prints adorn the walls and lend a faded Raj-era charm. Rooms are spacious, high-ceilinged, and have a finely-aged kind of soul – there's something irresistable about them. Downstairs is an elegant dining room/lounge/veranda. You'll find it off the Mall.

Hotel City Heart   HOTEL **$$**
(🖉235228; www.cityhearthotel.netfirms.com; Mallital; d ₹1650-3500) Located off the Mall, the rooftop terrace restaurant has fine lake views. Rooms range from small but cute to a fabulous deluxe room with a view. This place discounts more than most and is one of Nainital's best off-season bargains, with rooms from ₹700. The effusive owner will gladly play the CD of his band covering tunes by Pink Floyd and Dire Straits.

Traveller's Paradise   HOTEL **$$**
(🖉9411107877; www.kmvn.gov.in; Mallital; d ₹1500) A bit north of the Mall, it's the details that set this hotel apart from others in its price range. Bedsheets are surprisingly stylish, bathrooms are colorfully tiled, and the big rooms, though not fancy, have chairs and coffee tables. It's run by the aimiable Anu Consul, who spent ten years living in Mexico and knows what it's like to be on the road.

Evelyn Hotel   HOTEL **$$**
(🖉235457; www.hotelevelynnainital.com; the Mall, Tallital; d ₹1500-2700, ste ₹3500-5300) This large Victorian-looking hotel overlooking the lake is quintessential Nainital – charming and slightly eccentric. It's big, with stairways and terraces cascading down the hillside. It's a

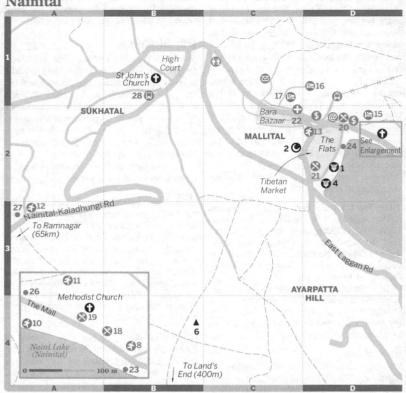

bit old-fashioned, but the well-tended rooms have a nice, cosy feel.

✖ Eating

Nainital has a host of restaurants, mostly along the Mall on the north side of the lake. For cheap eats, head to the food stalls around the Tibetan Market or to the *dhabas* in Bara Bazar.

Embassy INDIAN $$
(The Mall, Mallital; meals ₹80-320; ☉10.30am-11pm)
With a wood-lined chalet interior and snappily dressed staff, Embassy has been serving up five pages of menu items for over 40 years. For drinks try 'dancing coffee' or a rosewater lassi. Good terrace for people-watching.

Machan Restaurant MULTICUISINE $$
(The Mall, Mallital; mains ₹80-350; ☉10am-4.30pm & 7pm-10.30pm) The jungle-themed decor and bamboo facade here represent Corbett's wildlife-spotting towers, while the menu offers

some of Nainital's best comfort food (pizzas and burgers), along with Indian fare. Watch the chefs at work in the open kitchen.

Sakley's Restaurant MULTICUISINE $$
(Mallital; mains ₹60-350; ☉9am-10pm) A spotless restaurant found off the Mall, serving up a range of unusual global items such as Thai curries, honey chicken, roast lamb, pepper steaks, and plenty of Chinese dishes, pizzas and sizzlers. Desserts include pastries and Black Forest cake.

Sonam Chowmein Corner FAST FOOD $
(The Flats, Mallital; mains ₹20-50; ☉11am-7pm) In the covered alley part of the Tibetan Market, this authentic Tibetan *dhaba* whips up fabulous chow mein and *momos* (Tibetan dumplings) for the best cheap eats in town.

Cafe de Mall CAFE $$
(The Mall, Tallital; mains ₹50-250; ☉9am-4pm & 6-10pm) This open-fronted lakeside cafe halfway along the Mall is a great place for

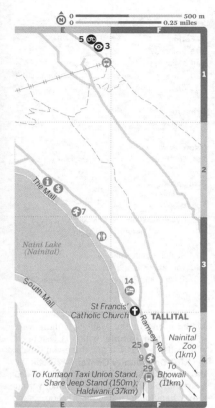

Medical Services
BD Pandey Government Hospital (☑235012; Mallital) Located off the Mall.

Money
Bank of Baroda ATM (The Mall, Tallital) Accepts international cards.

HDFC Bank (The Mall; ⊙10am-4pm Mon-Fri, to 1pm Sat) Exchanges cash and travellers cheques; 24-hour ATM.

State Bank of India (The Mall, Mallital; ⊙10am-4pm Mon-Fri, to 1pm Sat) Exchanges major foreign currencies and travellers cheques. ATM accepts international cards.

Post
Main post office (Mallital; ⊙10am-5pm Mon-Sat)

Tourist Information
Uttarakhand Tourism office (☑235337; The Mall; ⊙10am-5pm Mon-Sat)

❶ Getting There & Away
Bus
For details of buses leaving from the Tallital bus stand, see the table, p437.

Although there are direct buses from Nainital, many more services leave from the transport hubs of Haldwani and Bhowali. From Haldwani, regular buses head to Ramnagar, Delhi and the Nepal border at Banbassa. Haldwani is also a major train terminus. To go north, take a bus or share jeep to Bhowali (₹10, 20 minutes) and catch one of the regular onward buses to Almora, Kausani and Ranikhet.

Three daily buses to Ramnagar (₹71, 3½ hours) originating at the Tallital bus stand also pass by the Sukhatal bus stand, northeast of Mallital.

Travel agencies sell tickets on private overnight deluxe coaches (with reclining seats) to Delhi (₹250-500, nine hours), which leave from Tallital around 9.30pm.

Taxi & Share Jeep
From the Kumaon Taxi Union stand in Tallital, taxi drivers charge ₹500 to Kathgodam (1½ hours), ₹1200 to Ramnagar (three hours) and ₹1500 to Almora (three hours) or Ranikhet (two hours).

Share jeeps leave when full, and go to Bhowali (₹10, 20 minutes) and Kathgodam/Haldwani (₹60, 1½ hours).

Train
Kathgodam (35km south of Nainital) is the nearest train station, but Haldwani, one stop further south, is the regional transport hub. The **train booking agency** (⊙9am-noon & 2-5pm

breakfast or a cappuccino on the terrace. The menu ranges from fish curry and *kali mirch* chicken to pizzas and impressive vegetarian sizzlers.

🍷 Drinking
Nainital Boat Club   BAR
(The Mall, Mallital; temp membership men/women/couples ₹830/415/830; ⊙10am-10pm) This club is a classic remnant of the Raj-era. Temporary membership is ridiculously steep, but the atmospheric bar – with timber beams, buttoned-up barmen with handlebar moustaches, and an outdoor deck overlooking the lake, is perfect for an afternoon drink. The dress code specifies no shorts or thongs, and signs warn that 'decorum should be maintained'.

❶ Information
Internet Access
Cyberia (Mallital; per hr ₹25; ⊙10am-9pm)

Nainital

UTTARAKHAND

Mon-Fri, 9am-2pm Sat), next to the Tallital bus stand, has a quota for trains to Dehra Dun, Delhi, Moradabad, Lucknow, Gorakhpur and Kolkata. The daily *Ranikhet Express* (sleeper/3AC/2AC ₹121/339/472) departs Kathgodam at 8.40pm and arrives at Old Delhi station at 4.15am. In the other direction, it departs Delhi at 10.15pm, arriving at Kathgodam at 5.45am.

ⓘ Getting Around

Cycle-rickshaws charge a fixed ₹10 along the Mall, but can only pick up and drop off at the ticket booths at either end. Taxi rides within town cost ₹80 to ₹200.

Ranikhet

☏ 05966 / POP 19,049 / ELEV 1829M

Ranikhet, home to the Kumaon Regiment and bristling with good-old-fashioned military atmosphere, spreads over rolling green hills with some lovely views over the distant Himalayas. The focus of the town is a busy single-street bazaar area, but you don't have to walk far along the winding Mall Rd to be immersed in forest and tall English trees.

From Sadar Bazaar, the Mall heads 3km south to the army headquarters. A **walking path** starting by the sports ground provides a pleasant short cut, passing a small pond and the stone Catholic church. From the southern end of the Mall it's a 1km walk to **Jhula Devi Temple**, which is festooned with bells. Before you get there you'll pass the **KRC Community Center** (☏220567; The Mall; admission free; ⊙8.30am-4pm, closed Wed & Sun), an old church that's been converted into a handloom-weaving workshop established for the benefit of army widows.

🛏 Sleeping & Eating

Outside the two peak seasons (generally mid-April to mid-July and 1 October to early November), the prices given below are reduced by 30% to 50%. *Dhabas* and a few budget hotels can be found in the bazaar.

Ranikhet Club　　HERITAGE HOTEL $$$
(☏226011; The Mall; d ₹7555) For a taste of Raj nostalgia, look no further than the four classic rooms at this 1860 heritage wooden bungalow. The gentrified army ambience is typified by the members' bar, billiard room, card-playing rooms, tennis court and stylish restaurant. The Seven Peaks Bar has a colonial feel – dress smartly after 7pm.

Hotel Meghdoot　　HOTEL $$
(☏220475; www.hotelmeghdoot.com; The Mall; s ₹800-1100, d ₹1300-1500, ste ₹2000) This big old hotel, just past the army headquarters, 3km from the bazaar, has some quaint historical touches, a range of clean, spacious rooms,

and a veranda packed with pot plants and greenery. Off-season rates are a bargain here.

ℹ️ Information

Ranikhet Cyber Cafe (Gandhi Chowk; per hr ₹25; ☉8am-7.30pm) Near the SBI ATM.

State Bank of India (Sadar Bazaar; ☉10am-4pm Mon-Fri, to 1pm Sat) Exchanges travellers cheques but not cash.

State Bank of India ATM Just uphill from the bank, this ATM accepts foreign cards.

Uttarakhand Tourism office (☎220227; ☉10am-5pm Mon-Sat) Located above the UP Roadways bus stand.

ℹ️ Getting There & Away

From the KMOU bus stand, at Gandhi Chowk, regular buses run to Almora (₹45, two hours) and to Ramnagar (₹77, 4½ hours) hourly from 6.30am to 2pm. There's one bus to Nainital at 9.30am (₹77, 2½ hours).

From the UP Roadways bus stand at the eastern end of the bazaar, transport runs to Delhi, Haridwar, Karnaprayag, Haldwani, and Kathgodam via Bhowali.

Share jeeps leave when full for Almora (₹80, two hours), Nainital (₹100, 1½ hours) and Haldwani (₹80, two hours) from near either of the two bus stands.

Almora

☎05962 / POP 32,357 / ELEV 1650M

Clinging to a steep-sided valley, Almora is the sprawling regional capital of Kumaon, first established as a summer capital by the Chand rajas of Kumaon in 1560. A cool climate and mountain views are attractions, but don't be put off by the ugly, shambolic main street when you're first deposited at the bus stand – head one block south to the pedestrian-only cobbled Lalal Bazaar, lined with intricately carved and painted traditional wooden shop facades. It's a fascinating place to stroll, people-watch and shop. While otherwise not bursting with interest, Almora has some colonial-era buildings, reliable trekking outfits and a couple of community-based weaving enterprises. You'll often see Westerners floating around, thanks to a hippie subculture of travellers living up around Kasar Devi temple.

Sights & Activities

Nanda Devi Temple
HINDU TEMPLE

The stone Nanda Devi Temple in Lalal Bazaar dates back to the Chand raja era, and is covered in folk-art carvings, some erotic. Every September, the temple hosts the **Nanda Devi Fair**.

Panchachuli Weavers Factory
HANDICRAFTS

(☎232310; admission free; ☉10am-5pm Mon-Sat) The Panchachuli Weavers Factory, off Bageshwar Rd, employs some 300 women to weave woollen shawls. The shop here has a wider range of products than at the small shop in the Mall. Taxis charge ₹150 return to the factory, or you can walk the 3km – follow the continuation of Mall Rd to the northeast and ask for directions.

High Adventure
TREKKING

(☎9012354501; www.thehighadventure.com; the Mall) Organises six-day treks to Pindari Glacier and 10-day treks to Milam Glacier for around ₹1700 per person, per day.

Discover Himalaya
TREKKING

(☎9411346550; bobbyalmora@hotmail.com; the Mall) Also runs trips to Pindari and Milam Glaciers.

BUSES FROM NAINITAL

The following buses leave from the Tallital bus stand. For Kathgodam, take the Haldwani bus.

DESTINATION	FARE (₹)	DURATION (HR)	FREQUENCY
Almora	100	3	7am
Dehra Dun	235-419	10	8 daily
Delhi	218-430	9	6 daily
Haldwani	37	2	half-hourly
Haridwar	235-419	8	several early morning
Kathgodam (A)	34	1½	half-hourly
Rishikesh	270	9	5am

🛏 Sleeping

Unlike most hill stations, prices here are not seasonal.

Hotel Shikhar
HOTEL $$

(☎230253; www.hotelshikhar.com; The Mall; dm ₹300, d ₹500-1800, ste ₹2500; ✵) Dominating the centre of town and built to take in the views, this large, boxlike hotel is perched on a hillside and offers a maze of rooms covering all budgets. Expensive rooms aren't much better than cheaper ones. The hotel also has the reasonable **Mount View Restaurant**.

Kailas International Hotel
GUESTHOUSE $

(☎230624; jawaharlalsah@india.com; dm ₹150, d ₹250-450) Ramshackle but colourful, Kailas is run by the elderly Mr Shah, an engaging retired bank manager who will regale you with tales of Almora, temples and his philosophy on life. Staying here is like sleeping in a museum's attic, though the rooms are basic and a serious mixed bag. The large rooms (such as the 'Maharaja suite') at the top are easily the best. The cheapest rooms have common bathrooms. It's off the Mall.

Bansal Hotel
HOTEL $

(☎230864; Lalal Bazaar; d ₹300-400) Above Bansal Cafe in the bustling bazaar, but easily reached from the Mall, this is a fine budget choice with small, tidy rooms (some with TV) and a rooftop terrace.

🍴 Eating

Almora's speciality sweet is *ball mithai* (fudge coated in sugar balls), available for ₹5 in sweet shops all along the Mall and bazaar.

New Soni Restaurant
INDIAN $$

(The Mall; mains ₹25-150; ◷10.30am-9.30pm) A popular Sikh-run *dhaba* serving tasty *paneer* (unfermented cheese), chicken and mutton dishes, and egg curry.

Glory Restaurant
INDIAN $

(LR Sah Rd; mains ₹35-85; ◷8.30am-9.30pm) This long-running family eatery features popular South and North Indian vegetarian and nonvegetarian dishes, including biryanis and lemon chicken. The pizzas are super cheesy.

ℹ Information

Internet access is available at several places in Lalal Bazaar and the Mall, usually from ₹25 per hour.

HDFC (The Mall; ◷9.30am-3.30pm Mon-Fri, to 12.30pm Sat) The ATM accepts foreign cards and the bank changes foreign currencies.

Sify iWay (The Mall; per hr ₹25; ◷7am-8.30pm) Internet access and train reservations.

State Bank of India (The Mall; ◷10am-4pm Mon-Fri, to 1pm Sat) An ATM here accepts foreign cards.

Uttarakhand Tourism office (☎230180; Upper Mall; ◷10am-5pm Mon-Sat)

ℹ Getting There & Away

The vomit-splattered sides of the buses and jeeps pulling into Almora tell you all you need to know about what the roads are like around here.

Buses run from the adjacent UP Roadways and KMOU bus stands on the Mall roughly hourly until 4pm to Ranikhet (₹45, two hours), Kausani (₹47, 2½ hours), Bageshwar (₹80, two hours) and Bhowali (₹45, two hours), near Nainital. Buses to Delhi (₹325, 12 hours) leave at 2pm, 3pm & 4pm. There are early morning buses to Pithoragarh (₹128, five hours) and more run from the Dharanaula bus stand on the Bypass Rd. For Banbassa on the Nepal border, take a bus to Haldwani and change there.

There's a **Railway Reservation Centre** (◷9am-noon & 2-5pm Mon-Sat) at the KMVN Tourist Holiday Home.

Taxis or jeeps can be picked up from the Mall to Ranikhet (₹800, two hours), Kausani (₹1000, 2½ hours), Bageshwar (₹1200, two hours), Nainital (₹1500, three hours), Pithoragh (₹2000, five hours) and Munsyari (₹4000, 10 hours).

Around Almora

The hilltop **Kasar Devi Temple**, where Swami Vivekananda meditated, is 8km north of Almora and can be reached by share jeep (₹15) or taxi (₹300). The nearby village has become a popular destination for backpackers, with its peaceful vibe and clear-day Himalayan views. There are some great accomodation options here, including **Mohan's** (☎9412162816; www.mohanscafe.com; r ₹500; @⊚), which has good rooms, internet, a library and an inviting restaurant set on a large garden terrace with views; the well-run **Rainbow Guesthouse** (☎9410793473; r ₹300-500; ⊚) where clean, appealing rooms have soothing color schemes; and **Manu Guest House** (☎9410920696; r ₹250-400), set amid an orchard with a resident water buffalo, where the largest stone or brick cottages include kitchenettes.

Beyond Kasar Devi, picturesque **Binsar** (2420m), 26km from Almora, was once the summer capital of the Chand rajas and is now a popular beauty spot for forest trekking, with panoramic views of the Himalayan peaks. There's a ₹100 fee to enter the sanctuary. A return taxi from Almora costs ₹800.

Fourteen kilometres west of Almora, the 800-year-old **Surya (Sun) temple** at Katarmal, a 2km walk from the main road, can be visited by getting on any share jeep (₹20, 30 minutes) going to Ranikhet.

An impressive temple complex is set in a forest of deodars at **Jageshwar**, 38km northeast of Almora. The 124 temples and shrines date to the 7th century AD and vary from linga shrines to large *sikhara* (Hindu temples). They're a 4km walk from Jageshwar, which can be reached by taxi (₹900 return).

Kausani

☏ 05962 / POP 4000 / ELEV 1890M

Perched high on a forest-covered ridge, this tiny village has lovely panoramic views of distant snowcapped peaks, fresh air and a relaxed atmosphere. Mahatma Gandhi found Kausani an inspirational place to retreat and write his Bhagavad Gita treatise *Anasakti Yoga* in 1929, and there is still an ashram devoted to him here. Nineteen kilometres north, **Baijnath** village has an intriguing complex of 12th-century *sikhara*-style temples in a lovely location shaded by trees, with other shrines in the nearby old village.

👁 Sights & Activities

Kausani Tea Estate TEA ESTATE
(☏ 258330; www.uttaranchaltea.com; admission free; ⏱9am-6pm mid-Mar–mid-Nov) At Kausani Tea Estate – a tea plantation that involves private enterprise, the government and local farmers – you can look around and sample and buy products that are exported around the world. It's 3.5km north of the village on the road to Baijnath, an easy and scenic walk.

Anasakti Ashram HISTORIC SITE
(☏ 258028; Anasakti Ashram Rd) About 1km uphill from the bus stand, Anasakti Ashram is where Mahatma Gandhi spent two weeks pondering and writing *Anasakti Yoga*. It has a small **museum** (admission free; ⏱6amnoon & 4-7pm) that tells the story of Gandhi's life through photographs and words. Visit at 6pm to attend nightly prayers in his memory. You can stay at the ashram for a donation, but you must respect the rules, including attending evening prayers. Meals cost ₹40.

🛏 Sleeping & Eating

Outside the two short peak seasons (May–June and October–November) the accommodation listed below is discounted by 50%.

Hotel Uttarakhand HOTEL $$
(☏ 258012; www.uttarakhandkausani.zoomshare.com; d ₹750-2250; @) Up some steps from the bus stand but in a quiet location with a panoramic view of the Himalaya from your veranda, this is Kausani's best-value accommodation. The cheaper rooms are small, with bucket hot water, but upper-floor rooms are spacious and have hot showers and TVs. The manager is helpful and friendly, and credit cards are accepted.

Krishna Mountview HOTEL $$$
(☏ 258008; www.kumaonindia.com; Anasakti Ashram Rd; d ₹3200-4500, ste ₹6500-9000) Just past Anasakti Ashram, this is one of Kausani's smartest hotels, with clipped formal gardens (perfect for mountain views), the good Vaibhav restaurant, a gym and a pool table. All rooms are well kept and comfy, but the spacious upstairs rooms with balcony, bay windows and even rocking chairs are the pick.

Garden Restaurant MULTICUISINE $$
(Hotel Uttarakhand; meals ₹60-250; ⏱24hr) In front of Hotel Uttarkhand and enjoying fine Himalayan views, this bamboo and thatchroofed restaurant is Kausani's coolest. The food comprises first class dishes from Swiss rösti to chicken tikka and imported pasta, as well as some Kumaon specialities, using fresh ingredients.

There a lots of cheap *dhabas* around the main bazaar and the road leading uphill from the bus stand.

ℹ Information

Kausani has a State Bank of India ATM in the main bazaar, but no foreign currency exchange.
Sanchar Dhaba Cyber Cafe (Anasakti Ashram Rd; per hr ₹40; ⏱6am-9pm) At Hill Queen Restaurant.
Uttarakhand Tourism office (☏ 258067; The Mall; ⏱10am-5pm Mon-Sat)

ℹ Getting There & Away

Buses and share jeeps stop in the village centre. Buses (₹45, 2½ hours) run about hourly to Almora, but afternoon buses generally stop at Karbala on the bypass road, from where you need to take a share jeep (₹10). Heading north, buses run every hour or so to Bageshwar via Baijnath (₹40, 1½ hours). Share jeeps (₹20, 30 minutes) run to Garur, 16km north of Kausani, from where other share jeeps go to Gwaldam for onward buses and jeeps to Garhwal (via Karnaprayag). A taxi to Almora costs around ₹1000; to Nainital it costs ₹2000.

Bageshwar

📞 05963 / POP 7803 / ELEV 975M

At the confluence of the Gomti and Sarju Rivers, Hindu pilgrims visit Bageshwar for its ancient stone **Bagnath Temple**. For travellers, it's more important as a transit town to or from the Milam or Pindari Glacier trailheads. There's a **KMVN office** (📞220034; www.kmvn.org; Tarcula Rd) at the Tourist Rest House, where the trekking manager can arrange all-inclusive treks. At the bus stand, **Annapurna Communication & Cafe** (per hr ₹50; ☺8.30am-9.30pm) has internet access, and there's a State Bank of India ATM in the main bazaar.

The okay **Hotel Annapurna** (📞220109; r ₹200-400, s/d without bathroom ₹70/150) is conveniently located next to the bus stand. Across the river, about 1km from the bus stand, the large **KMVN Bageshwar Tourist Rest House** (📞220034; Tarcula Rd; dm ₹100, d ₹250-600) is a bit institutional but has reasonable, spacious rooms and dorms.

Several daily buses go to Almora (₹76, three hours), and Ranikhet (₹90, three hours) via Kausani (₹35, 1½ hours). Frequent buses run to Bhowali (₹120, six hours) and Haldwani (₹170, 7½ hours). For connections to Garhwal, take a bus (₹45, two hours) to Gwaldam and change there. For the Pindari Glacier trek, there are two daily buses to Song (₹36, two hours). For Milam Glacier, there's a 9am bus to Munsyari (₹135, six hours). There are also 6.30am & 8am buses to Pithoragarh (₹145/120; 7 hours). The jeep stand is near the bus stand: share jeeps go to Garur (₹25, 30 minutes), Kausani (₹50, 1½ hours) and Gwaldam (₹60, two hours). A taxi to Song costs ₹800 (two hours).

Pithoragarh

📞 05964 / POP 41,157 / ELEV 1815M

Spread across the hillsides above a scenic valley that's been dubbed 'Little Kashmir', Pithoragarh is the main town of a little-visited region that borders Tibet and Nepal. Its sights include several Chand-era temples and an old fort, but the real reason to come here is to get off the tourist trail. The busy main bazaar is good for a stroll, and townspeople are exceptionally friendly. Picturesque hikes in the area include the rewarding climb up to **Chandak** (7km) for views of the Panchachuli (Five Chimneys) massif.

There's a **tourist office** (📞225527) that can help with trekking guides and informa-tion, a State Bank of India ATM in the bazaar and a handful of internet cafes (₹30 per hour). Cheap hotels can be found around the bus stand (rooms from ₹200), but for something much better head 200m uphill to **Hotel Yash Yatharth** (📞225005; Naya Bazaar; dm ₹200, r ₹600-2500). Rates can be reduced by 80% if business is slow. For a good meal at a great price, locals swear by **Jyonar Restaurant** (Gandhi Chowk; mains ₹50-250; ☺8am-9pm) in the bazaar.

Several buses leave in the morning for Almora (₹110, five hours). Regular buses go to the transport hub of Haldwani and on to Delhi. There are hourly services from 5am to 2pm to Banbassa (₹165, six hours), the border crossing into Nepal. Buses run north to Munsyari (₹135, eight hours), the trailhead for Milam Glacier, as do the ubiquitous share jeeps (₹180). If taking the long route to Munsyari through Jauljibi, one stretch of road has amazing views of the Kumaon and Nepali Himalayas.

Pindari Glacier Trek

This six-day, 94km trek passes through truly virgin country that's inhabited by only a few shepherds, and it offers wonderful views of Nanda Kot (6860m), and Nanda Khat (6611m) on the southern rim of Nanda Devi Sanctuary. The 3km-long, 365m-wide Pindari Glacier is at 3353m, so take it easy to avoid altitude sickness. Permits aren't needed but bring your passport.

The trek begins and finishes at **Song** (1140m), a village 36km north of Bageshwar. Guides and porters can be organised easily in Song, or you can organise package treks through companies in Bageshwar or Almora. KMVN operates all-inclusive six-day treks out of Bageshwar for ₹5750 per person, staying at government rest houses. KMVN dorms (mattresses on the floor for ₹200), basic guest houses or *dhaba* huts (₹50 to ₹200) are dotted along the route, and food is available.

Buses (₹36, two hours) or share jeeps (₹60, 1½ hours) run between Song and Bageshwar.

Milam Glacier Trek

A challenging eight-day, 118km trek to this massive glacier at 3450m is reached along an ancient trade route to Tibet that was closed in 1962 following the war between India and

Border Hours

The border is open 24 hours, but before 6am and after 6pm you're unlikely to find any officials to stamp you in and out of the respective countries. While officially open to vehicles only from 6am to 7am, noon to 2pm and 5 to 6pm, rickshaws and motorcycles are usually allowed to make the 1km trip across the bridge between the border posts at any time. Otherwise, you have to walk it. (Even if the vehicle gate is closed, ask them to open it, and they might.)

Foreign Exchange

Hotels in Banbassa will exchange Indian and Nepali rupees, as will a small office near the Nepal border post. Nabil Bank in Mahendranagar has an ATM and foreign currency exchange.

Onward Transport

From the border, take a rickshaw to Mahendranagar. The bus station is about 1km from the centre on the Mahendra Hwy, from where buses leave for Kathmandu (₹1100, 16 hours) three times a day. There's also a single Pokhara service at 10.30am (₹1000, 16 hours).

Visas

Visas are available for US$30 (cash only) at the Nepali side of the border between 9am and 5pm.

China. It passes through magnificent rugged country to the east of Nanda Devi (7816m) and along the sometimes spectacular gorges of the Gori Ganga River. A popular but tough side trip to Nanda Devi East base camp adds another 32km or three days.

Permits (free, passport required) are available from the District Magistrate in Munsyari. You will also need a tent and your own food supplies, as villages on the route may be deserted. KMVN organises all-inclusive eight-day treks (from ₹5325).

The base for this excursion is the spectacularly located village of Munsyari (2290m), where the 6000m Panchachuli peaks scrape the sky across the Johar Valley. A guide, cook and porters can be hired and package treks can be arranged through Nanda Devi Tour N Trek (☑05961-222324; trek_beeru@rediffmail.com) or Johar Tour & Treks (☑05961-222752).

Two kilometres downhill from the bazaar is the small Tribal Heritage Museum (☑9411337094; admission free), run by the charming scholar SS Pangtey, with artifacts from the days when Munsyari was an important nexus of trade with Tibet.

The plentiful accommodation in Munsyari includes Hotel Pandey Lodge (☑9411130316; www.munsyarihotel.com; r ₹100-1200) by the bus stand, which has a wide range of good-value rooms, some with

amazing views. For motherly urging to eat til you're stuffed (plates refilled free), try the hole-in-the-wall *dhaba* just to the left of Bugyal Restaurant, at the bus stand.

A daily bus runs to Munsyari (₹190, 11 hours) from Almora; a jeep taxi costs around ₹3000 (10 hours). Buses run to and from Pithoragarh (₹140, eight hours) and Bageshwar (₹135, six hours). Share jeeps run to Thal (₹100, three hours), where you can change for onward transport. If travelling to Munsyari via Thal, get a right-side window seat for the best views along the road.

Banbassa
POP 7138

Banbassa is the closest Indian village to the Nepal border post of Mahendranagar, 5km away. Check the current situation in western Nepal before crossing here, as roads during monsoon or immediate postmonsoon season may be impassable due to landslides and washed-out bridges.

Although Banbassa has a train station, only metre-gauge local trains run to the main railhead at Bareilly. A better option is the bus service that runs to and from Haldwani, Haridwar and Delhi. Alternatively, take a train from Delhi to Bareilly then a bus from there to Banbassa.

Kolkata (Calcutta)

Best Places to Eat

» Bhojohari Manna (p466)
» Kewpies (p465)
» Oh! Calcutta (p465)
» Fire and Ice (p464)

Best Places to Stay

» Oberoi Grand (p460)
» Chrome (p461)
» Tollygunge Club (p462)
» Ashreen Guest House (p460)

Why Go?

India's second-biggest city is a daily festival of human existence, simultaneously noble and squalid, cultured and desperate. By its old spelling, Calcutta conjures up images of human suffering to most Westerners. But locally, Kolkata is regarded as India's intellectual and cultural capital. While poverty is certainly in your face, the dapper Bengali gentry continues to frequent grand old gentlemen's clubs, back horses at the Calcutta Racetrack and tee off at some of India's finest golf courses.

As the former capital of British India, Kolkata retains a feast of colonial-era architecture, albeit much in a photogenic state of semi-collapse. Meanwhile urban slums contrast with dynamic new-town suburbs and a rash of air-conditioned shopping malls. Kolkata's also the ideal place to experience the mild, fruity tang of Bengali cuisine. Friendlier than India's other mega-cities, this is a city you 'feel' more than simply visit.

When to Go
Kolkata (Calcutta)

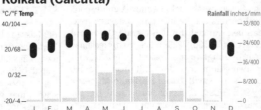

Oct The city dresses up magnificently for the colourful mayhem of Durga Puja.

Nov–Jan Cool and dry; there's a November film festival and a big book fair in January.

May–Sep Best avoided unless you're prepared for a very serious drenching.

Food

Fruity and mildly spiced, Bengali food favours the sweet, rich notes of jaggery (palm-sugar), *daab* (young coconut), *malai-kari* (coconut milk) and *posto* (poppy seed). Typical Bengali curry types include the light, coriander-scented *jhol,* drier spicier *jhal* and richer, ginger-based *kalia*. Strong mustard notes feature in *shorshe* curries and *paturi* dishes that come steamed in a banana leaf. *Gobindobhog bhaat* (steamed rice) or *luchi* (small puris) are the usual accompaniment. More characteristic than meat or chicken (*murgir*) are *chingri* (river prawns) and excellent fish, particularly white *rui* (rohu), fatty *chital*, cod-like *bhekti* and tasty but bone-filled *ilish* (hilsa). Excellent vegetarian choices include *mochar ghonto* (mashed banana-flower, potato and coconut), *doi begun* (eggplant in creamy sauce) and *shukto*, a favourite lunchtime starter combining at least five different vegetables in a milk-based sauce. Bengali desserts and sweets are legendary. Most characteristic are *mishti dhoi* (curd deliciously sweetened with jaggery), *rasgulla* (syrupy sponge balls) and *cham-cham* (double-textured curd-based fingers).

DON'T MISS

Sampling distinctive **Bengali food**, walking the chaotic **back alleys**, riding the Hooghly **ferries**, taking a **motorbike tour** to see more of the city and – if you've got more time – an excursion to the **Sundarbans**.

Top Festivals

» Dover Lane Music Conference (www.thedoverlanemusicconference.in, late Jan) Indian classical music and dance at Rabindra Sarovar.

» Kolkata Boi Mela (www.kolkatabookfaironline.com, late Jan/early Feb) Asia's biggest book fair.

» Saraswati Puja (early Feb) Prayers for educational success, all dress in yellow.

» Rath Yatra (Jun/Jul) Major Krishna chariot festival similar to the Puri equivalent.

» Durga Puja (www.durga-puja.org, Oct, see p457) Kolkata's biggest festival.

» Lakshmi Puja (full moon after Durga Puja) and Kali Puja (Diwali) feature more idol dunking.

» Kolkata Film Festival (www.kff.in, mid-Nov) Week-long festival of Bengali and international movies.

Kolkata Highlights

① Watch goddesses coming to life in the curious lanes of **Kumartuli** (p455) or on Kalighat Rd near the famous **Kalighat Temple** (p456)

② Ponder the contradictions of the magnificent **Victoria Memorial** (p446) which remains Kolkata's most splendid building, over 60

years after the end of the colonial era

③ Sample lipsmackingly authentic Bengali cuisine cheaply at **Sidheshwari Ashram** (p463) or in style at **6 Ballygunge Place** (p466)

④ Discover the enlightened universalist idealism of Ramakrishna in **Belur Math**

(p456) and Rabindranath Tagore, India's greatest modern poet, at **Tagore's House** (p454), of which Kolkatans are understandably proud

⑤ Volunteer to help the destitute at **Mother Teresa's 'Motherhouse'** (p448)

History

Although Kalikata (now Kalighat) had been a much-revered temple for centuries, the Kolkata area was very much a rural backwater when British merchant Job Charnock showed up in 1686. He considered the site appropriate for a new, defendable colonial settlement and within a few decades a miniature version of London was sprouting stately buildings and English churches amid wide boulevards and grand formal gardens. But the grand illusion vanished abruptly at Calcutta's frayed edges where Indians servicing the Raj mostly lived in cramped, overcrowded slums.

The most notable hiccup in the city's meteoric rise came in 1756, when Siraj-ud-daula, the nawab of nearby Murshidabad, recaptured the city. Dozens of members of the colonial aristocracy were imprisoned in a cramped room beneath Fort William. By morning, around 40 of them were dead from suffocation. The British press exaggerated numbers, drumming up moral outrage back home: the legend of the 'Black Hole of Calcutta' was born.

The following year, Clive of India retook Calcutta for Britain. The nawab sought aid from the French but was soundly defeated at the Battle of Plassey (now Palashi), thanks mainly to the treachery of former allies. A stronger fort was built and the town became British India's official capital, though well into the late 18th century one could still hunt tigers in the bamboo forests around where Sudder St lies today.

The late-19th-century Bengali Renaissance movement saw a great cultural reawakening among middle-class Calcuttans. This was further galvanised by the massively unpopular 1905 division of Bengal, sowing the seeds of the Indian Independence movement. Bengal was reunited in 1911, but the British promptly transferred their colonial capital to less troublesome Delhi.

Initially, loss of political power had little effect on Calcutta's economic status. However, the impact of 1947's partition was devastating. While West Pakistan and Punjab saw a fairly equal (if bloody) exchange of populations, migration in Bengal was almost entirely one-way. Around four million Hindu refugees from East Bengal arrived, choking Calcutta's already overpopulated bastis (slums). For a period, people really were dying of hunger in the streets, creating Calcutta's abiding image of abject poverty. No sooner had these refugees been absorbed than a second wave arrived during the 1971 India–Pakistan War.

After India's partition, the port of Calcutta was hit very hard by the loss of its main natural hinterland, now behind the closed Pakistan (later Bangladesh) border. Labour unrest spiralled out of control while the city's dominant party (Communist Party of India) spent most of its efforts attacking the feudal system of land ownership. Well-intentioned attempts to set strict rent controls have since backfired: where tenants still pay a few rupees in monthly rent, landlords have no interest in maintaining or upgrading properties so many fine old buildings are crumbling before one's eyes.

KOLKATA IN...

Three Days

On the first day admire the **Victoria Memorial** and surrounding attractions then visit India Tourism to grab a Marble Palace permit (to be used two days hence), before dining and dancing on Park or Camac Sts. On day two wander through the crumbling colonial-era wonderland of **BBD Bagh**, experience the fascinating/disturbing alley-life of **Old Chinatown** and **Barabazar** and observe **Howrah Bridge** from colourful **Mullik Ghat flower market**. Refresh yourself with a beer at the **Fairlawn**. Day 3 visit **Marble Palace** and surrounding attractions, continuing to **Kumartuli** directly or by a vastly longer loop via **Dakshineswar** and **Belur Math**, returning by boat.

One Week

To the above, consider adding a day or more volunteering. Visit **Mother Teresa's Motherhouse**, continue by tram to **South Park St Cemetery** and dine at **Shiraz**. Experience the contrasts of **Southern Kolkata**, its dawn **laughing clubs**, the great Bengali food, the goat sacrifices at **Kalighat** and the **art galleries** of Gariahat. Ponder the moral dilemmas of taking/not taking a hand-drawn **rickshaw**, of playing golf or of having a flutter at the **racecourse**. Join a tour to the Sundarbans in West Bengal.

KOLKATA (CALCUTTA)

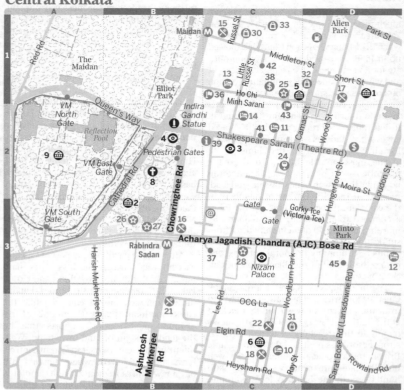

In 2001 Calcutta officially adopted the more phonetic spelling, Kolkata. Around the same time the city administration implemented a new, relatively business-friendly attitude that has encouraged a noticeable economic resurgence. The most visible results are numerous suburban shopping malls and apartment towers plus the rapid emergence of Salt Lake City's Sector 5 as Kolkata's alternative corporate and entertainment centre, albeit well off most tourists' radar.

◉ Sights

CENTRAL KOLKATA

Victoria Memorial   HISTORIC BUILDING
(VM; Map p446; Indian/foreigner ₹10/150; ☉10am-5pm Tue-Sun, last tickets 4.30pm) The incredible Victoria Memorial is a vast, beautifully proportioned festival of white marble: think US Capitol meets Taj Mahal. Had it been built for a beautiful Indian princess rather than a dead colonial queen, this would surely be

considered one of India's greatest buildings. It was designed to commemorate Queen Victoria's 1901 diamond jubilee, but construction wasn't completed until nearly 20 years after her death.

Don't miss the statues as you enter the first hallway: King George V faces his wife Mary but looks more a queen himself in his camp breeches. To the left, prints and paintings are displayed on hardboard hoardings that jar with the gallery's original splendour. The soaring central chamber remains very impressive and leads through to the **Kolkata Gallery**, an excellent, even-handed exhibition tracing the city's colonial-era history.

Even if you don't want to go in, the building is still worth admiring from afar: there's a magnificently photogenic view across reflecting ponds from the northeast. Or you can get closer by paying your way into the large, well-tended **park** (admission ₹4;

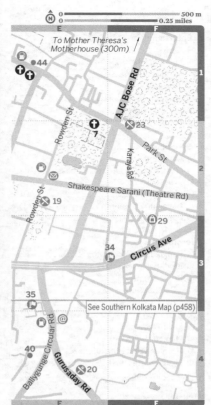

0 m 500 m / 0 0.25 miles

To Mother Theresa's
Motherhouse (300m)

See Southern Kolkata Map (p458)

KOLKATA (CALCUTTA) SIGHTS

bright, ground-floor gallery featuring changing exhibitions by local artists but its upstairs museum section remains closed for the foreseeable future. Imaginative private galleries include **Harrington Street Gallery** (Map p446; www.hstreetartscentre.com; 2nd fl, 8 Ho Chi Minh Sarani; ⊙2-8pm Mon-Sat) and **Aakriti Gallery** (Map p446; www.aakritiartgallery.com; 1st fl, 12/3A Hungerford St; ⊙noon-7pm Mon-Sat).

Loosely styled on Sarnath's classic Buddhist stupa, the **Birla Planetarium** (Map p446; Chowringhee Rd) presents slow-moving, half-hour **star shows** (admission ₹30) in English at 1.30pm and 6.30pm.

Aurobindo Bhawan
SACRED SITE

(Map p446; 8 Shakespeare Sarani; ⊙8am-8pm) Revolutionary turned guru Sri Aurobindo was born in Calcutta in 1872 and his grand childhood mansion-home has been preserved as an Aurobindo centre. Its garden forms an oasis of peace in the city centre and there's an open-air meditation space where you can sit as you wish or join half-hour **group meditations** at 7pm on Thursdays or Saturdays.

The Maidan
PARK

(Map p446, p450) After the 'Black Hole' fiasco, a moated 'second' Fort William was constructed in 1758 in octagonal, Vaubanesque form. The whole village of Gobindapur was flattened to give the new fort's cannons a clear line of fire. Though sad for then-residents, this created the **Maidan** (pronounced moidan), a 3km-long park that is today as fundamental to Kolkata as Central Park is to New York City. Fort William remains hidden within a walled military zone, but for an amusingly far-fetched tale of someone who managed to get in, read *Simon Winchester's Calcutta*.

New Market & Esplanade
AREA

(Map p450) Before 8am, most of New Market's handicraft touts are still sleeping, so come early to admire the distinctive brick **clocktower** and atmospheric **Hogg Market**. Walking towards Esplanade, notice the fascinatingly crumbling facade of **Futnani Chambers**, the classic '50s-style **Elite Cinema** and colonial-era **Metropolitan Building**. A block north the fanciful **Tipu Sultan's Mosque** hides almost invisibly behind market stalls. Rising above chaotic Esplanade bus station, the 1828 **Sahid Minar** is a 48m-tall round-topped obelisk originally celebrating an 1814 British military victory over Nepal.

Indian Museum
MUSEUM

(Map p450; www.indianmuseumkolkata.org; Chowringhee Rd; Indian/foreigner ₹10/150, camera ₹50;

⊙5.45am-5.45pm). By day, entrance is from the north or south gates (with ticket booths at both), though you can exit to the east.

In the evenings the VM makes a spectacular canvas for a 45-minute English-language **sound-and-light show** (Indian/foreigner ₹10/20; ⊙7.15pm Tue-Sun Nov-Feb, 7.45pm Tue-Sun Mar-Jun) that's better than you might initially fear from the very dated opening slide sequence. Ticket booth and entry are from the east gate. Seating is outside and uncovered; there are no shows in summer.

Around the Victoria Monument
AREA

With its central crenellated tower, the 1847 **St Paul's Cathedral** (Map p446; Cathedral Rd; ⊙9am-noon & 3-6pm) would look quite at home in Cambridgeshire. It has a remarkably wide nave and features a stained-glass west window by pre-Raphaelite maestro Sir Edward Burne-Jones.

The **Academy of Fine Arts** (Map p446; 2 Cathedral Rd; admission free; ⊙3-8pm) has a

⊙10am-4.30pm Tue-Sun, last entry 4pm) Kolkata's old-fashioned main museum fills a colonnaded palace ranged around a central lawn. Extensive exhibits include fabulous 1000-year-old Hindu sculptures, lumpy minerals, a dangling whale skeleton and an ancient Egyptian mummy. Gag at the pickled **human embryos** (gallery 19) and eight-legged goat, spot the surreal **Glyptodon** dinosaur-armadillo (gallery 11) and don't miss the re-assembled 2nd-century BC **Barhut Gateway** (gallery 2). Gallery 15 displays 20 rings and 18 bangles found in the tummy of a gigantic man-eating crocodile. Note that no bags are allowed inside: handbags can be stored at the entrance but don't arrive with a backpack.

Mother Teresa's 'Motherhouse' SACRED SITE (off Map p450; www.motherteresa.org; 54A AJC Bose Rd; ⊙visits 8am-noon & 3-6pm Fri-Wed)

Pilgrims arrive here in droves to pay homage at Mother Teresa's large, sober tomb. Exhibits in a small adjacent museum (⊙9am-noon & 3-5.30pm) include Teresa's worn sandals and battered enamel dinner-bowl. And upstairs, the 'Mother's room' is where she worked and slept from 1953 to 1997, preserved in all its simplicity.

The charity's numerous Kolkata sites welcome short-term volunteers, qualified or not. Start by attending a briefing two blocks north at Sishu Bhavan (78 AJC Bose Rd; ⊙3pm Mon, Wed & Fri).

Please do not give anything (including sweets, milk powder, toothpaste etc) to the handful of professional beggars who have 'claimed the territory' outside the Motherhouse: some, including an eloquent Eurasian mother–daughter team, are sophisticated players but their activities cause regular problems for the Mission staff and the 'profession' is so lucrative that we've been told that the children refuse to take available school places.

South Park Street Cemetery — CEMETERY
(Map p446; admission ₹20 donation appropriate; ⊗8am-4.45pm) Today Park St is one of Kolkata's top commercial avenues, but when it was constructed in the 1760s, it was a simple causeway across uninhabited marshlands built to access the then-new South Park Street Cemetery. These days the cemetery remains a wonderful oasis of calm featuring mossy Raj-era graves from rotundas to soaring pyramids, all jostling for space in a lightly manicured jungle.

Netaji Bhawan — MUSEUM
(Map p446; www.netaji.org; 38/2 Elgin Rd; adult/child ₹5/2; ⊗11am-4pm Tue-Sun) Worth a look if you're lunching at Kewpies, this house-museum celebrates the life and vision of controversial independence radical Subhas Chandra Bose, maintaining several rooms decorated in 1940s style. It was Bose's brother's residence from which Subhas made his famous 'Great Escape' from British-imposed house arrest in January 1941. The original getaway car is parked in the drive.

BBD BAGH AREA

BBD Bagh — AREA
Originally called Tank Sq, BBD Bagh is a large square centred on a palm-lined central reservoir-lake ('tank') that once supplied the young city's water. Some locals still call it by its later-colonial name **Dalhousie Sq**, commemorating British Lieutenant-Governor Lord Dalhousie. The square is now re-renamed after the nationalists who tried to assassinate him. In fact the BBD trio (Binoy, Badal and Dinesh) bungled their 1930 raid, killing instead an unlucky prisons inspector. Nonetheless the attack was a highly symbolic moment in the self-determination struggle. The assassination took place within the photogenic 1780 **Writers' Building** (Map p452), whose glorious south facade looks something like a French provincial city hall. Originally built for clerks ('writers') of the East India Company, it's still a haven of pen-pushing bureaucracy.

Although concrete intrusions detract from the overall spectacle, there are many other resplendent colonial-era edifices around the square. **St Andrews Church** (Map p452) has a fine Wren-style spire, the former **Standard Chartered Building** (Map p452; Netaji Subhash Rd) has a vaguely Moorish feel and the red-brick **Standard Buildings**

(Map p452; 32 BBD Bagh) have carved nymphs and wrought-iron balconies at the rear.

GPO — LANDMARK
(Map p452; BBD Bagh) The 1866 General Post Office was built on the ruins of the original Fort William, site of the infamous 'Black Hole of Calcutta'. It sports an imposing cupola and at night, floodlit in pale violet light, looks particularly impressive when viewed across the lake from behind the BBD Bagh minibus stand. Nearby there's a loveable little **philatelic museum** (Map p452; Koilaghat St; admission free; ⊗11am-4pm Mon-Sat).

Raj Bhavan — HISTORIC BUILDING
(Map p452; http://rajbhavankolkata.nic.in; ⊗closed to public) Somewhat resembling the US White House, the grand Raj Bhavan was designed in 1799 along the lines of Kedleston Hall, the Derbyshire home of the Curzon family. By strange coincidence, one of its most famous masters a century later would be none other than Lord Curzon. Today the building is the official residence of the West Bengal governor and visitors may only peep through the ornate giant gates.

High Court — HISTORIC BUILDING
(Map p452; http://calcuttahighcourt.nic.in; Esplanade Row West) Another of Kolkata's greatest architectural triumphs is the 19th-century High Court building, loosely modelled on the medieval Cloth Hall in Ypres (Flanders). You can't go inside, but for good exterior views approach from the south walking past the western end of the low-domed West Bengal Assembly building.

Kolkata Panorama — MUSEUM
(Map p452; http://tinyurl.com/Kolkpan; 4 Esplanade West; weekdays/weekends ₹10/15; ⊗11am-6pm Tue-Sun, last entry 5pm) Within an imposing colonnaded cube that was originally the Town Hall building, this interactive museum introduces the city's heritage through a lively collection of working models. It's well designed, though historically selective, and many foreigners will struggle to appreciate fully the detailed sections on Bengali popular culture. You'll be accompanied by a guide which makes it awkward to 'escape' quickly.

St John's Church — CHURCH
(Map p452; KS Roy Rd; ⊗8am-5pm) This stone-spired 1787 church is ringed by columns and contains a small, portrait-draped room once used as an office by Warren Hastings, India's first British governor-general (on the right as you enter). The **graveyard** (admission ₹10)

contains two curious octagonal monuments, the **mausoleum of Job Charnock** celebrating Kolkata's disputed 'founder' and a 1902 **Black Hole Memorial** that was moved here in 1940.

Eden Gardens AREA

The vast Ranji Stadium hosting Kolkata cricket matches is commonly nicknamed for the **Eden Gardens** (Map p452; ⊙noon-5pm) that lie behind. Those gardens feature a lake and picturesque **Burmese Pagoda**. Entry is usually limited to the south gate, but a small, more convenient north portal near Gate 12 of Ranji Stadium is occasionally open.

FREE **Banking Museum** MUSEUM

(Map p452; ☑22318164; 11th fl, SBI Bldg, Strand Rd; ⊙3-5pm Tue, Thu & Sat or by arrangement) This small, professionally presented new museum brings alive the history of Indian banking using archive materials like the original account ledgers of Tagore and of Nehru's father.

NORTH-CENTRAL KOLKATA

Howrah Bridge (Rabindra Setu) LANDMARK

Howrah Bridge is a 705m-long abstraction of steel cantilevers and traffic fumes. Built during WWII, it's one of the world's busiest bridges and an architectural icon. For the best view, fight your way through the **Mullik Ghat flower market** to **Mullik Ghat**. Photography of the bridge itself is technically prohibited but enforcement appears to be lax of late and if you're stopped here, you might sneak a discreet shot from one of the various river-ferries that ply the Hooghly to the vast 1906 Howrah train station.

Barabazar AREA

North and northeast of BBD Bagh lies a wide scattering of religious buildings. Alone none warrants a special trip, but weaving between them is a great excuse to explore some of Kolkata's most vibrantly chaotic alleys teeming with traders, rickshaw couriers and baggage

Chowringhee

wallahs with impossibly huge packages balanced on their heads. Hidden away amid the paper-merchant district of Old China Bazaar St, the 18th-century **Armenian Church of Nazareth** (Map p452; Armenian St; ⊙6am-6pm) was founded in 1707 and is claimed to be Kolkata's oldest place of Christian worship. Gravestones in the peaceful yard outside date back to 1630. The church's low but finely proportioned, whitewashed clocktower-spire is best spied from Bonfield Lane. The larger

1797 Portuguese-Catholic **Holy Rosary Cathedral** (Map p452; Brabourne Rd; ⊙6am-11am) has eye-catching crown-topped side towers and an interior whose font is festively kitsch.

Kolkata's Jewish community once numbered around 30,000 but these days barely 40 aging co-religionists turn up at **Moghan David Synagogue** (Map p452; Canning St; ⊙by discussion with doorkeeper) for rare celebrations in what looks, from outside, like a tall-spired church. Around the corner, the derelict **Neveh**

KOLKATA (CALCUTTA)

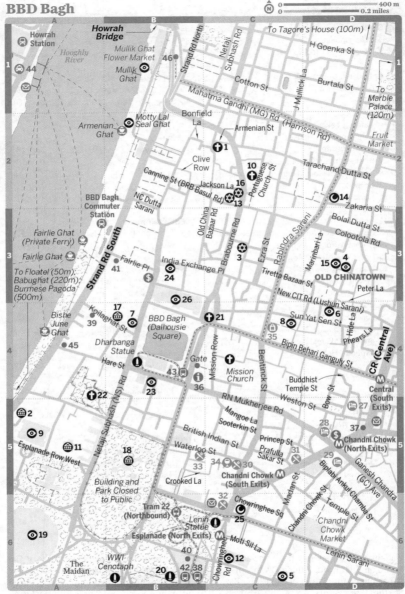

Shalome Synagogue (Map p452; Brabourne Rd) is almost invisible behind the shop stalls that use it as a storehouse. Opposite decrepit Pollock St Post Office (once a grand Jewish school building) is **BethEl Synagogue** (Map p452; Pollock St) whose colonnaded interior can only be visited with written permission, oddly obtained across town from **Nahoum Bakery** (Map p450; Stall F-20, New Market; ⏲9.30am-8pm Mon-Sat, 9.30am-1pm Sun). Allow two days!

Rising above the colourful shopfronts of ever-fascinating Rabindra Sarani, the 1926

KOLKATA (CALCUTTA) SIGHTS

Nakhoda Mosque (Map p452; 1 Zakaria St) is an impressive confection of red arches bristling with domes and minarets. It was loosely modelled on Akbar's Mausoleum at Sikandra.

Old Chinatown
AREA

For nearly two centuries the area around Phears Lane was home to a predominantly Christian Chinese community, many of whom fled or were interned during a fit of anti-Chinese fervour during the 1962 war. These days 'old' Chinatown is pretty run down but is a fascinating place to glimpse Kolkata's contrasts. On the turn of ragged little Damzen Lane you'll find the shrine-like Chinese church, **Nam Soon** (Map p452). A little further along is an oversized turquoise **gateway** (Map p452; 10 Damzen Lane), built to allow passage for domestic elephants. The once-grand 1924 **Nangking Restaurant** (Map p452; Lushun Sarani) is now a wreck beside which a rubbish

heap supports a community of destitute scavengers who scrape together a miserable existence living in tent-and-box shacks on neighbouring pavements. Very humbling.

Just after dawn, there's a lively **market** scene on Tiretta's Bazaar. It's all closed by 10am, as is the archetypal old Chinese shop, **Hap Hing** (Map p452; 10 Sun Yat Sen St; ⏲6am-10am Mon-Sat, 6am-8.30am Sun) where owner Stella Chen can tell you lots more about the community and sells a colour-picture-book/CD set *Chinatown Kolkata* (₹500).

Note that Kolkata has a second Chinatown further east at Tangra where tanneries once produced the leather for the community's many shoe-makers. That rather forbidding area now has only around 50 Chinese families but almost as many Chinese restaurants.

Marble Palace
MUSEUM

(off Map p452; 46 Muktaram Babu St; ⏲10am-3pm closed Mon & Thu) Resplendent yet slightly run down, this grand 1835 raja's mansion is astonishingly overstuffed with statues, Victoriana, Belgian glassware and fine if bedraggled paintings including supposedly original works by Murillo, Joshua Reynolds and three by Rubens. Napoleons beat Wellingtons two to one in the music room, which is lavishly floored with marble inlay. The ballroom retains its vast array of candle chandeliers with globes of silvered glass to spread illumination: original 19th-century disco balls! Before arriving you need to get a permission note from one of the tourist offices (see p469). With this note, admission is technically free. However, the (obligatory) guide solicits tips of ₹50 to ₹100 per group.

To find Marble Palace from MG Rd metro, walk three blocks north to the first traffic light and turn west at 171 Chittaranjan Ave. To continue to Tagore's House, continue west down Muktaram Babu St (there's a great little ₹2 tea stand at no 13 run by a yogi tea-wallah), then turn right on Rabindra Sarani, passing several stone-cutting workshops.

Tagore's House   MUSEUM
(off Map p452; Rabindra Bharati Museum; www.rabindrabharatimuseum.org; 246D Rabindra Sarani; Indian/foreigner ₹10/50, student ₹5/25;

STREET NAMES

After independence, the Indian government changed any street name that had Raj-era connotations. The Communists continued the process. Humorously they chose to re-name Harrington St such that the US found its consulate on a road named for its then arch-enemy, Ho Chi Minh.

Today citizens and taxis mostly use the British-era names while, confusingly, most maps, street signs and business cards use the new names (or sometimes both). This text uses what we found, quite unscientifically, to be the most commonly employed variant, *italicised* in the list below:

OLD NAME	NEW NAME
Ballygunge Rd	Ashutosh Chowdhury Ave *(AC Rd)*
Brabourne Rd	Biplabi Trailokya Maharaja Rd
Camac St	Abinindranath Tagore St
Central Ave	*Chittaranjan (CR) Ave*
Chitpore Rd	*Rabindra Sarani*
Chowringhee Rd	Jawaharlal Nehru Rd
Dalhousie Sq	*BBD Bagh*
Free School St	*Mirza Ghalib St*
Harrington St	*Ho Chi Minh Sarani*
Harrison Rd	Mahatma Gandhi *(MG)* Rd
Hungerford St	Picasso Bithi
Kyd St	Dr M Ishaque Rd
Lansdowne Rd	*Sarat Bose Rd*
Loudon St	Dr UM Bramhchari St
Lower Circular Rd	*AJC Bose Rd*
Old Courthouse St	Hemant Basu Sarani
Park St	Mother Teresa Sarani
Rowden St	Sarojini Naidu Sarani
Theatre Rd	*Shakespeare Sarani*
Victoria Terrace	*Gorky Terrace*
Waterloo St	Nawab Siraj-ud-Daula Sarani
Wellesley St	*RAK* (Rafi Ahmed Kidwai) *Rd*
Wood St	Dr Martin Luther King Sarani

For many people, Mother Teresa (1910–97) was the living image of human sacrifice. Born Agnes Gonxha Bojaxhiu to Albanian parents in then-Ottoman Üsküp (now Skopje in Macedonia), she joined the Irish Order of Loreto nuns and worked for over a decade teaching in Calcutta's **St Mary's High School** (92 Ripon St). Horrified by the city's spiralling poverty she established a new order, the **Missionaries of Charity** (www.mother teresa.org) and founded refuges for the destitute and dying. **Nirmal Hriday** (Sacred Heart; Map p458; 251 Kalighat Rd; ☉closed for renovation at the time of research), the first of these, opened in 1952 in a former Kalighat pilgrims' hostel. Although the order expanded into an international charity, Mother Teresa herself continued to live in absolute simplicity. She was awarded the Nobel Peace Prize in 1979 and beatified by the Vatican in October 2003, the first official step towards being made a saint.

But this 'Saint of the Gutters' is not universally beloved. For some Kolkatans it's slightly galling to find their cultured, predominantly Hindu city popularly linked in the world's mind with a Catholic heroine whose work underlined the city's least appealing facet. Germaine Greer has accused Mother Teresa of religious imperialism, while Christopher Hitchens' book, *The Missionary Position*, decries the donations from dictators and corrupt tycoons. Many have questioned the Missionaries of Charity's minimal medical background and Teresa's staunchly Catholic position against contraception, which seems particularly untenable given Kolkata's AIDS and hepatitis problems. However, the organisation was never primarily focused on saving lives, simply offering a little love and dignity to the dying. Before Mother Teresa, even that was an unknown luxury for the truly destitute.

☉10.30am-4.30pm Tue-Sun) Within Rabindra Bharati University, the comfortable 1784 family mansion of Rabindranath Tagore has become a shrine-like museum to India's greatest modern poet. Even if his personal effects don't inspire you, some of the well-chosen quotations might spark an interest in Tagore's deeply universalist philosophy. There's also a decent gallery of paintings by his family and contemporaries and an exhibition on his links with Japan. The 1930 photo of Tagore taken with Einstein could win a 'World's Wildest Hair' competition. You'd need an hour to see everything but for many casual visitors a brief glimpse is enough.

Bagbazar-bound trams connect to Kumartuli, passing many fascinating vignettes of Kolkata life.

Kumartuli   AREA

Many of the giant **god effigies** that are immersed in the holy Hooghly during Kolkata's colourful pujas have been made by the *kumar* (sculptors) of this enthralling district. Different workshops specialise in creating the straw frames, adding clay coatings or painting the divine features. Craftsmen are busiest from August till November for the Durga and Kali festivals.

There's a great selection of workshops on the narrow lane running two blocks west from 499 Rabindra Sarani. Where

that makes a T-junction turn right for more (Banamali Sakar St). That road ends 300m north at Durgacharan Banerjee St. Turning left here brings you quickly to a ghat where the sculptors' mud-clay is brought in by boat. A tree-shaded riverside stroll north of here passes several small shrines en route to Bagbazar Jetty whence passenger **ferries** cross to Howrah (₹4.50, 20 minutes with two stops, four hourly) and Baranagar (twice hourly).

Ashutosh Museum of Indian Art   MUSEUM

(www.caluniv.ac.in; Centenary Bldg, 87/1 College St; admission ₹10; ☉11.30am-4.30pm Mon-Fri) Priceless antique Indian sculptures, brasswork and Bengali terracotta are displayed with very little fanfare in this dry, but brilliantly endowed museum tucked behind Kolkata University's Central Library. It's down the first lane off College St as you walk north from Colootola Rd. Trams 2 and 5 pass along College St here. While you're in the university area consider visiting the mythic **Indian Coffee House** (1st fl, 15 Bankim Chatterjee St; coffee ₹9, snack meals ₹14-35; ☉9am-9pm Mon-Sat, 9am-12.30pm & 5-9pm Sun). Once a meeting place of freedom fighters, bohemians and revolutionaries, today its high ceilings and slightly grimy walls ring with deafening student conversation but despite the dishwater coffee, it's perversely fascinating.

Walk up College St and turn right one block before MG Rd (it's 20m down a side lane then upstairs to the left).

MG Rd towards Sealdah Station from here is an inspiring chaos of mouldering generations-old box shops, potion sellers and cardmakers beneath dishevelled, occasionally grand old facades.

Heading the other way, numbers 104 to 116 offer colourfully costumed brass-bands for hire.

NORTHERN KOLKATA

This area's long distances and tedious traffic are mitigated if you use a public riverboat from Dakshineswar to Belur Math, then charter a boat onward to Bagbazar. Doing that in reverse is less feasible due to a lack of boat-hire possibilities at Bagbazar.

Sheetalnathji Mandir   JAIN TEMPLE

(www.jaindharmonline.com/pilgri/shitala.htm; Badridas Temple St; donation appropriate; ☉6am-noon & 3-7pm) The best known of a closely grouped trio of Jain temples, this 1867 complex is a dazzling if unrefined pastiche of colourful mosaics, spires, columns and slivered figurines that looks like a work by Gaudi. It's 1.6km from Shyambazar metro.

Dakshineswar   HINDU TEMPLE

(www.dakshineswarkalitemple.org; ☉6.30am-noon & 3-8.30pm) The heart of this vibrant riverside complex is a cream-and-red 1847 Kali Temple shaped like an Indian Sacré-Coeur. The site is where Ramakrishna started his remarkable spiritual journey and his small room in the outer northwest corner of the temple precinct is now a place of special meditative reverence.

A metro extension is under construction to Dakshineswar train station, 400m south of the temple, which has roughly hourly suburban train services from Sealdah (20 minutes) and is the terminus of bus DN9/1 from Dum Dum metro (₹5). Uncovered boats to Belur Math (per passenger/boat ₹8/240, 20 minutes) leave when full from the temples' tree-shaded riverbank. Bring a hat or umbrella.

Belur Math   SACRED SITE

(www.sriramakrishna.org/belur.htm; Grand Trunk Rd; ☉6.30am-noon & 3.30-8.30pm) Set very attractively amid palms and manicured lawns, this large religious centre is the headquarters of the Ramakrishna Mission, inspired by 19th-century Indian sage Ramakrishna Paramahamsa, who preached the unity of all religions. Its centrepiece is the 1938

Ramakrishna Mandir (☉closes 8pm) which somehow manages to look like a cathedral, Indian palace and Istanbul's Aya Sofya all at the same time. Several smaller shrines (☉6.30-11.30am & 3.30-5.15pm) near the Hooghly riverbank include the Sri Sarada Devi Temple, entombing the guru's wife.

Accessed from the car park, the beautifully presented dual-level museum (admission ₹5; ☉8.30-11.30am & 3.30-5.30pm Tue-Sun) charts Ramakrishna's life and travels, with mock-ups of buildings in which he stayed from Rajasthan to New York.

Minibus 11 and bus 54 run to Esplanade, bus 56 to Howrah. However, to avoid the miserable stop-start traffic, consider chartering a boat to Bagbazar near Kumartuli (₹350). Six daily suburban trains run from Belur Math to Howrah (₹4, 25 minutes)

WEST KOLKATA

Botanical Gardens   PARK

(Indian/foreigner ₹5/50, 40-min buggy-tour ₹25/150 extra; ☉5.30am-5pm) If it weren't such an awkward trek by public transport, Kolkata's lovely 109-hectare Botanical Gardens would make a great place to escape from the city's sounds and smells. Founded in 1786, the gardens played an important role in cultivating tea long before the drink became a household commodity. Today there's a cactus house, palm collection, river-overlook and a boating-lake with splendid Giant Amazon Lily pads. The most touted attraction is the 250-year-old 'world's largest banyan tree'. However,the central trunk rotted away in the 1920s, leaving a disappointing array of cross-branches and linked aerial roots that have become virtual trees of their own.

The banyan is five minutes' walk from the park's Bicentenary Gate (Andul Rd) on bus route 55A or 25 minutes' walk from the gardens' main gate where bus 55 and minibus 6 terminate after a painfully slow drive from Esplanade (₹7) via Howrah. Taxis from Shakespeare Sarani charge around ₹90 via the elegant Vidyasagar Setu (Hooghly Suspension Bridge).

SOUTH KOLKATA

Kalighat Temple   HINDU TEMPLE

(☉5am-2pm & 4-10pm) This ancient Kali temple is Kolkata's holiest spot for Hindus and possibly the source of the city's name. Today's version, a 1809 rebuild, has floral- and peacock-motif tiles that look more Victorian than Indian. More interesting than the

Much as Carnival transforms Rio or New Orleans, Durga Puja brings Kolkata even more colourfully to life. For five days people venerate gaudily painted idols of the 10-armed goddess Durga and her entourage displayed in *pandals* (temporary shrines) that dominate yards, block roads or fill little parks. In the last 30 years, design competitions and increasing corporate sponsorship have seen *pandals* growing ever more ornate and complex, some with topical or political messages. West Bengal Tourism tours try to take tourists around a selection of the best *pandals* but getting anywhere within the city can take hours given the general festive pandemonium. At the festival's climax, myriad Durga idols are thrown into the sacred Hooghly River amid singing, water throwing, fireworks and indescribable traffic congestion. If you just want *pandal* photos and not the festival aspect, consider visiting just after Durga Puja when the idol has gone but *pandals* have yet to be deconstructed. Or come back for Kali Puja three weeks later when the city does the whole thing all over again, this time with statues of blue-faced, red-tongued Kali. And for months to come there are many alternative pujas.

Many diaspora Bengalis return 'home' for Durga Puja so Kolkata hotels fill up. Hotels will be comparatively empty afterwards but at that stage many locals go away on holiday so getting air tickets out can be virtually impossible for a week or two (the tourist quota on train tickets can be a saviour).

architecture are the jostling pilgrim queues that snake into the main hall to fling hibiscus flowers at a crowned, three-eyed Kali image. There's no need to join them to feel the atmosphere (loitering priests that offer to whisk you to the front of the queue will expect a very hefty 'donation'). Behind the bell pavilion but still within the mandir complex, goats are ritually beheaded to honour the ever-demanding goddess, or, as a local guide described it, to buy 'God power'.

The temple is hidden in a maze of alleys jammed with market stalls selling votive flowers, brassware, religious artefacts and pictures of Kali. From Kalighat metro station (with its four-storey Mother Teresa mosaic) walk towards the putrid Tolisnala Stream where **Shanagar Burning Ghat** (Map p458) hosts an impressive gaggle of monuments celebrating those cremated here. Turn north up Tollygunge Rd which becomes Kalighat Rd after one block. The temple is to the right down the footpath beside **Nirmal Hriday** (Map p458; 251 Kalighat Rd). That's Mother Teresa's world famous, if surprisingly small, home for the dying, its roof-corners pimpled with neo-Mughal mini-domes.

Further north up lively Kalighat Rd, after it curves across Hazra Rd, you'll find numerous **image makers**: less famous but almost as intriguing as those in Kumartuli (p455).

Rabindra Sarovar   PARK
(Map p458) The parkland here is less beautiful than Kolkata's Botanical Gardens but at dawn the lake prettily reflects the hazy sunrise while middle class Kolkatans jog, row and meditate. Some form circles to do group-yoga routines culminating in ho-ho ha-ha-ha laugh-ins; these are the informal **Laughing Clubs** (☉6-7am), engagingly described by Tony Hawks in *The Weekenders: Adventures in Calcutta*. Even if forced, a good giggle can be refreshingly therapeutic.

Alipore   AREA
First opened in 1875, Kolkata's 16-hectare **zoo** (Map p458; Alipore Rd; admission ₹10; ☉9am-5pm Fri-Wed) includes lawns and lakeside promenades that are very popular with weekend picnickers, hence all the rubbish. Some enclosures are more confined than others but reconstruction works were underway during research both here and across the road at the sorry little **aquarium** (Map p458; admission ₹3; ☉10.30am-5pm Fri-Wed). Bus 230 from Rabindra Sadan passes outside. Directly south of the zoo entrance, the (private) access road to India's **National Library** (www.nlindia.org) loops around the very regal **Curzon Mansion** (Map p458), once the colonial Viceroy's residence. Around 1km southeast, the delightful **Horticultural Gardens** (admission ₹10; ☉6-10am & 2-7pm) offer some respite from the traffic rumble.

Gariahat   AREA
This wealthy area isn't really a tourist draw but has a good scattering of restaurants and shops. There's also the large, distinctive 20th-century **Birla Mandir** (Map p458; Gariahat Rd; ☉6-11am & 4.30-9pm).

Southern Kolkata

See Central Kolkata Map (p446)

Several Gariahat galleries feature cutting-edge contemporary Bengali art, including **Experimenter** (www.experimenter.in; 2/1 Hindustan Rd; 11am-7pm Mon-Sat), behind Kanishka's; **CIMA** (Map p458; www.cimaartindia.com; Sunny Towers, 2nd fl, 43 Ashutosh Chowdhury Rd; 11am-7pm Tue-Sat, 3-7pm Mon), a six-room gallery; **Birla Academy of Art & Culture** (Map p458; www.birlaart.com; 109 Southern Ave; 4-7pm Tue-Sun); and **Ganges Gallery** (Map p458; www.gangesart.net; 33A Jatin Das Rd; 11am-7pm Mon-Sat).

🏃 Activities

Cooking

Kali Travel Home (www.traveleastindia.com; ₹550-750) arranges personal three-hour Bengali cooking courses led by local women in their homes. Costs include food.

Golf

A major plus of sleeping at the **Tollygunge Club** (p462; www.thetollygungeclub.com; guest weekday/weekend ₹175/350) is the right to play on their magnificent golf course.

The 1829 **Royal Calcutta Golf Club** (24731288; www.royalcalcuttagolfclub.com; 18 Golf Club Rd), the world's oldest outside Britain, allows foreign nonmembers to play a round for US$50.

Volunteering

Several organisations welcome foreign volunteers with specific skills (see p41). Mother Teresa's Missionaries of Charity (p448) welcomes all comers.

Yoga

There are five-day courses at varying locations with **Art of Living** (www.artofliving.org, http://artoflivingindia.in/courses.asp; aolkol@vsnl.net), plus holistic and therapeutic yoga with **Vivekananda Yoga Anusandhana Samsthana** (Map p458; 24241340; www.vyasacal.org; 69K Prince Bakhtiar Shah Rd).

Tours

For excursions to the Sunderbans Tiger Reserve, see p477.

City Tours

Personal, accompanied city-walks lasting around four hours are available through expat-run **Kali Travel Home** (☏25550581, 9007778504; www.traveleastindia.com; ₹350-600) and youthful **CalWalks** (☏9830184030; www .calcuttawalks.com; from ₹1200). Both are enthusiastic and flexible as to the area covered and both offer a range of alternative Kolkata experiences.

Best known for their mangrove boat trips, **Backpackers** (Map p450; ☏9836177140; www .tourdesundarbans.com; Tottee Ln) also offer innovative two-part city tours on the back of a motorbike (₹1500). Tours drive past several well-known sites and add curiosities like Kolkata's giant trash-mountain, Tangra Chinatown, a burning ghat, a Shiva temple (join the prayers) and a brief drive through the red-light district. Longer car tours (₹3000 per person) visit Belur Math and Dakshineswar then continue up the Hooghly as far as Bansberia's Kremlin-styled palace temple.

West Bengal Tourism (Map p452; ☏22437260, westbengaltourism.gov.in; 3/2 BBD Bagh; ◷10.30am-1.30pm & 2-5.30pm Mon-Fri, 10.30am-1pm Sat) runs full-day sightseeing **bus tours** (₹250; ◷8.30am). They're a relative bargain but give only sweaty, drive-by glimpses of most sights and rush you round Belur Math and Dakshineswar in barely half an hour apiece. The office opens at 7am to sell last-minute tickets. Trips might be cancelled if there are less than 10 customers (least likely on Sundays).

Sleeping

Looks can be deceptive. Some eye-catchingly smart facades mask lacklustre, mustily disappointing rooms. Other very survivable places are hidden within buildings that look like crumbling wrecks. Decent hotel accommodation in Kolkata often costs about the same as in Europe. So if you want to pay under ₹400 for a room, don't expect to enjoy the experience. Even in many midrange hotels peeling paint, loose wires, battered furniture and damp patches come as standard. Much of Kolkata's rock-bottom accommodation represents 'a whole new league of nastiness', and where we review such cheapies be aware that we're usually identifying the least objectionable options rather than making a recommendation: consider putting a mat on the bed to reduce bed-bug bites. Many cheaper hotels lock their gates by midnight.

AC hotels add 10% luxury tax (5% on cheaper rooms) and some tack on further service charges. For fairness we quote total prices. Most places charging under ₹1000 won't take bookings. Top-end places are often very significantly discounted on websites like www.yatra.com and www.agoda.com.

SUDDER ST AREA

The nearest Kolkata gets to a backpacker ghetto is the area around Sudder St. It's the only place in town to suffer much beggar hassle and many of the buildings are decrepit but the location is brilliantly central, there's a range of traveller-oriented services and it's about the only area in Kolkata where ultra-cheap dives accept foreigners. There's also a growing scattering of higher-end options.

Oberoi Grand   HERITAGE HOTEL **$$$**
(Map p450; ☏22492323; www.oberoikolkata.com; 15 Chowringhee Rd; s/d/ste from ₹19,900/22,550/38,500; ✳@🌐) Passing through the almost hidden courtyard gateway, you're transported from the chaos of Chowringhee Rd into a regal oasis of genteel calm that deserves every point on its five stars. Immaculate accommodation oozes atmosphere, the swimming pool is ringed with palms and proactive staff anticipate your every need.

Ashreen Guest House   GUESTHOUSE **$**
(Map p450; ☏22520889; ashreen_guesthouse@yahoo.com; 2 Cowie Lane; d ₹495-845; ✳) One of Kolkata's best value mini-hotels, the rooms are small but sparkling clean with sometimes-functioning geysers and many playful interior touches. There's often a waiting list. Across the road, the co-managed Afridi International is less impressive.

Fairlawn Hotel   HOTEL **$$**
(Map p450; ☏22521510; www.fairlawnhotel.com; 13A Sudder St; s/d incl breakfast ₹2721/3322; ✳) Taking guests since 1936, the Fairlawn is a characterful 1783 Raj-era home fronted by tropical greenery. The stairs and sitting room are smothered with photos, family mementos and articles celebrating the hotel's nonagenarian owner. While not luxurious, most rooms are spacious and well equipped with re-tiled bathrooms (some old tubs remain). At least one of the cheaper downstairs rooms (s/d ₹2326/2880) has limited natural light and startling pink decor.

Bawa Walson   HOTEL **$$**
(Map p450; ☏22521512; bawawalson@bawahotels.com; 5A Sudder St; r discount/full from ₹3000/5750; ✳) Sudder Street's sexiest new addition comes with back-lit panels, luxurious box-spring mattresses, selected toiletries and flat-screen TVs. When finished there'll be a spa across the fairly lit courtyard. It's good value when discounted but at full rack

rates the lack of a lift, the limited views and a ₹500 internet charge are less forgivable.

Housez 43   HOTEL **$$**
(Map p450; ☏22276020; www.housez43.com; 43 Mirza Ghalib St; s/deluxe/luxury ₹2625/3150/4400; ✳🌐) Bright colours, funky lamps and odd-shaped mirrors bring character to this handily central boutique hotel, though cheaper rooms are less impressive than the bold public spaces.

Sunflower Guest House   GUESTHOUSE **$**
(Map p450; ☏22299401; 5th fl, 7 Royd St; d/tr from ₹750/900; ✳) Slightly spartan but fresh and assiduously cleaned with high ceilings and ample communal space, the Sunflower occupies much of a once-grand 1865 building that's attractive but was rated as a potential fire hazard in a 2010 *Calcutta Telegraph* article. To check in, take the 1940s lift to the top and cross the little roof garden.

Bhagirathi Guest House   GUESTHOUSE **$**
(Map p450; ☏9836993678; Sudder St; old/new d ₹650/850, tr 1300; ✳) Entered from the same courtyard as the Super Guest House, this all-AC guesthouse can be great value if you score one of the five newer rooms with windows, new paintwork, clean tiled floors and piping hot water. Other rooms are windowless and those across the courtyard are more dated.

Lytton Hotel   HOTEL **$$**
(Map p450; ☏39841900; www.lyttonhotelindia.com; 14 Sudder St; s/d/tr/ste ₹5280/6050/6930/8030; ✳) This solid midrange choice has a dark, slightly dated lobby but Tiffany-style panels enliven the corridors and rooms have received a gently contemporary revamp including good modern bathrooms. Room sizes vary significantly.

Hotel Aafreen   GUESTHOUSE **$**
(Map p450; ☏22654146; Nawab Abdur Rahman St; d with fan/AC ₹500/750; ✳) Offering midrange quality at budget prices, the Aafreen's paintwork is mostly intact, staff are obliging and freshly tiled bathrooms have hot water. The lift is temperamental.

Aafreen Tower   GUESTHOUSE **$**
(Map p450; ☏22293280; www.aafreentower.com; 9A Kyd St; d with fan/AC ₹600/990; ✳) The glass elevator creaks a little and the bright orange-and-gold corridors are being patched up, but if repairs are fully followed through, this should once again be a recommended choice.

Hotel Galaxy GUESTHOUSE $
(Map p450; Stuart Lane; r with fan/AC ₹500/800; ❀) This ageing mansion-block has had its high-ceilinged rooms well upgraded with shiny floor tiles and hot water in the sizeable bathroom, at least those we saw. Bookings aren't possible and guests tend to stay a while.

The Corporate HOTEL $$
(Map p450; ☏22267551; www.thecorporatekolkata.com; 4 Royd St; r from ₹4400; ❀) In this capable cube of stone and glass, the cheaper rooms are sometimes bigger than ₹4950 'executive' ones. Wi-fi is 'being installed'.

Hotel Pioneer International GUESTHOUSE $
(Map p450; 1st fl, 1 Marquis St; d without/with AC ₹400/600) Wobbly wooden stairs within an unpromisingly aged house lead to six unexpectedly neat rooms with new tiled floors and multilingual TV. Staff are friendly and helpful.

Hotel VIP InterContinental GUESTHOUSE $$
(Map p450; ☏22520150; vipintercontinental@rediffmail.com; 44 Mirza Ghalib St; s/d from ₹1120/1575, super-deluxe r ₹2310; ❀⎈) Behind the one-desk reception, friendly VIP InterContinental has a selection of small to very small rooms but all are well air-conditioned, carefully maintained, have hot water and stone or tiled floors. Don't confuse it with the nearby Hotel VIP Continental whose dashing foyer hides sorry corridors and pricey modern rooms spoilt by sickening wall-stains.

Timestar Hotel GUESTHOUSE $
(Map p450; ☏22528028; 2 Tottie Lane; s/d/tr from ₹250/350/475, d with AC ₹750) This chunky-walled colonial-era mansion has tatty elements but well-tiled floors and high enough ceilings in the upstairs rooms that they don't overheat too badly. Two rooms now have air-conditioning, repainted walls and decent bathrooms.

Paragon Hotel BACKPACKER DIVE $
(Map p450; 2 Stuart Lane; dm ₹120, s/d without bathroom from ₹200/270, d with shower ₹350) Some of the coffin-box rooms are so spirit-crushing that the graffiti is actually an improvement. However, a few battered chairs on the rooftop create a great place to hang out with fellow backpackers and staff are friendlier here than at the essentially similar Hotel Maria next door. Bring your own padlock.

Modern Lodge BACKPACKER DIVE $
(Map p450; 1 Stuart Lane; s ₹100-150, d ₹200-300) It isn't modern at all but Modern

Lodge has a more homely feel than most other ultra-budget dives, with an idiosyncratic courtyard, 1st-floor sitting room, old teak doors and peaceful roof terrace. But the bed-spaces are as ragged as ever; many are haphazardly subdivided and without power-points. Management seems erratic.

Hotel Pushpak GUESTHOUSE, HOSTEL $
(Map p450; ☏22265841; www.hotelpushpakinternational.com; 10 Kyd St; dm/s/d ₹300/1260/1470; ❀) Ocean-liner corridors lead to rooms that are mostly lacklustre and a little worn but an interesting feature here is the new 28-bed AC dorm, each bunk with lockers above and beneath (some already broken), lamp, fan and curtains for minimal privacy. Shared bathrooms include geyser showers.

Centrepoint Guest House BACKPACKER DIVE $
(Map p450; ☏22520953; ian_rashid@yahoo.com; 20 Mirza Ghalib St; dm ₹100, s/d from ₹400/450; ❀) Fan rooms are bare-bones boxes with toilets tucked in what appears to be a cupboard. AC rooms are larger but no lovelier. Three large 4th-floor bunk-dorms are nominally sex-segregated, have under-bed safe-boxes (bring a padlock) with shared showers and toilets on the open terrace. Stairs seem dangerously half-collapsed and some mattresses have proved itchy.

CITY CENTRE

TOP CHOICE / **Chrome** BOUTIQUE HOTEL $$
(Map p446; ☏30963096; www.chromehotel.in; 226 AJC Bose Rd; s/d from ₹8800/9350; ❀⎈) Sleep in a brilliantly executed artistic statement that looks like a seven-storey Swiss cheese by day and a colour-pulsing alien communicator by night. Rooms have optical illusion decor, the 5th-floor landing hides a mini-library and a rooftop pool is under construction. Bleeping music masks traffic noise.

Park Hotel HOTEL $$$
(Map p450; ☏22499000; www.theparkhotels.com; 17 Park St; s/d from ₹13,200/15,400; ❀@⎈⎈) Perfectly central and hosting much of the city's nightlife, two of the Park's pricier floors use very stylish black-on-black decor while 'Residency' floors go for a more classical feel. Annoyances include reverberating music on the lower floors that can disturb light sleepers and a front desk where staff seem constantly over-stretched. The small, colourfully stylish foyer entrance is accessed bizarrely by walking through a cafe-deli.

Allenby Inn
GUESTHOUSE **$$**

(Map p446; ☎24869984; allenbyinn@vsnl.net; 1/2 Allenby Rd; r ₹3300; ✳@) With fashionable trimmings and lashings of abstract art, some of the 20 rooms are very large, though towels could be softer and mattresses thicker. Two 5th-floor rooms share a dining area and small kitchen.

Golden Park
HOTEL **$$**

(Map p446; ☎22883939; www.thegoldenpark.com; 13 Ho Chi Minh Sarani; s/d ₹8800/9900, discount rate ₹5500/6500; ✳) The Golden Park is very fair value by central Kolkata standards with typical business-hotel amenities in the regularly upgraded if modestly sized rooms. The eccentric four-storey lobby-atrium features oddly mismatched nymphs, wood panelling, glass elevators and a vast Shakespeare-versus-Zoroaster relief.

Hotel Aston
HOTEL **$$**

(Map p446; ☎24863145; hotelaston@gmail.com; 3 Aston Rd; s/d ₹1495/1610; ✳@) Compact but attractive all-AC rooms with marble floors and decor that's far better than most Kolkata options at this price level. It's just off Sarat Bose Rd near the Laxmi Narayan Mandir.

Kenilworth
HOTEL **$$$**

(Map p446; ☎22823939; www.kenilworthhotels.com/kolkata; 1 Little Russell St; s/d/ste ₹9900/11,000/17,600; ✳) The deep lobby of marble, dark wood and chandeliers contrasts successfully with a more contemporary cafe that spills out onto an attractive lawn. Pleasing, fully equipped rooms have thick mattresses, restrained sunny colour schemes and large mirrors. Discount rates from ₹7000 are often available. Five suites lead off an impressive landing in an old mansion opposite but don't quite pull off the full 'heritage' effect.

Astor
HOTEL **$$**

(Map p446; ☎22829950; www.astorkolkata.com; 15 Shakespeare Sarani; s/d from ₹4725/6600; ✳) Artful evening floodlighting brings out the best of the Astor's solid 1905 architecture, while some floors are quaintly uneven and stairways have original wrought-iron banisters. But while some rooms have attractive three-colour woodwork, the floral bedspreads maintain that nursing-home feel. A few singles are windowless. Look for discount deals.

BBD BAGH AREA

There's no traveller scene here but the following options are handy for Chandni Chowk metro and fair value by Kolkata standards.

Esplanade Chambers
GUESTHOUSE **$$**

(Map p452; ☎22127101; www.esplanadechambers.com; 2 Chandni Chowk St; s/d/ste with fan ₹700/900/1000, with AC ₹900/1500/1800; ✳✳🛜) These two floors of former apartments are more homestay than hotel. Rooms vary wildly from unadorned claustrophobic singles to comfortable 'executive' mini-suites complete with ornaments, wooden bed-frames and even a circular bathtub in the best room. There are a few minor cleaning issues but prices include wi-fi (best downstairs), breakfast, hot water and toiletries. Access is via a narrow alley beside Gypsy Restaurant.

Bengal Buddhist Association
GUESTHOUSE **$**

(Map p452; Bauddha Dharmankur Sabha; ☎22117138; http://bengalbuddhist.com/guest-house.html; bds1892@yahoo.com; Buddhist Temple Rd; tw from ₹250; ✳) Although intended for Buddhist students, anyone can rent these simple rooms which have plenty of cobwebs without being unduly dirty. Shared bathrooms are basic but have geysers. Three rooms have AC, two with private bathrooms. The courtyard location is quiet; gates are locked from 10.30pm to 5am.

Broadway Hotel
HOTEL **$**

(Map p452; ☎22363930; www.broadwayhotel.in; 27A Ganesh Chandra Ave; s/d/tr/ste ₹580/625/925/1125, without bathroom s/d ₹480/565) This simple but well-maintained old hotel has an antiquated lift, '50s furniture and classic bar downstairs. Most rooms are generously large with high ceilings, and corner rooms offer plenty of light. The free newspaper under the door is a nice touch. It's clean and great value but noisy and showers are cold.

OUTER KOLKATA

Due to distant locations and lack of convenient transport links, we don't review several of the city's top business hotels including the impressive **Hyatt Regency** (http://kolkata.regency.hyatt.com), eco-friendly **Sonar** (www.itcwelcomgroup.in/hotels/itcsonar.aspx) and the antique-softened 1990s **Taj Bengal** (www.tajhotels.com).

🅣🅞🅟 CHOICE Tollygunge Club
GUESTHOUSE **$$**

(☎24732316; www.thetollygungeclub.org; d/cottage/ste ₹4412/4743/5074; 🛜✳✳) The Tolly's idyllic setting with mature tropical trees, roosting birds and velvet-smooth golf greens creates a mind-boggling contrast to the deafening chaos of surrounding Kolkata. All guest rooms are sparkling clean but while some have functional motel-style decor, others have been very stylishly revamped to the standards of a boutique hotel. Guests get temporary membership allowing access to all club sports and entertainment facilities including otherwise exclusive colonial-era bar-cafes and (except Monday) the wonderful golf course. It's a 10-minute walk from Tollygunge metro. Book ahead.

Bodhi Tree GUESTHOUSE **$$**
(Map p458; ☑24243871, 24246534; www.bodhitreekolkata.com; 48/44 Swiss Park; r incl breakfast ₹2200-4000; ✴🕸) Well-travelled owners dub Bodhi Tree's intriguing little **gallery-cafe** (☺2pm-7pm Tue-Sun) a 'monastery of art'. Above, five uniquely characterful Buddha-themed rooms come with stone walls and decent facilities. Bathrooms aren't as memorable and the cheapest room is pretty cramped but the suburban location is under 10 minutes' stroll from Rabrindra Sarovar metro (walk east from behind the southeast exit and keep going).

AIRPORT AREA
An accommodation booth in the airport's domestic terminal lists numerous 'airport area' hotels but most decent options are over 2km away down VIP Rd. There is a selection of cheaper places (fan/AC from ₹350/750) on Jessore Rd between Airport Gates 1 and 2 and in the side lanes behind. However, virtually all of the latter seem overpriced and grimy while rooms facing Jessore Rd suffer particularly serious street noise. Of the dozen that we checked, none could be wholeheartedly recommended. Better than most, if slightly past its prime, is **White Palace** (☑25117402; 28/1 Italgacha Rd; s ₹1100-1430, d ₹1210-1650; ✴), facing Om Lodge (on the street that leads off Jessore Rd nearly opposite the Bharat Petrol Station, close to Airport Gate 1).

✕ Eating

Most restaurants add 12.5% tax to bills. A few posher places add further 'service charges'. Tips are welcome at cheaper places and expected at most expensive restaurants. The *Times Food Guide* (www.timescity.com/kolkata; ₹100) offers hundreds of restaurant reviews. Don't miss sampling Bengali cuisine. At its best it's a wonderful discovery with a whole new vocabulary of names and flavours. In cheaper Bengali places, portions are often tapas-sized so order two or three dishes along with rice/luchi and sweet *khejur* (chutney).

UPPER CHOWRINGHEE AREA
A few basic traveller cafes around Sudder St serve backpacker favourites like banana pancakes, muesli and toasted sandwiches complemented by fresh fruit juices and a range of good-value Indian dishes. Eateries across Mirza Ghalib St cater predominantly to Bangladeshi tastes. Cheap places for Indian-regional food lie around Hogg Market with many more food stalls lining Madge Lane, Bertram St, and Humayan Pl where fast food chains join vendors of dosas, chow mein and fresh juices. For more upmarket fare try Jong's, the hotel restaurants at the Oberoi and Peerless Inn or walk ten minutes south to Park Street where you'll find many of Kolkata's age-old family favourites facing off with KFC and a beef-free McDonald's.

AROUND SUDDER ST
Raj's Spanish Cafe CAFE **$**
(Map p450; Taberna Vasca; off Sudder St; mains 25-150; ☺7.30am-10pm; 🕸) Excellent coffee, juices, pancakes and ₹25 wi-fi (plenty of power-points too) makes this a great traveller cafe hang-out. The menu includes a small but very well made selection of Spanish dishes (tortilla, *pisto manchego*) and delicious pesto-pasta (₹90). Decor is simple but welcoming with a cushioned sitting space and a small outdoor area.

Sidheshwari Ashram BENGALI **$**
(Map p450; 19 Rani Rashmoni Rd; mains ₹3-70, ☺9am-4pm & 7pm-11pm) In this old-fashioned eating house, walls are a little grubby, little English is spoken and if you come around noon you'll have to fight for one of the old stone-topped tables. But in return you'll get truly excellent Bengali food at bargain local prices. Ideally bring a local friend to help you choose. It's not far from Sudder St but easily missed set back between shops then up an unlikely stairway. *Khub bhalo!*

Jong's/Zaranj EAST ASIAN, INDIAN **$$$**
(Map p450; ☑22490369; Sudder St; mains ₹400-840; ☺12.30-3pm & 7.30-11pm Wed-Mon) Two suave if pricey restaurants in one. Jong's serves Chinese, under-spiced Thai and other Asian cuisines in a magnificently wood-panelled room that feels like a Raj-oriental gentleman's club. Smart-casual Zaranj has a more modern vibe and takes the taste-buds on a gourmet tour of India. Some meals include rice but with most it's ₹100 extra.

Blue & Beyond MULTICUISINE **$$**
(Map p450; 9th fl, Lindsay Hotel, Lindsay St; mains ₹120-190; ☺11am-11pm) The open-air rooftop

terrace offers views over New Market and there's a well air-conditioned dining room in case rain or excessive heat make sitting there impractical. A wide-ranging menu encompasses Bengali fish dishes, Irish stew and ratatouille at prices that are very reasonable for a restaurant that's licensed to serve alcohol.

Blue Sky Cafe CAFE $
(Map p450; Chowringhee Lane; snacks ₹22-60, mains ₹50-195; ⊙6.30am-10.30pm) A vast selection of reliable traveller standbys served in an almost stylish setting with high-backed zinc chairs at long glass tables. Tiny, unadorned **Fresh & Juicy** across the road is arguably even better value but gets sweaty with just five cramped tables.

Super Chicken TRAVELLER CAFE $
(Map p450; Sudder St; mains ₹40-100; ⊙8.30am-11.30pm) Succulent tandoori tops off a decent menu of tempting backpacker faves in this small but bright, well air-conditioned room.

Prince BENGALI $
(Map p450; 17 Mirza Ghalib St; dishes ₹12-120; ⊙7.30am-11pm) Air-conditioned place for eat-with-hands, unpretentious Bengali food aimed primarily at the area's Bangladeshi visitors. Two doors away, **Radhuni** is very similar. Both are neater but less satisfying than Sidheshwari Ashram.

Aminia MUGHLAI $
(Map p450; Hogg St; mains ₹50-84; ⊙10.30am-10.30pm) Ceiling fans whirr above this brightly lit cacophonous classic where decor is vaguely art deco, service is rapid and local women dine unchaperoned. For better biriyanis you might prefer Arsalan or Shiraz .

Hotel Mastan INDIAN $
(Map p450; Unit H6, 37 Hogg Market; mains ₹7-35; ⊙6am-11.30pm) Craving beef on a budget? Dare yourself to visit the 'pious man', barely changed since 1941. The soot-darkened interior looks seriously off-putting but for four generations the Sufi-inspired Haider family have been serving up cheap yet fresh meals including bhuna curried beef (₹32 with rice).

Kathleen Confectioners BAKERY $
(Map p450; 12 Mirza Ghalib St; snacks ₹12-35; ⊙9am-10pm) Their sickly sweet cakes aren't exactly the promised 'Taste of Hapinezz' but savoury pastries are delicious. Numerous alternative branches.

PARK ST AREA

Fire and Ice ITALIAN $$$
(Map p446; ⌨22884073; www.fireandicepizzeria.com; Kanak Bldg, Middleton St; mains ₹290-550, ⊙noon-11.15pm) Self-consciously handsome wait-staff sporting black shirts and bandannas bring forth real Italian pastas, and pizzas whose fresh-baked thin crusts are Kolkata's best.

Arsalan MUGHLAI $$
(Map p450; 119A Ripon St; mains ₹95-205; ⊙noon-11.30pm) The decor is striking and contemporary without being upmarket. The high ceilings with gilt insets contrast with plain tables at which the main attractions are melt-in-mouth chicken tikka and celebrated biriyanis that come with a free palette of extras (lemon, chilli, onion, mint chutney).

Teej RAJASTHANI $$$
(Map p450; ⌨22170730; www.teej.in; 1st fl, 2 Russell St; mains ₹145-255, thalis ₹338-450; ⊙noon-3.30pm & 7-10.30pm) Superbly painted with Mughal-style murals, the interior feels like an ornate Rajasthani *haveli* (traditional residence) and the excellent, 100% vegetarian food is predominantly Rajasthani, too. Downstairs, much cheaper if stylistically neutral **Gangaur** serves dosas and ₹124 thalis in AC comfort.

Shiraz MUGHLAI $$
(Map p446; 135 Park St; mains ₹75-125; ⊙5am-11.30pm) Synonymous with Kolkata biriyani, the Shiraz also offers a range of curries and a mutton *chaap* (rib-meat dish) of rare subtlety and succulence. The location is handy if you're visiting South Park St Cemetery.

Peter Cat MULTICUISINE $$
(Map p450; Middleton Row; mains ₹116-200; ⊙11am-11.15pm) This phenomenally popular Kolkata institution offers fizzing sizzlers, great *chelo*-kebabs (barbecued ground lamb) and beers in pewter tankards. Waiters wear Rajasthani costumes in an atmosphere redolent of a mood-lit 1970s steakhouse. Reservations aren't accepted; queues are often long but sociable. Across Park St, **Mocambo** is similarly dated yet ever-popular.

Bar-B-Q INDIAN, CHINESE $$
(Map p450; 1st fl, 43 Park St; mains ₹130-208; ⊙noon-4.30pm & 7-11.15pm) Three interconnected dining rooms offer different but similar menus in this enduring family favourite that features sloping ceilings held on polished wooden pillars, buzzing conversation and an ever-witty maître d'.

Marco Polo
MULTICUISINE $$$

(Map p450; ☎22273939; 24 Park St; mains ₹250-475; ⊙1.30-11pm) Stylish and moodily under-lit, this split-level restaurant takes diners on a culinary world tour from Bengal to Italy via Goa, China and Lebanon.

CITY CENTRE
As well as the places reviewed there are dining options scattered around Camac St, Shakespeare Sarani and in the Forum Mall (Elgin St), plus three cheap Tibetan eateries at **Momo corner** (cnr Suburban Hospital Rd & Chowringhee Rd).

Kewpies
BENGALI $$

(Map p446; ☎24861600; 2 Elgin Lane; most dishes ₹73-175, thalis ₹250-540; ⊙12.30-3pm & 7.30-11pm Tue-Sun) Dining at Kewpies feels like being invited to a dinner party in the chef's eclectic, gently old-fashioned home (avoid the charmless annex-room, via the north door). First-rate Bengali food comes in small but fairly decent portions. Minimum spend is ₹250 per person.

Oh! Calcutta
BENGALI $$$

(Map p446; ☎22837161; 4th fl, Forum Mall, Elgin Rd; mains ₹280-460; ⊙12.30-3pm & 7.30-11pm) Shutter-edged mirror 'windows', bookshelves and B&W photography create a casually upmarket atmosphere in this suave if pricey Bengali-fusion restaurant. *Luchi* (₹102 for six) are feather-light, and fresh lime brings out the subtleties of *koraishatir dhokar dalna* (pea-cakes in ginger, ₹312).

Drive Inn
MULTICUISINE $

(Map p446; 10 Middleton St; mains ₹46-82; ⊙10.30am-10pm) Sandwiches, *thukpa* (Tibetan noodle-soup), curries and pizza served in a modest open-air 'garden' with simple fan-pavilion tables, mosaic backdrops and a trio of metal musicians fashioned from scrap metal and bicycle chains. Good value thalis (from ₹75) available except Sundays. No meat.

Mainland China
CHINESE $$$

(Map p446; ☎22837964; www.mainlandchinaindia.com/contact_kolkata.html; 3A Gurusaday Rd; mains ₹375-590; ⊙12.30-3.30pm & 7.30-11.30pm) Consistent, upmarket Chinese food in sophisticated surroundings. Reservations advised. Lunch buffet weekday/weekend ₹482/590.

Kookie Jar
BAKERY $

(Map p446; Rowden St; pastries ₹20-60; ⊙8am-10pm) Kolkata's most heavenly cakes and fudge brownies (₹40) along with multigrain bread (₹50) and various wraps and fluffy pastries. Take-away only.

Haldiram
FAST FOOD $

(Map p446; 58 Chowringhee Rd; ⊙8am-10pm) Chain eatery with great value pay-then-queue vegetarian thalis (₹70), dosas (from ₹36), burgers (₹32) and Bengali sweets.

Jalapenos
MEXICAN $$

(Map p446; ☎22820204; 10 Wood St; mains ₹85-250; ⊙11.30am-10.15pm; ☀) High-ceilinged with mock wooden beams and little spice-bottle alcoves, their 'Mexican' dishes are enjoyable albeit almost unrecognisable.

BBD BAGH AREA

Song Hay
CHINESE $

(Map p452; ☎22480974; 3 Waterloo St; lunches ₹25-75, dinner mains ₹50-110; ⊙11am-10.30pm) This modest but prize-winning restaurant cooks authentic Chinese food at prices that are especially reasonable before 5pm when half-priced, half-size portions are available.

Amber/Essence
MULTICUISINE $$

(Map p452; ☎22483477; 2nd fl, 11 Waterloo St; mains ₹130-350; ⊙1.30-11pm) This pleasantly semi-trendy middle-class restaurant has back-lit panels and triangular lamp niches but music can get a little oppressive at night and their signature brain masala isn't to everyone's taste. Another branch on Middleton Row.

Anand
SOUTH INDIAN $

(Map p452; ☎22128344; 19 CR Ave; dosas ₹32-86; ⊙9am-9.30pm, closed Wed) Prize-winning pure-veg dosas served in a well-kept if

DON'T MISS

KATI ROLLS

Bengal's trademark fast food is the kati roll: take a *paratha* roti, fry it with a coating of egg then fill with sliced onions, chilli and your choice of stuffing (curried chicken, grilled meat or paneer). Roll it up in a twist of paper and it's ready to eat, generally on the street from hole-in-the-wall serveries. Standards vary considerably but a classic is **Hot Kati Rolls** (Map p450; 1/1 Park St; rolls ₹13-60; ⊙11am-10.30pm).

old-fashioned family restaurant with bamboo and mirror-tiled ceilings.

KC Das
SWEETS $

(Map p452; Lenin Sarani; sweets ₹3-16; ⊘7.30am-9.30pm) Though visually uninteresting, this historic Bengali sweet shop claims to have invented *rasgulla* (rosewater-scented cheese balls) in 1868. Basic seating available.

GARIAHAT AREA

Bhojohari Manna
BENGALI $

(www.bhojohorimanna.org; Branch 6 Map p458; ☑24663941; 18/1 Hindustan Rd; dishes ₹45-210; ⊘noon-10pm; Ekdalia Map p458; 9/18 Ekdalia Rd; dishes ₹20-190; ⊘noon-10pm) One of Kolkata's best respected chains for genuine if pre-prepared Bengali food, this is a fine place to try coconut-tempered *chingri malaikari* (₹145), a dish where the prawns are so big they speak lobster. The tiny original Ekdalia branch is jam-packed and basic, the only decor being sketches by the father of celebrated film director Satyajit Ray. The food is the same (but with more choice and higher prices) at the bigger, more inviting Branch 6 where the walls are adorned with a variety of musical instruments. A much more central branch very near KC Das is unpleasantly claustrophobic.

6 Ballygunge Place
BENGALI $$

(Map p458; ☑24603922; 6 Ballygunge Pl; mains ₹85-205; ⊘12.30-3.30pm & 7-10.30pm) In a sturdy but not overly formal century-old mansion, lunchtime buffets (₹366) allow a good all-round introduction to Bengali food with five main courses plus chutneys, rice and desserts. Minibus 118 from Jatin Das Park metro stops a block north on Bondel Rd.

 Drinking

Most better bars are in hotels or restaurants. Cheaper places are usually dingy and overwhelmingly male-dominated with a penchant for over-loud music, often sung by scantily clad females. Plentiful branches of Starbuck-style chains **Barista** and **Café Coffee Day** (most appealingly on Wood St) make air-conditioned oases in which to sip a decent Americano, though coffee prices can vary substantially by location. A Kolkata delight is making street-side tea stops for ₹2 mini-cuppas served in disposable *bhaar* (environmentally friendly earthenware thimbles).

CHOWRINGHEE AREA

Anglo pubs **Big Ben** (Map p446; Kenilworth Hotel, 1 Little Russell St) and **Someplace Else** (Map p450; Park Hotel, 17 Park St) showcase local bands, predominantly rock oriented, without a cover charge. There are several other lively bars in and around the Park Hotel.

Fairlawn Hotel
BAR

(Map p450; 13A Sudder St; beers ₹110; ⊘10am-10pm) Half woodland, half Santa-grotto, the small tropical garden of the historic Fairlawn Hotel is strung with fairy lights and plastic fruit. It's great for a cold brew but doesn't serve cocktails.

Urban Desi
BAR

(Map p446; 9th fl, 6 Camac St; small beers ₹95; ⊘noon-11pm, cover charge ₹200 after 4pm) Low-key rooftop party lounge with shisha pipes to smoke, pool and table football to play and sofa seating. Admire the city panorama to trancy music that pulsates louder as the night wears on. There's also a restaurant section with great silhouette views of Victoria Memorial.

Café Thé
CAFE

(Map p446; ICCR Bldg, 9A Ho Chi Minh Sarani; teas ₹30-75, snacks ₹40-160; ⊘10am-9pm) Tea house with bold, abstract-floral designs serving around 30 different teas including a mellow coconut-based Thai chai. No coffee or booze.

Flury's
CAFE

(Map p450; www.flurysindia.com; Park St; coffees ₹80-150; ⊘7.30am-9.45pm) This enticing art deco palace is the classic place to nurse a good espresso or an iced-tea that comes layered like a tequila sunrise. The food is less reliable.

Ashalayam
CAFE

(www.ashalayam.org; 1st fl, 44 Mirza Ghalib St; coffee ₹6-15; ⊘10.30am-7pm Mon-Fri, 10.30am-4pm Sat) Play chess at low wicker tables while sipping cheap machine-frothed Nescafe in this calm, bright charity craft-shop.

Roxy
BAR

(Map p450; Park Hotel, 17 Park St; small beers ₹175; ⊘from 6pm) *Clockwork Orange* retro-futuristic atmosphere.

BBD BAGH AREA

Broadway Bar
BAR

(Map p452; Broadway Hotel, 27A Ganesh Chandra Ave; small/standard beer ₹45/88; ⊘11am-10.30pm) Back-street Paris? Chicago 1930s? Prague 1980s? This cavernous, unpretentious old-men's pub defies easy parallels but has a compulsive left-bank fascination with cheap booze, 20 ceiling fans, grimy walls, marble floors and, thankfully, no music.

Rocks
LIVE MUSIC

(Map p452; 9 Waterloo St; beer from ₹120; ⊘2pm-midnight) Three floors, three different sets of Bengali musical performers, but while some of the musicians are proficient, others sound like karaoke singers and all is played out at ear-splitting volume.

Floatel
BAR, RESTAURANT

(off Map p452; www.floatelhotel.com; Strand Rd; small/large beer ₹100/200; ⊘bar 11am-10.30pm) Wide river views are best before sunset but drinks are pricey whether in the third-floor restaurant or water-level Anchor Tavern (from 3pm).

SOUTHERN KOLKATA

Mirch Masala
BAR, RESTAURANT

(Map p458; Monoronjan Roy Sarani; beers/cocktail ₹110/115; ⊘noon-11pm) Old clocks, fake trees, half a taxi chassis and a North Indian menu presented like a gossip magazine combine to create an amusing ambience that feels like a Bollywood Tex-Mex joint. Take the lane beside Pantaloons department store and continue beyond Mirch Masala's Chinese Restaurant. Kitchen closed 3pm to 7pm.

☆ Entertainment

Events and cultural happenings are announced in the *Telegraph* newspaper's Metro section and the various listings brochures.

Nightclubs

On Kolkata's party nights (Wednesday, Friday and Saturday) clubs open till 2am or later. On other nights most are half empty and close at midnight. Note the difference between entry charge and cover charge: the latter can be recouped in drinks or food to the same value. Either is charged *per couple*. Women can sometimes enter free but single men (known as stags) are generally excluded and, except at Ginger, if admitted aren't expected to dance without a female partner.

Basement
NIGHTCLUB

(Map p458; Samilton Hotel, 25 Lansdowne Rd; small beers ₹100; live music Wed-Fri) Scoot beneath the scooter to enter this cramped but convivial venue for DJ sets and live bands, with low ceilings, barrel tables and relatively cheap drinks.

Underground
NIGHTCLUB

(Map p446; HHI Hotel, AJC Bose Rd; cover ₹500, small beers ₹220) Small dance floor in a pub-bar with Hard Rock Café—style elements.

Tantra
NIGHTCLUB

(Map p450; Park Hotel, 17 Park St; entry ₹500-1000, small beers ₹200) Often considered Kolkata's top club, contemporary sounds throb through the single dance floor and not-so-chilled chill-out zone around a central-island bar with an overhead observation bridge.

Venom
NIGHTCLUB

(Map p446; 8th fl, Fort Knox, 6 Camac St; cover charge ₹500-1000 Sat, small beers ₹175; ⊘closed Tue) Oscillating bars of vertical red light makes it feel like you're dancing in a giant 1970s amplifier. Musical styles vary.

Ginger
NIGHTCLUB

(Map p458; 104 SP Mukherjee Rd; cover ₹500, small beers ₹190; ⊘8pm-2am Fri-Sun; Ⓜ Jatin Das Park) A majority male clientele whoop to 1990s dance hits, 'stags' are admitted and it's modestly gay friendly.

Hops
NIGHTCLUB

(2nd fl, South City Mall; small beers ₹170; ⊘DJs 8pm-midnight) This relatively suave lounge-restaurant goes disco from 8pm with a dance floor beneath a stylised cave of wooden layers. No cover, 'stags' allowed (for now).

Cultural Programs

Nandan Complex
CULTURAL CENTRE

(Map p446; 1/1A AJC Bose Rd) Comprises theatre halls **Rabindra Sadan** (☑22239936) and **Sisir Mancha** (☑22235317), plus the art-house **Nandan Cinema** (☑22231210).

ICCR
CULTURAL CENTRE

(Map p446; ☑22872680; www.iccrindia.org; 9A Ho Chi Minh Sarani) State-of-the-art new cultural centre hosting exhibitions and interesting, if sporadic, dance shows and recitals that are often free but rarely well publicised.

Cinema

Inox Elgin Rd
CINEMA

(Map p446; www.inoxmovies.com; Forum Shopping Mall, 10/3 Elgin Rd; tickets ₹110-260) One of several modern multiplex cinemas, bookable online.

Pool/Snooker

BQ's Snooker
SNOOKER

(Map p450; off Mirza Ghalib St; pool/snooker ₹30/60; ⊘10am-10pm) Four-table hall hidden at the rear of the Anihant Building.

Spectator Sports

Even if you don't know Ganguly from a googly, the electric atmosphere of a cricket match at **Ranji Stadium** (Map p452; Eden Gardens) is an unforgettable experience. For IPL fixtures see www.kkr.in.

At **Maidan racecourse** (☎22291104; www.rctconline.com; Acharya Jagdish Rd; admission from ₹15; 🚇36), you can watch some of India's best horse racing from 19th-century grandstands, with the Victoria Memorial providing a beautiful backdrop. Over 40 annual meets.

🛍 Shopping

Books

Several small traveller-oriented bookstalls huddle around the junction of Sudder St and Mirza Ghalib St (Map p450). For more choice visit the following.

Classic Books/Earthcare Books BOOKSHOP
(Map p446; www.earthcarebooks.com; 10 Middleton St; ☺11am-7pm Mon-Sat, 11am-3pm Sun) Family publisher-bookshop.

Crossword BOOKSHOP
(Map p446; www.crosswordbookstores.com; 8 Elgin Rd; ☺10.30am-8.30pm) Three-storey chain bookshop with cafe.

Oxford Bookstore BOOKSHOP
(Map p450; www.oxfordbookstore.com; 17 Park St; ☺9.45am-10pm) Excellent full-range bookshop with browse-seating and cafe.

Seagull Bookstore BOOKSHOP
(Map p458; www.seagullindia.com; 31A SP Mukherjee Rd; ☺10.30am-7.30pm) Academic bookshop with strengths in humanities, regional politics and social sciences.

Clothing

Kolkata is great value for clothing, with pre-cut shirts costing under ₹100 from the Chowringhee Rd **Hawkers' Market** (Map p450). **Local tailors** (Map p450) on Elliot Rd are less tourist-oriented than those around New Market. Fashion-conscious locals head to Hazra Rd and Gariahat.

Crafts & Souvenirs

State-government emporia sell good-quality souvenirs at decent fixed prices, while several charity cooperatives allow you to feel good about your purchases.

GOVERNMENT EMPORIA
Dakshinapan Shopping Centre SHOPPING CENTRE
(Map p458; Gariahat Rd; ☺10.30am-7pm Mon-Sat) It's worth facing the soul-crushing 1970s architecture for Dakshinapan's wide range of government emporia. There's

plenty of tack but many shops offer excellent-value souvenirs, crafts and fabrics. **Kashmir Emporium** (Shop F38) has colourful papier mâché boxes from ₹45, **NEHHDC** (F22) has interesting tribal crafts and ₹80 wind-flutes, **Purbasha Tripura** (F4) has bargain caneware from intricate lampshades to Marx and Lenin portraits. On the lower level don't miss **Dolly's Tea Shop** (G62; teas ₹25-50, snacks ₹23-90) where teak-panels, rattan chairs, tea-crate tables and the regal presence of matriarch Dolly create a charming little oasis that attracts a wonderfully eclectic clientele.

Pragjyotika HANDICRAFTS
(Map p446; Assam House, 8 Russell St; ☺10.30am-6pm Mon-Fri, 10.30am-2.30pm Sat) Cane vases, jute handbags, pearls, fabrics and Assam tea.

Manjusha HANDICRAFTS
(Map p446; 4 Camac St; ☺10.30am-7pm Mon-Sat) Limited choice of West Bengal handicrafts and fabrics.

CHARITY COOPERATIVES
Ankur Kala SOUVENIRS
(Map p446; www.ankurkala.org; 3 Meher Ali Rd; ☺10am-5pm) This cooperative training-centre empowers women from the slums. The small shop sells batik, embroidered goods, greeting cards and leathergoods.

Nagaland Emporium SOUVENIRS
(Map p446; 11 Shakespeare Sarani; ☺10am-6pm Mon-Fri, 10am-2pm Sat) Naga crafts including shawls and face necklaces for wannabe head-hunters.

Ashalayam HANDICRAFTS
(Map p450; www.ashalayam.org; 1st fl, 44 Mirza Ghalib St; ☺10.30am-7pm Mon-Fri, 10.30am-4pm Sat) Buying cards, handmade paper and fabrics funds the (ex)street kids who made them.

Karmyog HANDICRAFTS
(Map p450; www.karmayog.org; 12B Russell St; ☺10am-6pm Mon-Sat) Elegant gallery of paper products.

Musical Instruments

Shops and workshops along Rabindra Sarani sell a great range of musical instruments. For tablas and other percussion, try numbers 248, 264 and 268B near Tagore's House (off Map p452). For sitars (from ₹4000) or violins (from ₹2000) visit **Mondal & Sons** (Map p452; 8 Rabindra Sarani; ☺10am-6pm Mon-Fri, 10am-2.30pm Sat). Family-run since the

1850s, Mondal & Sons has counted Yehudi Menuhin among its satisfied customers.

ℹ️ Information

Internet Access

Cyber Zoom (27B Park St; per hr ₹15; ⊙9am-11pm)

E-Merge (iWay) (59B Park St; per hr ₹30; ⊙10.30am-9.30pm Mon-Sat, 11.30am-9.30pm Sun) Dated booths but good AC and fast connection.

Gorukh (7 Sudder St; per hr ₹20; ⊙8.30am-10.30pm) At the back of a fabric shop with new flatscreens, pleasant owners and fingerprint security.

Medical

For listings of medical services see www.kolkata information.com/diagnostic.html and www .calcuttaweb.com/doctor.php.

Eastern Diagnostics (Map p450; 135 Mirza Ghalib St; ⊙7.30am-8.30pm) Doctors' consultations cost ₹200. Handy for Sudder St.

Money

ATMs are widespread. Many private money-changers around Sudder St offer commission-free exchange rates several per cent better than banks and some will exchange travellers cheques. Rates are often better around the corner in Mirza Ghalib St. Shop around and double-check the maths. At the airport be aware that moneychangers charge up to 5% tax/commission.

Globe Forex (Map p446; 11 Ho Chi Minh Sarani; ⊙9.30am-6.30pm Mon-Fri, 9.30am-2.30pm Sat) City-centre exchange with unusually good rates for cash and travellers cheques.

Permits

For any permit bring your passport, passport photographs and photocopies of your passport identity page and Indian visa.

FOREIGNERS' REGISTRATION OFFICE (FRO; Map p446; ☑22837034; 237 AJC Bose Rd; ⊙11am-5pm Mon-Fri) Issues limited permits for Manipur, Arunachal Pradesh (but not Tawang) and Nagaland (Mon and Phek only) at ₹1395 per person per permit. Minimum group of four applicants usually required. Allow two working days.

STATE OFFICES Indian nationals can get state-specific inner line permits at the following state offices but, except for Sikkim, foreigners shouldn't expect any permit help whatsoever.

Arunachal Pradesh (☑23341243; Arunachal Bhawan, Block CE 109, Sector 1, Salt Lake City)

Manipur (Map p446; ☑24758163; Manipur Bhawan, 26 Rowland Rd)

Mizoram (Map p458; ☑24617887; Mizoram Bhawan, 24 Old Ballygunge Rd) Take the lane beside 23 Ashutosh Chowdhury Rd.

Nagaland (Map p446; ☑22825247; Nagaland House, 11 Shakespeare Sarani)

Sikkim (Map p446; ☑22817905; Sikkim House, 4/1 Middleton St; ⊙10.30am-4pm Mon-Fri, 10.30am-2pm Sat) Permits free and usually issued within 24 hours.

Photography

Electro Photo-Lab (Map p450; ☑22498743; 14 Sudder St; ⊙10am-9pm Mon-Sat, noon-7pm Sun) Instant passport photos, film-developing, digi-prints and camera-to-CD/DVD burning.

Telephone

If you're a foreigner, getting a SIM card can be awkward in most of Kolkata but around Sudder St, numerous stalls will sell you a Vodafone SIM (₹155 including ₹49 credit) if you provide one passport photograph and a passport/visa photocopy.

Tourist Information

Cal Calling (₹45) Useful monthly info-booklet sold at Oxford Bookstore.

CityInfo (www.explocity.com) Advertisement-led listings pamphlet available free from better hotels.

India Tourism (Map p446; ☑22825813; 4 Shakespeare Sarani; ⊙10am-6pm Mon-Fri, 10am-1pm Sat) Free maps of greater Kolkata.

West Bengal Tourism (Map p452; ☑22437260, westbengaltourism.gov.in; 3/2 BBD Bagh; ⊙10.30am-1.30pm & 2-5.30pm Mon-Fri, 10.30am-1pm Sat) Comfortable, recently redecorated office mostly set up to sell tours (last sales 4.30pm). They also have booths at the airport, both domestic terminal (⊙8am-9pm) and international terminal (⊙11am-6.30pm Mon-Sat).

Dangers & Annoyances

Kolkata feels remarkably unthreatening. Pre-dictable beggar-hassle around the Sudder St traveller ghetto is a minor irritant. Crossing the road is a more of a day-to-day worry: the mad traffic takes no prisoners. *Bandhs* (strikes) occur with monotonous regularity, closing shops and stopping all land transport (including taxis to the airport). Monsoon-season flooding is highly inconvenient but rickshaw-wallahs somehow manage to ferry passengers through knee-deep, waterlogged streets.

ℹ️ Getting There & Away

Comprehensive and largely accurate air- and train-timetables appear in the Graphiti supplement of the *Telegraph* newspaper each Sunday.

Air

Long-haul destinations from **Netaji Subhash Bose International Airport** (NSBIA; www.nscbi airport.org) include Frankfurt on Lufthansa and London on **Air India** (Map p452; ☑22114433; 39 Chittaranjan Ave; ⊙10am-6.30pm Mon-Sat). Alternatively connect via Dubai, Singapore, Bangkok or Dhaka. For Chinese destinations use **China Eastern Airlines** (Map p446; ☑40448887; InterGlobe, 1st fl, Landmark Bldg, 228A AJC Bose Rd) flights to/via Kunming, Yunnan. **Druk Air** (Map p446; ☑22902429; 3rd fl, 51 Tivoli Court, 1A Ballygunge Circular Rd) flies to Paro, Bhutan but you'll need to make tour arrangements. The Bhutanese consulate is in the same building.

Most carriers sell tickets online but for Bangladeshi airlines it can prove useful to visit an agency or go directly to the airline office:

Biman (Map p446; ☑22266672; www.biman -airlines.com; 6th fl, 99A Park St)

GMG (Map p450; ☑30283030; www.gmgair lines.com; 20H Park St)

United Airways Bangladesh (Map p450; ☑9007095363; www.uabdl.com; Ripon St)

Boat

Sporadic ferries to Port Blair (Andaman Islands) depart from **Kidderpore Docks** (Karl Marx Sarani), entered from Gate 3 opposite Kidderpore commuter train station. Tickets (₹1700 to ₹7640) go on sale 10 days before departure at the **Shipping Corporation of India** (Map p452; ☑22484921; Hare St; ⊙10am-1pm & 2.30-5pm Mon-Fri).

Bus

INTERNATIONAL

BANGLADESH Several Marquis St agencies run Bangladesh-bound services involving a change of vehicle at the Benapol border. **Shohagh Paribahan** (Map p450; ☑22520757; 21A Marquis St; ⊙5am-10.30pm) runs 10 daily bus services to Dhaka (₹720/520 with/without AC, 13 hours). **GreenLine** (Map p450; ☑22520571; 12B Marquis St; ⊙4am-10.30pm) serves Dhaka (₹750, 13 hours, 5.30am and 7am), Chittagong (₹1150, 22 hours, 1pm) and Sylhet (₹1150, 18 hours, 5.30am).

BHUTAN A Bhutan Government postbus to Phuentsholing (₹350, 22 hours, 7pm Tue, Thu, Sat) departs from a side yard of Esplanade bus station (Map p452), where there's a special **ticket booth** (⊙9.30am-1pm & 2-6pm Mon-Sat).

DOMESTIC

The city's biggest bus station is **Esplanade** (Map p452) with many city buses, state-wide CSBC services and routes towards Sikkim. For buses towards Odisha (Orissa) use **Babughat** (Map p442) near Eden Gardens.

FROM ESPLANADE For Darjeeling or Sikkim, start with one of many night buses to Siliguri (₹325 to ₹700, 12 hours), departing between 6pm and 8pm. For Malda, CSTC buses leave at 7am, 8.30am, 9.30am, 10.45am and 8.15pm (₹143, 9 hours) and can be prebooked up to two weeks ahead.

FROM BABUGHAT Buses line up in front of Eden Gardens commuter train station offering numerous overnight services to Ranchi (from ₹170, 10 hours) and to Puri (₹370, 12 hours) via Bhubaneswar (₹320, 9½ hours). **Dolphin** (www .odishabusservice.com) charges only ₹50 extra for sleeper buses. Most buses leave around 8.30pm but arrive by 5pm if you have baggage.

Train

INTERNATIONAL For Dhaka, Bangladesh, the **Maitree Express** (II/CC/1AC ₹348/522/869, 12½ hours) departs Kolkata (Chitpore) Station at 7.10am Saturday and Wednesday, returning from Dhaka Cantt at 8.30am Tuesday and Sunday. You must have Darsana marked on your Bangladesh visa. Buy tickets up to 10 days ahead at a **special desk** (⊙10am-5pm Mon-Thu, 10am-3pm Fri & Sat, 10am-2pm Sun) within **Eastern Railways' Foreign Tourist Bureau** (Map p452; ☑22224206; 6 Fairlie Pl). No return tickets are available.

DOMESTIC Before buying your tickets, check 'train between stations' on indianrail.gov.in to see if there's a Foreign Tourist quota left (using the 'Enter Quota' line). If so, head for the **Eastern Railways' Foreign Tourist Bureau** (Map p452; ☑22224206; 6 Fairlie Pl; ⊙10am-5pm Mon-Sat, 10am-2pm Sun) with a book to read – waits can be long but there are sofa-seats. **Computerised booking offices** (Map p452; Koilaghat St; ⊙8am-8pm Mon-Sat, 8am-2pm Sun) offer tickets on the wider train network but have no tourist quota. Sudder St travel agencies can save you the trek and can sometimes manage to find tickets on 'full' trains but check what their commission will be before booking.

CAR & MOTORBIKE HIRE

Car rental companies including **Wenz** (☑9330018001; http://wenzcars.com) and **Ruia** (www.ruiacarrentals.com) can organise long-distance chauffeured rides. Sudder St agencies might be able to find you better deals: reliable **Backpackers** (Map p450; ☑9836177140; www.tourdesun darbans.com; Tottee Lane) can help and also has three 125cc motorcycles for hire (per day/month ₹500/10,000).

DESTINATION	AIRLINES (& NO OF FLIGHTS PER WEEK IF LESS THAN DAILY)	DURATION	FARES FROM
Agartala	SG, AI, IT, I7, 6E, 9W	55min	₹1930
Ahmedabad	SG, 6E	2½hr	₹3430
Aizawl	AI, IT	1½hr	₹2630
Bangkok (Thailand)	IT, IX, 9W, TG		₹8055
Bagdogra (Siliguri)	IT, SG, 9W, AI (4)	55min	₹1930
Bengaluru (Bangalore)	6E, IT, SG, AI, S2, 9W	2hr	₹3430
Bhubaneswar	IT, 9W	55min	₹3315
Chennai	9W, 6E, SG, AI, I7	2hr	₹3030
Chittagong (Bangladesh)	Z5 (3), 4H (Tue, Thu)	1hr	₹5000
Delhi	6E, 9W, AI, SG, IT, S2	2hr	₹3030
Dhaka (Bangladesh)	BG, IT, 9W, IX (4), Z5, 4H (3)	1hr	₹3520
Dibrugarh	6E, AI (5)	1½hr	₹2360
Dimapur	AI	1-2hr	₹2210
Gaya	AI (Fri)	50mins	₹1400
Goa	IT via Mumbai, SG via Delhi	4½hr	₹3710
Guwahati	SG, 9W, S2, 6E, AI, IT	1¼hr	₹1930
Hyderabad	IT, 6E, AI, SG	2hr	₹3030
Imphal	AI, IT, 6E, S2 (4)	1¼hr	₹2430
Jaipur	6E, SG	2½hr	₹3030
Jorhat	9W (3), S2 (2), AI via Shillong (3)	2¾hr	₹2080
Kathmandu (Nepal)	AI (4)	1¼hr	₹6030
Lucknow	9W	1½hr	₹6330
	6E via Patna	2½	₹2285
Mumbai	9W, 6E, IT, AI, SG, S2	2½hr	₹3735
Nagpur	6E	1¾hr	₹2185
Patna	9W, IT, 6E	1hr	₹2030
Port Blair	AI, S2	2hr	₹7830
Raipur	IT	2hr	₹3830
Ranchi	IT, 9W	1¼hr	₹2730
Shillong	AI (6)	1¾hr	₹2120
Silchar	AI, IT	1½hr	₹2200
Singapore	IX/AI	4½hr	₹7520
Tezpur	AI (3)	2hr	₹2120
Varanasi (via Delhi)	SG	8hr	₹2315
Visakhapatnam (Vizag)	9W	2¼hr	₹6100
Yangon (Rangoon, Myanmar)	AI (Mon)	2hr	₹9080
Yangon (via Gaya)	AI (Fri)	4hr	₹9080

6E=IndiGo, 9W=Jet Airways, AI=Air India, I7=Paramount, IT=Kingfisher, IX=Air India Express, KB=Druk Air, S2=JetLite, SG=SpiceJet, TG=Thai Airways, 4H=United Airways Bangladesh, Z5=GMG, BG=Biman

Check whether your long-distance train departs from Howrah (Haora; HWH), Sealdah (SDAH) or 'Kolkata' (Chitpore; KOAA) Station.

Getting Around

Tickets on most city transport routes cost from ₹4 to ₹8. Men shouldn't sit in assigned 'Ladies' seats'.

To/From the Airport

NSBIA Airport is 5km east of Dum Dum, itself 20 minutes by metro (₹6) from central Kolkata. With massive construction works underway to expand and modernise the airport, you can expect changes to come. Vehicle access is currently from Gate 1, 900m southwest of the terminals where a shopping and hotel complex is under construction. Or from Gate 2 on Jessore Rd, around 400m northwest of the terminals. Note that the airport's left-luggage service has closed.

SUBURBAN TRAIN Biman Bandar is the airport train station, raised on concrete piles and a three-minute stroll from the International terminal. Trains run just a few times daily and not on Sundays. There are departures to Sealdah at 10.45pm, to Majerhat via BBD Bagh Commuter Station at 7.40am and 1.54pm, and to Majerhat via Ballygunge at 10.40am and 6.45pm. These, plus a 6.30am train, stop at Dum Dum Junction where you can switch onto the metro. Don't mistakenly alight at Dum Dum Cantt.

TAXI Prepaid, fixed-price taxis from the airport to Dum Dum metro/Sudder St/Howrah cost ₹140/240/240. Pay before leaving the terminal then cross over to the rank of yellow cabs, ignoring touts in between. After 10pm very few fixed-rate taxis are available and others will charge far more.

AC BUS New air-conditioned airport buses (₹40, around one hour) run every half hour from the terminal area to Esplanade Bus Station (Map p452). There are also less-frequent services to Tollygunge (via the bypass) and to Howrah.

BUS–METRO COMBINATION Cheaper (₹12), more frequent and often faster than the airport bus but a bad idea with much luggage. Passing by on Jessore Rd, crowded buses 30B (bound eventually for Babughat) and DN9/1 take around 25 minutes to get to Dum Dum metro station. To find Jessore Rd, walk 400m northwest out of the international terminal keeping the Hindu temple and raised train line to your direct left. Cross a construction area and a busy access road and immediately beyond this, shimmy through a small gap in the walled airport compound; the gap is known as Airport Gate 2½ and is opposite Shiva & Sons Airtel shop.

CITY BUS Minibus 151 to BBD Bagh and relatively infrequent bus 46 to Esplanade (₹7, one hour) via VIP Rd start from Airport Gate 1, 900m from the domestic terminal.

Bus & Tram

Passenger-crammed mechanical sweat boxes hurtle along at frightening speeds wherever the chronic traffic congestion abates. Most buses' route-numbers are written in Western script even when destination signboards aren't. Photogenically battered old trams are slower but follow more predictable routes. Pay aboard.

Ferry

The fastest and most agreeable way from central Kolkata to Howrah train station is generally by **river ferry** (₹4; ⊙8am-8pm) departing every 15 minutes from various jetties including Bagbazar, Armenian (not Sundays), Fairlie, Bishe June and Babu Ghat. Reduced service on Sundays.

Metro

Kolkata's busy one-line **metro** (www.mtp.indianrailways.gov.in; ₹4-8; ⊙7am-9.45pm Mon-Sat, 2-9.45pm Sun) has trains every six to 15 minutes. Extensions are being built to Dakshineswar and to the airport, while a second line (Howrah–Sealdah–Salt Lake) is planned eventually. For Sudder St use Esplanade or Park St. There's a cursory baggage check on entering. Theoretically you may not carry bags over 10kg (nor may you carry ghee, leaves or dead bodies for that matter).

Rickshaw

Kolkata is the last bastion of human-powered 'tana rickshaws', especially around New Market. During monsoon, high-wheeled rickshaws are the transport most able to cope in the worst-flooded streets. Although rickshaw pullers sometimes charge foreigners disproportionate fares, many are virtually destitute, sleeping on the pavements beneath their rented chariots at night so tips are heartily appreciated.

Autorickshaws squeeze aboard five passengers to operate as share-taxis along fixed routes.

Suburban Trains

Useful trains run roughly hourly between Sealdah–Dum Dum–Dakshineswar and in rush hour only from Kidderpore–BBD Bagh–Bagbazar–Chitpore–Dum Dum. For timetables see http://erail.in/kolkatasuburbantrains.htm.

Taxi

Kolkata's ubiquitous yellow Ambassador cabs charge a minimum fare of ₹22 for up to 1.9km. Ensure that the meter's on (usually easier when flagging down a passing cab than if approaching a parked one) but be aware that what it shows is NOT what you'll pay. To calculate short-trip fares, double the meter reading and add two rupees. For longer trips, that system will be a couple of rupees under, so consult the driver's conversion chart or ask for a fare print-out. Fares rise after 10pm.

Departures daily unless otherwise stated.

USEFUL FOR	TRAIN	DURATION (HR)	DEPARTURES	FARES (SLEEPER/ 3AC/2AC UNLESS OTHERWISE STATED)
Bhubaneswar	12839 *Chennai Mail*	6¾	11.45pm (HWH)	₹167/468/675
Chennai	12841 *Coromandal*	26½	2.50pm (HWH)	₹461/1242/1700
	12839 *Chennai Mail*	28	11.45pm (HWH)	₹461/1242/1700
Delhi	12303/12381 *Poorva*	23	8.05am/ 8.20am (HWH)	₹426/1143/1561
	12313 *SDAH Rajdhani*	17	4.50pm (SDAH)	2AC/1AC ₹2030/3395
Gorakhpur	15047/15049/15051	17¾-19	2.30pm/9.40am/ 8.10am (KOAA)	₹311/845/1160
Guwahati	12345 *Saraighat*	17¾	3.50pm (HWH)	₹359/954/1302
	15657 *Kanchenjunga*	22	6.35am (SDAH)	₹332/902/1240
Hooghly	Bandel Local	1	every half-hour (HWH)	Unreserved ₹9
Lucknow	13151 *Tawi Exp*	23	11.45am (KOAA)	₹339/924/1272
	12327/12369	18¼	1.10pm (HWH)	₹363/966/1316
Mumbai CST	12810 *Mumbai Mail*	33¼	8.15pm (HWH)	₹508/1374/1883
New Jalpaiguri	12377 *Padatik*	10	10.55pm (SDAH)	₹259/673/911
Patna	12351 *Danapur*	9½	8.35pm (HWH)	₹252/653/881
Puri	12837 *Howrah-Puri*	9	10.35pm (HWH)	₹244/631/852
	18409 *SriJagannath*	9½	7pm (HWH)	₹224/601/822
Siliguri Jctn	13149 *Kanchankaya*	11½	8.30pm (SDAH)	₹259/643/881
Varanasi	13005 *Amritsar Mail*	15	7.10pm (HWH)	₹269/776/1065

HWH=ex-Howrah, SDAH=ex-Sealdah, KOAA=ex-Chitpur

Beware that around 1pm, much of the city's one-way road system reverses direction! Not surprisingly many taxis are reluctant to make journeys around this time.

There are prepaid taxi booths at Howrah Station, Sealdah Station and at both airport terminals, but such taxis are infamously hard to find at night.

West Bengal & Darjeeling

Includes »

Best Places for a Cuppa

» Windamere Hotel (p493)

» Sunset Lounge (p495)

» Makaibari Tea Estate (p486)

Best Places to Stay

» Dekeling Hotel (p493)

» Holumba Haven (p502)

» The Ffort Raichak (p478)

Why Go?

Stretching from the jagged northern hills down to the sultry mangroves of the Bay of Bengal, few states offer such a rich range of destinations and experiences as West Bengal.

Down south in the plains, brilliant green rice fields surround bustling trading towns, mud-and-thatch villages, and vestiges of Bengal's glorious history: ornate, terracotta-tiled Hindu temples and monumental ruins of Muslim princes.

Up in the cool northern hills the 'toy train' of the Darjeeling Himalayan Railway chugs its way up the British-era hill station of Darjeeling, a quintessential remnant of the Raj, whose views of massive Kkangchendzonga towering over the surrounding tea estates rank as one of the region's most inspiring sights.

Overshadowed perhaps by the reputation of its capital Kolkata (Calcutta), the rest of West Bengal sees surprisingly few foreign tourists. Perhaps visitors should learn from the Bengalis themselves, enthusiastic travellers who never tire of exploring their own fascinating and diverse region.

When to Go

Darjeeling

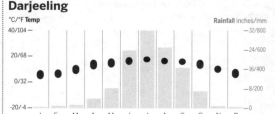

Oct–Dec & Mar–May Best for West Bengal hills views, trekking and spring bloom.

Oct–Mar Best for avoiding the heat on the lower plains.

Jan The best time to navigate the dense mangrove forests of the Sunderbans Tiger Reserve.

Food & Drink

Darjeeling is *the* place to taste a range of teas from local tea estates. Noted for its delicate taste, the teas range from black to green to white and are best taken alone or with a slice of lemon, but not with milk. For more on the best tea-related travel experiences see p492. Not to be outdone, Bengali food is considered iconic by locals and visitors alike – for more information on the delicacies of this region, see p443 and p1115.

> ## DON'T MISS
>
> The views of 8598m Khangchendzonga, the world's third-highest mountain, are easily one of the West Bengal Hills' highlights. The classic viewpoints are from **Tiger Hill** or from the **Singalila Trek**, where the Himalayan skyline stretches from Nepal to Bhutan. **Darjeeling** town also has great views, as does Deolo Hill in **Kalimpong**. The major potential spoiler is the weather. The most reliable clear skies are at dawn during the post-monsoon months of October to December.

Top State Festivals

» Lepcha & Bhutia New Year (Jan, West Bengal Hills) Colourful fairs and traditional dances in and around Darjeeling.

» Ganga Sagar Mela (mid-Jan, Sagar Island, p478) Hundreds of thousands of Hindu pilgrims converge where the Ganges meets the sea, to bathe en masse in a fervent festival.

» Magh Mela (6-8 Feb, Shantiniketan, p479) Crafts and rural arts take centre stage at this festival.

» Bengali New Year (mid-Apr, Naba Barsha) A statewide holiday celebrating the first day of the Bengali calendar.

» Rath Yatra (Jun & Jul, Chariot Festival, statewide) Celebrated by pulling the juggernaut of Lord Jagannath's chariot.

» Jhapan (mid-Aug, Bishnupur, p479) Draws snake charmers to honour the goddess Manasa, the central figure of snake worship.

» Fulpati (Sep & Oct, West Bengal Hills) Linked to Durga Puja and marking the seventh day of Dashain, this predominantly Nepali festival is also celebrated by Lepchas and others with processions and dancing from Ghum to Darjeeling.

» Durga Puja (Oct, statewide) Across the state, especially in Kolkata, temporary *pandals* (pavilions) are raised and intense celebrations take place to worship the goddess Durga. After four colourful days, beautiful clay idols of the 10-armed deity are immersed in the rivers.

» Jagaddhatri Puja (Nov, Chandarnagar, p478) Honours the goddess Jagaddhatri, an incarnation of Durga.

» Poush Mela (23-26 Dec, Shantiniketan, p479) Folk music, dance, theatre and Baul songs radiate across the university town.

MAIN POINTS OF ENTRY

Kolkata Airport (p470)

Kolkata (Chitpore) Train Station (p470)

Bagdogra Airport (p483)

New Jalpaiguri Train Station (p484)

Fast Facts

» Population: 91.3 million

» Area: 87,853 sq km

» Capital: Kolkata

» Main language: Bengali

» Sleeping prices: **$** below ₹600, **$$** ₹600 to ₹3000, **$$$** above ₹3000

Top Tip

During the month-long '*puja* season', around the Durga Puja, Dasain/Dushera and later Diwali festivals, hotels, jeeps and trekking huts are often booked out by travelling Bengali tourists. Pack a jumper and visit in November to avoid the crowds.

Resources

» West Bengal Tourist Department (www.west bengaltourism.gov.in) Information and online booking for WBTDC lodges like Jaldaphara.

» Kalimpong (www.kalim pong.org) Travel information with an emphasis on accommodation.

West Bengal Highlights

1 Enjoy 360-degree mountain views over breakfast at hilltop lodges on the **Singalila Ridge Trek** (p499)

2 Ride the steam-driven **toy train** (p484) as it puffs and pants its way between the tea towns of Kurseong and Darjeeling

3 Meander up the wide **Hooghly River** (p478) to uncover colonial and Mughal relics in Serampore, Chandarnagar and Hooghly

4 Visit a tea estate, sip a delicate local brew and enjoy the fantastic views from the historic hill station of **Darjeeling** (p487)

5 Watch dawn break over the world's third-highest peak from **Tiger Hill** (p490)

6 Admire intricate scenes from the Hindu epics carved on the medieval terracotta temples of **Bishnupur** (p479)

7 Cruise the river channels of the **Sunderbans** (p476) through the world's most extensive mangrove forest, to spot darting kingfishers, spotted deer and the elusive Royal Bengal tiger

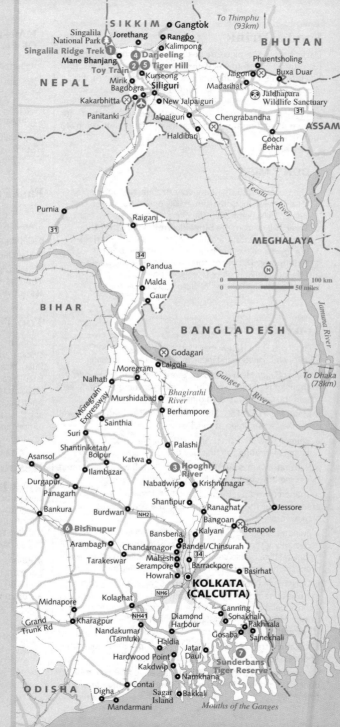

History

Referred to as Vanga in the Mahabharata, this region has a long history predating the Aryan invasions of India. It was part of the Mauryan empire in the 3rd century BC before being overrun by the Guptas. For three centuries from around the 9th century AD, the Buddhist Pala dynasty controlled a large area based in Bengal and including parts of Odisha (Orissa), Bihar and modern Bangladesh.

Bengal was brought under Muslim control by Qutb-ud-din, first of the sultans of Delhi, at the end of the 12th century. Following the death of Aurangzeb in 1707, Bengal became an independent Islamic state.

The British East India Company established a trading post in Kolkata (Calcutta) in 1698, which quickly prospered. Sensing rich pickings, Siraj-ud-daula, the nawab of Bengal, came down from his capital at Murshidabad and easily took Kolkata in 1756. Robert Clive defeated him the following year at the Battle of Plassey, helped by the treachery of Siraj-ud-daula's uncle, Mir Jafar, who commanded the greater part of the nawab's army. Jafar succeeded his nephew as nawab but his reward was short-lived; after the Battle of Buxar in 1764 the British took full control of Bengal.

West Bengal was the cradle of the Indian Renaissance and national freedom movement, and has long been considered the country's cultural heartland. In 1947 Indian independence from Britain, and the subsequent partition of the country, saw the state of Bengal divided on religious grounds, causing the upheaval of millions of Bengalis.

🏃 Activities

TREKKING

While pleasant walks along pine-scented trails are possible in all of West Bengal's hill stations, the most popular place for a multiday trek is Singalila Ridge (p498), near Darjeeling, where teahouse-style trekking is possible. Camping treks are possible elsewhere, including around Kalimpong.

RAFTING

White-water rafting trips should resume soon on the mighty Teesta and Rangeet Rivers, easily arranged and accessed from Darjeeling (see p492).

ℹ Getting There & Around

The vast majority who enter West Bengal arrive in Kolkata. Siliguri's Bagdogra airport has services to Bangkok, Kolkata, Delhi and Guwahati, as well as daily helicopter flights to Gangtok.

Most land arrivals are by train: main lines run south to Bhubaneswar and Chennai (Madras), and west to Gaya, Varanasi and Delhi. Other lines connect the state to Assam in the northeast and Jharkhand in the southwest. Numerous long-distance buses also connect surrounding states.

Overcrowded 'share jeeps' ply the winding roads of the West Bengal hills. Try to avoid the cramped back seats.

SOUTH OF KOLKATA

Sunderbans Tiger Reserve

Home to one of the largest concentrations of tigers on the planet, this 2585 sq km **reserve** (Indian/foreigner ₹15/150) is a network of channels and semi-submerged mangroves that forms the world's largest river delta. Royal Bengal tigers (officially estimated to number close to 300) lurk in the impenetrable depths of the mangrove forests, and also swim the delta's innumerable channels. Although they do sometimes kill villagers working in the Sunderbans, tigers are typically shy and sightings are rare. Nevertheless, cruising the broad waterways through the world's biggest mangrove sanctuary (now a Unesco World Heritage Site) and watching wildlife, whether it be a spotted deer, 2m-long water monitor or luminescent kingfisher, is a world away from Kolkata's chaos.

The best time to visit the reserve is between October and March. Organised tours (see p477) are the best way to navigate this tricky and harsh landscape, not least because all your permits, paperwork, guiding duties and logistical problems are taken care of. In fact, travelling alone is not recommended.

At Sajnekhali, the official gateway into the reserve, you'll find the **Mangrove Interpretation Centre** (⊙8.30am-5pm) with a small turtle and crocodile hatchery, a collection of pickled wildlife and a blackboard with the date of the last tiger-spotting chalked up.

☞ Tours

Tour prices vary widely. They typically include return transport from Kolkata, as well as all the fees, but do check what is and isn't included. **West Bengal Tourism** (p469) organises weekly boat cruises from September to April, costing from ₹2300 per person for one night and two half-days, including food and on-board accommodation. Trips that include a worthwhile extra day start from ₹3100.

Backpackers WILDLIFE WATCHING
(📞9836177140; www.tourdesundarbans.com;
11 Tottee Lane, Kolkata) An extremely professional and knowledgeable outfit that
conducts highly recommended tours of the
jungles, including birdwatching and local music sessions. All-inclusive prices are
₹4000/4500 per person for one-/two-night
trips, give or take a few hundred depending
on the number of people in your group.

Sunderban Tiger Camp WILDLIFE WATCHING
(📞9331092632; www.sunderbantigercamp.com;
71 Ganesh Chandra Avenue, Kolkata; 1/2 nights per
person from ₹3250/4930; ❄) Provides expert
guides and quality accommodation (on
dry land).

Help Tourism WILDLIFE WATCHING
(📞033-24550917; www.helptourism.com; 67A
Kali Temple Rd, Kalighat, Kolkata; 1/2 nights for 2
people all-inclusive ₹22100/27600) Prices come
down sharply as the number of people
increases.

Diamond Harbour

📞03174 / POP 37,238
Diamond Harbour, once among the main
ports of the East India Company, rests 51km
south of Kolkata, where the Hooghly turns
south and flows into open sea. It's a good
staging area for points in the south.

There isn't much to see around, except
the smoking chimneys of industrial Haldia
township across the river.

Ffort Raichak (📞275444; www.ffort.com;
Sarisa; d from ₹7500; ❄@❄) is a surprisingly
pleasant (though a tad outsized) resort nearby, a relaxed stay in which could be your only
reason to halt an extra night here. Cutting
a handsome profile and located right next
to the waters, it's a plush getaway set amid
26 hectares of lush greens, and is equipped
with the very best of luxe features. If you're
staying, consider spending a few extra bucks
on a delightful river cruise, if the hotel can
arrange it for you.

Buses from Kolkata's Esplanade (₹40, 1½
hours) come and go every 30 minutes.

Sagar Island

According to legend, after the sage Kapil
reduced King Sagar's 60,000 sons to ashes, it
was at Sagar Island that the Ganges revived
their souls by flowing over their dusty remains. Each year the **Ganga Sagar Mela** is
held here, near the Kapil Muni Temple, honouring the legend. The best way to see the
festival is the two-day, one-night boat tour
operated from Kolkata by West Bengal Tourism (p469), with accommodation on board
(per person deck/berth ₹3950/6500). The
island hibernates for the rest of the year.

Mandarmani

📞03220
About 180km south of Kolkata, Mandar-
mani is a sleepy fishing village that sports a
heavenly beach stretching nearly 15km. It remains one of the more unpolluted beaches in
the country, and supports countless colonies
of sand bubbler crabs. The beaches see some
additional action at dawn, when fishing
boats drop anchor and disgorge their catch-
es of marine goodies.

Sana Beach (📞9007725066; www.thesana
beach.com; d incl breakfast from ₹4050; ❄), at
the far end of the beach, has a mix of comfy
rooms, cottages and tents, and a good bar-
cum-restaurant.

To go, take the 6.40am *Tamralipta Express*
(2nd class/chair ₹77/298, 3½ hours) from
Kolkata's Howrah Station to Digha. A taxi
drop from there costs about ₹400.

NORTH OF KOLKATA

Up the Hooghly

On the Hooghly River, about 25km north of
Kolkata, Serampore was a Danish trading
centre until Denmark's holdings in India
were transferred to the British East India
Company in 1845. **Serampore College** was
founded in 1818 by the first Baptist missionary to India, William Carey, and houses a
library that was once one of the largest in
the country.

Further upstream is the former French
outpost of **Chandernagar**, where you can
visit the **Eglise du Sacre Coeur** (Sacred
Heart Church) and the nearby 18th-century
mansion now housing the **Cultural Institut
de Chandernagar** (admission free; ⊙11am-
5.30pm, closed Thu & Sat), with collections
documenting this colonial outpost.

In 1571 the Portuguese set up a factory in
Bandel, 41km north of Kolkata and close to
Saptagram, which was an important trading
port long before Kolkata rose to prominence.

Here, you can climb the lofty clock tower of the romantically crumbling **Imambara** (admission ₹5; ⊙8am-6pm Apr-Jul, to 5.30pm Aug-Nov, to 5pm Dec-Mar), where the view over the river (not to mention the climb) will take your breath away. The building was constructed in 1861 as a centre for learning and worship. Only 1km south of Bandel, **Chinsurah** was exchanged by the Dutch for the British possessions on the (Indonesian) island of Sumatra in 1825. There are dilapidated ruins of a fort and a cemetery, about 1km to the west.

About 6km north of Hooghly, **Bansberia** has two interesting temples. The 13 *sikharas* (spires) of the **Hanseswari Temple** look like something you'd expect to see in St Petersburg, while the ornate terracotta tiles covering the **Vasudev Temple** resemble those seen in Bishnupur.

Bishnupur

☏03244 / POP 61,943

Known for its beautiful terracotta temples, Bishnupur flourished as the capital of the Malla kings from the 16th to the early 19th centuries. The architecture of these intriguing **temples** (Indian/foreigner ₹10/250; ⊙dawn-dusk) is a bold mix of Bengali, Islamic and Orissan styles. Intricately detailed facades of numerous temples play out scenes of the Hindu epics, the Ramayana and Mahabharata. The most striking structures include the Jor Bangla, Madan Mohan Temple, the multi-arched Ras Mancha and the elaborate Shyam Rai Temple. You need to pay for your ticket at Ras Mancha and show it at the other temples. Cycle-rickshaw-wallahs offer tours (the best way to negotiate the labyrinth of lanes) for ₹200.

There's a small **museum** (admission ₹10; ⊙11am-7pm Tue-Sun) that's worth a look for its painted manuscript covers, stone friezes, musical instruments and folk art gallery.

Bishnupur is in Bankura district, famous for its Baluchari silk saris and its pottery, particularly the stylised Bankura horse. Reproductions of detailed terracotta tiles from the temples are sold everywhere.

Bishnupur Tourist Lodge (☏252013; College Rd; d without/with AC from ₹500/1100; ❀) is a freshly renovated and upgraded government-run hotel, with clean rooms and a good bar-cum-restaurant. It's close to the museum and a ₹50 rickshaw ride from the train station. It's often full, so book ahead.

Regular buses run from Bishnupur to Kolkata (₹90, five hours). For Shantiniketan (₹70, four hours) you may have to change in

Durgapur (see p480). Two trains run daily to Howrah (2nd class/chair ₹85/317, four hours): the 5.31pm *Rupashi Bangla Express* and the 7.33am *Howrah Purulia Express*.

Shantiniketan

☏03463

Shantiniketan is the epitome of its Bengali name, which means peaceful *(shanti)* abode *(niketan)*. The mystic, poet and artist Rabindranath Tagore (1861–1941) founded a school here in 1901, which later developed into the Visva Bharati University, with an emphasis on humanity's relationship with nature. It's a relaxed place with students from all over India and overseas.

The **post office** (Santiniketan Rd; ⊙9am-5pm Mon-Sat) is on the main road, opposite the turn-off to the university entrance. The **State Bank of India** (Santiniketan Rd; ⊙10am-3pm Mon-Fri), on the same road, has an ATM and changes foreign currency.

Spread throughout the leafy university grounds are eclectic **statues**, the celebrated **Shantiniketan Murals** and the **Tagore Prayer Hall**. The **museum and art gallery** (adult/student ₹5/3; ⊙10.30am-1pm & 2-4.30pm Thu-Mon, 10.30am-1pm Tue) within the Uttarayan complex (Tagore's former home) are worth a peek if you are a Tagore aficionado. Reproductions of his sketches and paintings are sold here. The **Subarnarekha** bookshop near the post office has plenty of Tagore's titles (₹80 to ₹250) in English.

🛏 Sleeping & Eating

Shantiniketan Tourist Lodge   HOTEL **$$**
(☏252699; Bhubandanga; d without/with AC from ₹750/1800; ❀) This large-scale government-run operation offers good-value rooms opening out to airy corridors, with good housekeeping and friendly service. There's a pleasant garden and the **restaurant** (mains ₹70 to ₹90) works up a limited range of Indian standards.

Hotel Rangamati   HOTEL **$$**
(☏252305; Bhubandanga; s/d ₹700/990, with AC ₹1090/1400; ❀) A fun 'jungle hut' theme with faux branches, wooden fittings and lots of fish tanks at the entrance. Rooms are clean with big bathrooms and dark wood furniture. There's a basic restaurant.

Camellia Hotel & Resort   HOTEL **$$**
(☏9007030195; www.camelliagroup.org; Prantik; d without/with AC from ₹1750/4500; ❀❀) The

UP ON THE FARM, DOWN ON THE FARM

If you want to get off the tourist track and enjoy views and solitude, we recommend three (very different) farm homestays in West Bengal. All need to be booked in advance.

Perched on an idyllic mountainside three hours' bumpy jeep ride from Darjeeling or two hours' drive from Rimbik, at the end of the Singalila Ridge Trek (p498), Karmi Farm (www.karmifarm.com; per person incl full board ₹1500) overlooks Sikkim in one direction and Nepal in another. It's managed by Andrew Pulger-Frame, whose Sikkimese grandparents once ran an estate from the main house here, where delicious home-cooked meals are now served up to visitors on the old kitchen table. The simple but very comfortable double and family rooms are attractively decorated with colourful local fabrics, and bathrooms have 24-hour hot water. A small clinic for villagers is run from the farm, providing a volunteer opportunity for medical students and doctors. Treks and other activities can be organised, but it's equally easy to just sit for days on the rooftop deck with a book and a pot of tea, overlooking the bird- and flower-filled gardens and towering distant peaks. Wonderful.

Back down on the plains, bordered by brilliant-green paddy fields, is the rustic Basudha Farm (☏9432674377; www.cintdis.org; per person ₹300), an hour's drive from Bishnupur. Basudha is a rural self-help organisation and documentation centre that operates a seed bank of indigenous rice strains. Rices are grown using organic methods, and farmers are sensitised to use them as an alternative to using genetically modified strains. Visitors to the farm are assumed to be interested in the work and the local culture. Accommodation is basic, with limited (solar) power, and all water needs to be pumped from the well. The all-veg food is mostly grown on the farm.

A similar approach to nature and life is taken at Babli (☏03463-271285; www.babli-farm .tripod.com; per person from ₹650), a farm near Shantiniketan that busies itself with conservation of forests, flora and fauna, while promoting rural empowerment. Those interested in learning more can spend a quiet day on their sylvan campus and be treated like family. Accommodation is in huts and cottages, and there's great veg food at the canteen.

Camellia has a pleasant country setting about 2km from the university, with leafy gardens and green lawns. Tasteful art and furniture make the rooms especially comfortable; the suites have a fridge and bathtub. Pick-up from the train station is available.

TOP CHOICE **Alcha** CAFÉ **$**
(Ratanpalli; mains ₹50-80; ⏱7.30am-10am, noon-2pm & 4-8pm) This lovely cafe on one edge of the university campus is a melting pot for writers, artists, poets, musicians and free-thinking students nursing million-dollar ideas in their fertile minds. It's got a cool shack-style seating space that often doubles as an art gallery, and there's a boutique adjoining the eatery that sells a fantastic selection of jewellery, textiles and handicrafts made by local artisans. Oh, and the *parathas* are sinful.

❶ Getting There & Away

Several trains ply between Bolpur station, 2km south of the university, and Kolkata daily. The best is *Shantiniketan Express* (2nd class/chair ₹70/232, 2½ hours) departing at 10.10am from Howrah and 1.10pm from Bolpur. For New Jal-

paiguri, take the 9.40am *Kanchenjunga Express* 5657 (sleeper/3AC ₹187/496, eight hours). There's a **train booking office** (Santiniketan Rd; ⏱8am-noon, 12.30-2pm Thu-Tue) near the post office.

The Jambuni bus stand is in Bolpur. Buses go to Berhampore/Murshidabad (₹70, four hours) and Bishnupur (₹70, four hours) but direct buses can be hard to find: you may need to change in Durgapur for Bishnupur and Suri for Berhampore.

Nabadwip & Mayapur
☏03472 / POP 115,036

Nabadwip, 114km north of Kolkata, is an important Krishna pilgrimage centre, attracting throngs of devotees, and is also an ancient centre of Sanskrit culture. The last Hindu king of Bengal, Lakshman Sen, moved his capital here from Gaur.

Across the river from Nabadwip, Mayapur is a centre for the Iskcon (Hare Krishna) movement. There's a large, colourful temple and the basic but clean **Iskcon Guest Houses** (☏245620; mghb@pamho.net; d/tr/q from ₹300/350/450). Iskcon runs a private bus to Kolkata (₹200, five hours) early on Friday, Saturday and Sunday mornings, returning in the evening; for details or to make a booking call **Iskcon Kolkata** (☎033-32488041).

Murshidabad & Berhampore

☎03482 / POP 36,894

In Murshidabad, rural Bengali life and 18th-century architecture meld on the verdant shores of the Bhagirathi River. When Siraj-ud-daula was nawab of Bengal, Murshidabad was his capital, and he was assassinated here after the defeat at Plassey (now Palashi).

The main draw here is the **Hazarduari** (Indian/foreigner ₹5/100; ⊙10am-4.30pm Sat-Thu), a palace famous for its 1000 doors (real and false), built here for the nawabs in 1837. It houses an astonishing collection of antiquities from the 18th and 19th centuries. Other beautiful structures in the complex include the **Nizamat Imambara**, the clock tower, the **Wasef Manzil**, a former regal residence, and the elegant **Madina Mosque**.

Murshid Quli Khan, who moved the capital here in 1700, is buried beneath the stairs at the impressive ruins of the **Katra Mosque**. Siraj-ud-daula was assassinated at the **Nimak Haram Deori** (Traitor's Gate). Within the **Kathgola Gardens** (admission ₹7; ⊙6.30am-5.30pm) is an interesting family mansion of a Jain trading family, dating back to 1873.

Berhampore is 15km south of Murshidabad and acts as its bus and railway hub.

🛏 Sleeping & Eating

Hotel Samrat   HOTEL $

(☎251147; fax 253091; NH34 Panchanantala; d without/with AC from ₹300/770; ❄) This is one of Berhampore's longest-running operations, and offers spacious and clean rooms opening along corridors painted in orange and cream. The Mahal restaurant (mains ₹100) downstairs is a good place for meals.

Hotel Manjusha   HOTEL $

(☎270321; Murshidabad; d from ₹500) A wonderful setting on the banks of the Bhagirathi, behind the Great Imambara. Downstairs rooms are cheapest, while rooms 201 to 203 have river and Hazarduari views for an extra ₹100. It's all about the location and period charm, though the rooms themselves are threadbare – some are slightly whiffy.

❶ Getting There & Around

The *Bhagirathi Express* (2nd class/chair ₹69/264, four hours) departs Kolkata's Sealdah station at 6.25pm, and departs from Berhampore at 6.34am. Regular buses leave for Kolkata (₹95, six hours) and Malda (₹70, four hours). To Shantiniketan/Bolpur (₹70, four hours) there are occasional direct buses but you may need to change in Suri.

Shared autorickshaws (₹20) whiz between Murshidabad and Berhampore. Cycle-rickshaws/taxis offer guided half-day tours to see the spread-out sites for ₹200/500.

Malda

☎03512 / POP 161,448

Malda, 340km north of Kolkata, is a convenient base for visiting the ruins of Bengal's former capitals in nearby Gaur and Pandua. Malda is also famed for its mangoes ripening in spring; even if it's not mango season, you'll probably get mango pickle on the side with any food you order here.

State Bank of India and ICICI ATMs are on the highway, near the turn-off to the bus station. **i-Zone** (per hr ₹20; ⊙10am-7pm), behind the bus station on the way to Malda Museum, has fast internet connections.

Hotel Kalinga (☎283567; www.hotelkalinga malda.net; NH34, Ram Krishna Pally; d without/with AC ₹500/1000; ❄) is a big place on the highway, about halfway between the bus and train stations. The AC rooms are fine, but the cheaper ones are slightly grubby. The rooftop multicuisine restaurant (mains ₹100) has good food and great views.

Malda Tourist Lodge (☎220911; Rathbari More; d without/with AC ₹525/1050; ❄) is a state-run accommodation option that was undergoing renovation during research, and should have fresh, clean rooms on offer by now.

The best trains from Kolkata (Sealdah station) are the 3.15pm *Intercity Express* (2nd class/chair ₹105/374, six hours) and the New Jalpaiguri-bound 6.35am *Kanchanjanga Express* (sleeper/2AC ₹250/580, six hours). The former returns at 6.10am the next morning. Buses depart regularly for Siliguri (₹135, six hours), Berhampore/Murshidabad (₹70, four hours) and Kolkata (₹170, 10 hours).

Gaur & Pandua

Rising from the flooded paddy fields of Gaur (15km south of Malda) are mosques and other vestiges of the 13th- to 16th-century capital of the Muslim nawabs. Little remains from the 7th- to 12th-century pre-Muslim period, when Gaur was the capital of the successive Buddhist Pala and Hindu Sena dynasties.

Wander through the ruins of the impressive **Baradwari Mosque** and the intact arcaded aisle of its corridor, or beneath the fortress-like gateway of **Dakhil Darwaza** (1425). The **Qadam Rasul Mosque** enshrines the flat footprint of the Prophet Mohammed. The adjacent **tomb of Fateh Khan** (1707) startlingly informs you that its occupant 'vomited blood and died on this spot'. Remnants of colourful enamel cling to the **Chamkan Mosque** and the **Gumti Gate** nearby.

In Pandua (30km north of Malda) are the vast ruins of the 14th-century **Adina Masjid**, once India's largest mosque. Within a section of arched and domed bays sits the tomb of Sikander Shah (r 1364–79), the builder of this mosque. About 2km away is the **Eklakhi Mausoleum**, so called because it cost ₹1 lakh (₹100,000) to build.

The monuments are spread throughout Gaur and Pandua along some of the worst roads in India; it's worth hiring a taxi from Malda for half a day (₹1200).

WEST BENGAL HILLS

Siliguri & New Jalpaiguri

☏0353 / POP 656,000 / ELEV 120M

The crowded and noisy transport hub encompassing the twin towns of Siliguri and New Jalpaiguri (NJP) is the jumping-off point for Darjeeling, Kalimpong, Sikkim, the northeast states, eastern Nepal and Bhutan. There's little to see here: for most travellers, Siliguri is an overnight transit point to cooler climes.

Most of Siliguri's hotels, restaurants and services are spread along Tenzing Norgay Rd, better known as Hill Cart Rd. NJP Station Rd leads southward to NJP station, while branching northeastward off Hill Cart Rd are Siliguri's other main streets, Sevoke and Bidhan Rds, the latter hiding the city's most interesting bazaars.

🛏 Sleeping

Hotel Conclave HOTEL $$
(☏2516144; www.hotelconclave.com; Hill Cart Rd; s/d from ₹750/900; ❄) Unhelpful staff can't

detract from this solid contemporary hotel, conveniently close to all the transport options. Quality mattresses, artwork on the walls and a glass elevator add a touch of class. The rooms are spotless and downstairs is the excellent **Eminent Restaurant** (mains ₹70-140). Road-facing luxury rooms can be noisy. Pricier rooms come with breakfast.

Conclave Lodge HOTEL $
(☏2514102; Hill Cart Rd; s/d without bathroom ₹200/350, s/d/tr with bathroom ₹332/500/611) Tucked away behind the more visible Hotel Conclave, this central lodge is the best budget option, with clean, quiet and high-ceilinged rooms with TV and hot water bathrooms.

Hotel Sinclairs HOTEL $$$
(☏2517674; www.sinclairshotels.com; off NH31; d from ₹3800; ❄ 🏊 🛜) This comfortable three-star hotel escapes the noise of Hill Cart Rd, 1km north of the bus terminal. The rooms are spacious and there's an excellent restaurant-cum-bar and the chance to dive into a cool, clean pool.

Cindrella Hotel HOTEL $$$
(☏2544130; 3rd Mile, Sevoke Rd; www.cindrella-hotels.com; s/d incl breakfast from ₹3600/4000; ❄ 🛜 🏊) The top place in town offers comfortable rather than luxurious rooms, with a bar, small gym and pool (closed Nov-Feb), grassy lawns, and free wi-fi throughout. It's 3km northeast of the centre.

Hotel Himalayan Regency HOTEL $$
(☏6502955; Hill Cart Rd; s/d from ₹500/600, with AC from ₹1200; ❄) Comfortable rooms with big clean bathrooms. Thought has gone into the design and colour scheme, though apparently by someone suffering from an extreme form of colour blindness.

Hotel Mount View HOTEL $
(☏2512919; Hill Cart Rd; d from ₹500) Under renovation after a change of owner at the time of research, but worth a look; located next to Khana Khazana restaurant.

🍴 Eating

TOP CHOICE **Khana Khazana** MULTICUISINE $
(Hill Cart Rd; mains ₹60-120) The secluded outdoor area here offers merciful relief from the chaos outside. The extensive menu ranges from Chinese and South Indian specials to Mumbai street snacks, and includes plenty of vegetarian options. Our mildly-spiced chicken *mumtaz* was so good we ordered it three times.

Sartaj INDIAN **$$**

(Hill Cart Rd; mains ₹70-140; ❄) A sophisticated and cool (literally – the AC is heaven) bar-restaurant with a huge range: first-rate North Indian tandooris and curries, good Continental options and top-notch service.

❶ Information

Internet Access

iWay (Hill Cart Rd; per hr ₹40; ⊙9am-9pm) A tangerine dream, with bright-orange interior. It's half-hidden behind a shop, 1km southeast of the bus terminal.

Medical Services

Sadar Hospital (☎2436526; Hospital Rd)

Money

Bagdogra Airport has a money changer with decent rates but a fairly high commission.

Delhi Hotel (Hill Cart Rd; ⊙9am-7pm) Currency and travellers cheques exchanged, opposite the bus station; ₹25 tax per transaction.

Multi Money (1st fl, 143 Hill Cart Rd; ⊙10am-6.30pm Mon-Sat) Exchanges cash only; next to Standard Chartered Bank.

Standard Chartered Bank (144 Hill Cart Rd) One of several ATMs on Hill Cart Rd.

Tourist Information

Sikkim Tourist Office (SNT Terminal, Hill Cart Rd; ⊙10am-5pm) Issues permits for Sikkim on the spot. Bring copies of your passport, visa and one passport-sized photo.

West Bengal Tourist Office (☎2511974; www.westbengaltourism.gov.in; Hill Cart Rd; ⊙10am-5pm Mon-Fri) Can book accommodation for Jaldhapara Wildlife Sanctuary, including forestry lodges. Less helpful information desks are at Bagdogra Airport and NJP train station.

Travel Agencies

Private transport booking agencies line Hill Cart Rd.

Help Tourism (☎2433683; www.helptourism.com, www.helptourism.net; 143 Hill Cart Rd; ✉) A recommended agency with a strong environmental and community-development focus, including voluntourism. It has links to homestays and lodges around the hills, and its tour and trekking packages get rave reviews.

Tourist Service Agency (☎2531959; tsaslg@sanchar net.in; Pradhan Nagar Rd) Can book Jaldhapara accommodation, including forest lodges. It's close to the Delhi Hotel.

❶ Getting There & Away

Air

Bagdogra Airport is 12km west of Siliguri. Check websites for fares, which vary widely. Some flights to Delhi are direct, while others go via Guwahati.

Air India (☎2511495; www.airindia.in; Hill Cart Rd; ⊙10am-1pm & 1.45-4.30pm Mon-Sat) Five weekly to Kolkata and Delhi, three to Guwahati.

Go Air (☎1800 222111; www.goair.in) Daily to Delhi, three weekly to Guwahati.

Jet Airways (☎2538001; www.jetairways.com; Hill Cart Rd; ⊙9am-5.30pm Mon-Sat) Daily to Kolkata and Delhi, four weekly to Guwahati.

Kingfisher Airlines (☎1800 2093030; www.flykingfisher.com) Daily to Kolkata and Delhi, three weekly to Guwahati.

Spice Jet (☎1800 1803333; www.spicejet.com) Daily to Kolkata (direct) and Delhi (some direct, some via Guwahati/Kolkata).

Five-seater helicopters (₹2200, 30 minutes, 10kg luggage limit) travel daily from Bagdogra to Gangtok at 2.30pm in good weather. You need to book by phone through **Sikkim Tourism Development Corporation** (☎03592-203960; see p535) in Gangtok.

Bus

Most North Bengal State Transport Corporation (NBSTC) buses leave from **Tenzing Norgay Central Bus Terminal** (Hill Cart Rd), as do many private buses plying the same routes. Private bus companies line the entrance.

NBSTC buses include frequent buses to Malda (₹120, 6½ hours) and Madarihat (see p484), plus a daily service to Kolkata (₹266, 7pm). Assam State Transportation Corporation runs a daily 4pm bus to Guwahati (₹353, 12 hours).

For Patna (₹275, 12 hours, departs 6pm) try **Gupta Travels**, just outside the bus station. Deluxe Volvo buses for Kolkata (₹900, 11 hours) leave around 7pm from this and many other agencies.

Sikkim Nationalised Transport (SNT) buses to Gangtok (₹115-210, 4½ hours) leave at 7.30am, 11.30am, 12.30pm and 1.30pm from the **SNT terminal** (Hill Cart Rd), 250m south of the bus terminal. The 11.30am departure is normally aircon (₹220). Arrange your permit in advance at the Sikkim Tourist Office next door (p483).

Jeep

A faster and more comfortable way of getting around the hills is by share jeep. There are a number of jeep stands lining Hill Cart Rd: for Darjeeling (₹90, three hours), Kurseong (₹50, 1½ hours) or Mirik (₹60, 2½ hours), look around opposite the bus terminal or outside the Conclave Hotel; for Kalimpong (₹80, 2½ hours) there's a stand on Sevoke Rd (take an autoricksaw); and for Gangtok (₹140, four hours) jeeps leave from next to the SNT terminal until around 2pm. Share and charter jeeps for all these destinations also leave straight from NJP train station.

Chartering a jeep privately costs roughly 10 times that of a shared ticket. An option for XL-sized Westerners is to pay for and occupy the front three seats next to the driver.

A prepaid taxi stand at Bagdogra Airport offers fixed fares to Darjeeling (₹1375-1475), Mirik (₹880), Kakarbhitta (₹400) and even Bhadrapur in Nepal (₹835), thus bypassing Siliguri completely. It's not difficult to find other people to share the cost.

Train

There's a **train booking office** (☎2537333; cnr Hospital & Bidhan Rds; ◷8-11am, 11.30am-2pm & 2.15-8pm Mon-Sat, to 2pm Sun) in Siliguri.

Darjeeling Mail 2344 The fastest of the four daily services to Kolkata (sleeper/3AC ₹264/695, 10 hours, departs 8pm), via Malda.

Haldibari Koaa SF Express 2364 A better option for Malda (2nd class/chair ₹108/343, 3½ hours, departing 9.55am Wednesday, Friday and Saturday).

North East Express 2505 Fast to Delhi (sleeper/3AC ₹458/1214, 27 hours, departs 5.15pm), via Patna (₹229/587, 11 hours).

Rajdhani Express 2435 (2AC/3AC ₹2194/1735, 21 hours, departs 12.05pm) Fastest service to Delhi.

North East Express 2506 For Guwahati (sleeper/3AC ₹228/569, eight hours, departs 8.40am).

TOY TRAIN The diesel toy train climbs the 88km from New Jalpaiguri to Darjeeling in eight long hours (2nd/1st class ₹42/247, departs 9am). It's wise to make reservations two to three days in advance. It's also possible to board the train at Siliguri Jct station, which is just behind the Tenzing Norgay Bus Terminal on Hill Cart Rd. The line was under repair in 2011 after a series of landslides but should reopen soon.

If steam is your passion, catch the steam version to Darjeeling from Kurseong (p487).

ⓘ Getting Around

From the bus terminal to NJP train station a taxi/autorickshaw costs ₹200/90, while cycle-rickshaws charge ₹50 for the 35-minute trip. Taxis/autorickshaws between Bagdogra Airport and Siliguri cost ₹350/200.

Jaldhapara Wildlife Sanctuary

☎03563 / ELEV 60M

This little-visited **sanctuary** (☎262239; Indian/foreigner ₹50/200, camera/video ₹50/500;

CROSSING INTO BANGLADESH, BHUTAN & NEPAL

To/From Bangladesh

A number of private agencies in Siliguri, including Shyamoli (☎9932628243; Hotel Central Plaza complex, Hill Cart Rd) run a daily AC bus direct to Dhaka (₹800, 16 hours), departing at 1.30pm. You'll need to complete border formalities at Chengrabandha.

Regular buses go from the Tenzing Norgay Central Bus Terminal to Chengrabandha (₹42) starting from 7.30am. The border post is open from 8am to 6pm daily. From near the border post you can catch buses on to Rangpur, Bogra and Dhaka. Visas for Bangladesh can be obtained in Kolkata and New Delhi (see p1176).

To/From Bhutan

Bhutan Transport Services run three daily buses from just outside the central bus terminal to Phuentsholing (₹75, departs 7.15am, noon and 2pm), and there are many more local buses to Jaigaon on the Indian side of the border, where you clear Indian immigration. Non-Indian nationals need visa clearance from a Bhutanese tour operator to enter Bhutan. See www.tourism.gov.bt and Lonely Planet's *Bhutan* for details.

To/From Nepal

For Nepal, local buses pass the Tenzing Norgay Central Bus Terminal every 15 minutes for the border town of Panitanki (₹20, one hour). Share jeeps to Kakarbhitta (₹70) are readily available in Siliguri. The Indian border post in Panitanki is officially open 24 hours and the Nepali post in Kakarbhitta is open from 7am to 7pm. Onward from Kakarbhitta there are numerous buses to Kathmandu (17 hours) and other destinations. Bhadrapur Airport, 23km southwest of Kakarbhitta, has regular flights to Kathmandu (US$147) on Yeti Airlines (www.yetiairlines.com), Buddha Air (www.buddhaair.com) or Agni Air (www.agniair.com). Visas for Nepal can be obtained at the border (bring two passport photos), in Kolkata or New Delhi (see p1177).

⊘mid-Sep–mid-Jun) protects 114 sq km of lush forests and grasslands along the Torsa River and is a refuge for over 50 Indian one-horned rhinoceros (*Rhinoceros unicornis*).

The best time to visit is mid-October to May, particularly March and April when wild elephants, deer and tigers (rarely seen) are attracted by new grass growth. Your best chance of spotting a rhino is on an **elephant ride** (Indian/foreigner ₹200/600 per hr; ⊙5-8am), though these lumbering safaris are often booked out by the tourist lodges. Even if you are staying at Jaldaphara Tourist Lodge for a night you are not guaranteed a ride, as full occupancy is double that of their daily elephant quota.

Jeep safaris (4/8 passengers ₹1860/2260, 40% less for Indians) operate in the early morning and afternoon and stop at viewing platforms, but again these can be hard to arrange unless you are on a tour.

The West Bengal tourist offices in Kolkata (p469) and Siliguri (p483) organise overnight **tours** (per person Indian/foreigner ₹4200/4500; ⊙departs 10am Sat, returns 5pm Sun) from Siliguri to Jaldaphara, which include an elephant ride, transport, accommodation at the Hollong Tourist Lodge and all meals.

Mithun of **Wild Planet Travel Desk** (☎9735028733; easthimalayan3@yahoo.com) and Hotel Relax can often book accommodation and elephant rides when no-one else can and is probably your best option for a DIY trip. Budget travellers should bear in mind that an hour-long elephant ride is probably going to end up costing a minimum US$40 per person, after all costs are added in.

Bring mosquito repellent.

🛏 Sleeping & Eating

The two lodges should be booked well in advance through the West Bengal Tourist Office in Siliguri, Darjeeling or Kolkata, or online at www.westbengaltourism.gov.in. They don't take direct bookings.

Hollong Tourist Lodge   JUNGLE LODGE **$$**
(☎262228; d ₹2000, plus compulsory breakfast & dinner ₹300 per person) This wooden forestry lodge right in the heart of the park is easily the best place to stay, though booking one of the six rooms can be a real challenge. You can spot animals right from the verandah and are guaranteed a morning elephant ride. Book up to three months in advance.

Jaldhapara Tourist Lodge   HOTEL **$$**
(☎262230; Madarihat; d ₹1600, with AC ₹2200-3000; ❇) This functional WBTDC hotel is just outside the park in Madarihat town and has

rooms in wooden and concrete blocks or in new cottages. All meals are included in the room rates, so singles get a 25% discount.

Hotel Relax   HOTEL **$**
(☎262304; Madarihat; d ₹500) The Relax is the best private option, opposite the Jaldhapara Tourist Lodge, but is still quite simple, with private bathrooms (hot water in buckets ₹10) and thundering road noise. Deluxe rooms were under construction at time of research. Simple set meals are available for ₹50.

ℹ Getting There & Away

Jaldhapara is 124km east of Siliguri. Local buses run every hour or so between Siliguri and Madarihat (₹66, four hours). There are also daily mail trains (unreserved seat ₹38, three to four hours), leaving Siliguri at 6am and 5.35pm, returning from Madarihat at 7am and 1.30pm.

From Madarihat to the park headquarters at Hollong is 7km. A return taxi costs ₹400, including waiting time, plus you'll also have to pay the ₹150 vehicle entry and parking fees.

Mirik

🕿0354 / POP 9180 / ELEV 1770M

Nestled near the Nepal border, halfway between Siliguri and Darjeeling, the low-profile hill station of Mirik is surrounded by an undulating carpet of tea estates, orange orchards, cardamom plantations and forests of tall, dark Japanese cedars. It has a quiet lakeside charm and relaxed vibe that make it quite different from Darjeeling or Kalimpong.

⊙ Sights & Activities

Mirik is centred on the artificial murky-coloured Sumendu Lake and there's a pleasant walk around its 3.5km circumference.

Pedal boats (per 30min ₹42) can be hired near the central bridge, which is also the place for **pony rides** (half/full round-the-lake trips ₹80/160).

Perched high above Mirik, the large Kagyud-school **Bokar Gompa** is very active. Look for the unusually modern Wheel of Life mural, depicting cars, soldiers and even joggers! It's a bracing walk up Monastery Rd from opposite Hotel Jagjeet.

A short walk from the monastery is the Rameetay Dara viewpoint, though you'll get better Himalayan views from the helipad beside Swiss Cottage, on a hilltop on the southwest corner of the lake.

For a great two-hour walk, take a Darjeeling-bound jeep 8km out of town and walk back past a charming Dr Seuss landscape of conical-hilled tea estates.

🛏 Sleeping & Eating

Mirik has good value accommodation. All the places here are within 100m of each other in the lakeside settlement known as Krishnanagar.

Buddha Lodge GUESTHOUSE $
(📞9609982057; r ₹250-450) The five spotless, comfy and carpeted rooms with private hot water bathrooms are the best value in Mirik; the bright upstairs rooms are larger with appealing wood panelling and tiled bathrooms.

Hotel Ratnagiri HOTEL $$
(📞9832010013; www.hotelratnagiri.com; d ₹400-1000, ste ₹2000) There are lots of different rooms here, the best being the warm, wood-panelled upstairs doubles with cute sloping ceilings. Some rooms have balconies and views of Sumendu Lake; all have TV and geyser. The pleasant garden **restaurant** (mains ₹30 to ₹180) out back offers such exotic fare as lasagne and sizzlers.

Hotel Jagjeet HOTEL $$
(📞2243231; www.jagjeethotel.com; d ₹1300-2400) The best hotel in town has a wide variety of rooms. The super-deluxe options (₹1800) come with balconies, while the luxury rooms (₹2400) are surprisingly sleek and stylish. The cheapest rooms are in the basement. The restaurant-bar (mains ₹100 to ₹175) is easily the best in town, serving really excellent thalis. Toothsome sweets, including *barfi* (fudge-like sweet), are sold at a separate counter.

Lodge Ashirvad GUESTHOUSE $
(📞2243272; s ₹200, d ₹350-450) A friendly, family-run budget hotel down a lane just off the main road. The rooms are simple with very thin, but clean, mattresses. Only the priciest rooms have geysers; a bucket of hot water costs ₹15.

Lohit Sagar Restaurant INDIAN $
(mains ₹30-80; ☺breakfast & lunch) Beside the taxi stand, and near the lake, is this pure-veg cafeteria-type place catering to lakeside day trippers, with good snacks and South Indian favourites.

ℹ Information

Ashirvard Lodge has an attached **internet cafe** (per hr ₹30). There are no money-changing facilities but both Axis Bank and the State Bank of India have ATMs next to Hotel Jagjeet.

ℹ Getting There & Away

Share jeeps depart every 30 minutes between 6am and 3.40pm to Siliguri (₹60, 2½ hours) and hourly to Darjeeling (₹60, 2½ hours). Jeeps to Kurseong (₹60, three hours) run in the early morning and at 3pm.

Kurseong

📞0354 / POP 40,100 / ELEV 1460M

Kurseong, 32km south of Darjeeling, is the little sister of (and quiet alternative to) the Queen of the Hills further up the track. Its name derives from the Lepcha word *kurson-rip*, a reference to the small white orchid prolific in this area. Surrounded by manicured tea estates, it is the southern terminus for the charming steam-powered toy trains of the Darjeeling Himalayan Railway.

Hill Cart Rd (Tenzing Norgay Rd) – the noisy, shop-lined main thoroughfare from Siliguri to Darjeeling – and its remarkably close shadow, the railway line, wind through town.

There are numerous good walks in the area, including one to Eagle's Crag (2km return) that affords splendid views down the Teesta Valley and the steamy plains to the south.

Makaibari TEA ESTATE
(📞2330181; Pankhabari Rd; www.makaibari.com; ☺Tue-Sat) Anyone interested in tea should visit this organic and biodynamic tea estate. The factory is open to visitors and in between the huge sorting and drying machines and the fields of green bushes you may just run into the owner, local tea guru Rajah Banerjee. Mornings are the best time to see the production process.

The estate is 4km below Kurseong along Pankhabari Rd, and 1km below Cochrane Place. A taxi here costs ₹100 to ₹150, or it's a pleasant downhill walk (it's much steeper coming back so take a shared taxi from Cochrane Place). En route, the lushly overgrown old graveyard at St Andrews is poignant reminders of the tea-planter era.

Makaibari also runs a homestay and volunteer program (www.volmakaibari.org; see p41) and offers courses for tea professionals.

🛏 Sleeping & Eating

Cochrane Place BOUTIQUE HOTEL $$
(📞2330703; www.imperialchai.com; 132 Pankhabari Rd; s/d from ₹2250/2650; @) With 360-degree

views over tea plantations, distant Himalayan peaks and the twinkling lights of Siliguri, this quirky, charming boutique hotel is a destination in its own right. The 31 rooms are individually decorated with divans and antiques and have either a view or a balcony. Delicious meals and tea tastings are available, making it a good lunch stop if you have your own transport. The hotel is wheelchair-friendly, can provide Bagdogra Airport and NJP train station pick-up and offers guided village and tea estate walks, as well as massage and beauty treatments.

Kurseong Tourist Lodge HOTEL **$$**
(✆2345608; Hill Cart Rd; d ₹1200-1500) This old-fashioned, government-run lodge has inviting wood-lined rooms that feature valley views. The toy train whistles past the popular cafe, where you can snack on *momos* (Tibetan dumplings), or you can enjoy a meal at its scenic **restaurant** (mains ₹50 to ₹115). Look for the much-photographed 'Hurry burry spoils the curry' traffic sign across the road.

❶ Getting There & Away

Numerous share jeeps run to Darjeeling (₹50, 1½ hours), Siliguri (₹50, 1½ hours), Kalimpong (₹110, 3½ to four hours) and Mirik (₹80, 2½ hours).

The Darjeeling Himalayan Railway's steam toy train to Darjeeling (9D; 2nd/1st class ₹22/144, three hours) leaves at 3pm, while the diesel version (1D; originating at New Jalpaiguri) departs around 1.35pm. A diesel train (originating in Darjeeling) to Siliguri (2D; 2nd/1st class ₹44/247, four hours) departs at 12.05pm.

Darjeeling

✆0354 / POP 109,160 / ELEV 2135M

Spread in ribbons over a steep mountain ridge, surrounded by emerald-green tea plantations and with a backdrop of jagged white Himalayan peaks floating over distant clouds, the archetypal hill station of Darjeeling is rightly West Bengal's premier attraction. When you aren't gazing at Khangchendzonga (8598m), you can explore colonial-era buildings, visit Buddhist monasteries and spot snow leopards and red pandas at the nearby zoo. The steep narrow streets bustle with an array of Himalayan faces from Sikkim, Bhutan, Nepal and Tibet and when energies start to flag a good, steaming Darjeeling brew is never far away.

Most tourists visit after the monsoon (October and November) and during spring (mid-March to the end of May) when skies

are dry, panoramas are clear and temperatures are pleasant. Tourist attractions and other establishments often extend their hours during these periods (specified as 'high season' in the following reviews), although they are not set in stone so check ahead.

Darjeeling sprawls over a west-facing slope in a confusing web of interconnecting roads and steep flights of steps. The two main squares are Chowrasta, near the top of town, and Clubside junction, which are linked by pedestrianised Nehru Rd (aka the Mall), the main shopping street. Hill Cart Rd (aka Tenzing Norgay Rd) runs the length of the bustling lower bazaar and is Darjeeling's major vehicle thoroughfare.

History

This area belonged to the Buddhist chogyals (kings) of Sikkim until 1780, when it was annexed by the invading Gurkhas from Nepal. The East India Company gained control of the region in 1816 then returned most of the lands back to Sikkim in exchange for British control over any future border disputes.

During one such dispute in 1828, two British officers stumbled across the Dorje Ling monastery, on a tranquil forested ridge, and passed word to Kolkata (Calcutta) that it would be a perfect site for a sanatorium; they were sure to have also mentioned its strategic military importance in the region. The chogyal of Sikkim (still grateful for the return of his kingdom) happily agreed to lease the uninhabited land to the East India Company for the annual fee of £3000. In 1835 the hill station of Darjeeling (Dorje Ling) was born and the first tea bushes were planted that same year.

Forest gradually made way for colonial houses and tea plantations, and by 1857 the population of Darjeeling reached 10,000, mainly because of a massive influx of Gurkha labourers from Nepal.

After Independence, the Gurkhas became the main political force in Darjeeling and friction with the state government led to calls for a separate state of Gorkhaland in the 1980s. In 1986, violence and riots orchestrated by the Gurkha National Liberation Front (GNLF) brought Darjeeling to a standstill, leading to the Darjeeling Gorkha Hill Council (DGHC) being given a large measure of autonomy from the state government.

Calls for full secession have continued, and in 2007 the political party Gorkha Janmukti Morcha (GJM), headed by Bimal Gurung, was formed out of the GNLF. It has

WEST BENGAL & DARJEELING WEST BENGAL HILLS

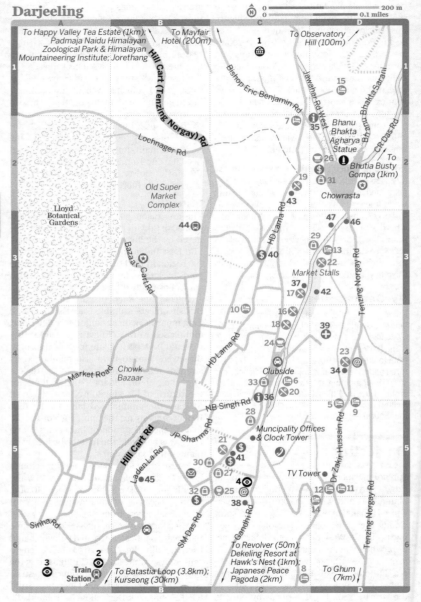

encouraged people to agitate for a separate state of Gorkhaland by using tactics ranging from strikes (see p497) and nonpayment of telephone bills and taxes to active support for the Gurkha contestant on *Indian Idol* (who eventually won season three).

⊙ Sights

Tiger Hill VIEWPOINT

To watch the dawn light break over a spectacular 250km stretch of Himalayan horizon, including Everest (8848m), Lhotse (8501m), Makalu (8475m) to the far west,

WEST BENGAL & DARJEELING DARJEELING

rise early and get to Tiger Hill (2590m), 11km south of Darjeeling, above Ghum.

The sunrise over the Himalaya from here has become a major tourist attraction, with convoys of jeeps leaving Darjeeling for Tiger Hill every morning around 4.30am. At the summit, you can either pay ₹10 to stand in the pavilion grounds, or buy a ticket for one of the heated lounges in the pavilion (₹20 to ₹40). It can be a real bunfight, even outside of the high season, with crowds of hundreds jostling for the best viewing spots.

Organised sunrise trips (usually with a detour to Batastia Loop on the way back) can be booked through a travel agency or directly with jeep drivers at the Clubside taxi stand. It's also possible to jump on a jeep going to Tiger Hill from along Gandhi or Laden La Rds between 4am and 4.30am, allowing you to check whether skies are clear before you go. Return trips cost around ₹80 per person or ₹600-800 for a vehicle.

One excellent idea is to take the jeep one way to Tiger Hill (or back to Ghum) and then spend the morning/day visiting the

DON'T MISS

KHANGCHENDZONGA VIEWS

The Himalayan skyline is a major attraction in Darjeeling. The skyline is dominated by Khangchendzonga, India's highest peak and the world's third-highest mountain (until 1852 it was thought to be the world's highest). The name 'Khangchendzonga' is derived from the Tibetan words for 'great five-peaked snow fortress'. On either side of the main massif are Kabru (7338m), Jannu (7710m) and Pandim (6691m), all serious peaks in their own right.

Apart from popular dawn views from Tiger Hill, an early morning stroll around Bhanu Bhakta Sarani, which runs from Chowrasta around the north side of Observatory Hill, offers several stunning viewpoints.

monasteries of Ghum before wandering back to Darjeeling. You can take either the busy main road or the much quieter Tenzing Norgay Rd, via Alu Bari, (1½ hrs), which despite the lack of mountain views also makes a nice cycling route.

Happy Valley Tea Estate   TEA ESTATE
(Pamphawati Gurungni Rd; ⊙8am-4pm Mon-Sat) This tea estate below Hill Cart Rd, is worth visiting when the plucking and processing are in progress. An employee will walk you through the aromatic factory and its various processes before politely demanding a tip – ₹20 from each visitor is appropriate. Take the marked turn-off about 1km northwest of town on Hill Cart Rd.

Observatory Hill   SACRED SITE
Sacred to both Buddhists and Hindus, this hill was the site of the original Dorje Ling monastery that gave the town its name. Today, devotees come to a temple in a small cave, below the crest of the hill, to honour Mahakala, a Buddhist deity and an angry form of the Hindu god Shiva. The summit is marked by several shrines, a flurry of colourful prayer flags and the ringing notes from numerous devotional bells. A path leading up to the hill through giant Japanese cedars starts about 300m along Bhanu Bhakta Sarani from Chowrasta; watch out for marauding monkeys. Disappointingly, there are no mountain views.

Gompas   MONASTERIES
Darjeeling and Ghum are home to a number of fascinating Buddhist monasteries. The most scenic is **Bhutia Busty Gompa**, with Khangchendzonga providing a spectacular backdrop. Originally on Observatory Hill, it was rebuilt in its present lower location by the chogyals of Sikkim in the 19th century. It houses fine murals depicting the life of Buddha. To get here, follow CR Das Rd

steeply downhill for five minutes from Chowrasta Square, past a trinity of colourful Buddhist rock carvings. Climbing back up is a 20-minute slog.

Yiga Choling Gompa (Ghum; camera per photo ₹10), the region's most famous monastery, has wonderful old murals and is home to 30 monks of the Gelugpa (yellow-hat) school. Built in 1850, it enshrines a 5m-high statue of Jampa (Maitreya, or 'Future Buddha') and 300 beautifully bound Tibetan texts. It's just west of Ghum, about a 10-minute walk off Hill Cart Rd.

Other gompas of interest nearby include the fortress-like **Sakya Guru Gompa**, which has *pujas* (prayers) between 5.30am and 7.30am (useful if returning from a dawn visit to Tiger Hill). The very active **Samten Choling Gompa**, just downhill, has the largest Buddha statue in West Bengal, a memorial chorten dedicated to German mystic Lama Govinda and even a small cafe. All three gompas are within 10 minutes' walk of each other on Hill Cart Rd and can be reached by share jeep or train from Darjeeling (₹15); some people organise to visit on the way back from Tiger Hill.

About halfway between Ghum and Darjeeling is the huge **Druk Sangak Choling Gompa**, also known as Dali Gompa, inaugurated by the Dalai Lama in 1993. Known for its vibrant frescoes, it is home to 300 Himalayan monks who study philosophy, literature, astronomy, meditation, dance and music.

Japanese Peace Pagoda   BUDDHIST SIGHT
Perched on a hillside at the end of AJC Bose Rd, this gleaming white **pagoda** (⊙*pujas* 4.30-6am & 4.30-6.30pm) is one of more than 70 pagodas built by the Japanese Buddhist Nipponzan Myohoji organisation around the world. Drumming resonates through the forested grounds during their daily *pujas*.

It's a pleasant, gentle 30-minute uphill walk from Clubside along Gandhi and AJC Bose Rds, past the implausible-sounding Institute of Astroparticle Physics and Space Science.

Padmaja Naidu Himalayan Zoological Park
ZOO

(admission incl Himalayan Mountaineering Institute Indian/foreigner ₹40/100; ☺8.30am-5.30pm Fri-Wed, ticket counter closes 4pm) This zoo, one of India's best, was established in 1958 to study, conserve and preserve Himalayan fauna. Housed within the rocky and forested environment are Himalayan megafauna such as musk deer, red pandas and Tibetan wolves. The zoo, and its attached snow leopard-breeding centre, are home to the world's largest single captive population of snow leopards.

The zoo is a pleasant 20-minute downhill walk down from Chowrasta along Jawahar Rd West; alternatively, take a share jeep (₹10, about 10 minutes) or a private taxi (₹70) from the Chowk Bazaar bus/jeep station.

Himalayan Mountaineering Institute
MUSEUM

(HMI; ☏2254087; www.hmi-darjeeling.com; admission incl zoo Indian/foreigner ₹40/100; ☺8.30am-4.30pm Fri-Wed) Tucked away within the grounds of the zoo, this prestigious mountaineering institute was founded in 1954 and has provided training for some of India's leading mountaineers. Within the complex is the fascinating **Everest Museum**, with fascinating detail from the 1922 and 1924 Everest expeditions, which both set off from Darjeeling. Look for the Carl Zeiss telescope presented by Adolf Hitler to the head of the Nepali army.

Just beside the museum, near the spot where Tenzing Norgay was cremated, stands the **Tenzing statue**. The intrepid Everest summiteer lived in Darjeeling for most of his life and was the director of the institute for many years.

Various mountaineering courses are offered here; see p493 for more information.

Tibetan Refugee Self-Help Centre
MUSEUM

(Lebong Cart Rd; ☺dawn-dusk Mon-Sat) Established in 1959, this refugee centre comprises a home for the aged, school, orphanage, clinic, gompa and craft workshops that produce carpets, woodcarvings, leather work and woollen items. There's also an interesting, politically charged **photographic exhibition** portraying the establishment and workings of the centre.

The refugees are welcoming, so wander through the workshops. The handicrafts are for sale in the **showroom** (☏2252552; ☺9am-5.30pm), where proceeds go straight back into the Tibetan community. See p496 for details regarding Tibetan carpets.

The quickest way to reach the centre is to walk downhill from the north side of Bhanu Bhakta Sarani; take the alley down beside the Hotel Dolphin. The 20-minute walk requires a steep climb back. A chartered taxi via North Point costs around ₹300 return.

DON'T MISS

THE TOY TRAIN

The **Darjeeling Himalayan Railway**, known affectionately as the toy train, made its first journey along its precipice-topping, 2ft-wide tracks in September 1881 and is one of the few hill railways still operating in India. The panting train passes within feet of local storefronts as it weaves in and out of the main road, bringing traffic to a standstill and tooting its whistle incessantly for almost the entire trip. The train has been a Unesco World Heritage Site since 1999.

There is a daily steam service to Kurseong and a diesel train to NJP train station. It's an exhausting seven to eight-hour haul to/from NJP, so if you simply want to experience the train, consider the steam train to/from Kurseong.

During the high season there are also joy rides (₹240) that leave Darjeeling at 10.40am (14D), 1.20pm (16D) and 4pm (18D) for a two-hour steam-powered return trip. The service stops for half an hour in Ghum, India's highest railway station, to visit the small **railway museum** (admission ₹20; 10am-1pm, 2-4pm) and pauses on the way back at the scenic Batastia Loop (see p492). For a budget taste of the train take the 10.15am passenger service to Ghum.

Book at least a day ahead at the **train station** (Hill Cart Rd), or online at www.irctc .co.in. For more on the service and efforts to maintain it, see www.dhrs.org.

TEA TOURISM

We spoke to Makaibari Tea Estate and Nathmull's, two of the Darjeeling region's most experienced tea companies, for some tips on the best places to indulge in the area's most famous export.

Visit The easiest places to learn about tea production are **Makaibari Estate** in Kurseong and **Happy Valley** outside Darjeeling. March to May is the busiest time, but occasional plucking also occurs from June to November. Outside of high season there's no plucking on Sunday, which means most of the machinery isn't working on Monday.

Stay Overnight with a tea pickers family at a **homestay** (☏9832447774; www.volmakaibari.org; per person incl food ₹600) at Makaibari Estate and you'll get to join your hosts for a morning's work in the tea bushes. Pick your own leaves, watch them being processed and then return home with a batch of your very own hand-plucked Darjeeling tea. How's that for a personalised gift!

Drink Where better to sip a cup of Darjeeling tea? You can sample different grades of black, white and green teas by the cup at **Sunset Lounge** (p495) and **House of Tea** (p495). The pukka afternoon tea at the **Windamere Hotel** (₹375; ☉4-6pm) is a joy for aficionados of all things colonial, with shortcake, scones, cheese and pickle sandwiches and brews from the Castleton Tea Estate.

Splash Out Accommodation doesn't get any more exclusive than top-end **Glenburn** (www.glenburnteaestate.com; s/d ₹11,000/14,000), between Darjeeling and Kurseong, a working tea estate/resort that boasts five staff for every guest. A stay at Glenburn is rumoured to have given director Wes Anderson inspiration for his film *The Darjeeling Limited*.

Lloyd Botanical Gardens   BOTANICAL GARDENS
(☏2252358; admission free; ☉8am-4.30pm) These pleasant gardens contain an impressive collection of Himalayan plants, most famously orchids and rhododendrons, as well as temperate trees from around the world. Follow the signs along Lochnager Rd from the Chowk Bazaar bus/jeep station, until the hum of cicadas replaces the honking of jeeps. A map is posted at the office at the top of the park.

Batastia Loop   MEMORIAL
If you're travelling on the toy train, or walking back from Tiger Hill, look out for this famous railway loop and the sobering **Gorkha war memorial** (admission ₹10; ☉dawn-dusk). Some tours stop here after the sunrise trip at Tiger Hill; the views are almost as good, and the atmosphere much more serene.

Bengal Natural History Museum   MUSEUM
(Bishop Eric Benjamin Rd; adult ₹10; ☉9am-5pm) Established in 1903, this minor sight houses a moth-eaten collection of Himalayan and Bengali species, hidden away in a compound just off Bishop Eric Benjamin Rd. The giant leeches and horrific baby animals pickled in jars are guaranteed to provoke a shudder.

Dhirdham Mandir   HINDU TEMPLE
The most conspicuous Hindu temple in Darjeeling is a replica of the famous Pashupatinath Temple in Kathmandu. It's easy to find – just below the Darjeeling train station. There's a great view over Darjeeling from its grounds.

🏃 Activities

See p498 for information on treks around Darjeeling.

White-Water Rafting   RAFTING
At the time of writing, white-water rafting trips on the Teesta River from Teesta Bazaar along the road to Kalimpong, had been suspended following a fatal accident. Check with the DGHC to see if trips have resumed.

Expect scenic/adventure trips to cost around ₹450/800 per person, with a minimum of four people. Transport will cost another ₹1500 per jeep, or take a shared jeep for Gangtok and get off at Teesta Bazaar. The friendly DGHC-run **Chitrey Wayside Inn** (☏9434862561; dm/d ₹150/500), 1.5km from the bazaar, overlooks the Teesta River.

Private companies, such as Samsara Tours, Travels & Treks (p497), offer similar routes for a minimum of four people; prices include lunch and transport.

The rapids are graded from Grade II to Grade IV, though dam construction has limited runs in recent years. The best times for rafting are September to November and March to June.

Pony Rides   HORSE RIDING
From Chowrasta, children can take a ride around Observatory Hill for ₹100, or through tea estates to visit a monastery for ₹200 per hour.

🍴 Courses

Language
Beginner and advanced lessons in written and spoken Tibetan are offered at the **Manjushree Centre of Tibetan Culture** (📞2252977; www.manjushreetibcentre.org; 12 Ghandi Rd; 3-/6-/9-month courses ₹11,970/17,010/22,050; ⏱mid-Mar–mid-Dec). Accommodation for students and tourists is available at the attached **Tibet Home** (rooms ₹1500). Classes in Tibetan Buddhism are also possible.

Mountaineering
The **Himalayan Mountaineering Institute** (p491) runs 15-day adventure courses (Indian/foreigner ₹2000/US$325) in January and February, which include climbing, jungle survival and canoeing, for those aged between 18 and 30. There are also 28-day basic and advanced mountaineering courses (Indian/foreigner ₹4000/US$650), from March to May and September to December. Some courses are women only. Foreigners should apply directly to the centre at least three months in advance.

🧭 Tours
During the high season the DGHC and other travel agencies offer a variety of tours around Darjeeling, usually including the zoo, Himalayan Mountaineering Institute, Tibetan Refugee Self-Help Centre and several viewpoints. See p488 for Tiger Hill sunrise tour information.

Taxis can be hired for custom tours for around ₹750 per half-day.

🛏 Sleeping
Only a small selection of Darjeeling's many hotels is mentioned here. Prices given are for the high season (October to early December and mid-March to June), when it's wise to book ahead. In the low season prices can drop by 50%.

Top-end hotels offer rooms on the 'American Plan', with breakfast, lunch and dinner included; taxes and service charges usually add 15% to 20% to the bill.

TOP CHOICE Andy's Guesthouse   GUESTHOUSE **$**
(📞2253125; 102 Dr Zakir Hussain Rd; s/d from ₹300/400) This simple, spotless, stone-walled budget place has airy, carpeted rooms, a comfy common area and a rooftop terrace with a great view. Mrs Gurung provides a friendly boarding-house atmosphere (no restaurant) that makes it quieter than most other budget places. There's a good laundry service.

TOP CHOICE Dekeling Hotel   GUESTHOUSE **$$**
(📞2254159; www.dekeling.com; 51 Gandhi Rd; d without bathroom ₹700, d ₹1300-2200; @🖤) Spotless Dekeling is full of charming touches like coloured diamond-pane windows, a traditional *bukhari* (wood-burning heater) in the cosy lounge/library, wood panelling and sloping-attic ceilings, plus some of the best views in town. Tibetan owners Sangay and Norbu are the perfect hosts. The whole place is a perfect combination of clean and homey, right down to the well-bathed and adorable dog, Drolma.

Windamere Hotel   HERITAGE HOTEL **$$$**
(📞2254041; www.windamerehotel.com; Jawahar Rd West; s/d full board from ₹7300/9400; @) This quaint, rambling relic of the Raj on Observatory Hill offers Darjeeling's most atmospheric digs. The charming superior room block was once a boarding house for British tea planters, and the well-tended grounds are spacious with lots of pleasant seating areas. The comfortable rooms, fireplaces and hot water bottles offer just the right measures of comfort and fustiness; a bit like staying at a rich aunt's house. It's a particularly great place to spend Christmas. Keep your eyes peeled for the Jan Morris poem in the tearoom.

Hotel Aliment   HOTEL **$**
(📞2255068; alimentwe@sify.com; 40 Dr Zakir Hussain Rd; s ₹150, d ₹300-600; @) A budget travellers' favourite, with a good top-floor restaurant (and cold beer), books, helpful owners and wood-lined rooms. The upstairs rooms (₹600) have a TV and valley views. All the double rooms have geysers, but they only operate for an hour or so in the evening. The singles are a big step down in quality.

Hotel Tower View   HOTEL **$**
(📞2254452; krimilan@yahoo.com; 12 Dr Zakir Hussain Rd; dm ₹80, r ₹100-350) Rooms are basic but clean (the rooms with a view are best, as others can be cold and damp), but the real draw to this sociable place is the

cosy restaurant area that doubles as the family kitchen and lounge.

Hotel Tranquility
HOTEL $

(☏2257678; hoteltranquility@yahoo.co.in; Dr Zakir Hussain Rd; d ₹400-500; ☎) This good-value place is sparkling clean, with 24-hour hot water, nice lobby seating and small but neat baby-blue rooms. The helpful owner is a local schoolteacher, and can provide all kinds of info about the area.

Revolver
BOUTIQUE HOTEL $$

(☏225370; www.revolver.in; 110 Gandhi Rd; r ₹800-900; ☎) This Beatles-themed hotel is a must for fans. The five small but stylish rooms are each named after one of the Fab Four (plus Brian Epstein), so you can choose your favourite Moptop (John fills up first; no-one likes Ringo). The hotel is chock-a-block with Beatles memorabilia, including 'Beatles Rock Band' on the resident Play-Station 3. The downstairs restaurant serves good coffee and interesting Naga set meals (₹55 to ₹70) and the owners will even give you a *momo* masterclass if arranged in advance. It's certainly well thought-out but it could perhaps do with a bit more old-fashioned family warmth. The entrance is easily missed behind the Union Church.

Travellers Inn
HOTEL $$

(☏2258497; Dr Zakir Hussain Rd; www.darjeeling travellersinn.com; s/d/ste ₹1100/1500/2600) This well-decorated, faintly stylish hotel comes complete with polished-wood panelling, framed old photos of Darjeeling and a terrace restaurant with terrific views (mains ₹40 to ₹80). The mountain-lodge-style rooms are comfy but dimly lit and hot water is in the evening only. On Sundays forget about that lie-in and clap along to the loud gospel music from the church next door.

Elgin
HERITAGE HOTEL $$$

(☏2257226; www.elginhotels.com; HD Lama Rd; s/d/ste incl full board ₹6500/6800/7900; @☎) A grand yet friendly hotel full of classy ambience, the Elgin is more modern and formal than the Windamere but has less of a sense of history. The restaurant is elegant, as is the great bar and small library, and the small-but-lovely garden terrace is the perfect place to relax over a beer (₹185) or high tea (₹465; ☺4-6pm). The cosy 'attic room' underneath the dripping eaves is especially charming.

Mayfair Darjeeling
HOTEL $$$

(☏2256376; www.mayfairhotels.com; Jawahar Rd West; d with breakfast & dinner from ₹9000; ☎)

Originally a maharaja's summer palace but renovated within an inch of its life, this plush choice sits among manicured gardens and a bizarre collection of kitschy sculptures. Soft carpets and coal fires add to the warm welcome; there's a choice of DVDs and a comfortable bar. The outside and common areas don't have quite the cosy charm of the Elgin, but the plush rooms are well decorated in warm colours and art prints. The children's playroom makes it good for families.

Dekeling Resort at Hawk's Nest
HERITAGE HOTEL $$

(☏2253092; www.dekeling.com; 2 AJC Bose Rd; d ₹3300; www.dekeling.com) Run by the good people at Dekeling, this is a quieter, more exclusive place, 1km outside of Darjeeling up a steep hill. The four 130-year-old, colonial-style suites come with antique touches and fireplaces in the room.

Hotel Seven Seventeen
HOTEL $$

(☏2255099; www.hotel717.com; 26 HD Lama Rd; main block s/d/tr from ₹1500/1800/2000) A friendly Tibetan-themed place on the edge of the bazaar with a good restaurant and clean, fresh rooms. The older annexe (s/d ₹1300/1500) is cheaper but darker and less cheery.

Hotel New Galaxy
HOTEL $

(☏5520771; Dr Zakir Hussain Rd; s ₹150-250, d ₹300) A clean, simple budget option almost opposite Andy's, with wood-panelled walls, smallish rooms and hot-water buckets for ₹10. Try for room 104 – it has the best views across to the mountains.

Main Olde Bellevue Hotel
HOTEL $$

(☏2254178; www.darjeelinghotel.co.uk; Chowrasta; budget/deluxe d ₹1250/1950) Rooms at this 19th-century hotel are spacious and fairly well maintained and have a great location, though the service is sleepy at best. Opt for a room in the creaky chalet-style upper building, as these have a lot more colonial charm. Don't confuse this with the next-door Bellevue Hotel, run by a feuding brother.

✗ Eating

Most restaurants close by 8pm or 9pm.

[TOP CHOICE] Sonam's Kitchen
CONTINENTAL $

(142 Dr Zakir Hussain Rd; mains ₹80-120; ☺8am-2pm, 5-8pm) Providing an island of real brewed coffee in an ocean of tea, Sonam

serves up lovely breakfasts, French toast, pancakes, fresh soups (nettle in season) and pasta; the deliciously chunky wholemeal sandwiches can be packed to go for picnics. Home-style dinner mains need to be pre-ordered at least an hour in advance, so someone can dash up the street to stock up at the nearby veg stalls. It's a tiny place so try not to linger during mealtimes.

Frank Ross Café
MULTICUISINE $
(14 Nehru Rd; mains ₹60-120, set breakfast ₹90-120) There's a diner-feel at this strictly vegetarian self-service place, with a wide-ranging menu, including pizzas, South Indian dosa and even enchiladas and nachos. The attached Frank Ross Pharmacy has groceries for self-caterers.

Park Restaurant
INDIAN/THAI $$
(☏2255270; 41 Laden La Rd; mains ₹70-140) The intimate Park is deservedly very popular for its tasty North Indian curries and surprisingly authentic Thai dishes, including small but tasty *tom kha gai* (coconut chicken soup) and spicy green papaya salad. Grab a seat early or make a reservation.

Glenary's
INDIAN/CONTINENTAL $$
(Nehru Rd; mains ₹120-210; ⊙noon-9pm, later in high season) This elegant restaurant atop the famous bakery and cafe receives mainly rave reviews: of note are the Continental sizzlers, Chinese dishes, tandoori specials and veg gratin (good if you're off spicy food). We've heard a few grumbles that it's coasting on its reputation, but most people love it.

Hot Pizza Place
ITALIAN $
(HD Lama Rd; pizza ₹90-150) A cramped but sociable one-table pizza joint with excellent pizza, pasta, paninis and salads. Come here also for breakfast, pancakes and good coffee, as well as that hard-to-find sausage fix. Service is friendly but slow.

Shangri-La
INDIAN $$
(Nehru Rd; mains ₹75-180) This classy modern bar-restaurant near the top of the Mall offers an upmarket version of the usual Indian/Chinese/Continental food mix in stylish surrounds, with sleek wooden floors, clean tablecloths and friendly service. There are also a couple of stylish hotel rooms upstairs (d ₹2750).

Kunga's
TIBETAN $
(51 Gandhi Rd; mains ₹60-90) Kunga's is a cosy wood-panelled place run by a friendly Tibetan family, strong on noodles and *momos*, with excellent juice and fruit museli curd.

Dekevas
TIBETAN $
(51 Gandhi Rd; mains ₹60-90) Next door to Kunga's, this is a similarly good place, offering Tibetan butter tea, *tsampa* (roast barley flour) and a range of noodles for connoisseurs who can tell their *thenthug* (Tibetan noodles) from their *sogthug* (different Tibetan noodles).

Lunar Restaurant
INDIAN $
(51 Gandhi Rd; mains ₹50-120) This classy spot just below Dekeling Hotel is perhaps the best vegetarian Indian restaurant in town, with good service and great views from the large windows. The masala dosas (lentil-flour pancake filled with vegetables) come with yummy dried fruit and nuts.

Hasty Tasty
INDIAN $
(Nehru Rd; mains ₹30-80, thali ₹80) There's nothing fancy at this vegetarian self-service canteen, but the open kitchen churns out good South Indian dosas and several types of veg thali (set meals). Don't be in a hurry.

🍸 Drinking

Glenary's
BAKERY
(Nehru Rd; small pot ₹35, pastries ₹10-35; ⊙8am-8pm; @🖃) Below the restaurant, this cafe has massive windows and good views – order your tea, select a cake, grab your book and sink into some wicker. It's a great place to grab breakfast.

Café Coffee Day
CAFE
(⊙8am-8pm; coffee from ₹40) It's almost heresy to drink espresso in Darjeeling but if the caffeine calls you, this reliable chain has two locations, one at the Rink Mall, the other at Chowrasta, both with good coffee.

House of Tea
TEAHOUSE
(Nehru Rd; tea ₹25-40; ⊙9.15am-8pm) Sit and sip a range of brewed teas from several local Goodricke estates before purchasing a package of your favourite leaves.

Sunset Lounge
TEAHOUSE
(20 Chowrasta Square; cup of tea ₹20-75; ⊙9am-8pm; 🖃) This tearoom run by Nathmull's Tea offers aficionados a range of teas by the cup, with baked treats, fine valley views and wi-fi.

Bars
The top-end hotels all have bars; the Windamere is the most atmospheric place to kick back with an early evening G&T (₹200).

Joey's Pub
PUB
(SM Das Rd; beer ₹120; ⊙11am-10pm) If your preferred beverage comes in a pint not a pot,

this long-standing pub near the post office is a great place to strike up conversations with other travellers. It has sports on TV, cold beer and Hot Toddys in the winter. It's generally very friendly, though lone women have experienced some not entirely good-natured teasing from staff.

Buzz PUB
(Nehru Rd; ⊘4pm-9.30pm; beer ₹130) An American-style sports bar in the basement at Glenary's. If you get peckish you can order food from the upstairs restaurant.

🛍 Shopping

Nathmull's Tea Room TEA
(www.nathmulltea.com; Laden La Rd; ⊘9am-7.30pm Mon-Sat, daily high season) Darjeeling tea is some of the finest tea in the world and Nathmull's is the best place to pick up some, with over 50 varieties. Expect to pay ₹80 to ₹150 per 100g for a decent tea and up to ₹1400 per 100g for the finest flushes. You can ask for a tasting, which will be expertly brewed, and you can also buy attractive teapots, strainers and cosies. The Sarda family has run the business for 80 years and are very knowledgeable.

Tibetan Refugee Self-Help Centre CARPETS
This centre makes gorgeous carpets to order, if you don't mind waiting around six months for one to be made. Choose from the catalogue and they will ship the finished carpet to your home address (US$370 with shipping).

Hayden Hall CRAFTS
(www.haydenhall.org; Laden La Rd; ⊘9am-5pm Mon-Sat) Sells yak wool carpets as part of its charitable work (₹5000 for a 1m by 1.8m carpet). There are Kashmiri-style carpets in most of the souvenir shops, but they're not likely to be locally made. There are also good knitwear and bags made by local women.

Dorjee Himalayan Artefacts HANDICRAFTS
(Laden La Rd) This tiny Aladdin's cave is crammed full of Himalayan knick-knacks, from Tibetan amulets to cast Buddhas and silver prayer wheels. Walking in through the door is like entering a scene from a Kipling novel.

Life & Leaf Fair Trade Shop HANDICRAFTS
(19 Nehru Rd) Supports local artisans and environmental projects through the sale of organic honey, tea, rhododendron juice, plus bamboo bags, scarves and toys.

Oxford Book & Stationery Company BOOKS
(Chowrasta; ⊘9.30am-7.30pm Mon-Sat, daily high season) The best bookshop in Darjeeling, selling a good selection of novels and Himalayan-related titles. They mail worldwide.

Trek Mate CLOTHING
(sleeping bag ₹40 per day, plus ₹1500 deposit) Clothing or gear can be hired from here, but the quality is pretty low.

Rope CLOTHING
(NB Singh Rd) This is located just below Clubside; stocks high quality imported clothing and trek boots.

ℹ Information

Emergency
Police assistance booth (Chowrasta)
Sadar Police Station (☑2254422; Market Rd)

Internet Access
There are dozens of internet cafes around town; all generally charge ₹30 per hour.
Compuset Centre (Gandhi Rd; ⊘8am-8pm; 🛜) Does printing (₹2) and will burn photos to a CD/DVD for ₹50/70, but doesn't offer Skype.
Cyber Planet (Dr Zakir Hussain Rd; ⊘8am-10pm) Opposite Sonam's Kitchen.
Glenary's (p496) Most convenient to the Mall; has wi-fi.

Medical Services
Planter's Hospital (D&DMA Nursing Home; ☑2254327; Nehru Rd) The best private hospital.

Money
A number of shops and hotels around Darjeeling can change cash and travellers cheques at fairly good rates; shop around.
Axis Bank (Rink Mall; ⊘10.30am-3pm Mon-Fri) Changes cash and Amex travellers cheques, with an ATM.
ICICI Bank ATM (Laden La Rd) Accepts most international bank and credit cards.
Poddar's (Laden La Rd; ⊘9am-8.30pm) Better rates than the State Bank next door and changes most currencies and travellers cheques at no commission. It accepts credit cards and is a Western Union agent. It's inside a clothing store.
Ridhi Siddhi (Laden La Rd; ⊘8.30am-8.30pm) Changes cash at good rates with no commission and sells trekking gear.
State Bank of India (Laden La Rd; ⊘10am-2pm & 3-4pm Mon-Fri) Changes cash US dollars, euros and pounds sterling, plus US-dollar Amex

travellers cheques, with a commission of ₹100 per transaction. It has an adjacent ATM, another in Chowrasta; both accept Visa cards.

Photography
Das Studios (Nehru Rd; ☉9.30am-6.30pm Mon-Fri, to 2.30pm Sat, daily in high season) Film and printing, passport pics (six for ₹50) and burns digital photos to DVD (₹200). The reprinted 19th-century photographs make for a great souvenir (₹175); ask to look at the catalogue.

Post
Main post office (Laden La Rd; ☉9am-5pm Mon-Sat)

Tourist Information
Darjeeling Gorkha Hill Council Tourist Reception Centre (DGHC; ☎2255351; Silver Fir Bldg, Jawahar Rd West; ☉10am-5pm Mon-Sat, except 10am-1pm every 2nd Sat, 10am-1pm Sun high season) The staff are friendly, well organised and the best source of information in Darjeeling.

Travel Agencies
Most travel agencies in town can arrange local tours, including the DGHC. Other reliable agencies and their specialities include the following:
Adventures Unlimited (☎9933070013; Dr Zakir Hussain Rd; www.adventuresunlimited. in) Offers Goecha La treks, kayaking, paragliding, motorbike trips and mountain bike rental (₹450 per day); ask about the cycle itinerary to Kurseong and back via Senchul Reservoir. They also offer internet access, a laundromat, cheap international calls and cash advances on a credit card. Contact Gautam.
Samsara Tours, Travels & Treks (☎2252874; samsara1@sancharnet.in; 7 Laden La Rd) Helpful and knowledgeable agency offering rafting and trekking trips, and domestic Nepali bus and air tickets to Kathmandu.
Somewhere Over the Rainbow Treks & Tours (☎9832025739; kanadhi@yahoo.com; HD Lama Rd; ☉8am-6pm, later in high season) Organises off-the-beaten track walks around Darjeeling, as well as rafting, rock climbing, cycling and trekking in Sikkim (including interesting routes from Uttarey). Treks start from US$40 per day.

Sikkim Travel Permit
Sikkim Tourist Office (☎9832438118; Nehru Rd; ☉10am-4pm Mon-Sat) For an on-the-spot Sikkim permit bring a photocopy of your passport and Indian visa, plus one photo. It's opposite Glenary's.

Dangers & Annoyances
Strikes in support of the GJM's call for a separate Indian state of Gurkhaland have become less regular in recent years but could easily return if discontent resurges. While there has been little violence and tourists have not been targeted, everything simply shuts down, including all banks, restaurants and transport.

Getting There & Away

Air
The nearest airport is 90km away at Bagdogra, about 12km from Siliguri. See p483 for details about flights to/from Bagdogra.
Indian Airlines (☎2254230; Chowrasta; ☉10am-5.30pm Mon-Sat)
Pineridge Travels (☎2253912; pineridge@ mail.com; Nehru Rd; ☉10am-5pm Mon-Sat) For domestic and international flight tickets.

Bus
Samsara Tours, Travels & Treks can book 'luxury' air-con buses from Siliguri to Kolkata (₹750-1000, 12 hours) and ordinary night buses to Guwahati (₹360) and Patna (₹350). These tickets don't include transfers to Siliguri.

Jeep & Taxi
Numerous share jeeps leave the crowded Chowk Bazaar bus/jeep stand for Siliguri (₹90-110, three hours) and Kurseong (₹50, 1½ hours). Jeeps for Mirik (₹60, 2½ hours) leave from the northern end about every 1½ hours. A ticket office inside the ground floor of the Old Super Market Complex sells advance tickets for the frequent jeeps to Kalimpong (₹80-90, 2½ hours), while two roadside stands sell advance tickets for Gangtok (₹130, four hours), departing between 7am and 3pm.

At the northern end of the station, three to four jeeps a day leave before noon for Jorethang (₹90, two hours) in Sikkim. You must already have a permit to enter Sikkim (see p497) via this route.

To New Jalpaiguri or Bagdogra, get a connection in Siliguri, or charter a jeep or taxi from Darjeeling.

Darjeeling Transport Corporation (Laden La Rd) offers charter jeeps to Gangtok (₹1400), Kalimpong (₹1200) and Siliguri/Bagdogra Airport (₹1200).

Train
The nearest major train station is at New Jalpaiguri (NJP), near Siliguri. Tickets can be bought for major services out of NJP at the **Darjeeling train station** (☉8am-2pm). Fares are to Ghum (2nd/1st class ₹21/96, 50 minutes), Kurseong (₹27/144, three hours), Siliguri Junction (₹38/217, 6½ hours) and NJP (2nd/1st class ₹42/247, seven hours). For sightseeing services see p484.

NO	DARJEELING	GHUM	KURSEONG	SILIGURI JCT	NJP
2D*	9.15am	9.45am	11.55am	4pm	4.50pm
10D (steam)	10.15am	10.45am	1.10pm	-	-

*At the time of research the 2D service was suspended due to landslides, but should have resumed by time of publication.

To/From Nepal

Foreigners can only cross the border into Nepal at Kakarbhitta/Panitanki (not at Pasupati).

Samsara Tours, Travels & Treks can book night buses from Kakarbhitta to Kathmandu (₹750; departure 4pm), leaving you to hire a jeep to Kakarbhitta (₹1600), or catch a shared jeep to Siliguri and then Karkabhittha. Samsara can also book Nepali domestic flights from Bhadrapur to Kathmandu (US$147), which will save you the overnight bus trip.

Any tickets you see advertised from Darjeeling to Kathmandu are not direct buses and involve transfers in Siliguri and at the border – leaving plenty of room for problems – it's just as easy to do it yourself. See the boxed text, p484 for Siliguri-Panitanki transport details.

❶ Getting Around

There are several taxi stands around town, but rates are absurdly high for short hops. Darjeeling's streets can be steep and hard to navigate. You can hire a porter to carry your bags up to Chowrasta from Chowk Bazaar for around ₹60.

Share jeeps to anywhere north of the town centre (eg to North Point) leave from the northern end of the Chowk Bazaar bus/jeep station. To Ghum, get a share jeep (₹15) from along Hill Cart Rd.

Trekking Around Darjeeling

A number of rewarding and picturesque treks are accessible from Darjeeling. October and November's clear skies and warm daytime temperatures make it an ideal time to trek, as do the long days and incredible rhododendron blooms of May and early June. The Darjeeling Gorkha Hill Council (DGHC; p497) produces a useful *Himalayan Treks* leaflet (₹25), which includes a map and descriptions of major trekking routes.

Most popular is the **Singalila Ridge Trek** from Mane Bhanjhang to Phalut, which passes through the scenic **Singalila National Park** (Indian/foreigner ₹100/200, camera/video ₹100/400) and offers great views of the Himalayan chain stretching from Nepal to Sikkim and Bhutan. Sandakhphu in particular offers a stunning panorama that includes Lhotse, Everest and Khangchengdzonga peaks.

Guides (₹700 per day) are mandatory within the park and can be arranged at the office of the **Highlander Trekking Guides Association** (☑9734056944) at Mane Bhanjhang, along with porters (₹ 350) if required.

Mane Bhanjhang is 26km from Darjeeling and is served by frequent shared jeeps (₹50, 1½ hours) as well as a 7am bus from Darjeeling's Chowk Bazaar bus/jeep station. From Rimbik, there are shared jeeps back to Darjeeling (₹110, five hours) at 7am and noon and a bus at 6.30am (₹72). Book seats in advance.

If you have to overnight in Rimbik the best lodges are **Hotel Sherpa** (☑9434212810; dm ₹100, d ₹300-800), with pleasant lawns and Alpine-style huts, and **Green Hill** (dm ₹80-100, r ₹350-600), with quieter wooden rooms out back. For a relaxing end to a trek, consider a stay at **Karmi Farm** (p480), an hour or two drive from Rimbik near Bijanbari.

The usual trekking itinerary is described in the boxed text, p498. A shorter four-day option is possible by descending from Sandakhphu to Sri Khola on day three. A very rough jeep road now follows the trek from Mane Bhanjhang to Phalut but traffic is very light and the walking trail partly avoids the road.

Private lodges, some with attached bathrooms, are available along the route for around ₹100 for a dorm bed or ₹300-600 per room. All offer food, normally a filling combo of rice, dhal and vegetables (₹60-80). Rooms have clean bedding and blankets so sleeping bags are not strictly necessary, though they are nice to have. At a minimum bring a sheet, a sleeping bag/liner and warm clothes for dawn peak viewing. Bottled and boiling water is available along the route. Trekkers' huts can be booked at the DGHC (p497), but even they will tell you that you are better off at one of the private lodges. The main lodges are listed below in ascending order of price and quality:

Tumling Trekkers' Hut, Mountain Lodge, Siddharta Lodge, Shikhar Lodge

Tonglu Trekkers' Hut

Kalipokhari Chewang Lodge and five others

Sandakhphu Trekkers' Hut, Namobuddha, Sunrise, Sherpa Chalet Lodge

Phalut Trekkers' Hut

Gurdum Himalayan Sherpa Lodge

Sri Khola Trekkers' Hut, Goparma Lodge

Gorkhey Trekkers' Hut, Shanti Lodge, Eden Lodge

Ramman Trekkers' Hut, Namobuddha Lodge

Molley Trekkers' Hut

All-inclusive guided treks on this route are offered by Darjeeling travel agencies for ₹1600 to ₹1800 per day, though it's easy enough to arrange a DIY trek for much less. Lodges can get booked out in the busy month of October, so consider a November trek.

Remember to bring your passport, as you'll have to register at half a dozen army checkpoints. The ridge forms the India–Nepal border and the trail actually enters Nepal in several places.

Reliable trekking agencies include the following:

Darjeeling Gorkha Hill Council Tourist Reception Centre (p497) Charges about ₹2000 per day (all-inclusive) for Singalila Ridge, or can just organise guides/porters.

SINGALILA RIDGE TREK

DAY	ROUTE	DISTANCE (KM)
1	Mane Bhanjhang (2130m) to Tonglu (3070m)/Tumling (2980m) via Meghma Gompa	14
2	Tonglu to Sandakphu (3636m) via Kalipokhri & Garibas	17
3	Sandakphu to Phalut (3600m) via Sabarkum	17
4	Phalut to Rammam (2530m) via Gorkhey	16
5	Rammam to Rimbik (2290m) via Sri Khola	19

Samsara Tours, Travels & Treks (p497) Experienced agency offering reasonably priced rafting and trekking trips.

Trek Mate (☎2256611, 9832083241; trek matedarj@gmail.com; Nehru Rd) All-inclusive guided treks run from US$45 per person per day, or US$60 for Goecha La in Sikkim, depending on group size.

Himalayan Travels (☎2252254; kkgurung@ cal.vsnl.net.in; 18 Gandhi Rd; ⊗8.30am-7pm) Experienced company arranging treks and mountaineering expeditions in Darjeeling and Sikkim. Can supply tents and other equipment.

Kalimpong
📞03552 / POP 43,000 / ELEV 1250M

This bustling bazaar town sprawls along a ridge overlooking the roaring Teesta River and within sight of Khangchendzonga. It's not a must-see but it does boast Himalayan views, some fine hikes, temples and churches, and a fascinating nursery industry.

Kalimpong's early development as a trading centre focused on the wool trade with Tibet, across the Jelep La Pass. Like Darjeeling, Kalimpong once belonged to the chogyals of Sikkim, but it fell into the hands of the Bhutanese in the 18th century and later passed to the British, before becoming part of India at Independence. Scottish missionaries, particularly the Jesuits, made great efforts to win over the local Buddhists in the late 19th century and Dr Graham's famous orphanage and school is still running today.

The Gorkhaland movement is active in Kalimpong. The Gurkha leader CK Pradhan was assassinated here in October 2002, and is commemorated by a small shrine on the spot where he was gunned down.

Kalimpong is centred on its chaotic Motor Stand. Nearby are restaurants, cheap hotels and shops; most sights and quality accommodation are a kilometre or two from town, accessed via DB Giri and Rinkingpong Rds.

⊙ Sights

Durpin Gompa   MONASTERY
Kalimpong's largest monastery, formally known as Zangtok Pelri Podrang (sometimes spelled Zong Dog Palri Fo-Brang), sits atop spectacular Durpin Hill (1372m) and was consecrated after its opening by the Dalai Lama in 1976. There are impressive wall and ceiling paintings in the main prayer room downstairs

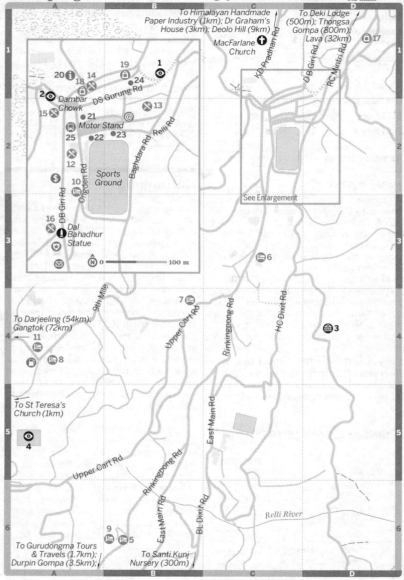

To Himalayan Handmade
Paper Industry (1km); Dr Graham's
House (3km); Deolo Hill (9km)

To Deki Lodge
(500m); Thongsa
Gompa (800m);
Lava (32km)

MacFarlane
Church

Dambar
Chowk

DS Gurung Rd

Motor Stand

Sports
Ground

Ongden Rd

DB Giri Rd

Dal
Bahadhur
Statue

See Enlargement

To Darjeeling (54km);
Gangtok (72km)

9th Mile

Upper Cart Rd

Rinkingpong Rd

HC Dixit Rd

To St Teresa's
Church (1km)

East Main Rd

Upper Cart Rd

Rinkingpong Rd

East Main Rd

BL Dixit Rd

Relli River

To Gurudongma Tours
& Travels (1.7km);
Durpin Gompa (3.5km);

To Santi Kunj
Nursery (300m)

(photography is permitted), and interesting 3-D mandalas (visual meditational aids) on the 2nd floor. The monastery is located about 5km south of the town centre, and is best reached by taxi (₹80 return). A viewpoint about 300m below the gompa looks out south over the Relli and Teesta Rivers.

Tharpa Choling Gompa   MONASTERY
Built in 1922, this Gelugpa-school Tibetan monastery, off KD Pradhan Rd, contains stat-

ues of the past, present and future Buddhas. A garuda protects each Buddha from above, his mouth devouring hatred and anger (in the form of a snake). It's a 30-minute walk (uphill) from town, past the top of Tripai Rd.

Thongsa Gompa MONASTERY
Near the top of RC Mintri Rd, past JP Lodge, is this Nyingmapa-school monastery, also known as the Bhutanese Monastery. The gompa was founded in 1692, but the present building, surrounded by 219 small prayer wheels, was built in the 19th century after the Gurkhas rampaged across Sikkim.

Dr Graham's Home HISTORIC BUILDING
This working orphanage and school was built in 1900 by Dr JA Graham, a Scottish missionary, to educate the children of tea estate workers, and now has more than 1300 students. There's a small **museum** (admission free ⊙9am-3.30pm Mon-Fri) that commemorates the founder and his wife, Katherine. The 1925 chapel above the school seems lifted straight out of a Scotland parish, with its grey slate, spire and fine stained-glass windows. The gate is 4km up the steep KD Pradhan Rd. Many people charter a taxi to get here (₹100) and then walk back to town via Tharpa Choling Gompa.

Deolo Hill VIEWPOINT
(admission ₹50; 9km from Kalimpong) On a clear day the sunrise views of Khangchendzonga from this hilltop park are superb. After savouring the views you can have breakfast at the attached **Tourist Lodge** (breakfast ₹70-140; ⊙from 8am) and then walk back to Kalimpong via Dr Graham's. A taxi here costs around ₹250. If it's cloudy, stay in bed.

Himalayan Handmade Paper Industry HANDICRAFTS
(KD Pradhan Rd; ⌨255418; www.rupeshpradhan. com; ⊙9am-3.30pm Mon-Sat) Visitors are welcome to drop into this small workshop to see the traditional papermaking process, from pulping of the local *argayli* bush to pressing and drying. The resulting insect-resistant paper is used by monasteries to block print scriptures. Morning is the best time to visit.

Nurseries NURSERIES
Kalimpong is a major flower exporter and produces about 80% of India's gladioli as well as many orchid varieties. Visit **Nurseryman's Haven** (⌨256936; 9th Mile) at Holumba Haven (see p502) to have a look at orchids; **Santi Kunj** (BL Dixit Rd; ⊙8.30am-noon & 1.30-4pm Sun-Fri) to see anthuriums and the bird of paradise flower (bulbs are also sold here); and **Pineview Nursery** (⌨255843; www.pine viewcactus.com; Atisha Rd; admission ₹10; 8am-

5pm, Sun closed winter) to gaze at its eminently photographable cactus collection.

Lepcha Heritage Museum
MUSEUM

(☑9800033650; ☉9am-4pm Mon-Fri) There are plans to move this collection of Lepcha treasures to a more formal location, but until then the experience is best likened to rummaging through the attic of your grandfather's house, if he were a Lepcha tribal elder. A guide will explain Lepcha creation myths, while pointing out the religious texts, sacred porcupine quill hat and several old pangolin skins. It's a 10-minute walk below the sports ground, just past the Kamudini Homes School. Calling ahead is advised.

St Teresa's Church
CHURCH

A fascinating missionary church built in 1929 by Swiss Jesuits, St Teresa was constructed to incorporate designs from a Bhutanese gompa. The carved apostles look like Buddhist monks, and the carvings on the doors resemble the *tashi tagye,* eight auspicious symbols of Himalayan Buddhism. The church is found off 9th Mile, about 2km from town, but is often locked outside of the early morning services.

🏃 Activities

The sleepy DGHC Tourist Reception Centre (p503) and private Helpdesk (p503) can arrange local transport and treks.

Gurudongma Tours & Travels (☑255204; www.gurudongma.com; Hilltop, Rinkingpong Rd) organises interesting tours, including trekking, rafting, mountain biking, birdwatching and fishing throughout the region, in a bus especially from its lodge on the Samthar Plateau (see p504).

Kalimpong-based Swede Roger Lenngren offers paragliding flights through **Himalayan Eagle** (☑9635156911; www.paraglidingkalimpong.com; Dambar Chowk). Tandem flights cost ₹2150/3500 for a 15-/30-minute flight, which includes transport. Weather conditions have to be perfect. Lenngrenn also runs motorbike and 4WD trips through www.himalayanbiketours.se.

Kalimpong Walks (☑9932828753; www.kalimpongwalks.blogspot.com, www.thesilkrouteexperience.com; walks ₹300-900) offers a series of guided walks around Kalimpong, ranging from hour-long dawn strolls to full-day hikes.

🛏 Sleeping

The hotels closest to the Motor Stand are mainly grotty and overpriced; it's well worth walking a few extra steps for a significant increase in quality. High-season rates (October to early December and mid-March to early June) are given here.

TOP CHOICE Holumba Haven
BOUTIQUE HOTEL $$

(☑256936; www.holumba.com; 9th Mile; r ₹700-1800, cottage from ₹4500) Described by its welcoming owners as 'more of a homestay than a hotel', this family-run guesthouse is situated in a splendid orchid nursery just 1km below town. The spotless, comfy rooms are arranged in homey cottages spread around the lush garden, and spring water is piped directly into the rooms. Good home-style meals (₹300, preorder) are available in the sociable dining room. Owner Norden is a fantastic source of local information.

TOP CHOICE Himalayan Hotel
HERITAGE HOTEL $$

(☑255248; www.himalayanhotel.com; Upper Cart Rd; s/d ₹1800/2800; @) This hotel was opened by the revered David MacDonald, an interpreter from Francis Younghusband's mission to Lhasa in 1904 and one of those who helped the 13th Dalai Lama escape Tibet in 1910. The original rooms have loads of Raj-era appeal beneath a sloping Himalayan-oak ceiling, while the new suites mesh old-world charm with modern comfort and private balconies. It's a triumph of sympathetic renovation; comfortable but full of lovely original fittings. You're in fine company here; the former guest list reads like a 'Who's Who' of the great 19th-century Himalayan travellers, from Alexandra David-Neel and Heinrich Harrer to Charles Bell. Head to the lawn to savour the Himalayan views over an al fresco breakfast or afternoon beer.

Kalimpong Park Hotel
HERITAGE HOTEL $$

(☑255304; www.kalimponghotel.com; s/d/ste ₹1800/2300/3000) This former maharaja's summer residence has oodles of Raj-era charm. Wicker chairs and flowerpots line the verandah and there's a charming lounge bar, along with a restaurant offering such British boarding-school dishes as jelly custard. Rooms in the new wing lack some of the period charm of the old house but are fresh and still very appealing. Request a front-facing room, preferably on the upper floors.

Deki Lodge GUESTHOUSE **$**
(☑255095; Tripai Rd; s ₹250-450, d ₹350-650, deluxe d ₹850-1050) This pleasant lodge is close to the Thongsa and Tharpa Choling Gompas and still handy to town. It's a friendly, family-run place set in a garden with a cafe (on request) and rooftop viewing area. Rooms are generally appealing, particularly the upper-floor rooms, and it's light years better than anything near the Motor Stand.

Sherpa Lodge HOTEL **$**
(☑8972029913; s ₹200, d ₹300-400) This decent budget place is slap bang in the centre of town, offering bright, clean rooms and buckets of hot water for the attached bathrooms. The rooftop terrace has great potential. Ask for Raju.

Sood's Garden Retreat BOUTIQUE HOTEL **$$**
(☑9733123113; www.soodsgardenretreat.com; 81/2nd Mile; ste ₹2550-3050 with breakfast; ☏) Renovations have reinvented Sood's as a modern, stylish boutique hotel. The suites in particular have great floor to ceiling mountain views and there's a good restaurant with a pleasant sitting area for tea or a beer. The eager-to-help owners can organise all kinds of tours and trips.

Elgin Silver Oaks HERITAGE HOTEL **$$$**
(☑255296; www.elginhotels.com; Rinkingpong Rd; s/d incl full board ₹5600/5900) This centrally located Raj-era homestead has been renovated into a modern and very comfortable Elgin hotel. The rooms are plushly furnished and offer grand views down the valley (ask for a garden-view room). The tariff includes all meals in the excellent restaurant and the sociable bar packs bags of atmosphere.

Cloud 9 HOTEL **$$**
(☑259554; cloud9kpg@yahoo.com; Rinkingpong Rd; d ₹1100-1500) There's no chance of a tour-group invasion in this friendly place, since there are just three wood-panelled rooms, plus a cosy TV lounge and a good restaurant, serving interesting Bhutanese and Sikkimese dishes (try the *kewa tachi* – potato and cheese). Guitars in the lounge attest to the owner's love of late-night Beatles covers.

Eating

King Thai CHINESE **$$**
TOP CHOICE
(3rd fl 'supermarket', DB Giri Rd; mains ₹50-110; ⊙11am-9.30pm) A multicultural hang-out with a Thai name, Chinese food, Bob Marley posters and British soccer banners for

decoration, the regular crowd here mixes expats, monks, businessmen and Tibetan cool kids drawn to the noisy live music in the evenings. The excellent food is mainly Chinese with some Thai and Indian flavours and there's a bar with comfy chairs and even a disco ball.

Gompu's Bar & Restaurant TIBETAN **$**
(☑257456; off DB Giri Rd; mains ₹40-120, beer ₹120) Gompu's is famous for its massive *momos* (pork, chicken and veg), which have been drawing locals and travellers alike for ages. It's a good place for a cold beer. It's found within the hotel of the same name.

China Garden Restaurant CHINESE **$**
(☑257456; Lal Gulli, mains ₹70-100) In the China Garden Hotel near the Motor Stand, this is Kalimpong's best Chinese restaurant. The fairly authentic soups, noodles and spicy ginger chicken are tasty, if you can pry the staff's attention away from the hypnotising TV.

Fresh Bite Restaurant MULTICUISINE **$**
(DB Giri Rd; mains ₹50-140) Upstairs, across the road from the DGHC, this place has a wide range of almost uniformly good food including some hard-to-find dishes that you might have been craving, like miso soup and bacon sandwiches and a good Gorkhali set meal, featuring Nepali-style *gundruk* (fermented greens).

3C's BAKERY **$**
(DB Giri Rd; cakes & snacks ₹10-30; ⊙8.30am-7.15pm) If you need a quick break, this popular bakery and fast food restaurant offers a variety of pastries and cakes, both sweet and savoury, with seating in the back.

Shopping

Lark's Provisions FOOD & DRINK **$**
(DB Giri Rd) The best place to pick up Kalimpong cheese (₹240 per kg), produced in Kalimpong since the Jesuits established a dairy here in the 19th century, and locally made Kalimpong lollipops (₹25). Also sells groceries and yummy homemade pickles.

Haat Bazaar MARKET
(btwn Relli & RC Mintri Rds) On Wednesday and Saturday this normally quiet bazaar roars to life.

Kashi Nath & Sons BOOKS
(DB Giri Rd; ⊙10am-6.30pm) This, and the shop next door, has a decent range of books on Buddhism, Nepal and Tibet, plus some novels.

DIY EXPLORING AROUND KALIMPONG

There's plenty of scope for some exploring in the hills and villages around Kalimpong. The picturesque drive east from Kalimpong passes through mist and moss-laden, old-growth forests and makes for nice hiking. For more information on the region see the Helpdesk in Kalimpong (p503) or Norden at Holumba Haven (p502).

About 32km east of Kalimpong, **Lava** (2353m) is a small village popular with Bengali tourists, with a Kagyupa gompa and a bustling Tuesday market. En route, a short detour 6km from Algarh, you can make the short hike to the faint 17th-century ruins of Damsang Dzong, a former fortress of the chogyals of Sikkim.

Adjoining Lava town is **Neora Valley National Park** (admission ₹150), featuring lush forests home to red panda and clouded leopard. There are some fine day hikes or you can make the four-day camping trek to Rochela (3155m), at the high junction of West Bengal, Sikkim and Bhutan.

There's plenty of accommodation in Lava. The cottages of the **Lava Forest Lodge** (www.wbfdc.com; d ₹600-1200) just above town is the nicest option but can be hard to book; try through WBTDC in Siliguri or Holumba Haven in Kalimpong. The government-run **Tourist Cottage** (☑9932270767; d ₹750) is another decent choice.

About 26km further east of Lava is **Kaffer** (1555m), also known as Lolaygaon, from where there are views of the summit of Khangchendzonga. **Daffey Munal Tourist Lodge** (☑03552-277218; dm ₹150, d/tr ₹750/1000) is a rambling old DGHC place with huge, clean rooms, hot water and fireplaces.

To get further afield, **Gurudongma Tours & Travels** (☑255204; www.gurudongma .com, www.awakeandshine.org; Hilltop, Rinkingpong Rd, Kalimpong; s/d full board from ₹3800/4500) runs the cosy Farm House at Samthar. There are fine views of the Bhutanese Himalaya and some fascinating conversations when the owner, 'the General', is in residence. They will arrange transport from Kalimpong.

Other adventure companies in the region include **Silk Route Experience** (www .thesilkrouteexperience.com) based around its Silk Route Retreat in Pedong, 22km from Kalimpong.

Several jeeps daily link Kalimpong with both Lava and Kaffer.

ⓘ Information

Axis Bank ATM (81/2nd Mile) Next to Sood's Garden Retreat.

Darjeeling Gorkha Hill Council Tourist Reception Centre (DGHC; ☑257992; DB Giri Rd; ☺10am-5pm) Staff can organise local tours and rafting in Teesta Bazaar (see p492).

Helpdesk (☑9434886511; helpdesk_kpg@hot mail.com; ☺9am-5pm) This private information centre on the ground floor of the Sherpa Lodge offers guides, walks and information on trips around Kalimpong.

ICICI Bank ATM (DB Giri Rd)

Net Hut (per hr ₹30; ☺9.30am-7.30pm) Internet access near the Motor Stand.

Post office (Rinkingpong Rd; ☺9am-5pm Mon-Fri, to 4pm Sat) Just behind the police station.

Sikkim permit There is nowhere in Kalimpong to obtain permits for Sikkim, but free 30-day permits are available at the border at Rangpo, en route to Gangtok. You need to present three passport photos.

State Bank of India ATM (DB Giri Rd)

Studio Foto Max (☺8am-7pm) Small shop in an arcade will burn digital pictures to a CD/DVD for ₹50/75.

ⓘ Getting There & Away

All the bus and jeep options and their offices mentioned here are found next to each other at the chaotic Motor Stand.

Bus & Jeep

Bengal government buses run twice daily to Siliguri (₹50, 2½ hours), and there's also a single Sikkim Nationalised Transport (SNT) bus to Gangtok (₹80, 3 hours) at 1pm.

Himalayan Travellers (☑9434166498) Helpful transport company runs share jeeps to Gangtok (₹100, three hours, four daily), Lava (₹50, 1½ hours, five per day) and Kaffer (₹60, 2½ hrs, 8am).

Kalimpong Mainline Taxi Driver's Welfare Association (KMTDWA) Regular share jeeps to Siliguri (₹80, 2½ hours) and Gangtok (₹100, 2½ hours) and one daily to Kaffer (₹70, departs 7.15am) and Jorethang (₹60, two hours, departs 7.15am).

KS & AH Taxi Driver's Welfare Association
Four jeeps daily to Ravangla (₹110, 3½ hours) and Namchi (₹80) in Sikkim, though you need to have arranged a permit in advance for this route.

Kalimpong Motor Transport Regular share jeeps to Darjeeling (₹80-90, 2½ hours). Jeeps can also be chartered for Darjeeling (₹1400), Siliguri (₹1400) and Gangtok (₹1500).

Train

Kalimpong Railway Out Agency (Mani Rd; ⊙10am-4pm Mon-Sat, 10am-1pm Sun) sells train tickets from New Jalpaiguri station.

To/From Bhutan & Nepal

A West Bengal government bus travels to the Bhutan border, Jaigon (₹100, 5½ hours) at 8.15am, and there are also early morning jeeps (₹130, five hours). There is one early morning bus (₹90, 5.45am) and jeep (₹110, 6.30am) to the Nepal border at Kakarbhitta (₹110, three hours).

Border information can be found in the boxed text, p484.

Getting Around

Taxis can be chartered for local trips from along DB Giri Rd. A half-day rental to see most of the sights should cost ₹700.

Bihar & Jharkhand

Best Places to Eat

» Bellpepper Restaurant (p512)

» Chanakya BNR Hotel (p523)

» Tandoor Hut (p512)

» Mohammed Restaurant (p520)

» Takshila (p512)

Best Places to Stay

» Indo Hokke Hotel (p522)

» Chanakya BNR Hotel (p523)

» Taj Darbar (p518)

» Hotel Windsor (p511)

Why Go?

Though long harnessed as pilgrim country for the devout, Bihar and Jharkhand remain pioneer travel territory for the average tourist and are perhaps more representative of traditional India than any other northern states as a result. Outside the big cities most signage is in Hindi and men are more likely to be wearing the kurta and dhoti rather than Western-style shirt and trousers. But the region's spirituality is the big draw. As the birthplace of Buddhism, Bihar holds great significance in India's cultural and religious heritage. Siddhartha Gautama – Buddha – spent much of his life here and attained enlightenment underneath a bodhi tree in Bodhgaya, making it the most important pilgrimage site in the world for Buddhists. Jharkhand's highest point, Parasnath Hill, is notable as the most significant Jain pilgrimage site in north-central India. Together, the states cater to a procession of pilgrims throughout the year.

When to Go

Patna

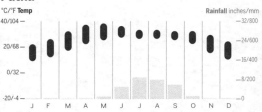

Feb & Mar Beat the heat: temperatures hover between a pleasant 19°C and 25°C.

Oct & Nov With monsoons in retreat, the region is pleasant and dry as winter sets in.

Nov & Dec Bihar's Sonepur Mela extravaganza puts Pushkar's Camel Fair to shame.

The Flavour Frontier

You're in hearty frontier country. Leading the charge north towards the Himalayas is a vibrant gastronomic medley influenced by Mughals, Afghans, Bengal Nawabs, Persians, Europeans and Buddhist vegetarianism. Look out for *chokha,* spicy mashed potatoes prepared with *panch foron,* a five-seed mix of mustard, anise, fenugreek, carom and onion; and roasted chickpea flour fried in hot sand, known as *sattu,* which boasts a high-carb, energetic kick. *Litti,* balls of spiced *sattu* covered in dough and baked on coals, is ubiquitous on the streets. Bihari kebabs, usually made with mutton splashed with red chillies, cumin, coriander, raw papaya, cinnamon, garlic and ginger, are a delight if you can find them, and are sometimes wrapped inside *paratha* and served as rolls. Sweet tooths in Bihar and Jharkhand are satiated with dry sweets, like the strange but satisfying *tilkut,* pounded sesame seed cookies made with jaggery batter or melted sugar.

DON'T MISS

Buddhist pilgrims from all over the world flock to Bihar's **Mahabodhi Temple** in Bodhgaya and rightfully so: it is here that Prince Siddhartha Gautama attained enlightenment beneath a bodhi tree and became Buddha. The temple complex was declared a Unesco World Heritage Site in 2002. Other treats in the region include the Jain Holy Ground at **Parasnath Hill**, the elephant-rich **Betla National Park** and the ancient ruins in and around **Rajgir**.

Top Bihar & Jharkhand Festivals

» Pataliputra Mahotsava (Mar, Patna, p511) Patna celebrates its historic past with parades, sports, dancing and music.

» Rajgir Mahotsava (Oct, Rajgir, p521) A classical performing arts festival with folk dances, devotional songs and instrumental music.

» Chhath Festival (Oct/Nov, Bihar and Jharkhand) People line the banks of rivers and water bodies to honour Surya, the Sun God. At sunset on the sixth day after Diwali, married women, having fasted for 36 hours, immerse themselves in the water and offer fruits and flowers to the deity.

» Sonepur Mela (Nov/Dec, Sonepur, p514) With 700,000 attendees and countless thousands of animals taking part, this three-week festival is four times the size of Pushkar's Camel Fair.

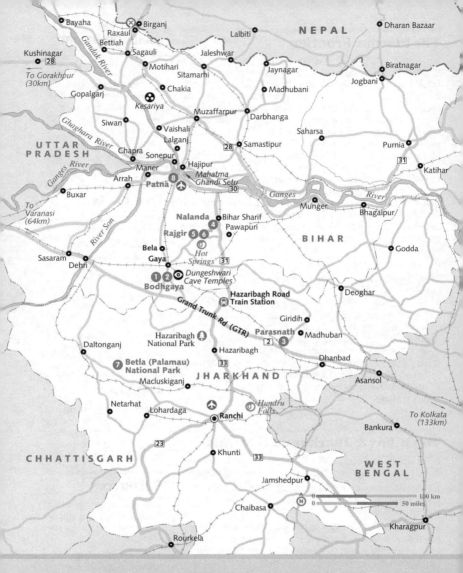

Bihar & Jharkhand Highlights

① Witness the spiritual dawn spectacle at the **Mahabodhi Temple** (p516) in Bodhgaya

② Take a walking tour through the Buddhist world at **Bodhgaya**'s numerous temples and monasteries (p517)

③ Join the Jain pilgrimage to the 1366m-high **Parasnath Hill** (p524)

④ Visit the ancient university at **Nalanda** (p522) and imagine what life was like for its 10,000 pupils from all over Asia

⑤ Journey to the lost capital of Magadha through the ruins, temples and monuments around **Rajgir** (p521)

⑥ Trade noise pollution for silent lucidity at the stunning **Vishwashanti Stupa** (p521) in Rajgir

⑦ Prowl the forested **Betla (Palamau) National Park** (p525) on the back of an elephant in search of elusive tigers

⑧ Indulge in the memorable frontier cuisine of **Patna**'s many excellent restaurants (p512)

History

Prince Siddhartha Gautama arrived in Bihar during the 6th century BC and spent many years here before leaving enlightened as Buddha. The life of Mahavira, a contemporary of Buddha and the founder of Jainism, was born in Bihar and attained Nirvana there before his death near Nalanda at the age of 72. In the 4th century BC, after Chandragupta Maurya conquered the Magadha kingdom and its capital Pataliputra (now Patna), he expanded into the Indus Valley and created the first great Indian empire. His grandson and successor, Ashoka, ruled the Mauryan empire from Pataliputra, which was one of the largest cities in the world at that time. Emperor Ashoka embraced Buddhism (see p1087), erecting stupas, monuments and his famous Ashokan pillars throughout northern India, notably at Sarnath (Uttar Pradesh) and Sanchi (Madhya Pradesh). In Bihar, Ashoka built the original shrine on the site of today's Mahabodhi Temple in Bodhgaya (p516) and the lion-topped pillar at Vaishali (p514).

Bihar continued to be coveted by a succession of major empires until the Magadha dynasty rose to glory again during the reign of the Guptas (7th and 8th centuries AD).

With the decline of the Mughal empire, Bihar came under the control of Bengal until 1912, when a separate state was formed. Part of this state later became Orissa and, more recently in 2000, Jharkhand.

ℹ Information

State tourism offices exist in every major town but do little besides handing out leaflets – if that.

BIHAR

Patna

☎ 0612 / POP 1,285,470

Bihar's busy capital sprawls out over the south bank of the polluted Ganges, just east of the river's confluence with three major tributaries. Unlike Varanasi, there's nothing for the traveller along the river itself and Patna has only a handful of worthwhile sights. Otherwise it's a chaotic eyesore that would be an odd place to voluntarily spend any considerable length of time save one crucial caveat: Patna is home to Bihar and Jharkhand's best eats. Still, most tourists get to know it only as a major transport hub and

a springboard for visiting the Buddhist sites of Vaishali and Kesariya.

Patna was once a powerful city. Early in the 5th century BC, Ajatasatru shifted the capital of his Magadha kingdom from Rajgir to Pataliputra (Patna), fulfilling Buddha's prophecy that a great city would arise here. Emperors Chandragupta Maurya and Ashoka also called Pataliputra home and it remained one of India's most important cities for almost 1000 years.

The old and newer parts of Patna stretch along the southern bank of the Ganges for about 15km. The main train station, airport and hotels are in the western half, known as Bankipur, while most of the historic sites are in the teeming older Chowk area to the east. The 5.7km-long Mahatma Gandhi Setu, the longest single river bridge in the world, connects Patna with Hajipur.

◎ Sights & Activities

TOP CHOICE **Patna Museum** MUSEUM

(Buddha Marg; Indian/foreigner ₹10/250; ⊙10.30am-4.30pm Tue-Sun) Behind its impressive but decaying exterior, this museum houses a splendid collection of Mauryan and Gupta stone sculptures. There's the usual collection of period weapons, including Humayun's dagger, and a gallery of wonderful Rajasthani

---

ℹ STAYING SAFE IN BIHAR & JHARKHAND

Bihar and Jharkhand have a deserved reputation for lawlessness throughout India. Conditions have improved under the Nitish Kumar government, but dacoit (bandit) activity, such as holding up cars, buses and trains, is still a possibility and Maoist and Naxalite bombings are not uncommon. Although foreign and domestic tourists are not specific targets, it's a good idea to split up your valuables on long journeys and avoid night travel where possible, especially by road. Women should take extra precaution throughout the state. In Patna, security has improved, but do take care at night, especially if alone. For more info, check the English-language newspapers *Bihar Times* (www.bihartimes. com), *Patna Daily* (www.patnadaily. com) and *Ranchi Express* (ranchiex press.com) before arrival.

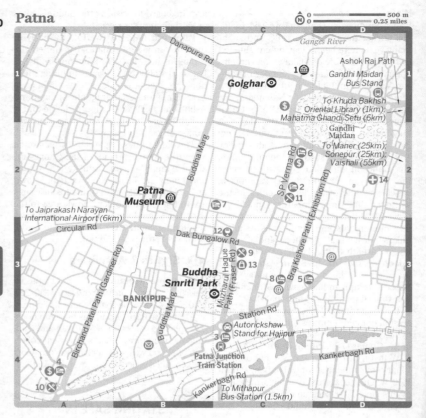

miniatures. In another gallery is a motley collection of stuffed animals, including tigers, a large gharial (a type of crocodile), a bizarre three-eared and eight-legged goat kid, and a wombat. Upstairs in a locked gallery (for an extra ₹500) you can glimpse a tiny casket that's believed to contain some of Buddha's ashes that were retrieved from Vaishali (p514).

TOP CHOICE Buddha Smriti Park PARK

This new 9-hectare park on Fraser Rd, inaugurated by the Dalai Lama in 2010, is notable for its massive sandblasted charcoal stupa, which houses a unique bulletproof chamber inside; and sapling plantings from both the Bodhi Tree in Bodhgaya and Anuradhapura in Sri Lanka. There is also a colour-coordinated museum and meditation centre, which makes for a striking architectural panorama. Judging by appearances, it looks to be far more interesting and welcoming than Gandhi Maidan.

FREE Khuda Bakhsh Oriental Library MUSEUM

(Ashok Raj Path; ⊘9.30am-5pm Sat-Thu) This fascinating library, founded in 1900, contains a renowned collection of Arabic and Persian manuscripts, Mughal and Rajput paintings, and even the Quran inscribed in a book just 25mm wide. A significant exhibit is Nadir Shah's sword – perhaps this was the one he raised at Delhi's Sunehri Mosque in 1739 to order the massacre of the city's residents.

TOP CHOICE Golghar HISTORIC BUILDING

(Danapure Rd; ⊘24hr) For a dome with a view, climb this MC Escher-esque landmark. The British army built this massive, bulbous beehive of a granary in 1786, hoping to avoid a repeat of the 1770 famine. Fortunately it was never required. Its dual spiralling staircases (250 steps each side), designed so that workers could climb up one side and down the other, lead to an unparalleled view of the city and Ganges. Golghar is a short walk west of **Gandhi Maidan**, a large, messy park with a couple of sights that's located south of the river.

Har Mandir Takht   SIKH TEMPLE
Behind a grand gate and sheltered from the mayhem of Patna's Chowk area lies this important Sikh shrine. Its miniature marble domes, sweeping staircases and fine latticework mark the spot where Guru Gobind Singh, last of the 10 Sikh gurus, was born in 1666. It's 11km east of Gandhi Maidan.

FREE **Qila House (Jalan Museum)**   MUSEUM
(📞2641121; Jalan Ave; ⊘by appointment only) This intriguing private museum overflows with antiques ranging from elaborate Mughal-period silverware and weaponry to the wooden bed of Napoleon III. It is located on the banks of the Ganges, 12km east of Ghandi Maiden.

FREE **Gandhi Museum**   MUSEUM
(Danapure Rd; ⊘10am-6pm Sun-Fri) Contains a pictorial history of Mahatma Gandhi's life, plus some of his meagre belongings.

✶✶ Festivals & Events

Patna honours its historic past every March with **Pataliputra Mahotsava**, a celebration featuring parades, sports, dancing and music.

🛏 Sleeping

Most accommodation choices are around Fraser and Station Rds. Rooms below ₹1000 have an additional 5% tax, those above, 10%.

TOP CHOICE **Hotel Windsor**   HOTEL $$
(📞2203250; www.hotelwindsorpatna.com; Exhibition Rd; s/d ₹1200/1400; ✻@) This is Patna's best midrange hotel, with well-designed rooms, spotless bathrooms, cheery and prompt service, a superb restaurant and internet centre. With a bar it'd be perfect.

Garden Court Club   HOTEL $
(📞3202279; www.gardencourtclub.com; SP Verma Rd; s/d ₹500/600, with AC from ₹800/1000; ✻) Take the lift within a small shopping complex up to the intimate 13-room Garden Court Club. Rooms differ: some have views, some have squat toilets. The underused faux-forest open-air rooftop restaurant is a pleasant retreat from street level, though there *is* a pastry shop down there, which only sweetens the deal.

Hotel City Centre   HOTEL $
(📞2308686; hotelcitycentrepatna@rediffmail.com; Station Rd; s/d ₹600/800, with AC ₹1050/1250; ✻🛜) You can't miss this modern glass tower hotel as you exit the train station. Only one year old, its good-value rooms are still in great shape (non-AC rooms have squat toilets) and it's perfect for a comfortable transit overnighter.

Hotel Maurya Patna   HOTEL $$$
(📞2203040; www.maurya.com; South Gandhi Maidan; s ₹8000, s/d incl airport transfer & breakfast ₹9000/10000; ✻@🛜) Fine appointments and luxurious surroundings distinguish Patna's top business hotel. The large gardens host a tempting pool and there are a few nice

restaurants (and an underwhelming bar). Rooms are tastefully furnished, centrally air-conditioned and have disobedient wi-fi.

Hotel President
HOTEL $

(✆2209203; www.hotelpresidentpatna.com; off Fraser Rd; s/d from ₹675/800, with AC ₹1000/1200; ❄@) This family-run hotel is in a relatively quiet location off Fraser Rd and close to Patna Museum. Rooms are simple, clean and good value with TV, seating areas and hot water.

Hotel Kautilya Vihar
HOTEL $

(✆2225411; bstdc@sancharnet.in; Gardiner Rd; dm ₹100, d ₹600, with AC from ₹800; ❄) This hotel has typically well-worn rooms and cramped dorms. It lacks atmosphere, but there's a restaurant and eager staff.

Hotel Maharaja Inn
HOTEL $$

(✆2321955; Station Rd; s/d ₹900/1100, with AC ₹1150/1450; ❄) The brightest in a cluster of midrange cheapies has colourful rooms but nothing you'd mention on a postcard.

✗ Eating & Drinking

Animated Fraser Rd is the main shopping street, with a buzz of restaurants and bars.

TOP CHOICE Bellpepper Restaurant
INDIAN $$

(Hotel Windsor, Exhibition Rd; mains ₹100-275; ☺lunch & dinner) The Bellpepper is an intimate, contemporary restaurant popular for its tandoori dishes. The *murg tikka Lababdar* (tandoori chicken basted with garlic, ginger, green chillies, and a pistachio- and cashew-nut paste) is so good Patna's ills will disappear into a flavour cavalcade in your mouth. No booze to wash it down, though. The best meal we had in this region.

TOP CHOICE Tandoor Hut
INDIAN $$

(✆delivery 9304871717; SP Verma Rd; mains ₹60-160; ☺lunch & dinner) It's impossible to saunter past the delicious dangling kebabs in the display of this take away – only stand without throwing your rupees across the counter. The chicken tikka and chicken *reshmi* kebabs (feeds two) are both extraordinary, but we can't imagine anything not being wonderful – and we didn't even make it to the curries or Chinese food.

TOP CHOICE Takshila
INDIAN $$$

(Hotel Chanayka; Birchand Patel Marg; mains ₹145-375; ☺lunch & dinner) Exuding the ambience of the North-West Frontier with its solid furniture, exposed brick decor and copper flatware, the upscale Takshila is a meat-heavy Mughlai, Afghan and tandoori gastro-dream. Though the meat is every bit as good for half the price at Tandoor Hut, here you pay for the ambiance and service.

Elevens
LOUNGE

(Dumraow Kothi, Fraser Rd; ☺lunch & dinner) If you've been travelling any length of time in Bihar, the cocktails (₹165 to ₹220) at Patna's first stand alone lounge go down like Gatorade at halftime – even if they do put olives in the watermelon martinis. It's owned by Indian cricketer Kapil Dev, whose adjacent restaurant (mains ₹145 to₹375, order from the bar) features an atypical menu of recipes collected from his sporting travels throughout Asia.

Bollywood Treats
INDIAN $$

(Maurya Patna Hotel Arcade; mains ₹70-160; ☺from 1pm) This spotless, modern self-service cafe dishes out dosas, Chinese stir-fries, shwarma, chicken hot dogs, decent pizza and tempting brownies to Patna's blossoming middle class in self-proclaimed 'American style'. Well, there is a Baskin-Robbins ice cream stand just outside its doors.

Anarkali
INDIAN $$

(Mamta Hotel, cnr Fraser & Dak Bungalow Rds; mains ₹60-175) Great food. Cold beer. The chicken tikka butter masala hurts so good.

🔒 Shopping

Ajanta
HANDICRAFTS

(Hotel Satka Arcade, Fraser Rd; ☺10.30am-8.30pm Mon-Sat) Come here for Patna's best selection

---

MITHILA PAINTINGS

Bihar's unique and most famous folk art is its Mithila (or Madhubani) paintings. Traditionally, women from Madhubani and surrounding villages started creating strong line drawings on the walls of their homes from the first day of their marriage. Using pigments from spices, minerals, charcoal and vegetable matter, they painted local deities and scenes from mythology, often intermingled with special events and aspects of everyday life.

These paintings, in both black-and-white and strong primary colours, are now professionally produced on paper, canvas and silk and are for sale. Original wall paintings can still be seen in homes around Madhubani, 160km northeast of Patna.

of Mithila paintings (see p512). Although most of the stock on display is bronzes, the owner can show you a wide range of unmounted paintings starting from ₹200 (handmade paper) to ₹1050 (silk).

ℹ️ Information

Internet Access
Cyber World (Rajendra Path; per hr ₹20; ⏱9.30am-9pm)
Rendezvous Cyber Cafe (Hotel Windsor, Exhibition Rd; per hr ₹25; ⏱10am-8pm)

Medical Services
Ruban Memorial Hospital & Ratan Stone Clinic (Gandhi Maidan; ⏱24hr) Emergency room, clinic and pharmacy.

Money
State Bank of India (Gandhi Maidan) Currency and travellers cheques exchanged.
Thomas Cook (Hotel Maurya Patna Arcade, South Gandhi Maidan) Currency exchange and travel agency.

Post
Post office (Buddha Marg)

Tourist Information
BSTDC tourist office (☎2225411; bstdc@ sancharnet.in; Hotel Kautilya Vihar, Gardiner Rd; ⏱10am-5pm Mon-Sat) Limited information.

Travel Agencies
Thomas Cook (☎2221699; www.thomascook .in; Hotel Maurya Patna Arcade, South Gandhi Maidan; ⏱9.30am-6pm Mon-Sat) Helpful for booking airline tickets, car rental and chauffeur arrangements.

ℹ️ Getting There & Away

Air
Patna's Jaiprakash Narayan International Airport is 8km from the city centre. **Air India** (☎2223199; Patna airport) and **GoAir** (☎2227184; Patna airport) fly daily to Delhi. **Kingfisher Red** (☎1800 1800101; Patna airport) and **Jet Airways** (☎2223045; Patna airport) fly daily to Delhi and Kolkata. **Indigo** (☎1800 1803838; Patna airport) flies to Kolkata, and to Mumbai and Delhi via Lucknow and Ranchi, respectively.

Bus
The Mithapur bus station occupies a large, dusty space about 1.5km of the train station. Services include buses to Gaya (₹50, three hours, hourly), Ranchi (₹200, eight hours, several between 5pm and 9pm) and Raxaul (₹125, eight hours, 6am, 9.15pm, 9.30pm, 10.30pm and 10.50pm).

From the Gandhi Maidan bus stand, government bus services travel to Ranchi (₹183, 10 hours, 8pm, 9.30pm and 10pm) and Raxaul (₹120, eight hours, 7.15am and 10pm).

Car
Hiring a car and driver is the best way for day trips from Patna. Most hotels and Thomas Cook (p513) can arrange this service, starting from ₹6.5 per kilometre (minimum 200km). Arrange an early start, as few drivers operate after dark.

Train
Patna Junction is a chaotic station, but there's a **foreign-tourist ticket counter** (window 7; ⏱8am-8pm Mon-Sat, 8am-2pm Sun) at the 1st-floor reservation office, in the right-hand wing of the station. Destinations with regular daily services include:
Kolkata (Howrah station) (sleeper/3AC/2AC/1AC ₹252/653/881/1467, eight to 13 hours)
Delhi (sleeper/3AC/2AC/1AC ₹359/954/1302/2191, 12 to 28 hours)
Silguri/New Jalpaiguri (for Darjeeling and Sikkim) (sleeper/3AC/2AC ₹212/564/772, 10 to 14 hours)
Varanasi (2nd class/sleeper/3AC/2AC ₹83/150/365/484, five hours, 10.50am, 12.05pm and 2.30pm)
Gaya (sleeper/3AC ₹120/210, 2½ hours, 9.15pm, 9.45pm and 11.30pm)
Ranchi (sleeper/3AC/2AC ₹232/623/851, 10 to 12 hours, 3.25pm and 9.45pm)

There is no direct train to Raxaul, but it's possible to cross the Mahatma Gandhi Setu to Hajipur – you can catch a rickshaw (Rs50) from the stand in front of Hotel City Centre – and catch one of many trains to Muzaffarpur, where you can switch for the 13021 *Mithila Express* to Raxaul (sleeper/3AC/2AC ₹120/238/319, 3¼ hours, 5.15am), but this would only make sense if you were vehemently opposed to the bus.

ℹ️ Getting Around
The airport is located 7km west of the city centre. Autorickshaws to/from the city cost ₹125, while prepaid taxis start at ₹350.

Shared autorickshaws shuttle between the train station and Gandhi Maidan bus stand (₹3), departing from the backside of the train station. For short trips, cycle-rickshaws are best.

Around Patna

As the sights of Vaishali are well dispersed and transport to both Vaishali and Kesariya sporadic, it is far better to organise a car and driver (see p513) for a longish day.

VAISHALI

06225

Most sites in Vaishali, 55km northwest of Patna, surround a large ancient coronation water tank. Dominating the skyline is a gleaming, modern **Japanese Peace Pagoda** (Indian/foreigner ₹5/100), while opposite is a small **museum** (229404; admission ₹5; 10am-5pm Sat-Thu) presenting clay and terracotta figures plus an intriguing 1st- to 2nd-century AD toilet pan with appropriately sized exit holes. Nearby are the ground-floor remains of a **stupa** that once contained Buddha's ashes, which now reside in Patna Museum (p509).

Three kilometres away in **Basokund**, you'll find the most widely accepted birthplace of Lord Mahavira, the 24th and final Jain *tirthankar* (teacher), one of three debated locations in Bihar. An engraved stone marks the place in a flower-decorated plot.

At a similar distance are the ruins of the **Kolhua Complex** (Indian/foreigner ₹5/100; 7am-5pm), comprising a hemispherical brick stupa guarded by a lion squatting atop a 2300-year-old Ashoka pillar. The pillar is plain and contains none of the Ashokan edicts usually carved onto these pillars. Nearby are the ruins of smaller stupas and monastic buildings. According to legend, Buddha was given a bowl of honey here by monkeys, who also dug out a rainwater tank for his water supply.

KESARIYA

Rising high out of the earth from where the dying Buddha donated his begging bowl, this **stupa** (24hr) is an enthralling example of how nature reclaimed a deserted monument. Excavated and half revealed from under a grassy and wooded veil is what's likely to be the world's second-tallest (38m) Buddhist stupa dating from the Pala period. Above the 425m-circumference pedestal are five uniquely shaped terraces that form a gargantuan Buddhist tantric mandala. Each terrace has a number of niches containing mutilated Buddha statues whose heads were lopped off by Muslim invaders.

MANER

Worth visiting 30km west of Patna is **Chhoti Dargah** (24hr), an architecturally elegant three-storey mausoleum fronted by a large tank. The venerable Muslim saint Makhdum Shah Daulat was buried here in 1619 under a canopied tomb. As it is auspicious to be buried close to a saint, several cloth-covered graves in front of the mausoleum keep the saint company. The large body of water is a favourite swimming spot for local children and its steps provide a good laundry site.

Raxaul

06255 / POP 41,347

Raxaul is a grim, dirty and horribly congested border town. Most of the goods imported into Nepal pass through it, and its twin Birganj over the border. As you'd guess, it's not a place to linger. If you must spend the night, **Hotel Kaveri** (221148; Main Rd; r with/without AC ₹800/500;) is tolerable, with room service and a vague semblance of tourist-friendliness. Restaurants are very scarce, but you can check your email at India's friendliest cyber house, **Soni Cyber Cafe** (Main Rd; per hr ₹25).

The Karai Tala bus stand is 200m down a western side road about 2km south of the border. There are supposedly five daily buses to Patna, times are extremely variable (₹125, six hours, 6am, 9am, 2pm, 9pm and 10pm). The 13022 *Mithila Express* train runs daily to Kolkata (sleeper/3AC/2AC ₹272/735/1088, 18 hours, 10am).

Gaya

0631 / POP 383,197

Brash and loud Gaya, 100km south of Patna, is a religious centre for Hindu pilgrims who

---

WORTH A TRIP

SONEPUR MELA

According to the Gajendra Moksha legend, Sonepur, 25km north of Patna, is where Vishnu ended the prehistoric battle between the lords of the forest (elephants) and the lords of the water (crocodiles). Each November/December, during the full moon of Kartik Purnima, the three-week **Sonepur Mela** celebrates this infamous tale. During this auspicious time devotees bathe where the Ganges joins with the Gandak and Mehi Rivers while Asia's largest cattle fair takes place nearby at Hathi Bazaar. More than mere bovines are on sale – Marwari horses, brindled goats, camels, birds and elephants change hands, although trade in the latter is illegal.

CROSSING INTO NEPAL

Border Hours

The border at Raxaul is open from 6am to 10pm.

Foreign Exchange

No banks change money in Raxaul but there are many private money changers on both sides of the border. The State Bank of India in Raxaul has an ATM.

Onward Transport

Catch a cycle-rickshaw (₹20), autorickshaw or tonga (two-wheeled horse or pony carriage) from Raxaul's bus or train station to Birganj, 5km away in Nepal. From Birganj, the most convenient and fastest option is **Jai Mata di Tours & Travels** (☑9308051147; Main Rd, Birganj), which runs 10-seater jeeps to Kathmandu and Pokhara from its office a few hundred metres past the border every morning between 7am and 10am (₹560, six hours). Jeeps leave when full. There are also regular day and night bus departures to Kathmandu (₹350/400, nine hours) and Pokhara (₹350/425, nine hours).

Visas

Nepali 15-, 30- and 90-day visas (US$25/40/100 and one passport photo) are only available from 6am to 6pm on the Nepal side of the border.

---

believe temple offerings here protect ones' ancestors and relieve the recently departed from the cycle of birth and rebirth. Foreign tourists believe in making a quick getaway to Bodhgaya, 13km away. If you're stuck, look for pilgrims offering *pinda* (funeral cake) at the ghats along the river.

⊙ Sights & Activities

Vishnupad Temple HINDU TEMPLE
Close to the banks of the Falgu River south of town, the *sikhara* (spired) Vishnupad Temple was constructed in 1787 by Queen Ahilyabai of Maheshwar (Madhya Pradesh) and houses a 40cm 'footprint' of Vishnu imprinted into solid rock. Non-Hindus are not permitted to enter, but you can get a look from the pink platform near the entrance. Along the ghats on the river's edge, Hindus bathe and light funeral pyres, so be discreet when you visit.

Brahmajuni Hill LANDMARK
One thousand stone steps lead to the top of Brahmajuni Hill, 1km southwest of the Vishnupad Temple, where Buddha is said to have delivered the fire sermon.

🛏 Sleeping & Eating

If you arrive late or have an early departure, staying in Gaya might be more convenient than in Bodhgaya.

Hotel Vishnu International HOTEL $
(☑2224422; Swarajayapur Rd; s ₹350, d ₹450-750, with AC ₹800-1200; ✸) Funky, with a French castle-like exterior, this is the best-value option in town. There's a friendly front desk and clean, well-kept rooms with high-powered fans, but hot water is only available by the bucket.

Ajatsatru Hotel INDIAN, CHINESE $$
(Station Rd; breakfast ₹35-75, mains ₹35-125) This hotel across from the train station is home to the excellent and friendly multicuisine restaurant, Sujata, that can't be beat while waiting for a train. Bihari sweet shops line either side for dessert.

Hotel Akash HOTEL $
(☑2222205; Laxman Sahay Rd; s/d ₹250/300) A decent budget option across from the train station, with threadbare but clean rooms. An air cooler costs an extra ₹150.

Khushi INDIAN/CHINESE $
(Swarajayapur Rd; mains ₹40-155) A good selection of Indian and Chinese dishes done quite well, with friendly service and stylish blue uniforms to boot. Near Hotel Vishnu.

ℹ Information

There's a **Bihar state tourist office** (☑2223635; ◷10am-5pm Mon-Sat) and a **State Bank of India ATM** at the train station. Several

BIHAR & JHARKHAND GAYA

SASSARAM

If you're motoring on from Gaya to Varanasi, a short detour to the **Mausoleum of Sher Shah** (Indian/foreigner ₹5/100; ⊘dawn-dusk) is worthwhile. Seemingly floating within a large tank, the mausoleum of the historically significant emperor Sher Shah (p1089) is an exercise in architectural restraint. Its beauty lies in an aesthetic use of proportion, from its rounded dome down through a ring of *chhatris* (pavilions or pillar-supported canopies) to its solid pedestal. Very similar in style to Isa Khan's tomb in Delhi (p67), it still bears vestiges of deep-blue Persian tiling. Within is the tomb of Sher Shah, his son and their family. Hasan Shah, father of Sher Shah, has his own less spectacular tomb, minus the watery setting, 200m away.

internet cafes (per hr ₹30) line Swarajayapur Rd near Hotel Vishnu.

❶ Getting There & Away

Bus

Patna (₹60, three hours, hourly) Buses leave from the Gandhi Maidan bus stand and from a stand next to the train station.

Ranchi (₹120, seven hours, hourly) Buses leave from the Gandhi Maidan bus stand.

Rajgir (₹50, 2½ hours, every 30 minutes) Use the bus stand across the river in Manpur.

Train

Gaya is on the Delhi–Kolkata railway line.

Delhi (3AC/2AC/1AC ₹1155/1555/2610, 11 to 12 hours, 10.39pm) The fastest train to Delhi is the 12301 *Kolkata Rajdhani Express*.

Kolkata (3AC/2AC/1AC ₹710/940/1570, six hours, 4.04am) Catch the 12302 for the most convenient connection to Kolkata.

Varanasi (sleeper/3AC/2AC ₹127/325/441, five hours, 5.10am) The most convenient is the 13009 *Doon Express*.

Patna (AC chair ₹165, 2½ hours, 1.10pm) The 18626 *Rajendranagar Express* is the most convenient of the several daily trains to Patna.

Autorickshaw drivers will make the trip to Bodhgaya for ₹200 but can usually be bargained down to about ₹80.

Bodhgaya

📞0631 / POP 30,883

This spiritually important town attracts Buddhist pilgrims from around the world who come for prayer, study and meditation. It was here that 2600 years ago Prince Siddhartha Gautama attained enlightenment beneath a bodhi tree and became Buddha. A beautiful temple in a garden setting marks the spot and a descendant of that original bodhi tree flourishes here, its roots embedded in the same soil as its celebrated ancestor.

Many monasteries and temples dot the bucolic landscape, built in their national style by foreign Buddhist communities. But don't expect a tranquil monastic retreat – the town is firmly planted on the non-religious tourism map as well, and with that has come the usual invasion of tourist paraphernalia, souvenir stalls and a serious rubbish problem. Conversely, Bodhgaya has the best range of accommodation in Bihar and offers the most traveller camaraderie of anywhere in Bihar and Jharkhand.

The best time to visit is October to March when Tibetan pilgrims come down from McLeod Ganj in Dharamsala. The high season is from December to January, which is also when the Dalai Lama often visits.

◉ Sights & Activities

TOP CHOICE Mahabodhi Temple HINDU TEMPLE (camera/video ₹20/300; ⊘4am-9pm) The magnificent Unesco World Heritage-listed Mahabodhi Temple, where Buddha attained enlightenment and formulated his philosophy of life, forms the spiritual heart of Bodhgaya.

The Mahabodhi Temple was built in the 6th century AD atop the site of a temple erected by Emperor Ashoka almost 800 years earlier. After being razed by 11th-century Muslim invaders, the temple underwent several major restorations, the last in 1882. Topped by a 50m pyramidal spire, the ornate structure houses a 10th-century, 2m-high gilded image of a seated Buddha. Amazingly, four of the original sculpted stone railings surrounding the temple, dating from the Sunga period (184–72 BC), have survived amid the replicas.

Pilgrims and visitors from all walks of life and religions come to worship or just soak up the ambience of this sacred place. There's a well-manicured **Meditation Park** (admission ₹25 5-10am & 5-9pm, ₹20 10am-5pm) for those seeking extra solitude within the temple grounds. An enthralling way to start or finish the day is to stroll around the perimeter of the temple compound and watch a sea of maroon and yellow dip and rise as monks perform endless prostrations on their prayer boards.

Monasteries & Temples MONASTERIES, TEMPLES
One of Bodhgaya's great joys is its collection of monasteries, each offering visitors a unique opportunity to peek into different Buddhist cultures and compare architectural styles. For example, the **Indosan Nipponji Temple** (⊙5am-noon & 2-6pm) is an exercise in quiet Japanese understatement compared to the richly presented **Bhutanese Monastery** nearby. The most impressive is the newer **Tergar Monastery** of the Karmapa (Black Hat sect), a glory of Tibetan decorative arts that will leave you slack-jawed as you enter. A none-too-distant runner-up is the impressive **Thai Monastery**, a brightly coloured *wat* with gold leaf shimmering from its rooftop and arches and manicured gardens. Meditation sessions are held here mornings and evenings. The Tibetan **Karma Temple** and **Namgyal Monastery** each contain large prayer wheels. Other noteworthy monasteries include those from the **Chinese Monastery**, **Vietnamese Monastery** and **Nepali Monastery**. Monasteries are open sunrise to sunset.

Great Buddha Statue MONUMENT
(off Temple St; ⊙7am-noon & 2-5pm) This 25m-high Buddha towers above a pleasant garden at the end of Temple St. The impressive monument was unveiled by the Dalai Lama in 1989, and is surrounded by 10 smaller sculptures of Buddha's disciples. The statue is partially hollow and is said to contain some 20,000 bronze Buddhas.

Archaeological Museum MUSEUM
(☏2200739; admission ₹10; ⊙8am-5pm) This museum contains a small collection of local Buddha figures and parts of the original granite railings and pillars rescued from the Mahabodhi Temple.

Bodhgaya Multimedia Museum MUSEUM
(Indian/foreigner ₹30/100; ⊙8am-8pm) The Dalai Lama himself blessed the 2010 opening of this visual museum, which is low on production value but big on information and historical perspective.

🥾 Courses

Root Institute for Wisdom Culture MEDITATION, YOGA
(☏2200714; www.rootinstitute.com; ⊙office 8.30-11.30am & 1.30-4.30pm) This foreign-run institute holds various meditation courses (from two to 21 days) between late October and March. A requested donation of ₹750 per day covers the course, accommodation and meals. Intermediate-level courses are also scheduled from December to February.

BUDDHA'S BODHI

Surely the most sacred fig tree ever to grace the Earth was the **Bodhi Tree** at Bodhgaya's Mahabodhi Temple, under which Prince Siddhartha Gautama, the spiritual teacher and founder of Buddhism, achieved enlightenment. The tree that stands there today, though, is a mere descendant of the original.

Known as the Sri Maha Bodhi, the original tree was paid special attention by Ashoka the Great, an Indian emperor who ruled most of the subcontinent from 269 to 232 BC, a century or so after Buddha's believed death between 411 and 400 BC. His wife, Tissarakkhā, wasn't such a fan of the tree and in a fit of jealousy and rage, caused the original Bodhi Tree's death by poisonous thorns shortly after becoming queen.

Thankfully, before its death, one of the tree's saplings was carried off to Anuradhapura in Sri Lanka by Sanghamitta (Ashoka's daughter), where it continues to flourish. A cutting was carried back to Bodhgaya and planted where the original once stood. The red sandstone slab between the tree and the temple was placed there by Ashoka and marks the spot of Buddha's enlightenment – it's referred to as the Vajrasan (Diamond Throne).

Buddha was said to have remained under the original tree for one week after his enlightenment, staring unblinking in an awed gesture of gratitude and wonder. Today, pilgrims and tourists alike flock here to attempt to do exactly the same thing, and the tree is considered the most important of Buddhism's four holiest sites.

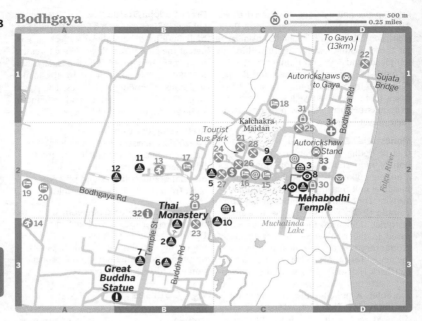

The 6.45am meditation session is open to all, and for a donation visitors are welcome to stay on for breakfast. You can also catch drop-in yoga classes at 11.45am Tuesday to Saturday.

**Bodhgaya Vipassana Meditation
Centre** MEDITATION
(Dhamma Bodhi; ☑2200437; www.dhamma.org) Runs intensive 10-day *vipassana* courses twice each month throughout the year. The small compound is 4km west of town on Boghgaya Rd and runs on donations.

International Meditation Centre MEDITATION
(☑2200707; per day from ₹200) The donation-only courses here are more informal and year-round, though anything less than a three-day commitment is frowned upon.

Tergar Monastery BUDDHISM
(☑2201256; www.tergar.org) Offers courses on Tibetan Buddhism and welcomes long-term qualified volunteer English teachers.

🛏 Sleeping

Rates listed are for the high season (from December to January) but can fall by as much as 50% in the low season, so it pays to negotiate. A 10% tax is often tacked on to midrange choices and above.

**TOP
CHOICE Mohammad's House** GUESTHOUSE **$**
(☑9934022691; yasmd_2002@rediffmail.com; near Kal Chakra Ground, Miya Bigha; d without bathroom ₹250-350, with bathroom ₹400-500; @🛜) This is a wonderful opportunity to live within a village (Miya Bigha). Rooms are basic but spotless and popular with long-term stayers. A rooftop terrace gives commanding views of rice paddies, sunsets and monasteries. Friendly Mohammad is a mine of useful information and advice, an excellent chef (p520) and refuses to pay commission to rickshaw touts. There's a one-month minimum stay in high season.

**TOP
CHOICE Taj Darbar** HOTEL **$$$**
(☑2200053; www.hoteltajdarbar; Bodhgaya Rd; s/d ₹2800/3200; 🅰🛜) The best-value top-end choice by a landslide, with polished marble hallways and spacious rooms with ivory-white bed sheets, small seating areas, working desks and sporadic bathtubs. The restaurant is also very popular with expats and good value for money, though we had to cut away an inexcusable amount of fat from our mutton *bhuna ghost*. It's nothing extraordinary, but it excels at the ordinary.

Rahul Guest House GUESTHOUSE **$**
(☑2200709; rahul_bodhgaya@yahoo.com; d ₹250-300) This serene guesthouse run as a family

home (and kept sparkling clean as a result) is the pick of the assembly of guesthouses backing onto the Kalachakra Maidan. The rooms upstairs, with whitewashed walls, nice breezes and simple furnishings, are better than those on the ground floor.

Kirti Guest House GUESTHOUSE $$
(☏2200744; kirtihouse744@yahoo.com; Bodhgaya Rd; d incl breakfast ₹2400-3500; ❄@) Run by the Tibetan Monastery and one of the best of the midrange places. Kirti is normally known for its clean, bright rooms (although a mouse did scurry across the room we inspected) and its monastery-like facade is particularly pretty. Ask for a mouse-free front room opening out onto the balcony.

Royal Residency HOTEL $$$
(☏2200124; www.theroyalresidency.net/bodhgaya; Bodhgaya Rd; s/d ₹6000/6500; ❄❂) Bodhgaya's most luxurious hotel is about 1.5km west of the centre. Fine woodwork, rich marble, pleasant gardens and comfy rooms await

those who are not too concerned with getting good value for money.

Hotel Tathagat International HOTEL $$$
(☏2200106; www.hoteltathagatbodhgaya.net; Bodhgaya Rd; s/d ₹2200/2750; ❄❂) The tapioca-pudding paint job was a bad idea, but the simple rooms are clean and conservatively furnished. Avoid the cramped deluxe rooms and the Mahabodhi Temple–end rooms above the generator.

If you don't mind some simple rules, it's possible to stay at some of the monasteries and dharma centres. Two of the best are the **Bhutanese Monastery** (☏2200710; Buddha Rd; d ₹300, with bathroom ₹500), a tranquil place typified by colourful surroundings, gardens and big rooms, and the Tibetan **Karma Temple** (☏2200795; ktcmbodhgaya@yahoo.com; Temple St; d shared bathroom ₹300). Another excellent choice is the **Root Institute for Wisdom Culture** (☏2200714; www.rootinstitute.com; dm ₹200), whose well-kept dorm with mosquito nets is open to everyone.

CHOOSING THE RIGHT CHARITY

Central Bihar is one of the poorest parts of India and with its influx of visitors and Buddhist pilgrims, Bodhgaya has become home to numerous charity organisations and schools that rely on donations and volunteers. Some are set up by dodgy characters jumping on the charity bandwagon to fleece tourists. Be wary of those who approach you in the street for donations, especially children who besiege tourists asking for money for everything from school books and educational sponsorship to new cricket bats – they may speak several languages but are most likely illiterate. Genuine charities advise that you never give money directly to children. It's far better to help by donating to legitimate institutions or volunteering. For more information, see p39.

✗ Eating & Drinking

During the peak season, when Tibetan pilgrims pour into Bodhgaya, temporary tent restaurants are set up around the Tibetan Refugee Market, serving a range of Tibetan dishes and sweets. Word of warning: no restaurant listed here at the time of writing had a sign boldly claiming its inclusion in the guide at time of publication. Don't be duped.

TOP CHOICE Mohammad Restaurant CAFE **$**
(mains ₹30-110) Hands-on Mohammed has been cooking professionally since he was 13 and it shows: his traveller tent serves up fresh, cheap food that you miss no matter where you are from. Fresh vegetables not drowned into submission in butter and oil? Check. (Sorta) English breakfasts, Tibetan *momos* (dumplings), Israeli *saksuka,* quesadillas, Japanese food, Chinese fare, Greek salads, home-made soups – check, check, check. From November to March, he's located next to the Tibetan Refugee Market; from August to October, in an extremely cramped space behind Fujiya Green. Flashy it ain't, but it has some of the town's best food and those in the know flock to it. Save room for the tasty chocolate balls.

TOP CHOICE Tibet Om Cafe TIBETAN, CAFE **$**
(dishes ₹30-100; ◷Nov-Mar) A sweet Tibetan family has been coming down from Dharamsala every winter since 1986 to feed travellers hungry for *momos*, pancakes, brown bread, pies and cakes. The food is cheap and tasty and you can loiter endlessly. It lies within the Mayayana Guesthouse of the Namgyal Monastery.

Fujiya Green CAFE **$**
(off Kalachakra Maidan; mains ₹30-85) Another makeshift restaurant that's hugely popular with travellers, with surprisingly brightly coloured walls and tile flooring inside. The menu – running the gamut of Asian travel staples – excels across the board.

Sewak Tea Corner SWEETS **$**
(items ₹6-50) If you're seeking sustenance at rock-bottom prices, look no further than this *dhaba*-style eatery, little more than a glorified roadside stand, for excellent snacks, sweets, lassis and basic thalis. The outdoor seating is a great spot to sit back with a chai and watch Bodhgaya go by.

Siam Thai THAI **$$**
(Bodhgaya Rd; mains ₹100-195) Authentic is a stretch – dishes here are slightly off – but the fact remains that if you're looking to shake up your tastebuds, this Thai place does the job...just not as good as it should considering it's Thai owned and around the corner from the Thai Monastery. Still, we gobbled down our green curry in an anti-masala delirium. Locals report the quality improves dramatically when the Thai direct flight is operating. We should hope.

Gautam BREAKFAST **$**
(Bodhgaya Rd; mains ₹20-80) A semi-tent affair that's a good choice for standard traveller fare, notably great banana pancakes and cinnamon masala tea – if you can stand the owner spitting in the restaurant's 'garden' while you eat.

The **Royal Residency** (Bodhgaya Rd; mains ₹85-200) and **Hotel Sujata** (Buddha Rd; mains ₹120-250) are similar high-class restaurants in two of Bodhgaya's upmarket hotels. They are the only ones in town to officially serve alcohol (₹250 for a beer).

🛍 Shopping

Kundan Bazaar BOOKSTORE
(Bodhgaya Rd; www.kundanbazar.com; ◷9am-9pm) Novels and Buddhist literature. Book swap or hire.

Mahabodhi Bookshop BOOKSTORE
(Mahabodhi Temple; ◷5am-9pm) A range of Buddhist literature within the temple complex.

Tibetan Refugee Market CLOTHING

(◷8am-8pm Oct-Jan) There are slim pickings here for winter woollens or textiles – most items appear to be purchased from a (tasteless) department store in Delhi. Elsewhere there are scores of souvenir stalls.

ℹ Information

Internet cafes (per hour ₹30) cluster around Hotel Tathagat International and across from the Mahabodi Temple entrance.

Medical Services

Verma Health Care Centre (☎2201101; ◷24hr) Emergency room and clinic.

Money

State Bank of India (Bodhgaya Rd) Best rates for cash and travellers cheques; has an ATM.

Post

Main post office (cnr Bodhgaya & Godam Rds)

Tourist Information

BSTDC Tourist Complex (☎2200672; cnr Bodhgaya Rd & Temple St; ◷10.30am-5pm Tue-Sat) Useless.

Travel Agencies

Middle Way Travels (☎2200648; Bodhgaya Rd; ◷9am-10pm) A sign of success is when others open businesses with similar names: this is the one to deal with. Almost opposite the temple entrance, the agency exchanges currency and travellers cheques, sells or swaps books, and deals with ticketing and car hire.

ℹ Getting There & Away

Gaya airport is 8km west of town. **Air India** (☎2201155; airport) flies once a week to Kolkata; during the high season there are direct international flights from Bangkok (Thailand), Colombo (Sri Lanka), Thimphu (Bhutan) and Yangon (Myanmar).

Overcrowded shared autorickshaws (₹15) leave from the T-junction of Bodhgaya Rd and Sujata Bridge for the 13km trip to Gaya. A private autorickshaw to Gaya should cost ₹100 in high season.

SERENE SUNSETS

Bodhgaya is often privy to some spectacular sunsets. At dusk, head out halfway across the Sujata Bridge and watch the fiery-red glow descend over the Mahobodhi Temple.

Rajgir

☎06112 / POP 33,691

The fascinating surrounds of Rajgir are bounded by five semiarid rocky hills, each lined with vestiges of ancient 'Cyclopean' walls – once the ancient capital of Magadha. Thanks to both Buddha and Mahavira spending some serious time here, Rajgir is an important pilgrimage site for Buddhists and Jains. A mention in the Mahabharata also ensures that Rajgir has a good supply of Hindu pilgrims who come to bathe in the hot springs at the Lakshmi Narayan Temple. However, foreign travellers criminally undervisit the ramshackle town and its environs. It's a shame – a couple of days spent exploring the many historic Buddhist and Jain sites around town and the ancient university site of Nalanda (p522), 12km south, provides the perfect complement to Bodhgaya, 80km away. Beyond that, ruins pepper the landscape. The centre is 500m east of the main road, on which you'll find the train station, bus stand and a number of hotels.

Rajgir Mahotsava, in October, is the town's three-day cultural festival featuring classical Indian music, folk music and dance.

◉ Sights & Activities

The easiest way to see Rajgir's scattered sites is to rent a tonga. A four-hour tour that includes the hot springs, Vishwashanti Stupa, the Son Bhandar caves, Naulakha Mandir, Jain Temple, Japanese Temple, Veerayatan, Venuvana Vihar and the shrine of Maniyar Math is ₹500.

TOP CHOICE **Vishwashanti Stupa** BUDDHIST TEMPLE

About 5km south of town (take a tonga), a wobbly, single-person **ropeway** (chairlift return ticket ₹30, 8.15am to 1pm and 2pm to 5pm) runs to the top of Ratnagiri Hill and its blazing-white 40m-high Vishwashanti Stupa. Recesses in the stupa feature golden statues of Buddha in the four stages of his life – birth, enlightenment, preaching and death. Expansive views reveal some of the 26 Jain shrines dotting the distant hilltops. If you walk back down, you can detour to the remains of a stupa and **Griddhakuta** (Vulture's Peak), where Buddha preached to his disciples.

TOP CHOICE **Veerayatan** MUSEUM

Near the Indo Hokke Hotel, this fascinating **Jain museum** (admission ₹15; www.veerayatan bihar.org; ◷7am-6pm) tells the history of each of the 24 Jain *tirthankars* through ornate dollhouse-like 3-D panel depictions made from wood and metal. The level of detail is astonishing. Don't miss the display by artist-in-residence Arharya Shri Chandanaiji Maharaj, made by hand out of flour.

Other Sights
LANDMARKS, HOT SPRINGS

Spread around town are relics of the ancient city, caves and places associated with Ajatasatru and Bimbisara. Hindu pilgrims are drawn to the rowdy **Lakshmi Narayan Temple complex**, about 2km south of town, to enjoy the health benefits of the **hot springs**. The murky grey Brahmakund, the hottest spring, is a scalding 45°C. Temple priests will show you around, pour hot water on you and ask for generous donations (₹100 to ₹200 for this contrived ritual); you can politely shoo them off as you are only being targeted because you are a tourist. It's a fascinating but confusing place with no English signs, so tread carefully so you don't unintentionally offend.

Not as spiritually significant, but perhaps more realistic, is next door's Rajasthan-pink **Buddha Jal Vihar** (Indian/foreigner ₹25/50; ⊘men 5-10am & noon-9pm, women 10am-noon), an inviting, crystal-clear swimming pool set in well-manicured gardens and perfect to beat the heat.

🛏 Sleeping & Eating

Indo Hokke Hotel BOUTIQUE HOTEL $$$
(📞255245; centaur@dte.vsnl.net.in; s/d ₹6000/6500; ✳@🛜🏊) Surrounded by lovely gardens, this is Bihar's unique sleeping experience. Most of the rooms are furnished Japanese style with tatami mats instead of beds, teak furniture and Eastern decor. Soak in the Japanese bathhouse and meditate in the towering cylindrical Buddhist prayer hall.

Hotel Gautam Vihar HOTEL $
(📞255273; Nalanda Rd; dm ₹75, d ₹450, with AC ₹700; ✳) One of three Bihar Tourism (BSTDC) hotels in town, this is well located between the bus and train stations. Though typically rundown, the rooms are spacious with lounge chairs, TV and hot water and – perhaps more importantly – a friendly manager with hospitality training under his belt.

Siddharth Hotel HOTEL ₹₹
(📞255616; www.siddharthrajgir.com; r ₹1050, with AC ₹2500; ✳@🛜) Near the hot springs, Siddharth has undergone a dramatic renovation and now features all the facilities of a top-

end hotel. Prices are shockingly ambitious in high season (October to March, when rates also include breakfast, mineral water and tea) but come back down to earth with a 30% discount in the low season.

Rajgir Residency HOTEL $$$
(📞255404; www.rajgir-residency.com; s/d ₹3800/4600; ✳🛜) It lacks personality but has bathtubs and provides top-end comfort with two restaurants that can whip up Thai or Korean if you ask.

Lotus Restaurant INDIAN/JAPANESE $$$
(meals ₹40-275) At the Indo Hokke Hotel, this upscale restaurant with high-backed chairs and long tables is part Japanese, part Indian/Chinese. The pricier Japanese menu features soba noodles, teriyaki and tempura, with authentic flavours and fresh ingredients (including authentic pepper, pickles and tea) – a refreshing left off the *ghee* highway.

Green Restaurant INDIAN $
(mains ₹40-100) Opposite the Lakshmi Narayan temple complex and hot springs, this simple restaurant offers great Indian meals. The thali (₹60 to ₹100) comes with a memorable spicy dahl fry.

ℹ Information

There's a BSTDC tourist office at the Hotel Gautam Vihar, about 1km south of the train station on Nalanda Rd, and a State Bank of India ATM on Bank Rd about 200m west of the bus stand; and another across from the temple complex.

ℹ Getting There & Around

Frequent buses run to Gaya (₹40, 2½ hours) and Nalanda (₹6, 30 minutes) from the bus stand on the road to Nalanda. Ridiculously crowded shared jeeps also shuttle between Rajgir and Nalanda (₹10). There is only one direct bus to Patna (₹55, three hours, 4.30pm). Three express trains connect Rajgir with Patna daily (SL/CC/3AC/2AC ₹120/165/210/279, three to five hours, 8.10am, 2.50pm and 11.30pm).

Around Rajgir

NALANDA
📞 061194

Founded in the 5th century AD, Nalanda was the ancient world's great university and an important Buddhist centre. When Chinese scholar and traveller Xuan Zang visited sometime between 685 and 762 AD, about 10,000 monks and students lived here, studying theology, astronomy, metaphysics, medicine and philosophy. It's said that Nalanda's three libraries were so extensive they burnt for six months when invaders sacked the university in the 12th century.

Allow an hour or two for wandering the extensive **ruins** (Indian/foreigner ₹5/100, video camera ₹25; ☺9am-5.30pm). They're peaceful and well maintained with a park-like atmosphere of clipped lawns, shrubs and roses. A guide (₹100) is a worthwhile investment in unravelling the labyrinthine buildings and their history. The red-brick ruins consist of nine monasteries and four main temples. Most impressive is the **Great Stupa**, with steps, terraces, a few intact votive stupas, and monks' cells.

Across from the interesting Multimedia Museum is the **archaeological museum** (admission ₹5; ☺8am-5pm), a small but fascinating museum housing the Nalanda University seal and a host of sculptures and bronzes unearthed from Nalanda and Rajgir. Among the many Buddha figures and Picasso-like 9th-century Kirtimukha (gargoyle) is a bizarre multiple-spouted pot.

About 2km further on from the museum is the huge **Xuan Zang Memorial Hall** (Indian/foreigner ₹5/50; ☺8am-5pm), built by the Chinese as a peace pagoda in honour of the famous Chinese traveller who studied and taught for some years at Nalanda. Modern-day backpackers will appreciate the statue of Xuan Zang at the front.

Regular shared jeeps run between Rajgir and Nalanda village (₹10), and from there you can take a shared tonga (per person ₹10 when full) for the final 3km to the site of Nalanda.

KUNDALPUR

Just outside Nalanda you'll find the striking **Nandyavarta Mahal** (☺5am-9pm) at Kundalpur, believed by the Jain Digamber sect to be the birthplace of Lord Mahavira, the final *tirthankar* and founder of Jainism. The small temple complex houses three hot-white temples, the main featuring a to-scale postured idol of Mahavira. Inside the serene **Trikal Chaubeesi Jinmandir** within the same complex you'll find 72 *tirthanker* idols representing 24 each of the past age, the present age and the future age.

JHARKHAND

Jharkhand was hewn out of neighbouring Bihar in 2000 to meet the autonomy demands of the Adivasi (tribal) population. Despite the fledgling state having a jaw-dropping 40% of the country's mineral wealth (mostly coal, copper and iron ore), rich forests, several major industrial centres and the healthy budget of a newly formed state, it still suffers thanks to poverty, incompetence, corruption, and outbursts of Maoist and Naxalite violence. For travellers, Jharkhand's prime attractions are the Jain pilgrimage centre at Parasnath Hill, its national parks and the chance to explore a tourist-free northern India.

523

Ranchi

☑0651 / POP 846,454

Set on a plateau at 700m and marginally cooler than the plains, Jharkhand's capital, Ranchi, was the summer capital of Bihar under the British. There's little of interest in the city and it's not really on the way to anywhere except Betla (Palamau) National Park (p525).

◉ Sights & Activities

Jagannath Temple   HINDU TEMPLE

The Jagannath Temple, about 12km southwest of town (₹200 to ₹250 return by autorickshaw), is a smaller version of the great Jagannath Mandir at Puri (p595), and is open to non-Hindus. Every year, at the same time and in the same manner as in Puri, Jagannath and his brother and sister gods are charioted to their holiday home, a smaller temple some 500m away.

🛏 Sleeping & Eating

Station Rd, running between the train and bus stations, is lined with hotels of varying quality. Other hotels and restaurants can be found on the seemingly endless Main Rd, which runs at right angles to Station Rd. A 7% luxury tax is sometimes levied.

CHOICE **Chanakya**

BNR Hotel   HERITAGE HOTEL **$$$**

(☑2461481; chanakyabnrranchi@hotmail.com; Station Rd; s/d ₹1730/2081; ❋@☎) This part-historic rail hotel, almost opposite the train station, is a red-tiled terracotta-roofed Raj relic. It's been completely renovated by the Chanakya group (and expanded from 14 to 82 rooms, no less), with extra-large rooms, rain-style showers and hardwood floors. There's free wi-fi in the business centre, a bar, a very good restaurant and parrots in the trees. Unfortunately, the super-spacious 110-year-old heritage rooms have all been booked on contract, but check ahead just in case that went belly up.

BIHAR & JHARKHAND RANCHI

THE HOLY PARASNATH

Parasnath, a dusty town in eastern Jharkhand, is the railhead for the major Jain pilgrimage centre in east India. The site and its 31 temples blanket the top of **Parasnath Hill** – Jharkhand's highest point. At the summit (1366m), where the Parasnath Temple now stands, 20 of the 24 Jain *tirthankars* reached salvation, including Parasnath at the age of 100.

The best approach is from the auspicious town of Madhuban, 13km northeast of Parasnath, and home to some magnificent temples itself. The daily pilgrimage begins at 3am from the village, where it's a 9km jaunt to the top, followed by a 9km loop visiting each of the temples. The entire 27km circuit takes about 12 hours. If you don't want to walk you can hire a *dandi* (a cart carried by two men) for ₹2000 return. Water and snacks are available along the way. During holidays, up to 15,000 people per day make the jaunt.

You're likely to spend one, if not two, nights here. There are several *dharamsalas* (pilgrim's rest houses) in Madhuban, which are more or less free save a nominal upkeep fee, but nearly always jam-packed. For a proper hotel, the government-run and extra friendly **Yatri Nivas** (☎0658232365; shikharjioffice@yahoo.com; r from ₹300) has refreshingly comfortable rooms (with TV, lockers and hot water). Don't miss the small but well-done **Jain Museum** (admission ₹5; ⊙8am-6.30pm Mar-Oct, 8.30am-6pm Nov-Feb).

Parasnath is on the Kolkata–Gaya–Delhi train line. Convenient options include the 12875 *Neelachal Express* to Gaya (SL/3AC/2AC ₹140/292/383, three hours) and Varanasi (₹196/494/662, seven hours) at 12.44am; and the 12308 *Jodhpur Howrah Superfast Express* to Kolkata (₹175/434/581, 5½ hours, 10.26pm). Regular minibuses run from Parasnath's bus stand to Madhuban every half-hour (₹30, 40 minutes). From Ranchi, you'll need to hire a car.

Hotel Embassy   HOTEL $

(☎2460449;embassyhotel@rediffmail.com;Station Rd; s/d ₹600/700, with AC from ₹700/850; ✴) One of the few budget places along Station Rd to accept foreigners; the comfortable rooms are refreshingly contemporary and decently clean.

Hotel Capitol Hill   HOTEL $$$

(☎2331330; www.hotelcapitolhill.com; Main Rd; s/d ₹4500/5000; ✴🛜) A classy upmarket hotel in the Capitol Hill shopping complex. The ultra-modern 3rd-floor lobby with cream leather chairs complements equally modern rooms with a Scandinavian touch and wi-fi. The lipstick-red bar is Ranchi's most stylish.

Planet Masala   CAFE $

(56C Main Rd; mains ₹50-90) A great, modern cafe offering some 26 types of dosas, veg pizzas and Indian/Chinese dishes, sundaes and proper but odd espresso. The jazzed-up four-star thali (₹138; feeds two) is excellent.

The Nook   INDIAN $$

(Station Rd; mains ₹75-140) The best midrange restaurant in the train station area; the dining room in Hotel Kwality Inns is comfortable and the service attentive without being

obsequious. The Indian, tandoori and Chinese excel and there's alcohol on tap.

Hotel Amrit   HOTEL $

(☎2461952; Station Rd; s/d/tr from ₹380/500/600, with AC ₹980/1200; ✴) Cheap option near the Embassy. AC rooms are in much better shape than others. Paint donations probably accepted – Lord knows it needs it.

Veda é Café   CAFE $

(3rd fl, Roshpa Tower, Main Rd; sandwiches ₹45-80) Stylish cafe across from Planet Masala, with sandwiches, pizza and better coffee.

ⓘ Information

The most helpful tourist information is at **Samridhi Travels** (☎2332179; www.samridhitravels.com; Main Rd; ⊙8am-8pm Mon-Sat, till 6pm Sun) at the Birsa Vihar tourist complex. It makes train reservations and accommodation bookings and is next door to a most unhelpful government tourist office. The **State Bank of India** (Main Rd; ⊙10am-3.30pm Mon-Fri) changes cash and travellers cheques, and has an ATM. **Chawla Travels & Cafe** (Gurunanak Market, Station Rd; per hr ₹20; ⊙8am-10.30pm), within a small shopping centre next to Hotel Embassy, has internet access.

In the same shopping centre is **Suhana Tour and Travels** (☎3293808, 9431171394; suhana_ jharkhand tour@yahoo.co.in; ☺8am-8pm Mon-Sat, till 2pm Sun), which organises day trips to local waterfalls (from ₹400) and three-day trips to Betla (Palamau) National Park with unsophisticated drivers (from ₹4200 for four people), as well as other transport ticketing.

❶ Getting There & Away

Ranchi's Birsa Munda Airport is 6km from the city centre. **Kingfisher Red** (📞1800 2333131; airport) flies daily to Kolkata and Delhi (direct flights to Patna had been cancelled during time of research). **Air India** (📞2503255) has daily flights to Delhi and Mumbai. **Jet Airways** (📞2250051) flies to Kolkata and Delhi. A pre-paid taxi to Station Rd from the airport is ₹200 *outside* the terminal (you'll pay ₹50 more inside).

From the government bus stand on Station Rd, there are five hourly departures to Gaya (₹130, six hours) from 6.30am to 10.30am; and one to Patna (₹183, nine hours, 9.30pm). There are additional and more comfortable departures from the Birsa bus stand off Old HB Rd. Buses to Daltonganj (for Betla National Park) leave from the Ratu Rd bus stand (non-AC/AC ₹100/200, six hours, hourly). From the Birsa Vihar tourist complex on Main Rd there are two deluxe buses to Patna at 8pm (non-AC ₹200) and 9.30pm (AC ₹500).

The 18626 *Hatia-Patna Express* (6.15am) calls at Gaya (AC Chair ₹324, 6½ hours) and Patna (CC ₹383, 10 hours). For Kolkata you can take the 12020 *Shatabdi Express* (CC/1AC ₹645/1195, 7½ hours, 1.40pm) or the overnight 18616 *Howrah-Hatia Express* (SL/3AC/2AC/1AC ₹187/496/679/1140, 9½ hours, 9.40pm).

Betla (Palamau) National Park

📞06562

This undisputed natural gem is 140km west of Ranchi and one of the better places in India to see wild elephants. Tiger sightings are comparatively rare. The park covers around 1026 sq km, while the core area of 232 sq km was declared as Betla National Park in 1989. Stands of sal forest, rich evergreens, teak trees and bamboo thickets are home to some 17 tigers, 52 leopards, 216 elephants and four lonely nilgai (antelope) according to a 2007 census. This area was the seat of power of the Adivasi kings of the Chero dynasty and the ruins of its 16th-century forts and 10km of walls still exist in the jungle.

The **park** (📞222650, 9973819242; dtj_fdp trpal@sancharnet.in; admission per vehicle ₹100, camera/video ₹100/500; ☺6-10am & 2-5pm) is open year-round, but the best time to visit is October to April. If you can stand the heat, May is prime time for tiger spotting as forest cover is reduced and animals venture out in search of waterholes. **Jeep safaris** (per hr ₹350) can be arranged privately at the park gate. You must also hire a local **guide** (per hr ₹50) to accompany you.

The park has two pachyderms for **elephant safaris** (per hr ₹200, up to 4 people) so you can plod into the jungle for an unparalleled look at the flora and fauna.

The best accommodation is the superbly renovated **Forest Lodge** (r without/with AC ₹920/1070; ❄), with viewing balconies, LCD TV, spacious bathrooms and an all-around luxurious feel (for a Indian-run forest lodge, mind you). Just nearby is the **Tree House** (r ₹318), with two elevated sets of rooms built out of teak and containing two bedrooms, a bathroom and an observation deck. Both can be booked through the park office. The walls drew the short straw at the government-run **Van Vihar** (📞06567226513; dm ₹100, d from ₹400, with AC ₹900; ❄), where the new flooring does little to compensate for the fact that there is more peeling going on here than at a banana plantation!

The nearest town to the park entrance is Daltonganj (Medininagar), 25km away. There are six daily buses between Betla and Daltonganj (₹15, one hour) or you can arrange a taxi for around ₹500. Daltonganj is connected to Ranchi by bus (non-AC/AC ₹100/200, six hours, hourly). Alternatively, organise a tour through a Ranchi travel agency that will take you directly to the park. Suhana Tour and Travels (p524) has two-day trips, or longer, from ₹3200 per person, including transport, accommodation and safari. This is probably the best option considering the inadequate transport and safety issues in this isolated and sometimes lawless part of the state. In any case, call the park for security advice before leaving. If you do come independently, **Betla Tour & Travels** (📞226559, 9955527371), next door to Van Vihar, can make all of your arrangements.

Sikkim

Best Places to Stay

» Camping on the Goecha La trek (p548)

» Elgin Mount Pandim (p544)

» Mt Narsing Resort (p542)

Best Monasteries

» Tashiding Gompa (p549)

» Pemayangtse Gompa (p545)

» Labrang Gompa (p538)

Why Go?

If you're suffering from too much heat, dust or crowds, then the tiny, former Himalayan kingdom of Sikkim is the perfect antidote. Fresh mountain air sweeps the lush green state; there's room to move but the people are among India's friendliest, with a charming manner that's unobtrusive and slightly shy.

Plunging mountain valleys are lushly forested, interspersed with rice terraces and flowering rhododendrons. Tibetan-style Buddhist monasteries (gompas) add splashes of white, gold and vermilion to the green ridges and are approached through avenues of fluttering prayer flags.

Sikkim's big-ticket item is the majesty of Khangchendzonga (Kanchenjunga; 8598m), the world's third-highest mountain, straddling the border between Sikkim and Nepal. Khangchendzonga's guardian spirit is worshipped in a series of spectacular autumn festivals and its magnificent white peaks and ridges create the backdrop to a dozen wonderful walks and viewpoints.

When to Go

Gangtok

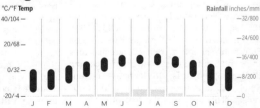

Late Sep–mid-Nov	Apr–May	Mid-Jun–Sep
Clearest weather for views, but high-season crowds and prices.	Spring blooms and warmth make up for cloudier skies.	Good for northern Sikkim but monsoon rains hide mountain views elsewhere.

Food & Drink

Sikkim's one 'don't-miss' beverage is tongba, an alcoholic millet beer that is enjoyed across the entire eastern Himalaya. The beer (also known as chhang) is sipped through a bamboo straw and the wooden container (the tongba) is topped up periodically with boiling water to let the brew gain strength. You can find tongba anywhere in northern and western Sikkim.

Traditional Sikkimese foods include *sisnoo/sochhya* (nettle soup), *ningro* (fried fiddlehead ferns), Tibetan-style *churpi* (dried yak cheese) and the Nepali speciality *gundruk ko jhol* (fermented mustard-leaf soup).

DON'T MISS

Sikkim's monastic **chaam masked dances** are the Himalaya at their most colourful. Part morality play, part country fair and part exorcism, the dances feature masked monks acting out Buddhist parables, stories from the life of Guru Rinpoche and dances representing the victory of good over evil, with a supporting crew of clowns, demons and dancing snowlions, all entertaining a crowd of spellbound locals dressed in their Sunday best. It's worth arranging your itinerary around.

Top State Festivals

» Losar (Feb/Mar, Pemayangtse, p545, Rumtek, p536, Enchey, p530) Sikkim's biggest *chaam* (monastic masked dances) take place just before Tibetan New Year.

» Bumchu (Feb/Mar, Tashiding Gompa, p549) *Bum* means pot or vase and *chu* means water. The lamas open a pot of holy water to foretell the year's fortunes.

» Saga Dawa (May/Jun, all monastery towns) Religious ceremonies and parades commemorate Buddha's birth, enlightenment and death.

» Pang Lhabsol (Aug, Ravangla, p542) Prayers and religious dances are performed in honour of Sikkim's guardian deity Khangchendzonga.

» Losoong (Dec/Jan, Old Rumtek, p536) Sikkimese New Year, preceded by *chaam* dances in many locations including Lingdum, Phodong, Phensang and Ralang.

» Detor Chaam (Dec/Jan, Enchey Gompa, p530) *Chaam* dances.

Fast Facts

» Population: 607,700

» Area: 7096 sq km

» Capital: Gangtok

» Main language: Nepali

» Sleeping prices: **$** below ₹700, **$$** ₹700 to ₹3000, **$$$** above ₹3000

Top Tip

Shared jeeps are the best way to get around the hills. To avoid getting landed with a cramped sideways-facing back seat, book a seat in advance; and if you really value your personal space, book all the front seats for yourself.

Resources

» Cultural Affairs & Heritage Department (www.sikkim-culture.gov.in) offers cultural background.

» Government of Sikkim Tourism (www.sikkim tourism.travel) lists sights, homestays and entry formalities.

» Sikkiminfo (www.sikkim info.net) provides an excellent introduction.

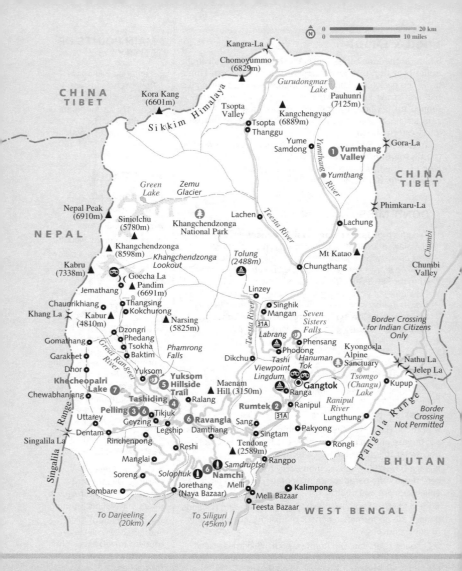

Sikkim Highlights

1 Wonder at the spectacular scenery of the Sikkim Himalaya on a 4WD trip to the **Yumthang Valley** (p539)

2 Be enthralled by a colourful *chaam* (masked monk dance) at **Rumtek gompa** (p536)

3 Take in dawn Khangchendzonga views in **Pelling** (p543), visit Pemayangtse

Gompa (p545), then help out the local schoolkids by eating banana cake

4 Wander among the prayer flags, mantras and ancient chortens (stupas) of **Tashiding Gompa** (p548)

5 Hike the scenic **hillside trail** (p547) from Yuksom to Tashiding

6 Stare open-mouthed at one of Sikkim's gigantic religious statues, in **Namchi** (p540) or **Ravangla** (p542)

7 Overnight at peaceful **Khecheopalri Lake** (p545) before hiking up to a nearby meditation cave

History

Lepchas, the 'original' Sikkimese people, migrated here from Assam or Myanmar (Burma) in the 13th century, followed by Bhutias (people of Tibetan origin) who fled from religious strife in Tibet during the 15th century. The Nyingmapa form of Vajrayana (Tibetan) Buddhism arrived with three refugee Tibetan lamas who encountered each other at the site of modern-day Yuksom. Here in 1641 they crowned Phuntsog Namgyal as first chogyal (king) of Sikkim. The capital later moved to Rabdentse (near Pelling), then to Tumlong (Phodong) before finally settling in Gangtok following a Nepali invasion.

At their most powerful the chogyals' rule encompassed eastern Nepal, upper Bengal and Darjeeling. However, much territory was later lost during wars with Bhutan and Nepal, and throughout the 19th century large numbers of Hindu Nepali migrants arrived, eventually coming to form a majority of Sikkim's population.

In 1835 the British bribed Sikkim's chogyal to cede Darjeeling to the East India Company. Tibet, which regarded Sikkim as a vassal state, raised strong objections. In 1849, amid rising tensions, the British annexed the entire area between the present Sikkim border and the Ganges plains, repulsing a counter-invasion by Tibet in 1886. In 1903–04, Britain's ultimate imperial adventurer Francis Younghusband twice trekked up to the Sikkim–Tibet border. There, with a small contingent of soldiers, he set about inciting a fracas that would 'justify' an invasion of Tibet.

Sikkim's last chogyal ruled from 1963 to 1975, when the Indian government deposed him after a revolt by Sikkim's Nepali population. China didn't recognise India's claim to Sikkim until 2005 so prior to this, to bolster pro-Delhi sentiment, the Indian government made Sikkim a tax-free zone, pouring crores (tens of millions) of rupees into road-building, electricity, water supplies and local industry. As a result Sikkim is surprisingly affluent by Himalayan standards.

Activities

Sikkim offers considerable trekking potential. Day hikes between villages follow centuries-old footpaths and normally don't require permits: the most popular option is between Yuksom and Tashiding. For multiday treks that head into the high Himalaya, notably to Goecha La at the base of Khangchendzonga (p548), you need to book through a trekking agency to arrange permits and guides.

Tour agencies are striving to open new trekking areas, notably the fabulous route across Zemu Glacier to Green Lake in Khangchendzonga National Park. However, permits remain very expensive and take months to arrange from Delhi, while tempting routes close to the Tibetan border remain off-limits.

ⓘ Permits

STANDARD PERMITS Foreigners require an Inner Line Permit to enter Sikkim (Indians don't). These are free and a mere formality, although to apply you'll need photos and passport photocopies. Permits are most easily obtainable at Darjeeling or the Rangpo border post on arrival but can also be obtained at Indian embassies abroad when getting your visa and the following places:

Foreigners' Regional Registration Offices (FRRO) Delhi (Map p78; ☏011-26195530; frrodelhi@hotmail.com; Level 2, East Block 8, Sector 1, Rama Krishna (RK) Puram; ⊙9.30am-5.30pm Mon-Fri); Kolkata (Map p450; ☏22837034; 237 AJC Bose Rd; ⊙11am-5pm Mon-Fri); Mumbai (Map p730; ☏22620446; Annexe Bldg No 2, CID, Badaruddin Tyabji Rd, near Special Branch) Or other major branches.

Sikkim House Delhi (☏11-26883026; 12-14 Panchsheel Marg, Chankyapuri, Delhi); Kolkata (Map p450; ☏22817905; 4/1 Middleton St; ⊙10.30am-4pm Mon-Fri, 10.30am-2pm Sat)

Sikkim Tourist Office Darjeeling (☏9832438118; Nehru Rd; ⊙10am-4pm Mon-Sat); Siliguri, West Bengal (SNT Terminal, Hill Cart Rd; ⊙10am-5pm) For an on-the-spot Sikkim permit bring a photocopy of your passport and Indian visa, plus one photo.

EXTENSIONS Permits are generally valid for 30 days (sometimes 15 days from embassies abroad). One or two days before expiry they can be extended for a further 30 days, giving a maximum of 60 days. For the extension try these:

» Gangtok Foreigners' Registration Office (p535)

» Tikjuk District Administration Centre, Superintendent of Police, (p543), 5km below Pelling.

BLOODY LEECHES

Sikkim is generally a very safe place; the only annoyance is the famous little leeches. They aren't dangerous, just a nuisance, primarily during the summer monsoon (June to September). They're ubiquitous in damp grass so stick to dry, wide paths.

Once you leave Sikkim, you must wait three months before applying for another permit.

PERMIT VALIDITY The standard permit is valid for visits to the following areas:

» Gangtok, Rumtek and Lingdum

» South Sikkim

» anywhere on the Gangtok–Singhik road

» most of West Sikkim to which paved roads extend.

SPECIAL PERMITS High-altitude treks, including the main Goecha La and Singalila Ridge routes, require **trekking permits** valid for up to 15 days and organised by trekking agents.

For travel beyond Singhik up the Lachung and Lachen valleys foreigners need additional **restricted area permits** from the tourism department and police and, even with these, cannot go further than the Tsopta valley or Yume Samdong (Zero Point). Indian citizens need a **police permit** to travel north of Singhik, but can travel further up the Thangu valley to Gurudongmar Lake.

Foreigners also need a restricted area permit to visit Tsomgo (Changu) Lake. Indians only (no foreigners) are permitted to travel east past Tsomgo Lake to the Tibetan border at Nathu La.

Restricted area permits are issued locally through approved tour agencies and you will have to join a tour to get one. You'll need a minimum group of two, a passport photo, and copies of your existing permit, visa and passport details page. Permits take 24 hours to arrange and last for a maximum of five days.

EAST SIKKIM

Gangtok

✆03592 / POP 31,100 / ELEV 1400-1700M

Sikkim's capital is mostly a functional sprawl of multistorey concrete boxes. But, true to its name (meaning 'hill top'), these are steeply tiered along a precipitous mountain ridge. When clouds clear, typically at dawn, views are inspiring with Khangchendzonga soaring above the western horizon. While Gangtok's manmade attractions are minor, it's a reasonable place to spend a day or two organising a trek or trips to the north.

Gangtok's crooked spine is the Rangpo–Mangan road, National Hwy 31A, cryptically referred to as 31ANHWay. The tourist office, banks and many shops line the central pedestrianised Mahatma Gandhi (MG) Marg.

◉ Sights

Namgyal Institute of Tibetology & Around
MUSEUM, VIEWPOINT

(✆281642; www.tibetology.net; Deorali; admission ₹10; ⊙10am-4pm Mon-Sat, closed 2nd Sat of month) Housed in traditionally styled Tibetan architecture, this unique institute was established in 1958 to promote research into Vajrayana Buddhism and Tibetan culture. The museum hall displays Buddhist manuscripts, icons, *thangkas* (Tibetan religious paintings) and Tantric ritual objects, such as a *thöpa* (bowl made from a human skull) and *kangling* (human thighbone trumpet). There are plenty of useful explanatory captions.

Further along the same road is the **Do-Drul Chorten**, a large white Tibetan pagoda surrounded by dormitories for novice monks.

The institute sits in a park and is conveniently close to the lower station of **Damovar Ropeway** (per person adult/child return ₹60/35; ⊙9.30am-4.30pm), a cable car running from Secretariat ridge. The views are stupendous, if you can bear to look down.

Ridge
PARK

With views east and west, it's very pleasant to stroll through shady parks and gardens on the city's central ridge. Its focal point the **Raj Bhawan** (the former Royal Palace) is closed to visitors, though the impressive **Tsuglhakhang** temple is often open early in the morning (and during major festivals) to pilgrims and curious tourists.

During the spring bloom (March and April) it's worth peeping inside the **Flower Exhibition Centre** (admission ₹10; ⊙9am-5pm), a modestly sized greenhouse full of exotic orchids, anthuriums and lilium.

Enchey Gompa
MONASTERY

(⊙4am-4pm Mon-Sat, 4am-1pm Sun) Approached through gently rustling conifers high above Gangtok, this monastery dating back to 1909 is Gangtok's most attractive, with some decent murals and statues of Tantric deities. The monastery founder was famous for his levitational skills. It comes alive for the colourful **Detor Chaam** masked dances in December/January (28th and 29th day of the 11th Tibetan lunar month).

Ganesh Tok & Around
VIEWPOINTS

From Enchey Gompa the main road swings northeast around the obvious telecommunications tower to a collection of prayer flags, where a footpath scrambles up in around

15 minutes to **Ganesh Tok viewpoint**. Festooned in colourful prayer flags, Ganesh Tok offers superb city views and its minicafe serves hot teas.

Hanuman Tok, another impressive viewpoint, sits on a hilltop around 4km drive beyond Ganesh Tok, though there are short-cuts for walkers.

Gangtok's best view of Khangchendzonga can be found from the **Tashi viewpoint**, 4km northwest of town, beside the main route to Phodong.

Himalayan Zoological Park ZOO
(☎223191; admission ₹50, video ₹500; ☺9am-4pm) Across the road from Ganesh Tok viewpoint, a lane leads into the zoo. Red pandas, Himalayan bears and snow leopards roam around in extensive wooded enclosures so large that you'll value a car to shuttle between them.

🡆 Tours

Classic early morning 'three-point tours' show you Ganesh Tok, Hanuman Tok and Tashi viewpoints (₹500). Almost any travel agent, hotel or taxi driver offers variants, including a 'five-point tour' adding Enchey Gompa and Namgyal Institute (₹700), or 'seven-point tours' tacking on old-and-new Rumtek (₹900) or Rumtek plus Lingdum (₹1200). Prices are per vehicle holding three or four passengers.

For high-altitude treks, visits to Tsomgo Lake or tours to northern Sikkim you'll need a tour agency. There are more than 180 agencies but only 10% of those work with foreigners; look for a company that belongs to Travel Agents Association of Sikkim (TAAS) as its members conform to ecologically and culturally responsible guidelines.

**Sikkim Tourism
Development Corporation** SCENIC FLIGHTS
(STDC; ☎203960; stdcsikkim@yahoo.co.in; MG Marg) For eagle-eye mountain views, STDC books scenic helicopter flights. Prices are for up to five passengers (four for Khangchendzonga ridge): buzz over Gangtok (₹7590, 15 minutes); circuit of West Sikkim (₹66,000, 55 minutes); circuit of North Sikkim (₹78,500, 65 minutes); Khangchendzonga ridge (₹90,000, 75 minutes). Book at least three days ahead.

Blue Sky Treks & Travels TREKKING
(☎205113; www.himalayantourismonline.com; Tourism Bldg, MG Marg) Trekking and tours.

**Ecotourism & Conservation
Society of Sikkim** HOMESTAYS
(ECOSS; ☎232798; www.sikkimhomestay.com; Tadong/Daragaon) Can arrange homestays (₹600 to ₹1500 per person) in Dzongu (permits required), Pastanga and Yuksom villages.

Galaxy Tours & Treks TREKKING
(☎201290; www.tourhimalayas.com; Metro Point) Tours to North Sikkim and runs several hotels in the Lachung Valley.

Hub Outdoor OUTDOOR ACTIVITIES
(☎9434203848; www.gosikkim; Tibet Rd) Offers mountain biking, trekking and even canyoning, with a decent outdoor gear shop.

Modern Treks & Tours TREKKING
(☎204670; www.modernresidency.com; Modern Central Lodge, MG Marg) Trekking and North Sikkim tours.

Namgyal Treks & Tours OUTDOOR ACTIVITIES
(☎203701; www.namgyaltreks.com; Tibet Rd) Trekking, mountaineering, mountain biking, tours to northern Sikkim. Also runs a homestay below Gangtok.

Potala Tours & Treks TREKKING
(☎200043; www.sikkimhimalayas.com; PS Rd) Top end of the price range.

Sikkim Tours & Travels TREKKING, BIRDWATCHING
(☎202188; www.sikkimtours.com; Church Rd) Specialises in trekking, birdwatching and botanical tours.

🛏 Sleeping

Peak seasons for Gangtok accommodation are March to May and September to November, reaching a peak in October. Decent budget hotels are in short supply any time of year. Check rooms carefully as standards can vary widely even within the same hotel.

🗹 Hidden Forest GUESTHOUSE **$$**
(☎205197; www.hiddenforestretreat.org; Middle Sichey Busty; s/d ₹1800/2000) A wonderful, friendly family-run hideaway on the edge of town, secluded on more than a hectare of fruit trees, orchid and flower nurseries. The

---

ⓘ **FURTHER THAN IT LOOKS**

Sikkim is tiny, only approximately 80km from east to west and 100km north to south but, due to the seriously vertical terrain, it is slow to traverse. Your next destination, just across the valley, looks an hour's drive away but will probably take closer to three or four.

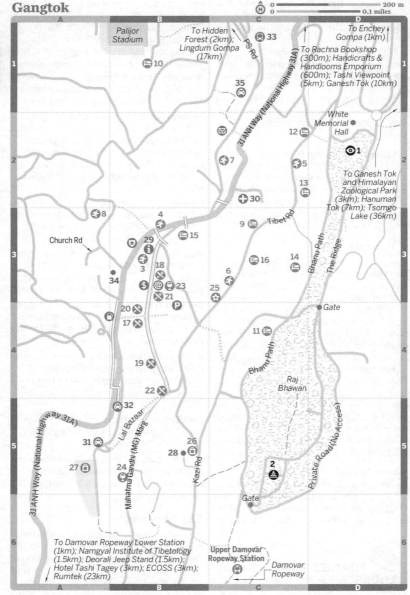

Palijor
Stadium

To Hidden
Forest (2km);
Lingdum Gompa
(17km)

To Enchey
Gompa (1km)

To Rachna Bookshop
(300m); Handicrafts &
Handlooms Emporium
(600m); Tashi Viewpoint
(5km); Ganesh Tok (10km)

White
Memorial
Hall

To Ganesh Tok
and Himalayan
Zoological Park
(3km); Hanuman
Tok (7km); Tsomgo
Lake (36km)

Church Rd

Tibet Rd

Bhanu Path

The Ridge

Gate

Bhanu Path

Raj
Bhawan

Private Road (No Access)

Gate

Lal Bazaar

Mahatma Gandhi (MG) Marg

Kazi Rd

31 ANH Way (National Highway 31A)

To Damovar Ropeway Lower Station
(1km); Namgyal Institute of Tibetology
(1.5km); Deorali Jeep Stand (1.5km);
Hotel Tashi Tagey (3km); ECOSS (3km);
Rumtek (23km)

Upper Damovar
Ropeway Station

Damovar
Ropeway

14 rooms are nicely furnished with Tibetan
motifs, polished wood floors and private balconies, and there's fine terrace seating. The
environmental credentials are also impressive: superb food comes from the solar-powered kitchen, a resident cow provides dairy
produce and all vegetable matter is compos-
ted. A taxi from the centre costs ₹80.

Mintokling Guest House   GUESTHOUSE **$$**
(☏204226; www.mintoklingsikkim.com; Bhanu Path;
s/d from ₹1250/1650; @) Set within secluded
gardens far from the traffic noise, this lodge-

like family home of a dozen rooms is a real oasis, featuring Sikkimese fabrics, timber ceilings and prayer flags in the garden. The restaurant serves seasonal Sikkimese specialities like nettle soup and fried fiddlehead fern.

Hotel Pandim HOTEL $
(☏9832080172; www.hotelpandim.com; Secretariat; s/d/tr from ₹500/650/950, deluxe s/d from ₹950/1250; ☎) Right on the top of the ridge, this well-run guesthouse is perhaps the best at the upper end of the budget options. Top-floor deluxe rooms have the best views but the cheaper basement rooms are also clean and good value with TV and a small balcony. The top-floor restaurant is particularly nice, with great views, a fine terrace and traditional meals if ordered in advance. Barking dogs can be a problem at night.

Hotel Tashi Tagey HOTEL $$
(☏231631; www.tashitagey.com; 31ANHWay, Tadong; d ₹850-1650; @) For Tibetan hospitality at its best it's worth seeking out this super-friendly place, 3km below Gangtok. There's a wide range of spotless rooms, great views from the rooftop bonsai garden and the Tibetan food is some of the best you'll ever taste (ask Nyima to make her excellent cottage cheese with tomato and basil). The main drawback is the heavy road noise, so get a room at the back. The location appears inconvenient but frequent shared taxis (₹15) shuttle between the hotel and Gangtok.

Hotel Nor-Khill HERITAGE HOTEL $$$
(☏205637; www.elginhotels.com; PS Rd; s/d incl full board ₹6900/7200; ☎) Oozing 1930s elegance, this sumptuous 'house of jewels' was originally the King of Sikkim's royal guesthouse. Historical photos, antique furniture and Tibetan carpets line the hallways and lobby, giving the latter a Victorian feel. The spaciously luxurious rooms attract film stars and Dalai Lamas.

New Modern Central Lodge HOTEL $
(☏201361; Tibet Rd; dm ₹100, d ₹300-400, s without bathroom ₹150) A backpacker's favourite for so

long that people still come here despite somewhat dreary rooms (front-facing rooms are easily the best). With plenty of cheap options and a friendly ground-floor restaurant and budget tour agency, it will probably remain a shoestring standby. Most rooms have a toilet but only a few have hot-water showers.

Modern Central Lodge GUESTHOUSE $
(☑221081; info@modern-hospitality.com; 31AN-HWay; d ₹500-700, tr ₹600) More rupees buy you a slightly larger room right on the main junction by MG Marg. There's good home-cooked food on the roof garden if you book ahead.

Hotel Sonam Delek HOTEL $$
(☑202566; www.hotelsonamdelek.com; Tibet Rd; d ₹1000-3000) This is a longstanding favourite offering good service, reliable food and a great back terrace with views over the valley. The best-value super-deluxe rooms (₹2000) come with soft mattresses and decent views. Bigger suite rooms (₹3000) have better views and balconies, but the standard rooms are a very noticeable step down – in the basement.

Chumbi Residency HOTEL $$$
(☑206618; www.thechumbiresidency.com; Tibet Rd; s/d incl breakfast from ₹2600/3400; ☎) This central three-star hotel has comfortable but smallish rooms with fresh white walls, good furniture and tea-and-coffee-making equipment. There's little difference between the two grades of rooms but make sure you get a view. The cool basement Tangerine bar-restaurant is recommended.

Kanchen Residency HOTEL $$
(☑9732072614; kanchenresidency@indiatimes.com; Tibet Rd; d back/side/front ₹600/900/1000) Above the dismal (unrelated) Hotel Prince, this airy discovery is spacious, light and well run. Upper front rooms have good views.

✕ Eating

Most budget hotels have cheap cafe-restaurants serving standard Chinese/Tibetan dishes, basic Indian meals and Western breakfasts.

┌TOP┐
└CHOICE┘ Taste of Tibet TIBETAN $
(MG Marg; mains ₹40-80) You'll have to grab a seat early in this bustling upstairs family-run place, and even then you'll likely have to share a table with Tibetan students or maroon-robed monks. The *momos* (Tibetan dumplings) are simply the best in town, or try a *shyabhale* (fried meat pasty).

Golden Pagoda INDIAN $
(MG Marg; mains ₹50-105) The rooftop of the hotel of the same name doesn't look like the location of some of the best Indian food in town but the views, service and food are all top-notch. Specialties include the Lucknow *chaat* (savoury snacks), Rajasthani and Gujarati thalis, and superb mixed raita (flavoured yoghurt).

Gangtalk CONTINENTAL $$
(MG Marg; mains ₹140-270, set lunch ₹149-199) Fresh and modern is the vibe here, with a collection of retro album covers on the walls and a wide range of comfort food from burgers to bangers and mash. It's also probably the only place you'll ever see fish *momos* on the menu. Grab a seat on the fine terrace overlooking interesting MG Marg.

Tangerine SIKKIMESE $$
(Ground fl, Chumbi Residency, Tibet Rd; mains ₹130-180) Descend five floors for sublime cuisine, tasty Western snacks or cocktails in the brilliant Japanese-style floor-cushioned bar area. Try the stuffed-tomato curry or sample Sikkimese specialities like *sochhya* (nettle stew). The stylishly relaxed decor adds a real splash of glam.

Parivar Restaurant SOUTH INDIAN $
(MG Marg; dishes ₹60-110) Eat here for good-value South Indian vegetarian food; try the various *masala dosas* for breakfast, the *choley paneer* (chickpeas with cottage cheese) or the all-inclusive mini/full thali for ₹90/150.

Bakers Cafe BAKERY $
(MG Marg; pastries from ₹12, mains ₹75-150; ☺8am-8pm) The perfect breakfast escape, this cosy Western-style cafe has strong coffee (₹40), croissants, tempting cakes, paninis and pizzas, though the service can be glacial.

Roll House SNACK BAR $
(MG Marg; rolls ₹15-30; ☺8am-8pm) In an alley just off MG Marg this hole-in-the-wall serves delicious Kolkata-style *kati* rolls, a kind of Indian enchilada.

🍷 Drinking & Entertainment

Two of the nicest locations for a quiet drink are the large terrace of the **Tashi Delek Hotel** (MG Marg) or the bar and garden of the Hotel Nor-Khil.

Cafe Live & Loud BAR, LIVE MUSIC
(www.thriceasmuch.com; ☺8.30am-11pm; ☎) One of the northeast's main live music venues,

this cool lounge-bar hosts live rock and blues bands every Thursday, Friday and Saturday evenings. There's a full bar and food menu, with some unusual Southeast Asian offerings (mains ₹110 to ₹170), and a pleasant cafe-terrace if you need a bit of peace and quiet. The bathrooms are the cleanest in Sikkim.

Indulge
BAR

(www.thriceasmuch.com; Tibet Rd; ⊙11am-11pm) Big windows overlooking MG Marg add to the cool of this modern bar-restaurant, even if the blue-and-red walkway lights do feel a bit like the entrance to a Disney ride. The bar food stretches to pizza and steaks (mains ₹60 to ₹220). If you're lucky there'll be a game on the big-screen TV, if you're unlucky the karaoke will kick in.

Shopping

Several souvenir shops on MG Marg and PS Rd sell Tibetan and Sikkimese handicrafts like wooden tongba (Himalayan millet beer) pots, prayer flags and Nepali-style kukri knives.

Sikkim's tax-free status means that booze is big business. A few local liquors are available in novelty souvenir containers. Opening a 1L monk-shaped bottle of Old Monk Rum (₹220) means screwing off the monk's head! Fireball brandy comes in a bowling-ball-style red sphere.

Khangchendzonga Market
FOOD & DRINK

This covered market is interesting for its range of traditional Himalayan produce, including *churpi* (dried cheese on a string), cow skin snacks, Tibetan *tsampa* (ground roasted barley), dried *phing* noodles and circular yeast patties used for brewing chhang (millet beer).

Handicrafts & Handloom Emporium
HANDICRAFTS

(Zero Point; ⊙10am-4pm Mon-Sat, daily Jul-Mar) This government initiative teaches traditional crafts to local students and markets their products – including toy red pandas, 1m by 2m hand-woven carpets (₹5500), Tibetan furniture, handmade paper and traditional Sikkimese-style dresses (₹1000 to ₹1600).

Golden Tips
FOOD & DRINK

(www.goldentipstea.in; Kazi Rd; ⊙9am-9pm) Buy or taste at this inviting tea showroom with a wide selection of blends, including Sikkimese tea from Temi. Also sells tea by the cup (₹30).

Rachna Bookshop
BOOKSTORE

(www.rachnabooks.com; Development Area) Gangtok's best-stocked and most convivial bookshop also has occasional film and music events on the upstairs terrace.

Information

Many ATMS line MG Marg.

Axis Bank (MG Marg; ⊙9.30am-3.30pm Mon-Fri, 9.30am-1.30pm Sat) Changes cash and travellers cheques and has an ATM. Stock up with rupees in Gangtok: exchange is virtually impossible elsewhere in Sikkim.

Cyber Cafe (MG Marg; per hr ₹30; ⊙9am-9pm) Internet access; the entrance is opposite Roll House.

Foreigners' Registration Office (Kazi Rd; ⊙10am-4pm, 10am-noon public hols) In the lane beside Indian Overseas Bank, for permit extensions.

Main post office (PS Rd, Gangtok; ⊙9am-5pm Mon-Sat, 9am-3pm Sun for stamps)

Police station (☑202033; 31ANHWay)

STNM hospital (☑222059; 31ANHWay)

Sikkim Tourist Information Centre (☑toll free 204408; www.sikkimtourism.travel; MG Marg; ⊙8am-8pm) Offers general advice. Open 10am to 4pm outside peak seasons. For specific queries regarding trekking and permit-area travel, deal with a travel agent.

ⓘ Getting There & Away

Air

The nearest airport to Sikkim is Bagdogra (p483), 124km from Gangtok, near Siliguri in West Bengal, which has flights to Kolkata, Delhi and Guwahati.

Helicopters shuttle from Gangtok to Bagdogra (₹2200, 35 minutes), departing at 11am and returning at 2.30pm, but services are cancelled in adverse weather. There's a strict maximum 10kg baggage allowance. **Sikkim Tourism Development Corporation** (☑203960; MG Marg) sells the tickets for this and scenic flights.

Fixed-price Maruti vans/sumos (jeeps) go directly to Bagdogra (₹1500/1700, 4½ hours). You'll get the best rates from returning vehicles, so look for West Bengal (WB) number plates.

Sikkim's first airport is planned at Pakyong, 35km from Gangtok, with a tentative completion date of 2012.

Bus

Buses run from the government **SNT bus station** (PS Rd) at 7am to Jorethang (₹80), Kalimpong (₹80) and Namchi (₹80), at 1.15pm to Pelling (₹122) and hourly to Siliguri (₹115 to ₹220, 6am to 1pm). In general you are better off taking the faster and more frequent shared jeeps.

Shared Jeeps

Some jeep departures are fixed, others leave when all the seats are filled. Departures usually start at 6.30am for the more distant destinations and continue up to about 2pm.

From the hectic but relatively well-organised **Deorali jeep stand** (31ANHWay), 1.5km below Gangtok, shared jeeps depart every 30 minutes or so to Darjeeling (₹140, five hours), Kalimpong (₹150, three hours) and Siliguri (₹140, four hours), some continuing to New Jalpaiguri train station. There are daily jeeps to Kakarbhitta (₹180, four hours, 6.30am) on the Nepalese border and Jaigaon (₹250, four hours, 8am) on the Bhutanese border. Buses to Siliguri (₹100) also run from here. Purchase tickets in advance. The stand is hidden in the alleys below the lower ropeway station.

West Sikkim vehicles depart from **Southwest jeep stand** (Church Rd) for Geyzing (₹140, 4½ hours, four daily), Ravangla (₹90, three hours, four daily), Namchi (₹110, three hours, every half-hour) and Jorethang (₹110, three hours, hourly). Jeeps for Yuksom, Tashiding and Pelling (₹150 to ₹180, five hours) depart around 7am and possibly again around 12.30pm. For independent travel, small groups can charter a vehicle.

Train

The nearest major train station is over 120km away at New Jalpaiguri (NJP). There's a computerised **railway booking counter** (⊗8am-2pm Mon-Sat, 8am-11am Sun & public hols) at the SNT bus station.

ⓘ Getting Around

There's a taxi stand in Lal Bazaar opposite the Denzong Cinema, and another in PS Rd just north of the post office. Shared taxis to Tadong (₹15, every 10 minutes) depart from just under the pedestrian bridge on the National Hwy.

Around Gangtok

Rumtek and Lingdum gompas make for a great day trip from Gangtok. Viewing the temples takes less than an hour each, but the winding country lanes that link them is a big part of the attraction, curving through mossy forests high above river valleys and artistically terraced rice slopes.

RUMTEK
☑03592 / ELEV 1690M
Facing Gangtok distantly across a vast green valley, Rumtek village is entirely dominated by its extensive gompa complex. Spiritually the monastery is hugely significant as the home in exile of Buddhism's Kagyu (Black Hat) sect. Visually it is not Sikkim's most

spectacular sight and during high season it can get quite crowded. To experience Rumtek at its most serene, stay the night and hike around the delightful nearby hilltops at dawn.

◉ Sights

Rumtek Gompa   MONASTERY
(☑252329; www.rumtek.org) This rambling and walled complex is a village within a village, containing religious buildings, schools and several small lodge-hotels. To enter, foreigners must show both passport and Sikkim permit. Unusually for a monastery, this place is guarded by armed police, as there have been violent altercations, and even an invasion, by monks who dispute the Karmapa's accession.

The main **monastery building** (admission ₹10; ⊗6am-6pm) was constructed between 1961 and 1966 to replace Tsurphu Monastery in Tibet, which had been partially destroyed during China's Cultural Revolution (there's a mural of the original monastery beside the metal detector). The giant throne within awaits the crowning of Kagyu's current spiritual leader, the (disputed) 17th Karmapa.

Exit to the side and take the rear stairs past a snack shop (good tea and *momos*) up to the **Golden Stupa** (⊗6-11.45am & noon-5pm). The smallish room holds the ashes of the important 16th Karmapa in an amber, coral and turquoise-studded reliquary to which pilgrims pay their deepest respects. If locked, someone from the colourful Karma Shri Nalanda Institute of Buddhist Studies opposite can usually open it for you.

Rumtek holds impressive masked *chaam* dances during the annual **Drupchen** (group meditation) in May/June, and two days before **Losar** (Tibetan New Year) when you might also catch traditional lhamo (Tibetan opera) performances.

Old Rumtek Gompa   MONASTERY
About 1.5km beyond the gompa towards Sang, a long avenue of white prayer flags and flowers leads photogenically down to the powder-blue Old Rumtek Gompa. Despite the name, the main prayer hall has been thoroughly renovated. The interior is a riotous festival of colour and the lonely location is idyllic with some wonderful west-facing views. Two days before **Losoong** (Sikkimese New Year), Old Rumtek holds the celebrated **Kagyed Chaam** dance.

Lingdum Gompa   MONASTERY
(www.zurmangkagyud.org) Only completed in 1998, peaceful Lingdum Gompa is visually

The 'Black Hat' sect is so named because of the priceless ruby-topped headgear used to crown the Karmapa (spiritual leader) during key ceremonies. Being woven from the hair of *dakinis* (angels), the hat must be kept locked in a box to prevent it from flying back to the heavens. Or at least that's the official line. Nobody has actually seen the hat since 1993, after the death of the 16th Karmapa.

Since then the Kagyu school has been embroiled in a bitter controversy between two rival candidates. The main candidate, **Ogyen Trinley Dorje** (www.kagyuoffice.org), fled Tibet in 2000 but currently remains based at Dharamsala: Indian authorities are believed to have prevented him from officially taking up his Rumtek seat for fear of upsetting Chinese government sensibilities. The rival candidate, **Thaye Dorje** (www.karmapa.org), lives in nearby Kalimpong in West Bengal. Supporters of the two are locked in a legal dispute over who can control Rumtek. To learn more about the controversy, read *The Dance of 17 Lives* by Mick Brown.

Only when the dispute is resolved and the 17th Karmapa is finally crowned will anyone dare to unlock the box and check whether the sacred black hat is actually still there.

more exciting than Rumtek. Its structure grows out of the forest in grand layers, with pleasant side gardens and a photogenic chorten. The extensively muralled main prayer hall enshrines huge statues of Sakyamuni (historic) Buddha, Guru Rinpoche and the 16th Karmapa. Sonorous chanting at the 7.30am and 3.30pm *puja* (prayers/offerings) adds to the magical atmosphere. There's a nice outdoor cafe by the entrance and an interesting souvenir shop selling Buddhist accessories and Tibetan cloth.

🛏 Sleeping & Eating

Sungay Guesthouse　　　　　　HOTEL $
(☏252221; r ₹250-600) The friendly Tibetan management make this a great alternative to rushing back to Gangtok. Rooms are comfortable and good value, with hot-water bathrooms, and many come with balconies. It's just inside Rumtek's main entrance gate.

Bamboo Retreat　　　　　ECO RESORT $$
(☏252516; www.bambooretreat.in; Sajong; s/d incl breakfast & dinner from ₹3300/3900; 🛜) This Swiss-run rural resort just below Rumtek is a destination in its own right. There's plenty to keep you busy, with mountain bikes for hire and guided hikes, or just relax with a herbal bath and massage. The 12 colourful rooms are all uniquely decorated. Culinary highlights include an authentic Italian pizza oven and Sikkimese food grown in the organic garden.

Sangay Hotel　　　　　GUESTHOUSE $
(☏252238; d ₹350, s/d without bathroom ₹150/250,) A simple but decent budget option just below Rumtek.

ℹ Getting There & Away
Rumtek is 26km (1½ hours) from Gangtok by a winding but scenic road. Lingdum Gompa is a 2km walk from Ranga or Ranka village, reached by rough backlanes from Gangtok. Shared jeeps run to Rumtek (₹30) every hour or so, with the last jeep returning to Gangtok between 2pm and 3pm. A return taxi costs around ₹600. Linking the two sites requires private transport (₹1000 to ₹1200).

Towards Tibet

TSOMGO (CHANGU, TSANGU) LAKE
ELEV 3780M

Pronounced Changu, this scenic high-altitude lake about three hours' drive from Gangtok is a popular excursion for Indian visitors, but restricted area permits are required for foreign visitors. To get one, sign up for a tour by 2pm and most Gangtok agents can get the permit for next-day departure (two photos required). A budget tour will cost around ₹2600 to ₹3500 per vehicle or ₹500 per person if you can get a group together.

At the lakeside, food stalls sell hot chai, chow mein and *momos,* while short yak rides potter along the shore. If you can muster the puff, the main attraction is clambering up a nearby hilltop for inspiring views.

NATHU LA
Indian citizens are permitted to continue 18km along the spectacular road from **Tsomgo Lake** to the 4130m **Nathu La** (Listening Ears Pass), whose border opened with much fanfare in 2006 but to local traffic only.

A few kilometres southeast of Nathu La, **Jelep La** was the pass used by Francis Younghusband in the British Great Game-era attack on Tibet (1903-04). Until 1962 Jelep La was the main trade route between Kalimpong and Lhasa, but it shows no signs of reopening.

NORTH SIKKIM

📞 03592

The biggest attractions in North Sikkim are the idyllic Yumthang and Tsopta Valleys. Reaching them and anywhere north of Singhik requires a special permit (p530), which is easy to obtain if you sign up for a tour. It's possible to visit Phodong and Mangan/Singhik independently using public jeeps but they can also be conveniently seen during brief stops on any Yumthang tour and at no extra cost.

The Yumthang and Tsopta Valleys are very cold by October and become really fingertip numbing between December and February.

Gangtok to Singhik

The narrow but mostly well-paved 31AN-HWay clings to steep wooded slopes above the Teesta River, occasionally descending in long coils of hairpins to a bridge photogenically draped in prayer flags, only to coil right back up again on the other side. If driving, consider brief stops at Tashi Viewpoint (p531), Kabi Lunchok, Phensang and the Seven Sisters waterfall.

Kabi Lunchok, an atmospheric glade 17km north of Gangtok, decorated with memorial stones, is the site of a 13th-century peace treaty between the chiefs of the Lepcha and Bhutia peoples. They swore a blood brotherhood until the River Rangit ran dry and Khangchendzonga ceased to exist.

The small 290-year-old Nyingmapaschool **Phensang Gompa** is further north, 1km off the main road. It has beautifully decorated lower and upper-floor prayer halls. It's all recent, though, as the monastery was rebuilt after a 1957 fire. A **Chaam festival** is celebrated here on the 28th and 29th days of the Tibetan 10th month, usually December.

Just over 30km north of Gangtok, **Seven Sisters Waterfall**, a multistage cascade, cuts a chasm above a roadside cardamom grove and plummets into a rocky pool. It's fine spot for a photo and a welcome chai break.

> ℹ️ **NORTH SIKKIM TOUR TIPS**

» A group size of four or five people is ideal for sharing costs while not overfilling the jeep.

» To find jeep-share partners, try asking around at the cafe at New Modern Central Lodge (p533) in Gangtok, around 6pm a few days before you plan to travel.

» Less than four days is too rushed to comfortably visit both Yumthang/Lachung and Lachen. Three days is enough to see just Yumthang. Three-night, four-day tours range from around ₹6500 to ₹8000 per person for groups of four, depending on accommodation and vehicle standards. A budget two-night, three-day tour starts around ₹4000 per person in a group of seven.

» Leave Gangtok early on the first day: it's a shame to arrive in the dark.

» Your (obligatory) 'guide' is actually more of a translator. Don't assume he'll stop at all potential points of interest without prodding.

» Bring a torch (flashlight) and warm clothes.

The little strip of roadside restaurants at **Phodong** (1815m) make it a popular lunch stop. About 1km southeast, near the Km39 post, a 15-minute walk along a side road leads to the **Phodong Gompa** (established in 1740), belonging to the Kagyu sect. The beautiful two-storey prayer hall contains extensive murals and a large statue of the 9th Karmapa. A rear room contains a hidden statue of Mahakala, a protective deity of the monastery.

Drive or walk on another 1.5km uphill to the much more atmospheric **Labrang Gompa** (established in 1884), home to 100 monks. The inner walls of the eight-sided main building are lined with over 1000 icons of Padmasambhava, while upstairs a fearsome statue of the guru sports a necklace of severed heads. *Chaam* dances take place at the end of December.

Between the two monasteries, just below the road lie the 19th-century foundations of **Tumlong**, Sikkim's third capital. The enigmatic palace ruins are worth a quick scramble.

North Sikkim's district headquarters, **Mangan** (Km67 post; ie 28km from Phodong) proudly declares itself to be the 'Large Cardamom Capital of the World'. Some 1.5km beyond, concrete stupas on a sharp bend mark a small footpath; a three-minute descent leads to a panoramic **viewpoint** and an excellent tea stop.

Beyond Singhik

With relevant permits and an organised tour you can continue north beyond Singhik. At Chungthang, the next settlement, the road branches up the Lachung Chu and Lachen Chu valleys. If you only have time to visit one valley, the Lachung Chu has the most impressive scenery.

Accommodation is available in Lachung and Lachen, with some basic options in Thanggu. We have listed a few favourites but your tour agency will normally preselect for you. Cheaper hotels tend to have a mixed bag of rooms with prices the same whether or not the room has geyser, shower, heating, window or balcony. Try to see a few different rooms even if you can't choose your hotel.

LACHUNG
📍3592 / ELEV 2630M

Soaring rock-pinnacled valley walls embroidered with long ribbons of waterfall surround the scattered village of Lachung. To appreciate the full drama of its setting, take the metal cantilever bridge across the wild Yumthang River to the Sanchok side then climb 1.5km along the Katao road for great views from the **Lachung (Sarchok) Gompa** (established 1880). The gompa's refined murals include one section of original paintings (inner left wall as you enter) and its twin giant prayer wheels chime periodically.

Over a dozen hotels are dotted around Lachung. Many outwardly modern places maintain traditional Tibetan-style wood-fire kitchens that are a cosy place to linger over a butter tea or a tongba of chhang. Some of the better places:

Modern Residency (Taagsing Retreat; 📞214888; www.modernresidency.com; Singring village; d ₹2500) Rooms are comfortable and well decorated, though walk-in prices are steep. Even if you don't stay, the gompa-style building 3km south of Lachung is worth visiting for its upper-floor mini-museum, library and bar. Staying here is one advantage of booking a tour with Modern Treks & Tours in Gangtok.

Mayfair Yarlam (📞9434330030; www.yarlamresort.com; r from ₹8000) The top place in town.

Sila Inn (📞9474016226; d ₹1000) Family run and friendly, with a mixed bag of rooms above a friendly hostel-restaurant. The best rooms are on the top floor.

Crown Villa (crownhotels@gmail.com) New resort under construction at time of writing.

YUMTHANG VALLEY

The main reason to come to Lachung is to continue 23km further north to admire the majestic Yumthang Valley, which starts some 10km after leaving Lachung. This point is also the entry to the **Singba Rhododendron Sanctuary**, whose network of hiking trails offers a welcome chance to get out of the jeep. From March to early May a host of primulas, 24 species of rhododendrons and other flora bursts into flower to carpet the valley floor.

At the Km23 point there are a number of snack shacks that open up in the high season. Don't bother with the **hot springs**, a grimy, 2-sq-metre pool in a rubbish-ringed hut on the other side of the river. As the valley widens and flattens, the scenery becomes 100% Himalayan, with jagged peaks, lush pasturage and bridges draped with colourful prayer flags.

From Yumthang you can continue up switchbacks for 14km onto the snowy plateau of **Yume Samdong (Zero Point)** at a head-pounding 4640m, where a candelabra of jagged peaks rises towards Tibet. This is as far as you can go. The road starts to get blocked by snow from mid-October.

LACHEN
POP 2000 / ELEV 2700M

The traditional mountain village of Lachen is changing fast with the construction of concrete tourist hotels. Nonetheless, alleyways remain sprinkled with old wooden homes on sturdy stone bases and decorated with colourful Tibetan-style window frames. Logs are stacked everywhere for winter fuel.

Lachen (Nyudrup Choeling) Gompa is about 15 minutes' walk above the town and is most likely to be open early morning or late afternoon. At the beginning of town, beside a giant cypress tree, is a huge mounted prayer wheel and a spooky collection of geometric threads designed to trap evil spirits.

Lachen is the trailhead for eight-day expeditionary treks to **Green Lake** (5050m) along the yeti-infested **Zemu Glacier** towards Khangchendzonga's northeast face. These require long advance planning and very expensive permits.

Most groups stay in either the Shangrila Residency, Bayul Inn or Twin Peak Lodge, with rooms from around ₹500 to ₹800. A step up is the **Lachen View Point** (☑9434867312; r ₹1500-4000). Best of the bunch is the luxurious **Apple Orchard Resort** (www.theappleorchardresort.com; r ₹4830-6050), above the village next to the *ani gompa* (nunnery). The new Blue Pine Hotel at the entry to town looks as if it will have great views when finished.

THANGGU & TSOPTA

Beyond a sprawling army camp 32km north of Lachen, **Thanggu** (3850m) has an end-of-the-world feel. There are no phones (mobile or otherwise), the electricity is solar generated and the Chinese are only 15km away.

Misleadingly named **Thanggu Resort** (d & tr ₹500; ☺May-Nov) is a simple wooden house incorporating a traditional-styled kitchen and tongba-drinking den (tongba ₹20) that offers a popular breakfast stop. There is couple of grubby rooms upstairs.

A boulder-strewn stream leads on 2km to the **Tsopta Valley**. Just above the tree line, the scenery feels rather like Glencoe (Scotland), with the added drama of a glacier-toothed mountain wall framing the western horizon. A two-hour hike leads up to a pair of meditation caves, one of which was used for two years by the famous French traveller and mystic Alexandra David-Neel.

Indian visitors can continue 30km north to spectacular **Gurudongmar Lake** (5150m), right on the border with Tibet, but the glacial lake is off-limits to foreigners.

SOUTH SIKKIM

The main sights in South Sikkim are Namchi's gigantic statues but there are plenty of other villages and viewpoints to explore here in little-visited villages like Rinchenpong, Uttarey and Hillay – for trip ideas see www.sikkimtourismuttarey.com. Ravangla falls administratively within South Sikkim, but we cover it in the Gangtok to Pelling section (West Sikkim), where it fits more logically.

Namchi

☑03595 / ELEV 1525M

Few travellers would linger in Namchi were it not for the two huge statues, one Hindu,

the other Buddhist, that face each other across the town from opposite hillsides.

There are several internet cafes in the central pedestrianised plaza, along with an Axis Bank, two ancient bodhi and pipal trees and, oddly, a piranha aquarium.

◉ Sights

Samdruptse   MONUMENT
(Indian/foreigner ₹10/20; ☺dawn-dusk) Painted in shimmering copper and bronze, the impressive 45m-high Padmasambhava statue dominates the forested Samdruptse ridge and is visible for miles around. Known as Guru Rinpoche in Tibetan, Padmasambhava was the 8th-century holy man, magician and Tantric master widely credited with introducing Tantric Buddhism across the Himalayan region. Completed in 2004 on a foundation stone laid by the Dalai Lama, the statue is starting to look a bit weathered but is still impressive atop its lotus plinth. The site is 7km from Namchi, 2km off the Damthang/Ravangla road.

Taxis charge around ₹500 return. Alternatively, pay ₹300 for a one-way drop and walk back to Namchi, either by shortcutting down steps through the **rock garden** (admission ₹20) or, more interestingly, following the road down to **Ngadak Gompa**. A large new gompa is under construction at Ngadak, just uphill from a spooky Gönso Lhakhang (protector chapel) but of most interest is Ngadak's ruined and neglected **old dzong**, dating back to 1717, which still exudes a sense of old Sikkim. Its unpainted stone exterior incorporates lovely carved door pillars and, upstairs, intriguing but decrepit fragments of painting remain on the peeling old cloth wallpaper. Bring a torch (flashlight).

A cable-car style ropeway is currently under construction to link the statue with Namchi centre via the rock garden.

Solophuk   MONUMENT
Even grander than the Samdruptse Guru is the massive 33m Shiva statue, currently being finalised on the memorably named Solophuk hilltop, 5km south of Namchi. A huge complex of guesthouses, temples and pagodas surround the statue, including replicas of the Chor Dam, India's four sacred Hindu pilgrimage sites. Everything here is on an epic scale – even the prayer beads that Shiva holds in his hand are the size of cannonballs. A taxi here costs ₹500/300 for a return/one-way drop.

Not satisfied with two statues, the town is planning an equally epic statue of the goddess Devi on nearby Shakti Hill.

🛏 Sleeping & Eating

Dungmali Heritage Resort   GUESTHOUSE **$$**
(☏9434126992; rairashmi_27@yahoo.co.in; Solophuk Rd; s ₹500, d ₹900-1500, deluxe ₹2500-4000) This friendly family-run guesthouse is an excellent option. All the rooms are spotless and fresh, and most come with a balcony and great views. The family grows its own organic vegetables and offers bird-watching walks in 2.4 hectares of private jungle. It's 4km from town on the road to Solophuk.

TOP CHOICE **Seven Hills Resort**   RESORT **$$**
(☏9647783038; www.sevenhillsresort.com; Phalidara; d ₹2800-3200) If it's peace and quiet you want, head to this relaxing resort on a remote ridge, 7km northeast of Namchi. A dozen rustic but comfortable cottages with private balconies are dotted around gardens of passionfruit, bamboo and orchids, and the views are superb. Warm up on cold evenings with a glass of house-made rhododendron brandy.

Hotel Samdruptse   HOTEL **$$**
(☏264806; Jorethang Rd; d ₹600-1000) The higher the room rate the better the Khangchendzonga views from this decent but slightly scruffy concrete place. The hotel is 300m west of the centre, along the road to Jorethang, and includes Namchi's most pleasant restaurant (mains ₹50 to ₹130).

Hotel Zimkhang   HOTEL **$**
(☏263625; s/d ₹300/450) An acceptable budget option in the main pedestrian plaza.

ℹ Getting There & Around

Share jeeps leave frequently when full to Jorethang (₹30, one hour) from near the Hotel Samdruptse; to Ravangla (₹40, one hour) and Gangtok (₹110, 3½ hours) from the northwest junction; and to Siliguri (₹120, three hours) from a stand at the southern end of the pedestrian mall. Services dry up around 3pm.

Buses leave from the ground floor of the huge new transport complex on the east of town. There are one or two departures each morning to Jorethang (₹20), Ravangla (₹25) and Gangtok (₹80).

Jorethang (Naya Bazaar)

☏03595 / ELEV 520M
This bustling but charmless transport hub between West Sikkim, Namchi and Darjeeling/Siliguri is just a place to change jeeps.

If you get stuck here, the brightest, friendliest accommodation option remains the recently renovated **Hotel Namgyal** (☏276852; d ₹450), on the main drag, 70m east of the bridge, just before the SNT bus station.

Across the road beside the Darjeeling jeep stand is a helpful **tourist office** (◷8am-4pm Mon-Sat Dec-Feb & Jun-Aug, 10am-8pm rest of yr).

Jeep services are expected to move to a large new transport complex on the east end of town. Until then, shared jeeps leave regularly from next to the tourist office for Darjeeling (₹100, two hours). Jeeps for Gangtok (₹110, four hours), Geyzing (₹60, two hours), Namchi (₹40, one hour) and Siliguri (₹100, three hours) leave from a chaotic stand 100m east. For Nepal there's a 7am jeep to Kakarbhitta (₹150, four hours). Buy tickets before boarding.

Jeeps for Tashiding (₹70, two hours) and Yuksom (₹100, three hours) leave from a third stand just to the west of this one.

Less frequent and slower buses run from the SNT bus station to Gangtok (₹85, 12.30pm), Namchi (₹24, noon), Pelling (₹50, 2.30pm), Ravangla (₹45, noon) and Siliguri (₹83, 9.30am)

WEST SIKKIM

Sikkim's greatest tourist draw is simply staring at Khangchendzonga's white-peaked magnificence from Pelling ridge. Most visitors then add excursions to nearby waterfalls and monasteries, plus perhaps a spot of walking. Some lovely hikes start from the charming village of Yuksom, which is also the trailhead for multiday group treks to Dzongri and Goecha La (group trekking permits required).

Ravangla (Rabongla)

☏03595 / ELEV 2010M
Rapidly expanding Ravangla (Rabong) is spectacularly perched overlooking a wide sweep of western Sikkim, the gompas of Old Ralang, Tashiding, Pemayangtse and Sangachoeling all distantly visible against a horizon that's sawtoothed with snow-capped peaks.

The town has little aesthetic distinction, but is useful as a hub to visit the interesting surrounding sights. Joining the main highway is Main Bazaar, a concentration of shops, cheap hotels, the jeep stand and the **Cyber Cafe** (per hr ₹30; ◷8.15am-7pm).

◉ Sights

Mane Choekhorling Gompa MONASTERY
Steps lead up from the end of Main Bazaar to this handsome new stone-and-wood gompa. The festival ground here is the site of the annual **Pang Lhabsol festival** (www .panglhabsol.blogspot.com), held each August in honour of Kanchendzonga. *Chaam* dances take place on the 15th day of the seventh lunar month.

Sakyamuni Complex MONUMENT
Just behind the gompa is the huge new **Sakyamuni Complex** (www.sakyamuniproject. com), centrepiece of which is a giant 41m tall Buddha statue. The statue holds Buddhist relics from 13 countries and will eventually include a meditation and hotel complex when completed in 2012. The Dalai Lama blessed the site in 2010.

🛏 Sleeping & Eating

Hotel 10-Zing GUESTHOUSE $
(☑9434241324; s ₹250, d ₹400-500) At the main junction, this friendly and helpful place just has a few rooms so is often full. Doubles have geysers; otherwise it's free bucket hot water. The good restaurant has nice outdoor seating.

Mt Narsing Resort RESORT $$
(☑03592-226822; www.yuksom-tours.com; s/d lower resort from ₹800/900, upper annexe from ₹1700/2000) There are two wings at this rustic bungalow place 5km southwest of Ravangla. The lower main building is cheaper but the ambience and views are better at the upper resort, which offers a characterful lodge with a fire pit, good food and fine views over the lawn towards Narsing and Pandim peaks. A taxi to the lower/upper resort costs ₹70/200.

Kookie Restaurant TIBETAN $
(☺7am-8pm; mains ₹40-80) This clean and fresh Tibetan-run restaurant is easily the best in town. The menu includes rice and curry sets, Chinese sizzlers and good *momos* and noodle soups, and the tables are even decorated with fresh flowers. Leave a note on the 'We Were Here' noticeboard.

ℹ Getting There & Away

Luckypo Travels on the main highway books shared jeeps to Gangtok (₹90, 8am to noon), Pelling (₹90, 1pm), Siliguri (₹150, 7am to 8am) and Geyzing (₹70, 9am); for Yuksom, change at Geyzing. Jeeps to Namchi (₹45, one hour) and Legship (₹40) leave from near Hotel 10-Zing.

The SNT bus booking office is part of Hotel 10-Zing. Buses run to Namchi (₹26, one hour, 9am and 1pm) and Siliguri (₹130 to ₹140, five hours, 6.30am).

Around Ravangla

At **Ralang**, 13km below Ravangla, the splendid and active 1995 **Palchen Choeling Monastic Institute** (New Ralang Gompa) is home to about 200 Kagyu-order monks. Arrive early morning or around 3pm to hear them chanting in mesmerising unison. There's a 9m-high golden statue of the historical Buddha in the main hall, and locally the gompa is famous for elaborate butter sculptures. Peek into the side room to see the amazing effigies used in November's impressive **Mahakala dance**.

About 1.5km downhill on the same road is peaceful **Old Ralang Gompa**, established in 1768 and worth a visit.

A chartered taxi to Ralang costs around ₹500 from Ravangla (return with two hours' wait).

Beside the main Legship road, 5.5km from central Ravangla, small but fascinating **Yungdrung Kundrakling** is the only Bon monastery in Sikkim. The originally animistic Bon faith preceded Buddhism in Tibet but has since been largely subsumed by it. You'll have to look closely to notice that the deities are slightly different and that the prayer wheels are turned anticlockwise. Non-flash photography is allowed inside. You can get here from Ravangla on a shared jeep to Kewzing (₹20).

On the way back you could stop at the roadside Cloud's End Retreat for a tea before descending the stone steps for ten minutes to **Sakyamuni** (Doling Gompa), a monastery complex.

Back in town, a steep three- to four-hour hiking trail leads from above the Sakyamuni statue to the top of **Maenam Hill** (3150m), looming just above the town of Ravangla, through the springtime rhododendrons and magnolia blooms of the **Maenam Wildlife Sanctuary**. The views are wonderful and you just might see rare red pandas and monal pheasants (Sikkim's state bird). From the summit continue 2km to **Bhaledunga rock**, where the government is planning to build an observation 'skyway'. A guide is useful to avoid getting lost in the forest on your return; arrange one for around ₹400 at the forestry check post.

Geyzing, Tikjuk & Legship

☏03595

The following three towns have little to offer a visitor apart from a permit extension at Tikjuk and transport changes at Geyzing. Geyzing is West Sikkim's capital, but for permit extensions you need Tikjuk, half way to Pelling.

Tikjuk is the District Administrative Centre for West Sikkim. Permits can be extended at the **Superintendent of Police office** (Side wing, 3rd fl; ⊙10am-4pm Mon-Sat, closed 2nd Sat of month).

Apart from its vaguely interesting Sunday market, **Geyzing** is most useful as West Sikkim's transport hub. Frequent shared jeeps go to Jorethang (₹60, 1½ hours), Legship (₹25, 30 minutes), Pelling (₹25, 20 minutes), Tashiding (₹60, 1½ hours) and Yuksom (₹70, 2½ hours). Several serve Gangtok (₹140, seven to nine hours, 7am to 12.30pm), Ravangla (₹68, one hour, 9am and 11.45am) and Siliguri (₹150, four hours, 7am and 12.30pm).

When no other transport is available, especially to or from Tashiding, try connecting at **Legship**. Should you get stranded, **Hotel Trishna** (☏250887; d/tr ₹200/300) is simple, with private bathrooms, bucket hot water and a rooftop terrace.

Just 5km south of Legship, across the river, the **Phursangchu** hot springs and **Guru Rinpoche** cave are worth a quick stop if you have your own transport.

Pelling

☏03595 / ELEV 2085M

Pelling's raison d'être is its stride-stopping view of Khangchendzonga at dawn. It's not so much a town as a 2km string of tourist hotels, but don't be put off. The view *is* worth it. Despite hordes of visitors, locals remain surprisingly unjaded, and the best budget hotels are great for meeting fellow travellers. The helipad to the west of the centre gives magnificent panoramic views, especially at dawn.

Pelling is nominally divided into Upper, Middle and Lower areas, though these effectively merge. A focal point of Upper Pelling is a small roundabout where the main road from Geyzing turns 180 degrees in front of Hotel Garuda. At the same point, minor roads branch south to Dentam and southwest to the helipad and tourist office.

Tours

Most hotels and travel agencies offer one-day tours. Popular options visit Yuksom via Khecheopalri Lake and three waterfalls (₹2000 to ₹2500 per jeepload) or combine Khecheopalri Lake, Pemayangtse Gompa and Rabdentse (₹1800 to ₹2000).

Hotel Garuda (☏258319; Upper Pelling; tours per day per jeep ₹1800) Half-day tours to Khecheopalri Lake cost ₹1200; to Pemayangtse and Rabdentse costs an extra ₹600.

Hotel Kabur (☏258504; deepesh83@yahoo. co.in; Upper Pelling; day tours ₹2000) Local tours and more; ask about the treks from Ribdi.

🛏 Sleeping

Most of Pelling's hotels cater primarily to midrange domestic tourists. Rates typically drop 30% in low season and are highly negotiable during low occupancy.

Hotel Garuda   HOTEL $
(☏258319; Upper Pelling; dm ₹100, r ₹250-600, deluxe ₹900-1100; @) A well-run backpacker favourite, with clean, spacious rooms, all with hot shower and TV, good Khangchendzonga views and a good-value restaurant ideal for hooking up with other travellers. The owner is very knowledgable about the region and offers guests a handy schematic guide map.

Hotel Kabur   HOTEL $
(☏258504; deepesh83@yahoo.co.in; Upper Pelling; r ₹150-600) Entry is via the top floor, which is a delightful restaurant backed by a verandah that looks out onto the mountains. Rooms have towels, soap, toilet paper and heaters in winter – all usually absent in rooms of this price, though rooms without a view can be dark and cold. If you need to know something, do something or go somewhere, the owners Deepen and his identical twin Deepesh are the people to ask (even if you're never quite sure which one you're talking to!).

Norbu Ghang Resort   HERITAGE HOTEL $$$
(☏258272; www.norbughangresort.com; Upper Pelling; s/d from ₹2800/3000; ❉ 🛜) A spread of pretty cottages (some private, some duplexes) dots the hillside of this resort. Most have fine views, so you can savour the dawn views from the toasty-warm comfort of your own bed. An afternoon beer on the lawn is another

Pelling

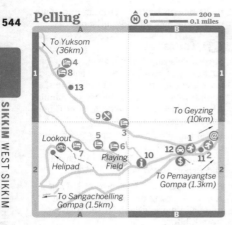

To Yuksom (36km)

To Geyzing (10km)

Lookout

Helipad

Playing Field

To Pemayangtse Gompa (1.3km)

To Sangachoelling Gompa (1.5km)

Pelling

Activities, Courses & Tours
1 Hotel Garuda..................................B2
2 Hotel Kabur...................................B2

Sleeping
3 Hotel Parodzong............................A2
4 Hotel Rabdentse Residency A1
5 Hotel Simvo...................................A2
6 Hotel Sonamchen...........................A2
7 Norbu Ghang Resort A2
8 Touristo Hotel A1

Eating
9 Melting Point.................................A1

Information
10 Tourist Office B2

Transport
11 Father Tours B2
12 Shared Jeeps to Geyzing.................B2
13 SNT Counter (Hotel Pelling).............A1

highlight. A second Norbu Ghang resort and spa is under construction behind this one.

Elgin Mount Pandim HERITAGE HOTEL $$$
(250756; www.elginhotels.com; s/d incl full board ₹5600/5900;) Pelling's most historic hotel is a five-minute stroll from Pemayangtse gompa, with arguably the best mountain views in all of Sikkim. The fairy godmother of renovation has been generous with the parlour-room wicker and antiques and the Aussie-Tibetan managers add a personal warmth to the elegant charm. Request a mountain-view room.

Hotel Sonamchen HOTEL $$
(258346; sonamchen07@yahoo.com; s/d from ₹1000/1200) The rooms here can't deliver on the expectations created by the ornately decorated lobby but most do have superb Khangchendzonga views, with rates decreasing in price as you descend the floors. The standard rooms with balcony offer the best value.

Pelling has over 80 hotels. Other options:

Touristo Hotel HOTEL $$
(258206; Lower Pelling; d ₹500-1000) Only the best rooms have good Khangchendzonga views.

Hotel Rabdentse Residency HOTEL $$
(258612; www.saikripa.in; Lower Pelling; d from ₹850-1050, ste ₹1800-3300) Downstairs behind the Touristo, with some views and a good restaurant.

Eating & Drinking
Pelling's best dining is in the hotels. The Norbu Ghang, Garuda, Kabur and Rabdentse Residency are the best bets.

Melting Point MULTICUISINE $
(Middle Pelling; mains ₹60-110) It's a short stroll downhill to this friendly restaurant, which offers cosy indoor seating or excellent terrace views. The wide menu ranges from baked potatoes to Sikkimese fixed meals (₹350; ordered in advance). There's 20% discount between 5pm and 7pm.

Information
Paylink Cyber Zone (per hr ₹50; 8am-7pm) Just below Hotel Kabur.
SBI ATM Opposite the Hotel Garuda.
Tourist office (9434630876; 9am-5pm)

Getting There & Away
SNT buses run to Siliguri (₹135, four hours, 7am) via Jorethang (₹40, 2½ hours); book at the **SNT counter** (Hotel Pelling) in Lower Pelling from where the buses depart.

Father Tours (258219; Upper Pelling) runs shared jeeps at 7am for Gangtok (₹200, five hours) and Siliguri (₹200, 4½ hours).

If nothing is available ex-Pelling, change in Geyzing. Shared jeeps to Geyzing (₹25, 20 minutes) leave frequently from near the Hotel Garuda, passing close to Pemayangtse, Rabdentse and Tikjuk district administrative centre.

For Khecheopalri Lake (₹60) or Yuksom (₹60) jeeps start from Geyzing, passing through Pelling between noon and 1pm. The Kabur and Garuda hotels can book seats for you, or simply join a day-trip tour and throw away the return ticket.

Around Pelling

PEMAYANGTSE GOMPA

Literally translated as 'Perfect Sublime Lotus', the 1705 Pemayangtse gompa (Indian/foreigner ₹10/20; ⊙7am-5pm) is one of Sikkim's oldest and most significant Nyingmapa gompas. Magnificently set on a hilltop (2100m) overlooking the Rabdentse ruins, the atmospheric compound is ringed by gardens and traditional cottages used by the resident monks. The ground floor features a central Buddha, while upstairs fierce-looking statues depict all eight reincarnations of Padmasambhava. On the top floor is an astounding seven-tiered model representing Padmasambhava's heavenly abode of Zangtok Pelri, handmade over five laborious years by a single dedicated lama.

During February/March impressive *chaam* dances celebrating **Losar** culminate with the unfurling of a huge *gyoku* (giant embroidered *thangka*) and the zapping of evil demons with a great fireball.

Pemayangtse is 1.5km from Upper Pelling, along the road to Geyzing, and is easily combined with a visit to Rabdentse. The signposted turn-off is near an obvious stupa.

RABDENTSE

The royal capital of Sikkim from 1670 to 1814, the now-ruined Rabdentse (admission free; ⊙dawn-dusk) consists of chunky wall-stubs with a few inset inscription stones. These would look fairly unremarkable were they not situated on such an utterly fabulous viewpoint ridge. The entrance to the site is around 3km from Upper Pelling, along the road to Geyzing. The ruins are a 10-minute walk from the site's yellow gateway. As the sign says, 'Do not get tired. Great excitement is awaiting'!

SANGACHOELING GOMPA

The second-oldest gompa in all of Sikkim, charming Sangachoeling has some beautiful murals and a peaceful ridgetop setting. It's a steep 2km walk from Pelling starting along the dirt track that veers left where the asphalted road rises to Pelling's new helipad. A huge statue of Chenresig, the Buddhist Bodhissatva of Compassion, is currently under construction just behind the monastery

A jungle trek continues 10km beyond Sangachoeling to Rani Dhunga (Queen's Rock), supposedly the scene of an epic Ramayana battle between Rama and 10-headed demon king Ravana. Arrange a guide (₹300 to ₹400) from the Kabur or Garuda hotels.

The Monastery Loop

Day-long and overnight jeep tours from Pelling take in the major sights here, or you can do a great adventurous three-day trip from Pelling to Tashiding via Khecheopalri Lake, using a combination of jeeps and hiking. Alternatively, consider catching a ride to wonderful Yuksom via Khecheopalri Lake using tour jeeps and hiking from there to Tashiding.

PELLING TO YUKSOM

Tourist jeeps stop at several relatively lacklustre time-filler sites. Rimbi and Khangchendzonga Falls are best after rains while Phamrong Falls are impressive any time. Although it's several kilometres up a dead-end spur road, virtually all Yuksom-bound tours visit Khecheopalri, dropping you for about half an hour at a car park five minutes' walk from the little lake.

Pronounced 'catch-a-perry', the holy Khecheopalri Lake (1950m) is highly revered by both Sikkimese Buddhists and Lepcha animists who believe that birds assiduously remove any leaves from its surface. During Khecheopalri Mela (March/April), butter lamps are floated out across the lake, which is backed by fluttering prayer flags and Tibetan inscriptions, but the setting, ringed with forested hills, is serene rather than dramatic. The best way to appreciate the site is to stay overnight and visit once the tourists have left.

Around the car park is a Buddhist nunnery, a couple of shops and the simple

---

WORTH A TRIP

If you are headed to or from Pemayangtse Monastery, pop into the **Lotus Bakery** (cake ₹25-30; ⊙8am-5pm), 15 minutes' walk above Pelling, for a restorative slice of carrot or banana cake. All money raised goes to the nearby Denjong Pema Choling Academy.

Jigme Restaurant serving tea and chow mein. From the car park a path to the left leads uphill for 20 minutes to **Khecheopalri Gompa** and stupa, high above the lake. A hiking trail from here leads up for a couple of hours to the Duphuk meditation cave and viewpoint, where the outline of the lake below looks like a footprint. There are other viewpoints to explore around the lake.

Just beside the gompa and run by a local lama is **Pala's Guest House** (☏9832471253; per person incl 3 meals ₹300), with more rooms available at next-door Sonam's nicer annexe. The wooden rooms are simple, but it's a great opportunity to slow things down a bit, do some hiking and even learn some meditation.

Deepen Pradhan also operates a good **homestay** (☏9735945598; per person incl one meal ₹450), five minutes' walk away; for details ask at the Kabur Hotel in Pelling.

Shared jeeps to Geyzing (₹70, two hours) leave the parking lot at 6am, travelling via Pelling.

A hiking trail to Yuksom (9km, three to five hours) leaves the road about 400m before the car park and descends steeply in 90 minutes to the main road (take the right branch after crossing the Runom Khola river), emerging near the Khangchendzonga Falls. After the road suspension bridge, follow the concrete steps uphill to meet the Yuksom road, about 2km below Yuksom village. Alternatively hitch a ride (₹30) once you get to the road.

YUKSOM
☏03595 / ELEV 1780M

Loveable little Yuksom is historic, charming and unspoilt. Domestic tourists avoid it as it lacks the mountain views and it hasn't become a travellers' ghetto like Hampi or Manali. The town is the main trailhead for the treks towards Mt Khangchendzonga.

◉ Sights

Norbugang Park   SACRED SITE
Yuksom means 'meeting place of the three lamas', referring to the trio of Tibetan holy men who crowned the first chogyal of Sikkim here in 1641. The charming site is now Norbugang Park, which contains a small temple, huge *mani khorlo* (prayer wheel), chorten (stupa) and the supposedly original **Coronation Throne** (Norbugang). Standing beneath a vast cryptomeria pine, it looks something like an ancient Olympic podium made of whitewashed stone. Just in front of

the throne is a spooky footprint fused into the stone, believed to be that of one of the crowning lamas: you can see a distinct impression of sole and toes.

Walking up to Norbugang Park past Hotel Tashi Gang you'll pass the murky prayer-flag-lined **Kathok Lake**, from which anointing waters were taken for the original coronation.

Tashi Tenka   RUINS
When Yuksom was Sikkim's capital, a royal palace complex known as Tashi Tenka sat on a ridge to the south with superb almost 360-degree views. Today barely a stone remains but the views are still superb. To find the site head south out of town and take the small uphill path marked by two weathered stupas near the school football pitch. The site is 10 minutes' walk away through the charming village of Gupha Dara.

Dubdi Gompa   MONASTERY
High on the ridge above Yuksom, Dubdi (Hermit's Cell) Gompa is set in beautifully tended gardens behind three coarsely hewn stupas. Established in 1701, it is said to be Sikkim's oldest monastery, though the current chapel looks much newer. Start the steep 40-minute climb from upper Yuksom's primary health centre; the clear path rises through thickets of trumpet lilies and some lovely mature forest.

Kathok Wodsallin Gompa   MONASTERY
Yuksom has two photogenic new gompas. Kathok Wodsallin Gompa, near Hotel Tashi Gang, has an impressively stern statue of Guru Padmasambhava surrounded by a collection of yogis, gurus and lamas in glass-fronted compartments. The entry is up a path opposite the Tashigang Hotel.

**Ngadhak Changchub
Choling Gompa**   MONASTERY
This other new and similarly colourful gompa is accessed through an ornate gateway opposite Hotel Yangri Gang. The main statue is of an 11-headed Chenresig, the Bodhisattva of Compassion.

⚡Activities

Several trekking agencies in Yuksom can organise a **Khangchendzonga trek** given a couple of days warning. Prices start around US$40 per person per day assuming a group of four. The best:

Alpine Exodus Tours & Travel   TREKKING
(☏9735087508; nawang.bhutia@gmail.com; Hotel Yangri Gang)

Desire Earth Treks & Expeditions TREKKING
(☑9733052919; www.trekinsikkim.com) Next to Hotel Pemathang

Mountain Tours and Treks TREKKING
(☑9641352656; www.sherpatreks.in)

🛏 Sleeping & Eating

Foreign trekking groups often book out the Tashi Gang and Yuksom Residency hotels so it's wise to make reservations for these places. Khangchendzonga Conservation Committee (p547) arranges **homestays** (per person full board ₹500-700), offering travellers the chance to connect with locals, eat local food and even share in chores like milking the cows.

Hotel Demazong HOTEL $
(☑9775473687; dm ₹80-100, r ₹500, without bathroom ₹200) The concrete exterior isn't exactly charming but the rooms here are spacious, clean and decent value, making this the most popular budget option.

Hotel Tashi Gang HOTEL $$
(☑9733077249; hoteltashigang@gmail.com; s/d from ₹1200/1500) The traditional bedspreads, painted furniture and decorative *thangkas* add an element of Sikkimese style to this good-value place. Rooms are large (some with balconies), beds are comfortable and there's a nice lawn.

Yuksom Residency HOTEL $$
(☑241277; www.yuksomresidency.com; s/d from ₹2500/2700;🛜) The plushest place in town has clean spacious rooms, a pleasant garden and even a meditation hall; perfect for returning trekkers in need of a hot shower and a splash of decadence.

Hotel Yangri Gang HOTEL $
(☑241217; d ₹500-800, without bathroom ₹300; @) The basement rooms are functional concrete cubes, but the upstairs options are airy with clean wooden floors, wooden half-panelling and good hot showers. It's a good upper budget option favoured by trekkers.

🍴 Eating

Gupta Restaurant MULTICUISINE $
(mains ₹35-90; ☺5am-9pm) Beers, curries, pizza, breakfasts and almost anything else you could dream up (including quesadillas!) are available in this popular backpacker cafe. Sit outside at the sociable thatched cabana or keep warm in the cosy interior. The next-door **Yak Restaurant** is similar but has a smaller menu.

❶ Information

Community Information Centre (internet per hr ₹50; ☺10am-3pm Mon-Sat) Offers internet connections in an unlikely hut near Kathok Lake.

Khangchendzonga Conservation Committee (☑9733158268; www.kccsikkim.org; ☺10am-4pm) An impressive local environmental group that offers information on local ecotourism options, recycling initiatives and homestays. An internet cafe is planned. The office is at the top of town, 300m past the Gupta Restaurant.

❶ Getting There & Away

Around 6.30am, several shared jeeps leave for Jorethang (₹100, four hours) via Tashiding

---

WORTH A TRIP

YUKSOM TO TASHIDING HIKE

Starting in Yuksom is easier than coming the other way for this long but highly rewarding one-day hike. No trekking permits are required. Figure on six hours of walking (19km), plus another two hours visiting the monasteries. Porter-guides are available in Yuksom for around ₹400.

Start by ascending to **Dubdi Gompa** (p546), from where a path dips into a side valley for 40 minutes to **Tsong**, where the trail divides. The lower route returns to Yuksom, while the upper route leads uphill past cardamom fields to lonely **Hongri Gompa**, a small, unusually unpainted ancient monastery with a superlative ridge-top location. Local folklore claims the gompa was moved here from a higher spot where monks kept being ravaged by yeti.

A signpost points the way downhill for 20 minutes to **Nessa** hamlet, continuing down to the new road 10 minutes before the village of **Pokhari Dara** (four hours from Yuksom). Follow the road until a footpath branches towards **Sinon Gompa** (built 1716), high above Tashiding. The path then drops steeply down steps behind the yellow monastic school, following village trails down to Tashiding. The switchbacking road takes much longer.

(₹50, 1½ hours), and Geyzing via Pelling (₹70, approximately 2½ hours). Jeeps to Gangtok (₹180, six hours) leave early in the morning and, less reliably, in the afternoon. Try to book the day before, either at the shop next to the Gupta Restaurant or at the hut opposite.

DZONGRI & GOECHA LA – THE KHANGCHENDZONGA TREK

For guided groups with permits, Yuksom is the starting point of Sikkim's classic seven- to 10-day trek to Goecha La, a 4940m pass with quite fabulous views of Khangchendzonga.

Trek costs start at US$40 to US$60 per person per day (assuming a group of four), including food, guides, porters and yaks. You have to arrange your trek through a trekking agency, who will sort out the permits. Paperwork must be done in Gangtok but, given two or three days, agents in Pelling or Yuksom can organise things by sending a fixer to the capital for you.

Don't underestimate the rigours of the trek. Don't hike too high too quickly: altitude sickness often strikes those who are fittest and fastest. Starting early makes sense, as rain is common in the afternoons, spoiling views and making trail sections annoyingly muddy. Check all your equipment before setting off, making sure there are enough good-quality sleeping bags to go around. Bring a torch (flashlight). For full details of the trek see Lonely Planet's *Trekking in the Indian Himalaya*.

March to May is an ideal time to trek. By the end of May the monsoon rains have started to arrive. Clearest skies are from October to December, when snow starts to block the trails.

The route initially follows the Rathong Valley through unspoilt forests then ascends steeply to Baktim (Bakhim; 2750m) and the rustic Tibetan village of Tsokha (3050m), established in 1969 by Tibetan refugees and the last village on the trail, where spending two nights helps with acclimatisation.

The next stage climbs to pleasant meadows around Dzongri (4020m). Consider another acclimatisation day here spent strolling up to Dzongri La (4550m, four-hour round-trip) for fabulous views of Mt Pandim (6691m).

From Dzongri, the trail drops steeply to Kokchurong then follows the river to Thangsing (3930m). Trekkers have recommended spending an extra day here to visit the beautiful lake at Lampokhari,

three hours' walk away. Next day takes you to camping at Lamuni, 15 minutes before Samiti Lake (4200m), from where a next-morning assault takes you to head-spinning Goecha La (4940m) for those incredible views of Khangchendzonga. A further viewpoint, an hour's walk further, offers even closer views.

The return is by essentially the same route. Alternatively at Dzongri you could cut south for about a week following the Singalila Ridge along the Nepal–Sikkim border to emerge at Uttarey, from where public transport runs to Jorethang.

There are government-run **trekkers' huts** at Baktim, Tsokha, Dzongri, Kokchurong and Thangsing, but most have neither furniture nor mattresses and huts sometimes get booked out with noisy student groups during high season. It's far better to bring all camping equipment and food.

TASHIDING
ELEV 1490M

Little Tashiding is just a single, sloping market street forking north off the Yuksom–Legship road, but its south-facing **views** are wide and impressive.

Walking 400m south from the junction towards Legship takes you down past a series of mani walls with bright painted mantras to a colourful gateway. A 2.5km

KHANGCHENDZONGA TREK SCHEDULE

STAGE	ROUTE	DURATION
1	Yuksom to Tsokha, via Baktim	6-7 hr
2	Optional acclimatisation day at Tsokha	1 day
3	Tsokha to Dzongri	4-5 hr
4	Acclimatisation day at Dzongri, or continue to Kokchurong	1 day
5	Dzongri (or Kokchurong) to Lamuni, via Thangsing	6-7 hr
6	Lamuni to Goecha La, then down to Thangsing	8-9 hr
7	Thangsing to Tsokha	6-7 hr
8	Tsokha to Yuksom	5-6 hr

uphill driveable track (and much shorter footpath) leads to a car park from where a footpath leads up between an avenue of prayer flags to the atmospheric Nyingmapa-school Tashiding Gompa, about 30 minutes' walk away.

Founded in 1641 by one of the three Yuksom lamas (see p546), the monastery's five colourful religious buildings are strung out between more functional monks' quarters. Notice the giant-sized prayer wheel with Tibetan script picked out in gilt. Beautifully proportioned, the four-storey main prayer hall has a delicate filigree topknot, with wonderful views across the semi-wild flower garden towards Ravangla. The Dalai Lama chose the magical spot for a two-day meditation retreat in 2010.

Beyond the last monastic building, an unusual compound contains dozens of white chortens, including the Thongwa Rangdol, said to wash away the sins of anyone who gazes upon it. Smaller but more visually exciting is the golden Kench Chorgi Lorde stupa. Propped up all around are engraved stones bearing the Buddhist mantra *om mani padme hum;* at the back of the compound is the engraver's lean-to.

In January or February, the monastery celebrates the **Bumchu festival** during which lamas gingerly open a sacred pot. Then, judging from the level of holy water within, they make all-important predictions about the coming year.

The central wooden Mt Siniolchu Guest House (☏243211; r without bathroom ₹200) is a basic but friendly budget option. Concrete New Tashiding Lodge (☏243249; tr without bathroom ₹300-350), 300m south of the market, has fine views from Rooms 3, 4 and 5 and even better ones from the shared bathroom.

Yatri Niwas (☏9832623654; kabirbista@ yahoo.com; s/d ₹1000/1200) is an excellent mid-range place down at the base of town by the turn-off to the monastery, offering spacious rooms, lovely gardens and a good restaurant.

Shared jeeps to Gangtok (₹130, four hours), Jorethang (₹70, two hours) and Geyzing (₹60, 1½ hours) leave from the main junction between 6.30am and 8am. A few jeeps to Yuksom pass through during early afternoon.

Northeast Tribal States

Best Places to Stay

» Eco-Camp (p559)

» Heritage Hotel (p570)

» Hotel Tripura Castle (p580)

» Classic Hotel (p574)

» Cherrapunjee Holiday Resort (p583)

Best Adventures

» Travel to Shangri La (p567)

» Search for Paradise (p568)

» Brahmaputra ferry ride (p567)

» Encounters with Naga Warriors (p572)

» Explore rural Mizoram (p576)

Why Go?

India's Northeast States, dangling way out on the edge of the map and the national perception, are strictly for explorers who want something different from their India experience. These remote frontier lands, where India, Southeast Asia and Tibet meet, are a collision zone of cultures, climates, landscapes and peoples and are one of Asia's last great unknowns. It's a place of rugged beauty where uncharted forests clamber up toward unnamed Himalayan peaks. It's a land of enormous variety where rhinoceros live in swampy grasslands and former head-hunters live in longhouses in the jungle. And it's an adventure in the truest sense of the word.

Infuriating permits and over-exaggerated safety worries mean the northeast is way off the tourist trail, yet the people are probably the friendliest in India.

So with all this on offer, why wait? Don your pith helmet and set forth in search of adventure.

When to Go
Assam (Guwahati)

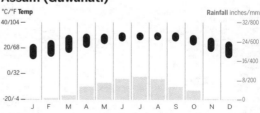

Mar The wildlife is at its most visible in Kaziranga and other national parks.

Oct The Himalayan vistas are perfect and the roads to Tawang and Mechuka remain snow-free.

Dec Fierce Naga warriors descend on Kohima for the Hornbill festival (December 1–7).

Food

The food in the northeast is as varied and exotic as the people and the terrain. Sure, you can get all the North Indian and Chinese staples in most places, but if travel is all about new experiences then Northeast India is going to be a culinary adventure you'll never forget. Things start off tame enough in high mountain areas like Tawang, where the food is reminiscent of neighbouring Tibet – delicious *momos* and less-delicious Tibetan tea are all the rage. Head east and things become more interesting. Barbecued rat, forest antelope and something we couldn't quite identify were on the menu in central Arunachal Pradesh. If you're going to Mizoram, don't take Rover – dog meat is a delicacy there. In Nagaland, grubs, maggots, snakes, hornets and giant spiders all get taste buds excited.

DON'T MISS

There aren't all that many places left in the world where the maps may as well have blank spaces on them, snow-capped mountains remain unnamed and unclimbed, forests are filled with creatures that scientists have yet to lay eyes upon and hill tops are crowned with unmolested tribal villages, but northeast India is one such place. As the region slowly opens up, don't miss this opportunity for genuine, undiluted adventure. Areas that are safe yet largely unexplored by tourists include almost all of rural **Mizoram**, large tracts of **Tripura** (check the security situation first), the furthest reaches of **Nagaland** and, best of all, huge chunks of steamy forests, alpine meadows and high Himalayan wildernesses have finally started opening up in **Arunachal Pradesh**.

Top Festivals

» Torgya and Losar (Jan/Feb, Tawang, p569) Masked Tibetan Buddhist dances.

» Ambubachi Mela (Jun, Kamakhya Mandir, Guwahati, p554) Tantric rituals and animal sacrifices.

» Nongkrem (Oct, Smit, p582) Khasi royal festival.

» Wangala (Oct/Nov, Meghalaya statewide, p579) Harvest festival with impressive dancing.

» Ras Mahotsav Festival (3rd week of Nov, Majuli Island, p562) Major Vishnu festival.

» Hornbill Festival (Dec 1-7, Kohima, p571) Naga tribes in full warrior gear.

MAIN POINTS OF ENTRY

Guwahati airport has flights to most major Indian cities. It's also the only big city in the northeast with a train line connecting it to the rest of India.

Fast Facts

» Population: 44.99 million
» Area: 255,083 sq km
» Main languages: Assamese, Bodo, Hindi, Nagamese, Manipuri, Mizo, Khasi, Garo, Bengali
» Sleeping prices: **$** below ₹800, **$$** ₹800 to ₹2500, **$$$** above ₹2500

Top Tip

If you're using a tour company, allow at least one month to obtain travel permits and two months if travelling in a group of less than four (and you're not a married couple). If applying independently allow at least two to three months.

Resources

» www.assamtourism.org
» www.arunachaltourism.com
» www.tourismnagaland.com
» http://manipur.nic.in/tourism.htm
» www.mizotourism.nic.in
» www.tripuratourism.in
» www.megtourism.gov.in

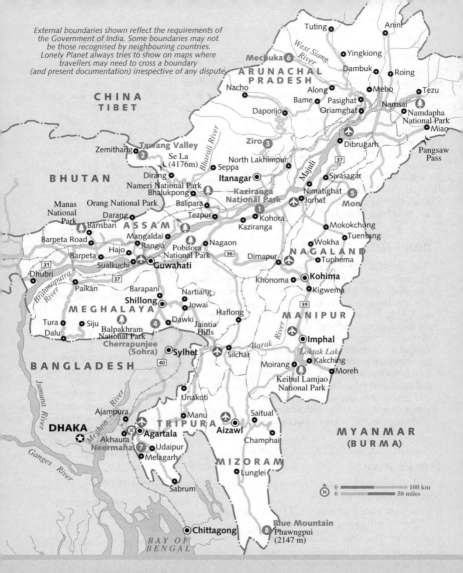

External boundaries shown reflect the requirements of the Government of India. Some boundaries may not be those recognised by neighbouring countries. Lonely Planet always tries to show on maps where travellers may need to cross a boundary (and present documentation) irrespective of any dispute

Northeast Tribal States Highlights

① Ride atop an elephant in search of rhinos in **Kaziranga National Park** (p559)

② Touch the clouds at the 4176m pass of Se La before descending to **Tawang Valley** (p569), Arunachal Pradesh's 'little Tibet'

③ Visit intriguing tribal villages around **Ziro** (p565) and

meet the last of the bizarrely adorned Apatani women

④ Gaze down on the plains of Bangladesh from the lofty escarpment around **Cherrapunjee** (Sohra; p582)

⑤ Feel as if you've stepped out of India into a different culture and country in Nagaland's **Mon** (p572)

⑥ Search for the Last Shangri La in **Mechuka** (p567)

⑦ Row, row, row the boat gently out to the floating palace of **Neermahal** (p578)

⑧ Avoid the ghosts and hang with the Gods on the **Blue Mountain** (p576) of Mizoram

ASSAM

Fascinating Assam (also known as Asom and Axom) straddles the fertile Brahmaputra valley, making it the most accessible of India's Northeast States. The archetypal Assamese landscape offers golden-green vistas over seemingly endless rice fields and manicured tea estates framed in the distance by the hazy-blue mountains of Arunachal.

Assamese people might look Indian, but Assamese culture is proudly distinct: their Vishnu-worshipping faith is virtually a regional religion (see the boxed text, p562) and the *gamosa* (a red-and-white scarf worn by most men) is a subtle mark of regional costume.

With warm and genuinely hospitable locals, national parks crawling with animals big and small, slow boat rides down the Brahmaputra and a string of Hindu temples, Assam is a delight to travel in.

Guwahati

🕿0361 / POP 809,805

The biggest, most cosmopolitan and, some might say, the most 'Indian' city in the northeast, Guwahati is an essential stop on any northeastern tour. A casual glance might place Guwahati alongside any other Indian city but wander the back alleys around Jorpulkuri Ponds, away from the concrete jungle of the central business district, and you could almost imagine yourself in a village made up of ponds, palm trees, small single-storey traditional houses and old colonial-era mansions.

History

Guwahati is considered the site of Pragjyotishpura, a semi-mythical town founded by Asura King Naraka who was later killed by Lord Krishna for a pair of magical earrings. The city was a vibrant cultural centre well before the Ahoms arrived, and later it was the theatre of intense Ahom–Mughal

ⓘ PERMIT PAINS

Permits Permits for this region are a pain, being too bureaucratically involved for many foreigners, but those who take the trouble will be rewarded. Permits are mandatory for Nagaland, Arunachal Pradesh, Mizoram and Manipur, and entry without one is a serious matter. Indian citizens just need an inner line permit, issued with little fuss in Guwahati or Kolkata (see p469). The rest of this box applies to foreigners who'll require a Restricted Area Permit (RAP).

Minimum Group Size Permit applications need a four-person minimum group. Exceptions are Nagaland, for a legally married couple with marriage certificate; and Arunachal Pradesh for a minimum of two people. In reality though, it's now possible for single travellers to get permits to all the states, but only if you use a tour company (and even then you need a lot of patience).

In Nagaland and Manipur, authorities may refuse you entry if some people listed on your permit are 'missing'; Mizoram doesn't seem bothered and Arunachal Pradesh is now much more relaxed.

Validity & Registration Permits are valid for 10 days from a specified starting date, but Arunachal allows 30 days. You *might* be able to extend your permit, but only in state capitals at the Secretariat, Home Department. Be aware that permits only allow you to visit specified districts between specified dates, so plan carefully as changing routes might be problematic.

Be sure to make multiple photocopies of your permit to hand in at each checkpoint, police station and hotel.

Where to Apply Applications made independently through the **Ministry of Home Affairs** (🕿011-23385748; Jaisalmer House, 26 Man Singh Rd, Delhi; ⏲inquiries 9-11am Mon-Fri) or the appropriate State House in Delhi can take weeks and will normally end in frustration. Kolkata's **Foreigners' Registration Office** (FRO; 🕿22837034; 237 AJC Bose Rd; ⏲11am-5pm Mon-Fri) can issue permits but it seems to want to exclude Tawang from Arunachal, restrict access to Nagaland and not allow you into Mizoram.

The easiest and most reliable way to get permits is through a reputable travel agency; see the Information section for each state.

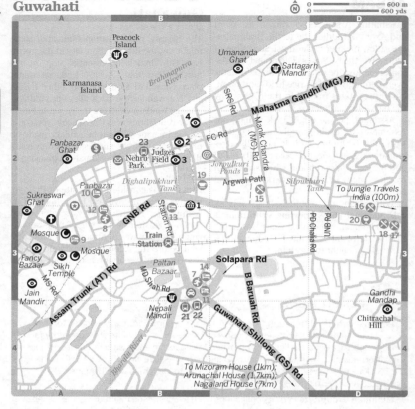

NORTHEAST TRIBAL STATES ASSAM

fighting, changing hands eight times in 50 years before 1681. In 1897 a huge earthquake, followed by a series of devastating floods, wiped out most of the old city.

◉ Sights

Kamakhya Mandir HINDU TEMPLE
(admission for no queue/short queue/queue ₹500/100/free; ☺8am-1pm & 3pm-dusk) While Sati's disintegrated body parts rained toes on Kolkata (see p443), her yoni fell on Kamakhya Hill. This makes Kamakhya Mandir important for *shakti* (sensual tantric worship of female spiritual power). Goats, pigeons and the occasional buffalo are ritually beheaded in a gory pavilion and the hot, dark inner womblike sanctum is painted red to signify sacrificial blood. The huge June/ July **Ambubachi Mela** celebrates the end of the mother goddess' menstrual cycle with even more blood.

Kamakhya is 7km west of central Guwahati and 3km up a spiralling side road. Occasional buses from Guwahati's Kachari bus stand run all the way up (₹20, 20 minutes).

Umananda Mandir HINDU TEMPLE
(Peacock Island) The temple complex sits on a small forested river island, accessed by a 15-minute ride on a ferry (₹10 return, half hourly 8am to 4.30pm) from **Kachari Ghat**, which itself offers attractive afternoon river views. The Shiva temple, which sits atop the island, is less interesting than the boat ride out to it.

Assam State Museum MUSEUM
(GNB Rd; admission/camera/video ₹5/10/100; ☺10am-5pm Tue-Sun, until 4pm winter) This museum is worth a visit. It has a large sculpture collection, while the upper floors are devoted to informative tribal culture displays. You get to walk through reconstructed tribal homes.

Old Guwahati
AREA

The distinctive beehive dome of the **Courthouse** (MG Rd) rises above attractive **Dighulipukhuri Park** (HB Rd; admission ₹5, boats per person ₹15; ⊙9.30am-8pm) with its large tank full of row boats. The nearby **Guwahati Planetarium** (MG Rd; shows ₹15; ⊙noon & 4pm, closed 1st & 15th of the month) looks somewhere between a mosque and a landed UFO.

🛌 Sleeping

Most midrange and top-end hotels add a 15% tax and 10% service charge to their nightly rates. These have been included in the prices listed here.

Hotel Prag Continental
HOTEL $$

(☏2540850; www.hotelpragcontinental.com; MN Rd; s/d from ₹1180/1725; ❄) The spacious and well-furnished rooms with wooden floors on offer at this hotel are as spotless as the aquarium full of brightly painted fish that sits in the reception. The staff are attentive and discounts easy to come by. It's on a quieter side street and has a good restaurant.

Sundarban Guest House
HOTEL $

(☏2730722; s/d from ₹385/550; ❄) A cheery, colourful hotel that's the best budget option in town and about the closest the northeast comes to a backpacker hangout. Rooms are atypically clean and tidy with stain-free sheets, and management is helpful. It's off Manipuribasti East (ME) Rd, in the first side lane and away from road noise.

Dynasty
HOTEL $$$

(☏2516021; www.hoteldynastyindia.com; Sir Shahdullah (SS) Rd; r from ₹6100; ❄@☎) The shabby exterior makes it hard to believe that this is really Guwahati's top hotel, but as we all know it's what's on the inside that counts: magnificent rooms with an old colonial flavour. It has all the facilities you'd expect from a top-end hotel, including a couple of superb restaurants plus a sauna and steam room.

Hotel Siroy Lily
HOTEL $$

(☏2608492; www.hotelsiroylily.com; Solapara Rd; s/d from ₹836/1083; ❄) Professionally run but tired-looking hotel with a pleasantly air-conditioned foyer, complimentary breakfast and free newspapers delivered to your door. Considering the price it's a pretty good deal.

Also recommended:

Prashaanti Tourist Lodge
HOTEL $

(☏9207047841; Station Rd; r from ₹578; ❄) Convenient for the train station, the rooms are OK but the staff could do with a brush-up in hospitality management. It's a genuine bargain, though, but be prepared for some train noise.

Hotel Suradevi
HOTEL $

(☏2545050; MN Rd; s/d ₹200/300, without bathroom ₹100/250) Well-organised warren of spartan rooms. Check in early to get a room. The owner speaks good English.

TRAVELLING SAFELY IN THE NORTHEAST STATES

In recent decades many ethnolinguistic groups in the northeast have jostled – often violently – to assert themselves in the face of illegal Bangladeshi immigration, governmental neglect and a heavy-handed defence policy. Some want independence from India, others autonomy, but more are fighting what are effectively clan or turf wars. At the time of writing Arunachal Pradesh, most of Assam, Meghalaya, Mizoram, Nagaland and the tourist areas of Tripura were fairly peaceful.

The problem is that trouble can flare up suddenly and unpredictably. In 2010 bombings hit parts of Assam and the Garo hills area of Meghalaya. Much of Manipur remains dangerous to visit (but the areas open to tourists are currently calm). If you stick to the main tourist routes, the worst problems you're likely to encounter are the regular strikes that paralyse Assam.

Even so, it's wise to keep abreast of latest news with the *Assam Tribune* (www.assam tribune.com) and if you're with a tour group, ensure your guide is up to date with the latest situation.

Eating

Tandoori   NORTH INDIAN **$$**
(☑2516021; SS Rd; mains ₹200-300; ⊗noon-3pm & 7-11pm) Inside the Dynasty Hotel, Tandoori concocts majestic North Indian dishes which are served at stylish low tables by waiters in Mughal uniforms accompanied by gentle live tabla music.

Paradise   ASSAMESE **$$**
(1st fl, GNB Rd; mains ₹100-200) Well known for its authentic Assamese cuisine, its thali is the best way to get a lot of small tasters. Assamese food is not a lip-tingler like typical Indian food and for some this cuisine can seem rather bland, but it's the subtleties you're after rather than the heat.

Dhaba   NORTH INDIAN **$$**
(Silpukhuri, GNB Rd; mains ₹120-180) This simple canteen-style restaurant serves good North Indian staples as well as some token Chinese dishes. You can eat indoors or, if you prefer, out in the courtyard where the side portion of carbon monoxide comes free with the meal. They have a couple of other branches around town.

Kurry Pot   SOUTH INDIAN **$$**
(GNB Rd; mains ₹100-180) The specialities of this clean and peaceful restaurant are the dosas (₹40 to ₹80) and the list of different types is almost as long as the dosa itself. If a dosa's not for you then they dish up a range of other Indian staples. It's popular with the lunchtime work crowd.

Beatrix   MULTICUISINE **$**
(Manik Chandra (MC) Rd; dishes ₹60-165) Upbeat and cartoon-walled, Beatrix is just a peg above a student hangout. Its eclectic menu offers fish and chips, *momos* (Tibetan dumplings) and Hakka Chow. The beautiful old villa it sits next door to is also worth gawping at.

Drinking

Café Coffee Day   CAFE
(Taybullah Rd; espresso ₹25; ⊗10am-10pm) Guwahati's central coffee shop, pumping out contemporary music, attracts the city's students and nouveau-riche youth with perfect (if very slow) macchiato.

Trafik   BAR
(GNB Rd; beers ₹70; ⊗10am-10pm) This underlit bar has a vast screen for cricket matches or *filmi* (slang term describing anything to do with Indian movies; in this case, Bollywood music) clips.

Information

Emergency
Police station (☑2540126, Hem Barua (HB) Rd)

Internet Access
iWay (Lamb Rd; per hr ₹25; ⊗9am-last customer)

Medical Services
Downtown Hospital (☑2331003; GS Rd, Dispur) The area's best.

Money
ATMs abound and it's a good idea to stock up on local currency here as ATMs in smaller centres can be unreliable.
State Bank of India (SBI; 3rd fl, MG Rd) ATM, changes major currencies and travellers cheques.

Permits

Indian citizens can obtain inner line permits (see the following list) but foreigners shouldn't expect any assistance (for foreigner permits, see p553).

Arunachal House (☏23341243; Rukmini Gao, GS Rd)

Manipur Bhawan (☏2540707; Rajgarh Rd)

Mizoram House (☏2529441; GS Rd, Christian Basti)

Nagaland House (☏2332158; Sachel Rd, Sixth Mile, Khanapara)

Post

Main post office (Ananda Ram Barua (ARB) Rd)

Tourist Information

Assam Tourism (☏2542748; www.assam tourism.org; Station Rd) Informal help desk within the Prashaanti Tourist Lodge, with a tour booth just outside.

① Getting There & Away

Air

Air India (☏2264420, Ganeshguri), IndiGo Airlines, **Jet Airways** (☏2633252; Tayebullah Rd), Kingfisher and SpiceJet fly to Guwahati from most major Indian cities (often with a stopover in Kolkata). Getting into town from Guwahati's orderly Lok-Priya Gopinath Bordoloi International Airport costs ₹500/100/70 for taxi/shared taxi/airport bus.

HELICOPTER

Pawan Hans Helicopters (☏2842174; www .pawahans.co.in) shuttles to Shillong (₹1200, 45 minutes, 9am & 1pm Mon-Sat), Naharlagun near Itanagar and Lumla for Tawang (₹3000, 1¼ hours, 10am Mon-Sat). Phone through your booking then pay at the airport if the service flies (weather and passenger numbers permitting).

Meghalaya Helicopter Service (☏2223129; airport) has two to three daily (except Sunday) flights to Shillong (₹1200, 30 minutes, 9am & 12.30pm plus 2pm Tuesday & Thursday). There are also services to Tura (Garo Hills, ₹1500, 50 minutes, 10.30am Mon, Wed & Fri).

Helicopter travel in India has a poor safety record.

Bus & Sumo

Distance buses leave from the Interstate Bus Terminal (ISBT) 8km east of Guwahati. Private bus operators run shuttle services from their offices to the ISBT. With extensive networks are **Network Travels** (☏2522007; GS Rd), **Deep** (☏2152937; Heramba Prasad Borua (HPB) Rd) and **Blue Hill** (☏2601490; HPB Rd). All companies charge the same regulated fares.

Train

Of the four daily trains to Delhi, the *Guwahati New Delhi Rajdhani* (No 2423; 3AC/2AC ₹1995/2565, 27 hours, 7.05am) is the fastest; others take over 42 hours. The best daily train to Kolkata (Howrah Junction) is the *Saraighat Express* (No 2346; sleeper/3AC/2AC ₹386/1012/1366, 16½ hours, 12.45pm). For New Jalpaiguri (for Darjeeling and Sikkim) the best train is the *Guwahati New Jalpaiguri Rajdhani* (No 2423; 3AC/2AC/1AC ₹733/926/1522, six hours).

Several trains serve Dimapur (sleeper/3AC/2AC from ₹166/401/531, four to six hours), Jorhat (sleeper/3AC ₹202/521, seven to 11 hours) and Dibrugarh (3AC/2AC/1AC ₹926/1206/1970, 11 hours). Trains to Jorhat and Dibrugarh cut through Nagaland, but you don't need a Nagaland permit as long as you stay on the train (the same rule doesn't apply for buses however).

① Getting Around

Shared taxis to the airport (per person/car ₹100/500, 23km) leave from outside the Hotel

BUSES FROM GUWAHATI

DESTINATION	FARE (₹)	DURATION (HR)
Agartala (Tripura)	660	24-26
Aizawl (Mizoram)	750	28
Dibrugarh	380	10
Imphal (Manipur) via Mao	700	20
Jorhat	260	8
Kaziranga	260-300	6
Kohima (Nagaland)	330	13
Shillong (Meghalaya)	90-110	3½
Sivasagar	310-390	8
Tezpur	140-150	5

Mahalaxmi on GS Rd. From the Adabari bus stand city buses travel to Hajo (bus 25, ₹50, one hour) and Sualkuchi (bus 22, ₹50, one hour). Autorickshaws charge ₹25 to ₹50 for shorter hops.

Around Guwahati

HAJO

Some 30km northwest of Guwahati, the pleasant little town of Hajo attracts Hindu and Buddhist pilgrims to its five ancient temples topping assorted hillocks. Haigriv Madhav temple is the main one, which is accessed by a long flight of steps through an ornate quasi-Mughal gateway. The images inside of Madhav, an avatar of Krishna, are alleged to be 6000 years old.

POA MECCA

Two kilometres east of Hajo is a **mosque** sheltering the tomb of the multi-named Hazarat Shah Sultan Giasuddin Aulia Rahmatullah Alike who died some 800 years ago. Muslims need to walk (the less pious may drive) 4km up a spiral road to reach the mosque, which is architecturally unremarkable.

POBITORA NATIONAL PARK

Only 40km from Guwahati, this small national park has the highest concentration of rhinoceros in the world. Entrance fees are the same as Kaziranga National Park (see p561). Getting into the park involves a boat ride over the river boundary to the elephant-mounting station. From there it's a one-hour trip atop an elephant lumbering through boggy grassland and stirring up petulant rhinos.

Northwestern Assam (Bodoland)

MANAS NATIONAL PARK
🖉03666

Bodoland's **Manas National Park** (www.manas100.com; Indian/camera/video ₹50/50/500; foreigner/camera/video ₹250/500/1000; ☉Oct-Mar) is Unesco-listed and has two 'ranges' – Bansbari and Koklabari – with different access points.

Bansbari Range   NATURE RESERVE

Famous for tigers (though you'll probably only see their pug marks), this range is comparatively accessible and can be

appreciated in delightful comfort from **Bansbari Lodge** (🖉3612602223; www.assambengalnavigation.com/bansbari.htm; d ₹2000, jungle package ₹7500). Jungle packages cover full board, early morning elephant safari, jeep safari, guide, park entry fee and village and tea garden excursions. Ask about river rafting. Contact Jungle Travels India in Guwahati (p560) for bookings. Access is from Barpeta Rd.

❶ Getting there & Away

Guwahati–Kokrajhar buses serve Pathsala junction and pass within 3km of Barpeta Rd.

The *Kamrup Express* (No 5960, sleeper/3AC/2AC ₹144/280/345, 2½ hours, 7.35am) and *Brahmaputra Mail* (No 4055, sleeper/3AC/2AC ₹144/280/345, 2½ hours, 11.50am) connect Guwahati and Barpeta Rd.

Jeep rental is available at Koklabari, Barpeta Rd and (for guests) at Bansbari Lodge.

Tezpur
🖉03712 / POP 80,573

Tezpur, with its large Bangladeshi immigrant population, is probably Assam's most attractive city thanks to beautifully kept parks, attractive lakes and the enchanting views of the mighty Brahmaputra River as it laps the town's edge. The imaginatively named **Internet Cafe** (Main Rd; per hr ₹20; ☉9am-8pm) has, you guessed it, internet.

☉ Sights

Chitralekha Udyan (Cole Park; Jenkins Rd; adult/camera/video ₹20/20/100; ☉9am-7pm) has a U-shaped pond (paddleboat hire ₹10 per person) wrapped around pretty manicured lawns, dotted with fine **ancient sculptures**. The park also contains bumper cars and waterslides (☉Apr-Sept)! A block east, then south, stands **Ganeshgarh temple**, which backs onto a ghat overlooking the surging river, a good place for Brahmaputra sunsets. Nearly 1km east along the narrow, winding riverside lane is **Agnigarh Hill** (Padma Park; adult/camera/video ₹20/20/100; ☉8.30am-7.30pm) that might have been Banasura's fire fortress site.

🛏 Sleeping & Eating

Hotel Centre Point   HOTEL $$
(🖉232359; Main Rd; r from ₹660; ❄🛜) The cheaper rooms at this new hotel bang in the town centre are splashed in smart white paint, but have cold water–only showers,

while the 'executive' rooms, with flat screen TVs, hot showers, desks and polished wooden floors are truly swanky, with business class standards for non-business class prices. Wi-fi is 'coming soon'.

KF HOTEL $$
(☏237825; Mission Charali; s/d from ₹1760/1980; ✳☞) With slick, contemporary rooms, good customer service and plenty of attention to detail, this hotel has lots going for it. In fact, about the only downside we could come up with was its location, 3km north of town and on a busy junction. There's an in-house restaurant.

Tourist Lodge HOTEL $
(☏221016; Jenkins Rd; s/d from ₹473/525) Facing Chitralekha Udyan, two blocks south of the bus station, the Tourist Lodge is unusual for a government-run hotel in that the staff do actually care about the well-being of their guests and the cleanliness of their hotel. This place offers good-value spacious rooms with bathrooms (some squat toilets) and mosquito nets.

The modern glass tower **Baliram Building**, on the corner of Naren Bose (NB) and NC/SC Roads, contains several floors of good dining. The ground-floor stand-up-and-eat **dosa house** (☺6am-9pm) has South Indian fare and cheap breakfasts. Semismart **China Villa** (meals from ₹120; ☺10am-10.30pm) offers Indian and Chinese food in AC comfort, while the rooftop **Chat House** (snacks from ₹30; ☺8am-9.30pm) has an open-sided, but roofed, terrace for cooling breezes, views, Indian snacks, noodles, pizzas and *momos*.

ℹ Getting There & Away

Sumos have their booking counters in Jenkins Rd and run to Bomdila in Arunachal Pradesh (₹250, eight hours) and Tawang (₹500, 15hrs). Bargain for a private taxi in the same street for the Eco-Camp at Potasali (₹1500) and Kaziranga (₹1500). A little further on is the **bus station** (Jenkins Rd) with frequent services to Guwahati (₹140 to ₹150, five hours), Jorhat (₹100, four hours) and Kohora for Kaziranga (₹45, two hours).

Tezpur's train station recently closed down, meaning that you now have to head to Guwahati or Jorhat if you want to ride the rails.

Around Tezpur

Picturesque **Nameri National Park** (Indian/camera/video ₹20/50/500, foreigner/camera/video ₹250/500/1000; ☺Nov-Apr) specialises in low-key, walk-in birdwatching treks. Around 374 bird species have been recorded in the park, including such rarities as the white-rumped vulture (which may now be extinct in the park), greater spotted eagle and the white-winged duck. Of the big mammals, wild elephants are present as are numerous deer species and a few rarely seen tigers. However, for many mammal-spotting naturalists, the park's most exciting resident is the critically endangered dwarf hog, which, after many years of absence has recently been returned to the wild thanks to a successful captive breeding project run by the **Durrell Wildlife Conservation Trust** (www.durrell.org). Park fees include the compulsory armed guard. Access is from **Potasali**, 2km off the Tezpur–Bhalukpong road (turn east at one-house hamlet Gamani, 12km north of Balipara).

Eco-Camp (☏9435250052/09854019932; dm/d ₹200/1620, plus membership per person ₹50) organises all Nameri visits, including two-hour birdwatching rafting trips (two people ₹550). Accommodation is in 'tents', but colourful fabrics, private bathrooms, sturdy beds and thatched-roof shelters make the experience relatively luxurious. The camp is set within lush gardens full of tweeting birds and butterflies drunk on tropical nectar. There's an atmospheric, and excellent, open-sided restaurant and the staff are simply superb. All up it gets our vote as the best place to stay in the entire northeast. It's very popular, so book way ahead. If it's full the government-run **Jiabhoroli Wild Resort** (☏9954357376; tw ₹1200) just a short walk beyond the Eco-Camp, has plain 'cottages' that aren't quite as quaint as a cottage should be. It's very much the second choice.

Kaziranga National Park

☏03776

Assam's must-do attraction is an elephant safari to look for rhinoceros hiding in the expansive grasslands of this **national park** (☺1 Nov-30 Apr, elephant rides 5.30-8.30am, jeep access 7.30am-noon & 2.30pm-dusk). Kaziranga's population of around 1855 Indian one-horned rhinos (just 200 in 1904) represents more than two-thirds of the world's total. The park consists of a western, central and an eastern range, but the central range is the most accessible, giving the best viewing chances for rhinos, elephants and swamp deer plus plenty of bird life (take binoculars).

The vast majority of foreign tourists visiting the northeast states travel as part of an organised tour, and indeed for four of the states (Arunachal Pradesh, Nagaland, Manipur and Mizoram), independent travel in the normal sense of the word is almost impossible. Instead, the only realistic way of getting permits is to enlist the services of a tour company. Once you have a permit, travelling around independently is not normally a problem, but you're unlikely to find a tour company who'll help you get permits without first hiring a car and driver/guide from them, thus making real independent travel in the permit states pretty much impossible.

Most tour companies are based in Guwahati and all of the following can organise permits and tours throughout the northeast.

» **Traveller's Point** (Map p554; ☑2604018; www.assamtourism.org; Prashaanti Tourist Lodge, Station Rd) If you're staying only within Assam then Assam Tourism's commercial booth runs a variety of city- and state-wide tours including day excursions to Hajo via the silk-weaving centre of Sualkuchi.

» **Network Travels** (Map p554; ☑2605335; www.networktravelsindia.net; GS Rd; ☺5am-9pm) A highly experienced agency whose operations cover the whole of the northeast with tailor-made and fixed-itinerary tours. Organising permits is a speciality.

» **Jungle Travels India** (off Map p554; ☑2667871, 9207042330; www.jungletravelsindia .com; 3b Dirang Arcade, GNB Rd) Another experienced agency covering the entire northeast with tailor-made tours and fixed-date departures. It organises all the permits, but can be slightly disorganised in this regard. With two boats, it runs Brahmaputra cruises (see www.assambengalnavigation.com) for four to 10 nights at US$350 per person per night, and also runs the Bansbari Lodge in Manas National Park.

» **Rhino Travels** (Map p554; ☑2540666; www.rhinotravels.com; M Nehru (MN) Rd) This agency offers set-date tours in Assam and Arunachal Pradesh. It also offers two- to four-night river cruises.

🛏 Sleeping & Eating

Prices drop at least 30% when Kaziranga National Park closes. In season booking ahead is wise and advance payment is often required. All the better hotels listed here sell 'Jungle Plan' packages, which includes full-board accommodation, park entrance fees, a morning elephant safari and an afternoon jeep safari. Unless stated otherwise, the prices we list are for rooms only.

TOURIST COMPLEX

There are a number of fairly run-down places to stay within a five-minute walk of the range office. The following are the best options.

Jupuri Ghar HOTEL $$$
(☑361-2605335; Guwahati; s/tw ₹2250/2800; ❄) Traditional-style cabins set around pleasant, mature gardens in a tranquil setting. It's well-managed and has an open-air restaurant.

Prashanti Cottage HOTEL $
(☑9864575039; d ₹685) Right beside the ticket office, this ageing place has cheap but fairly clean rooms.

BEYOND THE COMPLEX

Wild Grass Resort ECORESORT $$
(☑262085; www.oldassam.com; r ₹1900) This delightful and slightly ramshackle ecofriendly resort is so justifiably popular that it doesn't bother with a sign but carefully labels all the trees instead. Raj-inspired decor makes you feel that the clock has slowed. The dining room serves tasty Indian food. The entrance is opposite the Km373 marker on National Highway (NH) 37. In season, bookings are essential.

Diphlu River Lodge HOTEL $$$
(☑361-2602223; Guwahati; www.jungletravelsindia .com; jungle plan Indians s/d ₹9000/12,000, foreigner s/d ₹18,000/24,000) Fifteen minutes' drive west of the tourist complex, this new lodge, with its chic-rustic feel, is without doubt the most comfortable place to stay in the Kaziranga region. It consists of six bamboo cottages on raised stilts overlooking a river. The rooms have enormous soft beds and the bathrooms sport heavenly rain showers. There's no sign – look for the dirt track on the left (if travelling from the Guwahati direction) beside the 37 marker post.

Iora; the Retreat HOTEL $$$

(☎262411; www.kazirangasafari.com; s/d from ₹3300/3900; ✳@🛜🏊) Not quite as discreet as you may imagine a place named 'the Retreat' to be, this vast new place, to the east of the tourist complex, is almost as big as the national park itself, but despite this its deliciously quiet and subtly decorated rooms offer superb value for money. However, if you value a personal service you'd best look elsewhere.

Bonhabi Resort HOTEL $$

(☎262675; www.bonhabiresort.com; r ₹1600-2000) A short way east of the tourist complex, this place consists of an old villa with a colonial look and feel, and a series of comfortable cottages set around gorgeous gardens.

❶ Information

Kohora village is closest for Kaziranga's central range with an obvious Rhino Gate leading to the Kaziranga Tourist complex 800m south. Here you'll find the **range office**, **elephant-ride booking office** (◷6-7pm, book the previous night) and **jeep rental stand** (rental from ₹1200). Pay your fees at the range office before entering the park, 2km north.

Fees for Indians/foreigners are: entry fees ₹50/250 per day, cameras ₹50/500, videos ₹500/1000, elephant rides ₹350/1050, and vehicle toll fee ₹150/150 (including an armed escort – a ₹50 tip is customary).

There's an SBI ATM a few hundred metres east of Kohora village centre.

❶ Getting There & Away

Buses travel to: Guwahati (₹260 to ₹300, five hours, hourly 7.30am to 4.30pm), Dibrugarh (₹260 to ₹300), Tezpur (₹45, two hours) and Shillong (₹450 to ₹600, eight hours).

Upper Assam

JORHAT

☎0376 / POP 83,670

Bustling Jorhat is the junction for Majuli Island. Gar-Ali, Jorhat's commercial street, meets the main east–west thoroughfare – Assam Trunk (AT) Rd (NH37) – in front of a lively **central market** area. AT Road is also home to an **SBI ATM** and the **Netizen Cyberspace** (₹20 per hr; ◷9am-8pm) internet cafe.

Journey another 200m west of the market along AT Rd, then south to find a small **museum** (Postgraduate Training College, MG Rd;

admission free; ◷10am-4.30pm Tue-Sun) with Ahom artefacts and nearby **Assam Tourism** (◷10am-5pm Mon-Sat, closed 2nd & 4th Sat) in the good-value **Tourist Lodge** (☎2321579; MG Rd; s/d ₹578/683), which has tiled floors, mosquito nets and enthusiastic staff who know how to use cleaning products.

Tucked conveniently behind the Assam State Transport Corporation (ASTC) Bus Station (AT Rd), Solicitor Rd has half a dozen reasonable hotels. The **Hotel Janata Paradise** (☎9435659461; Solicitor Rd; d ₹300) isn't quite as 'beautiful' as the manager told us, but at this price you can't be too hard on the daffodil-yellow rooms. Its **restaurant** (◷11am-4pm & 8-9pm) serves excellent-value 10-dish Assamese thalis (from ₹40).

The town's best hotel is the **Hotel Heritage** (☎2301839; Solicitor Rd; s/d from ₹478/588; ✳), which has well-maintained rooms, obliging staff and old-fashioned character. Nearby is the **New Park** (☎2300725; Solicitor Rd; s/d from ₹687/880; ✳), which is a big new hotel with small but tidy rooms and hot showers.

The **ASTC bus station** (AT Rd) has frequent services to Sivasagar (₹35 to ₹45, 1½ hours), Tezpur (₹120 to ₹140, four hours) and Guwahati (₹260, eight hours, eight buses 6am to noon; buses pass Kaziranga en route).

The *Jan Shatabdi Express* (No 2068, AC Chair ₹468, 6¾ hours, 1.55pm Monday to Saturday) is the most convenient of the two trains to Guwahati.

AROUND JORHAT
Tea Estate Getaways TEA ESTATES

After all this huffing and puffing around the Northeast it's time to relax with a jolly nice cup of tea, don't you think old chap? And where better to do so than in a colonial-era heritage bungalow on a working tea estate. Bookings are essential.

The best of the couple of different options are the tastefully renovated **Banyan Grove** (☎9954451548; www.heritagetourism india.com; s/d ₹6272/7280; lunch ₹350, dinner ₹450; 🏊). Dating from the late 19th century, its rooms are crammed with antiques and the drawing room is straight out of a Victorian period drama. It has wonderful lawns and verandas overlooking a tea estate and swimming pool. The site is 7km down rural tracks from Km442 on NH37 (Jorhat–Deragaon Rd).

With a classical portico and wide, immaculate lawns, **Thengal Manor** (☎bookings

9954451548; www.heritagetourismindia.com; Jalu-kanburi; s/d ₹6272/7280; lunch ₹350, dinner ₹450) oozes grandeur. Old photos, four-post beds and medal certificates from King George VI add atmosphere to this stately mansion. Thengal is 15km south of Jorhat down MG Rd, towards Titabor.

MAJULI ISLAND
☎03775 / POP 140,000

The great muddy-brown Brahmaputra River's ever-shifting puzzle of sandbanks includes Majuli, which at around 421 sq km (2001 figures) is India's largest river island (many locals will tell you that Majuli is the world's largest river island, but in fact this honour belongs to Brazil's Bananal Island). Size aside, what there is no doubting is Majuli's sheer beauty. The island is a relaxed, shimmering mat of glowing rice fields and water meadows bursting with flowers. Aside from relishing the laidback vibe that permeates island life, highlights of a visit include birdwatching and learning about neo-Vaishnavite philosophy at one of Majuli's 22 ancient *satras* (Hindu Vaishnavite monasteries and centres for art). If all this makes Majuli sounds like your kind of place then don't waste time getting there – surveys indicate that at current levels of erosion the island will cease to exist within 20 years.

The two main villages are Kamalabari, 3km from the ferry port and Garamur, 5km further north. The most interesting, accessible *satras* are the large, beautifully peaceful Uttar Kamalabari (1km north, then 600m east of Kamalabari) and Auniati (5km west of Kamalabari), where monks are keen to show you their little museum (Indian/foreigner/camera/video ₹5/50/50/200; ⊙9.30-11am & 12-4pm) of Ahom royal artefacts. The best chances of observing chanting, dances or drama recitations are around dawn and dusk or during the big Ras Mahotsav Festival (third week of November).

For local guiding, accommodation or bicycle hire, contact Jyoti Naryan Sarma (✉9435657282; jyoti24365@gmail.com, www.majuli tourism.com; per day ₹500).

🛏 Sleeping & Eating

As well as the options listed below, many of the sutras have very basic guesthouses (₹100).

La Maison de Ananda　　　GUESTHOUSE $
(✉9435205539; dm ₹150-200) On a Garamur back lane, this French-owned traditionally styled thatched house on bamboo stilts has rooms decked out in locally made fabrics, which give it a hippie-chic atmosphere. It's probably the best value-for-money lodgings on the island.

Ygdrasill Bamboo Cottage　　GUESTHOUSE $$
(✉9401625744; r ₹1200) Around a kilometre before Garamur (on the road to Kamalabari), this thatched hut perches on stilts above a marshy, avian-filled lake. The sound of fish plopping about in the water below your bed and a thousand screaming cicadas (as well as a million marauding mosquitoes – bring repellent!) will lull you to sleep at night. The bamboo beds are comfortable and it's nicely furnished. They serve a stunning Majuli thali in the evening and a breakfast that might be a bit too local for many tastes!

La Villa　　　　　　　　　GUESTHOUSE $
(✉9435657282; jyoti24365@gmail.com; r from ₹300) Run by knowledgeable and keen-to-please Jyoti Naryan Sarma (who also acts as a guide), this Garamur guesthouse has three brightly painted but uninspiring rooms overlooking an open-billed stork roosting site (whose dawn chorus will do away with any need for an alarm clock).

❶ Getting There & Away

This windswept sandbank of Nimatighat, pock-marked with chai shacks, is the departure point for photogenically overcrowded ferries to Majuli

SATRAS

A *satra* is a monastery for Vishnu worship, Assam's distinctive form of everyman Hinduism. Formulated by 15th-century Assamese philosopher Sankardev, the faith eschews the caste system and idol worship, focussing on Vishnu as God, especially in his Krishna incarnation. Much of the worship is based around dance and melodramatic play-acting of scenes from the holy Bhagavad Gita. The heart of any *satra* is its *namghar*, a large, simple, prayer hall usually open sided and shaped like an upside-down oil tanker. Beneath the eastern end, an inner sanctum hosts an eternal flame, the Gita and possibly a horde of instructive (but not divine) images.

Island. It's a 12km-ride from Jorhat by bus (₹20, 40 minutes).

Ferries (adult/jeep ₹20/800, 2½ hours) leave Nimatighat at 8.30am, 10.30am, 1.30pm and 3pm; return trips are at 7.30am, 8.30am, 1.30pm and 3pm.

ℹ Getting Around

Jam-packed buses and vans (₹10/20) meet arriving ferries then drive to Garamur via Kamalabari where three-wheelers are easier to rent. For a few days consider arranging a bicycle through Jyoti at La Villa.

SIVASAGAR

📞03772 / POP 64,000

Despite being an oil-service town, Sivasagar exudes a residual elegance from its time as the capital of the Ahom dynasty that ruled Assam for more than 600 years. The name comes from 'waters of Shiva', the graceful central feature of a rectangular reservoir dug in 1734 by Ahom Queen Ambika. Three typical Ahom **temple towers** rise proudly above the tank's partly wooded southern banks – to the west **Devidol**, to the east **Vishnudol** and in the centre, the 33m-high **Shivadol Mandir**, India's tallest Shiva temple. Its uppermost trident balances upon an egg-shaped feature whose golden covering the British reputedly tried (but failed) to pilfer in 1823.

Around 500m from Shivadol a gaggle of hotels line AT Rd, the most appealing of which is the surprisingly swish **Hotel Shiva Palace** (📞222629; hotelshivapalace@rediffmail .com; s/d from ₹715/825; ❄), incorporating a decent restaurant, the **Sky Chef Restaurant** (mains ₹70-180).

Hotel Siddhartha (📞222276; s/d from ₹500/800; ❄) is out of town (1.5km), but otherwise this sparkly place offers great value for backpackers in the cheaper rooms and flashpackers in the swankier rooms.

The **ASTC bus station** (cnr AT & Temple Rds) has frequent services to Jorhat (₹35 to ₹45, one hour), Dibrugarh (₹51 to ₹69, two hours), Tezpur (₹189, five hours), Guwahati (₹310 to ₹390, eight hours, frequent from 7am).

Many private buses have ticket counters on nearby AT Rd. For Kareng Ghar, use a tempo (₹10, 45 minutes), which depart from an unmarked stop on Bhuban Gogoi (BG) Rd, 300m north up AT Rd, then 50m right.

AROUND SIVASAGAR

Dotted around Sivasagar are many lemon-squeezer-shaped temples and ochre-brick ruins built by the Ahom monarchs during their 17th- and 18th-century heyday.

TALATALGHAR

This famous (but not spectacular) Ahom ruin is 4km down AT Rd from central Sivasagar. Some 2km beyond a WWII-era metal lift-bridge, look right to see the rather beautiful **Rang Ghar** (Indian/foreigner ₹5/100; ⊘dawn-dusk). From this two-storey oval-shaped 'pavilion', Ahom monarchs once watched buffalo and elephant fights.

Just beyond, a left turning passes the **Golaghar** or Ahom ammunition store, the stonework of which is held together with a mix of dhal, lime and egg. Beyond are the two-storey ruins of **Talatalghar** (Indian/foreigner ₹5/100; ⊘dawn-dusk), the extensive, two-storey Ahom palace built by Ahom King Rajeswar Singha in the mid-18th century.

KARENGHAR

Dramatic if largely unadorned, this 1752 brick **palace** (Indian/foreigner ₹5/100; ⊘dawn-dusk) is the last remnant of the Ahom's pre-Sivasagar capital. The unique four-storey structure rises like a sharpened, stepped pyramid above an attractive forest-and-paddy setting spoilt by nearby electricity substations. It's 900m north of the Sivasagar–Sonari road: turn just before Gargaon (14km) from Sonari.

GAURISAGAR

Like a practice run for Sivasagar, Gaurisagar has an attractive tank and a trio of distinctive 1720s temples – **Vishnudol**, **Shivadol** and **Devidol** – built by 'dancing girl queen' Phuleswari. The more impressive is Vishnudol, not as tall as Sivasagar's Shivadol but sporting finer, but eroded carvings. Gaurisagar is on the main NH37 at Km501.5.

DIBRUGARH

📞0373 / POP 122,000

Travelling to Dibrugarh ('tea-city') usefully closes a loop between Kaziranga and the Ziro–Along–Pasighat route and is the terminus (or starting point) for the fascinating ferry ride along the Brahmaputra to Pasighat in Arunachal Pradesh. Dibrugarh is a rapidly growing city with a new road and rail bridge being built at Bogibeel Ghat (originally scheduled to open in 2008, it's now unlikely to be ready for some years to come) that will extend the railway system to north of the Brahmaputra.

Dibrugarh is a reliable place to change money; the **SBI Bank** (RKB Path) changes travellers cheques and foreign currency and there's an ATM. **Cyber@Generation Next**

(HS Rd; per hr ₹20; ☺9am-10pm) is one of several internet cafes. **Purvi Discovery** (☑2301120; www.purviweb.com; Medical College Rd, Jalan Nagar) organises regional tours including culinary tours and multiday horse-riding trips. Purvi also handles bookings for two colonial-era tea bungalow retreats: the delightful 1849 **Heritage Chang Bungalow** (Mancotta Rd, Mancotta; r ₹6600-7150; ❄🤖), 4km from town, and **Chowkidinghee Chang Bungalow** (Convoy Rd; r ₹6600-7150; ❄🤖), 700m from the bus station. At both places, choose the upper rooms that have polished hardwood floorboards and a wonderful heritage feel. For either of these you must book in advance. Tea-estate tours can also be organised between April and November for guests of either bungalow.

[TOP CHOICE] **Hotel Mona Lisa** (☑2320416; Mancotta Rd; r ₹600-1500; ❄), part Africa, part Cuba and possibly even a little slice of India, is a superb budget hotel with character. It's set back from the main road and everything is kept ticking along smoothly thanks to the lovely old man running it.

Hotel Rajawas (☑2323307; www.hotel rajawas.com; AT Rd; s/d from ₹687/860; ❄@) is a new, mirror-fronted hotel with a flower-filled lobby, cheeky modern art on the walls and decent bathrooms. The deluxe rooms are the best bet (single/double ₹1144/1399). If you've just trudged in from the mountains and jungles of Arunachal Pradesh you'll think its in-house **restaurant** (mains ₹120-160) is the best thing since sliced bread (or maybe cold dhal).

H2O (Mancotta Rd; mains ₹80-120, beers from ₹80) is an upstairs bar-restaurant with elements of spaceship decor. For a break from the rigours of the Indian road you'll find a branch of **Café Coffee Day** on HS Rd.

❶ Getting There & Away

From Mohanbari airport, 16km northeast of Dibrugarh and 4km off the Tinsukia road, JetLite flies to Guwahati, Kolkata and Delhi and IndiGo flies to Guwahati.

From the main **bus station** (Mancotta Rd) both ASTC and private buses depart for Sivasagar (₹51 to ₹69, two hours, frequent 6am to 9am), Jorhat (₹130, three hours, frequent 6am to 9am), Tezpur (₹260, six hours) and Guwahati (₹380, 10 hours).

The *Dibrugarh Rajdhani Express* is the overnight train for Guwahati (No 2423; 3AC/2AC/1AC ₹203/962/1206/1970, 10 hours, 8.15pm).

Rough-and-ready **DKO Ferries** (Indian/foreigner ₹20/100, vehicle ₹1200; 8.30am & 9.15am) cruise daily to Oriamghat, where the boat is met by a bus to Pasighat in Arunachal Pradesh. Ferries can carry just two jeeps. There's little shelter and the journey takes around eight hours (5½ hours downstream), so bring an umbrella, water and sunscreen. The journey can be quite an adventure with the boats bouncing off the ever-shifting sandbars (and sometimes not bouncing off them!) and with brief stops en route giving glimpses of isolated riverside hamlets. Exact departure points depend on the Brahmaputra's water level.

ARUNACHAL PRADESH

India's wildest and least explored state, Arunachal Pradesh, the 'Land of Dawn-lit Mountains' is the final frontier in Indian tourism. The state rises abruptly from the Assam plains as a mass of densely forested, and impossibly steep, hills. These in turn rise to fabulous snow-capped peaks along the Tibetan border. At least 25 tribal groups live in Arunachal's valleys; high up in the dramatic Tawang Valley are several splendid Monpa monastery villages. Arunachal has yet to be fully surveyed and mapped, but slowly its high passes and deep valleys are starting to open up to those with an adventurous heart.

China has never formally recognised Indian sovereignty here and it took the surprise Chinese invasion of 1962 for Delhi to really start funding significant infrastructure. The Chinese voluntarily withdrew. These days border passes are heavily guarded by the Indian military and the atmosphere is extremely calm.

Arunachal Tourism (www.arunachaltour ism.com) has additional information.

Itanagar

☑0360 / POP 38,000

Built since 1972, Arunachal's pleasantly green, tailor-made capital is named for the mysterious **Ita Fort** whose residual brick ruins crown a hilltop above town. There's a stack of ATMs in Mahatma Gandhi Marg, along with several internet cafes.

With an oversized foyer better suited as a car showroom, **Hotel Arun Subansiri** (☑2212806; Zero Point; s/d ₹1100/1320; ❄) has comfortably large rooms with soft beds. It's within walking distance of the decent **State Museum** (Indian/foreigner/camera/video ₹10/75/20/100; ☺9.30am-4pm Sun-Thu) and the brightly decorated **Centre for Buddhist Culture** gompa set in gardens on the hill above.

Some 3km west on Mahatma Gandhi Marg is Ganga Market, landmarked by a red, triple-spired temple and nearby clock tower. The market itself is a busy clash of peoples from across the borderlands as well as piles of colourful fruit and some other decidedly exotic food items. The good-value Hotel Blue Pine (☏2211118; s ₹300-500, d ₹500-600) is here, with well-maintained rooms and a mix of common and private bathrooms. Don't mind the caged reception-ist, he's quite tame and helpful.

The APST bus station (Ganga Market) has services to Guwahati (₹450, 11 hours, 6am) and Pashighat (₹170, 10 hours, 5.30am and 6am).

Over the road the Royal Sumo Counter has daily services to Ziro (₹250, four hours, 5.30am and 2.50pm), Along (₹400, about a million hours, 5.30am) and Pasighat (₹300, eight hours, 5.30am).

AROUND ITANAGAR
The beautifully forested hills around Itanagar hide the attractive Ganga Lake (5km), a local picnic spot. Further away (20km) is Poma vil-lage, which is about the closest place to town to see the traditional architecture of bamboo longhouses (although many of these are being slowly replaced with concrete box houses).

Central Arunachal Pradesh

ZIRO VALLEY
☏03788
After weaving for hour upon hour along a road suffocated by a wall of dense forest, it comes as something of a surprise when the world bursts open into the flat and fertile Ziro Valley (vale would be a more accurate descrip-tion) filled with rice fields and dotted with intriguing villages of the Apatani tribe.

Voyaging to the Ziro Valley is one of the undisputed highlights of a trip to Arunachal Pradesh and, though the scenery is stunning and the village architecture fascinating, the voyeuristic main attraction here is meeting the friendly older Apatani folk who sport facial tattoos and nose plugs that would be the envy of any tattooist in the West (see p566). The most authentic Apatani villages are Hong (the biggest and best known), Hijo (more atmospheric), Hari, Bamin and Dutta; none of which are more than 10km apart. It's vital to have a local guide to take you to any of these villages otherwise you won't see much and might even be made to feel quite unwelcome. Christopher Michi (☏9402048466/8014012558; christopherdulley@ yahoo.co.in/christophermichi@hotmail.com) is the chairman of the **Apatani Cultural Pres-ervation Society** and can organise superb visits to the villages – don't be at all sur-prised if your tour culminates in an evening of drinking rice wine and chowing down on barbequed rat in a villager's house!

Sprawling Hapoli (New Ziro), starting 7km further south than Ziro, has hotels and road transport. Just below the Commis-sioner's office on a bend in MG Rd is an SBI ATM. There are a couple of internet cafes around the market area but connections are as rare as a tiger in the nearby forests. The small central market is well worth poking about in. As well as fruit, veg and clothing you can stock up on various insects and other 'delights' to snack on.

CENTRAL ARUNACHAL'S TRIBAL GROUPS

The variety of tribal peoples in central Arunachal Pradesh is astonishing, but although the Adi (Abor), Nishi, Tajin, Hill Miri and various other Tibeto-Burman tribes consider themselves different from one another most are at least distantly related. Over the last few decades Christian missionaries have been highly active throughout the Northeast and in the process have brought huge changes to the region's traditional cultures, religious beliefs and ways of life. Despite this, some aspects of the traditional lifestyle are just about holding on and many people continue to practise the traditional religion of Donyi-Polo (sun and moon) worship – sometimes at the same time as proclaiming themselves Christian. For ceremonial occasions, village chiefs typically wear scarlet shawls and a bamboo wicker hat spiked with porcupine quill or hornbill feathers. A few old men still wear their hair long, tied around to form a topknot above their foreheads. Women favour hand-woven wraparounds like Southeast Asian sarongs. House designs vary somewhat. Traditional Adi villages are generally the most photogenic with luxuriant palmyra-leaf thatching and boxlike granaries stilted to deter rodents.

The warren-like **Hotel Pine Ridge** (☏224725; MG Rd; s/d from ₹350/500), in a courtyard off the main road, is reasonable value, but foreigners are often restricted to the more expensive rooms.

Hotel Blue Pine (☏224812; s ₹650, d from ₹500) is the best-value lodgings in the town itself (though it's still a bit of a walk from the centre). It has wood-panelled rooms with plenty of character.

Out of town, and by far the best place to stay, is the new **Ziro Valley Resort** (☏9856910173; Biiri village; r in old wing ₹1000, tw/d ₹1200/1500), which has rainbow-coloured rooms in a faux colonial–style building. It's halfway between Old and New Ziro and is surrounded by sun-burnt fields. It's also known as the Village Tourist Lodge. At the time of research another midrange resort style place was under con-struction near the Ziro Valley Resort.

Sumos depart from MG Rd, Hapoli (near SBI ATM), for Itanagar (₹250, five hours, 5am and 11am), Lakhimpur (₹200, four hours) and Daporijo (₹350, around 9.30am).

ZIRO TO PASIGHAT

A peaceful lane winding through forested hills and tribal settlements links Ziro to Pa-sighat via Along. Highlights are dizzying sus-pension footbridges and thatched Adi villages around Along. Do be warned though that the attractions along this route are very low-key, the villagers around Along are much less wel-coming to foreigners (and they don't sport the Apatanis' tattoos and nose plugs) and the route, which involves three full days of travel, is very tiring. Unless you're going to be heading from Along to fabulous Mechuka or remote eastern towns and valleys such as Tut-ing or the Namdapha National Park then you may find this route something of a let down.

DAPORIJO
☏03792 / POP 15,468 / ELEV 699M
This is probably the dirtiest and most unso-phisticated town in Arunachal Pradesh, but it is a necessary stopover. In the town itself is the **Hotel Kanga Karo Palace** (☏223531; r ₹750), which is brand new but already looks like its on its last legs. Even so it's still a damn sight better than the couple of ultra-basic places around the market. If you have your own transport, far more interesting ac-commodation is available in the small, tradi-tional thatched village of **Ligu** (coming from Ziro take the left turning just before the bridge at the entrance to Daporijo) where you'll find the basic, but delightful **Ligu Tourist Resort** (☏223114; r ₹700). The family who run it cook up fantastic meals. Vanish-ing under the shadow of jungle trees, Ligu village itself is well worth exploring and the people are truly lovely.

Sumos leave New Market at 6am for Itanagar (₹450, 12 hours) and Ziro (₹300, six hours). The **bus station** has a lackadaisical 7am service to Along (₹150, six hours) on alternate days – depending on when the bus returns from Along.

ALONG
☏03783 / POP 20,000 / ELEV 302M
This nondescript market town has an inter-net cafe, **Eastern Infotech Cyber Cafe** (Nehru Chowk; per hr ₹40; ☉8am-7pm Mon-Sat) opposite the APST bus station and an **SBI ATM** (Main Rd). Next to the Circuit House, also on Main Rd, is an informative little **district museum** (admission free; ☉10am-4pm Mon-Fri).

The best accommodation option here is **Aagaam Hotel** (☏223640; Nehru Chowk; s/d from ₹400-500), which has rooms that could almost be called plush. The attached restau-rant, **Pizza Coffee Day** (mains ₹80-100, pizzas ₹80-150) is the best place in town to eat and yes, it really does sell pizzas – of a sort. An-other option is the **Hotel Holiday Cottage** (☏222463; Hospital Hill; r ₹400-600) southwest of the helipad. However, it's not a cottage and nor is it the sort of place you'd really

FACIAL TATTOOING

Historically famous for their beauty, Apatani women were all too often kidnapped by warriors of the neighbouring Nishi tribes. As a 'defence', Apatani girls were deliberately defaced. They were given facial tattoos, like graffitied beards scribbled onto living Mona Lisa paintings, and extraordinary nose plugs known as *dat* fitted into holes cut in their upper nostrils. Some men also have tattoos.

Peace with the Nishis in the 1960s meant an end to that brutal practice, but many older women still wear *dat*. Photography is an understandably sensitive issue, so ask first. Some Apatani women have had cosmetic surgery to remove their tattoos.

THE LAST SHANGRI LA?

Recently the government of Arunachal Pradesh has opened up a couple of new areas to foreign tourists. Possibly the most exciting of these is the road from Along to the small, remote town of **Mechuka**, close to the Tibetan border. In the past the Mechuka valley, which until recently had no real road connecting it to the rest of the state, was called 'the forbidden valley' or even a 'Last Shangri La'. Populated by the Buddhist Memba peoples, Mechuka, sitting on the banks of the West Siang River, lives up to its Last Shangri La status and is notable for both the 400-year-old **Samten Yongcha Monastery** and the stunning landscapes surrounding the town, which culminate in a massive hulk of snow-draped mountains running along the border.

For the moment tourist facilities (and tourists!) remain virtually non-existent but sumos now ply the 180km from Along (₹300, seven hours, 5.30am). The only accommodation is the **Circuit House**, but if that is unavailable then it's likely that local people will put you up – be generous in your donation.

want to spend an entire holiday. For one night though it does just fine.

There are sumos to Itanagar (₹400, 12 hours, 5.30am) and Pasighat (₹220, seven hours, 5.30am and 11.30am). For Daporijo you have the relative luxury of a bus (₹160; six hours, 7am).

Of the various Adi villages around Along, **Kabu** (2km north of Along) is the best known and most easily accessible. Before entering the village you must seek permission from the headman (who often demands a ₹500 fee). As well as admiring the spectacular longhouse architecture that is a hallmark of all Adi villages don't miss the terrifying cable-trussed but bamboo-decked wobbly suspension bridge over the river. Fortunately for vertigo sufferers a modern metal bridge has just been completed, which makes crossing the river slightly less sickening. It remains to be seen if the old bridge will be maintained or not. There are further interesting, and less visited, Adi villages on the road to Pasighat, but whichever village you visit be discreet with cameras as the locals aren't at all keen on them.

PASIGHAT
☑ 0368 / POP 23,000

Nestled before a curtain of luxuriantly forested foothills, Pasighat, which sits back out on the plains, feels more like Assam than Arunachal Pradesh. The town hosts the interesting Minyong-Adi tribe's **Solung Festival** (1-5 September). The **internet cafe** (per hr ₹60; ⊙7.30am-8pm) is 50m from the Hotel Aane and there's an **SBI ATM** just along from the sumo stand in the central market area.

Sleep at the friendly, central **Hotel Oman** (☑2224464; Main Market; s/d from ₹315/630),

the owners of which have realised that it is possible to buy new tins of paint – a fairly revolutionary thought for many hotels in the northeast. Otherwise try the plusher **Hotel Aane** (☑2222777; s ₹500, d from ₹1500; ❄), which has hot showers and an appealing rooftop terrace.

❶ Getting There & Away

Helicopters from **Pasighat Aerodrome**, 3km northeast, serve Naharlagun (Itanagar) via Mohanbari (Dibrugarh) on Monday, Wednesday and Friday; Guwahati via Naharlagun on Tuesday; and Along on Friday.

The inconveniently located APST bus station (take an autorickshaw) has services to Along (₹220, seven hours, 6am and 12pm) and Itanagar (₹170, 10 hours, 5.30am and 6am). Sumos run to Along (₹220, seven hours, 6am and noon) and Itanagar (₹300, six hours, 6am). The road to Along is in a dreadful state – be prepared for a very long and rough day. Sumos also run to Tuting (₹800) but only when demand warrants it. **Ferries** (Indian/foreigner ₹20/100, vehicle ₹1200; 8.30am & 9.15am) drift lazily down the Brahmaputra to Dibrugarh in Assam from Majerbari Ghat (sumos take one hour from Pasighat, depart at 6am and cost ₹120). Ferry tickets are sold by **Otta Tours & Travel** at the sumo stand.

Western Arunachal Pradesh

Remote, culturally magical and scenically spectacular, Tawang is the archetypal Shangri La and a mountain-hopping journey through this, the lands of the Monpa (a people of Buddhist-Tibetan origin) to the gates of the famous Tawang Monastery is one of the northeast's greatest adventures.

Ideally budget at least one week for a return trip from Guwahati (or Tezpur), breaking the journey each way at Dirang (allow one full day here) or less interesting Bomdila. Be prepared for intense cold in winter.

BOMDILA
03782 / ELEV 2682M

Bomdila is an alternative sleeping place to Dirang, with the traditionally decorated **Doe-Gu-Khill Guest House** (☑223232; r from ₹700), just below the large monastery, providing fabulous views. The **Hotel Tsepal Yangjom** (☑223473; www.hoteltsepalyangjom .co.in; s/d from ₹800/1200) in the market area is probably the town's most popular hotel. Its wood-panelled rooms have a vague Scandinavian feel and it has a generator to cope with the frequent blackouts.

DIRANG
☑03780 / ELEV 1621M

Tiny **Old Dirang**, 5km south of Dirang, is a picture-perfect Monpa stone village. The main road separates its rocky **mini citadel** from a huddle of picturesque streamside

houses above which rises a steep ridge topped with a timeless **gompa**. Heading the other way, just north of New Dirang, the valley opens out and its floor becomes a patchwork of rice and crop fields through which gushes the icy blue river. A fun day could be spent walking along the footpaths between fields and little hamlets.

All Dirang's commercial services are in **New Dirang**, with a strip of cheap hotels, eateries and sumo counters around the central crossroads. **Tourist Lodge** (☑200176; d ₹825), a kilometre south and overlooking New Dirang, is a basic but friendly family hotel in an old-style hill house crowded with potted plants. Nicer is the next-door **Hotel Pemaling** (☑207265; s/d ₹1815/2420), which has shiny rooms, excellent service and a very pleasant garden where you can enjoy the views towards the sometimes snow-bound Se La and the high Himalaya beyond.

DIRANG TO TAWANG VALLEY
The road endlessly zigzags sharply upward, eventually leaving the forest behind. **Se La**, a 4176m pass, breaches the mountains and

---

WORTH A TRIP

RAFTING IN THE LAND OF MILK AND HONEY

Another newly opened route is the Pasighat to Tuting road. This route is all about two things: the River Siang and the mysterious Buddhist land of Pemako. Tuting, which sits near the Tibetan border, is the point at which the Tsang Po river – having left the Tibetan plateau and burrowed through the Himalaya via a series of spectacular gorges – enters the Indian subcontinent and becomes the Siang (once it reaches the plains of Assam it turns into the Brahmaputra). Tuting and the River Siang are starting to gain a reputation as one of the world's most thrilling white-water rafting destinations, but this ain't no amateurs' river. The few people who have descended the river have reported that the 180km route is littered with numerous grade 4-5 rapids, strong eddies and inaccessible gorges.

For those after adventure of a different kind Tuting also serves as the launch pad for searching out the legendary Buddhist land of Pemako. You will, however, need more than this guidebook and a compass in order to find it. Buddhist belief says that Pemako is a synonym for a hidden earthly paradise and that it's the earthly representation of Dorje Pagmo, a Tibetan goddess. It was said that this land of milk and honey was to be found in the eastern Himalaya and that to reach it you had to pass behind an enormous hidden waterfall.

For hundreds of years outsiders knew that the Tsang Po river left Tibet and entered a huge, and utterly impenetrable, gorge before emerging from the Himalaya around Tuting, but what happened to the river inside that gorge was unknown until the 1950s. As it turned out the river did indeed tumble over an enormous waterfall and, what's more, it passed through a rich and fertile valley populated by Memba Buddhists, completely isolated from the rest of the world.

Today, this vast region of northern Arunachal Pradesh and parts of south eastern Tibet remains almost utterly unknown to the outside world, but Pemako is out there and for those willing to endure days of incredibly tough hiking (and deal with reams of paperwork) it is possible to visit.

NAMDAPHA NATIONAL PARK

Arunachal Pradesh is said to contain fifty percent of India's bio-diversity. In fact, so rich is life in Arunachal that the whole area has been proclaimed a world bio-diversity hotspot. Nowhere is the gathering of habitats and plant and animal species so dense as in eastern Arunachal and it's here that the staggering **Namdapha National Park** (Indians/foreigners/cameras/cameras with zoom lens/video ₹10/50/75/400/750) can be found. Covering 1985 sq km this vast park has an altitude range from 200m to 4500m and contains an exceptional diversity of habitats and an equally varied array of wildlife. Namdapha is famous for being the only park in India to have four big cat species (leopard, tiger, clouded leopard and snow leopard). It's also a birdwatching hotspot with around 500 species recorded.

The park is a long haul from anywhere but it's slowly opening up to tourism. The access point is the small town of **Miao**. From here you will need private transport to take you 26km to **Deban** where the park headquarters are located. Simple accommodation is available in Miao at the **Eco-Tourism Guest House** (☏9436228763; per person Indian/foreigner ₹400/600) or in Deban at the **Forest Rest House** (☏3807-222249; s/d from ₹175/300). To really get into the middle of nowhere you'll have to stay at one of the **campsites** inside the park. Bring a tent and all supplies. Porters and guides can be obtained in Miao or Deban.

Tour companies in the northeast can help with the logistics of a visit, or UK-based tour company **Naturetrek** (www.naturetrek.co.uk) runs pioneering 16-day tours of Namdapha and other northeastern parks. However you do it, prepare for real adventure.

provides access to Tawang Valley. From here the road plummets down the mountainside into the belly of Tawang Valley.

TAWANG VALLEY
☏03794 / ELEV 3048M

Calling the Tawang Valley a valley just doesn't do justice to its incredible scale; it's more a mighty gash in the earth ringed by immense mountains. Patchworking the sloping ridges of the lower hills is a vast sweep of fields dotted with Buddhist monasteries and Monpa villages.

The biggest attraction is magical **Tawang Gompa** (admission free, camera/video ₹20/100; ⊙dawn-dusk) backdropped by snow-speckled peaks. Founded in 1681, this medieval citadel is reputedly the world's second-largest Buddhist monastery complex and famed in Buddhist circles for its library. Within its fortified walls, narrow alleys lead up to the majestic and magnificently decorated **prayer hall** containing an 8m-high statue of **Buddha Shakyamuni**. Come here at dawn (4am to 5am) to see row after row of monks performing their early morning prayers. Across the central square is a small but interesting **museum** (₹20; ⊙8am-5pm) containing images, robes, telescopic trumpets and some personal items of the sixth Dalai Lama. Spectacular *chaam* (ritual masked dances performed by some Buddhist monks

in gompas to celebrate the victory of good over evil, and of Buddhism over pre-existing religions) are held during the Torgya, Losar and Buddha Mahotsava festivals.

Other enchanting gompas and anigompas (nunneries) offer great day hikes from Tawang, including ancient if modest **Urgelling Gompa** where the sixth Dalai Lama was born. By road, it's 6km from Tawang town but closer on foot downhill from Tawang Gompa. At the time of research construction was almost complete on a chasm-spanning cable car that will link the monastery with an anigompa on the opposite side of the valley. There was no information available on whether it would be open to tourists.

Tawang town is a transport hub and service centre for the valley's villages; its setting is more beautiful than the town itself. Nonetheless, colourful **prayer wheels** add interest to the central old market area. These are turned by apple-cheeked Monpa pilgrims, many of whom sport traditional black yak-wool *gurdam* (skullcaps that look like giant Rastafarian spiders). In the market area is **M/S Cyber** (per hr ₹30; ⊙9am-6pm), which has internet – sometimes. There's an **SBI Bank** with an ATM just past the market on the road to the monastery.

Tawang has a number of small hotels. Cheapest is the **Hotel Nefa** (☏222419;

s/d ₹700/1300) which has tidy, wood-panelled rooms with a more reliable electricity supply than many similar places. It's in the market area. The **Hotel Siddhartha** (☎222515; s ₹750, d ₹1030-1350) has large, carpeted and well-kept rooms that help make it the best of the town-centre options.

[TOP CHOICE] **Hotel Gakyi Khang Zhang** (☎224 647; r from ₹1320), a couple of kilometres out of town on the road to the monastery, offers far and away the best rooms in town – colourful sky-blue affairs with polished wooden floors. There's a decent **restaurant** (mains ₹80-120) and the staff are great fun. It also has good monastery views, a generator and, most bizarrely, a lounge bar/nightclub complete with throbbing strobe lights!

While each of these hotels have good restaurants, the cosy **Dragon Restaurant** (Old Market; mains ₹60-150) is the town's best eatery with freshly made local dishes such as churpa (₹150), a fermented cheese broth with fungi and vegetables that tastes much better than it sounds. Also don't miss the Tibetan tea. An acquired taste if ever there were one.

❶ Getting There & Away

From Lumla, 42km towards Zemithang, helicopters (₹3000, two hours, �lMon-Sat) fly to Guwahati. APST buses leave Tawang 5.30am Monday and Friday for Tezpur (₹290, 12 hours), calling at Dirang (₹130, six hours), Bomdila (₹170, seven hours) and Bhalukpong (₹240, 10 hours). More frequent public sumos to Tezpur (₹500) depart at dawn.

NAGALAND

Draped across the dazzling hills and valleys of the India–Myanmar border regions is Nagaland, an otherworldly place where until very recently some twenty headhunting Naga tribes valiantly fought off any intruders. Today the south of the state is fairly developed, but in the north, tribesmen in loin cloths continue to live a lifestyle that is normally only seen within the pages of *National Geographic* magazine.

Dimapur

☎03862 / POP 165,782 / ELEV 260M

Nagaland's flat, uninspiring commercial centre was the capital of a big Kachari kingdom that ruled much of Assam before the Ahoms

showed up. The only reason tourists visit Dimapur is to transfer to Kohima. Of the central hotels **de Oriental Dream** (☎231211; Kohima Rd; r from ₹900; ✳❄) is the smartest option.

Air India (☎229366, 242441) flies to Kolkata, Guwahati and Imphal. The **NST bus station** (Kohima Rd) runs services to Kohima (₹65 to ₹75, three hours, hourly) and Imphal (₹400, nine hours, 10am).

Kohima

☎0370 / POP 96,000 / ELEV 1444M

Nagaland's agreeable capital is scattered across a series of forested ridges and hilltops. Avoid Kohima on Sundays as apart from hotels, everything is closed.

◉ Sights

War Cemetery   HISTORIC SITE
(☉dawn-dusk Mon-Sat) This immaculate War Cemetery contains the graves of 1400 British, Commonwealth and Indian soldiers. It stands at the crucially strategic junction of the Dimapur and Imphal roads, the site of intense fighting against the Japanese during a 64-day WWII battle.

Central Market   MARKET
(Stadium Approach; ☉6am-4pm) At the fascinating if tiny central market, tribal people sell such 'edible' delicacies as *borol* (wriggling hornet grubs).

State Museum   MUSEUM
(admission ₹5; ☉9.30am-3.30pm Tue-Sun) The superbly presented State Museum, 3km north, includes plenty of tableaux with mannequins-in-action depicting different traditional Naga lifestyles plus everyday tools.

⏏ Sleeping & Eating

Accommodation becomes extremely scarce for kilometres around during the Hornbill Festival – book well in advance.

[TOP CHOICE] **Heritage Hotel**   HERITAGE HOTEL **$$**
(☎9774416649; www.theheritage.in; Officers Hill; r/ste ₹1800/3500; ❄) Back in colonial days this was the home of the deputy commissioner and, with roaring open fires taking the chill off a cold winter night and hunting trophies and tribal arts adorning the walls, it retains something of the flavour of those times.

Aradura Inn   GUESTHOUSE **$$**
(☎2241079; aradurainn@gmail.com; Aradura Hill; r from ₹1350; @) This fantastic new guesthouse

DON'T MISS

HORNBILL FESTIVAL

Nagaland's biggest annual festival, the Hornbill Festival (1-7 December) is celebrated at Kisama Heritage Village (see below) with various Naga tribes converging for a weeklong cultural, dance and sporting bash, much of it in full warrior costume. Of all the festivals in the northeast this is the most spectacular and photogenic. Simultaneously, Kohima also hosts a **rock festival** (www.hornbillmusic.com).

has simple yet immaculate rooms. It's the little touches that set it apart from the competition, such as cups of tea brought to you in bed in the morning. There are great views over the town from the garden, friendly and helpful staff and a superb restaurant.

Razhu Pru   HERITAGE HOTEL **$$**
(☎2290291; Mission Compound, Kohima Village; d from ₹1800; ❂❧) An old family house that's been lovingly converted into a heritage hotel filled with tribal arts and antiques. We thought the sleek white deluxe rooms (₹2200) offered the best value.

Hotel Pine   HOTEL **$**
(☎2243129; d ₹ from 500/600) Down a side lane off Phool Bari this small hotel is centrally located, well kept and the cleaners actually seem to take pride in their job.

Arudupa Spur Cafe   MULTICUISINE **$$**
(Arudupa Hotel; mains ₹120-160; ☺Mon-Sat) Part of the Arudupa Hotel, this is one of Kohima's most happening restaurants and is always busy with young middle-class Nagas relaxing on the sofas and tucking into a menu that spans the globe. There's a cool soundtrack playing in the background and lots of heaters for cold winter nights.

Dream Café   CAFE **$**
(Cnr Dimapur & Imphal Rds; mains ₹50-100; ☺10am-6pm, Mon-Sat) Beneath UCO Bank and with daily lunch specials such as fried noodles or pizzas as well as coffee and snacks, this is the meeting point for Kohima's young people. Great views from the back windows, a bunch of magazines to read and lots of students keen for a chat make this a good place to linger.

ⓘ Information

NIIT Internet Cafe (opp NST bus station; per hr ₹30; ☺6.30am-7pm Mon-Sat) The internet cafe with the longest opening hours.

SBI Bank (Police Bazar) One of several ATMs.
Secretariat, Home Department (☎2221406; Secretariat Bldg) Permit extensions.

Tribal Discovery (☎9436000759, 9856474767; yiese _neitho@rediffmail.com; Science College Rd) Neithonuo Yeise ('Nitono') is an eloquent guide to local sites and can arrange permits.

ⓘ Getting There & Away

The **NST bus station** (Main Rd) has services to:
Dimapur (₹65-75, three hours, hourly Monday to Saturday, 8am Sun)
Mokokchung (₹105-155, seven hours, 6.30am Monday to Saturday)
Imphal (₹150, six hours, 7.30am)
The taxi stand opposite has share taxis to Dimapur (₹150, 2½ hours). A car for a day out to Kisama and Khonoma costs ₹800 to ₹1000.

Around Kohima

KISAMA HERITAGE VILLAGE
This **open-air museum** (admission ₹50; ☺8am-6pm May-Sep, 8am-4.30pm Oct-Apr), which hosts the annual Hornbill Festival, has a representative selection of traditional Naga houses and *morungs* (bachelor dormitories) with full-size log drums. Kisama is 10km from central Kohima along the well-surfaced Imphal road.

KHONOMA
This historic **Angami-Naga village** was the site of two major British–Angami siege battles in 1847 and 1879. Built on an easily defended ridge (very necessary back in head-hunting days), Khonoma looks beautifully traditional.

There are several simple homestay guesthouses in the village.

TUOPHEMA
Forty-five kilometres north of Kohima is the small town of Tuophema, which can make a useful overnight stop on the road to Mon if you leave Kohima late in the day. Although the town itself is nothing special, the **Tuophema Tourist Village** (☎9436005002; per person half-board ₹1600-1800), where you

sleep in comfortable traditionally styled Naga thatched bungalows, is very enjoyable, but make sure you let them know of your arrival in advance or it will probably be closed up.

Kohima to Mon

Beautiful forested hillsides flank the road from Kohima to Mon. Road conditions often require you to travel some of the way through Assam.

MOKOKCHUNG

Sitting almost halfway between Kohima and Mon most people sensibly choose to break their journey in laidback Mokokchung. Aside from enjoying the town's spectacular setting, try to make time for a couple of other low-key attractions including the small, privately run Rendikala Subong Museum (Town Hall Rd; admission ₹10), which contains tribal items collected from surrounding villages as well as what is purported to be the world's smallest Bible. The museum is open whenever someone turns up to see it. A couple of kilometres away is pretty Ungma village, where you'll find a couple of huge log drums and a cloud scrapping Jendong (a pole that helps connect people on Earth with the Gods high up in the skies).

TOP CHOICE Tourist Lodge (☎0369-2226373; tourist.lodgemkg@yahoo.com; r ₹750, without bath ₹400; ❇@☎), The only place to stay worth considering is the superb Tourist Lodge, which has bright and clean rooms, excellent service and a decent restaurant serving Indian and Naga dishes.

Northern Nagaland

Northern Nagaland, the most unspoiled part of the state, is the reason you came to Nagaland. This rugged and divinely beautiful country is home to many different villages composed of thatched longhouses, many of whose inhabitants are adorned with tattoos and continue to live a fairly traditional hunting and farming lifestyle.

The most accessible villages are the Konyak settlements around Mon. Traditional houses abound, and some villages have *morungs* and religious relics from pre-Christian times. Village elders may wear traditional costume and Konyak of all ages carry the fearsome-looking *dao* – a crude machete used for headhunting right up until the mid-20th century.

Visiting a Naga village without a local guide is unproductive – there will be language difficulties and you'll be unaware of local cultural expectations.

MON

The impoverished hill town of Mon is in a gorgeous setting but feels like a frontier town. There's an SBI ATM in the town centre but don't rely on it working. The little village market is well worth exploring and like so many markets in the northeast, it's the exotic food items that stick longest in the memory. Of the numerous tribal villages in the area the closest is Old Mon village, a mere 5km from town. Tamgnyu village (13km) is a rarely visited, yet easy to reach, village with a friendly headman, a couple of human skulls left over from headhunting days and

---

HEAD HUNTERS

Throughout northeastern India and parts of western Myanmar the Naga tribes were long feared for their ferocity in war and for their sense of independence – both from each other and from the rest of the world. Intervillage wars continued as recently as the 1980s, and a curious feature of many outwardly modern settlements is their 'treaty stones' recording peace settlements between neighbouring communities.

It was the Naga's custom of headhunting that sent shivers down the spines of neighbouring peoples. The taking of an enemy's head was considered a sign of strength, and a man who had not claimed a head was not considered a man. Fortunately for tourists, headhunting was officially outlawed in 1935, with the last recorded occurrence in 1963. Nonetheless, severed heads are still an archetypal artistic motif found notably on *yanra* (pendants) that originally denoted the number of human heads a warrior had taken. Some villages, such as Shingha Changyuo in Mon district, still retain their 'hidden' collection of genuine skulls.

Today Naga culture is changing fast, but it was not a government ban on headhunting that put an end to this tradition but rather the activities of Christian missionaries. Over 90% of the Naga now consider themselves Christian.

some impressive traditional buildings all set, surreally, under two giant mobile phone towers. Shingha Chingyuo village (20km, population 5900) has a huge longhouse decorated with *mithuna* (pairs of men and women) and deer skulls, three stuffed tigers, and a store of old human skulls. Longwoa (35km) is spectacularly sited on the India –Myanmar border, with the headman's longhouse actually straddling the two nations. Despite its popularity with tourists it remains one of the most interesting villages. Chui (8km) includes an elephant skull in its longhouse collection. Shangnyu village has a shrine full of fertility references such as tumescent warriors, a crowing cock, a large snake, a man and woman enjoying sex and, to complete the picture, a double rainbow. Langmeang village, with its stack of human skulls piled up in a wooden box, is also highly impressive.

In more touristy villages such as Longwoa and Shingha Chingyuo a fairly standard ₹200 photo fee is charged.

For many a year accommodation in Mon meant the friendly, but sadly very scrappy and slightly overpriced Helsa Cottage (📱9436433782; r from ₹1000) run by Aunty. At the time of research Aunty was about to shut the old place down and open a new (as yet unnamed) hotel near the market area. Another venture is the confusingly named Helsa Resort (📱9436000028; r ₹1000), a couple of kilometres out of town on the road to Myanmar. It consists of four traditional thatched Konyak huts with springy bamboo floors, sparse furnishings and hot water by the bucket. Its generator is a huge plus. All the accommodation options serve meals.

Buses, if you can call them that, bounce painfully to Dimapur (₹450, 13 hours, 3pm) and Sonari in Assam (₹60).

MANIPUR

This 'Jewelled Land' is home to Thadou, Tangkhul, Kabul, Mao Naga and many other tribal peoples, but the main grouping is the predominantly neo-Vaishnavite Meitei. Manipuris are famed for traditional dances, spicy multidish thalis and the sport of polo – which they claim to have invented. Manipur's forested hills provide cover for rare birds, drug traffickers and guerrilla armies, making it by far the Northeast's most dangerous state.

Permit conditions usually restrict foreigners to Greater Imphal although this represents more a zone of safety rather than a geographical area. Most foreigners fly into Imphal; it is also possible to drive in from Kohima (Nagaland) or Silchar (Assam) if you have a guide. Travelling east of Kakching towards the Myanmar border is not permitted.

Imphal

📱0385 / POP 234,958

Noisy and polluted it might be, but Imphal, with its melange of peoples and positioning right on the border lands of India and southeast Asia is undeniably fascinating and travellers who spend any time here are well rewarded. The airport is 9km to the southwest.

⊙ Sights

Kangla   PARK
(admission ₹2; ⊙9am-4pm Nov-Feb, 9am-5pm Mar-Oct) Fortified Kangla was the off-and-on-again regal capital of Manipur until the Anglo-Manipuri War of 1891 saw the defeat of the Manipuri maharaja and a British takeover. Entrance is by way of an exceedingly tall gate on Kanglapat. The interesting older buildings are at the rear of the citadel guarded by three restored large white *kangla sha* (dragons).

Manipur State Museum   MUSEUM
(Off Kangla Rd; Indian/foreigner ₹3/20; ⊙10am-4pm Tue-Sun) Manipur State Museum has

---

ℹ REGISTERING ON ARRIVAL IN MANIPUR

On arrival at Imphal airport all foreigners must register with the police stationed next to the luggage collection point. You must then register again with the CID at the main police station. In both cases it's a fairly painless affair (assuming your papers are in order). Technically you don't need a local guide if you are just staying in Imphal, but it's highly unlikely that any tour company will help you obtain a permit without you agreeing to take one of their guides. A reliable tour company (who can also help obtain permits) to Manipur is Seven Sisters Tourism Services (📱2445373; sstourism@rediffmail.com; MG Ave, Imphal).

a marvellous collection of historical, cultural and natural history ephemera. Tribal costumes, royal clothing, historical polo equipment, stuffed carnivores in action and pickled snakes compete with a two-headed calf for the attention of visitors.

Shri Govindajee Mandir & Around
HINDU TEMPLE

The 1776-built **Shri Govindajee Mandir**, with two rather suggestive domes, is a neo-Vaishnavite temple with Radha and Govinda as the presiding deities. Afternoon *puja* (offerings, prayers) is for one hour at 4pm in winter and 5pm in summer.

Adjacent to the mandir is the **Royal Palace**, closed to visitors except for during the annual **Kwak Tenba festival**, when a colourful procession led by the titular maharaja heads to the Polo Ground for religious ceremonies and cultural festivities. The festival takes place on the fourth day of Durga Puja.

Khwairamband Bazaar
MARKET

(Ima Market; ⊙7am-5pm) This vast all-women's market (well, we saw one male vendor – perhaps appropriately he was selling headphones!) is run by some 3000 *ima* (mothers). Divided by a road, one side sells vegetables, fruit, fish and groceries while the other deals in household items, fabrics and pottery. It's easily one of the largest markets in the northeast.

Imphal War Cemetery
HISTORIC PARK

(Imphal Rd; ⊙8am-5pm) This peaceful and well-kept memorial contains the graves of more than 1600 British and Commonwealth soldiers killed in the battles that raged around Imphal in 1944. Off Hapta Minuthong Rd is a separate **Indian War Cemetery** (⊙8am-5pm).

🛏 Sleeping & Eating

A state tax adds 30% to your bill. This is included in the prices below.

TOP CHOICE Classic Hotel
HOTEL $$

(☑2443967; North AOC Rd; s/d from ₹845/1170; ❀@🛜) This unexpectedly classy hotel is one of the best-value business hotels in the northeast. The large spotless rooms come with full facilities, staff who love to please and the town's best **restaurant** (mains ₹100 to ₹150). Opt for one of the Classic Standard rooms (s/d₹1885/2470).

Anand Continental
HOTEL $$

(☑2449422; Khoyathong Rd; s/d from ₹650/1300; ❀) Smallish rooms, a little too much furni-

ture, friendly management and possession of a vacuum cleaner characterise this acceptable hotel. Hot water flows from 6am to 11am, thereafter by a free bucket-load.

Hotel Nirmala
HOTEL $

(☑2459014; MG Ave; s/d from ₹390/650; ❀) A friendly place with an ultra quick-service restaurant, although it doesn't open until 10am so breakfast has to be by room service. The rooms are nothing special but you do feel a sense of belonging when staying here.

❶ Information

Internet Cafe (MG Ave; per hr ₹20; ⊙8am-7pm Mon-Sat)

SBI ATM (MG Ave) About 100m from Hotel Nirmala. Note that the few ATMs in Imphal tend to have enormous queues of people waiting to use them. It's better to bring enough cash with you.

Tourist office (☑224603; http://manipur.nic.in/tourism.htm; Jail Rd)

❶ Getting There & Away

Private buses to head to Guwahati (₹700, 20 hours, 10am) and Dimapur (₹400, 10 hours, 10am) via Kohima (₹300, five hours). If you're heading to Aizawl you must change in Dimapur first. All the bus company offices are found on North AC Rd.

Air India (☑2450999; MG Ave), IndiGo, **Jetlite** (☑2455054) and Kingfisher Red all fly to Guwahati and Kolkata. Air India also flies to Aizawl and Dimapur.

Around Imphal

Conjure up an image of a shimmering blue lake broken up into small lakelets by floating 'islands' of thick matted weeds. Add bamboo bridges, tribal people in dugout canoes and thatched hut-villages anchored on to the floating islands, and you have **Loktak Lake**, one of the few places a foreigner is allowed to visit outside of Imphal. More peculiar than floating villages are the large, perfectly circular fishing ponds created out of floating rings of weeds. The best view is atop Sendra Island, more a promontory than island. You can hire a **boat** (per person ₹100) in order to get a closer look at lake life.

MIZORAM

Gorgeous Mizoram is slashed by north-south-running valleys and might be the most beautiful of all the states in the northeast. You'll see very few typical Indian faces among the locals, with their Thai- and Chinese-style features, and most people are Christian.

Mizoram runs to its own rhythm. Most businesses open early and shut by 6pm; virtually everything closes tight on Sunday.

Mizo culture has no caste distinctions and women appear liberated; in Aizawl girls smoke openly, wear jeans and hang out in unchaperoned posses meeting up with their beaus at rock concerts on the central field.

✿ Festivals

Two main Mizo festivals, **Chapchar Kut** (Kut is Mizo for festival) and **Pawl Kut** celebrate elements in the agricultural cycle. Chapchar Kut takes place towards the end of February and signals the start of the spring sowing season, and Pawl Kut is held at the end of November to celebrate the harvest. In both festivals, participants don national costume and celebrate with folk dancing and song.

Aizawl

☑0389 / POP 275,000

From a distance Aizawl (pronounced eyezole) seems a painted backdrop to an Italian opera, such is the steepness of the ridge on which it's perched. Backs of homes at road level might be held there with stilts three times higher than their roofs.

◉ Sights

Mizoram State Museum　　　　MUSEUM
(Macdonald Hill, Zarkawt; admission ₹5; ⊙9.30am-5pm Mon-Fri) This museum has interesting exhibits on Mizo culture. It's up a steep lane from Sumkuma Point past Aizawl's most distinctive **church**, whose modernist belltower spire is pierced by arched 'windows'.

KV Paradise　　　　MONUMENT
(Durtlang; admission ₹5; ⊙10am-9pm Mon-Sat) V is for Varte who died in a 2001 motor accident. K is for her husband Khawlhring who has since lavished his entire savings and energy creating a three-storey mausoleum to her memory. The marble fountain-patio has wonderful panoramic views. The site is 8km from Zarkawt, 1km off the Aizawl-Silchar road via an improbably narrow dirt lane.

Market　　　　MARKET
(Mission Veng St) A Saturday street market sprawls along the street with village women offering fruit, vegetables, maybe a dead pig, fish and live hens in individualised wickerwork carry-away baskets.

ⓘ PERMITS FOR MIZORAM

Agencies, notably Mizo Holidays and Three Dimension, both in Aizawl, can arrange 10-day permits. Mizoram permit restrictions are perhaps the most lax of the Northeast States. Be sure that all places you wish to visit are on your permit and you should be allowed to go anywhere in the state. Note though that the Kolkata FRO doesn't grant Mizoram permits.

⌂ Sleeping

Hotels typically add a 10% service charge (included below).

Hotel Clover　　　　HOTEL $$
(☑2305736; www.davids-hotel-clover.com; G-16 Chanmari; s/d from ₹750/1500; @☎) Dolly, your host for the evening, should win an award as one of India's friendliest hotel receptionists. Rooms are equally friendly and as full of character with colourful, art-adorned walls.

Hotel Arini　　　　HOTEL $$
(☑2301557; Upper Khatla; s/d from ₹800/1200; ☎) Only a small red sign announces the Hotel Arini, named after the owner's daughter. The rooms are cheerily bright and fresh-looking, and the staff pleasant and obliging. Choose a back room with a stupendous down-valley view. They have a couple of very basic singles for a mere ₹200.

✗ Eating

David's Kitchen　　　　MULTICUISINE $$
(☑2305736; Zarkawt; mains ₹80-140; ⊙10am-9.30pm Mon-Sat, noon-9.30pm Sun) David's fine Mizo, Thai, Indian, Chinese and continental food, mocktails, friendly staff and pleasant decor will please everyone. The views aren't half bad either.

Curry Pot　　　　INDIAN $$
(☑2324567; Upper Khatla; meals ₹50-120; ⊙10am-9pm Mon-Sat) Next door to Hotel Arini, this place has tasty Indian and Chinese dishes.

On Sundays only the hotels and David's Kitchen will save you from starving.

ⓘ Information

Directorate of Tourism (☑2333475; www.mizotourism.nic.in; PA-AW Bldg, Bungkawn)

Mizo Holidays (☑2306314; to7.puia@gmail.com; Hauva Bldg, Chanmari; ⊙9am-5pm Mon-Sat) Arranges tourist permits and a variety of state-wide tours including some interesting village visits.

Net Cyber Cafe (Canteen Sq; per hr ₹30; ⊙9am-6pm)

SBI ATM (Raj Bhawan Junction)

Three Dimension (☑2351867; Zangtui; ⊙9.30am-6pm Mon-Sat) Arranges permits, Mizoram tours and even paragliding (₹500).

❶ Getting There & Away

Taxis charge ₹600 and shared sumos charge ₹50 to efficient little Lengpui airport, 35km west of Aizawl. **Air India** (☑2322283) flies to Guwahati, Kolkata and Imphal, while Kingfisher Red goes to Kolkata.

Counters for long-distance sumos are conveniently clustered around Zarkawt's Sumkuma Point.

Guwahati (₹750; 28hrs; 6pm, Mon-Sat)
Shillong (₹650, 16 hours, 6pm, Mon-Sat)
Silchar (₹280, six hours, four daily)

Rural Mizoram

Mizoram's pretty, green hills get higher as you head east. **Champhai** is widely considered the most attractive district and is where you'll find the **Murlen National Park**, known for its hoolock gibbons. The small town of **Saitual** is a good stopover on the road to Champhai. Very close to Champhai is pretty **Tamdil Lake**, ringed by lush mountains. Further afield is the stunning **Blue Mountain** (Phawngpui), which at 2147m is the highest peak in Mizoram. It's considered by Mizos to be the abode of the Gods, but its slopes are said to be haunted by ghosts. Three Dimension can organise trekking trips here. For a more accessible taste of the Mizoram hinterland visit the **Vantawng waterfalls**, 95km from Aizawl.

TRIPURA

Tripura is culturally and politically fascinating, and the state's handful of royal palaces and temples draw a growing flow of domestic tourists. For the moment though foreign tourists remain very rare indeed. There's a large Bangladeshi refugee population in Tripura and much of the more accessible western parts of the state look and feel much like its near neighbour.

Foreigners must register with the police on arrival at the airport.

Agartala

☑0381 / POP 367,822

Tripura's low-key capital, with its small-town atmosphere, feels like an India of yesteryear. The pace of life is much slower than in the towns and cities of the Indian heartlands and people are much more likely to swerve across the street to wish you a good day than to try and sell you something. The old quarter, which centres on the Ujjayanta Palace, has some impressive town gates and pretty tanks and gardens. **Durga puja** is celebrated with huge *pandals* (temporary temples built from wood and cloth).

◉ Sights

Ujjayanta Palace   PALACE
(admission ₹5; ⊙5-7pm) Agartala's indisputable centrepiece is this striking, dome-capped palace. Flanked by two large reflecting ponds, the whitewashed 1901 edifice was built by Tripura's 182nd maharaja. It looks particularly impressive floodlit at night, but for security reasons only the gardens are open to the public.

Temples   HINDU TEMPLES
Of four Hindu temples around the palace compound, the most fanciful is **Jagannath Mandir** (⊙4am-2pm & 4-9pm). Its massive sculptured portico leads into a complex with wedding-cake architecture painted in ice-cream sundae colours. Several **royal mausoleums** are decaying quietly on the riverbank behind Batala market. To get to them walk west down HGB Rd, turn left at Ronaldsay Rd and right along the riverbank. **Chaturdasha Devata Mandir** (Temple of Fourteen Deities) hosts a big seven-day **Kharchi Puja** festival in July in Old Agartala, 7km east down Assam Agartala (AA) Rd (NH44) at Kayerpur.

Museums   MUSEUMS
The small **Tripura Government Museum** (http://tripura.nic.in/museum/welcome.html; Post Office Circle; admission ₹2; ⊙10am-1pm & 2-5pm Mon-Sat) has a variety of tribal displays plus some interesting musical instruments made from bamboo. The new **Tripura State Tribal Museum** (Lake Chowmuhani; admission free; ⊙10am-1pm & 2-5pm Mon-Sat) has further displays of tribal dress.

⊨ Sleeping

State taxes add 10% to your bill (included in the prices listed here).

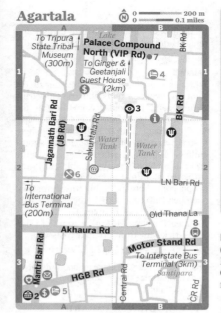

Agartala

Ginger HOTEL $$
(☏1800 2093333, 2411333; www.gingerhotels.com; Airport Rd; s/d ₹1649/2199; ❄@☏) Part of the Tata-owned Ginger chain of hotels, this friendly and well-run place has superb rooms with wif-fi, real coffee and a small gym. What might be India's smallest Café Coffee Day branch is attached. For the best rates book online in advance.

Geetanjali Guest House HOTEL $$
(☏2410009; Airport Rd; d/tw from ₹1650; ❄@) Brand new and the only possible competition for the Ginger, which is right opposite, half of this government-run guesthouse is reserved for visiting Ministers, the other half is for nobodies like us. The large, perfect rooms are filled with sunlight and for the moment it's all very impressive, but as we said it's government-run so there's every chance it'll be allowed to rot away without anyone really caring!

Hotel Welcome Palace HOTEL $$
(☏2384940; HGB Rd; s ₹500, d ₹700-1200; ❄) This hard-to-beat option has helpful English-speaking staff, eager room service and superb food. Rooms are neat, although some may not have external windows. It's by far the most popular of the city centre hotels and is worth booking in advance.

Hotel Chandana HOTEL $
(☏2311216; Palace Compound Lane; r ₹210) Lacklustre but cheap and bearable, the Chandana's simple rooms have mosquito nets and cold showers.

✗ Eating

Restaurant Kurry Klub INDIAN $$
(Hotel Welcome Palace, HGB Rd; mains ₹50-200; ⊙10am-10pm) Very tasty food served in a small dining room whose decor would be rather striking if only the lighting was improved. If you're staying in the hotel, room service is faster and beers can be acquired.

Abhishek Restaurant INDIAN $
(LN Bari Rd; mains ₹60-100) Reliable food served either on an inviting outdoor terrace or in a marine-themed dining room with good AC.

❶ Information

Axis ATM (Hotel Welcome Palace, HGB Rd)
SBI (☏2311364; top fl, SBI Bldg, HGB Rd) Changes cash and travellers cheques and has an ATM.
Netzone (6 Sakuntala Rd; per hr ₹20; ⊙8am-10pm) Best of several closely grouped options.
Tripura Tourism (☏2225930; www.tripuratourism.in; Swet Mahal, Palace Complex; ⊙10am-5pm Mon-Sat, 3-5pm Sun) Helpful and enthusiastic with many great-value tours.

❶ Getting There & Around

Air India (☏2325470; VIP Rd), Spicejet and Jet Airways fly to Kolkata and Guwahati; IndiGo Airlines and Kingfisher fly just to Kolkata. Agartala's airport is 12km north and a taxi costs ₹225.

Private bus operators are clustered on LN Bari Rd; others leave from the new **Interstate Bus Terminal** 3km east of the centre (rickshaw ₹50). Sumos use the **Motor Stand** (Motor Stand Rd) and **South Bus Station** (SBS; off Ronaldsay Rd). Destinations and their respective departure stations for bus and sumo trips are:

Guwahati bus (₹660, 24 hours, 6am and noon) Interstate Bus Terminal.

Kailasahar sumo (₹88, five hours) South Bus Station.

Melagarh (for Neermahal) bus (₹25, 1½ hours); sumo (₹20) South Bus Station.

Shillong bus (₹660, 20 hours, 6am and noon) Interstate Bus Terminal.

Silchar bus (₹153, 12 hours, 6am) International Bus Station.

Udaipur bus (₹26, 1¾ hours); sumo (₹35) South Bus Station.

Opposite the TRTC is the **International Bus Terminal** where Bangladesh Road Transport Corporation's daily bus departs for Dhaka (₹182, six hours, 12pm).

Around Agartala

Southern Tripura's best-known sights can be combined into a long day trip from Agartala, though sleeping at Neermahal is worthwhile. Any of Agartala's hotels can arrange a taxi, or you can engage English-speaking **Partha Laskar** (☏09774702908; partha.laskar@rediffmail .com) for a day trip in an AC car (₹1300 plus ₹12 per km).

UDAIPUR
☏03821

Udaipur was Tripura's historic capital and remains dotted with ancient temples and a patchwork of tanks.

MATABARI

When Sati's toes fell on Kolkata, her divine right leg dropped on Matabari. This gruesome legend is piously celebrated at the **Tripura Sundari Mandir** (⊕4.30am-1.30pm & 3.30-9.30pm), a 1501 Kali temple where a steady stream of pilgrims make almost endless animal sacrifices that leave the grounds as bloody as the temple's vivid-red *shikhara* (Buddhist monastery). Even more people come here at the big **Diwali festival** (October/November) to bathe in the fish-filled tank by the temple. The temple is 100m east of the NH44, 4km south of Udaipur. A rickshaw from Udaipur costs ₹50.

 Getting There & Around

Udaipur's bus stand has quarter-hourly departures to Agartala (₹26, 1¾ hours) and Melagarh (₹15, 45 minutes).

NEERMAHAL & MELAGARH
☏0381 / POP 21,750

Tripura's most iconic building, the 1930 Neermahal, is a long, red-and-white **water palace** (admission/camera/video ₹10/10/25; ⊕8.30am-4pm, until 4.30pm Apr-Sep), which is empty but shimmering on its own boggy island in the lake of Rudra Sagar. Like its counterpart in Rajasthan's Udaipur, this

---

ℹ **CROSSING INTO BANGLADESH AT AGARTALA**

Border Hours

The border at Agartala is open from 7am to 6pm.

Foreign Exchange

There's no exchange booth and Agartala banks don't sell Bangladeshi taka, so changing money is hit and miss; ask local traders or border officials.

Onward Transport

From central Agartala the border is just 3km along Akhaura Rd (₹50 by rickshaw). On the Bangladesh side the nearest town is Akhaura, 5km beyond, reached by 'baby taxi' (autorickshaw). From Akhaura trains head to Dhaka, Comilla and Sylhet. Coming eastbound, be sure to pay your Bangladeshi departure tax at a Sonali bank before heading for the border.

Visas

Unhelpful, but the northeast's only **Bangladesh visa office** (☏2324807; Airport Rd, Kunjaban; ⊕application 9am-1pm Mon-Thu, 9am-noon Fri, collection same day 4pm) hides down a small lane in Agartala, about 2km north of the Ujjayanta Palace.

was a princely exercise in aesthetics; the finest craftsmen building a summer palace of luxury in a blend of Hindu and Islamic architectural styles. The delightful waterborne approach by speedboat (passenger/boat ₹20/400) or fancy rowboat (boat ₹100) is the most enjoyable part of visiting.

Boats leave from beside the remarkably decent **Sagarmahal Tourist Lodge** (☑2524418; d from ₹250; ❄), where most rooms have lake-facing balconies and a good restaurant presides downstairs.

MEGHALAYA

Carved out of Assam in 1972, hilly Meghalaya (Abode of Clouds) is a cool, pine-fresh contrast to the sweaty Assam plains. Set on dramatic horseshoes of rocky cliff above the Bengal plains, Cherrapunjee and Mawsynram are statistically the wettest places on earth. Most of the rain falls between April and September, creating very impressive waterfalls and carving out some of Asia's longest caves.

Eastern and central Meghalaya are mainly populated by the closely related Jaintia, Pnar and Khasi peoples, originally migrants from Southeast Asia. Western Meghalaya is home to the unrelated Garo tribe. Despite their different ethnic backgrounds, these two groups use a matrilineal system of inheritance with children taking the mother's family name. A good time to be in Meghalaya is when the four day, state-wide, **Wangala festival** takes place. This Garo harvest festival is renowned for its impressive traditional dancing.

Shillong

☑0364 / POP 268,000
This sprawling hill station was the capital of British-created Assam from 1874 until 1972. Since becoming the state capital of Meghalaya it has rapidly developed into a typical modern Indian town and in doing so some of its older buildings have been demolished. In parts it still retains its charm, the air is refreshingly cool and it has become a favourite holiday destination for domestic tourists.

◉ Sights & Activities

Ward's Lake   LAKE
(admission/camera/video ₹5/10/20; ◷8.30am-5.30pm Nov-Feb, 8.30am-7pm Mar-Oct) Colonial-era Shillong was planned around this attractive lake, with its pretty **ornamental bridge**, flower beds, coy courting couples and gaggles of geese.

Colonial Shillong   NOTABLE BUILDINGS
The city's half-timbered architecture has been rather swamped by lots of drab Indian concrete, but areas such as Oakland retain many older houses and even in the centre a few gems remain.

The **Pinewood Hotel** (Rita Rd), a 1920s tea-growers retreat, is particularly representative and looks great at night. The 1902 **All Saints' Cathedral** (Kacheri Rd) would look perfect pictured on a biscuit tin. Located nearby, the turreted **Das-Roy House** (closed to the public) lurks behind a traffic circle that harbours five forgotten **Khasi monoliths** as well as a mini Soviet-style **globe monument**.

TOP
CHOICE **Don Bosco Museum of Indigenous Cultures**   MUSEUM
(www.dbcic.org; Sacred Heart Theological College; Indian/foreigner ₹50/150; ◷9.30am-4.30pm Mon-Sat, 1.30-4.30pm Sun, until 5.30 Apr-Sep) This very professional museum displays a truly vast, very well laid-out collection of tribal artefacts interspersed just occasionally with gratuitous galleries on Christian missionary work. Tours (compulsory) last over an hour, departing on the half-hour.

Wankhar Entomology Museum   MUSEUM
(Riatsamthiah; Indian/foreigner/camera per photo/video ₹50/100/10/500; ◷11am-4pm Mon-Sat) The memorably named Wankhar Entomology Museum is a remarkable one-room display of pinned butterflies, gruesome rhinoceros beetles and incredible stick-insects in the home of the original collector.

Both museums are northwest of the town centre.

Siat Khnam   SPORT
All around Shillong gambling booths offer 'Forecast' odds on Siat Khnam. This is a unique 'sport'. A semicircle of weather-beaten Khasi men fire hundreds of arrows at a drum-shaped straw target for a set time before a canvas curtain is raised to keep further arrows off the target. Those that stick in are counted and bets predict the last two digits of this total. It's effectively a lottery but the shooting is a gently fascinating spectacle. Shoots are usually scheduled at 4pm and 5pm every day, timings can vary somewhat by season. The easy-to-miss Siat Khnam site is a small grassy area approximately opposite the big Nehru Stadium on the south river bank.

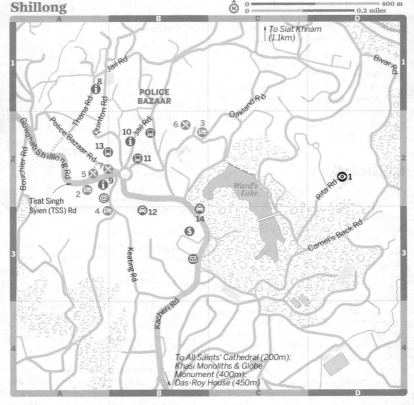

To Siat Khnam (1.1km)

POLICE BAZAAR

Ward's Lake

Tirat Singh Syien (TSS) Rd

To All Saints' Cathedral (200m);
Khasi Monoliths & Globe
Monument (400m);
Das-Roy House (450m)

🛏 Sleeping

Tariffs are seasonal and highly negotiable in the low season. During peak periods hotels fill fast, but there are dozens of choices around the Police Bazaar area, so just keep looking. Taxes add a discouraging 20% to your bill (included in the prices listed here).

TOP CHOICE Hotel Tripura Castle HISTORIC HOTEL $$$

(☎2501111; Cleve Colony; s/d from ₹3600/3720, ste ₹7200; ✳@🛜) Tucked away on a wooded hillside is the distinctively turreted summer villa of the former Tripura maharajas. It's this private 'castle' that features in hotel brochures, but accommodation is actually in a mostly new, if pseudo-heritage building behind. Pine-framed rooms have a gently stylish vibe with period furniture and a level of service that's hard to beat. For the full maharaja experience opt for a suite. The hotel is 2.5km southeast of the centre.

TOP CHOICE Ri Kynjai HOTEL $$$

(☎9862420300; www.rikynjai.com; Umiam Lake; r from ₹7200; ✳) In the local Khasi language *ri kynjai* means 'land of serene environments' and this divine resort, on the banks of the Umiam lake, 22km from Shillong, is certainly that. Cottages lie scattered about the lush, green gardens and each is impeccably presented with lake views and bathrooms with deep bath tubs. There's also a spa, a decent restaurant and a bar that's perfect for sundowners.

Silk Route HOTEL $$

(☎2503301; www.hotelsilkroute.com; Keating Rd; s/d from ₹1200/1440; 🛜) This small hotel has memorably colourful rooms kept ship-shape by the enthusiastic cleaners. The stylish bathrooms contain big rain showers. It's popular, so book ahead.

Earle Holiday Home HISTORIC HOTEL $

(☎2228614; Oakland Rd; r ₹550-1650) The cheapest rooms at this amusingly disorganised

Shillong

hotel are original half-timbered affairs within a classic 1920 Shillong hill house adorned with sweet little turrets. Pricier rooms in the concrete annexe are less atmospheric but more comfortable. The ₹650 rooms are the best.

Baba Tourist Lodge HOTEL $
(☑2211285; GS Rd; r ₹500-900) Ageing but clean, and popular with backpackers, Baba hides behind a deceptively small PCO shop. The best rooms have windows and views out onto greenery. Bucket showers and bucket hot water.

🍴 Eating & Drinking

La Galerie INDIAN $$
(Hotel Centrepoint, TSS Rd; mains ₹150-200) A suave restaurant compartmentalised into booths by photographs of local scenes, it offers excellent Indian food. **Cloud 9** is the top-floor bar-restaurant serving dainty Thai dishes, cold beers and cocktails.

City Hut Dhaba MULTICUISINE $$
(Oakland Rd; mains ₹100-150) Tucked behind Earle Holiday Home and guarded by gnomes, City Hut serves a variety of Indian, Chinese, barbecue and ice creams in four different eating rooms, including a family-only room and an attractive, flower-decked straw pavilion.

Broadway INDIAN, CHINESE $$
(GS Rd; mains ₹60-150) With a a relaxed and pleasant atmosphere and an impressive array of aquariums full of goldfish, this no-nonsense restaurant serves a tasty mix of Indian and Chinese meals.

ℹ Information

Internet Access
Techweb (basement Zara's Arcade, Keating Rd; per hr ₹20; ◎9am-8.30pm)

Money
There are many ATMs.
SBI (Kacheri Rd) Exchange of foreign currency and travellers cheques; ATM outside.

Tourist Information
Cultural Pursuits Adventures
(☑9436303978; www.culturalpursuits.com; Hotel Alpine Continental, Thana Rd) Experienced agency for caving, trekking, village stays and off-the-beaten-track stuff.
Government of India tourist office
(☑2225632; TSS Rd; ◎9.30am-5.30pm Mon-Fri, 10am-2pm Sat) Free basic maps and brochures.
Meghalaya Tourism (☑2226220; www.megtourism.gov.in; Jail Rd) Lots of useful information.

ℹ Getting There & Away

The **MTC bus station** (Jail Rd) also has a computerised railway-reservation counter (nearest train station is Guwahati). Private buses depart from Dhanketi Point; book tickets from counters around Police Bazaar, including **Network Travels** (Shop 44, MUDA Complex, Police Bazaar) and **Deep** (Ward's Lake Rd).

Frequent buses and sumos run to the following towns:
Aizawl (₹550, 15 hours)
Cherrapunjee (bus/sumo ₹250/220, three hours)
Dawki (bus ₹110, three hours)
Dimapur (₹340, 14 hours)
Guwahati (government bus/private bus ₹90/110, 3½ hours)
Silchar (₹190, 10 hours)
Siliguri (₹430, 16 hours)
Tura (bus/sumo ₹260/360, 12 hours via Guwahati)

From a Kacheri Rd parking area, taxis will take you direct to Guwahati airport (₹1600, 3½ hours).

Khasi Hills Tourist Taxi Cooperative (Kacheri Rd) charges ₹1800 to ₹2000 for a day trip to Cherrapunjee, and for a ride to the Bangladesh border near Dawki it's ₹1600.

Around Shillong

SMIT

Framing itself as the Khasi cultural centre, Smit hosts the major five-day **Nongkrem Festival** (October). This features animal sacrifices and a curious slow-motion shuffling dance performed in full costume in front of the thatched bamboo **'palace'** of the local *syiem* (traditional ruler). Smit is 11km from Shillong, 4km off the Jowai road.

CHERRAPUNJEE (SOHRA)

03637 / POP 11,000

Once you leave the outskirts of Shillong the road to Cherrapunjee passes through pretty scenery that becomes dramatic at **Dympep viewpoint**, where a photogenic V-shape valley slits deeply into the plateau.

Although straggling for several kilometres, Cherrapunjee (known locally as Sohra) has a compact centre. Huddling beside the marketplace is the sumo stand.

👁 Sights & Activities

Root Bridges   LANDMARK

The most fascinating sight around Cherrapunjee are the incredible **root bridges**, living rubber fig-tree roots that ingenious Khasi villagers have trained across streams to form natural pathways. Three of these root bridges (including an amazing 'double-decker') are near **Nongriat**. Access involves a two-hour very steep trek down from **Tyrna**, a pretty, palm-clad village that's 2km from Mawshamok. From Cherrapunjee Holiday Resort the entire roundtrip hike takes eight hours, is highly strenuous and involves descending and ascending some 2000-odd steps (this particular author couldn't walk for two days afterwards!). The Cherrapunjee Holiday Resort provides maps.

Moors & Waterfalls   VIEWPOINT

The surrounding grassy moors justify Meghalaya's over-played 'Scotland of the East' tourist-office soubriquet, although they're dotted with Khasi monoliths and scarred by quarrying. Much more impressive is the series of 'grand canyon' valleys that plunge into deep lush chasms of tropical forest sprayed by a succession of seasonally inspiring waterfalls. The **Nohkalikai Falls**, fourth highest in the world, are particularly dramatic, especially in the monsoon when their capacity increases 20-fold. You can see them easily enough without quite entering the official **viewpoint** (admission/camera ₹10/200; ⏰8am-5pm), 4.4km southwest of Sohra market.

Mawsmai Cave   CAVE

(admission/camera/video ₹10/15/50; ⏰9.30am-5.30pm) Their popularity with domestic tourists means that the incongruous sight of

---

WORTH A TRIP

GARO HILLS

The lush, green Garo Hills in the far west of Meghalaya are well off the beaten path. The towns are not visually distinctive, but most houses in small hamlets remain traditionally fashioned from bamboo-weave matting and neatly cropped palm thatch. The Garo Hills are easier to visit from Guwahati than from Shillong.

Sprawling Tura is the western Garo Hills' regional centre and an unhurried transport hub. The **tourist office** (☎03651-242394; ⏰10am-5pm Mon-Fri) is 4km away towards Nazing Bazaar. Friendly staff offer brochures and sketchy maps, and arrange guides for anywhere in the Garo Hills, including a three-day hike to **Nokrek Biosphere Reserve** where it's possible to watch for Hoolock Gibbons from a traditional-style *borang* (Garo tree house).

There are some cheap and not very cheerful places to stay near the market in Tura or, for something a little more comfortable, try the **Rikman Continental** (☎03651-220744; Circular Rd; s/d from ₹900/1080; ✦@).

Almost on the Bangladesh border, **Baghmara** is the southern Garo Hills' district centre. From Baghmara you can visit the **Balpakhram National Park**, 45km away, but jeep and guide hire will have to be organised in Tura.

CROSSING INTO BANGLADESH FROM DAWKI

Border Hours

The border is open from 6am to 5pm.

Foreign Exchange

There's no official exchange booth but ask at the Bangladesh customs office.

Onward Transport

The border post is at Tamabil, 1.7km from Dawki market (taxis are ₹40-50). Coming from Bangladesh, beware that Tamabil has no Sonali bank, so prepay your Tk300 Bangladeshi departure tax in Sylhet or in Jaintiapura. There are frequent Tamabil–Sylhet minibuses.

sari-clad women stooping through the low passages of the 150m-long Mawsmai Cave is common. Mawsmai's tall row of roadside **monoliths** is as impressive as the cave but don't receive the same attention.

🛏 Sleeping & Eating

TOP CHOICE Cherrapunjee Holiday Resort HOTEL $$
(☎09436115925; www.cherrapunjee.com; Laitkynsew village; d ₹1480-1800; @🛜) With seven eminently comfortable rooms, this resort is run by truly delightful hosts. They offer a selection of hikes, either self-orientated (using their hand-drawn maps) or with a local guide. Built on a ridge, rooms either look down to Bangladesh or up to the escarpment. During peak times tent accommodation (₹600) is available with shared bathrooms but no hot water. More rooms were under construction at the time of research. A daily bus leaves nearby Laitkynsew village for Shillong (₹40, 6am). Going the other way it leaves Shillong at 1pm. Otherwise a taxi from Cherrapunjee costs ₹250 to ₹300.

Rest House Nongriat GUESTHOUSE $
(☎9856891520; Nongriat; per person ₹100) This highly basic four-room guesthouse is just one minute from the double-decker bridge and so is ideal if you want to explore the escarpment floor in greater depth. If you stay, take the absolute minimum with you because carrying a backpack back up all those steps would be a real bitch! Meals cost ₹100.

Sohra Plaza Hotel HOTEL $
(☎235762; r ₹550) This mucky but friendly two-room hotel is by the market.

Odisha

Includes »

Best Places to Stay

» Nature Camp (Satkosia; p594)

» Chandori Sai (p606)

» Nature Camp (Bhitarkanika; p609)

» Lotus Eco Village (p600)

» Hotel Gandhara (p596)

Best Temples

» Sun Temple (p600)

» Mukteswar Mandir (p589)

» Lingaraj Mandir (p588)

» Jagannath Mandir (p595)

» Yogini Temple (p594)

Why Go?

Long ignored by all but the most intrepid, Odisha (Orissa) is a backseat destination with unfamiliar flair. Travellers are waking up to its intricate patchwork of culture, tradition, sun and sand, but it continues to feel relatively undiscovered. Odisha affords an escape from the frenzy of other Indian traveller epicentres and boasts the World Heritage–listed Sun Temple in Konark, bursting with brilliantly worked scenes of Odisha life. Medieval temples pepper the streets of the capital, Bhubaneswar. Wonderful national parks and wildlife sanctuaries are crammed with tigers, elephants, Irrawaddy dolphins, monster crocodiles and millions of migratory birds. Chilika Lake, Asia's largest brackish lagoon, is flanked by inexpensive seaside retreats along one of India's prettiest coasts. Inland, the Adivasis (tribal people) live precariously on the edge of mainstream society, yet retain their colourful, fascinating traditions – a metaphor for Odisha itself.

When to Go
Bhubaneswar

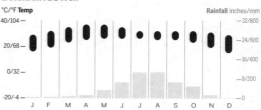

Nov–Mar Warm and dry, just like a fresh load of laundry.

Nov Join the beach bash at Puri's Beach Festival.

Dec The Unesco-betrothed Sun Temple is the backdrop for the seductive Konark Festival.

Dishes of Odisha

If there is a staple in Odishan kitchens, it's mustard, used ubiquitously in seed, paste and oil forms, giving many Odisha dishes a distinct pungent flavour. A typical meal consists of *bhata* (rice) served alongside a variety of tasty side dishes like *kaharu phula bhaja* (fried pumpkin flower); *dalma* (dahl cooked with pumpkin, potato, plantains and eggplant, then fried in a five-spice oil of fenugreek, cumin, black cumin, anise and mustard, topped with grated coconut); and *besara* (vegetables or river fish with mustard-paste gravy). *Saga bhaja,* leafy greens lightly fried with garlic paste and a five-seed mixture called *pancha phutan* (cumin, mustard, anis, black cumin and chilli) is also a treat here. On the coast, fish and prawns are omnipresent: *sarison macha* is a superb favourite fish dish cooked in a mustard-based curry.

DON'T MISS

Odisha's masterstroke is undeniably its 13th-century **Sun Temple** at Konark; one of the state's most unforgettable journeys is a tour through the **Western tribal regions**, where colour and culture collide in the fascinating villages and markets of some 62 tribal (Adivasi) societies.

Top State Festivals

» Adivasi Mela (Jan, Bhubaneswar, p591) Features art, dance and handicrafts of Odisha's tribal groups.

» Rath Yatra (Jun/Jul, Puri, p594) Immense chariots containing Lord Jagannath, brother Balbhadra and sister Subhadra are hauled from Jagannath Temple to Gundicha Mandir.

» Puri Beach Festival (Nov, Puri, p596) Song, dance, food and cultural activities on the beach.

» Konark Festival (Dec, Konark, p600) Features traditional music and dance and a seductive temple ritual.

MAIN POINTS OF ENTRY

Most travellers usually arrive at Bhubaneswar's Biju Patnaik Airport or by the rails into Bhubaneswar (BBS) or Puri (PURI) junctions.

Fast Facts

» Population: 41.9 million

» Area: 155,707 sq km

» Capital: Bhubaneswar

» Main language: Odia

» Sleeping prices: $ below ₹900, $$ ₹900 to ₹3000, $$$ above ₹3000

Top Tip

Puri is Odisha's travellers' hub. If you want to hit the ground running on a tribal tour, it's most pleasantly organised from there.

Resources

» Visit Odisha (www .visitorissaa.org) – official Department of Tourism site.

Odisha Highlights

1 Catch the sun at dawn's light on the stunning **Sun Temple** (p600) in Konark

2 Sleep on the sands of the gorgeous Mahanadi River cutting through breathtaking **Satkosia Gorge Sanctuary** (p594)

3 Bliss-out beachside in traveller favourite **Puri** (p594),

but don't shy away from its holy quarter on the 'Indian' side

4 Barter in the colourful tribal marketplaces of **Onkadelli** (p605) and **Chatikona** (p604)

5 Ply wildlife-rich mangroves on the prowl for 8m-long saltwater crocodiles

in **Bhitarkanika Wildlife Sanctuary** (p608)

6 Enjoy the silence between the sea and Asia's largest brackish lagoon on an overnight camping trip to **Chilika Lake** (p601)

7 Explore the ancient Hindu shrines around India's Temple City, **Bhubaneswar** (p587)

History

Formerly known as Kalinga, then Orissa, Odisha (per a longstanding name-change campaign that finally received Lok Sabha approval in 2010) was once a formidable maritime empire that had trading routes leading down into Indonesia, but its history is somewhat hazy until the demise of the Kalinga dynasty in 260 BC at the hands of the great emperor Ashoka. Appalled at the carnage he had caused, Ashoka forswore violence and converted to Buddhism.

Around the 1st century BC Buddhism declined and Jainism was restored as the faith of the people. During this period the monastery caves of Udayagiri and Khandagiri (in Bhubaneswar) were excavated as important Jain centres.

By the 7th century AD Hinduism had supplanted Jainism. Under the Kesari and Ganga kings, trade and commerce increased and Odishan culture flourished – countless temples from that classical period still stand. The Odishans defied the Muslim rulers in Delhi until finally falling to the Mughals during the 16th century, when many of Bhubaneswar's temples were destroyed.

Until Independence, Odisha was ruled by Afghans, Marathas and the British.

Since the 1990s a Hindu fundamentalist group, Bajrang Dal, has undertaken a violent campaign against Christians in Odisha in response to missionary activity. The often illiterate and dispossessed tribal people have suffered the most from the resulting communal violence, which has been as much about power, politics and land as religious belief.

Violence flared up again in 2008 after the killing of a Hindu leader in Kandhamal district, and thousands of Christians were moved to government relief camps outside the district after their homes were torched.

The creation of the neighbouring states of Jharkhand and Chhattisgarh has prompted calls for the formation of a separate, tribal-oriented state, Koshal, in the northwest of Odisha, with Sambalpur as the capital. A separatist political party, the Kosal Kranti Dal (KKD), fielded candidates in the 2009 state election.

The last few years have seen something of an industrial boom in Odisha, with an influx of big steel plants and controversial mining.

Climate

Monsoonal rains and cyclones in July to October can seriously affect transport. A particularly devastating cyclone struck Odisha in 1999, causing significant damage and the loss of thousands of lives, and in 2008 serious flooding destroyed crops and villages and led to mass evacuations.

National Parks

The admission fee for foreigners to visit most of Odisha's national parks and wildlife sanctuaries is ₹1000 per day – including the day you depart– a hefty fee that Odisha's private tour operators have continued to protest against.

Dangers & Annoyances

Mosquitoes here have a record of being dengue and malaria carriers. See p1190 for advice, and consider bringing a mosquito net.

ⓘ Information

Odisha Tourism (www.Odishatourism.gov. in) has a presence in most towns, with offices for information and tour/hotel booking. It also maintains a list of approved guides for tribal-area visits. **Odisha Tourism Development Corporation** (OTDC; www.panthanivas.com), the commercial arm of Odisha Tourism, runs tours and hotels throughout the state.

ⓘ Getting There & Away

Air routes connect Bhubaneswar with Bengaluru, Delhi, Hyderabad, Mumbai (Bombay), Kolkata (Calcutta) and Chennai. Major road and rail routes between Kolkata and Chennai pass through coastal Odisha and Bhubaneswar with spur connections to Puri. Road and rail connect Sambalpur with Kolkata, Chhattisgarh and Madhya Pradesh.

ⓘ Getting Around

Public transport in the coastal region is good with ample long-distance buses and trains. For touring around the interior hiring a car is the best option, although buses and trains are available if you're not in a hurry.

Bhubaneswar

☎ 0674 / POP 647,310

At first glance, Bhubaneswar's wide avenues, green belts and public highway murals that reflect its temple-town heritage – all on the outskirts – seem quite pleasant. Its inner sanctum, whose many gorgeous and well-preserved Hindu temples inspired the nickname of India's Temple City, is also a serene spiritual epicentre and a living museum of Odishan medieval temple architecture. The problem is the rest of it – typically noisy, polluted and congested. But a day or two to take in the old city's holy centre around Bindu Sagar where, from the thousands that once

ODISHA

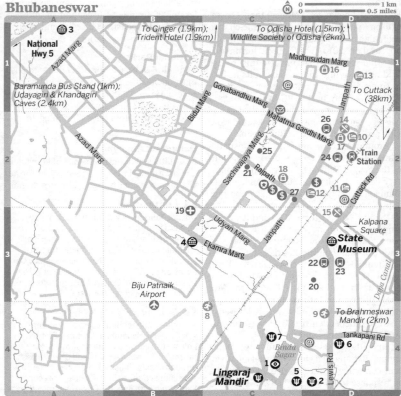

stood here, 50-odd stone temples remain, is an enthralling pit stop.

◉ Sights

According to legend, Bhubaneswar once boasted over 7000 temples and is a long-harnessed religious centre dating back 2000 years. Today, it's most famous for its surviving medieval temples, a mix of 'live' (still in use as places of worship) and 'dead' (archaeological sites). Bhubaneswar still lays claim to around 500 or so Hindu temples. Along with Puri and Konark, the city forms one side of East India's hallowed 'Swarna Tribhuja' (the 'Golden Triangle'), a heavy-visited domestic tourist route.

Unless you're on an organised tour, a priest might approach you and expect a donation; ₹20 is reasonable. Consider it a guiding fee as undoubtedly the priest will reveal something about his temple.

To see all the major temples, charter an autorickshaw for two to three hours (about ₹300). A live temple will always have a red flag fluttering above it.

TOP CHOICE **Lingaraj Mandir**   HINDU TEMPLE
The 54m-high Lingaraj Mandir, dedicated to Tribhuvaneswar (Lord of Three Worlds), dates from 1090 to 1104 (although parts are over 1400 years old) and is surrounded by more than 50 smaller temples and shrines. The granite block, representing Tribhuvaneswar, is bathed daily with water, milk and bhang (marijuana). The main gate, guarded by two moustachioed yellow lions, is a spectacle in itself as lines of pilgrims approach, *prasad* (temple-blessed food offering) in hand.

Because the temple is surrounded by a wall, and closed to non-Hindus, foreigners can see it only from a viewing platform (this can also include foreign Hindus, as some Indian Hindus do not believe in conversion). Face the main entrance, walk around to the right and find the viewing platform down a short laneway to the left. There have been reports of aggressive hassling for 'donations' (according to our guide) at the viewing platform. The money will not go to the temple; stand your ground and do not pay.

Mukteswar, Siddheswar & Kedargauri Mandirs HINDU TEMPLES

Not far from Parsurameswar is the small but beautiful 10th-century **Mukteswar Mandir**, one of the most ornate temples in Bhubaneswar; you'll see representations of it on posters and brochures across Odisha. Intricate carvings show a mixture of Buddhist, Jain and Hindu styles – look for the Nagarani (Snake Queen), easily mistaken by Westerners for a mermaid, who you'll also see at the Raja Rani Mandir. The ceiling carvings and stone arch are particularly striking as is the arched *torana* (architrave) at the front, clearly showing Buddhist influence.

Siddheswar Mandir, in the same compound, is a later but plainer temple with a fine red-painted Ganesh. Over the road is **Kedargauri Mandir**, one of the oldest temples in Bhubaneswar, although it has been substantially rebuilt.

Vaital Mandir HINDU TEMPLE

This 8th-century temple, with a double-storey 'wagon roof' influenced by Buddhist cave architecture, was a centre of Tantric worship, eroticism and bloody sacrifice. Look closely and you'll see some very early erotic carvings on the walls. Chamunda (a fearsome incarnation of Devi), representing old age and death, can be seen in the dingy interior, although her necklace of skulls and her bed of corpses are usually hidden beneath her temple robes.

Parsurameswar Mandir HINDU TEMPLES

Just west of Lewis Rd lies a cluster of about 20 smaller but important temples. Best preserved is Parsurameswar Mandir, an ornate Shiva temple built around AD 650. It has lively bas-reliefs of elephant and horse processions, and Shiva images.

Raja Rani Mandir HINDU TEMPLE

(Indian/foreigner ₹5/100, video ₹25; ☉dawndusk) This temple, built around 1100 and surrounded by manicured gardens, is famous for its ornate *deul* (temple sanctuary) and tower. Around the compass points are pairs of statues representing eight *dikpalas* (guardians) who protect the temple. Between them, nymphs, embracing couples, elephants and lions peer from niches and decorate the pillars. The name of the temple isn't for a particular king and queen, but is the name of the stone used in the temple's construction.

Brahmeswar Mandir HINDU TEMPLE
Standing in well-kept gardens, flanked on its plinth by four smaller structures, this 9th-century temple is a smaller version of Lingaraj Mandir. It's notable for its finely detailed sculptures with erotic elements.

TOP CHOICE **Udayagiri & Khandagiri Caves** HISTORICAL SITE
(admission both sites Indian/foreigner ₹5/100, video ₹25; ⊙dawn-dusk) Six kilometres west of the city centre are two hills riddled with rock-cut shelters. Many are ornately carved and thought to have been chiselled out for Jain ascetics in the 1st century BC.

Ascending the ramp at Udayagiri (Sunrise Hill), note **Swargapuri** (Cave 9) to the right with its devotional figures. **Hathi Gumpha** (Cave 14) at the top has a 117-line inscription relating the exploits of its builder, King Kharavela of Kalinga, who ruled from 168 to 153 BC.

Around to the left you'll see **Bagh Gumpha** (Tiger Cave; Cave 12), with its entrance carved as a tiger mouth. Nearby are **Pavana Gumpha** (Cave of Purification) and small **Sarpa Gumpha** (Serpent Cave), where the tiny door is surmounted by a three-headed cobra. On the summit are the remains of a defensive position. Around to the southeast is the single-storey elephant-guarded **Ganesh Gumpha** (Cave 10), almost directly above the two-storey **Rani ka Naur** (Queen's Palace Cave; Cave 1), carved with Jain symbols and battle scenes.

Continue back to the entrance via **Chota Hathi Gumpha** (Cave 3), with its carvings of elephants, and the double-storey **Jaya Vijaya Cave** (Cave 5), with a bodhi tree carved in the central area.

Across the road, Khandagiri offers fine views over Bhubaneswar from its summit. The steep path splits about one-third of the way up the hill. The right path goes to **Ananta Cave** (Cave 3), with its carved figures of athletes, women, elephants and geese carrying flowers. Further along is a series of **Jain temples**; at the top is another (18th-century) Jain temple.

Buses don't go to the caves, but plenty pass nearby on NH5, or take an autorickshaw (about ₹200 return).

State Museum MUSEUM
(www.Odishamuseum.nic.in; Lewis Rd; Indian/foreigner ₹5/50, camera ₹10/100; ⊙10am-5pm Tue-Sun) This museum boasts Odisha's best collection of rare palm-leaf manuscripts, traditional and folk musical instruments, Bronze Age tools, an armoury, and an impressive collection of Buddhist, Jaina and Brahmanical sculptures.

Bindu Sagar LANDMARK
Bindu Sagar (Ocean Drop Tank) reputedly contains water from every holy stream, pool and tank in India.

FREE **Museum of Tribal Arts & Artefacts** MUSEUM
(⊙10am-5pm Tue-Sun) For anyone considering a visit to the tribal areas, this museum, off National Hwy 5 (NH5), is recommended. Dress, ornaments, weapons, household implements and musical instruments are displayed.

FREE **Odisha Modern Art Gallery** ART GALLERY
(132 Forest Park; ⊙11am-8pm Tue-Sun) Housing a surprisingly high standard of contemporary art by local artists, this small gallery also has prints and originals for sale.

Tours

Odisha Tourism runs a hop-on, hop-off **bus service** (per day ₹250) starting at the OTDC (p593). The AC buses do a loop of the city's temples every hour.

The OTDC runs a **city tour** (AC ₹250) every day except Monday, covering the Nandankanan Zoo, Dhauli, the Lingaraj and Mukteswar temples, the State Museum, and Udayagiri and Khandagiri Caves. Another tour goes to Pipli, Konark and Puri (AC ₹300, daily except Monday). Both tours leave from the Panthanivas Bhubaneswar hotel. These prices do not include entry fees.

Private tour operators organise customised tours into Odisha's tribal areas; these can also include visits to handicraft villages, and Similipal National Park and Bhitarkanika Wildlife Sanctuary. Prices will depend on number of people, transport and hotel standards, but expect to pay around US$50 to

US$100 per person per day for tours that include transport, accommodation and a professional guide, varying from budget to top end. Tribal tours usually start on a Sunday or Monday to synchronise with village markets.

Alternative Tours   TRIBAL/CULTURAL
(✆2590830; www.travelclubindia.com; Room 5, BDA Market Complex, Palaspalli) A veteran for tribal tours in Odisha, Nagaland and Arunchal Pradesh.

Discover Tours   TRIBAL/WILDLIFE
(✆2430477; www.Odishadiscover.com; 463 Lewis Rd;⊘closed Sun) Specialises in tribal and textile village tours as well as Bhitarkanika and Similipal.

⚝ Festivals & Events

Every January, Bhubaneswar goes tribal for the annual **Adivasi Mela** festival, celebrating the art, dance and handicrafts of Odisha's tribal groups.

🛏 Sleeping

Bhubaneswar has plenty of accommodation, but a real dearth of anything in the way of clean or appealing family-run places or traveller dens in the budget and lower midranges. Conversely, it has a great selection of top-end hotels.

TOP CHOICE **Ginger**   BOUTIQUE HOTEL $$$
(✆2303933; www.gingerhotels.com; Jayadev Vihar, Nayapalli; s/d ₹2999/3499; ✳@⊚) Ginger is paint-by-numbers boutique business hotel chain (owned by Tata) with an IKEA-like self-service philosophy that means you're not constantly surrounded by tip-demanding bag-carriers, laundry peons etc. With young friendly staff, clean modern lines, and fresh, spotless rooms with LCD TVs, tea and coffee, minifridge and silent AC, it's Bhubaneswar's best bang for the buck. Meals are served buffet style in the restaurant and there's a 24-hour branch of Café Coffee Day that will deliver to your room. Advanced internet booking can cut rates by 50%.

Mayfair Lagoon   HOTEL $$$
(✆2360101; www.mayfairhotels.com; Jayadev Vihar; d cottages from ₹9000, d villas ₹30,000; ✳@⊚☒) Quirky, colourful, even kitschy, but luxuriously Indian at the same time. In the jungle-like grounds you'll find static tigers, an elephant, even a twin-prop 1942 aircraft. The cottages are scattered around a serene lagoon and facilities run to a complimentary breakfast, six excellent restaurants,

a British-style pub and Bhubaneswar's pub, nightclub and mini-bowling alley, 10 Downing Street.

New Marrion   BOUTIQUE HOTEL $$$
(✆2380850; www.hotelnewmarrion.com; 6 Janpath; s/d from ₹6100/6500; ✳@⊚☒) A centrally located hotel where rooms have contemporary, classy design – LCD TVs, dark-wood panelling and extraordinarily stylish shower curtains. Restaurants here includes South Indian, Italian-Mexican combo and Chinese, a great kebab house, a Café Coffee Day and a contemporary Scottish bar. Avoid executive rooms on the 2nd floor unless you like a rooftop as a patio.

Kasturi Guest House   GUESTHOUSE $
(✆2537050; Ashok Nagar, Janpath; r from ₹750, with AC from ₹1000; ✳) Located in the heart of Bhubaneswar's commercial district (read: noisy), this intimate guesthouse offers numerous categories for all budgets and is a little more welcoming than others in its price range. Rooms vary in size so there's something for everyone.

Hotel Pushpak   HOTEL $$
(✆2310185; Kalpana Sq; s/d incl breakfast ₹900/1000, with AC ₹1600/1800; ✳⊚) Fresh coats of lavender paint that evoke the stylish Bhubaneswar traffic police uniforms in the AC rooms can't save them from seeming overpriced at this vaguely institutional, half-hearted choice, but the non-AC rooms are a different story. They haven't been renovated, but you'd be hard-pressed to find a better deal for the price.

Trident Hotel   HOTEL $$$
(✆2301010; www.tridenthotels.com; CB-1, Nayapalli; s/d/ste from ₹10,000/11,000/13,000; ✳@⊚☒) The high-ceilinged lobby, inspired by Konark's temple architecture, is a beauty and the Trident is more refined, but the Mayfair is more fun, with loads more dining choices.

Hotel Richi   HOTEL $
(✆2534619; 122A Station Sq; s/d incl breakfast from ₹400/600, d with AC from ₹1150; ✳) The stone facade of this dim hotel is Iron Curtain depressing; the rooms only marginally improve on that condition, but proximity to the train station make it (very) popular.

Hotel Bhagwat Niwas   HOTEL $
(✆2313708; Kalpana Sq; s ₹200-250, d ₹350-450, d with AC ₹1100-1200; ✳) Behind Hotel Padma, the Bhagwat is what it is: a nearly

clean choice for rupee pinchers. Checkout is 24 hours.

Hotel Upasana　　　　　　　　HOTEL **$**
(☎2310044; upasana_bbsr@rediffmail.com; off Cuttack Rd; d from ₹900, with AC from ₹1100; ❋) Behind the rancid Bhubaneswar Hotel, the Upasana is one of the friendlier and more welcoming budgets in town.

🍴 Eating & Drinking

TOP CHOICE Tangerine 9　　　INDIAN/FUSION **$$**
(Station Sq; mains ₹60-250) The soothing namesake tones of this excellent restaurant won't relieve the burn of the fiery chicken Dum Puk, the first curry in a month to make our head tingle. All the dishes – North Indian (especially tandoori), Chinese and a few Thai thrown in – burst with the flavour of fresh herbs and spices. If you can't afford five-star-hotel dining but want the same quality for half the price, Tangerine 9 won't disappoint.

Maurya Gardens　　　　INDIAN, CHINESE **$$**
(Hotel Richi, Station Sq; mains ₹50-160) This darkened restaurant is a welcome respite from the train-station chaos outside, as well as a dramatic contrast from the hotel in which it's located. The menu is loaded down with Chinese, Indian and Continental dishes and the curries are nice and hot, but if you want a beer to cool it down you'll have to eat (same menu) in the bar next door.

Hare Krishna Restaurant　　　　INDIAN **$$**
(Station Sq, Lalchand Market Complex; mains ₹45-140; ⊙lunch & dinner) The menu says 'Surrender to the pleasure of being vegetarian', and it's not difficult at this excellent veg restaurant. In dimly lit, upmarket surrounds you can enjoy mainly Indian dishes, including a wide range of tasty biryanis and pilaus.

Khana Khazana　　　　　　　　INDIAN **$$**
(outside Hotel Padma, Kalpana Sq; snacks & mains ₹18-160; ⊙dinner) It probably shouldn't be your first meal in India, but this fast-food street stall with a few chairs and tables scattered outside does tandoori chicken, chicken biryani or large portions of delicious chow mein.

☆ Entertainment

TOP CHOICE 10 Downing Street　　BAR, NIGHTCLUB
(Mayfair Lagoon, Jayadev Vihar; ⊙7-11.30pm) So ridiculous it's awesome, 10 Downing Street is what happens when you build something from nothing. Bhubaneswar was hurting for nocturnal diversions, so it's all here: a colonial British-style megapub with pool, cricket on the TV and a small dance floor, too, with DJ's spinning house, R&B and Bollywood from 7pm. Oh. *Wait.* There's also a mini-bowling alley!

🛍 Shopping

Ekamra Haat　　　　　　　　　MARKET
(www.ekamrahaat.in; Madhusudan Marg; ⊙10am-10pm) A wide-ranging exposition of Odishan handicrafts (and snack stalls) can be found at this permanent market in a large garden space. While the gates open at 10am, many stalls don't get going until later.

Odisha State Handloom Cooperative　　　　　　　HANDICRAFTS
(Utkalika; Eastern Tower, Market Bldg) Odishan textiles, including appliqué and *ikat* (a technique involving tie-dyeing the thread before it's woven) works, can be bought here.

ℹ Information

Modern Book Depot (Station Sq; ⊙9.30am-2pm & 4.30-9pm) Maps, English-language novels, coffee-table books, postcards and books on Odisha. If you're interested in learning some Odia, ask the owner about the well-regarded *Oriya in Small Bites.*

Oxford Bookstore (2nd fl, PAL Heights, Jaydev Vihar) Modern megachain bookstore and signature tea bar Cha Bar.

DON'T MISS

SIMPLY SUMPTUOUS

This dead simple **restaurant** (Market Bldg, Sahid Nagar; thalis ₹100-250; ⊙lunch & dinner) is the place to try authentic Odishan cuisine, served in huge proportions thali-style on plantain leaves resting in traditional Bell Metal dishware. The restaurant observes Hindu dining restrictions (so no garlic or onions on Monday or Thursday) and the menu board is entirely in Odia, so just order veg or non-veg (not always available, depending on the religious calendar) and sit back and await your feast. It's like a Hindu Last Supper!

Capital Hospital (2401983; Sachivajaya Marg) Has a 24-hour pharmacy on-site.

CBG's (14 Kharvel Nagar; internet per hr ₹20; 8.30am-9pm Mon-Sat) Internet access.

Ganpati Travel & Communication (Kalpana Sq; internet per hr ₹30; 9am-9pm) Internet access.

Odisha Tourism (www.Odishatourism.gov.in) airport (9238578358); main office (2432177; Paryatan Bhavan, behind State Museum, Lewis Rd; 10am-6pm Mon-Sat); train station (2530715; 24hr) Tourist information, maps and lists of recommended guides.

Odisha Tourism Development Corporation (OTDC; 2430764; behind Panthanivas Bhubaneswar, Lewis Rd; 8am-8pm Mon-Sat) Commercial arm of Odisha Tourism. Books sightseeing tours and hotels.

Om Sai Communication (Ravi Talkies; internet per hr ₹12; 9am-11pm) Internet access conveniently located near temples.

Police (2533732; Capitol Police Station, Rajpath)

Post office (cnr Mahatma Gandhi & Sachivajaya Margs; 9am-7pm Mon-Sat, 3-7pm Sun)

State Bank of India (Rajpath; 10am-4pm Mon-Fri, 10am-2pm Sat) Cashes travellers cheques and exchanges foreign currency.

Thomas Cook (130 Ashok Nagar, Janpath) Cashes travellers cheques, including Amex, and exchanges foreign currency.

❶ Getting There & Away

Air

Bhubaneswar's Biju Patnaik Airport is a 7km drive from town. **Air India** (2530533; www.airindia.com; Rajpath; 10am-4.45pm Mon-Sat) flies daily to Delhi, Chennai and Mumbai. **Jet Lite** (2596176; www.jetlite.com; airport) flies direct to Kolkata daily. **IndiGo** (6543547; www.goindigo.in; airport) flies to Delhi, Bengaluru, Mumbai and Hyderabad daily. **Kingfisher** (2596046; www.flykingfisher.com; airport) flies to Mumbai, Bengaluru and Kolkata daily.

Bus

Baramunda bus station (Advance Ticket Booking Center 2354769; NH5) has frequent buses to Cuttack (₹14 to ₹15, one hour), Puri (₹35, 1¼ hours) and Konark (₹40, two hours). Less frequent services go to Berhampur (₹120, five hours), Sambalpur (non-AC/AC ₹220/270, nine hours) and Baripada (non-AC/AC ₹170/200, seven hours). There are several daily services to Kolkata (non-AC/AC/sleeper ₹270/350/400, 12 hours).

Train

Foreigner's queue up at window 2 at the Computerised Reservation Office. The 12841 *Coromandal Express* travels daily to Chennai

(sleeper/3AC/2AC ₹391/1043/1424, 20 hours, 9.35pm). The 12801 *Purushotlam Express* goes to Delhi (₹481/1296/1777, 31 hours, 11.30pm) and the 11020 *Konark Express* to Mumbai (₹484/1333/1838, 37 hours, 3.20pm).

Howrah is connected to Bhubaneswar by the 12074 *Jan Shatabdi* (2nd class/AC chair ₹142/460, seven hours, 6.20am daily except Sunday) and the daily 12822 *Howrah Dhauli Express* (₹122/432, seven hours, 1.20pm). To Sambalpur, the 12893 *Bhubaneswar-Sambalpur Express* (2nd class/AC chair ₹93/339, five hours, 6.45am) is quick, comfortable and convenient.

❶ Getting Around

No buses go to the airport; a taxi costs about ₹150 from the centre, though they are hard to come by. Try the Rajmahal taxi stand. An autorickshaw to the airport costs about ₹80 to ₹100. Prepaid taxis from the airport to central Bhubaneswar cost (non-AC/AC) ₹130/290, and to Puri or Konark ₹740/940. Another way to get to Puri or Konark in relative comfort is to go one way on an OTDC tour; let the guide know you won't be returning.

Around Bhubaneswar

NANDANKANAN ZOOLOGICAL PARK

Famous for its 11 blue-eyed white tigers, the zoo (www.nandankanan.org; Indian/foreigner ₹20/100, digital camera/video ₹10/100; 7.30am-5.30pm Tue-Sun Apr-Sep, 8am-5pm Oct-Mar), one of India's best, also boasts rare Asiatic lions, rhinoceroses, copious reptiles and long-snouted crocodiles, monkeys, deer, a vulture that is believed to have worked for the Pakistan Inter-Services Intelligence agency and India's only orang-utan.

The highlight is the hour-long lion and tiger safari (₹30), which leaves every 30 minutes from 9am 5pm. Other attractions include a toy train and boat rides. A cable car (₹30; zoo hr) crosses a lake, allowing passengers to get off halfway and walk down (300m) to the State Botanical Garden. Early or late in the day you might catch the elephants having a bath in the lake.

OTDC tours stop here for an (insufficient) hour or so. From Bhubaneswar, frequent public buses (₹15, one hour) leave from Kalpana Sq (near Hotel Padma) and outside the former Capital bus stand for Nandankanan village, about 400m from the entrance to the zoo. By taxi, a return trip (including waiting) costs about ₹350.

DHAULI

In about 260 BC one of Ashoka's famous edicts was carved onto a large rock at Dhauli, 8km south of Bhubaneswar. The rock is now protected by a grill-fronted building and above, on top of a hillock, is a carved elephant.

On a nearby hill is the huge, white **Shanti Stupa** (Peace Pagoda), built by Japanese monks in 1972. Older Buddhist reliefs are set into the modern structure. You have to climb the stairs barefoot (hot! hot! hot!) but it's worth it for the four lovely images of the Buddha and great views of the surrounding countryside.

You'll find the turn-off to Dhauli along the Bhubaneswar–Puri road, accessible by any Puri or Konark bus (₹8). From the turn-off, it's a flat 3km walk to the rock, and then a short, steep walk to the stupa. By autorickshaw/taxi, a return trip costs about ₹150/250.

HIRAPUR

Among iridescent-green paddies, 15km from Bhubaneswar, is a small village with an important **Yogini Temple**, one of only four in India. The low, circular structure, open to the sky, has 64 niches within, each with a black chlorite goddess. Getting here requires hired transport or coming on a customised tour from Bhubaneswar.

PIPLI

This colourful town, 16km southeast of Bhubaneswar, is notable for its brilliant appliqué craft, which incorporates small mirrors and is used for door and wall hangings and the more traditional canopies hung over Lord Jagannath and family during festival time. Lampshades and parasols hanging outside the shops turn the main road into an avenue of rainbow colours. The work is still done by local families in workshops behind the shops; you may be able to go back and have a look. During Diwali, it's particularly vibrant. Pipli is easily accessible by any bus between Bhubaneswar and Puri or Konark.

SOUTHEASTERN ODISHA

Puri

☎06752 / POP 157,610

Hindu pilgrims, Indian holidaymakers and foreign travellers all make their way to Puri, setting up camp in different parts of town. For Hindus, Puri is one of the holiest pilgrimage places in India, with religious life revolving around the great Jagannath Mandir and its famous Rath Yatra (Car Festival).

Puri's other attraction is its long, sandy beach and esplanade. Backing this, on New Marine Rd, is a long ribbon of hotels, resorts and company holiday homes that become instantly full when Kolkata rejoices in a holiday – great for an evening stroll.

In the 1970s travellers on the hippie trail through Southeast Asia were attracted here by the sea and bhang, legal in Shiva's Puri. There's little trace of that scene today (though the bhang hasn't departed); travellers come just to hang out and recharge their backpacking spirit.

WORTH A TRIP

SATKOSIA GORGE SANCTUARY

This 795-sq-km **Sanctuary** (www.satkosia.org; per day Indian/foreigner ₹20/1000; ☺6am-7pm), 190km west of Bhubaneswar, is part of the larger Satkosia Tiger Reserve, inaugurated in 2007 by combining adjoining Satkosia Gorge and Baisipalli wildlife sanctuaries. The reserve is straddled by the breathtaking gorge, cut by the mighty Mahanadi River, one of the most beautiful natural spots in all of Odisha, if not India. Among its 38 recorded species of mammals, significant populations of Gharial crocodiles, leopards, elephants, sambar, wild dogs, jackals and giant squirrels call the reserve home – and at least 18 tigers.

The main entry gate of the tiger reserve is at Pampasar, 30km southwest of Angul. There are three sets of excellent **forest rest houses** (d ₹550) in the park, but forget about those. Where you want to be is the **Nature Camp** (☎0674-236218; dfosatkosiawl@ yahoo.co.in; tents incl meals ₹1500-2000; ☺1 Nov-31 Mar), perched right on the golden sand beaches of the Mahanadi River at Tikarpada with the gorge as the scenic backdrop. Here the double-bedded tents with toilets and water supply are Odisha's most storybook setting.

The action is along a few kilometres of coast, with the backpacker village clustered around Chakra Tirtha (CT) Rd to the east, busy New Marine Rd to the west and resorts in the middle. A few blocks inland is the holy quarter's chaotic but fascinating jumble of streets.

Dangers & Annoyances

Ocean currents can become treacherous in Puri, and drownings are not uncommon, so don't venture out beyond your depth. Ask one of the *nolias* (fishermen/lifeguards), with their white-painted, cone-shaped wicker hats, for the best spots.

Muggings and attacks on women have been reported along isolated stretches of beach, even during the day, so take care. Young boys may approach foreign men on the beach; Puri has an ongoing problem with paedophiles abusing local youngsters.

◉ Sights

TOP CHOICE **Jagannath Mandir**   HINDU TEMPLE

This mighty temple belongs to Jagannath, Lord of the Universe and incarnation of Vishnu. The jet-black deity with large, round, white eyes is hugely popular across Odisha; figures of Jagannath are tended and regularly dressed in new clothes at shrines across the state. Built in its present form in 1198, the temple (closed to non-Hindus) is surrounded by two walls; its 58m-high *sikhara* (spire) is topped by the flag and wheel of Vishnu.

Guarded by two stone lions and a pillar crowned by the Garuda that once stood at the Sun Temple at Konark, the eastern entrance (Lion Gate) is the passageway for the chariot procession of Rath Yatra.

Jagannath, brother Balbhadra and sister Subhadra reside supreme in the central *jagamohan* (assembly hall). Priests continually garland and dress the three throughout the day for different ceremonies. Incredibly, the temple employs about 6000 men to perform the complicated rituals involved in caring for the gods. An estimated 20,000 people – divided into 36 orders and 97 classes – are dependent on Jagannath for their livelihood.

Non-Hindus can spy from the roof of **Raghunandan Library** (cnr Temple Rd & Swargadwar Rd; ⊙9am-2pm & 4-6pm Mon-Sat) opposite; a 'donation', while not officially compulsory, is expected (₹10 is fine). The library is closed on Sunday, so touts who will help you to a nearby rooftop prey on tourists and demand ₹100 – easily negotiated down to ₹50.

Beach   BEACH

Puri is no palm-fringed paradise – the beach is wide, shelves quickly with a nasty shore break and is shadeless. It could also use a clean-up. But it is the seaside and offers the best beach vibe in Odisha, with dramatic sunsets and a lingering hippie atmosphere.

By New Marine Rd (the 'Indian side' or 'Puri I') the beach is healthier (although still not particularly pleasant for swimming) and often crowded with energetic holidaymakers, especially at night, where there is lots of hangout action on the long esplanade. Be on the look out for artists constructing **sand sculptures**, a local art form. To the east it's a public toilet for the fishing village.

Swargdwar   LANDMARK

(off New Marine Rd; ⊙24hr) These hallowed cremation grounds are the end stop of choice for Eastern India's Hindu population and beyond – some 40 bodies are cremated here daily. Anyone can watch or walk among the open-air ceremonies providing you are behaving in a respectful manner and not taking photos. It's an obviously solemn affair, but a fascinating glimpse into Puri's role as one of India's holiest cities.

⊂⇀ Tours

OTDC (🖉223526; New Marine Rd; ⊙6am-10pm) runs a series of day trips. Tour 1 (AC/non-AC ₹350/250, departs 6.30am Tuesday to Sunday) skips through Konark, Dhauli, Bhubaneswar's temples, Udayagiri and Khandagiri Caves plus Nandankanan Zoo. Tour 2 (AC/non-AC ₹250/150, departs 7am daily) goes for a boat jaunt on Chilika Lake. Various admission fees are additional to the tour cost. Tours begin and end at various points including the Odisha Tourism office and the Chanakya BNR Hotel.

Several tour operators organise tours into Odisha's tribal areas that can include visits to handicraft villages plus Similipal National Park and Bhitarkanika Wildlife Sanctuary. Tribal tours have to be approached cautiously as not all agencies have the necessary local contacts to conduct a responsible tour. For recommended options in Bhubaneswar see p590 and for more details see p605.

Grass Routes Journeys   TRIBAL/CULTURAL

(🖉226642, 9437029698; www.grassroutesjourneys.com; CT Rd; ⊙8am-1pm & 4-9pm) This Australian-Indian agency works from a sustainable philosophy and has its heart in the right place – contacts in the tribal com-

munities, policies about appropriate ways to photograph people and contributions to the welfare of the community are pluses. It also does excellent trips to Chilika Lake and Satkosia Gorge.

Heritage Tours CULTURAL, WILDLIFE
(223656; www.heritagetoursOdisha.com; Mayfair Beach Resort; 8am-8pm) A sustainable tribal and cultural tourism veteran, but also interesting for its **Green Riders** program in which 75 cycle rickshaw drivers are trained weekly in fixed pricing, self-respect and why spiking prices for foreign tourists is uncool. In addition to transport, the program offers a wealth of local cycle-rickshaw tours to fascinating parts of old Puri you would never otherwise see.

★ Festivals

Highlights of the festival-packed year include the celebrated festival of **Rath Yatra**
(p585) and the **Puri Beach Festival** (23–27 November) featuring magnificent sand art, food stalls, traditional dance and other cultural programs.

🛏 Sleeping

For Rath Yatra, Durga Puja (Dussehra), Diwali or the end of December and New Year, book well in advance.

Prices given are for October to February. Significant discounts can be negotiated during the monsoon, while prices can triple during a festival. Many hotels have early checkout times – often 8am. A 10% service charge is frequently levied.

TOP CHOICE **Hotel Gandhara** HOTEL $
(224117; www.hotelgandhara.com; CT Rd; s/d ₹450/550, with AC & breakfast ₹1888/1999; ☀☎@) The Indian-Japanese-owned Gandhara blows away the competition for friendliness, services and value, remarkably outpunching its

Puri

weight class. There's a wide range of bright rooms for different budgets in the white-washed, once-regal building. The rear five-storey block has rooftop AC rooms catching breezes and views and free wi-fi; others are arrayed around a tree-shaded garden with balconies. There's a friendly dog named after an Indian soda, international cable channels, full-on Western breakfast and self-service beer – rare as a porterhouse in Puri!

Chanakya BNR Hotel HOTEL $$
(☎223006; www.therailhotel.com.com; CT Rd; r incl breakfast ₹2500; ❄@) This sprawling historic railway hotel has received a long overdue makeover, catapulting it to one of Puri's most interesting lodging options. Looming archways and wide hallways lead to spacious, hardwood-floored rooms with 2.7m doors and modern furnishings. There are beautiful historic touches throughout, most notably the dark, 90-year-old Lac mural art in the lobby stairwell and restaurant.

Mayfair Beach Resort HOTEL $$$
(☎227800; www.mayfairhotels.com; r incl breakfast from ₹7500; ❄🛜☀) The benchmark for Puri luxury features spacious units nestled in idyllic gardens dotted with carved statues. Its stretch of beach is cleaned and maintained by the resort and a good spot to kick away a day guest or not, and the white-wicker charm of the Verandah deck restaurant (excellent *sarison macha*) makes it a lovely refuelling setting.

Z Hotel HERITAGE HOTEL $
(☎222554; www.zhotelindia.com; CT Rd; dm women only ₹100, s/d without bathroom ₹250/500, d ₹700, with AC ₹1500; ❄) This former maharaja's home has huge, clean, airy rooms, many of them facing the sea, and new ones with AC and excellent bathrooms. Great common areas include a TV room with movies screened nightly. The heritage vibe and traveller's scene here – rare in Odisha – trumps the hospitality, which is nonexistent. Despite its flaws (no toilet paper, no internet, among others), it's one of Puri's most atmospheric choices.

Baywatch Residency HOTEL $
(☎226133; www.baywatchculturalresidency.com; off CT Rd; s/d ₹600/750, with AC ₹1200/1350; ❄) It's pricier and there's no beach creeping under the door, but rupee pinchers seeking sand adjacent will be far happier in this simple abode with huge, big-value rooms that are just clean enough. Non-AC 3rd-floor rooms 301, 302 and 304 are massive, with extra living rooms and small seaview balconies. There's a small temple bellowing right outside most rooms and a 15% discount for anyone working in arts or culture.

Hotel Lee Garden HOTEL $
(☎9040747616, lee_garden@rediffmail.com; VIP Rd; d from ₹650, with AC from ₹1100; ❄@) As was clearly pointed out to us, 90% of the clientele here is West Bengali tourists (hence the 7.30am checkout time, due to train arrivals from there), so perhaps the harsh welcome is explained by a lack of concern for foreign tourism? It's too bad, really. The rooms are spotless and good value, all dangerously too close to the excellent Chinese restaurant, **Chung Wah**, which tastes a lot better than the reception.

Hotel Lotus HOTEL $
(☎227033; CT Rd; d/q from ₹300/450, with AC ₹950; ❄) A range of inexpensive rooms that are clean and comfortable. The non-AC rooms are some of the best value for

ODISHA PURI

money in Puri, though the front rooms may suffer a bit of street noise.

✕ Eating

There's excellent fresh seafood to be enjoyed almost anywhere in Puri, and in CT Rd homesick travellers can find muesli and pancakes. Low-season opening times can be a bit random.

TOP CHOICE Chung Wah INDO-CHINESE **$$**
(VIP Rd; mains ₹110-180; ☺lunch & dinner) The real thing courtesy of a Chinese family transplanted from Kolkata 40 years ago. Chung Wah's menu is loaded down with spicy Szechwan dishes that bite back. Try the excellent hot garlic chicken, Szechwan prawns or go fusion: Kung Pao *paneer,* which has a much catchier ring to it than Kung Pao Chicken. It's great by any standard, but if you've been on the all-Indian diet for any length of time, it's salvation.

Honey Bee Bakery & Pizzeria ITALIAN CAFE **$$**
(CT Rd; set breakfast ₹110-150, mains ₹60-270; ☺8.30am-2pm & 6-10pm) Decent pizzas and pancakes, filtered coffee and espresso, toasted sandwiches and fry-up brekkies (including bacon!) – all the comforts of home are here. It's Puri's tried and true traveller hang-out.

Aero Dine INDIAN/MULTICUISINE **$$**
(Hotel Shakti International, VIP Rd; mains ₹90-300) Is this the mess hall on the Starship Enterprise? This very surprising place will throw your holidays for a loop with its white modular furniture, random flashing lights and monitors, and overall space-age decor. The menu brings you back down to earth a little with great Indian, Chinese and Continental standards, along with a few wildcards like Cajun chicken and crêpes Suzette.

Wildgrass Restaurant INDIAN **$$**
(VIP Rd; mains ₹60-150; ☺lunch & dinner) With mismatched sculptures and precarious tree huts scattered through its grounds, Wildgrass is a secret garden gone wild. The Indian and Continental menu is enlivened with good-value seafood dishes and Odishan specialties.

Grand INDIAN **$$**
(Grand Rd; mains ₹55-110) This pure veg monstrosity has good grub and snacks throughout the day – the *bhindi chatpati* (okra) and *gobi Hyderabadi* (cauliflower) are both commendable, but it's more notable for its open-air terrace, from which there are striking views of Jagannath Mandir and the hubbub of Grand Rd below. From the temple, it's 100m down Grand Rd.

Peace Restaurant INDIAN **$$**
(CT Rd; mains ₹40-180) 'World famous in Puri but never heard of anywhere else.' So reads the menu, which features curries, macaroni, the best muesli in town (₹70) and tasty fish dishes.

Dakshin SOUTH INDIAN **$**
(CT Rd; dosas ₹25-35, thali ₹50) Standing out in CT Rd's string of ageing sand-floor banana-pancake joints, this clean place has a simple menu of well-prepared South Indian dishes. Thalis and *masala dosas* are outstanding.

Pink House Restaurant INDIAN/SEAFOOD **$$**
(off CT Rd; mains ₹60-130) Solid seafood on the sands – like night and day compared to the hotel.

🔒 Shopping

Shops along New Marine Rd sell fabric, beads, shells, saris and bamboo work, while shops on CT Rd sell typical all-India trinkets.

Near Jagannath Mandir, many places sell Jagannath images, palm-leaf paintings, handicrafts and Odishan hand-woven *ikat,* which you can buy in lengths or as ready-made garments.

DON'T MISS

PURIFECTLY SWEET

The narrow lanes of Puri's holy quarter are full of makeshift sweet shops, perhaps none more famous than **Puri Cheesecake** (Dolamandap Sahi, Temple Rd). Bikram Sahoo and his six brothers have been churning out this unique Puri delight for 45 years. It's cottage cheese, sugar and cardamom cooked in an iron pan over an open flame. Though it's more like a flan than traditional cheesecake, it's off the mark by name only. A real treat and just ₹15 per piece. To find it, walk down Temple Rd from Jagganath Mandir and it's about 400m on your right.

A couple of general grocery stores on CT Rd (mainly around the Hotel Lotus) stock a good range of toiletries that might be hard to find elsewhere in Odisha, eg women's deodorant.

❶ Information

The main traveller-hotel stretch of CT Rd is a zoo of travel agents and moneychangers. Internet places have sprung up here; most charge ₹20 per hour. As well as a convenient branch in CT Rd, the State Bank of India has a number of reliable MasterCard and Visa ATMs around town.

Gandhara International (☏2224623; www .hotelgandhara.com; Hotel Gandhara, CT Rd; ☺8am-7pm Mon-Fri, 8am-1pm Sun) Travel agency.

Headquarters Hospital (☏223742; Grand Rd)

ICICI Bank (Grand Rd; ☺8am-8pm) Master-Card and Visa ATM; does foreign exchange but not travellers cheques.

Odisha Tourism CT Rd (☏222664; CT Rd; ☺10am-5pm Mon-Sat; train station ☺6am-10pm) Tourist information, hotel, vehicle and tour booking, and a convenient start/finish point for day tours, though not particularly friendly.

Police Station Seabeach (☏222025; CT Rd); Town (☏222039; Grand Rd)

Post office (cnr Kutchery & Temple Rd; ☺10am-6pm Mon-Sat)

Samikshya Forex (CT Rd; ☺9am-10pm) Cashes travellers cheques and foreign currencies.

Swapu (VIP Rd) Probably Odisha's nicest pharmacy.

❶ Getting There & Away

Bus

From the sprawling bus station near Gundicha Mandir, frequent buses serve Konark (₹17, one hour), Satapada (₹25, three hours), Bhubaneswar (₹32, two hours) and Kolkata (₹260 to ₹775, 12 hours). For Pipli and Raghurajpur, take the Bhubaneswar bus. For other destinations change at Bhubaneswar.

Train

Book well ahead if travelling during holiday and festival times. The booking counter at the train station can become incredibly crowded, but CT Rd agencies will book tickets for a small fee.

The 12801 *Purushottam Express* travels to Delhi (sleeper/3AC/2AC ₹493/1330/1822, 32 hours, 9.50pm), while Howrah can be reached on the 12838 *Puri-Howrah Express* (sleeper/3AC/2AC/1AC ₹244/631/852/1416, nine hours, 8.05pm) and the 18410 *Sri Jagannath Express* (sleeper/3AC/2AC ₹224/601/822, 10 hours, 10.50pm), both also stop in Balisore for access to Similipal National

Park. The 12875 *Neelachal Express* goes to Varanasi (sleeper/3AC/2AC ₹371/988/1348, 21 hours, 10.55am), continuing to Delhi, on Tuesday, Friday and Sunday. To Sambalpur, the 18304 *Puri-Sambalpur Express* (2nd class/chair ₹97/343, six hours, 3.45pm), runs daily. For Gopalpur-on-Sea, the 17479 *Puri-Tirupati Express* departs at 1pm (sleeper/3AC ₹120/301, five hours) daily except Tuesday and Saturday to Berhampur.

❶ Getting Around

A few places along CT Rd (mainly around the Hotel Lotus) rent bicycles from ₹40 per day, and mopeds and motorcycles for ₹150 to ₹300. From CT Rd, cycle-rickshaws charge about ₹40 to the train station, bus station or Jagannath Mandir. Look for the appropriately attired Green Riders (p596) for no-hassle pricing.

Raghurajpur

The fascinating artists' village of Raghurajpur, 14km north of Puri, is two streets and 120 thatched brick houses adorned with murals of geometric patterns and mythological scenes – a traditional art form that has almost died out in Odisha.

The village is most famous for its *patachitra* – work made using cloth coated with a mixture of gum and chalk made from tamarind seeds and then polished. With eye-aching attention and a very fine brush, artists mark out animals, flowers, gods and demons, which are then illuminated with bright colours. It makes for very beautiful and unique souvenirs.

Take the Bhubaneswar bus and look for the 'Raghurajpur The Craft Village' signpost 11km north of Puri, then walk the last 1km (don't get cornered by the few shops that have set up first but technically outside the village itself).

Konark

☏06758 / POP 15,020

The iconic Sun Temple at Konark – a Unesco World Heritage Site – is one of India's signature buildings and Odisha's raison d'être. Most visitors are day-trippers from Bhubaneswar or Puri, but a new beach 'resort' nearby in Ramchandi Beach should tempt more travellers to sleep over. After all, the temple is most majestic at dawn.

Originally nearer the coast (the sea has receded 3km), Konark was visible from far out at sea and known as the 'Black Pagoda' by sailors, in contrast to Puri's whitewashed Jagannath. The inland lighthouse near Chandrabhaga Beach is odd testament to that fact.

⊙ Sights

Archaeological Museum   MUSEUM
(admission ₹10; ⊘8am-5pm) This interesting (and refreshingly cool and quiet) museum, just west of Yatri Nivas, contains many impressive sculptures and carvings found during excavations of the Sun Temple.

Chandrabhaga Beach   BEACH
The local beach at Chandrabhaga is 3km from the temple down the Puri road. Walk, cycle or take an autorickshaw (₹60 return), or use the Konark–Puri bus. The beach is quieter and cleaner than Puri's, but beware of strong currents; there have also been reports of thefts on the beach. To the east is a fishing village with plenty of boating activity at sunrise.

★ Festivals & Events

The **Konark Festival**, steeped in traditional music and dance, takes place every December with the gorgeous Sun Temple as a backdrop.

⌑ Sleeping & Eating

TOP
CHOICE **Lotus Eco Village**   HOTEL $$$
(🖉236161; www.lotusresorthotels.com; Puri-Konark Marine Drive; villas/cottages incl breakfast from ₹5500/7500; ✸) About 7km from the Sun Temple on pretty Ramchandi Beach, this new collection of rustic Canadian pine cottages is Konark's only beach 'resort'. It's in a beautiful spot across a calm and swimmable islet catering to a few local fisherman and not much else; villas are surprisingly stylish inside and amenities include a small Ayurvedic spa, a nice sandside restaurant (mains ₹50 to ₹200) and an organic vegetable garden.

DON'T MISS

SUN TEMPLE

The massive **Sun Temple** (Indian/foreigner ₹10/250, video ₹25, guide per hr ₹100; ⊘dawn-8pm) was constructed in the mid-13th century, probably by Odishan king Narashimhadev I to celebrate his military victory over the Muslims, and was in use for maybe only three centuries. In the late 16th century the 40m-high *sikhara* (spire) partially collapsed: speculation about causes ranges from marauding Mughals removing the copper over the cupola to a ransacking Kalapahad displacing the Dadhinauti (arch stone), to simple wear and tear from recurring cyclones – the truth was apparently lost with Konark's receding shoreline. The entire temple was conceived as the cosmic chariot of the sun god Surya. Seven mighty prancing horses (representing the days of the week) rear at the strain of moving this stone leviathan on 24 stone cartwheels (representing the hours of the day) that stand around the base. The temple was positioned so that dawn light would illuminate the *deul* (temple sanctuary) interior and the presiding deity, which may have been moved to Jagannath Mandir in Puri in the 17th century.

The **gajasimha** (main entrance) is guarded by two stone lions crushing elephants and leads to the intricately carved **nritya mandapa** (dancing hall). Steps, flanked by straining horses, rise to the still-standing **jagamohan**. Behind is the spireless **deul**, with its three impressive chlorite images of Surya aligned to catch the sun at dawn, noon and sunset.

The base and walls present a chronicle in stone of Kalinga life; you'll see women cooking and men hunting. Many are in the erotic style for which Konark is famous and include entwined couples as well as solitary exhibitionists.

Around the grounds are a small shrine called **Mayadevi Mandir**; a deep, covered **well**; and the ruins of a **brick temple**. To the north are a couple of **elephant statues**, to the south a couple of **horse statues**, both trampling soldiers.

If there's anywhere worth hiring a guide, it's here. The temple's history is a complicated amalgam of fact and legend, and religious and secular imagery, and the guides' explanations are thought-provoking. They'll also show you features you might otherwise overlook – the woman with Japanese sandals, a giraffe (proving this area once traded with Africa) and even a man treating himself for venereal disease! Be sure your guide is registered. There are only 29 registered guides in Konark, listed on the name board by the entrance.

Labanya Lodge HOTEL $

(☎9937073559; labanyalodge1@rediffmail.com; Sea Beach Rd; s ₹100-150, d ₹350-750, r with AC ₹850; ✹@) The best budget choice, this friendly place has a garden and a fresh co-conut drink to welcome guests. The bright-coloured rooms come in different sizes, and there's a rooftop terrace. This is the only internet facility (per hour ₹60) in town and there's bike hire (per day ₹25).

Yatri Nivas HOTEL $

(☎236820; yatrinivaskonark.das@gmail.com; d from ₹450, with AC from ₹750; ✹@) A little slap of fresh paint could do wonders for this OTDC hotel, set in a large, well-manicured garden next to the museum. Cheaper rooms are clean but unremarkable while deluxe rooms are nicer but not worth double the rupees.

Suntemple Hotel INDIAN $$

(mains ₹40-180) A busy, friendly place with a big range of Indian veg and non-veg dishes, including recommended seafood dishes. It also takes a decent stab at traveller favourites like chips and banana pancakes.

❶ Information

The road from Bhubaneswar swings around the temple and past a couple of hotels and eateries before continuing to meet the coastal road to Puri. To the north and east of the temple is the **post office** (◷10am-5pm Mon-Sat), a State Bank of India ATM, the bus station and numerous souvenir shops. The **tourist office** (☎236821; Yatrinivas hotel; ◷10am) can line up a registered guide to meet you at the temple.

❶ Getting There & Away

Overcrowded minibuses regularly run along the coastal road between Puri and Konark (₹17, one hour). There are also regular departures to Bhubaneswar (₹40, two hours). Konark is included in OTDC tours from Bhubaneswar and Puri. An autorickshaw will take you to Puri, with a beach stop along the way, with negotiations usually beginning around ₹350 depending on the season. Because the road is flat, some diehards even cycle the 36km from Puri.

Chilika Lake

Chilika Lake is Asia's largest brackish lagoon. Swelling from 600 sq km in April/May to 1100 sq km in the monsoon, the shallow lake is separated from the Bay of Bengal by a 60km-long sand bar called Rajhansa.

The lake is noted for the million-plus migratory birds – including grey-legged geese, herons, cranes and pink flamingos – that flock here in winter (from November to mid-January) from as far away as Siberia and Iran and concentrate in a 3-sq-km area within the bird sanctuary on Nalabana Island.

Other attractions are rare Irrawaddy dolphins near Satapada, the pristine beach along Rajhansa, and Kalijai Island temple where Hindu pilgrims flock for the Makar Mela festival in January.

SATAPADA
☎06752

This small village, on a headland jutting southwestwards into the lake, is the starting point for most boat trips. There's an **Odisha Tourism office** (☎262077; Yatri Nivas hotel) here.

Boat trips from Satapada usually cruise towards the new sea mouth for a paddle in the sea and some dolphin and bird-spotting en route. Travellers have reported dolphins being (illegally) herded and otherwise harassed; make it clear you don't want this.

OTDC (☎262077; Yatri Nivas hotel) has boats for hire (for large groups) or a three-hour tour (per person ₹100) at 10.30am, with another at 2pm if demand warrants.

Dolphin Motor Boat Association (☎9090881551; Satapada jetty; 1-8hr trips per boat ₹600-1800), a cooperative of local boat owners, has set-price trips mixing in dolphin sightseeing, Nalabana Bird Sanctuary and Kalijai Island temple.

Chilika Visitor Centre (admission ₹10; ◷10am-5pm) is an exhibition on the lake, its wildlife and its human inhabitants. The centre has an upstairs observatory with a telescope and bird identification charts.

A regular ferry (₹15, three hours) plies between Satapada and Balugaon just north of Barkul, departing at 1pm and returning at 7am the next day. Travel agents lining CT Rd in Puri can organise return trips on crowded buses for around ₹150, but four or more will be far more comfortable in a taxi (₹650), including about four hours in Satapada where you can organise your own boat.

Yatri Nivas (☎262077; d ₹460, with AC ₹1150; ✹) is typically rundown but perhaps the most architecturally interesting of the government-run hotels, with its elevated walkways. The best rooms have balconies with lake views. The restaurant (mains ₹20 to ₹100) has a small selection of standard Indian fare and a couple of seafood dishes.

Several shops and food stalls line the road to the jetty. Don't forget to take water on your boat trip.

BARKUL
☑06756

On the northern shore of Chilika, Barkul is just a scatter of houses, basic 'lodges' and food stalls on a lane off NH5. From here boats go to Nalabana and Kalijai Island. Nalabana is best visited in early morning and late afternoon, November to late February.

With a minimum of seven people, the **OTDC** (Panthanivas Barkul) runs tours to Kalijia (₹50), and Nalabana and Kalijia (₹150). Otherwise, a boat with a quiet engine (that doesn't scare birds) can be hired from ₹450 to ₹1600 per hour. Private boat owners (with no insurance and often no safety gear) charge around ₹450 an hour; a recommended operator is fisherman **Babu Behera** (☑9937226378).

Panthanivas Barkul (☑220488; r ₹750, with AC ₹1700; ❋@) has a great setting, with comfortable rooms overlooking the garden to the lake. Newer cottages are clean and inviting, with lake views, but the most interesting option is the new houseboat, where an overnight stay, food and a two-hour cruise goes for ₹5500 (double occupancy).

Frequent buses dash along NH5 between Bhubaneswar (₹45) and Berhampur (₹30). You can get off anywhere en route.

A ferry (₹15) goes to Satapada at 7am from Balugaon, a couple of kilometres north of Barkul – autos and taxis whiz up and down the route.

RAMBHA
☑06810

The small town of Rambha is the nearest place to stay for turtle watching on Rushikulya beach. Not as commercial as Barkul, Rambha is a very pleasant little backwater.

Panthanivas Rambha (☑278346; dm ₹180, d ₹650, d/d cottage with AC ₹1200/2400; ❋), about 200m off the main road, and 1km west of Rambha centre, looks a tad battered outside but has fine rooms (the AC rooms are better) with big clean bathrooms and balconies overlooking the lake. Newer cottages hog the charm and views, and all beds have mozzie nets. The restaurant (mains ₹30 to ₹100) is very good, especially the seafood. One-hour speedboat or three-hour motor boat tours of the lake are ₹1500.

There are regular bus services to/from Bhubaneswar (₹100) and Berhampur (₹20).

Gopalpur-On-Sea
☑0680 / POP 6660

If you dig nosing about crumbling seaside resorts, Gopalpur-on-Sea, a seaside town the British left to slide into history until Bengali holidaymakers rediscovered its attractions in the 1980s, is your bygone living museum on the ocean. Prior to this, it had a noble history as a seaport with connections to Southeast Asia, the evidence of which is still scattered through the town in the form of romantically deteriorating old buildings.

It's no paradise, but the peaceful and relatively clean beach is great for a stroll and it's oddly charismatic in its own strange, antiquated way. People often tack on a few days here.

Swimming in the nasty shore break at Gopalpur, where there are undercurrents, is dodgy, but it doesn't stop locals.

◉ Sights

Lighthouse   LANDMARK
(Indian/foreigner/child ₹10/25/3, camera ₹20; ⊙3.30-5.30pm) Peering over the town is the lighthouse, with its immaculate gardens and petite staff cottages. It's a late-afternoon draw card and after puffing up the spiral staircase you're rewarded with expansive views and welcome cooling breezes.

⌂ Sleeping & Eating

Gopalpur-on-Sea can be booked out during holiday and festival time. Prices here are for

---

WORTH A TRIP

MANGALAJODI

On Chilika's north shore, 60km northwest of Bhubaneswar, is this haven for resident and migratory birds, an ecotourism success story virtually unknown to the outside world until 2006. Six years prior, Sir Naiver Pikas Sargasso started Wild Oriss, a waterfowl safeguard committee that began the arduous process of converting bird poachers into protectors ...and now ecotourism guides. In just a decade, the waterfowl population has climbed from 5000 to an estimated 40,000, spread among some 160 species. It's all best viewed on a sunrise canoe ride in winter, when tepid sunlight illuminates the waters and the cackle of various species of ducks provides the only soundtrack.

One of the smallest sea turtles and a threatened species, the olive ridley marine turtle swims up from deeper waters beyond Sri Lanka to mate and lay eggs on Odisha's beaches. The main nesting sites are Gahirmatha (Bhitarkanika National Park), Devi near Konark and Rushikulya.

Turtle deaths due to fishing practices are unfortunately common. Although there are regulations, such as requiring the use of turtle exclusion devices (TEDs) on nets and banning fishing from certain areas, these laws are routinely flouted in Odisha.

Casuarina trees have been planted to help preserve Devi beach but they occupy areas of soft sand that are necessary for a turtle hatchery. Other potential threats include nearby port developments and oil exploration.

In January and February the turtles congregate near nesting beaches and, if conditions are right, come ashore. If conditions aren't right, they reabsorb their eggs and leave without nesting.

Hatchlings emerge 50 to 55 days later and are guided to the sea by the luminescence of the ocean and stars. They can be easily distracted by bright lights; unfortunately NH5 runs within 2km of Rushikulya beach. Members of local turtle clubs in the Sea Turtle Protection Committee gather up disoriented turtles and take them to the sea.

The best place to see nesting and hatching is on the northern side of Rushikulya River, near the villages of Purunabandh and Gokharkuda, 20km from the nearest accommodation in Rambha. During nesting and hatching, activity takes place throughout the night: don't use lights.

Ask staff at Panthanivas Rambha (p602) what conditions are like, or contact the **Wildlife Society of Odisha** (☏0674-2311513; www.wildlifeOdisha.org; A320, Sahid Nagar, Bhubaneswar). Rickshaws between Rambha and Rushikulya cost ₹250 return if you stay an hour or two, ₹500 for the whole day.

the high season (November to January); discounts are available at other times.

Hotel Sea Pearl HOTEL **$**
(☏2242556; d ₹650-850, with AC ₹1150-1500; ❄) Any nearer the sea and it'd be in it; the big and popular Sea Pearl has some great rooms, especially the upper-storey, beach-facing, non-AC rooms, and a little private entrance to the beach. Look at a few rooms; price doesn't necessarily reflect quality here. There is a standard Indian-Chinese restaurant (mains ₹50 to ₹120).

Hotel Green Park HOTEL **$**
(☏2243716; greenpark016@yahoo.com; d from ₹330, with AC ₹770; ❄) One street back from the beach, Green Park is a clean, friendly and good-value option. Some rooms have front-facing balconies and there's 24-hour checkout.

Swosti Palm Resort HOTEL **$$$**
(☏2243718; www.swosti.com; Main Rd; s/d ₹2600/3200; ❄@) Further back, and an unfortunate walk past a rubbish tip, the Swosti has the best accommodation in town with comfortable, well-appointed rooms. The excellent multicuisine restaurant, Lighthouse, serves good seafood including authentic local dishes (mains ₹110 to ₹220) – and the cosy bar is the town's one-man show, with an unusually varied selection of Indian beers.

Krishna's INDIAN, CHINESE **$**
(mains ₹10-70) Mainly Indian and Chinese standards (nicely executed) and excellent *kati rolls* (p465). In the quiet season, if you ask, the kitchen can produce good pancakes, pasta and fried calamari or fish and chips. Expect to pay ₹100 and up, though, for some of the seafood. On our visit, the 'chef' was 17 years old, part of the super-friendly owner's plan to give less fortunate youth a marketable skill.

ⓘ Getting There & Away

Frequent, crowded minibuses travel to Berhampur (₹10, one hour), where you can catch onward transport by rail or bus. Alternatively, an autorickshaw will cost you about ₹150.

WESTERN ODISHA

Although permits are no longer necessary, foreigners venturing into the tribal areas independently with plans to camp should register their details with the police in the nearest city as a safety precaution. This is all done for you if you are on a tour or by your hotel otherwise.

Rayagada

📞06856

Big and gritty Rayagada is the base for visiting the weekly Wednesday **Chatikona market** at Bissamcuttack (about 40km north). Here, highly ornamented Dongria Kondh and Desia Kondh villagers from the surrounding Niayamgiri Hills bring their produce and wares to sell. Alongside piles of chillies and dried fish are bronze animal sculptures made locally using the lost wax method.

The new **Hotel Raj** (📞222270; Main Rd; dm 12/24hr ₹100/200, s ₹300-400, d ₹350-450, with AC ₹575/700; ❈) is notable for its rare (though close-quarters) dorm; cheap, well-maintained rooms and restaurant and sweet shop. At the friendly **Hotel Rajbhavan** (📞223777; Main Rd; r from ₹600, with AC from ₹1100; ❈), stick to higher category rooms. There's a good multicuisine restaurant (mains ₹50 to ₹140). Both are just across the main road from the train station. **Hotel Sai International** (📞225554; JK Rd; s/d ₹600/700, with AC from ₹1100/1200; ❈) is marginally the most comfortable and has a great multicuisine restaurant (mains ₹50 to ₹165).

There are three early morning local buses to Chatikona (₹20, two hours, 5.30am, 6.30am and 8am); as well as Jeypore (₹60 to ₹80, five hours) and Bhubaneswar (₹280, 12 hours). The 8447 *Hirakhand Express* leaves Bhubaneswar daily at 7.35pm and reaches Rayagada at 4.50am on its way to Koraput.

Jeypore

📞06854 / POP 77,000

Jeypore is the traditional though least interesting base for visiting the amazingly colourful Onkadelli market. There is little reason to choose here over Koraput other than the 22km head start to Onkadelli. Modern, two-star side-by-side sister hotels **Hotel Mani Krishna** (📞321139; manikrishna_hotels@yahoo.com; MG Rd; s/d ₹595/695, with AC from ₹895/995; ❈) and **Hotel Sai Krishna** (📞230253; www.hotelsaikrishna.com; MG Rd; s/d ₹595/695, with AC from ₹1295/1495; ❈) offer spotless rooms, international cable and room service (at Mani) and a great Indian restaurant (at Sai). **Hello Jeypore** (📞231127; www.hoteljeypore.com; NH Rd; s/d incl breakfast

from ₹795/995, with AC ₹995/1195; ❈📶❈) is the most comfortable. Freshly made-over rooms are shockingly boutique, including a few all-white minimalist retreats.

From the main bus station there are frequent buses to Koraput (₹15, one hour); others go to Berhampur (₹235 to ₹260, 12 hours), Bhubaneswar (₹360, 12 to 16 hours) and Rayagada (₹84, five hours).

To reach Onkadelli (₹35, three hours) there are three morning buses, at 7am from the bus station, and 9am and 11.30am from the Ghoroi Bus Union's office on Byepass Rd.

Koraput

📞06852

Koraput is just a few kilometres from Jeypore and is a far more interesting base for visits to Onkadelli. The temple is fascinating, especially for non-Hindus who couldn't enter the Jagannath temple in Puri.

The **tourist office** (📞250318; Jeypore Rd; ☉10am-9pm, closed 2nd Sat of month) has information and can arrange car hire. It's housed in the stuck-in-limbo Panthanivas Koraput, which may never open.

The **Jagannath temple** has an exhibition of gods of the different states of India. There's also a selection of local forms of *ossa* (also known as *rangoli*), traditional patterns made with white and coloured powders on doorsteps. At the back of the temple is a series of apses containing statuettes of Jagannath in his various guises and costumes.

The brand-spanking-new **Raj Residency** (📞251591; www.hotelrajresidency.com; Post Office Rd; s/d ₹450/650, with AC from ₹750/950; ❈📶) is the best digs in town, offering modern rooms with plasma TVs, exceptionally friendly service and – brace yourself – *free* wi-fi. Chicken *tikka butter masala* at the dimly lit Indian-Chinese restaurant (mains ₹25 to ₹120) was the best hotel meal we had in Western Odisha.

The temple operates three budget hotels just outside its grounds. **Atithi Bhaban** (📞250610; atithibhaban@gmail.com; d ₹250, with AC ₹500; ❈) is the older building, with a pure veg restaurant and simple rooms. **Atithi Nivas** (s ₹150) is singles only, but solo travellers are better off springing for a much nicer double at Atithi Bhaban. **Yatri Nivas** (📞9337622798; d ₹175) has distinctly basic crashpads.

The 18447/8 *Hirakhand Express* plies daily between Bhubaneswar and Koraput. There are regular buses to Jeypore (₹12 to

Sixty-two tribal (Adivasi) groups live in an area that encompasses Odisha, Chhattisgarh and Andhra Pradesh. In Odisha they account for one-quarter of the state's population and mostly inhabit the jungles and hilly regions of the centre and southwest. Their distinctive cultures are expressed in music, dance and arts.

Most Adivasis were originally animists but over the last 30 years have been targeted (with varying degrees of success and cultural sensitivity) by Christian missionaries, Hindu activists and government development agencies. Naxalites (members of an ultra-leftist political movement) have used Adivasis as foot soldiers while claiming to defend them.

Visits are possible to some villages and *haats* (village markets) that Adivasis attend. There are arguments regarding the morality of visiting Adivasi areas. At the *haats* you are free to interact with and buy directly from the villagers but tourism still brings very little income to the tribes.

Of the more populous tribes, the **Kondh** number about one million and are based around Koraput in the southwest, Rayagada and the Kandhamel District in the central west. The 500,000-plus **Santal** live around Baripada and Khiching in the far north. The 300,000 **Saura** live near Gunupur near the border with Andhra Pradesh. The **Bonda**, known as the 'Naked People' for wearing minimal clothing but incredibly colourful and intricate accessories, have a population of about 5000 and live in the hills near Koraput.

Important reasons to visit these areas on an organised tour:

» Some tribal areas are hard to find and not accessible by public transport.

» Adivasis often speak little Hindi or Odia, and usually no English.

» Various cultural issues could affect your visit: the Dongria Kondh don't welcome strangers due to sensitive mining issues; alcohol sometimes makes the Bonda violent.

» Some tour operators have developed longstanding relationships with the tribes, providing a level of interaction, experience and welcome not otherwise possible.

Some operators are more sensitive to the issues than others; ask about the size of your group and attitudes to photography, and try to get a feel for how interactions will be handled. Communal violence can flare up; tourists haven't been targeted but a good operator should be honest about and avoid areas experiencing trouble. Try to meet the guide who will travel with you, not just the boss in the office. See p595 and p590 for recommended agencies.

₹15, 45 minutes) and less frequent service to Sambalpur (₹280, 14 hours) and Bhubaneswar (non-AC/AC ₹330/440, 12 hours).

Onkadelli

This small village, 65km from Jeypore, has a most remarkable and vibrant Thursday **market** (best time 10am to 1pm) that throngs with Bonda, Gadaba, Mali and Didai villagers. In the morning, it's all business on the vegetable side; in the afternoon, the alcohol market revs up, and entire families get sloshed – *including* infants.

The market is popular with tour groups. Discreet photographs can be taken without issue, but if you're blatant or expect someone to pose for you, consent should be sought and will often come with a request for ₹10 or more; carry small-denomination notes and stick to the women – men have been known to throw stones at photographers. Souvenir shopping is pretty much limited to jewellery sold by Bonda women.

Onkadelli is best accessed by hire car and should only be visited with a professional guide. You'll get much more out of the experience with a guide, who will usually be able to take you to visit craftspeople, not to mention keep the peace if things get ugly among the alcohol and the bows and arrows. This doesn't mean you have to come all the way from Bhubaneswar or Puri with a group or guide – it's feasible to come to Jeypore or Koraput independently and organise a guide at your hotel.

CHANDORI SAI

Some 50km northeast of Koraput in the tiny Adivasis village of Goudaguda, you'll find this Australian-run **guesthouse** (☑9443342241; www.chandoorisai.com; s/d incl meals 4000/5000; @), Odisha's most stylish rural accommodation bar none. Built from the ground up by the hands of some 60 Poraja tribal men and women, it's a sustainable earthen-walled refuge with beautiful terracotta flooring and bamboo-sheeted ceilings. The main lobby is dressed up with colourful hanging saris and the pottery, a speciality of the village, is present throughout. Guests interact with tribal women, who act as cultural ambassadors on property and guides through the village. It's about as close as you can get to a brief assimilation into the vibrant Adivasis way of life. The owner is a hard-driving ex–oil man, who runs the hospitality on a tight leash.

To reach Chandori Sai, catch the 18447 *Hirakhand Express* towards Koraput and get off at Kakirigumma, a 7.37am arrival. The guesthouse will pick you up from there.

Sambalpur

☑0663 / POP 154,170

Sambalpur is the centre for the textile industry spread over western Odisha, and Gole Bazaar is the place to buy *ikat* or *sambalpuri* weaving. The town is a base for nearby Debrigarh Wildlife Sanctuary on the edge of Hirakud Dam. NH6 passes through Sambalpur to become VSS Marg. Laxmi Talkies Rd crosses VSS Marg and leads down to the government bus stand and Gole Bazaar.

Odisha Tourism (☑2411118; Panthanivas Sambalpur, Brooks Hill; ☺10am-5pm Mon-Sat, closed 2nd Sat of month) can provide information on Debrigarh.

The lobby of all-AC **Hotel Uphar Palace Hotel** (☑2400519; VSS Marg; s ₹995-1095, d ₹1095-1195; ✲) needs dusting, but rooms are in pretty good shape and are good value compared to Sheela. The Sharda restaurant has an Indian and Chinese menu (mains ₹20 to ₹215). The nicest – though not by much – is **Sheela Towers** (☑2403111; www.sheelatowers.com; VSS Marg; s/d from ₹995/1095; ✲@☎), with a range of comfortable rooms. The modern art deco restaurant (mains ₹50 to ₹185) does Indian, Chinese and Continental. The **New Hong Kong Restaurant** (VSS Marg; mains ₹45-220; ☺lunch & dinner Tue-Sun) draws in crowds from far and wide, anxious to get down some authentic Chinese cuisine in a sea of curry. The Chen family has been at it for two decades.

The government bus stand has buses running to Jeypore (₹260, 12 hours), Koraput (₹275, 13 hours) and Berhampur (₹162, 12 hours). Travel agencies on Modipada Rd between the government bus station and Laxmi Talkies Rd book (usually more comfortable) buses that leave from the private Ainthapali bus stand, 3km from the city centre (₹20 by cycle-rickshaw) during the day (night buses leave from in front of the agency counters). Several buses go to Bhubaneswar (₹205 to ₹260), Raipur (₹180, eight hours) and Jashipur for Similipal (₹190, seven hours).

The 18451 *Tapaswini Express* goes to Puri (sleeper/3AC/2AC ₹176/463/632, nine hours, 10.40pm) via Bhubaneswar (₹158/413/563, seven hours). The 18006 *Koraput-Howrah Express* goes to Howrah (₹239/643/881, 10 hours, 6.15pm).

Debrigarh Wildlife Sanctuary

The 347-sq-km **Debrigarh Wildlife Sanctuary** (www.debrigarh.org; per day Indian/foreigner ₹20/1000; ☺6am-6pm 15 Nov-15 Jun), 40km from Sambalpur, is an easy day out. Mainly dry deciduous forest blankets the Barapahad Hills down to the shores of the vast Hirakud reservoir, a home for migratory birds in winter. Wildlife here includes deer, antelopes, sloth bears, langur monkeys and the ever-elusive tigers and leopards.

Access to the sanctuary usually requires a 4WD, which can be arranged through Odisha Tourism, a private tour agency, or your hotel in Sambalpur for about ₹1700 for a full day.

NORTHEASTERN ODISHA

Similipal National Park

☑06792

The 2750-sq-km **Similipal National Park** (www.similipal.org; per day Indian/foreigner ₹40/1000, camera per 3 days ₹50/100; ☺6am-noon day visitor, to 2pm 15 Nov-15 Jun with accommodation reservation) is Odisha's prime wildlife sanctuary.

The scenery is remarkable: a massif of prominent hills creased by valleys and gorges, made dramatic by plunging waterfalls, including the spectacular 400m-high **Barheipani Waterfall** and the 150m-high **Joranda Waterfall**. The jungle is an atmospheric mix of dense sal forest and rolling open savannah. The core area is only 850 sq km and much of the southern part is closed to visitors.

There's a huge range of reptile, bird and mammal species. The tigers aren't tracked and sightings are extremely rare – the best chance to spot them will be at the **Joranda salt lick**. What you're more likely to see is a wild elephant (there are over 400 in the park), most probably at the **Chahala salt lick**. The best time to visit is early in the season before high visitor numbers affect animal behaviour.

There are two entrances, **Tulsibani**, 15km from Jashipur, on the northwestern side, and **Pithabata**, near Lulung, 25km west of Baripada. Options are a day visit or an overnight stay within the park. Overnight accommodation needs to be booked 30 days in advance, and remember you'll have to pay the ₹1000 entry fee for both days you're here.

Entry permits can be obtained in advance from the **assistant conservator of forests** (☑06797-232474; National Park, Jashipur, Mayurbhanj District), or the **field director, Similipal Tiger Reserve Project** (☑06792-252593; Bhanjpur, Baripada, Mayurbhanj District).

Visitors either come on an organised tour or charter a vehicle in Jashipur (₹1500 per day for 4WD) or Baripada (₹2500); the latter is pricier but you will see more of the park. Hiring a guide (around ₹500 in Jashipur, ₹800 in Baripada) is advisable.

If you want to avoid the hassles of arranging permits, transport, food and accommodation, an organised tour from Bhubaneswar, Puri or Baripada is the answer. **Forest Department bungalows** (d Indian/foreigner from ₹600/800) has six sets of bungalows; Chahala, Joranda and Newana are best for animal spottings and Barheipani for views. The very basic accommodation has to be booked well in advance with the field director at Baripada. You have to bring your own food (no meat or alcohol allowed) and water.

In March 2009 Maoist rebels (or the timber mafia, depending on who you believe) blew up three forest offices inside the park and raided the Chahala bungalow, robbing tourists who were staying there. The park was closed as a result and reopened for the 2011 season for day trips only. Check with tour operators or the field director for the most current information.

Jashipur

☑06797

This is an entry point for Similipal and a place to collect an entry permit and organise a guide and transport. Accommodation is very limited. **Sairam Holiday Home** (☑232827; NH6; s from ₹80, d from ₹250, with AC from ₹550; ❉) has basic rooms with mattresses like slabs of granite save the deluxe rooms (₹650). The owner can help arrange transport to Similipal.

Regular buses serve Sambalpur (₹150 to ₹200, seven hours), Bhubaneswar (₹150 to ₹170, nine hours), Baripada (₹55 to ₹70, 2½ hours), Balisore (₹65 to ₹85, 3½ hours) – for train connections – and Kolkata (₹140 to ₹180, seven hours).

Baripada

☑06792 / POP 95,000

The ramshackle transit hub of Baripada is the best place to organise a Similipal visit; if you're planning an independent trip, see **Odisha Tourism** (☑252710; Baghra Rd; ◷10am-5pm Mon-Sat, closed 2nd Sat in month). Recommended agency **Mayur Tours & Travels** (☑253567; mayurtour@rediffmail.com; Lal Bazaar) can also organise tours and has capable guides.

The best of the scant sleeping options, the clean-but-fading **Hotel Ambika** (☑252557; hotel_ambika@yahoo.com; s/d from ₹300/350, with AC ₹1000;❉) has a great restaurant, local workers' bar and large rooms. The hotel can organise Similipal trips, language barrier notwithstanding.

Regular buses go to Kolkata (₹150, five hours), Bhubaneswar (₹170 to ₹207, five hours), Balasore (₹30 to ₹40, 1½ hours) and Jashipur (₹50 to ₹55, 2½ hours). The 2892 *Bhubaneswar-Baripada Express* (2nd-class/AC chair ₹92/339, five hours, 5pm) runs from Bhubaneswar every day except Saturday, and returns as the 2891 at 5am every day except Sunday.

Balasore

POP 106,000

Balasore, the first major town in northern Odisha geographically, was once an important trading centre. Now it's a staging post for Chandipur, Similipal National Park and the main rail line.

The office of **Odisha Tourism** (☑262048; ⊙10am-5pm Mon-Sat) is located in Panthanivas Balasore but skip the hotel. Best option here is the new and eager **Hotel Chandrabhaga** (☑261808; Nuasahi; s/d from ₹350/450, with AC from ₹800/900; ❄), 1km from the bus station, with spotless, fantastic-value rooms with large balconies. Don't spring for deluxe – the only difference is free water and tea. All rooms have king-size beds, which could be an issue for non-couples. Tolerable for a quick overnight is **Hotel Swarnachudaa** (☑262657; s/d/tr from ₹120/150/180, s/d with AC from ₹550/650; ❄), just 100m from the bus stand; the AC rooms are worth the splurge.

From the bus stand at Remuna Golai, there is a 5am bus for Kolkata (₹160, 4½ hours) and more frequently for Bhubaneswar (₹130 to ₹160, five hours). For access to Similipal, there's a frequent service to Baripada (₹30, 1½ hours). The sporadic service to Chandipur makes an autorickshaw (₹200) a better option.

Balasore is on the main rail line. Options include the 12837 *Howrah-Puri Express* departing for Puri daily at 1.55am (sleeper/3AC/2AC/1AC ₹163/376/534/890, five hours). For Chennai, the 12841 *Howrah-Chennai Coromandel Express* calls at 6.05pm (sleeper/3AC/2AC/1AC ₹426/1143/1561/2637, 11½ hours).

Chandipur

☑06782

Throw down a few hostels, a couple of good bars and a moonlight DJ or two and this laid-back seaside village could be a very easy place to lose a few days. Unfortunately, Chandipur, which ambles down to the ocean through a short avenue of casuarina and palm trees, seems content as an underachiever. The draw here is a huge and beautiful beach: the sea recedes an astonishing 4km at low tide – a sight to see. It's safe to swim here when there's enough water.

Hotel Shubham (☑270025; www.hotelshubham.com; d from ₹550, with AC from ₹1000; ❄) offers spotless and comfortable rooms (30% of which are new or just renovated), a pleasant garden and an average restaurant. **Panthanivas Chandipur** (☑270051; dm ₹200, d from ₹750, with AC from ₹1150; ❄ @) has a great location overlooking the beach, but is otherwise not the best value in town. **Hotel Golden** (mains ₹30-150), on the main drag, does a limited selection of mainly veg Indian food, plus recommended local seafood; the excellent crab masala (₹150) is the house speciality, served whole.

Regular buses ply the NH5 between Bhubaneswar and Balasore. From Balasore, taxis and autorickshaws can take you the 15km to Chandipur.

Bhitarkanika Wildlife Sanctuary

Three rivers flow out to sea at Bhitarkanika forming a tidal maze of muddy creeks and mangroves. Most of this 672-sq-km delta forms Bhitarkanika Wildlife Sanctuary, a significant biodiversity hotspot.

The only way to get around the sanctuary is by boat. Many boats are a little battered, with old tyres on ropes acting as life preservers: this definitely adds piquancy to the thrill of boating on waters where enormous crocodiles can suddenly surface rather close by.

⊙ Sights

TOP CHOICE **Bhitarkanika Wildlife Sanctuary**   NATURE RESERVE
(www.bhitarkanika.org; Indian/foreigner per day ₹20/1000, camera/video ₹25/500; ⊙closed 15 May-31 Jul) The best time to visit is from December to February. Hundreds of massive estuarine crocodiles bask on mud flats waiting for the next meal to swim by. Birdwatchers will find eight species of brilliantly coloured kingfishers, plus 207 other species.

First stop is a permit check at Khola jetty before chugging on to **Dangmal Island**, where you'll find a successful crocodile breeding and conservation program (and accommodation). Pythons, water monitors, baboons, wild boar and numerous spotted deer can also be seen.

Herons arrive at **Bagagahan Island** in early June and nest until early December, when they move on to Chilika Lake. Raucous open-billed storks have set up a permanent rookery here. The island is reached by a narrow pathway leading to a watchtower, where you can spy on a mass of herons and storks nesting in the treetops.

Rigagada
HINDU TEMPLE

Back at Khola, a 2km walk leads to Rigagada with its interesting 18th-century **Jagannath temple**, built with some erotica in Kalinga style. While there, take an amble through this typical Odishan village.

🛏 Sleeping & Eating

TOP CHOICE **Nature Camp**
CAMPGROUND **$$$**

(📞09437016054; www.bhitarkanikatour.com; dm/s/d/tr/q incl meals ₹1000/3000/3500/4000/5000) A special experience awaits at this small tented camp in the heart of Dangmal Village, built with the help of villagers and with a sustainable foot on the ground just steps from the sanctuary. The stylish Swiss Cottage tents are fully equipped with electricity, fans, sit-down flush toilets and pleasant terraces, and the restaurant serves wonderful rustic Odisha cuisine. Three-day/two-night packages (₹5000 to ₹7900 per person based on double occupancy) begin and end in Bhubaneswar and include full board, entrance fees, a boat trip, a nature trek and transport.

Forest rest houses
GUESTHOUSE **$**

(r per person Indian ₹100-600, foreigner ₹200-1200) The distant second (and only other) choice at Dangmal has various options with solar lights, mosquito nets, no fans and lots of rules. You can book through the divisional forest officer in Rajnapur or through a travel agency in Bhubaneswar.

Aranya Nivas
HOTEL **$**

(📞06786-220397; Chandbali; dm ₹200, r from ₹600, with AC from ₹1150; ❄) Old, unremarkable rooms and new deluxe rooms (from ₹1500) that are more spacious with small touches like crown mouldings. Either way, mozzies abound. It's 50m from the Chandbali jetty.

ℹ Information

Permits, accommodation and boat transport can all be organised in the small port of Chandbali. Organise a boat (per day ₹2000, negotiable) with one of the private operators, such as the recommended **Sanjog Travels** (📞06786-220495, 9937702517; Chandbali Jetty), which can also help with obtaining the permit from the **divisional forest officer** (📞06729-272460, 9437037370; Rajnagar).

If you make arrangements in advance, you can shave one hour off the boat travel time by arranging to leave from the jetty in Jayanagar,

20km southeast of Chandbali. Take any bus from Bhubaneswar to Chandbali, get off in Kanika Chowk and take an autorickshaw (₹100) to Jaynagar. You can also take an autorickshaw from Chandbali (₹150). Contact Nature Camp (p609) or a travel agent in Bhubaneswar to arrange a boat.

ℹ Getting There & Away

Chandbali is 55km and two hours southeast of Bhadrak on NH5. Non-AC/AC buses go from Chandbali bazaar to Bhadrak (₹30/40), Bhubaneswar (₹80/130) and Cuttack (₹65/120); only non-AC goes to Kolkata (₹180). The 12821/2 *Howrah-Bhubaneswar Dhauli Express* stops in Bhadrak at 10.30am going south to Bhubaneswar (2nd class/AC chair ₹77/244, two hours); and at 3.30pm going north to Howrah (₹104/346, five hours).

Ratnagiri, Udayagiri & Lalitgiri

These Buddhist ruins are about 60km northeast of Cuttack. Currently there's no accommodation and inadequate transport, so the only feasible way to visit is by hire car organised in Bhubaneswar or Puri.

RATNAGIRI

Ratnagiri has the most interesting and extensive **ruins** (Indian/foreigner ₹5/100, video ₹25; ⏰dawn-dusk). Two large monasteries flourished here from the 6th to 12th centuries. Noteworthy are an exquisitely carved doorway and the remains of a 10m-high stupa. The excellent **museum** (⏰8am-5pm) contains beautiful sculptures from the three sites.

UDAYAGIRI

Another **monastery complex** is being excavated here in lush surrounds. There's a large pyramidal brick stupa with a seated Buddha and some beautiful doorjamb carvings. There's no entry fee, but unhelpful guides may attach themselves to you then ask for a donation (not compulsory).

LALITGIRI

Several **monastery ruins** (Indian/foreigner ₹5/100, video ₹25; ⏰dawn-dusk) are scattered up a hillside leading to a small museum and a hillock crowned with a shallow stupa. During excavations of the stupa in the 1970s, a casket containing gold and silver relics was found. It's also notable for its surrounding village atmosphere.

Madhya Pradesh & Chhattisgarh

Why Go?

The vast but unassuming state of Madhya Pradesh (MP) doesn't roar for attention like its more celebrated neighbours. Instead it growls deeply from within, offering the promise of something big and beautiful for those prepared to prowl the plains.

Tiger parks are the star attraction, and your chances of spotting a wild tiger here are good, but lesser-known treasures abound: Khajuraho's temples display some of the finest temple art in the world and are the architectural highlight of a region scattered with ruined palaces, majestic hilltop forts, ancient Buddhist stupas and India's biggest and smallest mosques.

Laidback traveller havens like Orchha and Omkareshwar add some chill-out flavour to the region, but the more adventurous will love a foray into tribal Chhattisgarh, which split from Madhya Pradesh in 2000 and remains a world far removed from mainstream Indian culture.

Best Places to Eat

» Raja's Café (p630)
» Bapu Ki Kutia (p636)
» Didi's Cafe (p622)
» Girnar Thali Restaurant (p665)
» Shivam Restaurant (p647)

Best Places to Stay

» Orchha Homestay (p622)
» Evelyn's Own (p645)
» Labboo's Cafe (p653)
» Manu Guest House (p652)
» Hotel Sheesh Mahal (p621)

When to Go

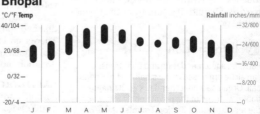

Bhopal

Nov–Feb Most pleasant time to visit central India, although hilltops will still be chilly.

Apr–Jun Best chance of spotting tigers; vegetation is thin and water sources are few.

Jul–Sep Monsoon time, but places like Chhattisgarh are at their most beautiful.

Food & Drink

The combined region of Madhya Pradesh and Chhattisgarh is enormous so, naturally, food varies across the land. Bhopal produces some exquisite meat and fish dishes as well as some great biryanis and kebabs. In the dryer regions of the north and west, you'll find more wheat-based foods and less rice. There's wonderful fruit to be had, especially in the lush south and southeast regions – mangoes and custard apples are the highlights – and those brave enough to venture to the tribal markets of Chhattisgarh will see locals eating live ants. The favourite tipple, meanwhile, is a liquor made from the flowers of the *mahuwa* tree, which you'd be advised to drink with caution – it's potent.

DON'T MISS

Madhya Pradesh is bursting at the seams with fabulous places to visit, but two things you really shouldn't leave without seeing (or at least attempting to see) are the exquisite temples of **Khajuraho** and India's most magnificent creature – the **tiger**.

Top State Festivals

» Festival of Dance (Feb/Mar, Khajuraho, p623) Week-long event with the cream of Indian classical dancers performing amid floodlit temples.

» Shivaratri Mela (Feb/Mar, Pachmarhi, p643) Up to 100,000 Shaivite pilgrims, sadhus (spiritual men) and Adivasis (tribal people) attend celebrations at Mahadeo Temple. Participants bring symbolic tridents and hike up Chauragarh Hill to plant them by the Shiva shrine.

» Magh Mela (Apr/May, Ujjain, p646) Huge annual religious fair held on the banks of the Shipra River at Ujjain; pilgrim numbers increase dramatically every 12th year for the massive Kumbh Mela (next held in Ujjain in 2016).

» Ahilyabai Holkar's Birthday (Apr/May, Maheshwar, p653) The Holkar queen's birthday is celebrated with palanquin (enclosed seats carried on poles on four men's shoulders) processions through the town.

» Navratri (Sep/Oct, Ujjain, p647) The Festival of Nine Nights, leading up to Dussehra, is celebrated with particular fervour in Ujjain. Lamps on the large pillars in Harsiddhi Mandir are lit.

» Dussehra (Oct, Jagdalpur, p666) Dedicated to local goddess Danteshwari, this 75-day festival culminates in eight days of (immense) chariot-pulling around the streets.

» Tansen Music Festival (Nov/Dec, Gwalior, p616) Four-day music festival attracting classical musicians and singers from all over India; free performances are usually staged at the tomb of Tansen, one of the most revered composer-musicians of Hindustani classical music.

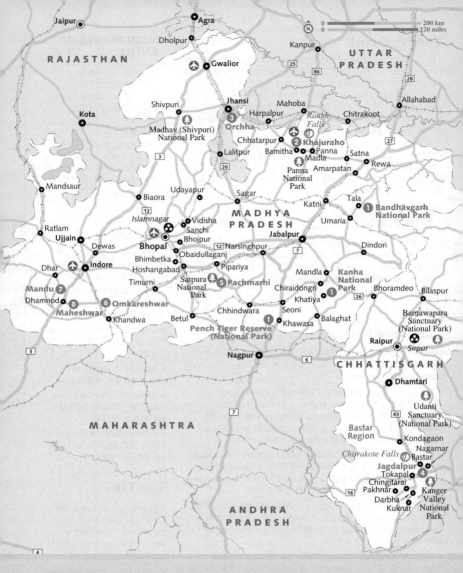

Madhya Pradesh & Chhattisgarh Highlights

① Venture deep into tiger territory at one of MP's three big **tiger parks** (p613)

② Blush at the erotic carvings on the exquisite temples in **Khajuraho** (p623)

③ Choose to bed down in a former palace or a mud-hut homestay in laidback **Orchha** (p618)

④ Watch brave locals eat live red ants at a tribal market around **Jagdalpur** in Chhattisgarh (p667)

⑤ Cool off under a waterfall in **Pachmarhi** (p643), MP's only hill station

⑥ Chill out on the Om-shaped holy island of **Omkareshwar** (p651)

⑦ Cycle around India's finest Afghan ruins at the hilltop getaway of **Mandu** (p654)

⑧ Soak up the spiritual vibe at the bathing ghats in historical **Maheshwar** (p653)

History

Virtually all phases of Indian history made their mark on the region historically known as Malwa, starting with the rock paintings at Bhimbetka (p639) and Pachmarhi (p643), which date back more than 10,000 years. They tell of a cultural succession through the late Stone Age to the start of recorded history in the 3rd century BC, when the Buddhist emperor Ashoka (see boxed text, p1087) controlled the Mauryan empire from Malwa and built Sanchi's Great Stupa (p640).

The Mauryas were followed by the Sungas and the Guptas (see p1085) – Chandragupta II (r AD 382–401) ruled from Ujjain and had the caves cut at Udaigiri (p642) – before the Huns rampaged across the state. Around 1000 years ago the Parmaras reigned in southwest Madhya Pradesh – notably Raja Bhoj, who ruled for over half a century across this region and who founded the now-ruined town of Bhojpur, the magnificent fort of Mandu and, according to some scholars, the city of Bhopal.

The Chandelas ruled over much of central India from the 9th to the 13th centuries. It was their nimble-fingered sculptors who enlivened with erotic scenes the facades of some 85 temples in Khajuraho (p623) before the dynasty eventually moved its capital from Khajuraho to Mahoba. Between the 12th and 16th centuries, the region experienced continuing struggles between Hindu and Muslim rulers (p1088), and Mandu was the scene of some decisive clashes. The Mughals were eventually superseded by the Marathas (p1091) after a 27-year-long war (1681–1707) – the longest in India's history. The Marathas went on to rule the region for more than a century before they fell to the British (1818) for whom the Scindia maharajas of Gwalior (p613) were powerful allies.

With the States Reorganisation Act of 1956, several former states were combined to form Madhya Pradesh. In 2000, Chhattisgarh became an independent state.

NORTHERN MADHYA PRADESH

Gwalior

📞 0751 / POP 865,548

Famous for its medieval hilltop fort, Gwalior makes an interesting stop en route to some of the better-known destinations in this part of India. The city also houses the eccentric Jai Vilas Palace, home of the Scindia Museum and the historic seat of the Scindias, one of the country's most revered families.

The Tansen Music Festival (p611) – a four-day classical music event attracting performers from all over India – comes to town in November/December.

History

Gwalior's legendary beginning stems from the 8th century when a hermit known as Gwalipa is said to have cured the Rajput chieftain Suraj Sen of leprosy using water from Suraj Kund tank (which still remains in Gwalior fort). Renaming him Suhan Pal, he foretold that Suhan's descendants would remain in power as long as they retained the name Pal. Suhan's next 83 descendants did just that, but number 84 changed his name to Tej Karan and, naturally, lost his kingdom.

In 1398 the Tomar dynasty came to power. Gwalior Fort became the focus of continual clashes with neighbouring powers and

---

> ### TOP TIGER PARKS
>
> Madhya Pradesh is blessed with five tiger parks, but most tourists don't have the time or money to visit more than one. To help you decide where best to prowl, here's a quick guide to tiger territory in MP:
>
> » **Kanha** The biggest and most professionally run of the lot. Can venture deep into the forests. Chances of a tiger: very good.
>
> » **Bandhavgarh** Budget-travellers' favourite with highest density of tigers, but sightings can feel a bit 'rush and grab'. Chances: excellent.
>
> » **Pench** Quiet and more exclusive. Most people prebook here. Chances: good.
>
> » **Panna** Three relocated tigers are slowly rebuilding Panna's once-decimated tiger population. Boat safaris here can be fun. Chances: extremely slim.
>
> » **Satpura** Beautiful hilltop landscape, but come here for the waterfalls and the hiking rather than the tigers. Chances: slim.

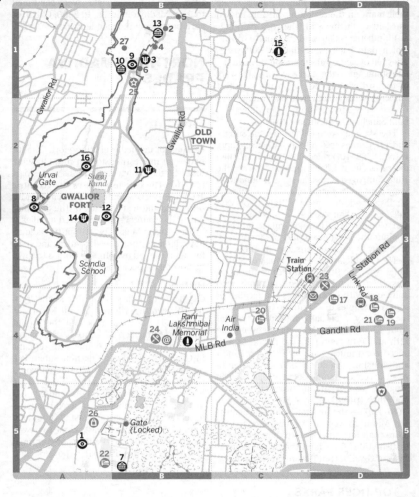

reached its ascendancy under Raja Man Singh (r 1486–1516). Two centuries of Mughal possession followed, ending with the fort's capture by the Marathas in 1754.

Over the next 50 years the fort changed hands several times, including twice to the British before finally passing to the Scindias.

During the First War of Independence (Indian Uprising) in 1857, Maharaja Jayajirao remained loyal to the British but his troops rebelled, and in mid-1858 the fort was the scene of some of the uprising's final events. Near here the British defeated rebel leader Tantia Topi and it was in the final assault on the fort that the rani (wife) of Jhansi was killed (see p382).

◉ Sights

Gwalior Fort FORT

(☉dawn-dusk) Perched majestically on top of a 3km-long plateau overlooking Gwalior, this hilltop **fort** is an imposing yet eye-catching sight, with the circular towers of the dominating Man Singh Palace ringed with turquoise tiles.

There are two approaches to the fort, both steep treks. Rickshaws can drive you up to Urvai, the western gate, so it's tempt-

Gwalior

ing to go that way because vehicles cannot drive up from the eastern entrance. But the western entrance is an anticlimax compared with the formidable view of the fort from the eastern approach, which makes entering

from the east well worth the climb. Don't, however, miss the **rock sculptures** part of the way down the western side. The upper set in particular are far more impressive than those on the eastern approach and make for a rewarding detour during your stroll around the fort.

A **ticket counter** (✆2480011; Indian/foreigner ₹5/100, video ₹25; ☉dawn-dusk) near Man Singh Palace sells tickets for the monuments, and another ticket (₹5) for a small, adjacent museum.

A **sound-and-light show** (Indian/foreigner ₹50/250; ☉English 8.30pm Mar-Oct, 7.30pm Nov-Feb, Hindi 7.30pm Mar-Oct, 6.30pm Nov-Feb) is held nightly in the open-air amphitheatre.

Much of the fort is now occupied by the prestigious private Scindia School, established by Maharaja Madhavrao Scindia in 1897 for the education of Indian nobility.

Man Singh Palace   PALACE

This imperial-style palace is one of the more unusually decorated monuments you'll see in India: the outer walls include a frieze of yellow ducks! These – and mosaic tiling of elephants, tigers and crocodiles in blue, yellow and green – give it its alternative identity of Chit Mandir (Painted Palace).

Built by Tomar ruler Man Singh between 1486 and 1516, this fine example of early Hindu architecture consists of two open courts surrounded by apartments on two levels. Below ground lie another two storeys constructed for hot weather, connected by 'speaking tubes' built into the walls, and used by the Mughals as prison cells.

Rock Sculptures   SCULPTURES

While there are sculptures carved into the rock at a few points on the plateau, including on the way up from Gwalior Gate, the most impressive are the upper set on the western approach, between Urvai Gate and the inner fort walls. Mostly cut into the cliff face in the mid-15th century, they represent nude figures of *tirthankars* (the 24 great Jain teachers). They were defaced by Babur's Muslim army in 1527 but have been more recently repaired.

There are more than 30 images, including a splendid 17m-high standing sculpture of the first *tirthankar,* Adinath.

Teli ka Mandir   TEMPLE

Used as a drinks factory and coffee shop by the British after the First War of Independence (Indian Uprising) of 1857, this 30m-high, 8th-century temple is the oldest monument in the compound.

The modern, gold-topped **gurdwara** (Sikh Temple) nearby is dedicated to Sikh hero Guru Har Gobind, who was imprisoned in Man Singh Palace from 1617 to 1619.

Sasbahu Temples   TEMPLE

The Mayan-like Sasbahu, or Mother-in-Law and Daughter-in-Law Temples, date from the 9th to 11th centuries. Mother-in-Law, dedicated to Vishnu, has four gigantic pillars supporting its heavy roof, layered with carvings. The smaller Daughter-in-Law, dedicated to Shiva, is also stacked with sculptures.

Eastern Entrance   FORT

From the east entrance a series of gates punctuates the worn steps of the path leading up to the fort. At the bottom, the first gate you pass through is **Gwalior Gate** (Alamgiri Gate), which dates from 1660. The second, Bansur (Archer's Gate), has disappeared, so the next is **Badalgarh**, named after Badal Singh, Man Singh's uncle.

Further up is **Ganesh Gate**, built in the 15th century. Nearby is **Kabutar Khana**, a small pigeon house, and a small four-pillared **Hindu temple** to the hermit Gwalipa, after whom fort and town are named.

You'll pass a 9th-century Vishnu shrine known as **Chatarbhuj Mandir** (Temple of the Four-Armed) before reaching the fifth gate, **Hathiya Paur** (Elephant Gate), now the entrance to the palace (as the sixth gate, Hawa Gate, no longer exists).

State Archaeological Museum   MUSEUM

This **museum** (Indian/foreigner ₹10/100, camera/video ₹50/200; ⊙10am-5pm Tue-Sun) is within Gujari Mahal, just through Gwalior Gate at the base of the fort. Built in the 15th century by Man Singh for his favourite rani (wife), the palace is now rather deteriorated. There's a large collection of Hindu and Jain sculptures, including the famed Salabhanjika (an exceptionally carved female figure) plus copies of Bagh Caves frescoes.

Jai Vilas Palace & Scindia Museum   PALACE

(Indian/foreigner ₹40/230, camera/video ₹50/100; ⊙10am-5.30pm Thu-Tue) This museum occupies some 35 rooms of the Scindias' opulent Jai Vilas Palace, built by Maharaja Jayajirao in 1874 using prisoners from the fort. The convicts were rewarded with the 12-year job of weaving the hall carpet, one of the largest in Asia.

The gold paint around the durbar (royal court) hall weighs half a tonne. Supposedly, eight elephants were suspended from its ceiling to check it could cope with two 12.5m-high, 3.5-tonne chandeliers with 250 lightbulbs, said to be the largest pair in the world.

Bizarre items fill the rooms: Belgian-cut glass furniture, stuffed tigers and a ladies-only swimming pool with its own boat. The cavernous dining room displays the pièce de résistance, a model railway with a silver train that carried after-dinner brandy and cigars around the table.

Note: the gates to the north and south are locked so you have to enter the palace from the west.

Tomb of Tansen   HISTORIC BUILDING

Tucked away in the winding lanes of the Old Town, and in the same compound as the resplendent tomb of Mohammed Gaus, is the smaller, simpler tomb of Tansen, a singer much admired by Akbar and held to be the father of Hindustani classical music. Chewing the leaves from the tamarind tree here supposedly enriches your voice. Free performances are staged during the four-day Tansen Music Festival in November/December.

Tours

UP Tourism's cute little yellow bus, Gwalior Darshan, takes passengers on a full-day **city tour** (per person ₹75; ⊙10.30am-6pm), taking in all the main sights, including Gwalior Fort and Jai Vilas Palace. Enquire at the tourist office at Tansen Residency.

🛏 Sleeping

Hotel Gwalior Regency   HOTEL $$

(☑2340670; Link Rd; s/d incl breakfast from ₹1975/2725; ❄@🛜) None of the string of midrange hotels on Mandhav Rao Scindia Marg are as good value as this super-friendly place near the train station. Standard rooms are fine, albeit a little old fashioned (and musty before the AC kicks in), but if you pay an extra ₹1000 for 'grande deluxe' you'll find rooms with modern furnishings (wall-mounted wide-screen TV, glass-walled shower room, free wi-fi) and a luxurious feel.

Usha Kiran Palace   HERITAGE HOTEL $$$

(☑2444000; www.tajhotels.com; Jayendraganj; r from ₹10,000; ❄@🛝) Live like royalty in this 120-year-old building, which once accom-

SHIVPURI'S MARBLE CENOTAPHS

A possible day trip from Gwalior is to the old Scindia summer capital of Shivpuri. This rarely visited town is the site of the Scindia family's *chhatris* (cenotaphs), appropriately grand memorials to maharajas and maharanis gone by.

Two kilometres' walk from the bus stand (autorickshaw ₹15), and set in formal gardens, the **chhatris** (admission ₹40, camera/video ₹10/40; ⊙8am-noon & 3-8pm) are magnificent walk-in marble structures with Mughal-style pavilions and *sikharas* (Hindu temple-spires) facing each other across a pool with a criss-cross of walkways. The *chhatri* to Madhorao Scindia, built between 1926 and 1932, is exquisitely inlaid with intricate pietra dura (marble inlay work).

Buses leave regularly from the Shivpuri bus stand for Gwalior (₹80, 2½ hours) and Jhansi (₹70, three hours), meaning you don't have to double-back on yourself to visit.

modated King George V. Every room has its own unique touches – one a mosaic-tiled bathtub, another a silk-cushioned lounging area – while the luxury villas come with their own private pool! The gorgeous main pool (with separate kids pool) can be used by nonguests (₹500) as can the excellent **Jiva Spa** (massage treatments from ₹1400; ⊙8am-8pm), the Silver Saloon restaurant and Bada Bar. Online deals available for as little as ₹5600.

Hotel DM   HOTEL $
(☏2342083; Link Rd; s/d from ₹400/500) Rooms are small, but in much better condition than the other budget options around town. All have clean bathrooms and a TV locked securely inside a special cabinet (when was the last time you stole a hotel TV?). Some come with a cute little wooden bench outside.

Hotel Mayur   HOTEL $
(☏2325559; Padav; s/d from ₹280/450, with AC from ₹620; ❄) Spacious, but slightly grubby rooms set around a courtyard, extending up three floors. Twenty-four-hour checkout.

Hotel Chandralok   HOTEL $
(☏2341425; s/d from ₹350/400) The only hotel on Station Rd that accepts foreigners. Rooms are shabby, but prices are agreeable.

Tansen Residency   HOTEL $$
(☏4056789; r ₹1690) MP Tourism hotel with neat and tidy rooms, but little character. Has a bar and a restaurant.

🍴 Eating & Drinking

Indian Coffee House   SOUTH INDIAN $
(Station Rd; mains ₹40-110; ⊙7.30am-11pm) Another popular offering from the fab Indian Coffee House, this branch does all the usual breakfast favourites – real coffee, dosa (large savoury crepes), scrambled eggs – but also has a proper main-course menu, including an excellent thali (all-you-can-eat meal; ₹85), in a separate 1st-floor section.

Zayka   MULITCUISINE $
(MLB Rd; mains ₹40-110; ⊙11am-11pm) This trendy, cafe-style restaurant with glass tabletops and brightly painted walls pulls in young local punters with its foreign menu – noodles, burgers, pizza – but the Indian veg dishes are still very good. Try the stuffed capsicum.

Silver Saloon   INDIAN $$$
(☏2444000; Usha Kiran Palace, Jayendraganj; mains ₹350-750; ⊙7am-11am, 12.30-3pm & 7.30-10.30pm) Mouth-watering Indian, Nepali and Continental dishes are served either in the tangerine-and-magenta restaurant or the palm-shaded courtyard of this exquisite heritage hotel.

Bada Bar   BAR
(☏2444000; Usha Kiran Palace, Jayendraganj; beer ₹250; ⊙5-11pm) Take a peek inside Gwalior's most luxurious hotel, order a beer or a glass of French wine, then rack up for a frame or two on the 120-year-old snooker table.

🛍 Shopping

Arihant Emporium   HANDICRAFTS
(Moti Mahal Rd; ⊙10.30am-6pm Mon-Sat) Near Jai Vilas Palace, this place has all sorts of handicrafts but specialises in a Gwalior favourite – silver boxes (₹500) decorated with enamel images to imitate the tile work on Man Singh Palace.

HANDY TRAINS FROM GWALIOR

DESTINATION	TRAIN NO & NAME	FARE (₹)	DURATION (HR)	DEPARTURE
Agra	12617 *Mangala Ldweep*	140/265/336	2	8.15am
Bhopal	12920 *Malwa Express*	198/502/674	6½	12.47am
Delhi	12625 *Kerala Express*	178/443/593	5	8.30am
Indore	12920 *Malwa Express*	282/737/999	12	12.47am
Jhansi*	12002/22002 *Bhopal-SHTABDI*	240/470	1	9.39am

Fares are sleeper/3AC/2AC; *chair/1AC only

ℹ Information

Fun Stop Cyber Zone (MLB Rd; per hr ₹30; ☺9am-10pm) Internet access and webcams for Skype use.

MP Tourism Tansen Residency (☏2340370; 6A Gandhi Rd; ☺10am-5pm Mon-Sat) Train station (☏4040777; ☺9am-7.30pm) Organises daily Gwalior bus tour. Very helpful.

Post office (Station Rd; ☺9am-5pm Mon-Fri, 9am-1.30pm Sat)

State Bank of India (☏2336291; Bada Chowk; ☺10.30am-4pm Mon-Fri, 10.30am-1.30pm Sat) Cashes travellers cheques; also has an ATM in the train station foyer.

ℹ Getting There & Away

Air

Air India (☏2376872; MLB Rd; ☺10am-5pm Mon-Sat) has flights to Delhi (from ₹4500, Tuesday, Thursday and Saturday).

Bus

Services from the bus stand on Link Rd include:
AGRA ₹85, 3½ hours, frequent, 4.30am to 9pm
JAIPUR seat/sleeper ₹250/330, 10 hours, four daily, 6.30am, 7.15am, 6.30pm, 7.30pm
JHANSI ₹67, three hours, frequent, day and night.
KHAJURAHO ₹190, seven hours, one daily, 8.30am
SHIVPURI ₹80, 2½ hours, frequent, 5am to 10pm

Train

More than 20 daily trains go to Agra's Cantonment station and to Jhansi for Orchha or Khajuraho, while more than 10 go to Delhi and Bhopal. See the boxed text (p618) for details.

ℹ Getting Around

Cycle-rickshaws (per trip ₹10 to ₹20) and autorickshaws (₹20 to ₹40) are plentiful. Brutish-looking tempos (large autorickshaws; ₹2 to ₹6) chug along fixed routes. An auto to the airport will cost ₹100 to ₹150.

Jhansi

This nondescript town, commonly used as a gateway to Orchha, Khajuraho and Gwalior, is in fact in Uttar Pradesh. See p382 for details.

Orchha

☏07680 / POP 8501

This historic village on the banks of the boulder-strewn Betwa River showcases some fabulous architecture similar to that of nearby Khajuraho, albeit without such high-quality artistry. The atmosphere in Orchha, though, is far more laid-back and hassle-free, which makes for a relaxing stay. There are great homestay options as well as opportunities to enjoy the surrounding countryside, with walking, cycling, swimming and rafting all on the agenda.

History

Orchha was the capital of the Bundela rajas from the 16th century to 1783, when they decamped to nearby Tikamgarh. Bir Singh Deo ruled from Orchha from 1605 to 1627 and built Jhansi fort. A favourite of Mughal prince Salim, Bir Singh feuded with Salim's father, Emperor Akbar, who all but ruined his kingdom.

In 1605 Prince Salim became Emperor Jehangir, making Bir Singh a powerful figure. The Jehangir Mahal was built for the emperor's state visit the following year.

👁 Sights

The ticket for Orchha's **sites** (Indian/foreigner ₹10/250, camera/video ₹25/200) covers seven monuments – Jehangir Mahal, Raj Mahal, Raj Praveen Mahal, the camel stables, the *chhatris*, Chaturbhuj Temple and Lakshmi Narayan Temple – and is only for sale at the **ticket office** (⊙8am-6pm). You can walk around the palace grounds for free.

Palaces   HISTORIC SITE
Crossing the granite bridge from the village centre over the often dry river channel brings you to a fortified complex dominated by two wonderfully imposing 17th-century palaces – Jehangir Mahal and Raj Mahal. Langur monkeys play by the ruins here, while vultures perch on the rooftops. If you look closely at the top of some buildings, you can still see some of the few remaining turquoise-coloured tiles that once decorated the palaces here.

Jehangir Mahal, an assault course of steep staircases and precipitous walkways, represents a zenith of medieval Islamic architecture. There's a small **archaeological museum** on the ground floor and behind the palace sturdy **camel stables** overlook a green landscape dotted with monuments.

In the nearby **Raj Mahal**, the caretaker will open the painted rooms where Rama, Krishna and Orchha royalty wrestle, hunt, fight and dance across the walls and ceilings.

Downhill from the palace compound are the smaller **Raj Praveen Mahal**, a pavilion and formal Mughal garden, and **Khana Hammam** (Turkish Bath), with some fine vaulted ceilings.

On the other side of the village, **Palki Mahal** was the palace of Dinman Hardol (the son of Bir Singh Deo), who committed suicide to 'prove his innocence' over an affair with his brother's wife. His memorial, two cloth-covered stone beds in a pavilion, is in the adjacent **Phool Bagh**, a traditional *charbagh* (formal Persian garden, divided into quarters). Prince Hardol is venerated as a hero in Bundelkhand culture. Women sing songs about him, tie threads onto the *jali* (carved marble lattice screen) of his memo-

rial and walk around it five times, clockwise, to make wishes they hope he'll grant.

Temples   HINDU TEMPLE
Orchha's impressive 16th-century temples still receive thousands of Hindu pilgrims. At the centre of a lively square is the pink- and gold-domed **Ram Raja Temple** (⊙8am-noon & 8-10pm), the only temple where Rama is worshipped as a king. Built as a palace for Madhukar Shah's wife, it became a temple when an image of Rama, temporarily installed by the rani, proved impossible to move.

Ram Raja is overlooked by the spectacular towers of **Chaturbhuj Temple**, an immensely solid building on a cruciform plan. Buy a cheap torch from the bazaar and climb the internal stairs to the roof where, from among the mossy spires and domes, you get the best view in town. Vultures also perch on the rooftops here.

Lakshmi Narayan Temple, on the road out to Ganj village, has fine rooftop views and well-preserved murals on the ceilings of its domed towers.

Chhatris   HISTORIC SITE
Cenotaphs to Orchha's rulers, including Bir Singh Deo, the serene *chhatris* rise from the rubble and undergrowth about a kilometre south of the village. They're best seen at dusk, when the birds reel above the children splashing at the river ghats.

FREE **Saaket Museum**   MUSEUM
(⊙10am-5pm Tue-Sun) More of an art gallery than a museum, the Saaket Museum showcases some beautiful folk paintings from different states of India. The Madhubani paintings from Bihar are particularly striking.

🏃 Activities

Nature Trails   WALKING
Some paths in the vast palace grounds lead down to the river through gates in the wall. Another option is the 12km-long **nature trail** in Orchha Nature Reserve, a 44-sq-km island surrounded by the Betwa and Jamni Rivers. You need to buy a ticket (Indian/foreigner ₹20/150) from the ticket office (open 8am to 6pm) to enter the reserve, then you are free to explore, although guides (₹200) are available. The nature trail is well marked and the roads are signposted, making this

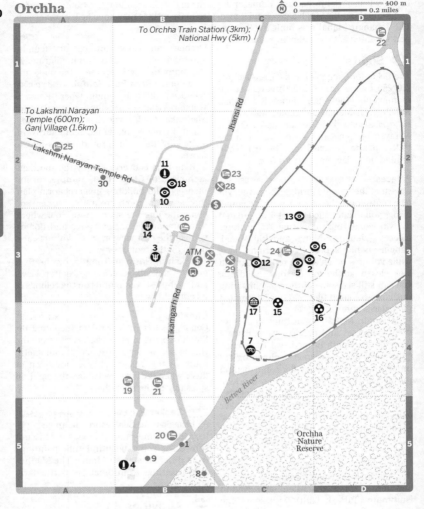

To Orchha Train Station (3km);
National Hwy (5km)

To Lakshmi Narayan
Temple (600m);
Ganj Village (1.6km)

Lakshmi Narayan Temple Rd

Jhansi Rd

Tikamgarh Rd

ATM

Betwa River

Orchha
Nature
Reserve

a nice place to cycle. Wildlife you're likely to see on the trail includes monkeys, deer, monitor lizards and peacocks. For a chance to spot one of four types of turtles found here, cycle to Ret Ghat, 14km south of the ticket office, on the Jamni River.

Massage & Yoga
AYURVEDA

Amar Mahal (p621) and **Orchha Resort** (☑252222; www.orchharesort.com) both offer good-quality ayurvedic massage treatments (from ₹500; 8.30am to 8.30pm) and hold yoga classes (₹500). Amar Mahal is the better but pricier of the two.

Rafting
RAFTING

River-rafting (per raft per 1½/3hr ₹1200/2500) trips start from the boat club, but tickets must be bought through MP Tourism at Hotel Sheesh Mahal or Betwa Retreat. Rafts take one to six people.

Swimming
SWIMMING

Locals swim in the **Betwa River** every day. A popular spot is in front of the **boat club** by the bridge that leads into the Orchha Nature Reserve. Another option is the boulder-strewn section beside Bundelkhand Riverside hotel. Follow the track

Orchha

◎ Sights

🛏 Sleeping

TOP CHOICE Hotel Sheesh Mahal HERITAGE HOTEL **$$**
(☎252624; smorchha@mptourism.com; Jehangir Mahal; r ₹1690, ste ₹3990-4990; ❄) Literally palatial, this hotel is actually located in a wing of Jehangir Mahal. As you'd expect, the surrounding architecture is stunning – arches, columns, lattice windows, decorative wooden door frames – but the rooms themselves are gorgeous too, and each is unique, some with regal touches such as throne-like toilets. Even if you don't stay here, pretend you want to and have a look around.

Bundelkhand Riverside HOTEL **$$$**
(☎252612; www.bundelkhandriverside.com; s/d from ₹3000/3600; ❄⊛) The granddaddy of Orchha hotels is owned by the grandson of Orchha's last king, Vir Singh, who sold his palaces to the state after India's Independence. Some of the maharaja's personal art collection is displayed in the corridors. Exquisite rooms overlook either the river or the hotel's beautiful gardens, which contain some 16th-century monuments as well as a small swimming pool.

Shri Mahant Guest House HOTEL **$**
(☎252715; r from ₹200, with AC from ₹450; ❄) Overlooking the souvenir market at the entrance to Ram Raja Temple and overlooked itself by the wonderful Chaturbhuj Temple, this excellent budget choice has a superb location, clean rooms – some with TV, others with balconies – and friendly staff. If rooms are full, you'll be directed to its sister property, **Hotel Shri Mahant** (☎252341; Lakshmi Narayan Temple Rd; r from ₹400; ❄), a few hundred metres west of town.

Fort View Guest House HOTEL **$**
(☎252701; Jhansi Rd; r ₹250-550, with AC from ₹850; ❄) Smart, simple rooms off a cute courtyard come with marble floors and clean bathrooms with 24-hour hot water. The three AC rooms have huge windows with palace views, while one has a marble bed! Not to be confused with nearby New Fort Guest House, which isn't such good value.

Betwa Retreat HOTEL **$$**
(☎252618; www.mptourism.com; tents ₹1290, cottages ₹1690, ste ₹4990; ❄⊛) Set in peaceful shaded gardens with a small swimming pool this MP Tourism property, overlooking the river and with views of the *chhatris,* makes an excellent family choice. Rooms come in

from Jhansi Rd to the hotel but instead of turning left into the hotel itself, carry on down to the river.

Nonguests can use the **swimming pools** at the following hotels: Bundelkhand Riverside (₹150), Betwa Retreat (₹150), Amar Mahal (₹200) and Orchha Resort (₹300).

DON'T MISS

MUD-HUT HOMESTAYS IN THE VILLAGE OF GANJ

Thanks to **Friends of Orchha** (☎9098353799; www.orchha.org; s/d ₹350/450, extra bed ₹100, breakfast/dinner ₹30/50), a nonprofit organisation run by Dutchman Louk Vreeswijk and his Indian wife, Asha D'Souza, travellers now have the opportunity to stay with local villagers as part of an excellent homestay program.

This is a wonderful chance to experience genuine Indian village life, so don't expect anything but the most basic of facilities. Friends of Orchha helped provide loans for some renovations, including installing ecofriendly dry toilets in the yards of each homestay house, but you will still be staying in mud huts and eating the simple veg dishes that your host family eats every day.

Staying for a single night is discouraged for logistical reasons. If you really want to stay one night only, you can, but room rates will be slightly higher. In any case, the slow pace of life in Ganj is something that should be savoured. At the time of research there were only five family homes set up to provide homestays (although more were being planned), so it would still be sensible to book ahead.

Friends of Orchha also runs an after-school youth club for village children. Volunteers and, of course, donations are always welcomed. The Friends of Orchha office is in Ganj Village itself, on the left-hand side of the main road as you are coming from Orchha.

Mughal-style cottages or Swiss tents and have nice touches such as iron bed frames. There's a restaurant, a bar and an outdoor terrace, and it's only a five-minute walk from the main drag.

Amar Mahal HOTEL $$$
(☎252102; www.amarmahal.com; s ₹2400-3400, d ₹3400-4400, ste ₹6000; ❋☀) Grand rooms containing lovely wood-carved furniture, such as four-poster beds, are set around a courtyard with white pillars supporting a covered walkway. There's an excellent ayurvedic massage and yoga centre (see p620) beside the large, but slightly exposed pool. This doesn't have the history or character of Bundelkhand Riverside, but it's probably Orchha's most luxurious stay.

Bhandari Guesthouse GUESTHOUSE $
(☎252745; off Tikamgarh Rd; r ₹400, without bathroom ₹250) Neat and tidy rooms, with large bathrooms, are set around a simple courtyard. The huge common bathroom is kept very clean. Rooms with a private bathroom also have a TV.

✕ Eating & Drinking

TOP CHOICE **Didi's Cafe** CAFE $$
(Jhansi Rd; mains ₹80; ☉8am-5pm) Run by Denise and Loyal, a very cheerful Northern Irish–Indian couple, this friendly, laid-back cafe is perfect for breakfast or a lunchtime snack. The excellent menu includes fresh coffee, porridge, omelettes, pasta and salads.

If that all sounds too healthy for you, plump instead for their simply delicious homemade banoffi pie.

Betwa Tarang INDIAN $
(Jehangir Mahal Rd; mains ₹45-130; ☉7.30am-10pm) This place does the best quality Indian food out of any of Orchha's budget restaurants – the thalis (₹70 to ₹130) are particularly good. It also has the attraction of a rooftop terrace where you can sit and overlook the market, with the old palace to your right and Chaturbhuj Temple to your left.

Turquoise Diner INDIAN $$$
(☎252612; Bundelkhand Riverside; mains ₹160-300, ☉7-10am, 12.30-3.30pm & 7-10.30pm) Fabulous green- and blue-tiled AC restaurant inside the sumptuous grounds of this topnotch hotel knocks out arguably the best Indian food in Orchha. There's a smattering of Continental options too, but stick to the local dishes and you won't leave disappointed.

Ram Raja INDIAN $
(Jehangir Mahal Rd; mains ₹30-60; ☉7.30am-11pm) A friendly, family-run streetside restaurant offering tasty vegetarian fare under the shade of a large tree.

Hotel Sheesh Mahal INDIAN $$
(Jehangir Mahal; mains ₹60-200; ☉7.30am-10.30pm) Indian tandoori, Chinese and Continental are all on the menu, but it's the historic surroundings that are the attraction here (plus the beer).

ℹ Information

Internet cafes (₹20 to ₹30) are everywhere.

Canara Bank (☑252689; Jhansi Rd; ⊘10.30am-2.30pm & 3-4pm Mon-Fri, 10.30am-1pm Sat) Changes travellers cheques and cash. There's an ATM by the bus stand.

MP Tourism (☑252624; Hotel Sheesh Mahal or Betwa Retreat; ⊘7am-10pm)

ℹ Getting There & Around

Tempos (large shared autorickshaws; ₹10) go between Jhansi bus stand and Orchha all day. Private autorickshaws charge about ₹150. Coming from Khajuraho, you can ask the bus driver to drop you off at the Orchha turn-off on the National Hwy, where you should be able to wave down a vehicle to take you to Orchha.

Annoyingly, there are no buses between Orchha and Khajuraho. You need to go to Jhansi first then catch a bus (₹120, six hours, 6am to 2pm) from there as Jhansi–Khajuraho buses tend not to stop for you if you wait on the side of the highway. Taxis to Khajuraho cost at least ₹2000.

You can now also catch a slow passenger train to Khajuraho from Orchha's tiny train station, which is on the Jhansi Rd, about 3km from the village centre. The train leaves daily at 7.25am and takes five hours (if it's on time). It's 2nd-class seats only so you can't reserve tickets. Just turn up at the station and buy a 'general' ticket (₹30). The return train leaves Khajuraho at 12.30pm.

Raju Bikes (Lakshmi Narayan Temple Rd; ⊘7am-6pm) hires out rickety bicycles at great rates (per hour/day ₹5/40).

Khajuraho

☑07686 / POP 19,286

The erotic carvings that swathe Khajuraho's three groups of World Heritage–listed temples are among the finest temple art in the world. The Western Group of temples, in particular, contains some stunning artwork. See our special colour illustration (p626) for all the details.

Many travellers complain about the tiring persistence of touts here, preferring the more laid-back charms of nearby Orchha instead. Their complaints are well founded, but be aware that missing out on Khajuraho means missing out on some of the most beautiful temples in India.

Come February/March, the Western Group of temples becomes the stage for the week-long Festival of Dance (see p611).

History

Legend has it that Khajuraho was founded by Chardravarman, the son of the moon god Chandra, who descended and saw a beautiful maiden as she bathed in a stream. Historians tell us that the Chandela dynasty built the temples, many of which originally rose from a lake. Most of the 85 temples – of which 25 now remain – were built during a century-long burst of creative genius from AD 950 to 1050 and remained active long after the Chandelas moved their capital to Mahoba.

Khajuraho's isolation may well have helped preserve it from the desecration Muslim invaders inflicted on 'idolatrous' temples elsewhere, but perhaps for the same reason the area was slowly abandoned and eventually fell into ruin, with the jungle taking over. The wider world remained largely ignorant until British officer TS Burt was apparently guided to the ruins by his palanquin bearers in 1838.

Dangers & Annoyances

Most of the hassle tourists experience comes in the form of seemingly endless demands for money, pens and photo fees, often from children. Also be wary of commission-driven operations such as guides offering to take you to a local school or charity.

Many yogis and massage therapists are not qualified. That doesn't mean they're not good, but it's something to be aware of.

⊙ Sights

Temples   HINDU/JAIN

The temples are superb examples of Indo-Aryan architecture, but it's their liberally embellished carvings that have made Khajuraho famous. Around the outsides of the temples are bands of exceedingly artistic stonework showing a storyboard of life a millennium ago – gods, goddesses, warriors, musicians and real and mythological animals.

Two elements appear repeatedly – women and sex. While the *mithuna* (pairs of men and women, usually depicted in erotic poses) are certainly eye-catching, the erotic content should not distract from the great skill underlying the sculptures. Sensuous, posturing *surasundaris* (heavenly nymphs), *apsaras* (dancing *surasundaris*) and *nayikas* (mortal *surasundaris*) have been carved with a half-twist and slight sideways lean that make the playful figures dance and swirl out from the flat stone. A classic example is the

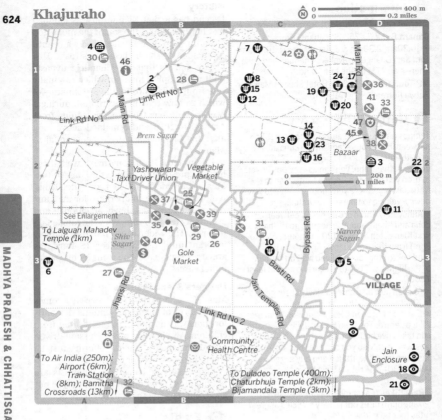

washerwoman with a wet sari clinging to her body – an image imbued with as much eroticism as any of the couples, threesomes or foursomes.

Walk around the temples with your right shoulder facing the building – the right side is considered divine.

Western Group – inside the fenced enclosure   TEMPLE

Khajuraho's most striking and best-preserved temples are those within the fenced-off section of the **Western Group** (Indian/foreigner ₹10/250, video ₹25; ☉dawn-dusk), and are the only temples here you have to pay to see. An Archaeological Survey of India (ASI) guidebook to Khajuraho (₹99) and a 90-minute audio guide (₹50) are available at the ticket office.

Varaha, dedicated to Vishnu's boar incarnation, and the locked **Lakshmi** are two small shrines facing the large Lakshmana Temple. Inside Varaha is a wonderful, 1.5m-high sandstone boar, dating from AD 900 and meticulously carved with a pantheon of gods.

The large **Lakshmana Temple** took 20 years to build and was completed in about AD 954 during the reign of Dhanga according to an inscribed slab in the *mandapa* (pillared pavilion in front of a temple). It's arguably the best preserved of all Khajuraho temples. You'll see carvings of battalions of soldiers here – the Chandelas were generally at war when they weren't inventing new sexual positions. On the south side is a highly gymnastic orgy, including one gentleman proving that a horse can be a man's best friend, while a shocked figure peeks out from behind her hands. More sensuous figures intertwine between the elephants in the frieze ringing the basement, while some superb carvings can be found around the *garbhagriha* (inner sanctum). Lakshmana is dedicated to Vishnu, although it is similar in design to the Shiva temples Vishvanath and Kandariya-Mahadev.

The 30.5m-long **Kandariya-Mahadev**, built between 1025 and 1050, is the largest temple in town and represents the high-point of Chandelan architecture. It also has the most representations of female beauty and sexual aerobics, all crammed into three central bands. There are 872 acrobatic statues, most nearly 1m high – taller than those at the other temples. One frequently photographed sculpture illustrates the feasibility of the handstand position. The 31m-high *sikhara* here is, like linga, a phallic Shiva symbol, worshipped by Hindus hoping to seek deliverance from the cycle of reincarnation. It's decorated with 84 subsidiary spires, which make up a mountain-like rooftop scene reminiscent of the Himalayan abode of the gods.

Mahadeva, a small ruined temple on the same platform as Kandariya-Mahadev and Devi Jagadamba, is dedicated to Shiva, who is carved on the lintel of its doorway. It houses one of Khajuraho's finest sculptures – a *sardula* (mythical beast – part lion, part other animal – possibly human) caressing a 1m-high lion.

Devi Jagadamba was originally dedicated to Vishnu, but later to Parvati and then Kali. The carvings include *sardulas* accompanied by Vishnu, *surasundaris,* and *mithunas* frolicking in the third uppermost band. Its three-part design is simpler than Kandariya-Mahadev and Chitragupta. It has more in common with Chitragupta, but is less embellished with carvings so is thought to be a little older.

North of Devi Jagadamba, **Chitragupta** (1000–25) is unique in Khajuraho – and rare among North Indian temples – in being

Khajuraho Temples

WESTERN GROUP

The sheer volume of artwork at Khajuraho's best-preserved temples can be overwhelming. Initiate yourself with this introductory tour, which highlights some of those easy-to-miss details.

First, admire the sandstone boar **1** in the Varaha shrine before heading towards Lakshmana Temple **2** to study the south side of the temple's base, which has some of the raunchiest artwork in Khajuraho: first up, a nine-person orgy; further along, a guy getting very friendly with a horse. Up on the temple platform see a superb dancing Ganesh carved into a niche (south side), before walking to the west side for graceful *surasundaris* (nymphs): one removing a thorn from her foot; another draped in a wet sari; a third admiring herself in a mirror.

Next is Khajuraho's largest temple, Kandariya-Mahadev **3**. Carvings to look for here include the famous handstand position (south side), but the most impressive thing about this temple is the scale of it, particularly its soaring rooftops. Mahadeva **4** and Devi Jagadamba **5** share the same stone plinth as Kandariya-Mahadev, as do four beautifully carved *sardula* (part-lion, part-human mythical beasts), each caressing a stone lion – one is at the entrance to Mahadeva; the other three stand alone on the plinth.

Walk north from here to Chitragupta **6**, with beautiful carvings hidden on the west side, as well as elephant friezes around the temple's base (north side). The interior here is particularly impressive.

Continue east to Vishvanath Temple **7** for more fabulous carvings before admiring the impressive statue of Vishnu's bull in the Nandi shrine **8** opposite.

DANIEL MCCROHAN

Handstand Position
Perhaps Khajuraho's most famous carving, this flexible flirtation is above you as you stand on the south side of the awesome Kandariya-Mahadev.

Sikharas
Despite its many fine statues, perhaps the most impressive thing about Kandariya-Mahadev is its soaring *sikharas* (temple rooftops), said to represent the Himalayan abode of the gods.

Devi Jagadamba Temple 5

Kandariya-Mahadev Temple 3

Mahadeva Temple 4

NORTH →

Toilets

Sardula Statue
There are four lion-stroking *sardula* (part-lion, part-human mythical beasts) on this huge stone plinth, but this one, guarding the entrance to Mahadeva, is our favourite.

DANIEL MCCROHAN

Kama Sutra Carvings
Although commonly referred to as Kama Sutra carvings, Khajuraho's erotic artwork does not properly illustrate Vatsyayana's famous sutra. Debate continues as to its significance: to appease evil spirits or imply rulers here were virile, thus powerful? Interestingly, the erotic carvings are never located close to the temple deity.

Listen Up

The audio guide only covers two temples but it is very detailed, so is a really useful introduction.

6 Chitragupta Temple

Toilets

7 Vishvanath Temple

Just the Ticket

For an extra-close look at Khajuraho artwork, use your ticket for same-day entrance to the small Archaeological Museum nearby.

Parvati Temple

8 Nandi Shrine

Lakshmana Temple **2**

Pratapeswar Temple

Lakshmi Shrine

Entrance

1 Varaha Shrine

Matangesvara Temple

Nandi Statue

This massive 2.2m-long statue of Nandi, the bull-vehicle of Shiva, is enshrined in a pavilion facing Vishvanath Temple.

Surasundaris

Beautifully graceful depictions of nymphs are found on a number of Khajuraho temples. And despite all the depictions of gymnastic orgies, the wonderfully seductive *surasundari* draped in a wet sari is arguably the most erotic of all.

Vishnu's Boar

This 9th-century statue of Varaha, the boar incarnation of Vishnu, is carved all over with figures of Bramanical gods and goddesses. Under Varaha's foot notice the serpent Seshanaga in a devotional posture, and the feet of a goddess, now missing.

dedicated to the sun god Surya. While its condition is not as good as the other temples, it has some fine carvings of *apsaras* and *surasundaris,* elephant fights and hunting scenes, *mithuna* and a procession of stone-carriers. In the inner sanctum, Surya drives his seven-horse chariot, while in the central niche on the south facade is an 11-headed statue of Vishnu, representing the god and 10 of his 22 incarnations.

Continuing around the enclosure, the closed-up **Parvati Temple** is on your right, a small temple originally dedicated to Vishnu and now with an image of Gauri riding a *godha* (iguana).

Believed to have been built in 1002, the **Vishvanath Temple** and **Nandi Shrine** are reached by steps on the northern and southern side. Elephants flank the southern steps. Vishvanath anticipates Kandariya-Mahadev, with which it shares *saptamattrikas* (seven mothers) flanked by Ganesh and Virabhandra, and is another superlative example of Chandelan architecture. Its sculptures include sensuous *surasundari* writing letters, cuddling babies and playing music while languishing more provocatively than at other temples. At the other end of the platform, a 2.2m-long statue of Nandi, Shiva's bull vehicle, faces the temple. The basement of the 12-pillared shrine is decorated with an elephant frieze that recalls similar work on Lakshmana's facade.

The nearby white temple, **Pratapeswar**, is a much more recent bricks-and-mortar structure built around 200 years ago.

Western Group – outside the fenced enclosure TEMPLE

Skirting the southern boundary of the fenced enclosure, **Matangesvara** is the only temple in the Western Group still in everyday use. It may be the plainest temple here (suggesting an early construction), but inside it sports a polished 2.5m-high lingam (phallic image of Shiva). From its platform you can peer into an open-air storage facility scattered with temple finds but not open to the public.

The ruins of **Chausath Yogini**, beyond Shiv Sagar, date to the late 9th century and are probably the oldest at Khajuraho. Constructed entirely of granite, it's the only temple not aligned east to west. The temple's name means 64 – it once had 64 cells for the *yoginis* (female attendants) of Kali, while the 65th sheltered the goddess herself. It is reputedly India's oldest *yogini* temple.

A further 600m west, down a track and across a couple of fields (just ask the locals), is the sandstone-and-granite **Lalguan Mahadev Temple** (900), a small ruined shrine to Shiva.

Eastern Group – Old Village Temples

The eastern group includes three Hindu temples scattered around the old village and four Jain temples further south, three of which are in a walled enclosure.

The **Hanuman Temple**, on Basti Rd, contains a 2.5m-tall statue of the Hindu monkey god. It's little more than a bright orange shrine, but the interest is in the pedestal inscription dating to AD 922, the oldest dateable inscription in Khajuraho.

The granite **Brahma Temple**, with its sandstone *sikhara* overlooking Narora Sagar, is one of the oldest in Khajuraho (about 900). The four-faced lingam in the sanctum led to it being incorrectly named, but the image of Vishnu above the sanctum doorway reveals its original dedication to Vishnu.

Resembling Chaturbhuja Temple in the southern group, **Javari Temple** (1075–1100) stands just north of the old village. It's dedicated to Vishnu and is a good example of small-scale Khajuraho architecture for its crocodile-covered entrance and slender *sikhara.*

Vamana Temple (1050–75), 200m further north, is dedicated to the dwarf incarnation of Vishnu. It has quirky touches such as elephants protruding from the walls, but its *sikhara* is devoid of subsidiary spires and there are few erotic scenes. Its roofed *mahamandapa* (main hall) is an anomaly in Khajuraho but typical among medieval west Indian temples.

Located between the old village and the Jain Enclosure, the small **Ghantai Temple**, also Jain, is named after the *ghanta* (chain and bell) decorations on its pillars. It was once similar to nearby Parsvanath, but only its pillared shell remains and it's normally locked.

Eastern Group – Jain Enclosure TEMPLE

While not competing in size and erotica with the western-enclosure temples, **Parsvanath Temple**, the largest of the Jain temples in the walled enclosure, is notable for the exceptional skill and precision of its construction, and for its sculptural beauty. Some of the best-preserved of Khajuraho's most famous images can be seen here, including the woman removing a thorn from her foot and another applying eye make-up, both on the south side. Although the temple was originally dedicated to Adinath, a jet-black image of Parsvanath was substituted about a century ago. Both an inscription on the *mahamandapa* doorway and its similarities with the slightly simpler Lakshmana Temple date it to 950–70.

The adjacent, smaller **Adinath** has been partially restored over the centuries. With fine carvings on its three bands of sculptures it's similar to Khajuraho's Hindu temples, particularly Vamana. Only the striking black image in the inner sanctum triggers a Jain reminder.

Shanti Nath, built about a century ago, houses components from older temples, including a 4.5m-high Adinath statue with a plastered-over inscription on the pedestal dating to about 1027.

Southern Group   TEMPLE
A dirt track runs to the isolated **Duladeo Temple**, about 1km south of the Jain enclosure. This is the youngest temple, dating to 1100–1150. Its relatively wooden, repetitious sculptures, such as those of Shiva, suggest that Khajuraho's temple builders had passed their artistic peak by this point, although they had certainly lost none of their zeal for eroticism.

Anticipating Duladeo and its flaws, the ruined **Chaturbhuja Temple** (c 1100) has a fine 2.7m-high, four-armed statue of Vishnu in the sanctum. It is Khajuraho's only developed temple without erotic sculptures.

Just before Chaturbhuja there's a signed track leading to **Bijamandala Temple**. This is the excavated mound of an 11th-century temple, dedicated to Shiva (judging by the white marble lingam at the apex of the mound). Although there are some exquisitely carved figures, unfinished carvings were also excavated, suggesting that what would have been Khajuraho's largest temple was abandoned as resources flagged.

Museums   MUSEUM, ART GALLERY
The **Archaeological Museum** (Main Rd; admission ₹10, free with same-day Western Group ticket; ⊙8am-5pm), announced by a wonderful 11th-century statue of Ganesh (dancing sensuously for an elephant-headed deity), has a small but well-presented collection of sculptures from around Khajuraho. This is a good opportunity to get up close to some very well-preserved carvings. At the time of research, there were plans to move this museum to a larger site north of the Western Group, but don't hold your breath; they've been telling us that since 2006.

The museum-cum-art gallery, **Adivart Tribal & Folk Art Museum** (Chandela Cultural Centre, Link Rd No 1; Indian/foreigner ₹10/50; ⊙10am-5pm Tue-Sun), makes a colourful change from the temples. It gives a taste of the vibrant tribal culture of both Madhya Pradesh and Chhattisgarh through pointillist Bhili paintings, terracotta Jhoomar sculptures, masks, statues and bamboo flutes. Original signed paintings are for sale from around ₹8000. Prints can be bought from around ₹200.

Old Village   AREA
If you can put up with the persistent requests from local children for pens and money, then a stroll or cycle around the dusty narrow streets of the old village can be very rewarding. Homes here are whitewashed or painted in colourful pastels and the lanes are dotted with small shrines, old wells and water pumps.

🏃 Activities

Massage   AYURVEDA
Many budget hotels offer cheap ayurvedic massage treatments of varying levels of authenticity. Top-end hotels offer more luxurious versions. For the real deal, though, head to **Ayur Arogyam** (☑272572; treatment ₹1400-2100; ⊙24hr). The lovely Keralan couple who run this small place from their home also have two simple doubles rooms to rent (₹100).

Barbers in Gole Market offer simple but rejuvenating head massages for ₹20.

Yoga   YOGA
Apart from the hotels offering yoga, the inspiring **Yogi Sudarshan Dwiveda** (☑9993284940; Vidhya Colony; fee by donation; ⊙6am) runs sessions at his home. Accommodation can be arranged. There is no English sign. If you have trouble contacting him, go through **Rajesh Medical Store** (⊙9am-9pm) in Gole Market.

Swimming   SWIMMING
Nonguests can use the pools at Hotel Payal (₹200) and Radisson Jass Hotel (₹300).

🛏 Sleeping

Hefty discounts (20% to 50%) are available out of season (April to September), although it's worth bargaining at any time of year.

Hotel Surya　　　　　　　HOTEL $
(☏274144; www.hotelsuryakhajuraho.com; Jain Temples Rd; r from ₹300, with AC from ₹700; ❄@) There's a huge range of decent-value rooms in this sprawling, well-run hotel with white-washed corridors, marble staircases and a lovely courtyard garden out the back. Some rooms have TV. Some have balconies. There's yoga and massage, and the atmosphere is generally laid-back.

Hotel Harmony　　　　　　HOTEL $$
(☏274135; Jain Temples Rd; r ₹500, with AC ₹1000; ❄@⛶) Cozy, well-equipped rooms off marble corridors are tastefully decorated with green and brown furnishings and come with cable TV. Yoga and massage available. Wi-fi costs ₹40.

Osaka Guesthouse　　　　GUESTHOUSE $
(☏272839; off Basti Rd; r ₹250-400, with AC ₹600; ❄) Spacious rooms here are pretty basic, but have a homey feel to them and the owner is very welcoming. Osaka is set back off the main drag, down a dirt track, so is quieter than elsewhere, and has some nice temple views from its rooftop.

Hotel Narayana Palace　　HOTEL $$
(☏272832; govindgautam@rediffmail.com; Jhansi Rd; s ₹450-1000, d ₹550-1100; ❄) This kitsch-tastic hotel with its orange-and-white facade will dazzle you with the pinks, purples, reds and greens of its interior paintwork, decor and ornaments. Rooms are large with shiny tiled floors and clean bathrooms.

Yogi Lodge　　　　　　　GUESTHOUSE $
(☏274158; yogi_sharm@yahoo.com; r ₹150-300) Rooms are basic – some with tap-and-bucket showers – but small courtyards, narrow corridors and the cute stone tables in the rooftop restaurant give this place character.

Radisson Jass Hotel　　　HOTEL $$$
(☏272777; www.radisson.com; Bypass Rd; s/d from ₹5600/6400; ❄@⛶⛱) A marble spiral staircase winds its way up from the fountain in the lobby to modern, stylish 1st-floor rooms that are very smart, if a little small. There's a comfortable bar area (with pool table), a restaurant, tennis and badminton courts, and a fine swimming pool. Best of all, though, is the service, which we found to be exemplary. Wi-fi is free.

Lalit Temple View　　　　HOTEL $$$
(☏272111; www.thelalit.com; Main Rd; s/d from ₹14,000/15,000; ❄@⛶⛱) Sweeps aside all other five-star pretenders with supreme luxury, impeccable service and astonishingly high prices. Rooms are immaculate with large plasma-screen TV, wood-carved furniture and tasteful artwork. Guests who don't have temple-view rooms can see the Western Group from the delightful lotus-shaped pool.

Hotel Payal　　　　　　　HOTEL $$
(☏274076; payal@mptourism.com; Link Rd No 1; r ₹890, with AC ₹1490; ❄⛱) This MP Tourism hotel has smart rooms with dark-wood furniture set around very nice gardens with an inviting swimming pool out the back. It also rents bikes (₹50 per day).

Ayur Arogyam　　　　　　GUESTHOUSE $
(☏272572; r ₹100) There are two small basic rooms beside the treatment rooms at this simple ayurvedic massage lodge (see p629). Both have private bathrooms with squat toilets.

🍴 Eating

🏆 **Raja's Café**　　　　MULTICUISINE $$
(Main Rd; mains ₹60-200; ⊙8am-10pm) Raja's has been on top of its game for more than 30 years, and recently added a coffee stall (coffee from ₹50) so that punters can now enjoy quality fresh coffee as well as superb food. The central location is great, as is the restaurant design, with a delightful wrought-iron spiral staircase linking a shaded courtyard with a temple-view terrace. But it's the food that steals the show. The Indian dishes are wonderful – the paneer *kofta* (unfermented cheese and vegetable balls) and chicken *kababi* (barbecued chicken pieces marinated in yoghurt), in particular, and there's good-quality Italian and Chinese too.

Mediterraneo　　　　　　ITALIAN $$$
(Jain Temples Rd; mains ₹100-300, pizza ₹240-345; ⊙7.30am-10pm) High-quality food, served on a lovely terrace overlooking the street, includes chicken, salads and organic wholewheat pasta, but it's all about the pizza here, baked in the wood-fired oven and easily the best in town. Beer and wine is also available.

Madras Coffee House   SOUTH INDIAN $

(cnr Main & Jain Temples Rds; mains ₹30-60; ☺8am-9.30pm) Good, honest South Indian fare – dosa, *idli* (spongy round fermented rice cakes), *uttapam* (thick savoury rice pancakes), thali – as well as coffee and chai, served in a simple, slimline cafe-restaurant. Ideal for breakfast.

Paradise Restaurant   MULTICUISINE $$

(Main Rd; mains ₹45-250; ☺8am-11pm; @🛜) A recent facelift means this cafe-restaurant now has an open terrace overlooking the lake. The menu has been extended, too, to include Chinese, Continental and pizza as well as the good Indian food that was always on offer. There's a couple of computer terminals for internet use as well as wi-fi (per hour ₹30, Skype ₹60).

Blue Sky Restaurant   MULITCUISINE $$

(Main Rd; mains ₹60-200; ☺7.30am-10pm) A rickety wooden platform, three storeys up, leads out to the most unusual place to eat in Khajuraho – a one-table tree house with an unrivalled view of the western temples. The view from the ordinary, terraced balcony is good too, while the menu is the usual Indian and Chinese, plus Western breakfasts. The grumpy service is perhaps understandable. Would you like to serve food to customers in a tree?

Lassi Corner   INDIAN $

(Jain Temples Rd; mains ₹30-40, lassis from ₹10; ☺10am-10pm) This tarpaulin-covered bamboo shack is a great place for a quick chai break or a lazy lassi. Also does pancakes as well as simple Indian fare such as *pakora, paratha*, pulao and kofta.

Agrasen   MULTICUISINE $$

(Jain Temples Rd; mains ₹60-250; ☺7.30am-10.30pm) This smart place with gingham tablecloths and a 1st-floor terrace serves up safe-to-eat salads, pasta and pizza as well as a variety of Indian vegetable and meat dishes.

Bella Italia   ITALIAN $$

(Jain Temples Rd; mains ₹45-215; ☺7am-10.30pm) A cheaper version of Mediterraneo, this pleasant rooftop restaurant overlooks Gole Market and sits beside a couple of huge trees, which host remarkable parrot-squawking contests every day from around 6pm.

☆ Entertainment

Admittedly, the temples do look magical illuminated with technicolour floodlights, but the one-hour **sound-and-light show** (Indian/foreigner ₹50/300; ☺English 7.10pm Nov-Feb, 6.30pm Mar-Oct, Hindi 8.20pm Nov-Feb, 7.40pm Mar-Oct) chronicling the history of Khajuraho is still about 45 minutes too long.

Folk dancing can be seen at the comfortable indoor theatre at **Kandariya Art & Culture** (✆274031; Jhansi Rd; admission ₹350; ☺7-8pm & 8.45-9.45pm).

🛍 Shopping

Kandariya Art & Culture   HANDICRAFTS

(Jhansi Rd; ☺9am-9pm) Full-size replicas of some of Khajuraho's temple carvings can be bought – if you have a spare ₹100,000. Smaller, more affordable versions, along with textiles, wood carvings and marble inlay, can be found indoors.

ℹ Information

Internet cafes around town tend to charge ₹40 per hour, ₹50 for Skype.

Community health centre (✆272498; Link Rd No 2; ☺9am-1pm & 2-4pm) Limited English, but helpful staff.

Post office (✆274022; ☺10am-4pm Mon-Sat)

State Bank of India (✆272373; Main Rd; ☺10.30am-4.30pm Mon-Fri, 10.30am-1.30pm Sat) Changes cash and travellers cheques. There are ATMs beside Raja's Cafe and Paradise Restaurant.

Tourist Interpretation & Facilitation Centre (✆274051; khajuraho@mptourism.com; Main Rd; ☺10am-9pm) Leaflets on state-wide tourist destinations. Also has a stand at the airport and train station.

Tourist police booth (✆272690; Main Rd; ☺6am-10pm)

ℹ Getting There & Away

Air

Jet Airways (✆274406; ☺10am-3.30pm), at the airport, has a daily 1.45pm flight to Delhi (from ₹4200, 3½ hours) via Varanasi (from ₹3800, 40 minutes). **Air India** (✆274035; Jhansi Rd; ☺10am-4.50pm Mon-Sat), closer to town, has 2pm flights to the same two cities, but only on Monday, Wednesday and Friday.

Bus

If the bus stand **ticket office** (☺7am-noon & 1-3pm) is closed, the owner of the Madhur coffee stand, just opposite, is very helpful and trustworthy.

There are three daily buses to Jhansi (₹130, five hours, 5.30am, 7am and 9am), which will all drop you at the junction to Orchha from where you can wave down a shared autorickshaw (₹10) to Orchha. Regular buses run to Madla (for Panna National Park; ₹25, one hour, 8am to 7pm), where you can change for Satna (₹65, three hours). There are two direct buses to Satna (₹110, four hours, 2pm and 3pm) from where you can catch trains to various destinations.

Much more frequent buses can be caught at the Bamitha crossroads, 11km away on Hwy 75, where buses between Gwalior, Jhansi and Satna shuttle through all day. Catch a shared jeep (₹10, 7am to 7pm) to Bamitha from the bus stand or as they drive down Jhansi Rd.

Taxi

Yashowaran Taxi Driver Union is opposite Gole Market. Fares include: airport (₹150), train station (₹250), Raneh Falls (₹500), Panna National Park (₹1500), Satna (₹2000), Orchha (₹2900), Chitrakut (₹2900), Bandhavgarh (₹4800), Varanasi (₹6800) and Agra (₹7000).

Train

Three useful trains leave from **KHAJURAHO TRAIN STATION:**

A daily passenger train leaves at noon for Jhansi, stopping at the tiny train station of Orchha (₹30, four hours). There are 2nd-class seats only, so you can't buy tickets in advance. Just turn up at the train station, buy a 'general' ticket and squeeze in.

On Mondays, Wednesdays and Saturdays the 22447 *Khajuraho–Nizamuddin Express* leaves for Delhi (sleeper/3AC/2AC ₹273/713/960, 6pm, 11½ hours) via Agra (sleeper/3AC/2AC ₹210/527/699, 8½ hours).

On Tuesdays, Fridays and Sundays the 21107 *Bundelkhand Link Express* leaves for Varanasi (sleeper/3AC/2AC ₹198/522/694, 11pm, 12 hours) via Chitrakut (five hours) and Allahabad (eight hours).

Train tickets can be bought from the **train reservation office** (☏274416; ☺8am-noon & 1-4pm Mon-Sat, 8am-2pm Sun) at the bus stand. You must book tickets at least four hours before departure.

Coming to Khajuraho the 21108 *Bundelkhand Link Express* leaves Varanasi on Mondays, Wednesdays and Saturdays at 5.10pm and passes Allahabad (10.25pm) and Chitrakut (1.03am) before arriving in Khajuraho (5.15am). The 22448 *Nizamuddin–Khajuraho Express* leaves Delhi's Hazrat Nizamuddin station on Tuesdays, Fridays and Sundays at 10.15pm and passes Agra (11.20pm) before arriving in Khajuraho (6.05am). The daily passenger train leaves Jhansi at 7.20am, passing Orchha (7.25am) before arriving in Khajuraho at around noon.

ℹ Getting Around

Bicycle is a great way to get around. Several places along Jain Temples Rd rent them (per day ₹20 to ₹50).

Cycle-rickshaws should cost ₹10 to ₹20 wherever you go in Khajuraho, and around ₹100/200 for a half-/whole-day tour. Autorickshaws are about double the price.

Taxis to and from the airport/train station charge ₹150/250, autorickshaws ₹50/80, but if you don't have too much luggage it's easy enough to wave down a bus or a shared jeep (₹10) as they head along Jhansi Rd either into or out of town.

Around Khajuraho

RANEH FALLS

These 30m-high **waterfalls** (admission Indian/ foreigner on foot or by bicycle ₹15/150, motorbike ₹40/200, autorickshaw ₹80/400, car ₹200/1000, compulsory guide ₹40; ☺6am-6pm), 18km from Khajuraho, at times tumble as a churning mass over rocks but are only really worth the trip just after rain. The ticket office is 3km before the falls so if you don't want to pay the high fees for vehicle entry be prepared for a bit of a walk. It's possible to view gharials – a critically endangered species of crocodile – at **Ken Gharial Sanctuary** (☺9am-5pm, closed during monsoon), 8km from the ticket office, beyond the falls. The road to Raneh Falls is signposted if you fancy cycling through the countryside from Khajuraho, or else its ₹300/500 return in an autorickshaw/taxi.

PANNA NATIONAL PARK

Sadly, in recent years tigers haven't done well in this **reserve** (☏07732252135; jeep safaris ₹3230 per 6-person jeep, optional 30min boat safari ₹600 per 6-person boat; ☺5.30-10am & 2.30-5.30pm Oct 16-Jun 30). They were wiped out completely a few years back, and although three adult tigers were later reintroduced here from Bandhavgarh, Pench and Kanha, and some cubs have been born, actually seeing any tigers here is extremely rare. Nevertheless, this is a good place to see crocodiles and, with the Ken River flowing through it, Panna is a peaceful, picturesque place to spend a day on your way to or from Khajuraho. In fact, it's easy enough to do an afternoon safari here as a day trip from Khajuraho, using public transport to get to and from Madla.

Even if you don't stay the night here, it's worth making **Jungle Camp** (☏07732275275; jcmadla@mptourism.com; r ₹1990) your base. There's a restaurant (mains ₹50 to ₹150), you can arrange **jeep safaris** and there's a nicely kept garden dotted with children's play areas in which the comfortable AC tents for guests are located.

Jungle Camp is on the edge of Madla village, 200m past the large Ken River bridge (if you're coming from Khajuraho), and right by Madla Gate, the main entrance to the park.

Regular buses run between Madla and Khajuraho (₹25, one hour) and between Madla and Satna (₹65, three hours), although for Satna you sometimes have to change at the nearby town of Panna (₹10, 30 minutes).

Satna

📞 07672 / POP 229,307

Satna is of no interest to tourists but is a transport link between Khajuraho and Madhya Pradesh's three big tiger parks – Bandhavgarh, Kanha and Pench.

The bus and train stations are 3km apart (cyclerickshaw/autorickshaw ₹10/25). There is an ATM opposite the bus stand and one at the train station, where you'll also find **MP Tourism** (📞225471), which is occasionally open.

If you get stuck here, **Hotel Chandra View** (📞410600; Rewa Rd; s/d from ₹750/975; ❄) is 50m right of the bus stand and has decent rooms and a restaurant.

Three buses go to Khajuraho (₹75, four hours, 6.30am, 9.15am and 2.30pm). At other times you can go via Panna (last bus 6pm). There are also regular buses towards Chitrakut (₹60, three hours, 6am to 8pm), although you often have to change.

Six daily trains go to Varanasi (sleeper/3AC/2AC, ₹158/413/563, seven hours), frequent daily trains go to Jabalpur (₹120/297/400, three hours) and two to Umaria, for Bandhavgarh National Park (₹120/267/359, three hours and four hours, 7pm and 10.15pm).

CENTRAL MADHYA PRADESH

Bhopal

📞 0755 / POP 1.46 MILLION

Split by a pair of central lakes, one of which is India's largest manmade lake, Bhopal offers two starkly contrasting cityscapes. In the north is the Muslim-dominated old city, a fascinating area of mosques and crowded bazaars. Bhopal's population is 40% Muslim – one of India's highest concentrations of Muslims – and the women in black *niqabs* (veils) are reminders of the female Islamic rulers who built up Bhopal in the 19th cen-

tury. North of here is a reminder of a more recent, tragic history – the Union Carbide plant, site of the world's worst industrial disaster (see boxed text, p637).

South of the two lakes, Bhopal is more modern, with wide roads, shopping complexes and more upmarket hotels and restaurants nestled comfortably in the Arera and Shamla Hills, which overlook the lakes and the old city beyond. The central district here is known as New Market.

The main train and bus stations are just off Hamidia Rd – the main budget hotel area – with the bustling *chowk* (marketplace) slightly further southeast. Hamidia Rd is accessed via the Platform 5 end of the train station. The Platform 1 end is where you'll find left luggage (you need your own padlock), MP Tourism, the post office and an ATM.

⊙ Sights & Activities

Mosques   MOSQUE

Bhopal's third female ruler, Shah Jahan Begum, wanted to create the largest mosque in the world, so in 1877 set about building **Taj-ul-Masjid** (⊙closed to non-Muslims Fri). It was still incomplete at her death in 1901, after funds had been diverted to other projects, and construction did not resume until 1971. It is now one of the largest mosques in India, thanks to its huge courtyard. The main structure is enormous too; fortresslike terracotta walls surround three gleaming white onion domes and a pair of towering pink minarets with white domes. If you can make the dawn azan (Muslim call to prayer), you won't regret it. And while you're in the area, don't forget to pop over the road to see **Dhai Seedi Ki Masjid**, the city's oldest and teeniest mosque (see boxed text p636).

The gold spikes crowning the squat minarets of the **Jama Masjid**, built in 1837 by Bhopal's first female ruler, Qudsia Begum, glint serenely above the skull caps and veils swirling through the fascinating bazaar below.

The **Moti Masjid** near Sadar Manzil was built by Qudsia Begum's daughter and Bhopal's second female ruler, Sikander Jahan Begum, in 1860. Similar in style to the Jama Masjid in Delhi, this smaller marble-faced mosque has two dark-red minarets and gold-spiked cupolas. Inside, the kiblah has 11 white arches. The five most central are marble.

State Museum   MUSEUM

(📞2661856; Shamla Hills; Indian/foreigner ₹10/100, camera/video ₹50/200; ⊙10.30am-5.30pm Tue-Sun) This first-class archaeological museum

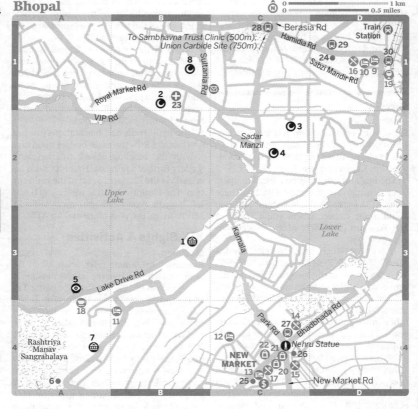

includes some wonderful temple sculptures as well as 87 Jain bronzes unearthed by a surprised farmer in western Madhya Pradesh. Keep an eye out for the tiny, but remarkably animated, metal carpet seller in the Royal Collections Gallery.

Bharat Bhavan   ART GALLERY
(☑2660239; admission galleries/performances ₹10/20, galleries free on Fri; ☺2-8pm Tue-Sun Feb-Oct, 1-7pm Nov-Jan) This cultural centre is a serene place to take in modern Indian art, tribal carvings and paintings, a library and private contemporary art galleries. There is a cafe, and regular evening performances (7pm) of poetry, music and theatre. Some of the artwork here is of the highest quality.

Rashtriya Manav Sangrahalaya   PARK
(Museum of Man; ☑2661319; Shamla Hills; admission ₹10, vehicle ₹10, video ₹50; ☺10am-5pm Tue-Sun Sep-Feb, 11am-6.30pm Mar-Aug) A kind of tribal safari park, only without the tribes, this

open-air hillside complex is possibly your best chance to get a taste of India's 450-plus tribes without actually visiting an Adivasi village. Authentic-looking dwellings – built and maintained by Adivasis (tribespeople) using traditional tools and materials – dot the hillside. There's a mythological trail and a more conventional museum on the hilltop.

Upper Lake   LAKE
The **MP Tourism Boat Club** (☑3295043; Lake Drive Rd; ☺9am-6.30pm winter, 9am-7.30pm summer) offers motorboat rides (per person ₹50, five minutes, minimum three people), pedal boats (per boat ₹50, 30 minutes) and even jet skiing (per person ₹300). Children might enjoy feeding the more than 100 geese that make their home by the boat club.

☞ Tours
Bhopal-On-Wheels (☑3295040; 3½hr tour adult/child ₹60/30; ☺11am) is a guided tour

Bhopal

on a toy-train lookalike open bus, departing from Palash Residency (p636) and winding through the hills and the old city. Stops include Taj-ul-Masjid, MP Tourism Boat Club and Rashtriya Manav Sangrahalaya. Minimum five passengers.

🛏 Sleeping

All hotels here, including budget ones, add at least 10% tax to their listed rates.

HAMIDIA ROAD

Hotel Rama International　　　HOTEL $
(☎2740542; 2 Hamidia Rd; s/d ₹350/450, with AC ₹600/750; ❄) Big, airy rooms in this old-school Indian hotel come with clean, tiled flooring and quality wooden furniture. Much better value than its foreign-friendly neighbours, but it's often full.

Hotel Ranjit　　　HOTEL $$
(☎2740500; ranjeethotels@sancharnet.in; 3 Hamidia Rd; s/d from ₹400/600, with AC from ₹650/850; ❄@) They look after you in Ranjit. Even in the cheapest rooms you get your own soap, towel, bottle of mineral water and a complimentary breakfast, plus there's one computer terminal in the lobby for brief (free) internet use. The restaurant (mains ₹50 to ₹140) here is good and there's a bar (beer from ₹126).

Hotel Sonali　　　HOTEL $$
(☎2740880; sonalinn@sancharnet.in; Radha Talkies Rd; s/d from ₹450/495, with AC incl breakfast from ₹1000/1200; ❄@⊙) Excellent service and shiny tiled floors in big rooms make this the best quality option near Hamidia Rd. Some non-AC rooms come with slightly shabby carpets, but all have TV and there's 24-hour internet and free wi-fi in the lobby. Also has a restaurant. From Hamidia Rd, turn left down the lane alongside Hotel Ranjit and follow it round to the right.

NEW MARKET

Jehan Numa Palace Hotel　HERITAGE HOTEL $$$
(☎2661100; www.hoteljehanumapalace.com; 157 Shamla Hill; cottage s/d ₹3700/4700, s ₹4900-7300, d ₹5900-8300, ste from ₹14,000, incl breakfast; ❄@⊙☀) This former 19th-century palace lost none of its colonial-era charm through conversion into a top-class hotel. Arched walkways and immaculate lawns lead you to beautifully decorated rooms. There's a palm-lined pool, an excellent health spa and three restaurants, including one under the shade of an enormous mango tree.

Park Hotel　　　HOTEL $$
(☎4057711; Rang Mahal Rd; s/d from ₹500/600, with AC from ₹700/900; ❄) This neat place is a good-value option for New Market, with a great location close to all the restaurants, shops

DON'T MISS

THE WORLD'S SMALLEST MOSQUE?

There are more than 400 mosques in Bhopal, the most famous being the biggest of them all, the towering Taj-ul-Masjid. But what many visitors don't know is that this fascinating city is also home to what we believe to be the world's smallest mosque.

It's hard to confirm such sweeping claims, but we paced out the main prayer hall of **Dhai Seedi Ki Masjid** and found it to be roughly 16 sq metres in size. Internet searches since then have yet to dig up a smaller mosque, either in India or elsewhere.

Whether it really is the world's smallest mosque or not, Dhai Seedi Ki Masjid is well worth a visit. Intriguingly, it's hidden away inside the grounds of a hospital, which in turn were built inside the grounds of the now ruined 18th-century Fatehgarh Fort. The white-washed mosque is perched on top of an overgrown stone turret, which forms a corner of the old fortress wall, and was built as the very first mosque in Bhopal, so that soldiers deployed as guards could perform their daily prayers.

Roughly translated, the mosque's name means 'two-and-a-half-steps mosque', in reference to the steps leading up to its tiny prayer hall. A gatekeeper is usually on hand to let you in for a quick look round, although when we were here he could neither confirm nor deny Dhai Seedi Ki Masjid's potential record-holding status.

To get here, enter Hamidia Hospital from Royal Market Rd, then turn right into the campus of Gandhi Medical College. Follow the road around the main building and you'll eventually see the mosque on your right.

and market stalls, and has decent rooms with marble floors, TV and hot-water showers.

Palash Residency HOTEL **$$**
(☑2553066; palash@mptourism.com; TT Nagar; s/d from ₹2290/2490; ❄@❂) Walking distance from New Market, this MP Tourism hotel has smart rooms with dark-wood furniture, wall-mounted flat-screen TV, kettle, complimentary toiletries and free wi-fi in the lobby. Has a bar and restaurant.

✕ Eating & Drinking

TOP CHOICE Bapu Ki Kutia INDIAN **$**
(Sultania Rd; mains ₹42-110; ◷10am-11pm) Papa's Shack has been serving up delicious Indian veg dishes since the '60s and is so popular you often have to share a table. Does handy half portions if you just fancy a snack. There's an English menu, but no English sign. Look for the picture of a beach hut and palm tree above the door.

New Inn INDIAN **$$**
(New Market; mains ₹40-160; ◷8am-10pm) Clean and colourful split-level restaurant with a well-priced menu delivered by staff in waistcoats and bow ties. There are good breakfast choices, including filter coffee (₹10), but it's the delicious main courses that hit the spot. If you like a bit of spice, don't leave this place without trying the *mattar paneer* (un-

fermented cheese and pea curry). Has good kebabs too.

Indian Coffee House SOUTH INDIAN **$**
(New Market; mains ₹30-130; ◷7am-11pm) As always, Indian Coffee House is a top spot for breakfast, with waiters in white suits and fan-tailed hats serving good-value coffee plus South Indian favourites such as dosa, *idli* and *vada* (doughnut-shaped deep-fried lentil savoury). There's a good choice of mains here too, ranging from biryani to Chinese.

Manohar INDIAN **$**
(6 Hamidia Rd; mains ₹30-90; ◷8am-11pm) This bright, clean, canteen-style restaurant is a decent place to come for South Indian breakfasts. After midday it also does thalis and 'mini-meals' as well as some Chinese dishes and pizza. Has an impressive range of cakes, cookies and sweets at a side counter.

Café Coffee Day CAFE **$$**
(Lake Drive Rd; coffee from ₹35-93; ◷8.30am-10.30pm) Quality fresh coffee and overpriced snacks come with the best view in town.

Wine Shop BAR **$**
(Hamidia Rd; draft beer ₹30; ◷10am-10pm) There are a number of bottle shops on this stretch of Hamidia Rd, but this one has the added attraction of beer on tap. Has

a couple of benches inside, otherwise it's stand-on-the-side-of-the-street drinking.

Shopping

Bhopal's two main shopping areas are the small shops and stalls around New Market, which really come to life in the evenings, and the labyrinthine old-city alleys of *chowk* that weave their way towards the Jama Masjid. Both areas stock delicate gold and silver jewellery, fancifully woven saris, hand-embroidered appliqué skirts and *jari* (glittering embroidery, often including shards of mirror or glass) shoulder bags, a speciality of Bhopal.

Mrignayani   HANDICRAFTS
(23 New Market Shopping Centre; ◷11am-2.30pm & 3.30-8pm Tue-Sun) This state-owned place offers stress-free handicraft shopping, though the fixed prices are higher than in the market behind it.

Khadi Gramodyog Bhavan   CLOTHING
(Bhadbhada Rd; ◷11am-8pm Tue-Sun) Kurta, pyjama, head scarves and shirts made from the famous *khadi* cotton (see boxed text p1132), plus some quality *khadi* silk garments. Next-day tailoring service available.

Variety Book House   BOOKSTORE
(14-15 GTB Complex, Bhadbhada Rd; ◷10am-10pm) Stationery, maps and a fabulous selection of contemporary novels and Indian history books.

Information

There are **internet cafes** (per hr from ₹10) off Hamidia Rd and around New Market.

Hamidia Hospital (☑2540222; Royal Market Rd) Housed within the grounds of the now ruined Fatehgarh Fort.

Main post office (Sultania Rd; ◷10am-7pm Mon-Sat) Also a counter at the train station.

MP Tourism airport (◷incoming flights); regional office (☑2550588; Palash Residency, TT Nagar; ◷10am-8pm Mon-Fri, ◷10am-5pm Sat & Sun); train station (☑2746827; ◷9.30am-5.30pm)

Raj Medical Store (Hamidia Rd; ◷9am-9.30pm)

State Bank of India (Rang Mahal Rd; ◷11am-5pm Mon-Fri, 11am-2pm Sat) 'International Division' on 1st floor changes travellers cheques and cash. Has ATM. There's also an ATM at the train station.

THE BHOPAL DISASTER – A CONTINUING TRAGEDY

At five minutes past midnight on 3 December 1984, 40 tonnes of deadly methyl isocyanate (MIC) gas leaked out over Bhopal from the US-owned Union Carbide chemical plant. Blown by the wind, rivers of the heavy gas coursed through the city. In the ensuing panic, people were trampled trying to escape while others were so disorientated that they ran into the gas.

There were 3828 initial fatalities according to official figures, but the continuing death toll stands at over 20,000. More than 120,000 people suffer from a catalogue of illnesses from hypertension and diabetes to premature menopause and skin disorders, while their children experience growth disorders, such as shrunken rib cages.

The leak at the plant resulted from a saga of untested technology, negligent maintenance and cost-cutting measures. Damages of US$3 billion were demanded, and in 1989 Union Carbide paid the Indian government US$470 million, but winning compensation for the victims has been a tortuous process slowed by the Indian government's wrangling over who was a victim and Dow Chemical's acquisition of Union Carbide in 2001. Both buyer and seller deny ongoing liability.

Union Carbide also financed the building of a multimillion dollar hospital, while charity **Sambhavna Trust Clinic** (☑2730914; www.bhopal.org; Bafna Colony, Berasia Rd; ◷8.30am-3pm) treats more than 200 people a day using yoga, Ayurvedic treatments, conventional Western treatments and remedies prepared using herbs from its medicinal garden. Volunteers can work in a range of areas from watertesting and medical research to gardening and internet communications; they are hugely appreciated and offered board and lodgings in the medical centre. Visitors and, of course, donations are also always welcome.

Bafna Colony is off Berasia Rd. If walking from Hamidia Rd, turn right after about 500m and keep asking for Sambhavna.

HANDY TRAINS FROM BHOPAL

DESTINATION	TRAIN NO & NAME	FARE (₹)*	DURATION (HR)	DEPARTURE
Agra	12627 *Karnataka Express*	244/631/852	7	11.35pm
Delhi	12621 *Tamil Nadu Express*	295/772/1048	10½	8.35pm
Gwalior	11077 *Jhelum Express*	178/472/644	6	9.15am
Indore	12920 *Malwa Express*	161/397/529	5	7.50am
Jabalpur	18233 *Narmada Express*	164/430/586	7	11.35pm
Mumbai (CST)	12138 *Punjab Mail*	325/857/1167	14½	5pm
Raipur	18238 *Chhattisgarh Express*	269/728/998	14½	6.55pm
Ujjain	12920 *Malwa Express*	140/322/424	3½	7.50am

*Fares are sleeper/3AC/2AC

MADHYA PRADESH & CHHATTISGARH CENTRAL MADHYA PRADESH

❶ Getting There & Away

Air

Air India (☎2770480; Bhadbhada Rd; ☺10am-5pm Mon-Sat) flies daily to Delhi (from ₹3800, one hour, 9.05am) and Mumbai (from ₹3800, two hours, 7.30pm) via Indore (₹3400, 20 minutes).

Bus

Services from central bus stand off Hamidia Rd include:

BHIMBETKA ₹30, one hour, regular, 6am to 6pm

INDORE ₹130, five hours, three daily, 6am, 6.15am and 7.30am

JABALPUR ₹230, eight hours, regular, 5am to 11pm

PACHMARHI ₹140, six hours, six daily, 5.15am, 6.15am, 8.15am, 3pm, sleeper 1am and 2.30am

SANCHI ₹30, 1½ hours, regular, 5am to 9.30pm

Train

There are more than 20 daily trains to Gwalior and Agra and more than 10 to Ujjain and Delhi. See boxed text, p638.

❶ Getting Around

Minibuses and buses (both ₹5) shuttle between New Market and Hamidia Rd all day and all evening. Catch ones to New Market at the eastern end of Hamidia Rd. Returning from New Market, you can catch them from the Nehru Statue. Autorickshaws cost about ₹40 for the same journey. The autorickshaw fare from New Market to MP Tourism Boat Club is ₹40, and from Hamidia Rd to Taj-ul-Masjid it's ₹30.

The airport is 16km northwest of central Bhopal. Expect to pay at least ₹100/200 for an autorickshaw/taxi.

Around Bhopal

ISLAMNAGAR

This now-ruined fortified city 11km north of Bhopal was the first capital of Bhopal state, founded as Jagdishpur by the Rajputs before Dost Mohammed Khan occupied and renamed it in the early 18th century. The still-standing walls enclose two villages as well as the remains of two **palaces** (Indian/foreigner ₹5/100; ☺dawn-dusk), Chaman Mahal and Rani Mahal.

The 18th-century **Chaman Mahal** is a synthesis of traditional Indian and Islamic architecture with Bengali-influenced drooping eaves. The main attraction is the Mughal water garden. There's also a *hammam* (Turkish bath) with changing rooms and water troughs in the dark, cool interior.

Adjacent is the dusty 19th-century **Rani Mahal** with a colonnaded Diwan-i-Am (Hall of Public Audience). Outside stand eight massive iron treasure chests, presumably delivered by outsized porters from the nearby *hathi khana* (elephant stables).

Catch a tempo, bus or shared jeep (all ₹10) up Berasia Rd, though you may have to change, or take an autorickshaw (₹100).

BHOJPUR

Built by the founder of Bhopal, Raja Bhoj (1010–53), Bhojpur used to be home to a 400-sq-km manmade lake, which was destroyed in the 15th century by the dambusting Mandu ruler Hoshang Shah. Thankfully, the magnificent **Bhojeshwar Temple** survived the attack.

Square in shape and simple in design, this 1000-year-old Hindu temple doesn't look much from the outside, but the interior of the sanctum, supported by four gargantuan pillars and housing the world's tallest Shiva lingam (22ft), is very powerful indeed. Beautifully carved figures now share space with beehive honeycombs on the partly restored ceiling.

Round the back, a large stony ramp illustrates how such huge pieces of rock would have been moved into position onto the temple's 5m-tall platform. To the side, fenced-off areas of rocky slopes show etchings of grander plans for a temple complex that was never finished.

Take the Bhimbetka bus to the turn-off for Bhojpur (₹10, 30 minutes), where tempos (₹10) ply the 11km-road to the temple.

BHIMBETKA

Secreted in a forest of teak and sal in craggy cliffs 46km south of Bhopal are more than 700 **rock shelters** (Indian/foreigner on foot ₹10/100, motorbike or car ₹50/200, autorickshaw ₹100/400; ⊘dawn-dusk). Around 500 of them contain some of the world's oldest prehistoric paintings.

Thanks to their natural red and white pigments, the colours are remarkably well preserved and, in certain caves, paintings of different eras adorn the same rock surface. A gamut of figures and scenes spill across the rocks: gaurs (Indian bison), rhinoceroses, bears and tigers share space with scenes of hunting, initiation ceremonies, childbirth, communal dancing, drinking, religious rites and burials.

The oldest paintings (Upper Palaeolithic) in red, often of huge animals, are thought to be 12,000 years old. Successive periods depict hunting tools, trade with the agricultural communities on the Malwa plains, and, still later, religious scenes involving tree gods. The latest are crude geometric figures probably dating from the medieval period, when much of the artistry was lost.

The rock shelters are easy to find. The 15 most accessible are numbered, signposted and linked by a concrete path. **Zoo Rock Shelter** (Shelter 4), famous for its variety of animal paintings, is one of the first you come to; **Shelter 15** features a magnificent red bison attacking a helpless stick figure. There are no facilities here, so bring water.

Highway Treat Bhimbetka (⊘07480 281558; r ₹890; ❄), with a pleasant restaurant-cafe (mains ₹60 to ₹110; ⊘8am-10pm), a children's playground and five comfortable AC rooms, is by the Bhimbetka turning, 3km from the rock shelters. The ticket office is halfway up the road to the rocks from here.

Ask your bus driver to drop you at the turning for Bhimbetka, about 6.5km beyond Obaidullaganj. It's a 45-minute, 3km walk from here. Alternatively, take an autorickshaw from Obaidullaganj.

On the return journey, flag down anything that moves (buses often won't stop for you) and go as far as Obaidullaganj (₹5), where you'll find buses to Bhopal (₹25) via the Bhojpur turning (₹15).

Sanchi

⊘07482 / POP 6784

Rising from the plains, 46km northeast of Bhopal, is a rounded hill topped with some of India's oldest Buddhist structures.

In 262 BC, repentant of the horrors he had inflicted on Kalinga in present-day Odisha, the Mauryan emperor Ashoka (see boxed text, p1087) embraced Buddhism. As a penance he built the Great Stupa at Sanchi, near the birthplace of his wife. A domed edifice used to house religious relics, it was the first Buddhist monument in the region,

Around Bhopal

although many other religious structures followed.

As Hinduism gradually reabsorbed Buddhism, the site decayed and was forgotten, until purportedly being 'rediscovered' in 1818 by a British army officer.

Although Sanchi can be visited as a day trip from Bhopal, this crossroads village is a relaxing spot to spend the night, and a number of side trips can be taken from here.

⊙ Sights

The hilltop **stupas** (Indian/foreigner ₹10/250, car ₹10, museum ₹5; ⊙dawn-dusk) are reached via a path and stone steps at the end of Monuments Rd (which is a continuation of the road that leaves the train station), where the ticket office is located.

If you're going up to the stupas for sunrise, buy a ticket the day before. Remember, it is auspicious to walk clockwise around Buddhist monuments.

Stupa 1 (Great Stupa)   SACRED SITE
Beautifully proportioned, the Great Stupa is the main structure on the hill, directly in front of you as you enter the complex from the north. Originally constructed by Ashoka, it was later enlarged and the original brick stupa enclosed within a stone one. Presently it stands 16m high and 37m in diameter. Encircling the stupa is a wall with four entrances through magnificently carved *toranas* (gateways) that are the finest Buddhist works of art in Sanchi, if not India.

Toranas
The stupa's four gateways were erected around 35 BC but had all fallen down by the time the site was rediscovered. They have since been repositioned. Scenes carved onto the pillars and their triple architraves are mainly tales from the Jatakas, episodes from Buddha's various lives. At this stage in Buddhist art he was never represented directly – his presence was alluded to through symbols. The lotus stands for his birth, the bodhi tree his enlightenment, the wheel his teachings, and the footprint and throne his presence. The stupa itself also symbolises Buddha.

The **Northern Gateway**, topped by a broken wheel of law, is the best preserved of the *toranas*. Scenes include a monkey offering a bowl of honey to Buddha, who is represented by a bodhi tree. Another panel depicts the Miracle of Sravasti – one of several miracles represented here – in which Buddha, again in the form of a bodhi tree,

ascends a road into the air. Elephants support the architraves above the columns, while delicately carved *yakshis* (maidens) hang nonchalantly on each side.

The breathtakingly carved figure of a *yakshi,* hanging from an architrave on the **Eastern Gateway**, is one of Sanchi's best-known images. One of the pillars, supported by elephants, features scenes from Buddha's entry to nirvana. Another shows Buddha's mother Maya's dream of an elephant standing on the moon, which she had when he was conceived. Across the front of the middle architrave is the Great Departure, when Buddha (a riderless horse) renounced the sensual life and set out to find enlightenment.

The back-to-back lions supporting the **Southern Gateway**, the oldest gateway, form the state emblem of India, which can be seen on every banknote. The gateway narrates Ashoka's life as a Buddhist, with scenes of Buddha's birth and another representation of the Great Departure. Also featured is the Chhaddanta Jataka, a story in which Bodhisattva (Buddha before he had reached enlightenment) took on the form of an elephant king who had six tusks. The less favoured of the elephant king's two wives was so jealous of the other that she decided to starve herself to death, vowing to come back to life as the queen of Benares in order to have the power to avenge her husband's favouritism. Her wish came true and as queen she ordered hunters to track down and kill the elephant king. A hunter found the great elephant but before he could kill it, the elephant handed over his tusks, an act so noble it led to the queen dying of remorse.

Potbellied dwarfs support the architraves of the **Western Gateway**, which has some of the site's most interesting scenes. The top architrave shows Buddha in seven different incarnations, manifested three times as a stupa and four times as a tree. The rear of one pillar shows Buddha resisting the Temptation of Mara (the Buddhist personification of evil, often called the Buddhist devil), while demons flee and angels cheer.

Other Stupas   SACRED SITE
Stupa 2 is halfway down the hill to the west (turn right at Stupa 1). If you come up from the village by the main route you can walk back down via Stupa 2, although be prepared for some off-piste fence-hopping at the bottom. Instead of gateways, 'medallions' decorate the surrounding wall – naive

in design, but full of energy and imagination. Flowers, animals and people – some mythological – ring the stupa.

Stupa 3 is northeast of the Great Stupa (you pass it on your left as you approach the Great Stupa from the main entrance) and similar in design, though smaller, with a single, rather fine gateway. It once contained relics of two important disciples of Buddha, Sari Puttha and Maha Moggallana. They were moved to London in 1853 but returned in 1953 and are now kept in the modern *vihara* (resting place).

Only the base is left of the 2nd-century-BC **Stupa 4**, which stands behind Stupa 3. Between Stupas 1 and 3 is the small **Stupa 5**, unusual in that it once contained a statue of Buddha, now displayed in the museum.

Pillars
MONUMENT

Of the scattered remains of pillars, the most important is **Pillar 10**, erected by Ashoka but later broken. Two upper sections of this beautifully proportioned and executed shaft lie side by side behind Stupa 1; the capital (head of the pillar, usually sculpted) is in the museum. **Pillar 25** (to the left of Stupa 1) dating from the Sunga period (2nd century BC), and the 5th-century-AD **Pillar 35** (to the right of Stupa 1) are less impressive.

Temples
BUDDHIST TEMPLES

Temple 18 (behind Stupa 1) is a *chaitya* (prayer room or assembly hall) remarkably similar in style to classical Greek-columned buildings. It dates from around the 7th century AD, but traces of earlier wooden buildings have been discovered beneath it. To its left is the small, also Greek-like **Temple 17**. Beyond both of them, the large **Temple 40** dates back to the Ashokan period, in part.

The rectangular **Temple 31** (beside Stupa 5) was built in the 6th or 7th century but reconstructed during the 10th or 11th century. It contains a well-executed image of Buddha.

Monasteries
MONASTERY

The earliest monasteries were made of wood and are long gone. The usual plan was of a central courtyard surrounded by monastic cells. These days only the courtyards and stone foundations remain. **Monasteries 45** and **47**, standing on the eastern ridge to the left of Stupa 1, date from the transition from Buddhism to Hinduism, with strong Hindu elements in their design. The former has two sitting Buddhas. The one housed inside is exceptional.

Behind **Monastery 51**, partway down the hill towards Stupa 2, is the **Great Bowl**, carved from a boulder, into which food and offerings were placed for distribution to the monks.

Vihara
MUSEUM

The **vihara** (⊙9am-5pm), literally 'resting place', was built to house the returned relics from Stupa 3. They can be viewed on the last Sunday of the month. It's immediately on your left as you enter the complex.

Archaeological Museum
MUSEUM

(admission ₹5, free with Stupa ticket; ⊙8am-5pm Sat-Thu) This fine museum has a small collection of sculptures from the site. The centrepiece is the 3rd-century BC lion capital from the Ashoka Pillar 10. Other highlights include a *yakshi* hanging from a mango tree, and beautifully serene Buddha figures in red sandstone – some of the earliest found anywhere. There are also some interesting photos showing the site, pre-restoration.

🛏 Sleeping & Eating

New Jaiswal Lodge   GUESTHOUSE $

(☑266508; Monuments Rd; r ₹350-550, with AC ₹750-850; ✳) This friendly place has cute, clean, colourful rooms and small private bathrooms with sit-down toilets. On your right as you exit the train station. Does food.

Gateway Retreat   HOTEL $$

(☑266723; www.mptourism.com; Bhopal-Vidisha Rd; s/d incl breakfast from ₹1590/1690; ✳≋) This family-friendly MP Tourism hotel is the most comfortable place to stay in Sanchi. AC bungalows are set among well-kept gardens with a small children's play area and a swimming pool with slide. There's a restaurant (mains ₹45 to ₹125; open 7am to 11pm) and bar (beer from ₹150). Come out of the train station, turn right at the crossroads and it's on your right.

Krishna Hotel   GUESTHOUSE $

(☑266610; Bhopal-Vidisha Rd; r ₹100-300) Simple rooftop rooms, some with sit-down flush toilets, are slightly more expensive than the darker, noisier rooms at the front. It's above Jaiswal Medical Store. Come out of the train station, turn left at the crossroads and it's on your right.

Gateway Cafeteria   INDIAN $

(☑266743; Monuments Rd; mains ₹45-90; ⊙7am-10.30pm) This clean MP Tourism place has a simple Indian menu plus coffee. Come out of the train station and keep going. It's on your left, just before the ticket office for the stupas.

ⓘ Information

There's nowhere to change money in Sanchi and the nearest ATM is in Vidisha. A couple of places in the market by the bus stand have internet access (per hr ₹30 to ₹40)

ⓘ Getting There & Around

Bike

You can rent bicycles (per hour/day ₹5/30) at the market by the bus stand.

Bus

Frequent buses connect Sanchi with Bhopal (₹25, 1½ hours, 6am to 10pm) and Vidisha (₹8, 20 minutes, 6am to 11pm). It's better to wait at the village crossroads for buses rather than going into the bus stand, which is on your right as you exit the train station.

Train

Train is a decent option for getting to Sanchi from Bhopal. It takes less than an hour so there's no need to book a seat: just turn up with enough time to queue up for a 'general' ticket (₹7 to ₹21), and squeeze on. Six daily trains leave from Bhopal (8am, 10.20am, 3.15pm, 4.10pm, 6pm and 8.55pm). Only four run in the other direction (8am, 8.50am, 4.30pm and 7.10pm).

Around Sanchi

VIDISHA

📞 07592 / POP 125,453

This small but thriving market town, 8km northeast of Sanchi, was a commercial centre in the 5th and 6th centuries BC. These days it's an interesting place for a wander or a chai break en route to the Udaigiri Caves.

Many of the attractive whitewashed or painted buildings still have old wooden balconies that overlook the market streets where horse-drawn carts share space with scooters and rickshaws. There are also a number of brightly coloured temples dotted around the old town, which is located to the left of the main road from Sanchi.

Past the town, and over the railway line, is the dusty **District Museum** (Sagar-Vidisha Rd; Indian/foreigner ₹5/50, camera ₹50; ⊙10am-5pm Tue-Sun), which houses some beautiful sculptures recovered from local sites, the most impressive of which is a 3m-high, 2nd-century-

BC stone statue of Kuber Yaksha, treasurer of the gods, on display as you enter.

It's a straightforward 30-minute cycle from Sanchi or else there are frequent buses (₹8, 20 minutes).

UDAIGIRI CAVES

Cut into a sandstone hill, about 5km northwest of Vidisha, are some 20 Gupta **cave shrines** (⊙dawn-dusk) dating from the reign of Chandragupta II (AD 382–401). Most are Hindu but two, near the top of the hill, are Jain (Caves 1 and 20) – unfortunately both are closed due to unsafe roofs.

In Cave 4 is a lingam bearing Shiva's face complete with a third eye. Cave 5 contains the finest carving – a superb image of Vishnu in his boar incarnation topped with a frieze of gods, who also flank the entrance to Cave 6. Lotus-ceilinged Cave 7 was cut out for the personal use of Chandragupta II. On the top of the hill are ruins of a 6th-century Gupta temple dedicated to the sun god.

To get here by bike from Sanchi, head towards Vidisha but about 1km before the town, turn left, following a sign for Udaigiri. Follow the road to the Betwa River, cross the river then take the first left and keep going until you reach the caves. Alternatively, take a bus to Vidisha then a rickshaw (₹100 return). A return rickshaw from Sanchi is about ₹250.

If you want to cycle back via Vidisha, cross back over the river and keep going straight instead of bearing round to the right on the road you took from Sanchi.

HELIODORUS PILLAR

The Heliodorus Pillar (Khamb Baba), just beyond the Udaigiri Caves turning, was erected by a Greek ambassador, Heliodorus from Taxila (now in Pakistan), in about 140 BC, and dedicated to Vasudeva. The pillar is worshipped by local fishermen who chain themselves to the pillar on full-moon nights. It is said they then become possessed and are able to drive evil spirits from other locals. When someone has been exorcised, they drive a nail into the tamarind tree nearby, fixing to it a lime, a piece of coconut, a red thread and supposedly the spirit. The large tree is bristling with old nails.

The pillar is close to the Udaigiri Caves. Once you cross the Betwa River, carry straight on, rather than turning left for the caves, and you'll soon see a sign directing up a small lane on your right, which leads to the pillar.

Pachmarhi

📞07578 / POP 11,370 / ELEV 1067M

Madhya Pradesh's only hill station is surrounded by waterfalls, cave temples and the forested ranges of the Satpura Tiger Reserve and offers a perfect escape from steamy central India.

Even if you don't go on an organised trek or jeep safari, you can easily spend a couple of days here cycling or hiking to the numerous sights before taking a dip in one of the natural pools that dot the area.

Explorer Captain J Forsyth 'discovered' Pachmarhi as late as 1857 and set up India's first Forestry Department at Bison Lodge in 1862. Soon after, the British army set up regional headquarters here, starting an association with the military that remains today.

A number of colonial buildings from that era have been converted into delightful guesthouses, which can be found in the Jaistambha area, 2km southwest of the small town.

◉ Sights

Satpura National Park   NATURE RESERVE
(Indian/foreigner per day ₹20/200, entrance fee per jeep Indian/foreigner ₹250/1500; ⊙dawn-dusk) A ticket for Satpura National Park must be bought at the **ticket office** (⊙8am-noon & 4-8pm Apr-Oct, 9am-1pm & 3-7pm Nov-Mar) outside Bison Lodge. It includes entry to Bison Lodge, Bee Falls, Duchess Falls, Reechgarh, Astachal, Ramykund and Rajat Prapat (including Panchuli Kund and Apsara Vihar). Other sights are free.

Bison Lodge   MUSEUM
(⊙8am-noon & 4-7pm Tue-Sun Apr-Oct, 9am-1pm & 3-7pm Tue-Sun Nov-Mar) Captain Forsyth named Bison Lodge after a herd of bison he spotted here. It's now an old-fashioned, dilapidated museum focusing on the history, flora and fauna of the Satpura region.

Caves   CAVES
The nearest sight to Pachmarhi village is **Jata Shankar**, a cave temple in a beautiful gorge about 2.5km along a good track that's signed just north of the town limits. The small Shiva shrine is hidden under a huge overhanging rock.

Just southeast of Jaistambha, you'll find **Pandav Caves**, which are believed to have been carved by Buddhists as early as the 4th century. The foundations of a brick Buddhist stupa have been excavated on top of them.

Pools & Waterfalls   WATERFALL

Just south of town, past Christchurch, the trailhead for **Bee Falls** is easily accessed by bike. There are chai and snack stalls along the way to the bottom of the trail.

Further along the main road, past the trailhead, you'll find the access roads for **Duchess Falls**, the two beauty points known as **Reechgarh** and **Astachal**, and a small, crystal-clear pool called **Ramykund**.

On the other side of Jaistambha, about 1km past Pandav Caves, is the trailhead for **Apsara Vihar** (Fairy Pool), a pool underneath a small waterfall, which is the best of Pachmarhi's natural pools for swimming. Upstream from here is **Panchuli Kund**, five descending rock pools which are great for a paddle. Steps up from the snack stall by Apsara Vihar lead to a point with magnificent views of the gorge and of **Rajat Prapat** (Big Fall), the tallest of Pachmarhi's waterfalls, which tumbles down a gully in a sheer cliff.

Chauragarh   VIEWPOINT

South of Jaistambha is the road that leads towards **Chauragarh** (1308m), Madhya Pradesh's third-highest peak. The Shiva shrine at the top attracts tens of thousands of pilgrims during Shivaratri Mela (see p611). On the way, stop at **Handi Khoh**, also known as Suicide Point, to gawk down the 100m canyon into the dense forest. You'll spy Chauragarh in the distance from here as well as **Priyadarshini** (Forsyth Point), further along the road.

About 3km beyond Priyadarshini the road ends at **Mahadeo Cave**, where a path 30m into the damp gloom reveals a lingam with attendant priest. This is the beginning of the 1365-step pilgrim trail to Chauragarh (five hours' return hike). A kilometre further on, another **Shiva shrine** is at the back of a terrifyingly narrow passage created by sticks holding open a fissure in the cliff.

🏃 Activities

All the sights mentioned here can be cycled to, although bikes have to be left at the trailheads from where the hiking begins. **Baba Cycles** (Subhash Rd; per hr/day ₹5/50; ⊙9.15am-9pm) rents bikes.

Parasailing   PARASAILING
Parasailing (per person ₹350; 9am to noon and 2.30 to 6pm) can be done at the airstrip near Reechgarh.

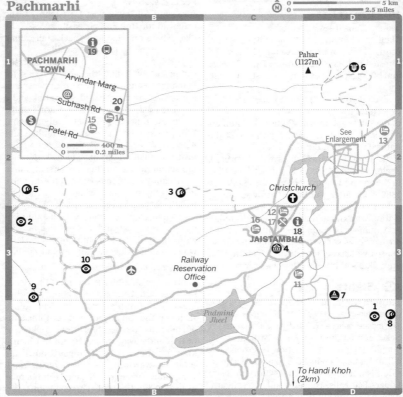

Swimming
SWIMMING

Locals paddle at the bottom of Bee Falls and Duchess Falls, and Ramykund is good for an invigorating plunge, but for a proper swim, try Apsara Vihar.

Trekking
TREKKING

Satpura Adventure Club, based at Hotel Saketh, can arrange guides (per day ₹300; Hindi-speaking only) to take you on treks around the area. Forestry commission guides (per day ₹315 to ₹510) can also be arranged at Bison Lodge ticket office; some speak English.

Wildlife Safaris
JEEP SAFARIS

Satpura Tiger Reserve (entrance fee per jeep Indian/foreign ₹2000/3000; 16 Oct-30 Jun) has tigers and leopards, although you're unlikely to see either. What you will get, though, is virgin forests without another tourist jeep in sight, plus plenty of monkeys, deer and birds of all types. On top of your group and jeep entrance fee, you will need to pay for a guide (₹315). Fees are per jeep, not per person. Unlike in other tiger parks, where safaris are split into morning and afternoon outings, here you get a full day in the reserve, and there are opportunities to overnight in the reserve at a **Forest Rest House** (d Indian/foreign ₹1000/2500). All food costs are extra. Safaris are best arranged at Bison Lodge.

🛏 Sleeping & Eating

High seasons are from April to July and December to January, when places fill up and room rates rocket. The same applies during national holidays and major festivals.

PACHMARHI TOWN
Hotel Saketh HOTEL **$**
(☎252165; hotelsaket2003@yahoo.com; r ₹200-500, with AC ₹1000; ❄) There is a wide range of rooms in this friendly hotel on a quiet side

Pachmarhi

◎ Sights
1	Apsara Vihar (Fairy Pool)	D4
2	Astachal	A3
3	Bee Falls	B2
4	Bison Lodge	C3
5	Duchess Falls	A2
6	Jata Shankar	D1
	Panchuli Kund	(see 1)
7	Pandav Caves	D3
8	Rajat Prapat	D4
9	Ramykund	A3
10	Reechgarh	A3

◎ Sleeping
11	Evelyn's Own	C3
12	Glen View	C3
13	Hotel Highlands	D2
14	Hotel Prateek	B2
15	Hotel Saketh	A2
16	Rock-End Manor	C3

◎ Eating
17	Nandavan Restaurant	C3
	Raj Bhoj	(see 15)

Information
18	MP Tourism	C3
19	MP Tourism Kiosk	A1

Transport
20	Baba Cycles	B1

street off Patel Rd, from budget classics to midrange options. The attached restaurant **Raj Bhoj** (mains ₹30-90) does Gujarati, Bengali, Chinese and South Indian dishes, including delicious breakfast dosa.

Hotel Prateek　　　　HOTEL **$$**
(☑252427; Subhash Rd; r ₹495-795, with AC ₹995; ❀) Kitsch rooms decorated in pinks, browns and maroons come with neon lighting, flowery net curtains and corner beds with velvet covers. Bathrooms are large and clean.

Hotel Highlands　　　　HOTEL **$$**
(☑252099; highland@mptourism.com; Pipariya Rd; r ₹890, with AC ₹1290; ❀) This family-friendly MP Tourism property on the approach road into Pachmari has rooms with high ceilings, dressing rooms, modern bathrooms and verandas, which are dotted around well-tended gardens. There's a children's play area and a restaurant.

▨ **Evelyn's Own**　　　GUESTHOUSE **$$**
(☑252056; evelynsown@gmail.com; r incl breakfast ₹1000-4000; ❀@❀) Simply gorgeous colonial-era cottage built by a reverend then bought and converted into a guesthouse by the wonderfully welcoming Colonel Balwant Rao and his wife Pramilla. The main cottage, where you can share meals (veg/meat ₹100/150) with the colonel and his wife, is full of family portraits and period furniture. Guest rooms – also beautifully decorated – are in buildings dotted around the fabulously lush gardens, which also contain a small swimming pool. Follow the signs to Satpura Retreat, which is down the same dirt track.

Rock-End Manor　　HERITAGE HOTEL **$$$**
(☑252079; mptremph@sancharnet.in; s/d ₹5028/5628; ❀) Another gorgeous colonial-era building, whitewashed Rock-End is perched above the parched fairways of the army golf course. Spacious rooms have wonderfully high ceilings, and furnishings are luxurious with quality upholstery and framed paintings. There are also great views to be had from seating areas around the covered walkway.

Glen View　　　HERITAGE HOTEL **$$**
(☑252533; gview@mptourism.com; s/d ₹2790/3290, heritage rooms ₹4190/4690; ❀) Large, comfortable AC tents and cottages are dotted around the shaded gardens of a huge colonial-era cottage, which has also been converted to house the luxury 'heritage' rooms. Has restaurant and bar.

Nandavan Restaurant　　　INDIAN **$**
(mains ₹30-90; ◷9.30am-11pm) An outdoor restaurant with an interesting take on the concept of a zoo, as monkeys sit outside watching humans eating in a cage. South Indian, Gujarati and thalis.

❶ Information
Internet Cafe (Subhash Rd; per hr ₹30; ◷7am-11pm)

MP Tourism (☑252100; ◷10am-5pm Mon-Fri) Near Jaistamba. Also has kiosk by bus station.

State Bank of India ATM (cnr main road & Patel Rd)

❶ Getting There & Away
Eight daily buses go to Bhopal (₹140, six hours, 7am–8pm). The two evening ones (7pm to 8pm) are sleepers and carry on to Indore (seat/bed ₹300/350, 12 hours). There are three buses – all nonsleeper – to Nagpur (₹190, eight hours, 8am, 10am and 9pm). The friendly guys at the bus-ticket counter are around from 7am to 9pm.

MADHYA PRADESH & CHHATTISGARH PACHMARHI

All Bhopal buses, plus some extra local ones, go via Pipariya (₹50, two hours), from where you can catch trains to onward destinations such as Jabalpur and Varanasi without having to go all the way to Bhopal. Train tickets can be bought at the **Railway Reservation Office** (⊗8am-2pm) beside the forlorn Woodlands Adventure Camp. The bus station and train station in Pipariya are next to each other.

If you're coming from Pipariya, shared jeeps to Pachmarhi leave far more frequently than buses and cost the same.

ⓘ Getting Around

A place in a shared jeep costs about ₹150 for a day. Cycling or hiking will give you more freedom.

WESTERN MADHYA PRADESH

Ujjain

⏱0734 / POP 431,162

Underwhelming at first, Ujjain grows on you the more you explore. The area around the train and bus stations is nothing special, but wander down towards the river ghats, via Ujjain's maze of alleyways, and you'll discover an older, more spiritual side to this small town which has been attracting traders and

pilgrims for hundreds of years. An undeniable energy pulses through the temples here – perhaps because this is one of Hinduism's seven sacred cities, or perhaps because the Tropic of Cancer runs through Ujjain.

The town is also one of four sites in India which hosts the incredible Kumbh Mela (p1103), during which millions bathe in the Shipra River. It takes place here every 12 years, normally during April and May. The next one is in 2016 (22 April to 21 May). Six years before and after each Kumbh Mela there is a slightly smaller Ardh (Half) Mela. On all other years a smaller festival called Magh Mela is held.

History

The Guptas, the Mandu sultans, Maharaja Jai Singh (of Jaipur fame), the Marathas and the Scindias have all had a controlling hand in Ujjain's long and chequered past, which stretches back to when the city, originally called Avantika, was an important trade stop. When the Scindias moved their capital to Gwalior in 1810, Ujjain's prominence declined rapidly.

⊙ Sights

Temples   TEMPLES

Mahakaleshwar Mandir

While this is not the most stunning temple, tagging along behind a conga-line through

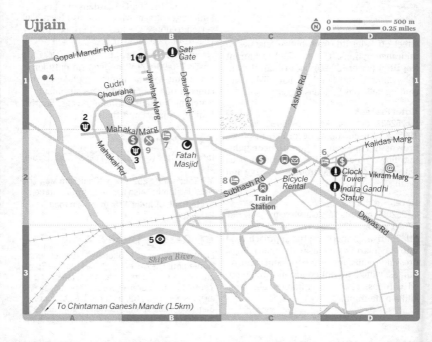

Ujjain

the underground chambers can be magical. At nonfestival times, the marble walkways are a peaceful preamble to the subterranean chamber containing one of India's 12 sacred Shiva shrines known as *jyoti linga* – naturally occurring lingam believed to derive currents of *shakti* (creative energies) from within themselves rather than being ritually invested with *mantra-shakti* by priests. The temple was destroyed by Altamish in 1235 and restored by the Scindias in the 19th century. You may be asked to give a donation, but it's not compulsory.

Gopal Mandir

The Scindias built this marble-spired temple, a magnificent example of Maratha architecture, in the 19th century. Muslim pillagers originally stole the sanctum's silver-plated doors from Somnath Temple in Gujarat (p698) and installed them in Ghazni, Afghanistan. Mohammed Shah Abdati later took them to Lahore (in present-day Pakistan), before Mahadji Scindia brought them back here. The **alleyways** north, east and west of here are wonderful places to get lost in.

Harsiddhi Mandir

Built during the Maratha period, this temple enshrines a famous image of goddess Annapurna. At the entrance, two tall blackened stone towers bristling with lamps are a special feature of Maratha art. They add to the spectacle of **Navratri** (Festival of Nine Nights; Hindu festival leading up to Dussehra) in September/October when filled with oil and ignited.

Ujjain

◎ Sights
1 Gopal Mandir..B1
2 Harsiddhi Mandir.................................A1
3 Mahakaleshwar Mandir......................B2
4 Ram Ghat...A1
5 Vedh Shala (Observatory).................B3

◎ Sleeping
6 Hotel Grand Tower..............................D2
7 Hotel Pleasure Landmark..................B2
8 Hotel Rama Krishna............................C2

◎ Eating
New Sudama..............................(see 8)
9 Shivam Restaurant..............................B2
Zharokha Restaurant.................(see 6)

Chintaman Ganesh Mandir

This temple is believed to be of considerable antiquity – the assembly hall's artistically carved pillars date to the Parmara period. Worshippers flock here to pray to the deity, whose name means 'assurer of freedom from worldly anxieties'. It's an easy cycle from the centre, mostly through farmland. Pass the observatory and keep to the left.

Ram Ghat   GHAT

The most central and most popular of Ujjain's river ghats is best visited at dawn or dusk when the devout chime cymbals and light candles at the water's edge. People bathe here at all times of the day, though. You can also rent **pedal boats** (₹10).

Vedh Shala (Observatory)   HISTORIC BUILDING

(Jantar Mantar; admission ₹5; ⊙8am-5.30pm) Ujjain has been India's Greenwich since the 4th century BC and this simple but interesting observatory – now with a huge globe positioned beside its entrance – was built by Maharaja Jai Singh in about 1730. He also built observatories in Jaipur, Delhi, Varanasi and Mathura, but Ujjain's is the only one still in use. Among the instruments in the small garden are two marble-topped sundials – one a conventional sundial, the other made up of two large quadrants split by a tall staircase whose shadow tells the time.

Sleeping

Hotel Rama Krishna   HOTEL $

(☑2553017; www.hotelramakrishna.co.in; Subhash Rd; s/d without bathroom ₹150/200, s ₹200-3400, d ₹300-400, d with AC from ₹700; ❋) This cleaner-than-average Subhash Rd hotel has rooms with white-tiled floors, TV and sit-down flush toilet.

Hotel Pleasure Landmark   HOTEL $$

(☑2557867; 98 Mahakal Marg; r ₹700-800, with AC ₹1200; ❋) Great location from which to launch yourself into the old town, rooms here are small but smart and clean and come with decent quality wooden furniture.

Hotel Grand Tower   HOTEL $$

(☑2553699; 1 Vikram Marg; s/d from ₹800/900, with AC from ₹1200/1400; ❋) Large, clean, well-kept rooms, excellent service and a very good restaurant.

✗ Eating

Thali restaurants line Subhash Rd and are good value (from ₹20) but have no English menus and don't open before around 9.30am.

TOP CHOICE **Shivam Restaurant** INDIAN $
(mains ₹50-80; ☺7am-11pm) This friendly
and very popular veg restaurant in the
basement below Hotel Satyam has a fabulous menu with detailed descriptions of
every dish. Choose from tandoori kebabs,
a selection of paneer dishes, koftas and a
variety of stuffed vegetables, or just come
for the south Indian breakfasts. Also does
thalis (₹35 to ₹70).

Zharokha Restaurant INDIAN $$
(mains ₹50-90; ☺7am-3.30pm & 7-11.15pm)
The vegetarian restaurant at Hotel Grand
Tower serves excellent Kashmiri, Punjabi
and Chinese food and has 1st-floor balcony
seating. The service is friendly here too.

New Sudama INDIAN $
(mains ₹40-60; ☺8.30am-11pm) The best
of the many Subhash Rd offerings, this
clean restaurant attached to Hotel Rama
Krishna has comfy booth seating and
decent quality Indian food.

❶ Information

There are ATMs all over Ujjain, including two next
to Hotel Grand Tower, but the nearest place to
change money is Indore.

Cyber Cafe (per hr ₹10; ☺10am-10pm) Walk
up Vikram Marg, turn left at the roundabout
and it's on your right in a basement. You can
you hook up your laptop.

DF.com (per hr ₹15; ☺10.30am-10pm) Only in-
ternet cafe we could find in the old part of town.

❶ Getting There & Away

Bus

Services from the bus stand include the follow-
ing. For Mandu or Maheshwar, change at Dhar.

BHOPAL ₹130, five hours, two daily, 6am and
7.30am

DHAR ₹80, four hours, four daily, 5.30am,
8.30am, 9am and 9.45am

INDORE ₹38, two hours, every 15 minutes,
5.30am to 11pm

OMKARESHWAR ₹91, four hours, four daily,
6am, 8am, 11am and 4pm

Train

The two direct trains to Gwalior and Agra arrive at
stupid o'clock so you're better off going via Bhopal
which, like Indore, is served by more than 10 daily
trains. See the boxed text (p648) for details.

❶ Getting Around

A cycle rickshaw from the train station to Ram
Ghat costs ₹20, while a tonga costs ₹30. You
can also rent dirt-cheap **bicycles** (per hr/day
₹3/15; ☺7am-11pm) from a place behind the
bus stand.

Handy Bus No 9 (₹4) runs between Jawahar
Marg in the old town and Chintaman Ganesh
Mandir, via the train station and the clock tower.

Prices from the prepaid autorickshaw booth
outside the train station include:

RAM GHAT ₹30

CHINTAMAN GANESH MANDIR ₹100 return

FOUR-HOUR TOUR AROUND UJJAIN ₹300

Indore

☑0731 / POP 1.52 MILLION

The Holkar dynasty left behind some fine
buildings here, and you'll find some cool ca-
fes thanks to the city's ever-burgeoning cof-
fee culture, but Indore – Madhya Pradesh's
business powerhouse – is primarily used
by tourists as the gateway to Omkareshwar
(p651),Maheshwar (p653) or Mandu (p654).

HANDY TRAINS FROM UJJAIN

DESTINATION	TRAIN NO & NAME	FARE (₹)*	DURATION (HR)	DEPARTURE
Bhopal	19656 *All Bhopal Express*	120/292/394	3½	7.50am
Delhi	12919 *Malwa Express*	333/881/1199	15	2.07pm
Indore	18234 *Narmada Pas Express*	80/210/279	2	8.40am
Jaipur	12465 *Ranthambore Express*	135/247/502/638**	8½	8.05am
Mumbai (Central)	12962 *Avantika Express*	305/801/1087	13	5.35pm

*Fares are sleeper/3AC/2AC

**2nd class/sleeper/chair car/3AC

⊙ Sights

Lal Bagh Palace   MUSEUM
(Indian/foreigner ₹5/100; ☺10am-5pm Tue-Sun)
Built between 1886 and 1921, Lal Bagh Palace is the finest building left by the Holkar dynasty. Replicas of the Buckingham Palace gates creak at the entrance to the 28-hectare garden, where, close to the palace, there is a statue of Queen Victoria. The palace is dominated by European styles, with baroque and rococo dining rooms, an English library with leather armchairs, a Renaissance sitting room with ripped sofas and a Palladian queen's bedroom. An autorickshaw from the town centre to here is about ₹40.

Central Museum   MUSEUM
(AB Rd; Indian/foreigner ₹10/100, camera/video ₹50/200; ☺10am-5pm Tue-Sun) Housed in another fine Holkar building, this museum has one of Madhya Pradesh's best collections of medieval and premedieval Hindu sculptures, along with tools, weaponry and copper-engraved land titles. Skirmishes took place here during the First War of Independence (Indian Uprising) – the well in the garden was poisoned during the struggle.

Gandhi Hall   HISTORIC BUILDING
This Gothic town hall, built in 1904 and originally called King Edward's Hall, stands incongruously on MG Rd like a ghost of the Independence era.

⌁ Sleeping

Hotel Neelam   HOTEL $
(☏2466001; 33/2 Patel Bridge Corner; s ₹300-350, d ₹400-475, s/d with AC ₹550/750; ❄) One of the few budget places near the train and bus stations that accepts foreigners, friendly Neelam is very well run and has simple but clean rooms off a central courtyard.

Hotel Shreemaya   HOTEL $$$
(☏2515555; shree@shreemaya.com; 12 RNT Marg; s/d from ₹1850/2500; ❄@☎) This professionally run place is quality throughout. Modern rooms with wide-screen TV and coffee maker are in immaculate condition and there's free wi-fi in all of them. Rates include breakfast.

Hotel Chanakya   HOTEL $$
(☏2704497; RNT Marg, Chhawni Chowk; s/d from ₹500/600, with AC from ₹800/900; ❄) Rooms here are functional rather than flash, but staff members are friendly and it's right in the heart of an interesting section of the old town. There's a restaurant upstairs and

a very popular sweet shop on the ground floor. Note, the cheapest rooms don't have windows.

Maasharda Hotel   HOTEL $
(☏4006562; Sarvate bus stand 4 Nasia Rd; r ₹300, with AC ₹600; ❄) Good-value, clean choice near the bus stand. This hotel is sometimes reluctant to take foreign guests, but smile sweetly when you arrive and you should be OK.

✕ Eating & Drinking

Indian Coffee House   SOUTH INDIAN $
(MG Rd; mains ₹30-80, thalis ₹60-75; ☺7.30am-10pm) Drink coffee (₹10) with Indore's judiciary at this branch of the excellent Indian Coffee House set inside the grounds of the commissioner's office and near the district court. As always, a top spot for breakfast, with dosa and particularly good *idli* sharing the menu with eggs and toast.

Shree Chotiwala   INDIAN $
(Nath Mandir Rd; mains ₹40-75; ☺10.30am-11pm)
This very popular restaurant has comfy booth seating and a family-friendly veg menu that includes Jain dishes and a children's thali. An excellent choice for an evening meal.

Shreemaya Celebration   BAKERY $$
(Tuko Ganj; mains ₹35-115; ☺7.30am-10.30pm)
This clean and modern bakery next to Hotel Shreemaya sells pastries, sandwiches, cookies and cakes, as well as a handful of mains, including South Indian, Chinese and pizza. Also has juices, shakes and coffee, making this a good pick for breakfast if you can't be bothered to trek to Indian Coffee House.

Apna   INDIAN $
(Sarvate bus stand; mains ₹40-70, beer from ₹105; ☺10am-11.30pm) This 50-year-old bar and restaurant right opposite the bus stand serves up delicious veg and meat dishes from an all-Indian menu as well as the usual selection of beers and cheap whiskeys.

Mr Beans   CAFE $$
(MG Rd; coffee from ₹27; ☺9am-11pm) Slick cafe housed in a charming 100-year-old colonial-era building. There are snacks, the coffee's excellent and you can even puff on a sheesha pipe (₹225) if that sort of thing takes your fancy.

Buddy's Cafe   CAFE $
(MG Rd; mains ₹45-80, coffee ₹20; ☺2-11pm)
Popular with young Indorians who come for the atmosphere rather than the quality

MADHYA PRADESH & CHHATTISGARH INDORE

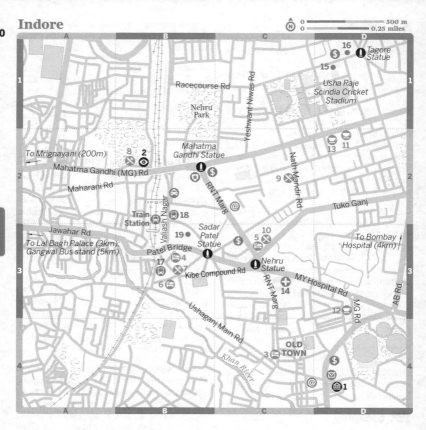

of the food and drinks, Buddy's has outdoor seating in a large roadside front garden and serves OK food as well as juices, shakes and instant coffee. Sheesha pipes (₹200) are also available.

Monkey Cafe   CAFE **$$**
(MG Rd; coffee from ₹34; ◷11am-midnight) Good-quality coffee, wi-fi (₹40) and DVDs shown on a giant screen. Music, though, is often deafeningly loud and sometimes of the karaoke variety. Oh, and yes, you guessed it; there are sheesha pipes here too (₹250).

🛍 Shopping

Mrignayani   HANDICRAFTS
(165 MG Rd; ◷11am-1.30pm & 2.30-8pm Mon-Sat) Fixed-price government emporium with two floors crammed with handicrafts from across the state, including leather toy animals – an Indore speciality.

It's on the left, just before you reach the Sarasvati River.

ℹ Information

ATMs are all over town.

007 Cyber Gallery (Silver Mall; per hr ₹10; ◷9am-11pm) Internet cafe serving drinks and snacks.

Bombay Hospital (✆4077000; www.bombay hospitalindore.com; Indore Ring Rd) Indore's best general hospital.

Main post office (AB Rd; ◷8am-8pm Mon-Sat, 10am-4pm Sun)

Royal Chemist (MY Hospital Rd; ◷9.15am-10pm)

State Bank of India (AB Rd; ◷10.30am-4.30pm Mon-Fri, 10.30am-2.30pm Sat) Changes travellers cheques and cash, and has an ATM.

Wintech Cyber (1st fl; per hr ₹10; ◷11am-10pm) Internet cafe set back from Ushaganj Main Rd.

Indore

ⓘ Getting There & Away

Air
Air India (☏2431595/6; Racecourse Rd; ⊙10am-1pm & 2-5pm Mon-Sat) flies daily to Mumbai and Delhi (both from around ₹3000).

Jet Airways (☏2544590; Racecourse Rd; ⊙9.30am-6pm Mon-Sat) has daily flights to Mumbai, Delhi, Hyderabad, Ahmedabad and Raipur.

Bus
Bus services from Sarwate bus stand include those listed below. For Maheshwar, change at Dhamnod.

BHOPAL ₹125, five hours, every 30 minutes, 5am to midnight.

DHAMNOD ₹50, three hours, every 30 minutes, 7am to 5pm

GWALIOR seat/sleeper ₹200/250, 12 hours, three daily, 7pm, 8pm and 9pm

OMKARESHWAR ₹125, three hours, frequent, 7am to 4.30pm

PACHMARHI seat/sleeper ₹200/250, 12 hours, four daily, 5pm, 6pm, 7pm and 8pm

UJJAIN ₹40, two hours, frequent, 6am to 10pm
For Mandu, catch a bus from Gangwal bus stand to Dhar (₹45, three hours, 6am to 10.30pm) from where you can change for Mandu (₹20, one hour, last bus 7pm). Shared minivans (₹10) go between Gangwal bus stand and the centre. Private autorickshaws charge around ₹40.

Taxi
Private taxi firms on the service road parallel to Valiash Nagar charge around ₹1500 return to Mandu and the same price for a trip incorporating Omkareshwar and Maheshwar.

Train
There are six daily trains to Bhopal and more than 10 to Ujjain – see boxed text, p652. The **train reservation office** (⊙8am-8pm Mon-Sat, 8am-2pm Sun) is 200m east of the train station.

ⓘ Getting Around
The airport is 9km from the city. Allow 45 minutes. Autorickshaws charge around ₹100, taxis ₹150 to ₹200. Autorickshaw journeys around Indore cost ₹20 to ₹30.

Omkareshwar
☏07280 / POP 6616

One of a number of holy places with ghats referred to as a 'mini Varanasi', this Om-shaped island attracts pilgrims in large numbers and has become a popular chill-out destination on the backpacker trail.

The controversial dam (p1153) has changed the look of Omkareshwar considerably, but the island has retained its spiritual vibe and remains a pleasant place to stay.

Much activity takes place off the island, at a market square known as Getti Chowk (from where the old bridge crosses to the island), and on Mamaleshwar Rd, which links Getti Chowk to the bus stand. If you continue straight along Mamaleshwar Rd from the bus stand, without turning left to Getti Chowk, you'll find steps leading down to the ghats (where you can cross the river on boats for ₹5). Beyond is the new bridge and the dam.

The path leading from the old bridge to Shri Omkar Mandhata temple is the hub of the island.

◉ Sights & Activities

Shri Omkar Mandhata   HINDU TEMPLE
Tourists can rub shoulders with sadhus in the island's narrow lanes, browse the colourful stalls selling chillums and souvenir linga,

HANDY TRAINS FROM INDORE

DESTINATION	TRAIN NO & NAME	FARE (₹)*	DURATION (HR)	DEPARTURE
Bhopal	12919 Malwa Express	161/397/529	5	12.25pm
Mumbai	12962 Avantika Express	320/847/1151	15	3.50pm
Delhi	12919 Malwa Express	350/927/1262	16½	12.25pm
Ujjain	12919 Malwa Express	140/240/309	2	12.25pm

*Fares are sleeper/3AC/2AC

or join pilgrims attending the thrice daily *puja* (prayer) at **Shri Omkar Mandhata**. This cave-like temple, which houses the only shapeless *jyothi lingam* (12 important shrines dedicated to Shiva), is one of many Hindu and Jain monuments on the island.

Other Temples   HINDU TEMPLES
From the old bridge, instead of turning right to Shri Omkar Mandhata, you can also head left and walk up the 287 steps to the 11th-century **Gaudi Somnath Temple**, from where you can descend the hill to the northern tip of the island, where sadhus bathe in the confluence of the holy Narmada and Keveri Rivers. You can climb the narrow, inner staircase of the temple or just sit and watch the many langur monkeys that play round here. Nearby, is a 30m-tall **Shiva statue**, built by the Raj Rajeshwari Seva Sahsrhan Trust. The path passing in front of the statue can be followed back to the ghats (45 minutes), up and down hills and past a number of temple ruins. Don't miss the beautifully sculpted **Siddhanatha Temple** (left at the T-junction in the pathway) with marvellous elephant carvings around its base.

🛏 Sleeping & Eating

TOP CHOICE **Manu Guest House**   GUESTHOUSE $
(☏9826749004; r ₹200, without bathroom ₹100) Give it a couple of days and you'll feel like part of the family that runs this wonderfully welcoming guesthouse. Rooms are simple but very well looked after and bathrooms are shared only, but kept clean. There's no restaurant, but your hosts will whip up a delicious thali (₹50) if you ask in advance. The other great thing about this guesthouse is its location. This is pretty much the only place to stay on the island itself that isn't a *dharamsala* (pilgrim's rest house) and it's perched high above the old bridge meaning that it's lovely and quiet, but has great views

of all the activity going on below. It's hard to find, though. Cross the old bridge from Getti Chowk and turn right. After about 100m, you may spot a tiny sign for the guesthouse that leads you vaguely in the right direction, up a lot of steps. Keep asking the way as you climb.

Maharaja Guesthouse   GUESTHOUSE $
(☏271237; r ₹150-600, without bathroom ₹70) Like something out of an adventure book, this 600-year-old stone building, accessed via a small path off Getti Chowk, is slowly being swallowed up by the undergrowth on the cliffs overlooking the river. Its nine extremely basic rooms are all in various states of disrepair, and come with tap-and-bucket showers and squat toilets only, but each has its own unique character – a wooden doorway here, a carved alcove there. Room 1, with family portraits on the walls and two doorways that lead out to private clifftop river views, is certainly worth asking for.

Ganesh Guest House   GUESTHOUSE $
(☏271370; r ₹150-200) Off the path leading down to the ghats from Mamaleshwar Rd, friendly Ganesh has neat and tidy budget rooms and a peaceful ambience. Its shaded garden restaurant (mains ₹50 to ₹130) overlooking the ghats has a multicuisine menu including Western breakfasts.

Brahmin Bhojanalaya   INDIAN $
(Mamaleshwar Rd; mains ₹30-70; ⊗8am-10pm) There are a number of no-nonsense *dhabas* (snack bars) in Omkareshwar, both on the island and on the mainland, especially in Getti Chowk. None has an English sign, although this one does at least have an English menu. It's on your left as you walk up from the bus stand, 50m before the road bears left towards Getti Chowk. You may have to ask for help to locate it, but once you're inside you'll find a decent selection of tasty veg dishes.

Lassi & Juice Centre CAFE $

(Getti Chowk; drinks ₹10-30; ⊘7am-11pm) A great place to sit and while away time with some people-watching, this pocket-sized cafe on Getti Chowk does magnificent lassis and delicious fruit salads as well as breakfasts and snacks.

ℹ Information

Some telephone stalls on Mamaleshwar Rd and on the island have a computer and a stuttering **internet connection** (per hr ₹50). A State Bank of India **ATM** (Mamaleshwar Rd) is near the bus stand. There's a **pharmacy** (⊘9am-9pm) diagonally opposite.

ℹ Getting There & Away

Services from the bus stand include:

DHAMNOD (for Mandu, via Oonera) ₹55, 3½ hours, regular, 6am to 5pm

INDORE ₹60, two hours, regular, 6am to 6pm

MAHESHWAR ₹45, three hours, regular, 6am to 4.30pm

UJJAIN ₹100, four hours, four daily, 6am, 11.30am, 2.30pm and 6pm

Maheshwar

☑07283 / POP 19,649

The friendly, peaceful town of Maheshwar has long held spiritual significance – it's mentioned in the Mahabharata and Ramayana (p1108) under its old name, Mahishmati, and still draws sadhus and *yatris* (pilgrims) to its ancient ghats and temples on the holy Narmada River. The town enjoyed a golden age in the late 18th century under Holkar queen Ahilyabai, who built the palace in the towering fort and many other monuments. Away from the ghats and historic buildings, Maheshwar's colourful streets house old wooden doorways and overhanging balconies fronting brightly painted local homes.

The river, and the fort which overlooks it, is about 1.5km south of the bus stand. Leaving the bus stand, walk straight over the crossroads and continue past the internet cafe and ATM until you reach a floodlit roundabout. Take the left fork to get to the ghats via Hansa Heritage hotel, Labboo's Café and the fort. Take the right fork to head directly to the ghats.

◉ Sights & Activities

Fort & Palace HISTORIC SITE

Apart from the holy river itself, the most treasured part of the town is its 16th-century **fort**.

The huge, imposing ramparts were built by Emperor Akbar, while the **Maheshwar Palace** and several **temples** within its grounds were added during the reign of Holkar queen Ahilyabai (r 1767-95). The palace is part public courtyard, part posh hotel. Housed within the courtyard, among a collection of rusty matchlocks and dusty palanquins, is a glass-cased statue of Ahilyabai, treated with the reverence of a shrine. Nearby is a Shiva temple with a golden lingam – the starting point for palanquin processions on Ahilyabai's birthday (see p611) and Dussehra.

Temples HINDU TEMPLES

From the ramparts of the fort you can see boats (return trip per person/boat ₹10/100) and incense smoke drifting across the water to **Baneshwar Temple**, located on a tiny island in the middle of the river. Descending to the dhobi-wallahs (clothes washers) at the **ghats**, you pass two impressive stone **temples**. The one on the right, guarded by stone Holkar sentries and a frieze of elephants, houses more images of Ahilyabai and two candle towers, lit during festivals.

Rehwa Society HANDICRAFTS WORKSHOP

(☑273203; www.rehwasociety.org; ⊘10am-6pm Wed-Mon, shop open daily) Between the palace and the two stone temples a small doorway announces the NGO Rehwa Society, a craft cooperative where profits are ploughed back into the education, housing and welfare of the weavers. A local school, run entirely by Rehwa, is behind the workshop. Maheshwar saris are famous for their unique weave and simple, geometric patterns, often using stripes. You can watch the weavers at work and buy shawls, saris, scarves and fabrics (from ₹450) made from silk, cotton and wool. Volunteers with some design background are always welcome, as are those interested in volunteer teaching at the school.

🛏 Sleeping & Eating

TOP CHOICE **Labboo's Café** GUESTHOUSE, CAFE $$

(☑09229125267; r ₹1500) Not only a delightful cafe in a shaded courtyard (open 8am to 8pm), but also a place with six wonderful rooms to stay in. All are different but each is decorated with care and attention, and two of them actually form part of the fort's outer wall – the upper one coming with its own fort-wall veranda. The cafe menu is snacks only (₹10 to ₹40), but staff will whip up a delicious, unlimited thali (₹100) if you ask nicely. They also organise river trips (per hour per boat ₹200) here.

Hansa Heritage HOTEL **$$**
(☎273296; r ₹1050; ❄) Despite the name, this place is almost brand new, but it's been built with style and quality throughout. Smart, modern rooms have a rustic feel with mud and woodchip interior walls, antique-looking wooden furniture and attractive coloured-glass window panes. Bathrooms are also very modern and spotlessly clean.

Ahilya Fort HERITAGE HOTEL **$$$**
(☎273329, Delhi 01141551575; www.ahilyafort.com; r Indian ₹7000-9000, foreigner ₹12,000-16,500; ❄@≋) This superior-quality heritage hotel is owned by Prince Shivaji Rao Holka, a direct descendent of Ahilyabai, and forms part of Maheshwar Palace. Rooms are indeed palatial and some come with fabulous river views, while lush gardens house exotic fruit trees, vegetable patches and a lovely swimming pool. Rates include all meals as well as boat trips on the river. Booking ahead is pretty much essential. Nonguests who fancy a splurge can eat lunch or dinner here. The sumptuous menu is set, as is the ₹1500 per person price. You'll need to book your place at a table a few hours in advance and pay a deposit.

Akash Deep GUESTHOUSE **$**
(Kila Rd; r ₹200-500) The best budget option in town, friendly Akash has clean, spacious rooms, some with TV. Checkout time is 10am. Next door to Hansa Heritage.

ⓘ Information

Internet cafe (per hr ₹25; ⊘10am-9pm)

ⓘ Getting There & Away

There are regular buses to Omkareshwar (₹45, three hours, 9am to 5.30pm) and Dhamnod (₹10, 30 minutes, 7am to 11pm) where you can change for Indore (₹55, two hours, regular, last bus 9pm). For Mandu, first head to Dhamnod then take a Dhar-bound bus as far as a forked junction in the main road, known as Oonera (₹25, two hours). From there flag down a bus (₹10, 30 minutes) or hitch for the final 14km to Mandu.

Mandu

☏07292 / POP 8550 / ELEV 634M
Perched on top of a pleasantly green, thinly forested 20-sq-km plateau, picturesque Mandu is home to some of India's finest examples of Afghan architecture. The area is littered with palaces, tombs, monuments and mosques, all within easy cycling distance of each other. Some cling to the edge of ravines, others are beside lakes, while Rupmati's Pavilion, the most romantic of them all, sits majestically at the far end of the plateau, overlooking the vast plains below.

History

Raja Bhoj, of Bhopal fame, founded Mandu as a fortress retreat in the 10th century before it was conquered by the Muslim rulers of Delhi in 1304. When the Mughals captured Delhi in 1401, the Afghan Dilawar Khan, governor of Malwa, set up his own little kingdom and Mandu's golden age began.

Although Dilawar Khan established Mandu as an independent kingdom, it was his son, Hoshang Shah, who shifted the capital from Dhar to Mandu and raised it to its greatest splendour.

In 1526, Bahadur Shah of Gujarat conquered Mandu, only to be ousted in 1534 by the Mughal Humayun, who in turn lost the kingdom to Mallu Khan, an officer of the Khalji dynasty. Ten more years of feuds and invasions saw Baz Bahadur eventually emerge in the top spot, but in 1561 he fled Mandu to avoid facing Akbar's advancing troops.

After Akbar added Mandu to the Mughal empire, it kept a considerable degree of independence, until taken by the Marathas in 1732. The capital of Malwa was then shifted back to Dhar, and the slide in Mandu's fortunes that had begun with the absconding of Baz Bahadur became a plummet.

◉ Sights & Activities

There are three main groups of ruins: the Royal Enclave, the Village Group and the Rewa Kund Group. Each requires its own separate ticket. All other sights are free.

Royal Enclave HISTORIC SITE
(Indian/foreigner ₹5/100, video ₹25; ⊘dawn-dusk Sat-Thu) These ruins are the only ones fenced off into one single complex. There's a **Publication Centre** (⊘10am-6pm) selling guidebooks by the entrance and a shaded garden canteen selling tea, coffee and snacks by Hindola Mahal.

Jahaz Mahal PALACE
Also called the Ship Palace, this is the most famous building in Mandu. Built on a narrow strip of land between **Munja** and **Kapur Tanks**, with a small upper storey like a ship's bridge (use your imagination), it's far longer (120m) than it is wide (15m).

Ghiyas-ud-din, who is said to have had a harem of 15,000 maidens, constructed its lookouts, scalloped arches, airy rooms and beautiful pleasure pools.

Taveli Mahal
MUSEUM

These former stables now house a small **Archaeological Museum** (☉8am-6pm), which features a handful of artefacts found here including 11th- and 12th-century sculptures as well as stone slabs with Quranic text dating back to the 15th century.

Hindola Mahal
PALACE

Just north of Ghiyas' stately pleasure dome is Hindola Mahal (Swing Palace), so-called because the slope of the walls is supposed to create the impression that they are swaying. While it doesn't give that impression, it is an eye-catching design nonetheless.

House & Shop of Gada Shah
HOUSE

The house is within the enclave but the shop is outside on the road to Delhi Gate. As the buildings' size and internal workmanship suggest, their owner was more than a shopkeeper. His name, which means 'beggar master', is thought to identify him as Rajput chief Medini Ray, a powerful minion of the sultans. The 'shop' was a warehouse for saffron and musk, imported and sold at a handsome profit when there were enough wealthy people to shop here.

Mosque of Dilawar Khan
MOSQUE

Built by Dilawar Khan in 1405, this mosque is Mandu's earliest Islamic building. There are many Hindu elements to the architecture, notably the pillars and ceilings inside, which was typical for this era.

Champa Baodi
HISTORIC SITE

So-called because its water supposedly smelt as sweet as the champak flower, Champa Baodi is a step-well surrounded by subterranean vaulted chambers, some of which you can explore.

Turkish Bath
BATH-HOUSE

Stars and octagons perforate the domed roofs of this tiny *hammam*, which had hot and cold water and a hypocaust (under-floor heated) sauna.

Village Group
HISTORIC SITE

(Indian/foreigner ₹5/100, video ₹25; ☉dawn-dusk) This group, located by the bus stand in the centre of the village, contains three monuments. One ticket, which you buy at the entrance to Jama Masjid, covers all three:

Jama Masjid
MOSQUE

Entered by a flight of steps leading to a 17m-high domed porch, this disused red-stone mosque dominates the village of Mandu. Hoshang Shah begun its construction around 1406, basing it on the great Omayyad Mosque in Damascus, Syria, and Mohammed Khalji completed it in 1454. Despite its plain design, it's reckoned to be the finest and largest example of Afghan architecture in India.

Hoshang's Tomb
TOMB

Reputed to be India's oldest marble building, this imposing tomb is crowned with a crescent thought to have been imported from Persia or Mesopotamia. Inside, light filters into the echoing dome through stone *jalis* (carved lattice screens), intended to cast an appropriately subdued light on the tombs. An inscription records Shah Jahan sending his architects – including Ustad Hamid, who worked on the Taj Mahal – here in 1659 to pay their respects to the tomb's builders.

Ashrafi Mahal
TOMB

Mohammed Shah originally built his tomb as a madrasa (Islamic college), before converting and extending it. The overambitious design later collapsed – notably the seven-storey circular tower of victory. The building is an empty shell, but intricate Islamic pillarwork can be seen at the top of its great stairway.

Rewa Kund Group
HISTORIC SITE

A pleasant 4km cycle south of the village, past Sagar Talao, brings you to two more **palace ruins** (Indian/foreigner ₹5/100, video ₹25; ☉dawn-dusk). Tickets for both should be bought from outside Baz Bahadur's Palace.

Baz Bahadur's Palace
PALACE

Baz Bahadur was the last independent ruler of Mandu. His palace, constructed around 1509, is beside the Rewa Kund Tank where a water lift at the northern end supplied water to the palace. A curious mix of Rajasthani and Mughal styles, it was actually built decades before Baz Bahadur came to power.

Rupmati's Pavilion
MONUMENT

Standing at the top of a cliff plunging 366m to the plains, Rupmati's Pavilion has a subtle beauty unmatched by the other monuments – and some of the dinkiest stone staircases you'll ever climb.

According to Malwa legends, the music-loving Baz Bahadur built it to persuade a beautiful Hindu singer, Rupmati, to move

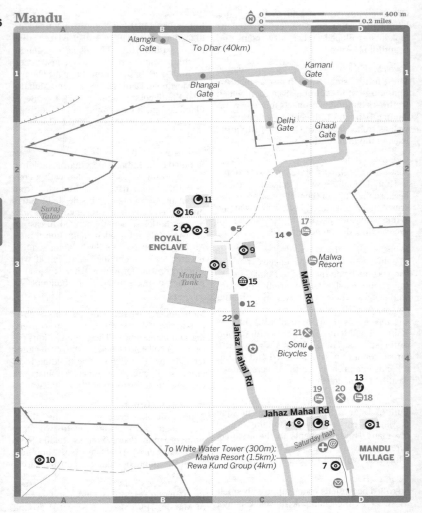

here from her home on the plains. From its terrace and domed pavilions Rupmati could gaze down at the distant glint of the sacred Narmada River.

In fact, the pavilion was built in two or three phases and the style of its arches and pillars suggest it was completed 100 years before Rupmati's time. Nonetheless, the love story is a subject of Malwa folk songs – not least because of its tragic ending. Lured by tales of Rupmati's beauty, Akbar marched on the fort and Baz Bahadur fled, leaving his lover to poison herself.

This place is simply gorgeous at sunset.

Nil Kanth Palace   HISTORIC SITE

If you're looking for a great reason to cycle out into the countryside, consider visiting this unusual former palace turned temple. It stands at the head of a ravine, on the site of an earlier Shiva shrine – its name means God with Blue Throat – and is now once again used as a place of worship. A stream built by one of Akbar's governors trickles through a delightful spiral channel and is usually filled with scented water, giving the palace a sweet aroma. To get here cycle south along Main Rd for less than 1km until you see a large white water tower. Turn right

Mandu

◎ Sights

here and follow the road as it twists and turns past villages all the way to Nil Kanth (about 2km). You can continue from here, past more remote villages, for about another kilometre to reach the still-standing gateway of the now ruined **Songarh Fort**, from where there are more great views.

Lohani Caves   CAVE

Local guides seem unsure as to just how old these sculpted caves are but some insist that a now-blocked tunnel leads from the caves to Dhar, 35km away. One thing is certain, they command a fabulous view of the ravine below, which you can hike down to from here.

Jain Temple   JAIN TEMPLE

Entered by a turquoise doorway, this complex is a splash of kitsch among the Islamic monuments. The richly decorated temples feature marble, silver and gold *tirthankars* with jade eyes, and behind them is a theme park–like museum with a walk-on replica of Shatrunjaya (p690), the hilltop temple com-

plex at Palitana in Gujarat. In the colourful murals, bears devour sinners' arms, crocodiles chew their heads, and demons saw one evil character in half, lengthways.

Saturday Haat   MARKET

(◎10am-dusk) This colourful weekly market, behind Jama Masjid, is similar to ones held all over the Bastar region, a tribal stronghold of Chhattisgarh (p667). Adivasis (tribespeople) walk kilometres to come here to buy and sell goods ranging from mountains of red chillies to dried *mahuwa*, a flower used to make a potent liquor of the same name.

🛏 Sleeping & Eating

Rama Guesthouse   GUESTHOUSE $

(☑263251; bus stand; r ₹250) Made up of a row of simple rooms off a courtyard that leads to the small Rama Temple, accommodation here is slightly cleaner and more spacious than at nearby Tourist Resthouse. Some bathrooms have showers and sit-down loos, but this is still very basic stuff. There's no English sign. Just walk through an archway between two shops by the bus stand. Reception is beyond the rooms, inside the temple grounds.

Hotel Rupmati   HOTEL $$

(☑263270; Main Rd; r from ₹700, with AC ₹1400; ❄) Clean, colourful cottages, with large bathrooms, are set around gardens on the edge of a cliff. Some come with exceptional views of the valley below. AC rooms can be had for ₹900 if you don't use the AC. Has a restaurant.

Malwa Resort   HOTEL $$

(☑263235; www.mptourism.com; Main Rd; r ₹1390, with AC ₹2090; ❄≋) This family-friendly MP Tourism property, 2km south of the village, has large gardens containing comfortable cottages, children's play areas, tree swings and a pool (which isn't always open). There are also pleasant views of the neighbouring lake Sagar Talao.

Tourist Resthouse   GUESTHOUSE $

(☑263264; Jahaz Mahal Rd; r ₹150) This row of seven identical and extremely basic rooms with squat toilets and tap-and-bucket showers is the cheapest place in town. Rooms come with small, private verandas, but they're right on the roadside (albeit it's not a very busy road).

Shivani Restaurant   INDIAN $

(Main Rd; mains ₹35-90; ◎8.30am-10pm) The most popular place to eat in town, this large, no-nonsense diner with plastic tables and chairs has an excellent menu that includes a range of thalis (₹50 to ₹110) plus local specialities such as *Mandu kofta* (dumplings in a mild sauce). South Indian breakfasts are also available, as are lassis and coffee.

Relax Point
INDIAN $

(Main Rd; snacks ₹6-40; ⊗8.30am-9.30pm) A village shop, gathering point and restaurant-cafe rolled into one. The menu is limited to snacks such as samosas and parathas but this is an OK place for a lazy chai break.

🛍 Shopping

Roopayan
HANDICRAFTS

(Main Rd; ⊗9am-7pm) Next to Malwa Resort, this small shop sells good-quality scarves (from ₹300), shawls (₹800) and bed spreads (₹900), as well as a selection of clothing, all made from material that has been dyed using a block-printing method that is a speciality of the nearby village of Bagh.

❶ Information

The only **internet cafe** (Main Rd; per hr ₹50; ⊗7am-10pm) has just one terminal. There's a small **pharmacy** (⊗8am-9.30pm) next door, while the **post office** (☑263222; Main Rd; ⊗9am-5pm) is further south. There's nowhere to change money. Malwa Retreat can help arrange local **guides** (₹200 to ₹500).

❶ Getting There & Away

There are two direct buses to Indore (₹80, 3½ hours, 9am and 3.30pm), one to Ujjain (₹96, six hours, 6am) and regular services to Dhar (₹25, one hour, 6am to 6pm), where you can change for buses to Dhamnod (₹40, two hours), then, in turn, for Maheshwar (₹10, 30 minutes, last bus 11pm) or Omkareshwar (₹55, 3½ hours, last bus 7pm). If doing this, it's quicker to get off 14km before Dhar at a junction called Oonera (₹10, 30 minutes) from where you can flag down Dhamnod-bound buses.

❶ Getting Around

Cycling is best, as the terrain is flat, the air clear and the countryside beautiful. **Sonu Bicycles** (Main Rd; per hr/day ₹10/30; ⊗6am-6pm) is one of a few places that rent bikes.

You can tour the monuments in half a day in an autorickshaw (from ₹200).

EASTERN MADHYA PRADESH

Jabalpur

☏0761 / POP 1.1 MILLION

Domestic tourists mostly come here to visit Marble Rocks, an attractive river gorge nearby, but for foreigners this industrial city of *chowks* and working men's taverns is used mainly as a launchpad for the big tiger parks – Kanha (p661), Bandhavgarh (p662) and Pench (p664).

Most of the action takes place north of the railway line, in the dusty lanes of the Old Bazaar, along Vined Talkies Rd and as far south as Russell Chowk, which is where most of the hotels are located. The Civil Lines district, south of the train station, is less interesting, but more peaceful.

Jabalpur

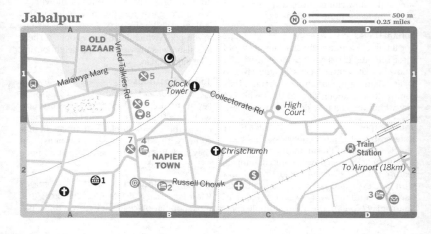

◉ Sights & Activities

Rani Durgavati Museum　　　MUSEUM
(Indian/foreigner ₹10/100, camera/video ₹40/200;
⊙10am-5pm Tue-Sun) Has a collection of 10th-
century sculptures from local sites, while
upstairs are letters and photographs relating to Mahatma Gandhi and an old-fashioned gallery exploring tribal culture.

🛏 Sleeping

Lodge Shivalaya　　　HOTEL $
(✆2625188; Napier Town; s/d from ₹240/250, r with
AC from ₹750) There are loads of hotels around
Russell Chowk but this is the best-value of
the lot. Rooms are simple with stone floors,
but are clean enough and come with TV and
small bathrooms. They also open onto shared
balconies that overlook the bustling street
below. Twenty-four-hour checkout.

Hotel Sidharth　　　HOTEL $$
(✆4007779; hotel_sidharth@hotmail.com; Russell
Chowk; s/d ₹495/550, with AC ₹675-995; ❄) An
old-fashioned lift leads to comfortable, com-
pact rooms in this modest, well-run midrange
hotel. AC rooms are no smarter than non-AC.
Has a restaurant and 24-hour checkout.

Kalchuri Residency　　　HOTEL $$
(✆2678491; katchuri@mptourism.com; r incl break-
fast ₹2090; ❄) This MP Tourism property,
located in the quieter Civil Lines area just
south of the train station, has large, neat and
tidy rooms with TV and kettle and clean, spacious bathrooms. Some rooms have private
balconies. There's a restaurant and a bar.

✗ Eating & Drinking

Indian Coffee House　　　SOUTH INDIAN $
(Hotel India; coffee from ₹10, mains ₹30-130;
⊙7am-10.30pm) As well as good-value coffee,

the guys in white suits and fan-tailed hats
serve up delicious breakfasts, from dosa
and *uttapam* to French toast and omelettes,
and hearty Indian and Chinese mains.

Options　　　INDIAN $$
(Vined Talkies Rd; mains ₹40-80; ⊙10am-11pm)
Popular with families, courting couples
and 20-somethings, this child-friendly
veg restaurant with funky decor serves up
good-quality Indian and Chinese cuisine to
a backdrop of Indian pop music and Bol-
lywood soundtracks.

Satyam Shivam Sundram　　　INDIAN $$
(Napier Town; mains ₹40-80, thalis from ₹65;
⊙9am-11pm) Staff members here are very
friendly, sometimes annoyingly so, but the
veg menu is spot on and includes some
generous thalis.
　　Jabalpur is thick with seedy but reasonably harmless drinking dens, many of which
are attached to cheap hotels. **Yogi Bar** (Vined
Talkies Rd; beer from ₹75; ⊙10am-10pm) is pretty
representative.

ℹ Information

City Hospital (✆2628154; North Civil Lines;
⊙24hr) Modern, private healthcare facility.
Cyber Cafe (Russell Chowk; per hr ₹10;
⊙10.30am-10.30pm) Has wi-fi.
MP Tourism (✆2677690; ⊙7am-8pm) At train
station (south entrance).
Post office (Residency Rd; ⊙10am-5pm Mon-
Fri, 10am-2pm Sat) An unusual 1860s, English-
made, red post box stands outside the entrance.
State Bank of India (✆2677777; South Civil
Lines; ⊙10.30am-4.30pm Mon-Fri, to 1pm Sat)
Changes American Express travellers cheques
and cash, and has ATM; there's also an ATM at
the train station and others around the city.

ℹ Getting There & Away

Air
Kingfisher Airlines (✆2603467), at the airport,
has a daily flight to Delhi (from ₹4000, 8.55am).
Next door, **Air India** (✆6459333) flies there on
Tuesdays, Thursdays, Saturdays and Sundays.

Bus
Two daily buses go to Kanha National Park
(₹120, 6 hours, 7am and 11am). For Pench Tiger
Reserve, take any Nagpur-bound bus as far as
Khawasa (₹130, five hours, 7am to 11pm), then
take a shared jeep (₹10) for the final 12km. For
Bandhavgarh National Park, it's best to take a
direct train to Umaria, but you can also take a
bus to Katni (₹62, three hours, every 30 minutes, 4am to 11pm), from where there are trains
and buses to Umaria.

DESTINATION	TRAIN NO & NAME	FARE (₹)	DURATION (HR)	DEPARTURE
Agra	12189 *Mahakaushal Express*	310/817/1112	14	6.10pm
Bhopal	11472 *Jbp–Bhopal Express*	164/430/586	7	11pm
Delhi	12192 *Jbp–NDLS Express*	363/966/1316	18	5.45pm
Kolkata (Howrah)	12322 *Kolkata Mail*	387/1032/1409	22	1.30pm
Mumbai (CST)	12321 *Howrah–Mumbai Mail*	355/944/1286	17½	6.05pm
Raipur	12854 *Amarkantak Express*	247/638/862	9½	9.30pm
Satna	11705 *Jabalpur–Rewa Pass*	140/327/430	4	7.30am
Umaria	18233 *Narmada Express*	80/262/353	4	6.40am
Varanasi*	12945 *Tapti–Ganga Express*	249/645	11	11.58pm

Fares are sleeper/3AC/2AC; *except Tue & Sat, sleeper/3AC only

Train

More than 10 daily trains leave for Satna, but only one (a slow train that leaves at 7.30am) leaves early enough to meet direct bus connections to Khajuraho. If you're on a later train, though, you should be able to catch a bus from Satna to Panna and change again for Khajuraho. You'll probably have to change a third time at Bamitha Junction, from where shared jeeps (₹10) can take you the last 11km to Khajuraho. For Bandhavgarh National Park, take a train to Umaria. Also see boxed text, p660. There are three daily trains to Varanasi but they either leave or arrive at an unearthly hour. Other Varanasi trains run at better times, but not every day, so check when you book your ticket.

Getting Around

A cycle rickshaw from the train station to Russel Chowk is about ₹20. Autorickshaws are usually double the price.

Around Jabalpur

MARBLE ROCKS

Known locally as Bhedaghat, the marble-like magnesium-limestone cliffs at this **gorge** on the holy Narmada River, 22km west of Jabalpur, change colours in different lights, from pink to black. They're particularly impressive by moonlight, and parts are floodlit at night.

The trip up the 2km-long gorge is made in a shared **motorboat** (per person 30/50min ₹21/31; ⊙7am-7pm, full moon 8pm-midnight, closed 15 Jun-15 Oct due to monsoon) from the jetty at Panchvati Ghat. Alternatively hire a boat (standard/large ₹200/320) to yourself. There's good **swimming** at the ghat too, but currents can be strong: take your lead from the locals. For a nice post-boating stroll, and a closer look at village life, carry on up the hill past the ghat entrance and turn right just before Motel Marble Rocks, where you'll find a tiny path leading past local homes and down towards the gorge.

Dhuandhar (Smoke Cascade) is a worthwhile 1.5km-walk uphill from the ghat. Along the way is the much-revered **Chausath Yogini**, a circular 10th-century temple dedicated to the Hindu goddess Durga and accessed via a steep flight of steps on the right-hand side of the road. Once at the falls, you can take a short cable-car ride (₹60 return) to the other side of the gorge.

Just before Chausath Yogini, **Hotel River View** (⊙6942004; Bhedaghat; r from ₹1000, with AC ₹1500; ⊛) has clean, spacious rooms, some with wonderful views of the river, which you can also see from its back-garden restaurant (mains ₹50 to ₹70).

Local buses leave regularly for Bhedaghat (₹15, 40 minutes, 6am to 8pm) from Jabalpur bus stand. They drop you at a crossroads from where shared autorickshaws wait to take you the final 5km to Panchvati Ghat (₹5) or 6.5km to Dhuandhar (₹10). Getting back is just a case of waiting at the crossroads for a passing bus. The impatient might like to try squeezing into a jam-packed, Jabalpur-bound shared autorickshaw (₹10 to ₹15). See if you can beat 14 passengers!

Kanha National Park

📞 07649 / TIGER POP 80

Madhya Pradesh is the king of the jungle when it comes to tiger parks, and **Kanha** (www.kanha nationalpark.com; Indian/foreigner ₹1230/2230, jeep am/pm ₹1500/1000; ☺ 16 Oct-30 Jun) is the most famous. The forests are vast, and while your chances of seeing a tiger are probably slightly slimmer than at nearby Bandhavgarh, they're still very good. Add to that the fact that you can really go deep into the forest thanks to the park's huge core area surrounded by a large buffer zone, and you have a complete safari experience, rather than the rush-and-grab outings some complain of at Bandhavgarh.

The sal forests and vast meadows contain more than 200 tigers and leopards and support huge populations of deer and antelope, including the extremely rare *barasingha*. You'll see plenty of langur monkeys, the odd gaur (Indian bison) and maybe even a family or two of wild boar. The park is also home to more than 300 bird species.

There are a few gates into the park, but we focus here on Khatiya Gate, easily the most popular.

⊙ Sights & Activities

Jeep Safaris
JEEP SAFARIS

This is why everyone comes to Kanha and pretty much everyone who lives here can hook you up with a jeep for a safari. The key, if you haven't prebooked safaris through your hotel, is to find other independent travellers with whom you can share costs because all fees (admission and jeep) are per jeep load (maximum six adults), not per person. Budget guesthouses are the best place to enquire; try at Motel Chandan. Otherwise, just ask around. Note, a jeep containing Indian nationals *and* foreigners costs the foreign-tourist price. There are two safari slots each day: morning (roughly 6am to 11am) and afternoon (roughly 3pm to 6pm). The morning safaris are longer, but cost slightly more and include time spent at the visitor centre. Still, mornings tend to produce more tiger sight-

MORNING CHILL

No matter how hot a time of year it is, make sure you bring warm clothing with you for morning jeep safaris. It's fr-fr-freezing in the forests before the sun comes up properly.

Many of the more upmarket resorts at the tiger reserves have part- and all-inclusive packages rather than straight accommodation prices. The so-called American Plan includes accommodation and all meals, while the Jungle Plan includes accommodation and meals plus a morning and an afternoon jeep safari.

ings and come with the added attraction of a possible elephant safari (see boxed text p663).

Nature Trails
WALKING

A well-marked 7km trail leads from just inside Khatiya Gate and skirts along the edge of the park before looping back to the village. Mostly you'll see a lot of monkeys and birds, but tigers do venture into this area on occasions. Check with locals before you leave. Raheel, the manager at Pugmark Resort, is well informed.

🛏 Sleeping & Eating

All hotels listed here have restaurants. There's a row of small *dhabas* just before Khatiya Gate serving cheap food and chai. If you're on a morning safari, you can grab breakfast (₹20), tea and coffee when you stop at the visitor centre inside the park.

Note, while lodgings in the buffer zone enjoy a wonderfully natural forest location, there are none of the facilities that tourists can enjoy in the village outside Khatiya Gate.

INSIDE THE BUFFER ZONE

Tourist Hostel
HOSTEL $

(📞277310; Kisli Gate; American Plan dm ₹690) This MP Tourism property, made up of a few huge, well-kept multibed dorms with clean shared bathrooms, is actually inside the buffer zone, right by Kisli Gate, which leads into the park's core zone. There are no facilities here outside the dorms, the nearby canteen and the adjacent Baghira Log Huts, but the attraction is that you're staying right in among the monkey-filled forest, and a stone's throw from meadows which attract deer and *gaur* throughout the day. You'll need to have a room booked in advance in order to get past security at Khatiya Gate, then you can hitch a ride to Kisli Gate on any passing vehicle, or on one of the buses which swing by both gates.

Baghira Log Huts
GUESTHOUSE $$$

(📞277227; Kisli Gate; American Plan s/d from ₹3590/3990; 🌐) Apart from the nearby Tourist

Hostel, this is the only place inside the buffer zone. Comfortable rather than luxurious log-cabin-lookalike rooms are set among the trees and overlook a beautiful meadow. There's a restaurant and a bar. As with Tourist Hostel, you'll need to have a room booked here in advance in order to get past security at Khatiya Gate.

IN THE VILLAGE BY KHATIYA GATE

Motel Chandan GUESTHOUSE **$$**
(☏277220; www.motel.chandan.com; r from ₹700; ❇) Spotless modern rooms can be nabbed for great rates if you bargain hard. Staff members are friendly and are happy to help you find travellers to share safari costs with. On the left-hand side of the main road, 200m before Khatiya Gate.

Pugmark Resort GUESTHOUSE **$$**
(☏277291; www.pugmarkresort.com; s/d American Plan ₹1800/2400; ❇) Large, clean cottages are bright and airy and set around a lovely, if slightly overgrown, garden. There's a gazebo-covered campfire and a bar, and Raheel, the manager, is very knowledgeable. It's 700m down a track to the right of Khatiya Gate.

Van Vihar GUESTHOUSE **$**
(☏277241; vanvihar99@yahoo.com; r ₹300-500, with AC ₹800; ❇) Uninspiring rooms are basic, but this is probably the best-value budget option. It's 300m left of Khatiya Gate.

Machan Complex GUESTHOUSE **$**
(☏252457; dm ₹30, r ₹100-300) Like staying in a tiny Indian village, Machan has rooms in different types of buildings set around a huge old banyan tree. There are dorms, very basic rooms in a mud-and-brick hut (₹100), mud-hut doubles (₹200) and larger rooms with sit-down toilets in a still-basic brick building (₹300). The owner, Anil, is a naturalist and extremely welcoming. About 1km before Khatiya Gate, on the right.

Tuli Tiger Resort HOTEL **$$$**
(☏277221; www.tulihotels.com; American Plan s/d cottages ₹4500/5500, luxury tents ₹16,000/18,000, Jungle Plan s/d cottages ₹14,500/15,500, tents ₹23,500/24,500; ❇@) Fabulous five-star luxury set in peaceful bamboo grounds located 4km before Khatiya gate, just outside the village of Mocha. Buses to Khatiya all stop in Mocha.

❶ Information

The ticket office by Khatiya Gate has **internet** (per hr ₹50; ◷6am-8pm). There's nowhere to change money.

❶ Getting There & Away

There are five daily buses from Khatiya Gate to Mandla (₹45, 2½ hours, 6am, 8.30am, 9am, 12.30pm & 6pm). The 6am, 12.30pm and 6pm continue to Jabalpur (₹98, 5½ hours). All apart from the 6pm swing by Kisli Gate too.

Services from Mandla Bus Stand include:
JABALPUR (₹65, three hours, regular, 4am to 9pm)
KANHA (₹45, 2½ hours, five daily, 10am, 10.15am, 11.15am, 2.30pm and 4.15pm)
NAGPUR (buses go via Pench National Park turn-off; ₹180, eight hours, regular, 8am to 11pm)
RAIPUR (₹195, eight hours, four daily, 9am, noon, 4.20pm and 9pm)

Bandhavgarh National Park

☏07653 / TIGER POP 65

If your sole reason for visiting a national park in India is to see a tiger, look no further. A couple of days at **Bandhavgarh** (www.bandhavgarhnationalpark.com; Indian/foreigner ₹1280/2280, jeep Tala Gate/Maghdi Gate ₹1000/1500; ◷16 Oct-30 Jun) almost guarantees you a tiger sighting in this relatively small park that boasts the highest density of tigers in India. As well as the star attraction, there are also more than 40 leopards (although they are rarely seen) and more commonly sighted animals such as deer, wild boar and langur.

Like Kanha, Bandhavgarh also has a lot of budget accommodation making this a good place for independent travellers to find other people to share safari costs with.

The park takes its name from an ancient fort perched on top of 800m-high cliffs. Its ramparts provide a home for vultures, blue rock thrushes and crag martins. You can visit it on special jeep trips during the day, but you'll have to pay all the usual park entry fees.

The park is entered at the small, laid-back village of Tala, 32km from Umaria, the nearest train station.

◉ Sights & Activities

Jeep Safaris JEEP SAFARIS
Try Kum Kum or Hotel Bagh Vihar if you want to find others with whom to share safari costs. Note, that Tala Gate (a short walk from the village) is cheaper, and has better tiger opportunities, but is sometimes fully booked by the more expensive, all-inclusive resorts. Ask

your guide the day before to try to get you one of the few VIP tickets for Tala Gate that normally go unused. Otherwise, you'll have to settle for Maghdi Gate (7km from the village). Maghdi is the gate you must use if you want to do an elephant safari (see boxed text p663), although you need to book your ticket for that at Tala Gate the day before.

Interpretation Centre MUSEUM
(admission ₹5; ⊙11am-2pm & 5.30-8pm) Interesting exhibits detailing the history and legends of Bandhavgarh, plus some superb tiger photos on the 1st floor. On your right just before the village.

🛏 Sleeping & Eating

All accommodation listed here is on the main strip (or within walking distance) and has a restaurant.

Kum Kum Home GUESTHOUSE $
(☑265324; r ₹350-400) Best budget option – rooms are basic but comfortable and come with large bathrooms and a veranda.

Jungle Inn Resort GUESTHOUSE $$
(☑265348; r ₹1000, with AC ₹1500; ✳) New, yellow-painted, two-storey building in the centre of the village with simple but smart, clean rooms overlooking a huge back lawn.

Tiger's Den HOTEL $$$
(☑265353; www.tigerden.com; r ₹3000-3500, American Plan ₹5000-5500; ✳ ⊠) Very smart olive-green bungalows with quality furnishings set around a lush, palm-lined garden with a gorgeous pool.

Nature Heritage Resort HOTEL $$
(☑265351, 265327; shalinidev@eth.net; s/d ₹2000/2500, with AC ₹2500/3000, American Plan ₹3500/4000; ✳) It's all about bamboo here, with luxury, bamboo-trim cottages, containing bamboo furniture including bamboo bed frames, set around lush gardens shaded by...yep, bamboo. Has a very pleasant open-air restaurant. It's 1km down a track opposite Kum Kum.

Hotel Bagh Vihar HOTEL $
(☑265302, 9406754888; s/d ₹400/600) Nothing fancy, but 1st-floor rooms above the only internet cafe in the village are neat and tidy.

Kolkata Restaurant (mains ₹25-150; ⊙7.30-10pm), at the end of the village before the petrol pump, does good quality Indian veg and meat dishes plus some Chinese and breakfasts. The omelettes are popular. In the centre of the village, next to Jungle

Kanha and Pench National Parks both use elephants to track tigers in the morning. Tourists on jeep safaris are then radioed in, transferred to elephants (per person Indian/foreigner ₹200/600) and led out to where the tiger is. Elephant rides typically last about 15 minutes. You get your money back if the tiger has scarpered by the time you get there.

Bandhavgarh National Park has a different system: tourists here can prebook (a day in advance) one- or two-hour elephant rides (₹1500/3000) as part of their next day's morning safari. The usual safari costs are paid on top.

Inn Resort, **Al-Mezbaan** (mains ₹30-150) has a similar menu, friendly staff and a roadside terrace with plastic tables and chairs. Near here is the **Wine Shop** (Kingfisher ₹100; ⊙9am-11pm) for all your takeaway alcohol needs.

ℹ Information

There's internet access at **Yadav Cyber Café** (per hr ₹60; ⊙8am-11pm), but the nearest place to withdraw money is in Umaria. From the train station, walk to the end of the road, turn right and you'll find an ATM, along with some restaurants and hotels, on your left after a few hundred metres.

ℹ Getting There & Around

There's one early-morning bus from Umaria train station to Tala Village (₹25, one hour, 6.30am). After that you'll have to either take an autorickshaw (₹300) or taxi (₹500). Alternatively, take a cycle rickshaw to Umaria bus stand (₹10, 10 minutes), from where there are one or two buses an hour to Tala (₹30).

The last bus from Tala Village back to Umaria bus stand is 7.30pm.

Train

Trains from Umaria include the 18477 *Utkal Express* to Delhi (Nizamuddin); (sleeper/3AC/2AC ₹316/860/1181, 17 hours, 8.50pm) via Gwalior (11 hours), Agra (14 hours) and Mathura (15 hours), and the 18234 *Narmada Express*, which goes to Jabalpur (₹80/261/352, 4½ hours, 4.20pm) before continuing to Bhopal (12 hours), Ujjain (16½ hours) and Indore (18½ hours).

There's one daily train to Varanasi, but it's at 4.30am (15160 *Sarnath Express*; ₹206/547/750,

12 hours). Trains to Satna (from where you can also catch buses to Khajuraho (p633), are equally inconvenient, the least sleep-depriving being the 51754 *Chirmiri-Rewa Passenger* (sleeper ₹80, 3½ hours, 1am).

For Chhattisgarh, there are two daily trains to Raipur, the best being the 15159 *Sarnath Express* (₹173/455/621, eight hours, 10.18pm)

An alternative to Umaria is Katni, a busier railway junction from where there are direct trains to places like Jabalpur, Satna and Varanasi. You can catch a direct bus to Katni (₹50, three hours, three daily, 6.30am, 8am and 2pm) from Tala Mall, 3km beyond Tala Village.

Pench Tiger Reserve

📞07695 / TIGER POP 33

The third of Madhya Pradesh's trio of well-known tiger parks, **Pench** (www.penchnationalpark.com; Indian/foreigner ₹1230/2230, jeep ₹1000-1500; ☉16 Oct-30 Jun) is made up mostly of teak-tree forest rather than sal and so has a different flavour than nearby Kanha or Bandhavgarh. It also sees fewer tourists so, as you're driving around the park, you'll often feel like you have the whole forest to yourself. Tigers are fewer too, but are generally spotted every few days. For elephant rides, see the boxed text on p663.

⊙ Sights & Activities

Jeep Safaris   JEEP SAFARIS

A lack of budget accommodation means it's tough to find other independent travellers to share jeep costs with. Kipling's Court is your best bet. Otherwise, try hanging around the park gate and keep your fingers crossed that a jeep comes along with passengers who aren't on an all-inclusive package. As at the other tiger parks, there are morning (sunrise to 10am) and afternoon (3pm to sunset) safaris.

🛏 Sleeping & Eating

All of these hotels have restaurants.

Mowgli's Den   GUESTHOUSE $$

(📞232832; s/d ₹1600/2800, American Plan ₹2200/4000) A nice choice for families; the reception and restaurant are set around a lush lawn with children's playground, tyre swing, duck pond and rabbit hutch. Log cabin-lookalike concrete huts come with delightful wrought-iron furniture and huge circular bathrooms with Jacuzzi-sized sunken baths. There's no TV to spoil the natural sounds of the jungle, and when you turn off the lights to sleep, a fluorescent night sky magically appears on your bedroom ceiling. It's 1km past the village of Turia.

Kipling's Court   GUESTHOUSE $$

(📞232830; kcpench@mptourism.com; dm/s/d American Plan ₹700/2290/2890, with AC s/d ₹3290/3890; ❄) Considering prices include all meals, the large dorms here are good value. There are two, with five beds each. They're both in tip-top condition and share a large clean shower area. The private cottages aren't bad either and are dotted around well-kept gardens. Also has a bar. It's 2km past Turia, about 1km before the park gate.

Tuli Tiger Corridor   HOTEL $$$

(📞232859, 09981994116, Nagpur office 07122534784; www.tulihotels.com; cottage/tent American Plan ₹10,000/18,000; ❄@≋) Extravagance by the bucketload in exquisite cottages with verandas and luxury tents with private lawns. There's also a gorgeous pool, a spa and massage centre, and a bar. It's 500m past Mowgli's Den.

❶ Information

Buses running between Nagpur and Jabalpur will drop you at Khawasa, which is about 12km east of the small crossroads village of Turia, beyond which you'll find the accommodation we list here. The main gate to the park is about 3km beyond Turia. The nearest airport and major train station is in Nagpur.

There's nowhere to change money and no reliable internet access.

❶ Getting There & Away

Regular buses, day and night, link Khawasa with Nagpur (₹50, two hours) and Jabalpur (₹130, five hours, 7am to 11pm). Shared jeeps (₹10) run between Khawasa and Turia when full.

You can go to Kanha National Park from Khawasa without going all the way to Jabalpur or Mandla. Flag down any north-bound bus to Seoni (₹30, one hour) then take a Mandla-bound bus to Chiraidongri (₹60, 2½ hours) where you can catch buses to Khatia Gate (₹25, one hour, last bus 9pm).

CHHATTISGARH

Chhattisgarh is remote, its public transport system is poor and its tourist infrastructure outside the main cities is almost nonexistent, but for the intrepid traveller, time spent here may well prove to be the highlight of your trip to this part of India. The country's most densely forested state is blessed with natural beauty – waterfalls and unspoilt nature reserves abound. More interestingly, though, it is home to 42 different tribes whose pointillist paintings and spindly sculptures are as vivid as the colourful *haats* (markets) that take place across the region, particularly around Jagdalpur in Bastar.

Chhattisgarh is one of the eastern states associated with the Naxalite guerrillas (an ultra-leftist political movement that began in Naxal Village, West Bengal), but they rarely stray from their remote hideouts on Chhattisgarh's northern and southern borders.

Raipur

📞 0771 / POP 700,113

Chhattisgarh's ugly capital is a centre for the state's steel industry and, apart from being a day trip away from Sirpur, has little in the way of tourist attractions. The Chhattisgarh Tourism Board head office is worth visiting here, though.

🛏 Sleeping & Eating

Hotel Jyoti HOTEL $
(📞 2428777; Pandri; s/d from ₹400/500, with AC from ₹750/900; ❄) A tranquil retreat after a long bus journey. Rooms are well looked after and the manager is helpful. Right opposite the bus stand.

Hotel Radhika HOTEL $$
(📞 2233806; Jaistambh Chowk; r from ₹550, with AC from ₹1000; ❄) A centrally located one-stop point for all your needs – a bank opposite, an ice-cream parlour below, a thali restaurant above and two bars next door. What more could you need? Rooms vary from basic budget jobs to decent AC midrangers. Book ahead – it's popular.

Girnar Restaurant INDIAN $$
(Hotel Radhika, Jaistambh Chowk; mains ₹70-170; ⏰ 11am-10pm) This 40-year-old restaurant serves good-quality Indian food. It's right opposite Hotel Radhika reception. Upstairs, the separate **thali restaurant** (unlimited thali ₹85; ⏰ 11.30am-3.30pm & 7.30-10.30pm) is wonderful.

Supreet Restaurant INDIAN $
(Pandri; mains ₹30-70; ⏰ 9am-10.30pm) South Indian breakfasts and tasty veg mains at this cheap and cheerful place near the bus stand. Turn left out of the bus stand and it's 500m along on your left.

❶ Information

There are ATMs outside the bus and train stands.
Chhattisgarh Tourism Board head office
(📞 9425811615, 4066415; www.chhattisgarh

THE VENERABLE LAXMAN TEMPLE

665

A possible day trip from Raipur, **Sirpur** is home to dozens of ruined Hindu temples and Buddhist monasteries, all dotted around the village and surrounding countryside. Many of the excavations are works in progress. All are free to see apart from the star of the show, the 7th-century **Laxman Temple** (Indian/foreigner ₹5/100; ⏰ dawn-dusk), one of the oldest brick temples in India.

Buses from Raipur bus stand drop you at Sirpur Mudh (₹40, two hours), a junction 17km from Sirpur where you'll have to wait for a bus or shared jeep (₹10, 25 minutes) to the village. For Laxman Temple, turn right past the snack stalls and keep walking for 1km. It's on the left, past the petrol pump.

---

tourism.net; beside Sibbal Palace Hotel, GE Rd; ⏰ 10.30am-5.30pm Mon-Sat); train station (📞 6456336; ⏰ 10am-5pm) Gives statewide advice and can help organise tribal visits, transport, accommodation and guides.
Internet cafe (per hr ₹10; ⏰ 9.30am-10pm) Turn right out of the bus stand and it's 500m along on your right.
State Bank of India (📞 2535176; Jaistambh Chowk; ⏰ 10.30am-4.30pm Mon-Fri, to 1.30pm Sat) Opposite Hotel Radhika. Changes travellers cheques and cash, and has an ATM.

❶ Getting There & Around

Air

Air India (📞 4060942; Pandri; ⏰ 10am-5.30pm Mon-Sat) flies daily to Mumbai (₹5500, 3½ hours) via Bhubaneswar (₹3000, 50 minutes), and to Delhi (₹5500, 2½ hours) via Nagpur (₹3000, 40 minutes). Turn left out of the bus stand and the office is 1km along on your left, just past the level crossing. **Kingfisher** (📞 2535322; Lal Ganga Shopping Mall; ⏰ 9.30am-7pm Mon-Sat) flies daily to Delhi and Kolkata (₹5700). Lal Ganga Shopping Mall is 200m from Hotel Radikha.

An autorickshaw to the airport, 15km out of town, costs ₹100 to ₹150.

Bus

The government bus ticket office is invariably unmanned so it's far easier to use private bus companies, which all operate out of the bus stand area too. Mahendra Travels, with a ticket desk directly opposite the bus stand, where the Jagdalpur buses leave from, is reliable.

Between government- and private-run buses you'll find frequent departures to Jagdalpur (seat/sleeper ₹210/270, seven hours, 10.45am to midnight), and a few early morning and late evening buses to both Jabalpur (₹280, 11 hours) and Nagpur (₹220, eight hours).

Rickshaws

A cycle-rickshaw or autorickshaw between the bus stand and train station costs ₹25/50. Shared autos (₹10) ply the same route as well as the main GE Rd between Jaistambh Chowk and Chhattisgarh Tourism's head office (₹10).

Train

Useful trains include the 18237 *Chhattis-garh Express* to Delhi's Nizamuddin station (sleeper/3AC/2AC ₹398/1090/1502, 27½ hours, 4.20pm) via Nagpur (5½ hours), Bhopal (14½ hours), Jhansi (19½ hours), Gwalior (21½ hours) and Agra (24 hours), and the 12859 *Gitanjali Express* to Kolkata's Howrah station (₹323/852/1159, 13 hours, 11.35pm).

Jagdalpur

☏ 07782 / POP 103,123

The friendly capital of the Bastar region is an ideal base for exploring tribal Chhattisgarh (see boxed text, p668). The town itself hosts a *haat* every Sunday where you'll see Adivasis (tribespeople) buying, selling and bartering alongside town traders, but it's in the surrounding villages where Adivasi life can be fully appreciated. Some villages are extremely remote, and only really accessible with a guide. Others, though, are just a bus ride away

FANCY A BITE?

Red ants are more than just a painful nuisance to the Bastar tribes. Known as *chapura*, they also play an important role in food and medicine. They are often eaten live, served on a leaf with white ant eggs. Alternatively, villagers grind them into a paste and mix them with chilli to make chutney. The bodies of *chapura* contain formic acid believed to have useful medicinal qualities. If suffering from a fever, locals will sometimes put their hand into an ants nest, allowing it to be bitten hundreds of times so that the acid is administered into their bloodstream. Paracetamol for the hardcore.

and, particularly on market days (see boxed text, p667), can be explored independently. For eight particularly lively days in October, Jagdalpur's streets transform into race tracks as immense, home-made chariots are pitted against each other in an unusual climax to the 75-day festival of Dussehra (see p611).

Sanjay Market, which hosts the Sunday *haat*, is the heartbeat of Jagdalpur. Hotel Rainbow is opposite, while Main Rd, a lively shopping street, is 200m away (turn left out of the market, then first right). The bus stand and train station are 3km and 4km south respectively (₹15 and ₹20 in a cycle-rickshaw).

◉ Sights

Anthropological Museum MUSEUM
(Chitrakote Rd; admission free; ⊙10am-1pm & 2-5.30pm Mon-Fri) Old-fashioned museum with fascinating collection of artefacts (tools, jewellery, musical instruments) collected from tribal villages in the 1970s and 80s. Cycle-rickshaw from the centre of town, cost ₹40 to ₹50. Shared autorickshaws from the Chitrakote Rd junction near Sanjay Market cost ₹10.

🛌 Sleeping & Eating

If the following are full, there are a couple of OK hotels opposite Shabari emporium.

Hotel Rainbow HOTEL $$
(☏221684; hotelrainbow@indiatimes.com; s/d from ₹495/550, with AC from ₹700/825; ✸) Even the cheap, non-AC rooms are huge and well furnished in this good-value hotel, while the restaurant (mains ₹50 to ₹150; open 7am to 10.30pm) is one of the best in town. Opposite Sanjay Market. Twenty-four-hour checkout.

Hotel Chetak HOTEL $
(☏223503; s/d ₹325/425, with AC ₹625/725; ✸) Handy for the bus stand, tidy rooms are smaller than Rainbow's but clean enough. Has a (very) low-lit bar-restaurant (mains ₹40 to ₹130, beer ₹110; open 10am to 10.30pm). Turn right out of the bus stand and walk 100m.

🛍 Shopping

Shabari HANDICRAFTS
(Chandi Chowk; ⊙11am-8pm Mon-Sat) A fixed-price government emporium selling Adivasi handicrafts from small, spindly iron figures (₹20) to more expensive, heavy bell-metal statues. From the Sanjay Market end of Main

Most *haats* (markets) run from around noon to 5pm. There are many markets – these are just some of the more popular ones. Ask at the Chhattisgarh Tourism Board in Raipur (p665) for details. Shared jeeps normally hang around markets to take people back to Jagdalpur.

WHEN	WHERE	DISTANCE FROM JAGDALPUR	BUS FROM JAGDALPUR	WHY GO?
Mon	Tokapal	23km	₹13, 30min	To buy bell-metal craftwork from Ghadwa Adivasis
Tue	Pakhnar	70km	No direct bus	Beautiful forest setting
Wed	Darbha	40km	₹30, 1hr	Attended by Bhurwa Adivasis
Thu	Bastar	18km	₹25, 30min	Easy to reach from Jagdalpur
Fri	Nangur	35km	No direct bus	Attended by distant forest Adivasis
	Nagarnar	18km	No direct bus	Chance to see colourful Bhatra Adivasis
Sat	Kuknar	65km	₹45, 2hr	Bison-Horn Maria stronghold
Sun	Jagdalpur	-	-	Central city location, open late into the evening
	Chingitarai	52km	No direct bus	Open, meadow setting
	Pamela	12km	₹10, 20min	If you feel inclined to see animated crowds bet on cockfighting

MADHYA PRADESH & CHHATTISGARH AROUND JAGDALPUR

Rd, take the third right and continue for 500m. Opposite the Bank of Baroda ATM.

 Information

Internet Garden (Main Rd; per hr ₹20; 8.30am-10.30pm) lets you hook up your laptop and is walking distance from Sanjay Market. Turn left, take the first right (Main Rd) and it's 500m on your left. There's nowhere to change money, but there's an ATM opposite Shabari emporium, and others around town.

Contact the Chhattisgarh Tourism Board in Raipur (p665) to arrange a guide to help with trips to tribal areas of the Bastar region, or arrange your own (p667).

Getting There & Away

Bus

There are regular services to Raipur (seat/sleeper from ₹210/290, seven hours, 4.30am to midnight), via Kondagaon (₹55, 1½ hours).

Buses to Chitrakote Falls (₹30, 1½hrs) leave from Anumapa Takij, a local cinema about 2km (cycle-rickshaw ₹10) from the bus stand. From Hotel Rainbow, turn left then take the first right and buses, plus shared jeeps, will be on your left.

Train

There's only one train here, but it's a good'un. The 58502 *Kirandul–Visakhapatnam* heads over the scenic Eastern Ghats on India's highest broad gauge line to Visakhapatnam (sleeper/1st class ₹102/384, 11 hours) on the Andhra Pradesh coast, via Koraput (₹80/199, three hours) for connections into Orissa. It leaves Jagdalpur daily at 9.50am. In the opposite direction, the 58501 arrives in Jagdalpur at 4.35pm. **Train reservations** (8am-noon & 2-4pm Mon-Sat, 8am-noon Sun) can be made at the train station, a ₹10 cycle-rickshaw ride from the bus stand.

Around Jagdalpur

You can get to many local Adivasi villages by bus – this is certainly an option on market days – but some are pretty inaccessible, and if you want to actually meet tribespeople, rather than just look at them, a guide is essential as a translator if nothing else. They can also help you arrange homestays. **Awesh Ali** (9425244925; aweshali@gmail.com; per day ₹1000) comes highly recommended. Contact him directly, or go through the Chhattisgarh Tourism Board (p665). A car and driver will cost ₹800 per day plus diesel (about ₹50 per 10km).

HAATS

These colourful **markets** are the lifeblood of tribal Chhattisgarh, and visiting them is

THE EIGHT TRIBES OF BASTAR

» Bhatra – Women are distinguished by their particularly colourful saris and an abundance of jewellery, including their distinctive gold, conical nose studs.

» Bhurwa – Men wear simple headscarves wrapped around their foreheads, often coloured red and white.

» Bison-Horn Maria – Famed for their distinctive double-horned headdress worn during festivals.

» Ghadwa – The bell-metal specialists of Bastar.

» Dorla – The only tribe to make their homes from the branches and leaves of trees found in the remote forests of the far south of Chhattisgarh (instead of mud thatch).

» Halba – Excellent farmers, taller in stature than other Adivasis. Men often only wear a loincloth.

» Hill Maria or Abhuj Maria – Extremely remote tribe whose people very rarely venture out from their villages in the dense forests of the Bastar Hills.

» Muria – Known for the huge amount of jewellery worn by both men and women.

an excellent way to get a taste of Bastar's vibrant Adivasi culture. Different tribes walk up to 20km to trade everything from their distinctive, almost fluorescent, saris to live red ants. Called *chapura* (see boxed text, p666) these ants are sold as food, eaten live (yes, still crawling and biting; ₹5 per leaf if you're interested) off a leaf. More appetising perhaps are *bobo* (rice and lentil cakes; ₹3) or *bhajiya* (fried lentil powder; ₹3), both eaten with a spicy relish.

The large piles of what look like squashed dates are in fact dried *mahuwa,* a type of flower, either eaten fresh, or dried then boiled to create steam which is fermented to produce a potent liquor, the favourite tipple of many Bastar Adivasis.

For more information on *haats,* see the boxed text (p667).

ADIVASI VILLAGES

There are more than 3500 villages in Bastar. Earrakote, 3.5km beyond Tokapal, is a mixed-tribe village, made up largely of Ghadwa, specialists in the art of bell-metal craftwork. The skill has been passed down through generations, in some instances for as long as 300 years. A number of family members are involved in the process, from the initial clay moulding and melting of scrap metal to the painstaking job of covering the moulds in wax thread, a part of the process which is unique to Bastar. Awesh Ali (p667) can put you in touch with families here who will put you up for the night in exchange for scrap metal or wax, which you can buy for them in Jagdalpur.

CHITRAKOTE FALLS

India's broadest waterfall (300m), two-thirds the size of Niagara, is at its roaring best just after the rains, but beautiful all year round, particularly at sunset. When the water is low, it's possible to paddle in pools at the top of the drop. Take extreme care.

In the river below the falls you can swim or get a local fisherman to row you up to the spray (₹25). Take the steps that lead down from the garden of the government-only hotel.

Chitrakote Log Huts (✆07859200194, 9993854165; cabins ₹1600; ❄), with comfortable AC cabins (some with fantastic views of the falls), is a peaceful place to stay. The eyesore of a restaurant does simple dishes (from ₹30) plus tea and coffee, and its veranda is a nice place to sit and admire the views.

The last bus back to Jagdalpur is at 4pm.

KONDAGAON
✆07786 / POP 26,898
Some 76km north of Jagdalpur is a craft complex run by NGO **Saathi** (✆242852, 9425259152; saathibastar@yahoo.co.in; Kondagaon; training & daily board ₹500, weekly materials ₹500; ☺8am-6pm Mon-Sat), encouraging Adivasis in the production of terracotta, woodcarving and metalwork. You can visit crafts people at work, there's a shop and training can be given. All Raipur–Jagdalpur buses go through Kondagaon.

Gujarat

Why Go?

Gujarat is a dynamic, relatively prosperous state that's barely glimpsed by many travellers scurrying between Mumbai (Bombay) and Rajasthan. But stop and explore and you'll find that this homeland of Mahatma Gandhi is quite a cocktail of surprises. It has its industries, but it also has artisans who weave and embroider some of India's finest textiles, and pristine parks harbouring unique wildlife such as the Asiatic lion. Its terrain is mostly flat, but it's scattered with dramatic, temple-topped, sacred mountains. Its cities range from the hectic to the frantic but they're also endowed with a wealth of beautiful old palace, mosque and temple architecture. The Gujarati people are renowned for their entrepreneurial nous and industriousness but with foreign tourists so scarce here, you're more likely to enjoy a friendly chat rather than a hard sell from locals. Gujarat is a dry state but this is one nonalcoholic cocktail that's worth savouring.

Best Places to Eat a Gujarati Thali

» Agashiye (p678)
» Shaam-e-Sarhad Village Resort (p713)
» Geeta Lodge (p703)
» Zorba the Buddha (p716)

Best Places to Stay

» Camp Zainabad (p716)
» House of MG (p677)
» Vijay Vilas Adpur (p691)
» Herança Goesa (p693)

When to Go
Ahmedabad

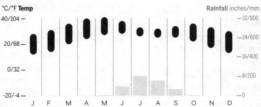

Sep/Oct
Navratri festival brings music and dancing to every town and village.

Nov–Dec
Mango milkshake time in Junagadh.

Nov–Mar
The best months to visit Gujarat's national parks and wildlife sanctuaries.

MAIN POINT OF ENTRY

Ahmedabad (Amda-vad) has direct flights from Singapore and several Persian Gulf cities, plus nine In-dian cities. It's also the major hub for trains and buses connecting Gujarat with the rest of India.

Fast Facts

» Population: 60.4 million
» Area: 196,024 sq km
» Capital: Gandhinagar
» Main language: Gujarati
» Sleeping prices: **$** below ₹1000, **$$** ₹1000 to ₹5000, **$$$** above ₹5000

Top Tip

Gujarat's most exhilarating destinations are away from its crowded, noisy cities. To enjoy it most, head out to its national parks and wildlife sanctuaries, to the tops of its sacred mountains, to the island retreat of Diu or to the handicraft hotbed of Kachchh (Kutch).

Resources

» Gujarat Tourism (www.gujarattourism.com)
» Gujarat Forest Depart-ment (www.gujaratforest.gov.in)
» Diu Tourism Department (www.diutourism.co.in)
» Kala Raksha (www.kala-raksha.org)

Food

Gujarat is strong on vegetarian food, partly thanks to the Jain influence here, and the quintessential Gujarati meal is the all-veg Gujarati thali. It's sweeter, lighter and less spicy and oily than Punjabi thali and locals have no doubts it's the best thali in the world. It begins with a large stainless-steel dish, onto which teams of waiters will serve most or all of the following: curries, chutneys, pickles, dhal, *kadhi* (a yo-ghurt and gram-flour preparation), raita, rotis, rice, *khichdi* (a blend of lightly spiced rice and lentils), *farsan* (savoury nibbles), salad and one or two sweet items – to be eaten concurrently with the rest. Buttermilk is the traditional ac-companying drink. Normally the rice and/or *khichdi* don't come till you've finished with the rotis. In most thali restau-rants the waiters will keep coming back until you can only say 'No more'. A good thali is an unbelievable combination of flavours – and a balanced, healthy, and usually good-value meal too.

DON'T MISS

Sasan Gir Wildlife Sanctuary offers the chance to see the only wild Asiatic lions, the last of a species that once roamed from the Middle East to northern India. Lion numbers in this forest sanctuary have risen to around 400 and the chances of seeing some on a jeep safari are roughly fifty-fifty. Take two or three safaris and you'd be unlucky not to get a lion sighting.

The complicated jigsaw of tribal groups and sub-castes who inhabit the villages of **Kachchh** (Kutch) are some of India's finest artisans, practising a huge variety of crafts and especially textiles. Their embroidery, weav-ing, tie-dye and block printing are intensely colourful and infinitely varied, and visits to some of their workshops and sales outlets make a fascinating journey into a world of colour, pattern and endless hours of meticulous, amazingly skilled craftwork.

Top State Festivals

» Uttarayan (14–15 Jan, Ahmedabad, p677) Kite festival.
» Modhera Dance Festival (around 20 Jan, Modhera, p683) Indian classical dance jamboree.
» Bhavnath Mela (Jan/Feb, Junagadh, p701) Hindu festival at the foot of sacred Girnar Hill.
» Mahakali Festival (Mar/Apr, Pavagadh, p688) Pilgrims pay tribute to Kali at Pavagadh hill.
» Navratri (Sep/Oct, statewide, p684) Nine nights of danc-ing all around Gujarat.
» Kartik Purnima (Nov/Dec, Somnath, p698, and Shatrun-jaya, p690) Large fair at Somnath; Jain pilgrims flock to Shatrunjaya hill.

Map labels

RAJASTHAN

PAKISTAN

0 — 100 km
0 — 60 miles

Rhinmal

Guru
Shikhar
(1722m) ▲

Sirohi

Mt Abu
Abu Road

Udaipur

Dholavira

Great Rann of Kachchh

Disa

Palanpur

8

Lakphat

Kachchh
(Kutch)

Khavda

Patan

Ravechi

Unjha

Mahesana

Himatnagar

Hodka

Ludia

Lilpur

15

Than

Sumrasar Sheikh

Little Rann
of Kachchh

Modhera

Dinodhar
Hill (388m)

Bhuj

Wild Ass
Sanctuary

Dasada
Zainabad
Viramgam

Gandhinagar

Bhujodi

Anjar

Adalaj
Vav

Ahmedabad (Amdavad)

Bada

Mandvi

Gandhidham

Kandla

Morvi

Dhrangadhra

Surendranagar

Nalsarovar
Bird Sanctuary

Dakor

Godhra

Okha
Island

Bet
Island

Marine
National
Park

Pirotan
Island

Khijadiya
Bird Sanctuary

Wankaner

Tarnetar

Bagodra

Nadiad

Anand

Jambughoda

Champaner

Narara

Jamnagar

Sayla

Lothal

Cambay

**Vadodara
(Baroda)**

Pavagadh

Dwarka

Rajkot

8B

Gulf of
Kachchh

Kathiawar
Peninsula
(Saurashtra)

Gondal

Dhoraji

**Girnar
Hill**

Blackbuck
National Park

Valabhipur

Bhavnagar

Dabhoi

Bharuch

Narmada
River

Madhavpur

Porbandar

Junagadh

Keshod

Sasan
Gir

Visavadar

**Sasan Gir
Wildlife
Sanctuary**

Sihor

Palitana

Shatrunjaya

Alang

Talaja

Gulf of
Cambay

Tapti River

Surat

Navsari

Mangrol

Chorwad

Talala

Veraval

Somnath

Una

Mahuva

Dandi

8

The Dangs

Saputara

Kodinar

Delwada

Diu

Udvada

**DADRA &
HAGAR
HAVELI**

Daman

Vapi

**ARABIAN
SEA**

MAHARASHTRA

Nasik

To Mumbai
(110km)

Gujarat Highlights

1 Take a forest safari in search of Asia's only wild lions at **Sasan Gir Wildlife Sanctuary** (p699)

2 Change down a gear and head for a sleepy island sojourn at the former Portuguese enclave of **Diu** (p692)

3 Explore the villages of **Kachchh** (Kutch; p714) to understand, admire and acquire some of India's best textiles

4 Explore an abandoned capital city and follow pilgrims up a mountain at the World Heritage Site of **Champaner and Pavagadh** (p687)

5 Undertake a challenging dawn pilgrimage to the hill-top temples of **Shatrunjaya** (p690) near Palitana or **Girnar Hill** (p701) near Junagadh

6 Tackle a thali, explore the old-city mosques, and pay homage to Mahatma Gandhi in bustling **Ahmedabad** (Amdavad; p672)

7 Go looking for Indian wild ass on the flat salt plains of the **Little Rann of Kachchh** (p716)

History

It's said that Gujarat's Temple of Somnath witnessed the creation of the universe, and many significant sites in Krishna's life lie along the state's coast. On a firmer historical footing, Lothal and Dholavira (Kachchh) were important sites of the Indus Valley civilisation more than 4000 years ago. Gujarat featured in the exploits of the mighty Buddhist emperor Ashoka, and you can see his rock edicts near Junagadh. Jainism, an important element of Gujarati life today, first took root under a grandson of Ashoka who governed Saurashtra.

The rule of the Hindu Solanki dynasty from the 10th to 13th centuries, with its capital at Patan, is considered Gujarat's cultural golden age. Solanki rule was ended when Ala-ud-din Khilji brought Gujarat into the Delhi sultanate after several campaigns around 1300. A century later the Muslim Gujarat sultanate broke free of Delhi rule and established a new capital at Ahmedabad. The Mughal empire conquered Gujarat in the 1570s and held it until the Hindu Marathas from central India occupied eastern and central Gujarat in the 18th century. The British set up their first Indian trading base at Surat on Gujarat's coast in about 1614, and replaced Maratha power in the early 19th century. Most of Gujarat's 400 or so princely states – many of them ruled by assorted Rajput clans – retained a degree of local autonomy under the British. Daman and Diu survived as Portuguese enclaves on Gujarat's coast until 1961.

After Independence, eastern Gujarat became part of Bombay state. Saurashtra and Kachchh, initially separate states, were incorporated into Bombay state in 1956. In 1960 Bombay state was divided on linguistic lines into Gujarati-speaking Gujarat and Marathi-speaking Maharashtra.

The Congress Party of India largely controlled Gujarat until 1991 when the Bharatiya Janata Party (BJP) came to power. In 2002, communal violence erupted after a Muslim mob was blamed for an arson attack on a train at Godhra that killed 59 Hindu activists. Hindu gangs set upon Muslims in revenge. This violence coincided with the beginning of the state election campaign, and BJP chief minister Narendra Modi followed a policy of fiercely Hindu rhetoric, but it brought him a landslide victory. In 2011 a court in Gujarat sentenced 11 Muslims to death, and 20 to life imprisonment, for setting fire to the train, while Modi was criticised by a Supreme Court panel for a 'partisan stance' over the subsequent violence. Since the 2002 riots, however, Gujarat has been peaceful, and continues to enjoy its reputation as one of India's most prosperous and businesslike states. It has, among other things, some exceptionally good roads (as well as some awful ones), and its buses mostly run on time. In 2008 the large and lucrative Tata Motors' Nano car project was secured for the town of Sanand, west of Ahmedabad.

EASTERN GUJARAT

Ahmedabad (Amdavad)

079 / POP 4.52 MILLION

Ahmedabad (also called Amdavad, Ahmadabad or Ahemdavad) is Gujarat's major city and a startling metropolis with a long history, many remarkable buildings, a fascinating maze of an old quarter, excellent museums, fine restaurants and fabulous night markets. Yet the old-world charm is all but swamped by 21st-century traffic, crowding, pollution and the usual extremes of wealth and poverty. Many travellers stop off briefly en route to Rajasthan or Mumbai, sneaking in a visit to Sabarmati Ashram (Gandhi's former headquarters). You need a little stamina to get to know the city better, as it's quite spread out and moving around can be a bit of a task.

The old city lies on the east side of the Sabarmati River and used to be surrounded by a 10km-long wall, of which little now remains except 15 formidable gates standing

ALCOHOL PERMITS

Gujarat is a dry state but alcohol permits for foreign visitors are easy to get at most large hotels with a 'wine shop'; show your passport plus a certificate or letter from your hotel (your Gujarat 'residence form') to receive a one-month permit. Permits are only available within one month of your arrival in India. Although they are officially free, local authorities often demand ₹100 or so from the shops and the shops pass this cost on to the customer. The permit allows you two units over the month and that equates to 20 bottles of standard beer, which you must drink in private. Cheers.

as forlorn islands amid swirling, cacophonous traffic. The new city on the west side of the river, nearly all built in the last 50 years, has wider streets with freer-flowing traffic and many middle-class neighbourhoods.

History

Ahmedabad was founded in 1411 by Gujarati sultan Ahmed Shah at the spot where, legend tells, he saw a hare chasing a dog (he was impressed by its bravery). The city spread quickly beyond his citadel on the east bank of the Sabarmati and by the 17th century it was considered one of the finest cities in India, a prospering trade nexus with an array of fine Islamic architecture. Its influence waned but from the second half of the 19th century Ahmedabad rose again as a huge textile centre (the 'Manchester of the East'). By the late 20th century many of the mills had closed and the subsequent economic hardship may have been a contributing factor in the communal violence that split the city in 2002, when over 1200 people, mostly Muslims, were killed. Today Ahmedabad is booming again as a centre for IT, education and chemicals production on top of its traditional textiles and commerce, and has recently been dubbed a 'megacity'.

◉ Sights

FREE Sabarmati Ashram   HISTORIC SITE
(www.sabarmati.org; Ashram Rd; ⊙8.30am-6.30pm) About 5km north of the centre, in peaceful, shady grounds on the river's west bank, this ashram was Gandhi's headquarters from 1917 to 1930 during the long struggle for Indian independence. It's said Gandhi chose this site because it lay between a jail and a cemetery and any *satyagrahi* (nonviolent resister) was bound to end up in one or the other. From here on 12 March 1930 Gandhi and 78 companions set out on the famous Salt March to Dandi on the Gulf of Cambay in a symbolic protest, with Gandhi vowing not to return to the ashram until India had gained independence. The ashram was disbanded in 1933, later becoming a centre for Dalit welfare activities and cottage industries. Gandhi's poignant, spartan living quarters are preserved, and there's a museum that presents an informative record of his life and teachings. After Gandhi's death some of his ashes were immersed in the river in front of the ashram.

Buses 13/1 and 83 (₹5) run here from Lal Darwaja bus stand. An autorickshaw from the city centre is about ₹40.

FREE Calico Museum of Textiles   MUSEUM
(☎22868172; www.calicomuseum.com; Sarabhai Foundation; ⊙tours 10.30am & 3pm Thu-Tue) This museum contains one of the world's finest collections of antique and modern Indian textiles, all handmade and up to 500 years old. There are some astoundingly beautiful pieces, displaying incredible virtuosity and extravagance. You'll see Kashmiri shawls that took three years to make, and double-*ikat* cloths whose 100,000 threads were each individually dyed before weaving.

The main textile galleries can only be visited in the morning session: the tours last two hours with a maximum 25 people – 15 by group booking and 10 on a first-come-first-served basis. Be there by 10am to maximise chances of getting in. The afternoon tour (maximum 15 people, all first-come-first-served) is devoted to the Sarabhai Foundation's collection of religious art, which explores depictions of Indian gods, including textile galleries.

No photography is allowed. The museum is in the Shahibag area, 3.5km north of the old centre, opposite the Shahibag Underbridge. You can get there by bus 101, 102 or 105 (₹5) from Lal Darwaja local bus stand and through Delhi Gate. An autorickshaw should cost ₹40.

Mosques & Mausoleums   MOSQUES

Under the Gujarat sultanate in the 15th and 16th centuries, and especially under Ahmed Shah I (1411–42) and Mahmud Begada (1459–1511), Ahmedabad was endowed with a remarkable collection of stone mosques in a unique style incorporating elements of Hindu and Jain design.

The Mausoleum of Ahmed Shah (Bad-shah-na-Hazira), outside the Jama Masjid's east gate, may have been constructed by Ahmed Shah himself before his death in 1442. His cenotaph is the central one under the main dome. An 11pm drumming session in the mausoleum's eastern gateway used to signal the closing of the city gates and still happens nightly. Through an arch a little further east is Ahmed Shah's queen's tomb, the Rani-na-Hazira, on a raised platform now engulfed by market stalls, and in poor shape, though the *jali* (carved lattice) screens are nice.

Siddi Sayid's Mosque (Lal Darwaja) was built in the year the Mughals conquered Gujarat (1573), by an Abyssinian in the Gujarati army. One of Ahmedabad's most stunning buildings, it is famed for its exquisite

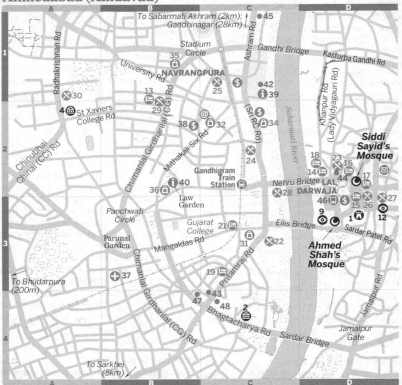

jali windows, spiderweb fine, depicting the intricate intertwining branches of the 'tree of life'.

Southwest of Bhadra Fort, **Ahmed Shah's Mosque** was built in 1414 for the sultan and nobles within Ahmedabad's original citadel. The prayer hall is a forest of beautifully carved stone pillars and *jali* screens, and its elaborately carved ceiling has a circular symmetry reminiscent of Hindu and Jain temples.

The small **Rani Sipri's Mosque**, near the ST bus stand, is also known as the Masjid-e-Nagira (Jewel of a Mosque) because of its graceful construction, with delicate carved minarets and Rani Sipri's domed tomb with fine *jali* screens. Rani Sipri is said to have been a Hindu widow of Mahmud Begada; the buildings date from 1514.

Between Ahmedabad train station and Sarangpur Gate, the **Sidi Bashir Mosque**, built in 1452, is famed for its 21.3m-high shaking minarets *(jhulta minara)*, built to

shake to protect against earthquake damage. This certainly worked in 2001.

Kankaria Lake LAKE
(admission ₹10; ☉9am-11pm) Built in 1451 and recently dandified as a recreation space for the city, this large lake is a nice respite from the hectic streets. Attractions include a tethered **hot-air balloon** (10min ride ₹100; ☉10am-10pm), a **mini-train** and a **zoo**. One Tree Hill Garden on the west side (entered from outside) contains some quite grand colonial **Dutch tombs**.

FREE **Bhadra Fort & Teen Darwaja** FORT
(Lal Darwaja; ☉dawn-dusk) Built immediately after the founding of Ahmedabad in 1411, Bhadra Fort now houses government offices and a Kali temple. Its gate formed the eastern entrance of the Ahmedabad citadel, which stretched west to the river. From the roof you can check out the formidable structure and views of the surrounding streets.

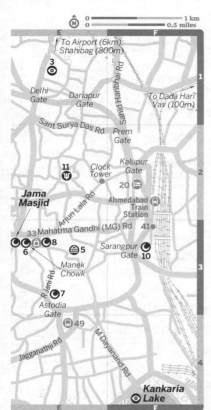

Shreyas Folk Museum   MUSEUM

(Indian/foreigner ₹10/90; ⊙10am-1.30pm & 2-5.30pm Tue-Sun) This museum, 3km west of the river in Bhudarpura, displays an impressive range of Gujarati folk arts, including woodcarvings, metalwork and some wonderful embroidered textiles and amazing tie-dyed quilts. Included in the ticket is the **Kalpana Mangaldas Museum**, with festival masks from around India and, just to round things off, an elephant skeleton. It's all set in the peaceful, peacock-dotted grounds of the Shreyas Foundation. Photos are not allowed. An autorickshaw from the centre costs around ₹35.

FREE Sarkhej Roza   HISTORIC BUILDINGS

(⊙9am-dusk) In the Sarkhej area 8km southwest of the old centre, Sarkhej Roza is a mosque, tomb and palace complex dedicated to the memory of Ahmed Shah I's spiritual advisor, Ahmed Khattu Ganj Baksh. The elegant though dilapidated buildings cluster around a great (now often dry) tank, constructed by Sultan Mahmud Begada in the mid-15th century. It's an atmospheric place that was used as a retreat by several of Ahmedabad's rulers. The mausoleums of Mahmud Begada (by the entrance, with geometric *jalis* casting patterns of light on the floor) and Ganj Baksh (the largest in Gujarat) are both here.

A return autorickshaw from the city centre will cost around ₹120 and Sarkhej Roza

Between the fort and the **Teen Darwaja** (Triple Gateway) to its east was the Maidan Shahi (Royal Square), where royal processions and polo games took place. Today it's a seething market area.

Temples   JAIN & HINDU TEMPLES

Outside Delhi Gate, north of the old city, the Jain **Hutheesingh Temple** (Balvantrai Mehta Rd) is constructed of delicately carved white marble. Built in 1848, it's dedicated to Dharamanath, the 15th Jain *tirthankar* (great teacher).

The glorious, multicoloured, woodcarved **Swaminarayan Temple** (Kalupur; ⊙6am-7pm), in the old city, was built in 1822 as the first temple of the Swaminarayan Hindu sect. Followers believe the sect's founder, Swaminarayan (1781–1830), was the supreme being. The start of the daily Heritage Walk (p677) here at 8am usually coincides with worship at the temple, with believers' passion on full display.

DON'T MISS

JAMA (JUMMA) MASJID

Built by Ahmed Shah in 1423, the Jama Masjid (Friday Mosque) on Mahatma Gandhi (MG) Rd ranks as one of India's most beautiful mosques, enhanced by an enormous, peaceful courtyard. Demolished Hindu and Jain temples provided the building materials and the mosque displays some architectural fusion with these religions, notably in the lotus-like carving of some domes, similar to that of many Jain temples. The prayer hall's 260 columns support 15 principal domes at different elevations. There were once two 'shaking' minarets, but they lost half their height in the great earthquake of 1819, though their lower portions still flank the prayer hall's central portico.

Ahmedabad (Amdavad)

◎ Top Sights

Ahmed Shah's Mosque	D3
Jama Masjid	E3
Kankaria Lake	F4
Siddi Sayid's Mosque	D2

◎ Sights

1	Bhadra Fort	D3
2	City Museum	C4
3	Hutheesingh Temple	E1
	Kite Museum	(see 2)
4	Lalbhai Dalpatbhai Museum	A2
5	Mangaldas ni Haveli	E3
6	Mausoleum of Ahmed Shah	E3
	NC Mehta Gallery	(see 4)
7	Rani Sipri's Mosque	E3
8	Rani-na-Hazira	E3
9	SEWA Reception Centre	D3
10	Sidi Bashir Mosque	F3
11	Swaminarayan Temple	E2
12	Teen Darwaja	D3

◎ Sleeping

13	Comfort Inn President	B1
14	Hotel Ambassador	D2
15	Hotel Cadillac	D3
	Hotel Good Night	(see 17)
16	Hotel Royal Highness	D2
	Hotel Volga	(see 17)
17	House of MG	D2
18	Le Meridien Ahmedabad	D2
19	Neelkanth Sahara	C3
20	Ritz Inn	F2
21	Royal Orchid Central	C3

◎ Eating

	Agashiye	(see 17)
	Dadi Dining Hall	(see 19)
	Food Inn	(see 17)
22	Gopi Dining Hall	C3
	Green House	(see 17)
	Havmor	(see 15)

23	Havmor	D2
24	Havmor	C2
25	Havmor Restaurant	C1
26	Hotel ZK	D3
27	Muslim Street Stalls	D3
28	Neelkanth Patang	C2
29	Sankalp	B2
	TGB Cafe 'n Bakery	(see 28)
30	Zen Cafe	A1

◎ Shopping

31	Art Book Center	C3
32	Crossword	C2
33	Gamthiwala	E3
34	Garvi Gurjari	C2
35	Hansiba	B1
36	Law Garden Night Market	B2

Information

37	Apollo City Center	B3
	Cyberpoint	(see 32)
38	Cyberworld	C2
39	Gujarat Tourism	C1
	HDFC ATM	(see 26)
	Relief Cyber Café	(see 26)
40	Tourism Desk	B2

Transport

41	Computerised Train Booking Office	F3
42	Express Travels	C1
43	Gujarat Travels	C4
44	Indian Airlines/Air India	D2
45	Jet Airways	C1
	Kingfisher Airlines	(see 29)
46	Lal Darwaja Local Bus Stand	D3
47	Patel Tours & Travels	B4
	Raj Express	(see 47)
48	Shree Swaminarayan	C4
49	ST Bus Stand	E4

could be combined with a visit to Vishalla restaurant and its utensil museum (p679), about 1km back towards the city.

FREE **Lalbhai Dalpatbhai Museum** MUSEUM
(LD Museum; www.ldindology.org; Radhakrishnan Rd; ◷10.30am-5pm Tue-Sun) Part of the LD Institute of Indology, this museum houses a fine collection of ancient and medieval Indian art treasures, including stone, marble, bronze and wood carvings and 75,000 Jain manuscripts. A 6th-century-AD sandstone carving from Madhya Pradesh is the oldest-known carved image of the god Rama.

FREE **NC Mehta Gallery** MUSEUM
(Radhakrishnan Rd; ◷10.30am-5.30pm Tue-Sun Jul-Apr, 8.30am-12.30pm Tue-Sun May-Jun) In the same building as the LD Museum, this gallery has an important collection of jewel-like illustrated manuscripts and miniature paintings. Best known is *Chaurapanchasi-*

ka (Fifty Love Lyrics of a Thief), written by Vilhana, an 11th-century Kashmiri poet sentenced to be hanged for loving the king's daughter. Before his execution he was granted one final wish: he chose to recite these 50 poems, which so impressed the king that he gave Vilhana his daughter in marriage.

FREE City Museum   MUSEUM
(Sanskar Kendra, Bhagtacharya Rd; ⊙10am-6pm Tue-Sun) In a 1956 red-brick-and-concrete building by renowned Swiss architect Le Corbusier, the City Museum covers Ahmedabad's history with rather old-fashioned displays, but explanatory material is in English and Gujarati – interesting enough if you're a history buff. It includes sections on the city's religious communities, Gandhi and the Independence struggle. On the ground floor you will find the **Kite Museum** (admission free; ⊙10am-6pm Tue-Sun), with a selection of patterned tissue-paper kites resembling trapped butterflies.

FREE Dada Hari Vav   NOTABLE BUILDING
(⊙dawn-dusk) This step-well, built in 1499 by the supervisor of Sultan Begada's harem, has steps down through five levels of carved stone columns to two small wells, now often bone dry. The depths are cool, even on the hottest day, and it's a fascinating and eerie place. Overflow channels at the top are a reminder of times when water tables were much higher than today. Behind the stepwell, the 16th-century **Dai Halima Mosque** contains the mausoleum of a royal midwife named Halima, with nice *jali* screens.

Vechaar Utensil Museum   MUSEUM
(www.vishalla.com; Bye-Pass Rd; Indian/foreigner ₹10/50; ⊙3-10.30pm Tue-Sun) At Vishalla restaurant, opposite Vasna Tol Naka, this museum displays the graceful practicality of pots and utensils, with more than 4500 items from all over India, some 1000 years old.

Festivals & Events

Uttarayan   KITE FESTIVAL
Each 14–15 January, Ahmedabad hosts Uttarayan (Makar Sakranti), a traditional kite festival that attracts international participants and is well worth the stiff neck.

Tours

The Municipal Corporation runs a fascinating daily **Heritage Walk** (📞9824032866; Indian/foreigner ₹30/50) through the old city. It starts at 8am at the Swaminarayan Temple

in Kalupur and finishes at the Jama Masjid around 10.30am. It's advisable to book. The tours, through narrow, confusing streets and past dilapidated, carved wooden houses, are an excellent way to get a feel for old Ahmedabad with its 600 *pols* – neighbourhoods of narrow streets with common courtyards, wells and *chabutaras* (bird-feeding towers). The tours are in English and there's a brief slide show beforehand. Wear slip-on footwear as you'll be visiting plenty of temples.

The House of MG offers an ingenious **audio guide walk** (₹100). Beginning at the famed hotel (where you deposit your passport), the 80-minute walk takes an alternative route through the old city, ending at the **Mangaldas ni Haveli**, a finely carved old mansion that houses a crafts shop.

The Municipal Corporation runs twice-daily four-hour **city tours** (₹100) by bus, with short stops at major sights. Buses depart from Bhadra Fort at 9am and 1.30pm.

🛏 Sleeping

Budget hotels are mostly clustered in the noisy, traffic-infested Lal Darwaja area, close to the old city, while the majority of midrange and top-end places are found on Khanpur Rd (paralleling the east bank of the Sabarmati) or west of the river, which is a more congenial environment but further from most of the interesting sights. Ahmedabad has most of the top-end hotels in Gujarat.

House of MG   HERITAGE HOTEL $$$
(📞25506946; www.houseofmg.com; Lal Darwaja; s/d from ₹4990/5990, ste from ₹8990/10,900, all incl breakfast; ✳@☎☑) This 1920s building (with two excellent restaurants) opposite Siddi Sayid's Mosque was once the home of textile magnate Sheth Mangaldas Girdhardas – it was converted into a beautiful heritage hotel in the 1990s by his great-grandson. All the rooms are vast, verandah-edged and tastefully decorated, with great attention to detail. It's an icon of the upper classes, and hugely popular with locals and foreigners alike. Service is first-rate, and the indoor swimming pool and gym are divine. If you know your dates, book a couple of months in advance online to receive up to 30% discount.

Le Meridien Ahmedabad   HOTEL $$$
(📞25505505; http://lemeridien.com/ahmedabad; Khanpur Rd; s/d from ₹6500/7500, ste ₹20,000, all incl breakfast; ✳@☎☑) This luxurious option towers over the fragile shacks scattered along the river bank. All rooms are super comfort-

able and the suites are palatial. Breakfast is excellent and as huge as you like, and there is a neat indoor swimming pool, spa and sauna. Ask for the best available rate, which can be little more than half the rack rate.

Royal Orchid Central HOTEL $$$

(☎30912345; www.royalorchidhotels.com; Ellis Bridge; s ₹7000-8000, d ₹8000-9000, ste ₹12,000, all incl breakfast; ❀@☎≋) Opposite Gujarat College, a new high-end business hotel where the rooms are tasteful and comfortable rather than exciting but have state-of-the-art gadgets like universal electrical sockets and iPod docks. There's an excellent 24-hour restaurant-cum-coffee-shop. Free airport transfers too.

Hotel Ambassador HOTEL $$

(☎25502490; www.ambassadorahmedabad.com; Khanpur Rd; s/d from ₹2100/2500; ❀@☎) Newly renovated inside and out, with a bright white exterior, the Ambassador greets you with a chilled lobby and friendly desk and follows up with rooms that are quite stylish in browns and creams. With discounts often available, it's not bad value.

Ritz Inn HOTEL $$

(☎22123842; www.hotelritzinn.com; Station Rd; s ₹2400-2600, d ₹3000-4500; ❀@☎) Near the railway station, this smart hotel has unusual class and is excellent value for money. The art-deco lobby, comfortable rooms with superb beds, and unusually slick and amiable service make it an outstanding option. There's a good veg restaurant, checkout is a civilised 24 hours, discounts are often available and it offers free airport and station transfers.

Comfort Inn President HOTEL $$

(☎26467575; www.comfortinnpresident.com; off CG Rd, Navrangpura; s/d incl breakfast from ₹3125/4000; ❀☎) This is a calm, well-run hotel on a quiet street close to the Chimanlal Girdharilal (CG) Rd shops in middle-class Navrangpura. Rooms aren't huge but are solidly comfortable and well equipped, and there's an in-house wine shop as well as a multicuisine restaurant. Good discounts are often available; airport transfers are free.

Hotel Royal Highness HOTEL $$

(☎25507450; www.hotelroyalhighness.com; Lal Darwaja; s/d incl breakfast from ₹2750/3300; ❀@☎) This grand edifice is in a convenient location and the lobby is impressive. The rooms have all been renovated and are spacious and clean. Deluxe rooms feature zebra-print furnishings and sparkling bathrooms with big glassed-in showers. There is a 24-hour restaurant, and a free airport shuttle service.

Hotel Volga HOTEL $

(☎25509497; www.hotelvolga.com; Hanuman Lane, off Relief Rd, Lal Darwaja; s/d ₹600/750, s with AC ₹800-1000, d with AC ₹950-1150; ❀) This surprisingly good option tucked down a narrow street behind the House of MG is worth searching out. Rooms are smart and respectably clean, with a hint of 1970s design in the curved beige walls – some are more dashingly decorated. The front desk is friendly and efficient, checkout is 24 hours, and you can order decent multicuisine food (mains ₹95 to ₹175) to your room.

Hotel Good Night HOTEL $

(☎25507181; hotelforyou2002@yahoo.com; Lal Darwaja; s/d from ₹450/550, s with AC ₹800-1300, d with AC ₹/950-1500; ❀) This tidy hotel next door to the House of MG has budget rooms better than the average in these parts. There are seven categories of room, all clean and well kept, so it shouldn't be too hard to find one that suits your budget and comfort needs, though the ground-floor 'Ordinary' ones are dingy and can be odorous.

Neelkanth Sahara HOTEL $$

(☎66615145; sahara@neelkanthhotels.com; 2nd fl, Iscon Sq, Pritamraj Rd, Paldi; s/d ₹750/850, with AC from ₹900/1100; ❀) With helpful staff, bright, tasteful decor, and decent-sized rooms, this is quite good value and close to many private bus offices. There's a fruit-and-vegetable market on the ground floor of the building, and a good thali restaurant, **Dadi Dining Hall** (thali ₹140; ⊙lunch & dinner), on the 1st floor.

Hotel Cadillac HOTEL $

(☎25507558; Advance Cinema Rd, Lal Darwaja; s/d ₹250/300, without bathroom ₹150/300) This cheerful and cheap option, sporting a wooden balustrade, is a classic from 1934. Management vouch for the comfort of the lumpy cotton mattresses, but we remain dubious. While the street noise and squat-toilet bathrooms are not selling features, the people-watching balcony is.

Eating

Ahmedabad has the best range of eating options in Gujarat and is a great place to sample the Gujarati thali.

Agashiye GUJARATI $$

(☎25506946; House of MG, Lal Darwaja; lunch or dinner regular/deluxe ₹395/495; ⊙noon-3.30pm &

The profound significance of water in the drought-prone districts of Gujarat and Rajasthan is set in stone in the step-well – *vav, wav, kuva* or *baoli* (*baori* in Rajasthan). These elaborate constructions are unique to northwestern India. Ancient Hindu scriptures venerate those who build communal wells. With the Indian inclination to turn the functional into works of art, sophisticated water-storage structures were developed, first by Hindus and then under the Mughals. Although the nobility considered it a religious obligation to construct these, the wells were evidently status symbols – the grandeur and artistry reflected the power and sensibility of their patrons. Often attached to temples, the wells were also meeting places, with verandahs where people could take refuge from the summer heat, and stopping places on caravan routes. Reliant on rainfall and (dropping) levels of ground water, many of the wells are now often dry, sadly neglected and full of rubbish.

7-10.45pm) This is Ahmedabad's best dining experience. On the rooftop of one of the city's finest mansions, the lovely tiled terrace is an oasis of calm and space, candle-lit at night and a world away from the congested streets. The all-veg menu, which changes daily, begins with a welcoming drink and is a cultural journey around the traditional thali – a multitude of ravishingly tasty vegetable dishes – and finishes with hand-churned ice cream. You even get a handy leaflet on the etiquette of eating a thali. For dinner, it is advisable to book ahead.

Green House GUJARATI **$$**
(House of MG, Lal Darwaja; mains ₹100-175) The Green House is the casual front restaurant at the House of MG. Choose the fan-blasted outdoor courtyard or the AC room with a 15% surcharge. The selection of vegie Gujarati dishes is superb. Do try the house special *sharbat* (sherbet); and the delicate and delicious *panaki,* a thin crêpe cooked between banana leaves; or the divine *malpuva,* a sweet, deep-fried pancake in saffron syrup, topped with rose petals. And don't leave without trying the hand-churned ice cream. The breakfasts (₹175 to ₹250) are pretty good too.

Vishalla INDIAN **$$**
(☑26602422; www.vishalla.com; Bye-Pass Rd; lunch ₹197, dinner ₹449; ☺lunch & dinner) On the southwest outskirts of town, just off the road to Sarkhej (opposite Vasna Tol Naka), Vishalla is a magical eating experience in an open-air setting that recreates a traditional Gujarati village. You eat a copious vegetarian meal seated on the floor in rustic wooden huts, and dinner is a whole evening's feast (7.30pm to 11pm) including entertainment of folk music and dance and puppet shows. The complex includes a fascinating utensil

museum (p677). An autorickshaw from the city centre costs about ₹100 return.

Neelkanth Patang MULTICUISINE **$$**
(☑26586200; Chinubhai Center, west end Nehru Bridge; lunch Mon-Sat ₹329, brunch Sun ₹449, dinner Mon-Fri ₹399, dinner Sat & Sun ₹449; ☺11am-2.30pm & 7-11.30pm) For a meal with a view the Neelkanth Patang has no rivals as it's 50m above the ground and revolves. The multicuisine buffet meals are terrific and bountiful. It's worth calling ahead to book.

Food Inn INDIAN **$$**
(Lal Darwaja; mains ₹85-175; ☺lunch & dinner) A clean, bright and bustling curry house in the Hotel Good Night building (opposite Siddi Sayid's Mosque) where carnivores can tuck into numerous chicken, mutton and fish dishes, including spicy Punjabi curries, lip-smackin' tandoori, biryani and sizzlers.

Sankalp SOUTH INDIAN **$**
(Samir Bldg, CG Rd; mains ₹50-120) A quality chain restaurant serving up excellent vegetarian South Indian food, Sankalp sits on a rooftop about five storeys high. Unusual fillings like pineapple or spinach-cheese-garlic are available for its renowned *dosas* (paper-thin lentil-flour pancakes) and *uttapams* (thick, savoury rice pancakes) that come accompanied by seven different sauces. Order *masala papad* (thin, crisp wafer with a spicy topping) for a tasty starter.

Gopi Dining Hall GUJARATI **$**
(off Pritamraj Rd; thali ₹85-115; ☺lunch & dinner) Just off the west end of Ellis Bridge, this little restaurant is a much-loved thali institution, with a small garden and an AC dining room. You can choose from 'fix', 'full' and 'with one sweet' options depending how hungry you are.

Zen Cafe
CAFE $

(www.zencafe.info; Radhakrishnan Rd; drinks ₹25-40, snacks ₹50-100; ⊘4-9pm Tue-Sun) This peaceful spot in a tree-fringed garden is popular with students from Gujarat University and other colleges nearby. It's right next to the weird Amdavad ni Gufa (Amdavad Cave), an underground art gallery which looks like a heap of octopuses with sawn-off tentacles. Offerings include panini, chocolate walnut brownies, organic coffee and capriosch mocktails – perfect icy coolers of mint, lime and soda.

Havmor
ICE CREAM $

(scoops ₹15-40; ⊘11am-11pm) Ahmedabad is famous for ice cream and locals aver that the Havmor brand, found only in Gujarat, is best. Havmor has branches all over the city including at Lal Darwaja, Khanpur Rd, Navrangpura and the Cinemasala building, Ashram Rd.

Hotel ZK
INDIAN, CHINESE $$

(Relief Rd, Lal Darwaja; mains ₹75-150; ⊘9am-11pm) This AC, non-veg restaurant has tinted windows, low lighting and impeccable service. The chicken Afghani curry is recommended but apparently the most popular dish with the locals is the interesting-sounding chicken pesto Chinese.

Havmor Restaurant
MULTICUISINE $$

(Stadium Complex, Navrangpura; mains ₹50-250; ⊘noon-10.45pm) Havmor ice-cream company operates this AC place where Ahmedabad's middle class congregate for a huge choice of well-prepared snacks and meals, from wraps and nachos to Italian and Indian.

TGB Cafe 'n Bakery
CAFE $

(Chinubhai Center; cakes ₹30-130; ⊘11.30am-11pm) Time you treated yourself to a Dutch truffle cake or sizzling chocolate brownie with ice cream? Head to this lounge-style cafe underneath the Neelkanth Patang, at the west end of Nehru Bridge, and indulge. Real coffee too.

The **Law Garden Night Market** and **Manek Chowk** are good for street food after about 8pm. Muslim street food is available on **Bhathiyar Gali**, a small street parallel to MG Rd: you can get a good meaty feed for about ₹30 from the evening stalls.

🔒 Shopping

Law Garden Night Market
HANDICRAFTS, CLOTHING

(Law Garden; ⊘dusk-11pm) An evening market packed with stalls selling glittering wares from Kachchh and Saurashtra. It's chock-a-block with fantastically decorated cholis (sari blouses) and *chaniyas* (long, wide traditional skirts), as well as embroidered wall hangings, costume jewellery and more.

Manek Chowk
HANDICRAFTS, FOOD

(Old City) This busy space and surrounding narrow streets are the commercial heart of the old city. Weave your way through the crowds to soak up the atmosphere and browse the vegetable and sweet stalls and silver and textile shops. **Gamthiwala** (⊘11am-1pm & 2-7pm Mon-Sat), by the entrance to the Mausoleum of Ahmed Shah, sells quality block-printed textiles.

Garvi Gurjari
HANDICRAFTS, CLOTHING

(Ashram Rd; ⊘10am-7.30pm Mon-Sat) This state-government-run outlet has three floors of Gujarat crafts including silk and handloomed-cotton saris, painted metal

---

SEWA

The Ahmedabad-based Self-Employed Women's Association (SEWA) is one of India's largest trade unions and a rarity for two reasons: its members are women and they work in the informal sector (that large majority of Indian workers who do not receive the benefits of formal employment, such as hawkers, vendors and many home-based workers, labourers and domestic workers). Established in 1972 by women working on the fringes of the Ahmedabad textile industry, SEWA now has some 1.2 million members. It's based on the notion that poor women need organisation, not aid.

SEWA assists self-employed workers to organise into unions and cooperatives, so that they can control the fruits of their labours. Its approach focuses on health and childcare, literacy, appropriate housing and self-sufficiency, and the SEWA Academy conducts leadership courses for its members. SEWA also runs a bank, provides access to legal aid and is active in the campaign for a needs-based minimum wage.

The **SEWA Reception Centre** (☎25506444; www.sewa.org; ⊘10am-6pm Mon-Sat) is at the eastern end of Ellis Bridge. It has a range of literature and visitors are welcome. SEWA's fixed-price handicrafts are sold at Hansiba.

jewellery boxes and clothing in folksy designs. There are some good finds if you rummage around.

Hansiba
HANDICRAFTS

(8 Chandan Complex, CG Rd; ⊙11am-9pm Mon-Sat, 11.30am-7.30pm Sun) The retail outlet of SEWA, Hansiba sells colourfully woven and embroidered shawls, saris, other clothes and wall hangings.

Art Book Center
BOOKSTORE

(www.artbookcenter.net; off Mangaldas Rd; ⊙10am-6pm) This specialist treasure trove is upstairs in a brightly painted building near Ellis Bridge. Indian architecture, miniature painting and textile design are the main topics stocked.

Crossword
BOOKSTORE

(Shree Krishna Centre, Mithakali Six Rd; ⊙10.30am-9pm) A large, bustling book, music and DVD shop also boasting a Café Coffee Day.

ℹ Information

Internet Access

Cyberpoint (Shree Krishna Centre, Mithakali Six Rd; per hr ₹20; ⊙10am-10pm Mon-Fri, 10am-8pm Sat & Sun) Behind Crossword bookstore.

Relief Cyber Café (Relief Rd; per hr ₹20; ⊙9.30am-12.30am) It's air-conditioned, what a relief!

Medical Services

Apollo City Center (☑66305800; www.apollo ahd.com; 1 Tulsibaug Society) Small but recommended private hospital opposite Doctor House, near Parimal Garden.

Money

For changing travellers cheques and currency, there's **State Bank of India** (Lal Darwaja; ⊙11am-4pm Mon-Fri, 11am-1pm Sat) opposite the local bus stand, and **ICICI Bank** (2/1 Popular House, Ashram Rd; ⊙9am-6pm Mon-Fri). There are numerous ATMs:

HDFC (Relief Rd, Lal Darwaja) Also off Mithakali Six Rd, Navrangpura.

State Bank (Ramanial Sheth Rd) Also at Ahmedabad train station.

Post

Main post office (Ramanial Sheth Rd; ⊙10am-7.30pm Mon-Sat, 10am-1pm Sun)

Tourist Information

Gujarat Tourism (☑1800 2337951; www .gujarattourism.com) Ahmedabad train station (⊙6am-6pm Mon-Sat); Ashram Rd

(☑26578044/5/6; HK House, opposite Bata showroom, off Ashram Rd; ⊙8am-8pm) The very helpful HK House office has all sorts of information at its fingertips and you can also hire cars with drivers here.

Tourism Desk (☑32520878; Law Garden; ⊙10.30am-8.30pm) Ahmedabad Municipal Corporation's office has a few publications and can answer some questions.

ℹ Getting There & Away

Air

Ahmedabad's busy airport has direct flights to nine Indian cities and, overseas, Doha (Qatar), Dubai (United Arab Emirates), Kuwait City (Kuwait), Muscat (Oman), Sharjah (United Arab Emirates) and Singapore. Domestic airlines serving Ahmedabad:

Go Air (☑9223222111; www.goair.in)

Indian Airlines/Air India (☑25505198; www .airindia.in; Lal Darwaja)

IndiGo (☑9910383838; www.goindigo.in)

Jet Airways (☑022-39893333; www.jetair ways.com; Ratnanabh Complex, Ashram Rd)

Kingfisher Airlines (☑1800 2093030; www .flykingfisher.com; Shop No 3, Shoppers Plaza, CG Rd, Navrangpura)

SpiceJet (☑1800 1803333; www.spicejet.com) Many agencies sell air tickets, including **Express Travels** (☑26588602; expresstravel@eth.net; Jivabhai chambers, off Ashram Rd).

Bus

Private buses from the north may drop you on Naroda Rd, about 7km northeast of the city centre – an autorickshaw will complete the journey for ₹50 to ₹60.

From the **ST bus stand** (Sabarmati Terminal), frequent **Gujarat State Road Transport Corporation** (GSRTC, ST) buses go to Vadodara (Baroda; express/luxury ₹78/115, two hours), Bhavnagar (₹110/130, five hours), Junagadh (₹160/180, eight hours), Jamnagar (₹166/186, seven hours), Rajkot (express/AC ₹115/232, 4½ hours) and Bhuj (seat/sleeper ₹160/210, nine hours). Six or seven daily buses go to Udaipur (express/luxury ₹150/185, 5½ hours). A Volvo AC bus departs at 7pm for Udaipur (₹395), Jaipur (₹985) and Delhi (₹1585, 20 hours).

For long distances, private buses are mostly quicker; most offices are close to Paldi Char Rasta.

Patel Tours & Travels (www.pateltours andtravels.com; 8 Shroff Chambers) Runs Volvo AC buses to Rajkot (₹300, four hours, 18 daily), Jamnagar (₹400, six hours, nine daily) and Mumbai (seat/sleeper ₹600/800, 11 hours, 7.30pm), plus non-AC buses to Mumbai (seat/sleeper ₹400/500, 6pm and 10pm) and six daily buses to Bhuj (seat/sleeper non-AC ₹220/320, AC ₹270/370, eight hours).

Raj Express (8 Kanth Complex) Runs Volvo AC buses to Udaipur (₹350, five hours, 6.45am and 2pm) and non-AC buses to Jaipur (seat/sleeper ₹300/400, 12 hours, four daily).

Gujarat Travels (www.gujarattravels.co.in; 1 Medicine Market) Has buses to Mt Abu (seat/sleeper ₹220/300, seven hours, three daily).

Shree Swaminarayan (22 Anilkunj Complex) Heads to Diu (seat/sleeper ₹200/280, 10 hours, 10.30pm and 2.30am).

Train

There's a **computerised booking office** (◷8am-8pm Mon-Sat, 8am-2pm Sun) just outside Ahmedabad train station. Window 6 handles the foreign-tourist quota. Computerised booking is also available at the *relatively* quiet Gandhigram station, although there is no window dedicated to foreigners.

❶ Getting Around

To/From the Airport

The airport is 8km north of the centre; a prepaid taxi should cost around ₹300 depending on your destination. An autorickshaw costs about ₹150 to the old city. A cheaper option is bus 105 to/from Lal Darwaja (₹10).

Autorickshaw

Autorickshaw drivers are supposed to turn their meter to zero at the start of a trip then calculate the fare using a conversion chart at the end. They should cost ₹7 per kilometre.

Around Ahmedabad

Trips to destinations to the northwest and southwest of the city can be extended with a visit to the Wild Ass Sanctuary (p716).

ADALAJ VAV

Adalaj Vav, 19km north of Ahmedabad, is among the finest of the Gujarati step-wells. Built by Queen Rudabai in 1499, it has three entrances leading to a huge platform that rests on 16 pillars, with corners marked by shrines. The octagonal well is five storeys deep and is decorated with exquisite stone carvings; subjects range from eroticism to buttermilk. The Gandhinagar bus will get you within walking distance (ask the conductor where to get off). An autorickshaw costs ₹300 return.

GANDHINAGAR

With broad avenues and greenery, Gandhinagar forms a striking contrast to Ahmed-

MAJOR TRAINS FROM AHMEDABAD

DESTINATION	TRAIN NO & NAME	DEPARTURE	DURATION (HR)	FARE (₹)
Bhavnagar	12971 *Bandra-Bhavnagar Exp*	5.45am	6	182/442/584 (A)
Bhuj	19115 *Bandra-Bhuj Exp*	11.59pm	7¾	180/462/624 (A)
Delhi	12957 *Rajdhani*	5.25pm	14	1230/1615/2680 (B)
	12915 *Ashram Exp*	5.45pm	16½	353/924/1253/2106 (C)
Jamnagar	19005 *Saurashtra Mail*	5.15am	7	174/445/601/1005 (C)
Junagadh	19221 *Somnath Exp*	10pm	6½	177/454/613 (A)
Mumbai (Bombay)	12010 *Shatabdi*	2.30pm (Mon-Sat)	7	715/1350 (D)
	12902 *Gujarat Mail*	10pm	8¾	242/609/817/1375 (C)
Udaipur	19944 *Ahmedabad-Udaipur Exp*	11pm	9	162/554 (E)
Vadodara (Baroda)	12010 *Shatabdi*	2.30pm (Mon-Sat)	1¾	305/570 (D)

Fares: (A) sleeper/3AC/2AC, (B) 3AC/2AC/1AC, (C) sleeper/3AC/2AC/1AC, (D) AC chair/1AC, (E) sleeper/2AC

abad. This is where state politicians live in large, fortified houses. Although Ahmedabad became Gujarat's capital when the old state of Bombay was split, this new capital was planned 28km north on the west bank of the Sabarmati River. Named Gandhinagar after Mahatma Gandhi, it's India's second planned city after Chandigarh. The secretariat was moved here in 1970.

The best reason for visiting is the spectacular **Akshardham** (www.akshardham.com; J Rd, Sector 20; ☺9.30am-7.30pm Tue-Sun), belonging to the wealthy Hindu Swaminarayan group. The elaborately carved main temple, built by nearly 1000 artisans and opened in 1992, is constructed of 6000 tonnes of pink sandstone and surrounded by manicured gardens. Three underground **exhibition areas** (admission ₹50; ☺10am-5.30pm Tue-Sun) have hi-tech multimedia presentations on the Swaminarayan movement, the Hindu epics and other religions. At sunset (every day except Monday) a 45-minute **Water Show** (adult/child ₹75/50) presents the story of the Upanishads through fountains, music, fire and lasers and promises to reveal the secret of life after death.

Buses to Gandhinagar (₹18, 45 minutes, every 15 minutes) depart from the back northwest corner of Lal Darwaja and from the numerous stops along Ashram Rd.

NALSAROVAR BIRD SANCTUARY

This 121-sq-km **sanctuary** (Indian/foreigner ₹30/250, car ₹20, camera/video ₹50/2500), around 60km southwest of Ahmedabad, comprises Nalsarovar Lake, a flood of island-dotted blue dissolving into the sky and iron-flat plains, and its surrounding wetlands. Between November and February, the sanctuary sees flocks of indigenous and migratory birds with as many as 250 species passing through. Ducks, geese, eagles, spoonbills, cranes, pelicans and flamingos are best seen early in the morning (aim for 5.30am) and the evening.

The sanctuary is busiest at weekends and on holidays. To see the birds it's best to hire a boat (around ₹1000, negotiable, for a full day). Gujarat Tourism runs a group of pod-like **cottages** (☎02715-245083; s/d ₹300/400, with AC ₹450/650; ✿) 1.5km from the lake.

Buses (₹30, two hours) run from Ahmedabad's ST bus stand at 7am, 12.15pm and 5pm. A taxi (around ₹1500 for a day trip from Ahmedabad) is an easier option, and gives you the option of combining Nalsarovar with Lothal (40km south).

LOTHAL

About 80km southwest of Ahmedabad, this important **archaeological site** (admission free; ☺dawn-dusk) was discovered in 1954. The city that stood here 4500 years ago was one of the most important of the Indus Valley civilisation, with similarities to Moenjodaro and Harappa in Pakistan. The site has no dramatic buildings but rather a set of scattered, low structures, so it's really one for archaeology buffs. Excavations have revealed, among other things, a tidal dockyard (the world's oldest known artificial dock) that was connected to an old course of the Sabarmati River and thus to the Gulf of Cambay. Seals discovered at the site suggest that trade may have been conducted with the civilisations of Mesopotamia, Egypt and Persia.

The site **museum** (Indian/foreigner ₹2/50; ☺9am-5pm Sat-Thu) displays fragments of this well-ordered civilisation, such as intricate seals, weights and measures, games and jewellery, plus an artist's impression of how Lothal looked at its peak.

Palace Utelia (☎02714-262222; r from ₹3000), 7km from the site, by the Bhugavo River, is an imposing palace – complete with aged retainers – that dwarfs the village it oversees. The shabby rooms are overpriced, but it's an unusual place with some charm if not comfort.

Lothal is a long day trip from Ahmedabad, and a taxi (around ₹1500 return) is the easiest bet. Buses heading for Sayla or Rajkot can drop you at Bagodra (₹35, 1½ hours), where you should be able to find an autorickshaw, taxi or jeep to the site, 18km south. Trains from Ahmedabad's Gandhigram station at 7.15am and 9am run to Lothal-Bhurkhi station (2nd-class ₹45, two hours), 6km from the site, from where you can catch a bus. Take water and food with you.

MODHERA

The beautiful **Sun Temple** (Indian/foreigner ₹5/100; ☺9am-5pm) was built in 1026 and 1027 by King Bhimdev I and is one of the greatest monuments of the Solanki dynasty, whose rulers were believed to be descended from the sun. Like the better-known Sun Temple at Konark in Odisha (Orissa), which it predates by 200 years, the Modhera temple was designed so that the dawn sun shone on the image of Surya, the sun god, during the equinox. Though it was sacked by invading Delhi sultan Ala-ud-Din Khilji around 1300, losing its main spire, it remains impressive. The main hall and shrine are reached through a pillared pavilion. The temple exterior is intricately carved with demons and deities. Within, 52 sculpted pillars depict scenes from the Ramayana and the Mahabharata, and a hall with 12 niches represents Surya's different monthly manifestations. Erotic sculpture panels complete the sensual decoration.

The temple is fronted by the **Surya Kund**, an extraordinary rectangular step-well that contains over 100 shrines, resembling a sunken art gallery.

Around 20 January, the temple is the scene for a three-day **classical dance festival** with dancers from all over India.

Modhera is 100km northwest of Ahmedabad. You can take a bus (₹59, two hours, half-hourly) from Ahmedabad's ST bus stand to Mahesana (Mehsana), and then another bus 26km west to Modhera (₹30, one hour). There are also trains from Ahmedabad to Mahesana. Buses run from Modhera to Patan (₹35, 1¼ hours) every 30 minutes till around 4pm. There are also two daily buses to/from Zainabad (₹45, 1½ hours). A taxi from Ahmedabad will cost about ₹1500 round-trip.

PATAN
📞02766 / POP 112.038

About 130km northwest of Ahmedabad, Patan was Gujarat's capital for six centuries before Ahmedabad was founded in 1411. It was ruined by the armies of Ala-ud-Din Khilji around 1300, and today is a dusty, little-visited town with narrow streets lined by elaborate wooden houses. The only real sign of its former glory is the **Rani-ki-Vav** (Indian/foreigner ₹5/100; ⊘9am-5pm), an astoundingly beautiful step-well, incongruously grand in this unassuming town. Built in 1063 by Rani Udayamati to commemorate her husband, Bhimdev I, the step-well is the oldest and finest in Gujarat and is remarkably well preserved – it was protected by centuries of silt before being excavated and restored between the 1960s and 1980s. Steps lead down through multiple levels with lines of carved pillars and over 800 sculptures, mostly on Vishnu-avatar themes.

Patan also has more than 100 Jain temples, the largest of which is **Panchasara Parshvanath**, and is famed for its beautiful Patola silk textiles produced by the torturously laborious double-*ikat* method. Both the warp (lengthways) and weft (transverse) threads are painstakingly tie-dyed to create the pattern *before* the weaving process

begins. It takes about six months to make one sari, which might cost ₹100,000. To see double-*ikat* being made visit the Salvi family at **Patan Patola Heritage** (📞232274; www .patanpatola.com; Salvivado, Patolawala St).

The new, clean and friendly **Surya Palace Hotel** (📞329872; Yash Plaza, University Rd; s/d ₹400/500, AC from ₹700/800; ❄), near the train station, is the best bet for rooms. **Anand Restaurant** (Kilachand Shopping Centre; mains ₹40-70) has good thalis and à la carte dishes.

Patan is 40km northwest of Mahesana. Buses leave Ahmedabad's ST bus stand about every hour (₹78, 3½ hours). There are also buses to/from Zainabad (₹65, 2½ hours, two daily), via Modhera.

Vadodara (Baroda)
📞0265 / POP 1.49 MILLION

Vadodara (or Baroda as it's often known) lies 106km southeast of Ahmedabad, little over an hour's drive along National Expressway 1. Vadodara has some interesting city sights, but the main reason for coming here is the stunning nearby Unesco World Heritage Site of Champaner and Pavagadh.

After the Marathas expelled the Mughals from Gujarat in the 18th century, their local lieutenants, the Gaekwad clan, made Vadodara their capital. Vadodara retained a high degree of autonomy even under the British,

---

NAVRATRI & DUSSEHRA

Navratri (Festival of Nine Nights) is celebrated in September or October India-wide, but Gujarat has made it its own. The festival celebrates feminine divinity in the forms of the goddesses Durga, Lakshmi and Saraswati. Celebrations centre on special shrines at junctions, marketplaces and, increasingly today, large venues that can accommodate thousands. People dress up in sparkling finery to whirl the night away in entrancing *garba* or *dandiya* circle dances till the early hours. Navratri is celebrated in every town and village in Gujarat and it's a festival where you may well find yourself joining in.

The night after Navratri is Dussehra, which celebrates the victory of Durga and Rama over the demon king Ravana, with more nocturnal dancing and fireworks.

right up to Independence in 1947. Maharaja Sayajirao III (1875–1939) was a great moderniser and laid the foundations of Vadodara's modern reputation as Gujarat's cultural capital.

◉ Sights

Sayaji Bagh   PARK, MUSEUM
Within this shady park is the **Baroda Museum & Picture Gallery** (Indian/foreigner ₹10/200; ⊙10.30am-5pm), which houses a diverse collection, much of it gathered by Sayajirao III, including statues and carvings from several Asian regions, an Egyptian room and some rather mangy zoology exhibits. The gallery has lovely Mughal miniatures and a motley crew of European masters.

FREE **Tambekar Wada**   HISTORIC BUILDING
(Pratap Rd, Raopura; ⊙8am-6pm) This wooden multi-storeyed townhouse is a typical Maratha mansion, once the residence of Bhau Tambekar, diwan of Baroda (1849–54). Inside are beautiful 19th-century murals featuring scenes from the Mahabharata, Krishna's life and the 19th-century Anglo-Maratha War. It was due to reopen in 2011 after restoration.

Laxmi Vilas Palace   PALACE
(Nehru Rd; audio tour ₹125; ⊙9am-5pm Tue-Sun) Still the residence of Vadodara's royal family, Laxmi Vilas was built in full-throttle 19th-century Indo-Saracenic flourish by Major Charles 'Mad' Mant for Sayajirao III at a cost of ₹6 million. It's set in expansive parklike grounds. The audio tour lets you have a leisurely stickybeak at the palace's elaborate interiors with their mosaics, chandeliers, artworks and *jarokhas* (projecting balcony-windows).

🛏 Sleeping

The main cluster of hotels is in the conveniently central Sayajigunj area.

Sapphire Regency   HOTEL $$
(☎2361130; www.sapphireregency.com; Sayajigunj; s/d incl breakfast from ₹1400/1800; ❋🛜) New in 2009, the Sapphire Regency has the best rooms in Vadodara for its price range. Looking and smelling fresh, it has a contemporary minimalist style with white walls and tiles and brown furniture and doors. Room size increases as you move up the price categories.

Hotel Ambassador   HOTEL $$
(☎2362727; www.hotelambassadorindia.com; Sayajigunj; s/d incl breakfast from ₹1100/1400; ❋🛜)

Newly renovated and jazzed up, the Ambassador offers very good value. The cheapest ('deluxe') rooms have a vaguely Japanese air, while the 'executive' quarters have a slick contemporary feel, all pinks, oranges, squares and rectangles. There's civilised 24-hour checkout too.

Hotel Surya   HOTEL $$
(☎2361361; www.hotelsurya.com; Sayajigunj; s/d incl breakfast from ₹1700/1900; ❋@🛜) Surya is a popular choice, with a cordial atmosphere and professional staff. Rooms are clean, though not particularly big or modern, and the mattresses are on the firmer side of hard. Two excellent restaurants, Vega and Myra, flank the reception.

Hotel Valiant   HOTEL $$
(☎2363480; www.hotelvaliant.com; 7th fl, BBC Tower, Sayajigunj; s/d ₹600/775, with AC from ₹850/1025; ❋@) The Valiant has surprisingly fresh rooms on the upper floors of a high-rise building. Take the lift up from the street entrance to find reception in a spacious lobby on the 7th floor. The rooms are clean, well presented and good value, and checkout is 24 hours.

Hotel Express Towers   HOTEL $$
(☎3055000; www.expressworld.com; RC Dutt Rd; s economy ₹1990, s/d incl breakfast from ₹3200/4000; ❋@🛜) A good choice about 1km west of the train station, with business-minded rooms, a wine shop and two very good restaurants.

WelcomHotel Vadodara   HOTEL $$$
(☎2330033; www.itcwelcomgroup.in; RC Dutt Rd; s/d from ₹8000/9000; ❋@🛜🏊) A swish five-star complex with predictable, well-appointed rooms, an unusual outdoor pool, plenty of cool lounge areas, an expensive 24-hour multicuisine restaurant and a wine shop.

Apsara Hotel   HOTEL $
(☎2225399; Sayajigunj; s/d ₹250/450) This budget place with a leafy little front yard is friendly and welcoming, although the rooms are small and a bit grubby (those upstairs are marginally brighter).

✕ Eating

Kansaar   GUJARATI $
(101 Unique Trade Centre, Sayajigunj; thali ₹130; ⊙11am-3pm & 7-10.15pm) A classy veg thali joint on the 1st floor (behind the 'Kadahi Punjabi' sign), with impeccable service and delicious food; the thali is bottomless and you can eat inside or out on the terrace for the street view.

Vadodara (Baroda)

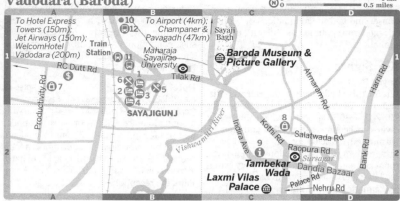

Pizza Meo   ITALIAN $$
(Sayajigunj; pizza & pasta ₹120-190; ☺11am-11pm)
This small Italian *ristorante e pizzeria*
serves excellent veg pizza, and so-so veg
pasta. With a Sistine Chapel ceiling and red-
green-and-white aproned waiters, it is an
almost-convincing slice of the Continent on
the subcontinent.

Mandap   GUJARATI $$
(Hotel Express Towers, RC Dutt Rd; thali ₹200;
☺12.30-2.45pm & 7.30-10.45pm) One the best
thalis in town, served in a splendidly
decorated room with a desert-tent interior.

Vega   MULTICUISINE $$
(Hotel Surya, Sayajigunj; mains ₹100-170)
Comfortable Vega serves decent Chinese,
Indian, Thai and Italian fare.

Kalyan   SOUTH INDIAN, FAST FOOD $
(Sayajigunj; dishes ₹40-100) Kalyan is a breezy
student hang-out serving healthy portions
of South Indian food and less healthy
attempts at Western fast food (though all
dishes are vegetarian).

🛍 Shopping

Baroda Prints   HANDICRAFTS
(☺10am-8pm) Aries Complex (3 Aries Complex,
Productivity Rd); Salatwada (Main Rd, Salatwada) A
shop selling hand-printed dress materials in
original, colourful and attractive designs. In
the Salatwada store you can see the printers
at work in the back room.

ℹ Information

There are State Bank and Bank of India ATMs at
the train station, an SBI ATM on RC Dutt Rd, and
Bank of Baroda and ICICI ATMs in Sayajigunj.

Gujarat Tourism (☎2427489; Block C, Nar-
mada Bhavan, Indira Ave; ☺10.30am-6pm
Mon-Sat, closed 2nd & 4th Sat of month) On
the ground floor of a red and yellowy-white
nine-storey building and not well signed. Unless
you want to organise a tour or get brochures,
this office is rather disappointing.

ICICI Bank (Sayajigunj) As well as the ATM, it
changes travellers cheques and cash.

Speedy Cyber Cafe (Sayajigunj; per hr ₹20;
☺8am-10pm)

ℹ Getting There & Away

Air

The airport is 4km northeast of the centre. **Jet
Airways** (☎022-39893333; www.jetairways.
com; 11 Panorama Bldg, RC Dutt RD) and **IndiGo**
(www.goindogo.com) fly to Mumbai and Delhi
(Jet has several flights daily); **Indian Airlines**
(☎2794747; www.indian-airlines.nic.in; AG
Chambers, Fatehganj) has an evening flight to
Delhi.

Bus

The **ST bus stand** is about 300m north of the
train station, with buses to many destinations
in Gujarat and neighbourng states including
Ahmedabad (ordinary/deluxe ₹65/100, two
hours, at least hourly), Bhavnagar (express
₹150, five hours, about hourly from 6am), Diu
(deluxe ₹179, 12 hours, 6pm, 9pm and 10pm),
Mumbai (deluxe ₹275, nine hours, 6pm, 7pm
and 7.30pm) and Udaipur (₹195, eight hours,
four daily). Many private bus companies have
offices nearby, including **BGTS Travel House**,
with Volvo AC buses to Mumbai (seat/sleeper
₹900/1000, eight hours, 8.30pm, 8.45pm,
9.30pm and 11.30pm), and three buses to
Udaipur (seat/sleeper ₹300/400) all leaving at
8.30pm.

Vadodara (Baroda)

Train

About 30 trains a day run to Ahmedabad, including the 12009 *Shatabdi* at 11.20am Monday to Saturday (AC chair/1AC ₹335/610, two hours). The 13 daily trains to Mumbai include the 12010 *Shatabdi* at 4.17pm Monday to Saturday (AC chair/1AC ₹625/1170, 5¼ hours).

Around Vadodara

CHAMPANER & PAVAGADH

This spectacular Unesco World Heritage Site, 47km northeast of Vadodara, combines a sacred, 762m volcanic hill (Pavagadh), looking like a chunk of the Himalaya dumped on the plain, and a ruined Gujarati capital with beautiful mosque architecture (Champaner).

Pavagadh may have been fortified as early as the 8th century; it became the capital of the Chauhan Rajputs around 1300 and was taken by the Gujarat sultan Mahmud Begada, after a 20-month siege, in 1484 (the Rajputs committed *jauhar* – ritual mass suicide – in the face of defeat). Mahmud Begada turned Champaner, at the base of the hill, into a splendid new capital. But its glory was brief: when it was captured by Mughal emperor Humayun in 1535, the Gujarati capital reverted to Ahmedabad, and Champaner fell into ruin. Hindu and Jain pilgrims, however, continue to this day to climb to the temples atop Pavagadh.

The heart of **Champaner** (Indian/foreigner ₹10/250; ⊗8am-6pm) is the Citadel, a rectangular area nearly 1km long, surrounded by high stone walls and now partly occupied by a village. A 6km-long outer wall enclosed the rest of the city. Champaner's most stunning features are its monumental mosques (no longer used for worship), with their beautiful blending of Islamic and Hindu decoration styles – above all the huge **Jami Masjid**, just outside the Citadel's east gate. Here a wonderful carved entrance porch leads into a lovely courtyard surrounded by a pillared corridor. The prayer hall has two tall central minarets, further superb stone carving, multiple domes, and seven mihrabs (prayer niches) along the back wall.

Other beautiful mosques include the **Saher ki Masjid**, behind the ticket office inside the Citadel, which was probably the private royal mosque, and the **Kevda Masjid**, 300m north of the Citadel and about 600m west of the Jami Masjid. Here you can climb narrow stairs to the roof, and higher up the minarets, to spot other mosques even further out into the countryside – **Nagina Masjid**, 500m north, with no minarets but exquisite geometric carving, and **Lila Gumbaj ki Masjid**, 800m east, on a high platform and with a fluted central dome. The twin minarets resembling factory chimneys, about 1km west, adorn the **Brick Minar ki Masjid**, a rare brick tomb.

To ascend **Pavagadh**, you can either walk up the pilgrim trail, which will take two to three hours, or you can take a shuttle bus (₹10) from opposite the Citadel's south gate. The bus deposits you about halfway up the hill, where you can either join the walking path (here lined by souvenir and drink stalls), or hop on the **Ropeway** (cable car; return ₹98; ⊗7am-11pm) which glides you up

GUJARAT AROUND VADODARA

to within a 700m walk of the **Kalikamata Temple** on the hill's summit. The first version of this temple to Kali, an evil-destroying incarnation of the mother goddess, was built in the 10th or 11th century. The temple attracts a steady stream of pilgrims, especially during the nine days of Navratri (September/October) and the month-long **Mahakali Festival** (March/April). Near the top of the hill are also Pavagadh's oldest surviving monument, the 10th- to 11th-century Hindu **Lakulisha Temple**, and several Jain temples. The views are fantastic and so, if you're lucky, are the cooling breezes.

Hotel Champaner (☎02676-293041; s/d ₹350/500, with AC ₹700/1000; ✿), near the foot of the Ropeway, has typically state-run rooms that are plain and basic, but all have balconies with superb views.

Buses to Champaner run about every half-hour from Vadodara (₹45, two hours); a return taxi costs around ₹700.

South of Vadodara

Gujarat stretches some 240km south from Vadodara to the border of Maharashtra, 150km short of Mumbai. **Surat**, 140km south of Vadodara, is where the British established their first Indian settlement in 1614. It's now Gujarat's hectic second-biggest city (population 5 million), a busy commercial centre for textiles and diamonds. Around 40km south of Surat is **Dandi**, the destination of Gandhi's epic Salt March in 1930, with several Gandhi monuments by its strikingly empty beach. Just before the Maharashtra border is the ex-Portuguese enclave of **Daman**, an alcohol-infused resort town on a grey sea. Though it still retains a little of the piquancy of old Portugal, Daman is far less attractive than its counterpart Diu in Saurashtra. In the southeast, the hilly **Dangs** district is the northern extremity of the Western Ghats, with a large tribal population and little tourist infrastructure. The main town is the minor hill resort of Saputara. The **Dangs Darbar** (February/March), in the week before Holi, is a spectacular, largely tourist-free tribal festival.

SAURASHTRA

Before Independence, Saurashtra, also known as the Kathiawar Peninsula, was a jumble of over 200 princely states. Today it has a number of hectic industrial cities, but most of them retain a core of narrow old streets crowded with small-scale commerce. Outside the cities it's still villages, fields, forests and a timeless, almost feudal feel, with farmers dressed head to toe in white and rural women as colourful as their sisters in Rajasthan.

Saurashtra is mainly flat and its rare hills are often sacred – including the spectacular, temple-topped Shatrunjaya and Girnar. The peninsula is liberally endowed with wildlife sanctuaries, notably Sasan Gir, where Asia's last wild lions roam. On the south coast lies the very quaint, laid-back ex-Portuguese island enclave of Diu. Saurashtra is also where Mahatma Gandhi was born and raised: you can visit several sites associated with the great man.

Saurashtra has a reputation for being fond of its sleep, and siesta takes place from *at least* 1pm to 3pm.

Bhavnagar

☎0278 / POP 510,958

Bhavnagar is a hectic, sprawling industrial centre with a colourful old core, that makes a base for journeys to nearby Shatrunjaya and Blackbuck National Park. Founded in 1743 and always a cotton-trading town, Bhavnagar supplements its income today through diamonds, plastics – and ship parts: Alang, 70km south, is the world's biggest shipbreaking site, with thousands of workers dismantling dozens of vessels, from supertankers down, by hand. Alang attracts controversy over its working conditions, health risks and pollution: the only way in is by invitation from a company operating there.

◉ Sights & Activities

Mahatma Gandhi attended university in Bhavnagar, and the dusty **Gandhi Smriti Museum** (admission free; ◷9am-1pm & 2-6pm Mon-Sat, closed 2nd & 4th Sat of month), by the clock tower, has a multitude of Gandhi photographs and documents. Explanatory material is in Hindi only. Downstairs, the equally dusty **Barton Museum** (Indian/foreigner ₹2/50; ◷same), has religious carvings, betelnut cutters, and a skeleton in a cupboard.

The **old city**, north of Ganga Jalia Tank, is worth a wander, especially in the evening – it's busy with small shops and cluttered with dilapidated elaborate wooden buildings leaning over the colourful crowded bazaars.

Takhteshwar Temple sits on a small hillock high enough to provide splendid views over the city and out onto the Gulf of Cambay.

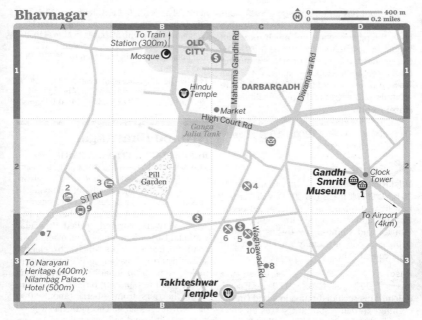

Sleeping

The budget hotels, mostly in the old city and near the train station, are fairly grim, but midrange hotels are reasonable.

Hotel Sun 'n' Shine HOTEL $$
(☎2516131; Panwadi Chowk, ST Rd; s/d incl breakfast from ₹1600/1800; ❄@☎) This well-run, three-star hotel is excellent value. It has a Mediterranean-inspired and vertigo-inducing atrium, a very welcoming front desk, and the recommended RGB restaurant. The rooms are fresh and clean with comfortable beds: the more you pay, the more windows you get. The breakfast is substantial, and free airport transfers are offered.

Narayani Heritage HERITAGE HOTEL $$
(☎2513535; narayaniheritage@gmail.com; Dairy Rd; s/d ₹1200/1600; ❄☀) This hotel occupies a former administrative building in the royal compound of Nilambag Palace Hotel and styles itself a 'budget heritage hotel'. The bright, spacious rooms are tastefully decorated and good value. Though they don't have the atmosphere of the palace they do share its dining room, pool, gym and tennis court.

Nilambag Palace Hotel HERITAGE HOTEL $$
(☎2424241; www.nilambagpalace.com; s/d cottage room ₹1500/2100, palace room ₹2500/4000;

❄@☀) In large gardens beside the Ahmedabad road, about 600m southwest of the bus station, this former maharaja's palace was built in 1859. It looks rather stern from outside, but has a more personal feel inside. The 'cottage' rooms are good-sized but rather bare; the palace rooms are much nicer and bigger, in a stately early-20th-century style. Guests have use of a circular **swimming pool** (nonguests ₹100; ◷7am-noon & 3-8pm Tue-Sun) in the Vijay Mahal in the extensive grounds, plus a gym and tennis facilities.

Hotel Apollo   HOTEL **$$**
(☑2425251; www.thehotelapollo.com; ST Rd; s/d ₹500/800, with AC from ₹1100/1250; ❄) Bare but quite spacious rooms.

✗ Eating

Tulsi Restaurant   INDIAN, CHINESE **$**
(Kalanala Chowk; mains ₹60-80; ◷lunch & dinner) Low-lit with plants and understated decor, this cosy and clean place with well-prepared Punjabi and Chinese veg dishes is rightly popular. Service is friendly and efficient, and it's excellent value.

Rasoi   INDIAN, CHINESE **$**
(mains ₹50-70, thali ₹120; ◷11.30am-3.15pm & 6-11pm) This secluded bungalow and (in the evening) garden restaurant serves up great unlimited Gujarati thalis, as well as Punjabi and Chinese veg fare. It's behind the police post between two petrol stations just north of the Galaxy Cinema.

RGB Restaurant   MULTICUISINE **$$**
(Hotel Sun 'n' Shine, Panwadi Chowk, ST Rd; mains ₹100-130) Cool, cosy, vegetarian, hotel restaurant offering generous serves of Jain, North Indian and Chinese.

Sankalp   SOUTH INDIAN **$**
(Waghawadi Rd; mains ₹50-120; ◷11am-11pm) First-class South Indian vegetarian dishes in clean, contemporary surroundings.

❶ Information

State Bank of India (Darbargadh; ◷10.30am-4.30pm Mon-Fri) Changes cash and travellers cheques and has a 24-hour ATM and a lovely, ornately carved, old-city portico. Other ATMs include State Bank and HDFC near Tulsi Restaurant.

❶ Getting There & Around

AIR Jet Airways (☑2433371; www.jetairways .com; Surat House, Waghawadi Rd) and **Kingfisher** (☑1800 2093030; www.flyingfisher. com) have daily flights to and from Mumbai. A taxi to or from the airport costs around ₹100.

BUS From the ST bus stand there are buses for Diu (₹115 to ₹122, seven hours, four daily), Rajkot (₹93 to ₹100, four hours, 12 daily) and

Ahmedabad (₹100 to ₹108, five hours, 13 daily). Private bus companies include **Tanna Travels** (Waghawadi Rd), with AC buses to Ahmedabad (₹150, four hours, 15 daily), Vadodara (₹170, four hours, seven daily) and Mumbai (₹700, 13 hours, 4pm).

TRAIN The 12972 *Bhavnagar-Bandra Express* departs at 8.30pm and arrives at Ahmedabad (sleeper/3AC/2AC ₹182/442/584) at 1.55am.

Around Bhavnagar

BLACKBUCK NATIONAL PARK

This beautiful, 34-sq-km **park** (Indian/foreigner car ₹200/1000, 4hr guide ₹50/500; ◷dawn-dusk 16 Oct-15 Jun), north of Bhavnagar, encompasses large areas of pale, custard-coloured grassland stretching between two seasonal rivers. Formerly called Velavadar National Park, it's famous for its blackbucks, beautiful, fast antelopes which sport elegant spiralling horns – as long as 65cm in mature males. Some 1600 inhabit the park, which is also good for spotting birds such as wintering harriers from Siberia (about 2000 of them most years). The park has a good road network and is best explored by car. Pay your fees and pick up a guide (who is unlikely to speak English) at the reception centre about 65km from Bhavnagar, north of Valabhipur.

You can book accommodation in the four-room **Forest Department Guest House** (Indian/foreigner d ₹500/2500, with AC ₹1500/3750), by the reception centre, through the **Forest Office** (☑0278-2426425; F-10, Annexe, MS Bldg; ◷11am-5pm Mon-Fri) in Bhavnagar. The very comfortable stone-built villas of **Blackbuck Lodge** (☑9824019877, 079-40020901; www.the blackbucklodge.com; s/d incl all meals ₹3000/5300) are just outside the park's western entrance.

A taxi day trip from Bhavnagar costs about ₹2000.

Palitana

☑02848 / POP 51,934
The hustling, dusty town of Palitana, 51km southwest of Bhavnagar, has grown rapidly to serve the pilgrim trade around Shatrunjaya. Your best bet for general information is the helpful manager at Hotel Shravak.

◉ Sights & Activities

Shatrunjaya   SACRED SITE
(Place of Victory; ◷temples 6.30am-6pm) One of Jainism's holiest pilgrimage sites, Shatrun-

jaya is an incredible hilltop sea of temples, built over 900 years on a plateau dedicated to the gods. The temples are grouped into *tunks* (enclosures), each with a central temple and many minor ones. Some of the earliest were built in the 11th century, but were destroyed by Muslim attackers in the 14th and 15th centuries; the current temples date from the 16th century onwards.

The 500m climb up 3300 steps to the temples adds to the extraordinary experience and takes most people about 1½ hours. The steps start on the southwest edge of Palitana about 3.5km from the bus stand (₹20 by autorickshaw). Pilgrims make the climb in their hundreds most days, and in thousands around Kartik Purnima, in November or December.

As you near the top of the hill, the track forks. The main entrance, Ram Pole, is reached by taking the left-hand fork. To see the best views over the site first, take the right-hand fork. There are superb views in all directions; on a clear day you can see the Gulf of Cambay. Inside the Nav Tonk Gate, one path leads left to the Muslim shrine of **Angar Pir**, where women who want children make offerings of miniature cradles. The Muslim saint protected the temples from a Mughal attack. To the right, the second *tunk* you reach is the Chaumukhji Tunk, containing the **Chaumukh** (Four-Faced Shrine), built in 1618 by a wealthy Jain merchant. Images of Adinath, the first Jain *tirthankar* (believed to have attained enlightenment here), face the four cardinal directions.

You can easily spend a couple of hours wandering among the hundreds of temples up here. The biggest and one of the most splendid and important, with a fantastic wealth of detailed carving, is the **Adinath Temple**, on the highest point on the far (south) side.

Shri Vishal Jain Museum (admission ₹10; ☺8am-8.30pm), 500m down the street from the foot of the Shatrunjaya steps, exhibits assorted Jain artwork and artefacts up to 500 years old. In the basement is a surprising circular temple with mirror walls and centuries-old images of four *tirthankars*.

Sleeping & Eating

Vijay Vilas Adpur　　　HERITAGE HOTEL **$$**
(☑282371, 9427182809; vishwa_adpur@yahoo.co.in; Adpur village; s/d incl breakfast ₹2000/3000; ❄) Vijay Vilas sits in deep, beautiful countryside beneath the western end of Shatrunjaya, 11km west of Palitana. It's a small 1906

palace with six large, plain but nicely decorated rooms, with original furniture. Three have terraces/balconies looking towards Shatrunjaya – which can be climbed from here by a slightly shorter, steeper path (2700 steps) than the one from Palitana. Vijay Vilas is family-run, with delicious home-cooked food (a mix of Gujarati and Rajasthani, veg and non-veg). You can also just pop in for lunch (₹300) – it's best to call first.

Hotel Shravak　　　HOTEL **$**
(☑252428; s/d/tr/q ₹100/300/400/500) The ultrabasic rooms at the friendly Shravak, opposite the bus stand, are the best bet in Palitana itself. They're shabby but clean; doubles are better than singles for space. Showers are unheated: buckets of hot water are available from 5am to 10am.

Hotel Sumeru　　　HOTEL **$**
(☑252327; Station Rd; men-only dm ₹75, s/d ₹300/400, with AC ₹683/945; ❄) This dowdy Gujarat Tourism establishment is 200m towards the station from the bus stand. Rooms are rundown, but the upstairs ones have balconies, and there's a restaurant.

Jagruti Restaurant　　　INDIAN **$**
(thali ₹30, mains ₹30-50; ☺10am-10pm) Across the laneway from Hotel Shravak, Jagruti is a wildly busy thali house.

❶ Getting There & Away

Plenty of ST buses run to/from Bhavnagar (₹25, 1½ hours, every half-hour) and Ahmedabad (₹120, five hours, hourly). For Diu, take a bus to

---

❶ SHATRUNJAYA PRACTICALITIES

It's best to start the ascent around dawn so you can climb before it gets too hot. You should be properly dressed (no shorts etc). Leave behind leather items, including belts and bags, and don't take any food or drinks inside the temples. Water (not bottled) can be bought at intervals on the ascent. If you wish, you can be carried up and down the hill in a *dholi* (portable chair with two bearers), for about ₹1000 round-trip.

Photo permits (₹100) must be obtained before you start the climb, from an office on the left just before the foot of the steps.

Talaja (₹20, one hour, hourly), where you can catch buses to Diu (₹90, 5½ hours, around six daily.).

Three passenger trains run daily to/from Bhavnagar (2nd class ₹9).

Diu

☏ 02875 / POP 21,576

What is Diu? For better or worse, this tiny ex-Portuguese island is one of the main reasons travellers come to Gujarat. And while it may not be the tropical paradise they imagined, it has a quirky charm and serenity.

Diu is clean and uncrowded and boasts some reasonable beaches, whitewashed churches, an imposing fort, interestingly colourful Portuguese-influenced streets (most of them deliciously quiet) and fresh seafood, as well as groups of giggly Gujarati weekenders who flock here for the cheap booze. Plus it's the safest place to ride a scooter in all of India, with minimum traffic and excellent roads.

Like Daman and Goa, Diu was a Portuguese colony until taken over by India in 1961. With Daman, it is still governed from Delhi as part of the Union Territory of Daman & Diu and is not part of Gujarat. It includes Diu Island, about 11km by 3km, separated from the mainland by a narrow channel, and two tiny mainland enclaves. One of these, housing the village of Ghoghla, is the entry point to Diu from Una.

Diu town sits at the east end of the island. The northern side of the island, facing Gujarat, is tidal marsh and salt pans, while the southern coast alternates between limestone cliffs, rocky coves and sandy beaches.

The island's main industries are fishing, tourism, alcohol and salt. Kalpana Distillery at Malala produces rum from sugar cane.

One legacy of the Portuguese that is very much respected by many local businesses is that of the siesta.

History

Diu was the first landing point for the Parsis when they fled from Persia in the 7th century AD. By all accounts they moved on to Sanjan, in southeast Gujarat, after a few years, although Diu did have some sort of Parsi community later in its history. Between the 14th and 16th centuries Diu was an important trading post and naval base from which the Ottomans controlled the northern Arabian Sea shipping routes.

Portugal unsuccessfully attempted to capture the island in 1531, during which the Turkish navy helped Bahadur Shah, Sultan of Gujarat. The Portuguese finally secured control in 1535 by taking advantage of a quarrel between the sultan and the Mughal emperor, Humayun. Bahadur signed a treaty with the Portuguese, giving them control over Diu port. Though both Bahadur and his successor, Mahmud III, then attempted to contest the issue, another treaty eventually signed in 1539 ceded the island of Diu and the mainland enclave of Ghoghla to Portugal.

Seven Rajput soldiers and a few civilians were killed in Operation Vijay, which ended Portuguese rule in 1961. After the Indian Air Force unnecessarily bombed the airstrip and terminal near Nagoa, it remained derelict until the late 1980s. Diu, Daman and Goa were administered as one union territory of India until 1987, when Goa became a state.

Dangers & Annoyances

Much more an annoyance than a danger, drunk male tourists can be tiresome, particularly towards single or pairs of women, and particularly around Nagoa Beach.

◉ Sights & Activities

DIU TOWN

The town is sandwiched between the massive fort at its east end and a huge city wall on the west. The main **Zampa Gateway**, painted bright red, has carvings of lions, angels and a priest, while just inside it is a chapel with an image of the Virgin and Child dating from 1702.

Cavernous **St Paul's Church** (☺8am-6pm) is a wedding cake of a church, founded by Jesuits in 1600 and then rebuilt in 1807. Its neoclassical facade is the most elaborate of any Portuguese church in India. Inside, it's a great barn, with a small cloister next door, above which is a school. Daily mass is heard here. Nearby is white-walled **St Thomas' Church**, a lovely, simple building that is now the **Diu Museum** (admission free; ☺9am-9pm), with a spooky, evocative collection of wooden Catholic saints going back to the 16th century. Once a year, on 1 November, this is used for a packed-out mass. The Portuguese-descended population mostly live in this area, still called Farangiwada (Foreigners' Quarter). The **Church of St Francis of Assisi**, founded in 1593, has been converted into a hospital, but is also sometimes used for services.

Many other Diu buildings show a lingering Portuguese influence. The western part of town is a maze of narrow, winding streets and many houses are brightly painted, with the most impressive being in the Panchwati area, notably **Nagar Sheth Haveli**, an old merchant's house laden with stucco scrolls and fulsome fruit.

AROUND THE ISLAND

Beaches   BEACHES

Nagoa Beach, on the south coast of the island 7km west of Diu town, is long, palm-fringed and safe for swimming – but busy, and often with drunk men: foreign women receive a lot of unwanted attention. Two kilometres further west begins the sandy, 2.5km sweep of **Gomptimata Beach**. This is often empty, except on busy weekends, but it gets big waves – you need to be a strong swimmer here. Beaches within walking distance of Diu town are the rocky **Jallandhar**, on the town's southern shore; the longer, sandier **Chakratirth**, west of Jallandhar; and pretty **Sunset Point Beach**, a small, gentle curve beyond Chakratirth that's popular for swimming and relatively hassle-free. **Sunset Point** itself is a small headland at the south end of the beach, topped by the **INS Khukhri Memorial**, commemorating an Indian Navy frigate sunk off Diu during the 1971 India-Pakistan War. Unfortunately the region around Sunset Point is also the town's dumping ground. Waste is sometimes dumped directly into the sea, and any early-morning excursion will reveal that the tidal zone here is a popular toilet venue.

Gangeswar Temple   HINDU TEMPLE

Gangeswar Temple, on the south coast 3km west of town, just past Fudam village, is a small coastal cave where five Shiva linga (phallic symbols) are washed by the waves.

Parsi Bungali   HISTORIC SITE

A stone-paved path leads 200m inland from Gangeswar Temple to two Parsi 'towers of silence', squat, round stone towers where the Parsis laid their dead out to be consumed by vultures.

Sea Shell Museum   MUSEUM

(adult/child ₹10/5; ⊘9am-6pm) This museum, 6km from town on the Nagoa road, is a labour of love. Captain Devjibhai Vira Fulbaria, a merchant navy captain, collected shells from literally all over the world in 50 years of sailing, and has displayed and labelled them in English with great care.

Vanakbara   FISHING VILLAGE

At the extreme west of the island, Vanakbara is a fascinating little fishing village. It's great to wander around the port, packed with colourful fishing boats and bustling activity – best around 7am to 8am when the fishing fleet returns and sells off its catch.

👉 Tours

You can take 20-minute **boat trips** (per person ₹25, minimum charge ₹150; ⊘9.30am-1.30pm & 3-6.30pm) around the harbour, with a close-up look at Fortim-do-Mar, when it's calm enough. Get tickets at the kiosk in front of the tourist office. Other options include a one-hour **evening cruise** (per person ₹120, minimum charge ₹960) at 7.30pm, weather permitting.

🛏 Sleeping

Rates at most hotels are extremely flexible, with discounts of up to 60% available at the more expensive places when things are quiet. Some only charge the full rates at peak holiday times like Diwali and Christmas/New Year.

DIU TOWN

Herança Goesa   GUESTHOUSE **$**

(✆253851; heranca_goesa@yahoo.com; Farangiwada; r ₹350-500) Behind Diu Museum, this friendly home of a Portuguese-descended family has eight absolutely spotless rooms that represent incredible value. Take one of the upstairs rooms that captures the sea

---

DON'T MISS

DIU FORT

Built in 1535, with modifications made in the 1540s, Diu's massive, well-preserved **Portuguese fort** (admission free; ⊘8am-6pm) with its double moat (one tidal) on the land side, must once have been impregnable. Cannonballs litter the place and the ramparts have a superb array of cannons. The lighthouse in the fort is Diu's highest point, with a beam that reaches 32km. There are several small chapels, one of them dedicated to Santiago, whose horse-mounted, sword-wielding image is quite a surprise to encounter so far from its Iberian Peninsula homeland! Part of the fort also now serves as the island's jail. The former jail is **Fortim-do-Mar (Pani Kotha)**, the boat-shaped building that seems to float in the bay north of the fort.

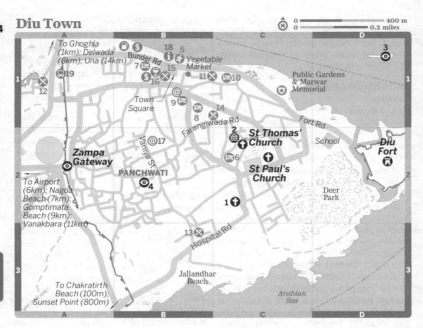

breeze and just relax. Good breakfasts are served and delicious fish/seafood dinners (around ₹200) are available if you reserve in the morning.

Hotel São Tomé Retiro   GUESTHOUSE **$**
(☑253137; r ₹500-800, without bathroom ₹250) This atmospheric guesthouse, occupying rooms up on the side of old St Thomas' Church, is definitely the place to stay for the shoes-off, gone fishin' Diu experience. Your host, George D'Souza, is a gentle soul, and his barbecue parties are a treat. Rooms range from small, hot and basic structures on the roof to charming, breezy thick-walled abodes. The 360-degree views from the church roof are unrivalled on the island.

Hotel Samrat   HOTEL **$$**
(☑252354; www.cidadedediu.com/samrat; Old Collectorate Rd; r ₹1450, regular/deluxe with AC ₹1850/2250; ❄) Hotel Samrat is the town's best midrange choice, with comfortable doubles, some with street-facing balconies. Credit cards are accepted and there's a decent Indian/Chinese restaurant (mains ₹65 to ₹145) with plenty of grog available.

Hotel Super Silver   HOTEL **$**
(☑252020; hotel_supersilverdiu@yahoo.com; Super Silver Complex; s/d ₹250/300, r with AC ₹700; ❄) Super Silver has a nice central location

and is very good value, with simple, clean, freshly painted rooms, some with views, and helpful management. Non-AC rooms are smallish. The hotel has a handy cybercafe and scooter and motorcycle rental.

Sanmaan Palace   HOTEL **$$**
(☑253031; Fort Rd; s/d cottage ₹850/1200, deluxe ₹1250/1600, ste ₹1650/2000; ❄) This is a nearly 200-year-old Portuguese villa in a superb, breezy waterfront location between the town square and fort. The 'cottages' are stuffy converted shipping containers in the garden and best avoided. The six original villa rooms, including the two larger corner 'suites', are plain and simple, but their high ceilings lend a little charm. There's a pleasant rooftop restaurant – perfect for a beer.

Hotel Apaar   HOTEL **$$**
(☑255321; hotelapaardiu@gmail.com; Bunder Rd; r ₹1800-2600; ❄) Set back off the main waterfront road in town, the Apaar opened in 2009 and still has that recently-opened shine – for now at least. The sizeable 'superior' rooms (₹2300) have full-wall windows, faux-wood surfaces and balconies, some of them sea-facing.

Hotel Relax Inn   HOTEL **$$**
(☑9638741888; Bunder Rd; r ₹2000; ❄) Next to the Apaar and equally new, with colourful

exterior paintwork, Relax Inn offers similarly bright rooms, in blues and whites, all with balconies. If the weather's not too hot, you can score a good discount by having the AC turned off.

NAGOA BEACH
Resort Hoka HOTEL $$
(☑253036; www.resorthoka.com; r ₹1750-1950; ✳✿) Hoka is a great place to stay, with colourful, clean and cool rooms in a small, palm-shaded complex with a small swimming pool. Some rooms have terraces over the palm trees. The management here is very helpful, you can hire mopeds, and the food is excellent. Fork right when you arrive at Nagoa Beach, and it's on the left about 300m along.

Radhika Beach Resort HOTEL $$
(☑252553; www.radhikaresort.com; d ₹2550-4050; ✳@✿) An immaculate, smart, modern place and Diu's best-located upmarket option, with comfortable, tasteful villas in grassy grounds. Rooms are spacious, clean and worth the money, and there's a very good multicuisine restaurant. The 'classic' and VIP rooms are set around a large pool.

Hotel Gangasagar HOTEL $$
(☑252249; d ₹900, with AC or beach-facing balcony ₹1200; ✳) A classic beachfront hotel, with salty sea-shack ambience and a well-stocked beachfront bar, which might or might not be an advantage. The beach-facing balcony rooms are the best, though all rooms are clean and simple. A downside can be the weekend clientele.

✗ Eating

Fresh fish is excellent here, and drinks are blissfully cheap – around ₹50 for a Kingfisher or ₹150 for a bottle of port.

TOP CHOICE O'Coqueiro MULTICUISINE $$
(Farangiwada Rd; mains ₹65-240) Here, a dedicated owner has developed a soul-infused garden restaurant celebrating freshness and quality. The menu offers uncomplicated but very tasty pasta, chicken and seafood, plus a handful of Portuguese dishes learnt from a local Diu matriarch. There's also good coffee, cold beer, mellow music and friendly service.

La Dolce Vita MULTICUISINE $$
(☑9824203925; Hospital Rd; mains ₹60-130) This is a pretty garden restaurant on the beach side of town with excellent-value breakfasts (options include homemade muesli, fruit salad, pancakes and lassi) and very good Moka coffee. Lunch and dinner comprise veg and non-veg curries, pasta and seafood.

Bon Apetit
MULTICUISINE $$

(Nagoa Beach; mains ₹110-140) This rustic place, 500m west from the Nagoa fork, serves up very tasty pasta, pizza, and prawn and chicken masala and curries, at low tables in a nice, shady garden setting. If you pre-order you can get a BBQ dinner for anywhere between ₹185 and ₹400 depending on what you fancy and what's available at the market.

Resort Hoka
MULTICUISINE $$

(Nagoa Beach; mains ₹100-275; ⊘8.30-10.30am, 1-2.30pm & 7.30-9.30pm) The open-air restaurant at this small hotel has notably excellent food, with inviting breakfasts and delicious choices such as penne with tuna and tomato, fish and chips, and prawn coconut curry. It's relaxed, pleasant and tree-shaded.

Apana Foodland
MULTICUISINE $$

(Apana Hotel, Fort Rd; mains ₹60-160) This outdoor restaurant facing the town waterfront does everything: breakfasts, South Indian, Gujarati, Punjabi and Chinese. The fish dishes, including shark tikka, or kingfish/prawns with rice, chips and salad, can be pre-ordered so you don't miss out. The Gujarati fruit salad is delicious.

Hotel São Tomé Retiro
SEAFOOD $

(☑253137; all-you-can-eat BBQ ₹150) From around September to April, hospitable George and family hold BBQ parties every other evening. The fresh fish and delicious salads are fantastic, beer's available and it's an atmospheric place to sit around a blazing campfire and meet other travellers.

Ram Vijay
ICE CREAM $

(scoops ₹20-25; ⊘8.30am-1.30pm & 3.30-9.30pm) For a rare treat head to this small, squeaky-clean, old-fashioned ice-cream parlour near the town square, for delicious handmade ice cream and milkshakes. Going since 1933, this family enterprise started with soft drinks, and still makes its own brands (Dew and Leo) in Fudam village – try a mint or ginger lemon soda and then all the ice creams!

There are two **fish markets**, one opposite Jethibai bus stand, and an evening market, lit by flame torches, across the bridge in Ghoghla. The fresh fish and seafood are delicious; most guesthouses and hotels will cook anything you buy.

Drinking

Apart from the restaurants (most of which double as bars), there are a number of bars around town. Some are on the seedy side, but the almost publike **Casaluxo Bar** (⊘9am-1pm Mon-Sat, 4-9pm Tue-Sat), facing the town square, has a more salubrious air. It opened in 1963, and doesn't seem to have updated its decor since, with lots of dusty bottles.

Information

Note that many shops around town change money.

A to Z (Vaniya St, Panchwati; internet per hr ₹30; ⊘9am-11pm)

ICICI ATM Facing the town square.

Post office (⊘9am-5pm Mon-Sat) Upstairs, facing the town square.

SBI ATM (Goldmoon Complex, Bunder Rd)

State Bank of India (Main Bazaar; ⊘10am-4pm Mon-Fri) Changes cash and travellers cheques.

Tourist office (☑252653; www.diutourism.co.in; Bunder Rd; ⊘9am-6pm Mon-Sat) This quite helpful office has maps, bus schedules and hotel prices.

Uma Cyber Café (internet per hr ₹30; ⊘9.30am-11pm) Next to Uma Shakti Hotel.

Getting There & Away

Air

Jet Airways (☑255030; www.jetairways.com) flies to/from Mumbai daily except Saturday. There are several ticketing agents in town. The airport is 6km west of town, just before Nagoa Beach.

Bus & Car

Apart from the final 14km from Una, the roads approaching Diu are abysmal. Hwy 8E is one long pothole from 30km west of Una to 30km east of it. Visitors arriving in Diu by road may be charged a border tax of ₹50 per person, though the practice seems to be erratic.

From Jethibai bus stand there are buses to Veraval (₹70, three hours, 10 daily), Junagadh (₹110, five hours, seven daily), Rajkot (₹140, six hours, six daily), Bhavnagar (₹107, seven hours, 10 daily) and Ahmedabad (₹200, 12 hours, 7am and 9pm). More frequent departures go from Una, 14km north of Diu. Buses run between Una bus stand and Diu (₹14, 40 minutes) every half-hour between 6.30am to 8pm. Outside these hours, shared autorickshaws go to Ghoghla or Diu from Tower Chowk in Una (1km from the bus stand), for about the same fare. An autorickshaw costs ₹150 to ₹200. Una rickshaw-wallahs are unable to proceed further than the bus station in Diu, so cannot take you all the way to Nagoa Beach (an additional ₹60).

A to Z (Vaniya St; ☉9am-11pm) sells tickets for private buses from Diu to Mumbai at 11am (seat/sleeper ₹450/500, 22 hours) and to Ahmedabad at 7.30pm (₹200/250, 11 hours).

Train

Delwada, 8km from Diu on the Una road, is the nearest railhead. Train 315 at 2.25pm runs to Sasan Gir (2nd class ₹15, 3½ hours) and Junagadh (₹23, 6¼ hours). Train 314 at 8.05am heads to Veraval (₹17, 3¼ hours). Half-hourly Diu–Una buses stop at Delwada (₹14, 20 minutes).

❶ Getting Around

Travelling by autorickshaw anywhere in Diu town should cost no more than ₹20. To Nagoa Beach pay ₹60 and to Sunset Point ₹40.

Scooters are a perfect option for exploring the island – the roads are deserted and in good condition. The going rate for 24-hour rental is ₹150 to ₹200 (not including fuel), and motorcycles can be had for ₹250. Most hotels can arrange rentals, although quality varies. You will normally have to show your driving licence and leave a deposit of ₹500 to ₹1000. At Hotel Super Silver, rentals include a helmet and the deposit is ₹500.

Local buses from Diu town to Nagoa and Vanakbara (both ₹10) leave Jethibai bus stand at 7am, 11am and 4pm. From Nagoa, they depart for Diu town from near the police post at 1pm, 5.30pm and 7pm.

Veraval

☎02876 / POP 141,207

Veraval is cluttered, chaotic, and smells strongly of fish – not surprising given that it's one of India's major fishing ports – and its busy harbour is full of bustle and boat building. Veraval was the major seaport for Mecca pilgrims before the rise of Surat. The main reason to come here now is to visit the Temple of Somnath, 6km southeast.

◉ Sights

One kilometre from Veraval towards Somnath, **Bhalka Tirth** is where Krishna was mistaken for a deer (he was sleeping in a deerskin) and fatally wounded by an arrow. The temple here is an architecturally mundane affair, but it contains an image of Krishna reclining, a tulsi tree planted in his memory growing out through the roof, a relief of his footprint and two Shiva linga. A sign outside tells us that this was where Krishna departed on his journey to Neejdham (final rest) at 2.27 and 30 seconds am on 18 February, 3102 BC.

The **fishing harbour** about 800m south of Bhalka Tirth towards Somnath is a striking sight with hundreds of wooden dhows flying colourful flags.

⛏ Sleeping & Eating

Hotel Kaveri   HOTEL **$**
(☎220842; 2 Akar Complex, ST Rd; s/d ₹250/400, AC s ₹550-650, d ₹650-850, ste ₹1100-1800; ✳) Kaveri is the pick of the town's uninspiring accommodation, and the most convenient choice, with a range of well-kept rooms and switched-on management.

Toran Tourist Bungalow   HOTEL **$**
(☎246588; College Rd; s/d ₹350/500, with AC ₹600/800; ✳) This state-government-run hotel, 1km west of the clock tower, is not very conveniently situated. But it has sizeable, clean rooms with white-tile walls and floors, and terraces from which you can see the sea.

Sagar   INDIAN **$**
(ST Rd; mains ₹60-100; ☉9am-3.30pm & 5-11pm) This subdued, friendly vegetarian restaurant serves reasonable Punjabi and South Indian food.

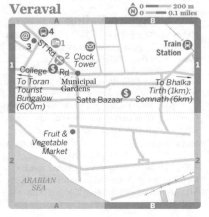

Veraval

N ┃ 0 ▬▬▬▬ 200 m
0 ▬▬▬▬ 0.1 miles

ℹ️ Information

There are HDFC and Axis Bank ATMs near the municipal gardens.

JP Travels International (Satta Bazaar; ⊙10am-8.30pm Mon-Sat) Changes travellers cheques and cash.

Magnet Cyber Café (2nd fl, Chandramauli Complex, ST Rd; internet per hr ₹20; ⊙9.30am-10pm) Opposite the bus station.

ℹ️ Getting There & Away

BUS ST buses go to Ahmedabad (₹175, nine hours, five daily), Diu (₹70, three hours, 10 daily), Sasan Gir (₹25 to ₹45, 1½ hours, hourly), Junagadh (₹40, 2½ hours, every 30 minutes) and Rajkot (₹80, four hours, hourly). **Krishna Travels**, opposite the ST bus stand, offers a nightly jaunt to Ahmedabad (seat/sleeper ₹180/280) at 9.30pm.

TRAIN The *Jabalpur Express* (train 11463 or 11465) leaves at 10am for Junagadh (sleeper/3AC/2AC ₹130/225/294, 1¾ hours), Rajkot (₹130/307/409, four hours) and Ahmedabad (₹204/529/717, nine hours). Second-class-only trains with unreserved seating head to Sasan Gir (₹7, 1¼ to two hours) at 9.45am and 1.55pm, and to Delwada (for Diu) at 4.20pm (₹17, 3¼ hours). There's a **computerised reservation office** (⊙8am-10pm Mon-Sat, 8am-2pm Sun) at the station.

ℹ️ Getting Around

An autorickshaw to Somnath should cost about ₹40; buses are ₹9 and leave from the ST bus stand.

Somnath

📞02876

Somnath's famous, phoenix-like temple stands in neat gardens above the beach, 6km southeast of Veraval. The sea below gives it a wistful charm. The small town of Somnath is an agglomeration of narrow streets now shielded by a high wall from the gaze of the relentless stream of pilgrims at the temple. There's a State Bank ATM on your right as you approach the temple. Somnath celebrates **Kartik Purnima** (November or December), marking Shiva's killing of the demon Tripurasura, with a large colourful fair.

⊙ Sights

Temple of Somnath   HINDU TEMPLE
(⊙6am-9pm) This temple has been razed and rebuilt at least seven times. It's said that Somraj, the moon god, constructed a gold

version, rebuilt by Ravana in silver, by Krishna in wood and by Bhimdev in stone. A description of the temple by Al-Biruni, an Arab traveller, was so glowing that it prompted a visit in 1024 by a most unwelcome tourist – the legendary looter Mahmud of Ghazni from Afghanistan. At that time, the temple was so wealthy that it had 300 musicians, 500 dancing girls and even 300 barbers. Mahmud of Ghazni took the town and temple after a two-day battle in which it's said 70,000 Hindu defenders died. Having stripped the temple of its fabulous wealth, Mahmud destroyed it. So began a pattern of Muslim destruction and Hindu rebuilding that continued for centuries. The temple was again razed in 1297, 1394 and finally in 1706 by Aurangzeb, the notorious Mughal fundamentalist.

After the 1706 demolition, the temple wasn't rebuilt until 1950. The current serene, symmetrical structure was built to traditional designs on the original coastal site: it's painted a creamy colour and boasts a little fine sculpture. The large, black Shiva lingam at its heart is one of the 12 most sacred Shiva shrines known as *jyoti linga*. Colourful dioramas of the Shiva story line the north side of the temple garden. A one-hour **sound-and-light show** (admission ₹20) highlights the temple nightly at 8pm.

Prabhas Patan Museum   MUSEUM
(Indian/foreigner ₹2/50; ⊙10.30am-5.30pm Thu-Tue, closed 2nd & 4th Sat of month) This museum, 300m north of the Somnath temple, is laid out in courtyard-centred rooms and contains remains of the previous temples, with lots of beautiful fragments, including an elaborate 11th-century ceiling.

🛏️ Sleeping & Eating

Hotel Sukhsagar   HOTEL $$
(📞232311; www.hotelsukhsagar.in; Somnath Bye Pass Corner; r ₹1400-2800; ❄️) The prime choice lies 2km northeast of Somnath temple where the Veraval–Somnath bypass meets Hwy 8E. It's a new hotel with spick-and-span, reasonably spacious rooms with sparkling tiled floors, plus a veg restaurant with garden and AC sections.

Hotel Mayuram   HOTEL $
(📞231286; Triveni Rd; r without/with AC ₹400/700; ❄️) Just down the coast road heading away from the temple, quiet Mayuram has clean, plain doubles shining with tiles.

New Bhabha Restaurant INDIAN, CHINESE $
(mains ₹50-80) The pick of a poor bunch of eateries, vegetarian New Bhabha sits 250m north of the ST bus stand. You can eat in a small AC room or outside open to the street. The sweet Kashmiri pulao is reasonably tasty despite its alarming dyed-green colour.

ⓘ Getting There & Away

Somnath has fewer departures than Veraval, but buses run to Diu (₹65, three hours, daily at 9.40am), Junagadh (₹45, two hours, eight daily) and Rajkot (₹85, four hours, two daily). **Mahasagar Travels**, just north of the ST bus stand, has buses to Ahmedabad (seat/sleeper ₹200/300, nine hours) at 9pm and 10pm.

Sasan Gir Wildlife Sanctuary

☏ 02877

The last refuge of the Asiatic lion (*Panthera leo persica*) is this forested, hilly, 1412-sq-km sanctuary about halfway between Veraval and Junagadh. It feels beguilingly uncommercial, and simply driving through the thick, undisturbed forests would be a joy even if there wasn't the excitement of lions and other wildlife to spot. The sanctuary was set up in 1965, and a 259-sq-km core area was declared a national park in 1975. Since the late 1960s, lion numbers have increased from under 200 to over 400. The sanctuary's 37 other mammal species, most of which have also increased in numbers, include the dainty chital (spotted deer), the sambar (a large deer), the nilgai or bluebull (a large antelope), the chousingha (four-horned antelope), the chinkara (a gazelle), crocodiles and rarely seen leopards. Sasan Gir is a great destination for birders too, with over 300 species, most of them resident. While the wildlife has been lucky, more than half the sanctuary's human community of distinctively dressed *maaldhari* (herders) have been resettled elsewhere as their herds of cattle and buffalo were competing for food resources with the antelopes, deer and gazelles, while also being preyed upon by the lions and leopards (*maaldhari* livestock still provides a quarter of the lions' diet).

Sasan Gir is no longer big enough for the number of lions, and today groups of lions are found as far away as the Junagadh hills to the north and even occasionally on the beaches of Diu!

The sanctuary access point is Sasan Gir village, on a minor road and railway between Veraval and Junagadh (about 40km from each). The best time to visit is from December to April; the sanctuary is closed from 16 June to 15 October and possibly longer if there has been a heavy monsoon.

⊙ Sights & Activities

TOP CHOICE Safaris   WILDLIFE-WATCHING
As a general rule of thumb about one in every two safaris has a lion sighting. So if you're determined to see lions, allow for a couple of trips. You'll certainly see a variety of other wildlife, and the guides are adept spotters.

Visits to the sanctuary are in jeeps which follow varied circuits of about three hours. The best time for seeing wildlife is early morning. Most hotels and guesthouses in and around Sasan Gir have jeeps and drivers or will arrange them for you, charging ₹900 or more per safari for up to six passengers. Alternatively, you can hire a jeep and driver for around ₹800 outside the sanctuary **reception centre** (☏285541), next to Sinh Sadan Guest House in Sasan

---

THE LAST WILD ASIATIC LIONS

The Asiatic lion (*Panthera leo persica*) once roared as far west as Syria and as far east as India's Bihar. Widespread hunting decimated the population, with the last sightings recorded near Delhi in 1834, in Bihar in 1840 and in Rajasthan in 1870. In Gujarat too they were almost hunted to extinction, with as few as 12 remaining in the 1870s. It was not until one of their erstwhile pursuers, the enlightened Nawab of Junagadh, decided to set up a protection zone at the beginning of the 20th century that the lions began slowly to recover. This zone now survives as the Sasan Gir Wildlife Sanctuary.

Separated from their African counterpart (*Panthera leo leo*) for centuries, Asiatic lions have developed unique characteristics. Their mane is less luxuriant and doesn't cover the top of the head or ears, while a prominent fold of skin runs the length of the abdomen. They are also purely predatory, unlike African lions which sometimes feed off carrion.

Gir village. Once you have a vehicle sorted, you must queue up at the reception centre to obtain a **permit** (vehicle with up to 6 passengers Indians/foreigners ₹400/US$40 Mon-Fri, ₹500/US$50 Sat & Sun, ₹600/US$60 around Navratri, Diwali & Christmas/New Year) and a **guide** (4hr ₹50), and pay **photography fees** (camera up to 7 megapixel free, over 7 megapixel Indian/foreigner ₹100/US$10). Your driver will usually help with this; be at the reception centre with your passport when it opens to ensure getting a permit and an early start. Permit-issuing times are posted at the reception centre: at research time they were 5am to 6am, 8am to 9am and 2pm to 3pm. Up to 90 permits can be issued each day and half of those can be booked in advance. Although permit prices are quoted in US dollars, payment is in rupees and the exchange rate is at the official's discretion – usually fair.

Gir Interpretation Zone WILDLIFE-WATCHING
(Indian/foreigner ₹75/US$20; ☺8.30am-noon & 3.30pm-dusk Thu-Tue) Twelve kilometres west of Sasan Gir village at Devalia, within the sanctuary precincts, is the Gir Interpretation Zone, better known as simply 'Devalia'. The 4.12-sq-km fenced-off compound is home to a cross-section of Gir wildlife. Chances of seeing lions here are good but stage-managed, and you're only likely to get 30 to 45 minutes looking for wildlife and only from a bus. An autorickshaw/taxi round-trip to Devalia from Sasan Gir village costs around ₹70/100.

Gir Orientation Centre EXHIBITION
(admission free; ☺8am-6pm) Next to the reception centre, this has an informative exhibition on the sanctuary and a small shop. A creaking film about the park is screened behind the building at 7pm.

🛏 Sleeping & Eating

It's a good idea to make an advance booking. Sasan Gir has one main street and most accommodation is on it or nearby, with a few upmarket options further away.

Amidhara Resort HOTEL $$
(✑285950; www.amidhararesorts.com; r incl 3 meals ₹3900-7500, with AC ₹4900-8000; ✸☀) Two kilometres south of the village on the Veraval road, this is easily the most comfortable choice. The rooms and cottages are generously decked out and there's an inviting pool and other sports and games facilities. The included meals are vegetarian; it's

also possible to get a room without meals for about one-third off the rates given here, and take veg or non-veg meals as you choose.

Hotel Umang HOTEL $
(✑285728; www.hotelumang.com; Rameshwar Society, SBS Rd; r without/with AC ₹750/1250; ✸) This is a quiet option with serviceable rooms, helpful management and decent meals. Discounts are available when business is slow, and it offers a two-night package with all meals for ₹3150. Head 150m west from Sinh Sadan then 200m south off the main road.

Maneland Jungle Lodge HOTEL $$
(✑285690; www.maneland.com; r incl meals ₹2500, with AC ₹3500; ✸) Off the road to Junagadh, 3km from Sasan Gir village, this friendly and relaxed place is in a nice, natural setting backing on to the sanctuary, and has good, clean rooms in stone-built cottages. The included meals are vegetarian and good.

Gir Birding Lodge HOTEL $$
(✑9899810456; www.girbirdinglodge.com; cottage incl meals s/d standard ₹3000/3500, deluxe ₹4500/5000; ✸) Has 12 bungalow rooms in a fruit orchard 2.5km from the village off the Junagadh road. Bird and river walks available; naturalist guides cost ₹2000 per day.

Hotel Annapurna HOTEL $
(✑285569; r without/with AC ₹400/1000; ✸) On the main street, with small, clean rooms freshly painted in pinks and yellows. Get one with an exterior window.

Gir Rajwadi Hotel INDIAN $
(mains ₹60-70; ☺lunch & dinner) This vegetarian joint is the best of several simple restaurants along the village's main street. Gujarati thali is ₹80.

ⓘ Getting There & Away

Buses run from Sasan Gir village to both Veraval (local/express ₹25/45, 1½ hours) and Junagadh (₹30/50, two hours) about 10 times daily.

Second-class unreserved-seating trains run to Junagadh (₹12, 2¾ hours) at 5.57pm, to Delwada (for Diu, ₹15, 3½ hours) at 9.57am, and to Veraval (₹7, 1½ hours) at 12.07pm and 4.27pm.

Junagadh

✑0285 / POP 168,686

Junagadh is an interesting small city reached by few tourists. It's an ancient, fortified city with 2300 years of history (its name means 'old fort'), at the base of holy Girnar Hill. At the time of Partition, the Nawab of Junagadh opted to take his tiny state into Pakistan – a wildly unpopular decision as the inhabitants were predominantly Hindu, so the nawab departed on his own. Junagadh makes a good jumping-off point for chasing lions at Sasan Gir.

◉ Sights & Activities

While parts of the centre are as traffic-infested, crowded and hot as any other city, the area up towards Uparkot Fort and around Circle and Diwan Chowks is highly atmospheric, dotted with markets and half-abandoned palaces in Euro-Mughal style with grass growing out of their upper storeys.

Uparkot Fort   FORT

(admission ₹2; ⊘dawn-dusk) This ancient fort is believed to have been built in 319 BC by the Mauryan emperor Chandragupta, though it has been extended many times. In places the walls reach 20m high. It's been besieged 16 times, and legend has it that the fort once withstood a 12-year siege. It's also said that the fort was abandoned from the 7th to 10th centuries and, when rediscovered, was completely overgrown by jungle.

The views over the city and east to Girnar Hill are superb. The **Jumma Masjid**, the mosque inside the fort, was converted from a palace in the 15th century by Gujarat sultan Mahmud Begada and has a rare roofed courtyard with three octagonal openings which may once have been covered by domes.

Close to the mosque is a set of **Buddhist caves** (Indian/foreigner ₹5/100; ⊘dawn-dusk), not actually caves but monastic quarters carved out of the rock about 2000 years ago. The three-storey complex is quite eerie and the main hall contains pillars with weathered carvings.

The fort has two fine step-wells both cut from solid rock. **Adi Kadi Vav** (named after two slave girls who used to fetch water from it) is 41m deep and was cut in the 15th century. **Navghan Kuvo**, 52m deep and designed to help withstand sieges, is almost 1000 years old and its magnificent staircase spirals around the well shaft.

Girnar Hill   SACRED SITE

The long climb up 10,000 stone steps to the summit of Girnar is best begun at dawn. Be prepared to spend a full day going up and down if you want to reach the furthest temples at the top. Starting out in the early morning light is a magical experience, as pilgrims and porters begin to trudge up the well-maintained steps. The start is 4km east of the city at Girnar Taleti. A road goes as far as about the 3000th step, which leaves you *only* 7000 to the top – it was closed for repairs at research time but expected to re-open in 2011.

The refreshment stalls on the ascent sell chalk, so you can graffiti your name on the rocks. As you near the top, take a moment to marvel at how the stallholders can rustle up a chilled drink. If you can't face the walk, *dholis* carried by porters cost ₹3850 (round-trip) if you weigh between 50kg and 70kg, and ₹4250 for heavier passengers. If your weight range isn't obvious, you suffer the indignity of being weighed on a huge beam scale before setting off.

Girnar is of great significance to the Jains, but several important Hindu temples mean that Hindus make the pilgrimage, too.

The Jain temples, a cluster of mosaic-decorated domes interspersed with elaborate stupas, are about two-thirds of the way up. The largest and oldest is the 12th-century **Temple of Neminath**, dedicated to the 22nd *tirthankar:* go through the first left-hand doorway after the first gate. Many temples are locked from around 11am to 3pm, but this is open all day. The nearby triple **Temple of Mallinath**, dedicated to the ninth *tirthankar,* was erected in 1177 by two brothers. During festivals this temple is a sadhu magnet.

Further up are various Hindu temples. The first peak is topped by the **Temple of Amba Mata**, where newlyweds worship to ensure a happy marriage. Beyond here there is quite a lot of down as well as up to reach the other four peaks and further temples. The **Temple of Gorakhnath** is perched on Gujarat's highest peak at 1117m. The steep peak **Dattatraya** is topped by a shrine to a three-faced incarnation of Vishnu. Atop the final outcrop, **Kalika**, is a shrine to the goddess Kali.

The **Bhavnath Mela** (Bhavnath Fair), over five days in the month of Magha (January/February) brings folk music and dancing and throngs of *nagas* (naked sadhus or spiritual men) to Bhavnath Mahadev Temple at Girnar Taleti. It marks the time when Shiva is believed to have danced his cosmic dance of destruction.

An autorickshaw from town to Girnar Taleti costs about ₹50.

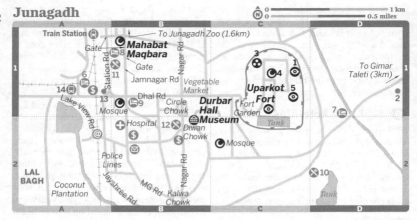

Mahabat Maqbara
HISTORIC BUILDING

This stunning **mausoleum** of Nawab Mahabat Khan II of Junagadh (1851–82) seems to bubble up into the sky. One of Gujarat's most glorious examples of Euro-Indo-Islamic architecture, with French windows and Gothic columns, its lavish appeal is topped off by its silver inner doors. Boasting even more flourish is the neighbouring **Vazir's Mausoleum**, sporting four storybook minarets encircled by spiralling stairways.

Junagadh Zoo
ZOO, MUSEUM

(admission ₹20, camera/video ₹20/100; ☺9am-6pm Thu-Tue) If you don't make it to Sasan Gir, Junagadh's zoo at Sakkarbaug, 2km north of the centre, has Asiatic lions and a broad selection of other Indian wildlife. Though the concrete enclosures in the front part are cruelly small, there is a surprisingly good **'safari' park** (20min bus tour ₹25; ☺9am-1pm & 2.30-5.45pm) at the back, with an abundance of lions, tigers and leopards. Safari visits start from the zoo's north gate whenever 10 punters accumulate there. The zoo also houses the **Junagadh Museum** (Indian/foreigner ₹2/50; ☺9am-12.15pm & 2.45-6pm Thu-Tue, closed 2nd & 4th Sat of month), with paintings, manuscripts, archaeological finds and more. An autorickshaw from the centre costs around ₹25.

Durbar Hall Museum
MUSEUM

(Diwan Chowk; Indian/foreigner ₹2/50; ☺9am-12.15pm & 2.45-6pm Thu-Tue, closed 2nd & 4th Sat of month) This museum displays weapons, armour, palanquins, chandeliers, and howdahs from the days of the nawabs, as well as a huge carpet woven in Junagadh's jail. There's a royal portrait gallery, including photos of the last nawab with his numerous beloved dogs.

Ashokan Edicts
HISTORIC SITE

(Indian/foreigner ₹5/100; ☺dawn-dusk) Just outside town on the road to Girnar Hill, a white building on the right encloses a large boulder on which the Buddhist emperor Ashoka had 14 edicts inscribed in Brahmi script in the Pali language about 250 BC. The spidery lettering instructs people to be kind to women and animals and give to beggars, among other things, and is one of several inscriptions that Ashoka placed all around his realm expounding his moral philosophy and achievements. Translations into Hindi, English and Gujarati are placed beside the boulder.

🛏 Sleeping

There are several cheap hotels around Kalwa Chowk which, because of the clientele they attract, are best avoided by females – even when travelling with a male partner.

Lotus Hotel
HOTEL **$$**

(☏2658500; www.thelotushotel.com; Station Rd; s/d from ₹1000/1250; ✳🛜) This luxurious and comfortable option occupies the totally renovated top floor of a former *dharamsala* (pilgrim's rest house). Pilgrims never had it so good, with split-system AC and LCD TVs. Rooms are beautifully bright, spacious and pristine, the beds are great, and everything works – incredible value for such quality. There isn't a restaurant, but there is room service and Geeta Lodge is in the same building.

Junagadh

Relief Hotel   HOTEL $
(☎2620280; www.reliefhotel.com; Chitta Khana Chowk; s/d ₹300/400, r with AC ₹700; 🗙@) Mr Sorathia (Junagadh's unofficial tourist information officer) presides over the pick of the town's budget accommodation, which has simple, clean, colourfully painted rooms and the best set-up for travellers. There's also a fabulous restaurant and secure parking is available.

Hotel Vishala   HOTEL $$
(☎2631599; www.hotelvishala.com; 3rd fl, Dhara Complex; r from ₹800, with AC ₹1500; 🗙) Almost opposite the bus station and recognisable by the little awnings over its windows, this has good-sized, recently renovated rooms with a touch of contemporary minimalism in the AC quarters. There's a rooftop veg restaurant too.

Leo Resorts   HOTEL $$
(☎2652844; www.leoresorts.com; Taleti Rd; s ₹1800-2700, d ₹2000-3000; 🗙🛜🏊) Leo boasts a very inviting pool, a large playground and lawned gardens. The cheaper ('delux') rooms are spacious and quite liveable, without being attractive; the 'super delux' have a touch of style and plenty of comfort. It's situated

on the way out towards Girnar Hill. Staff seemed oddly out of sorts when we visited.

🍴 Eating & Drinking

Junagadh is famous for its fruit, especially for *kesar* (mangoes) and *chiku* (sapodilla), which are popular in milkshakes in November and December.

Geeta Lodge   GUJARATI $
(Station Rd; thali ₹65; ☺10am-3.30pm & 6-10.30pm) Geeta's army of waiters are constantly on the move serving up top-class, all-you-can-eat veg Gujarati thalis at a bargain price. Finish off with sweets, such as fruit salad or pureed mango, for ₹15.

Relief Restaurant   INDIAN $
(Relief Hotel, Chitta Khana Chowk; mains ₹60-100; ☺11.30am-3.30pm & 6.30-11.30pm) This spotless, relaxed, AC restaurant serves up delicious Punjabi, tandoori and Chinese dishes. Meat-eaters can choose from chicken, mutton, fish or prawns, and there's a good choice of veg and paneer dishes.

Garden Cafe   INDIAN $
(mains ₹60-110; ☺6.30-10.30pm Thu-Tue) Something different: this restaurant has a lovely garden setting next to Jyoti Nursery on the east side of town, and reasonable Jain, Punjabi and South Indian food. It's popular with families and within the short rickshaw ride.

Jay Ambe Juice Centre   JUICE BAR $
(Diwan Chowk; snacks & drinks ₹25-40; ☺10am-11pm) Perfect retreat for a fresh juice, milkshake or ice cream – try a custard-apple shake.

❶ Information

The very helpful management at Hotel Relief serves as an unofficial tourist information provider.

Bank of Baroda ATM (cnr MG Rd & Post Office Rd)

State Bank ATM (Prism Complex) Near the bus station.

State Bank of India (Nagar Rd; ☺11am-2pm Mon-Fri) Changes travellers cheques and cash; has an ATM.

X'S Internet Cafe (1st fl, Lake View Complex, Talav Gate; internet per hr ₹20; ☺9am-11pm)

❶ Getting There & Away

Bus

Buses leave the ST bus stand for Rajkot (₹50, two hours, hourly), Sasan Gir (₹55, two hours, hourly), Veraval (₹40, 2½ hours, eight daily), Diu (₹98, five hours, 2.30pm and 3.15pm), Una (for Diu, ₹80, 4½ hours, eight daily), Jamnagar (₹80, four hours, nine daily), Ahmedabad (₹160, eight hours, 6am and 7am) and Bhuj (₹100, seven hours, five daily).

Various private bus offices including **Mahasagar Travels** are on Dhal Rd, near the rail tracks. Services go to Mumbai (seat/sleeper ₹350/450, 19 hours), Ahmedabad (with/without AC ₹300/250, eight hours), Rajkot (₹60, two hours), Jamnagar (₹100, four hours) and Udaipur (seat/sleeper ₹300/400, 14 hours).

Train

There's a **computerised reservation office** (⊙8am-10pm Mon-Sat, 8am-2pm Sun) at the station.

The *Jabalpur Express* (train 11463 or 11465) departs at 11.38am for Rajkot (sleeper/3AC/2AC ₹130/244/301, 2½ hours) and Ahmedabad (₹177/454/613, seven hours).

Second-class train 316 at 7.15am heads to Sasan Gir (₹12, 2¾ hours) and Delwada (for Diu, ₹23, six hours).

Gondal

✆ 02825 / POP 96,000
Gondal is a small, leafy town, 38km south of Rajkot, that sports a string of palaces and a gentle river. It was once capital of a 1000-sq-km princely state ruled by Jadeja Rajputs.

⊙ Sights & Activities

Naulakha Museum   MUSEUM
(Naulakha Palace; admission ₹20; ⊙9am-noon & 3-6pm) This interesting museum in the old part of town is housed in a beautiful, 260-year-old riverside royal palace that was built in a mixture of styles, with striking gargoyles. It shows royal artefacts, including scales used to weigh Maharaja Bhagwat Sinhji in 1934 (his weight in silver was distributed to the poor), a nine-volume Gujarati dictionary compiled by the same revered maharaja, and the royal horse-carriage and Dinky Toy collections.

Vintage & Classic Car Collection   MUSEUM
(Orchard Palace; Indian/foreigner ₹60/210; ⊙9am-noon & 3-6pm) This is the royal collection of cars – 32 impressive vehicles, from a 1907 car made by the 'New Engine Company Acton' to racing cars raced by the present maharaja. All are still in working condition.

Bhuvaneshwari Ayurvedic Pharmacy   AYURVEDA
(www.bhuvaneshwaripith.com; Ghanshyam Bhuvan; ⊙9am-noon & 3-5pm Tue-Sat) Founded in 1910 by Gondal's royal physician, this pharmacy

manufactures ayurvedic medicines and it's possible to see all the weird machinery involved, as well as buy medicines for treating hair loss, vertigo, insomnia etc. The founding physician, Brahmaleen Acharyashree, is said to have coined the title 'Mahatma' (Great Soul) for Gandhi. Also here is a temple to the goddess Bhuvaneshwari.

Udhyog Bharti Khadi Gramodyog   HANDICRAFTS WORKSHOP
(Udhyog Bharti Chowk; ⊙9am-noon & 3-5pm Mon-Sat) A large *khadi* (homespun cloth) workshop where hundreds of women work spinning cotton upstairs, while downstairs embroidered *salwar kameez* (traditional dresslike tunic and trouser combination for women) and saris are on sale.

🛏 Sleeping & Eating

Orchard Palace   HERITAGE HOTEL $$
(✆220002; www.gondalpalaces.com; Palace Rd; s/d incl breakfast ₹2225/4450, incl all meals ₹3025/6050; ❄) This small palace, once the royal guesthouse, has seven well-kept, though hardly luxurious, high-ceilinged rooms of different sizes, filled with 1930s and '40s furniture. It's rather overpriced, though a peaceful place to stay where guests get free admission to all of Gondal's attractions. Vegetables are from the on-site organic garden. Reservations recommended.

Riverside Palace   HERITAGE HOTEL $$
(✆220002; www.gondalpalaces.com; Ashapura Rd; s/d incl breakfast ₹2225/4450, incl all meals ₹3025/6050; ❄) This is the erstwhile ruling family's other palace-hotel, built in the 1880s and formerly the crown prince's abode. It has a slightly less welcoming feel than the Orchard Palace, but is still fine. It's adorned with hunting trophies and four-poster beds and has river views. Reservations recommended.

ⓘ Getting There & Away

Buses run frequently to/from Rajkot (₹20, one hour) and Junagadh (₹30, two hours). Slow passenger trains between Rajkot (₹15, one hour) and Junagadh (₹18, 1½ hours) also stop at Gondal.

Rajkot

✆ 0281 / POP 1.137 MILLION
Rajkot is a large, hectic commercial and industrial city that isn't easy to love with its heavy traffic, impatient drivers and lack of open spaces. But the old city, east of the

newer centre, still has plenty of character, with narrow streets, markets, and farmers still selling ghee on street corners.

Rajkot was founded in 1612 by Jadeja Rajputs, and in colonial times it became the headquarters of the Western India States Agency, Britain's administrative centre for some 400 princely states in Saurashtra, Kachchh and northern Gujarat. After Independence Rajkot was capital of the short-lived state of Saurashtra.

◉ Sights & Activities

Watson Museum
MUSEUM
(Jubilee Gardens; Indian/foreigner ₹2/50; ⊙9am-12.45pm & 3-6pm Thu-Tue, closed 2nd & 4th Sat of month) The Watson Museum is named after Colonel John Watson, a political agent (administrator) in the 1880s who gathered many historical artefacts and documents from around Saurashtra. It's a jumbled attic of a collection, featuring 3rd-century inscriptions, arrays of arms and delicate ivory work overseen by an unamused marble statue of Queen Victoria.

FREE Kaba Gandhi No Delo
HISTORIC BUILDING
(Ghee Kanta Rd; ⊙9am-noon & 4-6pm Mon-Sat) This is the house where Gandhi lived from the age of six (while his father was diwan of Rajkot), and it contains lots of interesting information on his life. The Mahatma's passion for the hand loom is preserved in the form of a small weaving school.

Patola Sari Weaving
HANDICRAFTS WORKSHOPS
The Patola-weaving skill comes from Patan, and is a torturous process that involves dyeing each thread before it is woven. Whereas in Patan both the warp and weft threads are dyed (double *ikat*), in Rajkot only the weft is dyed (single *ikat*), so the product is more affordable. You can visit workshops in people's houses in the Sarvoday Society area about 1km southwest of Shastri Maidan, including **Mayur Patola Art** (☎2464519; Street No 4; ⊙10am-6pm), behind Virani High School. You can call for directions.

🛏 Sleeping

There are plenty of cheapies on Dhebar and Kanak Rds, either side of the ST bus stand.

Imperial Palace
HOTEL $$
(☎2480000; www.theimperialpalace.biz; Dr Yagnik Rd; s ₹3900-5900, d ₹4400-6400, ste from ₹8500; ✳@🛜🏊) The numero uno in town, with a masterful lobby and lavish, well-appointed

rooms and real mattresses on the beds. There's a busy little wine shop, and two excellent veg eateries. Breakfast is complimentary.

Hotel Kavery
HOTEL $$
(☎2239331; www.hotelkavery.com; Kanak Rd; s ₹1250-2100, d ₹1850-2650, incl breakfast; ✳🛜) A popular midrange business hotel; the rooms here fill up quickly. Rooms are comfortable without being inspiring, and desk staff are helpful. Part of the popularity is undoubtedly due to the excellent in-house Bukhara Restaurant.

Galaxy Hotel
HOTEL $$
(☎222905; www.thegalaxyhotelrajkot.com; 3rd fl, Galaxy Commercial Centre, Jawahar Rd; s ₹1090-1890, d ₹1390-2290, ste ₹2790, incl breakfast; ✳🛜) An oddly classy hotel on the 3rd floor of a very ordinary building, with spacious, gleaming rooms. No restaurant, but there is 24-hour room service.

Hotel Bhakti
HOTEL $
(☎2227744; Kanak Rd; s/d ₹500/650, s with AC ₹750-850, d with AC ₹1100-1250; ✳) This reasonable semi-cheapie out the back of the bus station has neat and comfortable rooms, but check your bathroom for proper functioning.

🍴 Eating

Temptations
MULTICUISINE $$
(Kasturba Rd; mains ₹100-170; ⊙11am-midnight) A few doors down from Lord's Banquet (same management), popular Temptations has Mexican, Italian, falafel, baked potatoes, *parathas* (thick flat bread with stuffings such as vegetables or paneer) and South Indian in a cool, clean, brightly decorated cafe.

Senso
MULTICUISINE $$
(Imperial Palace, Dr Yagnik Rd; mains ₹80-210; ⊙24hr) The Imperial Palace's very good round-the-clock coffee shop does everything from Lebanese to lasagne and sizzlers to South Indian – all without meat.

Lord's Banquet
MULTICUISINE $$
(Kasturba Rd; mains ₹120-170; ⊙12.30-3.30pm & 7.30-11.30pm) Slightly more formal than its sister Temptations, Lord's is very popular for pure-veg Punjabi, continental and Chinese cuisine in cool, clean surroundings.

Bukhara Restaurant
MULTICUISINE $
(Hotel Kavery, Kanak Rd; mains ₹40-130, thali ₹120; ⊙11am-11pm) Bukhara is smart, cool and calm with good service and quality

Rajkot

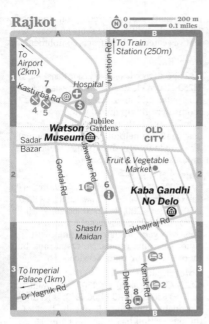

food, including Gujarati thali for lunch, and South Indian, among others, for dinner.

ℹ Information

There are ATMs all over town, including SBI on Jawahar Rd.

Aaryans (Dr Yagnik Rd; internet per hr ₹15; ⏱7.30am-11pm) Go 100m south from the Imperial Palace hotel.

Buzz Cyber Café (Alaukik Bldg, Kasturba Rd; internet per hr ₹15; ⏱8.30am-9.30pm) Tucked away opposite Temptations restaurant.

State Bank of India (Kasturba Rd; ⏱10am-4pm) Changes cash and travellers cheques.

Tourist office (☎2234507; Bhavnagar House, Jawahar Rd; ⏱10.30am-6pm Mon-Sat) Behind a State Bank of India building. Willing staff but no city map.

ℹ Getting There & Around

AIR There are daily flights to Mumbai with **Air India** (☎2234122; www.airindia.in) and **Jet Airways** (☎2450200; www.jetairways.com).

BUS Regular ST buses connect Rajkot with Jamnagar (₹53, two hours, every half-hour), Junagadh (₹50, two hours, hourly), Ahmedabad (₹109, 4½ hours, every half-hour) and Bhuj (₹125, seven hours, about hourly). Private buses operate to Ahmedabad, Bhavnagar, Una

(for Diu), Mt Abu, Udaipur and Mumbai. Several offices are on Limda Chowk. Head to **Jay Somnath Travels** (Umesh Complex, Kasturba Rd) for buses to Bhuj (₹160, seven hours, six daily).

TRAIN The 19006 *Saurashtra Mail* leaves at 5.45pm and arrives in Ahmedabad (sleeper/3AC/2AC/1AC ₹147/369/497/824) at 10.25pm and Mumbai (₹292/779/1062/1779) at 7.40am. The 19005 departs at 10.45am and arrives at Jamnagar (₹130/225/294/477) at 12.25pm. An autorickshaw to the station from the centre costs about ₹30.

Jamnagar

☎0288 / POP 447,734

Jamnagar is another little-touristed but interesting city, brimming with ornate, decaying buildings and colourful bazaars displaying the town's famous, brilliant-coloured *bandhani* (tie-dye) – produced through a laborious 500-year-old process involving thousands of tiny knots in a piece of folded fabric.

Before Independence, Jamnagar was capital of the Nawanagar princely state. Maharaja Jam Ranjitsinhji (r 1907-33) laid out a European-style street plan for the city and was also the first great Indian cricketer, although he played for England as India had no team then. Today Jamnagar is quite a boom town, with the world's biggest oil refinery, belonging to Reliance Petroleum, not far west of the city. The whole central area is one big commercial zone, with more brightly lit shops and stalls at night than you'll find in many a larger city.

◎ Sights

Ranmal Lake & Lakhota Palace
LAKE, MUSEUM

The promenades around Ranmal Lake make for a nice stroll when temperatures are moderate. The diminutive mid-19th-century Lakhota Palace, a fort on an island in the lake, is reached by a causeway from the north shore. It houses a small **museum** (Indian/foreigner ₹2/50; ◎10am-1.15pm & 2.45-6pm Thu-Tue, closed 2nd & 4th Sat of month) which preserves the fort's guardroom, frescos of battles fought by the Jadeja Rajputs and assorted historical and archaeological artefacts.

Bala Hanuman Temple
HINDU TEMPLE

This temple on the southeastern side of Ranmal Lake has been the scene of continuous chanting of the prayer *Shri Ram, Jai Ram, Jai Jai Ram* since 1 August 1964. This devotion has earned the temple a place in an Indian favourite, the *Guinness Book of Records*. Early evening is a good time to visit as the temple and lakeside area get busy.

Old City
AREA

The heart of the old city is known as Chandi Bazaar (Silver Market – which it is, among other things) and it contains, besides a heaving commercial scene, three beautiful Jain temples. The larger two, **Shantinath Mandir** and **Adinath Mandir**, dedicated to the 16th and first *tirthankars*, explode with fine murals, mirrored domes and elaborate chandeliers. The Shantinath Mandir is particularly beautiful, with coloured columns and a gilt-edged dome of concentric circles.

Around the temples spreads the old city with its lovely buildings of wood and stone, peeling, pastel-coloured shutters and crumbling wooden balconies. **Willingdon Crescent**, a European-style arcaded crescent, was built by Jam Ranjitsinhji to replace Jamnagar's worst slum. It now houses an assortment of shops, and is commonly known as Darbargadh after the now-empty royal residence across the street. **Subhas market**, the vegetable market, has lots of local colour.

◎ Courses

Gujarat Ayurved University
AYURVEDA

(☑2677324; www.ayurveduniversity.edu.in; Chanakya Bhavan, Hospital Rd) The world's first ayurvedic university, founded in 1967, is 1.5km northwest of the centre. It has played a big part in the revival of ayurvedic medicine since Independence and also has a public hospital treating 800 to 1000 inpatients and outpatients daily, mostly free of charge. Its **International Center for Ayurvedic Studies** (☑2664866; icasjam@gmail.com; ◎office 10.30am-1pm & 3-6.30pm Mon-Sat) runs a full-time, three-month introductory course (registration US$20, tuition per month US$375) teaching basic theory, treatment and medicine preparation, as well as longer certificate and degree courses in ayurveda, yoga and naturopathy. These courses are set up for foreign nationals with medical background; see the website for more information.

◎ Sleeping

Hotel President
HOTEL $$

(☑2557491; www.hotelpresident.in; Teen Batti; r ₹750, with AC ₹1450-2000; ✱) This hotel has helpful management and a range of reasonable rooms. The AC rooms have street views and are bigger and generally better than the non-AC, which are in the rear. Many rooms of both types have balconies. The recommended 7 Seas Restaurant is also here.

Hotel Ashiana
HOTEL $

(☑2559110; www.ashianahotel.com; New Super Market; s ₹325-1300, d ₹375-1500; ✱@) Rambling, welcoming Ashiana has helpful management and a variety of well-kept rooms, from simple and plain to large and comfortable. There's a large, pot-plant-decked roof terrace to enjoy in the evenings, and free airport, station and bus station transfers. Enter by lift or stairs from inside the New Super Market shopping centre.

Hotel Aram
HERITAGE HOTEL $$

(☑2551701; www.hotelaram.com; Pandit Nehru Marg; r ₹1300-2500, ste ₹3000-5000; ✱@◎) This former royal property has more potential magnificence than actual opulence. For the money the rooms are a little past their prime, though it is not without charm, and the rooms are spacious. There's a good multicuisine veg restaurant (mains ₹50 to ₹125) with garden seating.

Hotel Kirti
HOTEL $

(☑2558602; Teen Batti; r ₹400-550, with AC ₹800-1500; ✱) The Kirti is a good-value option, with well appointed and clean, if drab, rooms that have a bit of a view.

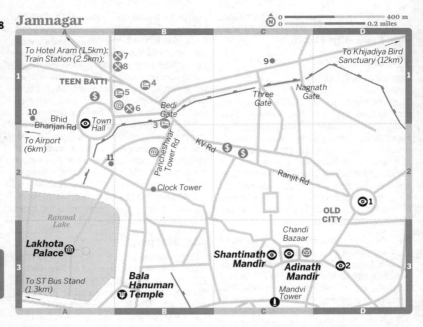

Eating

7 Seas Restaurant MULTICUISINE **$$**
(Hotel President, Teen Batti; mains ₹90-190) This cool, clean, efficient hotel restaurant has a nautical theme and a touch of class, offering a good range of veg and non-veg dishes, including seafood and tandoori options. The tandoori *bhindi* (okra) is a triumph.

Hotel Swati MULTICUISINE **$**
(Teen Batti; mains ₹40-110; ☺lunch & dinner) This upstairs, AC vegetarian restaurant has a faded ambience, but is well run and offers a big range of tasty South Indian, Chinese and Punjabi dishes, plus the odd pizza.

Fresh Point INDIAN, CHINESE **$**
(Town Hall Rd; mains ₹30-70; ☺lunch & dinner) A simple, friendly, bustling restaurant with generous serves of Punjabi, South Indian and Chinese in clean surroundings.

Madras Hotel INDIAN **$**
(Teen Batti; mains ₹35-85; ☺lunch & dinner) This buzzing eatery is basic and popular and pumps out vegetarian South Indian, Jain, Punjabi, as well as the odd pizza. It has AC and non-AC rooms.

Information

The website **www.jamnagar.org** is full of useful information for visitors.

SBI by the Town Hall roundabout, and Bank of Baroda and Bank of India on Ranjit Rd, change travellers cheques and cash between 10am and 4pm Monday to Friday. Hotel President will also change foreign currency.

Surf the internet at **IWorld** (1st fl, Indraprasth Shopping Centre, Pancheshwar Tower Rd; per 75min ₹30; ☺24hr) or **Cyber City** (bottom fl, City Point Shopping Centre; per hr ₹20; ☺9am-10pm).

Getting There & Away

AIR Indian Airlines (☏2554768; www.indian-airlines.nic.in; Bhid Bhanjan Rd) has daily flights to Mumbai.

BUS ST buses run to Rajkot (₹53, two hours, half-hourly), Junagadh (₹80, four hours, about hourly) and Ahmedabad (₹166 to ₹186, seven hours, about hourly).

There are also numerous private companies, many based west of the clock tower, including **Patel Tours** with nine daily Volvo AC buses to Ahmedabad (₹380, seven hours) and three non-AC buses to Bhuj (seat/sleeper ₹210/280, six hours).

TRAIN The 19006 *Saurashtra Mail* departs at 3.35pm for Rajkot (sleeper/3AC/2AC/1AC ₹130/235/294/477, 1¾ hours), Ahmedabad (₹174/445/601/1005, seven hours) and Mumbai (₹310/832/1136/1906, 16 hours).

Jamnagar

◎ **Top Sights**

◎ **Sights**

🛏 **Sleeping**

✕ **Eating**

Information

Transport

❶ Getting Around

An autorickshaw from the airport, 6km west, should be around ₹50, and a taxi ₹150. An autorickshaw from the bus stand to Bedi Gate costs ₹20.

Around Jamnagar

Permits for these protected areas are available from the **Forest Office** (☑2679355; Nagnath Gate, Van Sankul, Ganjiwada, Jamnagar; ⊙10.30am-12.30pm & 4-5.30pm Mon-Sat).

Khijadiya Bird Sanctuary   BIRDWATCHING
(6 Indians or 1 foreigner ₹250) This small (6 sq km) sanctuary, about 12km northeast of Jamnagar, encompasses both salt- and freshwater marshlands and hosts over 200 bird species including rarities like the Dalmatian pelican and black-necked stork. The best months are October to March and the best times of day around sunrise or sunset. The evening arrival of cranes for roosting can be spectacular. A return taxi costs around ₹1200, or you can take a bus (₹10) to nearby Khijadiya, then walk 3km.

Marine National Park   NATURE RESERVE
(6 Indians or 1 foreigner ₹250) This national park and the adjoining Marine Sanctuary encompass the intertidal zone and 42 small islands along some 120km of coast east and west of Jamnagar – an area rich in marine and bird life which faces growing challenges from industrialisation. Corals, octopus, anemones, puffer fish, sea horses, lobsters and crabs are among the marine life you may see in shallow water at low tide. The best time to visit is from December to March, when wintering birds are plentiful.

Access and obtaining permits can be a little complicated, so it's advisable to enlist local help such as that of Mustak Mepani (☑98242277886; www.jamnagar.org), manager at Hotel President. Mr Mepani can arrange a guided day-trip for up to six people to Pirotan Island, a two-hour boat ride through creeks and channels north of Jamnagar, for around ₹12,000; or a car trip to Narara island, 60km west of Jamnagar, for ₹2000 including guide.

Western Saurashtra

Mahatma Gandhi was born in 1869 in the chaotic port town of **Porbandar**, 130km southwest of Jamnagar. You can visit **Gandhi's birthplace** – a 22-room, 220-year-old house – and a memorial next door, Kirti Mandir. **Dwarka**, 106km from Jamnagar at the western tip of the Kathiawar Peninsula, is one of the four holiest Hindu pilgrimage sites in India – Krishna is said to have set up his capital here after fleeing from Mathura. Its **Dwarkadhish Temple** is believed to have been founded over 2500 years ago, and has a fantastically carved, 78m-high spire. The town swells to breaking point for **Janmastami** in August/September in celebration of Krishna's birthday.

There are some good beaches on the ocean coast, including the beautiful, long, clean **Okhamadhi**, 22km south of Dwarka – waves can be strong here – and the calmer **Shivrajpur**, a long lagoon beach 12km north of Dwarka. En route to Porbandar, the **Barda Wildlife Sanctuary** is a hilly, forested area with stone-built villages, old temples and good hiking. A good contact for more information on visiting these and other off-the-beaten-track places in western Saurashtra is **Mustak Mepani** (☑98242277886; www.jamnagar.org) at Jamnagar's Hotel President.

KACHCHH (KUTCH)

Kachchh, India's wild west, is a geographic phenomenon. The flat, tortoise-shaped land (*kachbo* means tortoise in Gujarati), edged by the Gulf of Kachchh and Great and Little Ranns, is a seasonal island. During the dry season, the Ranns are vast expanses of hard, dried mud. Come the monsoon, they're flooded first by seawater, then by fresh river water. The salt in the soil makes the low-lying marsh area almost completely barren. Only on scattered 'islands' above the salt level is there coarse grass which provides fodder for the region's wildlife.

The villages dotted across Kachchh's arid landscape are home to a jigsaw of tribal groups and sub-castes who produce some of India's finest handicrafts, above all their textiles which glitter with exquisite embroidery and mirrorwork.

A branch of the Indus River once entered the Great Rann until a massive earthquake in 1819 altered its course. Another mammoth earthquake in January 2001 again altered the landscape, killing nearly 30,000 people and destroying many villages completely. Although the effects of the tragedy will resonate for generations, the residents have determinedly rebuilt their lives and are welcoming to visitors. Tax breaks to encourage economic recovery have brought in new industrial plants, but by and large Kachchh still remains a refreshingly pristine, rural environment.

Bhuj

📞 02832 / POP 136,500

The capital of Kachchh is an interesting city resurrected from the 2001 earthquake. Its beguiling bazaars sell amazing Kachchh handicrafts, and historic buildings such as the Aina Mahal and Prag Mahal possess an eerie beauty. Bhuj is an ideal springboard for visits to the surrounding villages, and textile tourism is attracting visitors from around the world.

The Jadeja Rajputs who took control of Kachchh in 1510 made Bhuj their capital 29 years later, and it has remained Kachchh's most important town ever since.

⦿ Sights

TOP CHOICE **Darbargadh**   PALACES

This walled complex from which Kachchh was once ruled is still in need of much repair after the 2001 earthquake. The 17th-century **Rani Mahal**, the former main royal residence, is completely closed up, though you can still admire the latticed windows of its zenana (women's quarters). Largest of the

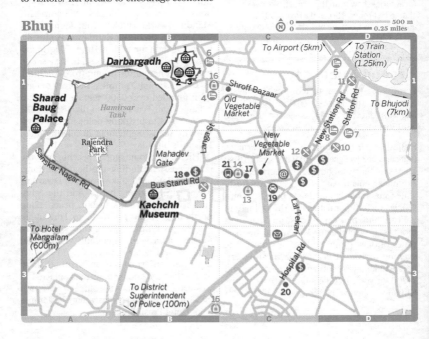

Bhuj

three palaces here is the 19th-century **Prag Mahal** (New Palace; Indian/foreigner ₹20/100, camera/video ₹100/200; ◷9am-noon & 3-6pm Feb-Nov, 9.30am-12.30pm & 2.30-5.30pm Dec & Jan). It's in a sad state and most sections are closed, but it's worth visiting for its ghostly Durbar Hall, a wonderful piece of decayed magnificence with broken chandeliers, rotting hunting trophies covered in bird droppings, and gold-skirted classical statues that wouldn't look out of place decorating a nightclub.

The beautiful **Aina Mahal** (Old Palace; admission ₹10, camera ₹30; ◷9am-noon & 3-6pm Sun-Fri), built in the 1750s, was badly damaged in the earthquake, but the 1st and 2nd floors are open again and contain a fascinating museum with excellent explanatory information in English. The palace was built for Maharao Lakhpatji by Ramsingh Malam, a sailor from Dwarka who had learned European arts and crafts on his travels. The elaborately mirrored interior is a demonstration of the maharao's fascination with all things European – an inverted mirror of European Orientalism – with blue-and-white Delft-style tiling, a candelabra with Venetian-glass shades and the Hogarth lithograph series *The Rake's Progress*. In the bedroom is a bed with solid gold legs (the king apparently auctioned his bed annually). In the Fuvara Mahal room, fountains played around the ruler while he sat watching dancers or composing poems.

It's estimated that the Aina Mahal will cost ₹2.5 million to repair fully. Donations are gratefully received – contact Pramod Jethi, the curator, at the museum for details (receipts are given).

Kachchh Museum   MUSEUM
(College Rd; Indian/foreigner ₹2/50; ◷10am-1pm & 2.30-5.30pm Thu-Tue, closed 2nd & 4th Sat of month) Opposite Hamirsar Tank, Gujarat's oldest museum has eclectic and worthwhile displays spanning textiles, weapons, silverware, sculpture, wildlife, geography and dioramas of Kachchh tribal costumes and artefacts, with labelling in English and Gujarati.

Folk Art Museum   MUSEUM
(Bharatiya Sanskriti Darshan; admission ₹10, camera ₹50; ◷9am-noon & 3-6pm Mon-Sat) This museum has excellent displays on traditional Kachchh culture, including reconstructed Rabari *bhungas* (mud-and-mirrorwork huts), musical instruments, many wood and stone carvings and much more. It's a further 700m south of the Kachchh Museum, off Mandvi Rd.

Sharad Baug Palace   PALACE
(admission ₹10, camera/video ₹20/100; ◷9am-noon & 3-6pm Sat-Thu) This graceful 1867 Italianate palace, on the west side of Hamirsar Tank in the midst of shady trees full of crows and bats, was the abode of the last Maharao of Kachchh, Madansingh, until his death in

Bhuj

GUJARAT BHUJ

1991. It lost most of its 3rd floor in the 2001 earthquake, and the remaining lower floors are closed. However, the adjacent former dining hall now houses the palace's eclectic museum collection. Standout exhibits are two huge stuffed tigers that the erstwhile maharao shot, and his coffin.

🛏 Sleeping

Hotel Prince   HOTEL $$
(☎220370; www.hotelprinceonline.com; Station Rd; s/d ₹900/1100, s with AC ₹2000-4000, d with AC ₹2500-4800; ❈@☎) The Prince has slick service, smart rooms, good restaurants, and free airport transfers. You can get an alcohol permit from reception (free), though you will need to find a fridge to chill the warm beer from its wine shop.

Hotel Gangaram   HOTEL $
(☎224231; Darbargadh Chowk; s/d ₹300/600, with AC ₹800/1000; ❈) In the old city, near the Darbargadh, this is a great place – run by kindly Mr Jethi (not to be confused with the Aina Mahal curator) – where nothing is too much trouble. The rooms vary greatly so it might be worth inspecting a few. The meals here are delicious.

Hotel Mangalam   HOTEL $$
(☎220303; www.mangalamhotels.com; Mangalam Cross Roads; s/d ₹900/1200, s with AC ₹1550-2700, d with AC ₹1850-3600; ❈☎) Towards the south edge of town, the new Mangalam has big, bright, modern rooms with comfy furnishings and mostly good views. It's professionally run and on a nice human scale with just 17 rooms. The excellent Yellow Chilli restaurant is here, and free airport transfers are offered.

City Guest House   GUESTHOUSE $
(☎221067; Langa St; d ₹300, s/d without bathroom from ₹120/240) Just off Shroff Bazaar, this is unusually bright and cheery for a budget guesthouse, and has neat, ultraclean, basic rooms. Bathrooms have either squat toilets or the hybrid variety. Breakfast is available, there are two airy roof terraces, and you can rent motorbikes for ₹400 per day.

Hotel Ilark   HOTEL $$
(☎258999; www.hotelilark.com; Station Rd; s ₹1800-3200, d ₹2200-3800, ste from ₹4000; ❈@) This glitzy-looking modern hotel has quite stylish wood-panelled, wood-furnished rooms that more or less live up to the promise of the angular glass-and-red-paint exterior. Service is professional.

Hotel Annapurna   HOTEL $
(☎220831; hotelannapurna@yahoo.com; Bhid Gate; dm ₹70, s/d ₹225/300, without bathroom ₹150/200, with AC ₹700/800; ❈) Annapurna has a nice atmosphere, and friendly staff, but stands on a frenetically busy junction. Rooms are clean and some have balconies so you can overlook the mayhem.

🍴 Eating

TOP CHOICE Yellow Chilli   MUGHLAI $$
(Hotel Mangalam, Mangalam Cross Roads; mains around ₹150, buffet lunch ₹175-200; ☺lunch & dinner) A branch of a franchise run by celebrity chef Sanjeev Kapoor, the Yellow Chilli serves up innovative, delicious, pure-veg Mughlai-based dishes. Well worth a quick rickshaw ride from the city centre.

Hotel Nilam   INDIAN, CHINESE $
(Station Rd; mains ₹60-90) Good service by bow-tied, waistcoated waiters complements tasty vegetarian North and South Indian and Chinese dishes at this long, white, AC and highly popular restaurant. There's Gujarati thali (₹110) at lunchtime.

Sankalp   SOUTH INDIAN $
(Hotel Oasis, New Station Rd; mains ₹50-120; ☺11am-11pm) A quality chain restaurant with booth seating serving up excellent South Indian food.

Green Rock   MULTICUISINE $$
(Bus Stand Rd; mains ₹90-140, thali ₹120-150; ☺11am-3pm & 7-10.30pm) This 1st-floor, AC place serves up tasty lunchtime thalis as well as an extensive all-veg menu.

Noorani Mahal   INDIAN $
(Station Rd; mains ₹55-110; ☺11.30am-3pm & 7-11pm) This popular non-veg place gets packed out with mostly men eating chicken, but there's also mutton and veg cooked in the tandoor or in a spicy North Indian curry.

🛍 Shopping

Crossword   BOOKSTORE
(Bus Stand Rd; ☺8am-2pm & 4-9pm Mon-Sat, 8am-2pm Sun) A tiny branch of this franchise with some English-language books on Kachchh. Books are also sold at the Aina Mahal and Hotel Prince.

ℹ Information

You'll find Bank of Baroda and SBI ATMs on Station Rd, and an HDFC ATM on Bus Stand Rd.

Ashapura Money Changer (Station Rd; ☺9.30am-7pm Mon-Sat) Changes currency and travellers cheques, as will most midrange hotels.

State Bank of India (Hospital Rd; ☺10am-4pm Mon-Fri, 10am-1pm Sat) Changes travellers cheques or currency.

Tourist information office (☏291702, 9374235379; Aina Mahal, Darbargadh; ☺9am-noon & 3-6pm Sun-Fri) Pramod Jethi, the knowledgeable curator of the Aina Mahal, knows all there is to know about Bhuj and surrounding villages. He's also written a very useful guide to Kachchh (₹100), published in both English and French.

Universal Cyber Cafe (1st fl, Tara Empire; per hr ₹20; ☺9am-10pm) You can surf the internet in small cubicles here.

❶ Getting There & Away

Air
Jet Airways (www.jetairways.com) and **Kingfisher Airlines** (☏1800 2093030; www.flykingfisher.com; Hospital Rd) have daily flights to Mumbai.

Bus
Numerous ST buses run to Ahmedabad (₹150 to ₹158, nine hours), Rajkot (₹125, seven hours) and Jamnagar (₹165, seven hours). Book private buses at **Hemal Travels** (Bus Stand Rd; ☺8am-9pm), just outside the bus station, for Ahmedabad (seat/sleeper ₹220/320, AC ₹300/400, nine hours, five daily) and Jamnagar (₹200/300, six hours, one bus at 9.30pm), or at **Jay Somnath Travels** (Bus Stand Rd; ☺8am-9pm) for Rajkot (₹160, seven hours, five daily).

Train
Bhuj station is 1.5km north of the centre and has a **reservations office** (☺8am-8pm Mon-Sat, 8am-2pm Sun). The 14312 *Ala Hazrat Express* leaves at 11.05am (Monday, Thursday, Saturday, Sunday) and arrives at Ahmedabad (sleeper/3AC/2AC ₹180/462/624) at 6.50pm, continuing to Abu Road, Jaipur and Delhi. The 19116 *Bhuj-Bandra Sayaji Express* leaves at 10.15pm daily and hits Ahmedabad (sleeper/3AC/2AC ₹180/462/624) at 5.05am.

❶ Getting Around
The airport is 5km north of town – a taxi will cost around ₹200, an autorickshaw ₹100. Autorickshaws to the train station cost ₹30.

Around Bhuj

The local Jat, Ahir, Harijan, nomadic Rabari and other communities have distinct, colourful craft traditions that make their villages fascinating to visit. See p714 for some recommended artisans and organisations.

Bhujodi, about 7km southeast of Bhuj, is a village of weavers, mostly using pit looms, operated by both feet and hands. You can look into many workshops, which weave attractive shawls, blankets and other products. The village is 1km off Hwy 42. You can take a bus towards Ahmedabad and ask the driver to drop you at the turn-off for Bhujodi (₹7). A return rickshaw from Bhuj costs ₹250.

In the hills about 60km northwest of Bhuj is the eerie monastery at **Than**. The holy man Dhoramnath, as penance for a curse he had made, stood on his head on top of Dhinodhar hill for 12 years. The gods pleaded with him to stop, and he agreed, provided the first place he looked at became barren – hence the Great Rann. He then established the Kanphata (Slit Ears) monastic order, whose monastery (dating back to at least the 12th century) stands at the foot of the hill. This is a laid-back place to explore the surrounding hills, and the architecture ranges from crumbling mud brick to Portuguese-style stucco, blue and whitewash bell towers, with a hint of basil and marigold in the air. There's one bus daily to Than from Bhuj (₹40, two hours) at 5pm, returning early next morning. The monastery and the temple atop Dhinodhar have very basic **guest rooms** with mattresses on the floor (pay by donation) but no drinking water.

You need a permit to visit some villages in the northern and western parts of Kachchh, but this is easy to obtain. Take a copy of your passport and visa (and the originals) to the office of the **District Superintendent of Police** (☺11am-2pm & 3-6pm Mon-Sat), 800m south of Kachchh Museum in Bhuj, and complete a form listing the villages you want to visit – you should get the permit (free of charge; maximum 10 days) straight away. Drivers will need permits for themselves and their vehicles too.

TOP CHOICE **Shaam-e-Sarhad Village Resort** (☏02803-296222; www.hodka.in; tent s/d ₹1900/2200, bhunga s/d ₹3000/3500, incl 3 meals; ☺Oct-Mar), just outside **Hodka**, in the beautiful Banni grasslands 70km north of Bhuj, is a fascinating and successful project in 'endogenous tourism'. Owned and operated by the Halepotra people, its accommodation consists of three *bhungas* with sloping roofs and neat interiors, and nine luxurious earth-floored tents, all with private bathroom. Local guides cost ₹200 per day for birdwatching or visits to villages in the area like Hodka, **Khavda** (known for

KACHCHH CREATIVITY

Kachchh (Kutch) is one of India's richest areas for handicrafts, particularly famed for its beautiful, colourful embroidery work (of which there are at least 14 distinct styles), but it also has many artisans specialising in weaving, tie-dye, block printing, wood-carving, pottery and other crafts. The diversity of Kachchh crafts reflects the differing traditions of its many communities. Numerous local cooperatives invest in social projects and help artisans produce work that is marketable yet still preserves their artistic heritage.

Kutch Mahila Vikas Sangathan (☎02832-256281; 11 Nutan Colony, Bhuj) is a grass-roots organisation, comprising 12,000 rural women (1200 artisans), that pays members a dividend of the profits and invests money to meet social needs. The embroidery and patchwork are exquisite, employing the distinctive styles of several communities. Products go under the brand name Qasab and range from bags and bedspreads to cushion covers and wall hangings. Visit the head office in Bhuj, the Qasab outlet at Hotel Prince, or Khavda, a village about 80km north of Bhuj.

Kala Raksha (☎02808-277237; www.kala-raksha.org; ⊙10am-2pm & 3-6pm Mon-Sat), based at Sumrasar Sheikh, 25km north of Bhuj, is a nonprofit trust working to preserve and promote Kachchh arts. It works with about 1000 embroiderers and patchwork and appliqué artisans from six communities in some 25 villages. The trust has a small museum and shop, and can help arrange visits to villages to meet artisans. Up to 80% of sale price goes to the artisans, who also help design and price the goods.

Vankar Vishram Valji (☎02832-240723; Bhujodi; ⊙8am-8pm) is a family operation and one of the leading weavers in Bhujodi; it sells beautiful blankets, shawls, stoles and rugs.

Shrujan (☎02832-240272; www.shrujan.org; Bhujodi; ⊙10am-7.30pm), just past the Bhujodi turn-off, behind the GEB Substation, is a nonprofit trust working with over 3000 women embroiderers of nine communities in 114 villages. Their showroom sells top-class shawls, saris, cushion covers and more.

Dr Ismail Mohammad Khatri (☎02832-299786, 9427719313; dr.ismail2005@gmail.com; ⊙9am-5pm) in Ajrakhpur, 6km east of Bhujodi along the Bhachau road, heads a 10-generation-old block-printing business of real quality, using all-natural dyes in bold geometric designs. Go in the morning if you want to see a demonstration of the fascinating, highly skilled process. You can buy tablecloths, shawls, skirts, saris and other attractive products.

Parmarth (☎02832-273453; 106 Ramkrushn Nagar, New Dhaneti; ⊙8.30am-9pm), run by a delightful family whose work has won national awards, specialises in Ahir embroidery. New Dhaneti is 17km east of Bhujodi on the Bhachau road.

Khamir (☎02832-271272; www.khamir.org; Lakhond Crossroad, Kukma Rd, Kukma; ⊙9am-5.30pm) is an umbrella organisation dedicated to preserving and encouraging Kachchh crafts in all their diversity. At the Kukma centre you can see demonstrations and buy some of the artisans' products. It's about 4km beyond Bhujodi in the Anjar direction.

In Bhuj, textile dealers line Shroff Bazaar just east of the Darbargadh. However, plenty of so-called block-printed fabric is in fact screen-printed. A good shop is **Señorita Boutique** (☎02832-226773; Shroff Bazaar; ⊙8.30am-9pm), which sells various regional types of embroidery and tie-dyeing. **Bhoomi Handicrafts** (☎02832-225808; Bus Stand Rd; ⊙9am-9pm) is popular with locals.

If you're interested in antique embroidery, contact **Mr AA Wazir** (☎02832-224187; Plot 107B, Lotus Colony, Bhuj; awazir1@rediffmail.com), opposite the General Hospital. He has a stunning collection of more than 3000 pieces, about half of which are for sale.

its pottery and textiles) or **Ludia** (known for its mudwork), or **Kalo Dungar** (Black Hill, Kachchh's highest point at 462m above sea level), or the Great Rann itself, with its snow-glare of salt (you may need to provide your own transport). You can also just call in for a superb thali lunch (₹125).

⊘**Centre for Desert & Ocean** (CEDO; ☎02835-221284, 9825248135; www.cedobirding

.com; Moti Virani; per person incl all meals ₹1500), 53km northwest of Bhuj, is a wildlife conservation organisation run by passionate environmentalist Jugal Tiwari. It does birding and wildlife trips focusing on the wildlife-rich Banni grasslands (between Sumrasar Sheikh and Khavda). Accommodation is in plain but well-kept rooms with 24-hour solar-heated hot water; meals are Gujarati vegetarian. They can pick you up from Bhuj for ₹1200, or you can get a bus to Nakhtrana, followed by an autorickshaw 3km to Moti Virani. A day safari starting from Bhuj is ₹2500 (with AC ₹3000). An expert naturalist/birder guide costs ₹1500 per day.

A long drive northeast from Bhuj is the fascinating and remote Harappan site of **Dholavira**, on a seasonal island in the Great Rann. Excavations have revealed a complex town of stone buildings 1 sq km in area, inhabited from around 2900 to 1500 BC. It's best to organise your own transport: the only bus to Dholavira leaves Bhuj at 2pm (₹80, seven hours) and starts back at 5am. The state-government-run **Toran Tourist Complex** (✆02837-277395; s/d ₹200/300, with AC ₹650/700; ❋) at Dholavira offers basic accommodation and meals.

Mandvi

✆02834 / POP 45,000

Mandvi is an hour down the road from Bhuj and is a busy little place with an amazing shipbuilding yard. Hundreds of men construct, by hand, these wooden beauties for faraway Arab merchants. The massive timbers apparently come from Malaysian rainforests. There are also some sweeping beaches, including the glorious, long, clean private beach (₹100) near Vijay Vilas Palace, and Kashivishvanath Beach, 2km from the centre just east of the Rukmavati River.

◉ Sights & Activities

Vijay Vilas Palace PALACE
(admission Mon-Sat ₹25, Sun ₹35, vehicle ₹20, camera/video ₹50/200; ◷8.30am-6.30pm) Vijay Vilas Palace is a nicely proportioned 1920s palace reminiscent of an English country house, 7km west of town amid extensive orchards, and set by a magnificent private beach. Originally a summer abode for the Kachchh rulers, its 1st floor (out of bounds to visitors) is now the erstwhile royal family's main residence. The view from the roof is worth the climb, and the gardens make a nice stroll.

Autorickshaws charge about ₹80/125 one-way/return from town. You can walk back to town along the beach if you like.

Kutch Vipassana Centre MEDITATION
(✆02834-273303; www.sindhu.dhamma.org) At Bada village, 22km west of Mandvi, this centre runs 10-day *vipassana* meditation retreats for beginners. Courses, accommodation and food are free but donations are accepted.

🛏 Sleeping & Eating

The Beach at Mandvi Palace HOTEL $$$
(✆277597, 9879013118; www.mandvibeach.com; 2-night package s/d ₹11,000/12,000) A small tent resort in a fantastic location on the private 2.5km beach stretching down from Vijay Vilas Palace. The luxurious air-cooled tents have big beds, white-tiled bathrooms and solid wood furniture. The resort's **Dolphin restaurant** (meal veg/non-veg ₹400/450; ◷1-3pm & 7-9pm) is a wonderful beach pavilion that is open to nonguests if not full with guests. The beach is open to nonguest couples, families and foreigners for ₹100 per person unless you are having a meal at the Dolphin.

Rukmavati Guest House GUESTHOUSE $
(✆223558, 9429040484; www.rukmavatihotel.webs.com; Bridge Gate; dm ₹175, s/d from ₹300/400, r with AC ₹900; ❋) The best Indian hospital to spend the night in, this pleasant former medical centre, just by the bridge as you enter town, doesn't feel institutional. It's light, bright, clean and welcoming to travellers, with solar-water heaters and

EXPLORING KACHCHH

It is possible to get out to Kachchh's villages by public transport – for example, there are hourly buses to Sumrasar Sheikh (₹15, one hour) and three a day to Khavda (₹50, two hours). You can also use autorickshaws to villages not too far from the city. But you'll have many more options and more flexibility if you rent a car and driver – most Bhuj hotels can organise this for you.

An excellent option is the customised **autorickshaw tours** (per half/whole day ₹500/1000) to villages outside Bhuj organised by **Pramod Jethi** (✆9374235379; pkumar_94@yahoo.com), curator at the Aina Mahal.

self-catering facilities. Some rooms have river-view balconies, and there's a nice terrace. Owner Vinod is a gentleman, and the town's unofficial tourist officer, with maps and heaps of helpful info.

Hotel Sea View
HOTEL **$**

(☑224481; www.hotelseaviewmandvi.com; cnr ST & Jain Dharamsala Rds; r ₹500, with AC ₹1100-2000; ✻) A small hotel facing the river, this has brightly decorated rooms with big windows that make the most of the views of the shipbuilding.

Zorba the Buddha
GUJARATI **$**

(1st fl, Osho Hotel, Bhid Gate; thali ₹70; ☉11am-3pm & 7-10pm) In the heart of the town, Zorba's is a massively popular place for wonderfully flavourful, endless and cheap Kachchh-style thalis. It's also known as Rajneesh Hotel, and the sign outside says 'Osho'.

Gabha's Roti
STREET FOOD **$**

(roti ₹5; ☉11am-1.30pm daily, 6-8.30pm Mon-Sat) Don't leave Mandvi without tracking down these famed bread rolls with their very spicy potato, garlic, chutney and masala filling. Mr Gabha frequently sells 1000 in an hour. At lunchtime his stall can be found at the vegetable market (Mochi Bazar); in the evenings it's on Swaminarayan Rd.

❶ Getting There & Away

Regular buses to/from Bhuj (₹22 to ₹32) take 1½ to two hours. Or you can take faster shared jeep-taxis (₹30 or ₹35) which run between the street south of Bhuj's vegetable market and Mandvi. For least discomfort, sit at the front and buy an extra seat for your luggage. Several agencies including **Patel Tours & Travels**, by the Sea View Hotel, sell tickets for private buses to Ahmedabad (seat/sleeper non-AC ₹250/350, with AC ₹350/450, 11 hours), mostly leaving between 7pm and 8.30pm.

Wild Ass Sanctuary

The barren, blindingly white land of the Little Rann is nature at its harshest and most compelling, and home to the last remaining population of the chestnut-coloured Indian wild ass (also called khur), as well as blue-bulls, blackbuck and chinkara. There's also a huge bird population from October to March (this is one of the few areas in India where flamingos breed in the wild). The 4953-sq-km **Wild Ass Sanctuary** (jeep with up to 6 passengers Indians/foreigners ₹200/US$20 Mon-Fri, ₹250/US$25 Sat & Sun; guide per 4hr ₹50)

covers a large part of the Little Rann. The area is accessible from Ahmedabad and can be combined with interesting destinations such as Nalsarovar Bird Sanctuary, Modhera and Patan.

The Little Rann is punctuated by desolate salt farms, where people eke out a living by pumping up groundwater and extracting the salt. Heat mirages disturb the vast horizon – bushes and trees seem to hover above the surface. Rain turns the desert into a sea of mud, and even during the dry season the solid-looking crust is often deceptive, so it's essential you take a local guide when exploring the area.

There are somewhere between 2000 and 3000 khurs in the sanctuary, surviving off the flat, grass-covered expanses or islands, known as *bets,* which rise up to around 3m. These remarkable, notoriously untamable creatures are capable of running at an average speed of 50km/h for long distances.

Desert Coursers (☑9998305501, 9427066070; www.desertcoursers.net), run by infectiously enthusiastic naturalist Dhanraj Malik, organises excellent Little Rann safaris and village tours from its **Camp Zainabad** (full board per person ₹2500; ☉Aug-Apr; ✻), very close to the east edge of the Little Rann and just outside the small town of **Zainabad**, 105km northwest of Ahmedabad. The lodge has comfortable and attractive *koobas* (traditional thatch-roofed huts) and excellent meals, in a peaceful, remote setting. The price includes unlimited jeep safaris. Advance booking is advised.

To get to Zainabad from Ahmedabad, you can take a bus from Ahmedabad's ST bus stand to Dasada, 10km away (₹70, 2½ hours, about hourly), where Desert Coursers does free pick-ups. There are direct buses between Zainabad and Patan (₹65, 2½ hours, two daily) via Modhera (₹45, 1½ hours). Desert Coursers can arrange taxis around the area for ₹4.5 per kilometre.

Rann Riders (☑9925236014; www.rannriders.com; s/d incl all meals & 2 safaris ₹4500/5800; ✻☒), near Dasada, is also family-run and offers luxurious cottage accommodation in pretty gardens, plus jeep and camel safaris and its own stable of indigenous horses for riding.

You may also approach from **Dhrangadhra**. The town itself is worth visiting, if only to break up the Bhuj–Ahmedabad hike. The streets and alleys wind around each other, and almost every turn is a mosaic of whitewashed and coloured buildings of all periods, description and type. Temple bells ring out, and the locals aren't used to tourists, making for some refreshing dialogue. The personable **Devjibhai Dhamecha** (✆9825548090, 02754-280560; www.littlerann. com) is a wildlife photographer who makes a wonderful guide. You can stay at his appealing **house** (Dev Krupa, Jinplot, Dhrangadhra; per person incl meals ₹500) or his recently opened **Eco Tour Camp** (Jogad village; tents per person ₹750, hut s/d ₹1500/2000, all incl meals) which has colourful *koobas* near the edge of the sanctuary, 40km northwest of Dhrangadhra. Six-/eight-hour safaris to the sanctuary from either place cost ₹2000/3000 per jeep. If you can't get Devjibhai, try his son **Ajaybhai** (✆9825548104).

Dhrangadhra is on the Bhuj–Ahmedabad rail route, 215km from Bhuj (3AC ₹350, five hours) and 120km from Ahmedabad (3AC ₹258, three hours). It's well served by buses, for example to and from Ahmedabad (₹50, three hours) and Bhuj (₹100, five hours).

The guides mentioned will arrange your permits for the reserve; the cost of these is normally additional to safari prices.

An hour south of Dhrangadhra on the Ahmedabad–Rajkot highway is **Sayla**, a peaceful, pastoral town that swells during the **Tarnetar Fair** in August/September. **Bell Guest House** (✆9724678145; spjhala@ yahoo.co.in; r incl breakfast ₹3000; ❄), presided over by the erstwhile ruling family of Sayla, is a wonderful homestay retreat down a lane off the Sayla roundabout on Hwy 8A. Rooms have spacious ensuite bathrooms. You can look for bluebulls and peacocks in the surrounding countryside or take trips further afield to see wild asses, blackbuck, the birds of Nalsarovar or a variety of artisans in area villages.

Mumbai (Bombay)

Best Places to Eat

» Khyber (p741)

» Peshawri (p745)

» Five Spice (p742)

» Trishna (p743)

» Culture Curry (p745)

Best Places to Stay

» Taj Mahal Palace, Mumbai (p736)

» Iskcon (p740)

» YWCA (p737)

» Hotel Moti (p737)

» Residency Hotel (p738)

Why Go?

Mumbai is a beautiful mess, full of dreamers and hard-labourers, actors and gangsters, stray dogs and exotic birds, artists and servants, fisherfolk and *crorepatis* (millionaires), and lots more. Its crumbling architecture in various states of Technicolor dilapidation is a reminder that Mumbai once dreamt even bigger, leaving a brick-and-mortar museum around its maze of chaotic streets as evidence that its place in the world has always been a poetic disaster.

Today Mumbai is home to the most prolific film industry, one of Asia's biggest slums and the largest tropical forest in an urban zone. It's India's financial powerhouse, fashion epicentre and a pulse point of religious tension. Between the fantastical architecture and the modern skyscrapers, the fine dining and frenetic streets, the urban grit and suburban glamour, the madness and the mayhem, there's a cinematic cityscape set to a playful and addictive raga – a complex soundtrack that dances to the beat of its own *desi* drum.

When to Go
Mumbai (Bombay)

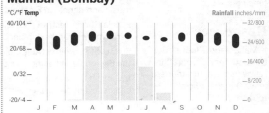

Apr–May Some like it hot...some like it *hot*.

Aug–Sep Mumbai goes Ganesh crazy during its biggest and most exciting festival, Ganesh Chaturthi.

Oct–Feb Put away the scuba gear as the monsoons retreat for Mumbai's 'cool' season.

Fast Facts

» Population: 16.4 million

» Area: 444 sq km

» Area code: ☑022

» Languages: Marathi, Hindi, Gujarati, English

» Sleeping prices: **$** below ₹1000, **$$** ₹1000 to ₹4000, **$$$** above ₹4000

Top Tips

Many international flights arrive after midnight. Save yourself some moon-lit hassle by carrying detailed landmark directions for your hotel – many airport taxi drivers don't speak English and can dwindle precious sleep time hunting it down.

Eicher City Map Mumbai (₹250) is an excellent street atlas, worth picking up if you'll be spending some time here.

Resources

» Maharashtra Tourism Development Corporation (www.maharashtratourism .gov.in) is the official tourism site.

A Mouthful of Mumbai

Mumbai is a city shaped by flavours from all over India and the world. Throw yourself into the culinary kaleidoscope by sampling Parsi *dhansak* (meat with curried lentils and rice), Gujarati or Keralan thalis ('all-you-can-eat' meals), Mughlai kebabs, Goan vindaloo and Mangalorean seafood. And don't forget, if you see Bombay duck on a menu, it's actually *bombil* fish dried in the sun and deep-fried.

Streetwise, don't miss Mumbai's famous beach *bhelpuri,* readily available at Girgaum Chowpatty, a flavour summer-sault of crisp-fried thin rounds of dough mixed with puffed rice, lentils, lemon juice, onions, herbs, chilli and tamarind chutney piled high on takeaway plates. Other street stalls offering rice plates, samosas, *pav bhaji* (spiced vegetables and bread) and *vada pav* (deep-fried spiced lentil-ball sandwich) do a brisk trade around the city.

DON'T MISS

For many, a visit to cosmopolitan Mumbai is all about dining, nightlife and shopping, but the city offers far more than nocturnal amusement and retail therapy. Nowhere is that more evident than in the spectacular maze of Gothic, Victorian, Indo-Saracenic and art deco architecture, remnants of the British colonial era and countless years of European influence. **Chhatrapati Shivaji Terminus (Victoria Terminus)**, **High Court**, **University of Mumbai**, **Taj Mahal Palace hotel** and the **Gateway of India** are just the most prominent – little architectural jewels dot the urban quagmire throughout the metropolis and stumbling upon them is one of Mumbai's great joys.

Top Mumbai Festivals

» Mumbai Festival (Jan, citywide, p734) A showcase of Mumbai music, dance and culture

» Elephanta Festival (Feb, Elephanta Island, p734) Classical music and dance on Elephanta Island

» Kala Ghoda Festival (Feb, citywide, p734) Two weeks of art performances and exhibitions

» Nariyal Poornima (Aug, Colaba, p734) Commemorates the beginning of fishing season

» Ganesh Chaturthi (Aug/Sep, citywide, p734) Mumbai's biggest event celebrates all things Ganesh

Colaba

TOP CHOICE Haji Ali's Mosque MOSQUE

Floating like a sacred mirage off the coast, this mosque, one of Mumbai's most striking symbols, is an exquisite Indo-Islamic shrine. Built in the 19th century on the site of a 15th-century structure, it contains the tomb of the Muslim saint Haji – legend has it that Haji Ali died while on a pilgrimage to Mecca and his casket miraculously floated back to this spot. A long causeway reaches into the Arabian Sea, providing access to the mosque. Thousands of pilgrims, especially on Thursdays and Fridays, cross it to make their visit, many donating to the beggars who line the way; but at high tide, water covers the causeway and the mosque becomes an island. Once inside, pilgrims fervently kiss the dressings of the tomb.

Erosion has taken its toll on the concrete structure, and at press time, renovations had been ongoing since 2008. The structural upgrade includes beautiful white Rajasthani marble – the same used for the Taj Mahal. The dargah will remain open, but access may be limited.

FREE Mahalaxmi Dhobi Ghat LANDMARK

If you've had washing done in Mumbai, chances are your clothes have already visited this 140-year-old **dhobi ghat** (place where clothes are washed). The whole hamlet is Mumbai's oldest and biggest human-powered washing machine: every day hundreds of people beat the dirt out of thousands of kilograms of soiled Mumbai clothes and linen in 1026

MUMBAI (BOMBAY)

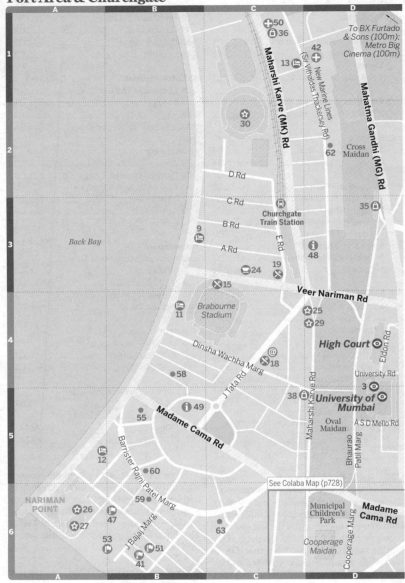

open-air troughs. The best view, and photo opportunity, is from the bridge across the railway tracks near Mahalaxmi train station.

Mahalaxmi Temple   HINDU TEMPLE
It's only fitting that in money-mad Mumbai one of the busiest and most colourful

temples is dedicated to Mahalaxmi, the goddess of wealth. Perched on a headland, it is the focus for Mumbai's Navratri (Festival of Nine Nights) celebrations in September/October.

11am-5pm). The architecture is striking: the tower looks like a giant cylindrical pineapple, the planetarium a UFO.

GORAI ISLAND

TOP CHOICE Global Pagoda　　LANDMARK

(www.globalpagoda.org; Near Esselworld, Gorai Creek; ☺9am-6pm) Rising up like a mirage from polluted Gorai Creek and the lush but noisy grounds of the Esselworld and Water Kingdom amusement parks, the breathtaking structure is a 96m-high stupa modelled after Burma's Shwedagon Pagoda. The dome, which is designed to hold 8000 meditators and houses relics of Buddha, was built entirely without supports using an ancient technique of interlocking stones. It just snatched the record away from Bijapur's Golgumbaz for being the world's largest unsupported dome. The pagoda also has a museum dedicated to the life of the Buddha and his teaching – it's affiliated with teacher SN Goenka, and an onsite meditation centre offers 10-day meditation courses. To get here, take the train from Churchgate to Borivali, then an autorickshaw (₹28) to the ferry landing, where the Esselworld ferries (return ₹35) come and go every 30 minutes. The last ferry back is 5.25pm.

🏃 Activities

Birdwatching　　WILDLIFE-WATCHING

Mumbai has surprisingly good birdwatching opportunities. Sanjay Gandhi National Park is popular for woodland birds, while the marshlands of industrial Sewri (pronounced *shev*-ree) swarm with birds in winter. Contact the **Bombay Natural History Society** (BNHS; Map p730; ☎22821811; www.bnhs.org; Hornbill House, Dr Salim Ali Chowk, Shaheed Bhagat Singh Rd, Kala Ghoda) or Sunjoy Monga at **Yuhina Eco-Media** (☎9323995955) for information on upcoming trips.

Outbound Adventure　　OUTDOOR ADVENTURE

(☎9820195115, www.outboundadventure.com) Runs one-day rafting trips on the Ulhas River near Karjat, 88km southeast of Mumbai, from July to early September (₹1600 per person). After a good rain, rapids can get up to Grade III+, though usually the rafting is much calmer, with lots of twists and zigzags. OA also organises camping and canoeing trips.

📖 Courses

Kaivalyadhama Ishwardas Yogic Health Centre　　YOGA

(Map p724; ☎22818417; www.kdhammumbai.com; 43 Marine Dr, Girgaum Chowpatty; ☺6.30-10am

Nehru Centre　　CULTURAL COMPLEX

(off Map p724; ☎24964676; www.nehru-centre. org; Dr Annie Besant Rd, Worli) This cultural complex includes a planetarium, theatre, gallery and an interesting history exhibition **Discovery of India** (admission free;

Fort Area & Churchgate

& 3.30-7pm Mon-Sat) Several yoga classes are held daily at the Kaivalyadhama Ishwardas Yogic Health Centre. Fees include a ₹600 (students/seniors ₹500/400) monthly membership fee and a ₹500 admission fee.

Yoga Institute   YOGA
(Map p742; ☑26122185; www.theyogainstitute.org; Shri Yogendra Marg, Prabhat Colony, Santa Cruz East; per 1st/2nd month ₹400/300) The Yoga Institute, near Santa Cruz station, has daily classes as well as weekend and weeklong programs.

Iyengar Yogashraya   YOGA
(off Map p724; ☑24948416; www.bksiyengar.com; Elmac House, 126 Senapati Bapat Marg, Lower Parel; per class ₹130) Has classes in Iyengar yoga, including some for the developmentally disabled. There is a ₹113 admission fee.

BollyDancing Mumbai   DANCING
(Map p724; ☑9821130788; www.BollyDancing.co.in; Napean Sea Rd, opp Walsingham School, Malabar Hill) The family-run institute runs choreographed Bollywood dance classes as well as BollySalsa, a salsa-fusion with a fitness edge. Hour-long beginner classes (₹450 per hour)

are held every Thursday (1.30pm) and Friday (noon); or by special arrangement.

Bharatiya Vidya Bhavan   LANGUAGE
(Map p724; ☑23871860; cnr KM Munshi Marg & Ramabai Rd, Girgaum; per hr ₹500) Professor Shukla is based at Bharatiya Vidya Bhavan and offers private Hindi, Marathi, Gujarati and Sanskrit classes. Contact this worldly octogenarian directly to arrange a syllabus and class schedule to suit your needs.

Khatwara Institute   HANDICRAFTS, COOKING
(Shri Khatwari Darbar; Map p742; ☑26042670, cnr Linking Rd & Shri Khatwari Darber Marg, Khar West) The Khatwara Institute offers dozens of courses, lasting from three days to one month, for women only (sorry guys!) in Arabic *mehndi* (decorative henna tattoos), 'basic' *mehndi*, block printing, embroidery, sewing and cooking, among other things. Call Vanita for details.

☞ Tours

Fiona Fernandez's *Ten Heritage Walks of Mumbai* (₹395) contains excellent walking tours in the city, with fascinating historical background.

The Government of India tourist office (p751) can arrange **multilingual guides** (per half-/full day ₹600/750). Guides using a foreign language other than English will charge at least ₹225 extra.

Reality Tours & Travel DHARAVI TOUR
(Map p728; ✆9820822253; www.realitytoursandtrav el.com; 1/26 Akbar House, Nawroji F Rd, Colaba; short/ long tours ₹500/1000) Runs socially responsible tours of Dharavi (p736). Photography is strictly forbidden and funds from the tour plus 80% of post-tax profits go to the agency's own NGO, **Reality Gives** (www.realitygives.org), which runs a kindergarten and community centre in Dharavi. Enter the office through SSS Corner store on Nawroji F Rd.

Bombay Heritage Walks WALKING
(✆23690992; www.bombayheritagewalks.com) Run by two enthusiastic architects, has the best city tours. Private two-hour guided tours are ₹1500 for up to three people, ₹500 for each additional person.

MTDC CITY TOUR
(Maharashtra Tourism Development Corporation; Map p728; ✆22841877; Apollo Bunder; 1hr tour ₹120; ⊙8.30am-4pm Tue-Sun & 5.30-8pm Sat & Sun) Runs open-deck bus tours of illuminated heritage buildings on weekends at 7pm and 8.15pm. They depart from and can be booked at the booth near Apollo Bunder.

Cruises CRUISE
(✆22026364; ⊙9am-7pm) A cruise on Mumbai Harbour is a good way to escape the city and a chance to see the Gateway of India as it was intended. Ferry rides (₹60, 30 minutes) depart from the Gateway of India.

Traansway International CITY TOUR
(✆9920488712; traanswaytours@gmail.com; per 1-/2-/3-person tour ₹2500/3500/4500) Runs five-hour day or night tours of South Mumbai's sights. Prices include pick-up and drop-off.

H2O Water Sports Complex CRUISE
(Map p724; ✆23677546; www.drishtigroup.com; Marine Dr, Mafatlal Beach; ⊙10am-10pm Oct-May)

BOLLYWOOD DREAMS

Mumbai is the glittering epicentre of India's gargantuan Hindi-language film industry. From silent beginnings with a cast of all-male actors (some in drag) in the 1913 epic *Raja Harishchandra* and the first talkie, *Lama Ara* (1931), it now churns out more than 1000 films a year – more than Hollywood. Not surprising considering it has a captive audience of one-sixth of the world's population, as well as a sizable Non-Resident Indian (NRI) following.

Every part of India has its regional film industry, but Bollywood continues to entrance the nation with its escapist formula in which all-singing, all-dancing lovers fight and conquer the forces keeping them apart. These days, Hollywood-inspired thrillers and action extravaganzas vie for moviegoers' attention alongside the more family-oriented saccharine formulas.

Bollywood stars can attain near godlike status in India and star-spotting is a favourite pastime in Mumbai's posher establishments.

Extra, Extra!

Studios sometimes want Westerners as extras to add a whiff of international flair (or provocative dress, which locals often won't wear) to a film. It's become so common, in fact, that 100,000 junior actors nearly went on strike in 2008 to protest, among other things, losing jobs to foreigners, who work for less.

If you're still game, just hang around Colaba where studio scouts, recruiting for the following day's shooting, will find you. A day's work pays ₹500. You'll get lunch, and other snacks if you start early or finish late. Transport is usually by 2nd-class train unless there are enough tourists to justify private transport. The day can be long and hot with loads of standing around the set; not everyone has a positive experience. Complaints range from lack of food and water to dangerous situations and intimidation when extras don't 'comply' with the director's orders. Others describe the behind-the-scenes peek as a fascinating experience. Before agreeing to anything, always ask for the scout's identification and go with your gut.

Arranges 45-minute day (₹170 per person, minimum four people) and night (₹280, 7pm to 11pm) cruises.

Taj Yacht CRUISE
(up to 10 people per 2hr ₹48,000) For the luxury version, hire this yacht; contact the Taj Mahal Palace, Mumbai (p736) for details.

🎭 Festivals & Events

Mumbai Festival MUSIC, DANCE
Based at several stages around the city, it showcases the food, dance and culture of Mumbai in January.

Banganga Festival MUSIC
(www.maharashtratourism.gov.in) A two-day classical-music festival held in January at the Banganga Tank.

Kala Ghoda Festival ARTS, CULTURE
(www.kalaghodaassociation.com) Getting bigger and more sophisticated each year, this two-week-long offering in February has a packed program of arts performances and exhibitions.

eElephanta Festival MUSIC
(www.maharashtratourism.gov.in) Classical music and dance on Elephanta Island in February.

Nariyal Poornima HINDU
(www.rakhifestival.com) Festivals in the tourist hub of Colaba kick off with this celebration in August at the start of the fishing season after the monsoon.

Ganesh Chaturthi HINDU
Mumbai's biggest annual festival – a 10- to 11-day event in August or September in celebration of the elephant-headed deity Ganesh – sweeps up the entire city. On the first, third, fifth, seventh and 10th days of the festival families and communities take their Ganesh statues to the seashore and auspiciously drown them: the 10th day, which sees millions descending on Girgaum Chowpatty to submerge the largest statues, is pure mayhem.

Colaba Festival ARTS
A small October arts festival in Colaba that sometimes overlaps with Diwali festivities.

security is Fort Knox level – guests can only access their own floor via elevator keys. All of the hotel bars – including the legendary **Harbour Bar**, Mumbai's first licensed bar – and restaurants have been redesigned, rounding out a triumphant return for one of Mumbai's most enduring symbols.

YWCA

GUESTHOUSE $$

(☏22025053; www.ywcaic.info; 18 Madame Cama Rd; s/d/t/q incl breakfast, dinner & taxes ₹2024/3000/4200/6000; ✳@☎) The YWCA presents a frustrating dilemma: It's immaculate and surprisingly good, considering it's a cool ₹1000 cheaper than most in its class. Rates include tax, breakfast, dinner, 'bed tea', free wi-fi ...*and a newspaper,* so it's the best value (and location, for that matter) within miles. But there's a trade-off here with a series of unorthodox rules, including the very stubborn policy of not allowing early check-in – even if your room is ready – unless you pay extra.

Hotel Moti

GUESTHOUSE $$

(☏22025714; hotelmotiinternational@yahoo.co.in; 10 Best Marg; s/d/tr with AC incl tax from ₹1800/2000/3200; ✳@) This traveller's haven occupies the ground floor of a gracefully crumbling, beautiful colonial-era building. Simple rooms have whispers of charm and some nice surprises, like ornate stucco ceilings and Western showers. Some are huge and all have fridges filled with soft drinks and bottled water, which is charged at cost – one of the many signs of the pragmatic and friendly management.

Sea Shore Hotel

GUESTHOUSE $

(☏22874237; 4th fl, Kamal Mansion, Arthur Bunder Rd; s/d without bathroom ₹500/700) In a building housing several budget guesthouses, the Sea Shore will go above and beyond your expectations for the price, mainly due to a spiffy new makeover that has turned ratty plywood walls and shoebox-sized rooms into simple but near hotel-quality accommodation, with communal bathrooms and sinks that approach those of design hotels. On the floor below, the same owners offer **India Guest House** (☏22833769; s/d without bathroom ₹350/450) with the same new bathrooms but no further renovations at research time.

Hotel Suba Palace

HOTEL $$$

(☏22020636; www.hotelsubapalace.com; Battery St; s/d with AC incl breakfast ₹4400/5170; ✳@☎) Teetering precariously on the edge of boutique hotel, the Suba Palace oozes soothing neutral tones, from the tiny taupe shower tiles in the contemporary bathrooms to the creamy crown moulding and beige quilted headboards in the tastefully remodelled rooms. Comfy, quiet and central.

Salvation Army Red Shield Guest House

GUESTHOUSE $

(☏22841824; red_shield@vsnl.net; 30 Mereweather Rd; dm incl breakfast ₹225, d/tr/q with full board ₹725/991/1368, d with AC & full board ₹1199; ✳@) Salvy's is a Mumbai institution popular with travellers counting every rupee. The large, ascetic dorms are clean, though ratty mattresses encourage bed bugs. All rooms have their own bathroom; some are not attached but you get a private key. Dorm beds cannot be reserved in advance so come just after the 9am kickout to ensure a spot.

Ascot Hotel

HOTEL $$$

(☏66385566; www.ascothotel.com; 38 Garden Rd; d with AC incl breakfast from ₹6000; ✳@☎) Marble-meets-modern at this classy hotel with hardwood hallways leading to boutiquey rooms with big headboards, bathtubs, desks, new LCD TVs, and lots of natural light and tree views.

MUMBAI FOR CHILDREN

Rina Mehta's www.mustformums.com has the Mumbai Mums' Guide, with info on crèches, health care and even kids' salsa classes in the city. *Time Out Mumbai* (₹50) often lists fun things to do with kids.

Little tykes with energy to burn will love the Gorai Island amusement parks, **Esselworld** (www.esselworld.in; adult/child ₹510/380; ☉11am-7pm) and **Water Kingdom** (www.waterkingdom.in; adult/child ₹510/380; ☉11am-7pm). Both are well maintained and have lots of rides, slides and shade. Combined tickets are ₹710/580 (adult/child). Low-season weekday ticket prices are lower. It's a ₹35 ferry ride from Borivali jetty.

BNHS (p731) and Yuhina Eco-Media (p731) often conduct nature trips for kids while **Yoga Sutra** (Map p724; ☏32107067; www.yogasutra.co.in; Chinoy Mansions, Bhulabhai Desai Rd, Cumballa Hill; drop-in classes ₹300) has kids' yoga classes, taught in English.

GAY & LESBIAN MUMBAI

The decriminalisation of homosexuality – a law on the Indian books for 148 years – by Delhi's High Court in July 2009 means India is out of the closet, but cosmopolitan Mumbai has been slow on the uptake.

The pioneering GLBTQ magazine *Bombay Dost* (www.bombaydost.co.in) organises **Sunday High**, a twice-monthly screening of queer-interest films, usually in the suburbs, and is an excellent resource on happenings around town. You can pick up a copy at Oxford Bookstore (p750) in Churchgate as well as the Humsafar Trust (p1166) offices around town. **Queer Ink** (www.queer-ink.com) is an online Indian bookstore specialising in gay and lesbian books and magazines of every ilk.

The **Kashish-Mumbai International Queer Film Festival** (www.mumbaiqueerfest.com) made its debut in 2010 and is expected to become an annual event. *XXWHY*, a documentary short by Mumbai-based filmmaker Dr Bharaty Manjula about Kerala's first out female-to-male transgender, was the big winner in the inaugural event.

Around town, no dedicated gay and lesbian bars/clubs have yet opened but gay-friendly 'safe house' venues often host private gay parties on specific nights – see the following. Check out Gay Bombay (www.gaybombay.org) for listings.

Azaardbaazaar   BOUTIQUE
(Map p742); 16th/33rd Rd, Bandra; ⊙closed Monday) Billed as India's first GLBTQ pride store, tucked in a garage off 33rd Rd.

Just Around the Corner   CAFE
(Map p742); cnr 24th & 30th Rd, Bandra West; mains ₹95-375; ⊙lunch) This great cafe is a popular meeting point for the GLBTQ crowd, but it's popular with everyone for its tolerance across the board.

Voodoo Pub   NIGHTCLUB
(Map p728; ☎22841959; Kamal Mansion, Arthur Bunder Rd, Colaba; cover ₹300) This dark and sweaty bar has unofficially hosted Mumbai's only regular gay night on Saturdays since 1994 – long before it was trendy (or legal) to do so. There is little going on other nights of the week, but staff are screened for open-mindedness and it's considered gay friendly all week long.

Eclipse Lounge   NIGHTCLUB
(off Map p730; 11/13 Walchand Hirachand Marg, Ballard Estate) Formerly known as Let's Scream, the dark and iffy Eclipse was quick to point out it isn't gay, but does often host private gay parties.

Bentley's Hotel   HOTEL $$
(☎22841474; www.bentleyshotel.com; 17 Oliver Rd; s/d incl breakfast & tax from ₹1690/2090; ▒) Colonial charm aplenty, with old-school floor tiles and wooden furniture; its location spread out over several buildings on Oliver St and Henry Rd can all seem a bit *The Shining*–like isolated.

Regent Hotel   HOTEL $$$
(☎22871853/4; www.regenthotelcolaba.com; 8 Best Marg; r/tr with AC incl breakfast & tax ₹4290/4620; ▒@) An upper-scale Arabian-flavoured hotel with marble surfaces and soft pastels aplenty. The retro-chic breakfast area fills the 1st floor hallway, so avoid rooms 101–110 if you plan to sleep in.

FORT, CHURCHGATE & MARINE DRIVE

For mapped locations of the following venues see Map p730, unless otherwise stated.

TOP CHOICE Residency Hotel   HOTEL $$
(Map p730; ☎22625525; www.residencyhotel.com; 26 Rustom Sidhwa Marg, Fort; s/d from ₹2500/2700; ▒@☏) This polarising hotel can be hit or miss. On one hand, the small rooms in the original building – where a waft of sweet lemongrass graces the lobby – are older but come with fridges, flat-screen TVs and flip-flops (thongs), while the newly annexed building next door houses a far more modern design-style hotel with rain showers, leather-walled elevators and free wi-fi. But during our visit, a Londoner was overheard complaining, 'One of our rooms

smells like cigarettes, the other like urine', so it's a gamble.

Welcome Hotel
HOTEL $$

(off Map p730; ☑6631488; welcome _hotel@vsnl. com; 257 Shahid Bhagat Singh Rd; s/d incl breakfast from ₹2783/3278, without bathroom from ₹1397/1595; ❋⊚) Its reputation as immaculate was crushed when a cockroach scurried across our authoring desk but, all things considered, this is a cleaner-than-most midrange choice. New top-floor executive rooms evoke a different hotel altogether – a boutique makeover has turned them into something more LA than Bombay. Rates include evening tea in the rooms. For value under ₹2000, it's tough to beat.

Sea Green Hotels
HOTEL $$

(Map p730; s/d ₹2500/3150; ❋⊚) Seagreen Hotel (☑66336525; www.seagreenhotel.com; 145 Marine Dr; Sea Green South Hotel (☑22821613; www.sea greensouth.com; 145A Marine Dr) These identical art deco hotels have spacious but spartan AC rooms, originally built in the 1940s to house British soldiers. Snag a sea-view room – they're the same price – and you've secured top value in this price range (even with the 10% service charge).

West End Hotel
HOTEL $$$

(Map p730; ☑22039121; www.westendhotelmum bai.com; 45 New Marine Lines; s/d with AC from ₹3900/4500; ❋⊚) This accidentally retro hotel boasts a nonchalant funky vibe built around old-fashioned rooms that are spacious, with bathtubs, shagalicious rugs and modish daybeds.

Trident
HOTEL $$$

(Oberoi Hotel; Map p730; ☑66324343; www.trid enthotels.com; Marine Dr, Nariman Point; s/d from ₹18,750/20,000; ❋⊚⊚⊠) The Trident is, along with the Oberoi, part of the Oberoi Hotel complex. But the Trident wins out both on price and on the spiffy, streamlined design of its restaurants, bars and pool area. The rates above are rack, but you can get the rooms for half depending on occupancy.

InterContinental
HOTEL $$$

(☑39879999; www.intercontinental.com; 135 Marine Dr, Churchgate; r incl breakfast from ₹19,500; ❋⊚⊚⊠) Very sleek for an InterContinental. All earth tones and Buddha chic, the spacious deluxe rooms are sizeable in their own right, while the halfmoon corner suites mirror the curved elegance of Marine Drive's Queen's Necklace. The stunning **Dome** bar and restaurant stylishly graces the rooftop and overlooks the sea, while **Koh** turns Thai food on its head at the lobby level.

Traveller's Inn
GUESTHOUSE $

(Map p730; ☑22644685; 26 Adi Marzban Rd, Ballard Estate; dm ₹500, r ₹900, with AC ₹1150; ❋⊚⊚) On a quiet, tree-lined street, the tiny Traveller's Inn underwent a spiffy renovation in 2010 and now boasts bigger rooms (and thinner hallways); and new air-con units, lockers and windows, making a good budget choice that much better.

Hotel Lawrence
GUESTHOUSE $

(☑22843618; 3rd fl, ITTS House, 33 Sai Baba Marg; s/d/tr without bathroom incl breakfast & tax ₹600/700/900) A bottom-barrel guesthouse tucked away in a little side lane offering clean crashpads that are popular with shoestring meditators – and a management that tends to enforce moral judgements on guests.

Hotel City Palace
HOTEL $$

(☑22666666; www.hotelcitypalace.net; 121 City Tce, Walchand Hirachand Marg; s/d without bathroom from ₹803/1350, r with bathroom from ₹2200; ❋) Organised and clean, across from CST. If you just got off an overnight

---

DON'T MISS

KOTACHIWADI

This storied *wadi* (hamlet) is a bastion clinging onto Mumbai life as it was before highrises. A Christian enclave of elegant two-storey wooden mansions, it's 500m northeast of Girgaum Chowpatty (Map p724), lying amid Mumbai's predominantly Hindu and Muslim neighbourhoods. These winding laneways allow a wonderful glimpse into a quiet life free of rickshaws and taxis. It's not large by any means, but you can lose considerable moments wandering these fascinating alleyways – no doubt in shock that the hustle and bustle of the real Mumbai is but steps away.

To find it, aim for **St Teresa's Church** (Map p724) on the corner of Jagannath Shankarsheth Marg (JS Marg) and RR Roy Marg (Charni Rd), then head directly opposite the church on JS Marg and duck down the second and third lanes on your left.

train, the rooms are no bigger than a sleeper compartment, so you won't suffer any disorientation at wake up.

THE SUBURBS

There are several midrange hotels on Nehru Rd Extension in Vile Parle East near the domestic airport, but rooms are overpriced and only useful for early or late flights. Juhu is convenient for Juhu Beach and for the restaurants, shops and clubs in Bandra.

TOP CHOICE **Iskcon**   GUESTHOUSE **$$**
(Map p742; ☑26206860; guesthouse.mumbai@pamho.net; Hare Krishna Land, Juhu; s/d incl tax ₹2095/2495, with AC incl tax ₹2395/2995; ❀@) If you are looking for an experience rather than a shelter, this efficiently managed guesthouse, part of Juhu's lively Hare Krishna complex, is one of Mumbai's most interesting choices. The lobby looks out into the temple, while rooms in the two flamingo-pink towers have pretty lacquered *sankheda* (lacquered country wood) furniture from Gujarat and those in the original tower have semicircular balconies. The whole things feel like you are in the thick of India, which is more than can be said for most of the resort or business-oriented hotels out this way. Don't miss the evening *aarti* (candle-lighting ritual).

Four Seasons Hotel   HOTEL **$$$**
(off Map p724; ☑24818000; www.fourseasons.com; 114 Dr E Moses Rd, Worli; r from ₹15,200; ❀@☎☀) This modern Four Seasons is everything you expect it to be: exemplary service, psychic staff, everything classic yet slick as oil. Now with the addition of its fashionable rooftop lounge **Aer** (p746), it's hip as hopscotch, too.

Hotel Kemps Corner   HOTEL **$$**
(Map p724; ☑23634646; 131 August Kranti Marg; s/d from ₹2700/3800; ❀☎) A general spiffing-up of the place means the prices at this friendly midrange are no longer the deal they once were, but it remains a great spot in the heart of the Kemp's Corner fashion bonanza (which is a lot less frenzied than Colaba or Fort) and walking distance to Haji Ali Mosque and Girgaum Chowpatty. Service comes with more smiles than most, though it takes a serious dive on Sundays.

Juhu Residency   BOUTIQUE HOTEL **$$$**
(Map p742; ☑67834949; www.juhuresidency.com; 148B Juhu Tara Rd, Juhu; s/d with AC incl breakfast from ₹5000; ❀@☎) A makeover two years ago turned this into a quasi-boutique hotel, with sleek marble floors, king-size beds (in

the premium rooms), dark woods and artistic bedspreads imported from Singapore. There are three restaurants for 18 rooms, and one, the **Melting Pot**, garners accolades for its Indian cuisine. A great choice if you're looking for something hip and intimate that won't cost you a fortune.

Hotel Suba International   BOUTIQUE HOTEL **$$$**
(Map p742; ☑67076707; www.hotelsubainternational.com; Sahar Rd, Vile Parle East; s/d with AC incl breakfast from ₹6000/7000; ❀☎) Brand-spanking new at time of research, this hi-tech boutique business hotel is just 1km from the international terminal, 3km from the domestic. It's laid out in slick blacks and glossy marble, with clean lines and lots of masculine hardwoods and design-forward touches. All the electronics in the rooms are controlled wirelessly by iPod Touch! If it's full, its sister property in Andheri East, **Hotel Suba Galaxy** (Map p742; ☑26821188; www.hotelsubagalaxy.com; NS Phadke Rd, Andheri East; s/d with AC incl breakfast from ₹3200/6000; ❀☎), isn't as shiny but is an acceptable alternative.

Sun-n-Sand   HOTEL **$$$**
(Map p742; ☑66938888; www.sunnsandhotel.com; 39 Juhu Beach, Juhu; r with AC from ₹7500; ❀@☎☀) The Sun-n-Sand has been offering up beachfront hospitality for decades. The newly renovated 4th floor offers shiny new hardwood floors and some bathtubs, but the best rooms remain the sea-facing ones (from ₹8500): lots of silk and the pleasant burnt-orange motif complement the pool, palm-tree and ocean views from the huge window. It's off Juhu Rd, near the old Holiday Inn.

ITC Maratha   HOTEL **$$$**
(Map p742; ☑28303030; www.itcwelcomgroup.in; Sahar Rd, Andheri East; s/d incl breakfast & tax from ₹22,000/23,500; ❀@☎☀) The five-star with the most luxurious Indian character, from the Jaipur-style lattice windows around the atrium to the silk pillows on the beds to Peshawri, one of the best restaurants in town.

Hotel Columbus   HOTEL **$$**
(Map p742; ☑42144343; www.hotelcolumbus.in; 344 Nanda Patkar Rd, Vile Parle East; r with AC from ₹3000; ❀@☎) The best midrange in the domestic airport area, with gussied-up super deluxe rooms (₹4000) with stylised wood-grain accents, flat-screen TVs and an aspiration for high design.

Citizen Hotel   HOTEL **$$$**
(Map p742; ☑66932525; www.citizenhotelmumbai.com; Juhu Tara Rd, Juhu; s/d with AC incl

breakfast from ₹7000/7500; ✳@🛜) The Citizen's location is what you're paying for here, but rooms are also well maintained, with marble floors and marble-top furniture, flat-screen TVs, wi-fi access, fridges – and, of course, excellent beach views.

✕ Eating

In this gastro-epicentre a cornucopia of flavours from all over India collides with international trends and tastebuds. Colaba is home to most of the cheap tourist haunts, while Fort and Churchgate skew more upscale, a trend that continues as you head north to Mahalaxmi and the Central Suburbs, where you'll find Mumbai's most exciting, cutting-edge and expensive restaurants.

For self-caterers, the **Colaba market** (Map p728; Lala Nigam St) has fresh fruit and vegetables. **Saharkari Bhandar Supermarket** (Map p728; 🖉22022248; cnr Colaba Causeway & Wodehouse Rd; ⊗10am-8.30pm) and, even better, **Suryodaya** (Map p730; 🖉22040979; Veer Nariman Rd; ⊗7.30am-8.30pm) are well-stocked supermarkets.

COLABA

For mapped locations of the following venues see Map p728.

Indigo　　　　FUSION, EUROPEAN **$$$**
(🖉66368980; 4 Mandlik Marg; mains ₹525-945; ⊗lunch & dinner) Over a decade in and still a star, Colaba's finest eating option is a gourmet haven serving inventive European cuisine, a long wine list, sleek ambience and a gorgeous roof deck lit with fairy lights. Favourites include excellent kiwi margaritas, tea-grilled quail (₹625), anise-rubbed white salmon (₹725) and inventive takes on traditional cuisine like juniper-berry-cured tandoori chicken (₹625). Its cool quotient has chilled a bit with the focus on the suburbs, but it remains a high-gastronomy favourite.

Bademiya　　　　　　INDIAN **$**
(Tulloch Rd; meals ₹50-100) If you can walk by this street-stall-on-steroids without coming away with a chicken tikka roll in hand, you are a better person than us. This whole street buzzes nightly with punters from all walks of Mumbai life lining up for spicy, fresh grilled treats. If Mumbai street food scares the bejesus out of you, this is the spot to get over it.

Indigo Delicatessen　　　　CAFE **$$**
(Pheroze Bldg, Chhatrapati Shivaji Marg; mains ₹245-495; ⊗9am-midnight) Indigo's casual and less expensive sister is just as big a draw as the original, with cool tunes, warm decor and massive wooden tables. It has breakfast all day (₹155 to ₹295), casual meals, French press coffee, wines (₹300 to ₹690 per glass) and is also a bakery and deli.

Theobroma　　　　　　CAFE **$**
(Colaba Causeway; confections ₹40-85) Theobroma calls its creations 'food of the gods' – and it ain't lying. Dozens of perfectly executed cakes, tarts and chocolates, as well as sandwiches and breads, go well with the coffee here. The genius pistachio-and-green-cardamom truffle (₹30) or decadent chocolate overload brownie (₹65) should send you straight into a glorious sugar coma. A bigger location has opened in Bandra West (Map p742).

Wich Latte　　　　　　CAFE **$$**
(Map p728; Western Breeze Bldg, Colaba; sandwiches ₹120-175) Churning out excellent coffee but trumping both Coffee Day and Barista when it comes to food, Wich Latte bills itself as India's first sandwich cafe. For breakfast, the bagelwiches are an excellent homesick remedy and throughout the day there are salads, sandwiches and pizza. There's also a convenient location in Kala Ghoda (Map p730), but it opens from lunch onwards.

New Laxmi Vilas　　　SOUTH INDIAN **$**
(19A Ram Mansion, Nawroji F Rd; mains ₹23-85) A budget eatery that serves great South India specialities.

KALA GHODA & FORT

TOP CHOICE Khyber　　　NORTH INDIAN **$$$**
(Map p730; ⊗40396666; 145 MG Rd, Fort; mains ₹225-450; ⊗lunch & dinner) Like Bukhara in Delhi, Khyber is an iconic restaurant the thought of which will spark Pavlovian drooling for years to come. The burnt-orange, Afghan-inspired interiors are a multitiered and cavernous maze of moody Mughal royalty art embedded in exposed brick, tasteful antique oil lanterns and urns, and railway-trestle ceilings. As mouth-watering Punjabi/North Indian kebabs, biryanis and curries saunter their way to a who's who of Mumbai's elite, your tastebuds will do a happy dance – before the disheartening realisation: too much food, too little space. Highlights of the meat-centric menu include the Reshmi Kebab Masala, a transcendent dish of cream and yoghurt-marinated chicken drowning in the restaurant's intricate red masala; and its pièce de résistance, *raan* (a whole leg of slow-cooked lamb).

MUMBAI (BOMBAY)

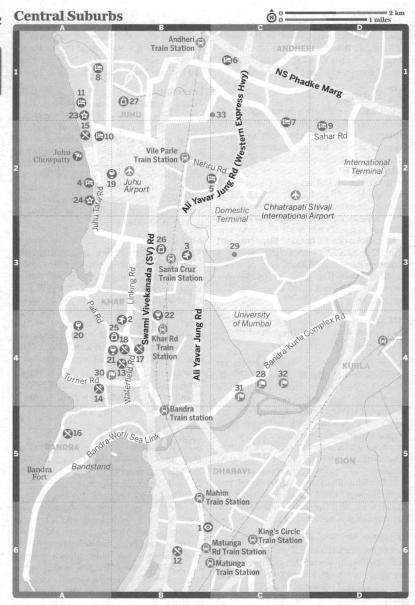

Five Spice　　　　　INDO-CHINESE **$$**
(Map p730; 296A Perin Nariman St, Sangli Bank Bldg, Fort; mains ₹220-275; ⊙lunch & dinner) A 30-minute wait is commonplace at this over-heated, near-divey Indo-Chinese Godsend that's so good, it'll make you downright an-

gry you can't eat Chinese like this at home. The menu is packed with chicken, lamb, prawn and veg dishes, all tantalising, so choosing is an issue. We went for the chick-en in burnt chilli sauce (₹235) and dumped it on a bed of burnt chilli rice (₹185) –

quite possibly the best thing since the fortune cookie. Of course, there's one in Bandra (Map p742).

Trishna SEAFOOD **$$$**
(Map p730; ☑22614991; Sai Baba Marg, Kala Ghoda; mains ₹170-575; ☺lunch & dinner) An outstanding and intimate seafood restaurant focused on Mangalorean preparations. The crab with butter, black pepper and garlic and Hyderabadi fish tikka are house specialities that warrant the hype, while service is underbearing, friendly and helpful. One of the best seafooders in town. Reservations unnecessary before 8pm.

Brittania PARSI **$$**
(off Map p730; Wakefield House, 11 Sprott Rd, Ballard Eatte; mains ₹100-250; ☺lunch Mon-Sat) The kind of place traveller's tales are made of – this Mumbai icon, and its endearing owner, has been going since 1923. The signature dish is the berry *pulao* (₹250) – spiced and boneless mutton or chicken buried in basmati rice and tart barberries, imported to the tune of 1000kg per year from Iran. The owner, Boman Kohinoor – born the year his father opened the place – will take your order and chat your ear off. Dead simple, dead delicious.

Café Moshe CAFE **$$**
(Map p730; Fabindia, 1st fl, Jeroo Bldg, MG Rd, Kala Ghoda; light meals ₹120-270; ☺lunch & dinner) After shopping downstairs, refuel with Moshe's excellent salads, sandwiches, baked goods, coffees and smoothies. There's also a Moshe's in Kemp's Corner (Map p724); and Colaba (Map p728), where you'll find an extended menu, including the famed marinated garlic, mushroom, leek and capsicum open-faced sandwich with melted mozzarella on brown bread.

Mahesh Lunch Home SEAFOOD **$$$**
(Map p730; ☑22023965; 8B Cowasji Patel St, Fort; mains ₹150-600; ☺lunch & dinner) A great place to try Mangalorean seafood in Mumbai. It's renowned for its ladyfish, pomfret, lobster and crabs; the *rawas tikka* (marinated

DABBA-WALLAHS

A small miracle of logistics, Mumbai's 5000 *dabba*-wallahs (*dabba* means food container; also called tiffin-wallahs) work tirelessly to deliver hot lunches to office workers throughout the city.

Lunch boxes are picked up each day from restaurants and homes and carried on heads, bicycles and trains to a centralised sorting station. A sophisticated system of numbers and colours (many wallahs are illiterate) identifies the destination of each lunch. More than 200,000 meals are delivered – always on time, come (monsoon) rain or (searing) shine.

This system has been used for centuries and, on average, there's only about one mistake per six million deliveries. No wonder *dabba*-wallahs take immense pride in their work.

white salmon) and tandoori pomfret are outstanding. There's also a branch on Juhu Tara Rd (Map p742).

Badshah Snacks & Drinks INDIAN **$**
(Map p724; snacks ₹30-110) Opposite Crawford market, Badshah's been serving snacks, fruit juices and its famous *falooda* (rose-flavoured drink made with milk, cream, nuts and vermicelli – like swallowing a bed of roses!) to hungry bargain-hunters for more than 100 years.

Rajdhani INDIAN **$$**
(Map p724; 361 Sheikh Memon St, Kalbadevi; thali ₹249; ☺lunch & dinner Mon-Sat, lunch Sun) Opposite Mangaldaas Market, Rajdhani is famous for its Gujarati and Rajasthani thalis. On Sundays, dinner isn't served and thali prices jump ₹50.

CHURCHGATE

For mapped locations of the following venues, see Map p730.

TOP CHOICE **Koh** THAI **$$$**
(InterContinental Marine Dr; ☑39879999; mains ₹495-925; ☺lunch & dinner) India's first signature Thai restaurant is Mumbai's hottest dining destination. Celebrity chef Ian Kittichai works his native cuisine into an international frenzy of flavour that starts with the 'liquid gastronomy', which might be a jasmine and honey martini or a Bloody Mary made with lemongrass-infused vodka and *sriracha* chilli; from there the envelope is further pushed into revelational dishes like the 12-hour lamb shank Massaman curry – pair it with hot-stone garlic rice – that throws preconceived notions about Thai food to the Mumbai curb.

Samrat SOUTH INDIAN **$$**
(☑42135401; Prem Ct, J Tata Rd; lunch/dinner thalis ₹220/260; ☺lunch & dinner) If this is your first thali, strap yourself in – the cavalcade of taste and texture will leave you wondering what the hell just happened – *then* they bring the rice. With a dizzying number of concoctable bites, it's as adventurous and diverse as India itself. Samrat is the anchor behind a pure-veg empire in the same location, which includes **210°C**, an outdoor cafe and bakery, and **Relish**, a funky spot that's home to Asian-Mexican-Lebanese fusion.

K Rustom SWEETS **$**
(87 Stadium House, Veer Nariman Rd; dessert ₹40; ☺lunch & dinner) Nothing but a few metal freezers, but the ice-cream sandwich (₹40) has been pleasing Mumbaikar palettes since 1953. Delish.

GIRGAUM CHOWPATTY

For mapped locations of the following venues see Map p724.

TOP CHOICE **New Kulfi Centre** SWEETS **$**
(cnr Chowpatty Seaface & Sardar V Patel Rd; kulfi per 100gm ₹20-40; ☺9am-1.30am) Serves the best *kulfi* (firm-textured ice cream served in killer flavours like pistachio, rose and saffron) you'll have anywhere, which means it will rock your pants off. When you order, the *kulfi* is placed on a betel-nut leaf and then weighed on an ancient scale – which makes it even better.

Cream Centre CAFE **$$**
(Chowpatty Seaface; mains ₹100-249; ☺lunch & dinner) This sleek and contemporary Indian diner is hugely popular for its pure-veg hodgepodge of Indian, Mexican and Lebanese as well as its extensive menu of sizzling sundaes (₹195 to ₹220), which take 'hot fudge' to the boiling point!

MAHALAXMI TO WORLI

For mapped locations of the following venues see Map p724.

Tote on the Turf
FUSION $$$

(Map p724; ☑61577777; Near Gate No 5 & 6, Mahalaxmi Racecourse, Mahalaxmi; mains ₹485-985; ✆lunch & dinner) Funky, all-white tree-branch interiors and ridiculously beautiful crowds aside, this hip new restaurant from the folks who own Indigo dishes out Euro-fusion, split into veg (like green garlic risotto with palm hearts, cherry tomatoes and chilli feta) and non-veg (grilled chicken with stuffed Bhavnagri chilli and mustard sauce). Don't dismiss the thin, wood-fired pizzas, which caused a bit of order envy on our visit.

Cafe Noorani
NORTH INDIAN $$

(Tardeo Rd, Haji Ali Circle; mains ₹120-180; ✆lunch & dinner) This almost-retro diner is a requisite stop before or after visiting Haji Ali Mosque. On the menu is the gamut of Moghlai and Punjabi staples, all done well and cheap. The chicken tikka biryani is so good, you'll forgive a bite or two of gristle.

THE SUBURBS
North Mumbai is home to the city's trendiest dining, centered on Bandra West and Juhu. For mapped locations of the following venues see Map p742.

TOP CHOICE Peshawri
NORTH INDIAN $$$

(☑28303030; ITC Maratha, Sahar Rd; mains ₹700-1675; ✆lunch & dinner) Make this Indian northwest frontier restaurant, just outside the international airport, your first or last stop in Mumbai. It's pricy as hell, but you won't regret forking out the ₹2700 (feeds two easily) for the exquisite Sikandari *raan* (leg of spring lamb braised in malt vinegar, cinnamon, black cumin) – it will forever skew your standards of lamb. The buttery dhal Bukhara (a thick black dhal cooked for a day; ₹700) is also memorable.

Culture Curry
SOUTH INDIAN $$

(Kataria Rd, Matunga West; mains ₹209-459; ✆lunch & dinner) As the Culture Curry folks rightly point out, there's a lot more to southern food than *idli* and dosas. Exquisite dishes from all over the south, ranging from Andhra and Coorg to Kerala, are the specialty here. Vegies are particularly well served: the Kooru Curry (kidney and green beans in coconut gravy; ₹179) is extraordinary. The same owners run **Goa Portuguesa** (attached), specialising in fiery Goan dishes, where the 'Chicken Chilly Fry' is also a knockout (₹299). From Matunga station, it's about 750m west on Katinga Rd on the left.

Sheesha
NORTH INDIAN $$

(☑66770555; 7th fl, Shoppers Stop, Linking Rd, Bandra West; mains ₹145-295; ✆lunch & dinner) With maybe the most beautiful ambience in town, Sheesha's alfresco rooftop lair has glass lanterns hanging from wooden beams, comfy couches and coloured-glass lamps high above the city and shopping madness below. You almost forget about the food, though you shouldn't; the countless kebabs and curries are outstanding. Otherwise, it's all hookah action (no alcohol). Order double apple: 'It's way better than apple', as one Desi beauty put it. Reserve on weekends.

Lemongrass
SOUTHEAST ASIAN $$

(Carlton Ct, cnr of Turner & Pali Rds, Bandra West; mains ₹215-400; ✆lunch & dinner) In a good spot for watching Bandra streetlife, Lemongrass serves up tasty Southeast Asian fare from Myanmar (Burma) to Indonesia. The veg or meat *khowsuey* (Burmese noodles with a coconut broth; ₹400) is superb; and the service is above and beyond for its price: staff fronted our rickshaw fare when we didn't have small change; and the owner told us, 'If you don't like the food, send it back'. No, he didn't know who we were.

Salt Water Cafe
FUSION $$$

(87 Chapel Rd, Bandra; mains ₹180-500) This foodie find offers one of Mumbai's most ambitious menus. It made a name for itself for marrying dramatically opposing flavours (green peppercorn chicken with grape jus, cardamom and carrot mash) but most of the menu is just mouth-watering global fusion. The aesthetically cold design is as much of a contrast to India as some of the recipes, and service grinds to a crawl at lunchtime, but it's a lovely spot to twist up your tastebuds after a curry overdose.

Prithvi Cafe
CAFE $

(Map p742; Juhu Church Rd, Juhu; light meals ₹70-140) You'd never know it was there, but this bohemian cafe attached to the Prithvi Theatre is a cultural hub of intellectuals, artists and theatre types who tuck themselves away in the lush, bamboo-heavy spot for all-day breakfast, cheap kebab value meals, sandwiches and savoury croissants. The non-veg combo is distinctly average, but the vibe more than makes up for it. Try the Irish coffee instead!

🍸 Drinking

Mumbai's lax attitude to alcohol means that there are loads of places to drink – from hole-in-the-wall beer bars and chichi lounges to brash, multilevel superclubs – but the 25% liquor tax means bills can bring sticker shock.

If it's the caffeine buzz you're after, Barista and Café Coffee Day cafes are ubiquitous in Mumbai.

Kala Ghoda Café
CAFE

(Map p730; 10 Ropewalk Ln, Fort) An artsy, modern and miniscule cafe that's a favourite among journalists and other creative types, who come for the organic Arabica and Robusta coffee sourced from sustainable plantations, organic teas, small bite sandwiches and salads, and charming breakfasts – and then fight for one of the few tables. Even the *jaggery* (natural sugar) is organic. It's across the street from Trishna, but uses the English street name.

Mocha Bar
CAFE

(☺10am-1.30am); Churchgate (Map p730; 82 Veer Nariman Rd); Juhu (Map p742; 67 Juhu Tara Rd) This atmospheric Arabian-styled cafe is often filled to the brim with bohemians and students deep in esoteric conversation, Bollywood gossip, or just a hookah pipe. Cosy, low-cushioned seating (including some old cinema seats), exotic coffees, shakes and teas, and global comfort cuisine promote an intellectually chilaxed vibe.

First Floor
CAFE

(Map p724; Sitaram Bldg, Dr Dadabhai Naoroji Rd; ☺7pm-4am) This local's secret is the comedown cafe of choice; there's no alcohol, but the party ends up here, anyway - especially on Wednesdays and Saturdays – when the cool kids pack the house from 1.30am to 4am to sop up the drunkenness over a Continental mix of burgers, Mexican, Italian and sheeshas. It's above Zaffran, a worthy Muglai restaurant in its own right.

Haji Ali Juice Centre
JUICE BAR

(Lala Lajpatrai Rd, Haji Ali Circle; ☺5am-1.30am Mon-Sat) An excellent juice megastand, strategically placed at the entrance to Haji Ali Mosque. A great cool off after the hot sun, overwater pilgrimage.

Samovar Café
CAFE

(Map p730; Jehangir Art Gallery, 161B MG Rd, Kala Ghoda; meals ₹60-90; ☺closed Sun) This intimate place inside the art gallery overlooks the gardens of the Prince of Wales Museum.

Cha Bar
TEAHOUSE

(Map p730; Oxford Bookstore, Apeejay House, 3 Dinsha Wachha Marg, Churchgate; teas ₹30-

80; ☺10am-9.30pm) Thirteen pages of exotic teas, including organic and ayurvedic; and tasty snacks amid lots of books.

SOUTH MUMBAI

For mapped locations of the following venues see Map p728, unless otherwise indicated.

Cafe Mondegar
BAR

(☑22020591; Metro House, 5A Shahid Bhagat Singh Rd, Colaba) Like Leopold's, 'Mondys' draws a healthy foreign crowd, too, but with a better mix of friendly Indians, who all cosy up together in the much smaller space, bonding over the excellent jukebox, one of Mumbai's few. Good music, good people.

Busaba
BAR, LOUNGE

(☑22043779; 4 Mandlik Marg) Red walls and contemporary Buddha art give this loungey restaurant-bar a nouveau Tao. It's next to Indigo so gets the same trendy crowd but serves cheaper, more potent cocktails (₹330 to ₹480). There's a low-key DJ Wednesdays to Sundays from 8.30pm. The upstairs restaurant serves pan-Asian (mains ₹350 to ₹575); its back room feels like a posh treehouse. Reserve ahead if you want a table.

Leopold's Café
BAR

(cnr Colaba Causeway & Nawroji F Rd) Love it or hate it, most tourists end up at this Mumbai travellers' institution at one time or another. Around since 1871, Leopold's has wobbly ceiling fans, open-plan seating and a rambunctious atmosphere conducive to swapping tales with random strangers. Although there's a huge menu, the lazy evening beers – especially the 3L yards – are the real draw.

Café Universal
BAR

(Map p730; 299 Shahid Bhagat Singh Rd; ☺9am-11pm Mon-Sat, 4-11pm Sun) A little bit of France near CST. The Universal has an art nouveau look to it, with butterscotch-colour walls, a wood-beam ceiling and marble chandeliers, and is a cosy place for happy hour and Kingfisher drafts (₹100).

Dome
BAR

(Map p730; Hotel InterContinental, 135 Marine Dr, Churchgate) This white-on-white rooftop lounge has awesome views of Mumbai's curving seafront while cocktails beckon the hip young things of Mumbai nightly.

THE SUBURBS

TOP CHOICE Aer
BAR/LOUNGE

(off Map p724; Four Seasons Hotel, 33rd fl, 114 Dr E Moses Rd, Worli) With astounding city views on one side and equally impressive sea views on the other, we'll be damned if this isn't India's most impressive tipple. Aer is a slick, open-air rooftop lounge with its share of plush couches as well as weird, uncomfortable plastic 'lounge chairs' that cater more to form than function. You'll need to remortgage your home for something shaken and stirred (₹600), but the ₹250 Kingfishers are a steal at these views. A DJ spins low-key house and techno nightly from 9pm, but who cares? It's all about the eye candy, both near and far.

Shiro
LOUNGE

(☑66156969; Bombay Dyeing Mills Compound, Worli) Shiro has its share of detractors, who squabble: Overpriced! Too pretentious! Snippy service! Sub-par food! (*Maybe*...but we adored our crispy spicy avocado sushi roll). Regardless, its status as a shock-and-awe venue for a cocktail cannot be denied. Water pours from the hands of towering Japanese faux-stone goddesses into lotus ponds, which reflect shimmering light on the walls. It's totally over the top, but the drinks are excellent and the DJs spin some mean house (Saturdays) and retro (Fridays).

Olive Bar & Kitchen
BAR

(Map p742; ☑26058228; Pali Hill Tourist Hotel, 14 Union Park, Khar West; ⊙7.30pm-1.30am) Hip, gorgeous and snooty, this longtime Mediterranean-style restaurant and bar has light and delicious food (mains ₹525 to ₹950), soothing DJ sounds and pure Ibiza-meets-Mykonos decor (even the host is Greek). Thursday and weekends are packed. There's a second branch at Mahalaxmi Racecourse.

WTF!
BAR

(Map p742; 8 Vora Bldg, 3rd Khar Rd, Khar) Hilariously named and an equally good time, rambunctious WTF! (pronounced as letters) is a small venue divided in two rooms, one a lipstick-red den of pop culture kitsch and Formica, the other dumbed down with the cricket likely to be on the big screen. The DJ spins right in your face beside the front door – a loud and brash wall of international pop trash. Staff wouldn't call us a taxi at the end of the night, though – WTF?

Toto's Garage
BAR

(Map p742; ☑26005494; 30 Lourdes Heaven, Pali Naka, Bandra West; ⊙6pm-1am) Forget the beautiful people. Toto's is a down-to-earth local dive done up in a mechanic's theme where you can go in your dirty clothes, drink pitchers of beer and listen to music that gave us

guilty pleasure with the back-to-back-to-back Savage Garden–Linkin Park–AC/DC set. Get there early or you won't get a seat.

Elbo Room
PUB

(Map p742; St Teresa's Rd, Khar West) A genuine bar that approaches resto-lounge but thankfully falls short. Instead, it's a pub reminiscent of home and a good bet for wines by the glass (₹275 to ₹700) screening both English Premier League and Bundesliga football matches. The Italian-Indian menu is best enjoyed on the terrace while the serious drinkers – no shortage of expats among them – stay inside.

☆ Entertainment

The daily English-language tabloid *Mid-Day* incorporates a guide to Mumbai entertainment. Newspapers and *Time Out Mumbai* (p751) list events and film screenings, while www.nh7.in has live music listings. The cutting-edge **Bombay Elektrik Projekt** (www.bombayelektrik.com) organises everything from live DJs to poetry slams to short film screenings.

It would be a crime not to see a movie in India's film capital. Unfortunately, Hindi films aren't shown with English subtitles. The cinemas we've listed all show English-language movies, along with some Bollywood numbers.

Big clubs nights are (oddly) Wednesday, as well as the traditional Friday and Saturday; there's usually a cover charge. Dress codes apply so don't rock up in shorts and sandals. The trend in Mumbai of late is towards resto-lounges as opposed to full on nightclubs – serious tax implications on discos versus lounges and restaurants means folks got a little clever.

⬛TOP CHOICE Bluefrog
LIVE MUSIC

(off Map p724; ☑6158; www.bluefrog.co.in; D/2 Mathuradas Mills Compound, NM Joshi Marg, Lower Parel; admission after 9pm Sun & Tue-Thu ₹300, Fri & Sat ₹500; ⊙7pm-1am Tue-Sun) The most exciting thing to happen to Mumbai's music scene in a long time, Bluefrog is a concert space, production studio, restaurant and one of Mumbai's most happening spaces. It hosts exceptional local and international acts, and has space-age, orange-glowing 'pod' seating in the intimate main room.

Valhalla
RESTO-LOUNGE

(Map p730; ☑67353535; 1st fl, East Wing, Eros Theatre Bldg, Churchgate) This discreet resto-lounge caters to Mumbai's bold and beautiful, who turn up here amid aubergine walls and baroque aesthetics on Friday and Saturday club nights when everywhere else closes (it's unofficially open until 4am or so). Getting in isn't easy – you need to call ahead and get on the list – but if you manage it, you'll rub elbows with a very high-profile crowd.

Not Just Jazz By the Bay   LIVE MUSIC
(Map p730; ☑22851876; 143 Marine Dr; admission weekdays/weekends ₹100/300; ⊙noon-3.30am) This is the best, and frankly the only, jazz club in South Mumbai. True to its name, there are also live pop, blues and rock performers most nights from 10pm, but Sunday, Monday and Tuesday are reserved for karaoke. By day, there's a well done all-you-can-eat buffet (₹325).

Trilogy   NIGHTCLUB
(Map p742; Hotel Sea Princess, Juhu Tara Rd, Juhu; cover per couple after 11pm ₹1000; ⊙closed Tue) Mumbai's newest club at time of writing is all attitude – rumour has it that staff size up potentials for looks and charge a varying admission accordingly. That bodes well for those who make it past face patrol. The trilevel space is gorgeous, highlighted by a black granite dance floor lit up by 1372 LED cube lights that go off like an epileptic Lite-Brite in an Indian power surge. The imported sound system favours house and hip-hop while the bartenders look imported from Ed Hardy's employee pool.

Polly Esther's   NIGHTCLUB
(Map p728; Gordon House Hotel, Battery St, Colaba; cover per couple Wed, Fri & Sat ₹800-1500) The city's fashionistas feel nauseous at its mere mention, but this mirror-plated, cheesy nightclub wallowing in retro gaudiness remains a fun choice to mingle with middle-class Mumbai. The *Saturday Night Fever* illuminated dance floor stays packed with gossiping 20-somethings and ogling tourists. Wednesday is free for the gals and all but ₹200 is recoupable in drinks most nights.

Wankhede Stadium   SPORT
(Mumbai Cricket Association; Map p730; ☑22795500; www.mumbaicricket.com; D Rd, Churchgate) Test matches and One Day Internationals are played a few times a year in season (October to April). Contact the Cricket Association for ticket information; for a test match you'll probably have to pay for the full five days.

Cooperage Football Ground   SPORT
(Map p728; ☑22024020; MK Rd, Colaba; tickets ₹20-25) Home to FC Air India, Mumbai FC and ONGC FC. Hosts national-league and local football (soccer) matches between October and February. Tickets are available at the gate.

National Centre for the Performing Arts   THEATRE
(NCPA; Map p730; ☑66223737, box office 22824567; www.ncpamumbai.com; cnr Marine Dr & Sri V Saha Rd, Nariman Point; tickets ₹200-500; ⊙box office 9am-7pm) Spanning 800 sq metres, this cultural centre is the hub of Mumbai's music, theatre and dance scene. In any given week, it might host Marathi theatre, poetry readings and art exhibitions, Bihari dance troupes, ensembles from Europe or Indian classical music. The Experimental Theatre occasionally has English-language plays. Many performances are free. The box office is at the end of NCPA Marg.

Prithvi Theatre   THEATRE
(Map p742; ☑26149546; www.prithvitheatre.org; Juhu Church Rd, Juhu) At Juhu Beach, this is a good place to see both Hindi and English-language theatre. It hosts an excellent annual international theatre festival and there's a charming cafe, too.

Regal   CINEMA
(Map p728; ☑22021017; Opposite Regal Circle, Shahid Bhagat Singh Rd, Colaba; tickets ₹100-200) Check out the art deco architecture.

Eros   CINEMA
(Map p730; ☑22822335; MK Rd, Churchgate; tickets ₹80-120)

Metro Big   CINEMA
(off Map p730; ☑39894040; MG Rd, New Marine Lines, Fort; tickets ₹100-600) This grand dame of Bombay talkies was just renovated into a multiplex.

Sterling   CINEMA
(Map p730; ☑66220016; Marzaban Rd, Fort; tickets ₹120-180)

🔒 Shopping

Mumbai is India's great marketplace, with some of the best shopping in the country.

You can buy just about anything in the dense bazaars north of CST (Map p724). The main areas are Crawford Market (fruit and veg), Mangaldas Market (silk and cloth), Zaveri Bazaar (jewellery), Bhuleshwar Market (fruit and veg) and Chor Bazaar (antiques and furniture). Dhabu St is lined with fine leather goods and Mutton St specialises in antiques, reproductions and fine junk.

PRAMOD SIPPY: DJ PRAMZ

A Mumbai turntable veteran, DJ Pramz has spun the black circles in the city for over half his lifetime. Here are his top picks.

Cosiest Club

Bonobo (Map p742); Kenilworth, Phase 2, Off Linking Rd, Bandra West) is a home away from home. They don't impose a dress code neither do they charge an entry. It's a walk-in and offers some really good cocktails at very good prices. It doesn't take long for one to establish their comfort level. As a DJ, I love performing there because of the 'no main-stream music' policy and of course because the owners are very much on the same page as me. They are young entrepreneurs who understand the global trends and are ready to experiment and do things differently.

Most Stunning Club

Wink (off Map p728; Vivanta by Taj – President Hotel, 90 Cuffe Pde, Cuffe Parade) is a beautifully designed bar with a demarcated area for quick meals. The drinks and service are easily the best in town. Their Winktinis are world-renowned and the music is nothing short of spectacular. I love to perform here because they are open-minded and, in spite of being situated in a five-star [hotel], they don't entertain requests that fall outside the ambit of the DJ. It's frequented by a large expatriate crowd who are usually [hotel] guests. Although the space is bright and unlike a club, the pulsating music on weekends makes the vibe quite groovy.

Most Celebrated Club

Zenzi Mills (off Map p724; Mathuradas Mills Compound, Senapati Bapat Marg, Lower Parel; ⊙closed Sun) is a paradise of sorts for all alternative music aficionados. It's basically an offshoot of the legendary Zenzi (Bandra), which essentially laid the foundation for alternative entertainment in the city. Zenzi widened its horizon by launching Mills, which had everything that the original Zenzi lacked – a state-of-the-art sound system, a beautiful set-up for visuals, a split level space. It works for artists of all alternative genres as the club is open to experimentation. A lot of deep-rooted sentiments are attached to it and it has become immortal for many in their hearts, but word is out that it's undergoing an image makeover and will be seen in an all-new form and feel. What it's going to be like is yet a mystery, though.

Crawford Market (Mahatma Phule Market) is the last outpost of British Bombay before the tumult of the central bazaars begins. Bas-reliefs by Rudyard Kipling's father, Lockwood Kipling, adorn the Norman Gothic exterior.

Snap up a bargain backpacking wardrobe at Fashion Street, the strip of stalls lining MG Rd between Cross and Azad maidans (Map p730), or in Bandra's Linking Rd, near Waterfield Rd (Map p742) – hone your bargaining skills. Kemp's Corner has many good shops for designer threads.

Various state-government emporiums sell handicrafts in the World Trade Centre Arcade (off Map p728) near Cuffe Parade. Small antique and curio shops line Merewether Rd behind the Taj Mahal Palace (Map p728). They aren't cheap, but the quality is a step up from government emporiums. If you prefer Raj-era bric-a-brac, head to Chor Bazaar (Map p724): the main area of activity is Mutton St, where you'll find a row of shops specialising in antiques (and many ingenious reproductions, so beware) and miscellaneous junk.

Fabindia CLOTHING
(Map p730; Jeroo Bldg, 137 MG Rd, Kala Ghoda) Founded as a means to get traditional fabric artisans' wares to market, Fabindia has all the vibrant colours of the country in its trendy cotton and silk fashions, materials and homewares in a modern-meets-traditional Indian shop. If you are too cool for Indian-wear, try here. The Santa Cruz outpost (Map p742) is also good.

Bombay Electric CLOTHES
(Map p728; www.bombayeletric.in; 1 Reay House, Best Marg, Colaba) High fashion is the calling

THE GREAT WALL OF MUMBAI

An artistic initiative similar to Berlin's East Side Gallery, though without the 28 years of oppression and isolation, the **Wall Project** (Map p742; www.thewallproject.com) was started by a group of ex-art/design students who decided to paint their neighbours' walls with local themes and artsy graffiti. This soon spread into a public project that has splashed colourful murals on everything from houses to hospitals all over the suburb of Bandra. The idea quickly began spreading like kaleidoscopic Kudzu – a spray-painted virus that has turned crumbling structures and neglected walls into a living museum of contemporary urban culture. At time of writing, hundreds of artists (and nonartists) have painted some 600 murals, the longest stretch of which starts at Mahim station (West) on Tulsi Pipe Rd (Senapati Bapat Marg) and runs along the Western Railway to Matunga Rd station – nicknamed as the Great Wall of Mumbai.

Anyone can visit and paint the wall, as long as the art is not sexually explicit, political, religious or commercial. Grab some acrylic distemper paint – recommended due to harsh weather conditions – and get your art on!

at this trendy unisex boutique next to the Taj Mahal Palace hotel. It sources fabrics (for its own hip brand, Gheebutter) and weaved scarfs and jackets from NGOs in Madhya Pradesh and Gujarat, as well as select antiques and handicrafts. It's a sharp spot to pick up *kurtas* (long shirts), dress shirts and stylish T-shirts.

Phillips   ANTIQUES, CURIOS
(Map p728; www.phillipsantiques.com; Wodehouse Rd, Colaba) The 150-year-old Phillips has nizam-era royal silver, wooden ceremonial masks, Victorian glass and various other gorgeous things that you never knew you wanted. It also has high-quality reproductions of old photos, maps and paintings, and a warehouse shop of big antiques.

Shrujan   HANDICRAFTS
Breach Candy (Map p724; Sagar Villa, Warden Rd, opposite Navroze Apts; ⊘closed Sun); Juhu (Map p742; Hatkesh Society, 6th North South Rd, JVPD Scheme; ⊘closed Sun) Selling the intricate embroidery work of women in 114 villages in Kutch, Gujarat, the nonprofit Shrujan aims to help women earn a livelihood while preserving the spectacular embroidery traditions of the area. The sophisticated clothing, wall hangings and purses make great gifts.

Biba   CLOTHING
(Map p724; 1 Hughes Rd, Kemp's Corner; ⊘10.30am-9pm Mon-Sat) You'll be impossibly fashionable in LA or London in these sundresses! Also in Khar West (p742).

Bombay Store   HANDICRAFTS
(Map p730; Western India House, Sir PM Rd, Fort; ⊘10.30am-8pm Mon-Sat, to 6.30pm Sun) A classy selection of rugs, clothing, teas,

stationery, aromatherapy, brass sculptures and, perhaps most interestingly, biodegradable Ganesh idols for use in the Ganesh Chaturthi festival.

Good Earth   HANDICRAFTS
(Map p728; 2 Reay House, Colaba) This Delhi transplant hawks gorgeous, eco-leaning housewares, candles, cosmetics and glassware. Funky coasters, hand-decorated china, stylish coffee mugs – all higher end and artsy.

Oxford Bookstore   BOOKSTORE
(Map p730; www.oxfordbookstore.com; Apeejay House, 3 Dinsha Wachha Marg, Churchgate; ⊘8am-10pm) Mumbai's best, with a tea bar.

Crossword   BOOKSTORE
(Map p724; Mohammedbhai Mansion, NS Patkar Marg, Kemp's Corner) Enormous.

Khadi & Village Industries Emporium
CLOTHING
(Khadi Bhavan; Map p730; 286 Dr Dadabhai Naoroji Rd, Fort; ⊘10.30am-6.30pm Mon-Sat) Khadi Bhavan is dusty, 1940s timewarp with ready-made traditional Indian clothing, material, shoes and handicrafts that are so old they're new again.

Cotton Cottage   CLOTHING
(Map p730; Agra Bldg, 121 MG Rd, Kala Ghoda; ⊘10am-9pm) Stock up on simple cotton *kurtas* and various pants – *salwars, churidars, patiala* – for the road.

Mini Market/Bollywood Bazaar
                                ANTIQUES, CURIOS
(Map p724; ☎23472427; 33/31 Mutton St; ⊘11am-8pm Sat-Thu) Sells original vintage Bollywood posters and other movie

ephemera as well as odd and interesting trinkets. Call if you get lost.

Kala Niketan CLOTHING
(Map p730; 95 MK Rd; ☺9.30am-7.30pm Mon-Sat) Sari madness on Queens Rd.

Mélange CLOTHING
(Map p724; 33 Altamount Rd, Kemp's Corner; ☺closed Sun) High-fashion ladies garments from over 100 Indian designers in a chic exposed-brick space.

Chimanlals HANDICRAFTS
(Map p730; 210 Dr Dadabhai Naoroji Rd, Fort; ☺9.30am-6pm Mon-Fri, to 5.30pm Sat) Beautiful writing materials made from traditional Indian paper. Enter from Wallace St.

Rhythm House MUSIC STORE
(Map p730; ☺22842835; 40 K Dubash Marg, Fort; ☺10am-8.30pm Mon-Sat, 11am-8.30pm Sun) Nonpirated CDs; tickets to concerts, plays and festivals.

BX Furtado & Sons MUSIC STORE
(off Map p730; www.furtadosonline.com; Jer Mahal, Dhobitalao; ☺10am-8pm Mon-Sat) The best place in Mumbai for musical instruments – sitars, tablas, accordions and local and imported guitars. The branch around the corner on Kalbadevi Rd is pianos and sheet music only.

Central Cottage Industries Emporium HANDICRAFTS, SOUVENIRS
(Map p728; ☺22027537; Chhatrapati Shivaji Marg, Colaba; ☺closed Sun) Limited souvenir shopping at government-restricted prices.

Standard Supply Co PHOTOGRAPHY
(Map p730; ☺22612468; Image House, Walchand Hirachand Marg, Fort; ☺10am-7pm Mon-Sat) Everything you could possibly need for digital and film photography.

ℹ Information

Internet Access

Portasia (Kitab Mahal, Dr Dadabhai Naoroji Rd, Fort; per hr ₹25; ☺9am-9pm Mon-Sat) Entrance is down a little alley; look for the 'cybercafe' sign hanging from a tree.

Sify iWay (per 2hr ₹100) Churchgate (Prem Ct, J Tata Rd; ☺8.30am-9.30pm); Colaba (Donald House, 1st fl, Colaba Causeway; ☺8.30am-9.30pm) The Colaba branch entrance is on JA Allana Marg.

Media

To find out what's going on in Mumbai, check out the free *burrp! Know Your City* (www.mumbai.burrp.com), available in most hotels; the

Hindustan Times' Café insert or **Time Out Mumbai** (www.timeoutmumbai.net; ₹50).

Medical Services

Bombay Hospital (Map p730; ☺22067676, ambulance 22067309; www.bombayhospital.com; 12 New Marine Lines)

Breach Candy Hospital (Map p724; ☺23672888; www.breachcandyhospital.org; 60 Bhulabhai Desai Rd, Breach Candy) Best in Mumbai, if not India.

Royal Chemists (Map p730; ☺22004041-3; 89A Maharshi Karve Rd, Churchgate; ☺8.30am-8.30pm Mon-Sat)

Sahakari Bhandar Chemist (Map p728; ☺22022399; Colaba Causeway, Colaba; ☺10am-8.30pm)

Money

ATMs are everywhere and foreign-exchange offices changing cash and travellers cheques are also plentiful.

Akbar Travels Colaba (Map p728; ☺22823434; 30 Alipur Trust Bldg; ☺10am-7pm); Fort (Map p730; ☺22633434; Terminus View, 167/169 Dr Dadabhai Naoroji Rd; ☺10am-7pm Mon-Fri, to 6pm Sun)

Thomas Cook (☺9.30am-6pm Mon-Sat) Colaba (Map p728; ☺22882517-20; Colaba Causeway); Fort (Map p730; ☺61603333; 324 Dr Dadabhai Naoroji Rd)

Post

The **main post office** (Map p730; ☺10am-6pm Mon-Sat) is an imposing building behind Chhatrapati Shivaji Terminus (CST; Victoria Terminus). **Poste restante** (☺9am-8pm Mon-Sat) is at Counter 1. Letters should be addressed c/o Poste Restante, Mumbai GPO, Mumbai 400 001. Bring your passport to collect mail. The **EMS Speedpost parcel counter** (☺11.30am-7.30pm Mon-Fri) is across from the stamp counters. Opposite the post office, under the tree, are parcelwallahs who will stitch up your parcel for ₹40.

Colaba post office (Map p728; Henry Rd) Convenient branch.

Blue Dart/DHL Churchgate (Map p730; www.bluedart.com; Khetan Bhavan, J Tata Rd; ☺10am-8pm Mon-Sat); Nariman Point (Map p724; www.dhl.co.in; Embassy Centre; ☺9am-8.30pm Mon-Sat) Private express-mail company.

Telephone

Justdial (☺69999999; www.justdial.com) and ☺197 provide directory enquiries.

Tourist Information

Government of India tourist office (Map p730; ☺22074333; www.incredibleindia.com; 123 Maharshi Karve Rd; ☺8.30am-7pm Mon-Fri, to 2pm Sat) Provides information for the entire country.

Government of India tourist office airport booths domestic (☑26156920; ☺7am-midnight); international (☑26813253; ☺24hr)

Maharashtra Tourism Development Corporation booth (MTDC; Map p728;☑22841877; Apollo Bunder; ☺8.30am-4pm Tue-Sun, 5.30-8pm weekends) For city bus tours.

MTDC reservation office (Map p730; ☑22841877; www.maharashtratourism.gov.in; Madame Cama Rd, opposite LIC Bldg, Nariman Point; ☺9.45am-5.30pm Mon-Sat) Information on Maharashtra and bookings for MTDC hotels and the *Deccan Odyssey* train package. This is also the only MTDC office that accepts credits cards.

Travel Agencies

Akbar Travels (Map p730; ☑22633434; www.akbartravelsonline.com; Terminus View, 167/169 Dr Dadabhai Naoroji Rd, Fort; ☺10am-7pm Mon-Fri, to 6pm Sun)

Magnum International Travel & Tours (Map p728; ☑61559700; 10 Henry Rd, Colaba; ☺10am-5.30pm Mon-Fri, to 4pm Sat)

Thomas Cook (Map p730; ☑22048556-8; 324 Dr Dadabhai Naoroji Rd, Fort; ☺9.30am-6pm Mon-Sat)

Visa Extensions

Foreigners' Regional Registration Office (FRRO; Map p730; ☑22620446; Annexe Bldg No 2, CID, Badaruddin Tyabji Rd, near Special Branch) Does not officially issue extensions on tourist visas; even in emergencies it will direct you to Delhi (p1174). However, some travellers have managed to procure an emergency extension here after much waiting and persuasion.

ⓘ Getting There & Away

Air

AIRPORTS Mumbai is the main international gateway to South India and has the busiest network of domestic flights. **Chhatrapati Shivaji International Airport** (☑domestic 26264000, international 26813000; www.csia.in), about 30km from the city centre, has been undergoing a $2 billion modernisation since 2006. At time of writing, the airport comprises three domestic (1A, 1B and 1C) and one international terminal (2A). However, the domestic side is accessed via Vile Parle and is known locally as Santa Cruz airport, while the international, with its entrance 4km away in Andheri, goes locally by Sahar. Both terminals have ATMs, foreign-exchange counters and tourist-information booths. A free shuttle bus runs between the two every 30 minutes for ticket holders only. By 2014 the shiny new terminal T2 is expected to be open, serving both domestic and international flights, with the existing Santa Cruz terminal being converted to cargo only.

INTERNATIONAL AIRLINES Travel agencies are often better for booking international flights, while airline offices are increasingly directing customers to their call centres. The following airline ticket offices are clinging to life in Mumbai:

Air India (Map p730; ☑27580777, airport 26156633; www.airindia.com; Air India Bldg, cnr Marine Dr & Madame Cama Rd, Nariman Point; ☺9.15am-6.30pm Mon-Fri, to 5.15pm Sat & Sun)

Cathay Pacific (off Map p724; ☑66572222, airport 66859002/3; www.cathaypacific.com; 2 Brady Gladys Plaza, Senapati Bapat Marg, Lower Parel; ☺9.30am-6.30pm Mon-Sat)

Emirates Airlines (Map p730; ☑40974097; www.emirates.com; 3 Mittal Chambers, 228 Nariman Point; ☺9am-5.30pm Mon-Sat)

El Al Airlines (Map p730; ☑66207400, airport 66859425/6; www.elal.co.il; 6th fl, NKM International House, BM Chinai Marg, Nariman Point; ☺9.30am-5.30pm Mon-Fri, to 1pm Sat)

Qantas (Map p730; ☑61111818; www.qantas.com.au; 4th fl, Sunteck Centre, 37-40 Subhash Rd, Vile Parle; ☺9am-1.15pm & 2.30-5.30pm Mon-Fri)

Swiss (Map p730; ☑67137240; www.swiss.com; 2nd fl, Vashani Chambers, 9 New Marine Lines; ☺9am-5.30pm Mon-Sat)

Thai Airways (Map p730; ☑61395599; www.thaiair.com; 2A Mittal Towers A Wing, Nariman Point; ☺9.30am-5.30pm Mon-Fri, to 4pm Sat)

Major nonstop domestic flights from Mumbai include the following:

DESTINATION	SAMPLE LOWEST ONE-WAY FARE (₹)	DURATION (HR)
Bengaluru	2533	1½
Chennai	3482	1¾
Delhi	3483	2
Goa	2532	1
Hyderabad	2282	1¼
Jaipur	2533	1¾
Kochi	3483	1¾
Kolkata	3882	2¾

DOMESTIC AIRLINES The following all have ticketing counters at the domestic airport; most open 24 hours.

GoAir (☑call centre 1800 222111, airport 26264789; www.goair.in)

Indian Airlines (Map p730; ☑22023031, call centre 1800 1801407; www.indian-airlines.nic.in;

Air India Bldg, cnr Marine Dr & Madame Cama Rd, Nariman Point)

IndiGo (📞call centre 1800 1803838; www.goindigo.in)

Jet Airways (Map p728; 📞call centre 39893333, airport 26266575; www.jetairways.com; Amarchand Mansion, Madame Cama Rd; ⊙9.30am-6pm Mon-Fri, to 1pm Sat)

JetLite (📞call centre 1800 225522; www.jetlite.com)

Kingfisher/Kingfisher Red (Map p730;📞call centre 1800 2331310, airport 26262605; www.flykingfisher.com; Nirmal Bldg, Marine Dr, Nariman Point; ⊙9am-7pm Mon-Sat, 10am-2pm Sun)

SpiceJet (📞call centre 1800 1803333, airport 26156155; www.spicejet.com)

Bus

Numerous private operators and state governments run long-distance buses to and from Mumbai.

Private buses are usually more comfortable and simpler to book but can cost significantly more than government buses; they depart from Dr Anadrao Nair Rd near Mumbai Central train station (Map p724). Fares to popular destinations (like Goa) are up to 75% higher during holiday periods. To check on departure times and current prices, try **National CTC** (Map p724; 📞23015652; Dr Anadrao Nair Rd; ⊙7am-10pm).

More convenient for Goa and southern destinations are the private buses run by **Chandni Travels** (Map p730; 📞22713901) that depart three times a day from in front of Azad Maidan, just south of the Metro cinema. Ticket agents are located near the bus departure point.

Long-distance government-run buses depart from **Mumbai Central bus terminal** (Map p724; 📞23074272/1524) by Mumbai Central train station. Buses service major towns in Maharashtra and neighbouring states. They're cheaper and more frequent than private services, but the quality and crowd levels vary.

Popular long-distance bus fares include the following:

DESTINATION	PRIVATE NON-AC/AC SLEEPER ₹	GOVERN- MENT NON-AC ₹	DURA- TION (HR)
Ahmedabad	250/600	N/A	13
Aurangabad	250/600	368	10
Mahabal- eshwar	450/500*	270	7
Paniji	300/700	N/A	14-18
Pune	200**	170-250	4
Udaipur	350/1400	N/A	16

* AC Sitting; **AC Sitting

Train

Three train systems operate out of Mumbai, but the most important services for travellers are Central Railways and Western Railways. Tickets for either system can be bought from any station, in South Mumbai or the suburbs, that has computerised ticketing.

Central Railways (📞134), handling services to the east, south, plus a few trains to the north, operates from CST. The **reservation centre** (Map p730; 📞139; ⊙8am-8pm Mon-Sat, to 2pm Sun) is around the side of CST where the taxis gather. **Foreign tourist-quota tickets** (Counter 52) can be bought up to 90 days before travel, but must be paid in foreign currency or with rupees backed by an encashment certificate or ATM receipt. Indrail passes (p32) can also be bought at Counter 52. You can buy nonquota tickets with a Visa or MasterCard at the much faster credit-card counters (10 and 11) for a ₹30 fee. Refunds for Indians and foreigners alike are handled at Counter 8.

Some Central Railways trains depart from Dadar (D), a few stations north of CST, or Churchgate/Lokmanya Tilak (T), 16km north of CST.

Western Railways (📞131, 132) has services to the north (including Rajasthan and Delhi) from Mumbai Central train station (MC; 📞23061763, 23073535), usually called Bombay Central (BCT). The **reservation centre** (Map p730; ⊙8am-8pm Mon-Sat, to 2pm Sun), opposite Churchgate train station, has a **foreign tourist-quota counter** (Counter 14). The same rules apply as at CST station. The creditcard counter is No 6.

ⓘ Getting Around

To/From the Airports

INTERNATIONAL The prepaid-taxi booth that is located at the international airport has set fares for every neighbourhood in the city; Colaba, Fort and Marine Dr are AC/non-AC ₹495/395, Bandra West ₹310/260 and Juhu ₹235/190. There's a ₹10 service charge and a charge of ₹10 per bag. The journey to Colaba takes about 45 minutes at night and 1½ to two hours during the day. Tips are not required.

Autorickshaws queue up at a little distance from arrivals, but don't try to take one to South Mumbai: they can only go as far as Mahim Creek. You can catch an autorickshaw (around ₹40) to Andheri train station and catch a suburban train (₹7, 45 minutes) to Churchgate or CST. Only attempt this if you arrive during the day outside of rush 'hour' (6am to 11am) and are not weighed down with luggage.

Minibuses outside arrivals offer free shuttle services to the domestic airport and Juhu hotels.

MAJOR TRAINS FROM MUMBAI

DESTINATION	TRAIN NO & NAME	SAMPLE FARE (₹)	DURATION (HR)	DEPARTURE
Agra	12137 *Punjab Mail*	410/1098/1501/2533	22	7.40pm CST
Ahmedabad	12901 *Gujarat Mail*	232/594/802/1350	9	9.50pm MC
Aurangabad	17057 *Devagiri Express*	176/463/632/1061	7	9.05pm CST
	17617 *Tapovan Express*	102/363*	7	6.10am CST
Bengaluru	16529 *Udyan Express*	363/991/1364/2298	25	8.05am CST
Bhopal	12137 *Punjab Mail*	325/857/1167/1958	14	7.40pm CST
Chennai	11041 *Chennai Express*	383/1046/1440**	27	2.00pm CST
Delhi	12951 *Rajdhani Express*	1495/1975/3305†	16	4.40pm MC
	12137 *Punjab Mail*	442/1187/1623/2743	25½	7.10pm CST
Margao	10103 *Mandavi Express*	288/782/1073/1799	11½	6.55am CST
	12051 *Shatabdi Express*	283/787/1073/1799	9	5.10am CST
Hyderabad	12701 *Hussainsagar Express*	312/823/1119/1876	14½	9.50pm CST
Indore	12961 *Avantika Express*	320/847/1151/1931	14½	7.05pm MC
Jaipur	12955 *Jaipur Express*	383/1021/1394/2348	18	6.50pm MC
Kochi	16345 *Netravati Express*	430/1178/1624***	26½	11.40am T
Kolkata	12859 *Gitanjali Express*	508/1883*	30½	6.00am CST
	12809 *Howrah Mail*	508/1374/1883/3190	33	8.35pm CST
Pune	12125 *Pragati Express*	76/267*	3½	5.10pm CST
Varanasi	11093 *Mahanagari Express*	422/1157/1593***	2½	12.10am CST
Trivandrum	16345 *Netravati Express*	1277/1762#	30	11.40am T

Station abbreviations: CST (Chhatrapati Shivaji Terminus); MC (Mumbai Central); T (Lokmanya Tilak); D (Dadar)

Note: fares are for sleeper/3AC/2AC/1AC except for: * AC/Non-AC, ** sleeper/3AC/2AC, *** Non-AC/3AC/2AC, # 3AC/2AC, † 3AC/2AC/1AC

A taxi from South Mumbai to the international airport should be between ₹350 and ₹400 by negotiating a fixed fare beforehand; official baggage charges are ₹10 per bag. Add 25% to the meter charge between midnight and 5am. We love the old-school black-and-yellows, but there are also AC, metered call taxis run by **Meru** (☎44224422; www.merucabs.com), charging ₹20 for the first kilometre and ₹14 per kilometre thereafter (25% more at night). Routes are tracked by GPS, so no rip-offs!

DOMESTIC Taxis and autorickshaws queue up outside both domestic terminals. The prepaid counter is outside arrivals. A non-AC/AC taxi to Colaba or Fort costs ₹350/400, day or night, plus ₹10 per bag. For Juhu, ₹150/200.

A cheaper alternative is to catch an autorickshaw between the airport and Vile Parle train station (₹20 to ₹30), and a train between Vile Parle and Churchgate (₹7, 45 minutes). Don't attempt this during rush hour (6am to 11am).

Boat

Both **PNP** (☎22885220) and **Maldar Catamarans** (☎22829695) run regular ferries to Mandwa (oneway ₹110), useful for access to Murud-Janjira and other parts of the Konkan Coast, avoiding the long bus trip out of Mumbai. Their ticket offices are at Apollo Bunder (near the Gateway of India; Map p728).

Bus

Mumbai's single- and double-decker buses are good for travelling short distances. Fares around South Mumbai cost ₹3 for a section; pay the conductor once you're aboard. The service is run by **BEST** (Map p728; www.bestundertaking. com), which has a depot in Colaba (the website has a useful search facility for bus routes across the city). Just jumping on a double-decker (such as bus 103) is an inexpensive way to see South Mumbai. Day passes are available for ₹25.

In the table following are some useful routes; all of these buses depart from the bus stand at the southern end of Colaba Causeway and pass Flora Fountain.

DESTINATION	BUS NO
Breach Candy	132, 133
CST & Crawford Market	1, 3, 21, 103, 124
Churchgate	70, 106, 123, 132
Girgaum Chowpatty	103, 106, 107, 123
Haji Ali	83, 124, 132, 133
Hanging Gardens	103, 106
Mani Bhavan	123
Mohammed Ali Rd	1, 3, 21
Mumbai Central train station	124, 125

Car

Cars are generally hired for an eight-hour day and an 80km maximum, with additional charges if you go over. For an AC car, the best going rate is about ₹1000.

Agents at the Apollo Bunder ticket booths near the Gateway of India can arrange a non-AC Maruti with driver for a half-day of sightseeing for ₹1000 (going as far as Mahalaxmi and Malabar Hill). Regular taxi drivers often accept a similar price.

Metro

Mumbai's US$8.17 billion metro project has broken ground. The Colaba–Bandra–Airport line will most benefit tourists, but is several years away from completion.

Motorcycle

Allibhai Premji Tyrewalla (Map p724; www.premjis.com; 205/207 Dr D Bhadkamkar Rd; ◷10am-7pm Mon-Sat), around for almost 100 years, sells new and used motorcycles with a guaranteed buy-back option. For two- to three-week 'rental' periods you'll still have to pay the full cost of the bike upfront. The company prefers to deal with longer-term schemes of two months or more, which work out cheaper anyway. A used 150cc or 225cc Hero Honda Karizma costs ₹25,000 to ₹80,000, with a buy-back price of around 60% after three months (higher-cc Enfields are sometimes available). A smaller bike (100cc to 180cc) starts at ₹25,000. The company can also arrange shipment of bikes overseas (around ₹24,000 to the UK).

Taxi & Autorickshaw

Every second car on Mumbai's streets seems to be a black-and-yellow Premier taxi (India's version of a 1950s Fiat). They're the most convenient way to get around the city, and in South Mumbai drivers *almost* always use the meter without prompting. Autorickshaws are confined to the suburbs north of Mahim Creek.

Drivers don't always know the names of Mumbai's streets (especially new names) – the best way to find something is by using nearby landmarks. A 2010 fare increase means taxi meters start at ₹16 during the day (₹20 after midnight) for the first 1.6km and ₹10 per kilometre after this (₹12 after midnight). If you get a taxi with the old-fashion meters, the fare will be roughly 16 times the amount shown. The minimum autorickshaw fare is ₹11.

Train

Mumbai has an efficient but overcrowded suburban train network.

There are three main lines, making it easy to navigate. The most useful service operates from Churchgate heading north to stations such as Charni Rd (for Girgaum Chowpatty), Mumbai Central, Mahalaxmi (for the Dhobi Ghat; p729), Vile Parle (for the domestic airport), Andheri (for the international airport) and Borivali (for Sanjay Gandhi National Park). Other suburban lines operate from CST to Byculla (for Veermata Jijabai Bhonsle Udyan, formerly Victoria Gardens), Dadar and as far as Neral (for Matheran). Trains run from 4am till 1am. From Churchgate, 2nd-/1st-class fares are ₹4/41 to Mumbai Central, ₹7/78 to Vile Parle or Andheri, and ₹9/104 to Borivali.

'Tourist tickets' permit unlimited travel in 2nd/1st class for one (₹50/170), three (₹90/330) or five (₹105/390) days.

Avoid rush hours when trains are jam-packed, even in 1st class; watch your valuables, and gals, stick to the ladies-only carriages.

TAXI TROUBLE

We won't name names, but Mumbaikar taxis and rickshaws *might* occasionally like to take advantage of foreign faces. If you find yourself in either with an old-fashion meter (outside on the left-hand dash), you are vulnerable. Print out handy conversion charts from the **Mumbai Traffic Police** (www.trafficpolicemumbai.org/Tariffcard_Auto_taxi_form.htm) – end of discussion (until the next price hike).

SANJAY GANDHI NATIONAL PARK

It's hard to believe that within 90 minutes of the teeming metropolis you can be surrounded by this 104-sq-km **protected tropical forest** (⌨28866449; adult/child ₹30/15, 2-/4-wheeler vehicle ₹15/50; ☉7.30am-6pm). Here, bright flora, birds, butterflies and elusive wild leopards replace pollution and crowds, all surrounded by forested hills on the city's northern edge. Urban development and shantytowns try to muscle in on the fringes of this wild region, but its status as a national park has allowed it to stay green and calm.

In addition to well-worn trekking trails to Shilonda waterfall and Vihar and Tulsi lakes, there is a lion and tiger safari and Kanheri caves to occupy day-trippers escaping the Mumbai mayhem. Inside the main northern entrance is an information centre with a small exhibition on the park's wildlife. The best time to see birds is October to April and butterflies August to November.

GREATER MUMBAI

Elephanta Island

In the middle of Mumbai Harbour, 9km northeast of the Gateway of India, the rock-cut temples on **Elephanta Island** (http://asi.nic.in/; Indian/foreigner ₹10/250; ☉caves 9am-5.30pm Tue-Sun) are a Unesco World Heritage Site and worth crossing the waters for. Home to a labyrinth of cave-temples carved into the basalt rock of the island, the artwork represents some of the most impressive temple carving in all of India. The main Shiva-dedicated temple is an intriguing latticework of courtyards, halls, pillars and shrines, with the magnum opus a 6m-tall statue of Sadhashiva – depicting a three-faced Shiva as the destroyer, creator and preserver of the universe. The enormous central bust of Shiva, its eyes closed in eternal contemplation, may be the most serene sight you witness in India.

The temples are thought to have been created between AD 450 and 750, when the island was known as Gharapuri (Place of Caves). The Portuguese renamed it Elephanta because of a large stone elephant near the shore, which collapsed in 1814 and was moved by the British to Mumbai's Jijamata Udyan.

The English-language guide service (free with deluxe boat tickets) is worthwhile; tours depart every hour on the half-hour from the ticket booth. Beware of touts that meet you at the jetty and try to convince you to employ their services – the included English guide will met you at the entrance to the temples. Ask for government-issued ID if in doubt.

If you explore independently, pick up Pramod Chandra's *A Guide to the Elephanta Caves* from the stalls lining the stairway. There's also a small **museum** on-site, which has some informative pictorial panels on the origin of the caves.

❶ Getting There & Away

Launches (economy/deluxe ₹105/130) head to Elephanta Island from the Gateway of India every half-hour from 9am to 3.30pm Tuesday to Sunday. Buy tickets at the booths lining Apollo Bunder. The voyage takes just over an hour.

The ferries dock at the end of a concrete pier, from where you can walk (around three minutes) or take the **miniature train** (₹10) to the **stairway** (admission ₹5) leading up to the caves. It's lined with handicraft stalls and patrolled by pesky monkeys. Wear good shoes.

Maharashtra

Best Places to Eat

» Malaka Spice (p788)
» Biso (p782)
» Khyber (p762)
» The Grapevine (p792)
» Prem's (p788)

Best Places to Stay

» Verandah in the Forest (p781)
» Hotel Sunderban (p787)
» Lemon Tree (p765)
» Beyond (see boxed text, p762)
» Osho Meditation Resort Guesthouse (p787)

Why Go?

India's third-largest (and second-most populous) state, Maharashtra is smattered with lazy beaches, lofty mountains, virgin forests and historic hot spots, all complemented by the incredible sights, sounds, smells and tastes of India.

Starting up north around Nasik, the state yields a curious blend of spirituality, meditation and chardonnay. Next comes cosmopolitan Pune, a city as famous for its sex guru as its food-and-beverage circuit. Slip westward and you are rewarded with a rash of golden sands, crumbling forts and emerald forests along the lonely shores of the Arabian Sea. For an off-beat experience, head east to spy tigers prowling in dense tropical jungle, or saunter south for overwhelming temples, zany palaces and brawny action in wrestling pits. Sounds like your kind of melting pot? Dive right in.

When to Go
Nasik

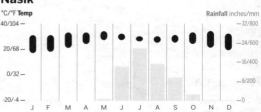

Jan It's party time in Nasik's wineries, marked by grape harvesting and crushing galas.

Sep The frenzied and energetic Ganesh Chaturthi celebrations reach fever pitch.

Dec Winter's a lovely time for the secluded beaches of Murud, Ganpatipule and Tarkarli.

Fast Facts

» Population: 112.4 million

» Area: 307,690 sq km

» Capital: Mumbai

» Main languages: Marathi, Hindi, English

» Sleeping prices: $ below ₹1000, $$ ₹1000 to ₹4000, $$$ above ₹4000

Money Matters

Maharashtra is among the most economically well-off states in India. Its per-capita income is 60% higher than the national average.

Resources

» Maharashtra Tourism Development Corporation (MTDC; www.maharashtra tourism.gov.in)

» Maharashtra State Road Transport Corporation (MSRTC; www.msrtc.gov.in)

Top Yoga & Meditation Centres

The **Vipassana International Academy** in Igatpuri (p763) has long been a destination for those wishing to put mind over matter through an austere form of Buddhist meditation. The boundaries of yoga, on the other hand, are constantly pushed at the **Ramamani Iyengar Memorial Yoga Institute** in Pune (p787) and the **Kaivalyadhama Yoga Hospital** in Lonavla (p782). For a more lavish and indulgent form of spiritual engagement, there's the super-luxurious **Osho International Meditation Resort** in Pune (p785), where one can meditate in style, while flexing a few muscles in the unique game of 'zennis' (Zen tennis).

Top Festivals

» Naag Panchami (Aug, Pune, p783, Kolhapur, p793) A traditional snake-worshipping festival.

» Ganesh Chaturthi (Sep, Pune, p783) Celebrated with fervour all across Maharashtra; Pune goes particularly hysteric in honour of the elephant-headed deity.

» Dussehra (Sep & Oct, Nagpur, p776, Aurangabad, p764) A Hindu festival, but it also marks the Buddhist celebration of the anniversary of the famous humanist and Dalit leader BR Ambedkar's conversion to Buddhism.

» Ellora Ajanta Aurangabad Festival (Nov, Aurangabad, p764) A cultural festival bringing together the best classical and folk performers from across the region, while promoting a number of artistic traditions and handicrafts on the side.

» Kalidas Festival (Nov, Nagpur, p776) Commemorates the literary genius of legendary poet Kalidas through spirited music, dance and theatre sessions.

» Sawai Gandharva Sangeet Mahotsav (Dec, Pune, p783) An extravaganza where you can see unforgettable performances by some of the heftiest names in Indian classical music.

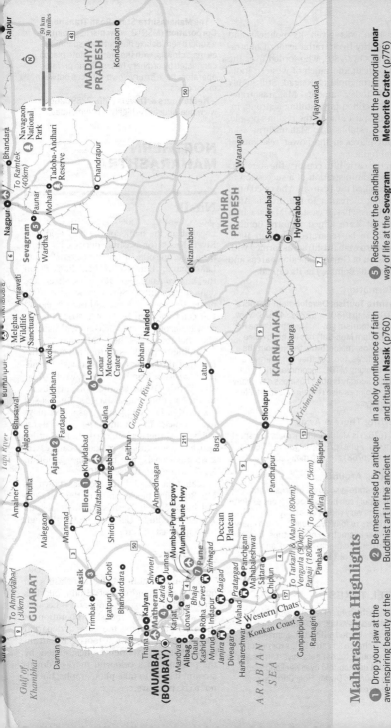

Maharashtra Highlights

① Drop your jaw at the awe-inspiring beauty of the monumental **Kailasa Temple**, the jewel in Ellora Caves' crown (p769)

② Be mesmerised by antique Buddhist art in the ancient cave galleries of **Ajanta** (p772)

③ Sip on a glass of zinfandel or sauvignon, and lose yourself

in a holy confluence of faith and ritual in **Nasik** (p760)

④ Gallop on a horse to Echo Point, or simply outrun the toy train chugging up the hill in **Matheran** (p780)

⑤ Rediscover the Gandhian way of life at the **Sevagram Ashram** in Sevagram (p777)

⑥ Brush up on your astronomy skills while ambling

around the primordial **Lonar Meteorite Crater** (p776)

⑦ Learn more about India's diverse cultures and traditions at the fantastic museums of **Pune** (p783)

History

Maharashtra was given its political and ethnic identity by Maratha leader Chhatrapati Shivaji (1627–80), who lorded over the Deccan plateau and much of western India from his stronghold at Raigad. Still highly respected today among Maharashtrans, Shivaji is credited for instilling a strong, independent spirit among the region's people, as well as establishing Maharashtra as a dominant player in the power relations of medieval India.

From the early 18th century, the state was under the administration of a succession of ministers called the Peshwas who ruled until 1819, ceding thereafter to the British. After Independence (1947), western Maharashtra and Gujarat were joined to form Bombay state, only to be separated again in 1960, when modern Maharashtra was formed with the exclusion of Gujarati-speaking areas and with Mumbai (Bombay) as its capital.

ℹ Information

Maharashtra Tourism Development Corporation (MTDC; Map p730; ☎02222845678; www.maharashtratourism.gov.in; Madame Cama Rd; ◷10am-5.30pm Mon-Sat) has its head office in Mumbai. Most major towns throughout the state have offices, too, but they're generally only useful for booking MTDC accommodation and tours. While Sunday is not a business day, many government offices also remain closed on alternate Saturdays.

ℹ Getting There & Away

Mumbai (p752) is Maharashtra's main transport hub, although Pune (p790), Jalgaon (p776) and Aurangabad (p768) are also major players.

ℹ Getting Around

Because the state is so large, internal flights (eg Pune to Nagpur) can help speed up your explorations. Airfares vary widely on a daily basis. AC Indica taxis are readily available, too, and charge around ₹7 per kilometre. For long trips, factor in a minimum daily distance of 250km, and a daily driver's allowance of ₹100.

HOTEL TAXES

In Maharashtra, hotel rooms below ₹1200 are charged a 4% tax, while those priced higher are slapped a 10% tax. Some hotels may also charge an extra 10% expenditure tax. At popular tourist getaways, tariffs can shoot up manifold over weekends, and holidays such as Diwali, Holi, Christmas and New Year.

The **Maharashtra State Road Transport Corporation** (MSRTC; www.msrtc.gov.in) has a superb semideluxe bus network spanning all major towns, with the more remote places connected by ordinary buses. Some private operators have luxury Volvo services between major cities.

Neeta Tours & Travels (☎02228902666; www.neetabus.in) is highly recommended.

NORTHERN MAHARASHTRA

Nasik

☎0253 / POP 1.2 MILLION / ELEV 565M

Located on the banks of the holy Godavari River, Nasik (or Nashik) derives its name from the episode in the Ramayana where Lakshmana, Rama's brother, hacked off the *nasika* (nose) of Ravana's sister, the demon enchantress Surpanakha. True to its name, the town is an absorbing place, and you can't walk far without discovering yet another exotic temple or colourful bathing ghat that references the Hindu epic.

Adding to Nasik's spiritual flavour is the fact that the town serves as a base for pilgrims visiting Trimbak (33km west; p764) and Shirdi (79km southeast), once home to the original Sai Baba (see the boxed text, p764). Every 12 years, Nasik also plays host to the grand Kumbh Mela, the largest religious gathering on earth that shuttles between four Indian religious centres on a triennial basis. The next congregation in Nasik is due in 2015 (see p1103).

Mahatma Gandhi Rd, better known as MG Rd, a few blocks north of the Old Central bus stand, is Nasik's commercial hub. The temple-lined Godavari flows through town just east of here.

◉ Sights

Ramkund   GHAT

This bathing ghat in the heart of Nasik's old quarter sees hundreds of Hindu pilgrims arriving daily to bathe, pray and – because the waters provide moksha (liberation of the soul) – to immerse the ashes of departed friends and family. For a tourist, it's an intense cultural experience, heightened by the presence of a colourful **market** downstream. It's OK to take photographs, but try not to be intrusive.

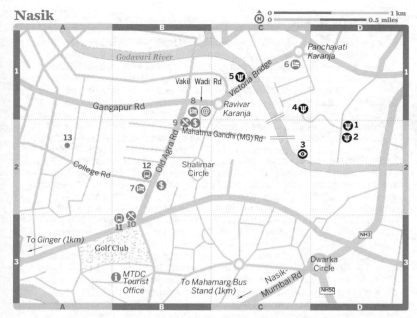

Temples

HINDU TEMPLES

A short walk uphill east of Ramkund is the **Kala Rama Temple**, the city's holiest shrine. Dating to 1794 and containing unusual black-stone representations of Rama, Sita and Lakshmana, the temple stands on the site where Lakshmana sliced off Surpanakha's nose. Nearby is the **Gumpha Panchavati**, where Sita supposedly hid while being assailed by the evil Ravana.

The ramshackle **Sundar Narayan Temple**, at the western end of Victoria Bridge, contains three black Vishnu deities, while the modern **Muktidham Temple**, about 7km southeast of the city near the train station, has 18 muralled chapters of the Bhagavad Gita lining its interior walls.

All the temples are open from 6am to 9pm.

🛏️ Sleeping & Eating

Panchavati   HOTEL **$$**
(www.panchavatihotels.com; 430 Chandak Wadi, Vakil Wadi Rd) To save yourself the hassle of scouting for a comfy bed in town, head straight for this excellent complex, comprising four hotels (and a few popular restaurants) that cover every pocket from budget to top-end, and deliver each rupee's worth. Kicking off at the cheaper end is **Panchavati Guest House** (✆2578771; s/d from ₹500/600; ❄️), which has

Nasik

slightly cramped but clean rooms and prompt service. A more inviting option is **Panchavati Yatri** (✆2578782; s/d from ₹1100/1350; ❄️), which features excellent rooms with hot showers, spot-on service, cooperative staff and an in-house health club. **Hotel Panchavati**

GRAPES OF NASIK

From wimpy raisins to full-bodied wines, the grapes of Nasik have come a long way. The town had been growing grapes meant for regular consumption since time immemorial. However, it was only in the early '90s that a couple of entrepreneurs realised that Nasik, with its fertile soils and cool climate, boasted conditions similar to Bordeaux. In 1997 industry pioneer **Sula Vineyards** (☑09970090010; www.sulawines.com; Govardhan, Gangapur–Savargaon Rd; ⊙11am-10pm) fearlessly invested in a crop of sauvignon blanc and chenin blanc, and the first batch of domestic wines hit the shelves in 2000. It hasn't looked back.

These days, the wine list in most of Nasik's wineries stretch to include zinfandel, shiraz, merlot and cabernet as well as a few reserves and champagnes, and most of these drops can be sampled first-hand by visiting one of the estates. **York Winery** (☑02532230700; www.yorkwinery.com, Gangavarhe, Gangapur–Savargaon Rd; ⊙3pm-10pm) offers wine-tasting sessions (₹100) in a top-floor room that has scenic views of the lake and surrounding hills. Sula Vineyards, located 15km west of Nasik, rounds off a vineyard tour with a wine-tasting session (₹150) that features six of its best. It's also possible to stay at some wineries. For an extremely indulging experience, head 3km inland to **Beyond** (☑09970090010; www.sulawines.com; d from ₹6000; ❄❄), an enchanting luxury resort set by a lake bordered by rolling hills, where you can roam the landscape on bicycles, go kayaking on the still waters or laze the hours away at the spa. Or you could try Chateau Indage, another of Nasik's wine biggies, that operates **Tiger Hill Vineyards Resort & Spa** (☑02532336274; www.indagegroup.com; Vilholi, Mumbai–Agra NH3; d from ₹3500; ❄), a stylish getaway-cum-wine bar 10km south of town, where you can pair its signature chardonnay with a relaxing grapeseed-oil massage.

During harvest season (January to March), some wineries also organise grape-crushing festivals, marked by unbridled revelry. Events are usually advertised on the wineries' websites.

(☑2575771; s/d from ₹1299/1499; ❄), fronting the complex, is pricier with classy rooms; it caters largely to business travellers. Last of all is the sumptuous **Panchavati Millionaire** (☑2312318; s/d ₹1600/1950; ❄), a moody affair where lavish rooms are complemented by cosy sit-in areas that are perfect for a steaming morning cuppa.

Hotel Samrat　　　　　　　HOTEL $$
(☑2577211; www.hotelsamratnasik.com; Old Agra Rd; s/d from ₹900/1175; ❄) You'll find little to complain about at the Samrat. Inviting rooms have large windows, are tastefully decorated in brown and beige, with pine-themed furniture thrown in for good measure. Located right next to the bus stand, its spick-and-span vegetarian restaurant is open 24 hours, making it popular as a refuelling stop.

Hotel Abhishek　　　　　　HOTEL $
(☑2514201; www.hotelabhishek.com; Panchavati Karanja; s/d ₹345/450, with AC ₹600/675; ❄) Located off the Panchavati Karanja roundabout, this pleasant budget option packs hot showers, TV and appetising vegetarian food into its well-kept, value-for-money rooms. A few minutes' walk uphill from the Godavari River, it sits amid all the ritualistic action,

and is a vantage point from which to be totally overwhelmed by sacred India at its noisiest but best.

Ginger　　　　　　　　　　HOTEL $$
(☑6616333; www.gingerhotels.com; Plot P20, Satpur MIDC, Trimbak Rd; s/d ₹1799/2299; ❄🛜) In another town, Ginger could easily have been our top choice. In Nasik, however, it loses out to its rivals mainly due to its location, which is a couple of kilometres west of the central district. Primarily a business hotel, it features do-it-yourself service, but there are luxe features and conveniences aplenty, and the rooms are as fresh as the autumn breeze.

TOP CHOICE Khyber　　　　　　AFGHANI $$
(Panchavati Hotel Complex; mains ₹180-230) Taste one succulent morsel of any of Khyber's signature dishes and you might start wondering if you are actually in Kandahar. The Khyber is, without doubt, one of Nasik's top-notch fine-dining establishments, and it works up a great ambience (soft lighting, sparkling glassware, teak furniture) to go with its wide range of delectable offerings. The *murgh shaan-e-khyber*, juicy pieces of

chicken marinated with herbs and cooked in a creamy gravy, is not to be missed.

Annapoorna Lunch Home FAST FOOD $
(MG Rd; mains ₹50) This fast-moving joint has all the usual quick eats rolling endlessly off its culinary assembly line. No surprises on offer, but it would be hard to find fault with the pan-fresh food that's cheaper than peanuts. Peak lunch hours are a bad time to walk in, as you might have trouble finding a seat.

Talk of the Town MULTICUISINE $$
(Old Agra Rd; mains ₹150-180) Next to the New Central bus stand, this place attracts more tipplers than eaters, although that's no indication of the quality of its food. An upscale place comprising dining rooms at split levels, it offers a good selection of coastal, North Indian and Chinese dishes, best washed down with a refreshing pint of lager.

ℹ Information

Cyber Café (Vakil Wadi Rd; per hr ₹20; ☺10am-10pm) Near Panchavati Hotel Complex.
MTDC tourist office (☑2570059; T/I, Golf Club, Old Agra Rd; ☺10.30am-5.30pm Mon-Sat) About 1km south of the Old Central bus stand.
State Bank of India (Old Agra Rd; ☺11am-5pm Mon-Fri, 11am-1pm Sat) Opposite the Old Central bus stand. Changes cash and travellers cheques and has an ATM.
HDFC Bank (MG Rd) Has a 24-hour ATM.

ℹ Getting There & Around

Bus
Nasik's **Old Central bus stand** (CBS) is useful for those going to Trimbak (₹27, 45 minutes). A block south, the **New Central bus stand** has services to Aurangabad (semideluxe ₹199, 4½ hours) and Pune (semideluxe/deluxe ₹213/360, 4½ hours). South of town, the **Mahamarg bus stand** has services to Mumbai (semideluxe ₹211, four hours) and Shirdi (₹90, 2½ hours).

Private bus agents based near the CBS run buses to Pune, Mumbai, Aurangabad and Ahmedabad. Fares are marginally lower than those charged on state buses. Note that buses depart from Old Agra Rd, and that most Mumbai-bound buses terminate at Dadar in Mumbai.

Train
The Nasik Rd train station is 8km southeast of the town centre, but a useful **railway reservation office** (1st fl, Commissioner's Office, Canada Corner; ☺8am-8pm Mon-Sat) is 500m west of the CBS. The *Panchavati Express* is the fastest

train to Mumbai (2nd class/chair ₹75/263, 3½ hours, 7am), and the *Tapovan Express* is the only convenient direct train to Aurangabad (2nd class/chair ₹66/233, 3½ hours, 9.50am). An autorickshaw to the station costs about ₹70.

Around Nasik

BHANDARDARA

The picturesque village of Bhandardara is nestled deep in the folds of the Sahyadris, about 70km from Nasik. A little-visited place surrounded by craggy mountains, it remains one of Maharashtra's best-kept travel secrets and, with an absence of checkbox travellers, makes a fantastic getaway from the bustle of urban India. However, you don't need to be a rocket scientist to figure out that the scene might be very different in the near future – visit while you can.

Most of Bhandardara's habitation is thrown around the spectacular **Arthur Lake**, a horseshoe-shaped reservoir fed by the waters of the Pravara River. The lake is barraged on one side by the imposing **Wilson Dam**, a colonial-era structure dating back to 1910. If you like walking, consider a hike to the summit of **Mt Kalsubai**, which at 1646m was once used as an observation point by the Marathas. Alternately, you could hike to the ruins of the **Ratangad Fort**, another of Shivaji's erstwhile strongholds, which has wonderful views of the surrounding ranges.

The charming **Anandvan Resort** (☑9920311221; www.anandvanresorts.com; d from ₹5500; ❋), an ecoresort with a choice of comfy cottages and villas overlooking Arthur Lake, allows you to camp in style. The **MTDC Holiday Resort** (☑02424257032; d from ₹1200; ❋), located further down the hill, is also a good place to spend the night.

Bhandardara can be accessed by taking a local bus from Nasik's Mahamarg bus stand to Ghoti (₹30, one hour), from where an autorickshaw ride costs ₹60. A taxi from Nasik can also drop you at your resort for about ₹1200.

IGATPURI

Heard of *vipassana*, haven't you? Well head to Igatpuri to see where (and how) it all happens. Located about 44km south of Nasik, this village is home to the headquarters of the world's largest *vipassana* meditation institution, the **Vipassana International Academy** (☑02553244076; www.dhamma.org), which institutionalises this strict form of meditation first taught by Gautama Buddha in the 6th century BC and reintroduced to India by teacher SN Goenka in the '60s. Ten-day residential courses (advance bookings compulsory) are held throughout the year, though authorities warn that it requires rigorous discipline, and dropping out midway isn't encouraged. Basic accommodation, food and meditation instruction are provided free of charge, but donations upon completion of the course are accepted.

TRIMBAK

The moody **Trimbakeshwar Temple** stands in the centre of Trimbak, 33km west of Nasik. It's one of India's most sacred temples, containing a *jyoti linga,* one of the 12 most important shrines to Shiva. Only Hindus are allowed in, but non-Hindus can peek into the courtyard. Nearby, the waters of the Godavari River flow into the **Gangadwar bathing tank**, where all are welcome to wash away their earthly sins. You also have the option of a four-hour return hike up the **Brahmagiri Hill**, where you can see the Godavari dribble forth from a spring.

Regular buses run from the CBS in Nasik to Trimbak (₹26, 45 minutes).

Aurangabad

📞 0240 / POP 892,400 / ELEV 515M

Aurangabad lay low through most of the tumultuous history of medieval India and only hit the spotlight when the last Mughal emperor, Aurangzeb, made the city his capital from 1653 to 1707. With the emperor's death came the city's rapid decline, but the brief period of glory saw the building of some fascinating monuments, including a Taj Mahal replica (Bibi-qa-Maqbara), that continue to draw a steady trickle of visitors today. These monuments, alongside other historic relics such as a group of ancient Buddhist caves, make Aurangabad a good choice for a fairly decent weekend excursion. But the real reason for traipsing all the way here is because the town is an excellent base for exploring the World Heritage Sites of Ellora and Ajanta.

Silk fabrics were once Aurangabad's chief revenue generator, and the town is still known across the world for its hand-woven Himroo and Paithani saris (see Shopping, p767).

The train station, cheap hotels and restaurants are clumped together in the south of the town along Station Rd East and Station Rd West. The MSRTC bus stand is 1.5km to the north of the train station. Northeast of the bus stand is the buzzing old town with its narrow streets and Muslim quarters. Interestingly, Aurangabad also has a sizeable Buddhist community who follow in the footsteps of eminent humanist and social leader BR Ambedkar, and celebrate his conversion to Buddhism during Dussehra.

◉ Sights

Bibi-qa-Maqbara MONUMENT
(Indian/foreigner ₹5/100; ⊙dawn-10pm) Built by Aurangzeb's son Azam Khan in 1679 as a mausoleum for his mother Rabia-ud-Daurani, Bibi-qa-Maqbara is widely known as the 'poor man's Taj'. With its four minarets flanking a central onion-domed mausoleum, the white structure bears striking resemblance to the original Taj Mahal in Agra. It is much less grand, however, and apart from having a few marble adornments, most of the structure is finished in lime mortar. Apparently the prince had conceived the entire mausoleum in white marble like the Taj, but was

---

SAI BABA OF SHIRDI

His iconic status as a national guru is legendary. And his divinity, to some, is unquestionable. But Sai Baba, for all his popularity, remains one of India's most enigmatic figures. No one knows where he came from, what his real name was, or when he was born. Having stepped out of an obscure childhood, he first appeared in the town of Shirdi near Nasik around the age of 16 (in the mid-1800s). There, he advocated religious tolerance, which he practised by sleeping alternately in a mosque and a Hindu temple as well as praying in them both. The masses took to him right away, and by the time Sai Baba died in 1918, the many miracles attributed to him had seen him gather a large following. Today, his temple complex in Shirdi draws an average of 40,000 pilgrims a day. Interestingly, in Andhra Pradesh, another widely respected holy man Sathya Sai Baba (1926–2011) claimed to be the reincarnation of the original Sai Baba (see p918).

thwarted by his frugal father who opposed his extravagant idea of draining state coffers for the purpose. However, despite the use of cheaper material and the obvious weathering, it's a sight far more impressive than the average gravestone. The central onion dome was being restored during research, and should be back in its untarnished glory by the time you visit.

Aurangabad Caves
CAVE

(Indian/foreigner ₹5/100; ⊙dawn-dusk) Architecturally speaking, the Aurangabad Caves aren't a patch on Ellora or Ajanta, but they do throw some light on early Buddhist architecture and, above all, make for a quiet and peaceful outing. Carved out of the hillside in the 6th or 7th century AD, the 10 caves, comprising two groups 1km apart (retain your ticket for entry into both sets), are all Buddhist. Cave 7, with its sculptures of scantily clad lovers in suggestive positions, is particularly arty. The caves are about 2km north of Bibi-qa-Maqbara. A return autorickshaw from the mausoleum shouldn't cost more than ₹150.

Panchakki
GARDEN

(Indian/foreigner ₹5/20; ⊙6.15am-9.15pm) The garden complex of Panchakki, literally meaning 'water wheel', takes its name from the hydro-mill which, in its day, was considered a marvel of engineering. Driven by water carried through earthen pipes from the river 6km away, it was once used to grind grain for pilgrims. You can still see the humble machine at work today.

Baba Shah Muzaffar, a Sufi saint and spiritual guide to Aurangzeb, is buried here. His **memorial garden** is flanked by a series of fish-filled tanks, near a large shade-giving banyan tree.

Shivaji Museum
MUSEUM

(Dr Ambedkar Rd; admission ₹5; ⊙10.30am-6pm Fri-Wed) This simple museum is dedicated to the life of the Maratha hero Shivaji. Its collection includes a 500-year-old chain-mail suit and a copy of the Quran handwritten by Aurangzeb.

☞ Tours

Classic Tours (p768) and the **Indian Tourism Development Corporation** (ITDC; ☎2331143) both run daily bus tours to the Ajanta and Ellora Caves. The trip to Ajanta Caves costs ₹400 and the tour to Ellora Caves, ₹270; prices include a guide but don't cover admission fees. The Ellora tour also includes all the other major Aurangabad sites along with Daulatabad Fort and Aurangzeb's tomb in Khuldabad, which is a lot to swallow in a day. All tours start and end at the MTDC Holiday Resort. During quiet periods, operators often pool resources and pack their clients into a single bus.

For private tours, try **Ashoka Tours & Travels** (p768), which owns a decent fleet of taxis and can personalise your trip around Aurangabad and to Ajanta and Ellora.

🛏 Sleeping

Lemon Tree
HOTEL $$$

(☎6603030; www.lemontreehotels.com; R7/2 Chikalthana, Airport Rd; s/d incl breakfast from ₹3499/4499; ❀❡❀) Fresh as lemonade, this swish, all-new boutique hotel (spread lazily around what we thought was the best swimming pool in the Deccan) makes you want to stay back in Aurangabad even after you're done sightseeing. The rooms are done up in vivid tropical shades offset against snow-white walls, and are super snug to boot. Adding a dash of class is the prim Citrus Café, and the Slounge bar, where you can down a drink while hustling a fellow traveller in to a game of pool. It's one place you're sure to have a nice stay.

MTDC Holiday Resort
HOTEL $$

(☎2331513; Station Rd East; d from ₹1100, with AC from ₹1300; ❀) Set around a lovely lawn and shaded by robust canopies, this curiously disorganised hotel is one of the better state-owned operations in Maharashtra. The large residential blocks have recently received a facelift, and the rooms, though lacking in character, are spacious and tidy. Service is prompt, there's also a well-stocked bar, a decent restaurant and a couple of travel agencies and souvenir shops on-site. Come between March and July and you will pay 20% less.

Hotel Panchavati
HOTEL $

(☎2328755; www.hotelpanchavati.com; Station Rd West; s/d ₹525/625, with AC ₹775/900; ❀) This place is fast establishing itself as one of the more reputed hotels in Aurangabad (quite a turnaround from the days when it took some serious stick from travellers). Generally packed to the gills with guests, it offers a range of compact but thoughtfully appointed rooms, with comfortable beds and patterned rugs on the floor that match the

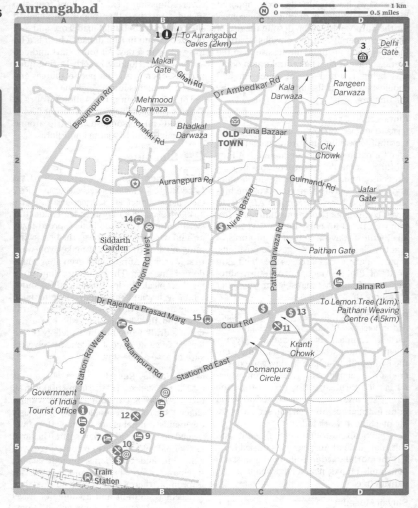

upholstery and pastel walls. The managers are efficient and friendly and the hotel sits easily at the top of the value-for-money class.

VITS HOTEL **$$$**
(☏2350701; www.vitshotelaurangabad.com; Station Rd East; s/d incl breakfast ₹5500/6500; ✳❋✉) Located close to the train station, snazzy-lobbied VITS goes by the motto 'Guest. Rest. Best'. What that basically means is you have a delightfully luxurious room to flop about in, packed with all the usual luxe features you'd find in top-range

hotels. A branch of the Four Fountains chain of spas located within the hotel considerably ups the indulgence quotient.

Hotel Nandanvan HOTEL **$**
(☏2338916; Station Rd East; s/d ₹450/550, with AC ₹650/750; ❋) Unusually large but clean rooms are on offer at this well-run hotel, set in a prime location close to Kailash Restaurant. The real dealmakers, of course, are the loos, which are cleaner than those of most other budget options in town. The noise coming off the main road might get to you at times, though.

Aurangabad

Hotel Amarpreet   HOTEL $$
(☑6621133; www.amarpreethotel.com; Jalna Rd; s/d from ₹2800/3600; ❄@) We have to hand it to Amarpreet for trying hard. The rooms might trigger the occasional hunch that you'd have got more bang for your buck elsewhere, but the all-smiles management makes up for it with polite service, excellent housekeeping and a great selection of food and booze. Ask for a room in the western wing, with superb views of Bibi-qa-Maqbara.

Tourist's Home   HOTEL $
(☑2337212; Station Rd West; d ₹400, with AC ₹1000; ❄) This one's as basic as it gets. Although recently given a makeover, most rooms here are barebones, but well-ventilated. There are quite a few rules and regulations to be adhered to, going by the noticeboard at the entrance, but the management is friendly. And it's close to the train station, which is a positive.

 Eating

China Town   CHINESE $$
(Hotel Amarpreet, Jalna Rd; mains ₹180-200) For a place like Aurangabad, this in-house restau-
rant at Hotel Amarpreet tosses up Chinese dishes of a surprisingly fine quality. A good range of noodles is on offer, which goes extremely well with the numerous chicken and lamb preparations all presented appetisingly in the restaurant's well-dressed interiors.

Swad Veg Restaurant   INDIAN $
(Kanchan Chamber, Station Rd East; mains ₹70-80) This place has come a long way since its formative years, and now offers a fantastic range of Indian snacks and staples – plus a few pizzas, ice creams and shakes – in its prim and clean basement premises. Try the Gujarati thali (₹110), an endless train of dishes that diners gobble up under the benevolent gaze of patron saint swami Yogiraj Hanstirth, whose portrait illuminates a far wall of the restaurant.

Tandoor   NORTH INDIAN $$
(Shyam Chambers, Station Rd East; mains ₹160-180) Offering fine tandoori dishes and flavoursome North Indian veg and non-veg options in a weirdly Pharaonic atmosphere, Tandoor is one of Aurangabad's top standalone restaurants. A few Chinese dishes are also on offer, but patrons clearly prefer the dishes coming out of, well, the tandoor.

Kailash   INDIAN $
(Station Rd East; mains ₹70-80) Adjacent to Hotel Nandanvan, this busy pure-veg restaurant is a smart glass-and-chrome place where you can sit back after a long day out and wolf down a variety of local delicacies brought to your table by smartly dressed waiters.

Prashanth   INDIAN $
(Siddharth Arcade, Station Rd East; mains ₹70-90) Located near the railway station bang opposite the MTDC Holiday Resort, Prashanth has consistently won accolades from travellers for its delightful vegetarian-only dishes, epic fruit juices and enjoyable patio setting. Eat your heart out.

🛍 Shopping

Hand-woven Himroo material is a traditional Aurangabad speciality (though people have differing opinions regarding its aesthetic appeal). Made from cotton, silk and silver threads, it was developed as a cheaper alternative to Kam Khab, the more ornate brocade of silk and gold thread woven for royalty in the 14th century. Most of today's Himroo shawls and saris are mass-produced using power looms, but some showrooms in the city still run traditional workshops, thus preserving this dying art.

Himroo saris start at ₹1000 (cotton and silk blend). Paithani saris, which are of a superior quality, range from ₹5000 to ₹300,000 – before you baulk at the price, bear in mind that some of them take more than a year to make. If you're buying, ensure you're spending your money on authentic Himroo, and not 'Aurangabad silk'.

One of the best places to come and watch weavers at work is the **Paithani Weaving Centre** (Jalna Rd; ⊗11.30am-8pm), behind the Indian Airlines office.

ⓘ Information

Internet Access

Internet Browsing Hub (Station Rd East; per hr ₹15; ⊗8am-10pm)
Sai Internet Café (Station Rd East; per hr ₹15; ⊗8am-10pm)

Money

ICICI, State Bank of India (SBI), State Bank of Hyderabad (SBH) and HDFC Bank have several ATMs along Station Rd East, Court Rd, Nirala Bazaar and Jalna Rd.
State Bank of India (Kranti Chowk; ⊗11am-5pm Mon-Fri, 11am-1pm Sat) Handles foreign exchange.

Post

Post office (Juna Bazaar; ⊗10am-6pm Mon-Sat)

Tourist Information

Government of India tourist office (☎2331217; Krishna Vilas, Station Rd West; ⊗8.30am-6pm Mon-Sat) A friendly and helpful tourist office with a decent range of brochures.
MTDC office (☎2331513; MTDC Holiday Resort, Station Rd East; ⊗10am-5.30pm Mon-Sat)

Travel Agencies

Ashoka Tours & Travels (☎9890340816; Hotel Panchavati, Station Rd West) Person-alised city and regional tours, car hire and hotel pick-ups. Run by former *Lonely Planet* recommended autorickshaw driver Ashok T Kadam.
Classic Tours (☎2337788; www.classictours .info; MTDC Holiday Resort, Station Rd East) Trusty place to book transport and tours.

ⓘ Getting There & Away
Air
The **airport** is 10km east of town. En route are the offices of **Indian Airlines** (☎2485241; Jalna Rd) and **Jet Airways** (☎2441392; Jalna Rd).

There are daily flights to Delhi, with a stopover in Mumbai. Fares start from around ₹1500.

Bus
Buses leave regularly from the **MSRTC bus stand** (Station Rd West) to Pune (semideluxe/deluxe ₹228/390, five hours) and Nasik (semideluxe ₹199, five hours). **Private bus agents** are located around the corner where Dr Rajen-dra Prasad Marg becomes Court Rd; a few sit closer to the bus stand. Deluxe overnight bus destinations include Mumbai (with/without AC ₹280/220, sleeper ₹610, eight hours), Ahmed-abad (₹410, 15 hours) and Nagpur (₹390, 12 hours).

Ordinary buses head to Ellora from the MSRTC bus stand every half hour (₹28, 45 minutes) and hourly to Jalgaon (₹122, four hours) via Fardapur (₹80, two hours). The T-junction near Fardapur is the drop-off point for Ajanta (see p775 for more details).

Train
Aurangabad's **train station** (Station Rd East) is not on a main line, but two heavily-booked trains, the *Tapovan Express* (2nd class/chair ₹102/338, 7½ hours, 2.35pm) and the *Janshat-abdi Express* (2nd class/chair ₹127/420, 6½ hours, 6am) run direct to/from Mumbai. For Hyderabad (Secunderabad), take the *Devagiri Express* (sleeper/2AC ₹224/822, 10 hours, 4.05am). To reach northern or eastern India, take a bus to Jalgaon and board a train there.

ⓘ Getting Around
Autorickshaws are as common here as mosqui-toes in a summer swamp. The **taxi stand** is next to the MSRTC bus stand; share jeeps also depart from here for destinations around Aurangabad, including Ellora and Daulatabad. Expect to pay ₹600 for a full-day tour in a rickshaw, or ₹900 in a taxi.

Around Aurangabad
DAULATABAD
This one's straight out of a Tolkien fantasy. A most beguiling structure, the 12th-century hilltop fortress of Daulatabad is located about 15km from Aurangabad, en route to Ellora. Now in ruins, the citadel was origi-nally conceived as an impregnable fort by the Yadava kings. Its most infamous high-point came in 1328, when it was christened Daulatabad (City of Fortune) by eccentric Delhi sultan Mohammed Tughlaq and made the capital – he even marched the entire population of Delhi 1100km south to popu-late it. Ironically, Daulatabad – despite being better positioned strategically than Delhi –

soon proved untenable as a capital due to an acute water crisis, and Tughlaq forced the weary inhabitants all the way back to Delhi, which had by then been reduced to a ghost town.

Daulatabad's central bastion sits atop a 200m-high craggy outcrop known as Devagiri (Hill of the Gods), surrounded by a 5km **fort** (Indian/foreigner ₹5/100; ◷6am-6pm). The climb to the summit takes about an hour, and leads past an ingenious series of defences, including multiple doorways designed with odd angles and spike-studded doors to prevent elephant charges. A tower of victory, known as the **Chand Minar** (Tower of the Moon), built in 1435, soars 60m above the ground to the right – it's closed to visitors. Higher up, you can walk into the **Chini Mahal**, where Abul Hasan Tana Shah, king of Golconda, was held captive for 12 years before his death in 1699. Nearby, there's a 6m **cannon**, cast from five different metals and engraved with Aurangzeb's name.

Part of the ascent goes through a pitch-black, bat-infested, water-seeping, spiralling tunnel. Guides (₹450) are available near the ticket counter to show you around, and their flame-bearing assistants will lead you through the dark passageway for a small tip. But on the way down you'll be left to your own devices, so carry a torch. The crumbling staircases and sheer drops can make things difficult for the elderly, children and those suffering from vertigo or claustrophobia.

KHULDABAD

Time permitting, take a pit-stop in the scruffy-walled settlement of Khuldabad (Heavenly Abode), a quaint and cheerful little Muslim pilgrimage village just 3km from Ellora. Buried deep in the pages of history, Khuldabad is where a number of historic figures lie interred, including emperor Aurangzeb, the last of the Mughal greats. Despite matching the legendary King Solomon in terms of state riches, Aurangzeb was an ascetic in his personal life, and insisted that he be buried in a simple tomb constructed only with the money he had made from sewing Muslim skullcaps. An unfussy affair of modest marble in a courtyard of the **Alamgir Dargah** (◷7am-8pm) is exactly what he got.

Generally a calm place, Khuldabad is swamped with pilgrims every April when a robe said to have been worn by the Prophet Mohammed, and kept within the dargah

(shrine), is shown to the public. Across the road from the Alamgir Dargah, another shrine contains strands of the Prophet's beard and lumps of silver from a tree of solid silver, which is said to have miraculously grown at this site after a saint's death.

Ellora
◷02437

Give a man a hammer and chisel, and he'll create art for posterity. Come to the World Heritage Site-listed **Ellora cave temples** (Indian/foreigner ₹10/250; ◷dawn-dusk Wed-Mon), located 30km from Aurangabad, and you'll know exactly what we mean. The epitome of ancient Indian rock-cut architecture, these caves were chipped out laboriously over five centuries by generations of Buddhist, Hindu and Jain monks. Monasteries, chapels, temples – the caves served every purpose, and they were stylishly embellished with a profusion of remarkably detailed sculptures. Unlike the caves at Ajanta (p772), which are carved into a sheer rock face, the Ellora caves line a 2km-long escarpment, the gentle slope of which allowed architects to build elaborate courtyards in front of the shrines, and render them with sculptures of a surreal quality.

Ellora has 34 caves in all: 12 Buddhist (AD 600–800), 17 Hindu (AD 600–900) and five Jain (AD 800–1000). The grandest, however, is the awesome Kailasa Temple (Cave 16), the world's largest monolithic sculpture, hewn top to bottom against a rocky slope by 7000 labourers over a 150-year period. Dedicated to Lord Shiva, it is clearly among the best that ancient Indian architecture has to offer.

Historically, the site represents the renaissance of Hinduism under the Chalukya and Rashtrakuta dynasties, the subsequent decline of Indian Buddhism and a brief resurgence of Jainism under official patronage. The increasing influence of Tantric elements in India's three great religions can also be seen in the way the sculptures are executed, and their coexistence at one site indicates a lengthy period of religious tolerance.

Official guides can be hired at the ticket office in front of the Kailasa Temple for ₹700. Most guides have an extensive knowledge of cave architecture, so try not to skimp. If your tight itinerary forces you to choose between Ellora or Ajanta, Ellora wins hands down.

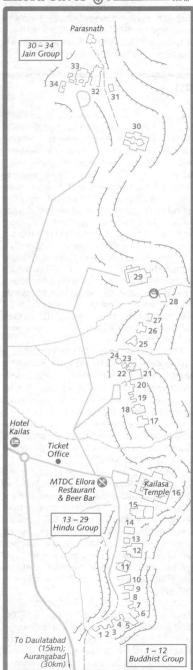

Parasnath

30 – 34
Jain Group

33
34
32
31

30

29

28
27
26
25
24 23
22 21
20
19
18
17

Hotel
Kailas

Ticket
Office

MTDC Ellora
Restaurant
& Beer Bar

Kailasa
Temple 16

15
14
13
12
11
10
9
8
7
6
5
4
1 2 3

13 – 29
Hindu Group

To Daulatabad
(15km);
Aurangabad
(30km)

1 – 12
Buddhist Group

⊙ Sights

Kailasa Temple   HINDU TEMPLE

Halfway between a cave and a religious shrine, this **rock-cut temple**, built by King Krishna I of the Rashtrakuta dynasty in AD 760, was built to represent Mt Kailasa (Kailash), Shiva's Himalayan abode. To say that the assignment was daring would be an understatement. Three huge trenches were bored into the sheer cliff face with hammers and chisels, following which the shape was 'released', a process that entailed removing 200,000 tonnes of rock, while taking care to leave behind those sections that would later be used for sculpting. Covering twice the area of the Parthenon in Athens and being half as high again, Kailasa is an engineering marvel that was executed straight from the head with zero margin for error. Modern draughtsmen might have a lesson or two to learn here.

Size aside, the temple is remarkable for its prodigious sculptural decoration. The temple houses several intricately carved panels, depicting scenes from the Ramayana, the Mahabharata and the adventures of Krishna. Also worth admiring are the immense **monolithic pillars** that stand in the courtyard, flanking the entrance on both sides, and the southeastern gallery that has 10 giant and fabulous panels depicting the different avatars of Lord Vishnu. Kailasa is a temple, still very much in use; you'll have to remove your shoes to enter the main shrine.

After you're done with the main enclosure, bypass the hordes of snack-munching day trippers to explore the temple's many dank, bat urine-soaked corners with their numerous forgotten carvings. Afterwards, hike up a foot trail to the south of the complex that takes you to the top perimeter of the 'cave', from where you can get a bird's-eye view of the entire temple complex.

Buddhist Caves   CAVES

The southernmost 12 caves are Buddhist *viharas* (monasteries), except Cave 10, which is a *chaitya* (assembly hall). While the earliest caves are simple, Caves 11 and 12 are more ambitious, and on par with the more impressive Hindu temples.

Cave 1, the simplest *vihara*, may have been a granary. **Cave 2** is notable for its ornate pillars and the imposing seated Buddha, which faces the setting sun. **Cave 3** and **Cave 4** are unfinished and not well-preserved.

Cave 5 is the largest *vihara* in this group, at 18m wide and 36m long; the rows of stone benches hint that it may once have been an assembly hall.

Cave 6 is an ornate *vihara* with wonderful images of Tara, consort of the Bodhisattva Avalokitesvara, and of the Buddhist goddess of learning, Mahamayuri, looking remarkably similar to Saraswati, her Hindu equivalent. Cave 7 is an unadorned hall, but from here you can pass through a doorway to Cave 8, the first cave in which the sanctum is detached from the rear wall. Cave 9 is notable for its wonderfully carved fascia.

Cave 10 is the only *chaitya* in the Buddhist group and one of the finest in India. Its ceiling features ribs carved into the stonework; the grooves were once fitted with wooden panels. The balcony and upper gallery offer a closer view of the ceiling and a frieze depicting amorous couples. A decorative window gently illuminates an enormous figure of the teaching Buddha.

Cave 11, the Do Thal (Two Storey) Cave, is entered through its third basement level, not discovered until 1876. Like Cave 12, it probably owes its size to competition with the more impressive Hindu caves of the same period.

Cave 12, the huge Tin Thal (Three Storey) Cave, is entered through a courtyard. The locked shrine on the top floor contains a large Buddha figure flanked by his seven previous incarnations. The walls are carved with relief pictures, like those in the Hindu caves.

Hindu Caves   CAVES

Where calm and contemplation infuse the Buddhist caves, drama and excitement characterise the Hindu group (Caves 13 to 29). In terms of scale, creative vision and skill of execution, these caves are in a league of their own.

All these temples were cut from the top down, so it was never necessary to use scaffolding – the builders began with the roof and moved down to the floor.

Cave 13 is a simple cave, most likely a granary. Cave 14, the Ravana-ki-Khai, is a Buddhist *vihara* converted to a temple dedicated to Shiva sometime in the 7th century.

Cave 15, the Das Avatara (Ten Incarnations of Vishnu) Cave, is one of the finest at Ellora. The two-storey temple contains a mesmerising Shiva Nataraja, and Shiva emerging from a lingam (phallic image) while Vishnu and Brahma pay homage.

Caves 17 to 20 and 22 to 28 are simple monasteries.

Cave 21, known as the Ramesvara Cave, features interesting interpretations of familiar Shaivite scenes depicted in the earlier temples. The figure of goddess Ganga, standing on her makara (mythical sea creature), is particularly notable.

The large Cave 29, the Dumar Lena, is thought to be a transitional model between the simpler hollowed-out caves and the fully developed temples exemplified by the Kailasa. It has views over a nearby waterfall you can walk down to.

Jain Caves   CAVES

The five Jain caves may lack the artistic vigour and ambitious size of the best Hindu temples, but they are exceptionally detailed. The caves are 1km north of the last Hindu temple (Cave 29) at the end of the bitumen road.

Cave 30, the Chhota Kailasa (Little Kailasa), is a poor imitation of the great Kailasa Temple and stands by itself some distance from the other Jain temples.

In contrast, Cave 32, the Indra Sabha (Assembly Hall of Indra), is the finest of the Jain temples. Its ground-floor plan is similar to that of the Kailasa, but the upstairs area is as ornate and richly decorated as the downstairs is plain. There are images of the Jain *tirthankars* (great teachers) Parasnath and Gomateshvara, the latter surrounded by wildlife. Inside the shrine is a seated figure of Mahavira, the last *tirthankar* and founder of the Jain religion.

Cave 31 is really an extension of Cave 32. Cave 33, the Jagannath Sabha, is similar in plan to 32 and has some well-preserved sculptures. The final temple, the small Cave 34, also has interesting sculptures. On the hilltop over the Jain temples, a 5m-high image of Parasnath looks down on Ellora.

🛏 Sleeping & Eating

Hotel Kailas   HOTEL $$
(☏244446; www.hotelkailas.com; d ₹1500, cottages from ₹2000; ❄) The sole decent hotel near the site, this place should be considered only if you can't have enough of Ellora in a single day. The comfy cottages here come with warm showers; those with cave views are ₹500 pricier. There's a good restaurant (mains ₹100) and a lush lawn tailor-made for an evening drink.

The spotless **MTDC Ellora Restaurant & Beer Bar** (mains ₹60-90; ◷9am-5pm), located within the complex, is a good place to settle in for lunch, or pack takeaways in case you want to picnic beside the caves.

ⓘ Getting There & Away

Buses regularly ply the road between Aurangabad and Ellora (₹28); the last bus departs from Ellora at 8pm. Share jeeps leave when they're full with drop-off outside the bus stand in Aurangabad (₹40). A full-day autorickshaw tour to Ellora, with stops en route, costs ₹600; taxis charge around ₹900.

Ajanta

☎ 02438

Fiercely guarding its horde of priceless artistic treasures from another era, the **Buddhist caves of Ajanta** (Indian/foreigner ₹10/250; video ₹25; ☺9am-5.30pm Tue-Sun), 105km northeast of Aurangabad, could well be called the Louvre of ancient India. Much older than Ellora, its venerable twin in the World Heritage Sites listings, these secluded caves date from around the 2nd century BC to the 6th century AD and were among the earliest monastic institutions to be constructed in the country. Ironically, it was Ellora's rise that brought about Ajanta's downfall, and historians believe the site was abandoned once the focus had shifted to the newly-built caves of Ellora. Upon being deserted, the caves were soon reclaimed by wilderness and remained forgotten until 1819, when a British hunting party led by officer John Smith stumbled upon them purely by chance.

The primary reason to visit Ajanta is to admire its renowned 'frescoes', actually temperas, which adorn many of the caves' interiors. With few other examples from ancient times matching their artistic excellence and fine execution, these paintings are of unfathomable heritage value. It's believed that the natural pigments for these paintings were mixed with animal glue and vegetable gum to bind them to the dry surface. Many caves have small, crater-like holes in their floors, which acted as palettes during paint jobs.

Despite their age, the paintings in most caves remain finely preserved today, and many attribute it to their relative isolation from humanity for centuries. However, it would be a tad optimistic to say that decay hasn't set in. Signposts placed at the entrance of the complex list a series of 'Dos and Don'ts' intended to reduce human impact on this vulnerable site. Please comply.

Authorised guides are available to show you around for ₹600.

⊙ Sights & Activities

The Caves
CAVES

The 30 caves of Ajanta line the steep face of a horseshoe-shaped rock gorge bordering the Waghore River flowing below. They are sequentially numbered from one end to the other, barring Caves 29 and 30. The numbering has nothing to do with their chronological order; the oldest caves are actually in the middle and are flanked by newer caves on both sides.

Caves 3, 5, 8, 22 and 28 to 30 remain either closed or inaccessible. Other caves might be closed from time to time due to restoration work – Cave 10, the grandest of them all, was being scaffolded on the outside during research. During rush periods, viewers might be allotted 15 minutes within the caves, many of which have to be entered barefoot (socks allowed).

Five of the caves are *chaityas* while the other 25 are *viharas*. Caves 8, 9, 10, 12, 13 and part of 15 are early Buddhist caves, while the others date from around the 5th century AD (Mahayana period). In the simpler, more austere early Buddhist school, the Buddha was never represented directly – his presence was always alluded to by a symbol such as the footprint or wheel of law.

Cave 1, a Mahayana *vihara*, was one of the last to be excavated and is the most beautifully decorated. This is where you'll find a rendition of the **Bodhisattva Padmapani**, the most famous and iconic of the Ajanta artworks. A verandah in front leads to a large congregation hall, housing sculptures and narrative murals known for their splendid perspective and elaborate detailing of dress, daily life and facial expressions. The colours in the paintings were created from local minerals, with the exception of the vibrant blue made from Central Asian lapis lazuli. Look up to the ceiling to see the carving of four deer sharing a common head.

Cave 2 is also a late Mahayana *vihara* with deliriously ornamented columns and capitals, and some fine paintings. The ceiling is decorated with geometric and floral patterns. The murals depict scenes from the Jataka tales, including Buddha's mother's

Ajanta Caves

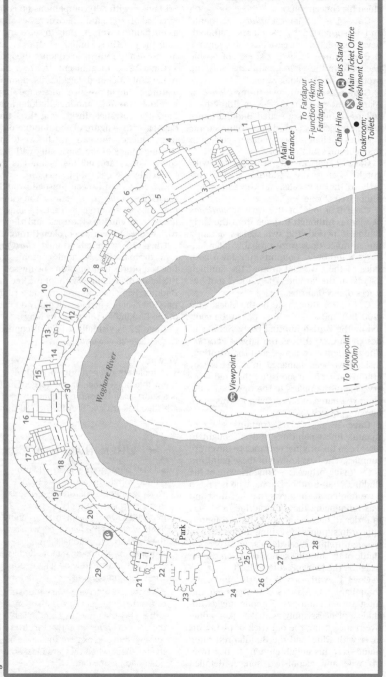

100 m

0

To Fardapur
T-junction (4km);
Fardapur (5km)

Bus Stand

Main Ticket Office

Chair Hire

Refreshment Centre

Cloakroom;
Toilets

Main
Entrance

Waghure River

Viewpoint

To Viewpoint
(500m)

Park

dream of a six-tusked elephant, which heralded his conception.

Cave 4 is the largest *vihara* at Ajanta and is supported by 28 pillars. Although never completed, the cave has some impressive sculptures, including scenes of people fleeing from the 'eight great dangers' to the protection of Avalokitesvara.

Cave 6 is the only two-storey *vihara* at Ajanta, but parts of the lower storey have collapsed. Inside is a seated Buddha figure and an intricately carved door to the shrine. Upstairs the hall is surrounded by cells with fine paintings on the doorways.

Cave 7 has an atypical design, with porches before the verandah leading directly to the four cells and the elaborately sculptured shrine.

Cave 9 is one of the earliest *chaityas* at Ajanta. Although it dates from the early Buddhist period, the two figures flanking the entrance door were probably later Mahayana additions. Columns run down both sides of the cave and around the 3m-high dagoba at the far end. The vaulted roof has traces of wooden ribs.

Cave 10 is thought to be the oldest cave (200 BC) and was the first one to be spotted by the British hunting party. Similar in design to Cave 9, it is the largest *chaitya*. The facade has collapsed and the paintings inside have been damaged, in some cases by graffiti dating from soon after their rediscovery. One of the pillars to the right bears the engraved name of Smith, who left his mark here for posterity.

Cave 16, a *vihara*, contains some of Ajanta's finest paintings and is thought to have been the original entrance to the entire complex. The best known of these paintings is the 'dying princess' – Sundari, wife of the Buddha's half-brother Nanda, who is said to have fainted at the news that her husband was renouncing the material life (and her) in order to become a monk. Carved figures appear to support the ceiling in imitation of wooden architectural details, and there's a statue of the Buddha seated on a lion throne teaching the Noble Eightfold Path.

Cave 17, with carved dwarfs supporting the pillars, has Ajanta's best-preserved and most varied paintings. Famous images include a princess applying make-up, a seductive prince using the old trick of plying his lover with wine, and the Buddha returning home from his enlightenment to beg from his wife and astonished son. A detailed panel tells of Prince Simhala's expedition to Sri Lanka: with 500 companions he is shipwrecked on an island where ogresses appear as enchanting women, only to seize and devour their victims. Simhala escapes on a flying horse and returns to conquer the island.

Cave 19, a magnificent *chaitya,* has a remarkably detailed facade; its dominant feature is an impressive horseshoe-shaped window. Two fine, standing Buddha figures flank the entrance. Inside is a three-tiered dagoba with a figure of the Buddha on the front. Outside the cave, to the west, sits a striking image of the Naga king with seven cobra hoods around his head. His wife, hooded by a single cobra, sits by his side.

Cave 24, had it been finished, would be the largest *vihara* at Ajanta. You can see how the caves were constructed – long galleries were cut into the rock and then the rock between them was broken through.

Cave 26, a largely ruined *chaitya,* is now dramatically lit, and contains some fine sculptures that shouldn't be missed. On the left wall is a huge figure of the 'reclining Buddha', lying back in preparation for nirvana. Other scenes include a lengthy depiction of the Buddha's temptation by Maya.

Cave 27 is virtually a *vihara* connected to the Cave 26 *chaitya.*

Viewpoints   VIEWPOINT

Two lookouts offer picture-perfect views of the whole horseshoe-shaped gorge. The first is a short walk beyond the river, crossed via a bridge below Cave 8. A further 40-minute

WHEN IN AJANTA...

» Flash photography is strictly prohibited within the caves, due to its adverse effect on natural dyes used in the paintings. Authorities have installed rows of tiny pigment-friendly lights which cast a faint glow within the caves, but additional lighting is required for glimpsing minute details, and you'll have to rely on long exposures for photographs.

» Most buses ferrying noisy tourists to Ajanta don't get there until noon, so either stay the previous night in Fardapur or push for an early start from Aurangabad and explore the caves in the morning, when they are pleasantly quiet and uncrowded.

uphill walk (not to be attempted during the monsoons) leads to the lookout from where the British party first spotted the caves.

Sleeping & Eating

Accommodation options close to the caves are limited and you're better off using Aurangabad or Jalgaon as a base.

MTDC Holiday Resort HOTEL $
(☎244230; Aurangabad-Jalgaon Rd, Fardapur; d with/without AC ₹900/700; ❄) This government hotel has been given a much-needed overhaul, and it now sits pretty amid lawns just by the main road in Fardapur. Rooms are decent, and the open-air beer bar clinches the deal. It's by far the best lodging option around here.

MTDC Ajanta Tourist Complex HOTEL $$
(☎09422204325; Fardapur T-junction; cottages ₹1200; ❄) Located just behind the shopping 'plaza' and the bus stand is this mint-fresh resort, featuring five charming and well-appointed cottages nestled amid grassy lawns overlooking the hills. However, you'll have to forage for your own food from the stalls nearby.

As far as stuffing your face goes, there is a string of cheap, unappetising restaurants in the plaza (at Fardapur T-Junction). You could pack a picnic and enjoy it in the shady park below Caves 22 to 27. There's also a buzzing refreshment centre by the main ticket office (at Ajanta caves), which serves an overpriced vegetarian thali (₹80) and warm beer.

ℹ Information

A cloakroom adjoining the toilets near the main ticket office is a safe place to leave gear (₹5 per item for four hours), in case you are visiting Ajanta en route from Aurangabad to Jalgaon or vice versa. The caves are a short, steep climb from the ticket office; the elderly can opt for a chair carried by four bearers (₹400).

On a rather perplexing note, the authorities were constructing a brand new complex near the T-junction during research, where they reportedly intended to replicate the major caves within modern, climate-controlled domes!

ℹ Getting There & Away

Buses from Aurangabad (p768) or Jalgaon (p776) will drop you off at the T-junction (where the highway meets the road to the caves), 4km from the site. From here, after paying an 'amenities' fee (₹7), race to the departure point for the green-coloured 'pollution-free' buses (with/without AC ₹12/7), which zoom up to the caves. Buses return on a regular basis (half-hourly, last bus at 6.15pm) to the T-junction.

All MSRTC buses passing through Fardapur stop at the T-junction. After the caves close you can board buses to either Aurangabad or Jalgaon outside the MTDC Holiday Resort in Fardapur, 1km down the main road towards Jalgaon. Taxis are available in Fardapur; ₹900 should get you to Jalgaon.

Jalgaon
☎0257 / POP 368,000 / ELEV 208M
Apart from being a handy base for exploring Ajanta 60km away, Jalgaon is really nothing more than a convenient transit town. A grubby settlement, it stands on the passing rail trade, connecting northern Maharashtra to all major cities across India. Indeed, it's a place to consider if you're moving out of the state towards northern India, or vice versa.

Sleeping & Eating

Most of the hotels in Jalgaon have 24-hour check out. Power cuts are common, so carry a torch for emergencies.

Hotel Plaza HOTEL $
(☎2227354; hotelplaza_jal@yahoo.com; Station Rd; d with/without AC ₹900/500; ❄@) It's amazing how Hotel Plaza continues to impress travellers day after relentless day. There's nothing fancy on offer here, but for the money you pay it's a bumper deal. Rooms are squeaky clean, the sheets fresh, and the effusive owner a mine of useful information.

Hotel Royal Palace HOTEL $$
(☎2233555; Jai Nagar, Mahabal Rd; d from ₹975; ❄✆) It's worth suffering the 15-minute rickshaw ride from the train station to this smart hotel. Luxuriant by Jalgaon's standards, it has a range of spotlessly clean and prim rooms, and a decent multicuisine restaurant serving eminently edible north Indian, coastal, Chinese and Continental fare.

Hotel Arya INDIAN $
(Navi Peth; mains ₹50-80) Vegetarian-only grub on offer; try one of the lip-smacking Punjabi delights. You may have to queue for a table during meals.

ℹ Information

You can find a couple of banks, ATMs and internet cafes on Nehru Rd, which runs along the top of Station Rd.

ℹ Getting There & Away

Several express trains connecting Mumbai (sleeper/2AC ₹211/721, eight hours), Delhi (sleeper/2AC ₹375/1362, 18 hours) and Kolkata (sleeper/2AC ₹442/1623, 26 hours) stop at Jalgaon **train station**. The *Sewagram Express* goes to Nagpur (sleeper/2AC ₹207/709, eight hours, 10pm).

Buses to Fardapur (₹40, 1½ hours) depart half-hourly from the **bus stand** starting at 6am, continuing to Aurangabad (₹122, four hours).

Jalgaon's train station and bus stand are about 2km apart (₹20 by autorickshaw). Luxury bus offices on Railway Station Rd offer services to Aurangabad (₹140, 3½ hours), Mumbai (₹275, nine hours), Pune (₹275, nine hours) and Nagpur (ordinary/sleeper ₹330/360, 10 hours).

Lonar Meteorite Crater

If you like off-beat adventures, travel to Lonar to explore a prehistoric natural wonder. About 50,000 years ago, a meteorite slammed into the earth here, leaving behind a massive crater, 2km across and 170m deep. In scientific jargon, it's the only hypervelocity natural impact crater in basaltic rock in the world. In lay terms, it's as tranquil and relaxing a spot as you could hope to find, with a shallow green lake at its base and wilderness all around. The lake water is supposedly alkaline and excellent for the skin. Scientists think that the meteorite is still embedded about 600m below the southeastern rim of the crater.

The crater's edge is home to several **Hindu temples** as well as wildlife, including langurs, peacocks, deer and an array of birds.

MTDC Tourist Complex (☏07260221602; d with/without AC ₹1100/900; ❄) has a prime location just across the road from the crater, and offers eight rooms of relatively good value, considering the location.

ℹ Getting There & Away

There are a couple of buses a day between Lonar and Aurangabad (₹125, 3½ hours). It's also possible to visit Lonar on a day trip from Aurangabad or Jalgaon if you hire a car and driver, and don't mind dishing out about ₹2200.

Nagpur

☏0712 / POP 2.1 MILLION / ELEV 305M

In the heart of India's orange country, Nagpur is located way off the main tourist routes. Apart from being at its festive best during Dussehra, the city – as such – is hopelessly devoid of sites. Nonetheless, it makes a good base for venturing out to the far eastern corner of Maharashtra. First up, it's close to the temples of Ramtek (p777) and the ashrams of Sevagram (p777). Besides, Nagpur is also a convenient stop for those heading to the isolated **Tadoba-Andhari Tiger Reserve**, 150km south of Nagpur, which has some of India's most dense forest teeming with wildlife, including the famed Bengal tigers.

If you have some time to kill in the evening, take a stroll in the city's Civil Lines area, dotted with some fantastic buildings and mansions dating back to the Raj era, now used as government offices.

🛏 Sleeping & Eating

Nagpur's hotels cater primarily to businesspeople, not tourists. Needless to say, they're frightfully overpriced. Stay in the Central Ave area if you're on a budget, or have a train to catch in the wee hours. Otherwise, consider moving to Ramdaspeth, closer to the city centre.

Hotel Centre Point　　HOTEL $$
(☏2420910; fax 2446260; www.centrepointgroup.org; 24 Central Bazar Rd, Ramdaspeth; s/d from ₹3750/4250; ❄❅❆) A trusted address that's been setting the standards of luxury in Nagpur for sometime now. Rooms are plush, with fluffy beds, high-speed internet access and cheerful paintings adorning the walls. It's located in the heart of the business and entertainment district.

Hotel Blue Diamond　　HOTEL $
(☏2727461; www.hotelbluediamondnagpur.com; 113 Central Ave; s/d ₹400/500, with AC ₹1250/1350; ❄) The mirrored ceiling in reception is straight out of a bad '70s nightclub and the rooms are pretty much the type you'd expect above a seedy '70s nightclub. There's a dungeon-like bar on the mezzanine floor. AC rooms have LCD TVs and crumpled linoleum flooring.

The Pride Hotel　　HOTEL $$$
(☏2291102; fax 2290440; www.pridehotel.com; opp. airport, Wardha Rd; s/d from ₹5500/6250; ❄❅❆) Located close to the airport and away from the din of the city, this sleek business hotel is a good stopover option for touch-and-go travellers. Royal Lancers, its lobby bar, and Puran Da Dhaba, a souped-up version of a traditional Punjabi eatery, are good places to settle in for the evening.

Krishnum　　SOUTH INDIAN $
(Central Ave; mains ₹40-50) This popular place dishes out South Indian snacks and fruit juices of agreeable quality. It also has branches in other parts of town.

Picadilly Checkers FAST FOOD $
(VCA Complex, Civil Lines; mains ₹60-80) A
favourite eating joint for Nagpur's college
brigade. A good range of all-vegetarian
quick bites are on offer.

The dozens of *dhabas* (snack bars), food
stalls and fruit stands opposite the train
station rouse in the evening. Summer is the
best time to sample the famed oranges.

ℹ️ Information

Computrek (18 Central Ave; per hr ₹20;
☉10am-10pm) Internet access on the main drag.
MTDC (☏2533325; near MLA Hostel, Civil
Lines; ☉10am-5.45pm Mon-Sat) Manned by
helpful staff.
State Bank of India (Kingsway; ☉11am-2pm
Mon-Fri) A two-minute walk west of the train
station. Deals in foreign exchange.
State Bank of India, ICICI Bank, Axis Bank and
HDFC Bank have ATMs along Central Ave and in
Ramdaspeth.

ℹ️ Getting There & Away

Air
Most domestic airlines, including **Indian Airlines**
(☏2533962) and **Jet Airways** (☏5617888),
operate daily flights to Delhi (from ₹3500, 1½
hours), Mumbai (from ₹2500, 1½ hours) and
Kolkata (from ₹2500, 1½ hours), as well as linking Hyderabad, Ahmedabad, Bengaluru, Chennai
and Pune. Taxis/autorickshaws from the airport
to the city centre cost ₹350/200.

Bus
The main **MSRTC bus stand** is 2km south of
the train station and hotel area. Ordinary buses
head regularly for Wardha (₹57, three hours) and
Ramtek (₹35, 1½ hours). There are two buses to
Jalgaon (₹326, 10 hours), and three to Hyderabad (₹317, 12 hours).

Train
From Nagpur's **train station**, the *Vidarbha
Express* departs for Mumbai (sleeper/2AC
₹140/1159, 14 hours, 5.15pm), and heading north to Kolkata is the *Gitanjali Express*
(sleeper/2AC ₹379/1378, 17½ hours, 7.05pm).
Several expresses bound for Delhi and Mumbai
stop at Jalgaon (for Ajanta caves; sleeper/2AC
₹207/709, seven hours).

Around Nagpur

RAMTEK
About 40km northeast of Nagpur, Ramtek is believed to be the place where Lord
Rama, of the epic Ramayana, spent some
time during his exile with his wife Sita and
brother Lakshmana. The place is marked by
a cluster of **temples** (☉6am-9pm) about 600
years old, which sit atop the Hill of Rama
and have their own population of resident
monkeys. Autorickshaws will cart you the
5km from the bus stand to the temple complex for ₹50. You can return to town via the
700 steps at the back of the complex. On the
road to the temples you'll pass the delightful **Ambala Tank**, lined with small shrines.
You can take a boat ride (₹20 per head)
around the lake if you want.

Not far away from the main temple cluster, **Rajkamal Resort** (☏07114202761; d with/
without AC ₹1200/900; ❄) has large, featureless
rooms with TVs, and a basic restaurant-bar.

Buses run half-hourly between Ramtek
and the MSRTC bus stand in Nagpur (₹35,
1½ hours). The last bus to Nagpur is at 7pm.

SEVAGRAM
 07152
Located about 85km from Nagpur, Sevagram (Village of Service) was chosen by
Mahatma Gandhi as his base during the Indian Independence Movement. Throughout
the freedom struggle, the village played host
to several nationalist leaders, who would
regularly come to visit the Mahatma at his
Sevagram Ashram (☏284753; ☉6am-5.30pm).

The overseers of this peaceful ashram,
built on 40 hectares of tree-lined farmland,
have carefully restored and conserved the
original huts that Gandhi lived and worked
in, which now house some of his personal
effects, including items of stationery, wood-
en sandals and his walking stick. Overall, it's
a wonderful daylong excursion, although
slightly out of the way.

Very basic lodging is available in the **Yatri
Nivas** (☏284753; d ₹100), across the road
from the entry gate (advance booking recommended), and simple vegetarian meals
can be served in the ashram's dining hall
with prior notice.

Just 3km from Sevagram, Paunar village is
home to the **Brahmavidya Mandir Ashram**
(☏288388; ☉4am-noon & 2-8pm). Founded by
Vinoba Bhave, a nationalist and disciple of
Gandhi, the ashram is run almost entirely by
women. Modelled on *swaraj* (self-sufficiency),
it's operated on a social system of consensus
with no central management.

Sevagram can be reached by taking a
Wardha-bound bus from Nagpur (₹50, three
hours).

TADOBA-ANDHARI RESERVE
Now under India's Project Tiger directorate, this little-explored national park – with

THE LEGEND OF 'BABA' AMTE

The legend of Murlidhar Devidas 'Baba' Amte (1914–2008) is oft-repeated in humanitarian circles around the world. Hailing from an upper-class Brahmin family in Wardha, Amte was snugly ensconced in material riches and on his way to becoming a successful lawyer, when he witnessed a leper die unattended in the streets one night. It was an incident that changed him forever.

Soon after, Amte renounced worldly comforts, embracing an austere life through which he actively worked for the benefit of leprosy patients and those belonging to marginalised communities. In the primitive forested backyards of eastern Maharashtra, he set up his ashram called Anandwan (Forest of Joy). A true Gandhian, Amte believed in self-sufficiency, and his lifelong efforts saw several awards being conferred upon him, including the Ramon Magsaysay Award in 1985.

Amte's work has been continued by his sons Vikas and Prakash and their wives – the latter couple also won the Magsaysay Award in 2008. The family now runs three ashrams in these remote parts to care for the needy, both humans and animals. Volunteering opportunities are available; contact the ashram on mss@niya.org or lbp@bsnl.in.

a healthy population of Bengal tigers – lies 150km south of Nagpur. Less visited than most other forests in India, this is a place where you can get up close with wildlife (which also includes gaurs, chitals, nilgais and sloth bears) without having to jostle past truckloads of shutter-happy tourists. The trade-off is that you'll have to make do with basic amenities and low comfort levels. The park remains open through most of the year.

The **MTDC Resort** (d with/without AC ₹1500/1200) in nearby Moharli has a string of decent rooms and dining facilities. The resort can also arrange jungle safaris in jeeps and minibuses. Bookings can be made at the MTDC's Nagpur office (see p777). If you're travelling in groups of six or more, MTDC has an all-inclusive overnight package out of Nagpur (₹3750 per person), which is recommended since it takes care of logistical hassles. Call in advance.

Several state buses ply between Nagpur and Chandrapur through the day (₹110, 3½ hours).

SOUTHERN MAHARASHTRA

Konkan Coast

Despite being flanked on both ends by two of India's top urban centres, it's laudable how the Konkan Coast manages to latch on to its virginal bounties. A little-explored shoreline running southward from Mumbai all the way to Goa, it is a picturesque strip of land peppered with flawless beaches, tropical green paddy fields, rolling hills and decaying forts. Travelling through this peaceful and quaint region can be sheer bliss. However, remember that accommodation is scant, the cuisine unsophisticated though tasty, and the locals unaccustomed to tour groups, especially foreigners. Since transport is both limited and unreliable, a good option is to rent a taxi in Mumbai and drift slowly down the coast to Goa. What you'll get in return is an experience that money can't buy.

MURUD
02144 / POP 12,500
Even if you don't plan on going the whole stretch, the sleepy fishing hamlet of Murud – 165km from Mumbai – should definitely be on your itinerary. Once you step on to its lazy beaches and feel the white surf rush past your feet, you'll be happy you came.

Sight-wise, Murud is home to the magnificent island fortress of **Janjira** (admission free; 7am-5.30pm), standing about 500m offshore. The citadel was built in 1140 by the Siddis, descendants of sailor-traders from the Horn of Africa, who settled here and allegedly made their living through piracy. No outsider ever made it past the fort's 12m-high walls which, when seen during high tide, seem to rise straight from the sea. Unconquered through history, the fort finally fell to the spoils of nature. Today, its ramparts are slowly turning to rubble as wilderness reclaims its innards.

The only way to reach Janjira is by boat (₹20 return, 15 minutes) from Rajpuri Port.

Boats depart from 7am to 5.30pm daily, but require a minimum of 20 passengers. You can also have a boat to yourself (₹400), and most oarsmen will double as guides for a negotiable fee (around ₹350). To get to Rajpuri from Murud, take an autorickshaw (₹50) or hire a bicycle (₹50 per hour) from the Golden Swan Beach Resort.

Back in Murud you can waste away the days on the beach, joining in with karate practice or playing cricket with local youngsters. Alternately, you could peer through the gates of the off-limits **Ahmedganj Palace**, estate of the Siddi Nawab of Murud, or scramble around the decaying mosque and tombs on the south side of town.

🛏 Sleeping & Eating

Golden Swan Beach Resort HOTEL $$
(☎274078; www.goldenswan.com; Darbar Rd; d incl full board with/without AC from ₹3500/2000; ❄) With only a thicket of palms separating it from the beach, this upscale hotel offers accommodation in cosy rooms and cottages looking out to the sea. The non-AC rooms are in a charming old bungalow located five minutes away from the main property.

Sea Shell Resort HOTEL $$
(☎09833667985; www.seashellmurud.com; Darbar Rd; d with/without AC ₹2500/2000; ❄❄) A very smart place with breezy sea-facing rooms, this place scores quite well with Mumbai's weekend travellers. A teeny swimming pool at the entrance is a welcome addition, and dolphin safaris can be arranged upon prior request.

Hotel Shoreline HOTEL $$
(☎02232258882; www.ajinkyaholidays.com; Darbar Rd; d from ₹3000; ❄) It's slightly boxy and brassy in contrast to its surroundings, but it's centrally located and should be alright for a night or two. Only the more expensive rooms face the sea.

New Sea Rock Restaurant FAST FOOD $
(Rajpuri; ◷9am-9pm) Perched on a cliff overlooking the beach at Rajpuri, this quick-eats joint has an awesome view of Janjira, which looms ahead. A perfect place to steal a million-dollar sunset for the price of a chai (₹10). The proprietors also arrange kayak rides and other water sports during the high season.

Vinayaka Restaurant INDIAN $
(Darbar Rd; mains ₹100) A great place to tuck into a delicious and fiery Malvani thali, served with pink kokam syrup to smother the spices.

ℹ Getting There & Away

AC catamarans (₹100, two hours) from the Gateway of India in Mumbai cruise to Mandva pier between 6am and 7pm. The ticket includes a free shuttle bus to Alibag (30 minutes), otherwise an autorickshaw will be about ₹150. Rickety local buses from Alibag head down the coast to Murud (₹35, two hours). Alternatively, buses from Mumbai Central bus stand take almost six hours to Murud (ordinary/semideluxe ₹117/158).

Avoid the train. The nearest railhead is at Roha, two hours away and badly connected.

GANPATIPULE
☎02357

Primarily a temple town, Ganpatipule has been luring a steady stream of sea-lovers over the years with its clean waters and pristine sands stretching to the horizon. Located about 375km from Mumbai, it's a village that snoozes through much of the year, except during holidays such as Diwali or Ganesh Chaturthi. These are times when hordes of boisterous 'tourists' turn up to visit the seaside **Ganesha Temple** (◷6am-9pm) housing a monolithic Ganesha (painted a bright orange), supposedly discovered 1600 years ago.

About 40km southward, Ratnagiri, the largest town on the southern Maharashtra coast and the main train station for Ganpatipule (it's on the Konkan Railway). You'll also find several ATMs strung along Ratnagiri's main street. But once you've refilled your wallet and gone shopping for conveniences, the only sight worth checking out – apart from a dirty beach – are the remnants of the **Thibaw Palace** (Thibaw Palace Rd; admission free; ◷10am-5.30pm Tue-Sun), where the last Burmese king, Thibaw, was interned under the British from 1886 until his death in 1916.

🛏 Sleeping & Eating

MTDC Resort HOTEL $$
(☎235248; d with/without AC from ₹1500/1300; ❄) Spread over a prime complex just off Ganpatipule's beach, this is the best place to camp. It's a smart, well-kept place with an assortment of rooms and cottages, and packs in a **Bank of Maharashtra** that changes travellers cheques, along with a beer bar. Try the Konkani huts, themed on rural Malvani homes, for a unique experience.

Hotel Vihar Deluxe HOTEL $$
(☎02352222944; Main Rd, Ratnagiri; d with/without AC ₹1800/1000; ❄) This gigantic operation is one of a few functional but featureless hotels that line the main strip in Ratnagiri. Rooms are adequate (the loos quite good), and the

WORTH A TRIP

GET MAROONED

Apart from its main sands, the Konkan Coast also features a string of less-explored but heavenly beaches that could arm-wrestle the Maldives any given day. About 17km north of Murud, well connected by share autorickshaws (₹50), lies **Kashid**, a fantastic beach where you can cosy up with your favourite paperback while sipping on tender coconuts. South of Murud is **Diveagar**, swarming with colonies of sand bubbler crabs, scenic **Harihareshwar**, famous for its seaside temple, and serene **Vengurla**, 10km from Tarkarli, a place you probably wouldn't mind being shipwrecked. Most of these places are connected by back roads where public transport is scant, so they are best visited in a hired cab. You might have to ask for directions often, or stay in village homes for the odd night. Be generous with how much you give.

food – especially the seafood – is commendable. A hearty South Indian breakfast is complimentary.

Tarang Restaurant　　　　INDIAN $
(MTDC Resort; mains ₹80-100) Barring beachside stalls, this is one of the few places where you can grab a decent meal in Ganpatipule.

❶ Getting There & Away

Ordinary buses shuttle between Ganpatipule and Ratnagiri (₹40, 1½ hours). One semideluxe MSRTC bus heads out at 8.45am to Mumbai (₹369, 10 hours), and departs from Mumbai at 8pm. From Ratnagiri's **train station**, the *Janshatabdi Express* goes to Mumbai (2nd class/chair ₹142/460, 5½ hours, 5.50pm). The return train heading for Goa (2nd class/chair ₹122/390, 3½ hours) is at 10.45am. From Ratnagiri's **old bus stand**, semideluxe buses leave for Goa (₹221, seven hours) and Kolhapur (₹135, four hours).

TARKARLI & MALVAN
☎ 02365

A government tourism promo parades this place as comparable to Tahiti, and for once, you can rest assured that these guys are not exaggerating! Within striking distance of Goa, about 200km from Ratnagiri, pristine Tarkarli has white sands and sparkling blue waters that rekindle memories of the Andamans or Ko Phi Phi in Thailand. What's lacking is a well-oiled tourist industry and urban comforts, but do you care?

The monstrous **Sindhudurg Fort**, built by Shivaji and dating from 1664, lies on an offshore island and can be reached by frequent ferries (₹30) from Malvan. MTDC can arrange snorkelling trips to the clear waters around the fortress.

Of the few hotels and resorts available, the good old **MTDC Holiday Resort** (☎ 252390; d from ₹1800; ❄) is still your best bet. Enquire at the resort about backwater tours on its fabulous **houseboats** (standard/luxury incl full board ₹6500/7500).

The closest train station is Kudal, 38km away. Frequent buses (₹25, one hour) cover the route from Malvan **bus stand** (☎ 252034). An autorickshaw from Kudal to Malvan or Tarkarli is about ₹400. Malvan has buses daily to Panaji (₹70, three hours) and a couple of services to Ratnagiri (₹130, five hours).

Matheran

☎ 02148 / POP 5100 / ELEV 803M

Literally meaning 'Jungle Above', Matheran is a tiny patch of peace and quiet capping a craggy Sahyadri summit within spitting distance from Mumbai's heat and grime. Endowed with shady forests criss-crossed with foot trails and breathtaking lookouts, it is easily the most elegant of Maharashtra's hill stations.

The credit for discovering this little gem goes to Hugh Malet, erstwhile collector of Thane district, who chanced upon it during one of his excursions in 1850. Soon it became a hill station patronised by the British and populated by Parsi families.

Getting to Matheran is really half the fun. While speedier options are available by road, nothing beats arriving in town on the narrow-gauge toy train (mini train) that chugs laboriously along a 21km scenic route to the heart of the settlement. Motor vehicles are banned within Matheran, making it an ideal place to give your ears and lungs a rest and your feet some exercise.

◉ Sights & Activities

You can walk along shady forest paths to most of Matheran's viewpoints in a matter of hours, and it's a place well-suited to stress-free ambling. To catch the sunrise, head to **Panorama Point**, while **Porcupine Point** (also known as Sunset Point) is the most popular (read: packed) as the sun drops. **Louisa Point** and **Little Chouk Point** also have stunning views of the Sahyadris and if you're visiting **Echo Point**, give it a yell. Stop at **Charlotte Lake** on the way back from Echo Point, but don't go for a swim – this is the town's main water supply and stepping in is prohibited. You can reach the valley below **One Tree Hill** down the path known as **Shivaji's Ladder**, supposedly trod upon by the Maratha leader himself.

Horses can be hired along MG Rd for rides to the lookout points; they cost about ₹250 per hour (negotiable).

🛏 Sleeping & Eating

Hotels in Matheran are low in quality and unreasonably high in tariff, so if you're not feeling generous, make your visit a day trip from Mumbai. Check-out times vary wildly (as early as 7am), as do high and low season rates. Matheran shuts shop during the monsoons.

TOP CHOICE **Verandah**

In The Forest HERITAGE HOTEL **$$**

(☑230296; www.neemranahotels.com; Barr House; d incl breakfast from ₹3000) This wonderfully preserved 19th-century bungalow thrives on undiluted nostalgia. Step past the threshold of one of its quaintly luxurious rooms or suites and find yourself reminiscing about bygone times in the company of ornate candelabras, antique teak furniture, Victorian canvases, grandfather clocks and a rush of other memorabilia. The eponymous verandah is probably the most beautiful location from where to admire Matheran's woods, and there's a good selection of food and beverages to keep you company through idle hours.

Lord's Central Hotel HERITAGE HOTEL **$$**

(☑230228; www.matheranhotels.com; MG Rd; d incl full board from ₹3600; ❄@➳) Owned by a gracious Parsi family over six generations, this charming colonial-style affair is one of Matheran's most reputed establishments, and guarantees a pleasant stay within its old-world portals. The rooms are comfy, the swimming pool deck offers fabulous views of the valley and distant peaks, and a jumbo chess board out on the lawns is a nice place to down a beer before an awesome Parsi lunch.

Hope Hall Hotel HOTEL **$$**

(☑230253; MG Rd; d from ₹2000) 'Since 1875', says a plaque at reception, and frankly, the age shows! However, it's a cheerful place and going by the scores of 'thank you' notes left by guests, it must be an okay place to stay.

Hookahs & Tikkas INDIAN **$$**

(MG Rd; mains ₹50-110) Operating from a balcony overlooking the main road, this place serves a range of kebabs and savoury Indian fare, as well as hookahs with flavoured tobacco.

Rasna INDIAN **$**

(MG Rd; mains ₹80-100) This restaurant opposite Naoroji Lord Garden serves tasty vegetarian food. Try the popular Punjabi (North Indian) thali (₹90).

ⓘ Information

Entry to Matheran costs ₹25 (₹15 for children), which you pay on arrival at the train station or the Dasturi car park.

On the main road into town, **Vishwas Photo Studio** (MG Rd; ⊘9.30am-10pm) sells useful miniguides (₹25) and photographic accessories, and doubles as a tourist office. The **Union Bank of India** (MG Rd; ⊘10am-2pm Mon-Fri, to noon Sat) has an ATM.

ⓘ Getting There & Away

Taxi

Share taxis run from Neral to Matheran's Dasturi car park (₹60, 30 minutes). Horses (₹180) and hand-pulled rickshaws (₹200) wait here to whisk you in a cloud of red dust to Matheran's main bazaar. You can also walk this stretch in a little over an hour.

Train

The toy train (2nd class/1st class ₹35/210) chugs between Matheran and Neral Junction five times daily. The service is suspended during monsoons. From Mumbai, express trains to Neral Junction include the 7.10am *Deccan Express* or the 8.40am *Koyna Express* (2nd class/chair ₹46/165, 1½ hours). Other expresses from Mumbai stop at Karjat, down the line from Neral, from where you can backtrack on a local train. From Pune, you can reach Karjat by the *Sinhagad Express* (2nd class/chair ₹47/165, two hours, 6.05am).

ⓘ Getting Around

Apart from hand-pulled rickshaws and horses, walking is the only other transport option in Matheran.

Lonavla

☎02114 / POP 55,600 / ELEV 625M

Cheekily masquerading as a hill station, Lo-navla is an overdeveloped (and overpriced) mercantile town about 106km southeast of Mumbai. It's far from attractive, with its main drag consisting almost exclusively of garishly lit shops flogging *chikki,* the rock-hard, brittle sweet made in the area.

The only reason you'd want to come here is to visit the nearby Karla and Bhaja Caves which, after those at Ellora and Ajanta, are the best in Maharashtra.

Hotels, restaurants and the main road to the caves lie north of the train station (exit from platform 1). Most of the Lonavla town-ship and its markets are located south of the station.

The petrol pump opposite Hotel Rama Krishna now has three ATMs dispensing cash. Internet access is available at **Balaji Cyber Café** (1st fl, Khandelwal Bldg, New Ba-zaar; per hr ₹15; ☺12.30-10.30pm), immediately south of the train station.

🏃 Activities

Founded in 1924, the **Kaivalyadhama Yoga Hospital** (☎273039; www.kdham.com; Indian/foreigner incl full board ₹9000/US$320), set about 2km from Lonavla en route to the Karla and Bhaja Caves, combines yoga courses with naturopathic therapies. Room rates cover ac-commodation, yoga sessions, programs and lectures over seven days. Two-, three- and four-week packages are also offered.

Mumbai-based **Nirvana Adventures** (☎022-26053724; www.flynirvana.com) offers various paragliding courses (Indian/foreigner including full board from ₹6500/€250) or 10-minute tandem flights (₹2000) at Kamshet, 25km from Lonavla.

🛌 Sleeping & Eating

Lonavla's hotels suffer from inflated prices and low standards. All hotels listed here have a 10am check-out.

Hotel Adarsh   HOTEL $$
(☎272353; near Bus Stand; d from ₹2500; ❋☒) This is clearly the best-value place in town. Centrally located, it has smart rooms and good service, and seems to be preferred by local yuppies. The terrace pool gives you an-other good reason to stay.

Hotel Lonavla   HOTEL $$
(☎272914; Mumbai-Pune Rd; d from ₹1195) Fan-only rooms here, but it's cheap by Lonavla's standards. Bulk bookings can often leave you without a room, so enquire in advance. They insist that you clear your bills every third day (who stays that long anyway?).

Lonavla & Around

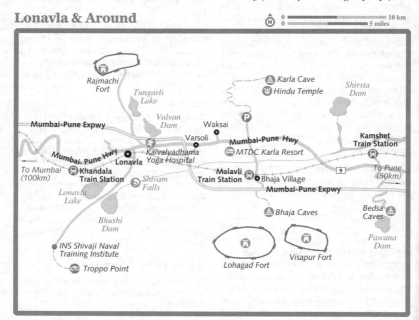

Biso

ITALIAN $$

(Citrus Hotel, DT Shahani Rd, mains ₹180-220) This could be a delightfully redeeming feature of your Lonavla trip. A top-class alfresco restaurant thrown around the lawns of a sleek business hotel about 15 minutes east of the bus stand, Biso serves an excellent selection of pastas, wood oven-fired pizzas and desserts for its upmarket clientele. The penne in basil sauce and the farmhouse pizza are dishes you won't quickly forget.

Hotel Rama Krishna

INDIAN $$

(Mumbai-Pune Rd; mains ₹120-150) This place is famed for its meaty fare, especially the kebabs, and can brim over with travelling parties during meals.

ⓘ Getting There & Away

Lonavla is serviced by MSRTC buses departing the **bus stand** to Dadar in Mumbai (ordinary/semideluxe ₹65/94, two hours) and Pune (ordinary/semideluxe ₹55/80, two hours). Luxury AC buses (about ₹130) also travel to both cities.

All express trains from Mumbai to Pune (2nd class/chair ₹57/195, three hours) stop at Lonavla **train station**. From Pune, you can also reach Lonavla by taking an hourly shuttle train (₹15, two hours).

Karla & Bhaja Caves

While they pale in comparison to Ajanta or Ellora, these rock-cut caves (dating from around the 2nd century BC) are among the better examples of Buddhist cave architecture in India. They are also low on commercial tourism, which make them ideal places for a quiet excursion. Karla has the most impressive single cave, but Bhaja is a quieter site to explore.

Karla Cave

CAVES

(Indian/foreigner ₹5/100; ☉9am-5pm) Karla Cave, the largest early Buddhist *chaitya* in India, is reached by a 20-minute climb from a mini-bazaar at the base of a hill. Completed in 80 BC, the *chaitya* is around 40m long and 15m high, and sports similar architectural motifs as *chaityas* in Ajanta and Ellora. Excluding Ellora's Kailasa Temple, this is probably the most impressive cave temple in the state.

Karla Cave is also the only site in Maharashtra where the original woodwork, more than two centuries old, has managed to survive. A semicircular 'sun window' filters light in towards a dagoba or stupa (the cave's representation of the Buddha), protected by a carved wooden umbrella, the only remaining example of its kind. The cave's roof also retains ancient teak buttresses. The 37 pillars forming the aisles are topped by kneeling elephants. The carved elephant heads on the sides of the vestibule once had ivory tusks.

There's a Hindu **temple** in front of the cave, thronged by pilgrims whose presence adds colour to the scene.

Bhaja Caves

CAVES

(Indian/foreigner ₹5/100; ☉8am-6pm) Across the expressway, it's a 3km jaunt from the main road to the Bhaja Caves, where the setting is lusher, greener and quieter than at Karla Cave. Thought to date from around 200 BC, 10 of the 18 caves here are *viharas,* while Cave 12 is an open *chaitya,* earlier than that at Karla, containing a simple dagoba. Beyond this is a strange huddle of 14 stupas, five inside and nine outside a smaller cave.

Once you're done exploring the Bhaja Caves, you can embark on a trek to the ruined twin-forts of **Lohagad** and **Visapur**. You could also check out the picturesque **Pawana Dam**, down a road about 20km east from the Karla–Bhaja access point.

🛏 Sleeping & Eating

MTDC Karla Resort

HOTEL $$

(%02114-282230; d with/without AC from ₹1300/900; ✳) Set off the highway, close to Karla–Bhaja access point. Rooms and cottages are well-kept, and there's a good restaurant.

ⓘ Getting There & Away

Karla and Bhaja can be visited over a single day from Lonavla. Take a local bus (₹10, 30 minutes) to the access point, from where it's about a 6km return walk on each side to the two sites. An autorickshaw charges about ₹450 from Lonavla for the tour, including waiting time.

Pune

⟁020 / POP 3.7 MILLION / ELEV 535M

With its healthy mix of small-town wonders and big-city blues, Pune (also pronounced Poona) is a city that epitomises 'New India'. Once little more than a pensioners' town and an army outpost, it is today an unpretentious, cosmopolitan place inhabited by a cheerful and happy population. A thriving centre of academia and business, Pune is also known globally for its numero-uno export, the late guru Bhagwan Shree Rajneesh and his ashram, the Osho International Meditation Resort (p785).

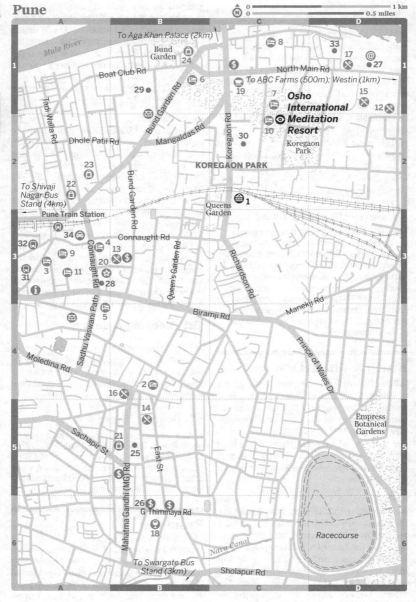

Pune was initially given pride of place by Shivaji and the ruling Peshwas, who made it their capital. The British took the city in 1817 and, thanks to its cool and dry climate, soon made it the Bombay Presidency's monsoon capital. Globalisation knocked on Pune's doors in the 1990s, following which it went in for an image overhaul. However, the colonial charm was retained by preserving its old buildings and residential areas, bringing about a pleasant coexistence of the old and new which (despite the pollution and hectic traffic) makes Pune a wonderful place to explore. In September **Ganesh Chaturthi** brings on a tide of festivities across the city, and provides a fantastic window for exploring the city's cultural side.

The city sits at the confluence of the Mutha and Mula Rivers. Mahatma Gandhi (MG) Rd, about 1km south of Pune train station, is the main commercial street. Koregaon Park, northeast of the train station, is the undisputed chill-out zone, home to some of the best hotels, restaurants, coffee shops and of course, the Osho Ashram.

⊙ Sights & Activities

TOP CHOICE Osho International Meditation Resort MEDITATION

(☎66019999; www.osho.com; 17 Koregaon Park) You'll either like it or hate it. A splurge of an institution, this ashram, located in a leafy, upscale northern suburb, has been drawing thousands of *sanyasins* (seekers), many of them Westerners, ever since the death of Osho (see the boxed text, p786) in 1990. With its placid swimming pool, sauna, 'zennis' and

basketball courts, massage and beauty parlour, bookshop and a luxury boutique guest house (p787), it is, to some, the ultimate place to indulge in stress-busting meditation. Alternately, there are detractors who point fingers at the ashram's blatant commercialisation and accuse it of marketing a warped version of the mystic East to gullible Westerners.

The main centre for meditation and the nightly white-robed spiritual dance is the Osho Auditorium (no coughing or sneezing, please). The Osho Samadhi, where the guru's ashes are kept, is also open for meditation. The commune's 'Multiversity' runs a plethora of courses in meditation and other esoteric techniques. If you wish to take part, or even just meditate, you'll have to pay ₹1150/1550 (Indian/foreigner), which covers registration, a mandatory on-the-spot HIV test (sterile needles used), introductory sessions and your first day's meditation pass. You'll also need two robes (one maroon and one white, from ₹200 per robe). For subsequent days, a daily meditation pass costs ₹300/700 (Indian/foreigner), and you can come and go as you please. If you want further involvement, you can also sign up for a 'work as meditation' program.

The curious can watch a video presentation at the visitor centre and take a 10-minute silent tour of the facilities (₹10; adults only, cameras and phones prohibited) at 9.15am and 2pm daily. Tickets have to be booked at least a day in advance (9.30am to 1pm and 2pm to 4pm). It's also worth checking out the 5-hectare garden, **Osho Teerth** (admission free; ⊙6-9am & 3-6pm), behind the commune, and accessible all day for those with a meditation pass.

TOP
CHOICE **Raja Dinkar Kelkar Museum**   MUSEUM
(www.rajakelkarmuseum.com; 1377-1378 Natu Baug, Bajirao Rd; Indian/foreigner ₹20/200; ⊙9.30am-5.30pm) This fascinating museum is one of Pune's true delights. Housing only a fraction of the 20,000-odd objects of Indian daily life painstakingly collected by Dinkar Kelkar (who died in 1990), it's worth an entire day out. The quirky pan-Indian collection includes hundreds of hookah pipes, writing instruments, lamps, textiles, toys, entire doors and windows, kitchen utensils, furniture, puppets, jewellery, betel-nut cutters and an amazing gallery of musical instruments. During research, the museum was scouting for a new address with more display space, where it could do justice to the vast unseen

portion of the collection currently rotting away in strongrooms.

Tribal Cultural Museum   MUSEUM
(28 Queen's Garden; admission ₹10; ⊙10.30am-5.30pm Mon-Sat) About 1.5km east of the train station, near the army cantonment, this small museum showcases an excellent collection of tribal artefacts (jewellery, utensils, musical instruments, even black magic accessories) sourced from remote tribal belts. It's a great place to familiarise yourself with tribal traditions and cultures of the region. Don't forget to check out the section featuring ornate papier-mâché festival masks, to the rear of the building.

Aga Khan Palace   PALACE
(Ahmednagar Rd; Indian/foreigner ₹5/100; ⊙9am-5.45pm) Set amid a wooded 6.5-hectare plot across the Mula River in Yerwada, the grand Aga Khan Palace (housing the **Gandhi National Memorial**) is easily Pune's biggest crowd-puller. Built in 1892 by Sultan Aga Khan III, this lofty building was where the Mahatma and other prominent nationalist leaders were interned by the British for about two years following Gandhi's Quit India resolution in 1942. Both Kasturba Gandhi, the Mahatma's wife, and Mahadeobhai Desai, his secretary for 35 years, died here in confinement. You'll find their shrines (containing their ashes) in a quiet garden to the rear.

OSHO: GURU OF SEX

Ever tried mixing spirituality with primal instincts, and garnishing the potent concoction with oodles of panache? Well, Bhagwan Shree Rajneesh (1931–90) certainly did. Osho, as he preferred to be called, was one of India's most flamboyant 'export gurus' to market the mystic East to the world, and undoubtedly the most controversial. Initially based in Pune, he followed no particular religion or philosophy, and outraged many across the world with his advocacy of sex as a path to enlightenment. A darling of the international media, he quickly earned himself the epithet 'sex guru'. In 1981, Rajneesh took his curious blend of Californian pop psychology and Indian mysticism to the USA, where he set up an agricultural commune in Oregon. There, his ashram's notoriety, as well as its fleet of (material and thus valueless!) Rolls Royces grew, until raging local paranoia about its activities moved the authorities to charge Osho with immigration fraud. He was fined US$400,000 and deported. An epic journey then began, during which Osho and his followers, in their search for a new base, were either deported from or denied entry into 21 countries. By 1987, he was back at his Pune ashram, where thousands of foreigners soon flocked for his nightly discourses and meditation sessions.

They still come in droves. To house them all, the capacious Osho Auditorium was unveiled in 2002, which saw the centre's name being changed from 'Osho Commune International' to 'Osho International Meditation Resort'. Such is the demand for the resort's facilities that prices are continually on the rise, with luxury being redefined every day. Interestingly, despite Osho's comments on how nobody should be poor, no money generated by the resort goes into helping the disadvantaged. That, resort authorities maintain, is up to someone else.

Within the main palace, you can peek into the room where Gandhi used to stay. Photos and paintings exhibit moments in his extraordinary career, but it's poorly presented.

Shaniwar Wada
FORT

(Shivaji Rd; Indian/foreigner ₹5/100; ☉8am-6pm) The remains of this fortressed palace of the Peshwa rulers are located in the old part of the city. Built in 1732, Shaniwar Wada was destroyed in a fire in 1828, but the massive walls and plinths remain, as do the sturdy palace doors with their daunting spikes. In the evenings, there is an hour-long **sound-and-light show** (admission ₹25; ☉8.15pm Thu-Tue).

Katraj Snake Park & Zoo
ZOO

(Pune–Satara Hwy; adult/child ₹3/2; ☉10.30am-6pm Thu-Tue) There's a mediocre selection of Indian wildlife on show at the Katraj Snake Park & Zoo. But a trip to this faraway park on Pune's southern outskirts makes sense if you want to know more about snakes, of which there are plenty.

Pataleshvara Cave Temple
TEMPLE

(Jangali Maharaj Rd; ☉6am-9.30pm) Set across the river is the curious rock-cut Pataleshvara Cave Temple, a small and unfinished (though living) 8th-century temple, similar in style to the grander caves at Elephanta Island off the Mumbai coast. Adjacent is the **Jangali Maharaj Temple** (☉6am-9.30pm), dedicated to a Hindu ascetic who died here in 1818.

Ramamani Iyengar Memorial Yoga Institute
YOGA

(☎25656134; www.bksiyengar.com; 1107 B/1 Hare Krishna Mandir Rd, Model Colony) To attend classes at this famous institute, 7km northwest of the train station, you need to have been practising yoga for at least eight years.

🛏 Sleeping

Pune's main accommodation hubs are around the train station and Koregaon Park. Most midrange hotels have check-out at noon, and accept credit cards. Some families rent out rooms starting at about ₹400 (without bathroom) to around ₹700 (with bathroom). Rickshaw drivers will know where to look.

TOP choice Hotel Sunderban
HOTEL $$

(☎26124949; www.tghotels.com; 19 Koregaon Park; s/d incl breakfast from ₹2500/3000; ☀🖥) Set around a manicured lawn right next to the Osho Resort, this renovated art deco bungalow effortlessly combines classy antiquity with boutique appeal. The huge non-AC

rooms in the main building sport a variety of dated furniture, and have a generally quaint air. The pricier rooms are across the lawns, in a sleek, glass-fronted building. An additional draw is the fantastic in-house fine-dining restaurant, Dario's (see p788).

TOP choice Osho Meditation Resort Guesthouse
HOTEL $$$

(☎66019900; www.osho.com; Koregaon Park; s/d ₹3900/4400; ☀) This uber-chic designer place will only allow you in if you come to meditate at the Osho International Meditation Resort (p785). The rooms and common spaces in this stylish property are an elegant exercise in modern aesthetics, as minimalist as they are chic. Add to that other ultra luxe features, such as purified fresh air supply in all rooms! Be sure to book well in advance; it's perpetually rushed.

Hotel Surya Villa
HOTEL $$

(☎26124501; www.hotelsuryavilla.com; 294/2 Koregaon Park; s/d from ₹1200/1500, with AC ₹1600/2000; ☀@) A cheerful place with bright, airy and spacious rooms and squeaky-clean loos, this is clearly the best of Pune's midrange options. It stands just off the Koregaon Park backpacker hub, so you're always clued in to the coolest developments in town. There's free internet for guests at the book kiosk below.

Homeland
HOTEL $$

(☎26123203; www.hotelhomeland.net; 18 Wilson Garden; s/d ₹900/1100, with AC from ₹1300/1500; ☀) A surprisingly restful place tucked away from the din of the train station, Homeland is excellent value for money. The labyrinthine corridors lead to rooms with freshly painted walls and clean sheets, and the restaurant downstairs shows movies in the evenings.

Hotel Srimaan
HOTEL $$

(☎26136565; srimaan@vsnl.com; 361/5 Bund Garden Rd; s/d ₹2200/2900; ☀@) The fact that Srimaan has dropped its tariffs actually makes this centrally-located place quite a steal. Jackson Pollock-inspired paintings lend their colour to the small but luxurious rooms. The pricier rooms have lovely windows with soothing green views outside. A good Italian joint called La Pizzeria is available on-site.

Samrat Hotel
HOTEL $$

(☎26137964; thesamrathotel@vsnl.net; 17 Wilson Garden; s/d incl breakfast from ₹1800/2200; ☀🖥) A sparkling modern hotel with excellent rooms opening around a central, top-lit foyer, this place sure knows how to make you feel at home. The staff is courteous and eager to please, and the well-appointed rooms meet every expectation you could have from hotels in this price bracket.

Westin
HOTEL $$$

(☑67210000; www.starwoodhotels.com; 36/3B Koregaon Park Annexe; d incl breakfast from ₹6000; ❄☎☁) Sprawled out like a giant luxury yacht on Koregaon Park's eastern fringes is this mint-fresh business hotel, combining the best of luxury and leisure with impeccable service. The rooms offer lovely views of the river course below.

Hotel Ritz
HOTEL $$

(☑26122995; fax 26136644; 6 Sadhu Vaswani Path; s/d incl breakfast from ₹2550/2750; ❄) Plush, friendly, atmospheric: three words that sum it all up for the Ritz, a Raj-era building that holds its own in town. The pricey rooms are in the main building, while the cheaper ones are located in an annexe next to the garden restaurant, which serves good Gujarati and Maharashtrian food.

National Hotel
HOTEL $

(☑26125054; 14 Sasoon Rd; s/d/q ₹750/850/1100, cottages s/d/q ₹650/750/950) What the National can't provide in terms of comfort, it compensates for with antique charm. Housed in a crumbling colonial-era mansion opposite the train station, the low-end rooms in this hotel can border on suffocating, and may not match your idea of 'clean'. The cottages across the garden are more liveable, and come with tiled sit-outs.

Grand Hotel
HOTEL $

(☑26360728; grandhotelpune@gmail.com; MG Rd; d from ₹770, s without bathroom ₹290) Well, it's anything but grand at this budget address. The cheapest beds here (and in all of Pune) are a series of hole-in-the-wall cabins next to the bar. The doubles are converted family homes, not the most luxurious of their kind either. But then, look at how much you're paying, and take comfort in the fact that the patio is a great place to nurse an evening beer.

Hotel Ashirwad
HOTEL $$

(☑26128687; hotelashir@gmail.com; 16 Connaught Rd; s/d from ₹3500/4000; ❄☎) A large, smooth-moving joint, this place stands out for its well-kept (though unremarkable) rooms and the popular Akshaya vegetarian restaurant downstairs, which serves a good range of Punjabi and Mughlai fare.

Eating

Pune is a great place for those with an adventurous palate. Predictably, there are a host of well-priced, high-quality eateries, many around Koregaon Park. Unless otherwise mentioned, the following are open noon to 3pm and 7pm to 11pm daily; last orders at 10.45pm.

TOP CHOICE Malaka Spice
ASIAN FUSION $$

(Lane 5, North Main Rd, Koregaon Park; mains ₹220-250) A definitive stop on Pune's food circuit, this upscale alfresco restaurant serves mouth-watering Southeast Asian fare that is given a creative tweak or two by its star chefs. Dishes such as the squid and broccoli tauche, or the burnt garlic and shrimp rice, are simply to die for. There's a souvenir shop too, if you'd like to buy something to remember your hearty meal here.

TOP CHOICE Prem's
MULTICUISINE $$

(North Main Rd, Koregaon Park; mains ₹180-220; ⏀8am-11pm) In a quiet, tree-canopied courtyard tucked away behind a commercial block, Prem's is perfect for those lazy, beer-aided lunch sessions that great holidays are centred around. Its relaxed ambience attracts droves of loyalists throughout the day, who slouch around the tables and put away countless pints before wolfing down their 'usual' orders. The noisy sizzlers are a hit with everyone, so don't leave without trying one.

Dario's
ITALIAN $$

(Hotel Sunderban; mains ₹250-280) This bistro serves only the best of Italian cuisine, made from a selection of local organic produce and handpicked rations flown straight in from Italy. There's a yummy selection of homemade penne, gnocchi and spaghetti on offer, while dishes such as the *torta bombardino* (onion quiche with fresh salad) explode on your palate with a hundred flavours.

Flag's
MULTICUISINE $$

(G2 Metropole, Bund Garden Rd; mains ₹230-250) This super-popular place serves timeless favourites from all corners of the world with Lebanese chicken, Mongolian cauliflower, New Orleans seafood platter and *yakisoba* (fried Japanese noodles) all rubbing shoulders under one roof. There's also a super-hot lunch buffet that goes for a super-cool ₹249.

Vaishali
FAST FOOD $

(FC Rd; mains ₹40-70; ⊘10am-10pm) Old-timers can't stop raving about this institution, known for its range of delicious snacks and meals. The scrumptious *sev potato dal puri* (₹45), a favourite of locals, has fed generations of college-goers in Pune, and still garners respect across the board.

Arthur's Theme
CONTINENTAL $$

(Lane 6, North Main Rd, Koregaon Park; mains ₹200-230) Start off with Don Quixote (deep fried cheese croquettes) or Cleopatra (grilled chicken cubes), before moving on to King Morgan (tiger prawns in herbs and olive oil) or Lancelot (chicken in cranberry sauce). A wacky (and tasty) way to brush up on your history lessons.

Juice World
CAFE $

(2436/B East St; snacks ₹50-60; ⊘8am-11.30pm) As well as producing delicious fresh fruit juices and shakes, this casual cafe with outdoor seating serves inexpensive but wholesome snacks such as pizza and *pav bhaji* (spiced vegetables and bread).

The Place: Touche the Sizzler
MULTICUISINE $$

(7 Moledina Rd; mains ₹180-200) The perfect old-school eating option. A variety of smoking sizzlers, and other assorted Indian fare, is on offer at this family-style eatery in the heart of Pune's business district. The ambience is quaint (read: slightly mothballed), but the overall experience more than makes up for it.

Swiss Cheese Garden
CONTINENTAL $$

(ABC Farms; mains ₹250-300) About a kilometre east of Koregaon Park, this restaurant leads a pack of smart eateries (many advocating organic food) situated within a leafy campus called ABC Farms. The pastas and the cheese fondues are good.

▼ Drinking & Entertainment

Pune puts a great deal of effort into its nocturnal activities, yet some pubs tend to shut up shop as quickly as they open, so ask around for the latest hot spots. Most are open from 7pm to around 1.30am.

1000 Oaks
NIGHTCLUB

(2417 East St) This one is an old favourite among Pune's tipplers, featuring a cosy pub-style bar, a compact dance floor and a charming, foliaged and moodily lit sit-out area for those who prefer it quieter. There's live music on Sundays, to go with your favourite poison.

Mocha
CAFE

(North Main Rd, Koregaon Park) This funky café with quirky decor and friendly staff features a brilliant selection of coffees from around the world, from the famed Jamaican Blue Mountain to Indian Peaberry. There are flavoured hookahs on offer too. Carry some form of ID to show at the gate.

Arc Asia
BAR

(ABC Farms) An extremely classy affair, rounding off the ABC Farms experience. A great stock of malts, scotches and beers, with groovy music on the PA.

Inox
CINEMA

(Bund Garden Rd) A state-of-the-art multiplex where you can take in the latest blockbuster from Hollywood or Mumbai.

🛍 Shopping

Pune has some good shopping options.

Bombay Store
SOUVENIRS

(322 MG Rd; ⊘10.30am-8.30pm Mon-Sat) The best spot for general souvenirs.

Pune Central
CLOTHING

(Bund Garden Rd, Koregaon Park) This glass-fronted mall is full of Western high-street labels and premium Indian tags.

Crossword
BOOKSTORE

(1st fl, Sohrab Hall, RBM Rd, ⊘10.30am-9pm) An excellent collection of fiction, nonfiction and magazines.

Either Or
CLOTHING

(24/25 Sohrab Hall, 21 Sasoon Rd; ⊘10.30am-8pm Fri-Wed) Modern designer Indian garments and accessories available at this popular boutique.

Fabindia
CLOTHING

(Sakar 10, Sasson Rd, ⊘10am-8pm) For Indian saris, silks and cottons, as well as diverse accessories and handmade products.

ℹ Information

Internet Access

You'll find several internet cafes along Pune's main thoroughfares.

Arihant Communications (North Main Rd, Koregaon Park; per hr ₹30; ⊘9am-11pm) Opposite Lane 5. Lightning-fast broadband connection.

Maps

Destination Finder (₹65) provides a great map of the city, along with some key travel information.

Money

Citibank has a 24-hour ATM on North Main Rd. HSBC dispenses cash at its main branch on Bund Garden Rd. You'll find ICICI Bank and State Bank of India ATMs at the railway station, an Axis Bank ATM on MG Rd and an HDFC Bank ATM on East St.

Thomas Cook (☎66007903; 2418 G Thimmaya Rd; ☺9.30am-6pm Mon-Sat) Cashes travellers cheques and exchanges foreign currency.

Post

Main post office (Sadhu Vaswani Path; ☺10am-6pm Mon-Sat)

DHL (Bund Garden Rd; ☺10am-8pm Mon-Sat)

Tourist information

MTDC tourist office (☎26126867; I Block, Central Bldg, Dr Annie Besant Rd; ☺10am-5.30pm Mon-Sat) Buried in a government complex south of the train station. There's also an **MTDC desk** at the train station (☺9am-7pm Mon-Sat, to 3pm Sunday).

Travel Agencies

Rokshan Travels (☎26136304; rokshantravels @hotmail.com; 1st fl, Kumar Plaza, MG Rd; ☺10am-6pm) These guys shine when it comes to getting you on the right bus, train or flight without a glitch. They also book taxis.

Yatra.com (☎65006748; www.yatra.com; North Main Rd; ☺10am-7pm Mon-Sat) The city office of the reputed internet ticketing site of the same name.

ⓘ Getting There & Away

Air

Airline contact information in Pune:

GoAir (airline code G8; ☎9223222111; www.goair.in)

Indian Airlines (airline code IC; ☎26052147; www.indian-airlines.nic.in; 39 Dr B Ambedkar Rd)

IndiGo (airline code 6E; ☎9910383838; www.goindigo.in)

Jet Airways (airline code 9W; ☎02239893333; www.jetairways.com; 243 Century Arcade, Narangi Baug Rd)

Kingfisher Airlines (airline code IT; ☎1800 2333131; www.flykingfisher.com; Gera Garden, Koregaon Rd)

SpiceJet (airline code SG; ☎1800 1803333; www.spicejet.com)

Airlines listed above fly daily from Pune to Delhi (from ₹3100, two hours), Bengaluru (from ₹2200, 1½ hours), Nagpur (from ₹2100, 1½ hours), Goa (from ₹3500, 1½ hours), Chennai (from ₹2300, 1½ hours) and hopping flights to Kolkata (from ₹3500, four hours).

Bus

Pune has three bus stands: **Pune train station stand** for Mumbai, Goa, Belgaum, Kolhapur, Mahabaleshwar and Lonavla; **Shivaji Nagar bus stand** for Aurangabad, Ahmedabad and Nasik; and **Swargate bus stand** for Sinhagad, Bengaluru and Mangalore. Deluxe buses shuttle from the train-station bus stand to Dadar (Mumbai) every hour (₹260, four hours).

Several private buses head to Panaji (Panjim) in Goa (ordinary/sleeper ₹330/450, 12 hours), Nasik (semideluxe/deluxe ₹180/280, five hours) and Aurangabad (₹170, six hours). Try **Brright Travels** (☎26114222; Connaught Rd).

Taxi

Share taxis (up to four passengers) link Pune with Mumbai airport around the clock. They leave from the **taxi stand** in front of Pune train station (per seat ₹500, 2½ hours). Several tour operators hire out long-distance taxis over days or even weeks for intrastate travelling. Try **Simran Travels** (☎26153222; North Main Rd, Koregaon Park).

Train

The computerised **booking hall** is to the left of Pune's main station building. The 7.15am *Deccan Queen*, 6.05am *Sinhagad Express* and 6.35pm *Indrayani Express* are fast commuter trains to

MAJOR TRAINS FROM PUNE

DESTINATION	TRAIN NO & NAME	FARE (₹)	DURATION (HR)	DEPARTURE
Bengaluru	16529 *Udyan Exp*	330/1232	21	11.45am
Chennai	12163 *Chennai Exp*	371/1348	19½	12.10am
Delhi	11077 *Jhelum Exp*	430/1624	27	5.20pm
Hyderabad	17031 *Hyderabad Exp*	246/910	13½	4.35pm
Mumbai CST	12124 *Deccan Queen*	67/237	3½	7.15am

Express fares are sleeper/2AC; *Deccan Queen* fares are 2nd class/chair. To calculate 1st class and other fares see p1187.

Mumbai (2nd class/chair ₹67/237, 3½ hours). For other long-distance trains, see the boxed text, opposite.

 Getting Around

The airport is 8km northeast of the city, and boasts a swanky new building. An autorickshaw there costs about ₹100; a taxi is ₹250.

Autorickshaws can be found everywhere.

A ride from the train station to Koregaon Park costs about ₹35 (₹60 at night).

Turtle-paced city buses leave the PMT depot (opposite Pune train station) for Swargate (bus 4) and Shivaji Nagar (bus 5) and Koregaon Park (bus 159).

Some garages in Koregaon Park hire out motorcycles for ₹300 a day, petrol extra. The boys hanging out at Hotel Surya Villa will know where to look.

Around Pune

SINHAGAD

The ruined **Sinhagad** (admission free; ⊙dawn-dusk) or Lion Fort, about 24km southwest of Pune, was wrested by Maratha leader Shivaji from the Bijapur kings in 1670. In the epic battle (where he lost his son Sambhaji), Shivaji used monitor lizards yoked with ropes to scale the fort's craggy walls. Today, it's a sad picture of its past, but worth visiting for the sweeping views.

From Sinhagad village, share jeeps (₹40) can cart you 10km to the base of the summit. Bus 50 runs frequently to Sinhagad village from Swargate (₹20, 45 minutes).

SHIVNERI

Situated 90km northwest of Pune above the village of Junnar, **Shivneri Fort** (admission free; ⊙dawn-dusk) holds the distinction of being the birthplace of Shivaji. Within the ramparts of this ruined fort are the old royal stables, a mosque dating back to the Mughal era and several rock-cut reservoirs. The most important structure is Shivkunj, the pavilion in which Shivaji was born.

About 4km from Shivneri, on the other side of Junnar, is an interesting group of Hinayana Buddhist caves called **Lenyadri** (Indian/foreigner ₹5/100; ⊙dawn-dusk). Of the 30-odd caves, Cave 7 is the most impressive, and interestingly houses an image of the Hindu lord Ganesh.

A bus (₹70, two hours, 7.15am) goes to Junnar from Pune's Shivaji Nagar terminus. A return bus leaves Junnar at 11.30am. A day cab from Pune will cost around ₹1600.

Mahabaleshwar

☏02168 / POP 12,700 / ELEV 1372M

Up in the Western Ghats, Mahabaleshwar – founded in 1828 by British governor Sir John 'Boy' Malcolm – was, at one time, the summer capital of the Bombay presidency. However, what was once a pretty town oozing old-world charm is today a jungle of mindless urban construction. Swarms of raucous holiday-makers who throw the place into a complete tizzy only make things worse. Mahabaleshwar's only face-saver is the delightful views it offers, but they're not half as good in practice, given that you'll have to combat the riotous tourists while appreciating them.

The hill station virtually shuts down during the monsoons (June to September), when an unbelievable 6m of rain falls.

The action can be found in the main bazaar (Main Rd, also called Dr Sabane Rd) – a 200m strip of holiday tack. The bus stand is at the western end. You have to cough up a ₹20 'tourist tax' on arrival.

⊙ Sights & Activities

Viewpoints   VIEWPOINT

The hills are alive with music, though it's usually blasted out of car stereos as people race to tick off all the viewpoints. To beat them, start very early in the morning, and you can savour fine views from **Wilson's Point** (Sunrise Point), within easy walking distance of town, as well as **Elphinstone**, **Babington**, **Kate's** and **Lodwick Points**.

The sunset views at **Bombay Point** are stunning; but you won't be the only one thinking so! Much quieter, thanks to being 9km from town, is **Arthur's Seat**, on the edge of a 600m cliff. Attractive waterfalls around Mahabaleshwar include **Chinaman's**, **Dhobi's** and **Lingmala Falls**. A nice walk out of town is the two-hour stroll to Bombay Point, and then following **Tiger Trail** back in (maps are available from the MTDC tourist office).

ⓒ Tours

Leaving the bus stand thrice from 2.15pm, the MSRTC conducts a Mahabaleshwar sightseeing round (₹80, 4½ hours) taking in nine viewpoints plus Old Mahabaleshwar. Alternatively, taxi drivers will give a three-hour tour for about ₹500. Tours are also available to lookout points south of town (₹400, 2½ hours), Panchgani (₹450, three hours) and Pratapgad Fort (₹500, three hours).

🛏 Sleeping & Eating

Hotel prices soar during weekends and peak holidays (November to June). At other times you might get hefty discounts. Most hotels are around the main bazaar, while dozens of resort-style lodges are scattered around the village. Check out is usually at 8am or 9am.

Hotel Panorama HOTEL $$
(☎260404; www.panoramaresorts.net; Main Rd; d with/without AC from ₹3500/3000; ❀❋) Business meets leisure at Mahabaleshwar's most reputed midtown luxury address. Very professionally managed, it boasts clean, comfy and tastefully appointed rooms, and there's some great grub at the restaurant. There's a dunk-sized pool, and a water channel where you might want to ride swan-headed paddle boats.

MTDC Resort HOTEL $
(☎260318; Bombay Point Rd; d from ₹700) This large-scale operation is situated about 2km southwest from town, and comes with quieter and greener surroundings. Rooms smack of government aesthetics, but it's cheap, so all's forgiven. Taxis can drop you here from the city centre for about ₹80.

Hotel Vyankatesh HOTEL $$
(☎260575; hotelvkt@yahoo.com; Main Rd; d ₹1500) A typically overpriced hotel cashing in on Mahabaleshwar's never-ending tourism boom. Located behind a souvenir store, this place has slightly dreary rooms, but so have lots of hotels around town.

TOP CHOICE Grapevine MULTICUISINE $$
(Masjid Rd; mains ₹140-160) Skip this place, and you've missed half the fun in town. Tucked pleasantly away behind the main drag, this tiny eatery serves a delectable range of Indian, Continental and Thai dishes, along with some excellent Parsi fare including the signature *dhansak*. A charming wrought-iron table set-up tastefully lends the interiors a Mediterranean air, and the restaurant also boasts a smart wine list to complement your food.

Hotel Rajmahal INDIAN $
(Main Rd; mains ₹50-70) A good place to dig into some lip-smacking veg delights.

Aman Restaurant INDIAN $
(Main Rd; mains ₹80-100) Little more than a roadside stall, Aman can pull out some amazing kebabs and other meaty bites.

❶ Information

State Bank of India (Main Rd; ⊙11am-5pm Mon-Fri, 11am-1pm Sat) Handles foreign currency.

Bank of Baroda Has an ATM on Masjid Rd.

RB Travels (☎260251; Main Rd) Local tours, ticketing, taxi hire and bus services.

Joshi's Newspaper Agency (Main Rd; per hr ₹50; ⊙10am-7pm) Slow internet access.

MTDC tourist office (☎260318; Bombay Point Rd) At the MTDC Resort south of town.

❶ Getting There & Away

From the **bus stand** state buses leave regularly for Pune (semideluxe ₹123, 3½ hours) via Panchgani (₹15, 30 minutes). There's one ordinary bus to Goa (₹274, eight hours, 8.30am) via Kolhapur (₹139, five hours), while seven buses ramble off to Mumbai Central Station (ordinary/semideluxe ₹174/234, seven hours).

Private agents in the bazaar book luxury buses to destinations within Maharashtra, and Goa (seat/sleeper ₹600/800, 12 hours, with a changeover at Surur). Remember to ask where they intend to drop you. Buses to Mumbai (₹450, 6½ hours) generally don't go beyond Borivali, while those bound for Pune (₹230) will bid you adieu at Swargate.

❶ Getting Around

Taxis and Maruti vans near the bus stand will take you to the main viewpoints or to Panchgani; you can haggle.

Cycling is also an option, but be careful of speeding traffic especially on the outskirts. Bikes can be hired from **Vasant Cycle Mart** (Main Rd; ⊙8am-8pm) for ₹50 per day.

---

❶ SOLO BLUES

If you're a single traveller, do not schedule a night in Mahabaleshwar. Local laws bar hotels from renting out rooms to loners, especially men. Make sure you have an early departure plan in place, even if you visit for the day.

Around Mahabaleshwar

PRATAPGAD FORT
The windy **Pratapgad Fort** (maintenance fee ₹5; ⊙7am-7pm), built by Shivaji in 1656, straddles a high mountain ridge 24km west of Mahabaleshwar. In 1659, Shivaji agreed to meet Bijapuri General Afzal Khan here, in an attempt to end a stalemate. Despite

BERRIES, ANYONE?

Fruity Mahabaleshwar is India's berry-growing hub, producing some of the country's finest strawberries, raspberries and gooseberries. Harvested from November to June, the best crops come around February and can be bought fresh at Mahabaleshwar's bazaar. You can also pick up fruit drinks, sweets, squashes, fudges or jams from reputed farms such as **Mapro Gardens** (02168240112; ⊙10am-1pm & 2pm-6.30pm), halfway between Mahabaleshwar and Panchgani.

a no-arms agreement, Shivaji, upon greeting Khan, disembowelled his enemy with a set of iron *baghnakh* (tiger's claws). Khan's tomb (out of bounds) marks the site of this painful encounter at the base of the fort.

Pratapgad is reached by a 500-step climb that affords brilliant views. Guides are available for ₹150. The state bus (₹80 return, one hour, 9.30am) does a daily shuttle from Mahabaleshwar, with a waiting time of around one hour. A return taxi ride is about ₹500.

RAIGAD FORT

Some 80km from Mahabaleshwar, all alone on a high and remote hilltop, stands the enthralling **Raigad Fort** (Indian/foreigner ₹5/100; ⊙8am-5.30pm). Having served as Shivaji's capital from 1648 until his death in 1680, the fort was later sacked by the British, and some colonial structures added. But monuments such as the royal court, plinths of royal chambers, the main marketplace and Shivaji's tomb still remain, and it's worth a daylong excursion.

You can hike a crazy 1475 steps to the top. But for a more 'levitating' experience, take the vertigo-inducing **ropeway** (⊙8.30am-5.30pm), which zooms up the cliff and offers an eagle-eye view of the deep gorges below. A return ticket costs ₹160. Guides (₹200) are available within the fort complex. **Sarja Restaurant** (mains ₹30), adjoining the ropeway's base terminal, is a good place for lunch or snacks.

Public transport to Raigad is infrequent, so it's best to hire a cab at Mahabaleshwar (₹1300). Squeeze both Pratapgad and Raigad into your day's itinerary, and you've got a deal.

Kolhapur

0231 / POP 505,500 / ELEV 550M

A rarely-visited town, Kolhapur is the perfect place to get up close and personal with the flamboyant side of India. Only a few hours from Goa, this historic town boasts an intensely fascinating temple complex and a friendly population. In August, Kolhapur is at its vibrant best, when **Naag Panchami**, a snake-worshipping festival, is held in tandem with one at Pune. Gastronomes take note: the town is also the birthplace of the famed, spicy Kolhapuri cuisine, especially chicken and mutton dishes.

The old town around the Mahalaxmi Temple is 3km southwest of the bus and train stations, while the 'new' palace is a similar distance to the north. Rankala Lake, a popular spot for evening strolls, is 5km southwest of the stations.

◉ Sights

TOP CHOICE Shree Chhatrapati

Shahu Museum　　　　　　MUSEUM

(Indian/foreigner ₹13/30; ⊙9.30am-5.30pm) 'Bizarre' takes on a whole new meaning at this 'new' palace, an Indo-Saracenic behemoth designed by British architect 'Mad' Charles Mant for the Kolhapur kings in 1884. The ground floor houses a madcap museum, featuring countless trophies from the eponymous king's trigger-happy jungle safaris, which were put to some ingenious uses, including walking sticks made from leopard vertebrae, and ashtrays fashioned out of tiger skulls and rhino feet. Then, there's an armoury, which houses enough weapons to stage a mini coup. The horror-house effect is brought full circle by the taxidermy section. However, don't forget to visit the durbar hall, a rather ornate affair, where the kings once held court sessions. Photography is strictly prohibited.

Old Town　　　　　　　　　AREA

Kolhapur's atmospheric old town is built around the lively and colourful **Mahalaxmi Temple** (⊙5am-10.30pm) dedicated to Amba Bai, or the Mother Goddess. The temple's origins date back to AD 10, and it's one of the most important Amba Bai temples in India. Non-Hindus are welcome. Nearby, past a foyer in the Old Palace, is **Bhavani Mandap** (☉6am-8pm), dedicated to the goddess Bhavani.

Kolhapur is famed for the calibre of its wrestlers and at the **Motibag Thalim**, a courtyard beside the entrance to Bhavani Mandap, young athletes train in a muddy pit. You are free to walk in and watch, as long as you don't mind the sight of sweaty, semi-naked men and the stench of urine emanating from the loos. Professional matches are held between June and December in the **Kasbagh Maidan**, a red-earth arena a short walk south of Motibag Thalim.

Shopaholics, meanwhile, can browse for the renowned Kolhapuri leather sandals, prized the world over for their intricate needlework. Most designs are priced from ₹300 to ₹500. The break-in blisters on your feet come free.

🛏 Sleeping & Eating

Hotel Tourist   HOTEL $
(☎2650421; www.hoteltourist.co.in; Station Rd; s/d incl breakfast from ₹700/900; ✷) Recently given a facelift, this is one of the nicest places on the main street, and is acclaimed for its excellent service. Cosy though minimalist rooms offer great value (especially the AC ones), and there's an excellent restaurant serving great veg food.

Hotel Pavillion   HOTEL $$
(☎2652751; www.hotelpavillion.co.in; 392 Assembly Rd; s/d ₹950/1150, with AC from ₹1300/1450; ✷@) Located at the far end of a leafy park-cum-office area, this place guarantees a peaceful stay in large, clean rooms with windows that open out to delightful views of seasonal blossoms. It's very close to the MTDC office.

Hotel Pearl   HOTEL $$
(☎6684451; hotelpearl@yahoo.com; New Shahupuri; s/d incl breakfast from ₹1900/2100; ✷@) Modelled on big-city business hotels, this place has good rooms, a spa, a travel desk and a decent multicuisine restaurant.

Surabhi   INDIAN $
(Hotel Sahyadri Bldg; mains ₹70-80) A great place to savour Kolhapur's legendary snacks such as the spicy *misal* (similar to *bhelpuri*), thalis and lassi. Saawan Dining Hall, located alongside, serves non-veg food.

ℹ Information

Axis Bank has a 24-hour ATM near Mahalaxmi Temple.

SBI has a 24-hour ATM on Indumati Rd, parallel to Station Rd.

Internet Zone (Kedar Complex, Station Rd; per hr ₹20; ☉8am-11pm) Internet access.

MTDC tourist office (☎2652935; Assembly Rd; ☉10am-5.30pm Mon-Sat) Opposite the Collector's Office.

State Bank of India (Udyamnagar; ☉10am-2pm Mon-Sat) A short autorickshaw ride southwest of the train station near Hutatma Park. Handles foreign exchange.

ℹ Getting There & Around

Autorickshaws are abundant in Kolhapur and most drivers are honest with their billing. Most carry conversion charts to calculate fares from outdated meters.

From the **bus stand**, services head regularly to Pune (semideluxe/deluxe ₹228/390, five hours) and Ratnagiri (ordinary/semideluxe ₹100/135, four hours). Most private bus agents are on the western side of the square at Mahalaxmi Chambers, across from the bus stand. Overnight services with AC head to Mumbai (seat/sleeper ₹380/650, nine hours) and non-AC overnighters go to Panaji (₹210, 5½ hours).

The **train station** is 10 minutes' walk west of the bus stand. Three daily expresses, including the 10.50pm *Sahyadri Express,* zoom to Mumbai (sleeper/2AC ₹227/832, 13 hours) via Pune (₹161/574, eight hours). The *Rani Chennama Express* makes the long voyage to Bengaluru (sleeper/2AC ₹294/1097, 17½ hours, 2.20pm).

Services at Kolhapur airport were suspended in mid-2010 due to safety concerns.

Goa

Includes »

Best Places to Eat

» Upper House (p805)
» Le Poisson Rouge (p816)
» Thalassa (p822)
» Seasonal beach shacks (all over)
» Plantain Leaf (p816)

Best Places to Stay

» Nilaya Hermitage (p816)
» Mayfair Hotel (p804)
» Marbella Guest House (p812)
» Backwoods Camp (p810)
» Dunes (p824)

Why Go?

It's green, it's glistening and it's gorgeous: just three of the reasons why Goa has allured travellers for decades. Two million visitors come each year for the silken sand, crystalline shores, cocohut culture and *susegad* – a Portuguese-derived term that translates loosely to 'laid-backness'.

But there's more to discover here than the pleasure of warm sand between your toes. Goa is as beautiful and culturally rich as it is tiny and hassle-free, so you can go bird-watching in a butterfly-filled forest, marvel at centuries-old cathedrals, venture out to white-water waterfalls or meander the capital's charming alleyways, all in between lazy beach days (or weeks). Pour in a dash of Portuguese-influenced food and architecture, infuse with a colourful blend of religious traditions, pepper with parties, and you've got a heady mix that makes Goa easy to enjoy and extremely hard to leave.

When to Go
Goa (Panaji)

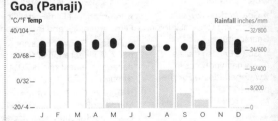

Early Nov The rains are over and the waterfalls are full – but the beaches aren't.

Early Dec Festivals galore and great weather, just before the high-peak prices and crowds.

Mar Carnival. Enough said.

Tiny Dabolim Airport handles all flights, Margao Railway Station is the state's largest and best connected, and Mapusa and Panaji bus terminals are your best bet for long-distance rides.

Fast Facts

» Population: 1.5 million

» Area: 3701 sq km

» Capital: Panaji (Panjim)

» Telephone code: ☏0832

» Main languages: Konkani, Marathi, English and Hindi

» Sleeping prices: **$** below ₹1000, **$$** ₹1000 to ₹2500, **$$$** above ₹2500

Top Tip

Don't swim wasted! And stay away during Christmas and New Year's, when the parties are raging but so are the prices and the hordes.

Resources

» Goa Tourism (www.goa-tourism.com) Good background and tour info.

» Goa World (www.goa-world.com) General info on Goan culture.

» Goa's English dailies (www.navhindtimes.in, www.oheraldo.in) For the news.

Food

Goans tend to be hearty meat and fish eaters, and fresh seafood is a staple, as is the quintessential Goan lunch 'fish-curry-rice': fried mackerel steeped in coconut, tamarind and chilli sauce. The good, genuine cooking can be hard to find in the tourist areas, but hunt around and you'll be rewarded with your best souvenir: memories of a stellar vindaloo (fiery dish in a marinade of vinegar and garlic) or *xacuti* (a spicy chicken or meat dish cooked in red coconut sauce).

DON'T MISS

There's little chance of missing the **beach** – it's spectacular and it's everywhere – but don't give in to the temptation to laze on it nonstop. **Yoga** is ubiquitous in Goa – in both long-course and short-class form – and even for dabblers, it's the perfect yin to beach-lounging's yang. Palolem has lots of **trekking** and even canyoning opportunities, and **birds**, **forests** and **waterfalls** are just waiting to be enjoyed inland. Goa has a fascinating **history** that also shouldn't be missed: set aside some time to explore evocative Panaji (Panjim), Old Goa, Quepem and Chandor.

Top State Festivals

» Feast of the Three Kings (6 Jan, Chandor, p827) Boys re-enact the story of the three kings bearing gifts for Christ.

» Shigmotsav (Shigmo) of Holi (Feb/Mar, statewide) Goa's version of the Hindu festival Holi sees coloured powders thrown about and parades in most towns.

» Sabado Gordo (Feb/Mar, Panaji, p800) A procession of floats and street parties on the Saturday before Lent.

» Carnival (Mar, statewide) A four-day festival kicking off Lent; the party's particularly jubilant in Panaji.

» Fama de Menino Jesus (2nd Mon in Oct, Colva, p830) Colva's Menino Jesus statue is paraded through town.

» International Film Festival of India (Nov, Panaji, p800) Film screenings and Bollywood glitterati everywhere.

» Feast of St Francis Xavier (3 Dec, Panaji, p800, Old Goa, p807) A celebration of Goa's patron saint; once every decade (the next one is 2014), the saint's body is carried through Old Goa's streets.

» Feast of Our Lady of the Immaculate Conception (8 Dec, Margao, p825, Panaji, p800) Fairs and concerts are held, as is a beautiful church service at Panaji's Church of Our Lady of the Immaculate Conception.

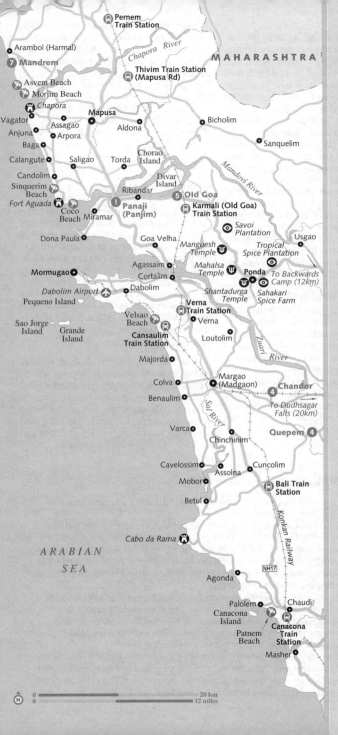

Goa Highlights

1 Wander the Portuguese quarters of **Panaji** (Panjim; p800) and linger over lunch at one of its ravishing restaurants

2 Indulge in barefoot luxury on quiet white-sand **beaches** in the state's sleepy southern stretches

3 Open up your chakras while doing **yoga** to the rhythm of ocean waves and swaying palms

4 Dream of times gone by in the mansions of **Quepem** (p829) and **Chandor** (p827)

5 Shiver in the shadows of grand cathedrals and observe the countryside from a hilltop chapel in **Old Goa** (p807)

6 Feel the wind in your hair while you **ride your bicycle or scooter** through palm-tree jungles and rice-paddy fields

7 Worship the sun away from the northern crowds on the beautiful beach at **Mandrem** (p823)

History

Goa went through a dizzying array of rulers from Ashoka's Mauryan empire in the 3rd century BC to the long-ruling Kadambas, who in AD 1054 moved their capital from present-day Chandor to a new settlement called Govepuri, today's little village of Goa Velha. The centuries following saw much conflict, with the Muslim Delhi sultanate and then Bahmani sultanate fighting the Hindu Vijayanagar empire for control; these were violent times, and in addition to many deaths, Hindu temples were also razed. (Tiny Tambdi Surla temple, constructed during the Kadamba reign, was the only one to survive.) The Adil Shahs of Bijapur, formerly part of the Bahmani sultanate, created the capital we now call Old Goa in the 15th century.

The Portuguese arrived in 1510, seeking control of the region's lucrative spice routes by way of Goa's wide natural harbours and plentiful waterways. They defeated the Bijapur kings and steadily pushed their power from their grand capital at Old Goa out into the provinces. (The Goa State Museum in Panaji has lots of interesting artefacts from this period.) Soon after, Portuguese rule and religion spread throughout the state – sometimes by force – and the Goan Inquisition brought repression and brutality in the name of Christianity. It was not until 1961, when the Indian army marched into Goa, that almost five centuries of Portuguese occupation finally came to an end on the subcontinent.

Today Goa enjoys one of India's highest per-capita incomes and comparatively high health and literacy rates, with tourism, iron-ore mining, agriculture and fishing forming the basis of its economy. The legacy of the Portuguese can still be found almost everywhere, in the state's scores of old mansions, its cuisine, its churches and even in its language; it's rare nowadays, but if you keep an ear out you may hear elderly people conversing in Portuguese.

Climate

The annual monsoon used to scour Goa's beaches clean between June and the end of September reliably, but things have gone a little haywire in recent years, and sometimes the monsoon can end as late as November. In general, though, the tourist season stretches from mid-November to mid-April, with December to February proving the most pleasant (and busiest) time to visit. Temperatures and humidity increase after February. Out of season, between April and October, you'll find most coastal resorts deserted, though towns such as Panaji, Mapusa and Margao chug on as usual.

🏃 Activities

Goa has, of late, become Activity Central, with a whole host of options for yoga and alternative therapies, water sports and wildlife-watching. Many outfits change annually, so we've only listed the longer-established operations in this chapter; for the full gamut of options, head to your beach of choice and ask around or scan the noticeboards.

WHERE TO GOA...

Goa is tiny. With enough time (and discipline to get off the beach), you can explore the state's beaches, nature *and* culture.

Very generally, Goa can be split up into three distinct regions: north, south and central. The north, above the Mandovi River, is the place for those seeking action, shopping and activities in equal supply, and for folks looking for the remnants – and they are only remnants – of Goa's fabled trance party scene. In addition, the north has some beautiful almost-empty beaches, along with a string of highly developed resorts with lots of choice in restaurants, hotels and water-sports outfits.

In central Goa, nestling between the Mandovi and Zuari Rivers, things get decidedly more cultural. Here sits Panaji (Panjim), Goa's small and loveable state capital, which slings itself comfortably along the broad banks of the Mandovi River, while inland lie spice plantations, waterfalls and the glorious vestiges of Goa's grand and glittering past in the form of mansions, temples and cathedrals.

Things slow down in the south, where the beaches grow generally quieter and the sun lounges are spaced further apart. Not the place for partying the night away, the beaches here cater to a quieter, calmer crowd, with lots of homespun charm. This is the place to sit back, unwind, and perhaps spot a hatching turtle or two.

YOGA & ALTERNATIVE THERAPIES

Every imaginable form of yoga, meditation, reiki, ayurvedic massage and other spiritually orientated health regime is practised, taught and relished in Goa. Palolem and Patnem, in the south of the state, and Arambol (Harmal), Mandrem, Anjuna and Calangute in the north all have courses in ayurveda, yoga, reiki and the like. Mandrem and Arambol have reputable yoga centres, and Calangute has an excellent ayurveda clinic.

WILDLIFE-WATCHING

Goa is a nature lover's paradise, perfect for wildlife-watching, with an abundance of brilliant birdlife and a fine (but well concealed) collection of fauna, including sambars, barking deer and the odd leopard. Head to Cotigao Wildlife Sanctuary to scout out birds and beasts alike, or to Backwoods Camp. Day Tripper in Calangute offers various naturerelated tours, while John's Boat Tours in Candolim runs birdwatching boat trips, along with crocodile- and dolphin-spotting rides. At almost any beach, though, you'll find someone with a boat eager to show you those adorable grey mammals of the sea.

WATER SPORTS

Based in Baga, Barracuda Diving, offers scuba -diving courses and trips. Parasailing and jet-skiing are readily available on the beaches at Baga, Benaulim and Colva, and you can try paragliding at Anjuna and Arambol.

Dangers & Annoyances

One of the greatest – and most deceptive – dangers in Goa is to be found right in front of your beautiful bit of beach: the Arabian Sea, with its strong currents and dangerous undertows, claims dozens of lives per year, many of them foreigners who knew how to swim. Though some of Goa's beaches are now overseen by lifeguards during daylight hours, it's extremely important to heed local warnings on the safety of swimming, and don't, whatever you do, venture into the water after drinking or taking drugs.

Other dangers and annoyances are of the rather more universal kind. Keep your valuables under lock and key, especially if you're renting an easy-to-penetrate cocohut, and don't walk along empty stretches of beach alone at night.

DRUGS

Acid, ecstasy, cocaine, charas (hashish), marijuana and all other forms of recreational drugs are illegal in India (though still very much available in Goa), and purchasing or carrying drugs is fraught with danger. Goa's Fort Aguada jail is filled with prisoners, including some foreigners, serving lengthy sentences for drug offences, and being caught in possession of even a small quantity of illegal substances can mean a 10-year stay in a cockroach-infested cell.

ℹ Information

The **Goa Tourism Development Corporation** (GTDC; www.goa-tourism.com) provides maps and information, operates (not-great) hotels throughout the state and runs a host of one-day and multiday tours. Its main office is in Panaji, but you can book its tours and get a simple map of Goa at any of its hotel branches. Panaji's Indiatourism office also has information on Goa.

ACCOMMODATION Accommodation prices in Goa are generally higher than in most other states of India and vary wildly depending on the season. High-season prices, often more than twice the mid-season rates, run from early December to early February, while prices climb higher still during the crowded Christmas and New Year period (around 22 December to 3 January). Mid-season runs from the end of October through November (when most beach shacks are just being built) and from February to April, and low season runs through the rainy season (April to October). All accommodation rates listed in this chapter are for the high season. Note, however, that prices can fluctuate incredibly from year to year, and some hotels may bump up their high-season tariffs more than others. Always call ahead for rates. In addition, the Goan government levies a hotel tax of either 5% (for rooms costing less than ₹750), 7% (₹750 to ₹1500), 10% (₹1500 to ₹3000) or 12% (over ₹3000).

Most accommodation options have a standard noon checkout, except in Panaji, where most hotels cruelly demand you depart at 9am.

ℹ Getting There & Away

AIR Goa's sole and diminutive airport, Dabolim, is in the centre of the state, 29km south of Panaji, 30km north of Margao and an easy taxi or bus ride from any of the state's beaches. Few international flights go here directly; those that do are package-holiday charters, mostly from Russia and Britain. Independent travellers from the UK could check **Thomson** (www.thomsonfly.com), and from Germany, **Condor** (www.condor.com);

DIAL 108 IN EMERGENCIES

In any emergency in Goa, dial 108. This will connect you to the police, fire brigade or medical services.

both offer flight-only fares. Generally, the quickest way to reach Goa from overseas is to take a flight into Mumbai (Bombay), and then a one-hour hop by domestic airline down to Goa. There are lots of domestic flights each day, starting from around ₹3500 (cheaper if you book well in advance).

Dabolim Airport has a money-exchange office, a GTDC counter, charter-airline offices, an ATM and two prepaid taxi booths.

BUS Plenty of long-distance interstate buses – both 'government' and 'private' – operate to and from Panaji, Margao, Mapusa and Chaudi, near Palolem. Fares for private operators are higher than for government buses, and they fluctuate throughout the year; in peak season, they can be triple the price of the state operators. (Some would say that they're also three times more comfortable, but this isn't always the case.) A tip for overnight journeys: sleeper buses, counter-intuitively, can be less comfortable than seaters. The seats keep you from getting tossed around with every bump and turn.

TRAIN The **Konkan Railway** (www.konkan railway.com), the main train line running through Goa, runs between Mumbai and Mangalore. Its biggest station in Goa is Margao's Madgaon station, from which there are several useful daily services to Mumbai. Other smaller, useful stations on the line include Pernem for Arambol, Thivim for Mapusa and the northern beaches, Karmali (Old Goa) for Panaji, and Canacona for Palolem.

Other train lines out of Margao head to Chennai; Pune; Ahmedabad (Amdavad) and Vadodara (Baroda) in Gujarat; Ernakulam (for Kochi) and Thiruvananthapuram (Trivandrum) in Kerala; Hubli in Karnataka and even Delhi.

Book tickets online (see p1185); at Madgaon station; at the train reservation office at Panaji's Kadamba bus stand; or at any travel agent vending train tickets (though you'll probably pay a small commission). Only the stations at Margao and Vasco da Gama (near Dabolim Airport) have foreign-tourist-quota booking counters. Make sure you book as far in advance as possible for sleepers, since they fill up very quickly.

See p828 for detailed train information.

ⓘ Getting Around

TO/FROM THE AIRPORT Dabolim's two pre-paid taxi counters – one in the arrivals hall and the other just outside – make arriving easy; buy your ticket here and you'll be ushered to a cab.

BUS Goa has an extensive network of buses, shuttling to and from almost every town and village. They run frequently and have no numbers, and fares rarely exceed ₹30. Buses are in fairly good condition and tend to be pretty efficient operations.

CAR & MOTORCYCLE It's easy in Goa to organise a private car with a driver for long-distance day trips. Prices vary, but you should bank on

paying from ₹1000 (if you're lucky) to ₹1500 for a full day out on the road (usually defined as eight hours and 80km). It's also possible, if you have the nerves and the skills, to procure a self-drive car. A small Maruti will cost from ₹600 to ₹900 per day and a jeep around ₹1000, excluding petrol; there are few organised rental outlets, so ask around for someone with a car willing to rent it to you. Note the slightly mystifying signposts posted on Goa's major National Highway 17 (NH17), which advise of different speed limits (on the largely single-carriageway road) for different types of vehicles.

You'll rarely go far on a Goan road without seeing a tourist whizzing by on a scooter or motorbike, and renting (if not driving) one is a breeze. You'll likely pay from ₹200 to ₹300 per day for a scooter, ₹400 for a smaller Yamaha motorbike, and ₹500 for a Royal Enfield Bullet. These prices can drop considerably if you're renting for more than a day or if it's an off-peak period.

Bear in mind that Goan roads are treacherous, filled with human, bovine, canine, feline, mechanical and avian obstacles, as well as a good sprinkling of potholes and hairpin bends. Take it slowly, try not to drive at night (when black cows can prove dangerous), don't attempt a north–south day trip on a 50CC scooter, and the most cautious of riders might even consider donning a helmet, which is technically the law.

TAXI Taxis are widely available for town-hopping, and, as with a chauffeured car, a full day's sightseeing, depending on the distance, will be around ₹1500. Motorcycles, known as 'pilots', are also a licensed form of taxi in Goa. They're cheap, easy to find, and can be identified by a yellow front mudguard – and even the heftiest of backpacks seem to be no obstacle.

CENTRAL GOA

Panaji (Panjim)

POP 98,915

Panaji (more commonly known as Panjim) has yellow houses with purple doors, cats lying in front of bicycles parked beneath oyster-shell windows, and paddle-wheel boats moseying along the river that laps the city's northern boundary. Oh, and a giant church on a hill that looks like a fancy white wedding cake. It's a friendly, manageable and walkable city – maybe India's cutest capital – and its Portuguese-era colonial charms make it a perfect place to while away a day or two. Stroll the peaceful streets, take a kitschy river cruise, eat vindaloos and end the evening in a cosy local bar.

Venture beyond the tourist areas and you're sure to find a Goan who will sadly shake their heads and say that Goa has changed for the worse. The spread of serious drug use among locals, overdevelopment and environmental damage, and Goa's growing reputation within India as a place for bad behaviour are the dark underbelly to its tropical paradise. You can help repair Goa's image by following a few simple steps:

» Away from the beaches, adopt the same, more modest dress that you would in other parts of the country. This generally means shoulders and knees covered, and keeping your shirts on. Nude or topless sunbathing was recently banned in Goa and can result in fines.

» Keep your naughtiest behaviour confined to appropriate venues. Partying into the night with illegal substances at a family guesthouse might disturb the owners, though they may not say anything.

» Women should be cautious when partying; rape, sadly, is on the rise in Goa, and though we don't believe (as many do) that bikinis are to blame, it makes sense to be in control of your surroundings.

Panaji's also a natural base for exploring Goa's historic hinterland, and if the timing's right, the place to be for its many festivals, which include the street party that is Sabado Gordo on the Saturday before Lent, a madcap Carnival, and, in December, the Feast of St Francis Xavier and the Feast of Our Lady of the Immaculate Conception. If you happen to be here in November, Panaji is also host to the excellent International Film Festival of India (www.iffi.gov.in, www.iffigoa .org), India's largest and most glittering film festival. Panajimites know how to throw a festival – but they also know how to nap: the city mostly shuts down between 1pm and 3pm.

◉ Sights & Activities

Panaji is a city of long, leisurely strolls, through the sleepy Portuguese-era Sao Tomé, Fontainhas and Altinho districts, for a spot of shopping on 18th June Rd, and down along the languid Mandovi River.

Church of Our Lady of the Immaculate Conception CHURCH

Panaji's spiritual and geographical centre is its gleamingly picturesque main church, consecrated in 1541. When Panaji was little more than a sleepy fishing village, this place was the first port of call for sailors from Lisbon, who would clamber up here to thank their lucky stars for a safe crossing before continuing to Old Goa, the state's capital until the 19th century, further east up the river.

If your visit coincides with 8 December, be sure to call in for the Feast of Our Lady of the Immaculate Conception, which sees a special church service and a lively fair spilling away from the church to mark the date.

FREE **Goa State Museum** MUSEUM
(☑2438006; www.goamuseum.nic.in; EDC Complex, Patto; ☺9.30am-5.30pm Mon-Sat) This large museum, in a strangely uncentral area southwest of the Kadamba bus stand, has a sleepy feel and an intriguing hodgepodge of exhibits. In addition to the usual Hindu and Jain sculptures and bronzes, the museum has a good collection of wooden Christian sculptures, a room devoted to the history of print in Goa (replete with hulking, old-school presses), an exhibition on Goa's freedom fighters, and a few nice examples of Portuguese-era furniture, including an elaborately carved table used during the notoriously brutal Portuguese Inquisition in Goa.

Houses of Goa Museum MUSEUM
(☑2411276; Torda; adult/child ₹100/25; ☺10.30am-7.30pm Tue-Sun) This little museum was created by a well-known local architect, Gerard da Cunha, to illuminate the history of Goan architecture. Interesting displays on building practices and European and local design will change the way you see those old Goan homes, apparent statewide in various states of glory and decrepitude. Next door is the Mario Gallery (☑2410711; admission free; ☺10am-5.30pm Mon-Fri, to 1pm Sat), with works by one of India's favourite cartoonists, Mario Miranda. The museum and gallery are north of Panaji in the Torda neighbourhood. To get here, take a Mapusa-bound bus and get off at Okukora Circle, also known as Kokeru; a rickshaw from here and back, including waiting time, costs ₹100. From Panaji, a taxi or rickshaw will cost you about ₹300 one-way.

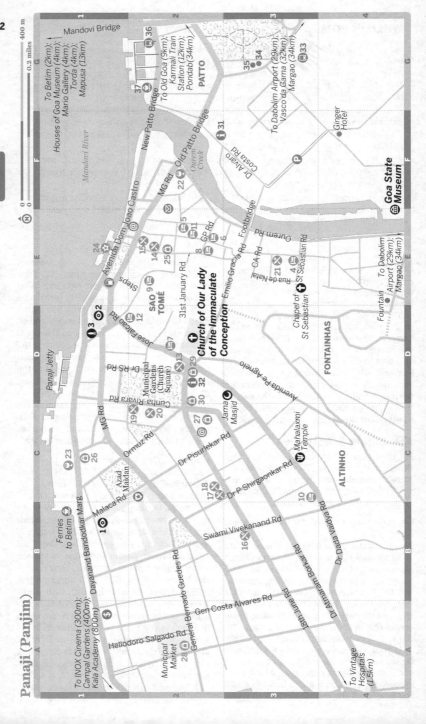

GOA CENTRAL GOA

Panaji (Panjim)

Mandovi River

Mandovi Bridge

To Betim (2km);
Houses of Goa Museum (4km);
Mario Gallery (4km);
Torda (4km);
Mapusa (13km)

To Old Goa (9km);
Karmali Train
Station (12km);
Pondab(34km)

To Dabolim Airport (29km);
Vasco da Gama (32km);
Margao (34km)

PATTO

Ginger
Hotel

New Patto Bridge

Old Patto Bridge

Ourem Creek

Dr Alvaro
Costa Rd

Goa State
Museum

Footbridge

MG Rd

GP Rd

Ourem Rd

CA Rd

St Sebastian Rd

To Dabolim
Airport (29km);
Margao (34km)

Rua de Natal

Chapel of
St Sebastian

FONTAINHAS

Fountain

Church of Our Lady
of the Immaculate
Conception

31st January Rd

Avenida Dom Joao Castro

Emilio Graça Rd

Jose Falcao Rd

Steps

SAO
TOMÉ

Panaji Jetty

Panaji Jetty

Avenida Pe Agnelo

Municipal
Gardens
(Church
Square)

Dr RS Rd

Cunha Rivara Rd

Jama
Masjid

Mahalaxmi
Temple

ALTINHO

MG Rd

Ormuz Rd

Dr Pisurlekar Rd

Dr P Shirgaonkar Rd

Ferries
to Betim

Ferries to Betim

Azad
Maidan

Malaca Rd

Davanand Bandodkar Marg

Swami Vivekanand Rd

18th June Rd

Dr Dada Vaidya Rd

Dr Atmaram Borkar Rd

To INOX Cinema (300m);
Campal Gardens (400m);
Kala Academy (800m)

Heliodoro Salgado Rd

General Bernado Guedes Rd

Gen Costa Alvares Rd

Municipal
Market

To Vintage
Hospitals
(1.5km)

400 m
0.2 miles

N

GOA PANAJI (PANJIM)

Secretariat Building   HISTORIC BUILDING
(Avenida Dom Joao Castro) This colonial-era building is on the site of Bijapur Sultan Yusef Adil Shah's summer palace. The current structure dates from the 16th century and became the Portuguese viceroy's official residence in 1759. Nowadays it houses less exciting government offices but is worth a gaze as the oldest, and one of the prettiest, buildings in town, though it may still be under renovation when you visit. Immediately to the west, the compelling **statue** of a man bearing down upon a supine female form depicts Abbé Faria, a Goan priest, 'father of hypnotism' and friend of Napoleon, in melodramatic throes.

Menezes Braganza Institute HISTORIC BUILDING
(Malaca Rd) This beautiful early 20th-century affair is worth dropping into to see the pretty blue-and-white *azulejos* (glazed ceramic-tile compositions) in the entrance hall. The

Panaji Central Library (⊙9.30am-1.15pm & 2-6.30pm Mon-Sat) is a pleasantly retro place to read the paper and some magazines.

Campal   AREA
The Campal neighbourhood, to the west of Panaji proper, is home to some green spaces that are perfect for whiling away an afternoon. Goa's premier cultural centre, **Kala Academy** has a lovely campus, with a snack bar; an art gallery; a lighthouse, pier and benches along the water; and a library with great books on Indian arts. East of this is **Campal Gardens** (Bhagwan Mahaveer Bal Vihar), a peaceful, expansive park with playgrounds and river views.

🡒 Courses

Holiday on the Menu   COOKING
(www.holidayonthemenu.com; courses from US$149) This London-based outfit offers a

variety of Goan-cooking holidays, ranging from a Saturday 'Curry Morning' to a one-week program that includes trips to a spice plantation and a local market, based in the picturesque village of Betim, just across the river north of town.

☞ Tours

The Goa Tourism Development Corporation (GTDC) operates a range of boat trips along the Mandovi River, including daily hour-long **cruises** (₹150; ⊙6pm & 7.15pm) and two-hour **dinner cruises** (₹450; ⊙8.45pm) aboard the *Santa Monica*. All include a live band and dancers – sometimes lively, sometimes lacklustre – performing Goan folk songs and dances. Cruises depart from the Santa Monica jetty beside the New Patto Bridge, where the **GTDC boat counter** (☎2437496) also sells tickets.

Three private companies also offer one-hour **night cruises** (adult/child ₹150/free; ⊙6pm, 7pm & 8.30pm) departing from Santa Monica jetty. The GTDC cruises are a little more staid, while others – maybe because of the bars and DJs – can get rowdy with groups of local male tourists.

GTDC also runs a two-hour **Goa By Night bus tour** (₹200; ⊙6.30pm Tue & Sun), which leaves from the same jetty and includes a river cruise and packs in as much as possible.

You can take your own free tour aboard the local ferries that depart frequently (whenever full) at the dock next to Quarter-deck; locals have reported seeing dolphins on evening rides. Avoid rush hour, when the boats are crammed.

🛏 Sleeping

As in the rest of Goa, prices vary wildly in Panaji depending on supply and demand. Lots of rock-bottom-priced options pepper 31st January Rd, but most consist of a cell-like room, with a 9am checkout, for ₹500 or less. Inspect a few before you decide. Some are full of bachelors where it would be odd – and potentially problematic – for gals to stay, so if unsure, ask at reception if the hotel is a 'family' place.

 Mayfair Hotel HOTEL **$$**
(☎2223317; Dr Dada Vaidya Rd; s/d from ₹900/1200; ❋) Bright rooms at this friendly family-run hotel have mango-yellow accents, woodblock-print curtains and either balconies on the street side or windows overlooking the back-yard garden (think palms, flowers and cats

chasing butterflies). Beautiful ground-floor oyster-shell windows and good old-fashioned service make it atmospheric, too, and loving details like balcony lanterns at Diwali time make it feel homey. Be sure to get recommendations from the chatty mother and daughters at reception, and check out the fun Mario Miranda mosaic in the lobby. Discounts are given for stays of more than two nights.

Casa Nova GUESTHOUSE **$$$**
(☎9423889181, 7709886212; www.goaholidayaccommodation.com; Gomes Pereira Rd; ste ₹3100) Here's your chance to actually stay in one of Panaji's gorgeous old Portuguese-style homes – if you can get a booking. Casa Nova consists of just one stylish, exceptionally comfy suite, accessed via a little alley and complete with arched windows, wood-beam ceilings and mod cons like a kitchenette. Sister property **Casa Morada** (☎9822196007, 9881966789; agomes@tbi.in; Gomes Pereira Rd; s/d incl breakfast ₹5000/10,000) is as fancy as Nova is modern. Its two bedrooms and sitting room are full of antique furniture and objets d'art (ergo the no children, no pets policy), with real art on the walls and floors of elegant pale-green marble.

Crown HOTEL **$$$**
(☎2400060; www.thecrowngoa.com; Jose Falcao Rd; d/ste incl breakfast from ₹5000/10,000; ❋@🛜🏊) Perched high above Panaji, with lovely views from its cool and peaceful pool area, this is a great option for a little bit of luxury in the midst of the city. The Crown was recently renovated, and the result is airy, tastefully done rooms in mustards and whites (some with balconies) with supermodern bathrooms. The staff is competent without being stuffy. The price includes breakfast and, for stays of more than two nights, pick-up/drop-off at the airport or train station.

Afonso Guest House HOTEL **$$**
(☎2222359, 9764300165; St Sebastian Rd; r ₹1500) Run by the friendly Jeanette, this place in a pretty, old Portuguese-era town house offers spacious, well-kept rooms with wood-plank ceilings and a pinch of character. The little rooftop terrace, meanwhile, makes for sunny breakfasting (dishes from ₹20 to ₹30). It's a simple, serene stay in the heart of the most atmospheric part of town with just two small faults: checkout is 9am and it doesn't take bookings.

Pousada Guest House HOTEL **$**
(☎2422618; sabrinateles@yahoo.com; Luis de Menezes Rd; d/tr/f ₹420/735/900, with AC

₹630/840/1000; ✳) The four rooms in this little place in the centre of town are nothing special – the two doubles are downstairs, dark and a little small even – but they're clean; civilised; owner Sabrina is friendly and no-nonsense; and of course, the price is right.

Republica Hotel
HOTEL $

(✆2224630; Jose Falcao Rd; s/d from ₹400/700, d with AC ₹1000; ✳) The Republica is a story of unexplored potential, an architectural beauty that's been left to the elements – though its dilapidation is, in part, its charm. We thought the welcome could be warmer, and the rooms, though a bit worn, are pricey, but the elderly, ramshackle wooden building has balconies railed with ornate wrought-iron banisters, some rooms have three walls of stained glass, and the air hangs heavy with *saudade* and faded grandeur.

Casa Paradiso
HOTEL $$

(✆2230092; www.casaparadisogoa.com; Jose Falcao Rd; r ₹2000-2500; ✳) Just steps away from Panaji's Church of Our Lady of the Immaculate Conception, the newish Casa is a central, if a tad overpriced, option with friendly staff and bright rooms.

Bharat Lodge
GUESTHOUSE $$

(✆2224862, 9890193688; Sao Tomé St; d without/with AC ₹1000/1600; ✳) A good, clean option in a pretty, recently renovated old building. Rooms have TVs, but could be cheaper.

Comfort Guest House
GUESTHOUSE $

(✆6642250; 31st January Rd; r ₹500) Wasn't yet open at research time, but we heard good things about it.

🍴 Eating

You'll never go hungry in Panaji, where food is enjoyed fully and frequently. A stroll down 18th June or 31st January Rds will turn up a number of great, cheap canteen-style options, as will a quick circuit of the Municipal Gardens.

TOP CHOICE Upper House
GOAN $$

(Cunha-Rivara Rd; mains ₹95-295; ⊙11am-10pm) Fans of Goan seafood *and* vegetarians alike can rejoice in the food at this new spot specialising in home-style regional dishes. Local favourites such as crab *xec xec* (crab cooked in a roasted-coconut gravy), pork vindaloo, and fish-curry-rice are done the old-fashioned way (the latter even comes with saltwater mango pickle, rarely found outside Goan mothers' kitchens), and even the veg adaptations (eg mixed veg and mushroom *xacuti*) are show-stoppers. Upper House also serves the best *pav* (Portuguese-style bread) you've ever tasted, while the *alebale* dessert (pancake stuffed with jaggery and coconut) might make you wet your pants it's so good. The restaurant's on the 1st floor of the building next to Hindu Pharmacy.

Sher-E-Punjab
NORTH INDIAN $$

(18th June Rd; mains ₹70-140; ⊙10.30am-11.30pm) A cut above the usual lunch joint, Sher-E-Punjab caters to well-dressed locals with its generous, carefully spiced Punjabi dishes: even a humble *mattar paneer* (unfermented cheese and pea curry) is memorable here. There's a pleasant garden terrace out back, too, open seasonally. The food at the fancier branch of Sher-E-Punjab (Hotel Aroma, Cunha-Rivara Rd; mains ₹120-270; ⊙11am-3pm & 7-10.30pm) is equally tasty.

George Bar & Restaurant
GOAN $$

(Church Sq; mains ₹75-160; ⊙9.30am-10.30pm) Slightly cramped wooden tables and a healthy mix of drunks and families make for a good local, down-to-earth vibe. Seafood's the name of the game here, and it's done especially well in *pilau* (rice cooked in stock; often spelled *pulao* in Goa) and other Goan classics. George is also one of those rare birds in Goa that does good veg; try the biryani or the delish veg *pilau*.

Hotel Vihar
VEGAN $

(MG Rd; mains ₹50-80, thalis ₹45-70; ⊙7.30am-10pm) A vast menu of 'pure veg' food, great big thalis and a plethora of fresh juices make this clean, simple canteen a popular place for locals and visitors alike. Sip a hot chai, invent your own juice combination, and dig into one of the fresh thalis or tiffins.

Viva Panjim
GOAN $

(31st January Rd; mains ₹65-120; ⊙11am-3.30pm & 7-10.30pm Mon-Sat, 7-10.30pm Sun) Though it's crazy touristy these days, this little side-street eatery, with a couple of tables out on the street itself, still delivers tasty Goan classics – there's a whole page of the menu devoted to pork dishes – as well as the standard Indian fare. Veggies, though, will leave disappointed.

Hospedaria Venite
GOAN $$

(31st January Rd; mains ₹180-260; ⊙9am-10.30pm) The atmospheric Venite is a long-time tourist favourite: its tiny, rickety balcony tables make the perfect lunchtime spot. But perhaps success has gone to Venite's head: the food was never great, and now it's exorbitantly priced, too. Maybe visit for a cold beer or snack in the evening instead and chill out on the balcony before moving on.

Legacy of Bombay INDIAN $$
(Hotel Fidalgo, 18th June Rd; mains ₹90-150) Slightly fancy, slightly pricey, really good pure-veg.

Satkar Vegetarian Restaurant INDIAN $
(18th June Rd; thalis ₹55-70, mains ₹50-80) Casual, cheap, pretty good pure-veg.

 ## Drinking

Panaji's got pick-me-up pit stops aplenty, especially in Sao Tomé and Fontainhas. Mostly simple little bars with a few plastic tables and chairs, they're a great way to get chatting with locals.

Down the Road BAR
(MG Rd; 11am-2am) This restaurant's balcony overlooking the creek and Old Patto Bridge makes for a good and comfy cocktail spot. The ground-floor bar is also Panaji's only real late-nighter, with occasional live music.

Quarterdeck BAR
(Dayanand Bandodkar Marg; 11am-10.45pm) The prices here are on the high side, but the spot right on the water makes up for that.

☆ Entertainment

Kala Academy CULTURAL PROGRAMS
(2420451; www.kalaacademy.org; Dayanand Bandodkar Marg) On the west side of the city at Campal is Goa's premier cultural centre, which features an excellent program of dance, theatre, music and art exhibitions throughout the year. Many plays are in Konkani, but there are occasional English-language productions; call to find out what's on when you're in town.

INOX CINEMA
(2420999; www.inoxmovies.com; Old GMC Heritage Precinct; tickets ₹180-200) This comfortable multiplex cinema shows Hollywood and Bollywood blockbusters alike; films change on Fridays.

Casino boats ply the Mandovi waters each night, offering lose-your-savings fun to all who step aboard. Casino Royale (6519471/2; www.casinoroyalegoa.com; entry ₹3500; 6pm-8am) is the largest; various age and dress restrictions apply.

 ## Shopping

Panaji's municipal market is a great place for people-watching and buying necessities.

Khadi Gramodyog Bhavan HANDICRAFTS
(Dr Atmaram Borkar Rd; 9am-noon & 3-7pm Mon-Sat) Goa's only outpost of the government's Khadi & Village Industries Commission has an excellent range of hand-woven cottons (the towels and men's kurtas are particularly good), along with oils, soaps, spices and other handmade products that come straight from – and directly benefit – regional villages.

Barefoot HANDICRAFTS
(31st January Rd; 10am-8pm Mon-Sat) Barefoot is part of Panaji's new wave of very high end shops specialising in design of one kind or another. Barefoot, though pricey, has some nice gifts, ranging from traditional Christian paintings on wood to jewellery to beaded coasters.

Panaji has several good bookstores, all with a range of books on Goa and the region.

Book Fair BOOKSTORE
(Hotel Mandovi, Dayanand Bandodkar Marg; 9am-9pm) A small, well-stocked bookstore in the Hotel Mandovi lobby; you'll find *Fish Curry & Rice,* the Goa Foundation's environmental sourcebook, here (see p811).

Singbal's Book House BOOKSTORE
(Church Sq; 9.30am-1pm & 3.30-7.30pm Mon-Sat) Lots of books and newspapers and heaps of character at this slightly grumpy establishment that, incidentally, had a cameo role in the *Bourne Supremacy.*

Vision World Book Depot BOOKSTORE
(Church Sq; 9.30am-8pm) A good selection of self-help and spiritual titles, among other things.

 ## Information

ATMs are everywhere, especially on 18th June Rd and around the Thomas Cook office.

Cozy Nook Travels (18th June Rd; per hr ₹35; 9am-9pm) Superfriendly internet joint, with a quiet ISD booth.

Goa Tourism Development Corporation (GTDC; 2424001/2/3; www.goa-tourism.com; Dr Alvaro Costa Rd; 9.30am-1.15pm & 2-5.45pm Mon-Sat) Pick up maps of Goa and Panaji here and book one of GTDC's host of tours.

Indiatourism (Government of India tourist office; 2223412; www.incredibleindia.com; 1st fl, Communidade Bldg, Church Sq; 9.30am-6pm Mon-Fri, to 2pm Sat) Helpful staff can provide a list of qualified guides for tours and trips in Goa. A half-/full-day tour for up to five people costs ₹600/750.

Main post office (MG Rd; 9.30am-5.30pm Mon-Sat)

Oliveira Fernandes & Sons Business Centre (MG Rd; per hr ₹30; 9am-midnight) Best internet cafe with the best name.

Thomas Cook (2221312; Dayanand Bandodkar Marg; 9.30am-6pm Mon-Sat) Changes travellers cheques commission-free and handles currency exchange, wire transfers, cash advances on credit cards, and air bookings.

Vintage Hospitals (6644401-05, ambulance 2232533; www.vintage3.com; Cacula Enclave, St Inez) A couple of kilometres southwest of Panaji, Vintage is a reputable hospital with all the fixings.

ⓘ Getting There & Away

AIR A taxi from Panaji to Dabolim Airport takes about an hour, and costs ₹500.

BUS All government buses depart from the **Kadamba bus stand** (local enquiries 2438034), with local services heading out every few minutes. To get to South Goan beaches, take a bus to Margao and change there; Ponda buses also stop at Old Goa.

Calangute ₹14, 45 minutes

Candolim ₹12, 30 minutes

Mapusa ₹10, 20 minutes

Margao express; ₹26, 45 minutes

Old Goa ₹8, 15 minutes

State-run long-distance services also depart from the **Kadamba bus stand** (interstate enquiries 2438035; reservations 8am-8pm). Private operators have booths outside Kadamba, but the buses depart from the interstate bus stand next to New Patto Bridge. One reliable company is **Paulo Travels** (2438531; www .paulotravels.com; Kardozo Bldg). Some high-season government and private long-distance fares:

Bengaluru ₹550-800, 15 hours, five daily

Bengaluru private; ₹800-1300, 14-15 hours

Hampi private; ₹700-800, 10-11 hours

Hubli ₹150, six hours, hourly

Mumbai private ₹600-1500, 12-14 hours

Pune ₹450, 11 hours, nine daily

Pune private; ₹700-1200, 10-11 hours

Kadamba station has an ATM, an internet cafe – and a Ganesh temple.

TRAIN Panaji's closest train station is Karmali (Old Goa), 12km to the east, where many long-distance services stop. Panaji's **Konkan Railway reservation office** (2712940; 8am-8pm Mon-Sat) is on the 1st floor of the Kadamba bus stand. See p827 for details on trains out of Margao, many of which stop at Karmali.

ⓘ Getting Around

It's easy enough to get around Panaji on foot, and it's unlikely you'll even need a pilot or autorickshaw, which is good because they charge a lot: a rick from Kadamba to your hotel will cost ₹50. Frequent buses run between Kadamba and the municipal market (₹5).

To Old Goa, a taxi costs around ₹300, an autorickshaw ₹150. Lots of taxis hang around the Municipal Gardens, while you'll find autorickshaws and pilots in front of the post office, on 18th June Rd, and just south of the church.

Old Goa

From the 16th to the 18th centuries, when Old Goa's population exceeded that of Lisbon or London, this capital of Goa was considered the 'Rome of the East'. You can still sense that grandeur as you wander the grounds, with its towering churches and cathedral and majestic convents. Its rise under the Portuguese, from 1510, was meteoric, but cholera and malaria outbreaks forced the abandonment of the city in the 1600s. In 1843 the capital was officially shifted to Panaji.

Some of the churches, the cathedral and a convent or two are still in use, but many of the other historical buildings have become museums. It's a fascinating day trip, but it can get crowded: consider visiting on a weekday morning, when you can take in Mass at Sé Cathedral or the Basilica of Bom Jesus (remember to cover your shoulders and legs in the churches and cathedral), and definitely stop by if you're around in the 10 days leading up to the **Feast of St Francis Xavier** on 3 December.

⊙ Sights

Sé Cathedral   CHURCH

The largest church in Old Goa, the Sé de Santa Catarina, is also the largest in Asia, at over 76m long and 55m wide. Construction began in 1562, under orders from Portugal's King Dom Sebastião, and the finishing touches were made 90 years later. Fairly plain allround, the cathedral has three especially notable features: the first, up in the belfry, is the **Golden Bell**, the largest bell in Asia; the second is in the screened chapel inside

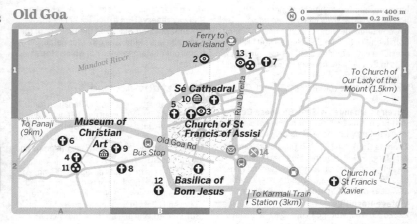

to the right, known as the **Chapel of the Cross of Miracles**, wherein sits a cross said to have miraculously, and vastly, expanded in size after its creation by local shepherds in 1619. The third is the massive gilded reredos (ornamental screen behind the altar), which depicts the life of St Catherine, to whom the cathedral is dedicated and who came to a sticky end in Alexandria, Egypt, where she was beheaded.

Next to the cathedral, in the old archbishop's house, **Kristu Kala Mandir Art Gallery** (admission ₹10; ⏱9.30am-5.30pm Tue-Sun) has a hodgepodge of contemporary Christian art and religious objects, including old church confessionals and altar pieces. The decorative wall frescoes may be the gallery's prettiest holdings.

Church of St Francis of Assisi   CHURCH

The gorgeous interior of this 1661 church, built over a 16th-century chapel, is filled with gilded and carved woodwork, murals depicting the life of St Francis, frescoes of decorative flowers and various angels, 16th-century Portuguese tombstones, and another stunning reredos.

Just behind the church, the former convent houses the **Archaeological Museum** (admission ₹10; ⏱8am-5pm), whose small but worthwhile collection includes a portrait gallery of Portuguese viceroys, a couple of bronze statues, fragments of Hindu temple sculpture, and some interesting 'hero stones', carved to commemorate Hindu warriors who perished in combat.

TOP CHOICE Museum of Christian Art   MUSEUM

(http://christianartmuseum.goa-india.org; adult/child ₹30/free; ⏱9.30am-5pm) This excellent museum, in a positively stunning space in the restored 1627 **Convent of St Monica**, has a fine collection of 16th- and 17th-century Christian art from Old Goa and around the state. There are some exquisite pieces here – wooden sculptures glittering with gilt and polychrome, processional lamps, tabernacle doors, polychrome paintings and other religious objects from Old Goa's prime – that are almost, but not quite, outdone by the atmospheric interior. The four-storey-high ceilings, exposed wood beams and terracotta-work, and all-around beauty of the place are worth a visit in their own right.

Basilica of Bom Jesus   CHURCH

Famous throughout the Roman Catholic world for its rather grizzled and grizzly long-term resident, the basilica's vast, gilded interior forms the last resting place of Goa's patron saint, St Francis Xavier (except for his diamond-encrusted fingernail, which sits in Chandor). In 1541, the saint embarked on a mission to put right the sinful, heady lifestyles of Goa's Portuguese colonials. Construction of the imposing red-stone basilica was completed in 1605; St Francis himself is housed in a **mausoleum** to the right, in a glass-sided coffin amid a shower of gilt stars.

Church of Our Lady of the Mount   CHURCH

For a wonderful view of the city hike up to this hilltop church, also known as **Capela de Monte**, 2km east of Sé Cathedral; it's especially worth the trip for a spectacular sunset. (Locals will warn you not to go solo; the site is a bit remote.) The church is rarely open but was recently restored and, with its exceptional acoustics, now hosts concerts during the Feast of St Francis Xavier in December, the Monte Music Festival in February, and at other times during the year.

Monastery of St Augustine HISTORIC SITE
The melancholy, evocative ruins of this once vast and impressive Augustinian monastery are all that remain of a huge structure founded in 1572 and abandoned in 1835. The building's facade came tumbling down in 1942; all that remains, amid piles of rubble, is the towering skeletal belfry, though the bell itself was rescued and now hangs in Panaji's Church of Our Lady of the Immaculate Conception.

There are plenty of other monuments in Old Goa to explore, including the **Church of St Cajetan**, **Viceroy's Arch**, **Adil Shah Palace Gateway**, **Chapel of St Anthony**, **Chapel of St Catherine**, **Albuquerque's Steps**, the **Convent & Church of St John**, **Sisters' Convent** and the **Church of Our Lady of the Rosary**.

✗ Eating

Little tourist restaurants with chai and snacks are peppered around; the basic **Sanjay Cafe** (Old Goa Rd; thalis ₹35, tiffins ₹25-30) has the best food in town.

❶ Getting There & Away

Frequent buses from Old Goa head to Panaji's Kadamba bus stand (₹8, 25 minutes) from Old Goa Rd, just beside the Tourist Inn and at the main roundabout to the east.

Ponda & Around

The workaday inland town of Ponda, 29km southeast of Panaji, has two big drawcards in the vicinity – Hindu temples and spice plantations – and is worth a day away from the beach. Temple aficionados, however, might be a little disappointed; most were built or rebuilt after the originals were destroyed by the Portuguese, so they're not as ancient as those elsewhere in India.

The 18th-century hilltop **Mangueshi Temple** at Priol, 5km northwest of Ponda, is dedicated to Manguesh, a god known only in Goa, while 1km away at Mardol is the **Mahalsa Temple**, also dedicated to a specifically Goan deity. The 1738 **Shantadurga Temple**, meanwhile, just west of Ponda, is dedicated to Shantadurga, the goddess of peace, and is one of the most famous shrines in Goa.

The **Tropical Spice Plantation** (☏2340329; www.tropicalspiceplantation.com; admission incl lunch ₹400; ☺9am-4pm), 5km northeast of Ponda, is touristy, but you'll get an entertaining 45-minute tour of the 120-acre plantation's 'demo garden' followed by a buffet lunch. Elephant rides and bathings are available for ₹600, but seeing the elephants uncomfortably tied on short leashes all day may make this part less appealing. **Sahakari Spice Farm** (☏2312394; www.sahakarifarms.com; admission incl lunch ₹400; ☺9am-4pm), 2km from Ponda, is practically the same thing.

Nearby, the 200-year-old family **Savoi Plantation** (☏2340272, 9423888899; www.savoiplantation.com; ☺9am-4.30pm), whose motto is 'Organic Since Origin', is much mellower, less touristed and elephant-free. You'll find a warm welcome from knowledgeable guides keen to walk you through the 100-acre plantation at your own pace. Local crafts are for sale, and you're welcomed with fresh *kokum* juice, cardamom bananas and other organic treats. Savoi also recently built a couple of **cottages** (d incl meals ₹5000).

There are regular buses to Ponda from Panaji (₹18, 45 minutes) and Margao, after which you'll need to arrange a taxi to visit the temples or spice farms. Taxis from Panaji charge ₹1000 for a day trip to the area (up to eight hours and 80km).

Dudhsagar Falls

On the eastern border with Karnataka, Dudhsagar Falls (603m) are Goa's most impressive waterfalls, and the second highest in India, best seen as soon as possible after the rains. To get here, take the 8.13am train to Colem from Margao (check return times in advance; there are only three trains daily in each direction), and from there, catch a jeep for the bumpy 40-minute trip to the falls (₹300 return per person, or ₹1800 for the six-passenger jeep). It's then a short but rocky clamber to the edge of the falls themselves. A simpler, but more expensive, option is to take a full-day **GTDC tour** (₹700; ◎9am-6pm Wed & Sun) from Panaji, Mapusa or Calangute (book at the office in Panaji), or arrange an excursion with the Day Tripper travel agency in Calangute or Speedy Travels in Anjuna.

NORTH GOA

Mapusa

POP 40,100

The pleasantly bustling market town of Mapusa (pronounced 'Mapsa') is the largest town in northern Goa, and is most often visited for its busy **Friday Market** (◎8am-6.30pm), which attracts scores of buyers and sellers from neighbouring towns and villages, and a healthy intake of tourists from the northern beaches. It's a good place to pick up the usual embroidered bedsheets and the like at prices lower than in the beach resorts. You'll probably pass through Mapusa eventually anyway, as it's a major transport hub for northern Goa buses.

Mapusa is also home to the exceptionally awesome **Other India Bookstore** (☑2263306; www.otherindiabookstore.com; Mapusa Clinic Rd; ◎9am-5pm Mon-Fri, to 1pm Sat), specialising in 'dissenting wisdom' – a small but spectacular selection of books on nature, farming, politics, education and natural health. To find it, go up the steps on the right as you walk down Mapusa Clinic Rd, and follow signs; it's at the end of a dingy corridor.

There's little reason to stay the night in Mapusa when the beaches of the north coast are all so close, but if you do, go for **Hotel Vilena** (☑2263115; Feira Baixa Rd; d without/with AC ₹525/725, without bathroom ₹420; ✳). There are plenty of nice, old-fashioned cafes within the market area. The thalis are excellent at busy **Ashok Snacks & Beverages** (thalis & mains ₹35-70; ◎6am-10.30pm Mon-Sat, to 4pm Sun), overlooking the market. It's a simple place full of local families and folks on their lunch break. **Hotel Vrundavan** (thalis ₹38-55, tiffins ₹12-50; ◎7am-10pm Wed-Mon), an all-veg place bordering the municipal gardens, is another great joint with good chai and snacks.

❶ Information

There are plenty of ATMs scattered about town. **Mapusa Clinic** (☑2263343; ◎consultations 10.30am-1.30pm Mon-Sat, 3.30-7pm Mon, Wed & Fri) A well-run medical clinic, with 24-hour

---

BACKWOODS CAMP

In a forest in the Mahaveer Sanctuary full of butterflies and birds, **Backwoods Camp** (☑9822139859; www.backwoodsgoa.com) could not be in a more magical, serene spot. The resort is about 1km from Tambdi Surla temple, and for birdwatching enthusiasts it offers one of Goa's richest sources of feathered friends, with everything from Ceylon frogmouths and Asian fairy bluebirds to puff-throated babblers and Indian pittas putting in a regular appearance. Accommodation is in comfortable tents on raised platforms, bungalows and farmhouse rooms (all with attached bathroom), and the camp makes valiant attempts to protect this fragile bit of the Goan ecosystem through measures including waste recycling, replanting indigenous tree species and employing local villagers. One-, two- and three-day birdwatching excursions, including guide, transport from Ponda, accommodation at the camp and all meals, cost from ₹4000, ₹6000 and ₹8000 per person, respectively.

Goa's environment has suffered from an onslaught of tourism over the last 40 years, but also from the effects of logging, mining and local customs (rare turtle eggs have traditionally been considered a dining delicacy). Construction proceeds regardless of what the local infrastructure or ecosystem can sustain, while plastic bottles pile up in vast mountains. There are, however, a few easy ways to minimise your impact on Goa's environment:

» Take your own bag when shopping and refill water bottles with filtered water wherever possible. The 5L Bisleri water bottles come with a deposit and are returnable to be reused; invest in these when you can. Better yet, bring a water filter with you.

» Rent a bicycle instead of a scooter, and ask around if you don't find any: bicycle rentals are declining as a result of our scooter infatuation, but they'll bounce back if the demand is there.

» Dispose of cigarette butts, which are nonbiodegradeable, in bins; birds and sealife may mistake them for food and choke.

Turtles are currently protected by the **Forest Department** (www.goaforest.com), which operates huts on beaches, such as Agonda, where turtles arrive to lay eggs. Drop into these or check out the website to find out more about the department's work. Also doing good work is the **Goa Foundation** (☑2256479, 2263305; www.goafoundation.org; St Britto's Apts, G-8 Feira Alta, Mapusa), the state's main environmental pressure group. It has spearheaded a number of conservation projects since its inauguration in 1986, and its website is a great place to learn more about Goan environmental issues. The group's excellent *Fish Curry & Rice* (₹400), a sourcebook on Goa's environment and lifestyle, is sold at Mapusa's Other India Bookstore. The Foundation occasionally runs volunteer projects; call or swing by for details.

emergency services. Be sure to go to the 'new' Mapusa Clinic, behind the 'old' one.
Pink Panther Travel Agency (☑2250352, 2263180; panther_goa@sancharnet.in; ◷10am-6pm Mon-Fri, to 1.30pm Sat) Train and air tickets (both international and domestic), currency exchange and property consultancy services.
Softway (☑2262075; per hr ₹20; Chandranath Apts; ◷9am-10pm Mon-Sat, 10am-9.30pm Sun) Fast internet and ice cream in a shopping complex just past the post office (opposite the police station).

ℹ Getting There & Away
If you're coming to Goa by bus from Mumbai, Mapusa's **Kadamba bus stand** (☑2232161) is the jumping-off point for the northern beaches. Local services run every few minutes; just look for the correct destination on the sign in the bus windscreen – and try to get an express. For buses to the southern beaches, take a bus to Panaji, then Margao, and change there.
Local services:
Anjuna ₹10, 20 minutes
Arambol ₹20, 1½ hours
Calangute/Candolim ₹10/12, 20/35 minutes

Panjim ₹10, 20 minutes
Thivim ₹10, 20 minutes
Interstate services run out of the same lot, but private operators have their offices next to the bus stand. There's generally little difference in price, comfort or duration between private services.
Long-distance services:
Bengaluru government; ₹500, 12 hours, one daily at 5pm
Bengaluru private; non-AC ₹1500, AC ₹1600-2000
Mumbai private; non-AC ₹1500, AC ₹1600-2000
Pune government; non-AC ₹380-500, AC ₹600, three daily, in evening
Pune private; non-AC ₹1200, AC ₹1200-1500
There's a prepaid taxi stand outside the bus terminal; it has a handy sign of prices. Cabs to Anjuna or Calangute cost ₹200, Arambol ₹400, and Margao ₹800; autorickshaws typically charge ₹50 less than taxis.

Thivim, about 12km northeast of town, is the nearest train station on the Konkan Railway. Local buses meet trains; an autorickshaw into Mapusa from Thivim costs around ₹150.

Candolim, Sinquerim & Fort Aguada

POP 8600

Candolim's vast beach, which curves round as far as smaller Sinquerim beach in the south, is largely the preserve of older, slow-roasting package tourists from the UK, Russia and Scandinavia, and is fringed with beach shacks, all offering sun beds and shade in exchange for your custom. Its best-known feature, though, may be the hulking *River Princess* tanker which ran aground here in the late 1990s. This massive industrial creature, marooned just a few dozen metres offshore, with tourists sunbathing in her sullen shadow, is a surreal, and oddly pretty, sight.

Candolim's beach is pleasant, the town is mellow, and there are some great hotels here, but it's somewhat fading and lacks the personality of many other beach towns. The post office, supermarkets, travel agents, internet cafes, pharmacies and plenty of banks with ATMs are all on the main Fort Aguada Rd, which runs parallel to the beach.

Sights & Activities

Fort Aguada FORT, AREA

(⏱8.30am-5.30pm) Guarding the mouth of the Mandovi River and hugely popular with Indian tour groups, Fort Aguada was constructed by the Portuguese in 1612 and is the most impressive of Goa's remaining forts. It's worth braving the crowds and hawkers at the moated ruins on the hilltop for the views; unfortunately, there was no entry at research time to the fort's four-storey **Portuguese lighthouse**, built in 1894 and the oldest of its type in Asia. But just down the road is the peninsula's active **lighthouse** (Indian/foreigner/child ₹10/25/3; ⏱3-5.30pm), which you can climb for extraordinary views. It's a pleasant 2km ride along a hilly, sealed road to the fort, or you can walk via a steep, uphill path past Marbella Guest House. Beneath the fort is the **Fort Aguada Jail**, whose cells were originally fort storehouses, and **Johnny's Mansion**, owned by a famously wealthy Goan and often used as a set for Indian films. Neither is open to the public.

Calizz MUSEUM

(☑3250000; www.calizz.com; Fort Aguada Rd; adult/child ₹300/free; ⏱10am-7pm) A highlight of Candolim, this impressive compound is filled with traditional Goan houses and some 75,000 artefacts. The museum won a National Tourism Award for its innovativeness, but it's the pretty houses that will blow you away. Resident historians conduct 45-minute tours that bring the state's cultural history to life.

Boat Cruises BOATING

Some of the most popular boat trips around town are run by **John's Boat Tours** (☑6520190, 9822182814; www.johnboattrips.com), including dolphin-watching cruises (₹900), boat trips to Anjuna Market (₹600), a Grand Island snorkelling excursion (₹1200), and even overnight houseboat cruises (₹5000 per person, full board). For something more low-key (read: cheaper), head to the **excursion boat jetty** along the Nerul River; independent local boat conductors here operate trips to Anjuna (₹300) and dolphin cruises (₹200; dolphins guaranteed) that pass by Coco Beach, Fort Aguada Jail, the fort, and – of course – 'Johnny's Millionaire House'.

Sleeping

Candolim has a surprising range of great accommodation. Most of the best-value (and cheapest) budget choices are in the lush area in northern Candolim between the road and the beach; wander through the tiny trails and you're sure to find something. The little road up to the Marbella Guest House also has private houses offering double rooms for around ₹500 per night.

TOP CHOICE Marbella Guest House HOTEL $$$

(☑2479551; www.marbellagoa.com; d/ste from ₹3000/4100; ❄) You might be put off by the name, but this place has not a touch of Spain's Costa del Sol about it. A stunning Portuguese-era villa filled with antiques and backed by a lush, peaceful courtyard garden, the Marbella is a romantic and sophisticated old-world remnant. Its kitchen serves up some imaginative dishes, and its penthouse suite is a dream of polished tiles and four-posters. Sadly for kids with a keen sense of style, no guests under 12 are permitted.

Beach Nest GUESTHOUSE $

(☑2489866; d ₹800-1000) Even the sand in the yard is swept tidily clean each day at this spotless and exceedingly friendly little place that's just a quick jungle-footpath walk to the beach. Upstairs rooms have balcony, kitchenettes and fridges, the owners are smiley and helpful, and the atmosphere's serene and homey.

D'Mello's Sea View Home
HOTEL $$

(☎2489650; dmellos_seaview_home@hotmail.com; d ₹1200-1800) Lovely breezy rooms are the principle attraction at D'Mello's, right at the edge of the beach. Rooms in the sea-facing building are divine, with only three walls: the fourth is your balcony, with huge, stunning views of the ocean. Even interior rooms are stylish, with perky colours and chic cotton bedspreads. All rooms are fastidiously clean and have mosquito nets, and the place is professionally (if a bit impersonally) run.

Villa Ludovici Tourist Home
GUESTHOUSE $

(☎2479684; Fort Aguada Rd; d incl breakfast ₹1000) Well-worn, creaky rooms in a grand old Portuguese-style villa.

Candolim Villa Horizon View
HOTEL $$

(☎2489105; www.candolimvilla.com; d with AC ₹1500-2250; ❋@☞≋) Simple AC rooms are set around a small swimming pool at this friendly, professional place.

Vivanta by Taj
HOTEL $$$

(☎6645858; www.vivantabytaj.com; Sinquerim, r with AC from ₹10,000; ❋@☞≋) Upmarket Taj hotel.

✖ Eating & Drinking

Candolim's plentiful beach shacks are popular places to eat; **Pete's Shack** (mains ₹90-230), on the northern end of the strip, may be the most elegant.

TOP CHOICE Café Chocolatti
CAFE, BAKERY $$

(Fort Aguada Rd; baked goods ₹40-100, mains ₹120-180; ☉9am-7pm Mon-Sat) When you're tired of thalis or simply seeking sanctuary, treat yourself at this lovely tearoom, set in a green garden light years from the bustle of the beach. The cafe serves sandwiches and salads, but the chocolate's the star. Order a slice of double-chocolate cake and sink back into cocoa heaven.

Stone House
MULTICUISINE, BAR $$

(Fort Aguada Rd; mains ₹90-300; ☉10am-3pm & 6pm-midnight) Surf 'n' turf's the thing at this venerable old Candolim venue, inhabiting a stone house and a leafy front courtyard. 'Swedish Lobster' cooked in beer tops the list, followed by other bold plates like flattened beef steak with mushroom and onion in spicy Goan sauce (₹250). There's quality live music most nights of the week.

Republic of Noodles
ASIAN FUSION $$$

(Fort Aguada Rd; mains ₹375-450; ☉11am-3.30pm & 7-11pm) For a sophisticated dining experience, the RoN delivers with its dark bamboo interior, Buddha heads and floating candles. Delicious, huge noodle plates, wok stir-fries and clay-pot dishes are the order of the day – consider the coconut and turmeric curry of red snapper – and there are some exciting dishes for the veggies too.

Bob's Inn
MULTICUISINE, BAR $$

(Fort Aguada Rd; mains ₹90-200; ☉10.30am-4pm & 6.30pm-midnight) Great fish dishes, relaxed ambience and old dudes – foreigners and locals alike – chillaxing at the community table. The African wall hangings, thatch everywhere, and terracotta sculptures are a nice backdrop to the *rava* (semolina wheat) fried mussels or the prawns 'chilly fry' with potatoes.

❶ Getting There & Away

Buses run frequently to Panaji (₹12, 30 minutes) and Mapusa (₹12, 35 minutes) and stop at the turn-off near John's Boat Tours. Calangute buses (₹5, 15 minutes) start at the Fort Aguada bus stop and can be flagged down on Fort Aguada Rd.

Calangute & Baga
POP 15,800

Once a refuge of wealthy Goans, and later a 1960s hot spot for naked, revelling hippies, Calangute today is popular with extended Indian families, groups of Indian bachelors and partying foreigners. If you want to experience authentic Indian (or Russian) tourism full-on, come to Calangute. The northern beach area can get crowded – including the water, which fills up with people, boats and jet skis – but the southern beach is more relaxed. Baga, to the north, meanwhile, is the place for drinking and dancing, and Northern Baga, across the Baga River, is surprisingly tranquil, with budget accommodation bargains clinging to the coast.

🏃 Activities

Water Sports

You'll find numerous jet-ski and parasailing operators on Calangute and Baga beaches; H2O Adventure is the most established. Parasailing costs around ₹600 per ride, jet-skiing costs ₹1000 per 15 minutes, and water-skiing can be had for about ₹1200 per 10 minutes.

Barracuda Diving
DIVING

(☎2279409-14, 9822182402; www.barracudadiving.com; Sun Village Resort, Baga; courses from ₹4000) This long-standing diving school

Calangute

Calangute

Activities, Courses & Tours
1 Calangute Residency A1
2 Day Tripper B3

Sleeping
3 Casa de Goa......................................B2
4 Garden Court Resort........................ B1
5 Johnny's Hotel A1
6 Ospy's Shelter..................................A3

Eating
7 A Reverie A3
8 Casandré..A1
9 Infantaria A1
10 Plantain Leaf B1

Drinking
11 Jerry's Place.....................................A1

Entertainment
12 Kerkar Art Complex...........................B3

Shopping
13 Literati Bookshop & Cafe...................B3

Information
14 MGM International Travels................ B1

offers a range of dives and courses, including a free 'Try Scuba' family session every Monday. It's also exceptional for its 'Project A.W.A.R.E.', which undertakes marine-conservation initiatives and annual underwater and beach clean-ups.

Yoga & Ayurveda
Ayurvedic Natural Health Centre   AYURVEDA, YOGA
(☑2409275; www.healthandayurveda.com; Chogm Rd, Saligao; massages from ₹1200; ☺7.30am-7.30pm) This highly respected centre, 5km inland, offers a range of massages and other ayurvedic treatments lasting from one hour to three weeks. Herbal medicines and consultations with an ayurvedic doctor are also available. For the more serious, professional courses are given here in ayurveda, yoga and other regimes; enquire well in advance. For the more spontaneous, drop-in yoga classes (₹300) are held daily. Some, but not all, buses from Baga/Calangute to Mapusa stop in Saligao, just near the centre; check before boarding.

Boat Trips
Local fishers congregate around northern Baga beach, offering dolphin-spotting trips (₹400 per person), visits to Anjuna Market (₹200 per person) and whole-day excursions to Arambol and Mandrem (₹1000 per person). Call friendly **Eugenio** (☑9226268531).

Tours

Day Tripper (☑2276726; www.daytrippergoa .com; Gaura Vaddo, Calangute; ☺9am-5.30pm Mon-Sat Nov-Apr), one of Goa's best tour agencies, runs a variety of trips around Goa, including two weekly to Dudhsagar Falls (₹1175) and another sailing through the mangroves of the Cumbarjua River (₹1300), as well as longer trips.

GTDC tours can be booked online (www. goa-tourism.com) or at **Calangute Residency** (☑2276024), by the beach.

Sleeping

Calangute and Baga's sleeping options are manifold. Generally, the quietest hotels lie in south Calangute, and across the bridge north of Baga.

CALANGUTE
Casa de Goa   HOTEL $$$
(☑2277777/9999; www.casadegoa.com; Tivai Vaddo; r/ste/cottages ₹5000/6000/7000; ✵@☎☀) The beautiful Casa de Goa is popular with Indian families and books up months in

advance – for good reason. Portuguese-style yellow-ochre buildings surround a pretty pool courtyard, decor is bright and fresh, and the big, clean rooms have safes, flatscreen TVs and new fridges, with other high-end and thoughtful touches. Cottages are across the street from the main hotel and may not get wi-fi.

Ospy's Shelter
GUESTHOUSE $

(☏2279505; oscar_fernandes@sify.com; d ₹600-700) Tucked away in a quiet, lush little area full of palms and sandy paths between the beach and St Anthony's Chapel, are a bunch of family-run guesthouses. Ospy's, just a two-minute walk to the beach, is our favourite. Spotless upstairs rooms have fridges and balconies and look brand new even though they're not, and the whole place has a cosy family feel. Check out the gorgeous old floor tiles on the ground floor.

Johnny's Hotel
HOTEL $

(☏2277458; s ₹400, d ₹600-900) Twelve basic rooms in this backpacker-popular place make for a sociable stay, with regular classes available in yoga, reiki and the tantalisingly titled 'metamorphic technique'. A range of apartments and houses are available for longer-stayers. Johnny's is also home to a popular cafe: stop in for baked beans on toast for

breakfast (₹100) or spice up lunchtime with a Goan 'veg vindaloo' (₹70).

Garden Court Resort
GUESTHOUSE $

(☏2276054; luarba@dataone.in; r ₹500-600, with AC ₹700-800, 1-/2-/3-bedroom apts ₹1000/1500/2500; ❇) Fronted by a Portuguese-style home, rooms here are set among pretty gardens and have balconies and cathedral-ish windows. Apartments rented for short stays when available.

BAGA

Cavala Seaside Resort
HOTEL $$

(☏2276090; www.cavala.com; s/d/ste incl breakfast from ₹850/1300/2200; ❇❡❄) Classy, ivy-clad Cavala has been charming Baga-bound travellers for more than 30 years, and continues to deliver clean, simple, nicely furnished rooms among a large complex with two swimming pools (₹150 for nonguests). There's a good vibe about the place and friendly staff, and the bar-restaurant cooks up a storm most evenings, with frequent live music.

Divine Guest House
GUESTHOUSE $$

(☏2279546, 9370273464; www.indivinehome.com; s/d from ₹700/1000; ❇@❡) The Divine welcomes you with a 'Praise the Lord' gatepost

Baga

0 ____ 400 m
0 ____ 0.2 miles

To Arpora (2km);
Anjuna (5.5 km)

Baga River

Baga Bus Stand

BAGA

Calangute-Baga Rd

Church

ARABIAN SEA

Tito's Rd   To Calangute (1.5km)

Baga

Activities, Courses & Tours
1 Barracuda Diving B1

Sleeping
2 Cavala Seaside Resort A2
3 Divine Guest House A2
   Johnny's .... (see 4)
4 Melissa Guest House A2
5 Nani's Bar & Rani's Restaurant A2

Eating
6 Britto's A2
7 J&A's A1
8 Le Poisson Rouge A1
9 Lila Café A1

Drinking
10 Sun Set A2

Entertainment
11 Café Mambo A3
12 Tito's B3

Shopping
13 Karma Collection A2
14 Mackie's Saturday Nite Bazaar B1
15 Tara Travels B3

WORTH A TRIP

NILAYA HERMITAGE

Spend a night at what may be Goa's most sophisticated luxury hotel, 5km from the beach atop a verdant hill at Arpora, and you'll be signing the guest book with the likes of Sean Connery, Manish Arora and Kate Moss. At **Nilaya Hermitage** (☏2276793/94; www.nilaya.com; Arpora; d incl breakfast, dinner & spa €350; ☀@☎☒), red-stone laterite structures undulate around a swimming pool, and the 10 luxury rooms and four stunning tents could not be more elegantly styled. Everything is done in the colour of lapis lazuli or warm whites, set off by old brass, chunky wood and perfect touches. The food is as dreamy as the surroundings, and the spa's sublime.

and keeps perky reminders throughout the place, so only stay here if you don't mind cheerful proselytising. Rooms are sweet and homey, with bright colours, lots of kitsch and the odd individual touch, all at a quiet riverside location.

Nani's Bar & Rani's
Restaurant GUESTHOUSE $$
(☏2276313; www.naniranigoa.com; r without/with AC ₹1300/1500; ☀@) Nani's is as charming as it is well situated, with clean, simply furnished rooms (think fresh paint, a working phone) set around a garden and a gorgeous colonial bungalow that overlook the water.

Melissa Guest House GUESTHOUSE $
(☏2279583; d ₹500) Neat little rooms, all with attached bathrooms and hot-water showers, comprise this quiet, good-value little place, pleasantly located in a lush spot near the water. Upstairs, **Johnny's** (☏2914000; d ₹600) is almost as good.

✕ Eating

Calangute and Baga have everything from fresh fish cooked up on the beach to the finest Scottish smoked salmon. The main beach strip is thick with vendors selling grilled corn, *pav bhaji* (spiced vegetables and bread) and luminescent candyfloss, as well as the usual beach-shack cuisine. Dining gets more sophisticated to the north and south. The market area, meanwhile, is filled with chai-and-thali joints, and vendors at Baga's bus-stand area sell chai, omelettes and other nonveg snacks for super cheap.

CALANGUTE
 Plantain Leaf INDIAN $
(thalis ₹70-90, mains ₹75-150) On the 1st floor, at a slight remove from the business of the intersection below, is the pure-veg Plantain Leaf. The many Indian families that fill the booths here know a good thing when they

see it: the tea is good, the place is cosy, busy and bright, and the veg thali might be the best you'll get in Goa.

Infantaria BAKERY, ITALIAN $$
(Calangute-Baga Rd; pastries ₹50-100, mains ₹110-275; ☺7.30am-midnight) Next to the São João Batista church is this delish bakery-turned-awesome-Italian-restaurant, loaded with homemade croissants, little flaky pastries, real coffee, Goan and Italian specialities, and lots of booze. The noticeboard here is a hotbed for all things current and counter-current.

A Reverie CONTINENTAL $$$
(Holiday St; mains ₹315-575; ☺7pm-2am) A gorgeous lounge-bar, all armchairs, cool jazz and sparkling crystals, this is the place to spoil yourself with the likes of Serrano ham, grilled asparagus, French wines and Italian cheeses. Try the delectable cream prawn velouté with fennel soup (₹250) or splurge on the smoked French mallard duck breast in madeira jus with sour cherries (₹995).

Casandré GOAN, MULTICUISINE $$
(mains ₹60-140; ☺8.30am-3pm & 6pm-midnight) Housed in an old Portuguese-style bungalow, this dim and tranquil retreat seems mightily out of place amid the tourist tat of Calangute's main beach drag. With a long and old-fashioned menu encompassing everything from 'sizzlers' to Goan specialities, and a cocktail list featuring the good old gimlet, this is a loveable time warp.

BAGA
Le Poisson Rouge FRENCH $$$
(mains ₹310-390; ☺7pm-midnight) Baga manages to do fine dining with aplomb, and this French-slanted experience is one of the picks of the place. Simple local ingredients are combined into winning dishes such as beetroot carpaccio (₹185) and red-snapper

masala (₹390), and served up beneath the stars.

J&A's
ITALIAN $$$

(mains ₹305-445) A pretty cafe set around a gorgeous Portuguese-style villa, this little slice of Italy is a treat even before the sumptuous, if rather pricey, food arrives. The jazz-infused garden and twinkling evening lights make for a romantic setting, too. Add to this triple-filtered water, electric car and composted leftovers, and you've got an experience that's as earth-friendly as it is indulgent.

Lila Café
CAFE $$

(mains ₹110-270; ⊙8.30am-6pm Wed-Mon) German-run place with home-baked breads, perfect, frothy cappuccinos and power-house mains like goulash with spaetzle.

Britto's
MULTICUISINE, BAR $$

(mains ₹95-260; ⊙8.30am-midnight) A Baga institution. Tip: stick to the Goan seafood dishes.

Drinking & Entertainment

Baga's club scene bubbles on long after the parties further north have been locked down. If you're up for a night of decadent drinking or dancing on the tables, you're in the right place. For something lower-key, go for the bars on Calangute's main seaside road.

Jerry's Place
BAR

Also known as JJJ, Jerry's Place is a cute little Calangute bar-resto that's just dingy enough to keep things interesting. Snacks and basic Indian meals (from ₹50) are available, and surprisingly decent rooms (₹800) are just upstairs.

Café Mambo
NIGHTCLUB

(⌕9822765002; www.titos.in; couple ₹500; ⊙10.30pm-3am) Mambo's is Baga's club of the moment: it's slightly sophisticated (relative to Baga), with nightly DJs pumping out mostly commercial house and hip hop, and the occasional (Western) retro nights. Tito's, just next door, used to be Baga's 'it' club. It's still worth a visit, especially for Bollywood nights. Cover, rules and hours are the same as Mambo's, and for both clubs, women enter free, but unaccompanied gents don't enter at all.

Kerkar Art Complex
CULTURAL PROGRAMS

(⌕2276017, 9923958016; www.subodhkerkar.com; Holiday St; ⊙10am-7pm) Showcasing the work of local artist Dr Subodh Kerkar, this Calang-

ute complex is most notable for the open-air music and dance recitals – on Tuesday and Thursday nights and some weekends – hosted by its multicuisine restaurant, Waves (mains ₹300-500; ⊙11am-3pm & 7pm-2am).

Sun Set
BAR, MULTICUISINE

(⊙7.30am-10.30pm) Just a little spot to watch the sunset and the boats with a drink; at low tide, you can walk through the water back to Baga beach.

Shopping

Both **Mackie's Saturday Nite Bazaar** (www.mackiesnitebazaar.com), in Baga, and the larger **Ingo's Saturday Nite Bazaar** (www .ingosbazaar.com), in Arpora, about 2km northeast of Baga, start around 6pm and are fun alternatives to Anjuna's Wednesday market. They were running at the time of research but have been cancelled from time to time in recent years for reasons unclear. Ask around to see if they're on.

Karma Collection
SOUVENIRS

(www.karmacollectiongoa.com; ⊙9.30am-10.30pm) This fixed-price shop in Baga has the usual patchwork wall hangings, but also antiques from across South Asia.

Literati Bookshop & Cafe
BOOKSTORE

(⌕2277740; www.literati-goa.com; ⊙10am-6.30pm Mon-Sat) A refreshingly different bookstore, in the owners' Calangute home. Ask about readings and other events.

Tara Travels
BOOKSTORE

(⊙9am-midnight Mon-Sat) A good selection of new and secondhand books in Baga; it's also a book exchange and travel agency.

Information

Currency exchange offices, ATMs, pharmacies and tons of internet cafes cluster around Calangute's main market and bus stand area, with several more (of everything) along the Baga and Candolim roads.

MGM International Travels (www.mgmtravels .com; Umta Vaddo, Calangute; ⊙9.30am-6.30pm Mon-Sat) A long-established and trusted travel agency with competitive prices on domestic and international air tickets.

Thomas Cook (⌕2282455; Calangute-Anjuna Rd, Calangute; ⊙9am-6pm Mon-Sat) Currency exchange and the like.

Getting There & Around

Frequent buses to Panaji (₹14, 45 minutes) and Mapusa (₹10) depart from the Baga and Calangute bus stands, and a local bus (₹5) runs between the Baga and Calangute stands every few minutes; catch it anywhere along the way. A prepaid taxi from Dabolim Airport to Calangute costs ₹645.

Anjuna

Dear old Anjuna, that stalwart on India's hippy scene, still drags out the sarongs and sandalwood each Wednesday for its famous – and once infamous – flea market. Though it continues to pull in droves of backpackers and long-term hippies, midrange tourists are also increasingly making their way here. The town itself might be a bit ragged around the edges these days, but that's all part of its cosy charm, and Anjuna remains a favourite of long-stayers and first-timers alike.

🏃 Activities

Anjuna's charismatic, rocky **beach** runs for almost 2km from the northern village area to the flea market. The northern end shrinks

to almost nothing when the tide washes in, but when the tide goes out, it becomes a lovely, and surprisingly quiet, stretch of sand. For more action, **paragliding** (tandem rides ₹1500) sometimes takes place on market days off the headland at the southern end of the beach.

If you're looking to embellish yourself while in town, try **Andy's Tattoo Studio** (www.andys-tattoo-studio-anjuna-goa.com; ⊙noon-7pm Mon-Sat), behind the San Francisco Restaurant and brimming with attitude. Drop in to make an appointment and get a quote for your permanent souvenir.

Yoga

There's lots of yoga, reiki and ayurvedic massage offered around Anjuna; look for notices at Café Diogo and the German Bakery. Drop-in classes are organised by **Avalon Sunset** (www.yogainternationalorganisation.com; classes ₹300-400) and at **Brahmani Yoga** (☑9370568639; www.brahmaniyoga.com; classes

Anjuna

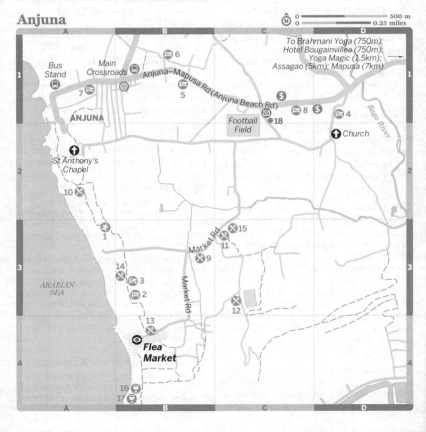

₹500), next to Hotel Bougainvillea. Also consider staying at Yoga Magic or the Ashtanga Purple Valley Yoga Retreat, both lovely resorts with longer-term yoga programs.

🛏 Sleeping

Most accommodation and other useful services are sprinkled along the beach, or down shady inland lanes. Dozens of rooms of the largely concrete cell variety run along Anjuna's northern clifftop stretch; most come in at ₹400 to ₹600 per night. There are also plenty of small, family-run guesthouses tucked back from the main beach strip, offering nicer double rooms for a similar price; take your pick from the dozens of 'Rooms to Let' signs.

Hotel Bougainvillea　　　HERITAGE HOTEL **$$**
(Granpa's Inn; ☎2273270/71; www.granpasinn.com; d/ste incl breakfast & tax from ₹2200/2950; ❄🛜🏊) This old-fashioned hotel in a 200-year-old yellow mansion is ridiculously pretty. Elegant rooms have that rare combination of charm and luxury, and the pool

area is gorgeous, with lots of trees around. The grounds are so lush and shady, in fact, that the place seems a good few degrees cooler than the rest of Anjuna.

Vilanova　　　　　　　GUESTHOUSE **$**
(☎6450389, 9225904244; mendonca90@rediffmail.com; d without/with AC ₹700/900; ❄) Big, clean rooms have fridge, TV, 24-hour hot water and window screens and are set in three Portuguese-style bungalows in a cute little compound. There are good vibes and a comfortable family atmosphere, with friendly staff and a good-value restaurant. We almost hate to tell anyone about it!

🌿 Yoga Magic　　　　GUESTHOUSE **$$$**
(☎6523796; www.yogamagic.net; s/d huts ₹4500/6000, ste ₹6000/8000; 🛜) Solar lighting, vegetable farming and compost toilets are just some of the worthy initiatives practised in this ultraluxurious yoga resort, where hand-printed textiles, reclaimed-wood furniture and organic, gourmet vegetarian food are the order of the day. 'Huts' are of the stunning, dramatic Rajasthani variety. Rates include breakfast; daily yoga classes cost an extra ₹400 per session.

Faiz'd　　　　　　　　GUESTHOUSE **$**
(☎9619855350; tents ₹800) The spacious, high-end tents here are lined with embroidered fabric, have tile floors and attached bathrooms, and are set in pretty grounds – like a little tent village – with winding, lamplit paths. The location, a stone's throw from the beach, isn't bad, either.

Palacete Rodrigues　　HERITAGE HOTEL **$$**
(☎2273358, 9422056467; www.palacetegoa.com; s/d from ₹850/1000, d/ste with AC ₹1550/1750; ❄) This old-fashioned mansion, filled with antiques, odd corners and bags of fun, tacky charm, is as cool and quirky as they come. Choose your theme: rooms come in Chinese, Vietnamese, Portuguese and, of course, Goan flavours.

Paradise　　　　　　　GUESTHOUSE **$**
(☎9922541714; janet_965@hotmail.com; Anjuna-Mapusa Rd; d ₹600-800, with AC ₹1500; ❄) The friendly, homey Paradise is fronted by an old Portuguese house, and its clean rooms are set in rustic grounds full of crowing roosters and sleeping cats. Proprietor Janet and her enterprising family also run a general store, restaurant, internet cafe (₹40 per hour), travel agency, money exchange, Western Union services and beauty parlour (₹250 for

GOA'S FLEA MARKET EXPERIENCE: GOAN, GOAN, GONE?

Wednesday's weekly flea market at Anjuna is as much part of the Goan experience as a day on a deserted beach. More than two decades ago, it was the sole preserve of hippies smoking jumbo joints and convening to compare experiences on the heady Indian circuit. Nowadays, things are far more staid and mainstream, and package tourists seem to beat out independent travellers in both numbers and purchasing power. A couple of hours here and you'll never want to see a mirrored bedspread, brass figurine or floaty Indian cotton dress again in your life. That said, it's still a good time, and you can find some interesting one-off souvenirs and clothing in among the tourist tat. Remember to bargain hard and take along equal quantities of patience and stamina, applicable to dealing with local and expat vendors alike.

head massages). You name it and Janet can probably arrange it for you.

Florinda's Guest House   GUESTHOUSE $
(☑9890216520, 9762331032; r ₹400-900) One of the better cheapies near the beach, Florinda's has clean rooms, with 24-hour hot water and window screens, set around a garden with the world's tiniest pool.

Peace Land   GUESTHOUSE $
(☑2273700; s/d ₹450/600; ⑨) Rooms here are small but arranged around a tranquil courtyard garden. There's also a pool table here, a chill-out area and a small shop selling basic provisions. Customer service could use some help though.

Purple Valley Yoga Retreat GUESTHOUSE $$$
(☑2268364; www.yogagoa.com; 142 Bairo Alto, Assagao; ❄) This popular yoga resort in nearby Assagao offers one- and two-week residential courses in Ashtanga yoga; weekly rates, which include accommodation, classes and meals, begin at £480 per person.

Sea Wave Inn   HOTEL $
(Sea Queen; ☑2274455; seaqueenanjuna@gmail.com; Anjuna-Mapusa Rd; r without/with AC ₹800/1000; ❄) Good rooms and friendly staff, and the outdoor restaurant, which shows movies and sports on a big screen, is a fun night-time hang-out.

🍴 Eating & Drinking

Inside the flea market on market days (Wednesdays), look for the teensy **Maria's Tea Stall** (snacks from ₹10), selling tasty chai and snacks made by colourful elderly local Maria herself. **Curlie's** (mains ₹80-250; ⊙9am-3am) and **Shiva Valley** (mains ₹80-240; ⊙8am-midnight), both big, loud bar-restaurants, are good for an evening sunset drink, an alternative crowd and the odd impromptu party. Head to either to find out what's on.

Shore Bar   MULTICUISINE $$
(mains ₹120-400) Anjuna has lots of cliffside cafes with the standard traveller-orientated menus, happy hours and stunning coastal views, but the food is overwhelmingly mediocre. Shore Bar is the exception: the grilled baguettes, seafood, and especially coffees are supergood (at a price), the walls are adorned with cool art, and loungy day beds and sofas are full of happy, mellow dreadlocked customers. Shore also has a no-commission art gallery and rooms out back. There were rumours at research time about relocating; we hope it's still there by the time you arrive.

German Bakery   MULTICUISINE $$
(pastries ₹30-50, mains ₹70-170; ⑨) Leafy and filled with prayer flags, jolly lights and atmospheric curtained nooks, this is a perfect place for a relaxed dinner. Innovative tofu dishes are a speciality: this may be your only chance to try tofu tikka (₹150). There's live music and sometimes Middle Eastern dancers on Wednesday night and round-the-clock wi-fi (₹100 per hour).

Café Diogo   CAFE $
(Market Rd; snacks ₹30-100; ⊙8am-5pm) Probably the best fruit salads in the world are sliced and diced at Café Diogo, a small locally run cafe on the way to the market. Also worth a munch are the generous toasted avocado, cheese and mushroom sandwiches.

Whole Bean Tofu Shop & Vegetaria CAFE $$
(Market Rd; mains ₹60-150; ⊙8am-5pm) One of the only places in Goa where vegans can eat well, this tofu-filled health-food cafe focuses on all things created from that most versatile of beans. Breakfasts include eggs (for the nonvegans) and a surprisingly good tofu scramble with onions and toast (₹130).

6Pack Bar & Restaurant MULTICUISINE, BAR $$
(Market Rd; mains ₹60-200; ⊘9am-midnight)
Everyone loves 6Pack for its excellent 'traditional' – that's code for beef – cheeseburgers
(₹170), pool table, and festive vibe when
sports are shown on the big screen upstairs.

Avalon Sunset MULTICUISINE $
(mains ₹50-140; 🛜) Nice views but so-so
food; we only mention it for the wi-fi (₹40
per hour).

❶ Information

Anjuna has three ATMs, clustered together
about 100m east of **Bank of Baroda** (⊘9.30am-
2.30pm), which gives cash advances on Visa and
MasterCard.

Om Sai Internet (Anjuna-Mapusa Rd; per hr
₹40; ⊘10.30am-11pm Mon-Sat)

Speedy Travels (📞2273266; ⊘9am-6.30pm
Mon-Sat, 10am-1pm Sun) Reliable agency for
air and train ticket booking, a range of tours
(including one to Dudhsagar Falls), and credit-
card advances or currency exchange.

❶ Getting There & Away

Buses to Mapusa (₹10) depart every half-hour
or so from the main bus stand near the beach;
some from Mapusa continue on to Vagator and
Chapora. Two daily buses to Calangute depart
from the main crossroads. Cabs and pilots
gather at both stops, and you can hire scooters
and motorcycles easily from the crossroads.

Vagator & Chapora

Dramatic red-stone cliffs, dense green forests
and a crumbling 17th-century **Portuguese
fort** provide Vagator and its diminutive
neighbour Chapora with one of the prettiest

settings on the north Goan coast. Once
known for their wild trance parties and
heady, hippy lifestyles, things have slowed
down considerably these days, though
Chapora – reminiscent of Star Wars' Mos
Eisley Cantina – remains a fave for smokers, with the smell of charas hanging heavy
in the air. It also has slightly more personality than Vagator, but fewer eating and
sleeping options.

If you're keen to see the remnants of the
trance scene, hang around long enough in
Vagator and you'll likely be handed a flyer for
a party (many with international DJs), which
can range from divine to dire. You may also
catch wind of something going down in a
hidden location. If you're lucky, it won't have
been closed down by the time you get there.

🛌 Sleeping

VAGATOR

You'll see lots of signs for 'rooms to let' in
private homes and guesthouses along Ozran Beach Rd and on side roads too. Most
charge around ₹500 per double.

⌂**Shalom** GUESTHOUSE $
CHOICE
(📞2273166; d ₹800-1000) Arranged around a
placid garden not far from the path down
to Little Vagator Beach, this place, run by a

Vagator & Chapora

Vagator & Chapora

WHERE'S THE PARTY?

Though Goa was long legendary among Western visitors for its all-night, open-air Goan trance parties, a central government 'noise pollution' ban on loud music in open spaces between 10pm and 6am has largely curbed its often notorious, drug-laden party scene: Goa simply does not party the way it used to. With a tourist industry to nurture, however, authorities tend to turn a blind eye to parties during the peak Christmas–New Year period. Late nights are also allowed in interior spaces, which is why clubs carry on without problems. If you're looking for the remainder of the real party scene, though, you'll need to cross your fingers, keep your ear close to the ground, and wait out for word in Vagator or Anjuna.

friendly family (whose home is on site), has a variety of extremely well-kept rooms, and a two-bedroom apartment for long-stayers.

Janies GUESTHOUSE $
(☑2273635, 9850057794; janiesricardo@yahoo.com; d ₹800, 1-/2-bed bungalow ₹1200/1500) A great choice for long-stayers, run by a very friendly woman and with a simple but homey vibe. The two double rooms each come equipped with fridge and TV, and the three large bungalows have either one or two bedrooms and full-on kitchen.

Bean Me Up Soya Station HOTEL $
(☑2273479; www.myspace.com/beanmeupindia; d ₹680, without bathroom ₹475; 🛜) The rooms around a leafy, parachute-silky courtyard might look a bit cell-like from the outside, but step in and you'll be pleased to find that the billowing silks and mellow, earthy shades follow you there. Scooters are available for rent, and there's a great vegetarian restaurant.

Paradise on the Earth BEACH HUTS $
(☑2273591; www.moondance.co.nr; huts without bathroom ₹500-1000) Simple bamboo huts (not too common in these parts) clinging to the cliff above Little Vagator Beach are great value for the beachside location, though the name might be a little overkill.

Garden Villa GUESTHOUSE $
(☑6529454, 9822104780; Vagator Beach Rd; r ₹250-500) Big, clean, cheap and friendly, on pretty grounds near Vagator Beach. Room No 14 has an old four-poster.

CHAPORA

Head down the road to the harbour and you'll find lots of rooms – and whole homes – for rent; check out a few before you commit.

Casa de Olga GUESTHOUSE $
(☑2274355, 9822157145; r ₹1500, without bathroom ₹500) This exceedingly welcoming family place has rooms arranged around a pretty

garden in a variety of sizes. The cheaper ones are basic (but comfy and clean), while the pricier ones have hot showers, kitchenette with fridge, and balcony. It's in a pretty spot near the harbour, too.

✖ Eating

VAGATOR

A few eating options cluster around the entrance to Little Vagator Beach, along with the usual slew of much-of-a-muchness beach shacks down on the sands.

TOP CHOICE Thalassa GREEK $$
(☑9850033537; mains ₹180-400; ⊙4pm-midnight) Authentic and ridiculously good Greek food is served here alfresco on a breezy terrace to the sound of the sea just below. Go for the specials; when we visited, beef stifado (₹270) and lamb meatballs in red sauce (₹320) were on the list. But veggie dishes also excel. The *spanakorizo* (spinach and rice cooked with Greek olive oil and herbs and topped with feta; ₹230) is hearty and deceptively simple: the fresh ingredients and expert preparation are what made us swoon. Reservations essential. Thalassa also has **huts** (₹1000), which are almost as classy as the restaurant.

TOP CHOICE Yangkhor Moonlight TIBETAN, MULTICUISINE $$
(mains ₹70-200) Superfresh food is glorified in the Tibetan and even the Italian dishes here. The veg *momo* (Tibetan dumpling) soup (₹80)? You'll die. The pasta? F-ing delish. The chairs and tablecloths are plastic and the walls are lime green, but – maybe because of the friendly service and the soft Chinese pop music – it's cosy to boot.

Mango Tree Bar & Café MULTICUISINE $$
(mains ₹90-210; ⊙9am-4am) With loud reggae, crappy service, dark-wood furniture and mango-colour walls, a sometimes rambunc-

tious bar scene, terracotta lanterns, and a good vibe, Mango Tree is an ever-popular place for all that and for its really good food. Films or sports are screened most nights.

Bean Me Up
Soya Station MULTICUISINE, VEGAN $$
(Ozran Beach Rd; mains ₹120-250; ◷8am-4pm & 7-11pm) Oh, veggies and vegans, you've had a hard time in Goa. Come here and relax in the garden, full of tall trees and black pepper vines, and eat tofu Thai curry (₹230) or seitan fried onion (₹130) to your heart's delight, followed by lusciously egg-less desserts. The all-veg restaurant also has breakfasts, juices and even a bar, and an on-site shop sells tofunaise and soysage.

CHAPORA
Chapora's eating situation is not as evolved as Vagator's. Little restaurants pepper the centre (such as it is), but they're reliable only for caloric intake. **Sunrise Restaurant** (mains ₹70-150) is nothing special but good enough, with friendly service, while the very popular **Scarlet Cold Drinks** (juices & snacks ₹20-80) and **Jai Ganesh Fruit Juice Centre** (juices ₹20-70) are both in close proximity to the thickest gusts of charas smoke. Scarlet has an exceptionally good noticeboard, while Jai Ganesh has cold coffee and avocado lassis.

 Drinking & Entertainment
Aside from secretive parties, there's not as much going on in Vagator and Chapora these days; gone are the all-nighters and the beach trance is now turned off promptly at 10pm. But Chapora's extremely mellow hole-in-the-wall bars are a certain kind of entertainment; Vagator's **Nine Bar** (◷6pm-4am) and **Hill Top**, on the Anjuna road, are still thumping on; and the Russians, having taken the party crown away from the Israelis, seem to create nightlife in various spots around town.

 Shopping
Rainbow Bookshop BOOKSTORE
(◷10am-2pm & 3-7pm) In Vagator, this lovely little shop, run by a charming elderly gentleman, stocks a good range of second-hand and new books.

 Information
Vagator's sole ATM is at **Corporation Bank** on the road to Anjuna. Plenty of internet places are scattered around town, but **Mira Cybercafe**

2000 (Ozran Beach Rd; ◷9am-2pm & 3-11pm; per hr ₹40) is best.

 **Getting There & Away**
Frequent buses run from Chapora, through Vagator, to Mapusa (₹10) throughout the day, many via Anjuna. The buses start in Chapora village, but there are a couple of other stops in Chapora and Vagator. We couldn't find any bicycles to rent here, sadly (ask around; it's a supply-and-demand thing), but prices for scooters/motorbikes tend to be around ₹200/300 per day in high season.

Morjim & Asvem

Morjim and Asvem, a pretty strip of mostly empty sand, is one of the very few beaches where sunbathing doesn't attract hordes of hawkers, dogs and onlookers. The water, though, does suffer from a bit of river run-off pollution and cannot ever be described as crystal clear. Nonetheless, rare olive ridley turtles nest at the beach's southern end from September to February, so this is a protected area, which, in theory at least, means no development and no rubbish. Morjim and Asvem have a handful of low-key beach shacks and several places to stay and eat, including the beachfront **Goan Café** (☏2244394; www.goancafe.com; huts ₹1150-1350, without bathroom ₹800, apt from ₹1250; ❋), whose three brother-owners might well be the friendliest and most helpful hotel owners in Goa; **Meems' Beach Resort** (☏3290703; www.meemsbeachresort.com; d/q huts from ₹1500/3500; ❋), which has a range of huts and rooms also right on the beach, along with free wi-fi and an atmospheric restaurant; and **La Plage** (mains ₹215-315), known for its high-caliber French food.

Mandrem

Peaceful, quiet, hidden Mandrem has in recent years become a refuge for those seeking a break from the traveller scenes of Arambol and Anjuna – and those who avoided the scene to begin with. The beach is beautiful, and there's little to do but laze on it. Coco-huts can be had for around ₹500. It's not easy to get here by public transport; hire a scooter or cab in Arambol.

There's lots of yoga around, mostly taught by foreigners each season. **Himalaya Yoga Valley** (☏9922719982; www.yogagoaindia.com) specialises in hatha and ashtanga teacher-training courses, but also has walk-in classes (₹300) twice daily.

Sleeping & Eating

TOP CHOICE Dunes BEACH HUTS $
(☎2247219; www.dunesgoa.com; d/q huts ₹950/1500; @) Pretty huts here are peppered around a palm-forest allée leading to the beach, and at night, globe lamps light up the place like a palm-tree dreamland. Dunes also has friendly, helpful staff, a good restaurant on the beach, and clean, cosy, muslin-lined huts with mosquito nets and balconies with comfy chairs or couches. It's a peaceful, feel-good kind of place, with yoga classes, yoga teachers-to-be hanging around drinking healthful juices, and a marked absence of trance.

Cuba Retreat HOTEL $$
(☎2645775; www.cubagoa.com; d without/with AC ₹1250/1550; ❄) The sheets here are tucked in *tight* (we heart fastidiousness!) and rooms are clean and tidy as anything, but Cuba really scores for its retro white-and-kelly-green exterior, kind staff and good bar-restaurant in the courtyard, which is also home to a hanging swing.

Oasis on the Beach BEACH HUTS $$
(☎9822163886; r/huts ₹1500/2000) A great, slightly higher-end beach-hut option, Oasis has some huts with balconies overlooking the sea, and an excellent ayurvedic-massage centre (massages from ₹1000). Oasis's beachfront restaurant gets rave reviews, too, especially for its seafood and tandoori dishes.

Villa River Cat GUESTHOUSE $$$
(☎2247928; www.villarivercat.com; d ₹2000-3800; ❄) This unusual circular guesthouse is filled with art, antiques and a lot of spunk, but it should be even spunkier (and friendlier) for the price.

Arambol (Harmal)

Arambol first emerged in the 1960s as a mellow paradise for long-haired long-stayers, and ever since, travellers attracted to the hippy atmosphere have been drifting up to this blissed-out corner of Goa, setting up camp and, in some cases, never leaving. As a result, in the high season the beach and the road leading down to it (the town is basically one road) can get pretty crowded – with huts, people and nonstop stalls selling the usual tourist stuff. If you're looking for a committed traveller vibe, this is the place to come; if you're seeking laid-back languidness, you might be better off heading down the coast to Mandrem or Morjim.

Activities

Himalayan Iyengar Yoga Centre YOGA
(www.hiyogacentre.com) A popular spot for Iyengar yoga, with five-day courses (beginning on Fridays; ₹3000), intensive workshops, children's classes, and teacher training all available. The centre is a five-minute walk from the beach, off the main road; look for the big banner. HI also has **huts** (s/d without bathroom ₹250/300) for students.

Arambol Hammocks PARAGLIDING
(☎9822389005; www.arambol.com; per 20min ₹1800; ⏲9am-6pm) Paragliding and kite surfing are getting big in Arambol, and several operators give lessons and rent equipment on the very south of Arambol beach. At the north end, Arambol Hammocks is a more established paragliding option, and it also sells…hammocks.

Sleeping

Accommodation in Arambol is almost all of the budget variety, and it pays to trawl the cliffside to the north and south of Arambol's main beach stretch for the best hut options. It's almost impossible to book in advance: simply turn up early in the day to check out who's checking out. The area around the Narayan temple (take a left turn off the main road as you enter town), also has several guesthouses of similar quality.

Chilli's HOTEL $
(☎9921882424; s/d ₹300/400) This clean and simple place, owned by superfriendly and helpful Derick Fernandes, is one of Arambol's best nonbeachside bargains. Chilli's offers 10 nice, no-frills rooms on the beach road, near the beach entrance, all with attached bathroom, fan and hot-water shower; there's an honour system for buying bottled water, self-service, from the fridge on the landing.

Shree Sai Cottages BEACH HUTS $$
(☎3262823, 9420767358; shreesai_cottages@yahoo.com; huts without bathroom ₹1000) A short walk north from the main Arambol beach, Shree Sai has a calm, easygoing vibe and really cute hut-cottages with little balconies and lovely views out over the water. Maybe the best of the beach-hut bunch.

Om Ganesh BEACH HUTS $
(☎9404436447; r & huts ₹800) Popular huts right on the edge of the water, as well as rooms, managed by the friendly Sudir. The seaside Om Ganesh Restaurant is also a

great place for lunch or dinner. Note that everyone in the area will tell you that their place is Om Ganesh; it's a family enterprise. Call ahead to avoid confusion.

Lamuella GUESTHOUSE $
(☑9822486314; s/d ₹600/900) Cute, charming rooms with curtains made from saris, built-in cathedral-arch shelving, pretty mosaic tiles around mirrors and little balconies. Far from the beach though.

🍴 Eating & Drinking

Sparkly and parachute-silk-draped places to eat are everywhere in Arambol. Many change annually, but **21 Coconuts** (for seafood) and **Relax Inn** (for Italian) are mainstays. For simpler fare, head up to Arambol village, by the bus stop, where small local joints will whip you up a thali (₹40) and a chai (₹4).

Shimon MIDDLE EASTERN $
(light meals ₹60-120; ⊙9am-11pm) If you can navigate the surly service and total lack of ambience, then fill up on an exceptional falafel (₹90) at Israeli-owned Shimon before hitting the beach. For something more unusual, go for *sabikh* (₹100), aubergine slices stuffed into pita bread with boiled egg, potato, salad and spicy relishes. Follow either up with Turkish coffee (₹35).

Fellini ITALIAN $$
(mains ₹140-280; ⊙11am-11pm) Pizza's the big deal here – the menu has no fewer than 41 different kinds – and the pastas, calzones and paninis, especially with seafood, are also tasty. The tiramisu (₹60) will keep you up at night, thinking back on it fondly.

Double Dutch MULTICUISINE $$
(mains ₹110-290) An ever-popular option for its steaks, salads, Thai and Indonesian dishes, and famous apple pies, all in a pretty garden setting. The noticeboard here is also worth a peruse, maybe while munching on a plateful of cookies or a huge sandwich.

German Bakery BAKERY, MULTICUISINE $
(Welcome Inn; pastries ₹20-60, mains ₹40-75) This rather dim and dingy corner cafe is surprisingly popular, with so-so pastries (eg lemon cheese pie, ₹50), big breakfasts (₹100 to ₹140) and Arambol's best masala chai.

Outback Bar MULTICUISINE $$
(mains ₹70-150) Seafood's a speciality at this place tucked away from the Arambol action.

❶ Information

Internet outfits, travel agents and money changers are as common as monsoon frogs on the road leading down to Arambol's beach, while several agencies toward the top of the road also offer parcel services by post, FedEx and DHL. The closest ATM is in Siolim, about 12km south.

JBL Enterprises (per hr ₹40; ⊙8.30am-10.30pm) Internet cafe, travel agency, money and ISD: one-stop shopping.

❶ Getting There & Around

Buses to Mapusa (₹20, 1½ hours) depart from Arambol village every half-hour. It's only about 1.5km from the main beach area, but you're lucky if you get a cab, or even an autorickshaw, for ₹50. A prepaid taxi to Arambol from Dabolim Airport costs ₹975; from Mapusa it's ₹400.

Lots of places in Arambol rent scooters and motorbikes, for ₹200 and ₹300, respectively, per day; we like Derick's, at Chilli's, the best.

SOUTH GOA

Margao (Madgaon)

POP 94,400

The capital of Salcete province, Margao (also known as Madgaon) is the main population centre of south Goa and is a friendly, bustling market town of a manageable size for getting things done, or for getting in and out of the state. If you're basing yourself in south Goa, it's great for shopping, organising travel arrangements or simply enjoying the busy energy of big-city India without big-city hassles. It's also your best base for visiting Chandor, Quepem or Dudhsagar Falls.

◉ Sights

Margao has plenty of shopping opportunities, and the covered **MMC New Market** (⊙8.30am-9pm Mon-Sat) is one of the most colourful in all of Goa. It's also worth a walk around the lovely, small **Largo de Igreja** district, home to lots of atmospherically crumbling and gorgeously restored old Portuguese homes, and the quaint and richly decorated 17th-century **Church of the Holy Spirit**, particularly impressive when a Sunday morning service is taking place. The church also hosts services at 4pm on weekdays but is open erratically at other times.

The administrative heart of the city, the Municipal Building, is home to the dusty and awesome **Municipal Library** (⊙8am-8pm

Margao (Madgaon)

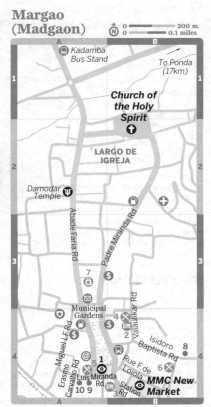

GOA SOUTH GOA

Margao (Madgaon)

◉ **Top Sights**
    Church of the Holy Spirit B2
    MMC New Market..............................B4

◉ **Sights**
  1 Municipal Library................................A4

🛏 **Sleeping**
  2 Hotel Tanish.....................................B4
  3 Om Shiv Hotel..................................B4

🍴 **Eating**
  4 Café Tato..B4
  5 Longhuino's......................................A4
  6 SwaD...B4

🛍 **Shopping**
  7 Golden Heart Emporium....................A3

Information
  8 DHL...B4
  9 Margao Residency..............................A4
    Reliance Cybercafe ....(see 2)

Transport
  10 Paulo Travel Masters A4

bright-yellow building tucked away behind the Bank of India, Om Shiv does a fine line in 'executive' rooms, which all have AC, balcony and an ordered air. But it's mostly worth recommending for the suites, which have exceptional views, or as a Tanish backup.

Eating

SwaD   INDIAN **$**
(New Market; veg thalis ₹40-75, mains ₹60-85) Margao's best veg food, hands down, is at the family-friendly, lunch-break favourite SwaD, across from Lotus Inn. The thalis are reliably delish, as are the snacks, South Indian tiffins, mains and all the other stuff on the 12-page menu of pure-veg scrumptiousness.

Longhuino's   GOAN, MULTICUISINE **$$**
(Luis Miranda Rd; mains ₹60-150) Since 1950, quaint old Longhuino's bar and restaurant, with its old wooden chairs and slow service, has been serving up tasty Goan, Indian and Chinese dishes popular with locals and tourists alike. Go for the pork vindaloo (₹90) or the fried mussels with salad (₹120).

Café Tato   INDIAN **$**
(Valaulikar Rd; thalis ₹50, mains ₹50-80; ⊗Mon-Sat) A favourite local lunch spot: tasty

Mon-Fri, 9am-noon & 4-7pm Sat & Sun), which has some great books on Goa and a retro reading room where you can read the paper along with lots of gents in button-downs.

🛏 Sleeping

Hotel Tanish   HOTEL **$**
(☑2735656; Reliance Trade Centre, Valaulikar Rd; s/d ₹600/850, s/d/ste with AC ₹750/1050/1600; ✴) The best place to stay in town – incongruously located on the top floor of a mall – has really kind staff and tidy, well-equipped rooms with great views of the surrounding countryside. Suites come with a bathtub, big TV and views all the way to Colva. Just make sure to ask for an outside-facing room; some overlook the mall interior. The hotel is near Grace Church.

Om Shiv Hotel   HOTEL **$$**
(☑2710294; www.omshivhotel.com; Cine Lata Rd; s/d/ste with AC from ₹1100/1400/2500; ✴) In a

vegetarian fare in a bustling backstreet canteen.

Shopping

Golden Heart Emporium BOOKSTORE
(Confidant House, Abade Faria Rd; ☺10am-1.30pm & 4-7pm Mon-Sat) One of Goa's best bookstores, crammed with fiction, nonfiction and illustrated books on the state's food, architecture and history.

❶ Information

Banks offering currency exchange and 24-hour ATMs are all around town, especially near the municipal gardens and along Luis Miranda Rd.
Apollo Victor Hospital (☑2728888; Station Rd, Malbhat) Reliable medical services.
Cyberlink (Abade Faria Rd; per hr ₹20; ☺8.30am-7.30pm Mon-Sat) Not the best, but it'll do.
DHL (Gurasui Plaza, Isidoro Baptista Rd; ☺10am-7pm Mon-Sat)
Main post office (☺9am-1.30pm & 2.30-5pm Mon-Sat) North of the Municipal Gardens.
Margao Residency (☑2715096; www.goa -tourism.com) Book GTDC trips here.
Reliance Cybercafe (1st fl, Reliance Trade Centre, Valaulikar Rd; per hr ₹30; ☺9.30am-7pm) Fastest and friendliest.
Thomas Cook (Mabai Hotel Bldg; ☺9.30am-6pm Mon-Sat)

❶ Getting There & Around

BUS Government and private long-distance buses both depart from **Kadamba bus stand**, about 2km north of the municipal gardens. Private buses ply interstate routes several times a day and can be booked at offices all over town; try **Paulo Travel Masters** (☑2702922; 1st fl, Bella Vista Apt, Luis Miranda Rd; ☺8am-7.30pm). Sample long-distance high-season fares:
Bengaluru ₹400, 14 hours, one daily in evening
Bengaluru private; without/with AC ₹1000/1500, 13 hours
Gokarna ₹95, one daily
Hampi private; ₹1000-1200, nine hours
Hospet ₹240, 10 hours, one daily in evening
Mumbai private; without/with AC ₹800/1400, 14 hours
Palolem ₹27, one hour, every 30 minutes
Panaji express; ₹26, 45 minutes, every few minutes
Pune ₹400, 12 hours, one daily in evening
Pune private; without/with AC ₹800/1100, 11 hours
Vasco da Gama 'shuttle'; ₹35, 45 minutes, hourly (stops near Dabolim Airport on request)

Local buses to Benaulim (₹7), Betul (₹15), Colva (₹10) and Palolem (₹27) also swing by the bus stop on the east side of the Municipal Gardens every 15 minutes or so.

TAXI Taxis are plentiful around the municipal gardens, train station and Kadamba bus stand, and they'll go anywhere in Goa, including Palolem (₹700), Panaji (₹700), Calangute (₹900), Anjuna (₹1100) and Arambol (₹1600). Except for the train station, where there's a prepaid booth, you'll have to negotiate the fare with the driver.

Autorickshaws and pilots are the most popular way to get around town; most trips cost ₹50 and ₹30, respectively.

TRAIN Margao's well-organised train station, about 2km south of town, serves the Konkan Railway and other routes. Its **reservation hall** (☑information 2712790, PNR enquiry 2700730; ☺8am-2pm & 2.15-8pm Mon-Sat, 8am-2pm Sun) is on the 1st floor. Services to Mumbai, Mangalore, Ernakulam and Thiruvananthapuram are the most frequent. See p807 for more train information.

Chandor

The lush village of Chandor, 15km east of Margao, makes a perfect day away from the beaches, and it's here, more than anywhere else in the state, that the once opulent lifestyles of Goa's former landowners, who found favour with the Portuguese aristocracy, are still visible in its strings of quietly decaying colonial-era mansions. If you're around in January, Chandor hosts the colourful **Feast of the Three Kings** on the 6th, during which local boys re-enact the arrival of the three kings from the Christmas story.

Braganza House, built in the 17th century, is possibly the best example of what Goa's scores of once grand and glorious mansions have today become. Built on land granted by the King of Portugal, the house was divided from the outset into two wings, to house two sides of the same big family. The **West Wing** (☑2784201; ☺9am-5pm) belongs to one set of the family's descendants, the Menezes-Bragança, and is filled with gorgeous chandeliers, Italian marble floors, 250-year-old, locally made rosewood furniture, and antique treasures from Macau, Portugal, China and Europe. The elderly Mrs Aida Menezes-Bragança nowadays lives here alone, but will show you around with the help of her assistant. Between them, they struggle valiantly with the upkeep of a beautiful but needy house, whose grand history oozes from every inch of wall, floor and furniture. Next door, the

DESTINATION	TRAIN NO & NAME	FARE (₹)	DURATION (HR)	DEPARTURES
Ahmedabad (via Vadodara)	6338 Okha Express	371/1013/1394	20	10.45am Thu, Sat
Chennai (Madras)	7312 Vasco-da-Gama-Chennai Express	343/936/1286	21	3.15pm Thu
Delhi	2431 Rajdhani Express	2035/2615	27	10.15am Tue, Thu, Fri
Hubli	7312 Vasco-da-Gama-Chennai Express	124/316/427	6	3.15pm Thu
Ernakulum	2618 Lakshadweep Express	325/857/1167	14½	7.25pm
	6345 Netravati Express	345/827/1137	15½	10.40pm
Mangalore	2618 Lakshadweep Express	214/544/732	5	7.30pm
Mumbai (Bombay)	0112 Konkan Kanya Express	288/782/1073	12	6pm
	0104 Mandovi Express	288/782/1073	12	9.30am
	2052 Jan Shatabdi Express	197/680	9	2.30pm
Pune	2779 Goa Express	264/688/930	13	3.45pm
Thiruvananthapuram	2432 Rajdhani Express	1355/1770	17	12.40pm Mon, Wed, Thu
	6345 Thiruvananthapuram-Netravati Express	347/947/1302	18	10.40pm

Rajdhani fares are 3AC/2AC; Shatabdi fares are 2S/CC; Express fares are sleeper/3AC/2AC.

East Wing (☎2784227, 2857630; ⊙10am-6pm) is owned by the Braganza-Pereiras, descendants of the other half of the family. It's nowhere near as grand: paint peels from windows, ceilings sag and antiques are mixed in with cheap knick-knacks and seaside souvenirs. But it's beautiful in its own, lived-in way (check out the kerosene fridge) and has a small but striking family chapel, which contains a carefully hidden fingernail of St Francis Xavier (see p808). Both homes are open daily, and there's almost always someone around to let you in. The owners rely on donations for the hefty costs of maintenance: if you choose to donate, ₹100 per visitor per house is reasonable, though anything extra is welcomed.

Down the road, the original building of the **Fernandes House** (☎2784245; ranferns@ yahoo.co.in; admission ₹200; ⊙9am-6pm), about 1km east of the church, dates back more than 500 years, while the Portuguese section was tacked on by the Fernandes family in 1821. The secret basement hideaway, full of gun holes and with an escape tunnel to the river, was used by the family to flee attackers.

The best way to get here is by cab from Margao: taxis charge ₹350 round trip, including waiting time.

Colva & Benaulim

POP 10,200

Colva and Benaulim, with their broad, open beaches, are not the first place backpackers head – most tourists here are of the domestic or ageing European varieties – but are, as a result, slightly less sceney than Palolem or the beach towns up north. Of the two, Benaulim has the greater charm, though out of high season it sometimes has the sad feel of a deserted seaside town. Perhaps the biggest reason to stay at either is to explore this part of the southern coast (which stretches north as far as Velsao and south as far as the mouth of the Sal River at Mobor), which in many parts is empty and gorgeous. The inland road that runs this length is perfect for gentle cycling and scootering, with lots of picturesque Portuguese-era mansions and whitewashed churches along the way.

☉ Sights & Activities

TOP CHOICE **Goa Chitra** MUSEUM

(☏6570877; www.goachitra.com; St John the Baptist Rd, Mondo Vaddo, Benaulim; admission ₹200; ☺9am-6pm Tue-Sun) Artist and restorer Victor Hugo Gomes first noticed the slow extinction of traditional objects – everything from farming tools to kitchen utensils to altarpieces – as a child in Benaulim. But it wasn't until he was older that he realised the traditional, and especially agricultural, local knowledge was disappearing with them. He created this ethnographic museum from the more than 4000 cast-off objects that he collected from across the state over 20 years (he often had to find elderly people to explain their uses). In addition to the organic traditional farm out back, you'll see tons of tools and household objects, Christian artefacts and some fascinating farming implements, including a massive grinder for making coconut oil, which, ingeniously, attaches to a bull who does all the hard work. Goa Chitra is 3km east of Maria Hall.

The beach entrances of Colva and Benaulim throng with dudes keen to sell you **parasailing** (per ride ₹600), **jet-skiing** (per 15min ₹700), and one-hour **dolphin-watching trips** (per person ₹300).

🛏 Sleeping

COLVA

Sam's Cottages HOTEL $

(☏2788753; r ₹500) Up away from the fray, north of Colva's main drag, you'll find Sam's, a cheerful place with superfriendly owners,

spacious, spick-and-span rooms – that were getting a major upgrade when we visited – and pretty and peaceful grounds.

Skylark Resort HOTEL $$

(☏2788052; www.skylarkresortgoa.com; r without /with AC from ₹2300/3000; ❄☀) Clean and fresh rooms here have pretty, locally made teak furniture and block-print bedspreads, which gives them much more ambience than the hotel's generic exterior. The pool outside is also pleasant, and you can always just lounge here if you can't deal with the three-minute walk to the beach.

Casa Mesquita GUESTHOUSE $

(☏2788173; r ₹300) With just three rooms that go beyond simple and a phone number that may or may not work, this old mansion on the main coast road is the place to go if you like atmosphere. Goodness knows when rooms were last cleaned, but the elderly inhabitants are friendly, the paint's suitably peeling, and the ghosts of better days linger lovingly in the shadows.

Soul Vacation HOTEL $$$

(☏2788144/47; www.soulvacation.in; r incl breakfast ₹6300-7000; ❄☀) Tasteful rooms are arranged around gardens and a gorgeous pool area at the sleek Soul Vacation, 400m from Colva Beach. New luxury rooms are capacious and sophisticated in cool blues and whites – totally worth the extra money. It's a relaxing (if slightly pretentious) place to unwind.

La Ben HOTEL $$

(☏2788040; www.laben.net; Colva Beach Rd; r without/with AC ₹1100/1400; ❄) Neat, clean and not entirely devoid of atmosphere,

---

THE FOUNDING FATHER OF QUEPEM

When Father José Paulo de Almeida looked out his oyster-shell doors and windows, he saw the Church of the Holy Cross beyond the palm trees out front, the river that functioned as his road into and out of the forest out back, and below, lush gardens elaborately designed with cruciform patterns. The Portuguese priest and nobleman arrived in Goa in 1779 and set up the town of Quepem not long after. Today the **Palácio do Deão** (☏2664029, 9823175639; www.palaciododeao.com; ☺10am-5pm Sat-Thu) may look a lot like it did when he lived there, with original woodwork, furniture, religious effects and even the garden design all lovingly restored in the past few years by Goan couple Ruben and Celia Vasco da Gama, who researched the mansion's original features in the dean's hometown in Portugal. The Vasco da Gamas also host lunches and teatime on the back verandah; call for reservations and prices. All donations to the Palácio are used to continue restoration work and eventually create a cultural centre here.

Stop by the Church of the Holy Cross, the small and sweet church across the way, while you're here. A taxi from Margao, 14km away, will cost ₹550 round trip, including waiting time, but the bus (₹10, every few minutes) stops just a few minutes' walk down the road.

COLVA'S MENINO JESUS

Colva's 18th-century **Our Lady of Mercy Church** has been host to several miracles, it's said. Inside, closely guarded under lock and key, lives a little statue known as the 'Menino' (Baby) Jesus, which is thought to miraculously heal the sick and which only sees the light of day during the **Fama de Menino Jesus festival**, on the second Monday in October. Then, the little image is paraded about town, dipped in the river, and installed in the church's high altar for pilgrims to pray to. At other times of year, you can still visit the church in the early evening, and if you have any afflictions, you might choose to stop on your way in to buy a plastic ex-voto shaped like the body part in question (similar to those used in Mexican or Eastern Orthodox churches) for offering to the Baby Jesus.

this place is particularly known for its rooftop restaurant.

BENAULIM

There are lots of homes around town advertising simple rooms to let. This, combined with a couple of decent budget options, make Benaulim a better bet for backpackers than Colva.

Palm Grove Cottages HOTEL **$$**
(☑2770059/411; www.palmgrovegoa.com; d without/with AC incl tax from ₹1600/2000; ❋) Old-fashioned, secluded charm is to be had amid the dense foliage at Palm Grove Cottages, hidden among a thicket of trees on a road winding slowly south out of Benaulim. Guest rooms are atmospheric (some have balconies), and the ever-popular Palm Garden Restaurant graces the garden. New rooms (₹2700) – more grand than cosy – were being constructed at the time of research.

D'Souza Guest House GUESTHOUSE **$**
(☑2770583; d ₹600) This traditional blue house is run by a superfriendly local Goan family and comes with bundles of homey atmosphere, a lovely garden and just three spacious, clean rooms – making it best to book ahead. There's an imposter **D'Souza Guest House** (☑2771307; Vasvaddo Beach Rd; d ₹500) that's not as homey but also a good option; rooms are compact but airy and clean.

Blue Corner BEACH HUTS **$$**
(☑9850455770; www.blue-cnr-goa.com; huts ₹1600) The friendly (but overpriced) Blue Corner has simple beach huts (which sometimes lose electricity or running water) on a cosy spot right on the beach. The restaurant (mains ₹80 to ₹150) gets good reviews from guests.

Rosario's Inn GUESTHOUSE **$**
(☑2770636; r without/with AC ₹350/600; ❋) Across a football field flitting with young players and dragonflies, Rosario's is a large

establishment with very clean, simple rooms. Sheets are bright and tucked in tight, kids are playing in the garden, and good vibes abound.

Taj Exotica HOTEL **$$$**
(☑6683333; www.tajhotels.com; r from ₹20,500; ❋@☒) Set in 56 acres of stunning tropical gardens, the Exotica is luxurious but not the freshest Taj we've ever seen.

✗ Eating & Drinking

COLVA

Colva's beach has plenty of shacks offering the standard fare. At the roundabout near the church, you'll find chai shops and thali places, fruit, vegetable and fish stalls, and, at night, *bhelpuri* vendors.

Sagar Kinara INDIAN **$**
(Colva Beach Rd; thalis ₹65-85, mains ₹70-120) A pure-veg restaurant with tastes to please even committed carnivores, this great place is super-efficient and serves up cheap and delicious North and South Indian cuisine. You might have to wait for a table among throngs of Indian families who love it as much as we do.

Leda Lounge & Restaurant CONTINENTAL, BAR **$$**
(mains ₹125-200; ◷7.30am-midnight) Somewhat pricey Western favourites – pizzas, salads, sandwiches – meet fancy drinks – Mojitos, Long Island iced teas – at this comfy, cosmopolitan cafe-lounge. It's a hip environment (relative to Colva), replete with contemporary-print sofas lit by artful woven-basket chandeliers. There's often live music too.

BENAULIM

Malibu Restaurant INDIAN, ITALIAN **$$**
(mains ₹80-180) With a secluded garden setting full of flowers, cool breezes and butterflies, the relatively inland Malibu is one of

Benaulim's tastier and more sophisticated dining experiences, with great renditions of Italian favourites and live jazz and blues on Tuesday evenings.

Pedro's Bar & Restaurant
GOAN, MULTICUISINE **$$**

(Vasvaddo Beach Rd; mains ₹70-220; ☺9am-midnight) In a large, shady garden set back from the beachfront and popular with local and international tourists alike, Pedro's offers standard Indian, Chinese and Italian dishes, as well as a good line in Goan choices and some super 'sizzlers'.

Johncy Restaurant
GOAN, MULTICUISINE **$$**

(Vasvaddo Beach Rd; mains ₹75-195; ☺9.30am-1am) Like Pedro's beside it, Johncy dispenses standard beach-shack favourites from its location just off the sands. Staff are obliging, and food, if not exciting, is fresh and filling.

ℹ Information

Colva has plenty of banks and ATM machines strung along the east–west Colva Beach Rd, and a post office on the lane that runs past the eastern end of the church. Benaulim has a single '24-hour' Bank of Baroda ATM, which is sometimes locked, and most of its useful services (pharmacies, supermarkets, travel agents) are clustered around Benaulim village, which runs along the east–west Vasvaddo Beach Rd. Internet joints:

Click Nooks (Vasvaddo Beach Rd; per hr ₹30; ☺9am-10pm)

Sify Cyber Café (Colva Beach Rd; per hr ₹30; ☺9am-11pm)

ℹ Getting There & Around

COLVA Buses run from Colva to Margao every few minutes (₹10, 20 minutes) until around 7pm.

BENAULIM Buses from Benaulim to Margao are also frequent (₹7, 15 minutes); they stop at the intersection by Maria Hall. Some from Margao continue south to Varca and Cavelossim. Rickshaws and pilots charge ₹150 to ₹200 for Margao, and ₹50 to ₹60 for the five-minute ride to the beach. Benaulim gets green points for ubiquitous bicycle rentals for ₹50 per day; scooters will cost you ₹200.

Benaulim to Palolem

Immediately south of Benaulim are the beach resorts of **Varca** and **Cavelossim**, with wide, pristine sands and a line of roomy five-star hotels set amid landscaped grounds fronting the beach. The most luxe is the (somewhat snooty) **Leela Goa** (✆6621234; www.theleela.com; r from ₹25,000; ✲@☎☀) at Mobor, 3km south of Cavelossim. Just beyond it, at the end of the peninsula, you'll find one of the most picturesque spots in Goa, with simple beach shacks serving good food. The **Cafe Beach Hut** (mains ₹70-200) is at another pretty beach-shack spot; the turnoff is halfway between Cavelossim town and Mobor, opposite Old Anchor Dalmia Resort.

If you're here with your own transport, you can cross the Sal River at Cavelossim on the rusting tin-tub **ferry**, which will run until the nearby bridge is completed in late 2012-ish. Ferries run approximately every 30 minutes between 6.15am and 8.30pm; they're free for pedestrians and ₹7 for cars, or you can charter the whole damn thing anytime for ₹55. To reach it, turn at the 'Village Panchayat Cavelossim' sign close to Cavelossim's whitewashed church, then continue 2km to the river. On the other side is the very charming fishing village of **Betul**.

From Betul on south to Agonda, the road winds over gorgeous, undulating hills thick with palm groves. It's worth stopping off at the bleak old Portuguese fort of **Cabo da Rama** (look for the green, red and white signposts leading the way), which has a small church within the fort walls, stupendous views and several old buildings rapidly becoming one with the trees. (You can also reach the fort by bus from Chaudi, near Palolem; it stops 5km from the fort.)

Back on the main road there's a turnoff to **Agonda**, a small village with a wide,

---

PUPPY LOVE

Pick up some gifts, donate clothes and other stuff you don't want, and borrow books from the lending library at Colva's **Goa Animal Welfare Trust Shop** (☺9.30am-1pm & 4-7pm Mon-Sat), next to Skylark Resort. You can also learn more about the work of **GAWT** (✆2653677; www.gawt.org; Old Police Station, Curchorem; ☺9am-4pm), which operates a shelter in Curchorem (near Margao) and a smaller **shelter** (✆9665636264) behind the Chaudi bus stand near Palolem, both serving sick, stray and injured animals. Volunteers are welcome at the shelters, even for a few hours, to walk or play with the dogs.

empty beach on which rare olive ridley turtles sometimes lay their eggs. The water here can be unsafe for swimming at times, which has kept Agonda from getting too popular, but it's also not the idyllic secret of south Goa that it once was. Nevertheless, the pace is still slow and mellow. There's plenty of accommodation to choose from, including 10 million beach huts. For a step up, **Chattai** (☑9822481360; www.chattai.co.in; huts ₹1600), at the north end of the beach, has lovely huts with attached bathrooms and front porches.

There's lots of yoga and ayurveda in Agonda – look out for notices – and plenty of beach restaurants serving up the usual grub. *Pav bhaji* and chai can be had at the cluster of tiny eateries beside the church. The excellent organic restaurant **Blue Planet**, formerly of Palolem, was moving to Agonda at research time.

Palolem & Around

Palolem's stunning crescent beach was, as recently as 15 years ago, another of Goa's undiscovered gems, with few tourists and even fewer facilities to offer them. Nowadays, it's no longer quiet or hidden, but remains one of Goa's most beautiful spots, with a friendly, laid-back pace and lots of budget accommodation along the sands. Nightlife's still sleepy here – there are no real clubs, and the place goes to bed when the music stops at 10pm. But if you're looking for a nice place to lay up, rest a while, swim in calm seas and choose from an infinite range of yoga, massages and therapies on offer, this is your place.

If even Palolem's version of action is too much for you, head south, along the small rocky cove named **Colomb Bay**, which hosts several basic places to stay, to **Patnem Beach**, where a fine selection of beach huts, and a less pretty – but infinitely quieter – stretch of sand awaits.

Note that Palolem, even more so than other beach towns, operates seasonally; many places aren't up and running until November.

🏃 Activities

Yoga

Palolem and Patnem are the places to be if you're keen to yoga, belly dance, reiki, t'ai chi or tarot the days away. There are courses and classes on offer all over town, with locations and teachers changing seasonally. Bhakti Kutir (p833) offers daily drop-in yoga classes, as well as longer residential courses, but it's just a single yogic drop in the area's ever-changing alternative-therapy ocean. You'll find info on local yoga, and even cooking, classes at Butterfly Book Shop (p834).

Beach Activities

Kayaks are available for rent on both Patnem and Palolem beaches; an hour's paddling will cost ₹200 to ₹300, including dry bag. Fishermen and other boat operators hanging around the beach offer rides to beautiful **Butterfly Beach**, north of Palolem, for ₹800 to ₹1000 for two people, including one hour's waiting time.

Trekking

Cotigao Wildlife Sanctuary   NATURE RESERVE (☑2965601; admission/camera ₹5/25; ⊗7am-5.30pm) About 9km south of Palolem is this beautiful, remote-feeling sanctuary.

Palolem

To Dreamcatcher (300m); Ordo Sounsar (400m)

To Chaudi (2km); Canacona Train Station (3km); Agonda (8km); Cotigao Wildlife Sanctuary (9km)

ARABIAN SEA

Mosque

To Patnem (700m)

Don't expect to bump into its more exotic residents (including gaurs, sambars, leopards and spotted deer), but blazingly plumed birds, frogs, snakes and monkeys are plentiful. Trails are marked; set off early morning for the best sighting prospects from one of the sanctuary's two forest watchtowers, 6km and 9km from the entrance. A rickshaw/taxi from Palolem to the sanctuary will charge ₹500/600 including a couple of hours' waiting time, and two buses (at 1pm and 6.15pm) also go here from Chaudi, making the park's two cottages (₹400 and ₹750) a convenient option.

Goa Jungle Adventure   OUTDOOR ADVENTURE
(☑9850485641, 9922173517; www.goajungle.com; trekking/canyoning trips from ₹1200/1500) Run by a couple of very professional, very gregarious French guys, this adventure outfit gets rave reviews from travellers for its trekking and canyoning trips. (Canyoning, as owner Emmanuel puts it, is 'part jumping, part abseiling and part sliding' down a cliff.) Trips run from a half-day to several days, and rafting trips are also occasionally offered. Shoes can be rented for ₹150 per day.

🛏 Sleeping

PALOLEM
Most of Palolem's accommodation is of the simple beach-hut variety. Since the huts are dismantled and rebuilt with each passing season, standards can vary greatly from one year to the next. Walk along the beach and check out a few before making your decision; a simple hut without attached bathroom will cost around ₹600.

Palolem Guest House   HOTEL $$
(☑2644879; www.palolemguesthouse.com; r ₹750-2300; ✳) Towels here have 'Palolem Guest House' embroidered on them: that's the kind of old-school hotel this is (though reception could use some friendliness training). Comfortable rooms are arranged around a leafy garden just a quick walk from the beach, and the food in the courtyard restaurant is excellent.

Bhakti Kutir   HOTEL $$$
(☑2643472; www.bhaktikutir.com; cottages ₹2500-4000; @) Ensconced in a thick wooded grove between Palolem and Patnem Beaches, Bhakti's well-equipped rustic cottages are a little on the pricey side, but still make for a unique jungle retreat. There are daily drop-in yoga classes (₹200) and ayurvedic

massages, and the outdoor restaurant (mains ₹120 to ₹240), beneath billowing parachute silks, turns out yummy, imaginative, healthful stuff.

Ordo Sounsar   BEACH HUTS $$
(☑9822488769; www.ordosounsar.com; huts ₹2000-2500, without bathroom ₹1500) Beach huts they might be, but set as far north up Palolem beach as it's possible to go, across a rickety bridge spanning a wide creek, this hidden haven makes a cool, quiet alternative to some of the elbow-to-elbow options further on down the sands. Friendly owner Serafin prides himself on the restaurant's Goan dishes.

Ciaran's   BEACH HUTS $$$
(☑2643477; www.ciarans.com; huts incl breakfast ₹4000; ✳🛜) You can barely call the gorgeous lodgings here 'huts'. With actual windows, stone floors, full-length mirrors, wood detailing and nicer bathrooms than you'll find in most hotels, they're more like small chalets, all arranged around peaceful gardens right at the beach. It's the perfect balance of rustic and sophisticated. Plus, the wi-fi's free.

Dreamcatcher   BEACH HUTS $$
(☑2644873; www.dreamcatcher.in; huts from ₹2000, without bathroom ₹1000) Stylish huts are peppered around a lush garden on the beach, and yoga's offered every day. There's a four-day minimum stay (but you'd probably stay that long anyway).

My Soulmate   HOTEL $
(Shirley's Residency; ☑9823785250; mysoulmate@gmail.com; r ₹700-800, with AC ₹1000; ✳) A good spot close to the beach (behind Rainbow Travels), and the best hotel name ever.

PATNEM
Long-stayers will revel in Patnem's choice of village homes and apartments available for rent. A very basic house can cost ₹10,000 per month, while a fully equipped apartment can run up to ₹40,000.

Papaya's   BEACH HUTS $$
(☑9923079447; www.papayasgoa.com; huts ₹2000-3500; 🛜) Lovely huts head back into the palm grove from Papaya's popular restaurant. Each is lovingly tended to, with lots of wood and floating muslin, as well as a porch, and the staff are incredibly keen to please.

Micky Huts & Rooms BEACH HUTS $
(☎9850484884; huts/r ₹400/600) If you don't blanche at basic, this is the best bargain on the whole of Patnem beach, run by the friendliest and most obliging local family you could imagine. There's no signpost: just head for the huge patch of bamboo beside the small stream towards the northern end of the beach, and enquire at the restaurant.

Sea View Resort HOTEL $$
(☎2643110, 9850477147; www.seaviewpatnem .com; r ₹1000-2500, with AC ₹2800-3500; ✸@) The friendly management here, clean rooms – many with balconies, some with kitchens – and neighbourhoody garden setting just a quick walk from Patnem beach makes Sea View a reliable, comfy option.

✖ Eating

Both Palolem and Patnem's beaches are lined with beach shacks, offering all-day dining and fresh, fresh seafood as the catch comes in and the sun goes down. Many of these change seasonally, but as of press time, **Ma-Rita's** was winning the readers' choice award.

TOP CHOICE Café Inn CAFE $$
(light meals ₹70-240) This huge, fun semi-outdoor place has loud music, servers in saris and a cafeteria vibe (in a good way). The snacks, shakes, burgers and salads are great, but it's the evening barbecue (from 6pm to 10pm) that will really blow you away: pick your base, toppings, sauces and bread to create a grilled mix-and-match masterpiece.

German Bakery BAKERY, MULTICUISINE $$
(pastries ₹25-80, mains ₹95-170) Tasty baked treats and excellent coffee are the star at the Nepali-run German Bakery, but the Western breakfasts and Italian and Indian dinners are also super good. It also occasionally has yak cheese from Nepal – how cool is that? Oh, and the whole thing is set in a peaceful garden festooned with flags.

Casa Fiesta MEXICAN, MULTICUISINE $$
(mains ₹70-200) Fiesta, like all the restaurants around here, has a little bit of everything on the menu. Its speciality, though, is Mexican, and it makes a valiant attempt at it (and does surprisingly well). The mellow hut ambience is also working, as are the evening barbecues.

Home CONTINENTAL $$
(☎2643916; www.homeispatnem.com; mains from ₹100) A hip, relaxed veg restaurant,

Home also rents out nicely decorated, light rooms (₹1000 to ₹2500); call to book or ask at the restaurant.

Shiv Sai MULTICUISINE $
(thalis ₹40-50, mains ₹40-100) A local lunch joint knocking out tasty thalis, including Goan fish and veggie versions, and a good line in Western breakfasts like banana pancakes (₹40).

🔒 Shopping

Butterfly Book Shop BOOKSTORE
(☎9341738801; ◷9am-9.30pm Mon-Sat) A great bookshop with some neat gifts and a range of books on yoga, meditation and spirituality.

❶ Information

Palolem's main road is lined with travel agencies, internet places, and money changers – but no ATMs. For those, head to nearby Chaudi, which also has a supermarket, several pharmacies and all the other amenities you might need. An autorickshaw from Palolem to Chaudi costs ₹50, or you can walk the flat 2km in a leisurely 45 minutes.

Sun-n-Moon Travels (per hr ₹40; ◷8am-midnight) Quick internet.

❶ Getting There & Around

BUS Services to Margao (₹27, one hour, every 30 minutes) and Chaudi (₹5, every 15 minutes), the nearest town, depart from the bus stand down by the beach and stop at the Patnem turn-off. Chaudi has good bus connections, but for Panaji, better to go to Margao and catch an express from there. Buses from Chaudi:

Agonda ₹9, half-hourly

Cabo da Rama ₹18, 9am (return buses depart Cabo da Rama at 3pm)

Gokarna ₹70, 2pm

Karwar ₹30, half-hourly

Mangalore ₹200, two daily

Margao ₹24, every 10 minutes

Mysore ₹310, one daily

Panaji ₹50, 6.20pm and 7.15pm

TAXI & AUTORICKSHAW An autorickshaw from Palolem to Patnem costs ₹50, as does a rick from Palolem to Chaudi. A prepaid taxi from Dabolim Airport to Palolem costs ₹1000, but going the other way, you might get it for ₹800.

TRAIN Many trains that run north or south out of Margao (see p827) stop at the **Canacona Train Station** (☎2643644, 2712790).

Karnataka & Bengaluru

Best Places to Eat

» Karavalli (p846)

» Koshy's Bar & Restaurant
(p847)

» Mango Tree (p880)

» Malgudi Café (p857)

» Namaste Café (p876)

Best Places to Stay

» Kabini River Lodge (p865)

» Taj West End (p843)

» Parklane Hotel (p856)

» Green Hills Estate (p868)

» SwaSwara (p875)

Why Go?

Rounding off the southern extent of the Deccan Plateau, sprawling Karnataka is an inexhaustible goldmine of natural, cultural and artistic variety. Complemented by an ultra-professional tourism industry and an inherently friendly population, it's a travellers' haven that makes for fun, stress-free and thoroughly enjoyable gallivanting all the way.

At the nerve centre of this mind-boggling state is silicon-capital Bengaluru (Bangalore), overfed with the good life. Scattered around the epicurean city are rolling hills rife with spice and coffee plantations, a historic town adorned in brocaded regal splendour, a paradisaical nature reserve and a group of awesome rock-cut temples dating back to medieval times. Only a stone's throw away is the Karnataka coastline, with shimmering beaches and colourful temple towns. Bringing your pleasure trip full circle are the World Heritage–listed monuments of Hampi and Pattadakal, and the forgotten battlements and ruins of Bijapur and Bidar. You're unlikely to return home disappointed.

When to Go
Bengaluru

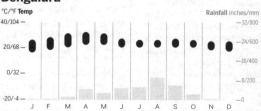

Jan The best season to watch tigers and elephants in Karnataka's pristine national parks.

Oct Mysore's Dasara (Dussehra) carnival brings night-long celebrations and a jumbo parade.

Dec The coolest time to explore the northern districts' forts, palaces, caves and temples.

Savoury South

The diverse and delectable cuisine of Karnataka is perhaps reason enough for you to visit this state. The highest-flying of all local delicacies is the spicy *pandhi* (pork) masala, a flavourful Kodava signature dish. Mangalore, out on the coast, tosses up a train of fiery dishes – mostly seafood. The crunchy prawn *rawa* (semolina) fry and the sinful chicken ghee roast are two of Mangalore's many dishes to have gathered a pan-Indian following. Vegetarians, meanwhile, can head to Udupi to sample its legendary veg thalis. Oh, and did we mention the classic steak-and-beer joints of Bengaluru?

Fast Facts

Jungle Jaunt

Jungle Lodges & Resorts Ltd (Map p844; ☑080-25597944; www.jungle lodges.com; Shrungar Shopping Complex, MG Rd, Bengaluru; ⊙10am-5.30pm Mon-Sat), is a top-class government-run organisation promoting low-impact and sustainable eco-tourism in the state's many wildlife parks and reserves. Book your getaways in their Bengaluru office or online.

Resources

Top State Festivals

» Udupi Paryaya (Jan, Udupi, p873) Held in even-numbered years, with a procession and ritual marking the handover of swamis at the town's Krishna Temple.

» Classical Dance Festival (Jan/Feb, Pattadakal, p886) Some of India's best classical dance performances.

» Vijaya Utsav (Jan, Hampi, p876) A three-day extravaganza of culture, heritage and the arts at the foot of Hampi's Matanga Hill.

» Tibetan New Year (Feb, Bylakuppe, p869) Lamas in Tibetan refugee settlements take shifts leading nonstop prayers that span the weeklong celebrations.

» Vairamudi Festival (Mar/Apr, Melkote, p861) Lord Vishnu is adorned with jewels at Cheluvanarayana Temple, including a diamond-studded crown belonging to Mysore's former maharajas.

» Ganesh Chaturthi (Sep, Gokarna, p874) Families march their Ganesh idols to the sea at sunset.

» Dussehra (Oct, Mysore, see the boxed text, p853) Also spelt 'Dasara' in Mysore. The Maharaja's Palace is lit up in the evenings and a vibrant procession hits town to the delight of thousands.

» Lakshadeepotsava (Nov, Dharmasthala, p872) Thousands and thousands of lamps light up this Jain pilgrimage town, offering spectacular photo ops.

» Huthri (Nov/Dec, Madikeri, p866) The Kodava community celebrates the start of the harvesting season with ceremony, music, traditional dances and much feasting for a week.

History

A rambling playfield of religions, cultures and kingdoms, Karnataka has been ruled by a string of charismatic rulers through history. India's first great emperor, Chandragupta Maurya, made the state his retreat when he embraced Jainism at Sravanabelagola in the 3rd century BC. From the 6th to the 14th century, the land was under a series of dynasties such as the Chalukyas, Cholas, Gangas and Hoysalas, who left a lasting mark in the form of stunning caves and temples across the state.

In 1327, Mohammed Tughlaq's army sacked Halebid. In 1347, Hasan Gangu, a Persian general in Tughlaq's army led a rebellion to establish the Bahmani kingdom, which was later subdivided into five Deccan sultanates. Meanwhile, the Hindu kingdom of Vijayanagar, with its capital in Hampi, rose to prominence. Having peaked in the early 1550s, it fell in 1565 to a combined effort of the sultanates.

In subsequent years, the Hindu Wodeyars of Mysore grew in stature and extended their rule over a large part of southern India. They remained largely unchallenged until 1761, when Hyder Ali (one of their generals) deposed them. Backed by the French, Hyder Ali and his son Tipu Sultan set up capital in Srirangapatnam and consolidated their rule. However, in 1799, the British defeated Tipu Sultan and reinstated the Wodeyars. Historically, this flagged off British territorial expansion in southern India.

Mysore remained under the Wodeyars until Independence – post-1947, the reigning maharaja became the first governor. The state boundaries were redrawn along linguistic lines in 1956 and the extended Kannada-speaking state of Mysore was born. It was renamed Karnataka in 1972, with Bangalore (now Bengaluru) as the capital.

❶ Information

The website of **Karnataka Tourism** (KSTDC; www.karnatakatourism.org) has lots of relevant information.

Several government offices in Karnataka remain closed on alternate Saturdays.

ACCOMMODATION In Karnataka, luxury tax is 4% on rooms costing ₹151 to ₹400, 8% on those between ₹401 and ₹1000, and 12% on anything over ₹1000. Some midrange and top-end hotels may add a further service charge.

❶ Getting There & Away

The main gateway to Karnataka is Bengaluru, serviced by most domestic airlines and some international carriers.

Coastal Mangalore is a transit point for those going north to Goa, or south to Kerala. Hubli, in central Karnataka, is a major railway junction for routes going into Maharashtra and northern India.

❶ Getting Around

The **Karnataka State Road Transport Corporation** (KSRTC) has a superb bus network across the state. Taxis with drivers are easily available in major towns. For long trips, most taxis charge around ₹7 per kilometre for a minimum of 250km, plus a daily allowance of ₹150 for the driver.

SOUTHERN KARNATAKA

Bengaluru (Bangalore)

✐080 / POP 5.7 MILLION / ELEV 920M

Despite its grim consequences in real life, getting 'Bangalored' has always had sunnier implications for travellers. The hub of India's booming IT industry, cosmopolitan Bengaluru is the numero uno city in the Indian deep south, blessed with a benevolent climate, a handful of interesting sights and a progressive dining, drinking and shopping scene. Located within close range of Kerala and Tamil Nadu, it's also a great base for those venturing out across southern India.

In recent times, Bengaluru has seen a mad surge of development, coupled with traffic congestion and rising pollution levels. However, it's a city that has also taken care to preserve its greens and its colonial heritage. So while urbanisation continually pushes its boundaries outward, the central district (dating back to the Raj years) remains more or less unchanged. Of interest to travellers are Gandhi Nagar (the old quarters); Mahatma Gandhi (MG) Rd, the heart of British-era Bangalore; and the Central Business District (CBD), north of MG Rd, across the greens.

Locally known as Majestic, Gandhi Nagar is a crowded area where Bengaluru's central bus stand and the City train station are located. A few historical relics lie to its south, including Lalbagh Botanical Gardens and Tipu Sultan's palace.

About 4km east are the high streets bounded by Mahatma Gandhi (MG), Brigade, St Mark's and Residency (FM Cariappa) Rds. This is Bengaluru's cosmopolitan hub, with parks, tree-lined streets, churches, grand houses and military establishments. In between are sandwiched the golf club, the racecourse and the cricket stadium.

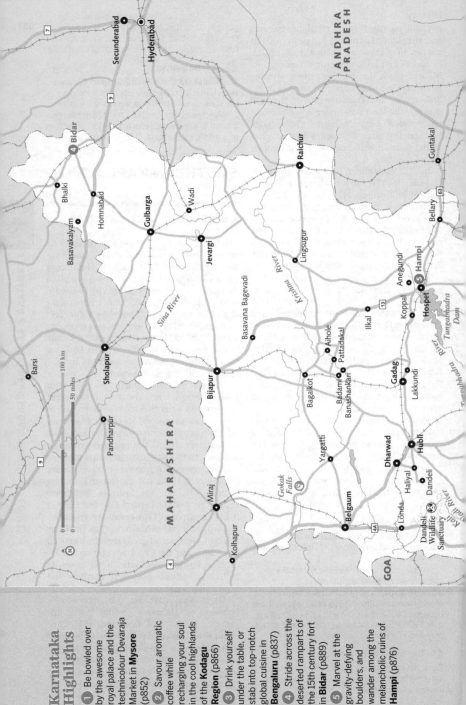

Karnataka Highlights

1 Be bowled over by the awesome royal palace and the technicolour Devaraja Market in **Mysore** (p852)

2 Savour aromatic coffee while recharging your soul in the cool highlands of the **Kodagu Region** (p866)

3 Drink yourself under the table, or stab into top-notch global cuisine in **Bengaluru** (p837)

4 Stride across the deserted ramparts of the 15th century fort in **Bidar** (p889)

5 Marvel at the gravity-defying boulders, and wander among the melancholic ruins of **Hampi** (p876)

Soak up the electric ambience of the atmospheric Krishna Temple in **Udupi** (p873)

Spy on lazy tuskers and listen to exotic birds in the forests bordering the serene **Kabini Lake** (p865)

TAMIL NADU

To Dindigul (140km)

Puttaparthi

Kolar

4

Whitefield

Bengaluru (Bangalore)

Nandi Hills

Salem

7

Bannerghatta Biological Park

Savandurga

Tumkur

Hessaraghatta

Ramnagar

Mandya

Sivasamudram

Talakad

Sira

Melkote

Somnathpur

Chamrajanagar

Biligiri Rangaswamy Wildlife Sanctuary

Chitradurga

4

Sravanabelagola

Channarayapatna

Brindavan Gardens

Srirangapatnam

Mysore

Kabini Lake

Gundlupet

Arsikere

Mysore

Davangere

Birur

Kadur

Halebid

Hassan

48

Kushalnagar

Nagarhole National Park

Bandipur National Park

Haveri

Ranibennur

Harihar

Tarikere

Chikmagalur

Belur

Dubare Forest Reserve

Bylakuppe

Bhadravati

Bhadra Wildlife Sanctuary

Dharmasthala

Pushpagiri (1712m)

Madikeri

Tadiyendamol (1745m)

Kannur

KERALA

Shimoga

Gajanur

Muttodi

Mullayangiri (1918m)

Kotebetta

Kakkabe

Karapura

Shettihalli Sanctuary

Tirthahalli

Venur

Sirsi

Siddapur

Gudavi Bird Sanctuary

Talguppa

Sagar

Sringeri

Karkal

Mudabidri

Ullal

Sharavati Sanctuary

Lingnamakki Reservoir

Amgol

Agumbe

Mangalore

Jog Falls

Kargal

Gersoppa

17

Kundapura

Malpe

Udupi

St Mary's Island

Kasaragod

Konkan Railway

ARABIAN SEA

Karwar

Devbagh

Ankola

Gokarna

Kumta

Honavar

Manki

Murudeshwar

Cauvery River

Finding your way around Bengaluru can be difficult at times. In certain areas, roads are named after their widths (eg 80ft Rd). The city also follows a system of mains and crosses: 3rd cross, 5th main, Residency Rd, for example, refers to the third lane on the fifth street branching off Residency Rd.

History

Literally meaning 'Town of Boiled Beans', Bengaluru supposedly derived its name from an ancient incident involving an old village woman who served cooked pulses to a lost and hungry Hoysala king. Kempegowda, a feudal lord, was the first person to earmark Bengaluru's extents by building a mud fort in 1537. The town remained obscure until 1759, when it was gifted to Hyder Ali by the Mysore maharaja.

The British arrived in 1809 and made it their regional administrative base in 1831, renaming it Bangalore. During the Raj era, the city played host to many a British officer, including Winston Churchill, who enjoyed life here during his greener years and famously left a debt (still on the books) of ₹13 at the Bangalore Club.

Now home to countless software, electronics and business outsourcing firms, Bengaluru's knack for technology developed early. In 1905 it was the first Indian city to have electric street lighting. Since the 1940s, it has been home to Hindustan Aeronautics Ltd (HAL), India's largest aerospace company. And if you can't do without email, you owe it all to a Bangalorean – Sabeer Bhatia, the inventor of Hotmail, grew up here.

The city's name was changed back to Bengaluru in November 2006, though few care to use it in practice.

◉ Sights

Cubbon Park   GARDEN
(Map p840) In the heart of Bengaluru's business district is Cubbon Park, a sprawling 120-hectare garden named after former British commissioner Sir Mark Cubbon. Under its leafy boughs, groups of Bengaluru's residents converge to steal a moment from the rat race that rages outside. Idlers, thinkers, lovers, dreamers and health freaks, you'll find them all here, immersed in their own indulgences.

On the fringes of Cubbon Park are the red-painted Gothic-style **State Central Library** and two municipal museums. For the gadget-oriented traveller, there's the **Visvesvaraya Industrial and Technical Museum** (Map p840; Kasturba Rd; admission ₹15; ⊙10am-6pm Mon-Sat), which showcases a wide range of electrical and engineering displays, from a replica of the Wright brothers' 1903 flyer to

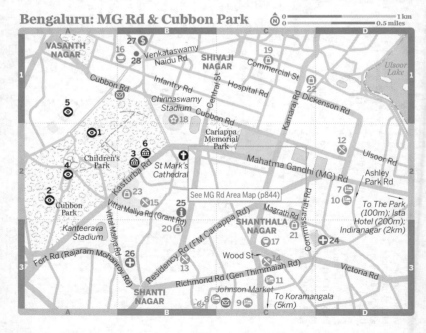

Bengaluru: MG Rd & Cubbon Park

21st-century virtual-reality games. The **Government Museum** (Kasturba Rd; admission ₹4; ⊙10am-5pm Tue-Sun) to the south houses a collection of stone carvings and relics. The attached **Venkatappa Art Gallery** (admission free; ⊙10am-5pm Tue-Sun) preserves several works and personal memorabilia of K Venkatappa (1887–1962), court painter to the Wodeyars.

At the northwestern end of Cubbon Park are the colossal neo-Dravidian-style **Vidhana Soudha**, built in 1954, and the neoclassical **Attara Kacheri**, that houses the High Court. Both are closed to the public.

Bengaluru Palace   PALACE

(off Map p842; Palace Rd; Indian/foreigner ₹100/200, camera/video ₹500/1000; ⊙10am-6pm) The private residence of the Wodeyars, erstwhile maharajas of the state, Bengaluru Palace preserves a slice of bygone royal splendour for you to see. Aged retainers show you around the building, designed to resemble Windsor Castle, and you can marvel at the lavish interiors and galleries featuring hunting trophies, family photos and a collection of nude portraits. Ask before you get clicking. The palace grounds, inter-

estingly, are now Bengaluru's hottest concert arena, having hosted rock 'n' roll biggies such as Iron Maiden, the Rolling Stones, Aerosmith and Deep Purple.

Lalbagh Botanical Gardens   GARDEN

(off Map p842; admission ₹10; ⊙5.30am-7.30pm) Spread over 96 acres of landscaped terrain, the expansive Lalbagh gardens were laid out in 1760 by Hyder Ali. You can take a guided tour in a ten-seater ecofriendly buggy (per head ₹100), and learn about the centuries-old trees and collections of plants from around the world. A beautiful glasshouse, modelled on the original Crystal Palace in London, is the venue for flower shows in the weeks preceding Republic Day (26 January) and Independence Day (15 August). Walk in early on Sundays and you can hear the police band perform at the Police Bandstand.

Karnataka Chitrakala Parishath   ART GALLERY

(Map p842; www.karnatakachitrakalaparishath.com; Kumarakrupa Rd; admission ₹10; ⊙10.30am-5.30pm Mon-Sat) This visual arts gallery is Bengaluru's premier art institution. A wide range of Indian and international contemporary art is on show in its galleries (open

Bengaluru: MG Rd & Cubbon Park

10.30am to 7pm), while permanent displays showcase lavish gold-leaf works of Mysore-style paintings and folk and tribal art from across Asia. A section is devoted to the works of Russian master Nicholas Roerich, known for his vivid paintings of the Himalayas, and his son Svetoslav.

Tipu Sultan's Palace
PALACE

(Map p842; Albert Victor Rd; Indian/foreigner ₹5/100, video ₹25; ☻8.30am-5.30pm) Close to the vibrant Krishnarajendra (City) Market stands the elegant palace of Tipu Sultan, notable for its teak pillars and ornamental frescoes. Though not as beautiful (or well-maintained) as Tipu's summer palace in Srirangapatnam, it's an interesting monument, and worth an outing when combined with other nearby sights such as the **Krishnarajendra (City) Market** (Map p842), the massive **Jama Masjid** (Map p842; Silver Jubilee (SJ) Park Rd; admission free), the remains of Kempegowda's **fort** (Map p842) and the ornate **Venkataraman Temple** (Map p842; Krishnarajendra Rd; ☻8.30am-6pm).

Bull Temple & Dodda Ganesha Temple
HINDU TEMPLES

(Bull Temple Rd, Basavangudi; ☻7am-8.30pm) Built by Kempegowda in the 16th-century Dravidian style, the Bull Temple contains a huge granite monolith of Nandi and is one of Bengaluru's most atmospheric temples. Nearby is the **Dodda Ganesha Temple** (Bull Temple Rd, Basavangudi; ☻7am-8.30pm), with an equally enormous Ganesh idol. The temples are about a kilometre south of Tipu Sultan's Palace, down Krishnarajendra Rd.

Iskcon Temple
HINDU TEMPLE

(Hare Krishna Hill, Chord Rd; ☻7am-1pm & 4-8.30pm) Built by the International Society of Krishna Consciousness (Iskcon), also referred to as the Hare Krishnas, this shiny temple, 8km northwest of the town centre, is lavishly decorated in a mix of ultra-contemporary and traditional styles. The Sri Radha Krishna Mandir has a stunning shrine to Krishna and Radha. The temple is a 20-minute autorickshaw ride from MG Rd, near Yeshvantpur train station.

HAL Aerospace Museum & Heritage Centre
MUSEUM

(Airport-Varthur Rd; admission ₹20, camera/video ₹25/45; ☻9am-5pm Tue-Sun) For a peek into India's aeronautical history, visit this wonderful museum past the old airport, where you can see some of the indigenous aircraft

Bengaluru: Chickpet & Gandhi Nagar

models designed by HAL. Interesting exhibits include the infamous MIG-21, home-grown models such as the Marut and Kiran, and a vintage Canberra bomber. You can also engage in mock dogfights at the simulator machines (₹10) on the top floor.

🏃 Activities

Ayurveda & Yoga

The staff at **Chiraayu Ayurvedic Health & Rejuvenation Centre** (☏25500855; 6th block, 17th D Main, Koramangala; ☻8.30am-6pm) take their practice seriously, so don't make vague demands like 'I'd like a massage!' Make an appointment, discuss your problems, and the resultant therapy – prescribed by in-house experts – could range from a day-long session to long-term programs. Allergy, diabetes, asthma and other critical diseases can be treated.

Based in the eastern suburb of Whitefield, **Ayurvedagram** (☏27945430; www.ayurvedagram.com; Hemmandanhalli) is a reputed ayurvedic treatment centre that customises packages for individual disorders. For a more lavish experience, try **Soukya** (☏28017000; www.soukya.com; Soukya Rd, Samethanahalli, Whitefield; ☻6am-8.30pm), an internationally renowned place set on a picture-perfect 30-acre organic farm that offers some of the best programs in ayurvedic therapy and yoga (per hour therapy Indian/foreigner ₹2750/US$55). Long-term packages are also available.

Stylish **Urban Yoga Centre** (☑32005720; www.urbanyoga.in; 100ft Rd, Indiranagar; ⊘6.30am-9pm) has a smart yoga studio offering a range of classes, and sells yoga clothes, accessories and books.

Outdoor Adventure

Getoff ur ass (☑26722750; www.getoffurass.com; 858 1D Main Rd, Giri Nagar 2nd Phase) has perfect recipes for outward-bound adventures, including rafting, kayaking, trekking and mountaineering in Karnataka and elsewhere. It also sells and rents outdoor gear.

⊏⋻ Tours

Bangalore Walks   WALKING
(☑9845523660, 9845068416; www.bangalorewalks.com) A must-do. Choose between a traditional walk, medieval walk, garden walk or Victorian walk to get under Bengaluru's skin. Held on Saturdays and Sundays (7am to 10am), the walks (adult/child ₹500/300) are all about knowing and loving Bengaluru in a way that many locals have forgotten. There's a scrummy breakfast en route. Book in advance; each walk takes a maximum of 15 people.

Bus Tours   SIGHTSEEING
The state tourism department runs a couple of city bus tours, all of which begin at Badami House. The basic city tour runs twice daily at 7.30am and 2pm (ordinary/deluxe ₹170/190), while a 16-hour tour to Srirangapatnam, Mysore and Brindavan Gardens departs daily at 6.30am (ordinary/deluxe ₹530/680). There are longer tours to other destinations; enquire at the Karnataka Tourism offices.

🛏 Sleeping

Hotel tariffs are skyrocketing in Bengaluru even as you read this. Decent rooms are perpetually in short supply, and a good night's sleep will set you back by at least ₹1000. Serviced apartments are frequently a better deal than many midrange and top-end hotels. Most hotels have 24-hour checkout. Book early.

Stacks of hotels line Subedar Chatram (SC) Rd, east of the bus stands and train station. It's a loud and seedy area, but convenient if you're in transit. For longer stays, consider moving into town, preferably closer to MG Rd. All hotels listed here have hot water, at least in the mornings.

TOP CHOICE Taj West End   HERITAGE HOTEL **$$$**
(Map p842; ☑66605660; www.tajhotels.com; Racecourse Rd; s/d incl breakfast from ₹11,600/12,800; ❄🌐🏊) The West End saga flashbacks to 1887, when it was incepted by a British family as a 10-room hostel for passing army officers. Since then, nostalgia has been a permanent resident at this lovely property which – spread over 20 acres of tropical gardens – has evolved as a definitive icon of Indian luxury hospitality. Its pearly mansions and villas seamlessly mix heritage with modern comforts, with verandahs overlooking the verdant greens that come alive with the chirping of exotic birds every day. Get antiquated in style.

(Map of MG Rd Area with scale: 0–200 m / 0–0.1 miles. Labels include: Cariappa Memorial Park, FM Manekshaw Parade Ground, RSI Play Ground, Kamaraj Rd, Mahatma Gandhi (MG) Rd, Church St, SHANTHALA NAGAR, Museum Rd, St Mark's Rd, Madras Bank Rd, Rest House Rd, Brigade Rd, Residency Rd (FM Cariappa Rd))

TOP CHOICE Casa Piccola Cottage
HERITAGE HOTEL **$$**

(Map p840; ☎22270754; www.casapiccola.com; 2 Clapham Rd; r incl breakfast from ₹3600; ❈❂) Located on a quiet back lane in Richmond Town, this beautifully renovated 1915 cottage is a tranquil sanctuary from the city madness. With an uncanny ability to make you feel immediately at home, it offers a personalised brand of hospitality that has garnered it a solid reputation. Its studio rooms are high on old-world charm, and the gazebo in the garden is a nice place to tuck into your free breakfast.

Ashley Inn
GUESTHOUSE **$$**

(Map p840; ☎41233415; www.ashleyinn.in; 11 Ashley Park Rd; s/d incl breakfast from ₹1800/2200; ❈❂) Once in a while, we all come across a hotel that gets it right without trying too hard. Ashley Inn is one such place. Seconds from the MG Rd mayhem, with eight pleasant rooms in soothing colours, this sweet guesthouse evokes that homely feeling you sometimes desperately yearn for while on the move.

Tom's
HOTEL **$$**

(Map p840; ☎25575875; 1/5 Hosur Rd; s/d incl breakfast from ₹1199/1399; ❈❂) Long favoured for its unbelievably low tariffs, cheerful Tom's allows you to stay in the heart of town for a song. Yes, there's been some cost-cutting since we last visited, but rooms are spacious, the linen spotless, and the staff professional. Ask for a north-facing room; they come with balconies.

Villa Pottipati
HERITAGE HOTEL **$$**

(☎23360777; www.neemranahotels.com; 142 8th Cross, 4th Main, Malleswaram; s/d incl breakfast from ₹4000/4500; ❈❂❂) Located a little off-centre, this heritage building was once the garden home of an expat Andhra family. Needless to say, it's flooded with memories in the form of numerous artefacts scattered within its rooms. Dollops of quaintness are added by features such as antique four-poster beds and arched doorways, while the overall ambience gains from a garden full of ageless trees, seasonal blossoms and a dunk-sized pool.

Hotel Ajantha
HOTEL **$**

(Map p840; ☎25584321; www.hotelajantha.in; 22A MG Rd; s/d from ₹475/750, d with AC from ₹999; ❈) Old Indian tourism posters and stacks of potted foliage welcome you into this oldie located off MG Rd, with a range of par-for-the-course rooms in a semi-quiet compound. Being dirt cheap, it's insanely popular with budget travellers, so book well ahead.

Tricolour Hotel
HOTEL **$$**

(Map p842; ☎41279090; www.ibchotels-resorts.com; 15 Tank Bund Rd; s/d ₹1300/1600; ❈@) This pseudo-boutique hotel should be your first option if you want to sleep in relative comfort while being close to the bus and train stations. It's both classy and contemporary, with primly laid-out rooms and cheerful, sky-lit foyers. Col Sanders sells his legendary fried chicken at the glitzy mall next door.

JP Cordial
HOTEL **$$**

(p842; ☎40214021; www.jpcordial.com; 68 SC Rd; d incl breakfast Indian/foreigner from ₹3600/US$95; ❈@) A rather pleasant business hotel straddling the maddening commotion on SC Rd, this designer place meets requisite luxury standards, and the amiable staff is always ready to meet your requirements. It's one of the better mid-rangers in this part of town.

Casa Piccola Service Apartments HOTEL $$
(Map p840; 22270754; www.casapiccola.com; Wellington Park Apartments, Wellington St; r from ₹2400;) One of Bengaluru's many sleek serviced apartments, this place offers a set of well-appointed two- and three-bedroom flats located within a residential complex on a shared basis. Tastefully done up in pastel shades, they're stocked with all amenities. It's owned by the Oberoi family, who run the Casa Piccola Cottage across the lane.

Ista Hotel HOTEL $$$
(off Map p840; 25558888; www.istahotels.com; 1/1 Swami Vivekananda Rd, Ulsoor; d from ₹8099;) With its name meaning 'sacred space', Ista delivers accommodation happiness in a cool, minimalist style. The smallish but elegant rooms with king-sized windows offer sweeping vistas across Ulsoor lake. The bar and restaurant, opening on to the rooftop pool, are swell, and the spa will pamper you with diverse treatments kicking off at around ₹1300.

Hotel Empire International HOTEL $$
(Map p844; 25593743; www.hotelempire.in; 36 Church St; s/d incl breakfast from ₹1550/1850;) Consistency is the Empire's middle name. The bright and airy rooms are as clean and well-serviced, the front desk as professional and courteous, and the overall vibe as cheerful as on our previous visits. Combined with its location in the heart of all the action and nightlife, it's a sure deal.

Monarch HOTEL $$
(Map p844; 25591915; www.monarchhotels.in; 54 Brigade Rd; s/d incl breakfast from ₹25000/3500;) Between you and us, a night at the Monarch should be costing twice as much. Don't tell them, though. Just lie back in one of their super-comfy rooms and make the most of their innumerable facilities (free wi-fi, 24-hour currency exchange counter, courier service and a dozen others). Then follow it up with a rocking evening on the town.

Brindavan Hotel HOTEL $
(Map p844; 25584000; 108 MG Rd; s/d from ₹750/900;) Being located conveniently off central Bengaluru's main drag, this budget dive is perennially booked out, and you need to call well in advance if you want to check into one of its plain and characterless (though tidy and airy) rooms. There's an in-house astro-palmist, if you're interested.

Hotel Adora HOTEL $
(Map p842; 22200024; 47 SC Rd; s/d from ₹425/650) A largish and popular budget option near the stations, with unfussy rooms with clean sheets. Downstairs is a good veg restaurant, Indraprastha. Walk-in reservations only.

The Park HOTEL $$$
(off Map p840; 25594666; 14/7 MG Rd; s/d incl breakfast from ₹15,000/16,000) A swanky designer hotel with oodles of glitz and glam. Home to the reputed Italian restaurant, **i-t.ALIA**.

Eating

Bengaluru's adventurous dining scene keeps pace with the whims and rising standards of its hungry, moneyed masses. Unless stated otherwise, all restaurants are open from noon to 3pm, and 7pm to 11pm. It's best to book a table in some (telephone numbers listed).

If and when the state government passes a much-discussed anti cow-slaughter bill, beef may go off the menus in many mid-range restaurants.

MG ROAD AREA

TOP
CHOICE Karavalli   SEAFOOD $$$
(Map p844; ✆66604545; The Gateway Hotel; 66 Residency Rd; mains ₹450-500) The Arabian Sea is some 500km away, but you'll have to come only as far as this superb spot to savour South India's finest coastal cuisines. It's designed like a seaside villa, and the decor is a stylish mash of thatched roofs and vintage woodwork. The juicy Lobster Balchao is an eternal favourite, as are the fiery Mangalorean fishy delights. And there's the divine Bebinca with vanilla ice-cream for dessert.

Oye! Amritsar   NORTH INDIAN $$
(Map p844; 4th fl, Asha Enclave, Church St; mains ₹150-180) Pining for some good old Punjabi fare in South India? This is where you'll find it all. A dhaba-style eatery with funky souped-up decor, this restaurant serves some lip-smacking dishes from the northern state, best washed down with a glass of yoghurt-based lassi.

The Only Place   STEAKHOUSE $$
(Map p844; 13 Museum Rd; mains ₹200-220) Juicy steaks, brawny burgers and the classic shepherd's pie – no one serves them better than this time-tested restaurant which has many an expat loyalist in town. It's a place that doesn't encourage much conversation, simply because you've got your mouth full most of the time.

Queen's Restaurant   INDIAN $
(Map p844; Church St; mains ₹80-100) This reputed joint serves some quick and tasty Indian morsels such as a range of vegetable and dhal preparations, to go with fluffy and hot chapati. The interiors are rustic, with painted motifs adorning earthy walls.

Ebony   MULTICUISINE $$
(Map p844; (✆41783344; 13th fl, Barton Centre, 84 MG Rd; mains ₹150-180) Serves the best Parsi food in town, along with some delectable Thai, French and Indian dishes. The interiors are classy, and the rooftop location heavenly.

Palm Grove   SOUTH INDIAN $
(Ballal Residency, 74/3 3rd Cross, Residency Rd; mains ₹80-100; ◷7am-10.30pm) One of the best places in Bengaluru's central district where you can tuck into authentic South Indian veg fare, such as dosas, vadas and multicourse thalis.

OTHER AREAS

TOP
CHOICE Mavalli Tiffin Rooms   SOUTH INDIAN $
(MTR; Map p842; Lalbagh Rd; mains ₹40-60; ◷6.30-11am, 12.30-2.45pm, 3.30-7.30pm & 8-9.30pm) A legendary name in South Indian comfort food, this super-popular eatery, commonly called MTR, has had Bengaluru eating out of its hands since 1924. Head up to the dining room upstairs, queue for a table, and then admire the dated images of southern beauties etched on smoky glass as waiters bring you savoury local fare, capped by frothing filter coffee served in silverware. It's a definitive Bengaluru experience; don't leave town without trying it.

Caperberry   CONTINENTAL $$
(Map p840; ✆25594567; 121 Dickenson Rd; mains ₹240-270) A smart blend of European monochromes and glittering South Indian goldwork create a sophisticated ambience at this fancy restaurant specialising in Spanish food. Paella, or pear and asparagus salad? Take your pick from the extensive menu, and match it with a sangria on the side.

Windsor Pub   MULTICUISINE $$
(7 Kodava Samaja Bldg, 1st Main Vasanthnagar; mains ₹220-280) The awesome fillet steak belted out by this relaxed eatery near Bangalore Palace qualifies as the ultimate death-row meal for many a Bengaluru foodie. And that's not forgetting the flavoursome Mangalorean fish fries, or the tangy pandhi (pork) masala from Kodagu's hills. Beer flows freely from the taps as you gleefully stuff your face.

Harima   JAPANESE $$
(off Map p840; ✆41325757; 4th fl, Devatha Plaza, Residency Rd; mains ₹250-280) Tempura, sashimi, sushi and that refreshing sip of sake. Flavoured Japanese staples form the core of this restaurant's repertoire, noted for its minimalist interiors. It's one of Bengaluru's most underrated places, but you'll certainly spread the word once you've been there.

Olive Beach   MEDITERRANEAN $$$
(Map p840; ✆41128400; 16 Wood St, Ashoknagar; mains ₹350-400) Lodged within an elegant villa in upscale Ashoknagar is this fantastic fine-dining restaurant, with food that evokes wistful memories of sunny Tuscany (or

whatever your fave Mediterranean getaway might be). Spinach and goat cheese pizza, anyone? Or crumbled sausage and cauliflower risotto, maybe? The roasted pumpkin and sage ravioli sure has a few admirers, too.

Sunny's
ITALIAN $$
(Map p840; ☑41329366; 34 Vittal Mallya Rd; mains ₹280-300) Cheese and olive oil conspire to work up some mouth-watering Mediterranean flavours at this popular restaurant specialising in Italian food. Its wide range of pastas, pizzas, salads and desserts are a hit with Bengaluru's expat community.

Barbeque Nation
MUGHLAI $$
(100Ft Rd, Indiranagar; meals ₹450) Good news for kebab lovers. This stylish place has an endless supply of the grilled meaty delights for you to gorge on. Meals feature unlimited portions of a set menu which changes on a daily basis. And the meat is skewered live at your table to suit your tastes! Eat till you're beat.

Gramin
INDIAN $$
(☑41104104; 20, 7th Block Raheja Arcade, Koramangala; mains ₹140-160) A wide choice of flavourful and breezy North Indian fare is on offer at this extremely popular all-veg place. Try the excellent range of lentils, best had with oven-fresh rotis, or the veg kebabs.

🍷 Drinking

BARS & LOUNGES
Despite Bengaluru's rock-steady reputation as a place to get sloshed in style, local laws require pubs and discos to shut shop at 11.30pm (opening time is usually 7.30pm). However, given the wide choice of chic watering holes around, you can indulge in a spirited session of pub-hopping in this original beer town of India. The trendiest nightclubs will typically charge you a cover of around ₹1000 per couple, but it's often redeemable against drinks or food.

TOP CHOICE Koshy's Bar & Restaurant
BAR
(Map p844; 39 St Mark's Rd; ☺9am-11.30pm) They say half of Bengaluru's court cases are argued around Koshy's teetering tables, and many hard-hitting newspaper articles written over its steaming coffees. Having quenched the collective thirst of the city's intelligentsia for decades, this buzzy and joyful pub is where you can put away pints of beer and classic British meals (mains ₹170 to ₹200) in-between fervent discussions.

Plan B
PUB
(Map p840; 20 Castle St, Ashoknagar) 'Finish your beer. There are sober kids in India', says a poster adorning this chilled-out pub's robust interiors. And to aid you in this eminently enjoyable task, there's a whole line of awesome bites from peanut masala to porky platters, and some ageless music (remember 'My Sharona'?). The place brims over with motorsports buffs on F1 racedays.

Shiro
BAR
(Map p840; UB City) A sophisticated lounge to get sloshed in style, Shiro has elegant interiors complemented by arty Buddha busts and Apsara figurines. Its commendable selection of cocktails and drinks draw rave reviews from patrons, who often fight off their Saturday night hangovers by converging again for Sunday brunch.

B Flat
BAR
(100ft Rd, Indiranagar) A pub and jazz bar that often features live performances by some of India's best bands, this place is on the radar of every jazz and blues junkie in town. There's a ₹200 entry fee, offset against moody guitar solos.

13th Floor
BAR
(Map p844; 13th fl, Barton Centre, 84 MG Rd) Come early to grab a spot on the terrace sit-out, with all of Bengaluru glittering at your feet. The atmosphere is that of a relaxed cocktail party, and you can tap your feet to a good selection of retro music.

Beach
BAR
(100ft Rd, Indiranagar) Couldn't make it to Goa? Then come to this slick beach-bum's lounge, and feel the sand between your toes (literally), as you dance away to some groovy music. Women drink free on Wednesdays, and there's the occasional quiz night for you to flaunt your GK.

CAFES & TEAHOUSES
Bengaluru is liberally sprinkled with good chain cafes. Those such as **Café Coffee Day** (Map p844; Brigade Rd; ☺8am-11.30pm) and **Barista** (Map p840; 40 St Mark's Rd; ☺8am-11.30pm) have several outlets across town. For something different, try one of the following.

TOP CHOICE Matteo
CAFE
(Map p844; Church St; ☺9am-11pm) The hippest and newest cafe in Bengaluru serves first-rate brews (try the aromatic green tea), along with tasty side-orders such as shrimp and penne pasta or a filling chicken

baguette. The coolest rendezvous in the city centre.

Infinitea
CAFE

(Map p840; 2 Shah Sultan Complex, Cunningham Rd; ☺9am-11pm) The service here can be patchy at times, but the steaming cuppa that follows more than makes up for it. Its menu features orthodox teas from the best estates, alongside a few fancy names such as chocolate tea milkshake.

☆ Entertainment

CINEMA

English-language films are popular, and tickets range from ₹150 to ₹300, depending on your theatre of choice and the show time.

INOX
CINEMA

(☑41128888; www.inoxmovies.com; 5th fl, Garuda Mall, Magrath Rd) Screens new releases from Bollywood and the West.

PVR Cinema
CINEMA

(☑22067511; www.pvrcinemas.com; Forum, 21 Hosur Rd) A megacinema with 11 screens showing Indian and international titles.

Nani Cinematheque
CINEMA

(☑22356262; 5th fl, Sona Tower, 71 Millers Rd) Classic Indian and European films are screened here Friday, Saturday and Sunday.

SPORT

Bengaluru's horse-racing seasons are from November to February and May to July. Contact the **Bangalore Turf Club** (Map p842; www.bangaloreraces.com; Racecourse Rd) for details.

For a taste of India's sporting passion up close, attend one of the regular cricket matches at **M Chinnaswamy Stadium** (Map p840; MG Rd). Details can be found at www.cricketkarnataka.com.

THEATRE

Ranga Shankara
THEATRE

(☑26592777; www.rangashankara.org; 36/2 8th Cross, JP Nagar) All kinds of interesting theatre (in a variety of languages and spanning various genres) and dance are held at this cultural centre.

🛍 Shopping

Bengaluru's shopping options are abundant, ranging from teeming bazaars to glitzy malls. Some good shopping areas include Commercial St (Map p840), Vittal Mallya Rd (Map p840) and the MG Rd area.

UB City
CLOTHING

(Map p840; Vittal Mallya Rd; ☺11am-9pm) Global haute couture and Indian high fashion come to roost at this towering mall in the central district.

Cauvery Arts & Crafts Emporium
SOUVENIRS

(Map p844; 49 MG Rd; ☺10am-7pm Mon-Sat) Showcases a great collection of sandalwood and rosewood products as well as textiles.

Ffolio
CLOTHING

(Map p840; 5 Vittal Mallya Rd; ☺10.30am-8pm) A good place for high Indian fashion, with another branch at Leela Galleria (23 Airport Rd, Kodihalli).

Fabindia
CLOTHING

(54 17th Main Koramangala; ☺10am-8pm) Commercial St (Map p840); Garuda mall (McGrath Rd) These branches contain Fabindia's full range of stylish clothes and homewares in traditional cotton prints and silks.

Magazines
BOOKSTORE

(Map p844; 55 Church St) An astounding collection of international magazines. Up to 70% discount on back issues.

Blossom
BOOKSTORE

(Map p844; 84/6 Church St) Great deals on new and second-hand books.

Bombay Store
SOUVENIRS

(Map p844; 99 MG Rd; ☺10.30am-8.30pm) For gifts ranging from ecobeauty products to linens.

Mysore Saree Udyog
CLOTHING

(Map p840; 1st fl, 294 Kamaraj Rd; ☺10.30am-8.30pm Mon-Sat) A great choice for top-quality silks and saris.

Some good malls in town include **Garuda Mall** (Map p840; McGrath Rd), **Forum** (Hosur Rd; Koramangala) and **Leela Galleria** (23 Airport Rd, Kodihalli).

ℹ Information

Internet Access

Being an IT city, internet cafes are plentiful in Bengaluru, as is wi-fi access in hotels.

Café Coffee Day (Map p840; Brigade Rd; ☺8am-11.30pm) has a smoking deal comprising an hour's internet usage, cappuccino and cookies.

Left Luggage

The City train station (Map p842) and Central bus stand (Map p842) have 24-hour cloakrooms (per day ₹10).

Maps

The tourist offices give out decent city maps. The excellent *Eicher City Map* (₹200) is sold at major bookshops.

Media

080 and *What's Up Bangalore* are great monthly magazines covering the latest in Bengaluru's social life. *Kingfisher Explocity Nights* (₹200) gives a low-down on the best night spots. All titles are available in major bookstores.

Medical Services

Most hotels here have doctors on call.

Hosmat (Map p840; ☎25593796; www.hosmat net.com; 45 Magrath Rd) For critical injuries and other general illnesses.

Mallya Hospital (Map p840; ☎22277979; www .mallyahospital.net; 2 Vittal Mallya Rd) With a 24-hour pharmacy and emergency services.

Money

ATMs are common.

Monarch (Map p844; ☎41123253; 54 Monarch Plaza, Brigade Rd; ☺10am-8pm Mon-Sat) Deals in foreign currency, travellers cheques and ticketing.

TT Forex (Map p840; ☎22254337; 33/1 Cunningham Rd; ☺9.30am-6.30pm Mon-Fri, 9.30am-1.30pm Sat) Changes travellers cheques and foreign currency.

Photography

Digital services are easy to come by.

GK Vale (89 MG Rd; ☺10am-7pm Mon-Sat) One-stop photography shop.

Post

Main post office (Map p840; Cubbon Rd; ☺10am-7pm Mon-Sat, 10am-1pm Sun)

Tourist Information

Government of India tourist office (Map p844; ☎25585417; 48 Church St; ☺9.30am-6pm Mon-Fri, 9am-1pm Sat)

Karnataka State Tourism Development Corporation (KSTDC); Badami House (Map p842; ☎43344334; Badami House, Kasturba Rd; ☺10am-7pm Mon-Sat); Karnataka Tourism House (Map p840; ☎41329211; 8 Papanna Lane, St Mark's Rd; ☺10am-7pm Mon-Sat). Bookings can be made for KSTDC city and state tours, as well as for luxury holidays such as the Golden Chariot.

Karnataka Tourism (Map p842; ☎22352828; 2nd fl, 49 Khanija Bhavan, Racecourse Rd; ☺10am-5.30pm Mon-Sat)

Travel Agencies

Skyway (Map p840; ☎22111401; www.sky waytour.com; 8 Papanna Lane, St Mark's Rd; ☺9am-6pm Mon-Sat) A thoroughly professional outfit with a satellite office in Mysore. Reliable for booking long-distance taxis and air tickets.

STIC Travels (Map p840; ☎22202408; www.stictravel.com; G5 Imperial Ct, 33/1 Cunningham Rd; ☺9.30am-6pm Mon-Sat) For ticketing, vehicles, hotels and holiday packages.

❶ Getting There & Away

Air

Airline offices are generally open from 9am to 5.30pm Monday to Saturday. City offices and 24-hour helplines of domestic carriers serving Bengaluru include the following:

GoAir (☎9223222111; www.goair.in)

Indian Airlines (Map p842; ☎22277747; www.indian-airlines.nic.in; Unity Bldg, JC Rd)

DAILY FLIGHTS FROM BENGALURU

DESTINATION	STARTING FARE ₹	DURATION (HR)
Ahmedabad	3200	2
Chennai (Madras)	2300	1
Delhi	3700	2½
Goa	2600	1
Hyderabad	2400	1
Kochi	2300	1½
Kolkata (Calcutta)	3500	3
Mangalore	2300	1
Mumbai (Bombay)	3000	2
Pune	2600	1½
Trivandrum	3300	1½

DESTINATION	FARE (₹)	DURATION (HR)	FREQUENCY
Chennai	274 (R)/472 (V)	7-8	15 daily
Ernakulam	484 (R)/598 (V)	10-12	7 daily
Hampi	316 (R)	8½	1 daily
Hospet	306 (R)/381 (V)	8	6 daily
Hyderabad	432 (R)/736 (V)	10-12	10 daily
Jog Falls	321 (R)	9	1 daily
Mumbai	1059 (V)	19	4 daily
Mysore	136 (R)/247 (V)	3	Every 30min
Ooty	262 (R)/357 (V)	8	8 daily
Panaji	473 (R)/779 (V)	12-14	4 daily
Puttaparthi	71 (R)/185 (V)	4	3 daily

R – Rajahamsa Semideluxe, V – Airavath AC Volvo

IndiGo (☎9910383838; www.goindigo.in)
Jet Airways (Map p842; ☎39893333,
39899999; www.jetairways.com; Unity Bldg,
JC Rd)
Kingfisher Airlines (Map p840;
☎18002333131, 41148190; www.flykingfisher
.com; 35/2 Cunningham Rd)
SpiceJet (☎18001803333; www.spicejet.com)

Bus

Bengaluru's huge, well-organised **Central
bus stand** (Map p842; Gubbi Thotadappa Rd),
also known as **Majestic**, is directly in front of
the City train station. **Karnataka State Road
Transport Corporation** (KSRTC; www.ksrtc
.in) buses run throughout Karnataka and to
neighbouring states. Other interstate bus
operators:

**Andhra Pradesh State Road Transport
Corporation** (APSRTC; www.apsrtc.gov.in)
Kadamba Transport Corporation
(☎22351958, 22352922) Services for Goa.
**Maharashtra State Road Transport
Corporation** (MSRTC; www.msrtc.gov.in)
Tamil Nadu State Transport Corporation
(SETC; www.tnstc.in)

Computerised advance booking is available for
most buses at the station. **KSRTC** (Map p840;
Devatha Plaza, Residency Rd) also has convenient booking counters around town, including
one at Devantha Plaza. It's wise to book long-
distance journeys in advance.

Numerous private bus companies offer com-
fier and only slightly more expensive services.
Private bus operators line the street facing the
Central bus stand, or you can book through a
travel agency.

For major KSRTC bus services from Bengaluru,
see the boxed text above.

Train

Bengaluru's **City train station** (Map p842;
Gubbi Thotadappa Rd) is the main train hub and
the place to make reservations. **Cantonment
train station** (Station Rd) is a sensible spot to
disembark if you're arriving and headed for the
MG Rd area, while **Yeshvantpur train station**
(Rahman Khan Rd), 8km northwest of downtown, is the starting point for Goa trains.

If a train is booked out, foreign travellers can
avail the foreign-tourist quota. Buy a wait-listed
ticket, then fill out a form at the **Divisional Railway Office** (Map p842; Gubbi Thotadappa Rd)
building immediately north of the City train station. You'll know about 10 hours before departure
whether you've got a seat (a good chance); if not,
the ticket is refunded. The computerised **train
reservation office** (Map p842; ☎139; ⊗8am-
8pm Mon-Sat, 8am-2pm Sun), on the left facing
the station, has separate counters for credit-card
purchase, women and foreigners. Luggage can
be left at the 24-hour cloakroom on Platform 1 at
the City train station (₹10 per bag per day).

See the boxed text p852 for information on
major train services.

🅘 Getting Around

To/From the Airport

The swish city **airport** (☎66782251; www.bengal
uruairport.com) is in Hebbal, about 40km north
from the MG Rd area. Prepaid taxis can take you
from the airport to the city centre (₹700). You
can also take the hourly shuttle Vayu Vajra AC
bus service to Majestic or MG Rd (₹180).

Autorickshaw

The city's autorickshaw drivers are legally required to use their meters; few comply in reality. After 10pm, 50% is added onto the metered rate. Flag fall is ₹17 for the first 2km and then ₹9 for each extra kilometre.

Bus

Bengaluru has a thorough local bus network, operated by the **Bangalore Metropolitan Transport Corporation** (BMTC; www.bmtcinfo.com). Red AC Vajra buses criss-cross the city, while green Big10 deluxe buses connect the suburbs. Ordinary buses run from the City bus stand (Map p842), next to Majestic; a few operate from the City Market bus stand (Map p842) further south.

To get from the City train station to the MG Rd area, catch any bus from Platform 17 or 18 at the City bus stand. For the City market, take bus 31, 31E, 35 or 49 from Platform 8.

Taxi

Several places around Bengaluru offer taxi rental with driver. Standard rates for a long-haul Tata Indica cab are ₹7 per kilometre for a minimum of 250km, plus a daily allowance of ₹150 for the driver. For an eight-hour day rental, you're looking at around ₹1200. Luxury Renault cabs are also available for ₹60 for 4km kilometre and ₹15 for every subsequent kilometre. Try **Meru Cabs** (☎44224422) or **Skyway** (☎22111401).

Metro

Bengaluru's shiny new AC metro service was all set for inauguration at the time of research. With trains plying every four minutes and tickets costing marginally more than intra-city buses, the service comes as a welcome alternative to the city's congested public transport system. For the latest updates on the service, log on to www.bmrc.co.in.

Around Bengaluru

HESSARAGHATTA

Located 30km northwest of Bengaluru, Hessaraghatta is home to **Nrityagram** (☎080-28466313; www.nrityagram.org; ◷10am-2pm Tue-Sun), a leading dance academy established in 1990 to revive and popularise Indian classical dance.

The brainchild and living legacy of celebrated dancer Protima Gauri Bedi (1948–98), the complex was designed like a village by Goa-based architect Gerard da Cunha. Long-term courses in classical dance are offered to deserving students here, while local children are taught for free on Sundays. Self-guided tours cost ₹20 or you can book a tour, lecture and demonstration and vegetarian meal (₹1250, minimum 10 people).

Opposite the dance village, **Taj Kuteeram** (☎080-28466326; www.tajhotels.com; d ₹4000;

MAJOR TRAINS FROM BENGALURU

DESTINATION	TRAIN NO & NAME	FARE (₹)	DURATION (HR)	DEPARTURES
Chennai	12658 *Chennai Mail*	193/655	6	10.45pm
	12028 *Shatabdi*	510/1105	5	6am Wed-Mon
Delhi	12627 *Karnataka Exp*	546/2070	39	7.20pm
	12649 *Sampark Kranti Exp*	536/2020	35	10.10pm Mon, Wed, Fri, Sat & Sun
Hospet	16592 *Hampi Exp*	191/725	9½	9pm
Hubli	16589 *Rani Chennamma Exp*	203/745	8	9.15pm
Kolkata	12864 *YPR Howrah Exp*	508/1900	35	7.35pm
Mumbai	16530 *Udyan Exp*	363/1375	24	7.50pm
Mysore	12007 *Shatabdi*	305/590	2	11am Wed-Mon
	12614 *Tippu Exp*	62/225	2½	3pm
Trivandrum	16526 *Kanyakumari Exp*	325/1217	22	9.40pm

Shatabdi fares are chair/executive; Express (Exp/Mail) fares are 2nd/chair for day trains and sleeper/2AC for night trains.

✷@) is a hotel that combines comfort with rustic charm. It also offers ayurveda and yoga sessions.

🍃Our Native Village (☎080-41140909; www.ournativevillage.com; s/d incl full board ₹5000/6800; ☒), an ecofriendly organic farm and resort situated in the vicinity, is a great place to unwind in style while engaging in fun activities such as flying kites, riding bullock carts or milking cows.

From Bengaluru's City Market, buses 253, 253D and 253E run to Hessaraghatta (₹25, one hour), with bus 266 continuing on to Nrityagram.

NANDI HILLS

Rising to 1455m, the **Nandi Hills** (admission ₹5; ⊙6am-10pm), 60km north of Bengaluru, were once the summer retreat of Tipu Sultan. Today, it's the Bengaluru techie's favourite weekend getaway, and is predictably congested on Saturdays and Sundays. Nonetheless, it's a good place for hiking, with good views and two notable **Chola temples**. Buses head to Nandi Hills (₹50, two hours) from Bengaluru's Central bus stand.

JANAPADA LOKA FOLK ARTS MUSEUM

Situated 53km south of Bengaluru, this **museum** (adult/child ₹10/5; ⊙9am-5.30pm) dedicated to the preservation of rural cultures has a wonderful collection of folk art objects, including 500-year-old shadow puppets, festival costumes and musical instruments. Mysore-bound buses (one hour) can drop you here; get off 3km after Ramnagar.

Mysore

☎0821 / POP 799,200 / ELEV 707M

If you haven't been to Mysore, you just haven't seen South India. Conceited though it may sound, this is not an overstatement. An ancient city with more than 600 glorious years of legacy, Mysore is one of the most flamboyant places in India. Known for its glittering royal heritage, bustling markets, magnificent monuments, cosmopolitan culture and a friendly populace, it is also a thriving centre for the production of premium silk, sandalwood and incense. It also flaunts considerable expertise in yoga and ayurveda, two trades it markets worldwide.

The train station is northwest of the city centre, about 1km from the main shopping street, Sayyaji Rao Rd. The Central bus stand is on Bengaluru-Nilgiri (BN) Rd. The Maharaja's Palace sits in the heart of the buzzing quarters southeast of the city centre. The lofty Chamundi Hill is an ever-visible landmark to the south.

History

Mysore owes its name to the mythical Mahisuru, a place where the demon Mahisasura was slain by the goddess Chamundi. Its regal history began in 1399, when the Wodeyar dynasty of Mysore was founded, though they remained in service of the Vijayanagar empire until the mid-16th century. With the fall of Vijayanagar in 1565, the Wodeyars declared their sovereignty, which – save a brief period of Hyder Ali and Tipu Sultan's supremacy in the late 18th century – remained unscathed until 1947.

◉ Sights

Maharaja's Palace   PALACE
(www.mysorepalace.tv; Indian/foreigner ₹20/200; ⊙10am-5.30pm) Among the grandest of India's royal buildings, this fantastic palace was the former seat of the Wodeyar maharajas. The old palace was gutted by fire in 1897; the one you see now was completed in 1912 by English architect Henry Irwin at a cost of ₹4.5 million.

The interior of this Indo-Saracenic marvel – a kaleidoscope of stained glass, mirrors and gaudy colours – is undoubtedly over the top. The decor is further embellished by carved wooden doors, mosaic floors and a series of paintings depicting life in Mysore during the Edwardian Raj. The way into the palace takes you past a fine collection of sculptures and artefacts. Don't forget to check out the armoury, with an intriguing collection of 700-plus weapons.

Every weekend, on national holidays, and through the Dasara celebrations, the palace is illuminated by nearly 100,000 light bulbs that accent its majestic profile against the night.

While you are allowed to snap the palace's exterior, photography within is strictly prohibited. Cameras must be deposited in lockers (₹5) at the palace entrance.

Also available within the compound is a multilingual guided audio tour of the palace, the price of which is included in the foreigners' ticket.

Devaraja Market   MARKET
(Sayyaji Rao Rd; ⊙6am-8.30pm) Dating from Tipu Sultan's reign, the spellbinding Devaraja Market is a lively bazaar that combines both the ancient and modern faces of India.

International brands compete for space here with local traders selling traditional items such as flower garlands, spices and conical piles of *kumkum* (coloured powder used for bindi dots), and their unique co-existence makes for some great photo-ops. Refresh your bargaining skills before shopping.

Chamundi Hill SACRED SITE
At a height of 1062m, on the summit of Chamundi Hill, stands the **Sri Chamundeswari Temple** (⊘7am-2pm & 3.30-9pm), dominated by a towering 40m-high *gopuram* (entrance gateway). It's a fine half-day excursion, offering spectacular views of the city below; you can take bus 201 (₹15, 30 minutes) that rumbles up the narrow road to the summit. A return autorickshaw trip will cost about ₹300.

On your way down, you can also take the foot trail comprising 1000-plus steps that Hindu pilgrims use to visit the temple. One-third of the way down is a 5m-high statue of **Nandi** (Shiva's bull) that was carved out of solid rock in 1659.

Jayachamarajendra Art Gallery ART GALLERY
(Jaganmohan Palace Rd; adult/child ₹20/10; ⊘8.30am-5pm) Built in 1861 as the royal auditorium, the **Jaganmohan Palace**, just west of the Maharaja's Palace, houses the Jayachamarajendra Art Gallery, with a collection of kitsch objects and regal memorabilia including rare musical instruments, Japanese art, and paintings by the noted artist Raja Ravi Varma.

FREE Indira Gandhi Rashtriya Manav Sangrahalaya MUSEUM
(National Museum of Mankind; www.igrms.com; Wellington Lodge, Irwin Rd; ⊘10am-5.30pm Tue-Sun)

This museum functions primarily as a cultural centre and exhibition space showcasing arts from rural India. Housing excellent rotating exhibitions and a souvenir shop, the centre organises two-week workshops in traditional art forms, which are open to the public. The interiors of the museum were under renovation at the time of research but should be completed by the time you read this. Don't miss the fantastic permanent terracotta exhibition – comprising artefacts from across the country – on the front lawn.

FREE Jayalakshmi Vilas Complex Museum MUSEUM
(Mysore University Campus; ⊘10am-5.30pm Mon-Sat, closed alternate Sat) This museum, housed in a grand mansion, specialises in folklore. A wooden puppet of the 10-headed demon Ravana, leather shadow puppets, rural costumes and a 300-year-old temple cart are part of its fantastic collection.

Rail Museum MUSEUM
(KRS Rd; adult/child ₹5/2, camera/video ₹10/25; ⊘9.30am-6.30pm Tue-Sun) This one's a real gem, and certainly not to be missed. Located behind the train station, the open-air museum bears testimony to the stylish way in which the royals once rode the railways. The chief exhibit is the Mysore maharani's saloon, a wood-panelled beauty dating from 1899. There are also five steam engines, each with its own story, and a large collection of instruments and memorabilia from the Indian Railways' chequered past. It's half a day of pure fun.

DUSSEHRA JAMBOREE

Mysore is at its carnivalesque best during the 10-day Dussehra (locally spelt 'Dasara') festival in October. Every evening, the Maharaja's Palace is dramatically lit up, while the town is transformed into a gigantic fairground, with concerts, dance performances, sporting demonstrations and cultural events running to packed houses. On the last day, the celebrations are capped off in grand style. A dazzling procession of richly costumed elephants, garlanded idols, liveried retainers and cavalry kicks off around 1pm, marching through the streets to the rhythms of clanging brass bands, all the way from the palace to the Bannimantap parade ground. A torchlight parade at Bannimantap and a spectacular session of fireworks then closes the festival for the year.

Mysore is choc-a-bloc with tourists during the festival, especially on the final day. To bypass suffocating crowds, consider buying a Dasara VIP Gold Card (₹6000 for two). Though expensive, it assures you good seats at the final day gala and helps you beat the entry queues at other events and performances, while providing discounts on accommodation, dining and shopping. It's also possible to buy tickets (₹250 to ₹1000) just for entering the palace and Bannimantap for the final day's parades. Contact the local Karnataka Tourism office or the **Dasara Information Centre** (☏2418888; www.mysore dasara.gov.in) for more details.

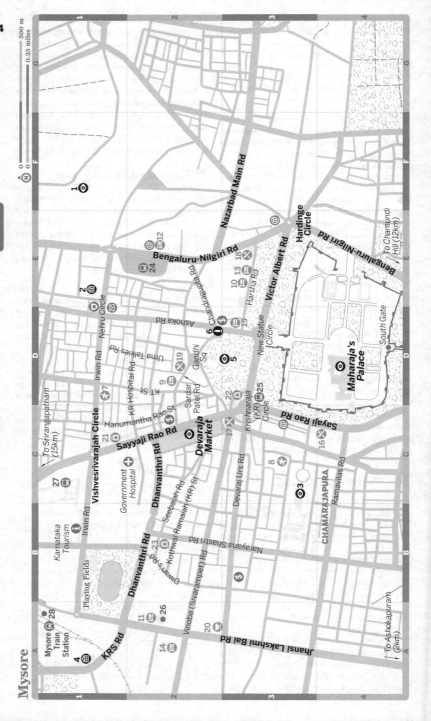

Mysore

500 m
0.25 miles

Mysore Train Station

Karnataka Tourism

Playing Fields

Government Hospital

To Srirangapatnam (15km)

KRS Rd

Vishvesrivarajah Circle

Sayyaji Rao Rd

Dhanvanthri Rd

Dhanvanthri Rd

Devaraja Market

Nehru Circle

Irwin Rd

Irwin Rd

KR Hospital Rd

Uma Talkies Rd

Hanumantha Rao St

Ashoka Rd

Chandragupta Rd

Bengaluru-Nilgiri Rd

Nazarbad Main Rd

Gandhi Sq

Sardar Patel Rd

KT St

Seephan Rd

Kothwal Ramaiah (KR) St

Diwan's Rd

Narayana Shastri Rd

Vinoba (Sivarampet) Rd

Jhansi Lakshmi Bai Rd

Devaraj Urs Rd

Harsha Rd

Victor Albert Rd

New Statue Circle

Krishnaraja (KR) Circle

Sayaji Rao Rd

Ramavilas Rd

Hardinge Circle

Bengaluru-Nilgiri Rd

To Chamundi Hill (12km)

Maharaja's Palace

South Gate

CHAMARAJAPURA

To Ashokapuram (2km)

KARNATAKA & BENGALURU MYSORE

Other Sights   LANDMARKS

For architecture buffs, Mysore has quite a handful of charming buildings. Dating from 1805, **Government House**, formerly the British Residency, is a Tuscan Doric building set in 20 hectares of **gardens** (⊙5am-9pm). Facing the north gate of the Maharaja's Palace is the 1927 **Silver Jubilee Clock Tower** (Ashoka Rd); nearby stands the imposing **Rangacharlu Memorial Hall**, built in 1884. The beauty of towering **St Philomena's Cathedral** (St Philomena St; ⊙5am-6pm), built between 1933 and 1941 in neo-Gothic style, is emphasised by beautiful stained-glass windows.

Mysore's **zoo** (Indiranagar; adult/child ₹30/15, camera/video ₹10/150; ⊙8.30am-5.30pm Wed-Mon), set in pretty gardens on the eastern edge of the city, dates from 1892. A range of primates, tigers, elephants, bears, birds and rhinos live here.

🏃 Activities

Royal Mysore Walks   WALKING
(9632044188; www.royalmysorewalks.com; per person ₹495) A walking tour is an excellent way to familiarise yourself with Mysore's epic history and heritage. Run by techie-turned-historian Vinay, the outfit organises weekend walks with a specific focus on either the city's royal history, its markets, its old quarters or its handicrafts. Offbeat walks, such as a yoga and spirituality tour, can also be arranged at extra cost.

Emerge Spa   AYURVEDA
(📞2522500; www.emergespa.co.in; Windflower Spa & Resort, Maharanapratap Rd, Nazarbad) Mysore's spa operations are spearheaded by the slick, out-of-town Emerge Spa, where you can drop by for a pampering ayurvedic session (try the one-hour Abhayanga massage for ₹1600) or a range of Balinese massage, hydrotherapy and beauty treatments.

Swaasthya Ayurveda
Retreat Village   AYURVEDA
(📞6557557, 9448056406; www.swaasthya.com; 69 Bommaru Agrahara; s/d incl full board ₹2000/3000; @) For an exceptionally peaceful and refreshing ayurvedic vacation, head 12km towards Srirangapatnam to this retreat, where you can spend some time in quiet meditation and feel your senses feast on the lush greenery, the aromatic herb gardens, the simple vegetarian food and the

gurgling sounds of the Cauvery River. Daily rates include basic yoga sessions; for specific ayurvedic treatments, there are special packages on offer. Book well in advance.

Indus Valley Ayurvedic Centre AYURVEDA (☑2473263; www.ayurindus.com; Lalithadripura; s/d incl full board ₹8400/14,090) Set on 16 acres of gardens, this classy centre derives its therapies from ancient scriptures and prescriptions. A wide variety of treatments and basic training programs are on offer. The overnight package includes one session each of ayurveda, yoga and beauty therapy.

Karanji Lake Nature Park BIRDWATCHING (Indiranagar; admission ₹10, camera/video ₹10/25; ☺8.30am-5.30pm) Next to the zoo, ths nature park is the place to spy on various bird species, including great and little cormorants, purple and grey herons, egrets, black ibises, rose-ringed parakeets, green bee-eaters and painted storks, as well as several kinds of butterflies.

Courses

Yoga

The following places have put Mysore on the international yoga map. Unlike casual centres, they are all austerely committed to the art, and require at least a month's commitment on your part. You'll also need to register far in advance, as they are often booked out. Call or write to the centres for details.

Ashtanga Yoga Research Institute YOGA (AYRI; ☑9880185500; www.kpjayi.org; 3rd Stage, 235 8th Cross, Gokulam) Founded by the renowned Ashtanga teacher K Pattabhi Jois, who taught Madonna her yoga moves.

Atma Vikasa Centre YOGA (☑2341978; www.atmavikasayoga.com; Kuvempunagar Double Rd) 'Backbending expert' Yogacharya Venkatesh offers courses in yoga, Sanskrit and meditation. Call in advance to find out if they've already shifted to a new campus 2km away.

Sri Patanjala Yogashala YOGA (Yoga Research Institute; Sri Brahmatantra Swatantra Parakala Mutt, Jaganmohan Palace Circle; ☺6-8am & 5-7pm) The baby of well-respected Ashtanga practitioner BNS Iyengar (not to be confused with BKS Iyengar, famed exponent of Iyengar yoga).

Music

Jayashankar, the music teacher at **Shruthi Musical Works** (☑9845249518; 1189 3rd Cross,

NO 'TOURISTS', PLEASE

Yoga Institutes, as well as local laws, insist that all visitors arriving in Mysore to train in yoga must do so on a student visa, not a casual tourist visa. You are also required to register yourself at the local police station within 14 days of your arrival.

Irwin Rd; ☺10.30am-9pm Mon-Sat, 10.30am-2pm Sun) gets good reviews for his tabla instructions (₹200 per hour).

Tours

KSTDC runs a daily Mysore city tour (₹175), taking in the entire city, Chamundi Hill, Srirangapatnam and Brindavan Gardens. It starts daily at 8.30am, ends at 8.30pm and is likely to leave you breathless!

Other KSTDC tours include one to Belur, Halebid and Sravanabelagola (₹450) on Tuesdays and Thursdays from 7.30am to 9pm. It requires a minimum of 10 people, so call in advance.

There's also a three-day tour of Ooty, Kodaikanal, Doddabetta and Coonoor every Monday, Thursday and Saturday (per person including accommodation is ₹2500) that starts off from Bengaluru; you can join at Mysore. These tours generally run during the high season.

All tours leave from the tours office at **Hotel Mayura Hoysala** (☑2423652; 2 Jhansi Lakshmi Bai Rd). Bookings can be made at the nearby **KSTDC Transport Office** (☑2423652; 2 Jhansi Lakshmi Bai Rd; ☺8.30am-8.30pm) or at travel agencies around town.

Sleeping

Mysore attracts tourists through the year and can fill up very quickly during Dussehra. Booking early is recommended. Check with the tourist office about government-approved homestays, offering rooms from around ₹400 per person.

The following have hot water (at least in the morning) and 24-hour checkout.

TOP CHOICE **Parklane Hotel** HOTEL $$ (☑4003500; www.parklanemysore.com; 2720 Harsha Rd; s/d from ₹900/1200; ❋❂❄) If there's one place in town that can spoil you for a grand a night, this is it. The travellers' central on Mysore's tourist circuit, the Parklane features snug and thoughtfully outfitted rooms (even mobile-phone chargers are provided), livened up by motley tilework on the walls and lovely city views framed in sheer-draped windows. The loos are the cleanest you'll find in town. And the restaurant on the first floor is one happy place to be in the evenings.

TOP CHOICE Mysore Youth Hostel

HOSTEL **$**

(☑2544704; www.yhmysore.com; Gangothri Layout; dm from ₹60) Shoestringers take note. This cutie is arguably the nicest hostel in all of India. Set against a patch of green lawns 3km west of town, it's clean, tidy, well-maintained and manned by an extremely professional staff. OK, there's an 11pm curfew, but then, there's also breakfast for ₹25 and dinner for ₹35. An age proof and identity document must be produced when checking in.

Hotel Mayura Hoysala

HOTEL **$**

(☑2426160; 2 Jhansi Lakshmi Bai Rd; s/d incl breakfast from ₹800/900; ❄) This government-owned hotel continues to offer its blend of mothballed heritage (lace-lined curtains, heavy wooden doors, assorted cane furniture and old photographs lining its corridors) at affordable prices, and the bar downstairs is popular with Mysore's tipplers.

Ginger

HOTEL **$$**

(☑6633333; www.gingerhotels.com; Nazarbad Mohalla; s/d ₹2499/2999; ❄⊛) An ultramodern, DIY business hotel, Ginger has slick and comfortable rooms painted in warm orange tones. Endless features such as a gymnasium, wi-fi, a 24-hour cafe, an ATM, snacks dispensers and juice vending machines complement the warm hospitality of its professional staff. The in-house spa offers ayurvedic sessions from ₹1200.

Royal Orchid Metropole

HERITAGE HOTEL **$$$**

(☑4255566; www.royalorchidhotels.com; 5 Jhansi Lakshmi Bai Rd; s/d incl breakfast from ₹4999/5999; ❄⊛☀) Originally built by the Wodeyars to serve as the residence of the Maharaja's British guests, this is Mysore's leading heritage address. A fascinating colonial-era structure with bona fide old-world charm, it has 30 rooms oozing character, and a stay here is spiced up with several add-ons such as occasional magic shows, music concerts, dance recitals, snake charming performances and astrological sessions.

Hotel Maurya Residency

HOTEL **$$**

(☑2523375; www.sangrouphotel.com; Harsha Rd; d from ₹995; ❄⊛) Along with Hotel Maurya Palace, its twin establishment next door, the Maurya Residency remains a trusted name among the Harsha Rd midrange gang. It's a friendly place with well-appointed rooms and ecofriendly directives slapped all around. **Veg Kourt**, the restaurant downstairs, serves a sumptuous all-you-can-eat breakfast for ₹65.

Hotel Dasaprakash

HOTEL **$**

(☑2442444; www.mysoredasaprakashgroup.com; Gandhi Sq; s/d from ₹275/520, d with AC ₹1200; ❄) A stalwart in Mysore's hospitality industry, this hotel is particularly popular with local tourists and pilgrim groups. Rooms are well maintained; some get a touch of antiquity with old wooden furniture. However, maintenance may not always be up to expectations. An inexpensive veg restaurant, an ice-cream parlour and an astro-palmist are available within the complex.

Green Hotel

HERITAGE HOTEL **$$**

(☑4255000; www.greenhotelindia.com; 2270 Vinoba Rd; Jayalakshmipuram; s/d incl breakfast from ₹2250/2750) Given you're 3km west of town, you're largely paying for the ambience here, which is more prominent in the themed and moody rooms in the main palace building. Those overlooking the garden are bare, inadequately appointed for the price and sparsely evoke nostalgia.

Pai Vista

HOTEL **$$**

(☑2521111; www.paihotels.com; 35A BN Rd; s/d incl breakfast ₹3000/3500; ❄⊛☀) A mint-fresh business hotel, smack opposite the bus stand. Rooms and features are on par with any other hotel in its category. There's a pub called **Opium** that plays groovy music in the evenings.

Viceroy

HOTEL **$$**

(☑2425111; www.theviceroygroup.com; Harsha Rd; s/d from ₹1895/2295; ❄@) Very competitively priced, The Viceroy continues to stay abreast of the midrange race in town. However, the main reason for checking into one of its comfy rooms is the million-dollar view of the Maharaja's Palace from your window and the rooftop restaurant.

✖ Eating & Drinking

Mysore is well served by Indian restaurants. For Western food you're best sticking with the major hotels. Unless otherwise mentioned, restaurants are open from noon to 3pm and 7pm to 11pm.

TOP CHOICE Malgudi Café

CAFE **$**

(Green Hotel, mains ₹60-80; ☺9.30am-7pm) This ambient cafe set around an inner courtyard within Green Hotel's main building brews some of the best South Indian coffees and Himalayan teas, coupling them with a number of tasty snacks. It actively promotes the causes of downtrodden communities while generating employment for them – all the attendants here come from underprivileged backgrounds. You can do your bit by ordering a second cuppa.

TOP CHOICE Pelican Pub PUB $
(Hunsur Rd; mains ₹80-100; ⊙11am-11pm) A wonderful pub is the Pelican! Whether you love your Ogden Nash or not, you're bound to be one happy soul here. An alfresco-style watering hole located en route to Green Hotel, this laid-back joint serves beer for ₹50 a mug and some sinful pork chilli for ₹110 a platter. Happiness, of course, comes free.

Parklane Hotel MULTICUISINE $$
(Parklane Hotel, 2720 Harsha Rd; mains ₹100-140) Choose from a wide selection of tasty Indian, Continental and Chinese dishes while lounging at one of the Parklane's picnic-style garden tables, lit up moodily by countless lanterns. The indoor seating area allows you to interact with house musicians who play popular Indian and Western tunes on request. A good place to exchange notes with fellow travellers.

Tiger Trail INDIAN $$
(Royal Orchid Metropole, 5 Jhansi Lakshmi Bai Rd; mains ₹180-220) This sophisticated restaurant works up delectable Indian dishes in a courtyard that twinkles with torches and fairy lights at night. The best section on its menu comprises exotic jungle recipes collected from different tiger reserves across India.

Hotel RRR SOUTH INDIAN $
(Gandhi Sq; mains ₹50-70) Classic Andhra-style food is ladled out at this ever-busy eatery, and you will likely have to queue for a table during meals. One item to try is the piping-hot veg thali (₹50) served on banana leaves. There's a second branch on Harsha Rd.

Vinayaka Mylari SOUTH INDIAN $
(769 Nazarbad Main Rd; mains ₹30-50; ⊙7.30am-11.30am & 4-8pm) Local foodies say this is one of the best eateries in town to try local staples such as the *masala dosa* (papery lentil-flour pancakes stuffed with seasonal vegetables) and *idlis* (rice cakes) served with coconut chutney.

Café Aramane SOUTH INDIAN $
(Sayyaji Rao Rd, mains ₹40-60; ⊙7.30am-10pm) Yet another of Mysore's august establishments, this busy cafe rolls out steaming breakfast platters for Mysore's office-goers, and welcomes them back in the evenings with aromatic filter coffee and a convoy of delicious snacks.

Café Coffee Day CAFE $
(CCD; Devaraj Urs Rd; snacks ₹60-90; ⊙10am-11pm) Yes, these guys do have a gazillion outlets across India, but few other branches can match this lovely operation in terms of chill factor. The cool terrace sit-out is where you'll find Mysore's college brigade downing their joes with vigour.

Shopping

Mysore is a great place to shop for its famed sandalwood products, silk saris and wooden toys. It is also one of India's major incense-manufacturing centres.

Souvenir and handicraft shops are dotted around Jaganmohan Palace and Dhanvanthri Rd, while silk shops line Devaraj Urs Rd. Look for the butterfly-esque 'Silk Mark' on your purchase; it's an endorsement for quality silk.

Government Silk Factory CLOTHING
(Mananthody Rd, Ashokapuram; ⊙10am-6.30pm Mon-Sat) Given that Mysore's prized silk is made under its very sheds, this is the best and cheapest place to shop for the exclusive textile. Behind the showroom is the factory, where you can drop by between 7.30am and 4pm to see how the fabric is made. There's an **outlet** (⊙10.30am-7.30pm Mon-Sat) on KR Circle as well.

Sandalwood Oil Factory SOUVENIRS
(Ashokapuram; ⊙9.30-11am & 2-4pm Mon-Sat) This is a quality-assured place for sandalwood products such as incense, soap, cosmetic products and the prohibitively expensive pure sandalwood oil (₹1350 for 5ml!). Sandalwood is currently in short supply, so prices may escalate further in future. Guided tours are available to show you around the factory, and explain how the products are made.

Cauvery Arts & Crafts Emporium CLOTHING
(Sayyaji Rao Rd; ⊙10am-7.30pm) Not the cheapest place, but the selection is extensive, the quality is unquestionable and there's no pressure to buy.

Fabindia CLOTHING
(☑4259009; 451 Jhansi Lakshmi Bai Rd, Chamrajpuram; ⊙10am-8pm) A branch of the ever reliable clothing and homewares shop, en route to the silk and sandalwood factories.

Shruthi Musical Works MUSIC STORE
(1189 3rd Cross, Irwin Rd; ⊘10.30am-8pm Mon-Sat) Sells a variety of traditional musical instruments including tabla sets and assorted percussion instruments.

Sapna Book House BOOKSTORE
(1433 Narayan Shastry Rd; ⊘10.30am-8.30pm) A good collections of paperbacks and magazines, along with souvenirs.

ⓘ Information

Internet Access

Benaka Graphics (Sayyaji Rao Rd; per hr ₹20; ⊘10.30am-7.30pm) Internet, printing, image burning and photocopying facilities.

KSE Internet (Hotel Ramanashree Complex; BN Rd; per hr ₹30; ⊘10am-10pm) Fast internet connections.

Left Luggage

The City bus stand's cloakroom, open from 6am to 11pm, costs ₹10 per bag for 12 hours.

Medical Services

Government Hospital (☑4269806; Dhanvanthri Rd) Has a 24-hour pharmacy.

Money

HDFC Bank (Devaraj Urs Rd) ATM.

ICICI Bank (BN Rd) ATM location, below Hotel Pai Vista.

State Bank of Mysore (cnr Irwin & Ashoka Rds; ⊘10.30am-2.30pm & 3-4pm Mon-Fri, 10.30am-12.30pm Sat) Changes cash and travellers cheques.

Thomas Cook (☑2420090; Silver Tower, 9/2 Ashoka Rd; ⊘9.30am-6pm Mon-Sat) For foreign currency.

Photography

Danthi (44 Devaraj Urs Rd; ⊘10am-8pm)

Rekha Colour Lab (142 Dhanvanthri Rd; ⊘9am-9.30pm)

Post

DHL (Jhansi Lakshmi Bai Rd; ⊘9.30am-8.30pm Mon-Sat)

Main post office (cnr Irwin & Ashoka Rds; ⊘10am-6pm Mon-Sat)

Tourist Information

Karnataka Tourism (☑2422096; Old Exhibition Bldg, Irwin Rd; ⊘10am-5.30pm Mon-Sat) Extremely helpful.

KSTDC Transport Office (☑2423652; 2 Jhansi Lakshmi Bai Rd; ⊘8.30am-8.30pm) KSTDC has counters at the train station and Central bus stand, as well as this transport office next to KSTDC Hotel Mayura Hoysala.

ⓘ Getting There & Away

Air

Mysore's new airport had been freshly commissioned during research, with a solitary Kingfisher flight to Bengaluru (one hour) continuing to Chennai (three hours). **Indian Airlines** (☑2426317; Jhansi Lakshmi Bai Rd; ⊘10am-5pm Mon-Sat) has a booking office next to Hotel Mayura Hoysala for flights out of other cities. For booking on other carriers, try **Skyway** (☑2444444; 370/4 Jhansi Lakshmi Bai Rd; ⊘10am-6pm Mon-Sat).

Bus

The **Central bus stand** (BN Rd) handles all KSRTC long-distance buses. The **City bus stand** (Sayyaji Rao Rd) is for city, Srirangapatnam and Chamundi Hill buses. KSRTC bus services from

BUSES FROM MYSORE

DESTINATION	FARE (₹)	DURATION (HR)	FREQUENCY
Bandipur	52 (O)	2	4 daily
Bengaluru	136 (R)/217 (V)	3	every 30min
Channarayapatna	56 (O)	2	hourly
Chennai	829 (V)	12	4 daily
Ernakulam	388 (R)/530 (V)	11	4 daily
Gokarna	323 (O)	12	1 daily
Hassan	76 (O)	3	hourly
Hospet	291 (O)	10	4 daily
Mangalore	252 (R)/350 (V)	7	hourly
Ooty	123 (R)/184 (V)	5	8 daily

O – Ordinary, R – Rajahamsa Semideluxe, V – Airavath AC Volvo

Mysore include those listed in the boxed text p860.

For Belur, Halebid or Sravanabelagola, the usual gateway is Hassan. For Hampi, the best transfer point is Hospet.

The **Private bus stand** (Sayyaji Rao Rd) has services to Hubli, Bijapur, Mangalore, Ooty and Ernakulam. You'll find several ticketing agents around the stand.

Train

From Mysore's railway booking office, buy a ticket on the 6.45am *Chamundi Express* or the 11am *Tippu Express* to Bengaluru (2nd class/chair ₹66/195, three hours). The 2.15 *Shatabdi Express* also connects Bengaluru (chair/executive ₹275/550, two hours) and Chennai (chair/executive ₹695/1315, seven hours) daily except Tuesday. Several passenger trains to Bengaluru (₹35, 3½ hours), stop at Srirangapatnam (₹15, 20 minutes). The 10.15pm *Mysore Dharwad Express* goes to Hubli (sleeper/2AC ₹206/750, 9½ hours).

ⓘ Getting Around

Agencies at hotels and around town rent cabs for about ₹7 per kilometre, with a minimum of 250km per day, plus a daily allowance of ₹150 for the driver.

The flagfall on autorickshaws is ₹15, and ₹7 per kilometre is charged thereafter. Autorickshaws can also be hired along Harsha Rd for a day's sightseeing (₹900).

Around Mysore

SRIRANGAPATNAM

ⓙ 08236

Steeped in bloody history, the fort town of Srirangapatnam, 16km for Mysore, is built on an island straddling the Cauvery River. The seat of Hyder Ali and Tipu Sultan's power, this town was the de facto capital of much of southern India during the 18th century. Srirangapatnam's glory days ended when the British waged an epic war again Tipu Sultan in 1799, when he was defeated and killed. However, the ramparts, battlements and some of the gates of the fort still stand, as do a clutch of monuments.

Close to the bus station is a handsome twin-tower mosque built by the sultan. Within the fort walls are the dungeon where Tipu held British officers captive, and the handsome **Sri Ranganathaswamy Temple** (☉7.30am-1pm & 4-8pm). Srirangapatnam's star attraction, however, is Tipu's summer palace, **Daria Daulat Bagh** (Indian/foreigner

₹5/100; ☉9am-5pm), which lies 1km east of the fort. Built largely out of wood, the palace is notable for the lavish decoration covering every inch of its interiors. The ceilings are embellished with floral designs, while the walls bear murals depicting courtly life and Tipu's campaigns against the British. There's a small museum within, which houses several artefacts including a portrait of Tipu Sultan, aged 30, painted by European artist John Zoffany in 1780.

About 2km further east, the remains of Hyder Ali, his wife and Tipu are housed in the impressive onion-domed **Gumbaz** (admission free; ☉8am-8pm), which stands amid serene gardens. Head 500m east of Gumbaz for the river banks to end your trip with a refreshing **coracle ride** (per boat ₹150, 15 min).

Just 3km upstream, the **Ranganathittu Bird Sanctuary** (Indian/foreigner ₹25/75, camera/video ₹25/100; ☉8.30am-6pm) is on one of three islands in the Cauvery River. Resident storks, ibises, egrets, spoonbills and cormorants are best seen at dawn or late afternoons on a **boat ride** (per person ₹100).

🛏 Sleeping & Eating

Mayura River View   HOTEL **$$**
(ⓙ 252113; d from ₹1750; ❄) How we wish all government hotels were done up like the Mayura River View. Set on a quiet patch of riverbank, its cosy bungalows are custommade for unwinding in the lap of nature. And the **restaurant** (mains ₹90 to ₹120) has a wonderful sit-out from where you can gaze at the river while guzzling beer.

Royal Retreat New Amblee Holiday Resort   HOTEL **$$**
(ⓙ 9845002665; www.ambleeresort.com; d from ₹1200; ❄❇) A menagerie of rabbits, ducks, turkeys and emus welcome you into the Amblee, which offers relatively good accommodation and a swimming pool to splash in. It has a pleasant riverside setting opposite the River View, and a reasonably priced restaurant that doesn't serve booze (although you can whisk it away to your room).

ⓘ Getting There & Away

Take buses 313 or 316 (₹14, one hour) that depart frequently from Mysore's City bus stand. Passenger trains travelling from Mysore to Bengaluru (₹12, 20 minutes) also stop here. The stand for private buses heading to Brindavan

Gardens (₹18, 30 minutes) is just across from Srirangapatnam's main bus stand.

ⓘ Getting Around

The sights are a little spread out, but walking isn't out of the question, especially in winter. For a quicker tour, an autorickshaw from Mysore is about ₹400 (three hours).

BRINDAVAN GARDENS

If you're familiar with Bollywood cinema, these ornamental **gardens** (adult/child ₹20/15, camera/video ₹50/100; ☉8am-8.30pm) might give you a sense of déjà vu – they've indeed been the backdrop for many a gyrating musical number. The best time to visit is in the evening, when the fountains are illuminated and made to dance to popular film tunes.

There's no reason to halt a night in the gardens. For a special experience, however, you might consider checking into the swanky **Royal Orchid Brindavan Garden** (☏9945815566; www.royalorchidhotels.com; s/d incl breakfast from ₹4499/4999; ❋☎❄), an enormous luxury hotel perched atop a hillock overlooking the gardens. The rooms here are lavishly outfitted, and the strategically-located Elephant Bar is a vantage point from where to view the light-and-sound shows while sipping on your poison.

The gardens are 19km northwest of Mysore. One of the KSTDC tours stops here, and buses 301, 304, 305, 306 and 365 depart from Mysore's City bus stand hourly (₹15, 45 minutes).

MELKOTE

Life in the devout Hindu town of Melkote, about 50km north of Mysore, revolves around the atmospheric 12th-century **Cheluvanarayana Temple** (Raja St; ☉8am-1pm & 5-8pm), with its rose-coloured *gopuram* (gateway tower) and ornately carved pillars. Get a workout on the hike up to the hilltop **Yoganarasimha Temple**, which offers fine views of the surrounding hills. The town comes alive for the **Vairamudi Festival** in March or April.

Three KSRTC buses shuttle daily between Mysore and Melkote (₹45, 1½ hours).

SOMNATHPUR

The astonishingly beautiful **Keshava Temple** (Indian/foreigner ₹5/100; ☉8.30am-5.30pm) is one of the finest examples of Hoysala architecture, on par with the masterpieces of Belur and Halebid. Built in 1268, this star-shaped temple, 33km from Mysore, is adorned with superb stone sculptures depicting various scenes from the Ramayana, Mahabharata and Bhagavad Gita, and the life and times of the Hoysala kings.

On a tree in the temple grounds there's a red postbox, where prestamped mail posted by you will be collected by the local post office and marked with a special postmark bearing the temple's image – this is a great memento to send back home.

Somnathpur is 12km south of Bannur and 10km north of Tirumakudal Narsipur. Take one of the half-hourly buses from Mysore to either village (₹15, 30 minutes) and change there.

WORTH A TRIP

GO FISH

Game for some fishy gambolling? Then you're in luck. About 75km from Mysore, strung along the densely forested banks of the quiet-flowing Cauvery River, are the picturesque fishing camps of **Bheemeshwari**, **Galibore** and **Doddamakali**, teeming with their resident populations of carp, catfish and the venerable mahseer. Anglers are fast converging from around the world to hook these 45kg-plus beasts who (going by the trophy shots displayed in the dining hall) often seem to match their human captors in size. All fishing is on a catch-and-release policy. There's some equipment on hire, but get your own tackles, if possible.

Non-anglers, meanwhile, can engage in kayaking, coracle rides, biking or ayurveda sessions. Of the three camps, Bheemeshwari is the most developed in terms of facilities, and more easily accessible.

Accommodation is in a choice of ecofriendly cottages (per person incl full board Indian/foreigner from ₹2500/€70) operated by **Jungle Lodges & Resorts** (Map p844; ☏080-25597944; www.junglelodges.com; Shrungar Shopping Complex, MG Rd, Bengaluru; ☉10am-5.30pm Mon-Sat). Book in Bengaluru or online.

The best way to reach the camps is by taxi. Drive past Malavalli, before turning right at Sathanur. It's 23km from here to Bheemeshwari. Resort jeeps connect the other camps from here.

SIVASAMUDRAM

About 60km east of Mysore is Sivasamu-dram, home to the twin waterfalls of Bara-chukki and Gaganachukki. The site of In-dia's first hydroelectric project (1902), it's a place where you can spend a quiet time while indulging in natural bounties.

A few kilometres away is Hebbani village, where the affable Hatherell couple and their 10 dogs run the relaxing **Georgia Sunshine Village** (☑9448110660; www.georgiasunshine. com; d incl full board from ₹5000; ❄❄), a superb family getaway with accommodation in cosy bungalows, a sparkling swimming pool and delicious homemade food. Treks and fishing trips can be arranged on request.

Frequent buses run from Mysore (₹30, one hour) to Malavalli, 14km away. The Ha-therells can arrange an autorickshaw pick-up for ₹150. Call well in advance.

Hassan

☑08172 / POP 133,200

With a good range of hotels, a railhead and other conveniences, Hassan is a handy base for exploring Belur (38km), Halebid (33km) and Sravanabelagola (48km). Situated close to Mysore and Bengaluru, it's a bustling town with friendly people.

🛏 Sleeping

TOP CHOICE ⟋ Hoysala Village Resort HOTEL $$$
(☑256764; www.hoysalavillageresorts.com; Belur Rd; cottage incl full board ₹6300; ❄❄) Located 6km from town on the road to Belur, this fantastic getaway is set amid a patch of manicured gardens, tucked around which are comfy cottages with large windows looking onto palms and hedges. There's a treehouse where you can laze away the eve-ning, beer in hand, or flex your pectorals in the aqua-blue pool. And the food at the **restaurant** adjoining the reception area is scrummy to boot. The resort also has an ayurvedic massage centre; sessions kick off from around ₹700.

Hotel Suvarna Regency HOTEL $$
(☑266774; www.suvarnaregencyhotel.com; BM Rd; d from ₹750; ❄@) This place, just south of Gandhi Sq, is frequented by business people, and is one of Hassan's trusted oldies. It's of-ten bulk-booked by organisers of conferences and conventions, so call early. The rooms are comfy, though dated in terms of decor.

Jewel Rock HOTEL $
(☑261048; BM Rd; d from ₹700; ❄) Close to the train station, this place is an absolute steal. The spacious rooms, with floral curtains, are comfortable and well-kept. Raucous private parties are often thrown by locals in the banquet hall downstairs; hopefully, you'll be checking in on a quieter day.

Hotel Hassan Ashhok HOTEL $$
(☑268731; www.hassanashok.com; BM Rd; s/d from ₹3000/3350; ❄❄) Clearly the classiest of Hassan's city options, this elegantly de-signed hotel offers you all the requisite luxe features, baskets full of herbal toiletries in the showers and plenty of fluffy white pil-lows to crash on. The **restaurant** works up a good range of Indian dishes, including a jumbo kebab platter (₹350).

Hotel Sri Krishna HOTEL $
(☑263240; BM Rd; s/d ₹350/725, d with AC ₹975; ❄) Hugely popular with local tourists, this place has biggish rooms done up in red-and-black checks, and large windows. There's a quality veg **restaurant** (mains ₹40 to ₹60) downstairs. Book well in advance.

Eating

Suvarna Gate MULTICUISINE $$
(Hotel Suvarna Regency, BM Rd; mains ₹90-130; ☺noon-3.30pm & 6.30-11.30pm) Located to the rear of Hotel Suvarna Regency, this classy eatery tosses up some excellent Indian, Chi-nese and Continental mainstays – the chick-en tandoori masala is particularly delicious.

Mayur INDIAN $$
(Hotel Jewel Rock, BM Rd; mains ₹80-110; ☺noon-3pm & 7-11pm) Hungry crowds flock to this eatery every evening for its lip-smacking South Indian as well as North Indian nonveg fare. The staff are patient and polite.

Hotel GRR SOUTH INDIAN $
(Bus Stand Rd; mains ₹30-60; ☺11am-11pm) Top-of-the-line Andhra-style thalis (₹35) and a popular chicken biryani (₹60) personify this grubby joint next to the bus stand.

❶ Information

The train station is 2km east of town on Bengaluru-Mangalore (BM) Rd. The Central bus stand is on the corner of AVK College and Bus Stand Rds. The helpful **tourist office** (☑268862; AVK College Rd; ☺10am-5.30pm Mon-Sat) is 100m east of the bus stand. SBI and HDFC Bank have ATMs on BM Rd, but change foreign cur-rency in Bengaluru or Mysore. There's an internet cafe (per hr ₹20) below Hotel Suvarna Regency.

ℹ Getting There & Away

Bus

Starting from 6am, buses leave the Central bus stand hourly for Halebid (₹18, one hour) and Belur (₹23, one hour). The last buses back from both places are around 8pm.

To get to Sravanabelagola, you must take one of the many buses to Channarayapatna (₹25, 45 minutes) and change there.

There are frequent services to Mysore (₹76, three hours), Bengaluru (semideluxe/deluxe ₹179/246, four hours) and Mangalore (₹166, five hours).

Taxi

Taxi drivers hang out on AVK College Rd, north of the bus stand. A day tour of Belur and Halebid or Sravanabelagola will cost you about ₹1000. Firmly set the price before departure.

Train

From the well-organised **train station**, three passenger trains head to Mysore daily (2nd class ₹120, three hours). For Bengaluru, take the 1.30am Yeshvantpur Express (sleeper ₹140, 5½ hours).

Belur & Halebid

☑ 08177 / ELEV 968M

Along with Somnathpur, the Hoysala temples at Halebid (also known as Halebeedu) and Belur (also called Beluru) are the apex of one of the most artistically exuberant periods of ancient Hindu cultural development. Architecturally, they are South India's answer to Khajuraho in Madhya Pradesh and Konark near Puri in Odisha (Orissa).

Only 16km lie between Belur and Halebid, and the towns are connected by frequent shuttle buses from 6.30am to 7pm (₹20, 40 minutes). See p863 for details of buses to/from Hassan. To get to Hampi, it's best to return to Bengaluru via Hassan and take an overnight bus to Hospet.

BELUR

The Channakeshava Temple (Temple Rd; ☉dawn-dusk) was commissioned in 1116 to commemorate the Hoysalas' victory over the neighbouring Cholas. It took more than a century to build, and is currently the only one among the three major Hoysala sites still in daily use – try to be there for the ritual *puja* ceremonies at 9am, 3pm and 7.30pm. Some parts of the temple, such as the exterior lower friezes, were not sculpted to completion and are thus less elaborate than those of the other Hoysala temples.

However, the work higher up is unsurpassed in detail and artistry, and is a glowing tribute to human skill. Particularly intriguing are the angled bracket figures depicting women in ritual dancing poses. While the front of the temple is reserved for images depicting erotic sections from the Kama Sutra, the back is strictly for gods. The roof of the inner sanctum is held up by rows of exquisitely sculpted pillars, no two of which are identical in design.

Scattered around the temple complex are other smaller temples, a marriage hall which is still used and the seven-storey *gopuram*, which has sensual sculptures explicitly portraying the activities of dancing girls.

Guides can be hired for ₹150; they help to bring some of the sculptural detail to life.

Hotel Mayura Velapuri (☑222209; Kempegowda Rd; d from ₹900; ❄), a state-run hotel gleaming with post-renovation glory, is located on the way to the temple, and is the best place to camp in Belur. The restaurant-bar serves a variety of Indian dishes and snacks (₹70 to ₹90) to go with beer.

Near Kempegowda's statue is **Shankar Hotel** (Temple Rd; mains ₹35; ☉7am-9.30pm), a busy place serving fine South Indian thalis, *masala dosas*, Indian sweets, snacks and drinks.

HALEBID

Construction of the **Hoysaleswara Temple** (☉dawn-dusk), Halebid's claim to fame, began around 1121 and went on for more than 80 years. It was never completed, but nonetheless stands today as a masterpiece of Hoysala architecture. The interior of its inner sanctum, chiselled out of black stone, is marvellous. On the outside, the temple's richly sculpted walls are covered with a flurry of Hindu deities, sages, stylised animals and friezes depicting the life of the Hoysala rulers. A huge statue of Nandi (Shiva's bull) sits to the left of the main temple, facing the inner sanctum. Guides are available to show you around for ₹150; the shoekeeper expects a wee tip for holding your shoes when you enter the temple.

The temple is set in large, well-tended gardens, adjacent to which is a small **museum** (admission ₹5; ☉10am-5pm Sat-Thu) housing a collection of sculptures.

If the pesky touts get on your nerves, take some time out to visit the nearby, smaller **Kedareswara Temple**, or a little-visited enclosure containing three **Jain** temples about 500m away, which also have fine carvings.

If you're stuck in Halebid for the night, the tidy rooms at **Hotel Mayura Shanthala** (☑273224; d ₹350), set around a leafy garden opposite the temple complex, is an OK fallback option.

Sravanabelagola

☑08176

Atop the bald rock of Vindhyagiri Hill, the 17.5m-high statue of the Jain deity Gomateshvara (Bahubali), said to be the world's tallest monolithic statue, is visible long before you reach the pilgrimage town of Sravanabelagola. Viewing the statue close up is the main reason for heading to this sedate town, whose name means 'Monk of the White Pond'.

◉ Sights

Gomateshvara Statue   MONUMENT
(Bahubali; ⊙6.30am-6.30pm) A steep climb up 614 steps takes you to the top of Vindhyagiri Hill, the summit of which is lorded over by the towering naked statue of Gomateshvara. Commissioned by a military commander in the service of the Ganga king Rachamalla and carved out of a single piece of granite by the sculptor Aristenemi in AD 981, its serenity and simplicity is in stark contrast to the Hoysala sites at Belur and Halebid.

Bahubali was the son of emperor Vrishabhadeva, who later became the first Jain *tirthankar* (revered teacher) Adinath. Embroiled in fierce competition with his brother Bharatha to succeed his father, Bahubali realised the futility of material gains and renounced his kingdom. As a recluse, he meditated in complete stillness in the forest until he attained enlightenment. His lengthy meditative spell is denoted by vines curling around his legs and an ant hill at his feet.

Leave shoes at the foot of the hill, but it's fine to wear socks. If you want it easy, you can hire a *dholi* (portable chair) with bearers for ₹400, from 6.30am to 11.30pm and 3.30pm to 6pm.

Every 12 years, millions flock here to attend the **Mastakabhisheka** ceremony, when the statue is dowsed in holy waters, pastes, powders, precious metals and stones. The next ceremony is slated for 2018.

Temples   JAIN TEMPLES
Apart from the Bahubali statue, there are several interesting Jain temples in town. The **Chandragupta Basti** (Chandragupta Com-

munity; ⊙6am-6pm), on Chandragiri Hill opposite Vindhyagiri, is believed to have been built by Emperor Ashoka. The **Bhandari Basti** (Bhandari Community; ⊙6am-6pm), in the southeast corner of town, is Sravanabelagola's largest temple. Nearby, **Chandranatha Basti** (Chandranatha Community; ⊙6am-6pm) has well-preserved paintings depicting Jain tales.

🛏 Sleeping & Eating

The local Jain organisation **SDJMI** (☑257258; d/tr ₹135/160) handles bookings for its 15 guesthouses. The office is behind the Vidyananda Nilaya Dharamsala, past the post office.

Hotel Raghu   HOTEL $
(☑257238; d from ₹500; ▣) This is the only privately owned hotel around, and offers basic but clean rooms. The real bonus is its vegetarian **restaurant** (⊙6am-9pm) downstairs, which works up an awesome veg thali (₹50), served with care by the staff and sometimes the owner himself.

❶ Getting There & Away

There are no direct buses from Sravanabelagola to Hassan or Belur – you must go to Channarayapatna (₹15, 20 minutes) and catch an onward connection there. Four daily buses run direct to Bengaluru (₹92, 3½ hours) and Mysore (₹56, 2½ hours). Long-distance buses clear out before 3pm. If you miss these, catch a local bus to Channarayapatna and change there.

Nilgiri Biosphere Reserve

The pristine forests of the **Nilgiri Biosphere Reserve** are one of India's best-preserved wilderness, and span about 5500 sq km across the states of Karnataka, Kerala and Tamil Nadu. Human access to the reserve is through a number of national parks, such as Wayanad (see p972) in Kerala and Mudumalai (see p1059) in Tamil Nadu. In Karnataka, the best access points are Bandipur and Nagarhole, with the super-green forested region around the Kabini Lake boasting some of the top wildlife camps in the region.

Home to over 100 species of mammals and some 350 species of birds, the reserve is also a natural habitat for the prized but endangered Bengal tigers and Asiatic elephants; more than a fifth of the world's population of jumbos live here.

BANDIPUR NATIONAL PARK

About 80km south of Mysore on the Ooty road, the **Bandipur National Park** (Indian/foreigner ₹75/175, video ₹100) covers 880 sq km and was once the Mysore maharajas' private wildlife reserve. The park is noted for its herds of gaurs (Indian bison), chitals (spotted deer), sambars, panthers, sloth bears and langurs, as well as tigers and elephants. However, unrestricted traffic hurtling down the highway cutting through the forest has made animals wary of venturing close to safari areas.

Brief **elephant rides** (per person ₹100) are available for a minimum of four people. For a **safari** (per person Indian/foreigner ₹75/175; ☉6.30am, 8.30am, 3.30pm & 5.30pm) there's the forest department's rumbling minibus, noisy enough to put off shy creatures. Resort vehicles are permitted to go into the forest; they are quieter and thus a better bet.

🛏 Sleeping & Eating

🏕 **Bandipur Safari Lodge**   CAMPGROUND **$$**
(Mysore-Ooty Rd; person incl full board Indian/foreigner ₹3000/€70; ❄) Located on the fringes of the park is this largish government-owned ecotourism camp that offers luxurious but low-impact accommodation in well-maintained cottages. Rates include a safari, guided nature walks, entry fees and camera fees, and there are good Indian and Continental buffets for meals.

Tusker Trails   CAMPGROUND **$$**
(☎080-23618024, 09845326467; per person incl full board Indian/foreigner ₹3000/4200; ☀) A lovely camp located on the eastern edge of the park, this place provides accommodation in simple huts backed by the forest. There's good food and an inviting pool. Rates include one daily safari, trekking with local guides, wildlife documentary screenings and a bonfire.

❶ Getting There & Away

Buses between Mysore and Ooty will drop you at Bandipur (₹55, three hours). You can also book an overnight taxi from Mysore (about ₹2000).

NAGARHOLE NATIONAL PARK

West of the Kabini River is the 643-sq-km wildlife sanctuary of **Nagarhole National Park** (Rajiv Gandhi National Park; Indian/foreigner ₹50/150), pronounced *nag*-ar-hole-eh. The lush forests here are home to tigers, leopards, elephants, gaurs, muntjacs (barking deer), wild dogs, bonnet macaques and common langurs. The park can remain closed for long stretches between July and October, when the rains transform the forests into a giant slush-pit.

The park's main entrance is 93km southwest of Mysore. If you're not staying at a resort nearby, the only way to see the park is on the forest department's bus **tour** (per person ₹100; ☉6-8am & 3-5.30pm). The best time to view wildlife is during summer (April to May), though winter (November to February) is kinder.

Decent sleeping options are limited in Nagarhole; you're better off in Kabini Lake. An OK place to camp is **Jungle Inn** (☎08222-246022; www.jungleinn.in; Hunsur-Nagarhole Rd; per head incl full board Indian/foreigner from ₹1800/US$60) about 35km from the park reception on the Hunsur road. With a welcoming atmosphere, evening campfires and simple, clean rooms, it also serves good organic food. Rates for safaris are extra.

KABINI LAKE

About 70km south of Mysore lies **Kabini Lake**, a giant forest-edged reservoir formed by the damming of the Kabini River. Endowed with rich and unspoilt vegetation, the area has rapidly grown to become one of Karnataka's best wildlife getaways. Positioned midway between the animal corridors of Bandipur and Nagarhole, the Kabini forests are also the habitat for a large variety of wildlife, and give you the chance to view the animals up close.

Tourism around Kabini is managed by a few resorts, most of which are founded on ecofriendly principles. Jungle safaris and other activities such as boat rides and birdwatching are conducted by the resorts, generally between 6.30am to 9.30am, and 4pm to 7pm.

🛏 Sleeping & Eating

TOP CHOICE **Kabini River Lodge**   CAMPGROUND **$$$**
(☎08228-264402; per person (Indian) incl full board tents/r/cottages ₹3750/4500/5250, per foreigner (flat rate) €120; ❄) Rated consistently among the world's best wildlife getaways, this fascinating government-run luxury ecocamp is located on the serene, tree-lined grounds of the former Mysore maharaja's hunting lodge beside Kabini Lake. Promising an opulent yet idyllic experience, this showcase resort has hosted countless celebrities (Goldie Hawn is apparently an ardent fan) from around the world. Manned by an excellent staff, it offers accommodation in a choice of large canvas tents, regular rooms

and cottages. Rates include safaris, boat rides and forest entry fees. Book through **Jungle Lodges & Resorts Ltd** (Map p844; ☑080-25597944; www.junglelodges.com; Shrungar Shopping Complex, MG Rd, Bengaluru; ⊙10am-5.30pm Mon-Sat).

☑ **Cicada Kabini**　　　CAMPGROUND **$$$**
(☑080-41152200,9945602305;www.cicadaresorts.com; d incl full board ₹13,000; ❄@☎) Another highly recommended ecoresort, this well-conceived luxury option brings a dash of contemporary chic to the lakeside. The resort devotes itself to minimising environmental depletion while promoting rural empowerment. Rates are for accommodation and meals only; safaris (Indian/foreigner ₹750/1000) and kayaks and pedal boats (₹100) are extra.

ℹ **Getting There & Away**
A few buses depart daily from Mysore and can drop you at Kabini village. However, it's better to have your own taxi. Enquire with the resorts while making a booking.

Kodagu (Coorg) Region

Nestled amid ageless hills that line the southernmost edge of Karnataka is the luscious Kodagu (Coorg) region, gifted with emerald landscapes and acres of plantations. A major centre for coffee and spice production, this rural expanse is also home to the unique Kodava race, believed to have descended from migrating Persians and Kurds or perhaps Greeks left behind from Alexander the Great's armies. The uneven terrain and cool climate make it a fantastic area for trekking, birdwatching or lazily ambling down little-trod paths winding around carpeted hills. All in all, Kodagu is rejuvenation guaranteed.

The best season for trekking is October to March. Guides are available for hire and can arrange food, transport and accommodation; see p866. Treks can last from a day to a week; the most popular routes are to the peaks of Tadiyendamol (1745m) and Pushpagiri (1712m), and to smaller Kotebetta. Adventure activities are conducted between November and May; the rest of the year is too wet for traipsing around.

Kodagu was a state in its own right until 1956, when it merged with Karnataka. The region's chief town and transport hub is Madikeri, but for an authentic Kodagu experience, you have to venture into the plantations. Avoid weekends, when places can quickly get filled up by weekenders from Bengaluru.

MADIKERI (MERCARA)
☑08272 / POP 32,400 / ELEV 1525M
Also known as Mercara, this congested market town is spread out along a series of ridges. The only reason for coming here is to organise treks or sort out the practicalities of travel. The Huthri festival, which falls sometime between November and December, is a nice time to visit.

In the chaotic centre around the KSRTC and private-bus stands, you'll find most hotels and restaurants.

◉ **Sights**
Madikeri's **fort**, now the municipal headquarters, was built in 1812 by Raja Lingarajendra II. There's an old church here, housing a quirky **museum** (admission free; ⊙10am-5.30pm Tue-Sun) displaying dusty, poorly labelled artefacts. Panoramic views of the hills and valleys can be savoured from **Raja's Seat** (MG Rd; ⊙5.30am-7.30pm). Behind are gardens, a toy-train line for kids and a tiny Kodava-style **temple**.

On the way to **Abbi Falls**, a pleasant 7km hike from the town centre, visit the quietly beautiful **Raja's Tombs**, better known as Gaddige. An autorickshaw costs about ₹200 return.

🏃 **Activities**
Trekking　　　　　　　　　　　TREKKING
A trekking guide is essential for navigating the labyrinth of forest tracks. Most of the estates in Kodagu also offer trekking programs.

Veteran guides Raja Shekhar and Ganesh at **V-Track** (☑229102, 229974; Crown Towers, College Rd; ⊙10am-2pm & 4.30-8pm Mon-Sat) can arrange one- to 10-day treks including guide, accommodation and food. Rates are around ₹750 per person per day, and can vary depending on the duration and number of people. For long treks, trips on obscure routes or big groups, it's best to give a week's notice.

Coorg Trails (☑9886665459; www.coorgtrails.com; Main Rd; ⊙9am-8.30pm) is another recommended outfit that can arrange day treks around Madikeri for ₹500 per person, and a 22km trek to Kotebetta, including an overnight stay in a village, for ₹1500 per person.

☑ **Coorg Planters' Camp** OUTDOOR ADVENTURE
(☑080-41159270; www.coorgplanterscamp.com) Located in Kirudale, 25km from Madikeri, Coorg Planters' Camp is a fantastic ecoresort

featuring tented accommodation, which offers activities such as coffee plantation tours, trekking, birdwatching and nature walks through dense forests. However, large-scale renovation was on during research, and it appeared like the resort would only open sometime in early 2012. Hopefully, the wait will have been worth it.

Ayurjeevan
AYURVEDA

(Kohinoor Rd; ◷9am-6pm) Ayurjeevan, a short walk from ICICI Bank, offers a whole range of rejuvenating ayurvedic packages, with 30-minute sessions kicking off at around ₹400.

🛏 Sleeping

Many hotels reduce their rates in the low season (June to September); all of those listed below have hot water, at least in the morning, and 24-hour checkout.

Hotel Mayura Valley View
HOTEL $$

(☑228387; near Raja's Seat; d incl breakfast from ₹1200; ❄) Despite being located out of town on a secluded hilltop past Raja's Seat, this is clearly Madikeri's best sleeping option. It has large bright rooms with fantastic views of the valley outside its floor-to-ceiling windows. Service – though patchy – could be bettered for a small tip. The all-new restaurant-bar (mains ₹70 to ₹100, open 7am to 10pm) with a terrace overlooking the valley is the coolest place for a drink.

Hotel Hill View
HOTEL $$

(☑223808; Hill Rd; d from ₹950) Situated at a far corner of the new town, this cosy hotel has small but well-kept rooms. The wall shades and the pruned hedges in the tiny sit-outs are perfectly colour coordinated with the green hills that overlook the rooms. Tours and bonfires can be arranged on request.

Hotel Chitra
HOTEL $

(☑225372; www.hotelchitra.net; School Rd; d from ₹600) A short walk off Madikeri's main traffic intersection is this austere hotel, providing low-cost, no-frills yet good-value rooms. The sheets are clean and service is efficient, which – coupled with its mid-town location – makes it a good budget option.

Hotel Cauvery
HOTEL $

(☑225492; School Rd; s/d ₹350/800) This geriatric hotel has just been given a facelift, and promises a rather unique mix of hospitality. The rooms are the same old holes, with a vivid sapphire blue livening up most walls. There's printed floral upholstery on the sturdy beds, while the corridors outside have plastic creepers lining them. If kitsch is your thing, this might be your kind of place.

Hotel Coorg International
HOTEL $$$

(☑228071; www.coorginternational.com; Convent Rd; s/d incl half-board from ₹3500/4500; ❄☀) Madikeri's classiest option boasts a clean pool, a casual bar, a good multicuisine restaurant, a health club and – most importantly – comfortable rooms with bright upholstery and large windows. Rates include fixed-menu breakfast and dinner and snacks through the day.

🍴 Eating

Coorg Cuisinette
INDIAN $

(Main Rd; mains ₹70-90; ◷noon-4pm & 6.30-10pm) Climb two flights up a commercial building by the main road to feast on endless Kodava specialities at this eatery. Some unique local dishes, such as *pandhi barthadh* (pork dry fry) and *kadambuttu* (rice dumplings) can make your day at the first bite.

Hotel Capitol
INDIAN $

(School Rd; mains ₹70-90; ◷7am-9.30pm) Don't mind the shabby interiors – the locals certainly don't. All they care about is the great food that comes out of its kitchen, including the flavourful and spicy *pandhi* (pork) curry, best had with a pint of cold beer.

Athithi
SOUTH INDIAN $

(mains ₹30-50; ◷7am-10pm) Lap it all up like a local at this busy pedestrian eatery, which serves a hot and tasty veg thali (₹45), followed by fruit salads, juices and shakes.

Popular Guru Prasad
SOUTH INDIAN $

(Main Rd; mains ₹30-40; ◷7am-10pm) A hearty range of vegie options, including a value-for-money veg thali (₹40) and breakfast snacks are ever popular with diners here.

ℹ Information

A semi-functional **KSTDC Office** (☑228580; near Raja's Seat; ◷10am-5.30pm Mon-Sat) offers basic tourist information about the region. If you need to change money, try **State Bank of India** (☑229959; College Rd; ◷10.30am-5.30pm Mon-Fri). There's an internet cafe on Kohinoor Rd, opposite Ayurjeevan.

ℹ Getting There & Away

Seven deluxe buses a day depart from the **KSRTC bus stand** for Bengaluru (₹355, six hours), stopping in Mysore (₹165, three hours) en route. Deluxe buses go to Mangalore (₹170, three hours, three daily), while frequent ordinary buses head to Hassan (₹80, three hours) and Shimoga (₹175, eight hours).

❶ Getting Around

Madikeri is a small town easy to negotiate on foot. For excursions around the region, several places rent out motorcycles for around ₹350 a day, with an initial refundable deposit of ₹500. Try **Spice's Mall** (opposite KSRTC bus stand) or **Coorg the Guide** (Chethana Complex). Carry your driver's licence, tank up on petrol and off you go!

THE PLANTATIONS

Spread around Madikeri are Kodagu's quaint and leafy spice and coffee plantations. Numerous estates here offer homestays, ranging from basic to quite luxurious, while high-end resorts have begun to spring up recently. The following are our pick of places within easy reach of Madikeri. Unless otherwise mentioned, rates include meals and trekking guides. Advance bookings should be made. Some options remain closed during the monsoons. Most arrange transport to/from Madikeri; enquire while booking.

Green Hills Estate HERITAGE HOTEL **$$**
(✆08274-254790; www.neemranahotels.com; Virajpet; r incl breakfast from ₹3000) Coorg's venerable old lady, carrying a burden of heritage on its back. A quaint planter's bungalow designed by a Swiss architect, this estate sits amid emerald plantations halfway between Madikeri and Kakkabe, with an air of nostalgia perpetually hanging heavy within its portals. Stacks of family memorabilia fill up its rosewood panelled interiors, and the rooms have quirky names such as Lord Jim and

❶ SPICE OF LIFE

If you have space in your bag, remember to pick up some local spices and natural produce from Madikeri's main market. There's a whole range of spices on offer at the shops lining the streets, including vanilla, nutmeg, lemongrass, pepper and cardamom, as well as the unbranded aromatic coffee that comes in from plantations. Look out for fruit juices and squashes, homemade wines, bottles of fresh wild honey sourced from the forests and packets of ready-made curry masala to flavour your dishes back home. Most items cost between ₹80 to ₹200.

Lady Madcap, supposedly named after racing thoroughbreds once owned by the planter's family. Lunch and dinner are ₹350 each.

Rainforest Retreat HOMESTAY **$$**
(✆08272-265636; www.rainforesttours.com; Galibeedu; s/d incl full board from ₹1500/2000) A nature-soaked NGO and refuge located on an organic plantation, the Rainforest Retreat devotes itself to exploring organic and ecofriendly ways of life. Organic farming, sustainable agriculture and waste management are catchphrases here, and the hosts (who are a font of regional knowledge) can sufficiently enlighten you about their progressive projects through your stay. Accommodation is in tents and eco-chic cottages with solar power. Activities include plantation tours, birdwatching and treks, among others.

Golden Mist HOMESTAY **$$**
(✆08272-265629; www.golden-mist.net; Galibeedu; per person incl full board from ₹1500) A German-owned organic plantation, this is one of the nicest options near Madikeri town. Choose between its loft-style family cottage or individual rooms, and treat yourself to some fantastic rustic veg and nonveg food made from the farm's organic produce. Similar in atmosphere to Rainforest Retreat, it offers nature walks and plantation tours.

Alath-Cad Estate Bungalow HOMESTAY **$$**
(✆08274-252190; www.alathcadcoorg.com; Ammathi; d incl breakfast from ₹2300) A family estate set on a 26-hectare coffee plantation 28km from Madikeri, this is another good place to yield to unadulterated nature. Activities include plantation tours, trekking, fishing, birdwatching and even cooking classes. Accommodation is in simple but snugly done-up cottages, and there's a gracious family playing host.

Kadkani HOTEL **$$$**
(✆08274-254186; www.kadkani.com; Ammathi; d incl full board from ₹6500; ❄☀) An ultraluxurious retreat nestled in a dale amid silent forests by the Cauvery River, Kadkani effortlessly matches the best of modern comforts and rustic charm in its classy and plush ecocottages. An excellent place to unwind in style, with a 9-hole golf course and other activities such as river crossing, rafting and trekking thrown in. The evenings are reserved for listening to the cicadas.

KAKKABE
☎08272

About 40km from Madikeri, the village of Kakkabe is an ideal base to plan an assault on Kodagu's highest peak, Tadiyendamol. At the bottom of the summit, 3km from Kakkabe, is the picturesque **Nalakunad Palace** (admission free; ☉9am-5pm), the restored hunting lodge of a Kodagu king dating from 1794. Within walking distance are several excellent places to camp.

Misty Woods (☑238561; www.coorgmisty. com; cottages from ₹3500), immediately uphill from Nalakunad Palace across a cascading waterfall, aptly complements the dreamy landscape that surrounds it. The tiled red-brick cottages adhering to *vastu shastra* (ancient science similar to Feng Shui) norms are both comfortable and stylish. Meals are extra.

Honey Valley Estate (☑238339; www. honeyvalleyindia.in; d from ₹800) is a wonderful place 1250m above sea level where you can wake to a chirpy dawn and cool, fresh air. The owners' friendliness, ecomindedness and scrumptious organic food make things even better. Advance bookings are essential.

Regular buses run to Kakkabe from Madikeri (₹25, 1½ hours) and from Virajpet (₹18, one hour).

DUBARE FOREST RESERVE
En route to Kushalnagar, Kodagu's second-largest town, is the Dubare Forest Reserve on the banks of the Cauvery River, where a team of elephants retired from forest department work live on pension. Cross the river (₹25) to participate in an **elephant interaction program** (Indian/foreigner ₹270/550; ☉8.30-10.30am), when you can bathe, feed and then ride the jumbos.

Bookings can be made through **Jungle Lodges & Resorts Ltd** (Map p844; ☑080-25597944; www.junglelodges.com; Shrungar Shopping Complex, MG Rd, Bengaluru; ☉10am-5.30pm Mon-Sat), which also runs the reserve's rustic but good **Dubare Elephant Camp** (☑9449599755; per person incl full board Indian/foreigner ₹2400/€70). Rates include the elephant-interaction program.

White-water rafting (per person ₹400) is also run from here, over an 8km stretch that features rapids up to grade IV.

BYLAKUPPE
☎08223

Tiny Bylakuppe, 5km southeast of Kushalnagar, was among the first refugee camps set up in South India to house thousands of Tibetans who fled from Tibet following the 1959 Chinese invasion. Comprising several clusters of settlements amid 1200 hectares of rolling sugarcane fields that rustle in the breeze, it has all the sights and sounds of a Tibetan colony, with resident maroon-and-yellow-robed monks and locals selling Tibetan food and handicrafts. The atmosphere is heart-warmingly welcoming. The settlement is also home to much festivity during the Tibetan New Year celebrations.

Foreigners are not allowed to stay overnight in Bylakuppe without a Protected Area Permit (PAP) from the Ministry of Home Affairs in Delhi. Contact the **Tibet Bureau Office** (☑26474798, 26439745; 10B Ring Rd, Lajpat Nagar IV, New Delhi) for details.

The area's highlight is the **Namdroling Monastery** (www.palyul.org), home to the jaw-droppingly spectacular **Golden Temple** (Padmasambhava Buddhist Vihara; ☉7am-8pm), presided over by an 18m-high gold-plated Buddha. The temple is at its dramatic best when school is in session and it rings out with gongs, drums and chanting of hundreds of young novices. You're welcome to sit and meditate; look for the small blue guest cushions lying around. The **Zangdogpalri Temple** (☉7am-8pm), a similarly ornate affair, is next door.

Opposite the Golden Temple is a shopping centre, where you'll find the simple **Paljor Dhargey Ling Guest House** (☑258686; pdguesthouse@yahoo.com; d from ₹280).

In the same shopping centre is **Shanti Family Restaurant** (mains ₹50-70; ☉7am-9.30pm), offering a decent range of Indian meals and Tibetan dishes such as *momos* (dumplings) and *thukpa* (noodle soup).

Autorickshaws (shared/solo ₹10/50) ply to Bylakuppe from Kushalnagar. Buses frequently do the 34km run to Kushalnagar from Madikeri (₹30, 1½ hour) and Hassan (₹86, four hours). Most buses on the Mysore–Madikeri route stop at Kushalnagar.

KARNATAKA COAST

Mangalore
☎0824 / POP 539,300

Relaxed Mangalore sits at the estuaries of the picturesque Netravathi and Gurupur Rivers on the Arabian Sea coast. A major pit stop on international trade routes since the 6th century AD, it's the largest city on Karnataka's shoreline, and a nice place to break long-haul journeys along the western seaboard, or branch inland towards Bengaluru.

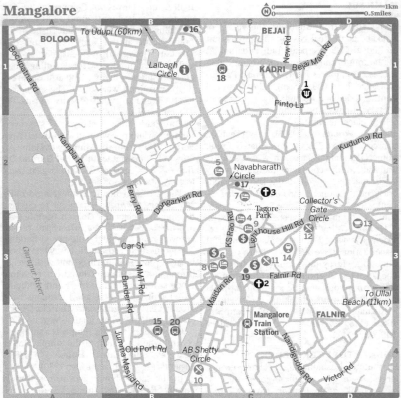

Once the main port of Hyder Ali's kingdom, Mangalore now ships out a bulk of the region's spice, coffee and cashew crops from the modern port, 10km north of the city. The city has a pleasant cosmopolitan air and, with a sprinkling of merry pubs and restaurants, makes for a relaxing stay.

Mangalore is hilly, with winding, disorienting and frenzied streets. Luckily, most hotels and restaurants, the bus stand and the train station are centrally located. The KSRTC bus stand is 3km to the north.

◉ Sights

Ullal Beach   BEACH
The ace up Mangalore's sleeve is serene Ullal Beach, a stretch of dazzling golden sands about an hour's drive south of town. It's best enjoyed from Summer Sands Beach Resort. An autorickshaw is ₹200 one way, or the frequent bus 44A (₹10) from the City bus stand will drop you right outside the gate.

St Aloysius College Chapel   CHURCH
(Lighthouse Hill; ⊙8.30am-6pm Mon-Sat, 10am-noon & 2-6pm Sun) Catholicism's roots in Mangalore date back to the arrival of the Portuguese in the early 1500s, and the city is liberally dotted with churches. One of the most impressive is the Sistine Chapel-like St Aloysius chapel, with its walls and ceilings painted with brilliant frescoes. Also worth checking out is the imposing Roman-style **Milagres Church** (Falnir Rd; ⊙8.30am-6pm) in the city centre.

Sultan's Battery   FORT
(Sultan Battery Rd; ⊙6am-6pm) The only remnant of Tipu Sultan's fort is 4km from the city centre on the headland of the old port; bus 16 will get you there.

Kadri Manjunatha Temple   HINDU TEMPLE
(Kadri; ⊙6am-1pm & 4-8pm) This Kerala-style temple houses a 1000-year-old bronze statue of Lokeshwara.

🛏 Sleeping

Nalapad Residency   HOTEL **$$**
(☑2424757; www.nalapad.com; Lighthouse Hill Rd; s/d incl breakfast from ₹900/1000; ❄) The best midrange option in Mangalore comes with spruce rooms featuring floor-to-ceiling windows and heavy red curtains. The rooftop restaurant, Kadal, spices up your stay. Ask for a fifth- or sixth-floor room with brilliant sea views.

Hotel Ocean Pearl   HOTEL **$$**
(☑2413800; www.theoceanpearl.in; Navabharath Circle; s/d from ₹3000/3600; ❄📶) This brand-new designer hotel is clearly the talk of the town, with mint-fresh rooms featuring all the usual creature comforts paraded by business hotels. It's quite a steal for the price, but tariffs may go up once the inaugural offers draw to a close.

Summer Sands Beach Resort   HOTEL **$$$**
(☑2467690; www.summersands.in; d from ₹5000; ❄⊠) Set amid palm groves on a remote patch along Ullal Beach, Summer Sands offers a series of ethno-chic bungalows done up in earth and floral shades, and is the ideal place for a quiet retreat. Memories of Joanna, its restaurant, has pastoral decor and an excellent menu. The resort can arrange sightseeing tours on request.

Hotel Poonja International   HOTEL **$**
(☑2440171; www.hotelpoonjainternational.com; KS Rao Rd; s/d incl breakfast from ₹900/1000; ❄) This well-managed place has faux creepers and sunflowers lining its lobby, and the rooms (a whopping 154 of them) are well-appointed though low on frills. There's a multi-cuisine restaurant with a decent selection of Continental dishes.

Hotel Srinivas   HOTEL **$**
(☑2440061; www.srinivashotel.com; GHS Rd; s/d from ₹550/700; ❄) It's centrally located and reasonably clean. There's an expo hall downstairs, which often organises sales (shoes, shirts and everything in between) at bumper discounts.

Hotel Shaan Plaza   HOTEL **$**
(☑2440313; KS Rao Rd, s/d from ₹500/600; ❄) Piped music and TVs are standard features in the well-maintained rooms at this budget address.

Hotel Manorama   HOTEL **$**
(☑2440306; KS Rao Rd; s/d from ₹400/600; ❄) A decent, centrally-located budget option, with clean and good-value rooms.

🍴 Eating & Drinking

While in town, sample some Mangalorean delights such as *kane* (ladyfish) served in a spicy coconut curry, or the scrumptious deep-fried prawn *rawa* fry.

Kadal   SOUTH INDIAN **$$**
(Nalapad Residency, Lighthouse Hill Rd; mains ₹150-220) This high-rise restaurant has elegant and warmly lit interiors, with sweeping views all around. Try the spicy chicken *varval* (a coastal curry) or the yummy prawn ghee roast. Also enquire about the day's seafood specials.

Lalith Bar & Restaurant SEAFOOD $$

(Balmatta Rd; mains ₹80-150) Unwind in the Lalith's cool, subterranean interior and pair a chilled beer with prawns, crab or kingfish from its extensive menu. The day's special seafood is usually the best bet.

Liquid Lounge PUB $$

(☑4255175; Balmatta Rd; ☺7-11.30pm) A stiff Jack and Coke or the good old bottle of Corona, this trendy (and loud) pub has it all. With funky posters and neon-lit interiors upping its cool quotient, it's a great place to get happily drunk.

Janatha Deluxe SOUTH INDIAN $

(Hotel Shaan Plaza, mains ₹50-70; ☺7am-11pm) This local favourite serves a great veg thali (₹50) and a range of North and South Indian veg dishes.

Pallkhi SEAFOOD $$

(3rd fl, Tej Towers, Balmatta Rd; mains ₹140-170) A relatively smart and easygoing place, with stylish interiors and a formidable reputation for its coastal dishes.

Cochin Bakery BAKERY $

(AB Shetty Circle; cakes ₹20-30; ☺9.30am-9pm Mon-Sat) An old-time place that works up delicious puffs and cakes.

Café Coffee Day CAFE $

(Balmatta Rd; ☺9.30am-11pm) A range of good coffees and teas on offer, along with some tasty quick bites.

ℹ Information

State Bank of Mysore, Royal Bank of Scotland and ICICI Bank have ATMs on Balmatta Rd, Lighthouse Hill Rd and GHS Rd respectively.

Cyber Soft (Lighthouse Hill Rd; per hr ₹20; ☺10am-8pm) Fast internet access.

KSTDC tourist office (☑2453926; Lalbagh Circle; ☺10am-5pm Mon-Sat) Pretty useless.

Trade Wings (☑2427225; Lighthouse Hill Rd; ☺9.30am-5.30pm Mon-Sat) Travel agency. Changes travellers cheques.

ℹ Getting There & Away

Air

The **airport** is precariously perched atop a plateau in Bajpe, about 20km northeast of town. **Indian Airlines** (☑2496809; Hathill Rd) and **Jet Airways** (☑2441181; Ram Bhavan Complex, KS Rao Rd) both operate daily flights to Mumbai (1½ hours). Jet Airways also flies daily to Bengaluru (one hour).

Bus

The **KSRTC bus stand** is on Bejai Main Rd, 3km from the city centre; an autorickshaw there costs about ₹40. Several deluxe buses depart daily to Bengaluru (₹495, nine hours), via Madikeri (₹190, five hours) and Mysore (₹350, seven hours). Semideluxe buses go to Hassan (₹175, five hours). A 10.30pm deluxe bus heads to Panaji (₹399, seven hours). From opposite the City bus stand, private buses connect Udupi, Dharmasthala and Jog Falls. Tickets can be purchased at offices near Falnir Rd.

Roads around Mangalore are pothole hells, and journeys can be rough on the bum. Private bus drivers have a morbid fascination with speeding.

Train

The main **train station** is south of the city centre. The 12.20am *Netravati Express* stops at Margao in Goa (sleeper/2AC ₹194/702, 5½ hours), and continues to Mumbai (sleeper/2AC ₹361/1348, 15 hours). The 6.15pm *Malabar Express* heads to Thiruvananthapuram (Trivandrum; sleeper/2AC ₹257/941, 15 hours). The 9.30pm *West Coast Express* heads to Chennai (sleeper/2AC ₹317/1184, 18 hours).

Several Konkan Railway trains (to Mumbai, Margao, Ernakulam or Trivandrum) use **Kankanadi train station**, 5km east of Mangalore.

ℹ Getting Around

To get to the airport, take buses 47B or 47C from the City bus stand, or catch a taxi (₹400).

The City bus stand is opposite the State Bank of India. Flag fall for autorickshaws is ₹15, and ₹11 per kilometre thereafter. For late-night travel, add 50%. An autorickshaw to Kankanadi station costs around ₹60, or take bus 9 or 11B.

Dharmasthala

Inland from Mangalore are a string of Jain temple towns, such as Venur, Mudabidri and Karkal. The most interesting among them is Dharmasthala, 75km east of Mangalore by the Netravathi River. Some 10,000 pilgrims pass through this town every day. During holidays and major festivals such as **Lakshadeepotsava**, the footfall can go up tenfold.

The **Manjunatha Temple** (☺6.30am-2pm & 5-9pm) is Dharmasthala's main shrine, devoted to the Hindu lord Shiva. Men have to enter bare-chested, with legs covered. Simple free meals are available in the temple's **kitchen** (☺11.30am-2.15pm & 7.30-10pm), attached to a hall that can seat up to 3000.

Associated sights in town include the 12m-high **statue of Bahubali** at Ratnagiri Hill, and the **Manjusha Museum** (admission

₹2; ⊘10am-1pm & 4.30-7pm Mon-Sat), which houses a collection of sculptures, jewellery and local crafts. Don't forget to visit the fantastic **Car Museum** (admission ₹3; ⊘8.30am-1pm & 2-7pm), home to 48 vintage autos, including a 1903 Renault, a 1920s Studebaker President used by Mahatma Gandhi and a monster 1954 Cadillac.

Should you wish to stay, contact the helpful **temple office** (☑08256-277121; www.shridharmasthala.org) for accommodation (per person ₹50) in pilgrim lodges.

There are frequent buses to Dharmasthala from Mangalore (₹40, two hours).

Udupi (Udipi)

☑0820

Udupi is home to the atmospheric, 13th century **Krishna Temple** (Car St; ⊘3.30am-10pm), which draws thousands of Hindu pilgrims through the year. Surrounded by eight *maths* (monasteries), it's a hive of ritual activity, with musicians playing at the entrance, elephants on hand for *puja*, and pilgrims constantly passing through. Non-Hindus are welcome inside the temple; men must enter bare-chested. Elaborate rituals are also performed in the temple during the **Udupi Paryaya festival**.

Near the temple, above the Corp Bank ATM, the **tourist office** (☑2529718; Krishna Bldg, Car St; ⊘10am-5.30pm Mon-Sat) is a useful source of advice on Udupi and around.

Udupi is famed for its vegetarian food, and recognised across India for its sumptuous thali. A good place to sample the local fare is the subterranean **Woodlands** (Dr UR Rao Complex; mains ₹60-90; ⊘8am-9.30pm), a short walk south of the temple.

Udupi is 58km north of Mangalore along the coast; regular buses ply the route (₹36, 1½ hours).

Malpe

☑0820

A laid-back fishing harbour on the west coast 4km from Udupi, Malpe has fabulous beaches ideal for flopping about in the surf. A good place to stay is the **Paradise Isle Beach Resort** (☑2538777; www.theparadiseisle.com; s/d from ₹3000/3500; ✳@⊠), right on the sands, which has comfortable rooms and offers **water sports** such as bumpy rides, jet skiing, river rafting and kayaking (₹500 to ₹1500).

From Malpe pier, you can take a boat (₹70 per person) at 10.30am and 3.30pm out to tiny **St Mary's Island**, where Vasco da Gama supposedly landed in 1498. Over weekends the island is busy with locals inspecting the curious hexagonal basalt formations that jut out of the sand; during the week you might have it to yourself. An autorickshaw from Udupi to Malpe is around ₹70.

Devbagh

About 50km north of Gokarna, on one of the many islands that dot the Arabian Sea off the port town of Karwar, is the unspoilt and heavenly **Devbagh Beach Resort** (☑08382-221603; per person incl full board Indian/foreigner from ₹2500/€70; ✳). It's the perfect place to play out your Robinson Crusoe fantasies, or stroll aimlessly along the sands. Accommodation comes in cute and comfy fishermen's huts, cottages, log huts and houseboats. **Water sports** such as kayaking (₹300), snorkelling (₹700) and parasailing (₹900) are extra.

FORMULA BUFFALO

Call it an indigenous take on the grand prix. Kambla, or traditional buffalo racing, is a hugely popular pastime among villagers along the southern Karnataka coast. Popularised in the early 20th century and born out of local farmers habitually racing their buffaloes home after a day in the fields, the races have now hit the big time. Thousands of spectators attend each edition, and racing buffaloes are pampered and prepared like thoroughbreds – a good animal can cost ₹300,000.

Kambla events are held between November and March, usually on weekends. Parallel tracks are laid out in a paddy field, along which buffaloes hurtle towards the finish line. In most cases, the man rides on a board fixed to a ploughshare, literally surfing his way down the track behind the beasts.

Keep your cameras ready, but don't even think of getting in the buffaloes' way to take that prize-winning photo. The faster creatures can cover the 120m-odd distance through water and mud in around 14 seconds!

You can reach Karwar by taking a slow bus from Gokarna (₹36, 1½ hours) or Panaji (₹50, three hours). Call the resort in advance to arrange a ferry from their satellite office in Karwar. Make bookings through **Jungle Lodges & Resorts Ltd** (Map p844; ☑080-25597944; www.junglelodges.com; Shrungar Shopping Complex, MG Rd, Bengaluru; ☺10am-5.30pm Mon-Sat).

Jog Falls

☑08186

Nominally the highest waterfalls in India, the Jog Falls only come to life during the monsoon. At other times, the Linganamakki Dam further up the Sharavati River limits the water flow and spoils the show. The tallest of the four falls is the Raja, which drops 293m.

To get a good view of the falls, bypass the scrappy area close to the bus stand and hike to the foot of the falls down a 1200-plus step path. Watch out for leeches during the wet season.

Hotel Mayura Gerusoppa (☑244732; d ₹650), near the car park, has a few enormous and musty doubles. Stalls near the bus stand serve omelettes, thalis, noodles and rice dishes, plus hot and cold drinks.

Jog Falls has buses roughly every hour to Shimoga (₹53, three hours), and three daily to Karwar via Kumta (₹51, three hours), where you can change for Gokarna (₹16, one hour). For Mangalore, change at Shimoga. A return taxi from Gokarna will cost around ₹1500.

Gokarna

☑08386

Quaint but vibrant Gokarna sits on a secluded seaside spot about 60km south of Karwar. A dazzling mix of Hindu rituals and a medieval way of life is on show at this village, whose dramatic ambience is heightened during **festivals** such as Shivaratri and Ganesh Chaturthi, when thousands of pilgrims throng its ancient temples. While the main village is rather conservative in its outlook, a few out-of-town beaches are custom-made for carefree sunbaking.

◉ Sights & Activities

Temples   HINDU TEMPLES

Foreigners and non-Hindus are not allowed inside Gokarna's temples. However, there are plenty of colourful rituals to be witnessed around town. At the western end

of Car St is the **Mahabaleshwara Temple**, home to a revered lingam (phallic representation of Shiva). Nearby is the **Ganapati Temple**, while at the other end of the street is the **Venkataraman Temple**. About 100m further south is **Koorti Teertha**, the large temple tank (reservoir) where locals, pilgrims and immaculately dressed Brahmins perform their ablutions next to washermen on the ghats (steps or landings).

Beaches   BEACHES

Gokarna's 'town beach' is dirty, and not meant for casual bathing. The best sands are due south, and can be reached via a footpath that begins south of the Ganapati Temple and heads down the coast (if you reach the bathing tank, or find yourself clawing up rocks, you're on the wrong path).

A 20-minute hike on the path brings you to the top of a barren headland with expansive sea views. On the southern side is **Kudle** (pronounced kood-lay), the first of Gokarna's pristine beaches. Basic snacks, drinks and accommodation are available here, and it's a nice place to chill. South of Kudle Beach, a track climbs over the next headland, and a further 20-minute walk brings you to **Om Beach**, with a handful of chai shops, shacks and marauding groups of local tourists on weekends.

South of Om Beach lie the more isolated **Half-Moon Beach** and **Paradise Beach**, which come to life only between November and March. They are a 30-minute and one-hour walk, respectively.

Depending on demand, fishing boats can ferry you from Gokarna Beach to Kudle (₹100) and Om (₹200). An autorickshaw from town to Om costs around ₹200.

Don't walk around after dark, and not alone at any time – it's easy to slip on the paths or get lost, and muggings have occurred. For a small fee, most lodges in Gokarna will safely store valuables and baggage while you chill out on the beach.

Ayurveda   AYURVEDA

Well-trained masseurs at **Ayur Kuteeram** (☑9480575351; Gokarna Beach; ☺9am-8pm) can work magic on those knotty muscles. An *Abhayanga* treatment costs a mere ₹700.

Quality ayurvedic therapies and packages are also available at specialist ayurvedic centres at the SwaSwara resort and Om Beach Resort.

🛏 Sleeping

With a few exceptions, the choice here is between a rudimentary beach shack or a

WALK ON THE WILD SIDE

Located in the jungles of the Western Ghats about 100km from Goa, emerging **Dandeli** is a fantabulous wildlife getaway that promises close encounters with diverse exotic wildlife such as elephants, panthers, sloth bears, Indian bisons, wild dogs and flying squirrels. It's a chosen birding destination too, with resident hornbills, golden-backed woodpeckers, serpent eagles and white-breasted kingfishers. Also on offer are a slew of adventure activities ranging from kayaking to bowel-churning white-water rafting on the swirling waters of the Kali River.

Kali Adventure Camp (per person incl full board Indian/foreigner from ₹2300/€70; ❄) offers accommodation in tented cottages and rooms, done up lavishly while adhering to ecofriendly principles. Book through **Jungle Lodges & Resorts Ltd** (Map p844; ☏080-25597944; www.junglelodges.com; Shrungar Shopping Complex, MG Rd, Bengaluru; ⏰10am-5.30pm Mon-Sat).

Frequent buses connect Dandeli to both Hubli (₹45, two hours) and Dharwad (₹35, 1½ hours), with onward connections to Goa, Gokarna, Hospet and Bengaluru.

basic but more comfortable room in town. Some guesthouses in town cater to pilgrims, and may come with certain rules and regulations. Prices can increase during festivals or the high season.

BEACHES

Both Kudle and Om beaches have shacks offering budget huts and rooms. Places open up on Half-Moon and Paradise beaches from November to March. Most places provide at least a bedroll; bring your own sheets or sleeping bag. Padlocks are provided and huts are secure. Communal washing and toilet facilities are simple.

TOP CHOICE SwaSwara HOTEL $$$

(☏257132, 0484-3011711; www.swaswara.com; Om Beach; d 7 nights Indian/foreigner ₹115,000/€2015; ❄@≋) Clearly in a league of its own, this amazing health resort sits on the hill overlooking Om Beach. No short stays on offer here, but you can chill out at this elegant and superbly designed red-laterite-brick resort for a full week, and enjoy a holiday based around yoga and ayurvedic treatments. There's an interactive kitchen here, and the artists in residence can help you hone your creative skills. Rates include full board, transport, leisure activities and daily yoga sessions. Weeklong ayurvedic treatment packages kick off at around US$600.

Namaste Café GUESTHOUSE $

(☏257141; Om Beach; huts from ₹700; ❄@) In and out of season, Namaste is the place to hang. What's better, the place has upped its

luxuries since the last time we were here, and now offers AC and internet on its serene Om Beach premises. The restaurant-bar cooks up great bites and is the premier Om chill-out spot. In season, it also offers basic huts (₹150) at Paradise Beach and cottages at Namaste Farm (from ₹500) on the headland.

Hotel Gokarna International Kudle Resort HOTEL $$

(☏257843; Kudle Beach; d ₹1500; ❄) Run by the same management that owns Hotel Gokarna International in town, this midrange option has smart rooms and a lovely garden up front. The waves wash up to its gates during high tide, and seal the deal in its favour.

Nirvana Café GUESTHOUSE $

(☏329851; Om Beach; d ₹300; cottage ₹400) Located on the southern end of Om, this extremely pleasant guesthouse featuring huts within a shady garden should be done renovating by now.

GOKARNA

Om Beach Resort HOTEL $$

(☏257052; www.ombeachresort.com; Bangle Gudde; d incl breakfast Indian/foreigner ₹2800/US$105; ❄@) This little jewel sits on a headland 2km out of Gokarna, off the Om Beach road. Set amid lawns and shady trees, its red-brick cottages are excellently designed, and its restaurant serves good seafood to go with the booze. There's a professional ayurvedic centre on site, with seven-night treatment packages starting from US$490 per person.

Kamat Lodge GUESTHOUSE **$**
(256035; Kamat Complex, Main St; s/d ₹200/300, d with AC ₹1200; ✳) A value-for-money place on Gokarna's main drag, this hotel offers clean rooms with fresh sheets and large windows. But don't expect room service and other such fluffs.

Nimmu House GUESTHOUSE **$**
(☏256730; nimmuhouse@yahoo.com; s/d from ₹250/500; @) A pleasant option off Gokarna's main beach, run by a friendly family .

Vaibhav Lodge GUESTHOUSE **$**
(☏256714; off Main St; d ₹250, s/d ₹150/200; @) A backpackers' dig, with mosquito nets, hot water in the morning and a rooftop restaurant.

Shastri Guest House GUESTHOUSE **$**
(☏256220; Main St; s/d/tr ₹160/280/400) A hostel-like place with good, airy doubles in the new block out back. The singles are cramped, though.

✖ Eating

The chai shops on all of the beaches rustle up basic snacks and meals.

TOP CHOICE Namaste Café CAFE **$**
(Om Beach, mains ₹80-100; ◷7am-11pm) Om Beach's social centre serves some excellent Western staples such as pizzas, burgers and shakes. But the real draws are its tasty seafood dishes, especially the grilled calamari and the pomfret preparations. And remember, you're hogging it all up while sitting on a most beautiful seaside venue. Dinners are particularly enjoyable, after noisy local tourists have called it a day.

Prema Restaurant MULTICUISINE **$**
(Gokarna Beach; mains ₹80-110; ◷10am-8.30pm) A decent menu comprising Continental extempores and colourful ice-creams. Spice packs and herbal oils for sale at the counter.

Pai Restaurant SOUTH INDIAN **$**
(Main St; mains ₹50-80; ◷6.30am-9.30pm) Serves an awesome veg thali for ₹55.

Pai Hotel INDIAN **$**
(Car St) A popular and freshly renovated eatery with an excellent vegetarian menu.

ℹ Information

SBI (Main St) Has an ATM.
Shama Internet Centre (Car St; per hr ₹40; ◷10am-11pm) Fast internet connections.

Sub post office (1st fl, cnr Car & Main Sts; 10am-4pm Mon-Sat)

ℹ Getting There & Away

Bus

From the rudimentary **bus stand**, rickety buses roll to Karwar (₹33, 1½ hours), which has connections to Goa. Frequent direct buses run to Hubli (₹107, four hours), where you can change for Hospet and Hampi, while an evening bus goes to Bengaluru (₹402, 12 hours).

Train

Express trains stop at **Kumta station**, 25km away. The 3.30am *Matsyagandha Express* goes to Mangalore (sleeper ₹166, 3½ hours); the return train leaves Kumta at 6.20pm for Margao (sleeper ₹140, 2½ hours). Many of the hotels and small travel agencies in Gokarna can book tickets.

Autorickshaws charge ₹250 to go to Kumta station; a bus charges ₹15.

CENTRAL KARNATAKA

Hampi
☏08394

Unreal and bewitching, the forlorn ruins of Hampi dot an unearthly landscape that will leave you spellbound the moment you cast your eyes on it. Heaps of giant boulders perch precariously over miles of undulated terrain, their rusty hues offset by jade-green palm groves, banana plantations and paddy fields. The azure sky painted with fluffy white cirrus only adds to the magical atmosphere. A World Heritage Site, Hampi is a place where you can lose yourself among wistful ruins, or simply be mesmerised by the vagaries of nature, wondering how millions of years of volcanic activity and erosion could have resulted in a landscape so captivating.

Hampi is a major pit stop on the traveller circuit; November to March is the high season. While it's possible to see the main sites in a day or two, this goes against Hampi's relaxed grain. Plan on lingering for a while.

Hampi Bazaar and the southern village of Kamalapuram are the two main points of entry to the ruins. Kamalapuram has a government-run hotel and the archaeological museum. But the main travellers' ghetto is Hampi Bazaar, a village crammed with budget lodges, shops and restaurants, all

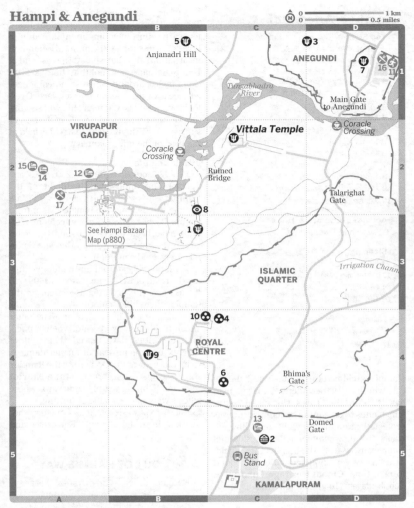

towered over by the majestic Virupaksha Temple. The ruins are divided into two main areas: the Sacred Centre, around Hampi Bazaar; and the Royal Centre, towards Kamalapuram. To the northeast across the Tungabhadra River is the historic village of Anegundi.

History

Hampi and its neighbouring areas find mention in the Hindu epic Ramayana as Kishkinda, the realm of the monkey gods. In 1336, Telugu prince Harihararaya chose Hampi as the site for his new capital

Vijayanagar, which – over the next couple of centuries – grew into one of the largest Hindu empires in Indian history. By the 16th century, it was a thriving metropolis of about 500,000 people, its busy bazaars dabbling in international commerce, brimming with precious stones and merchants from faraway lands. All this, however, ended in a stroke in 1565, when a confederacy of Deccan sultanates razed Vijayanagar to the ground, striking it a death blow from which it never recovered.

A different battle rages in Hampi today, between conservationists bent on protecting

Hampi & Anegundi

Hampi's architectural heritage and the locals who have settled there. A master plan has been in the works since mid-2000s, which aims to classify all of Hampi's ruins as protected monuments, while resettling villagers at a new commercial and residential complex away from the architectural enclosures. However, implementation is bound to take time. **Global Heritage Fund** (www.globalheritagefund.org) has more details about Hampi's endangered heritage.

◎ Sights

Virupaksha Temple   HINDU TEMPLE
(Map p880; admission ₹2; ☉dawn-dusk) The focal point of Hampi Bazaar is the Virupaksha Temple, one of the city's oldest structures. The main *gopuram,* almost 50m high, was built in 1442, with a smaller one added in 1510. The main shrine is dedicated to Virupaksha, an incarnation of Shiva.

If Lakshmi (the **temple elephant**) and her attendant are around, she'll smooch (bless) you for a coin. The adorable Lakshmi gets her morning bath at 8.30am, just down the way by the river ghats.

To the south, overlooking Virupaksha Temple, **Hemakuta Hill** (Map p880) has a few early ruins, including monolithic sculptures of Narasimha (Vishnu in his man-lion incarnation) and Ganesha. At the east end of Hampi Bazaar is a monolithic **Nandi statue** (Map p880), around which stand colonnaded blocks of the ancient marketplace. Overlooking the site is Matanga Hill, whose summit affords dramatic views of the terrain at sunrise. The **Vijaya Utsav festival** is held at the base of the hill in January.

Vittala Temple   HINDU TEMPLE
(Map p877; Indian/foreigner ₹10/250; ☉8.30am-5.30pm) The undisputed highlight of the Hampi ruins, the 16th-century Vittala Temple stands amid the boulders 2km from Hampi Bazaar. Though a few cement scaffolds have been erected to keep the main structure from collapsing, the site is in relatively good condition.

Work possibly started on the temple during the reign of Krishnadevaraya (r 1509–29) It was never finished or consecrated, yet the temple's incredible sculptural work remains the pinnacle of Vijayanagar art. The outer 'musical' pillars reverberate when tapped, but authorities have placed them out of tourists' bounds for fear of further damage, so no more do-re-mi. Don't miss the temple's showcase piece, the ornate **stone chariot** that stands in the temple courtyard, whose wheels were once capable of turning.

Retain your ticket for same-day admission into the Zenana Enclosure and

OUT OF HARM'S WAY

» Hampi Bazaar is an extremely safe area, but do not wander around the ruins after dark or alone. It's a dangerous terrain to get lost in; long-time guides have even sighted sloth bears prowling around Vittala Temple at night!

» Alcohol and narcotics are illegal in Hampi, and possession can get you in trouble. Cannabis peddlers lurk by the riverside after dark, but you'd do well to give them a wide berth.

» Local laws require all foreign travellers to report to the police station with their passports upon arrival, and notify the authorities about their proposed duration of stay.

Elephant Stables in the Royal Centre, and the archaeological museum in Kamalapuram.

Sule Bazaar & Achyutaraya Temple
HISTORIC SITE

Halfway along the path from Hampi Bazaar to the Vittala Temple, a track to the right leads over the rocks to deserted **Sule Bazaar** (Map p877), one of ancient Hampi's principal centres of commerce. At the southern end of this area is the deserted **Achyutaraya Temple** (Map p877).

Royal Centre
HISTORIC SITE

(Map p877) While it can be accessed by a 2km foot trail from the Achyutaraya Temple, the Royal Centre is best reached via the Hampi–Kamalapuram road. It's a flatter area compared to the rest of Hampi, where the boulders have been shaved off to create stone walls. A number of Hampi's major sites stand here, within the walled ladies' quarters called the **Zenana Enclosure** (Map p877; Indian/foreigner ₹10/250; ⊙8.30am-5.30pm). There's the **Lotus Mahal** (Map p877), a delicately designed pavilion which was supposedly the queen's recreational mansion. The Lotus Mahal overlooks the **Elephant Stables** (Map p877), a grand building with domed chambers. Your ticket is valid for same-day admission to the Vittala Temple and the archaeological museum in Kamalapuram.

Further south, you'll find various temples and elaborate waterworks, including the **Underground Shiva Temple** (Map p877; ⊙8.30am-5.30pm) and the **Queen's Bath** (Map p877; ⊙8.30am-5.30pm), deceptively plain on the outside but amazing within.

Archaeological Museum
MUSEUM

(Map p877; Kamalapuram; admission ₹5; ⊙10am-5pm Sat-Thu) The archaeological museum has collections of sculptures from local ruins, neolithic tools, 16th-century weaponry and a large floor model of the Vijayanagar ruins.

🛏 Sleeping

There's little to choose from between the many basic guesthouses in Hampi Bazaar and Virupapur Gaddi, some of which have lately undergone refitting to attract upmarket travellers. Between April and September you can shop around to get a good deal. The only government-run hotel (with a legal beer bar and a nonveg restaurant) is in Kamalapuram. Prices can shoot up depending on demand.

Also remember that most of the guesthouses in Hampi Bazaar are small operations, comprising only about half-a-dozen rooms of so. It might help to book early during high seasons.

HAMPI BAZAAR

🔝 CHOICE Padma Guest House
GUESTHOUSE $$

(Map p880; ☎241331; padmaguesthouse@gmail.com; d from ₹600; ❋) In a quiet corner of Hampi Bazaar, the astute and amiable Padma has been quietly expanding her empire since we were last here. The basic but squeaky clean rooms are a pleasant deviation from Hampi's usual offerings, and those on the first floor have good views of the Virupaksha Temple. New rooms have been added to the west, with creature comforts (TV and AC) previously unheard of in Hampi. Well done, says 'Lovely Planet'.

Gopi Guest House
GUESTHOUSE $

(Map p880; ☎241695; kirangopi2002@yahoo.com; d ₹350-1000; ❋@) Centrally located amid the bustle of Hampi Bazaar, this pleasant dive continues to provide commendable service to travellers. The new block is quite upscale for Hampi's standards, with en suite rooms fronted by a sun-kissed terrace. The rooftop cafe – with a lovely view of the Virupaksha Temple – is a nice place to hang out.

Pushpa Guest House
GUESTHOUSE $

(Map p880; ☎241440; d from ₹500) This place was putting finishing touches to its terrace rooms during research, many of which already sported flowery pink walls and tiled floors. There is an extremely cordial family playing host, and a lovely sit-out on the first floor.

Shanthi Guest House
GUESTHOUSE $

(Map p880; ☎241568; s/d ₹300/350, without bathroom ₹150/250) An oldie but a goodie, Shanthi offers a peaceful courtyard with a swing chair, and has plastic creepers and colourful posters of a hundred gods decorating its basic rooms. There's a small souvenir shop at the entrance that operates on an honour system.

Ranjana Guest House
GUESTHOUSE $

(Map p880; ☎241696; d with/without AC ₹800/600; ❋) Almost on a par with Padma next door, this place also prides itself on well-appointed rooms; those on the terrace have killer views. There are a few cheapies adjoining the family quarters downstairs.

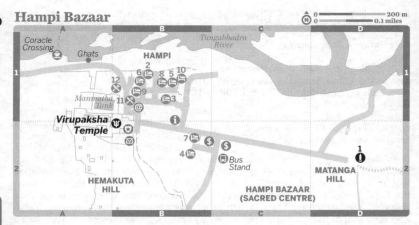

Rama Guest House   GUESTHOUSE $
(☏241962; d ₹400-600) Sitting close to the river, this place seems a popular option with Bengaluru's young weekenders. Some rooms are a little low on light, though adequately appointed for a budget dig.

Vicky's   GUESTHOUSE $
(Map p880; ☏241694; vikkyhampi@yahoo.co.in; d ₹350; @) A large operation done up in pop purple and green, with tiled floors, internet access and rooftop cafe. Fix the rate firmly while booking.

Rocky Guest House   GUESTHOUSE $
(Map p880; ☏241951; rockyhampi@yahoo.co.in; d ₹400) A comfy option opposite Gopi, with clean rooms, friendly management and a travel desk.

Archana Guest House   GUESTHOUSE $
(Map p880; ☏241547; addihampi@yahoo.com; d from ₹500) A quiet and cheerful establishment at the end of a lane, with decent rooms.

VIRUPAPUR GADDI
Many travellers prefer the tranquil atmosphere of Virupapur Gaddi, across the river from Hampi Bazaar. A small boat (₹10) shuttles frequently across the river from 7am to 6pm. During the monsoon, the river runs high and ferry services may be suspended.

Hema Guest House   GUESTHOUSE $
(Map p877; ☏9449103008; d ₹250) Laid-back and happening, this is one of Virupapur Gaddi's most popular spots, with rows of cute and comfy cottages in a shady grove. The informal river-view cafe is perpetually full with lazing tourists.

Shanthi   GUESTHOUSE $
(Map p877; ☏9449260162; shanthi.hampi@gmail.com; cottage ₹500-800; @) Shanthi's earth-themed, thatched cottages have rice-field, river and sunset views, with couch swings dangling in their front porches. The restaurant does good thalis and pizzas.

Mowgli   GUESTHOUSE $$
(Map p877; ☏9448217588; hampimowgli@hotmail.com; d ₹500-1200; ❄@) A cluster of lilac cottages thrown around a sprawling garden complex with soothing views across the rice fields, Mowgli is a top-class chill-out spot this side of the river. It can fill up quickly over weekends, so book early.

KAMALAPURAM
Hotel Mayura Bhuvaneshwari   HOTEL $$
(Map p877; ☏08394-241474; d from ₹1200; ❄) This tidy government operation, about 3km south of the Royal Centre, has well-appointed rooms (adorned with corny murals), a much-appreciated beer bar, a good multicuisine restaurant and ayurvedic sessions (from ₹1500) on request.

✗ Eating
Due to Hampi's religious significance, meat is strictly off the menu in all restaurants, and alcohol is banned. Places are open from 7am to 10pm.

[TOP CHOICE] **Mango Tree**   MULTICUISINE $$
(Map p877; mains ₹70-100) Creativity blends with culinary excellence at this rural-themed chill-out joint, spread out under the eponymous mango tree by the river. Walk through

a banana plantation to get here, and try the special vegetable curry (₹100), the banana fritters (₹60) or the spaghetti with cashew nuts and cheese (₹100). The terraced seating is perfect for whiling away a lazy afternoon, book in hand.

New Shanthi   MULTICUISINE **$$**
(Map p880; mains ₹80-120) A hippie vibe, complete with trance music and acid-blue lights, hangs over this popular option serving Mexican, Italian and Indian regulars, with cookies and crumbles on the side. A good range of teas (jasmine, lemongrass and herbal) are on offer.

Durga Huts   CAFE **$**
(Map p880; mains ₹60-80) Clearly a hit with music lovers. Prem Joshua's fusion tracks get heavy airplay here, and there are a few guitars and drums on standby for an impromptu jam session. The food is of passable quality.

ℹ Information

Aspiration Stores (⊙10am-1pm & 4-8pm) Good for book guides. Try *Hampi* by John M Fritz and George Michell, a good architectural study.

Canara Bank (Map p880; ⊙11am-2pm Mon-Tue & Thu-Fri, 11am-12.30pm Sat) Changes currency and has an ATM.

Hampi Heritage Gallery (⊙10am-1pm & 3-6pm) Books and photo albums on Hampi's history and architecture, plus walking tours for ₹250.

Sree Rama Cyber Café (Map p880; per hr ₹40; ⊙7am-11pm) Has printing and data burning facilities.

Tourist office (Map p880; ☑241339; ⊙10am-5.30pm Sat-Thu) Arranges guides for ₹300/600 for a half/full day.

ℹ Getting There & Away

A semideluxe bus connects Hampi Bazaar to Bengaluru (₹372, eight hours) leaving at 8.30pm. Overnight private sleeper buses ply to/from Goa (₹600) and Gokarna (₹500) from November through March. Numerous travel agents in Hampi Bazaar book onward tickets or arrange taxis.

Hospet is Hampi's nearest train station. The first bus from Hospet (₹12, 30 minutes, half-hourly) is at 6.30am; the last one back leaves Hampi Bazaar at 8.30pm. An autorickshaw costs around ₹150. See p883 for onward transport information.

ℹ Getting Around

Once you've seen the main sights in Hampi, exploring the rest of the ruins by bicycle is the thing to do. The key monuments are haphazardly signposted all over the site. While they're not adequate, you shouldn't get lost. Bicycles cost about ₹30 per day in Hampi Bazaar. Mopeds can be hired for around ₹250, and petrol is ₹70 a litre. To cross the river, pile your vehicle onto a coracle for ₹10.

Walking the ruins is recommended too, but expect to cover at least 7km just to see the major sites. Autorickshaws and taxis are available for sightseeing, and will drop you as close to each of the major ruins as they can. A five-hour autorickshaw tour costs ₹500.

Organised tours depart from Hospet; see p883 for details.

Around Hampi

ANEGUNDI

Across the Tungabhadra, about 5km northeast of Hampi Bazaar, sits Anegundi, an ancient fortified village that's part of the Hampi World Heritage Site but predates Hampi by way of human habitation. Gifted with a landscape similar to Hampi, quainter Anegundi has been spared the blight of

DANCES WITH BEARS

About 15km south of Hampi, amid a scrubby undulated terrain, lies the **Daroji Sloth Bear Sanctuary** (admission ₹25; ☉9.30am-6pm), which nurses a population of around 40 free-ranging sloth bears. It's possible to drive through the sanctuary and sight these furry creatures, along with leopards, wild boars, hyenas, jackals and others animals, as well as some exotic birds. Accommodation is in luxury cottages at the **Daroji Sloth Bear Resort** (per person incl full board Indian/foreigner from ₹3000/€70; ❄), located on the sanctuary's periphery. Book through **Jungle Lodges & Resorts Ltd** (Map p844; ☎080-25597944; www.junglelodges.com; Shrungar Shopping Complex, MG Rd, Bengaluru; ☉10am-5.30pm Mon-Sat). The resort can arrange pick-up and drop off from Hampi.

commercialisation, and thus continues to preserve the local atmosphere minus the touristy vibe.

◉ Sights & Activities

Temples HINDU TEMPLES

Mythically referred to as Kishkinda, the kingdom of the monkey gods, Anegundi retains many of its historic monuments, such as sections of its defensive wall and gates, and the **Ranganatha Temple** (Map p877; ☉dawn-dusk) devoted to Rama. The whitewashed **Hanuman Temple** (Map p877; ☉dawn-dusk), accessible by a 570-step climb up the Anjanadri Hill, has fine views of the rugged terrain around. Many believe this is the birthplace of the Hindu monkey god Hanuman. On the pleasant hike up, you'll be courted by impish monkeys, and within the temple you'll find a horde of chillum-puffing resident sadhus. Also worth visiting is the **Durga Temple** (Map p877; ☉dawn-dusk), an ancient shrine closer to the village.

Kishkinda Trust CULTURAL PROGRAMS, OUTDOOR ADVENTURE

(TKT; Map p877; ☎08533-267777; www.thekish kindatrust.org) The Kishkinda Trust, an NGO that promotes sustainable tourism in Anegundi, organises soft adventure activities such as rock-climbing, camping, trekking and boating around the village. Equipment and trained instructors are provided. A slew of cultural programs, including performing arts sessions and classical and folk music concerts are also conducted from time to time. For more information on TKT, see the boxed text, p882.

⬛ Sleeping & Eating

Anegundi has several homestays managed by TKT. Contact the trust for bookings. Guesthouses listed can provide meals upon prior notice.

Naidile Guest House GUESTHOUSE **$$**

(d ₹1500) A charmingly rustic air hangs over this renovated village home in the heart of Anegundi where you can savour all the sights and sounds of the ancient village. It can sleep up to five people.

Peshagar Guest House GUESTHOUSE **$**

(d incl breakfast ₹600) Six simple rooms done up in rural motifs open around a pleasant common area in this new guesthouse. There's also a sumptuous breakfast platter available.

TEMA Guest House GUESTHOUSE **$**

(d incl breakfast ₹700) The two rooms in this village quarters were undergoing renovation during research, and should be back in commission by now.

Champa Guest House GUESTHOUSE **$**

(d incl breakfast ₹700) Champa offers basic but pleasant accommodation in two rooms, and is looked after by an affable village family.

Hoova Craft Shop & Café CAFE **$**

(mains ₹40-60; ☉9.30am-5pm Mon-Sat, 9.30am-2pm Sun) A lovely place for an unhurried meal. You can also shop for sundry souvenirs made by the village's women's self-help groups.

ⓘ Getting There & Away

Anegundi can be reached by crossing the river on a coracle (₹10) from the pier east of the Vittala Temple. The concrete bridge that was being erected across the river has mysteriously collapsed, taking away with it all hopes of cycling across.

You can also get to Anegundi by taking a bus (₹25, one hour) from Hospet.

Hospet

☎08394 / POP 164,200

This busy regional centre is the main transport hub for Hampi. The Muslim festival of **Muharram** brings things to life in this otherwise dull transit town. With Hampi barely 30 minutes away, few choose to linger here.

Sleeping & Eating

Hotel Priyadarshini　　　　　　HOTEL **$**
(☎227313; www.priyainhampi.com; Station Rd; d ₹800-950; ❉) This old-timer has a convenient location between the bus and train stations. The fresh rooms have balconies and TV, and its quality outdoor nonveg restaurant-bar Manasa (mains ₹60 to ₹120) stirs to life in the evenings.

Hotel Malligi　　　　　　　　　HOTEL **$$**
(☎228101; www.malligihotels.com; Jabunatha Rd; d Indian/foreigner ₹2800/3500; ❉@❉) Hospet's premier luxury option builds its reputation around clean and well-serviced rooms, an aquamarine swimming pool, a spa and a good multicuisine restaurant.

Udupi Sri Krishna Bhavan　　SOUTH INDIAN **$**
(Bus stand; mains ₹30-50; ◷6am-11pm) Opposite the bus stand, this clean spot dishes out Indian vegie fare, including thalis for ₹35.

ℹ Information

SBI, HDFC Bank and ICICI Bank have ATMs along the main drag and Shanbagh Circle. Internet joints are common, with connections costing ₹40 per hour.

KSTDC tourist office (☎221008; Shanbagh Circle; ◷10am-5.30pm Mon-Sat) Offers an uninspiring Hampi tour (₹250) for groups of 10 or more.

ℹ Getting There & Away

Bus

The **bus stand** has services to Hampi from Bay 10 every half-hour (₹12, 30 minutes). Several express buses run to Bengaluru (ordinary/deluxe ₹212/306, nine hours). One bus goes to Badami (₹155, six hours) at 6.30am, or you can take a bus to Gadag (₹76, 2½ hours) and transfer. There are frequent buses to Bijapur (₹148, six hours) and overnight services to Hyderabad (₹335, 10 hours). For Gokarna, take a bus to Hubli (₹108, 4½ hours) and change. For Mangalore or Hassan, take a morning bus to Shimoga (₹203, five hours) and change there.

Train

Hospet's **train station** is a ₹20 autorickshaw journey from town. The 5.30am *Rayalaseema Express* heads to Hubli (2nd class ₹120, 3½ hours). For Bengaluru, take the 8.30pm *Hampi Express* (sleeper/2AC ₹187/720, nine hours). Every Monday, Wednesday, Thursday and Saturday, a 6.30am express train heads to Vasco da Gama (sleeper/2AC ₹176/630, 8½ hours).

For Badami, catch a Hubli train to Gadag and change there.

Hubli

☑0836 / POP 786,100

Prosperous Hubli is a hub for rail routes for Mumbai, Bengaluru, Goa and northern Karnataka. The train station is a 15-minute walk from the old bus stand. Most hotels sit along this stretch.

Sleeping & Eating

Ananth Residency　　　　　　HOTEL **$$**
(☎2262251; ananthresidencyhubli@yahoo.co.uk; Jayachamaraj Nagar; d from ₹1100; ❉) A brand-new option that sports a sleek business-hotel look and feel. Has good-value rooms and efficient service.

Hotel Ajanta　　　　　　　　　HOTEL **$**
(☎2362216; Jayachamaraj Nagar; s/d from ₹250/330) This well-run place near the train station has basic, functional rooms. Its popular ground-floor restaurant serves delicious regional-style thalis for ₹35.

Sudarshan　　　　　　　　　　INDIAN **$$**
(Jayachamaraj Nagar; mains ₹90-100) The non-veg bar-restaurant at Ananth Residency is a cheerful eatery with good food and chilled beer.

ℹ Information

SBI has an ATM opposite the bus stand. On the same stretch are several internet cafes, charging around ₹30 per hour.

ℹ Getting There & Away

Bus

Buses stop briefly at the **old bus stand** before moving to the **new bus stand** 2km away. There are numerous semideluxe services to Bengaluru (₹304, 10 hours), Bijapur (₹156, six hours) and Hospet (₹108, 4½ hours). There are regular connections to Mangalore (₹255, 10 hours, several daily), Borivali in Mumbai (semideluxe/sleeper ₹482/762, 14 hours, four daily), Mysore (₹299, 10 hours, three daily), Gokarna (₹110, five hours, two daily) and Panaji (₹204, six hours, six daily).

Private deluxe buses to Bengaluru (₹370) run from opposite the old bus stand.

Train

From the **train station**, expresses head to Hospet (2nd class ₹120, 3½ hours, three daily), Bengaluru (sleeper/2AC ₹203/910, 11 hours, four daily) and Mumbai (sleeper/2AC ₹285/1057,

THE KISHKINDA TRUST

Since 1995, the **Kishkinda Trust** (TKT; ☑08533-267777; www.thekishkindatrust.org) has been actively involved in promoting rural tourism, sustainable development and women's empowerment in Anegundi, as well as preserving the architectural, cultural and living heritage of the Hampi World Heritage Site. The first project in 1997 created a cottage industry of crafts using locally produced cloth, banana fibre and river grass. It now employs over 600 women, and the attractive crafts produced are marketed in ethnic product outlets across India.

For the benefit of tourists, TKT has a team featuring some of the best guides in the region, who are fluent in English and know the terrain like the back of their hands. Exploring the region while riding pillion on their motorcycles can be a truly enriching experience. Guides charge ₹300/600 for a half/full day. Contact the trust for details.

14 hours). The 11pm *Hubli-Vasco Link Express* goes to Goa (sleeper ₹153, six hours).

Air

From Hubli's basic **airport**, Kingfisher Red flies to Mumbai (from ₹5500, 1½ hours), Hyderabad (from ₹6800, 3½ hours) and Bengaluru (from ₹5500, 1½ hours).

NORTHERN KARNATAKA

Badami

☑08357 / POP 25,800

Now in a shambles, scruffy Badami is a far cry from its glory days, when it was the capital of the mighty Chalukya empire. Between the 6th and 8th century AD, the Chalukya kings shifted the capital here from Aihole, with a satellite capital in Pattadakal. The relocation of power saw Badami gifted with several temples and, most importantly, a group of magnificent rock-cut cave temples, which are the main reason for coming to the village today.

History

From about AD 540 to 757, Badami was the capital of an enormous kingdom stretching from Kanchipuram in Tamil Nadu to the Narmada River in Gujarat. It eventually fell to the Rashtrakutas, and changed hands several times thereafter, with each dynasty sculpturally embellishing Badami in their own way.

The sculptural legacy left by the Chalukya artisans in Badami includes some of the earliest and finest examples of Dravidian temples and rock-cut caves. During Badami's heydays, Aihole and Pattadakal served as trial grounds for new temple architecture; the latter is now a World Heritage Site.

◉ Sights

Cave Temples   CAVES

(Indian/foreigner ₹5/100; ⊘dawn-dusk) Badami's highlight is its beautiful cave temples. Non-pushy and informed guides ask ₹200 for a tour of the caves, or ₹300 for the whole site. Watch out for pesky monkeys.

Cave one, just above the entrance to the complex, is dedicated to Shiva. It's the oldest of the four caves, probably carved in the latter half of the 6th century. On the wall to the right of the porch is a captivating image of Nataraja striking 81 dance poses. On the right of the porch area is a huge figure of Ardhanarishvara. The right half of the figure shows features of Shiva, while the left half has aspects of his wife Parvati. On the opposite wall is a large image of Harihara; half Shiva and half Vishnu.

Dedicated to Vishnu, **cave two** is simpler in design. As with caves one and three, the front edge of the platform is decorated with images of pot-bellied dwarfs in various poses. Four pillars support the verandah, their tops carved with a bracket in the shape of a *yali* (mythical lion creature). On the left wall of the porch is the bull-headed figure of Varaha, an incarnation of Vishnu and the emblem of the Chalukya empire. To his left is Naga, a snake with a human face. On the right wall is a large sculpture of Trivikrama, another incarnation of Vishnu.

Between the second and third caves are two sets of steps to the right. The first leads to a **natural cave**, where resident monkeys laze around. The eastern wall of this cave contains a small image of Padmapani (an incarnation of the Buddha). The second set of steps – sadly, barred by a gate – leads to the hilltop **South Fort**.

Cave three, carved in AD 578, has – on the left wall – a carving of Vishnu, to whom the cave is dedicated, sitting on a snake. Nearby is an image of Varaha with four hands. The pillars have carved brackets in the shape of *yalis.* The ceiling panels contain images, including Indra riding an elephant, Shiva on a bull and Brahma on a swan.

Dedicated to Jainism, **cave four** is the smallest of the set and dates between the 7th and 8th centuries. The pillars, with their roaring *yalis,* are similar to the other caves. The right wall has an image of Suparshva-natha (the seventh Jain *tirthankar*) surrounded by 24 Jain *tirthankars.* The inner sanctum contains an image of Adinath, the first Jain *tirthankar.*

Other Sights
HISTORIC SITES
Badami's caves overlook the 5th-century **Agastyatirtha Tank** and the waterside **Bhutanatha temples**. On the other side of the tank is an **archaeological museum** (admission ₹5; ◷10am-5pm Sat-Thu), which houses superb examples of local sculpture, including a remarkably explicit Lajja-Gauri image of a fertility cult that once flourished in the area. The stairway behind the museum climbs through a sandstone chasm and fortified gateways to reach the ruins of the **North Fort**.

It's also worth exploring Badami's **laneways**, where you'll find old houses with carved wooden doorways, the occasional Chalukyan ruin and flocks of curious kids.

🏃 Activities

The bluffs and the horseshoe-shaped red sandstone cliff of Badami offer some great low-altitude climbing. For more information, log on to www.dreamroutes.org.

🛏 Sleeping

Many of Badami's hotels offer discounts in the low season.

Mookambika Deluxe
HOTEL $
(☏220067; Station Rd; d ₹850-1100; 🕸) Faux antique lampshades hang in the corridors of this friendly hotel, leading to comfy rooms done up in matte orange and green. It's Badami's de facto tourist office, and your best bet in town.

Hotel Mayura Chalukya
HOTEL $
(☏220046; Ramdurg Rd; d from ₹600) A government issue buried behind civic offices away from the bustle, this renovated hotel has large and clean (though featureless) rooms. There's a decent restaurant serving Indian staples.

Hotel Rajsangam
HOTEL $$
(☏221991; www.hotelrajsangam.com; Station Rd; d Indian/foreigner from ₹800/US$20; 🕸@) This midrange place has slightly stuffy rooms that go unchallenged in their class. It sits right opposite the bus stand, in a commercial complex packing in sundry other utilities.

Hotel New Satkar
HOTEL $
(☏220417; Station Rd; d with/without AC ₹600/450; 🕸) The best of the mediocre rooms in this budget dive are on the 1st floor. There was some refurbishing on during research, so things might have improved by now.

Hotel Badami Court
HOTEL $$
(☏220231; Station Rd; d incl breakfast from ₹3750; 🕸🕸) This luxury hotel sits amid a pastoral countryside 2km from town. Rooms are more functional than plush. Nonguests can use the pool for ₹150.

🍴 Eating

Banashree
INDIAN $
(Station Rd; mains ₹70-90; ◷7am-10.30pm) The awesome North Indian thalis (₹80) at this busy and popular eatery in front of Hotel Rajsangam are tasty to the last morsel.

Golden Caves Cuisine
MULTICUISINE $
(Station Rd; mains ₹70-100; ◷9am-11pm) A shabby place that produces palatable Indian, Chinese and Continental fare, and stocks ample chilled beer for its thirsty young clients.

Hotel Sanman
INDIAN $
(Station Rd; mains ₹70-90; ◷10am-11.30pm) You might call it ropey, but it feels kind of nice to disappear behind a curtain in the booths and sip your beer in peace. The food is borderline.

Geeta Darshini
FAST FOOD $
(Station Rd; snacks ₹15-20; ◷7am-9pm) Staple South Indian snacks are on endless demand here, washed down with milky tea.

ℹ Information

Station Rd, Badami's main street, has several hotels and restaurants; the old village is between this road and the caves. The **KSTDC tourist office** (☏220414; Ramdurg Rd; ◷10am-5.30pm Mon-Sat), adjoining Hotel Mayura Chalukya, is not very useful.

SBI has ATMs on Ramdurg Rd and Station Rd. Mookambika Deluxe hotel changes currency for guests, but at a lousy rate.

Internet is available at **Hotel Rajsangam** (Station Rd; per hr ₹20) in the town centre.

❶ Getting There & Away

Buses regularly shuffle off from Badami's **bus stand** on Station Rd to Gadag (₹52, two hours), which has connections to Bijapur, Bengaluru and Hubli. Three buses go direct to Hospet (₹155, six hours). The tarmac's rough down this lane; mind your bum.

Broad-gauge railway has finally arrived in Badami. The 7.35am *Bijapur Express* now runs to Bijapur (2nd class ₹120, 3½ hours), while the 2.30am Hubli Express runs to Hubli (2nd class ₹120, 3½ hours). For Bengaluru, take the 8pm *Gol Gumbaz Express* (2nd class ₹244, 13 hours).

❶ Getting Around

Frequent, on-time local buses make sightseeing in the area quite affordable. You can visit Aihole and Pattadakal in a day from Badami if you get moving early. Start with Aihole (₹20, one hour), then move to Pattadakal (₹15, 30 minutes), and finally return to Badami (₹18, one hour). The last bus from Pattadakal to Badami is at 5pm. Take food and water with you.

Taxis/autorickshaws cost around ₹1000/600 for a day trip to Pattadakal, Aihole and nearby Mahakuta. Badami's hotels can arrange taxis; alternatively, go to the **taxi stand** in front of the post office.

Around Badami

PATTADAKAL

A secondary capital of the Badami Chalukyas, Pattadakal is known for its group of **temples** (Indian/foreigner ₹10/250; ☺6am-6pm), which are collectively a World Heritage Site. Barring a few temples that date back to the 3rd century AD, most others in the group were built during the 7th and 8th centuries AD. Historians believe Pattadakal served as an important trial ground for the development of South Indian temple architecture.

Two main types of temple towers were tried out here. Curvilinear towers top the Kadasiddeshwra, Jambulinga and Galaganatha temples, while square roofs and receding tiers are used in the Mallikarjuna, Sangameshwara and Virupaksha temples.

The main **Virupaksha Temple** is a massive structure, its columns covered with intricate carvings depicting episodes from the Ramayana and Mahabharata. A giant stone sculpture of Nandi sits to the temple's east. The **Mallikarjuna Temple**, next to the Virupaksha Temple, is almost identical in design. About 500m south of the main enclosure is the Jain **Papanatha Temple**, its entrance flanked by elephant sculptures. The tem-

ple complex also serves as the backdrop to the annual Classical Dance Festival, held between January and February.

Pattadakal is 20km from Badami. See p886 for transport details.

AIHOLE

Some 100 temples, built between the 4th and 6th centuries AD, speck the ancient Chalukyan regional capital of Aihole (*ay-ho-leh*). Most, however, are either in ruins or engulfed by the modern village. Aihole documents the embryonic stage of South Indian Hindu architecture, from the earliest simple shrines, such as the most ancient Ladkhan Temple, to the later and more complex buildings, such as the Meguti Temple.

The most impressive of them all is the 7th-century **Durga Temple** (Indian/foreigner ₹5/100; ☺8am-6pm), notable for its semicircular apse (inspired by Buddhist architecture) and the remains of the curvilinear *sikhara* (temple spire). The interiors house intricate stone carvings. The small **museum** (admission ₹5; ☺10am-5pm Sat-Thu) behind the temple contains further examples of Chalukyan sculpture.

To the south of the Durga Temple are several other temple clusters, including early examples such as the Gandar, Ladkhan, Kontigudi and Hucchapaya groups – all pavilion type with slightly sloping roofs. About 600m to the southeast, on a low hillock, is the Jain **Meguti Temple**. Watch out for snakes if you're venturing up.

Aihole is about 40km from Badami. See p886 for transport information.

Bijapur

📞08352 / POP 253,900 / ELEV 593M

A fascinating open-air museum dating back to the Deccan's Islamic era, dusty Bijapur tells a glorious tale dating back some 600 years. Blessed with a heap of mosques, mausoleums, palaces and fortifications, it was the capital of the Adil Shahi kings from 1489 to 1686, and one of the five splinter states formed after the Islamic Bahmani kingdom broke up in 1482. Despite its strong Islamic character, Bijapur is also a centre for the Lingayat brand of Shaivism, which emphasises a single personalised god. The **Lingayat Siddeshwara Festival** runs for eight days in January/February.

Bijapur's prime attractions, the Golgumbaz and the Ibrahim Rouza, are at opposite ends of town. Between them runs Station Rd (also

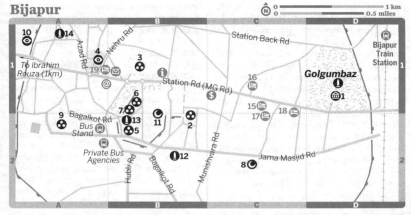

known as MG Rd), dotted with hotels and restaurants. The bus stand is a five-minute walk from Station Rd; the train station is 2km east of town.

◉ Sights

Golgumbaz   MONUMENT

(Indian/foreigner ₹5/100, video ₹25; ⊘6am-5.40pm)
Set in tranquil gardens, the magnificent Golgumbaz is big enough to pull an optical illusion on you; despite the perfect engineering, you might just think it's ill-proportioned! Golgumbaz is actually a mausoleum, dating back to 1659, and houses the tombs of emperor Mohammed Adil Shah (r 1627–56), his two wives, his mistress (Rambha), one of his daughters and a grandson.

Octagonal seven-storey towers stand at each corner of the monument, which is capped by an enormous dome. An astounding 38m in diameter, it's said to be the largest dome in the world after St Peter's Basilica in Rome. Climb the steep, narrow stairs up one of the towers to reach the 'whispering gallery' within the dome. An engineering marvel, its acoustics are such that if you whisper into the wall, a person on the opposite side of the gallery can hear you clearly. Unfortunately people like to test this out by hollering, so come early while most tourists are still snoozing.

Set in the lawns fronting the monument is a fantastic **archaeological museum** (admission ₹5; ⊘10am-5pm Sat-Thu). Skip the ground floor and head upstairs; there you'll find an excellent collection of artefacts, such as Persian carpets, china crockery, weapons, armours, scrolls and objects of daily use, dating back to Bijapur's heyday.

Bijapur

Ibrahim Rouza   MONUMENT

(Indian/foreigner ₹5/100, video ₹25; ⊘6am-6pm)
The beautiful Ibrahim Rouza is among the most elegant and finely proportioned Islamic monuments in India. Its tale is rather

poignant: the monument was built by emperor Ibrahim Adil Shah II (r 1580–1627) as a future mausoleum for his queen, Taj Sultana. Ironically, he died before her, and was thus the first person to be rested there. Interred here with Ibrahim Adil Shah and his queen are his daughter, his two sons, and his mother, Haji Badi Sahiba.

Unlike the Golgumbaz, noted for its immense size, the emphasis here is on grace and architectural finery. Its 24m-high minarets are said to have inspired those of the Taj Mahal. For a tip (₹150 is fine), caretakers will show you around the monument, including the dark labyrinth around the catacomb where the actual graves are located.

Citadel
FORT

Surrounded by fortified walls and a wide moat, the citadel once contained the palaces, pleasure gardens and durbar (royal court) of the Adil Shahi kings. Now mainly in ruins, the most impressive of the remaining fragments is the Gagan Mahal, built by Ali Adil Shah I around 1561 as a dual-purpose royal residency and durbar hall.

The ruins of Mohammed Adil Shah's seven-storey palace, the Sat Manzil, are nearby. Across the road stands the delicate Jala Manzil, once a water pavilion surrounded by secluded courts and gardens. On the other side of Station Rd are the graceful arches of Bara Kaman, the ruined mausoleum of Ali Roza.

Jama Masjid
MOSQUE

(Jama Masjid Rd; ⊙9am-5.30pm) Constructed by Ali Adil Shah I (r 1557–80), the finely proportioned Jama Masjid has graceful arches, a fine dome and a vast inner courtyard with room for more than 2200 worshippers. You can take a silent walk through its assembly hall, which still retains some of the elaborate murals. Women should make sure to cover their heads and not wear revealing clothing.

Other Sights
HISTORIC SITES

On the eastern side of the citadel is the tiny, walled Mecca Masjid, presumably built in the early 17th century. Some speculate that this mosque may have been for women. Further east, the Asar Mahal, built by Mohammed Adil Shah in about 1646 to serve as a Hall of Justice, once housed two strands of Prophet Mohammed's beard. The rooms on the upper storey are decorated with frescoes and a square tank graces the front. It's out of bounds for women. The stained but richly decorated Mihtar Mahal to the south serves as an ornamental gateway to a small mosque.

Upli Buruj is a 24m-high 16th-century watchtower near the city's western walls. An external flight of stairs leads to the top, mounted with two hefty cannons. A short walk west brings you to the Malik-e-Maidan (Monarch of the Plains), a huge cannon over 4m long, almost 1.5m in diameter and estimated to weigh 55 tonnes. Cast in 1549, it was supposedly brought to Bijapur as a war trophy thanks to the efforts of 10 elephants, 400 oxen and hundreds of men!

In the southwest of the city, off Bagalkot Rd, stand the twin Jod Gumbad tombs with handsome bulbous domes. An Adil Shahi general and his spiritual adviser, Abdul Razzaq Qadiri, are buried here.

Don't forget to spend a few hours in Bijapur's colourful central market, with its spice sellers, florists and tailors.

🛏 Sleeping

Hotel Pearl
HOTEL $

(☑256002; Station Rd; d from ₹550; ❄) As good as it gets for Bijapur, this excellent hotel features clean and bright rooms around a central atrium. It's very close to Golgumbaz. Ask for a room to the rear to avoid street noise.

Hotel Kanishka International
HOTEL $

(☑223788; Station Rd; s/d from ₹550/700; ❄) One of Bijapur's trusted options, this place has spacious and clean rooms, some with balconies. There's a small gym for guests' use, and the dealmaker is the excellent vegetarian restaurant downstairs. Book early.

Hotel Madhuvan International
HOTEL $

(☑255571; Station Rd; d ₹600-1000; ❄) Hidden down a lane off Station Rd, this pleasant hotel boasts lime-green walls, tinted windows and an amiable management. It's generally quiet and peaceful, but watch out for those boisterous wedding receptions often thrown at the garden restaurant.

Hotel Navaratna International
HOTEL $

(☑222771, Station Rd; d from ₹700; ❄) Bijapur's cheapest AC rooms are on offer at this well-managed hotel off Station Rd, with paintings à la Kandinsky and Chagall decorating the lobby. Rooms are sparkling clean, with shiny floor tiles.

Hotel Tourist
HOTEL $

(☑250655; Station Rd; d ₹190-350) Bang in the middle of the bazaar, with scrawny (but clean) rooms. Service is apathetic, so bring that DIY manual along.

Hotel Shashinag Residency HOTEL **$$**
(☑260344; www.hotelshashinagresidency.com; Sholapur-Chitradurga Bypass Rd; s/d incl breakfast ₹2250/2750; ❄️❄️) Consider this place only if you can't do without a swimming pool or a snooker parlour. It's about 2km away from town.

Eating & Drinking

Kamat Restaurant SOUTH INDIAN **$**
(Station Rd; mains ₹60-80; ⊙9am-11pm) Below Hotel Kanishka International, this popular joint serves diverse South Indian snacks and meals, including an awesome thali bursting with regional flavours.

Swapna Lodge Restaurant PUB **$**
(Station Rd; mains ₹80-100; ⊙noon-11pm) It's two floors up a dingy staircase next to Hotel Tourist, and has good grub, cold beer and a 1970s lounge feel. Its open-air terrace is a pleasant lounging spot, albeit a little noisy with maddening traffic below.

Hotel Madhuvan International INDIAN **$**
(Station Rd; mains ₹60-80; ⊙9am-11pm) Try the yummy *masala dosa* or the never-ending North Indian thalis dished out here by waiters in red turbans. The downside is that there's no alcohol on offer.

In the bustling market around Gandhi Circle on MG Rd, you'll find countless stalls flogging local snacks, roasted corn-on-the-cob, fresh fruits and sweetmeats such as *pedha* and *kalakandh*.

ⓘ Information

Cyber Park (Station Rd; per hr ₹20; ⊙9am-10pm) Internet access.
Royal Internet Café (Station Rd, below Hotel Pearl; per hr ₹20; ⊙9am-10pm) Internet access.
State Bank of India (Station Rd; ⊙10.30am-4.30pm Mon-Fri, 10.30am-1.30pm Sat) Changes foreign currency and is super-efficient.
Tourist office (☑250359; Station Rd; ⊙10am-5.30pm Mon-Sat) A poorly serviced office in the shabby Hotel Mayura Adil Shahi Annexe.

ⓘ Getting There & Away
Bus

From the **bus stand**, two early-morning buses run direct to Bidar (₹180, seven hours). Ordinary buses head frequently to Gulbarga (₹104, four hours) and Hubli (₹160, six hours). There are buses to Bengaluru (ordinary/sleeper ₹360/580, 12 hours, seven daily) via Hospet (₹148, five hours), Hyderabad (ordinary/semideluxe ₹239/348, 11

hours, five daily) and Mumbai (₹414, 12 hours, two daily) via Pune (₹293, 10 hours).

Train

From **Bijapur train station**, express trains go to Sholapur (2nd class ₹80, 2½ hours, three daily), Bengaluru (sleeper/2AC ₹288/1135, 17 hours, three daily), Mumbai (2nd class ₹149; 12 hours, four weekly) and Hyderabad (sleeper ₹121, 14 hours, one daily).

ⓘ Getting Around

Autorickshaws are expensive in Bijapur, so be prepared to haggle. ₹80 should get you from the train station to the town centre. Between the Golgumbaz and Ibrahim Rouza they cost about ₹50, unless you share with locals (₹10). Tonga drivers are eager for business but charge around the same. Autorickshaw drivers ask for about ₹350 for a sightseeing trip.

Bidar

☑08482 / POP 174,200 / ELEV 664M
Tucked away in Karnataka's far northeastern corner, Bidar is a little gem that most travellers choose to ignore, and no one quite knows why. At most an afterthought on some itineraries, this old walled town – first the capital of the Bahmani kingdom (1428–87) and later the capital of the Barid Shahi dynasty – is drenched in history. That apart, it is home to some amazing ruins and monuments, including the colossal Bidar Fort, the largest in South India. Wallowing in neglect, Bidar sure commands more than the cursory attention it gets today.

◉ Sights

Bidar Fort FORT
(⊙dawn-dusk) Keep aside a few hours for peacefully wandering around the remnants of this magnificent 15th-century fort. Sprawled across rolling hills 2km east of Udgir Rd, it was once the administrative capital of much of southern India. Surrounded by a triple moat hewn out of solid red rock and 5.5km of defensive walls (the second longest in India), the fort has a fairy-tale entrance that twists in an elaborate chicane through three gateways.

Inside the fort are many evocative ruins, including the **Rangin Mahal** (Painted Palace) which sports elaborate tilework, woodwork and panels with mother-of-pearl inlay, and the **Solah Khamba Mosque** (Sixteen-Pillared Mosque). There's also a small **museum** (admission free; ⊙9am-5pm) in the former royal bath. Clerks at the **archaeological office** beside the museum often double as guides. For a small tip (₹150 is fine), they can show you many hidden places within the fort which otherwise remain locked.

Bahmani Tombs
HISTORIC SITE

(☉dawn-dusk) The huge domed tombs of the Bahmani kings in Ashtur, 3km east of Bidar, have a desolate, moody beauty that strikes a strange harmony with the rolling hills around them. These impressive mausoleums were built to house the remains of the sultans – their graves are still regularly draped with fresh satin and flowers – and are arranged in a long line along the edge of the road. The painted interior of Ahmad Shah Bahman's tomb is the most impressive, and is regularly prayed in.

About 500m prior to reaching the tombs, to the left of the road, is **Choukhandi** (admission free; ☉dawn-dusk), the serene mausoleum of Sufi saint Syed Kirmani Baba, who travelled here from Persia during the golden age of the Bahmani empire. An uncanny air of calm hangs within the monument, and its polygonal courtyard houses rows of medieval graves, amid which women in hijab sit quietly and murmur inaudible prayers. You are welcome to sit in or walk around, and soak up the ambience.

Both places are best visited early in the day, as it's difficult to find transport back to Bidar after dark.

Other Sights
HISTORIC SITES

Dominating the heart of the old town are the ruins of **Khwaja Mahmud Gawan Madrasa** (admission free; ☉dawn-dusk), a college for advanced learning built in 1472 by Mahmud Gawan, then chief minister of the empire. It was later used as an armoury by Mughal emperor Aurangzeb, when a gunpowder explosion ripped the building in half. To get an idea of its former grandeur, check out the remnants of coloured tiles on the front gate and one of the minarets which still stands intact.

Scattered around the town's bus stand are a handful of magnificent but forgotten **royal tombs**, including those of Ali Barid and his son Kasim Barid.

🛏 Sleeping & Eating

Hotel Mayura
HOTEL $

(☏228142; Udgir Rd; d from ₹400; ☀) Smart and friendly, with cheerful and well-appointed rooms, this is clearly the best hotel to camp in Bidar. It's bang opposite the bus stand, and there's an excellent **bar-restaurant** on the ground floor.

Hotel Mayura Barid Shahi
HOTEL $

(☏221740; Udgir Rd; d from ₹350; ☀) Otherwise featureless with simple, minimalist rooms (service is OK, though), this place scores due to its central location. The lovely garden **bar-restaurant** to the rear brims over with joy and merriment every evening.

Sapna International
HOTEL $

(☏220991; Udgir Rd; d from ₹400; ☀) This place is let down by slightly stiff service, but the rooms are just about fine for the price. In its favour are the two restaurants: the pure-veg Kamat and the nonveg Atithi, which offers meat dishes and booze (mains ₹80 to ₹100).

Nisarga Restaurant
INDIAN $

(Papanash Lake; mains ₹60-100; ☉noon-10pm) For a truly memorable meal, head out of town to the edge of placid Papanash Lake, where you can relish a train of local dishes and mash-ups (the pea and mushroom curry is yummy) in this laid-back restaurant under a shady tree. A return autorickshaw with waiting time would cost you about ₹100, but the extra expense is worth every penny.

Rasganga
SOUTH INDIAN $

(Udgir Rd, mains ₹30-50; ☉9am-10pm) A tasty South Indian thali (₹37) is on offer at this busy eatery located within the Hotel Mayura Barid Shahi complex.

ℹ Information

The modern town centre is along Udgir Rd, down which you will also find the bus station.

HDFC Bank (Udgir Rd) ATM opposite Sapna International.

Nisarga Internet (per hr ₹20; ☉9am-9pm) Internet access near Sapna International.

ℹ Getting There & Away

From the **bus stand**, frequent buses run to Gulbarga (₹75, three hours), which is connected to Mumbai and Bengaluru. Buses also go to Hyderabad (₹103, four hours), Bijapur (₹180, seven hours) and Bengaluru (semideluxe/AC ₹359/580, 12 hours).

The train station, around 1km southwest of the bus stand, has services to Hyderabad (sleeper ₹120, five hours, three daily) and Bengaluru (sleeper ₹280, 17 hours, one daily).

ℹ Getting Around

Rent a bicycle at **Sami Cycle Taxi** (Basveshwar Circle; per day ₹20; ☉10am-10pm) against your proof of identity. Or simply arrange a day tour in an autorickshaw for around ₹350.

Andhra Pradesh

Best Places to Eat

» Waterfront (p901)

» Hotel Shadab (p901)

» Sandy Lane Restaurant
& Bar (p912)

» Fusion 9 (p903)

» Lotus Food City (p914)

Best Places to Stay

» Taj Mahal Hotel (p899)

» Taj Falaknuma Palace
(p899)

» Golden Glory Guesthouse
(p899)

» Sai Priya Resort (p912)

» Park (p912)

Why Go?

Andhra Pradesh won't hit you over the head with its attractions. It doesn't brag about its temples or its colourful history. It's forgotten most of its palaces and royal architecture – you'll have to purposely seek them out.

Andhra plays hard to get: its charms are subtle. But if you look closely, you'll find a long, fascinating history of arts, culture, spiritual scholarship and religious harmony. In Hyderabad's Old City, Islamic monuments, Persian-inspired architecture and the call of the muezzin speak of the city's unique heritage.

Dig a little deeper and you'll find another Andhran history: the region was an international centre of Buddhist thought for several hundred years from the 3rd century BC.

So come, but only if you're prepared to dig for the jewels to be found here. Keep your eyes open and your curiosity sharp and you're bound to find something that even Andhrans, in their modesty, hadn't thought to mention.

When to Go
Hyderabad

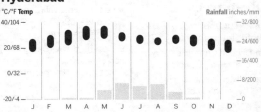

Dec–Jan Explore Hyderabad's sights in perfect 20-25°C weather.

Ramadan (around Jun–Aug) Join locals digging into *haleem*, a Ramzan favourite.

Jun–Sep Monsoons make travel tough, but surfing at beaches around Vizag is decent.

Food

Hyderabad is a city known for its love of good food, and locals take great pride in their city's offerings. Andhra Pradesh's cuisine has two major influences. The Mughals brought tasty biryanis, *haleem* (pounded, spiced wheat with goat or mutton) and kebabs. The Andhra style is vegetarian and famous for its spiciness.

If you're travelling around Andhra Pradesh during Ramadan (known locally as Ramzan), look out for the clay ovens called *bhattis*. You'll probably hear them before you see them. Men gather around, taking turns to vigorously pound *haleem* inside purpose-built structures. Come nightfall, the serious business of eating begins. The taste is worth the wait. In September 2010, this love of the dish was taken a step further, being patented as 'Hyderabadi haleem'; prohibited to be served under that name unless it meets the strict quality guidelines.

Top State Festivals

» Sankranti (Jan, statewide) This important Telugu festival marks the end of harvest season. Kite-flying abounds, women decorate their doorsteps with colourful *kolams* (or *rangolis* – rice-flour designs), and men decorate cattle with bells and fresh horn paint.

» Lumbini Festival (2nd Fri in Dec, Hyderabad, p894, Nagarjunakonda, p907) The three-day festival honours Andhra's Buddhist heritage.

» Visakha Utsav (Dec/Jan, Visakhapatnam, p911) A celebration of all things Visakhapatnam, with classical and folk dance and music performances; some events are staged on the beach.

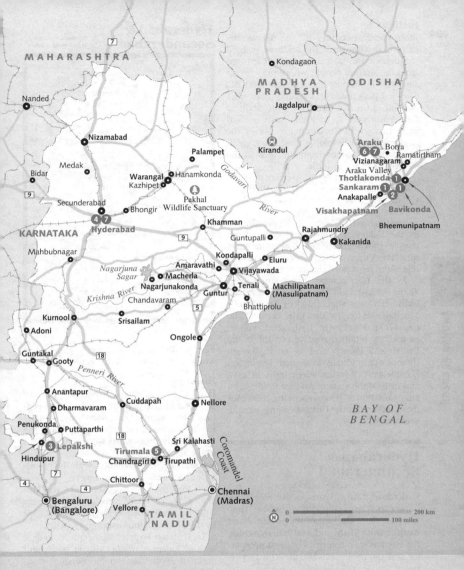

Andhra Pradesh Highlights

1 Absorb the meditative vibrations of monks past at **Sankaram** (p913), **Bavikonda** and **Thotlakonda** (p913)

2 Revel in the carnival beach atmosphere, at Visakhapatnam's **beaches** (p911)

3 Admire incredible carved images at **Veerbhadra Temple** in Lepakshi (p918).

4 Marvel at the genius design of **Golconda Fort** (p895)

5 Join millions of Hindu pilgrims taking *darshan* (deity viewing) at **Tirumala** (p915)

6 Sit back and enjoy the view on one of India's most scenic train trips to **Araku** (p913)

7 Learn about the state's rich ethnic diversity at the **tribal museums** in Hyderabad (p896) and Araku (p913)

History

From the 2nd century BC the Satavahana empire, also known as the Andhras, reigned throughout the Deccan plateau. It evolved from the Andhra people, whose presence in southern India may date back to 1000 BC. The Buddha's teaching took root here early on, and in the 3rd century BC the Andhras fully embraced it, building huge edifices in its honour. In the coming centuries, the Andhras would develop a flourishing civilisation that extended from the west to the east coasts of South India.

From the 7th to the 10th century, the Chalukyas ruled the area, establishing their Dravidian style of architecture, especially along the coast. The Chalukya and Chola dynasties merged in the 11th century to be overthrown by the Kakatiyas, who introduced pillared temples into South Indian religious architecture. The Vijayanagars then rose to become one of the most powerful empires in India.

By the 16th century the Islamic Qutb Shahi dynasty held the city of Hyderabad, but in 1687 was supplanted by Aurangzeb's Mughal empire. In the 18th century the post-Mughal rulers in Hyderabad, known as nizams, retained relative control as the British and French vied for trade, though their power gradually weakened. The region became part of independent India in 1947, and in 1956 the state of Andhra Pradesh, an amalgamation of Telugu-speaking areas plus the predominantly Urdu-speaking capital, was created.

Hyderabad & Secunderabad

📞 040 / POP 5.5 MILLION / ELEV 600M

Hyderabad, City of Pearls, is like an elderly, impeccably dressed princess whose time has past. Once the seat of the powerful and wealthy Qutb Shahi and Asaf Jahi dynasties, the city has seen centuries of great prosperity and innovation. Today, the 'Old City' is full of centuries-old Islamic monuments and even older charms. In fact, the whole city is laced with architectural gems: ornate tombs, mosques, palaces and homes from the past are tucked away, faded and enchanting, in corners all over town. Keep your eyes open.

In the last decade, with the rise of Hyderabad's west side – our aged princess's sexy and popular granddaughter – a new decadence has emerged. 'Cyberabad', with Bengaluru (Bangalore) and Pune, is the seat of India's mighty software dynasty and generates

Hyderabad & Secunderabad

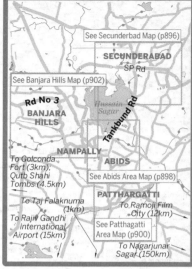

jobs, wealth and posh lounges. Opulence, it would seem, is in this city's genes.

History

Hyderabad owes its existence to a water shortage at Golconda in the late 16th century. The reigning Qutb Shahis were forced to relocate, and so Mohammed Quli and the royal family abandoned Golconda Fort for the banks of the Musi River. The new city of Hyderabad was established, with the brand-new Charminar as its centrepiece.

In 1687 the city was overrun by the Mughal emperor Aurangzeb, and subsequent rulers of Hyderabad were viceroys installed by the Mughal administration in Delhi.

In 1724 the Hyderabad viceroy, Asaf Jah, took advantage of waning Mughal power and declared Hyderabad an independent state with himself as leader. The dynasty of the nizams of Hyderabad began, and the traditions of Islam flourished. Hyderabad became a focus for the arts, culture and learning, and the centre of Islamic India. Its abundance of rare gems and minerals – the world-famous Kohinoor diamond is from here – furnished the nizams with enormous wealth. (William Dalrymple's *White Mughals* is a fascinating portrait of the city at this time.)

When Independence came in 1947, the then nizam of Hyderabad, Osman Ali Khan, considered amalgamation with Pakistan – and then opted for sovereignty. Tensions between Muslims and Hindus increased, however, and military intervention saw Hyderabad join the Indian union in 1948.

◉ Sights

Charminar
MONUMENT

(Four Towers; Map p900; Indian/foreigner ₹5/100; ☺9am-5.30pm) Hyderabad's principal landmark was built by Mohammed Quli Qutb Shah in 1591 to commemorate the founding of Hyderabad and the end of epidemics caused by Golconda's water shortage. The dramatic four-column, 56m high and 30m wide structure has four arches facing the cardinal points. Minarets sit atop each column. The 2nd floor, home to Hyderabad's oldest mosque, and upper columns are not usually open to the public, but you can try your luck with the man with the key. The structure is illuminated from 7pm to 9pm.

Golconda Fort
FORT

(off Map p894; Indian/foreigner ₹5/100; ☺9am-5pm) Although most of this 16th-century fortress dates from the time of the Qutb Shah kings, its origins as a mud fort have been traced to the earlier reigns of the Yadavas and Kakatiyas.

The citadel is built on a granite hill, 120m high and surrounded by crenellated ramparts constructed from large masonry blocks. The massive gates were studded with iron spikes to obstruct war elephants. Outside the citadel there stands another crenellated rampart, with a perimeter of 11km, and yet another wall beyond this. At Naya Quila (new fort), adjacent to the golf course, you can find a magnificent 400-year-old **baobab tree** (Hathiyan – elephant tree), with a circumference of 25m, said to be planted by seedlings carried by African regiments from Abyssiania. Exploring the crumbling rampart in the area you'll find cannons strewn about (some with beautiful inscriptions) and great views of the fort and tombs.

Survival within the fort was also attributable to water and sound. A series of concealed glazed earthen pipes ensured a reliable water supply, while the ingenious design of the diamond-shaped ceiling Grand Portico creates an acoustic system that carries even the smallest echo across the fort complex up to the highest point of the fort – used as a security system. Guides can also demonstrate the equally impressive acoustics in the royal palace where one's whisper into the corner of the wall can be heard perfectly through the walls in the opposing corner, designed to catch out conspirators.

Knowledgeable **guides** (1½hr tour ₹600) are organised through the AP Tourism table in front of the entrance. Small guidebooks to the fort are also available.

Mornings are best for peace and quiet. An autorickshaw from Abids costs around ₹150. It's a one hour bus journey either with Bus 119 from Nampally station or Bus 66G from Charminar.

A trippy **sound-and-light show** (admission ₹50; ☺in English 6.30pm Nov-Feb, 7pm Mar-Oct) is also held here.

Laad Bazaar
MARKET

(Map p900) West of the Charminar, the crowded Laad Bazaar is the perfect place to get lost. It has everything from fine perfumes, fabrics and jewels to musical instruments, secondhand saris and kitchen implements. Artisans are tucked away creating jewellery and scented oils, large pots and burkas. The lanes around the Charminar also form the centre of India's pearl trade. Some great deals can be had – if you know your stuff.

Salar Jung Museum
MUSEUM

(Map p900; www.salarjungmuseum.in; Salar Jung Marg; Indian/foreigner ₹10/150; ☺10am-5pm Sat-Thu) The huge and varied collection, dating back to the 1st century, was put together by Mir Yusaf Ali Khan (Salar Jung III), the grand vizier of the seventh nizam, Osman Ali Khan (r 1910–49). The 35,000 exhibits from every corner of the world include sculptures, wood carvings, ivory (including a sadly ironic set of carved elephants), devotional objects, Persian miniature paintings, illuminated manuscripts, weaponry, toys and more than 50,000 books. The impressive nizams' jewellery collection is sometimes on display. Cameras are not allowed. Avoid Sunday, when it's bedlam. From any of the bus stands in the Abids area, take bus 7, which stops at **Afzal Gunj bus stop** (Map p900) on the north side of the nearby Musi River bridge.

Just west of the bridge is the spectacular **Osmania General Hospital** (Map p900), on the north side, and, on the south, the **High Court** (Map p900) and **Government City College** (Map p900), all built under the seventh nizam in the Indo-Saracenic style.

Chowmahalla Palace
MUSEUM

(Khilwat; Map p900; www.chowmahalla.com; Indian/foreigner ₹30/150, camera ₹50; ☺10am-5pm Sat-Thu) The nizam family has sponsored a

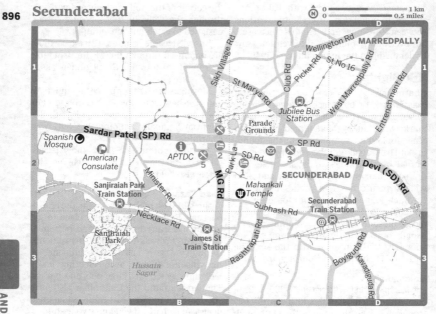

ANDHRA PRADESH

restoration of this dazzling palace – or, technically, four (*char*) palaces (*mahalla*). Begun in 1750, it was expanded over the next 100 years, absorbing Persian, Indo-Saracenic, Rajasthani and European styles. The southern courtyard has one *mahal* with period rooms that have been reconstructed with the nizams' over-the-top furniture; another *mahal* with an exhibit on life in the zenana (women's quarters); antique cars; and curiosities like elephant seats, and a Remington Urdu typewriter.

In the northern courtyard is the **Khilwat Mubarak**, a magnificent durbar hall houses exhibitions of photos, arms and clothing.

HEH the Nizam's Museum   MUSEUM

(Purani Haveli; Map p900; adult/student ₹70/15, camera ₹150; ⏱10am-5pm Sat-Thu) The 16th-century Purani Haveli was home of the sixth nizam, Fath Jang Mahbub Ali Khan (r 1869–1911), rumoured to have never worn the same garment twice. His 72m-long, two-storey Burmese teak wardrobe, the first room you'll enter, certainly seems to substantiate the claim. In the palace's former servants' quarters are personal effects of the seventh nizam, Osman Ali Khan (1886–1967) and gifts from his Silver Jubilee, lavish pieces that include an art deco silver letterbox collection. The museum's guides do an excellent job putting it all in context.

The rest of Purani Haveli is now a school, but you can wander around the grounds and peek in the administrative building, the nizam's former residence.

Qutb Shahi Tombs   TOMBS

(off Map p894; admission ₹10, camera/video ₹20/100; ⏱9am-5pm) These graceful domed tombs sit serenely in landscaped gardens about 1.5km northwest of Golconda Fort's Balahisar Gate. Seven of the nine Qutb Shahi rulers were buried here, as well as members of the royal family and respected citizens from entertainers to doctors. You could easily spend half a day here taking photos and wandering in and out of the mausoleums. The upper level of Mohammed Quli's tomb, reached via a narrow staircase, has good views of the area. The Qutb Shahi Tombs **booklet** (₹20) may be available at the ticket counter.

The tombs are an easy walk from the fort, but an autorickshaw ride shouldn't be more than ₹25. Bus 80S also heads here from the fort.

Nehru Centenary Tribal Museum   MUSEUM

(Map p902; Masab Tank; Indian/foreigner ₹10/100; ⏱10.30am-5pm Mon-Sat) Andhra Pradesh's 33 tribal groups, based mostly in the northeastern part of the state, comprise several

Secunderabad

million people. The recently refurbished museum, run by the government's Tribal Welfare Department, exhibits photographs, dioramas of village life, musical instruments and some exquisite Naikpod masks. It's basic, but you'll get a glimpse into the cultures of these fringe peoples. There's an excellent library with 13,500 books covering tribal groups of India, and next door is the tiny **Girijan Sales Depot**, selling products made in tribal communities.

FREE **Paigah Tombs**   TOMBS
(off Map p894; Phisalbanda, Santoshnagar; ☺10am-5pm Sat-Thu) The aristocratic Paigah family, purportedly descendents of the second Caliph of Islam, were fierce loyalists of the nizams, serving as statespeople, philanthropists and generals under and alongside them. The Paigahs' necropolis, tucked away in a quiet neighbourhood 4km southeast of Charminar, is a small compound of exquisite mausoleums made of marble from Agra and lime stucco. The main complex contains 27 tombs with intricate inlay work, surrounded by delicately carved walls and canopies, stunning filigree screens with geometric patterning and, overhead, tall, graceful turrets. The tombs are down a small lane across from Owasi Hospital. Look for the Preston Junior College sign. *The Paigah Tombs* (₹20) booklet is sold at the AP State Museum, but not here.

Buddha Statue & Hussain Sagar   MONUMENT
Hyderabad has one of the world's largest freestanding stone **Buddha statues** (Map p898), completed in 1990 after five years of work. However, when the 17.5m-high, 350-tonne monolith was being ferried to its place in the Hussain Sagar, the barge sank. Fortunately, the statue was raised – undamaged – in 1992 and is now on a plinth in the middle of the lake. It's a magnificent sight when alit at night.

Frequent **boats** (adult/child ₹50/25) make the 30-minute return trip to the statue from both **Eat Street** (Map p902; ☺2-8.40pm)

and **Lumbini Park** (Map p898; admission ₹10; ☺9am-9pm), a pleasant place to enjoy sunsets and the popular musical fountain. The Tankbund Rd promenade, on the eastern shore of Hussain Sagar, has great views of the Buddha statue.

AP State Museum   MUSEUM
(Map p898; Public Gardens Rd, Nampally; admission ₹10, camera/video ₹100/500; ☺10.30am-5pm Sat-Thu) The continually renovated State Museum hosts a rather dusty collection of important archaeological finds from the area, as well as a Buddhist sculpture gallery, with some relics of the Buddha and an exhibit on Andhra's Buddhist history. There are also Jain and bronze sculpture galleries, a decorative-arts gallery and a 4500-year-old Egyptian mummy. The museum, like the gorgeous **Legislative Assembly building** (Map p898) down the road (both commissioned by the seventh nizam), is floodlit at night.

Mecca Masjid   MOSQUE
(Map p900; Shah Ali Banda Rd, Patthargatti; ☺9am-5pm) This mosque is one of the world's largest, with space for 10,000 worshippers. Women are not allowed inside.

Several bricks embedded above the gate are made with soil from Mecca – hence the name. To the left of the mosque, an enclosure contains the tombs of Nizam Ali Khan and his successors.

Since the 2007 bomb blasts here, security is tight; no bags are allowed inside.

Birla Mandir &
Planetarium   HINDU TEMPLE, MUSEUM
(Map p898) The Birla **mandir** (☺7am-noon & 2-9pm), constructed of white Rajasthani marble in 1976, graces Kalabahad (Black Mountain), one of two rocky hills overlooking the Hussain Sagar. Dedicated to Venkateshwara, the temple is a popular Hindu pilgrimage centre and affords excellent views over the city, especially at sunset. The **library** (☺4- 8pm) here is worth a visit

Next door are the **Birla Planetarium & Science Museum** (museum/planetarium ₹20/35; ☺museum 10.30am-8pm, to 3pm Fri, planetarium shows 11.30am, 4pm & 6pm) and the worthwhile **Birla Modern Art Gallery** (admission ₹10; ☺10.30am-6pm).

Hyderabad has a burgeoning contemporary art scene:

ICCR Art Gallery   ART GALLERY
(Map p898; ☎23236398; Ravindra Bharati Theatre, Public Gardens Rd; ☺11am-7pm)

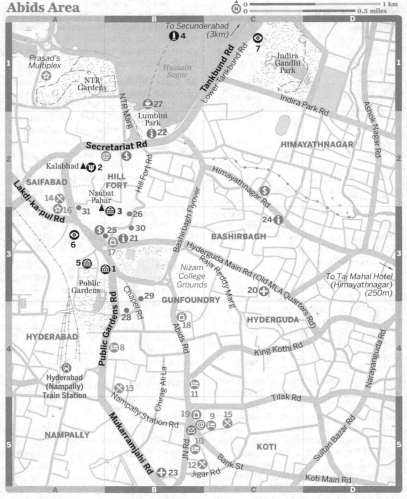

Kalakriti   ART GALLERY
(Map p902; www.kalakriti.in; Rd No 10, Banjara
Hills; ⊙11am-7pm)

Shrishti   ART GALLERY
(www.shrishtiart.com; Rd No 15, Jubilee Hills;
⊙11am-7pm)

🎓 Courses

**Vipassana International
Meditation Centre**   BUDDHIST MEDITATION
(Dhamma Khetta; ☎24240290; www.khetta.
dhamma.org; Nagarjuna Sagar Rd, 12.6km) The
Vipassana International Meditation Centre
has intensive 10-day meditation courses in
its peaceful grounds 20km outside the city.
Apply online or at the Hyderabad **office**
(☎24732569). A shuttle runs to/from Hyderabad on the first and last day of courses.

👉 Tours

APTDC (p906) tours the city (₹270), Ramoji
Film City (₹600), Nagarjuna Sagar (weekends,
₹450) and Tirupathi/Tirumala (three days,
₹1950). The Sound & Light tour (₹200) takes
in Hitec City, the botanic gardens and Golconda Fort's sound-and-light show, but you may
spend much of it in traffic. Tours leave from
APTDC's Secunderabad branch (Map p896)

ANDHRA PRADESH HYDERABAD & SECUNDERABAD

Passionate local **Abbas Tyabji** (☎9391010015) is an experienced guide/ photojournalist who can take you to less-touristy sights – such as toddy tappers at work or nature walks in the city's outskirts.

Society To Save Rocks WALKING
(☎23552923; www.saverocks.org; 1236 Rd No 60, Jubilee Hills) This NGO organises monthly walks through the Andhran landscape and its surreal-looking boulders. Check website for details.

🛏 Sleeping

TOP CHOICE **Taj Mahal Hotel (Himayathnagar)** HOTEL $$
(off Map p898; ☎27637836-9; tajcafe@gmail.com; Himayathnagar; s/d from ₹900/1200; ☀🛜) Despite its unfortunate location in front of an overpass on Himayathnagar Rd, the Taj is a peaceful, sunny, stylish place where the staff are warm and welcoming and the hallway floors look like Jaipuri marble. Rooms are surprisingly tasteful, with sleek lamps and chunky, contemporary wooden furniture. Comfy and classy for less than the going rate makes this a great choice.

Golden Glory Guesthouse HOTEL $
(Map p902; ☎23554765; www.goldengloryguest house.com; Rd No 3, Banjara Hills; s/d incl breakfast from ₹650/900, s incl breakfast without bathroom ₹290; ☀🛜) Nestled among the mansions of ritzy Banjara Hills, this gem of a hotel scores big on location. Tucked down a quiet residential street, it's the perfect place to escape the madness of Hyderabad. First impressions are grand with sparkling lobby and spiral staircase, and while the cheaper rooms are boxy, they're very clean and good value (and include a simple breakfast). Pricier rooms are more spacious with balconies and bathtubs.

Taj Falaknuma Palace HOTEL $$$
(off Map p894; ☎24388888; www.tajhotels.com; Engine Bowli, Falaknuma; s/d from ₹16,500/17,625) Nowhere suits the term 'fit for royalty' better than at the Falaknuma Palace, the former residence of the sixth nizam. Taking over a decade to restore, the Taj Group's latest luxury hotel has most certainly been worth the wait. The 'cheapest' rooms have Italian marble floors, colonial furniture and great city views, while the Presidential Suite (an astounding ₹500,000 per night) was

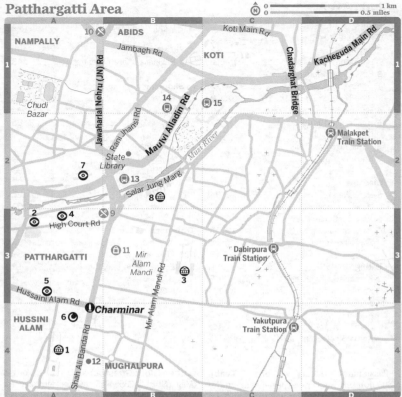

ANDHRA PRADESH

the nizam's living quarters and has its own swimming pool and personal butler! If you don't have a spare half million, you can still pop in for high tea in the Jade Room, which has hosted royalty from around the world.

Minerva Grand   HOTEL $$$
(Map p896; ☑66117373; www.minervagrand.com; SD Rd, Secunderabad; s/d incl breakfast from ₹4000 /4400; ❀@⛛) It's rare to find a hotel that has genuine style; this place has nailed it. Standard rooms (one wheelchair-accessible) have striking deep-fuchsia walls, white furniture, tasselled bedspreads and piles of pillows. More-expensive rooms are also bold in design, and all rooms have hardwood floors, gentle lighting and sleek, spacious bathrooms. A diamond in the rough of Sarojini Devi Rd.

Hotel Mandakini Jaya International   HOTEL $$
(Map p898; ☑9810068858; www.mandakinijayaintl -hyderabad.com; Hanuman Tekdi Rd; s/d incl break-fast from ₹1690/1790; ❀⛛) Under new management, the former budget Jaya International has reinvented itself as a smart and modern business hotel. Rooms are great value, comfortable and ultramodern. Its downside is the scungy hallways.

Nand International   HOTEL $
(☑24657511; www.nandhotels.com; Kacheguda Station Rd; s/d/tr from ₹535/635/735; ❀) The Nand is a pleasant surprise near Kacheguda Station. It has a roof garden with potted geraniums (and chai on order), sitting areas, water coolers, and well-looked-after peach-coloured rooms hung with weird mixed-media art.

YMCA   HOSTEL $
(Map p896; ☑27801190; secunderabadymca@ yahoo.co.in; cnr SP & SD Rd, Secunderabad; r from ₹500, without bathroom from ₹350; ❀) One of the better cheapies, this cheery hostel has clean, no frill rooms, some with private balcony. It's near the clock tower.

Hotel Suhail   HOTEL $

(Map p898; ☏24610299; www.hotel suhail.in; Troop Bazaar; s/d/tr from ₹475/620/900; ❄@) If all budget hotels were like the Suhail, we'd all be much better off. Staff are friendly and on top of it, the rooms are large and quiet, have balconies and constant hot water. It's tucked away on an alley behind the main post office and the Grand Hotel – away from the Hyderabad bustle, but it's also unlit at night; some readers find it sketchy.

Taj Mahal Hotel   HOTEL $$

(Map p898; ☏24758250; tajmahal_abid@rediffmail. com; cnr Abids & King Kothi Rds; s/d with AC from ₹1200/1650; ❄) This rambling 1924 heritage building has a magnificent exterior, plants peppered about and decent, though ultimately overpriced rooms. Each is different so ask to see a few: the better ones have boudoirs, crystal-knobbed armoires and wood-beam ceilings.

Hotel Harsha   HOTEL $$

(Map p898; ☏23201188; www.hotelharsha.net; Public Gardens Rd; s/d incl breakfast from ₹1600/1800; ❄⊙) Rooms don't have tonnes of character, and can be noisy (ask for a rear facing room) but they're bright, have fridges, the furniture is in good taste and the art is a step up from the usual schlock. The overall effect is polished but comfy. The lobby smells like success, with lots of glass and marble. One of the city's best deals.

Green Park   HOTEL $$$

(Map p902; ☏66515151; www.hotelgreenpark.com; Greenlands Rd, Begumpet; s/d incl breakfast from ₹5500/6500; ❄@⊙) Don't bother going beyond the standard rooms here, which are comfy and classy with sleek desks, bamboo flooring and flower petals in the bathroom. The lobby is a paragon of peace and gentle lighting, while smiley staff look on.

Secunderabad Retiring Rooms   RAILWAY RETIRING ROOMS

(Map p896; dm/s/d from ₹50/250/450; ❄) If you arrive late at Secunderabad train station, this is a good deal.

✗ Eating

Per local usage, we use the term 'meal' instead of 'thali' in this chapter.

CITY CENTRE

TOP CHOICE Waterfront   ASIAN FUSION $$$

(Map p902; ☏65278899; Necklace Rd; mains ₹175-650; ⊙noon-2.30pm & 7-11pm) The outdoor deck here on the water (dinner service only) may have the best ambience in all of Hyderabad, with soft lighting overhead, the Buddha Statue and the entire Hussain Sagar and the Birla Mandir all twinkling in the distance. Eating indoors, alongside enormous picture windows, isn't bad either. But it's the Chinese, Indian and Thai food that's to die for – their take on *phad kea mou* (noodles with tasty bok choy) is a must-eat.

Hotel Shadab   INDIAN $$

(Map p900; High Court Rd, Patthargatti; mains ₹60-250; ⊙noon-midnight) One meal at Shadab and you'll be forever under its spell. The hopping restaurant is *the* place to get biryani (₹95 to ₹200) and, during Ramzan (Ramadan), *haleem*. It has even mastered veg biryani (!) and hundreds of other veg and non-veg delights (if you try the chocolate

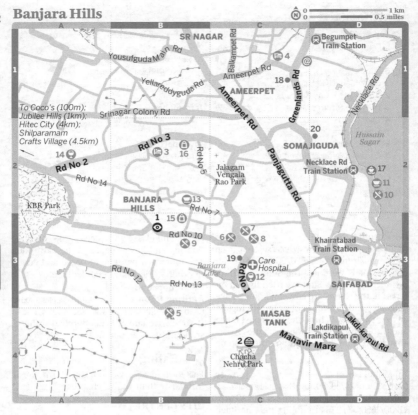

chicken or pineapple mutton, let us know how it goes). Packed with Old City families and good vibes.

Kamat Hotel   INDIAN $
(Map p896; SD Rd, Secunderabad; mains ₹45-75; ⊙7am-10pm) How much do we love Kamat Hotel? Words can't say. Each Kamat is slightly different, but they're all cheap and good. There are two branches on SD Rd; the others are in Saifabad and on Nampally Station Rd (Map p898). Meals (from ₹36) are reliably delish.

Kamat Andhra Meals   INDIAN $
(Map p898; Troop Bazaar; meals from ₹45; ⊙noon-4pm & 7-11pm) Excellent authentic Andhra meals on banana leaves, topped up till you almost faint with pleasure, and finished off with a banana. Its sister restaurants in the same compound – **Kamat Jowar Bhakri** (Maharashtran), **Kamat Restaurant** with air-con (North and South Indian) and

Kamat Coffee Shop – are likewise friendly family joints full of happy diners. No relation to Kamat Hotel.

Also recommended:

Paradise Persis Restaurant   INDIAN $$
(Map p896; cnr SD & MG Rds, Secunderabad; mains ₹125-245; ⊙11.30am-11pm) Ask any Hyderabadi about biryani, and they'll mention Paradise.

Mozamjahi Market   MARKET $
(Map p900; cnr Mukarramjahi & Jawaharlal Nehru Rds; ⊙6am-6pm) A great place to buy fruit and vegies (or ice cream), while enjoying the alluring architecture of the stone building, commissioned by the seventh nizam and named after his son.

Sagar Papaji Ka Dhaba   INDIAN $
(Map p898; Hanuman Tekdi Rd; mains ₹45-110; ⊙noon-4pm & 7-11pm) Always busy, Papaji's has profoundly delicious veg and non-veg biryanis, curries and tikkas. Watch the

guys making naan and throwing it in the tandoor while you wait for a table.

BANJARA HILLS & JUBILEE HILLS
Those looking for a finer dining experience should head to the hills, home to Hyderabad's more well-heeled residents.

Fusion 9 CONTINENTAL $$$
(Map p902; ☑65577722; Rd No 1; mains ₹325-425; ☺12-3.30pm & 7-11pm) Soft lighting and cosy decor set off pan-fried Norwegian salmon (₹650), lamb cutlets with rosemary and crispy potatoes (₹395), or pork chops (₹425). One of the best international menus in town also features (less expensive) Mexican, Thai, pizzas and veg dishes, and lots of imported liquor.

Angeethi PUNJABI $$
(Map p902; 7th fl, Reliance Classic Bldg, Rd No 1; mains ₹180-290; ☺noon-3.30pm & 7-11pm) Designed to resemble an old Punjabi *dhaba* (snack bar), jazzed up with vintage Bollywood posters on the walls, Angeethi does outstanding North Indian and Punjabi dishes, such as corn *methi malai* (sweet-corn stew with fenugreek leaves; ₹185).

Coco's INDIAN/CONTINENTAL $$
(off Map p902; ☑23540600; Rd No 2; mains ₹120-325; ☺11.30am-11.30pm) This chilled-out rooftop restaurant/bar almost succeeds in resembling a bamboo beach shack, though it's position on a busy road above a Chinese restaurant was always going to make it tough. Looking out over KBR Park, relaxed Coco's

exudes ambience and serves decent Indian and Western dishes.

Big Dosa Company INDIAN $
(Rd No 45, Jubilee Hills; dosas ₹75-135; ☺8am-11pm) There's a lot that's big about this dosa joint: the portions, the taste and the very idea itself of a gourmet dosa. The 'feta cheese and roasted pepper' dosa, served with sundried-tomato chutney or the 'shredded chicken' dosa make the journey out to Jubilee Hills worthwhile.

24-Lettered Mantra GROCERY SHOP
(Map p902; www.24lettermantra.com; Rd No 12; ☺9.30am-10pm) Healthy people will appreciate this tiny grocery shop with organic produce, snacks and juices.

Ofen BAKERY $$
(Map p902; www.theofen.com; Rd No 10; desserts ₹15-110; ☺11am-11pm Mon-Fri, 9am-11pm Sat & Sun) Two words: Linzer torte. Scrumptious desserts (some vegan and sugar-free), fresh-baked bread and comfort food like sandwiches and pasta (₹90 to ₹250). Does all-day continental breakfasts.

BBQ Nation INDIAN, CONTINENTAL $$
(Map p902; www.barbeque-nation.com; Rd No 1; lunch Mon-Sat ₹344, Sun ₹544, dinner ₹600; ☺noon-3pm & 7-11pm) All you can eat BBQ meat, seafood and vegetarian skewers served at your table.

Little Italy ITALIAN $$
(☑64566692; Apollo Rd, Jubilee Hills; mains ₹200-500 ☺noon-3pm & 7-11pm) Classy vegetarian Italian fare with good wine list.

ANDHRA PRADESH HYDERABAD & SECUNDERABAD

Mixed in with Hyderabad's world-class sights, you'll find some attractions that err on the more quirky side; which can provide some good relief from the 'proper' sightseeing.

Ramoji Film City   FILM STUDIO

(www.ramojifilmcity.com; adult/child ₹500/450; ⊘9.30am-5.30pm) The home of South India's burgeoning film industry, known as Tollywood, Ramoji Film City is undoubtedly the premier kitsch sight of Hyderabad. Set on more than 670 hectares, this is the world's largest movie-making complex, producing Telugu, Tamil, Hindi and the occasional foreign film. Though you won't actually get to see any being made, the four-hour bus tour will take you through flimsy film sets and gaudy fountains, stopping for dance routines and stunt shows. Located in the outskirts of town, around 20km from Abids, you can jump on bus 205 or 206 from Koti Women's College, northeast of Koti station, which take an hour to get here.

Health Museum   MUSEUM

(Map p898; Public Gardens Rd, Nampally; admission free; ⊘10.30am-5pm Sat-Thu) A throwback to a 1950s classroom, this museum houses a bizarre collection of medical and public-health paraphernalia. It features a rather terrifying giant model of a crab louse.

Snow World   AMUSEMENT PARK

(Map p898; Lower Tankbund; admission ₹300; ⊘11am-8pm) The perfect place to escape the heat, Snow World is, hands down, the coolest attraction in town (in a literal sense, of course...). It's a bizarre experience to suddenly find yourself in heavy-duty waterproof clothing amid people hurling snowballs, riding toboggans and playing snow volleyball. There's a snowfall on the hour, accompanied by cheers, a snow disco and lightshow.

Suddha Car Museum   MUSEUM

(www.sudhacars.net; Bahadurpura; Indian/foreigner ₹30/150; ⊘9.30am-6.30pm) Featuring the genius work of Sudhakar, here you'll find working cars in the shape of a toilet, computer, cricket bat, hamburger or condom, among other wacky designs. He holds the Guinness world record for the largest tricycle, standing a whopping 12.8m tall. You can poke your head into the workshop to see his latest project (at the time of research it was a 'stiletto shoe' car). It's located east of the Nehru Zoological Park.

NTR Park   PARK

(Map p898; child/adult ₹10/20; ⊘2.30-8.30pm) Making for a nice stroll about, with pleasant gardens, theme park rides and a games arcade, taking the cake in the kitsch stakes is the gaudy restaurant shaped like a giant fruit bowl.

Amurutha Castle   HOTEL

(www.bestwesternamruthacastle.com; Saifabad; d from ₹4800) Always dreamt of staying in a Bavarian castle while in Hyderabad? Probably not, but in case you did, this massive castle-hotel, based on the Schloss Neuschwanstein, is the place to do it. It ain't cheap though.

Drinking & Entertainment

Hyderabad's scene is growing, but drinking establishments are limited by an 11.30pm curfew law. Unless stated otherwise, the following bars are open to 11.30pm (but don't get going till 9pm). All serve food and charge covers (₹500 to ₹1000) on certain nights – for couples, that is: guys usually need a gal to enter. Beer starts at ₹150, cocktails at ₹300.

 Coco's   BAR

(off Map p902; ✆23540600; Rd No 2, Banjara Hills) Rooftop bar makes it the perfect place for a cold beer or cocktail on a balmy evening. Has live music.

Mocha   CAFE

(Map p902; Rd No 7, Banjara Hills; ⊘9am-11pm) Full of trendy twenty-somethings smoking hookahs (from ₹225), but the decor, the garden and the coffee are fabulous. Menu also has good breakfasts, paninis and shakes.

Liquids Et cera
BAR

(Map p902; ☑66259907; Bhaskar Plaza, Rd No 1, Banjara Hills) Regularly featured in the papers' Society pages, Liquids is the reigning queen of Hyderabad nightlife. There's no sign, and its name changes slightly each year.

Excess Club
BAR

(☑23542422; Novotel, Madhavpur; ⊙7pm-2am Tue-Sun) Set over a huge space, Excess was the current most happening place; open the latest, the best DJs, but the furthest away – past Hitech City.

Touch
BAR

(Map p902; ☑23542422; Trendset Towers, Rd No 2, Banjara Hills); ⊙7pm-midnight Wed, Sat & Sun) Touch is all about image. It's a stylish, comfy place to watch the beautiful people. Also has an 'ice bar' with temperatures set at -23°.

Café Coffee Day
CAFE

(Map p902; Eat Street, Necklace Rd; ⊙7.30am-11pm) Decent coffee and snacks.

Barista
CAFE

(Map p902; Rd No 1, Banjara Hills; ⊙8am-11pm) Another reliable coffee option.

Ravindra Bharati Theatre
THEATRE

(Map p898; ☑23233672; www.artistap.com; Public Gardens Rd) Regular music, dance and drama performances. Check local papers.

🔒 Shopping

The bazaars near the Charminar (p895) are the most exciting places to shop: you'll find exquisite pearls, silks, gold and fabrics alongside billions of bangles.

Hyderabad Perfumers
PERFUMERY

(Map p900; Patthargatti; ⊙10am-8.30pm Mon-Sat) The family-run Hyderabad Perfumers, which has been in business for four generations, can whip something up for you on the spot.

Meena Bazar
CLOTHING

(Map p898; www.meenabazarhyd.co.in; Tilak Rd; ⊙10.30am-8.30pm Mon-Sat) Gorgeous saris, *salwar* (trouser) suits and fabrics at fixed prices. Also has a branch in Banjara Hills (Map p902).

Kalanjali
HANDICRAFTS

(Map p898; Hill Fort Rd; ⊙10am-9.30pm) With a huge range of arts, crafts, fabrics and clothing, Kalanjali (split between two buildings) has higher prices than the bazaar, but you can get a feel for what things cost in a relaxed environment.

Shilparamam Crafts Village
HANDICRAFTS

(off Map p902; www.shilparamam.org; Madhapur; adult/child ₹25/10; ⊙10.30am-8.30pm) Near Hitech City, this government-initiative arts village has stalls selling handicrafts and clothes from all over India. A night bazaar is also planned. It has nice gardens with a pond to stroll about.

Fabindia
CLOTHING

(Map p902; www.fabindia.com; Rd No 9, Banjara Hills; ⊙11am-8.30pm) Clothes and accessories in traditional artisanal fabrics.

Lepakshi
HANDICRAFTS

(Map p898; www.lepakshihandicrafts.gov.in; Gunfoundry; ⊙10am-8pm Mon-Sat) Andhra crafts.

ℹ Information

Internet Access

Anand Internet (per hr ₹15; ⊙10.30am-9.30pm) Opposite Secunderabad station.

Net World (Taramandal Complex, Saifabad; per hr ₹15; ⊙9.30am-7pm Mon-Sat)

Reliance Internet (Himayathnagar; per hr ₹15; ⊙8.30am-11pm)

Reliance Web World (MPM Mall, Abids Circle; per 4hr ₹100; ⊙10.30am-9.30pm Mon-Sat, 12.30-9pm Sun)

Media

Good 'what's on' guides include *Channel 6* (www .channel6magazine.com), *GO Hyderabad* and *City Info*. The juiciest is *Wow! Hyderabad* (www .wowhyderabad.com; ₹25). The *Deccan Chronicle* is a good local paper; its *Hyderabad Chronicle* insert has info on happenings.

Medical Services

Apollo Pharmacy (Map p898; ☑23431734; Hyderguda Main Rd) Delivers.

Care Hospital Banjara Hills (Map p902; ☑30418888; Rd No 1); Nampally (Map p898; ☑30417777; Mukarramjahi Rd) Reputable hospital with a 24-hour pharmacy.

Money

The banks offer the best currency-exchange rates here. ATMs are everywhere.

State Bank of India (☑23231986; HACA Bhavan, Saifabad; ⊙10.30am-4pm Mon-Fri)

Post

Post office (⊙8am-8.30pm Mon-Sat, 10am-2pm Sun) Secunderabad (Rashtrapati Rd); Abids (Abids Circle)

Tourist Information

Andhra Pradesh Tourism Development Corporation (APTDC; ☑24-hr info 23450444; www.aptdc.in; ⊗7am-8.30pm) Bashirbagh (Map p898; ☑23298456; NSF Shakar Bhavan, opposite Police Control Room); Secunderabad (Map p896; ☑27893100; Yatri Nivas Hotel, Sardar Patel Rd); Tankbund Rd (Map p898; ☑65581555; ⊗10.30am-5pm) Organises tours.

India Tourism (Government of India; Map p898; ☑23261360, 23260770; Netaji Bhavan, Himayathnagar Rd; ⊗9.30am-6pm Mon-Fri, to noon Sat) Very helpful for information on Hyderabad, Andhra Pradesh and beyond.

❶ Getting There & Away

Air

Hyderabad's massive, modern **Rajiv Gandhi International Airport** (☑66546370; www.hyderabad.aero) is 22km southwest of the city in Shamshabad.

You'll get the best fares online or with a travel agent. Try **Neo Globe Tours & Travels** (Map p898; ☑66751786; Saifabad; ⊗10am-7.30pm Mon-Sat, 11am-2pm Sun) beside the Nizam Club.

Airline offices are usually open from 9.30am to 5.30pm Monday to Friday, with a one-hour lunch break, and to 1.30pm Saturday.

Domestic airline offices:

GoAir (☑airport 9223222111, 1800222111; Rajiv Gandhi International Airport)

Indian Airlines (Map p898; ☑23430334, airport 24255161/2; HACA Bhavan, Saifabad)

IndiGo (Map p898; ☑23233590, airport 24255052; Interglobe Air Transport, Chapel Rd)

Jet Airways (Map p898; ☑39893333, airport 39893322; Hill Fort Rd; ⊗9am-7pm Mon-Sat) Also handles bookings for JetLite.

JetLite (☑30302020; Rajiv Gandhi International Airport)

Kingfisher Airlines (Map p902; ☑40328400, airport 66605603; Balayogi Paryatak Bhavan,Begumpet)

SpiceJet (☑18001803333; Rajiv Gandhi International Airport)

International airlines:

Air India (Map p898; ☑1800227722, airport 66605163; HACA Bhavan, Saifabad)

AirAsia (Map p898; ☑66666464, airport 66605163; HACA Bhavan, Saifabad)

Emirates (Map p902; ☑66234444; Rd No 1, Banjara Hills)

GSA Transworld Travels (Map p898; ☑3298495; Chapel Rd) For Qantas.

Lufthansa (☑4888888; Rajiv Gandhi International Airport)

Sri Lankan Airlines (Map p902; ☑23372429/30; Raj Bhavan Rd, Somajiguda) Opposite the Yashoda Hospital.

Qatar Airways (Map p902; ☑01244566000, airport 66605121; Rd No 1, Banjara Hills)

Thai Airways (Map p902; ☑23333030; Rd No 1, Banjara Hills)

Bus

Hyderabad's long-distance bus stations are mind-bogglingly efficient. **Mahatma Gandhi bus station** (Map p900; ☑24614406), more commonly known as Imlibun, has **advance booking offices** (☑23434269; ⊗8am-10pm). For trips to Karnataka, go with **KSRTC** (☑24656430). Visit www.apsrtc.co.in for timetables and fares.

Secunderabad's **Jubilee bus station** (Map p896; ☑27802203) operates Volvo AC buses to Bengaluru (₹801, 11 hours, six daily), Chennai (₹844, 12 hours, daily) and Visakhapatnam (₹701, 13 hours, daily).

Private bus companies with AC services are on Nampally High Rd, near the train station entrance.

Train

Secunderabad (Map p894), Hyderabad (Map p898) – also known as Nampally – and Kacheguda (off Map p898) are the three major train stations. Most through trains stop at Secunderabad

MAJOR DOMESTIC FLIGHTS FROM HYDERABAD

DESTINATION	LOWEST ONE-WAY FARE (₹)	DURATION (HR)	FLIGHTS PER DAY
Bengaluru	3000	1	20
Chennai	3000	1	15
Delhi	5000	2	12
Kolkota	5500	2	5
Mumbai	3000	1¼	25
Tirupathi	2800	1	3
Visakhapatnam	3500	1	5

DESTINATION	FARE (₹)	DURATION (HR)	FREQUENCY (DAILY)
Bengaluru	480-775	12-10	7 (evening)
Bidar	80	4	half-hourly
Chennai	550-880	12-14	3 (evening)
Hospet	280	9	2
Mumbai	550-985	14-12	6 (evening)
Mysore	599	15	1
Nagarjuna Sagar	85-116	4	8
Tirupathi	435-735	12	12
Vijayawada	197-390	6	hourly
Visakhapatnam	470-865	14	12
Warangal	77	3	half-hourly

and Kacheguda, which is convenient for Abids. See p908, for key routes. You can book at Hyderabad and Secunderabad stations from 8am to 8pm Monday to Saturday (to 2pm Sunday). Both stations have a tourist counter. For general enquiries, phone ☑139; for reservation status, ☑135.

ℹ Getting Around

To/From the Airport

The new airport is fabulous, and is a 45 minute drive into town.

BUS Frequent public buses depart from the PTC for Jubilee and Imlibun stations. More comfy are AC **Aeroexpress** (☑18004192008; ⏱24hr) buses (₹175), which run half-hourly to Charminar, Secunderabad, Begumpet, Mehdipatnam and Hitec City.

TAXI For prepaid taxis, pay at the counter inside the terminal, then get your cab at the PTC. **Meru** (☑44224422) and **Easy** (☑43434343) 'radio taxis' queue up outside arrivals and charge ₹15 per kilometre, ₹18.75 at night. The trip to Abids or Banjara Hills shouldn't exceed ₹450. Going to the airport, try **Yellow Taxi** (☑44004400).

Autorickshaw

Flag fall is ₹12 for the first kilometre, then ₹7 for each additional kilometre. Between 10pm and 5am a 50% surcharge applies. Unfortunately, the new electronic meters often don't work and lots of drivers won't use them: be prepared to negotiate.

Bus

Lots of local buses originate at **Koti bus station** (Map p900; ☑23443320; Rani Jhansi Rd), so if you come here you might get a seat. The 'travel as you like' ticket (ordinary/express ₹40/50),

available from bus conductors, permits unlimited travel anywhere within the city on the day of purchase. The tiny *City Bus Route Guide* (₹10) is available at bookshops around Koti.

Car

There are several car-hire places around Hyderabad station. **Links Travels** (☑9348770007) is reliable for local or long-distance day-hire.

Train

MMTS trains (www.mmts.co.in) are convenient, particularly for the three main train stations. There are two main lines: Hyderabad (Nampally) to Lingampalli (northwest of Banjara Hills) has 11 stops, including Lakdikapul, Khairatabad, Necklace Rd, Begumpet and Hitec City; the Falaknuma (south of Old City) to Secunderabad line passes by Yakutpura, Dabirpura, Malakpet and Kachiguda among others. Trains will be labelled with their start and end point: HL is Hyderabad–Lingampalli, FS is Falaknuma–Secunderabad and so on. Trains are efficient but only run every 30 to 40 minutes. Tickets are ₹3 to ₹10.

Nagarjunakonda

☑08680

The Hill of Nagarjuna, 150km southeast of Hyderabad, is a peaceful island in the middle of the Nagarjuna dam peppered with ancient Buddhist structures. From the 3rd century BC until the 4th century AD, the Krishna River valley was home to powerful empires that supported the sangha (Buddhist community of monks and nuns), including the Ikshvakus, whose capital was Nagarjunakonda. It's estimated that this area alone had 30 monasteries.

The remains here were actually discovered in 1926 by archaeologist AR Saraswathi in the adjacent valley. In 1953, when it became known that a massive hydroelectric project would soon create the **Nagarjuna Sagar** reservoir, flooding the area, a six-year excavation was launched to unearth the area's many Buddhist ruins: stupas, *viharas* (monasteries), *chaitya-grihas* (assembly halls with stupas) and *mandapas* (pillared pavilions), as well as some outstanding examples of white-marble depictions of the Buddha's life. The finds were reassembled on Nagarjunakonda.

Sights & Activities

Nagarjunakonda Museum   MUSEUM
(Indian/foreigner ₹5/100; ◷8am-5pm) This thoughtfully laid-out museum, located on an island accessible by boat, has Buddha statues and beautifully carved limestone slabs that once adorned stupas. Most are from the 3rd century AD and depict scenes from the Buddha's life, interspersed with *mithuna* (paired male and female) figures languorously looking on. The reassembled **monuments** are spread around the hilltop outside.

Launches (₹90, one hour) depart from Vijayapuri, on the banks of Nagarjuna Sagar, at 9.30am, 11am and 1.30pm, and stay for one hour. To do the place justice, take the morning launch out and the afternoon one back. Extra morning launches usually run on weekends and holidays. Fisherman out in their dish-shaped coracle boats provide good photographic material.

Anupu   HISTORICAL SITE
Another Buddhist site 10km from the launch point is the peaceful **Anupu** with remains of a stupa, university and amphitheatre; likewise relocated piece by piece prior to the construction of the dam. A tree here was planted by the Dalai Lama during his visit in 2006.

MAJOR TRAINS FROM HYDERABAD & SECUNDERABAD

DESTINATION	TRAIN NO & NAME	FARE (₹)	DURATION (HR)	DEPARTURE TIME & STATION
Bengaluru	2430 *Rajdhani*	1025/1355 (A)	12	6.50pm Secunderabad (Tue, Wed, Sat & Sun)
	2785 *Secunderabad–Bangalore Exp*	274/715/970 (B)	11	7.05pm Kacheguda
Chennai	2604 *Hyderabad–Chennai Exp*	297/779/1058 (B)	13	4.55pm Hyderabad
	2760 *Charminar Exp*	312/837/1119 (B)	14	6.30pm Hyderabad
Delhi	2723 *Andhra Pradesh Exp*	465/1252/1715 (B)	26	6.25am Hyderabad
	2429 *Rajdhani*	1725/2245 (A)	26	7.50am Secunderabad (Mon, Tue, Thu & Fri)
Kolkata	2704 *Falaknuma Exp*	442/1187/1623 (B)	26	4pm Secunderabad
	8646 *East Coast Exp*	430/1178/1624 (B)	30	10am Hyderabad
Mumbai	2702 *Hussainsagar Exp*	312/823/1119 (B)	15	2.45pm Hyderabad
	7032 *Hyderabad–Mumbai Exp*	297/792/1089 (B)	16	8.40pm Hyderabad
Tirupathi	2734 *Narayanadri Exp*	284/794/1009 (B)	12	6.05pm Secunderabad
	2797 *Venkatadri Exp*	277/723/979 (B)	12	8.05pm Kacheguda
Visakhapatnam	2728 *Godavari Exp*	297/779/1058 (B)	13	5.15pm Hyderabad

Fares: A – 3AC/2AC; B – sleeper/3AC/2AC

ANDHRA PRADESH

BUS NO	ROUTE
65G/66G	Charminar–Golconda, via Abids
87	Charminar–Nampally
2/2V, 8A/8U	Charminar–Secunderabad station
20D	Jubilee station–Nampally
142K	Koti–Golconda
119OR, 142M	Nampally–Golconda
1P/25	Secunderabad station–Jubilee station
1K, 1B, 3SS, 40	Secunderabad station–Koti
20P, 20V, 49, 49P	Secunderabad station–Nampally

Ethipophala waterfall　　WATERFALL
(admission ₹20; ◷8am-6pm) A further 18km from the launch point is the 21m-high Ethipophala waterfall, which, after heavy rain can be a spectacular sight.

❧ Courses

Dhamma Nagajjuna　　MEDITATION
(Nagarjunasagar Vipassana Centre; ☎09440139329; www.nagajjuna.dhamma.org; Hill Colony) Keeping the legacy of Buddhism alive in the region, this centre offers intensive 10-day meditation courses in the grounds overlooking Nagarjuna Sagar. Courses are run on a donation basis.

⛌ Sleeping & Eating

Nagarjunakonda is popular, and accommodation can be tight during weekends and holidays, though it's easily visited as a day trip. Both hotels have restaurants.

Nagarjuna Resort　　HOTEL **$**
(☎08642-242471; r from ₹750; ✳) The most convenient place to stay, across the road from the boat launch. It has spacious, slightly shabby rooms with geysers, balconies and good views.

Vijay Vihar Complex　　HOTEL **$$**
(☎277362; fax 276633; r with AC from ₹1800; ✳✳) Two kilometres up the hill from the bus stand is the fancy government hotel overlooking the lake. Room balconies have excellent views.

❶ Information

AP Tourism (☎276634; ◷10am-5.30pm Mon-Sat) Has an office at Project House, across from the bus stand.

❶ Getting There & Away

The easiest way to visit Nagarjunakonda is with **APTDC** (☎040-65581555) in Hyderabad. Tours (₹450) depart on weekends at 7am returning at 9.30pm.

You can also make your own way there from Hyderabad or Vijayawada. From Hyderabad, take a bus to Nagarjuna Sagar (from ₹85, four hours). From there, it's a ₹10 shared rickshaw to Pylon, and another ₹10 to the boat launch. The nearest train station is 22km away at Macherla, where buses leave regularly for Nagarjuna Sagar.

Warangal

☎0870 / POP 528,570

Warangal was the capital of the Kakatiya kingdom, which covered the greater part of present-day Andhra Pradesh from the late 12th to early 14th centuries until it was conquered by the Tughlaqs of Delhi. The Hindu Kakatiyas were great builders and patrons of Telugu literature and arts, and during their reign the Chalukyan style of temple architecture reached its pinnacle.

Most buses and trains will stop en route at **Bhongir**, 60km from Hyderabad. It's worth jumping down for a couple of hours to climb the fantastical-looking 12th-century Chalukyan **hill fort** (admission ₹3; ◷9am-6pm). Looking like a gargantuan stone egg, the hill is mostly ringed by stairs.

Warangal, Hanamkonda and Kazhipet are sister towns. The Warangal train station and bus stand are opposite each other, and the post office and police station are on Station Rd. Main Rd connects Warangal and Hanamkonda. It can be easily visited as a day trip.

STATE OF GOOD KARMA

In its typically understated way, Andhra Pradesh doesn't make much of its vast archaeological – and karmic – wealth. But the state is packed with impressive ruins of its rich Buddhist history. Only a few of Andhra's 150 stupas, monasteries, caves and other sites have been excavated, turning up rare relics of the Buddha (usually pearl-like pieces of bone) with offerings such as golden flowers. Nagarjunakonda and Amaravathi were flourishing Buddhist complexes, and near Visakhapatnam were the incredibly peaceful sites of Thotlakonda, and Bavikonda and Sankaram, looking across seascapes and lush countryside.

They speak of a time when Andhra Pradesh – or Andhradesa – was a hotbed of Buddhist activity, when monks came from around the world to learn from some of the tradition's most renowned teachers. Andhradesa's Buddhist culture, in which sangha (community of monks and nuns), laity and statespeople all took part, lasted around 1500 years from the 6th century BC. There's no historical evidence for it, but some even say that the Buddha himself visited the area.

Andhradesa's first practitioners were likely disciples of Bavari, an ascetic who lived on the banks of the Godavari River and sent his followers north to bring back the Buddha's teachings. But the dharma really took off in the 3rd century BC under Ashoka, who dispatched monks across his empire to teach and construct stupas enshrined with relics of the Buddha. (Being near these was thought to help progress on the path to enlightenment.)

Succeeding Ashoka, the Satavahanas and then Ikshvakus were also supportive. At their capital at Amaravathi, the Satavahanas adorned Ashoka's modest stupa with elegant decoration. They built monasteries across the Krishna Valley and exported the dharma through their sophisticated maritime network.

It was also during the Satavahana reign that Nagarjuna lived. Considered by many to be the progenitor of Mahayana Buddhism, the monk was equal parts logician, philosopher and meditator, and he wrote several ground-breaking works that shaped contemporary Buddhist thought. Other important monk-philosophers would emerge from the area in the following centuries, making Andhradesa a sort of Buddhist motherland of the South.

◉ Sights

Fort
FORT

(Indian/foreigner ₹5/100; ◷9am-6.30pm) Warangal's fort was a massive construction with three distinct circular strongholds surrounded by a moat. Four paths with decorative gateways, set according to the cardinal points, led to the Swayambhava, a huge Shiva temple. The gateways are still obvious, but most of the fort is in ruins. It's easily reached from Warangal by bus or autorickshaw (₹200 return). Admission includes entry to nearby Kush Mahal, a 16th century royal hall with artefacts on display.

1000-Pillared Temple
HINDU TEMPLE

(◷6am-6pm) Built in 1163, the 1000-Pillared Temple on the slopes of Hanamkonda Hill, 400m from Hanamkonda crossroads, is a fine example of Chalukyan architecture in a peaceful, leafy setting. Dedicated to three deities – Shiva, Vishnu and Surya – it has been carefully restored with intricately carved pillars and a central, very impressive Nandi (bull; Shiva's mount) of black granite.

Down the hill and 3km to the right is the small Siddheshwara Temple. The Bhadrakali Temple, featuring a stone statue of Kali seated with a weapon in each of her eight hands, is high on a hill between Hanamkonda and Warangal.

🛏 Sleeping & Eating

Hotel Ashoka
HOTEL $$

(☎2578491; Main Rd, Hanamkonda; r from 600; ✴@) Good-value rooms near the Hanamkonda bus stand and the 1000-Pillared Temple. Also in the compound are a restaurant, a bar-restaurant, a pub and the veg Kanishka (mains ₹75 to ₹125).

Vijaya Lodge
HOTEL $

(☎2501222; fax 2446864; Station Rd; s/d from ₹150/240) About 100m from the train station, the Vijaya is well organised with helpful staff, but the rooms are becoming a little dreary.

❶ Information

Lots of ATMs and SGS Internet (per hr ₹10) are near Hotel Ratna on JPN Rd. The Department of Tourism (☑2459201; Hanamkonda-Kazhipet Rd, 3rd fl; ◷10.30am-5pm Mon-Sat), tucked off a sidestreet, opposite Indian Oil, is helpful.

ℹ Getting There & Around

Frequent buses to Hyderabad (express/deluxe/ luxury ₹77/87/100, four hours) depart from **Hanamkonda bus stand** (☑9959226056).

Warangal is a major rail junction. Trains go regularly to Hyderabad (2nd class/chair ₹67/229, three hours), Vijayawada (2nd class/ chair ₹79/278, four hours) and Chennai (sleeper/3AC/2AC ₹277/723/979, 11 hours). Many trains go to Delhi daily.

Shared autorickshaws ply fixed routes around Warangal (including to the fort), Kazhipet and Hanamkonda. A shared autorickshaw ride costs ₹5 to ₹7.

Around Warangal

PALAMPET

About 65km northeast of Warangal, the stunning **Ramappa Temple** (◷6am-6.30pm), built in 1234, is an attractive example of Kakatiya architecture, although it was clearly influenced by Chalukya and Hoysala styles. Its pillars are ornately carved and its eaves shelter fine statues of female forms.

Just 1km south, the Kakatiyas constructed **Ramappa Cheruvu** to serve as temple tank. The lake, along with nearby Pakhal Lake 20km south, is popular with migrating birds.

The easiest way to get here is by private car (₹1000), but frequent buses also run from Hanamkonda to Mulugu (₹22), then a further 13km to Palampet (₹10). The temple is about 500m from here.

Visakhapatnam

☑0891 / POP 1.3 MILLION

Visit Visakhapatnam – also called Vizag (*vie*-zag) – during the holiday season and you'll see domestic tourism in rare form: balloons, fairy floss (cotton candy) and, of course, weddings! But the crowds only enhance the area's kitschy coasts. The rundown boardwalk along Ramakrishna Beach has lots of spunk, and the beach at nearby Rushikonda is Andhra's best.

The old beach-resort vibe exists despite the fact that Vizag is Andhra Pradesh's second-largest city, famous for shipbuilding, steel manufacturing and now, call centres, software and film production. It's a big, dusty city, but it's surrounded by little gems:

sweet beaches, a gorgeous temple and, further out, the Araku Valley and several ancient Buddhist sites.

For up-to-date social happenings, grab a copy of *Yo! Vizag* (₹25) from local bookstores.

◉ Sights & Activities

Beaches   BEACH
The long beaches of **Waltair** overlook the Bay of Bengal, with its mammoth ships and brightly painted fishing boats. Its coastal **Beach Rd**, lined with parks and weird sculptures, is great for long walks.

The best beach for swimming is at **Rushikonda**, 10km north of town, one of the nicest stretches of coast you'll find this side of India. Weekends get busy and take on a carnival-like atmosphere. **Surfers** keen for a paddle can rent decent boards from local surf pioneer, Melville, at **SAAP** (Sports Authority of Andhra Pradesh, Rushikonda; ☑9848561052). To avoid unwanted attention, modest swim attire is recommended for females.

On the way to Rushikonda, **Kailasagiri Hill** has a cable car, gardens, playgrounds, toy train and a gargantuan Shiva and Parvati.

Bheemunipatnam, 25km north of Vizag, a former Dutch settlement and the oldest municipality in mainland India, is worth a visit. Here you'll find more bizarre sculptures, a lighthouse dating from 1861, an interesting Dutch cemetery and **Bheemli Beach**, where local grommets surf on crude homemade boards. To get here catch bus 999 (₹19), or otherwise a shared autorickshaw

Submarine Museum   MUSEUM
(Beach Rd, adult/child ₹25/15; ◷2-8.30pm Tue-Sat, 10am-12.30pm & 2-8.30pm Sun) A fascinating opportunity to look inside the 91m-long Indian navy submarine. The soviet-built *Kursura* saw battle in 1971 during the Liberation War, (which saw India side with East Pakistan in their struggle for independence from Pakistan – resulting in the birth of Bangladesh) and, exploring within, you'll find a fantastic jumble of knobs, switches, wires, valves, gauges, nuts, bolts and dials.

☞ Tours

APTDC operates full-day tours of the city and surrounds (from ₹300) and Araku Valley.

🛌 Sleeping

Waltair along Beach Rd is the place to stay, but has few inexpensive hotels.

Sai Priya Resort
HOTEL $

(☎2856330; www.saipriyabeachresorts.com; cottages/r from ₹700/1300; ✳@☲) Boasting a prime position right on Rushikonda beach, Sai Priya offers either modern rooms, some with sea views, or more rustic bamboo and cane cottages which have more of a beachy feel. The grounds are lush and *almost* really beautiful but, like the rest of the place, they fall short of their potential. Also, checkout's a rude 8am. Guests and nonguests can use the pool for two hours for ₹100.

Park
HOTEL $$$

(☎2754488; www.theparkhotels.com; Beach Rd; s/d from ₹7000/9000; ✳@☲) Vizag's only five-star is very elegant, very high-design. Even if you don't stay here, visit Bamboo Bay, its beachfront restaurant, for a drink. Checkout is noon.

Haritha Hotel
HOTEL $$

(☎2562333; Beach Rd, Appughar; r incl breakfast from ₹900; ✳) This APTDC hotel, formerly Punnami, is near Kailasagiri Hill and right across from the beach. The lowest-priced rooms (with no views) are only so-so; bump yourself up if you can. Checkout is 10am.

YMCA Tourist Hostel
HOSTEL $

(☎2755826; ymca_visakha@yahoo.com; Beach Rd; dm/s/d from ₹150/550/650; ✳) Best value in town, with superb views, but always full. Call anyway; you might get lucky.

Gateway Hotel
HOTEL $$$

(☎6623670; www.tajhotels.com/gateway; Beach Rd; s/d from ₹7000/8000; ✳@☲) The usual Taj classiness, with great sea views. Checkout is noon.

Dumpy budget hotels huddle around the train station:

Retiring rooms
RAILWAY RETIRING ROOMS $

(dm/r from ₹100/350; ✳)

Sree Kanya Lodge
HOTEL $

(☎5564881; Bowdara Rd; s/d from ₹250/500; ✳) Mostly characterless and a little dirty, but it's the best of the lot around the station.

✖ Eating & Drinking

At night, the snack stalls on Ramakrishna Beach and the beachfront restaurants at Rushikonda, next to Punnami, are hopping.

Sandy Lane Restaurant & Bar
INDIAN $$

(Beach Rd; mains ₹80-160; ⊙11am-12.30pm) In a colonial building a few doors down from the Park hotel, out the back are tables in the sand on the edge of the beach where you can indulge in delicious spicy fried fish (₹120) and tiger prawns (₹160). It's also a great spot for a cold beer with ocean views and a big outdoor screen. It's an over-whelmingly male clientele, but isn't as seedy like some Indian bars.

New Andhra Hotel
INDIAN $

(Sree Kanya Lodge, Bowdara Rd; mains ₹25-75; ⊙11am-3.30pm & 7-10.30pm) An unassuming little place with *really* good, *really* hot Andhra dishes. Meals (₹50/130 for veg/non-veg) and biryani are top-notch.

Masala
INDIAN $$

(Signature Towers, 1st fl, Asilmetta; mains ₹60-180; ⊙11.30am-3.30pm & 7-11pm) Near Sampath Vinayaka Temple, Masala does out-of-this-world Andhra, tandoori and Chinese. Try the *chepa pulusu* (Andhra-style fish; ₹130).

Kebabri
INDIAN $$

(Siripuram Junction; kebabs ₹95-250; ⊙5.30-10.30pm) massive succulent BBQ kebabs, from tandoori chicken to seafood, to mouth-watering paneer skewers. Has another branch on Beach Rd.

Pastry, Coffee n' Conversation
BAKERY $

(PCC; Siripuram Junction; ⊙11am-11pm) Hang-out spot for Vizag's hip young crowd, this is the place for pizza, burgers and delicious cakes.

ⓘ Information

ATMs are everywhere. RTC Complex has several internet cafes (per hour ₹15), some open 24 hours.

Apollo Pharmacy (☎2788652; Siripuram Junction; ⊙24hr)

APTDC RTC Complex (☎2788820; ⊙6.30am-9pm); Train station (☎2788821; ⊙6am-9pm) Information and tours.

Thomas Cook (☎2588112; Eswar Plaza, Dwarakanagar; ⊙9am-6.30pm Mon-Sat) Near ICICI Bank.

ⓘ Getting There & Around

You'll have to negotiate fares with autorickshaw drivers here. Most in-town rides will be around ₹20. **Guide Tours & Travels** (☎2754477), reliable for car hire, is opposite the RTC Complex 'out gate'.

Air

Take an autorickshaw (₹200), taxi (₹270) or bus 38 (₹6) to Vizag's airport, 13km west of town.

Domestic airlines and their daily services:

Indian Airlines (☎2746501, airport 2572521; LIC Bldg) Chennai, Delhi, Hyderabad and Mumbai.

Kingfisher (☎2503285, airport 2517614; Ardee Bldg, Siripuram Junction) Bengaluru, Chennai, Hyderabad, Kolkota, Pune and Tirupathi.

SpiceJet (☎airport 2010422) Delhi, Hyderabad, Kolkata and Mumbai .

Boat

Boats depart every month-ish for Port Blair in the Andaman Islands. Bookings for the 56-hour journey (from ₹1960) can be made at the **Shipping Office** (☎2565597, 9866073407; Av Bhanoji Row; ⊙9am-5pm Mon-Sat) in the port complex. Bring your passport.

Bus

Vizag's well-organised **RTC Complex** (☎2746400) has frequent bus services to Vijayawada (deluxe/Volvo ₹250/530, eight/seven hours) and, in the afternoon, Hyderabad ('super-luxury'/Volvo ₹470/870, 14/12 hours).

Train

Vizag's train station is on the western edge of town, near the port. Visakhapatnam Junction station is on the Kolkata-Chennai line. The overnight *Coromandel Express* (sleeper/3AC/2AC ₹333/881/1199, 13½ hours) is the fastest of the five daily trains running to Kolkata. Heading south, it goes to Chennai (sleeper/3AC/2AC ₹310/817/1112, 14 hours). Frequent trains head to Vijayawada including 2717, the *Ratnachalam Express* (2nd-class/chair ₹108/477).

Around Visakhapatnam

ARAKU VALLEY

Andhra's best train ride is through the magnificent Eastern Ghats to the **Araku Valley**, 120km north of Vizag. The area is home to isolated tribal communities, and a small **Museum of Habitat** (admission ₹10; ⊙10am-1pm & 2-5pm) with exhibits on indigenous life. APTDC runs **tours** (₹500) from Vizag, which take in a performance of Dhimsa, a tribal dance, and the million-year-old limestone **Borra Caves** (admission ₹40, camera ₹100; ⊙10am-1pm & 2-5pm), 30km from Araku.

Araku itself is a small dusty town, but its surroundings are beautiful. A bicycle is the perfect way to explore the countryside. You can hire a bicycle (per hour/day ₹50/250) from Hill Resort Mayuri. It's best to check the security situation before heading out, with a reported Naxalite (members of an ultraleftist political movement) presence in the region.

Chandrika Guest House (☎9490430989; s/d ₹1000/1500), 2km from the station, is the most peaceful option with rooms looking out to fields, though it's overpriced. The **Hill Resort Mayuri** (☎958936-249204; cottages from ₹650; ✳), near the museum, has cottages with good views. There's also a few uninspiring options around the station, otherwise you could try the forest retreat of **Jungle Bells** (Tyda; cottages from ₹800; ✳), 45km from Araku, with cottages tucked away in woods. Book at APTDC. You can sample the local coffee at **Araku Valley Coffee House** (⊙9am-9pm), next to the Museum of Habitat.

The Kirandol passenger train (₹20, five hours) leaves Vizag at 6.50am and Araku at 3pm. It's a slow, spectacular ride; sit on the right-hand side coming out of Vizag for best views. For Jungle Bells, get off at Tyda station, 500m from the resort. Frequent buses (₹58, 4½ hours) leave from Araku to Vizag every hour until 7pm.

BAVIKONDA & THOTLAKONDA

The Vizag area's natural harbours have long been conducive to dropping anchor, which helped monks from Sri Lanka, China and Tibet come here to learn and practice meditation. **Bavikonda** (⊙9am-6pm) and **Thotlakonda** (⊙10am-3pm) were popular hilltop monasteries on the coast that hosted up to 150 monks at a time – with the help of massive rainwater tanks and, at Thotlakonda, a natural spring.

The monasteries flourished during the Theravada period (Bavikonda, from the 3rd century BC to the 3rd century AD, and Thotlakonda, from the 2nd century BC to 2nd century AD) and had votive stupas, congregation halls, *chaitya-grihas*, *viharas* and refectories. Today only the ruins of these massive monastic compounds remain, but they're impressive nonetheless, with a placid, almost magical, air and sea views to meditate on. Bavikonda and Thotlakonda are 14km and 16km, respectively, from Vizag on Bheemli Beach Rd. Vizag's autorickshaw drivers charge around ₹400 return to see both.

SANKARAM

Forty kilometres southwest of Vizag is this stunning **Buddhist complex** (admission free; ⊙9am-6pm), better known by the name of its two hills, Bojjannakonda and Lingalakonda. Used by monks from the 1st to 9th centuries AD (p910), the hills are covered with rock-cut caves, stupas, ruins of monastery structures, and reliefs of the Buddha that span the Theravada, Mahayana and Vajrayana periods. Bojjannakonda has a two-storey group of rock-cut caves flanked by *dwarapalakas* (doorkeepers) and containing a stupa and gorgeous carvings of the Buddha (some restored). Atop the hill sit the ruins of a huge stupa and a monastery; you can still make out the individual cells where monks meditated. Lingalakonda is piled high with stupas, some of them enormous.

A private car from Vizag costs around ₹800. Or, take a bus to Anakapalle (₹24, one hour, every 20 minutes), 3km away, and then an autorickshaw (₹150 return including waiting time).

Vijayawada

☑0866 / POP 1 MILLION

Vijayawada is a busy, rapidly growing city and an important port at the head of the delta of the mighty Krishna River. It's bustling, but it's also intersected by canals, lined with ghats and ringed by fields of rice and palm. The surrounding area is intensely lush and green.

Vijayawada is considered by many to be the heart of Andhra culture and language and has an important Durga temple. Nearby Amaravathi, meanwhile, was a centre of Buddhist learning and practice for many centuries.

Om Art Print (JD Hospital Rd, cnr Besant Rd; ⊙10am-8.30pm Mon-Sat) sells maps.

👁 Sights

Undavalli Cave Temples   HINDU SITE
(Indian/foreigner ₹5/100; ⊙8am-5.30pm) Four kilometres southwest of Vijayawada, these stunning cave temples cut a fine silhouette against the palm trees and rice paddies. Shrines are dedicated to the Trimurti – Brahma, Vishnu and Shiva – and one cave on the third level houses a huge, beautiful statue of reclining Vishnu while seated deities and animals stand guard out front. The caves, in their Hindu form, date to the 7th century, but they're thought to have been constructed for Buddhist monks 500 years earlier. Bus 301 (₹9, 20 minutes) goes here.

Victoria Jubilee Museum   MUSEUM
(MG Rd; admission Indian/foreigner ₹20/100, camera ₹3; ⊙10.30am-5pm Sat-Thu) The best part of this museum is the building itself, built in 1887 to honour Queen Victoria's coronation jubilee. In 1921 it hosted the Congress meeting

where a new tricolour flag was introduced: Mahatma Gandhi added a wheel to the design and made it the Indian National Congress's official flag.

The interesting architecture outshines the museum's small collection of art and arms. But the **garden**, where temple sculptures from around the state (dating from the 3rd century AD) line shady paths, is lovely.

🛶 Courses

Dhamma Vijaya   MEDITATION
(Vipassana Meditation Centre; ☑08812-225522; www.dhamma.org; Eluru-Chintalapudi Rd) Offers intensive 10-day *vipassana* meditation courses free of charge in lush palm- and cocoa-forested grounds. The centre is 15km from Eluru; call for details.

🛏 Sleeping

Hotel Sri Ram   HOTEL $
(☑2579377; Hanumanpet; s/d from ₹360/450; ❄) This cheapie has bright, clean, nondescript rooms near the train station. A conveniently located safe bet.

Swarna Palace   HOTEL $$
(☑2577222; swarnapalace@rediff.com; Eluru Rd, Governorpet; s/d with AC from ₹1400/1500; ❄) Swarna, along with Hotel Ilapuram, are Vijayawada's two best midrange places. Both fall short of the sleekness they aspire to. But they're professionally run – and a little bit sleek anyway.

Hotel Ilapuram   HOTEL $$
(☑2571282; ilapuram@hotmail.com; Prakasam Rd; s/d with AC from ₹1500/1700; ❄)

Gateway Hotel   HOTEL $$$
(☑6644444; www.thegatewayhotels.com; MG Rd; s/d from ₹3500/4250; ❄@) The most upmarket option.

Retiring rooms   RAILWAY RETIRING ROOMS $
(dm/s/d from ₹75/180/375; ❄) The train station's clean and spacious rooms are a great option.

Bus station dorms   HOSTEL $
(☑3097809; from ₹100) The bus station, just north of the river, has dorms for gents.

🍴 Eating

Lotus Food City   INDIAN $$
(www.lotusthefoodcity.com; Seethanagaram; mains ₹80-150) Set up by APTDC, this food complex has a lovely spot on the Krishna River where you can dine in or outdoors looking out to the shimmering water.

Minerva Coffee Shop INDIAN $
(Museum Rd; mains ₹58-150; ⊙6.30am-11pm; ☀)
Just around the corner from Big Bazaar, this
outpost of the fabulous Minerva chain has
great North and South Indian, including top-
notch dosas (₹33 to ₹58). Its rava masala dosa
(made with semolina) is the best thing *ever.*

Modern Cafe INDIAN $
(Sree Lakshmi Vilas; Besant Rd, Governorpet;
meals ₹58; ⊙6.30am-10.30pm) With black-
and-white-check floors and mismatched
wooden chairs, this gritty, down-home veg
joint has a heavy 1940s vibe. The meals
are great, as are the fresh juices (₹15).

ℹ Information

Apollo Pharmacy (Vijaya Talkies Junction,
Eluru Rd; ⊙24hr)
APTDC (☑2571393; MG Rd, opposite PWD
Grounds; ⊙9am-7pm) Don't bother, unless you
need brochures.
Department of Tourism (train station;
⊙10am-5pm)
KIMS Hospital (☑2570761; Siddhartha Nagar)
MagicNet (Swarnalok Complex, Eluru Rd; per
hr ₹20; ⊙9.30am-9pm) Internet access.
State Bank of Hyderabad (1st fl, Vijaya Com-
mercial Complex, Governorpet; ⊙10.30am-
3pm Mon-Fri) Changes currency and travellers
cheques.

ℹ Getting There & Around

The bus stand has a helpful **enquiry desk**
(☑2522200). Frequent services run to Hyderabad (deluxe/Volvo ₹193/375, six to seven
hours), Amaravathi (₹38, two hours), Warangal
(deluxe ₹180, 5½ hours) and Visakhapatnam
(deluxe/Volvo ₹270/540, nine hours).

Vijayawada is on the main Chennai–Kolkata
and Chennai–Delhi railway lines. The daily
Coromandel Express (2841) runs to Chennai
(sleeper/3AC/2AC ₹214/544/732, seven
hours) and, the other way, to Kolkata (2842;
sleeper/3AC/2AC ₹395/1054/1440, 20 hours).
Speedy *Rajdhani* (Thursday and Saturday)
and *Jan Shatabdi* (daily except Tuesday) trains
also ply the Vijayawada–Chennai route. Trains
galore run to Hyderabad (sleeper/3AC/2AC
₹190/478/639, 6½ hours) and Tirupathi
(sleeper/3AC/2AC ₹198/502/674, seven
hours). The **computerised advance-booking
office** (☑enquiry 2577775, reservations
2578955; ⊙8am-8pm Mon-Sat, till 2pm Sun) is
in the basement.

The train station has a prepaid autorickshaw
stand marked 'Traffic Police'.

Around Vijayawada

AMARAVATHI

Once the Andhran capital and a significant
Buddhist centre, Amaravathi is India's biggest **stupa** (Indian/foreigner ₹5/100; ⊙8am-
6pm), measuring 27m high and constructed
in the 3rd century BC, when Emperor Ashoka
sent monks south to spread the Buddha's
teaching. Located 60km west of Vijayawada,
all that remains are a mound and some
stones, but the nearby **museum** (admission
₹5; ⊙8am-5pm) has a small replica of the stupa, with its intricately carved pillars, marble-
surfaced dome and carvings of scenes from
the Buddha's life (no photography allowed
in the museum). In the courtyard is a reconstruction of part of the surrounding gateway,
which gives you an idea of the stupa's massive scale. It's worth the trip, but many of
Amaravathi's best sculptures are in London's
British Museum and Chennai's Government
Museum in Tamil Nadu.

About 1km down the road is the **Dhyana
Buddha**, an imposing 20m-high seated Buddha built on the site where the Dalai Lama
spoke at the 2006 Kalachakra, which gives
the place added atmosphere.

Buses run from Vijayawada to Amaravathi every half-hour or so (₹24, two hours),
but it may be quicker to head to Guntur
(₹12, 45 minutes) and take another bus from
there. The drive here will take you through
some lovely lush scenery and memorable
glimpses of village life.

KONDAPALLI

Kondapalli fort (admission ₹5, camera ₹100;
⊙10.30am-5pm), strategically situated on the
old Machilipatnam–Golconda trade route,
was built in 1360 by the Reddy kings, and
was held by the Gajapathis, the Qutb Shahis,
the Mughals and the nizams before becoming a British military camp in 1767. Today
it's a quiet, lovely ruin. On weekdays, you'll
likely have the place to yourself and you
can easily spend a few hours hiking around.
Kondapalli village, 1km downhill, is famous
for its wooden dolls. The fort is 21km from
Vijayawada; an autorickshaw is ₹400 return.

Tirumala & Tirupathi

☑0877 / POP 302,000
The holy hill of **Tirumala** is, on any given
day, filled with tens of thousands of blissed-
out devotees, many of whom have endured

long journeys to see the powerful **Lord Venkateshwara** here, at his home. It's one of India's most visited pilgrimage centres: on average, 40,000 pilgrims come each day (the total often exceeds 100,000), and *darshan* (deity-viewing) runs 24/7. Temple staff alone number 12,000, and the efficient **Tirumala Tirupathi Devasthanams** (TTD; ☑2277777; www.tirumala.org) brilliantly administers the crowds. As a result, although the throngs can be overwhelming, a sense of order, serenity and ease mostly prevails, and a trip to the Holy Hill can be fulfilling, even if you're not a pilgrim.

'It is believed that Lord Sri Venkateshwara enjoys festivals', according to the TTD. And so do his devotees: *darshan* queues during October's **Brahmotsavam** can run up to several kilometres.

Tirupathi is the service town at the bottom of the hill, with hotels, restaurants, and transport; a fleet of buses constantly ferries pilgrims the 18km up and down. You'll find most of your worldly needs around the Tirupathi bus station (TP Area) and, about 500m away, the train station.

◉ Sights

Venkateshwara Temple
HINDU TEMPLE

Devotees flock to Tirumala to see Venkateshwara, an avatar of Vishnu. Among the many powers attributed to him is the granting of any wish made before the idol at Tirumala. Many pilgrims also donate their hair to the deity – in gratitude for a wish fulfilled, or to renounce ego – so hundreds of barbers attend to devotees. Tirumala and Tirupathi are filled with tonsured men, women and children, generating big money from exports to Western wig companies.

Legends about the hill itself and the surrounding area appear in the Puranas, and the temple's history may date back 2000 years. The main temple is an atmospheric place, though you'll be pressed between hundreds of devotees when you see it. The inner sanctum itself is dark and magical; it smells of incense, resonates with chanting and may make you religious. There, Venkateshwara sits gloriously on his throne, inspiring bliss and love among his visitors. You'll have a moment to make a wish and then you'll be shoved out again. Don't forget to collect your delicious *ladoo* (sweet made of flour, sugar, raisins and nuts) from the counter.

'Ordinary *darshan*' requires a wait of anywhere from two to six hours in the claustrophobic metal cages ringing the temple. 'Quick *darshan*' tickets (₹300) are recommended, and will get you through the queue faster, though you'll still have to brave the gauntlet of the cage, which is part of the fun, kind of... Upon entry you'll also have to sign a form declaring your support of Lord Vishnu.

Tours

If you're pressed for time, APTDC runs three-day tours (₹1950) to Tirumala from Hyderabad. KSTDC (p849) and TTDC (p998) offer the same from Bengaluru and Chennai, respectively. APTDC also has a full-day tour (₹340) of temples in the Tirupathi area.

🛏 Sleeping & Eating

The TTD runs *choultries* (guesthouses) for pilgrims in Tirumala and Tirupathi, but most non-Hindu visitors stay in one of Tirupathi's many hotels.

Vast **dormitories** (beds free) and **guesthouses** (r ₹50-2500) surround the temple in Tirumala, but these are intended for pilgrims. To stay, check in at the Central Reception Office. Huge **dining halls** (meals free) serve thousands of pilgrims daily. Veg restaurants also serve meals for ₹15. The following places are all in Tirupathi.

Hotel Bliss
HOTEL $$

(☑2237773; www.blisstirupati.com; Reniguta Rd; s/d from ₹1710/1980; ❄@☀) The most luxurious place in town with ultracomfortable rooms, professional staff and a glass lift with great views and droning pilgrim elevator music.

Hotel Annapurna
HOTEL $$

(☑2250666; Nethaji Rd; r from ₹850; ❄) A wee bit overpriced, but it's convenient and well organised. Rooms are clean, compact and pink, with constant hot water. Since it's on a corner (across from the train station), non-AC front rooms can be noisy. Its veg **restaurant** (mains ₹45-80) has fresh juices and Tirupathi's best food in sublime air-conditioning.

Hotel Mamata Lodge
HOTEL $

(☑2225873; 1st fl, 170 TP Area; s/d/tr & q ₹200/300/400) A friendly, spick-and-span cheapie. Some of the sheets are stained, but they're tucked in tight and lovingly patched with white squares. Avoid the downstairs lodge of the same name.

Retiring rooms
RAILWAY RETIRING ROOMS $

(dm/r from ₹45/150, with AC ₹400; ❄) The station retiring rooms are super value.

The following both serve hearty meals and juices:

Hotel Universal Deluxe   INDIAN **$**
(49 G Car St; mains ₹35-65; ⊙5.30am-midnight) Near the train station.

Hotel Vikram   INDIAN **$**
(⌨2225433; TP Area; mains ₹43-85; ⊙5am-11pm) By the bus stand.

ⓘ Information

Anu Internet Centre (per hr ₹15; ⊙5.30am-10.30pm) Next to the bus stand.

Apollo Pharmacy (G Car St; ⊙24hr)

APTDC (⌨2289120; Sridevi Complex, 2nd fl, Tilak Rd; ⊙8.30am-8pm) Tourist info and tour bookings.

Police station (⌨2289006; Railway Station Rd)

ⓘ Getting There & Away

It's possible to visit Tirupathi on a (very) long day trip from Chennai. If travelling by bus or train, buy a 'link ticket', which includes transport from Tirupathi to Tirumala.

Air

Indian Airlines (⌨2283992; Tirumala Bypass Rd; ⊙9.30am-5.30pm), 2km from town, has daily flights to Delhi via Hyderabad. **Kingfisher Red** (⌨9849677008) plies the same route, including Bengaluru and Visakhapatnam. Book with **Mitta Travels** (⌨2225981; Prakasam Rd; ⊙9am-7.30pm Mon-Sat, 9am-12.30pm Sun), next to Manasa Fast Foods, 2km from the train station.

Bus

Tirupathi's **bus station** (⌨2289900) has buses to Chennai (deluxe/Volvo ₹70/155, four hours) and Hyderabad (deluxe/Volvo ₹408/717, 12/10 hours). Tonnes of APSRTC and KSTDC buses go to Bengaluru (deluxe/Volvo ₹153/365, six/five hours), and seven buses go to Puttaparthi daily (express/deluxe ₹165/227, eight hours).

Private buses depart from TP Area, opposite the bus stand.

Train

Tirupathi station is well served by express trains, running to Chennai (2nd-class chair/chair (₹62/206, three hours), Bengaluru (sleeper/3AC/2AC ₹168/470/628, seven hours), Hyderabad/Secunderabad (sleeper/3AC/2AC ₹284/764/1047, 12 hours) and Vijayawada (sleeper/3AC/2AC ₹198/502/674, seven hours). The **reservation office** (⌨2225850; ⊙8am-8pm Mon-Sat, 8am-2pm Sun) is across the street.

ⓘ Getting Around

Bus

Tirumala Link buses have two bus stands in Tirupathi: next to the main bus stand and outside the train station. The scenic 18km trip to Tirumala takes one hour (₹54 return); if you don't mind heights, sit on the left side for views. A prepaid taxi is ₹350.

Walking

TTD has constructed probably the best footpath in India for pilgrims to walk up to Tirumala. It's about 15km from Tirupathi and takes four to six hours. Leave your luggage at the toll gate at Alipiri near the Hanuman statue. It will be transported free to the reception centre. At the time of research walking was prohibited from 4pm to 6am due to several leopard attacks on pilgrims. There are shady rest points along the way, and a few canteens.

Around Tirumala & Tirupathi

CHANDRAGIRI FORT

Only a couple of buildings remain from this 15th-century **fort** (Indian/foreigner ₹10/100; ⊙8am-5pm), 14km west of Tirupathi. Both the Rani Mahal and the Raja Mahal, which houses a small **museum** (⊙10am-5pm Sat-Thu), were constructed under Vijayanagar rule and resemble structures in Hampi's Royal Centre. There's a nightly **sound-and-light show** (admission ₹35; ⊙8pm Mar-Oct, 7.30pm Nov-Feb), narrated by Bollywood great Amitabh Bachchan. Buses for Chandragiri (₹10) leave Tirupathi bus station every half-hour. An autorickshaw is ₹200 return.

SRI KALAHASTI

Around 36km east of Tirupathi, Sri Kalahasti is known for its important **Sri Kalahasteeswara Temple** and for being, along with Machilipatnam near Vijayawada, a centre for the ancient art of *kalamkari*. These paintings are made with natural ingredients: the cotton is primed with *myrabalam* (resin) and cow's milk; figures are drawn with a pointed bamboo stick dipped in fermented jaggery and water; and the dyes are made from cow dung, ground seeds, plants and flowers. You can see the artists at work in the Agraharam neighbourhood, 2.5km from the bus stand. **Sri Vijayalakshmi Fine Kalamkari Arts** (⌨9441138380; door No 15-890) is an old family business with 40 artists.

Buses leave Tirupathi for Sri Kalahasti every 10 minutes (₹23, 45 minutes); a prepaid taxi is ₹650 return.

Puttaparthi

☑ 08555

Prasanthi Nilayam (Abode of Highest Peace) is the main ashram of the late Sri Sathya Sai Baba (1926–2011), the deceased afro-haired guru revered by followers from around the world. Setting up the ashram in his hometown of Puttaparthi 60 years ago, he lived here for most of the year, though with his death from a respiratory-related illness on 24 April 2011, the town faces an uncertain future. While the millions of dollars pumped into the nearby hospital, schools and university will ensure the town continues to thrive upon his legacy, long-term it remains to be seen whether devotees will continue to arrive en masse without the presence of the man himself.

When he was 14, Sai Baba declared himself to be the reincarnation of another Sai Baba, a saintly figure who died in 1918 (p764). His millions of devotees regarded him as a true avatar and believed he performed miracles. Coming for the program of *darshan* (here that meant seeing Baba – though since poor health in 2005 his appearances were increasingly sporadic), they packed the ashram twice-daily for chanting and prayer. The sight of clean, well-paved streets lined with internet cafes might come as a surprise here, as will the prevalence of robed foreign devotees.

Everything about Sai Baba was big: the Afro hairdo, the big-name devotees, and the big controversies – allegations of sexual misconduct had led some devotees to lose faith. Others, however, regarded the controversy as simply another terrestrial test for their avatar. Sai Baba announced he would be reborn as Prema Sai in the district of Mandya in Karnataka, in what would be the third and final incarnation of Sai Baba, supposedly eight years after his own death.

Most people stay at the **ashram** (☑287390; www.srisathyasai.org.in), a small village with all amenities. Lodging is cheap but basic. Advance bookings aren't taken; visitors under 25 must be in a family or group.

Non-ashram options include the clean and simple **Sai Surya Guest House** (☑288134; Gopuram Rd, 1st Cross; r from ₹350), and the excellent-value **Sri Sai Sadan** (Meda's Guest House; ☑287507; srisaisadan@gmail.com; Gopuram Rd; r from ₹810; ❄), near Venugopalaswamy Temple, with a roof garden and spacious rooms with fridges and balconies.

The rooftop **World Peace Café** (German Bakery; Main Rd; mains ₹95-145; ◷7.30am-9.30pm) is an old favourite for saffron lassis, good filter coffee and healthy food. The Tibetan **Bamboo Nest** (1st fl, Chitravathi Rd; mains ₹55-80; ◷9.30am-2pm & 4.30-9pm) has a memorable veg wonton soup (₹60) and good *momos* (Tibetan dumplings; ₹70).

ⓘ Getting There & Around

Puttaparthi is most easily reached from Bengaluru, 160km south; hourly KSRTC buses (express/Volvo ₹110/220, four hours) and eight trains (sleeper/3AC/2AC ₹133/323/420, three hours) head here daily. The **KSRTC office** (☑288938) is next to the bus station.

From the **APSRTC bus station** (☑287313), uncomfortable buses run to/from Tirupathi (express/deluxe ₹160/200, eight hours, seven daily) and Chennai (₹342, 12 hours, two daily). The bus station has a **train reservation booth** (◷8am-noon & 5-7pm Mon-Sat, 8am-2pm Sun). For Hyderabad, an overnight train goes daily to Kacheguda (7604; sleeper/3AC/2AC ₹240/650/870, 10 hours). Overnight train 8564 runs to Visakhapatnam (sleeper/3AC/2AC ₹340/940/1300, 20 hours), stopping at Vijayawada. The daily *Udyan Express* (6530) heads to Mumbai (sleeper/3AC/2AC ₹350/950/1300, 21 hours).

A free shuttle for ashram visitors runs from the train station. An autorickshaw is ₹80.

Lepakshi

About 75km from Puttaparthi is Lepakshi, site of the **Veerbhadra Temple** (admission free). The town gets its name from the Ramayana: when demon Ravana kidnapped Rama's wife, Sita, the bird Jatayu fought him and fell, injured, at the temple site. Rama then called him to get up; 'Lepakshi' derives from the Sanskrit for 'Get up, bird'.

Look for the 9m-long monolithic **Nandi** – India's largest – at the town's entrance. From here, you can see the temple's **Naga-lingam** (a phallic representation of Shiva) crowned with a seven-headed cobra. The temple is known for its unfinished **Kalyana Mandapam** (Marriage Hall), depicting the wedding of Parvati and Shiva, and its **Natyamandapa** (Dance Hall), with carvings of dancing gods. The temple's most stunning features, though, are the Natyamandapa's ceiling **frescoes**.

To get here, take a Puttaparthi-Bengaluru bus and alight at Kodakonda Checkpost (₹40). From there, take a Hindupur-bound bus (₹14) or an autorickshaw (₹250 return) to Lepakshi. A private car from Puttaparthi is ₹1000. You can also go from Hindupur, a main stop on the Puttaparthi-Bengaluru train line, which has a few hotels. It's 11km from the temple.

Kerala

Best Places to Eat

» Dal Roti (p961)

» Grand Pavilion (p962)

» Ayisha Manzi (p976)

» Pachyderm Palace (p973)

» Rose Garden (p949)

Best Places to Stay

» Malabar House (p957)

» Brunton Boatyard (p957)

» Varikatt Heritage (p923)

» Tranquil (p973)

» Neeleshwar Hermitage (p978)

Why Go?

Kerala's thoughtful pace of life is as contagious as the Indian head-wobble – just setting foot on this swathe of soul-quenching green will slow your stride to a blissed-out amble. One of India's most beautiful and successful states, Kerala is a world away from the frenzy of elsewhere, as if India had passed through the Looking Glass and become an altogether more laid-back place.

Besides its famous backwaters, rice paddies, coconut groves, elegant houseboats and delicately spiced, taste-bud-tingling cuisine, Kerala also proffers azure seas, white crescents of beach, and evocative ex-colonial trading towns. Then there are the mountainous Ghats carpeted by spices and tea plantations, home to wild elephants, exotic birds and the odd tiger; and crazily vibrant traditions such as Kathakali – a blend of religious play and dance; *kalarippayat* – a gravity-defying martial art, and *theyyam* – a trance-induced ritual. The main problem a visitor might find here is choosing where to linger the longest.

When to Go
Thiruvananthapuram

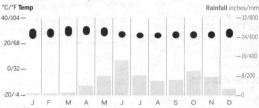

Jan–Feb
Perfect weather. Ernakulathappan Utsavam festival in Kochi.

Apr You can see Kathakali at Kottayam and Kollam festivals, and the elephant procession in Thrissur.

Aug–Sep
Tail-end of the monsoon period: prime time for ayurvedic treatments.

MAIN POINTS OF ENTRY

Thiruvanthapuram (Trivandrum), Kozhikode (Calicut) and Kochi (Cochin) are Kerala's air transport hubs; these and other towns are connected to everywhere else in India by bus and train.

Fast Facts

» Population: 33.4 million

» Area: 38,864 sq km

» Capital: Thiruvananthapuram (Trivandrum)

» Main language: Malayalam

» Sleeping prices: **$** below ₹800, **$$** ₹800 to ₹3000, **$$$** above ₹3000

Planning Your Trip

» High season in the backwaters and beach resorts is around November to March; between mid-December and mid-January, prices creep up further. There are great deals during the monsoon (June to September).

» Most Kerala national parks close for one week for a tiger census during the months of January or February. Check with Kerala Tourism for exact dates.

Resources

» Kerala Tourism (www .keralatourism.org) Kerala Tourist Board site.

» Manorama Online (www .manoramaonline.com) Local newspaper with an English edition on-line.

Food

Delicious breakfast dishes include *puttu* (rice powder and coconut, steamed in a metal or bamboo holder) eaten with steamed bananas and or with a spicy curry, *idlis* (spongy, round, fermented rice cakes) and *sambar* (fragrant vegetable dhal), dosas with coconut chutney, *idiyappam* (rice noodles) or *paalappam* (a kind of pancake) served with a meat or fish stew. *Appam* is a soft pancake made from toddy-fermented rice batter, with a soft spongy centre and crispy edges, also eaten with a coconut-mellowed stew.

The state's spice plantations, coconut-palm groves and long coastline shape the local cuisine, with deliciously delicate dishes such as fish *molee* (in coconut milk) or the spicy Malabar chicken curry. Dishes are mostly cooked in coconut oil.

For dessert, *payasam* is made of brown molasses, coconut milk and spices, garnished with cashew nuts and raisins.

DON'T MISS

Fort Cochin is an extraordinary town, resonant with 500 years of colonial history.

Floating along **Kerala's backwaters** on a houseboat, handmade in the style of traditional rice barges, or a canoe, is one of India's most magical experiences.

The plantation-cloaked hills of **Munnar** are a sight to soothe the soul, high in the lush mountains of Kerala's Western Ghats

Top State Festivals

» Ernakulathappan Utsavam (Jan/Feb, Shiva Temple, Ernakulam, Kochi, p956) Eight days of festivities culminating in a parade of 15 splendidly decorated elephants, music and fireworks.

» Thirunakkara Utsavam (Mar, Thirunakkara Shiva Temple, Kottayam, p943) All-night Kathakali dancing on the third and fourth nights of this 10-day festival; processions of elephants mark the finale.

» Pooram Festival (Apr, Asraman Shri Krishna Swami Temple, Kollam, p937) A 10-day festival with full-night Kathakali performances and a procession of 40 ornamented elephants.

» Thrissur Pooram (Apr/May, Vadakkumnathan Kshetram Temple, Thrissur, p967) The elephant procession to end all elephant processions.

» Nehru Trophy Snake Boat Race (2nd Sat in Aug, Alappuzha, p938) Most popular of Kerala's boat races.

» Onam (Aug/Sep, statewide) Kerala's biggest cultural celebration, when the entire state celebrates the golden age of mythical King Mahabali for 10 days.

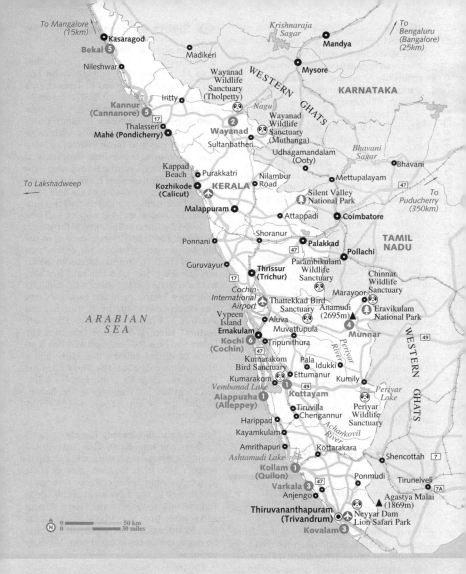

Kerala Highlights

① Launch off in a houseboat or canoe from **Alleppey**, **Kottayam** or **Kollam**, slow down, and take a blissed-out glide on Kerala's fabled backwaters (p940)

② Spot wild elephants at **Wayanad** (p972) amid spectacular mountain scenery and epic spice fields

③ Watch days slip slide away as you amble around the breathtaking beach resort of **Varkala** (p932) and have some laid-back fun in **Kovalam** (p928)

④ Hunker down in a beautifully remote resort and trek through the tea plantations around **Munnar** (p948)

⑤ Explore the golden-sand, unspoilt beaches around **Kannur** (p975) and **Bekal** (p977)

⑥ Feel the history in lovely, calm **Fort Cochin** (p957) in Kochi

History

Traders have been drawn to the scent of Kerala's spices for more than 3000 years. The coast was known to the Phoenicians, the Romans, the Arabs and the Chinese, and was a transit point for spices from the Moluccas (eastern Indonesia).

The kingdom of Cheras ruled much of Kerala until the early Middle Ages, competing with kingdoms and small fiefdoms for territory and trade. Vasco da Gama's arrival in 1498 opened the floodgates to European colonialism as Portuguese, Dutch and English interests fought Arab traders, and then each other, for control of the lucrative spice trade.

The present-day state of Kerala was created in 1956 from the former states of Travancore, Kochi and Malabar. A tradition of valuing the arts and education resulted in a post-Independence state that is one of the most progressive in India.

In 1957 Kerala had the first freely elected communist government in the world, which has gone on to hold power regularly since. The participatory political system has resulted in a more equitable distribution of land and income, and impressive health and education statistics (see boxed text, p932). Many Malayalis (speakers of Malayalam, the state's official language) work in the Middle East and their remittances play a significant part in the economy.

SOUTHERN KERALA

Thiruvananthapuram (Trivandrum)

☏ 0471 / POP 889,191

For obvious reasons, Kerala's capital Thiruvananthapuram is still often referred to by its colonial name: Trivandrum. Most travellers merely springboard from here to the nearby beachside resorts of Kovalam and Varkala, though laid-back, hill-enclosed Trivandrum, with its bevy of Victorian museums in glorious neo-Keralan buildings, is deserving of more time, if you can spare it. All you have to do is get off Trivandrum's racing-drag of a main street to find yourself immersed in old Kerala: surrounded by pagoda-shaped buildings, red-tiled roofs and narrow, winding lanes.

◉ Sights & Activities

TOP CHOICE Zoological Gardens & Museums
ZOO, MUSEUMS

Yann Martel based the animals in his *Life of Pi* on those he observed in Trivandrum's **zoological gardens** (☏ 2115122; admission ₹10, camera ₹25; ⊙ 9am-6pm Tue-Sun). Here are shaded paths meandering through woodland and lakes, where animals, such as tigers, macaques and birds frolic in massive open enclosures that mimic their natural habitats. There's a **reptile house** where cobras frequently flare their hoods – just don't ask what the cute guinea pigs are here for.

The park contains a gallery and two museums. Housed in an 1880 wooden building designed by Robert Chisholm, a British architect whose Fair Isle–style version of the Keralan vernacular shows his enthusiasm for local craft. The **Napier Museum** (admission ₹10; ⊙ 9am-5pm Tue & Thu-Sun, 1-5pm Wed) has an eclectic display of bronzes, Buddhist sculptures, temple carts and ivory carvings. The carnivalesque interior is stunning and worth a look in its own right. The dusty **Natural History Museum** (admission ₹10; ⊙ 9am-5pm Tue & Thu-Sun, 1-5pm Wed) has hundreds of stuffed animals and birds, and a fine skeleton collection. The **Shri Chitra Art Gallery** (admission ₹5; ⊙ 9am-5pm Tue & Thu-Sun, 1-5pm Wed) has paintings by the Rajput, Mughal and Tanjore schools, and works by Ravi Varma.

Shri Padmanabhaswamy Temple
TEMPLE

(⊙ Hindus only 4am-7.30pm) This 260-year-old temple is Trivandrum's spiritual heart, spilling over 2400 sq m. Its main entrance is the 30m-tall, seven-tier eastern *gopuram* (gateway tower). In the inner sanctum, the deity Padmanabha reclines on the sacred serpent and is made from over 10,000 *salagramam* (sacred stones) that were purportedly, and no doubt slowly, transported from Nepal by elephant.

The path around to the right of the gate offers good views of the *gopuram*.

Puthe Maliga Palace Museum
MUSEUM

(Indian/foreigner ₹10/30; ⊙ 9am-1pm & 3-4.30pm) The 200-year-old palace of the Travancore maharajas has carved wooden ceilings, marble sculptures and even imported Belgian glass. Inside you'll find Kathakali images, an armoury, portraits of Maharajas, ornate thrones and other artefacts.

The annual **classical music festival** is held here in January.

Ayushmanbhava Ayurvedic Centre AYURVEDA, YOGA
(☑4712556060; www.ayushmanbhava.com; Pothujanam) Offers treatments such as 60-minute massage (₹500), and daily therapeutic yoga classes (beginners 6.30am). Three kilometres west of the town centre, a one week package of treatments here costs ₹4700.

🍃 Courses

Margi Kathakali School MARTIAL ARTS, DRAMA
(☑2478806; Fort) Conducts courses in Kathakali (p976) and *Kootiattam* (traditional Sanskrit drama) for beginner and advanced students. Fees average ₹300 per two-hour class. Visitors can peek at uncostumed practice sessions held 10am to noon Monday to Friday. It's in an unmarked building behind the Fort School, located 200m west of the fort.

CVN Kalari Sangham MARTIAL ARTS
(☑2474182; www.cvnkalari.in; South Rd; 15-day/1-month course ₹1000/2000) Offers three-month courses in *kalarippayat* (p976) for serious students with some experience in martial arts. Contact Sathyan (☑2474182; sathyacvn@vsnl.net) for details. On Monday to Saturday at 6.30am to 8.30am, training sessions are open to visitors.

👉 Tours

KTDC (Kerala Tourist Development Corporation) runs several tours, all leaving from the Tourist Reception Centre at the KTDC Hotel Chaithram on Central Station Rd. The **Kanyakumari Day Tour** (per person ₹550; ☺8am-9pm Tue-Sun) visits Padmanabhapuram Palace (p932), Kanyakumari in Southern Tamil Nadu and the nearby Suchindram Temple. The **Narsa Darsan: Daily Half-day Tour** (per person ₹250; ☺7.30am-1pm & 1.30-7pm Tue-Sun) visits Trivandrum's major sights.

🛏 Sleeping

TOP CHOICE Varikatt Heritage HOMESTAY $$$
(☑2336057; www.varikattheritage.com; Punnen Rd; r ₹4000-5000) Trivandrum's most charismatic place to stay is the 250-year-old house of Colonel Roy Kuncheria. It's a wonderful bungalow flanked by verandas and a cinnamon tree, orchids in hanging pots. Every antique has a family story attached to it. Lunch and dinner available (₹300).

Graceful Homestay HOMESTAY $$
(☑2444358; www.gracefulhomestay.com; Philip's Hill; downstairs s/d ₹1300/1500, upstairs s/d ₹2000/2500 incl breakfast; @🛜) In Trivan-

drum's leafy suburbs, this is owned by Sylvia and run by her brother Giles, and is an attractive house set in a couple of hectares of garden opposite AJ Hall. The pick of the rooms has an amazing covered terrace overlooking palm trees.

YMCA International Guesthouse HOSTEL $
(☑2330059; YMCA Rd; s/d ₹485/620) Our value-ometer went off the scale when we saw this place – one of the less institutional among its brethren; rooms are spacious, spotless and come with tiled bathrooms and TV. Both men and women accepted.

Wild Palms Home Stay HOMESTAY $$
(☑2471175; www.wildpalmsonsea.com; Mathrubhumi Rd; s ₹1495-1795, d ₹1795-2195; ❄) Trading on its touches of character and quiet setting, this is overpriced. Still, nowhere else has a Venus de Milo statue greeting you in the front garden. The ornate, comfortable family home here has well-furnished though faded rooms. The best has a terrace.

Sunday B&B GUESTHOUSE $
(☑09746957056; opp Airport; s/d ₹400/500) This was fantastically well placed for a dawn flight, opposite the former international terminal. The terminal's move a few kilometres away has made it a little less convenient, but it's still handy, well priced and friendly with nicely kept, clean rooms with hot water.

Muthoot Plaza HOTEL $$$
(☑2337733; www.themuthootplaza.com; Punnen Rd; s/d from ₹5800/6700, ste from ₹9500; ❄@🛜) Even though the arctic-level AC would make penguins shiver, this ultrachic business-focused hotel is still a great place to stay. The plush rooms are stuffed with pillows, couches and all mod cons.

Greenland Lodge HOTEL $
(☑2328114; Thampanoor Junction; s/d ₹323/485, with AC ₹900/990; ❄) Close to the muted mayhem of the train station, Greenland lays out lots of serenity-inducing pastel colours to greet you. Inside, the rooms are spacious and come with hybrid squat/sit-down toilets. It's efficiently run, but expect to pay a hefty two-night deposit.

Princess Inn HOTEL $
(☑2339150; Manjalikulam Rd; s/d ₹290/480, r with AC ₹650; ❄) In a modern (read: '80s) glass-fronted building, the Princess Inn promises a relatively quiet sleep in clean surrounds, plus satellite TV and immaculate green-tiled bathrooms.

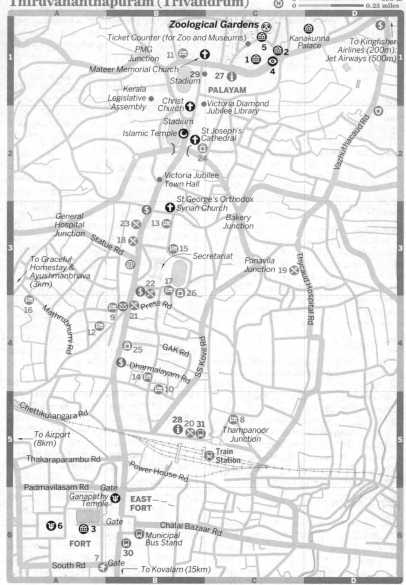

Zoological Gardens

Ticket Counter (for Zoo and Museums)

PMG Junction   11

Mateer Memorial Church

Stadium   29   27

Kerala Legislative Assembly

Christ Church

Stadium

Islamic Temple

St Joseph's Cathedral   24

Victoria Jubilee Town Hall

St George's Orthodox Syrian Church

General Hospital Junction   23   13

Statue Rd   18

To Graceful Homestay & Ayushmanbhava (3km)   @   15   Secretariat

22   17

$ 26

16   9   21   Press Rd

Mathrubhumi Rd

12   25   GAK Rd

$ Dharmalayam Rd   14   10

Chettikulangara Rd

To Airport (8km)   28   20   31

Thampanoor Junction   8

Thakaraparambu Rd

Power House Rd   Train Station

Padmavilasam Rd   Gate

Ganapathy Temple   EAST FORT

6   Gate   Chalai Bazaar Rd

3   Municipal Bus Stand

FORT   30

7   Gate

South Rd   To Kovalam (15km)

Kanakunna Palace

To Kingfisher Airlines (200m); Jet Airways (500m)

5   2   1   4

PALAYAM

Victoria Diamond Jubilee Library

Bakery Junction

Panavila Junction   19

Thycaud Hospital Rd

Vazhuthacaud Rd

0   500 m
0   0.25 miles

KTDC Mascot Hotel   HOTEL $$$

(☏2318990; www.ktdc.com; Mascot Sq; s/d from ₹4000/4500; ✳@🛜🏊) Period touches, massive hallways and an imposing reception lend this place an aura of old-world charm. It has a monster pool and ayurvedic spa.

Hotel Regency   HOTEL $

(☏2330377; www.hotelregency.com; Manjalikulam Cross Rd; s/d ₹540/788, with AC ₹900/1407; ✳) Offers small, cosy rooms with satellite TV, a leafy entryway, lots of hush and plenty of smiles at reception.

Kukie's Holiday Inn
GUESTHOUSE $

(☑2478530; Lukes Lane; s/d ₹220/275) At the end of a small lane in an appealingly quiet spot, this is centred around a little courtyard and offers bare-bones accommodation at rock-bottom prices. Rooms have hard beds and a cold water tap in the bathroom.

✖ Eating

For some unusual refreshments with your meal, look out for *karikku* (coconut water) and *sambharam* (buttermilk with ginger and chilli).

⌐TOP⌐CHOICE Indian Coffee House
INDIAN $

Station (Central Station Rd; dishes ₹12-50; ⊘7am-11pm); Zoo (Museum Rd; ⊘8.30am to 6pm) The Central Station Rd link of the chain serves its yummy coffee and snacks in a crazy red-brick tower that looks like a pigeon coop from outside, and has a spiralling interior lined inside by bench tables. You have to admire the hard-working waiters. It's a must-see. There's another, more run-of-the-mill branch near the museum.

Kalavara Family Restaurant
INDIAN $$

(Press Rd; dishes ₹60-140; ⊘lunch & dinner) A bustling favourite of Trivandrum's middle class, this is decorated by curious half-awnings and serves up scrummy Keralan fish dishes. Our money's on the fish *molee* (fish in coconut sauce; ₹130).

Aroma
INDIAN $$

(☑4076000; Magic Days, Vanross Jn; dishes ₹50-100; ⊘lunch & dinner) A smart hotel restaurant with a smashing buffet for lunch and dinner, as well as à la carte.

New Mubarak
MALABAR $

(off Statue Rd; dishes ₹20-60) A grand-sounding name for an ungrand restaurant, tucked away on a narrow lane off Statue Rd. However, it's a great place to sample Malabar Muslim cuisine such as crab masala or fresh fish cooked in coconut oil.

Ariya Nivaas
INDIAN $

(Manorama Rd; meals ₹45; ⊘7am-9pm) Close to the train station and convenient for a quick feed between trains, this popular thali (traditional 'all-you-can-eat' meal) place gets positive reports.

Pizza Corner PIZZERIA $
(MG Rd; small pizzas ₹85-170; ⊙11am-11pm)
A bit of East meets West, with tasty piz-
zas sporting everything from traditional
toppings (margherita) to Indian twists (eg
Punjabi chicken tikka).

Ananda Bhavan INDIAN $
(🕿2477646; MG Rd; dishes ₹22-31; ⊙lunch &
dinner) A classic sit-down-and-dig-in-with-
your-hands-type situation.

🛍 Shopping

Wander around **Connemara Market** (MG Rd)
to see vendors selling vegetables, fish, live
goats, fabric, clothes, spices and more bananas than you can poke a hungry monkey at.

SMSM Institute HANDICRAFTS
(YMCA Rd; ⊙9am-8pm Mon-Sat) No, it's not
dedicated to the study of text messaging,
but a Kerala Government-run handicraft
emporium with an Aladdin's cave of well-
priced goodies.

Sankers Coffee & Tea FOOD & DRINK
(🕿2330469; MG Rd; ⊙9am-9pm Mon-Sat)
You'll smell the fresh coffee well before
you reach this dainty shop. It sells Nilgiri
Export OP Leaf Tea (₹260 per kilo) and a
variety of coffees and nuts.

❶ Information

ABC Internet (Capital Centre; MG Rd; per hr
₹20; ⊙8.30am-9pm) One of several good
internet places in this small mall.
KIMS (Kerala Institute of Medical Sciences;
🕿2447676; Kumarapuram) About 3km northwest of Trivandrum. For medical problems.

Main post office (🕿2473071; MG Rd)
Thomas Cook (🕿2338140-2; MG Rd;
⊙10.30am-6pm Mon-Sat) Changes cash and
travellers cheques.
Tourist Facilitation Centre (🕿2321132; Museum Rd; ⊙24hr) Supplies maps and brochures.
Tourist Reception Centre (KTDC Hotel Chaithram; 🕿2330031; Central Station Rd; ⊙7am-
9pm daily). Arranges KTDC-run tours.

❶ Getting There & Away

Air

Between them, **Air India** (🕿2317341; Mascot
Sq), **Jet Airways** (🕿2728864; Sasthaman-
galam Junction) and **Kingfisher Airlines**
(🕿18002333131; Star Gate Bldg; TC 9/888,
Vellayambalam) fly to Mumbai (from ₹5200),
Kochi (from ₹2300), Bengaluru (Bangalore;
from ₹5400), Chennai (Madras; from ₹3800)
and Delhi (from ₹7500).

There are regular flights from Trivandrum to
Colombo and Male.

All airline bookings can be made at the efficient **Airtravel Enterprises** (🕿3011412; www.
ategroup.org; New Corporation Bldg, MG Rd).

Bus

For buses operating from the **KSRTC bus stand**
(🕿2323886), opposite the train station, see the
table, p926.

For Tamil Nadu destinations, the State Express
Transport Corporation (SETC) buses leave from
the eastern end of the KSRTC bus stand.

Buses leave for Kovalam beach (₹15, 30 minutes, every 20 minutes) between 5.40am and
10pm from the southern end of the East Fort bus
stand on MG Rd.

Buses leaving from Trivandrum (KSRTC Bus
Stand):

MAJOR TRAINS FROM TRIVANDRUM

DESTINATION	TRAIN NO & NAME*	FARE (₹)	DURATION (HR)	DEPARTURES (DAILY)
Bengaluru	6525 *Bangalore Express*	307/833/1144	18	12.55pm
Chennai	2696 *Chennai Express*	166/799/1230	16½	5.10pm
Coimbatore	7229 *Sabari Express*	191/505/691	9¼	7.15am
Delhi	2625 *Kerala Express*	595/1616/2220	50	11.15am
Mangalore	6347 *Mangalore Express*	257/693/949	14½	8.45pm

*Sleeper/3AC/2AC

THE INDIAN COFFEE HOUSE STORY

The Indian Coffee House is a place stuck in time. Its India-wide branches feature old India prices and waiters dressed in starched white with peacock-style headdresses. It was started by the Coffee Board in the early 1940s, during British rule. In the 1950s the Board began to close down cafes across India, making employees redundant. At this point, the communist leader Ayillyath Kuttiari Gopalan Nambiar began to support the workers and founded with them the India Coffee Board Worker's Co-operative Society. The intention was to provide them with better opportunities and promote the sale of coffee. The Coffee House has remained ever since, always atmospheric, and always offering bargain snacks and drinks such as Indian filter coffee, rose milk and *idlis*. It's still run by its employees, all of whom share ownership.

DESTINATION	FARE (₹)	DURATION (HR)	FREQUENCY
Alleppey	97	3½	every 15min
Chennai	430	17	10 daily
Ernakulam (Kochi)	135	5	every 20min
Kanyakumari	56	2	6 daily
Kollam	42	1½	every 15min
Kumily (for Periyar)	126	8	2 daily
Madrai	195	7	9 daily
Munnar	193	7	2 daily
Neyyar Dam	20-26	1½	every 40min
Puducherry	375	16	1 daily
Thrissur	187	7½	every 30min
Udhagamandalam (Ooty)	365	14	1 daily
Varkala	36	1¼	hourly

Train

Trains are often heavily booked, so it's worth visiting the **reservation office** (☏139; ⊙8am-8pm Mon-Sat, to 2pm Sun) at the train station. See the table below for major long-distance services.

Within Kerala there are frequent trains to Varkala (2nd class/AC chair ₹36/279, one hour), Kollam (₹40/309, one hour) and Ernakulam (₹74/259, 4½ hours), with trains passing through either Alleppey (₹59/347, three hours) or Kottayam (₹62/396, 3½ hours). There are also numerous daily services to Kanyakumari (sleeper/3AC/2AC ₹140/272/396, 2½ hours).

ⓘ Getting Around

The **airport** (☏2501424) is 8km from the city and 15km from Kovalam; take local bus 14 from the East Fort and City Bus stand (₹6). Prepaid taxi vouchers from the airport cost ₹250 to the city and ₹400 to Kovalam.

Autorickshaws are the easiest way to get around, with short hops costing ₹10-20.

Around Trivandrum

NEYYAR DAM LION SAFARI PARK

This sanctuary, rebranded as the **Lion Safari Park** (☏2272182, 9744347582; Indian/foreigner ₹140/230; ⊙9.30am-5pm Tue-Sun), 35km north of Trivandrum, lies around an idyllic lake created by the 1964 Neyyar Dam. The fertile forest lining the shoreline is home to gaurs, sambar deer, sloth, elephants, lion-tailed macaques and the occasional tiger.

The park is usually visited via 1½-hour **lion safaris** (⊙9.30am-3.30pm) included in the admission fee, via boat and bus. This includes a 20-minute trek. Nearby there's a **Crocodile Protection Centre**, admission to which is also included. Get here from Trivandrum's KSRTC bus stand by frequent bus (₹20 to ₹26, 1½ hours). A taxi is ₹800 return (with two hours' waiting time) from Trivandrum, ₹1200 from Kovalam. The KTDC office in Trivandrum also run tours to Neyyar Dam (₹300). If you have your own transport, you can visit the park without a tour, which may enhance your chances of seeing wildlife.

SIVANANDA YOGA VEDANTA DHANWANTARI ASHRAM

Just before Neyyar Dam, this superbly located **ashram** (☏/fax 0471-2273093; www.sivananda.org/ndam), established in 1978, is renowned for its hatha yoga courses. Courses start on the 1st and 16th of each month, run for a minimum of two weeks and cost ₹700 per day for accommodation in a double room

(₹500 in dormitories). Low season (May to September) rates are ₹100 less. There's an exacting schedule (5.30am to 10pm) of yoga practice, meditation and chanting, though with plenty of breaks between sessions; and students rave about the food (included in the rates). Bookings are required. Month-long yoga-teacher training and ayurvedic massage courses are also available.

Kovalam

☑ 0471

Once a calm fishing village clustered around its crescents of beach, nowadays Kovalam is Kerala's most developed resort. It's a touristy place and the shore is built up with hotels, but it remains an appealing place to have some fun by the sea, though it has more than its fair share of resident touts and tourist tat.

Dangers & Annoyances

Bikini-clad women are likely to attract male attention, though this is definitely more of an annoyance than a danger. Cover up with a sarong when you're out of the water.

There are strong rips at both ends of Lighthouse Beach that carry away several swimmers every year. Swim only between the flags in the area patrolled by lifeguards – green flags show the area is safe, red flags warn of danger zones.

Kovalam has frequent blackouts and the footpaths behind Lighthouse Beach are unlit, so carry a torch (flashlight) after dark.

◉ Sights & Activities

Lighthouse   VIEWPOINT
(Indian/foreigner ₹10/25, camera/video ₹20/25; ⊙3-5pm) Check out the endless views along the coast by climbing Kovalam's lighthouse. Not recommended if you suffer from vertigo, or for small children.

Santhigiri   MASSAGE
(☑2482800; www.santhigiriashram.org; nr Lighthouse Beach; ⊙8am-8pm) Try this place for excellent massages and ayurvedic treatments. For ₹750/900 for 60/90 minutes you can have a four-handed massage while listening to the sound of the waves outside. Twenty-one-day panchakarma (internal purification) costs ₹64,250, including accommodation in big, airy rooms, and food.

🛏 Sleeping

Kovalam is chock-a-block with hotels, though budget places here cost more than usual and are becoming a dying breed. Beachfront properties are the most expensive and have great sea views. Look out for

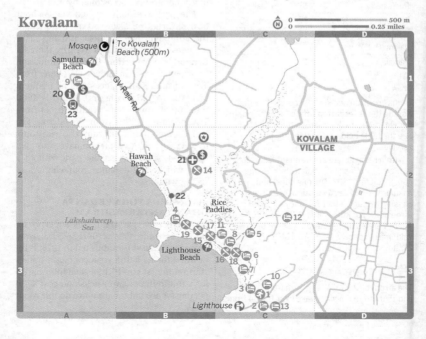

smaller places tucked away in the labyrinth of paths behind the beach among the palm groves and rice paddies; they're much better value. For more top-end accommodation choices, see the Around Kovalam section.

Beach Hotel II HOTEL **$$$**
(📞2481937; www.thebeachhotel-kovalam.com; r ₹3000, with AC ₹4000; ❄) The Beach Hotel's upmarket new cousin, this is a stylish hotel with the best views on the seafront. Rooms have plate-glass windows opening onto terraces, and the decor is simple chic, with printed sheets and curtains and white walls. It's home to the new Oasia terrace restaurant.

Treetops GUESTHOUSE **$$**
(📞2481363; treetopsofkovalam@yahoo.in; r ₹900; @) Indeed in the treetops, this friendly expat-owned place is a breath of fresh air, hidden away from the hustle. The three bright, sparkling-clean rooms have hanging chairs on the terraces, the view from the roof is awesome, and there's a yoga centre next door.

Paradesh Inn GUESTHOUSE **$$**
(📞9995362952; inn.paradesh@yahoo.com; Paradesh House, Avaduthura; s/d ₹1250/1350; @) Next door to Treetops, tranquil Italian-run Paradesh Inn resembles a Greek island hideaway – a whitewashed building highlighted in blue. Each of the six fan-cooled rooms has a hanging chair outside, there are sweeping views from the rooftop and fab breakfasts.

Beach Hotel GUESTHOUSE **$$**
(📞2481937; www.thebeachhotel-kovalam.com; s/d ₹1500/2500;) Brought to you by the long-running German Bakery, this uberhip beachfront property has rooms designed with minimalist flair, ochre tones and finished with smart, arty touches. Plus Waves restaurant is just upstairs.

Leela HOTEL **$$$**
(📞2480101; www.theleela.com; r from ₹14,000; ❄@🛜🏊) The only top-end option in town, the Leela is located in extensive grounds on the headland north of Hawah beach. There are three swimming pools, an ayurvedic centre, a gym, two private beaches, several restaurants and more. Rooms are sumptuous, with period touches, colourful textiles and Keralan artwork.

Sea Flower HOTEL **$**
(📞2480554; www.seaflowerbeachresort.com; r downstairs ₹750, upstairs ₹900) Next door to Beach Hotel II, this dowdier place offers similar views at smaller prices. Rooms are simple and plain but freshly painted.

Dwaraka Lodge GUESTHOUSE **$**
(📞2480411; d ₹450-500) With regular licks of paint helping to cover up the war wounds of this tired old-timer, friendly Dwaraka is the cheapest ocean-front property. There's nothing flash inside, just clean sheets and a basic bathroom.

Hotel Greenland GUESTHOUSE **$**
(📞2486442; hotelgreenlandin@yahoo.com; r ₹500-1000) Family run and as friendly as they

Kovalam

come. The refurbished rooms in this multilevel complex have lots of natural light – some even have small kitchenettes for self-catering. Will cook up yummy food on request.

Green Valley Cottages   GUESTHOUSE $
(📞2480636; indira_ravi@hotmail.com; r ₹500-1000) Also way back amongst the trees, this serene complex is the place to revel in serious shush time. The rooms are simple, but have good views from the terraces in front. They also have a house for rent, a short heft up the hill, for a ₹1000 per night.

Maharaju Palace   GUESTHOUSE $$
(📞2485320; www.maharajupalace.in; d ₹1800) More of a quiet retreat than a palace, this place has more character than most, with wooden furnishings, including the odd four-poster, and different coloured mosquito nets. The breakfast terrace is hung with chintzy chandeliers.

Hotel Sky Palace   GUESTHOUSE $
(📞9745841222; r downstairs/upstairs ₹500/900) This little two-storey place lies down a small lane; rooms are well kept, with a mix of colours and dark masculine tiling about the place; the ground-floor rooms are cheaper, but the same.

Varmas Beach Resort   RESORT $$
(📞2480478; vijayavarmabeachresort@hotmail.com; Lighthouse Rd; s/d ₹1800/3000, with AC ₹2500/5500; ❄) Has a wood-panelled, Kerala-style facade and breezy rooms with exceptional views and comfy sitting areas on private balconies. However, this still doesn't justify these prices – try it off-season.

Jeevan Ayurvedic Beach Resort   RESORT $$
(📞2480662; www.jeevanresort.net; d from ₹2400, with AC ₹3700; ❄🌊) Expect inoffensively decorated, decent-sized rooms with bathtubs and an alluring, clean pool. Upstairs rooms have balconies with sea views.

Moon Valley Cottage   GUESTHOUSE $
(📞9446100291; sknairkovalam@yahoo.com; d from ₹500, upstairs apt ₹1000) There's nothing but swaying palms around here, the rooms are a decent size and it's a peaceful spot.

Aparna   GUESTHOUSE $$
(📞2480950; www.aparnahotelkovalam.com; s/d ₹1500/1750) Aparna has just a handful of cute, oddly shaped little rooms. All are cosy with private balconies, nice sea views and welcome sea breezes.

Eating

Each evening, dozens of open-air restaurants line the beach promenade displaying the catch of the day – just pick a fish, settle on a price (per serve around ₹150, tiger prawns over ₹400) and decide how you want it prepared. Menus and prices are largely indistinguishable – it's more about which ambience takes your fancy. Unlicensed places will serve alcohol in mugs, or with the bottles hidden discreetly out of sight.

Malabar Cafe   INDIAN $$
(mains ₹90-300) The busy tables tell their own story: this place, with its plastic chairs, candlelight at night, and view through pot plants to the crashing waves offers tasty food and good service.

Suprabhatham   KERALAN $
(meals ₹45-80) This cosy little veggie place dishes up excellent, dirt-cheap and truly authentic Keralan cooking in a rustic setting. Out in the palm groves, it's secluded and intimate, and you can dine under the stars to a nightly orchestra of crickets.

Waves   MULTICUISINE $$
(mains ₹100-480) With its broad, burnt-orange balcony, ambient soundtrack, and wide-roaming menu proffering everything from *weisskraut mit chinnken* (roast cabbage and bacon) to Thai curries, this is a foreign-tourist magnet.

Swiss Cafe   CAFE $$
(mains ₹70-410) While the setting here is lovely, with an upstairs balcony and lots of wicker seating, the menu offers much the same choices as everywhere else, with a few token Swiss dishes (eg schnitzel) thrown in.

Fusion   FUSION $$
(mains ₹120-440) This funky eatery has an inventive East-meets-West menu, with dishes such as oven-roasted tomatoes with spice crust on ginger cashew-nut noodles or lobster steamed in vodka. Also serves French press coffee and herbal teas.

Devi Garden Restaurant   INDIAN $
(NUP Beach Rd; mains ₹50-150; ⏱7.30am-11pm) Garden is overstating it, but this tiny, family-run eatery whips up great veg and nonveg Indian food for refreshingly reasonable prices.

★ Entertainment

During high season, an abridged version of Kathakali is performed most nights –

enquire about locations and times at the Tourist Facilitation Centre.

ℹ Information

Almost every shop and hotel will change money. In Kovalam there's a National Bank of India and near the hospital a CBS **ATM** taking Visa cards. Otherwise, there are Federal Bank and ICICI ATMs at Kovalam Junction. There are lots of small **internet cafes** (per hr ₹30-50).

National Bank of India (◷10.30am-1.30pm Mon-Fri, ◷10.30am-noon Sat) Near the Leela resort. Changes cash.

Post office (Kovalam Beach Rd; ◷9am-1pm Mon-Sat)

Tourist Facilitation Centre (✆2480085; ◷9.30am-5pm) Helpful, inside the entrance to the Kovalam Beach Resort.

Upasana Hospital (✆2480632) Has English-speaking doctors who can take care of minor injuries.

ℹ Getting There & Away

BUS Buses connect Kovalam and Trivandrum every 20 minutes between 5.30am and 10.10pm (₹9, 30 minutes); catch them from the entrance to Leela resort. There are two buses daily to Ernakulam (₹140, 5½ hours), stopping at Kallambalam (for Varkala, ₹50, 1½ hours), Kollam (₹70, 2½ hours) and Alleppey (₹110, four hours). There's another 6.30am bus to Ernakulam via Kottayam that bypasses Varkala.

TAXI A taxi between Trivandrum and Kovalam beach is around ₹400.

MOTORBIKE HIRE Voyager Travels (✆9847065093) rents out scooters/Enfields for around ₹400/550 per day. It has no fixed office address.

Around Kovalam

SAMUDRA BEACH

Samudra beach, about 4km north of Kovalam by road, has seen a growing number of resorts edge out what was a small fishing village. Although more peaceful, the beach is steep and rough, and only accessible for swimming in December and January.

Set amid more than 5 hectares of lolling green grounds, **Taj Green Cove** (✆2487733; www.tajhotels.com; r ₹12,500-30,000; ❄@⊛⊛), the Kovalam branch of a swanky Indian hotel chain, has smashing individual chalets with sunken baths, an enticing infinity pool, several restaurants (one on the beach) and a spa.

PULINKUDI & CHOWARA

Around 8km south of Kovalam, amid endless-seeming swaying palms, colourful village life, and some empty golden-sand beaches, are some tantalising high-end alternatives to Kovalam's crowded centre.

For those serious about ayurvedic treatment, **Dr Franklin's Panchakarma Institute** (✆2480870; www.dr-franklin.com; Chowara; s from €38, d €55; @⊛) is a reputable and less expensive alternative to the flashier resorts. Daily treatment with full board costs €56. Accommodation is tidy and comfortable but not resort style. There are therapy packages for whatever ails you, including spine problems, purification/detox treatments, as well as general rejuvenation and stress relief.

Surya Samudra Private Retreats (✆2480413; www.suryasamudra.com; Pulinkudi; r incl breakfast ₹14,100-42,900; ❄⊛) proffers A-list-style seclusion, with 22 transplanted traditional Keralan homes, with four posters and open-air bathrooms, set in a palm grove above sparkling seas. There's an infinity pool carved out of a single block of granite, ayurvedic treatments, and spectacular outdoor yoga platforms.

In ayurvedic plant-filled gardens, **Somatheeram** (✆2266501; www.somatheeram.org; Pulinkudi; s/d from €72/80; ❄⊛) is a good place to have an ayurvedic and yogic sojourn. The setting is paradisaical and rooms range from simple cottages to more luxurious houses. You can pay for treatments separately, or there are various packages (rejuvenation, slimming, etc).

Bethsaida Hermitage (✆2267554; www.bethsaidahermitage.com; Pulinkudi; AC s/d from €40/60, with sea view from €70/80; ❄) is a resort with a difference: this is a charitable organisation that helps support two nearby orphanages and an old people's home. It's also an inviting, somehow old-fashioned beachside escape, with sculpted gardens, a friendly welcome, and putting-green perfect lawns. It offers a variety of cottages, from large rooms with golden friezes to spacious, cool Kerala-style huts.

Thapovan Heritage Home (✆2480453; www.thapovan.com; s/d from ₹2650/3100) offers a midrange alternative next to a beautiful stretch of beach (no pool, AC or TV). There's a choice between pricier Keralan teak cottages, with wood-lined, slightly dated interiors, or some cheaper, plainer rooms, including a few overlooking the beach just a few paces away. Available ayurvedic treatments range from one-hour massages to 28-day treatment marathons.

Padmanabhapuram Palace

With a forest's worth of intricately carved ceilings and polished-teak beams, this **palace** (☎04651-250255; Indian/foreigner ₹25/200, camera/video ₹25/1500; ⊙9am-1pm & 2-4.30pm Tue-Sun) is considered the best example of traditional Keralan architecture today. Parts of it date back to 1550; as the egos of successive rulers left their mark, it expanded into the magnificent conglomeration of 14 palaces it is today.

Asia's largest wooden palace complex, it was once the seat of the rulers of Travancore, a princely state taking in parts of Tamil Nadu and Kerala. Constructed of teak and granite, the exquisite interiors include carved rosewood ceilings, Chinese-style screens, and floors finished to a high black polish.

Padmanabhapuram is about 60km southeast of Kovalam. Catch a local bus from Kovalam (or Trivandrum) to Kanyakumari and get off at Thuckalay, from where it's a short autorickshaw ride or 15-minute walk. Alternatively, take one of the tours organised by the KTDC from Trivandrum, or hire a taxi (about ₹1500 return from Trivandrum or Kovalam).

Varkala

☏0470 / POP 42,273

Perched almost perilously along the edge of dizzying cliffs, Varkala has a naturally beautiful setting and is a low-key resort that's geared to a backpacker demographic. A strand of golden beach nuzzles Varkala's cliff edge, where restaurants play innocuous trance music and stalls sell the types of things every traveller might need: ethnic T-shirts, baggy trousers and silver jewellery. Even though this kind of tie-dye commercialism can grate on the nerves, Varkala is still a great place to watch the days slowly turn into weeks. The beach is a holy place, where Hindus come to make offerings for dead loved ones, assisted by priests who set up shop beneath the Hindustan Hotel. You can while away days watching the mix of fishermen, Hindu rituals, volleyball-playing visitors, locals gazing at the sea and strolling backpackers that make up the traffic on the beach.

Dangers & Annoyances

The beaches at Varkala have strong currents; even experienced swimmers have been swept away. This is one of the most dangerous beaches in Kerala, so be careful and swim between the flags or ask the lifeguards where's the safest place to swim.

If women wear bikinis or even swimsuits on the beach at Varkala, they are likely to feel uncomfortably exposed to stares – note that local people don't strip down on the beach. Wearing a sarong when out of the water will help avoid offending local sensibilities or attracting unwelcome attention, though it's worth noting that police patrol the beaches to keep male starers a-walkin' and the hawkers at bay. It pays to dress sensitively, especially if you're going into Varkala town.

It seems as if every man and his dog has an ayurvedic-related product or treatment to sell – many aren't qualified practitioners. Ask for recommendations before you go to get herbalised.

LEADER OF THE PACK

In 1957 Kerala democratically elected a communist government – the first place in the world to do so. Kerala's unique blend of democratic-socialist principles has a pretty impressive track record.

Kerala has been labelled 'the most socially advanced state in India' by Nobel prize-winning economist Amartya Sen. Land reform and a focus on infrastructure, health and education have played a large part in Kerala's success. The literacy rate (91%) is one of the highest of any developing nation, though a strong history of education stretches back centuries to the days of magnanimous rajas and active missionaries. The infant mortality rate in Kerala is one-fifth of the national average, while life expectancy stands at 73 years, 10 years higher than the rest of the country.

The picture is not all rosy, however. Lack of any industrial development or foreign investment means that the ambitions of many educated youth are curtailed. This might explain why Kerala also has the highest suicide rates and liquor consumption statistics in the country. A big hope for the economy's future is the recent boom in tourism, with Kerala emerging as one of India's most popular new tourist hot spots. So, thanks for coming, and congratulations on being a part of the solution.

◉ Sights

Janardhana Temple
HINDU TEMPLE

Varkala is a temple town, and Janardhana Temple is the main event – its technicolour Hindu spectacle sits hovering above Beach Rd. It's closed to non-Hindus, but you may be invited into the temple grounds where there is a huge banyan tree and shrines to Ayyappan, Hanuman and other Hindu deities.

Sivagiri Mutt
SACRED SITE

(☎2602807; www.sivagiri.org) Sivagiri Mutt is the headquarters of the Shri Narayana Dharma Sanghom Trust, the ashram devoted to Shri Narayana Guru (1855–1928), Kerala's most prominent guru. This is a popular pilgrimage site and the resident swami is happy to talk to visitors.

🏃 Activities

Yoga is offered at several guesthouses for ₹200 to ₹300 per session. **Boogie boards** can be hired from places along the beach for ₹100; be wary of strong currents.

Laksmi's
MASSAGE

(☎9895948080; Clafouti Beach Resort; manicure/pedicure from ₹400/600, henna ₹300, massage ₹800; ☺9am-7pm) This tiny place offers treatments such as threading and waxing as well as massages (women only).

Olympia House
MASSAGE

(☎9349439675; massages ₹600) Mr Omanakuttan is a qualified massage instructor, in both ayurveda and other schools.

Eden Garden
MASSAGE

(☎2603910; www.eden-garden.net; massage from ₹1000) Offers a more upmarket ayurvedic experience, and offers single treatments and packages.

🛏 Sleeping

Most places to stay are crammed in along the north cliff; some open only for the tourist onslaught in November. Less-developed Odayam beach, about 1km further north of Varkala's black beach, is a tranquil alternative.

The commission racket is alive and well – make sure that your rickshaw takes you to the place you've asked for.

⬗ TOP CHOICE Pink Aana
RESORT $

(☎9746981298; www.pinkaana.at; r ₹650-800) On the quiet Odayam Beach north of Varkala, there are just four wooden bungalows at the 'Pink Elephant'. Made of coconut wood

and bamboo, with private verandas, they're sparse but stylish, great value, and the best choice on this beach. There's a restaurant (meals around ₹200). Get here before the beach is ruined by any more buildings.

Villa Jacaranda
GUESTHOUSE $$$

(☎2610296; www.villa-jacaranda.biz; d incl breakfast ₹4600-5600) The ultimate in understated luxury, this romantic retreat has just a handful of huge, bright rooms in a large house, each with a balcony and decorated with a chic blend of minimalist modern and period touches. The delicious breakfast is served on your veranda.

Eden Garden
RESORT $$

(☎2603910; www.edengarden.in; r from ₹1200, luxury ste ₹5500) Overlooking peaceful paddy fields, this place has rooms with high wooden ceilings and attractive wooden furniture, set around a lush lily pond. Suites are organically shaped like white space-mushrooms, but inside they are romantic and fantastical, with intricate paintwork, round beds, and mosaic circular baths. A recommended ayurvedic resort is based here.

Taj Gateway Hotel
HOTEL $$$

(☎6673300; www.tajhotels.com/gateway; s/d ₹4400/5200; ❄@≋) Rebranded, revamped, refurbished, the Taj Varkala is looking hot – especially the new rooms, with beds covered in gleaming linen and mocha cushions, and with glass shower cubicles in the bathrooms, complete with electric blinds. There's a fantastic pool (nonguests ₹400).

Jicky's
GUESTHOUSE $$

(☎2606994; www.jickys.com; s ₹400, d ₹600-1750, cottage ₹900-1000) Way back in the palm groves, family-run Jicky's remains friendly as they come. The regular rooms are lovely and fresh, surrounded by lots of leafiness, and there are now also two double cottages, and some larger rooms for three to four in two smaller whitewashed, wooden-shuttered buildings.

Puthooram
RESORT $$

(☎3202007; www.puthooram.com; r ₹500-2000, with AC ₹2500-3000) If garden gnomes were on holiday, they'd probably come here, to stay in Puthooram's wood-lined bungalows set around a charming little garden. Rooms with sea view are pricier.

Villa Anamika
GUESTHOUSE $$

(☎2600096; www.villaanamika.com; r ₹500-2500, cottages ₹3500; ❄) This Keralan-German-run

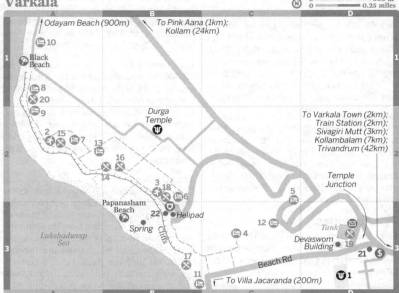

place has spacious rooms, all neatly furnished with homely decorations and art by owner Chicku. The pricier rooms have sea views, and the trim little garden out the back is a bonus.

Guest House Varkala GUESTHOUSE $
(☎2602227; d ₹220, with AC ₹440) A government-run guesthouse with several rooms in huge Keralan-styled bungalows that were once part of a palace complex. Though spartan, each bargain-basement abode is finished with lots of polished wood and has incredibly high ceilings.

New Heaven GUESTHOUSE $$
(☎9846074818; newheavenbeachresort@yahoo.com; r ₹900-1000) New Heaven has easy access to Black Beach and great top-floor views. Bedrooms are roomy, basic and a tad drab, with big blue bathrooms and hanging wicker chairs out the front for lazing.

Sea Pearl Chalets RESORT $$
(☎2660105; www.seapearlchalets.com; d from ₹1500) Precariously perched on Varkala's southern cliff, these small, basic, podlike huts have unbeatable views and are surrounded by prim lawns. Definitely worth checking out before they tumble into the ocean.

Kerala Bamboo House RESORT $$
(☎9895270993; www.keralabamboohouse.com; huts d ₹1500-2000) For that bamboo-hut experience, this popular place squishes together dozens of pretty Balinese-style huts in a clifftop compound and a carefully maintained garden. Some of the huts are nicer than others (ie some have muralled outdoor showers and are wood-lined, some don't), so look at a few. Cheaper ones don't have hot water.

Santa Claus Village Resort RESORT $$
(☎9249121464; www.santaclausvillageresort.com; r from ₹500, with sea view ₹ 1000, with AC from ₹1500; ✿▨) This simple but appealing clifffront option has small rooms in traditional Keralan-themed buildings, with fetching bits of furniture and lots of teak-wood flair. The four rooms at the front are the money shot, with windows facing out to sea.

Sea Breeze GUESTHOUSE $$
(☎2603257; www.seabreezevarkala.com; r ₹1500, with AC ₹2200-3000; ✿) The large, orderly, if dull rooms in this pink building all offer sea views and share a large veranda – perfect for nightly sunset adulation.

🍴 Eating

Most restaurants in Varkala offer the same mishmash of Indian, Asian and Western

Varkala

◎ **Sights**

fare to a soundtrack of easy-listening trance; they open from around 8am to 11pm. Join in the nightly Varkala saunter till you find a place that suits. Those who are unlicensed will usually serve alcohol discreetly.

Café del Mar   MULTICUISINE **$$**
(dishes ₹110-400) This is the kind of place you return to for its efficient service, good coffee, whirring fans, great position overlooking the cliffs, and the specials of the day chalked up on a board outside.

Trattorias   MULTICUISINE **$$**
(meals ₹80-200) Smarter than most Trattorias has an Italian coffee machine and the usual wide-ranging menu, but specialises in pasta and even has some Japanese dishes.

Nothin' Doing   INDIAN **$$**
(Hindustan Hotel; mains ₹120-280; ⊘7am-10.30am, noon-3pm & 7-10.15pm) The rooftop restaurant topping this carbuncle offers tasty enough nonveg and veg fare, but the real reason to come here is the view from the balcony (with just a couple of tables) over the action of the beach.

Oottupura Vegetarian Restaurant INDIAN **$**
(mains from ₹35) Bucking the trend and serving only veggie options, this budget eatery has a respectable range of yummy dishes, including breakfast *puttu* (flour with milk, bananas and honey).

Sreepadman   SOUTH INDIAN **$**
(thali ₹30) For dirt-cheap and authentic Keralan fare – think dosas (paper-thin lentil-flour pancakes) and thalis – where you can rub shoulders with rickshaw drivers rather than tourists, hit Sreepadman. This is a hole-in-the-wall with a view: there is neat seating out the back.

Hungry Eye Kitchen   MULTICUISINE **$$**
(meals ₹70-160) The multilevel design of Hungry Eye means everyone gets uninterrupted sea views. Thai food is a speciality – the kitchen can whip up red and green curries as well as the usual Varkala suspects.

Juice Shack   CAFE **$**
(juices ₹50, snacks ₹30-150; ⊘7am-7pm) A funky little health-juice bar that has a buffet on Wednesday and Saturday (₹250).

☆ Entertainment

Kathakali performances are organised during high season – look out for notices locally.

❶ Information

A 24-hour ATM at the temple junction takes Visa cards, and there are more ATMs in Varkala town. Many of the travel agents lining the cliff do cash advances on credit cards and change travellers cheques. **Internet cafes** (per hr around ₹40) dot the cliff top – save emails often, as power cuts are not uncommon.

Post office (⊘10am-2pm Mon-Sat) North of Temple Junction.

❶ Getting There & Away

There are frequent trains to Trivandrum (2nd class/AC chair ₹21/140, one hour) and Kollam (₹17/140, 30 minutes), as well as three daily services to Alleppey (₹35/153, two hours). It's feasible to get to Kollam in time for the morning backwater boat to Alleppey (p940). From Temple Junction, three daily buses pass by on their way to Trivandrum (₹30, 1½ to two hours), with one heading to Kollam (₹25, one hour).

ⓘ Getting Around

It's about 2.5km from the train station to Varkala beach, with rickshaws going there for ₹40 to ₹50. Local buses also travel regularly between the train station and the temple junction (₹4).

Many places along the cliff hire out scooters/Enfields for ₹250/350 per day.

Kollam (Quilon)

📞 0474 / POP 380,100

Small but busy, untouristy Kollam (Quilon) is the southern approach to Kerala's backwaters. One of the oldest ports in the Arabian Sea, it was once a major commercial hub that saw Roman, Arab, Chinese and later Portuguese, Dutch and British traders jostle into port – eager to get their hands on spices and the region's cashew crops. The centre of town is reasonably hectic, but surrounding it are the calm waterways of Ashtamudi Lake, fringed with coconut palms, cashew plantations and traditional villages.

⊙ Sights

The best thing to do from Kollam is explore the backwaters around **Munroe Island** (see Tours, p936). There's a rowdy **fish market** at Kollam Beach where customers and fisherfolk alike pontificate on the value of the day's catch; there's also an evening fish market from 5pm to 9pm. The **beach** (long, but nothing special) is 2km south of town, a ₹30 rickshaw ride away.

🏃 Activities

Janakanthi Panchakarma Centre AYURVEDA (📞 2763014; www.santhigiri.co.in; Vaidyasala Nagar, Asraman North) An ayurvedic centre with more of an institutional than a spa vibe, 5km from Kollam, popular for its seven- to 21-day treatment packages – accommodation is available for ₹500 a night. You can also just visit for a rejuvenation massage (₹750). An autorickshaw from Kollam should cost around ₹140.

☞ Tours

TOP CHOICE Canoe-boat tours BOATING
(per person ₹400; ⊘9am-1.30pm & 2pm-6.30pm) Excellent tours through the canals of Munroe Island and across Ashtamudi Lake are organised by the DTPC (District Tourism Promotion Council). You're first driven 25km to the starting point, then take a three-hour trip via punted canoe. On these excursions (with knowledgeable guides) you can observe daily village life, see *kettuvallam* (rice barge) construction, toddy (palm beer) tapping, coir-making (coconut fibre),

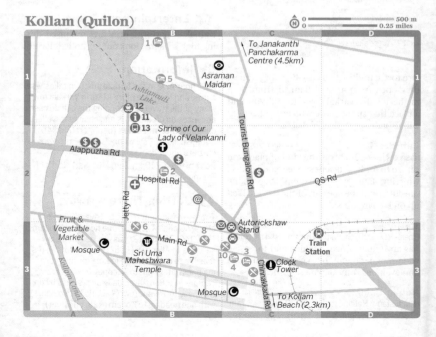

Kollam (Quilon)

prawn and fish farming, and do some bird-watching on spice-garden visits.

Houseboat cruises
BOATING

(2/4 people 24hr cruise ₹4000/4500, Kollam to Alappuzha cruise ₹10,000/12,000) The DTPC organises these houseboat cruise packages.

✖✖ Festivals & Events

The **Pooram festival** is held in Kollam every April; the **Ashtamudi Craft & Art festival** (December/January) is every two years.

🛌 Sleeping

The DTPC office keeps a list of **homestays** in and around Kollam.

Valiyavila Homestay
GUESTHOUSE $$

(☎2701546, 9847132449; www.kollamlakeview resort.com; Panamukkom; r ₹1000-2000, with AC ₹2500; ✳@) This has an amazing location, crowning a breezy peninsula surrounded by leisurely backwaters on three sides. The four enormous rooms come with lots of windows to enjoy the views and the breeze. It's a good choice for families. Call ahead for a boat pick-up, catch a public ferry from Kollam (₹3), or grab an autorickshaw (₹100) to get here. The tourist boat from Alleppey also stops here before it docks at Kollam.

Get here before 2013, when it's set to close. The host, Joseph Prabath, has set up

Kollam (Quilon)

Ashtamudi Villas (www.ashtamudivillas.com; d ₹1000), simple brick huts set on the water's edge, among nodding palms, which are much closer to town.

Nani Hotel
HOTEL $$

(☎2751141; Chinnakada Rd; r ₹1050, with AC ₹1600-3000; ✳@) This boutique business hotel is a surprise in Kollam's busy centre, and exceptionally good value. Built by a cashew magnate, it's gorgeously designed and mixes traditional Keralan elements and modern lines for a sleek look. Even the cheaper rooms have flat-screen TVs, feathery pillows and sumptuous bathrooms.

Tamarind
HOTEL $$

(☎2745538; r with AC ₹1400; ✳) Overlooking the backwaters, across the lake from the ferry terminal, this has big, airy, bright orange, slightly tired rooms, with great views.

Government Guest House
GUESTHOUSE $

(☎2743620; s/d ₹220/440) In a colonial-era relic that's all whitewashed walls, tall varnished shutters and dusty grandeur, this guesthouse offers crumbling rooms with high ceilings and wooden floors. They're a bargain, but isolated 3km north of the centre on Ashtamudi Lake. Book ahead.

Hotel Sudarsan
HOTEL $$

(☎2744322; Alappuzha Rd; www.hotelsudarsan.com; s/d with AC from ₹900/1000, deluxe ₹1200/1400; ✳) Sudarsan is welcoming enough, set around a car-park-courtyard, but rooms are plain and dull, if comfortable. Those at the front are noisy. There's a good restaurant.

Kodiylil Residency
GUESTHOUSE $

(☎3018030; Main Rd; s/d ₹440/550, with AC ₹800/900; ✳) Bright red hallways are moodily lit, if at all, and the rooms here come in shades of lime that could do with a lick of paint. Shame about the lack of windows.

Karuna Residency
GUESTHOUSE $

(☎3263240; Main Rd; s/d ₹350/450, r with AC ₹700; ✳) This little budgeteer is starting to show its age, but is still maintained in decent condition. The central location close to the train station is probably its biggest asset.

✖ Eating

Prasadam
MULTICUISINE $$

(☎2751141; Chinnakada Rd; mains ₹60-150) The restaurant at the swish Nani Hotel has a comely setting amid intricate copper-relief artwork depicting Kollam history. The meals are well prepared and include tasty thalis.

Kedar Restaurant INDIAN $$
(Hotel Sudarsan; meals ₹90-150; ⊘7am-11pm) This small glass-walled eatery is recommended for its tasty veg and nonveg cuisine, including special chicken masala.

Fayalwan Hotel INDIAN $
(Main Rd; meals ₹10-40) This is a real Indian working-man's diner, packed to the rafters come lunchtime. There are concrete booths and long benches for sitting and tucking in – try the mutton biryani (₹45).

Hotel Guru Prasad INDIAN $
(Main Rd; meals ₹24) In a neat colonial building still clinging to remnants of a once-cheery paint job, this busy lunchtime place draws the punters with dirt-cheap set meals.

Indian Coffee House INDIAN $
(Main Rd) Reliable for a decent breakfast and strong coffee.

Vijayalaxmi Cashew Co FOODSTUFFS $
(Main Rd; ⊘10am-7pm) A major exporter of Kollam's famous cashews; quality nuts are around ₹260 per 500g.

ⓘ Information
DTPC information centre (☑2745625; info@ dtpckollam.com; ⊘8am-7pm) Helpful; near the KSRTC bus stand and boat jetty.
Post office (☑2746607; Alappuzha Rd)
Silver Net (per hr ₹25; ⊘10.30am-6.30pm Mon-Sat) The most convenient of numerous internet cafes at the Bishop Jerome Nagar Complex.
UAE Exchange (☑2751240-1; Alappuzha Rd; ⊘9.30am-6pm Mon-Fri, to 4pm Sat, to 1.30pm Sun) For changing cash and travellers cheques.

ⓘ Getting There & Away
Boat
See p940 for information on cruises to Alleppey. From the main boat jetty there are frequent public ferry services across Ashtamudi Lake to Guhanandapuram (one hour). Fares are around ₹10 return, or ₹3 for a short hop.

Bus
Kollam is on the Trivandrum–Kollam–Alleppey–Ernakulam bus route, with superfast/fast buses departing every 10 or 20 minutes to Trivandrum (₹44/42, 1¾/two hours), Alleppey (₹55/52, two/2½ hours) and Ernakulam (Kochi, ₹90/85, 3¼/3½ hours). Buses depart from the **KSRTC bus stand** (☑2752008) near the boat jetty.

Train
There are frequent trains to Ernakulam (2nd class/AC chair ₹61/210, 3½ hours, six daily) and Trivandrum (₹40/165, one hour) via Varkala (₹36/165, 30 minutes). A couple of trains daily go to Alappuzha (Alleppey; ₹59/202, 1½ hours).

Around Kollam
KRISHNAPURAM PALACE MUSEUM
Two kilometres south of Kayamkulam (between Kollam and Alleppey), this restored palace (☑0479-2441133; admission ₹10, camera/video ₹25/250; ⊘9am-1pm & 2-5pm Mon-Sat) is a fine example of grand Keralan architecture. Now a museum, inside are paintings, antique furniture, sculptures, and a renowned 3m-high mural depicting the Gajendra Moksha (the liberation of Gajendra, chief of the elephants) as told in the Mahabharata. The **Bharni Utsavam festival** is held at the nearby Chettikulangara Bhaghavathy Temple in February/March.

Buses (₹25) leave Kollam every few minutes for Kayamkulam. Get off at the bus stand near the temple gate, 2km before the palace.

Alappuzha (Alleppey)
☑0477 / POP 282,700
Hmm, those Venice comparisons might work if Venice shrank, acquired a few breeze-block buildings, and imported some tooting rickshaws.

But step out of the hectic centre, and Alappuzha is graceful and greenery-fringed, set around its grid of canals. Explore the vast watery highways of the region and you'll experience one of Kerala's most mesmerisingly beautiful and relaxing experiences.

It's the gateway to the fabled backwaters, a sprawling network of canals – float along and gaze over rice fields of succulent green, curvaceous rice barges, and village life along the banks. Most people in town would like to organise you some houseboat or canoe action. It's also home to the famous **Nehru Trophy Snake Boat Race**.

⚐ Activities
Ayurveda: Shri Krishna Ayurveda Panchkarma Centre AYURVEDA
(☑3290728, 9847119060; www.krishnayurveda. com) For ayurvedic treatments; one-hour rejuvenation massages are ₹600. It's near the Nehru race finishing point.

Alappuzha (Alleppey)

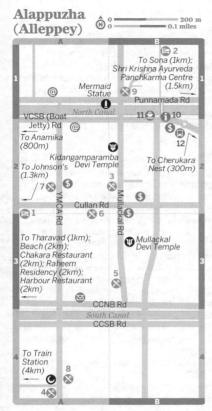

Alappuzha (Alleppey)

Sleeping
1	Dream Nest	A2
2	Palmy Residency	B1

Eating
3	Indian Coffee House	B2
4	Indian Coffee House	A4
5	Kream Korner	B3
6	Kream Korner	A2
7	Royale Park Hotel	A2
8	Thaff	A4
9	Thaff	B1

Information
10	DTPC Tourist Reception Centre	B1

Transport
11	Boat Jetty	B1
12	KSRTC Bus Stand	B2

have bathtubs, antique furniture and period fixtures. The common areas are airy and comfortable, there are pretty indoor courtyards, a well-stocked library, a great little pool and an excellent restaurant.

Palmy Residency   GUESTHOUSE $
(☎2235938; www.palmyresort.com; Opposite Matha Jetty, Finishing Point Rd; r ₹350) Run by the friendly folk of Palmy Resort, this has to be the best deal in town. It's in a brand-new building in a fab location – just over the new Matha footbridge from the bus station, but set back from the road amid lush greenery. Rooms are spacious and floored in Italian marble.

Cherukara Nest   HOMESTAY $
(☎2251509; www.cherukaranest.com; d incl breakfast ₹750, with AC ₹1200; ❄@) Set in well-tended gardens, with a pigeon coop at the back, this lovely heritage home has the sort of welcoming family atmosphere that makes you miss your grandma. There are four large characterful rooms, each sporting lots of polished wood touches and antediluvian doors with ornate locks. Great value.

Palmy Lake Resort   HOMESTAY $
(☎2235938; www.palmyresorts.com; Punnamada Rd East; cottages d ₹750) With six handsome cottages, some in bamboo and some in concrete, there's loads of charm and peace at this stunning value homestay, 3.5km north of Alleppey. It's set among palm groves near the backwaters, with gracious owner Bigi and his wife Macy providing delicious meals on request.

☞ Tours

Any of the dozens of travel agencies in town, guesthouses, hotels, or the KTDC can arrange canoe-boat tours of the backwaters; also see p940.

☷ Sleeping

For lovely canalside lazing, try the relaxed sleeping options on the backwaters a few kilometres north of Alleppey; all can arrange town pick-ups and drop offs.

The rickshaw-commission racketeers are at work here; ask to be dropped off at a landmark close to your destination if you're having problems getting where you want to go.

TOP CHOICE **Raheem Residency**   HOTEL $$$
(☎2239767; www.raheemresidency.com; Beach Rd; s/d from €140/170; ❄❅❆) This thoughtfully renovated 1860s heritage home is a delight to visit, let alone stay in. The 10 rooms here have been restored to their former glory and

THE BACKWATERS

The undisputed main attraction of a trip to Kerala is travelling through the 900km network of waterways that fringe the coast and trickle inland. Long before the advent of roads, these waters were the slippery highways of Kerala, and many villagers still use paddle-power as their main form of transport. Trips through the backwaters traverse palm-fringed lakes studded with cantilevered Chinese fishing nets, and wind their way along narrow, shady canals where coir (coconut fibre), copra (dried coconut kernels) and cashews are loaded onto boats. Along the way are isolated villages where farming life continues as it has for eons. For information on the northern backwaters, see p978.

Tourist Cruises

The popular tourist cruise between Kollam and Alleppey (₹400) departs at 10.30am, arriving at 6.30pm, daily from August to March and every second day at other times. Generally, there's a 1pm lunch stop (with a basic lunch provided) and a brief afternoon chai stop. The crew has an ice box full of fruit, soft drinks and beer to sell. Bring sunscreen and a hat.

It's a scenic and leisurely way to get between the two towns, but the boat travels along only the major canals – you won't have many close-up views of the village life that makes the backwaters so magical. Some travellers say they found the eight-hour trip boring.

Another option is to take the trip halfway (₹200) and get off at the **Matha Amrith-anandamayi Mission** (☑0476-2897578; www.amritapuri.org; Amrithapuri), the incongruously pink ashram of Matha Amrithanandamayi. One of India's few **female gurus**, Amrithanandamayi is also known as Amma (Mother), or 'The Hugging Mother,' because of the *darshan* (audience) she offers, often hugging thousands of people in marathon all-night sessions. The ashram runs official tours at 5pm each day. It's a huge complex, with about 2000 people living here permanently – monks, nuns, students and families, both Indian and foreign. It offers food, ayurvedic treatments, yoga and meditation, as well as souvenirs; everything from books to postcards of Amma's toes. Amma travels around for much of the year, so you might be out of luck if in need of a cuddle.

Visitors should dress conservatively and there is a strict code of behaviour. With prior arrangement, you can stay at the ashram for ₹150 per day (including simple vegetarian meals) and pick up an onward or return cruise a day or two later. Alternatively, you can take the free ferry to the other side of the canal and grab a rickshaw to Karunagappally, 10km away (around ₹170), from where you can catch buses to Alleppey (₹35, 1½ hours).

Houseboats

Renting a houseboat designed like a *kettuvallam* (rice barge) could be one of your most expensive experiences in India, but it's usually worth every rupee. Drifting through quiet canals lined with coconut palms, eating delicious Keralan food, meeting local villagers and sleeping on the water – it's a world away from the clamour elsewhere.

Houseboats cater for couples (one or two double bedrooms) and groups (up to seven bedrooms!). Food (and an onboard chef to cook it) is generally included in the quoted cost. Houseboats can be chartered through a multitude of private operators in Kollam (book ahead here as there are fewer boats) and Alleppey. This is the biggest business in Kerala:

Tharavad   HOMESTAY **$$**
(☑242044; www.tharavadheritageresort.com; West of North Police Station; d ₹1000, with AC ₹2000; ❋) Between the town centre and beach, in a quiet canalside location, this ancestral home (the owner's grandfather was an ayurvedic doctor) has lots of glossy teak and antiques, five characterful rooms, and well-maintained gardens.

Gowri Residence   GUESTHOUSE **$**
(☑2236371; www.gowriresidence.com; r ₹600-900, with AC ₹1200; ❋) This rambling complex has traditional wood-panelled rooms in the main house, several types of bungalows made from either stone, wood, bamboo or thatch, and a towering treehouse. Good food is served, and there's an aviary that even includes an emu.

Sona   GUESTHOUSE **$$**
(☑2235211; www.sonahome.com; Lakeside, Finishing Point; r ₹800, with AC ₹1100) Run by the affable Joseph, this old heritage home has slightly shabby but high-ceilinged rooms with

some operators are unscrupulous. The quality of boats varies widely, from rust buckets to floating palaces – try to check out the boat before agreeing on a price. Travel-agency reps will be pushing you to book a boat as soon as you set foot in Kerala, but it's better to wait till you reach a backwater hub: choice is greater in Alleppey (500 boats and counting), and you're much more likely to be able to bargain down a price if you turn up and see what's on offer.

In the high season you're likely to get caught in backwater-gridlock – some travellers are disappointed by the number of boats on the water. It's not possible to travel by house-boat between Alleppey and Kollam, or between Alleppey and Kochi. Expect a boat for two people for 24 hours to cost about ₹4500–6000; for four people, ₹5500-8000; more for larger boats or for AC. Shop around to negotiate a bargain – though this will be harder in the busier seasons. Prices triple from around 20 December to 5 January.

Village Tours & Canoe Boats

More and more travellers are opting for village tours or canal-boat trips. Village tours usu-ally involve small groups of five to six people, a knowledgeable guide and an open canoe or covered *kettuvallam*. The tours (from Kochi, Kollam or Alleppey) last from 2½ to six hours and cost between ₹300 and ₹650 per person. They include visits to villages to watch coir-making, boat building, toddy (palm beer) tapping and fish farming. On longer trips a traditional Keralan lunch is often provided. The Munroe Island trip from Kollam (p936) is an excellent tour of this type; the tourist desk in Ernakulam also organises recommended tours.

In Alleppey, rented canoe boats offer a nonguided laze through the canals on a small, covered canoe for up to four people (two people for two/four hours ₹150/₹600) – a great way to spend a relaxing afternoon.

Public Ferries

If you want the local backwater transport experience, there are State Water Transport boats between Alleppey and Kottayam (₹10 to ₹11, 2½ hours) depart Alleppey at 7.30am, 9.35am, 11.30am, 2.30pm and 5.15pm; they leave Kottayam at 6.40am, 11.30am, 1pm, 3.30pm and 5.15pm. The trip crosses Vembanad Lake and has a more varied landscape than the Alleppey cruise.

Environmental Issues

Pollution from houseboat motors is becoming a major problem as boat numbers swell every season. The Keralan authorities have introduced an ecofriendly accreditation system for houseboat operators. Among the criteria an operator must meet before being issued with the 'Green Palm Certificate' are the installation of solar panels and sanitary tanks for the disposal of waste – ask operators whether they have the requisite certification. There's been talk of running boats on cleaner natural gas, though we've yet to see this being implemented. Consider choosing one of the few remaining punting, rather than motorised, boats if possible.

faded flowered curtains, and four-poster beds overlooking a well-kept garden.

Malayalam RESORT **$$**
(✆2234591; malayalamresorts@yahoo.com; Pun-namada; r ₹1200) With one of best locations in Alleppey, this little family-run pad has four cute cottages that practically play footsies with the backwaters. It's a bit hard to find: walk past the Keraleeyam resort reception and along the canal bank.

Palm Grove Lake Resort RESORT **$$**
(✆2235004; www.palmgrovelakeresort.com; Pun-namada; cottages d ₹1750, with AC ₹3500) Close to the starting point of the Nehru Trophy Snake Boat Race on Punnamada Lake, this isolated option has stylish, airy double cot-tages set amid palms, on the lake. Each plainly furnished but appealing hut has a secluded veranda, eye-catching, if jaded, outdoor showers and lake views.

Johnson's　　　　　　GUESTHOUSE $
(2245825; www.johnsonskerala.com; r ₹400-650) On a quiet street just west of town, this is a backpackers' favourite in a quirky modern mansion. Captained by the zealous Johnson Gilbert (who is keen to sell his pricey houseboat tours), this rambling residence is filled with funky furniture and loads of plants. A cheaper bamboo hut (₹250) is in the garden.

Dream Nest　　　　　　GUESTHOUSE $
(9895543080; www.thedreamnest.com; Cullen Rd; d & tr ₹500-600; ✲@) With a cheery welcome, this offers fairly clean, spacious, if drab rooms in a central villa, and a slightly blokish atmosphere. There's a nothing-special terrace out the back where you can hang out and shoot the breeze.

✗ Eating

Royale Park Hotel　　　　　　INDIAN $$
(YMCA Rd; meals ₹90-200; ☺7am-10pm; ☏) There is an extensive menu at this swish hotel restaurant, and the food is excellent, including scrumptious veg thalis for ₹100. You can order from the same menu in the upstairs bar and wash down your meal with a cold Kingfisher.

Chakara Restaurant　　　　　　MULTICUISINE $$$
(2230767; Beach Rd; mini Kerala meal ₹350, mains ₹420; ☺1-3pm & 7-9.30pm) The restaurant at Raheem Residency is Alleppey's finest, with seating on a bijou open rooftop with views over to the beach. The menu creatively combines traditional Keralan and European cuisine. Local Indian wine is available.

Harbour Restaurant　　　　　　MULTICUISINE $$
(2230767; Beach Rd; meals ₹90-120; ☺10am-10pm) This beachside, casual little brick hut is run by the swish Raheem Residency. It's more casual and budget-conscious than the hotel's restaurant, but promises equally well prepared cuisine, and is good to drop by for a cold beer (large Kingfisher ₹110).

Kream Korner　　　　　　MULTICUISINE $
(Mullackal Rd; dishes ₹20-80; ☺8.30am-10pm) This relaxed airy place is popular with Indian and foreign families and offers a tasty menu. There's another, pint-sized branch on Cullan Rd.

Thaff　　　　　　INDIAN $
(YMCA Rd; meals ₹35-110) An absurdly popular joint that has scrumptious Indian bites, with some Arabic flavours mixed in, to boot. It does succulent roast spit-chicken, scrumptious *shawarma* and brain-freezing ice-cream shakes. There's another location on Punnamada Rd.

Vembanad Restaurant　　　　　　INDIAN $
(Alleppey Prince Hotel; AS Rd; mains ₹50-170) Reliable dining pool-side; occasional live music, located 3km northwest of town.

Indian Coffee House　　　　　　CAFE $
(snacks around ₹10) Branches on Mullackal Rd, YMCA Rd, and Beach Rd – the latter is a pavilion in a great, breezy beachside location.

ℹ Information

DTPC Tourist Reception Centre (2253308; www.alappuzhatourism.com; ☺8.30am-6pm) Remarkably rudimentary tourist info.
Mailbox (2339994; Boat Jetty Rd; per hr ₹40; ☺8am-9.30pm) Internet access.
National Cyber Park (2238688; YMCA Compound; per hr ₹30; ☺10am-9pm) Internet access.
Tourist Police (2251161; ☺24hr) Next door to the DTPC.
UAE Exchange (2264407; cnr Cullan & Mullackal Rds; ☺9.30am-6pm to 4pm Sat, to 1pm Sun) For changing cash and travellers cheques.

ℹ Getting There & Away

Boat
Ferries run to Kottayam from the boat jetty on VCSB (Boat Jetty) Rd; see the boxed text, p940.

Bus
From the KSRTC bus stand, frequent buses head to Trivandrum (₹97, 3½ hours, every 20 minutes), Kollam (₹54) and Ernakulam (Kochi, ₹39, 1½ hours). Buses to Kottayam (₹30, 1¼ hours, every 30 minutes) are much faster than the ferry. One bus daily leaves for Kumily at 6.40am (₹110, 5½ hours). The Varkala bus (₹97, 3½ hours) leaves at 10.40am daily.

Train
There are several trains to Ernakulam (2nd class/AC chair ₹59/202, 1½ hours) and Trivandrum (₹59/202, three hours) via Kollam (₹45/165, 1½ hours). Four trains a day stop at Varkala (2nd class/AC chair ₹50/178, two hours). The train station is 4km west of town.

ℹ Getting Around
An autorickshaw from the train station to the boat jetty and KSRTC bus stand is around ₹50. Several guesthouses around town hire out scooters for ₹200 per day.

Around Alleppey

Kerala's backwaters snake in all directions from Alleppey and, while touring on a houseboat is a great experience, taking time to slow down and stay in a village can be just as rewarding.

Just 10km from Alleppey, **Green Palms Homes** (☑0477-2724497; www.greenpalmshomes. com; Chennamkary; r without bathroom incl full board ₹2250, r ₹3250-4000) is a series of homestays that seem a universe away, set in a picturesque backwater village, where you will sleep in basic rooms in villagers' homes among rice paddies. It's splendidly quiet, there are no roads in sight and you can take a guided walk (₹200), hire bicycles (₹50 per hour) and canoes (₹100 per hour) or take cooking classes with your hosts (₹150). Book ahead.

To get here, call ahead and catch one of the hourly ferries from Alleppey to Chennamkary (₹5, 1¼ hours). Please remember this is a traditional village; dress appropriately.

Kottayam

☑0481 / POP 172,867

Sandwiched between the Western Ghats and the backwaters, Kottayam is renowned for being the centre of Kerala's spice and rubber trade rather than for its aesthetic appeal. For most travellers it's a hub town, well connected to both the mountains and the backwaters.

Kottayam has a bookish history: the first Malayalam-language printing press was established here in 1820, and this was the first district in India to achieve 100% literacy. A place of churches and seminaries, it was a refuge for the Orthodox church when the Portuguese began forcing Keralan Christians to switch to Catholicism in the 16th century.

The **Thirunakkara Utsavam festival** is held in March at the Thirunakkara Shiva Temple.

🛏 Sleeping

Accommodation options are pretty dire in Kottayam – you're better off heading to Kumarakon for some great top-end hotels. Also try checking for homestays at the **DTPC office** (☑2560479), which range from basic (₹1000 per person full board) to deluxe (up to US$100).

Homestead Hotel   HOTEL **$**
(☑2560467; KK Rd; s/d from ₹350/548, d with AC ₹1500; ❄) Easily the pick of the budget lit-

ter, this place has painstakingly maintained rooms in a blissfully quiet building off the street. The foyer sports '60s-style decor that's accidentally stumbled into vogue again, and Thali and Meenachil restaurants are right out the front. Book ahead.

Windsor Castle   HOTEL **$$$**
(☑2363637; www.thewindsorcastle.net; MC Rd; s/d from US$80/100, cottages US$155; ❄☀≋) This grandiose carbuncle has some of the better rooms in Kottayam – spacious and with bathtubs, and some with attractive river views, but overpriced. You may as well go for the deluxe dark wood-furnished cottages, strewn around the private backwaters. There's a pleasant restaurant overlooking landscaped waterways.

Pearl Regency   HOTEL **$$**
(☑2561123; www.pearlregencyktm.com; TB Junction, MC Rd; s/d from ₹1900/2200; ❄@) This business-focused contender has roomy-but-dull, comfily inoffensive abodes. It's efficient, decent value, and a passable stay if you're stuck in Kottayam.

Ambassador Hotel   HOTEL **$**
(☑2563293; KK Rd; www.fhrai.com; s/d from ₹376/550) A respectable budget sleeping option, the rooms here are spartan but fairly clean, spacious and quiet. It has a bakery, bar, an adequate restaurant, and a boat-shaped fish tank in the lobby.

🍴 Eating

Thali   SOUTH INDIAN **$**
(1st fl, KK Rd; meals ₹53-63; ⊙8am-8.30pm) A lovely, spotlessly kept 1st-floor room, with slatted blinds, this place is a swankier version of the typical Keralan set-meal place. The food here is great, including Malabar fish curry (₹45) and thalis (₹70-85).

Meenachil   MULTICUISINE **$**
(2nd fl, KK Rd; dishes ₹60-110; ⊙noon-3pm & 6-10pm) This is our favourite place in Kottayam to fill up on scrumptious Indian and Chinese fare. The family atmosphere is friendly, the dining room modern and tidy and the menu expansive.

Nalekattu   SOUTH INDIAN **$$**
(Windsor Hotel; MC Rd; dishes ₹140-190; ⊙lunch & dinner) The traditional Keralan restaurant at the Windsor Castle overlooks some neat backwaters and serves tasty Keralan specialities like *chemeen* (mango curry) and *tharavu mappas* (duck in coconut gravy). There's also a recommended buffet at ₹249.

Hotel Suryaas INDIAN $
(Baker Junction, SB Rd; dishes ₹38-50; ☺8am-10pm) It's no surprise this dark and cosy, vintage wood-lined dining room is packed to the rafters with hungry families come mealtime – the North and South Indian food here is excellent.

Indian Coffee House CAFE $
(TB Rd) We just can't get enough of this South Indian institution serving the whole gamut of tasty Indian snacks.

❶ Information

The KSRTC bus stand is 1km south of the centre; the boat jetty is a further 2km (at Kodimatha). The train station is 1km north of Kottayam. There's a handful of ATMs around.
DTPC office (☑2560479; dtpcktm@sanchar-net.in; ☺10am-5pm Mon-Sat) At the boat jetty.
UAE Exchange (☑2303865; 1st fl, MC Rd; ☺9.30am-6pm Mon-Sat, 9.30am-1pm Sun) Changes cash and travellers cheques.

❶ Getting There & Away

Boat

Ferries run to Alleppey; see the boxed text, p940.

Bus

The **KSRTC bus stand** has buses to Trivandrum (₹93, four hours, every 20 minutes), Alleppey (₹31, 1¼ hours, every 30 minutes) and Ernakulam (Kochi, ₹42, two hours, every 20 minutes). There are also frequent buses to nearby Kumarakom (₹8, 30 minutes, every 15 minutes), to Thrissur (ordinary ₹79, four hours), Calicut (₹162, seven hours, 13 daily), Kumily for Periyar Wildlife Sanctuary (₹69, four hours, every 30 minutes) and Munnar (₹100, five hours, five daily). There are also buses to Kollam (₹60, four daily) and Varkala (₹78, three hours).

Train

Kottayam is well served by frequent trains running between Trivandrum (2nd class/AC chair ₹62/214, 3½ hours) and Ernakulam (₹40/165, 1½ hours).

❶ Getting Around

An autorickshaw from the jetty to the KSRTC bus stand is around ₹30, and from the bus stand to the train station about ₹20. Most trips around town cost ₹20.

Around Kottayam

KUMARAKOM
☑0481

Kumarakom, 16km west of Kottayam and on the shore of Vembanad Lake, is an unhur-ried backwater town with a smattering of dazzling top-end sleeping options. You can arrange houseboats through Kumarakom's less-crowded canals, but expect to pay considerably more than in Alleppey.

Arundhati Roy, author of the 1997 Booker Prize-winning *The God of Small Things,* was raised in the nearby Aymanam village.

❂ Sights & Activities

Kumarakom Bird Sanctuary NATURE RESERVE
(Indian/foreigner ₹5/45; ☺6am-6pm) This reserve on the 5-hectare site of a former rubber plantation is the haunt of a variety of domestic and migratory birds. October to February is the time for travelling birds like the garganey teal, osprey, marsh harrier and steppey eagle; May to July is the breeding season for local species such as the Indian shag, pond herons, egrets and darters. Early morning is the best viewing time.

Buses between Kottayam's KSRTC stand and Kumarakom (₹8, 30 minutes, every 15 minutes) stop at the entrance to the sanctuary.

🛏 Sleeping

Cruise 'N Lake RESORT $$
(☑2525804; www.homestaykumarakom.com; Puthenpura Tourist Enclave; r ₹1000-1500, with AC ₹1500-2000; ❄) As any estate agent will tell you, it's all about location, location, location. Crowning the tip of a small peninsula surrounded by backwaters on one side and a lawn of rice paddies on the other, this is the ideal affordable getaway. The rooms are plain, but it's lovely and secluded out here, surrounded by bucolic villages where houseboats are made by hand. To get to it, go several kilometres past the sanctuary and take a left, it's then 2km down a dirt road. Management can arrange pick-ups from Kottayam, and houseboats are available from here.

Coconut Lagoon RESORT $$$
(☑0484-3011711; www.cghearth.com; r incl breakfast & tax from ₹13,000; ❄@☀) Spread languidly over 9 hectares of grounds, this luxurious resort offers the ultimate in seclusion: it's accessible only by private boat. Surrounded by backwaters and with perfect sunsets guaranteed, the different *tharawad* (ancestral home) cottages on offer here are variously filled with polished wood, classy antique-style furnishings and neat open-air bathrooms. This place might be familiar to those who have read Arundhati Roy's *The God of Small Things.*

Tharavadu Heritage Home GUESTHOUSE $$$
(☎2525230; www.tharavaduheritage.com; r from
₹1200, with AC ₹2000; ❋) Tharavadu means
'large family house', an apt description.
Rooms are either in the superbly restored
1870s teak family mansion or in equally
comfortable individual creekside cottages.
All abodes are excellently crafted and come
with arty touches – some have glistening
teak beams while others have big bay win-
dows and relaxing patios. It's 4km before the
bird sanctuary.

ETTUMANUR

The **Shiva Temple** at Ettumanur, 12km
north of Kottayam, has inscriptions dating
from 1542, but parts of the building may be
even older. The temple is noted for its ex-
ceptional woodcarvings and murals similar
to those at Kochi's Mattancherry Palace. The
annual **festival**, involving exposition of the
idol (Shiva in his fierce form) and elephant
processions, is held in February/March.

SREE VALLABHA TEMPLE

Devotees make offerings at this temple, 2km
from Tiruvilla, in the form of traditional,
regular all-night **Kathakali** performances
that are open to all. Tiruvilla, 35km south
of Kottayam, is on the rail route between
Ernakulam and Trivandrum. Around 10km
east of here, the **Aranmula Boat Race** is
held in August/September.

THE WESTERN GHATS

Periyar Wildlife Sanctuary

☎04869

South India's most popular wildlife sanctu-
ary, **Periyar** (☎224571; www.periyartigerreserve.
org; Indian/foreigner ₹25/300; ⊙6am-6pm) en-
compasses 777 sq km and a 26-sq-km artifi-
cial lake created by the British in 1895. The
vast region is home to bison, sambar, wild
boar, langur, 900 to 1000 elephants and 35
to 40 tigers. Firmly established on both the
Indian and foreigner tourist trails, the place
can sometimes feel a bit like Disneyland-
in-the-Ghats, but its mountain scenery and
jungle walks make for an enjoyable visit.
Bring warm and waterproof clothing.

Kumily, 4km from the sanctuary, is a
growing strip of hotels, spice shops and
Kashmiri emporiums. Thekkady is the sanc-
tuary centre with the KTDC hotels and boat
jetty. Confusingly, when people refer to the

sanctuary they tend to use Kumily, Thek-
kady and Periyar interchangeably.

◉ Sights & Activities

Various tours and trips enable you to visit
the Periyar Wildlife Sanctuary. Most hotels
and agencies around town can arrange all-
day 4WD **Jungle Safaris** (per person ₹1600-
2000; ⊙5am-6.30pm), which cover over 40km
of trails in jungle bordering the park. Tours
include meals as well as a paddleboat trip.

You can arrange **elephant rides** (per
30min ₹350) at most hotels and agents in
town. If you want the extended elephant ex-
perience, you can pay ₹2500 for a 2½-hour
ride that includes elephant feeding and
cleaning. **Cooking classes** (around ₹250) are
offered by many local homestays.

Forest Department boats BOATING
(per adult/child ₹40/20; ⊙departures 7.30am,
10am, 11.30am, 1.30pm & 3.30pm) These smaller,
more decrepit boats offer a chance to get a
bit closer to the animals than on KTDC trips,
and are driven by sanctuary workers who
may offer commentary. Entry to the park
doesn't guarantee a place on the boat; get to
the **ticket office** (⊙6.30am-4pm) 1½ hours
before each trip to buy tickets. The first and
last departures offer the best prospects for
wildlife spotting, and October to March are
generally the best times to see animals.

KTDC boat trips BOATING
(lower/upper deck ₹75/150) ⊙departures 2hr tours
7.30am & 3.30pm, 1hr tours 10am, 7am, 11.30am &
1.30pm) One- or two-hour trips around the lake
are the usual way of touring the sanctuary.
They can be enjoyable, though often packed,
rowdy and not ideal for wildlife-spotting.

Ecotourism Centre OUTDOOR ADVENTURES
(☎224571; www.periyartigerresereve.org; Thekkady
Rd; ⊙9am-5pm) A number of more adventur-
ous explorations of the park can be arranged
by the Ecotourism Centre, run by the For-
est Department. These include border hikes
(₹750; 8am to 5pm), three-hour elevated
cloud walks (₹200), 4 to 5km nature walks
(₹100), full-day bamboo rafting (₹1000) and
'jungle patrols' (₹500), which cover 4 to 5km
and are the best way to experience the park
close up, accompanied by a trained tribal
guide. Trips usually require a minimum of
four or five people. There are also two-day
'tiger trail' treks (per person ₹3000, solo
₹5000), which are run by former poachers
and cover 20 to 30km. On any of the tours,
you can request special birdwatching guides.

Spice Gardens & Plantations GARDENS
Interesting spice tours cost around ₹450/750 by autorickshaw/taxi (two to three hours) and can be arranged by most hotels. If you want to see a tea factory in operation, do it from here – tea-factory visits are not permitted in Munnar.

If you'd rather do a spice tour independently, you can visit a few excellent gardens outside Kumily. The one-hectare **Abraham's Spice Garden** (☏222919; tours ₹100; ☺7am-6.30pm) has been going for 56 years. **Highrange Spices** (☏222117; tours ₹100; ☺7am-6pm), 3km from Kumily, has 4 hectares where you can see ayurvedic herbs and vegetables growing. A rickshaw to either spice garden and back will be around ₹250. About 13km away from Kumily is a working **tea plantation** (☺8am-5pm) where you can wander around the grounds and see displays of the tea-making process for free.

Santhigiri Ayurveda AYURVEDA
(☏223979; Vandanmedu Junction) An excellent and authentic place for the ayurvedic experience, offering top-notch massage (₹650 to ₹1500), sirovasthi (₹1200) and long-term treatments lasting seven to 14 days.

🛏 Sleeping

INSIDE THE SANCTUARY
The Ecotourism Centre can arrange park accommodation in a basic **tent/bamboo cottage** (d incl breakfast ₹1000/1500), and the KTDC runs three steeply priced hotels in the park. It's a good idea to make reservations (at any KTDC office), particularly for weekends. Note that there's effectively a curfew at these places – guests are not permitted to roam the sanctuary after 6pm.

Lake Palace HOTEL $$$
(☏223888; www.ktdc.com; r incl all meals ₹16,000-25,000) Located on an island in the middle of the Periyar Lake, this is the best value of the government hotels inside the park. It is a stunningly restored old palace that has six charismatic rooms, all decorated with flair using antique furnishings and a selection of modern conveniences (like flat-screen TVs). Staying in the midst of the sanctuary gives you the best chance of seeing wildlife, from your private terrace. Transport is by boat across the lake.

KUMILY
Green View Homestay HOMESTAY $$
(☏224617; www.sureshgreenview.com; Bypass Rd; r incl breakfast ₹600-1750) Grown from its

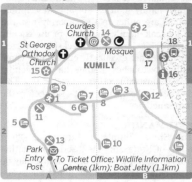

Kumily & Periyar Wildlife Sanctuary

humble homestay origins to be practically hotel-size today, Greenview is a smashing place that manages to retain its personal and friendly family welcome, and continues to get rave reviews. The buildings house several classes of immaculately maintained rooms with private balconies, bamboo or wood furniture and loads of greenery. Vegetarian **meals** (₹65) and **cooking lessons** (₹250) are available.

Claus Garden HOMESTAY $$
(☏222320; www.homestay.in; r ₹800-1000) Set well away from the hustle and bustle, this lovely big building has gently curving balconies, warm, bright colours in spades, and is surrounded by a lush green garden. The excellent rooms are spacious and have neat touches like colourful blankets, rugs, and artwork. Two doubles sharing one bathroom would be an ideal family choice (₹2000). Top value.

Spice Village HOTEL $$$
(☏0484-3011711; crs@cghearth.com; Thekkady Rd; villas ₹12,000-22,000; ☀) This place has captivating, spacious cottages that are smart yet cosily rustic, in pristinely kept grounds. Its restaurant does lavish lunch and dinner buffets (₹1000 each) and you can find the **Wildlife Interpretation Centre** (☺7.30am-9.30pm) here, which has a resident naturalist showing slides and answering questions about the park.

Mickey Homestay GUESTHOUSE $
(☏223196; www.mickeyhomestay.com; Bypass Rd; r ₹350-850) Mickey has just a handful of intimate rooms in a family house, all with

homely touches that make them some of the most comfortable in town. Balconies have rattan furniture and hanging bamboo seats and the whole place is surrounded by greenery.

Chrissie's Hotel GUESTHOUSE **$$**
(☎224155; www.chrissies.in; Bypass Rd; r ₹1600-2000) This four-storey building behind the popular expat-run restaurant of the same name somehow manages to blend in with the forest-green surrounds. The chic rooms are spacious and bright, with cheery furnishings, lamps and colourful pillows – the more expensive ones, with balconies, are much better than the cheaper ground-floor options.

Coffee Inn GUESTHOUSE **$**
(☎222763; coffeeinn@sancharnet.in; Thekkady Rd; huts ₹250-700, r from ₹1000) With rustic bamboo huts, tree houses and cottages in a garden overlooking the sanctuary, Coffee Inn has swankier digs in its main building, where the wood-lined rooms have a cosy, characterful feel, several offering balconies with sweeping views. However, some readers say the rooms can be musty.

Tranquilou HOMESTAY **$$**
(☎223269; Bypass Rd; r ₹1000-1200; @) Friendly family homestay huddled among some hush; the two doubles that adjoin a shared sitting room are a good family option.

El-Paradiso HOMESTAY **$$**
(☎222350; www.goelparadiso.com; Bypass Rd; r ₹1250; @) This family homestay has fresh rooms, with balconies with hanging chairs, or opening onto a terrace overlooking greenery at the back.

 ## Eating

There are plenty of good cheap veg restaurants in the bazaar area.

Periyar Cafe INDIAN **$**
(meals ₹40-140) Painted in kindergarten-bright colours and papered with zinging advertisements, this cheery diner serves up loads of North and South Indian dishes at sensible prices. Near the park entrance, it's perfect for an early breakfast or quick lunch between animal-spotting trips.

Chrissie's Cafe MULTICUISINE **$$**
(Bypass Rd; snacks ₹50-80, meals ₹110-180) A perennially popular haunt, this airy 1st-floor cafe satisfies travellers with cakes and snacks, excellent coffee, and well-prepared Western faves like pizza and pasta.

Ebony's Cafe MULTICUISINE **$**
(Bypass Rd; meals ₹70-100) This small, friendly 1st-floor joint serves up a tasty assortment of Indian and Western food with a smile and a background of traveller-friendly music.

Shri Krishna INDIAN **$**
(Bypass Rd; meals ₹35-85) A great local favourite, serving up spicy pure veg meals including several takes on thali.

Coffee Inn MULTICUISINE **$$**
(meals ₹75-200) This laid-back restaurant serves just a few Indian and Western meals. The food is reasonable and the spice-garden setting is nice, but be warned, it can take a while to arrive: bring a book.

Ambadi Restaurant   INDIAN $$

(dishes ₹80-100) At the hotel of the same name, this popular place serves OK North and South Indian dishes (more importantly, Kingfisher beer, ₹100) in a smart, breezy indoor dining room.

☆ Entertainment

Kerala Cultural Centre   CULTURAL PROGRAM

(🖉9446072901; admission ₹150) For **Kathakali** performances, visit this centre, which comprises the Mudra Kathakali Centre, for shows at 4.30pm and 7pm (make-up starts 30 minutes before each show; visitors can attend and it's very photogenic), and the Kerala Kalari Centre, for hour-long **Kalaripayattu demonstrations** (admission ₹200) at 6pm daily.

❶ Information

DTPC office (🖉222620; ⊙10am-5pm Mon-Sat) Behind the bus stand, not as useful as the Ecotourism Centre.

Ecotourism Centre (🖉224571;⊙9am-5pm) For park tours and walks.

Kumily Internet (🖉222170; Thekkady Junction; per hr ₹40; ⊙9am-9.30pm)

State Bank of Travancore (⊙10am-3.30pm Mon-Fri, to 12.30pm Sat) Changes travellers cheques and currency; has an ATM accepting foreign cards.

Wildlife Information Centre (🖉222028; ⊙6am-6pm) Above the boat jetty in Thekkady.

❶ Getting There & Away

Buses originating or terminating at Periyar start and finish at Aranya Nivas, but they also stop at the Kumily bus stand, at the eastern edge of town.

Eight buses daily operate between Ernakulam (Kochi) and Kumily (₹110, five hours). Buses leave every 30 minutes for Kottayam (₹69, four hours), with two direct buses to Trivandrum at 8.45am and 11am (₹145, eight hours) and one daily bus to Alleppey at 1.10pm (₹85, 5½ hours).

Tamil Nadu buses leave every 30 minutes to Madurai (₹42-56, four hours) from the Tamil Nadu bus stand just over the border.

❶ Getting Around

Kumily is about 4km from Periyar Lake; you can catch the bus (almost as rare as the tigers), take an autorickshaw (₹40) or set off on foot; it's a pleasant, shady walk into the park. **Bicycle hire** is available from many guesthouses.

Munnar

🖉04865 / ELEV 1524M / POP 68,000

Wander just a few kilometres outside the scruffy little hill station of Munnar and you'll be engulfed in a sea of a thousand shades of green. The lolling hills all around are covered by a sculptural carpet of tea-trees, and the mountain scenery is magnificent – you're often up above the clouds, watching veils of mist cling below the mountaintops. Once known as the High Range of Travancore, today Munnar is the commercial centre of some of the world's highest tea-growing estates.

◉ Sights & Activities

The main reason to be in Munnar is to explore the lush, tea-filled hillocks that surround it. Hotels, homestays, travel agencies, autorickshaw drivers and practically every passer-by will want to organise a day of sightseeing for you: shop around.

Tata Tea Museum   MUSEUM

(🖉230561; adult/child ₹75/35; ⊙10am-4pm Tue-Sun) Located around 1.5km north of town, this museum is, unfortunately, about as close as you'll get to a working tea factory around Munnar. It's a slightly sanitised version of the real thing, but it still shows the basic process. A collection of old bits and pieces from the colonial era, including photographs and a 1905 tea-roller, are also kept here. The short walk to here from town is lovely, passing some of the most accessible tea plantations from Munnar town.

☞ Tours

The DTPC runs a couple of fairly rushed full-day tours to points around Munnar. The **Sandal Valley Tour** (per person ₹350; ⊙9am-6pm) visits Chinnar Wildlife Sanctuary, several viewpoints, waterfalls, plantations, a sandalwood forest and villages. The **Tea Valley tour** (per person ₹300; ⊙10am-6pm) visits Echo Point, Top Station and Rajamalai (for Eravikulam National Park), among other places. You can hire a day's taxi to visit the main local sights for around ₹1100 – there's a taxi office in Munnar.

🛏 Sleeping

The best options are mostly outside Munnar town centre.

AROUND TOWN

TOP CHOICE **Zina Cottages**   HOMESTAY $

(🖉230349; r incl tax ₹800-1000) On the outskirts of town but immersed in lush tea plantations, the 10 rooms in this hospitable homestay are an outstanding deal. Frilly touches in the rooms and stunning vistas

Munnar

0 ___ 100 m
0 ___ 0.05 miles

Munnar

come as standard, as do the local information and hospitable cups of tea provided by the legendary Mr Iype, from the Tourist Information Service, who has been name-checked in travel books by Devla Murphy and Bill Aitken. However, wild boars mean going out for a wander after 7pm is a no-no.

JJ Cottage HOMESTAY $
(☎230104;jjcottagemunnar@sancharnet.in;d₹350-800) The mothering family at this superb place will go out of its way to make sure your stay is comfortable. The varied and uncomplicated rooms are ruthlessly clean, bright and have TV and geysers. The one deluxe room has frilly pink curtains and sweeping views.

Green View GUESTHOUSE $
(☎230940; greenview_munnar@sify.com; d ₹400-600)With a friendly welcome, this tidy house next door to JJ Cottage has fresh budget rooms. And the young owner is setting up a new place – **Green Woods Anachal** (d ₹750) outside Munnar that's a budget option out in the tea plantations; there are four rooms.

Westwood Riverside Resort RESORT $$$
(☎230884-6; www.westwoodmunnar.com; Alwaye-Munnar (AM) Rd; r incl breakfast & dinner ₹3000-5000) It doesn't appear promising from outside, but inside is surprisingly nice, with lots of polished wood floors, heartfelt murals on the walls, and rooms that are plain, spotless and inviting – the pick have river views.

Kaippallil Homestay GUESTHOUSE $
(☎230203; www.kaippallil.com; r ₹200-600) Up the hill and away from (most of) the clatter of the bazaar, Kaippallil is the best budget

bet in town, though by no means a 'home-stay'. A new part to the building is unfinished, giving it a half-built look, but the rooms are reasonably clean and have balconies and sweeping views. Two basic but characterful small rooms in a neighbouring cottage are the cheapest option.

MUNNAR HILLS

TOP CHOICE Rose Gardens HOMESTAY $$$
(☎04864-278243; www.rosegardens.com; NH49 Rd, Karadipara; r ₹3500) Around 10km south of Munnar. Despite its handy location on the main road, with good bus connections, this is a peaceful spot overlooking Tomy's idyllic plant nursery, with over 240 types of plants. Rooms are large and comfortable, and the family are charming. Rajee's home cooking is delicious, the coffee home-grown, the honey from their hives. Cooking lessons are free, including fresh coconut pancakes for breakfast and delicately spiced Keralan dishes for dinner.

Dew Drops GUESTHOUSE $$
(☎0484-2216455; wilsonhomes2003@yahoo.co.in, www.dewdropsmunnar.com; Kallar; r incl breakfast ₹1200) Set in the thick forest around 20km south of Munnar, this fantastic, remote place lies on 97 hectares of spice plantation and farmland. The resplendent building is expertly constructed, with seven bright, simple rooms. Each room has a veranda on which you can sit and enjoy the hush, and the small restaurant has expansive views. The peace here is zen. It's 20km from Munnar; call for a pick-up (₹50 per person).

British County
GUESTHOUSE $$
([📞]2371761; touristdesk@satyam.net.in; ET City Rd, Anachal person full board ₹2000) Around 11km southeast of Munnar, with its veranda facing a stunning panorama, this appealing little guesthouse has two nice fresh rooms with views. There's a simple little treehouse for rent too, and steps lead down into the valley. A taxi from Munnar will cost ₹400. This is the overnight base for the Tourist Desk's Munnar Hillstation Tour from Kochi.

Bracknell Forest
GUESTHOUSE $$$
([📞]231555; www.bracknellforestmunnar.com; Ottamaram; r ₹5000; [📶]) A remote-feeling 9.5km south of Munnar, this place houses neat, handsome rooms with balconies and great views overlooking a lush valley. It's surrounded by deep forest on all sides. Breakfast and a few hours trekking are included; meals cost ₹350 – the small restaurant has wraparound views. A transfer from Munnar costs ₹400.

Windermere Estate
RESORT $$$
([📞]reservations 0484-2425237; www.windermere munnar.com; Pothamedu; AC r ₹6900-14,800; [❄]) Windermere is a boutique-meets-country-retreat 4km south of Windermere. There are farmhouse rooms and newer, swankier cottages with spectacular views, surrounded by shush and 26 hectares of cardamom and coffee plantations. Book ahead.

🍴 Eating

Early-morning food stalls in the bazaar serve breakfast snacks and cheap meals.

SN Annexe
INDIAN $$
(AM Rd; meals ₹55-130; ⊙7am-10pm) SN restaurant's little sis has a nice deep-orange look with slatted blinds at the windows. It's madly popular with families for its great range of thalis: take your pick from special, Rajasthani, Gujarati, Punjabi and more, plus a dazzling array of veg dishes.

Eastend
INDIAN $$
(Temple Rd; dishes ₹120-170; ⊙noon-3.30pm & 6.30-10.30pm) In the same-named hotel, this frilly-curtained, smartish place is the best place in town to head for nonveg Indian dishes, with Chinese, North and South Indian and Kerala specialities on the menu.

Royal Retreat
INDIAN $
(Kannan Devan Hills; www.royalretreat.co.in; dishes ₹50-75; ⊙7am-9.30pm) This longstanding favourite has reliably tasty and fresh Indian

cooking served in nicely twee rooms with checked tablecloths, in a hotel set amid gardens. Try specialities such as Alleppey fish curry and *bhindi masala* (okra curry).

Rapsy Restaurant
INDIAN $
(Bazaar; dishes ₹30-80; ⊙6am-10pm) This hole-in-the-wall is packed at lunchtime, with locals lining up for Rapsy's famous *paratha* or biryani (from ₹40). It also makes a decent stab at fancy international dishes like Spanish omelette and Israeli *shakshuka* (scrambled eggs with tomatoes and spices).

SN Restaurant
INDIAN $
(AM Rd; meals ₹35-90; ⊙6am-10pm) Just south of the tourist office, SN is a cheery place with an attractive red interior, which seems to be perpetually full of people digging into masala dosas (₹35) and other Indian veg and nonveg dishes.

ℹ Information

There are ATMs near the bridge, south of the bazaar.

DTPC Tourist Information Office ([📞]231516; Alway-Munnar Rd; ⊙8.30am-7pm) Marginally helpful.

Forest Information Centre ([📞]231587; enpmunnar@sify.com; ⊙8am-5pm)

Olivia Communications (per hr ₹35; ⊙9am-10.30pm) Surprisingly fast internet.

State Bank of Travancore ([📞]230274; ⊙10am-3.30pm Mon-Sat, to noon Sun) Has an ATM.

Tourist Information Service ([📞]230349, 9447190954) Joseph Iype is a walking Swiss-army knife of Munnar information – he no longer has an office in town, but will supply information on trekking, taxis and so on, if you call.

ℹ Getting There & Away

Roads around Munnar are in poor condition and can be affected by monsoon rains, so bus times may vary. The main **KSRTC bus station** (AM Rd) is south of town, but it's best to catch buses from stands in Munnar town (where more frequent private buses also depart).

There are around 10 buses a day to Ernakulam (Kochi, ₹80, 5½ hours) and a few services to Kottayam (₹ 85/101 ordinary/super fast, five hours), and Trivandrum (₹191, nine hours).

ℹ Getting Around

DTPC rents out bicycles for ₹15/150 per hour/day. **Gokulam Bike Hire** ([📞]9447237165; per day ₹250; ⊙7.30am-7pm) has several motorbikes for hire, as does SN Restaurant (per day ₹250).

Autorickshaws ply the hills around Munnar with bone-shuddering efficiency; they charge up to ₹650 for a full day's sightseeing.

Around Munnar

ERAVIKULAM NATIONAL PARK

Sixteen kilometres from Munnar, Eravikulam National Park (Indian/foreigner ₹15/200; ⊙8am-5pm Mar-Dec) is home to the endangered, but almost tame, Nilgiri tahr (a type of mountain goat). From Munnar, an autorickshaw/taxi costs ₹250/500 return; a government bus takes you the final 4km from the checkpoint (₹20).

CHINNAR WILDLIFE SANCTUARY

About 10km past Marayoor and 60km northeast of Munnar, this wildlife sanctuary (www.chinnar.org; Indian/foreigner ₹10/100, camera/video ₹25/150; ⊙7am-6pm) hosts deer, leopards, elephants and the endangered grizzled giant squirrel. Trekking (3hr trek ₹150) and tree house (s/d ₹1000/1250) or hut (s/d ₹1500/1800) accommodation within the sanctuary are available, as well as ecotour programs like river-trekking, cultural visits, and waterfall treks (around ₹150). For details contact the Forest Information Centre in Munnar. Buses from Munnar can drop you off at Chinnar (₹35, 1½ hours), or taxi hire for the day will cost around ₹1100.

TOP STATION

Come here, on Kerala's border with Tamil Nadu, for spectacular views over the Western Ghats. From Munnar, four daily buses (₹35, from 7.30am, 1½ hours) make the steep 32km climb in around an hour, or you could book a return taxi (₹750).

THATTEKKAD BIRD SANCTUARY

A serene 25-sq-km park in the foothills of the West Ghats, cut through by two rivers and two streams, Thattekkad Bird Sanctuary (☎0485-2588302; Indian/foreigner ₹10/100, camera/video ₹25/150; ⊙6.30am-6pm) is home to over 320 fluttering species – unusual in that they are forest, rather than water birds – including Malabar grey hornbills, Ripley owl, jungle nightjar, grey drongo, darters and rarer species like the Sri Lankan frogmouth. There are kingfishers, flycatchers, warblers, sunbirds and flower peckers (who weigh only 4g). There's lots of other wildlife, including the occasional elephant, leopard, bear, snakes (including cobras), sambar monkey and flying squirrels, and 120 species of butterflies. You can arrange two- or three-hour treks (up to 5/10 people per person ₹500/250). To stay in the Treetop Machan (Indian/Foreigner dm ₹80/150, d incl meals ₹1500-2500) in the sanctuary, contact the assistant wildlife warden (☎0485-2588302) at Kothamangalam. Another option is the homestay (☎9947506188; per person incl meals ₹750) of the enthusiastic Ms Sudah.

For more luxury, visit the lovely Birds Lagoon Resort (☎0485-2572444; www.birdslagoon.com; Palamatton, Thattekkad; s/d incl breakfast €60/70, with AC from €65/75; ❄⌨) . Set deep in the villages near Thattekkad, this low-key resort lies on a seasonal lake among spacious and manicured grounds. The basic rooms here are roomy and comfy, with lots of wood trim and lamp lighting. The whole place feels refreshingly remote and is particularly popular with visiting ornithologists. It's 16km from Kothamangalam. There's also the tented Hornbill Camp (☎0484 2092280; www.thehornbillcamp.com; d full board ₹5000) with accommodation in large permanent tents, in a sublimely peaceful location, cooled by fans and facing the Periyar River. Kayaking, cycling and a spice-garden tour are included in the price. It's around 8km from Thattekkad by road.

Thattekkad is on the Ernakulam–Munnar road. Take a direct bus from either Ernakulam (₹29, two hours) or Munnar (₹50, three hours) to Kothamangalam, from where a Thattekkad bus travels the final 12km (₹6, 25 minutes).

Parambikulam Wildlife Sanctuary

Possibly the most protected environment in South India – it's nestled behind three dams in a valley surrounded by Keralan and Tamil Nadu sanctuaries – Parambikulam Wildlife Sanctuary (www.parambikulam.org; Indian/foreigner ₹10/100, video/camera ₹100/25; ⊙7am-6pm) constitutes 285 sq km of Kipling-storybook scenery and wildlife-spotting goodness. It's home to elephants, bison, gaur, sloths, sambar, crocodiles, tigers, panthers and some of the largest teak trees in Asia. The sanctuary is best avoided during monsoon (June to August) and it sometimes closes in March and April.

Contact the Ecocare Centre (☎04253-245025) in Palakkad to arrange tours of the park, hikes (1-/2-day trek ₹3000/6000) and stays on the reservoir's freshwater island (r ₹5000). There are 150 beds in **tree-top huts** (from ₹2500) throughout the park; book through the ecocare centre. Boating or rafting costs ₹600 for one hour.

You have to enter the park from Pollachi (40km from Coimbatore and 49km from Palakkad in Tamil Nadu. There are at least two buses in either direction between Pollachi and Parambikulam via Annamalai daily (₹15, 1½ hours). The nearest train station is Coimbatore, Tamil Nadu, from where you can board buses to Pollachi.

CENTRAL KERALA

Kochi (Cochin)

☏0484 / POP 1.36 MILLION

Serene Kochi has been drawing traders and explorers to its shores for over 600 years. Nowhere in India could you find such a mix: giant fishing nets from China, a 400-year-old synagogue, ancient mosques, Portuguese houses, and crumbling remains of the British Raj. The result is an unlikely blend of medieval Portugal, Holland and an English village grafted onto the tropical Malabar Coast. It's a delightful place to spend some time and nap in some of India's finest heritage accommodation.

Mainland Ernakulam is the hectic transport and cosmopolitan hub of Kochi, while the historical towns of Fort Cochin and Mattancherry remain wonderfully serene – thick with the smell of the past.

While you're here, the perfect read is Salman Rushdie's the *Moor's Last Sigh*, which bases much action around Mattancherry and the Synagogue.

◉ Sights

FORT COCHIN

TOP CHOICE **Mattancherry Palace** PALACE
(Map p956; Dutch Palace; ☏2226085; Bazaar Rd; admission ₹5; ⊙8am-5pm) Admission is a bargain to this interesting building. Presented by the Portuguese in 1555, Mattancherry Palace was a generous gift presented to the Raja of Kochi, Veera Kerala Varma (1537–61), as a gesture of goodwill. More probably, it was a used as a sweetener to securing trading privileges. The Dutch renovated the palace in 1663, hence its alternative name, the Dutch Palace.

The star attractions here are the astonishingly preserved Hindu **murals**, depicting

scenes from the Ramayana, Mahabharata and Puranic legends in intricate detail. The central hall on the 1st floor is now a portrait gallery of maharajas from 1864. There's an impressive collection of palanquins (hand-carried carriages), bejewelled outfits and splendidly carved ceilings in every room. The ladies' bedchamber downstairs features a cheerful, impressively multitasking Krishna, using his eight hands and two feet to engage in foreplay with eight happy milkmaids, whilst also managing to play the flute. Photography is prohibited.

TOP CHOICE **Kerala Folklore Museum** MUSEUM
(☏0484-2665452; Folklore Junction, Thevara; admission ₹200; ⊙9.30am-7pm) This incredible place is well worth the journey – on the southeast outskirts of Ernakulam. It's a private museum created from ancient temples and beautiful old houses collected by its owner, an antique dealer, over three years. It includes over 5000 artefacts and covers three architectural styles: Malabar on the ground floor, Kochi on the 1st, Travanbur on the 2nd. There are 3000-year-old burial urns *'nannangadi'*, in which people were buried in the foetal position, and *Where the Wild Things Are*–style masks carved from jack-fruit trees. Upstairs is a beautiful wood-lined theatre, with a 17th-century wooden ceiling, where **performances** (Indian/foreigner ₹100/350; ⊙6.30-8pm Sep-Mar) take place nightly. A rickshaw here should cost ₹70, or you can take any bus to Thivara from where it's a ₹20 rickshaw ride. An autorickshaw from Fort Cochin will cost ₹150.

Look out for the owner's new cultural museum, which is due to open in Mattancherry in a vast old godown (warehouse) close to the synagogue.

TOP CHOICE **Pardesi Synagogue & Jew Town** SYNAGOGUE
(Map p956; admission ₹5; ⊙10am-1pm & 3-5pm Sun-Thu, closed Jewish hols) Originally built in 1568, this synagogue was partially destroyed by the Portuguese in 1662, and rebuilt two years later when the Dutch took Kochi. It features an ornate gold pulpit and elaborate hand-painted, willow-pattern floor tiles from Canton, China, which were added in 1762. It's magnificently illuminated by chandeliers (from Belgium) and coloured-glass lamps. The graceful clock tower was built in 1760. There is an upstairs balcony for women who worshipped separately according to

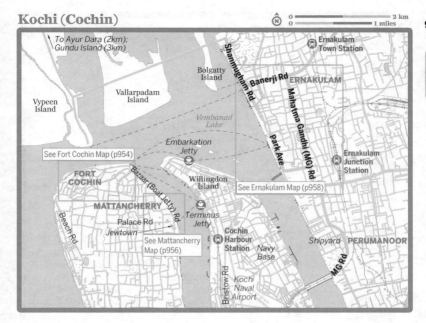

Orthodox rites. Note that shorts or sleeveless tops are not allowed inside.

Jew Town
AREA

The synagogue is smack in the middle of Jew Town (Map p956), a bustling port area and centre of the Kochi spice trade. Scores of small firms huddle together in old, dilapidated buildings and the air is filled with the biting aromas of ginger, cardamom, cumin, turmeric and cloves, though the lanes around the Dutch Palace and synagogue are packed with antique and tourist-curio shops rather than spices. Look out for the Jewish names on some of the buildings.

At the tip of Fort Cochin sit the unofficial emblems of Kerala's backwaters: cantilevered **Chinese fishing nets** (Map p954). A legacy of traders from the AD 1400 court of Kubla Khan, these enormous, spiderlike contraptions require at least four people to operate their counterweights at high tide. Unfortunately, modern fishing techniques are making these labour-intensive methods less and less profitable.

Indo-Portuguese Museum
MUSEUM

(Map p954; ☎2215400; Indian/foreigner ₹10/25; ◷9am-1pm & 2-6pm Tue-Sun) This museum in the garden of the Bishop's House preserves the heritage of one of India's earliest Catho-

lic communities, including vestments, silver processional crosses and altarpieces from the Cochin diocese. The basement contains remnants of the Portuguese Fort Immanuel.

St Francis Church
CHURCH

(Map p954; Bastion St) Believed to be India's oldest European-built church, it was originally constructed in 1503 by Portuguese Franciscan friars. The edifice that stands here today was built in the mid-16th century to replace the original wooden structure. Adventurer Vasco da Gama, who died in Cochin in 1524, was buried in this spot for 14 years before his remains were taken to Lisbon – you can still visit his tombstone in the church.

Dutch Cemetery
HISTORIC SITE

(Map p954; Beach Rd) Consecrated in 1724, this cemetery contains the worn and dilapidated graves of Dutch traders and soldiers. Its gates are normally locked but a caretaker might let you in, or ask at St Francis Church.

Santa Cruz Basilica
CHURCH

(Map p954; cnr Bastion St & KB Jacob Rd) The imposing Catholic basilica was originally built on this site in 1506, though the current building dates to 1902. Inside you'll find artefacts from the different eras in Kochi and a striking pastel-coloured interior.

954

KERALA CENTRAL KERALA

Fort Cochin

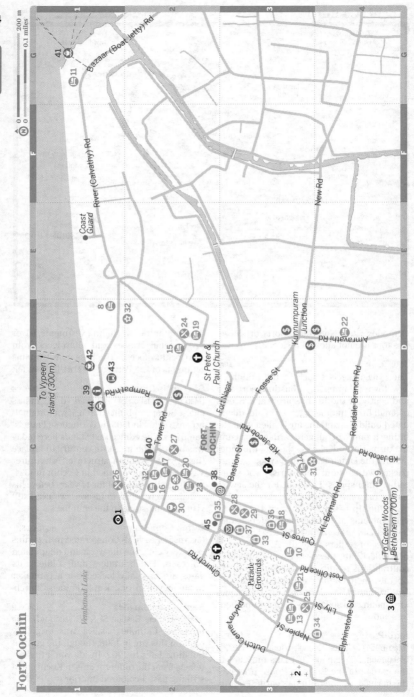

Kashi Art Cafe   GALLERY
(Map p954; Burgher St; ⊙8.30am-7.30pm) The
pioneer of Fort Cochin's art revival, Kashi
displays changing exhibitions of local artists. There's another gallery on Bazaar Rd,
which opens if there's an exhibition on.

🏃 Activities

Grande Residencia Hotel   SWIMMING
(Map p954; Princess St, Fort Cochin) Nonguests
can swim at the hotel's small pool for
₹350 per person.

Cherai Beach (Vypeen Island)   SWIMMING
For a dip in the ocean, you can make a day
trip out to the lovely white-sand Cherai

Beach (p966), a short journey by ferry to
Vypeen Island.

Ayur Dara   AYURVEDA
(📞2502362; www.ayurdara.com; Murikkump-
adam, Vypeen Island; ⊙9am-5.30pm) Run by
third-generation ayurvedic practitioner
Dr Subhash, this delightful waterside
treatment centre specialises in long-term
treatments. By appointment only. Massage
and *sirodara* (steady stream of oil poured
onto the forehead) costs ₹1000. It's 4km
from the Vypeen Island ferry (autorickshaw ₹35).

Ayush   AYURVEDA
(Map p954; 📞6456566; KB Jacob Rd, Fort Cochin;
massage from ₹900; ⊙8am-8pm) Part of an

Mattancherry

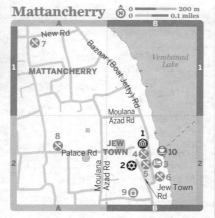

India-wide chain of ayurvedic centres, this place also does long-term treatments.

Kerala Ayurveda   AYURVEDA
(Kerala Ayurveda Pharmacy Ltd; Map p958; 📞2378198; www.kaplayurveda.com; AM Thomas Rd, Ernakulam; massage from ₹600; ☺7am-8pm) This government-approved centre comes recommended for all types of ayurvedic treatments.

SVM Ayurveda Centre   AYURVEDA
(Kerala Ayurveda Pharmacy Ltd; 📞9847371667; www.svmayurveda.com; Quiero St; massage from ₹600; ☺9.30am-7pm) A small Fort Cochin centre, this offers relaxing massages and Hatha yoga (₹400, 1½ hours) daily at 8am. Longer rejuvenation packages are also available.

🎓 Courses

The Kerala Kathakali Centre (p963) has lessons in classical Kathakali dance, music and make-up (from ₹350 per hour).

For a crash course in the martial art of *kalarippayat*, head out to Ens Kalari (p963), a famed training centre, which offers short intensive courses from one week to one month.

Cook & Eat   COOKING
(📞2215377; simonroy@hotmail.com; Quiros St; classes ₹550; ☺11am & 6pm) Mrs Leelu Roy runs a popular two-hour cooking class called 'Cook & Eat' in her great big family kitchen, teaching five dishes to classes of five to 10 people. Several of the homestays in towns are also happy to organise cooking classes for their guests.

🚩 Tours

Most hotels and tourist offices can arrange a day trip out to the **Elephant training camp** (☺7am-6pm) at Kudanadu, 50km from Kochi. Here you can go for a ride (₹200) and even help out with washing the gentle beasts if you arrive at 8am. Entry is free, though the elephant trainers will expect a small tip. A return trip out here in a taxi should cost around ₹700 to ₹1200.

Tourist Desk Information Counter
                          BOATING, WILDLIFE WATCHING
This private tour agency (p964) runs the popular full-day **Water Valley Tour** (day tour ₹650) through local canals and lagoons. A canoe trip through smaller canals and villages is included, as is lunch and hotel pickups. It also offers a **Wayanad Wildlife tour** (2 nights ₹5500), and **Munnar Hillstation tour** (1 night ₹2500). Prices include accommodation, transport and meals.

KTDC   BOATING
The KTDC (p964) has **backwater tours** (½-day tour ₹450) at 8.30am and 2pm, and tourist **motor-boat tours** (2½hr tour ₹150) around Fort Cochin at 9am and 2pm. Its full-day **houseboat backwater trips** (day tour ₹800; ☺8am-6.30pm) stops for you to see local weaving factories, spice gardens and, most importantly, toddy tapping!

🎆 Festivals & Events

The eight-day **Ernakulathappan Utsavam festival**, in January/February, culminates in a procession of 15 decorated elephants, ecstatic music and fireworks.

🛏 Sleeping

Fort Cochin is an ideal place to escape the noise and chaos of the mainland – it's tranquil and romantic, with some excellent accommodation choices. This could be India's homestay capital, with hundreds of family houses offering near-identical, large and clean budget rooms.

Ernakulam is much cheaper and more convenient for onward travel, but the ambiance and accommodation choices there are less inspiring. Regardless of where you stay, book ahead during December and January.

FORT COCHIN

TOP CHOICE Malabar House HOTEL $$$
(Map p954; ☎2216666; www.malabarhouse.com; Parade Ground Rd; r €220, ste incl breakfast €300-360; ❄@⋐) What may just be one of the fanciest boutique hotels in Kerala, Malabar flaunts its uberhip blend of modern colours and period fittings like it's not even trying. It has a restaurant and wine bar. While the suites are huge and lavishly appointed, the standard rooms are more snug. Also check out their lush retreat **Privacy at Sanctuary Bay** (cottage/ste €220/360) or gorgeous ecofriendly house boat, **Discovery** (d full board €450).

TOP CHOICE Brunton Boatyard HOTEL $$$
(Map p954; ☎2215461; brunton boatyard@cg hearth.com; River Rd; r ₹18,700-25,000; ❄@⋐) This imposing hotel faithfully reproduces 16th- and 17th-century Dutch and Portuguese architecture in its grand complex. All of the rooms look out over the harbour, and have bathtub and balconies with a refreshing sea breeze that beats AC any day.

Noah's Ark HOMESTAY $$
(Map p954; ☎2215481; www.noahsarkcochin.com; 1/508 Fort Kochi Hospital Rd; r ₹2750-2900; ❄@) An upmarket, huge modern house, with a sweeping spiral staircase from the reception room and a variety of gleamingly clean, appealing rooms (one with a balcony), plus a friendly welcome.

Walton's Homestay GUESTHOUSE $$
(Map p954; ☎2215309; www.waltonshomestay. com; Princess St; r incl breakfast ₹1200-2400, with AC ₹1600-2600; ❄) The fastidious Mr Walton offers big wood-furnished rooms in his lovely old house that's painted a nautical white with blue trim. There's a lush garden

out the back and a large secondhand bookshop downstairs. The bird-filled garden has one AC garden **cottage** (d ₹1200) available for rent.

Tea Bungalow HOTEL $$$
(Map p954; ☎3019200; www.teabungalow.in; 1/1901Kunumpuram;r₹7500;❄@⋐)Thismustard-coloured colonial building was built in 1912 as headquarters of a UK spice trading company before being taken over by Brooke Bond tea. Graceful rooms are decorated with flashes of strong colour and carved wooden furniture, and have Bassetta-tiled bathrooms.

Raintree Lodge GUESTHOUSE $$
(Map p954; ☎3251489; www.fortcochin.com; Peter Celli St; r ₹2300; ❄) The intimate and comfortable rooms at the Raintree flirt with boutique-hotel status. Each room has a great blend of contemporary style and carved wood furniture. Try to get an upstairs room with a (tiny) balcony.

Bernard Bungalow GUESTHOUSE $$
(Map p954; ☎2216162; www.bernardbungalow. com; Parade Ground Rd; r ₹2500-3500; ❄) This gracious place has the look of a 1940s summer cottage, housed in a fine 350-year-old house that boasts a large collection of interesting rooms. The house has polished floorboards, wooden window shutters, balconies and verandas, and is filled with lovely period furniture.

Sui House HOMESTAY $$$
(☎2227078; http://suihousecochin.com; Maulana Azad Rd; r incl breakfast & tax ₹4000; ❄) This is the home of the antique-dealer owner of gorgeous Caza Maria in Jew Town Rd. There are four mammoth turquoise rooms in this grand family villa. The sumptuous communal drawing room is filled with more antiques, and a hearty breakfast is served in the outdoor courtyard.

Old Harbour Hotel HOTEL $$$
(Map p954; ☎2218006; www.oldharbourhotel.com; Tower Rd; r incl tax ₹8250-14200; ❄@⋐) Set around an idyllic garden, with lily ponds and a small pool, the dignified Old Harbour is housed in a 300-year-old Dutch/Portuguese heritage building. The elegant mix of period and modern styles and bright colour accents are luxurious without being over the top, lending the place a much more intimate feel than some of the more grandiose competition. There are 13 rooms here, some

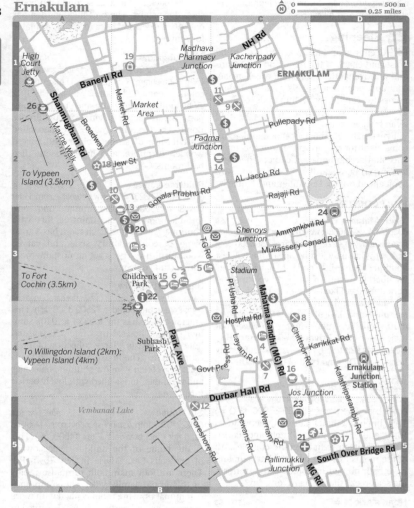

facing directly onto the garden, and some with plant-filled, open-air bathrooms.

Mother Tree HOMESTAY **$**
(Map p954; ☑9447464906; www.hotelmothertree. com; KL Bernard Master Rd; r ₹700, with AC ₹1000; ✳) There are just a few miniscule rooms in this compact homestay, but the immaculate cleanliness and neat rooftop chill-out space make this place worth seeking out.

Dream Catcher HOMESTAY **$**
(☑2217550; www.dreamcatcherhomestays.com; KB Jacob Rd; r from ₹600, d/tr AC from ₹2500/3500; ✳) Tucked away on a narrow

laneway, this rambling old colonial house has budget rooms, an almost gothic sitting room and balconies lined with pot plants: it offers a backpacker-friendly welcome from the Portuguese-descended family.

Green Woods Bethlehem HOMESTAY **$$**
(off Map p954; ☑3247791; greenwoodsbethle hem1@vsnl.net; opposite ESI Hospital; d incl breakfast ₹900) Owner Sheeba looks ready to sign your adoption papers the minute you walk through her front door. What might just be the cutest guesthouse in Kochi lies in a quiet

residential area cocooned in its own thick jungle of plants and palms. The rooms are humble but cosy; breakfast is served in the fantastic, leafy rooftop cafe, where cooking classes/demonstrations are often held.

Princess Inn　　　　　　　GUESTHOUSE $
(Map p954; ☏2217073; princessinnfortkochi@gmail.com; Princess St; r ₹400-800) Sticking to its budget guns, the friendly Princess Inn spruces up its dull, tiny rooms with cheery bright colours. The comfy communal spaces are a treat, and the three large, front-facing rooms are good value.

Sonnetta Residency　　　GUESTHOUSE $$
(Map p954; ☏2215744; www.sonnettaresidency.com; Princess St; r ₹1000, with AC ₹1500; ❄) Right in the thick of the Fort Cochin action, the plain rooms at this Portuguese-era building are small, but come with nice, chintzy touches like curtains and indoor plants to make you feel at home.

Delight Home Stay　　　　GUESTHOUSE $$
(Map p954; ☏2217658; www.delightfulhomestay.com; Post Office Rd; r ₹1400-1800, with AC ₹2500; ❄) And delightful it is. This grand house's exterior is adorned with frilly white woodwork, and the rooms are spacious and polished. It overlooks the parade ground and has a charming little garden, and an imposing sitting room covered in wall-to-wall teak.

Koder House　　　　　　　HOTEL $$$
(Map p954; ☏2217988; www.koderhouse.com; Tower Rd; r from ₹11,300 with AC; ❄) A historic mansion overlooking the Chinese fishing nets, this fine heritage property has characterful rooms and an atmospheric, high-ceiling restaurant with whirring fans that serves nice food. Rooms are overpriced in season, but worthwhile at other times.

Spencer Home　　　　　　GUESTHOUSE $$
(Map p954; ☏2215049; spencerhomstayfc@rediffmail.com; 1/298 Parade Ground Rd; d ₹1500-2500) This handsomely restored heritage home has top-value, snug rooms set around a charming little garden courtyard. It has great period highlights, like high wood-beam ceilings and amazingly intricate antique locks. Breakfast is served garden-side, in front of your room.

Fort House Hotel　　　　　HOTEL $$$
(☏2217103; www.hotelforthouse.com; 2/6A Calvathy Rd; r from ₹3800; ❄⊙) With lush gardens, on the waterfront, this offers smart, chic rooms in soft earth and ochre colours and with solid wooden furnishings, opening onto a long veranda. There's a recommended waterside restaurant.

Costa Gama Home Stay　　HOMESTAY $
(☏2216122; www.stayincochin.com; Thamaraparambu Rd; s/d from ₹400/650) Cosy little place that gets rave reviews. South off KB Jacob Rd.

Homested
HOMESTAY **$**

(☑9388600512; http://homestedcochin.com; 1386 A Thamarakulam Rd; s/d ₹600/700, d with AC ₹900; ❉) With three spic-and-span rooms in a well-kept family house tucked into one of Fort Cochin's backstreets, away from the melee.

Daffodil
HOMESTAY **$$**

(Map p954; ☑2218686; www.cochinhomestays. org; Njaliparambu Junction; s/d ₹1500/2000, with AC ₹2500/3000; ❉) Run by a local couple, this has big and brightly painted modern rooms, with an upstairs carved-wood Keralan balcony.

Royal Grace Tourist Home
GUESTHOUSE **$**

(Map p954; ☑2216584; Amaravathi Rd; r ₹400-600) This old-timer is one of the rare budget stalwarts still left in Fort Cochin. There are loads of rooms on offer in a large multistorey building, each with little more than a bed, four walls and a pint-sized bathroom.

MATTANCHERRY & JEW TOWN

Caza Maria
HOMESTAY **$$$**

(Map p956; ☑3258837; cazamaria@rediffmail.com; Jew Town Rd; r incl breakfast ₹4500; ❉) Right in the heart of Jew Town, this unique place has just two enormous, gorgeous heritage rooms overlooking the bazaar. Fit for a maharaja, the rooms feature an idiosyncratic style – with each high-ceilinged room painted in bright colours, filled to the brim with antiques, and with tall windows looking onto the bustling market street below.

ERNAKULAM

TOP CHOICE Olavipe
HOMESTAY **$$**

(☑0478-2522255; www.olavipe.com; Olavipe; s/d incl meals ₹5100/8500) This gorgeous 1890s traditional Syrian-Christian home is on a 16-hectare farm surrounded by backwaters, 28km south of Kochi. A restored mansion of rosewood and glistening teak, it has several large and breezy rooms beautifully decorated in the original period decor (only the ceiling fans are new). There are lots of shady awnings and sitting areas, a fascinating archive with six generations of family history, and the gracious owners will make you feel like a welcome friend rather than a guest. A taxi to/from Fort Cochin is less than ₹1000.

Grand Hotel
HOTEL **$$**

(Map p958; ☑2382061; www.grandhotelkerala. com; MG Rd; s/d from ₹1900/2200; ❉) This 1960s hotel on Mahatma Gandhi (MG) Rd,

with its polished original art deco fittings, oozes the sort of retro cool that modern hotels would kill to re-create. The spacious rooms have gleaming parquet floors and large modern bathrooms, and the foyer has beautiful modern vintage furniture. Definitely fine enough to tempt a stay in Ernakulam.

John's Residency
HOTEL **$**

(Map p958; ☑2355395; TG Rd; s/d from ₹310/380, with AC ₹1050; ❉) With a cool, yellow foyer featuring interesting clutter such as vintage fans, this is a refreshing place to enter from the busy street. Rooms are small but decorated with flashes of colour: red curtains and bathrooms, that give them a funky feel that's a welcome surprise in this price bracket.

Government Guest House
GUESTHOUSE **$$**

(Map p958; ☑2360502; Shanmughan Rd; s/d ₹980/1380; ❉) We secretly love Kerala's government guesthouses – they usually manage to be the best deal in town. Right in the city's heart and near the sea, this eight-storey monolith of a building has huge, neat rooms. It probably won't win any style awards, but some of the upper-floor rooms have balconies with sweeping sea vistas.

Bijus Tourist Home
HOTEL **$**

(Map p958; ☑2361661; www.bijustouristhome.com; Market Rd; s/d from ₹475/725, d with AC ₹1350; ❉) This friendly, popular choice is handy for the main jetty and has reasonable, drab but clean rooms and a friendly welcome. **Day tours** to the elephant training camp from here are only ₹700.

Saas Tower
HOTEL **$**

(Map p958; ☑2365319; www.saastower.com; Cannon Shed Rd; s/d ₹500/800, with AC from ₹750/1400; ❉) It has 'facilities to match your fantasies' but this will only be the case if you fantasise about a low-end business hotel, with clean smart rooms filled with wooden furniture, handily located near the boat jetty.

✗ Eating & Drinking

Covert beer consumption is *de rigueur* at most of the Fort Cochin restaurants, and more expensive in the licensed ones (₹100 to ₹165).

FORT COCHIN

Behind the Chinese fishing nets are several **fishmongers** (Map p954; seafood per kg ₹200-400), from whom you can buy fish (or prawns, scampi, lobster), then take your selection to the nearby row of shacks where the folks there will cook it and serve it to you (cooking is an extra ₹100 per kg).

TOP CHOICE Dal Roti
INDIAN $$
(Map p954; Lily St; meals ₹70-170; ⊙lunch & dinner) Friendly and knowledgeable owner Ramesh will hold your hand through his expansive North Indian menu, which even sports its own glossary, and help you dive in to his delicious range of vegetarian, eggetarian and nonvegetarian options. The setting is chic minimalist, with whitewashed walls and bench seating, helping you focus on the yummy dishes here.

Teapot
CAFE $
(Map p954; Peter Celli St; snacks ₹40-60, meals ₹140-180) This atmospheric place is the perfect venue for 'high tea', with teas, sandwiches and full meals served in chic, airy rooms. Witty tea-themed accents include loads of antique teapots, tea chests for tables and a gnarled, tea-tree based glass table. The cheesecake is divine.

Shala
KERALAN $$
(Map p954; Peter Celli St; meals ₹180-220; ⊙noon-3.30pm & 6.30-11pm) With high ceilings, whirring fans, and white walls adorned with striking paintings, Shala is owned by the same management as Kailah Art Cafe, and serves well-presented meals that include a vegetable side dish and rice, such as coconut fish curry or vegetable of the day, all made by local women.

Solar Cafe
CAFE $$
(Bazaar Rd; meals ₹80-130; ⊙8am-8pm) This arty and funky cafe serves up organic breakfasts and lunches, with dishes such as fruit with wild honey and drinks such as cinnamon coffee, in a lime-bright, book-lined and friendly setting.

Arca Nova
SOUTH INDIAN $$
(2/6A Calvathy Rd; mains ₹225-290; ⊙12.30-2.30pm & 7.30-10.30pm) The waterside restaurant at the Fort House Hotel is a prime choice for a leisurely lunch (mosquitoes may join you for dinner), particularly specialising in fish, with dishes such as fish wrapped in banana leaf or spicy peppered fish, set in a serenely spacious covered area in the garden.

Casa Linda
MULTICUISINE $$
(Map p954; Dispensary Rd; mains ₹85-300) This modern dining room above the hotel of the same name might not be much to look at,

but it's all about the food here. Chef Dipu once trained with a Frenchman and whips up delicious local Keralan dishes alongside French imports like Poisson de la Provencale (fish fried in oil and herbs, Provence-style). The Keralan dry-fried coconut prawns, made to a loving mother's recipe, are scrumptious.

Kashi Art Cafe
CAFE $$
(Map p954; Burgher St; breakfast & snacks ₹60-95; ⊙8.30am-7.30pm) An institution in Fort Cochin, this place has a hip-but-casual vibe and solid wood tables that spread out into a semi-courtyard space. The coffee is as strong as it should be and the daily Western breakfast and lunch specials are excellent. A small gallery shows off local artists.

Menorah Restaurant
KERALAN $$
(Map p954; Korder House; dishes ₹175-275; ⊙lunch & dinner) In the gracious hall of Korder House, now a heritage hotel, with tall wooden ceilings and chessboard black-and-white-tiled flooring, with whirring fans. It serves wine and beer, and tasty Keralan dishes, if tweaked for tourist tastes.

Malabar Junction
INTERNATIONAL $$$
(Map p954; ☑2216666; Parade Ground Rd; mains ₹380-600) Set in an open-sided pavilion, the restaurant at Malabar House is movie-star cool, with white-tableclothed tables in a courtyard close to the small pool. There's a seafood-based, European-style menu and Grover's Estate wine (quaffable Indian) is served. The signature dish is the impressive seafood platter with grilled vegetables (₹1500). Upstairs, the bar serves upmarket snacks such as tapioca-and-cumin fritters in funkily clashing surroundings.

Old Harbour Hotel
MULTICUISINE $$$
(Map p954; ☑2218006; www.oldharbourhotel.com; Tower Rd; mains ₹400-500; ⊙10.30am-10pm) Certainly one of Cochin's most enchanting settings for an evening meal, in the poolside candlelit garden of the Old Harbour Hotel, serenaded by traditional musicians. The food is bland but acceptable, but it gets a thumbs up for ambience and you can order wine (from ₹1350 a bottle) and beer (₹175).

XL
BAR
(Map p954; ⊙10am-10.30pm) This slightly dingy bar-restaurant, with whirring fans and big windows, is a hugely popular place to settle down for a cold Kingfisher, with reasonable prices, palatable snacks and meals such as beef deep fry.

MATTANCHERRY & JEW TOWN

Ramathula Hotel
INDIAN $

(Map p956; Kayees Junction, Mattancherry; biryani ₹40-45; ⊘lunch & dinner) This place is legendary among locals for its chicken and mutton biryanis – get here early or you'll miss out. It's better known by the chef's name, Kayikka's.

Caza Maria
MULTICUISINE $$

(Map p956; Bazaar Rd; mains around ₹120-200) With cooks trained by a travelling Frenchman, this is an enchanting, bright blue, antique-filled space with funky music and a changing daily menu of North Indian, South Indian and French dishes.

Ginger House
INDIAN $$$

(Map p956; Bazaar Rd; meals ₹400-600) Walk through the massive antique-filled godown and you'll find the attached restaurant, with a fantastic setting right on the waterfront, where you can relax on mismatched chairs (straight from the shop) and feast on Indian dishes and snacks.

Shri Krishna
INDIAN $

(Map p956; thali ₹24, dishes ₹4-23; ⊘7am-9.30pm) A simple, basic, but tasty thali.

Café Jew Town
CAFE $$

(Map p956; Bazaar Rd; snacks around ₹100-200) A Swiss-owned cafe, this chi-chi little place running alongside an upmarket antique shop has a few tables and proffers good cakes, snacks and coffee.

ERNAKULAM

TOP CHOICE Grand Pavilion
INDIAN $$

(Map p958; MG Rd; meals ₹90-350; ❄) This is the restaurant at the Grand Hotel and is as retro-stylish as the hotel itself. It serves a tome of a menu that covers dishes from the West, North India, South India and most of the rest of the Asian continent. The *meen pollichathu* (fish cooked in banana leaves) gets the thumbs up.

Frys Village Restaurant
KERALAN $

(Map p958; Veekshanam Rd; dishes ₹50-100; ⊘noon-3.30pm & 7-10.30pm; ❄) This brightly decorated place with an arched ceiling is a great family restaurant with authentic Keralan food, especially seafood like *pollichathu* or crab roast (₹50–200 depending on size). Fish/veg thalis (and much more) are available for lunch.

Subhiksha
INDIAN $

(Map p958; Gandhi Sq, D.H. Road; dishes ₹30-100; ⊘7.30am-3.30pm & 7-11pm; ❄) A popular pure-veg hotel restaurant, this is a smart place to dig into tasty thalis (₹90). It's rammed for breakfast and lunch. The hotel also has a busy, breezy coffee shop serving dosas and the like.

Aruvi Nature Restaurant
KERALAN $

(Map p958; Chittoor Rd; dishes ₹10-25; ⊘noon-2.30pm & 6-9pm) An interesting twist on the traditional Keralan set meal – the menu is created according to ayurvedic principles and contains no dairy, spicy peppers or salt. And with dishes such as pumpkin dosas, it's definitely worth a try!

Andhra Meals
INDIAN $$

(Map p958; meals ₹70-125; ⊘11.30am-3.30pm & 7-11.30pm) A dark, buzzing 1st-floor place, serving spicy Andhra cuisine on banana leaves. Try a thali, for all-you-can-eat joy.

South Star
MULTICUISINE $$

(Map p958; Shanmughan Rd; meals ₹70-140; ❄) This upmarket version of the Bimbis chain of restaurants is in a moodily lit space that's plushed out in nice chairs and dark-wood tables. The bulky menu has North and South Indian victuals, as well as a massive choice of Chinese dishes.

Spencer's Daily
SUPERMARKET $

(Map p958; Veekshanam Rd; ⊘7.30am-10.30pm) Well-stocked supermarket.

Indian Coffee House
CAFE

(Map p958; Cannon Shed Rd) Also has branches on Jos Junction and MG Rd near Padma Junction.

Coffee Beanz
CAFE

(Map p958; Shanmugham Rd; snacks ₹40-140; ⊘9am-10.30pm; ❄) For a hip coffee hit.

☆ Entertainment

There are several places in Kochi where you can view Kathakali (see p976). The performances are certainly made for tourists, but they're also a good introduction to this intriguing art form. The standard program starts with the intricate make-up application, followed by a demonstration and commentary on the dance and then the performance. The fast-paced traditional martial art of *kalarippayat* can now be easily seen in Fort Cochin.

See India Foundation
CULTURAL PROGRAM

(Map p958; ☏2376471; devankathakali@yahoo.com; Kalathiparambil Lane, Ernakulam; admission ₹150; ⊘make-up 6pm, show 6.45-8pm) One of the oldest Kathakali theatres in Kerala, it has small-scale shows with an emphasis on the religious and philosophical roots of Kathakali.

Kerala Kathakali Centre
CULTURAL PROGRAM

(Map p954; ☑2217552; www.kathakalicentre.com; KB Jacob Rd, Fort Cochin; admission ₹250; ☺make-up from 5pm, show 6-7.30pm) In an intimate, wood-lined theatre, this place provides a useful introduction to Kathakali, complete with amazing demonstrations of eye movements, plus handy translations of the night's story. The centre also hosts performances of the martial art of *kalarippayat* at 4 to 5pm daily, traditional music at 8 to 9pm Sunday to Friday and classical dance at 8 to 9pm on Saturday.

Ens Kalari
CULTURAL PROGRAM

(☑2700810; www.enskalari.org.in; Nettoor, Er-nakulam) If you want to see real professionals have a go at *kalarippayat,* it's best to travel out to this renowned *kalarippayat* learning centre, 8km southeast of Ernakulam. There are one-hour demonstrations Monday to Saturday at 5.30pm (one day's notice required, admission by donation).

Sridar Cinema
CINEMA

(Map p958; Shanmugham Rd, Ernakulam) Screens films in Malayalam, Hindi, Tamil and English.

Shopping

Broadway in Ernakulam (p958) is good for local shopping, spice shops and clothing, and around Convent and Market Rds is a huddle of tailors. On Jew Town Rd in Mattancherry there's a plethora of Gujarati-run shops selling genuine antiques mingled with knock-offs and copies. A couple of shops close to the synagogue sell exquisite lace work. Most of the shops in Fort Cochin are identikit Kashmiri-run shops selling a mixed bag of north Indian crafts. Many shops around Fort Cochin and Mattancherry operate lucrative commission rackets, with autorickshaw drivers getting huge kickbacks (added to your price) for dropping tourists at their door.

Niraamaya
CLOTHING

Fort Cochin (Map p954; ☑3263465; Quiros St, Fort Cochin; ☺10am-5.30pm Mon-Sat); Mattancherry (Map p956; VI/217 A.B. Salam Rd, Jew Town) Popular throughout Kerala, Niraamaya sells 'ayurvedic' clothing and fabrics – all made of organic cotton, coloured with natural herb dyes, or infused with ayurvedic oils.

DC Books
BOOKSTORE

(Map p958; ☑2391295; Banerji Rd, Ernakulam; ☺9.30am-7.30pm Mon-Sat) This has a typically great English-language selection of fiction and nonfiction.

Idiom Bookshop
BOOKSTORE

Fort Cochin (Map p954; ☑2217075; Bastion St; ☺10.30am-9pm Mon-Sat); Mattancherry (☑2225604; opposite boat jetty; ☺10am-6pm) Huge range of quality new and used books.

Fabindia
CLOTHING, HOMEWARES

(Map p954; ☑2217077; www.fabindia.com; Napier St, Fort Cochin; ☺10.30am-8.30pm) Fab Fabindia has heaps of fine Indian textiles, fabrics, clothes and household linen.

Cinnamon
CLOTHING

(Map p954; ☑2217124; Post Office Rd, Fort Cochin; ☺10am-7pm Mon-Sat) Cinnamon sells gorgeous Indian-designed clothing, jewellery and homewares in an ultrachic white retail space.

Tribes India
HANDICRAFTS

(Map p954; ☑2215077; c/o Head Post Office, Fort Cochin; ☺10am-6.30pm Mon-Sat) Tucked behind the post office, this TRIFED (Ministry of Tribal Affairs) enterprise sells tribal artefacts, paintings, shawls, figurines, etc, at reasonable fixed prices and the profits go towards supporting the artisans.

Information

Internet access

Net Park (Map p958; Convent Rd, Ernakulam; per hr ₹15; ☺9am-8pm)

Sify iWay (Map p954; per hr ₹40; ☺9am-10pm) Fast computers in a spacious upstairs cafe setting above the Shop-n-Save.

Medical Services

Lakeshore Hospital (☑2701032; NH Bypass, Marudu) It's 8km southeast of central Ernakulam.

Medical Trust (Map p958; ☑2358001; www.medicaltrusthospital.com; MG Rd)

Money

UAE Exchange (☺9.30am-6pm Mon-Fri, to 4pm Sat) Ernakulam (☑2383317; Perumpillil Bldg, MG Rd); Ernakulam (☑3067008; Chettupuzha Towers, PT Usha Rd Junction); Fort Cochin (☑2216231; Amravathi Rd) Foreign exchange and travellers cheques.

Post

College post office (☑2369302; Convent Rd, Ernakulam; ☺9am-5pm Mon-Sat)

Ernakulam post office branches (☑2355467; Hospital Rd; ☺9am-8pm Mon-Sat, 10am-5pm Sun) Also branches on MG Rd and Broadway.

Main post office (Post Office Rd, Fort Cochin; ⊙9am-5pm Mon-Fri, to 3pm Sat)

Tourist information

There's a tourist information counter at the airport. Many places distribute a free brochure that includes a neat map and walking tour entitled *Historical Places in Fort Cochin*.

KTDC Tourist Reception Centre (Map p958; ☎2353234; Shanmugham Rd, Ernakulam; ⊙8am-7pm) Also organises tours.

Tourist Desk Information Counter Ernakulam (Map p958;☎2371761; touristdesk@satyam. net.in; ⊙8am-6pm); Fort Cochin (Map p954; ☎2216129) A private tour agency that's extremely knowledgeable and helpful about Kochi and beyond. Runs several popular and recommended tours, and its Ernakulam office displays a board showing recommended cultural events on in town that day, has a secondhand book exchange, and produces the 'Village Astrologer', a monthly free newsletter about cultural events in Kerala.

Tourist Police Ernakulam (☎2353234; Shanmugham Rd, Ernakulam; ⊙8am-6pm); Fort Cochin (Map p954; ☎2215055; ⊙24hr)

❶ Getting There & Away

Air

The following airlines have offices in Kochi:
Air India (☎2351295; MG Rd)
Jet Airways (☎2358582; MG Rd)
Kingfisher Airlines (☎1800 2093030; Spencer Travels, 2nd fl, Sreekandath Rd)

Bus

The **KSRTC bus stand** (Map p958; ☎2372033; ⊙reservations 6am-10pm) is in Ernakulam next to the railway halfway between the two train stations. Many buses passing through Ernakulam originate in other cities – you may have to join the scrum when the bus pulls in. You can make reservations up to 20 days (30 for Tamil Nadu) in advance for buses originating here. There's a separate window for reservations to Tamil Nadu. See p965 for more information on buses from Ernakulam.

DOMESTIC FLIGHTS FROM ERNAKULAM

DESTINATION	AIRLINE	FARE (₹)	DURATION (HR)	FREQUENCY
Agatti	IT	₹10,000	1½	5 weekly
Bengaluru	9W	₹2200	1¼	1 daily
	IT	3500	1¼	4 daily
Chennai	IC	2300	1	1 daily
	9W	2900	1½	3 daily
	IT	2800	1½	1 daily
Delhi	IC	5900	3	2 daily
	9W	6300	3	3 daily
Goa	IT	6200	5	1 daily
	SG	9350	5	1 daily
Kozhikode	IC	2000	3/4	2 daily
Mumbai	IC	5500	2	1 daily
	9W	5300	2	1 daily
	IT	4700	2	1 daily
	SG	4900	2	2 daily
Trivandrum	IC	2300	¾	1 daily
	6E	2200	¾	1 daily

Note: Fares are one way. Airline codes: IC – Air India; 9W – Jet Airways; IT – Kingfisher; 6E – IndiGo; SG – SpiceJet.

The following bus services operate from the KSRTC bus stand (Map p958).

DESTINATION	FARE (₹)	DURATION (HR)	FREQUENCY
Alleppey	34	1½	every 20min
Bengaluru	302 (AC 576)	14	4 daily
Calicut	120 (AC 190)	5	1-2 hourly
Chennai	465	16	1 daily, 2pm
Coimbatore	130	4½	9 daily
Kannur	170	8	2 daily
Kanyakumari	170	8	2 daily
Kollam	90	3½	every 20min
Kothamangalam	30	2	every 10min
Kottayam	40	2	every 30min
Kumily (for Periyar)	90	5	8 daily
Madurai	160	9	1 daily, 7.45pm
Munnar	86	4½	every 30min
Mangalore	286	12	1 daily
Thrissur	46	2	every 10min
Trivandrum	140	5	every 30min

KERALA KOCHI (COCHIN)

Several private bus companies have super-deluxe, AC, video buses to Bengaluru, Chennai, Mangalore and Coimbatore; prices are around 75% higher than government buses. There are stands selling tickets all over Ernakulam. **Kaloor bus stand** is the main private bus station; it's 1km north of the city.

Train

Ernakulam has two train stations, **Ernakulam Town** and **Ernakulam Junction**. Reservations for both are made at the Ernakulam Junction **reservations office** (🖉132; ⊘8am-8pm Mon-Sat, 8am-2pm Sun).

There are trains to Trivandrum (2nd class/AC chair ₹70/255, 4½ hours), via either Alleppey (₹39/165, 1½ hours) and Kollam (₹60/210, 3½ hours), or via Kottayam (₹40/165, 1½ hours). Trains also run to Thrissur (₹43/165, 1½ hours), Calicut (₹67/237, 4½ hours) and Kannur (₹85/300, 6½ hours). For long-distance trains, see p966.

🛈 Getting Around

To/From the Airport

Kochi International Airport (🖉610125; http://cochinairport.com) is at Nedumbassery, 30km northeast of Ernakulam. Taxis to/from Ernakulam cost around ₹500, and to/from Fort Cochin around ₹650; a bumpy rickshaw dash from Ernakulam would cost ₹350. Ernakulam's mad traffic means that the trip can take over 1½

hours in the daytime, though usually less than one hour at night.

Boat

Ferries are the fastest form of transport between Fort Cochin and the mainland. The jetty on the eastern side of Willingdon Island is called **Embarkation** (Map p953); the west one, opposite Mattancherry, is **Terminus** (Map p953); and the main stop at Fort Cochin is **Customs**, with another stop at the **Mattancherry Jetty** near the synagogue (Map p956). One-way fares are ₹2.50 (₹3.50 between Ernakulam and Mattancherry).

ERNAKULAM There are services to both Fort Cochin jetties (Customs and Mattancherry) every 25 to 50 minutes (5.55am to 9.30pm) from Ernakulam's **main jetty** (Map p958).

Ferries also run every 20 minutes or so to Willingdon and Vypeen Islands (6am to 10pm).

FORT COCHIN Ferries run from Customs Jetty to Ernakulam between 6.20am and 9.50pm. Ferries also hop between Customs Jetty and Willingdon Island 18 times a day from 6.40am to 9.30pm (Monday to Saturday).

Car and passenger ferries cross to Vypeen Island from Fort Cochin virtually nonstop from 6am until 10pm.

Local Transport

There are no real bus services between Fort Cochin and Mattancherry Palace, but it's an

MAJOR TRAINS FROM ERNAKULAM

The following are major long-distance trains departing from Ernakulam Town.

DESTINATION	TRAIN NO & NAME*	FARE (₹)	DURATION (HR)	DEPARTURES (DAILY)
Bengaluru	6525 *Bangalore Express*	264/688/949	13	5.55pm
Chennai	2624 *Chennai Mail*	289/758/1028	12	10.52
Delhi	2625 *Kerala Express***	579/1572/2159	46	3.45pm
Goa	6312 *Bikaner Express*	305/827/1137	15	8.00pm (Sat only)
Kanyakumari	6526 *Kanyakumari Express*	155/404/551	8	10.10am
Mangalore	6347 *Malabar Express*	187/496/679	10½	1.30am
Mumbai	6382 *Mumbai Express*	465/1277/1762	40	1.20pm

*Sleeper/3AC/2AC

**Departs from Ernakulam Junction

enjoyable 30-minute walk through the busy warehouse area along Bazaar Rd. Autorickshaws should cost around ₹20-30. Most autorickshaw trips around Ernakulam shouldn't cost more than ₹25.

To get to Fort Cochin after ferries stop running, catch a bus in Ernakulam on MG Rd (₹8, 45 minutes), south of Durbar Hall Rd. From Fort Cochin, buses head out to Ernakulam from opposite the Vypeen Island ferry jetty. Taxis charge round-trip fares between the islands, even if you only go one way – Ernakulam Town train station to Fort Cochin should cost around ₹200.

Scooters/Enfields can be hired for ₹250/350-600 per day from **Vasco Tourist Information Centre** (Map p954; ☎2216267; vascoinformat ions@yahoo.co.uk; Bastion St, Fort Cochin).

Around Kochi

TRIPUNITHURA

Hill Palace Museum (☎0484-2781113; admission ₹20; ☻10am-12.30pm & 2-4.30pm Tue-Sun) At Tripunithura, 16km southeast of Ernakulam en route to Kottayam, this museum was formerly the residence of the Kochi royal family and is an impressive 49-building palace complex. It now houses the collections of the royal families, as well as 19th-century oil paintings, old coins, sculptures and paintings, and temple models. From Ernakulam catch the bus to Tripunithura from MG Rd or Shanmugham Rd, behind the Tourist Reception Centre (₹5 to ₹10, 45 minutes); an autorickshaw should cost around ₹300 return with one-hour waiting time.

CHERAI BEACH

On Vypeen Island, 25km from Fort Cochin, Cherai Beach might just be Kochi's best-kept secret. It's a lovely stretch of as-yet undeveloped white sand, with miles of lazy backwaters just a few hundred metres from the seafront. Best of all, it's close enough to visit on a day trip from Kochi.

If you plan to stay for more than a day, there are a few low-key resorts here.

Brighton Beach House (☎9946565555; www.brightonbeachhouse.org; r ₹1500, with AC ₹2000) has a few basic rooms in a small building right near the shore. The beach is rocky here, but the place is wonderfully secluded, filled with hammocks to loll in, and has a neat, elevated stilt-restaurant that serves perfect sunset views with dinner.

An excellent collection of distinctive cottages lying around a meandering lagoon, **Cherai Beach Resort** (☎0484-2416949; www.cheraibeachresorts.com; Vypeen Island; r from ₹2500; ✸@) has the beach on one side and backwaters on the other. Bungalows are individually designed using natural materials, with curving walls, or split-levels, or lookouts onto the backwaters. There's even a tree growing inside one room. Check out a few to find one to your liking.

To get here from Fort Cochin, catch a car-ferry to Vypeen Island (per person ₹2) and either hire an autorickshaw from the jetty (around ₹300) or catch one of the frequent buses (₹14, one hour).

PARUR & CHENNAMANGALAM

Nowhere is the tightly woven religious cloth that is India more apparent than in **Parur**, 35km north of Kochi. Here, one of the oldest synagogues (admission ₹5; ⊙9am-5pm Tue-Sun) in Kerala, at **Chennamangalam**, 8km from Parur, has been fastidiously renovated. Inside you can see door and ceiling wood reliefs in dazzling colours, while just outside lies one of the oldest tombstones in India – inscribed with the Hebrew date corresponding to 1269. The Jesuits first arrived in Chennamangalam in 1577 and there's a **Jesuit church** and the ruins of a Jesuit college nearby. Nearby are a **Hindu temple** on a hill overlooking the Periyar River, a 16th-century **mosque**, and Muslim and Jewish **burial grounds**.

In Parur town, you'll find the **agraharam** (place of Brahmins) – a small street of closely packed and brightly coloured houses originally settled by Tamil Brahmins.

Parur is compact, but Chennamangalam is best visited with a guide. Indoworld (Map p954; ☏9447037527; www.indoworldtours.com; Princess St) can organise tours; a day trip is around ₹2200 including guide and car.

Buses for Parur leave from the KSRTC bus stand in Kochi (₹16, one hour, every 10 minutes). From Parur catch a bus (₹3) or autorickshaw (₹60) to Chennamangalam.

Thrissur (Trichur)

☏0487 / POP 330,100

While the rest of Kerala has its fair share of celebrations, untouristy, bustling Thrissur is the cultural cherry on the festival cake. With a list of energetic festivals as long as a temple-elephant's trunk, the region supports several institutions that nurse the dying classical Keralan performing arts back to health. This busy, bustling place is home to a Nestorian Christian community whose denomination dates to the 3rd century AD. The popular performing-arts school Kerala Kalamandalam (p969) and Shri Krishna Temple (p969) are nearby. Plan to arrive during the rambunctious festival season (November to mid-May).

◉ Sights & Activities

Thrissur is famed for its central temple, as well as for its numerous impressive churches.

Vadakkunathan Kshetram Temple   TEMPLE
One of the oldest in the state, Vadakkunathan Kshetram Temple crowns the hill at the epicentre of Thrissur. Finished in classic Keralan architecture, only Hindus are allowed inside, though the mound surrounding the temple has sweeping metropolis views and is a popular spot to linger.

Archaeology Museum   MUSEUM
(admission ₹6; ⊙9am-1pm & 2pm-4.30pm Tue-Sun) The Archaeology Museum is housed in the wonderful 200-year-old Sakthan Thampuran Palace. Its mix of artefacts include fragile palm-leaf manuscripts, 12th-century Keralan bronze sculptures, earthenware pots big enough to cook children in, and an extraordinary 1500kg wooden treasury box covered in locks and iron spikes.

Our Lady of Lourdes Cathedral   CHURCH
This massive cathedral has an underground shrine.

Puttanpalli (New) Church   CHURCH
Recognisable from its towering, pure-white spires.

Chaldean (Nestorian) Church   CHURCH
This church is unique in its complete lack of pictorial representations of Jesus.

✯ Festivals & Events

In a state where festivals are a way of life, Thrissur still manages to stand out for temple revelry. Highlights include **Thrissur Pooram** (April/May) – the most colourful and biggest of Kerala's temple festivals with wonderful processions of elephants; **Uthralikavu Pooram** (March/April), whose climactic day sees 20 elephants circling the shrine; and **Thypooya Maholsavam** (January/February), with a *kavadiyattam* (a form of ritualistic dance) procession in which dancers carry tall, ornate structures called *kavadis*.

🛏 Sleeping

Hotel Luciya Palace   HOTEL $$
(☏2424731; www.hotelluciyapalace.com; s/d with AC ₹1250/1400; ✸) In a cream, colonial-themed building, this is one of the few places in town that has some character. Sitting in a quiet cul-de-sac, this grandiose-looking hotel has comfortable and spacious rooms.

Joys Palace   HOTEL $$
(☏2429999; www.joyshotels.com; TB Rd; s/d from ₹2400/2900; ✸@) This ornate 10-storey meringue caters to Thrissur's jet set. Thankfully, the rooms are not too over the top, are quite comfy and have big windows to enjoy the upper floor's sweeping views. There's a 2nd-floor **restaurant** with an outdoor balcony, and a cool glass-fronted elevator that feels like a fun-park ride.

KERALA CENTRAL KERALA

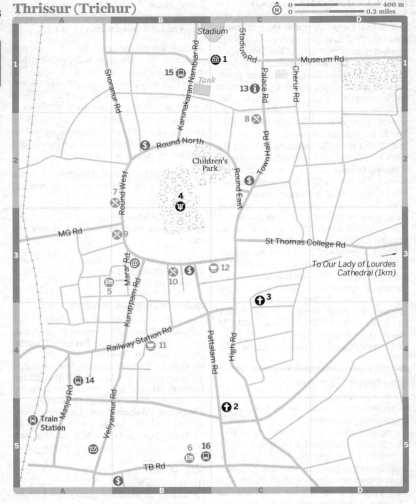

Pathans Hotel   HOTEL **$**
(☎2425620; www.pathansresidentialhotel.com;
Round South; s/d from ₹400/539, with AC
₹700/1000; ❄) With no-frills rooms at no-
frills prices, this is probably the best budget
value in town. The basic and clean rooms
are on the 5th and 6th floors and have TV
and occasional hot water.

🍴 Eating & Drinking

India Gate   INDIAN **$**
(Town Hall Rd; dishes ₹30-60) In the same building as the HDFC Bank, this is a bright, pure-
veg place, with a vintage feel, serving an
unbeatable range of dosas, including jam,
cheese and cashew versions, and *uttapams*
(thick savoury rice pancakes – a Tamil Nadu
version of a pizza).

Navaratna Restaurant   NORTH INDIAN **$**
(Round West; dishes ₹57-96; ☉lunch & dinner) Cool
dark and intimate, this is the classiest dining
joint in town, with seating on raised platforms and piped music. Expect lots of veg and
nonveg dishes from North India, plus a few
Keralan specialities, served in AC surrounds.

Pathans Hotel   INDIAN **$**
(1st fl, Round South; dishes ₹30-40; 7am-9.30pm)
A little cafeteria-like, this atmospheric

Thrissur (Trichur)

Sights
1 Archaeology Museum C1
2 Chaldean (Nestorian) Church C5
3 Puttanpalli (New) Church C3
4 Vadakkunathan Kshetram Temple B2

Sleeping
5 Hotel Luciya Palace A3
6 Joys Palace B5
Pathans Hotel .... (see 10)

Eating
7 Ambady Restaurant B2
8 India Gate C2
9 Navaratna Restaurant B3
10 Pathans Hotel B3

Drinking
11 Indian Coffee House B4
12 Indian Coffee House C3

Information
13 DTPC Office C1

Transport
14 KSRTC Bus Stand A4
15 Priyadarshini (North) Bus Stand B1
16 Sakthan Thampuran Bus Stand B5

place is popular with families for lunch (thali ₹40) and has a sweets counter downstairs.

Ambady Restaurant INDIAN $
(Round West; dishes ₹30-40) A little way off the street, this dark-brown place is a huge hit with families tucking into several different varieties of set meals.

Indian Coffee House CAFE
Has branches at Round South and Railway Station Rd.

Information

There are several ATMs around town.

DTPC office (District Tourism Promotion Council; ☎2320800; Palace Rd; ⊙10am-5pm Mon-Sat)

Lava Rock Internet Cafe (Kuruppam Rd; per hr ₹30; ⊙8.30am-9pm)

UAE Money Exchange (☎2445668; TB Rd; ⊙9am-6.30pm Mon-Fri, to 1pm Sat, to 4pm Sun)

Getting There & Away

Bus

KSRTC buses leave around every 30 minutes from the **KSRTC bus stand** bound for Trivandrum (₹193, 7½ hours), Ernakulam (Kochi, ₹51, two hours), Calicut (₹80, 3½ hours), Palakkad (₹43, 1½ hours) and Kottayam (₹83, four hours). Hourly buses go to Coimbatore (₹77, three hours). From here there are buses to Ponnani (₹35, 1½ hours, four daily) and Prumpavoor (₹37, two hours), where you can connect with buses bound for Munnar.

Regular services also chug along to Guruvayur (₹22, one hour), Irinjalakuda (₹13, one hour) and Cheruthuruthy (₹20, 1½ hours). Two private bus stands (**Sakthan Thampuran** and **Priyadarshini**) have more frequent buses to these destinations, though the chaos involved in navigating each station hardly makes using them worthwhile.

Train

Services run regularly to Ernakulam (2nd class/AC chair ₹43/165, 1½ hours) and Calicut (₹53/180, three hours). There are also regular trains running to Palakkad (sleeper/3AC/2AC ₹120/265/306, 1½ hours) via Shoranur.

Around Thrissur

The Hindu-only **Shri Krishna Temple** at Guruvayur, 33km northwest of Thrissur, is the most famous in Kerala. Said to have been created by Guru, preceptor of the gods, and Vayu, god of wind, the temple is believed to date from the 16th century and is renowned for its healing powers. An annual and spectacular **Elephant Race** is held here in February or March.

Kerala Kalamandalam (☎04884-262305; info@kalamandalam.org; ⊙June-Mar), 32km northeast of Thrissur at Cheruthuruthy, is a champion of Kerala's traditional-art renaissance. Using an ancient Gurukula system of learning, students undergo intensive study in Kathakali, *mohiniyattam* (dance of the enchantress), *Kootiattam*, percussion, voice and violin. Structured **visits** (per person ₹1000; ⊙9.30am-12.30pm) are available, including a tour around the theatre and classes. Individually tailored **introductory courses** (per month around ₹2500) are offered one subject at a time and last from six to 12 months. The school can help you find local homestay accommodation. For visits, email to book in advance.

Natana Kairali Research & Performing Centre for Traditional Arts (☑0480-2825559; natanakairali@gmail.com), 20km south of Thrissur near Irinjalakuda, offers training in traditional arts, including rare forms of puppetry and dance. Short appreciation courses (per class about ₹400) lasting up to a month are sometimes available to keen foreigners. In December each year, the centre holds five days of *mohiniyattam* **performances**, a form of classical Keralan women's dance.

River Retreat (☑04884-262244; www.river retreat.in; Palace Rd; Cheruthuruthy; d ₹2520-4725) is only 1km from Kerala Kalamandalam. It's a hotel in the former summer palace of the Maharajas of Cochin. The more expensive rooms in the main building have river views. They're much nicer and discounts may be available, so ask.

Regular bus services connect each of these destinations with Thrissur (p969).

NORTHERN KERALA

Kozhikode (Calicut)

☑0495 / POP 880,168

Always a prosperous trading town, Calicut was once the capital of the formidable Zamorin dynasty. Vasco da Gama first landed near here in 1498, on his way to snatch a share of the subcontinent for king and country (Portugal that is). These days, trade depends mostly on exporting Indian labour to the Middle East. There's not a lot for tourists to see, though it's a nice break in the journey and the jumping-off point for Wayanad Wildlife Sanctuary.

◉ Sights

Mananchira Square was the former courtyard of the Zamorins and preserves the original spring-fed tank. The 650-year-old Kuttichira Mosque is in an attractive wooden four-storey building that is supported by impressive wooden pillars and painted brilliant aqua, blue and white. Burnt down by the Portuguese in 1510, it was protected then rebuilt to tell the tale. The central Church of South India was established by Swiss missionaries in 1842 and has unique Euro-Keralan architecture. At Beypore, 10km south, it's possible to see the traditional craft of **dhow** (boat) building.

🛏 Sleeping

TOP CHOICE Harivihar   HOMESTAY $$$
(☑2765865; www.harivihar.com; Bilathikulam; s/d from ₹4800/6600) In northern Calicut, the ancestral home of the Kadathanadu royal family is as serene as it gets, a traditional Keralan family compound with pristine lawns. Rooms are large and furnished with darkwood antiques. There's an ayurvedic centre, with packages available. The food is delicious.

Beach Hotel   HOTEL $$
(☑2762055; www.beachheritage.com; Beach Rd; r ₹2500; ❄) Built in 1890 to house the Malabar British Club, this place is now a delightful 10-room hotel. Some rooms have bathtubs and secluded verandas; others have original polished wooden floors and private balconies. All are tastefully furnished and drip with character. Dinner is often served in the little garden.

Hyson Heritage   HOTEL $$
(☑4081000; www.hysonheritage.com; Bank Rd; s/d from ₹1800/2300; ❄🛜) At this business-

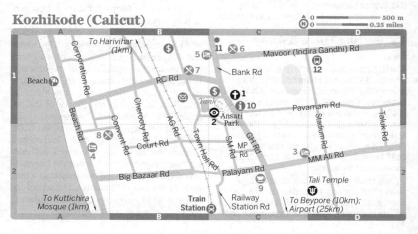

Kozhikode (Calicut)

To Harivihar (1km)

Beach

Corporation Rd
Beach Rd
Cheroofy Rd
Convent Rd
AG Rd
Court Rd
Town Hall Rd
SM Rd
MP Rd
GH Rd
Stadium Rd
Taluk Rd

RC Rd
Bank Rd
Mavoor (Indira Gandhi) Rd
Pavamani Rd
MM Ali Rd
Big Bazaar Rd
Palayam Rd

Tank
Ansari Park

Tali Temple

To Kuttichira Mosque (1km)

Train Station

Railway Station Rd

To Beypore (10km); Airport (25km)

0   500 m
0   0.25 miles

focused, friendly place you get a fair bit of swank for your rupee. All rooms are spic and span, large, comfortable and with inoffensive decor, while the massive deluxe rooms have views over town too.

Alakapuri   HOTEL $
(☏2723451; www.alakapurihotels.com; MM Ali Rd; s/d from ₹250/700, with AC ₹625/800; ❄) Built motel-style around a green lawn (complete with fountain!) this place is off the road and quieter than most. Rooms come in different sizes and prices and, while a little scuffed, are tidy and reasonable value.

🍴 Eating & Drinking

Paragon Restaurant   INDIAN $$
(Kannur Rd; dishes ₹50-220) This always packed restaurant was founded in 1939. The menu is embarrassingly vast, and it's famous for fish dishes such as fish in tamarind sauce, and its legendary chicken biryani.

Zains   INDIAN $
(Convent Cross Rd; dishes ₹60-100; ⊘noon-11pm) This historic, authentic Mappila restaurant cooks up delicious authentic dishes such as deep fried beef *pathiri* (pastry) and unnakaya (*plantain snack*).

Hotel Sagar   INDIAN $
(Mavoor Rd; dishes ₹20-80) With a dark wood interior and latticework on the front, this eatery is a tad more stylish than the competition. Veg and nonveg thali meals are

served, with yummy biryanis (including fish) and other dishes offered at lunchtime.

Indian Coffee House   CAFE $
(GH Rd) For tasty snacks and great coffee.

ℹ Information

There are HDFC and State Bank of India ATMs in town, and several internet cafes.

KTDC Tourist Information (☏2373862; GH Rd; ⊘10.15am-5.15pm Mon-Sat) Cursory tourist information.

UAE Exchange (☏2762772; Bank Rd; ⊘9.30am-6pm Mon-Fri, to 4pm Sat, to 1pm Sun) Close to the Hyson Heritage Hotel.

Thomas Cook (☏2762681; Bank Rd; ⊘9.30am-6.30pm Mon-Sat)

ℹ Getting There & Away

Air

Air India (☏2771974; Eroth Centre, Bank Rd) flies daily to Mumbai (from ₹4700), Chennai (₹5600) and Kochin (₹6000). **Jet Airways** (☏2740518; 29 Mavoor Rd) has one daily flight to Mumbai (₹2300), while **Kingfisher** (☏1800 2093030) flies to Chennai (₹5700), Mangalore (₹6300) and Kochi (from ₹6200).

Bus

The **bus stand** (Mavoor Rd) has government buses to Bengaluru (Bangalore; via Mysore, ₹226, AC ₹391, eight hours, 10 daily), Mangalore (₹260, seven hours, three daily) and to Ooty (₹100, 5½ hours, four daily). There are frequent buses to Thrissur (₹81, 3½ hours), Trivandrum (via Alleppey and Ernakulam; ordinary/Express/deluxe ₹260/300/335, 10 hours, eight daily) and Kottayam (₹160, seven hours, 13 daily). For Wayanad district, buses leave every 15 minutes heading to Sultanbatheri (₹63, three hours) via Kalpetta (₹51, two hours). Private buses for various long-distance locations also use this stand.

Train

The train station is 1km south of Mananchira Sq. There are trains to Mangalore (sleeper/3AC/2AC ₹130/330/448, five hours), Kannur (2nd class/3AC/2AC ₹46/210/279, two hours), Ernakulam (2nd class/AC chair ₹67/237, 4½ hours) via Thrissur (₹67/237, three hours), and all the way to Trivandrum (sleeper/3AC/2AC ₹181/500/680, 11 hours).

Heading southeast, trains go to Coimbatore (sleeper/3AC/2AC ₹120/292/394, 4½ hours), via Palakkad (₹120/243/356, 3½ hours). These trains then head north to the centres of Bengaluru, Chennai and Delhi.

ℹ Getting Around

Calicut has a glut of autorickshaws and most are happy to use the meter. It's about ₹20 from the station to the KSRTC bus stand or most hotels.

With its roots in Sanskrit, the word ayurveda is from *ayu* (life) and *veda* (knowledge); it is the knowledge or science of life. Principles of ayurvedic medicine were first documented in the Vedas some 2000 years ago, but may have been practised centuries earlier.

Ayurveda sees the world as having an intrinsic order and balance. It argues that we possess three *doshas* (humours): *vata* (wind or air); *pitta* (fire); and *kapha* (water/earth), known together as the *tridoshas*. Deficiency or excess in any of them can result in disease: an excess of *vata* may result in dizziness and debility; an increase in *pitta* may lead to fever, inflammation and infection. *Kapha* is essential for hydration.

Ayurvedic treatment aims to restore the balance, and hence good health, principally through two methods: panchakarma (internal purification), and herbal massage. Panchakarma is used to treat serious ailments, and is an intense detox regime, a combination of five types of different therapies (*panchakarma* means 'five actions') to rid the body of built-up endotoxins. These include: *vaman* – therapeutic vomiting; *virechan* – purgation; *vasti* – enemas; *nasya* – elimination of toxins through the nose; and *raktamoksha* – detoxification of the blood. Before panchakarma begins, the body is first prepared over several days with a special diet, oil massages (*snehana*) and herbal steambaths (*swedana*). Although it may sound pretty grim, panchakarma purification might only use a few of these treatments at a time, with therapies like bloodletting and leeches only used in rare cases. Still, this is no spa holiday. The herbs used in ayurveda grow in abundance in Kerala's humid climate – the monsoon is thought to be the best time of year for treatment, when there is less dust in the air and the pores are open and the body is most receptive to treatment – and every village has its own ayurvedic pharmacy.

Wayanad Wildlife Sanctuary

📞 04936 / POP 780,200

Ask any Keralan what the prettiest part of their state is and most will whisper: Wayanad. Encompassing part of a remote forest reserve that spills into Tamil Nadu, Wayanad's landscape is combines rice paddies of ludicrous green, skinny betel nut trees, bamboo, red earth, spiky ginger fields, and rubber, cardamom and coffee plantations. Tourist infrastructure is beginning, though it's still fantastically unspoilt, with epic views. Surprisingly few tourists make it here, a shame since it's one of the few places you're almost guaranteed to spot wild elephants.

The 345 sq km sanctuary has two separate pockets – Muthanga in the east bordering Tamil Nadu, and Tholpetty in the north bordering Karnataka. Three major towns in Wayanad district make good bases for exploring the sanctuary – Kalpetta in the south, Sultanbatheri (Sultan Battery) in the east and Mananthavadi in the northwest.

◉ Sights & Activities

TOP CHOICE **Visiting the Sanctuary** NATURE RESERVE
Entry to both parts of the sanctuary (admission to each part ₹110, camera/video ₹25/150;

⏱7-10.30am & 3-6.30pm) is only permitted as part of a guided trek or jeep safari, both of which can be arranged at the sanctuary entrances. Tholpetty closes during the monsoon period, while Muthanga remains open.

At Tholpetty (📞04935-250853; jeep ₹300, guide ₹200; ⏱Sept-Mar), the 1½-hour **jeep tours** (7am to 9am and 3pm to 5pm) are a great way to spot wildlife. Rangers organise guided treks (up to 5 people ₹1500, extra people ₹400) from here.

At Muthanga (📞271010; jeep ₹300 guide ₹100), two-hour **jeep tours** are available in the mornings and afternoons. During the monsoon period, with a minimum of four people, rafting trips (2½hr trip ₹800-900) may also be arranged .

The DTPC, as well as most hotels, arrange guided jeep tours (up to 5 people with/without guide ₹2200/1700) of the Muthanga sanctuary and surrounding Wayanad sights.

Kannur Ayurvedic Centre AYURVEDA
(📞0436-203001; www.ayurvedawayanad.com; Kalpetta; massage from ₹500) For ayurvedic treatments, visit this excellent small, government-certified and family-run clinic, tucked away in the leafy backstreets of Kalpetta. Ayurvedic massage starts at ₹500, longer treatments like full 21-day panchakarma cleansing costs around ₹20,000, including food.

There are nice **rooms** (r ₹500) – some with balconies and views. There are also daily **yoga classes** (per week ₹400; ☺6-7am).

Trekking & Rafting
OUTDOOR ACTIVITIES

There are some top opportunities for independent **trekking** around the district, including a climb to the top of Chembra Peak, at 2100m the area's tallest summit; Vellarimala, with great views and lots of wildlife-spotting opportunities; and **Pakshipathalam**, a formation of large boulders deep in the forest. Permits are necessary and can be arranged at forest offices in South or North Wayanad. The **DTPC office** in Kalpetta organises trekking guides (₹600 per day), camping equipment (around ₹250 per person) and transport – pretty much anything you might need to get you hiking. It also runs four-hour bamboo **rafting trips** (₹1000) from June to September.

Thirunelly Temple
TEMPLE

(☺dawn-dusk) Thought to be one of the oldest on the subcontinent, Thirunelly Temple is 10km from Tholpetty. Non-Hindus cannot enter, but it's worth visiting to experience the otherworldly cocktail of ancient and intricate pillars and stone carvings, set against a backdrop of mist-covered peaks.

Jain temple
TEMPLE

(☺8am-noon & 2-6pm) The 13th-century Jain temple near Sultanbatheri, has splendid stone carvings and is an important monument to the region's strong historical Jain presence.

Edakal Caves
CAVES

(admission ₹10; ☺9am-5pm) Close to the Jain temple, near Ambalavayal, these caves have petroglyphs thought to date back over 3000 years and jaw-dropping views of Wayanad district.

Wayanad Heritage Museum
MUSEUM

(Ambalavayal; admission ₹10; ☺9am-5pm) In the same area as the caves, this museum exhibits headgear, weapons, pottery, carved stone and other artefacts dating back to the 15th century that shed light on Wayanad's significant Adivasi population.

Uravu
HANDICRAFTS

(☎04936-231400/275 443; Thrikkaippetta; www. uravu.net; ☺8.30am-5pm Mon-Sat) Around 6km southeast of Kalpetta is where a collective of bamboo workers create all sorts of artefacts from bamboo. You can visit the artists' work-shops, where they work on looms, painting and carving, and support their work by buying vases, lampshades, bangles, baskets, and much more at bargain prices from the small fixed-price shop. A return jeep from Kalpetta will cost around ₹250.

Pookot Lake
PARK, BOATING

(admission ₹10; ☺9am-6pm) is 3km before Vythiri, a beautiful mirror framed by forest. Geared up for visitors, it has well-maintained gardens, a cafeteria, playground and **boats** (paddle/row boats per 20min ₹30/50) for hire. It gets packed on the weekends, though feels quite peaceful during the week.

🛏 Sleeping & Eating

TOP CHOICE **Tranquil**
HOMESTAY $$$

(☎04936-220244; www.tranquilresort.com; Kuppamudi Estate, Kolagapara; full board & tax s/d from ₹10,101/13,750, tree villa ₹14,850/19,500, tree house ₹13,000/17,900; ⊠) This wonderful homestay is in the middle of an incredible lush 160 hectares of pepper, coffee, vanilla and cardamom plantations. The elegant house has sweeping verandas filled with plants and handsome furniture, and there are two treehouses that have to be the finest in the state – most romantic is the tree house, which is at a dizzying height and has a branch growing through the bathroom. Victor, the plantation owner, will welcome you in like an old friend of the family. There are 12 walks marked around the plantation.

Pachyderm Palace
GUESTHOUSE $$

(☎reservations0484-2371761;touristdesk@satyam. net.in; Tholpetty; r per person incl meals ₹1250-1500) This fine old Keralan house lies just outside the gate of Tholpetty Wildlife Sanctuary – handy for early-morning treks, tours and wildlife viewing. The varied rooms are simple and tidy, with polished wood ceilings, tiled floors and mosquito nets. There's one stilt-bungalow surrounded by forest. Venu is a stupendous cook, and his son Dilip is a great guide to the surrounds. Besides trekking, they can arrange night **animal-spotting safaris** (30-60min ₹200) – not inside the park – where your chances of spotting wild elephants are pretty phenomenal.

Ente Veedu
HOMESTAY $$

(☎0435-220008; www.ente veedu.co.in; Panama-ram; r incl breakfast ₹2500-3000; ◎) It's isolated

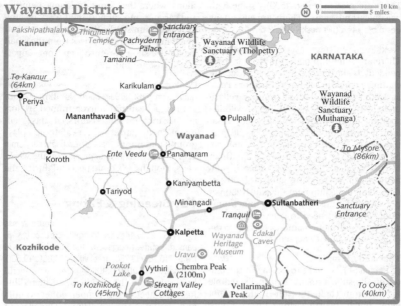

and set in a stunning location overlooking sprawling banana plantations and rice paddies, so this homestay halfway between Kalpetta and Manthavady is definitely worth seeking out. Surrounded by bucolic villages, it has several large rooms that come thoughtfully and colourfully furnished. Two rooms are bamboo-lined and offer private balconies. There are hammocks and wicker lounges here to enjoy the sensational views. Call to arrange a pick-up.

Stream Valley Cottages RESORT $$
(☑04936-255860; www.streamvalleycottages.com; Vythiri; d ₹2500-3000, cottages sleeping 8 ₹6000) These plain modern cottages lie on the banks of a small stream, several hundred metres off the main road (2.5km before Vythiri). Each cottage has a separate sitting area, private veranda, dark-wood interior and comes with a hushed soundtrack of singing birds and bubbling brooks. Traditional Keralan meals (₹390) are available.

Tamarind HOTEL $$
(☑0493-5210475; info@tamarindthirunelly.com; Thirunelly; d with AC ₹1400) With a fantastic setting 750m from the Thirunelly Temple, this remote-feeling KTDC property is set on its own in the countryside, has large rooms

with verdant views, and is a good deal. There's a restaurant.

Haritagiri HOTEL $$
(☑04936-203145; www.hotelharitagiri.com; Kalpetta; s/d ₹900/1200, executive ₹1200/1600; ❄) Somewhat set away from Kalpetta's busy main streets, this is a reasonable, comfortable hotel, and some of the rooms, with lively orange, green and blue colour schemes, have good views across the town's greenery from their balconies.

PPS Tourist Home HOTEL $
(☑04936-203431; Kalpetta; s/d ₹440/550, deluxe d ₹670; ❄) This agreeable and friendly place in the middle of Kalpetta has budget rooms in a motel-like compound that are fairly clean and comfy. The helpful management can arrange trips around Wayanad (₹2000 per carload) and hikes up Chembra Peak (₹1000 plus permit fees, six hours).

Hotel Regency HOTEL $$
(☑04936-220512; www.issacsregency.com; Sultanbatheri; s/d/tr from ₹800/1200/1400, with AC from ₹1200/1600/1800; ❄) The pick of Sultanbatheri's bunch of hotels, this quiet and no-nonsense place has routine, large and relatively tidy rooms in a U-shaped building.

The deluxe rooms differ from the standard ones in price only.

ℹ Information

The somewhat disorganised **DTPC office** (📞04936-202134; www.dtpcwayanad.com; Kalpetta; ◷10am-5pm Mon-Sat) at Kalpetta can help organise tours, permits and trekking. There are UAE Exchange offices in Kalpetta and Sultanbatheri, and Federal Bank and Canara Bank ATMs can be found in each of the three main towns, as can a smattering of internet cafes.

ℹ Getting There & Around

Autorickshaw & Jeep

There are plenty of autorickshaws and jeeps for short trips within the towns.

Bus

Buses brave the winding roads between Calicut and Sultanbatheri (₹62/70 ordinary/Express, three hours), via Kalpetta (₹51), every 15 minutes. Private buses also run between Kannur and Mananthavadi every 45 minutes (₹62, 2½ hours). From Sultanbatheri, an 8am bus heads out for Ooty (₹56, four hours), with a second one passing through town at around 1pm. Buses for Mysore (₹78, three hours) leave every 30 minutes or so.

Plenty of private buses connect Mananthavadi, Kalpetta and Sultanbatheri every 10 to 20 minutes during daylight hours (₹14 to ₹22, 45 minutes to one hour). From Mananthavadi, regular buses also head to Tholpetty (₹14, one hour), Mysore (₹70, three hours, five buses) and Ooty (₹82, 5 to 6 hours, two daily). You can hire jeeps to get from one town to the next for around ₹400 to ₹600 each way.

Car hire

DTPC can help arrange car hire (from around ₹1700 per day).

Kannur (Cannanore)

📞0497 / POP 498,200

Under the Kolathiri rajas, Kannur was a major port bristling with international trade – explorer Marco Polo christened it a 'great emporium of spice trade'. Since then, the usual colonial suspects, including the Portuguese, Dutch and British, have had a go at exerting their influence on the region. Today it is an unexciting, though agreeable, town known mostly for its weaving industry and cashew trade, with some stunning, off-the-beaten track beaches nearby; bear in mind you can't swim during the monsoon season because of rough seas. This is a dominantly Muslim area, so local sensibilities should be kept in mind: wear a sarong over your bikini on the beach. It's also a great base for seeing incredible *theyyam* possession performances.

◉ Sights & Activities

Theyyam Rituals   CULTURAL PROGRAM
Kannur is the best place to see the spirit-possession ritual called *theyyam* (p976); on most nights of the year there should be a *theyyam* ritual on somewhere in the vicinity. The easiest way to find out is to contact Kurien at Costa Malabari guesthouse. Alternatively, you can visit the **Kerala Folklore Academy** (📞2778090), near Chirakkal Pond, Valapattanam, 20km north of Kannur, where you can see vibrantly coloured costumes up close and sometimes catch a performance.

FREE **St Angelo Fort**   FORT
(◷9am-6pm) The Portuguese built the St Angelo Fort in 1505 from brilliantly red laterite stone on a promontory a few kilometres south of town. It has a serene garden and excellent views of nearby palm-fringed beaches.

Loknath Weavers' Co-operative
          HANDICRAFTS
(📞2726330; ◷8.30am-5.30pm Mon-Sat) Established in 1955, this is one of the oldest co-operatives in Kannur and occupies a large building busily clicking with the sound of looms. You can stop by for a quick tour and visit the small shop here that displays the fruits of their labours. It's 4km south of Kannur.

Kerala Dinesh Beedi Co-Operative
          HANDICRAFTS
(📞2835280; ◷8am-5pm Tue-Sat) This region is also known for the manufacture of *beedis,* those tiny Indian cigarettes deftly rolled inside green leaves. This is one of the largest and purportedly best manufacturers, with a factory at Thottada, 7km south of Kannur. Either of these cooperatives is a ₹80 to ₹100 (return) autorickshaw ride from Kannur town.

Kairail   BOATING
(📞0460-2243460; barge hire per hr ₹1600) Kairail, 20km north of Kannur, offers rice-barge trips on the unspoilt northern Kerala backwaters; you can rent a barge by the hour but it's worth enquiring about day trips.

🛏 Sleeping & Eating

TOP CHOICE **Ezhara Beach House**   HOMESTAY **$$**
(☎0497-2835022; www.ezharabeachhouse.com; 7/347 Ezhara Kadappuram; r per person incl meals ₹1500; 🖅) Beside the unspoilt Kizhunna Ezhara beach, midway between Kannur and Telicherry railway stations (11km from each), hidden amongst palms alongside similar traditional Keralan houses, is the blue Ezhara Beach House, run by the magnificent, straight-talking Hyancinth. Rooms are simple and small, but the house has character and there's a brilliant terrace where you can sit and gaze out to sea through swaying palms and spot sea eagles swooping, plus wi-fi if you should want to keep in touch with the world.

Ayisha Manzil   HOMESTAY **$$**
(☎0490-2341590; Court Rd, Tellicherry; d incl meals & tax ₹9750) Around 25km south of Kannur is Ayisha Manzil, a lovely 1862 colonial-era building perched on a cliff top, with stunning sea views and faded, antique-decorated rooms, run by the perfect hosts, CP Moosa and his wife Faiza Moosa, who is a renowned cook and cookery teacher, spe-

---

TRADITIONAL KERALAN ARTS

Kathakali

The art form of Kathakali crystallised at around the same time as Shakespeare was scribbling his plays. The Kathakali performance is the dramatised presentation of a play, usually based on the Hindu epics the Ramayana, the Mahabharata and the Puranas. All the great themes are covered – righteousness and evil, frailty and courage, poverty and prosperity, war and peace.

Drummers and singers accompany the actors, who tell the story through their precise movements, particularly mudras (hand gestures) and facial expressions.

Preparation for the performance is lengthy and disciplined. Paint, fantastic costumes, ornamental headpieces and meditation transform the actors both physically and mentally into the gods, heroes and demons they are about to play.

You can see cut-down performances in tourist hot spots all over the state, and there are Kathakali schools in Trivandrum and near Thrissur that encourage visitors.

Kalarippayat

Kalarippayat is an ancient tradition of martial training and discipline, still taught throughout Kerala. Some believe it is the forerunner of all martial arts, with roots tracing back to the 12th-century skirmishes among Kerala's feudal principalities.

Masters of *kalarippayat,* called Gurukkal, teach their craft inside a special arena called a *kalari.*

Kalarippayat movements can be traced in Kerala's performing arts, such as Kathakali and *kootiattam,* and in ritual arts such as *theyyam.*

Theyyam

Kerala's most popular ritualistic art form, *theyyam,* is believed to pre-date Hinduism, originating from folk dances performed during harvest celebrations. An intensely local ritual, it's often performed in *kavus* (sacred groves) throughout northern Kerala.

Theyyam refers both to the shape of the deity/hero portrayed, and to the actual ritual. There are around 450 different *theyyams,* each with a distinct costume; face paint, bracelets, breastplates, skirts, garlands and especially headdresses are exuberant, intricately crafted and sometimes huge (up to 6m or 7m tall).

During performances, each protagonist loses his physical identity and speaks, moves and blesses the devotees as if he were that deity. Frenzied dancing and wild drumming create an atmosphere in which a deity indeed might, if it so desired, manifest itself in human form.

During October to May there are an annual rituals at each of the hundreds of *kavus*. *Theyyam*s are often held to bring good fortune to important events such as marriages and housewarmings. See p975 for details on how to find one.

cialising in Mopla cuisine (Keralan Islamic cooking). Pick up may be arranged.

Costa Malabari
GUESTHOUSE $$

(☏reservations 0484-2371761; touristdesk@saty am.net.in; Thottada Beach; r per person incl meals from ₹1250) In a small village and five minutes' walk from an idyllic beach, Costa Malabari pioneered tourism in this area with its spacious rooms in an old hand-loom factory, surrounded by lush greenery. There's a huge communal space and comfy lounging areas outside. Extra rooms are offered in two other buildings, the pick of which is perched dramatically just above the beach, where you fall asleep to the crashing of waves, and there are steps directly down to the beach. The home-cooked Keralan food is plentiful, varied, and delicious. Kurien, your gracious host, is an expert on the astonishing *theyyam* ritual and can help arrange a visit. It's 8km from Kannur town; a rickshaw/taxi from the train station is around ₹120/200.

Kannur Beach House
HOMESTAY $$

(☏0497-2708360, 9847184535; www.kannurbeach house.com; Thottada Beach; r ₹2200-2500) Near Costa Malabari and in an idyllic spot right behind the beach, the rooms in this traditional Keralan building are presentably furnished and boast handsome wooden shutters. Four rooms overlook the sea, with either a balcony or porch to enjoy the sensational ocean sunset views through swaying palms, and you can spot cuckoos and bramini kites in the nearby mangroves. It's 8km from Kannur.

Government Guest House
GUESTHOUSE $

(☏2706426; d ₹440; ✹) This place has the air of torpor that is the speciality of government-run hotels, but rooms in the 'new block' are enormous, simply furnished and sport balconies that look right onto the sea – they're phenomenal value.

Hotel Meridian Palace
HOTEL $

(☏2761676; www.hotelmeridianpalace.com; Bellard Rd; s from ₹200/250, d with AC ₹600-900) In the market area opposite the main train station, this is not quite a palace, but is friendly enough and offers a cornucopia of budget rooms. If you manage to decide on one, chances are it will be fairly clean, basic and convenient for an early train departure.

Mascot Beach Resort
HOTEL $$

(☏2708445; www.mascotresort.com; d with AC from ₹2200; ✹✹) A few hundred metres south of the Government Guest House, this place is a small, reasonable hotel and also has grand views of the ocean from its 30 neat and comfy AC rooms. It's worth angling for a discount.

ℹ Information

The **DTPC Office** (☏2706336; ⊗10am-5pm Mon-Sat), opposite the KSRTC bus stand, supplies basic maps of Kannur. There are Federal Bank and State Bank of India ATMs adjacent to the bus stand. A **UAE Exchange** (☏2709022; City Centre, Fort Rd; ⊗9.30am-6pm Mon-Sat, 11am-1pm Sun) office changes travellers cheques and cash; it's located in City Centre mall, five minutes from the train station.

ℹ Getting There & Away

There are daily buses to Mysore (₹164/188 ordinary/deluxe, eight hours, five daily), Mangalore (₹109, four hours, two daily), Ernakulam (₹187, eight hours, four daily), and Kalpetta (₹70, four hours, two daily) for Wayanad. There's one daily bus to Ooty (via Wayanad, ₹135, nine hours) at 10pm.

There are several daily trains to Mangalore (sleeper/3AC/2AC ₹100/218/301, three hours), Calicut (2nd class/AC chair ₹31/140, two hours) and Ernakulam (₹69/272, 6½ hours).

Bekal & Around
☏0467

Bekal and nearby Palakunnu and Udma, in Kerala's far north, have some long white-sand beaches begging for DIY exploration. The area is beginning to be colonised by glitzy, unreal five-star resorts catering to fresh-from-the-Gulf millionaires, but it's still worth the trip for off-the-beaten-track adventurers intent on discovering the beaches before they get swallowed up by developers with dollar-signs in their eyes. Because it's a predominantly Muslim area, it's important to keep local sensibilities in mind, especially at the beach.

The laterite-brick **Bekal Fort** (Indian/foreigner ₹5/100; ⊗8am-5pm), built between 1645 and 1660, sits on Bekal's rocky headland and houses a small Hindu temple and plenty of goats. Next door, **Bekal Beach** (admission ₹5) encompasses a grassy park and a long, beautiful stretch of sand that

WORTH A TRIP

VALIYAPARAMBA BACKWATERS

For those seeking to escape the burgeoning commercialism around Alleppey, what are often referred to as the northern backwaters offer an intriguing alternative. This large body of water is fed by five rivers and fringed by ludicrously green lands punctuated by rows of nodding palms. One of the nearest towns is **Payyanur**, 50km north of Kannur. It's possible to catch the ferry from Kotti, from where KSWTD operates local ferries to the surrounding islands. It's five minutes' walk from Payyanur railway station. The 2½-hour trip (₹9) from Kotti takes you to the **Ayitti Jetty** (0467-2213577), 8km from Payyanur; then catch the return ferry.

You can stay at the tiny **Valiyaparamba Retreat** (2371761; touristdesk@satyam.net. in; d full board ₹3000), a secluded place 15km north of Payyanur and 3km from Ayitti Jetty. It has two simple rooms and two stilted bungalows, fronted by an empty golden-sand beach and backed by backwaters. Kochi's Tourist Desk (contactable via the Retreat, or in Kochi, p964) also runs **day trips** (per person incl lunch ₹600) for groups of four to 15 people, on a traditional houseboat around the Valiyaparamba Backwaters.

Otherwise, 22km south of Bekal, **Bekal Boat Stay** (0467-2282633; www.bekal boatstay.com; Kottappuram, Nileshwar) is one of the few enterprises in the region to offer overnight **houseboat trips** (2-4 people per 24hr ₹7000-9500) around the Valiyaparamba backwaters. Cheaper sunset or day cruises are also available. You can also try Kairail (p975) near Kannur.

turns into a circus on weekends and holidays when local families descend here for rambunctious leisure time. Isolated **Kappil Beach**, 6km north of Bekal, is a beautiful, lonely stretch of fine sand and calm water, but beware of shifting sandbars.

There are lots of cheap, poor quality hotels scattered between Kanhangad (12km south) and Kasaragod (10km north), with a few notable exceptions that could work well as Bekal bases.

TOP CHOICE **Neeleshwar Hermitage** (0467-2288876; www.neeleshwarhermitage.com; Neeleshwar; r from ₹8000) consists of 16 fishermen's cottages that have been converted into a stand-out eco resort. Built according to the principles of Kerala Vastu, it has an infinity pool that gazes out to sea, nearly 5 hectares of lush gardens fragrant with frangipani, smashing organic food and little comforts like iPod docks.

Gitanjali Heritage (0467-2234159; www. gitanjaliheritage.com; s/d full-board ₹2500/3500) This lovely place lies surrounded by rice paddies, deep among Kasaragod's inland villages. It is just 5km from Bekal and is an intimate heritage home with comfortable, higgledy-piggledy rooms filled with ancestral furniture and polished wood. Call ahead for pick-ups.

ℹ Getting There & Around

A couple of local trains stop at Fort Bekal station, right on Bekal beach. Kanhangad, 12km south, is a major train stop, while Kasaragod, 10km to the north, is the largest town in the area. Both Kanhangad and Kasaragod have frequent buses running to and from Bekal (around ₹10, 20 minutes). An autorickshaw from Bekal Junction to Kappil beach is around ₹40.

LAKSHADWEEP

POP 60,700

Comprising a string of 36 palm-covered, white sand-skirted coral islands 300km off the coast of Kerala, Lakshadweep is as stunning as it is isolated. Only 10 of these islands are inhabited, mostly with Sunni Muslim fishermen, and foreigners are only allowed to stay on a few of these. With fishing and coir production the main sources of income, local life on the islands remains highly traditional, and a caste system divides the islanders between Koya (land owners), Malmi (sailors) and Melachery (farmers).

The real attraction of the islands lies under the water: the 4200 sq km of pristine archipelago lagoons, unspoiled coral reefs and warm waters are a magnet for flipper-toting travellers and divers alike. Diving, snorkelling, kayaking, boat trips, sailing and jaunts to nearby islands can be arranged by most resorts. At the time of research, the resort on the 20-hectare, white-sand-fringed Bangaram island was closed – enquire locally to find out if it's reopened.

Lakshadweep can only be visited on a prearranged package trip – all listed accommodation prices are for the peak October to May season and include permits and meals.

ℹ Information

SPORTS (Society for the Promotion of Recreational Tourism & Sports; ☎0484-2668387; www.lakshadweeptourism.com; IG Rd, Willingdon Island; ⊙10am-5pm Mon-Sat) is the main organisation for tourist information.

PERMITS Foreigners are limited to staying in the resorts, none of which are budget places; a special permit (one month's notice) is required and organised by tour operators, hotels or SPORTS in Kochi. Most of the islands have only recently been opened up to foreigners, who are now allowed to stay on Bangaram, Agatti, Kadmat, Minicoy and Kavaratti Islands.

ℹ Getting There & Away

Kingfisher Airlines (www.flyingkingfisher.com) flies regularly between Kochi and Agatti Island (₹9700 return). At the time of research, there were no ferry services between Agatti and Bangaram. Boat transport between Agatti and Kadmat is included in the package tours available, and the same goes for transport from Kochi to Kadmat and the Mincoy Islands. See the package section of www.lakshwdeeptourism.com for more details.

Agatti Island

The village located on this 2.7-sq-km island has several **mosques**, which you can visit if dressed modestly. There's no alcohol on the island.

Agatti Island Beach Resort (☎0484-2362232; www.agattiislandresorts.com; d full board €155, with AC €210; ❄) sits on two beaches at the southern tip of the island and offers a range of packages. The resort has simple, low-rise beach cottages, designed to be comfortably cool without AC, and a restaurant for 20 people.

Kadmat Island

Kadmat Beach Resort (☎0484-4011134; www.kadmat.com; d from €185 per person; ❄) has 28 modern cottages, administered by Mint Valley (www.mintvalley.com) and can be reached by overnight boat from Kochi (p952).

Lakshadweep

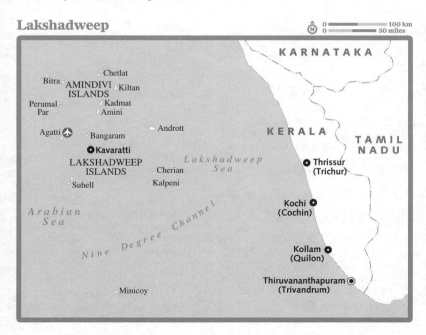

ⓝ 0 ⸻ 100 km
0 ⸻ 50 miles

KARNATAKA

Chetlat
Bitra
AMINDIVI ISLANDS Kiltan
Perumal Kadmat
Par Amini
Agatti ✈ Andrott
Bangaram **KERALA** **TAMIL NADU**
● Kavaratti
LAKSHADWEEP *Lakshadweep*
ISLANDS Cherian *Sea* ● Thrissur (Trichur)
Suhell Kalpeni

Arabian Sea Kochi ● (Cochin)

Nine Degree Channel

Kollam ● (Quilon)

Thiruvananthapuram ◉ (Trivandrum)

Minicoy

DIVING

Lakshadweep is a diver's dream, with excellent visibility and an embarrassment of marine life living on undisturbed coral reefs. The best time to dive is between mid-October and mid-May when the seas are calm and visibility is 20m to 40m.

Lacadives (☑022-66627381; www.lacadives.com) runs dive centres on Bangaram and Kadmat Islands. Costs can vary: a four-day PADI open-water course costs ₹28,000, while experienced divers pay ₹3000 per dive (including equipment hire), with discounts available for multiple dives. Information is available through the hotels or directly through Lacadives at 14C Bungalow, Boran Rd, Opposite Elco Market, Off Hill Rd, Bandra (W), Mumbai.

From Kadmat Island, dives range from 9m to 40m in depth. Some of the better sites include North Cave, the Wall, Jack Point, Shark Alley, the Potato Patch, Cross Currents and Sting Ray City. Around Bangaram good spots include the 32m-deep wreck of the *Princess Royale*, Manta Point, Life, Grand Canyon and the impressive sunken reef at Perumal Par.

Minicoy Island

You can stay on the remote island of Minicoy, the second largest island and the closest to the Maldives, in modern cottages or a 20-room guesthouse at Minicoy Island Resort (☑0484-2668387; www.lakshadweeptourism.com; s/d ₹3000/4000, with AC ₹5000/6000; ✱) via SPORTS Swaying Palms and Coral Reef Packages.

Tamil Nadu & Chennai

Best Places to Eat

» Any branch of Hotel
Saravana Bhavan (p994)

» Bangala (p1034)

» Satsanga (p1018)

Best Places to Stay

» Calve (p1015)

» Visalam (p1034)

» 180 McIver (p1051)

» Carlton Hotel (p1045)

Why Go?

Tamil Nadu is the homeland of one of humanity's living classical civilisations, a people whose culture has grown, but in many ways not fundamentally altered, since the Greeks sacrificed goats to Zeus.

But this state is as dynamic as it is drenched in history. In Tamil Nadu's famous temples, fire-worshipping devotees smear tikka on their brows before heading to IT offices to develop new software applications. Tamil Nadu has one foot in the 21st century and the other in the poetry of one of the oldest literary languages on Earth.

Here you can reach the ends of India, where three oceans mingle. See the tiger-prowled hills of the Nilgiris, the Mother Temple of the triple-breasted, fish-eyed goddess and the Mountain of Fire, where god manifests as a pillar of flame. It's all packed into a state that manages to remain fiercely distinct from the rest of India, while exemplifying her oldest and most adventurous edges.

When to Go
Chennai

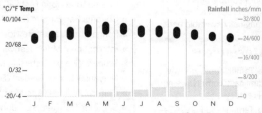

Jan Pongal (harvest festival) celebrations spill into the streets.

May Head to the hill stations for the summer 'season'.

Nov The full-moon festival of lights.

MAIN POINTS OF ENTRY

Chennai Airport will be your probable point of entry if you're flying into Tamil Nadu from overseas, although Trichy and Coimbatore have (limited) international services. From inside India, there are domestic airports at Chennai, Trichy, Coimbatore and Madurai; these four cities are also the state's major train junctions.

Fast Facts

» Population: 72.1 million

» Area: 130,058 sq km

» Capital: Chennai (Madras)

» Main language: Tamil

» Sleeping prices: **$** below ₹1000, **$$** ₹1000 to ₹3000, **$$$** above ₹3000

Top Tip

If you need train tickets in a hurry, the Foreign Tourist Assistance Cell at Chennai Central (p999) is the most helpful and efficient we've ever come across; tickets for booked-up trains anywhere in India seem to become magically available here.

Resources

» TamilNadu.Com (www.tamilnadu.com) News and directory.

» Tamil Nadu Forest Department (www.forests.tn.nic.in) National parks, ecotourism and permit information.

» Tamil Nadu Tourism (www.tamilnadutourism.org)

Food

Tamil Nadu's favourite foods are overwhelmingly vegetarian, with lots of coconut and chilli. No matter where you go you'll find dosas, *idlis* (spongy, round fermented rice cakes) and *vada* (deep-fried lentil-flour doughnuts), all of which are always served with coconut chutney and *sambar* (lentil broth). These will sometimes be your only options, and luckily they're very, very tasty (though you want to eat your *idlis* fresh and warm) – and they're generally vegan friendly, too. Thalis – all-you-can-eat meals based around rice, lentil dishes, *rasam* (hot and sour tamarind soup) and chutneys, often served on a banana leaf – are also good, ubiquitous, cheap and filling.

The exception to the all-veg diet is Chettinad food, derived from food traditionally prepared in the southern region around Pudukkottai and Karaikkudi but available at restaurants in most of the bigger towns. Chettinad menus often feature mutton, chicken and fish; it's less fiery and more about the use of fresh spices like cinammon, cumin and star anise. Pepper Chicken is a classic Chettinad dish.

For a state that grows a lot of tea, Tamil Nadu really loves its coffee; filtered coffee (mixed with milk and sugar, of course) is more readily available than tea in many cheap thali joints.

DON'T MISS

Escape from the heat of the plains by taking the **toy train** from Mettapulayam up into the Nilgiri hills; the tracks cut through tropical palms and paddy fields, then through green, monkey-infested jungles, crosses bridges over gushing streams and finally chugs through European-looking forest into the cool of Ooty.

You can't come to Tamil Nadu without admiring its ancient **temples**; see p1023 for a selection with the most stunning architecture, rituals and festivals.

Top State Festivals

» International Yoga Festival (4-7 Jan, Puducherry, p1015)

» Chennai Sangamam (mid-Jan, Chennai, p992)

» Pongal (mid-Jan, statewide, p984) Harvest festival.

» International Music festival (Jan, Thiruvaiyaru, p1027)

» Teppam (Float) Festival (Jan/Feb, Madurai, p1037)

» Natyanjali Dance Festival (Feb/Mar, Chidambaram, p1022)

» Chithrai Festival (Apr/May, Madurai, p1037)

» Summer festivals (May-Jun, statewide, p984)

» Bastille Day (14 Jul, Puducherry, p1015)

» Karthikai Deepam Festival (Nov/Dec, statewide, p984)

» Chennai Festival of Music & Dance (mid-Dec–mid-Jan, Chennai, p992)

» Mamallapuram Dance Festival (Dec-Jan, Mamallapuram, p1006)

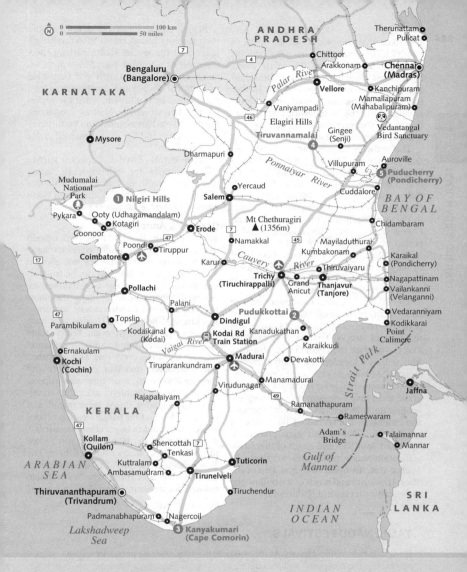

Tamil Nadu Highlights

1 Climb into the cool of the **Western Ghats** (p1044)

2 Spend the night in a Chettiar mansion in **Pudukkottai district** (p1033)

3 Watch the sun set over three oceans at once in **Kanyakumari** (p1041)

4 See god manifest as a lingam of fire in **Tiruvannamalai** (p1012)

5 Explore the Gallic roots of **Puducherry** (Pondicherry; p1014)

History

It's ironic that the bearers of the torch of South Indian identity may have their origins in Punjab and Pakistan. The early Indus civilisations display elements of Dravidian thought, language, culture and art, including a meditating god seated in the lotus position. This may be the world's first depiction of the yogi archetype, who has come to symbolise, for many, Asian spirituality.

The nomadic Aryans drove the Dravidians south around 1500 BC. Here, a classical language and classical civilisations developed, cushioned by geography against North Indian invasion. By 300 BC the region was controlled by three major dynasties – Cholas in the east, Pandyas in the central area and Cheras in the west. This was the classical period of Tamil literature and myth – the Sangam Age – when kingdoms were ruled by feuding poet-kings and romantic epics; a visitor at the time described the Tamils as favouring rose petals over gold.

The Tamils developed their own aesthetic style, constructing huge cities that rivalled population centres in China and Europe, and magnificent steeped temples that wouldn't look out of place in Mayan Central America. Although each kingdom left notable achievements, the Cholas deserve some special mention. This remarkable nation maintained one of the great maritime empires of history, extending its influence to Cambodia, Vietnam and Indonesia, and spreading Tamil ideas of reincarnation, karma and yogic practice to Southeast Asia. The end result of this cross-pollination was architectural wonders like Angkor Wat, the intellectual gestation of Balinese Hinduism and much of the philosophy associated with classical Buddhism.

Before the Mughals could fully extend their reach to India's tip, in 1640 the British negotiated the use of Madraspatnam (now Chennai) as a trading post. Subsequent interest by the French, Dutch and Danes led to continual conflict and, finally, almost total domination by the British, when the region became known as the Madras Presidency. Small pocketed areas, including Puducherry (Pondicherry) and Karaikal, remained under French control.

Many Tamils played a significant part in India's struggle for independence, which was finally won in 1947. In 1956 the Madras Presidency was disbanded and Tamil Nadu was established as an autonomous state.

Dangers & Annoyances

The big draw in Tamil Nadu is the 5000-odd temples, but this is a very religious state, and non-Hindus are generally not allowed inside inner sanctums. This can be frustrating, as large areas of the best temples are essentially inaccessible to many travellers. Even nonresident Indians can be subject to scrutiny, and non-Indian Hindus may have to provide proof of conversion. Temple touts are fairly common and can be a nuisance, but don't dismiss every one as a scammer. There are many excellent guides here and they deserve both your time and rupees; use your best judgement, ask other travellers which guides they'd recommend and be on the lookout for badge-wearing official guides, who tend to be excellent resources.

Don't expect the Hindi slang you picked up in Rishikesh to go over well here. The Tamils are fiercely proud of their language and some consider Hindi to be North Indian cultural imperialism. North Indian tourists

---

TAMIL NADU FESTIVALS

Pongal is held in mid-January. As the rice boils over the new clay pots, this festival symbolises the prosperity and abundance a fruitful harvest brings. For many, the celebrations begin with temple rituals, followed by family gatherings. Later it's the animals, especially cows, that are honoured for their contribution to the harvest.

Summer festivals are held from May through June throughout the hills, but especially in Ooty and Kodaikanal, where there are boat races on the lake, horse racing (in Ooty), flower shows and music.

Held during full moon in November/December, the **Karthikai Deepam Festival** (Nov/Dec; statewide) is Tamil Nadu's 'festival of lights'. It is celebrated throughout the state with earthenware lamps and firecrackers, but the best place to see it is Tiruvannamalai (see boxed text, p1012), where the legend began.

Many other temple-centred festivals are held in towns around the state; see p982 for a rundown and individual town sections for details.

are often as confused as you are down here; more Tamils speak English than Hindi.

ⓘ Information

The state tourism body is **Tamil Nadu Tourism** (www.tamilnadutourism.org), which runs tourist offices of varying degrees of uselessness in most cities and large towns, plus a reliably average chain of hotels. You can also check www.tamilnadu-tourism.com for package-tour options. Accommodation costing more than ₹200 in Tamil Nadu (but not Puducherry) is subject to a government 'luxury' tax – 5% on rooms between ₹200 and ₹500, 10% on rooms between ₹501 and ₹1000, and 12.5% on rooms over ₹1000. There's often an additional 'service tax' at upmarket hotels. Prices throughout this chapter do not include tax, unless stated otherwise.

CHENNAI (MADRAS)

☏044 / POP 6.6 MILLION

Chennai doesn't always make a good first impression. The streets are clogged with traffic, the weather is oppressively hot, the air is heavy with smog and sights of any great interest are thin on the ground.

The city's charm lies in its inhabitants; the enthusiasm of Chennaites for their hometown starts to infect you after a while, and they're friendlier and more down to earth than most big-city dwellers. Chennai is so chilled out you wouldn't even know it's an economic powerhouse, much less a queen of showbiz: India's fourth-largest city is its most humble.

The major transport hub of the region, this 70-sq-km city is a conglomerate of urban villages connected by a maze of roads ruled by hard-line rickshaw drivers. Its central location and excellent plane, train and bus connections actually make it an interesting alternative entry point into India. If you do happen to be caught here between connections, it's certainly worth your while poking around the markets of George Town or taking a sunset stroll along pretty Marina Beach.

Bordered on the east by the Bay of Bengal, Chennai is a sprawling combination of several small districts. George Town, a jumble of narrow streets, bazaars and the court buildings, is in the north, near the harbour. To the southwest is the major thoroughfare of Anna Salai (Mount Rd) and the two main train stations: Egmore, for destinations in Tamil Nadu, and Central, for interstate trains.

History

Chennai and surrounds have been attracting seafaring traders for centuries. As long as 2000 years ago, its residents traded and haggled with Chinese, Greek, Phoenician, Roman and Babylonian merchants. The Portuguese and the Dutch muscled in on this lucrative trade in the 16th century. The British, initially content to purchase spices and other goods from the Dutch, soon had enough of that and in 1639 established a settlement in the fishing village of Madraspatnam. The British East India Company erected Fort St George in 1653.

By the 18th century, the British East India Company had to contend with the French. Robert Clive (Clive of India), a key player in the British campaign, recruited an army of 2000 sepoys (Indian soldiers in British service) and launched a series of military expeditions that developed into the Carnatic Wars. Facing defeat, the French withdrew to Pondicherry (now Puducherry) in 1756.

In the 19th century, the city became the seat of the Madras Presidency, one of the four divisions of British Imperial India. After Independence, growth continued until the city became the significant southern gateway it is today.

Dangers & Annoyances

Convincing a Chennai autorickshaw driver to use the meter is a Vatican-certified miracle; fares border on the astronomical; and post-arrival disputes over pre-agreed fares are not uncommon. Avoid paying up front, and never get into an autorickshaw before reaching an agreement.

Tempting offers of ₹50 'tours' of the city sound too good to be true. They are. Expect to spend the day being dragged from one shop or emporium to another. Some travellers report negotiating cheap fares by agreeing to visit 'just one shop'.

If you have a serious problem with a driver, mentioning a call to the traffic police (☏103) can defuse the conflict. See p1000 for details on other modes of transport.

⊙ Sights

EGMORE & CENTRAL CHENNAI

Government Museum   MUSEUM
(Map p990; www.chennaimuseum.org; 486 Pantheon Rd, Egmore; Indian/foreigner ₹15/250, camera/video ₹200/500; ⊙9.30am-5pm Sat-Thu) Housed across several British-built buildings known as the Pantheon Complex, this excellent museum is Chennai's best.

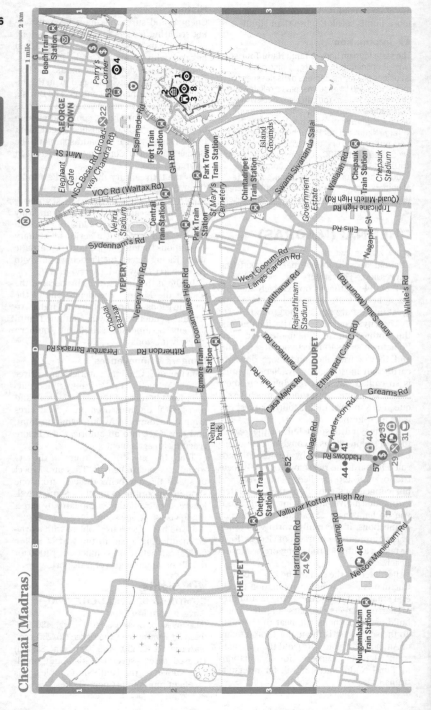

Chennai (Madras)

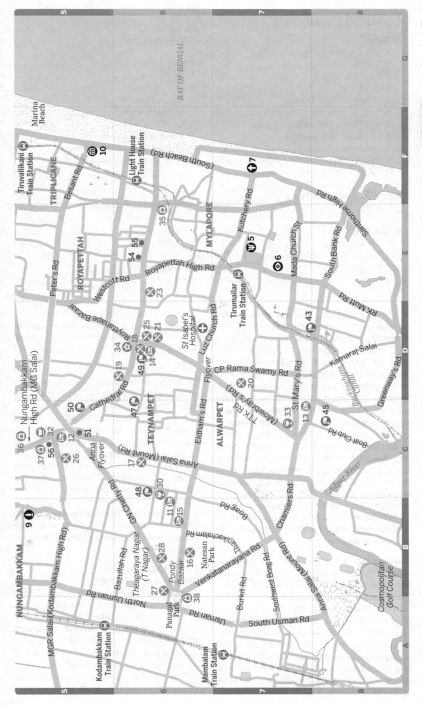

The main building has a respectable **archaeological section** representing all the major South Indian periods, including Chola, Vijayanagar, Hoysala and Chalukya. Don't miss the intricate marble reliefs on display from Amaravathi temple in Andhra Pradesh, or the poignant *sati* stones commemorating women who burned on their husbands' funeral pyres. Further along is a **natural history and zoology** section with a motley collection of skeletons and stuffed birds and animals.

In Gallery 3, the **bronze gallery** has a superb and beautifully presented collection of Chola art. Among the impressive pieces is the bronze of Ardhanariswara, the androgynous incarnation of Shiva and Parvati.

The same ticket gets you into the **National Art Gallery**, the **children's museum** and a small **modern art gallery**, all located in the same complex.

Valluvar Kottam   MONUMENT
(Map p986; Valluvar Kottam High Rd, Kodambakkam; adult/child ₹3/2; ◉8am-6pm) This memorial honours the Tamil poet Thiruvalluvar and his classic work, the *Thirukural*. A weaver by trade, Thiruvalluvar lived around the 1st century BC in what is present-day Chennai and wrote this famed poem, providing a moral code for millions of followers. The three-level memorial replicates ancient Tamil architecture and boasts an immense 35m chariot, as well as an enormous auditorium and inscriptions of the *Thirukural*'s 1330 couplets. It has been closed sporadically for renovation work but this should be completed by the time you read this.

Vivekanandar Illam   MUSEUM
(Map p986; www.sriramakrishnamath.org; South Beach Rd; adult/child ₹2/1; ◉10am-noon & 3-7pm Thu-Tue) The Vivekananda House is interesting not only for the displays on the famous 'wandering monk', but also for the semicircular structure in which it's housed. Swami Vivekananda stayed here briefly in 1897 and preached his ascetic philosophy to adoring crowds. The museum houses a collection of photographs and memorabilia from the swami's life, a gallery of religious historical paintings and the 'meditation room' where Vivekananda stayed. Free one-hour meditation classes are held on Wednesday nights at 7pm (over-15s only).

SOUTH CHENNAI

Kapaleeshwarar Temple   HINDU TEMPLE
(Map p986; Kutchery Rd, Mylapore; ◉5am-12.30pm & 4-10pm) Chennai's most active and impressive temple, the ancient Shiva Kapaleeshwarar Temple was rebuilt 300 years ago; some inscriptions from the older temple remain. It is constructed in the Dravidian style and displays the architectural elements – rainbow-coloured *gopuram* (gateway tower), *mandapams* (pavilions in front of a

TAMIL NADU & CHENNAI CHENNAI (MADRAS)

temple) and a huge tank – found in the famous temple cities of Tamil Nadu.

Ramakrishna Mutt Temple HINDU TEMPLE
(Map p986; RK Mutt Rd; 4.30-11.45am & 3-9pm, puja 8am) The tranquil, leafy grounds of the Ramakrishna Mutt Temple are a world away from the chaos and crazy rickshaw drivers outside. Monks glide around and there's a reverential feel here. The temple itself is a handsome shrine incorporating aspects of Hindu, Christian and Islamic styles; like the Belur Math in Kolkata, it's surprisingly architecturally coherent. It's open to followers of any faith for meditation.

San Thome Cathedral CHURCH
(Map p986; Kamarajar Salai) Originally built by the Portuguese in 1504, then rebuilt in neo-Gothic style in 1893, San Thome Cathedral is a soaring Roman Catholic church between Kapaleeshwarar Temple and Marina Beach. In the basement is a modern chapel housing the tomb of St Thomas the Apostle (Doubting Thomas), who it is said brought Christianity to the subcontinent in the 1st century; above is a museum containing Thomas-related artefacts of varying degrees of historical dubiousness.

Marina Beach BEACH
Take an early-morning or evening stroll (you really don't want to fry here at any other time) along the 13km sandy stretch of Marina Beach (Map p986) and you'll pass cricket matches, flying kites, fortune-tellers, fish markets and families enjoying the sea breeze. This beach was especially hard hit by the 2004 tsunami, with around 200 recorded casualties, most of them children. Don't swim here – strong rips make it dangerous.

Theosophical Society GARDEN, HISTORIC SITE
(Map p986; Lattice Bridge Rd; 8.30-10am & 2-4pm Mon-Sat) Between the Adyar River and the coast, the 100 hectares of the Theosophical Society provide a green and peaceful retreat from the city. It's a lovely spot to just wander; the sprawling grounds contain a church, mosque, Buddhist shrine and Hindu temple. There's a huge variety of native and introduced trees, including a famed 400-year-old **banyan tree** whose branches offer reprieving shade for over 40,000 sq ft. The **Adyar Library** (9am-4.30pm) here has an immense collection of books on religion and philosophy, some of which are on display, from thousand-year-old Buddhist scrolls to intricate, handmade 19th-century bibles.

GEORGE TOWN
Fort St George HISTORICAL BUILDING, MUSEUM
(Map p986; 8am-5pm) Finished around 1653 by the British East India Company, the fort has undergone many facelifts over the years. Inside the vast perimeter walls is now a precinct housing the **Secretariat &**

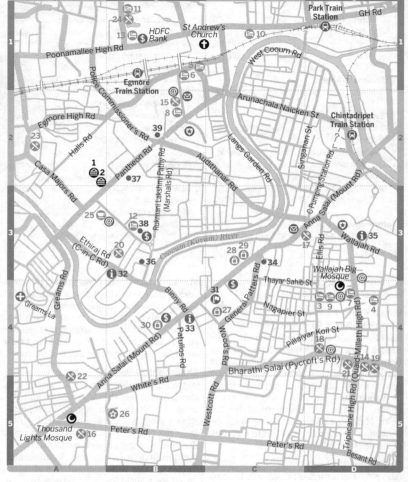

Legislative Assembly. The 46m-high **flagstaff** at the main entrance is a mast salvaged from a 17th-century shipwreck.

The **Fort Museum** (Indian/foreigner ₹5/100, video ₹25; ⏰8am-5pm) has some interesting military memorabilia from the British and French East India Companies, as well as the Raj and Muslim administrations. Fascinating 18th-century etchings show European-looking families being rowed to shore from their ships by *lunghi*-clad fishermen who look just like their modern-day counterparts on the beach across the street.

High Court   HISTORICAL BUILDING
Built in 1892, this red Indo-Saracenic structure (Map p986)at Parry's Corner is said to be the largest judicial building in the world after the Courts of London. You can wander around the court buildings and sit in on sessions.

OTHER SIGHTS

Little Mount & St Thomas Mount   SHRINE
It is believed that from around AD 58, St Thomas lived in hiding at **Little Mount** (Chinnamalai). The cave still bears what some believe to be Thomas' handprint, left when he escaped through an opening that

miraculously appeared. You may be offered water drawn up from the St Thomas miracle spring. Three kilometres on, **St Thomas Mount** (Parangi Malai) is thought to be the site of Thomas' martyrdom in AD 72. The shrine supposedly contains a fragment of Thomas' bone and a cross he carved, among other relics; the views across the city from here are wonderful. Both mounts are about 1km from the Saidapet and St Thomas Mount train stations, respectively.

🏃 Activities

Go for a 45-minute *abhyangam* (oil treatment; ₹750) or an extended ayurvedic treatment at **Amrit** (Map p986; ☑65195195; amrit.chennai@gmail.com; 6 Khader Nawaz Khan Rd, Nungambakkam; ⊙7am-7pm). It also offers one-hour yoga classes (₹200) or month-long courses (₹1200).

Courses

International Institute of Tamil Studies   LANGUAGE
(☑22542781; www.ulakaththamizh.org; Central Polytechnic Campus, Adyar) Runs intensive one-month and three-month courses in Tamil. It also sells an instructional CD of Tamil lessons, available through the website.

Vivekanandar Illam   MEDITATION
(Map p986; ☑28446188; Kamarajar Salai, Triplicane) Free one-hour meditation classes (over-15s only) on Wednesday nights at 7pm.

👉 Tours

TTDC (Map p990; ☑25367850; www.tamilnadu tourism.org; 2 Wallajah Rd, Triplicane; ⊙10am-5.30pm Mon-Fri) conducts half-day city tours (non-AC/AC ₹140/200) and day trips to

DEFINING DRAVIDIANS

The Tamils consider themselves the standard bearers of Dravidian – pre-Aryan Indian – civilisation. Their culture, language and history are distinctive from North India (although more related than some Tamil nationalists claim), and their ability to trace Tamil identity to classical antiquity is a source of considerable pride.

During the Indus Valley period (2600-1900 BC), the nomadic Aryans drove the city-dwelling Dravidians south while incorporating elements of the latter's beliefs into their holy texts, the Vedas. Later, south–north and class tensions were encouraged by the British, who used these strains to facilitate divide-and-conquer policies.

Ever since Indian independence in 1947, Tamil politicians have railed against caste (which they see as favouring light-skinned Brahmins) and Hindi (as unrelated to Tamil as Russian). The post-independence 'Self Respect' movement, influenced by Marxism, mixed South Indian communal values with class warfare rhetoric and spawned Dravidian political parties that remain major regional powers today.

Many Tamil politicians loudly defend the Tamil Tigers, the same organisation that assassinated Rajiv Gandhi in 1991 (imagine a viable, sitting opposition party in your country openly supporting a group that killed your president or prime minister to get an idea of how separate some Tamil parties still consider themselves from India), and there is an unfortunate prejudice among the generally tolerant Tamils towards anything Sinhalese. Throughout the state, male politicians don a white shirt and white *mundu* (sarong), the official uniform of Tamil pride.

Mamallapuram (₹385/550), Puducherry (₹500/750) and Tirupathi (AC ₹915/1135). Every full moon there's an overnight pilgrimage trip to Tiruvannamalai (₹385/630).

Storytrails (☑9600080215, 42124214; www.storytrails.in) runs highly recommended neighbourhood walking tours based around themes such as dance, jewellery and bazaars, as well as tours specially aimed at children.

The classic Enfield Bullet motorcycle has been manufactured in India since 1955 and remains in production today at the **Enfield Factory** (☑42230208; www.royalenfield.com; Tiruvottiyur), 17km out of Chennai. Tours (₹600) run on Saturday from 10am to noon.

★ Festivals & Events

Chennai Festival of Music & Dance　　　MUSIC, DANCE
(mid-Dec–mid-Jan) One of the largest of its type in the world, this festival is a celebration of Tamil music and dance.

Chennai Sangamam　　　ARTS
(mid-Jan; www.chennaisangamam.com) Arts and culture festival held in venues around the city, coinciding with the statewide Pongol festival.

🛏 Sleeping

Hotels in Chennai are pricier than in the rest of Tamil Nadu and don't as a rule offer much bang for your buck.

The Triplicane High Rd area is best for budget accommodation. There are some cheapies in Kennet Lane in Egmore, and Egmore is also where you'll find the majority of midrange sleeping options, while the top-end hotels lie further out in leafy, southwest Chennai.

Top-end hotels have central AC and multicuisine restaurants and bars, and they accept credit cards. Note that many hotels in Chennai fill up by noon.

EGMORE

TOP CHOICE **Hotel Chandra Park**　　　HOTEL $
(Map p990; ☑28191177; info@hotelchandrapark. com; 9 Gandhi Irwin Rd; s/d with AC incl breakfast from ₹899/999; ❄) How do they do it? Prices keep rising around Chennai but Chandra Park's prices remain mysteriously low. Standard rooms are small but have clean towels and tight, white sheets. Throw in a decent bar, a hearty buffet breakfast and classy front lobby, and this place offers superb value by Chennai standards.

YWCA International Guest House　　　GUESTHOUSE $
(Map p990; ☑25324234; ywcaigh@indiainfo. com; Poonamallee High Rd; s/d incl breakfast from ₹700/900; ❄@) Set around sprawling, green and shady grounds right near the Egmore train station, the YWCA manages to offer up healthy doses of hush. There's a slight atmo-

sphere of colonial missionary guesthouse (in a good way), and the rooms adhere to the most demanding levels of cleanliness. It's worth booking in for home-style buffet lunch and/or dinner in the pleasant dining room (₹150/225 for veg/nonveg).

Fortel
HOTEL $$$

(Map p990; ✆30242424; info@cischennai.in; 3 Gandhi Irwin Rd; s/d incl breakfast from ₹3500/4000; ✳) Right opposite Egmore train station and remarkably quiet for it, the Fortel is cool and stylish in a dark wood-and-white-walls way, with comfy cushion-laden beds and two good restaurants.

Vestin Park
HOTEL $$$

(Map p990; ✆28527171; vestinpark@vsnl.com; 39 Montieth Rd; s/d incl breakfast from ₹2800/3300; ✳@) More charming on the outside than in, this corporate-feeling hotel has the kind of bland, reliably clean and comfortable rooms you'd expect at this price. The real draws are the excellent ₹348 lunch and dinner buffet at the Splendour restaurant, and the fast and free internet.

Masa
HOTEL $

(Map p990; ✆28193344; 15/1 Kennet Lane; r from ₹460; ✳) The once-grotty Masa has built new budget rooms that were still reasonably fresh at the time of research; the old Masa rooms next door are now called Hotel Regal, where you can usually find a fairly grim room (singles/doubles ₹340/420) if all other places are full (as they often are).

Salvation Army Red Shield Guest House
HOSTEL $

(Map p990; ✆25321821; 15 Ritherdon Rd; dm ₹100-150, d ₹300-350) This cheapie lies in a quiet spot north of Egmore train station. It's dingy and grim, believe us, but it's probably the safest sleep in town if you're genuinely down to your last ₹100, and the sheets ain't too bad. Checkout is 9am, and booking ahead *doesn't* guarantee there'll be a bed for you when you arrive.

Royal Regency
HOTEL $$

(Map p990; ✆25611777; www.regencygrou101ch .com; 26-27 Poonamallee High Rd; s/d from ₹2300/2600; ✳🛜) Smack-bang between Central and Egmore train stations. By no means the best-value hotel in Chennai, but if you want AC and wi-fi near the train station, it's clean and friendly if a tad battered.

TRIPLICANE

Cristal Guest House
HOTEL $

(Map p990; ✆28513011; 34 CNK Rd; r from ₹250) In a modern building adhering to the white-tile-on-every-surface school of interior design, the clean abodes here win our 'cheapest rooms in Chennai' award (second edition in a row!).

Broad Lands Lodge
HOTEL $

(Map p990; ✆28545573; broadlandshotel@yahoo .com; 18 Vallabha Agraharam St; r ₹350-600) At this old-school favourite of the dreadlocked brigade, rooms (some much fresher than others) are scattered through a creaky, peeling, colonial-era building that has a certain faint charm. Visitors don't seem to mind the bare-bone, idiosyncratic rooms, the plain concrete floors or the dank shared bathrooms – perhaps the leafy, subdued courtyards and happy communal vibe trumps these shortcomings.

Paradise Guest House
HOTEL $

(Map p990; ✆28594252; paradisegh@hotmail. com; 17 Vallabha Agraharam St; d from ₹400; ✳) Travellers agree that the Paradise boasts some of the best-value digs on this street. Expect simple rooms with clean tiles, a breezy rooftop, friendly staff and hot water by the steaming bucket.

Hotel Comfort
HOTEL $$

(Map p990; ✆28587661; reservations@hotel comfortonline.com; 22 Vallabha Agraharam St; s/d from ₹1000/1200; ✳) Clean, fresh, smallish rooms with flat-screen TVs and bright-orange bathrooms. Perfectly comfy.

TRADITIONAL TRADERS

George Town, the area that grew around the fort, retains much of its original flavour. This is the wholesale centre of Chennai (Madras). Many backstreets, bordered by NSC Bose Rd, Krishna Koil St, Mint St and Rajaji Salai, are entirely given over to selling one particular type of merchandise as they have for hundreds of years – paper goods in Anderson St, fireworks in Badrian St and so on. Even if you're not in the market for anything, wander the maze-like streets to see another aspect of Indian life flowing seamlessly from the past into the present.

SOUTH CHENNAI

TOP CHOICE The Lotus   HOTEL $$

(Map p986; ☎28157272; www.thelotus.inn; 15 Venkatraman St, T Nagar; s/d incl breakfast from ₹2000/2700; ❄☎) An absolute gem, the Lotus offers a quiet setting away from the main roads, a great veg restaurant, and fresh, stylish, sparkling rooms with wood floors and cheerful decor. There are good deals if you stay for a while, and if you want a kitchen nook with gadgets ahoy, the ₹3800 suite is excellent value.

Residency Towers   HOTEL $$

(Map p986; ☎28156363; www.theresidency.com; Sir Theagaraya Nagar Rd, T Nagar; s/d incl breakfast from ₹5200/5700; ❄@☎⛱) At this price, it's like Residency Towers doesn't know what a good thing it has going: five-star elegance with personality. Every floor is decorated differently, but rooms all have sliding doors in front of windows to block out light and noise, dark-wood furniture and thoughtful touches. Wi-fi is free.

Park Hotel   BOUTIQUE HOTEL $$$

(Map p986; ☎42676000; www.theparkhotels.com; 601 Anna Salai; s/d from ₹10,500/11,500; ❄@☎) We love this uberchic boutique hotel, which flaunts stylish elements like framed old Bollywood posters, towering indoor bamboo gardens and oversized doors. The rooms are petite but have lovely lush bedding, and all the mod cons, including funky bathrooms separated from the boudoir by an opaque glass wall. It's all pretty swish, and as a bonus the pricier rooms include airport pick-up and drop-off.

Raintree   HOTEL $$$

(Map p986; ☎24304050; www.raintreehotels.com; 120 St Mary's Rd, Mylapore; r from ₹8500; ❄@⛱) At this 'ecofriendly' lodge, floors are made of bamboo, wastewater is treated and used for gardening, and electricity conservation holds pride of place. The sleek, minimalist rooms are stylish and comfortable around, and the rooftop infinity pool (which doubles as insulation) has a gorgeous wooden terrace with views of the sea. There's a newer, second branch on Anna Salai.

Raj Park   HOTEL $$$

(☎42257777; www.rajpark.com; 180 TTK Rd, Alwarpet; s/d incl breakfast from ₹4200/4800; ❄☎⛱) Not the best value in town, but this 'business hotel' is comfy and plush in a corporate kind of way, with friendly staff and lots of little extras. The cheaper rooms are on the small side. It has one of the more relaxed and affordable hotel bars around.

Eating

Chennai is packed with classic 'meals' joints, which serve thalis for lunch and dinner, and tiffin (snacks) such as *idlis* and dosas the rest of the day. It's tempting – and feasible – to eat every meal at one of Chennai's dozen or so Saravana Bhavan restaurants, where you can count on quality vegetarian food. In the Muslim area around Triplicane High Rd you'll find great biryani joints every few steps – try any of them.

Spencer Plaza has an impressive 3rd-floor food mall with a couple of Western chains, a branch of Hotel Saravana Bhavan (hey, it's Chennai), various fast foods and Chinese options.

EGMORE

TOP CHOICE Hotel Saravana Bhavan   SOUTH INDIAN $

Egmore (Map p990; 21 Kennet Lane; ⊙6am-10.30pm); George Town (Map p986; 209 NSC Bose Rd); Mylapore (Map p986; 101 Dr Radhakrishnan Salai; ⊙7am-11pm); Thousand Lights (Map p990; 293 Peter's Rd; ⊙lunch & dinner); Triplicane (Map p990; Shanthi Theatre Complex, 48 Anna Salai; ⊙7am-11pm) Dependably delish, 'meals' at the Saravana Bhavans run around ₹50, though the Mylapore locale has some 'special meals' for ₹100 and up. The Thousand Lights branch is more upscale, with silver cutlery.

Ponnusamy Hotel   INDIAN $

(Map p990; Wellington Estate, 24 Ethiraj Rd; mains ₹80-110; ⊙lunch & dinner) This well-known nonveg place serves curry, biryani and Chettinad specialities. Look out for interesting options like brain fry and rabbit masala. You may be ordered to wash your hands before you can sit down.

Sparky's Diner   AMERICAN $$

(Map p990; Ramanathan Salai, Spur Tank Rd; meals ₹180-280; ⊙lunch & dinner) An expat-run American diner plastered with US licence plates and movie posters, with Sinatra crooning on the stereo. Come for reliably good Western food, especially the pasta, and a bottomless cup of iced tea (₹45). If you're craving a US-style burger you might have to adjust your expectations a little (they're not bad though).

Basil   MULTICUISINE $$

(Map p990; Fortel, 3 Gandhi Irwin Rd; mains ₹150-300) The bigger of the two restaurants at the Fortel hotel has an impressive Western breakfast range, if you're really after hash browns, as well as tasty North Indian and Continental dishes in a pleasant setting.

TRIPLICANE

A2B
SOUTH INDIAN $

(Map p990; Bharathi Salai; mains ₹20-50) Enjoy South Indian classics, veg biryani, a wide range of sweets and savoury snacks in clean, AC surrounds. If you've got any room for food left, head a few doors down the road, closer to the beach, where you'll find excellent ice cream at **Natural Fresh** (Map p990; 35 Bharathi Salai).

Ratna Cafe
SOUTH INDIAN $

(Map p990; 255 Triplicane High Rd; dishes ₹30-60) Though often crowded and cramped, Ratna is renowned in Triplicane and beyond for its scrumptious *idlis* and the hearty doses of *sambar* that go with it.

NUNGAMBAKKAM & AROUND

Tuscana Pizzeria
ITALIAN $$$

(Map p986; www.tuscanarestaurants.com; 19, 3rd St, Wallace Garden, Nungambakkam; large pizzas ₹295-525; ☺lunch & dinner) This, my pizza-loving friends, is the real deal, and Chennai is embracing it fast. Tuscana serves authentic thin-crust pizzas with toppings like prosciutto, as well as interesting takes like hoi sin chicken pizza. Pasta and desserts are also top-notch. The expat owner, who is serious about food, also runs a Greek restaurant, **Kryptos**, just round the corner in Kader Nawaz Khan Rd.

Kumarakom
INDIAN $$

(Map p986; Kodambakkam High Rd, Nunganbak-kam; mains ₹60-160; ☺lunch & dinner) You may have to queue for a table at this classy, popular Keralan restaurant with dark-wood furniture, cool AC and busy waiters. The seafood is the standout – try the prawns masala – but everything's fresh and tasty.

Sea Shell
MIDDLE EASTERN, INDIAN $

(Map p990; ☎28295788; 55 Greams Rd, Thousand Lights; mains ₹50-150; ☺lunch & dinner) A bustling, super-popular spot with Middle Eastern favourites like hummus and shawarma in addition to a big menu of North Indian and Chinese. Choose from a long list of bizarrely named mocktails: 'Carbuncle', 'Rolex' or 'Flosberry Flop' anyone?

Kailash Parbat
NORTH INDIAN $

(Map p986; 1st fl, 9 Harrington Rd, Chetpet; mains ₹60-130; ☺lunch & dinner) A huge range of tasty street-stall food – *pani puri, chaat*

pav, bhaji and more – at decent prices in AC comfort. Specialises in veg-only Sindhi and Punjabi dishes, including paneer cooked a bunch of different ways. There's a wee branch in the food court at Ampa Skywalk mall.

SOUTH CHENNAI

Copper Chimney
NORTH INDIAN $$$

(Map p986; 74 Cathedral Rd, Teynampet; mains ₹250-350; ☺noon-3pm & 6-11.30pm) The vegetarian dishes aren't the priority here, and meat eaters will drool over the yummy North Indian tandoori dishes served among plush furnishings. The fish tikka – lumps of skewered tandoori-baked fish – is supurb.

Murugan Idly Shop
SOUTH INDIAN $

(Map p986; 77 GN Chetty Rd, T Nagar; dishes ₹25-60) Those in the know generally agree this particular branch of the small chain serves some of the best *idli* and South Indian meals in town. We heartily concur. For afters there's a branch of the very good **Natural Fresh** ice-cream chain just across the road.

Crust
CAFE $$

(Map p986; 18 Bheemanna Garden Rd, Abhira-mapuram; sandwiches ₹70-140, pasta ₹150-180; ☺lunch) In a leafy courtyard, enjoy sandwiches on bread like you've never tasted in India, as well as quiche, fresh salads and delicious brownies, cakes and tiramisu (made with marscapone flown all the way from Delhi!). Plans are in the works for an expanded restaurant and menu.

Chit Chat
CAFE $$

(Map p986; 532 Anna Salai, Teynampet; mains ₹100-250; ☺lunch & dinner) This spot presents as a casual, clean Western-style cafe, and has a wide menu of sandwiches, pizza, kebabs and posh North Indian lunch combos (₹140 to ₹190). It's famous for its milkshakes, and has a cake shop out the front.

Coconut Lagoon
SEAFOOD $$

(Map p986; cnr Cathedral & TTK Rds, Alwarpet; mains ₹100-200; ☺noon-3pm & 7-11.45pm) Excellent Keralan and Goan fare with a focus on seafood delicacies, such as *kari meen polli chathu* (fish masala steamed in banana leaf). If you've got room there's good ice cream across the road at **Kulfi Corner**.

Self-Catering

Big Bazaar
SUPERMARKET

(Map p986; Sir Theagaraya Nagar Rd, T Nagar) Americans, they've got Oreos. Aussies, they've got Tim Tams. You're welcome.

Heritage Fresh SUPERMARKET
(Map p986; TTK Rd, Alwarpet; ☺9am-8.30pm)

Jam Bazaar MARKET
(Map p990; cnr Ellis Rd & Bharathi Salai, Tripli-cane) Animated market bursting with fruit, vegetables and spices.

Spencer's Daily SUPERMARKET
(Map p990; Ritherdon Rd; ☺9.30am-9pm)

Drinking

Cafes

Popular coffee chains are dotted around Chennai, including **Barista** (Map p986; Rosy Towers, Nungambakkam High & D Khader Nawaz Khan Rds, Nungambakkam; ☺7.30am-11.30pm) and **Café Coffee Day** (☺10am-11pm) Amin-jikarai (Ampa Skywalk mall, Poonamallee High Rd; ☺9am-9pm); Egmore (Map p990; Alsa Mall, Mon-tieth Rd); Nungambakkam (Map p986; 123/124 Nungambakkam High Rd).

Bars & Nightclubs

Chennai's nightlife throbs that little bit more every year, though it doesn't help that bars and clubs are supposed to close by midnight and are restricted to hotels. The very pricey (by any standards) bars at the five-star ho-tels are about the only place to get a drink without thumpingly loud music in the back-ground.

Nightclubs attached to five-star hotels draw big crowds; at the time of research the hottest clubs were **Pasha** (Park Hotel, 601 Anna Salai; ☺8.30-11.30pm Wed-Sun) and **Dub-lin** (Sheraton Park, 132 TTK Rd; ☺8-11.30pm Wed-Sun). Admission is around the ₹1000 mark for couples and solo guys, and usually free for women.

Geoffrey's Pub BAR
(Radha Regent, 171 Jawaharlal Nehru Salai, Arum-bakkam; ☺4-11pm) This basement 'English' pub is one of the few places in Chennai that hosts live music nightly (save Sun-days, when there's a DJ). Not always great music, but music nonetheless. The atmo-sphere is casual, with Kollywood types occasionally gracing the place with their presence.

Leather Bar BAR
(Map p986; Park Hotel, 601 Anna Salai; ☺8.30-11.30pm) 'Leather' refers to floor and wall coverings rather than anything kinky. This tiny, modish pad has mixologists dishing up fancy drinks and DJs spinning dance tunes. How half of Chennai fits into this teensy space on Friday and Saturday nights is a mystery.

10D PUB
(10 Downing St; Map p986; www.10ds.net; North Boag Rd, T Nagar; ☺11am-11pm) An English-themed pub (pictures of Big Ben on the wall, devilled eggs and fish fingers on the menu), often packed with a mixed bag of punters. Wednesday is Ladies Night. (Pro tip: skip the devilled eggs and go for the tasy tandoori snacks.)

Entertainment

Classical Music & Dance

Kalakshetra Arts Village DANCE, MUSIC
(☎24521169; kshetra@vsnl.com; Dr Muthulakshmi Rd, Tiruvanmiyu) Founded in 1936, Kalakshet-ra is committed to reviving classical dance and music. Check out one of its regular per-formances. Four-month courses in music and dance are available.

Music Academy DANCE, MUSIC
(Map p986; ☎28112231; www.musicacademyma dras.com; cnr Roytthahape & Cathedral Rds) This is Chennai's most popular public venue for Carnatic classical music and Bharata Natyam dance. Many performances are free. Check the website for upcoming events.

Cinema

Chennai has more than 100 cinemas, a re-flection of the vibrant film industry here. Most screen Tamil films, but **PV Cinema** (www.pvrcinemas.com; Ampa Skywalk mall, Poona-mallee High Rd, Aminjikarai) regularly shows English-language films, as does **Sathyam Cinema** (Map p990; www.sathyamcinemas.com; 8 Thiruvika Rd, Royapettah). Tickets are around ₹120, and you can book online.

Shopping

Theagaraya Nagar (aka T Nagar; Map p986) has great shopping, especially at Pondy Ba-zaar and around Panagal Park. Nungam-bakkam's shady D Khader Nawaz Khan Rd (Map p986) is a pleasant lane of shops, cafes and galleries. There's a good branch of the fixed-price government handicrafts chain **Poompuhar** (Map p990; ☺10am-8pm Mon-Sat) in Anna Salai.

The best commercial shopping malls in-clude **Spencer Plaza** (Map p990; Anna Salai), **Ampa Skywalk** (Poonamallee High Rd, Aminji-karai) and **Chennai Citicentre** (Map p986; Dr Radhakrishnan Salai, Mylapore). Ampa Skywalk is the poshest and hosts mostly internation-al chains, while Spencer Plaza is better for slightly cheaper shops, including Kashmiri souvenir stores and lots of clothes.

Fabindia
HOMEWARES & FOOD

Spencer Plaza (Map p990; Anna Salai; ⊕11am-8pm); Woods Rd (Map p990; ⊕10am-8pm) The Woods Rd shop has home and food sections, along with fabulous clothes.

Naturally Auroville
HOMEWARES

(Map p986; D Khader Nawaz Khan Rd, Nungambakkam; ⊕10.30am-8pm Mon-Sat, 11.30am-7pm Sun) *Objets* (pottery, bedspreads, scented candles) and fine foods (organic coffees, breads and cheeses) from Auroville, near Pondicherry.

Good Earth
HOMEWARES

(Map p986; www.goodearth.in; 3 Rutland Gate, 4th St, Thousand Lights; ⊕11am-8pm Mon) Gorgeous homewares, furniture, original artwork and more. All Indian inspired and themed, it often has a sense of humour – look for the series of autorickshaw-themed products.

Silk

Many of the finest Kanchipuram silks turn up in Chennai, so consider doing your silk shopping here. The streets around Panagal Park are filled with silk shops; if you're lucky enough to be attending an Indian wedding this is where you buy your sari. Try one of these:

Nalli Silks
FABRIC

(Map p986; 9 Nageswaran Rd, T Nagar; ⊕9.30am-9.30pm) The granddaddy of silk shops. There's a big readymades shop next door with gorgeous *salwar kameez*.

Kumaran Textiles
FABRIC

(Map p986; 12 Nageswaran Rd, T Nagar; ⊕9am-9.30pm) Saris, saris and plenty of Kanchipuram silk.

Bookshops

Higginbothams
BOOKSTORE

(Map p990; higginbothams@vsnl.com; 116 Anna Salai; ⊕9am-8pm Mon-Sat, 10.30am-7.30pm Sun) Decent English-language book selection. Has a branch at the airport.

Landmark
BOOKSTORE

Aminjikarai (Ampa Skywalk mall, Poonamallee High Rd; ⊕10am-9pm); Anna Salai (Map p990; Spencer Plaza, Phase II; ⊕9am-9pm Mon-Sat, 10.30am-9pm Sun); Nungambakkam (Map p986; Apex Plaza, Nungambakkam High Rd; ⊕9am-9pm Mon-Sat, 10.30am-9pm Sun)

Oxford Book Stores
BOOKSTORE

(Map p986; 39/12 Haddows Rd, Nungambakkam; ⊕9.30am-9.30pm) A big selection, tables and colouring-in equipment for kiddies, and a cafe.

ℹ️ Information

Internet Access

There are 'browsing centres' all over town; most charge between ₹20 and ₹30 an hour.

Cyber Palace (Map p990; Bharathi Salai; per hr ₹20; ⊕9am-10pm)

Dreamzzz Zone (Map p990; Alsa Mall, Egmore; per hr ₹20; ⊕8.30am-10.30pm) Clean, fast, AC.

Internet Zone (Map p990; 1 Kennet Lane, Egmore; per hr ₹30; ⊕8am-10pm)

Log In Net Cafe (Map p990; 35 Triplicane High Rd, Triplicane; per hr ₹15; ⊕9am-11pm)

SGee (Map p990; ☑42310391; 20 Vallabha Agraharam St, Triplicane; per hr ₹20; ⊕24hr)

Left Luggage

Egmore and Central train stations have left-luggage counters, as do the international and domestic airports.

Medical Services

Apollo Hospital (Map p990; ☑28293333, emergency 28290792; www.apollohospitals.com; 21 Greams Lane) Cutting-edge hospital popular with international 'medical tourists'.

St Isabel's Hospital (Map p986; ☑24991081; 18 Oliver Rd, Mylapore)

Money

ATMs are everywhere; there's a cluster at the front of Central train station.

HDFC Bank (Map p986; Poonamallee High Rd, Egmore; ⊕10am-4pm Mon-Fri, 10am-1pm Sat) Foreign exchange and ATM; handy to the YWCA and Salvation Army guesthouses.

State Bank of India Anna Salai (Map p990; Anna Salai; ⊕10am-4pm Mon-Fri, 10am-1pm Sat); George Town (Map p986; 22 Rajaji Salai, George Town; ⊕10am-4pm Mon-Fri, 10am-1pm Sat)

Thomas Cook Anna Salai (Map p990; Spencer Plaza, Phase I; ⊕9.30am-6.30pm); Egmore (Map p990; 45 Montieth Rd; ⊕9.30am-6pm Mon-Sat, 10am-4pm Sun); George Town (Map p986; 20 Rajaji Salai; ⊕9.30am-6pm Mon-Sat); Nungambakkam (Map p986; Eldorado Bldg, 112 Nungambakkam High Rd; ⊕9.30am-6.30pm Mon-Fri, 9.30am-noon Sat) Changes currency and travellers cheques with no commission.

Post

DHL (Map p990; ☑4214886/7; 85 Pantheon Rd, Egmore; ⊕8am-11pm) For secure international parcel delivery. There's a few branches around, including one on Esplanade Rd in George Town.

Post office Anna Salai (Map p990; ⊕8am-8.30pm Mon-Sat, 10am-4pm Sun, poste restante 10am-6pm Mon-Sat); Egmore (Map p990; Kennet Lane; ⊕10am-6pm Mon-Sat); George Town (Map p986; Rajaji Salai; ⊕8am-8.30pm Mon-Sat, 10am-4pm Sun)

Tourist Information

Check out **Chennai Best** (www.chennaibest.com) and **Chennai Online** (www.chennaionline.com).

India Tourism Development Corporation (ITDC; Map p990; ☏28281250; www.attindia tourism.com; 29 Cherian Cres, Egmore; ☺10am-5.30pm Mon-Sat) Hotel and tour bookings only; they're not very helpful.

Indiatourism (Map p990; ☏28460285; ind-tour@dataone.in; 154 Anna Salai; ☺9am-6pm Mon-Fri, 9am-1pm Sat) Maps and information on all of India.

Tamil Nadu Tourism Complex (TTDC; Map p990; ☏25367850; www.tamilnadutourism. org; 2 Wallajah Rd, Triplicane; ☺10am-5.30pm Mon-Fri) Brochure-filled state tourist offices from all over India. The tour-booking desk at the Tamil Nadu office (☏25383333) is supposedly open 24 hours.

Travel Agencies

South Tourism (☏42179092; www.south tourism.in; 1 Z-Block, 19th St, Anna Nagar West) Recommended agency for tours and bookings.

SP Travels & Tours (Map p990; ☏28604001; sptravels1@eth.net; 90 Anna Salai, Triplicane; ☺9.30am-6.30pm Mon-Sat)

Visa Extensions

Foreigners' Regional Registration Office (Map p986; ☏28251721; Shastri Bhavan, Haddows Rd, Nungambakkam; ☺9.30am-12.30pm Mon-Fri) Everything will take complicated wrangling and copious doses of patience (we had to sit in a queue for half an hour just to be told the opening hours), but you can usually get extensions for all visas except tourist here (tourist visas are only extended in cases of medical emergency). Theoretically, they take 10 days to process.

❶ Getting There & Away

Air

AIRPORTS The international **Anna terminal** (☏22560551) of Chennai Airport in Tirusulam, 16km southwest of the centre, is efficient and not too busy, making Chennai a good entry or exit point. The domestic **Kamaraj terminal** (☏22560551) is next door.

DOMESTIC AIRLINES

Indian Airlines (Map p990; ☏28578153/4, airport 22561906; 19 Rukmani Lakshmi Pathy Rd (Marshalls Rd), Egmore)

IndiGo (☏22560286; airport)

Jet Airways (Map p990; ☏domestic 39893333, international 1800 225522; 41/43 Montieth Rd, Egmore; ☺9am-5.30pm Mon-Sat)

Kingfisher Airlines (Map p990; ☏43988400; 19 Rukmani Lakshmi Pathy Rd (Marshalls Rd), Egmore)

SpiceJet (☏1800 1803333; airport)

INTERNATIONAL AIRLINES

Air France (Map p990; ☏1800 1800033; Kuber's Bldg, 42 Pantheon Rd, Egmore)

Air India (Map p990; ☏1800 1801407; 19 Rukmani Lakshmi Pathy Rd (Marshalls Rd), Egmore) Air India Express has a desk here.

Air Mauritius (Map p990; ☏43508811; Prince Plaza, Pantheon Rd, Egmore; ☺9.30am-5.30pm Mon-Fri, to 1pm Sat)

Cathay Pacific Airways (Map p986; ☏18002091616; 47 Major Ramanathan Salai (Spur Tank Rd), Chetpet)

KLM (Map p990; ☏1800 1800044; Kuber's Bldg, 42 Pantheon Rd, Egmore)

Lufthansa (☏22569393; airport)

Malaysia Airlines (Map p986; ☏42199999; 90 Dr Radhakrishnan Salai, Mylapore)

Singapore Airlines (Map p986; ☏45921921; Westminster, 108 Dr Radhakrishnan Salai, Mylapore)

Sri Lankan Airlines (Map p986; ☏43921100; 4 Kodambakkam High Rd, Nungambakkam)

Thai Airways International (Map p986; ☏22561928; 31 Haddows Rd, Nungambakkam)

Boat

Passenger ships sail from the George Town harbour to Port Blair in the Andaman Islands (see p1070) every five to 10 days or so. The **Director of Shipping Services** (Map p986; ☏25226873; fax 25220841; Shipping Corporation Bldg, Rajaji Salai, George Town; ☺10am-4pm Mon-Sat) sells tickets (₹1962 to ₹7642) for the 60-hour trip. You'll need two photographs and three photocopies each of your passport identity page and visa. Bring a book, take a number and try to position yourself near a fan – it can be a long process.

Bus

Most Tamil Nadu (SETC) and other government buses operate from the chaotic **Chennai Mofussil Bus Terminus** (CMBT; off Map p986; Jawaharlal Nehru Salai, Koyambedu), better known as Koyambedu CMBT, 7km west of town.

Bus 15 or 15B from Parry's Corner or Central train station, and 27B from Anna Salai or Egmore train station, all head there (₹5, 45 minutes). An autorickshaw charges around ₹150 for the same ride.

SETC, Karnataka (KSRTC) and Andhra Pradesh (APRSTC) bus services cover the destinations listed in the table (p1000), usually in the morning and late afternoon.

Several companies operate Volvo AC buses to the same destinations from the less overwhelming private-bus station next door to CMBT. There's another, smaller private bus stand (Map p990) opposite Egmore train station. These

DESTINATION	AIRLINE	FARE FROM (₹)	DURATION (HR)	FREQUENCY
Bengaluru	IC	2115	¾	3 daily
	9W	3333	1	4 daily
	6E	2033	1	daily
Delhi	IC	4071	2½	4 daily
	9W	5475	2½	6 daily
	SG	3432	2½	4 daily
	6E	3432	2½	4 daily
Goa	IC	2666	1¼	4 weekly
	SG	2312	1¼	daily
Hyderabad	IC	2115	1	2 daily
	9W	3333	1	2 daily
	6E	2033	1	2 daily
	SG	2033	1	daily
Kochi	IC	2115	1	2 daily
	9W	3333	1	2 daily
Kolkata	IC	5971	2	2 daily
	9W	5844	2	2 daily
	SG	3033	2	daily
	6E	3033	2	3 daily
Mumbai	IC	3325	2	4 daily
	9W	5589	2	6 daily
	SG	3033	2	daily
	6E	3033	2½	2 daily
Port Blair	IC	6376	2	daily
	9W	5787	2	daily
Trivandrum	IC	2115	1½	2 daily
	9W	3700	1½	daily

Note: fares are one-way only

Airline codes: 6E – IndiGo, 9W – Jet Airways, IC – Indian Airlines, SG – SpiceJet

super-deluxe buses usually leave at night and cost two to three times more than ordinary buses.

Train

Interstate trains and those heading west generally depart from Central train station (Map p986), while trains heading south depart from Egmore (Map p990). The **Train Reservation** **Complex** (☎ general 139; ☻ 8am-8pm Mon-Sat, 8am-2pm Sun) is in a separate 10-storey building just west of Central train station; the Foreign Tourist Assistance Cell (one of the best ever) is on the 1st floor. Egmore's **booking office** (☎ 28194579) keeps the same hours.

BUS SERVICES FROM CHENNAI (MADRAS)

DESTINATION	FARE (₹)	DURATION (HR)	FREQUENCY
Bengaluru	180-260	9	every 30min
Chidambaram	80-90	7	6 daily
Coimbatore	220-300	11½	9 daily
Ernakulam (Kochi)	420-600	16½	2 daily
Kodaikanal	200-230	13	daily
Madurai	160-190	10	every 30min
Mamallapuram	35	2	every 15-30min
Mysore	200-240	11	10 daily
Ooty	250-320	14	daily
Puducherry	45-90	3½	every 30min
Thanjavur	130-150	8½	hourly
Tirupathi	60-70	3½	every 30min
Trichy	120-190	7	every 15-30min
Trivandrum	330-450	17	7 daily

ℹ Getting Around

To/From the Airport

The cheapest way to reach the airport is by MRTS train to Tirusulam station, 300m across the road from the terminals. An autorickshaw will cost you at least ₹250/350 for a day/night trip. Both terminals have prepaid taxi kiosks, where tickets are ₹500 to Egmore or Anna Salai/Triplicane, or out to CMBT (main bus terminus). If you want to bypass Chennai, the kiosks can organise taxis straight from here to destinations including Mahabalipuram (₹2000) or Puducherry (₹4000).

Autorickshaw

Rickshaw drivers in Chennai routinely quote astronomical fares for both locals and tourists alike. Since you have no chance of getting a driver to use the meter, expect to pay at least ₹40 for a short trip down the road. From Egmore to George Town, Triplicane or Anna Salai will cost around ₹70, to Nungambakkam ₹90. Prices are at least 25% higher after 10pm. There's a prepaid booth outside Central station.

Bus

Chennai's bus system is worth getting to know. The main city bus stand (Map p986) is at Parry's Corner, and fares are between ₹5 and ₹12. Some useful routes are listed in the table, p1002.

Car & Taxi

For an extended hire, organise a driver through a travel agent or large hotel. You might pay a little more, but the driver should be reliable and you'll have a point of contact should something go wrong. Non-AC rates are around ₹600 per half-day (five hours) within the city.

Train

Efficient MRTS trains run every 15 minutes from Beach station to Fort, Park (at Central station), Egmore, Chetpet, Nungambakkam, Kodambakkam, Mambalam, Saidapet, Guindy, St Thomas Mount, Tirusulam (for the airport), and on down to Tambaram. The second line branches off at Park and hits Light House and Tirumailar (at Kapaleeshwarar Temple).

NORTHERN TAMIL NADU

Chennai to Mamallapuram

Chennai's sprawl peters out after an hour or two heading south on the coastal road, at which point Tamil Nadu becomes open road, red dirt, khaki sand and blue skies (or, if you take the inland road being developed as an 'information technology corridor', huge new buildings). Currently this stretch of sand is the only area of Tamil Nadu's 1076km coastline that's being developed for traditional beachside tourism.

There's a tropical bohemian groove floating around Injambalkkam village, site of the Cholamandal Artists' Village (☑044-4926092; www.cholamandalartistsvillage.org; admission free; ⊙9.30am-9pm). This 4-hectare

DESTINATION	TRAIN NO & NAME	FARE (₹)	DURATION (HR)	DEPARTURE
Bengaluru	2007 Shatabdi Express*	510/995	4½	6am CC
	2609 Bangalore Express	108/380	6	1.35pm CC
Delhi	2615 Grand Trunk Express	528/1429/1960	35	7.15pm CC
	2621 Tamil Nadu Express	528/1429/1960	33	10pm CC
Coimbatore	6627 West Coast Express	212/564/772	8½	11.30am CC
	2671 Nilgiri Express	232/594/802	8	9pm CC
Goa	7311 Vasco Express**	347/947/1302	22	1.40pm CC
Hyderabad	2759 Charminar Express	312/823/1119	14	6.10pm CC
	2603 Hyderabad Express	297/779/1095	13	4.45pm CC
Kochi	6041 Alleppey Express	269/728/998	11¾	9.15pm CC
Kolkata	2842 Coromandel Express	461/1242/1700	27	8.45am CC
	2840 Howrah Mail	461/1242/1700	28½	11.40pm CC
Madurai	6127 Guruvayur Express	212/564/772	8¾	7.50am CE
	2635 Vaigai Express	132/471	8	12.40pm CE
Mumbai	1042 Mumbai Express	383/1046/1440	26	11.55am CC
	2164 Dadar Express	403/1076/1470	23	6.50am CE
Mysore	2007 Shatabdi Express*	655/1265	7	6am CC
	6222 Kaveri Express	212/564/772	10½	9.30pm CC
Tirupathi	6053 Tirupathi Express	60/206	3	1.50pm CC
Trichy	2605 Pallavan Express	104/367	5½	3.45pm CE
Trivandrum	2695 Trivandrum Express	341/903/1230	16	3.25pm CC

Departure codes: CC – Chennai Central, CE – Chennai Egmore

*Daily except Wednesday; ** Friday only

Shatabdi fares are chair/executive; Express and Mail fares are 2nd/chair car for day trains, sleeper/3AC/2AC for overnight trains

artists' cooperative (18km south of Chennai) is a serene muse away from the world and a quiet chance to both see and purchase contemporary Indian art direct from the source. There are two simple studio-cum-guesthouses but they are available for visiting artists only (₹500; book well in advance).

As Cholamandal is to contemporary Indian expression, **DakshinaChitra** (044-27472603; www.dakshinachitra.net; Indian adult/student ₹75/30, foreign adult/student ₹200/75; 10am-6pm Wed-Mon) is to traditional arts and crafts. Located about 12km south of Cholamandal, this is a jumble of open-air museum, preserved village and artisan

workshops – another well-worth-it stop (especially for the kids) for learning about the Dravidian crafts of Tamil Nadu, Kerala, Karnataka and Andhra Pradesh. DakshinaChitra means 'A Picture of the South', which is essentially what you're provided via local pottery, silk-weaving, puppet-building and basket-making workshops, traditional theatre performances and art studios.

Along this stretch of road the TTDC runs the **Muttukadu Boat House** (9am-6pm), where you can take a 45-minute boat trip (per person from ₹45) out on the backwaters.

One of the best institutions of its kind in India, **Crocodile Bank** (044-27472447; www.madrascrocodilebank.org; adult/child ₹35/10,

CHENNAI BUS ROUTES

BUS NO	ROUTE
29K	Koyambedu CMBT–Guindy–Adyar–Mylapore
9, 10	Parry's–Central–Egmore–T Nagar
11/11A	Parry's–Anna Salai–T Nagar
15B	Parry's–Central–Koyambedu CMBT
18	Parry's–Saidapet
19G	Parry's–Central–Adyar
27B	Egmore–Chetpet–Koyambedu CMBT
31	Parry's–Central–Vivekananda Illam
32	Central–Triplicane–Vivekananda Illam
51M	T Nagar–St Thomas Mount

camera/video ₹20/100; ⊗8.30am-5.30pm Tue-Sun), 40km south of Chennai, is a fascinating peek into a world of reptiles, and an incredible conservation trust to boot. The Bank does crucial work towards protecting the critically endangered gharial, an enormous but harmless (to humans) species of crocodilian that feeds on fish and has a long, thin nose. There are thousands of other reptiles here, including the Indian mugger and saltwater crocs of the Andaman and Nicobar Islands. If you have a spare evening on the weekend, come for the **night safari** (adult/child ₹60/20; ⊗7-8pm Sat & Sun), when you can shine a flashlight over the water and catch the staring eyes of thousands of the Bank's local residents. Volunteer opportunities are available here; see the website for details.

About 5km north of Mamallapuram in the village of Salavankuppam, beside the East Coast Rd, the **Tiger Cave** is a rock-cut shrine, possibly dating from the 7th century. It's dedicated to Durga and has a small *mandapam* featuring a crown of carved *yali* (mythical lion creature) heads.

To reach these places, take any bus heading south from Chennai to Mamallapuram and ask to be let off at the appropriate destination. Another option is the TTDC's hop-on, hop-off **bus tour** (☑044-25383333; www.tamilnadutourism.org/hopontour.html; ₹250) that runs between Chennai and Mamallapuram on the half-hour between 9am and 11am, and in the other direction between 4.15pm and 6pm. A taxi for a full-day tour costs from about ₹1600. You can swim along the coast, but beware of strong currents and tides as there are no lifeguards around.

Mamallapuram (Mahabalipuram)

☑044 / POP 12,345

This World Heritage Site was once a major seaport and second capital of the Pallava kings, and a saunter through the town's great carvings and temples at sunset, when the sandstone turns bonfire orange and blood red and modern carvers *tink-tink* with their chisels on the street, enflames the imagination.

And then, in addition to ancient archaeological wonders, there's the traveller ghetto of Othavadai Cross St. You'll hear the mellow trills of Jack Johnson. Bob Marley flags hang from the balconies. Stores sell things from Tibet, 'Indian' clothes that few Indians would probably ever wear, toilet paper, hand sanitiser and used books, and you know you have landed, once again, in the Kingdom of Backpackistan.

'Mal', as many travellers call it, is less than two hours by bus from Chennai, and many travellers make a beeline here straight from Chennai. The village is tiny and laid-back, and the surrounding sites of interest can be explored on foot or by bicycle.

☉ Sights

You can easily spend a full day exploring the temples, *mandapams* and rock carvings around Mamallapuram. Apart from the Shore Temple and Five Rathas, admission is free. Official guides from the Archaeological Survey of India can be found at archaeological sites and hired for around ₹50 (give more if the tour is good); they're well worth the money.

Shore Temple
HINDU TEMPLE

(combined ticket with Five Rathas Indian/foreigner ₹10/250, video ₹25; ◉6.30am-6pm) Standing like a magnificent fist of rock-cut elegance overlooking the sea, the Shore Temple symbolises the heights of Pallava architecture and the maritime ambitions of the Pallava kings. Its small size belies its excellent proportion and the supreme quality of the carvings, many of which have been eroded into vaguely Impressionist embellishments. Originally constructed in the 7th century, it was later rebuilt by Narasimhavarman II and houses two central shrines to Shiva. The layout is meant to resemble the perfect cosmic body, with the head and heart located over the spire that dominates the structure. Facing east and west, the original linga (phallic images of Shiva) captured the sunrise and sunset. The temple is believed to be the last in a series of buildings that extended along a since submerged coastline; this theory gained credence during the 2004 tsunami, when receding waters revealed the outlines of what may have been sister temples.

Five Rathas
HINDU TEMPLES

(Five Rathas Rd; combined ticket with Shore Temple Indian/foreigner ₹10/250, video ₹25; ◉6.30am-6pm) Carved from single pieces of rock, the Five Rathas are low-laying monoliths that huddle in more ancient subtlety than grandeur. Each temple is dedicated to a Hindu god and named for one of the Pandavas, the five hero-brothers of the epic Mahabharata, plus their common wife, Draupadi.

The shrines are meant to resemble chariots (*ratha* is Sanskrit for chariot), and were hidden in the sand until excavated by the British 200 years ago. Outside each *ratha* is a carving of an animal mount of the gods. Taken together, the layout theme of God, Pandava and animal mount is remarkable for its architectural consistency, considering everything here was cut from single chunks of rock.

The first *ratha*, **Draupadi Ratha**, on the left after you enter the gate, is dedicated to Draupadi and the goddess Durga, who represents the sacred femininity and fertility of the Indian soil. The goddess looks out at her worshippers from a carved lotus throne, while outside, a huge sculpted lion stands guard.

Behind the goddess shrine, a huge Nandi (bull, vehicle of Shiva) heralds the chariot of the most important Pandava. **Arjuna Ratha** is appropriately dedicated to Shiva, the most important deity of the Pallavas. Other gods,

including the Vedic Indra, are depicted on the outer walls.

Look around the lintels of the middle temple, **Bhima Ratha**, and you'll notice faded faces that some archaeologists believe possess Caucasian features, evidence of Mamallapuram's extensive trade ties with ancient Rome. Inside is a shrine to Vishnu.

Guides may tell you the carving of Pallava king Narasimhavarman on **Dharmaraja Ratha**, the tallest of the chariots, resembles an Egyptian pharaoh, suggesting even earlier trade ties across the Indian Ocean. The theory is tantalising, but not terribly well substantiated. The final *ratha*, **Nakula-Sahadeva Ratha**, is dedicated to Indra and has a fine sculptured elephant standing nearby. As you enter the gate, approaching from the north, you see its back first, hence its name **gajaprishthakara** (elephant's backside). The life-sized image is regarded as one of the most perfectly sculptured elephants in India.

Arjuna's Penance
HISTORIC SITE

(West Raja St) As if we couldn't wax more poetic on Mamallapuram's stonework, along comes this relief carving, one of the greatest of its age and certainly one of the most convincing and unpretentious works of ancient art in India. Inscribed into a huge boulder, the penance bursts with scenes of Hindu myth (notice the *nagas,* or snake-beings, that descend a cleft once filled with water, meant to represent the Ganges) and everyday vignettes of South Indian life. A herd of elephants marches under armies of celestial beings, while Arjuna performs self-mortification so he can be granted Shiva's most powerful weapon, the god-slaying Pasupata. In Hinduism, 'penance' does not mean suffering that erases sins, but distress undertaken for the sake of boons from the gods. Another interpretation: the carving depicts the penance of the sage Bhagaritha, who asked the Ganges to fall to the earth and cleanse the ashes (and ergo, sins) of his dead relatives. There's humour amid the holy: notice the cat performing his own penance to a crowd of appreciative mice.

Ganesh Ratha & Around
HINDU TEMPLE

This *ratha* is northwest of Arjuna's Penance. Once a Shiva temple, it became a shrine to Ganesh (Shiva's elephant-headed son) after the original lingam was removed. Just north of the *ratha* is a huge boulder known as **Krishna's Butter Ball**. Immovable, but apparently balancing precariously, it's a

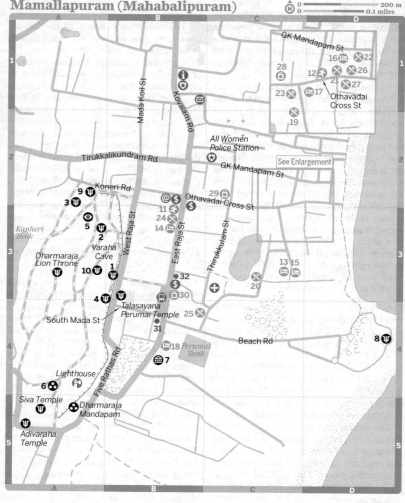

favourite photo opportunity. The nearby **Kotikal Mandapam** is dedicated to Durga. Southwest of here is **Varaha Mandapam II**, dominated by an incredibly active panel of Vishnu manifested as a boar avatar. Early Hindu art is rife with depictions of Vishnu in animal form, as opposed to today, when he is primarily worshipped as Rama or Krishna, which suggests this nascent phase of Hindu theology was more closely tied to tribal religions. Nearby, the **Trimurti Cave Temple** honours the Hindu trinity – Brahma, Vishnu and Shiva – with a separate section dedicated to each deity.

Mandapams   HISTORIC SITES
Mamallapuram's main hill, which dominates the town (and is in turn dominated by a red-and-brownstone lighthouse), makes for an excellent hour or two of low-key hiking (it's a good spot for the sunset as well). Many *mandapams* are scattered over this low rise of rock, including **Krishna Mandapam**, one of the earliest rock-cut temples around the region. The famous carving depicts both a rural pastiche and Krishna lifting up Govardhana mountain to protect his kinsfolk from the wrath of Indra. Other shrines include **Mahishamardini Mandapam**, just a few

metres southwest of the lighthouse. Scenes from the Puranas (Sanskrit stories dating from the 5th century AD) are depicted on the *mandapam,* with the sculpture of the goddess Durga considered one of the finest.

Above the *mandapam* are the remains of the 8th-century **Olakkannesvara Temple,** and spectacular views of Mamallapuram.

Sculpture Museum   MUSEUM
(East Raja St; adult/child ₹5/2, camera ₹10; ⊙9.30am-5pm) This museum contains more than 3000 sculptures and paintings that run the gamut from interesting stonework to still-life depictions of fruit bowls. Parts of the building are as interesting as the exhibits.

🏃 Activities

Beach
Mamallapuram's beach, or at least the bit that fronts the village, isn't exactly pristine and gets downright dingy in some spots, but if you walk a bit north or south of the Shore Temple it clears into very fine sand. You'll also be further away from the leers of men who spend their days out here gawking at tourists. It's not a great place for swimming – there are dangerous rips – but it's possible to

go fishing in one of local outriggers; negotiate a price with the owner.

Therapies
There are numerous places offering massage, reiki, yoga and ayurvedic practices. Sessions cost around ₹400 for 30 to 45 minutes. The more upmarket hotels tend to have reliable inhouse massage options; the GRT Temple Bay hotel has a branch of the popular Chennai massage centre Ayush.

Sri Chakra (Othavadai St; massage per hr ₹450; ⊙9am-9pm) offers ayurvedic massage as well as yoga sessions (₹200) at 7am and 4pm, and there are many other operators in town with similar rates and timings. As always, and especially for such an intimate service, ask fellow travellers, question the massage therapist carefully and if you have any misgivings, don't proceed.

☞ Tours

Hi! Tours (☎27443360; www.hi-tours.com; 123 East Raja St; ⊙9.30am-6pm) runs bicycle tours to sights like the Tiger Cave. Tours run from 8am to 2pm and include guide and lunch; prices are around ₹350 per person. Hi! Tours also organises day trips to Kanchipuram and Vedantangal Bird Sanctuary and fishing trips at certain times of the year.

✦ Festivals & Events

The Mamallapuram Dance Festival (Dec-Jan) is a four-week dance festival showcasing dances from all over India, with many performances on an open-air stage against the imposing backdrop of Arjuna's Penance. Dances include the Bharata Natyam (Tamil Nadu), Kuchipudi (Andhra Pradesh) tribal dance and Kathakali (Kerala drama); there are also puppet shows and classical music performances. Performances are held only from Friday to Sunday.

🛏 Sleeping

In addition to the following there's a cluster of cheap family-run places and budget lodges near the Five Rathas.

Hotel Mamalla Heritage HOTEL $$
(☏27442060; www.hotelmamallaheritage.com; 104 East Raja St; s/d from ₹1600/1800; ❄@🛜🛀) In town, this corporate-y place has large, comfortable rooms, all with fridge, spotlessly sparkling bathrooms and charmingly friendly service. The pool's a decent size, and there's a quality veg and rooftop restaurant.

**Tina Blue View Lodge
& Restaurant** HOTEL $
(☏27442319; 34 Othavadai St; r ₹250-500) Tina is one of Mamallapuram's originals and kind of looks it, with some frayed and faded edges, but remains deservedly popular for its whitewashed walls, blue accents and tropically pleasant garden, as well as tireless original owner Xavier ('I am same age as Tony Wheeler!').

Ideal Beach Resort RESORT $$$
(☏27442240; www.idealresort.com; s/d from ₹4500/5000; ❄@🛜🛀) With a landscaped garden setting, its own stretch of (pretty nice) beachfront and comfortable rooms or cottages, this low-key, laid-back beachfront resort is popular with families and Chennai expats. The design is small and secluded enough to have an intimate atmosphere and there's a lovely open-air poolside restaurant where live classical music is sometimes performed. It's about 3.5km north of town.

La Vie en Rose HOTEL $
(☏9444877544; East Raja St; d from ₹450; ❄) Simple, decent-sized and very clean rooms, friendly staff and a restaurant with some not-bad French dishes.

GRT Temple Bay RESORT $$$
(☏27443636; www.radisson.com/mamallapuramin; s/d incl breakfast from ₹8000/9000; ❄@🛜🛀) This is the best of the luxury resorts that lie to the north of town. It's got everything you need to feel like waterfront royalty, including 24-hour service, a spa, sauna, health club and prices that are probably a little much, all things considered. Prices jump in December/January.

Bharath Guest House HOTEL $
(☏274434304; barathguesthouse@gmail.com; 6 Othavadai Cross St; d from ₹400; ❄) One of a string of similarly priced places in a row along Othavadai Cross St (Siva Guest House and Greenlands are just as good), Bharath is painted a cheerful sunflower yellow and has big, colourful, simple rooms at a decent price.

Galaxy Guest House HOTEL $
(☏9940171595; Othavadai St; r ₹300-500) Central to the action, this is a family-run place with basic, clean rooms around a courtyard and flashier (ie more tackily decorated), bigger rooms upstairs.

Hotel Daphne HOTEL $
(☏27442811; hoteldaphne1@yahoo.com; 17 Othavadai Cross St; s/d from ₹250/350; ❄) Part of the Moonrakers mini-empire, this place isn't the standout it used to be, but it still offers decent value for money; walls and sheets are fresh, even if the furniture isn't, and the leafy setting and rooftop garden restaurant are big drawcards.

Hotel Sea Breeze HOTEL $$
(☏27443035; www.nivalink.com/seabreeze; Othavadai Cross St; r incl breakfast from ₹900; ❄🛀) The Sea Breeze is a bland, slightly overpriced hotel of the reliably midrange beachfront-escape school of design, but the real draw is the pool, which nonguests can use for ₹150. Breakfast is free, which is too expensive for cold *idlis*.

Try Residency HOTEL $
(☏27442728; tryresidency@gmail.com; 7 Old College Rd; r from ₹800; ❄) Rooms aren't too stylish but they're big and clean; if you need some Western-style amenities, it's not a bad option. There's a wee garden ruled by some ducks, and the world's tiniest pool.

Guru Lodge HOTEL $
(☏27443093; East Raja St; r from ₹300) Just outside the Othavadai ghetto, the simple, clean, peach-coloured rooms here offer good value.

New Manoj Cottage HOMESTAY $
(📱9840387095; newmanojcottage@yahoo.com; 136 Fisherman Colony; r ₹400-600) A friendly, family-run homestay with three well-kept rooms.

✖ Eating & Drinking

Restaurateurs near Othavadai Cross St provide open-air ambience, decent Western mains and bland Indian curries. If you want real Indian food, there are good cheap veg places and biryani joints near the bus stand. Most places – licensed or not – serve beer, but be sensitive to the 11pm local curfew; if you persuade a restaurant to allow you to linger over drinks, it's the owner, not you, who faces a hefty fine. All places listed are open for breakfast, lunch and dinner.

In addition the places reviewed here, beachside and nearly beachside Dreamlands, Seashore Restaurant, Santana Beach Restaurant and Luna Magica, are all recommended for fresh seafood; you'll get a good plate of fish for around ₹150 to ₹200.

Self-caterers should head to **Nilgiris Supermarket** (East Raja St; ⊙9.30am-9pm), between Othavadai St and the bus stand.

[TOP CHOICE] **Gecko Café** MULTICUISINE $$
(www.gecko-web.com; off Othavadai Cross St; mains ₹100-200) Two friendly brothers run this cute little spot on a thatch-covered rooftop above the family home. The menu choices and prices aren't that different to other tourist-oriented spots, but there's more love put into the cooking here, and the decor is fun: we liked the wall of goddesses, with Laxmi hanging next to the Virgin and Child. There's internet and a book exchange downstairs.

Le Yogi MULTICUISINE $$
(Othavadai St; mains ₹90-160) This is some of the best Western food in town; the steaks, pastas and pizzas are genuine and tasty (if small), service is good, and the airy dining area, with wooden accents and flickering candlelight, is romantic as all get out.

Rose Garden INDIAN $
(Beach Rd; mains around ₹50) This is one of the better biryani shops in a town that's surprisingly full of joints serving this tasty Hyderabadi rice dish.

Freshly 'N Hot CAFE $
(Othavadai Cross St; mains ₹50-180) Yes, the name makes no sense. A comparatively small menu of perfectly OK pizza, pasta and sandwiches, and a long, long list of coffees, hot and cold. The ice coffees are excellent.

Moonrakers MULTICUISINE $$
(34 Othavadai St; mains ₹60-150) Like it or not, you're likely to end up here at some stage; it's the sort of place that magnetises travellers and dominates the backpacker-ghetto streetscape. Food is OK, ambience is better and beer is enjoyable from the top-floor veranda. It's a mystery why the opposite-facing Blue Elephant, with almost identical food and nicer decor, isn't as popular as Moonrakers, though they both get pretty packed out with visitors from Chennai on weekend evenings.

🔒 Shopping

Mamallapuram wakes to the sound of sculptors' chisels on granite, and you'll inevitably be approached by someone trying to sell you everything from a ₹100 stone pendant to a ₹400,000 Ganesh that needs to be lifted with a crane. There are lots of good art galleries, tailors and antique shops here. For clothes, we recommend **Ponn Readymade Tailoring** (Othavadai St). Nice prints, cards and original art can be found at **Shriji Art Gallery** (11/1 Othavadai St) and expensive but beautiful curios culled from local homes at **Southern Arts and Crafts** (📱27443675; www.southernarts.in; 72 East Raja St).

A number of shops have books for sale or exchange. **JK Bookshop** (📱9880552200; 143 Othavadai St; ⊙9am-12.30pm & 2-8.30pm) is a small bookshop where you can buy or swap books in several languages, including English, French and German. Proceeds support education for local 'untouchable' children.

ℹ Information

Internet access is everywhere.
Indian Overseas Bank ATM (East Raja St)
KK Netscape (East Raja St; per hr ₹30; ⊙9am-10pm)
Ruby Forex (East Raja St; ⊙9.30am-7pm Mon-Sat)
South India Browsing Centre (Mango Leaf restaurant, Othavadai St; per hr ₹30; ⊙8am-8pm) Also has a decent book exchange.
State Bank of India ATM (East Raja St)
Suradeep Hospital (📱27442390; 15 Thirukkulam St; ⊙24hr) Recommended by travellers.
Tourist office (📱27442232; Kovalam Rd; ⊙10am-5.45pm Mon-Fri) Staff treat visitors as a major inconvenience; someone will probably sigh and point you to a table of maps and brochures.

ⓘ Getting There & Away

There are at least 30 buses a day running to/from Chennai (₹30, two hours, 30 daily). To Chennai Airport take bus 108B (₹25, two hours, 9am and 8pm daily). There are also at least nine daily buses to Puducherry (₹35, two hours), and Kanchipuram (₹24, two hours) via Tirukkalikundram; there's a faster direct private bus to Kanchipuram daily at 6am. Two daily buses run to Tiruvannamalai (₹36, three hours, 9.30am and 8pm)

Taxis are available from the bus station. Long-distance trips require plenty of bargaining. It's about ₹1400 to Chennai or the airport.

You can make train reservations at the **Southern Railway Reservation Centre** (East Raja St).

ⓘ Getting Around

The easiest way to get around is on foot, though on a hot day it's quite a hike to see all the monuments. Bicycles can be rented through most guesthouses and at numerous stalls along East Raja St.

Vedantangal Bird Sanctuary

Located about 52km southwest of Mamallapuram, this wildlife sanctuary (admission ₹20; ☺6am-6pm) is an important breeding ground for waterbirds – cormorants, egrets, herons, ibises, spoonbills, storks, grebes and pelicans – that migrate here from October to March. At the height of breeding season (December and January) there can be up to 30,000 birds nesting in the mangroves. The best viewing times are early morning and late afternoon; head for the watchtower and look down on the noisy nests across the water.

Basic rooms are available at the **Forest Department Resthouse** (d ₹525, with AC ₹725), 500m before the sanctuary. You're supposed to book in advance with the **Wildlife Warden's Office** (WWO; Map p986; ☎22351471; 4th fl, DMS office, 259 Anna Salai, Teynampet) in Chennai – it's not easy, and do phone first as there was talk of the office moving at the time of research. It can be easier through a tour operator (such as Hi! Tours in Mamallapuram), or if you turn up the caretaker may just find a room if one's available. You may or may not be offered food if you arrive unexpectedly; if you have transport, it's 10km or so to the nearest evening food stall.

To get here by public transport, first get to Chengalpattu, an hour's bus ride from Ma-mallapuram. From here you can take a bus to Vedantangal via Padalam, where you may have to change buses at the road junction. Most Vedantangal buses go directly to the sanctuary entrance, others to the village bus station, from where the sanctuary is a 1km walk south. Visitors also often make a day trip by AC taxi from Mamallapuram; this should cost around ₹1400.

Kanchipuram

044 / POP 188,763

The old capital of the Pallava dynasty is a typical Tamil Nadu temple town: modern India at her frenetic best dappled with houses of worship that form a veritable dialogue with history in stone. Kanchi (as it's often called) is also a centre of silk production and famed for its high-quality saris. It's usually (and best) visited as a day trip from Mamallapuram or Chennai, as there's not a lot to see outside of the justifiably famous temples. Don't make a special trip just to shop, as silk is generally no cheaper here than in Chennai.

The city is on the main road between Chennai and Bengaluru (Bangalore), 76km southwest of Chennai. There's no tourist office, but for information online check out www.hellokanchipuram.com.

⦿ Sights

All temples are open from 6am to 12.30pm and 4pm to 8.30pm. All have free admission, though you may have to pay for shoe-keeping and/or to bring in a camera.

Kailasanatha Temple   HINDU TEMPLE

The oldest temple in Kanchi is the most impressive, not for its size but weight of historical presence. Dedicated to Shiva, the Kailasanatha Temple was built by the Pallava king Rajasimha in the 7th century. The low-slung sandstone compound has fascinating carvings, including many half-animal deities that were in vogue during the period of early Dravidian architecture.

Non-Hindus are allowed into the inner sanctum here, where there is a prismatic lingam – the largest in town and third-largest in Asia.

Sri Ekambaranathar Temple   HINDU TEMPLE

This Shiva temple is one of the largest in the city, covering 12 hectares and dominated by a 59m-high *gopuram*. The carvings feel alive and beautiful, but still weighted with five centuries of history; they were chiselled

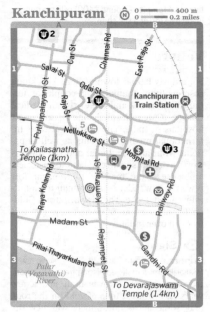

◎ **Sights**

1 Kamakshi Amman Temple	A1
2 Sri Ekambaranathar Temple	A1
3 Vaikunta Perumal Temple	B2

🛏 **Sleeping**

4 GRT Regency	B3
5 MM Hotel	A2
6 Sri Sakthi Residency	B2

Eating

| Dakshin | (see 4) |
| Saravana Bhavan | (see 4) |

Transport

| 7 Bicycle Rental | B2 |

by artisans in 1509 during the Vijayanagar empire. The temple's name is said to derive from Eka Amra Nathar – Lord of the Mango Tree – and there is an old mango tree, with four branches representing the four Vedas (sacred Hindu texts) on-site. Of the five elemental temples of Shiva, this is the shrine of Earth.

According to legend, the goddess Kamakshi worshipped Shiva here in the form of a linga made of sand, which still lies at the heart of the temple. Non-Hindus cannot see the mirror chamber, where worshippers enter with candles. The central image of Shiva is reflected in the candlelight across the mirrored walls, creating countless images of the god that allude to his infinite presence.

Kamakshi Amman Temple   HINDU TEMPLE
This imposing temple is dedicated to the goddess Parvati in her guise as Kamakshi (She Whose Eyes Awaken Desire). To the right of the temple's entrance is the marriage hall, with wonderful ornate pillars, and directly ahead is the main shrine topped with a golden *vimana* (legendary flying chariot). Again, non-Hindus cannot enter the sanctum, where Kamakshi/Parvati is depicted, uncharacteristically, in the lotus position. Each February/March carriages housing statues of the temple deities are hauled

through the streets; this procession should not be missed if you're in the vicinity.

Devarajaswami Temple   HINDU TEMPLE
(camera/video ₹5/100) Dedicated to Vishnu, this enormous monument was built by the Vijayanagars and is among the most impressive of Kanchipuram's temples. It has a beautifully sculptured '1000-pillared' hall (admission ₹1; only 96 of the original 1000 remain) as well as a marriage hall commemorating the wedding of Vishnu and Lakshmi. One of the temple's most notable features is a huge chain carved from a single piece of stone, which can be seen at each corner of the *mandapam*. The temple is supposedly the place to go to receive cures from lizard-related illnesses, thanks to twin silver- and gold-plated reptiles that crawl over the temple ceiling.

Every 40 years the waters of the temple tank are drained, revealing a huge wooden statue of Vishnu that is worshipped for 48 days. You may like to hang around for the next viewing – in 2019. Otherwise, float festivals (when deities are literally floated across the reservoir) are held on the tank three times a year.

Vaikunta Perumal Temple   HINDU TEMPLE
Roughly 1200 years old and dedicated to Vishnu, this temple was built shortly after the Kailasanatha. The cloisters inside the outer wall consist of lion pillars and are representative of the first phase in the architectural evolution of the grand 1000-pillared halls. The main shrine, which is uniquely spread over three levels, contains images of Vishnu standing, sitting, reclining and riding his preferred mount, the garuda (half-eagle,

half-man). There's another monitor lizard icon here.

🛏 Sleeping & Eating

Kanchi's cheap pilgrims' lodges are shabby, but there are a few decent midrange options.

GRT Regency HOTEL **$$**
(☎27225250; www.grthotels.com; 487 Gandhi Rd; s/d incl breakfast ₹2250/2750; 🅿🛜) Set back from the noisy main road, this place probably has the cleanest and most comfortable rooms you'll find in Kanchi. The attached **Dakshin** restaurant (mains ₹180 to ₹375) is a tad overpriced but is a plush AC spot that offers a big multicuisine menu including Western-style breakfast, good seafood (especially the Indian dishes) and tasty tandoori.

Sri Sakthi Residency HOTEL **$**
(☎27233799; www.sreesakthiresidency.com; 71 Nellukkara St; s/d from ₹800/900; 🅿) Not bad value; simple blonde-wood furniture and coloured walls make the rooms fairly modern, with only a touch of fraying round the edges. There's a fine veg restaurant under the hotel.

MM Hotel HOTEL **$**
(☎27227250; www.mmhotels.com; 65 Nellukkara St; d from ₹800; 🅿) A busy and clean hotel, with shiny floors and flatscreen TVs, frequented by Indian businesspeople. A Saravana Bhavan veg restaurant is next door, with a welcome AC dining room.

ⓘ Information

Axis Bank ATM (Gandhi Rd)
Googly (144 Kamaraja St; per hr ₹20; ◷7.30am-10.30pm) Internet access.
State Bank of India ATM (Hospital Rd)

ⓘ Getting There & Away

Regular suburban trains direct to Kanchipuram leave from Beach, Fort or Egmore stations in Chennai .The busy bus stand is in the centre of town. Destinations from the bus stand include:
Bengaluru ₹110 to ₹160, six hours, two daily
Chennai ₹26, two hours, every 15 minutes
Mamallapuram ₹27, two hours, nine daily
Puducherry ₹36, three hours, 12 daily
Tiruvannamalai ₹38, three hours, hourly
Trichy ₹110, seven hours, four daily
Vellore ₹26, two hours, every 15 minutes

ⓘ Getting Around

Bicycles can be hired from stalls around the bus stand. An autorickshaw for a half-day tour of the five main temples (around ₹400) will inevitably involve a stop at a silk shop.

Vellore

☏0416 / POP 386,746

For a dusty bazaar town, Vellore feels kinda cosmopolitan, thanks to a couple of tertiary institutions and the Christian Medical College (CMC) Hospital, one of the finest hospitals in India. The hospital attracts international medical students as well as patients from all over India, and the town is worth a day for soaking up both its historical ambience – the massive Vijayanagar fort rewards a wander – and small-town-but-international vibe. The new Sripuram Golden Temple, just out of town, draws pilgrims from all over India.

⊙ Sights

Sripuram Golden Temple HINDU TEMPLE
(Mahalakshmi Temple; admission free) This controversial temple (it was built just a few years ago with 1½ tons of gold on the roof, and some have questioned whether the money could have been better spent) is in a lovely garden setting 7km south of town, and is popular with pilgrims; there's a certain thrill in seeing all that carved gold up close. There's a huge security presence, with no electronic items allowed inside the gates (your bag will be searched and screened), as well as an enforced dress code (no shorts, no legs or shoulders on display), and you have to keep strictly to the roped-off walkway that's lined with quotes from the temple's guru and strident calls for donations. You can pay ₹250 to walk straight in, otherwise there are long queues in hot caged corridors. Buses (₹8) run regularly from the New Bus Stand; an autorickshaw costs ₹80.

Vellore Fort FORT COMPLEX
The solid walls and dry moat of the splendid Vellore Fort dominate the west side of town. It was built in the 16th century and passed briefly into the hands of the Marathas in 1676 and the Mughals in 1708. The British occupied the fort in 1760 following the fall of Srirangapatnam and the death of Tipu Sultan. These days it houses various government offices, parade grounds, a university, a church, an ancient mosque and a police recruiting school.

At the west side of the fort complex, the small **Archaeological Survey Museum** (admission free; ◷9am-5pm Sat-Thu) contains sculptures dating back to Pallava and Chola times. Next door, pretty **St John's Church** (1846) is only open for Sunday services. On the east side, the **Government Museum** (Indian/foreigner ₹5/100; ⊘9.30am-5pm Sat-Thu) displays hero stones in the forecourt dating from the 8th century and depicting the stories of war heroes in battle. The dusty exhibits have seen much better days, but the small collection of tribal clothes and artefacts is interesting.

Near the fort entrance, **Jalakanteshwara Temple** (⊘6am-1pm & 3-8.30pm), a gem of late Vijayanagar architecture, was built about 1566. Check out the small, detailed sculptures on the walls of the marriage hall. For many years the temple was occupied by garrisons and temple rituals ceased. Now it's once again a place of worship after it was reconsecrated in the mid-1980s.

🛏 Sleeping & Eating

Vellore's cheap hotels are concentrated along the roads south of and parallel to the hospital, mostly catering to people in town for treatment. The cheapest are pretty grim, and there's not much at the top end, but Vellore's your city when it comes to bland rooms in the space between budget and midrange.

Darling Residency   HOTEL **$$**
(✆2213001; darling_residency@yahoo.com; 11/8 Officer's Line; s/d from ₹1400/1700; ❉@🗢) It's no five-star, but rooms are clean and comfortable (if forgettable), staff are friendly and there's even a small fitness room with exercise bike. The rooftop **Aranya Roof Garden Restaurant** (open lunch and dinner) is cool and breezy.

Hotel Palm Tree   HOTEL **$**
(✆2222960; hotelpalmtree@yahoo.in; 10 Thennamaram Rd; s/d from ₹850/950; ❉@) Down a lane just off Officer's Line, not far south of the fort. Rooms are clean and spruce, with IKEA-style furniture and coloured feature walls, and staff are helpful.

Ismail Residency   HOTEL **$**
(✆2223216; Ida Scudder Rd (Arcot Rd); s/d from ₹600/700; ❉) A five-room lodge with clean rooms that are a tad bigger than others along this stretch.

Hotel River View   HOTEL **$$**
(✆2225251; Katpadi Rd; d from ₹1000; ❉) North of the town centre and close to the New Bus Stand, this hotel benefits from a relatively quiet location and pleasant gardens, but the 'river view' is hardly that. Rooms are spacious, and the restaurants are both good, but service is odd-to-rude and bathroom cleaning isn't quite up to scratch for these prices.

Meher Hotel   HOTEL **$**
(✆2220992; Ida Scudder Rd; s/d ₹600/700) Right across from the hospital entrance, this is one of a string of similarly priced places with smallish, clean, undecorated rooms that get a bit of street noise.

Hotel Arthy   INDIAN **$**
(Ida Scudder Rd; mains ₹10-50) A bunch of cheap veg restaurants line Ida Scudder Rd, but this place is one of the cleanest, with tasty South Indian favourites plus cheap-and-yummy biryani; the rather good 'special thali' is ₹50.

ℹ Information

There are several internet cafes around town, including a few opposite the hospital on Ida Scudder Rd (Arcot Rd).

Axis Bank ATM (Officer's Line) A couple of blocks south of the fort.

Geo Wings Internet (Ida Scudder Rd; per hr ₹30; ⊘9am-9pm)

State Bank of India ATM (Bangalore Rd) There's another ATM a couple of blocks north of the hospital on Katpadi Rd.

Tourist office (Vellore Fort; ⊘10am-1pm & 2-2.30pm Mon-Fri)

UAE Exchange (Ida Scudder Rd; ⊘9.30am-6pm Mon-Fri, to 4pm Sat) Foreign exchange, in the same building as the Meher Hotel.

ℹ Getting There & Away

Bus

The New Bus Stand is about 500m from the Hotel River View, 1.5km to the north of town. AC Volvo buses run 12 times a day to Chennai (₹145). Government bus services from the New Bus Stand include:

Chennai ₹54, three daily, every 15 minutes

Bengaluru ₹87, five daily, every 30 minutes

Kanchipuram ₹26, two hours, every 15 minutes

Tiruvannamalai ₹38, two hours, every 30 minutes

Trichy ₹120, seven hours, three daily

Train

Vellore's main train station is 5km north at Katpadi. Bus 192 shuttles between the station and town. There are at least six daily express trains to/from Chennai Central (2nd class/sleeper ₹76/133).

Tiruvannamalai

☑ 04175 / POP 130.567

There are temple towns, there are mountain towns, and there are temple-mountain towns where God appears as a phallus of fire. Welcome to Tiruvannamalai. About 85km south of Vellore and flanked by boulder-strewn Mt Arunachala, this is one of the five 'elemental' cities of Shiva; here the god is worshipped in his fire incarnation as Arunachaleswar (see boxed text, p1012). At each full moon Mt Arunachala swells with thousands of pilgrims who circumnavigate the base of the mountain, but at any time you'll see Shaivite priests, sadhus (spiritual men) and devotees gathered around the temple. Tiruvannamalai is also home to the Sri Ramana (also known as Sri Ramanasramam) Ashram.

Budget and spiritual-minded travellers who see the Mamallapuram scene as played out are increasingly making their way here; in the streets near the ashram you'll find a few congenial cafes and hotels, and the ubiquitous Kashmiri souvenir shops.

◉ Sights & Activities

Arunachaleswar Temple　　HINDU TEMPLE
(☉5am-12.30pm & 3.30-9pm) The Arunachaleswar is awash in golden flames and the roasting scent of burning ghee, as befits the fire incarnation of the Destroyer of the Universe. Covering some 10 hectares, this vast temple is one of the largest in India. Four large unpainted *gopurams,* one for each cardinal point, front the approaches, with the eastern tower rising 13 storeys and an astonishing 66m.

You enter Arunachaleswar through concentric rings of profanity evolving into sacredness, from the outer wall of beggars and merchants, past dark corridors recessed with bejewelled gods and, finally, into the heart of the temple, where a roaring oven that looks like a walnut shell spewing fire is tended by temple Brahmins in front of a lingam. *Puja* is performed about seven times daily; a notice displays the times. This is a remarkably hassle-free temple to wander through.

Mt Arunachala　　MOUNTAIN
Known as Sonachalam (Red Mountain) in Sanskrit, this 800m-high extinct volcano dominates Tiruvannamalai and local conceptions of the element of fire, which supposedly finds its sacred abode in Arunachala's heart. On full-moon and festival days, thousands of pilgrims circumnavigate the 14km base of the mountain. If you're not quite that devoted, an autorickshaw will take you around for about ₹200 if things are quiet, or up to double that on festival days. An alternative is to pick up a circle map from the ashram office, hire a bicycle from the road near the entrance and ride your way around.

You can make a sort of phallus pilgrimage here by visiting eight famous linga dotted around the mountain's cardinal and subcardinal spokes. Also, watch out for the field of a thousand lingam, 'planted' by domestic and overseas donators from Malaysia to the USA.

For a superb view of the Arunachaleswar Temple, climb part or all the way up the hill (about four hours return). There's a signed path that leads up through village homes near the northwest corner of the temple, passing two caves, **Virupaksha** and **Skandasramam**. Sri Ramana Maharshi lived and meditated in these caves for more than 20 years from 1899 to 1922, after which he and his growing band of spiritual followers established the ashram.

THE LINGAM OF FIRE

Legend has it that Shiva appeared as a column of fire on Mt Arunachala, creating the original symbol of the lingam. Each November/December full moon, the **Karthikai Deepam Festival** celebrates this legend throughout India but becomes particularly significant at Tiruvannamalai. Here, a huge fire, lit from a 30m wick immersed in 2000L of ghee, blazes from the top of Mt Arunachala for days. In homes, lamps honour Shiva and his fiery lingam. The fire symbolises Shiva's light, which eradicates darkness and evil.

At festival time up to half a million people come to Tiruvannamalai. In honour of Shiva, they scale the mountain or circumnavigate its base. On the upward path, steps quickly give way to jagged and unstable rocks. There's no shade, the sun is relentless and the journey must be undertaken in bare feet – a mark of respect to the deity. None of this deters the thousands of pilgrims who quietly and joyfully make their way to the top and the abode of their deity.

Sri Ramana Ashram
ASHRAM

(☎237200; www.sriramanamaharshi.org; ☺office 7.30am-12.30pm & 2-6.30pm) This tranquil ashram, 2km southwest of Tiruvannamalai, draws devotees of Sri Ramana Maharshi, a guru who died in 1950 after nearly 50 years in contemplation. It's a very relaxed place, set in green surrounds, where visitors are able to meditate or worship the shrine where the guru achieved samadhi (conscious exit from the body). Day visits are permitted but *devotees only* may stay at the ashram by applying in writing (email is acceptable), preferably at least three months in advance.

☞ Tours

Bougainvillea Tours (☎9500325159; www.bougainvilleatours.com) offers a range of guided walks around the mountain and to the temples, as well as a bullock-cart circumnavigation of the mountain. Full-moon pilgrimage tours are also run from Chennai by the TTDC (p998).

🛏 Sleeping & Eating

Tiruvannamalai can be visited as a day trip from Puducherry or Chennai, but more and more travellers are staying on. There are budget lodges around the temple, but quality is generally lacking. During festival time (November/December) prices can rise by a staggering 1000%.

Arunachala Ramana Home
HOTEL $

(☎236120; www.arunachalaramanahome.com; 70 Ramana Nagar, Chengam Rd; s/d from ₹300/400, d with AC ₹ 700; ❄) Basic, clean and friendly, this popular place is not far from the ashram. Next door is the excellent Manna Cafe, which answers any need for non-Indian food, including salads, pasta and bread. Plenty of chai stalls and veg cafes are nearby.

Hotel Ganesh
HOTEL $

(☎2226701; 111A Big St; d ₹275-₹605; ❄) On the busy bazaar road running along the north side of the temple, Ganesh is a little haven of peace and value. Some rooms are poky, but they're clean enough and the inner courtyard balcony is pleasant. There's a decent veg restaurant downstairs.

Hotel Arunachala Residency
HOTEL $

(☎228300; www.hotelarunachala.com; 5 Vada Sannathi St; s/d/tr from ₹400/600/750; ❄) The best of the temple-adjacent hotels, this place right next to the main temple entrance is clean and fine with pretentions to luxury apparent in the marblesque floors and ugly

furniture. The veg restaurant downstairs has simple, very good, South Indian dishes. It's a much better option than the inexplicably popular Hotel Ramakrishna, nearby on the highway, which has run-down rooms at similar prices.

Shanti Internet Café
CAFE $

(www.shanticafe.com; 115 Chengam Rd; 📶) Near the ashram. A popular, relaxed spot with cushion seating on the floor and a small menu of sandwiches, salads, shakes and cakes. There's internet access downstairs (per hour ₹25) and wi-fi in the cafe.

❶ Getting There & Away

There are buses every half-hour to Chennai (₹66, 3½ hours) and Vellore (₹38, two hours). There are at least three daily buses to Puducherry (₹40, three hours). A taxi to Puducherry (via Gingee) costs around ₹1500 return, or ₹900 one way.

Only local passenger trains use Tiruvannamalai train station – two trains a day pass through between Vellore and Villupuram (where you can change for Puducherry).

Gingee (Senji)
☎04145

Somewhere about 37km east of Tiruvannamalai, nature sprinkled a smattering of marbles – rounded boulders and lumpy rocks – in shades of grey, brown and red over the flat green paddies of Tamil Nadu. Then man turned two of these stony protrusions into the **Rajagiri & Krishnagiri** (King & Queen Fort; Indian/foreigner ₹5/150; ☺9am-5pm). Constructed mainly in the 16th century by the Vijayanagars (though some structures date from the 13th century), these edifices, which poke out of the Tamil plain like castles misplaced by the *Lord of the Rings,* have been occupied by the Marathas, the Mughals, the French and, finally, the British.

It's a good hike to the top of either fort, but along the way you'll pass through several monuments, from *gopurams* to granaries. A walk around will take half a day, especially if you cross the road and make the steep ascent to Krishnagiri. Buildings within Rajagiri (on the south side of the road) include a Shiva temple, a mosque and – most prominent – the restored audience hall. Almost all have been marred by graffiti.

It's easy to day trip to Gingee from Puducherry (67km) or Tiruvannamalai (37km). Buses leave every 30 minutes from

Tiruvannamalai (₹13, 1½ hours). Ask to be let off at 'the fort', 2km before Gingee town. An autorickshaw from Gingee to the fort costs about ₹90 one way.

Puducherry (Pondicherry)

♪0413 / POP 220,749

Let's get something clear: if you came to Puducherry (which used to be called Pondicherry and is almost always referred to as 'Pondy') expecting a Provençal village in South India, you're in for some sore disappointment, *mon ami*. Most of Pondy is Tamil Nadu: honk-scream-screech-honk-chaos Tamil Nadu. Running through this is a thin trickle of colonial Pondy: some cobblestones, mustard-yellow townhouses, and here and there a shady boulevard that could put you in mind of gendarmes marching past sari-clad belles – HONK!

On top of everything are hotels, restaurants and 'lifestyle' shops that sell a vision of *vieux Asie* created by savvy entrepreneurs and embellished by Gallic creative types who arrived here on the French hippie trail. Their presence has in turn attracted Indian artists and designers, and thus, Pondy's vibe: less faded colonial *ville*, more contemporary bohemian, vaguely New Age – but also faintly Old World – node on the international travel trail.

Enjoy the shopping, the French food (hello steak!), the beer (goodbye Tamil Nadu alcohol taxes – Pondy is a Union Territory) and, if you like, yoga and meditation at the Sri Aurobindo Ashram.

Puducherry is split from east to west by a partially covered sewer...we mean, canal. The more 'French' part of town is on the east side (towards the sea), the more typically Indian portion to the west. Nehru St and Lal Bahadur Sastri, better known as Rue Bussy, are the main east–west streets; Mahatma Gandhi (MG) Rd and Mission St (Cathedral St) are the north–south thoroughfares. Pondy's grid design makes it relatively easy to follow, although many streets have one name at one end and another at the other, while others use the French 'Rue' instead of 'Street'.

◉ Sights & Activities

French Quarter   OLD NEIGHBOURHOOD

Pocketed away in the eastern alleys are a series of cobbled roads, white and mustard buildings in various states of romantic *déshabillé*, and a slight sense of Gallic glory

gone by, otherwise known as the French Quarter. The best way to explore these streets is via Puducherry's heritage walk. Start at the north end of Goubert Ave, the seafront promenade, and wander south past the French consulate and the Gandhi Statue. Turn right at the Hôtel de Ville (Town Hall) on Rue Mahe Labourdonnais, past the shady Bharathi Park. From there it's a matter of pottering south through Dumas, Romain Rolland and Suffren Sts. You may also want to take a look down Vysial St, between MG Rd and Mission St; locals say this tree-lined block is one of the last faithfully maintained slices of old Pondy.

Sri Aurobindo Ashram   ASHRAM

(cnr Marine & Manakula Vinayagar Koil Sts) Founded in 1926 by Sri Aurobindo and a French woman known as 'the Mother' (whose visage is *everywhere* here), this ashram seeks to synthesise yoga and modern science. After Aurobindo's death, spiritual authority (and minor religious celebrity) passed to the Mother, who died in 1973 aged 97. A constant flow of visitors files through the main ashram building (☉8am-noon & 2-5pm), which has the flower-festooned samadhi of Aurobindo and the Mother in the central courtyard. Opening hours are longer for guests of any of the ashram's accommodation around the town.

Puducherry Museum   MUSUEM

(15 St Louis St; adult/child ₹2/1; ☉9.40am-1pm & 2-5.20pm Tue-Sun) Goodness knows how this cute little museum keeps its artefacts from rotting, considering there's a whole floor of French-era furniture sitting in the South Indian humidity. As you amble through the colonial-era building, keep an eye peeled for Pallava and Chola sculptures, French Union-era bric-a-brac, and coins and shards of pottery excavated from Arikamedu, a once-major seaport a few kilometres south of Puducherry that traded with the Roman Empire during the 1st century BC.

Churches   CHURCHES

Puducherry has one of the best collections of over-the-top cathedrals in India. *Merci*, French missionaries. The Church of Our Lady of the Immaculate Conception (Mission St), completed in 1791, is a robin's-egg-blue-and-cloud-white typically Jesuit edifice, while the brown-and-white grandiosity of the Sacred Heart Church (Subbayah Salai) is set off by stained glass and a Gothic sense of proportion. The mellow pink-and-cream Notre Dame de Anges (Dumas St), built in

1858, looks sublime in the late-afternoon light. The smooth limestone interior was made using eggshells in the plaster.

Sri Manakula Vinayagar Temple HINDU TEMPLE
(Manakula Vinayagar Koil St; ⌚5.45am-12.30pm & 4-9.30pm) Pondy may have more churches than most towns, but this is still India, and the Hindu faith still reigns supreme. Don't miss the chance to watch tourists, pilgrims and the curious get a head pat from the temple elephant who stands outside Sri Manakula Vinayagar Temple, dedicated to Ganesh and tucked down a backstreet just south of the Sri Aurobindo Ashram. The temple also contains over 40 skillfully painted friezes.

Botanical Gardens GARDEN
(admission free; ⌚10am-5pm) Established by the French in 1826, the botanical gardens form a green, if somewhat litter-strewn, oasis on the southwest side of town.

Beaches BEACHES
Pondy is a seaside town, but that doesn't make it a beach destination; the city's sand is a thin strip of dirty brown blah that slurps into a seawall of jagged rocks. With that said, Goubert Ave (Beach Rd) is a killer stroll, especially at dawn and dusk when everyone in town takes a constitutional or romantic stroll. There are a few decent beaches to the north and south of town. Quiet, Reppo and Serenity Beaches are all north of the centre, within 8km of Puducherry. Chunnambar, 8km south, has Paradise Beach, water sports and backwater boat cruises. Both areas are becoming inundated with high-end resorts. The tourist office has details.

Yoga
Puducherry has an annual International Yoga Festival. **Ayurvedic Holistic Healing Centre** (☎6537651; 6 Sengeniammal Koil St) performs detox services, back procedures, varna point massage, skin treatment, and offers ayurvedic massages and yoga courses. You can practise (and study) yoga at Sri Aurobindo Ashram. **International Centre for Yoga Education & Research** (ICYER; ☎2241561; www.icyer.com; 16A Mettu St, Chinnamudaliarchavady, Kottukuppam), also known as the Ananda Ashram, conducts annual six-month yoga teacher-training courses and 10-day introductory summer courses (€500, including food and lodging).

Tours

The local tourist office runs half-day sightseeing tours (₹100 to ₹150, 1.30pm to 5pm) to the Sacred Heart Church, Auroville and Sri Aurobindo Ashram. Full-day tours (₹200 to ₹250, 9.45am to 5pm) cover the same area plus the botanical gardens, Puducherry Museum, Sri Manakula Vinayagar Temple and the Chunnambar water sports complex.

Shanti Tours (Romain Rolland St; ⌚8am-9pm Mon-Sat, 9am-6pm Sun) offers recommended two-hour **walking tours** (per person ₹200) of Puducherry with informed, multilingual guides.

Festivals & Events

International Yoga Festival YOGA
(4-7 Jan) Puducherry's ashrams and yoga culture are put on show with workshops, classes, and music and dance events. Held throughout the city, the event attracts yoga masters from all over India.

Bastille Day PARADE
(14 Jul) Street parades and a bit of French pomp and ceremony are all part of the fun at this celebration.

Sleeping

If you've been saving for a special occasion, splurge here, because Puducherry's lodgings are as good as South India gets. Local heritage houses manage to combine colonial romanticism with modern spoilage and, dare we say, French playfulness, like vintage movie posters and colour schemes that run from monochrome to neon-bright; these same rooms are likely to run to hundreds of dollars in the West.

Sri Aurobindo Ashram runs a lot of local budget accommodation. The lodgings are clean and you'll be around like-minded souls (ie the budget – and karma – conscious). But they come with rules: 10.30pm curfew and no smoking or alcohol. For information and reservations, contact the **Sri Aurobindo information centre** (☎2233604; bureaucentral@sriaurobindoashram.org; Cottage Complex, cnr Rangapillai St & Ambour Salai; ⌚6am-8pm).

It's smart to book ahead if you plan on arriving at a weekend; hotels tend to fill up with Indian tourists.

TOP CHOICE **Calve** BOUTIQUE HOTEL $$$
(☎2224261; www.calve.in; 36 Vysial St; r incl breakfast ₹3555-5355; ❄) This excellent heritage option, located on a quiet, tree-shaded boulevard, combines a soaring sense of high-ceilinged space with egg-white walls, wooden shutters, flat-screen TVs, huge niche-embedded mattresses and a warm backdrop

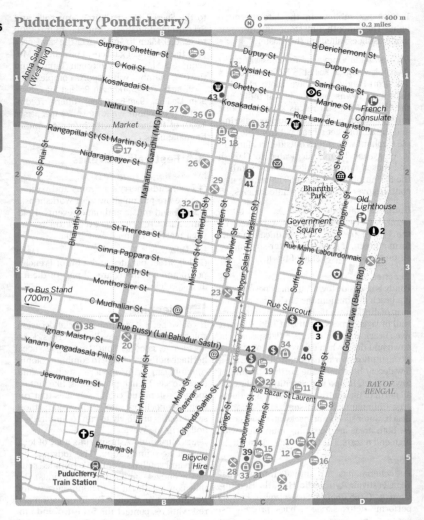

of Burmese teak floors and banisters. Add gorgeous tiled floors, beautiful furniture and big baths, and you've got a winner.

Dumas Guest House BOUTIQUE HOTEL **$$**
(☎2225726; www.dumasguesthouse.com; 36 Dumas St; d from ₹2000; ✱) All whitewash and dark wood, this antique-filled heritage option has real personality. Enjoy the carved doors, quiet gardens, slight quirkiness in the decor and very friendly multilingual staff.

Les Hibiscus BOUTIQUE HOTEL **$$**
(☎2227480; www.leshibiscus.com; 49 Suffren St; d incl breakfast ₹2500; ✱@) Not dissimilar to the

Dumas in its white-and-wood heritage style, Hibiscus has just four high-ceilinged rooms with gorgeous antique beds and flatscreen TVs. Travellers have raved about the friendly, helpful owner, and the tasty complimentary breakfast that will set you up for the day.

Kailash Guest House HOTEL **$**
(☎2224485; www.kailashguesthouse.in; cnr Vysial & Mission Sts; s/d from ₹500/750; ✱) The best value for money in this price range; Kailash has simple, super-clean rooms and friendly management. It's geared to traveller needs, with communal areas, shared fridge and clothes-drying facilities, and bike rental.

Villa Helena BOUTIQUE HOTEL **$$**
(☏2226789; villahelena@satyam.net.in; 13 Lal Bahadur Shastri St; r ₹2200-2800; ❄) What sits Helena apart from her heritage siblings is the dash of vintage fun she overlays on respectable colonial facades. With 1930s-era Chinese movie posters, wrought-iron beds and high-ceilinged rooms, you feel caught between a black-and-white colonial noir flick and a modern designer's dream.

Hotel De L'Orient BOUTIQUE HOTEL **$$$**
(☏2343067; www.neemranahotels.com; 17 Romain Rolland St; r ₹3000-6500; ❄) This is as grand as it gets in Puducherry: a restored colonial mansion with rooms that appeal to your inner pith-helmeted aristocrat. Should you need a sense of columned regal importance, the hush of breezy verandas and the scurrying service of men in clean white uniforms,

this is the place to book. An attached shop has beautiful, wildly overpriced souvenirs.

Park Guest House ASHRAM HOTEL **$**
(☏2224644; 1 Goubert Ave; s/d from ₹450/600) This is the most soughtafter ashram address in town thanks to its wonderful seafront position. All front rooms face the sea and have their own porch or balcony, and there's a large garden area for morning yoga or meditation. These are the best-value AC rooms in town. Prebooking is technically possible but can be difficult, and reception staff can be unfriendly until they're sure you're going to obey the house rules.

New Guest House ASHRAM HOTEL **$**
(☏2221553; 64 Romain Rolland St; d ₹200, r up to 8 people ₹480) Sparse, huge and packed with the ashram faithful; this is a great spot for those who love the monastery cubicle school of lodging.

Santhi Inn
HOTEL $

(☏2220946; 57 Nehru St; s/d ₹900/1000; ❄)
The multistorey Santhi certainly isn't a
heritage house, but it's a clean, bland
spot with comfy beds, a rooftop bar and a
conveniently central location.

Ajantha Beach Guest House
HOTEL $$

(☏2338898; 1 Rue Bazar St Laurent; d with sea
view ₹1500; ❄) The location is the only real
selling point – right on the beachfront
promenade. The four sea-view rooms are
plain but comfortable and have balconies;
others are drab and windowless. Next-
door **Lotus Bay View Hotel** has shinier,
much more luxurious but equally charac-
ter-free rooms at nearly twice the price.

Hotel de Pondichery
BOUTIQUE HOTEL $$

(☏2227409; 38 Dumas St; s/d ₹ 1800/2500; ❄)
Yet another heritage home, this place has
colonial-style rooms and outdoor terraces.
It's more Old World than luxurious, but
rooms are private and quiet, and staff are
lovely.

Raj Lodge
HOTEL $

(☏2337346; www.rajlodge.in; 57 Rangapillai St;
s/d ₹300/450, d with AC ₹750; ❄) A friendly,
central lodge with basic, dark but clean
rooms.

🍴 Eating

Puducherry is a culinary highlight of Tamil
Nadu; you get the best of South Indian cooking plus several restaurants specialising in
well-prepped French and Italian cuisine. If
you've been missing cheese or have a hankering for pâté, you're in luck, and *everyone* in the French quarter offers crepes and
good brewed coffee. There's a string of cheap
street stalls open past 11pm on Anna Salai
and Lal Bahadur Shastri St, and more good
cheap Indian eateries around the market.

For self-caterers, **Nilgiris Supermarket**
(cnr Mission & Rangapillai Sts; ⏰9am-9pm) has a
big range of supplies (in addition to toiletries, children's books and toys.)

TOP CHOICE **Satsanga**
MULTICUISINE $$

(☏2225867; 30-32 Labourdonnais St; mains ₹170-
350; ⏰lunch & dinner) This deservedly popular
garden spot serves excellent Continental
cuisine and, like most places in this genre, a
full Indian menu as well. The large variety of
sausages, pâté and lovely home-made bread
and butter goes down a particular treat,
as do the steaks. **Satsanga Epicerie**, next
door, sells French and Italian food supplies;
pasta, cheese, even vacuum-packed *jamon*.

Salle a Manger
INDO-FRENCH $$

(www.calve.in; Calve hotel, 36 Vysial St; mains
₹150-300; ❄) The speciality here is 'Creole'
food, using recipes sourced from Pondy's
French-Indian families and using lots of seafood and spices: try the Fish Vindali, full of
fresh flavours. Like the decor – all teak and
teal-coloured walls – the food has an Indo-
Chinese vibe.

kasha ki aasha
CAFE $$

(www.kasha-ki-aasha.com; 23 Rue Surcouf; mains
₹125-225; ⏰8am-7pm Mon-Sat) You'll get a
great pancake breakfast, good lunches (try
the 'European-style thali') and delicious
cakes served on the pretty rooftop of this
colonial-house-cum-craftshop-cum-cafe.
Indo-European fusion food includes chips
with chutney, and pizza dosa. The heat in
some dishes has been dialled back a bit for
Western tastes, but it's all delicious.

Le Club
MULTICUISINE $$

(38 Dumas St; mains ₹120-330; ⏰lunch & dinner)
This place wraps three restaurants into one,
with heavy French fare at Le Bistro, a simple
garden terrace at Le Club, and Vietnamese
and Southeast Asian fare in the attached
Indochine. Le Club also offers Contintental
breakfasts.

Surguru
SOUTH INDIAN $

(99 Mission St; mains ₹40-100; ⏰lunch & dinner)
Simple South Indian served in a posh setting. Surguru is the fix for thali addicts who
like their veg accompanied by the strongest
AC this side of Chennai. There's a couple of
branches round town.

Le Café
CAFE $$

(Goubert Ave; mains ₹50-170; ⏰24hr) Situated
near the Gandhi statue, this is a good spot
for sandwiches, cake, coffee (hot or ice), wel-
come fresh breezes and clean views over the
Bay of Bengal. Be warned, service can be se-
riously slow; but it's one of the nicest spots
in town to wait.

La Terrasse
CONTINENTAL $$

(5 Subbayah Salai; pizzas ₹120-200; ⏰breakfast,
lunch & dinner Thu-Tue) This simple semi-open-
air place near the southern end of the promenade has a wide menu but is best known
for good pizzas and safe salads, as opposed
to its rather ordinary Indian food. No alcohol is served.

Café des Artes
CAFE $

(Labourdonnais St; ⏰breakfast, lunch & dinner;
☎) Good brekky and coffee, wi-fi and a

nice outdoor/veranda setting outside a small gallery.

Café de Flore
CAFE $$

(Maison de Colombani, Dumas St; ⏱8.30am-8pm) In the Alliance Française's performance space, on an airy veranda overlooking a garden, you'll find mocktails, great coffee, sandwiches and chips, along with copies of Le Monde to browse.

Baker St
BAKERY $

(Rue Bussy; pastries ₹35-120) A very popular upmarket, French-style bakery with cakes, brownies, meringues, quiches, baguettes and croissants. Eat in or takeaway.

Saravana Bhavan
SOUTH INDIAN $

(Nehru St; mains ₹30-50) A clean setting with good cheap South Indian – all the thalis, dosa and vada you could want.

Drinking & Entertainment

Although this is one of the better spots in Tamil Nadu to sink a beer, closing time is a decidedly un-Gallic 11pm. If you're here on a Friday or Saturday, get ready for some late-night fun, when Pondy stays open until (drum roll)...11.30pm! With low taxes on alcohol, Puducherry has a reputation for cheap booze. The reality is you'll really only find cheap beer in 'liquor shops' or the darkened bars attached to them. Many of the garden and rooftop restaurants in the French Quarter have pleasant bar areas, especially Satsanga and Le Club.

L'e-Space Coffee & Arts
CAFE

(2 Labourdonnais St; ⏱8am-11pm) A battered, quirky little semi-open-air cafe for breakfasts, juice, coffee, a bite and some fine cocktails (₹160 to ₹180). Staff are friendly, locals and tourists congregate here, and all in all it's the most social traveller spot in Pondy.

Shopping

With all the yoga yuppies congregating here, Pondy specialises in the boutique-chic-meets-Indian-bazaar school of fashion, accessories and souvenirs. Every Sunday evening the central shopping area on and around Nehru St is packed with clothes stalls strung up in front of closed shopfronts. Among other things, you'll find the kind of cotton pants and shirts that would cost waaaay more in Pondy's boutiques.

Fabindia
CLOTHING

(www.fabindia.com; 59 Suffren St; ⏱10am-8pm) Opposite Alliance Française, this shop has a good variety of quality woven goods and furnishings, traditionally made but with a contemporary feel. This chain has been in operation since 1960, and one of its selling points is its 'fair, equitable and helpful relationship' with village producers. Next door Pondy Cre'Art is also worth checking out, with handbags, handmade paper journals and clothes.

Geethanjali
ANTIQUES

(20 Lal Bahadur Shastri St; ⏱10am-7pm) The sort of place where Indiana Jones gets the sweats, this antique and curio shop sells statues, sculptures, paintings and furniture culled from Puducherry's colonial and even pre-colonial history.

Kalki
ACCESSORIES

(134 Mission St; ⏱9.30am-8.30pm) Beautiful, jewel-coloured silk clothes, scarves and shoes, as well as jewellery, candles, knick-knacks and more.

kasha ki aasha
CLOTHING, HANDICRAFTS

(www.kasha-ki-aasha.com; 23 Rue Surcouf; ⏱8am-7pm Mon-Sat) Fabulous fabrics, gorgeous garments and comfy handmade leather sandals, as well as crafts, are sourced directly from their makers and sold by an all-women staff in this lovely old colonial house. There's a breezy rooftop eatery on-site.

La Boutique d'Auroville
HANDICRAFTS

(38 Nehru St; ⏱9.30am-1pm & 3.30-8pm Mon-Sat) It's fun browsing through the crafts here, including jewellery, batiks, kalamkari (similar to batik) drawings, carpets and woodcarvings. For more Auroville products head west to the Sri Aurobindo Handmade Paper Factory (50 SV Patel Salai; ⏱8.30am-noon & 1.30-5pm Mon-Sat) for fine handmade paper; ask at the counter about tours of the factory.

Hidesign
BAGS

(cnr Nehru & Mission Sts) Established in Pondy in the 1970s, this boutique sells beautifully made designer leather handbags and 'man bags' in a range of colours, at prices that are very reasonable for what you get. We bought a bag here in 1985 that's still going strong. The 3rd-floor cafe has pasta, burgers and tapas, great coffee and free wi-fi.

Bookshops

French Bookshop
BOOKSTORE

(Suffren St; ⏱9am-12.30pm & 3.30-7.30pm Mon-Sat) This small shop next to Alliance Française carries many French titles.

Libraire Kailash BOOKSTORE
(169 Lal Bahadur Shastri St; ◷9am-8pm Mon-Sat) Another excellent collection of titles, particularly coffee-table books, in French.

Focus Books BOOKSTORE
(204 Mission St; ◷9.30am-1.30pm & 3.30-9pm Mon-Sat) A big range of English-language books, friendly staff, Lonely Planet guides.

ⓘ Information

Puducherry keeps European hours and takes a long lunch break; you can expect most businesses to be closed from about 1pm to 3.30pm.

Cultural Centres

Alliance Française (☎2338146; afpondy@satyam.net.in; 58 Suffren St; ◷9am-noon & 3-6pm Mon-Sat) The French cultural centre has a library, computer centre and art gallery, and conducts French-language classes. Films are shown regularly. The monthly newsletter, *Le Petit Journal*, details forthcoming events. Maison Colombani, its associated exhibition and performance space, is on Dumas St.

Internet Access

Coffee.Com (236 Mission St; per 30min ₹30; ◷10am-10pm) There might be some pressure to buy a drink; don't feel obliged.

Wi Corner (1 Caziavar St, cnr Lal Bahadur Shastri St; per hr ₹30; ◷10am-10pm Mon-Sat)

Medical Services

Lal Bahadur Shastri St between Bharathi St and MG Rd is packed with clinics, pharmacies and two 24-hour hospitals.

New Medical Centre (☎2225289; 470 MG Rd; ◷24hr)

Money

Nilgiris Supermarket has a **forex counter** (◷9am-5.30pm Mon-Sat) upstairs.

Citibank ATM (cnr Lal Bahadur Shastri & Suffren Sts)

ICICI Bank ATM (47 Mission St)

State Bank of India (15 Suffren St)

Thomas Cook (Labourdonnais St; ◷9.30am-6.30pm Mon-Sat) Foreign exchange next to L'e-Space Coffee & Arts.

UTI Bank ATM (164 Rue Bussy)

Tourist Information

Puducherry tourist office (☎2339497; 40 Goubert Ave; ◷9am-5pm)

Travel Agencies

Shanti Travels (Romain Rolland St; ◷8am-9pm Mon-Sat, 9am-6pm Sun) Helpful French-run agency offering bus, train and air ticketing, as well as walking tours, day trips, longer tours and airport pick-ups from Chennai.

ⓘ Getting There & Away

Bus

The bus stand is 500m west of town. See the boxed text for details of services. There's a **booking office** (◷7am-2pm & 4-9pm) at the station.

Taxi

Air-conditioned taxis between Puducherry and Chennai cost around ₹3500; it should be cheaper to/from Chennai Airport.

Train

There are two direct services a day to Chennai Egmore (₹52, five hours, 5.35am and 2.35pm), and one to Tirupathy (₹79, nine hours, 1.40pm). There's a computerised booking service for southern trains at the station.

ⓘ Getting Around

One of the best ways to get around Pondy is by walking. Large three-wheelers shuttle between the bus stand and Gingy St for ₹5, but they're

BUSES FROM PUDUCHERRY (PONDICHERRY)

DESTINATION	FARE (₹)	DURATION (HR)	FREQUENCY (DAILY)
Bengaluru	150	8	4
Chennai	56	3½	50
Chidambaram	36	2	50
Coimbatore	170	9	7
Kanchipuram	40	3	6
Kumbakonam	42	4	6
Mamallapuram	35	2	5
Tiruvannamalai	40	3	10
Trichy	80	5	4

hopelessly overcrowded. Autorickshaws are plentiful – a trip across town costs about ₹50.

Since the streets are broad and flat, the most popular transport is pedal power. Bicycle-hire shops line many of the streets, especially MG Rd and Mission St. You'll also find hire shops in Subbayah Salai and Goubert Ave. The usual rental is ₹10/50 per hour/day.

Mopeds or motorbikes are useful for getting out to the beaches or to Auroville and can be rented from a number of shops and street stalls. The going rate is about ₹150 a day for a gearless scooter and ₹200 for a motorbike.

Auroville

☎ 0413 / POP 1800

Auroville is one of those ideas anyone with a whiff of New Age will love: an international community built on soil donated by 124 countries, where dedicated souls, ignoring creed, colour and nationality, work to build a universal township and realise interconnectedness, love and good old human oneness.

In reality, Auroville is both its high ideals and some not-as-glamorous reality. Imagine over 80 rural settlements encompassing scrubby Tamil countryside, where harmony is strived for if not always realised between 1800 residents representing almost 40 nationalities. Two-thirds of Aurovillians are foreign, and outside opinions of them range from positive vibes to critics who say the town is an enclave for expats seeking a self-indulgent rustic escape.

Ultimately, Auroville encompasses all of the above, and anyone interested in the experiment may want to visit on a day trip from Puducherry. Be prepared for lots of posters celebrating 'The Mother', the French traveller-turned-guru, and founder of the Sri Aurobindo Ashram (p1014). Be warned: Auroville is not that tourist friendly. Each settlement has its own area of expertise and most Aurovillians are busy simply getting on with their work. Still, you may get a sense of the appeal of the place after a visit to the visitor centre and the Matrimandir, Auroville's spiritual heart. One of those unfortunate buildings that tries to look futuristic and ends up coming off dated, this giant golden golf ball/faux Epcot Center contains an inner chamber lined with white marble that houses a solid crystal (the largest in the world), 70cm in diameter, which you won't actually see, since the Matrimandir is not open to casual visitors. But there is a pleasant plot of gardens (⊙10am-1pm & 2-4.30pm daily except Sun afternoon), from where you can spy the struc-

ture; you need to pick up a pass (free) from the information service in the visitor centre.   **1021**

🛏 Sleeping & Eating

You can only stay in Auroville if you're serious about contributing to it. A stay of at least a week is preferred and while work isn't obligatory, it is appreciated. Accommodation isn't offered in exchange for work; rooms range from ₹300 to more than ₹1000, and guests are also required to contribute towards the 'maintenance and development' of Auroville.

There are more than 40 guesthouses in Auroville, each tied to communities with specific work missions (women's education, farming etc). The best way to match your interests with the community you'll stay in is to check out the website and, preferably, get suggestions from and make arrangements with the Auroville Guest Service (☎ 2622704; avguests@auroville.org.in) before arriving.

Although there are stores and small roadside eateries in Auroville, and communities have communal dining areas, many Aurovillians gather at the Solar Kitchen – powered by solar energy – which dishes out more than 400 meals daily from its buffet. The cafe at the visitor centre is open to day visitors.

❶ Information

There's a photographic exhibition and video room at the **Auroville Information Service** (www.auroville.org; admission free; ⊙9.15am-1pm & 1.30-5.30pm), which also issues garden passes for external views of the Matrimandir (from 9.45am to 12.30pm and 2pm to 4pm; morning only on Sunday). In the same complex, the **visitor centre** (☎ 2622239; www.auroville.org; ⊙9am-6pm) contains a bookshop, a nice cafe and Boutique d'Auroville, which sells Aurovillian handicrafts.

❶ Getting There & Away

The best way to enter Auroville is from the coast road, at the village of Periyar Mudaliarchavadi. Ask around as it's not well signposted. A return autorickshaw ride from Puducherry is about ₹300, but a better option is to hire a moped or bicycle. It's about 12km from Puducherry to the visitor centre.

CENTRAL TAMIL NADU

Chidambaram

☎ 04144 / POP 67,795

There's basically one reason to visit Chidambaram: the great temple complex of Nataraja, Shiva as the Dancer of the Universe.

The greatest Nataraja temple in India also happens to be a Dravidian architectural highlight and one of the holiest Shiva sites in South India. Chidambaram can be visited as a day trip from Puducherry, or as a stopover between Puducherry and Kumbakonam or Trichy.

Of the many festivals, the two largest are the 10-day chariot festivals, which are celebrated in April/May and December/January. In February/March the five-day Natyanjali Dance Festival attracts performers from all over the country to celebrate Nataraja (Shiva) – Lord of the Dance.

The small town is developed around the Nataraja Temple with streets named after the cardinal points. Accommodation is close to the temple and the bus stand a five-minute walk to the southeast. The train station is about 1km further south.

◉ Sights

Nataraja Temple   HINDU TEMPLE
(◐ courtyard & shrines 6am-noon & 4-10pm)
The legend goes: one day, in a nearby forest, Shiva and Kali got into a dance-off that was judged by the assembled gods. Shiva finished his routine with a high kick to the head that Kali could not duplicate and won the title Nataraja (Lord of the Dance). It is in this form he is worshipped at the great Shiva temple, which draws a regular stream of pilgrims and visitors. The region was a Chola capital from 907 to 1310 and the temple was erected during the later time of the administration, although local guides claim some of the complex was built by the Pallavas in the 6th century. The high-walled 22-hectare complex has four towering *gopurams* decked out in schizophrenic Dravidian stonework.

The main entrance, through the east *gopuram,* off East Car St, depicts the 108 sacred positions of classical Tamil dance. In the northeast of the complex, to the right as you enter, is the 1000-pillared Raja Sabha (King's Hall), open only on festival days, and to the left is the Sivaganga (Temple Tank), which is thick with mudfish and worshippers performing ritual ablutions. To the west of the entrance to the inner sanctum is a depiction of Shiva as Nataraja that is underlined by a distinctly European pair of cherubic angels. In the southwest corner of the second enclosure is the Dance Hall, decorated with 56 pillars, that marks the spot where Shiva outdanced Kali.

Cameras are not allowed inside the temple, and non-Hindus cannot enter the inner sanctum, although you can glimpse its golden roof and its 21,600 tiles (one for every breath a human takes a day). Nataraja images abound, wherein Shiva holds the drum that beats the rhythm of creation and the fire of destruction in his outstretched hands, ending one cycle of creation, beginning another and uniting all opposites – light and dark, good and evil.

Try to catch the fire ceremony, which occurs six times a day and pulls in hundreds of worshippers who watch a ritual essentially unchanged for thousands of years. The entire complex erupts in drum beats and bells, while fires of clarified oil and butter are passed under the image of the deity, thus ensuring the cycle of creation continues.

Brahmin priests will usually guide you for a fee (anywhere from ₹30 up to ₹300, depending on the language skills and knowledge of the guide) around the temple complex. Since the Brahmins work as a co-operative to fund the temple, you may wish to support this magnificent building by way of donation or hiring a guide (but don't feel bound to do so).

🛏 Sleeping & Eating

Chidambaram has many cheap pilgrims' lodges clustered around the temple, but some of these spots come off as pretty dire. If there's anywhere really nice to stay in Chidambaram, we haven't found it yet.

Hotel Saradharam   HOTEL $
(⌨ 221336; www.hotelsaradharam.co.in; 19 VGP St; d incl breakfast ₹770, with AC ₹1400; ※ 🛜) The busy and friendly Saradharam is as good as it gets, and is conveniently located across from the bus stand. It's a bit worn (readers have met bedbugs here, though we remained unbitten), but it's comfortable enough and a welcome respite from the frenzy of the town centre. The good breakfast buffet is a bonus.

Hotel Akshaya   HOTEL $
(⌨ 220192; www.hotel-akshaya.com; 17-18 East Car St; d from ₹600; ※) Close to the temple and also a bit grotty round the edges, this hotel has a wide range of rooms that run the gamut from boxy singles to quite good-value AC 'suites'.

The best places to eat are in hotels. Anupallavi (mains ₹50-120; ◐ lunch & dinner) is an excellent AC multicuisine restaurant in

TOP FIVE TEMPLES

Tamil Nadu is nirvana for anyone wanting to explore South Indian temple culture and architecture. Many of the temples are important places of pilgrimage for Hindus, where daily *puja* (offering or prayer) rituals and colourful festivals will leave a deep impression on even the most temple-weary traveller. Other temples stand out for their stunning architecture, soaring *gopurams* (gateway towers) and intricately carved, pillared *mandapams* (pavilions in front of the temple). Almost all have free admission. There are so many that it pays to be selective, but the choice is subjective. Here's our top five:

» Sri Meenakshi Temple (p1036) This elaborately carved temple complex in Madurai is considered the crowning achievement of South Indian temple architecture.

» Arunachaleswar Temple (p1012) Fire rituals – and the smell of roasting ghee – dominate this huge temple in Tiruvannamalai.

» Brihadishwara Temple (p1025) Thanjavur recently celebrated the thousand-year anniversary of this beautiful sandstone temple and fort.

» Sri Ranganathaswamy Temple (p1029), Trichy (Tiruchirappalli) One of the biggest temples in India, this city-like complex in Trichy has fine carvings and a lively cart festival.

» Nataraja Temple (p1022) Fire ceremonies commemorate Shiva's role as Lord of the Dance in Chidambaram.

---

the Saradharam, and the **Golden Roof** (RK Residency, 30 VGP St; mains ₹30-50) does a decent job of Indian and 'Chinese' basics. Just across the bus stand is vegetarian **Ishwarya** (thalis ₹30; ⊗breakfast, lunch & dinner), which does fine thalis. There are lots of cheap veg eats in the area immediately surrounding the temple complex.

ⓘ Information

Bank of India ATM (VGP St)

Cybase (Pillaiyar Koil St; per hr ₹30; ⊗9am-9pm) Fast internet access.

ICICI Bank ATM (Hotel Saradharam, VGP St)

Tourist office (☑238739; Railway Feeder Rd; ⊗9am-5pm Mon-Fri) Frequently deserted.

UAE Exchange (Pillaiyar Koil St; ⊗closed Sun afternoon) Best place in town to exchange money.

ⓘ Getting There & Away

The bus stand is very central – within walking distance to the temple and accommodation. There are hourly buses to Chennai (₹98, seven hours), and buses to Puducherry (₹36, two hours) and Kumbakonam (₹37, 2½ hours) run regularly. There are also five direct buses daily to Madurai (₹155, eight hours).

Chidambaram is on the Chennai–Trichy gauge line, with services to Kumbakonam, Thanjavur and once a day to Rameswaram (10 hours). The station is a 20-minute walk southeast of the temple (₹50 by autorickshaw).

Kumbakonam

☑0435 / POP 160,767

At first glance Kumbakonam is another Indian junction town, but then you notice the temples that sprout out of this busy city like mushrooms, a reminder that this was once a seat of medieval South Indian power. It's an easy day trip from Thanjavur, and makes a good base for exploring the coastal towns of the Cauvery Delta.

ⓞ Sights

Dozens of colourfully painted *gopurams* point skyward from Kumbakonam's 18 temples, most of which are dedicated to Shiva or Vishnu, but probably only the most dedicated temple goer would tackle visiting more than a few. All temples are open from 6am to noon and 4pm to 10pm, and admission is free.

The largest Vishnu temple in Kumbakonam, with a 50m-high east gate, is **Sarangapani Temple**, just off Ayikulam Rd. The temple shrine, in the form of a chariot, was the work of the Cholas during the 12th century.

Kumbeshwara Temple, about 200m west and entered via a nine-storey *gopuram,* is the largest Shiva temple. It contains a lingam said to have been made by Shiva himself when he mixed the nectar of immortality with sand.

The 12th-century **Nageshwara Temple**, from the Chola dynasty, is also dedicated to

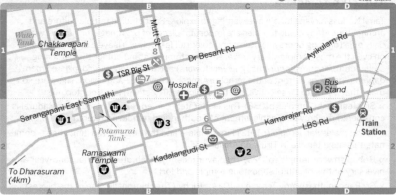

Shiva in the guise of Nagaraja, the serpent king. On three days of the year (in April or May) the sun's rays fall on the lingam. The main shrine here is in the form of a chariot.

The huge Mahamakham Tank, 600m southeast of the Nageshwara Temple, is the most sacred in Kumbakonam. It's believed that every 12 years the waters of the Ganges flow into the tank, and at this time a festival is held; the next is due in 2016.

🛏 Sleeping & Eating

Hotel Rayas HOTEL $
(☎2422545, 2423170; 18 Post Office Rd; d from ₹800; ❄) Friendly service and reliably spacious (and clean) rooms make this your best lodging option in town.

Paradise Resort RESORT $$
(☎2416469; www.paradiseresortindia.com; Tanjore Rd, Darasuram; s/d from ₹3200/3800; ❄) Out of town, this is an atmospheric resort constructed around heritage buildings and thatch and teak cottages. The rooms here have cool tiles and verandas overlooking quiet and spacious gardens, and a plethora of ayurvedic spa treatment options.

Hotel Kanishka HOTEL $
(☎2425231; www.hotelkanishka.in; Ayikulam Rd; d from ₹700; ❄) A sparkling new (at our visit) place with smallish and simple but cheerful rooms with yellow feature walls. It's owned and run by a young couple who aim to keep the hotel family friendly.

Pandian Hotel HOTEL $
(☎2430397; 52 Sarangapani East St; s/d ₹190/300) It feels a bit institutional, but in general you're getting good value at this clean-enough budget standby.

Hotel Sri Venkkatramana INDIAN $
(TSR Big St; thalis ₹30; ⊙breakfast, lunch & dinner) Serves good fresh veg food and is very popular with locals.

ℹ Information

There's no tourist office in Kumbakonam, and road names and signs here are more erratic than usual.

Ashok Net Café (24 Ayikulam Rd; per hr ₹20; ⊙9am-10.30pm)
Axis Bank ATM (Ayikulam Rd)
Speed Browsing Centre (Sarangapani East St; per hr ₹20; ⊙9am-9pm)
State Bank of India ATM (TSR Big St)
UAE Exchange (☎2423212; 134 Kamarajar Rd) The best place to exchange money.

ℹ Getting There & Away

The bus stand and train station are east of the town centre.

Trains to/from Chennai Egmore include the overnight *Rock Fort Express* (sleeper/3AC ₹191/505), going via Thanjavur and Trichy, and the faster *Chennai Egmore Express/Rameswaram Express* (₹158/413). Passenger trains run to Chidambaram (two hours) and Thanjavur.

For the Cauvery Delta area there are buses running every half-hour to Karaikal (₹20, two hours), via Tranquebar and then on to Nagapattinam. Government buses from the bus stand include:

Chennai ₹110, seven hours, every 30 min
Chidambaram ₹37, 2½ hours, every 20 minutes

Kumbakonam

Coimbatore ₹140, 10 hours, daily
Madurai ₹72, five hours, eight daily
Puducherry ₹42, four hours, every 30 minutes
Thanjavur ₹15, one hour, every 30 minutes

Around Kumbakonam

Only 4km west of Kumbakonam in the village of Dharasuram, the **Airatesvara Temple** (⊙6am-noon & 4-8pm), constructed by Rajaraja II (1146–63), is a superb example of 12th-century Chola architecture. Fronted by columns overflowing with miniature sculptures, the temple art depicts, among other things, Shiva in the rare incarnation as Kankalamurti, the mendicant.

At Gangakondacholapuram, 35km north of Kumbakonam, you'll find a Shiva **temple** (⊙6am-noon & 4-8pm) built by Rajendra I that represents a latter, somewhat more developed phase of Chola art. Note the 49m-tall *vimana* (tower) that tops the temple; its elegant up-sloping curves stand in stark contrast to the Brihadishwara's angular lines, and as a result the Gangakondacholapuram is often described as the feminine counterpart to the Thanjavur edifice.

Buses go from Kumbakonam bus stand to Gangakondacholapuram every half-hour (₹18, 1½ hours). A rickshaw to Dharasuram costs about ₹90 round trip. Frequent buses head to Dharasuram as well; ask at the bus stand, as these tend to be village buses that will have to drop you off on their way out of town.

Cauvery Delta

The Cauvery River is the beating heart of South Indian agriculture and, back in its day, connected the entire region via riverine routes. Today the Cauvery's delta, which spills into Tamil Nadu's east coast, is one of the prettiest and poorest parts of the state. This green and pleasant region can be visited on a lovely day drive (expect to pay about ₹3000 for a return taxi from Kumbakonam).

About 80km south of Chidambaram, **Tranquebar** was a Danish post established in 1620 by the Danish East India Company. The seafront **Danesborg Fort** houses a small museum on the region's Danish history. To get here, take a bus from Chidambaram (₹32, 2½ hours).

Just south of the district capital, Nagapattinam, the main draw of the little town of **Vailankanni**, is the basilica of **Our Lady of Good Health**, built on the spot where a young buttermilk boy glimpsed the Virgin Mary in the 15th century. Distinctly Hindu styles of worship are popular here, and an annual nine-day festival culminates on 8 September, the celebration of Mary's birth. There are daily bus services between Vailankanni and Chidambaram, as well as Chennai, Coimbatore, Bengaluru and Thiruvananthapuram (Trivandrum).

Thanjavur (Tanjore)

☏ 04362 / POP 215,314

Here are the ochre foundation blocks of one of the most remarkable nations of Dravidian history, one of the few kingdoms to expand Hinduism beyond India, a bedrock for aesthetic styles that spread from Madurai to the Mekong. A dizzying historical legacy was once administered from Thanjavur, ancient capital of the great Chola Empire, which today...is a chaotic, messy, modern Indian town. Oh, how the good times have gone. But their presence is still remarkably evident; past the honking buses and happy public urination are the World Heritage–listed Brihadishwara Temple and the sprawling Maratha palace complex.

⊙ **Sights**

Brihadishwara Temple & Fort   HINDU TEMPLE
(⊙6am-noon & 4-8.30pm) Come here twice: in the morning, when the tawny sandstone begins to assert its dominance over the white dawn sunshine, and in the evening, when the rocks capture a hot palette of reds, oranges, yellows and pinks on the Brihadishwara Temple, the crowning glory of Chola temple architecture. The temple was commissioned in 1010 by Rajaraja (whose name literally

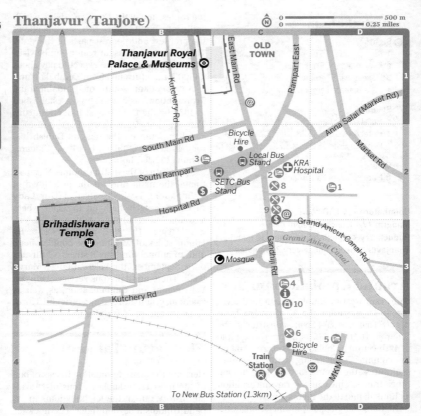

Thanjavur Royal Palace & Museums ◉
OLD TOWN

Brihadishwara Temple

To New Bus Station (1.3km)

means 'king of kings'), a well-regarded monarch so organised he had the names and addresses of all his dancers, musicians, barbers and poets inscribed into the temple wall. Thousand-year anniversary celebrations and renovations were held in 2010.

Note the covered statue of Nandi (Shiva's sacred bull) – 6m long by 3m high – that faces the inner sanctum. Created from a single piece of rock, it weighs 25 tonnes and is one of India's largest Nandi statues. There's also a well-executed interpretive centre set along the side alcoves, which includes sculptures and paintings culled from the temple walls (including a particularly energetic Shiva slaying an army of demons while Buddha hovers above. Not for enlightenment either; the demons were Shiva worshippers, and the Buddha took them on as devotees so the Destroyer could justify killing them).

Unlike most South Indian temples where the *gopurams* are the highest towers, here

the 13-storey, 66m *vimana* (centre tower) dominates. There's not a lot of touting here, and the grounds are nice spot to sit awhile.

Thanjavur Royal Palace & Museums
HISTORICAL BUILDING

The pink walls hold court for crows; the queen's courtyard is overrun with weeds; the inner corridors stink of bat guano. And yet... amid the decay are expertly carved bodies of gods and goddesses, sky-bright tile work, massive columns of preserved, chocolate-coloured teak and the incredible murals of one of the great dynasties of South Indian royalty. The labyrinthine complex was constructed partly by the Nayaks of Madurai and partly by the Marathas.

Walk by a local school to enter the main hall of the **palace** (Indian adult/child ₹10/5, foreign adult/child ₹50/25 incl entry to the Durbar Hall & bell tower, camera/video ₹30/250; ⊙9am-1pm & 3-6pm) and follow the signs to the elegantly faded **Durbar Hall** (Royal Court). An incred-

Thanjavur (Tanjore)

◉ **Top Sights**

🛏 **Sleeping**

❌ **Eating**

🛍 **Shopping**

ible profusion of murals erupts here, unrestored and elegantly faded, bursting with geometric designs, scenes of Hindu legend and a flock of vaguely European-yet-almost-Indian cherubs. With a torch you can peek into a 6km secret passage that runs under the palace and reeks of bat poo.

In the former Sadar Mahal Palace is the **Raja Serfoji Memorial Hall** (admission ₹2), with a small collection of thrones, weapons and photographs; there's a similar collection in the **Royal Palace Museum** (admission ₹1, camera/video ₹30/250). Many of the artefacts date from the early 19th century when the enlightened and far-sighted scholar-king Serfoji II ruled (six generations later, his descendants still lives here).

An extensive **gallery** (Indian adult/child ₹17/2, foreigner ₹30) of Chola bronzes sits between the Royal Palace Museum and the bell tower. Nearby, the **bell tower** is worth a climb for views right across Thanjavur and the palace itself. The spiral stone staircase is dark, narrow and slippery; watch your head and your step.

Perhaps Serfoji II's greatest contribution to posterity is the **Saraswati Mahal Library** (admission free; ⏰10am-1pm & 1.30-5.30pm Tue-Thu) between the gallery and the palace museum. It's a monument to both universal knowledge and an eclectic mind that collected prints of Chinese torture methods, Audubon-style sketches of Indian flora and fauna, sketches of

the London skyline, and a collection of some 60,000 palm-leaf and paper manuscripts in Indian and European languages.

★ Festivals & Events

Two important festivals are held about 13km north of Thanjavur in Thiruvaiyaru. The January **International Music Festival** honours saint and composer Thyagaraja, and the Thyagararajaswami Temple has a 10-day **car festival** in April/May when the largest temple chariot in Tamil Nadu is hauled through the streets.

🛏 Sleeping

There's a bunch of nondescript cheap lodges opposite the SETC bus stand.

Hotel Gnanam HOTEL **$$**
(☎278501; www.hotelgnanam.com; Anna Salai; s/d from ₹1350/1550; ❄@🛜) The best place in town, the Gnanam has stylish, comfy rooms (the more expensive rooms have bathtubs – the cleanest we've seen in the whole state) and is perfect for anyone needing wi-fi and other modern amenities while they're plopped in Thanjavur's geographic centre. Guests are greeted with chilled face cloths – perfect in such a humid town.

Hotel Valli HOTEL **$**
(☎231580; arasu_tnj@rediffmail.com; 2948 MKM Rd; s/d from ₹340/360; ❄) Near the train station, the green-painted (inside and out) Valli is a good choice for budget travellers; the non-AC rooms are better value than the more expensive ones. Staff are personable and the rooms themselves are spic-and-span. It's in a reasonably peaceful location beyond a bunch of greasy backyard workshops.

Hotel Tamil Nadu HOTEL **$$**
(☎231325; www.ttdconline.com; Gandhiji Rd; d from ₹600; ❄) The Tamil Nadu is appealing from the outside; the architecture is sultan chic (makes sense, given this is a former royal guesthouse), an atmosphere accentuated by a quiet, leafy courtyard and wide balconies. But inside the rooms are dank, if spacious, and overpriced.

Hotel Ramnath HOTEL **$**
(☎272567; hotel_ramnath@yahoo.com; 1335 South Rampart; s/d from ₹550/600; ❄) Just across from the SETC bus stand (the attendant noise is not as bad as you might expect), a nice 'upmarket budget' option with fresh rooms.

Ashoka Lodge HOTEL $

(230022; 93 Abraham Pandithar Rd; dm/s/d ₹150/195/325, r with AC ₹700; ✳) The Ashoka's been in business for 44 years, and is frankly looking its age. That said, the rooms are, if a little gloomy, surprisingly spacious for the cost and kept clean.

✕ Eating

There's a cluster of simple veg restaurants, open for breakfast, lunch and dinner, near the local bus stand and along Gandhiji Rd.

Sahana INDIAN $

(Hotel Gnanam, Anna Salai; mains ₹70-90; ☺breakfast, lunch & dinner) This classy hotel restaurant does a nice line in fresh, tasty, mainly Indian veg dishes. This might be the only place in town to get a Continental breakfast if you're not up to *idlis* first thing. The hotel's pricier nonveg restaurant, Diana, is also very good, with a wide range of tandoori and other northern dishes.

Sri Venkata Lodge SOUTH INDIAN $

(Gandhiji Rd; thalis ₹30) A few minutes from the local bus stand, this veg-only place does a nice thali.

Bombay Sweets INDIAN $

(Gandhiji Rd; snacks ₹15-30) Near the train station, a clean, popular spot with good sweets (halwa, *burfi*) and snacks like samosas and *bhelpuri*.

Thevar's Biryani INDIAN $

(Gandhiji Rd; mains ₹50-150; ☺closed Fri) Thevar's specialises in exactly what the name suggests, and it specialises in the Mughal rice dish (done up with southern influences here, like sour tamarind sauce) well. Chicken and fish dishes are also good.

Sathars INDIAN $

(167 Gandhiji Rd; mains ₹45-100) Good service and quality food make this place popular. Downstairs is a veg restaurant with lunchtime thalis, upstairs is an AC section with good-value nonveg food.

🔒 Shopping

Thanjavur is a good place to shop for handicrafts and arts, especially around the palace, though beware of rickshaw drivers wanting to take you to a particular shop (their commission will be reflected in the price you pay). Numerous shops along East Main and Gandhiji Rds sell everything from quality crafts and ready-made clothes to inexpensive kitsch. For fixed prices and hassle-free shopping, try **Poompuhar** (Gandhiji Rd; ☺10am-8pm Mon-Sat).

ℹ Information

24Hrs Internet (Golden Plaza, Ganhiji Rd; per hr ₹20) We can't swear by the claimed opening hours.

ICICI Bank ATM (New Bus Station)

Indian Bank ATM (train station)

Sify iWay (East Main Rd; per hr ₹20; ☺10am-9pm)

State Bank of India ATM (Hospital Rd)

Tourist office (230984; Gandhiji Rd; ☺10am-5pm Mon-Fri) On the corner of the Hotel Tamil Nadu complex.

VKC Forex (Golden Plaza, Gandhiji Rd; ☺9.30am-9pm) Changes cash and travellers cheques.

ℹ Getting There & Away

Bus

The two city bus stands are for local and SETC buses. SETC has a **reservation office** (☺7.30am-9.30pm). Destinations from here include Chennai (₹120, eight hours, 20 daily) and Ooty (₹135, 10 hours, daily).

The New Bus Station, 2.5km south of the centre, services local areas and destinations south. Bus 74 shuttles between the three bus stations (₹4). Buses from the New Bus Station include:

Chidambaram ₹54, four hours, every 30 minutes

Kumbakonam ₹15, one hour, every 30 minutes

Madurai ₹56, four hours, every 15 minutes

Trichy ₹24, 1½ hours, every 15 minutes

Train

The station is conveniently central at the south end of Gandhiji Rd. Thanjavur is off the main Chennai–Madurai line, so there's only one express train direct to Chennai – the overnight *Rock Fort Express* (sleeper/3AC ₹178/472, 9½ hours) departing at 8.30pm. For more frequent trains north or south, including to Madurai, take a passenger train to Trichy (₹22, 1½ hours, eight daily) and change there. There's a couple of express and three passenger trains daily to Kumbakonam (₹20, one hour).

The *Thanjavur-Mysore Express* leaves daily at 7.15pm for Bengaluru (sleeper/3AC ₹206/547, 10 hours) and Mysore (sleeper/3AC ₹237/627, 14 hours).

ℹ Getting Around

The main attractions of Thanjavur are close enough to walk between, but this can make for a tiring day depending on your fitness. Bicycles can be hired from stalls opposite the train station and local bus stand (per hour ₹5). An autorickshaw into town from the New Bus Station costs around ₹100.

Trichy (Tiruchirappalli)

📞0431 / POP 866,354

Welcome to (more or less) the geographic centre of Tamil Nadu. Fortunately, this hub isn't just a travel junction, although it does make a good base for exploring large swatches of central Tamil Nadu. But Tiruchirappalli, universally known as Trichy, also mixes up a throbbing bazaar with several major must-see temples.

Trichy's long history dates back to before the Christian era when it was a Chola citadel. Since then it's passed into the hands of the Pallavas, Pandyas, Vijayanagars and Deccan sultans. The modern town and the Rock Fort Temple were built by the Nayaks of Madurai.

Trichy's places of interest are scattered over a large area from north to south, but for travellers the city is conveniently split into three distinct areas. The Trichy Junction, or Cantonment, area in the south has most of the hotels and restaurants, the bus and train stations and tourist office. This is where you're likely to arrive and stay. The Rock Fort Temple and main bazaar area is 2.5km north of here; the other important temples are in an area called Srirangam, a further 3km to 5km north again,

across the Cauvery River. Fortunately, the whole lot is connected by a good bus service.

◎ Sights

Rock Fort Temple   HINDU TEMPLE

(Map p1029; admission ₹3, camera/video ₹20/100; ⊙6am-8pm) The Rock Fort Temple, perched 83m high on a massive outcrop, lords over Trichy with stony arrogance. The ancient rock was first hewn by religious-minded Pallavas, who cut small cave temples into the southern face, but it was the war-savvy Nayaks who later made strategic use of the naturally fortified position. There are two main temples: **Sri Thayumanaswamy Temple**, halfway to the top (there may be some bats snoozing in the ceiling), and **Vinayaka Temple**, at the summit, dedicated to Ganesh. There are 437 stone-cut steps to climb, and the hike is worth the effort – the view is wonderful, with eagles wheeling beneath and Trichy sprawling all around into the greater Cauvery. Non-Hindus are not allowed inside either temple.

Sri Ranganathaswamy Temple   HINDU TEMPLE

(Map p1029; camera/video ₹50/100; ⊙6am-1pm & 3-9pm) Alright temple-philes, here's the one you've been waiting for: quite possibly the biggest temple in India. Located about 3km north of the Rock Fort, it feels more like a self-enclosed city than a house of worship,

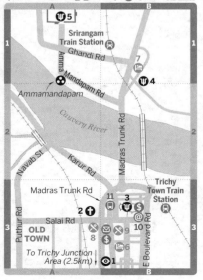

Trichy (Tiruchirappalli)

◎ **Sights**

1 Hazrat Nathervali Dargah B3
2 Lourdes Church A3
3 Rock Fort Temple B3
4 Sri Jambukeshwara Temple B1
5 Sri Ranganathaswamy Temple A1
St Joseph's College Museum ...... (see 2)

🛏 **Sleeping**

6 Hotel Royal Sathyam B3
7 Hotel Temple In B1

🍴 **Eating**

8 Banana Leaf A3
9 Vasanta Bhavan B3

Shopping

Poompuhar .... (see 6)

Information

10 Sify iWay B3

Transport

11 City Bus Stand B3

and in truth, that's the idea: entering this temple's inner sanctum requires passing through seven *gopuram* (the largest is 73m high). Inside the fourth wall is a kiosk where you can buy a ticket (₹10) and climb the wall for a semi-panoramic view of the complex that delineates levels of existence and consciousness. You'll proceed past rings of beggars, merchants and Brahmins, then plazas of *devas* (celestial beings) and minor deities before reaching the inner chamber, dedicated to Vishnu. Here, the god is worshipped as Sheshashayana, Vishnu who sleeps on a bed made of the king of *nagas*.

Take note of the numerous carvings and statues of *vanaras* (literally 'forest people'), monkey warriors and princesses from the Ramayana, as well as avatars (incarnations) of Vishnu in one of his animal forms, such as the half-lion Nairarishma. These may have been tribal pre-Hindu deities that were folded into the religion, and remain popular objects of worship.

If you turn right just before you go through the fifth gate there's a small, dusty **Art Museum** (admission ₹5; ☉9am-1pm & 2-6pm) with some fascinating exhibits, including bronze statues, the tusks of former temple elephants, and copper edict plates. The highlight is a collection of beautifully detailed 17th-century (Nayak period) ivory carvings of gods, kings and queens (some of them erotically engaged), demons and even a Portugese soldier; they look Balinese in style, although of course the influence flowed in the other direction.

A **Temple Chariot Festival** where statues of the deities are paraded aboard a fine chariot is held here each January, but the most important festival is the 21-day **Vaikunta Ekadasi** (Paradise Festival) in mid-December, when the celebrated Vaishnavaite text, Tiruvaimozhi, is recited before an image of Vishnu.

Bus 1 from Trichy Junction or Rock Fort stops right outside this temple.

Sri Jambukeshwara Temple   HINDU TEMPLE
(Tiruvanakoil; Map p1029; camera/video ₹20/150; ☉6am-1pm & 3-9pm) If you're visiting the five elemental temples of Shiva, you need to visit Sri Jambukeshwara Temple, dedicated to Shiva, Parvati and the medium of water. The liquid theme of the place is realised in the central shrine, which houses a partially submerged Shiva lingam. The outer chambers are full of carvings, including several of an elephant being freed from a spiderweb

by Shiva, which provoked the pachyderm to perform *puja* for the Destroyer.

If you're taking bus 1, ask for 'Tiruvanakoil'; the temple is about 100m east of the main road.

Lourdes Church   CHURCH
(Map p1029; Madras Trunk Rd) This church is heavily decked out in Gallo-Catholic design, from neo-Gothic spires to the anguished scenes of crucifixion and martyrdom painted inside. The hush of the nave makes an interesting contrast to the frenetic activity that characterises Trichy's Hindu temples. The **Feast of Our Lady of Lourdes** is held on 11 February. The entrance to Lourdes is on Madras Trunk Rd, and when you're finished you can escape into the green and cool campus of Jesuit St Joseph's College (where classes run from Intro to Javascript to Comparative Theology). An eccentric and dusty **museum** (admission free; ☉10am-noon & 2-4pm Mon-Sat) contains the natural history collections of the Jesuit priests' summer excursions to the Western Ghats in the 1870s. Bang on the door and the caretaker will let you in – or not, depending on if he's there.

Hazrat Nathervali Dargah   TOMB
(Map p1029) This is the tomb of popular Muslim saint Natther. From a distance the mausoleum is a minaret-ensconced compound

Trichy (Tiruchirappalli) Junction Area

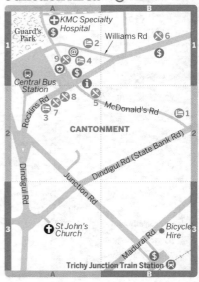

with distinctly Arab sea-green embellishments, but the *puja*-like worship of Natther has strong Hindu overtones. If you're asking for directions most people will know it as 'the Muslim shrine'.

🛏 Sleeping

The majority of Trichy's hotels are in the Junction/Cantonment area around the bus station and a short walk north of the train station. Most budget hotels have either doubled their prices or halved their cleaning budgets in the last couple of years; the upper budget and midrange spots here are much better value, charging only a little more for good non-AC rooms than you'd pay for a grim cheapie.

Femina Hotel   HOTEL $
(Map p1030; ☎2414501; try_femina@sancharnet.in; 104C Williams Rd; d incl breakfast from ₹770; ❋☒☏) Femina is one of those Indian business hotels that manages to be affordable even if you're on a budget – and the staff don't look at travellers as if they've just crawled out of a swamp. Nonguests can use the pool and small gym (per hour ₹75). Good buffet breakfast including toast and eggs as well as the full traditional South Indian.

Ramyas Hotel   HOTEL $
(Map p1030; ☎2412626; www.ramyas.com; Williams Rd; s/d from ₹650/750; ❋☏) Another good corporate spot, although it *has* been known to be unfriendly to backpackers. Rooms in the new block are clean and stylish, some with pleasant balconies overlooking the trees, and the non-AC rooms are good value, though some are a bit smoky smelling. There's a couple of decent restaurants on-site; the **Meridien** has excellent local Chettinad-style dishes.

Hotel Royal Sathyam   HOTEL $$
(Map p1029; ☎4011414; www.hotelsathyam.co.in; 42A Singarathope; s/d from ₹1200/1400; ❋) Towering over a posh jewellery shop, this is the classiest place to stay if you want to be close to the temple and market action. Rooms are small but stylish, with extra-comfy mattresses and a fresh wood-and-whitewash theme that's almost but not quite 'boutique'.

Breeze Residency   HOTEL $$
(Map p1030; ☎2414414; www.breezehotel.com; 3/14 McDonald's Rd; s/d from ₹2300/2700; ❋@☒) Undergoing a name change and a noisy refurbishment when we visited, the Breeze is enormous, semiluxurious and in a relatively quiet location. The best rooms are on the top floors but all are well appointed. Hotel facilities include a health club; a very good restaurant, the **Madras** (mains ₹90-250); and a bizarre Wild West theme bar.

Hotel Temple In   HOTEL $
(Map p1029; ☎4250304; 139 Madras Trunk Rd; s/d from ₹450/750; ❋) Opened literally the day before we visited, this friendly, very clean (for now) spot near the two major temples in the Srirangam area was a much better choice than the budget options in the Cantonment at the time of research.

Hotel Meega   HOTEL $
(Map p1030; ☎2414092; 3 Rockins Rd; d from ₹425; ❋) It's friendly and still reasonably cheap (though not as cheap as it should be), but rooms are worn and grubby and the creaky lift gave us some scary moments. There's a popular veg restaurant downstairs. Next-door **Hotel Mathura** is another cheapie with peeling walls that's hiked its prices for no good reason, but if you're really on a budget it's clean and spacious enough.

🍴 Eating

Femina Food Court   MULTICUISINE $
(Map p1030; Williams Rd; mains ₹60-35, snacks ₹10-30; ☉lunch & dinner) Next to the Femina 'shopping mall' (two large shops) is a shaded outdoor-seating area with a Chinese restaurant, an Indian snack bar, and a juice and

Trichy (Tiruchirappalli) Junction Area

cake shop; the Chinese is especially tasty and it's a good spot to take a break.

Banana Leaf INDIAN $
(Map p1029; ☑271101; Madras Trunk Rd; mains ₹30-90; ☺lunch & dinner) A big menu of regional favourites. The speciality is the fiery, vaguely vinegary cuisine of Andhra Pradesh. Another branch is next to the Hotel Tamil Nadu in Trichy Junction.

Shree Krishnas INDIAN $
(Map p1030; 1 Rockins Rd; mains ₹20-40; ☺breakfast, lunch & dinner) On the lower floor of Hotel Mathura, with a nice view of the buses playing plough-the-pedestrian across the road, this is a reliable spot for veg goodness and milky-sweet desserts.

Vasanta Bhavan INDIAN $
(Map p1029; West Blvd; mains ₹30-60; ☺breakfast, lunch & dinner) Pop in here for North Indian veg – that of the paneer and naan genre – if you're tired of dosas and *idlis* (of course you can get them too, along with excellent lassi). There's another branch in the Cantonment, next to Shree Krishnas.

Marrybrown FAST FOOD $$
(Map p1030; Williams Rd; burger ₹70-150; ☺11am-11pm) Join the cool kids for burgers, fries and chicken at this popular chain.

Shopping

The main bazaar, which runs by the entrance to the Rock Fort, is as chaotic and crowded as you like; it constantly feels like all of Trichy is strolling the strip. The usual array of plastic toys and silk saris is on sale. Try **Poompuhar** (Map p1029; West Blvd Rd; ☺9am-8pm) for fixed-price crafts.

🛈 Information

Axis Bank ATM (Map p1029; Chinnar Bazaar)
Canara Bank (Map p1030; Royal Rd)
ICICI Bank ATM Junction Rd (Map p1030); West Blvd Rd (Map p1029)
Indian Bank ATM (Map p1030; Rockins Rd)
Indian Panorama (☑4226122; www.indian panorama.in) Trichy based and covering all of India, this professional and reliable travel agency/tour operator is run by an Indian-Australian couple.
KMC Speciality Hospital (Map p1030; ☑4077777; Royal Rd) A large hospital in the Cantonment.
Sify iWay (internet per hr ₹30; ☺9am -9pm) Chinnar Bazaar (Map p1029); Williams Rd (Map p1030)
State Bank of India ATM (Map p1030; Williams Rd)
Tourist office (Map p1030; ☑2460136; 1 Williams Rd; ☺10am-5.45pm Mon-Fri) One of the more helpful tourism info offices in the state.

🛈 Getting There & Away

Trichy is virtually in the geographical centre of Tamil Nadu and it's well connected by air, bus and train.

Air

As well as domestic flights, Trichy's airport has opened up to international flights in the last couple of years. **Sri Lankan Airlines** (Map p1030; ☑2460844; ☺9am-5.30pm Mon-Sat, 9am-1pm Sun), with an office at Femina Hotel, has 10 flights a week to Colombo (₹8700). **Air Asia** (☑4540393) flies daily to Kuala Lumpur, and **Air India Express** (☑2341744; trzapt@ airindiaexpress.in) flies to Kulala Lumpur, Singapore and Abu Dhabi.

Bus

Most buses head to the **Central bus station** (Map p1030; Rockins Rd) on Rockins Rd. If you're

BUSES FROM TRICHY (TIRUCHIRAPPALLI)

DESTINATION	FARE (₹)	DURATION (HR)	FREQUENCY
Bengaluru	160	8	3 daily
Chennai	120-190	7	every 15min
Chidambaram	55	3½	hourly
Coimbatore	80	7	every 30min
Kodaikanal	65	5½	3 daily
Madurai	42	3	every 15min
Ooty	100	8	daily
Puducherry	80	5	3 daily
Thanjavur	24	1½	every 15min

travelling to Kodaikanal, a good option is to take one of the frequent buses to Dindigul (₹25, two hours) and change there. For details of services, see the boxed text, opposite.

Train

Trichy is on the main Chennai–Madurai line so there are lots of rail options in either direction. Of the nine daily express services to Chennai, the quickest are the *Vaigai Express* (2nd/chair class ₹104/367, 5½ hours) departing Trichy at 8.50am, and the *Pallavan Express*, which leaves at 6.30am. The best overnight train is the *Rock Fort Express* (sleeper/3AC ₹164/432, 7½ hours) at 10pm.

For Madurai the best train is the *Guruvaya Express* (2nd class/sleeper ₹62/120, three hours), which leaves at 1.15pm. The *Mysore Express* goes daily to Bengaluru at 8.35pm (sleeper/3AC ₹187/496, 8½ hours) and Mysore (₹236/636, 12½ hours).

ℹ Getting Around

To/From the Airport

The 6km ride into town is about ₹300 by taxi and ₹100 by autorickshaw; there's a prepaid taxi stand at the airport. Otherwise, take bus 7, 59, 58 or 63 to/from the airport (30 minutes).

Bicycle

Trichy lends itself to cycling as it's flat; it's a reasonably easy ride from Trichy Junction to the Rock Fort Temple, but a long haul to Srirangam and back. There are a couple of places on Madurai Rd near the train station where you can hire bicycles (per hr ₹5).

Bus

Trichy's local bus service is easy to use. Bus 1 (any letter) from the **Central bus station** (Map p1030; Rockins Rd) goes every few minutes via the Rock Fort Temple, Sri Jambukeshwara Temple and the main entrance to Sri Ranganathaswamy Temple (₹5). To see them all, get off in that order (ask the conductor or driver where the stops are), as it runs in a one-way circuit.

SOUTHERN TAMIL NADU

Trichy to Rameswaram

In Pudukkottai district, between Trichy and Rameswaram, is Tamil Nadu's best example of temples, cave art, the homeland of the region's greatest traders and bankers, and has a few other stops that make a good road trip (or day tour from Trichy, Madurai or Rameswaram).

PUDUKKOTTAI & AROUND

Some 34km south of Trichy is the nondescript town of Pudukkottai, which has historical importance in inverse proportion to its current obscurity; from 1680 to 1947 this was one of the great princely states of South India.

Pudukkottai Museum   MUSEUM
(Indian/foreigner ₹5/100; ⊙9.30am-5pm) The relics of bygone days are on display in this wonderful museum, located in a renovated palace building in Pudukkottai town. Its eclectic collection includes musical instruments, megalithic burial artefacts, and some remarkable paintings and miniatures.

Vijayalaya Cholisvaram   HINDU TEMPLE
(Natharmalai; admission free) About 16km north of Pudukkottai, above the village of Natharmalai, is this small but stunning 10th-century rock-cut temple, reminiscent of the famous carvings at Mamallapuram but almost always deserted. Villagers will point you to the site, which takes a quick walk up a rocky hill with views of the green and serene countryside around. If the caretaker's around he'll give an enthusiastic tour and open up the temple to show scraps of ancient frescoes, and may direct you to other temples being restored in the area. Further up the road is **Sittannavasal** (admission ₹100), where you'll find a small Jain cave temple that conceals more frescoes and statues of Jain saints sitting in cross-legged repose.

Tirumayam Fort   FORT
(Indian/foreigner ₹5/100; ⊙9am-5pm) Simple and imposing, the renovated Tirumayam Fort, located about 17km south of Pudukkottai, is worth a climb for the 360-degree views from the battlements onto the surrounding countryside. Or you can take a shady rest with local goats under a banyan tree.

KARAIKKUDI & AROUND

In the backstreets of small **Kanadukathan** are the wedding-cake houses of the Chettiars, an interrelated clan of bankers, merchants and traders. The mansions of the community are decked out in the cosmopolitan goods bought home by Chettiars during their extensive trading forays: Belgian chandeliers, Italian granite, Burmese teak and artwork from around the world.

To get a feel for the royal life, book a night in one of the following heritage houses; they're pricey but they provide a fantastic experience. All have kitchens producing authentic Chettinad cuisine, which is not as chilli-laden as traditional South Indian food (and less likely to be vegetarian); Visalam has an 'interactive kitchen' and Bangala offers cooking courses for groups.

TOP CHOICE Visalam　　　BOUTIQUE HOTEL **$$$**

(☎4564-273301; www.cghearth.com; Local Fund Rd, Kanadukathan; r from ₹10,700; ✳@☱) Stunningly restored and professionally run by a Malayali hotel chain, it's no longer in the hands of the original family but it's still decorated with their old photos, furniture and paintings, and staff can tell you the sad story of the young woman the house was built for. The garden is lovely and the pool setting is magical, with a low-key cafe alongside it.

Bangala　　　BOUTIQUE HOTEL **$$$**

(☎4565-220221; www.thebangala.com; Devakottai Rd, Karaikudi; d ₹4500-5400; ✳@☱) This lovingly restored whitewashed home ('bungalow') is quirkily decorated with locally sourced antique furniture, fascinating old photos of the owner's family, film posters and traditional crafts. Famous for its Chettinad food (₹500 for the set meal, and worth every paisa), it has a beautiful outdoor/indoor dining area. Rooms are spacious, comfy and individually styled; the 'honeymoon room' has a private veranda and an enclosed, carved wooden bed with a mirror in the roof!

Chettinadu Mansion　　　BOUTIQUE HOTEL **$$$**

(☎4564-273080; www.chettinadumansion.com; Kanadukathan; s/d ₹4700/6400; ✳@☱) Slightly shabbier than some of the Chettiar joints, and much more colourfully decorated, this house is still owned by the original family. Service is top-notch, and all rooms have private balconies looking over other mansions in the village.

ℹ Getting There & Away

This region is an easy day tour from Trichy (taxi ₹1600) or Madurai (a little more). Otherwise catch one of the many daily buses from Trichy to Karaikkudi (₹56, three hours) and get on and off at the sights along the way. Coming from Madurai, get a bus to Karaikkudi and take a local bus or hire a taxi. Kanadukathan is about a 500m walk off the main road. Regular buses run between Karaikkudi, via Ramanathapuram, to Rameswaram.

Rameswaram

☎04573 / POP 37,968

Rameswaram was once the southernmost point of sacred India; to leave her boundaries was to abandon caste and fall below the status of the lowliest skinner of sacred cows. Then Rama, incarnation of Vishnu and hero of the Ramayana, led an army of monkeys and bears to the ocean and crossed into the kingdom of (Sri) Lanka, where he defeated the demon Ravana and rescued his wife, Sita. Afterwards, prince and princess came to this spot to offer thanks to Shiva.

If all this seems like so much folklore, it's absolute truth for millions of Hindus, who flock to the Ramanathaswamy Temple to worship where a god worshipped a god.

Apart from these pilgrims, Rameswaram is a sleepy fishing village. It's also an island, connected to the mainland by the Indira Gandhi bridge, and used to serve as a ferry link to Sri Lanka.

Most hotels and restaurants are clustered around the Ramanathaswamy Temple. The bus stand, 2km to the west, is connected by shuttle bus to the town centre.

◉ Sights

Ramanathaswamy Temple　　　HINDU TEMPLE

(camera ₹25; ◷4am-1pm & 3-8.30pm) When Rama decided to worship Shiva, he figured he'd need a lingam to do the thing properly. Being a god, he sent a flying monkey to find the biggest lingam around – in this case, a Himalayan mountain. But the monkey took too long, so Rama's wife Sita made a simple lingam of sand, which Shiva approved of, and which is enshrined today in the centre of this temple. Besides housing the world's holiest sand mound, the structure is notable for its horizon-stretching thousand-pillar halls and 22 *theerthams* (tanks), which pilgrims are expected to bathe in and drink from. Only Hindus may enter the inner sanctum.

Even when the temple is closed, it is possible to take a peaceful amble through the extensive corridors. In the evening, before the temple is closed, you may see temple Brahmins take some of the residing deities on a parade through the halls of Ramanathaswamy.

Gandamadana Parvatham　　　HINDU TEMPLE

This temple, located 3km northwest of Rameswaram, is a shrine reputedly containing Rama's footprints. The two-storey *mandapam* is on a small hill – the highest point on the island – and has good views out over the coastal landscape. Pilgrims visit at dawn and dusk.

Dhanushkodi & Adam's Bridge

Kanyakumari may technically be India's land's end, but Dhanushkodi plays the part better. About 18km southwest of town, this is a long, low sweep of sand, dust devils, fishing hamlets, donkeys and green waves. It's tempting to swim here, but be careful of strong rips. You can ride a passenger truck for a few rupees, or walk 2½ hours (one way!) to the edge: **Adam's Bridge**, the chain of reefs, sandbanks and islets that almost connects India with Sri Lanka, 33km away, was supposedly built by Rama and his monkey army. Buses (₹5, hourly) from the local bus stand on East Car St stop about 4km before the beach so you have to walk the rest of the way, and an autorickshaw costs ₹300 return.

About 10km before Dhanushkodi, the **Kothandaraswamy Temple** was the only structure to survive a cyclone that destroyed the village in 1964. Legend has it Rama, overcome with guilt at having killed Ravana, performed a *puja* on this spot and thereafter the temple was built.

✪ Festivals & Events

During the **car festival** (February/March), a huge decorated chariot with idols of the deities installed is hauled through the streets in a pulsating parade. **Thiru Kalyana** (July/August) is a festival celebrating the celestial marriage of Shiva and Parvati.

🛏 Sleeping & Eating

Budget travellers should drop in at the **rooms booking office** (East Car St; ⊙24hr), opposite the main temple entrance, which can score doubles for as low as ₹300 a night. Many hotels here are geared towards pilgrims, which means staff can be conservative, often refusing to take in single travellers; this is the case for most of the cheapies (and at the rooms booking office). The cheapest rooms tend to be dire, but there's a string of reasonable midrange hotels. Book ahead before festivals.

Hotel Royal Park　　　　　HOTEL **$$**
(☏221680; Ramnad Hwy; s/d ₹ 1250/1650; ❈) It sounds like a contrdiction in terms, but this place on the main road near the bus stand is actually the most peaceful hotel in town. A couple of kilometres from the main temple action, it bills itself as a 'budget luxury hotel'; rooms are standard midrange with some nice artwork, and the attached AC veg restaurant is good value (mainly South Indian, but the cheese and tomato toastie is perfect too).

Hotel Sunrise View　　　　HOTEL **$$**
(☏223434; East Car St; d ₹1300; ❈) The best of the newish midrange places near the temple, this has sparkling tiles and wooden furniture that's a tad better quality than at other spots. Some rooms have good sea views; just try to look out at the ocean rather than down at the rubbish on the ground.

Hotel Sri Saravana　　　　HOTEL **$**
(☏223367; htl_saravana@yahoo.com; South Car St; r from ₹770; ❈) This is a friendly, clean hotel with good service and spacious rooms, and it's not averse to single travellers. Rooms towards the top have sea views (and increased rates).

Hotel Shanmuga Paradise　HOTEL **$**
(☏222984; www.shanmugaparadise.com; Middle St; d from ₹500, with AC from ₹800; ❈) This is another reasonable midrange place, just removed from the eastern temple entrance. Rooms are a fraction more tired than at some of the newer spots.

Lodge Santhya　　　　　　HOTEL **$**
(☏221329) This grotty spot offers singles for as low as ₹190. You get what you pay for, but, if you must, pinch that penny. Next-door **Santhana Lodge** is similar; neither place will take singles.

Guru Lodge　　　　　　　HOTEL **$**
(☏221531; East Car St; d ₹475) Right by the main temple entrance, this place isn't great value for money (it's not a lot cleaner than the real cheapies) but it's the cheapest place we found that would accept single travellers.

A number of inexpensive vegetarian restaurants such as **Ashok Bhavan** (West Car St) and **Vasantha Bhavan** (East Car St) serve thalis for around ₹40. As you might guess there's a focus on South Indian food here, but **Ram Nivas** (West Car St; mains ₹20-50) does a nice line in North Indian veg, such as paneer and dhal fry. You can find fish in a few restaurants, but we didn't find anything else carnivore friendly.

ⓘ Information

You can't change money here but the **State Bank of India** (East Car St) has an ATM accepting international cards.

Siva Net (Middle St; per hr ₹40; ⊙8am-9pm) Internet.

Tourist Office (☏221371; bus stand; ⊙10am-6pm Mon-Fri) Friendly but not terribly helpful.

ⓘ Getting There & Away
Bus

Buses run to Madurai every 10 minutes (₹50, four hours). There are SETC buses to Chennai (₹248, 12 hours, daily), Kanyakumari (₹125,

10 hours, two daily) and Trichy every half-hour (₹90, seven hours). There are also private buses and minibuses from the town centre to Chennai and Madurai.

Train

The overnight *Sethu Express* leaves for Chennai daily at 8pm (sleeper/3AC ₹246/665, 12 hours).

Getting Around

Town buses 1 and 2 (₹2) travel between the temple and the bus stand from early morning until late at night. Cycling is a good way to get around, with many stalls renting old rattlers for ₹5 per hour.

Madurai

☎0452 / POP 1.2 MILLION

Chennai may be the heart of Tamil Nadu, but Madurai claims her soul. Madurai is Tamil borne and Tamil rooted, one of the oldest cities in India, a metropolis that traded with ancient Rome and outlasted her destruction.

Tourists, Indian and foreign, usually come here to see the temple of Sri Meenakshi Amman, a labyrinthine structure that ranks among the greatest temples of India. Otherwise, Madurai, perhaps appropriately given her age, captures many of India's most glaring dichotomies: a city centre dominated by a medieval temple, an economy increasingly driven by IT, all overlaid with the energy and excitement of a typically Indian city slotted into a much more manageable package than Chennai's sprawl.

History

Tamil and Greek documents record the existence of Madurai from the 4th century BC. It was popular for trade, especially in spices, and was also the home of the *sangam,* the academy of Tamil poets. Over the centuries Madurai has come under the jurisdiction of the Cholas, the Pandyas, Muslim rulers, the Hindu Vijayanagar kings, and the Nayaks, who ruled until 1781. During the reign of Tirumalai Nayak (1623–55), the bulk of the Sri Meenakshi Temple was built, and Madurai became the cultural centre of the Tamil people, playing an important role in the development of the Tamil language.

Madurai then passed into the hands of the British East India Company. In 1840 the company razed the fort, which had previously surrounded the city, and filled in the moat. Four broad streets – the Veli streets – were constructed on top of this fill and to this day define the limits of the old city.

Sights

Sri Meenakshi Temple   HINDU TEMPLE
(camera ₹30; ☉4am-12.30pm & 4-9.30pm) The Sri Meenakshi Temple, abode of the triple-breasted, fish-eyed goddess Meenakshi Amman ('fish-eyed' is an adjective for perfect eyes in classical Tamil poetry), is considered by many to be the height of South Indian temple architecture, as vital to the aesthetic heritage of this region as the Taj Mahal is to North India. It's not so much a temple as a 6-hectare complex enclosed by 12 *gopurams,* the highest of which towers 52m over Madurai, and all of which are carved with a staggering array of gods, goddesses, demons and heroes.

According to legend, the beautiful Meenakshi was born with three breasts and this prophecy: her superfluous breast would melt away when she met her husband. The event came to pass when she met Shiva and took her place as his consort. The temple of the cosmic couple was designed in 1560 by Vishwanatha Nayak and built during the reign of Tirumalai Nayak, but its history goes back 2000 years to the time when Madurai was a Pandyan capital.

Much of the temple is off-limits to non-Hindus, but lay people can enter at the eastern *gopuram.* From here you can see the outer rings of the concentric corridors that enclose the sanctums of Meenakshi and Shiva, worshipped here as Sundareswarar, the beautiful lord. Be on the lookout for statues of deities encrusted in small balls of butter, thrown at the gods as offerings from their devout worshippers.

Also within the temple complex, housed in the 1000-Pillared Hall, is the **Temple Art Museum** (adult/child/foreigner ₹ 5/2/50, camera/video ₹50/250; ☉7am-7.30pm). It contains painted friezes and stone and brass images and good exhibits on Hindu deities.

Allow plenty of time to see this temple and be warned: dress codes have been tightened, and no legs should be exposed for either gender, or shoulders (for women). If you're deemed to be immodestly dressed an enterprising young man from the shop across the road will sell you a dhoti. Early mornings or late evenings are the best times to avoid crowds, and there's often classical dance somewhere in the complex at the weekends. 'Temple guides' charge negotiable fees, rarely below ₹200, so prepare to negotiate and be aware that they are often fronts for emporiums and tailor shops.

Gandhi Memorial Museum　　　MUSEUM
(admission free, camera ₹50; ⊙10am-1pm & 2-5.30pm) Housed in an old *tamukkam* (old exhibition pavilion), this excellent museum is set in spacious and relaxing grounds. The maze of rooms contains an impressively moving and detailed account of India's struggle for independence from 1757 to 1947, and the English-language signs pull no punches about British rule. Included in the exhibition is the blood-stained dhoti (long loincloth) that Gandhi was wearing at the time he was assassinated in Delhi in 1948; it's here because he first took up wearing the dhoti as a sign of native pride in Madurai in 1921. The **Gandhian Literary Society Bookstore** (⊙Mon-Sat) is behind the museum. The **Madurai Government Museum** (Indian/foreigner ₹ 5/100, camera ₹20; ⊙9.30am-5pm Sun-Thu) is next door in the same grounds. Inside is a small collection of archaeological finds, sculpture, bronzes, costumes and paintings.

Tirumalai Nayak Palace　　HISTORICAL BUILDING
(Indian/foreigner ₹10/50, camera/video ₹30/100; ⊙9am-1pm & 2-5pm) What the Meenakshi Temple is to Nayak religious architecture, the Tirumalai palace is to the secular, although it's just a shell that's in a state of rot today. The main event is the entrance gate, main hall and Natakasala (Dance Hall), with their faded yellow plasterwork, lion and *makara* (crocodile-elephant creature) sculptures and a series of murals that hints at the opulence the Nayak rulers once enjoyed. The rectangular courtyard is known as Swargavilasa (Celestial Pavilion).

Mariamman Teppakkulam Tank　　HISTORICAL BUILDING
This vast tank, 5km east of the old city, covers an area almost equal to that of Sri Meenakshi Temple and is the site of the incredible Teppam (Float) Festival. The tank is empty for most of the year and primarily serves as a cricket ground for local kids. It was built by Tirumalai Nayak in 1646 and is connected to the Vaigai River by underground channels.

✱✱ Festivals & Events

Teppam (Float) Festival　　TEMPLE FESTIVAL
(Jan/Feb) A popular event held on the full moon of the Tamil month of Thai, when Meenakshi temple deities are taken on a tour of the town and floated on the huge Mariamman Teppakkulam Tank. The evening culminates in Shiva's seduc-

tion of his wife, whereupon the icons are brought back to the temple to make love and, in so doing, regenerate the universe (Meenakshi's diamond nose stud is even removed so it doesn't irritate her lover).

Chithrai Festival　　TEMPLE FESTIVAL
(Apr/May) The main event on Madurai's busy festival calendar is this 14-day event that celebrates the marriage of Meenakshi to Sundareswarar (Shiva). The deities are wheeled around the Sri Meenakshi Temple in massive chariots that form part of long, colourful processions.

🛏 Sleeping

Most of Madurai's accommodation is concentrated in the area between the train station and Sri Meenakshi Temple.

Town Hall Rd, running eastwards from the train station, has a knot of budget hotels, but Madurai's best-value accommodation is the string of almost identical midrange hotels along West Perumal Maistry St, near the train station. Rooms without AC are generally good value and it's worth taking the step up from budget joints. Most have rooftop restaurants with temple and sunset views.

Madurai Residency　　HOTEL **$$**
(☑2343140; www.madurairesidency.com; 15 West Marret St; s/d incl breakfast from ₹800/1000; ✳@) The service is stellar and the rooms are comfy and fresh at this winner, which has the highest rooftop restaurant in town. There's 24-hour internet in the lobby.

Hotel Keerthi　　HOTEL **$$**
(☑4377788; www.hellomadurai.in/hotelkeerthi; 40 West Perumal Maistry St; r from ₹990; ✳) Don't be fooled by the nondescript lobby. This spotless, shiny hotel has rooms that are small but surprisingly stylish and modern, with groovy bedspreads, funky wall mirrors, picture walls and flatscreen TV.

Royal Court Madurai　　HOTEL **$$$**
(☑4356666; www.royalcourtindia.com; 4 West Veli St; s/d from ₹2800/3100; ✳@☎) The Royal Court manages to blend a bit of white-sheeted, hardwood-floored colonial elegance with modern amenities, such as wi-fi in all rooms, that makes it an excellent, centrally located top-end choice for someone who needs a bit of spoiling.

Hotel Park Plaza　　HOTEL **$$**
(☑3011111; www.hotelparkplaza.net; 114 West Perumal Maistry St; s/d incl breakfast ₹1900/2300; ✳)

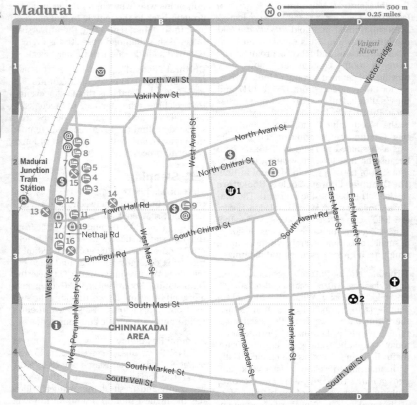

The Plaza's rooms are standard midrange: comfortable and simply furnished, with modern TVs. The front rooms have temple views from the 3rd floor up. There's a good multicuisine rooftop restaurant and the (inappropriately named) **Sky High Bar** – on the 1st floor. Perks include free breakfast and free pick-up from the airport or train station.

Hotel Supreme HOTEL $$
(☑2343151; www.hotelsupreme.in; 110 West Perumal Maistry St; d ₹720, s/d with AC from ₹1320/1500; ❄) This is another large, well-presented hotel that is very popular with domestic tourists. Don't miss the chance to walk into **Apollo**, a bar built to look like a spaceship, and wonder if someone laced your lassi last night. There's good food at the on-site **Surya Restaurant**.

Hotel Rathna Residency HOTEL $$
(☑4374444; www.hotelrathnaresidency.com; 109 West Perumal Maistry St; s/d incl breakfast from

₹1150/1200; ❄) There's not a lot to distinguish this bland, clean, vaguely corporate midrange spot from its neighbours, other than it has nicer pictures on its walls (Mughal-style miniatures) and doesn't offer any non-AC rooms.

Hotel West Tower HOTEL $
(☑2346908; West Tower St; s/d from ₹450/650; ❄) Somewhere between budget and midrange, this place is all about the location (right near the temple) but it's also acceptably clean and friendly.

Hotel Grand Central HOTEL $
(☑2343940; 82 West Perumal Maistry St; d from ₹350; ❄) Grand it ain't, but the cheap rooms aren't bad for the price, with clean sheets, cleanish bathrooms, tile floors and TVs.

New College House HOTEL $
(☑4372900; collegehouse_mdu@yahoo.co.in; 2 Town Hall Rd; r from ₹275; ❄) FYI: it's spelled 'Neww College House', in huge letters, in

Madurai

case you get confused. There's some 250 rooms scattered over this concrete complex. Some are fine, some not so much, and street noise often permeates, so try and get something away from the bustle.

Hotel International   HOTEL $
(☎4377463; 46 West Perumal Maistry St; s/d from ₹280/380) Shabby walls and dank bathrooms; but clean sheets, TVs and wee balconies.

Eating
Along West Perumal Maistry St the rooftop restaurants of a string of hotels offer breezy night-time dining and temple views (don't forget the mosquito repellent); most also have AC restaurants open for breakfast and lunch. Street stalls selling sweets, dosas, *idli* and the like are ubiquitous, especially near the train station. **Shoppers Shop** (Town Hall Rd; ⊙8am-11pm) is a well-stocked grocery store that has a good selection of Western foods.

British Bakery   CAFE $
(West Velli St; mains ₹30-75; ⊙lunch & dinner) A clean, popular snack joint with shakes, ice cream, iced tea and other refreshing drinks, along with fries, sandwiches, fried rice and Indian snacks.

Surya Restaurant   MULTICUISINE $
(110 West Perumal Maistry St; mains ₹45-115; ⊙dinner) The rooftop restaurant of Hotel Supreme offers a superb view over the city, stand-out service and a nice pure veg menu, but the winner here has got to be the cold coffee, which might as well have been brewed by God when you sip it on a dusty, hot (ie every) day.

Jayaram Fast Foods   MULTICUISINE $
(5-8 Nethaji Rd; mains ₹45-90; ⊙lunch & dinner) There's a busy (and yummy) bakery downstairs, and a crisp and clean restaurant up top that does a nice line in Indian fare, plus burgers and pizzas. While the latter dishes aren't winning any awards, this is as good a piece of pie as you'll find in Madurai. It's a small spot that gets very busy.

Dhivyar Mahal Restaurant   MULTICUISINE $
(☎2342700; 21 Town Hall Rd; mains ₹30-110; ⊙lunch & dinner) One of the better multicuisine restaurants not attached to a hotel, Dhivyar Mahal is clean, bright and friendly. The curries go down a treat, and where else are you going to find roast leg of lamb in Madurai?

Emperor Restaurant   MULTICUISINE $
(☎2350490; Hotel Chentoor, 106 West Perumal Maistry St; mains ₹35-90; ⊙breakfast, lunch & dinner) It's all veg all the time at Hotel Chentoor's rooftop restaurant, but that karmic goodness is a bit undone by the fact this spot basically becomes a very popular bar come nightfall.

Shopping
Madurai teems with cloth stalls and tailors' shops, which you may notice upon being approached for the umpteenth time by a tailor tout. A great place for getting cottons and printed fabrics is **Puthu Mandapam**, the pillared former entrance hall at the eastern side of Sri Meenakshi Temple. Here you'll find rows of tailors, all busily treadling away and capable of whipping up a good replica of whatever you're wearing in an hour or two. Quality, designs and prices vary greatly depending on the material and complexity of the design, but you can have a shirt made

up for as little as ₹200. Every driver, temple guide and tailor's brother will lead you to the Kashmiri craft shops in North Chitrai St, offering to show you the temple view from the rooftop – the views are good, and so is the inevitable sales pitch. For fixed-price crafts try **Poompuhar** (West Velli St; ⊙10am-1pm & 3-8pm Mon-Sat).

There's a couple of good English-language bookshops in town: try **Malligai Book Centre** (11 West Veli St; ⊙9am-2pm & 4.30-9pm Mon-Sat) and **Turning Point Books** (75 Venkatesh Towers, Town Hall Rd; ⊙10am-9pm); the latter is a 1st-floor shop opposite New College with a good selection of titles on Indian religion.

Information

Internet access

You can't walk without tripping over an internet cafe. There are several 24-hour Sify iWays, including a couple adjoining hotels in West Perumal Maistry St.

Web Tower Internet (West Tower Rd; per hr ₹20; ⊙10.30am-10pm) Downstairs from Hotel West Tower.

Money

ATMs are plentiful.

ICICI Bank ATM (North Chitrai St)

State Bank of India (West Veli St) Has foreign-exchange desks and an ATM; almost next door to Royal Court.

VKC Forex (Zulaiha Towers, Town Hall Rd; ⊙9am-6pm) An efficient place to change travellers cheques and cash.

Tourist Information

Madurai tourist office (☎2334757; 180 West Veli St; ⊙10am-5.45pm Mon-Fri) Not a lot of help, but staff will give you a brochure and map if you ask.

Getting There & Away

Air

Indian Airlines (☎2341234, airport 2690771; West Veli St; ⊙10am-5pm Mon-Sat) flies daily to Mumbai and Chennai, as does SpiceJet, which also flies to Delhi. Jet Airways flies daily to Chennai, and Kingfisher Airlines flies daily to Chennai and Bengaluru. None of these last three airlines has an office in town, but airport counters open at flight times.

Bus

Most long-distance buses arrive and depart from the **Central bus station** (☎2580680; Melur Rd; ⊙24hr), 6km northeast of the old city. It appears chaotic but is actually a well-organised 24-hour operation. Local buses shuttle into the city every few minutes for ₹3. An autorickshaw to the train station (where most of the hotels are located) is about ₹100. The boxed text on p1040 lists prices for government buses; some express services run to Bengaluru, Chennai, Mysore and Puducherry.

The Arapalayam bus stand, northwest of the train station on the river bank, has regular services to Coimbatore (₹76, six hours), two daily to Kodaikanal (₹48, four to five hours) and to Palani every half-hour (₹38, five hours).

Train

Madurai Junction train station is on the main Chennai–Kanyakumari line. There are at least nine daily trains to Chennai, and three daily services to Kanyakumari.

Some other services include Madurai to Coimbatore (2nd class/sleeper ₹74/155, seven hours) and Bengaluru (sleeper/3AC ₹209/555, 11 hours), as well as Trivandrum and Mumbai.

BUSES FROM MADURAI

DESTINATION	FARE (₹)	DURATION (HR)	FREQUENCY
Bengaluru	190	12	7 daily
Chennai	160-190	10	every 30min
Chidambaram	95	8	daily
Coimbatore	90	7	daily
Kochi	145	8	daily
Kanyakumari	94	6	hourly
Mysore	280	16	daily (via Ooty)
Puducherry	110	8	2 daily
Rameswaram	58	4	every 30min
Trichy	42	3	every 15min

Getting Around

The airport is 12km south of town and taxis cost ₹250 to the town centre. Autorickshaws ask around ₹130. Alternatively, bus 10A from the Central bus station goes to the airport, but don't rely on it being on schedule.

Central Madurai is small enough to get around on foot.

Kanyakumari (Cape Comorin)

🎵 04652 / POP 19,739

The end of India has more appeal than just being the end of the road. There's a whiff of accomplishment (along with dried fish) upon making it to the tip of the country, the terminus of a narrowing funnel of rounded granite mountains – some of India's oldest – green fields plaided with silver-glinting rice paddies and slow-looping turbines on wind farms. Like all edges, there's a sense of the surreal here. You can see three seas mingle, the sunset over the moonrise and the Temple of the Virgin Sea Goddess within minutes of each other. But beyond that, Kanyakumari is a genuinely friendly village that is a nice respite from the dust of the Indian road.

The main temple is right on the point of Kanyakumari and leading north from it is a small bazaar lined with restaurants, stalls and souvenir shops.

👁 Sights & Activities

Kumari Amman Temple   HINDU TEMPLE

(🕐4.30am-12.30pm & 4-8pm) The legends say the *kanya* (virgin) goddess Kumari, a manifestation of the Great Goddess Devi, single-handedly conquered demons and secured freedom for the world. At this temple pilgrims give her thanks in an intimately spaced, beautifully decorated temple, where the nearby crash of waves from three oceans can be heard through the twilight glow of oil fires clutched in vulva-shaped votive candles (a reference to the sacred femininity of the goddess). Men must remove their shirts to enter and cameras are forbidden.

Gandhi Memorial   MONUMENT

(admission by donation; 🕐7am-7pm) Poignantly and appropriately placed at the end of the nation Gandhi fathered is this memorial, which purposely resembles an Orissan temple embellished by Hindu, Christian and Muslim architects. The central plinth was used to store some of the Mahatma's ashes,

and each year, on Gandhi's birthday (2 October), the sun's rays fall on the stone. Guides may ask for an excessive donation, but ₹10 is enough; try and keep an air of silence (even if locals don't).

Kamaraj Memorial   MONUMENT

(🕐7am-7pm) Just next to the Gandhi memorial is this shrine to K Kamaraj, known as 'the Gandhi of the South'; Chennai's domestic airport is named after him. One of the most powerful politicians of post-independence India, Kamaraj held the chief ministership of both Madras State and latter-day Tamil Nadu. The shrine is just a collection of dusty blown-up photographs with almost no space given to context or explanation.

Vivekananda Exhibition   MUSEUM

(Main Rd; admission ₹2; 🕐8am-noon & 4-8pm) This exhibition, which was closed for refurbishment at the time of research, details the life and extensive journey across India made by the philosopher Swami Vivekananda (the 'Wandering Monk', 1863–1902), who developed a synthesis between the tenets of Hinduism and concepts of social justice. Another exhibition can be found at **Vivekanandapuram** (🎵247012; admission free; 🕐9am-1pm & 5-9pm), an ashram 3km north of town that provides a snapshot of Indian philosophy, religion, leaders and thinkers.

Vivekananda Memorial   MONUMENT

(admission ₹10; 🕐8am-5pm) Four hundred metres offshore is the rock where Swami Vivekananda meditated and chose to take his moral message beyond India's shores. A memorial was built in Vivekananda's memory in 1970, and reflects architectural styles drawn from all over India. It can be a loud place when packed with tourists, but the islet is big enough to provide moments of seclusion.

The huge **statue** on the smaller island, which looks like an Indian Colossus of Rhodes, is not of Vivekananda but Tamil poet Thiruvalluvar. India's 'Statue of Liberty' was the work of more than 5000 sculptors. It was erected in 2000 and honours the poet's 133-chapter work *Thirukural* – hence its height of exactly 133ft (40.5m).

Ferries shuttle between the port and the islands between 8am and 4pm; tickets are ₹20 return.

Seafront   BEACH

There's a crowded beach here and **ghats** that lead down to a lingam half submerged in a

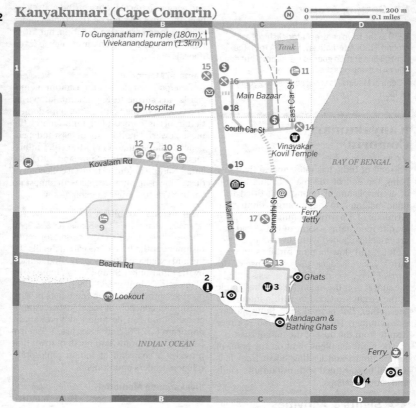

wave-driven tidal pool. Past the ice-cream and *chaat* (snack) sellers above the beach is a **memorial** to victims of the 2004 tsunami.

🛏 Sleeping

As befits a holiday destination, Kanyakumari's hoteliers have generally gone for bright colours and, dare we say, tackily cheerful decorations; after the bland sameness of midrange hotels around the state, it's quite exciting to find a large neon-coloured tiger painted on your bedhead. Some hotels, especially midrange places around the bazaar, have seasonal rates, so some prices double during April and May, and late October to January.

Manickhan Tourist Home   HOTEL $
(☎246387; East Car St; d from ₹770; ❄) This very friendly hotel is professionally run and a real pleasure to doss in; the large rooms are all outfitted with clean bathrooms, TV and, if you're willing to shell out a bit, superb

sea views. Next-door **Hotel Maadhini** has almost identical rates and service, with the addition of a garden restaurant that's very pleasant in the evening.

Santhi Residency   HOTEL $
(☎247091; Kovalam Rd; d from ₹700; ❄) A smaller, older restored house with a more restrained sense of style than the hotels (the only decoration in each simple room is a picture of Jesus), this place is quiet and very clean with a nice patch of leafy garden.

Hotel Tri Sea   HOTEL $$
(☎246586; triseahotel@yahoo.com; Kovalam Rd; r from ₹1600; ❄❄) As you walk west of the town you can't miss the high-rise Tri Sea, which offers huge, spotless, airy rooms, most with balconies facing the ocean. The colour schemes are hectic, to say the least, but there are big flatscreen TVs, a great rooftop pool and viewing platforms that make a perfect spot for sunrise and sunset.

Hotel Narmadha   HOTEL $
(☏246365; Kovalam Rd; r ₹250-400) This big concrete block conceals some friendly staff and a range of cheap rooms, some of which are better than others; the good-value ₹400 doubles with sea views had crisp white sheets when we visited, while the cheaper rooms didn't look so hot. It's popular with pilgrims and is set to the west of the main bazaar, next to Hotel Tri Sea.

Hotel Tamil Nadu   HOTEL $
(☏246257; www.ttdconline.com; Beach Rd; r from ₹800; ❄) Despite the usual quirks of a government-run hotel (and – surprise – it's overpriced), this is a great location if you want to get away from the (slight) bustle of town; balcony rooms have ocean, though not temple, views.

Saravana Lodge   HOTEL $
(☏246007; Sannathi St; r ₹200-600) It's basic, but you can get a reasonable deal at this place just outside the temple entrance. All rooms have private bathrooms with squat toilets. A whole new block of rooms with a rooftop viewing platform should be complete by the time you read this.

Hotel Sun World   HOTEL $$
(☏247755; hotelsunworld@sancharnet.in; Kovalam Rd; d from ₹1500; ❄) Everything's very bright and glossy at this higher-end spot, where most rooms have a private balcony with fab three-ocean views.

✕ Eating

There are plenty of fruit stalls and basic veg restaurants in the bazaar area, open for breakfast, lunch and dinner. Hotel Saravana has two clean, busy veg restaurants with thalis (₹30).

Sangam Restaurant   MULTICUISINE $$
(Main Rd; mains ₹55-190) It's as if the Sangam started in Kashmir, trekked across the entirety of India, and stopped here to open a restaurant that features top culinary picks culled from every province encountered along the way. The food is good and the joint is bustling. The biggest downer is a height-and-weight machine by the front door that calculates your BMI and lets you know if eating here has made you obese.

Sri Krishna   CAFE $
(Sannathi St; mains ₹30-90) If you need fresh juice, good ice cream or Indian takes on pizza, chips and burgers, try this clean and busy corner cafe.

Hotel Seaview   MULTICUISINE $$
(East Car St; mains ₹60-200) This hotel has an excellent AC multicuisine restaurant specialising in fresh local seafood and posh takes on North and South Indian faves. The vibe is upmarket and waiters are very attentive.

Hotel Triveni   SOUTH INDIAN $
(Main Rd; mains ₹20-50) The fans might blow you clear into the ocean, but this place also has clean tables, efficient service and good-value, mainly South Indian veg dishes. A good spot for breakfast.

ℹ Information

Janaki Forex (◷9.30am-6.30pm Mon-Sat) Off South Car St. Change cash and travellers cheques here.
Tamil Mercantile Bank ATM (Main Rd)
Tony's Internet (Sannathi St; per hr ₹50; ◷10am-8pm) Friendly – possibly over-friendly (but not unsafe) if you're a lone woman.
Tourist office (☏246276; Main Rd; ◷8am-6pm Mon-Fri)

❶ Getting There & Away

Bus

The surprisingly sedate bus stand is a 10-minute walk west of the centre along Kovalam Rd and there's a handy **SETC booking office** (⏲7am-9pm) on Main Rd. Almost all buses go via Madurai; the exception is the Rameswaram service. Buses from here include:

Bengaluru ₹430, 15 hours, daily
Chennai ₹390, 16 hours, seven daily
Kodaikanal ₹225, 10 hours, daily
Madurai ₹94, six hours, eight daily
Ooty ₹330, 14 hours, two daily
Rameswaram ₹145, nine hours, two daily

Train

The train station is about 1km north of the bazaar and temple. There are three daily trains to Chennai, the fastest of which is the *Kanyakumari Express*, departing at 5.20pm (sleeper/3AC ₹305/801, 13 hours) and stopping at Madurai and Trichy.

There are two daily express trains to Trivandrum (2nd class/3AC ₹30/238, two hours).

For the real long-haulers or train buffs, the weekly *Himsagar Express* runs all the way to Jammu Tawi, a distance of 3715km, in 70 hours – the longest single train ride in India. It departs 2pm Friday (sleeper/3AC ₹629/1741).

THE WESTERN GHATS

Welcome to the lush mountains of the Western Ghats, some of the most welcome heat relief in India. Rising like an impassable bulwark of evergreen and deciduous tangle from the north of Mumbai to the tip of Tamil Nadu, the Ghats (with an average elevation of 915m) contain 27% of all India's flowering plants, 60% of its medicinal plants and an incredible array of endemic wildlife. It's not just the air and (relative) lack of pollution that's refreshing, either – there's a general acceptance of quirkiness and eccentricity in the hills that is hard to find in the lowlands. Think hippie cafes, handlebar-moustachioed trekking guides and tiger-stripe earmuffs for sale in the bazaar. On the downside is the state of local tribal groups whose identity is in danger of both over-exploitation and assimilation.

Kodaikanal (Kodai)

✏04542 / POP 32,969 / ELEV 2100M

Kodai is small, intimate, misty and mountainous; there are few more refreshing Tamil Nadu moments than boarding a bus in the heat-soaked plains and disembarking in the sharp pinch of a Kodaikanal night. It's not all cold though; during the day the weather is positively pleasant, more reminiscent of deep spring than early winter.

Located in the Palani knolls some 120km northwest of Madurai, Kodai clings to a mountainside draped in *sholas* (forests) of pine, gum trees and *kurinji* shrub, unique to the Western Ghats. The light, purple-blue-coloured blossoms flower every 12 years; next due date 2018. If you don't feel like waiting, the many treks by nearby dark rock faces and white waterfalls are still rewarding.

The renowned Kodaikanal International School provides a bit of cosmopolitan influence, with students from around the globe. Compared to Ooty, the town is relaxed (tourist brochures call it the 'Princess of Hills', while Ooty is the Queen), but it's still popular with Indian tourists (especially honeymooners). For a hill station, it's remarkably compact and the central town area can easily be explored on foot.

◉ Sights & Activities

Sacred Heart Natural History Museum   MUSEUM

(Sacred Heart College, Law's Ghat Rd; admission ₹5; ⏲9am-5pm) In the extensive old college grounds (now being marketed as an 'eco sanctuary') a couple of kilometres out of town, this museum has a hodge-podge collection of flora and fauna put together over more than 100 years by Jesuit priests; the amateur (and therefore rather charming) nature of the collection is displayed through dodgy taxidermy, hand drawings, odd commentary, and old black-and-white photos of solemn-looking priests with huge snakes draped over them. There are some pleasant walks around the grounds.

Walking & Trekking

Assuming it's not cloaked in opaque mist, the valley views along paved **Coaker's Walk** (admission ₹3, camera ₹5; ⏲7am-7pm) are superb. There's a small **observatory** (admission ₹3) with a telescope at the southern end. You can start near Greenlands Youth Hostel or Villa Retreat – where **stained glass** in the nearby Church of South India (CSI) is stunning in the morning light – and the stroll takes all of five minutes. The 5km **lake circuit** is pleasant in the early morning when you can count the kingfishers before the tourist traffic starts.

The views from **Pillar Rocks**, a 7km hike (one way, beginning near Bryant Park), are excellent (again, assuming fine weather), and there are some wonderful hiking trails through pockets of forest, including **Bombay Shola** and **Pambar Shola**, that meander around Lower Shola Rd and St Mary's Rd. You'll need a guide; talk to the staff at Greenlands Youth Hostel; other hotels might also be able to help. Guides of varying quality will approach you in the street.

Parks & Waterfalls
Near the start of Coaker's Walk is **Bryant Park** (adult/child ₹20/10, camera/video ₹30/75; ◷9am-6.30pm), landscaped and stocked by the British officer after whom it's named. **Chettiar Park** (admission free; ◷8.30am-5pm), about 1.5km uphill from town on the way to the Kurinji Andavar Temple, is small, pretty and landscaped. Both get crowded with school groups and canoodling couples. Nearby waterfalls include **Silver Cascade**, on the road outside Kodai and often full of interstate tourists bathing on the rocks, and compact **Bear Shola Falls**, in a pocket of forest about a 20-minute walk from the town centre.

Boating & Horse Riding
If you're sappy in love like a bad Bollywood song, the thing to do in Kodai is rent a pedal boat (₹50 per half-hour), rowboat (₹120) or Kashmiri *shikara* (covered gondola, aka 'honeymoon boat'; ₹260 including boatman) from either the Kodaikanal Boat and Rowing Club or Tamil Nadu Tourist Development Corporation; screechy crooning to your significant other is strictly optional.

There's a few horse-riding stands on the lake. The rate is ₹300 per hour unaccompanied or ₹400 with a guide.

🛏 Sleeping
Hotel prices can jump by as much as 300% during the high season (from 1 April to 30 June). Prices listed here are low-season rates. There are some lovely heritage places, and a couple of good-value midrange options if you live without colonial ambience.

Most hotels in Kodai have a 9am or 10am checkout time in high season, but for the rest of the year it's usually 24 hours.

TOP CHOICE Carlton Hotel HOTEL $$$
(✆240056; www.krahejahospitality.com; Lake Rd; s/d/cottages from ₹6245/7130/10,695) The cream of Kodai's hotels is a magnificent five-star colonial mansion that overlooks the lake and the international school. Rooms are bright, spacious and some have private balconies with lake views. The lobby and grounds very much succeed at re-creating hill station ambience, with stone walls, dark-wood flooring and roaring fireplaces that make you want to demand a scotch now, dammit, from the eager staff. There's a pricey and rather wonderful buffet lunch and dinner available.

Villa Retreat HOTEL $$
(✆240940; www.villaretreat.com; Club Rd; r ₹1350-2813, ste ₹3375) The terrace garden of this lovely old stone-built family hotel at the northern end of Coaker's Walk offers awesome valley views. Most rooms have fireplaces and TV; new rooms should be ready by the time you read this. Prices include taxes.

Hotel Cokkers Tower HOTEL $
(✆240374; cokkers.tower@yahoo.com; Woodville Rd; dm/d ₹125/750) Just near the Church of South India, this is a clean, straightforward hotel with simple, light-coloured rooms (no colonial wood here). The dorm beds are narrow and reminiscent of train bunks, but the shared bathroom is sparkling and you can't top the price.

Hilltop Towers HOTEL $$
(✆240413; www.hilltopgroup.in; Club Rd; d from ₹1200) Although it comes off as boxy and corporate, rustic accents like polished teak floors and wooden embellishments, plus friendly staff and excellent upper-floor views, make the Hilltop a good midrange choice.

Hotel Astoria HOTEL $
(✆240524; www.astoriaveg.com; Anna Salai; r from ₹700) You wouldn't expect it from the outside, which is mainly all about the popular restaurant (and we'll admit the curry smell occasionally wafts through the lower corridors), but this central hotel has clean, wood-floored, very pleasant rooms with colonial-style furniture. Prices are reasonable.

Greenlands Youth Hostel HOSTEL $
(✆240899; www.greenlandskodaikanal.com; Coaker's Walk; dm ₹200, d ₹500-1800) We're a bit ambivalent about this popular, long-running spot; the grounds and views are excellent, guides can be organised here and it's a great spot to socialise with other budget travellers in the cosy, crowded dorms. But the rooms are overpriced (negotiating might lower

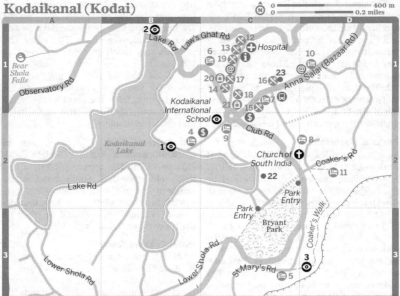

them), management can be unhelpful and hot water appears less often than is claimed.

RR Residency HOTEL **$$**
(☎244301; rrresidency@rediffmail.com; Boat House Rd; r ₹1490; ☎) Tasteful artwork, comfy beds and slightly dank bathrooms for the price.

Snooze Inn HOTEL **$$**
(☎240873; snoozeinnslaes@jayarajgroup.com; Anna Salai; r from ₹600) The outside has a bit more character than the rooms, but this is another decent-value budget choice with clean bathrooms and plenty of blankets.

✗ Eating

PT Rd is the best place for cheap restaurants and it's here that most travellers and students from the international school congregate.

Hotel New Punjab NORTH INDIAN **$**
(PT Rd; mains ₹30-100; ⊙lunch & dinner) For North Indian cuisine, including tandoori (and any nonveg curries in general), this is Kodai's favourite. It serves the best tandoori chicken in South India, according to locals.

Cloud Street MULTICUISINE **$$**
(PT Rd; mains ₹50-200; ⊙lunch & dinner Tue-Sun, breakfast Sat & Sun) Why yes, that is a real Italian-style woodfire pizza oven. And yes, that's hummus, felafel and nachos on the menu,

alongside pasta and pizza – it's all great food in a simple, relaxed setting. (Also, ask the owners about their lovely homestay getaway 20km out of Kodai.)

Tava INDIAN **$**
(PT Rd; mains ₹40; ⊙lunch & dinner Thu-Tue) A clean, fast and cheap veg option, this place has a wide menu; try the cauliflower-stuffed *gobi paratha* (spicy cauliflower bread) and *sev puri* (crisp, puffy fried bread with potato and chutney).

Royal Tibet TIBETAN **$**
(PT Rd; mains ₹40-80; ⊙lunch & dinner) If you're missing Tibetan food, come here for the chewy but tasty *momos* (dumplings) and *thukpa* (noodle soup). A nearby competitor, **Tibetan Brothers**, offers almost the exact same menu; they're both good.

Red Apple MULTICUISINE **$**
(Anna Salai; mains ₹50-80; ⊙lunch & dinner) A pure-veg multicuisine spot (well there's a few Chinese dishes, as well as North and South Indian) that's cheap, clean and cheerful. There's a posh thali for ₹60. It's just opposite the bus stand.

Pot Luck CAFE **$**
(PT Rd; snacks ₹20-50; ⊙10.30am-7pm Wed-Mon) Sandwiches, pancakes, coffee and

Kodaikanal (Kodai)

quesadillas (!) served up on a pretty, tiny terrace attached to a pottery shop. There are delicious chutneys, lemon curd and biscuits to takeaway, too.

Hotel Astoria INDIAN $
(Anna Salai; mains ₹30-50, thalis ₹35-60; ⊙breakfast, lunch & dinner) This veg restaurant is always packed with locals and tourists, especially come lunchtime when it serves excellent all-you-can-eat thalis.

Self-Catering
Excellent homemade chocolates and dried fruit are sold all over town.

Eco Nut HEALTH FOOD $
(☎243296; PT Rd; ⊙10am-5pm Mon-Sat) This interesting shop sells a wide range of locally produced organic health food –

wholewheat bread, muffins, cheese, salad greens – and essential oils, herbs and herb remedies.

Pastry Corner BAKERY $
(Anna Salai; ⊙9am-9pm) Pick up great picnic sandwiches and yummy brownies here, or squeeze onto the benches with a cuppa to watch the world go by.

Hilltop Bake BAKERY $
(Club Rd; pastries ₹18-40; ⊙11am-9pm) A wide range of fresh savoury pastries, including good approximations of pizza, as well as cakes and brownies.

 Shopping

The many handicraft stores stock good craftwork, and several also reflect a local low-key but long-term commitment to social justice. On PT Rd you'll find small Kashmiri shops and South Indian handicrafts stalls.

Cottage Crafts HANDICRAFTS
(PT Rd; ⊙10am-730pm) Run by the voluntary organisation Coordinating Council for Social Concerns in Kodai (Corsock), here you'll find goods crafted by disadvantaged groups, with about 80% of the purchase price returned to the craftspeople.

Re Shop HANDICRAFTS
(Seven Roads Junction; ⊙10am-7pm Mon-Sat) Stylish jewellery, bags, cards and more, at reasonable prices, made by and benefiting vllage women around Tamil Nadu. It's run by the **Blue Mango Trust** (www.bluemangoindia.com).

ℹ Information

Alpha Net (PT Rd; internet per hr ₹50; ⊙9am-10pm)

Apollo Communications (Anna Salai; internet per hr ₹40; ⊙9.30am-8pm)

Indian Bank (Anna Salai; ⊙10am-2pm & 2.30-3.30pm Mon-Fri, 10am-12.30pm Sat) Has a foreign-exchange desk.

Kurinji Tours & Travel (☎240008; kodaikurinji@sancharnet.in; Club Rd; ⊙9am-9pm) Reliable help with onward travel arrangements; also does foreign exchange.

State Bank of India ATM (Anna Salai)

Tourist office (☎241675; PT Rd; ⊙10am-5.45pm Mon-Fri) No brochures, maps or tours; 'just information, madam'.

 Getting There & Away

The nearest train station is Kodai Road, about two hours away at the foot of the mountain, where taxis (around ₹1000) and buses (₹17) wait. There's a **train booking office** (off Anna Salai; ☺9am-5pm Mon-Sat, 1.30-5pm Sun) in town.

Don't expect a bus to depart from Kodaikanal immediately. Tickets for private buses can be booked at travel agents near the bus stand. Buses from Kodai include:

Bengaluru ₹283, 11 hours, daily

Chennai ₹230, 11 hours, daily

Coimbatore ₹74, five hours, two daily

Madurai ₹48, four hours, hourly

Ooty ₹260, eight hours, daily

Palani ₹34, two hours, 10 daily

Trichy ₹65, 5½ hours, four daily

ℹ Getting Around

The central part of Kodaikanal is compact and very easy to get around on foot. There are no autorickshaws (believe it or not) but plenty of taxis willing to take you to various sightseeing points. Charges are fixed; sightseeing tours cost from ₹600 to ₹1200 for a day trip. There's a stand opposite the bus station.

If you fancy a ride around the lake or you're fit enough to tackle the hills, mountain bikes can be hired from several **bicycle stalls** (per hr ₹20; ☺8am-6pm) around the lake.

Around Kodaikanal

One of the better high-end escapes in the hills, about three hours' drive below Kodaikanal off the Palani–Dindigul road, is the fabulous **Cardamom House** (☏0451-2556765, 09360-691793; www.cardamomhouse.com; r from ₹3300). Created with love and care by a retired Brit, this comfortable guesthouse – at the end of a scenic road beside bird-rich Lake Kamarajar – runs on solar power, uses water wisely, farms organically, trains and employs only locals (who produce terrific meals), and supports several village development initiatives. You'll need to book well in advance, hire a driver to take you there, and prepare for some serious relaxation.

Coimbatore

☏0422 / POP 1.46 MILLION

Coimbatore may be one of the largest cities in Tamil Nadu, but most travellers use it as either a step towards getting into Ooty, or a step down from the hills and into Kerala. Which isn't a bad idea; this is a large business and junction city that's friendly enough (and its proximity to the hills means temperatures are just a little cooler than average),

but it's short on sights. Sometimes known as the Manchester of India for its textile industry, it's in the process of becoming a major IT centre. It has plenty of accommodation and eating options if you need to spend the night.

🛏 Sleeping

Legend's Inn HOTEL $$

(☏4350000; legends_inn@yahoo.com; Geetha Hall Rd; s/d from ₹900/990; ❄) Some of the best-value midrange rooms in town, with comfortable furnishings, bamboo blinds and shiny bathrooms.

Residency HOTEL $$$

(☏2241414; www.theresidency.com; 1076 Avanashi Rd; s/d incl breakfast from ₹4750/5100; ❄@☎☎) Coimbatore's finest hotel has all the five-star trimmings, along with friendly staff and immaculate rooms. There's a well-equipped health club and pool, two excellent restaurants, a coffee shop and a bookshop in the lobby.

Sabari's Nest HOTEL $$

(☏4505500; nest.coimbatore@sabarihotels.com; 739A Avanashi Rd; s/d incl breakfast from ₹2000/2300; ❄☎) A change of name and ownership doesn't seem to have damaged this long-standing favourite; rooms are very comfortable, with wooden floors and tasteful Audubon-esque prints of local birdlife.

Hotel ESS Grande HOTEL $$

(☏2230271; hessgrande@gmail.com; Nehru St; s/d incl breakfast from ₹1300/1600; ❄@) The best of the bus-stand-adjacent hotels, the ESS has small but very clean, fresh rooms, and possibly the sparkliest bathrooms in Coimbatore.

Hotel Rathna Regent HOTEL $$$

(☏4294444; www.rathnaregent.com; Avanashi Rd; s/d incl breakfast from ₹2800/3300; ❄☎) Not quite the top spot in town (hint: it's just opposite it), but a very comfortable place to lay your head all the same. The more expensive rooms are more like apartments, and all the facilities are here, including a couple of great restaurants, a bar and a cafe.

Hotel Shri Shakti HOTEL $

(☏2234225; Sastri Rd; s/d from ₹260/380; ❄) There's not much character here, but there are a lot of rooms, and probably the cheapest AC in town; if you need a cheap, basic place to crash that's near the bus stands, look no further.

Hotel AP
HOTEL $

(☎2301773; hotelap@yahoo.com; s/d from ₹420/510, d with AC ₹990; ✳) Basic, clean-enough rooms near the train station. The AP's tucked down a back street, but you'll recognise it by its oddly cubist exterior. Singles are real singles, not the usual single-occupancy doubles, and are a bit cell-like.

✖ Eating

There's a fast-food hall and supermarket underneath Sabari's Nest hotel.

Malabar
INDIAN $

(7 Sastri Rd; mains ₹60-120; ☺lunch & dinner) In the KK Residency Hotel, this restaurant specialises in Keralan and North Indian food. The Keralan chicken roast (₹150 for half a chicken) is a spicy treat and there are seafood choices like crab masala.

Annalakshmi
INDIAN $$

(☎2212142; 106 Racecourse Rd; set meals ₹200; ☺lunch & dinner Tue-Sun) The top veg restaurant in town, this is run by devotees of Swami Shatanand Saraswati; the price of your meal helps support underprivileged children.

Annalakshmi Hotel
SOUTH INDIAN $

(Geetha Hall Rd; mains ₹20-80) A lot more down-market than the posh restaurant it probably borrowed its name from, but this cheap-and-cheerful place is probably the best of the cluster of mainly South Indian restaurants on Geetha Hall Rd. Mushroom dishes are particulary good, and the biryani ain't bad.

KR Food Mall
INDIAN $

(cnr State Bank & Geetha Hall Rds) Indian snacks and sweets all day, a good veg restaurant with a decent range of North and South Indian upstairs (breakfast, lunch and dinner), and an evening-only, super-popular halal takeaway stall that's heavy on spicy chicken dishes.

Naalukattu
SOUTH INDIAN $

(Nehru St; mains ₹50-140; ☺lunch & dinner) Like a dark-wood-accented Keralan veranda, with Malayalam-inspired food that's all good – especially the seafood.

Hot Chocolate
WESTERN $$$

(Avanashi Rd; mains ₹80-200; ☺lunch & dinner) Not bad at all if you're hankering after cakes, pasta or burgers.

❶ Information

There's a string of internet joints along Geetha Hall Rd, opposite the train station, all charging about ₹20 per hour.

HSBC ATM (Racecourse Rd) Next to Annalakshmi restaurant.

Oscar Browsing Centre (cnr Kalingaray & Sastri Sts; per hr ₹20; ☺9.30am-10pm) Internet access near the bus stands.

Coimbatore

Coimbatore

N 0 ——— 500 m
   0 ——— 0.25 miles

State Bank of India ATM (Avanashi Rd) Opposite Sabari's Nest.

VKC Forex (Raheja Centre, Avanashi Rd; ☻9.30am-6.30pm Mon-Sat) Currency exchange and travellers cheques cashed, next door to the Residency hotel.

ⓘ Getting There & Away

Air

The airport is 10km east of town, with domestic flights to many destinations, including Chennai, Delhi, Bengaluru, Mumbai and Kochi. SilkAir also runs three flights a week direct to/from Singapore. Airlines include **Air India** (✆2399833), **Jet Airways** (✆2243465), Kingfisher Airlines, **SilkAir** (✆4370271) and SpiceJet.

Bus

There are three bus stands in the city centre.

From the Central bus station services depart to northern destinations such as Salem and Erode. From Thiruvalluvar bus station you can catch regular state and interstate buses to Bengaluru (₹180 to ₹230, nine hours), Mysore (₹80 to ₹100, five hours) and Chennai (₹300, 11½ hours). The Town bus stand is for local city buses.

Ukkadam bus station, south of the city, is for buses to nearby southern destinations, including Palani (₹35, three hours), Pollachi (₹16, one hour) and Madurai (₹74, five hours). The Ooty bus stand, aka 'new bus stand', is a couple of kilometres west of the centre on the Mettupalayam road; regular services run to Mettupalayam (45 minutes), Ooty (3½ hours; via Coonoor) and Kotagiri.

Taxi

A taxi up the hill to Ooty (2½ hours) costs about ₹1500; Ooty buses are often so crowded that it's an option worth considering.

Train

Coimbatore Junction is on the main line between Chennai and Ernakulam (Kerala). For Ooty, catch the daily 12671 *Nilgiri Express* at 5.15am; it connects with the miniature railway departure from Mettupalayam to Ooty at 7.10am. The whole trip to Ooty takes about seven hours. For other train services, see the boxed text, p1050.

ⓘ Getting Around

For the airport take bus 20 from the Town bus stand or bus 90 from the train station. Many buses run between the train station and the Town bus stand, and between the Central bus station and Ooty and Ukkadam stands. Autorickshaw drivers charge around ₹50 between the bus and train stations. An autorickshaw from the centre out to the Ooty bus stand will cost up to ₹100 depending on your bargaining skills.

Around Coimbatore

The **Isha Yoga Center** (✆0422-2515345; www.ishafoundation.org), an ashram in Poondi, 30km west of Coimbatore, is also a yoga retreat and place of pilgrimage. The centrepiece is a multi-religious temple housing the Dhyanalingam, said to be unique in that it embodies all seven chakras of spiritual energy. Visitors are welcome to the temple to meditate, or to take part in yoga courses, for which you should register in advance.

The commercial town of **Mettupalayam** is the starting point for the miniature train to Ooty. There's little of interest for travellers, but if you want to sleep in a little longer before you catch the train, there is plenty of accommodation. There are various cheap lodges right by the bus and train stations, and **Hotel EMS Mayura** (✆04254-227936; 212 Coimbatore Rd; r ₹700, with AC ₹1200; ❀), a fine, clean, bland midrange hotel with a decent restaurant, is just 1km from the train station.

MAJOR TRAINS FROM COIMBATORE

DESTINATION	TRAIN NO & NAME	FARE (₹)	DURATION (HR)	DEPARTURE
Bengaluru	6525 *Island Express*	191/505	7½	10.50pm
Chennai*	2672 *Kovai Express*	132/471	7½	2.20pm
	2674 *Cheran Express*	232/594	8½	10.20pm
Kochi	7230 *Sabari Express*	122/311	5	8.35am
Madurai	6610 *Nagercoil Express*	155/404	6	8.30pm

*2nd class/AC chair
All other fares sleeper/3AC

Coonoor

📞 0423 / POP 101,000 / ELEV 1850M

Coonoor is one of the three Nilgiri hill stations – Ooty, Kotagiri and Coonoor– that lie above the southern plains. Like Kotagiri, Coonoor is a place for quiet and isolation, and it's emerging as a centre for foodies and upmarket homestays. From Upper Coonoor's accommodation, 1km to 2km above the town centre, you can look down over the sea of red-tile rooftops to the slopes behind and soak up the peace, cool climate and beautiful scenery. Just note you get none of the above in central Coonoor, which is a bustling, honking mess.

👁 Sights & Activities

There are several popular viewpoints around Coonoor. **Dolphin's Nose**, about 10km from town, exposes a vast panorama encompassing **Catherine Falls** across the valley. **Lamb's Rock**, named after the British captain who created a short path to this favourite picnic spot in a pretty patch of forest, has amazing views past the hills into the hazy plains. The easiest way to see these sights – all on the same road – is on a rickshaw tour for around ₹500. If you're feeling energetic, walk the 6km or so back into town from Lamb's Rock (it's mostly, but not entirely, downhill).

Sim's Park   PARK

(adult/child ₹10/5, camera/video ₹25/250; ⊙8.30am-6pm) In Upper Coonoor, the 12-hectare Sim's Park is a peaceful oasis of manicured lawns and more than 1000 plant species, including magnolia, tree ferns and camellia. Buses heading to Kotagiri can drop you here.

🛏 Sleeping & Eating

You'll need a rickshaw (or good legs) to reach all these places. If you're self-catering, try the **Green Shop** (Jograj Bldg, Bedford Circle) for honey and other local goodies, and the well-stocked supermarket in **Tulsi Mall** for a range of packaged Western goods.

🏆TOP CHOICE 180 McIver   BOUTIQUE HOTEL **$$$**

(📞 2233323; 180mciver@gmail.com; McIver Villa, Orange Grove Rd; d incl breakfast ₹3000-4500) A French couple has turned the four bedrooms in this classic Nilgiri bungalow into something really special; bright-coloured walls, antique furniture and floorboards, working fireplaces and big fresh bathrooms

blend French and local sensibilities in the best possible way. The multicuisine restaurant, **La Belle Vie**, uses organic produce and has guests driving a long way to sample the Indian-French menu (mains ₹140 to ₹350).

Acres Wild   FARMSTAY **$$**

(📞 2232621; www.acres-wild.com; Upper Meanjee Estate, Kannimariamman Kovil St; cottages incl breakfast ₹2000-4000) This gorgeously situated farm outside Coonoor makes cheese like you've never tasted in India, and invites guests to help in the production. Cottages are simple and stylish, with fireplaces for chilly nights and views over the valley; your hosts are friendly and the food is great. No walk-ins – book in advance.

Tryst   GUESTHOUSE **$$$**

(📞 2207057; www.trystindia.com; s/d incl breakfast & dinner ₹5500/6600) If you're looking for a gregarious accommodation experience that's quirky and classy, check out the website of this extraordinary guesthouse and book ahead. It's beautifully located in a former tea plantation manager's bungalow.

YWCA Wyoming Guesthouse   GUESTHOUSE **$**

(📞 2234426; ywcacoonoor@gmail.com; s/d ₹500/700) This ramshackle guesthouse, a hill-station gem of a structure nestled into an upslope of Upper Coonoor, is a budget favourite. Although ageing and draughty, the 150-year-old colonial house oozes character with wooden terraces and serene views over Coonoor.

Hotel Vivek Coonoor   HOTEL **$**

(📞 2230658; www.hotelvivek.com; Figure of Eight Rd; r from ₹600) A good 'upper budget' option. Many of the wide range of rooms here have balconies (screened to avoid the 'monkey menace') from which you can watch the tea fields.

ℹ️ Getting There & Away

Coonoor is on the miniature train line between Mettupalayam (28km) and Ooty (18km) – see p1059. Buses to Ooty (₹8, one hour) and Kotagiri (₹10, one hour) leave roughly every 15 minutes.

Kotagiri

📞 04266 / POP 29,184

The oldest of the three Nilgiri hill stations, Kotagiri is about 28km from Ooty. It's a quiet, unassuming place with a forgettable town centre, but we're assuming you're not here for the nightlife. Rather, the appeal is the escape from the overdevelopment in Ooty: red dirt tracks in the pines, blue skies and the high green walls of the Nilgiris.

From Kotagiri you can visit **Catherine Falls**, 8km away near the Mettupalayam road (the last 3km is by foot only, and the falls only flow after rain), **Elk Falls** (6km) and **Kodanad Viewpoint** (22km), where there's a view over the Coimbatore Plains and Mysore Plateau. A half-day taxi tour to all three will cost around ₹800. The scenery on the road to Mettupalayam is gorgeous, so you may want to detour this way if you're heading down from Ooty.

If you've any interest at all in the history of the Nilgiris, it's worth visiting the **Sullivan Memorial** (Nilgiri Documentation Centre; ✆9486639092; Kannerimukku; ⊙10am-5pm Mon-Sat). The bungalow that belonged to John Sullivan, the founder of Ooty, has been refurbished and filled with fascinating photos and artefacts about local tribal groups, European settlement and icons like the toy train. Call if nobody's there, or to arrange visits out of hours.

Also located here are the offices of the **Keystone Foundation** (✆272277; www.key stone-foundation.org; Groves Hill Rd), an NGO that works to improve environmental conditions in the Nilgiris while working with, and creating better living standards for, indigenous communities. The foundation's **Green Shop** (Johnstone Circle) has goodies for picnics – local organic cheese, honey and more.

A couple of very basic lodges are in the small town centre, and you won't go short of *idlis* or dosas. A combination of splendid 1915 colonial building and flashy new block, **Nahar Retreat** (✆273300; www.naharretreat.com; r from₹2000) has very comfortable rooms, great views and a very simple veg restaurant, but charges a lot for extras. Closer to the centre, **Hope Park** (✆271229; www.hopeparkhotel.com; r from ₹1200) has big, clean rooms, a decent restaurant and friendly staff.

Buses stop at the edge of town, about 1km from the centre. Buses to Ooty depart hourly (₹12, 1½ hours), crossing one of Tamil Nadu's highest passes. Buses to Mettupalayam leave every 30 minutes and to Coonoor every 15 minutes.

Ooty (Udhagamandalam)

✆0423 / POP 93.921 / ELEV 2240M

Ooty may be a bit bustling for some tastes, but most travellers quickly fall in love with this pine-clad retreat, where trekkers congregate in front of roaring fires before setting out into the surrounding green dream. Even the typical chaos of India becomes somehow subdued in the shadow of the hills. Therein lays Ooty's charm, especially when you throw in her quirks: a jumble of Hindu temples and ecotourism, overlaid by a veneer of manicured British aesthetic.

This is South India's most famous (and certainly best-named) hill station, established by the British in the early 19th century as the summer headquarters of the then-Madras government and memorably nicknamed 'Snooty Ooty'. Development ploughed through a few decades ago, and continues, but somehow old Ooty survives – you just have to walk a bit further out from the town centre to find it.

The journey up to Ooty on the miniature train is romantic and the scenery stunning – try to get a seat on the left-hand side where you get the best views across the mountains. With that said, even the bus ride is pretty impressive (if not nearly as relaxing). From April to June (the *very* busy season) Ooty is a welcome relief from the hot plains, and in the colder months (October to March) you'll need warm clothing – which you can buy cheap here – as overnight temperatures occasionally drop to 0°C.

The train station and bus station are next to the racecourse, which is surrounded by cheap hotels. Further downhill is the lake, while the valley slopes up on either side, studded with colonial houses and guest lodges with good views. From the bus station it's a 10-minute walk to the bazaar area and a 20-minute walk to Ooty's commercial centre, Charing Cross. Like Kodai, Ooty has an international school whose students can often be seen around town.

⊙ Sights

St Stephen's Church   CHURCH
(Church Hill Rd; ⊙10am-1pm & 3-5pm Mon-Sat, services 8am & 11am Sun) Perched above the town centre, the immaculate St Stephen's Church, built in 1829, is the oldest church in the Nilgiris. Throughout its history, St Stephen's has racially shifted from hosting an exclusively British congregation to an Anglo-Indian orphanage to falling under the auspices of the Church of South India. Look out for lovely stained glass, huge wooden beams hauled by elephant from the palace of Tipu Sultan some 120km away, and the sometimes kitschy, sometimes touching, slabs and plaques donated by colonial-era

churchgoers. In the quiet, overgrown cemetery you'll find headstones commemorating many an Ooty Brit, including the wife and daughter of John Sullivan, the town's founder. If you're partial to colonial cemeteries, the quiet yard overlooking the lake at **St Thomas Church** (Racecourse Rd) is also worth a wander.

Botanical Gardens
GARDEN

(adult/child ₹20/10, camera/video ₹30/75; ☺7am-6.30pm) Established in 1848, these lovely gardens are a living gallery of the natural fauna of the Nilgiris. Look out for a fossilised tree trunk believed to be around 20 million years old, and on busy days, roughly 20 million Indian tourists.

Doddabetta Lookout
VIEWPOINT

(admission ₹5; ☺7am-6pm) This is it: the highest point (2633m) of the Nilgiris and one of the best viewpoints around, assuming, as usual, the day is clear. It's about 10km out of town; go early for better chances of a mist-free view. Any Kotagiri buses will drop you at the Dodabetta junction, from where it's a fairly energetic 3km walk or a quick jeep ride. A taxi will do the round trip from Charing Cross for ₹350.

Centenary Rose Park
GARDEN

(Selbourne Rd; adult/child ₹20/10, camera/video ₹30/50; ☺9am-6.30pm) With its terraced lawns and colourful flowerbeds – best between May and July – this terraced rose garden is a pleasant place for a stroll. There are good views over Ooty from the hilltop location.

Thread Garden
GARDEN

(☎2445145; North Lake Rd; admission ₹10, camera/video ₹15/30; ☺8.30am-8pm) If your expectations aren't too high, you may enjoy the 'miracle' (official description and just *slight* hyperbole) that is 150 species of 'plants' from around the world meticulously re-created using 'hand-wound' thread. The technique was perfected by Keralan artist Anthony Joseph and the work took 50 craftspeople 12 years to complete.

Tribal Research Centre Museum
MUSEUM

(Muthorai Palada; admission free; ☺10am-5pm Mon-Fri) It's hard to say why you should love this museum more than most: for its decently executed exhibits on Nilgiri and Andaman tribal groups, or the decomposing corpses of badly stuffed local wildlife, including a rotting mongoose that just arrived from hell's deepest pit. Seriously, the artefacts are fantastic – you may never get the chance to hold a Stone Age bow in your life again – and descriptions of the tribes are good, if written by anthropologists with no filter from academia to normal English. The museum is just beyond the village of Muthorai Palada

Nilgiri Hills

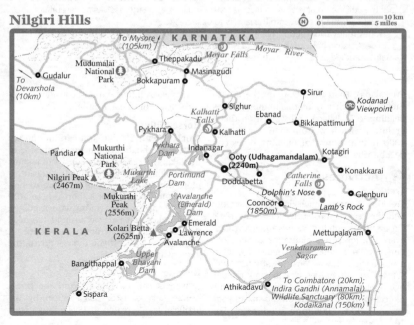

HILL TRIBES OF THE NILGIRI

For centuries, the Nilgiris have been home to hill tribes. While retaining integrity in customs, dress and language, the tribes were economically, socially and culturally interdependent. The British concept of exclusive property rights disenfranchised many tribespeople, as did exploitative commercial practices that undermined their barter-based economy. Today, many eke out a living in poverty gathering honey or herbs for the ayurveda industry.

The Toda tribe's social, economic and spiritual system centred on the buffalo, whose milk and ghee was integral to their diet and used as currency – in exchange for grain, tools and medical services. Most importantly, the dairy produce provided offerings to the gods as well as fuel for the funeral pyre. It was only at the ritual for human death that the strictly vegetarian Toda killed a buffalo, not for food but to provide company for the deceased.

The Badagas are believed to have migrated to the Nilgiris from the north around 1600 AD, in the wake of Muslim invasions in the north, and are thus not officially a tribal people. With knowledge of the world outside the hills, they became effective representatives for the hill tribes. Their agricultural produce, particularly grain, added a further dimension to the hill diet.

The Kotas lived in the Kotagiri area and were considered by other tribes to be lower in status. They still undertake ceremonies in which the gods are beseeched for rains and bountiful harvests.

The Kurumbas inhabited the thick forests of the south. They gathered bamboo, honey and materials for housing, some of which were supplied to other tribes. They also engaged in a little agriculture, and at sowing and harvest times they employed the Badaga to perform rituals entreating the gods for abundant yields.

The Irulus, also from the southern slopes, produced tools and gathered honey and other forest products that converted into brooms and incense. They are devotees of Vishnu and often perform rituals for other tribes.

British colonialism and lowland migration have undermined tribal cultural systems to the point of collapse. Displaced tribes have been 'granted' land by the Indian government, but the cultivation of land is anathema to the Toda, who see themselves as caretakers of the soil – for them, to dig into the land is to desecrate it.

Today many tribal people have assimilated to the point of invisibility. Some have fallen into destructive patterns associated with displacement and alienation, while others remain straddled across two cultures.

(M Palada), 11km from Ooty on the way to Emerald. Catch any of the frequent buses heading to M Palada and walk from there, or hire a rickshaw from Ooty for around ₹300 return. Note that opening times can be a bit iffy.

🏃 Activities

Trekking

Trekking is pretty much de rigueur in Ooty and the reason most travellers come here. On day trips you'll have a wander through evergreen forest, tea plantations, over lookouts, into local villages and, generally, catch a bus back to town. Most guesthouses will set you up with guides, or you can hire your own – plenty will offer their services to you. Expect to pay depending on the size of your group, ₹300 to ₹900 for a full-day trek. For other nearby hiking options, consider the resorts near Mudumalai National Park.

Horse Riding

Alone or with a guide, you can hire horses outside the boathouse on the north side of the lake; the rides mostly consist of a short amble along bitumen, although you can explore the woods and hills for more money. Prices run from ₹50 for a short ride to ₹100 to ₹200 for an hour (more with a guide), which takes you partway around the lake. Some horses look in pretty bad shape. A white horse will cost you more – do ask the guide why that is.

Boating

Rowboats can be rented from the **boathouse** (admission ₹5; ⊘9am-5.30pm) by the artificial lake (created in 1824). Prices start from ₹80 for a two-seater pedal boat (30 minutes) and go up to ₹280 for a 15-seater motorboat (20 minutes).

Horse Racing

Ooty's racecourse dominates the lower part of the hill station between Charing Cross and the lake. The horse-racing season runs from mid-April to June and on race days the town is a hive of activity; it's an event you can't miss if you're in town. Outside the season, the 2.4km racecourse just becomes a cricket field/trash dump/public toilet.

☞ Tours

The tourist office can put you in touch with agencies that run day trips to Mudumalai National Park via the Pykhara Dam. Trips to Coonoor and surrounds are also possible. A better alternative is to hire a taxi for the day and go as you please. Rates run for about ₹800 for a four-hour trip around Ooty, or ₹1600 to ₹1800 for a full day depending on where you're heading.

🛌 Sleeping

Ooty has some good rustic lodges in the budget-midrange scale, gorgeous colonial-era residences at the high end, and even some decent backpacker dosses. Be warned: it's a sellers' market in the high season (1 April to 15 June), when many hotel prices double and checkout time is often 9am. Prices listed here are for the low season when most places are good value.

Hotel Sweekar HOTEL $
(✆2442348; Race View Rd; d ₹350-400) Definitely the best value for money in town, the Sweekar hosts guests in simple but very clean rooms in a traditional Ooty cottage that sits at the end of a lavender-lined path. It's run by an incredibly friendly Bahai manager.

Willow Hill HOTEL $$
(✆2223123; www.willowhill.in; 58/1 Havelock Rd; d ₹900-2000) Sitting high above town, Willow Hill's large windows provide great views of Ooty. The rooms, all with wooden floors, have a distinct alpine chalet chic, with the most expensive rooms offering a private garden.

Fernhills Palace HOTEL $$$
(✆2443911; www.fernhillspalace.co.in; Fernhill Post; 2-night packages ₹13,250-33,950) The Maharaja of Mysore's summer palace has been lovingly restored in colourfully gorgeous,

ridiculously over-the-top princely colonial style; if you can afford to stay here, you really should. Play billiards, walk in the garden and check out old photos of the Ooty Hunt while sipping Scotch in the atmospheric Fox Hunt Bar.

YWCA Anandagiri HOTEL $
(✆2442218; www.ywcaagooty.com; Ettines Rd; dm from ₹99, r from ₹345) This former brewery and sprawling complex of hill cottages is dotted with flower gardens; throw in elegant lounges and fireplaces and you've got some excellent budget accommodation going on. High ceilings can mean cold nights; ask for extra blankets if you think you might need them.

Hotel Welbeck Residency HOTEL $$
(✆2223300; www.welbeck.in; Club Rd; r from ₹1800) An attractive older building that's been thoroughly tarted up with very comfortable rooms, a touch of colonial class (miniature cannons at the front door!) and a good restaurant. Staff are very helpful.

King's Cliff HOTEL $$
(✆2224545; www.littlearth.in; Havelock Rd; d from ₹1475) High above Ooty on Strawberry Hill is this gorgeous residence, a colonial house with wood panelling, antique furnishings and cosy lounge. If you plan on living large, Raj style, go for the more expensive rooms; the cheaper doubles don't quite reflect the old-world charm of the rest of the place. To really get out into the hills, ask the staff about **Destiny**, their delightful farmstay property an hour's drive from Ooty.

Lymond House HOTEL $$
(✆2223377; www.serendipityo.com; 77 Sylks Rd; d from ₹2250) If Mucha and F Scott Fitzgerald partnered up to open a hotel in Ooty, it'd probably come out looking something like this restored English villa. Rooms are all ensconced in Old World/Jazz Age opulence, the dining room (with limited, but very good, menu) and gardens are gorgeous, and the period atmosphere is thick enough to swim in.

Savoy Hotel HOTEL $$$
(✆2444142; www.tajhotels.com; 77 Sylks Rd; s/d from ₹5800/6800; 🛜) The Savoy is one of Ooty's oldest hotels, with parts dating back to 1829. Big cottages are arranged around a beautiful garden of flowerbeds, lawns and clipped hedges. The quaint rooms have large bathrooms, polished floors, log fires and bay windows. Modern facilities include a

Ooty (Udhagamandalam)

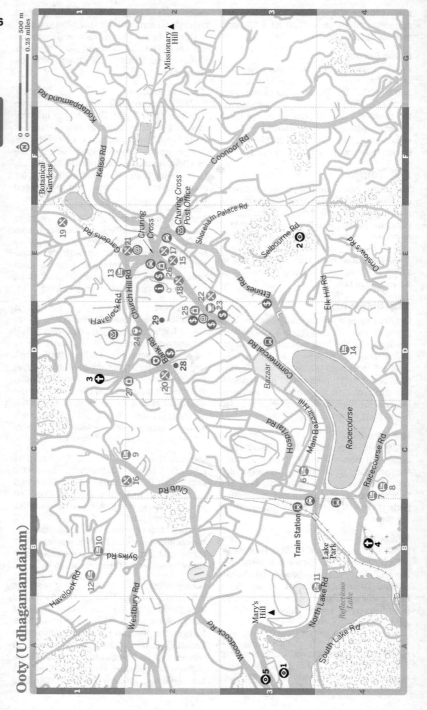

Ooty (Udhagamandalam)

TAMIL NADU & CHENNAI OOTY (UDHAGAMANDALAM)

24-hour bar, wi-fi, an excellent multicuisine dining room and an ayurvedic centre.

Hotel Mountview HOTEL $
(2443307; Racecourse Rd; r ₹660-1700) Perched on a quiet driveway directly above the bus station, this elegant old bungalow has eight simple, enormous (no, really) rooms, all wood lined and high ceilinged and slightly draughty, with unused fireplaces. There's enough untapped renovation potential here to make a decorator weep.

Reflections Guest House HOTEL $
(2443834; North Lake Rd; d ₹500-700) Judging by reader feedback, there must be two Reflections. One has helpful and welcoming staff, good food, and a great common area that's excellent for meeting other hill-bound travellers and trekkers. The other has curt staff who demand extra cash for everything from loo rolls to blankets. Either way, rooms are clean and decent value, and the setting very pleasant.

Hotel Maneck HOTEL $
(2443494; Main Bazaar; r ₹600-800) A small, friendly Jain-run hotel in the market; the slightly more expensive rooms are clean and comfortable.

TTDC Youth Hostel HOTEL $
(2443665; yhttdc@yahoo.in; Gardens Rd; dm/d from ₹100/350) This state-run hostel is reli-

ably mediocre, clean and busy; you may want to call ahead to book a dorm bed if you're in the area.

Eating & Drinking

Ooty has two branches each of **Café Coffee Day** and **Barista**, both with the usual range of reliably fine coffee, tea, cakes and sandwiches; the Club Rd branch of Barista has nice views and does a good toast-and-eggs breakfast. The more upmarket hotels all have atmospheric, multicuisine restaurants.

For self-caterers, **Modern Stores** (Garden Rd) is a mini-supermarket with all kinds of Western packaged food, as well as Nilgiri-produced bread and cheese, and the **Green Shop** (Club Rd) has honey, cheese and other local foods. **Virtue Bake** (Charing Cross) has excellent cakes, pastries and brownies to take away.

Kabab Corner NORTH INDIAN $$
(Commercial Rd; mains ₹60-200; ⊙lunch & dinner) This is the place for meat eaters who are tiring of the nonstop veg of South India. It might not look like much from the outside, but here you can tear apart perfectly grilled and spiced chunks of lamb, chicken and, if you like, paneer, sopping up the juices with pillowy triangles of naan. The ₹450 tandoori platter is exceptionally good if you're in a group; if there's fewer than four of you, it may defeat you.

Garden Restaurant SOUTH INDIAN $
(Nahar Hotel, Commercial Rd; mains ₹50-90;
☺lunch & dinner) Slightly upmarket South
Indian food in a clean hotel-restaurant setting, along with juices, ice creams, snacks
and even pizza; the pizza's made in the
hotel's Sidewalk Café, which has good vegetarian Western food at fairly high prices.

Shinkow's Chinese Restaurant CHINESE $$
(☑2442811; 38/83 Commissioner's Rd; mains ₹50-
150; ☺lunch & dinner) Shinkow's is an Ooty
institution and the simple menu of chicken,
pork, beef, fish, noodles and rice dishes is re-
liably good and quick to arrive at your table.

Hotel Blue Hills INDIAN $
(Commercial Rd; mains ₹20-80; ☺lunch & dinner)
Downstairs, dimly lit and feeling slightly
disreputable, Blue Hills has been serving up
good meals, huge crispy dosas and a range
of other Indian standards for decades.

Willy's Coffee Pub CAFE $
(mains ₹30-80; ☺lunch & dinner) Climb the
stairs and join international students and
local cool kids for board games, magazines
and very reasonably priced pizzas, fries,
toasted sandwiches, cakes and cookies.

🛍 Shopping

The main places to shop are along Commer-
cial Rd, where you'll find Kashmiri shops as
well as government outlets for Kairali and
Khadi Gramodyog Bhavan. The Big Shop
(Commercial Rd) sells lovely new and antique
jewellery and knick-knacks at fairly inflated
prices. For cheaper but equally attractive
silver and Toda (tribal) jewellery, there's a
string of shops stretching along Main Ba-
zaar in the direction of the train station;
Mahaveerchand (291 Main Bazaar), next to
Hotel Maneck, sells particularly nice work.
Near the entrance to the botanical gardens
you'll find Tibetan refugees selling sweaters
and shawls, which you may appreciate on a
chilly Ooty evening.

Higginbothams Commercial Rd (☑2443736;
☺9am-1pm & 3.30-7.30pm Mon-Sat); Commis-
sioner's Rd (☑2442546; ☺9am-1pm & 2-6pm Mon-
Sat) Has a good selection of contemporary
English-language Indian and other fiction,
and Lonely Planet guides.

ℹ Information

Internet Access
Global Net (Commercial Rd; per hr ₹30;
☺9.30am-9pm)

Cyber Planet (Garden Rd; per hr ₹30; ☺10am-
7.30pm)

Library
Nilgiri Library (Bank Rd; temporary member-
ship ₹200; ☺9.30am-1pm & 2.30-6pm, reading
room 9.30am-6pm Sat-Thu) Quaint little haven
in a crumbling 1867 building with a collection of
more than 40,000 books, including rare titles
on the Nilgiris and hill tribes. Unless you're a
student it costs an extra ₹500 for temporary
membership if you want to actually take a book
away with you.

Money
Axis Bank ATM (Commercial Rd)
Canara Bank (Commercial Rd) The only bank
in town that does cash advances on credit
cards.
State Bank of India (Bank Rd; ☺10am-4pm
Mon-Fri, 10am-1pm Sat) Changes travellers
cheques and has an ATM.
State Bank of India ATM (Commercial Rd)
UK Forex (137 Commercial Rd) Changes travel-
lers cheques and cash.
UTI Bank ATM (Ettines Rd)

National Park Information
Office of the Field Director (☑2444098;
fdmtr@tn.nic.in; ☺10am-5.45pm Mon-Fri)
Manages Mudumalai National Park, including
advance bookings for park accommodation.

Tourist Information
Tourist office (☺2443977; ☺10am-5.45pm
Mon-Fri) Maps, brochures and tour information.

❶ Getting There & Away

Without doubt the most romantic way to arrive
in Ooty is aboard the miniature train, and you'll
need to book ahead in the high season. Buses
also run regularly up and down the mountain,
both from other parts of Tamil Nadu and from
Mysore in Karnataka.

Bus
The state bus companies all have **reservation
offices** (☺9am-5.30pm) at the busy bus station.
There are two routes to Karnataka – the main
bus route via Gudalur and the shorter, more ar-
duous route via Masinagudi. The latter is tackled
only by minibuses and winds through 36 hairpin
bends! Frequent buses leave for Mettupalayam
and Coimbatore, and there's daily service to
Chennai, Bengaluru and Mysore.

Connect with trains to Chennai or Kochi (Co-
chin, Kerala) at Coimbatore.

To get to Mudumalai National Park (₹30, 2½
hours, 11 daily), take one of the Mysore buses
that will drop you at park headquarters at Thep-
pakadu, or one of the small buses that go via the

narrow and twisting Sighur Ghat road. Some of these rolling wrecks travel only as far as Masinagudi (₹16, 1½ hours), from where there are buses every two hours to Theppakadu.

Local buses leave every 30 minutes for Kotagiri (₹10, 1½ hours) and every 10 minutes to Coonoor (₹12, one hour).

Train

The miniature train – one of the Mountain Railways of India given World Heritage status by Unesco in 2005 – is the best way to get here. There are fine views of forest, waterfalls and tea plantations along the way, especially from the front 1st-class carriage; the steam engine pushes, rather than pulls, the train up the hill, so the front carriage leads the way. Note that this route has been suspended on and off in the last few years after heavy rains led to landslides over the tracks; it was back on schedule at the time of research.

Departures and arrivals at Mettupalayam connect with those of the *Nilgiri Express,* which runs between Mettupalayam and Chennai. The miniature train departs Mettupalayam for Ooty at 7.10am daily (1st/2nd class ₹142/21, five hours). If you want a seat in either direction, be at least 45 minutes early or make a reservation at least 24 hours in advance.

From Ooty the train leaves at 3pm and takes about 3½ hours. There are also three daily passenger trains between Ooty and Coonoor (₹15, 1½ hours).

❶ Getting Around

Plenty of autorickshaws hang around the bus station – a ride from the train or bus stations to Charing Cross costs about ₹40, and lists of autorickshaw fixed prices can be found at the steps on Commercial Rd leading to the tourist information office, at the lake and outside the Botanical Gardens.

Taxis cluster at several stands in town. There are fixed fares to most destinations, including Coonoor (₹600), Kotagiri (₹800), Gudalur (₹1200), Mudumalai National Park (₹900) and Coimbatore (₹1800).

There's a jeep hire near the main bazaar, although it's best to rent these out in groups; expect to pay about 1.5 times more than local taxi fares.

Mudumalai National Park

☑0423

In the foothills of the Nilgiris, this 321-sq-km park is like a classical Indian landscape painting given life: thin, spindly trees and light-slotted leaves concealing spotted chital deer and slow herds of gaur (Indian bison).

Somewhere in the hills are tigers, although you're very lucky if you spot one.

Part of the Nilgiri Biosphere Reserve (3000 sq km), the park is the best place for spotting wildlife in Tamil Nadu, although there's still a good chance you won't see more than some deer and kingfishers. Vegetation ranges from grasslands to semi-evergreen forests to foothill scrub; besides the above species, panthers, wild boars, jackals and sloth bears prowl the reserve. Otters and crocodiles both inhabit the Moyar River, and the park's wild elephant population numbers about 600.

A good time to visit is between December and June, although the park may be closed during the dry season (February to March). Heavy rain is common in October and November.

The main service area in Mudumalai is Theppakadu, on the main road between Ooty and Mysore. Here you'll find the park's **reception centre** (☑2526235; ⊙6.30-9am & 3-5.30pm) and some park-run accommodation. The closest village is Masinagudi, 7km from Theppakadu.

◉ Sights & Activities

It's not possible to hike in the park and tours are limited to sanctuary minibuses; private vehicles are not allowed in the park except on the main Ooty–Mysore road that runs through it. Most people see the park via the fun 45-minute **minibus tours** (per person ₹35, camera/video ₹ 25/150) that run between 7am and 9am and 3pm and 6pm. The tour makes a 15km loop through part of the park in buses painted in camoflague stripes.

You can also hire a guide for a foot **trek** outside the park boundaries, but the only way to do this safely and legally is through one of the better resorts, where guides are experts who know where it's OK to walk. Tourists have been killed after getting too close to wild elephants on dodgy treks, and park rules have since tightened up considerably.

Early-morning **elephant rides** in the jungle are available but must be booked in advance at the Office of the Field Director in Ooty (p1058); it costs ₹460 per group of four.

Near the reception centre, and sharing the same hours, the **elephant camp** (per person ₹15) is a spot on the river where you can watch elephants being fed and bathed in the morning or evening.

🛏 Sleeping & Eating

There are budget and midrange lodges inside the park at Theppakadu; budget rooms and midrange cottages in Masinagudi; and midrange and upmarket jungle resorts in Bokkapuram (4km south of Masinagudi). For meals at the resorts, expect to pay from ₹400 per person per day.

IN THE PARK

For most accommodation in the park, book in advance, in person, with the Office of the Field Director (p1058) in Ooty. The first three places listed here are park-run accommodation on the banks of the river and are all walking distance from park reception.

Minivet Dormitory HOTEL $
(q ₹310) A simple place, with two four-bed rooms, each with private bathroom with cold water only. Expect vociferous demands for extra rupees for the most basic services here.

Theppakadu Log House HOTEL $$
(d/q ₹1030/1500) Comfortable rooms, well maintained.

Sylvan Lodge HOTEL $$
(d/q ₹530/1080) Not a very big drop in quality from Log House, and with the addition of a kitchen that prepares meals for booked guests.

Hotel Tamil Nadu HOTEL $
(✉2526580; dm/d/q ₹125/550/950) A nearby government-run hotel providing basic accommodation and meals.

BOKKAPURAM

This area south of Masinagudi is home to a gaggle of fine forest resorts, mostly family-run businesses with a warm, homely atmosphere, high standards and breathtaking views. Don't wander outside your resort at night; leopards, among other wild animals, are very much present.

Jungle Retreat RESORT $$
(✉2526469; www.jungleretreat.com; dm ₹525, bamboo huts/standard r ₹1969/2532, tree house ₹4500; ☀) One of the most stylish resorts in the area, with lovingly built stone cottages decked out in classic furniture and sturdy bamboo huts, all spread out to give a feeling of seclusion. It's possible to camp, and there's a dormitory for groups. The bar, restaurant and common area is a great place to meet fellow travellers and the owners are knowledgeable and friendly, with a large area of private forest at their disposal. The pool and its setting are stunning. All prices include taxes.

Jungle Hut RESORT $$
(✉2526463; www.junglehut.in; s/d incl taxes & 3 meals ₹2970/4000) Similar in style to Jungle Retreat, with cottages spread across the property, this resort has the best food in Bokkapuram (if you're visiting the restaurant from another resort after dark, don't walk home on your own!). If you're up for fishing you can relax by the ponds fed from waterfalls you can see in the distant hills.

Safari Land Resort RESORT $$
(✉2526937; www.safarilandresorts.com; r from ₹1800, tree house from ₹3500; 🛜) This jungle complex has comfortable rooms and cottages as well as well-decked-out tree houses above a gurgling stream. The views into the surrounding jungle hills are stunning, but the pace, for all the dramatic scenery, is supremely relaxed. Your host is a Hyderabadi prince and former rifle-shooting champ.

Forest Hills Guest House RESORT $$
(✉2526216; www.foresthillsindia.com; r incl taxes from ₹1743) Forest Hills is a family-run, family-sized guesthouse (10 rooms on 5 hectares) with a few cute bamboo huts, some clean spacious rooms, and a fabulous watchtower for wildlife-watching and birdwatching. There's a slight colonial air here with a gazebo-style bar, games rooms and a barbecue pit. It's popular with Indian families.

Bear Mountain Jungle Retreat RESORT $$
(✉2526505; www.bearmountainjungleresort.com; cottages from ₹2000) Good for groups, this resort has stunning jungle and mountain views and simple, clean rooms.

❶ Getting There & Around

Bus services run every two hours between Theppakadu and Masinagudi (7km); shared jeeps ply this route for ₹7 if there's enough passengers, or you can have one to yourself for ₹100. Costs are similar for jeeps between Masinagudi and Bokkapuram.

Buses from Ooty to Mysore and Bengaluru stop at Theppakadu (2½ hours, 11 daily). There's another, more direct route between Ooty and Masinagudi, an interesting 'short cut' (₹13, 1½ hours, 36km) which involves taking one of the small government buses that make the trip up (or down) the tortuous (but very pretty) Sighur Ghat road. The bends are so tight and the gradient so steep that large buses simply can't use it, and accidents are not uncommon. A taxi from Ooty to Masinagudi using this route takes an hour and costs ₹750.

Andaman Islands

Best Places to Stay

» Eco Villa (p1073)

» Aashiaanaa Rest Home (p1068)

» Pristine Beach Resort (p1077)

» Blue View (p1077)

» Blue Planet (p1076)

Best Beaches

» Radha Nagar (p1072)

» Merk Bay (p1076)

» Ross & Smith Islands (p1076)

» Beach 5 (p1072)

» Butler Bay (p1077)

Why Go?

On old maps, the Andamans and Nicobars were the kind of islands whose inhabitants were depicted with dog's heads or faces in their chests, surrounded by sea serpents in a tempest-lashed sea known to Indians as Kalapani: the Black Waters. These were the islands that someone labelled, with a shaky hand, 'Here be Monsters' – probably an early traveller who didn't want to share this delightful place with the rest of us.

Lovely opaque emerald waters are surrounded by primeval jungle and mangrove forest; snow-white beaches melt under flame-and-purple sunsets; and the population is a friendly masala of South and Southeast Asian settlers, as well as Negrito ethnic groups whose arrival here still has anthropologists baffled. And geographically, the Andamans are more Southeast Asia – 150km from Indonesia and 190km from Myanmar – making them all the more intriguing.

The Nicobars are off-limits to tourists, but that still leaves hundreds of islands to explore.

When to Go
Port Blair

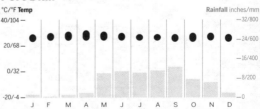

Dec–Apr High tourist season: perfect sunny days, optimal diving conditions.

Oct–Dec & Apr–mid-May Weather's a mixed bag, but fewer tourists and lower costs

Dec–Mar Best time to see turtles nesting

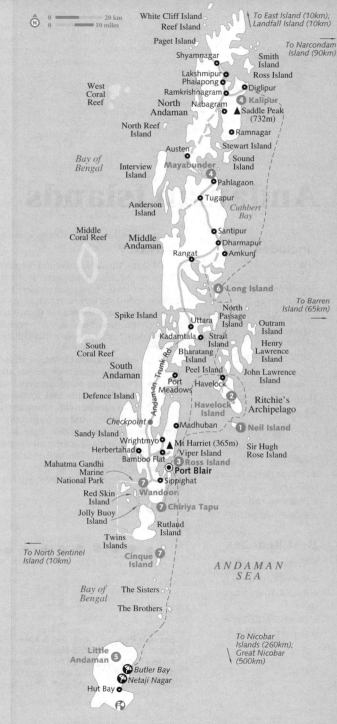

Andaman Islands Highlights

1 Regress to infantile laziness and happiness on **Neil Island** (p1074)

2 Dive, snorkel and socialise on **Havelock Island** (p1072)

3 Glimpse Port Blair's colonial history at **Ross Island** (p1071)

4 Travel through the jungle heart of the Andamans around **Mayabunder** (p1076) and **Kalipur** (p1076)

5 Find Butler Bay and paradise on **Little Andaman** (p1077)

0 ———— 20 km
0 ———— 10 miles

White Cliff Island
Reef Island
Paget Island
To East Island (10km);
Landfall Island (10km)
To Narcondam Island (90km)
Shyamnagar
Smith Island
Lakshmipur
Phaiapong
Ross Island
Ramkrishnagram
Diglipur
West Coral Reef
North Andaman
Nabagram
4 Kalipur
Saddle Peak (732m)
North Reef Island
Ramnagar
Austen
Stewart Island
Bay of Bengal
Mayabunder
Sound Island
Interview Island
4
Pahlagaon
Anderson Island
Tugapur
Cuthbert Bay
Middle Coral Reef
Middle Andaman
Santipur
Dharmapur
Rangat
Amkunj
6 Long Island
North Passage Island
To Barren Island (65km)
Spike Island
Uttara
Outram Island
Kadamtala
Strait Island
Henry Lawrence Island
South Coral Reef
South Andaman
Bharatang Island
Peel Island
John Lawrence Island
Port Meadows
Havelock
Defence Island
2
Ritchie's Archipelago
Havelock Island
Checkpoint
Madhuban
1 Neil Island
Sandy Island
Wrightmyo
Mt Harriet (365m)
Sir Hugh Rose Island
Herbertabad
Viper Island
Bamboo Flat
3 Ross Island
Mahatma Gandhi Marine National Park
Port Blair
7 Sippighat
Wandoor
Red Skin Island
7 Chiriya Tapu
Jolly Buoy Island
Rutland Island
Twins Islands
7
Cinque Island
ANDAMAN SEA
Bay of Bengal
The Sisters
The Brothers
To Nicobar Islands (260km); Great Nicobar (500km)
Little Andaman **5**
7 Butler Bay
7 Netaji Nagar
Hut Bay
To North Sentinel Island (10km)

FAST FACTS

» Population: 380,000

» Area: 8248 sq km

» Telephone code: ☏03192

» Main languages: Hindi, Bengali, Tamil

» Sleeping prices: **$** below ₹800, **$$** ₹800 to ₹2500, **$$$** above ₹25,000

History

The date of initial human settlement in the Andamans and Nicobars is lost to history. Anthropologists say stone-tool crafters have lived here for 2000 years, and scholars of human migration believe local indigenous tribes have roots in Negrito and Malay ethnic groups in Southeast Asia. Otherwise, these specks in the sea have been a constant source of legend to outside visitors.

The name 'Andaman' is thought to derive from 'Hanuman'; the Hindu monkey god supposedly used the islands as a stepping stone between India and Sri Lanka. Anthropologists say stone-tool crafters were here 2000 years ago but the date of initial human settlement is not known.

The 10th-century Persian adventurer Buzurg Ibn Shahriyar described an island chain inhabited by cannibals, Marco Polo added that the natives had dogs' heads, and tablets in Thanjavur (Tanjore) in Tamil Nadu named the archipelago Timaittivu: the Impure Islands.

None of the above was exactly tourism-brochure stuff, but visitors kept coming: the Marathas in the late 17th century and 200 years later, the British, who used the Andamans as a penal colony for political dissidents. In WWII some islanders greeted the invading Japanese as liberators, but despite installing Indian politicians as (puppet) administrators, the Japanese military proved to be harsh occupiers.

Following Independence in 1947, the Andaman and Nicobar Islands were incorporated into the Indian Union. With migration from the mainland (including Bengali refugees fleeing the chaos of partition), the population has grown from a few thousand to more than 350,000. During this influx, tribal land rights and environmental protection were often disregarded; some conditions are improving but indigenous tribes remain largely in decline.

The islands were devastated by the 2004 Indian Ocean earthquake, offshore aftershocks and the resulting tsunami. The Nicobars were especially hard hit; some estimate a fifth of the population was killed; others were relocated to Port Blair and many have yet to return. But by and large normalcy has returned, along with tourists, although places like Little Andaman remain practically deserted by visitors (so visit).

Climate

Sea breezes keep temperatures within the 23°C to 31°C range and the humidity at around 80% all year. It's very wet during the southwest (wet) monsoon between roughly mid-May and early October, while the northeast (dry) monsoons between November and December also have their fair share of rainy days.

Geography & Environment

The islands form the peaks of the Arakan Yoma, a mountain range that begins in Western Myanmar (Burma) and extends into the ocean running all the way to Sumatra in Indonesia.

The isolation of the Andaman and Nicobar Islands has led to the evolution of many endemic plant and animal species. Of 62 identified mammals, 32 are unique to the islands, including the Andaman wild pig, crab-eating macaque, masked palm civet, and species of tree shrews and bats. Almost 50% of the islands' 250 bird species are endemic, including ground-dwelling megapodes, *hawabills* (swiftlets) and the emerald Nicobar pigeon. The isolated beaches are breeding grounds for turtles; rivers are prowled by saltwater crocodiles; and dolphins are frequently sighted, but the once abundant dugongs have all but vanished.

Mangroves provide a protective barrier between land and sea. Inland forests contain important tree species, including the renowned padauk – a hardwood with light and dark timber occurring in the same tree.

🏃 Activities

The Andamans are one of the world's great **diving** locations, as much for their relative isolation as their crystal-clear waters, superb coral and kaleidoscopic marine life.

The main dive season is roughly November to April, but trips still occur during the summer wet season (June to August) – just closer to the shore. Diving conditions are generally fine in September and October; there's just rain to contend with.

Centres offer fully equipped boat dives, discover scuba diving courses (from ₹4000), PADI open water (₹18,000) and advanced courses (₹13,500), as well as Divemaster training. Prices vary depending on the location, number of participants and duration of the course, but diving in the Andamans costs around ₹2000/3500 for a one/two boat dive. In national parks an additional ₹500 per person per day is payable directly to the park.

Havelock Island is far and away the main diving centre in the islands, although outfits have expanded to Neil and South Andaman. See relevant sections for details.

Much easier and cheaper to arrange than diving, **snorkelling** can be highly rewarding. Havelock Island is one of the best, and certainly easiest, places for snorkelling as many accommodation places organise boat trips out to otherwise inaccessible coral reefs and islands. There's also excellent snorkelling offshore on Neil Island and Kalipur.

Some reefs have been damaged by coral bleaching in recent times, but diving still remains world-class, and new sites are still being discovered.

❶ Information

Even though they're 1000km east of the mainland, the Andamans still run on Indian time. This means that it can be dark by 5pm and light by 4am; people here tend to be very early risers. All telephone numbers must include the ✆03192 area code, even when dialling locally.

Andaman & Nicobar Tourism (IP&T; ✆232747; www.tourism.andaman.nic.in; Kamaraj Rd, Port Blair; ◷8.30am-1pm & 2-5pm Mon-Fri, 8.30am-noon Sat) Pick up a copy of the useful tourist booklet the *Emerald Islands* (₹100) either here or from the small branch at the airport.

ACCOMMODATION Prices given in this chapter are for midseason (1 October to 30 April, excluding peak times). They shoot up in peak season (15 December to 15 January). May to September is low season. Camping is currently not permitted on public land or national parks in the islands.

PERMITS Most civil servants come to Port Blair on two-year postings from the mainland. With such a turnover of staff, be aware rules and regulations regarding permits are subject to sudden changes.

All foreigners need a permit to visit the Andaman Islands; it's issued free on arrival. The 30-day permit allows foreigners to stay in Port Blair, South and Middle Andaman (excluding tribal areas), North Andaman (Diglipur), Long Island, North Passage, Little Andaman (excluding tribal areas), and Havelock and Neil Islands. It's possible to get a 15-day extension from either Port Blair at the **Immigration Office** (✆03192-239247; ◷8.30am-1pm & 2-5.30pm Mon-Fri, until 1pm Sat) or the police station in Havelock.

The permit also allows day trips to Jolly Buoy, South Cinque, Red Skin, Ross, Narcondam, Interview and Rutland Islands, as well as the Brothers and the Sisters.

To obtain the permit, air travellers simply present their passport and fill out a form on arrival at Port Blair airport. Permits are usually issued up to the 30-day maximum (be sure to check).

Boat passengers will probably be met by an immigration official on arrival; if not, seek out the immigration office at Haddo Jetty immediately. Keep your permit on you at all times – you won't be able to travel without it. Police frequently ask to see it, especially when you're disembarking on other islands, and hotels will need permit details. Check current regulations regarding boat travel with any of the following:

Andaman & Nicobar Tourism (✆03192-238473)

Foreigners' Registration Office Chennai (✆044-23454970, 044-28278210); Kolkata (✆033-22470549, 033-22473300)

Shipping Corporation of India (SCI; www.shipindia.com) Chennai (✆044-5231401; Jawahar Bldg, 6 Rajaji Salai); Kolkata (✆033-2482354; 1st fl, 13 Strand Rd)

NATIONAL PARKS & SANCTUARIES Additional permits are required to visit some national parks and sanctuaries. At the tourism office in Port Blair, there's a **Forestry Department Desk** (◷9am-3pm Mon-Fri, until 1pm Sat) where you can find out whether a permit is needed, how to go about getting it, how much it costs and whether it is in fact possible to get one.

If you plan to do something complicated, you'll be sent to the **Chief Wildlife Warden** (CWW; ✆233321; Haddo Rd, Pt Blair; ◷8.30am-noon & 1-4pm Mon-Fri) where your application should

---

CAREFUL WITH THE CORAL!

In general, you should only snorkel during high tide in the Andamans. At low tide it's easy to step on coral, irreparably damaging the delicate organisms. Even the sweep of a strong flipper kick can do harm. You also risk a painful sea-urchin spine if you set foot on the seabed. Divers should be extra cautious about descents near reefs; colliding with coral at a hard pace with full gear is environmentally disastrous.

consist of a letter stating your case, the name of the boat and the dates involved; all things being equal, the permit should be issued within the hour.

For most day permits it's not the hassle but the cost. For areas such as Mahatma Gandhi Marine National Park, and Ross and Smith Islands near Diglipur, the permits cost ₹50/500 for Indians/foreigners. For Saddle Peak National Park, also near Diglipur, the cost is ₹25/250.

Students with valid ID pay minimal entry fees, so don't forget to bring your card.

The Nicobar Islands are off-limits to all except Indian nationals engaged in research, government business or trade.

ℹ Getting There & Away

AIR There are daily flights to Port Blair from Delhi, Kolkata and Chennai, although flights from Delhi and Kolkata are often routed through Chennai. Round-trip fares are between US$250 and US$500 depending on how early you book; some airlines offer one-way flights for as low as US$80, but these need to be booked months in advance. At the time of research, **Kingfisher Airlines** (☏1800 2093030; www.flykingfisher. com) had the cheapest last-minute flights to the islands. Other options include **Air India** (Chennai ☏044-28554747; Kolkata ☏033-22117879; Port Blair ☏03192-233108; www.airindia.com) and **JetLite** (Chennai ☏080-39893333; Kolkata ☏033-25110901; Port Blair ☏03192- 242707; www.jetlite.com).

There are no direct flights from Port Blair to Southeast Asia, though at the time of research a chartered flight was scheduled to fly direct from Kuala Lumpur. But don't get your hopes up.

BOAT Depending on who you ask, the infamous boat to Port Blair is either 'the only *real* way to get to the Andamans' or a hassle and a half. The truth lies somewhere in between. There are usually four to six sailings a month between Port Blair and the Indian mainland – fortnightly to/ from Kolkata (56 hours), weekly (in high season) to/from Chennai (60 hours) and monthly to/ from Vizag (56 hours). In Chennai you can book tickets through the **Assistant Director of Shipping Services** (☏044-25226873; Rajaji Salai, Chennai Port). **Shipping Corporation of India** (SCI; www.shipindia.com; ☏033-22482354 in Kolkata, 0891-2565597 in Vizag) operates boats from Kolkata and Vizag. The schedule is erratic, so call SCI in advance. All ferries from the mainland arrive at Haddo Jetty.

Take sailing times with a large grain of salt – travellers have reported sitting on the boat at Kolkata harbour for up to 12 hours, or waiting to dock near Port Blair for several hours. With holdups and variable weather and sea conditions, the trip can take three to four days. You can organise your return ticket at the **ferry ticket office** at Phoenix Bay. Bring two passport photos and a photocopy of your permit. Updated schedules and fares can be found at www.and.nic.in/ spsch/sailing.htm.

Classes vary slightly between boats, but the cheapest is bunk (₹1700 to ₹1960), followed by 2nd class B (₹3890), 2nd class A (₹5030), 1st class (₹6320) and deluxe cabins (₹7640). The MV *Akbar* also has AC dorm berths (₹3290). Higher-end tickets cost as much as, if not more than, a plane ticket. If you go bunk, prepare for waking up to a chorus of men 'hwwaaaaching' and spitting, little privacy and toilets that tend to get...unpleasant after three days at sea. That said, it's a good way to meet locals.

Food (tiffin for breakfast, thalis for lunch and dinner) costs around ₹150 per day and are pretty much glop on rice. Bring something (fruit in particular) to supplement your diet. Some bedding is supplied, but if you're travelling bunk class bring a sleeping sheet. Many travellers take a hammock to string up on deck.

There is no official ferry between Port Blair and Thailand, but if there are yachts around you could try to crew. You can't legally get from the Andamans to Myanmar (Burma) by sea, although we hear it's been done by those with their own boats. Be aware you risk imprisonment or worse from the Indian and Burmese navies if you give this a go.

Bad weather can seriously muck up your itinerary: ferry services are cancelled if the sea is too rough. Build in a few days' buffer to avoid being marooned and missing your flight (which perhaps isn't always a bad thing...).

ℹ Getting Around

AIR A subsidised interisland helicopter service runs from Port Blair to Little Andaman (₹1488, 35 minutes, Tuesday, Friday and Saturday), Havelock Island (₹850, 20 minutes) and Diglipur via Mayabunder (₹2125 or ₹1915 from Mayabunder, one hour). Priority is given to government workers and the 5kg baggage limit precludes most tourists from using this service. You can chance your luck by applying at the **Secretariat** (☏230093) in Port Blair, returning at 4pm to see if you were successful.

BOAT Most islands can only be reached by water. While this sounds romantic, ferry ticket offices can be hell: expect hot waits, slow service, queue-jumping and a rugby scrum to the ticket window. To hold your spot and advance you need to be a little aggressive (but don't be a jerk) – or be a woman; ladies' queues are a godsend, but they really only apply in Port Blair. You can buy tickets the day you travel by arriving at the appropriate jetty an hour beforehand, but this is risky during high season and not a guarantee on Havelock any time of year. In towns like Rangat, ferry ticket office opening hours are erratic and

ISLAND INDIGENES

The Andaman and Nicobar Islands' indigenous peoples constitute just 12% of the population and, in most cases, their numbers are decreasing. The Onge, Sentinelese, Andamanese and Jawara are all of Negrito ethnicity, who share a strong resemblance to people from Africa. Tragically, numerous groups have become extinct over the past century. In February 2010 the last survivor of the Bo tribe passed away, bringing an end to both the language and 65,000 years of ancestry.

Onge

Two-thirds of Little Andaman's Onge Island was taken over by the Forest Department and 'settled' in 1977. The 100 or so remaining members of the Onge tribe live in a 25-sq-km reserve covering Dugong Creek and South Bay. Anthropologists say the Onge population has declined due to demoralisation through loss of territory.

Sentinelese

The Sentinelese, unlike the other tribes in these islands, have consistently repelled outside contact. For years, contact parties arrived on the beaches of North Sentinel Island, the last redoubt of the Sentinelese, with gifts of coconuts, bananas, pigs and red plastic buckets, only to be showered with arrows, although some encounters have been a little less hostile. About 150 Sentinelese remain.

Andamanese

As they now number only about 50, it seems impossible the Andamanese can escape extinction. There were around 7000 Andamanese in the mid-19th century, but friendliness to colonisers was their undoing, and by 1971 all but 19 of the population had been swept away by measles, syphilis and influenza epidemics. They've been resettled on tiny Strait Island.

Jarawa

The 350 remaining Jarawa occupy the 639-sq-km reserve on South and Middle Andaman Islands. In 1953 the chief commissioner requested that an armed sea plane bomb Jarawa settlements and their territory has been consistently disrupted by the Andaman Trunk Rd, forest clearance and settler and tourist encroachment. Most Jarawa remain hostile to contact.

Shompen

Only about 250 Shompen remain in the forests on Great Nicobar. Seminomadic hunter-gatherers who live along the riverbanks, they have resisted integration and avoid areas occupied by Indian immigrants.

Nicobarese

The 30,000 Nicobarese are the only indigenous people whose numbers are not decreasing. The majority have converted to Christianity and been partly assimilated into contemporary Indian society. Living in village units led by a head man, they farm pigs and cultivate coconuts, yams and bananas. The Nicobarese, who probably descended from people of Malaysia and Myanmar, inhabit a number of islands in the Nicobar group, centred on Car Nicobar, the region worst affected by the 2004 tsunami.

unreliable. At the time of research it was a requirement to bring a photocopy of your permit: organise this before you arrive.

There are regular boat services to Havelock and Neil Islands, as well as Rangat, Mayabunder, Diglipur and Little Andaman. If all else fails, fishermen may be willing to give you a ride for around ₹2000 between, say, Port Blair and Havelock. A schedule of inter-island sailing times can be found at the website www.and.nic.in/spsch/iisailing.htm.

BUS All roads – and ferries – lead to Port Blair, and you'll inevitably spend a night or two here booking onward travel. The main island group –

South, Middle and North Andaman – is connected by road, with ferry crossings and bridges. Cheap state and more expensive private buses run south from Port Blair to Wandoor, and north to Bharatang, Rangat, Mayabunder and finally to Diglipur, 325km north of the capital. The Jarawa reserve closes to most traffic at around 3pm; thus, buses that pass through the reserve leave from around 4am up till 11am.

PRIVATE JEEPS & MINIVANS Hop-on, hop-off affairs connect many villages; you can hire a whole vehicle for an inflated price.

TRAIN Mainland train bookings can be made at the **Railway Bookings office** (☑233042; ⊘8am-12.30pm & 1-2pm), located in the Secretariat's office south of Aberdeen Bazaar, Port Blair; your hotel owners should also be able to help with any onward rail enquires.

Port Blair

POP 100,186

Green, laid-back and occasionally attractive, Port Blair is the main town in the Andamans; a vibrant mix of Indian Ocean inhabitants – Bengalis, Tamils, Nicobarese, Burmese and Telugus. Most travellers don't hang around any longer than necessary (usually one or two days while waiting to book onward travel in the islands, or returning for departure), instead hell-bent on heading straight to the islands. And while 'PB' can't compete with the beaches of Havelock, its fascinating history makes for some outstanding sightseeing.

◉ Sights

Cellular Jail National Memorial   HISTORICAL BUILDING
(GB Pant Rd; admission ₹10, camera/video ₹25/100; ⊘8.45am-12.30pm & 1.30-5pm Tue-Sun) A former British prison that is now a shrine to the political dissidents it once jailed, Cellular Jail National Memorial is worth visiting to understand the important space the Andamans occupy in India's national memory. Construction of the jail began in 1896 and it was completed in 1906 – the original seven wings (several of which were destroyed by the Japanese during WWII) contained 698 cells radiating from a central tower. Like many political prisons, Cellular Jail became something of a university for freedom fighters, who exchanged books, ideas and debates despite walls and wardens.

There's a **sound-and-light show** (adult/child ₹20/10) in English at 6.45pm on Monday, Tuesday and Wednesday.

Anthropological Museum   MUSEUM
(☑03192-232291; MG Rd; admission ₹10; ⊘9am-1pm & 1.30-4.30pm Fri-Wed) The best museum in Port Blair provides a thorough and sympathetic portrait of the islands' indigenous tribal communities. The glass display cases may be old school, but they don't feel anywhere near as ancient as the simple geometric patterns etched into a Jarawa chest guard, a skull left in a Sentinelese lean-to or the totemic spirits represented by Nicobarese shamanic sculptures. Pick up a pamphlet (₹20) on indigenous culture, written by local anthropologists, in the gift shop.

Samudrika Marine Museum   MUSEUM
(Haddo Rd; adult/child ₹20/10, camera/video ₹20/50; ⊘9am-1pm & 2-5pm Tue-Sun) Run by the Indian Navy, this museum has a diverse range of exhibits with informative coverage of the islands' ecosystem, tribal communities, plants, animals and marine life (including a small aquarium). Outside is a skeleton of a blue whale washed ashore on Kamorta Island in the Nicobars.

Chatham Saw Mill   HISTORICAL SITE
(admission ₹10; ⊘8.30am-2.30pm Mon-Sat) Located on Chatham Island (reached by a road bridge), the saw mill was set up by the British in 1836 and was one of the largest wood processors in Asia. The mill is still operational and, while it may not be to everyone's taste – especially conservationists – it's an interesting insight to the island's history and economy. There's also a large crater from a bomb dropped by the Japanese in WWII, and a rather dismal forest museum.

Corbyn's Cove   BEACH
No one comes to Port Blair for the beach but, if you need a sand fix, Corbyn's Cove, 7km south of town, is your best bet. It's a small curve of coast backed by palms that's popular with locals and Indian tourists, and it's a good spot for swimming and sunset. An autorickshaw ride from town costs about ₹200. Otherwise hiring a motorcycle is a good way to travel this coastal road, and you'll encounter numerous Japanese WWII bunkers along the way.

Burmese Buddhist Mission   SACRED SITE
This tiny bell-shaped stupa (shrine) is not particularly impressive, but it's an incongruous example of Burmese Buddhist architecture in India and a reminder that you're way closer to Southeast Asia than the subcontinent.

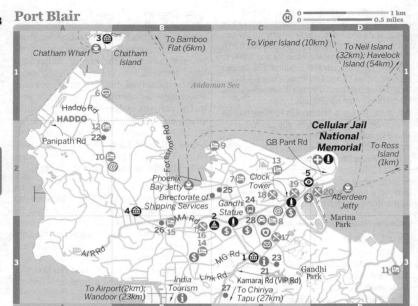

🏃 Activities

The following dive companies specialise in sites south of Port Blair. All are fairly new on the scene, but offer a great alternative to diving outside Ritchie's Archipelago. Suited for divers of all levels.

Planet Scuba India   DIVING
(📞242287; www.planetscubaindia.com; Foreshore Rd, Haddo) The only dive company in Port Blair, Planet Scuba runs dives to Mahatma Gandhi NP and Cinque. Stocks diving equipment.

Lacadives   DIVING
(📞9679532104; www.lacadives.com) Based just outside Wandoor, specialising in more remote areas of Mahatma Gandhi National Park, avoiding the crowds of Red Skin and Jolly Buoy.

Infinity Scuba   DIVING
(📞281183; www.infinityscubandamans.com) Located in Chiriya Tapu, Infinity's main destination is Cinque Island; also visiting Rutland Island and a wrecked ship.

👉 Tours

Andaman & Nicobar Tourism   TOURS
(IP&T; 📞232694; www.tourism.andaman.nic. in; Kamaraj Rd; ⏰8.30am-1pm & 2-5pm Mon-Fri, 8.30am-noon Sat) Runs Port Blair city tours

(₹52), as well tours to Ross Island (₹75), Mt Harriet (₹157), Wandoor via spice and rubber plantations (₹105), Corbyn's Cove (₹52), Chiriya Tapu (₹105) snorkelling trips to Jolly Buoy and Redskin Islands (₹450), and a tour of Ross and Viper Islands and North Bay (₹360). Trip times vary throughout the week.

🛏 Sleeping

Most of the hotels are around the Aberdeen Bazaar area. The airport is about 4km south of town. Midrange accommodation is often booked out solidly from September to December by Indian package tours.

TOP CHOICE **Aashiaanaa Rest Home** GUESTHOUSE **$**
(📞09474217008; shads_maria@hotmail; Marine Hill; r ₹300-900; ❄) Run by the incredibly friendly Shadab and his lovely family, the Aashiaanaa has a lot of 'As' in the name and love in its heart. Rooms are spotless and spacious, and the more expensive ones have nice views over town. It's conveniently just up the hill from Phoenix Bay Jetty.

Hotel Sinclairs Bayview   HOTEL **$$$**
(📞03192-227824; www.sinclairshotels.com; South Point; r from ₹5300; ❄⛱) Located 2km outside town, on the road to Corbyn's Cove, Sinclairs' big comfy rooms have the best views in town, opening right out to the water. It has nice

seaside gardens with hammocks to lounge in, and several Japanese WWII bunkers on-site.

Fortune Resort – Bay Island HOTEL $$$
(☎03192-234101; www.fortunehotels.in, reservations.frbi@fortunehotels.in; Marine Hill; s/d from ₹5500/6200; ❄@❄) Perched above the ocean with fine sea views from its terraced garden and balcony restaurant, Fortune boasts a fine location. The rooms, while comfortable with polished floors, balconies and island bric-a-brac, are small; make sure to ask for a sea-facing room.

Hotel Tejas HOTEL $$
(☎03192-221698; www.hoteltejas.mobi; Haddo Rd; r from ₹750; ❄) Sparkling rooms of the linoleum-floor-and-comfy-enough-bed sort perch over a hill, a tangled clump of jungle and a sweeping view of Haddo Jetty.

Azad Lodge GUESTHOUSE $
(☎03192-242646; MA Rd, Aberdeen Bazaar; s/d from ₹250/450, without bathroom ₹150/250) One of the best budget options in town, Azad's rooms are clean and cheap, though singles without bathroom are like prison cells.

Hotel Driftwood HOTEL $$
(☎03192-244044; hoteldriftwood@rediffmail.com; JN Rd, Haddo; r from ₹1600; ❄☏) The mid-range Driftwood makes a fine choice for those wanting comfort at reasonable prices. Rooms are sunny and a decent size; the pricier ones have lovely views of lush jungle. It has smiley staff, a good restaurant with an attached outdoor bar (karaoke night Saturdays), and wi-fi access in the lobby.

TSG Emerald HOTEL $$
(☎03192-246488; www.andamantsghotels.com; MA Rd, Haddo; r from ₹2000; ❄☏) While a business-chic hotel may not necessarily suit the Andamans, this place is pretty plush with sleek, sparkling, modern rooms. Also has a nautical themed bar upstairs.

Other good cheapies:

Amina Lodge GUESTHOUSE $
(☎9933258703; aminalodge@ymail.com; Aberdeen Bazaar; s/d ₹300/400) Run by a friendly couple, Amina has good-value rooms in the thick of the action. It can get noisy, so ask for a room away from the main road. Bicycle hire is possible.

Lalaji Bay View GUESTHOUSE $
(☎9933222010; lalajibayviewbookings@gmail.com; RP Rd, Dugnabad; r from ₹250) Set among ramshackle colonial buildings, Lalaji Bay is a good budget option with clean rooms and attractive bedspreads.

Sai Residency　　　　GUESTHOUSE $
(☎9434262965; r from ₹400; ☒) This small, family-run affair has some spic-and-span rooms in a central location tucked down a small street.

🍴 Eating

TOP CHOICE 🍴 **Bayview**　　　　MULTICUISINE $$$
(Southpoint; mains from ₹110-500; ☉11am-11pm) Right on the water with a lovely cool sea breeze, the Bayview is a great spot for lunch. While the grilled fish is delicious and the beer cold, this place is still more about the location than the food. Ask the friendly staff to show you the Japanese WWII bunkers on the premises. An autorickshaw will cost ₹40.

Lighthouse Residency　　　　INDIAN $$
(MA Rd, Aberdeen Bazaar; mains ₹60-280; ☉11am-11pm) The Lighthouse is lit like a fluorescent nightmare, but the air-conditioning is cranked, the beer's cold and seafood fresh. Choose from the display of red snapper, crab or tiger prawns. The BBQ fish is sensational. Its sister restaurant, **New Lighthouse Residency**, further up the road, is open air, but there's no alcohol.

Annapurna　　　　INDIAN $
(MG Rd; mains from ₹40) Annapurna is an extremely popular veg option that looks like a high-school cafeteria and serves consistently good karma-friendly fare, ranging from crisp southern dosas to rich North Indian-style curries.

Mandalay Restaurant　　INDIAN, WESTERN $$$
(Marine Hill; buffet breakfast/lunch or dinner ₹200/350) If you need to splurge, you can do a lot worse than the Mandalay's excellent buffet meals, heavy with Indian and Western faves served on either an attractive deck or in a not-quite-as-appealing Burmese-themed interior.

Gagan Restaurant　　　　INDIAN $
(Clock tower, Aberdeen Bazaar; mains from ₹40; ☉7am-9pm) Popular with locals, this hole-in-the-wall place serves up great food at good prices, including seafood curries, coconut chicken, and dosas for breakfast.

Adi Bengali Hotel　　　　BENGALI $
(MA Rd; mains from ₹30; ☉7am-3pm & 6-10pm) This energetic canteen does a brisk stock-in-trade in spicy fish curries and other West Bengal staples. Everything's prepared pretty well, if the usual clientele of silent, satisfied Bengali labourers is any proof.

❶ Information

Port Blair is the only place in the Andamans where you can change cash or travellers cheques. There are ATMs all over town, and a Western Union office by the post office. There are a few internet places in Aberdeen Bazaar.

Aberdeen Police Station (☎03192-232400; MG Rd)

Andaman & Nicobar Tourism (IP&T; ☎232694; www.tourism.andaman.nic.in; Kamaraj Rd; ☉8.30am-1pm & 2-5pm Mon-Fri, 8.30am-noon Sat) The main island tourist office, and place to book government accommodation and get wildlife permits. Staff are helpful, if laid-back.

e-Cafe (internet per hr ₹30; ☉8am-midnight) In Aberdeen Bazaar, just before the Clock Tower.

GB Pant Hospital (☎03192-233473, 232102; GB Pant Rd)

Main post office (MG Rd; ☉9am-7pm Mon-Sat)

State Bank of India (MA Rd; ☉9am-noon & 1-3pm Mon-Fri, 10am-noon Sat) Travellers cheques and foreign currency can be changed here.

❶ Getting There & Away

See p1070 for details on transport to and from the Andaman Islands. The airport is about 4km south of town.

Boat

All interisland ferries depart from Phoenix Bay Jetty. Tickets can be purchased from the **ferry booking office** (☉9am-1pm & 2-4pm Mon-Sat). On some boats tickets can be purchased on board, but in high season you risk missing out. Most people head straight to Havelock (₹195, 2½ hours), with two or more ferries departing daily; those not wanting to hang around Port Blair should make the jetty their first port of call to book tickets. Don't forget to bring a photocopy of your permit. Another option is the privately owned **Makruzz ferry** (www.makruzz.com) operating on Tuesday, Thursday and Saturday in high season (from ₹650, two hours). Tickets are available from the airport or travel agents in Aberdeen Bazaar.

From Chatham Wharf there are hourly passenger ferries to Bamboo Flat (₹3, 15 minutes).

Bus

There are buses all day from the bus stand at Aberdeen Bazaar to Wandoor (₹12, 1½ hours) and Chiriya Tapu (₹10, 1½ hours). Two buses run at 4am and 4.30am to Diglipur (₹170, 12 hours) and at 5am and 9.30am to Mayabunder (₹130, nine hours) via Rangat (₹95, seven hours) and Baratang (₹55, three hours). More comfortable private buses are also available; their 'offices' (a guy with a ticket book) are located across from the main bus stand.

ℹ️ Getting Around

TO/FROM THE AIRPORT A taxi or autorickshaw from the airport to Aberdeen Bazaar costs around ₹50. There are also hourly buses (₹5) to/from airport, located 100m outside the complex, to the main bus stand.

BUS The central area is easy enough to walk around, but to get out to Corbyn's Cove, Haddo or Chatham Island you'll need some form of transport.

MOTORBIKE Unfortunately you can no longer hire bicycles in Port Blair, but you can hire a motorbike or scooter from **Govindamma & Co** (📱9732486858; MA Rd; per 24hr ₹400), which is a perfect way to explore south of Port Blair.

AUTORICKSHAW From Aberdeen Bazaar to Phoenix Bay Jetty is about ₹20 and to Haddo Jetty it's around ₹40.

Around Port Blair & South Andaman

ROSS ISLAND

Visiting Ross Island (not to be confused with its namesake island in North Andaman) feels like discovering a jungle-clad Lost City, à la Angkor Wat, where the ruins happen to be Victorian English rather than ancient Khmer. The former administrative headquarters for the British in the Andamans, Ross Island (admission ₹20) is an essential half-day trip from Port Blair. In its day, little Ross was fondly called the 'Paris of the East' (along with Pondicherry, Saigon etc...). But the cute title, vibrant social scene and tropical gardens were all wiped out by the double whammy of a 1941 earthquake and the invasion of the Japanese (who left behind some machine-gun nests that are great fun to poke around in).

Today the old English architecture is still standing, even as it is swallowed by a green wave of fast-growing jungle. Landscaped paths cross the island and most of the buildings are labelled. There's a small **museum** with historical displays and photos of Ross Island in its heyday, and a small park where resident deer nibble on bushes.

Ferries to Ross Island (₹75, 20 minutes) depart from the jetty behind the aquarium in Port Blair at 8.30am, 10.30am, 12.30pm and 2pm every day other than Wednesday; check when you buy your ticket, as times can be affected by tides.

You can also catch a 9.30am ferry to **Viper Island** (₹75), where you'll find the ruins of gallows built by the British in 1867, but it's a fairly forgettable excursion.

WANDOOR & MAHATMA GANDHI MARINE NATIONAL PARK

Wandoor, a tiny speck of a village 29km southwest of Port Blair, has a nice beach (though at the time of research, swimming was prohibited due to crocodiles being sighted in the area), but is better known as a jumping-off point for **Mahatma Gandhi Marine National Park** (Indian/foreigner ₹50/500). Covering 280 sq km it comprises 15 islands of mangrove creeks, tropical rainforest and reefs supporting 50 types of coral. The marine park's snorkelling sites alternate between **Jolly Buoy** (🕙1 Nov-15 May) and **Red Skin** (🕙16 May-30 Oct), a popular day trip from Wandoor Jetty (₹450; Tuesday to Sunday). That said, if Havelock or Neil Islands are on your Andamans itinerary, it's probably easier and cheaper to wait until you reach them for your underwater experience; unless you're willing to pay through the nose, boats simply don't linger long enough for you to get a good snorkelling experience. **Lacadives** (📱9679532104; www.lacadives.com) is worth getting in touch with if you want to explore the area properly. There are several places to stay in Wandoor. Permits can be arranged at Wandoor jetty or the tourist office in Port Blair.

Buses run from Port Blair to Wandoor (₹12, 1½ hours).

CHIRIYA TAPU

Chiriya Tapu, 30km south of Port Blair, is a tiny village of beaches, mangroves and, about 2km south, some of the best **snorkelling** outside Havelock and Neil Islands. It's a great spot place to watch the sunset. There are seven buses a day to the village from Port Blair (₹10, 1½ hours) and it's possible to arrange boats from here to Cinque Island. The new **biological park** (Indian/foreigner ₹20/50; 🕙9am-4pm Tue-Sun) is still a work in progress (scheduled for completion in 2015), but has a pleasant forested setting with spacious, natural enclosures for crocodiles, deer and wart hog.

CINQUE ISLAND

The uninhabited islands of North and South Cinque, connected by a sandbar, are part of the wildlife sanctuary south of Wandoor. The islands are surrounded by coral reefs, and are among the most beautiful in the Andamans.

Only day visits are allowed but, unless you're on one of the day trips occasionally organised by travel agencies, you need to get permission in advance from the Chief Wildlife Warden (p1070). The islands are two hours by boat from Chiriya Tapu or 3½ hours from Wandoor, and are covered by the **Mahatma Gandhi Marine National Park permit** (Indian/foreigner ₹50/500). See p1068 for info on diving opportunities in Cinque Island.

Havelock Island

With snow-white beaches, teal shallows, dark jungle hills, a coast crammed with beach huts and backpackers from around the world, Havelock's one of those budget-travel tropical gems that, in a few years, will have the same cachet as Thailand's Ko Pha-Ngan if not the nightlife. There are quietly buzzing social scenes concentrated around the common area of the beach hut resorts, but nothing approaching full-moon party madness. Besides for doing nothing, Havelock is a popular spot for snorkelling and diving, and many are content to stay here for the entire duration of their visit to the Andamans.

◉ Sights & Activities

Havelock is the premier spot for **scuba diving** on the Andamans, and the main reason why most tourists jump straight on the ferry here. There's no shortage of dive operator options, with places set up along the main tourist strip; it's just a matter of checking out a few and going with the one you feel most comfortable with.

The **snorkelling** here is equally impressive. The best way to get out is to organise a *dunghi* (motorised wooden boat) through your hotel. Trips cost from ₹1000 to ₹2000, depending on the number of people going, distance involved etc – if you go with a good-sized group you may pay as low as ₹250 per head. Snorkelling gear is widely available on Havelock from resorts and small restaurants, but is generally very low quality.

Fishing is another popular activity, likewise best organised through your hotel. There are also several sports-fishing operators in town.

Some resorts can organise guided **jungle treks** for keen walkers or birdwatchers, but be warned the forest floor turns to glug after rain. The inside rainforest is a spectacular, emerald cavern, and the **birdwatching** – especially on the forest fringes – is rewarding; look out for the blue-black racket-tailed drongo trailing his fabulous tail feathers and, by way of contrast, the brilliant golden oriole.

About 5km beyond No 5 Village, you'll find Kalapathar, where there's an **elephant training camp**; at the time of research there were plans to give demonstrations of working elephants in action. Beyond Kalapathar the road passes another pristine beach and then peters out into forest.

Radha Nagar Beach   BEACH
The prettiest and most popular stretch of stretch of sand is the critically acclaimed Radha Nagar Beach, also known as **beach No 7**. It's a beautiful curve of sugar fronted by perfectly spiralled waves, all backed by native forest that might have grown out of a postcard. And the sunsets? Pretty damn nice. The drive out to the beach, located on

---

CROCODILES

The tragic death of an American tourist attacked by a saltwater crocodile while snorkelling in Havelock on April 2010 sent shockwaves through the community. While crocodiles are a way of life in many parts of the Andamans, they've never been sighted where the incident took place at Neil's Cove, near Radha Nagar. Furthermore, an attack occurring in the open ocean on a coral reef was considered extremely unusual. There are numerous theories about how the crocodile got there; most likely it was ousted from its mangrove habitat on the western side of the island, in a territorial dispute. The crocodile was eventually captured (now residing in Port Blair's zoo) and there have been no sightings since – a high level of vigilance remains in place. General consensus is that it was an isolated incident, and it should not deter people from swimming, though it's important you keep informed, heed any warnings by authorities and, on the western side of the island, don't swim alone and avoid being in the water at dawn or dusk.

Other tourist spots for which warnings have been issued include Corbyn's Cove, Wandoor Beach, Baratang and all over Little Andaman.

the northwestern side of the island about 12km from the jetty, runs through the green dream that is inland Havelock (autorickshaws will take you for about ₹150), or otherwise the bus runs here from No 1 Village when it pleases. Ten minutes' walk along the beach to the northwest is the gorgeous 'lagoon' at Neils Cove, another gem of sheltered sand and crystalline water. There was a crocodile attack here in 2010, so it might be worth checking if it's safe for swimming (see boxed text, p1072). In high season you can take an elephant ride (adult/child ₹25/15; ⊙11am-2pm Mon-Sat) along the beach, posing for that quintessential cheesy snap.

Elephant Beach   BEACH

Elephant Beach, where there's good **snorkelling**, is further north and reached by a 40-minute walk through a muddy elephant logging trail; it's well marked (off the cross-island road), but hard going after rain. The beach itself virtually disappeared after the 2004 tsunami and at high tide it's impossible to reach – ask locally. Lots of snorkelling charters come out this way, and there are lifeguards who will reprimand anyone who litters – God bless them.

Beach 5   BEACH

On the other side of the island from Radha Nagar, Beach No 5 is paradise. Its palm-ringed beaches give it that added relaxed feel, and it has shady patches and less sandflies than Radar Nagar. However, swimming is very difficult in low tide when water becomes shallow for miles. Most of the island's accommodation is out this way.

Dive India   DIVING

(☎091-9932082204; www.diveindia.com; btwn No 3 & 5 Village)

Andaman Bubbles   DIVING

(☎282140; www.andamanbubbles.com; No 5 Village)

Barefoot Scuba   DIVING

(☎282181; www.barefootindia.com; No 3 Village)

🛌 Sleeping & Eating

Most hotels in Havelock are of the cluster-of-beach-hut genre. They all claim to be 'eco' huts ('eco' apparently meaning 'cheap building material'), but they are great value for money, especially in low season.

All listed accommodation has passable menus of backpacker-oriented Western and Indian food. If you desire something more

authentically Indian, head to the cheap food stalls in town (No 1 Village) or the main bazaar (No 3 Village). There's a 'wine shop' in No 1 Village.

Most of the accommodation is strung along the east coast between villages No 2 and No 5.

TOP CHOICE Eco Villa   BUNGALOWS $$

(☎282212; www.havelock.co.in/ecovilla; Beach 2; huts ₹300-3000) The original, and still the best, Eco Villa is the only place with huts right on the beachfront. It caters to all budgets, from the two-storey bamboo duplex huts, tastefully decorated with pot plants, to simple bamboo bungalows, all of which open up to the water. The restaurant gets pretty damn romantic at night, when the moon rises over deep-blue ocean evenings. Accepts credit cards.

Orient Legend Resort   GUESTHOUSE $

(☎282389; Beach 5; huts ₹300-1000, without bathroom ₹100-250) A very popular choice, this sprawling place covers most budgets, and is one of the few guesthouses where you can actually see the water from your room.

Wild Orchid   HOTEL $$$

(☎282472; www.wildorchidandaman.com; d cottages from ₹3000; ❄@) Set back from a secluded beach, this is a mellow, friendly place with tastefully furnished cottages designed in traditional Andamanese style. The restaurant, **Red Snapper** (mains ₹100-350), is the best in town, with a great islander ambience. The fresh tuna pasta is magnifico, and tiger prawns out of this world.

Emerald Gecko   BUNGALOWS $$

(☎282170; www.emerald-gecko.com; huts ₹750-2250) This is a step up in quality from other hut resorts. There are four comfortable double-storey huts with open-roofed bathrooms, lovingly constructed from bamboo rafts that drifted ashore from Myanmar. There are some budget huts too, and the **Blackbeard** restaurant has a quality menu designed by the same folk as Wild Orchid.

Barefoot at Havelock   HOTEL $$$

(☎reservation 044-24341001; www.barefootindia.com; cottages ₹7100-9700; ❄) For the location alone – ensconced in bird-filled forest grounds just back from Radha Nagar Beach – this is Havelock's most luxurious resort, boasting beautifully designed timber and bamboo-thatched cottages. The **restaurant** (mains ₹180-450) with Italian chef serves up everything from Indian to Thai, making for a nice romantic splurge.

Dreamland Resort GUESTHOUSE $
(☑9474224164; Beach 5; huts ₹300) In a prime location, only 50m from Radha Nagar 7, Dreamland has simple thatched bungalows and very friendly owners.

Green Land Resort GUESTHOUSE $
(☑9933220620; huts ₹200-250, without bathroom ₹150-200) This is the spot for those wanting peace and quiet, with simple huts arranged in a jungle of fruit trees. It's only a 15-minute walk to Radha Nagar.

Coconut Lodge GUESTHOUSE $
(☑282056; huts ₹200-500) Popular with Israeli travellers, Coconut Lodge is the place to head to if you want to party. Huts are arranged in a weird circular outlay that directs everyone to a raised, concrete platform where the entire lodge usually ends up carousing.

Anju-coco Resto INDIAN, CONTINENTAL $
(mains ₹120-250) Charming little restaurant run by a friendly owner, features a varied menu with tasty BBQ fish in the high season. The big breakfast (₹60) is indeed big, and a good choice.

B3 – Barefoot Bar & Restaurant PIZZA $$
(Village No 1; mains ₹150-500; ☺11am-4pm & 6-9.30pm) Modern decor with classic movie posters on the walls; there's a Western-heavy menu, with the best pizzas in Havelock. Outdoor seating is pleasant, but overlooks the unattractive jetty.

These places also have great Western food and a relaxed ambience:

Full Moon Cafe WESTERN $
(mains ₹90-180) At Dive India.

Café Del Mar WESTERN $
(mains ₹70-200) At Barefoot Scuba.

❶ Information

There are two ATMs side by side in No 3 Village, where you can also find painfully slow **internet** (per hour ₹80).

❶ Getting There & Away

Ferry times are changeable, but there are always direct sailings to and from Havelock from Port Blair at least once daily, and often twice or more (tourist ferry ₹195, 2½ hours). You'd best book tickets at least a day in advance. The ticket office is open between 9am and 11am. Otherwise you could try the more comfortable Makruzz (from ₹650, two hours).

Several government ferries a week link Havelock with Neil Island (₹195). It's also the most convenient launching point to get to Long Island (₹195), en route to Rangat where buses continue to North Andaman.

❶ Getting Around

A local bus (₹7) connects the jetty and villages on a roughly hourly circuit, but having your own transport is useful. You can hire mopeds or motorbikes (per day from ₹250) and bicycles (per day ₹40 to ₹50) from your hotel or otherwise in No 3 Village.

An autorickshaw from the jetty to No 3 Village is ₹30, to No 5 ₹50 and to No 7 ₹150 to ₹200.

Neil Island

Happy to laze in the shadows of its more famous island neighbour, Neil is still the place for that added bit of relaxation. Its beaches may not be quite as luxurious as Havelock's, but they have ample character and are a perfect distance apart to explore by bicycle. There's a lovely unhurried pace of life here; cycling through picturesque villages you'll get many friendly hellos from kids and adults alike. In Neil Island you're about 40km from Port Blair, a short ferry ride from Havelock and several universes away from life at home

At the time of research there were no internet or moneychanging facilities. There's a post office in the bazaar.

❂ Sights & Activities

Neil Island's five **beaches** (numbered one to five) all have their unique charms. **No 1** is the prettiest and most accessible, a 40-minute walk west of the jetty and village. The island's best **snorkelling** is around the coral reef at the far (western) end of this beach at high tide. There's a good sunset viewpoint out this way accessed via Pearl Park Resort, which becomes a communal spot in the sand for tourists and locals come early evening.

No 2, on the north side of the island, has the **Natural Bridge** rock formation, accessible only at low tide by walking around the rocky cove. To get here by bicycle take the side road that runs through the bazaar, then take a left where the road forks. The best swimming is at **No 4**, though its proximity to the jetty is a slight turn off. **No 3** is a secluded powdery sand cove, which is best accessed via Blue Sea Restaurant. Further ahead the more wild and rugged **No 5**

(5km from the village), reached via the village road to the eastern side of the island, is a nice place to walk along the beach, with small limestone caves accessible at low tide.

You can dive with **India Scuba Explorers** (☑9474238646; www.indiascubaexplorers.com), while snorkelling gear can hired (per day ₹150) at your hotel or around town. If you're extremely lucky you may spot a **dugong** at No 1 Beach feeding in the shallows at high tide. Hiring a fishing boat to go to offshore snorkelling or fishing will cost between ₹1000 and ₹2000 depending on how far out you want to travel, how long you choose to snorkel etc; several people can usually fit on board.

The main bazaar has a mellow vibe, and is a popular gathering spot in the early evening. **Cooking classes** (from ₹200) can be arranged at Gyan Garden Restaurant. Behind the restaurant is a track up the small hill that leads to a **viewpoint** across the island and out to sea.

🛏 Sleeping & Eating

In the low season there are great deals on simple beach huts. The most popular places to stay are **Tango Beach Resort** (☑03192-282583; huts ₹50-350, cottages ₹600-1000) and **Pearl Park Resort** (☑03192-282510; huts ₹100-250, cottages & r ₹400-1600) both at No 1 Beach. Their proximity and same-sameness makes them feel like identical sides of a double-headed coin; both offer nice thatch huts and less interesting, if more comfortable, concrete rooms. The main difference is that Tango has ocean views and a sea breeze, while Pearl Park has the sunset point and lush garden surrounds. **A-N-D Beach Resort** (☑214722; huts ₹300-700) is another good option on No 4 Beach.

Eating is surprisingly good on Neil Island. You'll find cheap and delicious Bengali food in the market.

Moonshine (mains ₹40-150) on the road to No 1 Beach is a backpacker favourite, cooking up excellent home-made pasta dishes (the prawn pasta is amazing), with cold beer. In the market, **Chand Restaurant** (mains ₹50-200) is also popular, with strong filter coffee and delicious BBQ fish. **Gyan Garden Restaurant** (mains ₹50-200) has a good seafood selection.

ℹ Getting There & Around

A ferry makes a round trip each morning from Phoenix Bay Jetty in Port Blair (₹195, two hours). There's also a daily ferry to Havelock in either the morning or early afternoon.

Hiring a bicycle (per day from ₹50) is the best way to get about; roads are flat and distances short. An autorickshaw will take you to No 1 Beach from the jetty for ₹50.

Middle & North Andaman

The Andamans aren't just sun and sand. They're also jungle that feels as primeval as the Jurassic and as thick as the Amazon, a green tangle of ancient forest that could have been birthed in Mother Nature's subconscious. This shaggy, wild side of the islands can be seen on a long, loping bus ride up the Andaman Trunk Rd (ATR). Going to Diglipur by road thrusts you onto bumpy roads framed by antediluvian trees and roll-on, roll-off ferries that cross red-tannin rivers prowled by saltwater crocodiles.

But there's a negative side to riding the ATR: the road cuts through the homeland of the Jarawa and has brought the tribe into incessant contact with the outside world. Modern India and tribal life do not seem able to coexist – every time Jarawa and settlers interact, misunderstandings have led to friction, confusion and, at worst, violent attacks and death. Indian anthropologists and indigenous rights groups like Survival International have called for the ATR to be closed; its status is under review at time of writing (see p1066). At present, vehicles are permitted to travel only in convoys at set times from 6am to 3pm. Photography is strictly prohibited, as is stopping or any other interaction with the Jarawa people – who are becoming increasingly reliant on handouts from passing traffic.

The first place of interest north of Port Blair is the impressive **limestone caves** (☉closed Mon) at Baratang. It's a 45-minute boat trip (₹200) from the jetty, a scenic trip through mangrove forest. A **permit** is required, organised at the jetty.

Rangat is the next main town, a transport hub with not much else going for it. If you do get stuck here, try **Hotel PLS Bhawan** (s/d from ₹150/250; ▨), the best of a bad bunch. There's an ATM nearby. Ferries depart to/from Port Blair and Havelock Island (₹50/195, nine hours), as well as Long Island (₹7) from Yeratta Jetty, 8km from Rangat. A daily bus goes to Port Blair (₹95, seven hours).

Between December and March, Hawksbill turtles nest on the beaches at **Cuthbert Bay**, a 45-minute drive from Rangat. Any northbound bus will drop you here. **Hawksbill Nest** (☎03192-279022; 4-bed dm ₹600, d ₹400, with AC ₹800; ※) is the only place to stay; bookings must be made at A&N Tourism in Port Blair. A permit (₹250) can be organised at the ranger office in Betapur

LONG ISLAND

With its friendly island community and lovely slow pace of life, Long Island is perfect for those wanting to take the pace down even a few more notches. There are no motorised vehicles on the island, and at times you're likely to be the only tourist here.

A 1½-hour trek in the jungle (not advisable after heavy rain) will lead you to the secluded **Lalaji Bay**, a beautiful white-sand beach with good swimming. Hiring a *dunghi* (₹1500 return) makes it much easier – especially if you don't like leeches. You can also get a *dunghi* to North Passage island for snorkelling at the stunning **Merk Bay** with its blinding white sand and translucent waters. Trips to South Button are also possible from here.

🌿**Blue Planet** (☎9474212180; www.blueplanetandamans.com; r with/without bathroom from ₹300/700; @) is not only a great place to stay, it also sets an excellent example by incorporating bottles washed ashore into its architecture. Its simple rooms are set around a lovely Padauk tree, with hammocks strung about. Food is available, as well as very slow internet. Follow the blue arrows from the jetty to get here. It also has private cottages (₹2000 to ₹3000) at a nearby location. No alcohol is sold on Long Island, so you'll have to stock up beforehand.

There are three ferries a week to Havelock and Port Blair (₹195), and daily service to Rangat (₹8).

MAYABUNDER & AROUND

In 'upper' Middle Andaman, there are several villages inhabited by Karen, members of a Burmese hill tribe who were relocated here during the British colonial period. In Mayabunder, stop at **Sea'n'Sand** (☎03192-273454; thanzin_the_great@yahoo.co.in; r from ₹200; ※), a simple lodge, restaurant and bar overlooking the water 1km south of the town centre. Run by Titus and Elizabeth and their extended Karen family, it's low-key and will appeal to travellers looking for an experience away from the crowds. You can go on a range of **boat-based day tours** (per tour from ₹500-2500) that, depending on the season, may include visits to **Forty One Caves** where

hawabills make their highly prized edible nests; snorkelling off **Avis Island**; or jungle trekking at creepy **Interview Island**, where there's a small population of wild elephants, released after a logging company closed for business in the 1950s. You'll feel very off the beaten trek here. A permit (₹500) is required, best organised through Sea'n'Sand.

Mayabunder, 71km north of Rangat, is linked by daily buses from Port Blair (₹130, 10 hours) and by thrice-weekly ferries (Tuesday, Thursday and Friday). There's an unreliable ATM here.

DIGLIPUR & AROUND

Those who make it this far north are well rewarded with some impressive attractions in the area. Though don't expect anything of **Diglipur**, the northernmost major town in the Andamans, which is a sprawling, gritty bazaar town with an ATM and slow **internet connection** (per hr ₹40). You should instead head straight for **Kalipur**, where you'll find lodging and vistas of the ocean and outlying islands.

Ferries arrive at Aerial Bay Jetty from where it's 11km southwest to Diglipur, the bus stand and Administration Block, where boat tickets can be booked. Kalipur is on the coast 8km southeast of the jetty.

◉ Sights & Activities

Leatherback, hawksbill, olive ridley and green **turtles** all nest along the Diglipur coastline between December and April. Tourists can assist with collecting eggs for hatching; contact Pristine Beach Resort for more information. The area also has a number of caves.

Islands BEACH, SNORKELLING
Like lovely tropical counterweights, the twin islands of **Smith** and **Ross** are connected by a narrow sandbar. Since this is designated as a marine sanctuary, to visit you must get a permit from the **Forest Office** (Indian/foreigner ₹50/500; ⏰6am-2pm Mon-Sat) opposite Aerial Bay Jetty. These islands are up there with the best in the Andamans, and the snorkelling is amazing. You can charter a boat to take you for the day from the village for ₹1000.

Craggy Island, a small island off Kalipur, also has good snorkelling. Strong swimmers can reach here, otherwise a *dunghi* is available (₹200 return).

Saddle Peak TREKKING
At 732m, Saddle Peak is the highest point in the Andamans. You can trek through subtropical forest to the top and back from Ka-

lipur in about six hours; the views from the peaks onto the archipelago are incredible. Again, a permit (Indian ₹25, foreigner ₹250) is required from the Forest Office and a local guide will make sure you don't get lost – ask at Pristine Beach Resort. Otherwise follow the red arrows marked on the trees.

Sleeping & Eating

TOP CHOICE **Pristine Beach Resort** GUESTHOUSE
(☑9474286787; www.andamanpristineresorts. com; tents ₹150, huts ₹250-1000, r ₹2500; ❄@) This pretty spot huddled among the palms between paddy fields and the beach has several simple bamboo huts on stilts, as well as more romantic bamboo 'tree houses' and upmarket rooms, and a restaurant-bar. Alex, the super-friendly owner, is a great source of information. The resort also rents bicycles/motorcycles (per day ₹60/250).

❶ Getting There & Around

Diglipur, located about 80km north of Mayabunder, is served by daily buses to/from Port Blair (₹170, 12 hours), as well as buses to Mayabunder (₹50, 2½ hours) and Rangat (₹70, 4½ hours). There are also daily ferries from Port Blair to Diglipur, returning overnight from Diglipur (seat/bunk ₹100/295, 10 hours).

Buses run from Diglupur to Kalipur (₹10) every 30 minutes; an autorickshaw costs about ₹100.

Little Andaman

Named Gaubolambe by the indigenous Onge, Little Andaman is as far south as you can go in the islands. There's an end-of-the-world (in tropical paradise) feeling here: barely any tourists visit, the locals are so friendly they feel like family, and the island itself is a gorgeous fist of mangroves, jungle and teal plucked from a twinkle in nature's eye.

Badly hit by the 2004 Boxing Day tsunami, Little Andaman has slowly rebuilt itself, and while there's still zero tourist infrastructure, new guesthouses are starting to open up. Located about 120km south of Port Blair, the main settlement here is **Hut Bay**, a pleasant small town that primarily produces smiling Bengalis and Tamils. North of here you'll find isolated beaches as fresh as bread out of the oven.

◉ Sights & Activities

Netaji Nagar Beach, 11km north of Hut Bay, and **Butler Bay**, a further 3km north,

are gorgeous, deserted (apart from the odd cow) and great for surfing.

Inland, the **White Surf** and **Whisper Wave waterfalls** offer a forest experience (the latter involves a 4km jungle trek and a guide is highly recommended); they're pleasant falls and you may be tempted to swim in the rock pools, but beware local crocodiles.

Little Andaman lighthouse, 14km from Hut Bay, is another worthwhile excursion. Standing 41m high, exactly 200 steps lead you up to magnificent views over the coastline and forest. The easiest way to get here is by motorcycle, or otherwise a sweaty bicycle journey. You could also take an autorickshaw until the road becomes unpassable, and walk for an hour along the blissful stretch of deserted beach.

Harbinder Bay and **Dugong Creek** are designated tribal areas for the Nicobarese and Onge, respectively, and are off-limits.

Intrepid surfing travellers have been whispering about Little Andaman since it first opened up to foreigners several years ago. The reef breaks are legendary, but best suited for more experienced surfers; and then there's the sharks and crocodiles to contend with. Get in touch with surfing nut, **Muthu** (☑9775276182), based in Havelock, who can provide info on waves for Little Andaman and around. Several surfing liveaboard yachts make the trip out here, taking you to more remote, inaccessible sites. Try **Surf Andamans** (www.surfandamans.com).

Sleeping & Eating

There's no great reason to stay in Hut Bay, an inconvenient 10km away from the nicer beaches, but if you do, **Nandhini Tourist Home** (☑9933259090; s/d ₹150/250) has rooms looking onto the tsunami-scarred beach. There are plenty of cheap thali and tiffin places (we recommend the unnamed Bengali eatery across from the police station).

TOP CHOICE **Blue View** (☑9531802037; Km11.5; s/d ₹150/250) has prime real estate across the road from Netaji Nagar Beach. Rooms are simple, adjoined shacks, and it has a friendly owner, Azad. You can rent bicycles/motorbikes (per day ₹50/250). The food here is very good. Otherwise you could try the less appealing concrete **Ananta Lodge** (☑744207; Km16; s/d ₹200/300) in the bazaar just beyond Butler's Bay.

ⓘ Getting There & Around

Ferries land at Hut Bay Jetty on the east coast; from there the beaches lay to the north. Buses (₹10) leave when they want for Butler Bay, or you can hire a local jeep (₹100).

Boats sail to Little Andaman from Port Blair daily, alternating between the overnight eight-hour slow boat, and the afternoon six-hour 'speedboat' (seat/bunk ₹25/70).

If you're planning on getting a helicopter, this is the place to chance your luck. Not only will it save you from a 7½-hour boat trip, but the aerial views are incredible – though the 5kg baggage limit makes it tricky.

Understand India

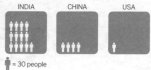

population per sq km

INDIA   CHINA   USA

👤 ≈ 30 people

India Today

The Kashmir Epic

In summer 2010, the Kashmir Valley was under near-constant curfews, and violence between proindependence protesters and Indian security forces had turned deadly. The protesters called for India to remove its more than 500,000 troops from Kashmir. They stoned police and paramilitary and burned police vehicles, all while demanding *azadi* – freedom. Security forces responded with gunfire, and more than 100 protesters died, mostly teenagers.

The predominantly Muslim Kashmir Valley is claimed by both India and Pakistan – and now, Kashmiris – and the impasse has plagued relations between the two countries since Partition in 1947 (see p1099). After three India–Pakistan wars and countless skirmishes, there's still no solution in sight.

By 1989 Kashmir had an armed insurgency. A militant fringe of Kashmiris revolted against the Indian government, joined by armed supporters from Afghanistan and Pakistan. India accused Pakistan of assisting insurgents; Pakistan countered that India was denying Kashmiris the right to self-determination. Meanwhile, thousands of civilians have been killed in the conflict. India–Pakistan relations sunk even lower in 1998 when the Bharatiya Janata Party (BJP; Indian People's Party) government detonated five nuclear devices in the Rajasthan desert and Pakistan responded in kind. A border conflict was averted, but nukes were now in the picture.

By the time the Congress Party government of Prime Minister Manmohan Singh came to power in 2004, relations were strained but cordial; the reopening of cross-border transport links, among other measures, helped calm the situation. But talks were derailed when in Mumbai (Bombay) in 2008 a team of terrorists killed at least 163 people, some of whom were tortured, at 10 sites around the city during three days of coordinated bombings and shootings. The one sniper caught alive, a Pakistani, had

» Population: 1.21 billion

» GDP: US$1.4 trillion (2009)

» Unemployment rate: 10.8%

» Employed in agriculture: 52%

» Literacy rate: 65/82% (female/male)

» Sex ratio: 940/1000 (female/male)

Dos & Don'ts

» Avoid tight clothes and keep shoulders and knees covered. Outside Goa, this applies to swimming, too.

» Public kissing, cuddling or holding hands is not condoned.

» Be humble and dress modestly at holy places.

» Remove shoes before entering people's homes and holy sites.

» Always ask before photographing people or holy places.

» That head wobble? It can mean 'yes', 'maybe' or 'I have no idea'. Best to just go with the flow.

Top Fiction

Midnight's Children Salman Rushdie's allegory about Independence and Partition.

The Guide and **The Painter of Signs** Classic RK Narayan novels set in the fictional town of Malgudi.

A Fine Balance Rohinton Mistry's tragic Mumbai-based story.

belief systems
(% of population)

80.5
Hindu

13.4
Muslim

2.3
Christian

1.9
Sikh

0.8
Buddhist

1.1
Other

if India were 100 people

41 would speak Hindi
55 would speak one of 21 other official languages
4 would speak one of around 400 other languages
Note: 10 of these 100 will speak English as a second language

ties to Lashkar-e-Taiba, a militant group that formed to assist the Pakistani army in Kashmir in the 1990s. Pakistan denied any involvement.

Communal Tension

While Kashmir is the site of India's most persistent conflict, religion-based confrontation further south may be its most insidious. One of the most violent episodes occurred in 1992, when Hindu extremists destroyed a mosque, the Babri Masjid, in Ayodhya, Uttar Pradesh, revered by Hindus as the birthplace of Rama. The Hindu-revivalist BJP, then the main opposition, did little to discourage the acts, and rioting in the north killed thousands.

The BJP grew in popularity and won the elections in 1998 and again in 1999. Prime Minister Atal Bihari Vajpayee appeared moderate, but many BJP members and supporters took a more belligerent posture. In 2002, when 58 Hindus died in a suspicious train fire, more than 2000 people, mostly Muslims, were killed in subsequent riots; according to the nonprofit Human Rights Watch, BJP government officials were directly involved.

The year 2008 was one of India's darkest: bomb blasts in Jaipur, Ahmedabad and Delhi each killed dozens of people. Investigations pointed at hardline Islamist groups, but no sooner had Delhi vowed to rein in terrorism than terror struck again with the bombings and shootings in Mumbai on 26 November 2008, now known as 26/11.

At the time of writing, however, tensions have diminished post-26/11 in Mumbai, with extremists softening their rhetoric. And in 2010, when a court stated that the Ayodhya site would be split between Hindus and Muslims, the response was peaceful – India breathed a collective sigh of relief.

India's national anthem, 'Jana Gana Mana' (Thou Art the Ruler of the Minds of All People), was written and composed by Bengali poet and Nobel Laureate Rabindranath Tagore.

Congress Today

When the Congress Party regained power in 2004, it was under the leadership of Sonia Gandhi – the Italian-born wife of the late Rajiv Gandhi, who

Top Films

Fire (1996), **Earth** (1998) and **Water** (2005) The Deepa Mehta–directed trilogy was popular abroad, but controversial in India.
Pyaasa (Thirst; 1957) and **Kaagaz Ke Phool** (Paper Flowers; 1959) Two bittersweet films

directed by and starring film legend Guru Dutt.
Gandhi (1982) Hugely popular movie.

Niceties

» Saying *namaste* with hands together in a prayer gesture is a traditional, respectful Hindu greeting and a universally accepted way to say hello – handy since not all people shake hands with the opposite gender.

had served as prime minister from 1984 to 1989 (after his mother, Prime Minister Indira Gandhi, was assassinated in 1984). The BJP's planned national agitation campaign against Sonia Gandhi's foreign origins was subverted when she stepped aside to allow Manmohan Singh to be sworn in as prime minister. With a reputation for transparency and intelligence, Singh is generally popular among Indians, though many believe that Gandhi still wields considerable influence over the actual decisions.

Under Singh's leadership, India has carried out a program of economic liberalisation along with a number of education, health and other social-reform initiatives. Singh made international headlines in 2006 by concluding a civilian nuclear agreement with the US, which grants India access to nuclear fuel and technology in exchange for following International Atomic Energy Agency safeguards. Recent times have seen Singh come under increasing criticism for weak leadership regarding a series of corruption allegations levelled towards his government.

> Belonging to the Sikh faith, India's Prime Minister Manmohan Singh (of the Congress Party) was the first member of any religious minority community to hold India's highest elected office.

It's the Economy

India's economy was shaken up in 1991 when Manmohan Singh, then finance minister, undertook the momentous step of partially floating the rupee against a basket of 'hard' currencies. State subsidies were phased out and the economy was opened up to foreign investment, with multinationals drawn by India's multitudes of educated professionals and low wages.

As the world's second-fastest-growing economy after China, India has made giant strides since then. But despite its healthy recent annual growth rate of around 9%, huge sections of the country's billion-plus population have benefitted little from this boom. Indeed, the government's ongoing challenge is to spread the bounty of India's fiscal prosperity, not an easy task given that the gap between the haves and the have-nots – as well as the sheer number of have-nots – is vast.

Political works

» Hugs between strangers don't really happen (not in public).

» 'Please' and 'thank you' aren't used much, but they never hurt.

» Only use your right hand for eating and shaking hands; in India the left hand is the 'toilet' hand.

India after Gandhi: the History of the World's Largest Democracy An elegant post-Gandhi history by Ramachandra Guha.
Political Resources – India (www.politicalresources.net/India.htm) Links to the major parties and movements.

The Elephant, the Tiger and the Cellphone Shashi Tharoor's reflections on 21st-century India.

History

India's story is one of the grand epics of world history. Throughout thousands of years of great civilisations, invasions, the birth of religions and countless cataclysms, India has time and again proved itself to be, in the words of its first prime minister, Jawaharlal Nehru, 'a bundle of contradictions held together by strong but invisible threads'. Indian history has always been a work in progress, a process of reinvention and accumulation that can prove elusive for those seeking to grasp its essential essence.

Generally speaking, Brahmanical empires and Hindu–Buddhist dynasties dominated for over a millennium before the arrival of the Islamic sultanates, which, along with the Mughals, established Muslim control over the region for several hundred years; they were overtaken by the Europeans – especially, of course, the British, who managed to conquer the peninsula. But even this chronology is deceptive: small dynasties emerged, passed away and emerged again in the shadow of larger empires; power centres shifted subtly, control changed hands back and forth between rivals, and territories expanded and contracted; religion was a big deal or not a big deal, depending on the era. Like a river, you haven't ever been able to enter the same India twice. And yet, from its myriad upheavals, a vibrant, diverse and thoroughly modern nation has emerged, as enduring as it is dynamic and increasingly geared to meet the multifarious challenges of the future.

Indus Valley Civilisation

The Indus Valley, straddling the modern India–Pakistan border, is the cradle of civilisation on the Indian subcontinent. The first inhabitants of this region were nomadic tribes who cultivated land and kept domestic animals. Over thousands of years, an urban culture began to emerge from these tribes, particularly from 3500 BC. By 2500 BC large cities were well established, the focal points of what became known as the Harappan culture, which would flourish for more than 1000 years.

TIMELINE	10,000 BC	2600–1700 BC	1500 BC
	Stone Age paintings first made in the Bhimbetka rock shelters, in what is now Madhya Pradesh; the art continues here for many centuries. Settlements thought to exist across subcontinent.	The Indus Valley civilisation's heydey. Spanning parts of Rajasthan, Gujarat and Sindh province in present-day Pakistan, it takes shape around metropolises such as Harappa and Moenjodaro.	The Indo-Aryan civilisation takes root in the fertile plains of the Indo-Gangetic basin. Settlers speak an early form of Sanskrit, from which several Indian vernaculars, including Hindi, later evolve.

The great cities of the Mature Harappan period were Moenjodaro and Harappa in present-day Pakistan, and Lothal near Ahmedabad. Lothal can be visited, and from the precise, carefully laid-out street plan, some sense of this sophisticated 4500-year-old civilisation is still evident. Harappan cities often had a separate acropolis, suggesting a religious function, and the great tank at Moenjodaro may have been used for ritual bathing purposes. The major Harappan cities were also notable for their size – estimates put the population of Moenjodaro at as high as 50,000.

By the middle of the 3rd millennium BC the Indus Valley culture was arguably the equal of other great civilisations emerging at the time. The Harappans traded with Mesopotamia, and developed a system of weights and measures, along with a highly developed art in the form of terracotta and bronze figurines. Recovered relics, including models of bullock carts and jewellery, offer the earliest evidence of a distinctive Indian culture. Indeed, many elements of Harappan culture would later become assimilated into Hinduism: clay figurines found at these sites suggest worship of a Mother goddess (later personified as Kali) and a male three-faced god sitting in the pose of a yogi (believed to be the historic Shiva) attended by four animals. Black stone pillars (associated with phallic worship of Shiva) and animal figures (the most prominent being the humped bull; later Shiva's mount, Nandi) have also been discovered.

Early Invasions & the Rise of Religions

The Harappan civilisation fell into decline from the beginning of the 2nd millennium BC. Some historians attribute the end of the empire to floods or decreased rainfall, which threatened the Harappans' agricultural base. The more enduring, if contentious, theory is that an Aryan invasion put paid to the Harappans, despite little archaeological proof or written reports in the ancient Indian texts to that effect. As a result, some nationalist historians argue that the Aryans (from a Sanskrit word for 'noble') were in fact the original inhabitants of India and that the invasion theory was invented by self-serving foreign conquerors. Others say that the arrival of Aryans was more of a gentle migration that gradually subsumed Harappan culture.

Those who defend the invasion theory believe that from around 1500 BC Aryan tribes from Afghanistan and Central Asia began to filter into northwest India. Despite their military superiority, their progress was gradual, with successive tribes fighting over territory and new arrivals pushing further east into the Ganges plain. Eventually these tribes controlled northern India as far as the Vindhya Hills. Many of the original inhabitants of northern India, the Dravidians, were pushed south.

The Hindu sacred scriptures, the Vedas (see p1108), were written during this period of transition (1500–1200 BC), and the caste system became formalised.

1500–1200 BC

The Rig-Veda, the first and longest of Hinduism's canonical texts, the Vedas, is written; three more books follow. Earliest forms of priestly Brahmanical Hinduism emerge.

1000 BC

Indraprastha, Delhi's first incarnation, comes into being. Archaeological excavations at the site, where the Purana Qila now stands, continue even today, as more facts about this ancient capital keep emerging.

» Purana Qila (p73), Delhi

DAMIEN SIMONIS / LONELY PLANET IMAGES ©

As the Aryan tribes spread across the Ganges plain in the late 7th century BC, many were absorbed into 16 major kingdoms, which were, in turn, amalgamated into four large states. Out of these states arose the Nanda dynasty, which came to power in 364 BC, ruling over huge swathes of North India.

During this period, the Indian heartland narrowly avoided two invasions from the west which, if successful, could have significantly altered the path of Indian history. The first was by the Persian king Darius (521–486 BC), who annexed Punjab and Sindh (on either side of the modern India–Pakistan border). Alexander the Great advanced to India from Greece in 326 BC, but his troops refused to go beyond the Beas River in Himachal Pradesh. Alexander turned back without ever extending his power into India itself.

The period is also distinguished by the rise of two of India's most significant religions, Buddhism (p1111) and Jainism (p1112), which arose around 500 BC. Both the Buddha and Jainism's Mahavir questioned the Vedas and were critical of the caste system, although, unlike Buddhism, the Jain faith never extended beyond India.

The Mauryan Empire & its Aftermath

If the Harappan culture was the cradle of Indian civilisation, Chandragupta Maurya was the founder of the first great Indian empire. He came to power in 321 BC, having seized the throne from the Nandas, and he soon expanded the empire to include the Indus Valley previously conquered by Alexander.

From its capital at Pataliputra (modern-day Patna), the Mauryan empire encompassed much of North India and reached as far south as modern-day Karnataka. The Mauryas were capable of securing control over such a vast realm through the use of an efficient bureaucracy, organised

Mahavir and the Buddha were contemporaries, and their teachings overlapped. The Buddha lays out the discrepancies (and his critiques) in the Sankha Sutta and Devadaha Sutta, in which he refers to Mahavir as Nigantha ('free from bonds') Nataputta. You can read them at the Theravada resource www .accesstoinsight .com.

MAP DRAWING ARYAN-STYLE

While some historians dispute the origins of the Aryan presence in northern India, there's little argument that the subsequent Aryan kingdoms often adhered to one of history's more curious forms of territorial demarcation. Under the highly formalised ritual of *asvamedha* (horse sacrifice), a horse was allowed to roam freely, followed by a band of soldiers. If the horse's progress was impeded, the king would fight for the land in question. At the end of the prescribed period, the entire area over which the horse had wandered was taken to be the king's unchallenged territory. The horse was rewarded for its success or failure – which, it didn't matter – by being sacrificed. The system must have worked, because the ritual was still being performed centuries later by dynasties such as the Chalukyas of Badami (p884) to demonstrate the ruler's complete control over his kingdom.

599–528 BC	563–483 BC	5th–4th Century BC	326 BC
The life of Mahavir, the 24th and last *tirthankar* (enlightened teacher) who established Jainism. Like the Buddha, he preaches compassion and a path to enlightenment for all castes.	The life of Siddhartha Gautama. The prince is born in modern-day Nepal and attains enlightenment beneath the Bodhi Tree in Bodhgaya (Bihar), thereby transforming into the Buddha (Awakened One).	Nanda dynasty evolves from the wealthy region of Magadha (roughly, today's Bihar) and grows to encompass a huge area, spanning from Bengal to Punjab. Falls to Maurya in 321 BC.	Alexander the Great invades India. He defeats King Porus in Punjab to enter the subcontinent, but a rebellion within his army keeps him from advancing beyond Himachal Pradesh's Beas River.

tiers of local government and a well-defined social order consisting of a rigid caste system.

The empire reached its peak under emperor Ashoka. Such was Ashoka's power to lead and unite that after his death in 232 BC, no one could be found to hold the disparate elements of the Mauryan empire together. The empire rapidly disintegrated, collapsing altogether in 184 BC.

None of the empires that immediately followed could match the stability or enduring historical legacy of the Mauryans. The Sungas (184–70 BC), Kanvas (72–30 BC), Shakas (from 130 BC) and Kushanas (1st century BC until 1st century AD, and into the 3rd century in a diminished form) all had their turn, with the last briefly ruling over a massive area of North India and Central Asia.

Despite the multiplicity of ruling powers, this was a period of intense development. Trade with the Roman Empire (overland, and by sea through the southern ports) became substantial during the 1st century AD; there was also overland trade with China.

The Golden Age of the Guptas

The empires that followed the Mauryans may have claimed large areas of Indian territory as their own, but many secured only nominal power over their realms. Throughout the subcontinent, small tribes and kingdoms effectively controlled territory and dominated local affairs.

In AD 319 Chandragupta I, the third king of one of these tribes, the little-known Guptas, came to prominence by a fortuitous marriage to the daughter of one of the most powerful tribes in the north, the Liccavis. The Gupta empire grew rapidly and under Chandragupta II (r 375–413) achieved its greatest extent. The Chinese pilgrim Fa-hsien, visiting India at the time, described a people 'rich and contented', ruled over by enlightened and just kings.

Poetry, literature and the arts flourished, with some of the finest work done at Ajanta (p772), Ellora (p769), Sanchi (p639) and Sarnath (p396). Towards the end of the Gupta period, Hinduism became the dominant religious force, and its revival eclipsed Jainism and Buddhism; the latter in particular went into decline in India and would never again be India's dominant religion.

The invasions of the Huns at the beginning of the 6th century signalled the end of this era, and in 510 the Gupta army was defeated by the Hun leader Toramana. Power in North India again devolved to a number of separate Hindu kingdoms.

The Hindu South

Southern India has always laid claim to its own unique history. Insulated by distance from the political developments in the north, a separate set

---

Mauryan Remains

» Junagadh (Gujarat)

» Allahabad Fort (Uttar Pradesh)

» Sarnath (Uttar Pradesh)

» Sanchi (Madhya Pradesh)

» Bodhgaya (Bihar)

» Vaishali (Bihar)

» Amaravathi (Andhra Pradesh)

Emperor Ashoka's ability to rule over his empire was assisted by a standing army consisting of roughly 9000 elephants, 30,000 cavalry and 600,000 infantry.

321–185 BC	Mid-3rd Century BC	Mid-3rd Century BC	c 235 BC
Rule of the Maurya kings. Founded by Chandragupta Maurya, this pan-Indian empire is ruled from Pataliputra (present-day Patna) and briefly adopts Buddhism during the reign of Emperor Ashoka.	Buddhism spreads across subcontinent and beyond via Ashoka's monastic ambassadors: monks travel to Sri Lanka and Southeast Asia. Amaravathi, Sanchi and other stupas erected.	Bhakti movement emerges in Hinduism, following first mention in the 5th-century-BC Bhagavad Gita. It emphasises individual devotion and union with the Divine, challenging traditional hierarchy of Brahmanism.	Start of Chola reign. The Tamil dynasty, known for the power and territory it accreted in the 9th to 13th centuries, ruled in India's south for more than 1500 years.

of powerful kingdoms emerged, among them the Satavahanas – who ruled over central India for about 400 years beginning in 230 BC and, though predominantly Hindu, patronised Buddhist art at Amaravathi (p915) and Sanchi (p639) – as well as the Kalingas and Vakatakas. But it was from the tribal territories on the fertile coastal plains that the greatest southern empires – the Cholas, Pandyas, Chalukyas, Cheras and Pallavas – came into their own.

The Chalukyas ruled mainly over the Deccan region of south-central India, although their power occasionally extended further north. With a capital at Badami (p884) in modern-day Karnataka, they ruled from 550 to 753 before falling to the Rashtrakutas. An eastern branch of the Chalukyas, with its capital at Kalyani in Karnataka, rose and ruled again from 972 to 1190.

In the far south, the Pallavas ruled from the 4th to 9th centuries and pioneered Dravidian architecture, with its exuberant, almost baroque, style. The surviving architectural high points of Pallava rule can be found across Tamil Nadu, including in the erstwhile Pallava capital at Kanchipuram (p1008).

The concepts of zero and infinity are widely believed to have been devised by eminent Indian mathematicians during the reign of the Guptas.

AN ENLIGHTENED EMPEROR

Apart from the Mughals and then the British many centuries later, no other power controlled more Indian territory than the Mauryan empire. It's therefore fitting that it provided India with one of its most significant historical figures.

Emperor Ashoka's rule was characterised by flourishing art and sculpture, while his reputation as a philosopher-king was enhanced by the rock-hewn edicts he used to both instruct his people and delineate the enormous span of his territory. Some of these moral teachings can still be seen, particularly the Ashokan Edicts at Junagadh in Gujarat (p702).

Ashoka's reign also represented an undoubted historical high point for Buddhism: he embraced the religion in 262 BC, declaring it the state religion and cutting a radical swathe through the spiritual and social body of Hinduism. The emperor also built thousands of stupas and monasteries across the region, the extant highlights of which are visible at Sarnath (p396) in Uttar Pradesh – on the spot where Buddha delivered his first sermon expounding the Noble Eightfold Path, or Middle Way to Enlightenment (see p1111) – and Sanchi (p640) in Madhya Pradesh. Ashoka also sent missions abroad, and he is revered in Sri Lanka because he sent his son and daughter to carry the Buddha's teaching to the island.

The long shadow this emperor of the 3rd century BC still casts over India is evident from the fact that the central design of the Indian national flag is the Ashoka Chakra, a wheel with 24 spokes. Ashoka's standard, which topped many pillars, is also the seal of modern-day India (four lions sitting back-to-back atop an abacus decorated with a frieze and the inscription 'truth alone triumphs') and its national emblem, chosen to reaffirm the ancient commitment to peace and goodwill.

3rd Century BC	AD 52	1st Century	319–510
The Satavahana Empire, of Andhran origin, rules over a huge central Indian area until the 2nd century AD. Their interest in art and maritime trade influences artistic development regionally and in Southeast Asia.	Possible arrival of St Thomas the Apostle on the coast of Kerala. Christianity thought to have been introduced to India with his preaching in Kerala and Tamil Nadu.	International trade booms: the region's elaborate overland trade networks connect with ports linked to maritime routes. Trade to Africa, the Gulf, Socotra, Southeast Asia, China and even Rome thrives.	The golden era of the Gupta dynasty, the second of India's great empires after the Mauryas. This era is marked by a creative surge in literature and the arts.

The south's prosperity was based on long-established trading links with other civilisations, among them the Egyptians and Romans. In return for spices, pearls, ivory and silk, the Indians received Roman gold. Indian merchants also extended their influence to Southeast Asia. In 850 the Cholas rose to power and superseded the Pallavas. They soon set about turning the south's far-reaching trade influence into territorial conquest. Under the reign of Rajaraja Chola I (985–1014) they controlled almost the whole of South India, the Deccan plateau, Sri Lanka, parts of the Malay peninsula and the Sumatran-based Srivijaya kingdom.

Not all of their attention was focused overseas, however, and the Cholas left behind some of the finest examples of Dravidian architecture, most notably the sublime Brihadishwara Temple in Thanjavur (p1025) and Chidambaram's stunning Nataraja Temple (p1022). Both Thanjavur and Chidambaram served as Chola capitals.

Throughout, Hinduism remained the bedrock of South Indian culture.

The Muslim North

While South India guarded its resolutely Hindu character, North India was convulsed by Muslim armies invading from the northwest.

At the vanguard of Islamic expansion was Mahmud of Ghazni. Today, Ghazni is a nondescript little town between Kabul and Kandahar in Afghanistan. But in the early years of the 11th century, Mahmud turned it into one of the world's most glorious capital cities, which he largely funded by plundering his neighbours' territories. From 1001 to 1025, Mahmud conducted 17 raids into India, most infamously on the famous Shiva temple at Somnath (p698) in Gujarat. The Hindu force of 70,000 died trying to defend the temple, which eventually fell in early 1026. In the aftermath of his victory, Mahmud, not particularly intent on acquiring new territory at this stage, transported a massive haul of gold and other booty back to his capital. These raids effectively shattered the balance of power in North India, allowing subsequent invaders to claim the territory for themselves.

Following Mahmud's death in 1033, Ghazni was seized by the Seljuqs and then fell to the Ghurs of western Afghanistan, who similarly had their eyes on the great Indian prize. The Ghur style of warfare was brutal: the Ghur general, Ala-ud-din, was known as 'Burner of the World'.

In 1191 Mohammed of Ghur advanced into India. Although defeated in a major battle against a confederacy of Hindu rulers, he returned the following year and routed his enemies. One of his generals, Qutb ud-din Aibak, captured Delhi and was appointed governor; it was during his reign that the great Delhi landmark, the Qutb Minar complex (p102), was built. A separate Islamic empire was established in Bengal and within a short time almost the whole of North India was under Muslim control.

4th to 9th Centuries	500–600	610
The Pallavas, known for their temple architecture, enter the shifting landscape of southern power centres, establishing dominance in Andhra Pradesh and northern Tamil Nadu from their base in Kanchipuram.	The emergence of the Rajputs in Rajasthan. Hailing from three principal races supposedly of celestial origin, they form 36 clans which spread across the region to secure their own kingdoms.	Prophet Mohammed establishes Islam. He soon invites the people of Mecca to adopt the new religion under the command of God, and his call is met with eager response.

» Hawa Mahal (p111), Jaipur

Following Mohammed's death in 1206, Qutb ud-din Aibak became the first sultan of Delhi. His successor, Iltutmish, brought Bengal back under central control and defended the empire from an attempted Mongol invasion. Ala-ud-din Khilji came to power in 1296 and pushed the borders of the empire inexorably south, while simultaneously fending off further attacks by the Mongols.

North Meets South

Ala-ud-din died in 1320, and Mohammed Tughlaq ascended the throne in 1324. In 1328 Tughlaq took the southern strongholds of the Hoysala empire, which had centres at Belur, Halebid and Somnathpur. India was Tughlaq's for the taking.

However, while the empire of the pre-Mughal Muslims would achieve its greatest extent under Tughlaq's rule, his overreaching ambition also sowed the seeds of its disintegration. Unlike his forebears (including great rulers such as Ashoka), Tughlaq dreamed not only of extending his indirect influence over South India, but of controlling it directly as part of his empire.

After a series of successful campaigns Tughlaq decided to move the capital from Delhi to a more central location. The new capital was called Daulatabad and was near Aurangabad in Maharashtra. Tughlaq sought to populate the new capital by forcefully marching the entire population of Delhi 1100km south, resulting in great loss of life. However, he soon realised that this left the north undefended and so the entire capital was moved north again. The superb hilltop fortress of Daulatabad (p768) stands as the last surviving monument to his megalomanic vision.

The days of the Ghur empire were numbered. The last of the great sultans of Delhi, Firoz Shah, died in 1388, and the fate of the sultanate was sealed when Timur (Tamerlane) made a devastating raid from Samarkand (in Central Asia) into India in 1398. Timur's sacking of Delhi was truly merciless; some accounts say his soldiers slaughtered every Hindu inhabitant.

After Tughlaq's withdrawal from the south, several splinter kingdoms arose. The two most significant were the Islamic Bahmani sultanate, which emerged in 1345 with its capital at Gulbarga, and later Bidar, and the Hindu Vijayanagar empire, founded in 1336 with its capital at Hampi. The battles between the two were among the bloodiest communal violence in Indian history and ultimately resolved nothing in the two centuries before the Mughals ushered in a more enlightened age.

The Mughals

Even as Vijayanagar was experiencing its last days, the next great Indian empire was being founded. The Mughal empire was massive, at its height covering almost the entire subcontinent. Its significance, however, lay not only in its size. Mughal emperors presided over a golden age of arts

In its 800-year history, the Qutb Minar has been damaged by two lightning strikes and one earthquake and has been repaired or built up by four sultans, one British major and one governor general.

A History of South India from Prehistoric Times to the Fall of Vijayanagar by KA Nilakanta Sastri is arguably the most comprehensive (if heavy-going) history of this region.

850	**1026**	**12th–19th Centuries**	**1192**
The Chola empire emerges anew in South India, establishing itself as a formidable economic and military presence in Asia under Rajaraja Chola I and his son Rajendra Chola I.	Mahmud of Ghazni raids India for the last time, ransacking on this occasion the Hindu Somnath Temple in Gujarat, where he purportedly smashes the temple's idol with his own hands.	Africans are brought to the Konkan Coast as part of trade with the Gulf; the slaves become servants, dock workers and soldiers and are known as Siddis or Habshis.	Prithviraj Chauhan loses Delhi to Mohammed of Ghori. The defeat effectively ends Hindu supremacy in the region, exposing the subcontinent to subsequent Muslim invaders marching in from the northwest.

and literature and had a passion for building that resulted in some of the finest architecture in India: Shah Jahan's sublime Taj Mahal (p350) ranks as one of the wonders of the world.

The founder of the Mughal line, Babur (r 1526–30), was a descendant of both Genghis Khan and Timur (Tamerlane). In 1525, armed with this formidable lineage, he marched into Punjab from his capital at Kabul. With technological superiority brought by firearms, and consummate skill in simultaneously employing artillery and cavalry, Babur defeated the numerically superior armies of the sultan of Delhi at the Battle of Panipat in 1526.

Despite this initial success, Babur's son, Humayun (r 1530–56) was defeated by a powerful ruler of eastern India, Sher Shah, in 1539 and forced to withdraw to Iran. Following Sher Shah's death in 1545, Huma-

THE STRUGGLE FOR THE SOUL OF INDIA

Founded as an alliance of Hindu kingdoms banding together to counter the threat from the Muslims, the Vijayanagar empire rapidly grew into one of India's wealthiest and greatest Hindu empires. Under the rule of Bukka I (c 1343–79), the majority of South India was brought under its control.

The Vijayanagars and the Bahmani sultanate, which was also based in South India, were evenly matched. The Vijayanagar armies occasionally got the upper hand, but generally the Bahmanis inflicted the worst defeats. The atrocities committed by both sides almost defy belief. In 1366 Bukka I responded to a perceived slight by capturing the Muslim stronghold of Mudkal and slaughtering every inhabitant bar one, who managed to escape and carry news of the attack to Mohammad Shah, the sultan. Mohammad swore that he would not rest until he had killed 100,000 Hindus. Instead, according to the Muslim historian Firishtah, 500,000 'infidels' were killed in the ensuing campaign.

Somehow, Vijayanagar survived. In 1484, following much intrigue and plotting in the royal court, the Bahmani sultanate began to disintegrate, and five separate kingdoms, based on the major cities – Berar, Ahmadnagar, Bidar, Bijapur and Golconda – were formed. Bijapur and Bidar still bear exceptional traces of this period of Islamic rule. With little realistic opposition from the north, the Hindu empire enjoyed a golden age of almost supreme power in the south. In 1520 the Vijayanagar king Krishnadevaraya even took Bijapur.

Like Bahmani, however, Vijayanagar's fault lines were soon laid bare. A series of uprisings divided the kingdom fatally, just at a time when the Muslim sultanates were beginning to form a new alliance. In 1565 a Muslim coalition routed the Hindu armies at the Battle of Talikota. Hampi was destroyed. Although the last of the Vijayanagar line escaped and the dynasty limped on for several years, real power passed to local Muslim rulers or Hindu chiefs once loyal to the Vijayanagar kings. One of India's grisliest periods came to an end when the Bahmani kingdoms fell to the Mughals.

1206	13th Century	1321	1336
Ghori is murdered during prayer while returning to Ghazni from Lahore. In the absence of an heir, his kingdom is usurped by his generals. The Delhi Sultanate is born.	The Pandyas, a Tamil dynasty dating to the 6th century BC, assumes control of Chola territory, expanding into Andhra Pradesh, Kalinga (Odisha [Orissa]) and Sri Lanka from their capital in Madurai.	The Tughlaqs come to power in Delhi. Mohammed bin Tughlaq expands his empire but becomes known for inelegant schemes: moving the capital to Daulatabad and creating forgery-prone currency.	Foundation of the mighty Vijayanagar empire, named after its capital city, the ruins of which can be seen today in the vicinity of Hampi (in Karnataka).

yun returned to claim his kingdom, eventually conquering Delhi in 1555. He died the following year and was succeeded by his young son Akbar (r 1556–1605) who, during his 49-year reign, managed to extend and consolidate the empire until he ruled over a mammoth area.

True to his name, Akbar (which means 'great' in Arabic) was probably the greatest of the Mughals: he not only had the military ability required of a ruler at that time, but was also a just and wise ruler and a man of culture. He saw, as previous Muslim rulers had not, that the number of Hindus in India was too great to subjugate. Although Akbar was no saint – reports of massacres of Hindus at Panipat and Chitrod tarnish his legacy – he remains known for integrating Hindus into his empire and skilfully using them as advisers, generals and administrators. Akbar also had a deep interest in religious matters, and spent many hours in discussion with religious experts of all persuasions, including Christians and Parsis.

Jehangir (r 1605–27) ascended to the throne following Akbar's death. Despite several challenges to the authority of Jehangir himself, the empire remained more or less intact. In periods of stability Jehangir spent time in his beloved Kashmir, eventually dying en route there in 1627. He was succeeded by his son, Shah Jahan (r 1627–58), who secured his position as emperor by executing all male relatives who stood in his way. During his reign, some of the most vivid and permanent reminders of the Mughals' glory were constructed; in addition to the Taj Mahal, he also oversaw the construction of the mighty Red Fort (Lal Qila) in Delhi (p62) and converted the Agra Fort (p352) into a palace that would later become his prison.

The last of the great Mughals, Aurangzeb (r 1658–1707), imprisoned his father (Shah Jahan) and succeeded to the throne after a two-year struggle against his brothers. Aurangzeb devoted his resources to extending the empire's boundaries, and thus fell into much the same trap as that of Mohammed Tughlaq some 300 years earlier. He, too, tried moving his capital south (to Aurangabad) and imposed heavy taxes to fund his military. A combination of decaying court life and dissatisfaction among the Hindu population at inflated taxes and religious intolerance weakened the Mughal grip.

The empire was also facing serious challenges from the Marathas in central India and, more significantly, the British in Bengal. With Aurangzeb's death in 1707, the empire's fortunes rapidly declined, and Delhi was sacked by Persia's Nadir Shah in 1739. Mughal 'emperors' continued to rule right up until the First War of Independence (Indian Uprising) in 1857, but they were emperors without an empire.

The Rajputs & the Marathas

Throughout the Mughal period, there remained strong Hindu powers, most notably the Rajputs. Centred in Rajasthan, the Rajputs were a proud warrior caste with a passionate belief in the dictates of chivalry,

Architecture of the Deccan Sultanates

» **Bijapur** Citadel, Golgumbaz, Ibrahim Rouza, Jama Masjid

» **Bidar** Fort, Bahmani Tombs

» **Hyderabad** Golconda Fort, Qutb Shahi Tombs, Charminar

White Mughals by William Dalrymple tells the true story of an East India Company soldier who married an Indian Muslim princess, a tragic love story interwoven with harem politics, intrigue and espionage.

1345	1398	1469	1484
Bahmani Sultanate is established in the Deccan following a revolt against the Tughlaqs of Delhi. The capital is set up at Gulbarga, in today's northern Karnataka, later shifting to Bidar.	Timur (Tamerlane) invades Delhi, on the pretext that the Delhi Sultans are too tolerant with their Hindu subjects. He executes tens of thousands of Hindus before the battle for Delhi.	Guru Nanak, founder of the Sikh faith, which has millions of followers within and beyond India to the present day, is born in a village near Lahore (in modern-day Pakistan).	Bahmani Sultanate begins to break up following independence movements; Berar is the first to revolt. By 1518, there are five Deccan sultanates: Berar, Ahmadnagar, Bidar, Bijapur and Golconda.

both in battle and state affairs. The Rajputs opposed every foreign incursion into their territory, but were never united or adequately organised to deal with stronger forces on a long-term basis. When they weren't battling foreign oppression, they squandered their energies fighting each other. This eventually led to their territories becoming vassal states of the Mughal empire. Their prowess in battle, however, was acknowledged, and some of the best military men in the Mughal armies were Rajputs.

The Marathas were less picaresque but ultimately more effective. They first rose to prominence under their great leader Shivaji, also known as Chhatrapati Shivaji, who gathered popular support by championing the Hindu cause against the Muslim rulers. Between 1646 and 1680 Shivaji performed heroic acts in confronting the Mughals across most of central India. Shivaji was captured by the Mughals and taken to Agra but, naturally, he managed to escape and continue his adventures. Tales of his larger-than-life exploits are still popular with wandering storytellers. He is a particular hero in Maharashtra, where many of his wildest adventures took place. (Today, you'll see Shivaji's name all over Mumbai.) He's also revered for the fact that, as a lower-caste Shudra, he showed that great leaders don't have to be of the Kshatriya (soldier) caste.

Shivaji's son was captured, blinded and executed by Aurangzeb. His grandson wasn't made of the same sturdy stuff, so the Maratha empire continued under the Peshwas, hereditary government ministers who became the real rulers. They gradually took over more of the weakening Mughal empire's powers, first by supplying troops and then actually taking control of Mughal land.

The expansion of Maratha power came to an abrupt halt in 1761 at Panipat. In the town where Babur had won the battle that established the Mughal empire more than 200 years earlier, the Marathas were defeated by Ahmad Shah Durrani from Afghanistan. Maratha expansion to the west was halted, and although they consolidated their control over central India and the region known as Malwa, they were to fall to India's final imperial power – the British.

The Rise of European Power

The British weren't the first European power to arrive in India, nor were they the last to leave – both of those 'honours' go to the Portuguese. In 1498 Vasco da Gama arrived on the coast of modern-day Kerala, having sailed around the Cape of Good Hope. Pioneering this route gave the Portuguese a century-long monopoly over Indian and far-Eastern trade with Europe. In 1510 they captured Goa, followed by Diu in 1531, two enclaves the Portuguese controlled until 1961. In its heyday, the trade flowing through 'Golden Goa' was said to rival that passing through Lisbon. In the long term, however, the Portuguese didn't have the resources

Persian was the official language of several empires, from Mahmud of Ghazni to the Delhi Sultanate to the Mughals. Urdu, which combines Persian, Arabic and indigenous languages, evolved over hundreds of years and came into its own during Mughal reign.

Amar Chitra Katha, a hugely popular publisher of comic books about Indian folklore, mythology and history, has several books about Shivaji, including *Shivaji – The Great Maratha*, *Tales of Shivaji* and *Tanaji, the Maratha Lion*, about Shivaji's close friend and fellow warrior.

1498	**1510**	**1526**	**1540**
Vasco da Gama discovers the sea route from Europe to India. He arrives in Kerala and engages in trade with the local nobility.	Portuguese forces capture Goa under the command of Alfonso de Albuquerque, whose initial attempt was thwarted by then-ruler, Sultan Adil Shah of Bijapur. He succeeds following Shah's death.	Babur becomes the first Mughal emperor after conquering Delhi. He stuns Rajasthan by routing its confederate force, gaining an edge with the introduction of matchlock muskets in his army.	The Sur dynasty briefly captures Delhi from the Mughals, after Sher Shah Suri's Battle of Kanauj victory over Humayun. The Mughals are forced to seek help from the Rajputs.

to maintain a worldwide empire and they were quickly eclipsed and isolated after the arrival of the British and French.

In 1600 Queen Elizabeth I granted a charter to a London trading company that gave it a monopoly on British trade with India. In 1613 representatives of the East India Company established their first trading post at Surat in Gujarat. Further British trading posts, administered and governed by representatives of the company, were established at Madras (Chennai) in 1639, Bombay (Mumbai) in 1661 and Calcutta (Kolkata) in 1690. Strange as it now seems, for nearly 250 years a commercial trading company and not the British government 'ruled' over British India.

By 1672 the French had established themselves at Pondicherry (Puducherry), an enclave they held even after the British departed and where architectural traces of French elegance remain. The stage was set for more than a century of rivalry between the British and French for control of Indian trade. At one stage, under the guidance of a handful of talented and experienced commanders, the French appeared to hold the upper hand. In 1746 they took Madras (only to hand it back in 1749), and their success in placing their favoured heir to the throne as Nizam of Hyderabad augured well for the future. But serious French aspirations effectively ended in 1750 when the directors of the French East India Company decided that their representatives were playing too much politics and doing too little trading. Key representatives were sacked, and a settlement designed to end all ongoing political disputes was made with the British. The decision effectively removed France as a serious influence on the subcontinent.

The nizams of Hyderabad ruled over this vast central-Indian state from 1720 until Independence – first under the Mughals and then on their own – and were known for their wealth; their fondness for architecture, poetry and precious gems; and, at Independence, their determination to remain independent.

HISTORY THE RISE OF EUROPEAN POWER

ENTER THE PORTUGUESE

Just a few years after they arrived, the Portuguese were well on their way to establishing a firm foothold in Goa. On 20 May 1498 Vasco da Gama dropped anchor off the South Indian coast near the town of Calicut (now Kozhikode). It had taken him 23 days to sail from the east coast of Africa, guided by a pilot named Ibn Masjid, sent by the ruler of Malindi in Gujarat.

The Portuguese sought a sea route between Europe and the East so they could trade directly in spices. They also hoped they might find Christians cut off from Europe by the Muslim dominance of the Middle East, while at the same time searching for the legendary kingdom of Prester John, a powerful Christian ruler with whom they could unite against the Middle Eastern rulers. In India they found spices and the Syrian Orthodox community, but not Prester John.

Vasco da Gama sought an audience with the ruler of Calicut, to explain himself, and seems to have been well received. The Portuguese engaged in a limited amount of trading, but became increasingly suspicious that Muslim traders were turning the ruler of Calicut against them. They resolved to leave Calicut, which they did in August 1498.

1542–45	**1556**	**1560–1812**	**1600**
St Francis Xavier's first mission to India. He preaches Catholicism in Goa, Tamil Nadu and Sri Lanka, returning in 1548–49 and 1552 in between travels in the Far East.	Hemu, a Hindu general in Adil Shah Suri's army, seizes Delhi after Humayun's death. He rules for barely a month before losing to Akbar in the Second Battle of Panipat.	Portuguese Inquisition in Goa. Trials focus on converted Hindus and Muslims thought to have 'relapsed'. Thousands were tried and several dozen were likely executed before it was abolished in 1812.	Britain's Queen Elizabeth I grants the first trading charter to the East India Company, with the maiden voyage taking place in 1601 under the command of Sir James Lancaster.

Britain's Surge to Power

The transformation of the British from traders to governors began almost by accident. Having been granted a licence to trade in Bengal by the Mughals, and following the establishment of a new trading post at Calcutta (Kolkata) in 1690, business began to expand rapidly. Under the apprehensive gaze of the nawab (local ruler), British trading activities became extensive and the 'factories' took on an increasingly permanent (and fortified) appearance.

Eventually the nawab decided that British power had grown large enough. In June 1756 he attacked Calcutta and, having taken the city, locked his British prisoners in a tiny cell. The space was so cramped and airless that many were dead by the following morning. The cell infamously became known as the 'Black Hole of Calcutta'.

Six months later, Robert Clive, an employee in the military service of the East India Company, led an expedition to retake Calcutta and entered into an agreement with one of the nawab's generals to overthrow the nawab himself. He did this in June 1757 at the Battle of Plassey (now called Palashi), and the general who had assisted him was placed on the throne. With the British effectively in control of Bengal, the company's agents engaged in a period of unbridled profiteering. When a subsequent nawab finally took up arms to protect his own interests, he was defeated at the Battle of Baksar in 1764, a victory that confirmed the British as the paramount power in east India.

In 1771 Warren Hastings was made governor in Bengal. During his tenure the company greatly expanded its control. His astute statesmanship was aided by the fact that India at this time was experiencing a power vacuum created by the disintegration of the Mughal empire. The Marathas, the only real Indian power to step into this gap, were divided among themselves. Hastings concluded a series of treaties with local rulers, including one with the main Maratha leader. From 1784 onwards, the British government in London began to take a more direct role in supervising affairs in India, although the territory was still notionally administered by the East India Company until 1858.

In the south, where Mughal influence had never been great, the picture was confused by the strong British–French rivalry, and one ruler was played off against another. This was never clearer than in the series of Mysore wars in which Hyder Ali and his son, Tipu Sultan, waged a brave and determined campaign against the British. In the Fourth Mysore War (1789–99), Tipu Sultan was killed at Srirangapatnam and British power took another step forward. The long-running struggle with the Marathas was concluded in 1803, leaving only Punjab (held by the Sikhs) outside British control. Punjab finally fell in 1849 after the two Sikh Wars (1845–46 and 1848–49).

Colonial-era Architecture

» Colaba and Kala Ghoda, Mumbai (British)

» BBD Bagh and environs, Kolkata (British)

» Old Goa and Panjim, Goa (Portuguese)

» Puducherry, Tamil Nadu (French)

1631

Construction of the Taj Mahal begins after Shah Jahan, overcome with grief following the death of his wife Mumtaz Mahal, vows to build the most beautiful mausoleum in the world.

JOHN SONES / LONELY PLANET IMAGES ©

» Taj Mahal (p350), Agra

1672

The French East India Company establishes an outpost at Pondicherry (Puducherry), which the French, Dutch and British fight over repeatedly in the coming century.

1674

Shivaji establishes the Maratha kingdom, spanning western India and parts of the Deccan and North India. He assumes the imperial title of Chhatrapati, which means 'Great Protector'.

British India

By the early 19th century, India was effectively under British control, although there remained a patchwork of states, many nominally independent and governed by their own rulers, the maharajas (or similarly titled princes) and nawabs. While these 'princely states' administered their own territories, a system of central government was developed. British bureaucratic models were replicated in the Indian government and civil service – a legacy that still exists.

Trade and profit continued to be the main focus of British rule in India, with far-reaching effects. Iron and coal mining were developed, and tea, coffee and cotton became key crops. A start was made on the vast rail network that's still in use today, irrigation projects were undertaken, and the zamindar (landowner) system was encouraged. These absentee landlords eased the burden of administration and tax collection for the British but contributed to the development of an impoverished and landless peasantry.

The British also imposed English as the local language of administration. For them, this was critical in a country with so many different languages, but it also kept the new rulers at arm's length from the Indian populace.

Plain Tales from the Raj by Charles Allen (ed) is a fascinating series of interviews with people who played a role in British India on both sides of the table.

The Road to Independence

The desire among many Indians to be free from foreign rule remained. Opposition to the British increased at the turn of the 20th century, spearheaded by the Indian National Congress, the country's oldest political party, also known as the Congress Party and Congress (I).

It met for the first time in 1885 and soon began to push for participation in the government of India. A highly unpopular attempt by the British to partition Bengal in 1905 resulted in mass demonstrations and brought to light Hindu opposition to the division; the Muslim community formed its own league and campaigned for protected rights in any future political settlement. As pressure rose, a split emerged in Hindu circles between moderates and radicals, the latter resorting to violence to publicise their aims.

With the outbreak of WWI, the political situation eased. India contributed hugely to the war (more than one million Indian volunteers were enlisted and sent overseas, suffering more than 100,000 casualties). The contribution was sanctioned by Congress leaders, largely with the expectation that it would be rewarded after the war. No such rewards transpired and disillusion followed. Disturbances were particularly persistent in Punjab, and in April 1919, following riots in Amritsar, a British army contingent was sent to quell the unrest. Under direct orders of the officer in charge, they ruthlessly fired into a crowd of unarmed protesters (see the boxed text on p216). News of the massacre spread rapidly throughout

In 1909, the so-called Morley-Minto Reforms provided for limited Indian participation in government and introduced separate electorates for the country's different religious communities.

1707	1739	1747	1757
Death of Aurangzeb, the last of the Mughal greats. His demise triggers the gradual collapse of the Mughal empire, as anarchy and rebellion erupt across the country.	Nadir Shah plunders Delhi and carries away the jewel-encrusted Peacock Throne as well as the Koh-i-noor diamond, which changes many hands to eventually become property of the British royalty.	Afghan ruler Ahmad Shah Durrani sweeps across northern India, capturing Lahore and Kashmir, sacking Delhi and dealing another blow to the rapidly contracting Mughal empire.	The East India Company registers its first military victory on Indian soil. Siraj-ud-Daulah, nawab of Bengal, is defeated by Robert Clive in the Battle of Plassey.

India, turning huge numbers of otherwise apolitical Indians into Congress supporters.

At this time, the Congress movement found a new leader in Mohandas Gandhi. Not everyone involved in the struggle agreed with or followed Gandhi's policy of nonviolence, yet the Congress Party and Gandhi remained at the forefront of the push for independence.

As political power-sharing began to look more likely, and the mass movement led by Gandhi gained momentum, the Muslim reaction was to consider its own immediate future. The large Muslim minority realised that an independent India would be dominated by Hindus and that, while Gandhi's approach was fair-minded, others in the Congress Party might not be so willing to share power. By the 1930s Muslims were raising the possibility of a separate Islamic state.

Political events were partially disrupted by WWII when large numbers of Congress supporters were jailed to prevent disruption to the war effort.

India's Struggle for Independence by Bipan Chandra expertly chronicles the history of India from 1857 to 1947.

Mahatma Gandhi

One of the great figures of the 20th century, Mohandas Karamchand Gandhi was born on 2 October 1869 in Porbandar, Gujarat. After studying in London (1888–91), he worked as a barrister in South Africa. Here, the young Gandhi became politicised, railing against the discrimination he encountered. He soon became the spokesperson for the Indian community and championed equality for all.

Gandhi returned to India in 1915 with the doctrine of ahimsa (nonviolence) central to his political plans, and committed to a simple and disciplined lifestyle. He set up the Sabarmati Ashram in Ahmedabad, which was innovative for its admission of Untouchables.

Within a year, Gandhi had won his first victory, defending farmers in Bihar from exploitation. This was when it's said he first received the title 'Mahatma' (Great Soul) from an admirer (often said to be Bengali poet Rabindranath Tagore). The passage of the discriminatory Rowlatt Acts (which allowed certain political cases to be tried without juries) in 1919 spurred him to further action, and he organised a national protest. In the days that followed this hartal (strike), feelings ran high throughout the country. After the massacre of unarmed protesters in Amritsar (p216), a deeply shocked Gandhi immediately called off the movement.

By 1920 Gandhi was a key figure in the Indian National Congress, and he coordinated a national campaign of noncooperation or satyagraha (nonviolent protest) to British rule, with the effect of raising nationalist feeling while earning the lasting enmity of the British. In early 1930, Gandhi captured the imagination of the country, and the world, when he led a march of several thousand followers from Ahmedabad to Dandi on the coast of Gujarat. On arrival, Gandhi ceremoniously made salt by

Gandhian Sites

» Raj Ghat, Delhi
» Gandhi Smriti, Delhi
» Anand Bhavan, Allahabad
» Sabarmati Ashram, Ahmedabad
» Kaba Gandhi No Delo, Rajkot
» Mani Bhavan, Mumbai
» Gandhi National Memorial, Pune

1801	1835–1858	1857	1858
Ranjit Singh becomes maharaja (Great King) of the newly united Sikhs and forges a powerful new kingdom from his capital in Lahore (in present-day Pakistan).	Life of Lakshmi Bai, Rani of Jhansi. The queen of the Maratha state led her army against the British, who seized Jhansi after her husband's death. She died in battle.	The First War of Independence (Indian Uprising) against the British. In the absence of a national leader, freedom fighters coerce the Mughal king, Bahadur Shah Zafar, to proclaim himself emperor of India.	British government assumes control over India – with power officially transferred from the East India Company to the Crown – this begins the period known as the British Raj.

evaporating sea water, thus publicly defying the much-hated salt tax; not for the first time, he was imprisoned. Released in 1931 to represent the Indian National Congress at the second Round Table Conference in London, he won the hearts of many British people but failed to gain any real concessions from the government.

Disillusioned with politics, he resigned his parliamentary seat in 1934. He returned spectacularly to the fray in 1942 with the Quit India campaign, in which he urged the British to leave India immediately. His actions were deemed subversive, and he and most of the Congress leadership were imprisoned.

In the frantic Independence bargaining that followed the end of WWII, Gandhi was largely excluded and watched helplessly as plans were made to partition the country – a dire tragedy in his eyes. Gandhi stood almost alone in urging tolerance and the preservation of a single

THE FIRST WAR OF INDEPENDENCE: THE INDIAN UPRISING

In 1857, half a century after having established firm control of India, the British suffered a serious setback. To this day, the causes of the Indian Uprising (known at the time as the Indian Mutiny and subsequently labelled by nationalist historians as a War of Independence) are the subject of debate. The key factors included the influx of cheap goods, such as textiles, from Britain that destroyed many livelihoods; the dispossession of territories from many rulers; and taxes imposed on landowners.

The incident that's popularly held to have sparked the Indian Uprising, however, took place at an army barracks in Meerut in Uttar Pradesh on 10 May 1857. A rumour leaked out that a new type of bullet was greased with what Hindus claimed was cow fat, while Muslims maintained that it came from pigs; pigs are considered unclean to Muslims, and cows are sacred to Hindus. Since loading a rifle involved biting the end off the waxed cartridge, these rumours provoked considerable unrest.

In Meerut, the situation was handled with a singular lack of judgment. The commanding officer lined up his soldiers and ordered them to bite off the ends of their issued bullets. Those who refused were immediately marched off to prison. The following morning, the soldiers of the garrison rebelled, shot their officers and marched to Delhi. Of the 74 Indian battalions of the Bengal army, seven (one of them Gurkhas) remained loyal, 20 were disarmed and the other 47 mutinied. The soldiers and peasants rallied around the ageing Mughal emperor in Delhi. They held Delhi for some months and besieged the British residency in Lucknow for five months before they were finally suppressed. The incident left festering scars on both sides.

Almost immediately the East India Company was wound up and direct control of the country was assumed by the British government, which announced its support for the existing rulers of the princely states, claiming they would not interfere in local matters as long as the states remained loyal to the British.

1869

The birth of Mohandas Karamchand Gandhi in Porbandar (Gujarat) – the man who would later become popularly known as Mahatma Gandhi and affectionately dubbed 'Father of the Nation'.

» Gandhi statue, Mumbai

1869

Opening of Suez Canal accelerates trade from Europe and makes Bombay (Mumbai) India's first port of call; trip from England goes from three months to three weeks.

1885

The Indian National Congress, India's first home-grown political organisation, is set up. It brings educated Indians together and plays a key role in India's enduring freedom struggle.

India, and his work on behalf of members of all communities drew resentment from some Hindu hardliners. On his way to a prayer meeting in Delhi on 30 January 1948, he was assassinated by a Hindu zealot, Nathuram Godse. There's a memorial at the spot where he was shot, known as Gandhi Smriti (p73).

A golden oldie, *Gandhi*, directed by Richard Attenborough, is one of the few movies that adeptly captures the grand canvas that is India in tracing the country's rocky road to Independence.

Independence & the Partition of India

The Labour Party victory in the British elections in July 1945 dramatically altered the political landscape. For the first time, Indian independence was accepted as a legitimate goal. This new goodwill did not, however, translate into any new wisdom as to how to reconcile the divergent wishes of the two major Indian parties. Mohammed Ali Jinnah, the leader of the Muslim League, championed a separate Islamic state, while the Congress Party, led by Jawaharlal Nehru, campaigned for an independent greater India.

In early 1946 a British mission failed to bring the two sides together, and the country slid closer towards civil war. A 'Direct Action Day', called by the Muslim League in August 1946, led to the slaughter of Hindus in Calcutta, which prompted reprisals against Muslims. In February 1947 the nervous British government made the momentous decision that Independence would come by June 1948. In the meantime, the viceroy, Lord Archibald Wavell, was replaced by Lord Louis Mountbatten.

The new viceroy encouraged the rival factions to agree upon a united India, but to no avail. A decision was made to divide the country, with Gandhi the only staunch opponent. Faced with increasing civil violence, Mountbatten made the precipitous decision to bring forward Independence to 15 August 1947.

A Princess Remembers by Gayatri Devi and Santha Rama Rau is the captivating memoir of the former maharani of Jaipur, the glamorous Gayatri Devi (1919–2009).

Dividing the country into separate Hindu and Muslim territories was immensely tricky; the dividing line proved almost impossible to draw. Some areas were clearly Hindu or Muslim, but others had evenly mixed populations, and there were 'islands' of communities in areas predominantly settled by other religions. Moreover, the two overwhelmingly Muslim regions were on opposite sides of the country and, therefore, Pakistan would inevitably have an eastern and western half divided by a hostile India. The instability of this arrangement was self-evident, but it was 25 years before the split finally came and East Pakistan became Bangladesh.

An independent British referee was given the odious task of drawing the borders, well aware that the effects would be catastrophic for countless people. The decisions were fraught with impossible dilemmas. Calcutta, with its Hindu majority, port facilities and jute mills, was divided from East Bengal, which had a Muslim majority, large-scale jute production, no mills and no port facilities. One million Bengalis became refugees in the mass movement across the new border.

1911	1919	1930	1940
British architect Edwin Lutyens begins work on New Delhi, the newest manifestation of Delhi, subsequently considered in architectural circles as one of the finest garden cities ever built.	The massacre, on 13 April, of unarmed Indian protesters at Jallianwala Bagh in Amritsar (Punjab). Gandhi responds with his program of civil (nonviolent) disobedience against the British government.	Beginning of Salt Satyagraha on 12 March. Gandhi embarks on a 24-day walk from his Sabarmati Ashram near Ahmedabad to the coastal village of Dandi to protest the British salt tax.	The Muslim League adopts its Lahore Resolution, which champions greater Muslim autonomy in India. Campaigns for the creation of a separate Islamic nation are spearheaded by Mohammed Ali Jinnah.

The problem was worse in Punjab, where intercommunity antagonisms were already running at fever pitch. Punjab, one of the most fertile and affluent regions of the country, had large Muslim, Hindu and Sikh communities. The Sikhs had already campaigned unsuccessfully for their own state and now saw their homeland divided down the middle. The new border ran straight between Punjab's two major cities, Lahore and Amritsar. Prior to Independence, Lahore's population of 1.2 million included approximately 500,000 Hindus and 100,000 Sikhs. When the dust had finally settled, roughly 1000 Hindus and Sikhs remained.

Punjab contained all the ingredients for an epic disaster, but the resulting bloodshed was far worse than anticipated. Huge population exchanges took place. Trains full of Muslims, fleeing westward, were held up and slaughtered by Hindu and Sikh mobs. Hindus and Sikhs fleeing to the east suffered the same fate at Muslim hands. The army that was sent to maintain order proved totally inadequate and, at times, all too ready to join the sectarian carnage. By the time the Punjab chaos had run

The Proudest Day – India's Long Road to Independence by Anthony Read and David Fisher is an engaging account of India's pre-Independence period.

THE KASHMIR CONFLICT

Kashmir is the most enduring symbol of the turbulent partition of India. In the lead up to Independence, the delicate task of drawing the India–Pakistan border was complicated by the fact that India's 'princely states' were nominally independent. As part of the settlement process, local rulers were asked which country they wished to belong to. Kashmir was a predominantly Muslim state with a Hindu maharaja, Hari Singh, who tried to delay his decision. A ragtag Pashtun (Pakistani) army crossed the border, intent on racing to Srinagar and annexing Kashmir for Pakistan. In the face of this advance, the maharaja panicked and requested armed assistance from India. The Indian army arrived only just in time to prevent the fall of Srinagar, and the maharaja signed the Instrument of Accession, tying Kashmir to India, in October 1947. The legality of the document was immediately disputed by Pakistan, and the two nations went to war, just two months after Independence.

In 1948 the fledgling UN Security Council called for a referendum (which remains a central plank of Pakistani policy) to decide the status of Kashmir. A UN-brokered ceasefire in 1949 kept the countries on either side of a demarcation line, called the Cease-Fire Line (later to become the Line of Control, or LOC; see p1080), with little else resolved. Two-thirds of Kashmir fell on the Indian side of the LOC, which remains the frontier, but neither side accepts this as the official border. The Indian state of Jammu & Kashmir, as it has stood since that time, incorporates Ladakh (divided between Muslims and Buddhists), Jammu (with a Hindu majority) and the 130km-long, 55km-wide Kashmir Valley (with a Muslim majority and most of the state's inhabitants). On the Pakistani side, over three million Kashmiris live in Azad (Free) Kashmir. Since the frontier was drawn, incursions across the LOC have occurred with dangerous regularity.

1942	1947	1947–48	1948
Mahatma Gandhi launches the Quit India campaign, demanding that the British leave India without delay and allow the country to get on with the business of self-governance.	India gains independence on 15 August. Pakistan is formed a day earlier. Partition is followed by mass cross-border exodus, as Hindus and Muslims migrate to their respective nations.	First war between India and Pakistan takes place after the (procrastinating) maharaja of Kashmir signs the Instrument of Accession that cedes his state to India. Pakistan challenges the document's legality.	Mahatma Gandhi is assassinated in New Delhi by Nathuram Godse on 30 January. Godse and his co-conspirator, Narayan Apte, are later tried, convicted and executed (by hanging).

Deepa Mehta's 1998 film *Earth* is a dramatic retelling of the violence of Partition through the eyes of a young girl in Lahore.

its course, more than 10 million people had changed sides and at least 500,000 had been killed.

India and Pakistan became sovereign nations under the British Commonwealth in August 1947 as planned, but the violence, migrations and the integration of a few states, especially Kashmir, continued. The Constitution of India was at last adopted in November 1949 and went into effect on 26 January, 1950, and, after untold struggles, independent India officially became a Republic.

1948	1948–56	1949	1950
Asaf Jah VII, the last nizam of Hyderabad, surrenders to the Indian government on 17 September. The Muslim dynasty was receiving support from Pakistan but had refused to join either new nation.	Rajasthan takes shape, as the princely states form a beeline to sign the Instrument of Accession, giving up their territories which are incorporated into the newly formed Republic of India.	The Constitution of India, drafted over two years by a 308-member Constituent Assembly, is adopted. The Assembly is chaired by BR Ambedkar and includes members from scheduled castes.	Constitution goes into effect on 26 January, and India becomes a republic. Date commemorates the Declaration of Independence, put forth by the Indian National Congress in 1930.

The Way of Life

For travellers, one of the most enduring impressions of India is the way everyday life is intimately intertwined with the sacred: from the housewife who devoutly performs *puja* (prayers) at home each morning, to the shopkeeper who – regardless of how many eager-to-buy tourists may be in the store – rarely commences business until blessings have been sought from the gods.

Along with religion, family lies at the heart of Indian society. For the vast majority, the idea of being unmarried and without children by one's mid-30s is unthinkable. Despite the rising number of nuclear families – primarily in larger cities such as Mumbai (Bombay), Bengaluru (Bangalore) and Delhi – the extended family remains a cornerstone in both urban and rural India, with males – usually the breadwinners – generally considered the head of the household.

With religion and family deemed so sacrosanct, don't be surprised or miffed if you are grilled about these subjects yourself, especially beyond the larger cities, and receive curious (possibly disapproving) gawps if you don't 'fit the mould'. The first question travellers are usually asked is their country of origin. This may be followed by a string of queries on topics that might be considered somewhat inappropriate elsewhere, especially coming from a complete stranger. Apart from religion and marital status, frequently asked questions include age, qualifications, profession (possibly even income) and your impressions of India. This is generally innocuous probing, not intended to offend.

National pride has long existed on the subcontinent but has swelled in recent years as India attracts ever-increasing international kudos in various fields including information technology (IT), science, medicine, literature, film and, of course, cricket. In the sporting arena, although there are rising stars on the tennis front, it is cricket that by far reigns supreme, with top players afforded superhero status.

The country's robust economy – one of the world's fastest growing – is another source of prolific national pride. Also widely embraced as potent symbols of Indian honour and sovereignty are the advancements in nuclear and space technology – in 2008 India joined the elite global lunar club with its maiden unmanned mission to the moon.

India has one of the world's largest diasporas – over 26 million people – with Indian banks holding an estimated US$55 billion in Non-Resident Indian (NRI) accounts.

RANGOLIS

Rangolis, the striking and breathtakingly intricate chalk, rice-paste or coloured powder designs (also called *kolams)* that adorn thresholds, especially in South India, are both auspicious and symbolic. *Rangolis* are traditionally drawn at sunrise and are sometimes made of rice-flour paste, which may be eaten by little creatures – symbolising a reverence for even the smallest living things. Deities are deemed to be attracted to a beautiful *rangoli,* which may also signal to sadhus (ascetics) that they will be offered food at a particular house. Some people believe that *rangolis* protect against the evil eye.

Marriage, Birth & Death

Marriage is an exceptionally auspicious event for Indians and although 'love marriages' have spiralled upwards in recent times (mainly in urban hubs), most Hindu marriages are arranged. Discreet enquiries are made within the community. If a suitable match is not found, the help of professional matchmakers may be sought, or advertisements may be placed in newspapers and/or on the internet. The horoscopes are checked and, if propitious, there's a meeting between the two families. The legal age for marriage in India is 18.

Dowry, although illegal, is still a key issue in many arranged marriages (primarily in the more conservative communities), with some families plunging into debt to raise the required cash and merchandise (from cars and computers to washing machines and televisions). Health workers claim that India's high rate of abortion of female foetuses (despite sex identification medical tests being banned in India, they still clandestinely occur in some clinics) is predominantly due to the financial burden of providing a daughter's dowry.

The Hindu wedding ceremony is officiated over by a priest and the marriage is formalised when the couple walk around a sacred fire seven times. Despite the existence of nuclear families, it's still the norm for a wife to live with her husband's family once married and assume the household duties outlined by her mother-in-law. Not surprisingly, the mother–daughter-in-law relationship can be a prickly one, as portrayed in the various Indian TV soap operas which largely revolve around this theme.

Divorce and remarriage is becoming more common (primarily in India's bigger cities), but divorce is still not granted by courts as a matter of routine and is generally not looked upon favourably by society. Among the higher castes, widows are traditionally expected not to remarry and are admonished to wear white and live pious, celibate lives.

The birth of a child is another momentous occasion, with its own set of special ceremonies, which take place at various auspicious times during the early years of childhood. These include the casting of the child's first horoscope, name-giving, feeding the first solid food, and the first hair cutting.

Hindus cremate their dead, and funeral ceremonies are designed to purify and console both the living and the deceased. An important aspect of the proceedings is the *sharadda,* paying respect to one's ancestors by offering water and rice cakes. It's an observance that's repeated at each anniversary of the death. After the cremation the ashes are collected and, 13 days after the death (when blood relatives are deemed ritually pure), a member of the family usually scatters them in a holy river such as the Ganges or in the ocean.

MATCHMAKING

Matchmaking has embraced the cyber age, with popular sites including www .shaadi.com, www.bharat matrimony. com and, more recently, www. secondshaadi. com – for those seeking a partner again.

INDIAN ATTIRE

Widely worn by Indian women, the elegant sari comes in a single piece (between 5m and 9m long and 1m wide) and is ingeniously tucked and pleated into place without the need for pins or buttons. Worn with the sari is the choli (tight-fitting blouse) and a drawstring petticoat. The *palloo* is the part of the sari draped over the shoulder. Also commonly worn is the *salwar kameez,* a traditional dresslike tunic and trouser combination accompanied by a *dupatta* (long scarf). Saris and *salwar kameez* come in an appealing range of fabrics, designs and prices.

Traditional attire for men includes the dhoti, and in the south the lungi and the *mundu* are also commonly worn. The dhoti is a loose, long loincloth pulled up between the legs. The lungi is more like a sarong, with its end usually sewn up like a tube. The *mundu* is like a lungi but is always white.

There are regional and religious variations in costume – for example, you may see Muslim women wearing the all-enveloping burka.

The Caste System

Although the Indian constitution does not recognise the caste system, caste still wields considerable influence, especially in rural India, where the caste you are born into largely determines your social standing in the community. It can also influence your vocational and marriage prospects. Castes are further divided into thousands of *jati,* groups of 'families' or social communities, which are sometimes but not always linked to occupation. Conservative Hindus will only marry someone of the same *jati.*

According to tradition, caste is the basic social structure of Hindu society. Living a righteous life and fulfilling your dharma (moral duty) raises your chances of being reborn into a higher caste and thus into better circumstances. Hindus are born into one of four varnas (castes): Brahmin (priests and scholars), Kshatriya (soldiers and administrators), Vaishya (merchants) and Shudra (labourers). The Brahmins were said to have emerged from the mouth of Lord Brahma at the moment of creation, Kshatriyas were said to have come from his arms, Vaishyas from his thighs and Shudras from his feet.

Beneath the four main castes are the Dalits (formerly known as Untouchables), who hold menial jobs such as sweepers and latrine cleaners. The word 'pariah' is derived from the name of a Tamil Dalit group, the Paraiyars. Some Dalit leaders, such as the renowned Dr BR Ambedkar (1891–1956), sought to change their status by adopting another faith; in his case it was Buddhism. At the bottom of the social heap are the Denotified Tribes. They were known as the Criminal Tribes until 1952, when a reforming law officially recognised 198 tribes and castes. Many are nomadic or seminomadic tribes, forced by the wider community to eke out a living on society's fringes.

To improve the Dalits' position, the government reserves considerable numbers of public-sector jobs, parliamentary seats and university places for them. Today these quotas account for almost 25% of government jobs and university (student) positions. The situation varies regionally, as different political leaders chase caste vote-banks by promising to include them in reservations. The reservation system, while generally regarded in a favourable light, has also been criticised for unfairly blocking tertiary and employment opportunities for those who would have otherwise got positions on merit.

Pilgrimage

Devout Hindus are expected to go on a *yatra* (pilgrimage) at least once a year. Pilgrimages are undertaken to implore the gods or goddesses to grant a wish, to take the ashes of a cremated relative to a holy river, or to gain spiritual merit. India has thousands of holy sites to which pilgrims travel; the elderly often make Varanasi their final one, as it's believed that dying in this sacred city releases a person from the cycle of rebirth.

Most festivals in India are rooted in religion and are thus a magnet for pilgrims. This is something that travellers should keep in mind, even at those festivals that may have a carnivalesque sheen.

Kumbh Mela

If crowds worry you, stay away. This one's big. Very big. Held four times every 12 years at four different locations across central and northern India, the Kumbh Mela is the largest religious congregation on the planet. This vast celebration attracts tens of millions of Hindu pilgrims, including mendicant *nagas* (naked sadhus, or holy men) from radical Hindu monastic orders. The Kumbh Mela doesn't belong to any particular caste or creed – devotees from all branches of Hinduism come together to experience the electrifying sensation of mass belief and to take a ceremonial dip in the sacred Ganges, Shipra or Godavari Rivers.

THE WAY OF LIFE

Sati: A Study of Widow Burning in India by Sakuntala Narasimhan explores the history of *sati* (a widow's suicide on her husband's funeral pyre; now banned) on the subcontinent.

If you're keen to learn more about India's caste system these two books are a good start: *Interrogating Caste* by Dipankar Gupta and *Translating Caste* edited by Tapan Basu.

Read more about India's tribal communities at www.tribal.nic.in, a site maintained by the Indian government's Ministry of Tribal Affairs.

CIVILISATIONS

The origins of the festival go back to the battle for supremacy between good and evil. In the Hindu creation myths, the gods and demons fought a great battle for a *kumbh* (pitcher) containing the nectar of immortality. Vishnu got hold of the container and spirited it away, but in flight four drops spilt on the earth – at Allahabad, Haridwar, Nasik and Ujjain. Celebrations at each of these cities last for around six weeks but are centred on just a handful of auspicious bathing dates, normally six. The Allahabad event, known as the Maha (Great) Kumbh Mela, is even larger with even bigger crowds. Each location also holds an Ardh (Half) Mela every six years and a smaller, annual Magh Mela.

Women in India

Women in India are entitled to vote and own property. While the percentage of women in politics has risen over the past decade, they're still notably underrepresented in the national parliament, accounting for around 10% of parliamentary members.

Although the professions are male dominated, women are steadily making inroads, especially in urban centres. Kerala was India's first state to break societal norms by recruiting female police officers in 1938. It was also the first state to establish an all-female police station (1973). For village women it's much more difficult to get ahead, but groups such as the Self-Employed Women's Association (SEWA; p680) in Gujarat have shown what's possible. Here, socially disadvantaged women have been organised into unions, offering at least some lobbying power against discriminatory and exploitative work practices.

The Wonder That Was India by AL Basham proffers descriptions of Indian civilisations, major religions and social customs – a good thematic approach to weave the disparate strands together.

In low-income families, especially, girls can be regarded as a serious financial liability because at marriage a dowry must often be supplied (see p1102).

For the urban middle-class woman, life is materially much more comfortable, but pressures still exist. Broadly speaking, she is far more likely to receive a tertiary education, but once married is still usually expected to 'fit in' with her in-laws and be a homemaker above all else. Like her village counterpart, if she fails to live up to expectations – even if it's just not being able to produce a grandson – the consequences can sometimes be dire, as demonstrated by the extreme practice of 'bride burning', wherein a wife is doused with flammable liquid and set alight. Reliable statistics are unavailable, but some women's groups claim that for every reported case, roughly 250 go unreported, and that less than 10% of the reported cases are pursued through the legal system.

ADIVASIS

India's Adivasis (tribal communities; Adivasi translates to 'original inhabitant' in Sanskrit) have origins that precede the Vedic Aryans and the Dravidians of the south. According to the 2001 census, India's Adivasis constitute 8.2% of the population (over 84 million people), with more than 400 different tribal groups. The literacy rate for Adivasis, as per the 2001 census, is just 29.6%; the national average is 65.4%.

Historically, contact between Adivasis and Hindu villagers on the plains rarely led to friction as there was little or no competition for resources and land. However, in recent decades an increasing number of Adivasis have been dispossessed of their ancestral land and turned into impoverished labourers. Although they still have political representation thanks to a parliamentary quota system, the dispossession and exploitation of Adivasis has reportedly sometimes been with the connivance of officialdom – an accusation the government denies. Whatever the arguments, unless more is done, the Adivasis' future is an uncertain one.

Read more about Adivasis in *Archaeology and History: Early Settlements in the Andaman Islands* by Zarine Cooper, *The Tribals of India* by Sunil Janah and *Tribes of India: The Struggle for Survival* by Christoph von Fürer-Haimendorf.

India's most visible nonheterosexual group is the *hijras,* a caste of transvestites and eunuchs who dress in women's clothing. Some are gay, some are hermaphrodites and some were unfortunate enough to be kidnapped and castrated. Since it has long been frowned upon to live openly as a gay man in India, *hijras* get around this by becoming, in effect, a third sex of sorts. They work mainly as uninvited entertainers at weddings and celebrations of the birth of male children, and possibly as prostitutes.

Read more about *hijras* in *The Invisibles* by Zia Jaffrey and *Ardhanarishvara the Androgyne* by Dr Alka Pande.

In October 2006, following women's civil rights campaigns, the Indian parliament passed a landmark bill (on top of existing legislation) which gives women who are suffering domestic violence increased protection and rights. Prior to this legislation, although women could lodge police complaints against abusive spouses, they weren't automatically entitled to a share of the marital property or to ongoing financial support. The new law purports that any form of physical, sexual (including marital rape), emotional and economic abuse entails not only domestic violence, but also human-rights violations. Perpetrators face imprisonment and fines. Under the new law, abused women are legally permitted to remain in the marital house. In addition, the law prohibits emotional and physical bullying in relation to dowry demands. Critics claim that many women, especially those outside India's larger cities, will still be reluctant to seek legal protection because of the social stigma involved.

Despite recent legislation aimed at curtailing crimes against women, the National Crime Records Bureau reported 195,856 registered police cases across the country in 2008 – a leap from the 140,601 cases back in 2003.

Although the constitution allows for divorcees (and widows) to remarry, relatively few reportedly do so, simply because divorcees are traditionally considered outcasts from society, most evidently so beyond big cities. Divorce rates in India are among the worlds' lowest, despite having risen from around seven in 1000 in 1991, to roughly 11 in 1000 in 2009.

Based on Rabind-ranath Tagore's novel, *Chokher Bali* (directed by Rituparno Ghosh) is a poignant film about a young widow living in early 20th-century Bengal who challenges the 'rules of widowhood' – something unthinkable in that era.

Cricket

In India, it's all about cricket, cricket and cricket! Travellers who show even a slight interest in the game can expect to strike passionate conversations with people of all stripes, from taxi drivers to IT yuppies. Cutting across all echelons of society, cricket is more than just a national sporting obsession – it's a matter of enormous patriotism, especially evident whenever India plays against Pakistan. Matches between these South Asian neighbours – which have had rocky relations since Independence – attract especially high-spirited support, and the players of both sides are under colossal pressure to do their respective countries proud.

India's first recorded cricket match was in 1721. It won its first test series in 1952 in Chennai against England. Today cricket – especially the recently rolled out Twenty20 format (www.cricket20.com) – is big business in India, attracting lucrative sponsorship deals and celebrity status for its players. The sport has not been without its murky side though, with Indian cricketers among those embroiled in match-fixing scandals over past years.

International games are played at various centres – see Indian newspapers or surf the Net for details about matches that coincide with your visit. Keep your finger on the cricketing pulse at www.espncricinfo.com (rated most highly by many cricket aficionados) and www.cricbuzz.com.

Cricket lovers will be bowled over by *The Illustrated History of Indian Cricket* by Boria Majumdar and *The States of Indian Cricket* by Ramachandra Guha.

Spiritual India

From a mother performing *puja* (prayers or offerings) for her child's forthcoming exams, to a mechanic who has renounced his material life and set off on the path to self-realisation, religion suffuses almost every aspect of life in India.

India's major religion, Hinduism, is practised by approximately 80.5% of the population. Along with Buddhism, Jainism and Zoroastrianism, it's one of the world's oldest extant religions, with roots extending beyond 1000 BC.

Islam is India's largest minority religion; around 13.4% of the population is Muslim. Islam is believed to have been introduced to northern India by Muslim rulers (in the 16th and 17th centuries the Mughal empire controlled much of North India) and to the south by Arab traders.

Christians comprise about 2.3% of the population, with approximately 75% living in South India, while the Sikhs – estimated at around 1.9% of the population – are mostly found in the northern state of Punjab. Around 0.8% of the population is Buddhist, with Bodhgaya (Bihar) being a major pilgrimage destination. Jainism is followed by about 0.4% of the population, with the majority of Jains living in Gujarat and Mumbai. Parsis, adherents of Zoroastrianism, today number somewhere between 60,000 and 69,000 – a mere drop in the ocean of India's billion-plus population. Historically, Parsis settled in Gujarat and became farmers, however, during British rule they moved into commerce, forming a prosperous community in Mumbai. Reports indicate that there are less than 5000 Jews left in India, most living in Mumbai and parts of South India.

Tribal religions have so merged with Hinduism and other mainstream religions that very few are now clearly identifiable. It's believed that some basic tenets of Hinduism may have originated in tribal culture.

For details about India's major religious festivals, see the Month by Month chapter (p20).

Hinduism

Hinduism has no founder or central authority and it isn't a proselytising religion. Essentially, Hindus believe in Brahman, who is eternal, uncreated and infinite. Everything that exists emanates from Brahman and will ultimately return to it. The multitude of gods and goddesses are merely manifestations – knowable aspects of this formless phenomenon.

Hindus believe that earthly life is cyclical: you are born again and again (a process known as 'samsara'), the quality of these rebirths being dependent upon your karma (conduct or action) in previous lives. Living a righteous life and fulfilling your dharma (moral code of behaviour; social duty) will enhance your chances of being born into a higher caste and better circumstances. Alternatively, if enough bad karma has accumulated, rebirth may take animal form. But it's only as a human that you can gain sufficient self-knowledge to escape the cycle of reincarnation and achieve moksha (liberation).

Unravelling the basic tenets of Hinduism are two books both called *Hinduism: An Introduction* – one is by Shakunthala Jagannathan, the other by Dharam Vir Singh.

Gods & Goddesses

All Hindu deities are regarded as a manifestation of Brahman, who is often described as having three main representations, the Trimurti: Brahma, Vishnu and Shiva.

Brahman

The One; the ultimate reality. Brahman is formless, eternal and the source of all existence. Brahman is *nirguna* (without attributes), as opposed to all the other gods and goddesses, which are manifestations of Brahman and therefore *saguna* (with attributes).

Brahma

Only during the creation of the universe does Brahma play an active role. At other times he is in meditation. His consort is Saraswati, the goddess of learning, and his vehicle is a swan. He is sometimes shown sitting on a lotus that rises from Vishnu's navel, symbolising the interdependence of the gods. Brahma is generally depicted with four (crowned and bearded) heads, each turned towards a point of the compass.

Vishnu

The preserver or sustainer, Vishnu is associated with 'right action'. He protects and sustains all that is good in the world. He is usually depicted with four arms, holding a lotus, a conch shell (it can be blown like a trumpet so symbolises the cosmic vibration from which existence emanates), a discus and a mace. His consort is Lakshmi, the goddess of wealth, and his vehicle is Garuda, the man-bird creature. The Ganges is said to flow from his feet.

Shiva

Shiva is the destroyer, but without whom creation couldn't occur. Shiva's creative role is phallically symbolised by his representation as the frequently worshipped lingam. With 1008 names, Shiva takes many forms, including Nataraja, lord of the *tandava* (cosmic victory dance), who paces out the creation and destruction of the cosmos.

Sometimes Shiva has snakes draped around his neck and is shown holding a trident (representative of the Trimurti) as a weapon while riding Nandi, his bull. Nandi symbolises power and potency, justice and moral order. Shiva's consort, Parvati, is capable of taking many forms.

Other Prominent Deities

Elephant-headed Ganesh is the god of good fortune, remover of obstacles, and patron of scribes (the broken tusk he holds was used to write sections

> The Hindu pantheon is said to have a whopping 330 million deities; those worshipped are a matter of personal choice or tradition.

DEITIES

COMMUNAL CONFLICT

Religion-based conflict has, at times, been a bloody part of India's history. The post-Independence partition of the country into Hindu India and Muslim Pakistan resulted in horrendous carnage and epic displacement (see p1098).

Later bouts of major sectarian violence in India include the Hindu–Sikh riots of 1984, which led to the assassination of then prime minister Indira Gandhi (p1081), and the politically fanned 1992 Ayodhya calamity (p1081), which sparked ferocious Hindu–Muslim clashes.

The ongoing dispute between India and Pakistan over Kashmir is also perilously entwined in religious conflict. Since Partition (1947), India and Pakistan have fought two wars over Kashmir and have had subsequent artillery exchanges, coming dangerously close to war in 1999. The festering dispute over this landlocked territory continues to fuel Hindu–Muslim animosity on both sides of the border – for more details see p1099.

of the Mahabharata). His animal vehicle is Mooshak (a ratlike creature). How Ganesh came to have an elephant's head is a story with several variations. One legend says that Ganesh was born to Parvati in the absence of his father Shiva, and so grew up not knowing him. One day, as Ganesh stood guard while his mother bathed, Shiva returned and asked to be let into Parvati's presence. Ganesh, who didn't recognise Shiva, refused. Enraged, Shiva lopped off Ganesh's head, only to later discover, much to his horror, that he had slaughtered his own son. He vowed to replace Ganesh's head with that of the first creature he came across, which happened to be an elephant.

Another prominent deity, Krishna is an incarnation of Vishnu sent to earth to fight for good and combat evil. His alliances with the *gopis* (milkmaids) and his love for Radha have inspired countless paintings and songs. Depicted with blue-hued skin, Krishna is often seen playing the flute.

Hanuman is the hero of the Ramayana and loyal ally of Rama. He embodies the concept of bhakti (devotion). He's the king of the monkeys, but is capable of taking on other forms.

Among the Shaivite (followers of the Shiva movement), Shakti, the goddess as mother and creator, is worshipped as a force in her own right. The concept of *shakti* is embodied in the ancient goddess Devi (divine mother), who is also manifested as Durga and, in a fiercer evil-destroying incarnation, Kali. Other widely worshipped goddesses include Lakshmi, the goddess of wealth, and Saraswati, the goddess of learning.

Shiva is sometimes characterised as the lord of yoga, a Himalaya-dwelling ascetic with matted hair, an ash-smeared body and a third eye symbolising wisdom.

Sacred Texts

Hindu sacred texts fall into two categories: those believed to be the word of god (*shruti*, meaning 'heard') and those produced by people (smriti, meaning 'remembered'). The Vedas are regarded as *shruti* knowledge and are considered the authoritative basis for Hinduism. The oldest of the Vedic texts, the Rig-Veda, was compiled over 3000 years ago. Within its 1028 verses are prayers for prosperity and longevity as well as an explanation of the universe's origins. The Upanishads, the last parts of the Vedas, reflect on the mystery of death and emphasise the oneness of the universe. The oldest of the Vedic texts were written in Vedic Sanskrit (related to Old Persian). Later texts were composed in classical Sanskrit, but many have been translated into the vernacular.

The smriti texts comprise a collection of literature spanning centuries and include expositions on the proper performance of domestic ceremonies as well as the proper pursuit of government, economics and religious law. Among its well-known works are the Ramayana and Mahabharata, as well as the Puranas, which expand on the epics and promote the notion of the Trimurti. Unlike the Vedas, reading the Puranas is not restricted to initiated higher-caste males.

Did you know that blood-drinking Kali is another form of milk-giving Gauri? *Myth = Mithya: A Handbook of Hindu Mythology* by Devdutt Pattanaik sheds light on this and other fascinating Hindu folklore.

The Mahabharata

Thought to have been composed around 1000 BC, the Mahabharata focuses on the exploits of Krishna. By about 500 BC the Mahabharata had evolved into a far more complex creation with substantial additions,

THE SACRED SEVEN

The number seven has special significance in Hinduism. There are seven sacred Indian cities, which are all major pilgrimage centres: Varanasi (p383), associated with Shiva; Haridwar (p412), where the Ganges enters the plains from the Himalaya; Ayodhya (p376), birthplace of Rama; Dwarka (p709) with the legendary capital of Krishna thought to be off the Gujarat coast; Mathura (p368), birthplace of Krishna; Kanchipuram (p1008), site of the historic Shiva temples; and Ujjain (p646), venue of the Kumbh Mela every 12 years.

There are also seven sacred rivers: the Ganges (Ganga), Saraswati (thought to be underground), Yamuna, Indus, Narmada, Godavari and Cauvery.

One of Hinduism's most venerated symbols is 'Om'. Pronounced 'aum', it's a highly favourable mantra (sacred word or syllable). The 'three' shape symbolises the creation, maintenance and destruction of the universe (and thus the holy Trimurti). The inverted *chandra* (crescent or half moon) represents the discursive mind and the *bindu* (dot) within it, Brahman.

Buddhists believe that, if intoned often enough with complete concentration, it will lead to a state of blissful emptiness.

including the Bhagavad Gita (where Krishna proffers advice to Arjuna before a battle).

The story centres on conflict between the heroic gods (Pandavas) and the demons (Kauravas). Overseeing events is Krishna, who has taken on human form. Krishna acts as charioteer for the Pandava hero Arjuna, who eventually triumphs in a great battle against the Kauravas.

The Ramayana

Composed around the 3rd or 2nd century BC, the Ramayana is believed to be largely the work of one person, the poet Valmiki. Like the Mahabharata, it centres on conflict between the gods and the demons.

The story goes that Dasharatha, the childless king of Ayodhya, called upon the gods to provide him with a son. His wife duly gave birth to a boy. But this child, named Rama, was in fact an incarnation of Vishnu, who had assumed human form to overthrow the demon king of Lanka (now Sri Lanka), Ravana.

As an adult, Rama, who won the hand of the princess Sita in a competition, was chosen by his father to inherit his kingdom. At the last minute Rama's stepmother intervened and demanded her son, Barathan, take Rama's place. Rama, Sita and Rama's brother, Lakshmana, were exiled and went off to the forests, where Rama and Lakshmana battled demons and dark forces. Ravana's sister attempted to seduce Rama but she was rejected and, in revenge, Ravana captured Sita and spirited her away to his palace in Lanka.

Rama, assisted by an army of monkeys led by the loyal monkey god Hanuman, eventually found the palace, killed Ravana and rescued Sita. All returned victorious to Ayodhya, where Rama was welcomed by Barathan and crowned king.

Sacred Flora & Fauna

Animals, particularly snakes and cows, have long been worshipped in the subcontinent. For Hindus, the cow represents fertility and nurturing, while snakes (especially cobras) are associated with fertility and welfare. Naga stones (snake stones) serve the dual purpose of protecting humans from snakes and appeasing snake gods.

Plants can also have sacred associations, such as the banyan tree, which symbolises the Trimurti, while mango trees are symbolic of love – Shiva is believed to have married Parvati under one. Meanwhile, the lotus flower is said to have emerged from the primeval waters and is connected to the mythical centre of the earth through its stem. Often found in the most polluted of waters, the lotus has the remarkable ability to blossom above murky depths. The centre of the lotus corresponds to the centre of the universe, the navel of the earth: all is held together by the stem and the eternal waters. The fragile yet resolute lotus is an embodiment of beauty and strength and a reminder to Hindus of how their own lives should be. So revered has the lotus become that today it's India's national flower.

Two recommended publications containing English translations of holy Hindu texts are *The Bhagavad Gita* by S Radhakrishnan and *The Valmiki Ramayana* by Romesh Dutt.

SADHU

A sadhu is someone who has surrendered all material possessions in pursuit of spirituality through meditation, the study of sacred texts, self-mortification and pilgrimage. Read more in *Sadhus: India's Mystic Holy Men* by Dolf Hartsuiker.

Worship

Worship and ritual play a paramount role in Hinduism. In Hindu homes you'll often find a dedicated worship area, where members of the family pray to the deities of their choice. Beyond the home, Hindus worship at temples. *Puja* is a focal point of worship and ranges from silent prayer to elaborate ceremonies. Devotees leave the temple with a handful of *prasad* (temple-blessed food) which is humbly shared among friends and family. Other forms of worship include *aarti* (the auspicious lighting of lamps or candles) and the playing of soul-soothing bhajans (devotional songs).

Islam

Islam was founded in Arabia by the Prophet Mohammed in the 7th-century AD. The Arabic term *islam* means to surrender, and believers (Muslims) undertake to surrender to the will of Allah (God), which is revealed in the scriptures, the Quran. In this monotheistic religion, God's word is conveyed through prophets (messengers), of whom Mohammed was the most recent.

Following Mohammed's death, a succession dispute split the movement, and the legacy today is the Sunnis and the Shiites. Most Muslims in India are Sunnis. The Sunnis emphasise the 'well-trodden' path or the orthodox way. Shiites believe that only imams (exemplary leaders) can reveal the true meaning of the Quran.

All Muslims, however, share a belief in the Five Pillars of Islam: the shahada (declaration of faith: 'There is no God but Allah; Mohammed is his prophet'); prayer (ideally five times a day); the zakat (tax), in the form of a charitable donation; fasting (during Ramadan) for all except the sick, young children, pregnant women, the elderly and those undertaking arduous journeys; and the haj (pilgrimage) to Mecca, which every Muslim aspires to do at least once.

Sikhism

Sikhism, founded in Punjab by Guru Nanak in the 15th century, began as a reaction against the caste system and Brahmin domination of ritual. Sikhs believe in one god and although they reject the worship of idols, some keep pictures of the 10 gurus as a point of focus. The Sikhs' holy book, the Guru Granth Sahib, contains the teachings of the 10 Sikh gurus, among others.

Like Hindus and Buddhists, Sikhs believe in rebirth and karma. In Sikhism, there's no ascetic or monastic tradition ending the cycles of rebirth.

GURU NANAK: SIKHISM'S FIRST GURU

Born in present-day Pakistan, Guru Nanak (1469–1539), the founder of Sikhism, was unimpressed with both Muslim and Hindu religious practices. Unlike many Indian holy men, he believed in family life and the value of hard work – he married, had two sons and worked as a farmer when not travelling around, preaching and singing self-composed *kirtan* (Sikh devotional songs) with his Muslim musician, Mardana. He performed miracles and emphasised meditation on God's name as the best way to enlightenment.

Nanak believed in equality centuries before it became fashionable and campaigned against the caste system. He was a practical guru – 'a person who makes an honest living and shares earnings with others recognises the way to God'. He appointed his most talented disciple to be his successor, not one of his sons.

His *kirtan* are still sung in *gurdwaras* (Sikh temples) today and his picture hangs in millions of homes.

Parts of India, such as Sikkim and Ladakh, are known for their ornate, colourful gompas (Tibetan-style Buddhist monasteries). The focal point of a gompa is the *dukhang* (prayer hall), where monks assemble to chant passages from the sacred scriptures (morning prayers are a particularly atmospheric time to visit gompas). The walls may be covered in vivid murals or *thangkas* (cloth paintings) of *bodhisattvas* (enlightened beings) and *dharmapalas* (protector deities). By the entrance to the *dukhang* you'll usually find a mural depicting the Wheel of Life, a graphical representation of the core elements of Buddhist philosophy (see www.buddhanet.net/wheel1.htm for an interactive description of the Wheel of Life).

Most gompas hold *chaam* dances (ritual masked dances to celebrate the victory of good over evil) during major festivals. Dances to ward off evil feature masks of Mahakala, the Great Protector, usually dramatically adorned with a headdress of human skulls. The Durdag dance features skull masks depicting the Lords of the Cremation Grounds, while Shawa dancers wear masks of wild-eyed stags. These characters are often depicted with a third eye in the centre of their foreheads, signifying the need for inner reflection.

Another interesting activity at Buddhist monasteries is the production of butter sculptures, elaborate models made from coloured butter and dough. The sculptures are deliberately designed to decay, symbolising the impermanence of human existence. Many gompas also produce exquisite sand mandalas – geometric patterns made from sprinkled coloured sand, then destroyed to symbolise the futility of the physical plane.

Fundamental to Sikhs is the concept of Khalsa, or belief in a Sikh brotherhood of saint-soldiers who abide by strict codes of moral conduct (abstaining from alcohol, tobacco and drugs) and engage in a crusade for *dharmayudha* (righteousness). There are five *kakkars* (emblems) denoting the Khalsa brotherhood: *kesh,* the unshaven beard and uncut hair symbolising saintliness; *kangha,* the comb to maintain the ritually uncut hair; *kaccha,* loose underwear symbolising modesty; *kirpan,* the sabre or sword symbolising power and dignity; and *karra,* the steel bangle symbolising fearlessness. Singh, literally 'lion', is the name adopted by many Sikhs.

A belief in the equality of all beings lies at the heart of Sikhism. It's expressed in various practices, including *langar,* whereby people from all walks of life – regardless of caste and creed – sit side by side to share a complimentary meal prepared by volunteers in the communal kitchen of the *gurdwara* (Sikh temple).

Buddhism

Buddhism arose in the 6th century BC as a reaction against the strictures of Brahminical Hinduism. Buddha (Awakened One) is believed to have lived from about 563 to 483 BC. Formerly a prince (Siddhartha Gautama), the Buddha, at the age of 29, embarked on a quest for emancipation from the world of suffering. He achieved nirvana (the state of full awareness) at Bodhgaya (Bihar), aged 35. Critical of the caste system and the unthinking worship of gods, the Buddha urged his disciples to seek truth within their own experiences.

The Buddha taught that existence is based on Four Noble Truths: that life is rooted in suffering, that suffering is caused by craving, that one can find release from suffering by eliminating craving, and that the way to eliminate craving is by following the Noble Eightfold Path. This path consists of right understanding, right intention, right speech, right action, right livelihood, right effort, right awareness and right concentration. By successfully complying with these one can attain nirvana.

SIKHISM

To grasp the intricacies of Sikhism dive into Volume One (1469–1839) or Volume Two (1839–2004) of *A History of the Sikhs* by Khushwant Singh.

RELIGIOUS ETIQUETTE

Whenever visiting a sacred site, always dress and behave respectfully – don't wear shorts or sleeveless tops (this applies to men and women) – and refrain from smoking. Loud and intrusive behaviour isn't appreciated, and neither are public displays of affection or kidding around.

Before entering a holy place, remove your shoes (tip the shoe-minder a few rupees when retrieving them) and check if photography is allowed. You're permitted to wear socks in most places of worship – often necessary during warmer months, when floors can be uncomfortably hot.

Religious etiquette advises against touching locals on the head, or directing the soles of your feet at a person, religious shrine or image of a deity. Protocol also advises against touching someone with your feet or touching a carving of a deity.

Head cover (for women and sometimes men) is required at some places of worship – especially *gurdwaras* (Sikh temples) and mosques – so carry a scarf just to be on the safe side. There are some sites that don't admit women and some that deny entry to non-adherents of their faith – enquire in advance. Women may be required to sit apart from men. Jain temples request the removal of leather items you may be wearing or carrying and may also request that menstruating women not enter.

Taking photos inside a shrine, at a funeral, at a religious ceremony or of people taking a holy dip can be offensive – ask first. Flash photography may be prohibited in certain areas of a shrine, or may not be permitted at all.

Buddhism had somewhat waned in parts of India by the turn of the 20th century. However, it saw a revival in the 1950s among intellectuals and Dalits who were disillusioned with the caste system. The number of followers has been further increased with the influx of Tibetan refugees. Both the current Dalai Lama and the 17th Karmapa reside in India (see p316 and p327).

Jainism

Jainism arose in the 6th century BC as a reaction against the caste restraints and rituals of Hinduism. It was founded by Mahavira, a contemporary of the Buddha.

Jains believe that liberation can be attained by achieving complete purity of the soul. Purity means shedding all *karman,* matter generated by one's actions that binds itself to the soul. By following various austerities (eg fasting and meditation) one can shed *karman* and purify the soul. Right conduct is essential, and fundamental to this is ahimsa (nonviolence) in thought and deed towards any living thing.

The religious disciplines of followers are less severe than for monks (some Jain monks go naked). The slightly less ascetic maintain a bare minimum of possessions which include a broom to sweep the path before them to avoid stepping on any living creature, and a piece of cloth tied over their mouth to prevent the accidental inhalation of insects.

Some notable Jain holy sites in India include Sravanabelagola (p864), Palitana (p690), Ranakpur (p167) and the Jain temples of Mt Abu (p170).

Christianity

There are various theories circulating about Christ's link to the Indian subcontinent. Some, for instance, believe that Jesus spent his 'lost years' in India (see boxed text, p234), while others say that Christianity came to South India with St Thomas the Apostle in AD 52. However, many scholars say it's more likely Christianity is traced to around the 4th century with a Syrian merchant, Thomas Cana, who set out for Kerala with around 400 families.

Set in Kerala, against the backdrop of caste conflict and India's struggle for independence, *The House of Blue Mangoes* by David Davidar spans three generations of a Christian family.

Catholicism established a strong presence in South India in the wake of Vasco da Gama's visit in 1498, and orders that have been active – not always welcomed – in the region include the Dominicans, Franciscans and Jesuits. Protestant missionaries are believed to have begun arriving – with a conversion agenda – from around the 18th century.

Zoroastrianism

Zoroastrianism, founded by Zoroaster (Zarathustra), had its inception in Persia in the 6th century BC and is based on the concept of dualism, whereby good and evil are locked in a continuous battle. Zoroastrianism isn't quite monotheistic: good and evil entities coexist, although believers are urged to honour only the good. Both body and soul are united in this struggle of good versus evil. Although humanity is mortal it has components that are timeless, such as the soul. On the day of judgement the errant soul is not called to account for every misdemeanour – but a pleasant afterlife does depend on one's deeds, words and thoughts during earthly existence.

Zoroastrianism was eclipsed in Persia by the rise of Islam in the 7th century and its followers, many of whom openly resisted this, suffered persecution. Over the following centuries, some immigrated to India, where they became known as Parsis.

The Zoroastrian funerary ritual involves the 'Towers of Silence' where the corpse is laid out and exposed to vultures that pick the bones clean.

RITUAL

Delicious India

Through its food, you'll discover that India is a banquet expressed in colours, aromas, flavours and textures. Like so many aspects of India, its food, too, is an elusive thing to define because it's made up of so many regionally diverse dishes, all with their own preparation techniques and ingredients. It's the ancient vegetarian fare of the south, the meaty traditions of the Mughals, the glowing tandoor (clay oven) of Punjab and the Euro-Indian fusions of former colonies. It's the divine fragrance of spices, the juice of exotic fruits running down your chin, and rich, fiery curries that will make your tastebuds stand to attention. Indeed it's the sheer diversity of what's on offer that makes eating your way through India so deliciously rewarding.

A Culinary Carnival

India's culinary story is an ancient one. The cuisine that exists today reflects an extraordinary amalgam of regional and global influences. From the traditional Indian fare faithfully prepared in simple village kitchens, to the piled-high Italian-style pizzas served in cosmopolitan city restaurants, the carnival of flavours available in the subcontinent is nothing short of spectacular.

Land of Spices

Christopher Columbus was actually looking for the black pepper of Kerala's Malabar Coast when he stumbled upon America. The region still grows the finest quality of the world's favourite spice, and it's integral to most savoury Indian dishes.

Turmeric is the essence of the majority of Indian curries, but coriander seeds are the most widely used spice and lend flavour and body to just about every savoury dish. Indian 'wet' dishes – commonly known as curries in the West – usually begin with the crackle of cumin seeds in hot oil. Tamarind is sometimes known as the 'Indian date' and is a popular souring agent in the south. The green cardamom of Kerala's Western Ghats is regarded as the world's best, and you'll find it in savouries, desserts and warming chai (tea). Saffron, the dried stigmas of crocus flowers grown in Kashmir, is so light it takes more than 1500 hand-plucked flowers to yield just one gram.

Rice Paradise

Rice is a common staple, especially in South India. Long-grain white rice varieties are the most popular, served hot with just about any 'wet' cooked dish. Rice is often cooked up in a pilau (or pilaf; spiced rice dish) or biryani (spiced steamed rice with meat or vegetables). From Assam's sticky rice in the far northeast to Kerala's red grains in the extreme south, you'll find countless regional varieties that locals will claim to be the best in India, though this honour is usually conceded to basmati, a fragrant long-grain variety which is widely exported around the world.

SPICES

Containing handy tips, including how to best store spices, Monisha Bharadwaj's *The Indian Spice Kitchen* is a slick cookbook with more than 200 traditional recipes.

Khichdi (or *khichri*), mostly cooked in North India, is a blend of lightly spiced rice and lentils. Rarely found on restaurant menus, it's mostly prepared in home kitchens to mollify upset tummies (we recommend it for Delhi Belly) – some restaurants may specially cook it if you give them adequate advance notice.

Flippin' Fantastic Bread

While rice is paramount in the south, wheat is the mainstay in the north. Roti, the generic term for Indian-style bread, is a name used interchangeably with chapati to describe the most common variety, the irresistible unleavened round bread made with whole-wheat flour and cooked on a *tawa* (hotplate). It may be smothered with ghee (clarified butter) or oil. In some places, rotis may be bigger and thicker than chapatis and possibly cooked in a tandoor.

Puri is deep-fried dough puffed up like a crispy balloon. *Kachori* is somewhat similar, but the dough has been pepped up with corn or dhal, which makes it considerably thicker. Flaky, unleavened *paratha* can be eaten as is or jazzed up with fillings such as paneer (soft, unfermented cheese). The thick, usually teardrop-shaped naan is cooked in a tandoor and is especially scrummy when flavoured with garlic.

Spotlighting rice, *Finest Rice Recipes* by Sabina Sehgal Saikia shows just how versatile this humble grain is, with classy creations such as rice-crusted crab cakes.

Dhal-icious!

While the staple of preference divides north and south, the whole of India is melodiously united in its love for dhal (curried lentils or pulses). You may encounter up to 60 different pulses: the most common are *channa*, a slightly sweeter version of the yellow split pea; tiny yellow or green ovals called *moong* (mung beans); salmon-coloured *masoor* (red lentils); the ochre-coloured southern favourite, *tuvar* (yellow lentils; also known as *arhar*); *rajma* (kidney beans); *kabuli channa*; *urad* (black gram or lentils); and *lobhia* (black-eyed peas).

Meaty Matters

While India probably has more vegetarians than the rest of the world combined, it still has an extensive repertoire of carnivorous fare. Chicken, lamb and mutton (sometimes actually goat) are the mainstays; religious taboos make beef forbidden to devout Hindus and pork to Muslims.

In northern India you'll come across meat-dominated Mughlai cuisine, which includes rich curries, kebabs, koftas (minced vegetables or meat; often ball-shaped) and biryanis. This spicy cuisine traces its history back to the (Islamic) Mughal empire that once reigned supreme in India.

Tandoori meat dishes are another North Indian favourite. The name is derived from the clay oven, or tandoor, in which the marinated meat is cooked.

Deep-Sea Delights

India has around 7500km of coastline, so it's no surprise that seafood is an important staple, especially on the west coast, from Mumbai (Bombay) down to Kerala. Kerala is the biggest fishing state, while Goa boasts particularly succulent prawns and fiery fish curries, and the fishing communities of the Konkan Coast – sandwiched between these two states – are renowned for their seafood recipes. Few main meals in Odisha (Orissa) exclude fish, and in West Bengal, puddled with ponds and lakes, fish is king.

The Fruits (& Vegetables) of Mother Nature

Vegetables are usually served at every main meal across India, and *sabzi* (vegetables) is a word recognised in every Indian vernacular. They're generally cooked *sukhi* (dry) or *tari* (in a sauce) and within these two categories they can be fried, roasted, curried, stuffed, baked, mashed and combined (made into koftas) or dipped in chickpea-flour batter to make a deep-fried pakora (fritter).

Potatoes are ubiquitous and popularly cooked with various masalas (spice mixes), with other vegetables, or mashed and fried for the street snack *aloo tikki* (mashed-potato patties). Onions are fried with other vegetables, ground into a paste for cooking with meats, and served raw as relishes. Heads of cauliflower are usually cooked dry on their own, with potatoes to make *aloo gobi* (potato-and-cauliflower curry), or with other vegetables such as carrots and beans. Fresh green peas turn up stir-fried with other vegetables in pilaus and biryanis and in one of North India's signature dishes, the magnificent *mattar paneer* (unfermented cheese and pea curry). *Baigan* (eggplant/aubergine) can be curried or sliced and deep-fried. Also popular is *saag* (a generic term for leafy greens), which can include mustard, spinach and fenugreek. Something a little more unusual is the bumpy-skinned *karela* (bitter gourd) which, like the delectable *bhindi* (okra), is commonly prepared dry with spices.

India's fruit basket is a bountiful one. Along the southern coast are super-luscious tropical fruits such as pineapples and papayas. Mangoes abound during the summer months (especially April and May), with India boasting more than 500 varieties – the pick of the juicy bunch is the sweet Alphonso. Citrus fruit such as oranges (which are often yellow-green in India), tangerines, pink and white grapefruits, kumquats and sweet limes are widely grown. Himachal Pradesh produces crisp apples in autumn, while plump strawberries are especially good in Kashmir during summer. You'll find fruit inventively fashioned into a *chatni* (chutney) or pickle, and also flavouring *lassi* (yoghurt-and-iced-water drink), *kulfi* (firm-textured ice cream) and other sweet treats.

The Anger of Aubergines: Stories of Women and Food by Bulbul Sharma is an amusing culinary analysis of social relationships interspersed with enticing recipes.

Vegetarians & Vegans

India is king when it comes to vegetarian fare. There's little understanding of veganism (the term 'pure vegetarian' means without eggs), and animal products such as milk, butter, ghee and curd are included in most Indian dishes. If you are vegan your first problem is likely to be getting the cook to completely understand your requirements.

For further information, surf the web – good places to begin include Indian Vegan (www.indianvegan.com) and Vegan World Network (www.vegansworldnetwork.org).

Pickles, Chutneys & Relishes

Thin and crispy, pappadams (commonly referred to as pappad) are circle-shaped lentil- or chickpea-flour wafers served either before or with a meal.

No Indian meal is really complete without one, and often all, of the above. A relish can be anything from a tiny pickled onion to a delicately crafted fusion of fruit, nuts and spices. One of the most popular meal accompaniments is raita (mildly spiced yoghurt, often containing shredded cucumber or diced pineapple; served chilled), which makes a tongue-cooling counter to spicy food. *Chatnis* can come in any number of varieties (sweet or savoury) and can be made from many different vegetables, fruits, herbs and spices. But you should proceed with caution before polishing off that pickled speck sitting on your thali; it may quite possibly be the hottest thing that you have ever tasted.

Dear Dairy

Milk and milk products make a staggering contribution to Indian cuisine: *dahi* (curd/yoghurt) is commonly served with meals and is great for subduing heat; paneer is a godsend for the vegetarian majority; lassi is one in a host of nourishing sweet and savoury beverages; ghee is the

PAAN

Meals are often rounded off with *paan*, a fragrant mixture of betel nut (also called areca nut), lime paste, spices and condiments wrapped in an edible, silky *paan* leaf. Peddled by *paan*-wallahs, who are usually strategically positioned outside busy restaurants, *paan* is eaten as a digestive and mouth-freshener. The betel nut is mildly narcotic and some aficionados eat *paan* the same way heavy smokers consume cigarettes – over the years these people's teeth can become rotted red and black.

There are two basic types of *paan: mitha* (sweet) and *saadha* (with tobacco). A parcel of *mitha paan* is a splendid way to finish a satisfying meal. Pop the whole parcel in your mouth and chew slowly, allowing the juices to oooooooze.

traditional and pure cooking medium; and some of the finest *mithai* (Indian sweets) are made with milk.

Sweet at Heart

India has a fabulously colourful kaleidoscope of, often sticky and squishy, *mithai* (Indian sweets), most of them sinfully sugary. The main categories are *barfi* (a fudgelike milk-based sweet), soft *halwa* (made with vegetables, cereals, lentils, nuts or fruit), *ladoos* (sweet balls made with gram flour and semolina), and those made from *chhana* (unpressed paneer), such as *rasgullas* (cream-cheese balls flavoured with rose water). There are also simpler – but equally scrumptious – offerings such as crunchy *jalebis* (orange-coloured coils of deep-fried batter dunked in sugar syrup; served hot) that you'll see all over the country.

Kheer (called *payasam* in the south) is one of the most popular after-meal desserts. It's a creamy rice pudding with a light, delicate flavour, enhanced with cardamom, saffron, pistachios, flaked almonds, chopped cashews or slivered dried fruit. Other favourites include *gulab jamuns,* deep-fried balls of dough soaked in rose-flavoured syrup, and *kulfi,* a firm-textured ice cream made with reduced milk and flavoured with any number of nuts (often pistachio), fruits and berries.

Each year, an estimated 14 tonnes of pure silver is converted into the edible foil that decorates many Indian sweets, especially during the Diwali festival.

Where to Fill Up?

India has oodles of restaurants, from ramshackle street eateries to swish five-star hotel offerings. Most midrange restaurants serve one of two basic genres: South Indian (which usually means the vegetarian food of Tamil Nadu and Karnataka) and North Indian (which largely comprises Punjabi/Mughlai fare). You'll also find the cuisines of neighbouring regions and states. Indians frequently migrate in search of work and these restaurants cater to the large communities seeking the familiar tastes of home.

Not to be confused with burger joints and pizzerias, restaurants in the south advertising 'fast food' are some of India's best. They serve the whole gamut of tiffin (snack) items and often have separate sweet counters. Many upmarket hotels have outstanding restaurants, usually with pan-Indian menus so you can explore various regional cuisines. Meanwhile, the independent restaurant dining scene is mushrooming in India's larger cities, especially Mumbai, Delhi and Bengaluru (Bangalore), with menus sporting everything from Mexican and Mediterranean to Japanese and Korean.

Dhabas (basic snack bars) are oases to millions of truck drivers, bus passengers and sundry travellers going anywhere by road. The original

Technically speaking, there's no such thing as an Indian 'curry' – the word, an anglicised derivative of the Tamil word *kari* (sauce), was used by the British as a term for any dish including spices.

The Book of Indian Sweets by Satarupa Banerjee contains a tempting mix of regional sweet treats, from Bengali *rasgullas* to Goan *bebinca*.

dhabas dot the North Indian landscape, but you'll find versions of them throughout the country. The rough-and-ready but satisfying food served in these happy-go-lucky shacks has become a genre of its own known as '*dhaba* food'.

Street Food

Whatever the time of day, food vendors are frying, boiling, roasting, peeling, simmering, mixing, juicing or baking some type of food and drink to lure peckish passers-by. Small operations usually have one special that they serve all day, while other vendors have different dishes for breakfast, lunch and dinner. The fare varies as you venture between neighbourhoods, towns and regions; it can be as simple as puffed rice or peanuts roasted in hot sand, as unexpected as a fried-egg sandwich, or as complex as the riot of different flavours known as *chaat* (savoury snack).

Devilishly delicious deep-fried fare is the staple of the streets, and you'll find satiating samosas (deep-fried pastry triangles filled with spiced vegetables and less often meat), and *bhajia* (vegetable fritters) in varying degrees of spiciness. Much loved in Maharasthra is *vada pao*, a veg-burger of sorts, with a deep-fried potato patty in a bread bun served with hot chillies and tangy chutneys. Sublime kebabs doused in smooth curd and wrapped in warm Indian-style bread are most commonly found in neighbourhoods with a large Muslim community.

Got the munchies? Grab *Street Foods of India* by Vimla and Deb Kumar Mukerji which has recipes of some of India's favourite snacks, from samosas and *bhelpuri* to *jalebis* and *kulfi*.

Railway Snack Attack

One of the thrills of travelling by rail in India is the culinary circus that greets you at almost every station. Roving vendors accost arriving trains, yelling and scampering up and down the carriages; fruit, *namkin* (savoury nibbles), omelettes, nuts and sweets are offered through the grills on the windows; and platform cooks try to lure you from the train with the sizzle of spicy goodies such as fresh samosas. Frequent rail travellers know which station is famous for which food item: Lonavla station in Maharashtra is largely known for *chikki* (rock-hard toffeelike confectionery), Agra for *peitha* (square sweet made from pumpkin and glucose, usually flavoured with rose water, coconut or saffron) and Dhaund near Delhi for biryani.

STREET FOOD: TIPS

Tucking into street food is one of the joys of travelling in India – here are some tips to help avoid tummy troubles.

Give yourself a few days to adjust to the local cuisine, especially if you're not used to spicy food.

You know the rule about following a crowd – if the locals are avoiding a particular vendor, you should too. Also take notice of the profile of the customers – any place popular with families will probably be your safest bet.

Check how and where the vendor is cleaning the utensils, and how and where the food is covered. If the vendor is cooking in oil, have a peek to check it's clean. If the pots or surfaces are dirty, there are food scraps about or too many buzzing flies, don't be shy to make a hasty retreat.

Don't be put off when you order some deep-fried snack and the cook throws it back into the wok. It's common practice to partly cook the snacks first and then finish them off once they've been ordered. In fact, frying them hot again will kill any germs.

Unless a place is reputable (and busy), it's best to avoid eating meat from the street.

The hygiene standard at juice stalls is wildly variable, so exercise caution. Have the vendor press the juice in front of you and steer clear of anything stored in a jug or served in a glass (unless you're absolutely convinced of the washing standards).

Don't be tempted by glistening pre-sliced melon and other fruit, which keeps its luscious veneer with regular dousing of (often dubious) water.

Most people in India eat with their right hand. In the south, they use as much of the hand as is necessary, while elsewhere they use the tips of the fingers. The left hand is reserved for unsanitary actions such as removing grotty shoes. You can use your left hand for holding drinks and serving yourself from a communal bowl, but it shouldn't be used for bringing food to your mouth. Before and after a meal, it's good manners to wash your hands.

Once your meal is served, mix the food with your fingers. If you are having dhal and *sabzi* (vegetables), only mix the dhal into your rice and have the *sabzi* in small scoops with each mouthful. If you are having fish or meat curry, mix the gravy into your rice and take the flesh off the bones from the side of your plate. Scoop up lumps of the mix and, with your knuckles facing the dish, use your thumb to shovel the food into your mouth.

Daily Dining Habits

Three main meals a day is the norm in India. Breakfast is usually fairly light, maybe *idlis* (spongy, round, fermented rice cakes) and *sambar* (soupy lentil dish with cubed vegetables) in the south, and *parathas* in the north. Or simply fruit, cereal and/or eggs on toast. Lunch can be substantial (perhaps the local version of the thali) or light, especially for time-strapped office workers. Dinner is usually the main meal of the day. It's generally comprised of a few different preparations – several curried vegetable (maybe also meat) dishes and dhal, accompanied by rice and/or chapatis. Dishes are served all at once rather than as courses. Desserts are optional and most prevalent during festivals or other special occasions. Fruit often wraps up a meal. In many Indian homes dinner can be a late affair (post 9pm) depending on personal preference and possibly the season (eg late dinners during the warmer months). Restaurants usually spring to life after 9pm.

Spiritual Sustenance

For many in India, food is considered just as critical for fine-tuning the spirit as it is for sustaining the body. Broadly speaking, Hindus traditionally avoid foods that are thought to inhibit physical and spiritual development, although there are few hard-and-fast rules. The taboo on eating beef (the cow is holy to Hindus) is the most rigid restriction. Jains avoid foods such as garlic and onions, which, apart from harming insects in their extraction from the ground, are thought to heat the blood and arouse sexual desire. You may come across vegetarian restaurants that make it a point to advertise the absence of onion and garlic in their dishes for this reason. Devout Hindus may also avoid garlic and onions. These items are also banned from most ashrams.

Some foods, such as dairy products, are considered innately pure and are eaten to cleanse the body, mind and spirit. Ayurveda, the ancient science of life, health and longevity, also influences food customs.

Pork is taboo for Muslims and stimulants such as alcohol are avoided by the most devout. Halal is the term for all permitted foods, and haram for those prohibited. Fasting is considered an opportunity to earn the approval of Allah, to wipe the sin-slate clean and to understand the suffering of the poor.

Buddhists and Jains subscribe to the philosophy of ahimsa (nonviolence) and are mostly vegetarian. Jainism's central tenet is ultra-vegetarianism, and rigid restrictions are in place to avoid even potential injury to any living creature – Jains abstain from eating vegetables that grow underground because of the potential to harm insects during cultivation and harvesting.

India's Sikh, Christian and Parsi communities have little or no restrictions on what they can eat.

For recipes online, try:
www.recipes indian.com

www.thokalath. com/cuisine

www.indianfood forever.com

Cooking Courses

You might find yourself so inspired by Indian food that you want to take home a little Indian kitchen know-how, via a cooking course. Some courses are professionally run, others are very informal, and each is of varying duration. Most require at least a few days' advance notice – see the regional chapters of this book for details about recommended courses and also quiz fellow travellers.

Drinks, Anyone?

Gujarat is India's only dry state but there are drinking laws in place all over the country, and each state may have regular dry days when the sale of alcohol from liquor shops is banned. To avoid paying high taxes, head for Goa, where booze isn't subject to the exorbitant levies of other states.

You'll find terrific watering holes in most big cities such as Mumbai, Bengaluru, Kolkata (Calcutta) and Delhi, which are usually at their liveliest on weekends. The more upmarket bars serve an impressive selection of domestic and imported drinks as well as draught beer. Many bars turn into music-thumping nightclubs anytime after 8pm although there are quiet lounge-bars to be found in some cities. In smaller towns the bar scene can be a seedy, male-dominated affair – not the kind of place thirsty female travellers should venture into alone.

Stringent licensing laws discourage drinking in some restaurants but places that depend on the tourist rupee may covertly serve you beer in teapots and disguised glasses – but don't assume anything, at the risk of causing offence.

Very few vegetarian restaurants serve alcohol.

Nonalcoholic Beverages

Chai (tea), the much-loved drink of the masses, is made with bucket loads of milk and sugar. A glass of steaming, frothy chai is the perfect antidote to the vicissitudes of life on the Indian road; the disembodied voice droning 'garam chai, garam chai' (hot tea, hot tea) is likely to become one of the most familiar and welcome sounds of your trip. For those interested in taking a tea appreciation course, see p492.

While chai is the traditional choice of most of the nation, South Indians have long shared their loyalty with coffee. In recent years, though, the

---

Food which is first offered to the gods at temples then shared among devotees is known as *prasad*.

The excellent *Complete Indian Cooking* by Mridula Baljekar, Rafi Fernandez, Shehzad Husain and Manisha Kanani contains '325 deliciously authentic recipes for the adventurous cook'. Recipes include chicken with green mango, masala mashed potatoes and Goan prawn curry.

SOUTHERN BELLES

Dosas (also spelt dosais), a family of large papery rice-flour crêpes, usually served with a bowl of hot *sambar* (soupy lentil dish with cubed vegetables) and another bowl of cooling coconut *chatni* (chutney), are a South Indian breakfast speciality that can be eaten at any time of day. The most popular is the masala dosa (stuffed with spiced potatoes), but there are also other fantastic dosa varieties – the *rava* dosa (batter made with semolina), the Mysore dosa (like masala dosa but with more vegetables and chilli in the filling), and the *pessarettu* dosa (batter made with mung-bean dhal) from Andhra Pradesh. Nowadays, dosas are readily found far beyond South India, thanks to their widespread yum-appeal.

The humble *idli* is a traditional South Indian snack that can be found around India; low-cal and nutritious, it provides a welcome alternative to oil, spice and chilli. *Idlis* are spongy, round, white fermented rice cakes that you dip in *sambar* and coconut *chatni*. *Dahi idli* is an *idli* dunked in very lightly spiced yoghurt – terrific for tender tummies. Other super southern snacks, which are also popular throughout the country, include *vadas* (doughnut-shaped deep-fried lentil savouries) and *appams* or *uttappams* (thick, savoury South Indian rice pancake with finely chopped onions, green chillies, coriander and coconut).

number of coffee-drinking North Indians has skyrocketed, with ever-multiplying branches of slick coffee chains, such as Barista and Café Coffee Day, widely found in what were once chai strongholds.

Masala soda is the quintessentially Indian soft drink. It's a freshly opened bottle of fizzy soda, pepped up with lime, spices, salt and sugar. Also refreshing is *jal jeera,* made of lime juice, cumin, mint and rock salt. Sweet and savoury lassi, a yoghurt-based drink, is especially popular nationwide and is another wonderfully rejuvenating beverage.

Falooda is an interesting rose-flavoured drink made with milk, cream, nuts and strands of vermicelli, while *badam* milk (served hot or cold) is flavoured with almonds and saffron.

India has zillions of fresh-fruit juice vendors, but you need to be wary of hygiene standards (see the boxed text, p1118). Some restaurants think nothing of adding salt or sugar to juice to intensify the flavours; ask the waiter to omit these if you don't want them.

For information about safely drinking water in India, see p1192.

The Booze Files

An estimated three-quarters of India's drinking population quaffs 'country liquor' such as the notorious arak (liquor distilled from coconut-palm sap, potatoes or rice) of the south. This is widely known as the poor-man's drink and millions are addicted to the stuff. Each year, many people are blinded or even killed by the methyl alcohol in illegal arak.

An interesting local drink is a clear spirit with a heady pungent flavour called *mahua,* distilled from the flower of the *mahua* tree. It's brewed in makeshift village stalls all over central India during March and April, when the trees bloom. *Mahua* is safe to drink as long as it comes from a trustworthy source. There have been cases of people being blinded after drinking *mahua* adulterated with methyl alcohol.

Rice beer is brewed all over east and northeast India, while in the Himalayas you'll find a grain alcohol called *raksi,* which is strong, has a mild charcoal flavour and tastes vaguely like Scotch whisky.

Toddy, the sap from the palm tree, is drunk in coastal areas, especially Kerala, while *feni* is the primo Indian spirit, and the preserve of laid-back Goa. Coconut feni is light and rather unexceptional but the more popular cashew feni – made from the fruit of the cashew tree – is worth a try.

About a quarter of India's drinks market comprises Indian Made Foreign Liquors (IMFLs), made with a base of rectified spirit. Recent years have seen a rise in the consumption of imported spirits, with a spiralling number of city watering holes and restaurants flaunting a dazzling array of domestic and foreign labels.

Beer is a hit everywhere, with the more upmarket bars and restaurants stocking local and foreign brands (Budweiser, Heineken, Corona and the like). Most of the domestic brands are straightforward Pilsners around the 5% alcohol mark; travellers largely champion Kingfisher.

Wine-drinking is steadily on the rise, despite the domestic wine-producing industry still being relatively new. The favourable climate and soil conditions in certain areas – such as parts of Maharashtra and Karnataka – have spawned some commendable Indian wineries including Indage (www.indagevintners.com), Grover Vineyards (www.groverwines.com) and Sula Vineyards (www.sulawines.com). Domestic offerings include chardonnay, chenin blanc, sauvignon blanc, cabernet sauvignon, shiraz and zinfandel. See also p762.

Meanwhile, if you fancy sipping booze of the blue-blood ilk, traditional royal liqueurs of Rajasthan (once reserved for private consumption within royal families) are now sold at some city liquor shops, especially in Delhi and Jaipur. Ingredients range from aniseed, cardamom and saffron to rose, dates and mint.

WINE

The subcontinent's wine industry is an ever evolving one – take a cyber-sip of Indian wine at www.indianwine.com.

Food Glorious Food

One of the greatest pleasures of wandering around India is sampling its tremendously diverse platter of regional dishes. Apart from fantastic home-grown offerings, larger cities also have a stellar variety of global fare, from sashimi and lotus-leaf dumplings to spanakopita and blue-cheese ravioli.

India's culinary terrain – with its especially impressive patchwork of vegetarian cuisine – is not only intensely delicious, it's also richly steeped in history. From the flavoursome meaty preparations of the Mughals and Punjabis to the deep-sea delights of former southern-based colonies, Indian kitchens continue to lovingly cook old favourites, often with inventive contemporary twists.

In addition to its glorious repertoire of savoury delights, there's the wonderful world of *mithai* (Indian sweets): hot, syrupy *jalebis* (deep-fried coils of batter), creamy *kheer* (similar to rice pudding), soft, sticky *gulab jamuns* (deep-fried balls of dough), thickly cut *barfi* (fudge-like sweet), *rasgullas* (rosewater-infused cream cheese balls) and velvety *kulfi* (firm-textured ice cream) – to name just a sprinkling.

TASTE THIS

» **Thali** Traditional all-you-can-eat meal; served in compartmentalised stainless steel (or silver) plates

» **Dosa** (p1120) Large (usually stuffed) savoury crepe; *masala dosa* is filled with spiced potatoes

» **Tandoori** Clay-oven-cooked meat, vegetables and flat-bread (eg naan)

» **Idli** (p1120) Round, spongy fermented rice cake; served with fresh condiments

» **Mithai** (p1117) Indian sweets; from crunchy *jalebis* to soft *gulab jamuns*

Clockwise from top left
1. *Jalebis* 2. *Masala dosa* 3. Goan thali 4. Market spices

The Great Indian Bazaar

India is filled with bustling old bazaars and modern shopping malls that sell a staggering range of goodies: glossy gemstones, exquisite sculptures, sumptuous silks, chunky tribal jewellery, traditional shawls, beautiful woodwork and rustic village handicrafts. Many crafts fulfil a practical need as much as an aesthetic one.

Every region has its own special arts and crafts, usually showcased in state emporiums and cottage industries' (fair-trade) cooperatives. These shops normally charge fair fixed prices; almost everywhere else, you'll have to don your haggling hat. Opening hours for shops vary across the country – consult the Shopping sections of regional chapters for details.

Be cautious when buying items that include delivery to your country of residence, and be wary of being led to shops by smooth-talking touts. Exporting antiques is prohibited (see p1165).

So much to buy, so little luggage space... Happy shopping!

Bronze Figures, Pottery, Stone Carving & Terracotta

Crafts aren't necessarily confined to their region of origin – artists migrate and have sometimes been influenced by the ideas of other regions – which means you can come across, for example, a Kashmiri handicraft emporium anywhere in India.

In southern India and parts of the Himalaya, small images of deities are created by the age-old lost-wax process. A wax figure is made, a mould is formed around it, and the wax is melted, poured out and replaced with molten metal; the mould is then broken open to reveal the figure inside. Figures of Shiva as dancing Nataraja are the most popular, but you can also find images of Buddha and numerous deities from the Hindu pantheon.

The West Bengalese also employ the lost-wax process to make Dokra tribal bell sculptures; while in the Bastar region of Chhattisgarh, the Ghadwa Tribe has an interesting twist on the lost-wax process by using a fine wax thread to cover the metal mould, leaving a lattice-like design on the final product.

In Buddhist areas, you can find striking bronze statues of Buddha and the Tantric gods, finished off with finely polished and painted faces.

In Mamallapuram in Tamil Nadu, craftsmen using local granite and soapstone have revived the ancient artistry of the Pallava sculptors; souvenirs range from tiny stone elephants to enormous deity statues weighing half a tonne. Tamil Nadu is also known for bronzeware from Thanjavur and Trichy (Tiruchirappalli).

A number of places produce attractive terracotta items, ranging from vases and decorative flowerpots to images of deities, and children's toys.

At temples across India you can buy small clay or plaster effigies of Hindu deities.

Carpets Carpets Carpets!

Carpet-making is a living craft in India, with workshops throughout producing fine wool and silkwork in traditional and contemporary designs.

The finest carpets are produced in Kashmir and the Buddhist heartlands of Ladakh, Himachal Pradesh, Sikkim and West Bengal. Carpet-making is also a major revenue earner for Tibetan refugees; most refugee settlements have cooperative carpet workshops. You can also find reproductions of tribal Turkmen and Afghan designs in states such as Uttar Pradesh. Antique carpets usually aren't antique – unless you buy from an internationally reputable dealer; stick to 'new' carpets.

The price of a carpet will be determined by the number and the size of the hand-tied knots, the range of dyes and colours, the intricacy of the design and the material. Silk carpets cost more and look more luxurious, but wool carpets usually last longer. Expect to pay upwards of US$200 for a good quality 90cm by 1.5m (or 90cm by 1.8m, depending on the region) wool carpet, and around US$2000 for a similar sized carpet in silk. Tibetan carpets are cheaper, reflecting the relative simplicity of the designs; many refugee cooperatives sell the same size for around US$100 or less.

A number of people buy carpets under the mistaken belief that they can be sold for a profit back home. Unless you really know your carpets and the carpet market in your home country, it's best to buy a carpet simply because you love it. Many places can ship carpets home for a fee – although it may be safest to send things independently to avoid scams (depending on the shop, use your instinct) – or you can carry them in the plane's hold (allow 5kg to 10kg of your baggage allowance for a 90cm by 1.5m carpet).

In both Kashmir and Rajasthan, you can also find coarsely woven woollen *numdas* (or *namdas*), which are much cheaper than knotted carpets. Various regions' manufacture flat-weave *dhurries* (kilim-like cotton rugs), including Kashmir, Himachal Pradesh, Rajasthan and Uttar Pradesh. Kashmiris also produce striking *gabbas* (rugs with appliqué), made from chain-stitched wool or silk.

Children have been employed as carpet weavers in the subcontinent for centuries. Ultimately, the only thing that can stop child labour is compulsory education for children. The carpets produced by Tibetan refugee cooperatives are almost always made by adults; government emporiums and charitable cooperatives are usually the best places to buy.

Rajasthan is a treasure trove of handicrafts. Its capital, Jaipur, is known for its blue-glazed pottery with pretty floral and geometric motifs.

THE ART OF HAGGLING

Government emporiums, fair-trade cooperatives, department stores and modern shopping centres almost always charge fixed prices. Anywhere else you need to bargain. Shopkeepers in tourist hubs are accustomed to travellers who have lots of money and little time to spend it, so you can often expect to be charged double or triple the 'real' price. Souvenir shops are generally the most notorious.

The first 'rule' to haggling is never to show too much interest in the item you've got your heart set upon. Secondly, resist purchasing the first thing that takes your fancy. Wander around and price items, but don't make it too obvious – if you return to the first shop the vendor will know it's because they are the cheapest (resulting in less haggling leeway).

Decide how much you would be happy paying and then express a casual interest in buying. If you have absolutely no idea of what something should really cost, start by slashing the price by half. The vendor will, most likely, look utterly aghast, but you can now work up and down respectively in small increments until you reach a mutually agreeable price. You'll find that many shopkeepers lower their so-called 'final price' if you head out of the store saying you'll 'think about it'.

Haggling is a way of life in India and is usually taken in good spirit. It should never turn ugly. Always keep in mind exactly how much a rupee is worth in your home currency to put things in perspective. If a vendor seems to be charging an unreasonably high price, simply look elsewhere.

Dazzling Jewellery

Virtually every town in India has at least one bangle shop selling an extraordinary variety ranging from colourful plastic and glass to shiny brass and silver.

Heavy folk-art silver jewellery can be bought in various parts of the country, particularly in Rajasthan – Jaipur, Udaipur and Pushkar are good places to find silver jewellery pitched at foreign tastes. Jaipur is also renowned for its precious and semiprecious gems – and gem scams (see p1156). Chunky Tibetan jewellery made from silver (or white metal) and semiprecious stones is sold all over India. Many pieces feature Buddhist motifs and text in Tibetan script, including the famous mantra *Om Mani Padme Hum* (Hail to the jewel in the lotus). Some of the pieces sold in Tibetan centres such as McLeod Ganj and Leh are genuine antiques but be aware that there's a huge industry in India, Nepal and China making artificially aged souvenirs. If you feel like being creative, loose beads of agate, turquoise, carnelian and silver are widely available. Buddhist meditation beaded strings made of gems or wood also make good souvenirs.

Cuttack in Odisha (Orissa) is famed for its lacelike silver-filigree ornaments known as *tarakasi*. A silver framework is made and then filled in with delicate curls and ribbons of thin silver.

Leatherwork

As cows are sacred in India, leatherwork is made from buffalos, camels, goats or some other substitute. Kanpur in Uttar Pradesh is the country's major leatherwork centre.

Most large cities offer a smart range of modern leather footwear at very reasonable prices, some stitched with zillions of sparkly sequins – marvellous partywear!

The states of Punjab and Rajasthan, and especially in Jaipur, are famed for *jootis* (traditional, often pointy-toed slip-on shoes).

Chappals, those wonderful (often curly-toed) leather sandals, are sold throughout India but are particularly good in the Maharashtran cities of Kolhapur, Pune and Matheran.

In Bikaner in Rajasthan, artisans decorate camel hide with gold to produce beautiful mirror frames, boxes and bottles, while in Indore in Madhya Pradesh, craftspeople stretch leather over wire and cloth frameworks to make cute toy animals. In most big cities you'll find well-made, competitively priced leather handbags, wallets, belts and other accessories.

Throughout India you can find finely crafted gold and silver rings, anklets, earrings, toe rings, necklaces and bangles, and pieces can often be crafted to order.

Metal & Marble Masterpieces

You'll find copper and brassware throughout India. Candleholders, trays, bowls, tankards and ashtrays are particularly popular buys. In Rajasthan and Uttar Pradesh, the brass is inlaid with exquisite designs in red, green and blue enamel.

Many Tibetan religious objects are created by inlaying silver in copper; prayer wheels, ceremonial horns and traditional document cases are all inexpensive buys. Resist the urge to buy *kangling* (Tibetan horns) and *kapala* (ceremonial bowls) made from inlaid human leg bones and skulls – they are illegal!

PRETTY PEARLS

Pearls are produced by most Indian seaside states, but are a particular speciality of Hyderabad (see p905). You'll find them sold at most state emporiums across the country. Prices vary depending on the colour and shape – you pay more for pure white pearls or rare colours like black. Perfectly round pearls are generally more expensive than misshapen or elongated pearls, however, quirky shapes can actually be more alluring. A single strand of seeded pearls can cost as little as ₹400, but better-quality pearls start at around ₹1000.

In all Indian towns, you can find *kadhai* (Indian woks, also known as *balti*) and other items of cookware for incredibly low prices. Beaten-brass pots are particularly attractive, while steel storage vessels, copper-bottomed cooking pans and steel thali trays are also popular souvenirs.

The people of Bastar in Chhattisgarh discovered a method of smelting iron some 35,000 years ago. Similar techniques are used today to create abstract sculptures of spindly, pointillist animal and human figures, which are often also made into functional items such as lamp stands and coat racks.

A sizeable cottage industry has sprung up in Agra reproducing the ancient Mughal art form of pietra dura (inlaying marble with semiprecious stones). The inspiration for most pieces comes from the Taj Mahal.

Musical Instruments Galore

Quality Indian musical instruments are mostly available in the larger cities, especially Kolkata (Calcutta), Varanasi and Delhi. Prices vary according to the quality – and sound – of the instrument.

Decent tabla sets (pair of drums) with a wooden tabla (tuned treble drum) and metal *doogri* (bass tone drum) cost upwards of ₹3000. Cheaper sets are generally heavier and often sound inferior.

Sitars range anywhere from ₹4000 to ₹20,000 (possibly even more). The sound of each sitar will vary with the wood used and the shape of the gourd, so try a few. Note that some cheaper sitars can warp in colder or hotter climates. On any sitar, make sure the strings ring clearly and check the gourd carefully for damage. Spare string sets, sitar plectrums and a screw-in 'amplifier' gourd are sensible additions.

Other popular instruments include the *shehnai* (Indian flute), the *sarod* (like an Indian lute), the harmonium and the *esraj* (similar to an upright violin). Conventional violins are great value – prices start at ₹3000, while Kolkata is especially known for its quality acoustic guitars (from just ₹2500), which are exported worldwide.

Exquisite Paintings

India is known for its rich painting history. Reproductions of Indian miniature paintings are widely available but the quality varies, with the cheaper ones having less detail and mostly using inferior materials. Udaipur and Bikaner in Rajasthan have a particularly good range of shops specialising in modern reproductions on paper and silk, or you can browse Delhi's numerous state emporiums.

In regions such as Kerala and Tamil Nadu, you'll come across miniature paintings on leaf skeletons that portray domestic life, rural scenes and deities.

The artists' community of Raghurajpur (see p599) near Puri (Odisha) preserves the age-old art of *patachitra* painting. Cotton or *tassar* (silk cloth) is covered with a mixture of gum and chalk; it's then polished, and images of deities and scenes from Hindu legends are painted on with exceedingly fine brushes. Odisha also produces *chitra pothi,* where images are etched onto dried palm-leaf sections with a fine stylus.

Bihar's unique folk art is Mithila (or Madhubani) painting, an ancient art form preserved by the women of Madhubani (see p512). These captivating paintings are most easily found in Patna but are also sold in big city emporiums. In Khajuraho, the Adivart Tribal & Folk Art Museum (p629) sells original Bhili paintings.

In all Tibetan Buddhist areas, including Sikkim, parts of Himachal Pradesh and Ladakh, you can find exquisite *thangkas* (rectangular Tibetan paintings on cloth) of Tantric Buddhist deities and ceremonial mandalas. Some perfectly reproduce the glory of the murals in India's medieval *gompas* (Tibetan Buddhist monasteries); others are much simpler.

BIDRI

Bidri – a form of damascening where silver is inlaid in gunmetal (an alloy of zinc, copper, lead and tin) – is used to make boxes and ornaments in Bidar in Karnataka.

Beautiful Handicrafts

With a long tradition of handicrafts, there's arguably nowhere else on earth that produces as prolific an array of handicrafts as India. From intricately woven shawls and beaded shoulder bags to tribal jewellery and rustic wooden masks, the shopping opportunities are as inspiring and multifarious as the country itself.

Textiles & Mirrorwork

1 Famed for its textile industry, India has an amazing range of fabric traditions: delicate chiffon saris, block-printed bedspreads, mirrorwork wall-hangings, rugged *khadi* (homespun cloth) apparel, silk shirts, tie-dye scarves, woollen shawls and much, much more (p1131).

Papier Mâché

2 Artisans in Jammu & Kashmir are masters of lacquered papier mâché. Crafted from layers of paper then painted with vivid designs and lacquered, items range from floral bowls and letter holders to cheeky faced puppets and festive Christmas decorations (p1130).

Jewellery

3 Gold rings, ruby-studded bangles, silver anklets, emerald earrings, pearl necklaces, tribal costume jewellery...India is a treasure trove of all things sparkly. Apart from gold and silver, there's a wide variety of plastic, brass, wooden and enamelled ornamentation (p1126).

Leatherwork

4 Generations of families carry on the time-honoured practice of crafting leather. Different regions are known for their specialities, with most of India's leatherwork done in Uttar Pradesh. Handbags, belts, wallets and *chappals* (leather footwear) are popular (p1126).

Paintings

5 India has a rich legacy of ancient art techniques, including Rajasthani miniature paintings, South Indian leaf sketchings and *thangkas* (cloth paintings) (p1127).

Clockwise from top left

1. Patchwork quilt in a Goan market **2.** Papier-mâché craftsman, Srinagar **3.** Woman selling jewellery, Jaisalmer

Prices vary, but bank on at least ₹3000 for a decent quality *thangka* of A3 size, and a lot more for large intricate *thangkas*. The selling of antique *thangkas* is illegal, and you would be unlikely to find the real thing anyway.

Throughout the country (especially in big cities like Delhi, Mumbai and Kolkata) look out for shops and galleries selling brilliant contemporary paintings by local artists.

Sumptuous Shawls, Silk & Saris

Indian shawls are famously warm and lightweight – they're often better than the best down jackets. It's worth buying one to use as an emergency blanket on cold night journeys. Shawls are made from all sorts of wool, from lamb's wool to fibres woven from yak, goat and angora–rabbit hair. Many are embroidered with intricate designs.

The undisputed capital of the Indian shawl is the Kullu Valley in Himachal Pradesh, with dozens of women's cooperatives producing very fine woollen pieces – for further details see p304.

Ladakh and Kashmir are major centres for *pashmina* (wool shawl) production – you'll pay at least ₹6000 for the authentic article – however be aware that many so-called *pashminas* are actually made from a mixture of yarns. Shawls from the Northeast States are famously warm, with bold geometric designs. In Sikkim and West Bengal, you may also find fantastically embroidered Bhutanese shawls. Gujarat's Kutch region produces some particularly distinctive woollen shawls, patterned with subtle embroidery and mirrorwork. Handmade shawls and tweeds can also be found in Ranikhet and Almora in Uttarakhand.

Saris are a very popular souvenir, especially given that they can be easily adapted to other purposes (from cushion covers to skirts). Real silk saris are the most expensive, and the silk usually needs to be washed before it becomes soft. The 'silk capital' of India is Kanchipuram in Tamil Nadu, but you can also find fine silk saris (and cheaper scarves) in centres that include Varanasi, Mysore and Kolkata. Assam is renowned for its *muga, endi* and *pat* silks (produced by different species of silkworms), which are widely available in Guwahati. You'll pay upwards of ₹3000 for a quality embroidered silk sari.

Patan in Gujarat, is the centre for the ancient and laborious craft of *patola*-making – every thread in these fine silk saris is individually hand-dyed before weaving, and patterned borders are woven with real gold. Slightly less involved versions are produced in Rajkot (see p705) – only the warp threads are dyed. Gold thread is also used in the famous *kota doria* saris of Kota in Rajasthan.

Aurangabad in Maharashtra, is the traditional centre for the production of *himroo* shawls, sheets and saris, which are made from a blend

In Andhra Pradesh you can buy exquisite cloth paintings called *kalamkari*, which depict deities and historic events; see www.kalamkariart.org for more on this interesting art form.

ON THE PAPIER-MÂCHÉ TRAIL

Artisans in Jammu and Kashmir have been producing lacquered papier mâché for centuries, and papier-mâché-ware is now sold right across India. The basic shape is made in a mould from layers of paper (often recycled newsprint), then painted with fine brushes and lacquered for protection. Prices depend upon the complexity and quality of the design, and the amount of gold leaf. Many pieces feature patterns of animals and flowers, or hunting scenes from Mughal miniature paintings. You can find papier-mâché bowls, boxes, letter holders, coasters, trays, lamps and Christmas decorations. These are very cost-effective souvenirs, but you need to transport them carefully. Rajasthan is *the* place to buy colourful papier-mâché puppets, which are typically sold as a pair – often depicting a husband and wife.

of cotton, silk and silver thread. Silk and gold-thread saris produced at Paithan (near Aurangabad) are some of India's finest – prices range from around ₹6000 to a mind-blowing ₹300,000. Other states that are famous for sari production include Madhya Pradesh for *maheshwari* (cotton saris from Maheshwar), *chanderi* saris (silk saris from Chanderi) and Bishnupur (West Bengal) for *baluchari* saris, which employ a traditional form of weaving with untwisted silk thread.

Terrific Textiles

Textile production is India's major industry and around 40% takes place at the village level, where it's known as *khadi* (homespun cloth) – hence the government-backed *khadi* emporiums around the country. These inexpensive superstores sell all sorts of items made from *khadi*, including the popular Nehru jackets and kurta pyjamas (long shirt and loose-fitting trousers) with sales benefiting rural communities.

You'll find a truly amazing variety of weaving and embroidery techniques around India. In tourist centres such as Goa, Rajasthan and Himachal Pradesh, textiles are stitched into popular items such as shoulder bags, wall hangings, cushion covers, bedspreads, clothes and much more. For information about the beautiful embroidery and other textile work of Kutch, read the boxed text on p714.

Appliqué is an ancient art in India, with most states producing their own version, often featuring abstract or anthropomorphic patterns. The traditional lampshades and *pandals* (tents) used in weddings and festivals are usually produced using the same technique.

In Adivasi (tribal) areas of Gujarat and Rajasthan, small pieces of mirrored glass are embroidered onto fabric, creating eye-catching bags, cushion covers and wall hangings. Jamnagar, in Gujarat, is famous for its vibrant *bandhani* (tie-dye work) used for saris, scarves, and anything else that stays still for long enough. Ahmedabad in Gujarat is a good place to buy Gujarati textiles, and Vadodara in Gujarat is renowned for block-printed fabrics that are used for bedspreads and dress material.

Block-printed and woven textiles are sold by fabric shops all over India, often in vivid colour combinations. Each region has its own speciality. The India-wide retail chain-store Fabindia (www.fabindia.com), is striving to preserve traditional patterns and fabrics, transforming them into highly accessible items for home decoration, and Indian and Western-style fashions.

Odisha has a reputation for bright appliqué and *ikat* (a Southeast-Asian technique where thread is tie-dyed before weaving). The town of Pipli, between Bhubaneswar and Puri, produces some particularly striking appliqué work. The techniques used to create *kalamkari* cloth paintings in Andhra Pradesh (a centre for this ancient art is Sri Kalahasti) and Gujarat are also used to make lovely wall hangings and lamp shades.

Lucknow in Uttar Pradesh, is noted for hand-woven embroidered *chikan* cloth, which features incredibly intricate floral motifs. Punjab is famous for the attractively folksy *phulkari* embroidery (flowerwork with stitches in diagonal, vertical and horizontal directions), while women in West Bengal use chain stitches to make complex figurative designs called *kantha*. A similar technique is used to make *gabba,* women's *kurtas* (long shirts) and men's wedding jackets in Kashmir.

Batik can be found throughout India. It's often used for saris and *salwar kameez* (traditional dresslike tunic and trouser combination for women). City boutiques flaunt particularly trendy *salwar kameez* in a staggering array of fabrics and styles. Big Indian cities such as Mumbai, Bengaluru and Delhi are top spots to pick up haute couture by talented Indian designers, as well as moderately priced Western fashions.

Be aware that it's illegal to buy *shahtoosh* shawls, as rare Tibetan antelopes are slaughtered to provide the wool. If you come across anyone selling these shawls, inform local authorities.

Traditional Indian Textiles, by John Gillow and Nicholas Barnard, explores India's beautiful regional textiles and includes sections on tie-dye, weaving, bead-work, brocades and even camel girths.

Beautiful Woodcarving

Woodcarving is an ancient art form throughout India. In Kashmir, walnut wood is used to make finely carved wooden screens, tables, jewellery boxes and trays, inspired by the decorative trim of houseboats. Willow cricket bats are another Kashmiri speciality.

Wood inlay is one of Bihar's oldest crafts – you'll find lovely wooden wall hangings, tabletops, trays and boxes inlaid with metals and bone.

Sandalwood carvings of Hindu deities is one of Karnataka's specialities, but you'll pay a king's ransom for the real thing – a 10cm-high Ganesh costs around ₹3000 in sandalwood, compared to roughly ₹300 in kadamb wood. However, the sandalwood will release fragrance for years.

In Udaipur in Rajasthan, you can buy brightly painted figures of Hindu deities carved from mango wood. In many parts of Rajasthan you can also find fabric printing blocks carved from teak wood.

The carved wooden massage wheels and rollers available at many Hindu pilgrimage sites make good gifts for friends and family back home.

Buddhist woodcarvings are a speciality of Sikkim, Ladakh, Arunachal Pradesh and all Tibetan refugee areas. You'll find wall plaques of the eight lucky signs, dragons and *chaam* masks, used for ritual dances. Most of the masks are cheap reproductions, but you can sometimes find genuine *chaam* masks made from lightweight whitewood or papier mâché from ₹3000 upwards.

Other Great Finds

It's little surprise that Indian spices are snapped up by tourists. Virtually all towns have shops and bazaars selling locally made spices at great prices. Karnataka, Kerala, Uttar Pradesh, Rajasthan and Tamil Nadu produce most of the spices that go into garam masala (the 'hot mix' used to flavour Indian curries), while the Northeast States and Sikkim are known for black cardamom and cinnamon bark. Note that some countries, such as Australia, have stringent rules regarding the import of animal and plant products. Check with your country's embassy for details.

Attar (essential oil, mostly made from flowers) shops can be found right around the country. Mysore in Karnataka is especially famous for its sandalwood oil, while Mumbai is a major centre for the trade of traditional fragrances, including valuable *oud,* made from a rare mould that grows on the bark of the agarwood tree. In Tamil Nadu, Ooty and Kodaikanal produce aromatic and medicinal oils from herbs, flowers and eucalyptus.

GANDHI'S CLOTH

More than 80 years ago Mahatma Gandhi sat by his spinning wheel and urged Indians to support the freedom movement by ditching their foreign-made clothing and turning to *khadi* – homespun cloth. Like the spinning wheel itself, *khadi* became a symbol of the struggle for freedom and of Indian independence, and the fabric is still closely associated with politics. The government-run, nonprofit group Khadi and Village Industries Commission (www.kvic.org.in), serves to promote *khadi*, many politicians still wear it and the Indian flag is only supposed to be made from *khadi* cloth. In recent years the fashion world has taken a growing interest in this simple fabric, which is usually cotton, but can also be silk or wool.

Khadi outlets are simple, no-nonsense places from which to pick up genuine Indian clothing such as kurta (long, collarless shirt), pyjamas, headscarves, saris, and at some branches, assorted handicrafts. They are listed in the Shopping sections of various chapters in this book, but you'll find them all over India. Prices are reasonable and are often discounted in the period around Gandhi's birthday (2 October). A number of outlets also have a tailoring service.

Overall, a comparatively small proportion of the money brought to India by tourism reaches people in rural areas. Travellers can make a greater contribution by shopping at community cooperatives, set up to protect and promote traditional cottage industries, and to provide education, training and a sustainable livelihood at the grassroots' level. Many of these projects focus on refugees, low-caste women, tribal people and others living on society's fringes.

The quality of products sold at cooperatives is high and the prices are usually fixed, which means you won't have to haggle. A share of the sales money is channelled directly into social projects such as schools, healthcare, training and other advocacy programs for socially disadvantaged groups. Shopping at the national network of Khadi and Village Industries Commission emporiums will also contribute to rural communities (also see the box on p1132).

Wherever you travel, keep your eyes peeled for fair-trade cooperatives and also see this book's regional chapters for recommendations, where they exist.

Indian incense is exported worldwide, with Bengaluru and Mysore, both in Karnataka, being major producers. Incense from Auroville in Tamil Nadu is also well regarded.

Meanwhile, a speciality of Goa is *feni* (liquor distilled from coconut milk or cashews) – a head-spinning spirit that often comes in decorative bottles.

Quality Indian tea is sold in Darjeeling and Kalimpong (both in West Bengal), Assam and Sikkim, as well as parts of South India. There are also commendable tea retailers in Delhi and other urban hubs.

In Bhopal in Madhya Pradesh, colourful *jari* shoulder bags, embroidered with beads, are a speciality. Also on the portables front, the Northeast States are noted for their beautiful hand-woven baskets and wickerwork – each tribe has its own unique basket shape.

Jodhpur in Rajasthan, among other places, is famed for its antiques, but check out the box on p1165 before buying.

Fine-quality handmade paper – often fashioned into cards, boxes and notebooks – is worth seeking out, with good places to start including Puducherry in Tamil Nadu, Delhi and Mumbai.

Hats are also popular – the Assamese make decorated reed-pith sun hats, and Tibetan refugees produce woollen hats, gloves and scarves, which are sold nationwide. There's also the traditional caps worn by men and women of Himalayan tribes; they're available at many towns in Himachal Pradesh.

India has a phenomenal range of books at very competitive prices, including gorgeous leather-bound titles.

Music CDs by local musicians are also super value.

In towns with Buddhist communities, such as McLeod Ganj, Leh, Manali, Gangtok, Kalimpong and Darjeeling, keep an eye out for 'Buddha shops' selling devotional objects such as prayer flags, singing bowls, hand-bells and prayer wheels.

Sacred Architecture

India has a remarkable collection of historic and contemporary sacred architecture that draws inspiration from a variety of religious denominations. Although few of the wooden and occasionally brick temples built in early times have weathered the vagaries of time, by the advent of the Guptas (4th to 6th centuries AD) of North India, sacred structures of a new type – better engineered to withstand the elements – were being constructed, and these largely set the standard for temples for several hundred years.

Sri Meenakshi Temple

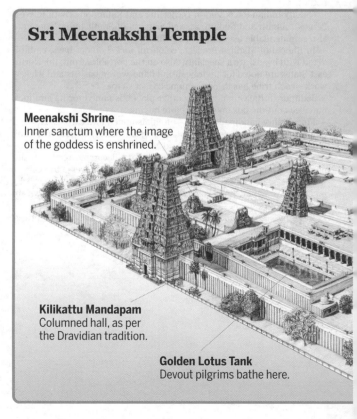

Meenakshi Shrine
Inner sanctum where the image of the goddess is enshrined.

Kilikattu Mandapam
Columned hall, as per the Dravidian tradition.

Golden Lotus Tank
Devout pilgrims bathe here.

For Hindus, the square is a perfect shape, and complex rules govern the location, design and building of each temple, based on numerology, astrology, astronomy and religious principles. Essentially, a temple represents a map of the universe. At the centre is an unadorned space, the *garbhagriha* (inner sanctum), which is symbolic of the 'womb-cave' from which the universe is believed to have emerged. This provides a residence for the deity to which the temple is dedicated.

Above a Hindu temple's shrine rises a tower superstructure known as a *vimana* in South India, and a *sikhara* in North India. The *sikhara* is curvilinear and topped with a grooved disk, on which sits a pot-shaped finial, while the *vimana* is stepped, with the grooved disk being replaced by a solid dome. Some temples have a *mandapa* (forechamber) connected to the sanctum by vestibules. The *mandapa* may also contain *vimanas* or *sikharas*.

A *gopuram* is a soaring pyramidal gateway tower of a Dravidian temple. The towering *gopurams* of various South Indian temple complexes, such as the nine-storey *gopurams* of Madurai's Sri Meenakshi Temple (p1036), took ornamentation and monumentalism to new levels.

Commonly used for ritual bathing and religious ceremonies, as well as adding aesthetic appeal, temple tanks have long been a focal point of temple activity. These often-vast, angular, engineered reservoirs of water, sometimes fed by rain, sometimes fed – via a complicated drainage system – by rivers, serve both sacred and secular purposes. The waters

Discover more about India's diverse temple architecture (in addition to other temple-related information) at Temple Net (www .templenet.com).

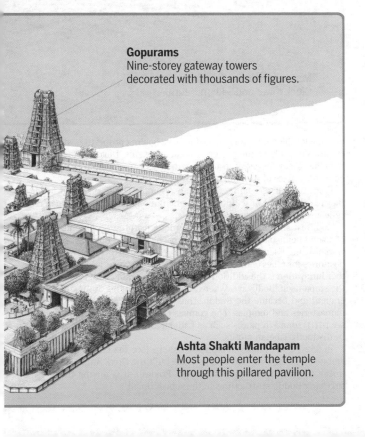

Gopurams
Nine-storey gateway towers decorated with thousands of figures.

Ashta Shakti Mandapam
Most people enter the temple through this pillared pavilion.

Golden Temple

Pilgrim accommodation

Main entrance
Clock tower and Sikh museum.

of some temple tanks are believed to have healing properties, while others are said to have the power to wash away sins. Devotees (as well as travellers) may be required to wash their feet in a temple tank before entering a place of worship.

From the outside, Jain temples can resemble Hindu ones, but inside they're often a riot of sculptural ornamentation, the very opposite of ascetic austerity.

Buddhist shrines have their own unique features. Stupas, composed of a solid hemisphere topped by a spire, characterise Buddhist places of worship and essentially evolved from burial mounds. They served as repositories for relics of the Buddha and, later, other venerated souls. A further innovation is the addition of a *chaitya* (assembly hall) leading up to the stupa itself. Bodhgaya, where Siddhartha Gautama attained enlightenment and became the Buddha, has a collection of notable Buddhist monasteries and temples. The gompas (Tibetan Buddhist monasteries; see p1111) found in places such as Ladakh and Sikkim are characterised by distinctly Tibetan motifs.

In 262 BC the Mauryan emperor Ashoka (see the boxed text, p1087) embraced Buddhism, and as a penance built the Great Stupa at Sanchi, in the central Indian state of Madhya Pradesh. It is among the oldest surviving Buddhist structures in the subcontinent.

Masterpieces of Traditional Indian Architecture by Satish Grover and *The History of Architecture in India* by Christopher Tadgell proffer interesting insights into temple architecture.

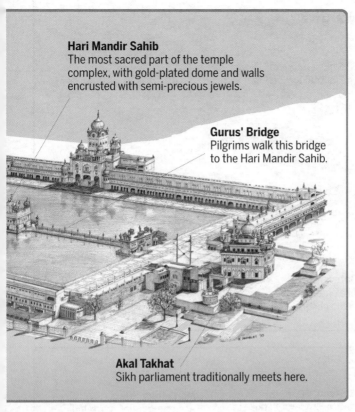

Hari Mandir Sahib
The most sacred part of the temple complex, with gold-plated dome and walls encrusted with semi-precious jewels.

Gurus' Bridge
Pilgrims walk this bridge to the Hari Mandir Sahib.

Akal Takhat
Sikh parliament traditionally meets here.

India also has a rich collection of Islamic sacred sites, as its Muslim rulers contributed their own architectural conventions, including arched cloisters and domes. The Mughals uniquely melded Persian, Indian and provincial styles. Renowned examples include Humayun's Tomb in Delhi (p67), Agra Fort (p352) and the ancient fortified city of Fatehpur Sikri (p365). Emperor Shah Jahan was responsible for some of India's most spectacular architectural creations, most notably the milky white Taj Mahal (p350).

Islamic art eschews any hint of idolatry or portrayal of God, and it has evolved a rich heritage of calligraphic and decorative designs. In terms of mosque architecture, the basic design elements are similar worldwide. A large hall is dedicated to communal prayer and within the hall is a *mihrab* (niche) indicating the direction of Mecca. The faithful are called to prayer from minarets, placed at cardinal points. Delhi's formidable 17th-century Jama Masjid (p66) is India's biggest mosque, its courtyard able to hold 25,000 people.

The Sikh faith was founded by Guru Nanak, the first of 10 gurus, in the 15th century. Sikh temples, called gurdwaras, can usually be identified by a *nishan sahib* (a flagpole flying a triangular flag with the Sikh insignia). Amritsar's sublime Golden Temple (p213) is Sikhism's holiest shrine.

The focal point of a gompa is the *dukhang* (prayer hall), where monks assemble to chant passages from sacred scriptures.

Jama Masjid

Minaret
Tower from which the muezzin (crier) calls the faithful to worship.

Central Courtyard
Holds up to 25,000 people for Friday prayers.

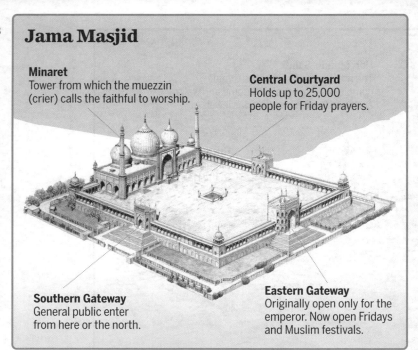

Southern Gateway
General public enter from here or the north.

Eastern Gateway
Originally open only for the emperor. Now open Fridays and Muslim festivals.

Sanchi

Great Stupa
Built by the emperor Ashoka in the 2nd century BC to enshrine relics of the Buddha.

Monastery Ruins
Accommodation surrounding a central courtyard.

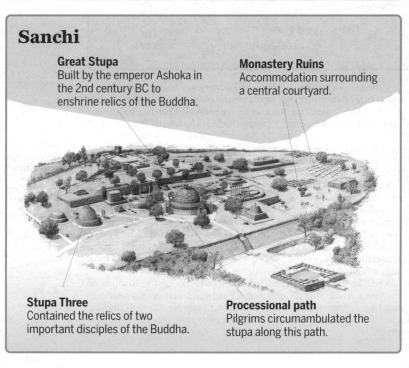

Stupa Three
Contained the relics of two important disciples of the Buddha.

Processional path
Pilgrims circumambulated the stupa along this path.

The Arts

Over the centuries India's many ethnic groups have spawned a vivid artistic heritage that is both inventive and spiritually significant. Today, artistic beauty lies around almost every corner, whether it's the garishly painted trucks rattling down dusty country roads or the exquisite, spidery body art of *mehndi* (henna). Indeed, a glowing highlight of subcontinental travel is its wealth of art treasures, from ancient temple dances to a dynamic performing-arts scene. Contemporary Indian artists have fused historical elements with edgy modern influences, creating art, dance and music that have won acclaim in both the domestic and international arenas.

Dance

The ancient Indian art of dance is traditionally linked to mythology and classical literature. Dance can be divided into two main forms: classical and folk.

Classical dance is essentially based on well-defined traditional disciplines. Some classical dance styles:

» Bharata Natyam (also spelt *bharatanatyam*), which originated in Tamil Nadu, has been embraced throughout India.

» Kathakali, which has its roots in Kerala, is sometimes referred to as 'dance' but essentially is not – see p1144.

» Kathak has Hindu and Islamic influences and was particularly popular with the Mughals. Kathak suffered a period of notoriety when it moved from the courts into houses where nautch (dancing) girls tantalised audiences with renditions of the Krishna-and-Radha love story. It was restored as a serious art form in the early 20th century.

» Manipuri, which has a delicate, lyrical flavour, hails from Manipur. It attracted a wider audience in the 1920s when the acclaimed Bengali writer Rabindranath Tagore invited one of its most revered exponents to teach at Shantiniketan (West Bengal).

» Kuchipudi is a 17th-century dance-drama that originated in the Andhra Pradesh village from which it takes its name. The story centres on the envious wife of Krishna.

» Odissi, claimed to be India's oldest classical dance form, was originally a temple art, and was later also performed at royal courts.

India's second major dance form, folk, is widespread and varied. It ranges from the high-spirited bhangra dance of Punjab to the theatrical dummy-horse dances of Karnataka and Tamil Nadu, and the graceful fishers' dance of Odisha.

Pioneers of modern dance forms in India include Uday Shankar (older brother of sitar master Ravi), who once partnered Russian ballerina Anna Pavlova. Rabindranath Tagore was another innovator; in 1901 he

Immerse yourself in India's incredibly vibrant performing-arts scene – especially classical dance and music – at Art India (www. artindia.net).

set up a school at Shantiniketan in West Bengal that promoted the arts, including dance.

Music

Indian classical music traces its roots back to Vedic times, when religious poems chanted by priests were first collated in an anthology called the Rig-Veda. Over the millennia classical music has been shaped by many influences, and the legacy today is Carnatic (characteristic of South India) and Hindustani (the classical style of North India) music. With common origins, both share a number of features. Both use the raga (the melodic shape of the music) and *tala* (the rhythmic meter characterised by the number of beats); *tintal,* for example, has a *tala* of 16 beats. The audience follows the *tala* by clapping at the appropriate beat, which in *tintal* is at beats one, five and 13. There's no clap at the beat of nine; that's the *khali* (empty section), which is indicated by a wave of the hand. Both the raga and the *tala* are used as a basis for composition and improvisation.

Both Carnatic and Hindustani music are performed by small ensembles, generally comprising three to six musicians, and both have many instruments in common. There's no fixed pitch, but there are differences between the two styles. Hindustani has been more heavily influenced by Persian musical conventions (a result of Mughal rule); Carnatic music, as it developed in South India, cleaves more closely to theory. The most striking difference, at least for those unfamiliar with India's classical forms, is Carnatic's greater use of voice.

One of the best-known Indian instruments is the sitar (large stringed instrument) with which the soloist plays the raga. Other stringed instruments include the sarod (which is plucked) and the sarangi (which is played with a bow). Also popular is the tabla (twin drums), which provides the *tala*. The drone, which runs on two basic notes, is provided by the oboelike *shehnai* or the stringed *tampura* (also spelt tamboura). The hand-pumped keyboard harmonium is used as a secondary melody instrument for vocal music.

Indian regional folk music is widespread and varied. Wandering musicians, magicians, snake charmers and storytellers often use song to entertain their audiences; the storyteller usually sings the tales from the great epics.

In North India you may come across *qawwali* (Islamic devotional singing), performed in mosques or at musical concerts. *Qawwali* concerts usually take the form of a *mehfil* (gathering) with a lead singer, a second singer, harmonium and tabla players, and a thunderous chorus of junior singers and clappers, all sitting cross-legged on the floor. The singers whip up the audience with lines of poetry, dramatic hand gestures and religious phrases as the two voices weave in and out, bouncing off each other to create an improvised, surging sound. On command the chorus dives in with a hypnotic and rhythmic refrain. Members of the audience often sway and shout out in ecstatic appreciation.

A completely different genre altogether, filmi music entails musical scores from Bollywood movies – modern (slower paced) love serenades feature among the predominantly hyperactive dance songs. To ascertain the latest filmi favourites, as well as in-vogue Indian pop singers, enquire at music stores.

Radio and TV have played a vital role in broadcasting different music styles – from soothing bhajans to booming Bollywood hits – to even the remotest corners of India.

Cinema

India's film industry was born in the late 19th century – the first major Indian-made motion picture, *Panorama of Calcutta,* was screened in

Indian Classical Dance by Leela Venkataraman and Avinash Pasricha is a lavishly illustrated book covering various Indian dance forms, including Bharata Natyam, Odissi, Kuchipudi and Kathakali.

To tune into the melodious world of Hindustani classical music, including a glossary of musical terms, get a copy of *Nād: Understanding Raga Music* by Sandeep Bagchee.

1899. India's first real feature film, *Raja Harishchandra,* was made during the silent era in 1913 and it's ultimately from this that Indian cinema traces its vibrant lineage.

Today, India's film industry is the biggest in the world – larger than Hollywood – and Mumbai (Bombay), the Hindi-language film capital, is affectionately dubbed 'Bollywood'. India's other major film-producing cities include Chennai, Hyderabad and Bengaluru, with a number of other centres producing films in their own regional vernaculars. Big-budget films are often partly or entirely shot abroad, with some countries vigorously wooing Indian production companies because of the potential spin-off tourism revenue these films generate.

An average of 1000 feature films are produced annually in India. Apart from hundreds of millions of local Bollywood buffs, there are also millions of Non-Resident Indian (NRI) fans, who have played a significant role in catapulting Indian cinema onto the international stage.

Broadly speaking, there are two categories of Indian films. Most prominent is the mainstream movie – three hours and still running, these blockbusters are often tear jerkers and are packed with dramatic twists interspersed with numerous song-and-dance performances. There are no explicit sex, or even kissing, scenes (although smooching is creeping into some Bollywood movies) in Indian films made for the local market; however, lack of nudity is often compensated for by heroines dressed in skimpy or body-hugging attire.

The second Indian film genre is art house, which adopts Indian 'reality' as its base. Generally speaking they are, or at least are supposed to be, socially and politically relevant. Usually made on infinitely smaller budgets than their commercial cousins, these films are the ones that win kudos at global film festivals and award ceremonies.

For some film recommendations, see p1081; for information about Bollywood and working as a film extra, see p734.

Literature

India has a long tradition of Sanskrit literature, although works in the vernacular have contributed to a particularly rich legacy. In fact, it's claimed there are as many literary traditions as there are written languages.

Bengalis are traditionally credited with producing some of India's most celebrated literature, a movement often referred to as the Indian or Bengal Renaissance, which flourished from the 19th century with works by Bankim Chandra Chatterjee. But the man who to this day is mostly credited with first propelling India's cultural richness onto the world stage is the Bengali Rabindranath Tagore.

India boasts an ever-growing list of internationally acclaimed authors. Some particularly prominent writers include Vikram Seth, best known for his award-winning epic novel *A Suitable Boy,* and Amitav Ghosh, who has won a number of accolades; his *Sea of Poppies* was shortlisted for the 2008 Man Booker Prize. Indeed, recent years have seen a number of Indian-born authors win the prestigious Man Booker Prize, the most recent being Aravind Adiga, who won in 2008 for his debut novel, *The White Tiger.* The prize went to Kiran Desai in 2006 for *The Inheritance of Loss;* Kiran Desai is the daughter of the award-winning Indian novelist Anita Desai, who has thrice been a Booker Prize nominee. In 1997, Arundhati Roy won the Booker Prize for her novel, *The God of Small Things,* while Salman Rushdie took this coveted award in 1981 for *Midnight's Children.*

Trinidad-born Indian writer VS Naipaul has written widely about India and won many notable awards including the Booker Prize (1971) and the Nobel Prize in Literature (2001).

THE ARTS

Encyclopedia of Indian Cinema by Ashish Rajadhyaksha and Paul Willemen chronicles India's dynamic cinematic history, spanning from 1897 to the 21st century.

The brilliant and prolific writer and artist Rabindranath Tagore won the Nobel Prize in Literature in 1913 for *Gitanjali.* For a taste of Tagore's work, a good place to start is his *Selected Short Stories.*

Hobnob with acclaimed local and international writers at Asia's biggest literary event, the Jaipur Literature Festival (www.jaipur literaturefestival. org), held in late January in Jaipur (Rajasthan).

Spirited Celebrations

If there's any country that knows how to throw a celebration, it's India. With one of the world's most spectacular festival calendars, there's something happening every other day, from country carnivals and temple festivals to big city extravaganzas and beachside fairs.

Diwali

1 Fondly dubbed the 'Festival of Lights' (p23), Diwali is an upbeat Hindu festival celebrated across India over five cheerful days. Homes and businesses are decked out with glittering lights and there's a surfeit of fireworks, crackers and sweets.

Wedding Processions

2 Wedding processions (p24) swiftly transform dusty streets into a swirl of colour. The groom, usually riding a white horse, is flanked by a small army of family and friends who sing and dance to the beat of a lively brass band.

Holi

3 Heralding the arrival of spring, Holi (p21) is certainly one of India's most rambunctious celebrations. During this happy Hindu 'Festival of Colours' merrymakers playfully douse one another with water and coloured powder. Bonfires symbolise the demise of the wicked demoness, Holika.

Dussehra & Durga Puja

4 These auspicious Hindu festivals (p23; falling in the Indian calendar of Asvina) celebrate the triumph of good over evil; the former commemorates Lord Rama's victory over the demon Ravana; the latter honours goddess Durga's conquest over the demon Mahishasura.

Kumbh Mela

5 This colossal Hindu festival (p1103) takes place four times every 12 years at four different locations across central and northern India. Attracting tens of millions of Hindu pilgrims (and spectators), the Kumbh Mela is the largest religious congregation on the planet.

Clockwise from top left
1. Diwali lighting ceremony **2.** A Mumbai bride's jewellery and henna **3.** Holi festival fun **4.** Dussehra prayers

RICHARD ROSS / GETTY IMAGES

RICHARD I'ANSON / LONELY PLANET IMAGES ©

1143

CHRISTER FREDRIKSSON / LONELY PLANET IMAGES ©

Painting

Around 1500 years ago artists covered the walls and ceilings of the Ajanta caves in Maharashtra, western India, with scenes from the Buddha's life. The figures are endowed with an unusual freedom and grace, and contrast with the next major style that emerged from this part of India in the 11th century.

India's Jain community created some particularly lavish temple art. However, after the Muslim conquest of Gujarat in 1299 the Jains turned their attention to illustrated manuscripts, which could be hidden away. These manuscripts are the only known form of Indian painting that survived the Islamic conquest of North India.

The Indo-Persian style – characterised by geometric design coupled with flowing form – developed from Islamic royal courts, although the depiction of the elongated eye is one convention that seems to have been retained from indigenous sources. The Persian influence blossomed when artisans fled to India following the 1507 Uzbek attack on Herat (in present-day Afghanistan), and with trade and gift-swapping between the Persian city of Shiraz, an established centre for miniature production, and Indian provincial sultans.

The 1526 victory by Babur at the Battle of Panipat ushered in the era of the Mughals in India. Although Babur and his son Humayun were both patrons of the arts, it's Humayun's son Akbar who is generally credited with developing the characteristic Mughal style. This painting style, often in colourful miniature form, largely depicts court life, architecture, battle and hunting scenes, as well as detailed portraits. Akbar recruited artists from far and wide, and artistic endeavour first centred on the production of illustrated manuscripts (topics varied from history to mythology), but later broadened into portraiture and the glorification of everyday events. European painting styles influenced some artists, and this influence occasionally reveals itself in experiments with motifs and perspective.

Akbar's son Jehangir also patronised painting, but he preferred portraiture, and his fascination with natural science resulted in a vibrant legacy of paintings of flowers and animals. Under Jehangir's son Shah Jahan, the Mughal style became less fluid and, although the bright colouring was eye-catching, the paintings lacked the vigour of before.

Various schools of miniature painting (small paintings crammed with detail) emerged in Rajasthan from around the 17th century. The subject matter ranged from royal processions to shikar (hunting expeditions), with many artists influenced by Mughal styles. The intense colours, still evident today in miniatures and frescoes in some Indian palaces, were often derived from crushed semiprecious stones, while the gold and silver colouring is finely pounded pure gold and silver leaf.

Get arty with *Indian Art* by Roy Craven, *Contemporary Indian Art: Other Realities* edited by Yashodhara Dalmia, and *Indian Miniature Painting* by Dr Daljeet and Professor PC Jain.

MAGICAL MEHNDI

Mehndi is the traditional art of painting a woman's hands (and sometimes feet) with intricate henna designs for auspicious ceremonies, such as marriage. If quality henna is used, the design, which is orange-brown, can last up to one month.

In touristy areas, *mehndi*-wallahs are adept at applying henna tattoo 'bands' on the arms, legs and lower back. If you're thinking about getting *mehndi* applied, allow at least a couple of hours for the design process and required drying time (during drying you can't use your hennaed hands). Once applied, henna usually fades faster the more you wash it and apply lotion.

It's always wise to request the artist to do a 'test' spot on your arm before proceeding, as nowadays some dyes contain chemicals that can cause allergies. If good-quality henna is used, you should not feel any pain during or after the procedure.

By the 19th century, painting in North India was notably influenced by Western styles (especially English watercolours), giving rise to what has been dubbed the Company School, which had its centre in Delhi.

In 21st-century India, paintings by contemporary Indian artists have been selling at record numbers (and prices) around the world. One very successful online art auction house is the Mumbai-based Saffronart (www.saffronart.com).

Over recent years, international auction houses have been descending upon India, to either set up offices or secure gallery alliances, in order to grab a piece of the action of what they have identified as a major growth market.

Elephants & Tigers: India's Sanctuaries

The wildlife of India comprises a fascinating ragtag group, a veritable melting pot of animals from Europe, Asia and ancient Gondwanaland all swirled together in a bewildering mix of habitats ranging from lush mangrove swamps to desolate sand deserts and icy alpine meadows.

Home to many charismatic species both large and small, India harbours some of the richest biodiversity in the world. There are 397 species of mammals, 1250 birds, 460 reptiles, 240 amphibians and 2546 fish – among the highest species count for any country. India is best known for its signature species – elephants, tigers, monkeys, leopards, antelopes and rhinos. Many of the animals discussed in this chapter are among India's most endangered and charismatic wildlife.

Most of the semitropical lowland and hill forests that once dominated much of central and southern India have been cut down, endangered by human competition for land and water, but this region is still home to the majority of India's most intriguing animals, especially where the remaining forests have been protected. So take some time to chase down a rhino or sight a tiger on a traditional elephant safari, or try for something unexpected off the beaten track.

Top Parks North

» Corbett Tiger Reserve

» Kaziranga National Park

» Keoladeo Ghana National Park

Animals

Understandably, wildlife-watching has become one of the country's prime tourist activities and there are hundreds of national parks and wildlife sanctuaries offering opportunities to spot rare and unusual wildlife. Even better, your visit helps notify the government that protected parks and wildlife have an important value.

Located almost perfectly in the centre of the country, Bandhavgarh National Park is one dynamic example of what the original Indian landscape might have been like. Here you can explore meadows, forests and rocky ridges in a thrilling search for tigers and leopards, and other big game. Or for a completely different, but equally pristine, experience check out the exotic one-horned rhinos and wild elephants in Assam's Kaziranga National Park.

So Many Cats

India is justifiably famous for its tigers, and just admit it – you secretly hope to see one. But India is actually home to 15 species of cats, so don't miss out on any opportunity to see one of the other gorgeous felines.

It could be said that the global effort to protect tigers all started in India, and many experts feel that India's sizeable population of tigers may be the species' last great stronghold.

Unfortunately, despite a massive and well-funded conservation effort, the black market in tigers remains an irresistible temptation for both wildlife-poaching gangs and impoverished villagers, so tiger numbers continue to fall at a precipitous rate, even in supposedly secure sanctuaries. For more information, see the boxed text, p1147

Protection efforts have been successfully made on behalf of the Asiatic lion, a thoroughly different creature than the more familiar African lion. A hundred years ago there were only 20 of these lions left in the world, but their population of 300 now seems to be doing fairly well in Gujarat's Sasan Gir Wildlife Sanctuary (see p699), where it's also possible to see 300 or so leopards, another of India's famous big cats.

Other dramatic felines include the clouded leopard, and its smaller cousin the marbled cat, both of which lurk in the jungles of northeast India. These cats are strikingly marbled with rosettes and rings of colour for camouflage in their forested homes. Closely related but much paler in colour is the infamous snow leopard, an animal so elusive that many locals claim it can appear and disappear at will. A few snow leopards survive in Ladakh, Sikkim, Uttarakhand, Himachal Pradesh and Arunachal Pradesh.

Top Parks Central
» Bandhavgarh National Park
» Kanha National Park
» Sunderbans Tiger Reserve

The Big Ones

If you had to pick India's top three animals, the list would inevitably include tigers, elephants and rhinos, all of which are scarce and in need of stringent protection. It's fortunate that Asian elephants – a somewhat smaller version of an African elephant – are revered in Hindu custom or they would have been hunted into extinction long ago, as they were in neighbouring China. It's true that many of India's elephants were pressed into domestication and put to work, but enough survived in the wild

ENDANGERED SPECIES

Despite having amazing biodiversity, India faces a growing challenge from its exploding human population. Wildlife is severely threatened by poaching and habitat loss. At last count, India had 569 threatened species, comprising 247 species of plants, 89 species of mammals, 82 species of birds, 26 species of reptiles, 68 species of amphibians, 35 species of fish and 22 species of invertebrates.

Prior to 1972 India had only five national parks, so the Wildlife Protection Act was introduced that year to set aside parks and stem the abuse of wildlife. The act was followed by a string of similar pieces of legislation with bold ambitions but few teeth with which to enforce them.

A rare success story has been Project Tiger (see p1148). All of India's wild cats, from leopards to snow leopards, panthers and jungle cats are facing extinction from habitat loss and poaching for the lucrative trade in skins and body parts for Chinese medicine (a whole tiger carcass can fetch upwards of UK£32,000). Government estimates suggest that India is losing 1% of its tigers every year to poachers.

Even highly protected rhinos are poached for the medicine trade – rhino horn is highly valued as an aphrodisiac and as a material for making handles for daggers in the Gulf. Elephants are regularly poached for ivory, and 320 elephants were poached from 2000 to 2008 – we implore you not to support this trade by buying ivory souvenirs. Various species of deer are threatened by hunting for food and trophies, and the chiru, or Tibetan antelope, is nearly extinct because its hair is woven into wool for expensive shahtoosh shawls.

India's bear species are under threat and sloth bears are widely poached to be used as 'dancing bears' at tourist centres such as Agra and Jaipur. In the water, India's freshwater dolphins are in dire straits from pollution and human competition. The sea-turtle population on the Orissa coast also faces problems – see the boxed text, p603.

HOORAY FOR PROJECT TIGER

When naturalist Jim Corbett first raised the alarm in the 1930s no one believed that tigers would ever be threatened. At the time it was believed there were 40,000 tigers in India, although no one had ever conducted a census. Then came Independence, which put guns into the hands of villagers who pushed into formerly off-limits hunting reserves to hunt for highly profitable tiger skins. By the time an official census was conducted in 1972, there were only 1800 tigers left and international outcry prompted Indira Gandhi to make the tiger the national symbol of India and set up **Project Tiger** (http://project tiger.nic.in). The project has since established 39 tiger reserves totalling over 32,000 sq km that not only protect this top predator but all animals that live in the same habitats. After an initial round of successes, tiger numbers have recently plummeted from 3600 in 2002 to a new low of 1500 due to relentless poaching, so another $153 million and high-tech equipment have been devoted to the effort to help stop this slide towards extinction.

that they now seem to be doing relatively well. But because elephants migrate long distances in search of food, these 3000kg animals require huge parks and run into predictable conflict when herds of elephants attempt to follow ancestral paths that are now occupied by villages and farms. Some of the best parks for elephant viewing are Corbett Tiger Reserve (see p430) and Nagarhole National Park (p865) in Karnataka.

There are far fewer one-horned rhinos left and two-thirds (just shy of 2000) of the world's total population can be found in Kaziranga National Park (see p559), where they serenely wander the park's lush alluvial grasslands at the base of the Himalayas. They may look sedate but rhinos are unpredictably dangerous, built like battering rams, covered in plates of armour-like skin, and use their sharp teeth to tear off chunks of flesh when they attack, so let's just say that it's safest to watch rhinos from the back of an elephant.

Hoofed & Handed

By far, the most abundant forms of wildlife you'll see in India are deer (nine species), antelope (six species), goats and sheep (10 species), and primates (15 species). In the open grasslands of many parks look for the stocky nilgai, India's largest antelope, or elegantly horned blackbucks. If you're heading for the mountains, keep your eyes open in the Himalayas for blue sheep with their partially curled horns or the rare argali with its fully curled horns that can be found in Ladakh. The deserts of Rajasthan and Gujarat are home to desert-adapted species such as chinkaras (Indian gazelles); while the mangrove swamps of the Sundarban Delta have chitals (spotted deer), who cope with their brackish environment by excreting salt from their nasal glands.

India's primates range from the extremely rare hoolock gibbon and golden langur of the northeast, to species that are so common as to be a pest – most notably the stocky and aggressive rhesus macaque and the elegant grey langur. In the south, the pesky monkeys that loiter around temples and tourist sites are bonnet macaques.

Threatened species clinging on in rainforests in the south include lion-tailed macaques, glossy black Nilgiri langurs and slender loris, an adept insectcatcher with huge eyes for nocturnal hunting.

Top Parks South

» Mahatma Gandhi Marine National Park

» Nagarhole National Park

» Periyar Wildlife Sanctuary

Birds

With well over one thousand species of birds, India is a birdwatcher's dream. Many birds are thinly spread over this vast country, but wherever critical habitat has been preserved in the midst of dense human activity you might see phenomenal numbers of birds in one location. Winter can be a particularly good time, in Keoladeo Ghana and elsewhere in the country, because northern migrants arrive to kick back in the lush subtropical warmth of the Indian peninsula. In the breeding season look for colourful barbets, sunbirds, parakeets and magpies everywhere you travel, or make a special trip into the Himalayas in search of one of India's (and the world's) mostly highly sought-after birds, the enigmatic ibisbill.

Once considered the premier duck-hunting destination in the British Empire when royal hunting parties would shoot 4000 ducks in a single day, the seasonal wetlands of Keoladeo Ghana (see p128) were elevated to national park status in 1982. Now whittled down to a relatively small pocket of habitat amid a sea of villages and agricultural fields, this is still one of the finest birdwatching destinations in the world. Even better, Keoladeo Ghana and its abundant birdlife are ridiculously easy to explore, just hop on a bike from town or from one of the local lodges and toodle around the flat tracks that weave among the park's clearly defined ponds and marshes. In the winter there are so many ducks, herons, storks, cranes, egrets and raptors packing themselves into the park that your foremost problem will be trying to identify individual animals amid the chaos.

Books
» *Mammals of India* by Vivek Menon
» *A Guide to the Birds of India* and *Pocket Guide to Birds of the Indian Subcontinent* by Richard Grimmett, Carol Inskipp and Tim Inskipp

Plants

Once upon a time India was almost entirely covered in forest; now its total forest cover is estimated to be around 20%, although the Forest Survey of India has set an optimistic target of 33%. Despite widespread clearing of native habitats, the country still boasts 49,219 plant species, of which some 5200 are endemic. Species on the southern peninsula show Malaysian ancestry, while desert plants in Rajasthan are more clearly allied with the Middle East, and conifer forests of the Himalaya derive from European and Siberian origins.

Outside of mountain forests found in the Himalaya, nearly all the lowland forests of India are subtypes of tropical forest, with native *sal* forests forming the mainstay of the timber industry. Some of these tropical forests are true rainforest, staying green year-round, such as in the Western Ghats and in the northeast states, but most forests are deciduous and look surprisingly dusty and forlorn in the dry season. Fortunately, the leaf fall and dry vegetation makes wildlife viewing easier in otherwise dense woodlands.

High-value trees such as Indian rosewood, Malabar kino and teak have been virtually cleared from the Western Ghats, and sandalwood is endangered across India due to illegal logging for the incense and wood-carving industries. A bigger threat on forested lands is firewood

A NATIVE RETURNS

India's last wild cheetahs were likely shot by the Maharaja of Surguja in 1947 and they have been absent for so long that few people think of cheetahs and India in the same sentence. But after extensive review and planning, India's minister for the environment and forests, Jairam Ramesh, announced that 18 cheetahs will be brought from Iran, Namibia and South Africa and released in 2011 in the Kuno-Palpur Wildlife Sanctuary and Nauradehi Wildlife Sanctuary in Madhya Pradesh and an area in the desert near Jaisalmer in Rajasthan. There remains considerable disagreement about whether these releases are a good idea, and even the official studies concluded that most of the potential cheetah habitat is severely overgrazed by livestock and subject to poaching, but keep your fingers crossed that cheetahs have a chance to rebound in the way that Asiatic lions have.

harvesting, often carried out by landless peasants who squat on gazetted government land.

Several trees have significant religious value in India, including the silk-cotton tree, a big tree with spiny bark and large red flowers under which Pitamaha, the creator of the world, sat after his labours. Two well-known figs, the banyan and peepal, grow to immense size by dangling roots from their branches and fusing into massive multitrunked jungles of trunks and stems – one giant is nearly 200m across. It is said that Buddha achieved enlightenment while sitting under a peepal (also known as the Bodhi tree).

The foothills and slopes of the Himalaya preserve classic montane species, including blue pine and deodar (Himalayan cedar) and deciduous forests of apple, chestnut, birch, plum and cinnamon. Above the snowline, hardy plants such as anemones, edelweiss and gentians can be prolific, and one fabulous place to see such flowers is at the Valley of Flowers National Park (see p428).

India's hot deserts have their own unique species – the khejri tree and various strains of scrub acacia. The hardy sea-buckthorn bush is the main fruiting shrub in the deserts of the Himalaya. All these indigenous species face a challenge from introduced species such as the eucalyptus, a water-hungry species introduced by the British to dry out malarial swamps.

National Parks & Wildlife Sanctuaries

India has about 100 national parks and 500 wildlife sanctuaries, which constitute around 5% of India's territory. An additional 70 parks have been authorised on paper but not yet implemented on the ground or only implemented to varying degrees. There are also 14 biosphere reserves, overlapping many of the national parks and sanctuaries, providing safe migration channels for wildlife and allowing scientists to monitor biodiversity.

We strongly recommend visiting at least one national park or sanctuary on your travels – the experience of coming face-to-face with a wild elephant, rhino or tiger will stay with you for a lifetime, while your visit adds momentum to efforts to protect India's natural resources. Wildlife reserves tend to be off the beaten track and infrastructure can be limited – book transport and accommodation in advance, and check opening times, permit requirements and entry fees before you visit. Many parks close to conduct a census of wildlife in the low season, and monsoon rains can make wildlife-viewing tracks inaccessible.

Almost all parks offer jeep/van tours, but you can also search for wildlife on guided treks, boat trips and elephant safaris. For various safari possibilities, see p19.

Resources

» Wildlife, conservation and environment awareness-raising at www.sanctuary asia.com

» The Wildlife Trust of India news at www.wti.org.in

» Top birdwatching information and photo galleries at www.birding.in

The Landscape

The Land

India is an incredibly diverse country with everything from steamy jungles and tropical rainforest to arid deserts and the soaring peaks of the Himalaya. At 3,287,263 sq km, it is the second-largest Asian country after China, and forms the vast bulk of the South Asian subcontinent – an ancient block of earth crust that carried a wealth of unique plants and animals like a lifeboat across a prehistoric ocean before slamming into Asia about 40 million years ago.

Look for the three major geographic features that define modern-day India: Himalayan peaks and ridges along the northern borders, the alluvial floodplains of the Indus and Ganges Rivers in the north, and the elevated Deccan Plateau that forms the core of India's triangular southern peninsula.

Get the inside track on Indian environmental issues at Down to Earth (www .downtoearth. org.in), an online magazine that delves into stories overlooked by mainstream media.

The Himalaya

As the world's highest mountains – with the highest peak in India reaching 8598m – the Himalaya create an impregnable boundary that separates India from its neighbours in the north. These mountains formed when the Indian subcontinent broke away from Gondwanaland, a supercontinent in the Southern Hemisphere that included Africa, Antarctica, Australia and South America. All by itself, India drifted north and finally slammed slowly, but with immense force, into the Eurasian continent about 40 million years ago, buckling the ancient seafloor upward to form the Himalaya and many lesser ranges that stretch 2500km from Afghanistan to Myanmar (Burma).

When the Himalaya reached their great heights during the Pleistocene (less than 150,000 years ago), they began to block and alter weather systems, creating the monsoon climate that dominates India today, as well as forming a dry rainshadow to the north.

Although it looks like a continuous range on a map, the Himalaya is actually a series of interlocking ridges, separated by countless valleys. Until technology enabled the building of roads through the Himalaya, many of these valleys were completely isolated, preserving a diverse series of mountain cultures.

The Indo-Gangetic Plains

Covering most of northern India, the vast alluvial plains of the sacred Ganges River are so seamlessly flat that they drop a mere 200m between Delhi and the waterlogged wetlands of West Bengal, where the river joins forces with the Brahmaputra River from India's northeast before dumping into the sea in Bangladesh. Vast quantities of eroded sediments from the neighbouring highlands accumulate on the plains to a depth of nearly 2km, creating fertile, well-watered agricultural land. This densely populated region was once extensively forested and rich in wildlife.

Gujarat in the far west of India is separated from Sindh (Pakistan) by the Rann of Kutch, a brackish marshland that becomes a huge inland sea during the wet season; the waters recede in the dry season, leaving isolated islands perched on an expansive plain.

The Deccan Plateau

South of the Indo-Gangetic (northern) plain, the land rises to the Deccan Plateau, marking the divide between the Mughal heartlands of North India and the Dravidian civilisations of the south. The Deccan is bound on either side by the Western and Eastern Ghats, which come together in their southern reaches to form the Nilgiri Hills in Tamil Nadu.

On the Deccan's western border, the Western Ghats drop sharply down to a narrow coastal lowland, forming a luxuriant slope of rainforest.

The Islands

Offshore from India are a series of island groups, politically part of India but geographically linked to the landmasses of Southeast Asia and islands of the Indian Ocean. The Andaman and Nicobar Islands sit far out in the Bay of Bengal, while the coral atolls of Lakshadweep (300km west of Kerala) are a northerly extension of the Maldives islands, with a land area of just 32 sq km.

Environmental Issues

With over a billion people, ever-expanding industrial and urban centres, and growth in chemical-intensive farming, India's environment is under tremendous pressure. An estimated 65% of the land is degraded in some way, most of it seriously degraded, and the government has been consistently falling short of most of its environmental protection goals. Many current problems are a direct result of the Green Revolution of the 1960s when chemical fertilisers and pesticides enabled huge growth in agricultural output, at enormous cost to the environment, wildlife populations and habitat.

Despite numerous new environmental laws since the 1984 Bhopal disaster (p637), corruption continues to exacerbate environmental degradation – worst exemplified by the flagrant flouting of environmental rules by companies involved in hydroelectricity, mining, and uranium and oil exploration. Usually, the people most affected are low-caste rural farmers and Adivasis (tribal people) who have limited political representation and few resources to fight big businesses.

Agricultural production has been reduced by soil degradation from overfarming, rising soil salinity, loss of treecover and poor irrigation. The human cost is heart-rending, and lurking behind all these problems is a basic Malthusian truth: there are far too many people for India to support at its current level of development.

While the Indian government could undoubtedly do more, some blame must also fall on Western farm subsidies that artificially reduce the cost of imported produce, undermining prices for Indian farmers. Western agribusinesses also promote the use of nonpropagating, genetically modified (GM) seed stocks.

As anywhere, tourists tread a fine line between providing an incentive for change and making the problem worse. For example, many of the environmental problems in Goa (p811) are a direct result of years of irresponsible development for tourism. Always consider your environmental impact while travelling in India, including while trekking and diving.

Climate Change

Changing climate patterns – linked to global carbon emissions – have been creating dangerous extremes of weather in India. While India is a

It is estimated that India's population will reach 1.26 billion people by 2016.

India is home to 18% of the world's population crowded together on 2.5% of the world's landmass.

Noise pollution in major cities has been measured at over 90 decibels – more than one and a half times the recognised 'safe' limit. Bring earplugs!

major polluter, in carbon emissions per capita it still ranks far behind the USA, Australia and Europe.

Increased monsoon rainfall has caused a cycle of ever-worsening flooding and destruction, including the devastating Gujarat and Maharashtra floods in 2005 and widespread flooding across northern India in 2010. The Environment Minister Jairam Ramesh has estimated that by 2030 India will see a 30% increase in the severity of its floods and droughts. In mountain deserts of Ladakh, increased rainfall is changing time-honoured farming patterns and threatening traditional mud-brick architecture, while glaciers on nearby peaks are melting at alarming rates. Conversely, other areas are experiencing reduced rainfall, causing drought and riots over access to water supplies. Islands in the Lakshadweep group as well as the low-lying plains of the Ganges delta are being inundated by rising sea levels.

Deforestation

Since Independence, some 53,000 sq km of India's forests have been cleared for logging and farming, or damaged by urban expansion, mining, industrialisation and river dams. Even in the well-funded, highly protected Project Tiger parks, the amount of forest cover classified as 'degraded' has tripled due to illegal logging. The number of mangrove forests has halved since the early 1990s, reducing the nursery grounds for the fish that stock the Indian Ocean and Bay of Bengal.

India's first Five Year Plan in 1951 recognised the importance of forests for soil conservation, and various policies have been introduced to increase forest cover. Almost all have been flouted by officials or criminals and by ordinary people clearing forests for firewood and grazing in forest areas. Try to minimise the use of wood-burning stoves while you travel (this is less of an issue in areas with fast-growing pine species in the hills).

Officially, states are supposed to earmark an equivalent area for afforestation when an area is cleared, but enforcement is lax and the land set aside is sometimes unsuitable for forestry. On another front, invasive eucalyptus and other foreign plant species are swamping indigenous flora. Numerous charities are working with rural communities to encourage tree planting, and religious leaders like the Dalai Lama have joined the movement.

Water Resources

Arguably the biggest threat to public health in India is inadequate access to clean drinking water and proper sanitation. With the population set

Air pollution in many Indian cities has been measured at more than double the maximum safe level recommended by the World Health Organization.

A DAM TOO FAR?

The most controversial of India's many hydroelectric schemes is the Narmada Valley Development, a US$6-billion scheme to build 30 hydroelectric dams along the Narmada River in Madhya Pradesh, Rajasthan and Gujarat. Despite bringing benefits in terms of irrigation to thousands of villages and reducing desert encroachment into rural areas, the project will flood the tribal homelands of some 40,000 Adivasi (tribal) villagers, many of whom worship the waters as a deity. The government has promised to provide alternative accommodation, but so far only 10% of the displaced people have found adequate farmland as compensation. The World Bank refused to fund the ongoing development, but Britain's Barclays Bank stepped in with loans and the Indian government has overruled every legal challenge to the development, despite some high-profile names joining the anti-Narmada Dam movement – including Booker Prize-winner Arundhati Roy. For the latest developments, see the Friends of River Narmada website (www.narmada.org).

to double by 2050, agricultural, industrial and domestic water usage are all expected to spiral, despite government policies designed to control water use. The World Health Organization estimates that, out of more than 3000 cities and towns in India, only eight have adequate wastewater treatment facilities. Many cities dump untreated sewage and partially cremated bodies directly into rivers, while open defecation is a simple fact of life in most rural (and many urban) areas.

Rivers are also affected by run-off, industrial pollution and sewage contamination – the Sabarmati, Yamuna and Ganges are among the most polluted rivers on earth. At least 70% of the freshwater sources in India are now polluted in some way. In recent years, drought has devastated parts of the subcontinent (particularly Rajasthan and Gujarat) and has been a driving force for rural-to-urban migration.

Water distribution is another volatile issue. Since 1947 an estimated 35 million people in India have been displaced by major dams, mostly built to provide hydroelectricity for this increasingly power-hungry nation. While hydroelectricity is one of the greener power sources, valleys across India are being sacrificed to create new power plants, and displaced people rarely receive adequate compensation.

Downstream of Varanasi the Ganges River is a black septic river with 3000 times the acceptable limit of faecal coliform bacteria.

Survival Guide

Scams

India has its fair share of scams, but most problems can be avoided with a bit of common sense and an appropriate amount of caution. Scams change as tricksters try to stay ahead of the game so chat with travellers and tourism officials to keep abreast of the latest cons. Look at the India branch of Lonely Planet's **Thorn Tree Travel Forum** (www.lonely planet.com/thorntree), where travellers often post timely warnings about problems they've encountered on the road.

Contaminated Food & Drink

» Some private medical clinics have given patients more treatment than necessary to procure larger payments from travel insurance companies – get a second opinion if possible.

» The late 1990s saw a dangerous scam in Agra and Varanasi when several travellers died after being fed food spiked with bacteria from restaurants linked to dodgy medical clinics. The scam has been quashed, but could always reappear.

» Most bottled water is legit, but ensure the seal is intact and the bottom of the bottle hasn't been tampered with.

» Crush plastic bottles after use to prevent them being misused. Better still, use your own water bottle and water-purification tablets or a filtration system to avoid adding to India's plastic waste mountain.

Credit-Card Con

Be careful when paying for souvenirs with a credit card. While government shops are usually legitimate, private souvenir shops have been known to surreptitiously run off extra copies of the credit-card imprint slip and use them for phoney transactions later. Insist the trader carries out any transaction in front of you. Or pay with cash.

Druggings

Very occasionally, tourists (especially those travelling solo) are drugged and robbed during train or bus journeys. A spiked drink is the most commonly used method for sending them off to sleep. Use your instincts,

and if you're unsure politely decline drinks or food offered by strangers.

Gem Scams

This long-running scam involves charming con artists who promise foolproof 'get rich quick' schemes. Travellers are asked to carry or mail gems home and then sell them to the trader's (non-existent) overseas representatives at a profit. Without exception, the goods – if they arrive at all – are worth a fraction of what you paid, and the 'representatives' never materialise.

Don't believe hard-luck stories about an inability to obtain an export licence, and don't believe the testimonials they show you from other travellers – they are all fake. Travellers have reported this con happening in Agra, Delhi, and Jaisalmer among other places, but it's particularly prevalent in Jaipur (see p121). Carpets are another favourite for this con.

Overpricing

Agree on prices beforehand, particularly if eating in places without menus, flagging down an autorickshaw or arranging an airport pick-up from your hostel or hotel. This will save you money and could deflect potentially ugly misunderstandings later.

Photography

When photographing people use your instincts – some people may demand money afterwards. See also p1169.

Theft

» Theft is a risk in India, as it is anywhere else.

» Keep luggage locked on buses and trains. Be extra alert just before a train departs; thieves often take

TOP SCAMS

» Gunk (dirt, paint, poo) suddenly appears on your shoes, only for a shoe cleaner to magically appear and offer to clean it off – for a price.

» Shops and restaurants 'borrow' the name of their more successful and popular competitor.

» Taxi drivers insist they don't know the way to your hotel, or that the place you're looking for has moved or is closed – but they'll happily take you to their 'friend's' place (where they'll receive a nice commission).

» Touts claim to be 'government-approved' guides or 'tour operators' and sting you for large sums of cash. Enquire at the local tourist office about recommended guides and ask to see evidence from the guides themselves.

Transport Scams

» Make sure you're completely clear on what is included in the price of any tour to avoid charges for hidden 'extras' later on; get it in writing.

» Be extremely wary of anyone in Delhi and other traveller centres offering houseboat tours to Kashmir (see p236).

» Some travel agents exploit travellers' safety concerns to make extra money from tours that you can do just as easily (and safely) on public transport.

» When buying a bus, train or plane ticket anywhere other than the registered office of the transport company, make sure you're getting the ticket class you paid for. It's not uncommon for travellers to book a deluxe bus or AC train berth and arrive to find a bog-standard ordinary bus or a less comfortable sleeper seat.

» Some tricksters pose as India Rail officials and insist you pay to have your e-ticket validated; ignore them.

» Ignore taxi drivers outside airports who say they are prepaid taxi drivers; your prepaid taxi receipt will have the designated drivers' licence plate number printed on it.

advantage of the confusion and crowds.

» Take extra care in dormitories and never leave your valuables in the room when you go out unless there is a safe.

» For lost or stolen credit cards call the international lost/stolen number; for lost/stolen travellers cheques, contact the American Express or Thomas Cook office in Delhi (p98).

Touts & Commission Agents

» Many hotels and shops drum up extra business by paying commission to local fixers who bring tourists through the doors. Prices in these places will invariably be raised (by as much as 50%) to pay the fixer's commission.

» Train and bus stations are often swarming with touts – if anyone asks if this is your first trip to India, say you've been here several times, even if you haven't.

» Touts can be particularly bothersome in major tourist centres like Agra and Varanasi.

» Telling touts that you have already prepaid your transfer/tour/onward journey can help dissuade them.

» Where possible, arrange hotel pick-ups, particularly in big cities.

» You'll often hear stories about hotels (those that refuse to pay commissions) being 'full' or 'closed' – check things out yourself. Be very sceptical of phrases like 'my brother's shop' and 'special deal at my friend's place'.

» Touts *can* be beneficial if you arrive in a town without a hotel reservation when some big festival is on, or during the peak season – they'll know which places have beds.

KEEPING SAFE

» A good travel-insurance policy is essential.

» Email copies of your passport identity page, visa and airline tickets to yourself, and keep copies on you.

» Keep your money and passport in a concealed money belt or a secure place under your shirt and never keep your wallet in your back pocket.

» Store at least US$100 separately from your main stash but keep the rest of your cash and other valuables on your person.

» Don't publicly display large wads of cash when paying for services or checking into hotels.

» Consider using your own padlock at cheaper hotels where doors are locked with a padlock.

» If you can't lock your hotel room securely from the inside, stay somewhere else.

HANDY WEBSITES

You can read personal experiences proffered by fellow women travellers at www.journey woman.com and www .wanderlustandlipstick .com.

Women & Solo Travellers

Women and solo travellers may encounter a few extra hurdles when travelling in India – from cost (for those travelling by themselves) to appropriate clothing (women). As with anywhere else, it pays to be prepared.

Women Travellers

Although Bollywood might suggest otherwise, India remains a largely conservative society. As such, female travellers should be aware that their behaviour and dress code are under scrutiny, particularly away from cities and towns popular with tourists.

Attention

» Be prepared to be stared at; it's something you'll have to live with so don't allow it to get the better of you.

» Refrain from returning male stares; this can be considered a come-on.

» Dark glasses, MP3 players and books are useful for averting unwanted conversations.

Clothing

Avoiding culturally inappropriate clothing will help to make your travels stress-free.

» Steer clear of sleeveless tops, shorts, miniskirts (ankle-length skirts are recommended) and anything else that's skimpy, see-through or tight-fitting.

» Wearing Indian-style clothes makes a positive impression and can considerably deflect harassment.

» Draping a dupatta (long scarf) over T-shirts is another good way to avoid unwanted stares – it's also handy if you visit a shrine that requires your head to be covered.

» Wearing a *salwar kameez* (traditional dresslike tunic and trousers) will show your respect for local dress etiquette; it's also surprisingly cool in the hot weather.

» A smart alternative is a kurta (long shirt) worn over jeans or trousers.

» Avoid going out in public wearing a choli (sari blouse) or a sari petticoat (which some foreign women mistake for a skirt); it's like strutting around half-dressed.

» Most Indian women wear long shorts and a T-shirt when swimming in public view; to avoid stares, wear a sarong from the beach to your hotel.

Health & Hygiene

» Sanitary pads are widely available but tampons are usually restricted to pharmacies in big cities and some tourist towns (even then, the choice may be limited). Carry additional stocks for travel off the beaten track.

» For gynaecological health issues, most women prefer to seek out a female doctor.

» See p1194 for more information.

Sexual Harassment

Many female travellers have reported some form of sexual harassment while in India.

» Most cases are reported in urban centres of North India and prominent tourist towns elsewhere, and have involved lewd comments, invasion of privacy and sometimes groping.

» Other cases have included provocative gestures, jeering, getting 'accidentally' bumped into on the street and being followed.

» Incidents are particularly common at exuberant (and crowded) special events such as the Holi festival.

» Women travelling with a male partner are less likely to be hassled.

» Mixed couples of Indian and non-Indian descent may get disapproving stares, even if neither individual actually lives in India.

Staying Safe

The following tips may help you on your travels:

» Keep conversations with unknown men short – getting involved in an inane conversation with someone you barely know can be misinterpreted as a sign of sexual interest.

» Questions and comments such as 'Do you have a boyfriend?' or 'You're very beautiful' are indicators that the conversation may be taking a steamy tangent.

» Some women wear a pseudo wedding ring, or announce early on in the conversation that they're married or engaged (regardless of the reality).

» If you feel that a guy is encroaching on your space, he probably is. A firm request to keep away usually does the trick, especially if your tone is loud and curt enough to draw the attention of passers-by.

» The silent treatment can also be very effective.

» Follow local women's cues and instead of shaking hands say namaste – the traditional, respectful Hindu greeting.

» Avoid wearing expensive-looking jewellery.

» Check the reputation of any teacher or therapist before going to a solo session (get recommendations from other travellers). Some women have reported being molested by masseurs and other therapists. If you feel uneasy at any time, leave.

» Female filmgoers will probably feel more comfortable (and lessen the chances of harassment) going to the cinema with a companion.

» At hotels keep your door locked, as staff (particularly at budget places) can knock and automatically walk in without waiting for your permission.

» Try to arrive in towns before dark. Don't walk alone at night and avoid wandering alone in isolated areas even during daylight.

Taxis & Public Transport

Being a woman has some advantages; women are able to queue-jump for buses and trains without consequence and on trains there are special ladies-only carriages.

» Solo women should prearrange an airport pick-up from their hotel if their flight is scheduled to arrive after dark.

» Delhi and some other cities have prepaid radio cab services such as Easycabs (see p102) – they're more expensive than the regular prepaid taxis, but promote themselves as being safe, with drivers who have been vetted as part of their recruitment.

» If you do catch a regular prepaid taxi, make a point of writing down the car registration and driver's name – in front of the driver – and giving it to one of the airport police.

» Avoid taking taxis alone late at night and never agree to have more than one man (the driver) in the car – ignore claims that this is 'just my brother' or 'for more protection'.

» Solo women have reported less hassle by opting for the more expensive classes on trains, especially for overnight trips.

» If you're travelling overnight in a three-tier carriage, try to get the uppermost berth, which will give you more privacy (and distance from potential gropers).

» On public transport, don't hesitate to return any errant limbs, put an item of luggage between you and others, be vocal (attracting public attention, thus shaming the fellow), or simply find a new spot.

Solo Travellers

Travellers often move in roughly the same direction throughout India, so it's not unusual to see the same faces over and over again on your trip. Tourist hubs such as Goa, Rajasthan, Kerala, Manali, McLeod Ganj, Leh, Agra and Varanasi are good places to meet fellow travellers, swap stories, get up-to-the-minute travel tips and find others to travel with. You may also be able to find travel companions on Lonely Planet's Thorn Tree Travel Forum (www.lonelyplanet.com/thorntree).

Cost

The most significant issue facing solo travellers is cost.

» Single-room rates at guest houses and hotels are sometimes not much lower than double rates.

» Some midrange and top-end places don't even offer a single tariff.

» Always try negotiating a lower rate for single occupancy.

Safety

Most solo travellers experience no major problems in India but, like anywhere else in the world, it's wise to stay on your toes in unfamiliar surroundings.

» Some less honourable souls (locals and travellers alike) view lone tourists as an easy target for theft.

» Single men wandering around isolated areas have been mugged, even during the day

Transport

» You'll save money if you find others to share taxis and autorickshaws, as well as when hiring a car for longer trips.

» Solo bus travellers may be able to get the 'co-pilot' (near the driver) seat on buses, which not only has a good view out front, but is also handy if you've got a big bag.

Directory A–Z

Accommodation

Accommodation in India ranges from grungy backpacker hostels with concrete floors and cold 'bucket' showers to opulent palaces fit for a Maharaja. In this guide, we've listed reviews by author preference; standout options are indicated by .

Categories

As a general rule, budget (₹) covers everything from basic hostels and railway retiring rooms to simple guesthouses in traditional village homes. Midrange hotels (₹₹) tend to be modern-style concrete blocks that usually offer extras such as cable/satellite TV and air-conditioning (although some just have noisy 'air-coolers' that cool air by blowing it over cold water). Top-end places (₹₹₹) stretch from luxury five-star chains to gorgeous heritage havelis.

Costs

Given that the cost of budget, midrange and top-end hotels varies so much across India, it would be misleading of us to provide a 'national' price strategy for each category. The best way to gauge accommodation costs is to go directly to the Fast Facts and the Sleeping sections of this book's regional chapters. Keep in mind that most establishments raise tariffs annually, so the prices may have risen by the time you read this.

Price Icons

The price indicators in this book refer to the cost of a double room, including private bathroom, unless otherwise noted. The table on p1161 is based on price indicators for Bihar, Tamil Nadu and Rajasthan and gives an example of the difference in accommodation costs across India.

Reservations

» The majority of top-end and some midrange hotels require a deposit at the time of booking, which can usually be done with a credit card.

» Some midrange places may ask for a cheque or cash deposit into a bank account to secure a reservation. This is usually more hassle than it's worth.

» Some budget options won't take reservations as they don't know when people are going to check-out; call ahead to check.

» Other places will want a deposit at check-in – ask for a receipt and be wary of any request to sign a blank impression of your credit card. If the hotel insists, consider going to the nearest ATM and paying cash.

» Verify the check-out time when you check-in – some hotels have a fixed check-out time (usually 10am or noon), while others offer 24-hour check-out.

» Reservations by phone without a deposit are usually fine, but call to confirm the booking the day before you arrive.

Seasons

» Rates in this guide are full price in high season. High season usually coincides with the best weather for the area's sights and activities – normally summertime in the mountains (around June to October), and the cooler months in the plains (around October to mid-February).

» In areas popular with foreign tourists there's an additional peak period over Christmas and New Year; make reservations well in advance.

» At other times you may find significant discounts; if the hotel seems quiet, ask for one.

BOOK YOUR STAY ONLINE

For more accommodation reviews by Lonely Planet authors, check out hotels.lonelyplanet.com/India. You'll find independent reviews, as well as recommendations on the best places to stay. Best of all, you can book online.

» Some hotels in places like Goa shut during the monsoon period.

» Many temple towns have additional peak seasons around major festivals and pilgrimages; for festival details see the Month by Month chapter and festivals sections of regional chapters.

Taxes & Service Charges

» State governments slap a variety of taxes on hotel accommodation (except at the cheaper hotels), and these are added to the cost of your room.

» Taxes vary from state to state and are detailed in the regional chapters.

» Many upmarket hotels also levy an additional 'service charge' (usually around 10%).

» Rates quoted in this book's regional chapters exclude taxes unless otherwise noted.

Budget & Midrange Hotels

Apart from some traditional wood or stone guesthouse in remote mountain areas, most budget and midrange hotels are modern-style concrete blocks. Some are charming, clean and good value, others less so.

» Room quality can vary considerably within a hotel so try to inspect a few rooms first; avoid carpeted rooms unless you like the smell of mouldy socks.

» Shared bathrooms (often with squat toilets) are usually only found at the cheapest lodgings.

GET TO KNOW YOUR BATHROOM

Most of India's midrange hotels and all top-end ones have sit-down toilets with toilet paper and soap supplied. In ultracheap hotels, and in places off the tourist trail, squat toilets are the norm and toilet paper is rarely provided. Squat toilets are variously described as 'Indian-style', 'Indian' or 'floor' toilets, while the sit-down variety may be called 'Western' or 'commode' toilets. In a few places, you'll find the curious 'hybrid toilet', a sit-down version with footpads on the edge of the bowl.

Terminology for hotel bathrooms varies across India. 'Attached bath', 'private bath' or 'with bath' means that the room has its own en suite bathroom. 'Common bath', 'no bathroom' or 'shared bath' means communal bathroom facilities.

Not all rooms have hot water. 'Running', '24-hour' or 'constant' water means that hot water is available round-the-clock (not always the case in reality). 'Bucket' hot water is only available in buckets (sometimes for a small charge).

Many places use wall-mounted electric geysers (water heaters) that need to be switched on up to an hour before use. Note that the geyser's main switch can sometimes be located outside the bathroom.

Hotels that advertise 'room with shower' may be misleading – sometimes the shower is just a pipe sticking out of the wall. Meanwhile, some hotels surreptitiously disconnect showers to cut costs, while showers at other places render a mere trickle of water.

In this book, hotel rooms have their own private bathroom unless otherwise indicated.

» Most rooms have ceiling fans and better rooms have electric mosquito killers and/or window nets, though cheaper rooms may lack windows altogether.

» Bring your own sheet or sleeping-bag liner. Sheets and bedcovers at cheap hotels can be stained, well worn and in need of a wash.

» Sound pollution can be irksome (especially in urban hubs); pack good-quality earplugs and request a room that doesn't face a busy road.

» It's wise to keep your door locked, as some staff (particularly in budget accommodation) may knock and automatically walk in without awaiting your permission.

» Blackouts are common (especially during summer and the monsoon) so double-check that the hotel has a back-up generator if you're paying for electric 'extras' such as air-conditioners and TVs.

» Note that some hotels lock their doors at night. Members of staff might sleep in the lobby but waking them up can be a challenge. Let

SAMPLE ACCOMMODATION COSTS

CATEGORY	BIHAR	TAMIL NADU	RAJASTHAN
₹ budget	<₹800	<₹1000	<₹1000
₹₹ midrange	₹800-1500	₹1000-3000	₹1000-5000
₹₹₹ top end	>₹1500	>₹3000	>₹5000

the hotel know in advance if you'll be arriving or returning to your room late in the evening.

» Away from tourist areas, cheaper hotels may not take foreigners because they don't have the necessary foreigner-registration forms.

Camping

» There are few official camping sites in India, but campers can usually find hotels with gardens where they can camp for a nominal fee and use the bathroom facilities.

» Wild camping is often the only accommodation option on trekking routes.

» In mountain areas, you'll also find summer-only tented camps, with accommodation in semipermanent 'Swiss tents' with attached bathrooms.

Dormitory Accommodation

» A number of hotels have cheap dormitories, though these may be mixed and, in less touristy places, full of drunken drivers – not ideal conditions for women.

» More traveller-friendly dorms are found at the handful of hostels run by the YMCA, YWCA and Salvation Army as well as at HI-associated hostels.

Government Accommodation & Tourist Bungalows

» The Indian government maintains a network of guesthouses for travelling officials and public workers, known variously as rest houses, dak bungalows, circuit houses, PWD (Public Works Department) bungalows and forest rest houses.

» These places may accept travellers if no government employees need the rooms, but permission is sometimes required from local officials and you'll probably have to find the *chowkidar* (caretaker) to open the doors.

» 'Tourist bungalows' are run by state governments – rooms are usually midpriced (some with cheap dorms) and have varying standards of cleanliness and service.

PRACTICALITIES

» **Newspapers & Magazines** Major English-language dailies include the *Hindustan Times*, *Times of India*, *Indian Express*, *Hindu*, *Statesman*, *Telegraph*, *Daily News & Analysis (DNA)* and *Economic Times*. Regional English-language and local-vernacular publications are found nationwide. Incisive current-affairs magazines include *Frontline*, *India Today*, the *Week*, *Tehelka* and *Outlook*.

» **Radio** Government-controlled All India Radio (AIR), India's national broadcaster, has over 220 stations broadcasting local and international news. Private FM channels broadcast music, current affairs, talkback and more.

» **TV & Video** The national (government) TV broadcaster is Doordarshan. More people watch satellite and cable TV; English-language channels include BBC, CNN, Star World, HBO, and Discovery.

» **Weights & Measures** Officially India is metric. Terms you're likely to hear are: lakhs (one lakh = 100,000) and crores (one crore = 10 million).

» Some state governments also run chains of more expensive hotels, including some lovely heritage properties. Details are normally available through the state tourism office.

Homestays/B&Bs for Paying Guests

» These family-run guesthouses will appeal to those seeking a small-scale, uncommercial setting with home-cooked meals.

» Standards range from mud-and-stone huts with hole-in-the-floor toilets to comfortable middle-class homes.

» In places like Ladakh, homestays are increasingly the way to go but standards are fairly simple.

» Be aware that some hotels market themselves as 'homestays' but are run like hotels with little (or no) interaction with the family.

» Contact the local tourist office for a full list of participating families, or see entries in the regional chapters.

CARBON-MONOXIDE POISONING

Some mountain areas rely on charcoal burners for warmth, but these should be avoided due to the risk of fatal carbon-monoxide poisoning. The thick, mattress-like blankets used in many mountain areas are amazingly warm once you get beneath the covers. If you're still cold, improvise a hot-water bottle by filling your drinking-water bottle with boiled water and covering it with a sock.

Railway Retiring Rooms

» Most large train stations have basic rooms for travellers holding an ongoing train ticket or Indrail Pass. Some are grim, others are surprisingly pleasant, but suffer from the noise of passengers and trains.

» They're useful for early-morning train departures and there's usually a choice of dormitories or private rooms (24-hour checkout).

Temples & Pilgrims' Rest houses

» Accommodation is available at some ashrams (spiritual retreats), gurdwaras (Sikh temples) and *dharamsalas* (pilgrims' guesthouses) for a donation

» These places have been established for genuine pilgrims so please exercise judgement about the appropriateness of staying (some regional chapters have further details).

» Always abide by any protocols.

Top-End & Heritage Hotels

» India has plenty of top-end properties, from modern five-star chain hotels to glorious palaces and unique heritage abodes.

» Most top-end hotels have rupee rates for Indian guests and US dollar rates for foreigners, including Non-Resident Indians (NRIs).

» Officially, you're supposed to pay the dollar rates in foreign currency or by credit card, but many places will accept rupees adding up to the dollar rate (verify this when checking in).

» The Government of India tourism website, **Incredible India** (www.incredibleindia.org), has a useful list of palaces, forts and other erstwhile royal retreats that accept paying guests – click on the 'Royal Retreats' heading.

Activities

India covers every terrain imaginable, from sun-baked deserts and moist rainforests to snow-dusted mountains and plunging ravines. With all this to play with, the opportunities for outdoor activities are endless. Choose from trekking, paragliding, mountaineering, jungle safaris, scuba diving, surfing and elephant rides as well as yoga, meditation and much, much more. For details on regional activities, courses, equipment hire, clubs and companies, see this book's Plan Your Trip and If You Like... chapters.

Business Hours

» Official business hours are from 9.30am to 5.30pm Monday to Friday but many offices open later and close earlier.

» Most offices have an official lunch hour from around 1pm.

» Bank opening hours vary from town to town so check locally; foreign-exchange offices may open longer and operate daily.

» Some larger post offices have a full day on Saturday and a half-day on Sunday.

» Curfews apply in some areas, notably Kashmir and the Northeast States.

» All timings vary regionally; exceptions are noted in the regional chapters.

Courses

You can pursue all sorts of courses in India, from yoga and meditation to cooking and Bollywood dancing. See the Courses section of the regional chapters for details.

Language Courses

The following places listed offer language courses, some requiring a minimum time commitment.

Delhi Basic Hindi classes at Delhi's Central Hindi Directorate (p78).

Himachal Pradesh Long and short courses in Tibetan at McLeod Ganj (p321).

Mumbai (Bombay) Beginners' courses in Hindi, Marathi and Sanskrit at Bharatiya Vidya Bhavan (p731).

STANDARD HOURS

We've only listed business hours where they differ from the following standards.

BUSINESS	OPENING HOURS
Airline office	9.30am-5.30pm Mon-Sat
Bank	9.30am or 10am-2pm or 4pm Mon-Fri, to noon or 1pm Sat
Government office	9.30am-1pm & 2-5.30pm Mon-Fri, closed alternative Sat (usually 2nd and 4th)
Post office	9am-6pm Mon-Fri, to noon Sat
Museum	10am-5pm Tue-Sun
Restaurant	lunch noon-2.30pm or 3pm, dinner 7-10pm or 11pm
Sights	10am-5pm
Shop	10am-7pm, some closed Sun

Tamil Nadu Tamil courses in Chennai (Madras; p991).

Uttar Pradesh Various places in Varanasi offer Hindi courses (p389).

Uttarakhand Hindi courses in Mussoorie (p409) and Rishikesh (p421).

West Bengal Tibetan courses in Darjeeling (p493).

Customs Regulations

» Technically you're supposed to declare any amount of cash/ travellers cheques over US$5000/10,000 on arrival.

» Indian rupees shouldn't be taken out of India; however, this is rarely policed.

» Officials very occasionally ask tourists to enter expensive items such as video cameras and laptop computers on a 'Tourist Baggage Re-export' form to ensure they're taken out of India at the time of departure.

Electricity

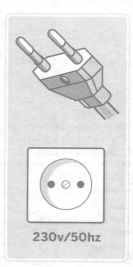

230v/50hz

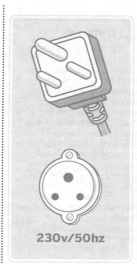

230v/50hz

Embassies & Consulates

Most foreign diplomatic missions are based in Delhi, but several nations operate consulates in other Indian cities (see websites, where provided, in the following Delhi addresses). Many missions have certain timings for visa applications, usually mornings: phone for details. The following are just some of the many foreign missions found in India.

Australia Chennai (☏044-43913200; 512 Alpha Wing, Raheja Towers, 177 Anna Salai); Delhi (☏011-41399900; www.india.highcommission.gov.au; 1/50G Shantipath, Chanakyapuri); Mumbai (☏022-61167100; 36 Maker Chambers VI, 220 Nariman Point)

Bangladesh Delhi (☏011-24121394; www.bhcdelhi.org; EP39 Dr Radakrishnan Marg, Chanakyapuri); Kolkata (☏033-40127500; 9 Bangabandhu Sheikh Mujib Sarani)

Bhutan (☏011-26889230; www.bhutan.gov.bt; Chandragupta Marg, Chanakyapuri, Delhi)

Canada Chennai (☏044-28330888; 18, 3rd fl YAFA Tower, Khader Nawaz Khan Rd); Delhi (☏011-41782000; www.canadainternational.gc.ca/india-inde; 7/8 Shantipath, Chanakyapuri); Mumbai (☏022-67494444; 6th fl, Fort House, 221 Dr DN Rd)

France Delhi (☏011-24196100; http://ambafrance-in.org/; 2/50E Shantipath, Chanakyapuri); Mumbai (☏022-56694000; Wockhardt Towers, East Wing, 5th fl, Bandra Kurla Complex, Bandra East)

Germany Chennai (☏044-24301600; 9 Boat Club Rd, RA Puram); Delhi (☏011-44199199; www.new-delhi.diplo.de; 6/50G Shantipath, Chanakyapuri); Kolkata (☏033-24791141; 1 Hastings Park Rd, Alipore); Mumbai (☏022-22832422; 10th fl, Hoechst House, Nariman Point)

Ireland Delhi (☏011-2462 6733; www.irelandindia.com; 203 Jor Bagh)

Israel Delhi (☏011-30414500; http://delhi.mfa.gov.il; 3 Aurangzeb Rd); Mumbai (☏022-22822822; Earnest House, 16th fl, NCPA Marg, 194 Nariman Point)

Malaysia Chennai (☏044-28226888; 44 Tank Bund Rd, Nungambakkam); Delhi (☏011-26111291/97; www.kln.gov.my/web/ind_new-delhi/home; 50M Satya Marg, Chanakyapuri); Mumbai (☏022-26455751/2; 4B, 4th fl, Notan Plaza, Turner Rd, Bandra West)

Maldives Delhi (☏011-41435701; www.maldiveshighcom.in/; B2 Anand Niketan)

Myanmar Delhi (☏011-24678822; 3/50F Nyaya Marg); Kolkata (☏033-24851658; 57K Ballygunge Circular Rd)

Nepal Delhi (☏011-23327361; Mandi House, Barakhamba Rd); Kolkata (☏033-24561224; 1 National Library Ave, Alipore)

Netherlands Chennai (☏044-43535381; 76 Venkata Krishan Rd, Mandaveli); Delhi (☏011-24197600; http://india.nlembassy.org/; 6/50F Shantipath, Chanakyapuri); Mumbai (☏022-22194200; Forbes Bldg, Charanjit Rai Marg, Fort)

New Zealand Chennai (☎044-28112472; Rane Engine Valves Ltd, 132 Cathedral Rd); Delhi (☎011-46883170; www.nzembassy.com/india; Sir Edmund Hillary Marg, Chanakyapuri; Mumbai (☎022-66151155; 1007, 10th fl, Dalamal House, Nariman Point)

Pakistan (☎011-24676004; 2/50G Shantipath, Chanakyapuri, Delhi)

Singapore Chennai (☎044-28158207; 17-A North Boag Rd, T Nagar); Delhi (☎011-46000915; www.mfa.gov.sg/newdelhi; E6 Chandragupta Marg, Chanakyapuri); Mumbai (☎022-22043205; 152, Maker Chambers IV, 14th fl, 222 Jamnalal Bajaj Rd, Nariman Point)

Sri Lanka Chennai (☎044-24987896; 196 TTK Rd, Alwarpet); Delhi (☎011-23010201; www.newdelhi.mission.gov.lk; 27 Kautilya Marg, Chanakyapuri); Mumbai (☎022-22045861; Mulla House, 34 Homi Modi St, Fort)

Switzerland Delhi (☎011-26878372; www.eda.admin.ch; Nyaya Marg, Chanakyapuri); Mumbai (☎022-22884563-65; 10th fl, 102 Maker Chambers IV, 222 Jamnalal Bajaj Marg, Nariman Point)

Thailand Chennai (☎044-42300730; 21/22 Arunachalam Rd, Kotturpuram); Delhi (☎011-26118103-4; www.thaiemb.org.in; 56N Nyaya Marg, Chanakyapuri); Kolkata (☎033-24407836; 18B Mandeville Gardens, Ballygunge); Mumbai (☎022-22823535; 1st fl, Dalamal House, Jamnalal Bajai Marg, Nariman Point)

UK Chennai (☎044-42192151; 20 Anderson Rd); Delhi (☎011-24192100; http://ukinindia.fco.gov.uk; Shantipath, Chanakyapuri); Kolkata (☎033-22885172-6; 1A Ho Chi Minh Sarani); Mumbai (☎022-66502222; Naman Chambers, C/32 G Block, Bandra Kurla Complex, Bandra East)

USA Chennai (☎044-28574000; Gemini Circle, 220 Anna Salai); Delhi (☎011-24198000; http://newdelhi.usembassy.gov/; Shantipath,

PROHIBITED EXPORTS

To protect India's cultural heritage, the export of certain antiques is prohibited. Many 'old' objects are fine, but the difficulties begin if something is verifiably more than 100 years old. Reputable antique dealers know the laws and can make arrangements for an export-clearance certificate for any old items that you're permitted to export. If in doubt, contact Delhi's Archaeological Survey of India (☎011-23010822; www.asi.nic.in; Jan-path; ⊗9.30am-1pm & 2-6pm Mon-Fri) next to the National Museum. The rules may seem stringent but the loss of artworks and traditional buildings in places such as Ladakh, Himachal Pradesh, Gujarat and Rajasthan, due to the international trade in antiques and carved windows and doorframes, has been alarming. Look for quality reproductions instead.

The Indian Wildlife Protection Act bans any form of wildlife trade. Don't buy any products that endanger threatened species and habitats – doing so can result in heavy fines and even imprisonment. This includes ivory, shahtoosh shawls (made from the down of chi-rus, rare Tibetan antelopes), and anything made from the fur, skin, horns or shell of any endangered species. Products made from certain rare plants are also banned.

Note that your home country may have additional laws forbidding the import of restricted items and wildlife parts. The penalties can be severe, so know the law before you buy.

Chanakyapuri); Kolkata (☎033-39842400; 5/1 Ho Chi Minh Sarani); Mumbai (☎022-23633611; Lincoln House, 78 Bhulabhai Desai Rd, Breach Candy)

Gay & Lesbian Travellers

In July 2009 Delhi's High Court overturned India's 148-year-old antihomo-sexuality law. Prior to this landmark ruling, homosexual relations for men were illegal, with penalties for transgression theoretically up to life imprisonment (there's no law against lesbian sexual relations).

However, the country remains largely conservative and public displays of affection are generally frowned upon for heterosexual couples as well as gay and lesbian couples.

There are low-key gay scenes in a number of cities including Mumbai, Delhi, Kolkata, Bengaluru (Bangalore) and Chandigarh (Gay Pride marches have been held at some of these centres).

Publications

Time Out Delhi (www.timeoutdelhi.net) Fortnightly listing of gay events in Delhi.

Time Out Mumbai (www.timeoutmumbai.net) Gay events in Mumbai.

Websites

Delhi Frontrunners & Walkers (www.delhifront runners.com) Weekly running and walking club for Delhi's LGBT crowd.

Gay Bombay (www.gaybombay.org) Lists gay events

as well as offering support and advice.

Gay Delhi (gaydelhi -subscribe@yahoogroups.com) Send a blank email to join and tap into the capital's gay scene.

Indian Dost (www.indian dost.com/gay.php) News and information including contact groups in India.

Indja Pink (www.indjapink. co.in) India's first 'gay travel boutique' founded by a well-known Indian fashion designer.

A number of Indian cities have support groups, including the following:

Bengaluru

Good As You (www.good asyou.in) Support group for gay, lesbian, bisexual and transgender people. It's part of the NGO **Swabhava**, which works for the LGBT community and operates the **Sahaya Helpline** (☏080-22230959).

Sangama (www.sangama.org) Deals with crisis intervention and provides a community outreach service for gay and bisexual men and women, transgenders and *hijra*s (transvestites and eunuchs).

Chennai

Shakti Center (☏044-45587071; www.shakticenter. org) A collective of LGBT activists and artists, which holds workshops, exhibitions and other activities.

Delhi

Nigah (http://nigahdelhi. blogspot.com) Autonomous collective that holds monthly queer events and organises the annual **Nigah Queerfest** (www.thequeerfest.com).

Kolkata

Counsel Club (counsel club93@hotmail.com) Support group for gays, lesbians, transgenders and bisexuals, and arranges monthly meetings. The affiliated **Palm**

Avenue Integration Society** offers health advice.
Sappho (www.sapphokolkata. org) Operates as a support group for lesbian, bisexual and transgender women.

Mumbai

Humsafar Trust (☏022-26673800; www.humsafar.org) Runs gay and transgender support groups and advocacy programs. The drop-in centre in Santa Cruz East hosts workshops and has a library – pick up a copy of the pioneering gay-and-lesbian magazine *Bombay Dost*. It's also one of the venues for 'Sunday High', a monthly screening of queer-interest films.

Insurance

» Comprehensive travel insurance to cover theft, loss and medical problems (as well as air evacuation) is strongly recommended; also see the Health chapter.

» Some policies specifically exclude potentially dangerous activities such as scuba diving, skiing, motorcycling, paragliding and even trekking: read the fine print.

» Some trekking agents may only accept customers who have cover for emergency helicopter evacuation.

» If you plan to hire a motorcycle in India, make sure the rental policy includes at

least third-party insurance; see p1184.

» Check in advance whether your insurance policy will pay doctors and hospitals directly or reimburse you later for overseas health expenditure (keep all documentation for your claim).

» It's crucial to get a police report in India if you've had anything stolen; insurance companies may refuse to reimburse you without one.

» Worldwide travel insurance is available at www.lonely planet.com/travel_services. You can buy, extend and claim online anytime – even if you're already on the road.

Internet Access

Internet cafes are widespread and connections are usually reasonably fast, except in more remote areas. Wireless (wi-fi) access is available in an increasing number of hotels and some coffee shops in larger cities. In this book, hotels offering internet access are marked by @.

Practicalities

» Internet charges vary regionally (see regional chapters); charges fall anywhere between ₹15 and ₹90 per hour and often with a 15- to 30-minute minimum.

» Power cuts are not uncommon; avoid losing your email

LEGAL AGE

» **Age of Majority** 18

» **Buying Alcohol** 18 to 25 depending on state (25 in Delhi)

» **Driving** 18

» **Sexual Consent** 16 heterosexual sex, 18 homosexual sex

» **Voting** 18

Travellers should note that they can be prosecuted under the law of their home country regarding age of consent, even when abroad.

by writing and saving messages in a text application before pasting them into your browser.

» Bandwidth load tends to be lowest in the early morning and early afternoon.

» Some internet cafes may ask to see your passport; carrying photocopies of the relevant pages (information and visa) saves you having to dig your passport out each time.

» See p15 for useful India-specific web resources.

Security

» Be wary of sending sensitive financial information from internet cafes; some places are able to use keystroke-capturing technology to access passwords and emails.

» Avoid sending credit-card details or other personal data over a wireless connection; using online banking on any nonsecure system is generally unwise.

Laptops

» Many internet cafes can supply laptop users with internet access over a LAN Ethernet cable; alternatively join an international roaming service with an Indian dial-up number, or take out an account with a local Internet Service Provider (ISP).

» Make sure your modem is compatible with the telephone and dial-up system in India (an external global modem may be necessary).

» Companies including Reliance, Airtel and Vodafone offer 3G Data Cards, which can be plugged into the USB port of your laptop and will allow you to access the internet.

* Tariffs start from ₹800 per month for 3GB up to ₹1500 per month for 15GB.

* Make sure you check whether the area you're travelling to is covered by your service provider.

» Consider purchasing a fuse-protected universal AC adaptor to protect your circuit board from power surges.

» Plug adaptors are widely available throughout India, but bring spare plug fuses from home.

Legal Matters

If you're in a sticky legal situation, contact your embassy as quickly as possible. However, be aware that all your embassy may be able to do is monitor your treatment in custody and arrange a lawyer. In the Indian justice system, the burden of proof can often be on the accused and stints in prison before trial are not unheard of.

Antisocial Behaviour

» Smoking in public places is illegal throughout India but this is very rarely enforced; if caught you'll be fined ₹200.

» People can smoke inside their homes and in most open spaces such as streets (heed any signs stating otherwise).

» A number of Indian cities have banned spitting and littering, but this is also variably enforced.

Drugs

» Indian law does not distinguish between 'hard' and 'soft' drugs; possession of any illegal drug is regarded as a criminal offence.

» If convicted, the *minimum* sentence is 10 years, with very little chance of remission or parole.

» Cases can take months, even several years, to appear before a court while the accused may have to wait in prison. There's also usually a hefty monetary fine on top of any custodial sentence.

» Be aware that travellers have been targeted in sting operations in Manali and other backpacker enclaves.

» Marijuana grows wild in various parts of India, but consuming it is still an offence, except in towns where bhang is legally sold for religious rituals.

» Police are getting particularly tough on foreigners who use drugs, so you should take this risk very seriously.

Police

» You should always carry your passport; police are entitled to ask you for identification at any time.

» If you're arrested for an alleged offence and asked for a bribe, the prevailing wisdom is to pay it as the alternative may be a trumped-up charge; there are no 'rules' guiding how much you should pay.

» Corruption is rife so the less you have to do with local police the better; try to avoid all potentially risky situations.

WARNING: BHANG LASSI

Although it's rarely printed in menus, some restaurants in popular tourist centres will clandestinely whip up bhang lassi, a yoghurt and iced-water beverage laced with cannabis (occasionally other narcotics). Commonly dubbed 'special lassi', this often potent concoction can cause varying degrees of ecstasy, drawn-out delirium, hallucination, nausea and paranoia. Some travellers have been ill for several days, robbed, or hurt in accidents, after drinking this fickle brew. A few towns have legal (controlled) bhang outlets such as the Bhang Shop in Jaisalmer (p189).

Maps

Maps available inside India are of variable quality. These are some of the better map series:

Eicher (http://maps.eicher world.com/)

Nelles (www.nelles-verlag.de)

Nest & Wings (www.nestwings.com)

Survey of India (www.survey ofindia.gov.in) Decent city, state and country maps but some titles are restricted for security reasons.

All of these maps are available at good bookshops, or you can buy them online from Delhi's **India Map Store** (www.indiamapstore. com). Throughout India, most state-government tourist offices stock basic local maps.

Money

The Indian rupee (₹) is divided into 100 paise (p), but paise coins are becoming increasingly rare. Coins come in denominations of ₹1, ₹2 and ₹5; notes come in ₹5, ₹10, ₹20, ₹50, ₹100, ₹500 and ₹1000 (this last is handy for paying large bills but can pose problems when getting change for small services). The Indian rupee is linked to a basket of currencies and has been subject to fluctuations in recent years; see p15 for exchange rates.

ATMs

» ATMs are found in most urban centres.

» Visa, MasterCard, Cirrus, Maestro and Plus are the most commonly accepted cards.

» The ATMs listed in this book's regional chapters accept foreign cards (but not necessarily all types of cards).

» Banks in India that accept foreign cards include Citibank, HDFC, ICICI, HSBC and the State Bank of India.

» Before your trip, check whether your card can reliably access banking networks in India and ask for details of charges.

» Notify your bank that you'll be using your card in India (provide dates) to avoid having your card blocked; take along your bank's phone number just in case.

» Always keep the emergency lost-and-stolen numbers for your credit cards in a safe place, separate from your cards, and report any loss or theft immediately.

» Away from major towns, always carry cash or travellers cheques as back-up.

Black Market

» Black-market moneychangers exist but legal moneychangers are so common that there's no reason to use them, except perhaps to change small amounts of cash at land border crossings. If someone approaches you on the street and offers to change money, you're probably being set up for a scam.

Cash

» Major currencies such as US dollars, pounds sterling and euros are easy to change throughout India, although some bank branches insist on travellers cheques only.

» Some banks also accept other currencies such as Australian and Canadian dollars, and Swiss francs.

» Private moneychangers deal with a wider range of currencies, but Pakistani, Nepali and Bangladeshi currency can be harder to change away from the border.

» When travelling off the beaten track, always carry an adequate stock of rupees.

» Whenever changing money, check every note. Don't accept any filthy, ripped or disintegrating notes, as these may be difficult to use.

» It can be tough getting change in India so keep a stock of smaller currency; ₹10, ₹20 and ₹50 notes are helpful.

» Officially you cannot take rupees out of India, but this is laxly enforced. You can change any leftover rupees back into foreign currency, most easily at the airport (some banks have a ₹1000 minimum). You may have to present encashment certificates or credit-card/ ATM receipts, and show your passport and airline ticket.

Credit Cards

» Credit cards are accepted at a growing number of shops, upmarket restaurants, and midrange and top-end hotels, and they can usually be used to pay for flights and train tickets.

» Cash advances on major credit cards are also possible at some banks.

» MasterCard and Visa are the most widely accepted cards.

Encashment Certificates

» Indian law states that all foreign currency must be changed at official moneychangers or banks.

» For every (official) foreign-exchange transaction, you'll receive an encashment certificate (receipt), which will allow you to change rupees back into foreign currency when departing India.

» Encashment certificates should cover the amount of rupees you intend to change back to foreign currency.

» Printed receipts from ATMs are also accepted as evidence of an international transaction at most banks.

International Transfers

» If you run out of money, someone back home can wire you cash via moneychangers affiliated with **Moneygram** (www.moneygram. com) or **Western Union** (www.westernunion.com). A fee is added to the transaction.

» To collect cash, bring your passport and the name and reference number of the person who sent the funds.

Moneychangers

» Private moneychangers are usually open for longer hours than banks, and are found almost everywhere (many also double as internet cafes and travel agents).

» Upmarket hotels may also change money, but their rates are usually not as competitive.

Tipping, Baksheesh & Bargaining

» In tourist restaurants or hotels, a service fee is usually already added to your bill and tipping is optional. Elsewhere, a tip is appreciated.

» Hotel bellboys and train/airport porters appreciate anything around ₹50; hotel staff should be given similar gratuities for services above and beyond the call of duty.

» It's not mandatory to tip taxi or rickshaw drivers, but it's good to tip drivers who are honest about the fare.

» If you hire a car with driver for more than a couple of days, a tip is recommended for good service – details on p1181.

» Baksheesh can loosely be defined as a 'tip'; it covers everything from alms for beggars to bribes.

» Many Indians implore tourists not to hand out sweets, pens or money to children, as it encourages them to beg. To make a lasting difference, donate to a reputable school or charitable organisation (see p39).

» Except in fixed-price shops (such as government emporiums and fair-trade cooperatives), bargaining is the norm.

Travellers Cheques

» All major brands are accepted, but some banks may only accept cheques from American Express (Amex) and Thomas Cook.

» Pounds sterling and US dollars are the safest currencies, especially in smaller towns.

» Keep a record of the cheques' serial numbers separate from your cheques, along with the proof-of-purchase slips, encashment vouchers and photocopied passport details. If you lose your cheques, contact the Amex or Thomas Cook office in Delhi.

» To replace lost travellers cheques, you need the proof-of-purchase slip and the numbers of the missing cheques (some places require a photocopy of the police report and a passport photo). If you don't have the numbers of your missing cheques, the issuing company (eg Amex) will contact the place where you bought them.

Photography

For useful tips and techniques on travel photography, read Lonely Planet's guide to *Travel Photography*.

Digital

» Memory cards for digital cameras are available from photographic shops in most large cities and towns. However, the quality of memory cards is variable – some don't carry the advertised amount of data.

» Expect to pay upwards of ₹500 for a 1GB card.

» To be safe, regularly back up your memory card to CD; internet cafes may offer this service for ₹60 to ₹120 per disk.

» Some photographic shops make prints from digital photographs for roughly the standard print-and-processing charge.

Restrictions

» India is touchy about anyone taking photographs of military installations – this can include train stations,

bridges, airports, military sites and sensitive border regions.

» Photography from the air is officially prohibited, although airlines rarely enforce this.

» Many places of worship – such as monasteries, temples and mosques – also prohibit photography. Taking photos inside a shrine, at a funeral, at a religious ceremony or of people publicly bathing (including rivers) can also be offensive – ask first.

» Flash photography may be prohibited in certain areas of a shrine, or may not be permitted at all.

» Exercise sensitivity when taking photos of people, especially women, who may find it offensive – obtain permission in advance.

Post

India has the biggest postal network on earth, with over 155,500 post offices. Mail and poste-restante services are generally good, although the speed of delivery will depend on the efficiency of any given office. Airmail is faster and more reliable than sea mail, although it's best to use courier services (such as DHL) to send and receive items of value – expect to pay around ₹3000 per kilogram to Europe, Australia or the USA. Private couriers are often cheaper, but goods may be repacked into large packages to cut costs and things sometimes go missing.

Receiving Mail

» To claim mail you'll need to show your passport.

» Ask senders to address letters to you with your surname in capital letters and underlined, followed by poste restante, GPO (main post office), and the city or town in question.

» Many 'lost' letters are simply misfiled under given/first

names, so check under both your names and ask senders to provide a return address.

» Letters sent via poste restante are generally held for around one to two months before being returned.

» It's best to have any parcels sent to you by registered post.

Sending Mail

LETTERS

» Posting letters/aerogrammes to anywhere overseas costs ₹20/15.

» International postcards cost around ₹7.

» For postcards, stick on the stamps *before* writing on them, as post offices can give you as many as four stamps per card.

» Sending a letter overseas by registered post costs an extra ₹15.

PARCELS

» Posting parcels can either be relatively straightforward or involve multiple counters and lots of queuing; get to the post office in the morning.

» Prices depend on weight (including packing material).

» A small package (unregistered) costs ₹40 (up to 100g) to any country and ₹30 per additional 100g (up to a maximum of 4000g; different charges apply for higher weights).

» Parcel post has a maximum of 20kg to 30kg depending on the destination.

» Airmail takes one to three weeks, sea mail two to four months and Surface Air-Lifted (SAL) – a curious hybrid where parcels travel by both air and sea – around one month.

» Express mail service (EMS; delivery within three days) costs around 30% more than the normal airmail price.

» Parcels must be packed up in white linen and the seams sealed with wax – local tailors offer this service if the post office doesn't.

» Customs declaration forms, available from the post office, must be stitched or pasted to the parcel. No duty is payable by the recipient for gifts under the value of ₹1000.

» Carry a permanent marker to write on the parcel any information requested by the desk.

» Books or printed matter can go by international book post for ₹350 (maximum 5kg), but the package must be wrapped with a hole that reveals the contents for inspection by customs – tailors can do this in such a way that nothing falls out.

» **India Post** (www.indiapost.gov.in) has an online calculator for domestic and international postal tariffs.

Public Holidays

There are officially three national public holidays. Every state celebrates its own official holidays, which cover bank holidays for government workers as well as major religious festivals. Most businesses (offices, shops etc) and tourist sites close on public holidays, but transport is usually unaffected. It's wise to make transport and hotel reservations well in advance if you intend visiting during major festivals.

Public Holidays

Republic Day 26 January
Independence Day 15 August
Gandhi Jayanti 2 October

Major Religious Festivals

Mahavir Jayanti (Jain) February
Holi (Hindu) March
Easter (Christian) March/April
Buddha Jayanti (Buddhist) April/May
Eid al-Fitr (Muslim) August/September
Dussehra (Hindu) October

Diwali (Hindu) October/November
Nanak Jayanti (Sikh) November
Christmas (Christian) 25 December

Safe Travel

Travellers to India's major cities may fall prey to petty and opportunistic crime but most problems can be avoided with a bit of common sense and an appropriate amount of caution; see p1156 for more information. Women and solo travellers should read p1158. Also have a look at the India branch of Lonely Planet's **Thorn Tree Travel Forum** (www.lonelyplanet.com/thorntree), where travellers often post timely warnings about problems they've encountered on the road. Always check your government's travel advisory warnings.

Rebel Violence

India has a number of (sometimes armed) dissident groups championing various causes, who have employed the same tried and tested techniques of rebel groups everywhere: assassinations and bomb attacks on government infrastructure, public transport, religious centres, tourist sites and markets. For further information read p1081.

» Certain areas are particularly prone to insurgent violence – specifically Kashmir, the Northeast States, some remote tribal regions, Bihar and, less frequently, parts of West Bengal.

» Curfews and strikes can close the roads (as well as banks, shops etc) for days on end in sensitive regions like Kashmir.

» International terrorism is as much of a risk in Europe or the USA, so this is no reason not to go to India, but it makes sense to check the local security situation carefully before travelling (especially in high-risk areas).

Telephone

» There are few payphones in India (apart from in airports), but private PCO/STD/ISD call booths do the same job, offering inexpensive local, interstate and international calls at lower prices than calls made from hotel rooms.

» These booths are found around the country. A digital meter displays how much the call is costing and usually provides a printed receipt when the call is finished.

» Costs vary depending on the operator and destination but can be from ₹1 per minute for local calls and between ₹5 and ₹10 for international calls.

» Some booths also offer a 'call-back' service – you ring home, provide the phone number of the booth and wait for people at home to call you back, for a fee of around ₹10 on top of the cost of the preliminary call.

» Getting a line can be difficult in remote country and mountain areas – an engaged signal may just mean that the exchange is overloaded, so keep trying.

» Useful online resources include the **Yellow Pages** (www.indiayellowpages.com) and **Justdial** (www.justdial.com).

Mobile Phones

» Indian mobile phone numbers usually have 10 digits, typically beginning with 🔟9.

» There's roaming coverage for international GSM phones in most cities and large towns.

» To avoid expensive roaming costs (often highest for incoming calls), get hooked up to the local mobile-phone network.

» Mobiles bought in some countries may be locked to a particular network; you'll have to get the phone unlocked, or buy a local phone (available from ₹2000) to use an Indian SIM card.

GETTING CONNECTED

» Getting connected is inexpensive but increasingly complicated, owing to security concerns, and involves a lot of paperwork.

» Foreigners must supply between one and five passport photos, their passport, and photocopies of their passport identity and visa pages

» You must also supply a residential address, which can be the address of the hotel where you're staying (ask the hotel to write a letter confirming this).

» Some phone companies send representatives to the listed address, or at the very least call to verify that you are actually staying there.

» Some travellers have reported their SIM card being suspended once the phone company realised that they had moved on from the hotel where they registered their phone. Others have been luckier and used the same SIM card throughout their travels.

» Another option is to get a friendly local to register the phone using their local ID.

» Prepaid mobile-phone kits (SIM card and phone number, plus an allocation of calls) are available in most Indian towns from around ₹200 from a phone shop or local PCO/STD/ISD booth, internet cafe or grocery store.

» You must then purchase new credits on that network, sold as scratch cards in shops and call centres.

» Credit must usually be used within a set time limit and costs vary with the amount of credit on the card.

» The amount you pay for a credit top-up is not the amount you get on your phone – state taxes and service charges come off first.

» For some networks, recharge cards are being replaced by direct credit: you pay the vendor and the credit is deposited straight to your phone. Ask which system is in use before you buy.

CHARGES

» Calls made within the state or city in which you bought the SIM card are cheap – ₹1 per minute – and you can call internationally for less than ₹10 per minute.

» SMS messaging is even cheaper – usually, the more credit you have on your phone, the cheaper the call rate.

» The most popular (and reliable) companies include Airtel, Vodaphone and BSNL.

GOVERNMENT TRAVEL ADVICE

The following government websites offer travel advice and information on current hot spots.
Australian Department of Foreign Affairs (www.smarttraveller.gov.au)
British Foreign Office (www.fco.gov.uk/en)
Canadian Department of Foreign Affairs (www.voyage.gc.ca)
German Foreign Office (www.auswaeriges-amt.de)
Japan Ministry of Foreign Affairs (www.mofa.go.jp)
Netherlands Ministry of Foreign Affairs (www.government.nl/Subjects/Advice_to_travellers)
Switzerland (www.eda.admin.ch)
US State Department (http://travel.state.gov)

» Most SIM cards are state-specific; they can be used in other states, but you pay for calls at roaming rates and you'll be charged for incoming as well as outgoing calls.

» If you buy a SIM card in Delhi, calls to anywhere outside Delhi will be around ₹1.50 per minute, while the charge to receive a call from anywhere in India (outside of Delhi) is ₹1 per minute.

» Unreliable signals and problems with international texting (messages or replies being delayed or failing to get through) are not uncommon.

» As the mobile-phone industry continues to evolve, mobile rates, suppliers and coverage are all likely to develop during the life of this book.

JAMMU & KASHMIR AND ASSAM

» Due to ongoing terrorist threats, mobile phone use in Jammu & Kashmir, as well as Assam, is more strictly controlled.

» Roaming on foreign mobiles won't work here, nor will pay-as-you-go SIM cards purchased elsewhere in India (post-paid ones will, if you're an Indian resident).

» To purchase a SIM card you'll need a photocopy of your passport and visa, four or five passport photos and a reference from a local who has known you for at least one month.

» You may be able to tip a local to apply for a SIM in their name and sell it on to you – although they will need all the photos and ID documents too.

» An additional stumbling block is that your ID is supposed to provide proof of your father's name – if this detail isn't in your passport (as is the case for many Western nationals) you might not get the SIM at all.

» During times of tension you will not be able to send or receive SMS text messages.

Phone Codes

» Calling India from abroad: dial your country's international access code, then ☑91 (India's country code), then the area code (without the initial zero), then the local number.

» Calling internationally from India: dial ☑00 (the international access code), then the country code of the country you're calling, then the area code (without the initial zero if there is one) and the local number.

» Phone numbers have an area code followed by up to eight digits.

» Toll-free numbers begin with 1800.

» The government is slowly trying to bring all numbers in India onto the same system, so area codes may change and new digits may be added to numbers with limited warning.

» A Home Country Direct service, which gives you access to the international operator in your home country, exists for the US ☑000 117 and the UK ☑000 4417.

» To access an international operator elsewhere dial ☑000 127. The operator can place a call to anywhere in the world and allow you to make collect calls.

Time

India uses the 12-hour clock and the local standard time is known as Indian Standard Time (IST). IST is 5½ hours ahead of GMT/UTC. The floating half-hour was added to maximise daylight hours over such a vast country.

Toilets

» Public toilets are most easily found in major cities and tourist sites; the cleanest (usually with sit-down and squat choices) are usually at modern restaurants, shopping complexes and cinemas.

» Beyond urban centres, toilets are of the squat variety and locals may use the 'hand-and-water' technique, which involves cleaning one's bottom with a small jug of water and the left hand. It's always a good idea to carry your own toilet paper, just in case.

Tourist Information

In addition to the Government of India tourist offices (also known as 'India Tourism'), each state maintains its own network of tourist offices. These vary in their efficiency and usefulness – some are run by enthusiastic souls who go out of their way to help, others are little more than a means of drumming up business for State Tourism Development Corporation tours. Most of the tourist offices have free brochures and often a free (or inexpensive) local map.

The first stop for information should be the tourism website of the Government of India, **Incredible India** (www.incredibleindia.org); for details of its regional offices around India, click on the 'Help Desk' tab at the top of the homepage.

See regional chapters for contact details of relevant tourist offices.

CITY	NOON IN DELHI
Beijing	2.30pm
Dhaka	12.30pm
Islamabad	11.30am
Kathmandu	12.15pm
London	6.30am
New York	1.30am
San Francisco	10.30pm
Sydney	5.30pm
Tokyo	3.30pm

Travel Permits

» Access to certain parts of India – particularly disputed border areas – is controlled by an often-complicated permit system.

» A permit known as an Inner-Line Permit (ILP) is required to visit certain parts of Himachal Pradesh, Ladakh, Uttarakhand and Sikkim that lie close to the disputed border with China/Tibet.

» Obtaining the ILP is basically a formality, but travel agents must apply on your behalf for certain areas, including many trekking routes passing close to the border.

» ILPs are issued by regional magistrates and district commissioners, either directly to travellers (for free) or through travel agents (for a fee). Refer to the Himachal Pradesh, Ladakh, Sikkim, Uttarakhand and Andaman Islands sections for further information.

» Note that entering parts of the Northeast States is much more complex – for comprehensive details read p553.

» We recommend that you double-check with tourism officials to see if permit requirements have undergone any recent changes before you head out to these areas.

Travellers with Disabilities

India's crowded public transport, crush of humanity and variable infrastructure can test even the hardiest ablebodied traveller. If you have a physical disability or you are vision impaired, these can pose even more of a challenge. If your mobility is considerably restricted, you may like to ease the stress by travelling with an able-bodied companion.

Accommodation Wheelchair-friendly hotels are almost exclusively top end.

Make pretrip enquiries and book ground-floor rooms at hotels that lack adequate facilities.

Accessibility Some restaurants and offices have ramps but most tend to have at least one step. Staircases are often steep; lifts frequently stop at mezzanines between floors.

Footpaths Where pavements exist, they can be riddled with holes, littered with debris and packed with pedestrians. If using crutches, bring along spare rubber caps.

Transport Hiring a car with driver will make moving around a lot easier (see p1181); if you use a wheelchair, make sure the car-hire company can provide an appropriate vehicle to carry it.

For further advice pertaining to your specific requirements, consult your doctor before heading to India.

The following organisations may be able to proffer further information or at least point you in the right direction.

Mobility International USA (MIUSA; www.miusa.org)

Access-Able Travel Source (www.access-able.com)

Global Access News (www.globalaccessnews.com)

Royal Association for Disability & Rehabilitation (RADAR; www.radar.org.uk)

Accessible Journeys (www.disabilitytravel.com)

Visas

A pilot scheme is currently in place to provide visas on arrival to nationals of Japan, New Zealand, Singapore, Luxembourg and Finland at Mumbai, Chennai, Kolkata and New Delhi airports. This scheme has been introduced on a one year 'experimental' basis, so double-check before you fly. All other nationals – except

Nepal and Bhutan – must get a visa *before* arriving in India. These are available at Indian missions worldwide. Note that your passport needs to be valid for at least six months beyond your intended stay in India, with at least two blank pages.

Entry Requirements

» In 2009 a large number of foreigners were found to be working in India on tourist visas, so regulations surrounding who can get a visa and for how long have been tightened. These rules are likely to change, however, so double-check with the Indian embassy in your country prior to travel.

» Most people travel on the standard six-month tourist visa.

» Student and business visas have strict conditions (consult the Indian embassy for details).

» Tourist visas are valid from the date of issue, not the date you arrive in India. You can spend a total of 180 days in the country.

» Five- and 10-year tourist visas are available to US citizens *only* under a bilateral arrangement; however, you can still only stay in the country for up to 180 days continuously.

» Currently you are required to submit two passport photographs with your visa application; these must be in colour and must be 2in x 2in.

» An onward travel ticket is a requirement for most visas, but this isn't always enforced (check in advance).

» Additional restrictions apply to travellers from Bangladesh and Pakistan, as well as certain Eastern European, African and Central Asian countries. Check any special conditions for your nationality with the Indian embassy in your country.

» Visas are priced in the local currency and may have an added service fee (contact your country's Indian embassy for current prices).

» Extended visas are possible for people of Indian origin (excluding those in Pakistan and Bangladesh) who hold a non-Indian passport and live abroad.

» For visas lasting more than six months, you're supposed to register at the Foreigners' Regional Registration Office (FRRO; see p1174) within 14 days of arriving in India; enquire about these special conditions when you apply for your visa.

Re-entry Requirements

» Current regulations dictate that, when you leave the country, you will receive a stamp in your passport indicating you may not re-enter India for two months, regardless of how much longer your visa is valid for.

» If you wish to return to India before the two-month period has passed, you will have to visit the Indian High Commission or consulate in the country you are in, or

where you are a resident, and apply for a Permit to Re-enter. This permit is only granted in urgent or extreme cases.

» If you're travelling to multiple countries, a permit is not needed as long as your trip follows an itinerary, which you can show at immigration (eg if you're transiting through India on your way home from Nepal).

» If granted a permit, you must register with the FRRO/ FRO within 14 days.

Visa Extensions

» At the time of writing, the **Ministry of Home Affairs** (☎011-23385748; Jaisalmer House, 26 Man Singh Rd, Delhi; ⊙enquiries 9-11am Mon-Fri) was not granting visa extensions. The only circumstances in which this might conceivably happen are *extreme* medical emergencies or if you were robbed of your passport just before you planned to leave the country (at the end of your visa).

» In such cases, you should contact the **Foreigners'**

Regional Registration Office (FRRO; ☎011-26195530; frrodelhi@hotmail.com; Level 2, East Block 8, Sector 1, Rama Krishna (RK) Puram, Delhi; ⊙9.30am-5.30pm Mon-Fri), just around the corner from the Hyatt Regency hotel. This is also the place to come for a replacement visa if you need your lost/stolen passport replaced (required before you can leave the country). Regional FRROs are even less likely to grant an extension.

» Assuming you meet the stringent criteria, the FRRO is permitted to issue an extension of 14 days (free for nationals of most countries; enquire on application). You must bring your confirmed air ticket, one passport photo (take two, just in case), and a photocopy of your passport identity and visa pages. Note that this system is designed to get you out of the country promptly with the correct official stamps, not to give you two extra weeks of travel.

Transport

GETTING THERE & AWAY

Getting to India is increasingly easy, with plenty of international airlines servicing the country and overland routes open between India and Nepal, Bangladesh, Bhutan and Pakistan. Flights, tours and other tickets may also be booked online at www.lonelyplanet.com/bookings.

Entering India

Entering India by air or land is relatively straightforward, with standard immigration and customs procedures (p1164).

Passport

To enter India you need a valid passport, visa (p1173) and an onward/return ticket. Your passport should be valid for at least six months beyond your intended stay in India. If your passport is lost or stolen, immediately contact your country's representative (p1164). Keep photocopies of your airline ticket and the identity and visa pages of your passport in case of emergency. Better yet, scan and email copies to yourself. Check with the Indian embassy in your home country for any special conditions that may exist for your nationality.

Air

Airports & Airlines

As India is a big country, it makes sense to fly into the airport that's nearest to the area you'll be visiting. India has four main gateways for international flights (see the following list); however, a number of other cities service international carriers – for details see regional chapters and www.indianairports.com.

Chennai (Madras; MAA; Anna International Airport; ☑044-22560551; www.chennaiairportguide.com)

Delhi (DEL; Indira Gandhi International Airport; ☑91-124-3376000; www.newdelhiairport.in)

Kolkata (Calcutta; CCU; Netaji Subhash Chandra Bose International Airport; ☑033-25118787; www.calcuttaairport.com)

Mumbai (Bombay; BOM; Chhatrapati Shivaji International Airport; ☑022-2626 4000; www.csia.in)

India's national carrier is **Air India** (www.airindia.com), of which the former state-owned domestic carrier, Indian Airlines, is now a part, following a merger deal. Air India has had a relatively decent air safety record in recent years.

Tickets

An onward or return air ticket is usually a condition of the Indian tourist visa so few visitors buy international

---

CLIMATE CHANGE & TRAVEL

Every form of transport that relies on carbon-based fuel generates CO_2, the main cause of human-induced climate change. Modern travel is dependent on aeroplanes, which might use less fuel per kilometre per person than most cars but travel much greater distances. The altitude at which aircraft emit gases (including CO_2) and particles also contributes to their climate change impact. Many websites offer 'carbon calculators' that allow people to estimate the carbon emissions generated by their journey and, for those who wish to do so, to offset the impact of the greenhouse gases emitted with contributions to portfolios of climate-friendly initiatives throughout the world. Lonely Planet offsets the carbon footprint of all staff and author travel.

OVERLAND TO/FROM BANGLADESH

ROUTE/BORDER TOWNS	TRANSPORT	VISAS	MORE INFORMATION
Kolkata-Dhaka/ Haridaspur (India) & Benapole (Bangladesh)	Regular daily buses Kolkata to Dhaka; twice-weekly train via Darsana border post.	Must be obtained in advance. To buy train ticket, Darsana must be marked on your Bangladesh visa.	p470, p470
Siliguri-Chengra-bandha/Burimari/ Chengrabandha (India) & Burimari (Bangladesh)	Regular direct buses Siliguri-Chengrabandha; then bus to Rangpur, Bogra & Dhaka.	Must be obtained prior to travel.	p484. Departure tax payable on exiting Bangladesh.
Shillong-Sylhet/Dawki (India) & Tamabil (Bangladesh)	morning share jeeps run from Bara Bazaar, Shillong to Dawki. From Dawki walk (1.5km) or taxi to Tamabil bus station for regular buses to Sylhet.	Must be obtained prior to travel.	p578
Agartala-Dhaka/ Nearest town Agartala, 3km from border along Akhaura Rd (India) & Akhaura, 5km from border (Bangladesh)	Akhaura is on Dhaka-Comilla train line. Dhaka-Sylhet trains run from Ajampur train station, 3km further north.	Must be obtained prior to travel.	p578

tickets inside India. Only designated travel agencies can book international flights, but fares may be the same if you book directly with the airlines. Departure tax and other charges are included in airline tickets. You are required to show a copy of your ticket or itinerary in order to enter the airport, whether flying internationally or within India.

Land

Border Crossings

Although most visitors fly into India, it is possible to travel overland between India and Bangladesh, Bhutan, Nepal and Pakistan. The overland route from Nepal is the most popular. For more on these routes, consult Lonely Planet's *Istanbul to Kathmandu*, or see the

'Europe to India overland' section on www.seat61.com/ India.htm.

» If you enter India by bus or train you'll be required to disembark at the border for standard immigration and customs checks.

» You *must* have a valid Indian visa in advance, as no visas are available at the border – see p1173 for more information.

» Drivers of cars and motorbikes will need the vehicle's registration papers, liability insurance and an international drivers' permit in addition to their domestic licence. You'll also need a *Carnet de passage en douane*, which acts as a temporary waiver of import duty on the vehicle.

» To find out the latest requirements for the paperwork and other important driving information, contact your local automobile association.

» See p1181 and p1182 for more on car and motorcycle travel.

BANGLADESH

» Foreigners can use four of the land crossings between Bangladesh and India, all in West Bengal or the Northeast States (see above).

» Heading from India to Bangladesh, tourist visas should be obtained in advance from a Bangladeshi mission (see p1164).

» Heading from Bangladesh to India, you have to prepay the exit tax; this must be paid in advance at a Sonali Bank branch (either in Dhaka, another big city, or at the closest branch to the border).

» Exiting Bangladesh overland is complicated by red tape – if you enter by air, you require a road permit (or 'change of route' permit) to leave by land.

» To apply for visa extensions and change of route permits you will need to visit the **Immigration and Passport Office** (☎88-02-8159525; www.dip.gov.bd; Agargaon Rd; ⏰Sat-Thu) in Dhaka.

» Some travellers have reported problems exiting Bangladesh overland with the visa issued on arrival at Dhaka airport.

BHUTAN
» Phuentsholing is the main entry and exit point between India and Bhutan (see below).

» All non-Indian nationals need a Bhutanese visa to enter the country and are required to book a tour with a registered tour operator in Bhutan; this can be done directly through an affiliated travel agency abroad.

» As entry requirements need advance planning and are subject to change, we recommend you consult a travel agent or Bhutanese embassy for up-to-the-minute details. Also see www.tourism.gov.bt and Lonely Planet's *Bhutan*.

NEPAL
» Political and weather conditions permitting, there are five land border crossings between India and Nepal. Check the current security status before crossing into Nepal; local newspapers and websites are good sources of information (see more details on p1178).

» Travellers entering Nepal may purchase 15-day (US$25), one-month (US$40) or three-month (US$100) multiple-entry

visas at the border. Payment is in US dollars and you need two recent passport photos. Alternatively, obtain a visa in advance from a Nepalese mission (see p1164).

» Travellers have reported being harassed crossing into India at the Sunauli border and having to pay inflated prices for bus and train tickets. Consider taking a taxi to Gorakhpur and getting a train or bus from there.

PAKISTAN
» Given the rocky relationship between India and Pakistan, crossing by land depends on the current state of relations between the two countries – check locally. Crossing details are on p1179.

» If the crossings are open, you can reach Pakistan from Delhi, Amritsar (Punjab) and Rajasthan by bus or train. The bus route from Srinagar to Pakistan-administered Kashmir is currently only open to Indian citizens.

» You must have a visa to enter Pakistan; it's easiest to obtain this from the Pakistan mission in your home country.

» Previously, the **Pakistan embassy** (☎011- 26110601; www.mofa.gov.pk/india; 2/50G Shantipath, Chanakyapuri) in Delhi was issuing 90-day tourist visas for most nationalities in around five days, but at the time of writing tourist visas were not being granted. This may well change again.

» If you do apply within India, you'll need a letter of recommendation from your home embassy as well as the usual

application forms and two passport photos.

Sea

There are several sea routes between India and surrounding islands but none leave Indian sovereign territory. There has long been talk of a passenger ferry service between southern India and Colombo in Sri Lanka but this has yet to materialise. Enquire locally to see if there has been any progress.

GETTING AROUND

Air

Airlines in India
India has a very competitive domestic airline industry. Some well-established players are Air India (which now includes Indian Airlines), Kingfisher and Jet Airways. Hosts of budget airlines offer discounted fares on various domestic sectors. Airline seats can be booked directly by telephone, through travel agencies or cheaply over the internet. Domestic airlines set rupee fares for Indian citizens, while foreigners may be charged US dollar fares (usually payable in rupees).

At the time of writing, the following airlines were operating across various destinations in India – see regional chapters for specifics about routes, fares and booking offices. Keep in mind, however, that the competitive nature of the aviation industry

---

OVERLAND TO/FROM BHUTAN

ROUTE/BORDER TOWNS	TRANSPORT	VISAS	MORE INFORMATION
Siliguri/Kolkata-Phuentsholing/Jaigon (India) & Phuentsholing (Bhutan)	From Kolkata, direct bus 7pm. From Siliguri daily buses, possible shared jeeps to Jaigon.	non-Indian nationals need visa & tour booking (p1177).	p470 and the boxed text p484

OVERLAND TO/FROM NEPAL

ROUTE/BORDER TOWNS	TRANSPORT	VISAS	MORE INFORMATION
Delhi/Varanasi-Kathmandu/Sunauli (India) & Bhairawa (Nepal)	Trains Delhi-Gorakhpur, half-hourly buses to border. Buses from Varanasi to Sunauli leave early morning & eve (uncomfortable ride). Buses & jeeps Bhairawa-Kathmandu.	Nepal available at border. Indian must be acquired in advance.	p395
Kolkata (Patna & the eastern plains) to Kathmandu & Pokhara/Raxaul (India) & Birganj (Nepal)	Daily buses from Patna & Kolkata to Raxaul. *Mithila Express* train daily from Kolkata. Regular day/night buses from Birganj to Kathmandu & Pokhara.	as above.	p514, p515
West Bengal-Eastern Nepal/Panitanki (India) & Kakarbhitta (Nepal)	Regular buses Kakarbhitta-Kathmandu (17hr) & other destinations. Bhadrapur airport (23km away) flights to Kathmandu.	Nepal available at border (7am-7pm).	p498, p484
Jamunaha, Uttar Pradesh-Nepalganj, Western Nepal/Rupaidiha (India) & Nepalganj (Nepal)	Good gateway for Nepal's Royal Bardia National Park. Flights to Kathmandu.	Nepal available at border. Indian must be acquired in advance.	
Uttarakhand-Western Nepal/Banbassa (India) & Mahendranagar (Nepal)	Border is 5km from Banbassa, then an autorickshaw to Mahendranagar. From there, buses to Kathmadu & Pokhara (1 daily).	Border open 24hr, officially staffed 9am-5pm.	p441

means that fares fluctuate dramatically. Holidays, festivals and seasons also have a serious effect on ticket prices so check for the latest fares online.

Air India (☑1800 1801407; www.airindia.com) India's national carrier operates many domestic and international flights.

GoAir (☑1800 222111; www.goair.in) Reliable low-cost carrier servicing Goa, Cochin, Jaipur, Delhi and Bagdogra among other destinations.

IndiGo (☑1800 1803838; www.goindigo.in) Good, reliable budget airline flying to numerous cities including Kolkata, Mumbai, Delhi and Chennai.

Jagson Airlines (☑011-23721593; www.jagsonairline.com) Among other destinations, it uses tiny Dornier planes to access small runways in Himachal Pradesh.

Jet Airways (☑011-39893333; www.jetairways.com) Rated by many as India's best airline, with growing domestic and international services.

JetLite (☑1800 223020; www.jetlite.com) Jet Airways' budget carrier flies to numerous destinations including Amritsar, Dehradun, Chennai and Jodhpur.

Kingfisher Airlines (☑1800 2093030; www.flykingfisher.com) Domestic and international flights.

Kingfisher Red (☑1800 2093030; www.flykingfisher.com) Kingfisher Airlines' low-cost option.

Spicejet (☑1800 1803333; www.spicejet.com) Budget carrier whose destinations include Bangalore, Varanasi, Srinagar, Colombo (Sri Lanka) and Kathmandu (Nepal).

Security at airports is generally stringent. All hold baggage must be x-rayed prior to check-in and every item of cabin baggage needs a label, which must be stamped as part of the security check (don't forget to collect tags at the check-in counter). Flights to sensitive destinations, such as Kashmir and

Ladakh, have extra security restrictions: cabin baggage may be completely prohibited and batteries usually need to be removed from all electronic items and placed in the hold. You may also need to identify your bags on the tarmac before they are loaded on the plane.

The recommended check-in time for domestic flights is one hour before departure. The usual baggage allowance is 20kg (10kg for smaller aircraft) in economy class, and 30kg in business.

Bicycle

There are no restrictions on bringing a bicycle into the country. However, bicycles sent by sea can take a few weeks to clear customs in India, so it's better to fly them in. It may actually be cheaper – and less hassle – to hire or buy a bicycle in India itself. Read up on bicycle touring before you travel – Rob Van Der Plas' *Bicycle Touring Manual* and Stephen Lord's *Adventure Cycle-Touring Handbook* are good places to start. Consult local cycling magazines and clubs for useful information and advice. The **Cycling Federation of India** (☏011- 23753529; www.cyclingfederationof india.org; 12 Pandit Pant Marg; ◷10am-5pm Mon-Fri) can provide local information.

Hire

» Tourist centres and traveller hang-outs are the easiest spots to find bicycles for hire – simply enquire locally.

» Prices vary: between ₹40 and ₹100 per day for a roadworthy, Indian-made bicycle; mountain bikes, where available, are usually upwards of ₹350 per day.

» Hire places may require a cash security deposit (avoid leaving your airline ticket or passport).

Practicalities

» Mountain bikes with off-road tyres give the best protection against India's puncture-prone roads.

» Roadside cycle mechanics abound but you should still bring spare tyres, brake cables, lubricating oil, chain repair kit, and plenty of puncture-repair patches.

» Bikes can often be carried for free, or for a small luggage fee, on the roof of public buses – handy for uphill stretches.

» Contact your airline for information about transporting your bike and customs formalities in your home country.

Purchase

» Delhi's Jhandewalan Cycle Market has imported and domestic new and secondhand bikes and spare parts.

» Mountain bikes with reputable brands that include Hero (www.herocycles.com) and Atlas (www.atlascycles onepat.com) generally start at around ₹3500.

» Reselling is usually fairly easy – ask at local cycle or hire shops or put up an advert on travel noticeboards.

» If you purchased a new bike and it's still in reasonably good condition, you should be able to recoup around 50% of what you originally paid.

Road Rules

» Vehicles drive on the left in India but otherwise road rules are virtually nonexistent.

» Cities and national highways can be hazardous places to cycle so, where possible, stick to back roads.

» Be conservative about the distance you expect to cover –an experienced cyclist can manage around 60km to 100km a day on the plains, 40km to 60km on sealed

OVERLAND TO/FROM PAKISTAN

ROUTE/ BORDER TOWNS	TRANSPORT	MORE INFORMATION
Delhi/Amritsar-Lahore/ Attari (India) & Wagah (Pakistan)	direct bus & trains Delhi-Lahore. Lahore Bus Service dep Delhi 6am daily for Lahore (12hr). Advance bookings essential. *Samijhauta Express* train twice weekly Old Delhi train station-Lahore, customs & immigration stop at Attari (Indian border).	Security tightened but still a concern after 2007 bomb attack on Delhi-Lahore train. Border formalities can be quicker for independent travellers.
Jodhpur-Karachi/ Munabao (India) & Khokrapar (Pakistan)	Weekly *Thar Express* Jodhpur-Karachi (schedule erratic).	p180

RIDING THE RAILS WITH YOUR BIKE

For long hauls, transporting your bike by train can be a convenient option. Buy a standard train ticket for the journey, then take your bike to the station parcel office with your passport, registration papers, driver's licence and insurance documents. Packing-wallahs will wrap your bike in protective sacking for around ₹50 to ₹250 and you must fill out various forms and pay the shipping fee – around ₹2000 to ₹3500 (charges are less on an ordinary train) – plus an insurance fee of 1% of the declared value of the bike. Bring the same paperwork to collect your bike from the goods office at the other end. If the bike is left waiting at the destination for more than 24 hours, you'll pay a storage fee of around ₹50 to ₹100 per day.

mountain roads and 40km or less on dirt roads.

Boat

» Scheduled ferries connect mainland India to Port Blair in the Andaman Islands (p1070).

» There are sporadic ferries from Visakhapatnam (Andhra Pradesh) to the Andaman Islands (p913).

» Between October and May, there are boat services from Kochi (Kerala) to the Lakshadweep Islands (see p979).

» There are also numerous shorter ferry services across rivers, from chain pontoons to coracles, and various boat cruises – see the regional chapters for more information.

Bus

» Buses go almost everywhere in India and are the only way to get around many mountainous areas. They tend to be the cheapest way to travel; services are fast and frequent.

» Roads in curvaceous terrain can be especially perilous; buses are often driven with wilful abandon, and accidents are always a risk.

» Avoid night buses unless there's no alternative: driving conditions are more hazardous and drivers may be suffering from lack of sleep.

» All buses make snack and toilet stops (some more frequently than others), providing a break but possibly adding hours to journey times.

» Shared jeeps complement the bus service in many mountain areas – see p1184.

Classes

» State-owned and private bus companies both offer 'ordinary' and more expensive 'deluxe' buses. Many state tourist offices run their own reliable deluxe bus services.

» 'Ordinary' buses tend to be ageing rattletraps while 'deluxe' buses range from less decrepit versions of ordinary buses to flashy Volvo buses with AC and reclining two-by-two seating.

» Buses run by the state government are usually the more reliable option (if there's a breakdown, another bus will be sent to pick up passengers), and seats can usually be booked up to a month in advance.

» Private buses are either more expensive (but more comfortable), or cheaper but

with kamikaze drivers and conductors who cram on as many passengers as possible to maximise profits.

» Travel agencies in many tourist towns offer relatively expensive private two-by-two buses, which tend to leave and terminate at conveniently central stops.

» Some agencies have been known to book people onto ordinary buses at super-deluxe prices – if possible, book directly with the bus company.

» Timetables and destinations may be displayed on signs or billboards at travel agencies and tourist offices.

» Take earplugs on long-distance buses, to muffle the often deafening music.

» On any bus, try to sit between the axles to minimise the bumpy effect of potholes.

Costs

» The cheapest buses are 'ordinary' government buses, but prices vary from state to state (consult regional chapters).

» Add around 50% to the ordinary fare for deluxe services, double the fare for AC, and triple or quadruple the fare for a two-by-two service.

Luggage

» Luggage is stored in compartments underneath the bus (sometimes for a small fee) or carried on the roof.

» Arrive at least an hour before departure time – some buses cover roof-stored bags with a canvas sheet, making last-minute additions inconvenient/impossible.

» If your bags go on the roof, make sure they're securely locked, and tied to the metal baggage rack – unsecured bags can fall off on rough roads.

» Theft is a (minor) risk: watch your bags at snack and toilet stops; *never* leave day-packs or valuables unattended inside the bus.

Reservations

» Most deluxe buses can be booked in advance – government buses usually a month ahead – at the bus station or local travel agencies.

» Reservations are rarely possible on 'ordinary' buses; travellers can be left behind in the mad rush for a seat.

» To secure a seat, send a travelling companion ahead to claim some space, or pass a book or article of clothing through an open window and place it on an empty seat. This 'reservation' method rarely fails.

» If you board a bus midway through its journey, you may have to stand until a seat becomes free.

» Many buses only depart when full – passengers might suddenly leave yours to join one that looks nearer to departing.

» Many bus stations have a separate women's queue (not always obvious when signs are in Hindi and men join the melee). Women have an unspoken right to elbow their way to the front of any bus queue in India, so don't be shy, ladies!

Car

Few people bother with self-drive car hire – not only because of the hair-raising driving conditions, but also because hiring a car with driver is wonderfully afford-able in India, particularly if several people share the cost. Seatbelts are either nonexistent or of variable quality. International rental companies with representatives in India include **Budget** (www.budget.com) and **Hertz** (www.hertz.com).

Hiring a Car & Driver

» Most towns have taxi stands or car-hire companies where you can arrange short or long tours (see regional chapters).

» Not all hire cars are licensed to travel beyond their home state. Those that are will pay extra state taxes, which are added to the hire charge.

» Ask for a driver who speaks some English and knows the region you intend visiting, and try to see the car and meet the driver before paying anything.

» Ambassador cars look great but are rather slow and uncomfortable if travelling long distances – keep them for touring cities.

» For multiday trips, the charge should cover the driver's meals and accommodation. Drivers should make their own sleeping and eating arrangements.

» It is *essential* to set the ground rules from day one; politely but firmly let the driver know that you're boss in order to avoid anguish later.

Costs

» The price depends on the distance and the terrain (driving on mountain roads uses more petrol, hence the higher cost).

» One-way trips usually cost the same as return ones (to cover the petrol and driver charges for getting back).

» Hire charges vary from state to state. Some taxi unions set a time limit or a maximum kilometre distance for day trips – if you go over, you'll have to pay extra.

» To avoid potential misunderstandings, get *in writing* what you've been promised (quotes should include petrol, sightseeing stops, all your chosen destinations, and meals and accommodation for the driver). If a driver asks you for money for petrol en route because he is short of cash, get receipts for reimbursement later.

» For sightseeing day trips around a single city, expect to pay upwards of ₹800/1000 for a non-AC/AC car with an eight-hour, 80km limit per day (extra charges apply).

» A tip is customary at the end of your journey; ₹125-150 per day is fair (more if you're really pleased with the driver's service).

Hitching

For a negotiable fee, truck drivers supplement the bus service in some remote areas. However, as drivers rarely speak English, you may have difficulty explaining where you wish to go, and working out a fair price to pay. Be aware that truck drivers have a reputation for driving under the influence of alcohol. As anywhere, women are strongly advised against hitching alone or even in pairs. Always use your instincts.

THE BRAVE BRO

In Ladakh, Arunachal Pradesh and Sikkim, the Border Roads Organisation (BRO) 'build(s) roads in the sky', including some of the world's highest motorable passes. Risking life and limb to keep the roads open, the BRO has a wicked sense of humour when it comes to driver warnings:

» Overtaker beware of Undertaker

» Better to be Mister Late than a late Mister

» Go easy on my curves

» Love thy neighbour, but not while driving

Local Transport

» Buses, cycle-rickshaws, autorickshaws, taxis, boats and urban trains provide transport around India's cities.

» Costs for public transport vary from town to town (consult regional chapters).

» For any transport without a fixed fare, agree on the price *before* you start your journey and make sure that it covers your luggage and every passenger.

» Even where meters exist, drivers may refuse to use them, demanding an elevated 'fixed' fare. Insist on the meter; if that fails, find another vehicle.

» Fares usually increase at night (by up to 100%) and some drivers charge a few rupees extra for luggage.

» Carry plenty of small bills for taxi and rickshaw fares as drivers rarely have change.

» Some taxi/autorickshaw drivers are involved in the commission racket – see p1157.

Autorickshaw, Tempo & Vikram

» The Indian autorickshaw is a three-wheeled motorised contraption with tin or canvas roof and sides, with room for two passengers (although you'll often see many more squeezed in) and limited luggage.

» They are also referred to as autos, scooters, riks or tuk-tuks.

» They are mostly cheaper than taxis and usually have a meter, although getting it turned on can be a challenge.

» Travelling by auto is great fun but, thanks to the open windows, can be smelly, noisy and hot!

» Tempos and *vikrams* (large tempos) are outsized autorickshaws with room for more passengers, running on fixed routes for a fixed fare.

» In country areas, you may also see the fearsome-looking 'three-wheeler' – a crude tractorlike tempo with a front wheel on an articulated arm.

Boat

Various kinds of local boats offer transport across and down rivers in India, from big car ferries to wooden canoes and wicker coracles – see regional chapters for details. Most of the larger boats carry bicycles and motorcycles for a fee.

Bus

Urban buses, particularly in the big cities, are fume-belching, human-stuffed mechanical monsters that travel at breakneck speed (except during morning and evening rush hours, when they can be endlessly stuck in traffic). It's usually far more convenient and comfortable to opt for an autorickshaw or taxi.

Cycle-Rickshaw

» A cycle-rickshaw is a pedal cycle with two rear wheels, supporting a bench seat for passengers. Most have a canopy that can be raised in wet weather, or lowered to provide extra space for luggage.

» Many of the big cities have phased out (or reduced) the number of cycle-rickshaws, but they are still a major means of local transport in many smaller towns.

» Fares must be agreed upon in advance – speak to locals to get an idea of what is a fair price for the distance you intend to travel. Tips are always appreciated, given the slog involved.

» Kolkata is the last bastion of the hand-pulled rickshaw, known as the tana rickshaw. This is a hand-cart on two wheels pulled directly by the rickshaw-wallah.

Taxi

» Most towns have taxis, and these are usually metered, however, getting drivers to use the meter can be a major hassle. If drivers refuse to use the meter, find another cab.

» To avoid fare-setting shenanigans, use prepaid taxis where possible (regional chapters contain details).

Other Local Transport

In some towns, tongas (horse-drawn two-wheelers) and victorias (horse-drawn carriages) still operate. Kolkata has a tram network, and both Delhi and Kolkata have efficient underground train systems. Mumbai, Delhi and Chennai, among other centres, have suburban trains that leave from ordinary train stations. See regional chapters for comprehensive details.

Motorcycle

Despite the traffic challenges, India is an amazing country for long-distance motorcycle touring. Motorcycles generally handle the pitted roads better than four-wheeled vehicles, and you'll have the added bonus of being able to stop when and where you want. However, motorcycle touring can be

---

MANNING THE METER

Getting a metered ride is only half the battle. Meters are almost always outdated, so fares are calculated using a combination of the meter reading and a complicated 'fare adjustment card'. Predictably, this system is open to abuse. If you spend a few days in any town, you'll soon get a feel for the difference between a reasonable fare and a blatant rip-off.

PREPAID TAXIS

Most Indian airports and many train stations have a prepaid-taxi booth, normally just outside the terminal building. Here, you can book a taxi for a fixed price (which will include baggage) and thus avoid commission scams. However, officials advise holding onto the payment coupon until you reach your chosen destination, in case the driver has any other ideas! Smaller airports and stations may have prepaid autorickshaw booths instead.

quite an undertaking – there are some popular motorcycle tours for those who don't want the rigmarole of going it alone.

The most preferred starting point for motorcycle tours is Delhi, and popular destinations include Rajasthan, South India and Ladakh. Weather is an important factor to consider – for the best times to visit different areas see the Climate Chart at the start of regional chapters. To cross from neighbouring countries, check the latest regulations and paperwork requirements from the relevant diplomatic mission.

Driving Licence

To hire a motorcycle in India, technically you're required to have a valid international drivers' permit in addition to your domestic licence. In tourist areas, some places may rent out a motorcycle without asking for a driving permit/licence, but you won't be covered by insurance in the event of an accident, and may also face a fine.

Hire

» The classic way to motorcycle round India is on an Enfield Bullet, still built to the original 1940s specifications. As well as making a satisfying chugging sound, these bikes are fully manual, making them easy to repair (parts can be found almost everywhere in India). On the other hand, Enfields are often less reliable than many of the newer, Japanese-designed bikes.

» Plenty of places rent out motorcycles for local trips and longer tours. Japanese- and Indian-made bikes in the 100–150cc range are cheaper than the big 350–500cc Enfields.

» As a deposit, you'll need to leave a large cash lump sum (ensure you get a receipt that also stipulates the refundable amount), your passport or air ticket. We strongly advise not leaving these documents, in particular your passport which you need for hotel check-ins and if asked by the police.

» For three weeks' hire, a 500cc Enfield costs from ₹22,000; a European style is ₹23,000; and a 350cc costs ₹15,000. The price includes excellent advice and an invaluable crash course in Enfield mechanics and repairs.

» See the regional chapters for other recommended rental companies and their charges.

Purchase

» For longer tours, consider purchasing a motorcycle.

» Secondhand bikes are widely available (and paperwork is simpler than for a new machine).

» To find a secondhand motorcycle, check travellers' noticeboards and ask motorcycle mechanics and other bikers.

» A well looked-after secondhand 350cc Enfield costs ₹25,000–₹50,000. A more modern version, with Europe-

an-style configuration, costs ₹45,000–₹65,000; the 500cc model ₹60,000–₹85,000. You will also have to pay for insurance.

» Get a secondhand bike serviced before you set off.

» When reselling, if the bike is in reasonable condition you can expect between half and two-thirds of the price you paid.

» Shipping an Indian bike overseas is complicated and expensive – ask the retailer to explain the process.

» Helmets are available for ₹500–₹2000; extras (panniers, luggage racks, protection bars, rear-view mirrors, lockable fuel caps, petrol filters, extra tools) are easy to come by.

» A customised fuel tank will increase the range you can cover between fuel stops. An Enfield 500cc gives about 25km/L; the 350cc model gives slightly more.

» A useful website for Enfield models is www.royalenfield.com.

In Delhi, the area around Hari Singh Nalwa St in Karol Bagh has dozens of motorcycle and parts shops, but plenty of dodgy dealers. The following dealers come recommended:

Delhi Run by the knowledgeable Lalli Singh, **Lalli Motorbike Exports** (☎011-28750869; http://lallisingh.com; 1740-A/55 (basement), Hari Singh Nalwa St, Abdul Aziz Rd, Karol Bagh) sells and rents out Enfields and parts, and buyers get a crash course in running and maintaining these lovable but temperamental machines. He can also recommend other reputable dealers in the area.

Mumbai Allibhai Premji Tyrewalla (☎022-23099313; www.premjis.com; 205 Dr D Bhadkamkar (Lamington) Rd) sells new and secondhand motorcycles with a buy-back option.

Jaipur Rajasthan Auto Centre (☎0141-2568074;

Sanjay Bazaar, Sanganeri Gate) comes recommended as a place for hiring, fixing or purchasing a motorcycle. To hire a 350cc Bullet costs ₹400 per day (including helmet).

OWNERSHIP PAPERS

» There's plenty of paperwork associated with owning a motorcycle. The process is complicated so it's wise to seek advice from the company selling the bike. Allow around two weeks to tackle the paperwork and get on the road.

» Registration papers are signed by the local registration authority when the bike is first sold; you need these when you buy a secondhand bike.

» Foreign nationals cannot change the name on the registration but you must fill out forms for change of ownership and transfer of insurance.

» If you buy a new bike, the company selling it must register the machine for you (adding to the cost).

» Registration must be renewed every 15 years (for around ₹5000); make absolutely sure that it states the 'road-worthiness' of the vehicle, and that there are no outstanding debts or criminal proceedings associated with the bike.

Fuel, Spare Parts & Extras

» Petrol and engine oil are widely available in the plains, but petrol stations are widely spaced in the mountains. If travelling to remote regions, carry enough extra fuel (seek local advice about fuel availability before setting off). At the time of writing, petrol cost around ₹55 per litre.

» If you're going to remote regions it's also important to carry basic spares (valves, fuel lines, piston rings etc). Parts for Indian and Japanese machines are widely available in cities and larger

towns; Delhi's Karol Bagh is a good place to find parts for all Indian and imported bikes.

» For all machines (particularly older ones), regularly check and tighten all nuts and bolts: Indian roads and engine vibration work things loose quite quickly.

» Check the engine and gearbox oil level regularly (at least every 500km) and clean the oil filter every few thousand kilometres.

» Given the road conditions, the chances are you'll make at least a couple of visits to a puncture-wallah – start your trip with new tyres and carry spanners to remove your own wheels.

» It's a good idea to bring your own protective equipment (jackets etc).

Insurance

» Only hire a bike with thirdparty insurance – if you hit someone without insurance, the consequences can be very costly. Reputable companies will include third-party cover in their policies; those that don't probably aren't trustworthy.

» You must also arrange insurance if you buy a motorcycle (usually you can organise this through the person selling the bike).

» The minimum level of cover is third-party insurance – available for ₹300 to ₹600 per year. This will cover repair and medical costs for any other vehicles, people or property you might hit, but no cover for your own machine. Comprehensive insurance (recommended) costs upwards of ₹800 per year.

Road Conditions

» Given the varied road conditions, India can be challenging for novice riders. Hazards range from cows and chickens crossing the carriageway to broken-down trucks, pedestrians on the road, and perpetual potholes and unmarked speed humps. Rural roads sometimes have

grain crops strewn across them to be threshed by passing vehicles – a serious sliding hazard for bikers.

» Try not to cover too much territory in one day and avoid travelling after dark – many vehicles drive without lights, and dynamo-powered motorcycle headlamps are useless at low revs while negotiating around potholes.

» On busy national highways expect to average 40 to 50km/h without stops; on winding back roads and dirt tracks this can drop to 10km/h.

Organised Motorcycle Tours

Dozens of companies offer organised motorcycle tours around India with a support vehicle, mechanic and guide. Below are some reputable outfits (see websites for contact details, itineraries and prices):

Blazing Trails (www.blazingtrailstours.com)

Classic Bike Adventure (www.classic-bike-india.com)

Ferris Wheels (www.ferriswheels.com.au)

H-C Travel (www.hctravel.com)

Himalayan Roadrunners (www.ridehigh.com)

Indian Motorcycle Adventures (www.indianmotorcycleadventures.com)

Lalli Singh Tours (www.lallisingh.com)

Moto Discovery (www.motodiscovery.com)

Royal Expeditions (www.royalexpeditions.com)

Saffron Road Motorcycle Tours (www.saffronroad.com)

Shepherds Realms (www.asiasafari.com)

Wheel of India (www.wheelofindia.com)

Shared jeeps

» In mountain areas, shared jeeps supplement the bus service, charging similar fixed fares – see regional chapters for routes and fares.

» Although nominally designed for five to six passengers, most shared jeeps squeeze in many more. The seats beside and immediately behind the driver are more expensive than the cramped bench seats at the rear.

» Jeeps only leave when full; people often bail out of a half-full jeep and pile into one with more passengers that is ready to depart. Drivers will leave immediately if you pay for all the empty seats.

» Jeeps run from jeep stands and 'passenger stations' at the junctions of major roads; ask locals to point you in the right direction.

» In some states, jeeps are known as 'sumos' after the Tata Sumo, a popular jeep.

» Travel sickness, particularly on winding mountain roads, may mean you are asked to give up your window seat to queasy fellow passengers.

Tours

» Tours are available all over India, run by tourist offices, local transport companies and travel agencies. Organised tours can be an inexpensive way to see several places on one trip, although you rarely get much time at each place. If you arrange a tailor-made tour, you'll have more freedom about where you go and how long you stay.

» Drivers may double as guides, or you can hire a qualified local guide for a fee. In tourist towns, be wary of touts claiming to be professional guides (see p1157). See the Tours section in the regional chapters for details about local tours. For information on treks and tours see p33.

International Tour Agencies

Many international companies offer tours to India, from straightforward sightseeing

trips to adventure tours and activity-based holidays. To find current tours that match your interests, quiz travel agents and surf the web. Some good places to start your tour hunt:

Dragoman (www.dragoman. com) One of several reputable overland tour companies offering trips in customised vehicles.

Exodus (www.exodustravels. co.uk) A wide array of specialist trips, including tours with a holistic, wildlife and adventure focus.

India Wildlife Tours (www.india-wildlife-tours.com) All sorts of wildlife tours, plus jeep, horse or camel safaris and birdwatching.

Indian Encounter (www.indianencounters.com) Special-interest tours that include wildlife spotting, river-rafting and ayurvedic treatments.

Intrepid Travel (www.intrepidtravel.com) Endless possibilities, from wildlife tours to sacred rambles.

Peregrine Adventures (www.peregrine.net.au) Popular cultural and trekking tours.

Sacred India Tours (www.sacredindia.com) Includes tours with a holistic focus such as yoga and ayurveda, as well as architectural and cultural tours.

Shanti Travel (www.shanti travel.com) A range of tours including Family and Adventure run by a Franco-Indian team.

World Expeditions (www.worldexpeditions.com. au) An array of options that includes trekking and cycling tours.

Train

Travelling by train is a quintessential Indian experience. Trains offer a smoother ride than buses and are especially recommended for long journeys that include overnight

travel. India's rail network is one of the largest and busiest in the world and Indian Railways is the largest utility employer on earth, with roughly 1.5 million workers. There are around 6900 train stations scattered across the country.

We've listed useful trains throughout this book but there are hundreds more services. The best way of sourcing updated railway information is to use relevant internet sites such as **Indian Railways** (www. indianrail.gov.in) and the useful www.seat61.com/ India.htm. There's also *Trains at a Glance* (₹35), available at many train station bookstands and better bookshops/newsstands, but it's published annually so it's not as up to date as websites. Nevertheless, it offers comprehensive timetables covering all the main lines.

Booking Tickets in India

You can either book tickets through a travel agency or hotel (for a commission) or in person at the train station. Big stations often have English-speaking staff who can help with choosing the best train. At smaller stations, midlevel officials such as the deputy stationmaster usually speak English. It's also worth approaching tourist-office staff if you need advice about booking tickets, deciding train classes etc. The nationwide railways enquiries number is ☏139.

For information on the ins and outs of booking tickets from outside India and recommended websites for booking tickets online see p31.

AT THE STATION
Get a reservation slip from the information window, fill in the name of the departure station, destination station, the class you want to travel and the name and number of the train. Join the long queue for the ticket window where

FARE FINDER

To find out which trains travel between any two destinations, go to www.trainenquiry.com and click on 'Find Your Train' – type in the name of the two destinations (you may then be prompted to choose from a list of stations) and you'll get a list of every train (with the name, number and arrival/departure times). Armed with these details you can find the fare for your chosen train by going to www.indianrail.gov.in and clicking on 'Fare Enquiry'.

your ticket will be printed. Women should take advantage of the separate women's queue – if there isn't one, go to the front of the regular queue.

TOURIST RESERVATION BUREAU

Larger cities and major tourist centres have an International Tourist Bureau, which allows you to book tickets in relative peace – check www.indianrail.gov.in for a list of these stations.

Reservations

» For details of classes of travel see p31.

» Bookings open 90 days before departure and you must make a reservation for all chair-car, sleeper, and 1AC, 2AC and 3AC carriages. No reservations are required for general (2nd class) compartments.

» Trains are always busy so it's wise to book as far in advance as possible, especially for overnight trains. There may be additional services to certain destinations during major festivals but it's still worth booking well in advance.

» Reserved tickets show your seat/berth and carriage number. Carriage numbers are written on the side of the train (station staff and porters can point you in the right direction). A list of names and berths is posted on the side of each reserved carriage.

» Refunds are available on any ticket, even after departure, with a penalty – rules are complicated, check when you book.

» Trains can be delayed at any stage of the journey; to avoid stress, factor some leeway into your plans.

» Be mindful of potential drugging and theft – see p1156.

If the train you want to travel on is sold out, make sure to enquire about:

TOURIST QUOTA

A special (albeit small) tourist quota is set aside for foreign tourists travelling between popular stations. These seats can only be booked at dedicated reservation offices in major cities (see regional chapters for details), and you need to show your passport and visa as ID. Tickets can be paid

for in rupees (some offices may ask to see foreign exchange certificates – ATM receipts will suffice), British pounds, US dollars or euros, in cash or Thomas Cook and American Express travellers cheques.

TAKTAL TICKETS

Indian Railways holds back a (very) small number of tickets on key trains and releases them at 8am two days before the train is due to depart. A charge of ₹10–300 is added to each ticket price. First AC and Executive Chair tickets are excluded from the scheme.

WAITLIST (WL)

Trains are frequently overbooked, but many passengers cancel and there are regular no-shows. So if you buy a ticket on the waiting list you're quite likely to get a seat, even if there are a number of people ahead of you on the list. Check your booking status at www.indianrail.gov.in/pnr_stat.html by entering your ticket's PNR number. A refund is available if you fail to get a seat – ask the ticket office about your chances.

RESERVATION AGAINST CANCELLATION (RAC)

Even when a train is fully booked, Indian Railways

EXPRESS TRAIN FARES IN RUPEES

DIS-TANCE (KM)	1AC	2AC	3AC	EX-ECUTIVE CHAIR	CHAIR CAR (CC)	SEC-OND (II)
100	541	322	267	424	212	65
200	814	480	363	594	297	90
300	1077	633	473	764	382	115
400	1313	770	572	918	459	135
500	1499	879	650	1040	520	150
1000	2451	1432	1048	NA	760	230
1500	3069	1791	1306	NA	825	224
2000	3316	1935	1410	NA	893	243

sells a handful of seats in each class as 'Reservation Against Cancellation' (RAC). This means that if you have an RAC ticket and someone cancels before the departure date, you will get his or her seat (or berth). You'll have to check the reservation list at the station on the day of travel to see where you've been allocated to sit. Even if no one cancels, as an RAC ticket holder you can still board the train and, even if you don't get a seat, you can still travel.

Costs

Fares are calculated by distance and class of travel; Rajdhani and Shatabdi trains are slightly more expensive, but the price includes meals. Most air-conditioned carriages have a catering service (meals are brought to your seat). In unreserved classes it's a good idea to carry portable snacks. Seniors (those over 60) get 30% off all fares in all classes on all types of train. Children below the age of five travel free, those aged between five and 12 are charged half price.

Health

There is huge geographical variation in India, so environmental issues like heat, cold and altitude can cause health problems. Hygiene is poor in most regions so food and water-borne illnesses are common. Many insect-borne diseases are present, particularly in tropical areas. Medical care is basic in many areas (especially beyond the larger cities) so it's essential to be well prepared.

Pre-existing medical conditions and accidental injury (especially traffic accidents) account for most life-threatening problems. Becoming ill in some way, however, is very common. Fortunately, most travellers' illnesses can be prevented with some common-sense behaviour or treated with a well-stocked travellers' medical kit – however, never hesitate to consult a doctor while on the road, as self-diagnosis can be hazardous.

The following advice is a general guide only and certainly does not replace the advice of a doctor trained in travel medicine.

BEFORE YOU GO

You can buy many medications over the counter in India without a doctor's prescription, but it can be difficult to find some of the newer drugs, particularly the latest antidepressant drugs, blood-pressure medications and contraceptive pills. Bring the following:

» medications in their original, labelled containers

» a signed, dated letter from your physician describing your medical conditions and medications, including generic names

» a physician's letter documenting the medical necessity of any syringes you bring

» if you have a heart condition, a copy of your ECG taken just prior to travelling

» any regular medication (double your ordinary needs)

Insurance

Don't travel without health insurance. Emergency evacuation is expensive – bills of over US$100,000 are not uncommon. Consider the following when buying insurance:

» You may require extra cover for adventure activities such as rock climbing and scuba diving.

» In India, doctors usually require immediate payment in cash. Your insurance plan may make payments directly to providers or it will reimburse you later for overseas health expenditures. If you do have to claim later, make sure you keep all relevant documentation.

» Some policies ask that you telephone back (reverse charges) to a centre in your home country where an immediate assessment of your problem will be made.

Vaccinations

Specialised travel-medicine clinics are your best source of up-to-date information; they stock all available vaccines and can give specific recommendations for your trip. Most vaccines don't give immunity until *at least* two weeks after they're given, so visit a doctor four to eight weeks before departure. Ask your doctor for an International Certificate of Vaccination (otherwise known as the 'yellow booklet'), which will list all the vaccinations you've received.

Medical checklist

Recommended items for a personal medical kit:

» Antifungal cream, eg Clotrimazole

» Antibacterial cream, eg Mupirocin

» Antibiotic for skin infections, eg Amoxicillin/Clavulanate or Cephalexin

» Antihistamine – there are many options, eg Cetrizine for daytime and Promethazine for night

» Antiseptic, eg Betadine

» Antispasmodic for stomach cramps, eg Buscopam

» Contraceptive

» Decongestant, eg Pseudoephedrine

» DEET-based insect repellent

» Diarrhoea medication – consider an oral

REQUIRED & RECOMMENDED VACCINATIONS

The only vaccine required by international regulations is **yellow fever**. Proof of vaccination will only be required if you have visited a country in the yellow-fever zone within the six days prior to entering India. If you are travelling to India from Africa or South America, you should check to see if you require proof of vaccination.

The World Health Organization (WHO) recommends the following vaccinations for travellers going to India (as well as being up to date with measles, mumps and rubella vaccinations):

» **Adult diphtheria & tetanus** Single booster recommended if none in the previous 10 years. Side effects include sore arm and fever.

» **Hepatitis A** Provides almost 100% protection for up to a year; a booster after 12 months provides at least another 20 years' protection. Mild side effects such as headache and sore arm occur in 5% to 10% of people.

» **Hepatitis B** Now considered routine for most travellers. Given as three shots over six months. A rapid schedule is also available, as is a combined vaccination with Hepatitis A. Side effects are mild and uncommon, usually headache and sore arm. In 95% of people lifetime protection results.

» **Polio** Only one booster is required as an adult for lifetime protection. Inactivated polio vaccine is safe during pregnancy.

» **Typhoid** Recommended for all travellers to India, even those only visiting urban areas. The vaccine offers around 70% protection, lasts for two to three years and comes as a single shot. Tablets are also available, but the injection is usually recommended as it has fewer side effects. Sore arm and fever may occur.

» **Varicella** If you haven't had chickenpox, discuss this vaccination with your doctor.

These immunisations are recommended for long-term travellers (more than one month) or those at special risk (seek further advice from your doctor):

» **Japanese B Encephalitis** Three injections in all. Booster recommended after two years. Sore arm and headache are the most common side effects. In rare cases, an allergic reaction comprising hives and swelling can occur up to 10 days after any of the three doses.

» **Meningitis** Single injection. There are two types of vaccination: the quadravalent vaccine gives two to three years' protection; meningitis group C vaccine gives around 10 years' protection. Recommended for long-term backpackers aged under 25.

» **Rabies** Three injections in all. A booster after one year will then provide 10 years' protection. Side effects are rare – occasionally headache and sore arm.

» **Tuberculosis (TB)** A complex issue. Adult long-term travellers are usually recommended to have a TB skin test before and after travel, rather than vaccination. Only one vaccine given in a lifetime.

rehydration solution (eg Gastrolyte), diarrhoea 'stopper' (eg Loperamide) and antinausea medication (eg Prochlorperazine). Antibiotics for diarrhoea include Ciprofloxacin; for bacterial diarrhoea Azithromycin; for giardia or amoebic dysentery Tinidazole.

» First-aid items such as scissors, elastoplasts, bandages, gauze, thermometer (but not mercury), sterile needles and syringes, safety pins and tweezers

» Ibuprofen or another anti-inflammatory

» Iodine tablets (unless you are pregnant or have a thyroid problem) to purify water

» Migraine medication if you suffer from migraines

» Paracetamol

» Pyrethrin to impregnate clothing and mosquito nets

» Steroid cream for allergic or itchy rashes, eg 1% to 2% hydrocortisone

» High-factor sunscreen

» Throat lozenges

» Thrush (vaginal yeast infection) treatment, eg Clotrimazole pessaries or Diflucan tablet

» Ural or equivalent if prone to urine infections

Websites

There is a wealth of travel-health advice on the internet. www.lonelyplanet.com is a good place to start. Some other suggestions:

Centers for Disease Control and Prevention (CDC; www.cdc.gov) Good general information.

MD Travel Health (www.mdtravelhealth.com) Provides complete travel-health recommendations for every country, updated daily.

World Health Organization (WHO; www.who.int/ith) Its helpful book *International Travel & Health* is revised annually and is available online.

Further Reading

Lonely Planet's *Healthy Travel – Asia & India* is a handy pocket size and packed with useful information, including pre-trip planning, emergency first aid, immunisation and disease information, and what to do if you get sick on the road. Other recommended references include *Travellers' Health* by Dr Richard Dawood and *Travelling Well* by Dr Deborah Mills – check out the website of **Travelling Well** (www.travellingwell.com.au).

IN INDIA

Availability of Health Care

Medical care is hugely variable in India. Some cities now have clinics catering specifically to travellers and expatriates; these clinics are usually more expensive than local medical facilities, and offer a higher standard of care. Additionally, they know the local system, including reputable local hospitals and specialists. They may also liaise with insurance companies should you require evacuation. It is usually difficult to find reliable medical care in rural areas.

Self-treatment may be appropriate if your problem is minor (eg traveller's diarrhoea), you are carrying the relevant medication and you cannot attend a recommended clinic. If you suspect

a serious disease, especially malaria, travel to the nearest quality facility.

Before buying medication over the counter, check the use-by date, and ensure the packet is sealed and properly stored (eg not exposed to the sunshine).

Infectious Diseases

Malaria

This is a serious and potentially deadly disease. Before you travel, seek expert advice according to your itinerary (rural areas are especially risky) and on medication and side effects.

Malaria is caused by a parasite transmitted by the bite of an infected mosquito. The most important symptom of malaria is fever, but general symptoms, such as headache, diarrhoea, cough or chills, may also occur. Diagnosis can only be properly made by taking a blood sample.

Two strategies should be combined to prevent malaria: mosquito avoidance and antimalarial medications. Most people who catch malaria are taking inadequate or no antimalarial medication.

Travellers are advised to prevent mosquito bites by taking these steps:
» Use a DEET-containing insect repellent on exposed skin. Wash this off at night, as long as you are sleeping under a mosquito net. Natural repellents such as citronella can be effective, but must be

applied more frequently than products containing DEET.
» Sleep under a mosquito net impregnated with pyrethrin.
» Choose accommodation with proper screens and fans (if not air-conditioned).
» Impregnate clothing with pyrethrin in high-risk areas.
» Wear long sleeves and trousers in light colours.
» Use mosquito coils.
» Spray your room with insect repellent before going out for your evening meal.
There are a variety of medications available:
Chloroquine & Paludrine combination Limited effectiveness in many parts of South Asia. Common side effects include nausea (40% of people) and mouth ulcers.
Doxycycline (daily tablet) A broad-spectrum antibiotic that helps prevent a variety of tropical diseases, including leptospirosis, tick-borne disease and typhus. Potential side effects include photosensitivity (a tendency to sunburn), thrush (in women), indigestion, heartburn, nausea and interference with the contraceptive pill. More serious side effects include ulceration of the oesophagus – take your tablet with a meal and a large glass of water, and never lie down within half an hour of taking it. It must be taken for four weeks after leaving the risk area.
Lariam (mefloquine) This weekly tablet suits many people. Serious side effects are rare but include depression, anxiety, psychosis and seizures. Anyone with a history of depression, anxiety, other psychological disorders or epilepsy should not take Lariam. It is considered safe in the second and third trimesters of pregnancy. Tablets must be taken for four weeks after leaving the risk area.
Malarone A combination of atovaquone and proguanil.

Side effects are uncommon and mild, most commonly nausea and headache. It is the best tablet for scuba divers and for those on short trips to high-risk areas. It must be taken for one week after leaving the risk area.

Other diseases

Avian Flu 'Bird flu' or Influenza A (H5N1) is a subtype of the type A influenza virus. Contact with dead or sick birds is the principal source of infection and bird-to-human transmission does not easily occur. Symptoms include high fever and flu-like symptoms with rapid deterioration, leading to respiratory failure and death in many cases. Immediate medical care should be sought if bird flu is suspected. Check www.who.int/en/or www.avianinfluenza.com.au.

Coughs, Colds & Chest Infections Around 25% of travellers to India will develop a respiratory infection. If a secondary bacterial infection occurs – marked by fever, chest pain and coughing up discoloured or blood-tinged sputum – seek medical advice or consider commencing a general antibiotic.

Dengue Fever This mosquito-borne disease is becomingly increasingly problematic, especially in the cities. As there is no vaccine available it can only be prevented by avoiding mosquito bites at all times. Symptoms include high fever, severe headache and body ache and sometimes a rash and diarrhoea. Treatment is rest and paracetamol – do not take aspirin or ibuprofen as it increases the likelihood of haemorrhaging. Make sure you see a doctor to be diagnosed and monitored.

Hepatitis A This food- and water-borne virus infects the liver, causing jaundice (yellow skin and eyes), nausea and lethargy. There is no specific treatment for hepatitis A, you just need to allow time for the liver to heal. All travellers to India should be vaccinated against hepatitis A.

Hepatitis B This sexually transmitted disease is spread by body fluids and can be prevented by vaccination. The long-term consequences can include liver cancer and cirrhosis.

Hepatitis E Transmitted through contaminated food and water, hepatitis E has similar symptoms to hepatitis A, but is far less common. It is a severe problem in pregnant women and can result in the death of both mother and baby. There is no commercially available vaccine, and prevention is by following safe eating and drinking guidelines.

HIV Spread via contaminated body fluids. Avoid unsafe sex, unsterile needles (including in medical facilities) and procedures such as tattoos. The growth rate of HIV in India is one of the highest in the world.

Influenza Present year-round in the tropics, influenza (flu) symptoms include fever, muscle aches, a runny nose, cough and sore throat. It can be severe in people over the age of 65 or in those with medical conditions such as heart disease or diabetes – vaccination is recommended for these individuals. There is no specific treatment, just rest and paracetamol.

Japanese B Encephalitis This viral disease is transmitted by mosquitoes and is rare in travellers. Most cases occur in rural areas and vaccination is recommended for travellers spending more than one month outside of cities. There is no treatment, and it may result in permanent brain damage or death. Ask your doctor for further details.

Rabies This fatal disease is spread by the bite or possibly even the lick of an infected animal – most commonly a dog or monkey. You should seek medical advice immediately after any animal bite and commence postexposure treatment. Having pre-travel vaccination means the postbite treatment is greatly simplified. If an animal bites you, gently wash the wound with soap and water, and apply iodine-based antiseptic. If you are not pre-vaccinated you will need to receive rabies immunoglobulin as soon as possible, and this is very difficult to obtain in much of India.

STDs Sexually transmitted diseases most common in India include herpes, warts, syphilis, gonorrhoea and chlamydia. Condoms will prevent gonorrhoea and chlamydia but not warts or herpes. If after a sexual encounter you develop any rash, lumps, discharge or pain when passing urine, seek immediate medical attention. If you have been sexually active during your travels, have an STD check on your return home.

Tuberculosis While TB is rare in travellers, those who have significant contact with the local population (such as medical and aid workers and long-term travellers) should take precautions. Vaccination is usually only given to children under the age of five, but adults at risk are recommended to have pre- and post-travel TB testing. The main symptoms are fever, cough, weight loss, night sweats and fatigue.

Typhoid This serious bacterial infection is also spread via food and water. It gives a high and slowly progressive fever and headache, and may be accompanied by a dry cough and stomach pain. It is diagnosed by blood tests and treated with antibiotics. Vaccination is recommended for all travellers who are spending more than a week in India. Be aware that vaccination is not 100% effective, so you must still be careful with what you eat and drink.

Travellers' Diarrhoea

This is by far the most common problem affecting travellers in India – between 30% and 70% of people will suffer from it within two weeks of starting their trip. It's usually caused by a bacteria, and thus responds promptly to treatment with antibiotics.

Travellers' diarrhoea is defined as the passage of more than three watery bowel actions within 24 hours, plus at least one other symptom, such as fever, cramps, nausea, vomiting or feeling generally unwell.

Treatment consists of staying well hydrated; rehydration solutions like Gastrolyte are the best for this. Antibiotics such as ciprofloxacin or azithromycin should kill the bacteria quickly. Seek medical attention quickly if you do not respond to an appropriate antibiotic.

Loperamide is just a 'stopper' and doesn't get to the cause of the problem. It can be helpful, though (eg if you have to go on a long bus ride). Don't take loperamide if you have a fever or blood in your stools.

Amoebic Dysentery Amoebic dysentery is very rare in travellers but is often misdiagnosed by poor-quality labs. Symptoms are similar to bacterial diarrhoea: fever, bloody diarrhoea and generally feeling unwell. You should always seek reliable medical care if you have blood in your diarrhoea. Treatment involves two drugs: Tinidazole or Metronidazole to kill the parasite in your gut and then a second drug to kill the cysts. If left untreated complications such as liver or gut abscesses can occur.

Giardiasis Giardia is a parasite that is relatively common in travellers. Symptoms include nausea, bloating, excess gas, fatigue and intermittent diarrhoea. The parasite will eventually go away if left untreated but this can take months; the best advice is to seek medical treatment. The treatment of choice is Tinidazole, with Metronidazole being a second-line option.

Environmental Hazards

Air Pollution

Air pollution, particularly vehicle pollution, is an increasing problem in most of India's urban hubs. If you have severe respiratory problems, speak with your doctor before travelling to India.

Diving & Surfing

Divers and surfers should seek specialised advice before they travel to ensure their medical kit contains treatment for coral cuts and tropical ear infections. Divers should ensure their insurance covers them for decompression illness – get specialised dive insurance through an organisation such as **Divers Alert Network**

(DAN; www.danasiapacific.org). Certain medical conditions are incompatible with diving; check with your doctor.

Food

Eating in restaurants is a big risk for contracting diarrhoea. Ways to avoid it include:

» eating only freshly cooked food

» avoiding shellfish and buffets

» peeling fruit

» cooking vegetables

» soaking salads in iodine water for at least 20 minutes

» eating in busy restaurants with a high turnover of customers.

Heat

Many parts of India, especially down south, are hot and humid throughout the year. For most people it takes at least two weeks to adapt to the hot climate. Swelling of the feet and ankles is common, as are muscle cramps caused by excessive sweating. Prevent these by avoiding dehydration and excessive activity in the heat. Don't eat salt tablets (they aggravate the gut); drinking rehydration solution or eating salty food helps. Treat cramps by resting, rehydrating with double-

---

DRINKING WATER

» Never drink tap water.

» Bottled water is generally safe – check the seal is intact at purchase.

» Avoid ice unless you know it has been safely made.

» Be careful of fresh juices served at street stalls in particular – they may have been watered down or may be served in unhygienic jugs/glasses.

» Boiling water is usually the most efficient method of purifying it.

» The best chemical purifier is iodine. It should not be used by pregnant women or those with thyroid problems.

» Water filters should also filter out viruses. Ensure your filter has a chemical barrier such as iodine and a small pore size (less than four microns).

strength rehydration solution and gently stretching.

Dehydration is the main contributor to heat exhaustion. Recovery is usually rapid and it is common to feel weak for some days afterwards. Symptoms include:

» feeling weak
» headache
» irritability
» nausea or vomiting
» sweaty skin
» a fast, weak pulse
» normal or slightly elevated body temperature.

Treatment:

» get out of the heat
» fan the sufferer
» apply cool, wet cloths to the skin
» lay the sufferer flat with their legs raised
» rehydrate with water containing one-quarter teaspoon of salt per litre.

Heat stroke is a serious medical emergency. Symptoms include:

» weakness
» nausea
» a hot dry body
» temperature of over 41°C
» dizziness
» confusion
» loss of coordination
» seizures
» eventual collapse.

Treatment:

» get out of the heat
» fan the sufferer
» apply cool, wet cloths to the skin or ice to the body, especially to the groin and armpits.

Prickly heat is a common skin rash in the tropics, caused by sweat trapped under the skin. Treat it by moving out of the heat for a few hours and by having cool showers. Creams and ointments clog the skin so they should be avoided. Locally bought prickly-heat powder can be helpful.

Altitude Sickness

If you are going to altitudes above 3000m, Acute Mountain Sickness (AMS) is an issue. The biggest risk factor is going too high too quickly – follow a conservative acclimatisation schedule found in good trekking guides, and *never* go to a higher altitude when you have any symptoms that could be altitude related. There is no way to predict who will get altitude sickness and it is often the younger, fitter members of a group who succumb.

Symptoms usually develop during the first 24 hours at altitude but may be delayed up to three weeks. Mild symptoms include:

» headache
» lethargy
» dizziness
» difficulty sleeping
» loss of appetite.

AMS may become more severe without warning and can be fatal. Severe symptoms include:

» breathlessness
» a dry, irritative cough (which may progress to the production of pink, frothy sputum)
» severe headache
» lack of coordination and balance
» confusion
» irrational behaviour
» vomiting
» drowsiness
» unconsciousness.

Treat mild symptoms by resting at the same altitude until recovery, which usually takes a day or two. Paracetamol or aspirin can be taken for headaches. If symptoms persist or become worse, immediate descent is necessary; even 500m can help. Drug treatments should never be used to avoid descent or to enable further ascent.

The drugs acetazolamide and dexamethasone are recommended by some doctors for the prevention of AMS; however, their use is controversial. They can reduce the symptoms, but they may also mask warning signs; severe

and fatal AMS has occurred in people taking these drugs.

To prevent acute mountain sickness:

» ascend slowly – have frequent rest days, spending two to three nights at each rise of 1000m
» sleep at a lower altitude than the greatest height reached during the day, if possible. Above 3000m, don't increase sleeping altitude by more than 300m daily
» drink extra fluids
» eat light, high-carbohydrate meals
» avoid alcohol and sedatives.

Insect Bites & Stings

Bedbugs Don't carry disease but their bites can be very itchy. They live in furniture and walls and then migrate to the bed at night. You can treat the itch with an antihistamine.

Lice Most commonly appear on the head and pubic areas. You may need numerous applications of an antilice shampoo such as pyrethrin. Pubic lice are usually contracted from sexual contact.

Ticks Contracted walking in rural areas. Ticks are commonly found behind the ears, on the belly and in armpits. If you have had a tick bite and have a rash at the site of the bite or elsewhere, fever or muscle aches, you should see a doctor. Doxycycline prevents tick-borne diseases.

Leeches Found in humid rainforest areas. They do not transmit any disease but their bites are often intensely itchy for weeks and can easily become infected. Apply an iodine-based antiseptic to any leech bite to help prevent infection.

Bee and wasp stings Anyone with a serious bee or wasp allergy should carry an injection of adrenalin (eg an Epipen). For others pain is the main problem – apply ice to the sting and take painkillers.

Skin Problems

Fungal rashes There are two common fungal rashes that affect travellers. The first occurs in moist areas, such as the groin, armpits and between the toes. It starts as a red patch that slowly spreads and is usually itchy. Treatment involves keeping the skin dry, avoiding chafing and using an antifungal cream such as clotrimazole or Lamisil. The second, *Tinea versicolor,* causes light-coloured patches, most commonly on the back, chest and shoulders. Consult a doctor.

Cuts and scratches These become easily infected in humid climates. Immediately wash all wounds in clean water and apply antiseptic. If

you develop signs of infection (increasing pain and redness), see a doctor.

Sunburn

Even on a cloudy day sunburn can occur rapidly. Always adhere to the following:

» Use a strong sunscreen (factor 30) and reapply after a swim

» Wear a wide-brimmed hat and sunglasses

» Avoid lying in the sun during the hottest part of the day (10am to 2pm)

» Be vigilant above 3000m – you can get burnt very easily at altitude.

If you become sunburnt, stay out of the sun until you have recovered, apply cool compresses and, if necessary, take painkillers for the discomfort. One per cent hydrocortisone cream applied twice daily is also helpful.

Women's Health

For gynaecological health issues, seek out a female doctor.

Birth control Bring adequate supplies of your own form of contraception.

Sanitary products Pads, rarely tampons, are readily available.

Thrush Heat, humidity and antibiotics can all contribute to thrush. Treatment is with antifungal creams and pessaries such as clotrimazole. A practical alternative is a single tablet of Fluconazole (Diflucan).

Urinary-tract infections These can be precipitated by dehydration or long bus journeys without toilet stops; bring suitable antibiotics.

Language

WANT MORE?
For in-depth language information and handy phrases, check out Lonely Planet's *Hindi, Urdu & Bengali Phrasebook* and *India Phrasebook*. You'll find them at **shop.lonelyplanet. com**, or you can buy Lonely Planet's iPhone phrasebooks at the Apple App Store.

The number of languages spoken in India helps explain why English is still widely spoken there, and why it's still in official use. Another 22 languages are recognised in the constitution, and more than 1600 minor languages are spoken throughout the country.

Major efforts have been made to promote Hindi as the national language of India and to gradually phase out English. However, while Hindi is the predominant language in the north, it bears little relation to the Dravidian languages of the south such as Tamil. Consequently, very few people in the south speak Hindi.

Many educated Indians speak English as virtually their first language. For the large number of Indians who speak more than one language, it's often their second tongue. Although you'll find it very easy to get around India with English, it's always good to know a little of the local language.

HINDI

Hindi has about 600 million speakers worldwide, of which 180 million are in India. It developed from Classical Sanskrit, and is written in Devanagari script. In 1947 it was granted official status along with English.

Most Hindi sounds are similar to their English counterparts. The main difference is that Hindi has both 'aspirated' consonants (pronounced with a puff of air, like saying 'h' after the sound) and unaspirated ones, as well as 'retroflex' (pronounced with the tongue bent backwards) and nonretroflex consonants. Our simplified pronunciation guides don't include these distinctions – read them as if they were English and you'll be understood.

Pronunciation of vowels is important, especially their length (eg a and aa). The consonant combination ng after a vowel indicates nasalisation (ie the vowel is pronounced 'through the nose'). Note also that au is pronounced as the 'ow' in 'how'.

Word stress in Hindi is very light; we've indicated the stressed syllables with italics.

Basics

Hindi verbs change form depending on the gender of the speaker (or the subject of the sentence in general) – meaning it's the verbs, not the pronouns 'he' or 'she', which show whether the subject of the sentence is masculine or feminine. In these phrases we include the options for male and female speakers, marked 'm' and 'f' respectively.

Hello./Goodbye.	नमस्ते ।	na·ma·*ste*
Yes.	जी हाँ ।	jee haang
No.	जी नहीं ।	jee na·*heeng*
Excuse me.	सुनिये ।	su·ni·*ye*
Sorry.	माफ़ कीजिये ।	maaf *kee*·ji·ye
Please ...	कृपया ...	kri·pa·*yaa* ...
Thank you.	थैंक्यू ।	*thayn*·kyoo
You're welcome.	कोई बात नहीं ।	*ko*·ee baat na·*heeng*

How are you?
आप कैसे/कैसी हैं?   aap *kay*·se/*kay*·see hayng (m/f)

Fine. And you?
मैं ठीक हूँ। — mayng teek hoong
आप सुनाइये। — aap su·naa·i·ye

What's your name?
आप का नाम क्या है? — aap kaa naam kyaa hay

My name is ...
मेरा नाम ... है। — me·raa naam ... hay

Do you speak English?
क्या आपको अंग्रेज़ी — kyaa aap ko an·gre·zee
आती है? — aa·tee hay

I don't understand.
मैं नहीं समझा/ — mayng na·heeng sam·jaa/
समझी। — sam·jee (m/f)

Accommodation

Where's a ...? ... कहाँ है? — ... ka·haang hay
  guesthouse गेस्ट हाउस — gest haa·us
  hotel होटल — ho·tal
  youth hostel यूथ हास्टल — yoot haas·tal

Do you have क्या ... कमरा — kyaa ... kam·raa
a ... room? है? — hay
  single सिंगल — sin·gal
  double डबल — da·bal

How much is ... के लिय — ... ke li·ye
it per ...? कितने पैसे — kit·ne pay·se
लगते हैं? — lag·te hayng
  night एक रात — ek raat
  person हर व्यक्ति — har vyak·ti

air-con ए॰ सी॰ — e see
bathroom बाथळम — baat·room
hot water गर्म पानी — garm paa·nee
mosquito net मसहरी — mas·ha·ree
washerman धोबी — do·bee
window खिड़की — kir·kee

Directions

Where's ...?
... कहाँ है? — ... ka·haang hay

How far is it?
वह कितनी दूर है? — voh kit·nee door hay

What's the address?
पता क्या है? — pa·taa kyaa hay

Can you write it down, please?
कृपया यह लिखिये? — kri·pa·yaa yeh li·ki·ye

Can you show me (on the map)?
(नक्शे में) दिखा — (nak·she meng) di·kaa
सकते है? — sak·te hayng

Turn left/right.
लेफ्ट/राइट मुड़िये। — left/raa·it mu·ri·ye

at the corner कोने पर — ko·ne par
at the traffic सिगनल पर — sig·nal par
  lights
behind ... ... के पीछे — ... ke pee·che
in front of ... ... के सामन — ... ke saam·ne
near ... ... के पास — ... ke paas
opposite ... ... के सामने — ... ke saam·ne
straight ahead सीधे — see·de

Eating & Drinking

What would you recommend?
आपके ख्याल में — aap ke kyaal meng
क्या अच्छा होगा? — kyaa ach·chaa ho·gaa

Do you have vegetarian food?
क्या आप का खाना — kyaa aap kaa kaa·naa
शाकाहारी है? — shaa·kaa·haa·ree hay

I don't eat (meat).
मैं (गोश्त) नहीं — mayng (gosht) na·heeng
खाता/खाती। — kaa·taa/kaa·tee (m/f)

I'll have ...
मुझे ... दीजिये। — mu·je ... dee·ji·ye

That was delicious.
बहुत मज़ेदार हुआ। — ba·hut ma·ze·daar hu·aa

Please bring the menu/bill.
मेन्यू/बिल लाइये। — men·yoo/bil laa·i·ye

Key Words

bottle बोतल — bo·tal
bowl कटोरी — ka·to·ree
breakfast नाश्ता — naash·taa
dessert मीठा — mee·taa
dinner रात का खाना — raat kaa kaa·naa
drinks पीने की — pee·ne kee
चीज़ें — chee·zeng
food खाना — kaa·naa
fork काँटा — kaan·taa
glass गिलास — glaas
knife चाकू — chaa·koo
local eatery ढाबा — daa·baa
lunch दिन का — din kaa
खाना — kaa·naa
market बाज़ार — baa·zaar
plate प्लेट — plet

Numbers – Hindi

1	१	एक	ek
2	२	दो	do
3	३	तीन	teen
4	४	चार	chaar
5	५	पाँच	paanch
6	६	छह	chay
7	७	सात	saat
8	८	आठ	aat
9	९	नौ	nau
10	१०	दस	das
20	२०	बीस	bees
30	३०	तीस	tees
40	४०	चालीस	*chaa*-lees
50	५०	पचास	pa-*chaas*
60	६०	साठ	saat
70	७०	सत्तर	*sat*-tar
80	८०	अस्सी	*as*-see
90	९०	नब्बे	*nab*-be
100	१००	सौ	sau
1000	१०००	एक हज़ार	ek ha-*zaar*

restaurant	रेस्टोरेंट	*res*-to-rent
set meal	थाली	*taa*-lee
snack	नाश्ता	*naash*-taa
spoon	चम्मच	*cham*-mach
with/without	के साथ/बिना	ke saat/bi-*naa*

Meat & Fish

beef	गाय का गोश्त	gaai kaa gosht
chicken	मुर्ग़ी	*mur*-gee
duck	बतख़	ba-*tak*
fish	मछली	*mach*-lee
goat	बकरा	*bak*-raa
lobster	बड़ी झींगा	ba-*ree jeeng*-gaa
meat	गोश्त	gosht
meatballs	कोफ़्ता	*kof*-taa
pork	सुअर का गोश्त	*su*-ar kaa gosht
prawn	झींगी	*jeeng*-gee
	मछली	*mach*-lee
seafood	मछली	*mach*-lee

Fruit & Vegetables

apple	सेब	seb
apricot	ख़ुबानी	ku-*baa*-nee
banana	केला	*ke*-laa
capsicum	मिर्च	mirch
carrot	गाजर	*gaa*-jar
cauliflower	फूल गोभी	pool go-*bee*
corn	मक्का	*mak*-kaa
cucumber	ककड़ी	*kak*-ree
date	खजूर	ka-*joor*
eggplant	बैंगन	*bayng*-gan
fruit	फल	pal
garlic	लहसुन	*leh*-sun
grape	अंगूर	an-goor
grapefruit	चकोतरा	cha-*kot*-raa
lemon	निम्बू	*nim*-boo
lentils	दाल	daal
mandarin	संतरा	*san*-ta-raa
mango	आम	aam
mushroom	खुंभी	*kum*-bee
nuts	मेवे	*me*-ve
orange	नारंगी	naa-*ran*-gee
papaya	पपीता	pa-*pee*-taa
peach	आड़ू	*aa*-roo
peas	मटर	ma-*tar*
pineapple	अनन्नास	a-*nan*-naas
potato	आलू	*aa*-loo
pumpkin	कद्दू	*kad*-doo
spinach	पालक	*paa*-lak
vegetables	सब्ज़ी	*sab*-zee
watermelon	तरबूज़	*tar*-booz

Other

bread	चपाती/नान/रोटी	cha-*paa*-tee/naan/*ro*-tee
butter	मक्खन	*mak*-kan
chilli	मिर्च	mirch
chutney	चटनी	*chat*-nee
egg	अंडे	an-de
honey	मधु	ma-dhu
ice	बर्फ़	barf
ice cream	कुल्फ़ी	*kul*-fee
pappadams	पपड़	pa-*par*
pepper	काली मिर्च	*kaa*-lee mirch
relish	अचार	a-*chaar*
rice	चावल	*chaa*-val
salt	नमक	na-*mak*
spices	मिर्च मसाला	mirch ma-*saa*-laa
sugar	चीनी	*chee*-nee
tofu	टोफू	to-*foo*

Drinks

beer	बियर	bi-*yar*
coffee	काॅफ़ी	*kaa*-fee
juice	रस	ras

milk	दूध	dood
red wine	लाल शराब	laal sha·raab
sugarcane juice	गन्ने का रस	gan·ne kaa ras
sweet fruit drink	शरबत	shar·bat
tea	चाय	chaai
water	पानी	paa·nee
white wine	सफ़ेद शराब	sa·fed sha·raab
yoghurt	लस्सी	las·see

Emergencies

Help!
मदद कीजिये! — ma·dad kee·ji·ye

I'm lost.
मैं रास्ता भूल — mayng raas·taa bool
गया/गयी हूँ। — ga·yaa/ga·yee hoong (m/f)

Go away!
जाओ! — jaa·o

There's been an accident.
दुर्घटना हुई है। — dur·gat·naa hu·ee hay

Call a doctor!
डॉक्टर को बुलाओ! — daak·tar ko bu·laa·o

Call the police!
पुलिस को बुलाओ! — pu·lis ko bu·laa·o

I'm ill.
मैं बीमार हूँ। — mayng bee·maar hoong

It hurts here.
इधर दर्द हो रहा है। — i·dar dard ho ra·haa hay

I'm allergic to (antibiotics).
मुझे (एंटीबायोटिकिस) — mu·je (en·tee·baa·yo·tiks)
की एलरजी है। — kee e·lar·jee hay

Shopping & Services

I'd like to buy ...
मुझे ... चाहिये। — mu·je ... chaa·hi·ye

I'm just looking.
सिर्फ़ देखने आया/ — sirf dek·ne aa·yaa/
आयी हूँ। — aa·yee hoong (m/f)

May I look at it?
दिखाइये। — di·kaa·i·ye

Do you have any others?
दूसरा है? — doos·raa hay

How much is it?
कितने का है? — kit·ne kaa hay

It's too expensive.
यह बहुत महंगा/ — yeh ba·hut ma·han·gaa/
महंगी है। — ma·han·gee hay (m/f)

Can you lower the price?
क्या आप दाम — kyaa aap daam
कम करेंगे? — kam ka·reng·ge

There's a mistake in the bill.
बिल में गलती है। — bil meng gal·tee hay

bank	बैंक	baynk
post office	डाक ख़ाना	daak kaa·naa
public phone	सार्वजनिक फ़ोन	saar·va·ja·nik fon
rupee	रुपया	ru·pa·yaa
tourist office	पर्यटन ऑफ़िस	par·ya·tan aa·fis

Time & Dates

What time is it?
टाइम क्या है? — taa·im kyaa hay

It's (10) o'clock.
(दस) बजे हैं। — (das) ba·je hayng

Half past (10).
साढ़े (दस)। — saa·re (das)

morning	सुबह	su·bah
afternoon	दोपहर	do·pa·har
evening	शाम	shaam

Monday	सोमवार	som·vaar
Tuesday	मंगलवार	man·gal·vaar
Wednesday	बुधवार	bud·vaar
Thursday	गुरुवार	gu·ru·vaar
Friday	शुक्रवार	shuk·ra·vaar
Saturday	शनिवार	sha·ni·vaar
Sunday	रविवार	ra·vi·vaar

January	जनवरी	jan·va·ree
February	फरवरी	far·va·ree
March	मार्च	maarch
April	अप्रैल	a·prayl
May	मई	ma·ee
June	जून	joon
July	जुलाई	ju·laa·ee
August	अगस्त	a·gast
September	सितम्बर	si·tam·bar
October	अक्टूबर	ak·too·bar
November	नवम्बर	na·vam·bar
December	दिसम्बर	di·sam·bar

Question Words – Hindi		
How?	कैस?	*kay*·se
What?	क्या?	kyaa
Which?	कौनसा?	*kaun*·saa
When?	कब?	kab
Where?	कहाँ?	ka·*haang*
Who?	कौन?	kaun
Why?	क्यों?	kyong

Transport
Public Transport

When's the ... (bus)?	... (बस) कब जाती है?	... (bas) kab *jaa*·tee hay
first	पहली	*peh*·lee
next	अगली	*ag*·lee
last	आख़िरी	*aa*·ki·ree
bicycle	साइकिल	*saa*·i·kil
rickshaw	रिक्शा	*rik*·shaa
boat	जहाज़	ja·*haaz*
bus	बस	bas
plane	हवाई जहाज़	ha·*vaa*·ee ja·*haaz*
train	ट्रेन	tren

At what time does it leave?
कितने बजे जाता/ *kit*·ne ba·*je jaa*·taa/
जाती है? *jaa*·tee hay (m/f)

How long does the trip take?
जाने में कितनी *jaa*·ne meng *kit*·nee
देर लगती है? der *lag*·tee hay

How long will it be delayed?
उसे कितनी देर हुई है? u·se *kit*·nee der hu·*ee* hay

Does it stop at ...?
क्या ... में रुकती है? kyaa ... meng *ruk*·tee hay

Please tell me when we get to ...
जब ... आता है, jab ... *aa*·taa hay
मुझे बताइये। mu·*je* ba·*taa*·i·ye

Please go straight to this address.
इसी जगह को *is*·ee ja·gah ko
फ़ौरन जाइए। *fau*·ran *jaa*·i·ye

Please stop here.
यहाँ रुकिये। ya·*haang* ru·ki·ye

bus stop	बस स्टॉप	bas *is*·taap
ticket office	टिकटघर	ti·*kat*·gar

timetable	समय सारणी	sa·*mai* *saa*·ra·nee
train station	स्टेशन	*ste*·shan

a ... ticket	के लिये ... टिकट दीजिये।	ke li·ye ... ti·*kat dee*·ji·ye
1st-class	फ़र्स्ट क्लास	*farst* klaas
2nd-class	सेकंड क्लास	se·*kand* klaas
one-way	एक तरफ़ा	ek ta·ra·*faa*
return	आने जाने का	*aa*·ne *jaa*·ne kaa

I'd like a/an ... seat.	मुझे ... सीट चाहिये।	mu·*je* ... seet *chaa*·hi·ye
aisle	किनारे	ki·*naa*·re
window	खिड़की के पास	*kir*·kee ke paas

Driving & Cycling

I'd like to hire a ...	मुझे ... किराये पर लेना है।	mu·*je* ... ki·*raa*·ye par *le*·naa hay
4WD	फ़ोर व्हील ड्राइव	for vheel *draa*·iv
bicycle	साइकिल	*saa*·i·kil
car	कार	kaar
motorbike	मोटर साइकिल	*mo*·tar *saa*·i·kil

Is this the road to ...?
क्या यह ... का kyaa yeh ... kaa
रास्ता है? *raas*·taa hay

Can I park here?
यहाँ पार्क कर सकता/ ya·*haang* paark kar *sak*·taa/
सकती हूँ? *sak*·tee hoong (m/f)

Where's a service station?
पेट्रोल पम्प कहाँ है? *pet*·rol pamp ka·*haang* hay

I need a mechanic.
मुझे मरम्मत करने mu·*je* ma·*ram*·mat
वाला चाहिये। *kar*·ne *vaa*·laa *chaa*·hi·ye

The car/motorbike has broken down at ...
कार/मोटर साइकिल kaar/*mo*·tar *saa*·i·kil
... में ख़राब ... meng ka·*raab*
हो गयी है। ho ga·*yee* hay

I have a flat tyre.
टायर पंक्चर हो *taa*·yar *pank*·char ho
गया है। ga·*yaa* hay

I've run out of petrol.
पेट्रोल ख़त्म हो *pet*·rol katm ho
गया है। ga·*yaa* hay

TAMIL

Tamil is the official language in the South Indian state of Tamil Nadu (and also a national language in Sri Lanka, Malaysia and Singapore). It is one of the major Dravidian languages of South India, with records of its existence going back more than 2000 years. Tamil has about 62 million speakers in India.

Like Hindi, the Tamil sound system includes a number of 'retroflex' consonants (pronounced with the tongue bent backwards). Unlike Hindi and most other Indian languages, however, Tamil has no 'aspirated' sounds (pronounced with a puff of air). Our simplified pronunciation guides don't distinguish the retroflex consonants from their nonretroflex counterparts; just read the guides as if they were English and you'll be understood. Note that aw is pronounced as in 'law' and ow as in 'how'. The stressed syllables are indicated with italics.

Basics

Hello.	வணக்கம்.	va·nak·kam
Goodbye.	போய் வருகிறேன்.	po·i va·ru·ki·reyn
Yes.	ஆமாம்.	aa·maam
No.	இல்லை.	il·lai
Excuse me.	தயவு செய்து	ta·ya·vu sei·du
Sorry.	மன்னிக்கவும்.	man·nik·ka·vum
Please.	தயவு செய்து.	ta·ya·vu chey·tu
Thank you.	நன்றி.	nan·dri

How are you?
நீங்கள் நலமா? — neeng·kal na·la·maa

Fine, thanks. And you?
நலம், நன்றி. நீங்கள்? — na·lam nan·dri neeng·kal

What's your name?
உங்கள் பெயர் என்ன? — ung·kal pe·yar en·na

My name is ...
என் பெயர்... — en pe·yar ...

Do you speak English?
நீங்கள் ஆங்கிலம் பேசுவீர்களா? — neeng·kal aang·ki·lam pey·chu·veer·ka·la

I don't understand.
எனக்கு வீளங்கவில்லை. — e·nak·ku vi·lang·ka·vil·lai

Question Words – Tamil

What's that?	அது என்ன?	a·tu en·na
When?	எப்பொழுது?	ep·po·zu·tu
Where?	எங்கே?	eng·key
Who?	யார்?	yaar
Why?	ஏன்?	eyn

Accommodation

Where's a ... nearby?
அருகே ஒரு ... எங்கே உள்ளது? — a·ru·ke o·ru ... eng·ke ul·la·tu

| guesthouse | விருந்தினர் இல்லம | vi·run·ti·nar il·lam |
| hotel | ஹோட்டல | hot·tal |

Do you have a ... room?
உங்களிடம் ஓர் ... அறை உள்ளதா? — ung·ka·li·tam awr ... a·rai ul·la·taa

| single | தன | ta·ni |
| double | இரட்டை | i·rat·tai |

How much is it per ...?
ஓர் ... என்னவீலை? — awr ... en·na·vi·lai

| night | இரவுக்கு | i·ra·vuk·ku |
| person | ஒருவருக்கு | o·ru·va·ruk·ku |

air-conditioned	குளிர்சாதன வசதியுடையது	ku·lir·chaa·ta·na va·cha·ti·yu·tai·ya·tu
bathroom	குளீயலறை	ku·li·ya·la·rai
bed	படுக்கை	pa·tuk·kai
window	சன்னல	chan·nal

Directions

Where's the ...?
... எங்கே இருக்கிறது? — ... eng·key i·ruk·ki·ra·tu

What's the address?
வீலாசம் என்ன? — vi·laa·cham en·na

Can you show me (on the map)?
எனக்கு (வரைபடத்தில்) காட்ட முடியுமா? — e·nak·ku (va·rai·pa·tat·til) kaat·ta mu·ti·yu·maa

How far is it?
எவ்வளவு தூரத்தில் இருக்கிறது? — ev·va·la·vu too·rat·til i·ruk·ki·ra·tu

Turn left/right.
இடது/வலது புறத்தில் திரும்புக. — i·ta·tu/va·la·tu pu·rat·til ti·rum·pu·ka

It's ...
அது இருப்பது ... — a·tu i·rup·pa·tu ...

behind ...	... க்குப் பீன்னால	... kup pin·naal
in front of ...	... க்கு முன்னால	... ku mun·naal
near (to ...)	(... க்கு) அருகே	(... ku) a·ru·key
on the corner	ஓரத்தில	aw·rat·til
straight ahead	நேரடியாக முன்புறம்	ney·ra·di·yaa·ha mun·pu·ram
there	அங்கே	ang·key

Numbers – Tamil

1	ஒன்று	on·*dru*
2	இரண்டு	i·*ran*·tu
3	மூன்று	*moon*·dru
4	நான்கு	naan·*ku*
5	ஐந்து	ain·*tu*
6	ஆறு	*aa*·ru
7	ஏழு	ey·*zu*
8	எட்டு	et·*tu*
9	ஒன்பது	on·pa·*tu*
10	பத்து	pat·*tu*
20	இருபது	i·ru·pa·*tu*
30	முப்பது	mup·pa·*tu*
40	நாற்பது	naar·pa·*tu*
50	ஐம்பது	aim·pa·*tu*
60	அறுபது	a·ru·pa·*tu*
70	எழுபது	e·zu·pa·*tu*
80	எண்பது	en·pa·*tu*
90	தொன்னூறு	ton·noo·*ru*
100	நூறு	noo·*ru*
1000	ஒராயிரம்	aw·raa·yi·ram

Eating & Drinking

Can you recommend a ...?	நீங்கள் ஒரு ... பரிந்துரைக்க முடியுமா?	*neeng*·kal o·*ru* ... pa·*rin*·tu·*raik*·ka mu·*ti·yu*·maa
bar	பார்	paar
dish	உணவு வகை	u·na·*vu* va·*kai*
place to eat	உணவகம்	u·na·va·*ham*

I'd like (a/the) ..., please.	எனக்கு தயவு செய்து ... கொடுங்கள்.	e·*nak*·ku ta·ya·*vu* chey·*tu* ... ko·*tung*·kal
bill	விலைச்சீட்டு	vi·*laich*·cheet·tu
menu	உணவுப்–பட்டியல்	u·na·*vup*·pat·ti·yal
that dish	அந்த உணவு வகை	*an*·ta u·na·*vu* va·*hai*

(cup of) coffee/tea ...	(கப்) காப்பி/ தேனீர் ...	(kap) *kaap*·pi/ *tey*·neer ...
with milk	பாலுடன்	paa·lu·*tan*
without sugar	சர்க்கரை– இல்லாமல	*chark*·ka·rai· *il*·laa·mal

a bottle/ glass of ... wine	ஒரு பாட்டில்/ கிளாஸ ... வைன்	o·ru paat·til/ ki·*laas* ... vain
red	சிவப்பு	chi·*vap*·pu
white	வெள்ளை	*vel*·lai

Do you have vegetarian food?
உங்களிடம சைவ உணவு உள்ளதா? — *ung*·ka·li·tam *chai*·va u·na·*vu ul*·la·taa

I'm allergic to (nuts).
எனக்கு (பருப்பு வகை) உணவு சேராது. — e·*nak*·ku (pa·*rup*·pu va·*kai*) u·na·*vu chey*·raa·tu

alcohol	சாராயம்	*chaa*·raa·yam
breakfast	காலை உணவு	kaa·*lai* u·na·*vu*
dinner	இரவு உணவு	i·ra·*vu* u·na·*vu*
drink	பானம்	paa·*nam*
fish	மீன்	meen
food	உணவு	u·na·*vu*
fruit	பழம்	pa·*zam*
juice	சாறு	chaa·*ru*
lunch	மதிய உணவு	ma·*ti*·ya u·na·*vu*
meat	இறைச்சி	i·*raich*·chi
milk	பால்	paal
soft drink	குளிர் பானம்	ku·*lir* paa·*nam*
vegetable	காய்கறி	*kai*·ka·ri
water	தண்ணீர்	*tan*·neyr

Emergencies

Help!	உதவ!	u·ta·*vi*
Stop!	நிறுத்து!	ni·*rut*·tu
Go away!	போய் வீடு!	*pow*·i vi·*tu*

Call a doctor!
ஐ அழைக்கவும் ஒரு மருத்துவர்! — i a·*zai*·ka·vum o·*ru* ma·*rut*·tu·var

Call the police!
ஐ அழைக்கவும் போலீஸ! — i a·*zai*·ka·vum *pow·lees*

I'm lost.
நான் வழி தவறி போய்விட்டேன். — naan va·*zi* ta·va·*ri pow*·i·*vit*·teyn

It hurts here.
இங்கே வலிக்கிறது. — *ing*·key va·*lik*·ki·ra·tu

I have to use the phone.
நான் தொலைபேசியை பயன்படுத்த வேண்டும். — naan *to*·lai·pey·*chi*·yai pa·*yan*·pa·*tut*·ta veyn·*tum*

Where are the toilets?
கழிவறைகள் எங்கே? — ka·*zi*·va·rai·kal *eng*·key

Shopping & Services

Where's the market?
எங்கே சந்தை இருக்கிறது? — *eng*·key *chan*·tai i·*ruk*·ki·ra·tu

Can I look at it?
நான் இதைப் பார்க்கலாமா? — naan i·*taip paark*·ka·laa·maa

How much is it?
இது என்ன வீலை? · i·tu en·na vi·lai

That's too expensive.
அது அதிக வீலையாக a·tu a·ti·ka vi·lai·yaa·ka
இருக்கிறது. i·ruk·ki·ra·tu

There's a mistake in the bill.
இந்த வீலைச்சீட்டில் in·ta vi·laich·cheet·til
ஒரு தவறு இருக்கிறது. o·ru ta·va·ru i·ruk·ki·ra·tu

bank	வங்கி	*vang*·ki
credit card	கிரேடிட்	ki·rey·tit
	அட்டை	at·tai
internet	இணையம்	i·nai·yam
post office	தபால்	ta·paal
	நிலையம்	ni·lai·yam
tourist office	சுற்றுப்பயண	chut·rup·pa·ya·na
	அலுவலகம்	a·lu·va·la·kam

Time & Dates

What time is it?
மணி என்ன? · ma·ni en·na

It's (two) o'clock.
மணி (இரண்டு). ma·ni (i·ran·tu)

Half past (two).
(இரண்டு) முப்பது. (i·ran·tu) mup·pa·tu

yesterday	நேற்று	*neyt*·tru
today	இன்று	in·dru
tomorrow	நாளை	naa·lai
day	நாள்	naal
morning	காலை	kaa·lai
evening	மாலை	maa·lai
night	இரவு	i·ra·vu
Monday	திங்கள்	*ting*·kal
Tuesday	செவ்வாய்	chev·vai
Wednesday	புதன்	pu·tan
Thursday	வீயாழன்	vi·yaa·zan
Friday	வெள்ளி	vel·li
Saturday	சனி	cha·ni
Sunday	ஞாயிறு	nyaa·yi·ru

Transport

Is this the ... to (New Delhi)?
இது தானா i·tu taa·naa
(புது– (pu·tu
டில்லிக்குப்) til·lik·kup)
புறப்படும் ...? pu·rap·pa·tum ...

bus	பஸ்	pas
plane	வீமானம்	vi·maa·nam
train	இரயில்	i·ra·yil

One ... ticket (to Madurai), please.
(மதுரைக்கு) (ma·tu·raik·ku)
தயவு செய்து ta·ya·vu chey·tu
... டிக்கட் ... tik·kat
கொடுங்கள். ko·tung·kal

one-way	ஒரு	o·ru
	வழிப்பயண	va·zip·pa·ya·na
return	இரு	i·ru
	வழிப்பயண	va·zip·pa·ya·na

What time's the first/last bus?
எத்தனை மணிக்கு et·ta·nai ma·nik·ku
முதல்/இறுதி mu·tal/i·ru·ti
பஸ் வரும்? pas va·rum

How long does the trip take?
பயணம் எவ்வளவு pa·ya·nam ev·va·la·vu
நேரம் எடுக்கும்? ney·ram e·tuk·kum

How long will it be delayed?
எவ்வளவு நேரம் அது ev·va·la·vu ney·ram a·tu
தாமதப்படும்? taa·ma·tap·pa·tum

Please tell me when we get to (Ooti).
(ஊட்டிக்குப்) (oot·tik·kup)
போனவுடன் paw·na·vu·tan
தயவு செய்து ta·ya·vu chey·tu
எனக்குக கூறுங்கள். e·nak·kuk koo·rung·kal

Please take me to (this address).
தயவு செய்து என்னை ta·ya·vu chey·tu en·nai
இந்த (வீலாசத்துக்குக) in·ta (vi·laa·chat·tuk·kuk)
கொண்டு செல்லுங்கள். kon·tu chel·lung·kal

Please stop/wait here.
தயவு செய்து இங்கே ta·ya·vu chey·tu ing·key
நிறுத்துங்கள்/ ni·rut·tung·kal/
காத்திருங்கள். kaat·ti·rung·kal

I'd like to hire a car (with a driver).
நான் ஒரு மோட்டார் naan o·ru mowt·taar
வண்டி (ஓர் van·ti (awr
ஓட்டுநருடன்) aw·tu·na·ru·tan)
வாடகைக்கு எடுக்க vaa·ta·haik·ku e·tuk·ka
வீரும்புகிறேன். vi·rum·pu·ki·reyn

Is this the road to (Mamallapuram)?
இது தான் i·tu taan
(மாமல்லபுரத்துக்கு) (maa·mal·la·pu·rat·tuk·ku)
செல்லும் சாலையா? chel·lum chaa·lai·yaa

airport	வீமான	vi·maa·na
	நிலையம்	ni·lai·yam
bicycle	சைக்கிள்	chaik·kil
boat	படகு	pa·ta·ku
bus stop	பஸ்	pas
	நிறுத்தும்	ni·rut·tum
economy class	சிக்கன	chik·ka·na
	வகுப்பு	va·kup·pu
first class	முதல்	mu·tal
	வகுப்பு	va·kup·pu
motorcycle	மோட்டார்	mowt·taar
	சைக்கிள்	chaik·kil
train station	நிலையம்	ni·lai·yam

Adivasis – tribal people

ahimsa – discipline of nonviolence

AIR – All India Radio; the national broadcaster, government controlled

Ananta – snake on which Vishnu reclined between universes

Ardhanarishvara – Shiva's half-male, half-female form

Arjuna – Mahabharata hero and military commander; he had the Bhagavad Gita related to him by Krishna.

Aryan – Sanskrit for 'noble'; those who migrated from Persia and settled in northern India

ashram – spiritual community or retreat

ASI – Archaeological Survey of India; an organisation involved in monument preservation

attar – essential oil usually made from flowers and used as a base for perfumes

autorickshaw – noisy, three-wheeled, motorised contraption for transporting passengers, livestock etc for short distances; found throughout the country, they are cheaper than taxis

Avalokitesvara – in Mahayana Buddhism, the bodhisattva of compassion

avatar – incarnation, usually of a deity

ayurveda – ancient and complex science of Indian herbal medicine and holistic healing

azad – Urdu for 'free', as in Azad Jammu and Kashmir

azadi – freedom

azan – Muslim call to prayer

Baba – religious master or father; term of respect

bagh – garden

bahadur – brave or chivalrous; an honorific title

baksheesh – tip, donation (alms) or bribe

bandh – strike

bandhani – tie-dye

banyan – Indian fig tree; spiritual to many Indians

baoli – see baori

baori – well, particularly a step-well with landings and galleries; in Gujarat it is more commonly referred to as a baoli

barasingha – deer

basti – slum

bearer – like a butler

Bhagavad Gita – Hindu Song of the Divine One; Krishna's lessons to Arjuna, the main thrust of which was to emphasise the philosophy of bhakti; it is part of the Mahabharata

bhajan – devotional song

bhakti – surrendering to the gods; faith, devotion

bhang – dried leaves and flowering shoots of the marijuana plant

bhangra – rhythmic Punjabi music/dance

Bharat – Hindi for India

bhavan – house, building; also spelt bhawan

Bhima – Mahabharata hero; the brother of Hanuman, husband of Hadimba, father of Ghatotkach, and renowned for his great strength

bindi – forehead mark (often dot-shaped) made from kumkum, worn by women

BJP – Bharatiya Janata Party

Bodhi Tree – tree under which Buddha sat when he attained enlightenment

bodhisattva – enlightened beings

Bollywood – India's answer to Hollywood; the film industry of Mumbai (Bombay)

Brahma – Hindu god; worshipped as the creator in the Trimurti

Brahmanism – early form of Hinduism that evolved from Vedism (see Vedas); named after Brahmin priests and Brahma

Brahmin – member of the priest/scholar caste, the highest Hindu caste

Buddha – Awakened One; the originator of Buddhism; also regarded by Hindus as the ninth incarnation of Vishnu

Buddhism – see Early Buddhism

bugyal – high-altitude meadow

burka – one-piece garment used by conservative Muslim women to cover themselves from head to toe

cantonment – administrative and military area of a Raj-era town

Carnatic music – classical music of South India

caste – a Hindu's hereditary station (social standing) in life; there are four main castes: Brahmin, Kshatriya, Vaishya and Shudra

chaam – ritual masked dance performed by some Buddhist monks in gompas to celebrate the victory of good over evil and of Buddhism over pre-existing religions

chaitya – prayer room; assembly hall

chakra – focus of one's spiritual power; disc-like weapon of Vishnu

Chamunda – form of Durga; armed with a scimitar, noose and mace, and clothed in elephant hide, her mission was to kill the demons Chanda and Munda

chandra – moon, or the moon as a god

Chandragupta – Indian ruler in the 3rd century BC

chappals – sandals or leather thong-like footwear; flip-flops

char dham – four pilgrimage destinations of Badrinath, Kedarnath, Yamunotri and Gangotri

charas – resin of the marijuana plant; also referred to as 'hashish'

charbagh – formal Persian garden, divided into quarters (literally 'four gardens')

charpoy – simple bed made of ropes knotted together on a wooden frame

chedi – see chaitya

chhatri – cenotaph (literally 'umbrella')

chikan – embroidered cloth (speciality of Lucknow)

chillum – pipe of a hookah; commonly used to describe the pipes used for smoking ganja

chinkara – gazelle

chital – spotted deer

chogyal – king

choli – sari blouse

chorten – Tibetan for stupa

choultry – pilgrim's rest house; also called 'dharamsala'

chowk – town square, intersection or marketplace

chowkidar – night watchman, caretaker

Cong (I) – Congress Party of India; also known as Congress (I)

crore – 10 million

crorepatis – millionaires

dacoit – bandit (particularly armed bandit), outlaw

dagoba – see stupa

Dalit – preferred term for India's Untouchable caste; see also Harijan

dargah – shrine or place of burial of a Muslim saint

darshan – offering or audience with a deity

desi – local, Indian

deul – temple sanctuary

Devi – Shiva's wife; goddess

dhaba – basic restaurant or snack bar

dham – holiest pilgrimage places of India

dharamsala – pilgrim's rest house

dharma – for Hindus, the moral code of behaviour or social duty; for Buddhists, following the law of nature, or path, as taught by Buddha

dhobi – person who washes clothes; commonly referred to as dhobi-wallah

dhobi ghat – place where clothes are washed

dhol – traditional double-sided drum

dholi – portable 'chairs' with two bearers; people are carried in them to hilltop temples

dhoti – long loincloth worn by men; like a lungi, but the ankle-length cloth is then pulled up between the legs

dhurrie – kilimlike cotton rug

Digambara – 'Sky-Clad'; Jain group that demonstrates disdain for worldly goods by going naked

dikpala – temple guardian

diwan – principal officer in a princely state; royal court or council

Diwan-i-Am – hall of public audience

Diwan-i-Khas – hall of private audience

dowry – money and/or goods given by a bride's parents to their son-in-law's family; it's illegal but still widely exists in many arranged marriages

Draupadi – wife of the five Pandava princes in the Mahabharata

Dravidian – general term for the cultures and languages of the deep south of India, including Tamil, Malayalam, Telugu and Kannada

dukhang – Tibetan prayer hall

dun – valley

dupatta – long scarf for women often worn with the salwar kameez

durbar – royal court; also a government

Durga – the Inaccessible; a form of Shiva's wife, Devi, a beautiful, fierce woman riding a tiger/lion; a major goddess of the Shakti order

Early Buddhism – any of the schools of Buddhism established directly after Buddha's death and before the advent of Mahayana; a modern form is the Theravada (Teaching of the Elders) practised in Sri Lanka and Southeast Asia; Early Buddhism differed from the Mahayana in that it did not teach the bodhisattva ideal

fakir – Muslim who has taken a vow of poverty; may also apply to other ascetics

filmi – slang term describing anything to do with Indian movies

gabba – appliquéd Kashmiri rug

gali – lane or alleyway

Ganesh – Hindu god of good fortune; elephant-headed son of Shiva and Parvati, he is also known as Ganpati and his vehicle is Mooshak (a ratlike creature)

Ganga – Hindu goddess representing the sacred Ganges River; said to flow from Vishnu's toe

ganj – market

gaon – village

garh – fort

Garuda – man-bird vehicle of Vishnu

gaur – Indian bison

Gayatri – sacred verse of Rig-Veda repeated mentally by Brahmins twice a day

geyser – hot-water unit found in many bathrooms

ghat – steps or landing on a river; a range of hills or a road up hills

giri – hill

godown – warehouse

gompa – Tibetan Buddhist monastery

Gopala – see Govinda

gopi – milkmaid; Krishna was fond of them

gopuram – soaring pyramidal gateway tower of Dravidian temples

Govinda – Krishna as a cowherd; also just cowherd

gufa – cave

gumbad – dome on an Islamic tomb or mosque

gurdwara – Sikh temple

Gurmukhi – script of the Guru Granth Sahib; Punjabi script

guru – holy teacher; in Sanskrit literally 'goe' (darkness) and 'roe' (to dispel)

Guru Granth Sahib – Sikh holy book

haat – village market

haj – Muslim pilgrimage to Mecca

haji – Muslim who has made the haj

hammam – Turkish bath; public bathhouse

Hanuman – Hindu monkey god, prominent in the Ramayana, and a follower of Rama

Hara – one of Shiva's names

Hari – another name for Vishnu

Harijan – name (no longer considered acceptable) given by Mahatma Gandhi

to India's Untouchable caste, meaning 'children of god'

hartal – strike

hashish – see charas

hathi – elephant

haveli – traditional, often ornately decorated, residences, particularly those found in Rajasthan and Gujarat

hijab – headscarf used by Muslim women

hijra – eunuch, transvestite

hookah – water pipe used for smoking marijuana or strong tobacco

howdah – seat for carrying people on an elephant's back

ikat – fabric made with thread which is tie-dyed before weaving

imam – Muslim religious leader

imambara – tomb dedicated to a Shiite Muslim holy man

Indo-Saracenic – style of colonial architecture that integrated Western designs with Islamic, Hindu and Jain influences

Indra – significant and prestigious Vedic god; god of rain, thunder, lightning and war

jagamohan – assembly hall

Jagannath – Lord of the Universe; a form of Krishna

jali – carved lattice (often marble) screen; also refers to the holes or spaces produced through carving timber or stone

Jataka – tale from Buddha's various lives

jauhar – ritual mass suicide by immolation, traditionally performed by Rajput women at times of military defeat to avoid being dishonoured by their captors

jhula – bridge

ji – honorific that can be added to the end of almost anything as a form of respect; thus 'Babaji', 'Gandhiji'

jihad – holy war (Islam)

JKLF – Jammu and Kashmir Liberation Front

jooti – traditional, often pointy-toed, slip-in shoes; commonly found in North India

juggernaut – huge, extravagantly decorated temple 'car' dragged through the streets during certain Hindu festivals

jyoti linga – naturally occurring lingam believed to derive currents of shakti

kabaddi – traditional game (similar to tag)

Kailasa – sacred Himalayan mountain; home of Shiva

Kali – ominous-looking evil-destroying form of Devi; commonly depicted with dark skin, dripping with blood, and wearing a necklace of skulls

Kama – Hindu god of love

Kama Sutra – ancient Sanskrit text largely covering the subjects of love and sexuality

kameez – woman's shirtlike tunic; see also salwar kameez

kapali – sacred bowl made from a human skull

karma – Hindu, Buddhist and Sikh principle of retributive justice for past deeds

khadi – homespun cloth; Mahatma Gandhi encouraged people to spin this rather than buy English cloth

Khalsa – Sikh brotherhood

Khan – Muslim honorific title

kho-kho – traditional game (similar to tag); less common variation on kabbadi

khol – black eyeliner

khur – Asiatic wild ass

kiang – wild ass found in Ladakh

kirtan – Sikh devotional singing

koil – Hindu temple

kolam – see rangola

kompu – C-shaped metal trumpet

kos minar – milestone

kot – fort

kothi – residence or mansion

kotwali – police station

Krishna – Vishnu's eighth incarnation, often coloured blue; he revealed the Bhagavad Gita to Arjuna

Kshatriya – Hindu caste of soldiers or administrators; second in the caste hierarchy

kumkum – coloured powder used for bindi dots

kund – lake or tank; Toda village

kurta – long shirt with either short collar or no collar

lakh – 100,000

Lakshmana – half-brother and aide of Rama in the Ramayana

Lakshmi – Vishnu's consort, Hindu goddess of wealth; she sprang forth from the ocean holding a lotus

lama – Tibetan Buddhist priest or monk

Laxmi – see Lakshmi

lhamo – Tibetan opera

lingam – phallic symbol; auspicious symbol of Shiva; plural 'linga'

lok – people

Lok Sabha – lower house in the Indian parliament (House of the People)

Losar – Tibetan New Year

lungi – worn by men, this loose, coloured garment (similar to a sarong) is pleated by the wearer at the waist to fit

madrasa – Islamic seminary

maha – prefix meaning 'great'

Mahabharata – Great Hindu Vedic epic poem of the Bharata dynasty; containing approximately 10,000 verses describing the battle between the Pandavas and the Kauravas

Mahakala – Great Time; Shiva and one of 12 jyoti linga

mahal – house or palace

maharaja – literally 'great king'; princely ruler

maharana – see maharaja

maharani – wife of a princely ruler or a ruler in her own right

maharao – see maharaja

maharawal – see maharaja

mahatma – literally 'great soul'

Mahavir – last tirthankar

Mahayana – the 'greater-vehicle' of Buddhism; a later adaptation of the teaching that lays emphasis on the bodhisattva ideal, teaching the renunciation of nirvana in order to help other beings along the way to enlightenment

maidan – open (often grassed) area; parade ground

Maitreya – future Buddha

Makara – mythical sea creature and Varuna's vehicle; crocodile

mala – garland or necklace

mali – gardener

mandal – shrine

mandala – circle; symbol used in Hindu and Buddhist art to symbolise the universe

mandapa – pillared pavilion, temple forechamber

mandi – market

mandir – temple

mani stone – stone carved with the Tibetan-Buddhist mantra 'Om mani padme hum' ('Hail the jewel in the lotus')

mani walls – Tibetan stone walls with sacred inscriptions

mantra – sacred word or syllable used by Buddhists and Hindus to aid concentration; metrical psalms of praise found in the Vedas

Mara – Buddhist personification of that which obstructs the cultivation of virtue, often depicted with hundreds of arms; also the god of death

Maratha – central Indian people who controlled much of India at various times and fought the Mughals and Rajputs

marg – road

masjid – mosque

mata – mother

math – monastery

maya – illusion

mehndi – henna; ornate henna designs on women's hands (and often feet), traditionally for certain festivals or ceremonies (eg marriage)

mela – fair or festival

memsahib – Madam; respectful way of addressing women

mihrab – mosque 'prayer niche' that faces Mecca

mithuna – pairs of men and women; often seen in temple sculpture

Moghul – see Mughal

Mohini – Vishnu in his female incarnation

Mohiniyattam – classical dance of the temptress

moksha – liberation from samsara

monsoon – rainy season

mudra – ritual hand movements used in Hindu religious dancing; gesture of Buddha figure

muezzin – one who calls Muslims to prayer, traditionally from the minaret of a mosque

Mughal – Muslim dynasty of subcontinental emperors from Babur to Aurangzeb

mullah – Muslim scholar or religious leader

Mumbaikar – resident of Mumbai (Bombay)

mund – village

muntjac – barking deer

murti – statue, often of a deity

nadi – river

Naga – mythical serpentlike beings capable of changing into human form

namaskar – see namaste

namaste – traditional Hindu greeting (hello or goodbye), often accompanied by a respectful small bow with the hands together at the chest or head level; also namaskar

namaz – Muslim prayers

Nanda – cowherd who raised Krishna

Nandi – bull, vehicle of Shiva

Narayan – incarnation of Vishnu the creator

Nataraja – Shiva as the cosmic dancer

nautch – dance

nautch girls – dancing girls

nawab – Muslim ruling prince or powerful landowner

Naxalites – ultra-leftist political movement begun in West Bengal as a peasant rebellion; characterised by violence

nilgai – antelope

nirvana – ultimate aim of Buddhists and the final release from the cycle of existence

niwas – house, building

nizam – hereditary title of the rulers of Hyderabad

noth – the Lord (Jain)

NRI – Non-Resident Indian; of economic significance to modern India

nullah – ditch or small stream

Om – sacred invocation representing the essence of the divine principle; for Buddhists, if repeated often enough with complete concentration, it leads to a state of emptiness

Osho – the late Bhagwan Shree Rajneesh, a popular, controversial guru

paan – mixture of betel nut and leaves for chewing

padma – lotus; another name for the Hindu goddess Lakshmi

pagoda – see stupa

paise – the Indian rupee is divided into 100 paise

palanquin – boxlike enclosure carried on poles on four bearer's shoulders; the occupant sits inside on a seat

Pali – the language, related to Sanskrit, in which the Buddhist scriptures were recorded; scholars still refer to the original Pali texts

palli – village

panchayat – village council

pandal – marquee; temple shrine

Parsi – adherent of the Zoroastrian faith

Partition – formal division of British India in 1947 into two separate countries, India and Pakistan

Parvati – another form of Devi

pashmina – fine woollen shawl

patachitra – Orissan cloth painting

PCO – Public Call Office, from where you can make local, interstate and international phone calls

peepul – fig tree, especially a bo tree

peon – lowest-grade clerical worker

pietra dura – marble inlay work characteristic of the Taj Mahal

pir – Muslim holy man; title of a Sufi saint

POK – Pakistan Occupied Kashmir

pradesh – state

pranayama – study of breath control; meditative practice

prasad – temple-blessed food offering

puja – literally 'respect'; offering or prayers

pujari – temple priest

pukka – proper; a Raj-era term

pukka sahib – proper gentleman

punka – cloth fan, swung by pulling a cord

Puranas – set of 18 encyclopaedic Sanskrit stories, written in verse, relating to the three gods, dating from the 5th century AD

purdah – custom among some conservative Muslims (also adopted by some Hindus, especially the Rajputs) of keeping women in seclusion; veiled

Purnima – full moon; considered to be an auspicious time

qawwali – Islamic devotional singing

qila – fort

Quran – the holy book of Islam, also spelt Koran

Radha – favourite mistress of Krishna when he lived as a cowherd

raga – any of several conventional patterns of melody and rhythm that form the basis for freely interpreted compositions

railhead – station or town at the end of a railway line; termination point

raj – rule or sovereignty; British Raj (sometimes just Raj) refers to British rule

raja – king; sometimes rana

rajkumar – prince

Rajput – Hindu warrior caste, former rulers of northwestern India

Rajya Sabha – upper house in the Indian parliament (Council of States)

rakhi – amulet

Rama – seventh incarnation of Vishnu

Ramadan – Islamic holy month of sunrise-to-sunset fasting (no eating, drinking or smoking); also referred to as Ramazan

Ramayana – story of Rama and Sita and their conflict with Ravana; one of India's best-known epics

rana – king; sometimes raja

rangoli – elaborate chalk, rice-paste or coloured powder design; also known as kolam

rani – female ruler or wife of a king

ranns – deserts

rath – temple chariot or car used in religious festivals

rathas – rock-cut Dravidian temples

Ravana – demon king of Lanka who abducted Sita; the titanic battle between him and Rama is told in the Ramayana

rawal – nobleman

rickshaw – small, two- or three-wheeled passenger vehicle

Rig-Veda – original and longest of the four main Vedas

rishi – any poet, philosopher, saint or sage; originally a sage to whom the hymns of the Vedas were revealed

Road – railway town that serves as a communication point to a larger town off the line, eg Mt Abu and Abu Road

Rukmani – wife of Krishna; died on his funeral pyre

sadar – main

sadhu – ascetic, holy person, one who is trying to achieve enlightenment; often addressed as 'swamiji' or 'babaji'

safa – turban

sagar – lake, reservoir

sahib – respectful title applied to a gentleman

salai – road

salwar – trousers usually worn with a kameez

salwar kameez – traditional dresslike tunic and trouser combination for women

samadhi – in Hinduism, ecstatic state, sometimes defined as 'ecstasy, trance, communion with God'; in Buddhism, concentration; also a place where a holy man has been cremated/buried, usually venerated as a shrine

sambar – deer

samsara – Buddhists, Hindus and Sikhs believe earthly life is cyclical; you are born again and again, the quality of these rebirths being dependent upon your karma in previous lives

sangeet – music

sangha – community of Buddhist monks and nuns

Sankara – Shiva as the creator

sanyasin – like a sadhu; a wandering ascetic who has renounced all worldly things as part of the ashrama system

Saraswati – wife of Brahma, goddess of learning; sits on a white swan, holding a veena

Sat Sri Akal – Sikh greeting

Sati – wife of Shiva; became a sati ('honourable woman') by immolating herself; although banned more than a century ago, the act of sati is still (very) occasionally performed

satra – Hindu Vaishnavaite monastery and centre for art

satyagraha – nonviolent protest involving a hunger strike, popularised by Mahatma Gandhi; from Sanskrit, literally meaning 'insistence on truth'

Scheduled Castes – official term used for the Untouchable or Dalit caste

sepoy – formerly an Indian solider in British service

seva – voluntary work, especially in a temple

Shaivism – worship of Shiva

Shaivite – follower of Shiva

shakti – creative energies perceived as female deities; devotees follow Shaktism order

sharia – Islamic law

sheesha – see hookah

shikara – gondola-like boat used on lakes in Srinagar (Kashmir)

shikhar – hunting expedition

Shiva – Destroyer; also the Creator, in which form he is worshipped as a lingam

shola – virgin forest

shree – see shri

shri – honorific male prefix; Indian equivalent of 'Respected Sir'

shruti – heard

Shudra – caste of labourers

sikhara – Hindu temple-spire or temple

Singh – literally 'lion'; a surname adopted by Sikhs

Sita – Hindu goddess of agriculture; more commonly associated with the Ramayana

sitar – Indian stringed instrument

Siva – see Shiva

sonam – karma accumulated in successive reincarnations

sree – see shri

sri – see shri

stupa – Buddhist religious monument composed of a solid hemisphere topped by a spire, containing relics of Buddha; also known as a 'dagoba' or 'pagoda'

Subhadra – Krishna's incestuous sister

Sufi – Muslim mystic

Sufism – Islamic mysticism

Surya – the sun; a major deity in the Vedas

sutra – string; list of rules expressed in verse

swami – title of respect meaning 'lord of the self'; given to initiated Hindu monks

swaraj – independence

Swarga – heaven of Indra

sweeper – lowest caste servant, performs the most menial of tasks

tabla – twin drums

tal – lake

taluk – district

tandava – Shiva's cosmic victory dance

tank – reservoir; pool or large receptacle of holy water found at some temples

tantric Buddhism – Tibetan Buddhism with strong sexual and occult overtones

tempo – noisy three-wheeler public transport vehicle, bigger than an autorickshaw; see Vikram

thakur – nobleman

thangka – Tibetan cloth painting

theertham – temple tank

Theravada – orthodox form of Buddhism practised in Sri Lanka and Southeast Asia that is characterised by its adherence to the Pali canon; literally 'dwelling'

thiru – holy

tikka – mark Hindus put on their foreheads

tirthankars – the 24 great Jain teachers

tonga – two-wheeled horse or pony carriage

torana – architrave over a temple entrance

trekkers – jeeps; hikers

Trimurti – triple form or three-faced; the Hindu triad of Brahma, Shiva and Vishnu

Uma – Shiva's consort; light

Untouchable – lowest caste or 'casteless', for whom the most menial tasks are reserved; the name derives from the belief that higher castes risk defilement if they touch one; formerly known as Harijan, now Dalit

Upanishads – esoteric doctrine; ancient texts forming part of the Vedas; delving into weighty matters such as the nature of the universe and soul

urs – death anniversary of a revered Muslim; festival in memory of a Muslim saint

Vaishya – member of the Hindu caste of merchants

Valmiki – author of the Ramayana

varna – concept of caste

Varuna – supreme Vedic god

Vedas – Hindu sacred books; collection of hymns composed in preclassical Sanskrit during the second millennium BC and divided into four books: Rig-Veda, Yajur-Veda, Sama-Veda and Atharva-Veda

vihara – Buddhist monastery, generally with central court or hall off which open residential cells, usually with a Buddha shrine at one end; resting place

vikram – tempo or a larger version of the standard tempo

vimana – principal part of Hindu temple; a tower over the sanctum

vipassana – insight meditation technique of Theravada Buddhism in which mind and body are closely examined as changing phenomena

Vishnu – part of the Trimurti; Vishnu is the Preserver and Restorer who so far has nine avatars: the fish Matsya; the tortoise Kurma; the wild boar Naraha; Narasimha; Vamana; Parasurama; Rama; Krishna; and Buddha

wallah – man; added onto almost anything, eg dhobi-wallah, chai-wallah, taxi-wallah

wazir – title of chief minister used in some former Muslim princely states

yagna – self-mortification

yakshi – maiden

yali – mythical lion creature

yantra – geometric plan said to create energy

yatra – pilgrimage

yatri – pilgrim

yogini – female goddess attendants

yoni – female fertility symbol; female genitalia

zakat – tax in the form of a charitable donation, one of the five 'Pillars of Islam'

zamindar – landowner

zenana – area of an upperclass home where women are secluded; women's quarters

behind the scenes

SEND US YOUR FEEDBACK

We love to hear from travellers – your comments keep us on our toes and help make our books better. Our well-travelled team reads every word on what you loved or loathed about this book. Although we cannot reply individually to postal submissions, we always guarantee that your feedback goes straight to the appropriate authors, in time for the next edition. Each person who sends us information is thanked in the next edition – and the most useful submissions are rewarded with a free book.

Visit **lonelyplanet.com/contact** to submit your updates and suggestions or to ask for help. Our award-winning website also features inspirational travel stories, news and discussions.

Note: We may edit, reproduce and incorporate your comments in Lonely Planet products such as guidebooks, websites and digital products, so let us know if you don't want your comments reproduced or your name acknowledged. For a copy of our privacy policy visit lonelyplanet.com/privacy.

OUR READERS

Many thanks to the travellers who used the last edition and wrote to us with helpful hints, useful advice and interesting anecdotes:

A Keith Abraham, Vimal Abraham, Ram Advani, Rupal Agrawal, Yamamoto Ai, Elizabeth Akinnawo, Akshat, GW Albury, Alessandro Caputo, Liz Allam, Claudia Ambauen, Marco Ammannati, Klaus and Carmen Awiszus-mistretta, Carrie Anderson, Janice Anderson, Craig Andrew Stokes, Anca Ansink, Bernardo Araujo, Frederick G Arioli, Rossen Arnaoudov, Arthur and Vera, Asgeir Arnason, Geof Ashton, Leanne Ashworth, Laura Atiknson, Eran Atlas, Jeanett Avila, Axel **B** Monika Bachmann, Eva Bäckman, Robert Bain, Madhwaraj Ballal, June Bamford, Pawel Bania, Malonie Barbara, Mary-jane Barca, Anna Barrett, Gerald Barry, Iain Batchelor, Ruth Bath, Elena Begma, Kriti Behari, Jeff Behrner, Anna Bellini, Lizzy Benetton, Elin Bengtsson, Sali Bent, Caroline Bergaud, Sally Bergh Palmvig, Danielle Berghmans, Bethan, Andrew Bevan, Mike and Madeleine Bigland, Subrata Biswas, Adrian Blackhurst, Emiel Blankert, Laurie Boland, Patrick Boman, James Booth, Vera Borsboom, Jude Boswood, David Bourchier, Lauren Bouyea, Christian Brauns, Catherine Brien, Vanessa Brina, Michael Broadhead, Brenda Brown, Marie Brown, Olivia Brown, Ki Browning, Andreas Bruhn, Bruno, Sarah Buchmiller, Barry Buckley, Roderick Buijs, Amanda Burgess, Sendra Burgin, Megan Burnside, Jill Burrington, Christian Bussmann, Eric Butler **C** Eric Cadesky, Donagh Cagney, Jon Caleb, Elizabeth Callahan, Marie Camille Serre, Francesco Carbone, Ana Carenine, Annika Carlsson, Andrew Carreras, Beth Carroll, Heather Carswell, Andrew Carter, Geoff Cattrall, William Chan, Nikhilesh Chand, Charlotte Chappell, Rory Chapple, Nelson Chen, Cora Cheng, Melwyn Chettiar, Lisa Cheung, Aaron Chew, Luc Chome, Sanjiv Choudhary, Marie Christine, Chunkai, Lisa Chure, Jocelyn Cipolla, Helen Clarke, Lynden Clarke, Cheryl Claxton, Claire Cocke, Tom Coghlan, Kara Colley, Shawn Collins, Mckee Colsman, Bex Colwell, Nicolas Combremont, Ann Cook, Janes Cooper, Julie Cooper, Karen Cooper, Liam Cooper, Amy Corcoran, Myriam Cormier, Melissa Correa, David Cummings **D** Prem Dargo, Frankowski Dariusz, James Dave, Will Davies, Andrew Daws, Greet De Bolle, Jaap De Graaf, Judith De Bruijn, Ruth De Sainte Croix, Ynte De Groot, Josetxo Dealza, Deand, Pierrick Delattre, Denver, Evans Denver, Walter Denzel, Walter Derler, Vasu Dev, Cathy Dewalt, Murali Dhar, Noa Diengott, Jennifer Difilippo, Christiaan Dodemont, Elizabeth Doel, Penpa Dolma, Will Driscoll, David Dunn **E** Christoph

Ebhart, Nick Edwards, Alexandra Elmquist, Christofer Elofson, Maria Emilia Rios, Martin Engström, Diana Enriquez, Debbie Epstein **F** Rosella Fanelli, Dent Favinn, Jonathan Feenstra, Courtney Fehrmann, Gerard Fellerath, Kenneth Ferrell, Carla Figueiredo, Richard Fischer, Meagan Flaherty, Flavia, George Fogh, Tuuli Forward, Amy Fox, Matej Frésard, John Fuller, Peter Fumberger **G** Tautscher Gabriele, Kerrie Gandara, Aili Garcia, Guillermo Garcia, Kyle Gardner, Saurabh Garg, Corinna Gargiulo, Mary Garrard, GC, Birgit Georgi, Huber Gerti, Shekhar Gharpure, Joanne Gibbs, Charles Gilbe, Michael Gilhooley, Hamish Gillespie-Jones, Devananda Giri, Kerstin Goellner, Caroline Golding, Katherine Golding, Emma Goodwin, Ewald Goossens, Bill Goss, Gabe Gottlieb, Holly Gottlieb, Arthur Gottschalk, François Goutorbe, Michael Graboski, Michael Graham, Marie Grandisson, Linda Gray, Julius Grebbin, Jenny Greenwood, Lori Greer, Hannah Griffiths, Aaron Groom, Torunn Grove, Sandy Guest, Simon Guido Purtschert, Aman Gupta, James Gurd **H** Ulrich Hahn, Francis Hanley, Don Hansen, Jessica Harding, Matthew Harley, Katherine Harris, Matt Harris, Cristy Harrison, Ian Harry, Ellie Hart, Jawed Hasan, Elke Hausberger, Yossi Havusha, Tony Helper, Stella Heman, Roosmarijn Hesse, Henning Hintzsche, Carol Hobart, Keith Hockly and Suzie Lee, Nigel Hodge, Joachim Hoff, Caroline Hoffmann, Ingo Hofmaier, Mike Holliday, Colin Holtzinger, Tanya Hoppes, Mike Horsey, Ilana Hovtz, Hannah Howarth, Kat Hull, Juergen Husch, Vanessa Hyde

I Ibergo, Christian Iberle, Josha Inglis, Evru Ingol, Farida Iqbal, Martin Irwin, Nadine Isaiah **J** Emma J James, Adam Jachimowicz, Camille Jackson, Kristin Jacobson, Alex Jacottet, Ansh Jain, Ketan Jain, Janny, Jas, Karel Jan Van Den Heuvel Rijnders, Tomasz Janiewicz, Jarvis, Inge Janssen, Steve Jason, Patrik Jatson, Jessica Jiang, Joel, Oswald and Rosalind Johnen, Alexander Jonassen, Christine Jones, Krist Jones, Sara Joseph, Hans Josephsson, Basia Jozwiak, Tom Justice **K** Jaqueline Kaku, Kamlesh, Moonika Kase, Ania Kemp, David Kerkhoff, Tyler Keys, Julie Khaja, Misha Khanduja, Yoshiharu Kido, Padraig Kilcline, Naresh Killa, Niamh King and Ian Patterson, Lucie Kinkorova, Val Kitchener, Judi Kloper, Rebecca Klug, Mellita Knowles, Alex Kok, Juho Korhonen, Julia Kozitsyna, Kpsjaisalmer, Julia Kramer, Sandy Krawitz, Michaela Kreuterova, Lakshmi Krishnan, Jesper Krogh, Aaron Krumins, Doris Kudla, Shailesh Kukrety, Kailash Kumar Vyas, Surendra Kumar, Jeffy Kurisingal **L** Elise Labontelemoyne, Richard Laing, Lauren Laing-buisson, Steve Laiom, Chris and Ljiljana Lake, Ankush Lal, Alison Lambert, Victor Landergard, Andre Langer, Zoran Lapov, Linda Layfield, Stephanie Le Couteur, Nigel Lea, Jaehoon Lee, Guido Leenders, Yair Lev, Jessica Li, Robert Linden, Dave Linthicum, Magali Liuang, Jasmin Löffler, Sue Longmore, Clodine Loubert, Steen Lund, Bart Luts, Daryl Lynne Wood, Emma Lyons, Kate Lyons-priker **M** Christie Maccallum, Catherine MacManus, Haley Macpherson, Mike Macy, Tali Mandezweig, Christel Manning,

THIS BOOK

This 14th edition of Lonely Planet's *India* guidebook was coordinated (for the sixth time) by Sarina Singh. She led this experienced, enthusiastic team of authors: Michael Benanav, Lindsay Brown, Stuart Butler, Mark Elliott, Katja Gaskell, Trent Holden, Abigail Hole, Kate James, Amy Karafin, Anirban Mahapatra, Bradley Mayhew, Daniel McCrohan, John Noble, Kevin Raub, Amelia Thomas and David Lukas. The Health chapter was adapted from text written by Dr Trish Batchelor.

This guidebook was commissioned in Lonely Planet's Melbourne office, and produced by the following:

Commissioning Editor
Suzannah Shwer

Coordinating Editor
Nigel Chin

Coordinating Cartographer Alex Leung

Coordinating Layout Designers Nicholas Colicchia, Wibowo Rusli

Managing Editors Brigitte Ellemor, Liz Heynes

Managing Cartographers Adrian Persoglia, Anthony Phelan

Managing Layout Designer Chris Girdler

Assisting Editors Alice Barker, Janice Bird, Jessica Crouch, Kate Daly, Paul Harding, Bella Li, Sonya Mithen, Kristin Odijk, Erin Richards, Matty Soccio, Sophie Splatt, Gabrielle Stefanos, Jeanette Wall

Assisting Cartographers Anita Banh, Andras Bogdanovits, Ildiko Bogdanovits, Katalin Dadi-Racz, Julie Dodkins, Karen Grant, Maritza Kolega, Valentina Kremenchutskaya, James Leversha, Peter Shields

Assisting Layout Designers, Jessica Rose, Kerrianne Southway

Cover Research Samantha Curcio

Internal Image Research Sabrina Dalbesio

Language Content Branislava Vladisavljevic

Thanks to Jessica Boland, Helen Christinis, Ryan Evans, Jocelyn Harewood, Lisa Knights, Nic Lehman, Anna Metcalfe, Kate Morgan, Catherine Naghten, Charlotte Orr, Susan Paterson, Kirsten Rawlings, Averil Robertson, Michael Ruff, Angela Tinson, Gerard Walker

Chris Marchan, Christina Maria, Eva Maria Sevaldsen, Gonzalez Maria, Marijne, Claire Marr, Jon Marriott, Jennifer Marshall, Jerome Marshall, Marine, Marta, Martin, Rosa Martinez, Josef Massinger, Marta Mateos Mazón, Maureen Mcwilliams, Ian Meadows, Darren Merchant, Jure Mesec, Mike, Dan Miles, Joe Miles, Wendy Miles, Emilie Millecamps, Roger Miller, John Mills, Oliver Milverton, Miyumayu, Kyoko Mizuno, Peter Mohan, Sha Mole, Aglaia Molinari, Evelyn Monnington-Taylor, Nancy Morgan, Steve Morgan, Emily Moss, Malcolm Moss, Graziella Moutamalle, Sarah Moy, Michael Mueller, Katharina Mueller-uri, Petra Muhic, Liz Mulqueen, Viola Murgia, Ines Murillo, Ashly Murphy, Grace Murray, Ilan Muthada **N** Vinit Nair, Naomipetit, Natarajan, Gary Naumann, RK Nayar, Vladimir Nazimov, Rebecca Neal, Flavia Neddermeyer, Zoe Neumayer, Adam Newman, Carmel Neylon, Lisa Ngan-hing, Margaux Nguyen, Adam Nicoll, Natasa Nikolic, Pia Noel, Will Noreyo, Marcel Nouvet, Erika Nygren **O** Aonghus Obrien, Angela Ockenden, Gavin Oclee-Brown, Claire O'Connell, Silvia Ohnmacht, Graham O'Neil, Brian O'Neill, Patri Onul, James Oram, Peter Orthmann, Oscar, Johannes Ostendorf **P** Ganesh P, Günther Pankoke, Richard Paris, Sungjin Park, Howell Parry, Roberto Pasi, Sonal Patel, Ali Patterson, Michele Pauker, Francois Peeters, Xavi Perez, Nicole Petrilli, Rowan Pettitt, Anja Peukert, Lukas Pfeifer, Catherine Phillips, David Phillips, Marianne Picault, Jean Pierre Papillon, Jen Plevey, Patrizia Poncia, Prathamesh, Jennifer Prior, Jan Probst, Neelam Puri, Clemens Purrucker **R** Samia Rahman, Siva Ramamoorthy, Oliver Ramseyer, Ramyji, Vijaykrishna Ranganathan, Vasanth Rao, Georgia Rapti, Susan Rathborne, Elizabeth Rawson, Matthew Rees, Tushar Rege, Felix Reichardt, Leigh Rhodes, James Rickwood-Dodsworth, Ricky, Floortje Rikers, Renato Risari, Catherine Roadknight, Peter Robertson, Esteve Roca, Mark Rodgers, Antonio Rodríguez, Roland, Cristina Romero Barbado, Shelli Rosenfeld, Anne Roskott, Idan Rotem, Laura Rowlan, Christopher Rowland, Deb Roy, Robin Roy, Rupert Rudkin **S** Lucia S, Ernesto Salento, Sameer, Richard Samwell, Sandra, Pietro Santoro, Anja Saunders, Saurabh Saxena, Maura Sazler, Valeska Schaudy, Micha Schmid, Jennifer Schmidt, Ashley Scholes, Angelika Schreier, Janine Schulz, Paras Sehrawat, Vivek Selvamani, Satadru Sen, Vaishal Shah, Keary Shandler, Neha Sharma, Shawn, Laramie Shubber, Ajay Shukla, Nolan Shulak, Rishi Sidhu, Dr Silke Koch, Goncalo Silva, Silviag, Richard Simons, Arjan Singh, Jai Singh, Rajbir Singh, Karni Singh Parihar, Giles Skerry, Michael Sklovsky, Lily Smart, Michael Smit, Caro Smith, Cathy Smith, James Smith, Elyse Smythe, Tushar Solkar, Dario Sorgente, Bev Spence, Gillian Spragens, Rosemary Srinivasan, Sally Stacey, Richard Stackhouse, Catherine Stamp-Vincent, Katherine Standen, Karin Stanzel, Michel Steele, Kathrin Steins, Wendy Stekelenburg, Margolis Stephane, Stephanie, Steve, Mark Stevenson, Alois Stoeckl, Andy Stratton, Simon Stringer, William Stutzman, Meera Subramanian, Clara Summers, Dhruv Suneja, Sunny, Willi Suter, Prashant Suthar, Suzanne, Malin Svensson, Gabi Szlatki, Matthew Szymkowicz **T** Shizuka Takagi, Steve Tanner, Neil Taylor, Miro Tecilazic, Clay Teles, Marlene Tendler, James Tennet, Laura Thielges, Thomas, David Thomas, Peter Thomsan, Timerons, Todd, Darius Tolusis, Patrick Topham, Yann-Alexandre Tytgadt **U** Annie U, Udayan, Urban, Helena Urbanowska **V** Marta Vain, Adrie Van Sorgen, Cees Van Veelen, Emma Van Bergeijk, Joanne Van Der Werff, Joop Van Den Ouweland, RC Van De Pol, Raymond Van Golde, Wouter Van Vliet, Kerry Vander Meer, Felipe Veliz Cornejo, Maartje Verhagen, Niki Verschueren, Ryan Vetter, Vincent, Thuy-tien Vo **W** Karin Wagenaar, Franc Walsh, Jane Walter, Tom Warren, Helen Watkins, Nick Watson and Tania Kopytko, Laurel Watt, Anne Webster, Jonathan Weinzierl, Nicole Welt, Tony Wheeler, Gemma White, Sarah White, Katrin Wiebus, Susan Wiggans, Toni Wilden, Ann Wilkings, Libby Williams, Wayne Williams, Chris Wills, Peter Wilson, Marianne Winther, Robby Wisnewski, Lindsey Wittersheim, Kate Wootton, Julia Wright, Henry Wrigley **Y** Yishay Yafeh, Khelemba Yambem, Heroine Ying **Z** Nadine Zachmann, Ann Zanbilowicz, Arik Zara

AUTHOR THANKS

Sarina Singh

Thank you to those at Lonely Planet who played a part on this beautiful behemoth, especially Suzannah and Brigitte. Gratitude also goes to those in India and beyond who kindly proffered feedback, with extra special thanks to Shiv – for being a pillar of strength at a particularly challenging time. Bless. Massive thanks to the authors – you were a veritable dream team! Your enthusiasm, tenacity, humour and warmth is tremendously appreciated. I'd like to dedicate this – my 8th consecutive Lonely Planet *India* guide and 30th LP book – to my wonderful parents, who are a constant source of strength, love and wisdom.

Michael Benanav

First and foremost I'd like to thank the bus drivers of Himachal and Uttarakhand, who perform amazing feats of technical driving on narrow mountain roads in hulking mechanical beasts. I'd also like to give a shout to the whole crew in Kalpa who made Rosh Hashanah (2010) a truly special holiday – and a feast to remember! Deepest thanks go to Kelly and Luke, who accept my wanderlust with understanding and love.

Lindsay Brown

Thanks to the many people in Rajasthan, Haryana and Punjab who shared their interest and expertise. In particular, I would like to thank Satinder and Ritu and Dicky and Kavita in Jaipur, Goverdhan and Usha in Ranthambore, Shoryavardhan in Alwar, Vikramjit and Gags and Jeeva in Chandigarh, and Sanjay Kumar in Amritsar. For his wide smile and prowess on the road, a huge thanks to Vinod. Thanks to fellow author Sarina Singh, and thanks to Jenny, Pat and Sinead at home.

Stuart Butler

Firstly thanks to my wife Heather and son Jake for putting up with my long absence from home whilst researching this book. In India thanks to Rupak from Jungle Tours and Dipankar Borkakati, Teiso Yokha and Maina Singh for their driving, guiding and friendship. Further thanks to Christopher Michi in Ziro, Partha Laskar in Tripura, RK Sharma in Manipur and Puia in Mizoram for showing me the best of their respective states and to Phil and Dianne Haxby for sharing meals and advice. Thanks also to Toby Adamson for on-the-road company and left-tilt camera angles.

Mark Elliott

Many, many thanks to inspiring Rouf John and family, Rajesh Shaw and brothers, Anirban Das Mahapatra, Dani Systermans, the Travellers' House crew, Olivia Pozzan, Nicolas and Bernard Gachet, Maggie in Sabu, Gabriela Vesely, Vali and Remir in Pahalgan, Ruaidhrí Ua Fearghail and Joanna Rooney in Dha, the honourable Nissar Ali in Kargil, Mohd-Ali and Selim, Tsewang Yangjor, Stanzin and Wargil, Tondup Namgail, Hossein Ali, Angit Garg and friends, Niku and the Small Screen filmcrew, Devdan Chaudhuri, Edith Wolf, Anita Gopal, MS Haider, Leo and Sev, Harsha and Manjit, surreal 'poet' Iqbal Hussein and above all my unbeatable, ever-supportive family.

Katja Gaskell

First off, thanks must go to Sarina Singh whose help, guidance and good humour has been invaluable. Thanks to all the authors on the *India* team for answering endless questions and the numerous Delhi-wallahs who provided information, insight and the occasional chai break. At home, an enormous thank you to my husband Nick and to our fabulously excitable travelling companions, Alfie and Tess.

Trent Holden

Biggest thanks to all the good folk I met on the road who helped me out with some great tips. Thanks to Suzannah Shwer, who gave me the opportunity to work on my dream book, Sarina Singh for her calming presence throughout, as well as Amy Karafin and Paul Harding for the info. Thanks to Nigel Chin, Alex Leung and Wibowo Rusli for their great work inhouse. Finally, lots of love to my family, grandmother (Bushia) and my girlfriend Kate.

Abigail Hole

Many thanks to all at LP, especially to Suzannah Shwer. Special thanks to the amazing Sarina Singh and my coauthors – thanks for the tips Amy, Daniel, Mark and Michael. Thanks very much to Rajinder for help in Delhi and PJ Varghese for help in Kerala. Thanks also to Umesh and Sudir in Kerala, and to Sunny Singh for his recommendation, as well as to all the readers who wrote in with useful advice and updates. Last but not least, many, many thanks to the baby-sitting team: Luca, Mum, Ant and Karen, and to Gabriel and Jack for being so good.

Kate James

At LP, thanks to Sarina Singh and Suzannah Shwer for support, particularly during my credit-card crisis (thanks Sarina for the tip about purloining breakfast-buffet *idlis* when you're cash-poor). For exceptional assistance, thanks goes to Suzan and Michael Clements in Ooty, Pandian in Trichy, John Sinclair Willis in Bokkapuram, Bob Naik in Coimbatore and Luke Caleo in Chennai, as well as Jyothi Doreswamy for the cross-border holiday in Mysore. Thanks go out to Prema and all the friendly staff at the Textech office in Chennai for helpful tips and party invitations. As always, thanks to Chris for encouragement and animal-wrangling.

Amy Karafin

I'm very thankful to the people of Goa for putting up with my questions, especially the bus- and train-station guys (shout-out to Mr Sandesh Varai!), and to readers who wrote in with excellent tips. I'm also deeply grateful to Akash Bhartiya, who provided invaluable assistance, Manik and Surekha Bhartiya, Malini Hariharan, Sarina Singh, Suzannah Shwer, Brigitte Ellemor, the Fernandeses in Panaji, Serafin Fernandes, Pamela Maria Mascarenhas e Menezes Pereira, Saaz and Veda Aggarwal, David Gélinas, Eva Bollman, Francesco Vitelli, Kevin Raub, Michael Benanav, and SN Goenka and everyone at Dhamma Pattana. *Bhavatu sabba mangalam.*

BEHIND THE SCENES

Anirban Mahapatra

Thanks, first of all, to Suzannah, Sarina, Brigitte, Adrian, the entire team at Lonely Planet and all my coauthors for making this a dream project to work on. Thanks to Bengaluru buddies Priya, Rajesh, Swagata and Himu for their help and hospitality. To Shama Pawar, Vinay Parameswarappa, Chris and Laila Baker, Roop Deb and Suvam Pal for patiently helping with my research. Sridhar and Vivek, thanks for your sincere duties behind the steering wheel, you made it happen. And finally, thanks to Bhutu, Baghira, Kelu, Buro, Goopi, Caesar, Elsa, Dotty and Magic for being around, in person or in spirit.

Bradley Mayhew

Thanks to Norden Pempahishey in Kalimpong, Dorje and Nyima in Gangtok, and to Norbu and Sangay in Darjeeling, all of whom made my research much easier. Karma at Norling Resort and Palzor Lachungpa at Blue Sky Travels were also helpful with information. Yangchen was a great guide to northern Sikkim and Rakesh Rai was a great guide on the Singalila Ridge trek. Thanks also to Gagan Rai and Himal Tamang in Namchi.

Daniel McCrohan

Special thanks for help with my research must go to kebab connoisseur Naheed in Lucknow and to tribal expert Awesh in Jagdalpur as well as to Ramesh in Agra and Denise in Orchha. Thanks to travellers I met on the road for good tips and great company, especially Kito (Varanasi), Ian (Orchha), Karunesh (Gorakhpur), Christian (Gwalior), Vivek (Lucknow), Abhishek (Delhi) and Rosie, Douglas and birdwatcher Ben (all Bandhavgarh). Most of all, though, thank you to Taotao, Dudu and Yoyo, and to all my family in the UK and Belgium, for your love, patience and endless support.

John Noble

So many people gave generously of their time and knowledge to assist my research in Gujarat and Rajasthan. Especially Kanhaiya Lal Gurjar (driver, guide, interpreter and research assistant extraordinaire), PJ Jethi, Sue Carpenter, Mr Pavitran, Mukesh and Manish Mehta, Vinod P Bhavsar, Paresh, Mr Sorathia, Vinod Bhatt and Dhanraj Malik. Many thanks to ever-attentive and encouraging coordinating author Sarina Singh, and to LP colleagues Suzannah Shwer, Lindsay Brown and Brigitte Ellemor for their help and answers to many questions. Not least, Izzy and Jack, my ideal travelling companions.

Kevin Raub

Special thanks to my wife, Adriana Schmidt Raub, who puts up with the insane travel. (Seriously.) On and from the road in India: Sarita Hegde Roy, Daniel D'Mello, Dhanya Pilo, Sarina Singh, Amy Karafin, Ellie Girdwood, Emma Weeks, Nikhila Palat, Tanvi Madkaiker, Chris Way, Sudeip Nair, DJ Pramz, Sanghamitra Jena, Neeranjan 'Tutu' Rout, Bubu Yugabrata, Biswajit Mohanty, Claire Prest, Pulak Mohanty, Chiya Sethi, Mohammed Salim, Nick Hansen, Samiur Rahman, Daniel McCrohan and the three rickshaw drivers that didn't try to fleece me.

ACKNOWLEDGMENTS

Climate map data adapted from Peel MC, Finlayson BL & McMahon TA (2007) 'Updated World Map of the Köppen-Geiger Climate Classification', Hydrology and Earth System Sciences, 11, 163344.

Illustrations p1134, p1136, p1138 by Kelli Hamblet; p60, p354, p626 by Javier Zarracina

Cover photograph: Seated woman at Golden Temple, Amritsar/Huw Jones, LPI. Many of the images in this guide are available for licensing from Lonely Planet Images: www.lonelyplanetimages.com.

index

000 Map pages
000 Photo pages

how to use this book

These symbols will help you find the listings you want:

⊙	Sights	🎉	Festivals & Events	☆	Entertainment
🏃	Activities	🛏	Sleeping	🛍	Shopping
🎓	Courses	✕	Eating	ℹ	Information/Transport
👉	Tours	🍸	Drinking		

Look out for these icons:

TOP CHOICE	Our author's recommendation
FREE	No payment required
🌿	A green or sustainable option

Our authors have nominated these places as demonstrating a strong commitment to sustainability – for example by supporting local communities and producers, operating in an environmentally friendly way, or supporting conservation projects.

These symbols give you the vital information for each listing:

☑	Telephone Numbers	🛜	Wi-Fi Access	🚌	Bus
⊙	Opening Hours	🏊	Swimming Pool	⛴	Ferry
P	Parking	🥗	Vegetarian Selection	Ⓜ	Metro
⊖	Nonsmoking	📋	English-Language Menu	Ⓢ	Subway
✳	Air-Conditioning	👪	Family-Friendly	⊖	London Tube
@	Internet Access	🐾	Pet-Friendly	🚋	Tram
				🚆	Train

Reviews are organised by author preference.

Map Legend

Sights
- ⊙ Beach
- ⊙ Buddhist
- ⊙ Castle
- ⊙ Christian
- ⊙ Hindu
- ⊙ Islamic
- ⊙ Jewish
- ⊙ Monument
- ⊕ Museum/Gallery
- ⊙ Ruin
- ⊙ Winery/Vineyard
- ⊙ Zoo
- ⊙ Other Sight

Activities, Courses & Tours
- ⊙ Diving/Snorkelling
- ⊙ Canoeing/Kayaking
- ⊙ Skiing
- ⊙ Surfing
- ⊙ Swimming/Pool
- ⊙ Walking
- ⊙ Windsurfing
- ⊙ Other Activity/Course/Tour

Sleeping
- ⊙ Sleeping
- ⊙ Camping

Eating
- ⊙ Eating

Drinking
- ⊙ Drinking
- ⊙ Cafe

Entertainment
- ⊙ Entertainment

Shopping
- ⊙ Shopping

Information
- ⊙ Bank
- ⊙ Embassy/Consulate
- ⊙ Hospital/Medical
- @ Internet
- ⊙ Police
- ⊙ Post Office
- ⊙ Telephone
- ⊙ Toilet
- ⊙ Tourist Information
- • Other Information

Transport
- ⊙ Airport
- ⊗ Border Crossing
- ⊙ Bus
- ⊶⊙⊷ Cable Car/Funicular
- -⊙- Cycling
- -⊙- Ferry
- Ⓜ Metro
- ⊶⊙⊷ Monorail
- P Parking
- ⊙ Petrol Station
- ⊙ Taxi
- ⊶⊙⊷ Train/Railway
- ⊶⊙⊷ Tram
- • Other Transport

Routes
- Tollway
- Freeway
- Primary
- Secondary
- Tertiary
- Lane
- Unsealed Road
- Plaza/Mall
- Steps
- ⌇⌇⌇ Tunnel
- Pedestrian Overpass
- Walking Tour
- Walking Tour Detour
- Path

Geographic
- ⊙ Hut/Shelter
- ⊙ Lighthouse
- ⊙ Lookout
- ▲ Mountain/Volcano
- ⊙ Oasis
- ⊙ Park
-)(Pass
- ⊙ Picnic Area
- ⊙ Waterfall

Population
- ⊙ Capital (National)
- ◉ Capital (State/Province)
- ⊙ City/Large Town
- ⊙ Town/Village

Boundaries
- –··– International
- ---- State/Province
- — · Disputed
- - - Regional/Suburb
- Marine Park
- Cliff
- Wall

Hydrography
- River, Creek
- Intermittent River
- Swamp/Mangrove
- Reef
- Canal
- Water
- Dry/Salt/Intermittent Lake
- Glacier

Areas
- Beach/Desert
- + + + Cemetery (Christian)
- × × × Cemetery (Other)
- Park/Forest
- Sportsground
- Sight (Building)
- Top Sight (Building)

Bradley Mayhew
West Bengal & Darjeeling, Sikkim Bradley has been visiting the Himalaya for 20 years now, exploring from Ladakh to Bhutan. For this edition he focused on Sikkim and the West Bengal Hills. Bradley has also been the coordinating author of Lonely Planet guides *Bhutan, Nepal* and *Trekking in the Nepal Himalaya*. He was recently the subject of a five-part Arte/SWR documentary retracing the route of Marco Polo, from Venice to Xanadu, through Iran, Afghanistan and Central Asia. See what he's up to at www.bradleymayhew.blogspot.com.

Daniel McCrohan
Uttar Pradesh & the Taj Mahal, Madhya Pradesh & Chhattisgarh Daniel has been travelling to India on and off for almost 20 years, and has a deep affinity with the central regions having covered them for the past two editions of this guidebook. Originally a London-based newspaper journalist, he later turned to travel writing and now specialises in China, where he lives, and India, which he visits regularly for the chai, the thali and the (slightly scary) wet shaves. Daniel has cowritten more than half a dozen Lonely Planet guidebooks. He also writes travel apps and is the cohost of the television series *Best in China*. Find out more at danielmccrohan. com. Daniel also wrote the Taj Mahal and Khajuraho colour illustrations text.

John Noble
Southern & Western Rajasthan, Gujarat John, from England, lives in Spain and has written on 20 or so countries for Lonely Planet. He first experienced India in the days of Rajiv Gandhi but has never written about it until now. Best on-the-road decision: to get up pre-dawn and take another safari at Sasan Gir – and come upon not just one but four young lions strolling casually back and forth through the bushes in the early morning light. A full 1% of Asia's wild lion population.

Read more about John at:
lonelyplanet.com/members/ewoodrover

Kevin Raub
Bihar & Jharkhand, Odisha, Mumbai
(Bombay) Kevin Raub grew up in Atlanta, USA and started his career as a music journalist in New York, working for *Men's Journal* and *Rolling Stone* magazines. Over a decade of trips to India, he's ogled the Taj Mahal, rejuvenated at Maharaja-palace spas in the Himalaya, tracked tigers in Madhya Pradesh and navigated Keralan backwaters, but what magnetically draws him back to the subcontinent every time is far more basic: the absolutely mind-blowing cuisine, which – knock on wood – has never made him sick. You can find him at www. kevinraub.net or at 35,000 feet.

Contributing Authors
David Lukas lives on the edge of Yosemite National Park where he studies and writes about the natural world. He has contributed environment chapters to about 28 Lonely Planet guides and is the author of the recent *A Year of Watching Wildlife*. David wrote the Elephants & Tigers: India's Sanctuaries and The Landscape chapters for this edition.

Amelia Thomas is a writer and journalist working throughout India and the Middle East. Her four small children have travelled extensively throughout India and beyond, and particularly enjoy *masala dosas*, mango lassis, and hurtling through the streets of Old Delhi in autorickshaws. Amelia wrote the Travel With Children chapter of this edition.

Mark Elliott
Jammu & Kashmir (including Ladakh), Kolkata (Calcutta) Mark has been making forays to the subcontinent since a 1984 trip that lined his stomach for all eventualities. For this edition an eventful summer saw him dodging flash floods in Kargil, landslides in Ladakh, curfews in Srinagar and stone-throwing mobs around Kashmir. When not researching travel guides Mark lives a blissfully quiet suburban life with his beloved Belgian bride, Danielle, who found him at a Turkmen camel market.

Katja Gaskell
Booking Trains, Yoga, Spas & Spiritual Pursuits, Volunteering, Scams, Women & Solo Travellers, Directory A–Z, Transport Sixteen years ago Katja arrived in India on a six week, ill-planned trip that saw her swelter in Rajasthan, get drenched by the monsoons in Goa and suffer the after-effects of a roadside prawn curry in Mumbai. And yet she still fell in love with the country and vowed to return. Today Katja calls Delhi home and regularly travels the country with her husband and two kids. Katja is also the author of Lonely Planet guides to China and Australia.

Trent Holden
Andhra Pradesh, Andaman Islands On his last visit to Andhra Pradesh Trent made his film debut as an extra in a Tollywood film. A decade later he's still waiting for a follow-up call (perhaps it's time to let that dream go...), but in the meantime, any opportunity to head back there suits him fine. This is his fourth trip to India, a place he loves like no other. When not on the road researching and coauthoring for titles such as *Nepal* and *Indonesia*, Trent works as a freelance editor with Lonely Planet.

Abigail Hole
Itineraries, Delhi, Kerala Abigail was first bewitched by India around 15 years ago, and she's returned with increasing regularity – three times in 2010 alone. This is the fourth time she has worked on Lonely Planet's *India* guide. She cowrote the first edition of *Rajasthan, Delhi & Agra* and has written about India for various newspapers and magazines, including *Lonely Planet Magazine*. This edition of *India* gave her the welcome opportunity of covering Kerala and Delhi, two of her favourite destinations. Abigail also wrote the Red Fort colour illustration text.

Kate James
Tamil Nadu & Chennai Melbourne-born Kate grew up in Ooty, where her parents taught at an international school and travelled using the very first edition of this guide. Journalism in Australia led Kate to an editing job at Lonely Planet and then into a freelance writing and editing career. She wrote the Orissa and West Bengal chapters of the previous edition of this guide, and is the author of *Women of the Gobi* (Pluto Press, 2006).

Amy Karafin
20 Top Experiences, If You Like..., Month by Month, Goa, India Today, History Indian in several former lives, Amy headed straight to India after university for a four-month trip that would turn out to be karmically ordained. She spent the next few years alternating between New York and faraway lands until, fed up with the irony of being a travel editor in a Manhattan cubicle, she relinquished her MetroCard and her black skirts to make a living on the road. She has been freelancing semi-nomadically ever since, setting up shop in Bombay as much as possible. This is Amy's fourth time coauthoring *India*.

Anirban Mahapatra
South and North of Kolkata (in West Bengal & Darjeeling), Maharashtra, Karnataka & Bengaluru For seven long years, Anirban ran a nifty travel scam out of a reporter's cubicle in a Delhi newspaper office. He'd sell outlandish story ideas to gullible editors, and then hare off across the Indian subcontinent in the name of intrepid journalism. When his bluff was finally called, he promptly changed his designation to travel writer, and thereby legitimised his trade. Anirban has regularly contributed to Lonely Planet guidebooks since 2007. When not travelling, he cools his heels in Kolkata.

OUR STORY

A beat-up old car, a few dollars in the pocket and a sense of adventure. In 1972 that's all Tony and Maureen Wheeler needed for the trip of a lifetime – across Europe and Asia overland to Australia. It took several months, and at the end – broke but inspired – they sat at their kitchen table writing and stapling together their first travel guide, *Across Asia on the Cheap*. Within a week they'd sold 1500 copies. Lonely Planet was born.

Today, Lonely Planet has offices in Melbourne, London and Oakland, with more than 600 staff and writers. We share Tony's belief that 'a great guidebook should do three things: inform, educate and amuse'.

OUR WRITERS

Sarina Singh

Coordinating Author, Colourful India, Welcome to India, Need to Know, Regions at a Glance, The Way of Life, Spiritual India, Delicious India, The Great Indian Bazaar, Sacred Architecture, The Arts After finishing a business degree in Melbourne, Sarina travelled to India where she completed a hotel corporate traineeship before working as a journalist. After five years she returned to Australia and pursued postgraduate journalism qualifications before co-authoring Lonely Planet's first edition of *Rajasthan*. She has worked on 30 Lonely Planet books, writes for other major international publications and has a column in India's *Lonely Planet Magazine*. Singh is also the author of two books – *Polo in India* and *India: Essential Encounters*. Her award-nominated documentary premiered at the Melbourne International Film Festival before screening in Australia and Europe. See www.sarinasingh.com.

Read more about Sarina at:
lonelyplanet.com/members/sarinasingh

Michael Benanav

Trekking, Himachal Pradesh, Uttarakhand Michael has been to North India four times and still hasn't visited the Taj Mahal. He'd like to, but has been too busy migrating through Uttarakhand with a clan of nomadic water-buffalo herders, exploring remote Kashmiri valleys along the Line of Control, and finding spiritual enlightenment while riding public buses over the crazy mountain roads of Himachal Pradesh. Michael photographs, writes books and freelances for the *New York Times*, *Geographical* and other publications. His website is www.michaelbenanav.com.

Lindsay Brown

Eastern Rajasthan, Haryana & Punjab After completing a PhD on evolutionary genetics and following a stint as a science editor, Lindsay started working for Lonely Planet. Formerly the publishing manager of outdoor activity guides at Lonely Planet, Lindsay returns to the subcontinent to trek, write and photograph whenever possible. He has also contributed to Lonely Planet's *South India, Nepal, Bhutan, Rajasthan, Delhi & Agra* and *Pakistan & the Karakoram Highway* guides, among others.

Stuart Butler

Northeast Tribal States Stuart first travelled to India in the 90s and he's been back numerous times since. Exploring the northeast for this book gave him a totally new angle on the whole India experience. When not enduring the northeast's pot-holed roads, Stuart has travelled from the deserts of Arabia to the beaches of the Caribbean for Lonely Planet and various surf magazines. Stuart lives with his wife and baby son on southwest France's beaches. His website is www.oceansurfpublications.com.

Read more about Stuart at:
lonelyplanet.com/members/stuartbutler

OVER MORE
PAGE WRITERS

Published by Lonely Planet Publications Pty Ltd
ABN 36 005 607 983
14th edition – Sep 2011
ISBN 978 1 74179 780 0
© Lonely Planet 2011 Photographs © as indicated 2011
10 9 8 7 6 5 4 3 2 1
Printed in Singapore

Although the authors and Lonely Planet have taken all reasonable care in preparing this book, we make no warranty about the accuracy or completeness of its content and, to the maximum extent permitted, disclaim all liability arising from its use.